D1536819

STATS
Major League Handbook
2002

STATS
Archivo de Grandes Ligas
2002

STATS, Inc.

STATS INC.
PUBLISHING

Published by STATS Publishing
A division of Sports Team Analysis & Tracking Systems, Inc.

Publicado por STATS Publishing
Una división de Sports Team Analysis & Tracking Systems, Inc.

Notice To Our Loyal Readers:

Beginning with our 2002 editions, many of your favorite STATS annuals will only be available directly from STATS, Inc. We are reducing the number of our titles to be sold in bookstores nationwide, but are not reducing the number of titles we publish.

You can visit our online bookstore at www.stats.com and order a free STATS Product Guide/Sports Calendar to be sent directly to you. This will allow us to include you in future product availability announcements.

If you would like to be added to our mailing list in order to be informed about releases of titles and special offers, please fill out the form below and return by mail to:

STATS, Inc.
8130 Lehigh Avenue
Morton Grove, IL 60053
ATTN: Pubs Mailing Request

Or, you may fax this page to (847) 470-9140. Please direct the fax to the attention of "Pubs Mailing Request."

Name_____

Address_____

City_____ State_____ Zip_____

Phone (   )_____ Ext._____ Fax (   )_____

E-mail_____

For more information regarding the mailing list, please call **1-800-63-STATS**.

Acknowledgments

The process of putting together the 13th edition of the *STATS Major League Handbook* requires a heavy dose of teamwork, and we'd like to thank those people who contribute to this effort.

The STATS team is successfully anchored by President Alan Leib. Senior Vice President Steve Byrd steers our consumer and TV divisions, while Vice President Robert Schur directs our commercial divisions.

Tony Nistler manages the publications unit that produces this book and all of our other sports titles. Tony oversaw editorial responsibilities, with help from Thom Henninger, Jim Henzler, Taylor Bechtold and Norm DeNosaquo. Getting the numbers programmed appropriately fell into the hands of Tim Coletta. Marc Carl manipulated the many columns and tables that are key to the book's design. Thanks also to Oscar Palacios for translating all of the introductory text into Spanish, with help from Judy Hutt. Getting the word out about and fulfulling orders for the *STATS Major League Handbook* and other STATS publications require the hard work of Walter Lis, Ryan Balock and Andy Degnan. Ryan designed this book's cover.

We couldn't publish this book without our Data Collection Department. Managing the collection of the numbers you'll find on these pages and in many of our other publications is Allan Spear. Special thanks go to Jeff Chernow, who oversees the accuracy of our major league baseball data.

Keeping STATS at the forefront of the sports information business on a daily basis are Jim Capuano, our Senior Vice President of Sales; Jeff Smith, who manages our technical operations; and Howard Lanin, who oversees our financial and administration areas.

Our Research Department for Fox Sports in Los Angeles is headed by Don Zminda, with help from Director of Operations Steve Vanderpool. Their team of sports researchers and technical staff provides many of the stats that are broadcast daily from the Fox Sports studios, as well as from remote pregame, postgame and live game telecasts on Fox and Fox Sports Net.

Agradecimientos

El proceso de crear la 13va edición del *STATS Major League Handbook* requirió mucho trabajo y queremos agradecer a todos los que contribuyeron en este trabajo.

STATS es dirigida por el Presidente Alan Leib. El Vice Presidente Steve Byrd guía las divisiones de Televisión y Productos para Consumidores. El Vice Presidente Robert Schur dirige la División Comercial.

Tony Nistler dirige la División de Publicaciones que produjo este y otros libros. Bajo Tony trabajan Thom Henninger, Jim Henzler, Taylor Bechtold y Norm DeNosaquo. El trabajo de programación es el área de Tim Coletta. Marc Carl diseñó el interior del libro. Gracias a Oscar Palacios por las traducciones y a Judy Hütt por su ayuda con ellas. Walter Lis, Ryan Balock y Andy Degnan están en control de la distribución de los libros. Ryan diseñó la portada de este libro.

Este libro no sería posible sin el trabajo de nuestro Departamento de Archivo. Allan Spear es el director de mantener ésta vasta colección de datos. Gracias especiales para Jeff Chernow, quien vigila la exactitud de los datos de Grandes Ligas.

Manteniendo a STATS como vanguardia en la industria de información de deportes es el trabajo diario de Jim Capuano, nuestro Vice Presidente de Ventas; Jeff Smith, director técnico de la compañía; y Howard Lanin, administrador de finanzas.

Nuestro Departamento de Investigaciones para Fox Sports en Los Angeles es dirigido por Don Zminda, con la asistencia de Steve Vanderpool. Su equipo de investigaciones provee muchas de las estadísticas televisadas diarias desde los estudios de Fox Sports, así como estadísticas en vivo y directo en las cadenas Fox y Fox Sports Net.

This book is dedicated to my parents, John and Shan Corelis. I cannot thank you enough for the love, support and guidance you've given me.

And to my wife Antoinette. May our life together be full of love, happiness and the jubilation of a World Series on the corner of Clark and Addison.

Go Cubs!

— Jim Corelis

Table of Contents

Indice

Introduction

Barry Bonds gave us one of those seasons for the ages. It was much more than just the home-run mark. In also surpassing the all-time single-season walks and slugging records, he showed us how he was in complete control at the plate. His dominance was even more apparent in the final three weeks of the season. After the brief break following the tragic events of September 11, Bonds was seeing fewer and fewer pitches in the strike zone, frequently as few as three or four hittable offerings in a game. Yet, he hit .408, slugged 1.082, homered 10 times, scored 19 runs and drove in 16 in those final 18 contests.

Obviously no one generated such stratospheric on-base and slugging percentages, and only Sammy Sosa hit as many homers during that span. It's as if Bonds was *toying* with pitchers until they finally had to offer up a pitch in the strike zone. And he was in charge of the proceedings all season long.

The San Francisco left fielder finished with 177 walks and an .863 slugging mark, surpassing Babe Ruth's single-season records of 170 free passes (in 1923) and an .847 slugging percentage (1920). Bonds' .515 on-base percentage marked the first time someone had posted a .500-plus OBP since Ted Williams and Mickey Mantle did it in 1957. When the Giants' star homered to wrap up play on the last Sunday of the 2001 campaign, he had slammed 73 bombs in just 476 at-bats to close the book on a very special summer.

Closing the book on Bonds' big year means it's time to present the newest edition of the book that documents his 2001 success. The *STATS Major League Handbook 2002* comes your way, filled with the usual goodies that provide a complete summary of the season just completed. You'll not only get the year-by-year career stats of every player who appeared in a major league game in 2001, but also lefty/right splits, fielding data for players by position, tons of leader boards, statistical analysis of the major league parks and player projections for 2002.

These pages make up the 13th edition of the *Handbook*. This will be the last time Cal Ripken and Tony Gwynn will grace them, and that may be true for Rickey Henderson, as well. While these future Hall of Famers may be passing from the scene, Bonds will be part of the *Major League Handbook* for years to come. And we'll be there to document each passing year.

—Thom Henninger

What's Official and What's Not

The statistics in this book technically are unofficial. The official Major League Baseball averages are not released until December, but we can't wait that long. If you compare these stats with the official ones, you'll find no major differences. That said, we do not agree with the unofficial stats released by Major League Baseball in the following instances:

- A.J. Pierzynski vs. Kip Wells, 3rd inning, and Corey Koskie vs. Kip Wells, 4th inning, CWS@Min 10/7/01. Pierzynski and Koskie drew intentional walks, though MLB credits these as non-intentional

In this case, we have confidence in the accuracy of our numbers and confirmed this with multiple STATS reporters and the individual teams involved. As always, we take extraordinary efforts to ensure the accuracy of our data.

Introducción

Barry Bonds nos brindó una temporada inolvidable. Fue más que el récord de cuadrangulareas. También superó la marca de bases por bolas y promedio de bases acumuladas durante una temporada. Eso nos muestra que Bonds tuvo una maestría de bateo completa. Su destreza fue claramente evidente en las últimas tres semanas de la temporada. Después de la pausa creada por los ataques terroristas del 11 de septiembre, Bonds vió menos strikes, frecuentemente solo tres o cuatros lanzamientos bateables por partido. Sin embargo, él bateó .408, tuvo un promedio de bases acumuladas de 1.082, disparó 10 cuadrangulares, anotó 19 carreras y empujó 16 en los últimos 18 juegos.

Nadie ha generado promedios de enbasamiento y de bases acumuladas a ese nivel, y solo Sammy Sosa conectó tantos cuadrangulares en esa misma estancia. Fue como si Bonds estaba *jugando* con los lanzadores hasta que le daban un lanzamiento sobre el plato.

El jardinero izquierdo de San Francisco terminó con 177 bases por bolas y un promedio de .863 bases por veces al bate, las dos marcas superando los récords de Babe Ruth de 170 bases por bolas (en 1923) y .847 promedio de bases (en 1920). El promedio de embasamiento de Bonds de .515 fue la primera vez que alguien se ha embasado más de la mitad de veces al bate desde Ted Williams y Mickey Mantle lo hicieron en 1957. Cuando la estrella de los Gigantes jonroneó el último domingo de la temporada del 2001, él había conectado 73 cuadrangulares en solo 476 veces al bate, para finalizar una temporada épica.

Celebrando la temporada histórica de Bonds significa que es hora de presentar la nueva edición del libro que documenta su éxito. El *STATS Major League Handbook 2002* (El Archivo de Grandes Ligas de STATS del 2002) viene repleto de un resumen estadístico de la temporada que acaba de terminar. No solo vas a recibir en desglose anual de cada pelotero que jugó en el 2001, pero también análisis de derechos contra zurdos, fildeo por cada posición, docenas de tablas de líderes, estadísticas por estadios y prognósticos para el 2002.

Estas páginas constituyen la 13va edición del *Handbook*. Esta es la última vez que Cal Ripken y Tony Gwynn apareceran en nuestro libro, y es posible que también sea la última vez para Rickey Henderson. Mientras estos futuros entrantes del Salón de la Fama se despiden de nosotros, nuevas estrellas serán parte del *Major League Handbook*. Y, cómo siempre, será un placer mostrarles a Uds. las estadísticas.

—Thom Henninger

Qué es Oficial y Qué Extra-oficial

Las estadísticas en este libro son técnicamente extra-oficiales. Las estadísticas oficiales no son divulgadas por las oficinas de las Grandes Ligas (MLB) hasta diciembre, pero no podemos esperar hasta entonces. Si comparan estas estadísticas con las oficiales, no verán muchas diferencias. Y nosotros no estamos siempre de acuerdo con las estadísticas divulgadas por MLB. Por ejemplo:

- A.J. Pierzynski contra Kip Wells, 3ra entrada, y Corey Koskie contra Kip Wells, 4ta entrada, Medias Blancas contra los Mellizos el 7/10/01. Pierzynski y Koskie recibieron bases por bolas intencionales, pero MLB dice que no son intencionales

En estos casos, nosotros tenemos confianza en nuestros números y los hemos confirmados con nuestros editores y los equipos involucrados. Nosotros siempre tomamos esfuerzos para asegurar estadísticas exactas.

Career Register

The Career Register includes the records of all players who saw major league action in 2001, plus the following 18 players who did not play in the majors in 2001, but who we feel are likely to play in 2002: Mike Benjamin, Kris Benson, Francisco Cordova, Gary DiSarcina, Scott Erickson, Seth Etherton, Juan Guzman, Carlos Hernandez, Bobby Jones, Kevin McGlinchy, Gil Meche, Mitch Meluskey, Jose Rosado, Bill Simas, Mike Sirotka, Garrett Stephenson, Todd Stottlemyre and Mo Vaughn.

The abbreviations used in the register are defined below:

For all players, **Age** is seasonal age as of June 30, 2002; **Ht** = Height; **Wt** = Weight; **Lg** = Major League (**AL** = American League; **NL** = National League) or minor league classification. Class-A (A+, A, A-) and Rookie (R+, R) have separate classifications to distinguish the level of competition. **IND** = independent minor league.

For Batters, **R** = bats or throws right; **L** = bats or throws left; **B** = bats both right and left; **Pos** = number of games played at each position in 2001; **DH** = designated hitter; **PH** = pinch hitter; **PR** = pinch runner; **G** = games; **AB** = at-bats; **H** = hits; **2B** = doubles; **3B** = triples; **HR** = home runs; **Hm** = home runs at home; **Rd** = home runs on the road; **TB** = total bases; **R** = runs; **RBI** = runs batted in; **TBB** = total bases on balls; **IBB** = intentional bases on balls; **SO** = strikeouts; **HBP** = times hit by pitches; **SH** = sacrifice hits; **SF** = sacrifice flies; **SB** = stolen bases; **CS** = times caught stealing; **SB%** = stolen base percentage; **GDP** = times grounded into double plays; **Avg** = batting average; **OBP** = on-base percentage; **SLG** = slugging percentage.

For pitchers, **Pos** = number of games pitched as a starter and as a reliever; **SP** = starting pitcher; **RP** = relief pitcher; **G** = games pitched; **GS** = games started; **CG** = complete games; **GF** = games finished; **IP** = innings pitched; **BFP** = batters facing pitcher; **H** = hits allowed; **R** = runs allowed; **ER** = earned runs allowed; **HR** = home runs allowed; **SH** = sacrifice hits allowed; **SF** = sacrifice flies allowed; **HB** = hit batsmen; **TBB** = total bases on balls; **IBB** = intentional bases on balls; **SO** = strikeouts; **WP** = wild pitches; **Bk** = balks; **W** = wins; **L** = losses; **Pct.** = winning percentage; **ShO** = shutouts; **Sv** = saves; **Op** = save opportunities; **Hld** = holds; **ERA** = earned run average.

An asterisk (*) by a player's minor league stats indicates that these are his 2001 minor league numbers only; previous minor league experience is not included. Figures in **boldface** indicate the player led the league in that category.

For players who played for more than one major league team in a season, stats for each team are shown just above the bottom-line career totals.

Archivo de Carreras

El Archivo de Carreras incluyen las estadísticas de todos los peloteros que jugaron en el 2001, más los siguientes jugadores que no jugaron en las Grandes Ligas en el 2001, pero que pueden jugar en el 2002: Mike Benjamin, Kris Benson, Francisco Córdova, Gary DiSarcina, Scott Erickson, Seth Etherton, Juan Guzmán, Carlos Hernández, Bobby Jones, Kevin McGlinchy, Gil Meche, Mitch Meluskey, José Rosado, Bill Simas, Mike Sirotka, Garrett Stephenson, Todd Stottlemyre y Mo Vaughn.

Las abreviaciones que ocupamos en el archivo son las siguientes:

Age (Edad) es la "edad de temporada" (la edad de los jugadores el 30 de junio del 2002); **Ht** = Altura en pies y pulgadas; **Wt** = Peso en libras; **Lg** = Grandes Ligas (**AL** = Liga Americana; **NL** = Liga Nacional) o clasificación de ligas menores. Clase-A (A+, A, A-) y Rookie (R+, R) tienen clasificaciones separadas para distinguir el nivel de competencia. **IND** = liga menor independiente.

Para Bateadores, **R** = batea o tira con su mano derecha; **L** = batea o tira con su izquierda; **B** = batea ambidiestro; **Pos** = número de partidos jugados en cada posición en el 2001; **DH** = bateador designado; **PH** = bateador emergente; **PR** = corredor emergente; **G** = partidos; **AB** = Veces-al-Bate; **H** = hits; **2B** = dobles; **3B** = triples; **HR** = cuadrangulares; **Hm** = cuadrangulares como local; **Rd** = cuadrangulares como visitante; **TB** = bases acumuladas; **R** = carreras; **RBI** = carreras empujadas; **TBB** = total de bases por bolas; **IBB** = bases por bolas intencionales; **SO** = ponches; **HBP** = golpeado por lanzador; **SH** = toques de sacrificio; **SF** = elevados de sacrificio; **SB** = bases robadas; **CS** = atrapado robando; **SB%** = promedio de bases robadas; **GDP** = arranques para doble plays; **Avg** = promedio de bateo; **OBP** = promedio de embasamiento; **SLG** = promedio de bases acumuladas.

Para Lanzadores, **Pos** = número de juegos lanzados como abridor y como relevista; **SP** = abridor; **RP** = relevista; **G** = juegos lanzados; **GS** = juegos abiertos; **CG** = juegos completos; **GF** = juegos cerrados; **IP** = entradas lanzadas; **BFP** = bateadores enfrentados; **H** = hits permitidos; **R** = carreras permitidas; **ER** = carreras limpias permitidas; **HR** = cuadrangulares permitidos; **SH** = toques de sacrificio permitidos; **SF** = elevados de sacrificio permitidos; **HB** = bateadores golpeados; **TBB** = total de bases por bolas; **IBB** = bases por bolas intencionales; **SO** = ponches; **WP** = lanzamiento salvajes; **Bk** = balks; **W** = victorias; **L** = derrotas; **Pct.** = porcentaje de ganados; **ShO** = blanqueadas; **Sv** = salvados; **Op** = oportunidades de salvar; **Hld** = Sujetón; **ERA** = efectividad.

Un asterisco (*) junto a las estadísticas de ligas menores de un jugador indica que estas son del 2001 solamente; número de temporadas menores previas no están incluidas. Números en **resaltado** indican que el jugador fue el líder de la liga en esa categoría.

Para peloteros que jugaron con más de un equipo en la temporada, las estadísticas para cada equipo están sobre la línea de los totales de carrera.

Andy Abad

Bats: Left **Throws:** Left **Pos:** 1B-1; PH/PR-1   **Ht:** 6'1" **Wt:** 184 **Born:** 8/25/72 **Age:** 29

							BATTING											BASERUNNING				PERCENTAGES		
Year Team	Lg	G	AB	H	2B	3B	HR	(Hm | Rd)	TB	R	RBI	TBB	IBB	SO	HBP	SH	SF	SB	CS	SB%	GDP	Avg	OBP	SLG
1993 Red Sox	R	59	230	57	9	2	1	—	—	73	24	28	25	0	27	2	2	4	2	2	.50	2	.248	.322	.317
1994 Sarasota	A+	111	354	102	20	0	2	—	—	128	39	35	42	4	58	5	5	5	2	12	.14	9	.288	.367	.362
1995 Trenton	AA	89	287	69	14	3	4	—	—	101	29	32	36	2	58	3	6	3	5	7	.42	6	.240	.328	.352
Sarasota	A+	18	59	17	3	0	0	—	—	20	5	10	6	0	13	0	0	0	4	3	.57	0	.288	.354	.339
1996 Sarasota	A+	58	202	58	15	1	2	—	—	81	28	41	37	1	28	3	2	2	10	3	.77	6	.287	.402	.401
Trenton	AA	65	213	59	22	1	4	—	—	95	33	39	33	2	41	0	0	3	5	3	.63	4	.277	.369	.446
1997 Trenton	AA	45	165	50	13	0	8	—	—	87	37	24	33	3	27	2	0	1	2	4	.33	2	.303	.423	.527
Pawtucket	AAA	68	227	62	7	0	9	—	—	96	28	32	36	1	47	2	1	1	3	2	.60	4	.273	.376	.423
1998 Pawtucket	AAA	111	365	112	18	1	16	—	—	180	71	66	68	2	70	3	4	5	10	6	.63	7	.307	.415	.493
1999 Pawtucket	AAA	102	377	112	21	4	15	—	—	186	61	65	51	5	50	2	2	3	7	2	.78	9	.297	.381	.493
2001 Sacramento	AAA	124	462	139	19	2	19	—	—	219	72	82	58	1	67	1	3	2	4	2	.67	12	.301	.379	.474
2001 Oakland	AL	1	1	0	0	0	0	(0 | 0)	0	0	0	0	0	0	0	0	0	0	0	—	0	.000	.000	.000

Jeff Abbott

Bats: R **Throws:** L **Pos:** PH/PR-16; CF-9; RF-8; LF-1   **Ht:** 6'2" **Wt:** 200 **Born:** 8/17/72 **Age:** 29

							BATTING											BASERUNNING				PERCENTAGES		
Year Team	Lg	G	AB	H	2B	3B	HR	(Hm	Rd)	TB	R	RBI	TBB	IBB	SO	HBP	SH	SF	SB	CS	SB%	GDP	Avg	OBP	SLG
2001 Brevard Cty *	A+	3	8	2	0	0	0	—	—	2	2	2	1	0	1	0	0	1	0	0	—	0	.250	.300	.250
Portland *	AA	8	26	12	1	0	2	—	—	19	4	6	2	1	0	0	0	0	0	1	.00	0	.462	.500	.731
Calgary *	AAA	47	175	56	9	0	9	—	—	92	25	24	6	0	33	0	1	3	1	2	.33	3	.320	.337	.526
1997 Chicago	AL	19	38	10	1	0	1	(0	1)	14	8	2	0	0	6	0	0	3	0	0	—	3	.263	.263	.368
1998 Chicago	AL	89	244	68	14	1	12	(5	7)	120	33	41	9	1	28	0	2	5	3	3	.50	2	.279	.298	.492
1999 Chicago	AL	17	57	9	0	0	2	(0	2)	15	5	6	5	0	12	0	1	1	1	1	.50	4	.158	.222	.263
2000 Chicago	AL	80	215	59	15	1	3	(1	2)	85	31	29	21	1	38	2	2	1	2	1	.67	0	.274	.343	.395
2001 Florida	NL	28	42	11	3	0	0	(0	0)	14	5	5	3	0	7	1	0	0	0	0	—	1	.262	.326	.333
5 ML YEARS		233	596	157	33	2	18	(6	12)	248	82	83	38	2	91	3	5	7	6	5	.55	12	.263	.307	.416

Kurt Abbott

Bats: Right **Throws:** Right **Pos:** PH/PR-5; 2B-1; SS-1   **Ht:** 6'0" **Wt:** 200 **Born:** 6/2/69 **Age:** 33

							BATTING											BASERUNNING				PERCENTAGES		
Year Team	Lg	G	AB	H	2B	3B	HR	(Hm	Rd)	TB	R	RBI	TBB	IBB	SO	HBP	SH	SF	SB	CS	SB%	GDP	Avg	OBP	SLG
2001 Greenville *	AA	2	6	0	0	0	0	—	—	0	0	0	1	0	1	0	0	0	0	0	—	0	.000	.143	.000
Richmond *	AAA	4	14	3	1	0	0	—	—	4	0	0	0	0	7	2	0	0	1	0	1.00	0	.214	.313	.286
1993 Oakland	AL	20	61	15	1	0	3	(0	3)	25	11	9	3	0	20	0	3	0	2	0	1.00	3	.246	.281	.410
1994 Florida	NL	101	345	86	17	3	9	(4	5)	136	41	33	16	1	98	5	3	2	3	0	1.00	5	.249	.291	.394
1995 Florida	NL	120	420	107	18	7	17	(12	5)	190	60	60	36	4	110	5	2	5	4	3	.57	6	.255	.318	.452
1996 Florida	NL	109	320	81	18	7	8	(6	2)	137	37	33	22	1	99	3	4	0	3	3	.50	7	.253	.307	.428
1997 Florida	NL	94	252	69	18	2	6	(1	5)	109	35	30	14	3	68	1	6	0	3	1	.75	5	.274	.315	.433
1998 Oak-Col		77	194	51	13	1	5	(3	2)	81	26	24	12	0	53	2	1	3	2	1	.67	5	.263	.308	.418
1999 Colorado	NL	96	286	78	17	2	8	(6	2)	123	41	41	16	0	69	0	2	1	3	2	.60	4	.273	.310	.430
2000 New York	NL	79	157	34	7	1	6	(3	3)	61	22	12	14	2	51	1	0	1	1	1	.50	2	.217	.283	.389
2001 Atlanta	NL	6	9	2	0	0	0	—	—	2	0	0	0	0	3	0	0	0	1	0	1.00	0	.222	.222	.222
1998 Oakland	AL	35	123	33	7	1	2	(1	1)	48	17	9	10	0	34	1	1	1	2	1	.67	3	.268	.326	.390
Colorado	NL	42	71	18	6	0	3	(2	1)	33	9	15	2	0	19	1	0	2	0	0	—	2	.254	.276	.465
9 ML YEARS		702	2044	523	109	23	62	(35	27)	864	273	242	133	11	571	17	21	12	22	11	.67	37	.256	.305	.423

Paul Abbott

Pitches: Right **Bats:** Right **Pos:** SP-27; RP-1   **Ht:** 6'3" **Wt:** 195 **Born:** 9/15/67 **Age:** 34

		HOW MUCH HE PITCHED						WHAT HE GAVE UP											THE RESULTS					
Year Team	Lg	G	GS	CG	GF	IP	BFP	H	R	ER	HR	SH	SF	HB	TBB	IBB	SO	WP	Bk	W	L	Pct.	ShO	Sv-Op	Hld	ERA
2001 Tacoma *	AAA	1	1	0	0	4	18	1	0	0	0	0	0	1	4	0	4	0	0	0	0	—	0	0-0	0	0.00
1990 Minnesota	AL	7	7	0	0	34.2	162	37	24	23	0	1	1	1	28	0	25	1	0	0	5	.000	0	0-0	0	5.97
1991 Minnesota	AL	15	3	0	1	47.1	210	38	27	25	5	7	3	0	36	1	43	5	0	3	1	.750	0	0-0	0	4.75
1992 Minnesota	AL	6	0	0	5	11	50	12	4	4	1	0	1	1	5	0	13	1	0	0	0	—	0	0-0	0	3.27
1993 Cleveland	AL	5	5	0	0	18.1	84	19	15	13	5	0	0	1	11	1	7	1	0	0	1	.000	0	0-0	0	6.38
1998 Seattle	AL	4	4	0	0	24.2	105	24	11	11	2	0	1	0	10	0	22	3	0	3	1	.750	0	0-0	0	4.01
1999 Seattle	AL	25	7	0	8	72.2	298	50	31	25	9	3	4	0	32	3	68	2	0	6	2	.750	0	0-2	3	3.10
2000 Seattle	AL	35	27	0	2	179	766	164	89	84	23	1	4	5	80	4	100	3	0	9	7	.563	0	0-0	4	4.22
2001 Seattle	AL	28	27	1	0	163	710	145	79	77	21	3	5	7	87	5	118	11	0	17	4	.810	0	0-0	0	4.25
8 ML YEARS		125	80	1	16	550.2	2385	489	280	262	66	15	19	14	289	14	396	27	0	38	21	.644	0	0-2	7	4.28

Brent Abernathy

Bats: Right **Throws:** Right **Pos:** 2B-79; PH/PR-1   **Ht:** 6'1" **Wt:** 185 **Born:** 9/23/77 **Age:** 24

							BATTING											BASERUNNING				PERCENTAGES		
Year Team	Lg	G	AB	H	2B	3B	HR	(Hm	Rd)	TB	R	RBI	TBB	IBB	SO	HBP	SH	SF	SB	CS	SB%	GDP	Avg	OBP	SLG
1997 Hagerstown	A	99	379	117	27	2	1	—	—	151	69	26	30	0	32	6	6	2	22	13	.63	6	.309	.367	.398
1998 Dunedin	A+	124	485	159	36	1	3	—	—	206	85	65	44	0	38	1	12	6	35	13	.73	11	.328	.381	.425
1999 Knoxville	AA	136	577	168	42	1	13	—	—	251	108	62	55	1	47	6	5	7	34	15	.69	11	.291	.355	.435
2000 Syracuse	AAA	92	358	106	21	2	4	—	—	143	47	35	26	1	32	1	3	3	14	13	.52	7	.296	.343	.399
Durham	AAA	27	91	24	6	0	1	—	—	33	14	15	11	0	11	4	3	5	9	2	.82	0	.264	.351	.363
2001 Durham	AAA	61	252	76	20	0	4	—	—	108	45	23	16	0	23	2	3	2	11	4	.73	3	.302	.346	.429
2001 Tampa Bay	AL	79	304	82	17	1	5	(3	2)	116	43	33	27	1	35	0	3	1	8	3	.73	3	.270	.328	.382

5

Bobby Abreu

Bats: Left **Throws:** Right **Pos:** RF-162; PH/PR-3   **Ht:** 6'0" **Wt:** 197 **Born:** 3/11/74 **Age:** 28

							BATTING											BASERUNNING				PERCENTAGES		
Year Team	Lg	G	AB	H	2B	3B	HR	(Hm | Rd)	TB	R	RBI	TBB	IBB	SO	HBP	SH	SF	SB	CS	SB%	GDP	Avg	OBP	SLG
1996 Houston	NL	15	22	5	1	0	0	(0 | 0)	6	1	1	2	0	3	0	0	0	0	0	—	1	.227	.292	.273
1997 Houston	NL	59	188	47	10	2	3	(3 | 0)	70	22	26	21	0	48	1	0	0	7	2	.78	0	.250	.329	.372
1998 Philadelphia	NL	151	497	155	29	6	17	(10 | 7)	247	68	74	84	14	133	0	4	4	19	10	.66	6	.312	.409	.497
1999 Philadelphia	NL	152	546	183	35	11	20	(13 | 7)	300	118	93	109	8	113	3	0	4	27	9	.75	13	.335	.446	.549
2000 Philadelphia	NL	154	576	182	42	10	25	(14 | 11)	319	103	79	100	9	116	1	0	3	28	8	.78	12	.316	.416	.554
2001 Philadelphia	NL	162	588	170	48	4	31	(13 | 18)	319	118	110	106	11	137	1	0	9	36	14	.72	13	.289	.393	.543
6 ML YEARS		693	2417	742	165	33	96	(53 | 43)	1261	430	383	422	42	550	6	4	20	117	43	.73	45	.307	.408	.522

Jose Acevedo

Pitches: Right **Bats:** Right **Pos:** SP-18   **Ht:** 6'0" **Wt:** 185 **Born:** 12/18/77 **Age:** 24

		HOW MUCH HE PITCHED						WHAT HE GAVE UP											THE RESULTS					
Year Team	Lg	G	GS	CG	GF	IP	BFP	H	R	ER	HR	SH	SF	HB	TBB	IBB	SO	WP	Bk	W	L	Pct.	ShO	Sv-Op	Hld	ERA
1997 Chstn-WV	A	15	8	0	3	57.1	245	61	29	25	8	2	1	5	9	0	34	4	1	3	3	.500	0	0--	—	3.92
1998 Chstn-WV	A	25	25	2	0	158.2	668	169	74	69	9	4	3	6	40	0	132	6	0	9	9	.500	0	0--	—	3.91
1999 Clinton	A	24	24	1	0	133.2	553	119	65	56	14	2	3	0	43	0	136	5	3	8	6	.571	1	0--	—	3.77
2000 Dayton	A	25	23	0	2	141	610	135	74	61	16	1	4	6	53	0	123	6	0	11	5	.688	0	0--	—	3.89
2001 Chattanooga	AA	16	11	0	1	78	319	68	34	32	6	5	1	3	25	1	82	2	0	4	4	.500	0	0--	—	3.69
2001 Cincinnati	NL	18	18	0	0	96	417	101	61	58	17	6	3	3	34	2	68	4	0	5	7	.417	0	0-0	0	5.44

Juan Acevedo

Pitches: Right **Bats:** Right **Pos:** RP-59   **Ht:** 6'2" **Wt:** 228 **Born:** 5/5/70 **Age:** 32

		HOW MUCH HE PITCHED						WHAT HE GAVE UP											THE RESULTS					
Year Team	Lg	G	GS	CG	GF	IP	BFP	H	R	ER	HR	SH	SF	HB	TBB	IBB	SO	WP	Bk	W	L	Pct.	ShO	Sv-Op	Hld	ERA
2001 Colo Sprngs *	AAA	6	0	0	3	7	28	3	2	1	0	1	0	0	4	0	7	1	0	0	0	—	0	1--	—	1.29
1995 Colorado	NL	17	11	0	0	65.2	291	82	53	47	15	4	2	6	20	2	40	2	1	4	6	.400	0	0-0	1	6.44
1997 New York	NL	25	2	0	4	47.2	215	52	24	19	6	2	5	4	22	2	33	0	1	3	1	.750	0	0-4	3	3.59
1998 St. Louis	NL	50	9	0	29	98.1	394	83	30	28	7	8	1	4	29	2	56	3	0	8	3	.727	0	15-16	3	2.56
1999 St. Louis	NL	50	12	0	21	102.1	457	115	71	67	17	4	6	4	48	3	52	5	0	6	8	.429	0	4-6	4	5.89
2000 Milwaukee	NL	62	0	0	18	82.2	347	77	38	35	11	1	1	1	31	9	51	3	2	3	7	.300	0	0-2	7	3.81
2001 Col-Fla	NL	59	0	0	20	60.1	282	68	35	28	6	3	3	2	35	9	47	1	0	2	5	.286	0	0-5	4	4.18
2001 Colorado	NL	39	0	0	14	32	153	37	24	20	4	2	1	1	19	6	26	0	0	0	2	.000	0	0-5	3	5.63
Florida	NL	20	0	0	6	28.1	129	31	11	8	2	1	2	1	16	3	21	1	0	2	3	.400	0	0-0	1	2.54
6 ML YEARS		263	34	0	92	457	1986	477	251	224	62	22	18	21	185	27	279	14	4	26	30	.464	0	19-33	22	4.41

Terry Adams

Pitches: Right **Bats:** Right **Pos:** SP-22; RP-21   **Ht:** 6'3" **Wt:** 215 **Born:** 3/6/73 **Age:** 29

		HOW MUCH HE PITCHED						WHAT HE GAVE UP											THE RESULTS					
Year Team	Lg	G	GS	CG	GF	IP	BFP	H	R	ER	HR	SH	SF	HB	TBB	IBB	SO	WP	Bk	W	L	Pct.	ShO	Sv-Op	Hld	ERA
1995 Chicago	NL	18	0	0	7	18	86	22	15	13	0	0	0	0	10	1	15	1	0	1	1	.500	0	1-1	0	6.50
1996 Chicago	NL	69	0	0	22	101	423	84	36	33	6	7	3	1	49	6	78	5	1	3	6	.333	0	4-8	11	2.94
1997 Chicago	NL	74	0	0	39	74	341	91	43	38	3	1	2	1	40	6	64	6	0	2	9	.182	0	18-22	11	4.62
1998 Chicago	NL	63	0	0	15	72.2	330	72	39	35	7	3	3	1	41	3	73	4	3	7	7	.500	0	1-7	13	4.33
1999 Chicago	NL	52	0	0	38	65	277	60	33	29	9	1	3	0	28	2	57	6	0	6	3	.667	0	13-18	3	4.02
2000 Los Angeles	NL	66	0	0	18	84.1	369	80	42	33	6	3	0	0	39	0	56	5	0	6	9	.400	0	2-7	15	3.52
2001 Los Angeles	NL	43	22	0	10	166.1	708	172	84	80	9	6	0	3	54	1	141	7	2	12	8	.600	0	0-1	4	4.33
7 ML YEARS		385	22	0	149	581.1	2534	581	292	261	40	21	11	6	261	19	484	34	6	37	43	.463	0	39-64	57	4.04

Benny Agbayani

Bats: Right **Throws:** Right **Pos:** LF-84; PH/PR-8   **Ht:** 6'0" **Wt:** 225 **Born:** 12/28/71 **Age:** 30

							BATTING											BASERUNNING				PERCENTAGES		
Year Team	Lg	G	AB	H	2B	3B	HR	(Hm	Rd)	TB	R	RBI	TBB	IBB	SO	HBP	SH	SF	SB	CS	SB%	GDP	Avg	OBP	SLG
2001 Norfolk *	AAA	4	16	5	1	0	1	—	—	9	3	3	1	0	0	0	0	0	0	0	—	1	.313	.353	.563
1998 New York	NL	11	15	2	0	0	0	(0	0)	2	1	0	1	0	5	0	0	0	0	2	.00	1	.133	.188	.133
1999 New York	NL	101	276	79	18	3	14	(10	4)	145	42	42	32	4	60	3	0	3	6	4	.60	8	.286	.363	.525
2000 New York	NL	119	350	101	20	1	15	(9	6)	168	59	60	54	2	68	7	0	3	5	5	.50	6	.289	.391	.480
2001 New York	NL	91	296	82	14	2	6	(4	2)	118	28	27	36	0	73	5	1	1	4	5	.44	11	.277	.364	.399
4 ML YEARS		322	937	264	52	6	35	(23	12)	433	130	129	123	6	206	15	1	7	15	16	.48	26	.282	.372	.462

Kurt Ainsworth

Pitches: Right **Bats:** Right **Pos:** RP-2   **Ht:** 6'3" **Wt:** 192 **Born:** 9/9/78 **Age:** 23

		HOW MUCH HE PITCHED						WHAT HE GAVE UP											THE RESULTS					
Year Team	Lg	G	GS	CG	GF	IP	BFP	H	R	ER	HR	SH	SF	HB	TBB	IBB	SO	WP	Bk	W	L	Pct.	ShO	Sv-Op	Hld	ERA
1999 Salem-Keizr	A-	10	10	1	0	44.2	187	34	18	8	1	3	2	3	18	0	64	3	0	3	3	.500	0	0--	—	1.61
2000 Shreveport	AA	28	28	0	0	158	667	138	67	58	12	4	5	3	63	3	130	7	1	10	9	.526	0	0--	—	3.30
2001 Fresno	AAA	27	26	0	0	149	634	139	91	84	22	4	6	7	54	1	157	10	0	10	9	.526	0	0--	—	5.07
2001 San Francisco	NL	2	0	0	2	2	12	3	3	3	1	0	0	1	2	0	3	0	0	0	0	—	0	0-0	0	13.50

Israel Alcantara

Bats: R **Throws:** R **Pos:** LF-6; 1B-4; RF-2; PH/PR-2; DH-1   **Ht:** 6'2" **Wt:** 180 **Born:** 5/6/73 **Age:** 29

							BATTING											BASERUNNING				PERCENTAGES		
Year Team	Lg	G	AB	H	2B	3B	HR	(Hm	Rd)	TB	R	RBI	TBB	IBB	SO	HBP	SH	SF	SB	CS	SB%	GDP	Avg	OBP	SLG
1992 Expos	R	59	224	62	14	2	3	—	—	89	29	37	17	4	35	1	0	2	6	5	.55	8	.277	.328	.397
1993 Burlington	A	126	470	115	26	3	18	—	—	201	65	73	20	2	125	7	1	5	6	7	.46	5	.245	.283	.428

6

BATTING																					BASERUNNING				PERCENTAGES		
Year Team	Lg	G	AB	H	2B	3B	HR	(Hm	Rd)	TB	R	RBI	TBB	IBB	SO	HBP	SH	SF		SB	CS	SB%	GDP		Avg	OBP	SLG
1994 Wst Plm Bch	A+	125	471	134	26	4	15	—	—	213	65	69	26	0	130	3	1	3		9	3	.75	6		.285	.324	.452
1995 Harrisburg	AA	71	237	50	12	2	10	—	—	96	25	29	21	1	81	2	1	1		1	1	.50	5		.211	.280	.405
Wst Plm Bch	A+	39	134	37	7	2	3	—	—	57	16	22	9	0	35	2	2	1		3	0	1.00	5		.276	.329	.425
1996 Harrisburg	AA	62	218	46	5	0	8	—	—	75	26	19	14	0	62	1	0	1		1	1	.50	5		.211	.261	.344
Expos	R	7	30	9	2	0	2	—	—	17	4	10	3	2	6	0	0	0		0	1	.00	1		.300	.364	.567
Wst Plm Bch	A+	15	61	19	2	0	4	—	—	33	11	14	3	0	13	1	0	1		0	0	—	1		.311	.348	.541
1997 Harrisburg	AA	89	301	85	9	2	27	—	—	179	48	68	29	1	84	3	0	3		4	5	.44	1		.282	.348	.595
1998 St. Pete	A+	38	141	47	5	0	10	—	—	82	21	26	21	2	29	2	0	0		1	0	1.00	6		.333	.427	.582
Reading	AA	53	203	63	12	2	15	—	—	124	36	44	17	2	37	2	0	1		0	1	.00	9		.310	.368	.611
Orlando	AA	15	55	13	4	0	3	—	—	26	8	18	7	0	15	0	0	3		0	1	.00	0		.236	.308	.473
1999 Trenton	AA	77	293	86	26	0	20	—	—	172	48	60	27	0	78	4	0	0		4	2	.67	0		.294	.361	.587
Pawtucket	AAA	24	81	22	3	0	9	—	—	52	13	23	9	0	29	3	0	0		0	0	—	0		.272	.366	.642
2000 Pawtucket	AAA	78	299	92	17	1	29	—	—	198	60	76	25	1	84	4	0	4		2	1	.67	3		.308	.364	.662
2001 Pawtucket	AAA	119	451	134	26	1	36	—	—	270	80	90	57	3	107	5	0	3		9	2	.82	9		.297	.380	.599
2000 Boston	AL	21	45	13	1	0	4	(1	3)	26	9	7	3	0	7	0	0	0		0	0	—	3		.289	.333	.578
2001 Boston	AL	14	38	10	1	0	0	(0	0)	11	3	3	3	0	13	0	0	0		1	0	1.00	0		.263	.317	.289
2 ML YEARS		35	83	23	2	0	4	(1	3)	37	12	10	6	0	20	0	0	0		1	0	1.00	3		.277	.326	.446

Cory Aldridge

Bats: L Throws: R Pos: PH/PR-4; RF-2; LF-1; CF-1   Ht: 6'0" Wt: 210 Born: 6/13/79 Age: 23

BATTING																					BASERUNNING				PERCENTAGES		
Year Team	Lg	G	AB	H	2B	3B	HR	(Hm	Rd)	TB	R	RBI	TBB	IBB	SO	HBP	SH	SF		SB	CS	SB%	GDP		Avg	OBP	SLG
1997 Braves	R	46	169	47	8	1	3	—	—	66	26	37	14	0	37	1	0	0		1	0	1.00	1		.278	.337	.391
1998 Danville	R+	60	214	63	16	1	3	—	—	90	37	33	29	1	48	2	1	1		16	2	.89	3		.294	.382	.421
1999 Macon	A	124	443	111	19	4	12	—	—	174	48	65	33	2	123	6	1	5		9	6	.60	9		.251	.308	.393
2000 Myrtle Bch	A+	109	401	100	18	5	15	—	—	173	51	64	33	2	118	1	0	9		10	5	.67	0		.249	.302	.431
2001 Greenville	AA	131	452	111	19	2	19	—	—	191	57	56	48	1	139	5	0	3		12	6	.67	6		.246	.323	.423
2001 Atlanta	NL	8	5	0	0	0	0	(0	0)	0	1	0	0	0	4	0	0	0		0	0	—	0		.000	.000	.000

Antonio Alfonseca

Pitches: Right Bats: Right Pos: RP-58   Ht: 6'5" Wt: 238 Born: 4/16/72 Age: 30

HOW MUCH HE PITCHED								WHAT HE GAVE UP												THE RESULTS						
Year Team	Lg	G	GS	CG	GF	IP	BFP	H	R	ER	HR	SH	SF	HB	TBB	IBB	SO	WP	Bk	W	L	Pct.	ShO	Sv-Op	Hld	ERA
1997 Florida	NL	17	0	0	2	25.2	123	36	16	14	3	1	0	1	10	3	19	1	0	1	3	.250	0	0-2	0	4.91
1998 Florida	NL	58	0	0	27	70.2	316	75	36	32	10	7	6	3	33	9	46	1	0	4	6	.400	0	8-14	9	4.08
1999 Florida	NL	73	0	0	49	77.2	325	79	28	28	4	3	1	4	29	6	46	1	0	5	4	.444	0	21-25	5	3.24
2000 Florida	NL	68	0	0	62	70	311	82	35	33	7	3	1	4	24	3	47	0	2	5	6	.455	0	**45-49**	1	4.24
2001 Florida	NL	58	0	0	52	61.2	268	68	24	21	6	5	1	5	15	3	40	2	0	4	4	.500	0	28-34	0	3.06
5 ML YEARS		274	0	0	192	305.2	1343	340	139	128	30	19	9	14	111	24	198	5	2	18	24	.429	0	102-124	14	3.77

Edgardo Alfonzo

Bats: Right Throws: Right Pos: 2B-122; PH/PR-3   Ht: 5'11" Wt: 187 Born: 11/8/73 Age: 28

BATTING																					BASERUNNING				PERCENTAGES		
Year Team	Lg	G	AB	H	2B	3B	HR	(Hm	Rd)	TB	R	RBI	TBB	IBB	SO	HBP	SH	SF		SB	CS	SB%	GDP		Avg	OBP	SLG
2001 Norfolk *	AAA	2	8	0	0	0	0	—	—	0	0	0	0	0	0	0	0	0		0	0	—	1		.000	.000	.000
1995 New York	NL	101	335	93	13	5	4	(0	4)	128	26	41	12	1	37	1	4	4		1	1	.50	7		.278	.301	.382
1996 New York	NL	123	368	96	15	2	4	(2	2)	127	36	40	25	2	56	0	9	5		2	0	1.00	8		.261	.304	.345
1997 New York	NL	151	518	163	27	2	10	(4	6)	224	84	72	63	0	56	5	8	5		11	6	.65	4		.315	.391	.432
1998 New York	NL	144	557	155	28	2	17	(8	9)	238	94	78	65	1	77	3	2	3		8	3	.73	11		.278	.355	.427
1999 New York	NL	158	628	191	41	1	27	(11	16)	315	123	108	85	2	85	3	1	9		9	2	.82	14		.304	.385	.502
2000 New York	NL	150	544	176	40	2	25	(13	12)	295	109	94	95	1	70	5	0	6		3	2	.60	12		.324	.425	.542
2001 New York	NL	124	457	111	22	0	17	(6	11)	184	64	49	51	0	62	5	1	5		1	0	1.00	7		.243	.322	.403
7 ML YEARS		951	3407	985	186	14	104	(44	60)	1511	536	482	396	7	443	22	25	37		39	14	.74	63		.289	.363	.443

Luis Alicea

Bats: B Throws: R Pos: 2B-67; DH-22; PH/PR-22; 3B-18   Ht: 5'9" Wt: 176 Born: 7/29/65 Age: 36

BATTING																					BASERUNNING				PERCENTAGES		
Year Team	Lg	G	AB	H	2B	3B	HR	(Hm	Rd)	TB	R	RBI	TBB	IBB	SO	HBP	SH	SF		SB	CS	SB%	GDP		Avg	OBP	SLG
1988 St. Louis	NL	93	297	63	10	4	1	(1	0)	84	20	24	25	4	32	2	4	2		1	1	.50	12		.212	.276	.283
1991 St. Louis	NL	56	68	13	3	0	0	(0	0)	16	5	0	8	0	19	0	0	0		0	1	.00	0		.191	.276	.235
1992 St. Louis	NL	85	265	65	9	11	2	(2	0)	102	26	32	27	1	40	4	2	4		2	5	.29	5		.245	.320	.385
1993 St. Louis	NL	115	362	101	19	3	3	(2	1)	135	50	46	47	2	54	4	1	7		11	1	.92	9		.279	.362	.373
1994 St. Louis	NL	88	205	57	12	5	5	(3	2)	94	32	29	30	4	38	3	1	3		4	5	.44	1		.278	.373	.459
1995 Boston	AL	132	419	113	20	3	6	(0	6)	157	64	44	63	0	61	7	13	9		13	10	.57	10		.270	.367	.375
1996 St. Louis	NL	129	380	98	26	3	5	(4	1)	145	54	42	52	10	78	5	4	6		11	3	.79	4		.258	.350	.382
1997 Anaheim	AL	128	388	98	16	7	5	(2	3)	143	59	37	69	3	65	8	4	2		22	8	.73	4		.253	.375	.369
1998 Texas	AL	101	259	71	15	3	6	(1	5)	110	51	33	37	0	40	5	4	3		4	3	.57	1		.274	.372	.425
1999 Texas	AL	68	164	33	10	0	3	(0	3)	52	33	17	28	0	32	0	3	1		2	1	.67	4		.201	.316	.317
2000 Texas	AL	139	540	159	25	8	6	(4	2)	218	85	63	59	1	75	5	7	7		1	3	.25	13		.294	.365	.404
2001 Kansas City	AL	113	387	106	16	4	4	(1	3)	142	44	32	23	0	56	4	3	1		8	6	.57	6		.274	.320	.367
12 ML YEARS		1247	3734	977	181	51	46	(20	26)	1398	523	399	468	25	590	47	46	45		79	47	.63	69		.262	.347	.374

Chad Allen

Bats: R Throws: R Pos: DH-23; LF-16; RF-15; PH/PR-12   Ht: 6'1" Wt: 195 Born: 2/6/75 Age: 27

BATTING																					BASERUNNING				PERCENTAGES		
Year Team	Lg	G	AB	H	2B	3B	HR	(Hm	Rd)	TB	R	RBI	TBB	IBB	SO	HBP	SH	SF		SB	CS	SB%	GDP		Avg	OBP	SLG
2001 Edmonton *	AAA	6	22	8	2	0	1	—	—	13	4	1	4	0	1	1	0	0		2	0	1.00	0		.364	.481	.591
1999 Minnesota	AL	137	481	133	21	3	10	(4	6)	190	69	46	37	1	89	2	1	2		14	7	.67	10		.277	.330	.395

			BATTING																	BASERUNNING				PERCENTAGES		
Year Team	Lg	G	AB	H	2B	3B	HR	(Hm	Rd)	TB	R	RBI	TBB	IBB	SO	HBP	SH	SF	SB	CS	SB%	GDP	Avg	OBP	SLG
2000 Minnesota	AL	15	50	15	3	0	0	(0	0)	18	2	7	3	0	14	1	0	1	0	2	.00	1	.300	.345	.360
2001 Minnesota	AL	57	175	46	13	2	4	(1	3)	75	20	20	19	1	37	0	0	1	1	2	.33	7	.263	.333	.429
3 ML YEARS		209	706	194	37	5	14	(5	9)	283	91	73	59	2	140	3	1	4	15	11	.58	18	.275	.332	.401

Armando Almanza

Pitches: Left **Bats:** Left **Pos:** RP-52 **Ht:** 6'3" **Wt:** 220 **Born:** 10/26/72 **Age:** 29

		HOW MUCH HE PITCHED						WHAT HE GAVE UP										THE RESULTS					
Year Team	Lg	G	GS	CG	GF	IP	BFP	H	R	ER	HR	SH	SF	HB	TBB	IBB	SO	WP	Bk	W	L	Pct.	ShO	Sv-Op	Hld	ERA
1999 Florida	NL	14	0	0	2	15.2	64	8	4	3	1	1	1	1	9	1	20	0	1	0	1	.000	0	0-0	3	1.72
2000 Florida	NL	67	0	0	8	46.1	216	38	27	25	3	2	2	2	43	6	46	1	0	4	2	.667	0	0-4	13	4.86
2001 Florida	NL	52	0	0	8	41	178	34	24	22	8	1	3	0	26	1	45	2	0	2	2	.500	0	0-2	12	4.83
3 ML YEARS		133	0	0	18	103	458	80	55	50	12	4	6	3	78	8	111	3	1	6	5	.545	0	0-6	28	4.37

Carlos Almanzar

Pitches: Right **Bats:** Right **Pos:** RP-10 **Ht:** 6'2" **Wt:** 200 **Born:** 11/6/73 **Age:** 28

		HOW MUCH HE PITCHED						WHAT HE GAVE UP										THE RESULTS					
Year Team	Lg	G	GS	CG	GF	IP	BFP	H	R	ER	HR	SH	SF	HB	TBB	IBB	SO	WP	Bk	W	L	Pct.	ShO	Sv-Op	Hld	ERA
2001 Columbus *	AAA	35	0	0	27	33.1	137	36	10	9	2	2	0	0	6	2	26	1	0	2	1	.667	0	18--	—	2.43
1997 Toronto	AL	4	0	0	2	3.1	12	1	1	1	1	0	0	0	1	0	4	0	0	0	1	.000	0	0-0	2	2.70
1998 Toronto	AL	25	0	0	8	28.2	129	34	18	17	4	1	0	1	8	2	20	0	0	2	2	.500	0	0-3	1	5.34
1999 San Diego	NL	28	0	0	11	37.1	173	48	32	31	6	2	1	3	15	2	30	2	0	0	0	—	0	0-0	0	7.47
2000 San Diego	NL	62	0	0	11	69.2	308	73	35	34	12	2	3	4	25	2	56	2	0	4	5	.444	0	0-3	8	4.39
2001 New York	AL	10	0	0	7	10.2	46	14	4	4	2	1	1	0	2	1	6	0	0	0	1	.000	0	0-2	0	3.38
5 ML YEARS		129	0	0	39	149.2	668	170	90	87	25	6	5	8	51	7	116	4	0	6	9	.400	0	0-8	9	5.23

Erick Almonte

Bats: Right **Throws:** Right **Pos:** SS-4; PH/PR-4; DH-3 **Ht:** 6'2" **Wt:** 180 **Born:** 2/1/78 **Age:** 24

			BATTING																	BASERUNNING				PERCENTAGES		
Year Team	Lg	G	AB	H	2B	3B	HR	(Hm	Rd)	TB	R	RBI	TBB	IBB	SO	HBP	SH	SF	SB	CS	SB%	GDP	Avg	OBP	SLG
1997 Yankees	R	52	180	51	4	4	3	—	—	72	32	31	21	1	27	0	1	2	8	2	.80	5	.283	.355	.400
1998 Greensboro	A	120	450	94	13	0	6	—	—	125	53	33	29	0	121	3	7	2	6	2	.75	17	.209	.260	.278
1999 Yankees	R	9	30	9	2	0	2	—	—	17	5	9	3	0	10	0	0	1	1	0	1.00	1	.300	.343	.567
Tampa	A+	61	230	59	8	2	5	—	—	86	36	25	18	0	49	2	5	2	3	1	.75	6	.257	.313	.374
2000 Norwich	AA	131	454	123	18	4	15	—	—	194	56	77	35	0	129	3	12	2	12	2	.86	3	.271	.326	.427
2001 Norwich	AA	3	12	3	0	0	0	—	—	3	2	0	1	0	6	0	0	0	1	0	1.00	1	.250	.308	.250
Columbus	AAA	97	345	99	19	3	12	—	—	160	55	55	44	1	90	2	7	2	4	5	.44	7	.287	.369	.464
2001 New York	AL	8	4	2	1	0	0	(0	0)	3	0	0	0	0	1	0	0	0	2	0	1.00	0	.500	.500	.750

Roberto Alomar

Bats: Both **Throws:** Right **Pos:** 2B-157 **Ht:** 6'0" **Wt:** 185 **Born:** 2/5/68 **Age:** 34

			BATTING																	BASERUNNING				PERCENTAGES		
Year Team	Lg	G	AB	H	2B	3B	HR	(Hm	Rd)	TB	R	RBI	TBB	IBB	SO	HBP	SH	SF	SB	CS	SB%	GDP	Avg	OBP	SLG
1988 San Diego	NL	143	545	145	24	6	9	(5	4)	208	84	41	47	5	83	3	16	0	24	6	.80	15	.266	.328	.382
1989 San Diego	NL	158	623	184	27	1	7	(3	4)	234	82	56	53	4	76	1	17	8	42	17	.71	10	.295	.347	.376
1990 San Diego	NL	147	586	168	27	5	6	(4	2)	223	80	60	48	1	72	2	5	5	24	7	.77	16	.287	.340	.381
1991 Toronto	AL	161	637	188	41	11	9	(6	3)	278	88	69	57	3	86	4	16	5	53	11	.83	5	.295	.354	.436
1992 Toronto	AL	152	571	177	27	8	8	(5	3)	244	105	76	87	5	52	5	6	2	49	9	.84	8	.310	.405	.427
1993 Toronto	AL	153	589	192	35	6	17	(8	9)	290	109	93	80	5	67	5	4	5	55	15	.79	13	.326	.408	.492
1994 Toronto	AL	107	392	120	25	4	8	(4	4)	177	78	38	51	2	41	2	7	3	19	8	.70	14	.306	.386	.452
1995 Toronto	AL	130	517	155	24	7	13	(7	6)	232	71	66	47	3	45	0	6	7	30	3	.91	16	.300	.354	.449
1996 Baltimore	AL	153	588	193	43	4	22	(14	8)	310	132	94	90	10	65	1	8	12	17	6	.74	14	.328	.411	.527
1997 Baltimore	AL	112	412	137	23	2	14	(10	4)	206	64	60	40	2	43	3	7	7	9	3	.75	10	.333	.390	.500
1998 Baltimore	AL	147	588	166	36	1	14	(7	7)	246	86	56	59	3	70	2	3	5	18	5	.78	11	.282	.347	.418
1999 Cleveland	AL	159	563	182	40	3	24	(12	12)	300	138	120	99	3	96	7	12	13	37	6	.86	13	.323	.422	.533
2000 Cleveland	AL	155	610	189	40	2	19	(8	11)	290	111	89	64	4	82	6	11	6	39	4	.91	14	.310	.378	.475
2001 Cleveland	AL	157	575	193	34	12	20	(7	13)	311	113	100	80	5	71	4	9	9	30	6	.83	9	.336	.415	.541
14 ML YEARS		2034	7796	2389	446	72	190	(100	90)	3549	1341	1018	902	55	949	45	127	87	446	106	.81	173	.306	.378	.455

Sandy Alomar Jr.

Bats: Right **Throws:** Right **Pos:** C-69; PH/PR-4 **Ht:** 6'5" **Wt:** 235 **Born:** 6/18/66 **Age:** 36

			BATTING																	BASERUNNING				PERCENTAGES		
Year Team	Lg	G	AB	H	2B	3B	HR	(Hm	Rd)	TB	R	RBI	TBB	IBB	SO	HBP	SH	SF	SB	CS	SB%	GDP	Avg	OBP	SLG
1988 San Diego	NL	1	1	0	0	0	0	(0	0)	0	0	0	0	0	1	0	0	0	0	0	—	0	.000	.000	.000
1989 San Diego	NL	7	19	4	1	0	1	(1	0)	8	1	6	3	1	3	0	0	0	0	0	—	1	.211	.318	.421
1990 Cleveland	AL	132	445	129	26	2	9	(5	4)	186	60	66	25	2	46	2	5	6	4	1	.80	10	.290	.326	.418
1991 Cleveland	AL	51	184	40	9	0	0	(0	0)	49	10	7	8	1	24	4	2	1	0	4	.00	4	.217	.264	.266
1992 Cleveland	AL	89	299	75	16	0	2	(1	1)	97	22	26	13	3	32	5	3	0	3	3	.50	7	.251	.293	.324
1993 Cleveland	AL	64	215	58	7	1	6	(3	3)	85	24	32	11	0	28	6	1	4	3	1	.75	3	.270	.318	.395
1994 Cleveland	AL	80	292	84	15	1	14	(4	10)	143	44	43	25	2	31	2	0	1	8	4	.67	7	.288	.347	.490
1995 Cleveland	AL	66	203	61	6	0	10	(4	6)	97	32	35	7	0	26	3	4	1	3	1	.75	8	.300	.332	.478
1996 Cleveland	AL	127	418	110	23	0	11	(3	8)	166	53	50	19	0	42	3	2	2	1	0	1.00	20	.263	.299	.397
1997 Cleveland	AL	125	451	146	37	0	21	(9	12)	246	63	83	19	2	48	3	6	1	0	2	.00	16	.324	.354	.545
1998 Cleveland	AL	117	409	96	26	2	6	(3	3)	144	45	44	18	0	45	5	3	5	0	3	.00	16	.235	.270	.352
1999 Cleveland	AL	37	137	42	13	0	6	(4	2)	73	19	25	4	0	23	0	1	0	1	0	1.00	15	.307	.322	.533
2000 Cleveland	AL	97	356	103	16	2	7	(5	2)	144	44	42	16	1	41	4	4	2	2	2	.50	9	.289	.324	.404
2001 Chicago	AL	70	220	54	8	1	4	(1	3)	76	17	21	12	1	17	2	3	2	1	2	.33	6	.245	.288	.345
14 ML YEARS		1063	3649	1002	203	9	97	(43	54)	1514	434	480	180	13	407	37	36	27	25	24	.51	107	.275	.313	.415

8

Moises Alou

Bats: Right **Throws:** Right **Pos:** RF-130; DH-4; PH/PR-2   **Ht:** 6'3" **Wt:** 195 **Born:** 7/3/66 **Age:** 35

Year Team	Lg	G	AB	H	2B	3B	HR	(Hm	Rd)	TB	R	RBI	TBB	IBB	SO	HBP	SH	SF	SB	CS	SB%	GDP	Avg	OBP	SLG
1990 Pit-Mon	NL	16	20	4	0	1	0	(0	0)	6	4	0	0	0	3	0	1	0	0	0	—	1	.200	.200	.300
1992 Montreal	NL	115	341	96	28	2	9	(6	3)	155	53	56	25	0	46	1	5	5	16	2	.89	5	.282	.328	.455
1993 Montreal	NL	136	482	138	29	6	18	(10	8)	233	70	85	38	9	53	5	3	7	17	6	.74	9	.286	.340	.483
1994 Montreal	NL	107	422	143	31	5	22	(9	13)	250	81	78	42	10	63	2	0	5	7	6	.54	7	.339	.397	.592
1995 Montreal	NL	93	344	94	22	0	14	(4	10)	158	48	58	29	6	56	9	0	4	4	3	.57	9	.273	.342	.459
1996 Montreal	NL	143	540	152	28	2	21	(14	7)	247	87	96	49	7	83	2	0	7	9	4	.69	15	.281	.339	.457
1997 Florida	NL	150	538	157	29	5	23	(12	11)	265	88	115	70	9	85	4	0	7	9	5	.64	13	.292	.373	.493
1998 Houston	NL	159	584	182	34	5	38	(19	19)	340	104	124	84	11	87	5	0	6	11	3	.79	14	.312	.399	.582
2000 Houston	NL	126	454	161	28	2	30	(17	13)	283	82	114	52	4	45	2	0	9	3	3	.50	21	.355	.416	.623
2001 Houston	NL	136	513	170	31	5	27	(15	12)	284	79	108	57	14	57	3	0	8	5	1	.83	18	.331	.396	.554
1990 Pittsburgh	NL	2	5	1	0	0	0	(0	0)	1	0	0	0	0	0	0	0	0	0	0	—	1	.200	.200	.200
Montreal	NL	14	15	3	0	1	0	(0	0)	5	4	0	0	0	3	0	1	0	0	0	—	0	.200	.200	.333
10 ML YEARS		1181	4238	1297	260	29	202	(106	96)	2221	696	834	446	70	578	33	9	58	81	33	.71	112	.306	.372	.524

Wilson Alvarez

Pitches: Left **Bats:** Left **Pos:** SP   **Ht:** 6'1" **Wt:** 245 **Born:** 3/24/70 **Age:** 32

Year Team	Lg	G	GS	CG	GF	IP	BFP	H	R	ER	HR	SH	SF	HB	TBB	IBB	SO	WP	Bk	W	L	Pct.	ShO	Sv-Op	Hld	ERA
2001 Orlando *	AA	5	5	0	0	20.1	92	24	10	10	2	0	1	1	6	0	18	1	0	1	3	.250	0	0--	—	4.43
Durham *	AAA	4	4	0	0	18	79	20	8	6	2	0	2	0	6	0	16	1	0	1	1	.500	0	0--	—	3.00
1989 Texas	AL	1	1	0	0	0	5	3	3	3	2	0	0	0	2	0	0	0	0	0	1	.000	0	0-0	0	—
1991 Chicago	AL	10	9	2	0	56.1	237	47	26	22	9	3	1	0	29	0	32	2	0	3	2	.600	1	0-0	0	3.51
1992 Chicago	AL	34	9	0	4	100.1	455	103	64	58	12	3	4	4	65	2	66	2	0	5	3	.625	0	1-1	3	5.20
1993 Chicago	AL	31	31	1	0	207.2	877	168	78	68	14	13	6	7	122	8	155	2	1	15	8	.652	1	0-0	0	2.95
1994 Chicago	AL	24	24	2	0	161.2	682	147	72	62	16	6	3	0	62	1	108	3	0	12	8	.600	1	0-0	0	3.45
1995 Chicago	AL	29	29	3	0	175	769	171	96	84	21	6	5	2	93	4	118	1	2	8	11	.421	0	0-0	0	4.32
1996 Chicago	AL	35	35	0	0	217.1	946	216	106	102	21	5	2	4	97	3	181	2	0	15	10	.600	0	0-0	0	4.22
1997 CWS-SF		33	33	2	0	212	896	180	97	82	18	10	6	4	91	4	179	5	1	13	11	.542	1	0-0	0	3.48
1998 Tampa Bay	AL	25	25	0	0	142.2	624	130	78	75	18	1	2	9	68	0	107	4	0	6	14	.300	0	0-0	0	4.73
1999 Tampa Bay	AL	28	28	1	0	160	703	159	92	75	22	3	3	6	79	1	128	3	0	9	9	.500	0	0-0	0	4.22
1997 Chicago	AL	22	22	2	0	145.2	613	126	61	49	9	6	5	3	55	1	110	4	0	9	8	.529	1	0-0	0	3.03
San Francisco	NL	11	11	0	0	66.1	283	54	36	33	9	4	1	1	36	3	69	1	1	4	3	.571	0	0-0	0	4.48
10 ML YEARS		250	224	11	4	1433	6194	1324	712	631	153	50	32	36	708	23	1074	24	4	86	77	.528	4	1-1	3	3.96

Brady Anderson

Bats: L **Throws:** L **Pos:** RF-66; LF-56; PH/PR-12; CF-6; DH-4   **Ht:** 6'1" **Wt:** 202 **Born:** 1/18/64 **Age:** 38

Year Team	Lg	G	AB	H	2B	3B	HR	(Hm	Rd)	TB	R	RBI	TBB	IBB	SO	HBP	SH	SF	SB	CS	SB%	GDP	Avg	OBP	SLG
1988 Bos-Bal	AL	94	325	69	13	4	1	(1	0)	93	31	21	23	0	75	4	11	1	10	6	.63	3	.212	.272	.286
1989 Baltimore	AL	94	266	55	12	2	4	(2	2)	83	44	16	43	6	45	3	5	0	16	4	.80	4	.207	.324	.312
1990 Baltimore	AL	89	234	54	5	2	3	(1	2)	72	24	24	31	2	46	5	4	5	15	2	.88	4	.231	.327	.308
1991 Baltimore	AL	113	256	59	12	3	2	(1	1)	83	40	27	38	0	44	5	11	3	12	5	.71	1	.230	.338	.324
1992 Baltimore	AL	159	623	169	28	10	21	(15	6)	280	100	80	98	14	98	9	10	9	53	16	.77	2	.271	.373	.449
1993 Baltimore	AL	142	560	147	36	8	13	(2	11)	238	87	66	82	4	99	10	6	6	24	12	.67	4	.263	.363	.425
1994 Baltimore	AL	111	453	119	25	5	12	(7	5)	190	78	48	57	3	75	10	3	2	31	1	.97	7	.263	.356	.419
1995 Baltimore	AL	143	554	145	33	10	16	(10	6)	246	108	64	87	4	111	10	4	2	26	7	.79	3	.262	.371	.444
1996 Baltimore	AL	149	579	172	37	5	50	(19	31)	369	117	110	76	1	106	22	6	4	21	8	.72	11	.297	.396	.637
1997 Baltimore	AL	151	590	170	39	7	18	(8	10)	277	97	73	84	6	105	19	2	1	18	12	.60	1	.288	.393	.469
1998 Baltimore	AL	133	479	113	28	3	18	(7	11)	201	84	51	75	1	78	15	4	1	21	7	.75	7	.236	.356	.420
1999 Baltimore	AL	150	564	159	28	5	24	(10	14)	269	109	81	96	7	105	24	1	7	36	7	.84	6	.282	.404	.477
2000 Baltimore	AL	141	506	130	26	0	19	(9	10)	213	89	50	92	5	103	8	5	7	16	9	.64	4	.257	.375	.421
2001 Baltimore	AL	131	430	87	12	3	8	(4	4)	129	50	45	60	4	77	8	2	1	12	4	.75	3	.202	.311	.300
1988 Boston	AL	41	148	34	5	3	0	(0	0)	45	14	12	15	0	35	4	4	1	4	2	.67	2	.230	.315	.304
Baltimore	AL	53	177	35	8	1	1	(1	0)	48	17	9	8	0	40	0	7	0	6	4	.60	1	.198	.232	.271
14 ML YEARS		1800	6419	1648	334	67	209	(96	113)	2743	1058	756	942	57	1167	152	74	49	311	100	.76	60	.257	.363	.427

Brian Anderson

Pitches: Left **Bats:** Right **Pos:** SP-22; RP-7   **Ht:** 6'1" **Wt:** 183 **Born:** 4/26/72 **Age:** 30

Year Team	Lg	G	GS	CG	GF	IP	BFP	H	R	ER	HR	SH	SF	HB	TBB	IBB	SO	WP	Bk	W	L	Pct.	ShO	Sv-Op	Hld	ERA
2001 Tucson *	AAA	2	2	0	0	12	44	7	2	2	0	0	0	0	2	0	8	0	0	1	0	1.000	0	0--	—	1.50
1993 California	AL	4	1	0	3	11.1	45	11	5	5	1	0	0	0	2	0	4	0	0	0	0	—	0	0-0	0	3.97
1994 California	AL	18	18	0	0	101.2	441	120	63	59	13	3	6	5	27	0	47	5	5	7	5	.583	0	0-0	0	5.22
1995 California	AL	18	17	1	0	99.2	433	110	66	65	24	5	5	3	30	2	45	1	3	6	8	.429	0	0-0	0	5.87
1996 Cleveland	AL	10	9	0	0	51.1	215	58	29	28	9	2	3	0	14	1	21	2	0	3	1	.750	0	0-0	1	4.91
1997 Cleveland	AL	8	8	0	0	48	199	55	28	25	7	0	5	0	11	0	22	1	0	4	2	.667	0	0-0	0	4.69
1998 Arizona	NL	32	32	2	0	208	845	221	109	100	39	8	3	1	24	2	95	3	6	12	13	.480	1	0-0	0	4.33
1999 Arizona	NL	31	19	2	4	130	549	144	69	66	18	4	0	1	28	3	75	0	2	8	2	.800	1	1-2	1	4.57
2000 Arizona	NL	33	32	2	0	213.1	876	226	101	96	38	6	6	3	39	7	104	1	4	11	7	.611	0	0-0	0	4.05
2001 Arizona	NL	29	22	1	1	133.1	571	156	93	77	25	7	4	1	30	2	55	2	1	4	9	.308	0	0-1	0	5.20
9 ML YEARS		183	158	8	8	996.2	4174	1101	563	521	174	35	32	17	205	17	468	15	21	55	47	.539	2	1-3	2	4.70

Garret Anderson

Bats: Left   Throws: Left   Pos: LF-144; DH-12; CF-12   Ht: 6'3"   Wt: 228   Born: 6/30/72   Age: 30

Year Team	Lg	G	AB	H	2B	3B	HR	(Hm	Rd)	TB	R	RBI	TBB	IBB	SO	HBP	SH	SF	SB	CS	SB%	GDP	Avg	OBP	SLG
1994 California	AL	5	13	5	0	0	0	(0	0)	5	0	1	0	0	2	0	0	0	0	0	—	0	.385	.385	.385
1995 California	AL	106	374	120	19	1	16	(7	9)	189	50	69	19	4	65	1	2	4	6	2	.75	8	.321	.352	.505
1996 California	AL	150	607	173	33	2	12	(7	5)	246	79	72	27	5	84	0	5	3	7	9	.44	22	.285	.314	.405
1997 Anaheim	AL	154	624	189	36	3	8	(5	3)	255	76	92	30	6	70	2	1	5	10	4	.71	20	.303	.334	.409
1998 Anaheim	AL	156	622	183	41	7	15	(4	11)	283	62	79	29	8	80	1	3	3	8	3	.73	13	.294	.325	.455
1999 Anaheim	AL	157	620	188	36	2	21	(10	11)	291	88	80	34	8	81	0	0	6	3	4	.43	15	.303	.336	.469
2000 Anaheim	AL	159	647	185	40	3	35	(20	15)	336	92	117	24	5	87	0	1	9	7	6	.54	21	.286	.307	.519
2001 Anaheim	AL	161	672	194	39	2	28	(13	15)	321	83	123	27	4	100	0	1	5	13	6	.68	12	.289	.314	.478
8 ML YEARS		1048	4179	1237	244	20	135	(66	69)	1926	530	633	190	40	569	4	12	35	54	34	.61	111	.296	.325	.461

Jimmy Anderson

Pitches: Left   Bats: Left   Pos: SP-34   Ht: 6'1"   Wt: 207   Born: 1/22/76   Age: 26

Year Team	Lg	G	GS	CG	GF	IP	BFP	H	R	ER	HR	SH	SF	HB	TBB	IBB	SO	WP	Bk	W	L	Pct.	ShO	Sv-Op	Hld	ERA
1999 Pittsburgh	NL	13	4	0	2	29.1	127	25	15	13	2	2	1	1	16	2	13	4	0	2	1	.667	0	0-0	0	3.99
2000 Pittsburgh	NL	27	26	1	0	144	648	169	94	84	13	5	3	7	58	2	73	6	0	5	11	.313	0	0-0	0	5.25
2001 Pittsburgh	NL	34	34	1	0	206.1	922	232	123	117	15	11	9	11	83	14	89	6	1	9	17	.346	0	0-0	0	5.10
3 ML YEARS		74	64	2	2	379.2	1697	426	232	214	30	18	13	19	157	18	175	16	1	16	29	.356	0	0-0	0	5.07

Marlon Anderson

Bats: Left   Throws: Right   Pos: 2B-140; PH/PR-8   Ht: 5'11"   Wt: 198   Born: 1/6/74   Age: 28

Year Team	Lg	G	AB	H	2B	3B	HR	(Hm	Rd)	TB	R	RBI	TBB	IBB	SO	HBP	SH	SF	SB	CS	SB%	GDP	Avg	OBP	SLG
1998 Philadelphia	NL	17	43	14	3	0	1	(1	0)	20	4	4	1	0	6	0	0	1	2	0	1.00	0	.326	.333	.465
1999 Philadelphia	NL	129	452	114	26	4	5	(4	1)	163	48	54	24	1	61	2	4	2	13	2	.87	6	.252	.292	.361
2000 Philadelphia	NL	41	162	37	8	1	1	(1	0)	50	10	15	12	0	22	0	0	0	2	2	.50	5	.228	.282	.309
2001 Philadelphia	NL	147	522	153	30	2	11	(7	4)	220	69	61	35	5	74	2	10	5	8	5	.62	12	.293	.337	.421
4 ML YEARS		334	1179	318	67	7	18	(13	5)	453	131	134	72	6	163	4	14	8	25	9	.74	23	.270	.312	.384

Matt Anderson

Pitches: Right   Bats: Right   Pos: RP-62   Ht: 6'4"   Wt: 200   Born: 8/17/76   Age: 25

Year Team	Lg	G	GS	CG	GF	IP	BFP	H	R	ER	HR	SH	SF	HB	TBB	IBB	SO	WP	Bk	W	L	Pct.	ShO	Sv-Op	Hld	ERA
1998 Detroit	AL	42	0	0	10	44	194	38	16	16	3	6	3	2	31	4	44	2	0	5	1	.833	0	0-4	6	3.27
1999 Detroit	AL	37	0	0	9	38	180	33	27	24	8	0	2	1	35	1	32	3	0	1	1	.667	0	0-2	3	5.68
2000 Detroit	AL	69	0	0	27	74.1	324	61	44	39	8	2	6	3	45	4	71	4	0	3	2	.600	0	1-1	9	4.72
2001 Detroit	AL	62	0	0	41	56	239	56	33	30	2	1	2	0	18	4	52	9	1	3	1	.750	0	22-24	9	4.82
4 ML YEARS		210	0	0	87	212.1	937	188	120	109	21	9	13	6	129	13	199	18	1	13	5	.722	0	23-31	27	4.62

Rick Ankiel

Pitches: Left   Bats: Left   Pos: SP-6   Ht: 6'1"   Wt: 210   Born: 7/19/79   Age: 22

Year Team	Lg	G	GS	CG	GF	IP	BFP	H	R	ER	HR	SH	SF	HB	TBB	IBB	SO	WP	Bk	W	L	Pct.	ShO	Sv-Op	Hld	ERA
2001 Memphis *	AAA	3	3	0	0	4.1	33	3	10	10	0	0	1	0	17	0	4	12	0	0	2	.000	0	0--	—	20.77
Johnson Cty *	R+	14	14	1	0	87.2	327	42	20	13	1	1	0	6	18	0	158	6	0	5	3	.625	0	0--	—	1.33
1999 St. Louis	NL	9	5	0	1	33	137	26	12	12	2	1	0	1	14	0	39	2	0	0	1	.000	0	0-0	0	3.27
2000 St. Louis	NL	31	30	0	0	175	735	137	80	68	21	8	6	6	90	2	194	12	2	11	7	.611	0	0-0	1	3.50
2001 St. Louis	NL	6	6	0	0	24	124	25	21	19	7	2	3	3	25	0	27	5	0	1	2	.333	0	0-0	0	7.13
3 ML YEARS		46	41	0	1	232	996	188	113	99	30	11	9	10	129	2	260	19	2	12	10	.545	0	1-1	1	3.84

Kevin Appier

Pitches: Right   Bats: Right   Pos: SP-33   Ht: 6'2"   Wt: 200   Born: 12/6/67   Age: 34

Year Team	Lg	G	GS	CG	GF	IP	BFP	H	R	ER	HR	SH	SF	HB	TBB	IBB	SO	WP	Bk	W	L	Pct.	ShO	Sv-Op	Hld	ERA
1989 Kansas City	AL	6	5	0	0	21.2	106	34	22	22	3	0	3	0	12	1	10	0	0	1	4	.200	0	0-0	0	9.14
1990 Kansas City	AL	32	24	3	1	185.2	784	179	67	57	13	5	9	6	54	2	127	6	1	12	8	.600	3	0-0	0	2.76
1991 Kansas City	AL	34	31	6	1	207.2	881	205	97	79	13	8	6	2	61	3	158	7	1	13	10	.565	3	0-0	1	3.42
1992 Kansas City	AL	30	30	3	0	208.1	852	167	59	57	10	8	3	2	68	5	150	4	0	15	8	.652	0	0-0	0	2.46
1993 Kansas City	AL	34	34	5	0	238.2	953	183	74	68	8	3	5	1	81	3	186	5	0	18	8	.692	1	0-0	0	2.56
1994 Kansas City	AL	23	23	1	0	155	653	137	68	66	11	9	7	4	63	7	145	11	1	7	6	.538	0	0-0	0	3.83
1995 Kansas City	AL	31	31	4	0	201.1	832	163	90	87	14	3	3	8	80	1	185	5	0	15	10	.600	1	0-0	0	3.89
1996 Kansas City	AL	32	32	5	0	211.1	874	192	87	85	17	7	4	5	75	2	207	10	1	14	11	.560	1	0-0	0	3.62
1997 Kansas City	AL	34	34	4	0	235.2	972	215	96	89	24	4	4	4	74	2	196	14	1	9	13	.409	1	0-0	0	3.40
1998 Kansas City	AL	3	3	0	0	15	69	21	13	13	3	0	1	1	5	1	9	1	0	1	2	.333	0	0-0	0	7.80
1999 KC-Oak	AL	34	34	1	0	209	926	230	131	120	27	7	5	7	84	4	131	10	1	16	14	.533	0	0-0	0	5.17
2000 Oakland	AL	31	31	1	0	195.1	884	200	109	98	23	5	6	9	102	10	129	6	0	15	11	.577	1	0-0	0	4.52
2001 New York	NL	33	33	1	0	206.2	856	181	89	82	22	6	7	15	64	4	172	12	0	11	10	.524	1	0-0	0	3.57
1999 Kansas City	AL	22	22	1	0	140.1	613	153	81	76	18	5	3	6	51	3	78	5	0	9	9	.500	0	0-0	0	4.87
Oakland	AL	12	12	0	0	68.2	313	77	50	44	9	2	2	1	33	1	53	5	1	7	5	.583	0	0-0	0	5.77
13 ML YEARS		357	345	34	2	2291.1	9642	2107	1002	923	188	65	63	64	823	45	1805	91	6	147	115	.561	12	0-0	1	3.63

Alex Arias

Bats: R Throws: R Pos: 3B-18; PH/PR-18; 1B-17; 2B-13; SS-13   Ht: 6'3"   Wt: 202   Born: 11/20/67   Age: 34

							BATTING													BASERUNNING				PERCENTAGES		
Year Team	Lg	G	AB	H	2B	3B	HR	(Hm	Rd)	TB	R	RBI	TBB	IBB	SO	HBP	SH	SF		SB	CS	SB%	GDP	Avg	OBP	SLG
1992 Chicago	NL	32	99	29	6	0	0	(0	0)	35	14	7	11	0	13	2	1	0		0	0	—	4	.293	.375	.354
1993 Florida	NL	96	249	67	5	1	2	(1	1)	80	27	20	27	0	18	3	1	3		1	1	.50	5	.269	.344	.321
1994 Florida	NL	59	113	27	5	0	0	(0	0)	32	4	15	9	0	19	1	1	1		0	1	.00	5	.239	.298	.283
1995 Florida	NL	94	216	58	9	2	3	(2	1)	80	22	26	22	1	20	2	3	3		1	0	1.00	8	.269	.337	.370
1996 Florida	NL	100	224	62	11	2	3	(1	2)	86	27	26	17	1	28	3	1	1		2	0	1.00	2	.277	.335	.384
1997 Florida	NL	74	93	23	2	0	1	(1	0)	28	13	11	12	0	12	3	4	0		0	1	.00	6	.247	.352	.301
1998 Philadelphia	NL	56	133	39	8	0	1	(1	0)	50	17	16	13	3	18	1	1	1		2	0	1.00	1	.293	.358	.376
1999 Philadelphia	NL	118	347	105	20	1	4	(4	0)	139	43	48	36	6	31	4	1	2		2	2	.50	12	.303	.373	.401
2000 Philadelphia	NL	70	155	29	9	0	2	(1	1)	44	17	15	16	2	28	3	3	3		1	0	1.00	3	.187	.271	.284
2001 San Diego	NL	70	137	31	9	0	2	(0	2)	46	19	12	17	1	22	1	1	2		1	0	1.00	1	.226	.312	.336
10 ML YEARS		769	1766	470	84	6	18	(10	8)	620	203	196	180	14	209	23	17	16		10	5	.67	47	.266	.339	.351

Tony Armas Jr.

Pitches: Right   Bats: Right   Pos: SP-34   Ht: 6'4"   Wt: 205   Born: 4/29/78   Age: 24

		HOW MUCH HE PITCHED						WHAT HE GAVE UP											THE RESULTS						
Year Team	Lg	G	GS	CG	GF	IP	BFP	H	R	ER	HR	SH	SF	HB	TBB	IBB	SO	WP	Bk	W	L	Pct.	ShO	Sv-Op	Hld	ERA
1999 Montreal	NL	1	1	0	0	6	28	8	4	1	0	0	1	0	2	1	2	2	0	0	1	.000	0	0-0	0	1.50
2000 Montreal	NL	17	17	0	0	95	403	74	49	46	10	7	3	3	50	2	59	3	0	7	9	.438	0	0-0	0	4.36
2001 Montreal	NL	34	34	0	0	196.2	851	180	101	88	18	15	6	10	91	6	176	9	1	9	14	.391	0	0-0	0	4.03
3 ML YEARS		52	52	0	0	297.2	1282	262	154	135	28	22	10	13	143	9	237	14	1	16	24	.400	0	0-0	0	4.08

Rolando Arrojo

Pitches: Right   Bats: Right   Pos: RP-32; SP-9   Ht: 6'4"   Wt: 220   Born: 7/18/68   Age: 33

		HOW MUCH HE PITCHED						WHAT HE GAVE UP											THE RESULTS						
Year Team	Lg	G	GS	CG	GF	IP	BFP	H	R	ER	HR	SH	SF	HB	TBB	IBB	SO	WP	Bk	W	L	Pct.	ShO	Sv-Op	Hld	ERA
2001 Sarasota *	A+	2	2	0	0	3	14	4	2	2	0	0	0	1	0	5	0	0	0	0	1	.000	0	0--	—	6.00
1998 Tampa Bay	AL	32	32	2	0	202	853	195	84	80	21	5	3	19	65	2	152	3	1	14	12	.538	2	0-0	0	3.56
1999 Tampa Bay	AL	24	24	2	0	140.2	630	162	84	81	23	5	3	14	60	2	107	2	0	7	12	.368	0	0-0	0	5.18
2000 Col-Bos	AL	32	32	0	0	172.2	771	187	118	108	24	4	7	16	68	6	124	4	2	10	11	.476	0	0-0	0	5.63
2001 Boston	AL	41	9	0	11	103.1	438	88	44	40	8	6	2	12	35	4	78	2	0	5	4	.556	0	5-7	3	3.48
2000 Colorado	NL	19	19	0	0	101.1	470	120	77	68	14	3	7	12	46	6	80	1	2	5	9	.357	0	0-0	0	6.04
Boston	AL	13	13	0	0	71.1	301	67	41	40	10	1	0	4	22	0	44	3	0	5	2	.714	0	0-0	0	5.05
4 ML YEARS		129	97	4	11	618.2	2692	632	330	309	76	20	15	61	228	14	461	11	3	36	39	.480	2	5-7	3	4.50

Bronson Arroyo

Pitches: Right   Bats: Right   Pos: SP-13; RP-11   Ht: 6'5"   Wt: 180   Born: 2/24/77   Age: 25

		HOW MUCH HE PITCHED						WHAT HE GAVE UP											THE RESULTS						
Year Team	Lg	G	GS	CG	GF	IP	BFP	H	R	ER	HR	SH	SF	HB	TBB	IBB	SO	WP	Bk	W	L	Pct.	ShO	Sv-Op	Hld	ERA
1995 Pirates	R	13	9	0	3	61.1	275	72	39	29	4	9	0	4	9	0	48	5	0	5	4	.556	0	0--	—	4.26
1996 Augusta	A	26	26	0	0	135.2	562	123	64	53	11	9	1	7	36	0	107	10	0	8	6	.571	0	0--	—	3.52
1997 Lynchburg	A+	24	24	3	0	160.1	658	154	69	59	17	7	0	3	33	0	121	9	0	12	4	.750	1	0--	—	3.31
1998 Carolina	AA	23	22	1	0	127	573	158	91	77	18	4	6	3	51	0	90	7	0	9	8	.529	0	0--	—	5.46
1999 Altoona	AA	25	25	2	0	153	668	167	73	62	15	5	2	7	58	1	100	6	0	15	4	.789	1	0--	—	3.65
Nashville	AAA	3	3	0	0	13	71	22	15	15	1	0	0	1	10	0	11	0	0	0	2	.000	0	0--	—	10.38
2000 Nashville	AAA	13	13	1	0	88.2	363	82	43	36	7	6	2	3	25	3	52	5	1	8	2	.800	0	0--	—	3.65
Lynchburg	A+	1	1	0	0	7	32	8	3	3	0	0	0	0	2	0	3	0	0	0	0	—	0	0--	—	3.86
2001 Nashville	AAA	9	9	2	0	66.1	276	63	32	29	6	2	1	2	15	1	49	4	0	6	2	.750	1	0--	—	3.93
2000 Pittsburgh	NL	20	12	0	1	71.2	338	88	61	51	10	5	2	4	36	6	50	3	1	2	6	.250	0	0-0	0	6.40
2001 Pittsburgh	NL	24	13	1	1	88.1	390	99	54	50	12	4	6	4	34	6	39	4	1	5	7	.417	0	0-0	2	5.09
2 ML YEARS		44	25	1	2	160	728	187	115	101	22	9	8	8	70	12	89	7	2	7	13	.350	0	0-0	2	5.68

Andy Ashby

Pitches: Right   Bats: Right   Pos: SP-2   Ht: 6'5"   Wt: 202   Born: 7/11/67   Age: 34

		HOW MUCH HE PITCHED						WHAT HE GAVE UP											THE RESULTS						
Year Team	Lg	G	GS	CG	GF	IP	BFP	H	R	ER	HR	SH	SF	HB	TBB	IBB	SO	WP	Bk	W	L	Pct.	ShO	Sv-Op	Hld	ERA
1991 Philadelphia	NL	8	8	0	0	42	186	41	28	28	5	1	3	3	19	0	26	6	0	1	5	.167	0	0-0	0	6.00
1992 Philadelphia	NL	10	8	0	0	37	171	42	31	31	6	2	2	1	21	0	24	2	0	1	3	.250	0	0-0	0	7.54
1993 Col-SD	NL	32	21	0	3	123	577	168	100	93	19	6	7	4	56	5	77	6	3	3	10	.231	0	1-1	0	6.80
1994 San Diego	NL	24	24	4	0	164.1	682	145	75	62	16	11	3	3	43	12	121	5	0	6	11	.353	0	0-0	0	3.40
1995 San Diego	NL	31	31	2	0	192.2	800	180	79	63	17	10	4	11	62	3	150	7	0	12	10	.545	2	0-0	0	2.94
1996 San Diego	NL	24	24	1	0	150.2	612	147	60	54	17	6	2	3	34	1	85	3	0	9	5	.643	0	0-0	0	3.23
1997 San Diego	NL	30	30	2	0	200.2	851	207	108	92	17	13	6	5	49	2	144	3	0	9	11	.450	0	0-0	0	4.13
1998 San Diego	NL	33	33	5	0	226.2	939	223	90	84	23	8	5	7	58	8	151	7	0	17	9	.654	1	0-0	0	3.34
1999 San Diego	NL	31	31	4	0	206	862	204	95	87	26	10	1	7	54	4	132	6	0	14	10	.583	3	0-0	0	3.80
2000 Phi-Atl	NL	31	31	3	0	199.1	867	216	124	109	29	18	10	6	61	9	106	6	1	12	13	.480	1	0-0	0	4.92
2001 Los Angeles	NL	2	2	0	0	11.2	49	14	5	5	2	0	0	0	1	0	7	0	0	2	0	1.000	0	0-0	0	3.86
1993 Colorado	NL	20	9	0	3	54	277	89	54	51	5	3	3	3	32	4	33	2	3	0	4	.000	0	1-1	0	8.50
San Diego	NL	12	12	0	0	69	300	79	46	42	14	3	4	1	24	1	44	4	0	3	6	.333	0	0-0	0	5.48
2000 Philadelphia	NL	16	16	1	0	101.1	455	113	75	64	17	11	9	5	38	5	51	4	0	4	7	.364	0	0-0	0	5.68
Atlanta	NL	15	15	2	0	98	412	103	49	45	12	7	1	1	23	4	55	2	1	8	6	.571	1	0-0	0	4.13
11 ML YEARS		256	243	21	3	1554	6596	1587	795	708	177	85	43	50	458	44	1023	51	4	86	87	.497	7	1-1	0	4.10

Pedro Astacio

Pitches: Right **Bats:** Right **Pos:** SP-26 **Ht:** 6'2" **Wt:** 210 **Born:** 11/28/69 **Age:** 32

Year Team	Lg	G	GS	CG	GF	IP	BFP	H	R	ER	HR	SH	SF	HB	TBB	IBB	SO	WP	Bk	W	L	Pct.	ShO	Sv-Op	Hld	ERA
1992 Los Angeles	NL	11	11	4	0	82	341	80	23	18	1	3	2	2	20	4	43	1	0	5	5	.500	4	0-0	0	1.98
1993 Los Angeles	NL	31	31	3	0	186.1	777	165	80	74	14	7	8	5	68	5	122	8	9	14	9	.609	2	0-0	0	3.57
1994 Los Angeles	NL	23	23	3	0	149	625	142	77	71	18	6	5	4	47	4	108	4	0	6	8	.429	1	0-0	0	4.29
1995 Los Angeles	NL	48	11	1	7	104	436	103	53	49	12	5	3	4	29	5	80	5	0	7	8	.467	1	0-1	2	4.24
1996 Los Angeles	NL	35	32	0	0	211.2	885	207	86	81	18	11	5	9	67	9	130	6	2	9	8	.529	0	0-0	0	3.44
1997 LA-Col	NL	33	31	2	2	202.1	862	200	98	93	24	9	7	9	61	0	166	6	3	12	10	.545	1	0-0	0	4.14
1998 Colorado	NL	35	34	0	0	209.1	938	245	160	145	39	12	3	17	74	0	170	2	0	13	14	.481	0	0-0	0	6.23
1999 Colorado	NL	34	34	7	0	232	1008	258	140	130	38	6	10	11	75	6	210	5	0	17	11	.607	0	0-0	0	5.04
2000 Colorado	NL	32	32	3	0	196.1	875	217	119	115	32	7	4	15	77	5	193	8	0	12	9	.571	0	0-0	0	5.27
2001 Col-Hou	NL	26	26	4	0	169.2	733	181	101	96	22	6	5	13	54	3	144	2	0	8	14	.364	1	0-0	0	5.09
1997 Los Angeles	NL	26	24	2	2	153.2	654	151	75	70	15	9	5	4	47	0	115	4	3	7	9	.438	1	0-0	0	4.10
Colorado	NL	7	7	0	0	48.2	208	49	23	23	9	0	2	5	14	0	51	2	0	5	1	.833	0	0-0	0	4.25
2001 Colorado	NL	22	22	4	0	141	617	151	91	86	21	5	4	10	50	3	125	2	0	6	13	.316	1	0-0	0	5.49
Houston	NL	4	4	0	0	28.2	116	30	10	10	1	1	1	3	4	0	19	0	0	2	1	.667	0	0-0	0	3.14
10 ML YEARS		308	265	27	9	1742.2	7480	1798	937	872	218	72	52	89	572	41	1366	47	14	103	96	.518	10	0-1	2	4.50

Justin Atchley

Pitches: Left **Bats:** Left **Pos:** RP-15 **Ht:** 6'3" **Wt:** 215 **Born:** 9/5/73 **Age:** 28

Year Team	Lg	G	GS	CG	GF	IP	BFP	H	R	ER	HR	SH	SF	HB	TBB	IBB	SO	WP	Bk	W	L	Pct.	ShO	Sv-Op	Hld	ERA
1995 Billings	R+	13	13	0	0	77	327	91	33	30	4	2	1	2	20	2	65	2	1	10	0	1.000	0	0--	—	3.51
1996 Chstn-WV	A	17	16	0	1	91	392	98	42	35	7	4	2	1	23	0	78	0	1	3	3	.500	1	1--	—	3.46
Winston-Sal	A+	12	12	0	0	69	290	74	48	39	13	3	3	2	16	0	50	2	0	3	3	.500	0	0--	—	5.09
1997 Chattanooga	AA	13	13	1	0	67	289	75	45	35	8	2	5	1	14	0	48	5	0	4	2	.667	0	0--	—	4.70
1999 Chattanooga	AA	17	17	0	0	97.1	416	114	48	37	9	1	6	1	22	1	70	1	1	4	9	.308	0	0--	—	3.42
Indianapolis	AAA	5	4	0	1	23.1	106	39	14	14	5	0	0	0	2	0	6	0	0	2	1	.667	0	0--	—	5.40
2000 Louisville	AAA	30	19	0	5	122.1	547	168	83	80	19	2	5	3	26	1	69	8	0	8	6	.571	0	1--	—	5.89
2001 Louisville	AAA	15	0	0	3	14	57	14	1	1	0	1	0	0	3	0	15	0	0	1	0	1.000	0	2--	—	0.64
2001 Cincinnati	NL	15	0	0	2	10.1	48	12	7	7	4	0	0	1	5	2	8	1	0	0	0	—	0	0-2	2	6.10

Rich Aurilia

Bats: Right **Throws:** Right **Pos:** SS-149; PH/PR-9 **Ht:** 6'1" **Wt:** 185 **Born:** 9/2/71 **Age:** 30

Year Team	Lg	G	AB	H	2B	3B	HR	(Hm	Rd)	TB	R	RBI	TBB	IBB	SO	HBP	SH	SF	SB	CS	SB%	GDP	Avg	OBP	SLG
1995 San Francisco	NL	9	19	9	3	0	2	(0	2)	18	4	4	1	0	2	0	1	1	1	0	1.00	1	.474	.476	.947
1996 San Francisco	NL	105	318	76	7	1	3	(1	2)	94	27	26	25	2	52	1	6	2	4	1	.80	1	.239	.295	.296
1997 San Francisco	NL	46	102	28	8	0	5	(1	4)	51	16	19	8	0	15	0	1	2	1	1	.50	3	.275	.321	.500
1998 San Francisco	NL	122	413	110	27	2	9	(5	4)	168	54	49	31	3	62	2	5	2	3	3	.50	3	.266	.319	.407
1999 San Francisco	NL	152	558	157	23	1	22	(9	13)	248	68	80	43	3	71	5	3	5	2	3	.40	16	.281	.336	.444
2000 San Francisco	NL	141	509	138	24	2	20	(12	8)	226	67	79	54	2	90	0	4	4	1	2	.33	15	.271	.339	.444
2001 San Francisco	NL	156	636	206	37	5	37	(15	22)	364	114	97	47	2	83	0	3	3	1	3	.25	14	.324	.369	.572
7 ML YEARS		731	2555	724	129	11	98	(43	55)	1169	350	354	209	12	375	8	23	19	13	13	.50	53	.283	.337	.458

Brad Ausmus

Bats: Right **Throws:** Right **Pos:** C-127; PH/PR-4 **Ht:** 5'11" **Wt:** 195 **Born:** 4/14/69 **Age:** 33

Year Team	Lg	G	AB	H	2B	3B	HR	(Hm	Rd)	TB	R	RBI	TBB	IBB	SO	HBP	SH	SF	SB	CS	SB%	GDP	Avg	OBP	SLG
1993 San Diego	NL	49	160	41	8	1	5	(4	1)	66	18	12	6	0	28	0	0	0	2	0	1.00	4	.256	.283	.413
1994 San Diego	NL	101	327	82	12	1	7	(6	1)	117	45	24	30	12	63	1	6	2	5	1	.83	8	.251	.314	.358
1995 San Diego	NL	103	328	96	16	4	5	(2	3)	135	44	34	31	3	56	2	4	4	16	5	.76	6	.293	.353	.412
1996 SD-Det	NL	125	375	83	16	0	5	(2	3)	114	46	35	39	1	72	5	6	2	4	8	.33	8	.221	.302	.304
1997 Houston	NL	130	425	113	26	1	4	(1	3)	152	45	44	38	4	78	3	6	6	14	6	.70	8	.266	.326	.358
1998 Houston	NL	128	412	111	10	4	6	(2	4)	147	62	45	53	11	60	3	3	1	10	3	.77	18	.269	.356	.357
1999 Detroit	AL	127	458	126	25	6	9	(5	4)	190	62	54	51	0	71	14	3	1	12	9	.57	11	.275	.365	.415
2000 Detroit	AL	150	523	139	25	3	7	(3	4)	191	75	51	69	0	79	6	4	2	11	6	.69	19	.266	.357	.365
2001 Houston	NL	128	422	98	23	4	5	(4	1)	144	45	34	30	6	64	1	6	2	4	1	.80	13	.232	.284	.341
1996 San Diego	NL	50	149	27	4	0	1	(0	1)	34	16	13	13	0	27	3	1	0	1	4	.20	4	.181	.261	.228
Detroit	AL	75	226	56	12	0	4	(2	2)	80	30	22	26	1	45	2	5	2	3	4	.43	4	.248	.328	.354
9 ML YEARS		1041	3430	889	160	24	53	(29	24)	1256	442	333	347	37	571	35	38	20	78	38	.67	93	.259	.332	.366

Jeff Austin

Pitches: Right **Bats:** Right **Pos:** RP-21 **Ht:** 6'0" **Wt:** 185 **Born:** 10/19/76 **Age:** 25

Year Team	Lg	G	GS	CG	GF	IP	BFP	H	R	ER	HR	SH	SF	HB	TBB	IBB	SO	WP	Bk	W	L	Pct.	ShO	Sv-Op	Hld	ERA
1999 Wilmington	A+	18	18	0	0	112.1	473	108	52	47	10	5	3	2	39	0	97	5	0	7	2	.778	0	0--	—	3.77
Wichita	AA	6	6	0	0	34.1	155	40	19	17	1	0	1	2	11	1	21	4	0	3	1	.750	0	0--	—	4.46
2000 Wichita	AA	6	6	0	0	43	168	33	16	14	3	0	2	5	4	0	31	2	0	2	2	.500	0	0--	—	2.93
Omaha	AAA	23	19	1	1	126.2	551	150	85	63	16	3	7	4	35	1	57	8	1	9	8	.529	1	0--	—	4.48
2001 Omaha	AAA	28	8	0	9	70.2	319	89	56	54	14	3	2	4	27	1	55	5	2	3	7	.300	0	2--	—	6.88
2001 Kansas City	AL	21	0	0	9	26	117	27	17	16	4	1	2	1	14	2	27	3	0	0	0	—	0	0-0	1	5.54

12

Bruce Aven

Bats: Right Throws: Right Pos: PH/PR-13; LF-5; RF-4   Ht: 5'9" Wt: 180 Born: 3/4/72 Age: 30

						BATTING												BASERUNNING				PERCENTAGES		
Year Team	Lg	G	AB	H	2B	3B	HR	(Hm | Rd)	TB	R	RBI	TBB	IBB	SO	HBP	SH	SF	SB	CS	SB%	GDP	Avg	OBP	SLG
2001 Las Vegas *	AAA	86	292	76	17	0	8	—	—	117	43	32	24	1	59	5	1	2	5	1	.83	10	.260	.325	.401
1997 Cleveland	AL	13	19	4	1	0	0	(0 | 0)	5	4	2	1	0	5	0	0	0	0	1	.00	0	.211	.250	.263
1999 Florida	NL	137	381	110	19	2	12	(3 | 9)	169	57	70	44	1	82	9	0	6	3	0	1.00	6	.289	.370	.444
2000 Pit-LA	NL	81	168	42	11	0	7	(4 | 3)	74	20	29	8	0	39	0	0	0	2	3	.40	4	.250	.284	.440
2001 Los Angeles	NL	21	24	8	2	0	1	(1 | 0)	13	3	2	0	0	5	2	0	0	0	0	—	0	.333	.385	.542
2000 Pittsburgh	NL	72	148	37	11	0	5	(4 | 1)	63	18	25	5	0	31	0	0	0	2	3	.40	4	.250	.275	.426
Los Angeles	NL	9	20	5	0	0	2	(0 | 2)	11	2	4	3	0	8	0	0	0	0	0	—	0	.250	.348	.550
4 ML YEARS		252	592	164	33	2	20	(8 | 12)	261	84	103	53	1	131	11	0	6	5	4	.56	10	.277	.344	.441

Manny Aybar

Pitches: Right Bats: Right Pos: RP-16; SP-1   Ht: 6'1" Wt: 177 Born: 10/5/74 Age: 27

		HOW MUCH HE PITCHED						WHAT HE GAVE UP												THE RESULTS					
Year Team	Lg	G	GS	CG	GF	IP	BFP	H	R	ER	HR	SH	SF	HB	TBB	IBB	SO	WP	Bk	W	L	Pct.	ShO	Sv-Op	Hld	ERA
2001 Iowa *	AAA	8	7	1	0	43	187	42	26	24	8	2	1	1	16	1	32	2	0	1	2	.333	1	0--	—	5.02
Durham *	AAA	11	3	0	1	31.2	140	40	25	20	5	2	4	0	9	0	29	1	2	1	3	.250	0	0--	—	5.68
1997 St. Louis	NL	12	12	0	0	68	295	66	33	32	8	7	4	4	29	0	41	1	1	2	4	.333	0	0-0	0	4.24
1998 St. Louis	NL	20	14	0	1	81.1	369	90	58	54	6	4	1	2	42	1	57	2	0	6	6	.500	0	0-0	0	5.98
1999 St. Louis	NL	65	1	0	22	69	430	104	67	59	13	4	3	4	36	3	74	1	2	4	5	.444	0	3-5	12	5.47
2000 Col-Cin-Fla	NL	54	0	0	20	79.1	349	74	42	38	11	5	4	2	35	3	45	7	1	2	2	.500	0	0-1	1	4.31
2001 Chicago	NL	17	1	0	1	22.2	113	28	19	16	5	1	1	2	17	0	16	2	0	2	1	.667	0	0-0	2	6.35
2000 Colorado	NL	1	0	0	0	1.2	10	5	3	3	1	0	0	0	0	0	0	0	0	0	1	.000	0	0-0	1	16.20
Cincinnati	NL	32	0	0	10	50.1	226	51	31	27	7	4	3	2	22	2	31	7	1	1	1	.500	0	0-0	0	4.83
Florida	NL	21	0	0	10	27.1	113	18	8	8	3	1	1	0	13	1	14	0	0	1	0	1.000	0	0-1	0	2.63
5 ML YEARS		168	28	0	44	348.1	1556	362	219	199	43	21	13	14	159	7	233	13	4	16	18	.471	0	3-6	15	5.14

Mike Bacsik

Pitches: Left Bats: Left Pos: RP-3   Ht: 6'3" Wt: 190 Born: 11/11/77 Age: 24

		HOW MUCH HE PITCHED						WHAT HE GAVE UP												THE RESULTS					
Year Team	Lg	G	GS	CG	GF	IP	BFP	H	R	ER	HR	SH	SF	HB	TBB	IBB	SO	WP	Bk	W	L	Pct.	ShO	Sv-Op	Hld	ERA
1996 Burlington	R+	13	13	1	0	69.2	276	49	23	17	3	0	2	1	14	0	61	3	1	4	2	.667	0	0--	—	2.20
1997 Columbus	A	28	28	0	0	139	622	163	94	84	16	7	3	9	47	1	100	12	2	4	14	.222	0	0--	—	5.44
1998 Kinston	A+	27	27	1	0	165.2	667	147	64	53	17	5	4	4	37	3	128	4	0	10	9	.526	0	0--	—	2.88
1999 Akron	AA	26	26	1	0	149.1	647	164	84	77	24	5	5	7	47	0	84	4	0	11	11	.500	0	0--	—	4.64
2000 Kinston	A+	11	11	0	0	65	269	72	36	33	4	1	2	2	8	0	56	0	0	3	6	.333	0	0--	—	4.57
Akron	AA	11	11	1	0	71.1	287	61	23	22	3	4	1	3	15	0	44	3	0	7	1	.875	0	0--	—	2.78
2001 Akron	AAA	5	5	0	0	29	124	31	20	18	7	0	2	0	7	0	9	0	0	3	3	.000	0	0--	—	5.59
Buffalo	AA	4	4	1	0	27.1	104	21	7	6	2	0	0	0	3	0	19	0	0	1	1	.500	1	0--	—	1.98
	AAA	21	20	2	0	121.1	501	115	47	44	13	2	0	3	25	0	81	0	0	12	5	.706	0	0--	—	3.26
2001 Cleveland	AL	3	0	0	0	9	45	13	10	9	0	0	1	1	3	1	4	0	0	0	0	—	0	0-0	0	9.00

Benito Baez

Pitches: Left Bats: Left Pos: RP-8   Ht: 6'0" Wt: 160 Born: 5/6/77 Age: 25

		HOW MUCH HE PITCHED						WHAT HE GAVE UP												THE RESULTS					
Year Team	Lg	G	GS	CG	GF	IP	BFP	H	R	ER	HR	SH	SF	HB	TBB	IBB	SO	WP	Bk	W	L	Pct.	ShO	Sv-Op	Hld	ERA
1995 Athletics	R	14	11	1	0	70	303	64	35	26	2	2	2	4	28	0	83	2	0	5	1	.833	0	0--	—	3.34
1996 W Michigan	A	32	20	0	4	129.2	557	123	60	50	6	5	6	2	52	1	92	4	1	8	4	.667	0	4--	—	3.47
1997 Visalia	A+	16	15	1	0	96.2	393	83	40	38	8	1	2	4	28	1	87	0	0	5	5	.500	0	0--	—	3.54
Huntsville	AA	15	7	0	4	42.1	206	64	47	43	8	2	4	1	22	1	27	3	2	2	4	.333	0	0--	—	9.14
1998 Huntsville	AA	34	17	0	11	122.2	579	161	92	79	12	3	5	4	64	0	83	7	1	3	8	.273	0	0--	—	5.80
1999 Midland	AA	37	0	0	9	54.1	243	68	35	33	5	3	7	0	15	2	51	2	2	5	1	.833	0	3--	—	5.47
Vancouver	AAA	11	0	0	4	18	76	18	7	7	2	0	0	0	7	0	19	1	1	0	2	.000	0	1--	—	3.50
2000 Midland	AA	37	0	0	9	53.1	246	61	35	29	4	1	1	1	27	3	50	4	0	5	4	.556	0	0--	—	4.89
2001 Calgary	AAA	49	0	0	15	59.1	232	53	22	20	5	3	0	1	7	1	56	4	0	7	1	.875	0	1--	—	3.03
2001 Florida	NL	8	0	0	3	9.1	55	22	14	14	3	0	0	0	6	0	14	0	0	0	0	—	0	0-0	0	13.50

Danys Baez

Pitches: Right Bats: Right Pos: RP-43   Ht: 6'3" Wt: 225 Born: 9/10/77 Age: 24

		HOW MUCH HE PITCHED						WHAT HE GAVE UP												THE RESULTS					
Year Team	Lg	G	GS	CG	GF	IP	BFP	H	R	ER	HR	SH	SF	HB	TBB	IBB	SO	WP	Bk	W	L	Pct.	ShO	Sv-Op	Hld	ERA
2000 Kinston	A+	9	9	0	0	49.2	221	45	29	26	5	3	1	6	20	0	56	4	1	2	2	.500	0	0--	—	4.71
Akron	AA	18	18	0	0	102.2	426	98	46	42	6	5	6	5	32	0	77	7	0	4	9	.308	0	0--	—	3.68
2001 Akron	AA	1	0	0	0	2	7	1	0	0	0	0	0	0	0	0	2	0	0	0	0	—	0	0--	—	0.00
Buffalo	AAA	16	0	0	8	25.1	100	18	9	9	2	0	1	0	9	0	30	0	1	2	0	1.000	0	3--	—	3.20
2001 Cleveland	AL	43	0	0	8	50.1	202	34	22	14	5	0	1	3	20	4	52	3	0	5	3	.625	0	0-1	14	2.50

Jeff Bagwell

Bats: Right Throws: Right Pos: 1B-160; PH/PR-2   Ht: 6'0" Wt: 195 Born: 5/27/68 Age: 34

						BATTING												BASERUNNING				PERCENTAGES		
Year Team	Lg	G	AB	H	2B	3B	HR	(Hm	Rd)	TB	R	RBI	TBB	IBB	SO	HBP	SH	SF	SB	CS	SB%	GDP	Avg	OBP	SLG
1991 Houston	NL	156	554	163	26	4	15	(6	9)	242	79	82	75	5	116	13	1	7	7	4	.64	12	.294	.387	.437
1992 Houston	NL	162	586	160	34	6	18	(8	10)	260	87	96	84	13	97	12	2	13	10	6	.63	17	.273	.368	.444
1993 Houston	NL	142	535	171	37	4	20	(9	11)	276	76	88	62	6	73	3	0	9	13	4	.76	20	.320	.388	.516
1994 Houston	NL	110	400	147	32	2	39	(23	16)	300	104	116	65	14	65	4	0	10	15	4	.79	12	.368	.451	.750
1995 Houston	NL	114	448	130	29	0	21	(10	11)	222	88	87	79	12	102	6	0	6	12	5	.71	9	.290	.399	.496
1996 Houston	NL	162	568	179	48	2	31	(16	15)	324	111	120	135	20	114	10	0	6	21	7	.75	15	.315	.451	.570

13

Year Team	Lg	G	AB	H	2B	3B	HR	(Hm	Rd)	TB	R	RBI	TBB	IBB	SO	HBP	SH	SF	SB	CS	SB%	GDP	Avg	OBP	SLG
1997 Houston	NL	162	566	162	40	2	43	(22	21)	335	109	135	127	27	122	16	0	8	31	10	.76	10	.286	.425	.592
1998 Houston	NL	147	540	164	33	1	34	(20	14)	301	124	111	109	8	90	7	0	5	19	7	.73	14	.304	.424	.557
1999 Houston	NL	162	562	171	35	0	42	(12	30)	332	143	126	149	16	127	11	0	7	30	11	.73	18	.304	.454	.591
2000 Houston	NL	159	590	183	37	1	47	(28	19)	363	152	132	107	11	116	15	0	7	9	6	.60	19	.310	.424	.615
2001 Houston	NL	161	600	173	43	4	39	(21	18)	341	126	130	106	5	135	6	0	5	11	3	.79	20	.288	.397	.568
11 ML YEARS		1637	5949	1803	394	26	349	(175	174)	3296	1199	1223	1098	137	1157	103	3	83	178	67	.73	166	.303	.415	.554

Cory Bailey

Pitches: Right **Bats:** Right **Pos:** RP-53   **Ht:** 6'1" **Wt:** 200 **Born:** 1/24/71 **Age:** 31

Year Team	Lg	G	GS	CG	GF	IP	BFP	H	R	ER	HR	SH	SF	HB	TBB	IBB	SO	WP	Bk	W	L	Pct.	ShO	Sv-Op	Hld	ERA
2001 Omaha *	AAA	5	0	0	4	10	37	2	0	0	0	1	0	0	5	0	7	0	0	1	0	1.000	0	1--	—	0.00
1993 Boston	AL	11	0	0	5	15.2	66	12	7	6	0	1	1	0	12	3	11	2	1	0	1	.000	0	0-0	0	3.45
1994 Boston	AL	5	0	0	2	4.1	24	10	6	6	2	0	0	0	3	1	4	0	0	0	1	.000	0	0-1	0	12.46
1995 St. Louis	NL	3	0	0	0	3.2	15	2	3	3	0	0	0	0	2	1	5	1	0	0	0	—	0	0-0	0	7.36
1996 St. Louis	NL	51	0	0	12	57	251	57	21	19	1	2	1	1	30	3	38	3	0	5	2	.714	0	0-1	10	3.00
1997 San Francisco	NL	7	0	0	4	9.2	45	15	9	9	1	0	1	0	4	0	5	0	0	1	0	1.000	0	0-0	0	8.38
1998 San Francisco	NL	5	0	0	1	3.1	13	2	1	1	1	0	0	0	1	0	2	0	0	0	0	—	0	0-0	0	2.70
2001 Kansas City	AL	53	0	0	13	67.1	283	57	28	26	3	3	3	0	33	2	61	4	0	1	1	.500	0	0-1	12	3.48
7 ML YEARS		135	0	0	37	161	697	155	75	70	8	6	6	1	85	10	126	10	1	6	6	.500	0	0-3	22	3.91

Harold Baines

Bats: Left **Throws:** Left **Pos:** DH-22; PH/PR-10   **Ht:** 6'2" **Wt:** 195 **Born:** 3/15/59 **Age:** 43

Year Team	Lg	G	AB	H	2B	3B	HR	(Hm	Rd)	TB	R	RBI	TBB	IBB	SO	HBP	SH	SF	SB	CS	SB%	GDP	Avg	OBP	SLG
2001 Charlotte *	AAA	2	8	0	0	0	0	—	—	0	0	0	0	0	1	0	0	0	0	0	—	0	.000	.000	.000
1980 Chicago	AL	141	491	125	23	6	13	(3	10)	199	55	49	19	7	65	1	2	5	2	4	.33	15	.255	.281	.405
1981 Chicago	AL	82	280	80	11	7	10	(3	7)	135	42	41	12	4	41	2	0	2	6	2	.75	6	.286	.318	.482
1982 Chicago	AL	161	608	165	29	8	25	(11	14)	285	89	105	49	10	95	0	2	9	10	3	.77	12	.271	.321	.469
1983 Chicago	AL	156	596	167	33	2	20	(12	8)	264	76	99	49	13	85	1	3	6	7	5	.58	15	.280	.333	.443
1984 Chicago	AL	147	569	173	28	10	29	(16	13)	308	72	94	54	9	75	0	1	5	1	2	.33	12	.304	.361	.541
1985 Chicago	AL	160	640	198	29	3	22	(13	9)	299	86	113	42	8	89	1	0	10	1	1	.50	23	.309	.348	.467
1986 Chicago	AL	145	570	169	29	2	21	(8	13)	265	72	88	38	9	89	2	0	8	2	1	.67	14	.296	.338	.465
1987 Chicago	AL	132	505	148	26	4	20	(12	8)	242	59	93	46	2	82	1	0	2	0	0	—	12	.293	.352	.479
1988 Chicago	AL	158	599	166	39	1	13	(5	8)	246	55	81	67	14	109	1	0	7	0	0	—	21	.277	.347	.411
1989 CWS-Tex	AL	146	505	156	29	1	16	(5	11)	235	73	72	73	13	79	1	0	4	0	3	.00	15	.309	.395	.465
1990 Tex-Oak	AL	135	415	118	15	1	16	(9	7)	183	52	65	67	10	80	0	0	7	0	3	.00	17	.284	.378	.441
1991 Oakland	AL	141	488	144	25	1	20	(11	9)	231	76	90	72	22	67	1	0	5	0	1	.00	16	.295	.383	.473
1992 Oakland	AL	140	478	121	18	0	16	(10	6)	187	58	76	59	6	61	0	0	6	1	3	.25	11	.253	.331	.391
1993 Baltimore	AL	118	416	130	22	0	20	(12	8)	212	64	78	57	9	52	0	1	6	0	0	—	14	.313	.390	.510
1994 Baltimore	AL	94	326	96	12	1	16	(11	5)	158	44	54	30	6	49	1	0	0	0	0	—	9	.294	.356	.485
1995 Baltimore	AL	127	385	115	19	1	24	(7	17)	208	60	63	70	13	45	0	0	4	0	2	.00	17	.299	.403	.540
1996 Chicago	AL	143	495	154	29	0	22	(9	13)	249	80	95	73	7	62	1	0	3	3	1	.75	20	.311	.399	.503
1997 CWS-Bal	AL	137	452	136	23	0	16	(6	10)	207	55	67	55	11	62	0	0	3	0	1	.00	12	.301	.375	.458
1998 Baltimore	AL	104	293	88	17	0	9	(5	4)	132	40	57	32	4	40	1	0	2	0	0	—	17	.300	.369	.451
1999 Bal-Cle	AL	135	430	134	18	1	25	(13	12)	229	62	103	54	3	48	0	0	2	1	2	.33	16	.312	.387	.533
2000 Bal-CWS	AL	96	283	72	13	0	11	(4	7)	118	26	39	36	7	50	0	0	1	0	0	—	6	.254	.338	.417
2001 Chicago	AL	32	84	11	1	0	0	(0	0)	12	3	6	8	0	16	0	0	2	0	0	—	4	.131	.202	.143
1989 Chicago	AL	96	333	107	20	1	13	(4	9)	168	55	56	60	13	52	1	0	3	0	1	.00	11	.321	.423	.505
Texas	AL	50	172	49	9	0	3	(1	2)	67	18	16	13	0	27	0	0	1	0	2	.00	4	.285	.333	.390
1990 Texas	AL	103	321	93	10	1	13	(6	7)	144	41	44	47	9	63	0	0	3	0	1	.00	13	.290	.377	.449
Oakland	AL	32	94	25	5	0	3	(3	0)	39	11	21	20	1	17	0	0	4	0	2	.00	4	.266	.381	.415
1997 Chicago	AL	93	318	97	18	0	12	(5	7)	151	40	52	41	10	47	0	0	2	0	1	.00	9	.305	.382	.475
Baltimore	AL	44	134	39	5	0	4	(1	3)	56	15	15	14	1	15	0	0	1	0	0	—	3	.291	.356	.418
1999 Baltimore	AL	107	345	111	16	1	24	(12	12)	201	57	81	43	3	38	0	0	2	1	2	.33	14	.322	.395	.583
Cleveland	AL	28	85	23	2	0	1	(1	0)	28	5	22	11	0	10	0	0	0	0	0	—	2	.271	.354	.329
2000 Baltimore	AL	72	222	59	8	0	10	(4	6)	97	24	30	29	6	39	0	0	1	0	0	—	6	.266	.349	.437
Chicago	AL	24	61	13	5	0	1	(0	1)	21	2	9	7	1	11	0	0	0	0	0	—	0	.213	.294	.344
22 ML YEARS		2830	9908	2866	488	49	384	(185	199)	4604	1299	1628	1062	187	1441	14	9	99	34	34	.50	298	.289	.356	.465

Paul Bako

Bats: Left **Throws:** Right **Pos:** C-60; PH/PR-1   **Ht:** 6'2" **Wt:** 205 **Born:** 6/20/72 **Age:** 30

Year Team	Lg	G	AB	H	2B	3B	HR	(Hm	Rd)	TB	R	RBI	TBB	IBB	SO	HBP	SH	SF	SB	CS	SB%	GDP	Avg	OBP	SLG
1998 Detroit	AL	96	305	83	12	1	3	(2	1)	106	23	30	23	4	82	0	1	4	1	1	.50	3	.272	.319	.348
1999 Houston	NL	73	215	55	14	1	2	(2	0)	77	16	17	26	3	57	0	3	3	1	1	.50	4	.256	.332	.358
2000 Hou-Fla-Atl	NL	81	221	50	10	1	2	(2	0)	68	18	20	27	10	64	1	1	1	0	0	—	6	.226	.312	.308
2001 Atlanta	NL	61	137	29	10	1	2	(0	2)	47	19	15	20	2	34	0	0	0	1	0	1.00	3	.212	.312	.343
2000 Houston	NL	1	2	0	0	0	0	(0	0)	0	0	0	0	0	1	0	0	0	0	0	—	0	.000	.000	.000
Florida	NL	56	161	39	6	1	0	(0	0)	47	10	14	22	7	48	1	1	1	0	0	—	4	.242	.335	.292
Atlanta	NL	24	58	11	4	0	2	(2	0)	21	8	6	5	3	15	0	0	0	0	0	—	2	.190	.254	.362
4 ML YEARS		311	878	217	46	4	9	(6	3)	298	76	82	96	19	237	1	5	8	3	2	.60	16	.247	.319	.339

James Baldwin

Pitches: Right **Bats:** Right **Pos:** SP-28; RP-1   **Ht:** 6'3" **Wt:** 235 **Born:** 7/15/71 **Age:** 30

Year Team	Lg	G	GS	CG	GF	IP	BFP	H	R	ER	HR	SH	SF	HB	TBB	IBB	SO	WP	Bk	W	L	Pct.	ShO	Sv-Op	Hld	ERA
2001 Charlotte *	AAA	2	2	0	0	12	48	12	7	7	2	1	1	0	2	0	11	0	0	1	0	1.000	0	0--	—	5.25
1995 Chicago	AL	6	4	0	0	14.2	81	32	22	21	6	0	0	0	9	1	10	1	0	0	1	.000	0	0-0	0	12.89
1996 Chicago	AL	28	28	0	0	169	719	168	88	83	24	2	2	4	57	3	127	12	1	11	6	.647	0	0-0	0	4.42

14

Year Team	Lg	HOW MUCH HE PITCHED						WHAT HE GAVE UP												THE RESULTS						
		G	GS	CG	GF	IP	BFP	H	R	ER	HR	SH	SF	HB	TBB	IBB	SO	WP	Bk	W	L	Pct.	ShO	Sv-Op	Hld	ERA
1997 Chicago	AL	32	32	1	0	200	879	205	128	117	19	3	6	5	83	3	140	**14**	**3**	12	15	.444	0	0-0	0	5.27
1998 Chicago	AL	37	24	1	3	159	712	176	103	94	18	3	5	10	60	2	108	5	1	13	6	.684	0	0-1	0	5.32
1999 Chicago	AL	35	33	1	1	199.1	886	219	119	113	34	4	7	7	81	1	123	11	1	12	13	.480	0	0-0	0	5.10
2000 Chicago	AL	29	28	2	0	178	758	185	96	92	34	6	5	8	59	3	116	4	1	14	7	.667	1	0-0	0	4.65
2001 CWS-LA		29	28	2	0	175	764	191	95	86	25	7	7	7	63	1	95	7	0	10	11	.476	1	0-0	0	4.42
2001 Chicago	AL	17	16	2	0	95.2	431	109	56	49	15	3	5	4	38	0	42	4	0	7	5	.583	0	0-0	0	4.61
Los Angeles	NL	12	12	0	0	79.1	333	82	39	37	10	4	2	3	25	1	53	3	0	3	6	.333	0	0-0	0	4.20
7 ML YEARS		196	177	7	4	1095	4799	1176	651	606	160	25	32	41	412	14	719	54	7	72	59	.550	2	0-1	0	4.98

John Bale

Pitches: Left **Bats:** Right **Pos:** RP-14   **Ht:** 6'4" **Wt:** 205 **Born:** 5/22/74 **Age:** 28

Year Team	Lg	HOW MUCH HE PITCHED						WHAT HE GAVE UP												THE RESULTS						
		G	GS	CG	GF	IP	BFP	H	R	ER	HR	SH	SF	HB	TBB	IBB	SO	WP	Bk	W	L	Pct.	ShO	Sv-Op	Hld	ERA
1996 St.Cathrnes	A-	8	8	0	0	33.1	148	39	21	18	2	0	1	0	11	0	35	4	2	3	2	.600	0	0--	—	4.86
1997 Hagerstown	A	25	25	0	0	140.1	603	130	83	67	11	4	3	1	63	1	155	11	0	7	7	.500	0	0--	—	4.30
1998 Dunedin	A+	24	9	0	5	66	290	68	39	34	5	3	5	4	23	1	78	6	1	4	5	.444	0	4--	—	4.64
Knoxville	AA	3	0	0	0	1.1	5	1	1	1	1	0	0	0	0	0	0	0	0	0	0	—	0	0--	—	6.75
1999 Knoxville	AA	33	4	0	9	62.1	265	64	32	26	7	1	0	6	16	1	91	4	0	2	2	.500	0	1--	—	3.75
Syracuse	AAA	6	4	0	0	22.2	92	16	14	10	1	2	3	0	10	0	10	1	0	0	3	.000	0	0--	—	3.97
2000 Syracuse	AAA	21	12	0	2	79	338	68	35	28	4	1	3	2	41	0	70	4	0	3	4	.429	0	0--	—	3.19
2001 Orioles	R	2	2	0	0	4	14	1	1	1	0	0	1	0	2	0	7	1	0	0	0	—	0	0--	—	2.25
Rochester	AAA	9	7	0	0	30.2	125	31	8	7	1	0	2	0	5	0	41	1	0	1	1	.500	0	0--	—	2.05
1999 Toronto	AL	1	0	0	0	2	10	2	3	3	1	0	0	0	2	0	4	0	0	0	0	—	0	0-0	0	13.50
2000 Toronto	AL	2	0	0	0	3.2	22	5	7	6	1	0	1	2	3	0	6	0	0	0	0	—	0	0-0	0	14.73
2001 Baltimore	AL	14	0	0	3	26.2	113	18	14	9	2	0	2	1	17	0	21	1	0	1	0	1.000	0	0-0	2	3.04
3 ML YEARS		17	0	0	3	32.1	145	25	24	18	4	0	3	3	22	0	31	1	0	1	0	1.000	0	0-0	2	5.01

Grant Balfour

Pitches: Right **Bats:** Right **Pos:** RP-2   **Ht:** 6'2" **Wt:** 175 **Born:** 12/30/77 **Age:** 24

Year Team	Lg	HOW MUCH HE PITCHED						WHAT HE GAVE UP												THE RESULTS						
		G	GS	CG	GF	IP	BFP	H	R	ER	HR	SH	SF	HB	TBB	IBB	SO	WP	Bk	W	L	Pct.	ShO	Sv-Op	Hld	ERA
1997 Twins	R	13	12	0	0	67	275	73	31	28	1	0	1	4	20	0	43	3	2	2	4	.333	0	0--	—	3.76
1998 Elizabethtn	R+	13	13	0	0	77.2	327	70	36	29	7	0	2	5	27	0	75	6	0	7	2	.778	0	0--	—	3.36
1999 Quad City	A	19	14	0	2	91.2	368	66	39	36	7	1	1	6	37	0	95	1	0	8	5	.615	0	1--	—	3.53
2000 Fort Myers	A+	35	10	0	13	89	392	91	46	42	8	3	1	8	34	2	90	10	1	8	5	.615	0	6--	—	4.25
2001 New Britain	AA	35	0	0	24	50	197	26	6	6	1	1	0	0	22	2	72	1	0	2	1	.667	0	13--	—	1.08
Edmonton	AAA	11	0	0	2	16.1	73	18	11	10	2	3	1	0	10	1	17	2	0	2	2	.500	0	0--	—	5.51
2001 Minnesota	AL	2	0	0	1	2.2	14	3	4	4	2	1	1	0	3	0	2	0	0	0	0	—	0	0-0	0	13.50

Willie Banks

Pitches: Right **Bats:** Right **Pos:** RP-5   **Ht:** 6'1" **Wt:** 200 **Born:** 2/27/69 **Age:** 33

Year Team	Lg	HOW MUCH HE PITCHED						WHAT HE GAVE UP												THE RESULTS						
		G	GS	CG	GF	IP	BFP	H	R	ER	HR	SH	SF	HB	TBB	IBB	SO	WP	Bk	W	L	Pct.	ShO	Sv-Op	Hld	ERA
2001 Syracuse *	AAA	24	23	0	0	146.2	636	151	63	53	12	1	2	11	53	0	121	11	0	8	5	.615	0	0--	—	3.25
Pawtucket *	AAA	2	2	0	0	12.2	50	8	3	2	0	0	0	1	3	0	12	0	0	2	0	1.000	0	0--	—	1.42
1991 Minnesota	AL	5	3	0	2	17.1	85	21	15	11	1	0	0	0	12	0	16	3	0	1	1	.500	0	0-0	0	5.71
1992 Minnesota	AL	16	12	0	2	71	324	80	46	45	6	2	2	5	37	0	37	5	1	4	4	.500	0	0-0	0	5.70
1993 Minnesota	AL	31	30	0	1	171.1	754	186	91	77	17	4	4	3	78	2	138	9	5	11	12	.478	0	0-0	0	4.04
1994 Chicago	AL	23	23	1	0	138.1	598	139	88	83	16	5	2	2	56	3	91	8	1	8	12	.400	1	0-0	0	5.40
1995 ChC-LA-Fla	NL	25	15	0	2	90.2	430	106	71	57	14	6	3	2	58	7	62	9	1	2	6	.250	0	0-1	1	5.66
1997 New York	AL	5	1	0	1	14	57	9	3	3	0	2	0	1	6	0	8	0	0	3	0	1.000	0	0-1	0	1.93
1998 NYY-Ari		42	0	0	13	58	265	54	37	31	6	6	1	2	37	4	40	5	1	2	3	.400	0	1-2	5	4.81
2001 Boston	AL	5	0	0	1	10.2	42	5	4	1	0	0	0	0	4	0	10	1	0	0	0	—	0	0-0	0	0.84
1995 Chicago	NL	10	0	0	2	11.2	73	27	23	20	5	1	1	0	12	4	9	3	0	0	1	.000	0	0-1	1	15.43
Los Angeles	NL	6	6	0	0	29	138	36	21	13	2	1	1	1	16	2	23	4	1	0	2	.000	0	0-0	0	4.03
Florida	NL	9	9	0	0	50	219	43	27	24	7	4	1	1	30	1	30	2	0	2	3	.400	0	0-0	0	4.32
1998 New York	AL	9	0	0	5	14.1	77	20	16	16	4	2	0	1	12	2	8	1	0	1	1	.500	0	0-0	0	10.05
Arizona	NL	33	0	0	8	43.2	188	34	21	15	2	4	1	1	25	2	32	4	1	1	2	.333	0	1-2	5	3.09
8 ML YEARS		152	84	1	22	571.1	2555	600	355	308	60	25	15	12	288	16	402	40	10	31	38	.449	1	1-4	6	4.85

Rod Barajas

Bats: Right **Throws:** Right **Pos:** C-50; PH/PR-3   **Ht:** 6'2" **Wt:** 229 **Born:** 9/5/75 **Age:** 26

Year Team	Lg	BATTING																		BASERUNNING				PERCENTAGES		
		G	AB	H	2B	3B	HR	(Hm	Rd)	TB	R	RBI	TBB	IBB	SO	HBP	SH	SF	SB	CS	SB%	GDP	Avg	OBP	SLG
1996 Visalia	A+	27	74	12	3	0	0	—	—	15	6	8	7	0	21	1	0	0	0	0	—	3	.162	.244	.203
Lethbridge	R+	51	175	59	9	3	10	—	—	104	47	50	12	0	24	2	0	4	2	1	.67	6	.337	.378	.594
1997 High Desert	A+	57	199	53	11	0	7	—	—	85	24	30	8	0	41	1	0	1	0	2	.00	7	.266	.297	.427
1998 High Desert	A+	113	442	134	26	0	23	—	—	229	67	81	25	2	81	7	0	7	1	1	.50	13	.303	.345	.518
1999 El Paso	AA	127	510	162	41	2	14	—	—	249	77	95	24	6	73	8	0	6	2	0	1.00	8	.318	.354	.488
2000 Tucson	AAA	110	416	94	25	0	13	—	—	158	43	75	14	0	65	5	0	11	4	3	.57	13	.226	.253	.380
2001 Tucson	AAA	45	162	52	13	0	9	—	—	92	23	32	9	2	23	3	1	1	3	1	.75	2	.321	.366	.568
1999 Arizona	NL	5	16	4	1	0	1	(1	0)	8	3	3	1	0	1	0	1	0	0	0	—	0	.250	.294	.500
2000 Arizona	NL	5	13	3	0	0	0	—	—	6	1	3	0	0	4	0	0	0	0	0	—	0	.231	.231	.462
2001 Arizona	NL	51	106	17	3	0	3	(2	1)	29	9	9	4	0	26	0	0	0	0	0	—	0	.160	.191	.274
3 ML YEARS		61	135	24	4	0	5	(4	1)	43	13	15	5	0	31	0	1	0	0	0	—	0	.178	.207	.319

Lorenzo Barcelo

Pitches: Right **Bats:** Right **Pos:** RP-17 **Ht:** 6'4" **Wt:** 230 **Born:** 8/10/77 **Age:** 24

Year Team	Lg	G	GS	CG	GF	IP	BFP	H	R	ER	HR	SH	SF	HB	TBB	IBB	SO	WP	Bk	W	L	Pct.	ShO	Sv-Op	Hld	ERA
1995 Bellingham	A-	12	11	0	0	47	198	43	23	18	3	0	1	2	19	0	34	1	1	3	2	.600	0	0--	—	3.45
1996 Burlington	A	26	26	1	0	152.2	633	138	70	60	19	5	5	5	46	0	139	5	5	12	10	.545	0	0--	—	3.54
1997 San Jose	A+	16	16	1	0	89	378	91	45	39	13	1	3	1	30	2	89	1	2	5	4	.556	1	0--	—	3.94
Shreveport	AA	5	5	0	0	31.1	132	30	19	14	4	1	0	0	8	0	20	0	2	2	0	1.000	0	0--	—	4.02
Birmingham	AA	6	6	0	0	33.1	147	36	20	18	2	0	1	4	9	0	29	1	0	2	1	.667	0	0--	—	4.86
1998 White Sox	R	3	3	0	0	6	24	6	1	1	0	1	0	0	0	0	9	0	0	0	1	.000	0	0--	—	1.50
1999 White Sox	R	9	9	0	0	42.2	171	36	14	8	0	1	0	1	6	0	57	3	2	2	1	.667	0	0--	—	1.69
Burlington	A	1	1	0	0	5	18	3	2	2	1	1	0	0	0	0	6	0	0	1	0	1.000	0	0--	—	3.60
Birmingham	AA	4	4	0	0	20	79	14	8	8	0	1	2	1	6	0	14	0	0	0	1	.000	0	0--	—	3.60
2000 Charlotte	AAA	17	17	0	0	99.1	433	114	53	47	20	1	4	4	17	1	62	3	2	5	6	.455	0	0--	—	4.26
2001 Charlotte	AAA	2	0	0	0	5	21	6	3	3	2	0	0	0	1	0	5	0	0	1	0	1.000	0	0--	—	5.40
2000 Chicago	AL	22	1	0	5	39	157	34	17	16	5	0	1	0	9	1	26	1	0	4	2	.667	0	0-1	0	3.69
2001 Chicago	AL	17	0	0	3	21	96	24	13	11	1	1	1	1	8	2	15	1	0	1	0	1.000	0	0-0	—	4.71
2 ML YEARS		39	1	0	8	60	253	58	30	27	6	1	2	1	17	3	41	2	0	5	2	.714	0	0-1	1	4.05

Glen Barker

Bats: Both **Throws:** Right **Pos:** CF-60; PH/PR-36 **Ht:** 5'10" **Wt:** 180 **Born:** 5/10/71 **Age:** 31

Year Team	Lg	G	AB	H	2B	3B	HR	(Hm	Rd)	TB	R	RBI	TBB	IBB	SO	HBP	SH	SF	SB	CS	SB%	GDP	Avg	OBP	SLG
2001 New Orleans *	AAA	46	168	47	2	4	2	—	—	63	28	20	12	0	45	2	4	1	7	3	.70	4	.280	.333	.375
1999 Houston	NL	81	73	21	2	0	1	(0	1)	26	23	11	11	0	19	1	4	1	17	6	.74	0	.288	.384	.356
2000 Houston	NL	84	67	15	2	1	2	(2	0)	25	18	6	7	0	23	1	2	0	9	6	.60	0	.224	.307	.373
2001 Houston	NL	70	24	2	0	0	0	(0	0)	2	12	1	3	0	6	2	0	1	4	6	.40	0	.083	.233	.083
3 ML YEARS		235	164	38	4	1	3	(2	1)	53	53	18	21	0	48	4	6	2	30	18	.63	0	.232	.330	.323

Andy Barkett

Bats: L **Throws:** L **Pos:** LF-9; 1B-4; PH/PR-4; RF-2; DH-1 **Ht:** 6'1" **Wt:** 205 **Born:** 9/5/74 **Age:** 27

Year Team	Lg	G	AB	H	2B	3B	HR	(Hm	Rd)	TB	R	RBI	TBB	IBB	SO	HBP	SH	SF	SB	CS	SB%	GDP	Avg	OBP	SLG
1995 Butte	R+	45	162	54	11	5	5	—	—	90	33	51	33	2	39	3	0	4	1	0	1.00	1	.333	.446	.556
Chston-SC	A	21	78	17	6	0	0	—	—	23	7	12	10	0	27	0	0	3	3	0	.00	3	.218	.297	.295
1996 Charlotte	A+	115	392	112	22	3	6	—	—	158	57	54	57	2	59	5	0	4	3	1	.75	6	.286	.380	.403
1997 Tulsa	AA	130	471	141	34	8	8	—	—	215	82	65	63	2	86	5	1	2	1	3	.25	15	.299	.386	.456
1998 Tulsa	AA	43	157	42	11	1	2	—	—	61	23	31	27	0	22	1	0	1	0	0	—	2	.268	.376	.389
Oklahoma	AAA	80	255	80	17	5	4	—	—	119	38	36	35	2	43	0	0	3	3	4	.43	6	.314	.392	.467
1999 Oklahoma	AAA	132	486	149	32	5	10	—	—	221	70	76	44	4	71	6	0	5	7	7	.50	18	.307	.368	.455
2000 Oklahoma	AAA	13	45	8	2	0	0	—	—	10	4	1	2	0	6	0	0	0	0	0	—	0	.178	.213	.222
Richmond	AAA	75	260	63	17	1	6	—	—	100	22	38	16	1	37	2	2	3	4	2	.67	6	.242	.288	.385
2001 Nashville	AAA	91	273	66	17	0	6	—	—	101	37	42	37	3	46	4	0	5	2	2	.50	5	.242	.335	.370
2001 Pittsburgh	NL	17	46	14	2	0	1	(0	1)	19	5	3	4	1	7	1	0	0	1	0	1.00	2	.304	.373	.413

John Barnes

Bats: Right **Throws:** Right **Pos:** RF-6; LF-3 **Ht:** 6'2" **Wt:** 205 **Born:** 4/24/76 **Age:** 26

Year Team	Lg	G	AB	H	2B	3B	HR	(Hm	Rd)	TB	R	RBI	TBB	IBB	SO	HBP	SH	SF	SB	CS	SB%	GDP	Avg	OBP	SLG
1996 Red Sox	R	30	101	28	4	0	1	—	—	35	9	17	5	0	17	6	0	5	4	0	1.00	3	.277	.333	.347
1997 Michigan	A	130	490	149	19	5	6	—	—	196	80	73	65	3	42	5	0	6	19	5	.79	7	.304	.387	.400
1998 Trenton	AA	100	380	104	18	0	14	—	—	164	53	36	40	3	47	3	2	4	3	8	.27	11	.274	.344	.432
New Britain	AA	20	71	19	4	1	0	—	—	25	9	8	9	0	9	1	0	1	1	1	.50	2	.268	.354	.352
1999 New Britain	AA	129	452	119	21	3	13	—	—	181	62	58	49	3	40	5	1	4	10	2	.83	15	.263	.339	.400
2000 Salt Lake	AAA	120	441	161	37	6	13	—	—	249	107	87	57	0	48	7	1	7	7	6	.54	10	.365	.439	.565
2001 Edmonton	AAA	81	311	91	21	2	8	—	—	140	42	42	27	2	28	11	0	2	3	2	.60	8	.293	.368	.450
2000 Minnesota	AL	11	37	13	4	0	0	(0	0)	17	5	2	2	0	6	2	0	0	0	1	.00	3	.351	.415	.459
2001 Minnesota	AL	9	21	1	0	0	0	(0	0)	1	1	0	1	0	3	1	0	0	0	0	—	0	.048	.130	.048
2 ML YEARS		20	58	14	4	0	0	(0	0)	18	6	2	3	0	9	3	0	0	0	1	.00	3	.241	.313	.310

Larry Barnes

Bats: Left **Throws:** Left **Pos:** 1B-16; PH/PR-2; LF-1 **Ht:** 6'1" **Wt:** 195 **Born:** 7/23/74 **Age:** 27

Year Team	Lg	G	AB	H	2B	3B	HR	(Hm	Rd)	TB	R	RBI	TBB	IBB	SO	HBP	SH	SF	SB	CS	SB%	GDP	Avg	OBP	SLG
1995 Angels	R	56	197	61	8	3	3	—	—	84	42	37	27	0	40	5	1	2	12	5	.71	1	.310	.403	.426
1996 Cedar Rapds	A	131	489	155	36	5	27	—	—	282	84	112	58	5	101	6	1	6	9	6	.60	8	.317	.392	.577
1997 Lk Elsinore	A+	115	446	128	32	2	13	—	—	203	68	71	43	4	84	5	1	5	3	4	.43	6	.287	.353	.455
1998 Lk Elsinore	A+	51	183	45	11	2	7	—	—	81	32	33	22	2	49	1	0	0	2	0	1.00	3	.246	.330	.443
Midland	AA	69	245	67	14	4	6	—	—	109	29	35	28	3	54	1	2	2	4	2	.67	5	.273	.348	.445
1999 Erie	AA	130	497	142	25	9	20	—	—	245	73	100	49	7	99	5	0	16	14	3	.82	7	.286	.346	.493
2000 Edmonton	AAA	103	397	102	22	11	7	—	—	167	56	54	48	5	81	0	0	3	3	6	.33	4	.257	.335	.421
2001 Salt Lake	AAA	100	404	117	21	8	18	—	—	208	78	73	29	1	90	1	0	2	6	1	.86	6	.290	.337	.515
2001 Anaheim	AL	16	40	4	0	0	1	(1	0)	7	2	2	1	0	9	0	0	0	0	0	—	1	.100	.122	.175

16

Michael Barrett

Bats: Right **Throws:** Right **Pos:** C-131; PH/PR-2   **Ht:** 6'2" **Wt:** 200 **Born:** 10/22/76 **Age:** 25

							BATTING											BASERUNNING				PERCENTAGES		
Year Team	Lg	G	AB	H	2B	3B	HR	(Hm | Rd)	TB	R	RBI	TBB	IBB	SO	HBP	SH	SF	SB	CS	SB%	GDP	Avg	OBP	SLG
1998 Montreal	NL	8	23	7	2	0	1	(0 | 1)	12	3	2	3	0	6	1	0	0	0	0	—	0	.304	.407	.522
1999 Montreal	NL	126	433	127	32	3	8	(5 | 3)	189	53	52	32	4	39	3	0	1	0	2	.00	18	.293	.345	.436
2000 Montreal	NL	89	271	58	15	1	1	(0 | 1)	78	28	22	23	5	35	1	1	1	0	1	.00	7	.214	.277	.288
2001 Montreal	NL	132	472	118	33	2	6	(3 | 3)	173	42	38	25	2	54	2	4	3	2	1	.67	14	.250	.289	.367
4 ML YEARS		355	1199	310	82	6	16	(8 | 8)	452	126	114	83	11	134	7	5	5	2	4	.33	39	.259	.309	.377

Kimera Bartee

Bats: Right **Throws:** Right **Pos:** LF-9; PH/PR-3; CF-2   **Ht:** 6'0" **Wt:** 200 **Born:** 7/21/72 **Age:** 29

							BATTING											BASERUNNING				PERCENTAGES		
Year Team	Lg	G	AB	H	2B	3B	HR	(Hm | Rd)	TB	R	RBI	TBB	IBB	SO	HBP	SH	SF	SB	CS	SB%	GDP	Avg	OBP	SLG
2001 Rancho Cuc *	A+	7	30	8	2	0	0	—	—	10	3	1	1	0	11	0	0	0	3	0	1.00	0	.267	.290	.333
Salt Lake *	AAA	40	167	46	13	2	3	—	—	72	23	27	19	2	26	0	2	1	5	1	.83	1	.275	.348	.431
Colo Sprngs *	AAA	24	78	15	2	0	5	—	—	32	14	15	6	0	31	1	1	1	3	0	1.00	0	.192	.256	.410
1996 Detroit	AL	110	217	55	6	1	1	(0 | 1)	66	32	14	17	0	77	0	13	0	20	10	.67	1	.253	.308	.304
1997 Detroit	AL	12	5	1	0	0	0	(0 | 0)	1	4	0	2	0	2	1	0	0	3	1	.75	0	.200	.500	.200
1998 Detroit	AL	57	98	19	5	1	3	(3 | 0)	35	20	15	6	0	35	0	0	1	9	5	.64	1	.194	.238	.357
1999 Detroit	AL	41	77	15	1	3	0	(0 | 0)	22	11	3	9	0	20	0	3	0	3	3	.50	2	.195	.279	.286
2000 Cincinnati	NL	11	4	0	0	0	0	(0 | 0)	0	2	0	0	0	2	1	0	0	1	0	1.00	0	.000	.200	.000
2001 Colorado	NL	12	15	0	0	0	0	(0 | 0)	0	0	1	2	1	5	1	0	1	0	0	—	0	.000	.158	.000
6 ML YEARS		243	416	90	12	5	4	(3 | 1)	124	69	33	36	1	141	3	16	2	36	19	.65	4	.216	.282	.298

Miguel Batista

Pitches: Right **Bats:** Right **Pos:** RP-30; SP-18   **Ht:** 6'2" **Wt:** 195 **Born:** 2/19/71 **Age:** 31

		HOW MUCH HE PITCHED						WHAT HE GAVE UP											THE RESULTS					
Year Team	Lg	G	GS	CG	GF	IP	BFP	H	R	ER	HR	SH	SF	HB	TBB	IBB	SO	WP	Bk	W	L	Pct.	ShO	Sv-Op	Hld	ERA
1992 Pittsburgh	NL	1	0	0	1	2	13	4	2	2	1	0	0	0	3	0	1	0	0	0	0	—	0	0-0	0	9.00
1996 Florida	NL	9	0	0	4	11.1	49	9	8	7	0	3	0	0	7	2	6	1	0	0	0	—	0	0-0	0	5.56
1997 Chicago	NL	11	6	0	2	36.1	168	36	24	23	4	4	4	1	24	2	27	2	0	0	5	.000	0	0-0	0	5.70
1998 Montreal	NL	56	13	0	12	135	598	141	66	57	12	7	5	6	65	7	92	6	1	3	5	.375	0	0-0	3	3.80
1999 Montreal	NL	39	17	2	3	134.2	606	146	88	73	10	8	11	7	58	2	95	6	0	8	7	.533	1	1-1	0	4.88
2000 Mon-KC		18	9	0	2	65.1	310	85	68	62	19	1	2	2	37	2	37	4	0	2	7	.222	0	0-2	0	8.54
2001 Arizona	NL	48	18	0	6	139.1	581	113	57	52	13	9	3	10	60	2	90	6	0	11	8	.579	0	0-0	4	3.36
2000 Montreal	NL	4	0	0	0	8.1	49	19	14	13	2	1	1	2	3	0	7	0	0	0	1	.000	0	0-2	0	14.04
Kansas City	AL	14	9	0	2	57	261	66	54	49	17	0	1	0	34	2	30	4	0	2	6	.250	0	0-0	0	7.74
7 ML YEARS		182	63	2	30	524	2325	534	313	276	59	32	25	26	254	17	348	25	1	24	32	.429	1	1-3	7	4.74

Tony Batista

Bats: R **Throws:** R **Pos:** 3B-101; DH-33; SS-20; PH/PR-3   **Ht:** 6'0" **Wt:** 185 **Born:** 12/9/73 **Age:** 28

							BATTING											BASERUNNING				PERCENTAGES		
Year Team	Lg	G	AB	H	2B	3B	HR	(Hm | Rd)	TB	R	RBI	TBB	IBB	SO	HBP	SH	SF	SB	CS	SB%	GDP	Avg	OBP	SLG
1996 Oakland	AL	74	238	71	10	2	6	(1 | 5)	103	38	25	19	0	49	1	0	2	7	3	.70	2	.298	.350	.433
1997 Oakland	AL	68	188	38	10	1	4	(0 | 4)	62	22	18	14	0	31	2	3	0	2	2	.50	8	.202	.265	.330
1998 Arizona	NL	106	293	80	16	1	18	(9 | 9)	152	46	41	18	0	52	3	0	4	1	1	.50	7	.273	.318	.519
1999 Ari-Tor		142	519	144	30	1	31	(10 | 21)	269	77	100	38	4	96	6	3	7	4	0	1.00	12	.277	.330	.518
2000 Toronto	AL	154	620	163	32	2	41	(25 | 16)	322	96	114	35	1	121	6	0	3	5	4	.56	15	.263	.307	.519
2001 Tor-Bal	AL	156	579	138	27	6	25	(14 | 11)	252	70	87	32	1	113	4	0	7	5	2	.71	9	.238	.280	.435
1999 Arizona	NL	44	144	37	5	0	5	(1 | 4)	57	16	21	16	3	17	2	0	2	2	0	1.00	2	.257	.335	.396
Toronto		98	375	107	25	1	26	(9 | 17)	212	61	79	22	1	79	4	3	5	2	0	1.00	11	.285	.328	.565
2001 Toronto	AL	72	271	56	11	1	13	(9 | 4)	108	29	45	13	1	66	4	0	3	0	1	.00	2	.207	.251	.399
Baltimore	AL	84	308	82	16	5	12	(5 | 7)	144	41	42	19	0	47	0	0	4	5	1	.83	7	.266	.305	.468
6 ML YEARS		700	2437	634	125	13	125	(59 | 66)	1160	349	385	156	6	462	22	6	23	24	12	.67	53	.260	.308	.476

Rick Bauer

Pitches: Right **Bats:** Right **Pos:** SP-6   **Ht:** 6'6" **Wt:** 212 **Born:** 1/10/77 **Age:** 25

		HOW MUCH HE PITCHED						WHAT HE GAVE UP											THE RESULTS					
Year Team	Lg	G	GS	CG	GF	IP	BFP	H	R	ER	HR	SH	SF	HB	TBB	IBB	SO	WP	Bk	W	L	Pct.	ShO	Sv-Op	Hld	ERA
1997 Bluefield	R+	13	13	0	0	72.1	294	58	31	23	1	0	4	4	20	0	67	8	0	8	3	.727	0	0--	—	2.86
Delmarva	A	1	0	0	1	2	7	0	0	0	0	0	0	0	1	0	2	0	0	0	0	—	0	1--	—	0.00
1998 Delmarva	A	22	22	1	0	118	505	127	69	62	11	5	2	8	44	0	81	6	0	5	8	.385	1	0--	—	4.73
1999 Frederick	A+	26	26	4	0	152	662	159	85	77	17	3	11	12	54	2	123	11	1	10	9	.526	0	0--	—	4.56
2000 Frederick	A+	3	3	0	0	19	79	20	13	11	1	0	1	0	6	0	15	2	0	1	0	1.000	0	0--	—	5.21
Bowie	AA	26	23	1	1	129	583	154	89	76	16	3	3	12	39	1	87	4	0	6	8	.429	0	1--	—	5.30
2001 Bowie	AA	9	9	2	0	61	247	52	27	24	8	1	2	5	10	0	34	1	0	2	6	.250	0	0--	—	3.54
Rochester	AAA	19	18	1	0	113.1	493	119	63	49	10	5	3	4	28	0	89	4	0	10	4	.714	1	0--	—	3.89
2001 Baltimore	AL	6	6	0	0	33	143	35	22	17	7	0	1	1	9	0	16	0	0	0	5	.000	0	0-0	0	4.64

Danny Bautista

Bats: R **Throws:** R **Pos:** PH/PR-47; RF-33; CF-28; LF-3   **Ht:** 5'11" **Wt:** 204 **Born:** 5/24/72 **Age:** 30

							BATTING											BASERUNNING				PERCENTAGES		
Year Team	Lg	G	AB	H	2B	3B	HR	(Hm | Rd)	TB	R	RBI	TBB	IBB	SO	HBP	SH	SF	SB	CS	SB%	GDP	Avg	OBP	SLG
1993 Detroit	AL	17	61	19	3	0	1	(0 | 1)	25	6	9	1	0	10	0	0	1	3	1	.75	1	.311	.317	.410
1994 Detroit	AL	31	99	23	4	1	4	(1 | 3)	41	12	15	3	0	18	0	0	0	1	2	.33	3	.232	.255	.414
1995 Detroit	AL	89	271	55	9	0	7	(3 | 4)	85	28	27	12	0	68	0	6	0	4	1	.80	6	.203	.237	.314
1996 Det-Atl		42	84	19	2	0	2	(1 | 1)	27	13	9	11	0	20	1	0	0	1	2	.33	4	.226	.323	.321
1997 Atlanta	NL	64	103	25	3	2	3	(1 | 2)	41	14	9	5	1	24	1	2	1	2	0	1.00	3	.243	.282	.398

17

Year Team	Lg	G	AB	H	2B	3B	HR	(Hm	Rd)	TB	R	RBI	TBB	IBB	SO	HBP	SH	SF	SB	CS	SB%	GDP	Avg	OBP	SLG
						BATTING													BASERUNNING				PERCENTAGES		
1998 Atlanta	NL	82	144	36	11	0	3	(2	1)	56	17	17	7	0	21	0	3	2	1	0	1.00	4	.250	.281	.389
1999 Florida	NL	70	205	59	10	1	5	(2	3)	86	32	24	4	0	30	1	0	1	3	0	1.00	5	.288	.303	.420
2000 Fla-Ari	NL	131	351	100	20	7	11	(5	6)	167	54	59	25	4	50	3	4	5	6	2	.75	11	.285	.333	.476
2001 Arizona	NL	100	222	67	11	2	5	(0	5)	97	26	26	14	1	31	1	2	0	3	2	.60	7	.302	.346	.437
1996 Detroit	AL	25	64	16	2	0	2	(1	1)	24	12	8	9	0	15	0	0	0	1	2	.33	1	.250	.342	.375
Atlanta	NL	17	20	3	0	0	0	(0	0)	3	1	1	2	0	5	1	0	0	0	0	—	3	.150	.261	.150
2000 Florida	NL	44	89	17	4	0	4	(1	3)	33	9	12	5	0	20	0	0	0	1	0	1.00	1	.191	.234	.371
Arizona	NL	87	262	83	16	7	7	(4	3)	134	45	47	20	4	30	3	4	5	5	2	.71	10	.317	.366	.511
9 ML YEARS		626	1540	403	73	13	41	(15	26)	625	202	195	82	6	272	7	17	10	24	10	.71	44	.262	.300	.406

Rod Beck

Pitches: Right **Bats:** Right **Pos:** RP-68　　　　**Ht:** 6'1" **Wt:** 235 **Born:** 8/3/68 **Age:** 33

		HOW MUCH HE PITCHED					WHAT HE GAVE UP											THE RESULTS						
Year Team	Lg	G	GS	CG	GF	IP	BFP	H	R	ER	HR	SH	SF	HB	TBB	IBB	SO	WP	Bk	W	L	Pct.	ShO	Sv-Op	Hld	ERA
1991 San Francisco	NL	31	0	0	10	52.1	214	53	22	22	4	4	2	1	13	2	38	0	0	1	1	.500	0	1-1	1	3.78
1992 San Francisco	NL	65	0	0	42	92	352	62	20	18	4	6	2	2	15	2	87	5	2	3	3	.500	0	17-23	4	1.76
1993 San Francisco	NL	76	0	0	71	79.1	309	57	20	19	11	6	3	3	13	4	86	4	0	3	1	.750	0	48-52	0	2.16
1994 San Francisco	NL	48	0	0	47	48.2	207	49	17	15	10	3	3	0	13	2	39	0	0	2	4	.333	0	28-28	0	2.77
1995 San Francisco	NL	60	0	0	52	58.2	255	60	31	29	7	4	3	2	21	3	42	2	0	5	6	.455	0	33-43	0	4.45
1996 San Francisco	NL	63	0	0	58	62	248	56	23	23	9	0	2	1	10	2	48	1	0	0	9	.000	0	35-42	0	3.34
1997 San Francisco	NL	73	0	0	66	70	281	67	31	27	7	1	0	2	8	2	53	1	0	7	4	.636	0	37-45	1	3.47
1998 Chicago	NL	81	0	0	70	80.1	349	86	33	27	11	2	5	2	20	4	81	2	0	3	4	.429	0	51-58	1	3.02
1999 ChC-Bos	NL	43	0	0	27	44	196	50	29	29	5	2	2	1	18	3	25	1	0	2	5	.286	0	10-15	3	5.93
2000 Boston	AL	34	0	0	8	40.2	169	34	15	14	2	2	0	2	12	1	35	1	0	3	0	1.000	0	0-3	7	3.10
2001 Boston	AL	68	0	0	28	80.2	342	77	42	35	15	3	2	3	28	6	63	5	1	4	6	.400	0	6-11	15	3.90
1999 Chicago	NL	31	0	0	19	30	141	41	26	26	5	2	2	0	13	3	13	1	0	2	4	.333	0	7-11	1	7.80
Boston	AL	12	0	0	8	14	55	9	3	3	0	0	0	1	5	0	12	0	0	0	1	.000	0	3-4	2	1.93
11 ML YEARS		642	0	0	479	708.2	2922	651	283	258	85	33	24	19	171	31	597	22	3	35	41	.461	0	266-321	32	3.28

Josh Beckett

Pitches: Right **Bats:** Right **Pos:** SP-4　　　　**Ht:** 6'4" **Wt:** 190 **Born:** 5/15/80 **Age:** 22

		HOW MUCH HE PITCHED					WHAT HE GAVE UP											THE RESULTS						
Year Team	Lg	G	GS	CG	GF	IP	BFP	H	R	ER	HR	SH	SF	HB	TBB	IBB	SO	WP	Bk	W	L	Pct.	ShO	Sv-Op	Hld	ERA
2000 Kane County	A	13	12	0	0	59.1	232	45	18	14	4	5	0	2	15	0	61	1	1	2	3	.400	0	0- -	—	2.12
2001 Brevard Cty	A+	13	12	0	0	65.2	238	32	13	9	0	2	1	0	15	0	101	1	1	6	0	1.000	0	0- -	—	1.23
Portland	AA	13	13	0	0	74.1	286	50	16	15	8	0	1	4	19	0	102	1	1	8	1	.889	0	0- -	—	1.82
2001 Florida	NL	4	4	0	0	24	99	14	9	4	3	0	0	1	11	0	24	1	0	2	2	.500	0	0-0	0	1.50

Joe Beimel

Pitches: Left **Bats:** Left **Pos:** RP-27; SP-15　　　　**Ht:** 6'2" **Wt:** 201 **Born:** 4/19/77 **Age:** 25

		HOW MUCH HE PITCHED					WHAT HE GAVE UP											THE RESULTS						
Year Team	Lg	G	GS	CG	GF	IP	BFP	H	R	ER	HR	SH	SF	HB	TBB	IBB	SO	WP	Bk	W	L	Pct.	ShO	Sv-Op	Hld	ERA
1998 Erie	A-	17	6	0	3	47	220	56	39	33	6	3	1	5	22	0	37	3	1	1	4	.200	0	0- -	—	6.32
1999 Hickory	A	29	22	0	3	130	570	146	81	64	12	4	5	12	43	0	102	10	2	5	11	.313	0	0- -	—	4.43
2000 Lynchburg	A+	18	18	2	0	120.2	515	111	49	45	6	7	6	8	44	1	82	2	0	10	6	.625	1	0- -	—	3.36
Altoona	AA	10	10	1	0	62.2	279	72	38	29	8	0	2	6	21	0	28	1	3	1	6	.143	0	0- -	—	4.16
2001 Pittsburgh	NL	42	15	0	9	115.1	511	131	72	67	12	3	1	6	49	4	58	3	0	7	11	.389	0	0-0	0	5.23

Kevin Beirne

Pitches: Right **Bats:** Left **Pos:** RP-5　　　　**Ht:** 6'4" **Wt:** 210 **Born:** 1/1/74 **Age:** 28

		HOW MUCH HE PITCHED					WHAT HE GAVE UP											THE RESULTS						
Year Team	Lg	G	GS	CG	GF	IP	BFP	H	R	ER	HR	SH	SF	HB	TBB	IBB	SO	WP	Bk	W	L	Pct.	ShO	Sv-Op	Hld	ERA
1995 White Sox	R	2	0	0	2	3.2	15	2	2	1	0	0	0	1	1	0	3	0	0	0	0	—	0	2- -	—	2.45
Bristol	R+	9	0	0	7	9	35	4	0	0	0	0	0	4	0	12	0	0	0	1	0	1.000	0	2- -	—	0.00
Hickory	A	3	0	0	1	4	16	7	2	2	0	0	0	0	0	0	4	0	0	0	0	—	0	2- -	—	4.50
1996 South Bend	A	26	25	1	0	145.1	627	153	85	67	5	5	5	9	60	0	110	12	3	4	11	.267	0	0- -	—	4.15
1997 Winston-Sal	A+	13	13	1	0	82.2	338	66	38	28	7	1	2	7	28	1	75	5	0	4	4	.500	0	0- -	—	3.05
Birmingham	AA	13	12	0	0	75	336	76	51	41	4	2	3	4	41	0	49	2	1	6	4	.600	0	0- -	—	4.92
1998 Birmingham	AA	26	26	2	0	167.1	702	142	77	64	12	6	6	6	87	2	153	4	2	13	9	.591	1	0- -	—	3.44
Calgary	AAA	2	2	0	0	8	38	12	5	4	1	1	1	1	4	0	6	0	0	0	0	—	0	0- -	—	4.50
1999 Charlotte	AAA	20	20	0	0	113	495	134	75	68	14	1	4	2	36	0	63	12	0	5	5	.500	0	0- -	—	5.42
2000 Charlotte	AAA	7	7	0	0	33.1	143	39	13	13	3	1	0	2	7	0	28	5	0	1	2	.333	0	0- -	—	3.51
2001 Auburn	A-	2	2	0	0	3.1	16	6	2	2	0	0	0	0	1	0	2	0	0	0	0	—	0	0- -	—	5.40
Syracuse	AAA	18	0	0	6	28.2	115	24	6	5	2	2	0	2	3	1	17	0	0	1	1	.500	0	0- -	—	1.57
2000 Chicago	AL	29	1	0	8	49.2	220	50	41	37	6	1	5	4	20	1	41	1	0	1	3	.250	0	0-1	0	6.70
2001 Toronto	AL	5	0	0	2	7	40	13	10	10	1	1	0	0	6	1	5	0	0	0	0	—	0	0-0	0	12.86
2 ML YEARS		34	1	0	10	56.2	260	63	51	47	10	2	5	4	26	2	46	1	0	1	3	.250	0	0-1	0	7.46

Todd Belitz

Pitches: Left **Bats:** Left **Pos:** RP-8　　　　**Ht:** 6'3" **Wt:** 200 **Born:** 10/23/75 **Age:** 26

		HOW MUCH HE PITCHED					WHAT HE GAVE UP											THE RESULTS						
Year Team	Lg	G	GS	CG	GF	IP	BFP	H	R	ER	HR	SH	SF	HB	TBB	IBB	SO	WP	Bk	W	L	Pct.	ShO	Sv-Op	Hld	ERA
1997 Hudson Val	A-	15	15	0	0	74	315	65	41	29	4	1	2	5	18	0	78	0	0	4	5	.444	0	0- -	—	3.53
1998 Chston-SC	A	21	21	0	0	130	530	99	44	35	8	6	1	8	48	0	123	11	1	6	4	.600	0	0- -	—	2.42
St. Pete	A+	7	7	0	0	44.2	188	39	28	25	3	2	2	1	14	0	40	2	0	2	2	.500	0	0- -	—	5.04
1999 Orlando	AA	28	28	0	0	160.2	712	169	114	103	23	3	6	11	65	1	118	2	4	9	9	.500	0	0- -	—	5.77
2000 Durham	AAA	43	0	0	6	47	199	33	24	20	1	1	3	2	28	1	46	1	0	1	1	.500	0	2- -	—	3.83
Sacramento	AAA	12	0	0	1	12.1	52	12	6	6	2	0	0	2	5	0	10	2	0	0	1	.000	0	1- -	—	4.38

Year Team	Lg	G	GS	CG	GF	IP	BFP	H	R	ER	HR	SH	SF	HB	TBB	IBB	SO	WP	Bk	W	L	Pct.	ShO	Sv-Op	Hld	ERA
2001 Sacramento	AAA	38	0	0	12	52.2	225	52	38	30	6	4	1	3	16	3	54	1	1	4	2	.667	0	0--	—	5.13
Colo Spngs	AAA	14	0	0	5	11	57	19	15	12	2	0	0	1	3	0	8	1	0	0	2	.000	0	2--	—	9.82
2000 Oakland	AL	5	0	0	3	3.1	19	4	2	1	0	0	0	0	4	0	3	1	0	0	0	—	0	0-0	0	2.70
2001 Colorado	NL	8	0	0	3	9.1	40	9	8	8	2	1	0	0	3	0	5	0	0	1	1	.500	0	0-0	0	7.71
2 ML YEARS		13	0	0	6	12.2	59	13	10	9	2	1	0	0	7	0	8	1	0	1	1	.500	0	0-0	0	6.39

David Bell

Bats: Right **Throws:** Right **Pos:** 3B-134; PH/PR-3; 1B-2   **Ht:** 5'10" **Wt:** 190 **Born:** 9/14/72 **Age:** 29

Year Team	Lg	G	AB	H	2B	3B	HR	(Hm	Rd)	TB	R	RBI	TBB	IBB	SO	HBP	SH	SF	SB	CS	SB%	GDP	Avg	OBP	SLG
1995 Cle-StL		41	146	36	7	2	2	(1	1)	53	13	19	4	0	25	2	0	1	1	2	.33	0	.247	.275	.363
1996 St. Louis	NL	62	145	31	6	0	1	(1	0)	40	12	9	10	2	22	1	0	1	1	1	.50	3	.214	.268	.276
1997 St. Louis	NL	66	142	30	7	2	1	(1	0)	44	9	12	10	2	28	0	2	1	1	0	1.00	0	.211	.261	.310
1998 StL-Cle-Sea		132	429	117	30	2	10	(2	8)	181	48	49	27	4	65	2	1	5	0	4	.00	11	.273	.315	.422
1999 Seattle	AL	157	597	160	31	2	21	(11	10)	258	92	78	58	0	90	2	3	7	7	4	.64	7	.268	.331	.432
2000 Seattle	AL	133	454	112	24	2	11	(4	7)	173	57	47	42	0	66	6	4	4	2	3	.40	11	.247	.316	.381
2001 Seattle	AL	135	470	122	28	0	15	(7	8)	195	62	64	28	1	59	3	5	4	2	1	.67	8	.260	.303	.415
1995 Cleveland	AL	2	2	0	0	0	0	(0	0)	0	0	0	0	0	0	0	0	0	0	0	—	0	.000	.000	.000
St. Louis	NL	39	144	36	7	2	2	(1	1)	53	13	19	4	0	25	2	0	1	1	2	.33	0	.250	.278	.368
1998 St. Louis	NL	4	9	2	1	0	0	(0	0)	3	0	0	0	0	3	0	0	0	0	0	—	0	.222	.222	.333
Cleveland	AL	107	340	89	21	2	10	(2	8)	144	37	41	22	4	54	2	1	5	0	4	.00	8	.262	.306	.424
Seattle	AL	21	80	26	8	0	0	(0	0)	34	11	8	5	0	8	0	0	0	0	0	—	3	.325	.365	.425
7 ML YEARS		726	2383	608	133	10	61	(27	34)	944	293	278	179	9	355	16	17	23	14	15	.48	42	.255	.309	.396

Derek Bell

Bats: R **Throws:** R **Pos:** RF-43; LF-5; CF-1; PH/PR-1   **Ht:** 6'2" **Wt:** 215 **Born:** 12/11/68 **Age:** 33

Year Team	Lg	G	AB	H	2B	3B	HR	(Hm	Rd)	TB	R	RBI	TBB	IBB	SO	HBP	SH	SF	SB	CS	SB%	GDP	Avg	OBP	SLG
2001 Nashville *	AAA	22	68	11	3	0	1	(—	—)	17	12	9	9	0	19	1	0	1	0	0	—	3	.162	.266	.250
1991 Toronto	AL	18	28	4	0	0	0	(0	0)	4	5	1	6	0	5	1	0	0	3	2	.60	0	.143	.314	.143
1992 Toronto	AL	61	161	39	6	3	2	(2	0)	57	23	15	15	1	34	5	2	1	7	2	.78	6	.242	.324	.354
1993 San Diego	NL	150	542	142	19	1	21	(12	9)	226	73	72	23	5	122	12	0	4	26	5	.84	7	.262	.303	.417
1994 San Diego	NL	108	434	135	20	0	14	(8	6)	197	54	54	29	5	88	1	0	2	24	8	.75	14	.311	.354	.454
1995 Houston	NL	112	452	151	21	2	8	(3	5)	200	63	86	33	2	71	8	0	6	27	9	.75	10	.334	.385	.442
1996 Houston	NL	158	627	165	40	3	17	(8	9)	262	84	113	40	8	123	8	0	9	29	3	.91	18	.263	.311	.418
1997 Houston	NL	129	493	136	29	3	15	(7	8)	216	67	71	40	3	94	12	0	2	15	7	.68	16	.276	.344	.438
1998 Houston	NL	156	630	198	41	2	22	(12	10)	309	111	108	51	0	126	4	0	10	13	3	.81	14	.314	.364	.490
1999 Houston	NL	128	509	120	22	0	12	(5	7)	178	61	66	50	1	129	4	0	5	18	6	.75	20	.236	.306	.350
2000 New York	NL	144	546	145	31	1	18	(8	10)	232	87	69	65	0	125	6	2	3	8	4	.67	14	.266	.348	.425
2001 Pittsburgh	NL	46	156	27	3	0	5	(4	1)	45	14	13	25	5	38	0	2	0	0	2	.00	4	.173	.287	.288
11 ML YEARS		1210	4578	1262	232	15	134	(69	65)	1926	642	668	377	30	955	61	6	46	170	51	.77	123	.276	.336	.421

Jay Bell

Bats: R **Throws:** R **Pos:** 2B-80; 3B-40; PH/PR-14; DH-3   **Ht:** 6'0" **Wt:** 184 **Born:** 12/11/65 **Age:** 36

Year Team	Lg	G	AB	H	2B	3B	HR	(Hm	Rd)	TB	R	RBI	TBB	IBB	SO	HBP	SH	SF	SB	CS	SB%	GDP	Avg	OBP	SLG
1986 Cleveland	AL	5	14	5	2	0	1	(0	1)	10	3	4	2	0	3	0	0	0	0	0	—	0	.357	.438	.714
1987 Cleveland	AL	38	125	27	9	1	2	(1	1)	44	14	13	8	0	31	1	3	0	2	0	1.00	0	.216	.269	.352
1988 Cleveland	AL	73	211	46	5	1	2	(2	0)	59	23	21	21	0	53	1	1	2	4	2	.67	3	.218	.289	.280
1989 Pittsburgh	NL	78	271	70	13	3	2	(1	1)	95	33	27	19	0	47	1	10	2	5	3	.63	9	.258	.307	.351
1990 Pittsburgh	NL	159	583	148	28	7	7	(1	6)	211	93	52	65	0	109	3	39	6	10	6	.63	14	.254	.329	.362
1991 Pittsburgh	NL	157	608	164	32	8	16	(7	9)	260	96	67	52	1	99	4	30	3	10	6	.63	15	.270	.330	.428
1992 Pittsburgh	NL	159	632	167	36	6	9	(5	4)	242	87	55	55	0	103	4	19	2	7	5	.58	12	.264	.326	.383
1993 Pittsburgh	NL	154	604	187	32	9	9	(3	6)	264	102	51	77	6	122	6	13	1	16	10	.62	16	.310	.392	.437
1994 Pittsburgh	NL	110	424	117	35	4	9	(8	5)	187	68	45	49	1	82	3	8	3	2	0	1.00	16	.276	.353	.441
1995 Pittsburgh	NL	138	530	139	28	4	13	(8	5)	214	79	55	55	1	110	4	3	1	2	5	.29	13	.262	.336	.404
1996 Pittsburgh	NL	151	527	132	29	3	13	(7	6)	206	65	71	54	5	108	5	6	6	6	4	.60	10	.250	.323	.391
1997 Kansas City	AL	153	573	167	28	3	21	(10	11)	264	89	92	71	2	101	4	3	9	10	6	.63	13	.291	.368	.461
1998 Arizona	NL	155	549	138	29	5	20	(11	9)	237	79	67	81	3	129	7	5	3	3	5	.38	14	.251	.353	.432
1999 Arizona	NL	151	589	170	32	6	38	(21	17)	328	132	112	82	2	132	4	4	9	7	3	.70	7	.289	.374	.557
2000 Arizona	NL	144	565	151	30	6	18	(9	9)	247	87	68	70	0	88	3	6	5	7	3	.70	7	.267	.348	.437
2001 Arizona	NL	129	428	106	24	1	13	(6	7)	171	59	46	65	3	79	4	8	4	0	1	.00	9	.248	.349	.400
16 ML YEARS		1959	7233	1934	392	67	193	(95	98)	3039	1109	846	826	24	1396	54	158	56	91	60	.60	159	.267	.344	.420

Rob Bell

Pitches: Right **Bats:** Right **Pos:** SP-27   **Ht:** 6'5" **Wt:** 225 **Born:** 1/17/77 **Age:** 25

Year Team	Lg	G	GS	CG	GF	IP	BFP	H	R	ER	HR	SH	SF	HB	TBB	IBB	SO	WP	Bk	W	L	Pct.	ShO	Sv-Op	Hld	ERA
1995 Braves	R	10	8	0	0	34	154	38	29	26	2	0	2	2	14	0	33	7	0	1	6	.143	0	0--	—	6.88
1996 Eugene	A-	16	16	0	0	81	356	89	49	46	5	5	3	3	29	1	74	2	0	5	6	.455	0	0--	—	5.11
1997 Macon	A	27	27	1	0	146.2	614	144	72	60	15	5	5	3	41	1	140	7	0	14	7	.667	0	0--	—	3.68
1998 Danville	A+	28	28	2	0	178.1	736	169	79	65	8	6	6	7	46	0	197	8	0	7	9	.438	0	0--	—	3.28
1999 Reds	R	2	2	0	0	8	26	3	1	1	0	1	0	0	0	0	11	1	0	0	0	—	0	0--	—	1.13
Chattanooga	AA	12	12	2	0	72	293	75	30	25	7	2	2	0	17	0	68	1	0	3	6	.333	1	0--	—	3.13
2000 Louisville	AAA	6	6	0	0	41	170	35	18	17	6	0	0	1	13	0	47	1	0	4	0	1.000	0	0--	—	3.73
2001 Louisville	AAA	5	4	0	0	27	118	32	10	10	4	1	1	1	4	0	26	1	0	2	2	.500	0	0--	—	3.33
2000 Cincinnati	NL	26	26	1	0	140.1	618	130	84	78	32	8	2	1	73	6	112	11	0	7	8	.467	0	0-0	0	5.00
2001 Cin-Tex		27	27	0	0	149.2	670	176	115	111	32	3	9	7	64	1	97	9	0	5	10	.333	0	0-0	0	6.67

19

		HOW MUCH HE PITCHED				WHAT HE GAVE UP			THE RESULTS			
Year Team	Lg	G GS CG GF	IP	BFP	H R ER HR SH SF HB	TBB IBB	SO WP Bk	W L	Pct.	ShO Sv-Op Hld	ERA
2001 Cincinnati	NL	9 9 0 0	44.1	188	46 28 27 9 0 1 3	17 1	33 1 0	0 5	.000	0 0-0 0	5.48
Texas	AL	18 18 0 0	105.1	482	130 87 84 23 3 8 4	47 0	64 8 0	5 5	.500	0 0-0 0	7.18
2 ML YEARS		53 53 1 0	290	1288	306 199 189 64 11 11 8	137 7	209 20 0	12 18	.400	0 0-0 0	5.87

Mark Bellhorn

Bats: B **Throws:** R **Pos:** PH/PR-16; 2B-12; 3B-9; SS-5; DH-4; RF-1   **Ht:** 6'1" **Wt:** 214 **Born:** 8/23/74 **Age:** 27

		BATTING																	BASERUNNING				PERCENTAGES		
Year Team	Lg	G	AB	H	2B	3B	HR	(Hm	Rd)	TB	R	RBI	TBB	IBB	SO	HBP	SH	SF	SB	CS	SB%	GDP	Avg	OBP	SLG
2001 Sacramento *	AAA	43	156	42	6	0	12	—		84	30	36	22	2	60	4	0	2	3	0	1.00	0	.269	.370	.538
1997 Oakland	AL	68	224	51	9	1	6	(3	3)	80	33	19	32	0	70	0	5	0	7	1	.88	1	.228	.324	.357
1998 Oakland	AL	11	12	1	1	0	0	(0	0)	2	1	1	3	0	4	1	0	0	2	0	1.00	0	.083	.313	.167
2000 Oakland	AL	9	13	2	0	0	0	(0	0)	2	2	0	2	0	6	0	0	0	0	0	—	0	.154	.267	.154
2001 Oakland	AL	38	74	10	1	2	1	(1	0)	18	11	4	7	0	37	0	1	0	0	0	—	1	.135	.210	.243
4 ML YEARS		126	323	64	11	3	7	(4	3)	102	47	24	44	0	117	1	6	0	9	1	.90	2	.198	.296	.316

Ronnie Belliard

Bats: Right **Throws:** Right **Pos:** 2B-96; PH/PR-5   **Ht:** 5'8" **Wt:** 180 **Born:** 4/7/75 **Age:** 27

		BATTING																	BASERUNNING				PERCENTAGES		
Year Team	Lg	G	AB	H	2B	3B	HR	(Hm	Rd)	TB	R	RBI	TBB	IBB	SO	HBP	SH	SF	SB	CS	SB%	GDP	Avg	OBP	SLG
1998 Milwaukee	NL	8	5	1	0	0	0	(0	0)	1	1	0	0	0	0	0	0	0	0	0	—	0	.200	.200	.200
1999 Milwaukee	NL	124	457	135	29	4	8	(5	3)	196	60	58	64	0	59	0	6	4	4	5	.44	16	.295	.379	.429
2000 Milwaukee	NL	152	571	150	30	9	8	(4	4)	222	83	54	82	4	84	3	4	7	5	5	.58	12	.263	.354	.389
2001 Milwaukee	NL	101	364	96	30	3	11	(7	4)	165	69	36	35	2	65	5	4	2	5	2	.71	5	.264	.335	.453
4 ML YEARS		385	1397	382	89	16	27	(16	11)	584	213	148	181	6	208	8	14	13	16	12	.57	33	.273	.357	.418

Clay Bellinger

Bats: R **Throws:** R **Pos:** 3B-17; LF-13; CF-10; PH/PR-10; 1B-6; SS-2; RF-2; DH-1   **Ht:** 6'3" **Wt:** 215 **Born:** 11/18/68 **Age:** 33

		BATTING																	BASERUNNING				PERCENTAGES		
Year Team	Lg	G	AB	H	2B	3B	HR	(Hm	Rd)	TB	R	RBI	TBB	IBB	SO	HBP	SH	SF	SB	CS	SB%	GDP	Avg	OBP	SLG
2001 Columbus *	AAA	26	98	21	10	0	1	—		34	13	9	5	1	22	1	0	0	3	0	1.00	0	.214	.260	.347
1999 New York	AL	32	45	9	2	0	1	(1	0)	14	12	2	1	0	10	0	0	0	1	0	1.00	1	.200	.217	.311
2000 New York	AL	98	184	38	8	2	6	(2	4)	68	33	21	17	1	48	5	1	2	5	0	1.00	1	.207	.288	.370
2001 New York	AL	51	81	13	1	1	5	(2	3)	31	12	12	4	0	23	1	1	1	1	2	.33	2	.160	.207	.383
3 ML YEARS		181	310	60	11	3	12	(5	7)	113	57	35	22	1	81	6	2	3	7	2	.78	4	.194	.258	.365

Carlos Beltran

Bats: Both **Throws:** Right **Pos:** CF-152; DH-3   **Ht:** 6'1" **Wt:** 190 **Born:** 4/24/77 **Age:** 25

		BATTING																	BASERUNNING				PERCENTAGES		
Year Team	Lg	G	AB	H	2B	3B	HR	(Hm	Rd)	TB	R	RBI	TBB	IBB	SO	HBP	SH	SF	SB	CS	SB%	GDP	Avg	OBP	SLG
1998 Kansas City	AL	14	58	16	5	3	0	(0	0)	27	12	7	3	0	12	1	0	1	3	0	1.00	2	.276	.317	.466
1999 Kansas City	AL	156	663	194	27	7	22	(12	10)	301	112	108	46	2	123	4	0	10	27	8	.77	17	.293	.337	.454
2000 Kansas City	AL	98	372	92	15	4	7	(4	3)	136	49	44	35	2	69	0	2	4	13	0	1.00	12	.247	.309	.366
2001 Kansas City	AL	155	617	189	32	12	24	(7	17)	317	106	101	52	2	120	5	1	5	31	1	.97	7	.306	.362	.514
4 ML YEARS		423	1710	491	79	26	53	(23	30)	781	279	260	136	6	324	10	3	20	74	9	.89	38	.287	.340	.457

Adrian Beltre

Bats: Right **Throws:** Right **Pos:** 3B-124; PH/PR-3; SS-2   **Ht:** 5'11" **Wt:** 170 **Born:** 4/7/79 **Age:** 23

		BATTING																	BASERUNNING				PERCENTAGES		
Year Team	Lg	G	AB	H	2B	3B	HR	(Hm	Rd)	TB	R	RBI	TBB	IBB	SO	HBP	SH	SF	SB	CS	SB%	GDP	Avg	OBP	SLG
2001 Vero Beach *	A+	3	9	4	1	0	0	—		5	0	1	2	0	1	1	0	0	0	0	—	0	.444	.583	.556
Las Vegas *	AAA	2	5	3	1	0	1	—		7	2	2	2	0	0	0	0	0	0	0	—	0	.600	.714	1.400
1998 Los Angeles	NL	77	195	42	9	0	7	(5	2)	72	18	22	14	0	37	3	2	0	3	1	.75	4	.215	.278	.369
1999 Los Angeles	NL	152	538	148	27	5	15	(6	9)	230	84	67	61	12	105	6	4	5	18	7	.72	4	.275	.352	.428
2000 Los Angeles	NL	138	510	148	30	2	20	(7	13)	242	71	85	56	2	80	2	3	4	12	5	.71	13	.290	.360	.475
2001 Los Angeles	NL	126	475	126	22	4	13	(4	9)	195	59	60	28	1	82	5	2	5	13	4	.76	9	.265	.310	.411
4 ML YEARS		493	1718	464	88	11	55	(22	33)	739	232	234	159	15	304	16	11	14	46	17	.73	30	.270	.335	.430

Marvin Benard

Bats: L **Throws:** L **Pos:** CF-75; RF-37; PH/PR-30; LF-15   **Ht:** 5'9" **Wt:** 185 **Born:** 1/20/70 **Age:** 32

		BATTING																	BASERUNNING				PERCENTAGES		
Year Team	Lg	G	AB	H	2B	3B	HR	(Hm	Rd)	TB	R	RBI	TBB	IBB	SO	HBP	SH	SF	SB	CS	SB%	GDP	Avg	OBP	SLG
1995 San Francisco	NL	13	34	13	2	0	1	(0	1)	18	5	4	1	0	7	0	0	0	1	0	1.00	1	.382	.400	.529
1996 San Francisco	NL	135	488	121	17	4	5	(2	3)	161	89	27	59	2	84	4	6	1	25	11	.69	8	.248	.333	.330
1997 San Francisco	NL	84	114	26	4	0	1	(0	1)	33	13	13	13	0	29	2	0	1	3	1	.75	2	.228	.315	.289
1998 San Francisco	NL	121	286	92	21	1	3	(2	1)	124	41	36	34	1	39	2	4	1	11	4	.73	3	.322	.396	.434
1999 San Francisco	NL	149	562	163	36	5	16	(9	7)	257	100	64	55	2	97	6	1	1	27	14	.66	5	.290	.359	.457
2000 San Francisco	NL	149	560	147	27	6	12	(6	6)	222	102	55	63	0	97	6	2	2	22	7	.76	4	.263	.342	.396
2001 San Francisco	NL	129	392	104	19	2	15	(3	12)	172	70	44	29	2	66	4	1	3	10	5	.67	3	.265	.320	.439
7 ML YEARS		780	2436	666	126	18	53	(22	31)	987	420	243	254	7	419	24	14	9	99	42	.70	26	.273	.347	.405

20

Alan Benes

Pitches: Right **Bats:** Right **Pos:** RP-8; SP-1 **Ht:** 6'5" **Wt:** 235 **Born:** 1/21/72 **Age:** 30

			HOW MUCH HE PITCHED						WHAT HE GAVE UP										THE RESULTS					
Year Team	Lg	G	GS	CG	GF	IP	BFP	H	R	ER	HR	SH	SF	HB	TBB	IBB	SO	WP	Bk	W	L	Pct.	ShO	Sv-Op	Hld	ERA
2001 Memphis *	AAA	25	25	1	0	142	637	164	71	56	13	7	2	7	51	1	96	2	0	7	6	.538	0	0--	—	3.55
1995 St. Louis	NL	3	3	0	0	16	76	24	15	15	2	1	0	1	4	0	20	3	0	1	2	.333	0	0-0	0	8.44
1996 St. Louis	NL	34	32	3	1	191	840	192	120	104	27	15	9	7	87	3	131	5	1	13	10	.565	1	0-0	0	4.90
1997 St. Louis	NL	23	23	2	0	161.2	666	128	60	52	13	5	4	4	68	3	160	9	2	9	9	.500	0	0-0	0	2.89
1999 St. Louis	NL	2	0	0	2	2	7	2	0	0	0	0	0	0	0	0	2	0	0	0	0	—	0	0-0	0	0.00
2000 St. Louis	NL	30	0	0	16	46	214	54	33	29	7	2	1	2	23	2	26	5	0	2	2	.500	0	0-1	2	5.67
2001 St. Louis	NL	9	1	0	4	14.2	68	14	12	12	5	0	0	0	12	0	10	0	0	2	0	1.000	0	0-0	0	7.36
6 ML YEARS		101	59	5	23	431.1	1871	414	240	212	54	23	14	14	194	8	349	22	3	27	23	.540	1	0-1	2	4.42

Andy Benes

Pitches: Right **Bats:** Right **Pos:** SP-19; RP-8 **Ht:** 6'6" **Wt:** 245 **Born:** 8/20/67 **Age:** 34

			HOW MUCH HE PITCHED						WHAT HE GAVE UP										THE RESULTS					
Year Team	Lg	G	GS	CG	GF	IP	BFP	H	R	ER	HR	SH	SF	HB	TBB	IBB	SO	WP	Bk	W	L	Pct.	ShO	Sv-Op	Hld	ERA
1989 San Diego	NL	10	10	0	0	66.2	280	51	28	26	7	6	2	1	31	0	66	0	3	6	3	.667	0	0-0	0	3.51
1990 San Diego	NL	32	31	2	1	192.1	811	177	87	77	18	5	6	1	69	5	140	2	5	10	11	.476	0	0-0	0	3.60
1991 San Diego	NL	33	33	4	0	223	908	194	76	75	23	5	4	4	59	7	167	3	4	15	11	.577	1	0-0	0	3.03
1992 San Diego	NL	34	34	2	0	231.1	961	230	90	86	14	19	6	5	61	6	169	1	1	13	14	.481	2	0-0	0	3.35
1993 San Diego	NL	34	34	4	0	230.2	968	200	111	97	23	10	6	4	86	7	179	14	2	15	15	.500	2	0-0	0	3.78
1994 San Diego	NL	25	25	2	0	172.1	717	155	82	74	20	11	1	1	51	2	189	4	0	6	14	.300	2	0-0	0	3.86
1995 SD-Sea		31	31	1	0	181.2	809	193	107	96	18	4	8	6	78	5	171	5	0	11	9	.550	1	0-0	0	4.76
1996 St. Louis	NL	36	34	3	1	230.1	963	215	107	98	28	2	6	6	77	7	160	6	0	18	10	.643	1	1-1	0	3.83
1997 St. Louis	NL	26	26	0	0	177	727	149	64	61	9	6	7	5	61	4	175	7	0	10	7	.588	0	0-0	0	3.10
1998 Arizona	NL	34	34	1	0	231.1	979	221	111	102	25	11	8	6	74	3	164	9	1	14	13	.519	0	0-0	0	3.97
1999 Arizona	NL	33	32	0	0	198.1	886	216	117	106	34	6	3	4	82	3	141	10	0	13	12	.520	0	0-0	0	4.81
2000 St. Louis	NL	30	27	1	1	166	719	174	95	90	30	9	8	1	68	0	137	1	0	12	9	.571	0	0-0	1	4.88
2001 St. Louis	NL	27	19	0	3	107.1	500	122	92	88	30	3	4	6	61	0	78	1	0	7	7	.500	0	0-1	0	7.38
1995 San Diego	NL	19	19	1	0	118.2	518	121	65	55	10	3	4	4	45	3	126	3	0	4	7	.364	1	0-0	0	4.17
Seattle	AL	12	12	0	0	63	291	72	42	41	8	1	4	2	33	2	45	2	0	7	2	.778	0	0-0	0	5.86
13 ML YEARS		385	370	20	6	2408.1	10228	2297	1167	1076	279	97	69	50	858	49	1936	63	16	150	135	.526	9	1-2	1	4.02

Armando Benitez

Pitches: Right **Bats:** Right **Pos:** RP-73 **Ht:** 6'4" **Wt:** 229 **Born:** 11/3/72 **Age:** 29

			HOW MUCH HE PITCHED						WHAT HE GAVE UP										THE RESULTS					
Year Team	Lg	G	GS	CG	GF	IP	BFP	H	R	ER	HR	SH	SF	HB	TBB	IBB	SO	WP	Bk	W	L	Pct.	ShO	Sv-Op	Hld	ERA
1994 Baltimore	AL	3	0	0	1	10	42	8	1	1	0	0	0	1	4	0	14	0	0	0	0	—	0	0-0	0	0.90
1995 Baltimore	AL	44	0	0	18	47.2	221	37	33	30	8	2	3	5	37	2	56	3	1	1	5	.167	0	2-5	6	5.66
1996 Baltimore	AL	18	0	0	8	14.1	56	7	6	6	2	0	1	0	6	0	20	1	0	1	0	1.000	0	4-5	1	3.77
1997 Baltimore	AL	71	0	0	26	73.1	307	49	22	20	7	2	4	1	43	5	106	1	0	4	5	.444	0	9-10	20	2.45
1998 Baltimore	AL	71	0	0	54	68.1	289	48	29	29	10	3	2	4	39	2	87	0	0	5	6	.455	0	22-26	3	3.82
1999 New York	NL	77	0	0	42	78	312	40	17	16	4	0	0	0	41	4	128	2	0	4	3	.571	0	22-28	17	1.85
2000 New York	NL	76	0	0	68	76	304	39	24	22	10	2	1	0	38	2	106	0	0	4	4	.500	0	41-46	0	2.61
2001 New York	NL	73	0	0	64	76.1	320	59	32	32	12	2	1	1	40	6	93	5	0	6	4	.600	0	43-46	0	3.77
8 ML YEARS		433	0	0	281	444	1851	287	164	156	53	11	12	12	248	21	610	12	1	25	27	.481	0	143-166	47	3.16

Mike Benjamin

Bats: Right **Throws:** Right **2000 Pos:** 3B-34; SS-30; 2B-27; PH/PR-16; 1B-1 **Ht:** 6'0" **Wt:** 172 **Born:** 11/22/65 **Age:** 36

					BATTING													BASERUNNING				PERCENTAGES		
Year Team	Lg	G	AB	H	2B	3B	HR	(Hm	Rd)	TB	R	RBI	TBB	IBB	SO	HBP	SH	SF	SB	CS	SB%	GDP	Avg	OBP	SLG
1989 San Francisco	NL	14	6	1	0	0	0	(0	0)	1	6	0	0	0	1	0	0	0	0	0	—	0	.167	.167	.167
1990 San Francisco	NL	22	56	12	3	1	2	(2	0)	23	7	3	3	1	10	0	0	0	1	0	1.00	2	.214	.254	.411
1991 San Francisco	NL	54	106	13	3	0	2	(0	2)	22	12	8	7	2	26	2	3	2	3	0	1.00	1	.123	.188	.208
1992 San Francisco	NL	40	75	13	2	1	1	(0	1)	20	4	3	4	1	15	0	3	0	1	0	1.00	1	.173	.215	.267
1993 San Francisco	NL	63	146	29	7	0	4	(3	1)	48	22	16	9	2	23	4	6	0	0	0	—	3	.199	.264	.329
1994 San Francisco	NL	38	62	16	5	1	1	(1	0)	26	9	9	5	1	16	3	5	0	5	0	1.00	1	.258	.343	.419
1995 San Francisco	NL	68	186	41	6	0	3	(1	2)	56	19	12	8	3	51	1	7	0	11	1	.92	3	.220	.256	.301
1996 Philadelphia	NL	35	103	23	5	1	4	(0	4)	42	13	13	12	5	21	2	1	0	3	1	.75	2	.223	.316	.408
1997 Boston	AL	49	116	27	9	1	0	(0	0)	38	12	7	4	0	27	1	1	1	2	3	.40	2	.233	.262	.328
1998 Boston	AL	124	349	95	23	0	4	(2	2)	130	46	39	15	1	73	6	13	2	3	0	1.00	11	.272	.312	.372
1999 Pittsburgh	NL	110	368	91	26	7	1	(1	0)	134	42	37	20	3	90	2	11	3	10	1	.91	3	.247	.288	.364
2000 Pittsburgh	NL	93	233	63	18	2	2	(0	2)	91	28	19	12	0	45	3	6	1	5	4	.56	3	.270	.313	.391
12 ML YEARS		710	1806	424	107	14	24	(10	14)	631	220	166	99	19	398	24	56	9	44	10	.81	33	.235	.282	.349

Gary Bennett

Bats: Right **Throws:** Right **Pos:** C-43; PH/PR-5 **Ht:** 6'0" **Wt:** 208 **Born:** 4/17/72 **Age:** 30

					BATTING													BASERUNNING				PERCENTAGES		
Year Team	Lg	G	AB	H	2B	3B	HR	(Hm	Rd)	TB	R	RBI	TBB	IBB	SO	HBP	SH	SF	SB	CS	SB%	GDP	Avg	OBP	SLG
2001 Norfolk *	AAA	20	67	20	5	0	2	—	—	31	7	14	4	1	12	1	0	1	0	0	—	0	.299	.342	.463
1995 Philadelphia	NL	1	1	0	0	0	0	(0	0)	0	0	0	0	0	1	0	0	0	0	0	—	0	.000	.000	.000
1996 Philadelphia	NL	6	16	4	0	0	0	(0	0)	4	0	1	2	1	6	0	0	0	0	0	—	0	.250	.333	.250
1998 Philadelphia	NL	9	31	9	0	0	0	(0	0)	9	4	3	5	0	5	0	0	1	0	0	—	1	.290	.378	.290
1999 Philadelphia	NL	36	88	24	4	0	1	(1	0)	31	7	21	4	0	11	0	0	2	0	0	—	7	.273	.298	.352
2000 Philadelphia	NL	31	74	18	5	0	2	(0	2)	29	8	5	13	0	15	2	0	0	0	0	—	1	.243	.371	.392
2001 Phi-NYM-Col	NL	46	131	32	6	1	2	(2	0)	46	15	10	12	4	24	1	2	2	0	0	—	1	.244	.308	.351
2001 Philadelphia	NL	26	75	16	3	1	1	(1	0)	24	8	6	9	1	19	0	1	1	0	0	—	0	.213	.294	.320
New York	NL	1	1	1	0	0	0	(0	0)	1	0	0	0	0	0	0	0	0	0	0	—	0	1.000	1.000	1.000
Colorado	NL	19	55	15	3	0	1	(1	0)	21	7	4	3	3	5	1	1	1	0	0	—	1	.273	.317	.382
6 ML YEARS		129	341	87	15	1	5	(2	3)	119	34	40	36	5	62	3	2	5	0	0	—	9	.255	.327	.349

21

Joaquin Benoit

Pitches: Right **Bats:** Right **Pos:** SP-1   **Ht:** 6'3" **Wt:** 205 **Born:** 7/26/79 **Age:** 22

		HOW MUCH HE PITCHED					WHAT HE GAVE UP											THE RESULTS					
Year Team	Lg	G	GS	CG	GF	IP	BFP	H	R	ER	HR	SH	SF	HB	TBB	IBB	SO	WP	Bk	W	L	Pct.	ShO	Sv-Op	Hld	ERA
1997 Rangers	R	10	10	1	0	44	177	40	14	10	0	1	0	1	11	0	38	1	0	3	3	.500	0	0- -	—	2.05
1998 Savannah	A	15	15	1	0	80	339	79	41	34	8	3	1	3	18	0	68	3	1	4	3	.571	0	0- -	—	3.83
1999 Charlotte	A+	22	22	0	0	105	483	117	67	62	5	1	7	11	50	0	83	3	2	7	4	.636	0	0- -	—	5.31
2000 Tulsa	AA	16	16	0	0	82.1	346	73	40	35	6	0	4	4	30	0	72	6	0	4	4	.500	0	0- -	—	3.83
2001 Tulsa	AA	4	4	0	0	21.2	94	23	8	8	1	0	0	1	6	0	23	2	0	1	0	1.000	0	0- -	—	3.32
Oklahoma	AAA	24	24	1	0	131	566	113	63	61	14	2	4	4	73	0	142	7	0	9	5	.643	1	0- -	—	4.19
2001 Texas	AL	1	1	0	0	5	26	8	6	6	3	0	1	0	3	0	4	0	0	0	0	—	0	0-0	0	10.80

Kris Benson

Pitches: Right **Bats:** Right **2000 Pos:** SP-32   **Ht:** 6'4" **Wt:** 200 **Born:** 11/7/74 **Age:** 27

		HOW MUCH HE PITCHED					WHAT HE GAVE UP											THE RESULTS					
Year Team	Lg	G	GS	CG	GF	IP	BFP	H	R	ER	HR	SH	SF	HB	TBB	IBB	SO	WP	Bk	W	L	Pct.	ShO	Sv-Op	Hld	ERA
1999 Pittsburgh	NL	31	31	2	0	196.2	840	184	105	89	16	6	7	6	83	5	139	2	1	11	14	.440	0	0-0	0	4.07
2000 Pittsburgh	NL	32	32	2	0	217.2	936	206	104	93	24	7	6	10	86	5	184	5	0	10	12	.455	1	0-0	0	3.85
2 ML YEARS		63	63	4	0	414.1	1776	390	209	182	40	13	13	16	169	10	323	7	1	21	26	.447	1	0-0	0	3.95

Jason Bere

Pitches: Right **Bats:** Right **Pos:** SP-32   **Ht:** 6'3" **Wt:** 225 **Born:** 5/26/71 **Age:** 31

		HOW MUCH HE PITCHED					WHAT HE GAVE UP											THE RESULTS					
Year Team	Lg	G	GS	CG	GF	IP	BFP	H	R	ER	HR	SH	SF	HB	TBB	IBB	SO	WP	Bk	W	L	Pct.	ShO	Sv-Op	Hld	ERA
1993 Chicago	AL	24	24	1	0	142.2	610	109	60	55	12	4	2	5	81	0	129	8	0	12	5	.706	0	0-0	0	3.47
1994 Chicago	AL	24	24	0	0	141.2	608	119	65	60	17	4	4	1	80	0	127	2	0	12	2	.857	0	0-0	0	3.81
1995 Chicago	AL	27	27	1	0	137.2	668	151	120	110	21	4	7	6	106	6	110	8	0	8	15	.348	0	0-0	0	7.19
1996 Chicago	AL	5	5	0	0	16.2	93	26	19	19	3	1	1	0	18	1	19	2	0	0	1	.000	0	0-0	0	10.26
1997 Chicago	AL	6	6	0	0	28.2	123	20	15	15	4	1	1	3	17	0	21	1	0	4	2	.667	0	0-0	0	4.71
1998 CWS-Cin		27	22	0	2	127.1	588	137	91	80	17	4	7	3	78	0	84	8	0	6	9	.400	0	0-0	0	5.65
1999 Cin-Mil	NL	17	14	0	0	66.2	322	79	52	45	9	6	2	2	50	3	47	6	0	5	0	1.000	0	0-0	0	6.08
2000 Mil-Cle		31	31	0	0	169.1	767	180	107	103	25	12	6	5	89	7	142	5	1	12	10	.545	0	0-0	0	5.47
2001 Chicago	NL	32	32	2	0	188	801	171	99	90	24	7	6	1	77	7	175	6	0	11	11	.500	0	0-0	0	4.31
1998 Chicago	AL	18	15	0	0	83.2	404	98	71	60	14	4	5	2	58	0	53	7	0	3	7	.300	0	0-0	0	6.45
Cincinnati	NL	9	7	0	2	43.2	184	39	20	20	3	0	2	1	20	0	31	1	0	3	2	.600	0	0-0	0	4.12
1999 Cincinnati	NL	12	10	0	0	43.1	220	56	37	33	6	5	1	2	40	3	28	2	0	3	0	1.000	0	0-0	0	6.85
Milwaukee	NL	5	4	0	0	23.1	102	23	15	12	3	1	1	0	10	0	19	4	0	2	0	1.000	0	0-0	0	4.63
2000 Milwaukee	NL	20	20	0	0	115	515	115	66	63	19	12	3	1	63	7	98	3	1	6	7	.462	0	0-0	0	4.93
Cleveland	AL	11	11	0	0	54.1	252	65	41	40	6	0	3	4	26	0	44	2	0	6	3	.667	0	0-0	0	6.63
9 ML YEARS		193	185	4	2	1018.2	4580	992	628	577	132	43	36	26	596	24	854	46	1	70	55	.560	0	0-0	0	5.10

Dave Berg

Bats: R **Throws:** R **Pos:** 2B-34; PH/PR-20; SS-19; 3B-16   **Ht:** 5'11" **Wt:** 185 **Born:** 9/3/70 **Age:** 31

		BATTING																	BASERUNNING				PERCENTAGES		
Year Team	Lg	G	AB	H	2B	3B	HR	(Hm	Rd)	TB	R	RBI	TBB	IBB	SO	HBP	SH	SF	SB	CS	SB%	GDP	Avg	OBP	SLG
1998 Florida	NL	81	182	57	11	0	2	(1	1)	74	18	21	26	1	46	0	4	3	3	0	1.00	1	.313	.393	.407
1999 Florida	NL	109	304	87	18	1	3	(1	2)	116	42	25	27	0	59	2	3	0	2	2	.50	7	.286	.348	.382
2000 Florida	NL	82	210	53	14	1	1	(1	0)	72	23	21	25	0	46	5	1	4	3	0	1.00	5	.252	.340	.343
2001 Florida	NL	82	215	52	12	1	4	(2	2)	78	26	16	14	0	39	2	2	2	0	1	.00	3	.242	.292	.363
4 ML YEARS		354	911	249	55	3	10	(5	5)	340	109	83	92	1	190	9	10	9	8	3	.73	16	.273	.343	.373

Brandon Berger

Bats: Right **Throws:** Right **Pos:** LF-5; DH-1; PH/PR-1   **Ht:** 5'11" **Wt:** 200 **Born:** 2/21/75 **Age:** 27

		BATTING																	BASERUNNING				PERCENTAGES		
Year Team	Lg	G	AB	H	2B	3B	HR	(Hm	Rd)	TB	R	RBI	TBB	IBB	SO	HBP	SH	SF	SB	CS	SB%	GDP	Avg	OBP	SLG
1996 Spokane	A-	71	283	87	12	1	13	—	—	140	46	58	31	0	64	2	1	3	17	5	.77	7	.307	.376	.495
1997 Lansing	A	107	304	115	22	6	12	—	—	185	64	73	42	1	79	7	0	4	13	1	.93	8	.293	.368	.471
1998 Wilmington	A+	110	338	75	18	3	8	—	—	123	53	50	53	1	94	5	7	5	13	3	.81	11	.222	.332	.364
1999 Wilmington	A+	119	450	132	27	4	16	—	—	215	73	73	45	0	93	8	6	6	29	7	.81	3	.293	.363	.478
2000 Wichita	AA	27	86	14	2	0	3	—	—	25	9	8	7	0	27	2	1	1	6	1	.86	2	.163	.240	.291
Wilmington	A+	102	379	108	18	4	15	—	—	179	63	71	40	2	71	17	4	3	12	4	.75	8	.285	.376	.472
2001 Wichita	AA	120	454	140	28	3	40	—	—	294	98	118	43	2	91	14	1	3	14	6	.70	9	.308	.383	.648
2001 Kansas City	AL	6	16	5	1	1	2	(1	1)	14	4	2	2	0	2	0	0	0	0	0	—	0	.313	.389	.875

Peter Bergeron

Bats: Left **Throws:** Right **Pos:** CF-101; PH/PR-1   **Ht:** 6'0" **Wt:** 185 **Born:** 11/9/77 **Age:** 24

		BATTING																	BASERUNNING				PERCENTAGES		
Year Team	Lg	G	AB	H	2B	3B	HR	(Hm	Rd)	TB	R	RBI	TBB	IBB	SO	HBP	SH	SF	SB	CS	SB%	GDP	Avg	OBP	SLG
2001 Ottawa *	AAA	52	206	49	5	3	0	—	—	60	29	8	20	0	42	1	2	1	15	7	.68	1	.238	.307	.291
1999 Montreal	NL	16	45	11	2	0	0	(0	0)	13	12	1	9	0	5	0	1	0	0	0	—	0	.244	.370	.289
2000 Montreal	NL	148	518	127	25	7	5	(3	2)	181	80	31	58	0	100	0	14	2	11	13	.46	4	.245	.320	.349
2001 Montreal	NL	102	375	79	11	4	3	(1	2)	107	53	16	28	2	87	5	8	0	10	7	.59	5	.211	.275	.285
3 ML YEARS		266	938	217	38	11	8	(4	4)	301	145	48	95	2	192	5	23	2	21	20	.51	9	.231	.305	.321

Lance Berkman

Bats: B **Throws:** L **Pos:** LF-128; CF-40; RF-7; PH/PR-3 — **Ht:** 6'1" **Wt:** 205 **Born:** 2/10/76 **Age:** 26

Year Team	Lg	G	AB	H	2B	3B	HR	(Hm	Rd)	TB	R	RBI	TBB	IBB	SO	HBP	SH	SF	SB	CS	SB%	GDP	Avg	OBP	SLG
1999 Houston	NL	34	93	22	2	0	4	(2	2)	36	10	15	12	0	21	0	0	1	5	1	.83	2	.237	.321	.387
2000 Houston	NL	114	353	105	28	1	21	(10	11)	198	76	67	56	1	73	1	0	7	6	2	.75	6	.297	.388	.561
2001 Houston	NL	156	577	191	55	5	34	(13	21)	358	110	126	92	5	121	13	0	6	7	9	.44	8	.331	.430	.620
3 ML YEARS		304	1023	318	85	6	59	(25	34)	592	196	208	160	6	215	14	0	14	18	12	.60	16	.311	.406	.579

Adam Bernero

Pitches: Right **Bats:** Right **Pos:** RP-5 — **Ht:** 6'4" **Wt:** 205 **Born:** 11/28/76 **Age:** 25

Year Team	Lg	G	GS	CG	GF	IP	BFP	H	R	ER	HR	SH	SF	HB	TBB	IBB	SO	WP	Bk	W	L	Pct.	ShO	Sv-Op	Hld	ERA
1999 W Michigan	A	15	15	2	0	95.2	386	75	36	27	8	0	2	4	23	0	80	3	3	8	4	.667	1	0--	—	2.54
2000 Jacksnville	AA	10	10	0	0	61.1	260	54	26	19	6	2	3	3	24	0	46	5	0	2	5	.286	0	0--	—	2.79
Toledo	AAA	7	7	1	0	47.1	182	34	16	13	5	0	0	3	10	0	37	1	0	3	1	.750	1	0--	—	2.47
2001 Toledo	AAA	26	25	1	1	140.1	641	172	90	80	13	7	3	10	54	0	99	1	5	6	11	.353	0	0--	—	5.13
2000 Detroit	AL	12	4	0	4	34.1	141	33	18	16	3	2	3	1	13	1	20	1	0	0	1	.000	0	0-0	1	4.19
2001 Detroit	AL	5	0	0	4	12.1	56	13	13	10	4	0	1	1	4	0	8	1	0	0	0	—	0	0-0	0	7.30
2 ML YEARS		17	4	0	8	46.2	197	46	31	26	7	2	4	2	17	1	28	2	0	0	1	.000	0	0-0	1	5.01

Angel Berroa

Bats: Right **Throws:** Right **Pos:** SS-14; PH/PR-1 — **Ht:** 5'11" **Wt:** 175 **Born:** 1/27/80 **Age:** 22

Year Team	Lg	G	AB	H	2B	3B	HR	(Hm	Rd)	TB	R	RBI	TBB	IBB	SO	HBP	SH	SF	SB	CS	SB%	GDP	Avg	OBP	SLG
1999 Athletics	R	46	169	49	11	4	2	—	—	74	42	24	16	0	26	7	0	2	11	4	.73	1	.290	.371	.438
Midland	AA	4	17	1	1	0	0	—	—	2	3	0	0	0	2	0	0	0	0	0	—	0	.059	.059	.118
2000 Visalia	A+	129	429	119	25	6	10	—	—	186	61	63	30	1	70	10	2	3	11	9	.55	10	.277	.337	.434
2001 Wilmington	A+	51	169	54	18	4	6	—	—	107	43	25	9	1	41	14	3	3	10	6	.63	7	.317	.382	.538
Wichita	AA	80	304	90	20	4	8	—	—	142	63	42	17	0	55	22	6	3	15	6	.71	6	.296	.373	.467
2001 Kansas City	AL	15	53	16	2	0	0	(0	0)	18	8	4	3	0	10	0	0	0	2	0	1.00	2	.302	.339	.340

Wilson Betemit

Bats: Both **Throws:** Right **Pos:** PH/PR-8; SS-1 — **Ht:** 6'2" **Wt:** 155 **Born:** 11/2/81 **Age:** 20

Year Team	Lg	G	AB	H	2B	3B	HR	(Hm	Rd)	TB	R	RBI	TBB	IBB	SO	HBP	SH	SF	SB	CS	SB%	GDP	Avg	OBP	SLG
1997 Braves	R	32	113	24	6	1	0	—	—	32	12	15	9	0	32	0	0	0	0	0	—	0	.212	.270	.283
1998 Braves	R	51	173	38	8	4	5	—	—	69	23	16	20	0	49	0	0	0	6	5	.55	1	.220	.301	.399
1999 Danville	R+	67	259	83	18	2	5	—	—	120	39	53	27	1	63	1	1	3	3	3	.67	4	.320	.383	.463
2000 Jamestown	A-	69	269	89	15	2	5	—	—	123	54	37	30	2	37	1	3	5	3	4	.43	4	.331	.393	.457
2001 Myrtle Bch	A+	84	318	88	20	1	7	—	—	131	38	43	23	1	71	1	0	4	8	5	.62	8	.277	.324	.412
Greenville	AA	47	183	65	14	0	5	—	—	94	22	19	12	0	36	1	1	2	6	2	.75	4	.355	.394	.514
2001 Atlanta	NL	8	3	0	0	0	0	(0	0)	0	0	1	0	0	2	0	0	0	1	0	1.00	0	.000	.400	.000

Dante Bichette

Bats: R **Throws:** R **Pos:** DH-46; LF-37; RF-16; PH/PR-11 — **Ht:** 6'2" **Wt:** 235 **Born:** 11/18/63 **Age:** 38

Year Team	Lg	G	AB	H	2B	3B	HR	(Hm	Rd)	TB	R	RBI	TBB	IBB	SO	HBP	SH	SF	SB	CS	SB%	GDP	Avg	OBP	SLG
1988 California	AL	21	46	12	2	0	0	(0	0)	14	1	8	0	0	7	0	0	4	0	0	—	0	.261	.240	.304
1989 California	AL	48	138	29	7	0	3	(2	1)	45	13	15	6	0	24	0	0	2	3	0	1.00	3	.210	.240	.326
1990 California	AL	109	349	89	15	1	15	(8	7)	151	40	53	16	1	79	3	1	2	5	2	.71	9	.255	.292	.433
1991 Milwaukee	AL	134	445	106	18	3	15	(6	9)	175	53	59	22	4	107	1	1	6	14	8	.64	9	.238	.272	.393
1992 Milwaukee	AL	112	387	111	27	2	5	(3	2)	157	37	41	16	3	74	3	2	3	18	7	.72	13	.287	.318	.406
1993 Colorado	NL	141	538	167	43	5	21	(11	10)	283	93	89	28	2	99	7	0	8	14	8	.64	7	.310	.348	.526
1994 Colorado	NL	116	484	147	33	2	27	(15	12)	265	74	95	19	3	70	4	0	2	21	8	.72	17	.304	.334	.548
1995 Colorado	NL	139	579	197	38	2	40	(31	9)	359	102	128	22	5	96	4	0	7	13	9	.59	16	.340	.364	.620
1996 Colorado	NL	159	633	198	39	3	31	(22	9)	336	114	141	45	4	105	6	0	10	31	12	.72	18	.313	.359	.531
1997 Colorado	NL	151	561	173	31	2	26	(20	6)	286	81	118	30	1	90	3	0	7	6	5	.55	19	.308	.343	.510
1998 Colorado	NL	161	662	219	48	2	22	(17	5)	337	97	122	28	2	76	1	0	4	14	4	.78	22	.331	.357	.509
1999 Colorado	NL	151	593	177	38	2	34	(20	14)	321	104	133	54	3	84	2	0	10	6	6	.50	15	.298	.354	.541
2000 Cin-Bos		155	575	169	32	2	23	(15	8)	274	80	90	49	3	91	4	1	7	5	2	.71	21	.294	.350	.477
2001 Boston	AL	107	391	112	30	1	12	(7	5)	180	45	49	20	1	76	3	0	1	2	2	.50	13	.286	.325	.460
2000 Cincinnati	NL	125	461	136	27	2	16	(11	5)	215	67	76	41	3	69	4	1	7	5	2	.71	18	.295	.353	.466
Boston	AL	30	114	33	5	0	7	(4	3)	59	13	14	8	0	22	0	0	0	0	0	—	3	.289	.336	.518
14 ML YEARS		1704	6381	1906	401	27	274	(177	97)	3183	934	1141	355	32	1078	41	5	73	152	73	.68	176	.299	.336	.499

Rocky Biddle

Pitches: Right **Bats:** Right **Pos:** SP-21; RP-9 — **Ht:** 6'3" **Wt:** 230 **Born:** 5/21/76 **Age:** 26

Year Team	Lg	G	GS	CG	GF	IP	BFP	H	R	ER	HR	SH	SF	HB	TBB	IBB	SO	WP	Bk	W	L	Pct.	ShO	Sv-Op	Hld	ERA
1997 Hickory	A	13	13	0	0	21.1	96	22	18	11	2	0	1	2	10	0	25	5	0	0	1	.000	0	1--	—	4.64
1998 White Sox	R	5	2	0	0	16	72	15	9	7	2	0	0	2	8	0	18	5	0	1	0	1.000	0	0--	—	3.94
Winston-Sal	A+	16	16	0	0	82.2	382	92	55	42	7	0	4	5	45	0	72	5	1	4	5	.444	0	0--	—	4.57
2000 Birmingham	AA	23	23	2	0	146.1	619	138	63	50	10	2	3	8	54	0	118	4	0	11	6	.647	2	0--	—	3.08
2000 Chicago	AL	4	4	0	0	22.2	105	31	25	21	5	0	2	0	8	0	7	2	0	1	2	.333	0	0-0	0	8.34
2001 Chicago	AL	30	21	0	1	128.2	571	137	87	77	16	4	3	8	52	3	85	6	0	7	8	.467	0	0-3	1	5.39
2 ML YEARS		34	25	0	1	151.1	676	168	112	98	21	4	5	8	60	3	92	8	0	8	10	.444	0	0-3	1	5.83

Nick Bierbrodt

Pitches: Left **Bats:** Left **Pos:** SP-16 **Ht:** 6'5" **Wt:** 185 **Born:** 5/16/78 **Age:** 24

Year Team	Lg	G	GS	CG	GF	IP	BFP	H	R	ER	HR	SH	SF	HB	TBB	IBB	SO	WP	Bk	W	L	Pct.	ShO	Sv-Op	Hld	ERA
1996 Diamndbcks	R	8	8	0	0	38	147	25	9	7	1	0	0	0	13	0	46	2	0	1	1	.500	0	0--	—	1.66
Lethbridge	R+	3	3	0	0	18	72	12	4	1	0	0	1	1	5	0	23	1	0	2	0	1.000	0	0--	—	0.50
1997 South Bend	A	15	15	0	0	75.2	340	77	43	34	4	3	1	9	37	0	64	6	1	2	4	.333	0	0--	—	4.04
1998 High Desert	A+	24	23	1	0	129.2	560	122	66	49	7	3	6	7	64	0	88	9	0	8	7	.533	0	0--	—	3.40
1999 El Paso	AA	14	14	2	0	76	341	78	45	39	3	2	1	8	37	0	55	5	0	5	6	.455	1	0--	—	4.62
Tucson	AAA	11	11	0	0	43.1	213	57	42	35	9	4	0	3	30	0	43	3	0	1	4	.200	0	0--	—	7.27
2000 Tucson	AAA	4	3	0	0	18.2	77	13	10	10	3	0	0	2	14	0	11	0	0	2	1	.667	0	0--	—	4.82
Diamndbcks	R	4	3	0	0	8	34	4	4	4	0	0	0	1	5	0	10	1	0	0	0	—	0	0--	—	4.50
El Paso	AA	7	7	0	0	35.1	166	37	30	28	1	2	1	3	24	0	36	5	0	1	3	.250	0	0--	—	7.13
2001 El Paso	AA	4	4	0	0	19.2	76	13	3	3	1	0	0	0	6	0	18	0	0	2	1	.667	0	0--	—	1.37
Tucson	AAA	7	6	0	0	45.1	185	48	15	11	0	3	1	1	9	1	56	1	0	4	1	.800	0	0--	—	2.18
2001 Ari-TB		16	16	0	0	84.1	389	100	59	52	17	0	2	4	39	1	73	3	0	5	6	.455	0	0-0	0	5.55
2001 Arizona	NL	5	5	0	0	23	108	29	21	21	6	0	1	0	12	0	17	0	0	2	2	.500	0	0-0	0	8.22
Tampa Bay	AL	11	11	0	0	61.1	281	71	38	31	11	0	1	4	27	1	56	3	0	3	4	.429	0	0-0	0	4.55

Larry Bigbie

Bats: L **Throws:** R **Pos:** CF-19; RF-17; PH/PR-9; LF-5 **Ht:** 6'4" **Wt:** 190 **Born:** 11/4/77 **Age:** 24

Year Team	Lg	G	AB	H	2B	3B	HR	(Hm	Rd)	TB	R	RBI	TBB	IBB	SO	HBP	SH	SF	SB	CS	SB%	GDP	Avg	OBP	SLG
1999 Bluefield	R+	8	30	8	0	0	0	—	—	8	3	4	3	0	8	1	0	1	1	3	.25	1	.267	.343	.267
Delmarva	A	43	165	46	7	3	2	—	—	65	18	27	29	0	42	0	0	3	3	1	.75	4	.279	.381	.394
2000 Frederick	A+	55	201	59	11	0	2	—	—	76	33	28	23	2	34	0	1	4	7	3	.70	3	.294	.360	.378
Bowie	AA	31	112	27	6	0	0	—	—	33	11	5	11	0	28	0	1	0	3	0	1.00	3	.241	.309	.295
2001 Bowie	AA	71	262	77	13	3	8	—	—	120	41	33	40	1	54	0	0	1	10	7	.59	5	.294	.386	.458
Rochester	AAA	10	42	13	4	0	1	—	—	20	5	2	3	0	8	0	0	0	1	1	.50	0	.310	.356	.476
2001 Baltimore	AL	47	131	30	6	0	2	(0	2)	42	15	11	17	1	42	0	1	0	4	1	.80	2	.229	.318	.321

Craig Biggio

Bats: Right **Throws:** Right **Pos:** 2B-154; DH-1; PH/PR-1 **Ht:** 5'11" **Wt:** 180 **Born:** 12/14/65 **Age:** 36

Year Team	Lg	G	AB	H	2B	3B	HR	(Hm	Rd)	TB	R	RBI	TBB	IBB	SO	HBP	SH	SF	SB	CS	SB%	GDP	Avg	OBP	SLG
1988 Houston	NL	50	123	26	6	1	3	(1	2)	43	14	5	7	2	29	0	1	0	6	1	.86	1	.211	.254	.350
1989 Houston	NL	134	443	114	21	2	13	(6	7)	178	64	60	49	8	64	6	6	5	21	3	.88	7	.257	.336	.402
1990 Houston	NL	150	555	153	24	2	4	(2	2)	193	53	42	53	1	79	3	9	1	25	11	.69	11	.276	.342	.348
1991 Houston	NL	149	546	161	23	4	4	(0	4)	204	79	46	53	3	71	2	5	3	19	6	.76	2	.295	.358	.374
1992 Houston	NL	162	613	170	32	3	6	(3	3)	226	96	39	94	9	95	7	5	2	38	15	.72	5	.277	.378	.369
1993 Houston	NL	155	610	175	41	5	21	(8	13)	289	98	64	77	7	93	10	4	5	15	17	.47	10	.287	.373	.474
1994 Houston	NL	114	437	139	44	5	6	(4	2)	211	88	56	62	1	58	8	2	2	39	4	.91	5	.318	.411	.483
1995 Houston	NL	141	553	167	30	2	22	(6	16)	267	123	77	80	1	85	22	11	7	33	8	.80	6	.302	.406	.483
1996 Houston	NL	162	605	174	24	4	15	(7	8)	251	113	75	75	0	72	27	8	8	25	7	.78	10	.288	.386	.415
1997 Houston	NL	162	619	191	37	8	22	(7	15)	310	146	81	84	6	107	34	0	7	47	10	.82	0	.309	.415	.501
1998 Houston	NL	160	646	210	51	2	20	(10	10)	325	123	88	64	6	113	23	1	4	50	8	.86	10	.325	.403	.503
1999 Houston	NL	160	639	188	56	0	16	(10	6)	292	123	73	88	9	107	11	5	6	28	14	.67	5	.294	.386	.457
2000 Houston	NL	101	377	101	13	5	8	(2	6)	148	67	35	61	3	73	16	7	5	12	2	.86	10	.268	.388	.393
2001 Houston	NL	155	617	180	35	3	20	(10	10)	281	118	70	66	4	100	28	0	6	7	4	.64	11	.292	.382	.455
14 ML YEARS		1955	7383	2149	437	46	180	(76	104)	3218	1305	811	913	60	1146	197	64	61	365	110	.77	93	.291	.381	.436

Willie Blair

Pitches: Right **Bats:** Right **Pos:** RP-5; SP-4 **Ht:** 6'1" **Wt:** 185 **Born:** 12/18/65 **Age:** 36

Year Team	Lg	G	GS	CG	GF	IP	BFP	H	R	ER	HR	SH	SF	HB	TBB	IBB	SO	WP	Bk	W	L	Pct.	ShO	Sv-Op	Hld	ERA
2001 Buffalo *	AAA	11	10	1	1	72	299	72	30	22	3	2	1	3	7	0	50	1	2	4	3	.571	0	0--	—	2.75
1990 Toronto	AL	27	6	0	8	68.2	297	66	33	31	4	0	4	1	28	4	43	3	0	3	5	.375	0	0-0	1	4.06
1991 Cleveland	AL	11	5	0	1	36	168	58	27	27	7	1	2	1	10	0	13	1	0	2	3	.400	0	0-1	0	6.75
1992 Houston	NL	29	8	0	1	78.2	331	74	47	35	5	4	3	2	25	2	48	2	0	5	7	.417	0	0-0	1	4.00
1993 Colorado	NL	46	18	1	5	146	664	184	90	77	20	10	8	3	42	4	84	6	1	6	10	.375	0	0-0	3	4.75
1994 Colorado	NL	47	1	0	19	77.2	365	98	57	50	9	3	1	4	39	3	68	4	0	0	5	.000	0	3-6	2	5.79
1995 San Diego	NL	40	12	0	11	114	485	112	60	55	11	8	2	2	45	3	83	4	0	7	5	.583	0	0-0	3	4.34
1996 San Diego	NL	60	0	0	17	88	377	80	52	45	13	4	3	7	29	5	67	2	0	2	6	.250	0	1-5	3	4.60
1997 Detroit	AL	29	27	2	0	175	739	186	85	81	18	3	6	3	46	2	90	6	1	16	8	.667	0	0-0	0	4.17
1998 Ari-NYM	NL	34	25	0	2	175.1	750	188	101	97	31	14	4	4	61	2	92	6	0	5	16	.238	0	0-0	0	4.98
1999 Detroit	AL	39	16	0	8	134	604	169	107	102	29	3	4	4	44	0	82	5	0	3	11	.214	0	0-0	0	6.85
2000 Detroit	AL	47	17	0	8	156.2	671	185	89	85	20	1	7	2	35	0	74	2	0	10	6	.625	0	0-2	2	4.88
2001 Detroit	AL	9	4	0	1	24	121	38	30	28	3	2	2	0	11	3	15	0	1	1	4	.200	0	0-0	0	10.50
1998 Arizona	NL	23	23	0	0	146.2	634	165	91	87	27	11	3	3	51	2	71	5	0	4	15	.211	0	0-0	0	5.34
New York	NL	11	2	0	2	28.2	116	23	10	10	4	3	1	1	10	0	21	1	0	1	1	.500	0	0-0	0	3.14
12 ML YEARS		418	139	3	75	1274	5572	1438	778	713	170	53	46	36	415	28	759	41	3	60	86	.411	0	4-14	15	5.04

Casey Blake

Bats: R **Throws:** R **Pos:** 1B-8; DH-5; 3B-5; PH/PR-3 **Ht:** 6'2" **Wt:** 200 **Born:** 8/23/73 **Age:** 28

Year Team	Lg	G	AB	H	2B	3B	HR	(Hm	Rd)	TB	R	RBI	TBB	IBB	SO	HBP	SH	SF	SB	CS	SB%	GDP	Avg	OBP	SLG
1996 Hagerstown	A	48	172	43	13	1	2	—	—	64	29	18	11	1	40	7	0	2	5	3	.63	3	.250	.318	.372
1997 Dunedin	A+	129	449	107	21	0	7	—	—	149	56	39	48	1	91	6	2	2	19	9	.68	5	.238	.319	.332
1998 Dunedin	A+	88	340	119	28	3	11	—	—	186	62	65	30	1	81	9	3	7	9	6	.60	5	.350	.409	.547
Knoxville	AA	45	172	64	15	4	7	—	—	108	41	38	22	0	25	2	0	3	10	0	1.00	6	.372	.442	.628

Year Team	Lg	G	AB	H	2B	3B	HR	(Hm	Rd)	TB	R	RBI	TBB	IBB	SO	HBP	SH	SF	SB	CS	SB%	GDP	Avg	OBP	SLG
1999 Syracuse	AAA	110	387	95	16	2	22	—	—	181	69	75	61	2	82	7	1	2	9	5	.64	10	.245	.357	.468
St.Cathrnes	A-	1	3	2	0	0	0	—	—	2	0	0	1	0	0	0	0	0	0	0	—	0	.667	.750	.667
2000 Syracuse	AAA	30	106	23	6	1	2	—	—	37	10	7	8	0	23	3	0	0	0	3	.00	2	.217	.291	.349
Salt Lake	AAA	80	293	93	22	2	12	—	—	155	59	52	39	0	59	6	2	2	7	2	.78	4	.317	.406	.529
2001 Edmonton	AAA	94	375	116	24	6	10	—	—	182	64	49	34	0	66	6	2	0	14	3	.82	11	.309	.376	.485
1999 Toronto	AL	14	39	10	2	0	1	(0	1)	15	6	1	2	0	7	0	0	0	0	0	—	1	.256	.293	.385
2000 Minnesota	AL	7	16	3	2	0	0	(0	0)	5	1	1	3	0	7	1	0	1	0	0	—	1	.188	.333	.313
2001 Min-Bal	AL	19	37	9	1	0	1	(0	1)	13	3	4	4	1	12	0	0	0	3	0	1.00	0	.243	.317	.351
2001 Minnesota	AL	13	22	7	1	0	0	(0	0)	8	1	2	3	1	8	0	0	0	1	0	1.00	0	.318	.400	.364
Baltimore	AL	6	15	2	0	0	1	(0	1)	5	2	2	1	0	4	0	0	0	2	0	1.00	0	.133	.188	.333
3 ML YEARS		40	92	22	5	0	2	(0	2)	33	10	6	9	1	26	1	0	1	3	0	1.00	2	.239	.311	.359

Henry Blanco

Bats: Right Throws: Right Pos: C-102; PH/PR-3   Ht: 5'11" Wt: 170 Born: 8/29/71 Age: 30

Year Team	Lg	G	AB	H	2B	3B	HR	(Hm	Rd)	TB	R	RBI	TBB	IBB	SO	HBP	SH	SF	SB	CS	SB%	GDP	Avg	OBP	SLG
1997 Los Angeles	NL	3	5	2	0	0	1	(0	1)	5	1	1	0	0	1	0	0	0	0	0	—	0	.400	.400	1.000
1999 Colorado	NL	88	263	61	12	3	6	(3	3)	97	30	28	34	1	38	1	3	2	1	1	.50	4	.232	.320	.369
2000 Milwaukee	NL	93	284	67	24	3	7	(3	4)	112	29	31	36	6	60	0	0	4	0	3	.00	9	.236	.318	.394
2001 Milwaukee	NL	104	314	66	18	3	6	(4	2)	108	33	31	34	6	72	2	5	2	3	1	.75	10	.210	.290	.344
4 ML YEARS		288	866	196	54	6	20	(10	10)	322	93	91	104	13	171	3	8	8	4	5	.44	23	.226	.309	.372

Matt Blank

Pitches: Left Bats: Left Pos: SP-4; RP-1   Ht: 6'2" Wt: 195 Born: 4/5/76 Age: 26

Year Team	Lg	G	GS	CG	GF	IP	BFP	H	R	ER	HR	SH	SF	HB	TBB	IBB	SO	WP	Bk	W	L	Pct.	ShO	Sv-Op	Hld	ERA
1997 Vermont	A-	16	15	2	0	95.2	375	74	26	18	2	1	3	2	14	0	84	0	0	6	4	.600	0	0--	—	1.69
1998 Cape Fear	A	21	21	2	0	134.2	539	121	45	39	6	4	2	9	24	0	114	1	1	9	2	.818	2	0--	—	2.61
Jupiter	A+	8	6	0	1	42.1	170	33	14	11	2	0	1	4	10	0	26	0	1	1	1	.833	0	0--	—	2.34
1999 Jupiter	A+	14	14	3	0	90	348	64	26	24	5	3	3	2	19	1	66	1	2	9	5	.643	1	0--	—	2.40
Harrisburg	AA	14	14	0	0	85	363	94	41	37	14	5	2	0	26	0	42	3	0	6	3	.667	0	0--	—	3.92
2001 Ottawa	AAA	14	14	1	0	81.2	367	89	52	47	13	3	5	8	30	0	58	3	2	6	7	.462	0	0--	—	5.18
2000 Montreal	NL	13	0	0	3	14	63	12	8	8	1	2	1	1	5	1	4	0	0	0	1	.000	0	0-1	0	5.14
2001 Montreal	NL	5	4	0	0	22.2	104	23	14	13	5	1	2	2	13	1	11	0	0	2	2	.500	0	0-0	0	5.16
2 ML YEARS		18	4	0	3	36.2	167	35	22	21	6	3	3	3	18	2	15	0	0	2	3	.400	0	0-1	0	5.15

Geoff Blum

Bats: B Throws: R Pos: 3B-72; LF-35; 2B-25; PH/PR-18; 1B-14; SS-4   Ht: 6'3" Wt: 195 Born: 4/26/73 Age: 29

Year Team	Lg	G	AB	H	2B	3B	HR	(Hm	Rd)	TB	R	RBI	TBB	IBB	SO	HBP	SH	SF	SB	CS	SB%	GDP	Avg	OBP	SLG
1999 Montreal	NL	45	133	32	7	0	8	(0	8)	67	21	18	17	3	25	0	3	0	1	0	1.00	3	.241	.327	.504
2000 Montreal	NL	124	343	97	20	2	11	(5	6)	154	40	45	26	2	60	3	3	4	1	4	.20	4	.283	.335	.449
2001 Montreal	NL	148	453	107	25	0	9	(6	3)	159	57	50	43	8	94	10	3	5	9	5	.64	12	.236	.313	.351
3 ML YEARS		317	929	236	52	4	28	(11	17)	380	118	113	86	13	179	13	9	9	11	9	.55	19	.254	.323	.409

Hiram Bocachica

Bats: R Throws: R Pos: PH/PR-43; 2B-19; LF-10; 3B-8; RF-3   Ht: 5'11" Wt: 165 Born: 3/4/76 Age: 26

Year Team	Lg	G	AB	H	2B	3B	HR	(Hm	Rd)	TB	R	RBI	TBB	IBB	SO	HBP	SH	SF	SB	CS	SB%	GDP	Avg	OBP	SLG
1994 Expos	R	43	168	47	9	0	5	—	—	71	31	16	15	0	42	2	2	0	11	4	.73	1	.280	.346	.423
1995 Albany	A	96	380	108	20	10	2	—	—	154	65	30	52	3	78	8	3	1	47	17	.73	4	.284	.381	.405
1996 Expos	R	9	32	8	3	0	0	—	—	11	11	2	5	1	3	1	0	0	2	1	.67	0	.250	.368	.344
Wst Plm Bch	A+	71	267	90	17	5	2	—	—	123	50	26	34	0	47	6	3	3	21	3	.88	6	.337	.419	.461
1997 Harrisburg	AA	119	443	123	19	3	11	—	—	181	82	35	41	1	98	13	1	3	29	12	.71	3	.278	.354	.409
1998 Harrisburg	AA	80	296	78	18	4	4	—	—	116	39	27	21	2	61	11	2	1	20	8	.71	1	.264	.334	.392
Ottawa	AAA	12	41	8	3	1	0	—	—	13	5	5	6	0	14	1	0	0	2	0	1.00	1	.195	.313	.317
Albuquerque	AAA	26	101	24	7	1	4	—	—	45	16	16	13	1	24	6	1	0	5	3	.63	1	.238	.358	.446
1999 San Antonio	AA	123	477	139	22	10	11	—	—	214	84	60	60	0	71	13	4	5	30	15	.67	5	.291	.382	.449
2000 Albuquerque	AAA	124	482	155	38	4	23	—	—	270	99	84	40	0	100	15	9	2	10	14	.42	7	.322	.390	.560
2000 Los Angeles	NL	8	10	3	0	0	0	(0	0)	3	2	0	0	0	2	0	0	0	0	0	—	0	.300	.300	.300
2001 Los Angeles	NL	75	133	31	11	1	2	(2	0)	50	15	9	9	0	33	1	0	0	4	1	.80	1	.233	.287	.376
2 ML YEARS		83	143	34	11	1	2	(2	0)	53	17	9	9	0	35	1	0	0	4	1	.80	1	.238	.288	.371

Brian Boehringer

Pitches: Right Bats: Both Pos: RP-51   Ht: 6'2" Wt: 190 Born: 1/8/70 Age: 32

Year Team	Lg	G	GS	CG	GF	IP	BFP	H	R	ER	HR	SH	SF	HB	TBB	IBB	SO	WP	Bk	W	L	Pct.	ShO	Sv-Op	Hld	ERA
1995 New York	AL	7	3	0	0	17.2	99	24	27	27	5	0	1	1	22	1	10	3	0	0	3	.000	0	0-1	0	13.75
1996 New York	AL	15	3	0	1	46.1	205	46	28	28	6	3	3	1	21	2	37	1	0	2	4	.333	0	0-1	0	5.44
1997 New York	AL	34	0	0	11	48	210	39	16	14	4	3	2	0	32	6	53	2	0	3	2	.600	0	0-3	5	2.63
1998 San Diego	NL	56	1	0	18	76.1	347	75	38	37	10	5	1	4	45	4	67	1	0	5	2	.714	0	0-1	7	4.36
1999 San Diego	NL	33	11	0	8	94.1	409	97	38	34	11	1	3	5	35	4	64	2	0	6	5	.545	0	0-2	3	3.24
2000 San Diego	NL	7	3	0	1	15.2	72	18	15	10	4	0	1	0	10	0	9	2	0	0	3	.000	0	0-1	0	5.74
2001 NYY-SF		51	0	0	17	69	311	67	35	28	7	2	4	5	29	5	60	0	0	0	4	.000	0	2-2	5	3.65
San Francisco	NL	29	0	0	17	34.1	156	32	20	16	4	1	2	2	15	5	27	0	0	0	1	.000	0	1-1	2	4.19
7 ML YEARS		203	21	0	56	367.1	1655	366	197	178	46	19	16	12	194	22	300	9	0	16	23	.410	0	2-11	22	4.36

Tim Bogar

Bats: R **Throws:** R **Pos:** PH/PR-7; 1B-3; SS-2; 3B-1 **Ht:** 6'2" **Wt:** 198 **Born:** 10/28/66 **Age:** 35

Year Team	Lg	G	AB	H	2B	3B	HR	(Hm	Rd)	TB	R	RBI	TBB	IBB	SO	HBP	SH	SF	SB	CS	SB%	GDP	Avg	OBP	SLG
2001 Las Vegas *	AAA	16	52	13	5	0	0	—	—	18	8	4	3	0	11	0	0	0	0	1	.00	1	.250	.291	.346
1993 New York	NL	78	205	50	13	0	3	(1	2)	72	19	25	14	2	29	3	1	1	0	1	.00	1	.244	.300	.351
1994 New York	NL	50	52	8	0	0	2	(0	2)	14	5	5	4	1	11	0	2	1	1	0	1.00	1	.154	.211	.269
1995 New York	NL	78	145	42	7	0	1	(0	1)	52	17	21	9	0	25	0	2	1	1	0	1.00	2	.290	.329	.359
1996 New York	NL	91	89	19	4	0	0	(0	0)	23	17	6	8	0	20	2	3	2	1	3	.25	1	.213	.287	.258
1997 Houston	NL	97	241	60	14	4	4	(3	1)	94	30	30	24	1	42	3	3	4	4	1	.80	4	.249	.320	.390
1998 Houston	NL	79	156	24	4	1	1	(0	1)	33	12	8	9	2	36	2	1	1	2	1	.67	5	.154	.208	.212
1999 Houston	NL	106	309	74	16	2	4	(2	2)	106	44	31	38	5	52	4	0	3	3	5	.38	10	.239	.328	.343
2000 Houston	NL	110	304	63	9	2	7	(3	4)	97	32	33	35	7	56	3	5	4	1	1	.50	15	.207	.292	.319
2001 Los Angeles	NL	12	15	5	2	0	2	(1	1)	13	4	2	2	0	1	0	0	0	0	0	—	0	.333	.412	.867
9 ML YEARS		701	1516	345	69	9	24	(10	14)	504	180	161	143	18	272	17	17	17	13	12	.52	39	.228	.298	.332

Brian Bohanon

Pitches: Left **Bats:** Left **Pos:** SP-19; RP-1 **Ht:** 6'2" **Wt:** 250 **Born:** 8/1/68 **Age:** 33

Year Team	Lg	G	GS	CG	GF	IP	BFP	H	R	ER	HR	SH	SF	HB	TBB	IBB	SO	WP	Bk	W	L	Pct.	ShO	Sv-Op	Hld	ERA
2001 Colo Sprngs *	AAA	1	1	0	0	5	23	8	1	1	0	0	0	0	1	0	2	0	0	0	0	—	0	0--	—	1.80
1990 Texas	AL	11	6	0	1	34	158	40	30	25	6	0	3	2	18	0	15	1	0	0	3	.000	0	0-0	0	6.62
1991 Texas	AL	11	11	1	0	61.1	273	66	35	33	4	2	5	2	23	0	34	3	1	4	3	.571	0	0-0	0	4.84
1992 Texas	AL	18	7	0	3	45.2	220	57	38	32	7	0	2	1	25	0	29	2	0	1	1	.500	0	0-0	0	6.31
1993 Texas	AL	36	8	0	4	92.2	418	107	54	49	8	2	5	4	46	3	45	10	0	4	4	.500	0	0-1	1	4.76
1994 Texas	AL	11	5	0	1	37.1	169	51	31	30	7	1	0	1	8	1	26	5	0	2	2	.500	0	0-0	0	7.23
1995 Detroit	AL	52	10	0	7	105.2	474	121	68	65	10	0	5	4	41	5	63	3	0	1	1	.500	0	1-1	10	5.54
1996 Toronto	AL	20	0	0	6	22	112	27	19	19	4	0	2	2	19	4	17	2	0	0	1	.000	0	1-1	2	7.77
1997 New York	NL	19	14	0	0	94.1	412	95	49	40	9	6	0	4	34	2	66	3	1	6	4	.600	0	0-0	0	3.82
1998 NYM-LA	NL	39	18	2	4	151.2	626	121	56	45	13	7	2	11	57	2	111	3	0	7	11	.389	0	0-1	1	2.67
1999 Colorado	NL	33	33	3	0	197.1	903	236	146	136	30	18	3	14	92	1	120	6	0	12	12	.500	1	0-0	0	6.20
2000 Colorado	NL	34	26	2	0	177	772	181	101	92	24	4	3	6	79	4	98	2	0	12	10	.545	1	0-0	2	4.68
2001 Colorado	NL	20	19	0	0	97	456	127	79	77	20	8	1	7	47	3	47	2	0	5	8	.385	0	0-0	0	7.14
1998 New York	NL	25	4	0	4	54.1	230	47	21	19	4	2	0	6	21	2	39	1	0	2	4	.333	0	0-1	1	3.15
Los Angeles	NL	14	14	2	0	97.1	396	74	35	26	9	5	2	5	36	0	72	2	0	5	7	.417	0	0-0	0	2.40
12 ML YEARS		304	157	8	26	1116	4993	1229	706	643	142	48	31	58	489	25	671	42	2	54	60	.474	2	2-4	16	5.19

Barry Bonds

Bats: Left **Throws:** Left **Pos:** LF-143; DH-6; PH/PR-5 **Ht:** 6'2" **Wt:** 210 **Born:** 7/24/64 **Age:** 37

Year Team	Lg	G	AB	H	2B	3B	HR	(Hm	Rd)	TB	R	RBI	TBB	IBB	SO	HBP	SH	SF	SB	CS	SB%	GDP	Avg	OBP	SLG
1986 Pittsburgh	NL	113	413	92	26	3	16	(9	7)	172	72	48	65	2	102	2	2	2	36	7	.84	4	.223	.330	.416
1987 Pittsburgh	NL	150	551	144	34	9	25	(12	13)	271	99	59	54	3	88	3	0	3	32	10	.76	4	.261	.329	.492
1988 Pittsburgh	NL	144	538	152	30	5	24	(14	10)	264	97	58	72	14	82	2	0	2	17	11	.61	3	.283	.368	.491
1989 Pittsburgh	NL	159	580	144	34	6	19	(7	12)	247	96	58	93	22	93	1	1	4	32	10	.76	9	.248	.351	.426
1990 Pittsburgh	NL	151	519	156	32	3	33	(14	19)	293	104	114	93	15	83	3	0	6	52	13	.80	8	.301	.406	.565
1991 Pittsburgh	NL	153	510	149	28	5	25	(12	13)	262	95	116	107	25	73	4	0	13	43	13	.77	8	.292	.410	.514
1992 Pittsburgh	NL	140	473	147	36	5	34	(15	19)	295	109	103	127	32	69	5	0	7	39	8	.83	9	.311	.456	.624
1993 San Francisco	NL	159	539	181	38	4	46	(21	25)	365	129	123	126	43	79	2	0	7	29	12	.71	11	.336	.458	.677
1994 San Francisco	NL	112	391	122	18	1	37	(15	22)	253	89	81	74	18	43	6	0	3	29	9	.76	3	.312	.426	.647
1995 San Francisco	NL	144	506	149	30	7	33	(16	17)	292	109	104	120	22	83	5	0	4	31	10	.76	12	.294	.431	.577
1996 San Francisco	NL	158	517	159	27	3	42	(25	17)	318	122	129	151	30	76	1	0	6	40	7	.85	11	.308	.461	.615
1997 San Francisco	NL	159	532	155	26	5	40	(24	16)	311	123	101	145	34	87	8	0	5	37	8	.82	13	.291	.446	.585
1998 San Francisco	NL	156	552	167	44	7	37	(21	16)	336	120	122	130	29	92	8	1	6	28	12	.70	15	.303	.438	.609
1999 San Francisco	NL	102	355	93	20	2	34	(16	18)	219	91	83	73	9	62	3	0	3	15	2	.88	6	.262	.389	.617
2000 San Francisco	NL	143	480	147	28	4	49	(25	24)	330	129	106	117	22	77	3	0	9	11	3	.79	6	.306	.440	.688
2001 San Francisco	NL	153	476	156	32	2	73	(37	36)	411	129	137	177	35	93	9	0	2	13	3	.81	5	.328	.515	.863
16 ML YEARS		2296	7932	2313	483	71	567	(281	286)	4639	1713	1542	1724	355	1282	65	4	80	484	138	.78	127	.292	.419	.585

Ricky Bones

Pitches: Right **Bats:** Right **Pos:** RP-61 **Ht:** 6'0" **Wt:** 202 **Born:** 4/7/69 **Age:** 33

Year Team	Lg	G	GS	CG	GF	IP	BFP	H	R	ER	HR	SH	SF	HB	TBB	IBB	SO	WP	Bk	W	L	Pct.	ShO	Sv-Op	Hld	ERA
1991 San Diego	NL	11	11	0	0	54	234	57	33	29	3	0	4	0	18	0	31	4	0	4	6	.400	0	0-0	0	4.83
1992 Milwaukee	AL	31	28	0	0	163.1	705	169	90	83	27	2	5	9	48	0	65	3	2	9	10	.474	0	0-0	0	4.57
1993 Milwaukee	AL	32	31	3	1	203.2	883	222	122	110	28	5	7	8	63	3	63	6	1	11	11	.500	0	0-0	0	4.86
1994 Milwaukee	AL	24	24	4	0	170.2	708	166	76	65	17	4	5	3	45	1	57	8	0	10	9	.526	1	0-0	0	3.43
1995 Milwaukee	AL	32	31	3	0	200.1	877	218	108	103	26	3	11	4	83	2	77	5	2	10	12	.455	0	0-0	0	4.63
1996 Mil-NYY	AL	36	24	0	2	152	699	184	115	105	30	5	5	10	68	2	63	2	0	7	14	.333	0	0-0	3	6.22
1997 Cin-KC		30	13	1	4	96	450	133	81	72	12	3	8	7	36	4	44	1	0	4	8	.333	0	0-1	2	6.75
1998 Kansas City	AL	32	0	0	12	53.1	231	49	18	18	4	5	0	1	24	5	38	2	0	2	0	1.000	0	1-2	3	3.04
1999 Baltimore	AL	30	2	0	7	43.2	207	59	29	29	7	2	1	2	19	0	26	3	0	0	3	.000	0	0-3	5	5.98
2000 Florida	NL	56	0	0	13	77.1	352	94	43	39	6	6	6	3	27	8	59	2	1	2	3	.400	0	0-3	6	4.54
2001 Florida	NL	61	0	0	19	64	288	71	39	36	7	2	2	3	33	9	41	0	0	4	4	.500	0	0-0	5	5.06
1996 Milwaukee	AL	32	23	0	2	145	658	170	104	94	28	4	4	9	62	2	59	2	0	7	14	.333	0	0-0	3	5.83
New York	AL	4	1	0	0	7	41	14	11	11	2	1	1	1	6	0	4	0	0	0	0	—	0	0-0	0	14.14
1997 Cincinnati	NL	9	2	0	2	17.2	98	31	22	20	2	1	2	2	11	2	8	0	0	0	1	.000	0	0-0	0	10.19
Kansas City	AL	21	11	1	2	78.1	352	102	59	52	10	2	6	5	25	2	36	1	0	4	7	.364	0	0-1	2	5.97
11 ML YEARS		375	164	11	58	1278.1	5634	1422	754	689	167	37	54	50	464	34	564	36	6	63	82	.434	1	1-9	23	4.85

Bobby Bonilla

Bats: B **Throws:** R **Pos:** PH/PR-54; 1B-33; RF-6; LF-4; DH-2; P-1 **Ht:** 6'3" **Wt:** 240 **Born:** 2/23/63 **Age:** 39

Year Team	Lg	G	AB	H	2B	3B	HR	(Hm	Rd)	TB	R	RBI	TBB	IBB	SO	HBP	SH	SF	SB	CS	SB%	GDP	Avg	OBP	SLG
1986 CWS-Pit		138	426	109	16	4	3	(2	1)	142	55	43	62	3	88	2	5	1	8	5	.62	9	.256	.352	.333
1987 Pittsburgh	NL	141	466	140	33	3	15	(7	8)	224	58	77	39	4	64	2	0	8	3	5	.38	8	.300	.351	.481
1988 Pittsburgh	NL	159	584	160	32	7	24	(9	15)	278	87	100	85	19	82	4	0	8	3	5	.38	4	.274	.366	.476
1989 Pittsburgh	NL	163	616	173	37	10	24	(13	11)	302	96	86	76	20	93	1	0	5	8	8	.50	10	.281	.358	.490
1990 Pittsburgh	NL	160	625	175	39	7	32	(13	19)	324	112	120	45	9	103	1	0	15	4	3	.57	11	.280	.322	.518
1991 Pittsburgh	NL	157	577	174	44	6	18	(9	9)	284	102	100	90	8	67	2	0	11	2	4	.33	14	.302	.391	.492
1992 New York	NL	128	438	109	23	0	19	(5	14)	189	62	70	66	10	73	1	0	1	4	3	.57	11	.249	.348	.432
1993 New York	NL	139	502	133	21	3	34	(18	16)	262	81	87	72	11	96	0	0	8	3	3	.50	12	.265	.352	.522
1994 New York	NL	108	403	117	24	1	20	(8	12)	203	60	67	55	9	101	0	0	2	1	3	.25	10	.290	.374	.504
1995 NYM-Bal		141	554	182	37	8	28	(14	14)	319	96	99	54	10	79	2	0	4	0	5	.00	22	.329	.388	.576
1996 Baltimore	AL	159	595	171	27	5	28	(9	19)	292	107	116	75	7	85	5	0	17	1	3	.25	13	.287	.363	.491
1997 Florida	NL	153	562	167	39	3	17	(8	9)	263	77	96	73	8	94	5	0	8	6	6	.50	18	.297	.378	.468
1998 Fla-LA	NL	100	333	83	11	1	11	(8	3)	129	39	45	41	4	59	0	0	6	1	2	.33	16	.249	.326	.387
1999 New York	NL	60	119	19	5	0	4	(2	2)	36	12	18	19	1	16	1	0	2	0	1	.00	4	.160	.277	.303
2000 Atlanta	NL	114	239	61	13	3	5	(4	1)	95	23	28	37	2	51	1	0	1	1	1	—	3	.255	.356	.397
2001 St. Louis	NL	93	174	37	7	0	5	(3	2)	59	17	21	23	3	53	1	0	0	1	1	.50	4	.213	.308	.339
1986 Chicago	AL	75	234	63	10	2	2	(2	0)	83	27	26	33	2	49	1	2	1	4	1	.80	4	.269	.361	.355
Pittsburgh		63	192	46	6	2	1	(0	1)	59	28	17	29	1	39	1	3	0	4	4	.50	5	.240	.342	.307
1995 New York	NL	80	317	103	25	4	18	(7	11)	190	49	53	31	10	48	1	0	2	0	3	.00	11	.325	.385	.599
Baltimore	AL	61	237	79	12	4	10	(7	3)	129	47	46	23	0	31	1	0	2	0	2	.00	11	.333	.392	.544
1998 Florida	NL	28	97	27	5	0	4	(3	1)	44	11	15	12	1	22	0	0	1	0	1	.00	6	.278	.355	.454
Los Angeles	NL	72	236	56	6	1	7	(5	2)	85	28	30	29	3	37	0	0	5	1	1	.50	10	.237	.315	.360
16 ML YEARS		2113	7213	2010	408	61	287	(132	155)	3401	1084	1173	912	128	1204	28	5	97	45	57	.44	169	.279	.358	.472

Aaron Boone

Bats: Right **Throws:** Right **Pos:** 3B-103; PH/PR-1 **Ht:** 6'2" **Wt:** 200 **Born:** 3/9/73 **Age:** 29

Year Team	Lg	G	AB	H	2B	3B	HR	(Hm	Rd)	TB	R	RBI	TBB	IBB	SO	HBP	SH	SF	SB	CS	SB%	GDP	Avg	OBP	SLG
2001 Louisville *	AAA	1	4	1	0	0	0	—	—	1	0	0	0	0	0	0	0	0	0	0	—	0	.250	.250	.250
1997 Cincinnati	NL	16	49	12	1	0	0	(0	0)	13	5	5	2	0	5	0	1	0	1	0	1.00	1	.245	.275	.265
1998 Cincinnati	NL	58	181	51	13	2	2	(2	0)	74	24	28	15	1	36	5	3	2	6	1	.86	3	.282	.350	.409
1999 Cincinnati	NL	139	472	132	26	5	14	(7	7)	210	56	72	30	2	79	8	5	5	17	6	.74	6	.280	.330	.445
2000 Cincinnati	NL	84	291	83	18	0	12	(5	7)	137	44	43	24	1	52	10	2	4	6	1	.86	5	.285	.356	.471
2001 Cincinnati	NL	103	381	112	26	2	14	(10	4)	184	54	62	29	1	71	8	3	6	6	3	.67	9	.294	.351	.483
5 ML YEARS		400	1374	390	84	9	42	(24	18)	618	183	210	100	5	243	31	14	17	36	11	.77	24	.284	.342	.450

Bret Boone

Bats: Right **Throws:** Right **Pos:** 2B-156; PH/PR-3; DH-2 **Ht:** 5'10" **Wt:** 180 **Born:** 4/6/69 **Age:** 33

Year Team	Lg	G	AB	H	2B	3B	HR	(Hm	Rd)	TB	R	RBI	TBB	IBB	SO	HBP	SH	SF	SB	CS	SB%	GDP	Avg	OBP	SLG
1992 Seattle	AL	33	129	25	4	0	4	(2	2)	41	15	15	4	0	34	1	1	0	1	1	.50	4	.194	.224	.318
1993 Seattle	AL	76	271	68	12	2	12	(7	5)	120	31	38	17	1	52	4	6	4	2	3	.40	6	.251	.301	.443
1994 Cincinnati	NL	108	381	122	25	2	12	(5	7)	187	59	68	24	1	74	8	5	6	3	4	.43	10	.320	.368	.491
1995 Cincinnati	NL	138	513	137	34	2	15	(6	9)	220	63	68	41	0	84	6	5	1	5	1	.83	14	.267	.326	.429
1996 Cincinnati	NL	142	520	121	21	3	12	(7	5)	184	56	69	31	0	100	3	5	9	3	2	.60	9	.233	.275	.354
1997 Cincinnati	NL	139	443	99	25	1	7	(4	3)	147	40	46	45	4	101	4	4	5	5	5	.50	11	.223	.298	.332
1998 Cincinnati	NL	157	583	155	38	1	24	(13	11)	267	76	95	48	3	104	4	9	4	6	4	.60	23	.266	.324	.458
1999 Atlanta	NL	152	608	153	38	1	20	(9	11)	253	102	63	47	0	112	5	9	2	14	9	.61	11	.252	.310	.416
2000 San Diego	NL	127	463	116	18	2	19	(8	11)	195	61	74	50	7	97	5	0	2	8	4	.67	11	.251	.326	.421
2001 Seattle	AL	158	623	206	37	3	37	(19	18)	360	118	141	40	5	110	9	5	13	5	5	.50	11	.331	.372	.578
10 ML YEARS		1230	4534	1202	252	17	162	(80	82)	1974	621	677	347	21	868	49	49	55	52	38	.58	110	.265	.321	.435

Pedro Borbon

Pitches: Left **Bats:** Left **Pos:** RP-71 **Ht:** 6'1" **Wt:** 205 **Born:** 11/15/67 **Age:** 34

Year Team	Lg	G	GS	CG	GF	IP	BFP	H	R	ER	HR	SH	SF	HB	TBB	IBB	SO	WP	Bk	W	L	Pct.	ShO	Sv-Op	Hld	ERA
1992 Atlanta	NL	2	0	0	2	1.1	7	2	1	1	0	0	0	0	1	1	1	0	0	0	0	.000	0	0-0	0	6.75
1993 Atlanta	NL	3	0	0	0	1.2	11	3	4	4	0	1	0	0	3	0	2	0	0	0	0	—	0	0-0	0	21.60
1995 Atlanta	NL	41	0	0	19	32	143	29	12	11	2	3	1	1	17	4	33	0	1	2	2	.500	0	2-4	6	3.09
1996 Atlanta	NL	43	0	0	19	36	140	26	12	11	1	4	0	1	7	0	31	0	0	3	0	1.000	0	1-1	4	2.75
1999 Los Angeles	NL	70	0	0	11	50.2	220	39	23	23	5	0	3	1	29	1	33	1	0	4	3	.571	0	1-2	15	4.09
2000 Toronto	AL	59	0	0	6	41.2	213	45	37	30	5	2	7	5	38	5	29	0	0	1	1	.500	0	1-1	12	6.48
2001 Toronto	AL	71	0	0	14	53.1	217	48	24	22	8	2	2	4	12	3	45	0	0	2	4	.333	0	0-5	13	3.71
7 ML YEARS		289	0	0	71	216.2	951	192	113	102	21	12	13	12	107	14	174	1	1	12	11	.522	0	5-13	50	4.24

Pat Borders

Bats: Right **Throws:** Right **Pos:** C-5; PH/PR-1 **Ht:** 6'2" **Wt:** 200 **Born:** 5/14/63 **Age:** 39

Year Team	Lg	G	AB	H	2B	3B	HR	(Hm	Rd)	TB	R	RBI	TBB	IBB	SO	HBP	SH	SF	SB	CS	SB%	GDP	Avg	OBP	SLG
2001 Durham *	AAA	87	313	74	15	1	1	—	—	97	26	28	16	0	61	1	2	1	3	2	.60	14	.236	.278	.310
Tacoma *	AAA	3	11	3	0	0	1	—	—	6	2	2	1	0	1	1	0	0	0	0	—	1	.273	.385	.545
1988 Toronto	AL	56	154	42	6	3	5	(2	3)	69	15	21	3	0	24	0	2	1	0	0	—	5	.273	.285	.448
1989 Toronto	AL	94	241	62	11	1	3	(1	2)	84	22	29	11	2	45	1	1	2	2	1	.67	7	.257	.290	.349
1990 Toronto	AL	125	346	99	24	2	15	(10	5)	172	36	49	18	2	57	0	1	3	0	1	.00	17	.286	.319	.497
1991 Toronto	AL	105	291	71	17	0	5	(2	3)	103	22	36	11	1	45	1	6	3	0	0	—	8	.244	.271	.354
1992 Toronto	AL	138	480	116	26	2	13	(7	6)	185	47	53	33	4	75	2	1	5	1	1	.50	11	.242	.290	.385
1993 Toronto	AL	138	488	124	30	4	16	(6	3)	181	38	55	20	2	66	2	7	3	2	2	.50	18	.254	.285	.371

					BATTING														BASERUNNING				PERCENTAGES		
Year Team	Lg	G	AB	H	2B	3B	HR	(Hm	Rd)	TB	R	RBI	TBB	IBB	SO	HBP	SH	SF	SB	CS	SB%	GDP	Avg	OBP	SLG
1994 Toronto	AL	85	295	73	13	1	3	(3	0)	97	24	26	15	0	50	0	1	0	1	1	.50	7	.247	.284	.329
1995 KC-Hou		63	178	37	8	1	4	(1	3)	59	15	13	9	2	29	0	0	0	0	0	—	3	.208	.246	.331
1996 StL-Cal-CWS		76	220	61	7	0	5	(3	2)	83	15	18	9	0	43	0	5	0	0	2	.00	4	.277	.306	.377
1997 Cleveland	AL	55	159	47	7	1	4	(0	4)	68	17	15	9	0	27	2	0	0	0	2	.00	5	.296	.341	.428
1998 Cleveland	AL	54	160	38	6	0	0	(0	0)	44	12	6	10	0	40	2	2	1	0	2	.00	3	.238	.289	.275
1999 Cle-Tor	AL	12	34	9	0	1	1	(1	0)	14	3	6	1	0	5	0	0	0	0	1	.00	0	.265	.286	.412
2001 Seattle	AL	5	6	3	0	0	0	(0	0)	3	1	0	0	0	1	0	1	0	0	0	—	0	.500	.500	.500
1995 Kansas City	AL	52	143	33	8	1	4	(1	3)	55	14	13	7	1	22	0	0	0	0	0	—	1	.231	.267	.385
Houston	NL	11	35	4	0	0	0	(0	0)	4	1	0	2	1	7	0	0	0	0	0	—	2	.114	.162	.114
1996 St. Louis	NL	26	69	22	3	0	0	(0	0)	25	3	4	1	0	14	0	1	0	0	1	.00	1	.319	.329	.362
California	AL	19	57	13	3	0	2	(2	0)	22	6	8	3	0	11	0	1	0	0	1	.00	1	.228	.267	.386
Chicago	AL	31	94	26	1	0	3	(1	2)	36	6	6	5	0	18	0	3	0	0	0	—	2	.277	.313	.383
1999 Cleveland	AL	6	20	6	0	1	0	(0	0)	8	2	3	0	0	3	0	0	0	0	1	.00	0	.300	.300	.400
Toronto	AL	6	14	3	0	0	1	(1	0)	6	1	3	1	0	2	0	0	0	0	0	—	0	.214	.267	.429
13 ML YEARS		1006	3052	782	155	12	67	(36	31)	1162	267	327	149	12	507	10	27	18	6	13	.32	88	.256	.291	.381

Mike Bordick

Bats: Right **Throws:** Right **Pos:** SS-58   **Ht:** 5'11" **Wt:** 175 **Born:** 7/21/65 **Age:** 36

					BATTING														BASERUNNING				PERCENTAGES		
Year Team	Lg	G	AB	H	2B	3B	HR	(Hm	Rd)	TB	R	RBI	TBB	IBB	SO	HBP	SH	SF	SB	CS	SB%	GDP	Avg	OBP	SLG
2001 Bowie *	AA	1	4	1	0	0	0	—		1	0	0	0	0	1	0	0	0	0	0	—	0	.250	.250	.250
Delmarva *	A	3	8	0	0	0	0	—	—	0	0	1	2	0	1	0	0	0	0	0	—	0	.000	.200	.000
1990 Oakland	AL	25	14	1	0	0	0	(0	0)	1	0	0	1	0	4	0	0	0	0	0	—	0	.071	.133	.071
1991 Oakland	AL	90	235	56	5	1	0	(0	0)	63	21	21	14	0	37	3	12	1	3	4	.43	3	.238	.289	.268
1992 Oakland	AL	154	504	151	19	4	3	(3	0)	187	62	48	40	2	59	9	14	5	12	6	.67	10	.300	.358	.371
1993 Oakland	AL	159	546	136	21	2	3	(2	1)	170	60	48	60	2	58	11	10	6	10	10	.50	9	.249	.332	.311
1994 Oakland	AL	114	391	99	18	4	2	(1	1)	131	38	37	38	1	44	3	3	5	7	2	.78	9	.253	.320	.335
1995 Oakland	AL	126	428	113	13	0	8	(2	6)	150	46	44	35	2	48	5	7	3	11	3	.79	8	.264	.325	.350
1996 Oakland	AL	155	525	126	18	4	5	(2	3)	167	46	54	52	0	59	1	4	5	5	6	.45	8	.240	.307	.318
1997 Baltimore	AL	153	509	120	19	1	7	(5	2)	162	55	46	33	1	66	2	12	4	0	2	.00	23	.236	.283	.318
1998 Baltimore	AL	151	465	121	29	1	13	(10	3)	191	59	51	39	0	65	10	15	4	6	7	.46	13	.260	.328	.411
1999 Baltimore	AL	160	631	175	35	7	10	(3	7)	254	93	77	54	1	102	5	8	10	14	4	.78	25	.277	.334	.403
2000 Bal-NYM		156	583	166	30	1	20	(9	11)	258	88	80	49	0	99	3	4	5	9	6	.60	16	.285	.341	.443
2001 Baltimore	AL	58	229	57	13	0	7	(2	5)	91	32	30	17	1	36	6	2	3	9	3	.75	4	.249	.314	.397
2000 Baltimore	AL	100	391	116	22	1	16	(6	10)	188	70	59	34	0	71	1	2	5	6	5	.55	12	.297	.350	.481
New York	NL	56	192	50	8	0	4	(3	1)	70	18	21	15	0	28	2	2	0	3	1	.75	4	.260	.321	.365
12 ML YEARS		1501	5060	1321	220	25	78	(39	39)	1825	600	536	432	10	677	58	91	51	86	53	.62	128	.261	.323	.361

Dave Borkowski

Pitches: Right **Bats:** Right **Pos:** RP-15   **Ht:** 6'1" **Wt:** 200 **Born:** 2/7/77 **Age:** 25

		HOW MUCH HE PITCHED						WHAT HE GAVE UP												THE RESULTS					
Year Team	Lg	G	GS	CG	GF	IP	BFP	H	R	ER	HR	SH	SF	HB	TBB	IBB	SO	WP	Bk	W	L	Pct.	ShO	Sv-Op	Hld	ERA
2001 Toledo *	AAA	18	0	0	4	28	118	22	14	11	1	3	0	3	9	1	22	2	0	1	2	.333	0	1-—	—	3.54
1999 Detroit	AL	17	12	0	2	76.2	351	86	58	52	10	1	2	4	40	0	50	3	0	2	6	.250	0	0-0	0	6.10
2000 Detroit	AL	2	1	0	0	5.1	34	11	13	13	2	0	1	0	7	1	1	0	0	0	1	.000	0	0-0	0	21.94
2001 Detroit	AL	15	0	0	7	29.2	135	30	21	21	5	0	2	3	15	3	30	0	0	0	2	.000	0	0-0	0	6.37
3 ML YEARS		34	13	0	9	111.2	520	127	92	86	17	1	5	7	62	4	81	3	0	2	9	.182	0	0-0	0	6.93

Toby Borland

Pitches: Right **Bats:** Right **Pos:** RP-2   **Ht:** 6'6" **Wt:** 193 **Born:** 5/29/69 **Age:** 33

		HOW MUCH HE PITCHED						WHAT HE GAVE UP												THE RESULTS					
Year Team	Lg	G	GS	CG	GF	IP	BFP	H	R	ER	HR	SH	SF	HB	TBB	IBB	SO	WP	Bk	W	L	Pct.	ShO	Sv-Op	Hld	ERA
2001 Salt Lake *	AAA	45	1	0	16	74.1	302	53	25	19	2	1	2	2	29	0	92	9	0	7	3	.700	0	3-—	—	2.30
1994 Philadelphia	NL	24	0	0	7	34.1	144	31	10	9	1	1	0	4	14	3	26	4	0	1	0	1.000	0	1-1	0	2.36
1995 Philadelphia	NL	50	0	0	18	74	339	81	37	31	3	3	2	5	37	7	59	12	0	1	3	.250	0	6-9	11	3.77
1996 Philadelphia	NL	69	0	0	11	90.2	399	83	51	41	9	4	1	3	43	3	76	10	0	7	3	.700	0	0-2	10	4.07
1997 NYM-Bos		16	0	0	5	16.2	89	17	14	14	2	0	0	3	21	0	8	3	0	0	1	.000	0	1-2	1	7.56
1998 Philadelphia	NL	6	0	0	3	9	39	8	5	5	1	1	0	0	5	0	9	2	0	0	0	—	0	0-0	0	5.00
2001 Anaheim	AL	2	0	0	1	3.1	19	8	5	4	1	1	0	0	1	0	0	0	0	0	0	—	0	0-1	0	10.80
1997 New York	NL	13	0	0	5	13.1	65	11	9	9	1	0	0	1	14	0	7	3	0	0	1	.000	0	1-2	1	6.08
Boston	AL	3	0	0	0	3.1	24	6	5	5	1	0	0	2	7	0	1	0	0	0	0	—	0	0-0	0	13.50
6 ML YEARS		167	0	0	45	228	1029	228	122	104	17	10	3	15	121	13	178	31	0	9	8	.529	0	8-15	22	4.11

Joe Borowski

Pitches: Right **Bats:** Right **Pos:** SP-1   **Ht:** 6'2" **Wt:** 225 **Born:** 5/4/71 **Age:** 31

		HOW MUCH HE PITCHED						WHAT HE GAVE UP												THE RESULTS					
Year Team	Lg	G	GS	CG	GF	IP	BFP	H	R	ER	HR	SH	SF	HB	TBB	IBB	SO	WP	Bk	W	L	Pct.	ShO	Sv-Op	Hld	ERA
2001 Iowa *	AAA	39	12	1	7	110	433	87	35	32	10	2	0	2	26	3	131	1	0	8	7	.533	1	1-—	—	2.62
1995 Baltimore	AL	6	0	0	3	7.1	30	5	1	1	0	0	0	0	4	0	3	0	0	0	0	—	0	0-0	0	1.23
1996 Atlanta	NL	22	0	0	8	26	121	33	15	14	4	5	0	1	13	4	15	1	0	2	4	.333	0	0-0	1	4.85
1997 Atl-NYY		21	0	0	9	26	123	29	13	12	2	1	0	0	20	5	8	0	0	2	3	.400	0	0-0	2	4.15
1998 New York	AL	8	0	0	6	9.2	42	11	7	7	0	0	0	0	4	0	7	0	0	1	0	1.000	0	0-0	0	6.52
2001 Chicago	NL	1	1	0	0	1.2	13	6	6	6	1	0	0	0	3	0	1	0	0	0	0	—	0	0-0	0	32.40
1997 Atlanta	NL	20	0	0	8	24	111	27	11	10	2	1	0	0	16	4	6	0	0	2	2	.500	0	0-0	2	3.75
New York	AL	1	0	0	1	2	12	2	2	2	0	0	0	0	4	1	2	0	0	0	0	—	0	0-0	0	9.00
5 ML YEARS		58	1	0	26	70.2	329	84	42	40	7	7	0	1	44	9	34	1	0	5	8	.385	0	0-0	3	5.09

Ricky Bottalico

Pitches: Right **Bats:** Left **Pos:** RP-66   **Ht:** 6'1" **Wt:** 215 **Born:** 8/26/69 **Age:** 32

		HOW MUCH HE PITCHED						WHAT HE GAVE UP												THE RESULTS					
Year Team	Lg	G	GS	CG	GF	IP	BFP	H	R	ER	HR	SH	SF	HB	TBB	IBB	SO	WP	Bk	W	L	Pct.	ShO	Sv-Op	Hld	ERA
2001 Reading *	AA	3	3	0	0	5	19	3	2	1	1	0	0	0	1	0	5	0	0	0	1	.000	0	0--	—	1.80
1994 Philadelphia	NL	3	0	0	3	3	13	3	0	0	0	0	0	0	1	0	3	0	0	0	0	—	0	0-0	0	0.00
1995 Philadelphia	NL	62	0	0	20	87.2	350	50	25	24	7	3	1	4	42	3	87	1	0	5	3	.625	0	1-5	20	2.46
1996 Philadelphia	NL	61	0	0	56	67.2	269	47	24	24	6	4	2	2	23	2	74	3	0	4	5	.444	0	34-38	0	3.19
1997 Philadelphia	NL	69	0	0	61	74	324	68	31	30	7	1	2	2	42	4	89	3	0	2	5	.286	0	34-41	0	3.65
1998 Philadelphia	NL	39	0	0	28	43.1	206	54	31	31	7	1	2	1	25	5	27	2	0	1	5	.167	0	6-7	3	6.44
1999 St. Louis	NL	68	0	0	40	73.1	347	83	45	40	8	3	0	3	49	1	66	6	0	3	7	.300	0	20-28	8	4.91
2000 Kansas City	AL	62	0	0	50	72.2	319	65	40	39	12	3	1	2	41	3	56	5	1	9	6	.600	0	16-23	1	4.83
2001 Philadelphia	NL	66	0	0	18	67	281	58	31	29	11	7	4	4	25	2	57	5	0	3	4	.429	0	3-7	22	3.90
8 ML YEARS		430	0	0	276	488.2	2109	428	227	217	58	22	12	18	248	20	459	25	1	27	35	.435	0	114-149	54	4.00

Kent Bottenfield

Pitches: Right **Bats:** Right **Pos:** SP-9; RP-4   **Ht:** 6'3" **Wt:** 240 **Born:** 11/14/68 **Age:** 33

		HOW MUCH HE PITCHED						WHAT HE GAVE UP												THE RESULTS					
Year Team	Lg	G	GS	CG	GF	IP	BFP	H	R	ER	HR	SH	SF	HB	TBB	IBB	SO	WP	Bk	W	L	Pct.	ShO	Sv-Op	Hld	ERA
2001 Round Rock *	AA	1	1	0	0	2.2	15	4	6	6	1	0	2	0	3	0	3	0	0	0	1	.000	0	0--	—	20.25
1992 Montreal	NL	10	4	0	2	32.1	135	26	9	8	1	1	2	1	11	1	14	0	0	1	2	.333	0	1-1	1	2.23
1993 Mon-Col	NL	37	25	1	2	159.2	710	179	102	90	24	21	4	6	71	3	63	4	1	5	10	.333	0	0-0	0	5.07
1994 Col-SF	NL	16	1	0	3	26.1	121	33	18	18	2	1	0	2	10	0	15	2	0	3	1	.750	0	1-1	0	6.15
1996 Chicago	NL	48	0	0	10	61.2	258	59	25	18	3	5	0	3	19	4	33	2	0	3	5	.375	0	1-3	4	2.63
1997 Chicago	NL	64	0	0	20	84	361	82	39	36	13	4	4	2	35	7	74	2	0	2	3	.400	0	2-4	8	3.86
1998 St. Louis	NL	44	17	0	11	133.2	578	128	72	66	13	11	3	4	57	3	98	3	2	4	6	.400	0	4-5	6	4.44
1999 St. Louis	NL	31	31	0	0	190.1	843	197	91	84	21	11	9	5	89	5	124	1	0	18	7	.720	0	0-0	0	3.97
2000 Ana-Phi	NL	29	29	1	0	171.2	765	185	106	103	30	2	7	3	77	4	106	1	0	8	10	.444	1	0-0	0	5.40
2001 Houston	NL	13	9	0	1	52	235	61	44	37	16	1	4	2	16	0	39	1	0	2	5	.286	0	1-1	0	6.40
1993 Montreal	NL	23	11	0	2	83	373	93	49	38	11	11	1	5	33	2	33	4	1	2	5	.286	0	0-0	0	4.12
Colorado	NL	14	14	1	0	76.2	337	86	53	52	13	10	3	1	38	1	30	0	0	3	5	.375	0	0-0	0	6.10
1994 Colorado	NL	15	1	0	3	24.2	112	28	16	16	1	1	0	2	10	0	15	2	0	3	1	.750	0	1-1	0	5.84
San Francisco	NL	1	0	0	0	1.2	9	5	2	2	1	0	0	0	0	0	0	0	0	0	0	—	0	0-0	0	10.80
2000 Anaheim	AL	21	21	0	0	127.2	571	144	82	81	25	2	5	3	56	4	75	1	0	7	8	.467	0	0-0	0	5.71
Philadelphia	NL	8	8	1	0	44	194	41	24	22	5	0	2	0	21	0	31	0	0	1	2	.333	1	0-0	0	4.50
9 ML YEARS		292	116	2	49	911.2	4006	950	506	460	123	57	33	28	385	27	566	16	3	46	49	.484	1	10-15	19	4.54

Brian Bowles

Pitches: Right **Bats:** Right **Pos:** RP-2   **Ht:** 6'5" **Wt:** 220 **Born:** 8/18/76 **Age:** 25

		HOW MUCH HE PITCHED						WHAT HE GAVE UP												THE RESULTS					
Year Team	Lg	G	GS	CG	GF	IP	BFP	H	R	ER	HR	SH	SF	HB	TBB	IBB	SO	WP	Bk	W	L	Pct.	ShO	Sv-Op	Hld	ERA
1995 Blue Jays	R	8	0	0	2	15	70	18	12	4	2	0	1	1	3	0	11	2	1	0	1	.000	0	0--	—	2.40
1996 Medcine Hat	R+	24	0	0	7	39.2	193	53	35	28	5	1	3	5	21	1	29	9	0	2	2	.500	0	1--	—	6.35
1997 Hagerstown	A	4	0	0	1	10.1	49	14	10	8	2	0	1	1	5	0	9	1	0	1	0	1.000	0	0--	—	6.97
Dunedin	A+	7	1	0	3	14.1	68	20	14	12	2	0	1	0	7	1	9	3	1	0	2	.000	0	0--	—	7.53
St.Cathrnes	A-	16	16	0	0	78.2	351	76	53	44	6	0	3	11	35	0	64	4	1	5	8	.385	0	0--	—	5.03
1998 Dunedin	A+	9	2	1	0	27	126	32	13	10	2	1	1	1	16	0	17	1	1	1	2	.333	0	0--	—	3.33
Hagerstown	A	31	4	0	9	67.2	306	80	41	34	4	2	3	9	18	1	48	6	0	2	4	.333	0	0--	—	4.52
1999 Hagerstown	A	48	1	0	22	79.1	355	73	41	35	4	3	4	12	39	3	80	9	0	6	2	.750	0	3--	—	3.97
2000 Tennessee	AA	49	0	0	12	81.2	343	64	31	27	1	2	3	8	36	1	72	11	0	4	4	.500	0	0--	—	2.98
2001 Syracuse	AAA	66	0	0	24	77.1	338	56	30	25	3	5	1	7	44	4	81	14	3	3	5	.375	0	6--	—	2.91
2001 Toronto	AL	2	0	0	0	3.2	15	4	0	0	0	0	0	0	1	0	4	1	0	0	0	—	0	0-0	0	0.00

Chad Bradford

Pitches: Right **Bats:** Right **Pos:** RP-35   **Ht:** 6'5" **Wt:** 205 **Born:** 9/14/74 **Age:** 27

		HOW MUCH HE PITCHED						WHAT HE GAVE UP												THE RESULTS					
Year Team	Lg	G	GS	CG	GF	IP	BFP	H	R	ER	HR	SH	SF	HB	TBB	IBB	SO	WP	Bk	W	L	Pct.	ShO	Sv-Op	Hld	ERA
2001 Sacramento *	AAA	12	0	0	3	23.2	87	15	2	1	0	0	0	2	2	0	24	0	0	0	0	—	0	2--	—	0.38
1998 Chicago	AL	29	0	0	8	30.2	125	27	16	11	0	0	0	0	7	0	11	1	1	2	1	.667	0	1-3	9	3.23
1999 Chicago	AL	3	0	0	0	3.2	24	9	8	8	1	0	0	0	5	0	0	1	0	0	0	—	0	0-0	0	19.64
2000 Chicago	AL	12	0	0	5	13.2	52	13	4	3	0	0	0	0	1	1	9	0	0	1	0	1.000	0	0-0	2	1.98
2001 Oakland	AL	35	0	0	19	36.2	154	41	12	11	6	1	0	1	6	0	34	0	0	2	1	.667	0	1-4	4	2.70
4 ML YEARS		79	0	0	32	84.2	355	90	40	33	7	1	0	1	19	1	54	2	1	5	2	.714	0	2-7	15	3.51

Milton Bradley

Bats: B **Throws:** R **Pos:** CF-60; LF-13; PH/PR-6; RF-3; DH-1   **Ht:** 6'0" **Wt:** 180 **Born:** 4/15/78 **Age:** 24

		BATTING																	BASERUNNING				PERCENTAGES		
Year Team	Lg	G	AB	H	2B	3B	HR	(Hm	Rd)	TB	R	RBI	TBB	IBB	SO	HBP	SH	SF	SB	CS	SB%	GDP	Avg	OBP	SLG
1996 Expos	R	31	109	27	7	1	1	—	—	39	18	12	13	0	14	1	1	1	7	4	.64	2	.248	.328	.358
1997 Vermont	A-	50	200	60	7	5	3	—	—	86	29	30	17	1	34	0	1	2	7	7	.50	6	.300	.352	.430
Expos	R	25	5	2	0	1	0	—	—	10	6	2	4	0	4	1	0	0	2	2	.50	0	.200	.333	.400
1998 Cape Fear	A	75	281	85	21	4	6	—	—	132	54	50	23	1	57	4	3	3	13	8	.62	7	.302	.360	.470
Jupiter	A+	67	261	75	14	1	5	—	—	106	55	34	30	2	42	5	1	2	17	9	.65	3	.287	.369	.406
1999 Harrisburg	AA	87	346	114	22	5	12	—	—	182	62	50	33	0	61	3	1	2	14	10	.58	5	.329	.391	.526
2000 Ottawa	AAA	88	342	104	20	1	6	—	—	144	58	29	45	3	56	1	1	2	10	15	.40	5	.304	.385	.421
2001 Ottawa	AAA	35	136	37	7	2	2	—	—	54	21	13	23	4	30	2	2	1	14	1	.93	3	.272	.383	.397
Buffalo	AAA	30	114	29	3	0	5	—	—	47	18	15	19	1	31	0	0	0	9	2	.82	0	.254	.361	.412
2000 Montreal	NL	42	154	34	8	1	2	(1	1)	50	20	15	14	0	32	1	1	1	2	1	.67	3	.221	.288	.325
2001 Mon-Cle		77	238	53	17	3	1	(0	1)	79	22	19	21	0	65	1	2	0	8	5	.62	7	.223	.288	.332

(continued)

Year Team	Lg	G	AB	H	2B	3B	HR	(Hm	Rd)	TB	R	RBI	TBB	IBB	SO	HBP	SH	SF	SB	CS	SB%	GDP	Avg	OBP	SLG
2001 Montreal	NL	67	220	49	16	3	1	(0	1)	74	19	19	19	0	62	1	2	0	7	4	.64	6	.223	.288	.336
Cleveland	AL	10	18	4	1	0	0	(0	0)	5	3	0	2	0	3	0	0	0	1	1	.50	1	.222	.300	.278
2 ML YEARS		119	392	87	25	4	3	(1	2)	129	42	34	35	0	97	2	3	1	10	6	.63	10	.222	.288	.329

Darren Bragg

Bats: L **Throws:** R **Pos:** RF-13; LF-8; PH/PR-8; CF-2   **Ht:** 5'9" **Wt:** 180 **Born:** 9/7/69 **Age:** 32

Year Team	Lg	G	AB	H	2B	3B	HR	(Hm	Rd)	TB	R	RBI	TBB	IBB	SO	HBP	SH	SF	SB	CS	SB%	GDP	Avg	OBP	SLG
2001 Norfolk *	AAA	32	99	33	4	0	4	—	—	49	22	7	23	1	22	2	0	0	5	2	.71	1	.333	.468	.495
Columbus *	AAA	53	199	58	11	2	7	—	—	94	30	21	27	3	51	1	0	0	3	2	.60	4	.291	.379	.472
1994 Seattle	AL	8	19	3	1	0	0	(0	0)	4	4	2	2	1	5	0	0	0	0	0	—	0	.158	.238	.211
1995 Seattle	AL	52	145	34	5	1	3	(1	2)	50	20	12	18	1	37	4	1	2	9	0	1.00	2	.234	.331	.345
1996 Sea-Bos	AL	127	417	109	26	2	10	(1	3)	169	74	47	69	6	74	4	2	7	14	9	.61	5	.261	.366	.405
1997 Boston	AL	153	513	132	35	2	9	(3	6)	198	65	57	61	5	102	3	5	4	10	6	.63	16	.257	.337	.386
1998 Boston	AL	129	409	114	29	3	8	(3	5)	173	51	57	42	0	99	6	4	4	5	3	.63	16	.279	.351	.423
1999 St. Louis	NL	93	273	71	12	1	6	(4	2)	103	38	26	44	1	67	3	5	0	3	0	1.00	5	.260	.369	.377
2000 Colorado	NL	71	149	33	7	1	3	(3	0)	51	16	21	17	1	41	0	0	3	4	1	.80	3	.221	.296	.342
2001 NYM-NYY		23	61	16	7	0	0	(0	0)	23	5	5	4	0	24	1	1	0	3	2	.60	0	.262	.318	.377
1996 Seattle	AL	69	195	53	12	1	7	(4	3)	88	36	25	33	4	35	2	1	4	8	5	.62	2	.272	.376	.451
Boston	AL	58	222	56	14	1	3	(3	0)	81	38	22	36	2	39	2	1	3	6	4	.60	3	.252	.357	.365
2001 New York	NL	18	57	15	6	0	0	(0	0)	21	4	5	4	0	23	1	1	0	3	2	.60	0	.263	.323	.368
New York	AL	5	4	1	1	0	0	(0	0)	2	1	0	0	0	1	0	0	0	0	0	—	0	.250	.250	.500
8 ML YEARS		656	1986	512	122	10	39	(21	18)	771	273	227	257	15	449	21	18	20	48	21	.70	47	.258	.346	.388

Jeff Branson

Bats: L **Throws:** R **Pos:** 2B-6; PH/PR-5; SS-2; 3B-1   **Ht:** 6'0" **Wt:** 180 **Born:** 1/26/67 **Age:** 35

Year Team	Lg	G	AB	H	2B	3B	HR	(Hm	Rd)	TB	R	RBI	TBB	IBB	SO	HBP	SH	SF	SB	CS	SB%	GDP	Avg	OBP	SLG
2001 Las Vegas *	AAA	96	289	79	18	0	4	—	—	109	28	20	26	2	71	2	3	3	3	2	.60	4	.273	.334	.377
1992 Cincinnati	NL	72	115	34	7	1	0	(0	0)	43	12	15	5	2	16	0	2	1	0	1	.00	4	.296	.322	.374
1993 Cincinnati	NL	125	381	92	15	1	3	(2	1)	118	40	22	19	2	73	0	8	4	4	1	.80	4	.241	.275	.310
1994 Cincinnati	NL	58	109	31	4	1	6	(1	5)	55	18	16	5	2	16	0	2	0	0	0	—	4	.284	.316	.505
1995 Cincinnati	NL	122	331	86	18	2	12	(9	3)	144	43	45	44	14	69	2	1	6	2	1	.67	9	.260	.345	.435
1996 Cincinnati	NL	129	311	76	16	4	9	(5	4)	127	34	37	31	4	67	1	7	3	2	0	1.00	6	.244	.312	.408
1997 Cin-Cle		94	170	34	7	1	3	(3	0)	52	14	12	14	1	40	1	1	2	1	2	.33	4	.200	.262	.306
1998 Cleveland	AL	63	100	20	4	1	1	(1	0)	29	6	9	3	0	21	0	1	1	0	0	—	1	.200	.221	.290
2000 Los Angeles	NL	18	17	4	1	0	0	(0	0)	5	3	0	1	0	6	0	0	0	0	0	—	1	.235	.278	.294
2001 Los Angeles	NL	13	21	6	0	0	0	(0	0)	6	3	0	0	0	4	0	0	0	0	0	—	0	.286	.286	.286
1997 Cincinnati	NL	65	98	15	3	1	1	(1	0)	23	9	5	7	1	23	0	1	0	1	0	1.00	3	.153	.210	.235
Cleveland	AL	29	72	19	4	0	2	(2	0)	29	5	7	7	0	17	1	0	2	0	2	.00	1	.264	.329	.403
9 ML YEARS		694	1555	383	72	11	34	(21	13)	579	173	156	122	25	312	4	22	17	9	5	.64	36	.246	.300	.372

Jeff Brantley

Pitches: Right **Bats:** Right **Pos:** RP-18   **Ht:** 5'10" **Wt:** 197 **Born:** 9/5/63 **Age:** 38

Year Team	Lg	G	GS	CG	GF	IP	BFP	H	R	ER	HR	SH	SF	HB	TBB	IBB	SO	WP	Bk	W	L	Pct.	ShO	Sv-Op	Hld	ERA
1988 San Francisco	NL	9	1	0	2	20.2	88	22	13	13	2	1	0	1	6	1	11	0	1	0	1	.000	0	1-1	0	5.66
1989 San Francisco	NL	59	1	0	15	97.1	422	101	50	44	10	7	3	2	37	8	69	3	2	7	1	.875	0	0-1	11	4.07
1990 San Francisco	NL	55	0	0	32	86.2	361	77	18	15	3	2	2	3	33	6	61	0	3	5	3	.625	0	19-24	8	1.56
1991 San Francisco	NL	67	0	0	39	95.1	411	78	27	26	8	4	4	5	52	10	81	6	0	5	2	.714	0	15-19	12	2.45
1992 San Francisco	NL	56	4	0	32	91.2	381	67	32	30	8	7	3	3	45	5	86	3	1	7	7	.500	0	7-9	3	2.95
1993 San Francisco	NL	53	12	0	9	113.2	496	112	60	54	19	5	5	7	46	2	76	3	4	5	6	.455	0	0-3	10	4.28
1994 Cincinnati	NL	50	0	0	35	65.1	262	46	20	18	6	5	1	0	28	5	63	1	0	6	6	.500	0	15-21	1	2.48
1995 Cincinnati	NL	56	0	0	49	70.1	283	53	22	22	11	2	3	1	20	3	62	2	2	3	2	.600	0	28-32	0	2.82
1996 Cincinnati	NL	66	0	0	61	71	288	54	21	19	7	4	5	0	28	6	76	2	0	1	2	.333	0	44-49	0	2.41
1997 Cincinnati	NL	13	0	0	9	11.2	53	9	5	5	2	0	0	2	7	1	16	2	0	1	1	.500	0	1-3	0	3.86
1998 St. Louis	NL	48	0	0	33	50.2	209	40	26	25	12	5	3	1	18	3	48	1	0	0	5	.000	0	14-22	3	4.44
1999 Philadelphia	NL	10	0	0	9	8.2	40	5	6	5	0	0	1	0	8	0	11	0	0	1	2	.333	0	5-6	0	5.19
2000 Philadelphia	NL	55	0	0	47	55.1	256	64	36	36	12	1	2	2	29	0	57	2	0	2	7	.222	0	23-28	1	5.86
2001 Texas	AL	18	0	0	7	21	94	26	12	12	5	0	1	0	9	1	11	1	0	0	0	.000	0	0-0	0	5.14
14 ML YEARS		615	18	0	379	859.1	3644	754	348	324	105	43	33	27	366	51	728	26	13	43	46	.483	0	172-218	49	3.39

Russell Branyan

Bats: L **Throws:** R **Pos:** 3B-72; LF-31; PH/PR-17; DH-7; RF-2   **Ht:** 6'3" **Wt:** 195 **Born:** 12/19/75 **Age:** 26

Year Team	Lg	G	AB	H	2B	3B	HR	(Hm	Rd)	TB	R	RBI	TBB	IBB	SO	HBP	SH	SF	SB	CS	SB%	GDP	Avg	OBP	SLG
1998 Cleveland	AL	1	4	0	0	0	0	(0	0)	0	0	0	0	0	2	0	0	0	0	0	—	0	.000	.000	.000
1999 Cleveland	AL	11	38	8	2	0	1	(0	1)	13	4	6	3	0	19	1	0	0	0	0	—	0	.211	.286	.342
2000 Cleveland	AL	67	193	46	7	2	16	(13	3)	105	32	38	22	1	76	4	0	1	0	0	—	2	.238	.327	.544
2001 Cleveland	AL	113	315	73	16	2	20	(11	9)	153	48	54	38	1	132	3	0	5	1	1	.50	2	.232	.316	.486
4 ML YEARS		192	550	127	25	4	37	(24	13)	271	84	98	63	2	229	8	0	6	1	1	.50	4	.231	.316	.493

Leslie Brea

Pitches: Right **Bats:** Right **Pos:** RP-2   **Ht:** 5'11" **Wt:** 170 **Born:** 10/12/78 **Age:** 23

		HOW MUCH HE PITCHED					WHAT HE GAVE UP												THE RESULTS						
Year Team	Lg	G	GS	CG	GF	IP	BFP	H	R	ER	HR	SH	SF	HB	TBB	IBB	SO	WP	Bk	W	L	Pct.	ShO	Sv-Op	Hld	ERA
1996 Mariners	R	7	0	0	3	10.2	47	7	10	6	1	0	1	0	6	0	12	1	1	1	0	1.000	0	0--	—	5.06
1997 Lancaster	A+	1	0	0	0	2	13	5	5	3	1	0	0	0	1	0	1	1	0	0	0	—	0	0--	—	13.50
Everett	A-	23	0	0	14	32.2	162	34	29	29	3	2	1	3	29	4	49	8	0	2	4	.333	0	3--	—	7.99
1998 Wisconsin	A	49	0	0	34	58.2	260	47	26	18	1	3	1	2	40	2	86	5	0	3	4	.429	0	12--	—	2.76
1999 St. Lucie	A+	32	18	0	9	120.2	516	95	64	50	4	2	2	4	68	1	136	7	3	1	7	.125	0	3--	—	3.73
2000 Norfolk	AAA	1	1	0	0	5	23	4	2	0	0	0	1	0	4	0	4	0	0	0	0	—	0	0--	—	0.00
Binghamton	AA	19	18	0	0	93.1	422	85	53	44	10	3	5	7	61	0	86	8	2	5	8	.385	0	0--	—	4.24
Bowie	AA	2	2	0	0	12.2	55	12	6	6	1	0	1	0	9	0	3	0	0	1	1	.500	0	0--	—	4.26
Rochester	AAA	4	4	0	0	19.1	95	27	18	13	3	0	1	1	8	0	13	2	0	1	2	.333	0	0--	—	6.05
2001 Rochester	AAA	63	0	0	22	82.1	367	80	44	35	6	4	2	2	35	3	98	6	1	2	6	.250	0	1--	—	3.83
2000 Baltimore	AL	6	1	0	3	9	49	12	11	11	1	0	1	1	10	0	5	1	0	0	1	.000	0	0-0	0	11.00
2001 Baltimore	AL	2	0	0	0	2	14	6	4	4	2	0	0	0	3	0	0	0	0	0	0	—	0	0-0	0	18.00
2 ML YEARS		8	1	0	3	11	63	18	15	15	3	0	1	1	13	0	5	1	0	0	1	.000	0	0-0	0	12.27

Chris Brock

Pitches: Right **Bats:** Right **Pos:** RP-24   **Ht:** 6'0" **Wt:** 185 **Born:** 2/5/70 **Age:** 32

		HOW MUCH HE PITCHED					WHAT HE GAVE UP												THE RESULTS						
Year Team	Lg	G	GS	CG	GF	IP	BFP	H	R	ER	HR	SH	SF	HB	TBB	IBB	SO	WP	Bk	W	L	Pct.	ShO	Sv-Op	Hld	ERA
2001 Scrantn-WB *	AAA	13	13	2	0	78.2	320	75	31	31	9	4	1	4	16	0	56	2	3	6	2	.750	0	0--	—	3.55
1997 Atlanta	NL	7	6	0	1	30.2	144	34	23	19	2	3	4	0	19	2	16	2	1	0	0	—	0	0-0	0	5.58
1998 San Francisco	NL	13	0	0	4	27.2	120	31	13	12	3	2	0	0	7	1	19	0	0	0	0	—	0	0-0	0	3.90
1999 San Francisco	NL	19	19	0	0	106.2	479	124	69	65	18	5	3	4	41	2	76	8	2	6	8	.429	0	0-0	0	5.48
2000 Philadelphia	NL	63	5	0	17	93.1	403	85	48	45	21	1	2	3	41	0	69	4	1	7	8	.467	0	1-3	16	4.34
2001 Philadelphia	NL	24	0	0	6	32.2	147	35	16	15	6	2	1	2	15	2	26	2	0	3	0	1.000	0	0-1	3	4.13
5 ML YEARS		126	30	0	28	291	1293	309	169	156	50	13	10	9	123	7	206	16	4	16	16	.500	0	1-4	19	4.82

Rico Brogna

Bats: Left **Throws:** Left **Pos:** 1B-67; PH/PR-7   **Ht:** 6'2" **Wt:** 203 **Born:** 4/18/70 **Age:** 32

		BATTING																	BASERUNNING				PERCENTAGES		
Year Team	Lg	G	AB	H	2B	3B	HR	(Hm Rd)	TB	R	RBI	TBB	IBB	SO	HBP	SH	SF	SB	CS	SB%	GDP	Avg	OBP	SLG
1992 Detroit	AL	9	26	5	1	0	1	(1 0)	9	3	3	3	0	5	0	0	0	0	0	—	0	.192	.276	.346
1994 New York	NL	39	131	46	11	2	7	(2 5)	82	16	20	6	0	29	0	1	0	1	0	1.00	0	.351	.380	.626
1995 New York	NL	134	495	143	27	2	22	(13 9)	240	72	76	39	7	111	2	2	2	0	0	—	10	.289	.342	.485
1996 New York	NL	55	188	48	10	1	7	(5 2)	81	18	30	19	1	50	0	0	4	0	0	—	4	.255	.318	.431
1997 Philadelphia	NL	148	543	137	36	1	20	(9 11)	235	68	81	33	4	116	0	0	4	12	3	.80	12	.252	.293	.433
1998 Philadelphia	NL	153	565	150	36	3	20	(11 9)	252	77	104	49	8	125	0	0	10	7	7	.50	12	.265	.319	.446
1999 Philadelphia	NL	157	619	172	29	4	24	(14 10)	281	90	102	54	7	132	2	0	4	8	5	.62	19	.278	.336	.454
2000 Phi-Bos		81	185	43	17	0	2	(2 0)	66	20	21	10	1	41	2	1	1	1	0	1.00	5	.232	.278	.357
2001 Atlanta	NL	72	206	51	9	0	3	(1 2)	69	15	21	14	1	46	1	1	1	3	1	.75	4	.248	.297	.335
2000 Philadelphia	NL	38	129	32	14	0	1	(1 0)	49	12	13	7	1	28	2	0	1	1	0	1.00	4	.248	.295	.380
Boston	AL	43	56	11	3	0	1	(1 0)	17	8	8	3	0	13	0	1	0	0	0	—	1	.196	.237	.304
9 ML YEARS		848	2958	795	176	13	106	(58 48)	1315	379	458	227	29	655	7	5	26	32	16	.67	73	.269	.320	.445

Troy Brohawn

Pitches: Left **Bats:** Left **Pos:** RP-59   **Ht:** 6'1" **Wt:** 190 **Born:** 1/14/73 **Age:** 29

		HOW MUCH HE PITCHED					WHAT HE GAVE UP												THE RESULTS						
Year Team	Lg	G	GS	CG	GF	IP	BFP	H	R	ER	HR	SH	SF	HB	TBB	IBB	SO	WP	Bk	W	L	Pct.	ShO	Sv-Op	Hld	ERA
1994 San Jose	A+	4	4	0	0	16.2	80	27	15	13	2	1	0	2	5	0	13	1	0	0	2	.000	0	0--	—	7.02
1995 San Jose	A+	11	10	0	1	65.1	246	45	14	12	4	1	1	1	20	0	57	5	1	7	3	.700	0	0--	—	1.65
1996 Shreveport	AA	28	28	0	0	156.2	668	163	99	80	30	7	3	6	49	0	82	8	3	9	10	.474	0	0--	—	4.60
1997 Shreveport	AA	26	26	1	0	169	695	148	57	48	10	3	1	2	64	0	98	4	3	13	5	.722	1	0--	—	2.56
1998 Fresno	AAA	30	19	0	4	121.2	528	144	75	71	18	11	5	3	36	1	87	8	0	10	8	.556	0	0--	—	5.25
1999 Tucson	AAA	3	2	0	0	13.2	67	22	8	5	1	3	0	0	3	0	12	0	0	1	0	1.000	0	0--	—	3.29
2000 Diamndbcks	R	3	3	0	0	4	16	5	1	0	0	0	0	0	1	0	6	0	0	0	0	—	0	0--	—	0.00
Tucson	AAA	11	1	0	2	16.2	71	18	7	7	5	1	2	1	5	0	16	0	1	0	0	—	0	0--	—	3.78
2001 Tucson	AAA	2	0	0	1	3.1	13	1	0	0	0	0	0	0	1	0	4	0	0	0	0	—	0	0--	—	0.00
2001 Arizona	NL	59	0	0	10	49.1	220	55	27	27	8	2	4	1	23	2	30	2	0	2	3	.400	0	1-3	10	4.93

Scott Brosius

Bats: Right **Throws:** Right **Pos:** 3B-120; CF-2   **Ht:** 6'1" **Wt:** 202 **Born:** 8/15/66 **Age:** 35

		BATTING																	BASERUNNING				PERCENTAGES		
Year Team	Lg	G	AB	H	2B	3B	HR	(Hm Rd)	TB	R	RBI	TBB	IBB	SO	HBP	SH	SF	SB	CS	SB%	GDP	Avg	OBP	SLG
1991 Oakland	AL	36	68	16	5	0	2	(1 1)	27	9	4	3	0	11	0	1	0	3	1	.75	2	.235	.268	.397
1992 Oakland	AL	38	87	19	2	0	4	(1 3)	33	13	13	3	1	13	2	0	1	3	0	1.00	0	.218	.258	.379
1993 Oakland	AL	70	213	53	10	1	6	(3 3)	83	26	25	14	0	37	1	3	2	6	0	1.00	6	.249	.296	.390
1994 Oakland	AL	96	324	77	14	1	14	(9 5)	135	31	49	24	0	57	2	4	6	2	6	.25	7	.238	.289	.417
1995 Oakland	AL	123	389	102	19	2	17	(12 5)	176	69	46	41	0	67	8	1	4	4	2	.67	5	.262	.342	.452
1996 Oakland	AL	114	428	130	25	0	22	(15 7)	221	73	71	59	4	85	7	1	5	7	2	.78	11	.304	.393	.516
1997 Oakland	AL	129	479	97	20	1	11	(7 4)	152	59	41	34	1	102	4	5	4	9	4	.69	9	.203	.259	.317
1998 New York	AL	152	530	159	34	0	19	(8 11)	250	86	98	52	1	97	10	8	3	11	8	.58	4	.300	.371	.472
1999 New York	AL	133	473	117	26	1	17	(4 13)	196	64	71	39	2	74	6	2	9	9	3	.75	13	.247	.307	.414
2000 New York	AL	135	470	108	20	0	16	(7 9)	176	57	64	45	1	73	2	0	3	3	0	1.00	17	.230	.299	.374
2001 New York	AL	120	428	123	25	2	13	(6 7)	191	57	49	34	2	83	5	6	5	3	1	.75	10	.287	.343	.446
11 ML YEARS		1146	3889	1001	200	8	141	(73 68)	1640	544	531	348	12	699	47	31	41	57	30	.66	84	.257	.323	.422

Jim Brower

Pitches: Right **Bats:** Right **Pos:** RP-36; SP-10 **Ht:** 6'2" **Wt:** 205 **Born:** 12/29/72 **Age:** 29

		HOW MUCH HE PITCHED					WHAT HE GAVE UP											THE RESULTS					
Year Team	Lg	G	GS	CG	GF	IP	BFP	H	R	ER	HR	SH	SF	HB	TBB	IBB	SO	WP	Bk	W	L	Pct.	ShO	Sv-Op	Hld	ERA
2001 Louisville *	AAA	2	2	0	0	11	47	12	5	5	1	0	0	1	2	0	11	0	0	1	0	1.000	0	0--	—	4.09
1999 Cleveland	AL	9	2	0	1	25.2	113	27	13	13	8	1	1	1	10	1	18	0	0	3	1	.750	0	0-0	0	4.56
2000 Cleveland	AL	17	11	0	1	62	293	80	45	43	11	1	0	2	31	1	32	3	0	2	3	.400	0	0-0	0	6.24
2001 Cincinnati	NL	46	10	0	13	129.1	559	119	65	57	17	9	3	5	60	5	94	5	1	7	10	.412	0	1-2	2	3.97
3 ML YEARS		72	23	0	15	217	965	226	123	113	36	11	4	8	101	7	144	8	1	12	14	.462	0	1-2	2	4.69

Adrian Brown

Bats: Both **Throws:** Right **Pos:** CF-7; PH/PR-1 **Ht:** 6'0" **Wt:** 185 **Born:** 2/7/74 **Age:** 28

		BATTING																BASERUNNING				PERCENTAGES		
Year Team	Lg	G	AB	H	2B	3B	HR	(Hm	Rd)	TB	R	RBI	TBB	IBB	SO	HBP	SH	SF	SB	CS	SB%	GDP	Avg	OBP	SLG
2001 Altoona *	AA	7	30	10	1	1	0	—	—	13	7	1	1	0	7	0	0	1	1	2	.33	0	.333	.344	.433
Lynchburg *	A+	4	18	6	0	0	0	—	—	6	2	1	1	0	3	1	0	0	2	0	1.00	0	.333	.400	.333
Williamsprt *	A-	4	18	6	0	1	0	—	—	8	4	4	1	0	2	0	0	0	2	0	1.00	0	.333	.368	.444
1997 Pittsburgh	NL	48	147	28	6	0	1	(0	1)	37	17	10	13	0	18	4	2	1	8	4	.67	3	.190	.273	.252
1998 Pittsburgh	NL	41	152	43	4	1	0	(0	0)	49	20	5	9	0	18	0	4	0	4	0	1.00	0	.283	.323	.322
1999 Pittsburgh	NL	116	226	61	5	2	4	(2	2)	82	34	17	33	2	39	1	6	1	5	3	.63	5	.270	.364	.363
2000 Pittsburgh	NL	104	308	97	18	3	4	(2	2)	133	64	28	29	1	34	0	2	1	13	1	.93	1	.315	.373	.432
2001 Pittsburgh	NL	8	31	6	0	0	1	(0	1)	9	3	2	3	0	3	0	0	0	2	1	.67	1	.194	.265	.290
5 ML YEARS		317	864	235	33	6	10	(4	6)	310	138	62	87	3	112	5	14	3	32	9	.78	13	.272	.341	.359

Dee Brown

Bats: L **Throws:** R **Pos:** LF-77; DH-20; PH/PR-5; CF-4; RF-3 **Ht:** 6'0" **Wt:** 215 **Born:** 3/27/78 **Age:** 24

		BATTING																BASERUNNING				PERCENTAGES		
Year Team	Lg	G	AB	H	2B	3B	HR	(Hm	Rd)	TB	R	RBI	TBB	IBB	SO	HBP	SH	SF	SB	CS	SB%	GDP	Avg	OBP	SLG
1996 Royals	R	7	20	1	1	0	0	—	—	2	1	1	0	0	6	1	0	0	0	2	.00	0	.050	.095	.100
1997 Spokane	A-	73	298	97	20	6	13	—	—	168	67	73	38	5	65	2	0	1	17	4	.81	5	.326	.404	.564
1998 Wilmington	A+	128	442	114	30	2	10	—	—	178	64	58	53	5	115	7	1	0	26	10	.72	12	.258	.347	.403
1999 Wilmington	A+	61	221	68	10	2	13	—	—	121	49	46	44	6	56	4	0	0	20	8	.71	10	.308	.431	.548
Wichita	AA	65	235	83	14	3	12	—	—	139	58	56	35	1	41	3	1	2	10	8	.56	7	.353	.440	.591
2000 Omaha	AAA	125	479	129	25	6	23	—	—	235	76	70	37	5	112	3	0	3	20	3	.87	14	.269	.324	.491
2001 Omaha	AAA	10	37	11	0	0	2	—	—	17	5	6	3	0	5	1	0	0	0	0	—	3	.297	.357	.459
1998 Kansas City	AL	5	3	0	0	0	0	(0	0)	0	2	0	0	0	1	0	0	0	0	0	—	0	.000	.000	.000
1999 Kansas City	AL	12	25	2	0	0	0	(0	0)	2	1	0	2	0	7	0	0	0	0	0	—	0	.080	.148	.080
2000 Kansas City	AL	15	25	4	1	0	0	(0	0)	5	4	4	3	0	9	0	0	0	0	0	—	0	.160	.250	.200
2001 Kansas City	AL	106	380	93	19	0	7	(4	3)	133	39	40	22	4	81	1	1	2	5	3	.63	12	.245	.286	.350
4 ML YEARS		138	433	99	20	0	7	(4	3)	140	46	44	27	4	98	1	1	2	5	3	.63	12	.229	.274	.323

Emil Brown

Bats: R **Throws:** R **Pos:** CF-57; PH/PR-23; LF-6; RF-4 **Ht:** 6'2" **Wt:** 193 **Born:** 12/29/74 **Age:** 27

		BATTING																BASERUNNING				PERCENTAGES		
Year Team	Lg	G	AB	H	2B	3B	HR	(Hm	Rd)	TB	R	RBI	TBB	IBB	SO	HBP	SH	SF	SB	CS	SB%	GDP	Avg	OBP	SLG
2001 Portland *	AAA	22	78	25	8	2	3	—	—	46	10	8	6	0	17	2	0	0	3	1	.75	2	.321	.384	.590
1997 Pittsburgh	NL	66	95	17	2	1	2	(1	1)	27	16	6	10	1	32	7	0	0	5	1	.83	1	.179	.304	.284
1998 Pittsburgh	NL	13	39	10	1	0	0	(0	0)	11	2	3	1	0	11	1	0	0	0	0	—	0	.256	.293	.282
1999 Pittsburgh	NL	6	14	2	1	0	0	(0	0)	3	0	0	0	0	3	0	0	0	0	0	—	0	.143	.143	.214
2000 Pittsburgh	NL	50	119	26	5	0	3	(2	1)	40	13	16	11	0	34	3	1	1	3	1	.75	3	.218	.299	.336
2001 Pit-SD	NL	74	137	26	4	1	3	(2	1)	41	21	13	16	1	49	2	0	0	12	4	.75	2	.190	.284	.299
2001 Pittsburgh	NL	61	123	25	4	1	3	(2	1)	40	18	13	15	1	42	2	0	0	10	4	.71	2	.203	.300	.325
San Diego	NL	13	14	1	0	0	0	(0	0)	1	3	0	1	0	7	0	0	0	2	0	1.00	0	.071	.133	.071
5 ML YEARS		209	404	81	13	2	8	(5	3)	122	52	38	38	2	129	13	1	1	20	6	.77	6	.200	.289	.302

Kevin Brown

Pitches: Right **Bats:** Right **Pos:** SP-19; RP-1 **Ht:** 6'4" **Wt:** 200 **Born:** 3/14/65 **Age:** 37

		HOW MUCH HE PITCHED						WHAT HE GAVE UP											THE RESULTS					
Year Team	Lg	G	GS	CG	GF	IP	BFP	H	R	ER	HR	SH	SF	HB	TBB	IBB	SO	WP	Bk	W	L	Pct.	ShO	Sv-Op	Hld	ERA
1986 Texas	AL	1	1	0	0	5	19	6	2	2	0	0	0	0	4	0	4	0	0	1	0	1.000	0	0-0	0	3.60
1988 Texas	AL	4	4	1	0	23.1	110	33	15	11	2	1	0	1	8	0	12	1	0	1	1	.500	0	0-0	0	4.24
1989 Texas	AL	28	28	7	0	191	798	167	81	71	10	3	6	4	70	2	104	7	2	12	9	.571	0	0-0	0	3.35
1990 Texas	AL	26	26	6	0	180	757	175	84	72	13	2	7	3	60	3	88	9	2	12	10	.545	2	0-0	0	3.60
1991 Texas	AL	33	33	0	0	210.2	934	233	116	103	17	6	4	13	90	5	96	12	3	9	12	.429	0	0-0	0	4.40
1992 Texas	AL	35	35	11	0	265.2	1108	262	117	98	11	7	8	10	76	2	173	8	2	21	11	.656	1	0-0	0	3.32
1993 Texas	AL	34	34	12	0	233	1001	228	105	93	14	5	3	15	74	5	142	8	1	15	12	.556	3	0-0	0	3.59
1994 Texas	AL	26	25	3	1	170	760	218	109	91	18	2	7	6	50	3	123	7	0	7	9	.438	0	0-0	0	4.82
1995 Baltimore	AL	26	26	3	0	172.1	706	155	73	69	10	5	2	9	48	1	117	3	0	10	9	.526	1	0-0	0	3.60
1996 Florida	NL	32	32	5	0	233	906	187	60	49	8	4	4	16	33	2	159	6	1	17	11	.607	3	0-0	0	1.89
1997 Florida	NL	33	33	6	0	237.1	976	214	77	71	10	5	1	14	66	2	205	7	1	16	8	.667	2	0-0	0	2.69
1998 San Diego	NL	36	35	7	0	257	1032	225	77	68	8	13	3	10	49	4	257	10	0	18	7	.720	3	0-0	0	2.38
1999 Los Angeles	NL	35	35	5	0	252.1	1018	210	99	84	19	7	1	7	59	1	221	4	1	18	9	.667	1	0-0	0	3.00
2000 Los Angeles	NL	33	33	5	0	230	921	181	76	66	21	13	4	9	47	1	216	4	0	13	6	.684	1	0-0	0	2.58
2001 Los Angeles	NL	20	19	1	0	115.2	465	94	41	34	8	5	0	2	38	2	104	3	1	10	4	.714	0	0-0	1	2.65
15 ML YEARS		402	399	72	1	2776.1	11511	2588	1132	982	169	78	50	119	768	38	2021	89	14	180	118	.604	17	0-0	1	3.18

Kevin Brown

Bats: Right Throws: Right Pos: C-16; PH/PR-1   Ht: 6'2" Wt: 215 Born: 4/21/73 Age: 29

Year Team	Lg	G	AB	H	2B	3B	HR	(Hm	Rd)	TB	R	RBI	TBB	IBB	SO	HBP	SH	SF	SB	CS	SB%	GDP	Avg	OBP	SLG
2001 Indianapols *	AAA	82	290	67	16	1	9	—	—	112	19	34	18	0	110	4	4	1	0	1	.00	8	.231	.284	.386
1996 Texas	AL	3	4	0	0	0	0	(0	0)	0	1	1	2	0	2	1	0	1	0	0	—	0	.000	.375	.000
1997 Texas	AL	4	5	2	0	0	1	(0	1)	5	1	1	0	0	0	0	0	0	0	0	—	0	.400	.400	1.000
1998 Toronto	AL	52	110	29	7	1	2	(1	1)	44	17	15	9	0	31	2	3	4	0	0	—	1	.264	.320	.400
1999 Toronto	AL	2	9	4	2	0	0	(0	0)	6	1	1	0	0	3	0	0	0	0	0	—	0	.444	.444	.667
2000 Milwaukee	NL	5	17	4	3	0	0	(0	0)	7	3	1	1	0	5	0	0	0	0	0	—	0	.235	.278	.412
2001 Milwaukee	NL	17	43	9	0	1	4	(0	4)	23	7	12	2	0	18	1	0	0	0	0	—	1	.209	.261	.535
6 ML YEARS		83	188	48	12	2	7	(1	6)	85	30	31	14	0	59	4	3	5	0	0	—	2	.255	.313	.452

Roosevelt Brown

Bats: L Throws: R Pos: LF-21; PH/PR-16; DH-3; RF-3; CF-1   Ht: 5'10" Wt: 200 Born: 8/3/75 Age: 26

Year Team	Lg	G	AB	H	2B	3B	HR	(Hm	Rd)	TB	R	RBI	TBB	IBB	SO	HBP	SH	SF	SB	CS	SB%	GDP	Avg	OBP	SLG
2001 Iowa *	AAA	88	364	126	34	1	22	—	—	228	68	77	14	1	67	8	0	2	3	5	.38	8	.346	.381	.626
1999 Chicago	NL	33	64	14	6	1	1	(0	1)	25	6	10	2	0	14	0	3	1	1	0	1.00	0	.219	.239	.391
2000 Chicago	NL	45	91	32	8	0	3	(1	2)	49	11	14	4	0	22	1	0	2	0	1	.00	0	.352	.378	.538
2001 Chicago	NL	39	83	22	6	1	4	(3	1)	42	13	22	7	0	12	1	0	1	0	0	—	3	.265	.326	.506
3 ML YEARS		117	238	68	20	2	8	(4	4)	116	30	46	13	0	48	2	3	4	1	1	.50	5	.286	.323	.487

Cliff Brumbaugh

Bats: Right Throws: Right Pos: RF-12; LF-6; PH/PR-6   Ht: 6'2" Wt: 205 Born: 4/21/74 Age: 28

Year Team	Lg	G	AB	H	2B	3B	HR	(Hm	Rd)	TB	R	RBI	TBB	IBB	SO	HBP	SH	SF	SB	CS	SB%	GDP	Avg	OBP	SLG
1995 Hudson Val	A-	74	282	101	19	4	2	—	—	134	44	45	39	4	51	2	0	2	15	3	.83	11	.358	.437	.475
1996 Chston-SC	A	132	458	111	23	7	6	—	—	166	70	45	47	2	103	1	1	2	20	7	.74	5	.242	.345	.362
1997 Charlotte	A+	139	522	136	27	4	15	—	—	216	78	70	47	2	99	6	0	4	13	11	.54	7	.261	.326	.414
1998 Tulsa	AA	132	483	125	34	4	15	—	—	206	65	76	54	5	77	4	3	5	1	3	.25	12	.259	.335	.427
1999 Tulsa	AA	135	513	144	35	3	25	—	—	260	94	89	71	1	88	2	0	4	18	4	.82	5	.281	.368	.507
Oklahoma	AAA	4	12	3	0	0	0	—	—	3	1	1	0	0	2	0	0	0	0	0	—	0	.250	.250	.250
2000 Tulsa	AA	7	27	6	1	0	2	—	—	13	5	3	9	0	10	0	0	0	1	0	1.00	0	.222	.417	.481
Oklahoma	AAA	127	454	126	28	4	10	—	—	192	81	56	85	1	72	1	4	3	9	12	.43	13	.278	.390	.423
2001 Oklahoma	AAA	54	202	62	11	3	8	—	—	103	38	42	33	0	41	2	0	3	3	3	.50	3	.307	.404	.510
Colo Sprngs	AAA	53	208	69	18	1	3	—	—	98	31	39	34	0	52	0	0	4	5	3	.63	1	.332	.419	.471
2001 Tex-Col		21	46	10	2	0	1	(0	1)	15	6	4	3	0	14	0	0	0	0	1	.00	3	.217	.265	.326
2001 Texas	AL	7	10	0	0	0	0	(0	0)	0	1	0	1	0	5	0	0	0	0	0	—	0	.000	.091	.000
Colorado	NL	14	36	10	2	0	1	(0	1)	15	5	4	2	0	9	0	0	0	0	1	.00	3	.278	.316	.417

Brian Buchanan

Bats: R Throws: R Pos: RF-39; DH-19; PH/PR-12; LF-7   Ht: 6'4" Wt: 230 Born: 7/21/73 Age: 28

Year Team	Lg	G	AB	H	2B	3B	HR	(Hm	Rd)	TB	R	RBI	TBB	IBB	SO	HBP	SH	SF	SB	CS	SB%	GDP	Avg	OBP	SLG
1994 Oneonta	A-	50	177	40	9	2	4	—	—	65	28	26	24	2	53	6	0	2	5	3	.63	2	.226	.335	.367
1995 Greensboro	A	23	96	29	3	0	3	—	—	41	19	12	9	1	17	1	0	0	7	1	.88	1	.302	.368	.427
1996 Tampa	A+	131	526	137	22	4	10	—	—	197	65	58	37	6	108	10	1	1	23	8	.74	14	.260	.321	.375
1997 Columbus	AAA	18	61	17	1	0	4	—	—	30	8	7	4	0	11	3	1	1	2	1	.67	3	.279	.348	.492
Norwich	AA	116	470	145	25	2	10	—	—	204	75	69	32	0	85	11	0	6	11	9	.55	11	.309	.362	.434
1998 Salt Lake	AAA	133	500	139	29	3	17	—	—	225	74	82	36	1	90	9	1	1	14	2	.88	7	.278	.337	.450
1999 Salt Lake	AAA	107	391	116	24	1	10	—	—	172	67	60	28	0	85	9	0	3	11	2	.85	14	.297	.355	.440
2000 Salt Lake	AAA	95	364	108	20	1	27	—	—	211	82	103	41	1	75	3	0	11	5	1	.83	16	.297	.363	.580
2000 Minnesota	AL	30	82	19	3	0	1	(1	0)	25	10	8	8	0	22	1	0	2	0	2	.00	3	.232	.301	.305
2001 Minnesota	AL	69	197	54	12	0	10	(7	3)	96	28	32	19	0	58	2	0	1	1	1	.50	2	.274	.342	.487
2 ML YEARS		99	279	73	15	0	11	(8	3)	121	38	40	27	0	80	3	0	3	1	3	.25	5	.262	.330	.434

Mike Buddie

Pitches: Right Bats: Right Pos: RP-31   Ht: 6'3" Wt: 215 Born: 12/12/70 Age: 31

Year Team	Lg	G	GS	CG	GF	IP	BFP	H	R	ER	HR	SH	SF	HB	TBB	IBB	SO	WP	Bk	W	L	Pct.	ShO	Sv-Op	Hld	ERA
2001 Indianapols *	AAA	27	0	0	12	46.2	194	36	13	12	4	0	2	0	25	4	31	4	0	4	1	.800	0	3- -	—	2.31
1998 New York	AL	24	2	0	8	41.2	180	46	29	26	5	1	1	3	13	1	20	2	1	4	1	.800	0	0-0	0	5.62
1999 New York	AL	2	0	0	0	2	9	3	1	1	0	0	0	0	0	0	1	0	0	0	0	—	0	0-0	0	4.50
2000 Milwaukee	NL	5	0	0	2	6	27	8	3	3	0	1	0	0	1	1	5	0	0	0	1	.000	0	2-2	2	3.89
2001 Milwaukee	NL	31	0	0	7	41.2	174	34	20	18	2	2	4	4	17	2	22	3	0	0	0	—	0	2-2	2	4.73
4 ML YEARS		62	2	0	17	91.1	390	91	53	48	8	2	3	7	31	4	48	5	1	4	2	.667	0	2-2	2	4.73

Mark Buehrle

Pitches: Left Bats: Left Pos: SP-32   Ht: 6'2" Wt: 200 Born: 3/23/79 Age: 23

Year Team	Lg	G	GS	CG	GF	IP	BFP	H	R	ER	HR	SH	SF	HB	TBB	IBB	SO	WP	Bk	W	L	Pct.	ShO	Sv-Op	Hld	ERA
1999 Burlington	A	20	14	1	4	98.2	412	105	49	45	8	2	2	5	16	1	91	3	6	7	4	.636	1	3- -	—	4.10
2000 Birmingham	AA	16	16	1	0	118.2	458	95	37	30	8	1	1	10	17	0	68	1	0	8	4	.667	1	0- -	—	2.28
2000 Chicago	AL	28	3	0	6	51.1	225	55	27	24	5	1	0	3	19	1	37	0	0	4	1	.800	0	0-2	3	4.21
2001 Chicago	AL	32	32	4	0	221.1	885	188	89	81	24	9	4	8	48	2	126	1	5	16	8	.667	2	0-0	0	3.29
2 ML YEARS		60	35	4	6	272.2	1110	243	116	105	29	10	4	11	67	3	163	1	5	20	9	.690	2	0-2	3	3.47

Damon Buford

Bats: Right **Throws:** Right **Pos:** CF-33; RF-1; PH/PR-1 **Ht:** 5'10" **Wt:** 180 **Born:** 6/12/70 **Age:** 32

Year Team	Lg	G	AB	H	2B	3B	HR	(Hm	Rd)	TB	R	RBI	TBB	IBB	SO	HBP	SH	SF	SB	CS	SB%	GDP	Avg	OBP	SLG
2001 Rochester *	AAA	39	149	38	10	0	4	—	—	60	20	12	22	0	26	3	0	2	3	1	.75	2	.255	.358	.403
Louisville *	AAA	13	54	20	5	1	3	—	—	36	14	14	10	0	17	0	0	1	0	1	.00	2	.370	.462	.667
1993 Baltimore	AL	53	79	18	5	0	2	(0	2)	29	18	9	9	0	19	1	1	0	2	2	.50	1	.228	.315	.367
1994 Baltimore	AL	4	2	1	0	0	0	(0	0)	1	2	0	0	0	1	0	0	0	0	0	—	0	.500	.500	.500
1995 Bal-NYM		68	168	34	5	0	4	(2	2)	51	30	14	25	0	35	5	3	3	10	8	.56	3	.202	.318	.304
1996 Texas	AL	90	145	41	9	0	6	(3	3)	68	30	20	15	0	34	0	1	1	8	5	.62	3	.283	.348	.469
1997 Texas	AL	122	366	82	18	0	8	(4	4)	124	49	39	30	0	83	3	3	2	18	7	.72	8	.224	.287	.339
1998 Boston	AL	86	216	61	14	4	10	(4	6)	113	37	42	22	1	43	1	0	2	5	5	.50	5	.282	.349	.523
1999 Boston	AL	91	297	72	15	2	6	(3	3)	109	39	38	21	0	74	2	1	3	9	2	.82	5	.242	.294	.367
2000 Chicago	NL	150	495	124	18	3	15	(9	6)	193	64	48	47	3	118	8	4	2	4	6	.40	9	.251	.324	.390
2001 Chicago	NL	35	85	15	2	0	3	(0	3)	26	11	8	4	0	23	0	0	0	0	0	—	3	.176	.213	.306
1995 Baltimore	AL	24	32	2	0	0	0	(0	0)	2	6	2	6	0	7	0	3	1	3	1	.75	0	.063	.205	.063
New York	NL	44	136	32	5	0	4	(2	2)	49	24	12	19	0	28	5	0	2	7	7	.50	3	.235	.346	.360
9 ML YEARS		699	1853	448	86	9	54	(25	29)	714	280	218	173	4	430	20	13	13	56	35	.62	37	.242	.311	.385

Jay Buhner

Bats: R **Throws:** R **Pos:** LF-10; PH/PR-5; DH-4; RF-2 **Ht:** 6'3" **Wt:** 210 **Born:** 8/13/64 **Age:** 37

Year Team	Lg	G	AB	H	2B	3B	HR	(Hm	Rd)	TB	R	RBI	TBB	IBB	SO	HBP	SH	SF	SB	CS	SB%	GDP	Avg	OBP	SLG
2001 Everett *	A-	3	10	6	1	0	2	—	—	13	3	3	1	0	2	0	0	0	0	0	—	0	.600	.636	1.300
Tacoma *	AAA	11	34	8	0	0	3	—	—	17	5	9	5	0	13	1	0	0	0	0	—	1	.235	.350	.500
1987 New York	AL	7	22	5	2	0	0	(0	0)	7	0	1	1	0	6	0	0	0	0	0	—	1	.227	.261	.318
1988 NYY-Sea	AL	85	261	56	13	1	13	(8	5)	110	36	38	28	1	93	6	1	3	1	1	.50	5	.215	.302	.421
1989 Seattle	AL	58	204	56	15	1	9	(7	2)	100	27	33	19	0	55	2	0	1	1	4	.20	0	.275	.341	.490
1990 Seattle	AL	51	163	45	12	0	7	(5	2)	78	16	33	17	1	50	4	0	1	2	2	.50	6	.276	.357	.479
1991 Seattle	AL	137	406	99	14	4	27	(14	13)	202	64	77	53	5	117	6	2	4	0	1	.00	10	.244	.337	.498
1992 Seattle	AL	152	543	132	16	3	25	(9	16)	229	69	79	71	2	146	6	1	8	0	6	.00	12	.243	.333	.422
1993 Seattle	AL	158	563	153	28	3	27	(13	14)	268	91	98	100	11	144	2	2	8	2	5	.29	12	.272	.379	.476
1994 Seattle	AL	101	358	100	23	4	21	(8	13)	194	74	68	66	3	63	5	2	5	0	1	.00	7	.279	.394	.542
1995 Seattle	AL	126	470	123	23	0	40	(21	19)	266	86	121	60	7	120	1	2	6	0	1	.00	15	.262	.343	.566
1996 Seattle	AL	150	564	153	29	0	44	(21	23)	314	107	138	84	5	159	9	0	10	0	1	.00	11	.271	.369	.557
1997 Seattle	AL	157	540	131	18	2	40	(13	27)	273	104	109	119	3	175	5	0	1	0	0	—	23	.243	.383	.506
1998 Seattle	AL	72	244	59	7	1	15	(8	7)	113	33	45	38	0	71	1	1	2	0	0	—	2	.242	.344	.463
1999 Seattle	AL	87	266	59	11	0	14	(5	9)	112	37	38	69	0	100	5	0	3	0	0	—	6	.222	.388	.421
2000 Seattle	AL	112	364	92	20	0	26	(15	11)	190	50	82	59	3	98	4	1	2	0	2	.00	10	.253	.361	.522
2001 Seattle	AL	19	45	10	2	0	2	(2	0)	18	4	5	8	0	9	0	0	0	0	0	—	3	.222	.340	.400
1988 New York	AL	25	69	13	0	0	3	(1	2)	22	8	13	3	0	25	3	0	1	0	0	—	1	.188	.250	.319
Seattle	AL	60	192	43	13	1	10	(7	3)	88	28	25	25	1	68	3	1	2	1	1	.50	4	.224	.320	.458
15 ML YEARS		1472	5013	1273	233	19	310	(146	164)	2474	798	965	792	41	1406	56	12	54	6	24	.20	123	.254	.359	.494

Dave Burba

Pitches: Right **Bats:** Right **Pos:** SP-27; RP-5 **Ht:** 6'4" **Wt:** 240 **Born:** 7/7/66 **Age:** 35

		HOW MUCH HE PITCHED						WHAT HE GAVE UP											THE RESULTS						
Year Team	Lg	G	GS	CG	GF	IP	BFP	H	R	ER	HR	SH	SF	HB	TBB	IBB	SO	WP	Bk	W	L	Pct.	ShO	Sv-Op	Hld	ERA
1990 Seattle	AL	6	0	0	2	8	35	8	6	4	0	2	0	1	2	0	4	0	0	0	0	—	0	0-0	0	4.50
1991 Seattle	AL	22	2	0	11	36.2	153	34	16	15	6	0	0	0	14	3	16	1	0	2	2	.500	0	1-1	0	3.68
1992 San Francisco	NL	23	11	0	4	70.2	318	80	43	39	4	2	4	2	31	2	47	1	1	2	7	.222	0	0-0	0	4.97
1993 San Francisco	NL	54	5	0	9	95.1	408	95	49	45	14	6	3	3	37	5	88	4	0	10	3	.769	0	0-0	10	4.25
1994 San Francisco	NL	57	0	0	13	74	322	59	39	36	5	3	1	6	45	3	84	3	0	3	6	.333	0	0-3	11	4.38
1995 SF-Cin	NL	52	9	1	7	106.2	451	90	50	47	9	4	1	0	51	3	96	5	0	10	4	.714	1	0-1	5	3.97
1996 Cincinnati	NL	34	33	0	0	195	849	179	96	83	18	5	12	2	97	9	148	9	1	11	13	.458	0	0-0	0	3.83
1997 Cincinnati	NL	30	27	2	1	160	706	157	88	84	22	6	3	9	73	10	131	6	0	11	10	.524	0	0-0	0	4.73
1998 Cleveland	AL	32	31	0	0	203.2	870	210	100	93	30	3	10	7	69	4	132	6	0	15	10	.600	0	0-0	0	4.11
1999 Cleveland	AL	34	34	1	0	220	940	211	113	104	30	2	3	8	96	3	174	13	0	15	9	.625	0	0-0	0	4.25
2000 Cleveland	AL	32	32	0	0	191.1	848	199	99	95	19	5	5	2	91	2	180	7	0	16	6	.727	0	0-0	0	4.47
2001 Cleveland	AL	32	27	1	4	150.2	684	188	112	104	16	5	7	3	54	2	118	6	0	10	10	.500	0	0-0	0	6.21
1995 San Francisco	NL	37	0	0	7	43.1	191	38	26	24	5	3	1	0	25	2	46	2	0	4	2	.667	0	0-1	5	4.98
Cincinnati	NL	15	9	1	0	63.1	260	52	24	23	4	1	0	0	26	1	50	3	0	6	2	.750	1	0-0	0	3.27
12 ML YEARS		408	211	5	51	1512	6584	1510	811	749	173	43	49	43	660	46	1218	61	2	105	80	.568	1	1-5	26	4.46

Jamie Burke

Bats: R **Throws:** R **Pos:** C-8; PH/PR-3; DH-1; 1B-1 **Ht:** 6'0" **Wt:** 195 **Born:** 9/24/71 **Age:** 30

Year Team	Lg	G	AB	H	2B	3B	HR	(Hm	Rd)	TB	R	RBI	TBB	IBB	SO	HBP	SH	SF	SB	CS	SB%	GDP	Avg	OBP	SLG
1993 Boise	A-	66	226	68	11	1	1	—	—	84	32	30	39	3	28	5	2	2	2	3	.40	4	.301	.412	.372
1994 Cedar Rapds	A	127	469	124	24	1	1	—	—	153	57	47	40	3	64	12	4	8	6	8	.43	15	.264	.333	.326
1995 Lk Elsinore	A+	106	365	100	15	6	2	—	—	133	47	56	32	1	53	9	11	4	6	4	.60	12	.274	.344	.364
1996 Midland	AA	45	144	46	8	2	2	—	—	64	24	16	20	1	22	2	1	0	1	1	.50	1	.319	.410	.444
Vancouver	AAA	41	156	39	5	0	1	—	—	47	12	14	7	0	18	1	1	2	2	1	.67	5	.250	.283	.301
1997 Midland	AA	116	428	141	44	3	6	—	—	209	77	72	40	0	46	8	0	3	2	3	.40	12	.329	.395	.488
Vancouver	AAA	8	27	8	1	0	0	—	—	9	4	3	3	0	2	1	0	0	0	0	—	3	.296	.387	.333
1998 Vancouver	AAA	61	162	35	6	0	2	—	—	47	14	14	13	0	25	6	2	2	0	1	.00	7	.216	.295	.290
Midland	AA	12	41	10	1	0	0	—	—	11	7	4	7	0	4	0	0	1	0	0	—	3	.244	.354	.268
1999 Edmonton	AAA	46	149	50	9	0	3	—	—	68	29	16	23	0	18	3	2	0	0	1	.00	3	.336	.434	.456
2000 Edmonton	AAA	75	263	63	12	0	0	—	—	75	25	17	19	2	42	5	2	1	1	1	.50	5	.240	.301	.285
2001 Salt Lake	AAA	61	215	47	10	3	0	—	—	63	25	27	19	0	28	5	2	4	1	0	1.00	6	.219	.292	.293
2001 Anaheim	AL	9	5	1	0	0	0	(0	0)	1	1	0	0	0	2	0	0	0	0	0	—	0	.200	.200	.200

John Burkett

Pitches: Right **Bats:** Right **Pos:** SP-34   Ht: 6'3" Wt: 215 Born: 11/28/64 Age: 37

Year Team	Lg	G	GS	CG	GF	IP	BFP	H	R	ER	HR	SH	SF	HB	TBB	IBB	SO	WP	Bk	W	L	Pct.	ShO	Sv-Op	Hld	ERA
1987 San Francisco	NL	3	0	0	1	6	28	7	4	3	2	1	0	1	3	0	5	0	0	0	0	—	0	0-0	0	4.50
1990 San Francisco	NL	33	32	2	1	204	857	201	92	86	18	6	5	4	61	7	118	3	3	14	7	.667	0	1-1	0	3.79
1991 San Francisco	NL	36	34	3	0	206.2	890	223	103	96	19	8	8	10	60	2	131	5	0	12	11	.522	1	0-0	1	4.18
1992 San Francisco	NL	32	32	3	0	189.2	799	194	96	81	13	11	4	4	45	6	107	0	0	13	9	.591	1	0-0	0	3.84
1993 San Francisco	NL	34	34	2	0	231.2	942	224	100	94	18	8	4	11	40	4	145	1	2	22	7	.759	0	0-0	0	3.65
1994 San Francisco	NL	25	25	0	0	159.1	676	176	72	64	14	12	5	7	36	7	85	2	0	6	8	.429	0	0-0	0	3.62
1995 Florida	NL	30	30	4	0	188.1	810	208	95	90	22	10	0	6	57	5	126	2	1	14	14	.500	1	0-0	0	4.30
1996 Fla-Tex		34	34	2	0	222.2	934	229	117	105	19	12	6	5	58	4	155	0	0	11	12	.478	1	0-0	0	4.24
1997 Texas	AL	30	30	2	0	189.1	828	240	106	94	20	4	7	4	30	1	139	1	0	9	12	.429	0	0-0	0	4.56
1998 Texas	AL	32	32	0	0	195	854	230	131	123	19	7	5	8	46	1	131	3	0	9	13	.409	0	0-0	0	5.68
1999 Texas	AL	30	25	0	1	147.1	656	184	95	92	18	5	3	3	46	1	96	4	0	9	8	.529	0	0-0	0	5.62
2000 Atlanta	NL	31	22	0	4	134.1	603	162	79	73	13	8	5	6	44	5	110	2	0	10	6	.625	0	0-1	0	4.89
2001 Atlanta	NL	34	34	1	0	219.1	902	187	83	74	17	6	7	6	70	13	187	5	1	12	12	.500	1	0-0	0	3.04
1996 Florida	NL	24	24	1	0	154	645	154	84	74	15	11	4	3	42	2	108	0	0	6	10	.375	1	0-0	0	4.32
Texas	AL	10	10	1	0	68.2	289	75	33	31	4	1	2	2	16	2	47	0	0	5	2	.714	1	0-0	0	4.06
13 ML YEARS		384	364	19	7	2293.2	9779	2465	1173	1077	212	98	59	73	603	53	1535	28	7	141	119	.542	5	1-2	1	4.23

Morgan Burkhart

Bats: Both **Throws:** Left **Pos:** DH-6; 1B-5; PH/PR-3   Ht: 5'11" Wt: 225 Born: 1/29/72 Age: 30

Year Team	Lg	G	AB	H	2B	3B	HR	(Hm	Rd)	TB	R	RBI	TBB	IBB	SO	HBP	SH	SF	SB	CS	SB%	GDP	Avg	OBP	SLG
1995 Richmond	IND	70	282	93	28	1	9	—	—	150	58	70	41	4	24	7	0	7	16	7	.70	5	.330	.418	.532
1996 Richmond	IND	74	266	95	27	1	17	—	—	175	60	64	49	4	24	14	0	6	22	4	.85	3	.357	.472	.658
1997 Richmond	IND	80	285	92	22	0	24	—	—	186	76	74	73	8	47	8	0	5	8	4	.67	6	.323	.466	.653
1998 Richmond	IND	80	280	113	18	1	36	—	—	241	97	98	85	9	38	13	0	1	13	1	.93	6	.404	.557	.861
1999 Sarasota	A+	68	245	89	18	0	23	—	—	176	56	67	37	6	33	6	0	7	5	2	.71	4	.363	.447	.718
Trenton	AA	66	239	55	14	1	12	—	—	107	40	41	31	1	43	10	0	3	3	0	1.00	2	.230	.339	.448
2000 Pawtucket	AAA	105	353	90	17	1	23	—	—	178	59	77	69	4	89	12	0	2	0	0	—	6	.255	.392	.504
2001 Pawtucket	AAA	120	412	111	19	1	25	—	—	207	64	62	68	4	113	8	0	1	1	0	1.00	4	.269	.382	.502
2000 Boston	AL	25	73	21	3	0	4	(1	3)	36	16	18	17	1	25	4	0	1	0	0	—	1	.288	.442	.493
2001 Boston	AL	11	33	6	1	0	1	(0	1)	10	3	4	1	0	11	0	0	0	0	0	—	1	.182	.206	.303
2 ML YEARS		36	106	27	4	0	5	(1	4)	46	19	22	18	1	36	4	0	1	0	0	—	2	.255	.380	.434

Ellis Burks

Bats: R **Throws:** R **Pos:** DH-102; LF-18; PH/PR-3; RF-2   Ht: 6'2" Wt: 205 Born: 9/11/64 Age: 37

Year Team	Lg	G	AB	H	2B	3B	HR	(Hm	Rd)	TB	R	RBI	TBB	IBB	SO	HBP	SH	SF	SB	CS	SB%	GDP	Avg	OBP	SLG
1987 Boston	AL	133	558	152	30	2	20	(12	8)	246	94	59	41	0	98	2	4	1	27	6	.82	1	.272	.324	.441
1988 Boston	AL	144	540	159	37	5	18	(8	10)	260	93	92	62	1	89	3	4	6	25	9	.74	8	.294	.367	.481
1989 Boston	AL	97	399	121	19	6	12	(6	6)	188	73	61	36	2	52	5	2	4	21	5	.81	8	.303	.365	.471
1990 Boston	AL	152	588	174	33	8	21	(10	11)	286	89	89	48	4	82	1	2	7	9	11	.45	18	.296	.349	.486
1991 Boston	AL	130	474	119	33	3	14	(8	6)	200	56	56	39	2	81	6	2	3	6	11	.35	7	.251	.314	.422
1992 Boston	AL	66	235	60	8	3	8	(4	4)	98	35	30	25	2	48	1	0	2	5	2	.71	5	.255	.327	.417
1993 Chicago	AL	146	499	137	24	4	17	(7	10)	220	75	74	60	2	97	4	3	8	6	9	.40	11	.275	.352	.441
1994 Colorado	NL	42	149	48	8	3	13	(7	6)	101	33	24	16	3	39	0	0	0	3	1	.75	3	.322	.388	.678
1995 Colorado	NL	103	278	74	10	6	14	(8	6)	138	41	49	39	0	72	2	1	1	7	3	.70	7	.266	.359	.496
1996 Colorado	NL	156	613	211	45	8	40	(23	17)	392	142	128	61	2	114	6	3	2	32	6	.84	19	.344	.408	.639
1997 Colorado	NL	119	424	123	19	2	32	(15	17)	242	91	82	47	0	75	3	1	2	7	2	.78	17	.290	.363	.571
1998 Col-SF	NL	142	504	147	28	6	21	(10	11)	250	76	76	58	1	111	6	5	9	11	8	.58	12	.292	.365	.496
1999 San Francisco	NL	120	390	110	19	0	31	(16	15)	222	73	96	69	2	86	6	0	4	7	5	.58	11	.282	.394	.569
2000 San Francisco	NL	122	393	135	21	5	24	(9	15)	238	74	96	56	5	49	1	0	8	5	1	.83	10	.344	.419	.606
2001 Cleveland	AL	124	439	123	29	1	28	(15	13)	238	83	74	62	2	85	5	0	4	5	1	.83	16	.280	.369	.542
1998 Colorado	NL	100	357	102	22	5	16	(8	8)	182	54	54	39	0	80	2	2	5	3	7	.30	10	.286	.355	.510
San Francisco	NL	42	147	45	6	1	5	(2	3)	68	22	22	19	1	31	4	3	4	8	1	.89	2	.306	.387	.463
15 ML YEARS		1796	6483	1893	363	62	313	(165	148)	3319	1128	1086	719	28	1178	50	28	61	176	80	.69	153	.292	.364	.512

A.J. Burnett

Pitches: Right **Bats:** Right **Pos:** SP-27   Ht: 6'5" Wt: 205 Born: 1/3/77 Age: 25

Year Team	Lg	G	GS	CG	GF	IP	BFP	H	R	ER	HR	SH	SF	HB	TBB	IBB	SO	WP	Bk	W	L	Pct.	ShO	Sv-Op	Hld	ERA
2001 Brevard Cty *	A+	2	2	0	0	9.1	35	4	2	2	0	0	0	0	4	0	10	0	0	0	0	—	0	0-	—	1.93
1999 Florida	NL	7	7	0	0	41.1	182	37	23	16	3	1	3	0	25	2	33	0	0	4	2	.667	0	0-0	0	3.48
2000 Florida	NL	13	13	0	0	82.2	364	80	46	44	8	6	3	2	44	3	57	2	0	3	7	.300	0	0-0	0	4.79
2001 Florida	NL	27	27	2	0	173.1	733	145	82	78	20	6	8	7	83	3	128	7	1	11	12	.478	1	0-0	0	4.05
3 ML YEARS		47	47	2	0	297.1	1279	262	151	138	31	13	14	9	152	8	218	9	1	18	21	.462	1	0-0	0	4.18

Jeromy Burnitz

Bats: Left **Throws:** Right **Pos:** RF-153; PH/PR-1   Ht: 6'0" Wt: 205 Born: 4/15/69 Age: 33

Year Team	Lg	G	AB	H	2B	3B	HR	(Hm	Rd)	TB	R	RBI	TBB	IBB	SO	HBP	SH	SF	SB	CS	SB%	GDP	Avg	OBP	SLG
1993 New York	NL	86	263	64	10	6	13	(6	7)	125	49	38	38	4	66	1	2	2	3	6	.33	2	.243	.339	.475
1994 New York	NL	45	143	34	4	0	3	(2	1)	47	26	15	23	0	45	1	1	0	1	1	.50	2	.238	.347	.329
1995 Cleveland	AL	9	7	4	1	0	0	(0	0)	5	4	0	0	0	0	0	0	0	0	0	—	0	.571	.571	.714
1996 Cle-Mil	AL	94	300	80	13	4	9	(5	4)	94	38	40	33	2	47	4	0	2	4	1	.80	4	.265	.377	.470
1997 Milwaukee	AL	153	494	139	37	8	27	(18	9)	273	85	85	75	8	111	5	3	0	20	13	.61	8	.281	.382	.553
1998 Milwaukee	NL	161	609	160	28	1	38	(17	21)	304	92	125	70	7	158	4	1	7	7	4	.64	9	.263	.339	.499
1999 Milwaukee	NL	130	467	126	33	2	33	(12	21)	262	87	103	91	7	124	16	0	6	7	3	.70	11	.270	.402	.561

						BATTING														BASERUNNING				PERCENTAGES		
Year Team	Lg	G	AB	H	2B	3B	HR	(Hm	Rd)	TB	R	RBI	TBB	IBB	SO	HBP	SH	SF	SB	CS	SB%	GDP	Avg	OBP	SLG
2000 Milwaukee	NL	161	564	131	29	2	31	(12	19)	257	91	98	99	10	121	14	0	9	6	4	.60	12	.232	.356	.456
2001 Milwaukee	NL	154	562	141	32	4	34	(16	18)	283	104	100	80	9	150	5	0	4	0	4	.00	6	.251	.347	.504
1996 Cleveland	AL	71	128	36	10	0	7	(4	3)	67	30	26	25	1	31	2	0	0	2	1	.67	3	.281	.406	.523
Milwaukee	AL	23	72	17	4	0	2	(1	1)	27	8	14	8	1	16	2	0	2	2	0	1.00	1	.236	.321	.375
9 ML YEARS		993	3309	852	188	23	188	(88	100)	1650	576	604	509	47	822	50	7	30	48	36	.57	56	.257	.362	.499

Pat Burrell

Bats: Right **Throws:** Right **Pos:** LF-146; PH/PR-6; DH-5   **Ht:** 6'4" **Wt:** 225 **Born:** 10/10/76 **Age:** 25

						BATTING														BASERUNNING				PERCENTAGES		
Year Team	Lg	G	AB	H	2B	3B	HR	(Hm	Rd)	TB	R	RBI	TBB	IBB	SO	HBP	SH	SF	SB	CS	SB%	GDP	Avg	OBP	SLG
1998 Clearwater	A+	37	132	40	7	1	7	—	—	70	29	30	27	2	22	0	0	2	2	0	1.00	3	.303	.416	.530
1999 Reading	AA	117	417	139	28	6	28	—	—	263	84	90	79	3	103	0	0	2	3	1	.75	13	.333	.438	.631
Scrantn-WB	AAA	10	33	5	0	0	1	—	—	8	4	4	4	0	8	1	0	0	1	0	1.00	0	.152	.263	.242
2000 Scrantn-WB	AAA	40	143	42	15	1	4	—	—	71	31	25	32	0	36	0	0	1	1	1	.50	1	.294	.420	.497
2000 Philadelphia	NL	111	408	106	27	1	18	(7	11)	189	57	79	63	2	139	1	0	2	0	0	—	5	.260	.359	.463
2001 Philadelphia	NL	155	539	139	29	2	27	(10	17)	253	70	89	70	7	162	5	0	4	2	1	.67	12	.258	.346	.469
2 ML YEARS		266	947	245	56	3	45	(17	28)	442	127	168	133	9	301	6	0	6	2	1	.67	17	.259	.352	.467

Homer Bush

Bats: Right **Throws:** Right **Pos:** 2B-78; PH/PR-1   **Ht:** 5'10" **Wt:** 180 **Born:** 11/12/72 **Age:** 29

						BATTING														BASERUNNING				PERCENTAGES		
Year Team	Lg	G	AB	H	2B	3B	HR	(Hm	Rd)	TB	R	RBI	TBB	IBB	SO	HBP	SH	SF	SB	CS	SB%	GDP	Avg	OBP	SLG
2001 Dunedin *	A+	4	17	6	0	0	0	—	—	6	4	2	2	0	3	0	0	0	1	0	1.00	1	.353	.421	.353
Syracuse *	AAA	9	32	8	0	0	0	—	—	10	11	3	3	0	6	2	0	1	0	0	—	1	.250	.342	.313
1997 New York	AL	10	11	4	0	0	0	(0	0)	4	2	3	0	0	0	0	0	0	0	0	—	0	.364	.364	.364
1998 New York	AL	45	71	27	3	0	1	(1	0)	33	17	5	5	0	19	0	2	0	6	3	.67	1	.380	.421	.465
1999 Toronto	AL	128	485	155	26	4	5	(2	3)	204	69	55	21	0	82	6	8	3	32	8	.80	9	.320	.353	.421
2000 Toronto	AL	76	297	64	8	0	1	(1	0)	75	38	18	18	0	60	5	4	1	9	4	.69	10	.215	.271	.253
2001 Toronto	AL	78	271	83	11	1	3	(2	1)	105	32	27	8	1	50	6	2	4	13	4	.76	2	.306	.336	.387
5 ML YEARS		337	1135	333	48	5	10	(6	4)	421	158	108	52	1	211	17	16	8	60	19	.76	22	.293	.332	.371

Brent Butler

Bats: R **Throws:** R **Pos:** 2B-23; PH/PR-19; SS-10; 3B-9   **Ht:** 6'0" **Wt:** 180 **Born:** 2/11/78 **Age:** 24

						BATTING														BASERUNNING				PERCENTAGES		
Year Team	Lg	G	AB	H	2B	3B	HR	(Hm	Rd)	TB	R	RBI	TBB	IBB	SO	HBP	SH	SF	SB	CS	SB%	GDP	Avg	OBP	SLG
1996 Johnson Cty	R+	62	248	85	21	1	8	—	—	132	45	50	25	1	29	2	1	2	8	1	.89	11	.343	.404	.532
1997 Peoria	A	129	480	147	37	2	15	—	—	233	81	71	63	6	69	4	0	6	6	4	.60	9	.306	.388	.485
1998 Pr William	A+	126	475	136	27	2	11	—	—	200	63	76	39	2	74	9	2	7	3	4	.43	12	.286	.347	.421
1999 Arkansas	AA	139	528	142	21	1	13	—	—	204	68	54	26	0	47	6	0	5	0	4	.00	16	.269	.308	.386
2000 Colo Sprngs	AAA	122	438	128	35	1	8	—	—	189	73	54	44	1	46	4	7	9	1	3	.25	15	.292	.356	.432
2001 Colo Sprngs	AAA	65	272	91	20	3	7	—	—	138	51	38	15	0	26	4	3	2	4	2	.67	13	.335	.375	.507
2001 Colorado	NL	53	119	29	7	1	1	(0	1)	41	17	14	7	0	7	1	2	2	1	1	.50	4	.244	.287	.345

Paul Byrd

Pitches: Right **Bats:** Right **Pos:** SP-16; RP-3   **Ht:** 6'1" **Wt:** 184 **Born:** 12/3/70 **Age:** 31

		HOW MUCH HE PITCHED						WHAT HE GAVE UP												THE RESULTS						
Year Team	Lg	G	GS	CG	GF	IP	BFP	H	R	ER	HR	SH	SF	HB	TBB	IBB	SO	WP	Bk	W	L	Pct.	ShO	Sv-Op	Hld	ERA
2001 Clearwater *	A+	4	4	0	0	23.2	98	24	10	9	1	1	1	1	5	0	17	1	0	0	3	.000	0	0- -	—	3.42
Scrantn-WB *	AAA	5	5	0	0	37	155	34	18	15	4	2	0	4	7	0	35	0	0	1	3	.250	0	0- -	—	3.65
1995 New York	NL	17	0	0	6	22	91	18	6	5	1	0	2	1	7	1	26	1	2	2	0	1.000	0	0-0	3	2.05
1996 New York	NL	38	0	0	14	46.2	204	48	22	22	7	1	1	0	21	4	31	3	0	1	2	.333	0	0-2	3	4.24
1997 Atlanta	NL	31	4	0	9	53	236	47	34	31	6	2	2	4	28	4	37	3	1	4	4	.500	0	0-0	1	5.26
1998 Atl-Phi	NL	9	8	2	0	57	233	45	19	17	6	2	1	0	18	1	39	2	0	5	2	.714	1	0-0	0	2.68
1999 Philadelphia	NL	32	32	1	0	199.2	872	205	119	102	34	5	6	17	70	2	106	11	3	15	11	.577	0	0-0	0	4.60
2000 Philadelphia	NL	17	15	0	0	83	371	89	67	60	17	3	1	3	35	2	53	1	0	2	9	.182	0	0-0	0	6.51
2001 Phi-KC		19	16	1	1	103.1	444	120	54	51	12	4	6	2	26	1	52	2	0	6	7	.462	0	0-0	0	4.44
1998 Atlanta	NL	1	0	0	0	2	11	4	3	3	0	0	0	0	1	0	1	0	0	0	0	—	0	0-0	0	13.50
Philadelphia	NL	8	8	2	0	55	222	41	16	14	6	2	1	0	17	1	38	2	0	5	2	.714	1	0-0	0	2.29
2001 Philadelphia	NL	3	1	0	1	10	45	10	9	9	1	2	2	1	4	0	3	1	0	1	0	1.000	0	0-0	0	8.10
Kansas City	AL	16	15	1	0	93.1	399	110	45	42	11	2	4	1	22	1	49	1	0	6	6	.500	0	0-0	0	4.05
7 ML YEARS		163	75	4	30	564.2	2451	572	321	288	83	17	19	27	205	15	344	23	6	35	35	.500	1	0-2	7	4.59

Eric Byrnes

Bats: R **Throws:** R **Pos:** LF-8; PH/PR-8; DH-5; RF-5; CF-2   **Ht:** 6'2" **Wt:** 205 **Born:** 2/16/76 **Age:** 26

						BATTING														BASERUNNING				PERCENTAGES		
Year Team	Lg	G	AB	H	2B	3B	HR	(Hm	Rd)	TB	R	RBI	TBB	IBB	SO	HBP	SH	SF	SB	CS	SB%	GDP	Avg	OBP	SLG
1998 Sou Oregon	A-	42	169	53	10	2	7	—	—	88	36	31	16	1	16	2	0	1	6	1	.86	3	.314	.378	.521
Visalia	A+	29	108	46	9	2	4	—	—	71	26	21	18	0	15	1	0	2	11	1	.92	2	.426	.504	.657
1999 Midland	AA	43	164	39	14	0	1	—	—	56	25	22	17	0	32	3	2	3	6	3	.67	5	.238	.316	.341
Modesto	A+	96	365	123	28	1	6	—	—	171	86	66	58	2	37	9	0	7	28	8	.78	14	.337	.433	.468
2000 Midland	AA	67	259	78	25	2	5	—	—	122	49	37	43	0	38	1	2	6	21	11	.66	5	.301	.395	.471
Sacramento	AAA	67	243	81	23	1	9	—	—	133	55	47	31	0	30	2	1	2	12	5	.71	3	.333	.410	.547
2001 Sacramento	AAA	100	415	120	23	2	20	—	—	207	81	51	33	1	66	5	2	7	25	3	.89	10	.289	.343	.499
2000 Oakland	AL	10	10	3	0	0	0	(0	0)	3	5	0	0	0	1	0	0	0	2	1	.67	0	.300	.364	.300
2001 Oakland	AL	19	38	9	1	0	3	(2	1)	19	9	5	4	0	6	1	0	0	1	0	1.00	0	.237	.326	.500
2 ML YEARS		29	48	12	1	0	3	(2	1)	22	14	5	4	0	7	1	0	0	3	1	.75	0	.250	.333	.458

Jolbert Cabrera

Bats: R **Throws:** R **Pos:** LF-36; CF-35; 2B-28; 3B-27; PH/PR-27; RF-18; SS-14; DH-1   **Ht:** 6'0" **Wt:** 177 **Born:** 12/8/72 **Age:** 29

Year Team	Lg	G	AB	H	2B	3B	HR	(Hm	Rd)	TB	R	RBI	TBB	IBB	SO	HBP	SH	SF	SB	CS	SB%	GDP	Avg	OBP	SLG
1998 Cleveland	AL	1	2	0	0	0	0	(0	0)	0	0	0	0	0	1	0	0	0	0	0	—	0	.000	.000	.000
1999 Cleveland	AL	30	37	7	1	0	0	(0	0)	8	6	0	1	0	8	1	0	0	3	0	1.00	1	.189	.231	.216
2000 Cleveland	AL	100	175	44	3	1	2	(2	0)	55	27	15	8	0	15	2	1	1	6	4	.60	1	.251	.290	.314
2001 Cleveland	AL	141	287	75	16	3	1	(1	0)	100	50	38	16	0	41	6	1	2	10	4	.71	4	.261	.312	.348
4 ML YEARS		272	501	126	20	4	3	(3	0)	163	83	53	25	0	65	9	2	3	19	8	.70	6	.251	.297	.325

Jose Cabrera

Pitches: Right **Bats:** Right **Pos:** RP-55   **Ht:** 6'0" **Wt:** 180 **Born:** 3/24/72 **Age:** 30

Year Team	Lg	G	GS	CG	GF	IP	BFP	H	R	ER	HR	SH	SF	HB	TBB	IBB	SO	WP	Bk	W	L	Pct.	ShO	Sv-Op	Hld	ERA
1997 Houston	NL	12	0	0	6	15.1	57	6	2	2	1	0	3	0	6	0	18	0	0	0	0	—	0	0-1	2	1.17
1998 Houston	NL	3	0	0	1	4.1	19	7	4	4	0	0	0	0	1	1	1	0	0	0	0	—	0	0-0	0	8.31
1999 Houston	NL	26	0	0	11	29.1	119	21	7	7	3	0	3	0	9	2	28	4	0	4	0	1.000	0	0-1	6	2.15
2000 Houston	NL	52	0	0	22	59.1	266	74	40	39	10	3	3	3	17	2	41	1	1	2	3	.400	0	2-3	5	5.92
2001 Atlanta	NL	55	0	0	23	59.1	253	52	24	19	5	2	6	2	25	4	43	3	1	7	4	.636	0	2-8	6	2.88
5 ML YEARS		148	0	0	63	167.2	714	160	77	71	19	5	15	5	58	9	131	8	2	13	7	.650	0	4-13	19	3.81

Orlando Cabrera

Bats: Right **Throws:** Right **Pos:** SS-162   **Ht:** 5'10" **Wt:** 175 **Born:** 11/2/74 **Age:** 27

Year Team	Lg	G	AB	H	2B	3B	HR	(Hm	Rd)	TB	R	RBI	TBB	IBB	SO	HBP	SH	SF	SB	CS	SB%	GDP	Avg	OBP	SLG
1997 Montreal	NL	16	18	4	0	0	0	(0	0)	4	4	2	1	0	3	0	1	0	1	2	.33	1	.222	.263	.222
1998 Montreal	NL	79	261	73	16	5	3	(2	1)	108	44	22	18	1	27	0	5	1	6	2	.75	6	.280	.325	.414
1999 Montreal	NL	104	382	97	23	5	8	(6	2)	154	48	39	18	4	38	3	4	0	2	2	.50	9	.254	.293	.403
2000 Montreal	NL	125	422	100	25	1	13	(7	6)	166	47	55	25	3	28	1	3	3	4	4	.50	12	.237	.279	.393
2001 Montreal	NL	162	626	173	41	6	14	(7	7)	268	64	96	43	5	54	4	4	7	19	7	.73	15	.276	.324	.428
5 ML YEARS		486	1709	447	105	17	38	(22	16)	700	207	214	105	13	150	8	17	11	32	17	.65	43	.262	.306	.410

Miguel Cairo

Bats: R **Throws:** R **Pos:** PH/PR-47; 3B-43; 2B-16; LF-6; SS-2; 1B-1   **Ht:** 6'1" **Wt:** 200 **Born:** 5/4/74 **Age:** 28

Year Team	Lg	G	AB	H	2B	3B	HR	(Hm	Rd)	TB	R	RBI	TBB	IBB	SO	HBP	SH	SF	SB	CS	SB%	GDP	Avg	OBP	SLG
2001 Iowa *	AAA	34	123	37	7	1	3	—	—	55	22	14	8	2	11	1	4	0	3	4	.43	3	.301	.348	.447
1996 Toronto	AL	9	27	6	2	0	0	(0	0)	8	5	1	2	0	9	1	0	0	0	0	—	1	.222	.300	.296
1997 Chicago	NL	16	29	7	1	0	0	(0	0)	8	7	1	2	0	3	1	0	0	0	0	—	0	.241	.313	.276
1998 Tampa Bay	AL	150	515	138	26	5	5	(3	2)	189	49	46	24	0	44	6	11	2	19	8	.70	9	.268	.307	.367
1999 Tampa Bay	AL	120	465	137	15	5	3	(1	2)	171	61	36	24	0	46	7	7	5	22	7	.76	13	.295	.335	.368
2000 Tampa Bay	AL	119	375	98	18	2	1	(0	1)	123	49	34	29	0	34	2	6	5	28	7	.80	7	.261	.314	.328
2001 ChC-StL	NL	93	156	46	8	1	3	(1	1)	65	25	16	18	1	23	0	7	1	4	2	.67	4	.295	.366	.417
2001 Chicago	NL	66	123	35	3	1	2	(1	1)	46	20	9	16	1	21	0	7	1	2	1	.67	3	.285	.364	.374
St. Louis	NL	27	33	11	5	0	1	(1	0)	19	5	7	2	0	2	0	0	0	2	1	—	1	.333	.371	.576
6 ML YEARS		507	1567	432	70	13	12	(6	6)	564	196	134	99	1	159	17	31	13	71	23	.76	34	.276	.323	.360

Mickey Callaway

Pitches: Right **Bats:** Right **Pos:** RP-2   **Ht:** 6'2" **Wt:** 190 **Born:** 5/13/75 **Age:** 27

Year Team	Lg	G	GS	CG	GF	IP	BFP	H	R	ER	HR	SH	SF	HB	TBB	IBB	SO	WP	Bk	W	L	Pct.	ShO	Sv-Op	Hld	ERA
1996 Butte	R+	16	11	0	1	63	274	70	37	26	5	0	3	3	25	0	57	7	0	6	2	.750	0	0- —	—	3.71
1997 St. Pete	A+	28	28	3	0	170.2	696	162	74	61	9	2	3	5	39	0	109	7	7	11	7	.611	0	0- —	—	3.22
1998 Orlando	AA	18	17	0	0	89.2	407	103	56	44	8	1	1	4	44	0	57	7	2	5	6	.455	0	0- —	—	4.42
Durham	AAA	9	8	0	0	47.2	209	49	27	24	6	1	0	1	17	0	19	2	0	5	3	.625	0	0- —	—	4.53
1999 Orlando	AA	2	2	0	0	10	44	15	6	5	1	0	0	0	2	0	7	1	0	1	1	.500	0	0- —	—	4.50
Durham	AAA	15	15	0	0	81.1	350	86	45	38	5	0	3	8	28	0	56	6	1	7	1	.875	0	0- —	—	4.20
2000 Durham	AAA	26	20	0	2	117.1	542	151	88	69	11	1	7	2	50	2	64	2	2	11	6	.647	0	0- —	—	5.29
2001 Durham	AAA	29	21	2	3	129	532	131	50	44	9	5	3	5	24	0	81	7	1	11	7	.611	1	0- —	—	3.07
1999 Tampa Bay	AL	5	4	0	0	19.1	99	30	20	16	2	0	1	0	14	1	11	1	0	1	2	.333	0	0-0	0	7.45
2001 Tampa Bay	AL	2	0	0	2	5	20	3	4	4	2	0	0	0	2	0	2	0	0	0	0	—	0	0-0	0	7.20
2 ML YEARS		7	4	0	2	24.1	119	33	24	20	4	0	1	0	16	1	13	1	0	1	2	.333	0	0-0	0	7.40

Mike Cameron

Bats: Right **Throws:** Right **Pos:** CF-149; PH/PR-2; DH-1   **Ht:** 6'2" **Wt:** 190 **Born:** 1/8/73 **Age:** 29

Year Team	Lg	G	AB	H	2B	3B	HR	(Hm	Rd)	TB	R	RBI	TBB	IBB	SO	HBP	SH	SF	SB	CS	SB%	GDP	Avg	OBP	SLG
1995 Chicago	AL	28	38	7	2	0	1	(0	1)	12	4	2	3	0	15	0	3	0	0	0	—	0	.184	.244	.316
1996 Chicago	AL	11	11	1	0	0	0	(0	0)	1	1	0	1	0	3	0	0	0	0	1	.00	0	.091	.167	.091
1997 Chicago	AL	116	379	98	18	3	14	(10	4)	164	63	55	55	1	105	5	2	5	23	2	.92	8	.259	.356	.433
1998 Chicago	AL	141	396	83	16	5	8	(5	3)	133	53	43	37	0	101	6	1	3	27	11	.71	6	.210	.285	.336
1999 Cincinnati	NL	146	542	139	34	9	21	(12	9)	254	93	66	80	2	145	6	5	6	38	12	.76	4	.256	.357	.469
2000 Seattle	AL	155	543	145	28	4	19	(5	14)	238	96	78	78	0	133	9	7	6	24	7	.77	10	.267	.365	.438
2001 Seattle	AL	150	540	145	30	5	25	(7	18)	259	99	110	69	3	155	10	1	13	34	5	.87	13	.267	.353	.480
7 ML YEARS		747	2449	617	128	26	88	(39	49)	1061	409	354	323	6	657	36	19	30	146	38	.79	41	.252	.344	.433

Ken Caminiti

Bats: B **Throws:** R **Pos:** 3B-66; 1B-33; PH/PR-19; DH-1 **Ht:** 6'0" **Wt:** 200 **Born:** 4/21/63 **Age:** 39

Year Team	Lg	G	AB	H	2B	3B	HR	(Hm	Rd)	TB	R	RBI	TBB	IBB	SO	HBP	SH	SF	SB	CS	SB%	GDP	Avg	OBP	SLG
1987 Houston	NL	63	203	50	7	1	3	(2	1)	68	10	23	12	1	44	0	2	1	0	0	—	6	.246	.287	.335
1988 Houston	NL	30	83	15	2	0	1	(0	1)	20	5	7	5	0	18	0	0	1	0	0	—	3	.181	.225	.241
1989 Houston	NL	161	585	149	31	3	10	(3	7)	216	71	72	51	9	93	3	3	4	4	1	.80	8	.255	.316	.369
1990 Houston	NL	153	541	131	20	2	4	(2	2)	167	52	51	48	7	97	0	3	4	9	4	.69	15	.242	.302	.309
1991 Houston	NL	152	574	145	30	3	13	(9	4)	220	65	80	46	7	85	5	3	4	4	5	.44	18	.253	.312	.383
1992 Houston	NL	135	506	149	31	2	13	(7	6)	223	68	62	44	13	68	1	2	4	10	4	.71	14	.294	.350	.441
1993 Houston	NL	143	543	142	31	0	13	(5	8)	212	75	75	49	10	88	0	1	3	8	5	.62	15	.262	.321	.390
1994 Houston	NL	111	406	115	28	2	18	(6	12)	201	63	75	43	13	71	2	0	3	4	3	.57	8	.283	.352	.495
1995 San Diego	NL	143	526	159	33	0	26	(16	10)	270	74	94	69	8	94	1	0	6	12	5	.71	11	.302	.380	.513
1996 San Diego	NL	146	546	178	37	2	40	(20	20)	339	109	130	78	16	99	4	0	10	11	5	.69	15	.326	.408	.621
1997 San Diego	NL	137	486	141	28	0	26	(15	11)	247	92	90	80	9	118	3	0	7	11	2	.85	12	.290	.389	.508
1998 San Diego	NL	131	452	114	29	0	29	(14	15)	230	87	82	71	4	108	4	0	8	6	2	.75	6	.252	.353	.509
1999 Houston	NL	78	273	78	11	1	13	(4	9)	130	45	56	46	3	58	3	0	7	6	2	.75	7	.286	.386	.476
2000 Houston	NL	59	208	63	13	0	15	(9	6)	121	42	45	42	8	37	1	0	2	3	0	1.00	7	.303	.419	.582
2001 Tex-Atl		118	356	81	17	1	15	(5	10)	145	36	41	43	3	85	2	0	3	0	1	.00	7	.228	.312	.407
2001 Texas	AL	54	185	43	8	1	9	(3	6)	80	24	25	22	2	41	2	0	2	0	0	—	3	.232	.318	.432
Atlanta	NL	64	171	38	9	0	6	(2	4)	65	12	16	21	1	44	0	0	1	0	1	.00	2	.222	.306	.380
15 ML YEARS		1760	6288	1710	348	17	239	(117	122)	2809	894	983	727	111	1163	29	14	67	88	39	.69	152	.272	.347	.447

Jose Canseco

Bats: Right **Throws:** Right **Pos:** DH-68; PH/PR-6; RF-2 **Ht:** 6'4" **Wt:** 240 **Born:** 7/2/64 **Age:** 37

Year Team	Lg	G	AB	H	2B	3B	HR	(Hm	Rd)	TB	R	RBI	TBB	IBB	SO	HBP	SH	SF	SB	CS	SB%	GDP	Avg	OBP	SLG
2001 Newark *	IND	41	134	38	9	0	7	—	—	68	30	27	40	2	39	6	0	3	10	1	.91	1	.284	.459	.507
1985 Oakland	AL	29	96	29	3	0	5	(4	1)	47	16	13	4	0	31	0	0	0	1	1	.50	1	.302	.330	.490
1986 Oakland	AL	157	600	144	29	1	33	(14	19)	274	85	117	65	1	175	8	0	9	15	7	.68	12	.240	.318	.457
1987 Oakland	AL	159	630	162	35	3	31	(16	15)	296	81	113	50	2	157	2	0	9	15	3	.83	16	.257	.310	.470
1988 Oakland	AL	158	610	187	34	0	42	(16	26)	347	120	124	78	10	128	10	1	6	40	16	.71	15	.307	.391	.569
1989 Oakland	AL	65	227	61	9	1	17	(8	9)	123	40	57	23	4	69	2	0	6	6	3	.67	4	.269	.333	.542
1990 Oakland	AL	131	481	132	14	2	37	(18	19)	261	83	101	72	8	158	5	0	5	19	10	.66	9	.274	.371	.543
1991 Oakland	AL	154	572	152	32	1	44	(16	28)	318	115	122	78	8	152	9	0	6	26	6	.81	16	.266	.359	.556
1992 Oak-Tex		119	439	107	15	0	26	(15	11)	200	74	87	63	2	128	6	0	4	6	7	.46	16	.244	.344	.456
1993 Texas	AL	60	231	59	14	1	10	(6	4)	105	30	46	16	2	62	3	0	3	6	6	.50	6	.255	.308	.455
1994 Texas	AL	111	429	121	19	2	31	(17	14)	237	88	90	69	8	114	5	0	2	15	8	.65	20	.282	.386	.552
1995 Boston	AL	102	396	121	25	1	24	(10	14)	220	64	81	42	4	93	7	0	5	4	0	1.00	9	.306	.378	.556
1996 Boston	AL	96	360	104	22	1	28	(17	11)	212	68	82	63	3	82	6	0	3	3	1	.75	7	.289	.400	.589
1997 Oakland	AL	108	388	91	19	0	23	(10	13)	179	56	74	51	1	122	3	0	4	8	2	.80	15	.235	.325	.461
1998 Toronto	AL	151	583	138	26	0	46	(25	21)	302	98	107	65	5	159	6	0	4	29	17	.63	7	.237	.318	.518
1999 Tampa Bay	AL	113	430	120	18	1	34	(12	22)	242	75	95	58	3	135	7	0	7	3	0	1.00	14	.279	.369	.563
2000 TB-NYY		98	329	83	18	0	15	(6	9)	146	47	49	64	2	102	4	0	4	2	0	1.00	7	.252	.377	.444
2001 Chicago	AL	76	256	66	8	0	16	(9	7)	122	46	49	45	1	75	1	0	4	2	1	.67	4	.258	.366	.477
1992 Oakland	AL	97	366	90	11	0	22	(12	10)	167	66	72	48	1	104	3	0	4	5	7	.42	15	.246	.335	.456
Texas	AL	22	73	17	4	0	4	(3	1)	33	8	15	15	1	24	3	0	0	1	0	1.00	1	.233	.385	.452
2000 Tampa Bay	AL	61	218	56	15	0	9	(4	5)	98	31	30	41	1	65	4	0	1	2	0	1.00	5	.257	.383	.450
New York	AL	37	111	27	3	0	6	(2	4)	48	16	19	23	1	37	0	0	3	0	0	—	2	.243	.365	.432
17 ML YEARS		1887	7057	1877	340	14	462	(219	243)	3631	1186	1407	906	64	1942	84	1	81	200	88	.69	178	.266	.353	.515

Javier Cardona

Bats: Right **Throws:** Right **Pos:** C-44; PH/PR-3; DH-1 **Ht:** 6'1" **Wt:** 185 **Born:** 9/15/75 **Age:** 26

Year Team	Lg	G	AB	H	2B	3B	HR	(Hm	Rd)	TB	R	RBI	TBB	IBB	SO	HBP	SH	SF	SB	CS	SB%	GDP	Avg	OBP	SLG
1994 Jamestown	A-	19	46	12	2	0	0	—	—	14	6	5	7	0	9	0	0	0	0	0	—	1	.261	.358	.304
1995 Fayettevlle	A	51	165	34	8	0	3	—	—	51	18	19	13	0	30	1	0	0	1	0	1.00	5	.206	.268	.309
1996 Fayettevlle	A	97	348	98	21	0	4	—	—	131	42	28	28	1	53	2	3	3	1	5	.17	9	.282	.330	.376
1997 Lakeland	A+	85	284	82	15	0	7	—	—	118	28	38	25	1	51	1	2	2	1	3	.25	8	.289	.346	.415
1998 Jacksnville	AA	46	163	54	16	1	4	—	—	84	31	40	15	1	29	1	0	2	0	0	—	6	.331	.387	.515
Toledo	AAA	47	162	31	4	0	5	—	—	50	12	16	9	1	32	1	4	0	0	0	—	3	.191	.238	.309
1999 Jacksnville	AA	108	418	129	31	0	26	—	—	238	84	92	46	0	69	8	0	5	4	2	.67	16	.309	.384	.569
2000 Toledo	AAA	56	218	60	10	0	11	—	—	103	29	43	15	0	33	2	0	2	0	0	—	7	.275	.325	.472
2001 Toledo	AAA	26	98	23	2	0	1	—	—	28	7	10	8	1	18	1	0	0	1	0	1.00	1	.235	.292	.286
2000 Detroit	AL	26	40	7	1	0	1	(1	0)	11	1	2	0	0	9	1	0	1	0	0	—	1	.175	.190	.275
2001 Detroit	AL	46	96	25	8	0	1	(0	1)	36	10	10	2	0	12	1	2	1	0	1	.00	2	.260	.280	.375
2 ML YEARS		72	136	32	9	0	2	(1	1)	47	11	12	2	0	21	2	2	2	0	1	.00	3	.235	.254	.346

Chris Carpenter

Pitches: Right **Bats:** Right **Pos:** SP-34 **Ht:** 6'6" **Wt:** 225 **Born:** 4/27/75 **Age:** 27

Year Team	Lg	G	GS	CG	GF	IP	BFP	H	R	ER	HR	SH	SF	HB	TBB	IBB	SO	WP	Bk	W	L	Pct.	ShO	Sv-Op	Hld	ERA
1997 Toronto	AL	14	13	1	1	81.1	374	108	55	46	7	1	2	2	37	0	55	7	1	3	7	.300	1	0-0	0	5.09
1998 Toronto	AL	33	24	1	4	175	742	177	97	85	18	4	5	5	61	1	136	5	0	12	7	.632	1	0-0	0	4.37
1999 Toronto	AL	24	24	4	0	150	663	177	81	73	16	4	6	3	48	1	106	9	1	9	8	.529	1	0-0	0	4.38
2000 Toronto	AL	34	27	2	1	175.1	795	204	130	122	30	3	1	5	83	1	113	3	0	12	12	.455	0	0-0	0	6.26
2001 Toronto	AL	34	34	3	0	215.2	930	229	112	98	29	3	1	16	75	5	157	5	0	11	11	.500	2	0-0	0	4.09
5 ML YEARS		139	122	11	6	797.1	3504	895	475	424	100	15	15	31	304	8	567	29	2	45	45	.500	5	0-0	0	4.79

Giovanni Carrara

Pitches: Right **Bats:** Right **Pos:** RP-44; SP-3 **Ht:** 6'2" **Wt:** 210 **Born:** 3/4/68 **Age:** 34

Year Team	Lg	G	GS	CG	GF	IP	BFP	H	R	ER	HR	SH	SF	HB	TBB	IBB	SO	WP	Bk	W	L	Pct.	ShO	Sv-Op	Hld	ERA
2001 Las Vegas *	AAA	6	6	0	0	29	122	27	10	10	5	1	0	3	9	0	35	0	1	1	2	.333	0	0- -	—	3.10
1995 Toronto	AL	12	7	1	2	48.2	229	64	46	39	10	1	2	1	25	1	27	1	0	2	4	.333	0	0-0	0	7.21
1996 Tor-Cin		19	5	0	4	38	188	54	36	34	11	1	0	2	25	3	23	1	0	1	1	.500	0	0-1	0	8.05
1997 Cincinnati	NL	2	2	0	0	10.1	49	14	9	9	4	1	0	0	6	1	5	0	0	0	1	.000	0	0-0	0	7.84
2000 Colorado	NL	8	0	0	2	13.1	72	21	19	19	5	0	1	1	11	2	15	0	0	0	1	.000	0	0-1	0	12.83
2001 Los Angeles	NL	47	3	0	2	85.1	348	73	30	30	12	6	1	1	24	3	70	0	0	6	1	.857	0	0-3	9	3.16
1996 Toronto	AL	11	0	0	3	15	76	23	19	19	5	0	0	0	12	2	10	1	0	0	1	.000	0	0-1	0	11.40
Cincinnati	NL	8	5	0	1	23	112	31	17	15	6	1	0	2	13	1	13	0	0	1	0	1.000	0	0-0	0	5.87
5 ML YEARS		88	17	1	10	195.2	886	226	140	131	42	9	4	5	91	10	140	2	0	9	8	.529	0	0-5	9	6.03

Hector Carrasco

Pitches: Right **Bats:** Right **Pos:** RP-56 **Ht:** 6'2" **Wt:** 220 **Born:** 10/22/69 **Age:** 32

Year Team	Lg	G	GS	CG	GF	IP	BFP	H	R	ER	HR	SH	SF	HB	TBB	IBB	SO	WP	Bk	W	L	Pct.	ShO	Sv-Op	Hld	ERA
1994 Cincinnati	NL	45	0	0	29	56.1	237	42	17	14	3	5	0	2	30	1	41	3	1	5	6	.455	0	6-8	3	2.24
1995 Cincinnati	NL	64	0	0	28	87.1	391	86	45	40	1	2	6	2	46	5	64	15	0	2	7	.222	0	5-9	11	4.12
1996 Cincinnati	NL	56	0	0	10	74.1	325	58	37	31	6	4	4	1	45	5	59	8	1	4	3	.571	0	0-2	15	3.75
1997 Cin-KC		66	0	0	22	86	388	80	46	42	7	4	3	8	41	5	76	11	2	2	8	.200	0	0-2	8	4.40
1998 Minnesota	AL	63	0	0	20	61.2	287	75	30	30	4	0	1	1	31	1	46	8	0	4	2	.667	0	1-2	10	4.38
1999 Minnesota	AL	39	0	0	10	49	204	48	29	27	3	0	1	1	18	0	35	4	0	2	3	.400	0	1-2	7	4.96
2000 Min-Bos	AL	69	1	0	20	78.2	364	90	46	41	8	8	4	4	38	1	64	14	1	5	4	.556	0	1-6	8	4.69
2001 Minnesota	AL	56	0	0	12	73.2	317	77	40	38	8	6	3	0	30	3	70	7	1	4	3	.571	0	1-2	1	4.64
1997 Cincinnati	NL	38	0	0	11	51.1	237	51	25	21	3	3	1	4	25	2	46	3	2	1	2	.333	0	0-0	5	3.68
Kansas City	AL	28	0	0	11	34.2	151	29	21	21	4	1	2	4	16	3	30	8	0	1	6	.143	0	0-2	3	5.45
2000 Minnesota	AL	61	0	0	18	72	324	75	38	34	6	4	3	4	33	0	57	14	0	4	3	.571	0	1-5	7	4.25
Boston	AL	8	1	0	2	6.2	40	15	8	7	2	2	0	1	5	1	7	0	1	1	1	.500	0	0-1	1	9.45
8 ML YEARS		458	1	0	151	567	2513	556	290	263	40	29	29	19	279	21	455	70	6	28	36	.438	0	15-33	63	4.17

Raul Casanova

Bats: Both **Throws:** Right **Pos:** C-56; PH/PR-18; DH-2 **Ht:** 6'0" **Wt:** 195 **Born:** 8/23/72 **Age:** 29

Year Team	Lg	G	AB	H	2B	3B	HR	(Hm	Rd)	TB	R	RBI	TBB	IBB	SO	HBP	SH	SF	SB	CS	SB%	GDP	Avg	OBP	SLG
1996 Detroit	AL	25	85	16	1	0	4	(1	3)	29	6	9	6	0	18	0	0	0	0	0	—	6	.188	.242	.341
1997 Detroit	AL	101	304	74	10	1	5	(5	0)	101	27	24	26	1	48	3	0	1	1	1	.50	10	.243	.308	.332
1998 Detroit	AL	16	42	6	2	0	1	(1	0)	11	4	3	5	0	10	1	0	0	0	0	—	0	.143	.250	.262
2000 Milwaukee	NL	86	231	57	13	3	6	(4	2)	94	20	36	26	1	48	4	2	2	1	2	.33	5	.247	.331	.407
2001 Milwaukee	NL	71	192	50	10	0	11	(7	4)	93	21	33	12	2	29	1	0	3	0	0	—	3	.260	.303	.484
5 ML YEARS		299	854	203	36	4	27	(18	9)	328	78	105	75	4	153	9	2	6	2	3	.40	24	.238	.304	.384

Sean Casey

Bats: Left **Throws:** Right **Pos:** 1B-136; PH/PR-8; DH-3 **Ht:** 6'4" **Wt:** 225 **Born:** 7/2/74 **Age:** 27

Year Team	Lg	G	AB	H	2B	3B	HR	(Hm	Rd)	TB	R	RBI	TBB	IBB	SO	HBP	SH	SF	SB	CS	SB%	GDP	Avg	OBP	SLG
1997 Cleveland	AL	6	10	2	0	0	0	(0	0)	2	1	1	1	0	2	1	0	0	0	0	—	0	.200	.333	.200
1998 Cincinnati	NL	96	302	82	21	1	7	(3	4)	126	44	52	43	3	45	3	0	3	1	1	.50	11	.272	.365	.417
1999 Cincinnati	NL	151	594	197	42	3	25	(11	14)	320	103	99	61	13	88	9	0	5	0	2	.00	15	.332	.399	.539
2000 Cincinnati	NL	133	480	151	33	2	20	(9	11)	248	69	85	52	4	80	7	0	6	1	0	1.00	16	.315	.385	.517
2001 Cincinnati	NL	145	533	165	40	0	13	(5	8)	244	69	89	43	8	63	9	0	3	3	1	.75	16	.310	.369	.458
5 ML YEARS		531	1919	597	136	6	65	(28	37)	940	286	326	200	28	278	29	0	17	5	4	.56	58	.311	.382	.490

Vinny Castilla

Bats: Right **Throws:** Right **Pos:** 3B-145; SS-3; PH/PR-1 **Ht:** 6'1" **Wt:** 205 **Born:** 7/4/67 **Age:** 34

Year Team	Lg	G	AB	H	2B	3B	HR	(Hm	Rd)	TB	R	RBI	TBB	IBB	SO	HBP	SH	SF	SB	CS	SB%	GDP	Avg	OBP	SLG
1991 Atlanta	NL	12	5	1	0	0	0	(0	0)	1	1	0	0	0	2	0	1	0	0	0	—	0	.200	.200	.200
1992 Atlanta	NL	9	16	4	1	0	0	(0	0)	5	1	1	1	1	4	1	0	0	0	0	—	0	.250	.333	.313
1993 Colorado	NL	105	337	86	9	7	9	(5	4)	136	36	30	13	4	45	2	0	5	2	5	.29	10	.255	.283	.404
1994 Colorado	NL	52	130	43	11	1	3	(1	2)	65	16	18	7	1	23	0	1	3	2	1	.67	3	.331	.357	.500
1995 Colorado	NL	139	527	163	34	2	32	(16	16)	297	82	90	30	2	87	4	4	6	2	8	.20	15	.309	.347	.564
1996 Colorado	NL	160	629	191	34	0	40	(27	13)	345	97	113	35	7	88	5	0	4	7	2	.78	20	.304	.343	.548
1997 Colorado	NL	159	612	186	25	2	40	(21	19)	335	94	113	44	9	108	8	0	4	2	4	.33	17	.304	.356	.547
1998 Colorado	NL	162	645	206	28	4	46	(26	20)	380	108	144	40	7	89	6	0	6	5	9	.36	24	.319	.362	.589
1999 Colorado	NL	158	615	169	24	1	33	(20	13)	294	83	102	53	7	75	1	0	5	2	3	.40	15	.275	.331	.478
2000 Tampa Bay	AL	85	331	73	9	1	6	(2	4)	102	22	42	14	3	41	3	0	6	1	2	.33	9	.221	.254	.308
2001 TB-Hou		146	538	140	34	1	25	(12	13)	251	69	91	35	3	108	4	0	4	1	4	.20	22	.260	.308	.467
2001 Tampa Bay	AL	24	93	20	6	0	2	(2	0)	32	7	9	3	0	22	1	0	0	0	0	—	3	.215	.247	.344
Houston	NL	122	445	120	28	1	23	(10	13)	219	62	82	32	3	86	3	0	4	1	4	.20	19	.270	.320	.492
11 ML YEARS		1187	4385	1262	209	19	234	(137	97)	2211	609	744	272	44	670	34	6	43	24	38	.39	135	.288	.331	.504

Alberto Castillo

Bats: Right **Throws:** Right **Pos:** C-66   **Ht:** 6'0" **Wt:** 185 **Born:** 2/10/70 **Age:** 32

Year Team	Lg	G	AB	H	2B	3B	HR	(Hm	Rd)	TB	R	RBI	TBB	IBB	SO	HBP	SH	SF	SB	CS	SB%	GDP	Avg	OBP	SLG
1995 New York	NL	13	29	3	0	0	0	(0	0)	3	2	0	3	0	9	1	0	0	1	0	1.00	0	.103	.212	.103
1996 New York	NL	6	11	4	0	0	0	(0	0)	4	1	0	0	4	0	0	0	0	0	0	—	0	.364	.364	.364
1997 New York	NL	35	59	12	1	0	0	(0	0)	13	3	7	9	0	16	0	2	1	0	1	.00	3	.203	.304	.220
1998 New York	NL	38	83	17	4	0	2	(0	2)	27	13	7	9	0	17	1	6	0	0	2	.00	1	.205	.290	.325
1999 St. Louis	NL	93	255	67	8	0	4	(2	2)	87	21	31	24	1	48	2	5	4	0	0	—	6	.263	.326	.341
2000 Toronto	AL	66	185	39	7	0	1	(1	0)	49	14	16	21	0	36	0	2	3	0	0	—	3	.211	.287	.265
2001 Toronto	AL	66	131	26	4	0	1	(0	1)	33	9	4	7	0	30	3	5	0	1	1	.50	2	.198	.255	.252
7 ML YEARS		317	753	168	24	0	8	(3	5)	216	63	65	73	1	160	7	20	8	2	4	.33	15	.223	.295	.287

Carlos Castillo

Pitches: Right **Bats:** Right **Pos:** RP-2   **Ht:** 6'2" **Wt:** 250 **Born:** 4/21/75 **Age:** 27

Year Team	Lg	G	GS	CG	GF	IP	BFP	H	R	ER	HR	SH	SF	HB	TBB	IBB	SO	WP	Bk	W	L	Pct.	ShO	Sv-Op	Hld	ERA
2001 Pawtucket *	AAA	28	21	5	3	163.2	684	179	78	62	12	3	8	4	24	1	114	3	2	9	11	.450	1	0--	—	3.41
1997 Chicago	AL	37	2	0	14	66.1	295	68	35	33	9	0	4	1	33	1	43	3	0	2	1	.667	0	1-1	3	4.48
1998 Chicago	AL	54	2	0	11	100.1	431	94	61	57	17	2	7	5	35	1	64	4	3	6	4	.600	0	0-2	5	5.11
1999 Chicago	AL	18	2	0	6	41	178	45	26	26	10	0	0	0	14	1	23	0	2	2	2	.500	0	0-0	1	5.71
2001 Boston	AL	2	0	0	1	3	12	3	2	2	1	0	1	0	0	0	0	0	0	0	0	—	0	0-0	0	6.00
4 ML YEARS		111	6	0	32	210.2	916	210	124	118	37	2	12	6	82	5	130	7	5	10	7	.588	0	1-3	7	5.04

Frank Castillo

Pitches: Right **Bats:** Right **Pos:** SP-26   **Ht:** 6'1" **Wt:** 200 **Born:** 4/1/69 **Age:** 33

Year Team	Lg	G	GS	CG	GF	IP	BFP	H	R	ER	HR	SH	SF	HB	TBB	IBB	SO	WP	Bk	W	L	Pct.	ShO	Sv-Op	Hld	ERA
2001 Pawtucket *	AAA	2	2	0	0	7.2	29	7	1	0	0	0	1	0	0	0	3	0	0	0	0	—	0	0--	—	0.00
1991 Chicago	NL	18	18	4	0	111.2	467	107	56	54	5	6	3	0	33	2	73	5	1	6	7	.462	0	0-0	0	4.35
1992 Chicago	NL	33	33	0	0	205.1	856	179	91	79	19	11	5	6	63	6	135	11	0	10	11	.476	0	0-0	0	3.46
1993 Chicago	NL	29	25	2	0	141.1	614	162	83	76	20	10	3	9	39	4	84	5	3	5	8	.385	0	0-0	0	4.84
1994 Chicago	NL	4	4	1	0	23	96	25	13	11	3	1	0	0	5	0	19	0	0	2	1	.667	0	0-0	0	4.30
1995 Chicago	NL	29	29	2	0	188	795	179	75	67	22	11	3	6	52	4	135	3	1	11	10	.524	2	0-0	0	3.21
1996 Chicago	NL	33	33	1	0	182.1	789	209	112	107	28	4	5	8	46	4	139	2	1	7	16	.304	1	0-0	0	5.28
1997 ChC-Col	NL	34	33	0	0	184.1	830	220	121	111	25	17	2	8	69	4	126	3	0	12	12	.500	0	0-0	0	5.42
1998 Detroit	AL	27	19	0	4	116	531	150	91	88	17	2	6	5	44	0	81	0	0	3	9	.250	0	1-1	0	6.83
2000 Toronto	AL	25	24	0	1	138	576	112	58	55	18	5	2	5	56	0	104	0	0	10	5	.667	0	0-0	0	3.59
2001 Boston	AL	26	26	0	0	136.2	580	138	72	64	14	3	6	4	35	2	89	3	1	10	9	.526	0	0-0	0	4.21
1997 Chicago	NL	20	19	0	0	98	446	113	64	59	9	11	0	4	44	1	67	1	0	6	9	.400	0	0-0	0	5.42
Colorado	NL	14	14	0	0	86.1	384	107	57	52	16	6	2	4	25	3	59	2	0	6	3	.667	0	0-0	0	5.42
10 ML YEARS		258	244	10	5	1426.2	6134	1481	772	712	171	70	35	52	442	26	985	32	7	76	88	.463	3	1-1	0	4.49

Luis Castillo

Bats: Both **Throws:** Right **Pos:** 2B-133; PH/PR-1   **Ht:** 5'11" **Wt:** 175 **Born:** 9/12/75 **Age:** 26

Year Team	Lg	G	AB	H	2B	3B	HR	(Hm	Rd)	TB	R	RBI	TBB	IBB	SO	HBP	SH	SF	SB	CS	SB%	GDP	Avg	OBP	SLG
1996 Florida	NL	41	164	43	2	1	1	(0	1)	50	26	8	14	0	46	0	2	0	17	4	.81	0	.262	.320	.305
1997 Florida	NL	75	263	63	8	0	0	(0	0)	71	27	8	27	0	53	0	1	0	16	10	.62	6	.240	.310	.270
1998 Florida	NL	44	153	31	3	2	1	(0	1)	41	21	10	22	0	33	1	1	0	3	0	1.00	1	.203	.307	.268
1999 Florida	NL	128	487	147	23	4	0	(0	0)	178	76	28	67	0	85	0	6	3	50	17	.75	3	.302	.384	.366
2000 Florida	NL	136	539	180	17	3	2	(1	1)	209	101	17	78	0	86	0	9	0	62	22	.74	11	.334	.418	.388
2001 Florida	NL	134	537	141	16	10	2	(1	1)	183	76	45	67	0	90	1	4	3	33	16	.67	6	.263	.344	.341
6 ML YEARS		558	2143	605	69	20	6	(2	4)	732	327	116	275	0	393	2	23	6	181	69	.72	27	.282	.364	.342

Juan Castro

Bats: R **Throws:** R **Pos:** SS-46; 2B-37; 3B-19; PH/PR-19; 1B-1   **Ht:** 5'10" **Wt:** 187 **Born:** 6/20/72 **Age:** 30

Year Team	Lg	G	AB	H	2B	3B	HR	(Hm	Rd)	TB	R	RBI	TBB	IBB	SO	HBP	SH	SF	SB	CS	SB%	GDP	Avg	OBP	SLG
1995 Los Angeles	NL	11	4	1	0	0	0	(0	0)	1	0	0	1	0	1	0	0	0	0	0	—	0	.250	.400	.250
1996 Los Angeles	NL	70	132	26	5	3	0	(0	0)	37	16	5	10	0	27	0	4	0	1	0	1.00	3	.197	.254	.280
1997 Los Angeles	NL	40	75	11	3	1	0	(0	0)	16	3	4	7	1	20	0	2	0	0	0	—	2	.147	.220	.213
1998 Los Angeles	NL	89	220	43	7	0	2	(0	2)	56	25	14	15	0	37	0	9	2	0	0	—	5	.195	.245	.255
1999 Los Angeles	NL	2	1	0	0	0	0	(0	0)	0	0	0	0	0	1	0	0	0	0	0	—	0	.000	.000	.000
2000 Cincinnati	NL	82	224	54	12	2	4	(1	3)	82	20	23	14	1	33	0	4	2	0	2	.00	9	.241	.283	.366
2001 Cincinnati	NL	96	242	54	10	0	3	(0	3)	73	27	13	13	2	50	0	4	2	0	0	—	9	.223	.261	.302
7 ML YEARS		390	898	189	37	6	9	(1	8)	265	91	59	60	4	169	0	23	6	1	2	.33	28	.210	.258	.295

Ramon Castro

Bats: Right **Throws:** Right **Pos:** C-4; PH/PR-4   **Ht:** 6'3" **Wt:** 225 **Born:** 3/1/76 **Age:** 26

Year Team	Lg	G	AB	H	2B	3B	HR	(Hm	Rd)	TB	R	RBI	TBB	IBB	SO	HBP	SH	SF	SB	CS	SB%	GDP	Avg	OBP	SLG
2001 Calgary *	AAA	108	390	131	33	0	27	(—	—)	245	81	90	38	3	74	1	0	4	1	1	.50	11	.336	.393	.628
1999 Florida	NL	24	67	12	4	0	2	(0	2)	22	4	4	10	3	14	0	0	1	0	0	—	1	.179	.282	.328
2000 Florida	NL	50	138	33	4	0	2	(0	2)	43	10	14	16	7	36	1	0	0	0	0	—	1	.239	.318	.312
2001 Florida	NL	7	11	2	0	0	0	(0	0)	2	0	1	1	0	1	0	0	0	0	0	—	0	.182	.250	.182
3 ML YEARS		81	216	47	8	0	4	(0	4)	67	14	19	27	10	51	1	0	3	0	0	—	2	.218	.304	.310

Frank Catalanotto

Bats: L **Throws:** R **Pos:** LF-78; PH/PR-25; RF-15; 2B-13; 3B-11; DH-5; 1B-5   **Ht:** 5'11"   **Wt:** 195   **Born:** 4/27/74   **Age:** 28

Year Team	Lg	G	AB	H	2B	3B	HR	(Hm	Rd)	TB	R	RBI	TBB	IBB	SO	HBP	SH	SF	SB	CS	SB%	GDP	Avg	OBP	SLG
1997 Detroit	AL	13	26	8	2	0	0	(0	0)	10	2	3	3	0	7	0	0	0	0	0	—	0	.308	.379	.385
1998 Detroit	AL	89	213	60	13	2	6	(3	3)	95	23	25	12	1	39	4	0	5	3	2	.60	4	.282	.325	.446
1999 Detroit	AL	100	286	79	19	0	11	(6	5)	131	41	35	15	1	49	9	0	5	3	4	.43	5	.276	.327	.458
2000 Texas	AL	103	282	82	13	2	10	(6	4)	129	55	42	33	0	36	6	3	2	6	2	.75	5	.291	.375	.457
2001 Texas	AL	133	463	153	31	5	11	(4	7)	227	77	54	39	3	55	8	1	1	15	5	.75	5	.330	.391	.490
5 ML YEARS		438	1270	382	78	9	38	(19	19)	592	198	159	102	5	186	27	4	13	27	13	.68	19	.301	.362	.466

Roger Cedeno

Bats: B **Throws:** R **Pos:** CF-67; RF-55; DH-7; PH/PR-4   **Ht:** 6'1"   **Wt:** 205   **Born:** 8/16/74   **Age:** 27

Year Team	Lg	G	AB	H	2B	3B	HR	(Hm	Rd)	TB	R	RBI	TBB	IBB	SO	HBP	SH	SF	SB	CS	SB%	GDP	Avg	OBP	SLG
1995 Los Angeles	NL	40	42	10	2	0	0	(0	0)	12	4	3	3	0	10	0	0	1	1	0	1.00	1	.238	.283	.286
1996 Los Angeles	NL	86	211	52	11	1	2	(0	2)	71	26	18	24	0	47	1	2	0	5	1	.83	0	.246	.326	.336
1997 Los Angeles	NL	80	194	53	10	2	3	(3	0)	76	31	17	25	2	44	3	3	2	9	1	.90	1	.273	.362	.392
1998 Los Angeles	NL	105	240	58	11	1	2	(2	0)	77	33	17	27	2	57	0	3	1	8	2	.80	1	.242	.317	.321
1999 New York	NL	155	453	142	23	4	4	(4	0)	185	90	36	60	3	100	3	7	2	66	17	.80	5	.313	.396	.408
2000 Houston	NL	74	259	73	2	5	6	(3	3)	103	54	26	43	0	47	0	2	1	25	11	.69	6	.282	.383	.398
2001 Detroit	AL	133	523	153	14	11	6	(3	3)	207	79	48	36	1	83	2	6	5	55	15	.79	5	.293	.337	.396
7 ML YEARS		671	1922	541	73	24	23	(15	8)	731	317	165	218	8	388	9	23	12	169	47	.78	19	.281	.355	.380

Shawn Chacon

Pitches: Right **Bats:** Right **Pos:** SP-27   **Ht:** 6'3"   **Wt:** 195   **Born:** 12/23/77   **Age:** 24

Year Team	Lg	G	GS	CG	GF	IP	BFP	H	R	ER	HR	SH	SF	HB	TBB	IBB	SO	WP	Bk	W	L	Pct.	ShO	Sv-Op	Hld	ERA
1996 Rockies	R	11	11	1	0	56.1	241	46	17	10	1	0	2	4	15	0	64	3	2	1	2	.333	0	0--	—	1.60
Portland	A-	4	4	0	0	19.2	92	24	18	15	2	0	0	1	9	0	17	5	0	0	2	.000	0	0--	—	6.86
1997 Asheville	A	28	27	1	0	162	701	155	80	70	13	5	3	14	63	1	149	15	1	11	7	.611	0	0--	—	3.89
1998 Salem	A+	12	12	0	0	56	258	53	35	33	5	3	2	6	31	0	54	8	1	0	4	.000	0	0--	—	5.30
1999 Salem	A+	12	12	0	0	72	316	69	44	33	3	1	3	2	34	0	66	5	0	5	5	.500	0	0--	—	4.13
2000 Carolina	AA	27	27	4	0	173.2	739	151	71	61	10	4	2	9	85	1	172	16	0	10	10	.500	3	0--	—	3.16
2001 Colo Sprngs	AAA	4	4	0	0	24	98	18	6	6	3	3	0	1	7	0	28	0	0	2	0	1.000	0	0--	—	2.25
2001 Colorado	NL	27	27	0	0	160	711	157	96	90	26	6	3	10	87	10	134	6	0	6	10	.375	0	0-0	0	5.06

Norm Charlton

Pitches: Left **Bats:** Both **Pos:** RP-44   **Ht:** 6'3"   **Wt:** 205   **Born:** 1/6/63   **Age:** 39

Year Team	Lg	G	GS	CG	GF	IP	BFP	H	R	ER	HR	SH	SF	HB	TBB	IBB	SO	WP	Bk	W	L	Pct.	ShO	Sv-Op	Hld	ERA
2001 Tacoma *	AAA	4	2	0	0	6	26	4	2	2	0	0	0	1	2	0	9	1	0	0	1	.000	0	0--	—	3.00
1988 Cincinnati	NL	10	10	0	0	61.1	259	60	27	27	6	1	2	2	20	2	39	2	4	4	5	.444	0	0-0	0	3.96
1989 Cincinnati	NL	69	0	0	27	95.1	393	67	38	31	5	9	2	2	40	7	98	2	4	8	3	.727	0	0-1	8	2.93
1990 Cincinnati	NL	56	16	1	13	154.1	650	131	53	47	10	7	4	4	70	4	117	9	1	12	9	.571	1	2-3	9	2.74
1991 Cincinnati	NL	39	11	0	10	108.1	438	92	37	35	6	7	1	6	34	4	77	11	0	3	5	.375	0	1-4	3	2.91
1992 Cincinnati	NL	64	0	0	46	81.1	341	79	39	27	7	7	3	3	26	4	90	8	0	4	2	.667	0	26-34	7	2.99
1993 Cincinnati	AL	34	0	0	29	34.2	141	22	12	9	4	0	1	0	17	0	48	6	0	1	3	.250	0	18-21	1	2.34
1995 Phi-Sea		55	0	0	22	69.2	284	46	31	26	4	4	2	4	31	3	70	6	1	4	6	.400	0	14-16	12	3.36
1996 Seattle	AL	70	0	0	50	75.2	323	68	37	34	7	3	2	1	38	1	73	9	0	4	7	.364	0	20-27	8	4.04
1997 Seattle	AL	71	0	0	38	69.1	343	89	59	56	7	7	0	4	47	2	55	7	1	3	8	.273	0	14-25	9	7.27
1998 Bal-Atl		49	0	0	19	48	231	53	29	29	5	2	2	1	33	0	47	7	0	2	1	.667	0	1-2	5	5.44
1999 Tampa Bay	AL	42	0	0	9	50.2	233	49	29	25	4	4	2	3	36	0	45	4	0	2	3	.400	0	0-1	15	4.44
2000 Cincinnati	NL	2	0	0	2	3	20	6	9	9	1	0	0	0	6	0	1	1	0	0	0	—	0	0-0	0	27.00
2001 Seattle	AL	44	0	0	10	47.2	189	36	16	16	4	3	1	4	11	0	48	4	0	4	2	.667	0	1-2	12	3.02
1995 Philadelphia	NL	25	0	0	5	22	102	23	19	18	2	1	1	3	15	3	12	1	0	2	5	.286	0	0-1	9	7.36
Seattle	AL	30	0	0	22	47.2	182	23	12	8	2	3	1	1	16	0	58	5	1	2	1	.667	0	14-15	3	1.51
1998 Baltimore	AL	36	0	0	11	35	178	46	27	27	5	1	1	0	25	0	41	5	0	2	1	.667	0	1-1	3	6.94
Atlanta	NL	13	0	0	8	13	53	7	2	2	0	1	1	1	8	0	6	2	0	0	0	—	0	0-1	2	1.38
13 ML YEARS		605	37	1	280	899.1	3845	798	419	371	70	52	21	32	409	27	808	77	9	51	54	.486	1	97-136	89	3.71

Endy Chavez

Bats: L **Throws:** L **Pos:** LF-22; CF-5; PH/PR-3; RF-2   **Ht:** 6'0"   **Wt:** 165   **Born:** 2/7/78   **Age:** 24

Year Team	Lg	G	AB	H	2B	3B	HR	(Hm	Rd)	TB	R	RBI	TBB	IBB	SO	HBP	SH	SF	SB	CS	SB%	GDP	Avg	OBP	SLG
1997 Mets	R	33	114	33	6	3	0	—	—	45	26	15	20	0	10	0	0	1	1	2	.33	2	.277	.379	.378
Kingsport	R+	19	73	22	4	0	0	—	—	26	16	4	13	0	10	0	2	0	5	2	.71	2	.301	.407	.356
1998 Kingsport	R+	33	114	33	8	4	0	—	—	49	26	16	17	0	17	0	3	3	10	5	.67	1	.289	.373	.430
1999 Capital Cty	A	73	253	64	8	1	0	—	—	74	40	15	34	0	36	0	2	1	20	12	.63	3	.253	.340	.292
St. Lucie	A+	45	183	57	8	3	2	—	—	77	33	18	22	2	22	0	2	1	9	3	.75	5	.311	.383	.421
2000 St. Lucie	A+	111	433	129	20	2	1	—	—	156	84	43	47	4	48	0	7	3	38	16	.70	3	.298	.364	.360
2001 Wichita	AA	43	168	50	6	1	1	—	—	61	27	13	16	0	13	0	3	2	11	6	.65	1	.298	.353	.363
Omaha	AAA	23	104	35	6	0	0	—	—	41	18	4	0	0	13	0	3	1	4	3	.57	1	.337	.333	.394
2001 Kansas City	AL	29	77	16	2	0	0	(0	0)	18	4	5	3	0	8	0	0	0	0	2	.00	3	.208	.238	.234

41

Eric Chavez

Bats: L Throws: R Pos: 3B-149; PH/PR-3; DH-1; 1B-1; SS-1   Ht: 6'0" Wt: 204 Born: 12/7/77 Age: 24

Year Team	Lg	G	AB	H	2B	3B	HR	(Hm	Rd)	TB	R	RBI	TBB	IBB	SO	HBP	SH	SF	SB	CS	SB%	GDP	Avg	OBP	SLG
1998 Oakland	AL	16	45	14	4	1	0	(0	0)	20	6	6	3	1	5	0	0	0	1	1	.50	1	.311	.354	.444
1999 Oakland	AL	115	356	88	21	2	13	(8	5)	152	47	50	46	4	56	0	0	5	1	1	.50	7	.247	.333	.427
2000 Oakland	AL	153	501	139	23	4	26	(15	11)	248	89	86	62	8	94	1	0	5	2	2	.50	9	.277	.355	.495
2001 Oakland	AL	151	552	159	43	0	32	(14	18)	298	91	114	41	9	99	4	0	7	8	2	.80	7	.288	.338	.540
4 ML YEARS		435	1454	400	91	7	71	(37	34)	718	233	256	152	22	254	5	0	12	12	6	.67	24	.275	.343	.494

Bruce Chen

Pitches: Left Bats: Left Pos: SP-27   Ht: 6'2" Wt: 210 Born: 6/19/77 Age: 25

Year Team	Lg	G	GS	CG	GF	IP	BFP	H	R	ER	HR	SH	SF	HB	TBB	IBB	SO	WP	Bk	W	L	Pct.	ShO	Sv-Op	Hld	ERA
2001 Reading *	AA	1	1	0	0	6	22	3	0	0	0	0	0	0	0	0	7	1	0	1	0	1.000	0	0--	—	0.00
Scrantn-WB *	AAA	3	3	0	0	18.2	74	14	8	8	2	2	0	1	5	0	14	2	0	1	0	1.000	0	0--	—	3.86
1998 Atlanta	NL	4	4	0	0	20.1	91	23	9	9	3	1	0	1	9	1	17	0	0	2	0	1.000	0	0-0	0	3.98
1999 Atlanta	NL	16	7	0	3	51	214	38	32	31	11	1	1	2	27	3	45	0	0	2	2	.500	0	0-0	0	5.47
2000 Atl-Phi	NL	37	15	0	4	134	559	116	54	49	18	8	3	2	46	4	112	4	1	7	4	.636	0	0-0	0	3.29
2001 Phi-NYM	NL	27	27	0	0	146	634	146	90	79	29	4	7	1	59	4	126	5	0	7	7	.500	0	0-0	0	4.87
2000 Atlanta	NL	22	0	0	4	39.2	176	35	15	11	4	3	2	1	19	2	32	0	1	4	0	1.000	0	0-0	0	2.50
Philadelphia	NL	15	15	0	0	94.1	383	81	39	38	14	5	1	1	27	2	80	4	0	3	4	.429	0	0-0	0	3.63
2001 Philadelphia	NL	16	16	0	0	86.1	381	90	53	48	19	2	4	1	31	4	79	2	0	4	5	.444	0	0-0	0	5.00
New York	NL	11	11	0	0	59.2	253	56	37	31	10	2	3	0	28	0	47	3	0	3	2	.600	0	0-0	0	4.68
4 ML YEARS		84	53	0	7	351.1	1498	323	185	168	61	14	11	6	141	12	300	9	1	18	13	.581	0	0-0	0	4.30

Scott Chiasson

Pitches: Right Bats: Right Pos: RP-6   Ht: 6'3" Wt: 200 Born: 8/14/77 Age: 24

Year Team	Lg	G	GS	CG	GF	IP	BFP	H	R	ER	HR	SH	SF	HB	TBB	IBB	SO	WP	Bk	W	L	Pct.	ShO	Sv-Op	Hld	ERA
1998 Royals	R	13	0	0	6	24.1	111	24	17	13	2	2	1	5	11	0	26	10	0	2	0	1.000	0	1--	—	4.81
1999 Sou Oregon	A-	15	13	0	1	69	318	80	52	40	6	3	2	5	39	0	51	3	0	2	2	.500	0	0--	—	5.22
2000 Visalia	A+	31	23	0	4	156	666	146	66	53	17	3	2	6	57	2	150	8	1	11	4	.733	0	2--	—	3.06
2001 West Tenn	AA	52	0	0	45	61.1	247	43	15	12	2	4	1	4	20	4	62	7	0	3	4	.429	0	24--	—	1.76
Iowa	AAA	11	0	0	10	12	49	11	3	3	1	0	0	2	0	0	14	0	0	0	0	—	0	10--	—	2.25
2001 Chicago	NL	6	0	0	3	6.2	28	5	2	2	0	0	0	1	2	0	6	1	0	1	1	.500	0	0-0	1	2.70

Randy Choate

Pitches: Left Bats: Left Pos: RP-37   Ht: 6'3" Wt: 180 Born: 9/5/75 Age: 26

Year Team	Lg	G	GS	CG	GF	IP	BFP	H	R	ER	HR	SH	SF	HB	TBB	IBB	SO	WP	Bk	W	L	Pct.	ShO	Sv-Op	Hld	ERA
1997 Oneonta	A-	10	10	0	0	62.1	242	49	12	12	1	0	0	2	12	1	61	0	2	5	1	.833	0	0--	—	1.73
1998 Tampa	A+	13	13	0	0	70	316	83	57	41	6	4	1	3	22	2	55	2	0	1	8	.111	0	0--	—	5.27
Greensboro	A	8	8	1	0	39	165	46	21	13	1	1	0	0	7	0	32	3	0	1	5	.167	0	0--	—	3.00
1999 Tampa	A+	47	0	0	17	50	224	51	25	25	4	4	0	2	24	5	62	4	0	2	2	.500	0	1--	—	4.50
2000 Columbus	AAA	33	0	0	0	35.1	151	34	8	8	2	0	0	3	14	3	37	0	0	2	0	1.000	0	1--	—	2.04
2001 Columbus	AAA	4	0	0	1	4.1	21	7	1	1	0	0	0	0	3	0	4	1	0	1	1	.500	0	0--	—	2.08
2000 New York	AL	22	0	0	6	17	75	14	10	9	3	0	1	1	8	0	12	1	0	1	0	1.000	0	0-0	2	4.76
2001 New York	AL	37	0	0	13	48.1	207	34	21	18	0	2	1	9	27	2	35	3	0	3	1	.750	0	0-0	3	3.35
2 ML YEARS		59	0	0	19	65.1	282	48	31	27	3	2	2	10	35	2	47	4	0	3	2	.600	0	0-0	5	3.72

Bobby Chouinard

Pitches: Right Bats: Right Pos: RP-8   Ht: 6'1" Wt: 189 Born: 5/1/72 Age: 30

Year Team	Lg	G	GS	CG	GF	IP	BFP	H	R	ER	HR	SH	SF	HB	TBB	IBB	SO	WP	Bk	W	L	Pct.	ShO	Sv-Op	Hld	ERA
2001 Colo Sprngs *	AAA	39	0	0	9	39.1	175	44	19	16	5	0	0	3	13	0	47	4	0	3	1	.750	0	1--	—	3.66
1996 Oakland	AL	13	11	0	0	59	278	75	41	40	10	3	3	3	32	3	32	0	0	4	2	.667	0	0-0	0	6.10
1998 Mil-Ari	NL	27	2	0	9	41.1	181	46	24	19	5	4	2	0	11	2	27	5	0	0	2	.000	0	0-1	6	4.14
1999 Arizona	NL	32	0	0	9	40.1	161	31	16	12	3	4	4	0	12	2	23	1	0	5	2	.714	0	1-2	7	2.68
2000 Colorado	NL	31	0	0	6	32.2	140	35	17	14	4	1	1	1	9	2	23	0	0	2	2	.500	0	0-2	3	3.86
2001 Colorado	NL	8	0	0	5	7.2	34	10	7	7	4	0	0	0	1	1	5	0	0	0	0	—	0	0-0	0	8.22
1998 Milwaukee	NL	1	0	0	0	3	12	5	1	1	0	0	1	0	0	0	1	0	0	0	0	—	0	0-0	0	3.00
Arizona	NL	26	2	0	9	38.1	169	41	23	18	5	4	1	0	11	2	26	5	0	0	2	.000	0	0-1	6	4.23
5 ML YEARS		111	13	0	29	181	794	197	105	92	26	12	10	4	65	10	110	6	0	11	8	.579	0	1-5	16	4.57

McKay Christensen

Bats: Left Throws: Left Pos: PH/PR-18; CF-17; LF-3   Ht: 5'11" Wt: 180 Born: 8/14/75 Age: 26

Year Team	Lg	G	AB	H	2B	3B	HR	(Hm	Rd)	TB	R	RBI	TBB	IBB	SO	HBP	SH	SF	SB	CS	SB%	GDP	Avg	OBP	SLG
1996 White Sox	R	35	133	35	7	5	1	—	—	55	17	16	10	0	23	3	0	1	10	3	.77	1	.263	.327	.414
Hickory	A	6	11	0	0	0	0	—	—	0	0	0	1	0	4	0	0	0	0	0	—	0	.000	.083	.000
1997 Hickory	A	127	503	141	12	12	5	—	—	192	95	47	52	0	61	11	4	6	28	20	.58	2	.280	.357	.382
1998 Winston-Sal	A+	95	361	103	17	6	4	—	—	144	69	32	53	1	54	11	4	2	20	10	.67	3	.285	.391	.399
1999 Birmingham	AA	75	293	85	8	6	3	—	—	114	53	28	31	0	46	8	4	1	18	6	.75	6	.290	.372	.389
Charlotte	AAA	1	4	1	0	0	0	—	—	1	0	0	0	0	0	0	0	0	1	0	1.00	0	.250	.250	.250
2000 Charlotte	AAA	90	337	89	13	2	6	—	—	124	49	29	32	1	51	1	7	5	28	6	.82	2	.264	.325	.368
2001 Charlotte	AAA	69	273	75	15	6	7	—	—	123	53	25	30	0	52	2	4	3	17	3	.85	3	.275	.347	.451
Las Vegas	AAA	16	57	14	2	1	1	—	—	21	8	3	5	0	11	1	0	0	3	1	.75	1	.246	.317	.368
1999 Chicago	AL	28	53	12	1	0	1	(1	0)	16	10	6	4	0	7	0	1	2	2	1	.67	1	.226	.271	.302

(continued)

Year Team	Lg	G	AB	H	2B	3B	HR	(Hm	Rd)	TB	R	RBI	TBB	IBB	SO	HBP	SH	SF	SB	CS	SB%	GDP	Avg	OBP	SLG
2000 Chicago	AL	32	19	2	0	0	0	(0	0)	2	4	1	2	0	6	1	0	0	1	1	.50	0	.105	.227	.105
2001 CWS-LA		35	53	17	2	0	1	(1	0)	22	7	7	3	0	12	4	0	0	3	2	.60	0	.321	.400	.415
2001 Chicago	AL	7	4	1	0	0	0	(0	0)	1	0	0	0	0	2	1	0	0	0	0	—	0	.250	.400	.250
Los Angeles	NL	28	49	16	2	0	1	(1	0)	21	7	7	3	0	10	3	0	0	3	2	.60	0	.327	.400	.429
3 ML YEARS		95	125	31	3	0	2	(2	0)	40	21	14	9	0	25	5	1	2	6	4	.60	1	.248	.319	.320

Ryan Christenson

Bats: R **Throws:** R **Pos:** PH/PR-19; LF-5; RF-3; CF-2; DH-1   **Ht:** 6'0" **Wt:** 191 **Born:** 3/28/74 **Age:** 28

Year Team	Lg	G	AB	H	2B	3B	HR	(Hm	Rd)	TB	R	RBI	TBB	IBB	SO	HBP	SH	SF	SB	CS	SB%	GDP	Avg	OBP	SLG
2001 Sacramento *	AAA	19	70	12	4	0	1	—	—	19	7	3	4	0	13	0	0	0	2	0	1.00	1	.171	.216	.271
Tucson *	AAA	57	215	62	17	0	6	—	—	97	32	27	23	0	43	0	2	3	5	2	.71	4	.288	.353	.451
1998 Oakland	AL	117	370	95	22	2	5	(2	3)	136	56	40	36	0	106	1	10	4	5	6	.45	1	.257	.321	.368
1999 Oakland	AL	106	268	56	12	1	4	(2	2)	82	41	24	38	0	58	1	8	4	7	5	.58	6	.209	.305	.306
2000 Oakland	AL	121	129	32	2	2	4	(3	1)	50	31	18	19	0	33	1	4	0	1	2	.33	1	.248	.349	.388
2001 Oak-Ari		26	8	1	1	0	0	(0	0)	2	4	1	1	0	2	0	0	0	1	0	1.00	0	.125	.222	.250
2001 Oakland	AL	7	4	0	0	0	0	(0	0)	0	1	0	0	0	1	0	0	0	0	0	—	0	.000	.000	.000
Arizona	NL	19	4	1	1	0	0	(0	0)	2	3	1	1	0	1	0	0	0	1	0	1.00	0	.250	.400	.500
4 ML YEARS		370	775	184	37	5	13	(7	6)	270	132	83	94	0	199	3	22	8	14	13	.52	8	.237	.319	.348

Jason Christiansen

Pitches: Left **Bats:** Right **Pos:** RP-55   **Ht:** 6'5" **Wt:** 241 **Born:** 9/21/69 **Age:** 32

Year Team	Lg	G	GS	CG	GF	IP	BFP	H	R	ER	HR	SH	SF	HB	TBB	IBB	SO	WP	Bk	W	L	Pct.	ShO	Sv-Op	Hld	ERA
2001 Memphis *	AAA	7	1	0	0	8	33	9	2	2	0	1	0	0	0	0	9	0	0	0	0	—	0	0--	—	2.25
1995 Pittsburgh	NL	63	0	0	13	56.1	255	49	28	26	5	6	3	3	34	9	53	4	1	1	3	.250	0	0-4	12	4.15
1996 Pittsburgh	NL	33	0	0	9	44.1	205	56	34	33	7	2	3	1	19	2	38	4	1	3	3	.500	0	0-2	2	6.70
1997 Pittsburgh	NL	39	0	0	9	33.2	154	37	11	11	2	0	0	2	17	3	37	4	0	3	3	.500	0	0-2	8	2.94
1998 Pittsburgh	NL	60	0	0	19	64.2	269	51	22	18	2	5	1	0	27	7	71	3	0	3	3	.500	0	6-10	15	2.51
1999 Pittsburgh	NL	39	0	0	17	37.2	158	26	17	17	2	2	1	2	22	4	35	0	0	2	3	.400	0	3-5	7	4.06
2000 Pit-StL	NL	65	0	0	19	48	210	41	29	27	3	4	1	2	27	5	53	3	0	3	8	.273	0	1-4	22	5.06
2001 StL-SF	NL	55	0	0	11	36.1	149	29	13	13	5	1	3	1	15	1	31	4	0	2	1	.667	0	3-4	11	3.22
2000 Pittsburgh	NL	44	0	0	17	38	164	28	22	21	2	3	1	0	25	4	41	3	0	2	8	.200	0	1-3	13	4.97
St. Louis	NL	21	0	0	2	10	46	13	7	6	1	1	0	2	2	1	12	0	0	1	0	1.000	0	0-1	9	5.40
2001 St. Louis	NL	30	0	0	8	19.1	83	15	10	10	4	0	1	1	10	1	19	0	0	1	1	.500	0	3-3	4	4.66
San Francisco	NL	25	0	0	3	17	66	14	3	3	1	1	2	0	5	0	12	4	0	1	0	1.000	0	0-1	7	1.59
7 ML YEARS		354	0	0	97	321	1400	289	154	145	26	20	12	11	161	31	318	22	2	17	21	.447	0	13-31	77	4.07

Tim Christman

Pitches: Left **Bats:** Left **Pos:** RP-1   **Ht:** 6'0" **Wt:** 195 **Born:** 3/31/75 **Age:** 27

Year Team	Lg	G	GS	CG	GF	IP	BFP	H	R	ER	HR	SH	SF	HB	TBB	IBB	SO	WP	Bk	W	L	Pct.	ShO	Sv-Op	Hld	ERA
1996 Portland	A-	21	0	0	7	40	176	30	23	19	6	1	3	1	23	0	56	2	1	1	2	.333	0	2--	—	4.28
1997 Asheville	A	29	0	0	11	63.1	263	55	32	24	8	5	3	3	18	1	87	7	4	7	3	.700	0	3--	—	3.41
1999 Salem	A+	38	0	0	7	48.1	188	38	18	13	0	1	2	2	12	0	64	1	0	1	2	.333	0	2--	—	2.42
2000 Carolina	AA	8	0	0	3	10.2	48	6	3	3	0	0	0	2	7	0	13	0	0	0	0	—	0	2--	—	2.53
2001 Colo Sprngs	AAA	38	0	0	10	40	195	52	31	28	4	0	2	3	21	1	42	4	0	2	5	.286	0	2--	—	6.30
2001 Colorado	NL	1	0	0	1	2	7	1	1	1	0	0	0	0	0	0	2	0	0	0	0	—	0	0-0	0	4.50

Alex Cintron

Bats: Both **Throws:** Right **Pos:** SS-7; PH/PR-2   **Ht:** 6'1" **Wt:** 170 **Born:** 12/17/78 **Age:** 23

Year Team	Lg	G	AB	H	2B	3B	HR	(Hm	Rd)	TB	R	RBI	TBB	IBB	SO	HBP	SH	SF	SB	CS	SB%	GDP	Avg	OBP	SLG
1997 Diamndbcks	R	43	152	30	6	1	0	—	—	38	23	20	21	0	32	2	3	1	1	4	.20	3	.197	.301	.250
Lethbridge	R+	1	3	1	0	0	0	—	—	1	0	0	0	0	1	0	1	0	0	0	—		.333	.333	.333
1998 Lethbridge	R+	67	258	68	11	4	3	—	—	96	41	34	20	0	32	2	3	2	8	4	.67	8	.264	.319	.372
1999 High Desert	A+	128	499	153	25	4	3	—	—	195	78	64	19	0	65	3	17	4	15	8	.65	14	.307	.333	.391
2000 El Paso	AA	125	522	157	30	6	4	—	—	211	83	59	29	0	56	2	13	7	9	9	.50	22	.301	.336	.404
2001 Tucson	AAA	107	425	124	24	3	3	—	—	163	53	35	15	1	48	2	20	6	9	6	.60	12	.292	.315	.384
2001 Arizona	NL	8	7	2	0	1	0	(0	0)	4	0	0	0	0	0	0	0	0	0	0	—	0	.286	.286	.571

Jeff Cirillo

Bats: Right **Throws:** Right **Pos:** 3B-137; PH/PR-1   **Ht:** 6'1" **Wt:** 190 **Born:** 9/23/69 **Age:** 32

Year Team	Lg	G	AB	H	2B	3B	HR	(Hm	Rd)	TB	R	RBI	TBB	IBB	SO	HBP	SH	SF	SB	CS	SB%	GDP	Avg	OBP	SLG
2001 Colo Sprngs *	AAA	1	4	3	1	0	0	—	—	4	2	3	1	0	0	0	0	0	0	0	—	0	.750	.800	1.000
1994 Milwaukee	AL	39	126	30	9	0	3	(1	2)	48	17	12	11	0	16	2	0	0	0	1	.00	4	.238	.309	.381
1995 Milwaukee	AL	125	328	91	19	4	9	(6	3)	145	57	39	47	0	42	4	1	4	7	2	.78	8	.277	.371	.442
1996 Milwaukee	AL	158	566	184	46	5	15	(6	9)	285	101	83	58	0	69	7	6	6	4	9	.31	14	.325	.391	.504
1997 Milwaukee	AL	154	580	167	46	2	10	(6	4)	247	74	82	60	0	74	14	4	3	4	3	.57	13	.288	.367	.426
1998 Milwaukee	NL	156	604	194	31	1	14	(6	8)	269	97	68	79	3	88	4	5	2	10	4	.71	26	.321	.402	.445
1999 Milwaukee	NL	157	607	198	35	1	15	(6	9)	280	98	88	75	4	83	5	3	7	7	4	.64	15	.326	.401	.461
2000 Colorado	NL	157	598	195	53	2	11	(9	2)	285	111	115	67	4	72	6	1	12	3	4	.43	19	.326	.392	.477
2001 Colorado	NL	138	528	165	26	4	17	(9	8)	250	72	83	43	6	63	5	1	9	12	2	.86	15	.313	.364	.473
8 ML YEARS		1084	3937	1224	265	19	94	(49	45)	1809	627	570	440	17	507	47	21	43	47	29	.62	114	.311	.383	.459

Stubby Clapp

Bats: Both **Throws:** Right **Pos:** PH/PR-18; 2B-4; LF-4   **Ht:** 5'8" **Wt:** 175 **Born:** 2/24/73 **Age:** 29

Year Team	Lg	G	AB	H	2B	3B	HR	(Hm	Rd)	TB	R	RBI	TBB	IBB	SO	HBP	SH	SF	SB	CS	SB%	GDP	Avg	OBP	SLG
1996 Johnson Cty	R+	29	94	21	3	2	1	—	—	31	25	15	26	0	15	1	1	1	9	2	.82	2	.223	.393	.330
1997 Pr William	A+	78	267	85	21	6	4	—	—	130	51	46	52	2	41	6	4	4	9	4	.69	2	.318	.435	.487
1998 Arkansas	AA	139	514	143	30	9	12	—	—	227	113	57	86	3	100	8	8	6	18	10	.64	10	.278	.386	.442
1999 Memphis	AAA	110	393	102	26	2	14	—	—	174	72	62	53	4	96	3	4	4	7	7	.50	9	.260	.349	.443
2000 Memphis	AAA	129	505	138	28	8	1	—	—	185	89	52	80	0	88	5	6	4	10	5	.67	7	.273	.375	.366
2001 Memphis	AAA	86	299	91	14	7	5	—	—	134	48	33	43	2	46	1	4	1	8	4	.67	4	.304	.392	.448
2001 St. Louis	NL	23	25	5	2	0	0	(0	0)	7	0	1	1	0	7	0	0	0	0	0	—	0	.200	.231	.280

Brady Clark

Bats: R **Throws:** R **Pos:** PH/PR-62; LF-26; RF-14; CF-7; DH-1   **Ht:** 6'2" **Wt:** 195 **Born:** 4/18/73 **Age:** 29

Year Team	Lg	G	AB	H	2B	3B	HR	(Hm	Rd)	TB	R	RBI	TBB	IBB	SO	HBP	SH	SF	SB	CS	SB%	GDP	Avg	OBP	SLG
1997 Burlington	A	126	459	149	29	7	11	—	—	225	108	63	76	3	71	4	1	3	31	18	.63	10	.325	.423	.490
1998 Chattanooga	AA	64	222	60	13	1	2	—	—	81	41	16	31	0	34	4	1	0	12	4	.75	11	.270	.370	.365
1999 Chattanooga	AA	138	506	165	37	4	17	—	—	261	103	75	89	6	58	2	5	5	25	17	.60	6	.326	.425	.516
2000 Louisville	AAA	132	487	148	41	6	16	—	—	249	90	79	72	0	51	9	0	9	12	8	.60	14	.304	.397	.511
2001 Louisville	AAA	49	167	44	5	1	2	—	—	57	24	18	18	1	17	6	0	1	6	2	.75	5	.263	.354	.341
2000 Cincinnati	NL	11	11	3	1	0	0	(0	0)	4	1	2	0	0	2	0	0	0	0	0	—	0	.273	.273	.364
2001 Cincinnati	NL	89	129	34	3	0	6	(4	2)	55	22	18	22	1	16	1	4	1	4	1	.80	6	.264	.373	.426
2 ML YEARS		100	140	37	4	0	6	(4	2)	59	23	20	22	1	18	1	4	1	4	1	.80	6	.264	.366	.421

Jermaine Clark

Bats: Left **Throws:** Right **Pos:** PH/PR-3; DH-2   **Ht:** 5'10" **Wt:** 175 **Born:** 9/29/76 **Age:** 25

Year Team	Lg	G	AB	H	2B	3B	HR	(Hm	Rd)	TB	R	RBI	TBB	IBB	SO	HBP	SH	SF	SB	CS	SB%	GDP	Avg	OBP	SLG
1997 Everett	A-	59	199	67	13	2	3	—	—	93	42	29	34	1	33	3	3	2	22	3	.88	1	.337	.437	.467
1998 Wisconsin	A	123	448	145	24	13	6	—	—	213	81	55	57	4	64	2	4	1	40	14	.74	3	.324	.402	.475
1999 Lancaster	A+	126	502	158	27	8	6	—	—	219	112	61	58	2	80	2	8	3	33	15	.69	10	.315	.386	.436
2000 New Haven	AA	133	447	131	23	9	2	—	—	178	80	44	87	3	69	14	18	3	38	8	.83	7	.293	.421	.398
2001 Tacoma	AAA	74	216	54	7	3	1	—	—	70	35	26	27	0	39	3	3	1	13	2	.87	6	.250	.340	.324
2001 Detroit	AL	3	0	0	0	0	0	(0	0)	0	1	0	0	0	0	0	0	0	0	0	—	0	—	—	—

Tony Clark

Bats: Both **Throws:** Right **Pos:** 1B-78; DH-42; PH/PR-10   **Ht:** 6'7" **Wt:** 245 **Born:** 6/15/72 **Age:** 30

Year Team	Lg	G	AB	H	2B	3B	HR	(Hm	Rd)	TB	R	RBI	TBB	IBB	SO	HBP	SH	SF	SB	CS	SB%	GDP	Avg	OBP	SLG
1995 Detroit	AL	27	101	24	5	1	3	(0	3)	40	10	11	8	0	30	0	0	0	0	0	—	2	.238	.294	.396
1996 Detroit	AL	100	376	94	14	0	27	(17	10)	189	56	72	29	1	127	0	0	6	0	1	.00	2	.250	.299	.503
1997 Detroit	AL	159	560	160	28	3	32	(18	14)	290	105	117	93	13	144	3	0	5	1	3	.25	11	.276	.376	.500
1998 Detroit	AL	157	602	175	37	0	34	(18	16)	314	84	103	63	5	128	3	0	5	3	3	.50	16	.291	.358	.522
1999 Detroit	AL	143	536	150	29	0	31	(12	19)	272	74	99	64	7	133	6	0	3	2	1	.67	14	.280	.361	.507
2000 Detroit	AL	60	208	57	14	0	13	(6	7)	110	32	37	24	2	51	0	0	0	0	0	—	10	.274	.349	.529
2001 Detroit	AL	126	428	123	29	3	16	(7	9)	206	67	75	62	10	108	1	0	6	0	1	.00	14	.287	.374	.481
7 ML YEARS		772	2831	783	156	7	156	(78	78)	1421	428	514	343	38	721	13	0	25	6	9	.40	74	.277	.355	.502

Royce Clayton

Bats: Right **Throws:** Right **Pos:** SS-133; PH/PR-6   **Ht:** 6'0" **Wt:** 185 **Born:** 1/2/70 **Age:** 32

Year Team	Lg	G	AB	H	2B	3B	HR	(Hm	Rd)	TB	R	RBI	TBB	IBB	SO	HBP	SH	SF	SB	CS	SB%	GDP	Avg	OBP	SLG
1991 San Francisco	NL	9	26	3	1	0	0	(0	0)	4	0	2	1	0	6	0	0	0	0	0	—	1	.115	.148	.154
1992 San Francisco	NL	98	321	72	7	4	4	(3	1)	99	31	24	26	3	63	0	3	2	8	4	.67	11	.224	.281	.308
1993 San Francisco	NL	153	549	155	21	5	6	(5	1)	204	54	70	38	2	91	5	8	7	11	10	.52	16	.282	.331	.372
1994 San Francisco	NL	108	385	91	14	6	3	(1	2)	126	38	30	30	2	74	3	3	2	23	3	.88	7	.236	.295	.327
1995 San Francisco	NL	138	509	124	29	3	5	(2	3)	174	56	58	38	1	109	3	4	3	24	9	.73	7	.244	.298	.342
1996 St. Louis	NL	129	491	136	20	4	6	(6	0)	182	64	35	33	4	89	1	2	4	33	15	.69	13	.277	.321	.371
1997 St. Louis	NL	154	576	153	39	5	9	(5	4)	229	75	61	33	4	109	3	2	5	30	10	.75	19	.266	.306	.398
1998 StL-Tex		142	541	136	31	2	9	(2	7)	198	89	53	53	1	83	3	6	5	24	11	.69	16	.251	.319	.366
1999 Texas	AL	133	465	134	21	5	14	(6	8)	207	69	52	39	1	100	4	9	3	8	6	.57	6	.288	.346	.445
2000 Texas	AL	148	513	124	21	5	14	(9	5)	197	70	54	42	1	92	3	12	3	11	7	.61	21	.242	.301	.384
2001 Chicago	AL	135	433	114	21	4	9	(6	3)	170	62	60	33	2	72	3	9	7	10	7	.59	16	.263	.315	.393
1998 St. Louis	NL	90	355	83	19	1	4	(1	3)	116	59	29	40	1	51	2	3	2	19	6	.76	10	.234	.313	.327
Texas	AL	52	186	53	12	1	5	(1	4)	82	30	24	13	0	32	1	3	3	5	5	.50	6	.285	.330	.441
11 ML YEARS		1347	4809	1242	225	43	79	(45	34)	1790	608	499	366	21	888	28	58	41	182	82	.69	133	.258	.312	.372

Roger Clemens

Pitches: Right **Bats:** Right **Pos:** SP-33   **Ht:** 6'4" **Wt:** 238 **Born:** 8/4/62 **Age:** 39

Year Team	Lg	G	GS	CG	GF	IP	BFP	H	R	ER	HR	SH	SF	HB	TBB	IBB	SO	WP	Bk	W	L	Pct.	ShO	Sv-Op	Hld	ERA
1984 Boston	AL	21	20	5	0	133.1	575	146	67	64	13	2	3	2	29	3	126	4	0	9	4	.692	1	0-0	0	4.32
1985 Boston	AL	15	15	3	0	98.1	407	83	38	36	5	1	2	3	37	0	74	1	3	7	5	.583	1	0-0	0	3.29
1986 Boston	AL	33	33	10	0	254	997	179	77	70	21	4	4	0	67	0	238	11	3	24	4	.857	1	0-0	0	2.48
1987 Boston	AL	36	36	18	0	281.2	1157	248	100	93	19	6	4	9	83	4	256	4	3	20	9	.690	7	0-0	0	2.97
1988 Boston	AL	35	35	14	0	264	1063	217	93	86	17	6	3	6	62	4	291	4	0	18	12	.600	8	0-0	0	2.93
1989 Boston	AL	35	35	8	0	253.1	1044	215	101	88	20	9	5	8	93	5	230	7	0	17	11	.607	3	0-0	0	3.13
1990 Boston	AL	31	31	7	0	228.1	920	193	59	49	7	7	5	7	54	3	209	8	0	21	6	.778	4	0-0	0	1.93

(continued)

Year Team	Lg	G	GS	CG	GF	IP	BFP	H	R	ER	HR	SH	SF	HB	TBB	IBB	SO	WP	Bk	W	L	Pct.	ShO	Sv-Op	Hld	ERA
1991 Boston	AL	35	35	13	0	271.1	1077	219	93	79	15	6	8	5	65	12	241	6	0	18	10	.643	4	0-0	0	2.62
1992 Boston	AL	32	32	11	0	246.2	989	203	80	66	11	5	5	9	62	5	208	3	0	18	11	.621	5	0-0	0	2.41
1993 Boston	AL	29	29	2	0	191.2	808	175	99	95	17	5	7	11	67	4	160	3	1	11	14	.440	1	0-0	0	4.46
1994 Boston	AL	24	24	3	0	170.2	692	124	62	54	15	2	5	4	71	1	168	4	0	9	7	.563	1	0-0	0	2.85
1995 Boston	AL	23	23	0	0	140	623	141	70	65	15	2	3	14	60	0	132	9	0	10	5	.667	0	0-0	0	4.18
1996 Boston	AL	34	34	6	0	242.2	1032	216	106	98	19	4	7	4	106	2	257	8	1	10	13	.435	2	0-0	0	3.63
1997 Toronto	AL	34	34	9	0	264	1044	204	65	60	9	5	2	12	68	1	292	4	0	21	7	.750	3	0-0	0	2.05
1998 Toronto	AL	33	33	5	0	234.2	961	169	78	69	11	8	2	7	88	0	271	6	0	20	6	.769	3	0-0	0	2.65
1999 New York	AL	30	30	1	0	187.2	822	185	101	96	20	10	5	9	90	0	163	8	0	14	10	.583	0	0-0	0	4.60
2000 New York	AL	32	32	1	0	204.1	878	184	96	84	26	1	2	10	84	0	188	2	1	13	8	.619	0	0-0	0	3.70
2001 New York	AL	33	33	0	0	220.1	918	205	94	86	19	4	4	5	72	1	213	14	0	20	3	.870	0	0-0	0	3.51
18 ML YEARS		545	544	116	0	3887	16007	3306	1479	1338	279	87	78	129	1258	45	3717	106	19	280	145	.659	45	0-0	0	3.10

Matt Clement

Pitches: Right **Bats:** Right **Pos:** SP-31   **Ht:** 6'3" **Wt:** 195 **Born:** 8/12/74 **Age:** 27

Year Team	Lg	G	GS	CG	GF	IP	BFP	H	R	ER	HR	SH	SF	HB	TBB	IBB	SO	WP	Bk	W	L	Pct.	ShO	Sv-Op	Hld	ERA
1998 San Diego	NL	4	2	0	0	13.2	62	15	8	7	0	2	0	0	7	1	13	2	0	2	1	1.000	0	0-0	0	4.61
1999 San Diego	NL	31	31	0	0	180.2	803	190	106	90	18	7	6	9	86	2	135	11	0	10	12	.455	0	0-0	0	4.48
2000 San Diego	NL	34	34	0	0	205	940	194	131	117	22	12	5	16	125	4	170	23	0	13	17	.433	0	0-0	0	5.14
2001 Florida	NL	31	31	0	0	169.1	760	172	102	95	15	14	3	15	85	2	134	15	0	9	10	.474	0	0-0	0	5.05
4 ML YEARS		100	98	0	0	568.2	2565	571	347	309	55	35	14	40	303	9	452	51	0	34	39	.466	0	0-0	0	4.89

Pasqual Coco

Pitches: Right **Bats:** Right **Pos:** RP-6; SP-1   **Ht:** 6'1" **Wt:** 160 **Born:** 9/24/77 **Age:** 24

Year Team	Lg	G	GS	CG	GF	IP	BFP	H	R	ER	HR	SH	SF	HB	TBB	IBB	SO	WP	Bk	W	L	Pct.	ShO	Sv-Op	Hld	ERA
1997 St.Cathrnes	A-	10	8	0	1	46	199	48	32	25	5	0	4	2	16	1	44	6	1	1	4	.200	0	0--	—	4.89
1998 St.Cathrnes	A-	15	15	1	0	81.2	353	62	52	29	4	2	1	9	32	0	84	10	3	3	7	.300	0	0--	—	3.20
1999 Hagerstown	A	14	14	0	0	97.2	384	67	29	24	4	1	1	8	25	1	83	2	0	11	1	.917	0	0--	—	2.21
Dunedin	A+	13	13	2	0	75	338	81	50	47	7	3	3	6	36	0	59	7	2	4	6	.400	0	0--	—	5.64
2000 Tennessee	AA	27	26	2	0	167.2	723	154	83	70	16	1	4	17	68	0	142	6	3	12	7	.632	0	0--	—	3.76
2001 Tennessee	AA	3	3	0	0	16	65	13	7	7	3	0	0	0	5	0	13	1	0	0	1	.000	0	0--	—	3.94
Syracuse	AAA	22	22	0	0	121.2	529	128	67	63	11	1	7	8	50	0	82	9	3	4	3	.571	0	0--	—	4.66
2000 Toronto	AL	1	1	0	0	4	23	5	4	4	1	0	0	1	5	0	2	1	0	0	0	—	0	0-0	0	9.00
2001 Toronto	AL	7	1	0	3	14.1	63	12	8	7	0	1	1	2	6	0	9	0	0	1	0	1.000	0	0-0	0	4.40
2 ML YEARS		8	2	0	3	18.1	86	17	12	11	1	1	1	3	11	0	11	1	0	1	0	1.000	0	0-0	0	5.40

Tony Cogan

Pitches: Left **Bats:** Left **Pos:** RP-39   **Ht:** 6'2" **Wt:** 195 **Born:** 12/21/76 **Age:** 25

Year Team	Lg	G	GS	CG	GF	IP	BFP	H	R	ER	HR	SH	SF	HB	TBB	IBB	SO	WP	Bk	W	L	Pct.	ShO	Sv-Op	Hld	ERA
1999 Spokane	A-	27	0	0	11	39.2	160	26	10	6	0	6	1	2	14	2	37	3	1	1	3	.250	0	4--	—	1.36
2000 Chstn-WV	A	13	13	0	0	78.2	303	65	19	16	3	1	1	5	14	0	51	5	1	6	2	.750	0	0--	—	1.83
Wilmington	A+	16	3	0	6	39.1	168	39	22	19	1	1	1	0	18	0	31	3	4	2	4	.333	0	1--	—	4.35
Wichita	AA	2	0	0	1	2.1	15	6	4	3	0	1	0	0	2	1	1	0	0	1	1	.500	0	0--	—	11.57
2001 Wichita	AA	8	0	0	4	17.1	68	13	6	4	2	1	1	1	4	0	12	1	1	1	1	.500	0	1--	—	2.08
Omaha	AAA	9	0	0	5	9.2	44	14	3	3	1	0	0	0	3	0	8	0	0	1	1	.500	0	2--	—	2.79
2001 Kansas City	AL	39	0	0	7	24.2	119	32	17	16	7	0	1	5	13	0	17	1	0	0	4	.000	0	0-2	6	5.84

Dave Coggin

Pitches: Right **Bats:** Right **Pos:** SP-17   **Ht:** 6'4" **Wt:** 195 **Born:** 10/30/76 **Age:** 25

Year Team	Lg	G	GS	CG	GF	IP	BFP	H	R	ER	HR	SH	SF	HB	TBB	IBB	SO	WP	Bk	W	L	Pct.	ShO	Sv-Op	Hld	ERA
1995 Martinsvlle	R+	11	11	0	0	48	209	45	25	16	1	1	1	5	31	0	37	8	1	5	3	.625	0	0--	—	3.00
1996 Piedmont	A	28	28	3	0	169.1	699	156	87	81	12	3	3	7	46	1	129	12	1	9	12	.429	3	0--	—	4.31
1997 Clearwater	A+	27	27	3	0	155	697	160	96	81	12	5	7	9	86	0	110	24	1	11	8	.579	2	0--	—	4.70
1998 Reading	AA	20	20	0	0	108.2	477	106	58	50	8	2	2	8	62	1	65	14	0	4	8	.333	0	0--	—	4.14
1999 Reading	AA	9	9	0	0	42	203	55	37	35	8	0	0	3	20	0	21	6	0	2	5	.286	0	0--	—	7.50
2000 Clearwater	A+	6	5	0	0	33.2	131	25	11	10	1	1	1	0	13	0	26	0	0	2	2	.500	0	0--	—	2.67
Reading	AA	7	7	0	0	42	181	49	24	23	5	2	0	1	13	0	30	2	0	2	3	.400	0	0--	—	4.93
2001 Scrantn-WB	AAA	9	9	0	0	45.2	204	35	27	22	2	3	1	5	33	0	27	4	0	3	2	.600	0	0--	—	4.34
2001 Scrantn-WB	AAA	15	15	0	0	97.1	406	93	36	33	6	2	2	4	31	0	53	4	0	5	5	.500	0	0--	—	3.05
2000 Philadelphia	NL	5	5	0	0	27	126	35	20	16	2	2	0	1	12	0	17	1	0	2	0	1.000	0	0-0	0	5.33
2001 Philadelphia	NL	17	17	0	0	95	415	99	46	44	7	4	3	5	39	6	62	3	0	6	7	.462	0	0-0	0	4.17
2 ML YEARS		22	22	0	0	122	541	134	66	60	9	6	3	6	51	6	79	4	0	8	7	.533	0	0-0	0	4.43

Mike Colangelo

Bats: R **Throws:** R **Pos:** LF-25; PH/PR-18; CF-14; RF-4   **Ht:** 6'1" **Wt:** 185 **Born:** 10/22/76 **Age:** 25

Year Team	Lg	G	AB	H	2B	3B	HR	(Hm	Rd)	TB	R	RBI	TBB	IBB	SO	HBP	SH	SF	SB	CS	SB%	GDP	Avg	OBP	SLG
1998 Cedar Rapds	A	22	83	23	8	0	4	--	--	43	13	8	12	1	16	2	0	1	5	1	.83	0	.277	.378	.518
Lk Elsinore	A+	36	145	55	11	3	5	--	--	87	33	21	13	0	24	6	0	1	2	6	.25	2	.379	.448	.600
1999 Erie	AA	28	109	37	10	3	1	--	--	56	24	14	14	0	22	4	0	0	3	3	.50	5	.339	.433	.514
Edmonton	AAA	26	105	38	7	1	0	--	--	47	13	9	13	1	18	2	1	0	2	1	.67	1	.362	.442	.448
2001 Mobile	AA	9	34	9	1	1	1	--	--	14	5	4	4	0	8	0	0	0	0	0	—	0	.265	.342	.412
Portland	AAA	61	180	47	11	1	3	--	--	69	27	22	31	1	44	6	1	1	5	3	.63	2	.261	.385	.383
1999 Anaheim	AL	1	2	1	0	0	0	(0	0)	1	0	0	1	0	0	0	0	0	0	0	—	0	.500	.667	.500

Year Team	Lg	BATTING																BASERUNNING				PERCENTAGES		
		G	AB	H	2B	3B	HR	(Hm | Rd)	TB	R	RBI	TBB	IBB	SO	HBP	SH	SF	SB	CS	SB%	GDP	Avg	OBP	SLG
2001 San Diego	NL	50	91	22	3	3	2	(1 | 1)	37	10	8	8	0	30	1	0	0	0	0	—	3	.242	.310	.407
2 ML YEARS		51	93	23	3	3	2	(1 | 1)	38	10	8	9	0	30	1	0	0	0	0	—	3	.247	.320	.409

Greg Colbrunn

Bats: Right Throws: Right Pos: PH/PR-37; 1B-14; 3B-10   Ht: 6'0" Wt: 212 Born: 7/26/69 Age: 32

Year Team	Lg	BATTING																BASERUNNING				PERCENTAGES		
		G	AB	H	2B	3B	HR	(Hm | Rd)	TB	R	RBI	TBB	IBB	SO	HBP	SH	SF	SB	CS	SB%	GDP	Avg	OBP	SLG
2001 Tucson *	AAA	5	13	5	1	0	0	—	—	6	1	4	2	0	0	0	0	0	0	0	—	1	.385	.467	.462
1992 Montreal	NL	52	168	45	8	0	2	(1 | 1)	59	12	18	6	1	34	2	0	4	3	2	.60	1	.268	.294	.351
1993 Montreal	NL	70	153	39	9	0	4	(2 | 2)	60	15	23	6	1	33	1	1	3	4	2	.67	1	.255	.282	.392
1994 Florida	NL	47	155	47	10	0	6	(3 | 3)	75	17	31	9	0	27	2	0	2	1	1	.50	3	.303	.345	.484
1995 Florida	NL	138	528	146	22	1	23	(12 | 11)	239	70	89	22	4	69	6	0	4	11	3	.79	15	.277	.311	.453
1996 Florida	NL	141	511	146	26	2	16	(7 | 9)	224	60	69	25	1	76	14	0	5	4	5	.44	22	.286	.333	.438
1997 Min-Atl		98	271	76	17	0	7	(3 | 4)	114	27	35	10	1	49	2	1	2	1	2	.33	8	.280	.309	.421
1998 Col-Atl	NL	90	166	51	11	2	3	(1 | 2)	75	18	23	10	0	34	4	0	0	4	3	.57	1	.307	.361	.452
1999 Arizona	NL	67	135	44	5	3	5	(2 | 3)	70	20	24	12	0	23	4	0	2	1	1	.50	3	.326	.392	.519
2000 Arizona	NL	116	329	103	22	1	15	(6 | 9)	172	48	57	43	2	45	10	0	3	0	1	.00	13	.313	.405	.523
2001 Arizona	NL	59	97	28	8	0	4	(4 | 0)	48	12	18	9	0	14	4	0	0	0	0	—	5	.289	.373	.495
1997 Minnesota	AL	70	217	61	14	0	5	(2 | 3)	90	24	26	8	1	38	1	0	2	1	2	.33	7	.281	.307	.415
Atlanta	NL	28	54	15	3	0	2	(1 | 1)	24	3	9	2	0	11	1	1	0	0	0	—	1	.278	.316	.444
1998 Colorado	NL	62	122	38	8	2	2	(1 | 1)	56	12	13	8	0	23	1	0	0	3	3	.50	1	.311	.359	.459
Atlanta	NL	28	44	13	3	0	1	(0 | 1)	19	6	10	2	0	11	3	0	0	1	0	1.00	0	.295	.367	.432
10 ML YEARS		878	2513	725	138	9	85	(41 | 44)	1136	299	387	152	10	404	49	2	25	29	20	.59	72	.288	.338	.452

Michael Coleman

Bats: R Throws: R Pos: CF-7; DH-3; RF-3; LF-1; PH/PR-1   Ht: 5'11" Wt: 215 Born: 8/16/75 Age: 26

Year Team	Lg	BATTING																BASERUNNING				PERCENTAGES		
		G	AB	H	2B	3B	HR	(Hm | Rd)	TB	R	RBI	TBB	IBB	SO	HBP	SH	SF	SB	CS	SB%	GDP	Avg	OBP	SLG
2001 Columbus *	AAA	29	101	24	3	4	4	—	—	45	16	17	13	0	35	2	0	0	3	3	.50	4	.238	.336	.446
1997 Boston	AL	8	24	4	1	0	0	(0 | 0)	5	2	2	0	0	11	0	1	0	1	0	1.00	0	.167	.167	.208
1999 Boston	AL	2	5	1	0	0	0	(0 | 0)	1	1	0	1	0	0	0	0	0	0	0	—	0	.200	.333	.200
2001 New York	AL	12	38	8	0	0	1	(0 | 1)	11	5	7	0	0	15	0	0	1	0	1	.00	0	.211	.205	.289
3 ML YEARS		22	67	13	1	0	1	(0 | 1)	17	8	9	1	0	26	0	1	1	1	1	.50	0	.194	.203	.254

Lou Collier

Bats: R Throws: R Pos: 3B-16; PH/PR-14; LF-12; CF-11; DH-1   Ht: 5'10" Wt: 182 Born: 8/21/73 Age: 28

Year Team	Lg	BATTING																BASERUNNING				PERCENTAGES		
		G	AB	H	2B	3B	HR	(Hm | Rd)	TB	R	RBI	TBB	IBB	SO	HBP	SH	SF	SB	CS	SB%	GDP	Avg	OBP	SLG
2001 Indianapolis *	AAA	86	312	90	17	2	14	—	—	153	48	36	24	1	64	7	3	3	9	3	.75	6	.288	.350	.490
1997 Pittsburgh	NL	18	37	5	0	0	0	(0 | 0)	5	3	3	1	0	11	0	0	0	1	0	1.00	1	.135	.158	.135
1998 Pittsburgh	NL	110	334	82	13	6	2	(1 | 1)	113	30	34	31	6	70	6	3	5	2	2	.50	8	.246	.316	.338
1999 Milwaukee	NL	74	135	35	9	0	2	(2 | 0)	50	18	21	14	0	32	0	1	2	3	2	.60	2	.259	.325	.370
2000 Milwaukee	NL	14	32	7	1	0	1	(0 | 1)	11	9	2	6	0	4	0	0	1	0	0	—	1	.219	.333	.344
2001 Milwaukee	NL	50	127	32	8	1	2	(1 | 1)	48	19	14	17	0	30	1	1	2	5	1	.83	0	.252	.340	.378
5 ML YEARS		266	665	161	31	7	7	(4 | 3)	227	79	74	69	6	147	7	5	10	11	5	.69	12	.242	.316	.341

Jesus Colome

Pitches: Right Bats: Right Pos: RP-30   Ht: 6'2" Wt: 170 Born: 6/2/80 Age: 22

Year Team	Lg	HOW MUCH HE PITCHED						WHAT HE GAVE UP											THE RESULTS						
		G	GS	CG	GF	IP	BFP	H	R	ER	HR	SH	SF	HB	TBB	IBB	SO	WP	Bk	W	L	Pct.	ShO	Sv-Op	Hld	ERA
1998 Athletics	R	12	11	0	0	56.2	229	47	27	20	1	0	1	6	16	0	62	5	3	2	5	.286	0	0--	—	3.18
1999 Modesto	A+	31	22	0	2	128.2	564	125	63	48	6	1	6	9	60	2	127	13	2	8	4	.667	0	1--	—	3.36
2000 Midland	AA	20	20	0	0	110.1	478	99	62	44	10	4	4	5	50	0	95	6	1	9	4	.692	0	0--	—	3.59
Orlando	AA	3	3	0	0	14.2	72	18	12	11	2	1	0	2	7	0	9	0	0	1	2	.333	0	0--	—	6.75
2001 Durham	AAA	13	0	0	3	17.1	79	22	13	12	1	1	1	2	6	0	18	3	0	0	3	.000	0	0--	—	6.23
2001 Tampa Bay	AL	30	0	0	9	48.2	209	37	22	18	8	2	2	2	25	4	31	2	0	2	3	.400	0	0-0	6	3.33

Bartolo Colon

Pitches: Right Bats: Right Pos: SP-34   Ht: 6'0" Wt: 230 Born: 5/24/75 Age: 27

Year Team	Lg	HOW MUCH HE PITCHED						WHAT HE GAVE UP											THE RESULTS						
		G	GS	CG	GF	IP	BFP	H	R	ER	HR	SH	SF	HB	TBB	IBB	SO	WP	Bk	W	L	Pct.	ShO	Sv-Op	Hld	ERA
1997 Cleveland	AL	19	17	1	0	94	427	107	66	59	12	4	1	3	45	1	66	5	0	4	7	.364	0	0-0	0	5.65
1998 Cleveland	AL	31	31	6	0	204	883	205	91	84	15	10	2	3	79	5	158	4	0	14	9	.609	2	0-0	0	3.71
1999 Cleveland	AL	32	32	1	0	205	858	185	97	90	24	5	4	7	76	5	161	4	0	18	5	.783	1	0-0	0	3.95
2000 Cleveland	AL	30	30	2	0	188	807	163	86	81	21	2	3	4	98	4	212	4	0	15	8	.652	1	0-0	0	3.88
2001 Cleveland	AL	34	34	1	0	222.1	947	220	106	101	26	8	4	2	90	2	201	4	0	14	12	.538	0	0-0	0	4.09
5 ML YEARS		146	144	11	0	913.1	3922	880	446	415	98	29	14	19	388	17	798	21	0	65	41	.613	4	0-0	0	4.09

David Cone

Pitches: Right Bats: Left Pos: SP-25   Ht: 6'1" Wt: 200 Born: 1/2/63 Age: 39

Year Team	Lg	HOW MUCH HE PITCHED						WHAT HE GAVE UP											THE RESULTS						
		G	GS	CG	GF	IP	BFP	H	R	ER	HR	SH	SF	HB	TBB	IBB	SO	WP	Bk	W	L	Pct.	ShO	Sv-Op	Hld	ERA
2001 Sarasota *	A+	1	1	0	0	4	14	2	0	0	0	0	0	0	0	0	6	0	0	0	0	—	0	0--	—	0.00
1986 Kansas City	AL	11	0	0	5	22.2	108	29	14	14	2	0	1	1	13	1	21	3	0	0	0	—	0	0-0	0	5.56
1987 New York	NL	21	13	1	3	99.1	420	87	46	41	11	4	3	5	44	1	68	2	4	5	6	.455	0	1-1	2	3.71
1988 New York	NL	35	28	8	0	231.1	936	178	67	57	10	11	5	4	80	7	213	10	10	20	3	.870	4	0-0	1	2.22

46

Year Team	Lg	G	GS	CG	GF	IP	BFP	H	R	ER	HR	SH	SF	HB	TBB	IBB	SO	WP	Bk	W	L	Pct.	ShO	Sv-Op	Hld	ERA
1989 New York	NL	34	33	7	0	219.2	910	183	92	86	20	6	4	4	74	6	190	14	4	14	8	.636	2	0-0	0	3.52
1990 New York	NL	31	30	6	1	211.2	860	177	84	76	21	4	6	1	65	1	233	10	4	14	10	.583	2	0-0	0	3.23
1991 New York	NL	34	34	5	0	232.2	966	204	95	85	13	13	7	5	73	2	241	17	1	14	14	.500	2	0-0	0	3.29
1992 NYM-Tor		35	34	7	0	249.2	1055	201	91	78	15	6	9	12	111	7	261	12	1	17	10	.630	5	0-0	0	2.81
1993 Kansas City	AL	34	34	6	0	254	1060	205	102	94	20	7	9	10	114	2	191	14	2	11	14	.440	1	0-0	0	3.33
1994 Kansas City	AL	23	23	4	0	171.2	690	130	60	56	15	1	5	7	54	0	132	5	1	16	5	.762	3	0-0	0	2.94
1995 Tor-NYY	AL	30	30	6	0	229.1	954	195	95	91	24	2	3	6	88	2	191	11	1	18	8	.692	2	0-0	0	3.57
1996 New York	AL	11	11	1	0	72	295	50	25	23	3	1	5	2	34	0	71	4	1	7	2	.778	0	0-0	0	2.88
1997 New York	AL	29	29	1	0	195	805	155	67	61	17	3	2	4	86	2	222	14	2	12	6	.667	0	0-0	0	2.82
1998 New York	AL	31	31	3	0	207.2	866	186	89	82	20	4	4	15	59	1	209	6	0	20	7	.741	0	0-0	0	3.55
1999 New York	AL	31	31	0	0	193.1	827	164	84	74	21	5	6	11	90	2	177	7	1	12	9	.571	1	0-0	0	3.44
2000 New York	AL	30	29	0	0	155	733	192	124	119	25	6	8	9	82	3	120	11	0	4	14	.222	0	0-0	0	6.91
2001 Boston	AL	25	25	0	0	135.2	614	148	74	65	17	2	6	10	57	4	115	9	0	9	7	.563	0	0-0	0	4.31
1992 New York	NL	27	27	7	0	196.2	831	162	75	63	12	6	6	9	82	5	214	9	1	13	7	.650	5	0-0	0	2.88
Toronto	AL	8	7	0	0	53	224	39	16	15	3	0	3	3	29	2	47	3	0	4	3	.571	0	0-0	0	2.55
1995 Toronto	AL	17	17	5	0	130.1	537	113	53	49	12	2	2	5	41	2	102	6	1	9	6	.600	2	0-0	0	3.38
New York	AL	13	13	1	0	99	417	82	42	42	12	0	1	1	47	0	89	5	0	9	2	.818	0	0-0	0	3.82
16 ML YEARS		445	415	56	9	2880.2	12099	2484	1209	1102	254	75	82	106	1124	41	2655	149	32	193	123	.611	22	1-1	3	3.44

Jeff Conine

Bats: R **Throws:** R **Pos:** 1B-80; LF-22; 3B-17; RF-16; DH-12; PH/PR-2   **Ht:** 6'1" **Wt:** 220 **Born:** 6/27/66 **Age:** 36

Year Team	Lg	G	AB	H	2B	3B	HR	(Hm	Rd)	TB	R	RBI	TBB	IBB	SO	HBP	SH	SF	SB	CS	SB%	GDP	Avg	OBP	SLG
1990 Kansas City	AL	9	20	5	2	0	0	(0	0)	7	3	2	2	0	5	0	0	0	0	0	—	1	.250	.318	.350
1992 Kansas City	AL	28	91	23	5	2	0	(0	0)	32	10	9	8	1	23	0	0	0	0	0	—	1	.253	.313	.352
1993 Florida	NL	162	595	174	24	3	12	(5	7)	240	75	79	52	2	135	5	0	6	2	2	.50	14	.292	.351	.403
1994 Florida	NL	115	451	144	27	6	18	(8	10)	237	60	82	40	4	92	1	0	4	1	2	.33	8	.319	.373	.525
1995 Florida	NL	133	483	146	26	2	25	(13	12)	251	72	105	66	5	94	1	0	12	2	0	1.00	13	.302	.379	.520
1996 Florida	NL	157	597	175	32	2	26	(15	11)	289	84	95	62	1	121	4	0	7	1	4	.20	17	.293	.360	.484
1997 Florida	NL	151	405	98	13	1	17	(7	10)	164	46	61	57	3	89	2	0	2	2	0	1.00	11	.242	.337	.405
1998 Kansas City	AL	93	309	79	26	0	8	(4	4)	129	30	43	26	1	68	2	0	6	3	0	1.00	8	.256	.312	.417
1999 Baltimore	AL	139	444	129	31	1	13	(7	6)	201	54	75	30	0	40	3	1	7	0	3	.00	12	.291	.335	.453
2000 Baltimore	AL	119	409	116	20	2	13	(7	6)	179	53	46	36	1	53	2	0	4	4	3	.57	14	.284	.341	.438
2001 Baltimore	AL	139	524	163	23	2	14	(5	9)	232	75	97	64	6	75	5	0	8	12	8	.60	12	.311	.386	.443
11 ML YEARS		1245	4328	1252	229	21	146	(70	76)	1961	562	694	443	24	795	25	1	56	27	22	.55	111	.289	.354	.453

Jason Conti

Bats: Left **Throws:** Right **Pos:** PH/PR-4; RF-1   **Ht:** 5'11" **Wt:** 180 **Born:** 1/27/75 **Age:** 27

Year Team	Lg	G	AB	H	2B	3B	HR	(Hm	Rd)	TB	R	RBI	TBB	IBB	SO	HBP	SH	SF	SB	CS	SB%	GDP	Avg	OBP	SLG
1996 Lethbridge	R+	63	226	83	15	1	4	—	—	112	63	49	30	0	29	6	0	3	30	7	.81	3	.367	.449	.496
1997 South Bend	A	117	458	142	22	10	3	—	—	193	78	43	45	2	99	11	4	3	30	18	.63	10	.310	.383	.421
High Desert	A+	14	59	21	5	1	2	—	—	34	15	8	10	0	12	1	0	0	1	2	.33	0	.356	.457	.576
1998 Tulsa	AA	130	530	167	31	12	15	—	—	267	125	67	63	4	96	9	1	2	19	13	.59	5	.315	.396	.504
1999 Tucson	AAA	133	520	151	23	8	9	—	—	217	100	57	55	1	89	5	3	6	22	8	.73	8	.290	.360	.417
2000 Tucson	AAA	93	383	117	20	5	11	—	—	180	75	57	23	1	57	5	2	5	11	3	.79	8	.305	.349	.470
2001 Tucson	AAA	92	362	120	23	6	9	—	—	182	68	52	33	1	54	12	3	3	2	5	.29	2	.331	.402	.503
Durham	AAA	38	157	48	12	0	5	—	—	75	24	18	9	1	31	1	1	0	3	1	.75	0	.306	.347	.478
2000 Arizona	NL	47	91	21	4	3	1	(1	0)	34	11	15	7	2	30	1	0	0	3	0	1.00	2	.231	.293	.374
2001 Arizona	NL	5	4	1	0	0	0	(0	0)	1	1	0	1	0	2	0	0	0	0	0	—	0	.250	.400	.250
2 ML YEARS		52	95	22	4	3	1	(1	0)	35	12	15	8	2	32	1	0	0	3	0	1.00	2	.232	.298	.368

Dennis Cook

Pitches: Left **Bats:** Left **Pos:** RP-62   **Ht:** 6'3" **Wt:** 190 **Born:** 10/4/62 **Age:** 39

Year Team	Lg	G	GS	CG	GF	IP	BFP	H	R	ER	HR	SH	SF	HB	TBB	IBB	SO	WP	Bk	W	L	Pct.	ShO	Sv-Op	Hld	ERA
2001 Scrantn-WB *	AAA	1	1	0	0	7	1	1	1	0	0	0	0	2	0	1	0	0	0	0	—	0	0--	—	9.00
1988 San Francisco	NL	4	4	1	0	22	86	9	8	7	1	0	3	0	11	1	13	1	0	2	1	.667	1	0-0	0	2.86
1989 San Francisco	NL	23	18	2	1	121	499	110	59	50	18	5	2	2	38	6	67	4	2	7	8	.467	1	0-0	1	3.72
1990 Phi-LA	NL	47	16	2	4	156	663	155	74	68	20	7	7	2	56	9	64	6	3	9	4	.692	1	1-2	6	3.92
1991 Los Angeles	NL	20	1	0	5	17.2	69	12	3	1	0	1	2	0	7	1	8	0	0	1	0	1.000	0	0-1	0	0.51
1992 Cleveland	AL	32	25	1	1	158	669	156	79	67	29	3	3	2	50	2	96	4	5	5	7	.417	0	0-0	0	3.82
1993 Cleveland	AL	25	6	0	2	54	233	62	36	34	9	3	2	2	16	1	34	0	1	5	5	.500	0	0-2	2	5.67
1994 Chicago	AL	38	0	0	8	33	143	29	17	13	4	3	0	0	14	3	26	0	1	3	1	.750	0	0-1	3	3.55
1995 Cle-Tex	AL	46	1	0	10	57.2	255	63	32	29	9	4	5	2	26	3	53	1	0	0	2	.000	0	2-2	6	4.53
1996 Texas	AL	60	0	0	12	70.1	298	53	34	32	2	3	5	7	35	7	64	0	0	5	2	.714	0	0-0	11	4.09
1997 Florida	NL	59	0	0	12	62.1	272	64	28	27	4	1	1	2	28	4	63	0	0	1	2	.333	0	0-2	13	3.90
1998 New York	NL	73	0	0	18	68	286	60	21	18	5	3	3	3	27	4	79	1	1	8	4	.667	0	1-5	21	2.38
1999 New York	NL	71	0	0	12	63	262	50	27	27	11	1	2	1	27	8	68	0	0	10	5	.667	0	3-6	19	3.86
2000 New York	NL	68	0	0	15	59	269	63	35	35	8	0	0	5	31	4	53	3	2	6	3	.667	0	2-8	10	5.34
2001 NYM-Phi	NL	62	0	0	14	45.2	194	43	24	23	8	3	1	2	14	3	38	3	1	1	1	.500	0	0-3	8	4.53
1989 San Francisco	NL	2	2	1	0	15	58	13	3	3	1	0	0	0	5	0	9	1	0	1	0	1.000	1	0-0	0	1.80
Philadelphia	NL	21	16	1	1	106	441	97	56	47	17	5	2	2	33	6	58	3	2	6	8	.429	1	0-0	1	3.99
1990 Philadelphia	NL	42	13	2	4	141.2	594	132	61	56	13	5	5	2	54	9	58	6	3	8	3	.727	1	1-2	3	3.56
Los Angeles	NL	5	3	0	0	14.1	69	23	13	12	7	2	2	0	2	0	6	0	0	1	1	.500	0	0-0	0	7.53
1995 Cleveland	AL	11	0	0	1	12.2	62	16	9	9	3	1	0	1	10	2	13	0	0	0	0	—	0	0-0	1	6.39
Texas	AL	35	1	0	9	45	193	47	23	20	6	3	5	1	16	1	40	1	0	0	2	.000	0	2-2	5	4.00
2001 New York	NL	43	0	0	11	36	148	28	18	17	6	1	1	1	10	1	34	3	1	1	1	.500	0	0-2	6	4.25
Philadelphia	NL	19	0	0	3	9.2	46	15	6	6	2	2	0	1	4	2	4	0	0	0	0	—	0	0-1	2	5.59
14 ML YEARS		628	71	6	111	987.2	4198	929	477	431	128	37	36	30	380	49	726	23	16	63	45	.583	3	9-34	99	3.93

Mike Coolbaugh

Bats: Right **Throws:** Right **Pos:** 3B-27; PH/PR-12; SS-3   **Ht:** 6'1" **Wt:** 190 **Born:** 6/5/72 **Age:** 30

						BATTING											BASERUNNING				PERCENTAGES		
Year Team	Lg	G	AB	H	2B	3B	HR	(Hm	Rd)	TB	R	RBI	TBB	IBB	SO	HBP	SH	SF	SB	CS	SB%	GDP	Avg	OBP	SLG
1990 Medcine Hat	R+	58	211	40	9	0	2	—	—	55	21	16	13	0	47	1	1	2	3	2	.60	8	.190	.238	.261
1991 St.Cathrnes	A-	71	255	58	13	2	3	—	—	84	28	26	17	0	40	3	4	4	4	5	.44	1	.227	.280	.329
1992 St.Cathrnes	A-	15	49	14	1	1	0	—	—	17	3	2	3	0	12	0	2	0	0	2	.00	1	.286	.327	.347
1993 Hagerstown	A	112	389	94	23	1	16	—	—	167	58	62	32	5	94	3	4	4	4	3	.57	9	.242	.301	.429
1994 Dunedin	A+	122	456	120	33	3	16	—	—	207	53	66	28	3	94	7	3	4	3	4	.43	14	.263	.313	.454
1995 Knoxville	AA	142	500	120	32	2	9	—	—	183	71	56	37	3	110	11	4	3	7	11	.39	13	.240	.305	.366
1996 Charlotte	A+	124	449	129	33	4	15	—	—	215	76	75	42	4	80	8	0	3	8	10	.44	10	.287	.357	.479
Tulsa	AA	7	23	8	3	0	2	—	—	17	6	9	2	0	3	2	0	0	1	0	1.00	0	.348	.444	.739
1997 Huntsville	AA	139	559	172	37	2	30	—	—	303	100	132	52	3	105	7	2	8	8	3	.73	17	.308	.369	.542
1998 Colo Sprngs	AAA	108	386	107	35	2	16	—	—	194	62	75	32	0	93	1	2	4	0	3	.00	13	.277	.331	.503
1999 Columbus	AAA	114	391	108	31	2	15	—	—	188	65	66	38	0	112	2	2	4	5	7	.42	5	.276	.340	.481
2000 Columbus	AAA	117	387	105	28	0	23	—	—	202	63	61	67	2	96	3	3	3	6	3	.67	5	.271	.380	.522
2001 Indianapols	AAA	94	347	93	24	3	10	—	—	153	49	50	39	1	92	5	6	4	3	2	.60	10	.268	.347	.441
2001 Milwaukee	NL	39	70	14	6	0	2	(2	0)	26	10	7	5	0	16	2	0	0	0	0	—	3	.200	.273	.371

Ron Coomer

Bats: R **Throws:** R **Pos:** 3B-76; 1B-36; PH/PR-17; DH-1   **Ht:** 6'0" **Wt:** 215 **Born:** 11/18/66 **Age:** 35

						BATTING											BASERUNNING				PERCENTAGES		
Year Team	Lg	G	AB	H	2B	3B	HR	(Hm	Rd)	TB	R	RBI	TBB	IBB	SO	HBP	SH	SF	SB	CS	SB%	GDP	Avg	OBP	SLG
2001 Iowa *	AAA	4	12	4	0	0	0	—	—	4	0	0	1	0	3	0	0	0	0	0	—	0	.333	.385	.333
1995 Minnesota	AL	37	101	26	3	1	5	(2	3)	46	15	19	9	0	11	1	0	0	0	1	.00	9	.257	.324	.455
1996 Minnesota	AL	95	233	69	12	1	12	(5	7)	119	34	41	17	1	24	0	0	3	3	0	1.00	10	.296	.340	.511
1997 Minnesota	AL	140	523	156	30	2	13	(4	9)	229	63	85	22	5	91	0	0	5	4	3	.57	11	.298	.324	.438
1998 Minnesota	AL	137	529	146	22	1	15	(6	9)	215	54	72	18	1	72	0	0	8	2	2	.50	22	.276	.295	.406
1999 Minnesota	AL	127	467	123	25	1	16	(6	10)	198	53	65	30	1	69	1	0	3	2	1	.67	16	.263	.307	.424
2000 Minnesota	AL	140	544	147	29	1	16	(3	13)	226	64	82	36	2	50	4	0	5	2	0	1.00	25	.270	.317	.415
2001 Chicago	NL	111	349	91	19	1	8	(3	5)	136	25	53	29	1	70	2	0	6	0	0	—	23	.261	.316	.390
7 ML YEARS		787	2746	758	140	8	85	(29	56)	1169	308	417	161	11	387	8	0	30	13	7	.65	116	.276	.315	.426

Brian Cooper

Pitches: Right **Bats:** Right **Pos:** RP-6; SP-1   **Ht:** 6'1" **Wt:** 185 **Born:** 8/19/74 **Age:** 27

		HOW MUCH HE PITCHED						WHAT HE GAVE UP										THE RESULTS						
Year Team	Lg	G	GS	CG	GF	IP	BFP	H	R	ER	HR	SH	SF	HB	TBB	IBB	SO	WP	Bk	W	L	Pct.	ShO	Sv-Op	Hld	ERA
2001 Salt Lake *	AAA	28	28	1	0	173	737	181	98	89	26	3	3	9	58	0	109	6	0	12	8	.600	0	0--	—	4.63
1999 Anaheim	AL	5	5	0	0	27.2	124	23	15	15	3	0	1	4	18	0	15	0	0	1	1	.500	0	0-0	0	4.88
2000 Anaheim	AL	15	15	1	0	87	396	105	66	57	18	4	4	2	35	1	36	1	0	4	8	.333	1	0-0	0	5.90
2001 Anaheim	AL	7	1	0	5	13.2	55	10	5	4	2	0	1	0	4	0	7	0	0	0	1	.000	0	0-0	0	2.63
3 ML YEARS		27	21	1	5	128.1	575	138	86	76	23	4	6	6	57	1	58	1	0	5	10	.333	1	0-0	0	5.33

Rocky Coppinger

Pitches: Right **Bats:** Right **Pos:** RP-5; SP-3   **Ht:** 6'5" **Wt:** 250 **Born:** 3/19/74 **Age:** 28

		HOW MUCH HE PITCHED						WHAT HE GAVE UP										THE RESULTS						
Year Team	Lg	G	GS	CG	GF	IP	BFP	H	R	ER	HR	SH	SF	HB	TBB	IBB	SO	WP	Bk	W	L	Pct.	ShO	Sv-Op	Hld	ERA
2001 Huntsville *	AA	16	0	0	7	29.2	125	28	9	7	1	2	0	2	11	0	24	1	0	2	0	1.000	0	4--	—	2.12
Indianapols *	AAA	15	5	0	3	48	182	25	10	10	2	2	1	1	20	1	42	2	0	6	1	.857	0	0--	—	1.88
1996 Baltimore	AL	23	22	0	1	125	548	126	76	72	25	2	5	2	60	1	104	4	0	10	6	.625	0	0-0	0	5.18
1997 Baltimore	AL	5	4	0	1	20	95	21	14	14	2	0	1	1	16	1	22	1	0	1	1	.500	0	0-0	0	6.30
1998 Baltimore	AL	6	1	0	3	15.2	72	16	9	9	3	0	0	0	7	1	13	0	0	0	0	—	0	0-0	0	5.17
1999 Bal-Mil		40	2	0	17	58.1	269	60	37	35	13	0	2	0	42	3	56	1	0	5	4	.556	0	0-2	9	5.40
2001 Milwaukee	NL	8	3	0	2	22.2	104	24	17	17	5	2	1	1	15	0	15	2	0	1	0	1.000	0	0-0	1	6.75
1999 Baltimore	AL	11	2	0	7	21.2	105	25	21	20	8	0	1	0	19	0	17	0	0	0	1	.000	0	0-0	0	8.31
Milwaukee	NL	29	0	0	10	36.2	164	35	16	15	5	0	1	0	23	3	39	1	0	5	3	.625	0	0-2	9	3.68
5 ML YEARS		82	32	0	24	241.2	1088	247	153	147	48	4	9	4	140	6	210	8	0	17	11	.607	0	0-2	10	5.47

Alex Cora

Bats: Left **Throws:** Right **Pos:** SS-132; PH/PR-4; 2B-1   **Ht:** 6'0" **Wt:** 180 **Born:** 10/18/75 **Age:** 26

						BATTING											BASERUNNING				PERCENTAGES		
Year Team	Lg	G	AB	H	2B	3B	HR	(Hm	Rd)	TB	R	RBI	TBB	IBB	SO	HBP	SH	SF	SB	CS	SB%	GDP	Avg	OBP	SLG
1998 Los Angeles	NL	29	33	4	0	1	0	(0	0)	6	1	0	2	0	8	1	2	0	0	0	—	0	.121	.194	.182
1999 Los Angeles	NL	11	30	5	1	0	0	(0	0)	6	2	3	0	0	4	1	0	0	0	0	—	1	.167	.194	.200
2000 Los Angeles	NL	109	353	84	18	6	4	(2	2)	126	39	32	26	4	53	7	6	2	4	1	.80	6	.238	.302	.357
2001 Los Angeles	NL	134	405	88	18	3	4	(2	2)	124	38	29	31	6	58	8	3	2	0	2	.00	16	.217	.285	.306
4 ML YEARS		283	821	181	37	10	8	(4	4)	262	80	64	59	10	123	17	11	4	4	3	.57	23	.220	.285	.319

Francisco Cordero

Pitches: Right **Bats:** Right **Pos:** RP-3   **Ht:** 6'2" **Wt:** 200 **Born:** 8/11/77 **Age:** 24

		HOW MUCH HE PITCHED						WHAT HE GAVE UP										THE RESULTS						
Year Team	Lg	G	GS	CG	GF	IP	BFP	H	R	ER	HR	SH	SF	HB	TBB	IBB	SO	WP	Bk	W	L	Pct.	ShO	Sv-Op	Hld	ERA
2001 Oklahoma *	AAA	12	0	0	12	15.1	57	8	2	1	0	0	0	0	3	0	20	0	0	0	1	.000	0	6--	—	0.59
1999 Detroit	AL	20	0	0	4	19	91	19	7	7	2	2	4	0	18	2	19	1	0	2	2	.500	0	0-0	6	3.32
2000 Texas	AL	56	0	0	13	77.1	365	87	51	46	11	2	6	4	48	3	49	7	0	1	2	.333	0	0-3	5	5.35
2001 Texas	AL	3	0	0	2	2.1	12	3	1	1	0	0	0	0	2	1	1	1	0	0	1	.000	0	0-0	1	3.86
3 ML YEARS		79	0	0	19	98.2	468	109	59	54	13	4	10	4	68	6	69	9	0	3	5	.375	0	0-3	11	4.93

Wil Cordero

Bats: R **Throws:** R **Pos:** LF-48; 1B-22; PH/PR-14; DH-12; RF-5   **Ht:** 6'2" **Wt:** 210 **Born:** 10/3/71 **Age:** 30

Year Team	Lg	G	AB	H	2B	3B	HR	(Hm	Rd)	TB	R	RBI	TBB	IBB	SO	HBP	SH	SF	SB	CS	SB%	GDP	Avg	OBP	SLG
1992 Montreal	NL	45	126	38	4	1	2	(1	1)	50	17	8	9	0	31	1	1	0	0	0	—	3	.302	.353	.397
1993 Montreal	NL	138	475	118	32	2	10	(8	2)	184	56	58	34	8	60	7	4	1	12	3	.80	12	.248	.308	.387
1994 Montreal	NL	110	415	122	30	3	15	(5	10)	203	65	63	41	3	62	6	2	3	16	3	.84	8	.294	.363	.489
1995 Montreal	NL	131	514	147	35	2	10	(2	8)	216	64	49	36	4	88	9	1	4	9	5	.64	11	.286	.341	.420
1996 Boston	AL	59	198	57	14	0	3	(2	1)	80	29	37	11	4	31	2	1	1	2	1	.67	8	.288	.330	.404
1997 Boston	AL	140	570	160	26	3	18	(11	7)	246	82	72	31	7	122	4	0	4	1	3	.25	11	.281	.320	.432
1998 Chicago	AL	96	341	91	18	2	13	(5	8)	152	58	49	22	0	66	3	1	4	2	1	.67	7	.267	.314	.446
1999 Cleveland	AL	54	194	58	15	0	8	(3	5)	97	35	32	15	0	37	6	0	2	2	0	1.00	7	.299	.364	.500
2000 Pit-Cle		127	496	137	35	5	16	(8	8)	230	64	68	32	1	76	7	0	1	1	2	.33	18	.276	.328	.464
2001 Cleveland	AL	89	268	67	11	1	4	(2	2)	92	30	21	22	2	50	4	2	3	0	0	—	6	.250	.313	.343
2000 Pittsburgh	NL	89	348	98	24	3	16	(8	8)	176	46	51	25	1	58	4	0	1	1	2	.33	11	.282	.336	.506
Cleveland	AL	38	148	39	11	2	0	(0	0)	54	18	17	7	0	18	3	0	0	0	0	—	7	.264	.310	.365
10 ML YEARS		989	3597	995	220	19	99	(47	52)	1550	500	457	253	29	623	49	12	23	45	18	.71	93	.277	.331	.431

Francisco Cordova

Pitches: Right **Bats:** Right **2000 Pos:** SP-17; RP-1   **Ht:** 6'1" **Wt:** 197 **Born:** 4/26/72 **Age:** 30

Year Team	Lg	G	GS	CG	GF	IP	BFP	H	R	ER	HR	SH	SF	HB	TBB	IBB	SO	WP	Bk	W	L	Pct.	ShO	Sv-Op	Hld	ERA
2001 Altoona *	AA	1	1	0	0	4.1	19	6	2	2	0	0	0	0	1	0	4	0	0	0	0	—	0	0--	—	4.15
Nashville *	AAA	1	1	0	0	1	5	2	2	1	0	0	0	0	0	0	1	0	0	0	0	—	0	0--	—	18.00
1996 Pittsburgh	NL	59	6	0	41	99	414	103	49	45	11	1	0	2	20	6	95	2	1	4	7	.364	0	12-18	3	4.09
1997 Pittsburgh	NL	29	29	2	0	178.2	744	175	80	72	14	3	7	9	49	4	121	4	0	11	8	.579	2	0-0	0	3.63
1998 Pittsburgh	NL	33	33	3	0	220.1	921	204	91	81	22	9	6	3	69	5	157	1	1	13	14	.481	2	0-0	0	3.31
1999 Pittsburgh	NL	27	27	2	0	160.2	682	166	83	79	16	7	4	4	59	6	98	5	0	8	10	.444	0	0-0	0	4.43
2000 Pittsburgh	NL	18	17	0	0	95	421	107	63	55	12	3	3	2	38	4	66	3	1	6	8	.429	0	0-0	0	5.21
5 ML YEARS		166	112	7	41	753.2	3182	755	366	332	75	23	20	20	235	25	537	15	3	42	47	.472	4	12-18	3	3.96

Marty Cordova

Bats: R **Throws:** R **Pos:** LF-84; RF-29; PH/PR-11; DH-7; CF-2   **Ht:** 6'0" **Wt:** 206 **Born:** 7/10/69 **Age:** 32

Year Team	Lg	G	AB	H	2B	3B	HR	(Hm	Rd)	TB	R	RBI	TBB	IBB	SO	HBP	SH	SF	SB	CS	SB%	GDP	Avg	OBP	SLG
1995 Minnesota	AL	137	512	142	27	4	24	(16	8)	249	81	84	52	1	111	10	0	5	20	7	.74	10	.277	.352	.486
1996 Minnesota	AL	145	569	176	46	1	16	(10	6)	272	97	111	53	4	96	8	0	9	11	5	.69	18	.309	.371	.478
1997 Minnesota	AL	103	378	93	18	4	15	(4	11)	164	44	51	30	2	92	3	0	2	5	3	.63	13	.246	.305	.434
1998 Minnesota	AL	119	438	111	20	2	10	(6	4)	165	52	69	50	3	103	5	0	6	3	6	.33	14	.253	.333	.377
1999 Minnesota	AL	124	425	122	28	3	14	(9	5)	197	62	70	48	2	96	9	0	6	13	4	.76	22	.285	.365	.464
2000 Toronto	AL	62	200	49	7	0	4	(3	1)	68	23	18	18	0	35	3	0	0	3	2	.60	6	.245	.317	.340
2001 Cleveland	AL	122	409	123	20	2	20	(9	11)	207	61	69	23	0	81	8	0	2	0	3	.00	9	.301	.348	.506
7 ML YEARS		812	2931	815	166	16	103	(57	46)	1322	420	472	274	12	614	46	0	30	55	30	.65	92	.278	.346	.451

Mark Corey

Pitches: Right **Bats:** Right **Pos:** RP-2   **Ht:** 6'3" **Wt:** 210 **Born:** 11/16/74 **Age:** 27

Year Team	Lg	G	GS	CG	GF	IP	BFP	H	R	ER	HR	SH	SF	HB	TBB	IBB	SO	WP	Bk	W	L	Pct.	ShO	Sv-Op	Hld	ERA
1995 Princeton	R+	4	3	0	0	14.2	61	12	7	6	1	0	0	0	6	0	8	0	0	1	1	.500	0	0--	—	3.68
1997 Chstn-WV	A	26	26	1	0	136	602	169	87	69	7	8	5	4	42	3	97	14	0	8	13	.381	0	0--	—	4.57
1998 Burlington	A	20	20	6	0	140	577	125	55	38	9	3	3	6	36	0	109	10	1	12	6	.667	2	0--	—	2.44
Indianapls	AAA	1	1	1	0	6	24	4	3	3	1	1	0	0	3	0	2	0	0	0	1	.000	0	0--	—	4.50
Chattanooga	AA	6	6	0	0	26.1	127	32	25	24	6	1	2	2	16	1	6	0	0	0	4	.000	0	0--	—	8.20
1999 Binghamton	AA	29	27	0	0	155	698	175	108	93	18	4	1	9	64	0	111	1	1	7	13	.350	0	0--	—	5.40
2000 Binghamton	AA	14	2	0	2	25.2	101	15	5	3	0	1	1	0	11	0	19	2	0	0	0	—	0	0--	—	1.05
Norfolk	AAA	20	11	0	2	63.2	303	80	52	48	11	2	3	8	29	1	43	4	0	3	7	.300	0	1--	—	6.79
2001 Binghamton	AA	25	0	0	23	35	137	23	10	7	1	2	0	1	12	0	50	2	0	1	2	.333	0	17--	—	1.80
Norfolk	AAA	28	0	0	20	36.2	147	24	7	6	1	3	0	0	22	0	42	0	0	8	2	.800	0	10--	—	1.47
2001 New York	NL	2	0	0	0	1.2	13	5	3	3	0	0	0	0	3	1	3	0	0	0	0	0-0	0			16.20

Rheal Cormier

Pitches: Left **Bats:** Left **Pos:** RP-60   **Ht:** 5'10" **Wt:** 187 **Born:** 4/23/67 **Age:** 35

Year Team	Lg	G	GS	CG	GF	IP	BFP	H	R	ER	HR	SH	SF	HB	TBB	IBB	SO	WP	Bk	W	L	Pct.	ShO	Sv-Op	Hld	ERA
2001 Reading *	AA	1	1	0	0	2	7	0	0	0	0	0	0	0	1	0	2	0	0	0	0	—	0	0--	—	0.00
1991 St. Louis	NL	11	10	2	1	67.2	281	74	35	31	5	1	3	2	8	1	38	2	1	4	5	.444	0	0-0	0	4.12
1992 St. Louis	NL	31	30	3	1	186	772	194	83	76	15	11	3	5	33	2	117	4	2	10	10	.500	1	0-0	0	3.68
1993 St. Louis	NL	38	21	1	4	145.1	619	163	80	70	18	10	4	4	27	3	75	6	0	7	6	.538	0	0-0	0	4.33
1994 St. Louis	NL	7	7	0	0	39.2	169	40	24	24	6	1	2	3	7	0	26	2	0	3	2	.600	0	0-0	0	5.45
1995 Boston	AL	48	12	0	3	115	488	131	60	52	12	6	2	3	31	2	69	4	0	7	5	.583	0	0-2	9	4.07
1996 Montreal	NL	33	27	1	1	159.2	674	165	80	74	16	4	8	9	41	3	100	8	0	7	10	.412	1	0-0	0	4.17
1997 Montreal	NL	1	1	0	0	1.1	9	4	5	5	1	0	0	0	1	0	0	0	0	0	1	.000	0	0-0	0	33.75
1999 Boston	AL	60	0	0	7	63.1	275	61	34	26	4	1	3	5	18	2	39	1	0	0	1	.000	0	0-3	15	3.69
2000 Boston	AL	64	0	0	12	68.1	293	74	40	35	7	5	2	0	17	2	43	1	0	3	3	.500	0	0-2	9	4.61
2001 Philadelphia	NL	60	0	0	16	51.1	222	49	26	24	5	3	0	4	17	4	37	1	0	5	6	.455	0	1-6	12	4.21
10 ML YEARS		353	108	7	45	897.2	3802	955	467	417	89	42	27	35	200	19	544	29	3	48	48	.500	1	1-13	45	4.18

Nate Cornejo

Pitches: Right **Bats:** Right **Pos:** SP-10 | **Ht:** 6'5" **Wt:** 200 **Born:** 9/24/79 **Age:** 22

Year Team	Lg	HOW MUCH HE PITCHED					WHAT HE GAVE UP												THE RESULTS						ERA
		G	GS	CG	GF	IP	BFP	H	R	ER	HR	SH	SF	HB	TBB	IBB	SO	WP	Bk	W	L	Pct.	ShO	Sv-Op	Hld	
1998 Tigers	R	5	0	0	2	14.1	58	12	2	2	0	0	0	1	2	0	9	1	0	1	0	1.000	0	1--	—	1.26
1999 W Michigan	A	28	28	4	0	174.2	750	173	87	72	4	10	9	12	67	0	125	11	5	9	11	.450	1	0--	—	3.71
2000 Lakeland	A+	12	12	1	0	77	322	67	37	26	5	0	1	4	31	0	60	2	1	5	5	.500	0	0--	—	3.04
Jacksnville	AA	16	16	0	0	91.2	389	91	52	47	6	3	3	4	43	1	60	1	1	5	7	.417	0	0--	—	4.61
2001 Erie	AA	19	19	3	0	124.1	519	107	47	37	12	3	0	7	41	0	105	4	0	12	3	.800	1	0--	—	2.68
Toledo	AAA	4	4	0	0	29.2	113	24	8	7	1	1	0	0	7	0	22	1	0	4	0	1.000	0	0--	—	2.12
2001 Detroit	AL	10	10	0	0	42.2	217	63	38	35	10	2	0	3	28	4	22	1	0	4	4	.500	0	0-0	0	7.38

Humberto Cota

Bats: Right **Throws:** Right **Pos:** PH/PR-4; C-3 | **Ht:** 6'0" **Wt:** 175 **Born:** 2/7/79 **Age:** 23

Year Team	Lg	BATTING																		BASERUNNING				PERCENTAGES		
		G	AB	H	2B	3B	HR	(Hm	Rd)	TB	R	RBI	TBB	IBB	SO	HBP	SH	SF	SB	CS	SB%	GDP	Avg	OBP	SLG
1997 Devil Rays	R	44	133	32	6	1	2	—	—	46	14	20	17	0	27	3	1	3	3	1	.75	1	.241	.333	.346
Hudson Val	A-	3	9	2	0	0	0	—	—	2	0	2	0	0	1	0	0	0	0	0	—	0	.222	.222	.222
1998 Princeton	R+	67	245	76	13	4	15	—	—	142	48	61	32	1	59	6	1	3	4	4	.50	3	.310	.399	.580
1999 Chston-SC	A	85	336	94	21	1	9	—	—	144	42	61	20	1	51	2	1	5	1	1	.50	9	.280	.320	.429
Hickory	A	37	133	36	11	2	2	—	—	57	28	20	21	1	20	0	0	2	3	1	.75	0	.271	.365	.429
2000 Altoona	AA	112	429	112	20	1	8	—	—	158	49	44	21	1	80	3	1	5	6	4	.60	8	.261	.297	.368
2001 Nashville	AAA	111	377	112	22	2	14	—	—	180	61	72	25	1	74	8	1	3	7	2	.78	8	.297	.351	.477
2001 Pittsburgh	NL	7	9	2	0	0	0	(0	0)	2	0	1	0	0	5	0	0	0	0	0	—	0	.222	.222	.222

Craig Counsell

Bats: L **Throws:** R **Pos:** SS-58; 2B-55; 3B-38; PH/PR-18; 1B-2 | **Ht:** 6'0" **Wt:** 175 **Born:** 8/21/70 **Age:** 31

Year Team	Lg	BATTING																		BASERUNNING				PERCENTAGES		
		G	AB	H	2B	3B	HR	(Hm	Rd)	TB	R	RBI	TBB	IBB	SO	HBP	SH	SF	SB	CS	SB%	GDP	Avg	OBP	SLG
1995 Colorado	NL	3	1	0	0	0	0	(0	0)	0	0	0	0	0	0	0	0	0	0	0	—	0	.000	.500	.000
1997 Col-Fla	NL	52	164	49	9	2	1	(1	0)	65	20	16	18	2	17	3	3	1	1	1	.50	5	.299	.376	.396
1998 Florida	NL	107	335	84	19	5	4	(2	2)	125	43	40	51	7	47	4	8	1	3	0	1.00	5	.251	.355	.373
1999 Fla-LA	NL	87	174	38	7	0	0	(0	0)	45	24	11	14	0	24	0	5	2	1	0	1.00	5	.218	.274	.259
2000 Arizona	NL	67	152	48	8	1	2	(0	2)	64	23	11	20	0	18	2	1	1	3	3	.50	4	.316	.400	.421
2001 Arizona	NL	141	458	126	22	3	4	(4	0)	166	76	38	61	3	76	2	6	6	6	8	.43	9	.275	.359	.362
1997 Colorado	NL	1	0	0	0	0	0	(0	0)	0	0	0	0	0	0	0	0	0	0	0	—	0	—	—	—
Florida	NL	51	164	49	9	2	1	(1	0)	65	20	16	18	2	17	3	3	1	1	1	.50	5	.299	.376	.396
1999 Florida	NL	37	66	10	1	0	0	(0	0)	11	4	2	5	0	10	0	2	0	0	0	—	0	.152	.211	.167
Los Angeles	NL	50	108	28	6	0	0	(0	0)	34	20	9	9	0	14	0	3	2	1	0	1.00	1	.259	.311	.315
6 ML YEARS		457	1284	345	65	11	11	(7	4)	465	186	116	165	12	182	11	23	11	14	12	.54	25	.269	.354	.362

Steve Cox

Bats: L **Throws:** L **Pos:** 1B-78; PH/PR-18; LF-6; DH-4; RF-2 | **Ht:** 6'4" **Wt:** 222 **Born:** 10/31/74 **Age:** 27

Year Team	Lg	BATTING																		BASERUNNING				PERCENTAGES		
		G	AB	H	2B	3B	HR	(Hm	Rd)	TB	R	RBI	TBB	IBB	SO	HBP	SH	SF	SB	CS	SB%	GDP	Avg	OBP	SLG
2001 Orlando *	AA	4	14	3	1	0	1	—	—	7	2	3	2	1	1	0	0	0	0	0	—	0	.214	.313	.500
1999 Tampa Bay	AL	6	19	4	1	0	0	(0	0)	5	0	0	0	0	2	0	0	0	0	0	—	2	.211	.211	.263
2000 Tampa Bay	AL	116	318	90	19	1	11	(7	4)	144	44	35	46	2	47	4	0	1	1	2	.33	9	.283	.379	.453
2001 Tampa Bay	AL	108	342	88	22	0	12	(3	9)	146	37	51	24	0	75	10	0	2	2	2	.50	11	.257	.323	.427
3 ML YEARS		230	679	182	42	1	23	(10	13)	295	81	86	70	2	124	14	0	3	3	4	.43	22	.268	.347	.434

Tim Crabtree

Pitches: Right **Bats:** Right **Pos:** RP-21 | **Ht:** 6'4" **Wt:** 220 **Born:** 10/13/69 **Age:** 32

Year Team	Lg	HOW MUCH HE PITCHED						WHAT HE GAVE UP												THE RESULTS						ERA
		G	GS	CG	GF	IP	BFP	H	R	ER	HR	SH	SF	HB	TBB	IBB	SO	WP	Bk	W	L	Pct.	ShO	Sv-Op	Hld	
2001 Tulsa *	AA	2	2	0	0	3	13	3	1	1	0	0	0	0	1	0	0	0	1	0	1	.000	0	0--	—	3.00
1995 Toronto	AL	31	0	0	19	32	141	30	16	11	1	0	1	2	13	0	21	2	0	0	2	.000	0	0-2	1	3.09
1996 Toronto	AL	53	0	0	21	67.1	284	59	26	19	4	2	3	2	22	4	57	3	0	5	3	.625	0	1-5	17	2.54
1997 Toronto	AL	37	0	0	16	40.2	199	65	32	32	7	4	2	2	17	3	26	4	0	3	3	.500	0	2-5	8	7.08
1998 Texas	AL	64	0	0	14	85.1	371	86	40	34	3	1	6	3	35	2	60	6	0	6	1	.857	0	0-1	10	3.59
1999 Texas	AL	68	0	0	21	65	275	71	26	25	4	1	1	1	18	1	54	5	0	5	1	.833	0	0-3	14	3.46
2000 Texas	AL	68	0	0	28	80.1	352	86	52	46	7	1	4	2	31	6	54	4	0	2	7	.222	0	2-9	11	5.15
2001 Texas	AL	21	0	0	14	23.1	117	37	18	17	3	3	3	1	14	2	16	3	0	0	5	.000	0	4-6	0	6.56
7 ML YEARS		342	0	0	133	394	1739	434	210	184	29	12	19	14	150	18	288	27	0	21	22	.488	0	9-31	61	4.20

Paxton Crawford

Pitches: Right **Bats:** Right **Pos:** SP-7; RP-1 | **Ht:** 6'3" **Wt:** 205 **Born:** 8/4/77 **Age:** 24

Year Team	Lg	HOW MUCH HE PITCHED						WHAT HE GAVE UP												THE RESULTS						ERA
		G	GS	CG	GF	IP	BFP	H	R	ER	HR	SH	SF	HB	TBB	IBB	SO	WP	Bk	W	L	Pct.	ShO	Sv-Op	Hld	
1995 Red Sox	R	12	7	1	4	46	184	38	17	14	2	0	0	1	12	0	44	6	0	1	3	.333	0	2--	—	2.74
1996 Michigan	A	22	22	1	0	128.1	548	120	62	51	5	2	5	8	42	1	105	8	1	6	11	.353	0	0--	—	3.58
1997 Sarasota	A+	12	11	2	0	65.1	289	69	42	33	6	4	2	1	27	2	56	3	0	4	8	.333	1	0--	—	4.55
1998 Trenton	AA	22	20	1	1	108	457	104	53	50	8	3	1	6	39	1	82	7	0	6	5	.545	0	0--	—	4.17
1999 Trenton	AA	28	28	1	0	163.1	696	151	81	74	12	7	4	10	59	1	111	10	1	7	8	.467	1	0--	—	4.08
2000 Trenton	AA	9	9	0	0	52.1	211	50	20	18	3	1	0	0	6	0	54	2	0	2	3	.400	0	0--	—	3.10
Pawtucket	AAA	12	11	1	1	61.1	252	47	32	31	6	6	2	6	22	1	47	0	0	7	4	.636	0	0--	—	4.55
2001 Pawtucket	AAA	6	6	1	0	29.1	133	43	19	18	4	0	1	2	7	1	15	1	0	1	3	.250	0	0--	—	5.52
2000 Boston	AL	7	4	0	2	29	123	25	15	11	0	4	2	1	13	2	17	0	0	2	1	.667	0	0-0	0	3.41

		HOW MUCH HE PITCHED			WHAT HE GAVE UP		THE RESULTS		
Year Team	Lg	G GS CG GF	IP	BFP	H R ER HR SH SF HB	TBB IBB	SO WP Bk	W L	Pct.	ShO Sv-Op Hld	ERA
2001 Boston	AL	8 7 0 1	36	161	40 19 19 3 0 1 2	13 0	25 2 0	3 0	1.000	0 0-0 0	4.75
2 ML YEARS		15 11 0 3	65	284	65 34 30 3 0 5 4	26 2	42 2 0	5 1	.833	0 0-0 0	4.15

Joe Crede

Bats: Right **Throws:** Right **Pos:** 3B-15; PH/PR-4 **Ht:** 6'2" **Wt:** 195 **Born:** 4/26/78 **Age:** 24

Year Team	Lg	G	AB	H	2B	3B	HR	(Hm	Rd)	TB	R	RBI	TBB	IBB	SO	HBP	SH	SF	SB	CS	SB%	GDP	Avg	OBP	SLG
1996 White Sox	R	56	221	66	17	1	4	—	—	97	30	32	9	0	41	2	1	4	1	1	.50	8	.299	.326	.439
1997 Hickory	A	113	402	109	25	0	5	—	—	149	45	62	24	0	83	5	0	2	3	1	.75	6	.271	.319	.371
1998 Winston-Sal	A+	137	492	155	32	3	20	—	—	253	92	88	53	3	98	12	0	11	9	7	.56	10	.315	.387	.514
1999 Birmingham	AA	74	291	73	14	1	4	—	—	101	37	42	22	1	47	1	0	3	2	6	.25	15	.251	.303	.347
2000 Birmingham	AA	138	533	163	35	0	21	—	—	261	84	94	56	10	111	15	1	5	3	4	.43	18	.306	.384	.490
2001 Charlotte	AAA	124	463	128	34	1	17	—	—	215	67	65	46	3	88	7	1	3	2	1	.67	5	.276	.349	.464
2000 Chicago	AL	7	14	5	1	0	0	(0	0)	6	2	3	0	0	3	0	0	1	0	0	—	0	.357	.333	.429
2001 Chicago	AL	17	50	11	1	1	0	(0	0)	14	1	7	3	0	11	1	0	1	1	0	1.00	1	.220	.273	.280
2 ML YEARS		24	64	16	2	1	0	(0	0)	20	3	10	3	0	14	1	0	2	1	0	1.00	1	.250	.286	.313

Doug Creek

Pitches: Left **Bats:** Left **Pos:** RP-66 **Ht:** 6'0" **Wt:** 200 **Born:** 3/1/69 **Age:** 33

		HOW MUCH HE PITCHED			WHAT HE GAVE UP		THE RESULTS		
Year Team	Lg	G GS CG GF	IP	BFP	H R ER HR SH SF HB	TBB IBB	SO WP Bk	W L	Pct.	ShO Sv-Op Hld	ERA
1995 St. Louis	NL	6 0 0 1	6.2	24	2 0 0 0 0 0 0	3 0	10 0 0	0 0	—	0 0-0 0	0.00
1996 San Francisco	NL	63 0 0 15	48.1	220	45 41 35 11 1 0 2	32 2	38 2 0	0 2	.000	0 0-1 7	6.52
1997 San Francisco	NL	3 3 0 0	13.1	64	12 12 10 1 0 0 2	14 0	14 0 0	1 2	.333	0 0-0 0	6.75
1999 Chicago	NL	3 0 0 2	6	32	6 7 7 1 0 1 0	8 1	6 1 0	0 0	—	0 0-0 0	10.50
2000 Tampa Bay	AL	45 0 0 8	60.2	265	49 33 31 10 2 3 2	39 3	73 3 0	1 3	.250	0 1-3 6	4.60
2001 Tampa Bay	AL	66 0 0 16	62.2	279	51 34 30 7 1 3 4	49 5	66 4 0	2 5	.286	0 0-3 15	4.31
6 ML YEARS		186 3 0 42	197.2	884	165 127 113 30 4 7 8	145 11	207 10 0	4 12	.250	0 1-7 24	5.15

Cesar Crespo

Bats: B **Throws:** R **Pos:** 2B-34; CF-11; LF-6; PH/PR-4; 3B-2; RF-2; SS-1 **Ht:** 5'11" **Wt:** 170 **Born:** 5/23/79 **Age:** 23

Year Team	Lg	G	AB	H	2B	3B	HR	(Hm	Rd)	TB	R	RBI	TBB	IBB	SO	HBP	SH	SF	SB	CS	SB%	GDP	Avg	OBP	SLG
1998 Capital City	A	116	428	108	18	4	6	—	—	152	61	48	44	1	114	3	7	1	47	14	.77	6	.252	.326	.355
1999 Brevard Cty	A+	115	427	122	17	2	6	—	—	161	63	40	62	2	86	1	7	1	22	8	.73	4	.286	.376	.377
2000 Portland	AA	134	482	124	21	6	9	—	—	184	96	60	77	3	118	2	8	5	41	15	.73	8	.257	.359	.382
2001 Portland	AAA	78	273	71	18	3	8	—	—	119	46	29	39	1	66	1	5	1	23	3	.88	4	.260	.354	.436
2001 San Diego	NL	55	153	32	6	0	4	(0	4)	50	27	12	25	0	50	0	1	0	6	2	.75	2	.209	.320	.327

Felipe Crespo

Bats: B **Throws:** R **Pos:** PH/PR-52; 1B-18; LF-4; 2B-3; DH-1; RF-1 **Ht:** 5'11" **Wt:** 200 **Born:** 3/5/73 **Age:** 29

Year Team	Lg	G	AB	H	2B	3B	HR	(Hm	Rd)	TB	R	RBI	TBB	IBB	SO	HBP	SH	SF	SB	CS	SB%	GDP	Avg	OBP	SLG
2001 Fresno *	AAA	3	8	3	1	0	1	—	—	7	2	1	0	0	3	0	0	0	0	0	—	0	.375	.375	.875
1996 Toronto	AL	22	49	9	4	0	0	(0	0)	13	6	4	12	0	13	3	0	0	1	0	1.00	0	.184	.375	.265
1997 Toronto	AL	12	28	8	0	1	1	(0	1)	13	3	5	2	0	4	0	1	0	0	0	—	1	.286	.333	.464
1998 Toronto	AL	66	130	34	8	1	1	(0	1)	47	11	15	15	1	27	2	4	2	4	3	.57	1	.262	.342	.362
2000 San Francisco	NL	89	131	38	6	1	4	(1	3)	58	17	29	10	2	23	4	2	3	3	2	.60	3	.290	.351	.443
2001 SF-Phi	NL	73	107	20	4	1	4	(4	0)	38	9	15	11	1	34	2	1	4	1	1	.50	2	.187	.266	.355
2001 San Francisco	NL	40	66	13	1	0	4	(4	0)	26	8	10	7	1	26	2	1	2	1	1	.50	2	.197	.286	.394
Philadelphia	NL	33	41	7	3	1	0	(0	0)	12	1	5	4	0	8	0	0	2	0	0	—	0	.171	.234	.293
5 ML YEARS		262	445	109	22	4	10	(5	5)	169	46	68	50	4	101	11	8	9	9	6	.60	7	.245	.330	.380

Jack Cressend

Pitches: Right **Bats:** Right **Pos:** RP-44 **Ht:** 6'1" **Wt:** 185 **Born:** 5/13/75 **Age:** 27

		HOW MUCH HE PITCHED			WHAT HE GAVE UP		THE RESULTS		
Year Team	Lg	G GS CG GF	IP	BFP	H R ER HR SH SF HB	TBB IBB	SO WP Bk	W L	Pct.	ShO Sv-Op Hld	ERA
1996 Lowell	A-	9 8 0 1	45.2	189	37 15 12 0 2 2 4	17 1	57 6 1	3 2	.600	0 0-- —	2.36
1997 Sarasota	A+	28 25 2 1	165.2	718	163 98 70 15 8 6 2	56 1	149 14 4	8 11	.421	1 0-- —	3.80
1998 Trenton	AA	29 29 1 0	149.1	646	168 86 72 13 10 2 5	55 0	130 6 0	10 11	.476	1 0-- —	4.34
1999 Trenton	AA	3 3 0 0	15	71	19 12 12 3 0 1 0	7 0	11 2 0	1 0	1.000	0 0-- —	7.20
New Britain	AA	25 24 2 0	145	629	152 79 70 10 3 5 5	50 0	125 4 2	7 10	.412	2 0-- —	4.34
2000 Salt Lake	AAA	54 1 0 20	86.1	380	87 40 33 3 4 3 1	39 4	87 6 0	4 4	.500	0 8-- —	3.44
2001 Edmonton	AAA	12 0 0 3	18	78	19 12 7 2 3 0 1	7 2	9 0 0	2 2	.500	0 1-- —	3.50
2000 Minnesota	AL	11 0 0 4	13.2	60	20 8 8 0 0 0 0	6 0	6 0 0	0 0	—	0 0-0 0	5.27
2001 Minnesota	AL	44 0 0 9	56.1	232	50 24 23 6 2 2 1	16 0	40 2 0	3 2	.600	0 0-2 5	3.67
2 ML YEARS		55 0 0 13	70	293	70 32 31 6 2 2 1	22 0	46 2 0	3 2	.600	0 0-2 5	3.99

D.T. Cromer

Bats: Left **Throws:** Left **Pos:** PH/PR-42; 1B-8; DH-1 **Ht:** 6'2" **Wt:** 220 **Born:** 3/19/71 **Age:** 31

Year Team	Lg	G	AB	H	2B	3B	HR	(Hm	Rd)	TB	R	RBI	TBB	IBB	SO	HBP	SH	SF	SB	CS	SB%	GDP	Avg	OBP	SLG
1992 Sou Oregon	A-	50	168	35	7	0	4	—	—	54	17	26	13	1	34	1	1	2	4	3	.57	2	.208	.268	.321
1993 Madison	A	98	321	84	20	4	4	—	—	124	37	41	22	0	72	1	1	7	8	6	.57	5	.262	.309	.386
1994 W Michigan	A	102	349	89	20	5	10	—	—	149	50	54	33	1	76	4	3	2	11	10	.52	5	.255	.325	.427
1995 Modesto	A+	108	378	98	18	5	14	—	—	168	59	52	36	1	66	4	6	6	5	7	.42	10	.259	.325	.444

51

Year Team	Lg	G	AB	H	2B	3B	HR	Hm	Rd	TB	R	RBI	TBB	IBB	SO	HBP	SH	SF	SB	CS	SB%	GDP	Avg	OBP	SLG
1996 Modesto	A+	124	505	166	40	10	30	—	—	316	100	130	32	4	67	6	3	4	20	7	.74	5	.329	.373	.626
1997 Huntsville	AA	134	545	176	40	6	15	—	—	273	100	121	60	4	102	3	0	6	12	7	.63	8	.323	.389	.501
1998 Edmonton	AAA	125	504	148	30	3	16	—	—	232	75	85	32	3	93	4	0	4	12	6	.67	9	.294	.338	.460
1999 Indianapols	AAA	136	535	166	37	4	30	—	—	301	83	107	44	3	98	3	0	7	4	2	.67	12	.310	.362	.563
2000 Louisville	AAA	106	415	112	26	3	14	—	—	186	58	67	33	1	84	1	0	7	6	4	.60	11	.270	.320	.448
2001 Louisville	AAA	62	242	69	12	2	11	—	—	118	35	49	15	3	48	2	0	2	4	2	.67	7	.285	.330	.488
2000 Cincinnati	NL	35	47	16	4	0	2	(0	2)	26	7	8	1	1	14	1	1	1	0	0	—	0	.340	.360	.553
2001 Cincinnati	NL	50	57	16	3	0	5	(1	4)	34	7	12	3	0	19	0	0	3	0	0	—	0	.281	.302	.596
2 ML YEARS		85	104	32	7	0	7	(1	6)	60	14	20	4	1	33	1	1	4	0	0	—	0	.308	.327	.577

Deivi Cruz

Bats: Right **Throws:** Right **Pos:** SS-109; 3B-7; PH/PR-1   **Ht:** 6'0" **Wt:** 184 **Born:** 11/6/75 **Age:** 26

Year Team	Lg	G	AB	H	2B	3B	HR	Hm	Rd	TB	R	RBI	TBB	IBB	SO	HBP	SH	SF	SB	CS	SB%	GDP	Avg	OBP	SLG
2001 Erie *	AA	4	12	5	1	0	1	—	—	9	2	3	0	0	0	0	0	0	1	0	1.00	0	.417	.417	.750
1997 Detroit	AL	147	436	105	26	0	2	(0	2)	137	35	40	14	0	55	0	14	3	3	6	.33	9	.241	.263	.314
1998 Detroit	AL	135	454	118	22	3	5	(5	0)	161	52	45	13	0	55	3	5	2	3	4	.43	11	.260	.284	.355
1999 Detroit	AL	155	518	147	35	0	13	(9	4)	221	64	58	12	0	57	4	14	5	1	4	.20	10	.284	.302	.427
2000 Detroit	AL	156	583	176	46	5	10	(1	9)	262	68	82	13	2	43	4	8	7	1	4	.20	25	.302	.318	.449
2001 Detroit	AL	110	414	106	28	1	7	(2	5)	157	39	52	17	0	46	4	1	2	4	1	.80	13	.256	.291	.379
5 ML YEARS		703	2405	652	157	9	37	(17	20)	938	258	277	69	2	256	15	42	19	12	19	.39	68	.271	.293	.390

Jacob Cruz

Bats: L **Throws:** L **Pos:** PH/PR-35; LF-21; CF-16; RF-11   **Ht:** 6'0" **Wt:** 210 **Born:** 1/28/73 **Age:** 29

Year Team	Lg	G	AB	H	2B	3B	HR	Hm	Rd	TB	R	RBI	TBB	IBB	SO	HBP	SH	SF	SB	CS	SB%	GDP	Avg	OBP	SLG
2001 Colo Sprngs *	AAA	20	86	28	5	2	6	—	—	55	18	25	1	0	23	1	0	1	1	0	1.00	2	.326	.337	.640
1996 San Francisco	NL	33	77	18	3	0	3	(3	0)	30	10	10	12	0	24	2	1	0	0	1	.00	2	.234	.352	.390
1997 San Francisco	NL	16	25	4	1	0	0	(0	0)	5	3	3	3	0	4	0	0	1	0	0	—	3	.160	.241	.200
1998 SF-Cle		4	4	0	0	0	0	(0	0)	0	0	0	0	0	3	0	0	0	0	0	—	0	.000	.000	.000
1999 Cleveland	AL	32	88	29	5	1	3	(0	0)	45	14	17	5	0	13	1	1	1	0	2	.00	4	.330	.368	.511
2000 Cleveland	AL	11	29	7	3	0	0	(0	0)	10	3	5	5	0	4	1	0	1	1	0	1.00	0	.241	.361	.345
2001 Cle-Col		72	144	31	5	0	4	(2	2)	48	19	18	15	0	50	4	1	2	0	4	.00	4	.215	.303	.333
1998 San Francisco	NL	3	3	0	0	0	0	(0	0)	0	0	0	0	0	2	0	0	0	0	0	—	0	.000	.000	.000
Cleveland	AL	1	1	0	0	0	0	(0	0)	0	0	0	0	0	1	0	0	0	0	0	—	0	.000	.000	.000
2001 Cleveland	AL	28	68	15	4	0	3	(2	1)	28	12	11	5	0	23	3	0	0	0	2	.00	3	.221	.303	.412
Colorado	NL	44	76	16	1	0	1	(0	1)	20	7	7	10	0	27	1	1	2	0	2	.00	1	.211	.303	.263
6 ML YEARS		168	367	89	17	1	10	(8	2)	138	49	53	40	0	98	8	3	5	1	7	.13	13	.243	.326	.376

Jose Cruz

Bats: B **Throws:** R **Pos:** CF-133; LF-14; PH/PR-5; DH-1   **Ht:** 6'0" **Wt:** 200 **Born:** 4/19/74 **Age:** 28

Year Team	Lg	G	AB	H	2B	3B	HR	Hm	Rd	TB	R	RBI	TBB	IBB	SO	HBP	SH	SF	SB	CS	SB%	GDP	Avg	OBP	SLG
1997 Sea-Tor	AL	104	395	98	19	1	26	(11	15)	197	59	68	41	2	117	0	1	5	7	2	.78	5	.248	.315	.499
1998 Toronto	AL	105	352	89	14	3	11	(4	7)	142	55	42	57	3	99	0	0	4	11	4	.73	0	.253	.354	.403
1999 Toronto	AL	106	349	84	19	3	14	(8	6)	151	63	45	64	5	91	0	1	0	14	4	.78	6	.241	.358	.433
2000 Toronto	AL	**162**	603	146	32	5	31	(15	16)	281	91	76	71	3	129	2	2	3	15	5	.75	11	.242	.323	.466
2001 Toronto	AL	146	577	158	38	4	34	(15	19)	306	92	88	45	4	138	1	2	2	32	5	.86	8	.274	.326	.530
1997 Seattle	AL	49	183	49	12	1	12	(7	5)	99	28	34	13	0	45	0	1	1	1	0	1.00	3	.268	.315	.541
Toronto	AL	55	212	49	7	0	14	(4	10)	98	31	34	28	2	72	0	0	4	6	2	.75	2	.231	.316	.462
5 ML YEARS		623	2276	575	122	16	116	(53	63)	1077	360	319	278	17	574	3	6	14	79	20	.80	30	.253	.333	.473

Juan Cruz

Pitches: Right **Bats:** Right **Pos:** SP-8   **Ht:** 6'2" **Wt:** 155 **Born:** 10/15/80 **Age:** 21

Year Team	Lg	G	GS	CG	GF	IP	BFP	H	R	ER	HR	SH	SF	HB	TBB	IBB	SO	WP	Bk	W	L	Pct.	ShO	Sv-Op	Hld	ERA
1998 Cubs	R	12	5	0	0	41.1	210	61	48	28	2	1	5	3	14	0	36	8	3	2	4	.333	0	0--	—	6.10
1999 Eugene	A-	15	15	0	0	80.1	374	97	59	53	11	1	4	9	33	0	65	4	0	5	6	.455	0	0--	—	5.94
2000 Lansing	A	17	17	2	0	96	423	75	50	35	6	1	0	13	60	0	106	8	1	5	5	.500	1	0--	—	3.28
Daytona	A+	8	7	1	0	44.1	182	30	22	16	5	0	0	3	18	0	54	4	0	3	0	1.000	0	0--	—	3.25
2001 West Tenn	AA	23	23	0	0	121.1	534	107	56	54	6	6	2	16	60	0	137	4	0	9	6	.600	0	0--	—	4.01
2001 Chicago	NL	8	8	0	0	44.2	185	40	16	16	4	2	0	2	17	1	39	0	0	3	1	.750	0	0-0	0	3.22

Nelson Cruz

Pitches: Right **Bats:** Right **Pos:** RP-66   **Ht:** 6'1" **Wt:** 185 **Born:** 9/13/72 **Age:** 29

Year Team	Lg	G	GS	CG	GF	IP	BFP	H	R	ER	HR	SH	SF	HB	TBB	IBB	SO	WP	Bk	W	L	Pct.	ShO	Sv-Op	Hld	ERA
1997 Chicago	AL	19	0	0	5	26.1	116	29	19	19	6	1	0		9	1	23	3	0	0	2	.000	0	0-0	6	6.49
1999 Detroit	AL	29	6	0	10	66.2	295	74	44	42	11	2	4	3	23	1	46	2	0	2	5	.286	0	0-0	4	5.67
2000 Detroit	AL	27	0	0	12	41	172	39	14	14	4	0	2	3	13	3	34	2	0	5	2	.714	0	0-1	2	3.07
2001 Houston	NL	66	0	0	16	82.1	342	72	41	38	11	3	2	9	24	4	75	0	1	3	3	.500	0	2-4	10	4.15
4 ML YEARS		141	6	0	43	216.1	925	214	118	113	32	6	8	15	69	9	178	7	1	10	12	.455	0	2-5	22	4.70

Darwin Cubillan

Pitches: Right **Bats:** Right **Pos:** RP-29   **Ht:** 6'2" **Wt:** 170 **Born:** 11/15/74 **Age:** 27

		HOW MUCH HE PITCHED					WHAT HE GAVE UP											THE RESULTS						
Year Team	Lg	G	GS	CG	GF	IP	BFP	H	R	ER	HR	SH	SF	HB	TBB	IBB	SO	WP	Bk	W	L	Pct.	ShO	Sv-Op	Hld	ERA
1994 Yankees	R	13	8	1	1	57.1	222	45	16	15	1	4	1	0	16	0	48	2	1	4	2	.667	1	0- -	—	2.35
Greensboro	A	1	0	0	0	2	15	6	5	4	1	0	0	0	2	0	1	0	0	0	0	—	0	0- -	—	18.00
1995 Greensboro	A	22	14	1	3	97	409	86	50	39	5	3	1	4	38	1	78	5	0	5	5	.500	1	0- -	—	3.62
1997 Yankees	R	1	1	0	0	1.2	7	1	0	0	0	0	0	0	1	0	2	0	0	0	0	—	0	0- -	—	0.00
1998 Tampa	A+	45	1	0	13	65	310	79	45	34	3	1	7	1	36	9	70	8	1	9	2	.818	0	1- -	—	4.71
1999 Tampa	A+	55	0	0	28	75.1	311	57	27	21	6	4	1	3	32	6	76	2	0	7	4	.636	0	3- -	—	2.51
2000 Syracuse	AAA	24	0	0	14	32.2	123	14	2	2	0	1	0	1	13	1	41	1	0	3	1	.750	0	6- -	—	0.55
Oklahoma	AAA	8	0	0	6	16.2	61	9	2	2	0	0	0	0	4	0	12	0	0	0	0	—	0	2- -	—	1.08
2001 Oklahoma	AAA	9	0	4	4	13	72	20	16	15	4	1	0	2	12	0	8	0	0	1	1	.500	0	2- -	—	10.38
Ottawa	AAA	17	4	0	8	30.2	137	31	22	18	2	2	2	2	15	1	29	4	0	2	2	.500	0	2- -	—	5.28
2000 Tor-Tex	AL	20	0	0	6	33.1	172	52	36	35	9	0	3	1	25	0	27	1	0	1	0	1.000	0	0-0	0	9.45
2001 Montreal	NL	29	0	0	11	26.1	121	31	13	12	1	1	3	0	12	1	19	1	0	0	0	—	0	0-0	1	4.10
2000 Toronto	AL	7	0	0	1	15.2	75	20	14	14	5	0	0	1	11	0	14	0	0	1	0	1.000	0	0-0	0	8.04
Texas	AL	13	0	0	5	17.2	97	32	22	21	4	0	3	0	14	0	13	1	0	0	0	—	0	0-0	0	10.70
2 ML YEARS		49	0	0	17	59.2	293	83	49	47	10	1	6	1	37	1	46	2	0	1	0	1.000	0	0-0	1	7.09

Mike Cuddyer

Bats: Right **Throws:** Right **Pos:** 1B-5; 3B-2; DH-1   **Ht:** 6'2" **Wt:** 202 **Born:** 3/27/79 **Age:** 23

		BATTING															BASERUNNING				PERCENTAGES		
Year Team	Lg	G	AB	H	2B	3B	HR	(Hm | Rd)	TB	R	RBI	TBB	IBB	SO	HBP	SH	SF	SB	CS	SB%	GDP	Avg	OBP	SLG
1998 Fort Wayne	A	129	497	137	37	7	12	—	—	224	82	81	61	3	107	10	0	4	16	7	.70	13	.276	.364	.451
1999 Fort Myers	A+	130	466	139	24	4	16	—	—	219	87	82	76	0	91	10	2	6	14	4	.78	20	.298	.403	.470
2000 New Britain	AA	138	490	129	30	8	6	—	—	193	72	61	55	2	93	12	6	2	5	4	.56	16	.263	.351	.394
2001 New Britain	AA	141	509	153	36	3	30	—	—	285	95	87	75	3	106	6	0	3	5	9	.36	6	.301	.395	.560
2001 Minnesota	AL	8	18	4	2	0	0	(0 | 0)	6	1	1	2	0	6	0	0	0	1	0	1.00	1	.222	.300	.333

Midre Cummings

Bats: Left **Throws:** Right **Pos:** PH/PR-18; LF-3; RF-1   **Ht:** 6'0" **Wt:** 195 **Born:** 10/14/71 **Age:** 30

		BATTING															BASERUNNING				PERCENTAGES		
Year Team	Lg	G	AB	H	2B	3B	HR	(Hm | Rd)	TB	R	RBI	TBB	IBB	SO	HBP	SH	SF	SB	CS	SB%	GDP	Avg	OBP	SLG
2001 Tucson *	AAA	77	263	87	23	9	5	—	—	143	38	38	24	1	49	0	0	3	2	3	.40	4	.331	.383	.544
1993 Pittsburgh	NL	13	36	4	1	0	0	(0 | 0)	5	5	3	4	0	9	0	0	1	0	0	—	1	.111	.195	.139
1994 Pittsburgh	NL	24	86	21	4	0	1	(1 | 0)	28	11	12	4	0	18	1	0	1	0	0	—	0	.244	.283	.326
1995 Pittsburgh	NL	59	152	37	7	1	2	(1 | 1)	52	13	15	13	3	30	1	0	1	1	0	1.00	1	.243	.303	.342
1996 Pittsburgh	NL	24	85	19	3	1	3	(2 | 1)	33	11	7	0	0	16	0	1	0	0	0	—	0	.224	.221	.388
1997 Pit-Phi	NL	115	314	83	22	6	4	(3 | 1)	129	35	31	31	0	56	1	2	2	2	3	.40	3	.264	.330	.411
1998 Boston	AL	67	120	34	8	0	5	(4 | 1)	57	20	15	17	0	19	2	1	0	3	3	.50	2	.283	.381	.475
1999 Minnesota	AL	16	38	10	0	0	1	(1 | 0)	13	1	9	3	0	7	0	0	1	2	0	1.00	0	.263	.310	.342
2000 Min-Bos	AL	98	206	57	10	0	4	(2 | 2)	79	29	24	17	1	28	3	1	0	0	0	—	5	.277	.341	.383
2001 Arizona	AL	20	20	6	1	0	0	(0 | 0)	7	1	1	0	0	4	0	0	1	0	0	—	2	.300	.286	.350
1997 Pittsburgh	NL	52	106	20	6	2	3	(2 | 1)	39	11	8	8	0	26	1	1	0	0	0	—	1	.189	.252	.368
Philadelphia	NL	63	208	63	16	4	1	(1 | 0)	90	24	23	23	0	30	0	1	2	2	3	.40	2	.303	.369	.433
2000 Minnesota	AL	77	181	50	10	0	4	(2 | 2)	72	28	22	11	1	25	3	1	0	0	0	—	4	.276	.328	.398
Boston	AL	21	25	7	0	0	0	(0 | 0)	7	1	2	6	0	3	0	0	0	0	0	—	1	.280	.419	.280
9 ML YEARS		436	1057	271	56	8	20	(14 | 6)	403	126	117	89	4	187	7	5	7	8	6	.57	14	.256	.316	.381

Will Cunnane

Pitches: Right **Bats:** Right **Pos:** RP-30; SP-1   **Ht:** 6'2" **Wt:** 200 **Born:** 4/24/74 **Age:** 28

		HOW MUCH HE PITCHED						WHAT HE GAVE UP											THE RESULTS						
Year Team	Lg	G	GS	CG	GF	IP	BFP	H	R	ER	HR	SH	SF	HB	TBB	IBB	SO	WP	Bk	W	L	Pct.	ShO	Sv-Op	Hld	ERA
2001 Indianapolis *	AAA	7	3	0	3	23.1	98	25	10	10	2	0	1	1	6	1	25	0	0	1	1	.000	0	1- -	—	3.86
1997 San Diego	NL	54	8	0	16	91.1	430	114	69	59	11	1	1	5	49	3	79	3	0	6	3	.667	0	0-2	4	5.81
1998 San Diego	NL	3	0	0	1	3	14	4	2	2	1	0	0	0	1	1	1	0	0	0	0	—	0	0-0	0	6.00
1999 San Diego	NL	24	0	0	2	31	130	34	19	18	8	2	0	0	12	3	22	3	0	2	1	.667	0	0-0	5	5.23
2000 San Diego	NL	27	3	0	4	38.1	169	35	21	18	2	1	1	1	21	0	34	1	0	1	1	.500	0	0-0	1	4.23
2001 Milwaukee	NL	31	1	0	6	51.2	238	66	34	31	6	7	1	2	22	6	37	0	0	0	3	.000	0	0-0	1	5.40
5 ML YEARS		139	12	0	29	215.1	981	253	145	128	28	11	3	8	105	13	173	7	0	9	8	.529	0	0-2	11	5.35

Chad Curtis

Bats: R **Throws:** R **Pos:** CF-16; LF-10; RF-9; PH/PR-5; DH-2   **Ht:** 5'10" **Wt:** 185 **Born:** 11/6/68 **Age:** 33

		BATTING															BASERUNNING				PERCENTAGES		
Year Team	Lg	G	AB	H	2B	3B	HR	(Hm | Rd)	TB	R	RBI	TBB	IBB	SO	HBP	SH	SF	SB	CS	SB%	GDP	Avg	OBP	SLG
2001 Oklahoma *	AAA	4	14	4	0	0	0	—	—	4	3	1	2	0	2	0	0	0	0	0	—	1	.286	.375	.286
Tulsa *	AA	6	22	4	0	0	1	—	—	7	3	2	5	0	6	2	0	0	1	0	1.00	0	.182	.379	.318
1992 California	AL	139	441	114	16	2	10	(5 | 5)	164	59	46	51	2	71	6	5	4	43	18	.70	10	.259	.341	.372
1993 California	AL	152	583	166	25	3	6	(3 | 3)	215	94	59	70	2	89	4	7	7	48	24	.67	16	.285	.361	.369
1994 California	AL	114	453	116	23	4	11	(8 | 3)	180	67	50	37	0	69	5	7	4	25	16	.61	10	.256	.317	.397
1995 Detroit	AL	144	586	157	29	3	21	(11 | 10)	255	96	67	70	3	93	7	0	7	27	15	.64	10	.268	.349	.435
1996 Det-LA	AL	147	504	127	25	1	12	(3 | 9)	190	85	46	70	0	88	1	6	6	18	11	.62	15	.252	.341	.377
1997 Cle-NYY	AL	115	349	99	22	1	15	(4 | 11)	168	59	55	43	1	59	5	2	9	12	6	.67	7	.284	.362	.481
1998 New York	AL	151	456	111	21	1	10	(6 | 4)	164	79	56	75	3	80	7	1	6	21	5	.81	11	.243	.355	.360
1999 New York	AL	96	195	51	8	0	5	(0 | 5)	72	37	24	43	0	35	3	1	3	8	4	.67	6	.262	.398	.369
2000 Texas	AL	108	335	91	25	1	8	(5 | 3)	142	48	42	37	0	71	1	5	3	3	3	.50	12	.272	.343	.424
2001 Texas	AL	38	115	29	3	0	3	(1 | 2)	41	24	10	14	0	21	1	0	0	7	1	.88	3	.252	.338	.357
1996 Detroit	AL	104	400	105	20	1	10	(2 | 8)	157	65	37	53	0	73	1	6	6	16	10	.62	14	.263	.346	.393
Los Angeles	NL	43	104	22	5	0	2	(1 | 1)	33	20	9	17	0	15	0	0	0	2	1	.67	1	.212	.322	.317

Year Team	Lg	G	AB	H	2B	3B	HR	(Hm	Rd)	TB	R	RBI	TBB	IBB	SO	HBP	SH	SF	SB	CS	SB%	GDP	Avg	OBP	SLG
1997 Cleveland	AL	22	29	6	1	0	3	(1	2)	16	8	5	7	0	10	0	0	0	0	0	—	1	.207	.361	.552
New York	AL	93	320	93	21	1	12	(3	9)	152	51	50	36	1	49	5	2	9	12	6	.67	6	.291	.362	.475
10 ML YEARS		1204	4017	1061	195	16	101	(46	55)	1591	648	461	510	11	676	40	34	49	212	98	.68	102	.264	.349	.396

Jack Cust

Bats: Left **Throws:** Right **Pos:** PH/PR-2; LF-1   **Ht:** 6'1" **Wt:** 205 **Born:** 1/16/79 **Age:** 23

Year Team	Lg	G	AB	H	2B	3B	HR	(Hm	Rd)	TB	R	RBI	TBB	IBB	SO	HBP	SH	SF	SB	CS	SB%	GDP	Avg	OBP	SLG
1997 Diamndbcks	R	35	121	37	11	1	3	—	—	59	26	33	31	0	39	0	0	0	2	0	1.00	4	.306	.447	.488
1998 South Bend	A	16	62	15	3	0	0	—	—	18	5	4	5	1	20	0	0	1	0	1	.00	0	.242	.294	.290
Lethbridge	R+	73	223	77	20	2	11	—	—	134	75	56	86	3	71	4	0	2	15	8	.65	3	.345	.530	.601
1999 High Desert	A+	125	455	152	42	3	32	—	—	296	107	112	96	2	145	2	0	3	1	4	.20	5	.334	.450	.651
2000 El Paso	AA	129	447	131	32	6	20	—	—	235	100	75	117	12	150	2	0	2	12	9	.57	10	.293	.440	.526
2001 Tucson	AAA	135	442	123	24	2	27	—	—	232	81	79	102	3	160	5	0	5	6	3	.67	10	.278	.415	.525
2001 Arizona	NL	3	2	1	0	0	0	(0	0)	1	0	0	1	0	0	0	0	0	0	0	—	0	.500	.667	.500

Omar Daal

Pitches: Left **Bats:** Left **Pos:** SP-32   **Ht:** 6'3" **Wt:** 195 **Born:** 3/1/72 **Age:** 30

Year Team	Lg	G	GS	CG	GF	IP	BFP	H	R	ER	HR	SH	SF	HB	TBB	IBB	SO	WP	Bk	W	L	Pct.	ShO	Sv-Op	Hld	ERA
1993 Los Angeles	NL	47	0	0	12	35.1	155	36	20	20	5	2	2	0	21	3	19	1	2	2	3	.400	0	0-1	7	5.09
1994 Los Angeles	NL	24	0	0	5	13.2	55	12	5	5	1	1	0	0	5	0	9	1	1	0	0	—	0	0-0	3	3.29
1995 Los Angeles	NL	28	0	0	10	20	100	29	16	16	1	1	1	1	15	4	11	0	1	4	0	1.000	0	0-1	4	7.20
1996 Montreal	NL	64	6	0	9	87.1	366	74	40	39	10	2	2	1	37	3	82	1	1	4	5	.444	0	0-4	9	4.02
1997 Mon-Tor		42	3	0	6	57.1	270	82	48	45	7	7	1	2	21	3	44	2	0	2	3	.400	0	1-3	3	7.06
1998 Arizona	NL	33	23	3	4	162.2	664	146	60	52	12	9	6	3	51	3	132	0	1	8	12	.400	1	0-0	1	2.88
1999 Arizona	NL	32	32	2	0	214.2	895	188	92	87	21	4	7	7	79	3	148	3	2	16	9	.640	1	0-0	0	3.65
2000 Ari-Phi	NL	32	28	0	1	167	775	208	128	114	26	6	6	9	72	11	96	0	2	4	19	.174	0	0-0	0	6.14
2001 Philadelphia	NL	32	32	0	0	185.2	801	199	100	92	26	7	5	5	56	3	107	0	3	13	7	.650	0	0-0	0	4.46
1997 Montreal	NL	33	0	0	6	30.1	150	48	35	33	4	5	1	2	15	3	16	1	0	1	2	.333	0	1-3	3	9.79
Toronto	AL	9	3	0	0	27	120	34	13	12	3	2	0	0	6	0	28	1	0	1	1	.500	0	0-0	0	4.00
2000 Arizona	NL	20	16	0	1	96	460	127	88	77	17	3	5	7	42	11	45	0	1	2	10	.167	0	0-0	0	7.22
Philadelphia	NL	12	12	0	0	71	315	81	40	37	9	3	1	2	30	0	51	0	1	2	9	.182	0	0-0	0	4.69
9 ML YEARS		334	124	5	37	943.2	4081	974	509	470	109	39	30	28	357	33	648	8	13	53	58	.477	2	1-9	27	4.48

Mark Dalesandro

Bats: Right **Throws:** Right **Pos:** C-1   **Ht:** 6'0" **Wt:** 195 **Born:** 5/14/68 **Age:** 34

Year Team	Lg	G	AB	H	2B	3B	HR	(Hm	Rd)	TB	R	RBI	TBB	IBB	SO	HBP	SH	SF	SB	CS	SB%	GDP	Avg	OBP	SLG
2001 Charlotte *	AAA	75	262	68	18	0	4	—	—	98	16	23	6	0	24	3	3	3	0	1	.00	6	.260	.281	.374
1994 California	AL	19	25	5	1	0	1	(1	0)	9	5	2	2	0	4	0	0	0	0	0	—	2	.200	.259	.360
1995 California	AL	11	10	1	1	0	0	(0	0)	2	1	0	0	0	2	0	0	0	0	0	—	0	.100	.100	.200
1998 Toronto	AL	32	67	20	5	0	2	(1	1)	31	8	14	1	0	6	0	0	1	0	0	—	3	.299	.304	.463
1999 Toronto	AL	16	27	5	0	0	0	(0	0)	5	3	1	0	0	2	1	0	1	1	0	1.00	1	.185	.207	.185
2001 Chicago	AL	1	0	0	0	0	0	(0	0)	0	0	0	0	0	0	0	0	0	0	0	—	0	—	—	—
5 ML YEARS		79	129	31	7	0	3	(2	1)	47	17	17	3	0	14	1	0	2	1	0	1.00	6	.240	.259	.364

Jeff D'Amico

Pitches: Right **Bats:** Right **Pos:** SP-10   **Ht:** 6'7" **Wt:** 250 **Born:** 12/27/75 **Age:** 26

Year Team	Lg	G	GS	CG	GF	IP	BFP	H	R	ER	HR	SH	SF	HB	TBB	IBB	SO	WP	Bk	W	L	Pct.	ShO	Sv-Op	Hld	ERA
2001 Huntsville *	AA	1	1	0	0	7	25	3	2	2	0	0	0	0	2	0	5	0	0	1	0	1.000	0	0--	0	2.57
Beloit *	A	2	2	0	0	8.1	37	11	6	5	1	0	0	0	1	0	6	0	0	0	0	—	0	0--	0	5.40
1996 Milwaukee	AL	17	17	0	0	86	367	88	53	52	21	3	3	0	31	0	53	1	1	6	6	.500	0	0-0	0	5.44
1997 Milwaukee	AL	23	23	1	0	135.2	585	139	81	71	25	4	4	8	43	2	94	3	1	9	7	.563	0	0-0	0	4.71
1999 Milwaukee	NL	1	0	0	1	4		1	0	0	0	0	0	0	0	0	1	0	0	0	0	—	0	0-0	0	0.00
2000 Milwaukee	NL	23	23	1	0	162.1	667	143	55	48	14	10	3	6	46	5	101	5	0	12	7	.632	1	0-0	0	2.66
2001 Milwaukee	NL	10	10	0	0	47.1	216	60	42	32	11	2	1	1	16	4	32	2	0	2	4	.333	0	0-0	0	6.08
5 ML YEARS		74	73	2	1	432.1	1839	431	231	203	71	19	11	15	136	11	281	11	2	29	24	.547	2	0-0	0	4.23

Johnny Damon

Bats: L **Throws:** L **Pos:** CF-86; LF-67; RF-5; PH/PR-2; 1B-1   **Ht:** 6'2" **Wt:** 190 **Born:** 11/5/73 **Age:** 28

Year Team	Lg	G	AB	H	2B	3B	HR	(Hm	Rd)	TB	R	RBI	TBB	IBB	SO	HBP	SH	SF	SB	CS	SB%	GDP	Avg	OBP	SLG
1995 Kansas City	AL	47	188	53	11	5	3	(1	2)	83	32	23	12	0	22	1	2	3	7	0	1.00	2	.282	.324	.441
1996 Kansas City	AL	145	517	140	22	5	6	(3	3)	190	61	50	31	3	64	3	10	5	25	5	.83	4	.271	.313	.368
1997 Kansas City	AL	146	472	130	12	8	8	(3	5)	182	70	48	42	2	70	3	6	1	16	10	.62	3	.275	.338	.386
1998 Kansas City	AL	161	642	178	30	10	18	(11	7)	282	104	66	58	4	84	4	3	4	26	12	.68	4	.277	.339	.439
1999 Kansas City	AL	145	583	179	39	9	14	(5	9)	278	101	77	67	5	50	3	4	4	36	6	.86	13	.307	.379	.477
2000 Kansas City	AL	159	655	214	42	10	16	(10	6)	324	136	88	65	4	60	1	8	12	46	9	.84	7	.327	.382	.495
2001 Oakland	AL	155	644	165	34	4	9	(7	2)	234	108	49	61	1	70	5	5	4	27	12	.69	7	.256	.324	.363
7 ML YEARS		958	3701	1059	190	51	74	(35	39)	1573	612	401	336	19	420	20	37	32	183	54	.77	40	.286	.346	.425

54

Vic Darensbourg

Pitches: Left **Bats:** Left **Pos:** RP-58   **Ht:** 5'10" **Wt:** 165 **Born:** 11/13/70 **Age:** 31

Year Team	Lg	G	GS	CG	GF	IP	BFP	H	R	ER	HR	SH	SF	HB	TBB	IBB	SO	WP	Bk	W	L	Pct.	ShO	Sv-Op	Hld	ERA
1998 Florida	NL	59	0	0	10	71	287	52	29	29	5	3	3	0	30	6	74	4	0	0	7	.000	0	1-2	13	3.68
1999 Florida	NL	56	0	0	5	34.2	180	50	36	34	3	5	2	5	21	1	16	1	3	0	0	.000	0	0-1	10	8.83
2000 Florida	NL	56	0	0	17	62	274	61	32	28	7	3	6	2	28	1	59	1	0	5	3	.625	0	0-1	3	4.06
2001 Florida	NL	58	0	0	19	48.2	202	52	24	23	4	1	2	1	10	6	33	0	0	1	2	.333	0	1-3	11	4.25
4 ML YEARS		229	0	0	51	216.1	943	215	121	114	19	12	13	8	89	14	182	6	3	6	13	.316	0	2-7	37	4.74

Mike Darr

Bats: L **Throws:** R **Pos:** RF-69; CF-29; PH/PR-18; LF-5   **Ht:** 6'3" **Wt:** 205 **Born:** 3/21/76 **Age:** 26

Year Team	Lg	G	AB	H	2B	3B	HR	(Hm	Rd)	TB	R	RBI	TBB	IBB	SO	HBP	SH	SF	SB	CS	SB%	GDP	Avg	OBP	SLG
2001 Mobile *	AA	2	5	1	0	0	0	—	—	1	1	0	2	0	4	0	0	0	0	0	—	0	.200	.429	.200
1999 San Diego	NL	25	48	13	1	0	2	(1	1)	20	6	3	5	0	18	0	0	0	2	1	.67	1	.271	.340	.417
2000 San Diego	NL	58	205	55	14	4	1	(1	0)	80	21	30	23	1	45	0	0	0	9	1	.90	9	.268	.342	.390
2001 San Diego	NL	105	289	80	13	1	2	(2	0)	101	36	34	39	3	72	1	0	2	6	2	.75	8	.277	.363	.349
3 ML YEARS		188	542	148	28	5	5	(4	1)	201	63	67	67	4	135	1	0	2	17	4	.81	18	.273	.353	.371

Brian Daubach

Bats: L **Throws:** R **Pos:** 1B-106; RF-8; LF-6; PH/PR-6   **Ht:** 6'1" **Wt:** 201 **Born:** 2/11/72 **Age:** 30

Year Team	Lg	G	AB	H	2B	3B	HR	(Hm	Rd)	TB	R	RBI	TBB	IBB	SO	HBP	SH	SF	SB	CS	SB%	GDP	Avg	OBP	SLG
2001 Pawtucket *	AAA	1	4	1	0	0	0	—	—	1	0	0	0	0	2	0	0	0	0	0	—	0	.250	.250	.250
Lowell *	A-	1	2	0	0	0	0	—	—	0	0	1	1	0	1	0	0	0	0	0	—	0	.000	.333	.000
1998 Florida	NL	10	15	3	1	0	0	(0	0)	4	0	3	1	0	5	1	0	0	0	0	—	0	.200	.294	.267
1999 Boston	AL	110	381	112	33	3	21	(11	10)	214	61	73	36	0	92	3	0	0	0	1	.00	5	.294	.360	.562
2000 Boston	AL	142	495	123	32	2	21	(10	11)	222	55	76	44	2	130	6	0	4	1	1	.50	6	.248	.315	.448
2001 Boston	AL	122	407	107	28	3	22	(11	11)	207	54	71	53	7	108	5	1	6	1	0	1.00	10	.263	.350	.509
4 ML YEARS		384	1298	345	94	8	64	(32	32)	647	170	223	134	9	335	15	1	10	2	2	.50	21	.266	.339	.498

Jeff DaVanon

Bats: B **Throws:** R **Pos:** RF-17; CF-13; PH/PR-11; DH-6   **Ht:** 6'0" **Wt:** 185 **Born:** 12/8/73 **Age:** 28

Year Team	Lg	G	AB	H	2B	3B	HR	(Hm	Rd)	TB	R	RBI	TBB	IBB	SO	HBP	SH	SF	SB	CS	SB%	GDP	Avg	OBP	SLG
1995 Sou Oregon	A-	57	167	42	6	2	1	—	—	55	29	17	34	0	49	0	5	1	6	5	.55	1	.251	.376	.329
1996 W Michigan	A	89	289	70	13	4	2	—	—	97	43	33	49	2	66	1	2	1	5	7	.42	6	.242	.353	.336
1997 Visalia	A+	119	408	104	17	3	6	—	—	145	70	38	81	1	101	0	10	2	23	14	.62	7	.255	.377	.355
1998 Modesto	A+	84	301	101	17	4	5	—	—	141	66	60	59	1	69	1	0	6	33	10	.77	4	.336	.439	.468
1999 Midland	AA	100	374	128	29	11	11	—	—	212	87	60	53	3	68	4	4	5	18	10	.64	6	.342	.424	.567
Edmonton	AAA	34	132	43	8	3	6	—	—	75	35	19	20	0	27	1	1	1	11	4	.73	1	.326	.416	.568
2001 Salt Lake	AAA	69	256	80	19	8	10	—	—	145	46	48	32	2	57	3	1	4	8	3	.73	4	.313	.390	.566
1999 Anaheim	AL	7	20	4	0	1	1	(1	0)	9	4	4	2	0	7	0	0	0	0	1	.00	0	.200	.273	.450
2001 Anaheim	AL	40	88	17	2	1	5	(3	2)	36	7	9	11	0	29	0	0	1	1	3	.25	1	.193	.280	.409
2 ML YEARS		47	108	21	2	2	6	(4	2)	45	11	13	13	0	36	0	0	1	1	4	.20	1	.194	.279	.417

Joe Davenport

Pitches: Right **Bats:** Right **Pos:** RP-7   **Ht:** 6'5" **Wt:** 225 **Born:** 3/24/76 **Age:** 26

Year Team	Lg	G	GS	CG	GF	IP	BFP	H	R	ER	HR	SH	SF	HB	TBB	IBB	SO	WP	Bk	W	L	Pct.	ShO	Sv-Op	Hld	ERA
1994 Blue Jays	R	7	1	0	2	11	48	12	5	4	0	0	1	1	7	0	2	1	1	0	0	—	0	0--	—	3.27
1995 Hagerstown	A	13	0	0	2	17.2	91	22	19	12	3	0	4	1	13	0	13	6	0	0	1	.000	0	0--	—	6.11
Blue Jays	R	15	10	1	1	55.2	267	67	47	35	2	3	2	3	30	0	29	9	3	2	3	.400	0	1--	—	5.66
1996 St.Cathrnes	A-	20	8	0	3	66.2	295	71	44	38	5	4	3	5	23	0	43	8	0	2	4	.333	0	0--	—	5.13
1997 Hagerstown	A	37	0	0	29	51.1	225	43	26	21	0	4	1	4	24	2	43	8	0	4	6	.400	0	10--	—	3.68
1998 Winston-Sal	A+	20	0	0	15	26	106	25	9	4	0	1	0	2	4	0	26	3	0	2	0	1.000	0	2--	—	1.38
Birmingham	AA	26	0	0	15	38.2	202	54	36	31	2	1	4	2	30	0	22	5	0	3	2	.600	0	1--	—	7.22
1999 Charlotte	AAA	6	0	0	1	9	40	13	8	8	0	0	0	1	1	0	6	0	0	0	0	—	0	0--	—	8.00
Birmingham	AA	40	0	0	33	49.1	213	43	26	17	3	4	3	2	19	1	24	8	0	3	5	.375	0	10--	—	3.10
2000 Charlotte	AAA	59	0	0	33	70.2	314	74	41	36	6	7	4	11	27	2	42	7	1	1	4	.200	0	9--	—	4.58
2001 Colo Sprngs	AAA	31	0	0	9	34	181	62	38	32	3	1	1	5	15	0	23	3	0	2	2	.500	0	0--	—	8.47
1999 Chicago	AL	3	0	0	2	1.2	7	1	0	0	0	0	0	0	2	0	0	0	0	0	0	—	0	0-0	0	0.00
2001 Colorado	NL	7	0	0	3	10.1	44	8	7	4	1	1	0	0	7	0	8	0	0	0	0	—	0	0-0	0	3.48
2 ML YEARS		10	0	0	5	12	51	9	7	4	1	1	0	0	9	0	8	0	0	0	0	—	0	0-0	0	3.00

Tom Davey

Pitches: Right **Bats:** Right **Pos:** RP-39   **Ht:** 6'7" **Wt:** 230 **Born:** 9/11/73 **Age:** 28

Year Team	Lg	G	GS	CG	GF	IP	BFP	H	R	ER	HR	SH	SF	HB	TBB	IBB	SO	WP	Bk	W	L	Pct.	ShO	Sv-Op	Hld	ERA
1999 Tor-Sea	AL	45	0	0	15	65	298	62	34	34	5	1	2	7	40	1	59	6	0	2	1	.667	0	1-1	5	4.71
2000 San Diego	NL	11	0	0	2	12.2	50	12	1	1	0	0	0	0	2	0	6	1	0	2	1	.667	0	0-1	2	0.71
2001 San Diego	NL	39	0	0	8	38	169	41	22	19	3	0	0	1	17	3	37	3	1	2	4	.333	0	0-4	12	4.50
1999 Toronto	AL	29	0	0	10	44	198	40	28	23	5	1	2	3	26	0	42	6	0	1	1	.500	0	1-1	3	4.70
Seattle	AL	16	0	0	5	21	100	22	13	11	0	0	0	4	14	1	17	0	0	1	0	1.000	0	0-0	1	4.71
3 ML YEARS		95	0	0	25	115.2	517	115	64	54	8	1	2	8	59	4	102	10	1	6	6	.500	0	1-6	18	4.20

Ben Davis

Bats: Both **Throws:** Right **Pos:** C-135; PH/PR-4; 1B-2 **Ht:** 6'4" **Wt:** 215 **Born:** 3/10/77 **Age:** 25

Year Team	Lg	G	AB	H	2B	3B	HR	(Hm	Rd)	TB	R	RBI	TBB	IBB	SO	HBP	SH	SF	SB	CS	SB%	GDP	Avg	OBP	SLG
1998 San Diego	NL	1	1	0	0	0	0	(0	0)	0	0	0	0	0	0	0	0	0	0	0	—	0	.000	.000	.000
1999 San Diego	NL	76	266	65	14	1	5	(1	4)	96	29	30	25	3	70	0	0	2	2	1	.67	9	.244	.307	.361
2000 San Diego	NL	43	130	29	6	0	3	(1	2)	44	12	14	14	1	35	0	3	1	1	1	.50	2	.223	.297	.338
2001 San Diego	NL	138	448	107	20	0	11	(3	8)	160	56	57	66	5	112	4	1	7	4	4	.50	13	.239	.337	.357
4 ML YEARS		258	845	201	40	1	19	(5	14)	300	97	101	105	9	217	4	4	10	7	6	.54	24	.238	.322	.355

Doug Davis

Pitches: Left **Bats:** Right **Pos:** SP-30 **Ht:** 6'4" **Wt:** 190 **Born:** 9/21/75 **Age:** 26

		HOW MUCH HE PITCHED						WHAT HE GAVE UP										THE RESULTS						
Year Team	Lg	G	GS	CG	GF	IP	BFP	H	R	ER	HR	SH	SF	HB	TBB	IBB	SO	WP	Bk	W	L	Pct.	ShO	Sv-Op	Hld	ERA
2001 Oklahoma *	AAA	2	2	0	0	15.2	59	10	5	5	1	0	1	1	4	0	14	0	0	2	0	1.000	0	0- -	—	2.87
1999 Texas	AL	2	0	0	0	2.2	20	12	10	10	3	0	0	0	0	0	3	0	0	0	0	—	0	0-0	0	33.75
2000 Texas	AL	30	13	1	4	98.2	450	109	61	59	14	6	4	3	58	3	66	5	1	7	6	.538	0	0-3	2	5.38
2001 Texas	AL	30	30	1	0	186	828	220	103	92	14	4	6	3	69	1	115	7	2	11	10	.524	0	0-0	0	4.45
3 ML YEARS		62	43	2	4	287.1	1298	341	174	161	31	10	10	6	127	4	184	12	3	18	16	.529	0	0-3	2	5.04

Eric Davis

Bats: Right **Throws:** Right **Pos:** RF-48; PH/PR-31; DH-1 **Ht:** 6'3" **Wt:** 185 **Born:** 5/29/62 **Age:** 40

Year Team	Lg	G	AB	H	2B	3B	HR	(Hm	Rd)	TB	R	RBI	TBB	IBB	SO	HBP	SH	SF	SB	CS	SB%	GDP	Avg	OBP	SLG
1984 Cincinnati	NL	57	174	39	10	1	10	(3	7)	81	33	30	24	0	48	1	0	1	10	2	.83	1	.224	.320	.466
1985 Cincinnati	NL	56	122	30	3	3	8	(1	7)	63	26	18	7	0	39	0	2	0	16	3	.84	1	.246	.287	.516
1986 Cincinnati	NL	132	415	115	15	3	27	(12	15)	217	97	71	68	5	100	1	0	3	80	11	.88	6	.277	.378	.523
1987 Cincinnati	NL	129	474	139	23	4	37	(17	20)	281	120	100	84	8	134	1	0	3	50	6	.89	6	.293	.399	.593
1988 Cincinnati	NL	135	472	129	18	3	26	(14	12)	231	81	93	65	10	124	3	0	3	35	3	.92	11	.273	.363	.489
1989 Cincinnati	NL	131	462	130	14	2	34	(15	19)	250	74	101	68	12	116	1	0	11	21	7	.75	16	.281	.367	.541
1990 Cincinnati	NL	127	453	118	26	2	24	(13	11)	220	84	86	60	6	100	2	0	3	21	3	.88	7	.260	.347	.486
1991 Cincinnati	NL	89	285	67	10	0	11	(5	6)	110	39	33	48	5	92	5	0	2	14	2	.88	4	.235	.353	.386
1992 Los Angeles	NL	76	267	61	8	1	5	(1	4)	86	21	32	36	2	71	3	0	2	19	1	.95	9	.228	.325	.322
1993 LA-Det		131	451	107	18	1	20	(10	10)	187	71	68	55	7	106	1	0	4	35	7	.83	12	.237	.319	.415
1994 Detroit	AL	37	120	22	4	0	3	(0	3)	35	19	13	18	0	45	0	0	0	5	0	1.00	4	.183	.290	.292
1996 Cincinnati	NL	129	415	119	20	0	26	(8	18)	217	81	83	70	3	121	6	1	4	23	9	.72	8	.287	.394	.523
1997 Baltimore	AL	42	158	48	11	0	8	(1	7)	83	29	25	14	0	47	1	0	3	6	0	1.00	4	.304	.358	.525
1998 Baltimore	AL	131	452	148	29	1	28	(16	12)	263	81	89	44	0	108	5	0	7	7	6	.54	13	.327	.388	.582
1999 St. Louis	NL	58	191	49	9	2	5	(2	3)	77	27	30	30	1	49	1	0	1	5	4	.56	1	.257	.359	.403
2000 St. Louis	NL	92	254	77	14	0	6	(2	4)	109	38	40	36	0	60	1	0	2	1	1	.50	7	.303	.389	.429
2001 San Francisco	NL	74	156	32	7	3	4	(3	1)	57	17	22	13	0	38	1	0	1	1	1	.50	4	.205	.269	.365
1993 Los Angeles	NL	108	376	88	17	0	14	(7	7)	147	57	53	41	6	88	1	0	4	33	5	.87	8	.234	.308	.391
Detroit	AL	23	75	19	1	1	6	(3	3)	40	14	15	14	1	18	0	0	0	2	2	.50	4	.253	.371	.533
17 ML YEARS		1626	5321	1430	239	26	282	(132	150)	2567	938	934	740	59	1398	33	3	50	349	66	.84	112	.269	.359	.482

Kane Davis

Pitches: Right **Bats:** Right **Pos:** RP-57 **Ht:** 6'3" **Wt:** 194 **Born:** 6/25/75 **Age:** 27

		HOW MUCH HE PITCHED						WHAT HE GAVE UP										THE RESULTS						
Year Team	Lg	G	GS	CG	GF	IP	BFP	H	R	ER	HR	SH	SF	HB	TBB	IBB	SO	WP	Bk	W	L	Pct.	ShO	Sv-Op	Hld	ERA
1993 Pirates	R	11	4	0	5	28	140	34	30	22	0	3	2	0	19	1	24	2	0	0	4	.000	0	0- -	—	7.07
1994 Welland	A-	15	15	2	0	98.1	400	90	36	29	4	2	2	3	32	1	74	7	1	5	5	.500	0	0- -	—	2.65
1995 Augusta	A	26	25	1	0	139.1	602	136	73	58	4	3	4	9	43	0	78	10	1	12	6	.667	0	0- -	—	3.75
1996 Lynchburg	A+	26	26	3	0	157.1	684	160	84	75	12	12	3	10	56	0	116	11	2	11	9	.550	1	0- -	—	4.29
1997 Carolina	AA	6	6	0	0	28.2	128	22	17	12	2	2	1	3	16	1	23	2	0	3	0	1.000	0	0- -	—	3.77
1998 Augusta	A	2	2	0	0	9	36	8	6	6	0	1	1	0	3	0	6	0	2	0	0	—	0	0- -	—	6.00
Carolina	AA	18	16	0	0	74	362	102	84	76	12	4	0	7	38	2	39	10	1	1	11	.083	0	0- -	—	9.24
1999 Altoona	AA	16	16	0	0	95.1	421	97	51	40	5	2	4	3	41	1	53	4	0	6	4	.600	0	0- -	—	3.78
Nashville	AAA	12	9	0	1	49.1	224	65	38	37	8	2	1	3	17	1	31	2	0	3	2	.600	0	0- -	—	6.75
2000 Akron	AA	5	5	0	0	20	78	17	7	6	2	0	0	0	5	0	13	3	0	1	0	1.000	0	0- -	—	2.70
Buffalo	AAA	6	4	0	1	30	131	30	16	14	2	2	0	1	12	0	19	2	0	2	0	1.000	0	0- -	—	4.20
Indianapols	AAA	4	4	0	0	20.1	83	19	8	8	2	0	0	1	7	0	12	0	0	1	1	.500	0	0- -	—	3.54
2001 Colo Sprngs	AAA	4	0	0	1	5	22	5	2	2	0	0	0	0	3	1	7	0	0	0	0	—	0	0- -	—	3.60
2000 Cle-Mil		8	2	0	1	15	85	27	24	21	4	0	0	2	13	0	4	0	1	0	3	.000	0	0-0	0	12.60
2001 Colorado	NL	57	0	0	6	68.1	301	66	36	33	11	2	4	1	32	4	47	4	0	2	4	.333	0	0-5	9	4.35
2000 Cleveland	AL	5	2	0	0	11	61	20	21	18	3	0	0	1	8	0	2	0	1	0	3	.000	0	0-0	0	14.73
Milwaukee	NL	3	0	0	1	4	24	7	3	3	1	0	0	1	5	0	2	0	0	0	0	—	0	0-0	0	6.75
2 ML YEARS		65	2	0	7	83.1	386	93	60	54	15	2	4	3	45	4	51	4	1	2	7	.222	0	0-5	9	5.83

Lance Davis

Pitches: Left **Bats:** Right **Pos:** SP-20 **Ht:** 5'11" **Wt:** 165 **Born:** 9/1/76 **Age:** 25

		HOW MUCH HE PITCHED						WHAT HE GAVE UP										THE RESULTS						
Year Team	Lg	G	GS	CG	GF	IP	BFP	H	R	ER	HR	SH	SF	HB	TBB	IBB	SO	WP	Bk	W	L	Pct.	ShO	Sv-Op	Hld	ERA
1995 Princeton	R+	15	9	0	0	58	271	77	39	25	2	2	1	3	25	2	43	6	2	3	7	.300	0	0- -	—	3.88
1996 Chstn-WV	A	4	0	0	2	3.2	17	4	1	1	0	0	0	0	2	0	5	0	0	1	0	1.000	0	0- -	—	2.45
Billings	R+	16	5	0	1	45.2	232	59	41	34	5	1	2	1	33	0	43	5	2	2	3	.400	0	0- -	—	6.70
Princeton	R+	2	2	1	0	15	55	6	4	2	0	0	0	0	3	0	19	0	0	2	0	1.000	1	0- -	—	1.20
1997 Burlington	A	30	13	0	8	97	452	121	78	71	6	4	3	1	55	0	51	8	3	6	4	.600	0	0- -	—	6.59
1998 Burlington	A	25	4	0	6	54.1	216	35	17	12	3	5	0	2	29	4	38	6	0	4	2	.667	0	0- -	—	1.99
1999 Rockford	A	22	20	1	0	127.1	550	135	62	54	9	5	2	4	49	1	95	2	0	7	5	.583	0	0- -	—	3.82
2000 Chattanooga	AA	25	16	1	3	115.2	484	96	41	28	4	6	2	2	52	3	98	9	1	7	5	.583	1	0- -	—	2.18
Louisville	AAA	5	5	0	0	32	136	32	19	12	4	0	4	1	8	1	14	0	0	1	0	1.000	0	0- -	—	3.38

Year Team	Lg	G	GS	CG	GF	IP	BFP	H	R	ER	HR	SH	SF	HB	TBB	IBB	SO	WP	Bk	W	L	Pct.	ShO	Sv-Op	Hld	ERA
2001 Louisville	AAA	13	13	1	0	79.2	328	81	31	27	7	3	0	1	15	1	47	1	0	7	2	.778	1	0---	—	3.05
2001 Cincinnati	NL	20	20	1	0	106.1	461	124	60	56	12	4	0	1	34	0	53	2	0	8	4	.667	0	0-0	0	4.74

Russ Davis

Bats: Right **Throws:** Right **Pos:** 3B-46; PH/PR-6; DH-1   **Ht:** 6'0" **Wt:** 195 **Born:** 9/13/69 **Age:** 32

Year Team	Lg	G	AB	H	2B	3B	HR	(Hm	Rd)	TB	R	RBI	TBB	IBB	SO	HBP	SH	SF	SB	CS	SB%	GDP	Avg	OBP	SLG
1994 New York	AL	4	14	2	0	0	0	(0	0)	2	0	1	0	0	4	0	0	0	0	0	—	1	.143	.143	.143
1995 New York	AL	40	98	27	5	2	2	(2	0)	42	14	12	10	0	26	1	0	0	0	0	—	0	.276	.349	.429
1996 Seattle	AL	51	167	39	9	0	5	(3	2)	63	24	18	17	1	50	2	4	0	2	0	1.00	1	.234	.312	.377
1997 Seattle	AL	119	420	114	29	1	20	(11	9)	205	57	63	27	2	100	2	3	2	6	2	.75	11	.271	.317	.488
1998 Seattle	AL	141	502	130	30	1	20	(7	13)	222	68	82	34	1	134	3	2	9	4	3	.57	10	.259	.305	.442
1999 Seattle	AL	124	432	106	17	1	21	(12	9)	188	55	59	32	1	111	5	7	2	3	3	.50	13	.245	.304	.435
2000 San Francisco	NL	80	180	47	5	0	9	(5	4)	79	27	24	9	0	29	2	0	1	0	3	.00	1	.261	.302	.439
2001 San Francisco	NL	53	167	43	13	1	7	(1	6)	79	16	17	17	2	49	1	2	2	1	0	1.00	5	.257	.326	.473
8 ML YEARS		612	1980	508	108	6	84	(41	43)	880	261	276	146	7	503	16	18	16	16	11	.59	42	.257	.310	.444

Mike DeJean

Pitches: Right **Bats:** Right **Pos:** RP-75   **Ht:** 6'2" **Wt:** 212 **Born:** 9/28/70 **Age:** 31

Year Team	Lg	G	GS	CG	GF	IP	BFP	H	R	ER	HR	SH	SF	HB	TBB	IBB	SO	WP	Bk	W	L	Pct.	ShO	Sv-Op	Hld	ERA
1997 Colorado	NL	55	0	0	15	67.2	295	74	34	30	4	3	1	3	24	2	38	2	0	5	0	1.000	0	2-4	13	3.99
1998 Colorado	NL	59	1	0	9	74.1	307	78	29	25	4	4	4	1	24	1	27	3	0	3	1	.750	0	2-3	11	3.03
1999 Colorado	NL	56	0	0	17	61	288	83	61	57	13	3	3	2	32	8	31	3	0	2	4	.333	0	0-4	9	8.41
2000 Colorado	NL	54	0	0	15	53.1	235	54	31	29	9	3	1	0	30	6	34	5	0	4	4	.500	0	0-4	7	4.89
2001 Milwaukee	NL	75	0	0	19	84.1	371	75	31	26	4	1	4	9	39	7	68	8	0	4	2	.667	0	2-4	8	2.77
5 ML YEARS		299	1	0	75	340.2	1496	364	186	167	34	14	13	15	149	24	198	21	0	18	11	.621	0	6-19	48	4.41

Tomas de la Rosa

Bats: Right **Throws:** Right **Pos:** PH/PR-1   **Ht:** 5'10" **Wt:** 155 **Born:** 1/28/78 **Age:** 24

Year Team	Lg	G	AB	H	2B	3B	HR	(Hm	Rd)	TB	R	RBI	TBB	IBB	SO	HBP	SH	SF	SB	CS	SB%	GDP	Avg	OBP	SLG
1996 Expos	R	53	184	46	7	1	0	—	—	55	34	21	22	0	25	2	4	1	8	5	.62	2	.250	.335	.299
Vermont	A-	3	8	2	0	0	0	—	—	2	1	1	0	0	3	0	0	0	0	0	—	1	.250	.250	.250
1997 Wst Plm Bch	A+	4	9	2	0	0	0	—	—	2	1	0	2	0	3	0	0	0	2	0	1.00	0	.222	.364	.222
Vermont	A-	69	271	72	14	6	2	—	—	104	46	40	32	0	47	2	3	4	19	6	.76	1	.266	.343	.384
1998 Jupiter	A+	117	390	98	22	1	3	—	—	131	56	43	37	0	61	6	10	3	27	7	.79	5	.251	.323	.336
1999 Harrisburg	AA	135	467	122	22	3	6	—	—	168	70	43	42	2	64	1	7	5	28	15	.65	10	.261	.320	.360
2000 Ottawa	AAA	103	340	69	10	1	1	—	—	84	27	36	31	0	43	2	12	5	10	3	.77	9	.203	.270	.247
2001 Ottawa	AAA	121	420	100	24	0	7	—	—	145	56	30	40	4	63	5	9	4	12	9	.57	13	.238	.309	.345
2000 Montreal	NL	32	66	19	3	1	2	(1	1)	30	7	9	7	0	11	1	3	0	2	1	.67	2	.288	.355	.455
2001 Montreal	NL	1	1	0	0	0	0	(0	0)	0	0	0	0	0	0	0	0	0	0	0	—	0	.000	.000	.000
2 ML YEARS		33	67	19	3	1	2	(1	1)	30	7	9	7	0	11	1	3	0	2	1	.67	2	.284	.360	.448

Carlos Delgado

Bats: Left **Throws:** Right **Pos:** 1B-161; PH/PR-1   **Ht:** 6'3" **Wt:** 225 **Born:** 6/25/72 **Age:** 30

Year Team	Lg	G	AB	H	2B	3B	HR	(Hm	Rd)	TB	R	RBI	TBB	IBB	SO	HBP	SH	SF	SB	CS	SB%	GDP	Avg	OBP	SLG
1993 Toronto	AL	2	1	0	0	0	0	(0	0)	0	0	0	1	0	0	0	0	0	0	0	—	0	.000	.500	.000
1994 Toronto	AL	43	130	28	2	0	9	(5	4)	57	17	24	25	4	46	3	0	1	1	1	.50	5	.215	.352	.438
1995 Toronto	AL	37	91	15	3	0	3	(2	1)	27	7	11	6	0	26	0	0	2	0	0	—	1	.165	.212	.297
1996 Toronto	AL	138	488	132	28	2	25	(12	13)	239	68	92	58	2	139	9	0	8	0	0	—	13	.270	.353	.490
1997 Toronto	AL	153	519	136	42	3	30	(17	13)	274	79	91	64	9	133	8	0	4	0	3	.00	6	.262	.350	.528
1998 Toronto	AL	142	530	155	43	1	38	(20	18)	314	94	115	73	13	139	11	0	6	3	0	1.00	8	.292	.385	.592
1999 Toronto	AL	152	573	156	39	0	44	(17	27)	327	113	134	86	7	141	15	0	7	1	1	.50	11	.272	.377	.571
2000 Toronto	AL	162	569	196	57	1	41	(30	11)	378	115	137	123	18	104	15	0	4	0	1	.00	12	.344	.470	.664
2001 Toronto	AL	162	574	160	31	1	39	(13	26)	310	102	102	111	22	136	16	0	3	1	0	1.00	9	.279	.408	.540
9 ML YEARS		991	3475	978	245	8	229	(116	113)	1926	595	706	547	75	864	77	0	35	6	6	.57	65	.281	.388	.554

Wilson Delgado

Bats: B **Throws:** R **Pos:** SS-6; PH/PR-5; 3B-3; 2B-2   **Ht:** 5'11" **Wt:** 165 **Born:** 7/15/75 **Age:** 26

Year Team	Lg	G	AB	H	2B	3B	HR	(Hm	Rd)	TB	R	RBI	TBB	IBB	SO	HBP	SH	SF	SB	CS	SB%	GDP	Avg	OBP	SLG
2001 Omaha *	AAA	76	255	63	11	2	4	—	—	90	24	30	16	2	43	1	2	1	8	3	.73	10	.247	.293	.353
1996 San Francisco	NL	6	22	8	0	0	0	(0	0)	8	3	2	1	0	5	2	0	0	1	0	1.00	0	.364	.440	.364
1997 San Francisco	NL	8	7	1	1	0	0	(0	0)	2	1	0	0	0	2	0	1	0	0	0	—	0	.143	.143	.286
1998 San Francisco	NL	10	12	2	1	0	0	(0	0)	3	1	1	1	0	3	0	0	0	0	0	—	0	.167	.231	.250
1999 San Francisco	NL	35	71	18	2	1	0	(0	0)	22	7	3	5	0	9	1	1	0	1	0	1.00	3	.254	.312	.310
2000 NYY-KC	AL	64	128	33	2	0	1	(0	1)	38	21	11	11	0	26	0	0	2	2	1	.67	2	.258	.312	.297
2001 Kansas City	AL	14	25	3	0	0	0	(0	0)	3	1	1	3	0	10	0	0	0	0	0	—	1	.120	.214	.120
2000 New York	AL	31	45	11	1	0	1	(0	1)	15	6	4	5	0	9	0	0	1	1	0	1.00	1	.244	.314	.333
Kansas City	AL	33	83	22	1	0	0	(0	0)	23	15	7	6	0	17	0	0	1	1	1	.50	1	.265	.311	.277
6 ML YEARS		137	265	65	6	1	1	(0	1)	76	34	18	21	0	55	3	2	2	4	1	.80	5	.245	.306	.287

David Dellucci

Bats: L **Throws:** L **Pos:** PH/PR-67; RF-35; CF-18; LF-8　　　　　　**Ht:** 5'10" **Wt:** 198 **Born:** 10/31/73 **Age:** 28

								BATTING											BASERUNNING				PERCENTAGES		
Year Team	Lg	G	AB	H	2B	3B	HR	(Hm Rd)	TB	R	RBI	TBB	IBB	SO	HBP	SH	SF	SB	CS	SB%	GDP	Avg	OBP	SLG
1997 Baltimore	AL	17	27	6	1	0	1	(0 1)	10	3	3	4	1	7	1	0	0	0	0	—	2	.222	.344	.370
1998 Arizona	NL	124	416	108	19	12	5	(1 4)	166	43	51	33	2	103	3	0	1	3	5	.38	6	.260	.318	.399
1999 Arizona	NL	63	109	43	7	1	1	(0 1)	55	27	15	11	0	24	3	0	0	2	0	1.00	3	.394	.463	.505
2000 Arizona	NL	34	50	15	3	0	0	(0 0)	18	2	2	4	0	9	0	0	0	0	2	.00	1	.300	.352	.360
2001 Arizona	NL	115	217	60	10	2	10	(5 5)	104	28	40	22	4	52	2	0	0	2	1	.67	2	.276	.349	.479
5 ML YEARS		353	819	232	40	15	17	(6 11)	353	103	111	74	7	195	9	0	1	7	8	.47	14	.283	.349	.431

Valerio de los Santos

Pitches: Left **Bats:** Left **Pos:** RP-1　　　　　　**Ht:** 6'2" **Wt:** 180 **Born:** 10/6/75 **Age:** 26

			HOW MUCH HE PITCHED							WHAT HE GAVE UP									THE RESULTS						
Year Team	Lg	G	GS	CG	GF	IP	BFP	H	R	ER	HR	SH	SF	HB	TBB	IBB	SO	WP	Bk	W	L	Pct.	ShO	Sv-Op	Hld	ERA
1998 Milwaukee	NL	13	0	0	3	21.2	75	11	7	7	4	0	0	0	2	0	18	1	0	0	0	—	0	0-0	0	2.91
1999 Milwaukee	NL	7	0	0	3	8.1	43	12	6	6	1	0	0	1	7	0	5	1	0	0	1	.000	0	0-0	0	6.48
2000 Milwaukee	NL	66	2	0	15	73.2	320	72	43	42	15	2	1	1	33	7	70	3	1	2	3	.400	0	0-1	9	5.13
2001 Milwaukee	NL	1	0	0	0	1	5	1	1	1	0	0	0	0	1	0	1	0	0	0	0	—	0	0-0	0	9.00
4 ML YEARS		87	2	0	21	104.2	443	96	57	56	20	2	1	2	43	7	94	5	1	2	4	.333	0	0-1	9	4.82

Ryan Dempster

Pitches: Right **Bats:** Right **Pos:** SP-34　　　　　　**Ht:** 6'1" **Wt:** 201 **Born:** 5/3/77 **Age:** 25

			HOW MUCH HE PITCHED							WHAT HE GAVE UP									THE RESULTS						
Year Team	Lg	G	GS	CG	GF	IP	BFP	H	R	ER	HR	SH	SF	HB	TBB	IBB	SO	WP	Bk	W	L	Pct.	ShO	Sv-Op	Hld	ERA
1998 Florida	NL	14	11	0	1	54.2	272	72	47	43	6	5	6	9	38	1	35	5	0	1	5	.167	0	0-1	0	7.08
1999 Florida	NL	25	25	0	0	147	666	146	77	77	21	3	6	6	93	2	126	8	0	7	8	.467	0	0-0	0	4.71
2000 Florida	NL	33	33	2	0	226.1	974	210	102	92	30	4	5	5	97	7	209	4	0	14	10	.583	1	0-0	0	3.66
2001 Florida	NL	34	34	2	0	211.1	954	218	123	116	21	15	7	10	112	5	171	5	0	15	12	.556	1	0-0	0	4.94
4 ML YEARS		106	103	4	1	639.1	2866	646	349	328	78	27	24	30	340	15	541	22	0	37	35	.514	2	0-1	0	4.62

Mark DeRosa

Bats: R **Throws:** R **Pos:** SS-48; PH/PR-16; 2B-5; DH-3; 3B-1; LF-1　　　　　　**Ht:** 6'1" **Wt:** 195 **Born:** 2/26/75 **Age:** 27

								BATTING											BASERUNNING				PERCENTAGES		
Year Team	Lg	G	AB	H	2B	3B	HR	(Hm Rd)	TB	R	RBI	TBB	IBB	SO	HBP	SH	SF	SB	CS	SB%	GDP	Avg	OBP	SLG
2001 Richmond *	AAA	49	186	55	18	0	2	(— —)	79	31	17	17	0	22	1	1	4	7	3	.70	6	.296	.351	.425
1998 Atlanta	NL	5	3	1	0	0	0	(0 0)	1	2	0	0	0	1	0	0	0	0	0	—	0	.333	.333	.333
1999 Atlanta	NL	7	8	0	0	0	0	(0 0)	0	0	0	0	0	2	0	0	0	0	0	—	0	.000	.000	.000
2000 Atlanta	NL	22	13	4	1	0	0	(0 0)	5	9	3	2	0	1	0	0	0	0	0	—	0	.308	.400	.385
2001 Atlanta	NL	66	164	47	8	0	3	(3 0)	64	27	20	12	6	19	5	1	2	2	1	.67	3	.287	.350	.390
4 ML YEARS		100	188	52	9	0	3	(3 0)	70	38	23	14	6	23	5	1	2	2	1	.67	3	.277	.340	.372

Delino DeShields

Bats: L **Throws:** R **Pos:** LF-79; PH/PR-25; 2B-16; DH-8; 3B-5; 1B-1; CF-1　　　　　　**Ht:** 6'1" **Wt:** 175 **Born:** 1/15/69 **Age:** 33

								BATTING											BASERUNNING				PERCENTAGES		
Year Team	Lg	G	AB	H	2B	3B	HR	(Hm Rd)	TB	R	RBI	TBB	IBB	SO	HBP	SH	SF	SB	CS	SB%	GDP	Avg	OBP	SLG
1990 Montreal	NL	129	499	144	28	6	4	(3 1)	196	69	45	66	3	96	4	1	2	42	22	.66	10	.289	.375	.393
1991 Montreal	NL	151	563	134	15	4	10	(3 7)	187	83	51	95	2	151	2	8	5	56	23	.71	6	.238	.347	.332
1992 Montreal	NL	135	530	155	19	8	7	(1 6)	211	82	56	54	4	108	3	9	3	46	15	.75	10	.292	.359	.398
1993 Montreal	NL	123	481	142	17	7	2	(2 0)	179	75	29	72	3	64	3	4	2	43	10	.81	6	.295	.389	.372
1994 Los Angeles	NL	89	320	80	11	3	2	(1 1)	103	51	33	54	0	53	0	1	1	27	7	.79	5	.250	.357	.322
1995 Los Angeles	NL	127	425	109	18	3	8	(2 6)	157	66	37	63	4	83	1	3	1	39	14	.74	6	.256	.353	.369
1996 Los Angeles	NL	154	581	130	12	8	5	(3 2)	173	75	41	53	7	124	1	2	5	48	11	.81	12	.224	.288	.298
1997 St. Louis	NL	150	572	169	26	14	11	(6 5)	256	92	58	55	1	72	0	1	1	55	14	.80	5	.295	.357	.448
1998 St. Louis	NL	117	420	122	21	8	7	(3 4)	180	74	44	56	2	61	0	4	4	26	10	.72	6	.290	.371	.429
1999 Baltimore	AL	96	330	87	11	2	6	(4 2)	120	46	34	37	0	52	1	5	1	11	8	.58	5	.264	.339	.364
2000 Baltimore	AL	151	561	166	43	5	10	(4 6)	249	84	86	69	2	82	1	3	9	37	10	.79	16	.296	.369	.444
2001 Bal-ChC	NL	126	351	82	17	5	5	(3 2)	124	55	37	59	1	77	1	4	2	23	2	.92	8	.234	.344	.353
2001 Baltimore	AL	58	188	37	8	2	3	(1 2)	58	29	21	31	1	42	1	1	1	11	1	.92	3	.197	.312	.309
Chicago	NL	68	163	45	9	3	2	(2 0)	66	26	16	28	0	35	0	3	1	12	1	.92	5	.276	.380	.405
12 ML YEARS		1548	5633	1520	238	73	77	(35 42)	2135	852	551	733	29	1023	20	51	41	453	146	.76	99	.270	.354	.379

Elmer Dessens

Pitches: Right **Bats:** Right **Pos:** SP-34　　　　　　**Ht:** 6'0" **Wt:** 187 **Born:** 1/13/72 **Age:** 30

			HOW MUCH HE PITCHED							WHAT HE GAVE UP									THE RESULTS						
Year Team	Lg	G	GS	CG	GF	IP	BFP	H	R	ER	HR	SH	SF	HB	TBB	IBB	SO	WP	Bk	W	L	Pct.	ShO	Sv-Op	Hld	ERA
1996 Pittsburgh	NL	15	3	0	1	25	112	40	23	23	2	3	1	0	4	0	13	0	0	0	2	.000	0	0-0	3	8.28
1997 Pittsburgh	NL	3	0	0	1	3.1	13	2	0	0	0	0	0	1	0	0	2	0	0	0	0	—	0	0-0	0	0.00
1998 Pittsburgh	NL	43	5	0	8	74.2	332	90	50	47	10	4	3	0	25	2	43	1	0	2	6	.250	0	0-1	6	5.67
2000 Cincinnati	NL	40	16	1	6	147.1	640	170	73	70	10	12	7	3	43	7	85	4	0	11	5	.688	0	1-1	0	4.28
2001 Cincinnati	NL	34	34	1	0	205	862	221	103	102	32	7	7	1	56	1	128	4	1	10	14	.417	1	0-0	0	4.48
5 ML YEARS		135	58	2	16	455.1	1959	523	249	242	54	26	18	5	128	10	271	9	1	23	27	.460	1	1-2	10	4.78

Matt DeWitt

Pitches: Right **Bats:** Right **Pos:** RP-16   **Ht:** 6'4" **Wt:** 220 **Born:** 9/4/77 **Age:** 24

		HOW MUCH HE PITCHED					WHAT HE GAVE UP											THE RESULTS					
Year Team	Lg	G	GS	CG	GF	IP	BFP	H	R	ER	HR	SH	SF	HB	TBB	IBB	SO	WP	Bk	W	L	Pct.	ShO	Sv-Op	Hld	ERA
1995 Johnson Cty	R+	13	12	0	0	62.2	305	84	56	49	10	0	3	1	32	0	45	5	6	2	6	.250	0	0--	—	7.04
1996 Johnson Cty	R+	14	14	0	0	79.2	353	96	53	48	17	1	0	3	26	0	58	7	0	5	5	.500	0	0--	—	5.42
1997 Peoria	A	27	27	1	0	158.1	672	152	84	72	16	7	8	9	57	2	121	6	1	9	9	.500	0	0--	—	4.09
1998 Pr William	A+	24	24	1	0	148.1	588	132	65	60	13	3	3	7	18	0	118	5	0	6	9	.400	0	0--	—	3.64
1999 Arkansas	AA	26	26	0	0	148.1	644	153	87	73	21	4	3	1	59	0	107	3	1	9	8	.529	0	0--	—	4.43
2000 Syracuse	AAA	31	7	0	23	64.2	296	78	42	35	6	2	5	2	25	0	41	0	0	4	5	.444	0	15--	—	4.87
2001 Syracuse	AAA	53	0	0	47	58.1	239	45	20	18	4	3	0	1	17	1	44	2	0	3	2	.600	0	27--	—	2.78
2000 Toronto	AL	8	0	0	4	13.2	68	20	13	13	4	0	0	2	9	0	6	1	0	1	0	1.000	0	0-0	—	8.56
2001 Toronto	AL	16	0	0	9	19	87	22	8	8	2	1	0	1	10	5	13	2	0	0	2	.000	0	0-0	—	3.79
2 ML YEARS		24	0	0	13	32.2	155	42	21	21	6	1	0	3	19	5	19	3	0	1	2	.333	0	0-0	—	5.79

Einar Diaz

Bats: Right **Throws:** Right **Pos:** C-134; PH/PR-3; 2B-1   **Ht:** 5'10" **Wt:** 185 **Born:** 12/28/72 **Age:** 29

		BATTING																	BASERUNNING				PERCENTAGES		
Year Team	Lg	G	AB	H	2B	3B	HR	(Hm	Rd)	TB	R	RBI	TBB	IBB	SO	HBP	SH	SF	SB	CS	SB%	GDP	Avg	OBP	SLG
1996 Cleveland	AL	4	1	0	0	0	0	(0	0)	0	0	0	0	0	0	0	0	0	0	0	—	0	.000	.000	.000
1997 Cleveland	AL	5	7	1	1	0	0	(0	0)	2	1	1	0	0	2	0	0	0	0	0	—	0	.143	.143	.286
1998 Cleveland	AL	17	48	11	1	0	2	(1	1)	18	8	9	3	0	2	2	0	3	0	0	—	2	.229	.286	.375
1999 Cleveland	AL	119	392	110	21	1	3	(2	1)	142	43	32	23	0	41	5	6	1	11	4	.73	10	.281	.328	.362
2000 Cleveland	AL	75	250	68	14	2	4	(2	2)	98	29	25	11	0	29	8	6	0	4	2	.67	7	.272	.323	.392
2001 Cleveland	AL	134	437	121	34	1	4	(0	4)	169	54	56	17	0	44	16	8	0	1	2	.33	11	.277	.328	.387
6 ML YEARS		354	1135	311	71	4	13	(5	8)	429	135	123	54	0	118	31	20	4	16	8	.67	30	.274	.324	.378

R.A. Dickey

Pitches: Right **Bats:** Right **Pos:** RP-4   **Ht:** 6'3" **Wt:** 205 **Born:** 10/29/74 **Age:** 27

		HOW MUCH HE PITCHED						WHAT HE GAVE UP												THE RESULTS					
Year Team	Lg	G	GS	CG	GF	IP	BFP	H	R	ER	HR	SH	SF	HB	TBB	IBB	SO	WP	Bk	W	L	Pct.	ShO	Sv-Op	Hld	ERA
1997 Charlotte	A+	8	6	0	2	35	162	51	32	27	8	0	0	0	12	1	32	5	3	1	4	.200	0	0--	—	6.94
1998 Charlotte	A+	57	0	0	54	60	260	58	31	22	9	4	1	0	23	3	53	2	1	1	5	.167	0	38--	—	3.30
1999 Tulsa	AA	35	11	0	21	95	419	105	60	48	13	1	4	2	40	1	59	9	0	6	7	.462	0	10--	—	4.55
Oklahoma	AAA	6	2	0	1	22.2	99	23	12	11	1	3	0	1	7	1	17	2	0	2	2	.500	0	0--	—	4.37
2000 Oklahoma	AAA	30	23	2	2	158.1	680	167	83	79	14	4	9	7	65	1	85	5	2	8	9	.471	0	1--	—	4.49
2001 Oklahoma	AAA	24	24	3	0	163	687	164	77	68	14	7	2	7	45	1	120	3	0	11	7	.611	0	0--	—	3.75
2001 Texas	AL	4	0	0	1	12	53	13	9	9	3	0	0	0	7	1	4	1	0	0	1	.000	0	0-0	—	6.75

Mike DiFelice

Bats: Right **Throws:** Right **Pos:** C-60   **Ht:** 6'2" **Wt:** 205 **Born:** 5/28/69 **Age:** 33

		BATTING																	BASERUNNING				PERCENTAGES		
Year Team	Lg	G	AB	H	2B	3B	HR	(Hm	Rd)	TB	R	RBI	TBB	IBB	SO	HBP	SH	SF	SB	CS	SB%	GDP	Avg	OBP	SLG
2001 Tucson *	AAA	7	26	9	0	0	1	—	—	12	6	2	3	0	6	0	0	0	0	0	—	2	.346	.414	.462
1996 St. Louis	NL	4	7	2	1	0	0	(0	0)	3	0	2	0	0	1	0	0	0	0	0	—	0	.286	.286	.429
1997 St. Louis	NL	93	260	62	10	1	4	(1	3)	86	16	30	19	0	61	3	6	1	1	1	.50	11	.238	.297	.331
1998 Tampa Bay	AL	84	248	57	12	3	3	(1	2)	84	17	23	15	0	56	1	3	2	0	0	—	12	.230	.274	.339
1999 Tampa Bay	AL	51	179	55	11	0	6	(5	1)	84	21	27	8	0	23	3	0	1	0	0	—	1	.307	.346	.469
2000 Tampa Bay	AL	60	204	49	13	1	6	(4	2)	82	23	19	12	0	40	0	5	2	0	0	—	8	.240	.280	.402
2001 TB-Ari		60	170	32	5	1	2	(0	2)	45	14	10	8	0	49	4	3	2	1	1	.50	3	.188	.239	.265
2001 Tampa Bay	AL	48	149	31	5	1	2	(0	2)	44	13	9	8	0	39	3	2	2	1	1	.50	3	.208	.295	.295
Arizona	NL	12	21	1	0	0	0	(0	0)	1	1	1	0	0	10	1	1	0	0	0	—	0	.048	.091	.048
6 ML YEARS		352	1068	257	52	6	21	(11	10)	384	91	111	62	0	230	11	17	8	2	2	.50	35	.241	.287	.360

Craig Dingman

Pitches: Right **Bats:** Right **Pos:** RP-7   **Ht:** 6'4" **Wt:** 215 **Born:** 3/12/74 **Age:** 28

		HOW MUCH HE PITCHED						WHAT HE GAVE UP												THE RESULTS					
Year Team	Lg	G	GS	CG	GF	IP	BFP	H	R	ER	HR	SH	SF	HB	TBB	IBB	SO	WP	Bk	W	L	Pct.	ShO	Sv-Op	Hld	ERA
1994 Yankees	R	17	1	0	11	32	135	27	17	12	0	7	2	3	10	0	51	4	0	0	5	.000	0	1--	—	3.38
1996 Oneonta	A-	20	0	0	15	35.1	137	17	11	8	0	1	1	1	9	0	52	0	1	0	2	.000	0	9--	—	2.04
1997 Tampa	A+	19	0	0	11	22.1	92	15	14	13	2	1	0	0	14	2	26	3	0	0	4	.000	0	6--	—	5.24
Greensboro	A	30	0	0	27	33	131	19	7	7	0	2	1	1	12	0	41	3	0	2	0	1.000	0	19--	—	1.91
1998 Tampa	A+	50	0	0	28	70.2	293	48	29	25	8	3	2	1	39	9	95	2	0	5	4	.556	0	7--	—	3.18
1999 Norwich	AA	55	0	0	21	74.1	288	56	16	13	2	2	0	2	12	2	90	2	0	8	6	.571	0	9--	—	1.57
2000 Columbus	AAA	47	2	0	10	73.2	304	60	31	25	5	3	8	0	20	2	65	1	1	6	1	.857	0	1--	—	3.05
2001 Colo Sprngs	AAA	46	0	0	29	48	210	57	28	20	4	2	1	4	9	1	51	1	0	3	5	.375	0	7--	—	3.75
2000 New York	AL	10	0	0	4	11	51	18	8	8	1	0	0	0	3	0	8	0	0	0	0	—	0	0-0	—	6.55
2001 Colorado	NL	7	0	0	4	7.1	37	11	11	11	4	1	0	2	3	2	2	0	0	0	0	—	0	1-1	0	13.50
2 ML YEARS		17	0	0	8	18.1	88	29	19	19	5	1	0	2	6	2	10	0	0	0	0	—	0	1-1	0	9.33

Gary DiSarcina

Bats: Right **Throws:** Right **2000 Pos:** SS-12   **Ht:** 6'2" **Wt:** 205 **Born:** 11/19/67 **Age:** 34

		BATTING																	BASERUNNING				PERCENTAGES		
Year Team	Lg	G	AB	H	2B	3B	HR	(Hm	Rd)	TB	R	RBI	TBB	IBB	SO	HBP	SH	SF	SB	CS	SB%	GDP	Avg	OBP	SLG
1989 California	AL	2	0	0	0	0	0	(0	0)	0	0	0	0	0	0	0	0	0	0	0	—	0	—	—	—
1990 California	AL	18	57	8	1	1	0	(0	0)	11	8	0	3	0	10	0	1	0	1	0	1.00	3	.140	.183	.193
1991 California	AL	18	57	12	2	0	0	(0	0)	14	5	3	0	0	4	2	2	0	0	0	—	0	.211	.274	.246
1992 California	AL	157	518	128	19	0	3	(2	1)	156	48	42	20	0	50	7	5	3	9	7	.56	15	.247	.283	.301
1993 California	AL	126	416	99	20	1	3	(2	1)	130	44	45	15	0	38	6	5	3	5	7	.42	13	.238	.273	.313

59

(continued)

Year Team	Lg	G	AB	H	2B	3B	HR	(Hm	Rd)	TB	R	RBI	TBB	IBB	SO	HBP	SH	SF	SB	CS	SB%	GDP	Avg	OBP	SLG
1994 California	AL	112	389	101	14	2	3	(2	1)	128	53	33	18	0	28	2	10	2	3	7	.30	10	.260	.294	.329
1995 California	AL	99	362	111	28	6	5	(1	4)	166	61	41	20	0	25	2	7	3	7	4	.64	10	.307	.344	.459
1996 California	AL	150	536	137	26	4	5	(2	3)	186	62	48	21	0	36	2	16	1	2	1	.67	16	.256	.286	.347
1997 Anaheim	AL	154	549	135	28	2	4	(2	2)	179	52	47	17	0	29	4	8	5	7	8	.47	18	.246	.271	.326
1998 Anaheim	AL	157	551	158	39	3	3	(0	3)	212	73	56	21	0	51	8	12	3	11	7	.61	11	.287	.321	.385
1999 Anaheim	AL	81	271	62	7	1	1	(1	0)	74	32	29	15	0	32	2	9	1	2	2	.50	8	.229	.273	.273
2000 Anaheim	AL	12	38	15	2	0	1	(1	0)	20	6	11	1	0	3	1	2	0	0	1	.00	1	.395	.425	.526
12 ML YEARS		1086	3744	966	186	20	28	(13	15)	1276	444	355	154	0	306	36	77	21	47	44	.52	105	.258	.292	.341

Chris Donnels

Bats: L **Throws:** R **Pos:** PH/PR-44; 3B-14; 1B-7; P-1   **Ht:** 6'0" **Wt:** 185 **Born:** 4/21/66 **Age:** 36

Year Team	Lg	G	AB	H	2B	3B	HR	(Hm	Rd)	TB	R	RBI	TBB	IBB	SO	HBP	SH	SF	SB	CS	SB%	GDP	Avg	OBP	SLG
2001 Las Vegas *	AAA	39	137	32	5	0	7	(—	—)	58	17	25	21	0	24	0	0	1	1	0	1.00	7	.234	.333	.423
1991 New York	NL	37	89	20	2	0	0	(0	0)	22	7	5	14	1	19	0	1	0	1	1	.50	0	.225	.330	.247
1992 New York	NL	45	121	21	4	0	0	(0	0)	25	8	6	17	0	25	0	1	0	1	0	1.00	1	.174	.275	.207
1993 Houston	NL	88	179	46	14	2	2	(0	2)	70	18	24	19	0	33	0	0	1	2	0	1.00	6	.257	.327	.391
1994 Houston	NL	54	86	23	5	0	3	(2	1)	37	12	5	13	0	18	0	0	0	1	0	1.00	1	.267	.364	.430
1995 Hou-Bos		59	121	32	2	2	2	(0	2)	44	17	13	12	2	24	0	0	0	0	0	—	2	.264	.328	.364
2000 Los Angeles	NL	27	34	10	3	0	4	(3	1)	25	8	9	6	1	7	0	0	0	0	0	—	3	.294	.390	.735
2001 Los Angeles	NL	66	88	15	2	0	3	(2	1)	26	8	8	12	2	25	1	0	0	0	0	—	2	.170	.277	.295
1995 Houston	NL	19	30	9	0	0	0	(0	0)	9	4	2	3	2	6	0	0	0	0	0	—	1	.300	.364	.300
Boston	AL	40	91	23	2	2	2	(0	2)	35	13	11	9	0	18	0	0	1	0	0	—	1	.253	.317	.385
7 ML YEARS		376	718	167	32	4	14	(7	7)	249	78	70	93	6	151	1	2	3	5	1	.83	15	.233	.320	.347

Octavio Dotel

Pitches: Right **Bats:** Right **Pos:** RP-57; SP-4   **Ht:** 6'0" **Wt:** 175 **Born:** 11/25/75 **Age:** 26

Year Team	Lg	G	GS	CG	GF	IP	BFP	H	R	ER	HR	SH	SF	HB	TBB	IBB	SO	WP	Bk	W	L	Pct.	ShO	Sv-Op	Hld	ERA
1999 New York	NL	19	14	0	1	85.1	368	69	52	51	12	3	5	6	49	1	85	3	2	8	3	.727	0	0-0	0	5.38
2000 Houston	NL	50	16	0	25	125	563	127	80	75	26	7	8	7	61	3	142	6	0	3	7	.300	0	16-23	0	5.40
2001 Houston	NL	61	4	0	20	105	438	79	35	31	5	2	2	2	47	2	145	4	0	7	5	.583	0	2-4	14	2.66
3 ML YEARS		130	34	0	46	315.1	1369	275	167	157	43	12	15	15	157	6	372	13	2	18	15	.545	0	18-27	14	4.48

Sean Douglass

Pitches: Right **Bats:** Right **Pos:** SP-4   **Ht:** 6'6" **Wt:** 200 **Born:** 4/28/79 **Age:** 23

Year Team	Lg	G	GS	CG	GF	IP	BFP	H	R	ER	HR	SH	SF	HB	TBB	IBB	SO	WP	Bk	W	L	Pct.	ShO	Sv-Op	Hld	ERA
1997 Orioles	R	9	1	0	5	17.2	80	20	14	12	2	4	0	2	9	0	10	1	0	1	3	.250	0	0--	—	6.11
1998 Bluefield	R+	10	10	0	0	53	210	45	20	19	6	0	1	0	14	0	62	3	0	2	2	.500	0	0--	—	3.23
1999 Frederick	A+	16	16	1	0	97.2	425	101	48	36	9	4	3	5	35	0	89	3	0	5	6	.455	0	0--	—	3.32
2000 Bowie	AA	27	27	1	0	160.2	687	155	79	72	17	3	2	5	55	1	118	5	0	9	8	.529	0	0--	—	4.03
2001 Rochester	AAA	27	27	0	0	162.1	710	160	79	63	13	5	4	5	61	0	156	6	0	8	9	.471	0	0--	—	3.49
2001 Baltimore	AL	4	4	0	0	20.1	94	21	12	12	3	0	1	1	11	0	17	1	1	2	1	.667	0	0-0	0	5.31

Kelly Dransfeldt

Bats: Right **Throws:** Right **Pos:** SS-3; 3B-1; PH/PR-1   **Ht:** 6'2" **Wt:** 195 **Born:** 4/16/75 **Age:** 27

Year Team	Lg	G	AB	H	2B	3B	HR	(Hm	Rd)	TB	R	RBI	TBB	IBB	SO	HBP	SH	SF	SB	CS	SB%	GDP	Avg	OBP	SLG
1996 Hudson Val	A-	75	284	67	17	1	7	—	—	107	42	29	27	1	76	4	1	3	13	4	.76	2	.236	.308	.377
1997 Charlotte	A+	135	466	106	20	7	6	—	—	158	64	58	42	0	115	3	4	3	25	16	.61	8	.227	.294	.339
1998 Charlotte	A+	67	245	79	17	0	18	—	—	150	46	76	29	1	67	2	0	6	7	2	.78	4	.322	.390	.612
Tulsa	AA	58	226	57	15	4	9	—	—	107	43	36	18	0	79	2	0	3	8	1	.89	4	.252	.309	.473
1999 Oklahoma	AAA	102	359	85	21	2	10	—	—	140	55	44	24	0	108	3	3	3	6	3	.67	12	.237	.288	.390
2000 Oklahoma	AAA	117	441	109	22	3	8	—	—	161	60	42	38	0	123	4	1	3	10	5	.67	7	.247	.311	.365
2001 Oklahoma	AAA	143	551	138	29	5	9	—	—	204	76	63	50	1	116	3	1	1	12	9	.57	9	.250	.313	.370
1999 Texas	AL	16	53	10	1	0	1	(1	0)	14	3	5	3	0	12	0	1	0	0	0	—	2	.189	.232	.264
2000 Texas	AL	16	26	3	2	0	0	(0	0)	5	2	1	4	0	14	0	0	0	0	0	—	0	.115	.148	.192
2001 Texas	AL	4	3	0	0	0	0	(0	0)	0	0	0	0	0	0	0	0	0	0	0	—	0	.000	.000	.000
3 ML YEARS		36	82	13	3	0	1	(1	0)	19	5	7	4	0	26	0	1	0	0	0	—	2	.159	.198	.232

Darren Dreifort

Pitches: Right **Bats:** Right **Pos:** SP-16   **Ht:** 6'2" **Wt:** 211 **Born:** 5/3/72 **Age:** 30

Year Team	Lg	G	GS	CG	GF	IP	BFP	H	R	ER	HR	SH	SF	HB	TBB	IBB	SO	WP	Bk	W	L	Pct.	ShO	Sv-Op	Hld	ERA
1994 Los Angeles	NL	27	0	0	15	29	148	45	21	20	0	3	0	4	15	3	22	1	0	0	5	.000	0	6-9	3	6.21
1996 Los Angeles	NL	19	0	0	5	23.2	106	23	13	13	2	3	1	0	12	4	24	2	1	1	4	.200	0	0-2	1	4.94
1997 Los Angeles	NL	48	0	0	15	63	265	45	21	20	3	5	2	1	34	2	63	3	1	5	2	.714	0	4-7	9	2.86
1998 Los Angeles	NL	32	26	1	0	180	752	171	84	80	12	11	6	10	57	2	168	9	0	8	12	.400	0	0-0	0	4.00
1999 Los Angeles	NL	30	29	1	0	178.2	773	177	105	95	20	8	2	7	76	2	140	9	4	13	13	.500	1	0-0	0	4.79
2000 Los Angeles	NL	32	32	1	0	192.2	842	175	105	89	31	9	0	12	87	1	164	17	3	12	9	.571	1	0-0	0	4.16
2001 Los Angeles	NL	16	16	0	0	94.2	416	89	62	54	11	7	1	6	47	0	91	10	0	4	7	.364	0	0-0	0	5.13
7 ML YEARS		204	103	3	35	761.2	3302	725	411	371	79	46	12	40	328	14	672	51	9	43	52	.453	3	10-18	13	4.38

Ryan Drese

Pitches: Right **Bats:** Right **Pos:** RP-5; SP-4   **Ht:** 6'3" **Wt:** 220 **Born:** 4/5/76 **Age:** 26

Year Team	Lg	G	GS	CG	GF	IP	BFP	H	R	ER	HR	SH	SF	HB	TBB	IBB	SO	WP	Bk	W	L	Pct.	ShO	Sv-Op	Hld	ERA
1998 Watertown	A-	9	9	0	0	42	179	40	21	19	1	0	2	3	14	0	40	4	0	2	5	.286	0	0--	—	4.07
1999 Mahoning Vy	A-	5	5	0	0	17	66	8	6	5	1	0	2	1	7	0	26	0	1	0	2	.000	0	0--	—	2.65
Columbus	A	2	2	0	0	12	49	9	6	6	2	0	0	0	4	0	15	3	0	0	2	.000	0	0--	—	4.50
Kinston	A+	15	15	1	0	69.1	310	46	47	38	2	3	1	10	52	0	81	7	1	5	4	.556	0	0--	—	4.93
2000 Kinston	A+	1	1	0	0	2.1	9	2	1	1	0	1	0	0	1	0	4	1	0	0	1	.000	0	0--	—	3.86
2001 Akron	AA	14	13	1	1	86	340	64	34	32	4	7	1	6	29	0	73	4	0	5	7	.417	1	0--	—	3.35
Buffalo	AAA	11	10	0	0	60.2	255	60	28	27	7	2	1	6	17	0	52	1	1	5	1	.833	0	0--	—	4.01
2001 Cleveland	AL	9	4	0	2	36.2	149	32	15	14	2	1	0	1	15	0	24	0	0	1	2	.333	0	0-0	0	3.44

J.D. Drew

Bats: L **Throws:** R **Pos:** RF-97; CF-20; PH/PR-4; LF-1   **Ht:** 6'1" **Wt:** 195 **Born:** 11/20/75 **Age:** 26

Year Team	Lg	G	AB	H	2B	3B	HR	(Hm	Rd)	TB	R	RBI	TBB	IBB	SO	HBP	SH	SF	SB	CS	SB%	GDP	Avg	OBP	SLG
2001 Peoria *	A	3	11	6	2	0	0	—	—	8	3	0	1	0	0	0	0	0	0	0	—	1	.545	.583	.727
1998 St. Louis	NL	14	36	15	3	1	5	(4	1)	35	9	13	4	0	10	0	0	1	0	0	—	0	.417	.463	.972
1999 St. Louis	NL	104	368	89	16	6	13	(5	8)	156	72	39	50	0	77	6	3	3	19	3	.86	4	.242	.340	.424
2000 St. Louis	NL	135	407	120	17	2	18	(11	7)	195	73	57	67	4	99	6	5	1	17	9	.65	3	.295	.401	.479
2001 St. Louis	NL	109	375	121	18	5	27	(15	12)	230	80	73	57	4	75	4	3	4	13	3	.81	6	.323	.414	.613
4 ML YEARS		362	1186	345	54	14	63	(35	28)	616	234	182	178	8	261	16	11	9	49	15	.77	17	.291	.388	.519

Tim Drew

Pitches: Right **Bats:** Right **Pos:** SP-6; RP-2   **Ht:** 6'1" **Wt:** 195 **Born:** 8/31/78 **Age:** 23

Year Team	Lg	G	GS	CG	GF	IP	BFP	H	R	ER	HR	SH	SF	HB	TBB	IBB	SO	WP	Bk	W	L	Pct.	ShO	Sv-Op	Hld	ERA
1997 Burlington	R+	4	4	0	0	11.2	63	16	15	8	0	0	0	6	4	0	14	4	1	0	1	.000	0	0--	—	6.17
Watertown	A-	1	1	0	0	4.2	20	4	1	1	0	0	0	0	3	0	9	0	0	0	0	—	0	0--	—	1.93
1998 Columbus	A	13	13	0	0	71.1	311	68	43	30	5	0	4	6	26	0	64	5	2	4	3	.571	0	0--	—	3.79
Kinston	A+	15	15	0	0	90	392	105	58	52	9	3	5	5	31	1	67	5	2	3	8	.273	0	0--	—	5.20
1999 Kinston	A+	28	28	2	0	169	713	154	79	70	12	5	3	10	60	0	125	7	0	13	5	.722	0	0--	—	3.73
2000 Akron	AA	9	9	0	0	52	210	41	19	14	1	3	2	1	15	0	22	3	1	3	2	.600	0	0--	—	2.42
Buffalo	AAA	16	16	2	0	95	432	122	69	62	12	3	6	1	31	0	53	5	1	7	8	.467	0	0--	—	5.87
2001 Buffalo	AAA	18	18	1	0	108	467	115	54	47	13	2	0	8	27	1	75	6	1	8	6	.571	1	0--	—	3.92
2000 Cleveland	AL	3	3	0	0	9	51	17	12	10	1	0	2	1	8	0	5	0	0	1	0	1.000	0	0-0	0	10.00
2001 Cleveland	AL	8	6	0	0	35	173	51	39	31	9	1	2	4	16	0	15	5	0	0	2	.000	0	0-0	0	7.97
2 ML YEARS		11	9	0	0	44	224	68	51	41	10	1	4	5	24	0	20	5	0	1	2	.333	0	0-0	0	8.39

Rob Ducey

Bats: L **Throws:** R **Pos:** PH/PR-40; LF-10; CF-4; RF-4; DH-3   **Ht:** 6'2" **Wt:** 183 **Born:** 5/24/65 **Age:** 37

Year Team	Lg	G	AB	H	2B	3B	HR	(Hm	Rd)	TB	R	RBI	TBB	IBB	SO	HBP	SH	SF	SB	CS	SB%	GDP	Avg	OBP	SLG
2001 Scrantn-WB *	AAA	4	20	6	1	0	1	—	—	10	3	5	2	1	6	0	0	0	0	0	—	0	.300	.364	.500
1987 Toronto	AL	34	48	9	1	0	1	(1	0)	13	12	6	8	0	10	0	0	1	2	0	1.00	0	.188	.298	.271
1988 Toronto	AL	27	54	17	4	1	0	(0	0)	23	15	6	5	0	7	0	2	2	1	0	1.00	1	.315	.361	.426
1989 Toronto	AL	41	76	16	4	0	0	(0	0)	20	5	7	9	1	25	0	1	0	2	1	.67	2	.211	.294	.263
1990 Toronto	AL	19	53	16	5	0	0	(0	0)	21	7	7	7	0	15	1	0	1	1	1	.50	0	.302	.387	.396
1991 Toronto	AL	39	68	16	2	2	1	(0	1)	25	8	4	6	0	26	0	1	0	2	0	1.00	1	.235	.297	.368
1992 Tor-Cal	AL	54	80	15	4	0	0	(0	0)	19	7	2	5	0	22	0	0	1	2	4	.33	1	.188	.233	.238
1993 Texas	AL	27	85	24	6	3	2	(2	0)	42	15	9	10	2	17	0	2	2	2	3	.40	1	.282	.351	.494
1994 Texas	AL	11	29	5	1	0	0	(0	0)	6	1	1	2	0	1	0	0	0	0	0	—	1	.172	.226	.207
1997 Seattle	AL	76	143	41	15	2	5	(0	5)	75	25	10	6	0	31	0	0	2	3	3	.50	3	.287	.311	.524
1998 Seattle	AL	97	217	52	18	2	5	(2	3)	89	30	23	23	2	61	9	0	1	4	3	.57	4	.240	.336	.410
1999 Philadelphia	NL	104	188	49	10	2	8	(3	5)	87	29	33	38	1	57	0	0	1	2	1	.67	1	.261	.383	.463
2000 Phi-Tor	NL	117	165	32	5	1	6	(4	2)	57	26	26	31	1	49	0	0	1	1	0	1.00	1	.194	.318	.345
2001 Phi-Mon	NL	57	73	17	3	0	3	(2	1)	29	10	12	16	0	25	1	2	1	0	0	1.00	0	.233	.374	.397
1992 Toronto	AL	23	21	1	1	0	0	(0	0)	2	3	0	0	0	10	0	0	0	0	0	1.00	0	.048	.048	.095
California	AL	31	59	14	3	0	0	(0	0)	17	4	2	5	0	12	0	0	1	2	3	.40	1	.237	.292	.288
2000 Philadelphia	NL	112	152	30	4	1	6	(4	2)	54	24	25	29	1	47	0	0	1	1	0	1.00	1	.197	.322	.355
Toronto	AL	5	13	2	1	0	0	(0	0)	3	2	1	2	0	2	0	0	0	0	0	—	0	.154	.267	.231
2001 Philadelphia	NL	30	27	6	1	0	1	(1	0)	10	4	4	6	0	11	0	1	0	0	0	—	0	.222	.364	.370
Montreal	NL	27	46	11	2	0	2	(1	1)	19	6	8	10	0	14	1	1	1	0	1	.00	0	.239	.379	.413
13 ML YEARS		703	1279	309	78	13	31	(14	17)	506	190	146	166	7	346	11	8	14	22	17	.56	16	.242	.331	.396

Justin Duchscherer

Pitches: Right **Bats:** Right **Pos:** RP-3; SP-2   **Ht:** 6'3" **Wt:** 164 **Born:** 11/19/77 **Age:** 24

Year Team	Lg	G	GS	CG	GF	IP	BFP	H	R	ER	HR	SH	SF	HB	TBB	IBB	SO	WP	Bk	W	L	Pct.	ShO	Sv-Op	Hld	ERA
1996 Red Sox	R	13	8	0	2	54.2	232	52	26	19	0	3	4	3	14	0	45	4	6	2	0	.000	0	1--	—	3.13
1997 Red Sox	R	10	8	0	0	44.2	190	34	18	9	0	2	1	3	17	0	59	5	4	2	3	.400	0	0--	—	1.81
Michigan	A	4	4	0	0	24	109	26	17	15	1	0	1	3	10	0	19	0	0	1	1	.500	0	0--	—	5.63
1998 Michigan	A	30	26	0	0	142.2	627	166	84	76	9	7	3	13	47	3	106	7	1	7	12	.368	0	0--	—	4.79
1999 Augusta	A	6	6	0	0	41	150	21	1	1	0	0	0	0	8	0	39	1	0	4	0	1.000	0	0--	—	0.22
Sarasota	A+	20	18	0	0	112.1	475	101	62	56	14	2	5	12	30	0	105	5	0	7	7	.500	0	0--	—	4.49
2000 Trenton	AA	24	24	2	0	143.1	593	134	59	54	7	3	6	6	35	1	126	6	1	7	9	.438	2	0--	—	3.39
2001 Trenton	AA	12	12	1	0	73.2	293	59	25	20	6	0	0	5	14	1	69	0	0	6	3	.667	1	0--	—	2.44
Tulsa	AA	6	6	1	0	43.1	176	39	14	10	3	1	2	2	10	0	55	0	0	4	0	1.000	0	0--	—	2.08
Oklahoma	AAA	7	7	1	0	50.2	205	48	20	16	6	2	1	4	10	0	52	0	0	3	3	.500	1	0--	—	2.84
2001 Texas	AL	5	2	0	1	14.2	76	24	20	20	5	0	0	4	4	0	11	1	0	1	1	.500	0	0-0	0	12.27

Brandon Duckworth

Pitches: Right **Bats:** Right **Pos:** SP-11　　　　　　　**Ht:** 6'2" **Wt:** 185 **Born:** 1/23/76 **Age:** 26

Year Team	Lg	G	GS	CG	GF	IP	BFP	H	R	ER	HR	SH	SF	HB	TBB	IBB	SO	WP	Bk	W	L	Pct.	ShO	Sv-Op	Hld	ERA
1998 Piedmont	A	21	21	5	0	147.2	577	116	58	46	10	1	5	7	24	0	119	8	2	9	8	.529	3	0--	—	2.80
Clearwater	A+	9	9	1	0	53	235	64	25	22	2	1	1	2	22	0	46	4	0	6	2	.750	1	0--	—	3.74
1999 Clearwater	A+	27	17	0	1	132	602	164	84	71	13	5	7	5	40	0	101	10	1	11	5	.688	0	1--	—	4.84
2000 Reading	AA	27	27	1	0	165	688	145	70	58	17	5	2	7	52	0	178	6	3	13	7	.650	0	0--	—	3.16
2001 Scrantn-WB	AAA	22	20	2	1	147	584	122	46	43	14	5	2	7	36	2	150	5	0	13	2	.867	1	0--	—	2.63
2001 Philadelphia	NL	11	11	0	0	69	289	57	29	27	2	7	3	6	29	0	40	2	0	3	2	.600	0	0-0	0	3.52

Courtney Duncan

Pitches: Right **Bats:** Left **Pos:** RP-36　　　　　　　**Ht:** 6'0" **Wt:** 185 **Born:** 10/9/74 **Age:** 27

Year Team	Lg	G	GS	CG	GF	IP	BFP	H	R	ER	HR	SH	SF	HB	TBB	IBB	SO	WP	Bk	W	L	Pct.	ShO	Sv-Op	Hld	ERA
1996 Williamsprt	A-	15	15	1	0	90.1	360	58	28	22	6	3	0	5	34	0	91	8	0	11	1	.917	0	0--	—	2.19
1997 Daytona	A+	19	19	1	0	121.2	489	90	35	22	3	6	1	8	35	0	120	8	1	8	4	.667	0	0--	—	1.63
Orlando	AA	8	8	0	0	45	196	37	28	17	2	1	2	1	29	5	45	4	0	2	2	.500	0	0--	—	3.40
1998 West Tenn	AA	29	29	0	0	162.2	730	141	89	77	7	9	7	14	108	5	157	9	2	7	9	.438	0	0--	—	4.26
1999 West Tenn	AA	11	8	0	2	41.2	210	44	42	33	3	2	6	2	42	4	42	8	0	1	7	.125	0	0--	—	7.13
Daytona	A+	15	11	1	3	65	300	70	60	40	6	3	2	4	34	1	48	5	0	4	5	.444	1	1--	—	5.54
2000 West Tenn	AA	61	0	0	41	73.1	307	57	32	25	2	4	3	0	33	2	72	3	0	5	4	.556	0	25--	—	3.07
2001 Iowa	AAA	7	0	0	1	8.1	36	7	3	3	1	0	0	0	5	1	15	0	0	1	0	1.000	0	0--	—	3.24
2001 Chicago	NL	36	0	0	15	42.2	193	42	24	24	5	1	3	2	25	3	49	2	0	3	3	.500	0	0-2	7	5.06

Adam Dunn

Bats: Left **Throws:** Right **Pos:** RF-38; LF-30; PH/PR-3　　　　**Ht:** 6'6" **Wt:** 240 **Born:** 11/9/79 **Age:** 22

Year Team	Lg	G	AB	H	2B	3B	HR	(Hm	Rd)	TB	R	RBI	TBB	IBB	SO	HBP	SH	SF	SB	CS	SB%	GDP	Avg	OBP	SLG
1998 Billings	R+	34	125	36	3	1	4	—	—	53	26	13	22	1	23	3	0	1	4	2	.67	3	.288	.404	.424
1999 Rockford	A	93	313	96	16	2	11	—	—	149	62	44	46	3	64	10	0	3	21	10	.68	6	.307	.409	.476
2000 Dayton	A	122	420	118	29	1	16	—	—	197	101	79	100	4	101	12	0	6	24	5	.83	10	.281	.428	.469
2001 Chattanooga	AA	39	140	48	9	0	12	—	—	93	30	31	24	3	31	3	1	0	6	3	.67	1	.343	.449	.664
Louisville	AAA	55	210	69	13	0	20	—	—	142	44	53	38	3	51	5	0	1	5	1	.83	1	.329	.441	.676
2001 Cincinnati	NL	66	244	64	18	1	19	(8	11)	141	54	43	38	2	74	4	0	0	4	2	.67	4	.262	.371	.578

Shawon Dunston

Bats: R **Throws:** R **Pos:** PH/PR-37; RF-26; CF-23; LF-12; DH-1; 1B-1　　**Ht:** 6'1" **Wt:** 180 **Born:** 3/21/63 **Age:** 39

Year Team	Lg	G	AB	H	2B	3B	HR	(Hm	Rd)	TB	R	RBI	TBB	IBB	SO	HBP	SH	SF	SB	CS	SB%	GDP	Avg	OBP	SLG
1985 Chicago	NL	74	250	65	12	4	4	(3	1)	97	40	18	19	3	42	0	1	2	11	3	.79	3	.260	.310	.388
1986 Chicago	NL	150	581	145	37	3	17	(10	7)	239	66	68	21	5	114	3	4	2	13	11	.54	5	.250	.278	.411
1987 Chicago	NL	95	346	85	18	3	5	(3	2)	124	40	22	10	1	68	1	0	2	12	3	.80	6	.246	.267	.358
1988 Chicago	NL	155	575	143	23	6	9	(5	4)	205	69	56	16	8	108	2	4	2	30	9	.77	6	.249	.271	.357
1989 Chicago	NL	138	471	131	20	6	9	(3	6)	190	52	60	30	15	86	1	6	4	19	11	.63	7	.278	.320	.403
1990 Chicago	NL	146	545	143	22	8	17	(7	10)	232	73	66	15	1	87	3	4	6	25	5	.83	9	.262	.283	.426
1991 Chicago	NL	142	492	128	22	7	12	(7	5)	200	59	50	23	5	64	4	4	11	21	6	.78	9	.260	.292	.407
1992 Chicago	NL	18	73	23	3	1	0	(0	0)	28	8	2	3	0	13	0	0	0	2	3	.40	0	.315	.342	.384
1993 Chicago	NL	7	10	4	2	0	0	(0	0)	6	3	2	0	0	1	0	0	0	0	0	—	0	.400	.400	.600
1994 Chicago	NL	88	331	92	19	0	11	(2	9)	144	38	35	16	3	48	2	5	2	3	8	.27	4	.278	.313	.435
1995 Chicago	NL	127	477	141	30	6	14	(8	6)	225	58	69	10	3	75	6	7	3	10	5	.67	8	.296	.317	.472
1996 San Francisco	NL	82	287	86	12	2	5	(3	2)	117	27	25	13	0	40	1	5	1	8	0	1.00	8	.300	.331	.408
1997 ChC-Pit	NL	132	490	147	22	5	14	(10	4)	221	71	57	8	0	75	3	5	5	32	8	.80	9	.300	.312	.451
1998 Cle-SF		98	207	46	13	3	6	(2	4)	83	36	20	6	0	28	4	1	3	9	4	.69	3	.222	.255	.401
1999 StL-NYM	NL	104	243	78	11	3	5	(4	1)	110	35	41	2	0	39	5	3	2	10	4	.71	8	.321	.337	.453
2000 St. Louis	NL	98	216	54	11	2	12	(6	6)	105	28	43	6	0	47	3	4	1	3	1	.75	11	.250	.278	.486
2001 San Francisco	NL	88	186	52	10	3	9	(3	6)	95	26	25	2	0	32	2	2	1	3	1	.75	2	.280	.293	.511
1997 Chicago	NL	114	419	119	18	4	9	(7	2)	172	57	41	8	0	64	3	3	4	29	7	.81	7	.284	.300	.411
Pittsburgh	NL	18	71	28	4	1	5	(3	2)	49	14	16	0	0	11	0	2	1	3	1	.75	2	.394	.389	.690
1998 Cleveland	AL	62	156	37	11	3	3	(1	2)	63	26	12	6	0	18	1	0	3	9	4	.82	2	.237	.265	.404
San Francisco	NL	36	51	9	2	0	3	(1	2)	20	10	8	0	0	10	3	1	0	0	0	.00	1	.176	.222	.392
1999 St. Louis	NL	62	150	46	5	2	5	(4	1)	70	23	25	2	0	23	3	2	1	6	3	.67	4	.307	.327	.467
New York	NL	42	93	32	6	1	0	(0	0)	40	12	16	0	0	16	2	1	1	4	1	.80	4	.344	.354	.430
17 ML YEARS		1742	5780	1563	287	62	149	(76	73)	2421	729	659	200	44	967	40	55	48	211	82	.72	98	.270	.297	.419

Todd Dunwoody

Bats: L **Throws:** L **Pos:** LF-15; PH/PR-9; RF-7; CF-6　　　　**Ht:** 6'1" **Wt:** 210 **Born:** 4/11/75 **Age:** 27

Year Team	Lg	G	AB	H	2B	3B	HR	(Hm	Rd)	TB	R	RBI	TBB	IBB	SO	HBP	SH	SF	SB	CS	SB%	GDP	Avg	OBP	SLG
2001 Iowa *	AAA	75	251	71	18	3	8	—	—	119	31	32	17	3	75	2	0	2	6	4	.60	1	.283	.331	.474
1997 Florida	NL	19	50	13	2	2	2	(0	2)	25	7	7	7	0	21	1	0	0	2	0	1.00	1	.260	.362	.500
1998 Florida	NL	116	434	109	27	7	5	(2	3)	165	53	28	21	0	113	4	3	0	5	1	.83	6	.251	.292	.380
1999 Florida	NL	64	186	41	6	3	2	(1	1)	59	20	20	12	0	41	1	0	1	3	4	.43	1	.220	.270	.317
2000 Kansas City	AL	61	178	37	9	0	1	(1	0)	49	12	23	8	0	42	1	2	6	3	0	1.00	4	.208	.238	.275
2001 Chicago	NL	33	61	13	4	0	1	(0	1)	20	6	3	3	0	14	0	0	0	0	1	.00	0	.213	.250	.328
5 ML YEARS		293	909	213	48	12	11	(4	7)	318	98	81	51	0	231	7	5	7	13	6	.68	12	.234	.278	.350

Erubiel Durazo

Bats: L Throws: L Pos: PH/PR-49; 1B-38; DH-7; RF-2   Ht: 6'3" Wt: 240 Born: 1/23/74 Age: 28

								BATTING										BASERUNNING				PERCENTAGES		
Year Team	Lg	G	AB	H	2B	3B	HR	(Hm | Rd)	TB	R	RBI	TBB	IBB	SO	HBP	SH	SF	SB	CS	SB%	GDP	Avg	OBP	SLG
2001 Tucson *	AAA	3	11	3	0	0	1	—	—	6	3	1	1	0	3	0	0	0	0	0	—	0	.273	.333	.545
1999 Arizona	NL	52	155	51	4	2	11	(4 | 7)	92	31	30	26	1	43	1	0	3	1	1	.50	1	.329	.422	.594
2000 Arizona	NL	67	196	52	11	0	8	(3 | 5)	87	35	33	34	2	43	1	0	2	1	0	1.00	3	.265	.373	.444
2001 Arizona	NL	92	175	47	11	0	12	(4 | 8)	94	34	38	28	1	49	2	0	2	0	0	—	1	.269	.372	.537
3 ML YEARS		211	526	150	26	2	31	(11 | 20)	273	100	101	88	4	135	4	0	7	2	1	.67	5	.285	.387	.519

Chad Durbin

Pitches: Right Bats: Right Pos: SP-29   Ht: 6'2" Wt: 200 Born: 12/3/77 Age: 24

		HOW MUCH HE PITCHED						WHAT HE GAVE UP										THE RESULTS					
Year Team	Lg	G	GS	CG	GF	IP	BFP	H	R	ER	HR	SH	SF	HB	TBB	IBB	SO	WP	Bk	W	L	Pct.	ShO	Sv-Op	Hld	ERA
2001 Omaha *	AAA	5	5	0	0	27	112	22	11	10	4	1	1	2	6	0	35	0	1	2	2	.500	0	0- -	—	3.33
1999 Kansas City	AL	1	0	0	0	2.1	9	1	0	0	0	0	0	0	1	0	3	1	0	0	0	—	0	0-0	0	0.00
2000 Kansas City	AL	16	16	0	0	72.1	349	91	71	66	14	1	3	0	43	1	37	7	0	2	5	.286	0	0-0	0	8.21
2001 Kansas City	AL	29	29	2	0	179	777	201	109	98	26	2	7	11	58	0	95	6	0	9	16	.360	0	0-0	0	4.93
3 ML YEARS		46	45	2	0	253.2	1135	293	180	164	40	3	10	11	102	1	135	14	0	11	21	.344	0	0-0	0	5.82

Ray Durham

Bats: Both Throws: Right Pos: 2B-150; PH/PR-3; DH-1   Ht: 5'8" Wt: 180 Born: 11/30/71 Age: 30

								BATTING										BASERUNNING				PERCENTAGES		
Year Team	Lg	G	AB	H	2B	3B	HR	(Hm	Rd)	TB	R	RBI	TBB	IBB	SO	HBP	SH	SF	SB	CS	SB%	GDP	Avg	OBP	SLG
1995 Chicago	AL	125	471	121	27	6	7	(1	6)	181	68	51	31	2	83	6	5	4	18	5	.78	6	.257	.309	.384
1996 Chicago	AL	156	557	153	33	5	10	(3	7)	226	79	65	58	4	95	10	7	7	30	4	.88	6	.275	.350	.406
1997 Chicago	AL	155	634	172	27	5	11	(3	8)	242	106	53	61	0	96	6	2	8	33	16	.67	14	.271	.337	.382
1998 Chicago	AL	158	635	181	35	8	19	(10	9)	289	126	67	73	3	105	6	6	3	36	9	.80	5	.285	.363	.455
1999 Chicago	AL	153	612	181	30	8	13	(7	6)	266	109	60	73	1	105	4	3	2	34	11	.76	9	.296	.373	.435
2000 Chicago	AL	151	614	172	35	6	12	(5	12)	276	121	75	75	0	105	7	5	8	25	13	.66	13	.280	.361	.450
2001 Chicago	AL	152	611	163	42	10	20	(9	11)	285	104	65	64	3	110	4	6	6	23	10	.70	10	.267	.337	.466
7 ML YEARS		1050	4134	1143	229	51	97	(38	59)	1765	713	436	435	13	699	43	34	38	199	68	.75	65	.276	.349	.427

Mike Duvall

Pitches: Left Bats: Right Pos: RP-8   Ht: 6'0" Wt: 200 Born: 10/11/74 Age: 27

		HOW MUCH HE PITCHED						WHAT HE GAVE UP										THE RESULTS					
Year Team	Lg	G	GS	CG	GF	IP	BFP	H	R	ER	HR	SH	SF	HB	TBB	IBB	SO	WP	Bk	W	L	Pct.	ShO	Sv-Op	Hld	ERA
2001 Edmonton *	AAA	55	0	0	19	62.2	277	73	32	31	7	4	3	1	21	1	63	4	0	2	2	.500	0	3- -	—	4.45
1998 Tampa Bay	AL	3	0	0	4	4	17	4	3	3	0	0	0	0	2	0	1	0	0	0	0	—	0	0-0	0	6.75
1999 Tampa Bay	AL	40	0	0	7	40	188	46	21	18	5	1	1	2	27	1	18	4	1	1	1	.500	0	0-1	0	4.05
2000 Tampa Bay	AL	2	0	0	0	2.1	12	5	2	2	0	0	0	0	1	0	0	0	0	0	0	—	0	0-0	0	7.71
2001 Minnesota	AL	8	0	0	0	4.2	22	7	4	4	1	0	1	0	2	0	4	1	0	0	0	—	0	0-1	0	7.71
4 ML YEARS		53	0	0	7	51	239	62	30	27	6	1	2	2	32	1	23	5	1	1	1	.500	0	0-2	1	4.76

Jermaine Dye

Bats: Right Throws: Right Pos: RF-153; DH-4; CF-2   Ht: 6'5" Wt: 220 Born: 1/28/74 Age: 28

								BATTING										BASERUNNING				PERCENTAGES		
Year Team	Lg	G	AB	H	2B	3B	HR	(Hm	Rd)	TB	R	RBI	TBB	IBB	SO	HBP	SH	SF	SB	CS	SB%	GDP	Avg	OBP	SLG
1996 Atlanta	NL	98	292	82	16	0	12	(4	8)	134	32	37	8	0	67	3	0	3	1	4	.20	11	.281	.304	.459
1997 Kansas City	AL	75	263	62	14	0	7	(3	4)	97	26	22	17	0	51	1	1	1	2	1	.67	6	.236	.284	.369
1998 Kansas City	AL	60	214	50	5	1	5	(3	2)	72	24	23	11	2	46	1	0	4	2	2	.50	8	.234	.270	.336
1999 Kansas City	AL	158	608	179	44	8	27	(15	12)	320	96	119	58	4	119	1	0	6	2	3	.40	17	.294	.354	.526
2000 Kansas City	AL	157	601	193	41	2	33	(15	18)	337	107	118	69	6	99	3	0	6	0	1	.00	12	.321	.390	.561
2001 KC-Oak	AL	158	569	169	31	1	26	(16	10)	280	91	106	57	6	112	7	1	11	9	1	.90	8	.282	.346	.467
2001 Kansas City	AL	97	367	100	14	0	13	(8	5)	153	50	47	30	3	68	6	1	6	7	1	.88	2	.272	.333	.417
Oakland	AL	61	232	69	17	1	13	(8	5)	127	41	59	27	3	44	1	0	5	2	0	1.00	6	.297	.366	.547
6 ML YEARS		706	2577	735	151	12	110	(56	54)	1240	376	425	220	18	494	16	2	31	16	12	.57	62	.285	.341	.481

Damion Easley

Bats: Right Throws: Right Pos: 2B-153; PH/PR-1   Ht: 5'11" Wt: 185 Born: 11/11/69 Age: 32

								BATTING										BASERUNNING				PERCENTAGES		
Year Team	Lg	G	AB	H	2B	3B	HR	(Hm	Rd)	TB	R	RBI	TBB	IBB	SO	HBP	SH	SF	SB	CS	SB%	GDP	Avg	OBP	SLG
1992 California	AL	47	151	39	5	0	1	(1	0)	47	14	12	8	0	26	3	2	1	9	5	.64	2	.258	.307	.311
1993 California	AL	73	230	72	13	2	2	(0	2)	95	33	22	28	2	35	3	1	2	6	6	.50	5	.313	.392	.413
1994 California	AL	88	316	68	16	1	6	(4	2)	104	41	30	29	0	48	4	4	2	4	5	.44	8	.215	.288	.329
1995 California	AL	114	357	77	14	2	4	(1	3)	107	35	35	32	1	47	6	6	4	5	2	.71	11	.216	.288	.300
1996 Cal-Det	AL	49	112	30	2	0	4	(1	3)	44	14	17	10	0	25	1	5	1	3	1	.75	0	.268	.331	.393
1997 Detroit	AL	151	527	139	37	3	22	(12	10)	248	97	72	68	3	102	16	4	5	28	13	.68	18	.264	.362	.471
1998 Detroit	AL	153	594	161	38	2	27	(19	8)	284	84	100	39	2	112	16	0	2	15	5	.75	8	.271	.332	.478
1999 Detroit	AL	151	549	146	30	1	20	(12	8)	238	83	65	51	2	124	19	2	6	11	3	.79	15	.266	.346	.434
2000 Detroit	AL	126	464	120	27	2	14	(5	9)	193	76	58	55	1	79	11	4	1	13	4	.76	11	.259	.350	.416
2001 Detroit	AL	154	585	146	27	7	11	(4	7)	220	77	65	52	3	90	13	4	4	10	5	.67	10	.250	.323	.376
1996 California	AL	28	45	7	1	0	2	(1	1)	14	4	7	6	0	12	0	3	0	0	0	—	0	.156	.255	.311
Detroit	AL	21	67	23	1	0	2	(0	2)	30	10	10	4	0	13	1	2	1	3	1	.75	0	.343	.384	.448
10 ML YEARS		1106	3885	998	209	20	111	(59	52)	1580	554	476	372	14	688	92	32	28	104	49	.68	88	.257	.334	.407

Adam Eaton

Pitches: Right Bats: Right Pos: SP-17
Ht: 6'2" Wt: 190 Born: 11/23/77 Age: 24

Year Team	Lg	G	GS	CG	GF	IP	BFP	H	R	ER	HR	SH	SF	HB	TBB	IBB	SO	WP	Bk	W	L	Pct.	ShO	Sv-Op	Hld	ERA
1997 Piedmont	A	14	14	0	0	71.1	318	81	38	33	2	0	2	4	30	0	57	4	2	5	6	.455	0	0--	—	4.16
1998 Clearwater	A+	24	23	1	0	131.2	578	152	68	65	9	3	5	5	47	1	89	9	1	9	8	.529	0	0--	—	4.44
1999 Clearwater	A+	13	13	0	0	69	308	81	39	30	2	2	2	4	24	0	50	1	2	5	5	.500	0	0--	—	3.91
Reading	AA	12	12	2	0	77	317	60	30	25	9	1	2	5	28	1	67	1	2	5	4	.556	0	0--	—	2.92
Scrantn-WB	AAA	3	3	0	0	21	83	17	10	7	1	0	0	1	6	0	10	0	0	1	1	.500	0	0--	—	3.00
2000 Mobile	AA	10	10	1	0	57	238	47	20	17	3	1	3	1	18	0	58	4	1	4	1	.800	1	0--	—	2.68
2000 San Diego	NL	22	22	0	0	135	583	134	63	62	14	1	3	2	61	3	90	3	0	7	4	.636	0	0-0	0	4.13
2001 San Diego	NL	17	17	2	0	116.2	499	108	61	56	20	3	2	5	40	3	109	3	0	8	5	.615	0	0-0	0	4.32
2 ML YEARS		39	39	2	0	251.2	1082	242	124	118	34	4	5	7	101	6	199	6	0	15	9	.625	0	0-0	0	4.22

Angel Echevarria

Bats: R Throws: R Pos: PH/PR-44; LF-19; 1B-10; RF-5; DH-1
Ht: 6'3" Wt: 226 Born: 5/25/71 Age: 31

Year Team	Lg	G	AB	H	2B	3B	HR	(Hm	Rd)	TB	R	RBI	TBB	IBB	SO	HBP	SH	SF	SB	CS	SB%	GDP	Avg	OBP	SLG
1996 Colorado	NL	26	21	6	0	0	0	(0	0)	6	2	6	2	0	5	1	0	2	0	0	—	0	.286	.346	.286
1997 Colorado	NL	15	20	5	0	0	0	(0	0)	7	4	0	2	0	5	0	0	0	0	0	—	0	.250	.318	.350
1998 Colorado	NL	19	29	11	3	0	1	(1	0)	17	7	9	2	0	3	2	0	0	0	0	—	4	.379	.455	.586
1999 Colorado	NL	102	191	56	7	0	11	(5	6)	96	28	35	17	0	34	3	0	0	1	3	.25	11	.293	.360	.503
2000 Col-Mil	NL	41	51	10	2	0	1	(1	0)	15	3	6	7	0	11	0	0	0	0	0	—	1	.196	.293	.294
2001 Milwaukee	NL	75	133	34	11	0	5	(3	2)	60	12	13	8	0	29	3	0	1	0	1	.00	2	.256	.310	.451
2000 Colorado	NL	10	9	1	0	0	0	(0	0)	1	2	0	2	0	2	0	0	0	0	0	—	0	.111	.111	.111
Milwaukee	NL	31	42	9	2	0	1	(1	0)	14	3	4	7	0	9	0	0	0	0	0	—	1	.214	.327	.333
6 ML YEARS		278	445	122	25	0	18	(10	8)	201	56	69	38	0	87	9	0	3	1	4	.20	18	.274	.341	.452

David Eckstein

Bats: R Throws: R Pos: SS-126; DH-14; 2B-14; PH/PR-2
Ht: 5'8" Wt: 170 Born: 1/20/75 Age: 27

Year Team	Lg	G	AB	H	2B	3B	HR	(Hm	Rd)	TB	R	RBI	TBB	IBB	SO	HBP	SH	SF	SB	CS	SB%	GDP	Avg	OBP	SLG
1997 Lowell	A-	68	249	75	11	4	4	—	—	106	43	39	33	1	29	12	8	1	21	5	.81	2	.301	.407	.426
1998 Sarasota	A+	135	503	154	29	4	3	—	—	200	99	58	87	3	51	22	1	2	45	16	.74	8	.306	.428	.398
1999 Trenton	AA	131	483	151	22	5	6	—	—	201	109	52	89	0	48	25	13	5	32	13	.71	6	.313	.440	.416
2000 Pawtucket	AAA	119	422	104	20	0	1	—	—	127	77	31	60	0	45	20	9	4	11	8	.58	8	.246	.364	.301
Edmonton	AAA	15	52	18	8	0	3	—	—	35	17	8	9	0	5	0	0	1	5	3	.63	0	.346	.485	.673
2001 Anaheim	AL	153	582	166	26	2	4	(3	1)	208	82	41	43	0	60	21	16	2	29	4	.88	11	.285	.355	.357

Jim Edmonds

Bats: Left Throws: Left Pos: CF-147; PH/PR-6; 1B-2
Ht: 6'1" Wt: 212 Born: 6/27/70 Age: 32

Year Team	Lg	G	AB	H	2B	3B	HR	(Hm	Rd)	TB	R	RBI	TBB	IBB	SO	HBP	SH	SF	SB	CS	SB%	GDP	Avg	OBP	SLG
1993 California	AL	18	61	15	4	1	0	(0	0)	21	5	4	2	1	16	0	0	0	0	2	.00	1	.246	.270	.344
1994 California	AL	94	289	79	13	1	5	(3	2)	109	35	37	30	3	72	1	1	1	4	2	.67	3	.273	.343	.377
1995 California	AL	141	558	162	30	4	33	(16	17)	299	120	107	51	4	130	5	1	5	1	4	.20	10	.290	.352	.536
1996 California	AL	114	431	131	28	3	27	(17	10)	246	73	66	46	2	101	4	0	2	4	0	1.00	8	.304	.375	.571
1997 Anaheim	AL	133	502	146	27	0	26	(14	12)	251	82	80	60	5	80	4	0	5	5	7	.42	8	.291	.368	.500
1998 Anaheim	AL	154	599	184	42	1	25	(9	16)	303	115	91	57	7	114	1	1	1	7	5	.58	16	.307	.368	.506
1999 Anaheim	AL	55	204	51	17	2	5	(3	2)	87	34	23	28	0	45	0	0	1	5	4	.56	3	.250	.339	.426
2000 St. Louis	NL	152	525	155	25	0	42	(22	20)	306	129	108	103	3	167	6	1	8	10	3	.77	5	.295	.411	.583
2001 St. Louis	NL	150	500	152	38	1	30	(16	14)	282	95	110	93	12	136	4	1	10	5	5	.50	8	.304	.410	.564
9 ML YEARS		1011	3669	1075	224	13	193	(100	93)	1904	688	626	470	37	861	25	5	33	41	32	.56	62	.293	.374	.519

Joey Eischen

Pitches: Left Bats: Left Pos: RP-24
Ht: 6'1" Wt: 200 Born: 5/25/70 Age: 32

Year Team	Lg	G	GS	CG	GF	IP	BFP	H	R	ER	HR	SH	SF	HB	TBB	IBB	SO	WP	Bk	W	L	Pct.	ShO	Sv-Op	Hld	ERA
2001 Ottawa *	AAA	34	1	0	17	52.1	205	42	16	13	6	1	0	2	11	0	54	1	0	2	3	.400	0	7--	—	2.24
1994 Montreal	NL	1	0	0	0	0.2	7	4	4	4	0	0	0	1	0	0	1	0	0	0	0	—	0	0-0	0	54.00
1995 Los Angeles	NL	17	0	0	8	20.1	95	19	9	7	1	0	2	0	11	1	15	1	0	0	0	—	0	0-0	1	3.10
1996 LA-Det		52	0	0	14	68.1	308	75	36	32	7	3	2	4	34	7	51	4	0	1	2	.333	0	0-2	2	4.21
1997 Cincinnati	NL	1	0	0	0	1.1	7	2	2	1	0	0	0	0	1	0	2	1	0	0	0	—	0	0-0	0	6.75
2001 Montreal	NL	24	0	0	7	29.2	131	29	17	16	4	1	0	1	16	1	19	1	0	0	0	.000	0	0-2	2	4.85
1996 Los Angeles	NL	28	0	0	11	43.1	198	48	25	23	4	3	1	4	20	4	36	1	0	0	1	.000	0	0-0	1	4.78
Detroit	AL	24	0	0	3	25	110	27	11	9	3	0	1	0	14	3	15	3	0	1	1	.500	0	0-2	1	3.24
5 ML YEARS		95	0	0	29	120.1	548	129	68	60	12	4	2	8	62	9	88	7	0	1	3	.250	0	0-4	5	4.49

Scott Elarton

Pitches: Right Bats: Right Pos: SP-24
Ht: 6'7" Wt: 240 Born: 2/23/76 Age: 26

Year Team	Lg	G	GS	CG	GF	IP	BFP	H	R	ER	HR	SH	SF	HB	TBB	IBB	SO	WP	Bk	W	L	Pct.	ShO	Sv-Op	Hld	ERA
2001 Colo Sprngs *	AAA	2	2	0	0	7.2	39	14	6	6	2	0	0	2	0	0	8	1	0	0	1	.000	0	0--	—	7.04
1998 Houston	NL	28	2	0	7	57	227	40	21	21	5	1	1	1	20	0	56	1	0	2	1	.667	0	2-3	2	3.32
1999 Houston	NL	42	15	0	8	124	524	111	55	48	8	7	4	4	43	0	121	3	0	9	5	.643	0	1-4	5	3.48
2000 Houston	NL	30	30	2	0	192.2	855	198	117	103	29	5	7	6	84	1	131	8	0	17	7	.708	0	0-0	0	4.81
2001 Hou-Col	NL	24	24	0	0	132.2	595	146	105	104	34	7	2	6	59	2	87	5	0	4	10	.286	0	0-0	0	7.06

Year Team	Lg	G	GS	CG	GF	IP	BFP	H	R	ER	HR	SH	SF	HB	TBB	IBB	SO	WP	Bk	W	L	Pct.	ShO	Sv-Op	Hld	ERA
		HOW MUCH HE PITCHED						WHAT HE GAVE UP												THE RESULTS						
2001 Houston	NL	20	20	0	0	109.2	499	126	88	87	26	7	2	6	49	1	76	5	0	4	8	.333	0	0-0	0	7.14
Colorado	NL	4	4	0	0	23	96	20	17	17	8	0	0	0	10	1	11	0	0	0	2	.000	0	0-0	0	6.65
4 ML YEARS		124	71	2	15	506.1	2201	495	298	276	76	20	14	17	206	3	395	17	0	32	23	.582	0	3-7	7	4.91

Cal Eldred

Pitches: **Right** Bats: **Right** Pos: SP-2   Ht: 6'4" Wt: 235 Born: 11/24/67 Age: 34

Year Team	Lg	G	GS	CG	GF	IP	BFP	H	R	ER	HR	SH	SF	HB	TBB	IBB	SO	WP	Bk	W	L	Pct.	ShO	Sv-Op	Hld	ERA
1991 Milwaukee	AL	3	3	0	0	16	73	20	9	8	2	0	0	0	6	0	10	0	0	2	0	1.000	0	0-0	0	4.50
1992 Milwaukee	AL	14	14	2	0	100.1	394	76	21	20	4	1	0	2	23	0	62	3	0	11	2	.846	1	0-0	0	1.79
1993 Milwaukee	AL	36	36	8	0	258	1087	232	120	115	32	5	12	10	91	5	180	2	0	16	16	.500	1	0-0	0	4.01
1994 Milwaukee	AL	25	25	6	0	179	769	158	96	93	23	5	7	4	84	0	98	2	0	11	11	.500	0	0-0	0	4.68
1995 Milwaukee	AL	4	4	0	0	23.2	104	24	10	9	4	1	0	1	10	0	18	1	1	1	1	.500	0	0-0	0	3.42
1996 Milwaukee	AL	15	15	0	0	84.2	363	82	43	42	8	0	4	4	38	0	50	1	0	4	4	.500	0	0-0	0	4.46
1997 Milwaukee	AL	34	34	1	0	202	885	207	118	112	31	4	6	9	89	0	122	5	0	13	15	.464	1	0-0	0	4.99
1998 Milwaukee	NL	23	23	0	0	133	602	157	82	71	14	5	3	4	61	3	86	6	0	4	8	.333	0	0-0	0	4.80
1999 Milwaukee	NL	20	15	0	2	82	392	101	75	71	19	2	3	1	46	0	60	8	1	2	8	.200	0	0-0	0	7.79
2000 Chicago	AL	20	20	2	0	112	492	103	61	57	12	3	2	5	59	0	97	4	0	10	2	.833	1	0-0	0	4.58
2001 Chicago	AL	2	2	0	0	6	34	12	9	9	1	0	0	3	3	1	6	0	0	0	1	.000	0	0-0	0	13.50
11 ML YEARS		196	191	19	2	1196.2	5195	1172	644	607	150	26	37	43	510	9	789	32	2	74	68	.521	4	0-0	0	4.57

Robert Ellis

Pitches: **Right** Bats: **Right** Pos: SP-17; RP-2   Ht: 6'5" Wt: 220 Born: 12/15/70 Age: 31

Year Team	Lg	G	GS	CG	GF	IP	BFP	H	R	ER	HR	SH	SF	HB	TBB	IBB	SO	WP	Bk	W	L	Pct.	ShO	Sv-Op	Hld	ERA
1991 Utica	A-	15	15	1	0	87.2	407	87	66	45	4	6	5	6	61	0	66	13	0	3	9	.250	1	0--	—	4.62
1992 White Sox	R	1	1	0	0	5	24	10	6	6	0	0	0	0	1	0	4	0	0	1	0	1.000	0	0--	—	10.80
South Bend	A	18	18	1	0	123	481	90	46	32	3	4	2	4	35	0	97	7	2	6	5	.545	1	0--	—	2.34
1993 Sarasota	A+	15	15	8	0	104	414	81	37	29	3	4	3	3	31	1	79	6	1	7	8	.467	2	0--	—	2.51
Birmingham	AA	12	12	2	0	81.1	336	68	33	28	2	1	1	4	21	0	77	6	0	6	3	.667	1	0--	—	3.10
1994 Nashville	AAA	19	19	1	0	105	483	126	77	71	19	5	6	2	55	1	76	1	4	4	10	.286	0	0--	—	6.09
1995 Nashville	AAA	4	4	0	0	20.2	85	16	7	5	2	0	1	1	10	0	9	1	0	1	1	.500	0	0--	—	2.18
1996 Nashville	AAA	19	13	1	2	70.1	327	78	49	47	6	5	3	7	45	3	35	8	0	3	8	.273	0	0--	—	6.01
Birmingham	AA	2	2	0	0	7.1	35	9	9	9	1	0	1	1	8	0	8	1	0	0	1	.000	0	0--	—	11.05
Vancouver	AAA	7	7	1	0	44.1	186	30	19	16	2	2	2	0	28	0	29	5	0	2	3	.400	0	0--	—	3.25
1997 Vancouver	AAA	29	23	3	1	149	698	185	108	98	15	6	6	7	83	1	70	15	1	9	10	.474	0	0--	—	5.92
1998 Louisville	AAA	30	28	0	0	150.1	693	171	103	94	21	7	2	8	78	1	79	13	0	10	10	.500	0	0--	—	5.63
1999 New Orleans	AAA	27	27	1	0	155.2	690	176	106	94	20	5	6	5	51	1	105	11	2	7	12	.368	0	0--	—	5.43
2000 Syracuse	AAA	16	0	0	10	18	85	17	10	9	2	3	0	2	15	1	18	3	1	1	1	.500	0	2--	—	4.50
2001 Tucson	AAA	5	5	0	0	26.1	106	25	12	9	2	0	0	1	5	0	13	0	1	1	1	.500	0	0--	—	3.08
1996 California	AL	3	0	0	3	5	19	0	0	0	0	0	0	0	4	0	5	1	0	0	0	—	0	0-0	0	0.00
2001 Arizona	NL	19	17	0	1	92	413	106	61	59	12	6	7	4	34	2	41	3	2	6	5	.545	0	0-0	0	5.77
2 ML YEARS		22	17	0	4	97	432	106	61	59	12	6	7	4	38	2	46	4	2	6	5	.545	0	0-0	0	5.47

Alan Embree

Pitches: **Left** Bats: **Left** Pos: RP-61   Ht: 6'2" Wt: 190 Born: 1/23/70 Age: 32

Year Team	Lg	G	GS	CG	GF	IP	BFP	H	R	ER	HR	SH	SF	HB	TBB	IBB	SO	WP	Bk	W	L	Pct.	ShO	Sv-Op	Hld	ERA
2001 Fresno *	AAA	7	0	0	4	8	30	5	3	1	0	0	0	1	1	0	6	0	0	1	0	1.000	0	1--	—	1.13
1992 Cleveland	AL	4	4	0	0	18	81	19	14	14	3	0	2	1	8	0	12	1	1	0	2	.000	0	0-0	0	7.00
1995 Cleveland	AL	23	0	0	8	24.2	111	23	16	14	2	2	2	0	16	0	23	1	0	0	2	.600	0	1-1	6	5.11
1996 Cleveland	AL	24	0	0	2	31	141	30	26	22	10	1	3	0	21	3	33	3	0	1	1	.500	0	0-0	1	6.39
1997 Atlanta	NL	66	0	0	15	46	190	36	13	13	1	4	1	2	20	2	45	3	1	3	1	.750	0	0-0	16	2.54
1998 Atl-Ari	NL	55	0	0	16	53.2	237	56	32	25	7	4	1	1	23	0	43	3	0	4	2	.667	0	1-3	12	4.19
1999 San Francisco	NL	68	0	0	13	58.2	244	42	22	22	6	3	2	3	26	2	53	3	0	3	2	.600	0	0-3	22	3.38
2000 San Francisco	NL	63	0	0	21	60	263	62	34	33	4	4	5	3	25	2	49	1	0	3	5	.375	0	2-5	9	4.95
2001 SF-CWS		61	0	0	17	54	245	65	47	44	14	0	6	3	17	2	59	3	0	1	4	.200	0	0-3	9	7.33
1998 Atlanta	NL	20	0	0	5	18.2	87	23	14	9	2	1	1	0	10	0	19	0	0	1	0	1.000	0	0-1	6	4.34
Arizona	NL	35	0	0	11	35	150	33	18	16	5	3	0	1	13	0	24	3	0	3	2	.600	0	1-2	6	4.11
2001 San Francisco	NL	22	0	0	7	20	106	34	26	25	7	0	3	2	10	2	25	1	0	0	2	.000	0	0-1	0	11.25
Chicago		39	0	0	10	34	139	31	21	19	7	0	3	1	7	0	34	2	0	1	2	.333	0	0-2	9	5.03
8 ML YEARS		364	4	0	92	346	1512	333	204	187	47	18	22	13	156	11	317	18	2	18	19	.486	0	4-15	75	4.86

Juan Encarnacion

Bats: R Throws: R Pos: RF-63; CF-56; PH/PR-4; DH-2   Ht: 6'3" Wt: 187 Born: 3/8/76 Age: 26

							BATTING												BASERUNNING				PERCENTAGES		
Year Team	Lg	G	AB	H	2B	3B	HR	(Hm	Rd)	TB	R	RBI	TBB	IBB	SO	HBP	SH	SF	SB	CS	SB%	GDP	Avg	OBP	SLG
1997 Detroit	AL	11	33	7	1	1	1	(1	0)	13	3	5	3	0	12	1	0	0	3	1	.75	1	.212	.316	.394
1998 Detroit	AL	40	164	54	9	4	7	(4	3)	92	30	21	7	0	31	1	0	3	7	4	.64	2	.329	.354	.561
1999 Detroit	AL	132	509	130	30	6	19	(6	13)	229	62	74	14	1	113	9	4	2	33	12	.73	12	.255	.287	.450
2000 Detroit	AL	141	547	158	25	6	14	(4	10)	237	75	72	29	1	90	7	3	4	16	4	.80	15	.289	.330	.433
2001 Detroit	AL	120	417	101	19	7	12	(4	8)	170	52	52	25	1	93	6	5	4	9	5	.64	9	.242	.292	.408
5 ML YEARS		444	1670	450	84	24	53	(19	34)	741	222	224	78	3	339	25	12	13	68	26	.72	39	.269	.310	.444

Mario Encarnacion

Bats: Right **Throws:** Right **Pos:** LF-14; RF-6   **Ht:** 6'2" **Wt:** 205 **Born:** 9/24/77 **Age:** 24

Year Team	Lg	G	AB	H	2B	3B	HR	(Hm	Rd)	TB	R	RBI	TBB	IBB	SO	HBP	SH	SF	SB	CS	SB%	GDP	Avg	OBP	SLG
1996 W Michigan	A	118	401	92	14	3	7	—	—	133	55	43	49	0	131	5	4	0	23	8	.74	12	.229	.321	.332
1997 Modesto	A+	111	364	108	17	9	18	—	—	197	70	78	42	1	121	6	0	1	14	11	.56	7	.297	.378	.541
1998 Huntsville	AA	110	357	97	15	2	15	—	—	161	70	61	60	1	123	4	3	1	11	8	.58	9	.272	.382	.451
1999 Midland	AA	94	353	109	21	4	18	—	—	192	69	71	47	4	86	1	0	2	9	9	.50	6	.309	.390	.544
Vancouver	AAA	39	145	35	5	0	3	—	—	49	18	17	6	0	44	2	0	2	5	4	.56	7	.241	.277	.338
2000 Modesto	A+	5	15	3	0	0	0	—	—	3	1	1	1	0	4	0	0	0	0	0	—	2	.200	.250	.200
Sacramento	AAA	81	301	81	16	3	13	—	—	142	51	61	36	2	95	3	1	5	15	7	.68	8	.269	.348	.472
2001 Sacramento	AAA	51	186	53	8	2	12	—	—	101	29	33	17	2	61	4	0	1	4	3	.57	5	.285	.356	.543
Colo Sprngs	AAA	16	45	17	5	0	2	—	—	28	8	10	4	0	8	1	0	0	0	1	.00	1	.378	.440	.622
2001 Colorado	NL	20	62	14	1	0	0	(0	0)	15	3	3	5	0	14	0	0	0	2	1	.67	3	.226	.284	.242

Todd Erdos

Pitches: Right **Bats:** Right **Pos:** RP-10   **Ht:** 6'1" **Wt:** 204 **Born:** 11/21/73 **Age:** 28

	HOW MUCH HE PITCHED						WHAT HE GAVE UP												THE RESULTS						
Year Team	Lg	G	GS	CG	GF	IP	BFP	H	R	ER	HR	SH	SF	HB	TBB	IBB	SO	WP	Bk	W	L	Pct.	ShO	Sv-Op	Hld	ERA
2001 Pawtucket *	AAA	49	0	0	21	67.2	282	59	25	23	3	2	5	1	24	4	54	1	1	5	1	.833	0	7- -	—	3.06
1997 San Diego	NL	11	0	0	2	13.2	64	17	9	8	1	0	0	2	4	0	13	3	0	2	0	1.000	0	0-0	0	5.27
1998 New York	AL	2	0	0	1	2	11	5	2	2	0	0	0	0	1	1	0	0	0	0	0	—	0	0-0	0	9.00
1999 New York	AL	4	0	0	1	7	31	5	4	3	2	0	1	0	4	0	4	1	0	0	0	—	0	0-0	0	3.86
2000 NYY-SD		36	0	0	14	54.2	260	63	38	36	7	1	4	7	28	1	34	2	0	0	0	—	0	2-3	1	5.93
2001 Boston	AL	10	0	0	3	16.1	71	15	9	9	2	0	3	3	8	1	7	0	0	0	0	—	0	0-0	1	4.96
2000 New York	AL	14	0	0	6	25	114	31	14	14	2	0	0	1	11	0	18	1	0	0	0	—	0	1-1	0	5.04
San Diego	NL	22	0	0	8	29.2	146	32	24	22	5	1	4	6	17	1	16	1	0	0	0	—	0	1-2	1	6.67
5 ML YEARS		63	0	0	21	93.2	437	105	62	58	12	1	8	12	45	3	58	6	0	2	0	1.000	0	2-3	2	5.57

Scott Erickson

Pitches: Right **Bats:** Right **2000 Pos:** SP-16   **Ht:** 6'4" **Wt:** 230 **Born:** 2/2/68 **Age:** 34

	HOW MUCH HE PITCHED						WHAT HE GAVE UP												THE RESULTS						
Year Team	Lg	G	GS	CG	GF	IP	BFP	H	R	ER	HR	SH	SF	HB	TBB	IBB	SO	WP	Bk	W	L	Pct.	ShO	Sv-Op	Hld	ERA
1990 Minnesota	AL	19	17	1	1	113	485	108	49	36	9	5	2	5	51	4	53	3	0	8	4	.667	0	0-0	0	2.87
1991 Minnesota	AL	32	32	5	0	204	851	189	80	72	13	5	7	6	71	3	108	4	0	20	8	.714	3	0-0	0	3.18
1992 Minnesota	AL	32	32	5	0	212	888	197	86	80	18	9	7	8	83	3	101	6	1	13	12	.520	3	0-0	0	3.40
1993 Minnesota	AL	34	34	1	0	218.2	976	266	138	126	17	10	13	10	71	1	116	5	0	8	19	.296	0	0-0	0	5.19
1994 Minnesota	AL	23	23	2	0	144	654	173	95	87	15	3	4	9	59	0	104	10	0	8	11	.421	1	0-0	0	5.44
1995 Min-Bal	AL	32	31	7	1	196.1	836	213	108	105	18	3	3	5	67	0	106	3	2	13	10	.565	2	0-0	0	4.81
1996 Baltimore	AL	34	34	6	0	222.1	968	262	137	124	21	5	5	11	66	4	100	1	0	13	12	.520	0	0-0	0	5.02
1997 Baltimore	AL	34	33	3	0	221.2	922	218	100	91	16	3	4	5	61	5	131	11	0	16	7	.696	2	0-0	0	3.69
1998 Baltimore	AL	36	36	11	0	251.1	1102	284	125	112	23	7	2	13	69	4	186	4	0	16	13	.552	2	0-0	0	4.01
1999 Baltimore	AL	34	34	6	0	230.1	995	244	127	123	27	7	6	11	99	4	106	10	0	15	12	.556	3	0-0	0	4.81
2000 Baltimore	AL	16	16	1	0	92.2	446	127	81	81	14	3	5	5	48	0	41	3	0	5	8	.385	0	0-0	0	7.87
1995 Minnesota	AL	15	15	0	0	87.2	390	102	61	58	11	2	1	4	32	0	45	1	0	4	6	.400	0	0-0	0	5.95
Baltimore	AL	17	16	7	1	108.2	446	111	47	47	7	1	2	1	35	0	61	2	2	9	4	.692	2	0-0	0	3.89
11 ML YEARS		326	322	48	2	2106.1	9123	2281	1126	1037	191	60	58	88	745	28	1152	60	3	135	116	.538	16	0-0	0	4.43

Darin Erstad

Bats: Left **Throws:** Left **Pos:** CF-146; 1B-12; DH-4   **Ht:** 6'2" **Wt:** 220 **Born:** 6/4/74 **Age:** 28

Year Team	Lg	G	AB	H	2B	3B	HR	(Hm	Rd)	TB	R	RBI	TBB	IBB	SO	HBP	SH	SF	SB	CS	SB%	GDP	Avg	OBP	SLG
1996 California	AL	57	208	59	5	1	4	(1	3)	78	34	20	17	1	29	0	1	3	3	3	.50	3	.284	.333	.375
1997 Anaheim	AL	139	539	161	34	4	16	(8	8)	251	99	77	51	4	86	4	5	6	23	8	.74	5	.299	.360	.466
1998 Anaheim	AL	133	537	159	39	3	19	(9	10)	261	84	82	43	7	77	6	1	3	20	6	.77	2	.296	.353	.486
1999 Anaheim	AL	142	585	148	22	5	13	(7	6)	219	84	53	47	3	101	1	2	3	13	7	.65	16	.253	.308	.374
2000 Anaheim	AL	157	676	240	39	6	25	(11	14)	366	121	100	64	9	82	1	2	4	28	8	.78	8	.355	.409	.541
2001 Anaheim	AL	157	631	163	35	1	9	(3	6)	227	89	63	62	7	113	10	1	7	24	10	.71	8	.258	.331	.360
6 ML YEARS		785	3176	930	174	20	86	(39	47)	1402	511	395	284	31	488	22	12	26	111	42	.73	42	.293	.352	.441

Alex Escobar

Bats: Right **Throws:** Right **Pos:** CF-9; RF-7; PH/PR-5   **Ht:** 6'1" **Wt:** 180 **Born:** 9/6/78 **Age:** 23

Year Team	Lg	G	AB	H	2B	3B	HR	(Hm	Rd)	TB	R	RBI	TBB	IBB	SO	HBP	SH	SF	SB	CS	SB%	GDP	Avg	OBP	SLG
1996 Mets	R	24	75	27	4	0	0	—	—	31	15	10	4	0	9	3	0	1	7	1	.88	0	.360	.410	.413
1997 Kingsport	R+	10	36	7	3	0	0	—	—	10	6	3	3	1	8	0	0	1	1	0	1.00	3	.194	.250	.278
Mets	R	26	73	18	4	1	1	—	—	27	12	11	10	0	17	1	0	1	0	0	—	1	.247	.341	.370
1998 Capital Cty	A	112	416	129	23	5	27	—	—	243	90	91	54	1	133	5	5	3	49	7	.88	1	.310	.393	.584
1999 Mets	R	2	8	3	2	0	0	—	—	5	1	1	1	0	2	0	0	0	0	0	—	0	.375	.444	.625
St. Lucie	A+	1	3	2	0	0	1	—	—	5	1	3	1	0	1	0	0	0	1	1	.50	0	.667	.600	1.667
2000 Binghamton	AA	122	437	126	25	7	16	—	—	213	79	67	57	5	114	7	0	5	24	5	.83	8	.288	.375	.487
2001 Norfolk	AAA	111	397	106	21	4	12	—	—	171	55	52	35	2	146	3	1	5	18	3	.86	10	.267	.327	.431
2001 New York	NL	18	50	10	1	0	3	(3	0)	20	3	8	3	0	19	0	0	0	1	0	1.00	1	.200	.245	.400

Kelvim Escobar

Pitches: Right **Bats:** Right **Pos:** RP-48; SP-11

Ht: 6'1" **Wt:** 210 **Born:** 4/11/76 **Age:** 26

		HOW MUCH HE PITCHED						WHAT HE GAVE UP									THE RESULTS					
Year Team	Lg	G	GS	CG	GF	IP	BFP	H	R	ER	HR	SH	SF	HB	TBB	IBB	SO	WP	Bk	W	L	Pct.	ShO	Sv-Op	Hld	ERA
1997 Toronto	AL	27	0	0	23	31	139	28	12	10	1	2	0	0	19	2	36	0	0	3	2	.600	0	14-17	1	2.90
1998 Toronto	AL	22	10	0	2	79.2	342	72	37	33	5	0	3	0	35	0	72	0	0	7	3	.700	0	0-1	5	3.73
1999 Toronto	AL	33	30	1	2	174	795	203	118	110	19	2	8	10	81	2	129	6	1	14	11	.560	0	0-0	0	5.69
2000 Toronto	AL	43	24	3	8	180	794	186	118	107	26	5	4	3	85	3	142	4	0	10	15	.400	1	2-3	3	5.35
2001 Toronto	AL	59	11	1	15	126	517	93	51	49	8	2	5	3	52	5	121	2	0	6	8	.429	1	0-0	13	3.50
5 ML YEARS		184	75	5	50	590.2	2587	582	336	309	59	11	20	16	272	12	500	12	1	40	39	.506	2	16-21	22	4.71

Bobby Estalella

Bats: Right **Throws:** Right **Pos:** C-31; PH/PR-1

Ht: 6'1" **Wt:** 205 **Born:** 8/23/74 **Age:** 27

		BATTING															BASERUNNING				PERCENTAGES		
Year Team	Lg	G	AB	H	2B	3B	HR	(Hm | Rd)	TB	R	RBI	TBB	IBB	SO	HBP	SH	SF	SB	CS	SB%	GDP	Avg	OBP	SLG
2001 Fresno *	AAA	6	22	7	1	0	1	—	—	11	3	4	1	0	9	0	0	0	0	0	—	1	.318	.348	.500
Columbus *	AAA	48	171	44	10	1	10	—	—	86	26	38	21	1	45	2	0	3	0	2	.00	7	.257	.340	.503
1996 Philadelphia	NL	7	17	6	0	0	2	(0 | 2)	12	5	4	1	0	6	0	0	0	1	0	1.00	0	.353	.389	.706
1997 Philadelphia	NL	13	29	10	1	0	4	(1 | 3)	23	9	9	7	0	7	0	0	0	0	0	—	2	.345	.472	.793
1998 Philadelphia	NL	47	165	31	6	1	8	(3 | 5)	63	16	20	13	0	49	1	0	3	0	0	—	4	.188	.247	.382
1999 Philadelphia	NL	9	18	3	0	0	0	(0 | 0)	3	2	1	4	0	7	0	0	0	0	1	.00	0	.167	.318	.167
2000 San Francisco	NL	106	299	70	22	3	14	(6 | 8)	140	45	53	57	9	92	2	0	3	3	0	1.00	4	.234	.357	.468
2001 SF-NYY		32	97	19	5	1	3	(2 | 1)	35	12	10	12	2	30	2	0	0	0	0	—	2	.196	.297	.361
2001 San Francisco	NL	29	93	19	5	1	3	(2 | 1)	35	11	10	11	2	28	1	0	0	0	0	—	2	.204	.295	.376
New York	AL	3	4	0	0	0	0	(0 | 0)	0	1	0	1	0	2	1	0	0	0	0	—	0	.000	.333	.000
6 ML YEARS		214	625	139	34	5	31	(12 | 19)	276	89	97	94	11	191	5	0	6	4	1	.80	12	.222	.326	.442

Shawn Estes

Pitches: Left **Bats:** Right **Pos:** SP-27

Ht: 6'2" **Wt:** 195 **Born:** 2/18/73 **Age:** 29

		HOW MUCH HE PITCHED						WHAT HE GAVE UP										THE RESULTS					
Year Team	Lg	G	GS	CG	GF	IP	BFP	H	R	ER	HR	SH	SF	HB	TBB	IBB	SO	WP	Bk	W	L	Pct.	ShO	Sv-Op	Hld	ERA
1995 San Francisco	NL	3	3	0	0	17.1	76	16	14	13	2	0	0	1	5	0	14	4	0	0	3	.000	0	0-0	0	6.75
1996 San Francisco	NL	11	11	0	0	70	305	63	30	28	3	5	0	2	39	0	60	4	0	3	5	.375	0	0-0	0	3.60
1997 San Francisco	NL	32	32	3	0	201	849	162	80	71	12	13	2	8	100	2	181	10	2	19	5	.792	2	0-0	0	3.18
1998 San Francisco	NL	25	25	1	0	149.1	661	150	89	84	14	15	4	5	80	6	136	6	1	7	12	.368	1	0-0	0	5.06
1999 San Francisco	NL	32	32	1	0	203	914	209	121	111	21	14	3	5	112	2	159	15	1	11	11	.500	1	0-0	0	4.92
2000 San Francisco	NL	30	30	4	0	190.1	829	194	99	90	11	7	6	3	108	1	136	11	0	15	6	.714	2	0-0	0	4.26
2001 San Francisco	NL	27	27	0	0	159	693	151	78	71	11	5	9	5	77	7	109	10	2	9	8	.529	0	0-0	0	4.02
7 ML YEARS		160	160	9	0	990	4327	945	511	468	74	59	24	29	521	21	795	60	6	64	50	.561	6	0-0	0	4.25

Horacio Estrada

Pitches: Left **Bats:** Left **Pos:** RP-4

Ht: 6'0" **Wt:** 160 **Born:** 10/19/75 **Age:** 26

		HOW MUCH HE PITCHED						WHAT HE GAVE UP										THE RESULTS					
Year Team	Lg	G	GS	CG	GF	IP	BFP	H	R	ER	HR	SH	SF	HB	TBB	IBB	SO	WP	Bk	W	L	Pct.	ShO	Sv-Op	Hld	ERA
1995 Brewers	R	8	1	0	3	17	73	13	9	7	1	1	1	0	8	0	21	4	2	0	1	.000	0	2--	—	3.71
Helena	R+	13	0	0	1	30	144	27	21	18	3	5	0	3	24	0	30	2	0	1	2	.333	0	0--	—	5.40
1996 Beloit	A	17	0	0	9	29.1	113	21	8	4	2	2	0	0	11	1	34	5	1	2	1	.667	0	1--	—	1.23
Stockton	A+	29	0	0	11	51	214	43	29	26	7	1	1	2	21	2	62	3	0	1	3	.250	0	3--	—	4.59
1997 El Paso	AA	29	23	1	2	153.2	694	174	93	81	11	4	4	4	70	0	127	8	3	8	10	.444	0	1--	—	4.74
1998 El Paso	AA	8	8	0	0	49.2	206	50	27	25	3	6	2	2	21	0	37	4	0	5	0	1.000	0	0--	—	4.53
Louisville	AAA	2	2	0	0	12	50	10	4	4	1	0	0	0	5	0	4	0	0	0	0	—	0	0--	—	3.00
1999 Louisville	AAA	25	24	1	0	131.2	575	128	87	83	21	3	8	9	65	1	112	8	1	6	6	.500	0	0--	—	5.67
2000 Indianapols	AAA	25	25	3	0	159.1	663	149	63	59	14	7	2	7	45	0	103	9	0	14	4	.778	2	0--	—	3.33
2001 Colo Sprngs	AAA	16	16	0	0	91.1	387	102	51	48	11	2	2	3	20	0	77	8	1	8	4	.667	0	0--	—	4.73
1999 Milwaukee	NL	4	0	0	2	7.1	36	10	6	6	4	0	0	0	4	0	5	0	0	0	0	—	0	0-0	0	7.36
2000 Milwaukee	NL	7	4	0	2	24.1	123	30	18	17	5	0	1	2	20	4	13	3	0	3	0	1.000	0	0-0	0	6.29
2001 Colorado	NL	4	0	0	2	4.1	22	8	7	7	1	0	0	1	1	0	4	0	0	1	1	.500	0	0-0	0	14.54
3 ML YEARS		15	4	0	6	36	181	48	31	30	10	0	1	3	25	4	22	3	0	4	1	.800	0	0-0	0	7.50

Johnny Estrada

Bats: Both **Throws:** Right **Pos:** C-89; PH/PR-5

Ht: 5'11" **Wt:** 195 **Born:** 6/27/76 **Age:** 26

		BATTING															BASERUNNING				PERCENTAGES		
Year Team	Lg	G	AB	H	2B	3B	HR	(Hm | Rd)	TB	R	RBI	TBB	IBB	SO	HBP	SH	SF	SB	CS	SB%	GDP	Avg	OBP	SLG
1997 Batavia	A-	58	223	70	17	2	6	—	—	109	28	43	9	1	15	1	2	5	0	0	—	9	.314	.336	.489
1998 Piedmont	A	77	303	94	14	2	7	—	—	133	33	44	6	1	19	5	0	3	0	1	.00	11	.310	.331	.439
Clearwater	A+	37	117	26	8	0	0	—	—	34	8	13	5	0	7	0	2	2	0	0	—	2	.222	.250	.291
1999 Clearwater	A+	98	346	96	15	0	9	—	—	138	35	52	14	3	26	2	6	8	1	0	1.00	12	.277	.303	.399
2000 Reading	AA	95	356	105	18	0	12	—	—	159	42	42	10	2	20	4	2	0	1	0	1.00	6	.295	.322	.447
2001 Scrantn-WB	AAA	32	131	38	13	0	0	—	—	51	13	16	6	1	6	1	0	1	0	0	—	5	.290	.319	.389
2001 Philadelphia	NL	89	298	68	15	0	8	(7 | 1)	107	26	37	16	6	32	4	2	4	0	0	—	15	.228	.273	.359

Seth Etherton

Pitches: Right **Bats:** Right **2000 Pos:** SP-11

Ht: 6'1" **Wt:** 200 **Born:** 10/17/76 **Age:** 25

		HOW MUCH HE PITCHED						WHAT HE GAVE UP										THE RESULTS					
Year Team	Lg	G	GS	CG	GF	IP	BFP	H	R	ER	HR	SH	SF	HB	TBB	IBB	SO	WP	Bk	W	L	Pct.	ShO	Sv-Op	Hld	ERA
1998 Midland	AA	9	7	1	1	48.1	211	57	36	33	9	3	2	1	12	0	35	1	0	0	0	—	0	0--	—	6.14
1999 Erie	AA	24	24	4	0	167.2	694	153	72	61	14	7	5	3	43	0	153	4	4	10	10	.500	1	0--	—	3.27
Edmonton	AAA	4	4	0	0	21.1	94	25	13	13	7	1	1	0	6	0	19	1	0	0	2	.000	0	0--	—	5.48

			HOW MUCH HE PITCHED						WHAT HE GAVE UP										THE RESULTS					
Year Team	Lg	G	GS	CG	GF	IP	BFP	H	R	ER	HR	SH	SF	HB	TBB	IBB	SO	WP	Bk	W	L	Pct.	ShO	Sv-Op	Hld	ERA
2000 Edmonton	AAA	9	9	0	0	58.1	248	60	30	26	6	0	1	1	19	0	50	3	0	3	2	.600	0	0-	—	4.01
2000 Anaheim	AL	11	11	0	0	60.1	270	68	38	37	16	1	1	1	22	0	32	2	0	5	1	.833	0	0-0	0	5.52

Tony Eusebio

Bats: Right **Throws:** Right **Pos:** C-48; PH/PR-13   **Ht:** 6'2" **Wt:** 210 **Born:** 4/27/67 **Age:** 35

					BATTING													BASERUNNING				PERCENTAGES		
Year Team	Lg	G	AB	H	2B	3B	HR	(Hm	Rd)	TB	R	RBI	TBB	IBB	SO	HBP	SH	SF	SB	CS	SB%	GDP	Avg	OBP	SLG
1991 Houston	NL	10	19	2	1	0	0			3	4	0	6	0	8	0	0	0	0	0	—	1	.105	.320	.158
1994 Houston	NL	55	159	47	9	1	5	(1	4)	73	18	30	8	0	33	0	2	5	0	1	.00	4	.296	.320	.459
1995 Houston	NL	113	368	110	21	1	6	(5	1)	151	46	58	31	1	59	3	1	5	0	2	.00	12	.299	.354	.410
1996 Houston	NL	58	152	41	7	2	1	(1	0)	55	15	19	18	2	20	0	0	0	0	1	.00	5	.270	.343	.362
1997 Houston	NL	60	164	45	2	0	1	(0	1)	50	12	18	19	1	27	4	0	0	0	1	.00	4	.274	.364	.305
1998 Houston	NL	66	182	46	6	1	1	(1	0)	57	13	36	18	2	31	1	0	2	1	0	1.00	8	.253	.320	.313
1999 Houston	NL	103	323	88	15	0	4	(2	2)	115	31	33	40	4	67	0	0	0	0	0	—	9	.272	.353	.356
2000 Houston	NL	74	218	61	18	0	7	(2	5)	100	24	33	25	2	45	4	0	2	0	0	—	8	.280	.361	.459
2001 Houston	NL	59	154	39	8	0	5	(3	2)	62	16	14	17	3	34	3	0	0	0	0	—	2	.253	.339	.403
9 ML YEARS		598	1739	479	87	5	30	(15	15)	666	179	241	182	15	324	15	3	16	1	5	.17	53	.275	.346	.383

Adam Everett

Bats: Right **Throws:** Right **Pos:** PH/PR-7; SS-6   **Ht:** 6'0" **Wt:** 156 **Born:** 2/2/77 **Age:** 25

					BATTING													BASERUNNING				PERCENTAGES		
Year Team	Lg	G	AB	H	2B	3B	HR	(Hm	Rd)	TB	R	RBI	TBB	IBB	SO	HBP	SH	SF	SB	CS	SB%	GDP	Avg	OBP	SLG
1998 Lowell	A-	21	71	21	6	2	0	—	—	31	11	9	11	0	13	3	1	1	2	1	.67	2	.296	.407	.437
1999 Trenton	AA	98	338	89	11	0	10	—	—	130	56	44	41	0	64	10	9	4	21	5	.81	3	.263	.356	.385
2000 New Orleans	AAA	126	453	111	25	2	5	—	—	155	82	37	75	0	100	11	4	4	13	4	.76	6	.245	.363	.342
2001 New Orleans	AAA	114	441	110	20	8	5	—	—	161	69	40	39	0	74	16	9	4	24	5	.83	4	.249	.330	.365
2001 Houston	NL	9	3	0	0	0	0	(0	0)	0	1	0	0	0	1	0	0	0	1	0	1.00	0	.000	.000	.000

Carl Everett

Bats: B **Throws:** R **Pos:** CF-84; RF-9; DH-7; PH/PR-3   **Ht:** 6'0" **Wt:** 215 **Born:** 6/3/71 **Age:** 31

					BATTING													BASERUNNING				PERCENTAGES		
Year Team	Lg	G	AB	H	2B	3B	HR	(Hm	Rd)	TB	R	RBI	TBB	IBB	SO	HBP	SH	SF	SB	CS	SB%	GDP	Avg	OBP	SLG
2001 Sarasota *	A+	2	7	3	0	0	0	—	—	3	0	0	2	2	0	0	0	0	0	0	—	0	.429	.556	.429
Red Sox *	R	3	10	2	0	0	2	—	—	8	2	2	1	1	3	0	0	0	0	0	—	0	.200	.273	.800
1993 Florida	NL	11	19	2	0	0	0	(0	0)	2	0	1	0	0	9	0	0	0	1	0	1.00	0	.105	.150	.105
1994 Florida	NL	16	51	11	1	0	2	(0	2)	18	7	6	3	0	15	0	0	0	4	0	1.00	0	.216	.259	.353
1995 New York	NL	79	289	75	13	1	12	(9	3)	126	48	54	39	2	67	2	1	0	2	5	.29	11	.260	.352	.436
1996 New York	NL	101	192	46	8	1	1	(1	0)	59	29	16	21	2	53	4	1	1	6	0	1.00	4	.240	.326	.307
1997 New York	NL	142	443	110	28	3	14	(11	3)	186	58	57	32	3	102	7	3	2	17	9	.65	3	.248	.308	.420
1998 Houston	NL	133	467	138	34	4	15	(5	10)	225	72	76	44	2	102	3	3	2	14	12	.54	11	.296	.359	.482
1999 Houston	NL	123	464	151	33	3	25	(11	14)	265	86	108	50	5	94	11	2	8	27	7	.79	5	.325	.398	.571
2000 Boston	AL	137	496	149	32	4	34	(17	17)	291	82	108	52	5	113	8	0	5	11	4	.73	4	.300	.373	.587
2001 Boston	AL	102	409	105	24	4	14	(6	8)	179	61	58	27	3	104	13	0	5	9	2	.82	9	.257	.323	.438
9 ML YEARS		844	2830	787	173	20	117	(62	55)	1351	443	483	269	22	659	48	10	18	91	39	.70	41	.278	.349	.477

Scott Eyre

Pitches: Left **Bats:** Left **Pos:** RP-17   **Ht:** 6'1" **Wt:** 200 **Born:** 5/30/72 **Age:** 30

			HOW MUCH HE PITCHED						WHAT HE GAVE UP										THE RESULTS					
Year Team	Lg	G	GS	CG	GF	IP	BFP	H	R	ER	HR	SH	SF	HB	TBB	IBB	SO	WP	Bk	W	L	Pct.	ShO	Sv-Op	Hld	ERA
2001 Syracuse *	AAA	62	2	0	12	79.1	334	67	30	28	8	1	3	5	26	4	96	6	0	4	6	.400	0	0--	—	3.18
1997 Chicago	AL	11	11	0	0	60.2	267	62	36	34	11	1	2	1	31	1	36	2	0	4	4	.500	0	0-0	0	5.04
1998 Chicago	AL	33	17	0	10	107	491	114	78	64	24	2	3	2	64	0	73	7	0	3	8	.273	0	0-0	0	5.38
1999 Chicago	AL	21	0	0	8	25	129	38	22	21	6	0	1	1	15	2	17	1	0	1	1	.500	0	0-0	1	7.56
2000 Chicago	AL	13	1	0	3	19	93	29	15	14	3	0	2	1	12	0	16	0	0	1	1	.500	0	0-0	0	6.63
2001 Toronto	AL	17	0	0	5	15.2	66	15	6	6	1	0	1	1	7	2	16	2	0	1	2	.333	0	2-3	3	3.45
5 ML YEARS		95	29	0	26	227.1	1046	258	157	139	45	3	9	6	129	5	158	12	0	10	16	.385	0	2-3	4	5.50

Jorge Fabregas

Bats: Left **Throws:** Right **Pos:** C-53   **Ht:** 6'3" **Wt:** 220 **Born:** 3/13/70 **Age:** 32

					BATTING													BASERUNNING				PERCENTAGES		
Year Team	Lg	G	AB	H	2B	3B	HR	(Hm	Rd)	TB	R	RBI	TBB	IBB	SO	HBP	SH	SF	SB	CS	SB%	GDP	Avg	OBP	SLG
1994 California	AL	43	127	36	3	0	0	(0	0)	39	12	16	7	1	18	0	1	0	2	1	.67	5	.283	.321	.307
1995 California	AL	73	227	56	10	0	1	(1	0)	69	24	22	17	0	28	0	3	1	0	2	.00	9	.247	.298	.304
1996 California	AL	90	254	73	6	0	2	(1	1)	85	18	26	17	3	27	0	3	5	0	1	.00	7	.287	.326	.335
1997 Ana-CWS	AL	121	360	93	11	1	7	(1	6)	127	33	51	14	0	46	1	6	4	1	1	.50	16	.258	.285	.353
1998 Ari-NYM	NL	70	183	36	4	0	2	(0	2)	46	11	20	14	1	32	1	1	2	0	0	—	4	.197	.255	.251
1999 Fla-Atl	NL	88	231	46	10	2	3	(1	2)	69	20	21	26	6	27	2	4	5	0	0	—	9	.199	.280	.299
2000 Kansas City	AL	43	142	40	4	0	3	(1	2)	53	13	17	8	1	11	0	2	0	1	0	1.00	1	.282	.320	.373
2001 Anaheim	AL	53	148	33	4	2	2	(0	2)	47	9	16	3	0	15	0	4	2	0	0	—	5	.223	.235	.318
1997 Anaheim	AL	21	38	3	0	0	0	(0	0)	4	2	3	3	0	3	0	2	0	0	0	—	2	.079	.146	.105
Chicago	AL	100	322	90	10	1	7	(1	6)	123	31	48	11	0	43	1	4	4	1	1	.50	14	.280	.302	.382
1998 Arizona	NL	50	151	30	4	0	1	(0	1)	37	8	15	13	1	26	1	0	2	0	0	—	3	.199	.263	.245
New York	NL	20	32	6	0	0	1	(0	1)	9	3	5	1	0	6	0	1	0	0	0	—	1	.188	.212	.281
1999 Florida	NL	82	223	46	10	2	3	(1	2)	69	20	21	26	6	27	2	4	5	0	0	—	8	.206	.289	.309
Atlanta	NL	6	8	0	0	0	0	(0	0)	0	0	0	0	0	0	0	0	0	0	0	—	2	.000	.000	.000
8 ML YEARS		581	1672	413	52	5	20	(6	14)	535	140	189	106	12	204	4	24	19	4	5	.44	56	.247	.290	.320

Kyle Farnsworth

Pitches: Right **Bats:** Right **Pos:** RP-76   **Ht:** 6'4" **Wt:** 220 **Born:** 4/14/76 **Age:** 26

Year Team	Lg	HOW MUCH HE PITCHED						WHAT HE GAVE UP											THE RESULTS						
		G	GS	CG	GF	IP	BFP	H	R	ER	HR	SH	SF	HB	TBB	IBB	SO	WP	Bk	W	L	Pct.	ShO	Sv-Op	Hld	ERA
1999 Chicago	NL	27	21	1	1	130	579	140	80	73	28	6	2	3	52	1	70	7	1	5	9	.357	1	0-0	0	5.05
2000 Chicago	NL	46	5	0	8	77	371	90	58	55	14	4	4	4	50	8	74	3	0	2	9	.182	0	1-6	6	6.43
2001 Chicago	NL	76	0	0	24	82	339	65	26	25	8	2	2	1	29	2	107	2	2	4	6	.400	0	2-3	24	2.74
3 ML YEARS		149	26	1	33	289	1289	295	164	153	50	12	8	8	131	11	251	12	3	11	24	.314	1	3-9	30	4.76

Sal Fasano

Bats: Right **Throws:** Right **Pos:** C-37; PH/PR-2; DH-1   **Ht:** 6'2" **Wt:** 230 **Born:** 8/10/71 **Age:** 30

Year Team	Lg	BATTING																BASERUNNING				PERCENTAGES		
		G	AB	H	2B	3B	HR	(Hm	Rd)	TB	R	RBI	TBB	IBB	SO	HBP	SH	SF	SB	CS	SB%	GDP	Avg	OBP	SLG
2001 Omaha *	AAA	13	46	11	1	0	2			18	6	7	4	0	11	5	0	0	0	0	—	1	.239	.364	.391
Colo Sprngs *	AAA	26	82	25	4	0	7			50	16	23	9	1	26	4	1	1	0	0	—	4	.305	.396	.610
1996 Kansas City	AL	51	143	29	2	0	6	(1	5)	49	20	19	14	0	25	2	1	0	1	1	.50	3	.203	.283	.343
1997 Kansas City	AL	13	38	8	2	0	1	(0	1)	13	4	1	1	0	12	0	0	0	0	0	—	1	.211	.231	.342
1998 Kansas City	AL	74	216	49	10	0	8	(4	4)	83	21	31	10	1	56	16	3	2	1	0	1.00	4	.227	.307	.384
1999 Kansas City	AL	23	60	14	2	0	5	(2	3)	31	11	16	7	0	17	7	0	1	0	1	.00	4	.233	.373	.517
2000 Oakland	AL	52	126	27	6	0	7	(4	3)	54	21	19	14	0	47	3	0	1	0	0	—	3	.214	.306	.429
2001 Oak-KC-Col		39	85	17	5	0	3	(3	0)	31	12	9	5	0	31	4	2	0	0	0	—	3	.200	.277	.365
2001 Oakland	AL	11	21	1	0	0	0	(0	0)	1	2	0	1	0	12	1	0	0	0	0	—	1	.048	.130	.048
Kansas City	AL	3	1	0	0	0	0	(0	0)	0	0	0	0	0	0	0	0	0	0	0	—	0	.000	.000	.000
Colorado	NL	25	63	16	5	0	3	(3	0)	30	10	9	4	0	19	3	2	0	0	0	—	1	.254	.329	.476
6 ML YEARS		252	668	144	27	0	30	(14	16)	261	89	95	51	1	188	32	6	4	2	2	.50	15	.216	.301	.391

Jeff Fassero

Pitches: Left **Bats:** Left **Pos:** RP-82   **Ht:** 6'1" **Wt:** 200 **Born:** 1/5/63 **Age:** 39

Year Team	Lg	HOW MUCH HE PITCHED						WHAT HE GAVE UP											THE RESULTS						
		G	GS	CG	GF	IP	BFP	H	R	ER	HR	SH	SF	HB	TBB	IBB	SO	WP	Bk	W	L	Pct.	ShO	Sv-Op	Hld	ERA
1991 Montreal	NL	51	0	0	30	55.1	223	39	17	15	1	6	0	1	17	1	42	4	0	2	5	.286	0	8-11	7	2.44
1992 Montreal	NL	70	0	0	22	85.2	368	81	35	27	1	5	2	2	34	6	63	7	1	8	7	.533	0	1-7	12	2.84
1993 Montreal	NL	56	15	1	10	149.2	616	119	50	38	7	7	4	0	54	0	140	5	0	12	5	.706	0	1-3	6	2.29
1994 Montreal	NL	21	21	1	0	138.2	569	119	54	46	13	7	2	1	40	4	119	6	0	8	6	.571	0	0-0	0	2.99
1995 Montreal	NL	30	30	1	0	189	833	207	102	91	15	19	7	2	74	3	164	7	1	13	14	.481	0	0-0	0	4.33
1996 Montreal	NL	34	34	5	0	231.2	967	217	95	85	20	16	5	3	55	3	222	5	2	15	11	.577	1	0-0	0	3.30
1997 Seattle	AL	35	35	2	0	234.1	1010	226	108	94	21	7	10	3	84	6	189	13	2	16	9	.640	1	0-0	0	3.61
1998 Seattle	AL	32	32	7	0	224.2	954	223	115	99	33	8	8	10	66	2	176	12	0	13	12	.520	0	0-0	0	3.97
1999 Sea-Tex	AL	37	27	0	2	156.1	751	208	135	125	35	2	7	4	83	3	114	9	0	5	14	.263	0	0-0	2	7.20
2000 Boston	AL	38	23	0	4	130	577	153	72	69	16	7	2	1	50	2	97	2	0	8	8	.500	0	0-0	5	4.78
2001 Chicago	NL	82	0	0	30	73.2	308	66	31	28	6	1	2	1	23	5	79	3	0	4	4	.500	0	12-17	25	3.42
1999 Seattle	AL	30	24	0	1	139	669	188	123	114	34	1	6	4	73	3	101	7	0	4	14	.222	0	0-0	0	7.38
Texas	AL	7	3	0	1	17.1	82	20	12	11	1	1	1	0	10	0	13	2	0	1	0	1.000	0	0-0	0	5.71
11 ML YEARS		486	217	17	98	1669	7176	1658	814	717	168	85	49	28	580	35	1405	73	6	104	95	.523	2	22-38	57	3.87

Carlos Febles

Bats: Right **Throws:** Right **Pos:** 2B-78; PH/PR-3   **Ht:** 5'11" **Wt:** 185 **Born:** 5/24/76 **Age:** 26

Year Team	Lg	BATTING																BASERUNNING				PERCENTAGES		
		G	AB	H	2B	3B	HR	(Hm	Rd)	TB	R	RBI	TBB	IBB	SO	HBP	SH	SF	SB	CS	SB%	GDP	Avg	OBP	SLG
2001 Omaha *	AAA	25	98	33	7	1	2			48	23	9	9	0	14	4	0	0	6	2	.75	0	.337	.414	.490
1998 Kansas City	AL	11	25	10	1	2	0	(0	0)	15	5	2	4	0	7	0	0	0	2	1	.67	0	.400	.483	.600
1999 Kansas City	AL	123	453	116	22	9	10	(5	5)	186	71	53	47	0	91	9	12	3	20	4	.83	16	.256	.336	.411
2000 Kansas City	AL	100	339	87	12	1	2	(2	0)	107	59	29	36	1	48	10	13	1	17	6	.74	10	.257	.345	.316
2001 Kansas City	AL	79	292	69	9	2	8	(6	2)	106	45	25	22	0	58	1	1	1	5	2	.71	7	.236	.291	.363
4 ML YEARS		313	1109	282	44	14	20	(13	7)	414	180	109	109	1	204	20	26	5	44	13	.77	33	.254	.331	.373

Pedro Feliz

Bats: Right **Throws:** Right **Pos:** 3B-86; PH/PR-14; DH-1   **Ht:** 6'1" **Wt:** 180 **Born:** 4/27/77 **Age:** 25

Year Team	Lg	BATTING																BASERUNNING				PERCENTAGES		
		G	AB	H	2B	3B	HR	(Hm	Rd)	TB	R	RBI	TBB	IBB	SO	HBP	SH	SF	SB	CS	SB%	GDP	Avg	OBP	SLG
1994 Giants	R	38	119	23	0	0	0			23	7	3	2	0	20	2	3	0	2	3	.40	3	.193	.220	.193
1995 Bellingham	A-	43	113	31	2	1	0			35	14	16	7	0	33	0	2	2	1	1	.50	2	.274	.311	.310
1996 Burlington	A	93	321	85	12	2	5			116	36	36	18	0	65	1	0	3	5	2	.71	11	.265	.303	.361
1997 Bakersfield	A+	135	515	140	25	4	14			215	59	56	23	0	90	7	3	3	5	7	.42	15	.272	.310	.417
1998 Shreveport	AA	100	364	96	23	2	12			159	39	50	9	0	62	2	0	4	0	1	.00	15	.264	.282	.437
Fresno	AAA	3	7	3	1	0	1			7	1	3	1	0	0	0	0	0	0	0	—	1	.429	.500	1.000
1999 Shreveport	AA	131	491	124	24	6	13			199	52	77	19	0	90	3	1	5	4	2	.67	18	.253	.282	.405
2000 Fresno	AAA	128	503	150	34	2	33			287	85	105	30	4	94	2	0	2	1	1	.50	18	.298	.337	.571
2000 San Francisco	NL	8	7	2	0	0	0	(0	0)	2	1	0	0	0	1	0	0	0	0	0	—	0	.286	.286	.286
2001 San Francisco	NL	94	220	50	9	1	7	(3	4)	82	23	22	10	2	50	2	3	3	2	1	.67	5	.227	.264	.373
2 ML YEARS		102	227	52	9	1	7	(3	4)	84	24	22	10	2	51	2	3	3	2	1	.67	5	.229	.264	.370

Jared Fernandez

Pitches: Right **Bats:** Right **Pos:** RP-3; SP-2   **Ht:** 6'2" **Wt:** 223 **Born:** 2/2/72 **Age:** 30

Year Team	Lg	HOW MUCH HE PITCHED						WHAT HE GAVE UP											THE RESULTS						
		G	GS	CG	GF	IP	BFP	H	R	ER	HR	SH	SF	HB	TBB	IBB	SO	WP	Bk	W	L	Pct.	ShO	Sv-Op	Hld	ERA
1994 Utica	A-	21	1	0	15	30	144	43	18	12	4	0	0	0	8	2	24	0	1	1	1	.500	0	4--	—	3.60
1995 Utica	A-	5	5	1	0	38	148	30	11	8	2	0	1	1	9	1	23	1	0	3	2	.600	0	0--	—	1.89
Trenton	AA	11	10	1	0	67	290	64	32	29	4	3	1	5	28	1	40	2	0	5	4	.556	0	0--	—	3.90

69

Year Team	Lg	G	GS	CG	GF	IP	BFP	H	R	ER	HR	SH	SF	HB	TBB	IBB	SO	WP	Bk	W	L	Pct.	ShO	Sv-Op	Hld	ERA
1996 Trenton	AA	30	29	3	0	179	798	185	115	101	19	5	9	10	83	5	94	10	0	9	9	.500	0	0--	—	5.08
1997 Pawtucket	AAA	11	11	0	0	60.2	281	76	45	39	7	2	2	5	28	1	33	4	0	3	3	.000	0	0--	—	5.79
Trenton	AA	21	16	1	4	121.1	560	138	90	73	12	2	2	0	66	0	73	14	0	4	6	.400	0	0--	—	5.41
1998 Trenton	AA	36	7	0	10	118.1	527	132	80	69	8	8	3	3	51	3	70	15	1	3	7	.300	0	1--	—	5.25
Pawtucket	AAA	5	2	0	2	24.2	107	26	16	13	5	0	2	3	7	0	15	4	0	1	1	.500	0	0--	—	4.74
1999 Trenton	AA	7	0	0	4	18.2	80	18	9	7	4	0	0	0	8	0	10	1	0	3	0	1.000	0	1--	—	3.38
Pawtucket	AAA	27	20	3	2	163.1	687	172	88	77	20	7	5	5	39	0	76	3	1	12	9	.571	0	4--	—	4.24
2000 Pawtucket	AAA	31	9	2	17	113.1	464	103	51	38	10	4	4	5	36	0	65	11	1	10	4	.714	0	4--	—	3.02
2001 Louisville	AAA	33	28	4	2	196.1	843	218	105	90	24	3	1	9	54	0	118	20	0	10	9	.526	1	0--	—	4.13
2001 Cincinnati	NL	5	2	0	2	12.1	57	13	9	6	1	0	0	2	6	0	5	1	0	0	1	.000	0	0-0	0	4.38

Jose Fernandez

Bats: R **Throws:** R **Pos:** DH-7; PH/PR-5; 1B-2; 3B-2   **Ht:** 6'2" **Wt:** 195 **Born:** 11/2/74 **Age:** 27

Year Team	Lg	G	AB	H	2B	3B	HR	(Hm	Rd)	TB	R	RBI	TBB	IBB	SO	HBP	SH	SF	SB	CS	SB%	GDP	Avg	OBP	SLG
1994 Expos	R	44	168	39	8	0	5	—	—	62	27	23	13	0	33	2	0	1	11	1	.92	2	.232	.293	.369
1995 Vermont	A-	66	270	74	6	7	4	—	—	106	38	41	13	2	51	1	1	2	29	4	.88	2	.274	.308	.393
1996 Delmarva	A	126	421	115	23	6	12	—	—	186	72	70	50	5	76	7	0	3	23	13	.64	5	.273	.358	.442
1997 Wst Plm Bch	A+	97	350	108	21	3	9	—	—	162	49	58	37	3	76	7	0	0	22	14	.61	8	.309	.386	.463
Harrisburg	AA	29	96	22	3	1	4	—	—	39	10	11	11	0	28	1	0	0	2	0	1.00	4	.229	.315	.406
1998 Harrisburg	AA	104	369	109	27	1	17	—	—	189	59	58	36	3	73	9	1	5	16	6	.73	3	.295	.368	.512
Ottawa	AAA	21	60	16	4	1	0	—	—	22	8	4	5	0	14	0	1	1	3	1	.75	2	.267	.318	.367
1999 Ottawa	AAA	124	465	126	30	2	14	—	—	202	73	68	31	0	136	5	1	3	14	7	.67	11	.271	.321	.434
2000 Indianapolis	AAA	133	468	134	37	4	11	—	—	212	70	68	49	0	93	6	1	6	10	3	.77	11	.286	.357	.453
2001 Salt Lake	AAA	122	452	153	37	1	30	—	—	282	99	114	55	2	91	12	0	3	9	7	.56	9	.338	.421	.624
1999 Montreal	NL	8	24	5	2	0	0	(0	0)	7	0	1	1	0	7	0	0	0	0	0	—	1	.208	.240	.292
2001 Anaheim	AL	13	25	2	1	0	0	(0	0)	3	1	0	2	0	10	0	0	0	0	1	.00	0	.080	.148	.120
2 ML YEARS		21	49	7	3	0	0	(0	0)	10	1	1	3	0	17	0	0	0	0	1	.00	1	.143	.192	.204

Osvaldo Fernandez

Pitches: Right **Bats:** Right **Pos:** SP-14; RP-6   **Ht:** 6'2" **Wt:** 193 **Born:** 11/4/68 **Age:** 33

Year Team	Lg	G	GS	CG	GF	IP	BFP	H	R	ER	HR	SH	SF	HB	TBB	IBB	SO	WP	Bk	W	L	Pct.	ShO	Sv-Op	Hld	ERA
2001 Louisville *	AAA	9	9	0	0	53.2	220	54	26	23	6	3	0	6	12	1	31	1	1	3	2	.600	0	0--	—	3.86
1996 San Francisco	NL	30	28	2	1	171.2	760	193	95	88	20	12	5	10	57	4	106	6	2	7	13	.350	0	0-0	0	4.61
1997 San Francisco	NL	11	11	0	0	56.1	256	74	39	31	9	4	1	0	15	2	31	2	1	3	4	.429	0	0-0	0	4.95
2000 Cincinnati	NL	15	14	1	0	79.2	327	69	33	32	6	1	3	2	31	2	36	1	1	4	3	.571	0	0-0	0	3.62
2001 Cincinnati	NL	20	14	0	2	79.1	366	103	62	61	8	4	3	0	33	3	35	0	0	5	6	.455	0	0-1	0	6.92
4 ML YEARS		76	67	3	3	387	1709	439	229	212	43	21	12	12	136	11	208	9	4	19	26	.422	0	0-1	0	4.93

Tony Fernandez

Bats: Both **Throws:** Right **Pos:** PH/PR-60; DH-13; 3B-13   **Ht:** 6'2" **Wt:** 195 **Born:** 6/30/62 **Age:** 40

Year Team	Lg	G	AB	H	2B	3B	HR	(Hm	Rd)	TB	R	RBI	TBB	IBB	SO	HBP	SH	SF	SB	CS	SB%	GDP	Avg	OBP	SLG
1983 Toronto	AL	15	34	9	1	1	0	(0	0)	12	5	2	2	0	2	1	1	0	0	1	.00	1	.265	.324	.353
1984 Toronto	AL	88	233	63	5	3	3	(1	2)	83	29	19	17	0	15	0	2	2	5	7	.42	3	.270	.317	.356
1985 Toronto	AL	161	564	163	31	10	2	(1	1)	220	71	51	43	2	41	2	7	2	13	6	.68	12	.289	.340	.390
1986 Toronto	AL	163	687	213	33	9	10	(4	6)	294	91	65	27	0	52	4	5	4	25	12	.68	8	.310	.338	.428
1987 Toronto	AL	146	578	186	29	8	5	(1	4)	246	90	67	51	3	48	5	4	4	32	12	.73	14	.322	.379	.426
1988 Toronto	AL	154	648	186	41	4	5	(3	2)	250	76	70	45	3	65	4	3	4	15	5	.75	9	.287	.335	.386
1989 Toronto	AL	140	573	147	25	9	11	(2	9)	223	64	64	29	1	51	3	2	10	22	6	.79	9	.257	.291	.389
1990 Toronto	AL	161	635	175	27	17	4	(2	2)	248	84	66	71	4	70	7	2	6	26	13	.67	17	.276	.352	.391
1991 San Diego	NL	145	558	152	27	5	4	(1	3)	201	81	38	55	0	74	0	7	1	23	9	.72	12	.272	.337	.360
1992 San Diego	NL	155	622	171	32	4	4	(3	1)	223	84	37	56	4	62	4	3	3	20	20	.50	6	.275	.337	.359
1993 NYM-Tor		142	526	147	23	11	5	(1	4)	207	65	64	56	3	45	1	8	3	21	10	.68	16	.279	.348	.394
1994 Cincinnati	NL	104	366	102	18	6	8	(3	5)	156	50	50	44	8	40	5	4	3	12	7	.63	5	.279	.361	.426
1995 New York	AL	108	384	94	20	2	5	(3	2)	133	57	45	42	4	40	4	3	6	6	6	.50	11	.245	.322	.346
1997 Cleveland	AL	120	409	117	21	1	11	(7	4)	173	55	44	22	0	47	2	6	3	6	6	.50	11	.286	.323	.423
1998 Toronto	AL	138	486	156	36	2	9	(4	5)	223	71	72	45	5	52	13	3	6	13	8	.62	11	.321	.387	.459
1999 Toronto	AL	142	485	159	41	0	6	(5	1)	218	73	75	77	11	62	10	0	4	6	7	.46	10	.328	.427	.449
2001 Mil-Tor		76	123	36	4	0	2	(1	1)	46	11	15	8	0	17	1	1	1	1	3	.25	3	.293	.338	.374
1993 New York	NL	48	173	39	5	2	1	(0	1)	51	20	14	25	0	19	1	3	2	6	2	.75	3	.225	.323	.295
Toronto		94	353	108	18	9	4	(1	3)	156	45	50	31	3	26	0	5	1	15	8	.65	13	.306	.361	.354
2001 Milwaukee	NL	28	64	18	0	0	1	(0	1)	21	6	3	7	0	9	0	1	0	1	2	.33	1	.281	.352	.328
Toronto	AL	48	59	18	4	0	1	(1	0)	25	5	12	1	0	8	1	0	1	0	1	.00	2	.305	.323	.424
17 ML YEARS		2158	7911	2276	414	92	94	(42	52)	3156	1057	844	690	48	784	64	67	61	246	138	.64	161	.288	.347	.399

Mike Fetters

Pitches: Right **Bats:** Right **Pos:** RP-54   **Ht:** 6'4" **Wt:** 226 **Born:** 12/19/64 **Age:** 37

Year Team	Lg	G	GS	CG	GF	IP	BFP	H	R	ER	HR	SH	SF	HB	TBB	IBB	SO	WP	Bk	W	L	Pct.	ShO	Sv-Op	Hld	ERA
1989 California	AL	1	0	0	0	3.1	16	5	4	3	1	0	0	0	1	0	4	2	0	0	0	—	0	0-0	0	8.10
1990 California	AL	26	2	0	10	67.2	291	77	33	31	9	1	0	2	20	0	35	3	0	1	1	.500	0	1-1	1	4.12
1991 California	AL	19	4	0	8	44.2	206	53	29	24	4	1	0	3	28	2	24	4	0	2	5	.286	0	0-1	0	4.84
1992 Milwaukee	AL	50	0	0	11	62.2	243	38	15	13	3	5	2	7	24	2	43	4	1	5	1	.833	0	2-5	8	1.87
1993 Milwaukee	AL	45	0	0	14	59.1	246	59	29	22	4	5	5	2	22	4	23	0	0	3	3	.500	0	0-0	0	3.34
1994 Milwaukee	AL	42	0	0	31	46	202	41	16	13	0	2	3	1	27	5	31	3	1	1	4	.200	0	17-20	3	2.54
1995 Milwaukee	AL	40	0	0	34	34.2	163	40	16	13	3	2	1	0	20	4	33	5	0	0	3	.000	0	22-27	1	3.38
1996 Milwaukee	AL	61	0	0	55	61.1	268	65	28	23	4	0	4	1	26	4	53	5	0	3	3	.500	0	32-38	1	3.38
1997 Milwaukee	AL	51	0	0	20	70.1	298	62	30	27	4	6	4	1	33	3	62	1	1	1	5	.167	0	6-11	11	3.45

Year Team	Lg	G	GS	CG	GF	IP	BFP	H	R	ER	HR	SH	SF	HB	TBB	IBB	SO	WP	Bk	W	L	Pct.	ShO	Sv-Op	Hld	ERA
		HOW MUCH HE PITCHED						WHAT HE GAVE UP													THE RESULTS					
1998 Oak-Ana	AL	60	0	0	28	58.2	264	62	34	28	5	4	2	1	25	2	43	6	0	2	8	.200	0	5-9	11	4.30
1999 Baltimore	AL	27	0	0	10	31	151	35	23	20	5	1	0	2	22	2	22	1	1	1	0	1.000	0	0-3	2	5.81
2000 Los Angeles	NL	51	0	0	20	50	201	35	18	18	7	3	0	2	25	2	40	3	0	6	2	.750	0	5-7	11	3.24
2001 LA-Pit	NL	54	0	0	21	47.1	223	49	32	29	7	1	3	4	26	1	37	7	0	3	2	.600	0	9-12	14	5.51
1998 Oakland	AL	48	0	0	22	47.1	214	48	26	21	3	4	2	1	21	2	34	3	0	1	6	.143	0	5-8	10	3.99
Anaheim	AL	12	0	0	6	11.1	50	14	8	7	2	0	0	0	4	0	9	3	0	1	2	.333	0	0-1	1	5.56
2001 Los Angeles	NL	34	0	0	7	29.2	139	33	23	20	6	1	3	1	13	0	26	6	0	2	1	.667	0	1-3	14	6.07
Pittsburgh	NL	20	0	0	14	17.2	84	16	9	9	1	0	0	3	13	1	11	1	0	1	1	.500	0	8-9	0	4.58
13 ML YEARS		527	6	0	262	637	2772	621	307	264	56	31	24	26	299	31	450	45	4	28	37	.431	0	99-134	72	3.73

Robert Fick

Bats: L Throws: R Pos: C-78; 1B-26; PH/PR-20; DH-8; RF-8   Ht: 6'1" Wt: 189 Born: 3/15/74 Age: 28

Year Team	Lg	G	AB	H	2B	3B	HR	(Hm	Rd)	TB	R	RBI	TBB	IBB	SO	HBP	SH	SF	SB	CS	SB%	GDP	Avg	OBP	SLG
		BATTING																	BASERUNNING				PERCENTAGES		
1998 Detroit	AL	7	24	8	1	0	3	(0	3)	18	6	7	2	0	7	0	0	0	1	0	1.00	1	.364	.417	.818
1999 Detroit	AL	15	41	9	0	0	3	(1	2)	18	6	10	7	0	6	0	0	1	1	0	1.00	1	.220	.327	.439
2000 Detroit	AL	66	163	41	7	2	3	(0	3)	61	18	22	22	2	39	1	0	2	2	1	.67	4	.252	.340	.374
2001 Detroit	AL	124	401	109	21	2	19	(8	11)	191	62	61	39	3	62	4	0	4	0	3	.00	10	.272	.339	.476
4 ML YEARS		212	627	167	29	4	28	(9	19)	288	92	100	70	5	114	5	0	7	4	4	.50	16	.266	.341	.459

Luis Figueroa

Bats: Both Throws: Right Pos: 2B-3; PH/PR-1   Ht: 5'9" Wt: 152 Born: 2/16/74 Age: 28

Year Team	Lg	G	AB	H	2B	3B	HR	(Hm	Rd)	TB	R	RBI	TBB	IBB	SO	HBP	SH	SF	SB	CS	SB%	GDP	Avg	OBP	SLG
		BATTING																	BASERUNNING				PERCENTAGES		
1997 Augusta	A	71	248	56	8	0	0	—	—	64	38	21	35	0	29	1	9	2	22	6	.79	2	.226	.322	.258
Lynchburg	A+	26	89	25	5	0	0	—	—	30	12	2	7	0	6	0	0	0	1	2	.33	5	.281	.333	.337
1998 Carolina	AA	117	350	87	9	3	0	—	—	102	54	24	71	3	46	2	10	2	6	5	.55	12	.249	.376	.291
1999 Altoona	AA	131	418	110	15	5	3	—	—	144	61	50	52	0	44	3	16	3	9	9	.50	7	.263	.347	.344
2000 Altoona	AA	94	342	97	10	4	1	—	—	118	45	28	37	1	32	2	10	1	14	5	.74	8	.284	.356	.345
Nashville	AAA	23	64	16	1	0	3	—	—	26	6	8	1	0	8	0	0	0	2	1	.67	2	.250	.262	.406
2001 Nashville	AAA	92	347	104	11	1	4	—	—	129	45	29	31	1	26	1	6	2	8	5	.62	8	.300	.357	.372
Norfolk	AAA	17	58	15	3	1	1	—	—	23	7	5	5	0	6	0	1	0	0	0	—	1	.259	.317	.397
2001 Pittsburgh	NL	4	2	0	0	0	0	(0	0)	0	0	0	0	0	0	0	0	0	0	0	—	0	.000	.000	.000

Nelson Figueroa

Pitches: Right Bats: Right Pos: SP-13; RP-6   Ht: 6'1" Wt: 155 Born: 5/18/74 Age: 28

Year Team	Lg	G	GS	CG	GF	IP	BFP	H	R	ER	HR	SH	SF	HB	TBB	IBB	SO	WP	Bk	W	L	Pct.	ShO	Sv-Op	Hld	ERA
		HOW MUCH HE PITCHED						WHAT HE GAVE UP													THE RESULTS					
1995 Kingsport	R+	12	12	2	0	76.1	304	57	31	26	3	3	2	5	22	1	79	5	0	7	3	.700	2	0--	—	3.07
1996 Capital Cty	A	26	25	8	1	185.1	723	119	55	42	10	3	2	2	58	1	200	9	2	14	7	.667	4	0--	—	2.04
1997 Binghamton	AA	33	22	0	3	143	617	137	76	69	14	7	2	6	68	1	116	7	0	5	11	.313	0	0--	—	4.34
1998 Binghamton	AA	21	21	3	0	123.2	531	133	73	64	19	2	1	0	44	2	116	1	1	12	3	.800	2	0--	—	4.66
Tucson	AAA	7	7	0	0	41.1	180	46	22	17	8	0	2	2	16	1	29	1	0	2	2	.500	0	0--	—	3.70
1999 Diamndbcks	R	1	1	0	0	3	11	3	1	0	0	0	0	0	0	0	2	0	0	0	1	.000	0	0--	—	0.00
Tucson	AAA	24	21	1	0	128	541	128	59	56	16	3	1	5	41	0	106	6	0	11	6	.647	1	0--	—	3.94
2000 Tucson	AAA	17	16	1	0	112	455	101	41	35	9	2	2	0	28	2	78	8	0	9	4	.692	0	0--	—	2.81
Scrantn-WB	AAA	8	8	1	0	50	209	50	28	21	9	2	1	2	11	0	35	2	0	4	3	.571	0	0--	—	3.78
2001 Scrantn-WB	AAA	13	12	3	0	87.1	359	74	33	24	6	4	1	5	18	2	74	3	0	4	2	.667	0	0--	—	2.47
2000 Arizona	NL	3	3	0	0	15.2	68	17	13	13	4	1	2	0	5	0	7	2	0	0	1	.000	0	0-0	0	7.47
2001 Philadelphia	NL	19	13	0	1	89	393	95	40	39	8	4	0	7	37	3	61	2	0	4	5	.444	0	0-0	0	3.94
2 ML YEARS		22	16	0	1	104.2	461	112	53	52	12	5	2	7	42	3	68	4	0	4	6	.400	0	0-0	0	4.47

Jeremy Fikac

Pitches: Right Bats: Right Pos: RP-23   Ht: 6'2" Wt: 185 Born: 4/8/75 Age: 27

Year Team	Lg	G	GS	CG	GF	IP	BFP	H	R	ER	HR	SH	SF	HB	TBB	IBB	SO	WP	Bk	W	L	Pct.	ShO	Sv-Op	Hld	ERA
		HOW MUCH HE PITCHED						WHAT HE GAVE UP													THE RESULTS					
1998 Idaho Falls	R+	12	0	0	6	20	82	11	6	5	0	0		1	8	1	19	1	0	2	0	1.000	0	1--	—	2.25
1999 Rancho Cuc	A+	40	6	0	13	85	381	94	50	48	7	0	2	4	43	0	75	8	2	8	3	.727	0	0--	—	5.08
2000 Rancho Cuc	A+	61	0	0	43	75	298	46	19	15	2	4	1	4	24	0	101	6	0	5	3	.625	0	20--	—	1.80
2001 Portland	AAA	1	0	0	0	3	13	3	1	1	0	0	0		1	0	3	0	0	0	0	—	0	0--	—	3.00
Mobile	AA	53	0	0	33	68.2	276	54	16	15	3	4	2	3	20	4	75	3	0	6	0	1.000	0	18--	—	1.97
2001 San Diego	NL	23	0	0	5	26.1	99	15	6	4	2	2	0	1	5	1	19	0	0	2	0	1.000	0	0-2	6	1.37

Bob File

Pitches: Right Bats: Right Pos: RP-60   Ht: 6'4" Wt: 215 Born: 1/28/77 Age: 25

Year Team	Lg	G	GS	CG	GF	IP	BFP	H	R	ER	HR	SH	SF	HB	TBB	IBB	SO	WP	Bk	W	L	Pct.	ShO	Sv-Op	Hld	ERA
		HOW MUCH HE PITCHED						WHAT HE GAVE UP													THE RESULTS					
1998 Medcine Hat	R+	28	0	0	26	32	124	24	7	5	1	1	2	2	5	0	28	1	0	2	1	.667	0	16--	—	1.41
1999 Dunedin	A+	47	0	0	42	53	203	30	13	10	2	3	0	4	14	0	48	1	1	4	1	.800	0	26--	—	1.70
2000 Tennessee	AA	36	0	0	32	34.2	153	29	20	12	1	2	1	2	13	0	40	1	0	4	3	.571	0	20--	—	3.12
Syracuse	AAA	20	0	0	11	19.1	69	14	2	2	1	0	0	1	2	0	10	0	0	2	0	1.000	0	8--	—	0.93
2001 Tennessee	AA	3	0	0	3	3	10	3	1	1	1	0	0	0	0	0	2	0	0	0	0	—	0	0--	—	3.00
Syracuse	AAA	2	0	0	1	4	14	1	0	0	0	0	0	2	0	0	3	0	0	0	0	—	0	0--	—	0.00
2001 Toronto	AL	60	0	0	18	74.1	299	57	28	27	6	3	1	7	29	8	38	2	0	5	3	.625	0	0-2	6	3.27

Chuck Finley

Pitches: Left Bats: Left Pos: SP-22   Ht: 6'6" Wt: 225 Born: 11/26/62 Age: 39

Year Team	Lg	G	GS	CG	GF	IP	BFP	H	R	ER	HR	SH	SF	HB	TBB	IBB	SO	WP	Bk	W	L	Pct.	ShO	Sv-Op	Hld	ERA
2001 Akron *	AA	2	2	0	0	11	41	7	3	1	0	2	0	0	2	0	11	1	0	1	1	.500	0	0- -	—	0.82
1986 California	AL	25	0	0	7	46.1	198	40	17	17	2	4	0	1	23	1	37	2	0	3	1	.750	0	0-0	1	3.30
1987 California	AL	35	3	0	17	90.2	405	102	54	47	7	2	2	3	43	3	63	4	3	2	7	.222	0	0-2	0	4.67
1988 California	AL	31	31	2	0	194.1	831	191	95	90	15	7	10	6	82	7	111	5	8	9	15	.375	0	0-0	0	4.17
1989 California	AL	29	29	9	0	199.2	827	171	64	57	13	7	3	2	82	0	156	4	2	16	9	.640	1	0-0	0	2.57
1990 California	AL	32	32	7	0	236	962	210	77	63	17	12	3	2	81	3	177	9	0	18	9	.667	2	0-0	0	2.40
1991 California	AL	34	34	4	0	227.1	955	205	102	96	23	4	3	8	101	1	171	6	3	18	9	.667	2	0-0	0	3.80
1992 California	AL	31	31	4	0	204.1	885	212	99	90	24	10	10	3	98	2	124	6	0	7	12	.368	1	0-0	0	3.96
1993 California	AL	35	35	13	0	251.1	1065	243	108	88	22	11	7	6	82	1	187	8	1	16	14	.533	2	0-0	0	3.15
1994 California	AL	25	25	7	0	183.1	774	178	95	88	21	9	6	3	71	0	148	10	0	10	10	.500	2	0-0	0	4.32
1995 California	AL	32	32	9	0	203	880	192	106	95	20	4	5	7	93	1	195	13	1	15	12	.556	1	0-0	0	4.21
1996 California	AL	35	35	4	0	238	1037	241	124	110	27	7	9	11	94	5	215	17	2	15	16	.484	1	0-0	0	4.16
1997 Anaheim	AL	25	25	3	0	164	690	152	79	77	20	3	4	5	65	0	155	10	2	13	6	.684	1	0-0	0	4.23
1998 Anaheim	AL	34	34	1	0	223.1	976	210	97	84	20	3	5	6	109	1	212	8	0	11	9	.550	1	0-0	0	3.39
1999 Anaheim	AL	33	33	1	0	213.1	913	197	117	105	23	7	3	8	94	2	200	15	0	12	11	.522	0	0-0	0	4.43
2000 Cleveland	AL	34	34	3	0	218	936	211	108	101	23	5	4	2	101	3	189	9	0	16	11	.593	0	0-0	0	4.17
2001 Cleveland	AL	22	22	1	0	113.2	495	131	78	70	14	2	5	2	35	0	96	1	0	8	7	.533	0	0-0	0	5.54
16 ML YEARS		492	435	61	24	3006.2	12829	2886	1420	1278	291	97	79	75	1254	30	2436	127	22	189	158	.545	14	0-2	1	3.83

Steve Finley

Bats: Left Throws: Left Pos: CF-131; PH/PR-13; P-1   Ht: 6'2" Wt: 195 Born: 3/12/65 Age: 37

Year Team	Lg	G	AB	H	2B	3B	HR	(Hm	Rd)	TB	R	RBI	TBB	IBB	SO	HBP	SH	SF	SB	CS	SB%	GDP	Avg	OBP	SLG
1989 Baltimore	AL	81	217	54	5	2	2	(0	2)	69	35	25	15	1	30	1	6	2	17	3	.85	3	.249	.298	.318
1990 Baltimore	AL	142	464	119	16	4	3	(1	2)	152	46	37	32	3	53	2	10	5	22	9	.71	8	.256	.304	.328
1991 Houston	NL	159	596	170	28	10	8	(0	8)	242	84	54	42	5	65	2	10	6	34	18	.65	8	.285	.331	.406
1992 Houston	NL	162	607	177	29	13	5	(5	0)	247	84	55	58	6	63	3	16	2	44	9	.83	10	.292	.355	.407
1993 Houston	NL	142	545	145	15	13	8	(1	7)	210	69	44	28	1	65	3	6	3	19	6	.76	8	.266	.304	.385
1994 Houston	NL	94	373	103	16	5	11	(4	7)	162	64	33	28	0	52	2	13	1	13	7	.65	3	.276	.329	.434
1995 San Diego	NL	139	562	167	23	8	10	(4	6)	236	104	44	59	5	62	3	4	2	36	12	.75	8	.297	.366	.420
1996 San Diego	NL	161	655	195	45	9	30	(15	15)	348	126	95	56	5	87	4	1	5	22	8	.73	20	.298	.354	.531
1997 San Diego	NL	143	560	146	26	5	28	(5	23)	266	101	92	43	2	92	3	2	7	15	3	.83	10	.261	.313	.475
1998 San Diego	NL	159	619	154	40	6	14	(8	6)	248	92	67	45	0	103	3	3	4	12	3	.80	9	.249	.301	.401
1999 Arizona	NL	156	590	156	32	10	34	(17	17)	310	100	103	63	7	94	3	2	5	8	4	.67	4	.264	.336	.525
2000 Arizona	NL	152	539	151	27	5	35	(17	18)	293	100	96	65	7	87	8	2	9	12	6	.67	9	.280	.361	.544
2001 Arizona	NL	140	495	136	27	4	14	(8	6)	213	66	73	47	9	67	1	2	3	11	7	.61	8	.275	.337	.430
13 ML YEARS		1830	6822	1873	329	94	202	(85	117)	2996	1071	818	581	51	920	38	77	54	265	95	.74	108	.275	.332	.439

Tony Fiore

Pitches: Right Bats: Right Pos: RP-7   Ht: 6'4" Wt: 210 Born: 10/12/71 Age: 30

Year Team	Lg	G	GS	CG	GF	IP	BFP	H	R	ER	HR	SH	SF	HB	TBB	IBB	SO	WP	Bk	W	L	Pct.	ShO	Sv-Op	Hld	ERA
1992 Martinsvlle	R+	17	2	0	9	32.1	161	32	20	15	0	2	1	3	31	1	30	11	0	2	3	.400	0	0- -	—	4.18
1993 Batavia	A-	16	16	1	0	97.1	411	82	51	33	7	3	4	4	40	0	55	15	0	2	8	.200	0	0- -	—	3.05
1994 Spartanburg	A	28	28	9	0	166.2	719	162	94	76	10	2	5	4	77	1	113	19	1	12	13	.480	1	0- -	—	4.10
1995 Clearwater	A+	24	10	0	3	70.1	323	70	41	29	4	3	5	2	44	2	45	9	3	6	2	.750	0	0- -	—	3.71
1996 Clearwater	A+	22	23	8	0	128	533	102	61	45	4	1	1	5	56	1	80	13	1	8	4	.667	1	0- -	—	3.16
Reading	AA	5	5	0	0	31	146	32	21	15	2	0	1	1	18	0	19	6	0	1	2	.333	0	0- -	—	4.35
1997 Reading	AA	17	16	0	0	104.2	434	89	47	35	6	8	4	5	40	0	64	10	1	8	3	.727	0	0- -	—	3.01
Scrantn-WB	AAA	9	9	1	0	60.2	268	60	34	26	3	3	1	0	26	1	56	6	1	3	5	.375	0	0- -	—	3.86
1998 Scrantn-WB	AAA	41	7	0	12	94.2	418	92	53	47	4	3	3	1	52	1	71	6	0	4	7	.364	0	1- -	—	4.47
1999 Scrantn-WB	AAA	13	0	0	2	20.1	102	28	19	15	0	0	1	0	15	1	13	4	0	0	0	—	0	0- -	—	6.64
Salt Lake	AAA	40	0	0	35	46.2	205	45	21	18	1	2	2	2	26	3	38	3	1	2	1	.667	0	19- -	—	3.47
2000 Durham	AAA	53	1	0	26	75	317	62	22	19	3	6	0	3	38	6	39	3	1	5	3	.615	0	8- -	—	2.28
2001 Durham	AAA	15	0	0	9	20.1	76	7	0	0	0	0	0	0	8	0	11	0	0	1	0	1.000	0	0- -	—	0.00
Edmonton	AAA	32	6	0	12	80.2	344	85	35	33	4	1	1	5	25	0	58	3	1	5	0	1.000	0	1- -	—	3.68
2000 Tampa Bay	AL	11	0	0	3	15	74	21	16	14	3	0	0	2	9	2	8	1	0	1	1	.500	0	0-1	0	8.40
2001 TB-Min	AL	7	0	0	5	9.2	41	9	6	6	0	0	0	1	3	0	8	1	0	0	0	1.000	0	0-0	0	5.59
2001 Tampa Bay	AL	3	0	0	3	3.1	15	4	2	2	0	0	0	1	1	0	3	1	0	0	0	—	0	0-0	0	5.40
Minnesota	AL	4	0	0	2	6.1	26	5	4	4	0	0	0	0	2	0	5	0	0	0	0	1.000	0	0-0	0	5.68
2 ML YEARS		18	0	0	8	24.2	115	30	22	20	3	0	0	3	12	2	16	2	0	1	2	.333	0	0-1	0	7.30

John Flaherty

Bats: Right Throws: Right Pos: C-78   Ht: 6'1" Wt: 200 Born: 10/21/67 Age: 34

Year Team	Lg	G	AB	H	2B	3B	HR	(Hm	Rd)	TB	R	RBI	TBB	IBB	SO	HBP	SH	SF	SB	CS	SB%	GDP	Avg	OBP	SLG
1992 Boston	AL	35	66	13	2	0	0	(0	0)	15	3	2	3	0	7	0	1	1	0	0	—	0	.197	.229	.227
1993 Boston	AL	13	25	3	2	0	0	(0	0)	5	3	2	2	0	6	1	1	0	0	0	—	0	.120	.214	.200
1994 Detroit	AL	34	40	6	1	0	0	(0	0)	7	2	4	1	0	10	1	1	0	0	1	.00	1	.150	.167	.175
1995 Detroit	AL	112	354	86	22	1	11	(6	5)	143	39	40	18	0	47	3	8	2	0	0	—	8	.243	.284	.404
1996 Det-SD	AL	119	416	118	24	0	13	(8	5)	181	40	64	17	2	61	3	4	4	3	3	.50	13	.284	.314	.435
1997 San Diego	NL	129	439	120	21	1	9	(4	5)	170	38	46	33	7	62	0	2	2	4	4	.50	11	.273	.323	.387
1998 Tampa Bay	AL	91	304	63	11	0	3	(1	2)	83	21	24	22	0	46	1	4	3	0	5	.00	4	.207	.261	.273
1999 Tampa Bay	AL	117	446	124	19	0	14	(3	11)	185	53	71	19	0	64	6	1	10	0	2	.00	14	.278	.310	.415
2000 Tampa Bay	AL	109	394	103	15	0	10	(7	3)	148	36	39	20	2	57	0	2	2	0	0	—	11	.261	.296	.376
2001 Tampa Bay	AL	78	248	59	17	1	4	(3	1)	90	20	29	10	1	33	1	5	1	0	1	1.00	9	.238	.269	.363
1996 Detroit	AL	47	152	38	12	0	4	(2	2)	62	18	23	8	1	25	1	3	1	1	0	1.00	5	.250	.290	.408
San Diego	NL	72	264	80	12	0	9	(6	3)	119	22	41	9	1	36	2	1	3	2	3	.40	8	.303	.327	.451
10 ML YEARS		837	2732	695	134	3	64	(32	32)	1027	255	321	145	12	394	15	30	26	8	15	.35	76	.254	.293	.376

Darrin Fletcher

Bats: Left **Throws:** Right **Pos:** C-129; PH/PR-11; DH-1   **Ht:** 6'2" **Wt:** 205 **Born:** 10/3/66 **Age:** 35

Year Team	Lg	G	AB	H	2B	3B	HR	(Hm	Rd)	TB	R	RBI	TBB	IBB	SO	HBP	SH	SF	SB	CS	SB%	GDP	Avg	OBP	SLG
1989 Los Angeles	NL	5	8	4	0	0	1	(1	0)	7	1	2	1	0	0	0	0	0	0	0	—	0	.500	.556	.875
1990 LA-Phi	NL	11	23	3	1	0	0	(0	0)	4	3	1	0	0	6	0	0	0	0	0	—	0	.130	.167	.174
1991 Philadelphia	NL	46	136	31	8	0	1	(1	0)	42	5	12	5	0	15	0	1	0	0	1	.00	2	.228	.255	.309
1992 Montreal	NL	83	222	54	10	2	2	(0	2)	74	13	26	14	3	28	2	2	4	0	2	.00	8	.243	.289	.333
1993 Montreal	NL	133	396	101	20	1	9	(5	4)	150	33	60	34	2	40	6	5	4	0	0	—	7	.255	.320	.379
1994 Montreal	NL	94	285	74	18	1	10	(4	6)	124	28	57	25	4	23	3	0	12	0	0	—	6	.260	.314	.435
1995 Montreal	NL	110	350	100	21	1	11	(8	3)	156	42	45	32	1	23	4	1	2	0	1	.00	15	.286	.351	.446
1996 Montreal	NL	127	394	105	22	0	12	(7	5)	163	41	57	27	4	42	6	1	3	0	0	—	13	.277	.323	.414
1997 Montreal	NL	96	310	86	20	1	17	(10	7)	159	39	55	17	3	35	5	0	2	1	1	.50	6	.283	.328	.513
1998 Toronto	AL	124	407	115	23	1	9	(3	6)	167	37	52	25	7	39	6	1	7	0	1	.00	19	.283	.328	.410
1999 Toronto	AL	115	412	120	26	0	18	(10	8)	200	43	80	26	0	47	6	0	4	0	0	—	16	.291	.339	.485
2000 Toronto	AL	124	416	133	19	1	20	(10	10)	214	43	58	20	3	45	5	0	4	1	0	1.00	8	.320	.355	.514
2001 Toronto	AL	134	416	94	20	0	11	(7	4)	147	36	56	24	1	43	6	1	6	0	1	.00	18	.226	.274	.353
1990 Los Angeles	NL	2	1	0	0	0	0	(0	0)	0	0	0	0	0	0	1	0	0	0	0	—	0	.000	.000	.000
Philadelphia	NL	9	22	3	1	0	0	(0	0)	4	3	1	0	0	5	0	0	0	0	0	—	0	.136	.174	.182
13 ML YEARS		1200	3775	1020	208	8	121	(61	60)	1607	369	561	251	31	386	49	12	48	2	6	.25	118	.270	.320	.426

Bryce Florie

Pitches: Right **Bats:** Right **Pos:** RP-7   **Ht:** 5'11" **Wt:** 192 **Born:** 5/21/70 **Age:** 32

Year Team	Lg	G	GS	CG	GF	IP	BFP	H	R	ER	HR	SH	SF	HB	TBB	IBB	SO	WP	Bk	W	L	Pct.	ShO	Sv-Op	Hld	ERA
2001 Sarasota *	A+	2	0	0	0	4.2	21	3	0	0	0	0	0	0	5	0	7	0	0	0	0	—	0	0--	—	0.00
Trenton *	AA	6	1	0	2	11	47	5	4	2	0	1	0	3	6	0	17	2	0	0	1	.000	0	2--	—	1.64
Toledo *	AAA	10	0	0	5	11.2	59	14	8	8	1	0	0	0	13	0	10	3	0	2	1	.667	0	0--	—	6.17
1994 San Diego	NL	9	0	0	4	9.1	37	8	1	1	0	0	0	0	3	0	8	1	0	0	0	—	0	0-0	—	0.96
1995 San Diego	NL	47	0	0	10	68.2	290	49	30	23	8	5	1	4	38	3	68	7	2	2	2	.500	0	1-4	9	3.01
1996 SD-Mil		54	0	0	16	68.1	312	61	40	36	4	1	3	6	40	5	63	6	1	2	3	.400	0	0-3	8	4.74
1997 Milwaukee	AL	32	8	0	6	75	332	74	43	36	4	1	4	3	42	2	53	4	1	4	4	.500	0	0-1	0	4.32
1998 Detroit	AL	42	16	0	6	133	580	141	80	71	16	3	2	4	59	6	97	9	0	8	9	.471	0	0-0	4	4.80
1999 Det-Bos	AL	41	5	0	10	81.1	368	94	50	42	8	3	2	2	35	5	65	8	0	4	1	.800	0	0-0	3	4.65
2000 Boston	AL	29	0	0	14	49.1	223	57	30	25	5	6	3	1	19	6	34	0	0	0	4	.000	0	1-2	1	4.56
2001 Boston	AL	7	0	0	1	8.2	45	12	11	11	1	0	0	0	7	3	7	0	0	0	1	.000	0	0-0	0	11.42
1996 San Diego	NL	39	0	0	11	49.1	222	45	24	22	1	0	1	6	27	3	51	3	1	2	2	.500	0	0-1	4	4.01
Milwaukee	AL	15	0	0	5	19	90	20	16	14	3	1	2	0	13	2	12	3	0	1	1	.000	0	0-2	4	6.63
1999 Detroit	AL	27	3	0	6	51.1	234	61	31	26	6	3	1	1	20	2	40	4	0	2	1	.667	0	0-0	2	4.56
Boston	AL	14	2	0	4	30	134	33	19	16	2	0	1	1	15	3	25	4	0	2	0	1.000	0	0-0	1	4.80
8 ML YEARS		261	29	0	67	493.2	2187	500	285	245	46	19	16	20	243	30	395	35	4	20	24	.455	0	2-10	25	4.47

Cliff Floyd

Bats: Left **Throws:** Right **Pos:** LF-142; PH/PR-5; DH-3   **Ht:** 6'4" **Wt:** 235 **Born:** 12/5/72 **Age:** 29

Year Team	Lg	G	AB	H	2B	3B	HR	(Hm	Rd)	TB	R	RBI	TBB	IBB	SO	HBP	SH	SF	SB	CS	SB%	GDP	Avg	OBP	SLG
1993 Montreal	NL	10	31	7	0	0	1	(0	1)	10	3	2	0	0	9	0	0	0	0	0	—	0	.226	.226	.323
1994 Montreal	NL	100	334	94	19	4	4	(2	2)	133	43	41	24	0	63	3	2	3	10	3	.77	3	.281	.332	.398
1995 Montreal	NL	29	69	9	1	0	1	(1	0)	13	6	8	7	0	22	1	0	0	3	0	1.00	1	.130	.221	.188
1996 Montreal	NL	117	227	55	15	4	6	(3	3)	96	29	26	30	1	52	5	1	1	7	1	.88	3	.242	.340	.423
1997 Florida	NL	61	137	32	9	1	6	(2	4)	61	23	19	24	0	33	2	1	1	6	2	.75	3	.234	.354	.445
1998 Florida	NL	153	588	166	45	3	22	(10	12)	285	85	90	47	7	112	3	0	3	27	14	.66	10	.282	.337	.481
1999 Florida	NL	69	251	76	19	1	11	(4	7)	130	37	49	30	5	47	2	0	2	5	6	.45	8	.303	.379	.518
2000 Florida	NL	121	420	126	30	0	22	(13	9)	222	75	91	50	5	82	8	0	9	24	3	.89	4	.300	.378	.529
2001 Florida	NL	149	555	176	44	4	31	(16	15)	321	123	103	59	19	101	10	0	5	18	3	.86	9	.317	.390	.578
9 ML YEARS		809	2612	741	182	17	104	(51	53)	1269	424	429	271	37	521	34	4	26	100	32	.76	41	.284	.355	.486

Josh Fogg

Pitches: Right **Bats:** Right **Pos:** RP-11   **Ht:** 6'2" **Wt:** 205 **Born:** 12/13/76 **Age:** 25

Year Team	Lg	G	GS	CG	GF	IP	BFP	H	R	ER	HR	SH	SF	HB	TBB	IBB	SO	WP	Bk	W	L	Pct.	ShO	Sv-Op	Hld	ERA
1998 White Sox	R	2	0	0	0	4	13	0	0	0	0	0	1	0	1	0	5	1	0	1	0	1.000	0	0--	—	0.00
Hickory	A	8	8	0	0	41.1	173	36	17	10	4	1	0	1	13	0	29	1	1	1	3	.250	0	0--	—	2.18
Winston-Sal	A+	1	0	0	1	7	6	2	2	0	0	0	0	0	0	0	2	1	0	0	1	.000	0	0--	—	0.00
1999 Winston-Sal	A+	17	17	1	0	103.1	441	93	44	34	3	1		11	33	0	109	2	0	10	5	.667	1	0--	—	2.96
Birmingham	AA	10	10	0	0	55	249	66	37	36	8	1	2	5	18	0	40	2	1	3	2	.600	0	0--	—	5.89
2000 Birmingham	AA	27	27	2	0	192.1	787	190	68	55	7	5	4	6	44	2	136	9	1	11	7	.611	0	0--	—	2.57
2001 Charlotte	AAA	40	16	0	19	114.2	497	129	68	61	19	6	1	4	30	1	89	4	0	4	7	.364	0	4--	—	4.79
2001 Chicago	AL	11	0	0	4	13.1	53	10	3	3	0	0	1	1	3	1	17	0	0	0	0	—	0	0-0	2	2.03

P.J. Forbes

Bats: Right **Throws:** Right **Pos:** PH/PR-2; 2B-1   **Ht:** 5'10" **Wt:** 160 **Born:** 9/22/67 **Age:** 34

Year Team	Lg	G	AB	H	2B	3B	HR	(Hm	Rd)	TB	R	RBI	TBB	IBB	SO	HBP	SH	SF	SB	CS	SB%	GDP	Avg	OBP	SLG
1990 Boise	A-	43	170	42	9	1	0	—	—	53	29	19	23	1	20	0	7	1	11	4	.73	5	.247	.335	.312
1991 Palm Spring	A+	94	349	93	14	2	2	—	—	117	45	26	36	1	44	4	12	0	18	8	.69	7	.266	.342	.335
1992 Quad City	A	105	376	106	16	5	2	—	—	138	53	46	44	1	51	2	24	5	15	6	.71	4	.282	.356	.367
1993 Midland	AA	126	498	159	23	2	15	—	—	231	90	64	26	1	50	4	14	2	6	8	.43	13	.319	.357	.464
Vancouver	AAA	5	16	4	2	0	0	—	—	6	1	3	0	0	3	0	1	0	0	0	—	1	.250	.250	.375
1994 Angels	R	2	6	0	0	0	0	—	—	0	1	0	0	0	1	0	0	0	0	0	—	0	.000	.000	.000
Vancouver	AAA	90	318	91	21	2	1	—	—	119	39	40	20	0	42	0	7	5	2	1	.67	6	.286	.331	.374

Year Team	Lg	G	AB	H	2B	3B	HR	(Hm	Rd)	TB	R	RBI	TBB	IBB	SO	HBP	SH	SF	SB	CS	SB%	GDP	Avg	OBP	SLG
1995 Vancouver	AAA	109	369	101	22	3	1	—	—	132	47	52	21	0	46	2	7	10	4	6	.40	4	.274	.308	.358
1996 Vancouver	AAA	117	409	112	24	2	0	—	—	140	58	46	42	3	44	5	10	4	4	3	.57	13	.274	.346	.342
1997 Rochester	AAA	116	434	118	22	2	8	—	—	168	67	54	35	0	42	6	8	3	15	4	.79	11	.272	.333	.387
1998 Rochester	AAA	116	460	135	37	3	6	—	—	196	74	52	36	1	54	5	8	3	10	2	.83	15	.293	.349	.426
1999 Oklahoma	AAA	22	67	7	1	0	0	—	—	8	4	2	5	0	12	1	2	0	0	0	—	2	.104	.178	.119
Rochester	AAA	88	349	92	16	1	0	—	—	110	49	19	26	0	40	3	11	2	5	0	1.00	1	.264	.318	.315
2000 Scrantn-WB	AAA	99	334	92	22	1	2	—	—	122	51	32	30	0	29	4	0	4	7	2	.78	10	.275	.339	.365
2001 Scrantn-WB	AAA	133	514	157	29	2	5	—	—	205	79	61	48	0	72	3	9	2	5	0	1.00	9	.305	.367	.399
1998 Baltimore	AL	9	10	1	0	0	0	(0	0)	1	0	2	0	0	0	0	0	0	0	0	—	0	.100	.100	.100
2001 Philadelphia	NL	3	7	2	0	0	0	(0	0)	2	1	1	0	0	2	0	0	0	0	0	—	0	.286	.286	.286
2 ML YEARS		12	17	3	0	0	0	(0	0)	3	1	3	0	0	2	0	0	0	0	0	—	0	.176	.176	.176

Brook Fordyce

Bats: Right **Throws:** Right **Pos:** C-95   **Ht:** 6'0" **Wt:** 190 **Born:** 5/7/70 **Age:** 32

Year Team	Lg	G	AB	H	2B	3B	HR	(Hm	Rd)	TB	R	RBI	TBB	IBB	SO	HBP	SH	SF	SB	CS	SB%	GDP	Avg	OBP	SLG
1995 New York	NL	4	2	1	1	0	0	(0	0)	2	1	0	1	0	0	0	0	0	0	0	—	0	.500	.667	1.000
1996 Cincinnati	NL	4	7	2	1	0	0	(0	0)	3	0	1	3	0	1	0	0	0	0	0	—	0	.286	.500	.429
1997 Cincinnati	NL	47	96	20	5	0	1	(1	0)	28	7	8	8	1	15	0	0	1	2	0	1.00	1	.208	.267	.292
1998 Cincinnati	NL	57	146	37	9	0	3	(3	0)	55	8	14	11	3	28	0	1	0	0	1	.00	2	.253	.306	.377
1999 Chicago	AL	105	333	99	25	1	9	(5	4)	153	36	49	21	0	48	3	3	2	2	0	1.00	5	.297	.343	.459
2000 CWS-Bal	AL	93	302	91	18	1	14	(8	6)	153	41	49	17	0	50	4	2	5	0	0	—	4	.301	.341	.507
2001 Baltimore	AL	95	292	61	18	0	5	(0	5)	94	30	19	21	1	56	3	3	1	1	2	.33	7	.209	.268	.322
2000 Chicago	AL	40	125	34	7	1	5	(3	2)	58	18	21	6	0	23	2	2	1	0	0	—	1	.272	.313	.464
Baltimore	AL	53	177	57	11	0	9	(5	4)	95	23	28	11	0	27	2	0	4	0	0	—	3	.322	.361	.537
7 ML YEARS		405	1178	311	77	2	32	(17	15)	488	123	140	82	5	198	10	9	9	5	3	.63	18	.264	.315	.414

Casey Fossum

Pitches: Left **Bats:** Both **Pos:** SP-7; RP-6   **Ht:** 6'1" **Wt:** 160 **Born:** 1/9/78 **Age:** 24

Year Team	Lg	G	GS	CG	GF	IP	BFP	H	R	ER	HR	SH	SF	HB	TBB	IBB	SO	WP	Bk	W	L	Pct.	ShO	Sv-Op	Hld	ERA
1999 Lowell	A-	5	5	0	0	14.1	56	6	2	2	1	0	0	2	5	0	16	0	4	0	1	.000	0	0- -	—	1.26
2000 Sarasota	A+	27	27	3	0	149.1	623	147	71	57	7	2	6	7	36	0	143	3	0	9	10	.474	3	0- -	—	3.44
2001 Trenton	AA	20	20	0	0	117.2	483	102	47	37	5	0	0	12	28	0	130	2	0	3	7	.300	0	0- -	—	2.83
2001 Boston	AL	13	7	0	3	44.1	197	44	26	24	4	0	1	6	20	1	26	1	1	3	2	.600	0	0-0	0	4.87

Kevin Foster

Pitches: Right **Bats:** Right **Pos:** RP-9   **Ht:** 6'1" **Wt:** 175 **Born:** 1/13/69 **Age:** 33

Year Team	Lg	G	GS	CG	GF	IP	BFP	H	R	ER	HR	SH	SF	HB	TBB	IBB	SO	WP	Bk	W	L	Pct.	ShO	Sv-Op	Hld	ERA
2001 Oklahoma *	AAA	16	3	0	5	54.2	213	33	18	17	6	1	1	0	22	0	65	1	0	3	1	.750	0	0- -	—	2.80
1993 Philadelphia	NL	2	1	0	0	6.2	40	13	11	11	3	0	0	0	7	0	6	2	0	0	1	.000	0	0-0	0	14.85
1994 Chicago	NL	13	13	0	0	81	337	70	31	26	7	1	1	1	35	1	75	1	1	3	4	.429	0	0-0	0	2.89
1995 Chicago	NL	30	28	0	1	167.2	703	149	90	84	32	4	6	6	65	4	146	2	2	12	11	.522	0	0-0	0	4.51
1996 Chicago	NL	17	16	1	0	87	386	98	63	60	16	5	4	2	35	3	53	2	0	7	6	.538	0	0-0	0	6.21
1997 Chicago	NL	26	25	1	0	146.1	637	141	79	75	27	9	7	2	66	4	118	3	0	10	7	.588	0	0-0	0	4.61
1998 Chicago	NL	3	0	0	1	3.1	20	8	6	6	1	0	2	0	2	0	3	0	0	0	0	—	0	0-0	0	16.20
2001 Texas	AL	9	0	0	3	17.2	82	21	14	13	2	0	1	3	10	0	16	1	0	0	1	.000	0	0-0	0	6.62
7 ML YEARS		100	83	2	5	509.2	2205	500	294	275	88	19	21	14	220	12	417	11	3	32	30	.516	0	0-0	0	4.86

Kris Foster

Pitches: Right **Bats:** Right **Pos:** RP-7   **Ht:** 6'1" **Wt:** 200 **Born:** 8/30/74 **Age:** 27

Year Team	Lg	G	GS	CG	GF	IP	BFP	H	R	ER	HR	SH	SF	HB	TBB	IBB	SO	WP	Bk	W	L	Pct.	ShO	Sv-Op	Hld	ERA
1993 Expos	R	17	3	0	7	44.2	195	44	26	17	0	3	2	6	16	0	30	6	3	1	6	.143	0	1- -	—	3.43
1994 Expos	R	18	5	0	5	52.1	229	34	21	9	1	0	1	5	32	0	65	3	2	4	2	.667	0	4- -	—	1.55
1995 Yakima	A-	15	10	0	5	56	241	38	27	18	2	2	4	2	38	3	55	8	1	2	3	.400	0	3- -	—	2.89
1996 San Berndno	A+	30	8	0	9	81.2	355	66	46	35	5	3	4	3	54	3	78	10	4	3	5	.375	0	2- -	—	3.86
1997 Vero Beach	A+	17	17	2	0	89.2	414	97	69	53	8	3	3	7	44	1	77	5	1	6	3	.667	0	0- -	—	5.32
1998 Vero Beach	A+	24	6	0	7	53	249	59	45	40	8	2	1	1	27	0	52	6	5	3	5	.375	0	1- -	—	6.79
1999 Vero Beach	A+	8	0	0	3	15.1	59	10	5	3	1	0	2	0	2	0	15	0	6	1	1	.500	0	0- -	—	1.76
San Antonio	AA	33	0	0	19	52.2	228	43	24	21	3	2	2	0	26	1	53	6	0	0	2	.000	0	4- -	—	3.59
2000 San Berndno	A+	10	1	0	5	11.2	42	7	2	1	0	0	0	1	1	0	19	0	0	0	0	—	0	2- -	—	0.77
2001 Jacksnville	AA	17	0	0	17	18	64	6	2	2	1	0	0	1	2	0	29	0	0	3	0	1.000	0	7- -	—	1.00
Las Vegas	AAA	21	0	0	17	21	92	25	13	9	0	0	1	2	4	0	17	3	1	0	1	.000	0	12- -	—	3.86
Rochester	AAA	9	0	0	9	10	47	11	8	6	1	2	0	1	6	1	11	1	0	0	0	—	0	6- -	—	5.40
2001 Baltimore	AL	7	0	0	0	10	47	9	4	3	1	0	0	0	8	0	8	0	0	0	0	—	0	0-0	0	2.70

Keith Foulke

Pitches: Right **Bats:** Right **Pos:** RP-72   **Ht:** 6'0" **Wt:** 210 **Born:** 10/19/72 **Age:** 29

Year Team	Lg	G	GS	CG	GF	IP	BFP	H	R	ER	HR	SH	SF	HB	TBB	IBB	SO	WP	Bk	W	L	Pct.	ShO	Sv-Op	Hld	ERA
1997 SF-CWS		27	8	0	5	73.1	326	88	52	52	13	3	1	4	23	2	54	1	0	4	5	.444	0	3-6	6	6.38
1998 Chicago	AL	54	0	0	18	65.1	267	51	31	30	9	2	2	4	20	3	57	3	1	3	2	.600	0	1-2	13	4.13
1999 Chicago	AL	67	0	0	31	105.1	411	72	28	26	11	3	0	3	21	4	123	1	0	3	3	.500	0	9-13	22	2.22
2000 Chicago	AL	72	0	0	58	88	350	66	31	29	9	5	2	2	22	2	91	1	0	3	1	.750	0	34-39	3	2.97
2001 Chicago	AL	72	0	0	**69**	81	322	57	21	21	3	4	1	8	22	1	75	1	0	4	9	.308	0	42-45	0	2.33

		HOW MUCH HE PITCHED			WHAT HE GAVE UP			THE RESULTS		
Year Team	Lg	G GS CG GF	IP	BFP	H R ER HR SH SF HB	TBB IBB	SO WP Bk	W L Pct.	ShO Sv-Op Hld	ERA
1997 San Francisco	NL	11 8 0 0	44.2	209	60 41 41 9 2 0 4	18 1	33 1 0	1 5 .167	0 0-1 0	8.26
Chicago	AL	16 0 0 5	28.2	117	28 11 11 4 1 0 0	5 1	21 0 0	3 0 1.000	0 3-5 5	3.45
5 ML YEARS		292 8 0 181	413	1676	334 163 158 45 17 6 21	108 12	400 7 1	17 20 .459	0 89-105 43	3.44

Andy Fox

Bats: L **Throws:** R **Pos:** PH/PR-33; SS-12; 3B-9; 2B-2; LF-1; CF-1   **Ht:** 6'4" **Wt:** 202 **Born:** 1/12/71 **Age:** 31

		BATTING																	BASERUNNING				PERCENTAGES		
Year Team	Lg	G	AB	H	2B	3B	HR	(Hm	Rd)	TB	R	RBI	TBB	IBB	SO	HBP	SH	SF	SB	CS	SB%	GDP	Avg	OBP	SLG
2001 Calgary *	AAA	11	42	18	2	1	2	—	—	28	10	8	3	0	2	1	0	0	1	1	.50	1	.429	.478	.667
1996 New York	AL	113	189	37	4	0	3	(1	2)	50	26	13	20	1	28	1	9	0	11	3	.79	2	.196	.276	.265
1997 New York	AL	22	31	7	1	0	0	(0	0)	8	13	1	7	0	9	0	2	0	2	1	.67	1	.226	.368	.258
1998 Arizona	NL	139	502	139	21	6	9	(5	4)	199	67	44	43	0	97	18	0	1	14	7	.67	2	.277	.355	.396
1999 Arizona	NL	99	274	70	12	2	6	(4	2)	104	34	33	33	10	61	9	1	3	4	1	.80	4	.255	.351	.380
2000 Ari-Fla	NL	100	250	58	8	2	4	(2	2)	82	29	20	22	4	53	3	0	0	10	4	.71	2	.232	.302	.328
2001 Florida	NL	54	81	15	0	1	3	(3	0)	26	8	7	15	1	17	1	0	0	1	0	1.00	2	.185	.327	.321
2000 Arizona	NL	31	86	18	4	0	1	(1	0)	25	10	10	4	1	16	0	0	0	2	1	.67	1	.209	.244	.291
Florida	NL	69	164	40	4	2	3	(1	2)	57	19	10	18	3	37	3	0	0	8	3	.73	1	.244	.330	.348
6 ML YEARS		527	1327	326	46	11	25	(15	10)	469	177	118	140	15	265	33	12	4	42	16	.72	13	.246	.332	.353

Chad Fox

Pitches: Right **Bats:** Right **Pos:** RP-65   **Ht:** 6'3" **Wt:** 190 **Born:** 9/3/70 **Age:** 31

		HOW MUCH HE PITCHED			WHAT HE GAVE UP			THE RESULTS		
Year Team	Lg	G GS CG GF	IP	BFP	H R ER HR SH SF HB	TBB IBB	SO WP Bk	W L Pct.	ShO Sv-Op Hld	ERA
2001 Indianapolis *	AAA	4 0 0 4	6	25	4 1 1 0 1 0 0	3 0	8 0 0	3 0 1.000	0 0- –	1.50
1997 Atlanta	NL	30 0 0 8	27.1	120	24 12 10 4 0 0 0	16 0	28 4 0	1 0 1.000	0 0-1 7	3.29
1998 Milwaukee	NL	49 0 0 12	57	242	56 27 25 4 6 0 1	20 0	64 5 0	1 4 .200	0 0-2 20	3.95
1999 Milwaukee	NL	6 0 0 2	6.2	31	8 8 8 1 0 0 1	4 0	12 1 1	0 0 —	0 0-0 1	10.80
2001 Milwaukee	NL	65 0 0 9	66.2	287	44 16 14 6 2 1 5	36 7	80 5 1	5 2 .714	0 2-4 20	1.89
4 ML YEARS		150 0 0 31	157.2	685	135 63 57 15 8 1 7	76 7	184 15 2	6 7 .462	0 2-7 48	3.25

John Franco

Pitches: Left **Bats:** Left **Pos:** RP-58   **Ht:** 5'10" **Wt:** 185 **Born:** 9/17/60 **Age:** 41

		HOW MUCH HE PITCHED			WHAT HE GAVE UP			THE RESULTS		
Year Team	Lg	G GS CG GF	IP	BFP	H R ER HR SH SF HB	TBB IBB	SO WP Bk	W L Pct.	ShO Sv-Op Hld	ERA
1984 Cincinnati	NL	54 0 0 30	79.1	335	74 26 23 3 4 4 2	36 4	55 2 0	6 2 .750	0 4-8 2	2.61
1985 Cincinnati	NL	67 0 0 33	99	407	83 27 24 5 11 1 1	40 8	61 4 0	12 3 .800	0 12-14 11	2.18
1986 Cincinnati	NL	74 0 0 52	101	429	90 40 33 7 8 3 2	44 12	84 4 2	6 6 .500	0 29-38 2	2.94
1987 Cincinnati	NL	68 0 0 **60**	82	344	76 26 23 6 5 2 0	27 6	61 1 0	8 5 .615	0 32-41 0	2.52
1988 Cincinnati	NL	70 0 0 **61**	86	336	60 18 15 3 5 1 0	27 3	46 1 2	6 6 .500	0 **39-42** 1	1.57
1989 Cincinnati	NL	60 0 0 50	80.2	345	77 35 28 3 7 3 0	36 8	60 3 2	4 8 .333	0 32-39 1	3.12
1990 New York	NL	55 0 0 48	67.2	287	66 22 19 4 3 1 0	21 6	56 7 2	5 3 .625	0 33-39 0	2.53
1991 New York	NL	52 0 0 48	55.1	247	61 27 18 2 3 0 1	18 4	45 6 0	5 9 .357	0 30-35 0	2.93
1992 New York	NL	31 0 0 30	33	128	24 6 6 1 0 2 0	11 2	20 0 0	6 2 .750	0 15-17 1	1.64
1993 New York	NL	35 0 0 30	36.1	172	46 24 21 6 4 1 1	19 3	29 5 0	4 3 .571	0 10-17 0	5.20
1994 New York	NL	47 0 0 43	50	216	47 20 15 2 2 1 1	19 0	42 1 0	1 4 .200	0 **30-36** 0	2.70
1995 New York	NL	48 0 0 41	51.2	213	48 17 14 4 4 1 0	17 2	41 0 0	5 3 .625	0 28-36 0	2.44
1996 New York	NL	51 0 0 44	54	235	54 15 11 2 6 0 0	21 0	48 2 0	4 3 .571	0 28-36 1	1.83
1997 New York	NL	59 0 0 53	60	244	49 18 17 3 5 1 1	20 2	53 6 0	5 3 .625	0 36-42 0	2.55
1998 New York	NL	61 0 0 54	64.2	289	66 28 26 4 4 5 4	29 7	59 2 0	0 8 .000	0 38-46 1	3.62
1999 New York	NL	46 0 0 34	40.2	182	40 14 13 1 3 1 2	19 1	41 0 0	0 2 .000	0 19-21 1	3.40
2000 New York	NL	62 0 0 14	55.2	239	46 24 21 6 3 0 2	26 6	56 2 0	5 4 .556	0 4-4 20	3.40
2001 New York	NL	58 0 0 16	53.1	232	55 25 24 8 2 1 2	19 2	50 4 1	6 2 .750	0 2-7 17	4.05
18 ML YEARS		998 0 0 741	1150.1	4880	1062 414 351 70 79 28 19	449 72	907 50 9	88 76 .537	0 422-518 56	2.75

Julio Franco

Bats: Right **Throws:** Right **Pos:** 1B-23; PH/PR-3   **Ht:** 6'1" **Wt:** 190 **Born:** 8/23/61 **Age:** 40

		BATTING																	BASERUNNING				PERCENTAGES		
Year Team	Lg	G	AB	H	2B	3B	HR	(Hm	Rd)	TB	R	RBI	TBB	IBB	SO	HBP	SH	SF	SB	CS	SB%	GDP	Avg	OBP	SLG
1982 Philadelphia	NL	16	29	8	1	0	0	(0	0)	9	3	3	2	1	4	0	1	0	0	2	.00	1	.276	.323	.310
1983 Cleveland	AL	149	560	153	24	8	8	(6	2)	217	68	80	27	1	50	2	3	6	32	12	.73	21	.273	.306	.388
1984 Cleveland	AL	160	**658**	188	22	5	3	(1	2)	229	82	79	43	1	68	6	1	10	19	10	.66	23	.286	.331	.348
1985 Cleveland	AL	160	636	183	33	4	6	(3	3)	242	97	90	54	2	74	4	0	9	13	9	.59	26	.288	.343	.381
1986 Cleveland	AL	149	599	183	30	5	10	(4	6)	253	80	74	32	1	66	0	0	5	10	7	.59	**28**	.306	.338	.422
1987 Cleveland	AL	128	495	158	24	3	8	(5	3)	212	86	52	57	2	56	3	0	5	32	9	.78	23	.319	.389	.428
1988 Cleveland	AL	152	613	186	23	6	10	(3	7)	251	88	54	56	4	72	2	1	4	25	6	.81	19	.303	.361	.409
1989 Texas	AL	150	548	173	31	5	13	(9	4)	253	80	92	66	11	69	1	0	6	21	3	**.88**	27	.316	.386	.462
1990 Texas	AL	157	582	172	27	1	11	(4	7)	234	96	69	82	3	83	2	2	2	31	10	.76	12	.296	.383	.402
1991 Texas	AL	146	589	201	27	3	15	(7	8)	279	108	78	65	8	78	3	0	2	36	9	.80	13	**.341**	.408	.474
1992 Texas	AL	35	107	25	7	0	2	(2	0)	38	19	8	15	2	17	0	1	0	1	1	.50	3	.234	.328	.355
1993 Texas	AL	144	532	154	31	3	14	(6	8)	233	85	84	62	4	95	1	5	7	9	3	.75	16	.289	.360	.438
1994 Chicago	AL	112	433	138	19	2	20	(10	10)	221	72	98	62	4	75	5	0	5	8	0	.89	14	.319	.406	.510
1996 Cleveland	AL	112	432	139	20	1	14	(7	7)	203	72	76	61	0	82	3	0	3	8	8	.50	14	.322	.407	.470
1997 Cle-Mil	AL	120	430	116	16	1	7	(5	2)	155	68	44	69	4	116	1	1	4	15	6	.71	17	.270	.369	.360
1999 Tampa Bay	AL	1	1	0	0	0	0	(0	0)	0	0	0	0	0	0	0	0	0	0	0	—	0	.000	.000	.000
2001 Atlanta	NL	25	90	27	4	0	3	(2	1)	40	13	11	10	1	20	1	0	0	8	5	.62	3	.300	.376	.444
1997 Cleveland	AL	78	289	82	13	1	3	(2	1)	106	46	25	38	2	75	0	1	0	8	5	.62	13	.284	.367	.367
Milwaukee	AL	42	141	34	3	0	4	(3	1)	49	22	19	31	2	41	1	0	4	7	1	.88	4	.241	.373	.348
17 ML YEARS		1916	7334	2204	339	47	144	(74	70)	3069	1117	992	763	51	1026	34	15	68	260	101	.72	258	.301	.366	.418

Ryan Franklin

Pitches: Right Bats: Right Pos: RP-38

Ht: 6'3" Wt: 165 Born: 3/5/73 Age: 29

		HOW MUCH HE PITCHED						WHAT HE GAVE UP									THE RESULTS					
Year Team	Lg	G	GS	CG	GF	IP	BFP	H	R	ER	HR	SH	SF	HB	TBB	IBB	SO	WP	Bk	W	L	Pct.	ShO	Sv-Op	Hld	ERA
1993 Bellingham	A-	15	14	1	0	74	321	72	38	24	2	2	1	3	27	0	55	7	3	5	3	.625	1	0- --	---	2.92
1994 Appleton	A	18	18	5	0	118	493	105	60	41	6	3	1	17	23	0	102	6	3	9	6	.600	1	0- --	---	3.13
Calgary	AAA	1	1	0	0	5.2	28	9	6	5	2	0	0	1	0	0	2	0	0	0	0			0- --	---	7.94
Riverside	A+	8	8	1	0	61.2	261	61	26	21	5	1	3	4	8	0	35	0	1	4	2	.667	1	0- --	---	3.06
1995 Port City	AA	31	21	1	2	146	627	153	84	70	13	11	3	12	43	4	102	6	2	6	10	.375	1	0- --	---	4.32
1996 Port City	AA	28	27	2	0	182	764	186	99	81	23	6	3	16	37	0	127	4	2	6	12	.333	0	0- --	---	4.01
1997 Memphis	AA	11	8	2	2	59.1	234	45	22	20	4	0	3	1	14	1	49	1	0	4	2	.667	2	0- --	---	3.03
Tacoma	AAA	14	14	0	0	90.1	386	97	48	42	11	7	2	8	24	1	59	1	1	5	5	.500	0	0- --	---	4.18
1998 Tacoma	AAA	34	16	1	10	127.2	561	148	75	64	18	4	8	10	32	2	90	0	0	5	6	.455	0	1- --	---	4.51
1999 Tacoma	AAA	29	19	2	4	135.2	574	142	81	71	17	2	4	9	33	1	94	1	1	6	9	.400	1	2- --	---	4.71
2000 Tacoma	AAA	31	22	4	2	164	665	147	85	71	28	3	3	12	35	1	142	2	0	11	5	.688	0	0- --	---	3.90
2001 Tacoma	AAA	1	0	0	1	3.2	13	2	0	0	0	0	0	0	0	0	3	0	0	0	0			0- --	---	0.00
1999 Seattle	AL	6	0	0	2	11.1	51	10	6	6	2	0	0	1	8	1	6	0	0	0	0		0	0-0	---	4.76
2001 Seattle	AL	38	0	0	14	78.1	335	76	32	31	13	1	2	4	24	4	60	2	0	5	1	.833	0	0-1	5	3.56
2 ML YEARS		44	0	0	16	89.2	386	86	38	37	15	1	2	5	32	5	66	2	0	5	1	.833	0	0-1	6	3.71

Wayne Franklin

Pitches: Left Bats: Left Pos: RP-11

Ht: 6'2" Wt: 195 Born: 3/9/74 Age: 28

		HOW MUCH HE PITCHED						WHAT HE GAVE UP									THE RESULTS					
Year Team	Lg	G	GS	CG	GF	IP	BFP	H	R	ER	HR	SH	SF	HB	TBB	IBB	SO	WP	Bk	W	L	Pct.	ShO	Sv-Op	Hld	ERA
1996 Yakima	A-	20	0	0	5	25	115	32	10	7	2	0	0	0	12	3	22	3	1	0	1	1.000	0	1- --	---	2.52
1997 Savannah	A	28	7	1	10	82	362	79	41	29	10	1	1	4	35	0	58	2	1	5	3	.625	0	2- --	---	3.18
San Berndno	A	1	0	0	0	2	7	2	0	0	0	0	0	0	0	0	1	0	0	0	0		0	0- --	---	0.00
1998 Vero Beach	A+	48	0	0	26	86.2	369	81	43	34	7	3	5	2	26	0	78	3	2	9	3	.750	0	10- --	---	3.53
1999 Kissimmee	A+	12	0	0	7	17.2	69	11	4	3	0	1	0	1	6	0	22	0	0	3	0	1.000	0	1- --	---	1.53
Jackson	AA	46	0	0	40	50.1	200	31	11	9	3	3	4	3	16	3	40	1	0	3	1	.750	0	20- --	---	1.61
2000 New Orleans	AAA	48	0	0	15	44.2	208	51	29	18	4	3	1	2	19	3	37	1	0	3	3	.500	0	4- --	---	3.63
2001 New Orleans	AAA	41	0	0	8	49.2	216	47	28	21	6	2	0	3	18	2	51	2	0	2	1	.667	0	0- --	---	3.81
2000 Houston	NL	25	0	0	4	21.1	103	24	14	13	2	0	2	4	12	1	21	0	1	0	0		0	0-0	8	5.48
2001 Houston	NL	11	0	0	3	12	60	17	9	9	4	0	0	0	9	0	9	0	0	0	0		0	0-0	1	6.75
2 ML YEARS		36	0	0	7	33.1	163	41	23	22	6	0	2	4	21	1	30	0	1	0	0		0	0-0	9	5.94

John Frascatore

Pitches: Right Bats: Right Pos: RP-12

Ht: 6'1" Wt: 223 Born: 2/4/70 Age: 32

		HOW MUCH HE PITCHED						WHAT HE GAVE UP									THE RESULTS					
Year Team	Lg	G	GS	CG	GF	IP	BFP	H	R	ER	HR	SH	SF	HB	TBB	IBB	SO	WP	Bk	W	L	Pct.	ShO	Sv-Op	Hld	ERA
2001 Syracuse *	AAA	37	0	0	12	37	167	47	20	17	4	4	0	1	9	1	18	2	0	1	4	.200	0	2- --	---	4.14
1994 St. Louis	NL	1	1	0	0	3.1	18	7	6	6	2	0	0	0	2	0	2	1	0	0	1	.000	0	0-0	0	16.20
1995 St. Louis	NL	14	4	0	3	32.2	151	39	19	16	3	1	1	2	16	1	21	0	0	1	1	.500	0	0-0	0	4.41
1997 St. Louis	NL	59	0	0	17	80	348	74	25	22	5	5	5	6	33	5	58	4	0	5	2	.714	0	0-4	3	2.48
1998 St. Louis	NL	69	0	0	15	95.2	415	95	48	44	11	4	1	3	36	3	49	2	0	3	4	.429	0	0-2	13	4.14
1999 Ari-Tor	NL	59	0	0	24	70	297	73	32	29	11	6	3	2	21	8	37	5	0	8	5	.615	0	1-3	10	3.73
2000 Toronto	AL	60	0	0	15	73	335	87	51	44	14	2	4	7	33	2	30	3	0	2	4	.333	0	0-5	13	5.42
2001 Toronto	AL	12	0	0	2	16.1	69	16	4	4	4	0	0	0	4	1	9	0	0	1	0	1.000	0	0-1	1	2.20
1999 Arizona	NL	26	0	0	10	33	136	31	16	15	6	1	1	1	12	4	15	0	0	1	4	.200	0	0-1	4	4.09
Toronto		33	0	0	14	37	161	42	16	14	5	5	2	1	9	4	22	5	0	7	1	.875	0	1-2	6	3.41
7 ML YEARS		274	5	0	76	371	1633	391	185	165	50	18	14	20	145	20	206	15	0	20	17	.541	0	1-15	40	4.00

Ryan Freel

Bats: Right Throws: Right Pos: 2B-7; PH/PR-2; LF-1

Ht: 5'10" Wt: 185 Born: 3/8/76 Age: 26

		BATTING																	BASERUNNING				PERCENTAGES		
Year Team	Lg	G	AB	H	2B	3B	HR	(Hm	Rd)	TB	R	RBI	TBB	IBB	SO	HBP	SH	SF	SB	CS	SB%	GDP	Avg	OBP	SLG
1995 St.Cathrnes	A-	65	243	68	10	5	3	—	—	97	30	29	22	0	49	7	7	5	12	7	.63	3	.280	.350	.399
1996 Dunedin	A+	104	381	97	23	3	4	—	—	138	64	41	33	0	76	5	14	2	19	15	.56	4	.255	.321	.362
1997 Knoxville	AA	33	94	19	1	1	0	—	—	22	18	4	19	0	13	2	1	0	5	3	.63	3	.202	.348	.234
Dunedin	A+	61	181	51	8	2	3	—	—	72	42	17	46	2	28	9	6	1	24	5	.83	3	.282	.447	.398
1998 Knoxville	AA	66	252	72	17	3	4	—	—	107	47	36	33	0	32	1	3	4	18	9	.67	3	.286	.366	.425
Syracuse	AAA	37	118	27	4	0	2	—	—	37	19	12	26	0	16	4	0	3	4	.69	3	.229	.377	.314
1999 Knoxville	AA	11	46	13	5	1	1	—	—	23	9	9	8	0	4	0	0	1	4	2	.67	0	.283	.382	.500
Syracuse	AAA	20	77	23	3	2	1	—	—	33	15	11	8	0	13	4	1	0	10	3	.77	3	.299	.393	.429
2000 Dunedin	A+	4	18	9	1	0	3	—	—	19	7	6	0	0	1	0	0	0	0	0	—	0	.500	.500	1.056
Tennessee	AA	12	44	13	3	1	0	—	—	18	11	8	8	0	6	1	0	2	2	3	.40	3	.295	.400	.409
Syracuse	AAA	80	283	81	14	5	10	—	—	135	62	30	35	1	44	9	4	2	30	7	.81	3	.286	.380	.477
2001 Syracuse	AAA	85	319	83	21	3	5	—	—	125	60	33	42	0	42	7	6	2	22	9	.71	8	.260	.357	.392
2001 Toronto	AL	9	22	6	1	0	0	(0	0)	7	1	3	1	0	4	1	0	0	2	1	.67	0	.273	.333	.318

Jeff Frye

Bats: R Throws: R Pos: 2B-47; 3B-27; PH/PR-11; SS-2; LF-1

Ht: 5'9" Wt: 170 Born: 8/31/66 Age: 35

		BATTING																	BASERUNNING				PERCENTAGES		
Year Team	Lg	G	AB	H	2B	3B	HR	(Hm	Rd)	TB	R	RBI	TBB	IBB	SO	HBP	SH	SF	SB	CS	SB%	GDP	Avg	OBP	SLG
2001 Dunedin *	A+	4	12	6	0	0	0	—	—	6	4	1	2	0	1	0	0	0	0	1	1.00	1	.500	.571	.500
1992 Texas	AL	67	199	51	9	1	1	(0	1)	65	24	12	16	0	27	3	11	1	1	3	.25	2	.256	.320	.327
1994 Texas	AL	57	205	67	20	3	0	(0	0)	93	37	18	29	0	23	1	5	3	6	1	.86	1	.327	.408	.454
1995 Texas	AL	90	313	87	15	2	4	(2	2)	118	38	29	24	0	45	5	8	4	3	3	.50	7	.278	.335	.377
1996 Boston	AL	105	419	120	27	2	4	(3	1)	163	74	41	54	0	57	5	5	3	18	4	.82	6	.286	.372	.389
1997 Boston	AL	127	404	126	36	2	3	(1	2)	175	56	51	27	1	44	2	2	7	19	8	.70	12	.312	.352	.433
1999 Boston	AL	41	114	32	3	0	1	(1	0)	38	14	12	14	1	11	1	1	1	2	2	.50	2	.281	.362	.333

Year Team	Lg	G	AB	H	2B	3B	HR	(Hm	Rd)	TB	R	RBI	TBB	IBB	SO	HBP	SH	SF	SB	CS	SB%	GDP	Avg	OBP	SLG
2000 Bos-Col		106	326	100	19	0	1	(0	1)	122	49	16	36	0	54	2	5	2	5	3	.63	8	.307	.377	.374
2001 Toronto	AL	74	175	43	6	1	2	(2	0)	57	24	15	12	0	18	3	4	0	2	1	.67	2	.246	.305	.326
2000 Boston	AL	69	239	69	13	0	1	(0	1)	85	35	13	28	0	38	1	4	1	1	3	.25	5	.289	.364	.356
Colorado	NL	37	87	31	6	0	0	(0	0)	37	14	3	8	0	16	1	1	1	4	0	1.00	3	.356	.412	.425
8 ML YEARS		667	2155	626	135	11	16	(10	6)	831	316	194	212	2	279	22	41	21	56	25	.69	40	.290	.357	.386

Travis Fryman

Bats: R Throws: R Pos: 3B-96; DH-2; PH/PR-2; SS-1   Ht: 6'1" Wt: 205 Born: 3/25/69 Age: 33

Year Team	Lg	G	AB	H	2B	3B	HR	(Hm	Rd)	TB	R	RBI	TBB	IBB	SO	HBP	SH	SF	SB	CS	SB%	GDP	Avg	OBP	SLG
2001 Akron *	AA	6	25	9	2	0	1	—	—	14	3	3	2	0	5	0	0	0	0	0	—	0	.360	.407	.560
Buffalo *	AAA	8	27	13	1	0	2	—	—	20	9	8	5	0	6	0	0	1	1	0	1.00	0	.481	.545	.741
1990 Detroit	AL	66	232	69	11	1	9	(5	4)	109	32	27	17	0	51	1	1	0	3	3	.50	3	.297	.348	.470
1991 Detroit	AL	149	557	144	36	3	21	(8	13)	249	65	91	40	0	149	3	6	6	12	5	.71	13	.259	.309	.447
1992 Detroit	AL	161	659	175	31	4	20	(9	11)	274	87	96	45	1	144	6	5	6	8	4	.67	13	.266	.316	.416
1993 Detroit	AL	151	607	182	37	5	22	(13	9)	295	98	97	77	1	128	4	1	4	9	4	.69	8	.300	.379	.486
1994 Detroit	AL	114	464	122	34	5	18	(10	8)	220	66	85	45	1	128	5	1	13	2	2	.50	6	.263	.326	.474
1995 Detroit	AL	144	567	156	21	5	15	(9	6)	232	79	81	63	4	100	3	0	7	4	2	.67	18	.275	.347	.409
1996 Detroit	AL	157	616	165	32	3	22	(10	12)	269	90	100	57	2	118	4	1	10	4	3	.57	18	.268	.329	.437
1997 Detroit	AL	154	595	163	27	3	22	(13	9)	262	90	102	46	5	113	5	0	11	16	3	.84	15	.274	.326	.440
1998 Cleveland	AL	146	557	160	33	2	28	(16	12)	281	74	96	44	0	125	3	0	4	10	8	.56	12	.287	.340	.504
1999 Cleveland	AL	85	322	82	16	2	10	(6	4)	132	45	48	25	1	57	1	0	2	2	1	.67	13	.255	.309	.410
2000 Cleveland	AL	155	574	184	38	4	22	(9	13)	296	93	106	73	2	111	1	0	10	1	5	.50	15	.321	.392	.516
2001 Cleveland	AL	98	334	88	15	0	3	(3	0)	112	34	38	30	1	63	3	0	3	1	2	.33	8	.263	.327	.335
12 ML YEARS		1580	6084	1690	331	37	212	(111	101)	2731	853	967	562	18	1287	39	15	78	72	38	.65	142	.278	.339	.449

Brian Fuentes

Pitches: Left Bats: Left Pos: RP-10   Ht: 6'4" Wt: 220 Born: 8/9/75 Age: 26

		HOW MUCH HE PITCHED						WHAT HE GAVE UP										THE RESULTS						
Year Team	Lg	G	GS	CG	GF	IP	BFP	H	R	ER	HR	SH	SF	HB	TBB	IBB	SO	WP	Bk	W	L	Pct.	ShO	Sv-Op	Hld	ERA
1996 Everett	A-	13	2	0	3	26.2	114	23	14	13	2	0	1	0	13	0	26	5	0	0	1	.000	0	0--	—	4.39
1997 Wisconsin	A	22	22	0	0	118.2	486	84	52	47	6	3	3	8	59	0	153	11	3	6	7	.462	0	0--	—	3.56
1998 Lancaster	A+	24	22	0	1	118.2	541	121	73	55	8	1	6	9	81	0	137	14	2	7	7	.500	0	0--	—	4.17
1999 New Haven	AA	15	14	0	0	60	272	53	36	33	5	2	5	11	46	0	66	1	1	3	3	.500	0	0--	—	4.95
2000 New Haven	AA	26	26	1	0	139.2	610	127	80	70	7	4	7	13	70	0	152	14	0	7	12	.368	0	0--	—	4.51
2001 Tacoma	AAA	35	0	0	13	52	205	35	19	17	4	3	1	6	25	0	70	3	0	3	2	.600	0	6--	—	2.94
2001 Seattle	AL	10	0	0	3	11.2	47	6	6	6	2	0	1	3	8	0	10	1	0	1	1	.500	0	0-1	1	4.63

Brad Fullmer

Bats: Left Throws: Right Pos: DH-135; PH/PR-10; 1B-1   Ht: 6'0" Wt: 215 Born: 1/17/75 Age: 27

Year Team	Lg	G	AB	H	2B	3B	HR	(Hm	Rd)	TB	R	RBI	TBB	IBB	SO	HBP	SH	SF	SB	CS	SB%	GDP	Avg	OBP	SLG
1997 Montreal	NL	19	40	12	2	0	3	(1	2)	23	4	8	2	1	7	1	0	0	0	0	—	0	.300	.349	.575
1998 Montreal	NL	140	505	138	44	2	13	(3	10)	225	58	73	39	4	70	2	0	1	6	6	.50	12	.273	.327	.446
1999 Montreal	NL	100	347	96	34	2	9	(4	5)	161	38	47	22	6	35	2	0	3	2	3	.40	14	.277	.321	.464
2000 Toronto	AL	133	482	142	29	1	32	(16	16)	269	76	104	30	3	68	6	0	6	3	1	.75	14	.295	.340	.558
2001 Toronto	AL	146	522	143	31	2	18	(8	10)	232	71	83	38	8	88	6	0	7	5	2	.71	13	.274	.326	.444
5 ML YEARS		538	1896	531	140	7	75	(32	43)	910	247	315	131	22	268	17	0	17	16	12	.57	53	.280	.329	.480

Aaron Fultz

Pitches: Left Bats: Left Pos: RP-66   Ht: 6'0" Wt: 196 Born: 9/4/73 Age: 28

		HOW MUCH HE PITCHED						WHAT HE GAVE UP										THE RESULTS						
Year Team	Lg	G	GS	CG	GF	IP	BFP	H	R	ER	HR	SH	SF	HB	TBB	IBB	SO	WP	Bk	W	L	Pct.	ShO	Sv-Op	Hld	ERA
1992 Giants	R	14	14	0	0	67.2	282	51	24	16	0	4	1	4	33	0	72	7	0	3	2	.600	0	0--	—	2.13
1993 Clinton	A	26	25	2	0	148	641	132	63	56	8	12	2	11	64	2	144	10	2	14	8	.636	1	0--	—	3.41
Fort Wayne	A	1	1	0	0	4	21	10	4	4	0	0	0	0	0	0	3	0	0	0	0	—	0	0--	—	9.00
1994 Fort Myers	A+	28	28	3	0	168.1	745	193	95	81	9	6	4	7	60	5	132	9	2	9	10	.474	0	0--	—	4.33
1995 Hardware Cy	AA	3	3	0	0	15	64	11	12	11	1	0	2	0	9	0	12	0	0	0	2	.000	0	0--	—	6.60
Fort Myers	A+	21	21	2	0	122	516	115	52	44	10	4	3	8	41	1	127	7	1	3	6	.333	2	0--	—	3.25
1996 San Jose	A+	36	12	0	11	104.2	460	101	52	46	7	9	3	8	54	2	103	13	0	9	5	.643	0	1--	—	3.96
1997 Shreveport	AA	49	0	0	20	70	293	65	30	22	6	4	5	2	19	0	60	4	1	6	3	.667	0	1--	—	2.83
1998 Shreveport	AA	54	0	0	34	62	273	58	40	26	4	8	3	3	29	10	61	5	1	5	7	.417	0	15--	—	3.77
Fresno	AAA	10	0	0	3	16	68	22	10	9	2	0	0	0	2	1	13	1	0	0	0	—	0	0--	—	5.06
1999 Fresno	AAA	37	20	1	7	137.1	601	141	87	76	32	3	9	7	51	1	151	11	0	9	8	.529	0	0--	—	4.98
2000 San Francisco	NL	58	0	0	18	69.1	299	67	38	36	8	7	6	3	28	0	62	0	2	5	2	.714	0	1-3	7	4.67
2001 San Francisco	NL	66	0	0	17	71	300	70	40	36	9	3	4	1	21	3	67	1	0	3	1	.750	0	1-2	12	4.56
2 ML YEARS		124	0	0	35	140.1	599	137	78	72	17	10	10	4	49	3	129	1	2	8	3	.727	0	2-5	19	4.62

Rafael Furcal

Bats: Both Throws: Right Pos: SS-79   Ht: 5'10" Wt: 165 Born: 8/24/80 Age: 21

Year Team	Lg	G	AB	H	2B	3B	HR	(Hm	Rd)	TB	R	RBI	TBB	IBB	SO	HBP	SH	SF	SB	CS	SB%	GDP	Avg	OBP	SLG
1997 Braves	R	50	190	49	5	4	1	—	—	65	31	9	20	0	21	2	0	0	15	2	.88	1	.258	.335	.342
1998 Danville	R+	66	268	88	15	4	0	—	—	111	56	23	36	0	29	3	1	1	60	15	.80	2	.328	.412	.414
1999 Macon	A	83	335	113	15	1	1	—	—	133	73	29	41	1	36	5	1	0	73	22	.77	4	.337	.417	.397
Myrtle Bch	A+	43	184	54	9	3	0	—	—	69	32	12	14	0	42	0	4	0	23	8	.74	3	.293	.343	.375
2000 Greenville	AA	3	10	2	0	0	1	—	—	5	1	3	1	0	0	0	0	0	0	0	—	0	.200	.273	.500
2000 Atlanta	NL	131	455	134	20	4	4	(1	3)	174	87	37	73	0	80	3	9	2	40	14	.74	2	.295	.394	.382

77

Year Team	Lg	G	AB	H	2B	3B	HR	(Hm	Rd)	TB	R	RBI	TBB	IBB	SO	HBP	SH	SF	SB	CS	SB%	GDP	Avg	OBP	SLG
2001 Atlanta	NL	79	324	89	19	0	4	(3	1)	120	39	30	24	1	56	1	4	6	22	6	.79	5	.275	.321	.370
2 ML YEARS		210	779	223	39	4	8	(4	4)	294	126	67	97	1	136	4	13	8	62	20	.76	7	.286	.365	.377

Mike Fyhrie

Pitches: Right **Bats:** Right **Pos:** RP-18

Ht: 6'2" **Wt:** 203 **Born:** 12/9/69 **Age:** 32

Year Team	Lg		HOW MUCH HE PITCHED						WHAT HE GAVE UP											THE RESULTS					
		G	GS	CG	GF	IP	BFP	H	R	ER	HR	SH	SF	HB	TBB	IBB	SO	WP	Bk	W	L	Pct.	ShO	Sv-Op	Hld	ERA
2001 Cubs *	R	2	2	0	0	2	7	1	0	0	0	0	0	0	0	0	4	0	0	0	0	—	0	0--	—	0.00
Iowa *	AAA	13	0	0	4	15	69	14	8	8	1	0	0	1	8	0	15	1	0	0	1	1.000	0	2--	—	4.80
1996 New York	NL	2	0	0	0	2.1	14	4	4	4	0	0	0	0	3	0	0	0	0	0	1	.000	0	0-0	0	15.43
1999 Anaheim	AL	16	7	0	5	51.2	235	61	32	29	8	0	1	0	21	1	26	0	0	0	4	.000	0	0-0	1	5.05
2000 Anaheim	AL	32	0	0	7	52.2	220	54	14	14	4	1	3	0	15	4	43	0	0	0	0	—	0	0-0	2	2.39
2001 ChC-Oak		18	0	0	5	20	81	18	7	7	1	0	0	0	8	0	11	0	0	0	2	.000	0	0-0	5	3.15
2001 Chicago	NL	15	0	0	4	15	64	16	7	7	1	0	0	0	7	0	6	0	0	0	2	.000	0	0-0	5	4.20
Oakland	AL	3	0	0	1	5	17	2	0	0	0	0	0	0	1	0	5	0	0	0	0	—	0	0-0	0	0.00
4 ML YEARS		68	7	0	17	126.2	550	137	57	54	13	1	4	0	47	5	80	0	0	0	7	.000	0	0-0	8	3.84

Eric Gagne

Pitches: Right **Bats:** Right **Pos:** SP-24; RP-9

Ht: 6'2" **Wt:** 195 **Born:** 1/7/76 **Age:** 26

Year Team	Lg		HOW MUCH HE PITCHED						WHAT HE GAVE UP											THE RESULTS					
		G	GS	CG	GF	IP	BFP	H	R	ER	HR	SH	SF	HB	TBB	IBB	SO	WP	Bk	W	L	Pct.	ShO	Sv-Op	Hld	ERA
2001 Las Vegas *	AAA	4	4	0	0	23.2	87	15	4	4	2	2	0	0	8	0	31	2	0	3	0	1.000	0	0--	—	1.52
1999 Los Angeles	NL	5	5	0	0	30	119	18	8	7	3	1	0	0	15	0	30	1	0	1	1	.500	0	0-0	0	2.10
2000 Los Angeles	NL	20	19	0	0	101.1	464	106	62	58	20	5	3	3	60	1	79	4	0	4	6	.400	0	0-0	0	5.15
2001 Los Angeles	NL	33	24	0	3	151.2	649	144	90	80	24	6	8	16	46	1	130	3	1	6	7	.462	0	0-0	0	4.75
3 ML YEARS		58	48	0	3	283	1232	268	160	145	47	12	11	19	121	2	239	8	1	11	14	.440	0	0-0	0	4.61

Andres Galarraga

Bats: Right **Throws:** Right **Pos:** 1B-66; DH-39; PH/PR-19

Ht: 6'3" **Wt:** 250 **Born:** 6/18/61 **Age:** 41

Year Team	Lg	G	AB	H	2B	3B	HR	(Hm	Rd)	TB	R	RBI	TBB	IBB	SO	HBP	SH	SF	SB	CS	SB%	GDP	Avg	OBP	SLG
1985 Montreal	NL	24	75	14	1	0	2	(0	2)	21	9	4	3	0	18	1	0	0	1	2	.33	0	.187	.228	.280
1986 Montreal	NL	105	321	87	13	0	10	(4	6)	130	39	42	30	5	79	3	1	1	6	5	.55	8	.271	.338	.405
1987 Montreal	NL	147	551	168	40	3	13	(7	6)	253	72	90	41	13	127	10	0	4	7	10	.41	11	.305	.361	.459
1988 Montreal	NL	157	609	184	42	8	29	(14	15)	329	99	92	39	9	153	10	0	3	13	4	.76	12	.302	.352	.540
1989 Montreal	NL	152	572	147	30	1	23	(13	10)	248	76	85	48	10	158	13	0	3	12	5	.71	12	.257	.327	.434
1990 Montreal	NL	155	579	148	29	0	20	(6	14)	237	65	87	40	8	169	4	0	5	10	1	.91	14	.256	.306	.409
1991 Montreal	NL	107	375	82	13	2	9	(3	6)	126	34	33	23	5	86	2	0	0	5	6	.45	6	.219	.268	.336
1992 St. Louis	NL	95	325	79	14	2	10	(4	6)	127	38	39	11	0	69	8	0	3	5	4	.56	8	.243	.282	.391
1993 Colorado	NL	120	470	174	35	4	22	(13	9)	283	71	98	24	12	73	6	0	6	2	4	.33	9	.370	.403	.602
1994 Colorado	NL	103	417	133	21	0	31	(16	15)	247	77	85	19	8	93	6	0	5	8	3	.73	10	.319	.356	.592
1995 Colorado	NL	143	554	155	29	3	31	(18	13)	283	89	106	32	6	146	13	0	5	12	2	.86	14	.280	.331	.511
1996 Colorado	NL	159	626	190	39	3	47	(32	15)	376	119	150	40	3	157	17	0	8	18	8	.69	6	.304	.357	.601
1997 Colorado	NL	154	600	191	31	3	41	(21	20)	351	120	140	54	2	141	17	0	3	15	8	.65	16	.318	.389	.585
1998 Atlanta	NL	153	555	169	27	1	44	(16	28)	330	103	121	63	11	146	25	0	5	7	6	.54	8	.305	.397	.595
2000 Atlanta	NL	141	494	149	25	1	28	(14	14)	260	67	100	36	5	126	17	0	1	3	5	.38	15	.302	.369	.526
2001 Tex-SF		121	399	102	28	1	17	(8	9)	183	50	69	31	2	117	12	0	3	1	3	.25	12	.256	.326	.459
2001 Texas	AL	72	243	57	16	0	10	(5	5)	103	33	34	18	1	68	9	0	1	1	0	1.00	9	.235	.310	.424
San Francisco	NL	49	156	45	12	1	7	(3	4)	80	17	35	13	1	49	3	0	2	0	3	.00	3	.288	.351	.513
16 ML YEARS		2036	7522	2172	417	32	377	(189	188)	3784	1128	1341	534	99	1858	166	1	55	125	76	.62	161	.289	.347	.503

Gus Gandarillas

Pitches: Right **Bats:** Right **Pos:** RP-16

Ht: 6'1" **Wt:** 183 **Born:** 7/19/71 **Age:** 30

Year Team	Lg		HOW MUCH HE PITCHED						WHAT HE GAVE UP											THE RESULTS					
		G	GS	CG	GF	IP	BFP	H	R	ER	HR	SH	SF	HB	TBB	IBB	SO	WP	Bk	W	L	Pct.	ShO	Sv-Op	Hld	ERA
1992 Elizabethtn	R+	29	0	0	29	36	148	24	14	12	1	0	0	0	10	2	34	4	1	1	2	.333	0	13--	—	3.00
1993 Fort Wayne	A	52	0	0	48	66.1	295	66	37	24	8	5	5	1	22	2	59	4	0	5	5	.500	0	25--	—	3.26
1994 Fort Myers	A+	37	0	0	34	46.2	190	37	7	4	0	3	2	2	13	4	39	5	0	4	1	.800	0	20--	—	0.77
Nashville	AA	28	0	0	20	37	156	34	13	13	1	2	1	4	10	0	29	6	0	2	2	.500	0	8--	—	3.16
1995 Salt Lake	AAA	22	0	0	13	29.1	135	34	23	21	5	3	1	1	19	4	17	5	0	2	3	.400	0	2--	—	6.44
Hardware Cy	AA	25	0	0	18	32.1	152	38	26	22	1	7	0	3	16	0	25	3	0	2	4	.333	0	7--	—	6.12
1996 Twins	R	3	1	0	2	9	43	10	3	1	1	1	0	0	3	0	14	1	0	0	0	—	0	2--	—	1.00
Fort Myers	A+	4	0	0	3	6	35	9	7	6	0	0	1	0	8	0	3	1	0	0	0	—	0	1--	—	9.00
1997 New Britain	AA	17	7	1	2	61.1	253	67	34	32	6	0	2	3	15	0	29	5	0	2	4	.333	0	0--	—	4.70
Salt Lake	AAA	11	2	0	2	22.2	93	22	8	8	1	0	0	1	6	1	13	1	0	1	0	1.000	0	2--	—	3.18
1998 Salt Lake	AAA	53	1	0	24	70	322	88	47	41	4	1	2	0	24	5	42	9	0	4	5	.444	0	4--	—	5.27
1999 New Britain	AA	18	0	0	5	32.1	155	38	32	31	3	2	1	2	21	2	26	5	0	1	3	.250	0	2--	—	8.63
Salt Lake	AAA	42	0	0	8	61.1	279	73	37	31	8	0	0	2	20	4	47	7	1	2	2	.500	0	2--	—	4.55
2000 Salt Lake	AAA	63	1	0	26	89.2	399	105	50	43	9	4	7	2	33	4	75	6	0	9	4	.692	0	7--	—	4.32
2001 Pawtucket	AAA	12	0	0	7	14.2	70	19	9	7	0	1	1	0	10	1	7	3	0	2	1	.667	0	1--	—	4.30
Indianapolis	AAA	28	5	0	11	66.2	271	62	30	20	4	2	3	3	13	1	52	6	1	2	2	.500	0	1--	—	2.70
2001 Milwaukee	NL	16	0	0	6	19.2	91	25	13	12	2	3	0	0	10	3	7	1	0	0	0	—	0	0-0	0	5.49

Ron Gant

Bats: Right **Throws:** Right **Pos:** LF-62; PH/PR-25; DH-21   **Ht:** 6'0" **Wt:** 195 **Born:** 3/2/65 **Age:** 37

						BATTING													BASERUNNING				PERCENTAGES		
Year Team	Lg	G	AB	H	2B	3B	HR	(Hm	Rd)	TB	R	RBI	TBB	IBB	SO	HBP	SH	SF	SB	CS	SB%	GDP	Avg	OBP	SLG
1987 Atlanta	NL	21	83	22	4	0	2	(1	1)	32	9	9	1	0	11	0	1	1	4	2	.67	3	.265	.271	.386
1988 Atlanta	NL	146	563	146	28	8	19	(7	12)	247	85	60	46	4	118	3	2	4	19	10	.66	7	.259	.317	.439
1989 Atlanta	NL	75	260	46	8	3	9	(5	4)	87	26	25	20	0	63	1	2	2	9	6	.60	0	.177	.237	.335
1990 Atlanta	NL	152	575	174	34	3	32	(18	14)	310	107	84	50	0	86	1	1	4	33	16	.67	8	.303	.357	.539
1991 Atlanta	NL	154	561	141	35	3	32	(18	14)	278	101	105	71	8	104	5	0	5	34	15	.69	6	.251	.338	.496
1992 Atlanta	NL	153	544	141	22	6	17	(10	7)	226	74	80	45	5	101	7	0	6	32	10	.76	10	.259	.321	.415
1993 Atlanta	NL	157	606	166	27	4	36	(17	19)	309	113	117	67	2	117	2	0	7	26	9	.74	14	.274	.345	.510
1995 Cincinnati	NL	119	410	113	19	4	29	(12	17)	227	79	88	74	5	108	3	1	5	23	8	.74	11	.276	.386	.554
1996 St. Louis	NL	122	419	103	14	2	30	(17	13)	211	74	82	73	5	98	3	1	4	13	4	.76	9	.246	.359	.504
1997 St. Louis	NL	139	502	115	21	4	17	(11	6)	195	68	62	58	3	162	1	0	1	14	6	.70	2	.229	.310	.388
1998 St. Louis	NL	121	383	92	17	1	26	(14	12)	189	60	67	51	2	92	2	0	2	8	0	1.00	6	.240	.331	.493
1999 Philadelphia	NL	138	516	134	27	5	17	(6	11)	222	107	77	85	0	112	1	0	3	13	3	.81	6	.260	.364	.430
2000 Phi-Ana		123	425	106	19	3	26	(14	12)	209	69	54	56	1	91	1	1	4	6	6	.50	7	.249	.335	.492
2001 Col-Oak		93	252	65	13	3	10	(7	3)	114	46	35	35	2	80	0	2	3	5	1	.83	0	.258	.345	.452
2000 Philadelphia	NL	89	343	87	16	2	20	(9	11)	167	54	38	36	1	73	1	1	3	5	4	.56	7	.254	.324	.487
Anaheim	AL	34	82	19	3	1	6	(5	1)	42	15	16	20	0	18	0	0	1	1	2	.33	0	.232	.379	.512
2001 Colorado	NL	59	171	44	8	2	8	(6	2)	80	31	22	24	2	56	0	2	2	3	1	.75	0	.257	.345	.468
Oakland	AL	34	81	21	5	1	2	(1	1)	34	15	13	11	0	24	0	0	1	2	0	1.00	0	.259	.344	.420
14 ML YEARS		1713	6099	1564	288	49	302	(157	145)	2856	1018	945	732	37	1343	30	11	51	239	96	.71	89	.256	.337	.468

Rich Garces

Pitches: Right **Bats:** Right **Pos:** RP-62   **Ht:** 6'0" **Wt:** 245 **Born:** 5/18/71 **Age:** 31

		HOW MUCH HE PITCHED						WHAT HE GAVE UP											THE RESULTS						
Year Team	Lg	G	GS	CG	GF	IP	BFP	H	R	ER	HR	SH	SF	HB	TBB	IBB	SO	WP	Bk	W	L	Pct.	ShO	Sv-Op	Hld	ERA
2001 Lowell *	A-	2	2	0	0	2	7	1	0	0	0	0	0	0	0	1	1	0	0	0	0	—	0	0--	—	0.00
1990 Minnesota	AL	5	0	0	3	5.2	24	4	2	1	0	0	0	0	4	0	1	0	0	0	0	—	0	2-2	0	1.59
1993 Minnesota	AL	3	0	0	1	4	18	4	2	0	0	0	0	0	2	0	3	0	0	0	0	—	0	0-0	0	0.00
1995 ChC-Fla	NL	18	0	0	7	24.1	108	25	15	12	1	1	0	0	11	2	22	0	0	0	2	.000	0	0-1	1	4.44
1996 Boston	AL	37	0	0	9	44	205	42	26	24	5	0	5	0	33	5	55	0	0	3	2	.600	0	0-2	4	4.91
1997 Boston	AL	12	0	0	4	13.2	66	14	9	7	2	0	1	1	9	0	12	0	0	0	1	.000	0	0-2	1	4.61
1998 Boston	AL	30	0	0	11	46	201	36	19	17	6	2	1	2	27	3	34	1	1	1	1	.500	0	1-3	6	3.33
1999 Boston	AL	30	0	0	4	40.2	164	25	9	7	1	0	0	2	18	1	33	0	0	5	1	.833	0	2-3	2	1.55
2000 Boston	AL	64	0	0	9	74.2	309	64	28	27	7	1	4	1	23	5	69	3	0	8	1	.889	0	1-5	17	3.25
2001 Boston	AL	62	0	0	5	67	284	55	32	29	6	3	1	4	25	1	51	2	1	6	1	.857	0	1-2	17	3.90
1995 Chicago	NL	7	0	0	4	11	46	11	6	4	0	0	0	0	3	0	6	0	0	0	0	—	0	0-0	1	3.27
Florida	NL	11	0	0	3	13.1	62	14	9	8	1	1	0	0	8	2	16	0	0	0	2	.000	0	0-1	1	5.40
9 ML YEARS		261	0	0	53	320	1379	269	142	124	28	7	12	8	152	17	280	6	2	23	9	.719	0	7-20	48	3.49

Freddy Garcia

Pitches: Right **Bats:** Right **Pos:** SP-34   **Ht:** 6'4" **Wt:** 235 **Born:** 10/6/76 **Age:** 25

		HOW MUCH HE PITCHED						WHAT HE GAVE UP											THE RESULTS						
Year Team	Lg	G	GS	CG	GF	IP	BFP	H	R	ER	HR	SH	SF	HB	TBB	IBB	SO	WP	Bk	W	L	Pct.	ShO	Sv-Op	Hld	ERA
1999 Seattle	AL	33	33	2	0	201.1	888	205	96	91	18	3	6	10	90	4	170	12	3	17	8	.680	1	0-0	0	4.07
2000 Seattle	AL	21	20	0	0	124.1	538	112	62	54	16	6	1	2	64	4	79	4	2	9	5	.643	0	0-0	0	3.91
2001 Seattle	AL	34	34	4	0	**238.2**	971	199	88	81	16	8	5	5	69	6	163	3	1	18	6	.750	3	0-0	0	**3.05**
3 ML YEARS		88	87	6	0	564.1	2397	516	246	226	50	17	12	17	223	14	412	19	6	44	19	.698	4	0-0	0	3.60

Jesse Garcia

Bats: Right **Throws:** Right **Pos:** PH/PR-20; 2B-4; SS-2   **Ht:** 5'10" **Wt:** 171 **Born:** 9/24/73 **Age:** 28

						BATTING													BASERUNNING				PERCENTAGES		
Year Team	Lg	G	AB	H	2B	3B	HR	(Hm	Rd)	TB	R	RBI	TBB	IBB	SO	HBP	SH	SF	SB	CS	SB%	GDP	Avg	OBP	SLG
1993 Orioles	R	48	156	37	4	0	0	—	—	41	20	16	21	1	32	1	8	3	14	6	.70	1	.237	.326	.263
1995 Frederick	A+	124	365	82	11	3	3	—	—	108	52	27	49	0	75	9	7	2	5	10	.33	5	.225	.329	.296
1996 High Desert	A+	137	459	122	21	5	10	—	—	183	94	66	57	0	81	8	20	4	25	7	.78	7	.266	.354	.399
1997 Bowie	AA	141	437	103	18	1	5	—	—	138	52	42	38	0	71	6	24	2	7	7	.50	9	.236	.304	.316
1998 Bowie	AA	86	258	73	13	1	2	—	—	94	46	20	34	1	37	1	6	0	12	3	.80	3	.283	.369	.364
Rochester	AAA	44	160	47	6	4	0	—	—	61	20	18	7	0	22	3	2	3	7	5	.58	3	.294	.329	.381
1999 Rochester	AAA	62	220	56	10	2	2	—	—	76	25	23	11	0	21	0	11	1	9	6	.60	5	.255	.289	.345
2000 Rochester	AAA	106	372	90	12	2	1	—	—	109	44	23	27	0	60	4	16	1	9	4	.69	8	.242	.300	.293
2001 Richmond	AAA	105	375	100	22	3	2	—	—	134	50	22	22	1	54	4	21	1	18	6	.75	9	.267	.313	.357
1999 Baltimore	AL	17	29	6	0	0	2	(1	1)	12	6	2	2	0	3	0	3	0	0	0	—	1	.207	.258	.414
2000 Baltimore	AL	14	17	1	0	0	0	(0	0)	1	2	0	2	0	2	0	0	0	0	0	—	0	.059	.158	.059
2001 Atlanta	NL	22	5	1	0	0	0	(0	0)	1	3	0	0	0	1	0	1	0	6	2	.75	0	.200	.200	.200
3 ML YEARS		53	51	8	0	0	2	(1	1)	14	11	2	4	0	6	0	4	0	6	2	.75	1	.157	.218	.275

Karim Garcia

Bats: Left **Throws:** Left **Pos:** RF-13; LF-6; 1B-2   **Ht:** 6'0" **Wt:** 195 **Born:** 10/29/75 **Age:** 26

						BATTING													BASERUNNING				PERCENTAGES		
Year Team	Lg	G	AB	H	2B	3B	HR	(Hm	Rd)	TB	R	RBI	TBB	IBB	SO	HBP	SH	SF	SB	CS	SB%	GDP	Avg	OBP	SLG
2001 Buffalo *	AAA	125	462	122	16	4	31	—	—	239	85	85	44	6	106	1	1	6	4	4	.50	9	.264	.326	.517
1995 Los Angeles	NL	13	20	4	0	0	0	(0	0)	4	1	0	0	0	4	0	0	0	0	0	—	0	.200	.200	.200
1996 Los Angeles	NL	1	0	0	0	0	0	(0	0)	0	0	0	0	0	0	0	0	0	0	0	—	0	.000	.000	.000
1997 Los Angeles	NL	15	39	5	0	0	1	(0	1)	8	5	8	6	1	14	0	0	0	0	0	—	0	.128	.239	.205
1998 Arizona	NL	113	333	74	10	8	9	(4	5)	127	39	43	18	1	78	0	0	3	5	4	.56	6	.222	.260	.381
1999 Detroit	AL	96	288	69	10	3	14	(4	10)	127	38	32	20	1	67	0	0	3	2	4	.33	2	.240	.288	.441
2000 Det-Bal		16	33	3	0	0	0	(0	0)	3	1	0	0	0	10	0	0	0	0	0	—	1	.091	.091	.091
2001 Cleveland	AL	20	45	14	3	0	5	(1	4)	32	8	9	3	0	13	1	0	1	0	0	—	1	.311	.360	.711

						BATTING												BASERUNNING				PERCENTAGES		
Year Team	Lg	G	AB	H	2B	3B	HR	(Hm | Rd)	TB	R	RBI	TBB	IBB	SO	HBP	SH	SF	SB	CS	SB%	GDP	Avg	OBP	SLG
2000 Detroit	AL	8	17	3	0	0	0	(0 | 0)	3	1	0	0	0	4	0	0	0	0	0	—	1	.176	.176	.176
Baltimore	AL	8	16	0	0	0	0	(0 | 0)	0	0	0	0	0	6	0	0	0	0	0	—	0	.000	.000	.000
7 ML YEARS		274	759	169	23	11	29	(9 | 20)	301	92	92	47	3	187	1	0	6	7	8	.47	10	.223	.267	.397

Nomar Garciaparra

Bats: Right **Throws:** Right **Pos:** SS-21   **Ht:** 6'0" **Wt:** 180 **Born:** 7/23/73 **Age:** 28

						BATTING												BASERUNNING				PERCENTAGES		
Year Team	Lg	G	AB	H	2B	3B	HR	(Hm	Rd)	TB	R	RBI	TBB	IBB	SO	HBP	SH	SF	SB	CS	SB%	GDP	Avg	OBP	SLG
2001 Pawtucket *	AAA	4	16	7	2	0	1	—	—	12	3	4	1	0	2	1	0	0	0	0	—	0	.438	.500	.750
1996 Boston	AL	24	87	21	2	3	4	(3	1)	41	11	16	4	0	14	0	1	1	5	0	1.00	0	.241	.272	.471
1997 Boston	AL	153	684	209	44	11	30	(11	19)	365	122	98	35	2	92	6	2	7	22	9	.71	9	.306	.342	.534
1998 Boston	AL	143	604	195	37	8	35	(17	18)	353	111	122	33	1	62	8	0	7	12	6	.67	20	.323	.362	.584
1999 Boston	AL	135	532	190	42	4	27	(14	13)	321	103	104	51	7	39	8	0	4	14	3	.82	11	.357	.418	.603
2000 Boston	AL	140	529	197	51	3	21	(7	14)	317	104	96	61	20	50	2	0	7	5	2	.71	8	.372	.434	.599
2001 Boston	AL	21	83	24	3	0	4	(3	1)	39	13	8	7	0	9	1	0	0	0	1	.00	1	.289	.352	.470
6 ML YEARS		616	2519	836	179	29	121	(55	66)	1436	464	444	191	30	266	25	3	26	58	21	.73	49	.332	.381	.570

Mark Gardner

Pitches: Right **Bats:** Right **Pos:** SP-15; RP-8   **Ht:** 6'1" **Wt:** 220 **Born:** 3/1/62 **Age:** 40

		HOW MUCH HE PITCHED						WHAT HE GAVE UP											THE RESULTS						
Year Team	Lg	G	GS	CG	GF	IP	BFP	H	R	ER	HR	SH	SF	HB	TBB	IBB	SO	WP	Bk	W	L	Pct.	ShO	Sv-Op	Hld	ERA
2001 Fresno *	AAA	3	3	0	0	6	28	10	4	4	1	0	0	0	1	0	7	0	0	0	1	.000	0	0--	—	6.00
1989 Montreal	NL	7	4	0	1	26.1	117	26	16	15	2	0	0	2	11	1	21	0	0	0	3	.000	0	0-0	0	5.13
1990 Montreal	NL	27	26	3	1	152.2	642	129	62	58	13	4	7	9	61	5	135	2	4	7	9	.438	3	0-0	0	3.42
1991 Montreal	NL	27	27	0	0	168.1	692	139	78	72	17	7	2	4	75	1	107	2	1	9	11	.450	0	0-0	0	3.85
1992 Montreal	NL	33	30	0	1	179.2	778	179	91	87	15	12	7	9	60	2	132	2	0	12	10	.545	0	0-0	0	4.36
1993 Kansas City	AL	17	16	0	0	91.2	387	92	65	63	17	1	7	4	36	0	54	2	0	4	6	.400	0	0-0	0	6.19
1994 Florida	NL	20	14	0	3	92.1	391	97	53	50	14	4	5	1	30	2	57	3	1	4	4	.500	0	0-0	0	4.87
1995 Florida	NL	39	11	1	7	102.1	456	109	60	51	14	7	0	5	43	5	87	3	1	5	5	.500	1	1-1	4	4.49
1996 San Francisco	NL	30	28	4	0	179.1	782	200	105	88	28	6	5	8	57	3	145	2	0	12	7	.632	0	0-0	1	4.42
1997 San Francisco	NL	30	30	2	0	180.1	764	188	92	86	28	10	6	1	57	6	136	3	3	12	9	.571	1	0-0	0	4.29
1998 San Francisco	NL	33	33	4	0	212	886	203	106	102	29	6	7	6	65	5	151	5	1	13	6	.684	2	0-0	0	4.33
1999 San Francisco	NL	29	21	1	2	139	613	142	103	100	27	6	10	8	57	2	86	3	1	5	11	.313	0	0-1	1	6.47
2000 San Francisco	NL	30	20	0	3	149	634	155	72	67	16	6	6	5	42	2	92	2	1	11	7	.611	0	0-0	0	4.05
2001 San Francisco	NL	23	15	0	2	91.2	398	93	57	55	17	4	4	3	34	3	53	0	0	5	5	.500	0	0-0	0	5.40
13 ML YEARS		345	275	15	20	1764.2	7540	1752	960	894	237	73	66	65	628	37	1256	29	13	99	93	.516	8	1-2	6	4.56

Jon Garland

Pitches: Right **Bats:** Right **Pos:** RP-19; SP-16   **Ht:** 6'6" **Wt:** 205 **Born:** 9/27/79 **Age:** 22

		HOW MUCH HE PITCHED						WHAT HE GAVE UP											THE RESULTS						
Year Team	Lg	G	GS	CG	GF	IP	BFP	H	R	ER	HR	SH	SF	HB	TBB	IBB	SO	WP	Bk	W	L	Pct.	ShO	Sv-Op	Hld	ERA
1997 Cubs	R	10	7	0	0	40	161	37	14	12	3	0	0	1	10	0	39	3	3	3	2	.600	0	0--	—	2.70
1998 Rockford	A	19	19	1	0	107.1	467	124	69	60	11	1	1	8	45	0	70	5	1	4	7	.364	0	0--	—	5.03
Hickory	A	5	5	0	0	26.2	126	36	20	16	2	1	2	2	13	0	19	2	0	1	4	.200	0	0--	—	5.40
1999 Winston-Sal	A+	19	19	2	0	119	502	109	57	44	7	4	5	8	39	2	84	7	0	5	7	.417	1	0--	—	3.33
Birmingham	AA	7	7	0	0	39	175	39	22	19	4	2	1	3	18	0	27	4	0	3	1	.750	0	0--	—	4.38
2000 Charlotte	AAA	16	16	2	0	103.2	433	99	28	26	3	4	0	2	32	2	63	2	0	9	2	.818	1	0--	—	2.26
Birmingham	AA	1	1	0	0	6	22	4	0	0	0	1	0	0	1	0	10	0	0	0	0	—	0	0--	—	0.00
2001 Charlotte	AAA	5	5	1	0	33	134	31	10	10	1	2	1	1	11	1	26	0	0	0	3	.000	0	0--	—	2.73
2000 Chicago	AL	15	13	0	1	69.2	324	82	55	50	10	0	2	4	40	0	42	4	0	4	8	.333	0	0-0	1	6.46
2001 Chicago	AL	35	16	0	8	117	510	123	59	48	16	2	5	4	55	2	61	3	0	6	7	.462	0	1-1	2	3.69
2 ML YEARS		50	29	0	9	186.2	834	205	114	98	26	2	7	5	95	2	103	7	0	10	15	.400	0	1-1	3	4.73

Chris George

Pitches: Left **Bats:** Left **Pos:** SP-13   **Ht:** 6'1" **Wt:** 165 **Born:** 9/16/79 **Age:** 22

		HOW MUCH HE PITCHED						WHAT HE GAVE UP											THE RESULTS						
Year Team	Lg	G	GS	CG	GF	IP	BFP	H	R	ER	HR	SH	SF	HB	TBB	IBB	SO	WP	Bk	W	L	Pct.	ShO	Sv-Op	Hld	ERA
1998 Royals	R	5	4	0	0	15.2	65	14	9	5	1	1	0	0	4	0	10	0	0	0	1	.000	0	0--	—	2.87
1999 Wilmington	A+	27	27	0	0	145	618	142	65	58	8	3	4	5	53	0	142	5	1	9	7	.563	0	0--	—	3.60
2000 Wichita	AA	18	18	0	0	97.1	429	92	41	34	5	3	6	6	51	1	80	2	2	8	5	.615	0	0--	—	3.14
Omaha	AAA	8	8	0	0	44.2	194	47	29	24	8	0	1	1	20	0	27	1	1	3	2	.600	0	0--	—	4.84
2001 Omaha	AAA	20	20	0	0	117.1	489	103	54	46	14	2	1	1	51	0	84	0	1	11	3	.786	0	0--	—	3.53
2001 Kansas City	AL	13	13	1	0	74	313	83	48	46	14	3	4	0	18	0	32	3	2	4	8	.333	0	0-0	0	5.59

Jason Giambi

Bats: Left **Throws:** Right **Pos:** 1B-136; DH-17; PH/PR-1   **Ht:** 6'3" **Wt:** 235 **Born:** 1/8/71 **Age:** 31

						BATTING												BASERUNNING				PERCENTAGES		
Year Team	Lg	G	AB	H	2B	3B	HR	(Hm	Rd)	TB	R	RBI	TBB	IBB	SO	HBP	SH	SF	SB	CS	SB%	GDP	Avg	OBP	SLG
1995 Oakland	AL	54	176	45	7	0	6	(3	3)	70	27	25	28	0	31	3	1	2	2	1	.67	4	.256	.364	.398
1996 Oakland	AL	140	536	156	40	1	20	(6	14)	258	84	79	51	3	95	5	1	5	0	1	.00	15	.291	.355	.481
1997 Oakland	AL	142	519	152	41	2	20	(14	6)	257	66	81	55	3	89	6	0	8	0	1	.00	11	.293	.362	.495
1998 Oakland	AL	153	562	166	28	0	27	(12	15)	275	92	110	81	7	102	5	0	9	2	2	.50	16	.295	.384	.489
1999 Oakland	AL	158	575	181	36	1	33	(16	17)	318	115	123	105	6	106	7	0	8	1	1	.50	11	.315	.422	.553
2000 Oakland	AL	152	510	170	29	1	43	(23	20)	330	108	137	137	6	96	9	0	8	2	0	1.00	9	.333	.476	.647
2001 Oakland	AL	154	520	178	47	2	38	(27	11)	343	109	120	129	24	83	13	0	9	2	0	1.00	17	.342	.477	.660
7 ML YEARS		953	3398	1048	228	7	187	(102	85)	1851	601	675	586	49	602	48	2	49	9	6	.60	83	.308	.412	.545

Jeremy Giambi

Bats: L **Throws:** L **Pos:** DH-61; RF-37; PH/PR-20; LF-11; 1B-10   **Ht:** 6'0" **Wt:** 200 **Born:** 9/30/74 **Age:** 27

Year Team	Lg	G	AB	H	2B	3B	HR	(Hm	Rd)	TB	R	RBI	TBB	IBB	SO	HBP	SH	SF	SB	CS	SB%	GDP	Avg	OBP	SLG
2001 Sacramento *	AAA	9	27	9	1	0	0	—	—	10	1	1	1	0	6	0	0	0	0	0	—	1	.333	.357	.370
1998 Kansas City	AL	18	58	13	4	0	2	(0	2)	23	6	8	11	0	9	0	0	1	0	1	.00	3	.224	.343	.397
1999 Kansas City	AL	90	288	82	13	1	3	(2	1)	106	34	34	40	5	67	3	1	4	0	0	—	7	.285	.373	.368
2000 Oakland	AL	104	260	66	10	2	10	(3	7)	110	42	50	32	2	61	3	3	4	0	0	—	7	.254	.338	.423
2001 Oakland	AL	124	371	105	26	0	12	(5	7)	167	64	57	63	1	83	4	3	2	0	1	.00	13	.283	.391	.450
4 ML YEARS		336	977	266	53	3	27	(10	17)	406	146	149	146	8	220	10	7	11	0	2	.00	30	.272	.369	.416

Jay Gibbons

Bats: L **Throws:** L **Pos:** DH-28; LF-28; PH/PR-12; 1B-7   **Ht:** 6'0" **Wt:** 200 **Born:** 3/2/77 **Age:** 25

Year Team	Lg	G	AB	H	2B	3B	HR	(Hm	Rd)	TB	R	RBI	TBB	IBB	SO	HBP	SH	SF	SB	CS	SB%	GDP	Avg	OBP	SLG
1998 Medcine Hat	R+	73	290	115	29	1	19	—	—	203	66	98	37	1	25	3	0	9	2	1	.67	7	.397	.457	.700
1999 Hagerstown	A	71	292	89	20	2	16	—	—	161	53	69	32	1	56	1	0	5	3	0	1.00	12	.305	.370	.551
Dunedin	A+	60	212	66	14	0	9	—	—	107	34	39	25	0	38	0	0	1	2	1	.67	4	.311	.382	.505
2000 Tennessee	AA	132	474	152	38	1	19	—	—	249	85	75	61	5	67	10	0	7	3	1	.75	10	.321	.404	.525
2001 Baltimore	AL	73	225	53	10	0	15	(9	6)	108	27	36	17	0	39	4	0	0	0	1	.00	7	.236	.301	.480

Benji Gil

Bats: R **Throws:** R **Pos:** SS-44; PH/PR-24; 2B-21; 1B-18; DH-14; CF-1   **Ht:** 6'2" **Wt:** 210 **Born:** 10/6/72 **Age:** 29

Year Team	Lg	G	AB	H	2B	3B	HR	(Hm	Rd)	TB	R	RBI	TBB	IBB	SO	HBP	SH	SF	SB	CS	SB%	GDP	Avg	OBP	SLG
1993 Texas	AL	22	57	7	0	0	0	(0	0)	7	3	2	5	0	22	0	4	0	1	2	.33	0	.123	.194	.123
1995 Texas	AL	130	415	91	20	3	9	(5	4)	144	36	46	26	0	147	1	10	2	2	4	.33	5	.219	.266	.347
1996 Texas	AL	5	5	2	0	0	0	—	—	2	0	1	0	1	0	1	0	0	1	.00	0	.400	.500	.400
1997 Texas	AL	110	317	71	13	2	5	(3	2)	103	35	31	17	0	96	1	6	4	1	2	.33	3	.224	.263	.325
2000 Anaheim	AL	110	301	72	14	1	6	(4	2)	106	28	23	30	0	59	5	5	2	10	6	.63	7	.239	.317	.352
2001 Anaheim	AL	104	260	77	15	4	8	(6	2)	124	33	39	14	0	57	0	2	2	3	4	.43	6	.296	.330	.477
6 ML YEARS		481	1355	320	62	10	28	(18	10)	486	135	142	93	0	382	7	28	10	17	19	.47	21	.236	.287	.359

Geronimo Gil

Bats: Right **Throws:** Right **Pos:** C-17   **Ht:** 6'2" **Wt:** 195 **Born:** 8/7/75 **Age:** 26

Year Team	Lg	G	AB	H	2B	3B	HR	(Hm	Rd)	TB	R	RBI	TBB	IBB	SO	HBP	SH	SF	SB	CS	SB%	GDP	Avg	OBP	SLG
1996 Savannah	A	79	276	67	13	1	7	—	—	103	29	38	8	3	69	5	1	3	0	2	.00	6	.243	.274	.373
1997 Vero Beach	A+	66	213	53	13	1	6	—	—	86	30	24	15	0	41	4	1	0	3	0	1.00	5	.249	.310	.404
1998 San Antonio	AA	75	241	70	17	3	6	—	—	111	27	29	15	0	43	0	2	2	2	1	.67	8	.290	.329	.461
1999 San Antonio	AA	106	343	97	26	1	15	—	—	170	47	59	49	1	58	2	0	4	2	0	1.00	15	.283	.372	.496
2000 San Antonio	AA	100	352	100	19	1	11	—	—	154	42	58	33	3	65	6	1	5	3	2	.60	8	.284	.351	.438
Albuquerque	AAA	15	50	19	5	0	2	—	—	30	9	22	5	0	8	0	0	2	0	1	.00	1	.380	.421	.600
2001 Las Vegas	AAA	82	281	83	15	0	9	—	—	125	40	40	16	1	56	2	0	3	0	1	.00	9	.295	.334	.445
Rochester	AAA	23	82	22	6	1	2	—	—	36	7	14	0	0	23	1	0	2	0	0	—	1	.268	.271	.439
2001 Baltimore	AL	17	58	17	2	0	0	(0	0)	19	3	6	5	0	7	2	1	0	0	0	—	1	.293	.369	.328

Brian Giles

Bats: Left **Throws:** Left **Pos:** LF-124; CF-61   **Ht:** 5'10" **Wt:** 200 **Born:** 1/20/71 **Age:** 31

Year Team	Lg	G	AB	H	2B	3B	HR	(Hm	Rd)	TB	R	RBI	TBB	IBB	SO	HBP	SH	SF	SB	CS	SB%	GDP	Avg	OBP	SLG
1995 Cleveland	AL	6	9	5	0	0	1	(0	1)	8	6	3	0	0	1	0	0	0	0	0	—	0	.556	.556	.889
1996 Cleveland	AL	51	121	43	14	1	5	(2	3)	74	26	27	19	4	13	0	0	3	0	1	1.00	6	.355	.434	.612
1997 Cleveland	AL	130	377	101	15	3	17	(7	10)	173	62	61	63	2	50	1	3	7	13	3	.81	10	.268	.368	.459
1998 Cleveland	AL	112	350	94	19	0	16	(10	6)	161	56	66	73	8	75	3	1	3	10	5	.67	7	.269	.396	.460
1999 Pittsburgh	NL	141	521	164	33	3	39	(24	15)	320	109	115	95	7	80	3	0	8	6	2	.75	14	.315	.418	.614
2000 Pittsburgh	NL	156	559	176	37	7	35	(16	19)	332	111	123	114	13	69	7	0	8	6	0	1.00	15	.315	.432	.594
2001 Pittsburgh	NL	160	576	178	37	7	37	(18	19)	340	116	95	90	14	67	4	0	4	13	6	.68	10	.309	.404	.590
7 ML YEARS		756	2513	761	155	21	150	(77	73)	1408	486	490	454	48	355	18	4	33	51	16	.76	62	.303	.409	.560

Marcus Giles

Bats: Right **Throws:** Right **Pos:** 2B-62; PH/PR-9   **Ht:** 5'8" **Wt:** 180 **Born:** 5/18/78 **Age:** 24

Year Team	Lg	G	AB	H	2B	3B	HR	(Hm	Rd)	TB	R	RBI	TBB	IBB	SO	HBP	SH	SF	SB	CS	SB%	GDP	Avg	OBP	SLG
1997 Danville	R+	55	207	72	13	3	8	—	—	115	53	45	32	0	47	3	1	3	5	2	.71	4	.348	.437	.556
1998 Macon	A	135	466	136	38	3	29	—	—	321	111	108	85	4	103	10	0	3	12	5	.71	15	.329	.433	.636
1999 Myrtle Bch	A+	126	497	162	40	7	13	—	—	255	80	73	54	5	89	4	0	5	9	6	.60	9	.326	.393	.513
2000 Greenville	AA	132	458	133	28	2	17	—	—	216	73	62	72	6	71	2	0	1	25	5	.83	11	.290	.388	.472
2001 Richmond	AAA	67	252	84	19	1	6	—	—	123	48	44	22	1	48	2	0	3	13	5	.72	4	.333	.387	.488
2001 Atlanta	NL	68	244	64	10	2	9	(5	4)	105	36	31	28	0	37	0	1	0	2	5	.29	8	.262	.338	.430

Bernard Gilkey

Bats: R **Throws:** R **Pos:** PH/PR-38; LF-28; RF-8; DH-1   **Ht:** 6'0" **Wt:** 200 **Born:** 9/24/66 **Age:** 35

Year Team	Lg	G	AB	H	2B	3B	HR	(Hm	Rd)	TB	R	RBI	TBB	IBB	SO	HBP	SH	SF	SB	CS	SB%	GDP	Avg	OBP	SLG
2001 Richmond *	AAA	13	48	13	3	0	0	—	—	16	5	2	4	0	8	0	0	2	0	1	.00	3	.271	.315	.333
1990 St. Louis	NL	18	64	19	5	2	1	(0	1)	31	11	3	8	0	5	0	0	0	6	1	.86	1	.297	.375	.484
1991 St. Louis	NL	81	268	58	7	2	5	(2	3)	84	28	20	39	0	33	1	1	2	14	8	.64	14	.216	.316	.313
1992 St. Louis	NL	131	384	116	19	4	7	(3	4)	164	56	43	39	1	52	1	3	4	18	12	.60	5	.302	.364	.427
1993 St. Louis	NL	137	557	170	40	5	16	(7	9)	268	99	70	56	2	66	4	0	5	15	10	.60	16	.305	.370	.481
1994 St. Louis	NL	105	380	96	22	1	6	(0	6)	138	52	45	39	2	65	10	0	3	15	8	.65	6	.253	.336	.363
1995 St. Louis	NL	121	480	143	33	4	17	(5	12)	235	73	69	42	3	70	5	1	3	12	6	.67	17	.298	.358	.490
1996 New York	NL	153	571	181	44	3	30	(14	16)	321	108	117	73	7	125	4	0	8	17	9	.65	18	.317	.393	.562
1997 New York	NL	145	518	129	31	1	18	(7	11)	216	85	78	70	1	111	6	0	12	7	11	.39	9	.249	.338	.417
1998 NYM-Ari	NL	111	365	85	15	0	5	(2	3)	115	41	33	43	1	80	5	3	3	9	3	.75	11	.233	.320	.315
1999 Arizona	NL	94	204	60	16	1	8	(4	4)	102	28	39	29	2	42	2	1	5	2	2	.50	7	.294	.379	.500
2000 Ari-Bos	NL	74	164	29	6	1	3	(1	2)	46	17	15	17	2	28	3	0	1	0	0	—	8	.177	.265	.280
2001 Atlanta	NL	69	106	29	6	0	2	(1	1)	41	8	14	11	0	31	1	0	3	0	1	.00	4	.274	.339	.387
1998 New York	NL	82	264	60	15	0	4	(1	3)	87	33	28	32	1	66	4	2	3	5	1	.83	6	.227	.317	.330
Arizona	NL	29	101	25	0	0	1	(1	0)	28	8	5	11	0	14	1	1	0	4	2	.67	5	.248	.327	.277
2000 Arizona	NL	38	73	8	1	0	2	(1	1)	15	6	6	7	2	16	0	0	1	0	0	—	3	.110	.185	.205
Boston	AL	36	91	21	5	1	1	(0	1)	31	11	9	10	0	12	3	0	0	0	0	—	5	.231	.327	.341
12 ML YEARS		1239	4061	1115	244	24	118	(46	72)	1761	606	546	466	21	708	42	9	48	115	71	.62	116	.275	.352	.434

Keith Ginter

Bats: Right **Throws:** Right **Pos:** PH/PR-1   **Ht:** 5'10" **Wt:** 190 **Born:** 5/5/76 **Age:** 26

Year Team	Lg	G	AB	H	2B	3B	HR	(Hm	Rd)	TB	R	RBI	TBB	IBB	SO	HBP	SH	SF	SB	CS	SB%	GDP	Avg	OBP	SLG
1998 Auburn	A-	71	241	76	22	1	8	—	—	124	55	41	60	0	68	7	0	2	10	7	.59	1	.315	.461	.515
1999 Jackson	AA	9	34	13	1	0	1	—	—	17	9	6	4	0	6	2	0	1	0	0	—	0	.382	.463	.500
Kissimmee	A+	103	376	99	15	4	13	—	—	161	66	46	61	1	90	12	2	2	9	10	.47	7	.263	.381	.428
2000 Round Rock	AA	125	462	154	30	3	26	—	—	268	108	92	82	3	127	24	0	1	24	11	.69	9	.333	.457	.580
2001 New Orleans	AAA	132	457	123	31	5	16	—	—	212	76	70	61	1	147	23	2	4	8	6	.57	6	.269	.380	.464
2000 Houston	NL	5	8	2	0	0	1	(1	0)	5	3	3	1	0	3	0	0	0	0	0	—	0	.250	.300	.625
2001 Houston	NL	1	1	0	0	0	0	(0	0)	0	0	0	0	0	0	0	0	0	0	0	—	0	.000	.000	.000
2 ML YEARS		6	9	2	0	0	1	(1	0)	5	3	3	1	0	3	0	0	1	0	0	—	0	.222	.273	.556

Matt Ginter

Pitches: Right **Bats:** Right **Pos:** RP-20   **Ht:** 6'1" **Wt:** 220 **Born:** 12/24/77 **Age:** 24

		HOW MUCH HE PITCHED							WHAT HE GAVE UP											THE RESULTS					
Year Team	Lg	G	GS	CG	GF	IP	BFP	H	R	ER	HR	SH	SF	HB	TBB	IBB	SO	WP	Bk	W	L	Pct.	ShO	Sv-Op	Hld	ERA
1999 White Sox	R	3	0	0	1	8.1	33	5	4	3	0	0	1	0	3	0	10	0	0	1	0	1.000	0	1- -	—	3.24
Burlington	A	9	9	0	0	40	173	38	20	18	3	1	0	3	19	0	29	1	0	4	2	.667	0	0- -	—	4.05
2000 Birmingham	AA	27	26	0	0	179.2	741	153	72	45	6	5	5	13	60	2	126	12	0	11	8	.579	0	0- -	—	2.25
2001 Charlotte	AAA	22	10	0	2	76.1	319	62	26	22	3	2	3	7	24	4	67	5	0	2	3	.400	0	0- -	—	2.59
2000 Chicago	AL	7	0	0	3	9.1	52	18	14	14	5	0	1	0	7	0	6	1	0	1	0	1.000	0	0-1	0	13.50
2001 Chicago	AL	20	0	0	7	39.2	167	34	23	23	2	0	3	7	14	2	24	2	0	1	0	1.000	0	0-0	0	5.22
2 ML YEARS		27	0	0	10	49	219	52	37	37	7	0	4	7	21	2	30	3	0	2	0	1.000	0	0-1	0	6.80

Charles Gipson

Bats: R **Throws:** R **Pos:** LF-41; PH/PR-34; CF-14; DH-11; RF-11; 3B-9; SS-6; 2B-1   **Ht:** 6'2" **Wt:** 180 **Born:** 12/16/72 **Age:** 29

Year Team	Lg	G	AB	H	2B	3B	HR	(Hm	Rd)	TB	R	RBI	TBB	IBB	SO	HBP	SH	SF	SB	CS	SB%	GDP	Avg	OBP	SLG
1998 Seattle	AL	44	51	12	1	0	0	(0	0)	13	11	2	5	1	9	1	0	0	2	1	.67	1	.235	.316	.255
1999 Seattle	AL	55	80	18	5	2	0	(0	0)	27	16	9	6	0	13	1	2	0	3	4	.43	2	.225	.287	.338
2000 Seattle	AL	59	29	9	1	1	0	(0	0)	12	7	3	4	0	9	0	0	0	2	3	.40	0	.310	.394	.414
2001 Seattle	AL	94	64	14	2	2	0	(0	0)	20	16	5	4	0	20	2	1	1	1	1	.50	2	.219	.282	.313
4 ML YEARS		252	224	53	9	5	0	(0	0)	72	50	19	19	1	51	4	3	1	8	9	.47	5	.237	.306	.321

Joe Girardi

Bats: Right **Throws:** Right **Pos:** C-71; PH/PR-10   **Ht:** 5'11" **Wt:** 200 **Born:** 10/14/64 **Age:** 37

Year Team	Lg	G	AB	H	2B	3B	HR	(Hm	Rd)	TB	R	RBI	TBB	IBB	SO	HBP	SH	SF	SB	CS	SB%	GDP	Avg	OBP	SLG
1989 Chicago	NL	59	157	39	10	0	1	(0	1)	52	15	14	11	5	26	2	1	1	2	1	.67	4	.248	.304	.331
1990 Chicago	NL	133	419	113	24	2	1	(1	0)	144	36	38	17	11	50	3	4	4	8	3	.73	13	.270	.300	.344
1991 Chicago	NL	21	47	9	2	0	0	(0	0)	11	3	6	6	1	6	0	1	0	0	0	—	0	.191	.283	.234
1992 Chicago	NL	91	270	73	3	1	1	(1	0)	81	19	12	19	3	38	1	0	1	0	2	.00	8	.270	.320	.300
1993 Colorado	NL	86	310	90	14	5	3	(2	1)	123	35	31	24	0	41	3	12	1	6	6	.50	6	.290	.346	.397
1994 Colorado	NL	93	330	91	9	4	4	(1	3)	120	47	34	21	1	48	2	6	2	3	3	.50	13	.276	.321	.364
1995 Colorado	NL	125	462	121	17	2	8	(6	2)	166	63	55	29	0	76	2	12	1	3	3	.50	15	.262	.308	.359
1996 New York	AL	124	422	124	22	3	2	(1	1)	158	55	45	30	1	55	5	11	3	13	4	.76	11	.294	.346	.374
1997 New York	AL	112	398	105	23	1	1	(0	1)	133	38	50	26	1	53	2	5	3	2	3	.40	15	.264	.311	.334
1998 New York	AL	78	254	70	11	4	3	(1	2)	98	31	31	14	1	38	2	8	1	2	4	.33	10	.276	.317	.386
1999 New York	AL	65	209	50	16	1	2	(1	1)	74	23	27	10	0	26	5	3	2	3	1	.75	16	.239	.271	.354
2000 Chicago	NL	106	363	101	16	1	6	(4	2)	136	47	40	32	3	61	3	6	3	1	0	1.00	12	.278	.339	.375
2001 Chicago	NL	78	229	58	10	1	3	(1	2)	79	22	25	21	4	50	0	2	1	0	1	.00	2	.253	.315	.345
13 ML YEARS		1171	3870	1044	176	25	35	(20	15)	1375	434	408	260	31	568	25	76	22	43	31	.58	125	.270	.318	.355

Doug Glanville

Bats: Right **Throws:** Right **Pos:** CF-150; PH/PR-4   **Ht:** 6'2" **Wt:** 172 **Born:** 8/25/70 **Age:** 31

								BATTING											BASERUNNING				PERCENTAGES		
Year Team	Lg	G	AB	H	2B	3B	HR	(Hm Rd)	TB	R	RBI	TBB	IBB	SO	HBP	SH	SF	SB	CS	SB%	GDP	Avg	OBP	SLG
1996 Chicago	NL	49	83	20	5	1	1	(1 0)	30	10	10	3	0	11	0	2	1	2	0	1.00	0	.241	.264	.361
1997 Chicago	NL	146	474	142	22	5	4	(2 2)	186	79	35	24	0	46	1	9	2	19	11	.63	9	.300	.333	.392
1998 Philadelphia	NL	158	**678**	189	28	7	8	(3 5)	255	106	49	42	1	89	6	5	4	23	6	.79	7	.279	.325	.376
1999 Philadelphia	NL	150	628	204	38	6	11	(5 6)	287	101	73	48	1	82	6	5	5	34	2	**.94**	9	.325	.376	.457
2000 Philadelphia	NL	154	637	175	27	6	8	(3 5)	238	89	52	31	1	76	2	12	7	31	8	.79	11	.275	.307	.374
2001 Philadelphia	NL	153	634	166	24	3	14	(6 8)	238	74	55	19	1	91	4	10	7	28	6	.82	7	.262	.285	.375
6 ML YEARS		810	3134	896	144	28	46	(20 26)	1234	459	274	167	4	395	19	43	26	137	33	.81	43	.286	.323	.394

Troy Glaus

Bats: R **Throws:** R **Pos:** 3B-159; DH-2; SS-2; PH/PR-1   **Ht:** 6'5" **Wt:** 245 **Born:** 8/3/76 **Age:** 25

								BATTING											BASERUNNING				PERCENTAGES		
Year Team	Lg	G	AB	H	2B	3B	HR	(Hm Rd)	TB	R	RBI	TBB	IBB	SO	HBP	SH	SF	SB	CS	SB%	GDP	Avg	OBP	SLG
1998 Anaheim	AL	48	165	36	9	0	1	(0 1)	48	19	23	15	0	51	0	0	2	1	0	1.00	3	.218	.280	.291
1999 Anaheim	AL	154	551	132	29	0	29	(12 17)	248	85	79	71	1	143	6	0	3	5	1	.83	9	.240	.331	.450
2000 Anaheim	AL	159	563	160	37	1	47	(24 23)	340	120	102	112	6	163	2	0	1	14	11	.56	14	.284	.404	.604
2001 Anaheim	AL	161	588	147	38	2	41	(22 19)	312	100	108	107	7	158	6	0	0	10	3	.77	16	.250	.367	.531
4 ML YEARS		522	1867	475	113	3	118	(58 60)	948	324	312	305	14	515	14	0	13	30	15	.67	42	.254	.361	.508

Tom Glavine

Pitches: Left **Bats:** Left **Pos:** SP-35   **Ht:** 6'0" **Wt:** 185 **Born:** 3/25/66 **Age:** 36

		HOW MUCH HE PITCHED						WHAT HE GAVE UP												THE RESULTS					
Year Team	Lg	G	GS	CG	GF	IP	BFP	H	R	ER	HR	SH	SF	HB	TBB	IBB	SO	WP	Bk	W	L	Pct.	ShO	Sv-Op	Hld	ERA
1987 Atlanta	NL	9	9	0	0	50.1	238	55	34	31	5	2	3	3	33	4	20	1	1	2	4	.333	0	0-0	0	5.54
1988 Atlanta	NL	34	34	1	0	195.1	844	201	111	99	12	17	11	8	63	7	84	2	1	7	17	.292	0	0-0	0	4.56
1989 Atlanta	NL	29	29	6	0	186	766	172	88	76	20	11	4	2	40	3	90	2	0	14	8	.636	4	0-0	0	3.68
1990 Atlanta	NL	33	33	1	0	214.1	929	232	111	102	18	**21**	2	1	78	10	129	8	1	10	12	.455	0	0-0	0	4.28
1991 Atlanta	NL	34	34	**9**	0	246.2	989	201	83	70	17	7	6	2	69	6	192	10	2	**20**	11	.645	1	0-0	0	2.55
1992 Atlanta	NL	33	33	7	0	225	919	197	81	69	6	2	6	2	70	7	129	5	0	**20**	8	.714	**5**	0-0	0	2.76
1993 Atlanta	NL	36	**36**	4	0	239.1	1014	236	91	85	16	10	2	2	90	7	120	4	0	**22**	6	.786	2	0-0	0	3.20
1994 Atlanta	NL	25	25	2	0	165.1	731	173	76	73	10	9	6	1	70	10	140	8	1	13	9	.591	0	0-0	0	3.97
1995 Atlanta	NL	29	29	3	0	198.2	822	182	76	68	9	7	5	5	66	0	127	3	0	16	7	.696	1	0-0	0	3.08
1996 Atlanta	NL	36	**36**	1	0	235.1	994	222	91	78	14	15	2	0	85	7	181	4	0	15	10	.600	0	0-0	0	2.98
1997 Atlanta	NL	33	33	5	0	240	972	197	86	79	20	11	6	4	79	9	152	3	0	14	7	.667	2	0-0	0	2.96
1998 Atlanta	NL	33	33	4	0	229.1	934	202	67	63	13	6	2	2	74	2	157	3	0	**20**	6	.769	3	0-0	0	2.47
1999 Atlanta	NL	35	**35**	2	0	234	1023	**259**	115	107	18	**22**	10	4	83	14	138	2	0	14	11	.560	0	0-0	0	4.12
2000 Atlanta	NL	35	**35**	4	0	241	992	222	101	91	24	9	5	4	65	6	152	0	0	**21**	9	.700	2	0-0	0	3.40
2001 Atlanta	NL	35	**35**	1	0	219.1	929	213	92	87	24	5	8	2	97	10	116	2	0	16	7	.696	1	0-0	0	3.57
15 ML YEARS		469	469	50	0	3120	13094	2964	1303	1178	226	154	78	42	1062	102	1927	57	7	224	132	.629	21	0-0	0	3.40

Gary Glover

Pitches: Right **Bats:** Right **Pos:** RP-35; SP-11   **Ht:** 6'5" **Wt:** 205 **Born:** 12/3/76 **Age:** 25

		HOW MUCH HE PITCHED						WHAT HE GAVE UP												THE RESULTS					
Year Team	Lg	G	GS	CG	GF	IP	BFP	H	R	ER	HR	SH	SF	HB	TBB	IBB	SO	WP	Bk	W	L	Pct.	ShO	Sv-Op	Hld	ERA
1994 Blue Jays	R	2	0	0	0	1.1	13	4	8	7	1	0	0	1	4	0	2	1	1	0	0	—	0	0--	—	47.25
1995 Blue Jays	R	12	10	2	0	62.1	279	62	48	34	4	4	3	11	26	0	46	8	0	3	7	.300	0	0--	—	4.91
1996 Medcine Hat	R+	15	15	2	0	83.2	410	119	94	72	14	2	4	6	29	1	54	8	1	3	12	.200	0	0--	—	7.75
1997 Hagerstown	A	28	28	3	0	173.2	751	165	94	72	9	3	5	10	58	1	155	20	4	6	17	.261	0	0--	—	3.73
1998 Knoxville	AA	8	8	0	0	37.1	183	41	36	28	2	1	3	3	28	0	14	2	0	0	5	.000	0	0--	—	6.75
Dunedin	A+	19	18	0	0	109.1	484	117	66	52	8	1	6	7	36	0	88	11	1	7	6	.538	0	0--	—	4.28
1999 Knoxville	AA	13	13	1	0	86	346	70	39	34	5	2	1	4	27	0	77	4	0	8	2	.800	0	0--	—	3.56
Syracuse	AAA	14	14	0	0	76.1	347	93	50	44	10	0	3	0	35	0	57	3	1	4	6	.400	0	0--	—	5.19
2000 Syracuse	AAA	27	27	1	0	166.2	731	181	104	93	21	2	4	2	62	0	119	5	0	9	9	.500	0	0--	—	5.02
2001 Charlotte	AAA	6	6	1	0	38.1	139	21	8	8	3	0	0	1	5	0	29	0	0	2	1	.667	1	0--	—	1.88
1999 Toronto	AL	1	0	0	1	1	3	0	0	0	0	0	0	0	1	0	0	0	0	0	0	—	0	0-0	0	0.00
2001 Chicago	AL	46	11	0	10	100.1	429	98	61	55	16	2	2	4	32	3	63	4	0	5	5	.500	0	0-1	7	4.93
2 ML YEARS		47	11	0	11	101.1	432	98	61	55	16	2	2	4	33	3	63	4	0	5	5	.500	0	0-1	7	4.88

Ryan Glynn

Pitches: Right **Bats:** Right **Pos:** SP-9; RP-3   **Ht:** 6'3" **Wt:** 200 **Born:** 11/1/74 **Age:** 27

		HOW MUCH HE PITCHED						WHAT HE GAVE UP												THE RESULTS					
Year Team	Lg	G	GS	CG	GF	IP	BFP	H	R	ER	HR	SH	SF	HB	TBB	IBB	SO	WP	Bk	W	L	Pct.	ShO	Sv-Op	Hld	ERA
2001 Oklahoma *	AAA	13	13	1	0	79	357	87	62	57	10	1	2	5	41	0	52	2	0	2	6	.250	0	0--	—	6.49
1999 Texas	AL	13	10	0	0	54.2	262	71	46	44	10	0	1	1	35	0	39	3	1	2	4	.333	0	0-0	0	7.24
2000 Texas	AL	16	16	0	0	88.2	412	107	65	55	15	3	0	3	41	2	33	3	0	5	7	.417	0	0-0	0	5.58
2001 Texas	AL	12	9	0	0	46	219	59	38	36	7	0	2	0	26	1	15	5	0	1	5	.167	0	0-0	0	7.04
3 ML YEARS		41	35	0	0	189.1	893	237	149	135	32	3	3	4	102	3	87	11	1	8	16	.333	0	0-0	0	6.42

Wayne Gomes

Pitches: Right **Bats:** Right **Pos:** RP-55   **Ht:** 6'2" **Wt:** 227 **Born:** 1/15/73 **Age:** 29

		HOW MUCH HE PITCHED						WHAT HE GAVE UP												THE RESULTS					
Year Team	Lg	G	GS	CG	GF	IP	BFP	H	R	ER	HR	SH	SF	HB	TBB	IBB	SO	WP	Bk	W	L	Pct.	ShO	Sv-Op	Hld	ERA
2001 Lakewood *	A	2	2	0	0	2	13	2	1	1	0	0	0	0	3	0	3	0	0	0	0	—	0	0--	—	3.00
1997 Philadelphia	NL	37	0	0	13	42.2	191	45	26	25	4	2	0	1	24	0	24	2	0	5	1	.833	0	0-1	3	5.27
1998 Philadelphia	NL	71	0	0	16	93.1	408	94	48	44	9	5	1	3	35	4	86	6	0	9	6	.600	0	1-8	13	4.24
1999 Philadelphia	NL	73	0	0	58	74	341	70	38	35	5	3	2		56	2	58	3	1	5	5	.500	0	19-24	9	4.26

			HOW MUCH HE PITCHED						WHAT HE GAVE UP									THE RESULTS					
Year Team	Lg	G	GS	CG	GF	IP	BFP	H	R	ER	HR	SH	SF	HB	TBB	IBB	SO	WP	Bk	W	L	Pct.	ShO	Sv-Op	Hld	ERA
2000 Philadelphia	NL	65	0	0	26	73.2	324	72	41	36	6	7	4	3	35	3	49	10	0	4	6	.400	0	7-11	4	4.40
2001 Phi-SF	NL	55	0	0	16	63	285	72	37	37	7	6	4	1	29	6	52	4	0	6	3	.667	0	1-5	10	5.29
2001 Philadelphia	NL	42	0	0	12	48	215	51	23	23	4	4	3	1	22	4	35	2	0	4	3	.571	0	1-5	9	4.31
San Francisco	NL	13	0	0	4	15	70	21	14	14	3	2	1	0	7	2	17	2	0	2	0	1.000	0	0-0	1	8.40
5 ML YEARS		301	0	0	129	346.2	1549	353	190	177	31	25	12	10	179	15	269	25	1	29	21	.580	0	28-49	39	4.60

Chris Gomez

Bats: Right **Throws:** Right **Pos:** SS-94; 2B-8; PH/PR-2   **Ht:** 6'1" **Wt:** 195 **Born:** 6/16/71 **Age:** 31

				BATTING														BASERUNNING				PERCENTAGES		
Year Team	Lg	G	AB	H	2B	3B	HR	(Hm	Rd)	TB	R	RBI	TBB	IBB	SO	HBP	SH	SF	SB	CS	SB%	GDP	Avg	OBP	SLG
2001 Portland *	AAA	11	40	12	3	0	1	—	—	18	5	5	2	0	4	0	0	0	1	0	1.00	1	.300	.333	.450
Durham *	AAA	23	93	28	5	1	4	—	—	47	16	17	11	0	5	0	0	0	1	1	.50	5	.301	.375	.505
1993 Detroit	AL	46	128	32	7	1	0	(0	0)	41	11	11	9	0	17	1	3	0	2	2	.50	2	.250	.304	.320
1994 Detroit	AL	84	296	76	19	0	8	(5	3)	119	32	53	33	0	64	3	4	1	5	3	.63	6	.257	.336	.402
1995 Detroit	AL	123	431	96	20	2	11	(5	6)	153	49	50	41	0	96	3	3	4	4	1	.80	13	.223	.292	.355
1996 Det-SD		137	456	117	21	1	4	(2	2)	152	53	45	57	1	84	7	6	2	3	3	.50	16	.257	.347	.333
1997 San Diego	NL	150	522	132	19	2	5	(2	3)	170	62	54	53	1	114	5	3	3	5	8	.38	16	.253	.326	.326
1998 San Diego	NL	145	449	120	32	3	4	(3	1)	170	55	39	51	7	87	5	7	3	1	3	.25	11	.267	.346	.379
1999 San Diego	NL	76	234	59	8	1	1	(1	0)	72	20	15	27	3	49	1	2	1	1	2	.33	6	.252	.331	.308
2000 San Diego	NL	33	54	12	0	0	0	(0	0)	12	4	3	7	0	5	0	1	0	0	0	—	1	.222	.306	.222
2001 SD-TB		98	301	78	19	0	8	(5	3)	121	37	43	17	0	38	2	6	5	4	0	1.00	9	.259	.298	.402
1996 Detroit	AL	48	128	31	5	0	1	(1	0)	39	21	16	18	0	20	1	3	0	1	1	.50	5	.242	.340	.305
San Diego	NL	89	328	86	16	1	3	(1	2)	113	32	29	39	1	64	6	3	2	2	2	.50	11	.262	.349	.345
2001 San Diego	NL	40	112	21	3	0	0	(0	0)	24	6	7	9	0	14	0	2	2	1	0	1.00	5	.188	.244	.214
Tampa Bay	AL	58	189	57	16	0	8	(5	3)	97	31	36	8	0	24	2	4	3	3	0	1.00	4	.302	.332	.513
9 ML YEARS		892	2871	722	145	10	41	(23	18)	1010	323	313	295	12	554	27	34	20	25	22	.53	82	.251	.325	.352

Alex Gonzalez

Bats: Right **Throws:** Right **Pos:** SS-142; PH/PR-3; C-1   **Ht:** 6'0" **Wt:** 170 **Born:** 2/15/77 **Age:** 25

				BATTING														BASERUNNING				PERCENTAGES		
Year Team	Lg	G	AB	H	2B	3B	HR	(Hm	Rd)	TB	R	RBI	TBB	IBB	SO	HBP	SH	SF	SB	CS	SB%	GDP	Avg	OBP	SLG
1998 Florida	NL	25	86	13	2	0	3	(1	2)	24	11	7	9	0	30	1	2	0	0	0	—	2	.151	.240	.279
1999 Florida	NL	136	560	155	28	8	14	(7	7)	241	81	59	15	0	113	12	1	3	3	5	.38	13	.277	.308	.430
2000 Florida	NL	109	385	77	17	4	7	(5	2)	123	35	42	13	0	77	2	5	2	7	1	.88	7	.200	.229	.319
2001 Florida	NL	145	515	129	36	1	9	(5	4)	194	57	48	30	6	107	10	3	3	2	2	.50	13	.250	.303	.377
4 ML YEARS		415	1546	374	83	13	33	(18	15)	582	184	156	67	6	327	25	11	8	12	8	.60	35	.242	.283	.376

Alex Gonzalez

Bats: Right **Throws:** Right **Pos:** SS-154   **Ht:** 6'0" **Wt:** 200 **Born:** 4/8/73 **Age:** 29

				BATTING														BASERUNNING				PERCENTAGES		
Year Team	Lg	G	AB	H	2B	3B	HR	(Hm	Rd)	TB	R	RBI	TBB	IBB	SO	HBP	SH	SF	SB	CS	SB%	GDP	Avg	OBP	SLG
1994 Toronto	AL	15	53	8	3	1	0	(0	0)	13	7	1	4	0	17	1	1	0	3	0	1.00	2	.151	.224	.245
1995 Toronto	AL	111	367	89	19	4	10	(8	2)	146	51	42	44	1	114	1	9	4	4	4	.50	7	.243	.322	.398
1996 Toronto	AL	147	527	124	30	5	14	(3	11)	206	64	64	45	0	127	5	7	3	16	6	.73	12	.235	.300	.391
1997 Toronto	AL	126	426	102	23	2	12	(4	8)	165	46	35	34	1	94	5	11	2	15	6	.71	9	.239	.302	.387
1998 Toronto	AL	158	568	136	28	1	13	(7	6)	205	70	51	28	1	121	6	13	3	21	6	.78	13	.239	.281	.361
1999 Toronto	AL	38	154	45	13	0	2	(1	1)	64	22	12	16	0	23	3	0	0	4	2	.67	4	.292	.370	.416
2000 Toronto	AL	141	527	133	31	2	15	(5	10)	213	68	69	43	0	113	4	16	1	4	4	.50	14	.252	.313	.404
2001 Toronto	AL	154	636	161	25	5	17	(9	8)	247	79	76	43	0	149	7	7	10	18	11	.62	16	.253	.303	.388
8 ML YEARS		890	3258	798	172	20	83	(37	46)	1259	407	350	257	3	758	32	64	23	85	39	.69	77	.245	.304	.386

Dicky Gonzalez

Pitches: Right **Bats:** Right **Pos:** RP-9; SP-7   **Ht:** 5'11" **Wt:** 170 **Born:** 12/21/78 **Age:** 23

			HOW MUCH HE PITCHED						WHAT HE GAVE UP									THE RESULTS					
Year Team	Lg	G	GS	CG	GF	IP	BFP	H	R	ER	HR	SH	SF	HB	TBB	IBB	SO	WP	Bk	W	L	Pct.	ShO	Sv-Op	Hld	ERA
1996 Mets	R	11	8	2	1	47.1	195	50	19	14	1	2	0	2	3	0	51	1	0	4	2	.667	1	0--	—	2.66
Kingsport	R+	1	1	0	0	5	20	4	2	1	0	1	0	0	0	0	7	1	0	1	0	1.000	0	0--	—	1.80
1997 Capital Cty	A	10	7	1	2	47.1	204	50	28	26	8	2	1	1	15	0	49	2	0	1	4	.200	0	0--	—	4.94
Kingsport	R+	12	12	1	0	66	282	70	38	32	7	4	2	4	10	0	76	0	0	3	6	.333	0	0--	—	4.36
1998 St. Lucie	A+	8	8	0	0	46.2	193	46	22	16	8	1	0	1	13	0	23	1	0	2	5	.667	0	0--	—	3.09
Capital Cty	A	18	18	1	0	111.1	449	104	57	41	9	5	1	9	14	1	107	5	1	10	3	.769	0	0--	—	3.31
1999 Norfolk	AAA	1	1	0	0	6.2	23	5	2	2	0	0	0	0	1	0	3	0	0	1	0	1.000	0	0--	—	2.70
St. Lucie	A+	25	25	3	0	168.2	673	156	66	53	11	4	0	6	30	1	143	4	1	14	9	.609	0	0--	—	2.83
2000 Binghamton	AA	26	25	2	0	147.2	609	130	75	63	14	4	2	11	36	0	138	6	0	13	5	.722	1	0--	—	3.84
2001 Norfolk	AAA	17	16	2	0	96	392	96	35	33	10	4	6	4	20	1	70	2	0	6	5	.545	2	0--	—	3.09
2001 New York	NL	16	7	0	2	59	261	72	33	32	4	2	6	1	17	3	31	5	0	3	2	.600	0	0-0	1	4.88

Juan Gonzalez

Bats: Right **Throws:** Right **Pos:** RF-119; DH-21   **Ht:** 6'3" **Wt:** 220 **Born:** 10/16/69 **Age:** 32

				BATTING														BASERUNNING				PERCENTAGES		
Year Team	Lg	G	AB	H	2B	3B	HR	(Hm	Rd)	TB	R	RBI	TBB	IBB	SO	HBP	SH	SF	SB	CS	SB%	GDP	Avg	OBP	SLG
1989 Texas	AL	24	60	9	3	0	1	(1	0)	15	6	7	6	0	17	0	2	0	0	0	—	4	.150	.227	.250
1990 Texas	AL	25	90	26	7	1	4	(3	1)	47	11	12	2	0	18	2	0	1	0	1	.00	2	.289	.316	.522
1991 Texas	AL	142	545	144	34	1	27	(7	20)	261	78	102	42	7	118	5	0	3	4	4	.50	10	.264	.321	.479
1992 Texas	AL	155	584	152	24	2	43	(19	24)	309	77	109	35	1	143	5	0	8	0	1	.00	16	.260	.304	.529
1993 Texas	AL	140	536	166	33	1	46	(24	22)	339	105	118	37	7	99	13	0	1	4	1	.80	9	.310	.368	.632
1994 Texas	AL	107	422	116	18	4	19	(6	13)	199	57	85	30	10	66	7	0	4	6	4	.60	18	.275	.330	.472
1995 Texas	AL	90	352	104	20	2	27	(15	12)	209	57	82	17	3	66	0	0	5	0	0	—	15	.295	.324	.594

Year Team	Lg	G	AB	H	2B	3B	HR	(Hm	Rd)	TB	R	RBI	TBB	IBB	SO	HBP	SH	SF	SB	CS	SB%	GDP	Avg	OBP	SLG
								BATTING											BASERUNNING				PERCENTAGES		
1996 Texas	AL	134	541	170	33	2	47	(23	24)	348	89	144	45	12	82	3	0	3	2	0	1.00	10	.314	.368	.643
1997 Texas	AL	133	533	158	24	3	42	(18	24)	314	87	131	33	7	107	3	0	10	0	0	—	12	.296	.335	.589
1998 Texas	AL	154	606	193	50	2	45	(21	24)	382	110	157	46	9	126	6	0	11	2	1	.67	20	.318	.366	.630
1999 Texas	AL	144	562	183	36	1	39	(14	25)	338	114	128	51	7	105	4	0	12	3	3	.50	10	.326	.378	.601
2000 Detroit	AL	115	461	133	30	2	22	(8	14)	233	69	67	32	3	84	2	0	1	1	2	.33	13	.289	.337	.505
2001 Cleveland	AL	140	532	173	34	1	35	(22	13)	314	97	140	41	5	94	6	0	16	1	0	1.00	18	.325	.370	.590
13 ML YEARS		1503	5824	1727	346	22	397	(181	216)	3308	957	1282	417	71	1125	56	2	75	23	17	.58	160	.297	.345	.568

Luis Gonzalez

Bats: Left **Throws:** Right **Pos:** LF-161; PH/PR-1 **Ht:** 6'2" **Wt:** 195 **Born:** 9/2/67 **Age:** 34

Year Team	Lg	G	AB	H	2B	3B	HR	(Hm	Rd)	TB	R	RBI	TBB	IBB	SO	HBP	SH	SF	SB	CS	SB%	GDP	Avg	OBP	SLG
								BATTING											BASERUNNING				PERCENTAGES		
1990 Houston	NL	12	21	4	2	0	0	(0	0)	6	1	0	2	1	5	0	0	0	0	0	—	0	.190	.261	.286
1991 Houston	NL	137	473	120	28	9	13	(4	9)	205	51	69	40	4	101	8	1	4	10	7	.59	9	.254	.320	.433
1992 Houston	NL	122	387	94	19	3	10	(4	6)	149	40	55	24	3	52	2	1	2	7	7	.50	6	.243	.289	.385
1993 Houston	NL	154	540	162	34	3	15	(8	7)	247	82	72	47	7	83	10	3	10	20	9	.69	9	.300	.361	.457
1994 Houston	NL	112	392	107	29	4	8	(3	5)	168	57	67	49	6	57	3	0	6	15	13	.54	10	.273	.353	.429
1995 Hou-ChC	NL	133	471	130	29	8	13	(6	7)	214	69	69	57	8	63	6	1	6	6	8	.43	16	.276	.357	.454
1996 Chicago	NL	146	483	131	30	4	15	(6	9)	214	70	79	61	8	49	4	1	6	9	6	.60	13	.271	.354	.443
1997 Houston	NL	152	550	142	31	2	10	(4	6)	207	78	68	71	7	67	5	0	5	10	7	.59	12	.258	.345	.376
1998 Detroit	AL	154	547	146	35	5	23	(15	8)	260	84	71	57	7	62	8	0	8	12	7	.63	9	.267	.340	.475
1999 Arizona	NL	153	614	206	45	4	26	(10	16)	337	112	111	66	6	63	7	1	5	9	5	.64	13	.336	.403	.549
2000 Arizona	NL	162	618	192	47	2	31	(14	17)	336	106	114	78	6	85	12	2	12	2	4	.33	12	.311	.392	.544
2001 Arizona	NL	162	609	198	36	7	57	(26	31)	419	128	142	100	24	83	14	0	5	1	1	.50	14	.325	.429	.688
1995 Houston	NL	56	209	54	10	4	6	(1	5)	90	35	35	18	3	30	3	1	3	1	3	.25	8	.258	.322	.431
Chicago		77	262	76	19	4	7	(5	2)	124	34	34	39	5	33	3	0	3	5	5	.50	8	.290	.384	.473
12 ML YEARS		1599	5705	1632	365	51	221	(100	121)	2762	878	917	652	87	770	79	10	69	101	74	.58	123	.286	.363	.484

Raul Gonzalez

Bats: Right **Throws:** Right **Pos:** PH/PR-9; LF-2 **Ht:** 5'9" **Wt:** 190 **Born:** 12/27/73 **Age:** 28

Year Team	Lg	G	AB	H	2B	3B	HR	(Hm	Rd)	TB	R	RBI	TBB	IBB	SO	HBP	SH	SF	SB	CS	SB%	GDP	Avg	OBP	SLG
								BATTING											BASERUNNING				PERCENTAGES		
1991 Royals	R	47	160	47	5	3	0	—	—	58	24	17	19	0	21	0	1	2	3	4	.43	4	.294	.365	.363
1992 Appleton	A	119	449	115	32	1	9	—	—	176	82	51	57	1	58	2	4	6	13	5	.72	4	.256	.339	.392
1993 Wilmington	A+	127	461	124	30	3	11	—	—	193	59	55	54	1	58	4	1	4	13	5	.72	8	.269	.348	.419
1994 Wilmington	A+	115	414	108	19	8	9	—	—	170	60	51	45	2	50	2	2	4	0	4	.00	8	.261	.333	.411
1995 Wichita	AA	22	79	23	3	2	2	—	—	36	14	11	8	0	13	0	0	0	4	0	1.00	1	.291	.356	.456
Wilmington	A+	86	308	90	19	3	11	—	—	148	36	49	14	3	34	2	3	7	6	4	.60	3	.292	.320	.481
1996 Wichita	AA	23	84	24	5	1	1	—	—	34	17	9	5	0	12	1	0	0	1	2	.33	3	.286	.333	.405
1997 Wichita	AA	129	452	129	30	4	13	—	—	206	66	74	36	0	52	2	3	8	12	8	.60	12	.285	.335	.456
1998 Wichita	AA	118	455	148	31	1	17	—	—	232	84	86	58	3	53	2	1	4	12	8	.60	15	.325	.401	.510
1999 Trenton	AA	127	505	169	33	4	18	—	—	264	80	103	51	3	71	3	1	7	12	3	.80	14	.335	.394	.523
2000 Iowa	AAA	69	241	64	13	1	4	—	—	91	35	33	21	1	20	2	0	1	5	5	.50	6	.266	.328	.378
2001 Louisville	AAA	142	539	161	39	1	11	—	—	235	90	66	64	2	70	1	0	5	6	8	.43	20	.299	.371	.436
2000 Chicago	NL	3	2	0	0	0	0	(0	0)	0	0	0	0	0	2	0	0	0	0	0	—	0	.000	.000	.000
2001 Cincinnati	NL	11	14	3	0	0	0	(0	0)	3	0	1	0	0	3	0	0	0	0	0	—	0	.214	.267	.214
2 ML YEARS		14	16	3	0	0	0	(0	0)	3	0	1	0	0	5	0	0	0	0	0	—	0	.188	.235	.188

Wiki Gonzalez

Bats: Right **Throws:** Right **Pos:** C-47; PH/PR-19; DH-1 **Ht:** 5'11" **Wt:** 203 **Born:** 5/17/74 **Age:** 28

Year Team	Lg	G	AB	H	2B	3B	HR	(Hm	Rd)	TB	R	RBI	TBB	IBB	SO	HBP	SH	SF	SB	CS	SB%	GDP	Avg	OBP	SLG
								BATTING											BASERUNNING				PERCENTAGES		
2001 Lk Elsinore *	A+	4	13	2	0	0	0	—	—	2	1	1	2	0	4	0	0	1	0	0	—	0	.154	.250	.154
1999 San Diego	NL	30	83	21	2	1	3	(1	2)	34	7	12	1	0	8	1	0	0	0	0	—	5	.253	.271	.410
2000 San Diego	NL	95	284	66	15	1	3	(1	4)	98	25	30	30	4	31	3	1	1	1	2	.33	5	.232	.311	.345
2001 San Diego	NL	64	160	44	6	0	8	(5	3)	74	16	27	11	1	28	4	0	1	2	0	1.00	3	.275	.335	.463
3 ML YEARS		189	527	131	23	2	16	(7	9)	206	48	69	42	5	67	8	1	2	3	2	.60	13	.249	.313	.391

Tom Goodwin

Bats: Left **Throws:** Right **Pos:** CF-70; PH/PR-28; LF-8 **Ht:** 6'1" **Wt:** 175 **Born:** 7/27/68 **Age:** 33

Year Team	Lg	G	AB	H	2B	3B	HR	(Hm	Rd)	TB	R	RBI	TBB	IBB	SO	HBP	SH	SF	SB	CS	SB%	GDP	Avg	OBP	SLG
								BATTING											BASERUNNING				PERCENTAGES		
2001 Wilmington *	A	2	5	2	0	1	0	—	—	4	2	1	1	0	0	0	0	1	0	0	—	0	.400	.429	.800
1991 Los Angeles	NL	16	7	1	0	0	0	(0	0)	1	3	0	0	0	0	0	0	0	1	1	.50	0	.143	.143	.143
1992 Los Angeles	NL	57	73	17	1	1	0	(0	0)	20	15	3	6	0	10	0	0	0	7	3	.70	0	.233	.291	.274
1993 Los Angeles	NL	30	17	5	1	0	0	(0	0)	6	6	1	1	0	4	0	0	0	1	2	.33	1	.294	.333	.353
1994 Kansas City	AL	2	2	0	0	0	0	(0	0)	0	0	0	0	0	1	0	0	0	0	0	—	0	.000	.000	.000
1995 Kansas City	AL	133	480	138	16	3	4	(2	2)	172	72	28	38	0	72	5	14	0	50	18	.74	7	.288	.346	.358
1996 Kansas City	AL	143	524	148	14	4	1	(0	1)	173	80	35	39	0	79	2	21	1	66	22	.75	3	.282	.334	.330
1997 KC-Tex	AL	150	574	149	26	6	2	(0	2)	193	90	39	44	1	88	3	11	3	50	16	.76	7	.260	.314	.336
1998 Texas	AL	154	520	151	13	3	2	(2	0)	176	102	33	73	0	90	2	10	3	38	20	.66	2	.290	.378	.338
1999 Texas	AL	109	405	105	12	6	3	(1	2)	138	63	33	40	0	61	0	7	3	39	11	.78	7	.259	.324	.341
2000 Col-LA	NL	147	528	139	11	9	6	(4	2)	186	94	58	68	2	117	1	5	4	55	10	.85	5	.263	.346	.352
2001 Los Angeles	NL	105	286	66	8	5	4	(1	3)	96	51	22	23	0	58	0	1	2	22	8	.73	3	.231	.286	.336
1997 Kansas City	AL	97	367	100	13	4	2	(0	2)	127	51	22	19	0	51	2	11	1	34	10	.77	5	.272	.311	.346
Texas	AL	53	207	49	13	2	0	(0	0)	66	39	17	25	1	37	1	0	2	16	6	.73	2	.237	.319	.319
2000 Colorado	NL	91	317	86	8	8	5	(4	1)	125	65	47	50	2	76	1	5	4	39	7	.85	3	.271	.368	.394
Los Angeles	NL	56	211	53	3	1	1	(0	1)	61	29	11	18	0	41	0	0	0	16	3	.84	4	.251	.310	.289
11 ML YEARS		1046	3416	919	102	37	22	(10	12)	1161	576	252	332	3	580	13	69	16	329	111	.75	37	.269	.335	.340

85

Flash Gordon

Pitches: Right **Bats:** Right **Pos:** RP-47   **Ht:** 5'10" **Wt:** 190 **Born:** 11/18/67 **Age:** 34

Year Team	Lg	HOW MUCH HE PITCHED						WHAT HE GAVE UP											THE RESULTS					
		G	GS	CG	GF	IP	BFP	H	R	ER	HR	SH	SF	HB	TBB	IBB	SO	WP	Bk	W	L	Pct.	ShO	Sv-Op	Hld	ERA
2001 Daytona *	A+	2	2	0	0	2	6	0	0	0	0	0	0	0	0	0	3	0	0	0	0	—	0	0--	—	0.00
Iowa *	AAA	2	0	0	0	2	7	1	0	0	0	0	0	0	1	0	2	0	0	0	0	—	0	0--	—	0.00
1988 Kansas City	AL	5	2	0	0	15.2	67	16	9	9	1	0	0	0	7	0	18	0	0	0	2	.000	0	0-0	2	5.17
1989 Kansas City	AL	49	16	1	16	163	677	122	67	66	10	4	4	1	86	4	153	12	0	17	9	.654	1	1-7	3	3.64
1990 Kansas City	AL	32	32	6	0	195.1	858	192	99	81	17	8	2	3	99	1	175	11	0	12	11	.522	1	0-0	0	3.73
1991 Kansas City	AL	45	14	1	11	158	684	129	76	68	16	5	3	4	87	6	167	5	0	9	14	.391	0	1-4	4	3.87
1992 Kansas City	AL	40	11	0	13	117.2	516	116	67	60	9	2	6	4	55	4	98	5	2	6	10	.375	0	0-2	0	4.59
1993 Kansas City	AL	48	14	2	18	155.2	651	125	65	62	11	6	6	1	77	5	143	17	0	12	6	.667	0	1-6	2	3.58
1994 Kansas City	AL	24	24	0	0	155.1	675	136	79	75	15	3	8	3	87	3	126	12	1	11	7	.611	0	0-0	0	4.35
1995 Kansas City	AL	31	31	2	0	189	843	204	110	93	12	7	11	4	89	4	119	9	0	12	12	.500	0	0-0	0	4.43
1996 Boston	AL	34	34	4	0	215.2	998	249	143	**134**	28	2	11	4	105	5	171	6	1	12	9	.571	1	0-0	0	5.59
1997 Boston	AL	42	25	2	16	182.2	774	155	85	76	10	3	4	3	78	1	159	5	0	6	10	.375	1	11-13	6	3.74
1998 Boston	AL	73	0	0	**69**	79.1	317	55	24	24	2	2	2	0	25	1	78	9	0	7	4	.636	0	**46**-47	2	2.72
1999 Boston	AL	21	0	0	15	17.2	82	17	11	11	2	0	0	1	12	2	24	0	0	0	2	.000	0	11-13	1	5.60
2001 Chicago	NL	47	0	0	40	45.1	187	32	18	17	4	0	0	1	16	1	67	2	0	1	2	.333	0	27-31	5	3.38
13 ML YEARS		491	203	18	198	1690.1	7329	1548	853	776	137	42	57	29	823	37	1498	93	4	105	98	.517	4	98-123	12	4.13

Mark Grace

Bats: Left **Throws:** Left **Pos:** 1B-135; PH/PR-10   **Ht:** 6'2" **Wt:** 200 **Born:** 6/28/64 **Age:** 38

Year Team	Lg	BATTING																	BASERUNNING				PERCENTAGES		
		G	AB	H	2B	3B	HR	(Hm	Rd)	TB	R	RBI	TBB	IBB	SO	HBP	SH	SF	SB	CS	SB%	GDP	Avg	OBP	SLG
1988 Chicago	NL	134	486	144	23	4	7	(0	7)	196	65	57	60	5	43	0	0	4	3	3	.50	12	.296	.371	.403
1989 Chicago	NL	142	510	160	28	3	13	(8	5)	233	74	79	80	13	42	0	3	3	14	7	.67	13	.314	.405	.457
1990 Chicago	NL	157	589	182	32	1	9	(4	5)	243	72	82	59	5	54	5	1	8	15	6	.71	10	.309	.372	.413
1991 Chicago	NL	160	**619**	169	28	5	8	(5	3)	231	87	58	70	7	53	3	4	7	3	4	.43	6	.273	.346	.373
1992 Chicago	NL	158	603	185	37	5	9	(4	5)	259	72	79	72	8	36	4	2	8	6	1	.86	14	.307	.380	.430
1993 Chicago	NL	155	594	193	39	4	14	(5	9)	282	86	98	71	14	32	1	1	9	8	4	.67	**25**	.325	.393	.475
1994 Chicago	NL	106	403	120	23	3	6	(5	1)	167	55	44	48	5	41	0	0	3	0	1	.00	10	.298	.370	.414
1995 Chicago	NL	143	552	180	**51**	3	16	(4	12)	285	97	92	65	9	46	2	1	7	6	2	.75	10	.326	.395	.516
1996 Chicago	NL	142	547	181	39	1	9	(4	5)	249	88	75	62	8	41	1	0	6	2	3	.40	18	.331	.396	.455
1997 Chicago	NL	151	555	177	32	5	13	(6	7)	258	87	78	88	3	45	2	1	8	2	4	.33	18	.319	.409	.465
1998 Chicago	NL	158	595	184	39	3	17	(7	10)	280	92	89	93	8	56	3	0	7	4	7	.36	11	.309	.401	.471
1999 Chicago	NL	161	593	183	44	5	16	(8	8)	285	107	91	83	4	44	2	0	**10**	3	4	.43	14	.309	.390	.481
2000 Chicago	NL	143	510	143	41	1	11	(3	8)	219	75	82	95	11	28	6	2	8	1	2	.33	7	.280	.394	.429
2001 Arizona	NL	145	476	142	31	2	15	(6	9)	222	66	78	67	6	36	4	1	5	1	0	1.00	7	.298	.386	.466
14 ML YEARS		2055	7632	2343	487	45	163	(70	93)	3409	1123	1082	1013	106	597	33	16	93	68	48	.59	181	.307	.386	.447

Tony Graffanino

Bats: R **Throws:** R **Pos:** 3B-38; PH/PR-26; 2B-20; SS-5; DH-3; LF-3; 1B-1   **Ht:** 6'1" **Wt:** 190 **Born:** 6/6/72 **Age:** 30

Year Team	Lg	BATTING																	BASERUNNING				PERCENTAGES		
		G	AB	H	2B	3B	HR	(Hm	Rd)	TB	R	RBI	TBB	IBB	SO	HBP	SH	SF	SB	CS	SB%	GDP	Avg	OBP	SLG
1996 Atlanta	NL	22	46	8	1	1	0	(0	0)	11	7	2	4	0	13	1	0	1	0	0	—	0	.174	.250	.239
1997 Atlanta	NL	104	186	48	9	1	8	(5	3)	83	33	20	26	1	46	1	3	5	6	4	.60	3	.258	.344	.446
1998 Atlanta	NL	105	289	61	14	1	5	(3	2)	92	32	22	24	0	68	2	1	1	1	4	.20	7	.211	.275	.318
1999 Tampa Bay	AL	39	130	41	9	4	2	(0	2)	64	20	19	9	0	22	1	2	0	3	2	.60	1	.315	.364	.492
2000 TB-CWS	AL	70	168	46	6	1	2	(1	1)	60	33	17	22	0	27	2	1	1	7	4	.64	2	.274	.363	.357
2001 Chicago	AL	74	145	44	9	0	2	(1	1)	59	23	15	16	0	29	1	4	3	4	1	.80	4	.303	.370	.407
2000 Tampa Bay	AL	13	20	6	1	0	0	(0	0)	7	8	1	1	0	2	1	0	0	0	0	—	1	.300	.364	.350
Chicago	AL	57	148	40	5	1	2	(1	1)	53	25	16	21	0	25	1	1	1	7	4	.64	1	.270	.363	.358
6 ML YEARS		414	964	248	48	8	19	(10	9)	369	148	95	101	1	205	8	11	11	21	15	.58	17	.257	.329	.383

Danny Graves

Pitches: Right **Bats:** Right **Pos:** RP-66   **Ht:** 5'11" **Wt:** 185 **Born:** 8/7/73 **Age:** 28

Year Team	Lg	HOW MUCH HE PITCHED						WHAT HE GAVE UP											THE RESULTS					
		G	GS	CG	GF	IP	BFP	H	R	ER	HR	SH	SF	HB	TBB	IBB	SO	WP	Bk	W	L	Pct.	ShO	Sv-Op	Hld	ERA
1996 Cleveland	AL	15	0	0	5	29.2	129	29	16	15	2	0	1	0	10	0	22	1	0	2	0	1.000	0	0-1	0	4.55
1997 Cle-Cin		15	0	0	3	26	134	41	22	16	2	3	2	0	20	1	11	1	0	0	0	—	0	0-0	1	5.54
1998 Cincinnati	NL	62	0	0	35	81.1	340	76	31	30	6	2	5	2	28	4	44	4	0	2	1	.667	0	8-8	6	3.32
1999 Cincinnati	NL	75	0	0	56	111	454	90	42	38	10	5	2	2	49	4	69	3	0	8	7	.533	0	27-36	0	3.08
2000 Cincinnati	NL	66	0	0	57	91.1	388	81	31	26	8	6	4	3	42	7	53	3	1	10	5	.667	0	30-35	0	2.56
2001 Cincinnati	NL	66	0	0	54	80.1	337	83	41	37	7	3	2	4	18	6	49	2	1	6	5	.545	0	32-39	0	4.15
1997 Cleveland	AL	5	0	0	2	11.1	56	15	8	6	2	0	1	0	9	0	4	0	0	0	0	—	0	0-0	0	4.76
Cincinnati	NL	10	0	0	1	14.2	78	26	14	10	0	3	1	0	11	1	7	1	0	0	0	—	0	0-0	1	6.14
6 ML YEARS		299	0	0	210	419.2	1782	400	185	162	35	19	16	11	167	22	248	14	2	28	18	.609	0	97-119	7	3.47

Craig Grebeck

Bats: Right **Throws:** Right **Pos:** SS-23   **Ht:** 5'7" **Wt:** 155 **Born:** 12/29/64 **Age:** 37

Year Team	Lg	BATTING																	BASERUNNING				PERCENTAGES		
		G	AB	H	2B	3B	HR	(Hm	Rd)	TB	R	RBI	TBB	IBB	SO	HBP	SH	SF	SB	CS	SB%	GDP	Avg	OBP	SLG
1990 Chicago	AL	59	119	20	3	1	1	(1	0)	28	7	9	8	0	24	2	3	3	0	0	—	3	.168	.227	.235
1991 Chicago	AL	107	224	63	16	3	6	(3	3)	103	37	31	38	0	40	1	4	1	1	3	.25	3	.281	.386	.460
1992 Chicago	AL	88	287	77	21	2	3	(2	1)	111	24	35	30	0	34	3	10	3	0	0	.00	5	.268	.341	.387
1993 Chicago	AL	72	190	43	5	0	1	(0	1)	51	25	12	26	0	26	0	7	0	1	2	.33	9	.226	.319	.268
1994 Chicago	AL	35	97	30	5	0	0	(0	0)	35	17	5	12	0	5	1	3	0	0	0	—	4	.309	.391	.361
1995 Chicago	AL	53	154	40	12	0	1	(1	0)	55	19	18	21	0	23	3	4	0	0	0	—	0	.260	.360	.357
1996 Florida	NL	50	95	20	1	0	1	(0	1)	24	8	9	4	1	14	1	1	2	0	0	—	2	.211	.245	.253
1997 Anaheim	AL	63	126	34	9	0	1	(1	0)	46	12	6	18	1	11	0	5	1	0	1	.00	6	.270	.359	.365

Year Team	Lg	G	AB	H	2B	3B	HR	(Hm	Rd)	TB	R	RBI	TBB	IBB	SO	HBP	SH	SF	SB	CS	SB%	GDP	Avg	OBP	SLG
							BATTING												BASERUNNING				PERCENTAGES		
1998 Toronto	AL	102	301	77	17	2	2	(2	0)	104	33	27	29	0	42	4	8	2	2	2	.50	8	.256	.327	.346
1999 Toronto	AL	34	113	41	7	0	0	(0	0)	48	18	10	15	0	13	2	3	1	0	0	—	2	.363	.443	.425
2000 Toronto	AL	66	241	71	19	0	3	(2	1)	99	38	23	25	0	33	2	1	1	0	0	—	7	.295	.364	.411
2001 Boston	AL	23	41	2	1	0	0	(0	0)	3	1	2	2	0	9	0	0	0	0	0	—	0	.049	.093	.073
12 ML YEARS		752	1988	518	116	8	19	(11	8)	707	239	187	228	2	274	19	49	14	4	11	.27	49	.261	.340	.356

Shawn Green

Bats: L **Throws:** L **Pos:** RF-159; CF-2; 1B-1; PH/PR-1   **Ht:** 6'4" **Wt:** 200 **Born:** 11/10/72 **Age:** 29

Year Team	Lg	G	AB	H	2B	3B	HR	(Hm	Rd)	TB	R	RBI	TBB	IBB	SO	HBP	SH	SF	SB	CS	SB%	GDP	Avg	OBP	SLG
							BATTING												BASERUNNING				PERCENTAGES		
1993 Toronto	AL	3	6	0	0	0	0	(0	0)	0	0	0	0	0	1	0	0	0	0	0	—	0	.000	.000	.000
1994 Toronto	AL	14	33	3	1	0	0	(0	0)	4	1	1	1	0	8	0	0	0	1	0	1.00	1	.091	.118	.121
1995 Toronto	AL	121	379	109	31	4	15	(5	10)	193	52	54	20	3	68	3	0	3	1	2	.33	4	.288	.326	.509
1996 Toronto	AL	132	422	118	32	3	11	(7	4)	189	52	45	33	3	75	8	0	2	5	1	.83	9	.280	.342	.448
1997 Toronto	AL	135	429	123	22	4	16	(10	6)	201	57	53	36	4	99	1	1	4	14	3	.82	4	.287	.340	.469
1998 Toronto	AL	158	630	175	33	4	35	(21	14)	321	106	100	50	2	142	5	1	3	35	12	.74	6	.278	.334	.510
1999 Toronto	AL	153	614	190	45	0	42	(20	22)	361	134	123	66	4	117	11	0	5	20	7	.74	13	.309	.384	.588
2000 Los Angeles	NL	162	610	164	44	4	24	(15	9)	288	98	99	90	9	121	8	0	6	24	5	.83	18	.269	.367	.472
2001 Los Angeles	NL	161	619	184	31	4	49	(19	30)	370	121	125	72	10	107	5	0	5	20	4	.83	10	.297	.372	.598
9 ML YEARS		1039	3742	1066	239	23	192	(97	95)	1927	621	600	368	35	738	41	2	28	120	34	.78	65	.285	.353	.515

Steve Green

Pitches: Right **Bats:** Right **Pos:** SP-1   **Ht:** 6'2" **Wt:** 195 **Born:** 1/26/78 **Age:** 24

Year Team	Lg	G	GS	CG	GF	IP	BFP	H	R	ER	HR	SH	SF	HB	TBB	IBB	SO	WP	Bk	W	L	Pct.	ShO	Sv-Op	Hld	ERA
				HOW MUCH HE PITCHED						WHAT HE GAVE UP												THE RESULTS				
1998 Cedar Rapds	A	18	10	1	5	83.1	356	86	49	42	9	3	3	8	25	0	61	9	1	2	6	.250	0	0- —		4.54
1999 Lk Elsinore	A+	19	19	4	0	120.2	526	130	70	53	9	4	1	6	37	2	91	1	3	7	6	.538	4	0- —		3.95
Erie	AA	6	6	1	0	40.2	176	34	25	15	4	1	2	2	19	0	32	1	0	3	1	.750	0	0- —		3.32
2000 Erie	AA	13	13	0	0	79.1	330	71	34	30	7	2	0	3	34	0	66	1	0	7	4	.636	0	0- —		3.40
Edmonton	AAA	8	8	0	0	42	208	55	35	34	4	1	0	2	27	1	24	1	2	0	4	.000	0	0- —		7.29
2001 Salt Lake	AAA	10	10	1	0	59	247	59	30	24	3	0	1	3	13	0	40	3	1	6	2	.750	0	0- —		3.66
2001 Anaheim	AL	1	1	0	0	6	27	4	2	2	0	0	0	0	6	0	4	2	0	0	0	—	0	0-0	0	3.00

Todd Greene

Bats: Right **Throws:** Right **Pos:** C-34; DH-2; PH/PR-1   **Ht:** 5'10" **Wt:** 208 **Born:** 5/8/71 **Age:** 31

Year Team	Lg	G	AB	H	2B	3B	HR	(Hm	Rd)	TB	R	RBI	TBB	IBB	SO	HBP	SH	SF	SB	CS	SB%	GDP	Avg	OBP	SLG
							BATTING												BASERUNNING				PERCENTAGES		
2001 Columbus *	AAA	34	131	33	8	0	6	—	—	59	16	17	4	0	19	1	0	0	3	2	.60	3	.252	.279	.450
1996 California	AL	29	79	15	1	0	2	(1	1)	22	9	9	4	0	11	1	0	0	2	0	1.00	4	.190	.238	.278
1997 Anaheim	AL	34	124	36	6	0	9	(5	4)	69	24	24	7	1	25	0	0	0	2	0	1.00	1	.290	.328	.556
1998 Anaheim	AL	29	71	18	4	0	1	(0	1)	25	3	7	2	0	20	0	0	0	0	0	—	0	.254	.274	.352
1999 Anaheim	AL	97	321	78	20	0	14	(7	7)	140	36	42	12	0	63	3	0	2	1	4	.20	8	.243	.275	.436
2000 Toronto	AL	34	85	20	2	0	5	(2	3)	37	11	10	5	0	18	0	0	0	0	0	—	4	.235	.278	.435
2001 New York	AL	35	96	20	4	0	1	(1	0)	27	9	11	3	0	21	1	0	0	0	0	—	3	.208	.240	.281
6 ML YEARS		258	776	187	37	0	32	(16	16)	320	92	103	33	1	158	5	0	2	5	4	.56	20	.241	.276	.412

Rusty Greer

Bats: Left **Throws:** Left **Pos:** LF-60; PH/PR-2; DH-1   **Ht:** 6'0" **Wt:** 195 **Born:** 1/21/69 **Age:** 33

Year Team	Lg	G	AB	H	2B	3B	HR	(Hm	Rd)	TB	R	RBI	TBB	IBB	SO	HBP	SH	SF	SB	CS	SB%	GDP	Avg	OBP	SLG
							BATTING												BASERUNNING				PERCENTAGES		
2001 Tulsa *	AA	1	3	0	0	0	0	—	—	0	1	0	1	0	1	0	0	0	0	0	—	0	.000	.250	.000
1994 Texas	AL	80	277	87	16	1	10	(3	7)	135	36	46	46	2	46	2	2	4	0	0	—	3	.314	.410	.487
1995 Texas	AL	131	417	113	21	2	13	(7	6)	177	58	61	55	1	66	1	2	3	3	1	.75	9	.271	.355	.424
1996 Texas	AL	139	542	180	41	6	18	(9	9)	287	96	100	62	4	86	3	0	10	9	0	1.00	9	.332	.397	.530
1997 Texas	AL	157	601	193	42	3	26	(18	8)	319	112	87	83	4	87	3	1	2	9	5	.64	11	.321	.405	.531
1998 Texas	AL	155	598	183	31	5	16	(8	8)	272	107	108	80	1	93	4	0	9	2	4	.33	18	.306	.386	.455
1999 Texas	AL	147	556	167	41	3	20	(10	10)	274	101	101	96	2	67	5	0	5	2	2	.50	17	.300	.405	.493
2000 Texas	AL	105	394	117	34	3	8	(3	5)	181	65	65	51	0	61	3	0	5	4	1	.80	14	.297	.377	.459
2001 Texas	AL	62	245	67	23	0	7	(2	5)	111	38	29	27	1	32	1	1	5	1	2	.33	5	.273	.342	.453
8 ML YEARS		976	3630	1107	249	23	118	(60	58)	1756	619	597	500	16	538	22	6	43	30	15	.67	86	.305	.388	.484

Ben Grieve

Bats: L **Throws:** R **Pos:** RF-64; LF-56; DH-32; PH/PR-2   **Ht:** 6'4" **Wt:** 230 **Born:** 5/4/76 **Age:** 26

Year Team	Lg	G	AB	H	2B	3B	HR	(Hm	Rd)	TB	R	RBI	TBB	IBB	SO	HBP	SH	SF	SB	CS	SB%	GDP	Avg	OBP	SLG
							BATTING												BASERUNNING				PERCENTAGES		
1997 Oakland	AL	24	93	29	6	0	3	(3	0)	44	12	24	13	1	25	1	1	0	0	0	—	1	.312	.402	.473
1998 Oakland	AL	155	583	168	41	2	18	(5	13)	267	94	89	85	3	123	9	0	1	2	2	.50	18	.288	.386	.458
1999 Oakland	AL	148	486	129	21	0	28	(13	15)	234	80	86	63	2	108	8	0	1	4	0	1.00	5	.265	.358	.481
2000 Oakland	AL	158	594	166	40	1	27	(13	14)	289	92	104	73	2	130	3	0	5	3	0	1.00	32	.279	.359	.487
2001 Tampa Bay	AL	154	542	143	30	2	11	(5	6)	210	72	72	87	2	159	8	0	2	7	1	.88	13	.264	.372	.387
5 ML YEARS		639	2298	635	138	5	87	(39	48)	1044	350	375	321	10	545	29	1	9	16	3	.84	81	.276	.371	.454

Ken Griffey Jr.

Bats: Left **Throws:** Left **Pos:** CF-90; PH/PR-19; DH-2   **Ht:** 6'3" **Wt:** 205 **Born:** 11/21/69 **Age:** 32

						BATTING													BASERUNNING				PERCENTAGES		
Year Team	Lg	G	AB	H	2B	3B	HR	(Hm	Rd)	TB	R	RBI	TBB	IBB	SO	HBP	SH	SF	SB	CS	SB%	GDP	Avg	OBP	SLG
1989 Seattle	AL	127	455	120	23	0	16	(10	6)	191	61	61	44	8	83	2	1	4	16	7	.70	4	.264	.329	.420
1990 Seattle	AL	155	597	179	28	7	22	(8	14)	287	91	80	63	12	81	2	0	4	16	11	.59	12	.300	.366	.481
1991 Seattle	AL	154	548	179	42	1	22	(16	6)	289	76	100	71	21	82	1	4	9	18	6	.75	10	.327	.399	.527
1992 Seattle	AL	142	565	174	39	4	27	(16	11)	302	83	103	44	15	67	5	0	3	10	5	.67	15	.308	.361	.535
1993 Seattle	AL	156	582	180	38	3	45	(21	24)	359	113	109	96	25	91	6	0	7	17	9	.65	14	.309	.408	.617
1994 Seattle	AL	111	433	140	24	4	40	(18	22)	292	94	90	56	19	73	2	0	2	11	3	.79	9	.323	.402	.674
1995 Seattle	AL	72	260	67	7	0	17	(13	4)	125	52	42	52	6	53	0	0	2	4	2	.67	4	.258	.379	.481
1996 Seattle	AL	140	545	165	26	2	49	(26	23)	342	125	140	78	13	104	7	1	7	16	1	.94	7	.303	.392	.628
1997 Seattle	AL	157	608	185	34	3	56	(27	29)	393	125	147	76	23	121	8	0	12	15	4	.79	12	.304	.382	.646
1998 Seattle	AL	161	633	180	33	3	56	(30	26)	387	120	146	76	11	121	7	0	4	20	5	.80	14	.284	.365	.611
1999 Seattle	AL	160	606	173	26	3	48	(27	21)	349	123	134	91	17	108	7	0	2	24	7	.77	8	.285	.384	.576
2000 Cincinnati	NL	145	520	141	22	3	40	(22	18)	289	100	118	94	17	117	9	0	8	6	4	.60	7	.271	.387	.556
2001 Cincinnati	NL	111	364	104	20	2	22	(12	10)	194	57	65	44	6	72	4	1	4	2	0	1.00	8	.286	.365	.533
13 ML YEARS		1791	6716	1987	362	35	460	(246	214)	3799	1220	1335	885	193	1173	60	7	68	175	64	.73	124	.296	.379	.566

Jason Grilli

Pitches: Right **Bats:** Right **Pos:** SP-5; RP-1   **Ht:** 6'4" **Wt:** 185 **Born:** 11/11/76 **Age:** 25

			HOW MUCH HE PITCHED					WHAT HE GAVE UP									THE RESULTS					
Year Team	Lg	G	GS	CG	GF	IP	BFP	H	R	ER	HR	SH	SF	HB	TBB	IBB	SO	WP	Bk	W	L	Pct.	ShO	Sv-Op	Hld	ERA
1998 Shreveport	AA	21	21	3	0	123.1	511	113	60	52	11	6	3	4	37	0	100	6	3	7	10	.412	0	0--	--	3.79
Fresno	AAA	8	8	0	0	42	193	49	30	24	7	0	1	5	18	0	37	1	1	2	3	.400	0	0--	--	5.14
1999 Fresno	AAA	19	19	1	0	100.2	461	124	69	62	22	2	3	6	39	0	76	3	0	7	5	.583	0	0--	--	5.54
Calgary	AAA	8	8	0	0	41	205	56	48	35	7	2	1	2	23	0	27	5	1	1	5	.167	0	0--	--	7.68
2000 Calgary	AAA	8	8	0	0	41.1	204	58	37	33	4	3	3	2	23	0	21	6	0	1	4	.200	0	0--	--	7.19
2001 Marlins	R	2	2	0	0	4	15	2	0	0	0	0	0	1	0	0	6	0	0	0	0	--	0	0--	--	0.00
Portland	AA	1	1	0	0	4	15	3	1	1	1	0	0	0	0	0	3	0	0	0	1	.000	0	0--	--	2.25
Brevard Cty	A+	3	3	0	0	13.2	57	12	4	3	0	0	0	0	5	0	14	0	0	2	1	.333	0	0--	--	1.98
Calgary	AAA	8	8	0	0	47	205	46	26	21	4	0	3	2	20	0	35	1	0	1	2	.333	0	0--	--	4.02
2000 Florida	NL	1	1	0	0	6.2	35	11	4	4	0	2	0	2	2	0	3	0	0	1	0	1.000	0	0-0	0	5.40
2001 Florida	NL	6	5	0	1	26.2	115	30	18	18	6	1	0	2	11	0	17	0	0	3	2	.500	0	0-0	0	6.08
2 ML YEARS		7	6	0	1	33.1	150	41	22	22	6	3	0	4	13	0	20	0	0	3	2	.600	0	0-0	0	5.94

Jason Grimsley

Pitches: Right **Bats:** Right **Pos:** RP-73   **Ht:** 6'3" **Wt:** 205 **Born:** 8/7/67 **Age:** 34

			HOW MUCH HE PITCHED					WHAT HE GAVE UP									THE RESULTS					
Year Team	Lg	G	GS	CG	GF	IP	BFP	H	R	ER	HR	SH	SF	HB	TBB	IBB	SO	WP	Bk	W	L	Pct.	ShO	Sv-Op	Hld	ERA
1989 Philadelphia	NL	4	4	0	0	18.1	91	19	13	12	2	1	0	0	19	1	7	2	0	1	3	.250	0	0-0	0	5.89
1990 Philadelphia	NL	11	11	0	0	57.1	255	47	21	21	1	2	1	2	43	0	41	6	1	3	2	.600	0	0-0	0	3.30
1991 Philadelphia	NL	12	12	0	0	61	272	54	34	33	4	3	2	3	41	3	42	14	0	1	7	.125	0	0-0	0	4.87
1993 Cleveland	AL	10	6	0	1	42.1	194	52	26	25	3	1	0	1	20	1	27	2	0	3	4	.429	0	0-0	1	5.31
1994 Cleveland	AL	14	13	1	0	82.2	368	91	47	42	7	4	2	6	34	1	59	6	1	5	2	.714	0	0-0	0	4.57
1995 Cleveland	AL	15	2	0	2	34	165	37	24	23	4	1	2	2	32	1	25	7	0	0	0	--	0	1-1	0	6.09
1996 California	AL	35	20	2	4	130.1	620	150	110	99	14	4	5	13	74	5	82	11	0	5	7	.417	1	0-0	0	6.84
1999 New York	AL	55	0	0	25	75	336	66	39	30	7	3	3	4	40	5	49	8	0	7	2	.778	0	1-4	8	3.60
2000 New York	AL	63	4	0	18	96.1	428	100	58	54	10	2	6	5	42	1	53	16	0	3	2	.600	0	1-4	4	5.04
2001 Kansas City	AL	73	0	0	24	80.1	327	71	32	27	8	2	1	2	28	5	61	4	0	1	5	.167	0	0-7	26	3.02
10 ML YEARS		292	72	3	74	677.2	3056	687	404	366	60	23	22	38	373	23	446	76	2	29	34	.460	1	3-16	39	4.86

Marquis Grissom

Bats: R **Throws:** R **Pos:** CF-95; LF-26; PH/PR-23; RF-3; DH-2   **Ht:** 5'11" **Wt:** 188 **Born:** 4/17/67 **Age:** 35

						BATTING													BASERUNNING				PERCENTAGES		
Year Team	Lg	G	AB	H	2B	3B	HR	(Hm	Rd)	TB	R	RBI	TBB	IBB	SO	HBP	SH	SF	SB	CS	SB%	GDP	Avg	OBP	SLG
1989 Montreal	NL	26	74	19	2	0	1	(0	1)	24	16	2	12	0	21	0	1	0	1	0	1.00	1	.257	.360	.324
1990 Montreal	NL	98	288	74	14	2	3	(2	1)	101	42	29	27	2	40	0	4	1	22	2	.92	3	.257	.320	.351
1991 Montreal	NL	148	558	149	23	9	6	(3	3)	208	73	39	34	0	89	1	4	0	76	17	.82	6	.267	.310	.373
1992 Montreal	NL	159	653	180	39	6	14	(8	6)	273	99	66	42	6	81	5	3	4	78	13	.86	12	.276	.322	.418
1993 Montreal	NL	157	630	188	27	2	19	(9	10)	276	104	95	52	6	76	3	0	8	53	10	.84	9	.298	.351	.438
1994 Montreal	NL	110	475	137	25	4	11	(4	7)	203	96	45	41	4	66	1	0	4	36	6	.86	10	.288	.344	.427
1995 Atlanta	NL	139	551	142	23	3	12	(5	7)	207	80	42	47	4	61	1	9	5	29	9	.76	8	.258	.317	.376
1996 Atlanta	NL	158	671	207	32	10	23	(11	12)	328	106	74	41	6	73	3	4	4	28	11	.72	12	.308	.349	.489
1997 Cleveland	AL	144	558	146	27	6	12	(5	7)	221	74	66	43	1	89	6	6	9	22	13	.63	12	.262	.317	.396
1998 Milwaukee	NL	142	542	147	28	1	10	(2	8)	207	57	60	24	2	78	2	2	2	13	8	.62	12	.271	.304	.382
1999 Milwaukee	NL	154	603	161	27	1	20	(9	11)	250	92	83	49	4	109	0	4	5	24	6	.80	12	.267	.320	.415
2000 Milwaukee	NL	146	595	145	18	2	14	(4	10)	209	67	62	39	2	99	0	2	4	20	10	.67	9	.244	.288	.351
2001 Los Angeles	NL	135	448	99	17	1	21	(9	12)	181	56	60	16	0	107	2	0	2	7	5	.58	12	.221	.250	.404
13 ML YEARS		1716	6646	1794	302	47	166	(71	95)	2688	962	723	467	37	989	26	31	47	409	110	.79	120	.270	.318	.404

Buddy Groom

Pitches: Left **Bats:** Left **Pos:** RP-70   **Ht:** 6'2" **Wt:** 207 **Born:** 7/10/65 **Age:** 36

			HOW MUCH HE PITCHED					WHAT HE GAVE UP									THE RESULTS					
Year Team	Lg	G	GS	CG	GF	IP	BFP	H	R	ER	HR	SH	SF	HB	TBB	IBB	SO	WP	Bk	W	L	Pct.	ShO	Sv-Op	Hld	ERA
1992 Detroit	AL	12	7	0	3	38.2	177	48	28	25	4	3	2	0	22	4	15	0	1	0	5	.000	0	1-2	0	5.82
1993 Detroit	AL	19	3	0	6	36.2	170	48	25	25	4	2	4	2	13	5	15	2	1	0	2	.000	0	0-0	1	6.14
1994 Detroit	AL	40	0	0	10	32	139	31	14	14	4	0	3	2	13	2	27	0	0	1	0	1.000	0	1-1	11	3.94
1995 Det-Fla		37	4	0	11	55.2	274	81	47	46	8	2	2	2	32	4	35	3	0	2	5	.286	0	1-3	0	7.44
1996 Oakland	AL	72	1	0	16	77.1	341	85	37	33	8	2	0	3	34	3	57	5	0	5	0	1.000	0	2-4	10	3.84
1997 Oakland	AL	78	0	0	7	64.2	285	75	38	37	9	4	0	4	24	1	45	3	0	2	2	.500	0	3-5	12	5.15

Year Team	Lg	G	GS	CG	GF	IP	BFP	H	R	ER	HR	SH	SF	HB	TBB	IBB	SO	WP	Bk	W	L	Pct.	ShO	Sv-Op	Hld	ERA
					HOW MUCH HE PITCHED					WHAT HE GAVE UP												THE RESULTS				
1998 Oakland	AL	75	0	0	13	57.1	251	62	30	27	4	1	3	1	20	1	36	1	0	3	1	.750	0	0-6	16	4.24
1999 Oakland	AL	76	0	0	6	46	196	48	29	26	1	2	0	1	18	5	32	2	1	3	2	.600	0	0-3	27	5.09
2000 Baltimore	AL	70	0	0	14	59.1	260	63	37	32	5	5	5	0	21	2	44	1	0	2	4	.667	0	4-11	27	4.85
2001 Baltimore	AL	70	0	0	35	66	265	64	28	26	4	0	1	1	9	0	54	2	0	1	4	.200	0	11-13	16	3.55
1995 Detroit	AL	23	4	0	6	40.2	203	55	35	34	6	2	2	2	26	4	23	3	0	1	3	.250	0	1-3	0	7.52
Florida	NL	14	0	0	5	15	71	26	12	12	2	0	0	0	6	0	12	0	0	1	2	.333	0	0-0	0	7.20
10 ML YEARS		549	15	0	123	533.2	2358	605	313	291	51	17	24	12	206	27	360	19	3	22	25	.468	0	23-48	120	4.91

Mark Grudzielanek

Bats: Right **Throws:** Right **Pos:** 2B-133   **Ht:** 6'1" **Wt:** 185 **Born:** 6/30/70 **Age:** 32

Year Team	Lg	G	AB	H	2B	3B	HR	(Hm	Rd)	TB	R	RBI	TBB	IBB	SO	HBP	SH	SF	SB	CS	SB%	GDP	Avg	OBP	SLG
							BATTING												BASERUNNING				PERCENTAGES		
1995 Montreal	NL	78	269	66	12	2	1	(1	0)	85	27	20	14	4	47	7	3	0	8	3	.73	7	.245	.300	.316
1996 Montreal	NL	153	657	201	34	4	6	(5	1)	261	99	49	26	3	83	9	1	3	33	7	.83	10	.306	.340	.397
1997 Montreal	NL	156	649	177	54	3	4	(1	3)	249	76	51	23	0	76	10	3	3	25	9	.74	13	.273	.307	.384
1998 Mon-LA	NL	156	589	160	21	1	10	(5	5)	213	62	62	26	2	73	11	8	7	18	5	.78	18	.272	.311	.362
1999 Los Angeles	NL	123	488	159	23	5	7	(4	3)	213	72	46	31	1	65	10	2	3	6	6	.50	13	.326	.376	.436
2000 Los Angeles	NL	148	617	172	35	6	7	(4	3)	240	101	49	45	0	81	9	2	3	12	3	.80	16	.279	.335	.389
2001 Los Angeles	NL	133	539	146	21	3	13	(8	5)	212	83	55	28	0	83	11	3	5	4	4	.50	9	.271	.317	.393
1998 Montreal	NL	105	396	109	15	1	8	(3	5)	150	51	41	21	1	50	9	5	4	11	5	.69	11	.275	.323	.379
Los Angeles	NL	51	193	51	6	0	2	(2	0)	63	11	21	5	1	23	2	3	3	7	0	1.00	7	.264	.286	.326
7 ML YEARS		947	3808	1081	200	24	48	(28	20)	1473	520	332	193	10	508	67	22	24	106	37	.74	86	.284	.328	.387

Eddie Guardado

Pitches: Left **Bats:** Right **Pos:** RP-67   **Ht:** 6'0" **Wt:** 194 **Born:** 10/2/70 **Age:** 31

Year Team	Lg	G	GS	CG	GF	IP	BFP	H	R	ER	HR	SH	SF	HB	TBB	IBB	SO	WP	Bk	W	L	Pct.	ShO	Sv-Op	Hld	ERA
					HOW MUCH HE PITCHED					WHAT HE GAVE UP												THE RESULTS				
1993 Minnesota	AL	19	16	0	2	94.2	426	123	68	65	13	1	3	1	36	2	46	0	0	3	8	.273	0	0-0	0	6.18
1994 Minnesota	AL	4	4	0	0	17	81	26	16	16	3	1	2	0	4	0	8	0	0	2	0	.000	0	0-0	0	8.47
1995 Minnesota	AL	51	5	0	10	91.1	410	99	54	52	13	6	5	0	45	2	71	5	1	4	9	.308	0	2-5	5	5.12
1996 Minnesota	AL	83	0	0	17	73.2	313	61	45	43	12	6	4	3	34	4	74	3	0	6	5	.545	0	4-7	18	5.25
1997 Minnesota	AL	69	0	0	20	46	201	45	23	20	7	2	1	2	17	2	54	2	0	0	4	.000	0	1-1	13	3.91
1998 Minnesota	AL	79	0	0	12	65.2	286	66	34	33	10	3	6	0	28	6	53	2	0	3	1	.750	0	0-4	16	4.52
1999 Minnesota	AL	63	0	0	13	48	197	37	24	24	6	2	1	2	25	4	50	0	0	2	5	.286	0	2-4	15	4.50
2000 Minnesota	AL	70	0	0	36	61.2	262	55	27	27	14	3	2	1	25	3	52	1	1	7	4	.636	0	9-11	8	3.94
2001 Minnesota	AL	67	0	0	26	66.2	270	47	27	26	5	5	3	1	23	4	67	4	0	7	1	.875	0	12-14	14	3.51
9 ML YEARS		505	25	0	136	564.2	2446	559	318	306	83	29	27	10	236	27	475	17	2	32	39	.451	0	30-46	89	4.88

Vladimir Guerrero

Bats: Right **Throws:** Right **Pos:** RF-158   **Ht:** 6'3" **Wt:** 205 **Born:** 2/9/76 **Age:** 26

Year Team	Lg	G	AB	H	2B	3B	HR	(Hm	Rd)	TB	R	RBI	TBB	IBB	SO	HBP	SH	SF	SB	CS	SB%	GDP	Avg	OBP	SLG
							BATTING												BASERUNNING				PERCENTAGES		
1996 Montreal	NL	9	27	5	0	0	1	(0	1)	8	2	1	0	0	3	0	0	0	0	0	—	1	.185	.185	.296
1997 Montreal	NL	90	325	98	22	2	11	(5	6)	157	44	40	19	2	39	7	0	3	3	4	.43	11	.302	.350	.483
1998 Montreal	NL	159	623	202	37	7	38	(19	19)	367	108	109	42	13	95	7	0	5	11	9	.55	15	.324	.371	.589
1999 Montreal	NL	160	610	193	37	5	42	(23	19)	366	102	131	55	14	62	7	0	2	14	7	.67	18	.316	.378	.600
2000 Montreal	NL	154	571	197	28	11	44	(25	19)	379	101	123	58	23	74	8	0	4	9	10	.47	15	.345	.410	.664
2001 Montreal	NL	159	599	184	45	4	34	(21	13)	339	107	108	60	24	88	9	0	3	37	16	.70	24	.307	.377	.566
6 ML YEARS		731	2755	879	169	29	170	(93	77)	1616	464	512	234	76	361	38	0	17	74	46	.62	84	.319	.378	.587

Wilton Guerrero

Bats: B **Throws:** R **Pos:** PH/PR-29; SS-16; 2B-11; LF-6; 3B-4; DH-1   **Ht:** 6'0" **Wt:** 175 **Born:** 10/24/74 **Age:** 27

Year Team	Lg	G	AB	H	2B	3B	HR	(Hm	Rd)	TB	R	RBI	TBB	IBB	SO	HBP	SH	SF	SB	CS	SB%	GDP	Avg	OBP	SLG
							BATTING												BASERUNNING				PERCENTAGES		
2001 Louisville *	AAA	54	227	69	14	2	0	—	—	87	23	28	12	0	30	1	3	0	12	5	.71	4	.304	.342	.383
1996 Los Angeles	NL	5	2	0	0	0	0	(0	0)	1	0	0	0	0	2	0	0	0	0	0	—	0	.000	.000	.000
1997 Los Angeles	NL	111	357	104	10	9	4	(2	2)	144	39	32	8	1	52	0	13	2	6	5	.55	7	.291	.305	.403
1998 LA-Mon	NL	116	402	114	14	9	2	(0	2)	152	50	27	14	0	63	1	6	3	8	2	.80	4	.284	.307	.378
1999 Montreal	NL	132	315	92	15	7	2	(0	2)	127	42	31	13	0	38	2	10	0	7	6	.54	4	.292	.324	.403
2000 Montreal	NL	127	288	77	7	2	2	(2	0)	94	30	23	19	0	41	0	6	1	8	1	.89	6	.267	.312	.326
2001 Cincinnati	NL	60	142	48	5	1	1	(1	0)	58	16	8	3	0	17	0	2	0	5	2	.71	1	.338	.352	.408
1998 Los Angeles	NL	64	180	51	4	3	0	(0	0)	61	21	7	4	0	33	1	3	2	5	2	.71	3	.283	.299	.339
Montreal	NL	52	222	63	10	6	2	(0	2)	91	29	20	10	0	30	0	3	1	3	0	1.00	1	.284	.313	.410
6 ML YEARS		551	1506	435	51	28	11	(5	6)	575	178	121	57	1	213	3	37	6	34	16	.68	22	.289	.315	.382

Carlos Guillen

Bats: Both **Throws:** Right **Pos:** SS-137; PH/PR-7; DH-1   **Ht:** 6'1" **Wt:** 180 **Born:** 9/30/75 **Age:** 26

Year Team	Lg	G	AB	H	2B	3B	HR	(Hm	Rd)	TB	R	RBI	TBB	IBB	SO	HBP	SH	SF	SB	CS	SB%	GDP	Avg	OBP	SLG
							BATTING												BASERUNNING				PERCENTAGES		
1998 Seattle	AL	10	39	13	1	1	0	(0	0)	16	9	5	3	0	9	0	0	0	2	0	1.00	0	.333	.381	.410
1999 Seattle	AL	5	19	3	0	0	1	(1	0)	6	2	3	1	0	6	0	1	0	0	0	—	0	.158	.200	.316
2000 Seattle	AL	90	288	74	15	2	7	(3	4)	114	45	42	28	0	53	2	7	3	1	3	.25	6	.257	.324	.396
2001 Seattle	AL	140	456	118	21	4	5	(2	3)	162	72	53	53	0	89	1	7	6	4	1	.80	9	.259	.333	.355
4 ML YEARS		245	802	208	37	7	13	(6	7)	298	128	103	85	0	157	3	15	9	7	4	.64	16	.259	.329	.372

Jose Guillen

Bats: Right **Throws:** Right **Pos:** RF-36; PH/PR-5; DH-4   **Ht:** 5'11" **Wt:** 195 **Born:** 5/17/76 **Age:** 26

						BATTING												BASERUNNING				PERCENTAGES		
Year Team	Lg	G	AB	H	2B	3B	HR	(Hm | Rd)	TB	R	RBI	TBB	IBB	SO	HBP	SH	SF	SB	CS	SB%	GDP	Avg	OBP	SLG
2001 Durham *	AAA	33	119	35	9	0	7			65	18	29	3	0	28	0	0	2	0	0	—	3	.294	.306	.546
1997 Pittsburgh	NL	143	498	133	20	5	14	(5 | 9)	205	58	70	17	0	88	8	0	3	1	2	.33	16	.267	.300	.412
1998 Pittsburgh	NL	153	573	153	38	2	14	(10 | 4)	237	60	84	21	0	100	6	1	4	3	5	.38	7	.267	.298	.414
1999 Pit-TB		87	288	73	16	0	3	(1 | 2)	98	42	31	20	2	57	7	1	2	1	0	1.00	16	.253	.315	.340
2000 Tampa Bay	AL	105	316	80	16	5	10	(5 | 5)	136	40	41	18	1	65	13	2	0	3	1	.75	6	.253	.320	.430
2001 Tampa Bay	AL	41	135	37	5	0	3	(0 | 3)	51	14	11	6	2	26	3	0	1	2	3	.40	2	.274	.317	.378
1999 Pittsburgh	NL	40	120	32	6	0	1	(1 | 1)	41	18	18	10	1	21	0	1	1	1	0	1.00	7	.267	.321	.342
Tampa Bay	AL	47	168	41	10	0	2	(1 | 1)	57	24	13	10	1	36	7	0	1	0	0	—	9	.244	.312	.339
5 ML YEARS		529	1810	476	95	12	44	(21 | 23)	727	214	237	82	5	336	37	4	10	10	11	.48	47	.263	.307	.402

Mike Gulan

Bats: Right **Throws:** Right **Pos:** PH/PR-5; 3B-1   **Ht:** 6'1" **Wt:** 190 **Born:** 12/18/70 **Age:** 31

						BATTING												BASERUNNING				PERCENTAGES		
Year Team	Lg	G	AB	H	2B	3B	HR	(Hm | Rd)	TB	R	RBI	TBB	IBB	SO	HBP	SH	SF	SB	CS	SB%	GDP	Avg	OBP	SLG
1992 Hamilton	A-	62	242	66	8	4	7	—	—	103	33	36	23	0	53	1	0	4	12	4	.75	7	.273	.333	.426
1993 Springfield	A	132	455	118	28	4	23	—	—	223	81	76	34	0	135	9	3	3	8	4	.67	4	.259	.321	.490
1994 St. Pete	A+	120	466	113	30	2	8	—	—	171	39	56	26	2	108	2	0	6	2	8	.20	8	.242	.282	.367
1995 Arkansas	AA	64	242	76	16	3	12	—	—	134	47	48	11	1	52	6	0	1	4	2	.67	4	.314	.358	.554
Louisville	AAA	58	195	46	10	4	5	—	—	79	21	27	10	1	53	3	0	2	2	2	.50	6	.236	.281	.405
1996 Louisville	AAA	123	419	107	27	4	17	—	—	193	47	55	26	1	119	7	1	2	7	2	.78	10	.255	.308	.461
1997 Louisville	AAA	116	412	110	20	6	14	—	—	184	50	61	28	0	121	3	1	3	5	2	.71	12	.267	.316	.447
1998 Portland	AA	46	160	49	16	2	5	—	—	84	24	23	10	0	40	1	0	1	3	2	.60	6	.306	.349	.525
1999 Calgary	AAA	84	286	79	23	2	13	—	—	145	41	51	10	0	82	4	1	3	2	1	.67	9	.276	.307	.507
2000 Calgary	AAA	119	426	135	40	2	17	—	—	230	66	74	27	1	94	8	0	3	5	1	.83	12	.317	.367	.540
2001 Calgary	AAA	124	485	157	44	2	22	—	—	271	78	92	35	1	145	8	0	5	2	6	.25	12	.324	.375	.559
1997 St. Louis	NL	5	9	0	0	0	0	(0 | 0)	0	2	1	1	0	5	0	0	0	0	0	—	0	.000	.100	.000
2001 Florida	NL	6	6	0	0	0	0	(0 | 0)	0	1	0	2	0	2	0	0	0	0	0	—	0	.000	.250	.000
2 ML YEARS		11	15	0	0	0	0	(0 | 0)	0	3	1	3	0	7	0	0	0	0	0	—	0	.000	.167	.000

Mark Guthrie

Pitches: Left **Bats:** Right **Pos:** RP-54   **Ht:** 6'4" **Wt:** 215 **Born:** 9/22/65 **Age:** 36

		HOW MUCH HE PITCHED						WHAT HE GAVE UP										THE RESULTS						
Year Team	Lg	G	GS	CG	GF	IP	BFP	H	R	ER	HR	SH	SF	HB	TBB	IBB	SO	WP	Bk	W	L	Pct.	ShO	Sv-Op	Hld	ERA
1989 Minnesota	AL	13	8	0	2	57.1	254	66	32	29	7	1	5	1	21	1	38	1	0	2	4	.333	1	0-0	0	4.55
1990 Minnesota	AL	24	21	3	0	144.2	603	154	65	61	8	6	0	1	39	3	101	9	0	7	9	.438	1	0-0	0	3.79
1991 Minnesota	AL	41	12	0	13	98	432	116	52	47	11	4	3	1	41	2	72	7	0	7	5	.583	0	2-2	5	4.32
1992 Minnesota	AL	54	0	0	15	75	303	59	27	24	7	4	2	0	23	7	76	2	0	2	3	.400	0	5-7	19	2.88
1993 Minnesota	AL	22	0	0	2	21	94	20	11	11	2	1	2	0	16	2	15	1	3	2	1	.667	0	0-1	8	4.71
1994 Minnesota	AL	50	2	0	13	51.1	234	65	43	35	8	2	6	2	18	2	38	7	0	4	2	.667	0	1-3	12	6.14
1995 Min-LA		60	0	0	14	62	272	66	33	29	6	4	0	2	25	5	67	5	1	5	5	.500	0	0-2	15	4.21
1996 Los Angeles	NL	66	0	0	16	73	302	65	21	18	3	4	4	1	22	2	56	1	0	2	3	.400	0	1-3	12	2.22
1997 Los Angeles	NL	62	0	0	18	69.1	305	71	44	41	12	10	3	0	30	6	42	2	1	1	4	.200	0	1-4	13	5.32
1998 Los Angeles	NL	53	0	0	11	54	241	56	26	21	3	5	0	2	24	1	45	2	0	2	1	.667	0	0-1	8	3.50
1999 Bos-ChC		57	0	0	15	58.2	254	57	38	35	10	2	3	2	24	5	45	3	0	1	3	.250	0	2-2	14	5.37
2000 ChC-TB-Tor		76	0	0	15	71.1	315	70	41	37	8	4	4	2	37	9	63	13	0	3	6	.333	0	0-4	10	4.67
2001 Oakland	AL	54	0	0	11	52.1	225	49	29	26	7	1	3	4	20	1	52	3	0	6	2	.750	0	1-3	12	4.47
1995 Minnesota	AL	36	0	0	7	42.1	181	47	22	21	5	2	0	1	16	3	48	3	1	5	3	.625	0	0-2	10	4.46
Los Angeles	NL	24	0	0	7	19.2	91	19	11	8	1	2	0	1	9	2	19	2	0	0	2	.000	0	0-0	5	3.66
1999 Boston	AL	46	0	0	15	46.1	207	50	32	30	9	0	3	2	20	3	36	2	0	1	1	.500	0	2-2	12	5.83
Chicago	NL	11	0	0	0	12.1	47	7	6	5	1	2	0	0	4	2	9	1	0	0	2	.000	0	0-0	2	3.65
2000 Chicago	NL	19	0	0	3	18.2	82	17	11	10	1	2	3	1	10	4	17	4	0	2	3	.400	0	0-0	3	4.82
Tampa Bay	AL	34	0	0	7	32	145	33	18	16	4	1	0	0	18	5	26	7	0	1	1	.500	0	0-3	4	4.50
Toronto	AL	23	0	0	5	20.2	88	20	12	11	3	1	1	1	9	0	20	2	0	0	2	.000	0	0-1	3	4.79
13 ML YEARS		632	43	3	145	888	3834	914	462	414	92	48	35	18	340	46	710	56	5	44	48	.478	1	13-32	128	4.20

Ricky Gutierrez

Bats: Right **Throws:** Right **Pos:** SS-144; PH/PR-5   **Ht:** 6'1" **Wt:** 190 **Born:** 5/23/70 **Age:** 32

						BATTING												BASERUNNING				PERCENTAGES		
Year Team	Lg	G	AB	H	2B	3B	HR	(Hm | Rd)	TB	R	RBI	TBB	IBB	SO	HBP	SH	SF	SB	CS	SB%	GDP	Avg	OBP	SLG
1993 San Diego	NL	133	438	110	10	5	5	(5 | 0)	145	76	26	50	2	97	5	1	1	4	3	.57	7	.251	.334	.331
1994 San Diego	NL	90	275	66	11	2	1	(1 | 0)	84	27	28	32	1	54	2	2	3	2	6	.25	8	.240	.321	.305
1995 Houston	NL	52	156	43	6	0	0	(0 | 0)	49	22	12	10	3	33	1	1	1	5	0	1.00	4	.276	.321	.314
1996 Houston	NL	89	218	62	8	1	1	(1 | 0)	75	28	15	23	3	42	3	4	1	6	1	.86	4	.284	.359	.344
1997 Houston	NL	102	303	79	14	4	3	(0 | 3)	110	33	34	21	2	50	3	0	0	5	2	.71	17	.261	.315	.363
1998 Houston	NL	141	491	128	24	3	2	(1 | 1)	164	55	46	54	5	84	6	3	7	13	7	.65	20	.261	.337	.334
1999 Houston	NL	85	268	70	7	5	1	(1 | 0)	90	33	25	37	4	45	2	3	1	2	5	.29	9	.261	.354	.336
2000 Chicago	NL	125	449	124	19	2	11	(7 | 4)	180	73	56	66	0	58	7	16	4	8	2	.80	10	.276	.375	.401
2001 Chicago	NL	147	528	153	23	3	10	(7 | 3)	212	76	66	40	0	56	10	17	11	4	3	.57	13	.290	.345	.402
9 ML YEARS		964	3126	835	122	25	34	(23 | 11)	1109	423	308	333	20	519	39	47	29	49	29	.63	92	.267	.342	.355

Cristian Guzman

Bats: Both **Throws:** Right **Pos:** SS-118; PH/PR-2   **Ht:** 6'0" **Wt:** 195 **Born:** 3/21/78 **Age:** 24

						BATTING												BASERUNNING				PERCENTAGES		
Year Team	Lg	G	AB	H	2B	3B	HR	(Hm | Rd)	TB	R	RBI	TBB	IBB	SO	HBP	SH	SF	SB	CS	SB%	GDP	Avg	OBP	SLG
2001 Twins *	R	5	16	4	0	1	0	—	—	6	4	0	2	0	4	1	0	0	1	0	1.00	1	.250	.368	.375
1999 Minnesota	AL	131	420	95	12	3	1	(1 | 0)	116	47	26	22	0	90	3	7	4	9	7	.56	5	.226	.267	.276
2000 Minnesota	AL	156	631	156	25	20	8	(3 | 5)	245	89	54	46	1	101	2	7	4	28	10	.74	5	.247	.299	.388

90

<table>
<tr><td colspan="26">BATTING</td><td colspan="4">BASERUNNING</td><td colspan="3">PERCENTAGES</td></tr>
</table>

Year Team	Lg	G	AB	H	2B	3B	HR	(Hm	Rd)	TB	R	RBI	TBB	IBB	SO	HBP	SH	SF	SB	CS	SB%	GDP	Avg	OBP	SLG
2001 Minnesota	AL	118	493	149	28	14	10	(7	3)	235	80	51	21	0	78	5	8	0	25	8	.76	6	.302	.337	.477
3 ML YEARS		405	1544	400	65	37	19	(11	8)	596	216	131	89	1	269	10	22	8	62	25	.71	16	.259	.302	.386

Edwards Guzman

Bats: L **Throws:** R **Pos:** C-26; PH/PR-24; 1B-7; 3B-7; 2B-3; LF-2   **Ht:** 5'10" **Wt:** 205 **Born:** 9/11/76 **Age:** 25

Year Team	Lg	G	AB	H	2B	3B	HR	(Hm	Rd)	TB	R	RBI	TBB	IBB	SO	HBP	SH	SF	SB	CS	SB%	GDP	Avg	OBP	SLG
1996 San Jose	A+	106	367	99	19	5	1	—	—	131	41	40	39	4	60	5	6	5	3	5	.38	6	.270	.344	.357
1997 Shreveport	AA	118	380	108	15	4	3	—	—	140	52	42	33	4	57	1	5	3	3	1	.75	6	.284	.341	.368
1998 Fresno	AAA	102	325	99	17	0	9	—	—	143	50	48	24	4	47	3	3	1	1	0	1.00	4	.305	.357	.440
1999 Fresno	AAA	90	358	98	13	0	7	—	—	132	48	48	17	0	50	3	4	4	6	5	.55	11	.274	.309	.369
2000 Fresno	AAA	115	421	118	24	1	6	—	—	162	52	52	17	0	43	5	4	3	1	5	.17	17	.280	.314	.385
2001 Fresno	AAA	18	72	26	3	2	0	—	—	33	13	11	4	1	3	0	2	0	0	1	.00	1	.361	.395	.458
1999 San Francisco	NL	14	15	0	0	0	0	(0	0)	0	0	0	0	0	4	0	1	0	0	0	—	0	.000	.000	.000
2001 San Francisco	NL	61	115	28	6	0	3	(1	2)	43	8	7	5	2	16	0	0	1	0	0	—	2	.243	.273	.374
2 ML YEARS		75	130	28	6	0	3	(1	2)	43	8	7	5	2	20	0	1	1	0	0	—	2	.215	.243	.331

Geraldo Guzman

Pitches: Right **Bats:** Right **Pos:** RP-4   **Ht:** 6'2" **Wt:** 186 **Born:** 11/28/72 **Age:** 29

Year Team	Lg	G	GS	CG	GF	IP	BFP	H	R	ER	HR	SH	SF	HB	TBB	IBB	SO	WP	Bk	W	L	Pct.	ShO	Sv-Op	Hld	ERA
2000 Tucson	AAA	6	6	1	0	38	148	23	7	6	3	0	0	3	10	1	44	0	0	4	1	.800	1	0- -	—	1.42
El Paso	AA	17	7	0	5	50.1	220	47	23	21	2	3	0	3	22	2	53	3	0	3	3	.500	0	3- -	—	3.75
2001 Tucson	AAA	20	14	0	1	94.2	403	92	56	51	9	4	4	4	30	1	85	3	3	3	6	.333	0	0- -	—	4.85
2000 Arizona	NL	13	10	0	0	60.1	259	66	36	36	8	3	1	2	22	0	52	3	0	5	4	.556	0	0-1	0	5.37
2001 Arizona	NL	4	0	0	0	9.1	37	7	4	3	2	0	0	0	3	1	4	0	0	0	0	—	0	0-0	0	2.89
2 ML YEARS		17	10	0	0	69.2	296	73	40	39	10	3	1	2	25	1	56	3	0	5	4	.556	0	0-1	0	5.04

Juan Guzman

Pitches: Right **Bats:** Right **2000 Pos:** SP-1   **Ht:** 5'11" **Wt:** 195 **Born:** 10/28/66 **Age:** 35

Year Team	Lg	G	GS	CG	GF	IP	BFP	H	R	ER	HR	SH	SF	HB	TBB	IBB	SO	WP	Bk	W	L	Pct.	ShO	Sv-Op	Hld	ERA
2001 Orlando *	AA	2	2	0	0	12	45	8	1	1	0	0	0	0	4	0	9	0	0	2	0	1.000	0	0- -	—	0.75
Durham *	AAA	10	10	0	0	60.1	259	50	35	32	7	5	4	5	30	0	42	4	0	4	2	.667	0	0- -	—	4.77
1991 Toronto	AL	23	23	1	0	138.2	574	98	53	46	6	2	5	4	66	0	123	10	0	10	3	.769	0	0-0	0	2.99
1992 Toronto	AL	28	28	1	0	180.2	733	135	56	53	6	5	3	1	72	2	165	14	2	16	5	.762	0	0-0	0	2.64
1993 Toronto	AL	33	33	2	0	221	963	211	107	98	17	5	9	3	110	2	194	26	1	14	3	.824	1	0-0	0	3.99
1994 Toronto	AL	25	25	2	0	147.1	671	165	100	93	20	1	6	3	76	1	124	13	1	12	11	.522	0	0-0	0	5.68
1995 Toronto	AL	24	24	3	0	135.1	619	151	101	95	13	3	2	3	73	6	94	8	0	4	14	.222	0	0-0	0	6.32
1996 Toronto	AL	27	27	4	0	187.2	756	158	68	61	20	2	2	7	53	3	165	7	0	11	8	.579	1	0-0	0	2.93
1997 Toronto	AL	13	13	0	0	60	261	48	42	33	14	1	2	2	31	0	52	4	0	3	6	.333	0	0-0	0	4.95
1998 Tor-Bal	AL	33	33	2	0	211	918	193	117	102	23	2	5	8	98	2	168	11	0	10	16	.385	0	0-0	0	4.35
1999 Bal-Cin	AL	33	33	2	0	200	864	194	96	83	28	7	4	4	86	6	155	12	2	11	12	.478	1	0-0	0	3.74
2000 Tampa Bay	AL	1	1	0	0	1.2	14	7	8	8	2	1	0	0	3	0	0	0	0	1	0	1.000	0	0-0	0	43.20
1998 Toronto	AL	22	22	2	0	145	632	133	83	71	19	2	3	6	65	1	113	6	0	6	12	.333	0	0-0	0	4.41
Baltimore	AL	11	11	0	0	66	286	60	34	31	4	0	2	2	33	1	55	5	0	4	4	.500	0	0-0	0	4.23
1999 Baltimore	AL	21	21	1	0	122.2	544	124	63	57	18	4	3	3	65	3	95	7	2	5	9	.357	1	0-0	0	4.18
Cincinnati	NL	12	12	1	0	77.1	320	70	33	26	10	3	1	1	21	3	60	5	0	6	3	.667	0	0-0	0	3.03
10 ML YEARS		240	240	17	0	1483.1	6373	1360	750	672	149	29	38	35	667	22	1243	105	6	91	79	.535	3	0-0	0	4.08

Tony Gwynn

Bats: Left **Throws:** Left **Pos:** PH/PR-53; RF-17; DH-1   **Ht:** 5'11" **Wt:** 225 **Born:** 5/9/60 **Age:** 42

Year Team	Lg	G	AB	H	2B	3B	HR	(Hm	Rd)	TB	R	RBI	TBB	IBB	SO	HBP	SH	SF	SB	CS	SB%	GDP	Avg	OBP	SLG
1982 San Diego	NL	54	190	55	12	2	1	(0	1)	74	33	17	14	0	16	0	4	1	8	3	.73	5	.289	.337	.389
1983 San Diego	NL	86	304	94	12	2	1	(0	1)	113	34	37	23	5	21	0	4	3	7	4	.64	9	.309	.355	.372
1984 San Diego	NL	158	606	213	21	10	5	(3	2)	269	88	71	59	13	23	2	6	2	33	18	.65	15	.351	.410	.444
1985 San Diego	NL	154	622	197	29	5	6	(3	3)	254	90	46	45	4	33	2	1	1	14	11	.56	17	.317	.364	.408
1986 San Diego	NL	160	642	211	33	7	14	(8	6)	300	107	59	52	11	35	3	2	2	37	9	.80	20	.329	.381	.467
1987 San Diego	NL	157	589	218	36	13	7	(5	2)	301	119	54	82	26	35	3	2	4	56	12	.82	13	.370	.447	.511
1988 San Diego	NL	133	521	163	22	5	7	(3	4)	216	64	70	51	13	40	0	4	2	26	11	.70	11	.313	.373	.415
1989 San Diego	NL	158	604	203	27	7	4	(1	3)	256	82	62	56	16	30	1	11	7	40	16	.71	12	.336	.389	.424
1990 San Diego	NL	141	573	177	29	10	4	(2	2)	238	79	72	44	20	23	1	7	4	17	8	.68	13	.309	.357	.415
1991 San Diego	NL	134	530	168	27	11	4	(1	3)	229	69	62	34	8	19	0	0	5	8	8	.50	11	.317	.355	.432
1992 San Diego	NL	128	520	165	27	3	6	(4	2)	216	77	41	46	12	16	0	0	3	3	6	.33	13	.317	.371	.415
1993 San Diego	NL	122	489	175	41	3	7	(4	3)	243	70	59	36	11	19	1	1	7	14	1	.93	18	.358	.398	.497
1994 San Diego	NL	110	419	165	35	1	12	(4	8)	238	79	64	48	16	19	2	1	5	5	0	1.00	20	.394	.454	.568
1995 San Diego	NL	135	535	197	33	1	9	(5	4)	259	82	90	35	10	15	1	0	6	17	5	.77	20	.368	.404	.484
1996 San Diego	NL	116	451	159	27	2	3	(2	1)	199	67	50	39	12	17	1	1	6	11	4	.73	17	.353	.400	.441
1997 San Diego	NL	149	592	220	49	2	17	(8	9)	324	97	119	43	12	28	3	1	12	12	5	.71	12	.372	.409	.547
1998 San Diego	NL	127	461	148	35	0	16	(5	11)	231	65	69	35	6	18	1	0	8	3	1	.75	14	.321	.364	.501
1999 San Diego	NL	111	411	139	27	0	10	(5	5)	196	59	62	29	5	14	2	0	4	7	2	.78	15	.338	.381	.477
2000 San Diego	NL	36	127	41	12	0	1	(1	0)	56	17	17	9	2	4	1	0	3	0	1	.00	4	.323	.364	.441
2001 San Diego	NL	71	102	33	9	1	1	(0	1)	47	5	17	10	1	9	0	0	0	1	0	1.00	5	.324	.384	.461
20 ML YEARS		2440	9288	3141	543	85	135	(66	69)	4259	1383	1138	790	203	434	24	45	85	319	125	.72	260	.338	.388	.459

Luther Hackman

Pitches: Right Bats: Right Pos: RP-35
Ht: 6'4" Wt: 195 Born: 10/10/74 Age: 27

		HOW MUCH HE PITCHED						WHAT HE GAVE UP										THE RESULTS						
Year Team	Lg	G	GS	CG	GF	IP	BFP	H	R	ER	HR	SH	SF	HB	TBB	IBB	SO	WP	Bk	W	L	Pct.	ShO	Sv-Op	Hld	ERA
1994 Rockies	R	12	12	0	0	55.2	234	50	21	13	1	0	0	1	16	0	63	5	1	1	3	.250	0	0--	—	2.10
1995 Asheville	A	28	28	2	0	165	710	162	95	85	11	3	3	14	65	0	108	9	7	11	11	.500	0	0--	—	4.64
1996 Salem	A+	21	21	1	0	110.1	484	93	60	52	2	4	7	5	69	1	83	6	2	5	7	.417	0	0--	—	4.24
1997 New Haven	AA	10	10	0	0	50.2	241	58	49	44	11	5	2	5	34	1	34	4	3	0	6	.000	0	0--	—	7.82
Salem	A+	15	15	2	0	80.2	384	99	60	52	14	4	5	9	37	0	59	8	0	1	4	.200	0	0--	—	5.80
1998 New Haven	AA	28	23	1	2	139	640	169	102	84	18	7	7	10	54	1	90	10	2	3	12	.200	0	0--	—	5.44
1999 Carolina	AA	11	10	0	0	62.1	271	53	33	28	4	2	1	4	28	0	50	4	0	4	3	.571	0	0--	—	4.04
Colo Sprngs	AAA	15	15	1	0	101	445	106	49	42	7	4	3	6	44	2	88	2	2	7	6	.538	1	0--	—	3.74
2000 Memphis	AAA	21	21	0	0	119.2	522	134	71	63	11	5	3	5	36	1	66	1	0	8	9	.471	0	0--	—	4.74
2001 New Haven	AA	3	1	0	0	4	15	2	2	1	0	0	1	0	1	0	5	0	0	0	0	—	0	0--	—	2.25
Memphis	AAA	16	0	0	5	22.2	86	21	7	7	2	1	0	1	1	0	12	0	0	0	2	.000	0	0--	—	2.78
1999 Colorado	NL	5	3	0	0	16	84	26	19	19	5	2	0	0	12	0	10	0	0	1	2	.333	0	0-0	0	10.69
2000 St. Louis	NL	1	0	0	0	2.2	17	4	3	3	0	2	0	1	4	1	0	0	0	0	0	—	0	0-0	0	10.13
2001 St. Louis	NL	35	0	0	8	35.2	149	28	18	17	7	1	0	2	14	0	24	1	1	1	2	.333	0	1-3	5	4.29
3 ML YEARS		41	3	0	8	54.1	250	58	40	39	12	5	0	3	30	1	34	1	1	2	4	.333	0	1-3	5	6.46

Jerry Hairston Jr.

Bats: Right Throws: Right Pos: 2B-156; PH/PR-3
Ht: 5'10" Wt: 175 Born: 5/29/76 Age: 26

		BATTING																	BASERUNNING				PERCENTAGES		
Year Team	Lg	G	AB	H	2B	3B	HR	(Hm	Rd)	TB	R	RBI	TBB	IBB	SO	HBP	SH	SF	SB	CS	SB%	GDP	Avg	OBP	SLG
1998 Baltimore	AL	6	7	0	0	0	0	(0	0)	0	2	0	0	0	1	0	0	0	0	0	—	0	.000	.000	.000
1999 Baltimore	AL	50	175	47	12	1	4	(1	3)	73	26	17	11	0	24	3	4	0	9	4	.69	2	.269	.323	.417
2000 Baltimore	AL	49	180	46	5	0	5	(2	3)	66	27	19	21	0	22	6	5	0	8	5	.62	8	.256	.353	.367
2001 Baltimore	AL	159	532	124	25	5	8	(5	3)	183	63	47	44	0	73	13	9	4	29	11	.73	12	.233	.305	.344
4 ML YEARS		264	894	217	42	6	17	(8	9)	322	118	83	76	0	120	22	18	4	46	20	.70	22	.243	.316	.360

John Halama

Pitches: Left Bats: Left Pos: SP-17; RP-14
Ht: 6'5" Wt: 210 Born: 2/22/72 Age: 30

		HOW MUCH HE PITCHED						WHAT HE GAVE UP										THE RESULTS						
Year Team	Lg	G	GS	CG	GF	IP	BFP	H	R	ER	HR	SH	SF	HB	TBB	IBB	SO	WP	Bk	W	L	Pct.	ShO	Sv-Op	Hld	ERA
2001 Tacoma *	AAA	3	3	1	0	19	65	9	2	1	1	0	0	0	0	0	22	0	0	2	0	1.000	1	0--	—	0.47
1998 Houston	NL	6	6	0	0	32.1	147	37	21	21	0	3	4	2	13	0	21	2	1	1	1	.500	0	0-0	0	5.85
1999 Seattle	AL	38	24	1	7	179	763	193	88	84	20	5	9	7	56	3	105	4	0	11	10	.524	1	0-0	1	4.22
2000 Seattle	AL	30	30	1	0	166.2	736	206	108	94	19	4	6	2	56	0	87	4	1	14	9	.609	1	0-0	0	5.08
2001 Seattle	AL	31	17	0	6	110.1	485	132	69	58	18	3	4	6	26	0	50	2	0	10	7	.588	0	0-0	1	4.73
4 ML YEARS		105	77	2	13	488.1	2131	568	286	257	57	15	23	17	151	3	263	12	2	36	27	.571	2	0-0	2	4.74

Toby Hall

Bats: Right Throws: Right Pos: C-46; PH/PR-3
Ht: 6'3" Wt: 205 Born: 10/21/75 Age: 26

		BATTING																	BASERUNNING				PERCENTAGES		
Year Team	Lg	G	AB	H	2B	3B	HR	(Hm	Rd)	TB	R	RBI	TBB	IBB	SO	HBP	SH	SF	SB	CS	SB%	GDP	Avg	OBP	SLG
1997 Hudson Val	A-	55	200	50	3	0	1	—	—	56	25	27	13	1	33	1	1	3	0	0	—	3	.250	.295	.280
1998 Chston-SC	A	105	377	121	25	1	6	—	—	166	59	50	39	2	32	5	0	6	3	7	.30	15	.321	.386	.440
1999 St. Pete	A+	56	212	63	13	1	4	—	—	90	24	36	17	0	9	2	1	3	0	2	.00	7	.297	.350	.425
Orlando	AA	46	173	44	7	0	9	—	—	78	20	34	4	1	10	1	1	4	1	1	.50	7	.254	.269	.451
2000 Orlando	AA	68	271	93	14	0	9	—	—	134	37	50	17	2	24	1	0	5	3	2	.60	6	.343	.378	.494
Durham	AAA	47	184	56	15	0	7	—	—	92	21	35	3	0	19	2	0	5	0	0	—	9	.304	.314	.500
2001 Durham	AAA	94	351	125	28	1	19	—	—	212	59	72	29	7	22	3	0	3	1	3	.25	15	.335	.385	.568
2000 Tampa Bay	AL	4	12	2	0	0	1	(0	1)	5	1	1	1	0	0	0	0	0	0	0	—	0	.167	.231	.417
2001 Tampa Bay	AL	49	188	56	16	0	4	(1	3)	84	28	30	4	0	16	3	0	1	2	2	.50	5	.298	.321	.447
2 ML YEARS		53	200	58	16	0	5	(1	4)	89	29	31	5	0	16	3	0	1	2	2	.50	5	.290	.316	.445

Roy Halladay

Pitches: Right Bats: Right Pos: SP-16; RP-1
Ht: 6'6" Wt: 225 Born: 5/14/77 Age: 25

		HOW MUCH HE PITCHED						WHAT HE GAVE UP										THE RESULTS						
Year Team	Lg	G	GS	CG	GF	IP	BFP	H	R	ER	HR	SH	SF	HB	TBB	IBB	SO	WP	Bk	W	L	Pct.	ShO	Sv-Op	Hld	ERA
2001 Dunedin *	A+	13	0	0	5	22.2	99	28	12	10	1	1	1	2	3	0	15	3	0	0	1	.000	0	2--	—	3.97
Tennessee *	AA	5	5	3	0	34	132	25	9	8	2	0	0	2	6	0	29	2	0	2	1	.667	0	0--	—	2.12
Syracuse *	AAA	2	2	0	0	14	55	12	5	5	2	1	0	0	0	0	13	2	0	1	0	1.000	0	0--	—	3.21
1998 Toronto	AL	2	2	1	0	14	53	9	4	3	2	0	0	0	2	0	13	0	0	1	0	1.000	0	0-0	0	1.93
1999 Toronto	AL	36	18	1	2	149.1	668	156	76	65	19	3	4	4	79	1	82	6	0	8	7	.533	1	1-1	2	3.92
2000 Toronto	AL	19	13	0	4	67.2	349	107	87	80	14	2	3	2	42	0	44	6	1	4	7	.364	0	0-0	0	10.64
2001 Toronto	AL	17	16	1	0	105.1	432	97	41	37	3	3	1	1	25	0	96	4	1	5	3	.625	1	0-0	0	3.16
4 ML YEARS		74	49	3	6	336.1	1502	369	208	185	38	8	8	7	148	1	235	16	2	18	17	.514	2	1-1	2	4.95

Shane Halter

Bats: R Throws: R Pos: 3B-74; SS-62; 1B-8; DH-1; PH/PR-1
Ht: 6'0" Wt: 180 Born: 11/8/69 Age: 32

		BATTING																	BASERUNNING				PERCENTAGES		
Year Team	Lg	G	AB	H	2B	3B	HR	(Hm	Rd)	TB	R	RBI	TBB	IBB	SO	HBP	SH	SF	SB	CS	SB%	GDP	Avg	OBP	SLG
1997 Kansas City	AL	74	123	34	5	1	2	(1	1)	47	16	10	10	0	28	2	4	0	4	3	.57	1	.276	.341	.382
1998 Kansas City	AL	86	204	45	12	0	2	(0	2)	63	17	13	12	0	38	1	7	2	2	5	.29	3	.221	.265	.309
1999 New York	NL	7	0	0	0	0	0	(0	0)	0	0	0	0	0	0	0	0	0	0	0	—	0			
2000 Detroit	AL	105	238	62	12	2	3	(0	3)	87	26	27	14	0	49	1	10	2	5	2	.71	5	.261	.302	.366
2001 Detroit	AL	136	450	128	32	7	12	(4	8)	210	53	65	37	2	100	7	7	6	3	3	.50	14	.284	.344	.467
5 ML YEARS		408	1015	269	61	10	19	(5	14)	407	112	115	73	2	215	11	28	10	14	13	.52	23	.265	.318	.401

Darryl Hamilton

Bats: L **Throws:** R **Pos:** LF-24; PH/PR-18; CF-11; RF-3   **Ht:** 6'1" **Wt:** 192 **Born:** 12/3/64 **Age:** 37

Year Team	Lg	G	AB	H	2B	3B	HR	(Hm	Rd)	TB	R	RBI	TBB	IBB	SO	HBP	SH	SF	SB	CS	SB%	GDP	Avg	OBP	SLG
2001 Colo Sprngs *	AAA	4	13	2	0	0	0	(—	—)	2	0	0	2	0	2	0	0	0	0	0	—	1	.154	.267	.154
1988 Milwaukee	AL	44	103	19	4	0	1	(1	0)	26	14	11	12	0	9	1	0	1	7	3	.70	2	.184	.274	.252
1990 Milwaukee	AL	89	156	46	5	0	1	(1	0)	54	27	18	9	0	12	0	3	0	10	3	.77	2	.295	.333	.346
1991 Milwaukee	AL	122	405	126	15	6	1	(0	1)	156	64	57	33	2	38	0	7	3	16	6	.73	10	.311	.361	.385
1992 Milwaukee	AL	128	470	140	19	7	5	(1	4)	188	67	62	45	0	42	1	4	7	41	14	.75	10	.298	.356	.400
1993 Milwaukee	AL	135	520	161	21	1	9	(5	4)	211	74	48	45	5	62	3	4	1	21	13	.62	9	.310	.367	.406
1994 Milwaukee	AL	36	141	37	10	1	1	(0	1)	52	23	13	15	1	17	0	2	1	3	0	1.00	2	.262	.331	.369
1995 Milwaukee	AL	112	398	108	20	6	5	(3	2)	155	54	44	47	3	35	3	8	3	11	1	.92	9	.271	.350	.389
1996 Texas	AL	148	627	184	29	4	6	(2	4)	239	94	51	54	4	66	2	7	6	15	5	.75	15	.293	.348	.381
1997 San Francisco	NL	125	460	124	23	3	5	(1	4)	168	78	43	61	1	61	0	6	2	15	10	.60	6	.270	.354	.365
1998 SF-Col	NL	148	561	173	28	3	6	(3	3)	225	95	51	82	1	73	3	12	3	13	9	.59	6	.308	.398	.401
1999 Col-NYM	NL	146	505	159	19	4	9	(5	4)	213	82	45	57	0	39	2	3	1	6	8	.43	9	.315	.386	.422
2000 New York	NL	43	105	29	4	1	0	(0	1)	38	20	6	14	0	20	0	0	1	2	0	1.00	3	.276	.358	.362
2001 New York	NL	52	126	27	7	1	1	(0	1)	39	15	5	19	3	20	2	2	2	3	1	.75	2	.214	.322	.310
1998 San Francisco	NL	97	367	108	19	2	1	(1	0)	134	65	26	59	1	53	2	6	2	9	8	.53	6	.294	.393	.365
Colorado	NL	51	194	65	9	1	5	(2	3)	91	30	25	23	1	20	1	6	1	4	1	.80	0	.335	.406	.469
1999 Colorado	NL	91	337	102	11	3	4	(2	2)	131	63	24	38	0	21	1	2	1	4	5	.44	7	.303	.374	.389
New York	NL	55	168	57	8	1	5	(3	2)	82	19	21	19	0	18	1	1	0	2	3	.40	2	.339	.410	.488
13 ML YEARS		1328	4577	1333	204	37	51	(23	28)	1764	707	454	493	20	494	17	58	31	163	73	.69	82	.291	.360	.385

Joey Hamilton

Pitches: Right **Bats:** Right **Pos:** SP-26   **Ht:** 6'4" **Wt:** 230 **Born:** 9/9/70 **Age:** 31

Year Team	Lg	G	GS	CG	GF	IP	BFP	H	R	ER	HR	SH	SF	HB	TBB	IBB	SO	WP	Bk	W	L	Pct.	ShO	Sv-Op	Hld	ERA
2001 Louisville *	AAA	1	1	0	0	5	20	4	3	3	1	0	1	0	1	0	1	0	0	1	0	1.000	0	0--	—	5.40
1994 San Diego	NL	16	16	1	0	108.2	447	98	40	36	7	4	2	6	29	3	61	6	0	9	6	.600	1	0-0	0	2.98
1995 San Diego	NL	31	30	2	1	204.1	850	189	89	70	17	12	4	11	56	5	123	2	0	6	9	.400	2	0-0	0	3.08
1996 San Diego	NL	34	33	3	0	211.2	908	206	100	98	19	6	5	9	83	3	184	14	1	15	9	.625	0	0-0	1	4.17
1997 San Diego	NL	31	29	1	1	192.2	831	199	100	91	22	8	8	12	69	2	124	7	0	12	7	.632	0	0-0	0	4.25
1998 San Diego	NL	34	34	0	0	217.1	958	220	113	103	15	13	6	8	106	10	147	4	0	13	13	.500	0	0-0	0	4.27
1999 Toronto	AL	22	18	0	1	98	440	118	73	71	13	0	2	3	39	0	56	4	1	7	8	.467	0	0-0	1	6.52
2000 Toronto	AL	6	6	0	0	33	135	28	13	13	3	0	1	2	12	0	15	0	0	2	1	.667	0	0-0	0	3.55
2001 Tor-Cin		26	26	0	0	139.2	633	193	100	92	20	6	8	4	44	1	92	5	0	6	10	.375	0	0-0	0	5.93
2001 Toronto	AL	22	22	0	0	122.1	554	170	88	80	17	4	8	3	38	1	82	5	0	5	8	.385	0	0-0	0	5.89
Cincinnati	NL	4	4	0	0	17.1	79	23	12	12	3	2	0	1	6	0	10	0	0	1	2	.333	0	0-0	0	6.23
8 ML YEARS		200	192	7	3	1205.1	5202	1251	628	574	116	49	36	55	438	24	802	42	2	70	63	.526	4	0-0	2	4.29

Jeffrey Hammonds

Bats: Right **Throws:** Right **Pos:** CF-46; PH/PR-3   **Ht:** 6'0" **Wt:** 200 **Born:** 3/5/71 **Age:** 31

Year Team	Lg	G	AB	H	2B	3B	HR	(Hm	Rd)	TB	R	RBI	TBB	IBB	SO	HBP	SH	SF	SB	CS	SB%	GDP	Avg	OBP	SLG
2001 Brewers *	R	1	3	1	0	0	0	(—	—)	1	0	0	0	0	0	0	0	0	0	0	—	0	.333	.333	.333
1993 Baltimore	AL	33	105	32	8	0	3	(2	1)	49	10	19	2	1	16	0	1	2	4	0	1.00	3	.305	.312	.467
1994 Baltimore	AL	68	250	74	18	2	8	(6	2)	120	45	31	17	1	39	2	0	5	5	0	1.00	3	.296	.339	.480
1995 Baltimore	AL	57	178	43	9	1	4	(2	2)	66	18	23	9	0	30	1	1	2	4	2	.67	3	.242	.279	.371
1996 Baltimore	AL	71	248	56	10	1	9	(3	6)	95	38	27	23	1	53	4	6	1	3	3	.50	7	.226	.301	.383
1997 Baltimore	AL	118	397	105	19	3	21	(9	12)	193	71	55	32	1	73	3	0	2	15	1	.94	6	.264	.323	.486
1998 Bal-Cin		89	257	72	16	2	6	(1	5)	110	50	39	39	1	56	3	3	4	8	3	.73	2	.280	.376	.428
1999 Cincinnati	NL	123	262	73	13	0	17	(5	12)	137	43	41	27	0	64	1	2	1	3	6	.33	4	.279	.347	.523
2000 Colorado	NL	122	454	152	24	2	20	(14	6)	240	94	106	44	4	83	5	2	6	14	7	.67	11	.335	.395	.529
2001 Milwaukee	NL	49	174	43	11	1	6	(3	3)	74	20	21	14	1	42	4	0	2	5	3	.63	2	.247	.314	.425
1998 Baltimore	AL	63	171	46	12	1	6	(1	5)	78	36	28	26	1	38	3	0	3	7	2	.78	2	.269	.369	.456
Cincinnati	NL	26	86	26	4	1	0	(0	0)	32	14	11	13	0	18	0	3	1	1	1	.50	0	.302	.390	.372
9 ML YEARS		730	2325	650	128	12	94	(45	49)	1084	389	362	207	10	456	23	15	25	61	25	.71	41	.280	.341	.466

Mike Hampton

Pitches: Left **Bats:** Right **Pos:** SP-32   **Ht:** 5'10" **Wt:** 180 **Born:** 9/9/72 **Age:** 29

Year Team	Lg	G	GS	CG	GF	IP	BFP	H	R	ER	HR	SH	SF	HB	TBB	IBB	SO	WP	Bk	W	L	Pct.	ShO	Sv-Op	Hld	ERA
1993 Seattle	AL	13	3	0	2	17	95	28	20	18	3	1	1	0	17	3	8	1	1	1	3	.250	0	1-1	2	9.53
1994 Houston	NL	44	0	0	7	41.1	181	46	19	17	4	0	0	2	16	1	24	5	1	2	1	.667	0	0-1	10	3.70
1995 Houston	NL	24	24	0	0	150.2	641	141	73	56	13	11	5	4	49	3	115	3	1	9	8	.529	0	0-0	0	3.35
1996 Houston	NL	27	27	2	0	160.1	691	175	79	64	12	10	3	4	49	1	101	7	2	10	10	.500	1	0-0	0	3.59
1997 Houston	NL	34	34	7	0	223	941	217	105	95	16	11	7	2	77	2	139	6	1	15	10	.600	2	0-0	0	3.83
1998 Houston	NL	32	32	1	0	211.2	917	227	92	79	18	7	7	5	81	1	137	4	2	11	7	.611	1	0-0	0	3.36
1999 Houston	NL	34	34	3	0	239	979	206	86	77	12	10	9	5	101	2	177	9	0	22	4	.846	2	0-0	0	2.90
2000 New York	NL	33	33	3	0	217.2	929	194	89	76	10	11	5	8	99	5	151	10	0	15	10	.600	1	0-0	0	3.14
2001 Colorado	NL	32	32	2	0	203	904	236	138	122	31	8	6	8	85	7	122	6	0	14	13	.519	1	0-0	0	5.41
9 ML YEARS		273	219	18	9	1463.2	6278	1470	701	604	119	69	43	37	574	25	974	51	8	99	66	.600	8	1-2	12	3.71

Dave Hansen

Bats: L **Throws:** R **Pos:** PH/PR-55; 1B-25; 3B-21; DH-1; SS-1   **Ht:** 6'0"   **Wt:** 195   **Born:** 11/24/68   **Age:** 33

Year Team	Lg	G	AB	H	2B	3B	HR	(Hm	Rd)	TB	R	RBI	TBB	IBB	SO	HBP	SH	SF	SB	CS	SB%	GDP	Avg	OBP	SLG
2001 Vero Beach *	A+	3	9	0	0	0	0	—	—	0	1	0	1	0	2	0	0	0	0	0	—	0	.000	.100	.000
1990 Los Angeles	NL	5	7	1	0	0	0	(0	0)	1	0	1	0	0	3	0	0	0	0	0	—	0	.143	.143	.143
1991 Los Angeles	NL	53	56	15	4	0	1	(0	1)	22	3	5	2	0	12	0	0	0	1	0	1.00	2	.268	.293	.393
1992 Los Angeles	NL	132	341	73	11	0	6	(1	5)	102	30	22	34	3	49	1	0	2	0	2	.00	9	.214	.286	.299
1993 Los Angeles	NL	84	105	38	3	0	4	(2	2)	53	13	30	21	3	13	0	0	1	0	1	.00	0	.362	.465	.505
1994 Los Angeles	NL	40	44	15	3	0	0	(0	0)	18	3	5	5	0	5	0	0	0	0	0	—	0	.341	.408	.409
1995 Los Angeles	NL	100	181	52	10	0	1	(0	1)	65	19	14	28	4	28	1	0	1	0	0	—	0	.287	.384	.359
1996 Los Angeles	NL	80	104	23	1	0	0	(0	0)	24	7	6	11	1	22	0	0	1	0	0	—	4	.221	.293	.231
1997 Chicago	NL	90	151	47	8	2	3	(1	2)	68	19	21	31	1	32	1	2	1	1	2	.33	0	.311	.429	.450
1999 Los Angeles	NL	100	107	27	8	1	2	(2	0)	43	14	17	26	0	20	2	0	1	0	0	—	2	.252	.404	.402
2000 Los Angeles	NL	102	121	35	6	2	8	(4	4)	69	18	26	26	0	32	0	0	0	0	1	.00	3	.289	.415	.570
2001 Los Angeles	NL	92	140	33	10	0	2	(1	1)	49	13	20	32	5	29	0	0	3	0	1	.00	3	.236	.371	.350
11 ML YEARS		**878**	**1357**	**359**	**64**	**5**	**27**	**(11**	**16)**	**514**	**139**	**167**	**216**	**17**	**245**	**5**	**2**	**10**	**2**	**7**	**.22**	**27**	**.265**	**.365**	**.379**

Pete Harnisch

Pitches: Right   **Bats:** Right   **Pos:** SP-7   **Ht:** 6'0"   **Wt:** 228   **Born:** 9/23/66   **Age:** 35

Year Team	Lg	G	GS	CG	GF	IP	BFP	H	R	ER	HR	SH	SF	HB	TBB	IBB	SO	WP	Bk	W	L	Pct.	ShO	Sv-Op	Hld	ERA
2001 Louisville *	AAA	1	1	0	0	0.1	4	3	3	2	0	0	0	0	0	0	0	0	0	0	1	.000	0	0--	—	54.00
1988 Baltimore	AL	2	2	0	0	13	61	13	8	8	1	2	0	0	9	1	10	1	0	0	2	.000	0	0-0	0	5.54
1989 Baltimore	AL	18	17	2	1	103.1	468	97	55	53	10	4	5	5	64	3	70	5	1	5	9	.357	0	0-0	0	4.62
1990 Baltimore	AL	31	31	3	0	188.2	821	189	96	91	17	6	5	1	86	5	122	2	2	11	11	.500	0	0-0	0	4.34
1991 Houston	NL	33	33	4	0	216.2	900	169	71	65	14	9	7	5	83	3	172	5	2	12	9	.571	2	0-0	0	2.70
1992 Houston	NL	34	34	0	0	206.2	859	182	92	85	18	5	5	5	64	3	164	4	1	9	10	.474	0	0-0	0	3.70
1993 Houston	NL	33	33	5	0	217.2	896	171	84	72	20	9	4	6	79	5	185	3	1	16	9	.640	4	0-0	0	2.98
1994 Houston	NL	17	17	1	0	95	419	100	59	57	13	3	2	3	39	1	62	2	0	8	5	.615	0	0-0	0	5.40
1995 New York	NL	18	18	0	0	110	462	111	55	45	13	4	6	3	24	4	82	0	1	2	8	.200	0	0-0	0	3.68
1996 New York	NL	31	31	2	0	194.2	839	195	103	91	30	13	9	7	61	5	114	7	3	8	12	.400	1	0-0	0	4.21
1997 NYM-Mil		10	8	0	0	39.2	186	48	33	31	6	0	2	1	23	1	22	2	0	1	2	.333	0	0-0	0	7.03
1998 Cincinnati	NL	32	32	2	0	209	854	176	79	73	24	8	5	6	64	4	157	4	1	14	7	.667	1	0-0	0	3.14
1999 Cincinnati	NL	33	33	2	0	198.1	833	190	86	81	25	10	6	5	57	2	120	3	0	16	10	.615	2	0-0	0	3.68
2000 Cincinnati	NL	22	22	3	0	131	562	133	76	69	23	1	4	1	46	1	71	10	0	8	6	.571	1	0-0	0	4.74
2001 Cincinnati	NL	7	7	0	0	35.1	172	48	29	25	9	0	3	1	17	0	17	2	0	1	3	.250	0	0-0	0	6.37
1997 New York	NL	6	5	0	0	25.2	121	35	24	23	5	0	2	1	11	1	12	1	0	0	1	.000	0	0-0	0	8.06
Milwaukee	AL	4	3	0	0	14	65	13	9	8	1	0	0	0	12	0	10	1	0	1	1	.500	0	0-0	0	5.14
14 ML YEARS		**321**	**318**	**24**	**1**	**1959**	**8332**	**1822**	**926**	**846**	**223**	**74**	**63**	**49**	**716**	**38**	**1368**	**50**	**12**	**111**	**103**	**.519**	**11**	**0-0**	**0**	**3.89**

Travis Harper

Pitches: Right   **Bats:** Left   **Pos:** SP-2   **Ht:** 6'4"   **Wt:** 190   **Born:** 5/21/76   **Age:** 26

Year Team	Lg	G	GS	CG	GF	IP	BFP	H	R	ER	HR	SH	SF	HB	TBB	IBB	SO	WP	Bk	W	L	Pct.	ShO	Sv-Op	Hld	ERA
1998 Hudson Val	A-	13	10	0	1	56.1	228	38	14	12	2	1	1	8	20	0	81	4	0	6	2	.750	0	0--	—	1.92
1999 St. Pete	A+	14	14	0	0	81.1	347	82	36	31	4	1	4	10	23	0	79	8	0	4	5	.556	0	0--	—	3.43
Orlando	AA	14	14	1	0	72	319	73	45	43	10	4	5	10	26	0	68	7	0	6	3	.667	1	0--	—	5.38
2000 Orlando	AA	9	9	0	0	51.1	215	49	19	15	1	2	3	7	11	0	33	2	1	3	1	.750	0	0--	—	2.63
Durham	AAA	17	17	0	0	104	435	98	53	49	15	1	0	9	26	1	48	5	0	7	4	.636	0	0--	—	4.24
2001 Durham	AAA	25	25	1	0	155.2	642	140	70	64	25	5	7	12	38	0	115	7	2	12	6	.667	1	0--	—	3.70
2000 Tampa Bay	AL	6	5	1	0	32	141	30	17	17	5	1	1	1	15	0	14	1	0	1	2	.333	1	0-0	0	4.78
2001 Tampa Bay	AL	2	2	0	0	7	36	15	11	6	5	0	0	0	3	0	2	1	0	0	2	.000	0	0-0	0	7.71
2 ML YEARS		**8**	**7**	**1**	**0**	**39**	**177**	**45**	**28**	**23**	**10**	**1**	**1**	**1**	**18**	**0**	**16**	**2**	**0**	**1**	**4**	**.200**	**1**	**0-0**	**0**	**5.31**

Lenny Harris

Bats: L **Throws:** R **Pos:** PH/PR-95; 3B-11; 1B-7; LF-5; RF-3; DH-2; 2B-1   **Ht:** 5'10"   **Wt:** 220   **Born:** 10/28/64   **Age:** 37

Year Team	Lg	G	AB	H	2B	3B	HR	(Hm	Rd)	TB	R	RBI	TBB	IBB	SO	HBP	SH	SF	SB	CS	SB%	GDP	Avg	OBP	SLG
1988 Cincinnati	NL	16	43	16	1	0	0	(0	0)	17	7	8	5	0	4	0	1	2	4	1	.80	0	.372	.420	.395
1989 Cin-LA	NL	115	335	79	10	1	3	(1	2)	100	36	26	20	0	33	2	1	6	14	9	.61	14	.236	.283	.299
1990 Los Angeles	NL	137	431	131	16	4	2	(0	2)	161	61	29	29	2	31	1	3	1	15	10	.60	8	.304	.348	.374
1991 Los Angeles	NL	145	429	123	16	1	3	(1	2)	150	59	38	37	5	32	5	12	2	12	3	.80	16	.287	.349	.350
1992 Los Angeles	NL	135	347	94	11	0	0	(0	0)	105	28	30	24	3	24	1	6	2	19	7	.73	10	.271	.318	.303
1993 Los Angeles	NL	107	160	38	6	1	2	(0	2)	52	20	11	15	4	15	0	1	0	3	1	.75	4	.238	.303	.325
1994 Cincinnati	NL	66	100	31	3	1	0	(0	0)	36	13	14	5	0	13	0	0	1	7	2	.78	0	.310	.340	.360
1995 Cincinnati	NL	101	197	41	8	3	2	(0	2)	61	32	16	14	0	20	0	3	1	10	1	.91	6	.208	.259	.310
1996 Cincinnati	NL	125	302	86	17	2	5	(2	3)	122	33	32	21	1	31	1	6	3	14	6	.70	3	.285	.330	.404
1997 Cincinnati	NL	120	238	65	13	1	3	(2	1)	89	32	28	18	1	18	2	3	2	4	3	.57	10	.273	.327	.374
1998 Cin-NYM	NL	132	290	75	15	0	6	(2	4)	108	30	27	17	3	21	2	4	4	6	5	.55	13	.259	.300	.372
1999 Col-Ari	NL	110	187	58	13	0	1	(1	0)	74	17	20	6	0	7	0	0	1	2	1	.67	5	.310	.330	.396
2000 Ari-NYM	NL	112	223	58	7	4	4	(2	2)	85	31	26	20	2	22	0	2	3	13	1	.93	7	.260	.317	.381
2001 New York	NL	110	135	30	5	1	0	(0	0)	37	12	9	8	0	9	0	0	2	3	2	.60	3	.222	.266	.274
1989 Cincinnati	NL	61	188	42	4	0	2	(0	2)	52	17	11	9	0	20	1	1	0	10	6	.63	5	.223	.263	.277
Los Angeles	NL	54	147	37	6	1	1	(1	0)	48	19	15	11	0	13	1	0	6	4	3	.57	9	.252	.308	.327
1998 Cincinnati	NL	57	122	36	8	0	0	(0	0)	44	12	10	8	2	9	1	0	2	1	3	.25	8	.295	.338	.361
New York	NL	75	168	39	7	0	6	(2	4)	64	18	17	9	1	12	1	4	2	5	2	.71	5	.232	.272	.381
1999 Colorado	NL	91	158	47	12	0	0	(0	0)	59	15	13	6	0	6	0	0	0	1	1	.50	7	.297	.323	.373
Arizona	NL	19	29	11	1	0	1	(1	0)	15	2	7	0	0	1	0	0	1	1	0	1.00	0	.379	.367	.517
2000 Arizona	NL	36	85	16	1	1	1	(1	0)	22	9	13	3	1	5	0	0	3	5	0	1.00	3	.188	.209	.259
New York	NL	76	138	42	6	3	3	(1	2)	63	22	13	17	1	17	0	2	0	8	1	.89	4	.304	.381	.457
14 ML YEARS		**1531**	**3417**	**925**	**141**	**19**	**31**	**(11**	**20)**	**1197**	**411**	**314**	**239**	**21**	**280**	**14**	**42**	**22**	**126**	**52**	**.71**	**101**	**.271**	**.319**	**.350**

94

Willie Harris

Bats: Left **Throws:** Right **Pos:** CF-8; PH/PR-2 **Ht:** 5'9" **Wt:** 175 **Born:** 6/22/78 **Age:** 24

Year Team	Lg	G	AB	H	2B	3B	HR	Hm	Rd	TB	R	RBI	TBB	IBB	SO	HBP	SH	SF	SB	CS	SB%	GDP	Avg	OBP	SLG
1999 Bluefield	R+	5	22	6	1	0	0	—	—	7	3	3	4	0	2	0	0	1	1	0	1.00	1	.273	.370	.318
Delmarva	A	66	272	72	13	3	2	—	—	97	42	32	20	0	41	1	4	4	17	11	.61	4	.265	.313	.357
2000 Delmarva	A	133	474	130	27	10	6	—	—	195	106	60	89	4	89	9	7	4	38	15	.72	3	.274	.396	.411
2001 Bowie	AA	133	525	160	27	4	9	—	—	222	83	49	46	3	71	5	10	4	54	16	.77	6	.305	.364	.423
2001 Baltimore	AL	9	24	3	1	0	0	(0	0)	4	3	0	0	0	7	0	1	0	0	0	—	0	.125	.125	.167

Ken Harvey

Bats: Right **Throws:** Right **Pos:** 1B-3; DH-1 **Ht:** 6'2" **Wt:** 240 **Born:** 3/1/78 **Age:** 24

Year Team	Lg	G	AB	H	2B	3B	HR	Hm	Rd	TB	R	RBI	TBB	IBB	SO	HBP	SH	SF	SB	CS	SB%	GDP	Avg	OBP	SLG
1999 Spokane	A-	56	204	81	17	0	8	—	—	122	49	41	23	4	30	8	0	0	7	1	.88	3	.397	.477	.598
2000 Wilmington	A+	46	164	55	10	0	4	—	—	77	20	25	14	0	29	7	0	0	0	2	.00	4	.335	.411	.470
2001 Wilmington	A+	35	137	52	9	1	6	—	—	81	22	27	13	0	21	6	0	0	3	1	.75	5	.380	.455	.591
Wichita	AA	79	314	106	20	3	9	—	—	159	54	63	18	0	60	4	0	8	3	0	1.00	12	.338	.372	.506
2001 Kansas City	AL	4	12	3	1	0	0	(0	0)	4	1	2	0	0	4	0	0	0	0	0	—	1	.250	.250	.333

Chad Harville

Pitches: Right **Bats:** Right **Pos:** RP-3 **Ht:** 5'9" **Wt:** 180 **Born:** 9/16/76 **Age:** 25

Year Team	Lg	G	GS	CG	GF	IP	BFP	H	R	ER	HR	SH	SF	HB	TBB	IBB	SO	WP	Bk	W	L	Pct.	ShO	Sv-Op	Hld	ERA
1997 Sou Oregon	A-	3	0	0	1	5	23	3	0	0	0	1	0	2	3	0	6	0	0	1	0	1.000	0	0--	—	0.00
Visalia	A+	14	0	0	1	18.2	92	25	14	12	2	1	1	0	13	1	24	1	3	0	0	—	0	0--	—	5.79
1998 Visalia	A+	24	7	0	12	69	294	59	25	23	0	0	2	5	31	0	76	6	2	4	3	.571	0	4--	—	3.00
Huntsville	AA	12	0	0		14.2	63	6	4	4	0	0	1	0	13	1	24	1	0	0	0	—	0	8--	—	2.45
1999 Midland	AA	17	0	0	16	22.1	90	13	6	5	1	0	1	1	9	0	35	2	0	2	0	1.000	0	7--	—	2.01
Vancouver	AAA	22	0	0	19	25.2	114	24	5	5	0	0	0	3	11	1	36	4	0	1	0	1.000	0	11--	—	1.75
2000 Sacramento	AAA	53	0	0	29	64	280	53	35	32	8	2	1	3	35	0	77	8	0	5	3	.625	0	9--	—	4.50
2001 Visalia	A+	1	1	0	0	3	12	3	0	0	0	0	0	0	0	0	3	0	0	0	0	—	0	0--	—	0.00
Modesto	A+	2	1	0	0	3	12	2	2	1	0	1	0	0	0	0	3	0	0	0	0	—	0	0--	—	3.00
Sacramento	AAA	33	0	0	23	40.2	169	35	20	18	5	1	2	2	12	0	55	5	0	5	2	.714	0	8--	—	3.98
1999 Oakland	AL	15	0	0	8	14.1	69	18	11	11	2	0	1	0	10	1	15	3	1	0	2	.000	0	0-0	0	6.91
2001 Oakland	AL	3	0	0	1	3	11	2	0	0	0	0	0	0	0	0	2	1	0	0	0	—	0	0-0	1	0.00
2 ML YEARS		18	0	0	9	17.1	80	20	11	11	2	0	1	0	10	1	17	4	1	0	2	.000	0	0-0	1	5.71

Shigetoshi Hasegawa

Pitches: Right **Bats:** Right **Pos:** RP-46 **Ht:** 5'11" **Wt:** 178 **Born:** 8/1/68 **Age:** 33

Year Team	Lg	G	GS	CG	GF	IP	BFP	H	R	ER	HR	SH	SF	HB	TBB	IBB	SO	WP	Bk	W	L	Pct.	ShO	Sv-Op	Hld	ERA
2001 Rancho Cuc *	A+	2	2	0	0	2	10	3	1	0	0	2	0	0	0	0	1	0	0	0	0	—	0	0--	—	0.00
1997 Anaheim	AL	50	7	0	17	116.2	497	118	60	51	14	5	5	3	46	6	83	2	1	3	7	.300	0	0-1	3	3.93
1998 Anaheim	AL	61	0	0	20	97.1	401	86	37	34	14	4	6	2	32	2	73	5	2	8	3	.727	0	5-7	10	3.14
1999 Anaheim	AL	64	1	0	26	77	333	80	45	42	14	3	4	2	34	2	44	4	0	4	6	.400	0	2-5	6	4.91
2000 Anaheim	AL	66	0	0	26	95.2	415	100	42	37	11	2	3	2	38	6	59	2	1	10	5	.667	0	9-18	19	3.48
2001 Anaheim	AL	46	0	0	10	55.2	235	52	28	25	5	1	2	2	20	5	41	2	0	5	6	.455	0	0-6	12	4.04
5 ML YEARS		287	8	0	99	442.1	1881	436	212	189	58	15	20	11	170	21	300	15	4	30	27	.526	0	16-37	50	3.85

Bill Haselman

Bats: Right **Throws:** Right **Pos:** C-47; PH/PR-1 **Ht:** 6'3" **Wt:** 225 **Born:** 5/25/66 **Age:** 36

Year Team	Lg	G	AB	H	2B	3B	HR	Hm	Rd	TB	R	RBI	TBB	IBB	SO	HBP	SH	SF	SB	CS	SB%	GDP	Avg	OBP	SLG
2001 Oklahoma *	AAA	8	28	4	0	0	0	—	—	4	2	1	1	0	10	1	0	1	0	0	—	3	.143	.194	.143
1990 Texas	AL	7	13	2	0	0	0	(0	0)	2	5	3	1	0	5	0	0	0	0	3	.00	0	.154	.214	.154
1992 Seattle	AL	8	19	5	0	0	0	(0	0)	5	1	0	0	0	7	0	0	0	0	0	—	1	.263	.263	.263
1993 Seattle	AL	58	137	35	8	0	5	(3	2)	58	21	16	12	0	19	1	2	2	2	1	.67	5	.255	.316	.423
1994 Seattle	AL	38	83	16	7	1	1	(1	0)	28	11	8	3	0	11	1	1	0	1	0	1.00	2	.193	.230	.337
1995 Boston	AL	64	152	37	6	1	5	(1	5)	60	17	23	17	0	30	2	0	3	0	2	.00	4	.243	.322	.395
1996 Boston	AL	77	237	65	13	1	8	(5	3)	104	33	34	19	3	52	1	0	0	4	2	.67	13	.274	.331	.439
1997 Boston	AL	67	212	50	15	0	6	(3	3)	83	22	26	15	2	44	2	1	2	0	0	—	8	.236	.290	.392
1998 Texas	AL	40	105	33	6	0	6	(4	2)	57	11	17	3	0	17	0	0	2	0	0	—	2	.314	.327	.543
1999 Detroit	AL	48	143	39	8	0	4	(1	0)	59	13	14	10	1	26	0	0	0	2	0	1.00	2	.273	.320	.413
2000 Texas	AL	62	193	53	18	0	6	(3	3)	89	23	26	15	0	36	1	0	1	0	1	.00	5	.275	.329	.461
2001 Texas	AL	47	130	37	6	0	3	(2	1)	52	12	25	8	0	27	1	1	0	0	0	—	5	.285	.331	.400
11 ML YEARS		516	1424	372	87	3	44	(26	18)	597	169	192	103	6	274	9	5	10	9	9	.50	45	.261	.313	.419

Scott Hatteberg

Bats: Left **Throws:** Right **Pos:** C-72; PH/PR-20; DH-8 **Ht:** 6'1" **Wt:** 205 **Born:** 12/14/69 **Age:** 32

Year Team	Lg	G	AB	H	2B	3B	HR	Hm	Rd	TB	R	RBI	TBB	IBB	SO	HBP	SH	SF	SB	CS	SB%	GDP	Avg	OBP	SLG
1995 Boston	AL	2	2	1	0	0	0	(0	0)	1	1	0	0	0	0	0	0	0	0	0	—	1	.500	.500	.500
1996 Boston	AL	10	11	2	1	0	0	(0	0)	3	3	0	3	0	2	0	0	0	0	0	—	2	.182	.357	.273
1997 Boston	AL	114	350	97	23	1	10	(5	5)	152	46	44	40	2	70	2	2	1	0	1	.00	11	.277	.354	.434
1998 Boston	AL	112	359	99	23	1	12	(4	8)	160	46	43	43	3	58	5	0	3	0	0	—	11	.276	.359	.446
1999 Boston	AL	30	80	22	5	0	1	(1	0)	30	12	11	18	0	14	1	0	1	0	0	—	2	.275	.410	.375
2000 Boston	AL	92	230	61	15	0	8	(2	6)	100	21	36	38	3	39	0	1	2	0	0	—	8	.265	.367	.435

			BATTING															BASERUNNING				PERCENTAGES		
Year Team	Lg	G	AB	H	2B	3B	HR	(Hm	Rd)	TB	R	RBI	TBB	IBB	SO	HBP	SH	SF	SB	CS	SB%	GDP	Avg	OBP	SLG
2001 Boston	AL	94	278	68	19	0	3	(2	1)	96	34	25	33	0	26	4	0	1	1	1	.50	7	.245	.332	.345
7 ML YEARS		454	1310	350	86	2	34	(14	20)	542	163	159	175	8	209	12	3	8	1	3	.25	42	.267	.357	.414

LaTroy Hawkins

Pitches: Right **Bats:** Right **Pos:** RP-62   **Ht:** 6'5" **Wt:** 204 **Born:** 12/21/72 **Age:** 29

		HOW MUCH HE PITCHED					WHAT HE GAVE UP											THE RESULTS						
Year Team	Lg	G	GS	CG	GF	IP	BFP	H	R	ER	HR	SH	SF	HB	TBB	IBB	SO	WP	Bk	W	L	Pct.	ShO	Sv-Op	Hld	ERA
1995 Minnesota	AL	6	6	1	0	27	131	39	29	26	3	0	3	1	12	0	9	1	1	2	3	.400	0	0-0	0	8.67
1996 Minnesota	AL	7	6	0	1	26.1	124	42	24	24	8	1	1	0	9	0	24	1	1	1	1	.500	0	0-0	0	8.20
1997 Minnesota	AL	20	20	0	0	103.1	478	134	71	67	19	2	2	4	47	0	58	6	3	6	12	.333	0	0-0	0	5.84
1998 Minnesota	AL	33	33	0	0	190.1	840	227	126	111	27	4	10	5	61	1	105	10	2	7	14	.333	0	0-0	0	5.25
1999 Minnesota	AL	33	33	1	0	174.1	803	238	136	129	29	1	5	1	60	2	103	9	0	10	14	.417	0	0-0	0	6.66
2000 Minnesota	AL	66	0	0	38	87.2	370	85	34	33	7	4	1	1	32	1	59	6	0	2	5	.286	0	14-14	7	3.39
2001 Minnesota	AL	62	0	0	51	51.1	248	59	34	34	3	1	4	1	39	3	36	7	0	1	5	.167	0	28-37	1	5.96
7 ML YEARS		227	98	2	90	660.1	2994	824	454	424	96	13	26	13	260	7	394	40	7	29	54	.349	0	42-51	8	5.78

Charlie Hayes

Bats: R **Throws:** R **Pos:** PH/PR-19; 3B-11; 1B-2; DH-1   **Ht:** 6'0" **Wt:** 215 **Born:** 5/29/65 **Age:** 37

			BATTING															BASERUNNING				PERCENTAGES		
Year Team	Lg	G	AB	H	2B	3B	HR	(Hm	Rd)	TB	R	RBI	TBB	IBB	SO	HBP	SH	SF	SB	CS	SB%	GDP	Avg	OBP	SLG
1988 San Francisco	NL	7	11	1	0	0	0	(0	0)	1	0	0	0	0	3	0	0	0	0	0	—	0	.091	.091	.091
1989 SF-Phi	NL	87	304	78	15	1	8	(3	5)	119	26	43	11	1	50	0	2	3	3	1	.75	6	.257	.280	.391
1990 Philadelphia	NL	152	561	145	20	0	10	(3	7)	195	56	57	28	3	91	2	0	6	4	4	.50	12	.258	.293	.348
1991 Philadelphia	NL	142	460	106	23	1	12	(6	6)	167	34	53	16	3	75	1	2	1	3	3	.50	13	.230	.257	.363
1992 New York	NL	142	509	131	19	2	18	(7	11)	208	52	66	28	0	100	3	3	6	3	5	.38	12	.257	.297	.409
1993 Colorado	NL	157	573	175	45	2	25	(17	8)	299	89	98	43	6	82	5	1	8	11	6	.65	25	.305	.355	.522
1994 Colorado	NL	113	423	122	23	4	10	(4	6)	183	46	50	36	4	71	3	0	1	3	6	.33	11	.288	.348	.433
1995 Philadelphia	NL	141	529	146	30	4	11	(6	5)	215	58	85	50	2	88	4	0	6	5	1	.83	22	.276	.340	.406
1996 Pit-NYY	NL	148	526	133	24	2	12	(5	7)	197	58	75	37	4	90	0	3	3	6	0	1.00	17	.253	.300	.375
1997 New York	AL	100	353	91	16	0	11	(5	6)	140	39	53	40	2	66	1	0	4	3	2	.60	13	.258	.332	.397
1998 San Francisco	NL	111	329	94	8	0	12	(5	7)	138	39	62	34	0	61	0	1	2	2	1	.67	4	.286	.351	.419
1999 San Francisco	NL	95	264	54	9	1	6	(2	4)	83	33	48	33	0	41	1	0	3	3	1	.75	8	.205	.292	.314
2000 Milwaukee	NL	121	370	93	17	0	9	(2	7)	137	46	46	57	4	84	1	0	6	1	1	.50	11	.251	.348	.370
2001 Houston	NL	31	50	10	2	0	0	(0	0)	12	4	4	7	1	16	0	0	1	0	0	—	1	.200	.293	.240
1989 San Francisco	NL	3	5	1	0	0	0	(0	0)	1	0	0	0	0	1	0	0	0	0	0	—	0	.200	.200	.200
Philadelphia	NL	84	299	77	15	1	8	(3	5)	118	26	43	11	1	49	0	2	3	3	1	.75	6	.258	.281	.395
1996 Pittsburgh	NL	128	459	114	21	2	10	(5	5)	169	51	62	36	4	78	0	2	3	6	0	1.00	16	.248	.301	.368
New York	AL	20	67	19	3	0	2	(0	2)	28	7	13	1	0	12	0	1	0	0	0	—	1	.284	.294	.418
14 ML YEARS		1547	5262	1379	251	16	144	(67	77)	2094	580	740	420	30	918	21	12	50	47	31	.60	155	.262	.316	.398

Jimmy Haynes

Pitches: Right **Bats:** Right **Pos:** SP-29; RP-2   **Ht:** 6'4" **Wt:** 203 **Born:** 9/5/72 **Age:** 29

		HOW MUCH HE PITCHED					WHAT HE GAVE UP											THE RESULTS						
Year Team	Lg	G	GS	CG	GF	IP	BFP	H	R	ER	HR	SH	SF	HB	TBB	IBB	SO	WP	Bk	W	L	Pct.	ShO	Sv-Op	Hld	ERA
1995 Baltimore	AL	4	3	0	0	24	94	11	6	6	2	1	0	0	12	1	22	0	0	2	1	.667	0	0-0	0	2.25
1996 Baltimore	AL	26	11	0	8	89	435	122	84	82	14	4	5	2	58	1	65	5	0	3	6	.333	0	1-1	0	8.29
1997 Oakland	AL	13	13	0	0	73.1	329	74	38	36	7	1	4	2	40	1	65	4	1	3	6	.333	0	0-0	0	4.42
1998 Oakland	AL	33	33	1	0	194.1	875	229	124	110	25	5	9	5	88	4	134	11	0	11	9	.550	1	0-0	0	5.09
1999 Oakland	AL	30	25	0	2	142	652	158	112	100	21	4	5	2	80	3	93	7	2	7	12	.368	0	0-0	0	6.34
2000 Milwaukee	NL	33	33	0	0	199.1	897	228	128	118	21	10	6	7	100	7	88	7	0	12	13	.480	0	0-0	0	5.33
2001 Milwaukee	NL	31	29	0	0	172.2	756	182	98	93	20	14	7	4	78	17	112	8	0	8	17	.320	0	0-0	0	4.85
7 ML YEARS		170	147	1	10	894.2	4038	1004	590	545	110	39	36	22	456	34	579	42	3	46	64	.418	1	1-1	0	5.48

Rick Helling

Pitches: Right **Bats:** Right **Pos:** SP-34   **Ht:** 6'3" **Wt:** 220 **Born:** 12/15/70 **Age:** 31

		HOW MUCH HE PITCHED					WHAT HE GAVE UP											THE RESULTS						
Year Team	Lg	G	GS	CG	GF	IP	BFP	H	R	ER	HR	SH	SF	HB	TBB	IBB	SO	WP	Bk	W	L	Pct.	ShO	Sv-Op	Hld	ERA
1994 Texas	AL	9	9	1	0	52	228	62	34	34	14	0	0	0	18	0	25	4	1	3	2	.600	1	0-0	0	5.88
1995 Texas	AL	3	3	0	0	12.1	62	17	11	9	2	0	2	2	8	0	5	0	0	0	2	.000	0	0-0	0	6.57
1996 Tex-Fla		11	6	0	2	48	198	37	23	23	9	1	1	0	16	0	42	1	1	3	3	.500	0	0-0	1	4.31
1997 Fla-Tex		41	16	0	9	131	550	108	67	65	17	3	9	6	69	2	99	3	0	5	9	.357	0	0-1	6	4.47
1998 Texas	AL	33	33	4	0	216.1	922	209	109	106	27	6	10	1	78	6	164	10	0	20	7	.741	0	0-0	0	4.41
1999 Texas	AL	35	35	3	0	219.1	943	228	127	118	41	5	10	6	85	5	131	6	0	13	11	.542	0	0-0	0	4.84
2000 Texas	AL	35	35	0	0	217	963	212	122	108	29	4	9	9	99	2	146	2	0	16	13	.552	0	0-0	0	4.48
2001 Texas	AL	34	34	2	0	215.2	941	256	134	124	38	3	10	4	63	2	154	6	0	12	11	.522	1	0-0	0	5.17
1996 Texas	AL	6	2	0	2	20.1	92	23	17	17	7	0	1	0	9	0	16	1	0	1	2	.333	0	0-0	1	7.52
Florida	NL	5	4	0	0	27.2	106	14	6	6	2	1	0	0	7	0	26	0	1	2	1	.667	0	0-0	0	1.95
1997 Florida	NL	31	8	0	8	76	324	61	38	37	12	2	7	4	48	2	53	0	0	2	6	.250	0	0-1	6	4.38
Texas	AL	10	8	0	1	55	226	47	29	28	5	1	2	2	21	0	46	3	0	3	3	.500	0	0-0	0	4.58
8 ML YEARS		201	171	10	11	1111.2	4807	1129	627	587	177	22	51	28	436	17	766	34	2	72	58	.554	4	0-1	7	4.75

Wes Helms

Bats: R **Throws:** R **Pos:** 1B-77; PH/PR-27; 3B-17; LF-1   **Ht:** 6'4" **Wt:** 230 **Born:** 5/12/76 **Age:** 26

			BATTING															BASERUNNING				PERCENTAGES		
Year Team	Lg	G	AB	H	2B	3B	HR	(Hm	Rd)	TB	R	RBI	TBB	IBB	SO	HBP	SH	SF	SB	CS	SB%	GDP	Avg	OBP	SLG
1994 Braves	R	56	184	49	15	1	4	—	—	78	22	29	22	0	36	4	0	1	6	1	.86	3	.266	.355	.424
1995 Macon	A	136	539	149	32	1	11	—	—	216	89	85	50	0	107	10	0	3	2	2	.50	8	.276	.347	.401

Year Team	Lg	G	AB	H	2B	3B	HR	(Hm	Rd)	TB	R	RBI	TBB	IBB	SO	HBP	SH	SF	SB	CS	SB%	GDP	Avg	OBP	SLG
1996 Durham	A+	67	258	83	19	2	13	—	—	145	40	54	12	0	51	7	0	1	1	1	.50	7	.322	.367	.562
Greenville	AA	64	231	59	13	2	4	—	—	88	24	22	13	2	48	4	1	0	2	1	.67	6	.255	.306	.381
1997 Richmond	AAA	32	110	21	4	0	3	—	—	34	11	15	10	1	34	5	0	1	1	1	.50	4	.191	.286	.309
Greenville	AA	86	314	93	14	1	11	—	—	142	50	44	33	2	50	6	0	3	3	4	.43	14	.296	.371	.452
1998 Richmond	AAA	125	451	124	27	1	13	—	—	192	56	75	35	2	103	13	0	4	6	2	.75	11	.275	.342	.426
1999 Braves	R	9	33	15	2	0	0	—	—	17	1	10	5	0	4	1	0	0	0	1	.00	1	.455	.538	.515
Greenville	AA	30	113	34	6	0	8	—	—	64	15	26	7	1	34	1	0	0	1	0	1.00	0	.301	.347	.566
2000 Richmond	AAA	136	539	155	27	7	20	—	—	256	74	88	27	2	92	6	2	6	0	6	.00	10	.288	.325	.475
1998 Atlanta	NL	7	13	4	1	0	1	(0	1)	8	2	2	0	0	4	0	0	0	0	0	—	0	.308	.308	.615
2000 Atlanta	NL	6	5	1	0	0	0	(0	0)	1	0	0	0	0	2	0	0	0	0	0	—	0	.200	.200	.200
2001 Atlanta	NL	100	216	48	10	3	10	(6	4)	94	28	36	21	2	56	1	0	1	1	1	.50	3	.222	.293	.435
3 ML YEARS		113	234	53	11	3	11	(6	5)	103	30	38	21	2	62	1	0	1	1	1	.50	3	.226	.292	.440

Todd Helton

Bats: Left **Throws:** Left **Pos:** 1B-157; PH/PR-2   **Ht:** 6'2" **Wt:** 204 **Born:** 8/20/73 **Age:** 28

Year Team	Lg	G	AB	H	2B	3B	HR	(Hm	Rd)	TB	R	RBI	TBB	IBB	SO	HBP	SH	SF	SB	CS	SB%	GDP	Avg	OBP	SLG
1997 Colorado	NL	35	93	26	2	1	5	(3	2)	45	13	11	8	0	11	0	0	0	0	1	.00	1	.280	.337	.484
1998 Colorado	NL	152	530	167	37	1	25	(13	12)	281	78	97	53	5	54	6	1	5	3	3	.50	15	.315	.380	.530
1999 Colorado	NL	159	578	185	39	5	35	(23	12)	339	114	113	66	6	77	6	0	4	7	6	.54	14	.320	.395	.587
2000 Colorado	NL	160	580	216	59	2	42	(27	15)	405	138	147	103	22	61	4	0	10	5	3	.63	14	.372	.463	.698
2001 Colorado	NL	159	587	197	54	2	49	(27	22)	402	132	146	98	15	104	5	1	5	7	5	.58	14	.336	.432	.685
5 ML YEARS		665	2368	791	191	11	156	(93	63)	1472	475	514	330	48	307	21	2	24	22	18	.55	56	.334	.416	.622

Rickey Henderson

Bats: Right **Throws:** Left **Pos:** LF-104; PH/PR-22; DH-1   **Ht:** 5'10" **Wt:** 190 **Born:** 12/25/58 **Age:** 43

Year Team	Lg	G	AB	H	2B	3B	HR	(Hm	Rd)	TB	R	RBI	TBB	IBB	SO	HBP	SH	SF	SB	CS	SB%	GDP	Avg	OBP	SLG
2001 Portland *	AAA	9	40	11	3	0	0	—	—	14	5	2	1	0	9	0	1	0	1	0	1.00	1	.275	.293	.350
1979 Oakland	AL	89	351	96	13	3	1	(1	0)	118	49	26	34	0	39	2	8	3	33	11	.75	4	.274	.338	.336
1980 Oakland	AL	158	591	179	22	4	9	(3	6)	236	111	53	117	7	54	5	6	3	100	26	.79	6	.303	.420	.399
1981 Oakland	AL	108	423	135	18	7	6	(5	1)	185	89	35	64	4	68	2	0	4	56	22	.72	7	.319	.408	.437
1982 Oakland	AL	149	536	143	24	4	10	(5	5)	205	119	51	116	1	94	2	0	2	130	42	.76	5	.267	.398	.382
1983 Oakland	AL	145	513	150	25	7	9	(5	4)	216	105	48	103	8	80	4	1	1	108	19	.85	11	.292	.414	.421
1984 Oakland	AL	142	502	147	27	4	16	(7	9)	230	113	58	86	1	81	5	1	3	66	18	.79	7	.293	.399	.458
1985 New York	AL	143	547	172	28	5	24	(8	16)	282	146	72	99	1	65	3	0	5	80	10	.89	8	.314	.419	.516
1986 New York	AL	153	608	160	31	5	28	(13	15)	285	130	74	89	2	81	2	0	2	87	18	.83	12	.263	.358	.469
1987 New York	AL	95	358	104	17	3	17	(10	7)	178	78	37	80	1	52	2	0	0	41	8	.84	10	.291	.423	.497
1988 New York	AL	140	554	169	30	2	6	(2	4)	221	118	50	82	1	54	3	2	6	93	13	.88	6	.305	.394	.399
1989 NYY-Oak	AL	150	541	148	26	3	12	(7	5)	216	113	57	126	5	68	3	0	4	77	14	.85	8	.274	.411	.399
1990 Oakland	AL	136	489	159	33	3	28	(8	20)	282	119	61	97	2	60	4	2	2	65	10	.87	13	.325	.439	.577
1991 Oakland	AL	134	470	126	17	1	18	(8	10)	199	105	57	98	7	73	7	0	3	58	18	.76	7	.268	.400	.423
1992 Oakland	AL	117	396	112	18	3	15	(10	5)	181	77	46	95	5	56	6	0	3	48	11	.81	5	.283	.426	.457
1993 Oak-Tor	AL	134	481	139	22	2	21	(10	11)	228	114	59	120	2	65	4	1	4	53	8	.87	9	.289	.432	.474
1994 Oakland	AL	87	296	77	13	0	6	(4	2)	108	66	20	72	1	45	5	1	2	22	7	.76	6	.260	.411	.365
1995 Oakland	AL	112	407	122	31	1	9	(3	6)	182	67	54	72	2	66	4	1	3	32	10	.76	8	.300	.407	.447
1996 San Diego	NL	148	465	112	17	2	9	(6	3)	160	110	29	125	2	90	10	0	4	37	15	.71	5	.241	.410	.344
1997 SD-Ana		120	403	100	14	0	8	(6	2)	138	84	34	97	2	85	6	1	2	45	8	.85	10	.248	.400	.342
1998 Oakland	AL	152	542	128	16	1	14	(6	8)	188	101	57	118	0	114	5	2	3	66	13	.84	5	.236	.376	.347
1999 New York	NL	121	438	138	30	0	12	(1	11)	204	89	42	82	1	82	2	1	3	37	14	.73	4	.315	.423	.466
2000 NYM-Sea		123	420	98	14	2	4	(2	2)	128	75	32	88	1	75	4	3	4	36	11	.77	11	.233	.368	.305
2001 San Diego	NL	123	379	86	17	3	8	(2	6)	133	70	42	81	0	84	3	0	2	25	7	.78	8	.227	.366	.351
1989 New York	AL	65	235	58	13	1	3	(1	2)	82	41	22	56	0	29	1	0	1	25	8	.76	0	.247	.392	.349
Oakland	AL	85	306	90	13	2	9	(6	3)	134	72	35	70	5	39	2	0	3	52	6	.90	8	.294	.425	.438
1993 Oakland	AL	90	318	104	19	1	17	(8	9)	176	77	47	85	2	46	2	0	4	31	6	.84	8	.327	.469	.553
Toronto	AL	44	163	35	3	1	4	(2	2)	52	37	12	35	1	19	2	1	2	22	2	.92	1	.215	.356	.319
1997 San Diego	NL	88	288	79	11	0	6	(5	1)	108	63	27	71	2	62	4	0	2	29	4	.88	7	.274	.422	.375
Anaheim	AL	32	115	21	3	0	2	(1	1)	30	21	7	26	0	23	2	1	0	16	4	.80	3	.183	.343	.261
2000 New York	NL	31	96	21	1	0	0	(0	0)	22	17	2	25	1	20	2	0	1	5	2	.71	2	.219	.387	.229
Seattle	AL	92	324	77	13	2	4	(2	2)	106	58	30	63	0	55	2	3	3	31	9	.78	9	.238	.362	.327
23 ML YEARS		2979	10710	3000	503	65	290	(132	158)	4503	2248	1094	2141	61	1631	93	30	66	1395	333	.81	169	.280	.402	.420

Doug Henry

Pitches: Right **Bats:** Right **Pos:** RP-53   **Ht:** 6'4" **Wt:** 205 **Born:** 12/10/63 **Age:** 38

Year Team	Lg	G	GS	CG	GF	IP	BFP	H	R	ER	HR	SH	SF	HB	TBB	IBB	SO	WP	Bk	W	L	Pct.	ShO	Sv-Op	Hld	ERA
1991 Milwaukee	AL	32	0	0	25	36	137	16	4	4	1	1	2	0	14	1	28	0	0	2	1	.667	0	15-16	3	1.00
1992 Milwaukee	AL	68	0	0	56	65	277	64	34	29	6	1	2	0	24	4	52	4	0	1	4	.200	0	29-33	1	4.02
1993 Milwaukee	AL	54	0	0	41	55	260	67	37	34	7	5	4	3	25	8	38	4	0	4	4	.500	0	17-24	0	5.56
1994 Milwaukee	AL	25	0	0	7	31.1	143	32	17	16	7	1	0	1	23	1	20	3	0	2	3	.400	0	0-0	4	4.60
1995 New York	NL	51	0	0	20	67	273	48	23	22	7	3	2	1	25	6	62	6	1	3	6	.333	0	4-7	6	2.96
1996 New York	NL	58	0	0	33	75	293	82	48	39	7	3	3	1	36	6	58	6	0	2	8	.200	0	9-14	8	4.68
1997 San Francisco	NL	75	0	0	25	70.2	317	70	45	37	5	4	3	1	41	6	69	3	0	4	5	.444	0	3-6	21	4.71
1998 Houston	NL	59	0	0	25	71	296	55	25	24	9	3	3	0	35	5	59	7	0	8	2	.800	0	2-5	11	3.04
1999 Houston	NL	35	0	0	17	40.2	188	45	24	21	8	1	0	3	24	0	36	0	0	2	3	.400	0	2-4	2	4.65
2000 Hou-SF	NL	72	0	0	21	78.1	335	57	36	36	12	5	2	4	49	3	62	5	0	4	4	.500	0	1-4	12	4.14
2001 Kansas City	AL	53	0	0	20	75.2	342	75	53	51	14	5	3	3	45	2	57	5	0	2	2	.500	0	0-2	5	6.07
2000 Houston	NL	45	0	0	13	53	225	39	26	26	10	2	1	3	28	2	46	2	0	1	3	.250	0	1-2	6	4.42
San Francisco	NL	27	0	0	8	25.1	110	18	10	7	2	3	1	1	21	1	16	1	0	3	1	.750	0	0-2	6	2.49
11 ML YEARS		582	0	0	290	665.2	2911	611	346	310	83	32	24	17	341	42	541	41	2	34	42	.447	0	82-115	71	4.19

97

Pat Hentgen

Pitches: Right **Bats:** Right **Pos:** SP-9   **Ht:** 6'2" **Wt:** 195 **Born:** 11/13/68 **Age:** 33

Year Team	Lg	G	GS	CG	GF	IP	BFP	H	R	ER	HR	SH	SF	HB	TBB	IBB	SO	WP	Bk	W	L	Pct.	ShO	Sv-Op	Hld	ERA
1991 Toronto	AL	3	1	0	1	7.1	30	5	2	2	1	1	0	2	3	0	3	1	0	0	0	—	0	0-0	0	2.45
1992 Toronto	AL	28	2	0	10	50.1	229	49	30	30	7	2	2	0	32	5	39	2	1	5	2	.714	0	0-1	1	5.36
1993 Toronto	AL	34	32	3	0	216.1	926	215	103	93	27	6	5	7	74	0	122	11	1	19	9	.679	0	0-0	0	3.87
1994 Toronto	AL	24	24	6	0	174.2	728	158	74	66	21	6	3	3	59	1	147	5	1	13	8	.619	3	0-0	0	3.40
1995 Toronto	AL	30	30	2	0	200.2	913	236	129	114	24	2	1	5	90	6	135	7	2	10	14	.417	0	0-0	0	5.11
1996 Toronto	AL	35	35	10	0	265.2	1100	238	105	95	20	5	8	5	94	3	177	8	0	20	10	.667	3	0-0	0	3.22
1997 Toronto	AL	35	35	9	0	264	1085	253	116	108	31	9	3	7	71	2	160	6	2	15	10	.600	3	0-0	0	3.68
1998 Toronto	AL	29	29	0	0	177.2	795	208	109	102	28	5	7	5	69	1	94	7	1	12	11	.522	0	0-0	0	5.17
1999 Toronto	AL	34	34	1	0	199	869	225	115	106	32	3	11	3	65	1	118	8	1	11	12	.478	0	0-0	0	4.79
2000 St. Louis	NL	33	33	1	0	194.1	846	202	107	102	24	13	8	3	89	4	118	4	0	15	12	.556	1	0-0	0	4.72
2001 Baltimore	AL	9	9	1	0	62.1	252	51	25	24	7	1	1	0	19	3	33	1	0	2	3	.400	0	0-0	0	3.47
11 ML YEARS		294	264	33	11	1812.1	7773	1840	915	842	222	53	49	40	665	26	1146	60	9	122	91	.573	10	0-1	1	4.18

Felix Heredia

Pitches: Left **Bats:** Left **Pos:** RP-48   **Ht:** 6'0" **Wt:** 185 **Born:** 6/18/76 **Age:** 26

Year Team	Lg	G	GS	CG	GF	IP	BFP	H	R	ER	HR	SH	SF	HB	TBB	IBB	SO	WP	Bk	W	L	Pct.	ShO	Sv-Op	Hld	ERA
1996 Florida	NL	21	0	0	5	16.2	78	21	8	8	1	0	1	0	10	1	10	2	0	1	1	.500	0	0-0	2	4.32
1997 Florida	NL	56	0	0	10	56.2	259	53	30	27	3	2	2	5	30	1	54	2	0	5	3	.625	0	0-1	7	4.29
1998 Fla-ChC	NL	71	2	0	18	58.2	268	57	39	33	2	1	2	1	38	3	54	6	1	3	3	.500	0	2-5	17	5.06
1999 Chicago	NL	69	0	0	15	52	237	56	35	28	7	1	4	1	25	2	50	2	0	3	1	.750	0	1-7	12	4.85
2000 Chicago	NL	74	0	0	24	58.2	250	46	31	31	6	4	2	2	33	4	52	5	0	7	3	.700	0	2-5	12	4.76
2001 Chicago	NL	48	0	0	9	35	165	45	27	24	6	1	3	2	16	1	28	3	0	2	2	.500	0	0-3	8	6.17
1998 Florida	NL	41	2	0	12	41	194	38	30	25	1	1	2	1	32	2	38	5	1	0	3	.000	0	2-3	9	5.49
Chicago	NL	30	0	0	6	17.2	74	19	9	8	1	0	0	0	6	1	16	1	0	3	0	1.000	0	0-2	8	4.08
6 ML YEARS		339	2	0	81	277.2	1257	278	170	151	25	9	14	11	152	12	248	20	1	21	13	.618	0	5-21	58	4.89

Gil Heredia

Pitches: Right **Bats:** Right **Pos:** SP-18; RP-6   **Ht:** 6'1" **Wt:** 221 **Born:** 10/26/65 **Age:** 36

Year Team	Lg	G	GS	CG	GF	IP	BFP	H	R	ER	HR	SH	SF	HB	TBB	IBB	SO	WP	Bk	W	L	Pct.	ShO	Sv-Op	Hld	ERA
1991 San Francisco	NL	7	4	0	1	33	126	27	14	14	4	2	1	0	7	2	13	1	0	2	0	.000	0	0-0	0	3.82
1992 SF-Mon	NL	20	5	0	4	44.2	187	44	23	21	4	2	1	1	20	1	22	1	0	2	3	.400	0	0-0	1	4.23
1993 Montreal	NL	20	9	1	2	57.1	246	66	28	25	4	4	1	2	14	2	40	0	0	4	2	.667	0	2-3	1	3.92
1994 Montreal	NL	39	3	0	8	75.1	325	85	34	29	7	3	4	2	13	3	62	4	1	6	3	.667	0	0-0	5	3.46
1995 Montreal	NL	40	18	0	5	119	509	137	60	57	7	9	4	5	21	1	74	1	0	5	6	.455	0	1-3	1	4.31
1996 Texas	NL	44	0	0	21	73.1	320	91	50	48	12	1	2	1	14	2	43	2	0	2	5	.286	0	1-4	7	5.89
1998 Oakland	AL	8	6	0	2	42.2	175	43	14	13	4	1	0	3	3	0	27	0	0	3	3	.500	0	0-0	0	2.74
1999 Oakland	AL	33	33	1	0	200.1	852	228	119	107	22	3	0	8	34	4	117	2	1	13	8	.619	0	0-0	0	4.81
2000 Oakland	AL	32	32	0	0	198.2	860	214	106	91	24	4	6	4	66	5	101	3	0	15	11	.577	0	0-0	0	4.12
2001 Oakland	AL	24	18	0	2	109.2	493	144	75	68	27	3	4	2	29	3	48	1	0	7	8	.467	0	0-0	1	5.58
1992 San Francisco	NL	13	4	0	3	30	132	32	20	18	3	0	0	1	16	1	15	1	0	2	3	.400	0	0-0	1	5.40
Montreal	NL	7	1	0	1	14.2	55	12	3	3	1	2	1	0	4	0	7	0	0	0	0	—	0	0-0	0	1.84
10 ML YEARS		267	128	4	45	954	4093	1079	523	473	115	32	23	28	221	23	547	15	2	57	51	.528	0	4-10	16	4.46

Matt Herges

Pitches: Right **Bats:** Left **Pos:** RP-75   **Ht:** 6'0" **Wt:** 200 **Born:** 4/1/70 **Age:** 32

Year Team	Lg	G	GS	CG	GF	IP	BFP	H	R	ER	HR	SH	SF	HB	TBB	IBB	SO	WP	Bk	W	L	Pct.	ShO	Sv-Op	Hld	ERA
1999 Los Angeles	NL	17	0	0	9	24.1	104	24	13	11	5	1	0	1	8	0	18	0	0	2	0	.000	0	0-2	1	4.07
2000 Los Angeles	NL	59	4	0	17	110.2	461	100	43	39	7	9	4	6	40	5	75	4	0	11	3	.786	0	1-3	4	3.17
2001 Los Angeles	NL	75	0	0	22	99.1	435	97	39	38	8	4	3	8	46	12	76	2	0	9	8	.529	0	1-8	15	3.44
3 ML YEARS		151	4	0	48	234.1	1000	221	95	88	20	14	7	15	94	17	169	6	0	20	13	.606	0	2-13	20	3.38

Chad Hermansen

Bats: Right **Throws:** Right **Pos:** RF-15; CF-6; PH/PR-5   **Ht:** 6'2" **Wt:** 185 **Born:** 9/10/77 **Age:** 24

Year Team	Lg	G	AB	H	2B	3B	HR	(Hm	Rd)	TB	R	RBI	TBB	IBB	SO	HBP	SH	SF	SB	CS	SB%	GDP	Avg	OBP	SLG
2001 Nashville *	AAA	123	447	110	22	6	17	—	—	195	75	63	41	1	154	5	3	3	22	5	.81	5	.246	.315	.436
1999 Pittsburgh	NL	19	60	14	3	0	1	(0	1)	20	5	1	7	1	19	1	1	0	2	2	.50	0	.233	.324	.333
2000 Pittsburgh	NL	33	108	20	4	1	2	(2	0)	32	12	8	6	0	37	0	2	1	0	0	—	3	.185	.226	.296
2001 Pittsburgh	NL	22	55	9	1	0	2	(1	1)	16	5	5	1	0	18	0	0	0	0	1	.00	0	.164	.179	.291
3 ML YEARS		74	223	43	8	1	5	(3	2)	68	22	14	14	1	74	1	3	1	2	3	.40	3	.193	.243	.305

Dustin Hermanson

Pitches: Right **Bats:** Right **Pos:** SP-33   **Ht:** 6'2" **Wt:** 200 **Born:** 12/21/72 **Age:** 29

Year Team	Lg	G	GS	CG	GF	IP	BFP	H	R	ER	HR	SH	SF	HB	TBB	IBB	SO	WP	Bk	W	L	Pct.	ShO	Sv-Op	Hld	ERA
1995 San Diego	NL	26	0	0	6	31.2	151	35	26	24	8	3	0	1	22	1	19	3	0	3	1	.750	0	0-0	1	6.82
1996 San Diego	NL	8	0	0	4	13.2	62	18	15	13	3	2	3	0	4	0	11	0	1	1	0	1.000	0	0-0	0	8.56
1997 Montreal	NL	32	28	1	0	158.1	656	134	68	65	15	10	6	1	66	2	136	4	1	8	8	.500	1	0-0	0	3.69
1998 Montreal	NL	32	30	1	0	187	768	180	65	65	21	9	3	3	56	3	154	4	3	14	11	.560	0	0-0	0	3.13
1999 Montreal	NL	34	34	0	0	216.1	928	225	110	101	20	16	7	7	69	4	145	4	1	9	14	.391	0	0-0	0	4.20
2000 Montreal	NL	38	30	2	7	198	876	226	128	105	26	10	9	4	75	5	94	5	0	12	14	.462	1	4-7	1	4.77

	HOW MUCH HE PITCHED						WHAT HE GAVE UP										THE RESULTS						
Year Team	Lg	G	GS	CG	GF	IP	BFP	H	R	ER	HR	SH	SF	HB	TBB	IBB	SO	WP	Bk	W	L	Pct.	ShO	Sv-Op	Hld	ERA
2001 St. Louis	NL	33	33	0	0	192.1	830	195	106	95	34	7	2	8	365	3	123	6	0	14	13	.519	0	0-0	0	4.45
7 ML YEARS		203	155	4	17	997.1	4271	996	533	468	127	57	30	24	365	18	682	26	6	61	61	.500	2	4-7	3	4.22

Adrian Hernandez

Pitches: Right **Bats:** Right **Pos:** SP-3; RP-3   **Ht:** 6'2" **Wt:** 185 **Born:** 3/25/75 **Age:** 27

	HOW MUCH HE PITCHED						WHAT HE GAVE UP										THE RESULTS						
Year Team	Lg	G	GS	CG	GF	IP	BFP	H	R	ER	HR	SH	SF	HB	TBB	IBB	SO	WP	Bk	W	L	Pct.	ShO	Sv-Op	Hld	ERA
2000 Tampa	A+	1	1	0	0	6.2	24	3	1	1	0	0	0	0	1	0	13	1	0	1	0	1.000	0	0--	—	1.35
Norwich	AA	6	6	1	0	35.2	159	34	17	16	1	0	1	3	18	0	44	2	2	5	1	.833	0	0--	—	4.04
Columbus	AAA	5	5	2	0	30.2	134	24	18	15	2	1	2	3	18	0	29	2	2	2	1	.667	1	0--	—	4.40
2001 Columbus	AAA	21	21	0	0	117.2	515	116	75	72	13	4	4	10	60	1	97	10	5	8	7	.533	0	0--	—	5.51
2001 New York	AL	6	3	0	1	22	91	15	10	9	7	0	0	2	10	1	10	4	0	0	3	.000	0	0-0	0	3.68

Alex Hernandez

Bats: Left **Throws:** Left **Pos:** RF-4; PH/PR-4; 1B-2   **Ht:** 6'4" **Wt:** 190 **Born:** 5/28/77 **Age:** 25

	BATTING																BASERUNNING				PERCENTAGES		
Year Team	Lg	G	AB	H	2B	3B	HR	(Hm | Rd)	TB	R	RBI	TBB	IBB	SO	HBP	SH	SF	SB	CS	SB%	GDP	Avg	OBP	SLG
1995 Pirates	R	49	186	50	5	3	1	—	—	64	24	17	17	1	33	1	1	2	4	4	.50	3	.269	.330	.344
1996 Erie	A-	61	225	65	13	4	4	—	—	98	38	30	20	1	47	0	1	2	7	8	.47	1	.289	.344	.436
1997 Lynchburg	A+	131	520	151	37	4	5	—	—	211	75	68	27	2	140	2	2	7	13	8	.62	6	.290	.324	.406
1998 Carolina	AA	115	452	117	22	7	8	—	—	177	62	48	41	2	81	0	5	6	11	4	.73	12	.259	.317	.392
1999 Altoona	AA	126	475	122	26	3	15	—	—	199	76	63	54	1	110	2	3	3	11	8	.58	3	.257	.333	.419
2000 Altoona	AA	50	199	67	16	1	4	—	—	97	28	34	13	2	42	0	1	1	1	2	.33	4	.337	.376	.487
Nashville	AAA	76	276	76	17	2	8	—	—	121	29	37	11	1	60	1	0	0	6	3	.67	6	.275	.306	.438
2001 Nashville	AAA	88	342	101	16	1	8	—	—	143	45	36	13	2	65	4	1	4	3	4	.43	10	.295	.325	.418
2000 Pittsburgh	NL	20	60	12	3	0	1	(1 | 0)	18	4	5	0	0	13	0	0	0	1	1	.50	0	.200	.200	.300
2001 Pittsburgh	NL	7	11	1	0	0	0	(0 | 0)	1	0	0	0	0	2	0	0	0	0	0	—	1	.091	.091	.091
2 ML YEARS		27	71	13	3	0	1	(1 | 0)	19	4	5	0	0	15	0	0	0	1	1	.50	1	.183	.183	.268

Carlos Hernandez

Bats: Right **Throws:** Right **2000 Pos:** C-70; PH/PR-4; 1B-1   **Ht:** 5'10" **Wt:** 215 **Born:** 5/24/67 **Age:** 35

	BATTING																BASERUNNING				PERCENTAGES		
Year Team	Lg	G	AB	H	2B	3B	HR	(Hm | Rd)	TB	R	RBI	TBB	IBB	SO	HBP	SH	SF	SB	CS	SB%	GDP	Avg	OBP	SLG
2001 Memphis *	AAA	2	4	2	0	0	1	—	—	5	1	1	0	0	0	0	0	0	0	0	—	0	.500	.500	1.250
1990 Los Angeles	NL	10	20	4	1	0	0	(0 | 0)	5	2	1	0	0	2	0	0	0	0	0	—	0	.200	.200	.250
1991 Los Angeles	NL	15	14	3	1	0	0	(0 | 0)	4	1	1	0	0	5	1	0	1	1	0	1.00	2	.214	.250	.286
1992 Los Angeles	NL	69	173	45	4	0	3	(1 | 2)	58	11	17	11	1	21	4	0	2	0	1	.00	8	.260	.316	.335
1993 Los Angeles	NL	50	99	25	5	0	2	(1 | 1)	36	6	7	2	0	11	0	1	0	0	0	—	0	.253	.267	.364
1994 Los Angeles	NL	32	64	14	2	0	2	(0 | 2)	22	6	6	1	0	14	0	0	0	0	0	—	0	.219	.231	.344
1995 Los Angeles	NL	45	94	14	1	0	2	(1 | 1)	21	3	8	7	0	25	1	1	0	0	0	—	5	.149	.216	.223
1996 Los Angeles	NL	13	14	4	0	0	0	(0 | 0)	4	1	0	2	0	2	0	0	0	0	0	—	0	.286	.375	.286
1997 San Diego	NL	50	134	42	7	1	3	(2 | 1)	60	15	14	3	0	27	0	1	0	0	2	.00	5	.313	.328	.448
1998 San Diego	NL	129	390	102	15	0	9	(7 | 2)	144	34	52	16	2	54	9	0	2	2	2	.50	19	.262	.305	.369
2000 SD-StL	NL	75	242	62	15	0	3	(2 | 1)	86	23	35	21	1	35	4	0	3	2	3	.40	4	.256	.322	.355
2000 San Diego	NL	58	191	48	11	0	2	(1 | 1)	65	16	25	16	1	26	3	0	2	1	3	.25	4	.251	.316	.340
St. Louis	NL	17	51	14	4	0	1	(1 | 0)	21	7	10	5	0	9	1	0	1	1	0	1.00	0	.275	.345	.412
10 ML YEARS		488	1244	315	51	1	24	(14 | 10)	440	102	141	63	4	196	19	3	8	5	8	.38	43	.253	.298	.354

Carlos Hernandez

Pitches: Left **Bats:** Both **Pos:** SP-3   **Ht:** 5'10" **Wt:** 145 **Born:** 4/22/80 **Age:** 22

	HOW MUCH HE PITCHED						WHAT HE GAVE UP										THE RESULTS						
Year Team	Lg	G	GS	CG	GF	IP	BFP	H	R	ER	HR	SH	SF	HB	TBB	IBB	SO	WP	Bk	W	L	Pct.	ShO	Sv-Op	Hld	ERA
1999 Martinsvlle	R+	13	9	0	0	55.1	227	36	21	9	2	1	1	6	23	0	82	6	0	5	1	.833	0	0--	—	1.46
2000 Michigan	A	22	22	2	0	110.2	490	92	57	47	8	5	3	11	63	0	115	10	1	6	6	.500	1	0--	—	3.82
2001 Round Rock	AA	24	23	0	0	139	591	115	60	57	11	7	4	7	69	0	167	3	0	12	3	.800	0	0--	—	3.69
2001 Houston	NL	3	3	0	0	17.2	70	11	2	2	1	1	0	0	7	0	17	2	0	1	0	1.000	0	0-0	0	1.02

Jose Hernandez

Bats: R **Throws:** R **Pos:** SS-150; LF-1; CF-1; PH/PR-1   **Ht:** 6'1" **Wt:** 180 **Born:** 7/14/69 **Age:** 32

	BATTING																BASERUNNING				PERCENTAGES		
Year Team	Lg	G	AB	H	2B	3B	HR	(Hm | Rd)	TB	R	RBI	TBB	IBB	SO	HBP	SH	SF	SB	CS	SB%	GDP	Avg	OBP	SLG
1991 Texas	AL	45	98	18	2	1	0	(0 | 0)	22	8	4	3	0	31	0	6	0	1	1	.00	2	.184	.208	.224
1992 Cleveland	AL	3	4	0	0	0	0	(0 | 0)	0	0	0	0	0	2	0	0	0	0	0	—	0	.000	.000	.000
1994 Chicago	NL	56	132	32	2	3	1	(0 | 1)	43	18	9	8	0	29	1	5	0	2	2	.50	4	.242	.291	.326
1995 Chicago	NL	93	245	60	11	4	13	(6 | 7)	118	37	40	13	3	69	0	8	2	1	0	1.00	8	.245	.281	.482
1996 Chicago	NL	131	331	80	14	1	10	(4 | 6)	126	52	41	24	4	97	1	5	2	4	1	.80	10	.242	.293	.381
1997 Chicago	NL	121	183	50	8	5	7	(4 | 3)	89	33	26	14	2	42	0	1	1	5	5	.29	5	.273	.323	.486
1998 Chicago	NL	149	488	124	23	7	23	(11 | 12)	230	76	75	40	3	140	1	2	1	4	6	.40	12	.254	.311	.471
1999 ChC-Atl	NL	147	508	135	20	2	19	(6 | 13)	216	79	62	52	6	145	5	2	1	11	3	.79	10	.266	.339	.425
2000 Milwaukee	NL	124	446	109	22	1	11	(3 | 8)	166	51	59	41	3	125	6	0	3	3	7	.30	12	.244	.315	.372
2001 Milwaukee	NL	152	542	135	26	2	25	(9 | 16)	240	67	78	39	8	185	2	5	4	5	4	.56	9	.249	.300	.443
1999 Chicago	NL	99	342	93	12	2	15	(5 | 10)	154	57	43	40	3	101	5	1	0	7	2	.78	5	.272	.357	.450
Atlanta	NL	48	166	42	8	0	4	(1 | 3)	62	22	19	12	3	44	0	1	1	4	1	.80	5	.253	.302	.373
10 ML YEARS		1021	2977	743	128	26	109	(48 | 61)	1250	421	394	234	29	865	16	34	15	32	28	.53	72	.250	.306	.420

99

Livan Hernandez

Pitches: Right **Bats:** Right **Pos:** SP-34 **Ht:** 6'2" **Wt:** 222 **Born:** 2/20/75 **Age:** 27

		HOW MUCH HE PITCHED						WHAT HE GAVE UP												THE RESULTS						
Year Team	Lg	G	GS	CG	GF	IP	BFP	H	R	ER	HR	SH	SF	HB	TBB	IBB	SO	WP	Bk	W	L	Pct.	ShO	Sv-Op	Hld	ERA
1996 Florida	NL	1	0	0	0	3	13	3	0	0	0	0	0	0	2	0	2	0	0	0	0	—	0	0-0	0	0.00
1997 Florida	NL	17	17	0	0	96.1	405	81	39	34	5	4	7	3	38	1	72	0	0	9	3	.750	0	0-0	0	3.18
1998 Florida	NL	33	33	9	0	234.1	1040	265	133	123	37	8	5	6	104	8	162	4	3	10	12	.455	0	0-0	0	4.72
1999 Fla-SF	NL	30	30	2	0	199.2	886	227	110	103	23	7	6	2	76	5	144	2	2	8	12	.400	0	0-0	0	4.64
2000 San Francisco	NL	33	33	5	0	240	1030	254	114	100	22	12	9	4	73	3	165	3	0	17	11	.607	2	0-0	0	3.75
2001 San Francisco	NL	34	34	2	0	226.2	1008	266	143	132	24	12	12	3	85	7	138	7	0	13	15	.464	0	0-0	0	5.24
1999 Florida	NL	20	20	2	0	136	612	161	78	72	17	3	4	2	55	3	97	2	1	5	9	.357	0	0-0	0	4.76
San Francisco	NL	10	10	0	0	63.2	274	66	32	31	6	4	2	0	21	2	47	0	1	3	3	.500	0	0-0	0	4.38
6 ML YEARS		148	147	18	0	1000	4382	1096	539	492	111	43	39	18	378	24	683	16	5	57	53	.518	2	0-0	0	4.43

Orlando Hernandez

Pitches: Right **Bats:** Right **Pos:** SP-16; RP-1 **Ht:** 6'2" **Wt:** 220 **Born:** 10/11/69 **Age:** 32

		HOW MUCH HE PITCHED						WHAT HE GAVE UP												THE RESULTS						
Year Team	Lg	G	GS	CG	GF	IP	BFP	H	R	ER	HR	SH	SF	HB	TBB	IBB	SO	WP	Bk	W	L	Pct.	ShO	Sv-Op	Hld	ERA
2001 Tampa *	A+	2	2	0	0	7	29	6	2	0	0	0	0	0	1	0	8	0	0	0	0	—	0	0- -	—	0.00
Staten Ilnd *	A-	1	1	0	0	6	21	2	0	0	0	0	0	0	0	0	11	0	0	1	0	1.000	0	0- -	—	0.00
1998 New York	AL	21	21	3	0	141	574	113	53	49	11	3	5	6	52	1	131	5	2	12	4	.750	1	0-0	0	3.13
1999 New York	AL	33	33	2	0	214.1	910	187	108	98	24	3	11	8	87	2	157	4	0	17	9	.654	1	0-0	0	4.12
2000 New York	AL	29	29	3	0	195.2	820	186	104	98	34	4	5	6	51	2	141	1	0	12	13	.480	0	0-0	0	4.51
2001 New York	AL	17	16	0	0	94.2	414	90	51	51	19	2	2	5	42	1	77	0	0	4	7	.364	0	0-0	0	4.85
4 ML YEARS		100	99	8	0	645.2	2718	576	316	296	88	12	23	25	232	6	506	10	2	45	33	.577	2	0-0	0	4.13

Ramon Hernandez

Bats: Right **Throws:** Right **Pos:** C-135; PH/PR-4; 1B-2 **Ht:** 6'0" **Wt:** 227 **Born:** 5/20/76 **Age:** 26

		BATTING																	BASERUNNING				PERCENTAGES		
Year Team	Lg	G	AB	H	2B	3B	HR	(Hm	Rd)	TB	R	RBI	TBB	IBB	SO	HBP	SH	SF	SB	CS	SB%	GDP	Avg	OBP	SLG
1999 Oakland	AL	40	136	38	7	0	3	(1	2)	54	13	21	18	0	11	1	1	2	1	0	1.00	5	.279	.363	.397
2000 Oakland	AL	143	419	101	19	0	14	(7	7)	162	52	62	38	1	64	7	10	5	1	0	1.00	14	.241	.311	.387
2001 Oakland	AL	136	453	115	25	0	15	(5	10)	185	55	60	37	3	68	6	9	4	1	1	.50	10	.254	.316	.408
3 ML YEARS		319	1008	254	51	0	32	(13	19)	401	120	143	93	4	143	14	20	11	3	1	.75	29	.252	.321	.398

Roberto Hernandez

Pitches: Right **Bats:** Right **Pos:** RP-63 **Ht:** 6'4" **Wt:** 250 **Born:** 11/11/64 **Age:** 37

		HOW MUCH HE PITCHED						WHAT HE GAVE UP												THE RESULTS						
Year Team	Lg	G	GS	CG	GF	IP	BFP	H	R	ER	HR	SH	SF	HB	TBB	IBB	SO	WP	Bk	W	L	Pct.	ShO	Sv-Op	Hld	ERA
1991 Chicago	AL	9	3	0	1	15	69	18	15	13	1	0	0	0	7	0	6	1	0	1	0	1.000	0	0-0	0	7.80
1992 Chicago	AL	43	0	0	27	71	277	45	15	13	4	0	3	4	20	1	68	2	0	7	3	.700	0	12-16	6	1.65
1993 Chicago	AL	70	0	0	67	78.2	314	66	21	20	6	2	2	0	20	1	71	2	0	3	4	.429	0	38-44	0	2.29
1994 Chicago	AL	45	0	0	43	47.2	206	44	29	26	5	0	1	1	19	1	50	1	0	4	4	.500	0	14-20	0	4.91
1995 Chicago	AL	60	0	0	57	59.2	272	63	30	26	9	4	0	3	28	4	84	1	0	3	7	.300	0	32-42	0	3.92
1996 Chicago	AL	72	0	0	61	84.2	355	65	21	18	2	2	2	0	38	5	85	6	0	6	5	.545	0	38-46	0	1.91
1997 CWS-SF		74	0	0	50	80.2	340	67	24	22	7	2	1	1	38	5	82	3	0	10	3	.769	0	31-39	9	2.45
1998 Tampa Bay	AL	67	0	0	58	71.1	310	55	33	32	5	4	0	5	41	4	55	1	0	2	6	.250	0	26-35	0	4.04
1999 Tampa Bay	AL	72	0	0	66	73.1	321	68	27	25	1	2	3	4	33	1	69	3	0	2	3	.400	0	43-47	0	3.07
2000 Tampa Bay	AL	68	0	0	58	73.1	315	76	33	26	9	7	3	3	23	1	61	2	1	4	7	.364	0	32-40	1	3.19
2001 Kansas City	AL	63	0	0	55	67.2	287	69	34	31	7	1	0	1	26	3	46	6	0	5	6	.455	0	28-34	0	4.12
1997 Chicago	AL	46	0	0	43	48	203	38	15	13	5	1	1	1	24	4	47	2	0	5	1	.833	0	27-31	0	2.44
San Francisco	NL	28	0	0	7	32.2	137	29	9	9	2	1	0	0	14	1	35	1	0	5	2	.714	0	4-8	9	2.48
11 ML YEARS		643	3	0	543	723	3066	636	282	252	56	24	15	22	293	26	677	28	1	47	48	.495	0	294-363	16	3.14

Junior Herndon

Pitches: Right **Bats:** Right **Pos:** SP-8; RP-4 **Ht:** 6'1" **Wt:** 190 **Born:** 9/11/78 **Age:** 23

		HOW MUCH HE PITCHED						WHAT HE GAVE UP												THE RESULTS						
Year Team	Lg	G	GS	CG	GF	IP	BFP	H	R	ER	HR	SH	SF	HB	TBB	IBB	SO	WP	Bk	W	L	Pct.	ShO	Sv-Op	Hld	ERA
1997 Padres	R	14	14	0	0	77.1	348	80	51	38	2	3	3	5	32	0	65	6	2	3	2	.600	0	0- -	—	4.42
Idaho Falls	R+	1	1	0	0	5	20	5	0	0	0	0	0	0	1	0	3	0	0				0	0- -	—	0.00
1998 Clinton	A	21	21	3	0	132.1	543	119	59	44	3	4	5	8	34	0	101	2	0	10	8	.556	1	0- -	—	2.99
Rancho Cuc	A+	6	6	0	0	39.2	165	37	18	15	5	2	2	2	13	0	29	1	0	3	2	.600	0	0- -	—	3.40
1999 Mobile	AA	26	26	2	0	163	706	172	96	85	24	9	1	8	52	3	87	10	0	10	9	.526	2	0- -	—	4.69
2000 Las Vegas	AAA	26	26	3	0	135	610	151	90	77	13	5	2	4	65	2	75	5	0	10	11	.476	0	0- -	—	5.13
2001 Portland	AAA	21	21	0	0	116	515	132	72	59	18	4	7	4	39	0	47	2	0	9	5	.643	0	0- -	—	4.58
2001 San Diego	NL	12	8	0	2	42.2	201	55	34	30	5	2	0	3	25	5	14	1	0	2	6	.250	0	0-0	0	6.33

Phil Hiatt

Bats: Right **Throws:** Right **Pos:** 3B-17; PH/PR-11; 1B-6 **Ht:** 6'3" **Wt:** 200 **Born:** 5/1/69 **Age:** 33

		BATTING																	BASERUNNING				PERCENTAGES		
Year Team	Lg	G	AB	H	2B	3B	HR	(Hm	Rd)	TB	R	RBI	TBB	IBB	SO	HBP	SH	SF	SB	CS	SB%	GDP	Avg	OBP	SLG
2001 Las Vegas *	AAA	113	436	144	29	5	44	(—	—)	315	107	99	52	6	109	5	0	2	6	4	.60	9	.330	.406	.722
1993 Kansas City	AL	81	238	52	12	1	7	(4	3)	87	30	36	16	0	82	7	0	2	6	3	.67	8	.218	.285	.366
1995 Kansas City	AL	52	113	23	6	0	4	(1	3)	41	11	12	9	0	37	0	2	0	1	0	1.00	3	.204	.262	.363
1996 Detroit	AL	7	21	4	0	1	0	(0	0)	6	3	1	2	0	11	0	0	0	0	0	—	1	.190	.261	.286
2001 Los Angeles	NL	30	50	12	3	0	2	(0	2)	21	6	6	3	1	19	0	0	0	0	0	—	0	.240	.283	.420
4 ML YEARS		170	422	91	21	2	13	(5	8)	155	50	55	30	1	149	7	2	2	7	3	.70	12	.216	.278	.367

100

Richard Hidalgo

Bats: R **Throws:** R **Pos:** CF-128; RF-37; LF-23; PH/PR-4   Ht: 6'3" **Wt:** 190 **Born:** 7/2/75 **Age:** 26

Year Team	Lg	G	AB	H	2B	3B	HR	(Hm	Rd)	TB	R	RBI	TBB	IBB	SO	HBP	SH	SF	SB	CS	SB%	GDP	Avg	OBP	SLG
1997 Houston	NL	19	62	19	5	0	2	(0	2)	30	8	6	4	0	18	1	0	0	1	0	1.00	0	.306	.358	.484
1998 Houston	NL	74	211	64	15	0	7	(3	4)	100	31	35	17	0	37	2	0	4	3	3	.50	5	.303	.355	.474
1999 Houston	NL	108	383	87	25	2	15	(5	10)	161	49	56	64	2	73	4	0	5	8	5	.62	5	.227	.328	.420
2000 Houston	NL	153	558	175	42	3	44	(16	28)	355	118	122	56	3	110	21	0	9	13	6	.68	13	.314	.391	.636
2001 Houston	NL	146	512	141	29	3	19	(13	6)	233	70	80	54	3	107	16	0	11	3	5	.38	15	.275	.356	.455
5 ML YEARS		500	1726	486	116	8	87	(37	50)	879	276	299	187	8	345	44	0	29	28	19	.60	38	.282	.361	.509

Bobby Higginson

Bats: Left **Throws:** Right **Pos:** LF-142; DH-5   Ht: 5'11" **Wt:** 195 **Born:** 8/18/70 **Age:** 31

Year Team	Lg	G	AB	H	2B	3B	HR	(Hm	Rd)	TB	R	RBI	TBB	IBB	SO	HBP	SH	SF	SB	CS	SB%	GDP	Avg	OBP	SLG
1995 Detroit	AL	131	410	92	17	5	14	(10	4)	161	61	43	62	3	107	5	2	7	6	4	.60	5	.224	.329	.393
1996 Detroit	AL	130	440	141	35	0	26	(15	11)	254	75	81	66	7	66	1	3	6	6	3	.67	7	.320	.404	.577
1997 Detroit	AL	146	546	163	30	5	27	(16	11)	284	94	101	70	2	85	3	0	4	12	7	.63	10	.299	.379	.520
1998 Detroit	AL	157	612	174	37	4	25	(10	15)	294	92	85	63	2	.101	6	0	4	3	3	.50	16	.284	.355	.480
1999 Detroit	AL	107	377	90	18	0	12	(8	4)	144	51	46	64	2	66	2	0	2	4	6	.40	2	.239	.351	.382
2000 Detroit	AL	154	597	179	44	4	30	(12	18)	321	104	102	74	6	99	2	2	3	15	3	.83	5	.300	.377	.538
2001 Detroit	AL	147	541	150	28	6	17	(7	10)	241	84	71	80	3	65	2	1	9	20	12	.63	8	.277	.367	.445
7 ML YEARS		972	3523	989	209	24	151	(78	73)	1699	561	529	478	25	589	21	8	35	66	38	.63	53	.281	.367	.482

Erik Hiljus

Pitches: Right **Bats:** Right **Pos:** SP-11; RP-5   Ht: 6'5" **Wt:** 230 **Born:** 12/25/72 **Age:** 29

Year Team	Lg	G	GS	CG	GF	IP	BFP	H	R	ER	HR	SH	SF	HB	TBB	IBB	SO	WP	Bk	W	L	Pct.	ShO	Sv-Op	Hld	ERA
1991 Mets	R	9	9	1	0	38	183	31	27	18	1	0	1	1	37	0	38	5	1	2	3	.400	1	0- -	—	4.26
1992 Kingsport	R+	12	11	0	1	70.2	317	66	49	40	5	2	2	2	40	0	63	7	2	3	6	.333	0	0- -	—	5.09
1993 Capital Cty	A	27	27	1	0	145.2	640	114	76	70	8	2	7	4	111	1	157	17	4	7	10	.412	0	0- -	—	4.32
1994 St. Lucie	A+	26	26	3	0	160.2	709	159	85	71	8	6	10	5	90	3	140	10	8	11	10	.524	1	0- -	—	3.98
1995 St. Lucie	A+	17	17	0	0	111.1	453	85	46	37	4	6	5	3	50	2	98	10	6	8	4	.667	0	0- -	—	2.99
Binghamton	AA	10	10	0	0	55.1	252	60	38	36	8	2	1	1	32	1	40	4	2	2	4	.333	0	0- -	—	5.86
1996 Arkansas	AA	10	10	0	0	45.2	221	62	37	31	6	3	2	0	30	1	21	4	0	3	5	.375	0	0- -	—	6.11
1998 Jacksonville	AA	42	0	0	17	65.2	280	49	31	27	7	2	3	0	35	0	85	4	0	2	3	.400	0	2- -	—	3.70
1999 Lakeland	A+	3	0	0	1	4	15	4	1	1	0	0	0	0	0	0	9	0	1	0	0	—	0	0- -	—	2.25
Jacksnville	AA	10	0	0	3	17.1	65	5	4	2	1	3	1	1	5	0	28	1	1	1	0	1.000	0	0- -	—	1.04
Toledo	AAA	33	0	0	9	59.1	239	49	31	29	5	5	2	2	16	0	73	5	0	2	3	.400	0	5- -	—	4.40
2000 Toledo	AAA	46	0	0	15	70.2	297	67	33	27	3	2	5	0	20	1	81	3	0	5	3	.625	0	2- -	—	3.44
2001 Sacramento	AAA	15	15	3	0	101.2	402	79	46	41	18	1	2	1	26	2	108	2	0	8	5	.615	1	0- -	—	3.63
1999 Detroit	AL	6	0	0	0	8.2	35	7	5	5	2	0	1	0	5	0	1	0	0	0	0	—	0	0-0	—	5.19
2000 Detroit	AL	3	0	0	2	3.2	16	5	3	3	1	0	0	0	1	0	2	0	0	0	0	—	0	0-0	—	7.36
2001 Oakland	AL	16	11	0	3	66	290	70	29	25	7	2	1	0	21	1	67	2	1	5	0	1.000	0	0-0	—	3.41
3 ML YEARS		25	11	0	5	78.1	341	82	37	33	10	2	2	0	27	1	70	2	1	5	0	1.000	0	0-0	1	3.79

Glenallen Hill

Bats: Right **Throws:** Right **Pos:** DH-16   Ht: 6'3" **Wt:** 230 **Born:** 3/22/65 **Age:** 37

Year Team	Lg	G	AB	H	2B	3B	HR	(Hm	Rd)	TB	R	RBI	TBB	IBB	SO	HBP	SH	SF	SB	CS	SB%	GDP	Avg	OBP	SLG
2001 Rancho Cuc *	A+	3	12	2	1	0	1			6	1	3	0	0	5	0	0	0	0	0	—	0	.167	.167	.500
1989 Toronto	AL	19	52	15	0	0	1	(1	0)	18	4	7	3	0	12	0	0	0	2	1	.67	0	.288	.327	.346
1990 Toronto	AL	84	260	60	11	3	12	(7	5)	113	47	32	18	0	62	0	0	0	8	3	.73	5	.231	.281	.435
1991 Tor-Cle	AL	72	221	57	8	2	8	(3	5)	93	29	25	23	0	54	0	1	3	6	4	.60	7	.258	.324	.421
1992 Cleveland	AL	102	369	89	16	1	18	(7	11)	161	38	49	20	0	73	4	0	1	9	6	.60	11	.241	.287	.436
1993 Cle-ChC		97	261	69	14	2	15	(5	10)	132	33	47	17	1	71	1	1	4	8	3	.73	4	.264	.307	.506
1994 Chicago	NL	89	269	80	12	1	10	(7	3)	124	48	38	29	0	57	0	0	1	19	6	.76	5	.297	.365	.461
1995 San Francisco	NL	132	497	131	29	4	24	(13	11)	240	71	86	39	4	98	1	0	2	25	5	.83	11	.264	.317	.483
1996 San Francisco	NL	98	379	106	26	0	19	(9	10)	189	56	67	33	3	95	6	0	3	6	3	.67	6	.280	.344	.499
1997 San Francisco	NL	128	398	104	28	4	11	(8	3)	173	47	64	19	0	87	4	0	7	7	4	.64	8	.261	.297	.435
1998 Sea-ChC		122	390	121	25	2	20	(11	9)	210	63	56	28	2	79	3	0	1	1	1	.50	16	.310	.360	.538
1999 Chicago	NL	99	253	76	9	1	20	(11	9)	147	43	55	22	1	61	0	0	5	1	0	.83	7	.300	.353	.581
2000 ChC-NYY		104	300	88	9	1	27	(17	10)	180	45	58	19	2	76	1	0	1	0	1	.00	6	.293	.336	.600
2001 Anaheim	AL	16	66	9	0	0	1	(0	1)	12	4	2	0	0	20	0	0	0	0	0	—	3	.136	.136	.182
1991 Toronto	AL	35	99	25	5	2	3	(2	1)	43	14	11	7	0	24	0	1	0	2	2	.50	2	.253	.296	.434
Cleveland	AL	37	122	32	3	0	5	(1	4)	50	15	14	16	0	30	0	1	1	4	2	.67	5	.262	.345	.410
1993 Cleveland	AL	66	174	39	7	2	5	(0	5)	65	19	25	11	1	50	1	1	4	7	3	.70	3	.224	.268	.374
Chicago	NL	31	87	30	7	0	10	(5	5)	67	14	22	6	0	21	0	0	0	1	0	1.00	1	.345	.387	.770
1998 Seattle	AL	74	259	75	20	2	12	(5	7)	135	37	33	14	1	45	3	0	1	1	1	.50	13	.290	.332	.521
Chicago	NL	48	131	46	5	0	8	(6	2)	75	26	23	14	1	34	0	0	0	0	0	—	3	.351	.414	.573
2000 Chicago	NL	64	168	44	4	1	11	(6	5)	83	23	29	10	2	43	0	0	0	0	1	.00	5	.262	.303	.494
New York	AL	40	132	44	5	0	16	(11	5)	97	22	29	9	0	33	1	0	1	0	0	—	1	.333	.378	.735
13 ML YEARS		1162	3715	1005	187	21	186	(91	95)	1792	528	586	270	13	845	20	2	26	96	38	.72	89	.271	.321	.482

Ken Hill

Pitches: Right **Bats:** Right **Pos:** RP-5   Ht: 6'2" **Wt:** 215 **Born:** 12/14/65 **Age:** 36

Year Team	Lg	G	GS	CG	GF	IP	BFP	H	R	ER	HR	SH	SF	HB	TBB	IBB	SO	WP	Bk	W	L	Pct.	ShO	Sv-Op	Hld	ERA
2001 Louisville *	AAA	6	6	0	0	31.1	141	33	19	16	4	3	2	2	12	0	16	2	0	2	1	.667	0	0- -	—	4.60
Pawtucket *	AAA	8	8	0	0	31.2	148	42	27	23	5	2	0	0	11	0	17	4	0	2	1	.667	0	0- -	—	6.54
1988 St. Louis	NL	4	1	0	0	14	62	16	9	8	0	0	0	0	6	0	6	1	0	0	1	.000	0	0-0	0	5.14

101

Year Team	Lg	HOW MUCH HE PITCHED						WHAT HE GAVE UP												THE RESULTS						
		G	GS	CG	GF	IP	BFP	H	R	ER	HR	SH	SF	HB	TBB	IBB	SO	WP	Bk	W	L	Pct.	ShO	Sv-Op	Hld	ERA
1989 St. Louis	NL	33	33	2	0	196.2	862	186	92	83	9	14	5	5	99	6	112	11	2	7	15	.318	1	0-0	0	3.80
1990 St. Louis	NL	17	14	1	1	78.2	343	79	49	48	7	5	5	1	33	1	58	5	0	5	6	.455	0	0-0	1	5.49
1991 St. Louis	NL	30	30	0	0	181.1	743	147	76	72	15	7	7	6	67	4	121	7	1	11	10	.524	0	0-0	0	3.57
1992 Montreal	NL	33	33	3	0	218	908	187	76	65	13	15	3	3	75	4	150	11	4	16	9	.640	3	0-0	0	2.68
1993 Montreal	NL	28	28	2	0	183.2	780	163	84	66	7	9	7	6	74	7	90	6	2	9	7	.563	0	0-0	0	3.23
1994 Montreal	NL	23	23	2	0	154.2	647	145	61	57	12	6	6	6	44	7	85	3	0	16	5	.762	1	0-0	0	3.32
1995 StL-Cle		30	29	1	0	185	817	202	107	95	21	12	3	1	77	4	98	6	0	10	8	.556	0	0-0	0	4.62
1996 Texas	AL	35	35	7	0	250.2	1061	250	110	101	19	4	7	6	95	3	170	5	4	16	10	.615	3	0-0	0	3.63
1997 Tex-Ana	AL	31	31	1	0	190	833	194	103	96	19	3	7	3	95	3	106	7	0	9	12	.429	0	0-0	0	4.55
1998 Anaheim	AL	19	19	0	0	103	458	123	60	57	6	7	5	3	47	0	57	3	0	9	6	.600	0	0-0	0	4.98
1999 Anaheim	AL	26	22	0	2	128.1	569	129	72	68	14	3	8	4	76	1	76	5	0	4	11	.267	0	0-0	1	4.77
2000 Ana-CWS	AL	18	17	0	0	81.2	399	107	67	65	16	3	8	2	59	1	50	6	0	5	8	.385	0	0-0	0	7.16
2001 Tampa Bay	AL	5	0	0	1	7.1	38	10	11	10	4	2	0	1	5	2	2	2	0	0	1	.000	0	0-1	0	12.27
1995 St. Louis	NL	18	18	0	0	110.1	493	125	71	62	16	9	2	0	45	4	50	3	0	6	7	.462	0	0-0	0	5.06
Cleveland	AL	12	11	1	0	74.2	324	77	36	33	5	3	1	1	32	0	48	3	0	4	1	.800	0	0-0	0	3.98
1997 Texas	AL	19	19	0	0	111	499	129	69	64	11	2	6	2	56	3	68	5	0	5	8	.385	0	0-0	0	5.19
Anaheim	AL	12	12	1	0	79	334	65	34	32	8	1	1	1	39	0	38	2	0	4	4	.500	0	0-0	0	3.65
2000 Anaheim	AL	16	16	0	0	78.2	380	102	59	57	16	2	7	2	53	1	50	6	0	5	7	.417	0	0-0	0	6.52
Chicago	AL	2	1	0	0	3	19	5	8	8	0	1	1	0	6	0	0	0	0	0	1	.000	0	0-0	0	24.00
14 ML YEARS		332	315	19	4	1973	8520	1938	977	891	162	90	71	47	852	43	1181	78	13	117	109	.518	8	0-1	2	4.06

Shea Hillenbrand

Bats: R **Throws:** R **Pos:** 3B-129; PH/PR-7; 1B-6; DH-1   **Ht:** 6'1" **Wt:** 200 **Born:** 7/27/75 **Age:** 26

Year Team	Lg	BATTING																	BASERUNNING				PERCENTAGES		
		G	AB	H	2B	3B	HR	(Hm	Rd)	TB	R	RBI	TBB	IBB	SO	HBP	SH	SF	SB	CS	SB%	GDP	Avg	OBP	SLG
1996 Lowell	A-	72	279	88	18	2	2	—	—	116	33	38	18	1	32	8	0	2	4	3	.57	6	.315	.371	.416
1997 Michigan	A	64	224	65	13	3	3	—	—	93	28	39	9	1	20	1	0	4	1	3	.25	2	.290	.315	.415
Sarasota	A+	57	220	65	12	0	2	—	—	83	25	28	7	1	29	2	1	2	9	8	.53	4	.295	.320	.377
1998 Michigan	A	129	498	174	33	4	19	—	—	272	80	92	19	2	49	10	1	3	13	7	.65	11	.349	.383	.546
1999 Trenton	AA	69	282	73	15	0	7	—	—	109	41	36	14	3	27	3	0	3	6	5	.55	6	.259	.298	.387
2000 Trenton	AA	135	529	171	35	3	11	—	—	245	77	79	19	0	39	8	0	2	3	3	.50	15	.323	.355	.463
2001 Boston	AL	139	468	123	20	2	12	(5	7)	183	52	49	13	3	61	7	1	4	3	4	.43	12	.263	.291	.391

A.J. Hinch

Bats: Right **Throws:** Right **Pos:** C-43; DH-2; PH/PR-2   **Ht:** 6'1" **Wt:** 207 **Born:** 5/15/74 **Age:** 28

Year Team	Lg	BATTING																	BASERUNNING				PERCENTAGES		
		G	AB	H	2B	3B	HR	(Hm	Rd)	TB	R	RBI	TBB	IBB	SO	HBP	SH	SF	SB	CS	SB%	GDP	Avg	OBP	SLG
2001 Omaha *	AAA	45	168	54	14	0	10	—	—	98	28	33	11	0	33	1	0	1	1	0	1.00	5	.321	.365	.583
1998 Oakland	AL	120	337	78	10	0	9	(4	5)	115	34	35	30	0	89	4	13	7	3	0	1.00	6	.231	.296	.341
1999 Oakland	AL	76	205	44	4	1	7	(3	4)	71	26	24	11	0	41	2	9	1	6	2	.75	4	.215	.260	.346
2000 Oakland	AL	6	8	2	0	0	0	(0	0)	2	1	0	1	0	1	0	0	0	0	0	—	—	.250	.333	.250
2001 Kansas City	AL	45	121	19	3	0	6	(4	2)	40	10	15	8	1	26	3	1	1	1	1	.50	5	.157	.226	.331
4 ML YEARS		247	671	143	17	1	22	(11	11)	228	71	74	50	1	157	9	23	9	10	3	.77	15	.213	.273	.340

Brett Hinchliffe

Pitches: Right **Bats:** Right **Pos:** SP-1   **Ht:** 6'5" **Wt:** 190 **Born:** 7/21/74 **Age:** 27

Year Team	Lg	HOW MUCH HE PITCHED						WHAT HE GAVE UP												THE RESULTS						
		G	GS	CG	GF	IP	BFP	H	R	ER	HR	SH	SF	HB	TBB	IBB	SO	WP	Bk	W	L	Pct.	ShO	Sv-Op	Hld	ERA
1992 Mariners	R	24	0	0	20	35	161	42	17	9	0	3	0	3	9	0	26	1	1	5	4	.556	0	3--	—	2.31
1993 Mariners	R	10	9	0	0	44.1	190	55	32	25	4	1	3	3	5	0	29	4	1	0	4	.000	0	0--	—	5.08
1994 Appleton	A	27	27	3	0	173.2	721	140	79	62	16	7	4	10	50	4	160	5	2	11	7	.611	1	0--	—	3.21
1995 Riverside	A+	15	15	0	0	77.2	373	140	69	57	10	5	3	8	35	3	68	4	0	3	8	.273	0	0--	—	6.61
1996 Lancaster	A+	27	26	0	0	163.1	731	179	105	77	19	6	5	9	64	1	146	10	1	10	10	.500	1	0--	—	4.24
1997 Memphis	AA	24	24	5	0	145.2	627	159	81	72	20	3	4	9	45	2	107	2	1	10	10	.500	1	0--	—	4.45
1998 Lancaster	A+	3	3	0	0	17	62	8	5	3	2	0	0	0	5	0	26	1	0	1	1	.500	0	0--	—	1.59
Tacoma	AAA	25	25	2	0	159.2	681	132	80	71	22	1	5	4	88	2	100	4	2	10	8	.556	1	0--	—	5.15
1999 Tacoma	AAA	21	21	3	0	131	563	141	78	75	17	4	5	5	44	1	107	9	0	9	7	.563	0	0--	—	5.15
2000 Edmonton	AAA	27	3	0	10	64	272	63	29	27	6	1	2	2	24	0	30	8	1	2	3	.400	0	2--	—	3.80
Iowa	AAA	7	4	1	0	32	133	32	10	10	4	0	1	0	8	1	22	0	0	2	1	.000	1	0--	—	2.81
2001 Norfolk	AAA	11	10	0	1	59.2	257	67	30	20	7	0	0	0	1	1	46	0	0	3	2	.600	0	0--	—	3.02
1999 Seattle	AL	11	4	0	2	30.2	153	41	31	30	10	1	0	4	21	0	14	2	0	0	5	.000	0	0-0	0	8.80
2000 Anaheim	AL	2	0	0	0	1.2	7	1	1	1	0	0	0	5	1	0	0	0	0	0	0	—	0	0-0	0	5.40
2001 New York	NL	1	1	0	0	2	17	9	8	8	2	1	0	1	1	0	2	0	0	0	1	.000	0	0-0	1	36.00
3 ML YEARS		14	5	0	2	34.1	177	51	40	39	12	2	0	5	23	0	16	2	0	0	5	.000	0	0-0	1	10.22

Sterling Hitchcock

Pitches: Left **Bats:** Left **Pos:** SP-12; RP-1   **Ht:** 6'0" **Wt:** 205 **Born:** 4/29/71 **Age:** 31

Year Team	Lg	HOW MUCH HE PITCHED						WHAT HE GAVE UP												THE RESULTS						
		G	GS	CG	GF	IP	BFP	H	R	ER	HR	SH	SF	HB	TBB	IBB	SO	WP	Bk	W	L	Pct.	ShO	Sv-Op	Hld	ERA
2001 Lk Elsinore *	A+	6	6	0	0	26.1	116	33	18	12	3	1	1	0	1	0	31	1	0	0	2	.000	0	0--	—	4.10
Portland *	AAA	3	3	0	0	17	70	20	7	7	1	2	0	1	2	0	11	0	0	2	0	1.000	0	0--	—	3.71
1992 New York	AL	3	3	0	0	13	68	23	12	12	2	0	0	1	6	0	6	0	0	0	2	.000	0	0-0	0	8.31
1993 New York	AL	6	6	0	0	31	135	32	18	16	4	0	2	1	14	1	26	3	2	1	2	.333	0	0-0	0	4.65
1994 New York	AL	23	5	1	4	49.1	218	48	24	23	3	1	7	0	29	1	37	5	0	4	1	.800	0	2-2	0	4.20
1995 New York	AL	27	27	4	0	168.1	719	155	91	88	22	5	9	5	68	1	121	6	1	11	10	.524	1	0-0	3	4.70
1996 Seattle	AL	35	35	0	0	196.2	885	245	131	117	27	3	8	7	73	4	132	4	1	13	9	.591	0	0-0	0	5.35
1997 San Diego	NL	32	28	1	1	161	693	172	102	93	24	7	3	8	55	2	106	6	2	10	11	.476	0	0-0	0	5.20
1998 San Diego	NL	39	27	2	3	176.1	743	169	83	77	29	9	3	9	48	2	158	11	1	9	7	.563	1	1-2	3	3.93
1999 San Diego	NL	33	33	1	0	205.2	892	202	99	94	29	6	9	6	76	6	194	**15**	2	12	14	.462	0	0-0	1	4.11
2000 San Diego	NL	11	11	0	0	65.2	292	69	38	36	12	2	1	5	26	1	61	4	0	1	6	.143	0	0-0	0	4.93

Year Team	Lg	G	GS	CG	GF	IP	BFP	H	R	ER	HR	SH	SF	HB	TBB	IBB	SO	WP	Bk	W	L	Pct.	ShO	Sv-Op	Hld	ERA
2001 SD-NYY		13	12	1	0	70.1	323	89	46	44	6	2	4	3	21	0	43	3	1	6	5	.545	0	0-0	0	5.63
2001 San Diego	NL	3	3	0	0	19	85	22	9	7	1	1	0	1	3	0	15	1	0	2	1	.667	0	0-0	0	3.32
New York	AL	10	9	1	0	51.1	238	67	37	37	5	1	4	2	18	0	28	2	1	4	4	.500	0	0-0	0	6.49
10 ML YEARS		222	187	10	8	1137.1	4968	1204	644	600	158	38	44	40	416	18	884	56	11	67	67	.500	2	3-4	6	4.75

Denny Hocking

Bats: B **Throws:** R **Pos:** SS-47; PH/PR-30; 2B-17; 1B-11; DH-10; 3B-6; LF-6; CF-5; RF-5   **Ht:** 5'10" **Wt:** 183 **Born:** 4/2/70 **Age:** 32

								BATTING										BASERUNNING				PERCENTAGES		
Year Team	Lg	G	AB	H	2B	3B	HR	(Hm	Rd)	TB	R	RBI	TBB	IBB	SO	HBP	SH	SF	SB	CS	SB%	GDP	Avg	OBP	SLG
1993 Minnesota	AL	15	36	5	1	0	0	(0	0)	6	7	0	6	0	8	0	0	0	1	0	1.00	1	.139	.262	.167
1994 Minnesota	AL	11	31	10	3	0	0	(0	0)	13	3	2	0	0	4	0	0	0	2	0	1.00	1	.323	.323	.419
1995 Minnesota	AL	9	25	5	0	2	0	(0	0)	9	4	3	2	1	2	0	1	0	1	0	1.00	1	.200	.259	.360
1996 Minnesota	AL	49	127	25	6	0	1	(0	1)	34	16	10	8	0	24	0	1	1	3	3	.50	3	.197	.243	.268
1997 Minnesota	AL	115	253	65	12	4	2	(0	2)	91	28	25	18	0	51	1	5	1	3	5	.38	6	.257	.308	.360
1998 Minnesota	AL	110	198	40	6	1	3	(1	2)	57	32	15	16	1	44	0	3	2	2	1	.67	2	.202	.259	.288
1999 Minnesota	AL	136	386	103	18	2	7	(2	5)	146	47	41	22	1	54	3	4	6	11	7	.61	10	.267	.307	.378
2000 Minnesota	AL	134	373	111	24	4	4	(1	3)	155	52	47	48	1	77	0	7	5	7	5	.58	5	.298	.373	.416
2001 Minnesota	AL	112	327	82	16	2	3	(1	2)	111	34	25	29	1	67	2	4	1	6	1	.86	7	.251	.315	.339
9 ML YEARS		691	1756	446	86	15	20	(5	15)	622	223	168	149	5	331	6	25	16	36	22	.62	33	.254	.312	.354

Trevor Hoffman

Pitches: Right **Bats:** Right **Pos:** RP-62   **Ht:** 6'0" **Wt:** 215 **Born:** 10/13/67 **Age:** 34

			HOW MUCH HE PITCHED						WHAT HE GAVE UP									THE RESULTS						
Year Team	Lg	G	GS	CG	GF	IP	BFP	H	R	ER	HR	SH	SF	HB	TBB	IBB	SO	WP	Bk	W	L	Pct.	ShO	Sv-Op	Hld	ERA
1993 Fla-SD	NL	67	0	0	26	90	391	80	43	39	10	4	5	1	39	13	79	5	0	4	6	.400	0	5-8	15	3.90
1994 San Diego	NL	47	0	0	41	56	225	39	16	16	4	1	2	0	20	6	68	3	0	4	4	.500	0	20-23	1	2.57
1995 San Diego	NL	55	0	0	51	53.1	218	48	25	23	10	0	0	0	14	3	52	1	0	7	4	.636	0	31-38	0	3.88
1996 San Diego	NL	70	0	0	62	88	348	50	23	22	6	2	2	2	31	5	111	2	0	9	5	.643	0	42-49	0	2.25
1997 San Diego	NL	70	0	0	59	81.1	322	59	25	24	9	2	1	0	24	4	111	7	0	6	4	.600	0	37-44	0	2.66
1998 San Diego	NL	66	0	0	61	73	274	41	12	12	2	3	0	1	21	2	86	8	0	4	2	.667	0	53-54	0	1.48
1999 San Diego	NL	64	0	0	54	67.1	263	48	23	16	5	1	3	0	15	2	73	4	0	2	3	.400	0	40-43	0	2.14
2000 San Diego	NL	70	0	0	59	72.1	291	61	29	24	7	3	5	0	11	4	85	4	0	4	7	.364	0	43-50	0	2.99
2001 San Diego	NL	62	0	0	55	60.1	248	48	25	23	10	2	2	1	21	2	63	3	0	3	4	.429	0	43-46	0	3.43
1993 Florida	NL	28	0	0	13	35.2	152	24	13	13	5	2	1	0	19	7	26	3	0	2	2	.500	0	2-3	8	3.28
San Diego	NL	39	0	0	13	54.1	239	56	30	26	5	2	4	1	20	6	53	2	0	2	4	.333	0	3-5	7	4.31
9 ML YEARS		571	0	0	468	641.2	2580	474	221	199	63	18	20	5	196	41	728	37	0	43	39	.524	0	314-355	16	2.79

Todd Hollandsworth

Bats: L **Throws:** L **Pos:** LF-25; CF-12; RF-5; PH/PR-3   **Ht:** 6'2" **Wt:** 207 **Born:** 4/20/73 **Age:** 29

								BATTING										BASERUNNING				PERCENTAGES		
Year Team	Lg	G	AB	H	2B	3B	HR	(Hm	Rd)	TB	R	RBI	TBB	IBB	SO	HBP	SH	SF	SB	CS	SB%	GDP	Avg	OBP	SLG
1995 Los Angeles	NL	41	103	24	2	0	5	(3	2)	41	16	13	10	2	29	1	0	1	2	1	.67	1	.233	.304	.398
1996 Los Angeles	NL	149	478	139	26	4	12	(2	10)	209	64	59	41	1	93	2	3	2	21	6	.78	2	.291	.348	.437
1997 Los Angeles	NL	106	296	73	20	2	4	(1	3)	109	39	31	17	2	60	0	2	2	5	5	.50	8	.247	.286	.368
1998 Los Angeles	NL	55	175	47	6	4	3	(1	2)	70	23	20	9	0	42	1	2	0	4	3	.57	2	.269	.308	.400
1999 Los Angeles	NL	92	261	74	12	2	9	(5	4)	117	39	32	24	1	61	1	0	1	5	2	.71	2	.284	.345	.448
2000 LA-Col	NL	137	428	115	20	0	19	(13	6)	192	81	47	41	3	99	1	0	1	18	7	.72	8	.269	.333	.449
2001 Colorado	NL	33	117	43	15	1	6	(3	3)	78	21	19	8	2	20	0	0	0	5	0	1.00	1	.368	.408	.667
2000 Los Angeles	NL	81	261	61	12	0	8	(6	2)	97	42	24	30	2	61	1	0	1	11	4	.73	4	.234	.314	.372
Colorado	NL	56	167	54	8	0	11	(7	4)	95	39	23	11	1	38	0	0	0	7	3	.70	4	.323	.365	.569
7 ML YEARS		613	1858	515	101	13	58	(28	30)	816	283	221	150	11	404	6	7	7	60	24	.71	24	.277	.332	.439

Dave Hollins

Bats: Both **Throws:** Right **Pos:** DH-2   **Ht:** 6'1" **Wt:** 232 **Born:** 5/25/66 **Age:** 36

								BATTING										BASERUNNING				PERCENTAGES		
Year Team	Lg	G	AB	H	2B	3B	HR	(Hm	Rd)	TB	R	RBI	TBB	IBB	SO	HBP	SH	SF	SB	CS	SB%	GDP	Avg	OBP	SLG
2001 Buffalo *	AAA	89	316	86	25	2	16	—	—	163	50	67	45	8	79	7	0	2	0	0	—	7	.272	.373	.516
1990 Philadelphia	NL	72	114	21	0	0	5	(2	3)	36	14	15	10	3	28	1	0	2	0	0	—	1	.184	.252	.316
1991 Philadelphia	NL	56	151	45	10	2	6	(3	3)	77	18	21	17	1	26	3	0	1	1	1	.50	2	.298	.378	.510
1992 Philadelphia	NL	156	586	158	28	4	27	(14	13)	275	104	93	76	4	110	19	0	4	9	6	.60	8	.270	.369	.469
1993 Philadelphia	NL	143	543	148	30	4	18	(9	9)	240	104	93	85	5	109	5	0	7	2	3	.40	15	.273	.372	.442
1994 Philadelphia	NL	44	162	36	7	1	4	(1	3)	57	28	26	23	0	32	4	0	3	1	0	1.00	6	.222	.328	.352
1995 Phi-Bos		70	218	49	12	2	7	(5	2)	86	48	26	57	4	45	5	0	4	1	1	.50	4	.225	.391	.394
1996 Min-Sea	AL	149	516	135	29	2	16	(7	9)	212	88	78	84	7	117	13	1	2	6	6	.50	11	.262	.377	.411
1997 Anaheim	AL	149	572	165	29	2	16	(15	1)	246	101	85	62	2	124	8	1	5	16	6	.73	12	.288	.363	.430
1998 Anaheim	AL	101	363	88	16	2	11	(4	7)	141	60	39	44	2	69	7	2	2	11	3	.79	5	.242	.334	.388
1999 Toronto	AL	27	99	22	5	0	2	(1	1)	33	12	6	5	0	22	0	0	0	2	1	.67	2	.222	.260	.333
2001 Cleveland	AL	2	5	1	0	0	0	(0	0)	1	0	0	1	0	2	0	1	0	0	0	—	0	.200	.333	.200
1995 Philadelphia	NL	65	205	47	12	2	7	(5	2)	84	46	25	53	4	38	5	0	4	1	1	.50	4	.229	.393	.410
Boston	AL	5	13	2	0	0	0	(0	0)	2	2	1	4	0	7	0	0	0	0	0	—	0	.154	.353	.154
1996 Minnesota	AL	121	422	102	26	0	13	(6	7)	167	71	53	71	5	102	10	0	0	6	4	.60	9	.242	.364	.396
Seattle	AL	28	94	33	3	0	3	(1	2)	45	17	25	13	2	15	3	1	2	0	2	.00	2	.351	.438	.479
11 ML YEARS		969	3329	868	166	17	112	(61	51)	1404	577	482	464	28	684	65	5	30	47	26	.64	66	.261	.359	.422

103

Chris Holt

Pitches: Right **Bats:** Right **Pos:** SP-22; RP-8 **Ht:** 6'4" **Wt:** 205 **Born:** 9/18/71 **Age:** 30

Year Team	Lg	G	GS	CG	GF	IP	BFP	H	R	ER	HR	SH	SF	HB	TBB	IBB	SO	WP	Bk	W	L	Pct.	ShO	Sv-Op	Hld	ERA
1996 Houston	NL	4	0	0	3	4.2	22	5	3	3	0	0	0	0	3	1	0	1	0	0	1	.000	0	0-0	0	5.79
1997 Houston	NL	33	32	0	0	209.2	883	211	98	82	17	7	5	8	61	4	95	1	0	8	12	.400	0	0-0	0	3.52
1999 Houston	NL	32	26	0	2	164	720	193	92	85	12	9	8	8	57	1	115	5	0	5	13	.278	0	1-2	0	4.66
2000 Houston	NL	34	32	3	1	207	916	247	131	123	22	7	12	8	75	2	136	10	1	8	16	.333	1	0-0	0	5.35
2001 Detroit	AL	30	22	1	3	151.1	695	197	102	97	18	8	5	8	57	5	80	3	0	7	9	.438	0	0-0	0	5.77
5 ML YEARS		133	112	4	9	736.2	3236	853	426	390	69	31	30	32	253	13	426	20	1	28	51	.354	1	1-2	0	4.76

Mike Holtz

Pitches: Left **Bats:** Left **Pos:** RP-63 **Ht:** 5'9" **Wt:** 185 **Born:** 10/10/72 **Age:** 29

Year Team	Lg	G	GS	CG	GF	IP	BFP	H	R	ER	HR	SH	SF	HB	TBB	IBB	SO	WP	Bk	W	L	Pct.	ShO	Sv-Op	Hld	ERA
2001 Rancho Cuc *	A+	2	2	0	0	2	9	3	2	2	1	0	0	0	3	0	3	0	0	0	0	—	0	0--	0	9.00
1996 California	AL	30	0	0	8	29.1	127	21	11	8	1	1	1	3	19	2	31	1	0	3	3	.500	0	0-0	5	2.45
1997 Anaheim	AL	66	0	0	11	43.1	187	38	21	16	7	1	2	2	15	4	40	1	0	3	4	.429	0	2-8	14	3.32
1998 Anaheim	AL	53	0	0	9	30.1	137	38	16	16	0	1	2	1	15	1	29	4	0	2	2	.500	0	1-2	13	4.75
1999 Anaheim	AL	28	0	0	9	22.1	106	26	20	20	3	1	0	2	15	1	17	3	0	2	3	.400	0	0-0	1	8.06
2000 Anaheim	AL	61	0	0	6	41	176	37	26	23	4	4	3	2	18	2	40	1	0	3	4	.429	0	0-0	10	5.05
2001 Anaheim	AL	63	0	0	11	37	167	40	24	20	5	3	1	2	15	4	38	5	0	1	2	.333	0	0-1	15	4.86
6 ML YEARS		301	0	0	54	203.1	900	200	118	103	20	11	9	12	97	14	195	15	0	14	18	.438	0	3-11	58	4.56

Paul Hoover

Bats: Right **Throws:** Right **Pos:** C-2; PH/PR-1 **Ht:** 6'1" **Wt:** 210 **Born:** 4/14/76 **Age:** 26

Year Team	Lg	G	AB	H	2B	3B	HR	Hm	Rd	TB	R	RBI	TBB	IBB	SO	HBP	SH	SF	SB	CS	SB%	GDP	Avg	OBP	SLG
1997 Princeton	R+	66	251	76	16	4	4	—	—	112	55	37	20	0	37	6	3	4	7	4	.64	3	.303	.363	.446
1998 Chston-SC	A	40	124	36	10	1	3	—	—	57	24	19	22	1	29	5	0	0	2	1	.67	0	.290	.417	.460
Hudson Val	A-	73	269	76	20	1	4	—	—	110	51	37	39	3	44	11	0	6	26	3	.90	5	.283	.388	.409
1999 St. Pete	A+	118	408	111	13	6	8	—	—	160	66	54	54	3	81	16	0	4	23	7	.77	13	.272	.376	.392
2000 Orlando	AA	106	360	90	20	4	3	—	—	127	54	44	67	2	66	13	1	5	9	8	.53	5	.250	.382	.353
Durham	AAA	4	10	3	0	0	0	—	—	3	0	0	0	0	5	1	0	0	1	0	1.00	0	.300	.364	.300
2001 Durham	AAA	89	293	63	18	4	3	—	—	98	37	21	11	0	66	7	8	1	5	3	.63	7	.215	.260	.334
2001 Tampa Bay	AL	3	4	1	0	0	0	(0	0)	1	1	0	0	0	1	0	0	0	0	0	—	0	.250	.250	.250

Tyler Houston

Bats: Left **Throws:** Right **Pos:** 3B-62; PH/PR-13; 1B-3 **Ht:** 6'1" **Wt:** 210 **Born:** 1/17/71 **Age:** 31

Year Team	Lg	G	AB	H	2B	3B	HR	Hm	Rd	TB	R	RBI	TBB	IBB	SO	HBP	SH	SF	SB	CS	SB%	GDP	Avg	OBP	SLG
2001 Beloit *	A	1	3	0	0	0	0	—	—	0	0	0	0	0	1	0	0	0	0	0	—	0	.000	.000	.000
1996 Atl-ChC	NL	79	142	45	9	1	3	(1	2)	65	21	27	9	1	27	0	0	0	3	2	.60	5	.317	.358	.458
1997 Chicago	NL	72	196	51	10	0	2	(0	2)	67	15	28	9	1	35	0	0	2	1	0	1.00	4	.260	.290	.342
1998 Chicago	NL	95	255	65	7	1	9	(4	5)	101	26	33	13	1	53	0	1	1	2	2	.50	6	.255	.290	.396
1999 ChC-Cle	NL	113	276	62	10	1	10	(2	8)	104	28	30	31	4	78	0	1	1	1	1	.50	7	.225	.302	.377
2000 Milwaukee	NL	101	284	71	15	0	18	(6	12)	140	30	43	17	3	72	0	4	0	2	1	.67	13	.250	.292	.493
2001 Milwaukee	NL	75	235	68	7	0	12	(6	6)	111	36	38	18	1	62	1	2	0	0	0	—	3	.289	.343	.472
1996 Atlanta	NL	33	27	6	2	1	1	(1	0)	13	3	8	1	0	9	0	0	0	0	0	—	1	.222	.250	.481
Chicago	NL	46	115	39	7	0	2	(0	2)	52	18	19	8	1	18	0	0	0	3	2	.60	4	.339	.382	.452
1999 Chicago	NL	100	249	58	9	1	9	(2	7)	96	26	27	28	4	67	0	1	1	1	1	.50	7	.233	.309	.386
Cleveland	AL	13	27	4	1	0	1	(0	1)	8	2	3	3	0	11	0	0	0	0	0	—	0	.148	.233	.296
6 ML YEARS		535	1388	362	58	3	54	(19	35)	588	156	199	97	11	327	1	8	4	9	6	.60	38	.261	.309	.424

Bob Howry

Pitches: Right **Bats:** Left **Pos:** RP-69 **Ht:** 6'5" **Wt:** 220 **Born:** 8/4/73 **Age:** 28

Year Team	Lg	G	GS	CG	GF	IP	BFP	H	R	ER	HR	SH	SF	HB	TBB	IBB	SO	WP	Bk	W	L	Pct.	ShO	Sv-Op	Hld	ERA
1998 Chicago	AL	44	0	0	15	54.1	217	37	20	19	7	2	3	2	19	2	51	2	0	0	3	.000	0	9-11	19	3.15
1999 Chicago	AL	69	0	0	54	67.2	298	58	34	27	8	1	3	3	38	3	80	3	1	5	3	.625	0	28-34	1	3.59
2000 Chicago	AL	65	0	0	29	71	289	54	26	25	6	2	4	4	29	2	60	2	0	2	4	.333	0	7-12	14	3.17
2001 Chicago	AL	69	0	0	23	78.2	346	85	41	41	11	4	3	4	30	9	64	6	0	4	5	.444	0	5-11	21	4.69
4 ML YEARS		247	0	0	121	271.2	1150	234	121	112	32	11	13	13	116	16	255	13	1	11	15	.423	0	49-68	55	3.71

Mike Hubbard

Bats: Right **Throws:** Right **Pos:** C-5 **Ht:** 6'1" **Wt:** 205 **Born:** 2/16/71 **Age:** 31

Year Team	Lg	G	AB	H	2B	3B	HR	Hm	Rd	TB	R	RBI	TBB	IBB	SO	HBP	SH	SF	SB	CS	SB%	GDP	Avg	OBP	SLG
2001 Oklahoma *	AAA	35	129	40	8	1	6	—	—	68	22	23	11	0	20	2	2	0	0	1	.00	3	.310	.373	.527
1995 Chicago	NL	15	23	4	0	0	0	(0	0)	4	2	1	2	0	2	0	0	0	0	0	—	1	.174	.240	.174
1996 Chicago	NL	21	38	4	0	0	0	(1	0)	7	1	4	0	0	15	0	0	1	0	0	—	1	.105	.103	.184
1997 Chicago	NL	29	64	13	0	0	1	(0	1)	16	4	2	2	1	21	0	0	1	0	0	—	1	.203	.227	.250
1998 Montreal	NL	32	55	8	1	0	1	(0	1)	12	3	3	0	0	17	1	0	0	0	0	—	1	.145	.161	.218
2000 Atlanta	NL	2	5	0	0	0	0	(0	0)	0	0	0	0	0	1	0	0	0	0	0	—	0	.000	.000	.000
2001 Texas	AL	5	11	3	1	0	1	(0	1)	7	1	1	1	0	4	0	0	0	0	0	—	0	.273	.273	.636
6 ML YEARS		104	192	32	2	0	4	(2	2)	46	11	11	4	1	60	1	0	1	0	0	—	4	.167	.187	.240

Trenidad Hubbard

Bats: Right **Throws:** Right **Pos:** CF-2; PH/PR-2; RF-1   **Ht:** 5'9" **Wt:** 203 **Born:** 5/11/66 **Age:** 36

					BATTING														BASERUNNING				PERCENTAGES		
Year Team	Lg	G	AB	H	2B	3B	HR	(Hm	Rd)	TB	R	RBI	TBB	IBB	SO	HBP	SH	SF	SB	CS	SB%	GDP	Avg	OBP	SLG
2001 Omaha *	AAA	49	175	50	9	1	10	—	—	91	35	28	30	0	34	2	0	2	8	5	.62	1	.286	.392	.520
Iowa *	AAA	49	171	54	11	3	6	—	—	89	38	31	37	1	27	2	0	2	17	5	.77	4	.316	.439	.520
1994 Colorado	NL	18	25	7	1	1	1	(1	0)	13	3	3	3	0	4	0	0	0	0	0	—	1	.280	.357	.520
1995 Colorado	NL	24	58	18	4	0	3	(2	1)	31	13	9	8	0	6	0	1	0	2	1	.67	2	.310	.394	.534
1996 Col-SF	NL	55	89	19	5	2	2	(2	0)	34	15	14	11	0	27	1	0	0	2	0	1.00	3	.213	.307	.382
1997 Cleveland	AL	7	12	3	1	0	0	(0	0)	4	3	0	1	0	3	0	0	0	2	0	1.00	0	.250	.308	.333
1998 Los Angeles	NL	94	208	62	9	1	7	(2	5)	94	29	18	18	0	46	3	3	3	9	5	.64	5	.298	.358	.452
1999 Los Angeles	NL	82	105	33	5	0	1	(0	1)	41	23	13	13	1	24	0	1	1	4	3	.57	2	.314	.387	.390
2000 Atl-Bal		92	108	20	2	2	1	(0	1)	29	18	6	11	0	23	1	3	0	4	2	.67	3	.185	.267	.269
2001 Kansas City	AL	5	12	3	0	1	0	(0	0)	5	2	0	0	0	2	0	0	0	0	0	—	0	.250	.250	.417
1996 Colorado	NL	45	60	13	5	1	1	(1	0)	23	12	12	9	0	22	1	0	0	2	0	1.00	1	.217	.329	.383
San Francisco	NL	10	29	6	0	1	1	(1	0)	11	3	2	2	0	5	0	0	0	0	0	—	2	.207	.258	.379
2000 Atlanta	NL	61	81	15	2	1	1	(0	1)	22	15	6	11	0	20	1	3	0	2	1	.67	1	.185	.290	.272
Baltimore	AL	31	27	5	0	1	0	(0	0)	7	3	0	0	0	3	0	0	0	2	1	.67	2	.185	.185	.259
8 ML YEARS		377	617	165	27	7	15	(7	8)	251	106	63	65	1	135	5	8	4	23	11	.68	16	.267	.340	.407

Ken Huckaby

Bats: Right **Throws:** Right **Pos:** C-1   **Ht:** 6'1" **Wt:** 205 **Born:** 1/27/71 **Age:** 31

					BATTING														BASERUNNING				PERCENTAGES		
Year Team	Lg	G	AB	H	2B	3B	HR	(Hm	Rd)	TB	R	RBI	TBB	IBB	SO	HBP	SH	SF	SB	CS	SB%	GDP	Avg	OBP	SLG
1991 Great Falls	R+	57	213	55	16	0	3	—	—	80	39	37	17	0	38	4	1	3	3	2	.60	4	.258	.321	.376
1992 Vero Beach	A+	73	261	63	9	0	0	—	—	72	14	21	7	0	42	1	2	2	1	1	.50	5	.241	.262	.276
1993 Vero Beach	A+	79	281	75	14	1	4	—	—	103	22	41	11	1	35	2	3	2	2	1	.67	3	.267	.297	.367
San Antonio	AA	28	82	18	1	0	0	—	—	19	4	5	2	1	7	2	0	1	0	0	—	0	.220	.253	.232
1994 San Antonio	AA	11	41	11	1	0	1	—	—	15	3	9	1	1	1	0	0	0	1	0	1.00	0	.268	.286	.366
Bakersfield	A+	77	270	81	18	1	2	—	—	107	29	30	10	0	37	2	0	1	2	3	.40	7	.300	.329	.396
1995 Albuquerque	AAA	89	278	90	16	2	1	—	—	113	30	40	12	1	26	4	3	1	3	1	.75	16	.324	.359	.406
1996 Albuquerque	AAA	103	286	79	16	2	3	—	—	108	37	41	17	1	35	2	3	1	0	0	—	10	.276	.320	.378
1997 Albuquerque	AAA	69	201	40	5	1	0	—	—	47	14	18	9	1	36	0	3	2	1	0	1.00	5	.199	.231	.234
1998 Tacoma	AAA	16	49	11	2	0	0	—	—	13	4	1	5	0	6	0	0	0	0	2	.00	3	.224	.296	.265
Columbus	AAA	36	101	21	3	1	1	—	—	29	13	10	11	0	14	0	3	0	0	2	.00	3	.208	.286	.287
1999 Tucson	AAA	107	355	107	20	1	2	—	—	135	44	42	13	2	33	2	4	5	0	0	—	11	.301	.325	.380
2000 Tucson	AAA	76	243	67	11	1	4	—	—	92	31	33	10	2	30	2	0	3	2	2	.50	10	.276	.306	.379
2001 El Paso	AA	30	104	36	4	0	2	—	—	46	14	14	3	0	16	3	1	4	0	0	—	3	.346	.368	.442
Tucson	AAA	78	262	76	15	1	2	—	—	99	31	34	7	2	62	2	0	1	1	3	.25	3	.290	.313	.378
2001 Arizona	NL	1	1	0	0	0	0	(0	0)	0	0	0	0	0	1	0	0	0	0	0	—	0	.000	.000	.000

Tim Hudson

Pitches: Right **Bats:** Right **Pos:** SP-35   **Ht:** 6'0" **Wt:** 160 **Born:** 7/14/75 **Age:** 26

		HOW MUCH HE PITCHED					WHAT HE GAVE UP											THE RESULTS						
Year Team	Lg	G	GS	CG	GF	IP	BFP	H	R	ER	HR	SH	SF	HB	TBB	IBB	SO	WP	Bk	W	L	Pct.	ShO	Sv-Op	Hld	ERA
1999 Oakland	AL	21	21	1	0	136.1	580	121	56	49	8	1	2	4	62	2	132	6	0	11	2	.846	0	0-0	0	3.23
2000 Oakland	AL	32	32	2	0	202.1	847	169	100	93	24	5	7	7	82	5	169	7	0	20	6	.769	2	0-0	0	4.14
2001 Oakland	AL	35	35	3	0	235	980	216	100	88	20	12	8	6	71	5	181	9	1	18	9	.667	0	0-0	0	3.37
3 ML YEARS		88	88	6	0	573.2	2407	506	256	230	52	18	17	17	215	12	482	22	1	49	17	.742	2	0-0	0	3.61

Aubrey Huff

Bats: L **Throws:** R **Pos:** 3B-73; DH-20; 1B-19; PH/PR-1   **Ht:** 6'4" **Wt:** 221 **Born:** 12/20/76 **Age:** 25

					BATTING														BASERUNNING				PERCENTAGES		
Year Team	Lg	G	AB	H	2B	3B	HR	(Hm	Rd)	TB	R	RBI	TBB	IBB	SO	HBP	SH	SF	SB	CS	SB%	GDP	Avg	OBP	SLG
1998 Chston-SC	A	69	265	85	19	1	13	—	—	145	38	54	24	0	40	0	0	5	3	1	.75	5	.321	.371	.547
1999 Orlando	AA	133	491	148	40	3	22	—	—	260	85	78	64	4	77	4	0	2	2	3	.40	14	.301	.385	.530
2000 Durham	AAA	108	408	129	36	3	20	—	—	231	73	76	51	4	72	2	2	1	2	3	.40	15	.316	.394	.566
2001 Durham	AAA	17	66	19	6	0	3	—	—	34	14	10	5	0	7	0	0	0	0	0	—	3	.288	.338	.515
2000 Tampa Bay	AL	39	122	35	7	0	4	(3	1)	54	12	14	5	1	18	1	0	1	0	0	—	6	.287	.318	.443
2001 Tampa Bay	AL	111	411	102	25	1	8	(5	3)	153	42	45	23	2	72	0	0	0	1	3	.25	18	.248	.288	.372
2 ML YEARS		150	533	137	32	1	12	(8	4)	207	54	59	28	3	90	1	0	1	1	3	.25	24	.257	.295	.388

Todd Hundley

Bats: Both **Throws:** Right **Pos:** C-70; PH/PR-12   **Ht:** 5'11" **Wt:** 195 **Born:** 5/27/69 **Age:** 33

					BATTING														BASERUNNING				PERCENTAGES		
Year Team	Lg	G	AB	H	2B	3B	HR	(Hm	Rd)	TB	R	RBI	TBB	IBB	SO	HBP	SH	SF	SB	CS	SB%	GDP	Avg	OBP	SLG
2001 West Tenn *	AA	4	12	4	2	0	0	—	—	6	1	1	1	0	3	0	0	0	0	0	—	1	.333	.385	.500
Iowa *	AAA	15	51	10	1	0	3	—	—	20	7	8	4	0	23	1	0	1	0	0	—	0	.196	.263	.392
1990 New York	NL	36	67	14	6	0	0	(0	0)	20	8	2	6	0	18	0	1	0	0	0	—	1	.209	.274	.299
1991 New York	NL	21	60	8	0	1	1	(1	0)	13	5	7	6	0	14	1	1	1	0	0	—	3	.133	.221	.217
1992 New York	NL	123	358	75	17	0	7	(2	5)	113	32	32	19	4	76	4	7	2	3	0	1.00	8	.209	.256	.316
1993 New York	NL	130	417	95	17	2	11	(5	6)	149	40	53	23	7	62	2	2	4	1	1	.50	10	.228	.269	.357
1994 New York	NL	91	291	69	10	1	16	(8	8)	129	45	42	25	4	73	3	3	1	2	1	.67	3	.237	.303	.443
1995 New York	NL	90	275	77	11	0	15	(6	9)	133	39	51	42	5	64	5	1	3	1	0	1.00	4	.280	.382	.484
1996 New York	NL	153	540	140	32	1	41	(20	21)	297	85	112	79	15	146	3	0	2	1	3	.25	9	.259	.356	.550
1997 New York	NL	132	417	114	21	2	30	(14	16)	229	78	86	83	16	116	3	0	5	2	3	.40	10	.273	.394	.549
1998 New York	NL	53	124	20	4	0	3	(1	2)	33	8	12	16	0	55	1	0	1	1	1	.50	0	.161	.261	.266
1999 Los Angeles	NL	114	376	78	14	0	24	(10	14)	164	49	55	44	3	113	4	1	3	1	0	1.00	5	.207	.295	.436
2000 Los Angeles	NL	90	299	85	16	0	24	(10	14)	173	49	70	45	6	69	2	1	6	0	1	.00	5	.284	.375	.579
2001 Chicago	NL	79	246	46	10	0	12	(4	8)	92	23	31	25	0	89	3	0	2	0	0	—	7	.187	.268	.374
12 ML YEARS		1112	3470	821	158	7	184	(81	103)	1545	461	553	413	60	895	31	17	30	14	10	.58	65	.237	.321	.445

Brian Hunter

Bats: R **Throws:** R **Pos:** PH/PR-46; LF-22; CF-18; RF-5; DH-1   **Ht:** 6'3" **Wt:** 180 **Born:** 3/5/71 **Age:** 31

Year Team	Lg	G	AB	H	2B	3B	HR	(Hm	Rd)	TB	R	RBI	TBB	IBB	SO	HBP	SH	SF	SB	CS	SB%	GDP	Avg	OBP	SLG
2001 Scrantn-WB *	AAA	2	9	1	0	0	0	—	—	1	1	0	1	0	3	0	0	0	0	0	—	0	.111	.200	.111
1994 Houston	NL	6	24	6	1	0	0	(0	0)	7	2	0	1	0	6	0	1	0	2	1	.67	0	.250	.280	.292
1995 Houston	NL	78	321	97	14	5	2	(0	2)	127	52	28	21	0	52	2	2	3	24	7	.77	2	.302	.346	.396
1996 Houston	NL	132	526	145	27	2	5	(1	4)	191	74	35	17	0	92	2	1	7	35	9	.80	6	.276	.297	.363
1997 Detroit	AL	162	658	177	29	7	4	(2	2)	232	112	45	66	1	121	1	8	5	74	18	.80	13	.269	.334	.353
1998 Detroit	AL	142	595	151	29	3	4	(1	3)	198	67	36	36	0	94	2	2	1	42	12	.78	8	.254	.298	.333
1999 Det-Sea	AL	139	539	125	13	6	4	(0	4)	162	79	34	37	0	91	2	4	7	44	8	.85	8	.232	.280	.301
2000 Col-Cin	NL	104	240	64	5	1	1	(1	0)	74	47	14	27	0	40	1	5	1	20	3	.87	2	.267	.342	.308
2001 Philadelphia	NL	83	145	40	6	0	2	(2	0)	52	22	16	16	0	25	0	3	2	14	3	.82	3	.276	.344	.359
1999 Detroit	AL	18	55	13	2	1	0	(0	0)	17	8	0	5	0	11	1	1	0	0	3	.00	1	.236	.311	.309
Seattle		121	484	112	11	5	4	(0	4)	145	71	34	32	0	80	1	3	7	44	5	.90	8	.231	.277	.300
2000 Colorado	NL	72	200	55	4	1	1	(1	0)	64	36	13	21	0	31	1	4	0	15	3	.83	2	.275	.347	.320
Cincinnati	NL	32	40	9	1	0	0	(0	0)	10	11	1	6	0	9	0	1	1	5	0	1.00	0	.225	.319	.250
8 ML YEARS		846	3048	805	124	24	22	(7	15)	1043	455	208	221	1	521	10	26	26	255	61	.81	42	.264	.313	.342

Torii Hunter

Bats: Right **Throws:** Right **Pos:** CF-147; PH/PR-1   **Ht:** 6'2" **Wt:** 205 **Born:** 7/18/75 **Age:** 26

Year Team	Lg	G	AB	H	2B	3B	HR	(Hm	Rd)	TB	R	RBI	TBB	IBB	SO	HBP	SH	SF	SB	CS	SB%	GDP	Avg	OBP	SLG
1997 Minnesota	AL	1	0	0	0	0	0	(0	0)	0	0	0	0	0	0	0	0	0	0	0	—	0	—	—	—
1998 Minnesota	AL	6	17	4	1	0	0	(0	0)	5	0	2	2	0	6	0	0	0	0	1	.00	1	.235	.316	.294
1999 Minnesota	AL	135	384	98	17	2	9	(2	7)	146	52	35	26	1	72	6	1	5	10	6	.63	9	.255	.309	.380
2000 Minnesota	AL	99	336	94	14	7	5	(4	1)	137	44	44	18	2	68	2	0	2	4	3	.57	13	.280	.318	.408
2001 Minnesota	AL	148	564	147	32	5	27	(13	14)	270	82	92	29	0	125	8	1	1	9	6	.60	12	.261	.306	.479
5 ML YEARS		389	1301	343	64	14	41	(19	22)	558	178	173	75	3	271	16	2	8	23	16	.59	35	.264	.310	.429

Chad Hutchinson

Pitches: Right **Bats:** Right **Pos:** RP-3   **Ht:** 6'5" **Wt:** 230 **Born:** 2/21/77 **Age:** 25

		HOW MUCH HE PITCHED					WHAT HE GAVE UP											THE RESULTS						
Year Team	Lg	G	GS	CG	GF	IP	BFP	H	R	ER	HR	SH	SF	HB	TBB	IBB	SO	WP	Bk	W	L	Pct.	ShO	Sv-Op	Hld	ERA
1998 New Jersey	A-	3	3	0	0	15.1	67	15	7	6	0	0	0	2	4	0	20	0	0	0	1	.000	0	0--	—	3.52
Pr William	A+	5	5	0	0	29	118	20	12	9	4	1	0	1	11	0	31	0	2	2	0	1.000	0	0--	—	2.79
1999 Arkansas	AA	25	25	0	0	141	624	127	79	74	12	8	5	4	85	0	150	20	3	7	11	.389	0	0--	—	4.72
Memphis	AAA	2	2	0	0	12.1	48	4	3	3	2	0	0	0	8	0	16	0	0	2	0	1.000	0	0--	—	2.19
2000 Memphis	AAA	5	4	0	0	8.1	63	10	24	24	1	2	3	3	27	0	9	3	0	1	0	.000	0	0--	—	25.92
Arkansas	AA	11	11	1	0	48	206	40	21	18	1	0	1	2	27	0	54	2	0	2	3	.400	1	0--	—	3.38
2001 Memphis	AAA	27	20	0	1	97.2	492	99	91	86	8	3	5	10	104	0	111	17	1	4	9	.308	0	0--	—	7.92
2001 St. Louis	NL	3	0	0	0	4	27	9	11	11	3	0	0	1	6	0	2	1	0	0	0	—	0	0-0	0	24.75

Adam Hyzdu

Bats: R **Throws:** R **Pos:** PH/PR-22; RF-18; LF-8; 1B-4; CF-1   **Ht:** 6'2" **Wt:** 220 **Born:** 12/6/71 **Age:** 30

Year Team	Lg	G	AB	H	2B	3B	HR	(Hm	Rd)	TB	R	RBI	TBB	IBB	SO	HBP	SH	SF	SB	CS	SB%	GDP	Avg	OBP	SLG
1990 Everett	A-	69	253	62	16	1	6	—	—	98	31	34	28	1	78	2	0	5	2	4	.33	4	.245	.319	.387
1991 Clinton	A	124	410	96	14	5	5	—	—	135	47	50	64	1	131	3	7	2	4	5	.44	10	.234	.340	.329
1992 San Jose	A+	128	457	127	25	5	9	—	—	189	60	60	55	4	134	1	1	8	10	5	.67	6	.278	.351	.414
1993 San Jose	A+	44	165	48	11	3	13	—	—	104	35	38	29	0	53	0	1	2	1	1	.50	3	.291	.393	.630
Shreveport		86	302	61	17	0	6	—	—	96	30	25	20	2	82	1	1	1	0	5	.00	5	.202	.253	.318
1994 Winston-Sal	A+	55	210	58	11	1	15	—	—	116	30	39	18	0	33	2	0	2	1	5	.17	3	.276	.336	.552
Chattanooga	AA	38	133	35	10	0	3	—	—	54	17	9	8	0	21	1	1	0	0	2	.00	1	.263	.310	.406
Indianapolis	AAA	12	25	3	2	0	0	—	—	5	3	3	1	0	5	0	0	2	0	0	—	0	.120	.143	.200
1995 Chattanooga	AA	102	312	82	14	1	13	—	—	137	55	48	45	2	56	4	2	1	3	2	.60	4	.263	.362	.439
1996 Trenton	AA	109	374	126	24	3	25	—	—	231	71	80	56	6	75	2	0	2	1	8	.11	7	.337	.424	.618
1997 Pawtucket	AAA	119	413	114	21	1	23	—	—	206	77	84	72	0	113	4	1	2	10	6	.63	6	.276	.387	.499
1998 Tucson	AAA	34	100	34	7	1	4	—	—	55	21	14	15	0	23	0	1	2	0	1	.00	2	.340	.419	.550
1999 Pawtucket	AAA	12	35	8	0	0	1	—	—	11	4	6	4	0	13	0	0	0	0	0	—	0	.229	.308	.314
Altoona	AA	91	345	109	26	2	24	—	—	211	64	78	40	1	62	3	0	0	8	4	.67	2	.316	.392	.612
Nashville	AAA	14	44	11	1	0	5	—	—	27	6	13	4	0	11	0	0	0	0	0	—	2	.250	.313	.614
2000 Altoona	AA	142	514	149	39	2	31	—	—	285	96	106	94	7	102	8	0	3	3	7	.30	6	.290	.405	.554
2001 Nashville	AAA	69	261	76	17	2	11	—	—	130	38	39	17	3	68	0	0	2	1	3	.25	3	.291	.332	.498
2000 Pittsburgh	NL	12	18	7	2	0	1	(0	1)	12	2	4	0	0	4	0	0	0	0	0	—	0	.389	.389	.667
2001 Pittsburgh	NL	51	72	15	1	0	5	(0	5)	31	7	9	4	0	18	1	0	0	0	1	.00	1	.208	.260	.431
2 ML YEARS		63	90	22	3	0	6	(0	6)	43	9	13	4	0	22	1	0	0	0	1	.00	1	.244	.284	.478

Raul Ibanez

Bats: L **Throws:** R **Pos:** DH-33; PH/PR-27; RF-24; LF-17; 1B-10; CF-2; 3B-1   **Ht:** 6'2" **Wt:** 200 **Born:** 6/2/72 **Age:** 30

Year Team	Lg	G	AB	H	2B	3B	HR	(Hm	Rd)	TB	R	RBI	TBB	IBB	SO	HBP	SH	SF	SB	CS	SB%	GDP	Avg	OBP	SLG
2001 Omaha *	AAA	8	27	4	1	0	2	—	—	11	3	5	1	0	10	0	1	0	0	0	—	0	.148	.179	.407
1996 Seattle	AL	4	5	0	0	0	0	(0	0)	0	0	0	0	0	1	1	0	0	0	0	—	0	.000	.167	.000
1997 Seattle	AL	11	26	4	0	1	1	(1	0)	9	3	4	0	0	6	0	0	0	0	0	—	0	.154	.154	.346
1998 Seattle	AL	37	98	25	7	1	2	(1	1)	40	12	12	5	0	22	0	0	0	0	0	—	4	.255	.291	.408
1999 Seattle	AL	87	209	54	7	0	9	(3	6)	88	23	27	17	1	32	0	0	1	5	1	.83	4	.258	.313	.421
2000 Seattle	AL	92	140	32	8	0	2	(2	0)	46	21	15	14	1	25	1	0	1	2	0	1.00	1	.229	.301	.329
2001 Kansas City	AL	104	279	78	11	5	13	(5	8)	138	44	54	32	2	51	0	0	1	0	2	.00	6	.280	.353	.495
6 ML YEARS		335	757	193	33	7	27	(12	15)	321	103	112	68	4	137	2	0	3	7	3	.70	15	.255	.317	.424

Brandon Inge

Bats: Right **Throws:** Right **Pos:** C-79; PH/PR-4   **Ht:** 5'11" **Wt:** 185 **Born:** 5/19/77 **Age:** 25

							BATTING										BASERUNNING				PERCENTAGES		
Year Team	Lg	G	AB	H	2B	3B	HR	(Hm | Rd)	TB	R	RBI	TBB	IBB	SO	HBP	SH	SF	SB	CS	SB%	GDP	Avg	OBP	SLG
1998 Jamestown	A-	51	191	44	10	1	8	—	—	80	24	29	17	1	53	6	0	1	8	8	.50	4	.230	.312	.419
1999 W Michigan	A	100	352	86	25	2	9	—	—	142	54	46	39	0	87	3	2	6	15	3	.83	7	.244	.320	.403
2000 Jacksnville	AA	78	298	77	25	1	6	—	—	122	39	53	26	1	73	0	1	5	10	3	.77	10	.258	.313	.409
Toledo	AAA	55	190	42	9	3	5	—	—	72	24	20	15	0	51	1	1	1	2	1	.67	5	.221	.280	.379
2001 Tigers	R	3	10	1	0	0	1	—	—	4	1	2	2	0	2	0	0	0	0	0	—	0	.100	.250	.400
W Michigan	A	4	16	3	1	0	0	—	—	4	3	2	2	0	5	1	0	0	0	0	—	0	.188	.316	.250
Toledo	AAA	27	90	26	11	1	2	—	—	45	11	15	7	0	24	1	1	3	1	0	1.00	2	.289	.337	.500
2001 Detroit	AL	79	189	34	11	0	0	(0 | 0)	45	13	15	9	0	41	0	2	2	1	4	.20	2	.180	.215	.238

Hideki Irabu

Pitches: Right **Bats:** Right **Pos:** SP-3   **Ht:** 6'4" **Wt:** 240 **Born:** 5/5/69 **Age:** 33

		HOW MUCH HE PITCHED						WHAT HE GAVE UP											THE RESULTS					
Year Team	Lg	G	GS	CG	GF	IP	BFP	H	R	ER	HR	SH	SF	HB	TBB	IBB	SO	WP	Bk	W	L	Pct.	ShO	Sv-Op	Hld	ERA
2001 Jupiter *	A+					9	39	5	3	3	1	0	1	1	4	0	9	0	0	0	0	—	0	0- -	—	3.00
Ottawa *	AAA	4	4	0	0	22.1	92	22	12	11	2	0	0	2	6	0	21	4	1	1	2	.333	0	0- -	—	4.43
1997 New York	AL	13	9	0	0	53.1	246	69	47	42	15	1	2	1	20	0	56	4	3	5	4	.556	0	0-0	1	7.09
1998 New York	AL	29	28	2	0	173	732	148	79	78	27	6	6	9	76	1	126	6	1	13	9	.591	1	0-0	0	4.06
1999 New York	AL	32	27	2	2	169.1	733	180	98	91	26	4	4	6	46	0	133	7	0	11	7	.611	1	0-0	0	4.84
2000 Montreal	NL	11	11	0	0	54.2	247	77	45	44	9	3	2	1	14	0	42	5	2	2	5	.286	0	0-0	0	7.24
2001 Montreal	NL	3	3	0	0	16.2	74	22	9	9	3	0	1	0	3	0	18	0	0	0	2	.000	0	0-0	0	4.86
5 ML YEARS		88	78	4	2	467	2032	496	278	264	80	12	15	17	159	1	375	22	6	31	27	.534	2	0-0	1	5.09

Jason Isringhausen

Pitches: Right **Bats:** Right **Pos:** RP-65   **Ht:** 6'3" **Wt:** 210 **Born:** 9/7/72 **Age:** 29

		HOW MUCH HE PITCHED						WHAT HE GAVE UP											THE RESULTS					
Year Team	Lg	G	GS	CG	GF	IP	BFP	H	R	ER	HR	SH	SF	HB	TBB	IBB	SO	WP	Bk	W	L	Pct.	ShO	Sv-Op	Hld	ERA
1995 New York	NL	14	14	1	0	93	385	88	29	29	6	3	3	2	31	2	55	4	1	9	2	.818	0	0-0	0	2.81
1996 New York	NL	27	27	2	0	171.2	766	190	103	91	13	7	9	8	73	5	114	14	0	6	14	.300	1	0-0	0	4.77
1997 New York	NL	6	6	0	0	29.2	146	40	27	25	3	1	2	1	22	0	25	3	0	2	2	.500	0	0-0	0	7.58
1999 NYM-Oak		33	5	0	20	64.2	286	64	35	34	9	0	1	3	34	4	51	4	0	1	4	.200	0	9-9	0	4.73
2000 Oakland	AL	66	0	0	57	69	304	67	34	29	6	2	1	3	32	5	57	5	1	6	4	.600	0	33-40	0	3.78
2001 Oakland	AL	65	0	0	54	71.1	293	54	24	21	5	3	1	0	23	5	74	2	0	4	3	.571	0	34-43	0	2.65
1999 New York	NL	13	5	0	2	39.1	179	43	29	29	7	0	1	2	22	2	31	2	0	1	3	.250	0	1-1	0	6.41
Oakland	AL	20	0	0	18	25.1	107	21	6	5	2	0	0	1	12	2	20	2	0	0	1	.000	0	8-8	0	2.13
6 ML YEARS		211	52	3	131	499.1	2179	503	252	229	42	16	17	17	215	21	376	32	2	28	29	.491	1	76-92	0	4.13

Cesar Izturis

Bats: Both **Throws:** Right **Pos:** 2B-41; SS-6; PH/PR-3   **Ht:** 5'9" **Wt:** 155 **Born:** 2/10/80 **Age:** 22

							BATTING											BASERUNNING				PERCENTAGES		
Year Team	Lg	G	AB	H	2B	3B	HR	(Hm	Rd)	TB	R	RBI	TBB	IBB	SO	HBP	SH	SF	SB	CS	SB%	GDP	Avg	OBP	SLG
1997 St.Cathrnes	A-	70	231	44	3	0	1	—	—	50	32	11	15	0	27	1	8	2	6	3	.67	3	.190	.241	.216
1998 Hagerstown	A	130	413	108	13	1	1	—	—	126	56	38	20	0	43	2	9	2	20	9	.69	5	.262	.297	.305
1999 Dunedin	A+	131	536	165	28	12	3	—	—	226	77	77	22	4	58	6	17	9	32	16	.67	9	.308	.337	.422
2000 Syracuse	AAA	132	435	95	16	5	0	—	—	121	54	27	20	0	44	1	13	2	21	11	.66	5	.218	.253	.278
2001 Syracuse	AAA	87	342	100	16	3	2	—	—	128	32	35	10	0	22	1	4	5	24	9	.73	4	.292	.310	.374
2001 Toronto	AL	46	134	36	6	2	2	(1	1)	52	19	9	2	0	15	0	4	0	8	1	.89	0	.269	.279	.388

Damian Jackson

Bats: R **Throws:** R **Pos:** 2B-118; SS-3; CF-2; PH/PR-2   **Ht:** 5'11" **Wt:** 185 **Born:** 8/16/73 **Age:** 28

							BATTING											BASERUNNING				PERCENTAGES		
Year Team	Lg	G	AB	H	2B	3B	HR	(Hm	Rd)	TB	R	RBI	TBB	IBB	SO	HBP	SH	SF	SB	CS	SB%	GDP	Avg	OBP	SLG
2001 Portland *	AAA	3	10	3	3	0	0	—	—	6	4	0	3	0	1	0	0	0	0	1	.00	0	.300	.462	.600
1996 Cleveland	AL	5	10	3	2	0	0	(0	0)	5	2	1	1	0	4	0	0	0	0	0	—	0	.300	.364	.500
1997 Cle-Cin		20	36	7	2	1	1	(0	1)	14	8	2	4	1	8	1	1	0	2	1	.67	0	.194	.293	.389
1998 Cincinnati	NL	13	38	12	5	0	0	(0	0)	17	4	7	6	0	4	0	0	1	2	0	1.00	1	.316	.400	.447
1999 San Diego	NL	133	388	87	20	2	9	(6	3)	138	56	39	53	3	105	3	0	3	34	10	.77	2	.224	.320	.356
2000 San Diego	NL	138	470	120	27	6	6	(5	1)	177	68	37	62	2	108	3	4	2	28	6	.82	7	.255	.345	.377
2001 San Diego	NL	122	440	106	21	6	4	(1	3)	151	67	38	44	2	128	6	2	3	23	6	.79	6	.241	.316	.343
1997 Cleveland	AL	8	9	1	0	0	0	—	—	1	2	0	0	0	1	1	0	0	1	0	1.00	0	.111	.200	.111
Cincinnati	NL	12	27	6	2	1	1	(0	1)	13	6	2	4	1	7	0	1	0	1	1	.50	0	.222	.323	.481
6 ML YEARS		431	1382	335	77	15	20	(12	8)	502	205	124	170	8	357	13	7	9	89	23	.79	16	.242	.329	.363

Mike Jackson

Pitches: Right **Bats:** Right **Pos:** RP-67   **Ht:** 6'2" **Wt:** 225 **Born:** 12/22/64 **Age:** 37

		HOW MUCH HE PITCHED						WHAT HE GAVE UP											THE RESULTS					
Year Team	Lg	G	GS	CG	GF	IP	BFP	H	R	ER	HR	SH	SF	HB	TBB	IBB	SO	WP	Bk	W	L	Pct.	ShO	Sv-Op	Hld	ERA
1986 Philadelphia	NL	9	0	0	4	13.1	54	12	5	5	2	0	0	2	4	1	3	0	0	0	0	—	0	0-1	0	3.38
1987 Philadelphia	NL	55	7	0	8	109.1	468	88	55	51	16	3	4	3	56	6	93	6	8	3	10	.231	0	1-2	6	4.20
1988 Seattle	AL	62	0	0	29	99.1	412	74	37	29	10	3	10	2	43	10	76	6	0	6	5	.545	0	4-11	10	2.63
1989 Seattle	AL	65	0	0	27	99.1	431	81	43	35	8	6	2	6	54	6	94	1	2	4	6	.400	0	7-10	9	3.17
1990 Seattle	AL	63	0	0	28	77.1	338	64	42	39	8	8	5	2	44	12	69	9	2	5	7	.417	0	3-12	13	4.54
1991 Seattle	AL	72	0	0	35	88.2	363	64	35	32	5	4	0	6	34	11	74	3	0	7	7	.500	0	14-22	9	3.25
1992 San Fran	NL	67	0	0	24	82	346	76	35	34	7	5	2	4	33	10	80	1	0	6	6	.500	0	2-3	9	3.73
1993 San Fran	NL	81	0	0	17	77.1	317	58	28	26	7	4	2	3	24	6	70	2	2	6	6	.500	0	1-6	34	3.03
1994 San Fran	NL	36	0	0	12	42.1	158	23	8	7	4	4	1	2	11	0	51	0	0	3	2	.600	0	4-6	9	1.49

		HOW MUCH HE PITCHED					WHAT HE GAVE UP											THE RESULTS						
Year Team	Lg	G	GS	CG	GF	IP	BFP	H	R	ER	HR	SH	SF	HB	TBB	IBB	SO	WP	Bk	W	L	Pct.	ShO	Sv-Op	Hld	ERA
1995 Cincinnati	NL	40	0	0	10	49	200	38	13	13	5	1	1	1	19	1	41	1		6	1	.857	0	2-4	9	2.39
1996 Seattle	AL	73	0	0	23	72	302	61	32	29	11	0	1	6	24	3	70	2	0	1	1	.500	0	6-8	15	3.63
1997 Cleveland	AL	71	0	0	38	75	313	59	33	27	3	3	3	4	29	5	74	2	0	2	5	.286	0	15-17	14	3.24
1998 Cleveland	AL	69	0	0	57	64	239	43	11	11	4	1	0	4	13	0	55	1	3	1	1	.500	0	40-45	1	1.55
1999 Cleveland	AL	72	0	0	65	68.2	291	60	32	31	11	2	2	2	26	1	55	0	1	3	4	.429	0	39-43	0	4.06
2001 Houston	NL	67	0	0	16	69	292	68	36	36	14	4	2	2	22	3	46	2	0	5	3	.625	0	4-9	19	4.70
15 ML YEARS		902	7	0	393	1086.2	4524	869	445	405	115	48	35	49	436	75	951	36	25	58	64	.475	0	142-199	157	3.35

Ryan Jackson

Bats: L Throws: L Pos: 1B-35; PH/PR-29; LF-19; RF-15; DH-5

Ht: 6'2" Wt: 205 Born: 11/15/71 Age: 30

		BATTING																	BASERUNNING				PERCENTAGES		
Year Team	Lg	G	AB	H	2B	3B	HR	(Hm	Rd)	TB	R	RBI	TBB	IBB	SO	HBP	SH	SF	SB	CS	SB%	GDP	Avg	OBP	SLG
2001 Toledo *	AAA	9	35	10	1	0	1	—	—	14	2	9	5	0	6	0	0	0	0	0	—	0	.286	.375	.400
1998 Florida	NL	111	260	65	15	1	5	(3	2)	97	26	31	20	0	73	1	2	1	1	1	.50	3	.250	.305	.373
1999 Seattle	AL	32	68	16	3	0	0	(0	0)	19	4	10	6	0	19	1	0	2	3	3	.50	3	.235	.299	.279
2001 Detroit	AL	79	118	25	4	2	2	(1	1)	39	19	11	5	0	26	1	2	0	3	1	.75	1	.212	.250	.331
3 ML YEARS		222	446	106	22	3	7	(4	3)	155	49	52	31	0	118	3	4	3	7	5	.58	7	.238	.290	.348

John Jaha

Bats: Right Throws: Right Pos: DH-12

Ht: 6'1" Wt: 224 Born: 5/27/66 Age: 36

		BATTING																	BASERUNNING				PERCENTAGES		
Year Team	Lg	G	AB	H	2B	3B	HR	(Hm	Rd)	TB	R	RBI	TBB	IBB	SO	HBP	SH	SF	SB	CS	SB%	GDP	Avg	OBP	SLG
2001 Sacramento *	AAA	23	84	16	5	0	4	—	—	33	9	11	11	1	32	0	0	0	0	0	—	2	.190	.284	.393
1992 Milwaukee	AL	47	133	30	3	1	2	(1	1)	41	17	10	12	1	30	2	1	4	10	0	1.00	1	.226	.291	.308
1993 Milwaukee	AL	153	515	136	21	0	19	(5	14)	214	78	70	51	4	109	8	4	4	13	9	.59	6	.264	.337	.416
1994 Milwaukee	AL	84	291	70	14	0	12	(5	7)	120	45	39	32	3	75	10	1	4	3	3	.50	8	.241	.332	.412
1995 Milwaukee	AL	88	316	99	20	2	20	(8	12)	183	59	65	36	0	66	4	0	1	2	1	.67	8	.313	.389	.579
1996 Milwaukee	AL	148	543	163	28	1	34	(17	17)	295	108	118	85	1	118	5	0	3	3	1	.75	16	.300	.398	.543
1997 Milwaukee	AL	46	162	40	7	0	11	(1	10)	80	25	26	25	1	40	3	0	2	1	0	1.00	6	.247	.354	.494
1998 Milwaukee	NL	73	216	45	6	1	7	(2	5)	74	29	38	49	3	66	6	0	2	1	3	.25	5	.208	.354	.343
1999 Oakland	AL	142	457	126	23	0	35	(18	17)	254	93	111	101	2	129	6	0	3	2	0	1.00	14	.276	.414	.556
2000 Oakland	AL	33	97	17	1	0	1	(0	1)	21	14	15	33	0	38	3	0	0	1	0	1.00	4	.175	.398	.216
2001 Oakland	AL	12	45	4	3	0	0	(0	0)	7	2	8	6	0	15	0	0	0	0	0	—	3	.089	.192	.156
10 ML YEARS		826	2775	730	126	5	141	(57	84)	1289	470	490	430	15	686	50	6	24	36	17	.68	71	.263	.369	.465

Mike James

Pitches: Right Bats: Right Pos: RP-40

Ht: 6'3" Wt: 205 Born: 8/15/67 Age: 34

		HOW MUCH HE PITCHED						WHAT HE GAVE UP												THE RESULTS						
Year Team	Lg	G	GS	CG	GF	IP	BFP	H	R	ER	HR	SH	SF	HB	TBB	IBB	SO	WP	Bk	W	L	Pct.	ShO	Sv-Op	Hld	ERA
2001 Memphis *	AAA	10	0	0	11	9	42	10	6	4	1	1	2	2	4	1	9	0	0	0	2	.000	0	0--	--	4.00
1995 California	AL	46	0	0	11	55.2	237	49	27	24	6	2	0	3	26	2	36	1	0	3	0	1.000	0	1-2	3	3.88
1996 California	AL	69	0	0	23	81	353	62	27	24	7	6	5	10	42	7	65	5	0	5	5	.500	0	1-6	18	2.67
1997 Anaheim	AL	58	0	0	22	62.2	284	69	32	30	3	6	1	5	28	4	57	1	0	5	5	.500	0	7-13	12	4.31
1998 Anaheim	AL	11	0	0	3	14	55	10	3	3	0	0	0	0	7	0	12	0	0	0	0	.000	0	0-0	2	1.93
2000 St. Louis	NL	51	0	0	11	51.1	213	40	22	18	7	2	1	3	24	2	41	2	0	2	2	.500	0	2-5	12	3.16
2001 St. Louis	NL	40	0	0	11	38	173	43	24	22	5	3	1	5	17	2	26	3	0	1	2	.333	0	0-0	4	5.21
6 ML YEARS		275	0	0	80	302.2	1315	273	135	121	28	19	8	26	144	17	237	12	0	16	14	.533	0	11-26	51	3.60

Kevin Jarvis

Pitches: Right Bats: Left Pos: SP-32

Ht: 6'2" Wt: 200 Born: 8/1/69 Age: 32

		HOW MUCH HE PITCHED						WHAT HE GAVE UP												THE RESULTS						
Year Team	Lg	G	GS	CG	GF	IP	BFP	H	R	ER	HR	SH	SF	HB	TBB	IBB	SO	WP	Bk	W	L	Pct.	ShO	Sv-Op	Hld	ERA
1994 Cincinnati	NL	6	3	0	0	17.2	79	22	14	14	4	1	2	0	5	0	10	1	0	1	1	.500	0	0-0	0	7.13
1995 Cincinnati	NL	19	11	1	2	79	354	91	56	50	13	2	5	3	32	2	33	2	0	3	4	.429	1	0-0	0	5.70
1996 Cincinnati	NL	24	20	2	2	120.1	552	152	93	80	17	6	2	2	43	5	63	3	0	8	9	.471	0	0-0	0	5.98
1997 Cin-Min-Det	AL	32	5	0	13	68	329	99	62	58	17	2	1	1	29	0	48	4	0	0	4	.000	0	1-1	0	7.68
1999 Oakland	AL	4	1	0	0	14	75	28	19	18	6	0	1	1	6	0	11	0	0	0	1	.000	0	0-0	0	11.57
2000 Colorado	NL	24	19	0	0	115	505	138	83	76	26	6	2	4	33	3	60	2	0	3	4	.429	0	0-0	0	5.95
2001 San Diego	NL	32	32	1	0	193.1	809	189	107	103	37	7	4	5	49	4	133	1	0	12	11	.522	1	0-0	0	4.79
1997 Cincinnati	NL	9	0	0	3	13.1	70	21	16	15	4	1	0	1	7	0	12	2	0	0	1	.000	0	1-1	0	10.13
Minnesota	AL	6	2	0	1	13	70	23	18	18	4	0	1	0	8	0	9	2	0	0	0	—	0	0-0	0	12.46
Detroit	AL	17	3	0	9	41.2	189	55	28	25	9	1	1	0	14	0	27	0	0	0	3	.000	0	0-0	0	5.40
7 ML YEARS		141	91	4	17	607.1	2703	719	434	399	120	24	15	16	197	14	358	13	0	27	34	.443	3	1-1	0	5.91

Stan Javier

Bats: B Throws: R Pos: LF-62; PH/PR-19; CF-13; RF-11; 1B-6; DH-2

Ht: 6'0" Wt: 200 Born: 1/9/64 Age: 38

		BATTING																	BASERUNNING				PERCENTAGES		
Year Team	Lg	G	AB	H	2B	3B	HR	(Hm	Rd)	TB	R	RBI	TBB	IBB	SO	HBP	SH	SF	SB	CS	SB%	GDP	Avg	OBP	SLG
1984 New York	AL	7	7	1	0	0	0	(0	0)	1	1	0	0	0	1	0	0	0	0	0	—	0	.143	.143	.143
1986 Oakland	AL	59	114	23	8	0	0	(0	0)	31	13	8	16	0	27	1	0	0	8	0	1.00	2	.202	.305	.272
1987 Oakland	AL	81	151	28	3	1	2	(1	1)	39	22	9	19	3	33	0	6	0	3	2	.60	2	.185	.276	.258
1988 Oakland	AL	125	397	102	13	3	2	(0	2)	127	49	35	32	1	63	2	6	3	20	1	.95	13	.257	.313	.320
1989 Oakland	AL	112	310	77	12	3	1	(1	0)	98	42	28	31	1	45	1	4	2	12	2	.86	6	.248	.317	.316
1990 Oak-LA		123	309	92	9	6	3	(1	2)	122	60	27	40	2	50	0	6	2	15	7	.68	6	.298	.376	.395
1991 Los Angeles	NL	121	176	36	5	3	1	(0	1)	50	21	11	16	0	36	0	3	2	7	1	.88	4	.205	.268	.284
1992 LA-Phi	NL	130	334	83	17	1	1	(0	1)	105	42	29	37	2	54	3	3	2	18	3	.86	4	.249	.327	.314
1993 California	AL	92	237	69	10	4	3	(0	3)	96	33	28	27	1	33	1	1	3	12	2	.86	7	.291	.362	.405
1994 Oakland	AL	109	419	114	23	0	10	(1	9)	167	75	44	49	1	76	2	7	3	24	7	.77	7	.272	.349	.399

Year Team	Lg	G	AB	H	2B	3B	HR	(Hm	Rd)	TB	R	RBI	TBB	IBB	SO	HBP	SH	SF	SB	CS	SB%	GDP	Avg	OBP	SLG
1995 Oakland	AL	130	442	123	20	2	8	(3	5)	171	81	56	49	3	63	4	5	4	36	5	.88	8	.278	.353	.387
1996 San Francisco	NL	71	274	74	25	0	2	(1	1)	105	44	22	25	0	51	2	5	0	14	2	.88	4	.270	.336	.383
1997 San Francisco	NL	142	440	126	16	4	8	(6	2)	174	69	50	56	1	70	5	2	7	25	3	.89	5	.286	.368	.395
1998 San Francisco	NL	135	417	121	13	5	4	(1	3)	156	63	49	65	4	63	1	4	3	21	5	.81	13	.290	.385	.374
1999 SF-Hou	NL	132	397	113	19	2	3	(2	1)	145	61	34	38	4	63	1	8	2	16	7	.70	6	.285	.347	.365
2000 Seattle	AL	105	342	94	18	5	5	(5	0)	137	61	40	42	2	64	0	4	4	4	3	.57	7	.275	.351	.401
2001 Seattle	AL	89	281	82	14	1	4	(2	2)	110	44	33	36	1	47	2	3	1	11	1	.92	7	.292	.375	.391
1990 Oakland	AL	19	33	8	0	2	0	(0	0)	12	4	3	3	0	6	0	0	0	0	0		0	.242	.306	.364
Los Angeles	NL	104	276	84	9	4	3	(1	2)	110	56	24	37	2	44	0	6	2	15	7	.68	6	.304	.384	.399
1992 Los Angeles	NL	56	58	11	3	0	1	(1	0)	17	6	5	6	2	11	1	1	0	1	2	.33	0	.190	.277	.293
Philadelphia	NL	74	276	72	14	1	0	(0	0)	88	36	24	31	0	43	2	2	2	17	1	.94	4	.261	.338	.319
1999 San Francisco	NL	112	333	92	15	1	3	(2	1)	118	49	30	29	4	55	1	7	1	13	6	.68	4	.276	.335	.354
Houston	NL	20	64	21	4	1	0	(0	0)	27	12	4	9	0	8	0	1	1	3	1	.75	2	.328	.405	.422
17 ML YEARS		1763	5047	1358	225	40	57	(25	32)	1834	781	503	578	26	839	25	67	38	246	51	.83	102	.269	.345	.363

Geoff Jenkins

Bats: Left **Throws:** Right **Pos:** LF-104; PH/PR-1   **Ht:** 6'1" **Wt:** 204 **Born:** 7/21/74 **Age:** 27

Year Team	Lg	G	AB	H	2B	3B	HR	(Hm	Rd)	TB	R	RBI	TBB	IBB	SO	HBP	SH	SF	SB	CS	SB%	GDP	Avg	OBP	SLG
2001 Beloit *	A	1	3	1	1	0	0	—	—	2	1	1	1	0	1	0	0	0	0	0		0	.333	.500	.667
1998 Milwaukee	NL	84	262	60	12	1	9	(4	5)	101	33	28	20	4	61	2	0	1	1	3	.25	7	.229	.288	.385
1999 Milwaukee	NL	135	447	140	43	3	21	(10	11)	252	70	82	35	7	87	7	3	1	5	1	.83	10	.313	.371	.564
2000 Milwaukee	NL	135	512	155	36	4	34	(15	19)	301	100	94	33	6	135	15	0	4	11	1	.92	9	.303	.360	.588
2001 Milwaukee	NL	105	397	105	21	1	20	(11	9)	188	60	63	36	7	120	8	0	5	4	2	.67	11	.264	.334	.474
4 ML YEARS		459	1618	460	112	9	84	(40	44)	842	263	267	124	24	403	32	3	11	21	7	.75	37	.284	.345	.520

Jason Jennings

Pitches: Right **Bats:** Right **Pos:** SP-7   **Ht:** 6'2" **Wt:** 242 **Born:** 7/17/78 **Age:** 23

Year Team	Lg	G	GS	CG	GF	IP	BFP	H	R	ER	HR	SH	SF	HB	TBB	IBB	SO	WP	Bk	W	L	Pct.	ShO	Sv-Op	Hld	ERA
1999 Portland	A-	2	2	0	0	9	33	5	1	1	0	0	0	0	2	0	11	0	0	1	0	1.000	0	0--	—	1.00
Asheville	A	12	12	0	0	58.1	242	55	27	24	3	3	2	6	8	0	69	4	0	2	2	.500	0	0--	—	3.70
2000 Salem	A+	22	22	3	0	150.1	632	136	66	58	6	3	5	2	42	0	133	8	1	7	10	.412	1	0--	—	3.47
Carolina	AA	6	6	0	0	36.2	149	32	19	14	4	1	0	0	11	0	33	1	0	1	3	.250	0	0--	—	3.44
2001 Carolina	AA	4	4	0	0	25	106	25	9	8	1	0	0	1	8	0	24	0	0	1	0	1.000	0	0--	—	2.88
Colo Sprngs	AAA	22	22	4	0	131.2	572	145	80	69	9	6	2	7	41	0	110	3	2	7	8	.467	0	0--	—	4.72
2001 Colorado	NL	7	7	1	0	39.1	174	42	21	20	2	1	1	1	19	0	26	1	0	4	1	.800	1	0-0	—	4.58

Robin Jennings

Bats: L **Throws:** L **Pos:** RF-27; 1B-14; PH/PR-12; LF-4; DH-2   **Ht:** 6'2" **Wt:** 210 **Born:** 4/11/72 **Age:** 30

Year Team	Lg	G	AB	H	2B	3B	HR	(Hm	Rd)	TB	R	RBI	TBB	IBB	SO	HBP	SH	SF	SB	CS	SB%	GDP	Avg	OBP	SLG
1992 Geneva	A-	72	275	82	12	2	7	—	—	119	39	47	20	5	43	2	0	6	10	3	.77	7	.298	.350	.433
1993 Peoria	A	132	474	146	29	5	3	—	—	194	65	65	46	2	73	4	5	3	11	11	.50	9	.308	.372	.409
1994 Daytona	A+	128	476	133	24	5	8	—	—	191	54	60	45	5	54	4	4	4	2	10	.17	13	.279	.344	.401
1995 Orlando	AA	132	490	145	27	7	17	—	—	237	71	79	44	6	61	4	0	5	7	14	.33	11	.296	.355	.484
1996 Iowa	AAA	86	331	94	15	6	18	—	—	175	53	56	32	1	53	1	0	3	2	0	1.00	6	.284	.346	.529
1997 Iowa	AAA	126	464	128	25	5	20	—	—	223	67	71	56	5	73	5	0	2	5	3	.63	7	.276	.359	.481
1998 West Tenn	AA	2	6	0	0	0	0	—	—	0	0	0	0	0	2	0	0	0	0	0		0	.000	.000	.000
Iowa	AAA	81	298	74	23	2	16	—	—	149	57	62	33	1	49	6	1	0	4	4	.50	9	.248	.335	.500
1999 West Tenn	AA	13	53	17	3	0	5	—	—	35	11	17	5	0	7	1	0	2	1	0	1.00	1	.321	.377	.660
Iowa	AAA	67	259	80	20	5	9	—	—	137	47	35	25	0	34	1	0	0	6	4	.60	7	.309	.372	.529
2000 Salt Lake	AAA	91	345	107	33	6	11	—	—	185	70	61	35	1	45	3	4	8	4	2	.67	4	.310	.371	.536
Louisville	AAA	32	122	46	14	1	5	—	—	77	18	27	9	3	15	2	2	3	0	2	.00	3	.377	.419	.631
2001 Sacramento	AAA	38	144	44	11	3	5	—	—	76	26	26	9	0	26	2	0	1	5	2	.71	4	.306	.353	.528
Colo Sprngs	AAA	11	39	11	1	0	2	—	—	18	8	5	1	0	10	1	0	0	1	0	1.00	1	.282	.317	.462
Louisville	AAA	28	113	34	6	0	8	—	—	64	18	15	9	5	22	0	1	0	2	2	.50	1	.301	.352	.566
1996 Chicago	NL	31	58	13	5	0	0	(0	0)	18	7	4	3	0	9	1	0	0	1	0	1.00	0	.224	.274	.310
1997 Chicago	NL	9	18	3	1	0	0	(0	0)	4	1	2	0	0	2	0	0	1	0	0		0	.167	.158	.222
1999 Chicago	NL	5	5	1	0	0	0	(0	0)	1	0	0	0	0	2	0	0	0	0	0		0	.200	.200	.200
2001 Oak-Col-Cin	NL	48	132	35	8	2	3	(2	1)	56	14	18	7	1	18	0	0	1	0	0		0	.265	.300	.424
2001 Oakland	AL	20	52	13	3	0	0	(0	0)	16	4	4	2	0	6	0	0	1	0	0		0	.250	.273	.308
Colorado	NL	1	3	0	0	0	0	(0	0)	0	0	0	0	0	1	0	0	0	0	0		0	.000	.000	.000
Cincinnati	NL	27	77	22	5	2	3	(2	1)	40	10	14	5	1	11	0	0	0	0	0		0	.286	.329	.519
4 ML YEARS		93	213	52	14	2	3	(2	1)	79	22	24	10	1	31	1	0	2	1	0	1.00	0	.244	.279	.371

Marcus Jensen

Bats: Both **Throws:** Right **Pos:** C-12   **Ht:** 6'4" **Wt:** 204 **Born:** 12/14/72 **Age:** 29

Year Team	Lg	G	AB	H	2B	3B	HR	(Hm	Rd)	TB	R	RBI	TBB	IBB	SO	HBP	SH	SF	SB	CS	SB%	GDP	Avg	OBP	SLG
2001 Pawtucket *	AAA	27	102	24	7	2	4	—	—	47	11	12	6	0	27	0	0	0	0	0		4	.235	.278	.461
Oklahoma *	AAA	53	188	56	10	1	8	—	—	92	42	25	46	1	46	1	0	0	0	0		0	.298	.438	.489
1996 San Francisco	NL	9	19	4	1	0	0	(0	0)	5	4	4	8	0	7	0	0	0	0	0		1	.211	.444	.263
1997 SF-Det	NL	38	85	13	2	0	1	(1	0)	18	6	4	8	1	28	0	0	0	0	0		1	.153	.226	.212
1998 Milwaukee	NL	2	2	0	0	0	0	(0	0)	0	0	0	0	0	2	0	0	0	0	0		0	.000	.000	.000
1999 St. Louis	NL	16	34	8	5	0	1	(0	1)	16	5	1	6	1	12	0	2	0	0	0		1	.235	.350	.471
2000 Minnesota	AL	52	139	29	7	1	3	(2	1)	47	16	14	24	0	36	0	1	0	0	1	.00	3	.209	.325	.338
2001 Bos-Tex	AL	12	29	5	1	0	0	(0	0)	6	0	2	0	0	10	0	0	0	0	0		1	.172	.172	.207
1997 San Francisco	NL	30	74	11	2	0	1	(1	0)	16	5	3	7	1	23	0	0	0	0	0		2	.182	.250	.182
Detroit	AL	8	11	2	0	0	0	(0	0)	2															

109

Year Team	Lg	G	AB	H	2B	3B	HR	(Hm Rd)	TB	R	RBI	TBB	IBB	SO	HBP	SH	SF	SB	CS	SB%	GDP	Avg	OBP	SLG
2001 Boston	AL	1	4	1	0	0	0	(0 0)	1	0	0	0	0	1	0	0	0	0	0	—	0	.250	.250	.250
Texas	AL	11	25	4	1	0	0	(0 0)	5	0	2	0	0	9	0	0	0	0	0	—	1	.160	.160	.200
6 ML YEARS		129	308	59	16	1	5	(3 2)	92	31	25	46	2	95	0	3	0	0	1	.00	8	.192	.297	.299

Ryan Jensen

Pitches: Right **Bats:** Right **Pos:** SP-7; RP-3

Ht: 6'0" **Wt:** 205 **Born:** 9/17/75 **Age:** 26

Year Team	Lg	G	GS	CG	GF	IP	BFP	H	R	ER	HR	SH	SF	HB	TBB	IBB	SO	WP	Bk	W	L	Pct.	ShO	Sv-Op	Hld	ERA
1996 Bellingham	A-	13	11	0	0	47	208	35	30	26	4	1	0	1	38	0	31	7	0	2	4	.333	0	0- -	—	4.98
1997 Bakersfield	A+	1	1	0	0	1.1	7	3	2	2	1	0	1	0	0	0	2	0	0	0	0	—	0	0- -	—	13.50
Salem-Keizr	A-	16	16	0	0	80.1	353	87	55	46	10	2	2	4	32	0	67	2	1	7	3	.700	0	0- -	—	5.15
1998 Bakersfield	A+	29	27	0	1	168.1	726	162	89	63	14	6	1	8	61	3	164	10	2	11	12	.478	0	0- -	—	3.37
Fresno	AAA	2	1	0	0	5.2	25	4	5	3	2	0	1	0	4	0	6	0	0	0	0	—	0	0- -	—	4.76
1999 Fresno	AAA	27	27	0	0	156.1	688	160	96	89	17	6	6	6	68	1	150	13	0	11	10	.524	0	0- -	—	5.12
2000 Fresno	AAA	26	26	1	0	135.1	628	167	106	87	18	4	9	4	63	0	114	3	1	5	8	.385	0	0- -	—	5.79
2001 Fresno	AAA	20	17	1	2	106	445	97	43	41	11	4	1	5	34	0	95	2	0	11	2	.846	1	0- -	—	3.48
2001 San Francisco	NL	10	7	0	2	42.1	193	44	21	20	5	0	0	4	25	0	26	2	0	1	2	.333	0	0-0	0	4.25

Derek Jeter

Bats: Right **Throws:** Right **Pos:** SS-150

Ht: 6'3" **Wt:** 195 **Born:** 6/26/74 **Age:** 28

Year Team	Lg	G	AB	H	2B	3B	HR	(Hm Rd)	TB	R	RBI	TBB	IBB	SO	HBP	SH	SF	SB	CS	SB%	GDP	Avg	OBP	SLG
1995 New York	AL	15	48	12	4	1	0	(0 0)	18	5	7	3	0	11	0	0	0	0	0	—	0	.250	.294	.375
1996 New York	AL	157	582	183	25	6	10	(3 7)	250	104	78	48	1	102	9	6	9	14	7	.67	13	.314	.370	.430
1997 New York	AL	159	654	190	31	7	10	(5 5)	265	116	70	74	0	125	10	8	2	23	12	.66	14	.291	.370	.405
1998 New York	AL	149	626	203	25	8	19	(9 10)	301	127	84	57	1	119	5	3	3	30	6	.83	13	.324	.384	.481
1999 New York	AL	158	627	219	37	9	24	(15 9)	346	134	102	91	5	116	12	3	6	19	8	.70	12	.349	.438	.552
2000 New York	AL	148	593	201	31	4	15	(8 7)	285	119	73	68	4	99	12	3	3	22	4	.85	14	.339	.416	.481
2001 New York	AL	150	614	191	35	3	21	(13 8)	295	110	74	56	3	99	10	5	1	27	3	.90	13	.311	.377	.480
7 ML YEARS		936	3744	1199	188	38	99	(53 46)	1760	715	488	397	14	671	58	28	24	135	40	.77	79	.320	.392	.470

D'Angelo Jimenez

Bats: Both **Throws:** Right **Pos:** SS-85; PH/PR-2

Ht: 6'0" **Wt:** 194 **Born:** 12/21/77 **Age:** 24

Year Team	Lg	G	AB	H	2B	3B	HR	(Hm Rd)	TB	R	RBI	TBB	IBB	SO	HBP	SH	SF	SB	CS	SB%	GDP	Avg	OBP	SLG
1995 Yankees	R	57	214	60	14	8	2	— —	96	41	28	23	1	31	1	3	4	6	3	.67	6	.280	.347	.449
1996 Greensboro	A	138	537	131	25	5	6	— —	184	68	48	56	2	113	3	4	3	15	17	.47	7	.244	.317	.343
1997 Columbus	AAA	2	7	1	0	0	0	— —	1	1	0	0	1	0	0	0	1	0	0	—	0	.143	.125	.143
Tampa	A+	94	352	99	14	6	6	— —	143	52	48	50	4	50	2	3	6	8	14	.36	3	.281	.368	.406
1998 Norwich	AA	40	152	41	6	2	2	— —	57	21	21	25	1	26	2	2	1	5	5	.50	3	.270	.378	.375
Columbus	AAA	91	344	88	19	4	8	— —	139	55	51	46	0	67	1	1	5	6	6	.50	7	.256	.341	.404
1999 Columbus	AAA	126	526	172	32	5	15	— —	259	97	88	59	1	75	1	6	6	26	14	.65	8	.327	.392	.492
2000 Yankees	R	4	10	1	0	0	0	— —	1	2	0	5	0	1	0	0	0	0	0	—	0	.100	.400	.100
Tampa	A+	12	41	8	1	1	1	— —	14	8	2	8	1	7	0	0	1	0	0	—	1	.195	.320	.341
Columbus	AAA	21	73	17	3	1	1	— —	25	11	5	7	1	12	1	0	0	2	0	1.00	2	.233	.309	.342
2001 Columbus	AAA	56	214	56	11	1	5	— —	84	33	19	24	0	31	1	2	4	5	6	.45	2	.262	.333	.393
1999 New York	AL	7	20	8	2	0	0	(0 0)	10	3	4	3	0	4	0	0	0	0	0	—	0	.400	.478	.500
2001 San Diego	NL	86	308	85	19	0	3	(2 1)	113	45	33	39	4	68	0	0	2	3	3	.40	9	.276	.355	.367
2 ML YEARS		93	328	93	21	0	3	(2 1)	123	48	37	42	4	72	0	0	2	3	3	.40	9	.284	.363	.375

Jose Jimenez

Pitches: Right **Bats:** Right **Pos:** RP-56

Ht: 6'3" **Wt:** 228 **Born:** 7/7/73 **Age:** 28

Year Team	Lg	G	GS	CG	GF	IP	BFP	H	R	ER	HR	SH	SF	HB	TBB	IBB	SO	WP	Bk	W	L	Pct.	ShO	Sv-Op	Hld	ERA
1998 St. Louis	NL	4	3	0	0	21.1	94	22	8	7	0	1	1	0	8	0	12	0	0	3	0	1.000	0	0-0	0	2.95
1999 St. Louis	NL	29	28	2	0	163	727	173	114	106	16	10	6	11	71	2	113	10	1	5	14	.263	2	0-1	0	5.85
2000 Colorado	NL	72	0	0	55	70.2	301	63	27	25	4	4	2	3	28	6	44	5	0	5	2	.714	0	24-30	2	3.18
2001 Colorado	NL	56	0	0	49	55	237	56	27	25	6	2	1	0	22	4	37	3	0	6	1	.857	0	17-22	0	4.09
4 ML YEARS		161	31	2	104	310	1359	314	176	163	26	17	10	14	129	12	206	18	1	19	17	.528	2	41-53	2	4.73

Brett Jodie

Pitches: Right **Bats:** Right **Pos:** RP-5; SP-3

Ht: 6'4" **Wt:** 208 **Born:** 3/25/77 **Age:** 25

Year Team	Lg	G	GS	CG	GF	IP	BFP	H	R	ER	HR	SH	SF	HB	TBB	IBB	SO	WP	Bk	W	L	Pct.	ShO	Sv-Op	Hld	ERA
1998 Oneonta	A-	15	15	1	0	94	381	87	40	27	7	1	3	0	21	0	73	3	1	7	6	.538	1	0- -	—	2.59
1999 Greensboro	A	25	20	2	3	120.1	497	125	59	51	10	0	1	1	18	0	106	9	0	9	6	.600	0	1- -	—	3.81
2000 Tampa	A+	25	18	3	2	143.2	582	134	53	41	4	5	3	3	29	5	122	5	1	11	4	.733	1	0- -	—	2.57
Norwich	AA	3	3	1	0	20	77	16	8	7	3	0	1	3	5	0	9	0	0	2	1	.667	1	0- -	—	3.15
2001 Norwich	AA	2	2	0	0	14	52	10	1	1	0	1	0	1	2	0	14	0	0	2	0	1.000	1	0- -	—	0.64
Columbus	AAA	19	19	2	0	119.2	498	123	46	40	9	3	3	3	25	0	59	3	1	10	4	.714	1	0- -	—	3.01
Portland	AAA	5	5	0	0	30.1	128	33	16	16	7	1	0	0	8	1	19	1	0	2	1	.667	0	0- -	—	4.75
2001 NYY-SD		8	3	0	0	25.1	109	26	18	18	10	1	0	0	13	1	13	1	0	0	2	.000	0	0-0	0	6.39
2001 New York	AL	1	1	0	0	2	13	7	6	6	3	0	0	0	1	0	0	0	0	0	1	.000	0	0-0	0	27.00
San Diego	NL	7	2	0	0	23.1	96	19	12	12	7	1	0	0	12	1	13	1	0	0	1	.000	0	0-0	0	4.63

Adam Johnson

Pitches: Right **Bats:** Right **Pos:** SP-4; RP-3   **Ht:** 6'2" **Wt:** 210 **Born:** 7/12/79 **Age:** 22

Year Team	Lg	G	GS	CG	GF	IP	BFP	H	R	ER	HR	SH	SF	HB	TBB	IBB	SO	WP	Bk	W	L	Pct.	ShO	Sv-Op	Hld	ERA
2000 Fort Myers	A+	13	12	1	0	69.1	267	45	21	19	2	0	2	3	20	1	92	2	1	5	4	.556	1	0--	—	2.47
2001 New Britain	AA	18	18	0	0	113	481	105	53	48	10	4	5	9	39	2	110	5	0	5	6	.455	0	0--	—	3.82
Edmonton	AAA	4	4	0	0	23.2	98	19	15	15	0	2	1	1	10	0	25	0	0	1	1	.500	0	0--	—	5.70
2001 Minnesota	AL	7	4	0	0	25	119	32	25	23	6	1	1	5	13	0	17	1	0	1	2	.333	0	0-0	0	8.28

Brian Johnson

Bats: Right **Throws:** Right **Pos:** C-2; PH/PR-1   **Ht:** 6'2" **Wt:** 210 **Born:** 1/8/68 **Age:** 34

Year Team	Lg	G	AB	H	2B	3B	HR	(Hm	Rd)	TB	R	RBI	TBB	IBB	SO	HBP	SH	SF	SB	CS	SB%	GDP	Avg	OBP	SLG
2001 Dodgers *	R	5	18	8	0	0	2	—	—	14	4	3	2	0	0	0	0	0	0	0	—	0	.444	.500	.778
Las Vegas *	AAA	48	166	50	12	0	6	—	—	80	21	31	11	0	39	2	0	3	0	0	—	1	.301	.346	.482
1994 San Diego	NL	36	93	23	4	1	3	(3	0)	38	7	16	5	0	21	0	2	1	0	0	—	4	.247	.283	.409
1995 San Diego	NL	68	207	52	9	0	3	(1	2)	70	20	29	11	2	39	1	1	4	0	0	—	2	.251	.287	.338
1996 San Diego	NL	82	243	66	13	1	8	(3	5)	105	18	35	4	2	36	4	2	4	0	0	—	8	.272	.290	.432
1997 Det-SF		101	318	83	13	3	13	(8	5)	141	32	45	19	8	45	2	5	4	1	1	.50	11	.261	.303	.443
1998 San Francisco	NL	99	308	73	8	1	13	(7	6)	122	34	34	28	4	67	5	4	1	0	2	.00	11	.237	.310	.396
1999 Cincinnati	NL	45	117	27	7	0	5	(3	2)	49	12	18	9	0	31	0	1	0	0	0	—	2	.231	.286	.419
2000 Kansas City	AL	37	125	26	6	0	4	(3	1)	44	9	18	4	0	28	0	1	2	0	0	—	4	.208	.229	.352
2001 Los Angeles	NL	3	4	1	0	0	0	(0	0)	1	0	1	0	0	1	0	0	0	0	0	—	0	.250	.250	.250
1997 Detroit	AL	45	139	33	6	1	2	(2	0)	47	13	18	5	1	19	0	2	1	1	0	1.00	3	.237	.262	.338
San Francisco	NL	56	179	50	7	2	11	(6	5)	94	19	27	14	7	26	2	3	3	0	1	.00	8	.279	.333	.525
8 ML YEARS		471	1415	351	60	6	49	(28	21)	570	132	196	80	16	268	12	16	16	1	3	.25	42	.248	.291	.403

Charles Johnson

Bats: Right **Throws:** Right **Pos:** C-125; PH/PR-8   **Ht:** 6'2" **Wt:** 220 **Born:** 7/20/71 **Age:** 30

Year Team	Lg	G	AB	H	2B	3B	HR	(Hm	Rd)	TB	R	RBI	TBB	IBB	SO	HBP	SH	SF	SB	CS	SB%	GDP	Avg	OBP	SLG
1994 Florida	NL	4	11	5	1	0	1	(1	0)	9	5	4	1	0	4	0	0	1	0	0	—	1	.455	.462	.818
1995 Florida	NL	97	315	79	15	1	11	(3	8)	129	40	39	46	2	71	4	4	2	0	2	.00	11	.251	.351	.410
1996 Florida	NL	120	386	84	13	1	13	(9	4)	138	34	37	40	6	91	2	2	4	1	0	1.00	20	.218	.292	.358
1997 Florida	NL	124	416	104	26	1	19	(7	12)	189	43	63	60	6	109	3	3	2	0	2	.00	13	.250	.347	.454
1998 Fla-LA	NL	133	459	100	18	0	19	(14	5)	175	44	58	45	1	129	1	0	1	0	2	.00	12	.218	.289	.381
1999 Baltimore	AL	135	426	107	14	1	16	(8	8)	176	58	54	55	2	107	4	4	3	0	0	—	13	.251	.340	.413
2000 Bal-CWS	AL	128	421	128	24	0	31	(19	12)	245	76	91	52	0	106	1	1	3	2	0	1.00	8	.304	.379	.582
2001 Florida	NL	128	451	117	32	0	18	(5	13)	203	51	75	38	2	133	4	0	3	0	0	—	8	.259	.321	.450
1998 Florida	NL	31	113	25	5	0	7	(5	2)	51	13	23	16	0	30	0	0	1	0	1	.00	3	.221	.315	.451
Los Angeles	NL	102	346	75	13	0	12	(9	3)	124	31	35	29	1	99	1	0	0	0	1	.00	9	.217	.279	.358
2000 Baltimore	AL	84	286	84	16	0	21	(12	9)	163	52	55	32	0	69	0	1	1	2	0	1.00	8	.294	.364	.570
Chicago	AL	44	135	44	8	0	10	(7	3)	82	24	36	20	0	37	1	0	2	0	0	—	0	.326	.411	.607
8 ML YEARS		869	2885	724	148	4	128	(66	62)	1264	351	421	337	19	750	19	14	19	3	6	.33	86	.251	.331	.438

Jason Johnson

Pitches: Right **Bats:** Right **Pos:** SP-32   **Ht:** 6'6" **Wt:** 235 **Born:** 10/27/73 **Age:** 28

Year Team	Lg	G	GS	CG	GF	IP	BFP	H	R	ER	HR	SH	SF	HB	TBB	IBB	SO	WP	Bk	W	L	Pct.	ShO	Sv-Op	Hld	ERA
1997 Pittsburgh	NL	3	0	0	0	6	27	10	4	4	2	0	1	0	1	0	3	0	0	0	0	—	0	0-0	0	6.00
1998 Tampa Bay	AL	13	13	0	0	60	274	74	38	38	9	1	1	3	27	0	36	2	0	2	5	.286	0	0-0	0	5.70
1999 Baltimore	AL	22	21	0	0	115.1	515	120	74	70	16	2	4	3	55	0	71	5	1	8	7	.533	0	0-0	0	5.46
2000 Baltimore	AL	25	13	0	3	107.2	501	119	95	84	21	3	5	4	61	2	79	0	0	1	10	.091	0	0-0	2	7.02
2001 Baltimore	AL	32	32	2	0	196	856	194	109	89	28	6	6	13	77	3	114	9	0	10	12	.455	0	0-0	0	4.09
5 ML YEARS		95	79	2	3	485	2173	517	320	285	76	12	17	23	221	5	303	19	1	21	34	.382	0	0-0	2	5.29

Jonathan Johnson

Pitches: Right **Bats:** Right **Pos:** RP-5   **Ht:** 6'0" **Wt:** 180 **Born:** 7/16/74 **Age:** 27

Year Team	Lg	G	GS	CG	GF	IP	BFP	H	R	ER	HR	SH	SF	HB	TBB	IBB	SO	WP	Bk	W	L	Pct.	ShO	Sv-Op	Hld	ERA
1995 Charlotte	A+	8	7	1	1	43.1	178	34	14	13	2	2	0	1	16	0	25	3	3	1	5	.167	0	0--	—	2.70
1996 Okla City	AAA	1	1	0	0	9	29	2	0	0	0	0	0	0	1	0	6	0	0	1	0	1.000	1	0--	—	0.00
Tulsa	AA	26	25	6	1	174.1	728	176	86	69	15	3	5	6	41	1	97	2	3	13	10	.565	0	0--	—	3.56
1997 Okla City	AAA	13	12	1	1	58	276	83	54	47	6	1	3	1	29	3	33	2	1	1	8	.111	0	1--	—	7.29
Tulsa	AA	10	10	4	0	71.2	297	70	35	28	3	1	3	2	15	0	47	4	0	5	4	.556	0	0--	—	3.52
1998 Charlotte	A+	3	3	0	0	11.2	51	10	6	6	2	0	1	2	4	0	11	0	0	0	2	.000	0	0--	—	4.63
Oklahoma	AAA	19	18	1	1	112	474	109	66	61	15	0	4	11	32	0	94	6	2	6	6	.500	0	1--	—	4.90
1999 Rangers	R	1	1	0	0	5	18	3	1	1	0	0	0	0	0	0	4	0	0	0	0	—	0	0--	—	1.80
Tulsa	AA	1	1	0	0	5.2	28	12	6	6	3	1	1	0	0	0	4	0	0	0	0	—	0	0--	—	9.53
Oklahoma	AAA	21	8	0	5	67.2	308	91	53	47	9	2	3	2	23	0	38	6	0	8	4	.667	0	2--	—	6.25
2000 Oklahoma	AAA	36	2	0	18	56.2	243	55	38	32	8	1	2	0	26	2	63	3	1	4	7	.364	0	5--	—	5.08
2001 Tucson	AAA	15	12	0	0	73.2	324	63	48	43	7	2	2	3	42	0	51	6	0	4	4	.500	0	0--	—	5.25
1998 Texas	AL	1	1	0	0	4.1	22	5	4	4	0	0	1	0	5	0	3	0	0	0	0	—	0	0-0	0	8.31
1999 Texas	AL	1	0	0	0	3	21	9	5	5	0	0	1	1	2	0	3	0	0	0	0	—	0	0-0	0	15.00
2000 Texas	AL	15	0	0	3	29	144	34	23	20	3	0	2	6	19	2	23	2	0	1	1	.500	0	0-0	0	6.21
2001 Texas	AL	5	0	0	2	10.1	53	13	11	11	2	1	3	1	7	1	11	0	0	0	0	—	0	0-0	0	9.58
4 ML YEARS		22	1	0	5	46.2	240	61	43	40	5	1	7	8	33	3	40	2	0	1	1	.500	0	0-0	0	7.71

Mark Johnson

Bats: Left **Throws:** Right **Pos:** C-61   **Ht:** 6'0" **Wt:** 185 **Born:** 9/12/75 **Age:** 26

Year Team	Lg	G	AB	H	2B	3B	HR	(Hm	Rd)	TB	R	RBI	TBB	IBB	SO	HBP	SH	SF	SB	CS	SB%	GDP	Avg	OBP	SLG
2001 Charlotte *	AAA	55	196	53	5	2	4	—		74	24	24	29	1	34	0	2	1	2	1	.67	4	.270	.363	.378
1998 Chicago	AL	7	23	2	0	2	0	(0	0)	6	2	1	1	0	8	0	0	0	0	0	—		.087	.125	.261
1999 Chicago	AL	73	207	47	11	0	4	(2	2)	70	27	16	36	0	58	2	1	2	3	1	.75	2	.227	.344	.338
2000 Chicago	AL	75	213	48	11	0	3	(2	1)	68	29	23	27	0	40	1	10	0	3	2	.60	3	.225	.315	.319
2001 Chicago	AL	61	173	43	6	1	5	(2	3)	66	21	18	23	1	31	2	10	3	2	1	.67	5	.249	.338	.382
4 ML YEARS		216	616	140	28	3	12	(6	6)	210	79	58	87	1	137	5	21	5	8	4	.67	10	.227	.325	.341

Mark Johnson

Bats: L **Throws:** L **Pos:** PH/PR-36; 1B-21; LF-12; RF-7; DH-3   **Ht:** 6'4" **Wt:** 230 **Born:** 10/17/67 **Age:** 34

Year Team	Lg	G	AB	H	2B	3B	HR	(Hm	Rd)	TB	R	RBI	TBB	IBB	SO	HBP	SH	SF	SB	CS	SB%	GDP	Avg	OBP	SLG
2001 Norfolk *	AAA	42	152	48	15	0	8	—		87	27	25	22	0	20	2	0	1	2	1	.67	5	.316	.407	.572
1995 Pittsburgh	NL	79	221	46	6	1	13	(7	6)	93	32	28	37	2	66	2	0	1	5	2	.71	2	.208	.326	.421
1996 Pittsburgh	NL	127	343	94	24	0	13	(10	3)	157	55	47	44	3	64	5	0	4	6	4	.60	5	.274	.361	.458
1997 Pittsburgh	NL	78	219	47	10	0	4	(2	2)	69	30	29	43	1	78	2	0	3	1	1	.50	1	.215	.345	.315
1998 Anaheim	AL	10	14	1	0	0	0	(0	0)	1	1	0	0	0	6	0	0	0	0	0	—	1	.071	.071	.071
2000 New York	NL	21	22	4	0	0	1	(1	0)	7	2	6	5	0	9	0	0	0	0	0	—	1	.182	.333	.318
2001 New York	NL	71	118	30	6	1	6	(2	4)	56	17	23	16	1	31	0	0	2	0	2	.00	1	.254	.338	.475
6 ML YEARS		386	937	222	46	2	37	(22	15)	383	137	133	145	7	254	9	0	10	12	9	.57	10	.237	.342	.409

Mike Johnson

Pitches: Right **Bats:** Left **Pos:** RP-10   **Ht:** 6'2" **Wt:** 170 **Born:** 10/3/75 **Age:** 26

Year Team	Lg	G	GS	CG	GF	IP	BFP	H	R	ER	HR	SH	SF	HB	TBB	IBB	SO	WP	Bk	W	L	Pct.	ShO	Sv-Op	Hld	ERA
2001 Ottawa *	AAA	2	2	0	0	10	38	7	5	5	1	1	0	0	3	0	8	2	0	2	0	1.000	0	0--	—	4.50
Oklahoma *	AAA	23	8	1	6	88.1	382	101	48	45	12	2	3	3	22	0	67	3	0	3	5	.375	0	2--	—	4.58
1997 Bal-Mon		25	16	0	5	89.2	403	106	70	68	20	2	4	1	37	4	57	5	0	2	6	.250	0	2-2	0	6.83
1998 Montreal	NL	2	0	0	0	7.1	40	16	12	12	4	0	0	1	2	0	4	0	0	0	2	.000	0	0-0	0	14.73
1999 Montreal	NL	3	1	0	0	8.1	44	12	8	8	2	0	0	0	7	1	6	2	0	0	0	—	0	0-0	0	8.64
2000 Montreal	NL	41	13	0	5	101.1	466	107	73	72	18	4	2	9	53	1	70	8	0	5	6	.455	0	0-0	0	6.39
2001 Montreal	NL	10	0	0	0	11.1	50	13	6	6	3	0	0	2	4	0	10	2	0	0	0	—	0	0-2	2	4.76
1997 Baltimore	AL	14	5	0	5	39.2	183	52	36	35	12	0	2	1	16	2	29	1	0	0	1	.000	0	2-2	0	7.94
Montreal	NL	11	11	0	0	50	220	54	34	33	8	2	2	0	21	2	28	4	0	2	5	.286	0	0-0	0	5.94
5 ML YEARS		81	32	0	10	218	1003	254	169	166	47	6	6	13	103	6	147	17	0	7	14	.333	0	2-4	2	6.85

Nick Johnson

Bats: Left **Throws:** Left **Pos:** 1B-15; DH-6; PH/PR-5   **Ht:** 6'3" **Wt:** 224 **Born:** 9/19/78 **Age:** 23

Year Team	Lg	G	AB	H	2B	3B	HR	(Hm	Rd)	TB	R	RBI	TBB	IBB	SO	HBP	SH	SF	SB	CS	SB%	GDP	Avg	OBP	SLG
1996 Yankees	R	47	157	45	11	1	2	—		64	31	34	30	0	35	9	0	3	0	0	—	5	.287	.422	.408
1997 Greensboro	A	127	433	118	23	1	16	—		191	77	75	76	1	99	18	0	6	16	3	.84	5	.273	.398	.441
1998 Tampa	A+	92	303	96	14	1	17	—		163	69	58	68	3	76	19	0	3	1	4	.20	5	.317	.466	.538
1999 Norwich	AA	132	420	145	33	5	14	—		230	114	87	123	6	88	37	0	1	8	6	.57	9	.345	.525	.548
2001 Columbus	AAA	110	359	92	20	0	18	—		166	68	49	81	3	105	14	0	5	9	2	.82	6	.256	.407	.462
2001 New York	AL	23	67	13	2	0	2	(1	1)	21	6	8	7	0	15	4	0	0	0	0	—	3	.194	.308	.313

Randy Johnson

Pitches: Left **Bats:** Right **Pos:** SP-34; RP-1   **Ht:** 6'10" **Wt:** 232 **Born:** 9/10/63 **Age:** 38

Year Team	Lg	G	GS	CG	GF	IP	BFP	H	R	ER	HR	SH	SF	HB	TBB	IBB	SO	WP	Bk	W	L	Pct.	ShO	Sv-Op	Hld	ERA
1988 Montreal	NL	4	4	1	0	26	109	23	8	7	2	0	0	0	7	0	25	3	0	3	0	1.000	0	0-0	0	2.42
1989 Mon-Sea		29	28	2	1	160.2	715	147	100	86	13	10	13	3	96	2	130	7	7	7	13	.350	0	0-0	0	4.82
1990 Seattle	AL	33	33	5	0	219.2	944	174	103	89	26	7	6	5	120	2	194	4	2	14	11	.560	2	0-0	0	3.65
1991 Seattle	AL	33	33	2	0	201.1	889	151	96	89	15	9	8	12	152	0	228	12	2	13	10	.565	1	0-0	0	3.98
1992 Seattle	AL	31	31	6	0	210.1	922	154	104	88	13	3	8	18	144	1	241	13	1	12	14	.462	2	0-0	0	3.77
1993 Seattle	AL	35	34	10	1	255.1	1043	185	97	92	22	8	7	16	99	1	308	8	2	19	8	.704	3	1-1	0	3.24
1994 Seattle	AL	23	23	9	0	172	694	132	65	61	14	3	1	6	72	2	204	5	0	13	6	.684	4	0-0	0	3.19
1995 Seattle	AL	30	30	6	0	214.1	866	159	65	59	12	2	1	6	65	1	294	5	2	18	2	.900	3	0-0	0	2.48
1996 Seattle	AL	14	8	0	2	61.1	256	48	27	25	8	1	0	2	25	0	85	3	1	5	0	1.000	0	1-2	0	3.67
1997 Seattle	AL	30	29	5	0	213	850	147	60	54	20	4	1	10	77	2	291	4	0	20	4	.833	2	0-0	0	2.28
1998 Sea-Hou		34	34	10	0	244.1	1014	203	102	89	23	5	2	14	86	1	329	7	2	19	11	.633	6	0-0	0	3.28
1999 Arizona	NL	35	35	12	0	271.2	1079	207	86	75	30	4	3	9	70	3	364	4	2	17	9	.654	2	0-0	0	2.48
2000 Arizona	NL	35	35	8	0	248.2	1001	202	89	73	23	14	5	6	76	1	347	5	2	19	7	.731	3	0-0	0	2.64
2001 Arizona	NL	35	34	3	1	249.2	994	181	74	69	19	10	5	18	71	2	372	8	1	21	6	.778	2	0-0	0	2.49
1989 Montreal	NL	7	6	0	1	29.2	143	29	25	22	2	3	4	0	26	1	26	2	2	0	4	.000	0	0-0	0	6.67
Seattle	AL	22	22	2	0	131	572	118	75	64	11	7	9	3	70	1	104	5	5	7	9	.438	0	0-0	0	4.40
1998 Seattle	AL	23	23	6	0	160	685	146	90	77	19	5	1	11	60	0	213	7	2	9	10	.474	2	0-0	0	4.33
Houston	NL	11	11	4	0	84.1	329	57	12	12	4	0	1	3	26	1	116	0	0	10	1	.909	4	0-0	0	1.28
14 ML YEARS		401	391	79	5	2748.1	11376	2113	1076	956	241	80	60	125	1160	18	3412	88	24	200	101	.664	30	2-3	0	3.13

Russ Johnson

Bats: R Throws: R Pos: 3B-36; 2B-33; PH/PR-22; SS-6; DH-2   Ht: 5'10" Wt: 180 Born: 2/22/73 Age: 29

								BATTING											BASERUNNING				PERCENTAGES		
Year Team	Lg	G	AB	H	2B	3B	HR	(Hm Rd)	TB	R	RBI	TBB	IBB	SO	HBP	SH	SF	SB	CS	SB%	GDP	Avg	OBP	SLG
2001 Orlando *	AA	1	3	2	0	0	0	— —	2	0	0	1	0	0	0	0	0	0	0	—	1	.667	.750	.667
1997 Houston	NL	21	60	18	1	0	2	(2 0)	25	7	9	6	0	14	0	1	0	1	1	.50	2	.300	.364	.417
1998 Houston	NL	8	13	3	1	0	0	(0 0)	4	2	0	1	0	5	1	0	0	1	0	1.00		.231	.333	.308
1999 Houston	NL	83	156	44	10	0	5	(2 3)	69	24	23	20	0	31	0	4	3	2	3	.40	3	.282	.358	.442
2000 Hou-TB		100	230	55	8	0	2	(2 0)	69	32	20	27	0	40	1	4	1	5	2	.71	7	.239	.320	.300
2001 Tampa Bay	AL	85	248	73	19	2	4	(1 3)	108	32	33	34	0	57	1	4	1	2	2	.50	2	.294	.380	.435
2000 Houston	NL	26	45	8	0	0	0	(0 0)	8	4	3	2	0	10	0	1	0	1	1	.50	3	.178	.213	.178
Tampa Bay	AL	74	185	47	8	0	2	(2 0)	61	28	17	25	0	30	1	3	1	4	1	.80	4	.254	.344	.330
5 ML YEARS		297	707	193	39	2	13	(7 6)	275	97	85	88	0	147	3	13	5	11	8	.58	15	.273	.354	.389

Andruw Jones

Bats: Right Throws: Right Pos: CF-161   Ht: 6'1" Wt: 210 Born: 4/23/77 Age: 25

								BATTING											BASERUNNING				PERCENTAGES		
Year Team	Lg	G	AB	H	2B	3B	HR	(Hm Rd)	TB	R	RBI	TBB	IBB	SO	HBP	SH	SF	SB	CS	SB%	GDP	Avg	OBP	SLG
1996 Atlanta	NL	31	106	23	7	1	5	(3 2)	47	11	13	7	0	29	0	0	0	3	0	1.00	1	.217	.265	.443
1997 Atlanta	NL	153	399	92	18	1	18	(5 13)	166	60	70	56	2	107	4	5	3	20	11	.65	11	.231	.329	.416
1998 Atlanta	NL	159	582	158	33	8	31	(16 15)	300	89	90	40	8	129	4	1	4	27	4	.87	10	.271	.321	.515
1999 Atlanta	NL	162	592	163	35	5	26	(10 16)	286	97	84	76	11	103	9	0	2	24	12	.67	12	.275	.365	.483
2000 Atlanta	NL	161	656	199	36	6	36	(15 21)	355	122	104	59	0	100	9	0	5	21	6	.78	12	.303	.366	.541
2001 Atlanta	NL	161	625	157	25	2	34	(16 18)	288	104	104	56	3	142	3	0	9	11	4	.73	10	.251	.312	.461
6 ML YEARS		827	2960	792	154	23	150	(65 85)	1442	483	465	294	24	610	29	6	23	106	37	.74	56	.268	.337	.487

Bobby Jones

Pitches: Right Bats: Right Pos: SP-33   Ht: 6'4" Wt: 225 Born: 2/10/70 Age: 32

				HOW MUCH HE PITCHED			WHAT HE GAVE UP												THE RESULTS						
Year Team	Lg	G	GS	CG	GF	IP	BFP	H	R	ER	HR	SH	SF	HB	TBB	IBB	SO	WP	Bk	W	L	Pct.	ShO	Sv-Op	Hld	ERA
1993 New York	NL	9	9	0	0	61.2	265	61	35	25	6	5	3	2	22	3	35	1	0	2	4	.333	0	0-0	0	3.65
1994 New York	NL	24	24	1	0	160	685	157	75	56	10	11	4	4	56	9	80	1	3	12	7	.632	1	0-0	0	3.15
1995 New York	NL	30	30	3	0	195.2	839	209	107	91	20	11	6	7	53	6	127	2	1	10	10	.500	1	0-0	0	4.19
1996 New York	NL	31	31	3	0	195.2	826	219	102	96	26	12	5	3	46	6	116	2	0	12	8	.600	1	0-0	0	4.42
1997 New York	NL	30	30	2	0	193.1	806	177	88	78	24	6	4	2	63	3	125	3	1	15	9	.625	0	0-0	0	3.63
1998 New York	NL	30	30	0	0	195.1	804	192	94	88	23	4	7	8	53	2	115	2	2	9	9	.500	0	0-0	0	4.05
1999 New York	NL	12	9	0	0	59.1	253	69	37	37	3	3	3	2	11	0	31	0	0	3	3	.500	0	0-0	0	5.61
2000 New York	NL	27	27	1	0	154.2	676	171	90	87	25	7	6	5	49	3	85	2	1	11	6	.647	0	0-0	0	5.06
2001 San Diego	NL	33	33	1	0	195	880	250	137	111	37	9	9	4	38	6	113	3	0	8	19	.296	0	0-0	0	5.12
9 ML YEARS		226	223	11	0	1410.2	6034	1505	765	669	174	68	47	37	391	38	827	16	8	82	75	.522	4	0-0	0	4.27

Bobby Jones

Pitches: Left Bats: Right 2000 Pos: RP-10; SP-1   Ht: 6'0" Wt: 178 Born: 4/11/72 Age: 30

				HOW MUCH HE PITCHED			WHAT HE GAVE UP												THE RESULTS						
Year Team	Lg	G	GS	CG	GF	IP	BFP	H	R	ER	HR	SH	SF	HB	TBB	IBB	SO	WP	Bk	W	L	Pct.	ShO	Sv-Op	Hld	ERA
2001 St. Lucie *	A+	4	4	0	0	9.2	40	6	2	1	0	1	0	0	4	0	9	0	0	0	1	.000	0	0--	—	0.93
Binghamton *	AA	2	1	0	0	5	15	0	0	0	0	0	0	0	0	0	6	0	0	0	0	—	0	0--	—	0.00
Norfolk *	AAA	1	1	0	0	2	6	0	0	0	0	0	0	0	0	0	0	0	0	0	0	—	0	0--	—	0.00
1997 Colorado	NL	4	4	0	0	19.1	96	30	18	18	2	2	3	0	12	0	5	0	0	1	1	.500	0	0-0	0	8.38
1998 Colorado	NL	35	20	1	1	141.1	630	153	87	82	12	9	6	6	66	0	109	4	1	7	8	.467	0	0-0	0	5.22
1999 Colorado	NL	30	20	0	1	112.1	546	132	91	79	24	7	4	6	77	0	74	4	0	6	10	.375	0	0-0	0	6.33
2000 New York	NL	11	1	0	4	21.2	99	18	11	10	2	0	1	3	14	1	20	0	0	0	1	.000	0	0-0	1	4.15
4 ML YEARS		80	45	1	6	294.2	1371	333	207	189	40	18	14	15	169	1	208	8	1	14	20	.412	0	0-0	1	5.77

Chipper Jones

Bats: B Throws: R Pos: 3B-149; LF-8; PH/PR-2; DH-1   Ht: 6'4" Wt: 210 Born: 4/24/72 Age: 30

								BATTING											BASERUNNING				PERCENTAGES		
Year Team	Lg	G	AB	H	2B	3B	HR	(Hm Rd)	TB	R	RBI	TBB	IBB	SO	HBP	SH	SF	SB	CS	SB%	GDP	Avg	OBP	SLG
1993 Atlanta	NL	8	3	2	1	0	0	(0 0)	3	2	0	1	0	1	0	0	0	0	0	—	0	.667	.750	1.000
1995 Atlanta	NL	140	524	139	22	3	23	(15 8)	236	87	86	73	1	99	0	1	4	8	4	.67	10	.265	.353	.450
1996 Atlanta	NL	157	598	185	32	5	30	(18 12)	317	114	110	87	0	88	0	1	7	14	1	.93	14	.309	.393	.530
1997 Atlanta	NL	157	597	176	41	3	21	(7 14)	286	100	111	76	8	88	0	0	6	20	5	.80	19	.295	.371	.479
1998 Atlanta	NL	160	601	188	29	5	34	(17 17)	329	123	107	96	1	93	1	1	8	16	6	.73	17	.313	.404	.547
1999 Atlanta	NL	157	567	181	41	1	45	(25 20)	359	116	110	126	18	94	2	0	6	25	3	.89	20	.319	.441	.633
2000 Atlanta	NL	156	579	180	38	1	36	(18 18)	328	118	111	95	10	64	2	0	10	14	7	.67	14	.311	.404	.566
2001 Atlanta	NL	159	572	189	33	5	38	(19 19)	346	113	102	98	20	82	2	0	5	9	10	.47	13	.330	.427	.605
8 ML YEARS		1094	4041	1240	237	23	227	(119 108)	2204	773	737	652	58	609	7	3	46	106	36	.75	107	.307	.400	.545

Jacque Jones

Bats: L Throws: L Pos: LF-137; PH/PR-22; DH-5; CF-2; RF-2   Ht: 5'10" Wt: 176 Born: 4/25/75 Age: 27

								BATTING											BASERUNNING				PERCENTAGES		
Year Team	Lg	G	AB	H	2B	3B	HR	(Hm Rd)	TB	R	RBI	TBB	IBB	SO	HBP	SH	SF	SB	CS	SB%	GDP	Avg	OBP	SLG
1999 Minnesota	AL	95	322	93	22	2	9	(5 4)	148	54	44	17	1	63	4	1	3	3	4	.43	7	.289	.329	.460
2000 Minnesota	AL	154	523	149	26	5	19	(11 8)	242	66	76	26	4	111	0	1	0	7	5	.58	17	.285	.319	.463
2001 Minnesota	AL	149	475	131	25	0	14	(5 9)	198	57	49	39	2	92	3	2	0	12	9	.57	10	.276	.335	.417
3 ML YEARS		398	1320	373	75	7	42	(21 21)	588	177	169	82	7	266	7	4	3	22	18	.55	34	.283	.327	.445

Terry Jones

Bats: B Throws: R Pos: CF-13; PH/PR-11; LF-10; RF-2 Ht: 5'10" Wt: 165 Born: 2/15/71 Age: 31

Year Team	Lg	G	AB	H	2B	3B	HR	(Hm	Rd)	TB	R	RBI	TBB	IBB	SO	HBP	SH	SF	SB	CS	SB%	GDP	Avg	OBP	SLG
2001 Jupiter *	A+	7	25	4	1	0	0	—	—	5	4	1	1	0	3	0	0	0	0	0	—	0	.160	.192	.200
Ottawa *	AAA	17	68	20	2	0	0	—	—	22	6	5	3	0	13	0	1	1	2	3	.40	4	.294	.319	.324
1996 Colorado	NL	12	10	3	0	0	0	(0	0)	3	6	1	0	0	3	0	0	1	0	0	—	0	.300	.273	.300
1998 Montreal	NL	60	212	46	7	2	1	(1	0)	60	30	15	21	1	46	0	15	0	16	4	.80	2	.217	.288	.283
1999 Montreal	NL	17	63	17	1	1	0	(0	0)	20	4	3	3	0	14	0	0	0	1	2	.33	0	.270	.303	.317
2000 Montreal	NL	108	168	42	8	2	0	(0	0)	54	30	13	10	1	32	0	3	0	7	2	.78	3	.250	.292	.321
2001 Montreal	NL	30	77	20	5	0	0	(0	0)	25	8	2	2	0	11	0	0	0	3	0	1.00	2	.260	.278	.325
5 ML YEARS		227	530	128	21	5	1	(1	0)	162	78	34	36	2	106	0	18	1	27	8	.77	7	.242	.289	.306

Todd Jones

Pitches: Right Bats: Left Pos: RP-69 Ht: 6'3" Wt: 230 Born: 4/24/68 Age: 34

Year Team	Lg	G	GS	CG	GF	IP	BFP	H	R	ER	HR	SH	SF	HB	TBB	IBB	SO	WP	Bk	W	L	Pct.	ShO	Sv-Op	Hld	ERA
1993 Houston	NL	27	0	0	8	37.1	150	28	14	13	4	2	1	1	15	2	25	1	1	1	2	.333	0	2-3	6	3.13
1994 Houston	NL	48	0	0	20	72.2	288	52	23	22	3	3	1	1	26	4	63	1	0	5	2	.714	0	5-9	8	2.72
1995 Houston	NL	68	0	0	40	99.2	442	89	38	34	8	5	4	6	52	17	96	5	0	6	5	.545	0	15-20	8	3.07
1996 Houston	NL	51	0	0	37	57.1	263	61	30	28	5	2	1	5	32	6	44	3	0	6	3	.667	0	17-23	1	4.40
1997 Detroit	AL	68	0	0	51	70	301	60	29	24	3	1	4	1	35	2	70	7	0	5	4	.556	0	31-36	5	3.09
1998 Detroit	AL	65	0	0	53	63.1	279	58	38	35	7	2	6	2	36	4	57	5	0	1	4	.200	0	28-32	0	4.97
1999 Detroit	AL	65	0	0	62	66.1	287	64	30	28	7	3	1	1	35	1	64	2	0	4	4	.500	0	30-35	0	3.80
2000 Detroit	AL	67	0	0	60	64	271	67	28	25	6	1	1	1	25	1	67	2	0	2	4	.333	0	42-46	0	3.52
2001 Det-Min	AL	69	0	0	36	68	314	87	39	32	9	3	3	0	29	1	54	3	0	5	5	.500	0	13-21	10	4.24
2001 Detroit	AL	45	0	0	28	48.2	225	60	31	25	6	2	3	0	22	1	39	3	0	4	5	.444	0	11-17	3	4.62
Minnesota	AL	24	0	0	8	19.1	89	27	8	7	3	1	0	0	7	0	15	0	0	1	0	1.000	0	2-4	7	3.26
9 ML YEARS		528	0	0	367	598.2	2595	566	269	241	52	22	22	18	285	38	540	29	1	35	33	.515	0	183-225	38	3.62

Brian Jordan

Bats: R Throws: R Pos: RF-144; PH/PR-3; DH-2; CF-1 Ht: 6'1" Wt: 205 Born: 3/29/67 Age: 35

Year Team	Lg	G	AB	H	2B	3B	HR	(Hm	Rd)	TB	R	RBI	TBB	IBB	SO	HBP	SH	SF	SB	CS	SB%	GDP	Avg	OBP	SLG
1992 St. Louis	NL	55	193	40	9	4	5	(3	2)	72	17	22	10	1	48	1	0	0	7	2	.78	6	.207	.250	.373
1993 St. Louis	NL	67	223	69	10	6	10	(4	6)	121	33	44	12	0	35	4	0	3	6	6	.50	6	.309	.351	.543
1994 St. Louis	NL	53	178	46	8	2	5	(4	1)	73	14	15	16	0	40	1	0	2	4	3	.57	6	.258	.320	.410
1995 St. Louis	NL	131	490	145	20	4	22	(14	8)	239	83	81	22	4	79	11	0	2	24	9	.73	5	.296	.339	.488
1996 St. Louis	NL	140	513	159	36	1	17	(3	14)	248	82	104	29	4	84	7	2	9	22	5	.81	6	.310	.349	.483
1997 St. Louis	NL	47	145	34	5	0	0	(0	0)	39	17	10	10	1	21	6	0	0	6	1	.86	4	.234	.311	.269
1998 St. Louis	NL	150	564	178	34	7	25	(9	16)	301	100	91	40	1	66	9	0	4	17	5	.77	18	.316	.368	.534
1999 Atlanta	NL	153	576	163	28	4	23	(11	12)	268	100	115	51	2	81	9	0	9	13	8	.62	9	.283	.346	.465
2000 Atlanta	NL	133	489	129	26	0	17	(7	10)	206	71	77	38	1	80	5	0	5	10	2	.83	12	.264	.320	.421
2001 Atlanta	NL	148	560	165	32	3	25	(14	11)	278	82	97	31	3	88	6	0	8	3	2	.60	18	.295	.334	.496
10 ML YEARS		1077	3931	1128	208	31	149	(69	80)	1845	599	656	259	17	622	59	2	42	112	43	.72	90	.287	.337	.469

Kevin Jordan

Bats: R Throws: R Pos: PH/PR-44; 1B-10; 2B-10; 3B-10 Ht: 6'1" Wt: 201 Born: 10/9/69 Age: 32

Year Team	Lg	G	AB	H	2B	3B	HR	(Hm	Rd)	TB	R	RBI	TBB	IBB	SO	HBP	SH	SF	SB	CS	SB%	GDP	Avg	OBP	SLG
1995 Philadelphia	NL	24	54	10	1	0	2	(1	1)	17	6	6	2	1	9	1	0	0	0	0	—	0	.185	.228	.315
1996 Philadelphia	NL	43	131	37	10	0	3	(2	1)	56	15	12	5	0	20	1	3	2	2	1	.67	3	.282	.309	.427
1997 Philadelphia	NL	84	177	47	8	0	6	(4	2)	73	19	30	3	0	26	0	0	3	0	1	.00	5	.266	.273	.412
1998 Philadelphia	NL	112	250	69	13	0	2	(1	1)	88	23	27	8	1	30	2	0	1	0	0	—	5	.276	.303	.352
1999 Philadelphia	NL	120	347	99	17	3	4	(2	2)	134	36	51	24	1	34	6	0	3	0	0	—	12	.285	.339	.386
2000 Philadelphia	NL	109	337	74	16	2	5	(2	3)	109	30	36	17	0	41	1	0	3	0	1	.00	11	.220	.257	.323
2001 Philadelphia	NL	68	113	27	5	0	1	(1	0)	35	9	13	14	2	21	0	0	0	0	0	—	1	.239	.323	.310
7 ML YEARS		560	1409	363	70	5	23	(13	10)	512	138	175	73	5	181	11	3	12	2	3	.40	37	.258	.297	.363

Wally Joyner

Bats: Left Throws: Left Pos: 1B-39; PH/PR-10; DH-9 Ht: 6'2" Wt: 200 Born: 6/16/62 Age: 40

Year Team	Lg	G	AB	H	2B	3B	HR	(Hm	Rd)	TB	R	RBI	TBB	IBB	SO	HBP	SH	SF	SB	CS	SB%	GDP	Avg	OBP	SLG
1986 California	AL	154	593	172	27	3	22	(11	11)	271	82	100	57	8	58	2	10	12	5	2	.71	11	.290	.348	.457
1987 California	AL	149	564	161	33	1	34	(19	15)	298	100	117	72	12	64	5	2	10	8	2	.80	14	.285	.366	.528
1988 California	AL	158	597	176	31	2	13	(6	7)	250	81	85	55	14	51	5	0	8	8	2	.80	16	.295	.356	.419
1989 California	AL	159	593	167	30	2	16	(8	8)	249	78	79	46	7	58	6	1	8	3	2	.60	15	.282	.335	.420
1990 California	AL	83	310	83	15	0	8	(5	3)	122	35	41	41	4	34	1	1	5	2	1	.67	10	.268	.350	.394
1991 California	AL	143	551	166	34	3	21	(10	11)	269	79	96	52	4	66	1	2	5	2	0	1.00	11	.301	.360	.488
1992 Kansas City	AL	149	572	154	36	2	9	(1	8)	221	66	66	55	4	50	4	0	2	11	5	.69	19	.269	.336	.386
1993 Kansas City	AL	141	497	145	36	3	15	(4	11)	232	83	65	66	13	67	3	2	5	5	9	.36	6	.292	.375	.467
1994 Kansas City	AL	97	363	113	20	3	8	(2	6)	163	52	57	47	3	43	0	2	5	3	2	.60	12	.311	.386	.449
1995 Kansas City	AL	131	465	144	28	0	12	(6	6)	208	69	83	69	10	65	2	5	9	3	2	.60	10	.310	.394	.447
1996 San Diego	NL	121	433	120	29	1	8	(5	3)	175	59	65	69	8	71	3	1	4	5	3	.63	6	.277	.377	.404
1997 San Diego	NL	135	455	149	29	2	13	(6	7)	221	59	83	51	5	51	2	0	10	3	5	.38	14	.327	.390	.486
1998 San Diego	NL	131	439	131	30	1	12	(4	8)	199	58	80	51	8	44	1	0	3	1	2	.33	11	.298	.370	.453
1999 San Diego	NL	110	323	80	14	2	5	(2	3)	113	34	43	58	6	54	2	0	3	0	1	.00	8	.248	.363	.350
2000 Atlanta	NL	119	224	63	12	0	5	(2	3)	90	24	32	31	3	31	1	0	4	0	0	—	2	.281	.365	.402
2001 Anaheim	AL	53	148	36	5	1	3	(0	3)	52	14	14	13	0	18	0	0	0	1	1	.50	3	.243	.304	.351
16 ML YEARS		2033	7127	2060	409	26	204	(91	113)	3133	973	1106	833	109	825	38	26	91	60	39	.61	168	.289	.362	.440

Mike Judd

Pitches: Right **Bats:** Right **Pos:** RP-9; SP-3   **Ht:** 6'1" **Wt:** 217 **Born:** 6/30/75 **Age:** 27

Year Team	Lg	G	GS	CG	GF	IP	BFP	H	R	ER	HR	SH	SF	HB	TBB	IBB	SO	WP	Bk	W	L	Pct.	ShO	Sv-Op	Hld	ERA
2001 Oklahoma *	AAA	2	0	0	1	2.2	16	6	3	3	0	1	0	0	2	0	3	0	0	0	1	.000	0	0--	—	10.13
1997 Los Angeles	NL	1	0	0	0	2.2	11	4	0	0	0	0	0	0	2	0	4	0	0	0	0	—	0	0-0	0	0.00
1998 Los Angeles	NL	7	0	0	3	11.1	63	19	19	19	4	2	0	1	9	1	14	0	0	0	0	—	0	0-0	0	15.09
1999 Los Angeles	NL	7	4	0	0	28	120	30	17	17	4	0	0	1	12	0	22	3	0	3	1	.750	0	0-0	0	5.46
2000 Los Angeles	NL	1	1	0	0	4	20	4	7	7	2	0	0	1	3	0	5	0	0	0	1	.000	0	0-0	0	15.75
2001 TB-Tex	AL	12	3	0	3	29	137	34	24	17	4	0	3	1	15	0	16	1	0	1	1	.500	0	0-0	0	5.28
2001 Tampa Bay	AL	8	2	0	2	20	90	19	14	9	2	0	3	1	10	0	11	0	0	1	0	1.000	0	0-0	0	4.05
Texas	AL	4	1	0	1	9	47	15	10	8	2	0	0	0	5	0	5	1	0	0	1	.000	0	0-0	0	8.00
5 ML YEARS		28	8	0	6	75	351	91	67	60	14	2	3	4	39	1	61	4	0	4	3	.571	0	0-0	0	7.20

Jorge Julio

Pitches: Right **Bats:** Right **Pos:** RP-18   **Ht:** 6'1" **Wt:** 190 **Born:** 3/3/79 **Age:** 23

Year Team	Lg	G	GS	CG	GF	IP	BFP	H	R	ER	HR	SH	SF	HB	TBB	IBB	SO	WP	Bk	W	L	Pct.	ShO	Sv-Op	Hld	ERA
1997 Expos	R	15	8	0	4	55.1	248	57	25	22	0	1	2	1	21	0	42	3	0	5	6	.455	0	1--	—	3.58
Wst Plm Bch	A+	1	0	0	0	0	2	2	1	1	0	0	0	0	0	0	0	0	0	0	0	—	0	0--	—	0.00
1998 Vermont	A-	7	7	0	0	42	173	30	12	12	1	1	1	3	15	0	52	1	1	3	1	.750	0	0--	—	2.57
Cape Fear	A	6	6	0	0	31.2	134	33	20	20	4	0	1	1	12	0	20	1	0	2	2	.500	0	0--	—	5.68
1999 Jupiter	A+	23	22	0	1	114.2	491	116	62	50	6	3	5	3	34	0	80	11	1	4	8	.333	0	0--	—	3.92
2000 Jupiter	A+	21	15	0	3	79.1	363	93	60	52	4	1	5	4	35	0	67	1	3	2	10	.167	0	1--	—	5.90
2001 Bowie	AA	12	0	0	12	12.1	44	5	1	1	0	0	1	1	2	1	14	0	0	0	0	—	0	7--	—	0.73
Rochester	AAA	34	0	0	24	43.1	196	39	27	18	4	2	2	5	19	3	48	5	1	1	2	.333	0	12--	—	3.74
2001 Baltimore	AL	18	0	0	8	21.1	99	25	13	9	2	2	0	1	9	0	22	1	0	1	1	.500	0	0-1	3	3.80

David Justice

Bats: L **Throws:** L **Pos:** DH-85; LF-16; RF-11; PH/PR-3   **Ht:** 6'3" **Wt:** 200 **Born:** 4/14/66 **Age:** 36

Year Team	Lg	G	AB	H	2B	3B	HR	(Hm	Rd)	TB	R	RBI	TBB	IBB	SO	HBP	SH	SF	SB	CS	SB%	GDP	Avg	OBP	SLG
2001 Norwich *	AA	2	8	0	0	0	0	(—	0)	0	0	0	0	0	1	0	0	0	0	0	.000	0	.000	.000	.000
1989 Atlanta	NL	16	51	12	3	0	1	(1	0)	18	7	3	3	1	9	1	1	0	2	1	.67	1	.235	.291	.353
1990 Atlanta	NL	127	439	124	23	2	28	(19	9)	235	76	78	64	4	92	0	0	1	11	6	.65	2	.282	.373	.535
1991 Atlanta	NL	109	396	109	25	1	21	(11	10)	199	67	87	65	9	81	3	0	5	8	8	.50	4	.275	.377	.503
1992 Atlanta	NL	144	484	124	19	5	21	(10	11)	216	78	72	79	8	85	2	0	6	2	4	.33	1	.256	.359	.446
1993 Atlanta	NL	157	585	158	15	4	40	(18	22)	301	90	120	78	12	90	3	0	4	3	5	.38	9	.270	.357	.515
1994 Atlanta	NL	104	352	110	16	2	19	(9	10)	187	61	59	69	5	45	2	0	1	2	4	.33	8	.313	.427	.531
1995 Atlanta	NL	120	411	104	17	2	24	(15	9)	197	73	78	73	5	68	2	0	5	4	2	.67	5	.253	.365	.479
1996 Atlanta	NL	40	140	45	9	0	6	(5	1)	72	23	25	21	1	22	1	0	2	1	1	.50	5	.321	.409	.514
1997 Cleveland	AL	139	495	163	31	1	33	(17	16)	295	84	101	80	11	79	0	0	7	3	5	.38	12	.329	.418	.596
1998 Cleveland	AL	146	540	151	39	2	21	(7	14)	257	94	88	76	7	98	0	0	9	9	3	.75	9	.280	.363	.476
1999 Cleveland	AL	133	429	123	18	0	21	(11	10)	204	75	88	94	11	90	2	0	5	1	3	.25	14	.287	.413	.476
2000 Cle-NYY	AL	146	524	150	31	1	41	(24	17)	306	89	118	77	3	91	1	0	3	2	1	.67	13	.286	.377	.584
2001 New York	AL	111	381	92	16	1	18	(8	10)	164	58	51	54	5	83	0	0	4	1	2	.33	6	.241	.333	.430
2000 Cleveland	AL	68	249	66	14	1	21	(10	11)	145	46	58	38	2	49	0	0	1	1	1	.50	7	.265	.361	.582
New York	AL	78	275	84	17	0	20	(14	6)	161	43	60	39	1	42	1	0	2	1	0	1.00	6	.305	.391	.585
13 ML YEARS		1492	5227	1465	262	21	294	(155	139)	2651	875	968	833	82	933	17	1	52	49	45	.52	89	.280	.378	.507

Gabe Kapler

Bats: Right **Throws:** Right **Pos:** CF-133; PH/PR-2; DH-1   **Ht:** 6'2" **Wt:** 208 **Born:** 8/31/75 **Age:** 26

Year Team	Lg	G	AB	H	2B	3B	HR	(Hm	Rd)	TB	R	RBI	TBB	IBB	SO	HBP	SH	SF	SB	CS	SB%	GDP	Avg	OBP	SLG
2001 Tulsa *	AA	5	15	5	1	0	0	(—	—)	6	2	0	6	0	1	0	0	0	0	1	.00	0	.333	.524	.400
1998 Detroit	AL	7	25	5	1	0	0	(0	0)	7	3	0	1	0	4	0	0	0	2	0	1.00	0	.200	.231	.280
1999 Detroit	AL	130	416	102	22	4	18	(12	6)	186	60	49	42	0	74	2	4	4	11	5	.69	7	.245	.315	.447
2000 Texas	AL	116	444	134	32	1	14	(11	3)	210	59	66	42	2	57	0	2	3	8	4	.67	12	.302	.360	.473
2001 Texas	AL	134	483	129	29	1	17	(11	6)	211	77	72	61	2	70	3	2	7	23	6	.79	10	.267	.348	.437
4 ML YEARS		387	1368	370	83	7	49	(34	15)	614	199	187	146	4	205	5	8	14	44	15	.75	29	.270	.340	.449

Jason Karnuth

Pitches: Right **Bats:** Right **Pos:** RP-4   **Ht:** 6'2" **Wt:** 190 **Born:** 5/15/76 **Age:** 26

Year Team	Lg	G	GS	CG	GF	IP	BFP	H	R	ER	HR	SH	SF	HB	TBB	IBB	SO	WP	Bk	W	L	Pct.	ShO	Sv-Op	Hld	ERA
1997 New Jersey	A-	7	7	0	0	38.2	158	33	8	8	0	1	1	2	9	0	23	2	0	4	1	.800	0	0--	—	1.86
Peoria	A	4	4	0	0	23	102	29	19	17	1	1	1	1	7	1	12	2	1	0	3	.000	0	0--	—	6.65
1998 Pr William	A+	16	15	2	1	108	411	86	26	20	3	6	0	7	14	0	53	4	0	8	1	.889	2	0--	—	1.67
1999 Arkansas	AA	26	26	2	0	160.1	696	175	105	93	16	5	7	11	55	0	71	2	0	7	11	.389	0	0--	—	5.22
2000 Arkansas	AA	8	8	1	0	50.1	220	59	30	21	3	1	2	1	14	0	31	5	1	2	3	.400	0	0--	—	3.75
Memphis	AAA	16	13	0	1	78	341	89	44	35	7	4	2	5	27	0	28	3	0	5	4	.556	0	0--	—	4.04
2001 Memphis	AAA	55	0	0	17	73.2	324	82	37	35	7	3	2	6	24	0	42	2	0	4	4	.500	0	3--	—	4.28
2001 St. Louis	NL	4	0	0	1	5	24	6	1	1	1	0	0	1	4	0	1	0	0	0	0	—	0	0-0	0	1.80

Eric Karros

Bats: Right **Throws:** Right **Pos:** 1B-119; PH/PR-2 **Ht:** 6'4" **Wt:** 226 **Born:** 11/4/67 **Age:** 34

				BATTING																BASERUNNING				PERCENTAGES		
Year Team	Lg	G	AB	H	2B	3B	HR	(Hm	Rd)	TB	R	RBI	TBB	IBB	SO	HBP	SH	SF	SB	CS	SB%	GDP	Avg	OBP	SLG
1991 Los Angeles	NL	14	14	1	1	0	0	(0	0)	2	0	1	1	0	6	0	0	0	0	0	—	0	.071	.133	.143
1992 Los Angeles	NL	149	545	140	30	1	20	(6	14)	232	63	88	37	3	103	2	0	5	2	4	.33	15	.257	.304	.426
1993 Los Angeles	NL	158	619	153	27	2	23	(13	10)	253	74	80	34	1	82	2	0	3	0	1	.00	17	.247	.287	.409
1994 Los Angeles	NL	111	406	108	21	1	14	(5	9)	173	51	46	29	1	53	2	0	11	2	0	1.00	13	.266	.310	.426
1995 Los Angeles	NL	143	551	164	29	3	32	(19	13)	295	83	105	61	4	115	4	0	4	4	4	.50	14	.298	.369	.535
1996 Los Angeles	NL	154	608	158	29	1	34	(16	18)	291	84	111	53	2	121	1	0	8	8	0	1.00	**27**	.260	.316	.479
1997 Los Angeles	NL	**162**	628	167	28	0	31	(13	18)	288	86	104	61	2	116	2	0	9	15	7	.68	10	.266	.329	.459
1998 Los Angeles	NL	139	507	150	20	1	23	(9	14)	241	59	87	47	1	93	3	0	7	7	2	.78	7	.296	.355	.475
1999 Los Angeles	NL	153	578	176	40	0	34	(17	17)	318	74	112	53	0	119	2	0	6	8	5	.62	18	.304	.362	.550
2000 Los Angeles	NL	155	584	146	29	0	31	(16	15)	268	84	106	63	2	122	4	0	12	4	3	.57	18	.250	.321	.459
2001 Los Angeles	NL	121	438	103	22	0	15	(7	8)	170	42	63	41	2	101	3	0	3	3	1	.75	15	.235	.303	.388
11 ML YEARS		1459	5478	1466	276	9	257	(121	136)	2531	700	903	480	18	1031	25	0	68	53	27	.66	154	.268	.326	.462

Steve Karsay

Pitches: Right **Bats:** Right **Pos:** RP-74 **Ht:** 6'3" **Wt:** 215 **Born:** 3/24/72 **Age:** 30

		HOW MUCH HE PITCHED						WHAT HE GAVE UP											THE RESULTS						
Year Team	Lg	G	GS	CG	GF	IP	BFP	H	R	ER	HR	SH	SF	HB	TBB	IBB	SO	WP	Bk	W	L	Pct.	ShO	Sv-Op	Hld	ERA
1993 Oakland	AL	8	8	0	0	49	210	49	23	22	4	0	2	2	16	1	33	1	0	3	3	.500	0	0-0	0	4.04
1994 Oakland	AL	4	4	1	0	28	115	26	8	8	1	2	1	1	8	0	15	0	0	1	1	.500	0	0-0	0	2.57
1997 Oakland	AL	24	24	0	0	132.2	609	166	92	85	20	2	5	9	47	3	92	7	0	3	12	.200	0	0-0	0	5.77
1998 Cleveland	AL	11	1	0	4	24.1	111	31	16	16	3	1	2	2	6	1	13	2	0	0	2	.000	0	0-0	2	5.92
1999 Cleveland	AL	50	3	0	13	78.2	324	71	29	26	6	2	3	2	30	3	68	5	0	10	2	.833	0	1-3	9	2.97
2000 Cleveland	AL	72	0	0	46	76.2	329	79	33	32	5	2	2	3	25	4	66	0	0	5	9	.357	0	20-29	11	3.76
2001 Cle-Atl		74	0	0	29	88	356	73	27	23	5	6	4	1	25	10	83	3	0	3	5	.375	0	8-12	12	2.35
2001 Cleveland	AL	31	0	0	8	43.1	166	29	6	6	1	3	1	0	8	2	44	2	0	0	1	.000	0	1-1	8	1.25
Atlanta	NL	43	0	0	21	44.2	190	44	21	17	4	3	3	1	17	8	39	1	0	3	4	.429	0	7-11	4	3.43
7 ML YEARS		243	40	1	92	477.1	2054	495	228	212	44	15	19	20	157	22	370	18	0	25	34	.424	0	29-44	34	4.00

Randy Keisler

Pitches: Left **Bats:** Left **Pos:** SP-10 **Ht:** 6'3" **Wt:** 190 **Born:** 2/24/76 **Age:** 26

		HOW MUCH HE PITCHED						WHAT HE GAVE UP											THE RESULTS						
Year Team	Lg	G	GS	CG	GF	IP	BFP	H	R	ER	HR	SH	SF	HB	TBB	IBB	SO	WP	Bk	W	L	Pct.	ShO	Sv-Op	Hld	ERA
1998 Oneonta	A-	6	2	0	1	9.2	51	14	10	8	0	0	3	0	7	1	11	0	0	1	1	.500	0	1- -	—	7.45
1999 Greensboro	A	4	4	0	0	22.2	91	12	6	6	1	0	1	0	10	0	42	0	0	1	1	.500	0	0- -	—	2.38
Tampa	A+	15	15	1	0	90	375	67	43	33	2	3	1	3	40	0	77	4	1	10	3	.769	0	0- -	—	3.30
Norwich	AA	8	8	0	0	43.1	189	45	24	22	2	1	3	3	17	0	33	2	0	3	4	.429	0	0- -	—	4.57
2000 Norwich	AA	11	11	0	0	72.2	313	63	29	21	4	0	1	1	34	1	70	4	1	6	2	.750	0	0- -	—	2.60
Columbus	AAA	17	17	1	0	113.1	479	104	44	38	9	3	4	4	42	1	86	5	3	8	3	.727	1	0- -	—	3.02
2001 Columbus	AAA	18	18	3	0	97.1	444	111	67	56	10	3	3	3	39	0	88	2	0	5	7	.417	1	0- -	—	5.18
2000 New York	AL	4	1	0	0	10.2	52	16	14	14	1	0	0	0	8	0	6	0	0	1	0	1.000	0	0-0	0	11.81
2001 New York	AL	10	10	0	0	50.2	236	52	36	35	12	0	1	0	34	0	36	0	0	1	2	.333	0	0-0	0	6.22
2 ML YEARS		14	11	0	0	61.1	288	68	50	49	13	0	1	0	42	0	42	0	0	2	2	.500	0	0-0	0	7.19

Jason Kendall

Bats: R **Throws:** R **Pos:** C-133; LF-18; RF-10; PH/PR-3 **Ht:** 6'0" **Wt:** 195 **Born:** 6/26/74 **Age:** 28

				BATTING																BASERUNNING				PERCENTAGES		
Year Team	Lg	G	AB	H	2B	3B	HR	(Hm	Rd)	TB	R	RBI	TBB	IBB	SO	HBP	SH	SF	SB	CS	SB%	GDP	Avg	OBP	SLG
1996 Pittsburgh	NL	130	414	124	23	5	3	(2	1)	166	54	42	35	11	30	15	3	4	5	2	.71	7	.300	.372	.401
1997 Pittsburgh	NL	144	486	143	36	4	8	(5	3)	211	71	49	49	2	53	31	1	5	18	6	.75	11	.294	.391	.434
1998 Pittsburgh	NL	149	535	175	36	3	12	(6	6)	253	95	75	51	3	51	**31**	2	8	26	5	.84	6	.327	.411	.473
1999 Pittsburgh	NL	78	280	93	20	3	8	(5	3)	143	61	41	38	3	32	12	0	4	22	3	.88	8	.332	.428	.511
2000 Pittsburgh	NL	152	579	185	33	6	14	(7	7)	272	112	58	79	3	79	15	1	4	22	12	.65	13	.320	.412	.470
2001 Pittsburgh	NL	157	606	161	22	2	10	(3	7)	217	84	53	44	4	48	20	0	2	13	14	.48	18	.266	.335	.358
6 ML YEARS		810	2900	881	170	23	55	(28	27)	1262	477	318	296	26	293	124	7	27	106	42	.72	63	.304	.389	.435

Adam Kennedy

Bats: Left **Throws:** Right **Pos:** 2B-131; PH/PR-8; DH-5 **Ht:** 6'1" **Wt:** 192 **Born:** 1/10/76 **Age:** 26

				BATTING																BASERUNNING				PERCENTAGES		
Year Team	Lg	G	AB	H	2B	3B	HR	(Hm	Rd)	TB	R	RBI	TBB	IBB	SO	HBP	SH	SF	SB	CS	SB%	GDP	Avg	OBP	SLG
2001 Rancho Cuc *	A+	3	8	3	2	0	0	—	—	5	3	1	2	0	1	1	0	0	3	0	1.00	0	.375	.545	.625
1999 St. Louis	NL	33	102	26	10	1	1	(1	0)	41	12	16	3	0	8	2	1	2	0	1	.00	1	.255	.284	.402
2000 Anaheim	AL	156	598	159	33	11	9	(7	2)	241	82	72	28	5	73	3	8	4	22	8	.73	10	.266	.300	.403
2001 Anaheim	AL	137	478	129	25	3	6	(4	2)	178	48	40	27	3	71	11	7	9	12	7	.63	7	.270	.318	.372
3 ML YEARS		326	1178	314	68	15	16	(12	4)	460	142	128	58	8	152	16	16	15	34	16	.68	18	.267	.306	.390

Joe Kennedy

Pitches: Left **Bats:** Right **Pos:** SP-20 **Ht:** 6'4" **Wt:** 225 **Born:** 5/24/79 **Age:** 23

		HOW MUCH HE PITCHED						WHAT HE GAVE UP											THE RESULTS						
Year Team	Lg	G	GS	CG	GF	IP	BFP	H	R	ER	HR	SH	SF	HB	TBB	IBB	SO	WP	Bk	W	L	Pct.	ShO	Sv-Op	Hld	ERA
1998 Princeton	R+	13	13	0	0	67.1	282	66	37	28	5	1	2	3	26	0	44	4	2	6	4	.600	0	0- -	—	3.74
1999 Hudson Val	A-	16	16	1	0	95	376	78	33	28	2	1	1	4	26	0	101	7	1	6	5	.545	1	0- -	—	2.65
2000 Chston-SC	A	22	22	3	0	136.1	546	122	59	50	6	2	6	4	29	1	142	9	2	11	6	.647	2	0- -	—	3.30
2001 Orlando	AA	7	7	0	0	47	170	29	3	1	0	1	1	2	3	0	52	2	0	4	0	1.000	0	0- -	—	0.19
Durham	AAA	4	4	0	0	26	109	22	8	7	2	1	0	2	9	0	23	7	0	2	0	1.000	0	0- -	—	2.42
2001 Tampa Bay	AL	20	20	0	0	117.2	498	122	63	58	16	2	5	3	34	0	78	5	1	7	8	.467	0	0-0	0	4.44

Jeff Kent

Bats: Right **Throws:** Right **Pos:** 2B-140; 1B-30; PH/PR-1 **Ht:** 6'1" **Wt:** 205 **Born:** 3/7/68 **Age:** 34

Year Team	Lg	G	AB	H	2B	3B	HR	(Hm Rd)	TB	R	RBI	TBB	IBB	SO	HBP	SH	SF	SB	CS	SB%	GDP	Avg	OBP	SLG
1992 Tor-NYM		102	305	73	21	2	11	(4 7)	131	52	50	27	0	76	7	0	4	2	3	.40	5	.239	.312	.430
1993 New York	NL	140	496	134	24	0	21	(9 12)	221	65	80	30	2	88	8	6	4	4	4	.50	11	.270	.320	.446
1994 New York	NL	107	415	121	24	5	14	(10 4)	197	53	68	23	3	84	10	1	3	1	4	.20	7	.292	.341	.475
1995 New York	NL	125	472	131	22	3	20	(11 9)	219	65	65	29	3	89	8	1	4	3	3	.50	9	.278	.327	.464
1996 NYM-Cle		128	437	124	27	1	12	(4 8)	189	61	55	31	1	78	2	1	6	6	4	.60	8	.284	.330	.432
1997 San Francisco	NL	155	580	145	38	2	29	(13 16)	274	90	121	48	6	133	13	0	10	11	3	.79	14	.250	.316	.472
1998 San Francisco	NL	137	526	156	37	3	31	(17 14)	292	94	128	48	4	110	9	1	10	9	4	.69	16	.297	.359	.555
1999 San Francisco	NL	138	511	148	40	2	23	(11 12)	261	86	101	61	3	112	5	0	8	13	6	.68	12	.290	.366	.511
2000 San Francisco	NL	159	587	196	41	7	33	(14 19)	350	114	125	90	6	107	9	0	9	12	9	.57	17	.334	.424	.596
2001 San Francisco	NL	159	607	181	49	6	22	(8 14)	308	84	106	65	4	96	11	0	13	7	6	.54	11	.298	.369	.507
1992 Toronto	AL	65	192	46	13	1	8	(2 6)	85	36	35	20	0	47	6	0	4	2	1	.67	3	.240	.324	.443
New York	NL	37	113	27	8	1	3	(2 1)	46	16	15	7	0	29	1	0	0	0	2	.00	2	.239	.289	.407
1996 New York	NL	89	335	97	20	1	9	(2 7)	146	45	39	21	1	56	1	1	3	4	3	.57	7	.290	.331	.436
Cleveland	AL	39	102	27	7	0	3	(2 1)	43	16	16	10	0	22	1	0	3	2	1	.67	1	.265	.328	.422
10 ML YEARS		1350	4936	1409	323	31	216	(101 115)	2442	764	899	452	32	973	82	10	71	68	46	.60	110	.285	.351	.495

Bobby Kielty

Bats: B **Throws:** R **Pos:** RF-17; LF-11; CF-11; PH/PR-6; DH-1 **Ht:** 6'1" **Wt:** 215 **Born:** 8/5/76 **Age:** 25

Year Team	Lg	G	AB	H	2B	3B	HR	(Hm Rd)	TB	R	RBI	TBB	IBB	SO	HBP	SH	SF	SB	CS	SB%	GDP	Avg	OBP	SLG
1999 Quad City	A	69	245	72	13	1	13	— —	126	52	43	43	1	56	3	2	3	12	3	.80	7	.294	.401	.514
2000 New Britain	AA	129	451	118	30	3	14	— —	196	79	65	98	4	109	5	0	4	6	4	.60	16	.262	.396	.435
Salt Lake	AAA	9	33	8	4	0	0	— —	12	8	2	7	0	10	0	0	0	0	0	—	0	.242	.375	.364
2001 Edmonton	AAA	94	341	98	25	2	12	— —	163	58	50	53	1	76	6	2	2	5	0	1.00	11	.287	.391	.478
2001 Minnesota	AL	37	104	26	8	0	2	(1 1)	40	8	14	8	2	25	1	0	5	3	0	1.00	2	.250	.297	.385

Brooks Kieschnick

Bats: L **Throws:** R **Pos:** PH/PR-28; LF-8; RF-4; 1B-1 **Ht:** 6'4" **Wt:** 230 **Born:** 6/6/72 **Age:** 30

Year Team	Lg	G	AB	H	2B	3B	HR	(Hm Rd)	TB	R	RBI	TBB	IBB	SO	HBP	SH	SF	SB	CS	SB%	GDP	Avg	OBP	SLG
2001 Colo Sprngs *	AAA	71	252	74	9	3	13	— —	128	44	45	24	3	72	2	0	0	3	2	.60	7	.294	.360	.508
1996 Chicago	NL	25	29	10	2	0	1	(0 1)	15	6	6	3	0	8	0	0	0	0	0	—	0	.345	.406	.517
1997 Chicago	NL	39	90	18	2	0	4	(3 1)	32	9	12	12	0	21	0	0	0	1	0	1.00	0	.200	.294	.356
2000 Cincinnati	NL	14	12	0	0	0	0	(0 0)	0	0	0	1	0	5	0	0	0	0	0	—	0	.000	.077	.000
2001 Colorado	NL	35	42	10	2	1	3	(1 2)	23	5	9	3	0	13	0	0	0	0	0	—	1	.238	.289	.548
4 ML YEARS		113	173	38	6	1	8	(4 4)	70	20	27	19	0	47	0	0	0	1	0	1.00	3	.220	.297	.405

Darryl Kile

Pitches: Right **Bats:** Right **Pos:** SP-34 **Ht:** 6'5" **Wt:** 212 **Born:** 12/2/68 **Age:** 33

Year Team	Lg	G	GS	CG	GF	IP	BFP	H	R	ER	HR	SH	SF	HB	TBB	IBB	SO	WP	Bk	W	L	Pct.	ShO	Sv-Op	Hld	ERA
1991 Houston	NL	37	22	0	5	153.2	689	144	81	63	16	9	5	6	84	4	100	5	4	7	11	.389	0	0-1	0	3.69
1992 Houston	NL	22	22	2	0	125.1	554	124	61	55	8	5	6	4	63	4	90	3	4	5	10	.333	0	0-0	0	3.95
1993 Houston	NL	32	26	4	0	171.2	733	152	73	67	12	5	7	15	69	1	141	9	3	15	8	.652	2	0-0	0	3.51
1994 Houston	NL	24	24	0	0	147.2	664	153	84	75	13	14	2	9	82	6	105	10	0	9	6	.600	0	0-0	0	4.57
1995 Houston	NL	25	21	0	1	127	570	114	81	70	5	7	3	12	73	2	113	11	1	4	12	.250	0	0-0	0	4.96
1996 Houston	NL	35	33	4	1	219	975	233	113	102	16	10	9	16	97	8	219	13	3	12	11	.522	0	0-0	0	4.19
1997 Houston	NL	34	34	6	0	255.2	1056	208	87	73	19	17	10	10	94	2	205	7	1	19	7	.731	4	0-0	0	2.57
1998 Colorado	NL	36	35	4	1	230.1	1020	257	141	132	28	15	8	7	96	4	158	12	0	13	17	.433	1	0-0	0	5.20
1999 Colorado	NL	32	32	1	0	190.2	888	225	150	140	33	9	9	6	109	5	116	13	1	8	13	.381	0	0-0	0	6.61
2000 St. Louis	NL	34	34	5	0	232.1	960	215	109	101	33	11	8	13	58	1	192	8	1	20	9	.690	1	0-0	0	3.91
2001 St. Louis	NL	34	34	2	0	227.1	956	228	83	78	22	13	5	11	65	3	179	6	1	16	11	.593	1	0-0	0	3.09
11 ML YEARS		345	317	28	8	2080.2	9065	2053	1063	957	205	115	72	109	890	40	1618	97	19	128	115	.527	9	0-1	0	4.14

Byung-Hyun Kim

Pitches: Right **Bats:** Right **Pos:** RP-78 **Ht:** 5'11" **Wt:** 177 **Born:** 1/19/79 **Age:** 23

Year Team	Lg	G	GS	CG	GF	IP	BFP	H	R	ER	HR	SH	SF	HB	TBB	IBB	SO	WP	Bk	W	L	Pct.	ShO	Sv-Op	Hld	ERA
1999 Arizona	NL	25	0	0	10	27.1	121	20	15	14	2	1	0	5	20	2	31	4	1	1	2	.333	0	1-4	3	4.61
2000 Arizona	NL	61	1	0	30	70.2	320	52	39	35	9	2	3	9	46	5	111	3	2	6	6	.500	0	14-20	5	4.46
2001 Arizona	NL	78	0	0	44	98	392	58	32	32	10	5	0	8	44	3	113	5	1	5	6	.455	0	19-23	11	2.94
3 ML YEARS		164	1	0	84	196	833	130	86	81	21	8	3	22	110	10	255	12	4	12	14	.462	0	34-47	19	3.72

Sun-Woo Kim

Pitches: Right **Bats:** Right **Pos:** RP-18; SP-2 **Ht:** 6'2" **Wt:** 180 **Born:** 9/4/77 **Age:** 24

Year Team	Lg	G	GS	CG	GF	IP	BFP	H	R	ER	HR	SH	SF	HB	TBB	IBB	SO	WP	Bk	W	L	Pct.	ShO	Sv-Op	Hld	ERA
1998 Sarasota	A+	26	24	5	0	153	655	159	88	82	18	2	8	2	40	1	132	11	0	12	8	.600	0	0-—	—	4.82
1999 Trenton	AA	26	26	1	0	149	641	160	86	81	16	2	5	9	44	2	130	4	0	9	8	.529	1	0-—	—	4.89
2000 Pawtucket	AAA	26	25	0	0	134.1	603	170	98	90	17	2	4	5	42	1	116	5	0	11	7	.611	0	0-—	—	6.03
2001 Pawtucket	AAA	19	14	0	3	89	384	93	55	53	10	7	2	6	27	1	79	4	1	6	7	.462	0	0-—	—	5.36
2001 Boston	AL	20	2	0	7	41.2	201	54	27	27	1	3	0	4	21	5	27	5	0	0	2	.000	0	0-0	1	5.83

Ray King

Pitches: Left Bats: Left Pos: RP-82 Ht: 6'1" Wt: 230 Born: 1/15/74 Age: 28

		HOW MUCH HE PITCHED						WHAT HE GAVE UP									THE RESULTS					
Year Team	Lg	G	GS	CG	GF	IP	BFP	H	R	ER	HR	SH	SF	HB	TBB	IBB	SO	WP	Bk	W	L	Pct.	ShO	Sv-Op	Hld	ERA
1999 Chicago	NL	10	0	0	0	10.2	50	11	8	7	2	1	0	1	10	0	5	1	0	0	0	—	0	0-0	2	5.91
2000 Milwaukee	NL	36	0	0	8	28.2	111	18	7	4	1	0	1	0	10	1	19	1	0	3	2	.600	0	0-1	5	1.26
2001 Milwaukee	NL	82	0	0	19	55	234	49	22	22	5	3	2	1	25	7	49	2	0	0	4	.000	0	1-4	18	3.60
3 ML YEARS		128	0	0	27	94.1	395	78	37	33	8	4	3	2	45	8	73	4	0	3	6	.333	0	1-5	25	3.15

Gene Kingsale

Bats: B Throws: R Pos: LF-5; PH/PR-4; RF-3; CF-2 Ht: 6'3" Wt: 194 Born: 8/20/76 Age: 25

		BATTING															BASERUNNING				PERCENTAGES		
Year Team	Lg	G	AB	H	2B	3B	HR	(Hm | Rd)	TB	R	RBI	TBB	IBB	SO	HBP	SH	SF	SB	CS	SB%	GDP	Avg	OBP	SLG
2001 Rochester *	AAA	64	244	49	12	2	0	—	—	65	31	15	26	0	44	2	3	0	16	2	.89	6	.201	.283	.266
Tacoma *	AAA	51	215	63	14	4	3	—	—	94	30	24	8	0	25	3	2	0	12	4	.75	1	.293	.327	.437
1996 Baltimore	AL	3	0	0	0	0	0	(0 | 0)	0	0	0	0	0	0	0	0	0	0	0	—	0	—	—	—
1998 Baltimore	AL	11	2	0	0	0	0	(0 | 0)	0	1	0	0	0	1	0	0	0	0	0	—	0	.000	.000	.000
1999 Baltimore	AL	28	85	21	2	0	0	(0 | 0)	23	9	7	5	0	13	2	2	1	1	3	.25	3	.247	.301	.271
2000 Baltimore	AL	26	88	21	2	1	0	(0 | 0)	25	13	9	2	0	14	0	0	1	1	2	.33	4	.239	.253	.284
2001 Bal-Sea	AL	13	19	5	0	0	0	(0 | 0)	5	4	1	2	0	4	1	0	0	3	1	.75	1	.263	.364	.263
2001 Baltimore	AL	3	4	0	0	0	0	(0 | 0)	0	0	0	0	0	2	0	0	0	1	1	.50	0	.000	.000	.000
Seattle	AL	10	15	5	0	0	0	(0 | 0)	5	4	1	2	0	2	1	0	0	2	0	1.00	1	.333	.444	.333
5 ML YEARS		81	194	47	4	1	0	(0 | 0)	53	27	17	9	0	32	3	2	2	5	6	.45	8	.242	.284	.273

Mike Kinkade

Bats: R Throws: R Pos: LF-29; PH/PR-16; DH-10; 3B-10; 1B-3; RF-3; C-2 Ht: 6'1" Wt: 210 Born: 5/6/73 Age: 29

		BATTING															BASERUNNING				PERCENTAGES		
Year Team	Lg	G	AB	H	2B	3B	HR	(Hm | Rd)	TB	R	RBI	TBB	IBB	SO	HBP	SH	SF	SB	CS	SB%	GDP	Avg	OBP	SLG
1995 Helena	R+	69	266	94	19	1	4	—	—	127	76	39	43	2	38	10	0	6	26	9	.74	6	.353	.452	.477
1996 Beloit	A	135	499	151	33	4	15	—	—	237	105	100	47	7	69	32	3	6	23	12	.66	10	.303	.394	.475
1997 El Paso	AA	125	468	180	35	12	12	—	—	275	112	109	52	0	66	13	1	6	17	4	.81	13	.385	.455	.588
1998 Louisville	AAA	80	291	90	24	6	7	—	—	147	57	46	36	1	52	6	1	2	10	2	.83	7	.309	.394	.505
Norfolk	AAA	30	125	35	5	0	1	—	—	43	12	18	3	0	24	5	1	2	6	1	.86	5	.280	.319	.344
1999 Norfolk	AAA	84	312	96	20	2	7	—	—	141	53	49	21	2	31	5	0	2	7	1	.88	9	.308	.359	.452
2000 Binghamton	AA	90	317	116	24	3	10	—	—	176	66	67	35	4	39	9	0	3	18	7	.72	6	.366	.440	.555
Bowie	AA	8	27	7	1	0	3	—	—	17	4	5	3	1	7	2	0	0	0	0	—	2	.259	.375	.630
Rochester	AAA	15	55	20	5	0	1	—	—	28	10	10	11	0	11	1	0	1	0	1	.00	0	.364	.471	.509
1998 New York	NL	3	2	0	0	0	0	(0 | 0)	0	2	0	0	0	0	0	0	0	0	0	—	0	.000	.000	.000
1999 New York	NL	28	46	9	2	1	2	(1 | 1)	19	3	6	3	0	9	2	0	0	1	0	1.00	1	.196	.275	.413
2000 NYM-Bal	NL	5	9	3	1	0	0	(0 | 0)	4	0	1	0	0	1	1	0	0	0	0	—	0	.333	.400	.444
2001 Baltimore	AL	61	160	44	5	0	4	(2 | 2)	61	19	16	14	0	31	3	0	0	2	1	.67	9	.275	.345	.381
2000 New York	NL	2	2	0	0	0	0	(0 | 0)	0	0	0	0	0	1	0	0	0	0	0	—	0	.000	.000	.000
Baltimore	AL	3	7	3	1	0	0	(0 | 0)	4	0	1	0	0	1	0	0	0	0	0	—	0	.429	.500	.571
4 ML YEARS		97	217	56	8	1	6	(3 | 3)	84	24	23	17	0	41	6	0	0	3	1	.75	9	.258	.329	.387

Ryan Klesko

Bats: Left Throws: Left Pos: 1B-145; PH/PR-2 Ht: 6'3" Wt: 220 Born: 6/12/71 Age: 31

		BATTING															BASERUNNING				PERCENTAGES		
Year Team	Lg	G	AB	H	2B	3B	HR	(Hm | Rd)	TB	R	RBI	TBB	IBB	SO	HBP	SH	SF	SB	CS	SB%	GDP	Avg	OBP	SLG
1992 Atlanta	NL	13	14	0	0	0	0	(0 | 0)	0	0	1	0	0	5	1	0	0	0	0	—	0	.000	.067	.000
1993 Atlanta	NL	22	17	6	1	0	2	(0 | 2)	13	3	5	3	1	4	0	0	0	0	0	—	0	.353	.450	.765
1994 Atlanta	NL	92	245	68	13	3	17	(7 | 10)	138	42	47	26	3	48	1	0	4	1	0	1.00	8	.278	.344	.563
1995 Atlanta	NL	107	329	102	25	2	23	(15 | 8)	200	48	70	47	10	72	2	0	3	5	4	.56	8	.310	.396	.608
1996 Atlanta	NL	153	528	149	21	4	34	(20 | 14)	280	90	93	68	10	129	2	0	4	6	3	.67	10	.282	.364	.530
1997 Atlanta	NL	143	467	122	23	6	24	(10 | 14)	229	67	84	48	5	130	4	1	2	4	4	.50	12	.261	.334	.490
1998 Atlanta	NL	129	427	117	29	1	18	(8 | 10)	202	69	70	56	5	66	3	0	4	5	3	.63	9	.274	.359	.473
1999 Atlanta	NL	133	404	120	28	2	21	(12 | 9)	215	55	80	53	8	69	2	0	7	5	2	.71	6	.297	.376	.532
2000 San Diego	NL	145	494	140	33	2	26	(17 | 9)	255	88	92	91	9	81	1	0	4	23	7	.77	10	.283	.393	.516
2001 San Diego	NL	146	538	154	34	6	30	(15 | 15)	290	105	113	88	7	89	3	0	9	23	4	.85	16	.286	.384	.539
10 ML YEARS		1083	3463	978	207	26	195	(98 | 97)	1822	567	655	480	58	693	19	1	37	72	27	.73	79	.282	.369	.526

Steve Kline

Pitches: Left Bats: Both Pos: RP-89 Ht: 6'1" Wt: 215 Born: 8/22/72 Age: 29

		HOW MUCH HE PITCHED						WHAT HE GAVE UP									THE RESULTS					
Year Team	Lg	G	GS	CG	GF	IP	BFP	H	R	ER	HR	SH	SF	HB	TBB	IBB	SO	WP	Bk	W	L	Pct.	ShO	Sv-Op	Hld	ERA
1997 Cle-Mon		46	1	0	7	52.2	248	73	37	35	10	4	2	2	23	4	37	4	1	4	4	.500	0	0-3	5	5.98
1998 Montreal	NL	78	0	0	18	71.2	319	62	25	22	4	1	2	4	41	7	76	5	0	3	6	.333	0	1-2	18	2.76
1999 Montreal	NL	82	0	0	18	69.2	297	56	32	29	8	3	1	3	33	6	69	2	0	7	4	.636	0	0-2	16	3.75
2000 Montreal	NL	83	0	0	42	82.1	349	88	36	32	8	2	1	3	27	2	64	4	0	1	5	.167	0	14-18	12	3.50
2001 St. Louis	NL	89	0	0	26	75	303	53	16	15	3	4	5	4	29	7	54	1	0	3	3	.500	0	9-10	17	1.80
1997 Cleveland	AL	20	1	0	0	26.1	130	42	19	17	6	1	0	1	13	1	17	3	1	3	1	.750	0	0-2	4	5.81
Montreal	NL	26	0	0	7	26.1	118	31	18	18	4	3	2	1	10	3	20	1	0	1	3	.250	0	0-1	1	6.15
5 ML YEARS		378	1	0	111	351.1	1516	332	146	133	33	14	11	15	153	26	300	16	1	18	22	.450	0	24-35	68	3.41

118

Brandon Knight

Pitches: Right **Bats:** Left **Pos:** RP-4   **Ht:** 6'0" **Wt:** 170 **Born:** 10/1/75 **Age:** 26

Year Team	Lg	G	GS	CG	GF	IP	BFP	H	R	ER	HR	SH	SF	HB	TBB	IBB	SO	WP	Bk	W	L	Pct.	ShO	Sv-Op	Hld	ERA
1995 Rangers	R	3	2	0	0	12	54	12	7	7	0	0	1	0	6	0	11	2	0	2	1	.667	0	0--	—	5.25
Chston-SC	A	9	9	0	0	54.2	218	37	22	19	5	0	4	0	21	0	52	4	1	4	2	.667	0	0--	—	3.13
1996 Hudson Val	A-	9	9	0	0	53	236	59	29	26	1	2	1	1	21	0	52	2	1	2	2	.500	0	0--	—	4.42
Charlotte	A+	19	17	2	0	102	463	118	65	58	9	4	7	2	45	0	74	6	0	4	10	.286	0	0--	—	5.12
1997 Charlotte	A+	14	12	3	1	92.2	380	82	33	23	9	3	2	1	22	0	91	0	2	7	4	.636	1	0--	—	2.23
Tulsa	AA	14	14	2	0	90	383	83	52	45	12	0	4	2	35	0	84	9	4	6	4	.600	0	0--	—	4.50
1998 Tulsa	AA	14	14	0	0	86.1	379	94	54	49	11	1	3	0	37	0	87	12	0	6	6	.500	0	0--	—	5.11
Oklahoma	AAA	16	12	0	0	64.2	315	100	75	70	16	0	2	1	29	0	52	9	1	0	7	.000	0	0--	—	9.74
1999 Oklahoma	AAA	27	26	5	0	163	706	173	96	89	23	1	3	10	47	2	97	9	3	9	8	.529	0	0--	—	4.91
2000 Columbus	AAA	28	28	8	0	184.2	783	172	105	91	21	5	7	3	61	3	138	10	3	10	12	.455	1	0--	—	4.44
2001 Columbus	AAA	25	25	3	0	162.1	681	174	77	66	16	4	1	2	45	0	173	9	1	12	7	.632	0	0--	—	3.66
2001 New York	AL	4	0	0	2	10.2	52	18	12	12	5	0	0	0	3	0	7	0	0	0	0	—	0	0-0	0	10.13

Chuck Knoblauch

Bats: Right **Throws:** Right **Pos:** LF-108; DH-24; PH/PR-9   **Ht:** 5'9" **Wt:** 175 **Born:** 7/7/68 **Age:** 33

Year Team	Lg	G	AB	H	2B	3B	HR	(Hm	Rd)	TB	R	RBI	TBB	IBB	SO	HBP	SH	SF	SB	CS	SB%	GDP	Avg	OBP	SLG
1991 Minnesota	AL	151	565	159	24	6	1	(1	0)	198	78	50	59	0	40	4	1	5	25	5	.83	8	.281	.351	.350
1992 Minnesota	AL	155	600	178	19	6	2	(0	2)	215	104	56	88	1	60	5	2	12	34	13	.72	8	.297	.384	.358
1993 Minnesota	AL	153	602	167	27	4	2	(0	2)	208	82	41	65	1	44	9	4	5	29	11	.73	11	.277	.354	.346
1994 Minnesota	AL	109	445	139	45	3	5	(1	4)	205	85	51	41	2	56	10	0	3	35	6	.85	13	.312	.381	.461
1995 Minnesota	AL	136	538	179	34	8	11	(4	7)	262	107	63	78	3	95	10	0	3	46	18	.72	15	.333	.424	.487
1996 Minnesota	AL	153	578	197	35	14	13	(7	6)	299	140	72	98	6	74	19	0	6	45	14	.76	9	.341	.448	.517
1997 Minnesota	AL	156	611	178	26	10	9	(2	7)	251	117	58	84	6	84	17	0	4	62	10	.86	11	.291	.390	.411
1998 New York	AL	150	603	160	25	4	17	(5	12)	244	117	64	76	1	70	18	2	7	31	12	.72	13	.265	.361	.405
1999 New York	AL	150	603	176	36	4	18	(11	7)	274	120	68	83	0	57	21	3	5	28	9	.76	7	.292	.393	.454
2000 New York	AL	102	400	113	22	2	5	(5	0)	154	75	26	46	0	45	8	1	2	15	7	.68	6	.283	.366	.385
2001 New York	AL	137	521	130	20	3	9	(6	3)	183	66	44	58	1	73	14	5	2	38	9	.81	10	.250	.339	.351
11 ML YEARS		1552	6066	1776	313	64	92	(44	48)	2493	1091	593	776	21	698	135	18	54	388	114	.77	111	.293	.382	.411

Randy Knorr

Bats: Right **Throws:** Right **Pos:** C-27; PH/PR-7   **Ht:** 6'2" **Wt:** 230 **Born:** 11/12/68 **Age:** 33

Year Team	Lg	G	AB	H	2B	3B	HR	(Hm	Rd)	TB	R	RBI	TBB	IBB	SO	HBP	SH	SF	SB	CS	SB%	GDP	Avg	OBP	SLG
1991 Toronto	AL	3	1	0	0	0	0	(0	0)	0	0	0	1	0	1	0	0	0	0	0	—	0	.000	.500	.000
1992 Toronto	AL	8	19	5	0	0	1	(0	1)	8	1	2	1	1	5	0	0	0	0	0	—	0	.263	.300	.421
1993 Toronto	AL	39	101	25	3	2	4	(2	2)	44	11	20	9	0	29	0	2	0	0	0	—	0	.248	.309	.436
1994 Toronto	AL	40	124	30	2	0	7	(4	3)	53	20	19	10	0	35	1	0	1	0	0	—	7	.242	.301	.427
1995 Toronto	AL	45	132	28	8	0	3	(2	1)	45	18	16	11	0	28	0	1	0	0	0	—	5	.212	.273	.341
1996 Houston	NL	37	87	17	5	0	1	(1	0)	25	7	7	5	2	18	1	0	1	0	1	.00	1	.195	.245	.287
1997 Houston	NL	4	8	3	0	0	1	(0	1)	6	1	1	0	0	2	0	0	0	0	0	—	0	.375	.375	.750
1998 Florida	NL	15	49	10	4	1	2	(0	2)	22	4	11	1	0	10	0	0	1	0	0	—	0	.204	.216	.449
1999 Houston	NL	13	30	5	1	0	0	(0	0)	6	2	0	1	0	8	0	0	0	0	0	—	1	.167	.194	.200
2000 Texas	AL	15	34	10	2	0	2	(2	0)	18	5	2	0	0	3	0	3	0	0	0	—	2	.294	.294	.529
2001 Montreal	NL	34	91	20	2	0	3	(3	0)	31	13	10	8	0	22	1	2	1	0	0	—	4	.220	.287	.341
11 ML YEARS		253	676	153	27	3	24	(15	9)	258	82	88	47	3	161	3	8	4	0	1	.00	20	.226	.278	.382

Eric Knott

Pitches: Left **Bats:** Left **Pos:** RP-2; SP-1   **Ht:** 6'0" **Wt:** 188 **Born:** 9/23/74 **Age:** 27

Year Team	Lg	G	GS	CG	GF	IP	BFP	H	R	ER	HR	SH	SF	HB	TBB	IBB	SO	WP	Bk	W	L	Pct.	ShO	Sv-Op	Hld	ERA
1997 Lethbridge	R+	21	3	0	7	47	195	41	21	15	4	2	1	0	9	1	62	2	0	0	4	.000	0	3--	—	2.87
1998 High Desert	A+	28	22	1	3	143.1	616	175	84	72	16	3	4	1	28	1	96	3	3	12	7	.632	0	0--	—	4.52
1999 El Paso	AA	27	27	3	0	161.1	711	198	105	82	11	4	5	5	42	0	83	3	2	7	11	.389	0	0--	—	4.57
2000 Tucson	AAA	11	7	0	1	39.2	180	59	30	28	6	2	3	1	8	0	21	0	0	3	2	.600	0	0--	—	6.35
2001 El Paso	AA	17	0	0	2	26	116	29	13	9	2	2	0	1	8	2	20	1	0	4	1	.800	0	0--	—	3.12
Tucson	AAA	25	8	0	9	73.1	303	82	34	31	6	4	3	0	8	1	43	1	1	6	2	.750	0	1--	—	3.80
2001 Arizona	NL	3	1	0	0	4.2	25	8	9	1	0	0	0	2	0	0	4	0	0	0	1	.000	0	0-0	0	1.93

Gary Knotts

Pitches: Right **Bats:** Right **Pos:** SP-1; RP-1   **Ht:** 6'4" **Wt:** 235 **Born:** 2/12/77 **Age:** 25

Year Team	Lg	G	GS	CG	GF	IP	BFP	H	R	ER	HR	SH	SF	HB	TBB	IBB	SO	WP	Bk	W	L	Pct.	ShO	Sv-Op	Hld	ERA
1996 Marlins	R	12	9	1	2	57.1	227	35	16	13	0	2	2	6	17	0	46	5	0	4	2	.667	1	0--	—	2.04
1997 Kane County	A	7	7	0	0	20	113	33	34	29	2	2	0	3	17	0	19	8	1	1	5	.167	0	0--	—	13.05
Utica	A-	12	12	1	0	69.2	304	70	34	28	3	1	2	8	27	1	65	3	0	3	5	.375	0	0--	—	3.62
1998 Kane County	A	27	27	3	0	158.1	686	144	68	61	14	6	11	6	66	1	148	7	0	8	8	.500	0	0--	—	3.87
1999 Brevard Cty	A+	16	16	3	0	94	402	101	52	48	7	1	3	8	29	0	65	1	0	6	4	.600	2	0--	—	4.60
Portland	AA	12	12	1	0	81.2	358	79	39	34	12	4	3	8	33	0	63	4	0	6	3	.667	1	0--	—	3.75
2000 Portland	AA	27	27	2	0	156.1	687	161	102	81	15	3	5	7	63	1	113	8	0	9	8	.529	0	0--	—	4.66
2001 Calgary	AAA	21	21	1	0	118.2	528	136	77	72	16	3	3	2	43	0	104	5	0	6	7	.462	1	0--	—	5.46
2001 Florida	NL	2	1	0	0	6	28	7	4	4	1	0	0	2	1	0	9	0	0	0	1	.000	0	0-0	0	6.00

Billy Koch

Pitches: Right   Bats: Right   Pos: RP-69   Ht: 6'3"   Wt: 205   Born: 12/14/74   Age: 27

Year Team	Lg	G	GS	CG	GF	IP	BFP	H	R	ER	HR	SH	SF	HB	TBB	IBB	SO	WP	Bk	W	L	Pct.	ShO	Sv-Op	Hld	ERA
1999 Toronto	AL	56	0	0	48	63.2	272	55	26	24	5	4	1	3	30	5	57	0	0	0	5	.000	0	31-35	0	3.39
2000 Toronto	AL	68	0	0	62	78.2	326	78	28	23	6	4	0	2	18	4	60	1	0	9	3	.750	0	33-38	0	2.63
2001 Toronto	AL	69	0	0	56	69.1	308	69	39	37	7	5	4	6	33	7	55	5	0	2	5	.286	0	36-44	0	4.80
3 ML YEARS		193	0	0	166	211.2	906	202	93	84	18	13	5	11	81	16	172	6	0	11	13	.458	0	100-117	0	3.57

Ryan Kohlmeier

Pitches: Right   Bats: Right   Pos: RP-33; SP-1   Ht: 6'2"   Wt: 223   Born: 6/25/77   Age: 25

Year Team	Lg	G	GS	CG	GF	IP	BFP	H	R	ER	HR	SH	SF	HB	TBB	IBB	SO	WP	Bk	W	L	Pct.	ShO	Sv-Op	Hld	ERA
1997 Bowie	AA	2	0	0	1	2.2	9	0	0	0	0	0	0	2	0	5	0	1	0	0	0	—	0	1-—	—	0.00
Delmarva	A	50	0	0	41	74.2	276	48	22	22	8	2	2	1	17	1	99	2	1	2	2	.500	0	24-—	—	2.65
1998 Bowie	AA	42	0	0	28	50	219	52	37	34	13	1	1	3	16	1	56	2	1	4	4	.500	0	7-—	—	6.12
Frederick	A+	9	0	0	9	9.2	44	10	9	8	1	0	2	1	3	0	15	0	1	1	2	.333	0	5-—	—	7.45
1999 Bowie	AA	55	0	0	49	62.2	256	44	23	22	10	4	2	1	29	1	78	2	1	3	7	.300	0	23-—	—	3.16
2000 Rochester	AAA	37	0	0	28	46.2	192	33	14	13	4	2	3	2	16	2	49	2	0	1	4	.200	0	10-—	—	2.51
2001 Rochester	AAA	14	7	0	6	42	170	36	15	11	4	2	1	0	8	0	28	1	2	1	4	.200	0	4-—	—	2.36
2000 Baltimore	AL	25	0	0	22	26.1	120	30	9	7	1	1	1	0	15	2	17	0	0	0	1	.000	0	13-14	0	2.39
2001 Baltimore	AL	34	1	0	21	40.2	188	48	33	33	13	2	0	2	19	2	29	2	0	1	2	.333	0	6-10	3	7.30
2 ML YEARS		59	1	0	43	67	308	78	42	40	14	3	1	2	34	4	46	2	0	1	3	.250	0	19-24	3	5.37

Brandon Kolb

Pitches: Right   Bats: Right   Pos: RP-10   Ht: 6'1"   Wt: 190   Born: 11/20/73   Age: 28

Year Team	Lg	G	GS	CG	GF	IP	BFP	H	R	ER	HR	SH	SF	HB	TBB	IBB	SO	WP	Bk	W	L	Pct.	ShO	Sv-Op	Hld	ERA
1995 Idaho Falls	R+	9	8	0	0	38.1	181	42	33	30	1	2	2	2	29	0	21	5	0	2	3	.400	0	0-—	—	7.04
Padres	R	4	4	1	0	23	100	13	10	3	0	0	0	3	13	0	21	4	0	1	1	.500	1	0-—	—	1.17
1996 Clinton	A	27	27	3	0	181.1	776	170	84	69	7	6	7	8	76	1	138	19	0	16	9	.640	0	0-—	—	3.42
1997 Rancho Cuc	A+	10	10	0	0	63	261	60	29	21	0	1	1	2	22	0	49	5	0	3	2	.600	0	0-—	—	3.00
1998 Rancho Cuc	A+	4	4	0	0	20.2	92	14	8	7	3	0	0	1	18	0	16	0	1	2	0	.000	0	0-—	—	3.05
Mobile	AA	21	6	0	4	62	274	46	33	31	4	3	3	1	40	0	58	6	0	4	3	.571	0	1-—	—	4.50
1999 Mobile	AA	7	0	0	6	11.1	52	8	4	1	0	1	0	1	4	0	14	1	0	2	0	.000	0	2-—	—	0.79
Las Vegas	AAA	42	0	0	16	61.2	281	72	36	27	3	1	3	3	29	1	63	7	0	2	1	.667	0	4-—	—	3.94
2000 Las Vegas	AAA	47	0	0	35	56.1	250	53	35	28	2	0	1	5	21	0	59	2	0	3	3	.500	0	16-—	—	4.47
2001 Indianapols	AAA	40	0	0	29	54.2	236	49	28	26	7	2	0	0	22	4	57	2	0	3	5	.375	0	14-—	—	4.28
2000 San Diego	NL	11	0	0	5	14	66	16	8	7	0	0	1	0	11	1	12	3	0	0	1	.000	0	0-1	0	4.50
2001 Milwaukee	NL	10	0	0	3	9.2	53	16	16	14	6	0	2	0	8	1	8	1	0	0	0	—	0	0-0	0	13.03
2 ML YEARS		21	0	0	8	23.2	119	32	24	21	6	0	3	0	19	1	20	4	0	0	1	.000	0	0-1	0	7.99

Danny Kolb

Pitches: Right   Bats: Right   Pos: RP-17   Ht: 6'4"   Wt: 215   Born: 3/29/75   Age: 27

Year Team	Lg	G	GS	CG	GF	IP	BFP	H	R	ER	HR	SH	SF	HB	TBB	IBB	SO	WP	Bk	W	L	Pct.	ShO	Sv-Op	Hld	ERA
2001 Charlotte *	A+	7	3	0	2	18.2	78	21	8	8	1	0	0	0	2	0	16	0	0	1	2	.333	0	0-—	—	3.86
Tulsa *	AA	1	0	0	0	2	7	0	0	0	0	0	0	0	1	0	0	0	0	1	0	1.000	0	0-—	—	0.00
Oklahoma *	AAA	12	0	0	8	19	74	13	3	3	1	1	0	0	4	0	21	1	0	1	0	1.000	0	3-—	—	1.42
1999 Texas	AL	16	0	0	6	31	139	33	18	16	2	0	0	1	15	0	15	2	0	2	1	.667	0	0-0	0	4.65
2000 Texas	AL	1	0	0	0	0.2	9	5	5	5	0	0	1	0	2	0	0	0	0	0	0	—	0	0-0	0	67.50
2001 Texas	AL	17	0	0	1	15.1	70	15	8	8	2	1	1	0	10	1	15	3	0	0	0	—	0	0-0	7	4.70
3 ML YEARS		34	0	0	7	47	218	53	31	29	4	1	2	1	27	1	30	5	0	2	1	.667	0	0-0	7	5.55

Paul Konerko

Bats: Right   Throws: Right   Pos: 1B-144; DH-11; PH/PR-1   Ht: 6'2"   Wt: 215   Born: 3/5/76   Age: 26

Year Team	Lg	G	AB	H	2B	3B	HR	(Hm	Rd)	TB	R	RBI	TBB	IBB	SO	HBP	SH	SF	SB	CS	SB%	GDP	Avg	OBP	SLG
1997 Los Angeles	NL	6	7	1	0	0	0	(0	0)	1	0	0	1	0	2	0	0	0	0	0	—	1	.143	.250	.143
1998 LA-Cin	NL	75	217	47	4	0	7	(2	5)	72	21	29	16	0	40	3	0	3	0	1	.00	10	.217	.276	.332
1999 Chicago	AL	142	513	151	31	4	24	(16	8)	262	71	81	45	0	68	2	1	3	1	0	1.00	19	.294	.352	.511
2000 Chicago	AL	143	524	156	31	1	21	(10	11)	252	84	97	47	0	72	10	0	5	1	0	1.00	22	.298	.363	.481
2001 Chicago	AL	156	582	164	35	0	32	(19	13)	295	92	99	54	6	89	9	0	5	1	0	1.00	17	.282	.349	.507
1998 Los Angeles	NL	49	144	31	1	0	4	(2	2)	44	14	16	10	0	30	2	0	2	0	1	.00	5	.215	.272	.306
Cincinnati	NL	26	73	16	3	0	3	(0	3)	28	7	13	6	0	10	1	0	1	0	0	—	5	.219	.284	.384
5 ML YEARS		522	1843	519	101	5	84	(47	37)	882	268	306	163	6	271	24	1	16	3	1	.75	69	.282	.345	.479

Mike Koplove

Pitches: Right   Bats: Right   Pos: RP-9   Ht: 6'0"   Wt: 160   Born: 8/30/76   Age: 25

Year Team	Lg	G	GS	CG	GF	IP	BFP	H	R	ER	HR	SH	SF	HB	TBB	IBB	SO	WP	Bk	W	L	Pct.	ShO	Sv-Op	Hld	ERA
1998 Diamndbcks	R	2	0	0	1	4	19	4	4	4	0	0	0	1	0	0	5	0	0	0	0	—	0	0-—	—	9.00
Lethbridge	R+	12	1	0	4	28	114	23	12	11	2	0	1	4	3	0	22	0	0	1	2	.333	0	2-—	—	3.54
1999 South Bend	A	45	0	0	19	84	351	70	23	19	5	3	0	11	29	0	98	4	0	5	2	.714	0	7-—	—	2.04
2000 High Desert	A+	20	0	0	19	25.1	100	14	4	4	0	3	0	1	10	0	31	2	0	2	0	1.000	0	8-—	—	1.42
El Paso	AA	35	0	0	16	46.1	197	38	28	20	2	0	2	7	19	1	47	1	1	4	3	.571	0	6-—	—	3.88
2001 El Paso	AA	34	0	0	14	44	193	44	18	13	3	3	2	2	13	3	43	0	0	3	2	.600	0	4-—	—	2.66
Tucson	AAA	17	0	0	13	22.1	92	17	7	7	1	0	0	0	10	1	22	2	0	4	1	.800	0	9-—	—	2.82
2001 Arizona	NL	9	0	0	1	10	50	8	7	4	1	1	0	2	9	1	14	1	0	0	1	.000	0	0-0	1	3.60

Corey Koskie

Bats: Left **Throws:** Right **Pos:** 3B-150; DH-2; PH/PR-2   **Ht:** 6'3" **Wt:** 217 **Born:** 6/28/73 **Age:** 29

Year Team	Lg	G	AB	H	2B	3B	HR	(Hm	Rd)	TB	R	RBI	TBB	IBB	SO	HBP	SH	SF	SB	CS	SB%	GDP	Avg	OBP	SLG
1998 Minnesota	AL	11	29	4	0	0	1	(1	0)	7	2	2	2	0	10	0	0	0	0	0	—	0	.138	.194	.241
1999 Minnesota	AL	117	342	106	21	0	11	(4	7)	160	42	58	40	4	72	5	2	3	4	4	.50	6	.310	.387	.468
2000 Minnesota	AL	146	474	142	32	4	9	(1	8)	209	79	65	77	7	104	4	1	3	5	4	.56	11	.300	.400	.441
2001 Minnesota	AL	153	562	155	37	2	26	(11	15)	274	100	103	68	9	118	12	0	7	27	6	.82	16	.276	.362	.488
4 ML YEARS		427	1407	407	90	6	47	(17	30)	650	223	228	187	20	304	21	3	13	36	14	.72	33	.289	.378	.462

Mark Kotsay

Bats: L **Throws:** L **Pos:** CF-106; PH/PR-13; RF-5; LF-1   **Ht:** 6'0" **Wt:** 190 **Born:** 12/2/75 **Age:** 26

Year Team	Lg	G	AB	H	2B	3B	HR	(Hm	Rd)	TB	R	RBI	TBB	IBB	SO	HBP	SH	SF	SB	CS	SB%	GDP	Avg	OBP	SLG
1997 Florida	NL	14	52	10	1	1	0	(0	0)	13	5	4	4	0	7	0	1	0	3	0	1.00	1	.192	.250	.250
1998 Florida	NL	154	578	161	25	7	11	(5	6)	233	72	68	34	2	61	1	7	3	10	5	.67	17	.279	.318	.403
1999 Florida	NL	148	495	134	23	9	8	(5	3)	199	57	50	29	5	50	0	2	4	7	6	.54	11	.271	.306	.402
2000 Florida	NL	152	530	158	31	5	12	(5	7)	235	87	57	42	2	46	0	2	4	19	9	.68	17	.298	.347	.443
2001 San Diego	NL	119	406	118	29	1	10	(3	7)	179	67	58	48	1	58	2	1	3	13	5	.72	11	.291	.366	.441
5 ML YEARS		587	2061	581	109	23	41	(18	23)	859	288	237	157	10	222	3	13	19	52	25	.68	57	.282	.331	.417

Chad Kreuter

Bats: Both **Throws:** Right **Pos:** C-70; PH/PR-2; DH-1   **Ht:** 6'2" **Wt:** 200 **Born:** 8/26/64 **Age:** 37

Year Team	Lg	G	AB	H	2B	3B	HR	(Hm	Rd)	TB	R	RBI	TBB	IBB	SO	HBP	SH	SF	SB	CS	SB%	GDP	Avg	OBP	SLG
1988 Texas	AL	16	51	14	2	1	1	(0	1)	21	3	5	7	0	13	0	0	0	0	0	—	1	.275	.362	.412
1989 Texas	AL	87	158	24	3	0	5	(2	3)	42	16	9	27	0	40	0	6	1	0	1	.00	4	.152	.274	.266
1990 Texas	AL	22	22	1	1	0	0	(0	0)	2	2	2	8	0	9	0	1	1	0	0	—	0	.045	.290	.091
1991 Texas	AL	3	4	0	0	0	0	(0	0)	0	0	0	0	0	1	0	0	0	0	0	—	0	.000	.000	.000
1992 Detroit	AL	67	190	48	9	0	2	(2	0)	63	22	16	20	1	38	0	3	2	0	1	.00	5	.253	.321	.332
1993 Detroit	AL	119	374	107	23	3	15	(9	6)	181	59	51	49	4	92	3	2	3	2	1	.67	5	.286	.371	.484
1994 Detroit	AL	65	170	38	8	0	1	(1	0)	49	17	19	28	0	36	0	2	4	0	1	.00	3	.224	.327	.288
1995 Seattle	AL	26	75	17	5	0	1	(0	1)	25	12	8	5	0	22	2	1	0	0	0	—	0	.227	.293	.333
1996 Chicago	AL	46	114	25	8	0	3	(2	1)	42	14	18	13	0	29	2	2	1	0	0	—	2	.219	.308	.368
1997 CWS-Ana	AL	89	255	59	9	2	5	(3	2)	87	25	21	29	0	66	0	1	0	0	3	.00	7	.231	.310	.341
1998 CWS-Ana	AL	96	252	63	10	1	2	(2	0)	81	27	33	33	1	49	3	5	1	1	0	1.00	8	.250	.343	.321
1999 Kansas City	AL	107	324	73	15	0	5	(2	3)	103	31	35	34	1	65	6	2	2	0	0	—	16	.225	.309	.318
2000 Los Angeles	NL	80	212	56	13	0	6	(4	2)	87	32	28	54	0	48	2	2	1	1	0	1.00	6	.264	.416	.410
2001 Los Angeles	NL	73	191	41	11	1	6	(4	2)	72	21	17	41	2	52	1	0	1	0	0	—	5	.215	.355	.377
1997 Chicago	AL	19	37	8	2	1	1	(1	0)	15	6	3	8	0	9	0	0	0	0	1	.00	0	.216	.356	.405
Anaheim	AL	70	218	51	7	1	4	(2	2)	72	19	18	21	0	57	0	1	0	0	2	.00	7	.234	.301	.330
1998 Chicago	AL	93	245	62	9	1	2	(2	0)	79	26	33	32	1	45	3	5	1	1	0	1.00	8	.253	.345	.322
Anaheim	AL	3	7	1	1	0	0	(0	0)	2	1	0	1	0	4	0	0	0	0	0	—	0	.143	.250	.286
14 ML YEARS		896	2392	566	117	8	52	(31	21)	855	281	262	348	9	560	19	27	17	4	7	.36	65	.237	.336	.357

Tim Laker

Bats: Right **Throws:** Right **Pos:** C-14; PH/PR-2; P-1   **Ht:** 6'3" **Wt:** 225 **Born:** 11/27/69 **Age:** 32

Year Team	Lg	G	AB	H	2B	3B	HR	(Hm	Rd)	TB	R	RBI	TBB	IBB	SO	HBP	SH	SF	SB	CS	SB%	GDP	Avg	OBP	SLG
2001 Buffalo *	AAA	86	320	79	13	0	20	—	—	152	45	57	28	2	53	4	0	2	2	1	.67	10	.247	.314	.475
1992 Montreal	NL	28	46	10	3	0	0	(0	0)	13	8	4	2	0	14	0	0	0	1	1	.50	1	.217	.250	.283
1993 Montreal	NL	43	86	17	2	1	0	(0	0)	21	3	7	2	0	16	1	3	1	2	0	1.00	2	.198	.222	.244
1995 Montreal	NL	64	141	33	8	1	3	(1	2)	52	17	20	14	4	38	1	1	1	0	1	.00	5	.234	.306	.369
1997 Baltimore	AL	7	14	0	0	0	0	(0	0)	0	0	1	2	0	9	0	0	1	0	0	—	0	.000	.118	.000
1998 TB-Pit		17	29	10	1	0	1	(0	1)	14	3	2	2	0	4	0	0	1	0	1	.00	1	.345	.375	.483
1999 Pittsburgh	NL	6	9	3	0	0	0	(0	0)	3	0	0	0	0	2	0	0	0	0	0	—	0	.333	.333	.333
2001 Cleveland	AL	16	33	6	0	0	1	(0	1)	9	5	5	6	0	8	0	1	0	0	0	—	1	.182	.308	.273
1998 Tampa Bay	AL	3	5	1	0	0	0	(0	0)	1	1	0	1	0	1	0	0	0	0	1	.00	0	.200	.333	.200
Pittsburgh	NL	14	24	9	1	0	1	(0	1)	13	2	2	1	0	3	0	0	1	0	0	—	1	.375	.385	.542
7 ML YEARS		181	358	79	14	2	5	(1	4)	112	36	39	28	4	91	2	6	4	3	3	.50	10	.221	.278	.313

Mike Lamb

Bats: Left **Throws:** Right **Pos:** 3B-74; PH/PR-4   **Ht:** 6'1" **Wt:** 195 **Born:** 8/9/75 **Age:** 26

Year Team	Lg	G	AB	H	2B	3B	HR	(Hm	Rd)	TB	R	RBI	TBB	IBB	SO	HBP	SH	SF	SB	CS	SB%	GDP	Avg	OBP	SLG
1997 Pulaski	R+	60	233	78	19	3	9	—	—	130	59	47	31	2	18	4	2	6	7	2	.78	6	.335	.412	.558
1998 Charlotte	A+	135	536	162	35	3	9	—	—	230	83	93	45	5	63	4	2	8	18	7	.72	10	.302	.356	.429
1999 Tulsa	AA	137	544	176	51	5	21	—	—	300	98	100	53	5	65	7	1	8	4	3	.57	11	.324	.386	.551
Oklahoma	AAA	2	2	1	0	0	0	—	—	1	0	0	1	1	0	1	0	0	0	1	.00	0	.500	.750	.500
2000 Oklahoma	AAA	14	55	14	5	1	2	—	—	27	8	5	5	0	6	0	0	0	2	1	.67	5	.255	.317	.491
2001 Oklahoma	AAA	69	273	81	19	3	8	—	—	130	35	40	13	0	31	3	2	4	0	2	.00	8	.297	.331	.476
2000 Texas	AL	138	493	137	25	2	6	(4	2)	184	65	47	34	6	60	4	5	2	0	2	.00	10	.278	.328	.373
2001 Texas	AL	76	284	87	18	0	4	(1	3)	117	42	35	14	1	27	5	1	2	2	1	.67	6	.306	.348	.412
2 ML YEARS		214	777	224	43	2	10	(5	5)	301	107	82	48	7	87	9	6	4	2	3	.40	16	.288	.335	.387

Tom Lampkin

Bats: L **Throws:** R **Pos:** C-71; PH/PR-12; DH-1; RF-1   **Ht:** 5'11" **Wt:** 195 **Born:** 3/4/64 **Age:** 38

Year Team	Lg	G	AB	H	2B	3B	HR	(Hm	Rd)	TB	R	RBI	TBB	IBB	SO	HBP	SH	SF	SB	CS	SB%	GDP	Avg	OBP	SLG
1988 Cleveland	AL	4	4	0	0	0	0	(0	0)	0	0	0	1	0	0	0	0	0	0	0	—	1	.000	.200	.000
1990 San Diego	NL	26	63	14	0	1	1	(1	0)	19	4	4	4	1	9	0	0	0	0	1	.00	2	.222	.269	.302
1991 San Diego	NL	38	58	11	3	1	0	(0	0)	16	4	3	3	0	9	0	0	0	0	0	—	0	.190	.230	.276
1992 San Diego	NL	9	17	4	0	0	0	(0	0)	4	3	0	6	0	1	1	0	0	2	0	1.00	0	.235	.458	.235
1993 Milwaukee	AL	73	162	32	8	0	4	(1	3)	52	22	25	20	3	26	0	2	4	7	3	.70	2	.198	.280	.321
1995 San Francisco	NL	65	76	21	2	0	1	(1	0)	26	8	9	9	1	8	1	0	0	2	0	1.00	1	.276	.360	.342
1996 San Francisco	NL	66	177	41	8	0	6	(5	1)	67	26	29	20	2	22	5	0	2	1	5	.17	2	.232	.324	.379
1997 St. Louis	NL	108	229	56	8	1	7	(2	5)	87	28	22	28	5	30	4	4	2	2	1	.67	8	.245	.335	.380
1998 St. Louis	NL	93	216	50	12	1	6	(4	2)	82	25	28	24	5	32	7	1	0	3	2	.60	5	.231	.328	.380
1999 Seattle	AL	76	206	60	11	2	9	(5	4)	102	29	34	13	1	32	5	1	2	1	3	.25	2	.291	.345	.495
2000 Seattle	AL	36	103	26	6	1	7	(3	4)	55	15	23	9	1	17	3	0	2	0	0	—	7	.252	.325	.534
2001 Seattle	AL	79	204	46	10	0	5	(1	4)	71	28	22	18	1	41	7	1	1	1	0	1.00	4	.225	.309	.348
12 ML YEARS		673	1515	361	68	7	46	(23	23)	581	192	199	155	20	227	33	9	13	19	15	.56	34	.238	.320	.383

Ray Lankford

Bats: L **Throws:** L **Pos:** LF-106; CF-16; PH/PR-14; RF-2   **Ht:** 5'11" **Wt:** 200 **Born:** 6/5/67 **Age:** 35

Year Team	Lg	G	AB	H	2B	3B	HR	(Hm	Rd)	TB	R	RBI	TBB	IBB	SO	HBP	SH	SF	SB	CS	SB%	GDP	Avg	OBP	SLG
1990 St. Louis	NL	39	126	36	10	1	3	(2	1)	57	12	12	13	0	27	0	0	0	8	2	.80	1	.286	.353	.452
1991 St. Louis	NL	151	566	142	23	15	9	(4	5)	222	83	69	41	1	114	1	4	3	44	20	.69	4	.251	.301	.392
1992 St. Louis	NL	153	598	175	40	6	20	(13	7)	287	87	86	72	6	147	5	2	5	42	24	.64	5	.293	.371	.480
1993 St. Louis	NL	127	407	97	17	3	7	(6	1)	141	64	45	81	7	111	3	1	3	14	14	.50	5	.238	.366	.346
1994 St. Louis	NL	109	416	111	25	5	19	(8	11)	203	89	57	58	3	113	4	0	4	11	10	.52	0	.267	.359	.488
1995 St. Louis	NL	132	483	134	35	2	25	(16	9)	248	81	82	63	6	110	2	0	5	24	8	.75	10	.277	.360	.513
1996 St. Louis	NL	149	545	150	36	8	21	(8	13)	265	100	86	79	10	133	3	1	7	35	7	.83	12	.275	.366	.486
1997 St. Louis	NL	133	465	137	36	3	31	(10	21)	272	94	98	95	10	125	0	0	5	21	11	.66	9	.295	.411	.585
1998 St. Louis	NL	154	533	156	37	1	31	(20	11)	288	94	105	86	5	151	3	0	4	26	5	.84	4	.293	.391	.540
1999 St. Louis	NL	122	422	129	32	1	15	(8	7)	208	77	63	49	3	110	3	0	2	14	4	.78	6	.306	.380	.493
2000 St. Louis	NL	128	392	99	16	3	26	(18	8)	199	73	65	70	1	148	4	0	6	5	6	.45	6	.253	.367	.508
2001 StL-SD	NL	131	389	98	28	4	19	(10	9)	191	58	58	62	9	145	4	1	3	10	2	.83	6	.252	.358	.491
2001 St. Louis	NL	91	264	62	18	3	15	(7	8)	131	38	39	44	8	105	2	1	3	4	2	.67	4	.235	.345	.496
San Diego	NL	40	125	36	10	1	4	(3	1)	60	20	19	18	1	40	2	0	0	6	0	1.00	2	.288	.386	.480
12 ML YEARS		1528	5342	1464	335	52	226	(123	103)	2581	912	826	769	61	1434	32	9	47	254	113	.69	68	.274	.366	.483

Mike Lansing

Bats: Right **Throws:** Right **Pos:** SS-76; 2B-31; PH/PR-6   **Ht:** 6'0" **Wt:** 195 **Born:** 4/3/68 **Age:** 34

Year Team	Lg	G	AB	H	2B	3B	HR	(Hm	Rd)	TB	R	RBI	TBB	IBB	SO	HBP	SH	SF	SB	CS	SB%	GDP	Avg	OBP	SLG
1993 Montreal	NL	141	491	141	29	1	3	(1	2)	181	64	45	46	2	56	5	10	3	23	5	.82	16	.287	.352	.369
1994 Montreal	NL	106	394	105	21	2	5	(3	2)	145	44	35	30	3	37	7	2	2	12	8	.60	10	.266	.328	.368
1995 Montreal	NL	127	467	119	30	2	10	(4	6)	183	47	62	28	2	65	3	1	3	27	4	.87	14	.255	.299	.392
1996 Montreal	NL	159	641	183	40	2	11	(3	8)	260	99	53	44	1	85	10	9	1	23	8	.74	19	.285	.341	.406
1997 Montreal	NL	144	572	161	45	2	20	(11	9)	270	86	70	45	2	92	5	6	3	11	5	.69	9	.281	.338	.472
1998 Colorado	NL	153	584	161	39	2	12	(7	5)	240	73	66	39	4	88	5	7	3	10	3	.77	18	.276	.325	.411
1999 Colorado	NL	35	145	45	9	0	4	(2	2)	66	24	15	7	0	22	1	1	1	2	0	1.00	3	.310	.344	.455
2000 Col-Bos		139	504	121	18	6	11	(9	2)	184	72	60	38	2	75	0	3	3	8	2	.80	20	.240	.292	.365
2001 Boston	AL	106	352	88	23	0	8	(5	3)	135	45	34	22	1	50	1	4	3	3	3	.50	7	.250	.294	.384
2000 Colorado	NL	90	365	94	14	6	11	(9	2)	153	62	47	31	1	49	0	3	1	8	2	.80	13	.258	.315	.419
Boston	AL	49	139	27	4	0	0	(0	0)	31	10	13	7	1	26	0	0	2	0	0	—	7	.194	.230	.223
9 ML YEARS		1110	4150	1124	254	17	84	(45	39)	1664	554	440	299	17	570	37	43	22	119	38	.76	116	.271	.324	.401

Barry Larkin

Bats: Right **Throws:** Right **Pos:** SS-44; PH/PR-1   **Ht:** 6'0" **Wt:** 185 **Born:** 4/28/64 **Age:** 38

Year Team	Lg	G	AB	H	2B	3B	HR	(Hm	Rd)	TB	R	RBI	TBB	IBB	SO	HBP	SH	SF	SB	CS	SB%	GDP	Avg	OBP	SLG
1986 Cincinnati	NL	41	159	45	4	3	3	(3	0)	64	27	19	9	1	21	0	0	1	8	0	1.00	2	.283	.320	.403
1987 Cincinnati	NL	125	439	107	16	2	12	(6	6)	163	64	43	36	3	52	5	5	8	21	6	.78	8	.244	.306	.371
1988 Cincinnati	NL	151	588	174	32	5	12	(9	3)	252	91	56	41	3	24	8	10	5	40	7	.85	7	.296	.347	.429
1989 Cincinnati	NL	97	325	111	14	4	4	(1	3)	145	47	36	20	5	23	2	2	8	10	5	.67	7	.342	.375	.446
1990 Cincinnati	NL	158	614	185	25	6	7	(4	3)	243	85	67	49	3	49	7	7	4	30	5	.86	14	.301	.358	.396
1991 Cincinnati	NL	123	464	140	27	4	20	(16	4)	235	88	69	55	1	64	3	3	2	24	6	.80	7	.302	.378	.506
1992 Cincinnati	NL	140	533	162	32	6	12	(8	4)	242	76	78	63	8	58	4	2	7	15	4	.79	13	.304	.377	.454
1993 Cincinnati	NL	100	384	121	20	3	8	(4 .	4)	171	57	51	51	6	33	1	1	3	14	1	.93	13	.315	.394	.445
1994 Cincinnati	NL	110	427	119	23	5	9	(6	3)	179	78	52	64	3	58	0	5	5	26	2	.93	6	.279	.369	.419
1995 Cincinnati	NL	131	496	158	29	6	15	(8	7)	244	98	66	61	2	49	3	3	4	51	5	**.91**	6	.319	.394	.492
1996 Cincinnati	NL	152	517	154	32	4	33	(14	19)	293	117	89	96	3	52	7	0	7	36	10	.78	20	.298	.410	.567
1997 Cincinnati	NL	73	224	71	17	3	4	(0	4)	106	34	20	47	6	24	3	1	1	14	3	.82	3	.317	.440	.473
1998 Cincinnati	NL	145	538	166	34	10	17	(8	9)	271	93	72	79	5	69	2	4	3	26	3	**.90**	12	.309	.397	.504
1999 Cincinnati	NL	161	583	171	30	4	12	(7	5)	245	108	75	93	5	57	2	5	4	30	8	.79	12	.293	.390	.420
2000 Cincinnati	NL	102	396	124	26	5	11	(6	5)	193	71	41	48	0	31	1	2	0	14	6	.70	10	.313	.389	.487
2001 Cincinnati	NL	45	156	40	12	0	2	(1	1)	58	29	17	27	2	25	2	0	0	3	2	.60	2	.256	.373	.372
16 ML YEARS		1854	6843	2048	373	70	181	(98	83)	3104	1163	851	839	56	689	50	50	57	362	73	.83	142	.299	.377	.454

Brandon Larson

Bats: Right **Throws:** Right **Pos:** 3B-9; PH/PR-5   **Ht:** 6'0" **Wt:** 210 **Born:** 5/24/76 **Age:** 26

Year Team	Lg	G	AB	H	2B	3B	HR	(Hm	Rd)	TB	R	RBI	TBB	IBB	SO	HBP	SH	SF	SB	CS	SB%	GDP	Avg	OBP	SLG
1997 Chattanooga	AA	11	41	11	5	1	0	—	—	18	4	6	1	0	10	0	0	1	0	0	—	1	.268	.279	.439
1998 Burlington	A	18	68	15	3	0	2	—	—	24	5	9	4	0	16	0	0	0	2	1	.67	1	.221	.264	.353
1999 Rockford	A	69	250	75	18	1	13	—	—	134	38	52	25	1	67	3	0	3	12	2	.86	7	.300	.367	.536
Chattanooga	AA	43	172	49	10	0	12	—	—	95	28	42	10	1	51	0	0	2	4	5	.44	3	.285	.332	.552
2000 Louisville	AAA	17	63	18	7	1	2	—	—	33	11	4	4	0	16	0	0	0	0	0	—	1	.286	.328	.524
Chattanooga	AA	111	427	116	26	0	20	—	—	202	61	64	31	5	122	8	0	3	15	5	.75	8	.272	.330	.473
2001 Louisville	AAA	115	424	108	22	2	14	—	—	176	61	55	24	1	123	12	0	2	5	6	.45	15	.255	.312	.415
2001 Cincinnati	NL	14	33	4	2	0	0	(0	0)	6	2	1	2	0	10	0	0	0	0	0	—	1	.121	.171	.182

Jason LaRue

Bats: R **Throws:** R **Pos:** C-107; PH/PR-12; 3B-3; LF-2; 1B-1   **Ht:** 5'11" **Wt:** 200 **Born:** 3/19/74 **Age:** 28

Year Team	Lg	G	AB	H	2B	3B	HR	(Hm	Rd)	TB	R	RBI	TBB	IBB	SO	HBP	SH	SF	SB	CS	SB%	GDP	Avg	OBP	SLG
1999 Cincinnati	NL	36	90	19	7	0	3	(1	2)	35	12	10	11	1	32	2	0	0	4	1	.80	4	.211	.311	.389
2000 Cincinnati	NL	31	98	23	3	0	5	(1	4)	41	12	12	5	2	19	4	0	0	0	0	—	3	.235	.299	.418
2001 Cincinnati	NL	121	364	86	21	2	12	(3	9)	147	39	43	27	4	106	9	1	2	3	3	.50	11	.236	.303	.404
3 ML YEARS		188	552	128	31	2	20	(5	15)	223	63	65	43	7	157	15	1	2	7	4	.64	16	.232	.304	.404

Chris Latham

Bats: B **Throws:** R **Pos:** LF-15; PH/PR-15; RF-14; CF-2   **Ht:** 6'0" **Wt:** 205 **Born:** 5/26/73 **Age:** 29

Year Team	Lg	G	AB	H	2B	3B	HR	(Hm	Rd)	TB	R	RBI	TBB	IBB	SO	HBP	SH	SF	SB	CS	SB%	GDP	Avg	OBP	SLG
2001 Syracuse *	AAA	79	288	80	20	9	13	—	—	157	57	54	51	5	90	1	0	6	14	11	.56	6	.278	.382	.545
1997 Minnesota	AL	15	22	4	1	0	0	(0	0)	5	4	1	0	0	8	0	0	0	0	0	—	0	.182	.182	.227
1998 Minnesota	AL	34	94	15	1	0	1	(1	0)	19	14	5	13	0	36	0	1	0	4	2	.67	0	.160	.262	.202
1999 Minnesota	AL	14	22	2	0	0	0	(0	0)	2	1	3	0	0	13	0	0	2	0	0	—	0	.091	.083	.091
2001 Toronto	AL	43	73	20	3	1	2	(1	1)	31	12	10	10	1	28	1	0	0	4	1	.80	1	.274	.369	.425
4 ML YEARS		106	211	41	5	1	3	(2	1)	57	31	19	23	1	85	1	1	2	8	3	.73	1	.194	.274	.270

Brian Lawrence

Pitches: Right **Bats:** Right **Pos:** SP-15; RP-12   **Ht:** 6'2" **Wt:** 195 **Born:** 5/14/76 **Age:** 26

Year Team	Lg	G	GS	CG	GF	IP	BFP	H	R	ER	HR	SH	SF	HB	TBB	IBB	SO	WP	Bk	W	L	Pct.	ShO	Sv-Op	Hld	ERA
1998 Idaho Falls	R+	4	4	2	0	22	92	22	7	6	1	0	1	2	5	0	21	0	0	3	0	1.000	1	0--	—	2.45
Clinton	A	12	12	2	0	80.1	323	67	34	25	5	2	1	4	13	0	79	0	0	5	3	.625	0	0--	—	2.80
1999 Rancho Cuc	A+	27	27	4	0	175.1	723	178	72	66	6	7	5	10	30	1	166	7	5	12	8	.600	3	0--	—	3.39
2000 Mobile	AA	21	21	0	0	126.2	496	99	40	34	6	1	0	10	28	0	119	1	0	7	6	.538	0	0--	—	2.42
Las Vegas	AAA	8	8	0	0	46.2	193	48	13	10	6	0	0	4	7	0	46	0	0	4	0	1.000	0	0--	—	1.93
2001 Portland	AAA	9	8	0	1	45	196	42	22	19	3	1	0	2	17	2	42	2	0	1	3	.250	0	1--	—	3.80
2001 San Diego	NL	27	15	1	5	114.2	484	107	53	44	10	4	3	5	34	5	84	1	0	5	5	.500	0	0-0	0	3.45

Matt Lawton

Bats: Left **Throws:** Right **Pos:** RF-142; DH-7; PH/PR-6   **Ht:** 5'10" **Wt:** 186 **Born:** 11/3/71 **Age:** 30

Year Team	Lg	G	AB	H	2B	3B	HR	(Hm	Rd)	TB	R	RBI	TBB	IBB	SO	HBP	SH	SF	SB	CS	SB%	GDP	Avg	OBP	SLG
1995 Minnesota	AL	21	60	19	4	1	1	(1	0)	28	11	12	7	0	11	3	0	0	1	1	.50	1	.317	.414	.467
1996 Minnesota	AL	79	252	65	7	1	6	(1	5)	92	34	42	28	1	28	4	0	2	4	4	.50	6	.258	.339	.365
1997 Minnesota	AL	142	460	114	29	3	14	(8	6)	191	74	60	76	3	81	10	1	1	7	4	.64	7	.248	.366	.415
1998 Minnesota	AL	152	557	155	36	6	21	(11	10)	266	91	77	86	6	64	15	0	4	16	8	.67	10	.278	.387	.478
1999 Minnesota	AL	118	406	105	18	0	7	(2	5)	144	58	54	57	7	42	6	0	7	26	4	.87	11	.259	.353	.355
2000 Minnesota	AL	156	561	171	44	2	13	(5	8)	258	84	88	91	8	63	7	0	5	23	7	.77	10	.305	.405	.460
2001 Min-NYM		151	559	155	36	1	13	(5	8)	232	95	64	85	6	80	11	0	2	29	8	.78	16	.277	.382	.415
2001 Minnesota	AL	103	376	110	25	0	10	(4	6)	165	71	51	63	6	46	3	0	2	19	6	.76	14	.293	.396	.439
New York	NL	48	183	45	11	1	3	(1	2)	67	24	13	22	0	34	8	0	0	10	2	.83	2	.246	.352	.366
7 ML YEARS		819	2855	784	174	14	75	(36	39)	1211	447	397	430	31	369	56	1	21	106	36	.75	61	.275	.378	.424

Jalal Leach

Bats: Left **Throws:** Left **Pos:** PH/PR-7; RF-2; LF-1   **Ht:** 6'2" **Wt:** 200 **Born:** 3/14/69 **Age:** 33

Year Team	Lg	G	AB	H	2B	3B	HR	(Hm	Rd)	TB	R	RBI	TBB	IBB	SO	HBP	SH	SF	SB	CS	SB%	GDP	Avg	OBP	SLG
1990 Oneonta	A-	69	257	74	7	1	2	—	—	89	41	18	37	3	52	0	4	0	33	13	.72	1	.288	.378	.346
1991 Ft. Laud	A+	122	468	119	13	9	2	—	—	156	48	42	44	3	122	0	3	3	28	12	.70	5	.254	.317	.333
1992 Pr William	A+	128	462	122	22	7	5	—	—	173	61	65	47	4	114	0	3	5	18	9	.67	8	.264	.329	.374
1993 Albany-Col	AA	125	457	129	19	9	14	—	—	208	64	79	47	3	113	1	0	4	16	12	.57	5	.282	.348	.455
1994 Columbus	AAA	132	444	116	18	9	6	—	—	170	56	56	39	3	106	1	3	4	14	12	.54	8	.261	.320	.383
1995 Columbus	AAA	88	272	66	12	5	6	—	—	106	37	31	22	1	60	2	1	4	11	4	.73	5	.243	.300	.390
1996 Harrisburg	AA	83	268	88	22	3	6	—	—	134	38	48	21	4	55	0	2	4	3	7	.30	6	.328	.372	.500
Ottawa	AAA	37	101	32	4	0	3	—	—	45	12	9	8	1	17	0	0	1	0	0	—	1	.317	.367	.446
1997 Tacoma	AAA	115	415	128	26	3	9	—	—	187	56	55	32	2	74	1	3	3	6	6	.50	11	.308	.357	.451
1998 Shreveport	AA	72	253	87	17	2	10	—	—	138	43	45	36	3	35	0	0	5	10	2	.83	6	.344	.418	.545
Fresno	AAA	35	130	46	8	2	9	—	—	85	23	26	8	1	26	0	0	1	3	2	.60	1	.354	.388	.654
1999 Fresno	AAA	116	371	109	19	5	15	—	—	183	58	75	27	2	67	0	2	4	8	7	.53	8	.294	.338	.493
2000 Scrantn-WB	AAA	65	180	48	9	2	4	—	—	73	24	21	19	3	34	0	1	1	8	3	.44	4	.267	.335	.406
Fresno	AAA	51	198	75	16	5	12	—	—	137	34	45	18	1	28	0	0	0	8	3	.73	2	.379	.431	.692

Year Team	Lg	G	AB	H	2B	3B	HR	(Hm	Rd)	TB	R	RBI	TBB	IBB	SO	HBP	SH	SF	SB	CS	SB%	GDP	Avg	OBP	SLG
								BATTING											**BASERUNNING**				**PERCENTAGES**		
2001 Fresno	AAA	130	467	133	30	3	16	—	—	217	68	70	31	3	94	1	0	3	13	6	.68	11	.285	.329	.465
2001 San Francisco	NL	8	10	1	0	0	0	(0	0)	1	0	1	2	0	3	0	0	0	0	0	—	0	.100	.250	.100

Matt LeCroy

Bats: R **Throws:** R **Pos:** DH-9; C-3; PH/PR-3; 1B-2 **Ht:** 6'2" **Wt:** 225 **Born:** 12/13/75 **Age:** 26

Year Team	Lg	G	AB	H	2B	3B	HR	(Hm	Rd)	TB	R	RBI	TBB	IBB	SO	HBP	SH	SF	SB	CS	SB%	GDP	Avg	OBP	SLG
1998 Fort Wayne	A	64	225	62	17	1	9	—	—	108	33	40	34	1	45	8	0	2	0	0	—	9	.276	.387	.480
Fort Myers	A+	51	200	61	9	1	12	—	—	108	32	51	21	1	35	4	0	6	2	1	.67	6	.305	.372	.540
Salt Lake	AAA	3	13	4	1	0	2	—	—	11	2	4	0	0	7	0	0	0	0	0	—	0	.308	.308	.846
1999 Fort Myers	A+	89	333	93	20	1	20	—	—	175	54	69	42	3	51	3	0	1	0	1	.00	10	.279	.364	.526
Salt Lake	AAA	29	119	36	4	1	10	—	—	72	23	30	5	0	22	1	0	2	0	1	.00	8	.303	.331	.605
2000 New Britain	AA	54	195	55	12	1	10	—	—	99	33	38	29	3	34	6	0	0	0	0	—	8	.282	.391	.508
Salt Lake	AAA	16	65	20	5	0	5	—	—	40	15	15	4	0	11	0	0	0	0	0	—	4	.308	.348	.615
2001 Edmonton	AAA	101	396	130	17	0	20	—	—	207	53	80	36	1	95	6	0	3	0	2	.00	8	.328	.390	.523
2000 Minnesota	AL	56	167	29	10	0	5	(2	3)	54	18	17	17	2	38	2	1	3	0	0	—	6	.174	.254	.323
2001 Minnesota	AL	15	40	17	5	0	3	(0	3)	31	6	12	0	0	8	1	0	1	0	1	.00	0	.425	.429	.775
2 ML YEARS		71	207	46	15	0	8	(2	6)	85	24	29	17	2	46	3	1	4	0	1	.00	6	.222	.286	.411

Ricky Ledee

Bats: L **Throws:** L **Pos:** RF-60; PH/PR-12; CF-10; LF-6 **Ht:** 6'1" **Wt:** 190 **Born:** 11/22/73 **Age:** 28

Year Team	Lg	G	AB	H	2B	3B	HR	(Hm	Rd)	TB	R	RBI	TBB	IBB	SO	HBP	SH	SF	SB	CS	SB%	GDP	Avg	OBP	SLG
2001 Oklahoma *	AAA	4	16	8	1	0	1	—	—	12	4	3	1	0	1	0	0	0	0	0	—	1	.500	.529	.750
1998 New York	AL	42	79	19	5	2	1	(0	1)	31	13	12	7	0	29	0	0	1	3	1	.75	1	.241	.299	.392
1999 New York	AL	88	250	69	13	5	9	(4	5)	119	45	40	28	5	73	0	0	2	4	3	.57	2	.276	.346	.476
2000 NYY-Cle-Tex	AL	137	467	110	19	5	13	(6	7)	178	59	77	59	4	98	2	0	3	13	6	.68	17	.236	.322	.381
2001 Texas	AL	78	242	56	21	1	2	(1	1)	85	33	36	23	0	58	3	1	3	3	3	.50	3	.231	.303	.351
2000 New York	AL	62	191	46	11	1	7	(2	5)	80	23	31	26	2	39	1	0	2	7	3	.70	7	.241	.332	.419
Cleveland	AL	17	63	14	2	1	2	(2	0)	24	13	8	8	0	9	0	0	0	0	0	—	3	.222	.310	.381
Texas	AL	58	213	50	6	3	4	(2	2)	74	23	38	25	2	50	1	0	1	6	3	.67	7	.235	.317	.347
4 ML YEARS		345	1038	254	58	13	25	(11	14)	413	150	165	117	9	258	5	1	9	23	13	.64	23	.245	.322	.398

Carlos Lee

Bats: Right **Throws:** Right **Pos:** LF-130; DH-17; PH/PR-6 **Ht:** 6'2" **Wt:** 235 **Born:** 6/20/76 **Age:** 26

Year Team	Lg	G	AB	H	2B	3B	HR	(Hm	Rd)	TB	R	RBI	TBB	IBB	SO	HBP	SH	SF	SB	CS	SB%	GDP	Avg	OBP	SLG
1999 Chicago	AL	127	492	144	32	2	16	(10	6)	228	66	84	13	0	72	4	1	7	4	2	.67	11	.293	.312	.463
2000 Chicago	AL	152	572	172	29	2	24	(12	12)	277	107	92	38	1	94	3	1	5	13	4	.76	17	.301	.345	.484
2001 Chicago	AL	150	558	150	33	3	24	(12	12)	261	75	84	38	2	85	6	1	2	17	7	.71	15	.269	.321	.468
3 ML YEARS		429	1622	466	94	7	64	(34	30)	766	248	260	89	3	251	13	3	14	34	13	.72	43	.287	.327	.472

David Lee

Pitches: Right **Bats:** Right **Pos:** RP-41 **Ht:** 6'1" **Wt:** 202 **Born:** 3/12/73 **Age:** 29

Year Team	Lg	G	GS	CG	GF	IP	BFP	H	R	ER	HR	SH	SF	HB	TBB	IBB	SO	WP	Bk	W	L	Pct.	ShO	Sv-Op	Hld	ERA
					HOW MUCH HE PITCHED						**WHAT HE GAVE UP**												**THE RESULTS**			
2001 Portland *	AAA	9	0	0	2	12	45	5	1	1	0	1	1	0	5	1	14	1	0	1	0	1.000	0	1- —	—	0.75
Mobile *	AA	2	0	0		2	7	2	0	0	0	0	0	0	0	0	3	1	0	0	0	—	0	0- —	—	0.00
1999 Colorado	NL	36	0	0	11	49	212	43	21	20	4	3	2	4	29	1	38	3	1	3	2	.600	0	0-0	2	3.67
2000 Colorado	NL	7	0	0	3	5.2	35	10	9	7	3	0	0	1	6	0	6	0	0	0	1	—	0	1-1	1	11.12
2001 San Diego	NL	41	0	0	11	48.2	222	52	20	20	6	1	1	6	27	1	42	1	1	1	0	1.000	0	0-0	4	3.70
3 ML YEARS		84	0	0	25	103.1	469	105	50	47	13	4	3	11	62	2	86	4	2	4	2	.667	0	1-1	7	4.09

Derrek Lee

Bats: Right **Throws:** Right **Pos:** 1B-156; PH/PR-6 **Ht:** 6'5" **Wt:** 225 **Born:** 9/6/75 **Age:** 26

Year Team	Lg	G	AB	H	2B	3B	HR	(Hm	Rd)	TB	R	RBI	TBB	IBB	SO	HBP	SH	SF	SB	CS	SB%	GDP	Avg	OBP	SLG
1997 San Diego	NL	22	54	14	3	0	1	(0	1)	20	9	4	9	0	24	0	0	0	0	0	—	1	.259	.365	.370
1998 Florida	NL	141	454	106	29	1	17	(4	13)	188	62	74	47	1	120	10	0	2	5	2	.71	12	.233	.318	.414
1999 Florida	NL	70	218	45	9	1	5	(0	5)	71	21	20	17	1	70	0	0	1	2	1	.67	3	.206	.263	.326
2000 Florida	NL	158	477	134	18	3	28	(9	19)	242	70	70	63	6	123	4	0	2	0	3	.00	14	.281	.368	.507
2001 Florida	NL	158	561	158	37	4	21	(8	13)	266	83	75	50	1	126	8	0	6	4	2	.67	18	.282	.346	.474
5 ML YEARS		549	1764	457	96	9	72	(21	51)	787	245	243	186	9	463	22	0	11	11	8	.58	48	.259	.335	.446

Travis Lee

Bats: Left **Throws:** Left **Pos:** 1B-156; PH/PR-4 **Ht:** 6'3" **Wt:** 214 **Born:** 5/26/75 **Age:** 27

Year Team	Lg	G	AB	H	2B	3B	HR	(Hm	Rd)	TB	R	RBI	TBB	IBB	SO	HBP	SH	SF	SB	CS	SB%	GDP	Avg	OBP	SLG
1998 Arizona	NL	146	562	151	20	2	22	(12	10)	241	71	72	67	5	123	0	0	1	8	1	.89	13	.269	.346	.429
1999 Arizona	NL	120	375	89	16	2	9	(7	2)	136	57	50	58	4	50	0	0	3	17	3	.85	10	.237	.337	.363
2000 Ari-Phi	NL	128	404	95	24	4	9	(2	7)	148	53	54	65	4	79	2	0	2	8	1	.89	12	.235	.342	.366
2001 Philadelphia	NL	157	555	143	34	2	20	(11	9)	241	75	90	71	5	109	4	1	9	3	4	.43	15	.258	.341	.434
2000 New York	NL	72	224	52	13	0	8	(1	7)	89	34	40	25	1	46	0	0	1	5	1	.83	6	.232	.308	.397
Philadelphia	NL	56	180	43	11	1	1	(1	0)	59	19	14	40	0	33	2	0	1	3	0	1.00	6	.239	.381	.328
4 ML YEARS		551	1896	478	94	7	60	(32	28)	766	256	266	261	15	361	6	1	15	36	9	.80	50	.252	.342	.404

Al Leiter

Pitches: Left **Bats:** Left **Pos:** SP-29   **Ht:** 6'3" **Wt:** 220 **Born:** 10/23/65 **Age:** 36

Year Team	Lg	G	GS	CG	GF	IP	BFP	H	R	ER	HR	SH	SF	HB	TBB	IBB	SO	WP	Bk	W	L	Pct.	ShO	Sv-Op	Hld	ERA
1987 New York	AL	4	4	0	0	22.2	104	24	16	16	2	1	0	0	15	0	28	4	0	2	2	.500	0	0-0	0	6.35
1988 New York	AL	14	14	0	0	57.1	251	49	27	25	7	1	0	5	33	0	60	1	4	4	4	.500	0	0-0	0	3.92
1989 NYY-Tor	AL	5	5	0	0	33.1	154	32	23	21	2	1	1	2	23	0	26	2	1	1	2	.333	0	0-0	0	5.67
1990 Toronto	AL	4	0	0	2	6.1	22	1	0	0	0	0	0	0	2	0	5	0	0	0	0	—	0	0-0	0	0.00
1991 Toronto	AL	3	0	0	1	1.2	13	3	5	5	0	1	0	0	5	0	1	0	0	0	0	—	0	0-0	0	27.00
1992 Toronto	AL	1	0	0	0	1	7	1	1	1	0	0	0	0	2	0	0	0	0	0	0	—	0	0-0	0	9.00
1993 Toronto	AL	34	12	1	4	105	454	93	52	48	8	3	3	4	56	2	66	2	2	9	6	.600	1	2-3	3	4.11
1994 Toronto	AL	20	20	1	0	111.2	516	125	68	63	6	3	8	2	65	3	100	7	5	6	7	.462	0	0-0	0	5.08
1995 Toronto	AL	28	28	2	0	183	805	162	80	74	15	6	4	6	108	1	153	14	0	11	11	.500	1	0-0	0	3.64
1996 Florida	NL	33	33	2	0	215.1	896	153	74	70	14	7	3	11	119	3	200	5	0	16	12	.571	2	0-0	0	2.93
1997 Florida	NL	27	27	0	0	151.1	668	133	78	73	13	10	3	12	91	4	132	2	0	11	9	.550	0	0-0	0	4.34
1998 New York	NL	28	28	4	0	193	789	151	55	53	8	6	2	11	71	2	174	4	1	17	6	.739	2	0-0	0	2.47
1999 New York	NL	32	32	1	0	213	923	209	107	100	19	13	10	9	93	8	162	4	1	13	12	.520	1	0-0	0	4.23
2000 New York	NL	31	31	2	0	208	874	176	84	74	19	10	6	11	76	1	200	4	0	16	8	.667	1	0-0	0	3.20
2001 New York	NL	29	29	0	0	187.1	772	178	81	69	18	9	6	4	46	3	142	5	2	11	11	.500	0	0-0	0	3.31
1989 New York	AL	4	4	0	0	26.2	123	23	20	18	1	1	1	2	21	0	22	1	1	1	2	.333	0	0-0	0	6.08
Toronto	AL	1	1	0	0	6.2	31	9	3	3	1	0	0	0	2	0	4	1	0	0	0	—	0	0-0	0	4.05
15 ML YEARS		293	263	13	7	1690	7248	1490	751	692	131	71	46	77	805	27	1449	54	17	117	90	.565	7	2-3	3	3.69

Mark Leiter

Pitches: Right **Bats:** Right **Pos:** RP-17; SP-3   **Ht:** 6'3" **Wt:** 220 **Born:** 4/13/63 **Age:** 39

Year Team	Lg	G	GS	CG	GF	IP	BFP	H	R	ER	HR	SH	SF	HB	TBB	IBB	SO	WP	Bk	W	L	Pct.	ShO	Sv-Op	Hld	ERA
2001 Beloit *	A	1	0	0	0	3.2	16	4	1	1	0	0	2	0	0	0	4	0	0	0	1	.000	0	0- -	—	2.45
1990 New York	AL	8	3	0	2	26.1	119	33	20	20	5	2	1	2	9	0	21	0	0	1	1	.500	0	0-0	0	6.84
1991 Detroit	AL	38	15	1	7	134.2	578	125	66	63	16	5	6	6	50	4	103	2	0	9	7	.563	0	1-2	2	4.21
1992 Detroit	AL	35	14	1	7	112	475	116	57	52	9	2	8	3	43	5	75	3	0	8	5	.615	0	0-0	3	4.18
1993 Detroit	AL	27	13	1	4	106.2	471	111	61	56	17	3	5	3	44	5	70	5	0	6	6	.500	0	0-1	1	4.73
1994 California	AL	40	7	0	15	95.1	425	99	56	50	13	4	4	9	35	6	71	2	0	4	7	.364	0	2-3	3	4.72
1995 San Francisco	NL	30	29	7	0	195.2	817	185	91	83	19	10	6	17	55	4	129	9	3	10	12	.455	1	0-0	0	3.82
1996 SF-Mon	NL	35	34	2	0	205	904	219	128	112	37	12	6	16	69	8	164	6	4	8	12	.400	0	0-0	0	4.92
1997 Philadelphia	NL	31	31	3	0	182.2	832	216	132	115	25	11	8	9	64	4	148	11	2	10	17	.370	0	0-0	0	5.67
1998 Philadelphia	NL	69	0	0	50	88.2	378	67	36	35	8	9	4	8	47	5	84	5	0	7	5	.583	0	23-35	1	3.55
1999 Seattle	AL	2	0	0	0	1.1	6	2	1	1	0	0	0	0	0	0	1	0	0	0	0	—	0	0-0	0	6.75
2001 Milwaukee	NL	20	3	0	3	36	149	32	16	15	6	1	2	0	8	2	26	3	0	2	1	.667	0	0-0	0	3.75
1996 San Francisco	NL	23	22	1	0	135.1	602	151	93	78	25	7	3	9	50	7	118	2	3	4	10	.286	0	0-0	0	5.19
Montreal	NL	12	12	1	0	69.2	302	68	35	34	12	5	3	7	19	1	46	4	1	4	2	.667	0	0-0	0	4.39
11 ML YEARS		335	149	15	88	1184.1	5154	1205	664	602	155	59	48	75	424	43	892	46	9	65	73	.471	1	26-41	11	4.57

Curtis Leskanic

Pitches: Right **Bats:** Right **Pos:** RP-70   **Ht:** 6'0" **Wt:** 186 **Born:** 4/2/68 **Age:** 34

Year Team	Lg	G	GS	CG	GF	IP	BFP	H	R	ER	HR	SH	SF	HB	TBB	IBB	SO	WP	Bk	W	L	Pct.	ShO	Sv-Op	Hld	ERA
1993 Colorado	NL	18	8	0	1	57	260	59	40	34	7	5	4	2	27	1	30	8	2	1	5	.167	0	0-0	0	5.37
1994 Colorado	NL	8	3	0	2	22.1	98	27	14	14	2	2	0	0	10	0	17	2	0	1	1	.500	0	0-0	0	5.64
1995 Colorado	NL	76	0	0	27	98	406	83	38	37	7	3	2	0	33	1	107	6	1	6	3	.667	0	10-16	19	3.40
1996 Colorado	NL	70	0	0	32	73.2	334	82	51	51	12	3	3	2	38	1	76	6	2	7	5	.583	0	6-10	9	6.23
1997 Colorado	NL	55	0	0	23	58.1	248	59	36	36	8	2	4	0	24	0	53	4	0	4	0	1.000	0	2-4	6	5.55
1998 Colorado	NL	66	0	0	20	75.2	332	75	37	37	9	0	0	1	40	2	55	3	1	6	4	.600	0	2-5	12	4.40
1999 Colorado	NL	63	0	0	5	85	382	87	54	48	7	5	3	5	49	4	77	5	0	6	2	.750	0	0-3	8	5.08
2000 Milwaukee	NL	73	0	0	39	77.1	333	58	23	22	7	1	4	3	51	5	75	5	0	9	3	.750	0	12-13	11	2.56
2001 Milwaukee	NL	70	0	0	58	69.1	297	63	30	28	11	3	0	2	31	5	64	2	0	2	6	.250	0	17-24	2	3.63
9 ML YEARS		499	11	0	207	616.2	2690	593	323	307	70	24	20	15	303	19	554	41	6	42	29	.592	0	49-75	67	4.48

Al Levine

Pitches: Right **Bats:** Left **Pos:** RP-63; SP-1   **Ht:** 6'3" **Wt:** 190 **Born:** 5/22/68 **Age:** 34

Year Team	Lg	G	GS	CG	GF	IP	BFP	H	R	ER	HR	SH	SF	HB	TBB	IBB	SO	WP	Bk	W	L	Pct.	ShO	Sv-Op	Hld	ERA
1996 Chicago	AL	16	0	0	5	18.1	85	22	14	11	1	0	1	1	7	1	12	0	0	0	1	.000	0	0-1	0	5.40
1997 Chicago	AL	25	0	0	6	27.1	133	35	22	21	4	1	2	2	16	1	22	2	0	2	2	.500	0	0-1	3	6.91
1998 Texas	AL	30	0	0	11	58	251	68	30	29	6	1	3	1	16	1	19	5	0	0	1	.000	0	0-0	0	4.50
1999 Anaheim	AL	50	1	0	12	85	349	76	40	32	13	2	7	3	29	2	37	3	0	1	1	.500	0	0-1	3	3.39
2000 Anaheim	AL	51	5	0	12	95.1	426	98	44	41	10	3	3	2	49	5	42	1	0	3	4	.429	0	2-2	5	3.87
2001 Anaheim	AL	64	1	0	21	75.2	316	71	25	20	7	5	5	2	28	4	40	6	0	8	10	.444	0	2-6	17	2.38
6 ML YEARS		236	7	0	67	359.2	1560	370	175	154	41	12	21	10	145	14	172	17	0	14	19	.424	0	4-11	28	3.85

Jesse Levis

Bats: Left **Throws:** Right **Pos:** C-11; PH/PR-1   **Ht:** 5'9" **Wt:** 200 **Born:** 4/14/68 **Age:** 34

Year Team	Lg	G	AB	H	2B	3B	HR	(Hm	Rd)	TB	R	RBI	TBB	IBB	SO	HBP	SH	SF	SB	CS	SB%	GDP	Avg	OBP	SLG
2001 Richmond *	AAA	67	192	57	6	0	1	—	—	66	18	27	24	2	15	2	3	0	2	0	1.00	6	.297	.381	.344
Indianapolis *	AAA	12	40	6	1	0	2	—	—	13	4	7	2	0	6	1	0	0	0	0	—	3	.150	.209	.325
1992 Cleveland	AL	28	43	12	4	0	1	(0	1)	19	2	3	0	0	5	0	1	0	0	0	—	0	.279	.279	.442
1993 Cleveland	AL	31	63	11	2	0	0	(0	0)	13	7	4	2	0	10	0	1	1	0	0	—	0	.175	.197	.206
1994 Cleveland	AL	1	1	1	0	0	0	(0	0)	1	0	0	0	0	0	0	0	0	0	0	1.000	0	1.000	1.000	1.000
1995 Cleveland	AL	12	18	6	2	0	0	(0	0)	8	1	3	1	0	0	0	1	0	0	0	—	1	.333	.333	.444
1996 Milwaukee	AL	104	233	55	6	1	1	(0	1)	66	27	21	38	0	15	2	1	0	0	0	—	7	.236	.348	.283

BATTING														BASERUNNING	PERCENTAGES		
Year Team	Lg	G AB H	2B 3B HR	(Hm Rd)	TB	R RBI	TBB	IBB	SO	HBP	SH	SF	SB CS SB% GDP	Avg	OBP	SLG
1997 Milwaukee	AL	99 200 57	7 0 1	(1 0)	67	19 19	24	0	17	1	5	2	1 0 1.00 4	.285	.361	.335
1998 Milwaukee	NL	22 37 13	0 0 0	(0 0)	13	4 4	7	2	6	2	1	1	1 0 1.00 3	.351	.468	.351
1999 Cleveland	AL	10 26 4	0 0 0	(0 0)	4	0 3	1	0	6	1	1	0	0 0 — 1	.154	.214	.154
2001 Milwaukee	NL	12 33 8	2 0 0	(0 0)	10	6 3	3	0	7	0	0	0	0 0 — 1	.242	.306	.303
9 ML YEARS		319 654 167	23 1 3	(1 2)	201	66 60	76	2	66	6	10	6	2 0 1.00 18	.255	.336	.307

Allen Levrault

Pitches: Right **Bats:** Right **Pos:** SP-20; RP-12 **Ht:** 6'3" **Wt:** 230 **Born:** 8/15/77 **Age:** 24

HOW MUCH HE PITCHED					WHAT HE GAVE UP						THE RESULTS						
Year Team	Lg	G GS CG GF	IP	BFP	H R ER	HR SH SF HB	TBB IBB	SO	WP	Bk	W L Pct.	ShO	Sv-Op	Hld	ERA
1996 Helena	R+	18 11 0 2	71	302	70 43 42	9 0 0 8	22 0	68	4	3	4 3 .571	0	1- -	—	5.32
1997 Beloit	A	24 24 1 0	131.1	561	141 89 77	18 1 2 6	40 1	112	3	12	3 10 .231	0	0- -	—	5.28
1998 Stockton	A+	16 15 4 0	97.1	388	76 33 31	8 4 3 2	27 0	86	2	1	9 3 .750	1	0- -	—	2.87
El Paso	AA	11 11 0 0	62.2	281	77 51 41	7 2 2 1	17 0	46	1	1	1 5 .167	0	0- -	—	5.89
1999 Huntsville	AA	16 16 2 0	99.2	404	77 44 38	11 3 2 5	33 0	82	3	3	9 2 .818	1	0- -	—	3.43
Louisville	AAA	9 5 0 1	34.1	169	48 37 33	9 1 2 3	16 0	33	1	0	3 3 .250	0	0- -	—	8.65
2000 Indianapols	AAA	21 18 1 1	108.1	460	98 55 51	9 7 5 6	46 3	78	5	2	6 8 .429	0	0- -	—	4.24
2001 Indianapols	AAA	5 5 0 0	30.2	120	22 9 9	1 1 0 1	8 1	30	0	0	2 1 .667	0	0- -	—	2.64
2000 Milwaukee	NL	5 1 0 2	12	51	10 7 6	0 1 1 0	7 0	9	0	0	0 1 .000	0	0-0	0	4.50
2001 Milwaukee	NL	32 20 1 0	130.2	593	146 93 88	27 3 4 7	59 7	80	2	1	6 10 .375	0	0-0	0	6.06
2 ML YEARS		37 21 1 2	142.2	644	156 100 94	27 4 5 7	66 7	89	2	1	6 11 .353	0	0-0	0	5.93

Darren Lewis

Bats: R **Throws:** R **Pos:** RF-29; LF-27; CF-21; PH/PR-21; DH-6 **Ht:** 6'0" **Wt:** 189 **Born:** 8/28/67 **Age:** 34

BATTING														BASERUNNING	PERCENTAGES		
Year Team	Lg	G AB H	2B 3B HR	(Hm Rd)	TB	R RBI	TBB	IBB	SO	HBP	SH	SF	SB CS SB% GDP	Avg	OBP	SLG
1990 Oakland	AL	25 35 8	0 0 0	(0 0)	8	4 1	7	0	4	1	3	0	2 0 1.00 2	.229	.372	.229
1991 San Francisco	NL	72 222 55	5 3 1	(0 1)	69	41 15	36	0	30	2	7	0	13 7 .65 1	.248	.358	.311
1992 San Francisco	NL	100 320 74	8 1 1	(1 0)	87	38 18	29	0	46	1	10	2	28 8 .78 3	.231	.295	.272
1993 San Francisco	NL	136 522 132	17 7 2	(2 0)	169	84 48	30	0	40	7	12	1	46 15 .75 4	.253	.302	.324
1994 San Francisco	NL	114 451 116	15 9 4	(4 0)	161	70 29	53	0	50	4	4	1	30 13 .70 6	.257	.340	.357
1995 SF-Cin		132 472 118	13 3 1	(1 0)	140	66 24	34	0	57	8	12	1	32 18 .64 9	.250	.311	.297
1996 Chicago	AL	141 337 77	12 2 4	(0 4)	105	55 53	45	1	40	3	15	5	21 5 .81 9	.228	.321	.312
1997 CWS-LA		107 154 41	4 1 1	(0 1)	50	22 15	17	0	31	0	7	0	14 6 .70 3	.266	.339	.325
1998 Boston	AL	155 585 157	25 3 8	(5 3)	212	95 63	70	0	94	8	2	5	29 12 .71 12	.268	.352	.362
1999 Boston	AL	135 470 113	14 6 2	(1 1)	145	63 40	45	0	52	5	14	4	16 10 .62 5	.240	.311	.309
2000 Boston	AL	97 270 65	12 0 2	(0 2)	83	44 17	22	0	34	3	8	0	10 5 .67 2	.241	.305	.307
2001 Boston	AL	82 164 46	9 1 1	(0 1)	60	18 12	8	0	25	3	5	5	5 5 .50 2	.280	.326	.366
1995 San Francisco	NL	74 309 78	10 3 1	(1 0)	97	47 16	17	0	37	6	7	1	21 7 .75 6	.252	.303	.314
Cincinnati	NL	58 163 40	3 0 0	(0 0)	43	19 8	17	0	20	2	5	0	11 11 .50 3	.245	.324	.264
1997 Chicago	AL	81 77 18	1 0 0	(0 0)	19	15 5	11	0	14	0	5	0	11 4 .73 2	.234	.330	.247
Los Angeles	NL	26 77 23	3 1 1	(0 1)	31	7 10	6	0	17	0	2	0	3 2 .60 1	.299	.349	.403
12 ML YEARS		1296 4002 1002	134 36 27	(14 13)	1289	600 335	396	1	503	45	99	19	246 104 .70 58	.250	.323	.322

Mark Lewis

Bats: Right **Throws:** Right **Pos:** 3B-4; 2B-3; PH/PR-2 **Ht:** 6'1" **Wt:** 195 **Born:** 11/30/69 **Age:** 32

BATTING														BASERUNNING	PERCENTAGES		
Year Team	Lg	G AB H	2B 3B HR	(Hm Rd)	TB	R RBI	TBB	IBB	SO	HBP	SH	SF	SB CS SB% GDP	Avg	OBP	SLG
2001 Buffalo *	AAA	48 184 55	10 1 4	—	79	22 29	18	2	26	4	1	0	0 1 .00 9	.299	.372	.429
1991 Cleveland	AL	84 314 83	15 1 0	(0 0)	100	29 30	15	0	45	0	2	5	2 2 .50 12	.264	.293	.318
1992 Cleveland	AL	122 413 109	21 0 5	(2 3)	145	44 30	25	1	69	3	1	4	4 5 .44 12	.264	.308	.351
1993 Cleveland	AL	14 52 13	2 0 1	(1 0)	18	6 5	0	0	7	0	1	0	3 0 1.00 1	.250	.250	.346
1994 Cleveland	AL	20 73 15	5 0 1	(1 0)	23	6 8	2	0	13	0	1	0	1 0 1.00 2	.205	.227	.315
1995 Cincinnati	NL	81 171 58	13 1 3	(1 2)	82	25 30	21	2	33	0	0	2	0 3 .00 1	.339	.407	.480
1996 Detroit	AL	145 545 147	30 3 11	(8 3)	216	69 55	42	0	109	5	4	3	6 1 .86 12	.270	.326	.396
1997 San Francisco	NL	118 341 91	14 6 10	(4 6)	147	50 42	23	2	62	4	1	3	3 2 .60 8	.267	.318	.431
1998 Philadelphia	NL	142 518 129	21 2 9	(4 5)	181	52 54	48	2	111	3	3	8	3 3 .50 17	.249	.312	.349
1999 Cincinnati	NL	88 173 44	16 0 6	(2 4)	78	18 28	7	1	24	0	2	2	0 0 — 8	.254	.280	.451
2000 Cin-Bal		82 182 46	18 0 2	(1 1)	70	20 24	13	0	34	1	1	1	7 2 .78 6	.253	.305	.385
2001 Cleveland	AL	6 13 1	0 0 0	(0 0)	1	1 0	0	0	4	0	0	0	0 0 — 1	.077	.077	.077
2000 Cincinnati	NL	11 19 2	1 0 0	(0 0)	3	1 3	1	0	3	0	0	0	0 0 — 1	.105	.150	.158
Baltimore	AL	71 163 44	17 0 2	(1 1)	67	19 21	12	0	31	1	1	1	7 2 .78 5	.270	.322	.411
11 ML YEARS		902 2795 736	155 13 48	(24 24)	1061	320 306	196	8	511	16	16	28	29 18 .62 79	.263	.312	.380

Cory Lidle

Pitches: Right **Bats:** Right **Pos:** SP-29 **Ht:** 5'11" **Wt:** 180 **Born:** 3/22/72 **Age:** 30

HOW MUCH HE PITCHED					WHAT HE GAVE UP						THE RESULTS						
Year Team	Lg	G GS CG GF	IP	BFP	H R ER	HR SH SF HB	TBB IBB	SO	WP	Bk	W L Pct.	ShO	Sv-Op	Hld	ERA
2001 Sacramento *	AAA	1 1 0 0	6	26	6 2 2	0 0 0 0	3 0	2	2	0	1 0 1.000	0	0- -	—	3.00
1997 New York	NL	54 2 0 20	81.2	345	86 38 32	7 4 4 3	20 4	54	2	0	7 2 .778	0	2-3	9	3.53
1999 Tampa Bay	AL	5 1 0 1	5	24	8 4 4	0 0 0 0	2 0	4	0	0	1 0 1.000	0	0-0	0	7.20
2000 Tampa Bay	AL	31 11 0 5	96.2	424	114 64 54	13 3 1 3	29 3	62	6	0	4 6 .400	0	0-0	2	5.03
2001 Oakland	AL	29 29 1 0	188	762	170 84 75	23 2 1 10	47 7	118	5	0	13 6 .684	0	0-0	0	3.59
4 ML YEARS		119 43 1 26	371.1	1555	378 187 165	43 9 6 16	98 14	238	13	0	25 14 .641	0	2-3	11	4.00

126

Jon Lieber

Pitches: Right **Bats:** Left **Pos:** SP-34   **Ht:** 6'2" **Wt:** 230 **Born:** 4/2/70 **Age:** 32

Year Team	Lg	G	GS	CG	GF	IP	BFP	H	R	ER	HR	SH	SF	HB	TBB	IBB	SO	WP	Bk	W	L	Pct.	ShO	Sv-Op	Hld	ERA
1994 Pittsburgh	NL	17	17	1	0	108.2	460	116	62	45	12	3	3	1	25	3	71	2	3	6	7	.462	0	0-0	0	3.73
1995 Pittsburgh	NL	21	12	0	3	72.2	327	103	56	51	7	5	6	4	14	0	45	3	0	4	7	.364	0	0-1	3	6.32
1996 Pittsburgh	NL	51	15	0	6	142	600	156	70	63	19	7	2	3	28	2	94	0	0	9	5	.643	0	1-4	9	3.99
1997 Pittsburgh	NL	33	32	1	0	188.1	799	193	102	94	23	6	7	1	51	8	160	3	1	11	14	.440	0	0-0	0	4.49
1998 Pittsburgh	NL	29	28	2	1	171	731	182	93	78	23	7	4	3	40	4	138	0	3	8	14	.364	0	1-1	0	4.11
1999 Chicago	NL	31	31	3	0	203.1	875	226	107	92	28	7	11	1	46	6	186	2	2	10	11	.476	1	0-0	0	4.07
2000 Chicago	NL	35	35	6	0	251	1047	248	130	123	36	9	7	10	54	3	192	2	2	12	11	.522	1	0-0	0	4.41
2001 Chicago	NL	34	34	5	0	232.1	958	226	104	98	25	13	9	7	41	4	148	4	1	20	6	.769	1	0-0	0	3.80
8 ML YEARS		251	204	18	10	1369.1	5797	1450	724	644	173	57	49	30	299	30	1034	16	12	80	75	.516	3	2-6	12	4.23

Mike Lieberthal

Bats: Right **Throws:** Right **Pos:** C-33; PH/PR-1   **Ht:** 6'0" **Wt:** 190 **Born:** 1/18/72 **Age:** 30

Year Team	Lg	G	AB	H	2B	3B	HR	(Hm	Rd)	TB	R	RBI	TBB	IBB	SO	HBP	SH	SF	SB	CS	SB%	GDP	Avg	OBP	SLG
1994 Philadelphia	NL	24	79	21	3	1	1	(1	0)	29	6	5	3	0	5	1	1	0	0	0	—	4	.266	.301	.367
1995 Philadelphia	NL	16	47	12	2	0	0	(0	0)	14	1	4	5	0	5	0	2	0	0	0	—	1	.255	.327	.298
1996 Philadelphia	NL	50	166	42	8	0	7	(4	3)	71	21	23	10	0	30	2	0	4	0	0	—	4	.253	.297	.428
1997 Philadelphia	NL	134	455	112	27	1	20	(11	9)	201	59	77	44	1	76	4	0	7	3	4	.43	10	.246	.314	.442
1998 Philadelphia	NL	86	313	80	15	3	8	(5	3)	125	39	45	17	1	44	7	0	5	2	1	.67	4	.256	.304	.399
1999 Philadelphia	NL	145	510	153	33	1	31	(10	21)	281	84	96	44	7	86	11	1	8	0	0	—	15	.300	.363	.551
2000 Philadelphia	NL	108	389	108	30	0	15	(8	7)	183	55	71	40	3	53	6	0	3	2	0	1.00	12	.278	.352	.470
2001 Philadelphia	NL	34	121	28	8	0	2	(0	2)	42	21	11	12	2	21	3	0	0	0	0	—	2	.231	.316	.347
8 ML YEARS		597	2080	556	126	6	84	(39	45)	946	286	332	175	14	320	34	4	27	7	5	.58	52	.267	.330	.455

Jeff Liefer

Bats: L **Throws:** R **Pos:** LF-35; 1B-15; 3B-15; PH/PR-11; DH-10; RF-4   **Ht:** 6'3" **Wt:** 210 **Born:** 8/17/74 **Age:** 27

Year Team	Lg	G	AB	H	2B	3B	HR	(Hm	Rd)	TB	R	RBI	TBB	IBB	SO	HBP	SH	SF	SB	CS	SB%	GDP	Avg	OBP	SLG
2001 Charlotte *	AAA	32	119	34	7	0	6			59	23	21	15	1	41	4	0	1	3	1	.75	1	.286	.381	.496
1999 Chicago	AL	45	113	28	7	1	0	(0	0)	37	8	14	8	0	28	0	0	1	2	0	1.00	3	.248	.295	.327
2000 Chicago	AL	5	11	2	0	0	0	(0	0)	2	0	0	0	0	4	0	0	0	0	0	—	0	.182	.182	.182
2001 Chicago	AL	83	254	65	13	0	18	(10	8)	132	36	39	20	1	69	2	1	2	0	1	.00	6	.256	.313	.520
3 ML YEARS		133	378	95	20	1	18	(10	8)	171	44	53	28	1	101	2	1	3	2	1	.67	9	.251	.304	.452

Kerry Ligtenberg

Pitches: Right **Bats:** Right **Pos:** RP-53   **Ht:** 6'2" **Wt:** 215 **Born:** 5/11/71 **Age:** 31

Year Team	Lg	G	GS	CG	GF	IP	BFP	H	R	ER	HR	SH	SF	HB	TBB	IBB	SO	WP	Bk	W	L	Pct.	ShO	Sv-Op	Hld	ERA
2001 Richmond *	AAA	1	0	0	1	1	4	0	0	0	0	0	0	0	1	0	2	0	0	0	0	—	0	0-	—	0.00
1997 Atlanta	NL	15	0	0	9	15	61	12	5	5	4	0	0	0	4	2	19	0	0	1	0	1.000	0	1-1	0	3.00
1998 Atlanta	NL	75	0	0	56	73	290	51	24	22	6	1	1	0	24	1	79	3	0	3	2	.600	0	30-34	11	2.71
2000 Atlanta	NL	59	0	0	19	52.1	217	43	21	21	7	2	1	0	24	5	51	0	0	2	3	.400	0	12-14	12	3.61
2001 Atlanta	NL	53	0	0	24	59.2	254	50	22	20	4	1	2	0	30	8	56	3	0	3	3	.500	0	1-2	0	3.02
4 ML YEARS		202	0	0	108	200	822	156	72	68	21	4	4	0	82	16	205	6	0	9	8	.529	0	44-51	23	3.06

Ted Lilly

Pitches: Left **Bats:** Left **Pos:** SP-21; RP-5   **Ht:** 6'0" **Wt:** 185 **Born:** 1/4/76 **Age:** 26

Year Team	Lg	G	GS	CG	GF	IP	BFP	H	R	ER	HR	SH	SF	HB	TBB	IBB	SO	WP	Bk	W	L	Pct.	ShO	Sv-Op	Hld	ERA
2001 Columbus *	AAA	5	5	0	0	25.1	101	16	10	8	2	0	1	1	8	0	30	1	0	0	0	—	0	0--	—	2.84
1999 Montreal	NL	9	3	0	1	23.2	110	30	20	20	7	0	1	3	9	0	28	1	0	0	1	.000	0	0-0	0	7.61
2000 New York	AL	7	0	0	1	8	39	8	6	5	1	0	0	1	5	0	11	1	1	0	0	—	0	0-0	0	5.63
2001 New York	AL	26	21	0	2	120.2	537	126	81	72	20	2	5	7	51	1	112	9	2	5	6	.455	0	0-0	0	5.37
3 ML YEARS		42	24	0	4	152.1	686	164	107	97	28	2	6	10	65	1	151	11	3	5	7	.417	0	0-0	0	5.73

Jose Lima

Pitches: Right **Bats:** Right **Pos:** SP-27; RP-5   **Ht:** 6'2" **Wt:** 205 **Born:** 9/30/72 **Age:** 29

Year Team	Lg	G	GS	CG	GF	IP	BFP	H	R	ER	HR	SH	SF	HB	TBB	IBB	SO	WP	Bk	W	L	Pct.	ShO	Sv-Op	Hld	ERA
1994 Detroit	AL	3	1	0	1	6.2	34	11	10	10	2	0	0	0	3	1	7	1	0	0	1	.000	0	0-0	0	13.50
1995 Detroit	AL	15	15	0	0	73.2	320	85	52	50	10	2	1	4	18	4	37	5	0	3	9	.250	0	0-0	0	6.11
1996 Detroit	AL	39	4	0	15	72.2	329	87	48	46	13	5	3	5	22	4	59	3	0	5	6	.455	0	3-7	6	5.70
1997 Houston	NL	52	1	0	15	75	321	79	45	44	9	6	3	5	16	2	63	2	0	1	6	.143	0	2-2	3	5.28
1998 Houston	NL	33	33	3	0	233.1	950	229	100	96	34	11	5	7	32	1	169	4	0	16	8	.667	1	0-0	0	3.70
1999 Houston	NL	35	35	3	0	246.1	1024	256	108	98	30	7	5	2	44	2	187	8	0	21	10	.677	0	0-0	0	3.58
2000 Houston	NL	33	33	0	0	196.1	895	251	152	145	48	12	12	2	68	3	124	3	0	7	16	.304	0	0-0	0	6.65
2001 Hou-Det		32	27	2	2	165.2	719	197	114	102	35	5	9	9	38	3	84	4	0	6	12	.333	0	0-0	0	5.54
2001 Houston	NL	14	9	0	3	53	249	77	48	43	12	4	4	5	16	1	41	3	0	1	2	.333	0	0-0	0	7.30
Detroit	AL	18	18	2	0	112.2	470	120	66	59	23	1	5	4	22	2	43	1	0	5	10	.333	0	0-0	0	4.71
8 ML YEARS		242	149	8	34	1069.2	4592	1195	629	591	181	46	40	34	241	20	730	30	0	59	68	.465	1	5-9	9	4.97

Mike Lincoln

Pitches: Right **Bats:** Right **Pos:** RP-31   **Ht:** 6'2" **Wt:** 210 **Born:** 4/10/75 **Age:** 27

Year Team	Lg	HOW MUCH HE PITCHED						WHAT HE GAVE UP												THE RESULTS					
		G	GS	CG	GF	IP	BFP	H	R	ER	HR	SH	SF	HB	TBB	IBB	SO	WP	Bk	W	L	Pct.	ShO	Sv-Op	Hld	ERA
2001 Nashville *	AAA	18	13	1	1	91.2	388	90	39	35	10	1	0	4	25	0	71	3	1	5	4	.556	0	0- -	—	3.44
1999 Minnesota	AL	18	15	0	0	76.1	353	102	59	58	11	2	6	1	26	0	27	4	0	3	10	.231	0	0- -	1	6.84
2000 Minnesota	AL	8	4	0	1	20.2	109	26	25	25	10	0	0	2	13	0	15	1	0	0	3	.000	0	0-0	0	10.89
2001 Pittsburgh	NL	31	0	0	5	40.1	168	34	16	12	3	1	1	4	11	0	24	2	0	2	1	.667	0	0-2	7	2.68
3 ML YEARS		57	19	0	6	137.1	630	172	100	95	24	3	7	7	50	0	66	7	0	5	14	.263	0	0-2	8	6.23

Scott Linebrink

Pitches: Right **Bats:** Right **Pos:** RP-9   **Ht:** 6'3" **Wt:** 185 **Born:** 8/4/76 **Age:** 25

Year Team	Lg	HOW MUCH HE PITCHED						WHAT HE GAVE UP												THE RESULTS					
		G	GS	CG	GF	IP	BFP	H	R	ER	HR	SH	SF	HB	TBB	IBB	SO	WP	Bk	W	L	Pct.	ShO	Sv-Op	Hld	ERA
1997 Salem-Keizr	A-	3	3	0	0	10	42	7	5	5	1	0	0	0	6	0	6	1	0	0	0	—	0	0- -	—	4.50
San Jose	A+	6	6	0	0	28.1	120	29	11	10	2	0	0	0	10	0	40	2	0	2	1	.667	0	0- -	—	3.18
1998 Shreveport	AA	21	21	0	0	113	494	101	66	63	12	6	5	7	58	1	128	8	0	10	8	.556	0	0- -	—	5.02
1999 Shreveport	AA	10	10	0	0	43.1	190	48	31	31	7	0	4	0	14	0	33	1	0	1	8	.111	0	0- -	—	6.44
2000 Fresno	AAA	28	7	0	14	62	255	54	42	36	10	0	2	1	12	0	49	3	1	1	4	.200	0	4- -	—	5.23
New Orleans	AAA	11	0	0	4	15	66	15	4	3	0	0	1	0	7	0	22	3	0	2	0	1.000	0	1- -	—	1.80
2001 New Orleans	AAA	50	0	0	20	72	287	52	28	28	4	4	2	2	24	6	72	9	0	7	6	.538	0	8- -	—	3.50
2000 SF-Hou	NL	11	0	0	4	12	63	18	8	8	4	0	0	3	8	0	6	0	0	0	0	—	0	0-0	0	6.00
2001 Houston	NL	9	0	0	2	10.1	44	6	4	3	0	1	1	2	6	0	9	1	0	0	0	—	0	0-0	0	2.61
2000 San Francisco	NL	3	0	0	1	2.1	16	7	3	3	1	0	0	0	2	0	0	0	0	0	0	—	0	0-0	0	11.57
Houston	NL	8	0	0	3	9.2	47	11	5	5	3	0	0	3	6	0	6	0	0	0	0	—	0	0-0	0	4.66
2 ML YEARS		20	0	0	6	22.1	107	24	12	11	4	1	1	5	14	0	15	1	0	0	0	—	0	0-0	0	4.43

Felipe Lira

Pitches: Right **Bats:** Right **Pos:** RP-4   **Ht:** 6'1" **Wt:** 205 **Born:** 4/26/72 **Age:** 30

Year Team	Lg	HOW MUCH HE PITCHED						WHAT HE GAVE UP												THE RESULTS					
		G	GS	CG	GF	IP	BFP	H	R	ER	HR	SH	SF	HB	TBB	IBB	SO	WP	Bk	W	L	Pct.	ShO	Sv-Op	Hld	ERA
2001 Ottawa *	AAA	42	0	0	19	60.2	243	56	17	14	4	7	0	0	10	2	47	1	0	5	4	.556	0	6- -	—	2.08
Scrantn-WB *	AAA	2	2	0	0	8.2	42	17	5	5	0	1	0	0	0	0	6	0	0	1	0	1.000	0	0- -	—	5.19
1995 Detroit	AL	37	22	0	7	146.1	635	151	74	70	17	4	9	8	56	7	89	5	1	9	13	.409	0	1-3	1	4.31
1996 Detroit	AL	32	32	3	0	194.2	850	204	123	113	30	5	11	10	66	2	113	7	0	6	14	.300	2	0-0	0	5.22
1997 Det-Sea	AL	28	18	1	3	110.2	516	132	82	78	18	2	4	6	55	2	73	7	0	5	11	.313	1	0-0	1	6.34
1998 Seattle	AL	7	0	0	3	15.2	75	22	10	8	5	0	1	0	5	0	16	1	0	1	0	1.000	0	0-0	1	4.60
1999 Detroit	AL	2	0	0	0	3.1	20	7	5	4	2	0	0	0	2	0	3	0	0	0	0	—	0	0-0	0	10.80
2000 Montreal	NL	53	7	0	8	101.2	468	129	71	61	11	3	9	4	36	6	51	2	1	5	8	.385	0	0-0	2	5.40
2001 Montreal	NL	4	0	0	1	5	28	11	7	7	1	1	0	0	2	0	3	0	0	0	0	—	0	0-0	0	12.60
1997 Detroit	AL	20	15	1	1	92	415	101	61	59	15	2	2	2	45	2	64	7	0	5	7	.417	1	0-0	0	5.77
Seattle	AL	8	3	0	2	18.2	101	31	21	19	3	0	2	4	10	0	9	0	0	0	4	.000	0	0-0	1	9.16
7 ML YEARS		163	79	4	22	577.1	2592	656	372	341	84	15	34	28	222	17	348	22	2	26	46	.361	3	1-3	4	5.32

Mark Little

Bats: R **Throws:** R **Pos:** PH/PR-28; CF-14; LF-13; RF-6   **Ht:** 6'0" **Wt:** 195 **Born:** 7/11/72 **Age:** 29

Year Team	Lg	BATTING																BASERUNNING				PERCENTAGES		
		G	AB	H	2B	3B	HR	(Hm	Rd)	TB	R	RBI	TBB	IBB	SO	HBP	SH	SF	SB	CS	SB%	GDP	Avg	OBP	SLG
1994 Hudson Val	A-	54	208	61	15	5	3	—	—	95	33	27	22	1	38	1	0	4	14	5	.74	4	.293	.357	.457
1995 Charlotte	A+	115	438	112	31	8	9	—	—	186	75	50	51	1	108	14	2	2	20	14	.59	4	.256	.350	.425
1996 Tulsa	AA	101	409	119	24	2	13	—	—	186	69	50	48	0	88	10	5	3	22	10	.69	5	.291	.377	.455
1997 Okla City	AAA	121	415	109	23	4	15	—	—	185	72	45	39	1	100	8	8	0	21	9	.70	8	.263	.338	.446
1998 Oklahoma	AAA	69	274	81	20	4	8	—	—	133	58	46	16	0	60	10	0	5	9	6	.60	8	.296	.351	.485
Memphis	AAA	19	63	17	3	3	0	—	—	26	9	6	6	1	10	2	0	2	0	3	.00	0	.270	.342	.413
1999 Memphis	AAA	51	196	58	11	5	3	—	—	88	40	22	10	1	48	6	1	1	12	5	.71	3	.296	.347	.449
2000 Memphis	AAA	107	424	120	29	7	15	—	—	208	70	64	51	1	98	11	1	2	22	11	.67	2	.283	.373	.491
2001 Colo Sprngs	AAA	9	40	15	2	0	0	—	—	17	6	4	3	0	9	1	0	0	5	2	.71	0	.375	.432	.425
1998 St. Louis	NL	7	12	1	0	0	0	(0	0)	1	0	0	2	0	5	0	1	0	1	0	1.00	1	.083	.214	.083
2001 Colorado	NL	51	85	29	6	0	3	(3	0)	44	18	13	1	1	20	4	0	0	5	2	.71	0	.341	.378	.518
2 ML YEARS		58	97	30	6	0	3	(3	0)	45	18	13	3	1	25	4	1	0	6	2	.75	0	.309	.356	.464

Graeme Lloyd

Pitches: Left **Bats:** Left **Pos:** RP-84   **Ht:** 6'7" **Wt:** 225 **Born:** 4/9/67 **Age:** 35

Year Team	Lg	HOW MUCH HE PITCHED						WHAT HE GAVE UP												THE RESULTS					
		G	GS	CG	GF	IP	BFP	H	R	ER	HR	SH	SF	HB	TBB	IBB	SO	WP	Bk	W	L	Pct.	ShO	Sv-Op	Hld	ERA
1993 Milwaukee	AL	55	0	0	12	63.2	269	64	24	20	5	1	2	3	13	3	31	4	0	3	4	.429	0	0-4	6	2.83
1994 Milwaukee	AL	43	0	0	21	47	203	49	28	27	4	1	2	3	15	6	31	2	0	2	3	.400	0	3-6	3	5.17
1995 Milwaukee	AL	33	0	0	14	32	127	28	16	16	4	1	4	0	8	2	13	3	0	0	5	.000	0	4-6	9	4.50
1996 Mil-NYY	AL	65	0	0	15	56.2	252	61	30	27	4	5	3	1	22	4	30	4	0	2	6	.250	0	0-5	17	4.29
1997 New York	AL	46	0	0	17	49	217	55	24	18	6	3	5	1	20	7	26	3	0	1	1	.500	0	1-1	2	3.31
1998 New York	AL	50	0	0	8	37.2	145	26	10	7	3	0	1	2	6	2	20	2	0	3	0	1.000	0	0-2	9	1.67
1999 Toronto	AL	74	0	0	25	72	301	68	36	29	11	1	1	4	23	4	47	1	0	5	3	.625	0	3-9	22	3.63
2001 Montreal	NL	84	0	0	28	70.1	303	74	38	34	6	2	2	6	21	2	44	1	0	9	5	.643	0	1-3	11	4.35
1996 Milwaukee	AL	52	0	0	15	51	217	49	19	16	3	5	1	1	17	3	24	0	0	2	4	.333	0	0-3	15	2.82
New York	AL	13	0	0	0	5.2	35	12	11	11	1	0	2	0	5	1	6	4	0	0	2	.000	0	0-2	2	17.47
8 ML YEARS		450	0	0	140	428.1	1817	425	206	178	43	14	20	20	128	30	242	20	0	25	27	.481	0	12-36	79	3.74

128

Esteban Loaiza

Pitches: Right **Bats:** Right **Pos:** SP-30; RP-6   **Ht:** 6'3" **Wt:** 210 **Born:** 12/31/71 **Age:** 30

		HOW MUCH HE PITCHED						WHAT HE GAVE UP										THE RESULTS						
Year Team	Lg	G	GS	CG	GF	IP	BFP	H	R	ER	HR	SH	SF	HB	TBB	IBB	SO	WP	Bk	W	L	Pct.	ShO	Sv-Op	Hld	ERA
1995 Pittsburgh	NL	32	31	1	0	172.2	762	205	115	99	21	10	9	5	55	3	85	6	1	8	9	.471	0	0-0	0	5.16
1996 Pittsburgh	NL	10	10	1	0	52.2	236	65	32	29	11	3	1	2	19	2	32	0	2	2	3	.400	1	0-0	0	4.96
1997 Pittsburgh	NL	33	32	1	0	196.1	851	214	99	90	17	10	7	12	56	9	122	2	3	11	11	.500	0	0-0	0	4.13
1998 Pit-Tex		35	28	1	3	171	751	199	107	98	28	7	12	5	52	4	108	4	2	9	11	.450	0	0-1	0	5.16
1999 Texas	AL	30	15	0	4	120.1	517	128	65	61	10	7	4	0	40	2	77	2	0	9	5	.643	0	0-0	0	4.56
2000 Tex-Tor	AL	34	31	1	2	199.1	871	228	112	101	29	4	5	13	57	1	137	1	0	10	13	.435	1	1-1	0	4.56
2001 Toronto	AL	36	30	1	1	190	837	239	113	106	27	6	4	9	60	1	110	1	1	11	11	.500	1	0-0	0	5.02
1998 Pittsburgh	NL	21	14	0	3	91.2	394	96	50	46	13	5	7	3	30	1	53	1	2	6	5	.545	0	0-1	0	4.52
Texas	AL	14	14	1	0	79.1	357	103	57	52	15	2	5	2	22	3	55	3	0	3	6	.333	0	0-0	0	5.90
2000 Texas	AL	20	17	0	2	107.1	480	133	67	64	21	2	4	3	31	1	75	1	0	5	6	.455	0	1-1	0	5.37
Toronto	AL	14	14	1	0	92	391	95	45	37	8	2	1	10	26	0	62	0	0	5	7	.417	1	0-0	0	3.62
7 ML YEARS		210	177	6	10	1102.1	4825	1278	643	584	143	47	42	46	319	22	671	16	7	60	63	.488	3	1-2	0	4.77

Keith Lockhart

Bats: Left **Throws:** Right **Pos:** PH/PR-63; 2B-47; 3B-4   **Ht:** 5'10" **Wt:** 170 **Born:** 11/10/64 **Age:** 37

		BATTING																		BASERUNNING				PERCENTAGES		
Year Team	Lg	G	AB	H	2B	3B	HR	(Hm	Rd)	TB	R	RBI	TBB	IBB	SO	HBP	SH	SF	SB	CS	SB%	GDP	Avg	OBP	SLG
1994 San Diego	NL	27	43	9	0	0	2	(2	0)	15	4	6	4	0	10	1	1	1	1	0	1.00	2	.209	.286	.349
1995 Kansas City	AL	94	274	88	19	3	6	(3	3)	131	41	33	14	2	21	4	1	7	8	1	.89	2	.321	.355	.478
1996 Kansas City	AL	138	433	118	33	3	7	(4	3)	178	49	55	30	4	40	2	1	5	11	6	.65	7	.273	.319	.411
1997 Atlanta	NL	96	147	41	5	3	6	(3	3)	70	25	32	14	0	17	1	3	4	0	0	—	4	.279	.337	.476
1998 Atlanta	NL	109	366	94	21	0	9	(4	5)	142	50	37	29	0	37	1	2	3	2	2	.50	2	.257	.311	.388
1999 Atlanta	NL	108	161	42	3	1	1	(0	1)	50	20	21	19	0	21	1	0	3	3	1	.75	2	.261	.337	.311
2000 Atlanta	NL	113	275	73	12	3	2	(1	1)	97	32	32	29	7	31	0	5	4	4	1	.80	10	.265	.331	.353
2001 Atlanta	NL	104	178	39	6	0	3	(0	3)	54	17	12	16	1	22	2	2	1	1	2	.33	1	.219	.289	.303
8 ML YEARS		789	1877	504	99	13	36	(17	19)	737	238	228	155	14	199	12	15	28	30	13	.70	30	.269	.324	.393

Paul Lo Duca

Bats: R **Throws:** R **Pos:** C-99; 1B-33; PH/PR-7; LF-4; DH-1; RF-1   **Ht:** 5'10" **Wt:** 185 **Born:** 4/12/72 **Age:** 30

		BATTING																		BASERUNNING				PERCENTAGES		
Year Team	Lg	G	AB	H	2B	3B	HR	(Hm	Rd)	TB	R	RBI	TBB	IBB	SO	HBP	SH	SF	SB	CS	SB%	GDP	Avg	OBP	SLG
2001 Las Vegas *	AAA	3	9	3	2	0	0	—	—	5	3	3	1	0	0	0	0	0	0	0	—	0	.333	.400	.556
1998 Los Angeles	NL	6	14	4	1	0	0	(0	0)	5	2	1	0	0	1	0	0	0	0	0	—	0	.286	.286	.357
1999 Los Angeles	NL	36	95	22	1	0	3	(1	2)	32	11	11	10	4	9	2	1	2	1	2	.33	3	.232	.312	.337
2000 Los Angeles	NL	34	65	16	2	0	2	(0	2)	24	6	8	6	0	8	0	2	0	0	2	.00	2	.246	.301	.369
2001 Los Angeles	NL	125	460	147	28	0	25	(11	14)	250	71	90	39	2	30	6	5	9	2	4	.33	11	.320	.374	.543
4 ML YEARS		201	634	189	32	0	30	(12	18)	311	90	110	55	6	48	8	8	13	3	8	.27	16	.298	.355	.491

Carlton Loewer

Pitches: Right **Bats:** Right **Pos:** SP-2   **Ht:** 6'6" **Wt:** 211 **Born:** 9/24/73 **Age:** 28

		HOW MUCH HE PITCHED						WHAT HE GAVE UP											THE RESULTS						
Year Team	Lg	G	GS	CG	GF	IP	BFP	H	R	ER	HR	SH	SF	HB	TBB	IBB	SO	WP	Bk	W	L	Pct.	ShO	Sv-Op	Hld	ERA
2001 Lk Elsinore *	A+	4	4	0	0	11.1	47	6	7	2	0	0	0	1	4	0	14	0	0	0	1	.000	0	0--	—	1.59
Portland *	AAA	14	12	0	0	81.1	341	97	42	35	7	2	1	4	15	0	64	1	0	5	4	.556	0	0--	—	3.87
1998 Philadelphia	NL	21	21	1	0	122.2	549	154	86	83	18	5	8	3	39	1	58	4	0	7	8	.467	0	0-0	0	6.09
1999 Philadelphia	NL	20	13	2	2	89.2	385	100	54	51	9	5	6	0	26	0	48	3	0	2	6	.250	1	0-0	1	5.12
2001 San Diego	NL	2	2	0	0	4.1	29	13	12	12	2	1	0	0	3	0	1	0	0	0	2	.000	0	0-0	0	24.92
3 ML YEARS		43	36	3	2	216.2	963	267	152	146	29	11	14	3	68	1	107	7	0	9	16	.360	1	0-0	1	6.06

James Lofton

Bats: Both **Throws:** Right **Pos:** SS-7; PH/PR-2   **Ht:** 5'9" **Wt:** 170 **Born:** 3/6/74 **Age:** 28

		BATTING																		BASERUNNING				PERCENTAGES		
Year Team	Lg	G	AB	H	2B	3B	HR	(Hm	Rd)	TB	R	RBI	TBB	IBB	SO	HBP	SH	SF	SB	CS	SB%	GDP	Avg	OBP	SLG
1993 Princeton	R+	50	174	39	4	2	1	—	—	50	26	13	19	0	41	0	6	3	11	5	.69	2	.224	.296	.287
1994 Billings	R+	66	282	91	11	10	4	—	—	134	64	47	26	0	46	1	4	3	18	5	.78	2	.323	.378	.475
1995 Winston-Sal	A+	38	123	27	5	1	0	—	—	34	15	14	8	1	22	1	2	0	1	4	.20	0	.220	.273	.276
Chstn-WV	A	65	192	40	10	1	0	—	—	52	20	14	18	1	43	3	2	0	8	5	.62	2	.208	.286	.271
1996 Winston-Sal	A+	82	277	62	9	0	3	—	—	80	27	33	27	1	55	1	5	2	14	8	.64	7	.224	.293	.289
1997 Burlington	A	129	483	128	18	3	4	—	—	164	83	45	54	1	89	4	9	3	20	12	.63	9	.265	.342	.340
1998 Tri-City	IND	89	394	112	20	3	3	—	—	147	69	34	22	1	64	0	8	1	33	14	.70	5	.284	.321	.373
1999 Tri-City	IND	87	353	105	13	3	2	—	—	130	66	48	24	0	40	0	12	3	25	11	.69	4	.297	.339	.368
2000 Tri-City	IND	90	389	118	20	4	7	—	—	167	67	52	32	1	52	1	3	3	44	12	.79	4	.303	.355	.429
Nashua	IND	22	87	21	6	0	3	—	—	36	17	12	10	0	19	1	3	0	2	1	.67	0	.241	.327	.414
2001 Sonoma Cty	IND	12	52	11	2	0	0	—	—	13	10	2	6	0	11	1	0	0	1	0	1.00	1	.212	.305	.250
Trenton	AA	29	111	35	7	0	5	—	—	57	22	11	10	0	23	1	1	0	3	1	.75	0	.315	.377	.514
Pawtucket	AAA	42	151	48	8	0	6	—	—	74	19	13	10	1	29	0	3	0	3	3	.50	4	.318	.360	.490
2001 Boston	AL	8	26	5	1	0	0	(0	0)	6	1	1	1	0	4	0	0	1	2	1	.67	1	.192	.214	.231

Kenny Lofton

Bats: Left **Throws:** Left **Pos:** CF-130; PH/PR-6 **Ht:** 6'0" **Wt:** 190 **Born:** 5/31/67 **Age:** 35

Year Team	Lg	G	AB	H	2B	3B	HR	(Hm	Rd)	TB	R	RBI	TBB	IBB	SO	HBP	SH	SF	SB	CS	SB%	GDP	Avg	OBP	SLG
1991 Houston	NL	20	74	15	1	0	0	(0	0)	16	9	0	5	0	19	0	0	0	2	1	.67	0	.203	.253	.216
1992 Cleveland	AL	148	576	164	15	8	5	(3	2)	210	96	42	68	3	54	2	4	1	66	12	.85	7	.285	.362	.365
1993 Cleveland	AL	148	569	185	28	8	1	(1	0)	232	116	42	81	6	83	1	2	4	70	14	.83	8	.325	.408	.408
1994 Cleveland	AL	112	459	160	32	9	12	(10	2)	246	105	57	52	5	56	2	4	6	60	12	.83	5	.349	.412	.536
1995 Cleveland	AL	118	481	149	22	13	7	(5	2)	218	93	53	40	6	49	1	4	3	54	15	.78	6	.310	.362	.453
1996 Cleveland	AL	154	662	210	35	4	14	(7	7)	295	132	67	61	3	82	0	7	6	75	17	.82	7	.317	.372	.446
1997 Atlanta	NL	122	493	164	20	6	5	(3	2)	211	90	48	64	5	83	2	2	3	27	20	.57	10	.333	.409	.428
1998 Cleveland	AL	154	600	169	31	6	12	(6	6)	248	101	64	87	1	80	2	3	6	54	10	.84	7	.282	.371	.413
1999 Cleveland	AL	120	465	140	28	6	7	(1	6)	201	110	39	79	2	84	6	5	5	25	6	.81	6	.301	.405	.432
2000 Cleveland	AL	137	543	151	23	5	15	(10	5)	229	107	73	79	3	72	4	6	8	30	7	.81	11	.278	.369	.422
2001 Cleveland	AL	133	517	135	21	4	14	(9	5)	206	91	66	47	1	69	2	5	5	16	8	.67	5	.261	.322	.398
11 ML YEARS		1366	5439	1642	256	69	92	(55	37)	2312	1050	551	663	35	731	22	42	47	479	122	.80	75	.302	.377	.425

Kyle Lohse

Pitches: Right **Bats:** Right **Pos:** SP-16; RP-3 **Ht:** 6'2" **Wt:** 190 **Born:** 10/4/78 **Age:** 23

		HOW MUCH HE PITCHED						WHAT HE GAVE UP										THE RESULTS					
Year Team	Lg	G	GS	CG	GF	IP	BFP	H	R	ER	HR	SH	SF	HB	TBB	IBB	SO	WP	Bk	W	L	Pct.	ShO	Sv-Op	Hld	ERA
1997 Cubs	R	12	11	0	0	47.2	210	46	22	16	0	1	1	1	22	0	49	3	0	2	2	.500	0	0--	—	3.02
1998 Rockford	A	28	26	3	1	170.2	712	158	76	61	8	8	5	11	45	1	121	13	1	13	8	.619	1	0--	—	3.22
1999 Daytona	A+	9	9	1	0	53	217	48	21	17	4	2	1	0	16	0	41	1	0	5	3	.625	1	0--	—	2.89
Fort Myers	A+	7	7	0	0	41.2	180	47	28	24	5	2	4	4	9	0	33	1	0	2	3	.400	0	0--	—	5.18
New Britain	AA	11	11	1	0	70.1	311	87	49	46	9	3	4	5	23	0	41	2	0	3	4	.429	0	0--	—	5.89
2000 New Britain	AA	28	28	0	0	167	744	196	123	112	23	5	6	3	55	0	124	6	0	3	18	.143	0	0--	—	6.04
2001 New Britain	AA	6	6	0	0	38	145	32	10	10	5	0	0	2	4	0	32	0	0	3	1	.750	0	0--	—	2.37
Edmonton	AAA	8	8	1	0	49	208	50	21	17	3	0	0	4	13	0	48	3	0	4	2	.667	1	0--	—	3.12
2001 Minnesota	AL	19	16	0	2	90.1	402	102	60	57	16	1	5	8	29	0	64	5	0	4	7	.364	0	0-0	0	5.68

Rich Loiselle

Pitches: Right **Bats:** Right **Pos:** RP-18 **Ht:** 6'5" **Wt:** 253 **Born:** 1/12/72 **Age:** 30

		HOW MUCH HE PITCHED						WHAT HE GAVE UP										THE RESULTS					
Year Team	Lg	G	GS	CG	GF	IP	BFP	H	R	ER	HR	SH	SF	HB	TBB	IBB	SO	WP	Bk	W	L	Pct.	ShO	Sv-Op	Hld	ERA
2001 Nashville *	AAA	26	1	0	12	33.2	157	33	24	23	2	3	0	6	23	3	18	3	0	0	2	.000	0	0--	—	6.15
1996 Pittsburgh	NL	5	3	0	0	20.2	90	22	8	7	3	0	0	0	8	1	9	3	0	1	0	1.000	0	0-0	1	3.05
1997 Pittsburgh	NL	72	0	0	58	72.2	312	76	29	25	7	2	2	1	24	3	66	4	0	1	5	.167	0	29-34	5	3.10
1998 Pittsburgh	NL	54	0	0	43	55	258	56	26	21	2	5	1	2	36	9	48	0	0	2	7	.222	0	19-27	1	3.44
1999 Pittsburgh	NL	13	0	0	6	15.1	69	16	9	9	2	1	0	2	9	2	14	1	0	3	2	.600	0	0-1	3	5.28
2000 Pittsburgh	NL	40	0	0	13	42.1	203	43	27	24	5	3	3	3	30	5	32	1	0	2	3	.400	0	0-6	7	5.10
2001 Pittsburgh	NL	18	0	0	9	18	101	28	24	23	3	2	0	4	17	4	9	3	0	0	1	.000	0	1-1	1	11.50
6 ML YEARS		202	3	0	129	224	1033	241	123	109	22	13	6	12	124	24	178	12	0	9	18	.333	0	49-69	18	4.38

Terrence Long

Bats: L **Throws:** L **Pos:** CF-74; LF-62; RF-28; PH/PR-3 **Ht:** 6'1" **Wt:** 190 **Born:** 2/29/76 **Age:** 26

Year Team	Lg	G	AB	H	2B	3B	HR	(Hm	Rd)	TB	R	RBI	TBB	IBB	SO	HBP	SH	SF	SB	CS	SB%	GDP	Avg	OBP	SLG
1999 New York	NL	3	3	0	0	0	0	(0	0)	0	0	0	0	0	2	0	0	0	0	0	—	1	.000	.000	.000
2000 Oakland	AL	138	584	168	34	4	18	(9	9)	264	104	80	43	1	77	1	0	3	5	0	1.00	18	.288	.336	.452
2001 Oakland	AL	162	629	178	37	4	12	(6	6)	259	90	85	52	8	103	0	0	6	9	3	.75	17	.283	.335	.412
3 ML YEARS		303	1216	346	71	8	30	(15	15)	523	194	165	95	9	182	1	0	9	14	3	.82	36	.285	.335	.430

Braden Looper

Pitches: Right **Bats:** Right **Pos:** RP-71 **Ht:** 6'5" **Wt:** 225 **Born:** 10/28/74 **Age:** 27

		HOW MUCH HE PITCHED						WHAT HE GAVE UP										THE RESULTS					
Year Team	Lg	G	GS	CG	GF	IP	BFP	H	R	ER	HR	SH	SF	HB	TBB	IBB	SO	WP	Bk	W	L	Pct.	ShO	Sv-Op	Hld	ERA
1998 St. Louis	NL	4	0	0	3	3.1	16	5	4	2	1	0	1	0	1	0	4	1	0	0	0	.000	0	0-2	0	5.40
1999 Florida	NL	72	0	0	22	83	370	96	43	35	7	5	5	1	31	6	50	2	2	3	3	.500	0	0-4	8	3.80
2000 Florida	NL	73	0	0	23	67.1	311	71	41	33	3	3	2	5	36	6	29	5	0	5	1	.833	0	2-5	18	4.41
2001 Florida	NL	71	0	0	21	71	295	63	28	28	8	0	3	2	30	3	52	0	0	3	3	.500	0	3-6	16	3.55
4 ML YEARS		220	0	0	69	224.2	992	235	116	98	19	8	11	8	98	15	135	8	2	11	8	.579	0	5-17	42	3.93

Albie Lopez

Pitches: Right **Bats:** Right **Pos:** SP-33 **Ht:** 6'2" **Wt:** 240 **Born:** 8/18/71 **Age:** 30

		HOW MUCH HE PITCHED						WHAT HE GAVE UP										THE RESULTS					
Year Team	Lg	G	GS	CG	GF	IP	BFP	H	R	ER	HR	SH	SF	HB	TBB	IBB	SO	WP	Bk	W	L	Pct.	ShO	Sv-Op	Hld	ERA
1993 Cleveland	AL	9	9	0	0	49.2	222	49	34	33	7	1	1	1	32	1	25	0	0	3	1	.750	0	0-0	0	5.98
1994 Cleveland	AL	4	4	1	0	17	76	20	11	8	3	0	0	1	6	0	18	3	0	1	2	.333	1	0-0	0	4.24
1995 Cleveland	AL	6	2	0	0	23	92	17	8	8	4	0	1	1	7	1	22	2	0	0	0	—	0	0-0	0	3.13
1996 Cleveland	AL	13	10	0	0	62	282	80	47	44	14	0	1	2	22	1	45	2	0	5	4	.556	0	0-0	0	6.39
1997 Cleveland	AL	37	6	0	10	76.2	364	101	61	59	11	3	2	4	40	9	63	5	0	3	7	.300	0	0-1	4	6.93
1998 Tampa Bay	AL	54	0	0	12	79.2	335	73	31	23	7	4	3	3	32	4	62	5	0	7	4	.636	0	1-5	4	2.60
1999 Tampa Bay	AL	51	0	0	14	64	281	66	40	33	8	1	4	1	24	2	37	3	0	3	2	.600	0	1-3	12	4.64
2000 Tampa Bay	AL	45	24	4	10	185.1	798	199	95	85	24	6	3	1	70	3	96	4	1	11	13	.458	1	2-4	1	4.13
2001 TB-Ari		33	33	3	0	205.2	896	226	123	110	26	8	6	4	75	3	136	2	1	9	19	.321	3	0-0	0	4.81
2001 Tampa Bay	AL	20	20	1	0	124.2	567	152	87	74	16	5	3	4	51	1	67	1	0	5	12	.294	1	0-0	0	5.34
Arizona	NL	13	13	2	0	81	329	74	36	36	10	3	2	0	24	2	69	1	0	4	7	.364	2	0-0	0	4.00
9 ML YEARS		252	88	8	46	763	3346	831	450	403	104	23	20	18	308	24	504	26	2	42	52	.447	5	4-13	21	4.75

Felipe Lopez

Bats: Both **Throws:** Right **Pos:** 3B-47; SS-3   **Ht:** 6'1" **Wt:** 175 **Born:** 5/12/80 **Age:** 22

Year Team	Lg	G	AB	H	2B	3B	HR	(Hm	Rd)	TB	R	RBI	TBB	IBB	SO	HBP	SH	SF	SB	CS	SB%	GDP	Avg	OBP	SLG
1998 St.Cathrnes	A-	19	83	31	5	2	1	—	—	43	14	11	3	0	14	0	0	0	4	2	.67	1	.373	.395	.518
Dunedin	A+	4	13	5	0	1	1	—	—	10	3	1	0	0	3	0	0	0	0	0	—	0	.385	.385	.769
1999 Hagerstown	A	134	537	149	27	4	14	—	—	226	87	80	61	0	157	3	0	6	21	14	.60	7	.277	.351	.421
2000 Tennessee	AA	127	463	119	18	4	9	—	—	172	52	41	31	0	110	1	8	3	12	11	.52	6	.257	.303	.371
2001 Tennessee	AA	19	72	16	2	1	2	—	—	26	12	4	9	0	23	0	0	0	4	4	.50	1	.222	.309	.361
Syracuse	AAA	89	358	100	19	7	16	—	—	181	65	44	30	4	94	3	2	4	13	5	.72	5	.279	.337	.506
2001 Toronto	AL	49	177	46	5	4	5	(3	2)	74	21	23	12	1	39	0	1	2	4	3	.57	2	.260	.304	.418

Javy Lopez

Bats: Right **Throws:** Right **Pos:** C-127; PH/PR-10   **Ht:** 6'3" **Wt:** 200 **Born:** 11/5/70 **Age:** 31

Year Team	Lg	G	AB	H	2B	3B	HR	(Hm	Rd)	TB	R	RBI	TBB	IBB	SO	HBP	SH	SF	SB	CS	SB%	GDP	Avg	OBP	SLG
1992 Atlanta	NL	9	16	6	2	0	0	(0	0)	8	3	2	0	0	1	0	0	0	0	0	—	0	.375	.375	.500
1993 Atlanta	NL	8	16	6	1	1	1	(0	1)	12	1	2	0	0	2	1	0	0	0	0	—	0	.375	.412	.750
1994 Atlanta	NL	80	277	68	9	0	13	(4	9)	116	27	35	17	0	61	5	2	2	0	2	.00	12	.245	.299	.419
1995 Atlanta	NL	100	333	105	11	4	14	(8	6)	166	37	51	14	0	57	2	0	3	0	1	.00	13	.315	.344	.498
1996 Atlanta	NL	138	489	138	19	1	23	(10	13)	228	56	69	28	5	84	3	1	5	1	6	.14	17	.282	.322	.466
1997 Atlanta	NL	123	414	122	28	1	23	(11	12)	221	52	68	40	10	82	5	1	4	1	1	.50	9	.295	.361	.534
1998 Atlanta	NL	133	489	139	21	1	34	(18	16)	264	73	106	30	1	85	6	1	8	5	3	.63	22	.284	.328	.540
1999 Atlanta	NL	65	246	78	18	1	11	(1	10)	131	34	45	20	2	41	3	0	0	0	3	.00	6	.317	.375	.533
2000 Atlanta	NL	134	481	138	21	1	24	(12	12)	233	60	89	35	3	80	4	0	5	0	0	—	20	.287	.337	.484
2001 Atlanta	NL	128	438	117	16	1	17	(10	7)	186	45	66	28	3	82	10	1	5	1	0	1.00	12	.267	.322	.425
10 ML YEARS		918	3199	917	146	11	160	(74	86)	1565	388	533	212	24	575	39	6	32	8	16	.33	111	.287	.335	.489

Luis Lopez

Bats: B **Throws:** R **Pos:** 3B-46; PH/PR-28; SS-17; 2B-15   **Ht:** 5'11" **Wt:** 166 **Born:** 9/4/70 **Age:** 31

Year Team	Lg	G	AB	H	2B	3B	HR	(Hm	Rd)	TB	R	RBI	TBB	IBB	SO	HBP	SH	SF	SB	CS	SB%	GDP	Avg	OBP	SLG
1993 San Diego	NL	17	43	5	1	0	0	(0	0)	6	1	1	0	0	8	0	0	1	0	0	—	0	.116	.114	.140
1994 San Diego	NL	77	235	65	16	1	2	(2	0)	89	29	20	15	2	39	3	2	1	3	2	.60	7	.277	.325	.379
1996 San Diego	NL	63	139	25	3	0	2	(1	1)	34	10	11	9	1	35	1	1	1	0	0	—	7	.180	.233	.245
1997 New York	NL	78	178	48	12	1	1	(1	0)	65	19	19	12	2	42	4	2	0	2	4	.33	2	.270	.330	.365
1998 New York	NL	117	266	67	13	2	2	(1	1)	90	37	22	20	3	60	4	3	2	2	2	.50	10	.252	.312	.338
1999 New York	NL	68	104	22	4	0	2	(1	1)	32	11	13	12	0	33	3	1	1	1	1	.50	1	.212	.308	.308
2000 Milwaukee	NL	78	201	53	14	0	6	(3	3)	85	24	27	9	1	35	5	8	2	1	2	.33	2	.264	.309	.423
2001 Milwaukee	NL	92	222	60	8	3	4	(2	2)	86	22	18	14	2	44	5	5	1	0	1	.00	6	.270	.326	.387
8 ML YEARS		590	1388	345	71	7	19	(11	8)	487	153	131	91	11	296	25	22	10	9	12	.43	35	.249	.304	.351

Luis Lopez

Bats: R **Throws:** R **Pos:** 3B-28; PH/PR-10; 1B-5; DH-4   **Ht:** 6'0" **Wt:** 205 **Born:** 10/5/73 **Age:** 28

Year Team	Lg	G	AB	H	2B	3B	HR	(Hm	Rd)	TB	R	RBI	TBB	IBB	SO	HBP	SH	SF	SB	CS	SB%	GDP	Avg	OBP	SLG
1995 Ogden	R+	46	182	65	15	0	7	—	—	101	36	39	16	0	20	2	3	2	1	1	.50	5	.357	.411	.555
1996 St.Cathrnes	A-	74	260	74	17	2	7	—	—	116	36	40	27	1	31	7	4	3	2	3	.40	4	.285	.364	.446
1997 Hagerstown	A	136	503	180	47	4	11	—	—	268	96	99	60	4	45	8	0	6	5	8	.38	14	.358	.430	.533
1998 Syracuse	AAA	11	41	9	0	0	1	—	—	12	6	3	6	0	6	0	0	1	0	0	—	2	.220	.313	.293
Knoxville	AA	119	450	141	27	1	15	—	—	215	70	85	58	3	55	3	0	8	0	2	.00	18	.313	.389	.478
1999 Syracuse	AAA	136	531	171	35	2	4	—	—	222	76	69	40	2	58	1	2	8	1	0	1.00	22	.322	.366	.418
2000 Syracuse	AAA	130	491	161	27	1	7	—	—	211	64	79	48	1	33	2	0	8	3	1	.75	10	.328	.384	.430
2001 Syracuse	AAA	87	339	110	26	2	10	—	—	170	57	73	39	7	31	2	0	6	1	1	.50	9	.324	.391	.501
2001 Toronto	AL	41	119	29	4	0	3	(2	1)	42	10	10	8	1	16	0	1	0	0	0	—	10	.244	.291	.353

Mendy Lopez

Bats: R **Throws:** R **Pos:** 2B-12; PH/PR-12; 3B-6; SS-6   **Ht:** 6'2" **Wt:** 190 **Born:** 10/15/74 **Age:** 27

Year Team	Lg	G	AB	H	2B	3B	HR	(Hm	Rd)	TB	R	RBI	TBB	IBB	SO	HBP	SH	SF	SB	CS	SB%	GDP	Avg	OBP	SLG
2001 New Orleans *	AAA	63	208	58	11	1	14	—	—	113	37	36	18	0	49	3	0	1	2	2	.50	5	.279	.343	.543
1998 Kansas City	AL	74	206	50	10	2	1	(1	0)	67	18	15	12	0	40	1	5	1	5	2	.71	6	.243	.286	.325
1999 Kansas City	AL	7	20	8	0	1	0	(0	0)	10	2	3	0	0	5	1	0	0	0	0	—	0	.400	.429	.500
2000 Florida	NL	4	3	0	0	0	0	(0	0)	0	0	0	1	0	1	0	0	0	0	0	—	0	.000	.250	.000
2001 Hou-Pit	NL	32	58	14	3	1	1	(0	1)	22	8	7	6	1	20	1	0	1	0	0	—	0	.241	.318	.379
2001 Houston	NL	10	15	4	0	0	1	(0	1)	7	3	3	2	0	4	1	0	0	0	0	—	0	.267	.389	.467
Pittsburgh	NL	22	43	10	3	1	0	(0	0)	15	5	4	4	1	16	0	0	1	0	0	—	0	.233	.292	.349
4 ML YEARS		117	287	72	13	4	2	(1	1)	99	28	25	19	1	66	3	5	2	5	2	.71	6	.251	.302	.345

Mark Loretta

Bats: R **Throws:** R **Pos:** 2B-52; 3B-39; SS-9; DH-4; PH/PR-2; P-1   **Ht:** 6'0" **Wt:** 180 **Born:** 8/14/71 **Age:** 30

Year Team	Lg	G	AB	H	2B	3B	HR	(Hm	Rd)	TB	R	RBI	TBB	IBB	SO	HBP	SH	SF	SB	CS	SB%	GDP	Avg	OBP	SLG
2001 Indianapols *	AAA	8	31	3	0	0	0	—	—	3	4	1	2	0	4	0	0	0	0	0	—	1	.097	.152	.097
1995 Milwaukee	AL	19	50	13	3	0	1	(0	1)	19	13	3	4	0	7	1	1	0	1	1	.50	1	.260	.327	.380
1996 Milwaukee	AL	73	154	43	3	0	1	(0	1)	49	20	13	14	0	15	0	2	0	2	1	.67	7	.279	.339	.318
1997 Milwaukee	AL	132	418	120	17	5	5	(2	3)	162	56	47	47	2	60	2	5	10	5	5	.50	15	.287	.354	.388
1998 Milwaukee	NL	140	434	137	29	0	6	(3	3)	184	55	54	42	1	47	7	4	4	9	6	.60	14	.316	.382	.424
1999 Milwaukee	NL	153	587	170	34	5	5	(2	3)	229	93	67	52	1	59	10	9	6	4	1	.80	14	.290	.354	.390

Year Team	Lg	G	AB	H	2B	3B	HR	(Hm	Rd)	TB	R	RBI	TBB	IBB	SO	HBP	SH	SF	SB	CS	SB%	GDP	Avg	OBP	SLG
2000 Milwaukee	NL	91	352	99	21	1	7	(3	4)	143	49	40	37	2	38	1	8	1	0	3	.00	9	.281	.350	.406
2001 Milwaukee	NL	102	384	111	14	2	2	(0	2)	135	40	29	28	0	46	7	7	3	1	2	.33	6	.289	.346	.352
7 ML YEARS		710	2379	693	121	13	27	(10	17)	921	326	253	224	6	272	28	36	24	22	19	.54	66	.291	.356	.387

Derek Lowe

Pitches: Right **Bats:** Right **Pos:** RP-64; SP-3   **Ht:** 6'6" **Wt:** 200 **Born:** 6/1/73 **Age:** 29

Year Team	Lg	G	GS	CG	GF	IP	BFP	H	R	ER	HR	SH	SF	HB	TBB	IBB	SO	WP	Bk	W	L	Pct.	ShO	Sv-Op	Hld	ERA
1997 Sea-Bos	AL	20	9	0	1	69	298	74	49	47	11	4	2	4	23	3	52	2	0	2	6	.250	0	0-2	1	6.13
1998 Boston	AL	63	10	0	8	123	527	126	65	55	5	4	5	4	42	5	77	8	0	3	9	.250	0	4-9	12	4.02
1999 Boston	AL	74	0	0	32	109.1	436	84	35	32	7	1	2	4	25	1	80	1	0	6	3	.667	0	15-20	22	2.63
2000 Boston	AL	74	0	0	64	91.1	379	90	27	26	6	4	1	2	22	5	79	2	1	4	4	.500	0	42-47	0	2.56
2001 Boston	AL	67	3	0	50	91.2	404	103	39	36	7	5	1	5	29	9	82	4	0	5	10	.333	0	24-30	4	3.53
1997 Seattle	AL	12	9	0	1	53	234	59	43	41	11	2	1	2	20	2	39	2	0	2	4	.333	0	0-0	1	6.96
Boston	AL	8	0	0	0	16	64	15	6	6	0	2	1	2	3	1	13	0	0	0	2	.000	0	0-2	1	3.38
5 ML YEARS		298	22	0	155	484.1	2044	477	215	196	36	18	11	19	141	23	370	17	1	20	32	.385	0	85-108	39	3.64

Sean Lowe

Pitches: Right **Bats:** Right **Pos:** RP-34; SP-11   **Ht:** 6'2" **Wt:** 215 **Born:** 3/29/71 **Age:** 31

Year Team	Lg	G	GS	CG	GF	IP	BFP	H	R	ER	HR	SH	SF	HB	TBB	IBB	SO	WP	Bk	W	L	Pct.	ShO	Sv-Op	Hld	ERA
2001 Charlotte *	AAA	2	2	0	0	10	42	9	6	5	0	0	0	1	2	0	8	0	0	1	1	.500	0	0--	—	4.50
1997 St. Louis	NL	6	4	0	1	17.1	89	27	21	18	2	1	2	1	10	0	8	0	0	0	2	.000	0	0-0	0	9.35
1998 St. Louis	NL	4	1	0	2	5.1	31	11	9	9	1	1	0	0	5	0	2	0	0	0	3	.000	0	0-0	0	15.19
1999 Chicago	AL	64	0	0	13	95.2	406	90	39	39	10	3	9	4	46	1	62	4	0	4	1	.800	0	0-3	6	3.67
2000 Chicago	AL	50	5	0	8	70.2	325	78	47	43	10	4	1	6	39	3	53	3	0	4	1	.800	0	0-0	6	5.48
2001 Chicago	AL	45	11	0	9	127	529	123	55	51	12	3	7	7	32	2	71	6	0	9	4	.692	0	3-3	3	3.61
5 ML YEARS		169	21	0	33	316	1380	329	171	160	35	12	19	18	132	6	196	13	0	17	11	.607	0	3-6	15	4.56

Mike Lowell

Bats: Right **Throws:** Right **Pos:** 3B-144; PH/PR-2   **Ht:** 6'4" **Wt:** 205 **Born:** 2/24/74 **Age:** 28

Year Team	Lg	G	AB	H	2B	3B	HR	(Hm	Rd)	TB	R	RBI	TBB	IBB	SO	HBP	SH	SF	SB	CS	SB%	GDP	Avg	OBP	SLG
1998 New York	AL	8	15	4	0	0	0	(0	0)	4	1	0	0	0	1	0	0	0	0	0	—	0	.267	.267	.267
1999 Florida	NL	97	308	78	15	0	12	(7	5)	129	32	47	26	1	69	5	0	5	0	0	—	8	.253	.317	.419
2000 Florida	NL	140	508	137	38	0	22	(11	11)	241	73	91	54	4	75	9	0	11	4	0	1.00	4	.270	.344	.474
2001 Florida	NL	146	551	156	37	0	18	(12	6)	247	65	100	43	3	79	10	0	10	1	2	.33	9	.283	.340	.448
4 ML YEARS		391	1382	375	90	0	52	(30	22)	621	171	238	123	8	224	24	0	26	5	2	.71	21	.271	.336	.449

Julio Lugo

Bats: R **Throws:** R **Pos:** SS-133; PH/PR-8; LF-6; 2B-2; RF-2   **Ht:** 5'10" **Wt:** 165 **Born:** 11/16/75 **Age:** 26

Year Team	Lg	G	AB	H	2B	3B	HR	(Hm	Rd)	TB	R	RBI	TBB	IBB	SO	HBP	SH	SF	SB	CS	SB%	GDP	Avg	OBP	SLG
1995 Auburn	A-	59	230	67	6	3	1	—	—	82	36	16	26	0	31	2	2	0	17	7	.71	7	.291	.368	.357
1996 Quad City	A	101	393	116	18	2	10	—	—	168	60	50	32	0	75	3	4	4	24	11	.69	7	.295	.350	.427
1997 Kissimmee	A+	125	505	135	22	14	7	—	—	206	89	61	46	1	99	2	8	4	35	8	.81	8	.267	.329	.408
1998 Kissimmee	A+	128	509	154	20	14	7	—	—	223	81	62	49	3	72	4	6	2	51	18	.74	13	.303	.367	.438
1999 Jackson	AA	116	445	142	24	5	10	—	—	206	77	42	44	0	53	3	1	4	25	11	.69	6	.319	.381	.463
2000 New Orleans	AAA	24	101	33	4	1	3	—	—	48	22	12	11	0	20	0	2	0	12	7	.63	2	.327	.393	.475
2000 Houston	NL	116	420	119	22	5	10	(6	4)	181	78	40	37	0	93	4	3	1	22	9	.71	9	.283	.346	.431
2001 Houston	NL	140	513	135	20	3	10	(6	4)	191	93	37	46	0	116	5	15	7	12	11	.52	7	.263	.326	.372
2 ML YEARS		256	933	254	42	8	20	(12	8)	372	171	77	83	0	209	9	18	8	34	20	.63	16	.272	.335	.399

Mark Lukasiewicz

Pitches: Left **Bats:** Left **Pos:** RP-24   **Ht:** 6'5" **Wt:** 240 **Born:** 3/8/73 **Age:** 29

Year Team	Lg	G	GS	CG	GF	IP	BFP	H	R	ER	HR	SH	SF	HB	TBB	IBB	SO	WP	Bk	W	L	Pct.	ShO	Sv-Op	Hld	ERA
1994 Hagerstown	A	29	17	0	5	98	449	108	70	52	8	6	4	7	51	0	84	8	0	3	6	.333	0	0--	—	4.78
1995 Dunedin	A+	31	13	0	11	88.1	383	80	62	55	13	1	2	7	42	0	71	7	0	3	6	.333	0	1--	—	5.60
1996 Dunedin	A+	23	0	0	5	31.1	144	28	20	16	1	1	1	4	22	1	31	1	0	2	1	.667	0	1--	—	4.60
Bakersfield	A+	7	0	0	3	12.2	66	17	14	13	2	1	0	1	11	0	9	1	0	0	2	.000	0	0--	—	9.24
Hagerstown	A	9	1	0	4	15.2	63	8	5	4	0	0	0	1	7	0	20	1	0	0	0	—	0	0--	—	2.30
1997 Knoxville	AA	27	0	0	8	37	149	26	17	15	2	1	1	1	14	1	43	4	0	2	0	1.000	0	7--	—	3.65
Syracuse	AAA	30	0	0	9	31.1	146	37	22	18	7	1	2	2	13	1	31	1	0	2	3	.400	0	0--	—	5.17
1998 Dunedin	A+	9	0	0	1	10.2	42	7	2	1	0	0	1	0	4	0	8	0	0	1	1	.500	0	0--	—	0.84
Knoxville	AA	5	0	0	2	9.1	33	6	2	2	0	0	0	1	0	16	0	0	0	0	—	0	1--	—	1.93
Syracuse	AAA	22	4	0	3	47.2	201	38	18	18	8	0	0	3	24	1	30	3	0	2	2	.500	0	1--	—	3.40
1999 Syracuse	AAA	37	9	1	6	97.2	431	109	59	58	20	1	2	0	40	1	77	5	1	4	4	.500	0	3--	—	5.34
2000 Tennessee	AA	3	0	0	1	4.2	22	4	3	3	1	0	0	0	4	0	6	0	0	0	0	—	0	0--	—	5.79
Syracuse	AAA	42	0	0	12	41.1	176	34	17	16	7	2	0	0	25	1	52	3	0	2	1	.667	0	0--	—	3.48
2001 Salt Lake	AAA	20	0	0	8	30.1	105	12	5	5	4	0	0	0	2	0	41	0	0	3	0	1.000	0	2--	—	1.48
2001 Anaheim	AL	24	0	0	11	22.1	98	21	17	15	6	1	1	2	9	2	25	2	0	0	2	.000	0	0-0	0	6.04

Fernando Lunar

Bats: Right **Throws:** Right **Pos:** C-64; PH/PR-2   **Ht:** 6'1" **Wt:** 190 **Born:** 5/25/77 **Age:** 25

							BATTING											BASERUNNING				PERCENTAGES		
Year Team	Lg	G	AB	H	2B	3B	HR	(Hm | Rd)	TB	R	RBI	TBB	IBB	SO	HBP	SH	SF	SB	CS	SB%	GDP	Avg	OBP	SLG
1994 Braves	R	33	100	24	5	0	2	—	—	35	9	12	1	0	13	3	1	1	0	0	—	1	.240	.267	.350
1995 Macon	A	39	134	24	2	0	0	—	—	26	13	9	10	0	38	3	3	0	1	0	1.00	3	.179	.252	.194
Eugene	A-	38	131	32	6	0	2	—	—	44	13	16	9	0	28	0	2	0	1	1	.00	2	.244	.293	.336
1996 Macon	A	104	343	63	9	0	7	—	—	93	33	33	20	0	65	12	3	2	3	2	.60	1	.184	.252	.271
1997 Macon	A	105	380	99	26	2	7	—	—	150	41	37	18	1	42	5	2	1	0	1	.00	11	.261	.302	.395
1998 Danville	A+	91	286	63	9	0	3	—	—	81	19	28	6	0	52	12	2	0	1	1	.50	8	.220	.266	.283
1999 Greenville	AA	105	343	77	15	1	3	—	—	103	33	35	12	5	64	12	0	0	0	1	.00	7	.224	.275	.300
2000 Greenville	AA	31	102	17	3	0	0	—	—	20	6	4	8	0	15	0	0	0	0	0	—	2	.167	.227	.196
Bowie	AA	22	80	23	7	1	0	—	—	32	12	8	6	0	8	3	0	0	0	0	—	2	.288	.360	.400
2000 Atl-Bal	AL	31	70	12	1	0	0	(0 | 0)	13	5	6	3	1	19	4	0	0	0	2	.00	2	.171	.247	.186
2001 Baltimore	AL	64	167	41	7	0	0	(0 | 0)	48	8	16	7	0	32	3	2	1	0	0	—	8	.246	.287	.287
2000 Atlanta	NL	22	54	10	1	0	0	(0 | 0)	11	5	5	3	1	15	3	0	0	0	2	.00	2	.185	.267	.204
Baltimore	AL	9	16	2	0	0	0	(0 | 0)	2	0	1	0	0	4	1	0	0	0	0	—	0	.125	.176	.125
2 ML YEARS		95	237	53	8	0	0	(0 | 0)	61	13	22	10	1	51	7	2	1	0	2	.00	10	.224	.275	.257

David Lundquist

Pitches: Right **Bats:** Right **Pos:** RP-17   **Ht:** 6'2" **Wt:** 200 **Born:** 6/4/73 **Age:** 29

		HOW MUCH HE PITCHED						WHAT HE GAVE UP									THE RESULTS						
Year Team	Lg	G	GS	CG	GF	IP	BFP	H	R	ER	HR	SH	SF	HB	TBB	IBB	SO	WP	Bk	W	L	Pct.	ShO	Sv-Op	Hld	ERA
1993 White Sox	R	11	10	0	0	63	267	70	26	22	0	1	1	4	15	0	40	2	2	5	3	.625	0	0- —	—	3.14
1994 Hickory	A	27	27	3	0	178.2	759	170	88	69	15	4	3	12	43	0	133	8	2	13	10	.565	2	0- —	—	3.48
1995 South Bend	A	18	18	5	0	118	492	107	54	47	4	7	3	5	38	0	60	3	0	8	4	.667	1	0- —	—	3.58
1996 White Sox	R	3	3	0	0	13.2	49	8	4	4	1	0	0	0	2	0	16	0	0	1	1	.500	0	0- —	—	2.63
Pr William	A+	5	5	0	0	27	125	31	17	17	2	1	0	1	14	1	23	2	1	0	2	.000	0	0- —	—	5.67
1997 Winston-Sal	A+	20	6	0	6	48	228	65	41	36	7	1	2	3	23	3	39	2	2	3	1	.750	0	0- —	—	6.75
Birmingham	AA	7	0	0	5	13.1	73	26	20	13	3	0	1	0	5	0	15	0	0	0	0	—	0	0- —	—	8.78
1998 Winston-Sal	A+	6	0	0	2	10.2	42	9	4	3	0	1	0	0	3	0	9	0	0	1	0	1.000	0	0- —	—	2.53
Birmingham	AA	33	0	0	21	41	165	28	15	15	1	2	1	2	15	1	41	1	0	1	1	.500	0	10- —	—	3.29
Calgary	AAA	12	0	0	8	15	64	12	6	6	0	0	2	1	7	0	12	1	0	3	0	1.000	0	2- —	—	3.60
1999 Charlotte	AAA	3	0	0	1	3.2	14	3	0	0	0	0	0	0	1	0	4	1	0	0	0	—	0	0- —	—	0.00
2000 Aberdeen	IND	21	0	0	8	41.2	213	69	49	42	11	0	2	4	17	3	32	5	0	4	3	.571	0	0- —	—	9.07
2001 Portland	AAA	50	0	0	22	63.2	266	59	25	22	6	3	2	1	20	0	67	3	0	4	7	.364	0	7- —	—	3.11
1999 Chicago	AL	17	0	0	7	22	106	28	21	21	3	2	1	1	12	0	18	0	0	1	1	.500	0	0-0	0	8.59
2001 San Diego	NL	17	0	0	9	19.2	86	20	13	13	1	0	1	1	7	1	19	2	1	0	1	.000	0	0-1	0	5.95
2 ML YEARS		34	0	0	16	41.2	192	48	34	34	4	2	2	2	19	1	37	2	1	1	2	.333	0	0-1	0	7.34

Brandon Lyon

Pitches: Right **Bats:** Right **Pos:** SP-11   **Ht:** 6'1" **Wt:** 170 **Born:** 8/10/79 **Age:** 22

		HOW MUCH HE PITCHED						WHAT HE GAVE UP									THE RESULTS						
Year Team	Lg	G	GS	CG	GF	IP	BFP	H	R	ER	HR	SH	SF	HB	TBB	IBB	SO	WP	Bk	W	L	Pct.	ShO	Sv-Op	Hld	ERA
2000 Queens	A-	15	13	0	0	60.1	230	43	20	16	1	2	2	2	6	0	55	1	1	5	3	.625	0	0- —	—	2.39
2001 Tennessee	AA	9	9	0	0	58.2	241	57	25	24	7	2	1	3	9	0	45	1	0	5	0	1.000	0	0- —	—	3.68
Syracuse	AAA	11	11	2	0	68.1	279	68	33	28	7	1	2	1	10	0	53	0	0	5	3	.625	0	0- —	—	3.69
2001 Toronto	AL	11	11	0	0	63	261	63	31	30	6	2	6	1	15	0	35	0	1	5	4	.556	0	0-0	0	4.29

John Mabry

Bats: L **Throws:** R **Pos:** PH/PR-50; RF-36; 1B-3; LF-3; CF-2; DH-1; P-1   **Ht:** 6'4" **Wt:** 210 **Born:** 10/17/70 **Age:** 31

							BATTING											BASERUNNING				PERCENTAGES		
Year Team	Lg	G	AB	H	2B	3B	HR	(Hm	Rd)	TB	R	RBI	TBB	IBB	SO	HBP	SH	SF	SB	CS	SB%	GDP	Avg	OBP	SLG
2001 Brevard Cty *	A+	4	13	2	0	0	0	—	—	2	0	4	2	0	1	0	0	1	0	0	—	0	.154	.250	.154
1994 St. Louis	NL	6	23	7	3	0	0	(0	0)	10	2	3	2	0	4	0	0	0	0	0	—	0	.304	.360	.435
1995 St. Louis	NL	129	388	119	21	1	5	(2	3)	157	35	41	24	5	45	2	0	4	0	3	.00	6	.307	.347	.405
1996 St. Louis	NL	151	543	161	30	2	13	(3	10)	234	63	74	37	11	84	3	3	5	3	2	.60	21	.297	.342	.431
1997 St. Louis	NL	116	388	110	19	0	5	(5	0)	144	40	36	39	9	77	3	4	2	1	0	1.00	11	.284	.352	.371
1998 St. Louis	AL	142	377	94	22	0	9	(4	5)	143	41	46	30	6	76	1	3	2	0	2	.00	6	.249	.305	.379
1999 St. Louis	AL	87	262	64	14	0	9	(4	5)	105	34	33	20	1	60	0	2	1	2	1	.67	6	.244	.297	.401
2001 StL-Fla	NL	87	154	32	7	0	6	(2	4)	57	14	20	13	1	46	5	0	2	1	0	1.00	6	.208	.287	.370
2000 Seattle	AL	48	103	25	5	0	1	(0	1)	33	18	7	10	0	31	2	0	1	1	0	1.00	1	.243	.322	.320
San Diego	NL	48	123	28	8	0	3	(3	4)	57	17	25	5	0	38	0	0	1	0	0	—	3	.228	.256	.463
2001 St. Louis	NL	5	7	0	0	0	0	(0	0)	0	0	0	0	0	2	0	0	0	0	0	—	0	.000	.000	.000
Florida	NL	82	147	32	7	0	6	(2	4)	57	14	20	13	1	44	5	0	2	1	0	1.00	6	.218	.299	.388
8 ML YEARS		814	2361	640	129	3	55	(24	31)	940	264	285	180	33	461	16	10	17	6	10	.38	60	.271	.325	.398

Mike MacDougal

Pitches: Right **Bats:** Right **Pos:** SP-3   **Ht:** 6'4" **Wt:** 195 **Born:** 3/5/77 **Age:** 25

		HOW MUCH HE PITCHED						WHAT HE GAVE UP									THE RESULTS						
Year Team	Lg	G	GS	CG	GF	IP	BFP	H	R	ER	HR	SH	SF	HB	TBB	IBB	SO	WP	Bk	W	L	Pct.	ShO	Sv-Op	Hld	ERA
1999 Spokane	A-	11	11	0	0	46.1	196	43	25	23	3	1	1	6	17	0	57	8	1	2	2	.500	0	0- —	—	4.47
2000 Wilmington	A+	26	25	0	1	144.2	620	115	79	63	5	5	1	14	76	0	129	21	4	9	7	.563	0	1- —	—	3.92
Wichita	AA	2	2	0	0	11.2	54	16	10	10	0	0	1	1	7	0	9	1	0	0	0	—	0	0- —	—	7.71
2001 Omaha	AAA	28	27	1	0	144.1	649	144	90	75	13	3	2	11	76	0	110	15	2	8	8	.500	0	0- —	—	4.68
2001 Kansas City	AL	3	3	0	0	15.1	67	18	10	8	2	0	1	1	4	0	7	3	0	1	1	.500	0	0-0	0	4.70

Robert Machado

Bats: Right **Throws:** Right **Pos:** C-47; PH/PR-8   **Ht:** 6'1" **Wt:** 205 **Born:** 6/3/73 **Age:** 29

Year Team	Lg	G	AB	H	2B	3B	HR	(Hm	Rd)	TB	R	RBI	TBB	IBB	SO	HBP	SH	SF	SB	CS	SB%	GDP	Avg	OBP	SLG
2001 Iowa *	AAA	53	180	51	11	0	8			86	20	30	11	2	36	2	2	0	0	0	—	5	.283	.332	.478
1996 Chicago	AL	4	6	4	1	0	0	(0	0)	5	1	2	0	0	0	0	0	0	0	0	—	1	.667	.667	.833
1997 Chicago	AL	10	15	3	0	1	0	(0	0)	5	1	2	1	0	6	0	1	0	0	0	—	0	.200	.250	.333
1998 Chicago	AL	34	111	23	6	0	3	(2	1)	38	14	15	7	0	22	0	3	0	0	0	—	3	.207	.254	.342
1999 Montreal	NL	17	22	4	1	0	0	(0	0)	5	3	0	2	0	6	0	0	0	0	0	—	0	.182	.250	.227
2000 Seattle	AL	8	14	3	0	0	1	(1	0)	6	2	1	1	0	4	0	0	0	0	0	—	0	.214	.267	.429
2001 Chicago	NL	52	135	30	10	0	2	(2	0)	46	13	13	7	3	26	1	0	0	0	0	—	4	.222	.266	.341
6 ML YEARS		125	303	67	18	1	6	(5	1)	105	34	33	18	3	64	1	7	0	0	0	—	8	.221	.267	.347

Jose Macias

Bats: B **Throws:** R **Pos:** 3B-89; CF-22; 2B-18; PH/PR-12; RF-4; LF-3; DH-2   **Ht:** 5'10" **Wt:** 173 **Born:** 1/25/74 **Age:** 28

Year Team	Lg	G	AB	H	2B	3B	HR	(Hm	Rd)	TB	R	RBI	TBB	IBB	SO	HBP	SH	SF	SB	CS	SB%	GDP	Avg	OBP	SLG
1999 Detroit	AL	5	4	1	0	0	1	(1	0)	4	2	2	0	0	1	0	0	0	0	0	—	0	.250	.250	1.000
2000 Detroit	AL	73	173	44	3	5	2	(2	0)	63	25	24	18	0	24	1	4	0	2	0	1.00	3	.254	.328	.364
2001 Detroit	AL	137	488	131	24	6	8	(7	1)	191	62	51	32	0	54	3	8	3	21	6	.78	7	.268	.316	.391
3 ML YEARS		215	665	176	27	11	11	(10	1)	258	89	77	50	0	79	4	12	3	23	6	.79	10	.265	.319	.388

Rob Mackowiak

Bats: L **Throws:** R **Pos:** RF-40; PH/PR-24; 2B-21; LF-10; 3B-2; 1B-1   **Ht:** 5'10" **Wt:** 168 **Born:** 6/20/76 **Age:** 26

Year Team	Lg	G	AB	H	2B	3B	HR	(Hm	Rd)	TB	R	RBI	TBB	IBB	SO	HBP	SH	SF	SB	CS	SB%	GDP	Avg	OBP	SLG
1996 Pirates	R	27	86	23	6	1	0	—	—	31	8	14	13	1	11	1	0	1	3	1	.75	3	.267	.366	.360
1997 Erie	A-	61	203	58	14	2	1	—	—	79	26	25	21	0	47	7	3	1	1	7	.13	5	.286	.371	.389
1998 Augusta	A	25	70	17	4	0	1	—	—	24	16	8	13	0	19	1	1	0	4	2	.67	2	.243	.369	.343
Lynchburg	A+	86	292	80	24	6	3	—	—	125	30	31	17	0	65	4	4	2	6	3	.67	4	.274	.321	.428
1999 Lynchburg	A+	74	263	80	7	4	7	—	—	116	51	30	18	0	57	6	4	0	9	4	.69	5	.304	.362	.441
Altoona	AA	53	195	51	15	3	3	—	—	81	21	27	8	1	34	7	2	4	0	2	.00	6	.262	.308	.415
2000 Altoona	AA	134	526	156	33	4	13	—	—	236	82	87	22	0	96	9	4	7	18	5	.78	8	.297	.332	.449
2001 Nashville	AAA	32	118	31	5	0	4	—	—	48	14	14	7	0	39	0	2	1	1	1	.50	0	.263	.302	.407
2001 Pittsburgh	NL	83	214	57	15	2	4	(3	1)	88	30	21	15	5	52	3	2	3	4	3	.57	3	.266	.319	.411

Scott MacRae

Pitches: Right **Bats:** Right **Pos:** RP-24   **Ht:** 6'3" **Wt:** 205 **Born:** 8/13/74 **Age:** 27

Year Team	Lg	G	GS	CG	GF	IP	BFP	H	R	ER	HR	SH	SF	HB	TBB	IBB	SO	WP	Bk	W	L	Pct.	ShO	Sv-Op	Hld	ERA
1995 Billings	R+	18	0	0	4	27	135	32	24	17	0	0	5	3	20	4	9	2	1	0	1	.000	0	1- -	—	5.67
1996 Chstn-WV	A	29	20	1	2	123.2	530	118	61	46	3	4	3	7	53	0	82	8	0	8	7	.533	0	0- -	—	3.35
1997 Burlington	A	27	26	4	0	160.1	694	159	76	68	9	7	4	9	57	0	89	18	1	11	4	.733	1	0- -	—	3.82
1998 Chattanooga	AA	49	5	0	6	113.2	492	105	70	56	5	3	2	3	56	2	67	10	0	9	4	.692	0	0- -	—	4.43
1999 Chattanooga	AA	39	17	0	2	128.1	555	139	76	63	18	3	2	5	49	1	81	6	0	8	7	.533	0	0- -	—	4.42
2000 Chattanooga	AA	55	0	0	17	77.2	339	75	32	31	4	8	1	5	40	9	61	4	0	4	1	.800	0	1- -	—	3.59
2001 Chattanooga	AA	19	8	1	3	58.2	248	60	29	24	4	3	1	0	14	0	42	2	0	5	2	.714	0	0- -	—	3.68
Louisville	AAA	11	0	0	3	22	83	14	5	3	1	1	0	1	6	2	15	0	0	2	2	.500	0	2- -	—	1.23
2001 Cincinnati	NL	24	0	0	7	31.1	136	33	15	14	0	0	2	2	8	0	18	1	0	0	1	.000	0	0-0	1	4.02

Greg Maddux

Pitches: Right **Bats:** Right **Pos:** SP-34   **Ht:** 6'0" **Wt:** 185 **Born:** 4/14/66 **Age:** 36

Year Team	Lg	G	GS	CG	GF	IP	BFP	H	R	ER	HR	SH	SF	HB	TBB	IBB	SO	WP	Bk	W	L	Pct.	ShO	Sv-Op	Hld	ERA
1986 Chicago	NL	6	5	1	0	31	144	44	20	19	3	1	0	1	11	2	20	2	0	2	4	.333	0	0-0	0	5.52
1987 Chicago	NL	30	27	1	2	155.2	701	181	111	97	17	7	1	4	74	13	101	4	7	6	14	.300	0	0-0	0	5.61
1988 Chicago	NL	34	34	9	0	249	1047	230	97	88	13	11	2	9	81	16	140	3	6	18	8	.692	3	0-0	0	3.18
1989 Chicago	NL	35	35	7	0	238.1	1002	222	90	78	13	18	6	6	82	13	135	5	3	19	12	.613	1	0-0	0	2.95
1990 Chicago	NL	35	35	8	0	237	1011	242	116	91	11	18	5	4	71	10	144	3	3	15	15	.500	2	0-0	0	3.46
1991 Chicago	NL	37	37	7	0	263	1070	232	113	98	18	16	3	6	66	9	198	6	3	15	11	.577	2	0-0	0	3.35
1992 Chicago	NL	35	35	9	0	268	1061	201	68	65	7	15	3	14	70	7	199	5	0	20	11	.645	4	0-0	0	2.18
1993 Atlanta	NL	36	36	8	0	267	1064	228	85	70	14	15	7	6	52	7	197	5	1	20	10	.667	1	0-0	0	2.36
1994 Atlanta	NL	25	25	10	0	202	774	150	44	35	4	6	5	6	31	3	156	3	1	16	6	.727	3	0-0	0	1.56
1995 Atlanta	NL	28	28	10	0	209.2	785	147	39	38	8	9	1	4	23	3	181	1	0	19	2	.905	3	0-0	0	1.63
1996 Atlanta	NL	35	35	5	0	245	978	225	85	74	11	8	5	3	28	11	172	4	0	15	11	.577	1	0-0	0	2.72
1997 Atlanta	NL	33	33	5	0	232.2	893	200	58	57	9	11	7	6	20	6	177	0	0	19	4	.826	2	0-0	0	2.20
1998 Atlanta	NL	34	34	9	0	251	987	201	75	62	13	15	5	7	45	10	204	4	0	18	9	.667	5	0-0	0	2.22
1999 Atlanta	NL	33	33	4	0	219.1	940	258	103	87	16	15	5	4	37	8	136	1	0	19	9	.679	0	0-0	0	3.57
2000 Atlanta	NL	35	35	6	0	249.1	1012	225	91	83	19	8	5	10	42	12	190	1	2	19	9	.679	3	0-0	0	3.00
2001 Atlanta	NL	34	34	3	0	233	927	220	86	79	20	12	11	7	27	10	173	2	0	17	11	.607	3	0-0	0	3.05
16 ML YEARS		505	501	102	3	3551	14396	3206	1281	1121	196	185	71	97	760	140	2523	49	26	257	146	.638	34	0-0	0	2.84

Calvin Maduro

Pitches: Right **Bats:** Right **Pos:** SP-12; RP-10   **Ht:** 6'0" **Wt:** 180 **Born:** 9/5/74 **Age:** 27

Year Team	Lg	G	GS	CG	GF	IP	BFP	H	R	ER	HR	SH	SF	HB	TBB	IBB	SO	WP	Bk	W	L	Pct.	ShO	Sv-Op	Hld	ERA
2001 Rochester *	AAA	12	11	1	0	67	286	61	37	30	9	2	2	4	22	0	48	4	0	2	7	.222	0	0- -	—	4.03
1996 Philadelphia	NL	4	2	0	0	15.1	62	13	6	6	1	1	0	2	3	0	11	1	0	0	1	.000	0	0-0	0	3.52
1997 Philadelphia	NL	15	13	0	0	71	331	83	59	57	12	1	4	3	41	5	31	6	2	3	7	.300	0	0-0	0	7.23

		HOW	MUCH	HE	PITCHED			WHAT	HE	GAVE	UP								THE	RESULTS				
Year Team	Lg	G	GS	CG	GF	IP	BFP	H	R	ER	HR	SH	SF	HB	TBB	IBB	SO	WP	Bk	W	L	Pct.	ShO	Sv-Op	Hld	ERA
2000 Baltimore	AL	15	2	0	6	23.1	113	29	25	25	8	1	2	2	16	1	18	1	0	0	0	—	0	0-0	1	9.64
2001 Baltimore	AL	22	12	0	3	93.2	386	83	44	44	10	0	0	4	36	0	51	1	0	5	6	.455	0	0-0	1	4.23
4 ML YEARS		56	29	0	9	203.1	892	208	134	132	31	3	6	11	96	6	111	9	2	8	14	.364	0	0-0	2	5.84

Dave Magadan

Bats: L **Throws:** R **Pos:** PH/PR-64; 3B-22; 1B-9; DH-2; 2B-1; SS-1   **Ht:** 6'4" **Wt:** 215 **Born:** 9/30/62 **Age:** 39

							BATTING										BASERUNNING				PERCENTAGES		
Year Team	Lg	G	AB	H	2B	3B	HR	(Hm | Rd)	TB	R	RBI	TBB	IBB	SO	HBP	SH	SF	SB	CS	SB%	GDP	Avg	OBP	SLG
1986 New York	NL	10	18	8	0	0	0	(0 | 0)	8	3	3	3	0	1	0	0	0	0	0	—	1	.444	.524	.444
1987 New York	NL	85	192	61	13	1	3	(2 | 1)	85	21	24	22	2	22	0	1	1	0	0	—	5	.318	.386	.443
1988 New York	NL	112	314	87	15	0	1	(1 | 0)	105	39	35	60	4	39	2	1	3	0	1	.00	9	.277	.393	.334
1989 New York	NL	127	374	107	22	3	4	(3 | 1)	147	47	41	49	6	37	1	1	4	1	0	1.00	11	.286	.367	.393
1990 New York	NL	144	451	148	28	6	6	(2 | 4)	206	74	72	74	4	55	2	4	10	2	1	.67	11	.328	.417	.457
1991 New York	NL	124	418	108	23	0	4	(2 | 2)	143	58	51	83	3	50	2	7	7	1	1	.50	5	.258	.378	.342
1992 New York	NL	99	321	91	9	1	3	(2 | 1)	111	33	28	56	3	44	0	2	0	1	0	1.00	6	.283	.390	.346
1993 Fla-Sea		137	455	124	23	0	5	(3 | 2)	162	49	50	80	7	63	1	2	6	2	1	.67	12	.273	.378	.356
1994 Florida	NL	74	211	58	7	0	1	(1 | 0)	68	30	17	39	0	25	1	0	3	0	0	—	8	.275	.386	.322
1995 Houston	NL	127	348	109	24	0	2	(2 | 0)	139	44	51	71	9	56	0	1	2	2	1	.67	9	.313	.428	.399
1996 Chicago	NL	78	169	43	10	0	3	(2 | 1)	62	23	17	29	3	23	0	1	2	0	2	.00	3	.254	.360	.367
1997 Oakland	AL	128	271	82	10	1	4	(2 | 2)	106	38	30	50	1	40	2	4	1	0	1	1.00	4	.303	.414	.391
1998 Oakland	AL	35	109	35	8	0	1	(0 | 1)	46	12	13	13	1	12	0	0	1	0	1	.00	5	.321	.390	.422
1999 San Diego	NL	116	248	68	12	1	2	(1 | 1)	88	20	30	45	2	36	0	0	7	1	3	.25	10	.274	.377	.355
2000 San Diego	NL	95	132	36	7	0	2	(1 | 1)	49	13	21	32	1	23	0	0	2	0	0	—	4	.273	.410	.371
2001 San Diego	NL	91	128	32	7	0	1	(0 | 1)	42	12	12	12	0	20	1	0	1	0	0	—	1	.250	.317	.328
1993 Florida	NL	66	227	65	12	0	4	(3 | 1)	89	22	29	44	4	30	1	0	3	0	1	.00	3	.286	.400	.392
Seattle	AL	71	228	59	11	0	1	(0 | 1)	73	27	21	36	3	33	0	2	3	2	0	1.00	9	.259	.356	.320
16 ML YEARS		1582	4159	1197	218	13	42	(22 | 20)	1567	516	495	718	46	546	12	24	50	11	11	.50	98	.288	.390	.377

Wendell Magee

Bats: R **Throws:** R **Pos:** CF-36; LF-21; RF-19; PH/PR-15; DH-11   **Ht:** 6'0" **Wt:** 220 **Born:** 8/3/72 **Age:** 29

							BATTING										BASERUNNING				PERCENTAGES		
Year Team	Lg	G	AB	H	2B	3B	HR	(Hm | Rd)	TB	R	RBI	TBB	IBB	SO	HBP	SH	SF	SB	CS	SB%	GDP	Avg	OBP	SLG
2001 Toledo *	AAA	2	9	4	0	0	0	—	—	4	0	1	0	0	0	0	0	0	0	0	—	2	.444	.444	.444
1996 Philadelphia	NL	38	142	29	7	0	2	(2 | 0)	42	9	14	9	0	33	0	0	0	0	0	—	2	.204	.252	.296
1997 Philadelphia	NL	38	115	23	4	0	1	(0 | 1)	30	7	9	9	1	20	0	0	2	1	4	.20	4	.200	.254	.261
1998 Philadelphia	NL	20	75	22	6	1	1	(0 | 1)	33	9	11	7	0	11	0	0	0	0	0	—	4	.293	.354	.440
1999 Philadelphia	NL	12	14	5	1	0	2	(1 | 1)	12	4	5	1	0	4	0	0	0	1	0	1.00	7	.357	.400	.857
2000 Detroit	AL	91	186	51	4	2	7	(2 | 5)	80	31	31	10	0	28	0	0	1	1	0	1.00	7	.274	.310	.430
2001 Detroit	AL	90	207	44	11	4	5	(3 | 2)	78	26	17	23	1	44	1	1	4	3	0	1.00	8	.213	.293	.377
6 ML YEARS		289	739	174	33	7	18	(8 | 10)	275	86	87	59	2	140	1	1	4	5	4	.56	30	.235	.291	.372

Mike Magnante

Pitches: Left **Bats:** Left **Pos:** RP-65   **Ht:** 6'1" **Wt:** 185 **Born:** 6/17/65 **Age:** 37

		HOW	MUCH	HE	PITCHED			WHAT	HE	GAVE	UP								THE	RESULTS				
Year Team	Lg	G	GS	CG	GF	IP	BFP	H	R	ER	HR	SH	SF	HB	TBB	IBB	SO	WP	Bk	W	L	Pct.	ShO	Sv-Op	Hld	ERA
1991 Kansas City	AL	38	0	0	10	55	236	55	19	15	3	4	2	1	23	4	42	1	0	0	1	.000	0	0-2	2	2.45
1992 Kansas City	AL	44	12	0	11	89.1	403	115	53	49	5	5	7	2	35	5	31	2	0	4	9	.308	0	0-3	4	4.94
1993 Kansas City	AL	7	6	0	0	35.1	145	37	16	16	3	1	1	1	11	1	16	1	0	1	2	.333	0	0-0	0	4.08
1994 Kansas City	AL	36	1	0	10	47	211	55	27	24	5	2	3	0	16	1	21	3	0	2	3	.400	0	0-0	6	4.60
1995 Kansas City	AL	28	0	0	7	44.2	190	45	23	21	6	2	2	2	16	1	28	2	0	1	1	.500	0	0-1	5	4.23
1996 Kansas City	AL	38	0	0	9	54	238	58	38	34	5	0	4	4	24	1	32	3	0	2	2	.500	0	0-1	5	5.67
1997 Houston	NL	40	0	0	14	47.2	191	39	16	12	2	3	2	0	11	2	43	2	2	3	1	.750	0	1-5	3	2.27
1998 Houston	NL	48	0	0	20	51.2	237	56	28	28	2	3	1	4	26	4	39	3	0	4	7	.364	0	2-4	8	4.88
1999 Anaheim	AL	53	0	0	13	69.1	299	68	30	26	2	0	7	3	29	4	44	3	1	5	2	.714	0	0-3	4	3.38
2000 Oakland	AL	55	0	0	6	39.2	189	50	22	19	3	6	0	4	19	7	17	1	0	1	1	.500	0	0-3	14	4.31
2001 Oakland	AL	65	0	0	10	55.1	223	50	23	17	7	0	4	1	13	3	23	3	0	3	1	.750	0	0-1	18	2.77
11 ML YEARS		452	19	0	110	589	2562	628	295	261	43	24	32	19	223	32	336	24	3	26	30	.464	0	3-21	64	3.99

Chris Magruder

Bats: B **Throws:** R **Pos:** LF-8; PH/PR-7; RF-3; CF-1   **Ht:** 5'11" **Wt:** 200 **Born:** 4/26/77 **Age:** 25

							BATTING										BASERUNNING				PERCENTAGES		
Year Team	Lg	G	AB	H	2B	3B	HR	(Hm | Rd)	TB	R	RBI	TBB	IBB	SO	HBP	SH	SF	SB	CS	SB%	GDP	Avg	OBP	SLG
1998 Bakersfield	A+	22	92	28	7	0	1	—	—	38	21	4	13	1	16	0	0	0	3	0	1.00	2	.304	.390	.413
Salem-Keizr	A-	47	177	59	8	5	3	—	—	86	43	18	37	1	21	8	2	2	14	7	.67	2	.333	.464	.486
1999 Shreveport	AA	133	476	122	21	4	6	—	—	169	78	60	69	4	85	6	4	3	17	12	.59	15	.256	.358	.355
2000 Shreveport	AA	134	496	140	33	3	4	—	—	191	85	39	67	2	75	8	6	3	18	10	.64	11	.282	.375	.385
2001 Shreveport	AA	40	149	38	6	3	2	—	—	56	22	11	15	2	27	3	4	0	5	3	.63	2	.255	.335	.376
Fresno	AAA	54	214	60	7	1	10	—	—	99	37	30	18	0	45	7	0	1	3	1	.75	2	.280	.354	.463
Oklahoma	AAA	33	127	46	14	4	5	—	—	83	28	21	21	3	19	4	4	1	1	2	.33	3	.362	.464	.654
2001 Texas	AL	17	29	5	0	0	0	(0 | 0)	5	3	1	1	0	5	1	0	0	0	0	—	1	.172	.226	.172

Ron Mahay

Pitches: Left **Bats:** Left **Pos:** RP-17   **Ht:** 6'2" **Wt:** 190 **Born:** 6/28/71 **Age:** 31

		HOW	MUCH	HE	PITCHED			WHAT	HE	GAVE	UP								THE	RESULTS				
Year Team	Lg	G	GS	CG	GF	IP	BFP	H	R	ER	HR	SH	SF	HB	TBB	IBB	SO	WP	Bk	W	L	Pct.	ShO	Sv-Op	Hld	ERA
2001 Portland *	AAA	14	0	0	5	16.2	69	13	9	7	2	2	0	0	5	0	18	0	0	1	2	.333	0	0--	—	3.78
Iowa *	AAA	36	0	0	30	46.2	176	29	12	12	5	3	2	2	10	1	52	3	0	3	1	.750	0	14--	—	2.31
1997 Boston	AL	28	0	0	7	25	105	19	7	7	3	1	0	0	11	0	22	3	0	3	0	1.000	0	0-1	5	2.52

Year Team	Lg	G	GS	CG	GF	IP	BFP	H	R	ER	HR	SH	SF	HB	TBB	IBB	SO	WP	Bk	W	L	Pct.	ShO	Sv-Op	Hld	ERA
1998 Boston	AL	29	0	0	6	26	120	26	16	10	2	0	4	2	15	1	14	3	0	1	1	.500	0	1-2	7	3.46
1999 Oakland	AL	6	1	0	2	19.1	68	8	4	4	2	0	0	0	3	0	15	0	0	2	0	1.000	0	1-1	0	1.86
2000 Oak-Fla		23	2	0	7	41.1	199	57	35	33	10	1	2	0	25	1	32	4	0	1	1	.500	0	0-0	2	7.19
2001 Chicago		17	0	0	4	20.2	86	14	6	6	4	0	0	0	15	1	24	1	0	0	0	—	0	0-2	2	2.61
2000 Oakland	AL	5	2	0	1	16	82	26	18	16	4	1	1	0	9	0	5	2	0	0	1	.000	0	0-0		9.00
Florida	NL	18	0	0	6	25.1	117	31	17	17	6	0	1	0	16	1	27	2	0	1	0	1.000	0	0-0	2	6.04
5 ML YEARS		103	3	0	26	132.1	578	124	68	60	21	2	6	2	69	3	107	11	0	7	2	.778	0	2-4	16	4.08

Pat Mahomes

Pitches: Right **Bats:** Right **Pos:** RP-52; SP-4 **Ht:** 6'4" **Wt:** 212 **Born:** 8/9/70 **Age:** 31

Year Team	Lg	G	GS	CG	GF	IP	BFP	H	R	ER	HR	SH	SF	HB	TBB	IBB	SO	WP	Bk	W	L	Pct.	ShO	Sv-Op	Hld	ERA
1992 Minnesota	AL	14	13	0	1	69.2	302	73	41	39	5	0	3	0	37	0	44	2	1	3	4	.429	0	0-0	0	5.04
1993 Minnesota	AL	12	5	0	4	37.1	173	47	34	32	8	1	3	1	16	0	23	3	0	1	5	.167	0	0-0	0	7.71
1994 Minnesota	AL	21	21	0	0	120	517	121	68	63	22	1	4	1	62	1	53	3	0	9	5	.643	0	0-0	0	4.73
1995 Minnesota	AL	47	7	0	16	94.2	423	100	74	67	22	3	2	2	47	1	67	6	0	4	10	.286	0	3-7	9	6.37
1996 Min-Bos	AL	31	5	0	10	57.1	271	72	46	44	13	2	2	0	33	0	36	2	0	3	4	.429	0	2-2	4	6.91
1997 Boston	AL	10	0	0	2	10	54	15	10	9	2	0	1	2	10	1	5	1	0	1	0	1.000	0	0-0	1	8.10
1999 New York	NL	39	0	0	12	63.2	265	44	26	26	7	1	2	2	37	5	51	2	0	8	0	1.000	0	0-1	1	3.68
2000 New York	NL	53	5	0	12	94	439	96	63	57	15	3	3	2	66	4	76	5	0	5	3	.625	0	0-1	5	5.46
2001 Texas	AL	56	4	0	14	107.1	475	115	71	68	17	2	7	0	55	9	61	3	0	7	6	.538	0	0-1	6	5.70
1996 Minnesota	AL	20	5	0	5	45	220	63	38	36	10	0	2	0	27	0	30	2	0	1	4	.200	0	0-0	3	7.20
Boston		11	0	0	5	12.1	51	9	8	8	3	2	0	0	6	0	6	0	0	2	0	1.000	0	2-2	1	5.84
9 ML YEARS		283	60	0	71	654	2919	683	433	405	111	13	27	10	363	21	416	27	1	41	37	.526	0	5-12	24	5.57

Jim Mann

Pitches: Right **Bats:** Right **Pos:** RP-4 **Ht:** 6'3" **Wt:** 225 **Born:** 11/17/74 **Age:** 27

Year Team	Lg	G	GS	CG	GF	IP	BFP	H	R	ER	HR	SH	SF	HB	TBB	IBB	SO	WP	Bk	W	L	Pct.	ShO	Sv-Op	Hld	ERA
1994 Blue Jays	R	11	9	0	0	53	236	54	28	22	1	3	1	3	26	1	41	0	1	3	2	.600	0	0--	—	3.74
1995 Medcine Hat	R+	14	14	1	0	77.2	347	78	47	37	5	3	2	7	37	0	66	6	0	5	4	.556	1	0--	—	4.29
1996 St.Cathrnes	A-	26	0	0	23	27.1	117	22	12	11	3	2	2	3	10	1	37	0	1	2	1	.667	0	17--	—	3.62
1997 Hagerstown	A	19	0	0	16	26.2	122	35	18	15	4	0	1	1	11	0	30	2	0	1	0	1.000	0	4--	—	5.06
Dunedin	A+	12	0	0	4	18	88	27	12	12	2	0	1	1	6	1	13	1	0	1	0	1.000	0	0--	—	6.00
1998 Dunedin	A+	51	0	0	47	50.1	206	31	19	17	4	0	2	0	24	1	59	2	0	2	0	.000	0	25--	—	3.04
1999 Knoxville	AA	6	0	0	4	9.2	39	6	2	1	1	3	1	2	1	0	12	0	0	1	2	.333	0	0--	—	0.93
Syracuse	AAA	47	0	0	20	66	287	53	35	34	11	1	1	2	39	1	72	6	0	6	5	.545	0	5--	—	4.64
2000 Norfolk	AAA	49	0	0	19	81.2	326	61	27	27	8	3	2	2	33	3	74	3	1	3	4	.429	0	3--	—	2.98
2001 New Orleans	AAA	53	0	0	50	68	272	52	21	19	7	5	2	2	17	2	81	4	0	6	3	.667	0	27--	—	2.51
2000 New York	NL	2	0	0	2	2.2	15	6	3	3	1	0	0	0	1	0	0	0	0	0	0	—	0	0-0	0	10.13
2001 Houston	NL	4	0	0	1	5.1	23	3	2	2	0	0	0	2	4	0	5	0	0	0	0	—	0	0-0	0	3.38
2 ML YEARS		6	0	0	3	8	38	9	5	5	1	0	0	2	5	0	5	0	0	0	0	—	0	0-0	0	5.63

Matt Mantei

Pitches: Right **Bats:** Right **Pos:** RP-8 **Ht:** 6'1" **Wt:** 200 **Born:** 7/7/73 **Age:** 28

Year Team	Lg	G	GS	CG	GF	IP	BFP	H	R	ER	HR	SH	SF	HB	TBB	IBB	SO	WP	Bk	W	L	Pct.	ShO	Sv-Op	Hld	ERA
1995 Florida	NL	12	0	0	3	13.1	64	12	8	7	1	1	1	0	13	0	15	1	0	0	1	.000	0	0-0	0	4.73
1996 Florida	NL	14	0	0	1	18.1	89	13	13	13	2	1	0	1	21	1	25	2	0	1	0	1.000	0	0-1	0	6.38
1998 Florida	NL	42	0	0	23	54.2	224	38	19	18	1	3	4	7	23	3	63	0	0	3	4	.429	0	9-12	2	2.96
1999 Fla-Ari	NL	65	0	0	60	65.1	284	44	21	20	5	1	1	5	44	1	99	2	0	1	3	.250	0	32-37	0	2.76
2000 Arizona	NL	47	0	0	38	45.1	200	31	24	23	4	2	0	2	35	1	53	5	0	1	1	.500	0	17-20	0	4.57
2001 Arizona	NL	8	0	0	7	7	31	6	2	2	0	0	0	4	0	0	12	2	0	0	0	—	0	2-2	1	2.57
1999 Florida	NL	35	0	0	32	36.1	157	24	11	11	4	0	1	2	25	1	50	0	0	1	2	.333	0	10-12	0	2.72
Arizona	NL	30	0	0	28	29	127	20	10	9	1	1	0	3	19	0	49	2	0	0	1	.000	0	22-25	0	2.79
6 ML YEARS		188	0	0	132	204	892	144	87	83	15	8	6	15	140	6	267	12	0	6	9	.400	0	60-72	3	3.66

Josias Manzanillo

Pitches: Right **Bats:** Right **Pos:** RP-71 **Ht:** 6'0" **Wt:** 205 **Born:** 10/16/67 **Age:** 34

Year Team	Lg	G	GS	CG	GF	IP	BFP	H	R	ER	HR	SH	SF	HB	TBB	IBB	SO	WP	Bk	W	L	Pct.	ShO	Sv-Op	Hld	ERA
1991 Boston	AL	1	0	0	1	1	8	2	2	2	0	0	0	0	3	0	1	0	0	0	0	—	0	0-0	0	18.00
1993 Mil-NYM		16	1	0	6	29	140	30	27	22	2	3	3	2	19	3	21	1	0	1	1	.500	0	1-2	0	6.83
1994 New York	NL	37	0	0	14	47.1	186	34	15	14	4	0	0	3	13	2	48	2	0	3	2	.600	0	2-5	11	2.66
1995 NYM-NYY		23	0	0	8	33.1	154	37	19	18	4	2	1	2	15	4	25	6	0	1	2	.333	0	0-0	0	4.86
1997 Seattle	AL	16	0	0	4	18.1	88	19	13	11	3	0	2	0	17	1	18	2	0	0	1	.000	0	0-1	1	5.40
1999 New York	NL	12	0	0	1	18.2	80	19	12	12	5	1	1	2	4	1	25	0	0	0	0	—	0	0-0	1	5.79
2000 Pittsburgh	NL	43	0	0	11	58.2	246	50	23	22	6	4	2	0	32	4	39	1	0	2	2	.500	0	0-2	5	3.38
2001 Pittsburgh	NL	71	0	0	25	79.2	329	60	32	30	4	5	8	5	26	3	80	4	0	3	2	.600	0	2-7	9	3.39
1993 Milwaukee	AL	10	1	0	4	17	86	22	20	18	1	2	2	2	10	3	10	1	0	1	1	.500	0	1-2	0	9.53
New York	NL	6	0	0	2	12	54	8	7	4	1	1	1	0	9	0	11	0	0	0	0	—	0	0-0	0	3.00
1995 New York	NL	12	0	0	4	16	73	18	15	14	3	0	1	0	6	2	14	5	0	1	2	.333	0	0-0	0	7.88
New York	AL	11	0	0	4	17.1	81	19	4	4	1	2	0	2	9	2	11	1	0	0	0	—	0	0-0	0	2.08
8 ML YEARS		219	1	0	70	286	1231	251	143	131	28	15	17	14	129	18	257	16	0	10	10	.500	0	5-17	27	4.12

Jason Marquis

Pitches: Right Bats: Left Pos: RP-22; SP-16   Ht: 6'1" Wt: 185 Born: 8/21/78 Age: 23

		HOW MUCH HE PITCHED						WHAT HE GAVE UP												THE RESULTS						
Year Team	Lg	G	GS	CG	GF	IP	BFP	H	R	ER	HR	SH	SF	HB	TBB	IBB	SO	WP	Bk	W	L	Pct.	ShO	Sv-Op	Hld	ERA
1996 Danville	R+	7	4	0	0	23.1	113	30	18	12	0	0	0	1	7	0	24	2	0	1	1	.500	0	0--	—	4.63
1997 Macon	A	28	28	0	0	141.2	627	156	78	69	10	2	7	2	55	1	121	8	2	14	10	.583	0	0--	—	4.38
1998 Danville	A+	22	22	1	0	114.2	500	120	65	62	3	4	3	6	41	0	135	7	0	2	12	.143	0	0--	—	4.87
1999 Myrtle Bch	A+	6	6	0	0	32	134	22	2	1	0	0	1	1	17	0	41	2	0	3	0	1.000	0	0--	—	0.28
Greenville	AA	12	12	1	0	55	248	52	33	28	7	0	1	2	29	0	35	1	0	3	4	.429	0	0--	—	4.58
2000 Greenville	AA	11	11	0	0	68	287	68	35	27	10	1	2	1	23	0	49	2	1	4	2	.667	0	0--	—	3.57
Richmond	AAA	6	6	0	0	20	97	26	21	20	2	1	0	2	13	0	18	7	0	0	3	.000	0	0--	—	9.00
2000 Atlanta	NL	15	0	0	7	23.1	103	23	16	13	4	1	1	1	12	1	17	1	0	1	0	1.000	0	0-1	1	5.01
2001 Atlanta	NL	38	16	0	9	129.1	556	113	62	50	14	6	5	4	59	4	98	1	2	5	6	.455	0	0-2	2	3.48
2 ML YEARS		53	16	0	16	152.2	659	136	78	63	18	7	6	5	71	5	115	2	2	6	6	.500	0	0-3	3	3.71

Eli Marrero

Bats: R Throws: R Pos: C-65; PH/PR-21; LF-8; RF-7; 1B-6   Ht: 6'1" Wt: 180 Born: 11/17/73 Age: 28

		BATTING																	BASERUNNING				PERCENTAGES		
Year Team	Lg	G	AB	H	2B	3B	HR	(Hm	Rd)	TB	R	RBI	TBB	IBB	SO	HBP	SH	SF	SB	CS	SB%	GDP	Avg	OBP	SLG
1997 St. Louis	NL	17	45	11	2	0	2	(0	2)	19	4	7	2	1	13	0	0	1	4	0	1.00	1	.244	.271	.422
1998 St. Louis	NL	83	254	62	18	1	4	(2	2)	94	28	20	28	5	42	0	1	1	6	2	.75	5	.244	.318	.370
1999 St. Louis	NL	114	317	61	13	1	6	(3	3)	94	32	34	18	4	56	1	4	3	11	2	.85	14	.192	.236	.297
2000 St. Louis	NL	53	102	23	3	1	5	(2	3)	43	21	17	9	0	16	3	0	2	5	0	1.00	3	.225	.302	.422
2001 St. Louis	NL	86	203	54	11	3	6	(2	4)	89	37	23	15	2	36	0	3	3	6	3	.67	4	.266	.312	.438
5 ML YEARS		353	921	211	47	6	23	(9	14)	339	122	101	72	12	163	4	8	10	32	7	.82	27	.229	.285	.368

Damaso Marte

Pitches: Left Bats: Left Pos: RP-23   Ht: 6'0" Wt: 170 Born: 2/14/75 Age: 27

		HOW MUCH HE PITCHED						WHAT HE GAVE UP												THE RESULTS						
Year Team	Lg	G	GS	CG	GF	IP	BFP	H	R	ER	HR	SH	SF	HB	TBB	IBB	SO	WP	Bk	W	L	Pct.	ShO	Sv-Op	Hld	ERA
1995 Everett	A-	11	5	0	1	36.2	141	25	11	9	2	1	1	1	10	0	39	3	0	2	2	.500	0	0--	—	2.21
1996 Wisconsin	A	26	26	2	0	142.1	626	134	82	71	8	1	3	6	75	5	115	4	3	8	6	.571	1	0--	—	4.49
1997 Lancaster	A+	25	25	2	0	139.1	609	144	75	64	15	4	4	8	62	1	127	8	4	8	8	.500	1	0--	—	4.13
1998 Orlando	AA	22	20	0	0	121.1	541	136	82	71	14	2	6	2	47	0	99	6	2	7	6	.538	0	0--	—	5.27
1999 Tacoma	AAA	31	11	0	4	73.2	335	79	43	42	13	1	1	2	40	1	59	1	2	3	3	.500	0	0--	—	5.13
2000 Mariners	R	2	2	0	0	5	17	1	0	0	0	0	0	1	0	0	6	0	0	0	0	—	0	0--	—	0.00
New Haven	AA	4	0	0	2	5.2	23	6	1	1	1	0	0	0	2	0	4	0	1	0	0	—	0	0--	—	1.59
2001 Norwich	AA	23	0	0	4	36	147	29	16	14	3	1	2	2	7	0	36	0	1	3	1	.750	0	1--	—	3.50
Nashville	AAA	4	0	0	1	5.1	19	3	2	2	1	0	0	0	4	0	4	0	0	0	0	—	0	0--	—	3.38
1999 Seattle	AL	5	0	0	2	8.2	47	16	9	9	3	0	0	0	6	0	3	0	0	0	1	.000	0	0-0	0	9.35
2001 Pittsburgh	NL	23	0	0	4	36.1	154	34	21	19	5	1	2	3	12	3	39	1	0	0	1	.000	0	0-0	0	4.71
2 ML YEARS		28	0	0	6	45	201	50	30	28	8	1	2	3	18	3	42	1	0	0	2	.000	0	0-0	0	5.60

Al Martin

Bats: L Throws: L Pos: LF-72; DH-16; PH/PR-15; CF-1; RF-1   Ht: 6'2" Wt: 214 Born: 11/24/67 Age: 34

		BATTING																	BASERUNNING				PERCENTAGES		
Year Team	Lg	G	AB	H	2B	3B	HR	(Hm	Rd)	TB	R	RBI	TBB	IBB	SO	HBP	SH	SF	SB	CS	SB%	GDP	Avg	OBP	SLG
1992 Pittsburgh	NL	12	12	2	0	1	0	(0	0)	4	1	2	0	0	5	0	0	1	0	0	—	0	.167	.154	.333
1993 Pittsburgh	NL	143	480	135	26	8	18	(15	3)	231	85	64	42	5	122	1	2	3	16	9	.64	5	.281	.338	.481
1994 Pittsburgh	NL	82	276	79	12	4	9	(6	3)	126	48	33	34	3	56	2	0	1	15	6	.71	3	.286	.367	.457
1995 Pittsburgh	NL	124	439	124	25	3	13	(8	5)	194	70	41	44	6	92	2	1	0	20	11	.65	5	.282	.351	.442
1996 Pittsburgh	NL	155	630	189	40	1	18	(8	10)	285	101	72	54	2	116	2	1	7	38	12	.76	9	.300	.354	.452
1997 Pittsburgh	NL	113	423	123	24	7	13	(8	5)	200	64	59	45	7	83	3	1	5	23	7	.77	7	.291	.359	.473
1998 Pittsburgh	NL	125	440	105	15	2	12	(5	7)	160	57	47	32	2	91	5	0	2	20	3	.87	13	.239	.296	.364
1999 Pittsburgh	NL	143	541	150	36	8	24	(12	12)	274	97	63	49	5	119	1	0	2	20	3	.87	6	.277	.337	.506
2000 SD-Sea		135	480	137	15	10	15	(10	5)	217	81	36	36	5	85	4	0	3	10	9	.53	3	.285	.338	.452
2001 Seattle	AL	100	283	68	15	2	7	(2	5)	108	41	42	37	4	59	2	0	2	9	3	.75	2	.240	.330	.382
2000 San Diego	NL	93	346	106	13	6	11	(8	3)	164	62	27	28	5	54	2	0	2	6	8	.43	2	.306	.360	.474
Seattle	AL	42	134	31	2	4	4	(2	2)	53	19	9	8	0	31	2	0	1	4	1	.80	1	.231	.283	.396
10 ML YEARS		1132	4004	1112	208	46	129	(74	55)	1799	645	459	373	39	828	22	5	26	171	63	.73	55	.278	.341	.449

Tom Martin

Pitches: Left Bats: Left Pos: RP-14   Ht: 6'1" Wt: 200 Born: 5/21/70 Age: 32

		HOW MUCH HE PITCHED						WHAT HE GAVE UP												THE RESULTS						
Year Team	Lg	G	GS	CG	GF	IP	BFP	H	R	ER	HR	SH	SF	HB	TBB	IBB	SO	WP	Bk	W	L	Pct.	ShO	Sv-Op	Hld	ERA
2001 Brooklyn *	A-	1	1	0	0	1	4	2	0	0	0	0	0	0	0	0	0	0	0	0	0	—	0	0--	—	0.00
Norfolk *	AAA	23	0	0	8	23	108	31	17	16	4	0	2	2	10	0	24	1	0	2	1	.667	0	1--	—	6.26
1997 Houston	NL	55	0	0	18	56	236	52	13	13	2	6	1	1	23	2	36	3	0	5	3	.625	0	2-3	7	2.09
1998 Cleveland	AL	14	0	0	1	14.2	85	29	21	21	3	1	1	0	12	0	9	2	0	1	1	.500	0	0-0	3	12.89
1999 Cleveland	AL	6	0	0	0	9.1	44	13	9	9	2	0	1	0	3	1	8	0	0	1	0	1.000	0	0-0	0	8.68
2000 Cleveland	AL	31	0	0	7	33.1	143	32	16	15	3	0	1	0	15	2	21	1	0	1	0	1.000	0	0-0	0	4.05
2001 New York	NL	14	0	0	2	17	85	23	22	19	4	1	1	1	10	2	12	0	0	1	0	1.000	0	0-0	1	10.06
5 ML YEARS		120	0	0	28	130.1	593	149	81	77	14	8	5	3	63	7	86	6	0	8	5	.615	0	2-3	11	5.32

Dave Martinez

Bats: L Throws: L Pos: PH/PR-68; RF-28; LF-27; 1B-10; DH-1   Ht: 5'10" Wt: 175 Born: 9/26/64 Age: 37

		BATTING																	BASERUNNING				PERCENTAGES		
Year Team	Lg	G	AB	H	2B	3B	HR	(Hm	Rd)	TB	R	RBI	TBB	IBB	SO	HBP	SH	SF	SB	CS	SB%	GDP	Avg	OBP	SLG
1986 Chicago	NL	53	108	15	1	1	1	(1	0)	21	13	7	6	0	22	1	0	1	4	2	.67	1	.139	.190	.194

Year Team	Lg	G	AB	H	2B	3B	HR	(Hm	Rd)	TB	R	RBI	TBB	IBB	SO	HBP	SH	SF	SB	CS	SB%	GDP	Avg	OBP	SLG
1987 Chicago	NL	142	459	134	18	8	8	(5	3)	192	70	36	57	4	96	2	1	1	16	8	.67	4	.292	.372	.418
1988 ChC-Mon	NL	138	447	114	13	6	6	(2	4)	157	51	46	38	8	94	2	2	5	23	9	.72	3	.255	.313	.351
1989 Montreal	NL	126	361	99	16	7	3	(1	2)	138	41	27	27	2	57	0	7	1	23	4	.85	1	.274	.324	.382
1990 Montreal	NL	118	391	109	13	5	11	(5	6)	165	60	39	24	2	48	1	3	2	13	11	.54	8	.279	.321	.422
1991 Montreal	NL	124	396	117	18	5	7	(3	4)	166	47	42	20	3	54	3	5	3	16	7	.70	3	.295	.332	.419
1992 Cincinnati	NL	135	393	100	20	5	3	(3	0)	139	47	31	42	4	54	0	6	4	12	8	.60	6	.254	.323	.354
1993 San Francisco	NL	91	241	58	12	1	5	(1	4)	87	28	27	27	3	39	0	0	0	6	3	.67	5	.241	.317	.361
1994 San Francisco	NL	97	235	58	9	3	4	(1	3)	85	23	27	21	1	22	2	2	0	3	4	.43	6	.247	.314	.362
1995 Chicago	AL	119	303	93	16	4	5	(2	3)	132	49	37	32	2	41	1	9	4	8	2	.80	6	.307	.371	.436
1996 Chicago	AL	146	440	140	20	8	10	(3	7)	206	85	53	52	1	52	3	2	1	15	7	.68	4	.318	.393	.468
1997 Chicago	AL	145	504	144	16	6	12	(5	7)	208	78	55	55	7	69	3	5	6	12	6	.67	4	.286	.356	.413
1998 Tampa Bay	AL	90	309	79	11	0	3	(2	1)	99	31	20	35	4	52	2	0	1	8	7	.53	5	.256	.334	.320
1999 Tampa Bay	AL	143	514	146	25	5	6	(2	4)	199	79	66	60	3	76	5	10	5	13	6	.68	6	.284	.361	.387
2000 4 ML Teams	AL	132	457	125	19	5	5	(3	2)	169	60	47	50	3	73	2	1	3	8	7	.53	12	.274	.346	.370
2001 Atlanta	NL	120	237	68	11	3	2	(0	2)	91	33	20	21	0	44	1	0	0	3	3	.50	10	.287	.347	.384
1988 Chicago	NL	75	256	65	10	1	4	(2	2)	89	27	34	21	5	46	2	0	4	7	3	.70	2	.254	.311	.348
Montreal		63	191	49	3	5	2	(0	2)	68	24	12	17	3	48	0	2	1	16	6	.73	1	.257	.316	.356
2000 Tampa Bay	AL	29	104	27	4	2	1	(1	0)	38	12	12	10	1	17	0	1	2	1	4	.20	1	.260	.319	.365
Chicago	NL	18	54	10	1	1	0	(0	0)	13	5	1	2	0	8	0	0	0	1	0	1.00	0	.185	.214	.241
Texas	AL	38	119	32	4	1	2	(1	1)	44	14	12	14	2	20	1	0	0	2	1	.67	8	.269	.351	.370
Toronto	AL	47	180	56	10	1	2	(1	1)	74	29	22	24	0	28	1	0	1	4	2	.67	3	.311	.393	.411
16 ML YEARS		1919	5795	1599	238	72	91	(39	52)	2254	795	580	567	47	893	28	53	37	183	94	.66	84	.276	.341	.389

Edgar Martinez

Bats: Right **Throws:** Right **Pos:** DH-127; PH/PR-4; 1B-1   **Ht:** 5'11" **Wt:** 200 **Born:** 1/2/63 **Age:** 39

Year Team	Lg	G	AB	H	2B	3B	HR	(Hm	Rd)	TB	R	RBI	TBB	IBB	SO	HBP	SH	SF	SB	CS	SB%	GDP	Avg	OBP	SLG
1987 Seattle	AL	13	43	16	5	2	0	(0	0)	25	6	5	2	0	5	1	0	0	0	0	—	0	.372	.413	.581
1988 Seattle	AL	14	32	9	4	0	0	(0	0)	13	0	5	4	0	7	0	1	1	0	0	—	0	.281	.351	.406
1989 Seattle	AL	65	171	41	5	0	2	(0	2)	52	20	20	17	1	26	3	2	3	2	1	.67	3	.240	.314	.304
1990 Seattle	AL	144	487	147	27	2	11	(3	8)	211	71	49	74	3	62	5	1	3	1	4	.20	13	.302	.397	.433
1991 Seattle	AL	150	544	167	35	1	14	(8	6)	246	98	52	84	9	72	8	2	4	0	3	.00	19	.307	.405	.452
1992 Seattle	AL	135	528	181	46	3	18	(11	7)	287	100	73	54	2	61	4	1	5	14	4	.78	15	.343	.404	.544
1993 Seattle	AL	42	135	32	7	0	4	(1	3)	51	20	13	28	1	19	0	1	1	0	0	—	4	.237	.366	.378
1994 Seattle	AL	89	326	93	23	1	13	(4	9)	157	47	51	53	3	42	3	2	3	6	2	.75	2	.285	.387	.482
1995 Seattle	AL	145	511	182	52	0	29	(16	13)	321	121	113	116	19	87	8	0	4	4	3	.57	11	.356	.479	.628
1996 Seattle	AL	139	499	163	52	2	26	(14	12)	297	121	103	123	12	84	8	0	4	3	3	.50	15	.327	.464	.595
1997 Seattle	AL	155	542	179	35	1	28	(12	16)	300	104	108	119	11	86	11	0	6	2	4	.33	21	.330	.456	.554
1998 Seattle	AL	154	556	179	46	1	29	(17	12)	314	86	102	106	4	96	3	0	7	1	1	.50	13	.322	.429	.565
1999 Seattle	AL	142	502	169	35	1	24	(12	12)	278	86	86	97	6	99	6	0	3	7	2	.78	12	.337	.447	.554
2000 Seattle	AL	153	556	180	31	0	37	(19	18)	322	100	145	96	8	95	5	0	8	3	0	1.00	13	.324	.423	.579
2001 Seattle	AL	132	470	144	40	1	23	(10	13)	255	80	116	93	9	90	9	0	9	4	1	.80	11	.306	.423	.543
15 ML YEARS		1672	5902	1882	443	15	258	(127	131)	3129	1060	1041	1066	88	931	74	10	61	47	28	.63	152	.319	.425	.530

Felix Martinez

Bats: Both **Throws:** Right **Pos:** SS-67; 2B-10; PH/PR-3   **Ht:** 6'0" **Wt:** 180 **Born:** 5/18/74 **Age:** 28

Year Team	Lg	G	AB	H	2B	3B	HR	(Hm	Rd)	TB	R	RBI	TBB	IBB	SO	HBP	SH	SF	SB	CS	SB%	GDP	Avg	OBP	SLG
2001 Orlando *	AA	3	10	1	1	0	0	(—	—)	2	1	0	0	0	2	0	0	0	0	0	1.00	1	.100	.100	.200
1997 Kansas City	AL	16	31	7	1	1	0	(0	0)	10	3	3	6	0	8	0	1	0	0	0	—	1	.226	.351	.323
1998 Kansas City	AL	34	85	11	1	1	0	(0	0)	14	7	5	5	0	21	1	4	0	3	1	.75	1	.129	.187	.165
1999 Kansas City	AL	6	7	1	0	0	0	(0	0)	1	1	0	0	0	0	0	0	0	0	0	—	1	.143	.143	.143
2000 Tampa Bay	AL	106	299	64	11	4	2	(0	2)	89	42	17	32	0	68	8	12	2	9	3	.75	4	.214	.305	.298
2001 Tampa Bay	AL	77	219	54	13	1	1	(0	1)	72	24	14	10	0	46	5	3	1	6	5	.55	8	.247	.294	.329
5 ML YEARS		239	641	137	26	7	3	(0	3)	186	77	39	53	0	143	14	20	3	18	9	.67	15	.214	.287	.290

Pedro Martinez

Pitches: Right **Bats:** Right **Pos:** SP-18   **Ht:** 5'11" **Wt:** 170 **Born:** 10/25/71 **Age:** 30

		HOW MUCH HE PITCHED						WHAT HE GAVE UP										THE RESULTS						
Year Team	Lg	G	GS	CG	GF	IP	BFP	H	R	ER	HR	SH	SF	HB	TBB	IBB	SO	WP	Bk	W	L	Pct.	ShO	Sv-Op	Hld	ERA
1992 Los Angeles	NL	2	1	0	1	8	31	6	2	2	0	0	0	0	1	0	8	0	0	0	1	.000	0	0-0	0	2.25
1993 Los Angeles	NL	65	2	0	20	107	444	76	34	31	5	0	5	4	57	4	119	3	1	10	5	.667	0	2-3	14	2.61
1994 Montreal	NL	24	23	1	1	144.2	584	115	58	55	11	2	3	11	45	3	142	6	0	11	5	.688	1	1-1	0	3.42
1995 Montreal	NL	30	30	2	0	194.2	784	158	79	76	21	7	3	11	66	1	174	5	2	14	10	.583	2	0-0	0	3.51
1996 Montreal	NL	33	33	4	0	216.2	901	189	100	89	19	9	6	3	70	3	222	6	0	13	10	.565	1	0-0	0	3.70
1997 Montreal	NL	31	31	13	0	241.1	947	158	65	51	16	9	1	9	67	5	305	3	1	17	8	.680	4	0-0	0	1.90
1998 Boston	AL	33	33	3	0	233.2	951	188	82	75	26	4	7	8	67	3	251	9	0	19	7	.731	2	0-0	0	2.89
1999 Boston	AL	31	29	5	1	213.1	835	160	56	49	9	3	6	9	37	1	313	6	0	23	4	.852	1	0-0	0	2.07
2000 Boston	AL	29	29	7	0	217	817	128	44	42	17	2	1	14	32	0	284	1	0	18	6	.750	4	0-0	0	1.74
2001 Boston	AL	18	18	1	0	116.2	456	84	33	31	5	2	0	6	25	0	163	4	0	7	3	.700	0	0-0	0	2.39
10 ML YEARS		296	229	36	23	1693	6750	1262	553	501	129	38	32	75	467	20	1981	43	4	132	59	.691	15	3-4	14	2.66

Ramon Martinez

Pitches: Right **Bats:** Both **Pos:** SP-4   **Ht:** 6'4" **Wt:** 184 **Born:** 3/22/68 **Age:** 34

		HOW MUCH HE PITCHED						WHAT HE GAVE UP										THE RESULTS						
Year Team	Lg	G	GS	CG	GF	IP	BFP	H	R	ER	HR	SH	SF	HB	TBB	IBB	SO	WP	Bk	W	L	Pct.	ShO	Sv-Op	Hld	ERA
1988 Los Angeles	NL	9	6	0	0	35.2	151	27	17	15	0	4	0	0	22	1	23	1	0	1	3	.250	0	0-0	1	3.79
1989 Los Angeles	NL	15	15	2	0	98.2	410	79	39	35	11	4	0	5	41	1	89	1	0	6	4	.600	2	0-0	0	3.19
1990 Los Angeles	NL	33	33	12	0	234.1	950	191	89	76	22	7	5	4	67	5	223	3	3	20	6	.769	3	0-0	0	2.92
1991 Los Angeles	NL	33	33	6	0	220.1	916	190	89	80	18	8	4	7	69	4	150	6	0	17	13	.567	4	0-0	0	3.27

138

	HOW MUCH HE PITCHED							WHAT HE GAVE UP													THE RESULTS						
Year Team	Lg	G	GS	CG	GF	IP	BFP	H	R	ER	HR	SH	SF	HB	TBB	IBB	SO	WP	Bk	W	L	Pct.	ShO	Sv-Op	Hld	ERA
1992 Los Angeles	NL	25	25	1	0	150.2	662	141	82	67	11	12	1	5	69	4	101	9	0	8	11	.421	1	0-0	0	4.00
1993 Los Angeles	NL	32	32	1	0	211.2	918	202	88	81	15	12	5	4	104	9	127	2	2	10	12	.455	3	0-0	0	3.44
1994 Los Angeles	NL	24	24	4	0	170	718	160	83	75	18	6	8	6	56	2	119	2	0	12	7	.632	2	0-0	0	3.97
1995 Los Angeles	NL	30	30	4	0	206.1	859	176	95	84	19	7	5	5	81	5	138	3	0	17	7	.708	2	0-0	0	3.66
1996 Los Angeles	NL	28	27	2	1	168.2	732	153	76	64	12	7	6	8	86	5	133	2	1	15	6	.714	2	0-0	0	3.42
1997 Los Angeles	NL	22	22	1	0	133.2	590	123	64	54	14	5	4	6	68	1	120	1	1	10	5	.667	0	0-0	0	3.64
1998 Los Angeles	NL	15	15	1	0	101.2	418	76	41	32	8	2	3	3	41	1	91	2	0	7	3	.700	0	0-0	0	2.83
1999 Boston	AL	4	4	0	0	20.2	84	14	8	7	2	0	1	2	8	0	15	0	0	2	1	.667	0	0-0	0	3.05
2000 Boston	AL	27	27	0	0	127.2	590	143	94	87	16	2	7	9	67	3	89	0	0	10	8	.556	0	0-0	0	6.13
2001 Pittsburgh	NL	4	4	0	0	15.2	77	16	15	15	4	0	1	2	16	0	9	1	0	0	2	.000	0	0-0	0	8.62
14 ML YEARS		301	297	37	1	1895.2	8075	1691	880	772	170	76	50	66	795	41	1427	33	7	135	88	.605	20	0-0	1	3.67

Ramon Martinez

Bats: R **Throws:** R **Pos:** 3B-70; 2B-42; SS-24; PH/PR-10   **Ht:** 6'1" **Wt:** 187 **Born:** 10/10/72 **Age:** 29

	BATTING																		BASERUNNING				PERCENTAGES		
Year Team	Lg	G	AB	H	2B	3B	HR	(Hm	Rd)	TB	R	RBI	TBB	IBB	SO	HBP	SH	SF	SB	CS	SB%	GDP	Avg	OBP	SLG
1998 San Francisco	NL	19	19	6	1	0	0	(0	0)	7	4	0	4	0	2	0	1	0	0	0	—	0	.316	.435	.368
1999 San Francisco	NL	61	144	38	6	0	5	(3	2)	59	21	19	14	0	17	0	6	1	1	2	.33	2	.264	.327	.410
2000 San Francisco	NL	88	189	57	13	2	6	(4	2)	92	30	25	15	1	22	1	4	1	3	2	.60	6	.302	.354	.487
2001 San Francisco	NL	128	391	99	18	3	5	(1	4)	138	48	37	38	6	52	5	6	6	1	2	.33	11	.253	.323	.353
4 ML YEARS		296	743	200	38	5	16	(8	8)	296	103	81	71	7	93	6	17	8	5	6	.45	19	.269	.335	.398

Sandy Martinez

Bats: Left **Throws:** Right **Pos:** C-1   **Ht:** 6'2" **Wt:** 215 **Born:** 10/3/72 **Age:** 29

	BATTING																		BASERUNNING				PERCENTAGES		
Year Team	Lg	G	AB	H	2B	3B	HR	(Hm	Rd)	TB	R	RBI	TBB	IBB	SO	HBP	SH	SF	SB	CS	SB%	GDP	Avg	OBP	SLG
1995 Toronto	AL	62	191	46	12	0	2	(1	1)	64	12	25	7	0	45	1	0	1	0	0	—	1	.241	.270	.335
1996 Toronto	AL	76	229	52	9	3	3	(2	1)	76	17	18	16	0	58	4	1	1	0	0	—	4	.227	.288	.332
1997 Toronto	AL	3	2	0	0	0	0	(0	0)	0	1	0	1	0	1	0	0	0	0	0	—	0	.000	.333	.000
1998 Chicago	NL	45	87	23	9	1	0	(0	1)	34	7	7	13	0	21	1	0	1	1	0	1.00	3	.264	.363	.391
1999 Chicago	NL	17	30	5	0	0	1	(0	1)	8	1	1	0	0	11	0	0	0	0	0	—	0	.167	.167	.267
2000 Florida	NL	10	18	4	2	0	0	(0	0)	6	1	0	0	0	8	0	0	0	0	0	—	1	.222	.222	.333
2001 Montreal	NL	1	1	0	0	0	0	(0	0)	0	0	0	0	0	0	0	0	0	0	0	—		.000	.000	.000
7 ML YEARS		214	558	130	32	4	6	(3	3)	188	39	51	37	0	144	6	1	3	1	0	1.00	9	.233	.286	.337

Tino Martinez

Bats: Left **Throws:** Right **Pos:** 1B-149; PH/PR-6; DH-3   **Ht:** 6'2" **Wt:** 210 **Born:** 12/7/67 **Age:** 34

	BATTING																		BASERUNNING				PERCENTAGES		
Year Team	Lg	G	AB	H	2B	3B	HR	(Hm	Rd)	TB	R	RBI	TBB	IBB	SO	HBP	SH	SF	SB	CS	SB%	GDP	Avg	OBP	SLG
1990 Seattle	AL	24	68	15	4	0	0	(0	0)	19	4	5	9	0	9	0	0	1	0	0	—	0	.221	.308	.279
1991 Seattle	AL	36	112	23	2	0	4	(3	1)	37	11	9	11	0	24	0	0	2	0	0	—	2	.205	.272	.330
1992 Seattle	AL	136	460	118	19	2	16	(10	6)	189	53	66	42	9	77	2	1	8	2	1	.67	24	.257	.316	.411
1993 Seattle	AL	109	408	108	25	1	17	(8	9)	186	48	60	45	9	56	5	3	3	0	3	.00	7	.265	.343	.456
1994 Seattle	AL	97	329	86	21	0	20	(8	12)	167	42	61	29	2	52	1	4	3	1	2	.33	9	.261	.320	.508
1995 Seattle	AL	141	519	152	35	3	31	(14	17)	286	92	111	62	15	91	4	2	6	0	0	—	10	.293	.369	.551
1996 New York	AL	155	595	174	28	0	25	(9	16)	277	82	117	68	4	85	2	1	5	2	1	.67	18	.292	.364	.466
1997 New York	AL	158	594	176	31	2	44	(18	26)	343	96	141	75	14	75	3	0	13	3	1	.75	15	.296	.371	.577
1998 New York	AL	142	531	149	33	1	28	(12	16)	268	92	123	61	3	83	6	0	10	2	1	.67	18	.281	.355	.505
1999 New York	AL	159	589	155	27	2	28	(7	21)	270	95	105	69	7	86	3	0	4	3	4	.43	14	.258	.328	.422
2000 New York	AL	155	569	147	37	4	16	(12	4)	240	69	91	52	9	74	8	0	3	4	1	.80	16	.258	.328	.422
2001 New York	AL	154	589	165	24	2	34	(22	12)	295	89	113	42	2	89	2	0	2	1	2	.33	12	.280	.329	.501
12 ML YEARS		1466	5363	1468	286	17	263	(124	139)	2577	773	1002	565	74	801	36	11	60	18	16	.53	145	.274	.343	.481

Henry Mateo

Bats: Both **Throws:** Right **Pos:** PH/PR-3; 2B-2   **Ht:** 5'11" **Wt:** 180 **Born:** 10/14/76 **Age:** 25

	BATTING																		BASERUNNING				PERCENTAGES		
Year Team	Lg	G	AB	H	2B	3B	HR	(Hm	Rd)	TB	R	RBI	TBB	IBB	SO	HBP	SH	SF	SB	CS	SB%	GDP	Avg	OBP	SLG
1995 Expos	R	38	122	18	0	0	0	—	—	18	11	6	14	0	47	5	5	1	2	7	.22	2	.148	.261	.148
1996 Expos	R	14	44	11	3	0	0	—	—	14	8	3	5	0	11	3	2	0	5	1	.83	0	.250	.365	.318
1997 Vermont	A-	67	228	56	9	3	1	—	—	74	32	31	30	1	44	7	3	2	21	11	.66	4	.246	.348	.325
1998 Cape Fear	A	114	416	115	20	5	4	—	—	157	72	41	40	2	111	13	15	4	22	16	.58	5	.276	.355	.377
Jupiter	A+	12	43	12	3	1	0	—	—	17	11	6	2	0	6	2	1	1	3	0	1.00	0	.279	.333	.395
1999 Jupiter	A+	118	447	116	27	7	4	—	—	169	69	58	44	3	112	10	17	6	32	16	.67	4	.260	.335	.378
2000 Harrisburg	AA	140	530	152	25	11	5	—	—	214	91	63	58	0	97	6	4	2	48	16	.75	4	.287	.362	.404
2001 Ottawa	AAA	118	500	134	14	12	5	—	—	187	71	43	33	3	89	7	11	1	47	14	.77	2	.268	.322	.374
2001 Montreal	NL	5	9	3	1	0	0	(0	0)	4	1	0	0	0	1	0	0	0	0	0	—	0	.333	.333	.444

Ruben Mateo

Bats: Right **Throws:** Right **Pos:** RF-39; PH/PR-1   **Ht:** 6'0" **Wt:** 185 **Born:** 2/10/78 **Age:** 24

	BATTING																		BASERUNNING				PERCENTAGES		
Year Team	Lg	G	AB	H	2B	3B	HR	(Hm	Rd)	TB	R	RBI	TBB	IBB	SO	HBP	SH	SF	SB	CS	SB%	GDP	Avg	OBP	SLG
2001 Oklahoma *	AAA	14	51	11	3	0	1	—	—	17	3	8	2	0	8	0	0	1	1	2	.33	1	.216	.241	.333
Louisville *	AAA	65	251	63	16	4	2	—	—	93	35	25	13	0	45	8	0	2	2	0	1.00	7	.251	.307	.371
1999 Texas	AL	32	122	29	9	1	5	(2	3)	55	16	18	4	0	28	1	0	0	3	0	1.00	5	.238	.268	.451
2000 Texas	AL	52	206	60	11	0	7	(3	4)	92	32	19	10	1	34	5	1	0	6	0	1.00	5	.291	.339	.447
2001 Texas	AL	40	129	32	5	2	1	(0	1)	44	18	13	9	0	28	6	1	2	1	0	1.00	0	.248	.322	.341
3 ML YEARS		124	457	121	25	3	13	(5	8)	191	66	50	23	1	90	12	2	2	10	0	1.00	11	.265	.316	.418

Mike Matheny

Bats: Right **Throws:** Right **Pos:** C-121; 1B-2

Ht: 6'3" **Wt:** 205 **Born:** 9/22/70 **Age:** 31

Year Team	Lg	G	AB	H	2B	3B	HR	(Hm	Rd)	TB	R	RBI	TBB	IBB	SO	HBP	SH	SF	SB	CS	SB%	GDP	Avg	OBP	SLG
1994 Milwaukee	AL	28	53	12	3	0	1	(1	0)	18	3	2	3	0	13	2	1	0	0	1	.00	1	.226	.293	.340
1995 Milwaukee	AL	80	166	41	9	1	0	(0	0)	52	13	21	12	0	28	2	1	0	2	1	.67	3	.247	.306	.313
1996 Milwaukee	AL	106	313	64	15	2	8	(5	3)	107	31	46	14	0	80	3	7	4	3	2	.60	9	.204	.243	.342
1997 Milwaukee	AL	123	320	78	16	1	4	(2	2)	108	29	32	17	0	68	7	9	3	0	1	.00	9	.244	.294	.338
1998 Milwaukee	NL	108	320	76	13	0	6	(4	2)	107	24	27	11	0	63	7	3	0	1	0	1.00	6	.238	.278	.334
1999 Toronto	AL	57	163	35	6	0	3	(1	2)	50	16	17	12	0	37	1	2	1	0	0	—	3	.215	.271	.307
2000 St. Louis	NL	128	417	109	22	1	6	(2	4)	151	43	47	32	8	96	4	7	4	0	0	—	11	.261	.317	.362
2001 St. Louis	NL	121	381	83	12	0	7	(4	3)	116	40	42	28	5	76	4	8	3	0	1	.00	11	.218	.276	.304
8 ML YEARS		751	2133	498	96	5	35	(19	16)	709	199	234	129	13	461	30	38	15	6	6	.50	53	.233	.285	.332

T.J. Mathews

Pitches: Right **Bats:** Right **Pos:** RP-30

Ht: 6'1" **Wt:** 214 **Born:** 1/19/70 **Age:** 32

Year Team	Lg	G	GS	CG	GF	IP	BFP	H	R	ER	HR	SH	SF	HB	TBB	IBB	SO	WP	Bk	W	L	Pct.	ShO	Sv-Op	Hld	ERA
2001 Memphis *	AAA	15	0	0	11	15	62	16	4	3	0	0	0	1	1	0	14	0	0	1	1	.500	0	4- -	—	1.80
1995 St. Louis	NL	23	0	0	12	29.2	120	21	7	5	1	4	0	0	11	1	28	2	0	1	1	.500	0	2-2	7	1.52
1996 St. Louis	NL	67	0	0	23	83.2	345	62	32	28	8	5	0	2	32	4	80	1	0	2	6	.250	0	6-11	9	3.01
1997 StL-Oak		64	0	0	26	74.2	329	75	32	25	9	8	1	2	30	4	70	1	0	10	6	.625	0	3-9	12	3.01
1998 Oakland	AL	66	0	0	15	72.2	319	71	44	37	6	2	9	4	29	3	53	1	0	7	4	.636	0	1-4	19	4.58
1999 Oakland	AL	50	0	0	15	59	242	46	28	25	9	5	1	2	20	4	42	2	0	9	5	.643	0	3-5	17	3.81
2000 Oakland	AL	50	0	0	19	59.2	273	73	40	40	10	1	4	2	25	5	42	2	0	2	3	.400	0	0-1	9	6.03
2001 Oak-StL		30	0	0	7	37.2	164	39	20	18	4	2	1	0	12	3	29	1	0	1	1	.500	0	1-1	5	4.30
1997 St. Louis	NL	40	0	0	12	46	197	41	14	11	4	6	0	1	18	3	46	1	0	4	4	.500	0	0-3	8	2.15
Oakland	AL	24	0	0	14	28.2	132	34	18	14	5	2	1	1	12	1	24	0	0	6	2	.750	0	3-6	4	4.40
2001 Oakland	AL	20	0	0	4	23	108	28	14	13	2	2	0	0	11	3	19	1	0	0	1	.000	0	1-1	3	5.09
St. Louis	NL	10	0	0	3	14.2	56	11	6	5	2	0	1	0	1	0	10	0	0	1	0	1.000	0	0-0	2	3.07
7 ML YEARS		350	0	0	117	417	1792	387	203	178	47	27	16	12	159	24	344	10	0	32	26	.552	0	16-33	78	3.84

Luis Matos

Bats: R **Throws:** R **Pos:** CF-23; RF-10; PH/PR-3; LF-1

Ht: 6'0" **Wt:** 179 **Born:** 10/30/78 **Age:** 23

Year Team	Lg	G	AB	H	2B	3B	HR	(Hm	Rd)	TB	R	RBI	TBB	IBB	SO	HBP	SH	SF	SB	CS	SB%	GDP	Avg	OBP	SLG
1996 Orioles	R	43	130	38	2	0	0	—	—	40	21	13	15	0	18	2	4	0	12	7	.63	3	.292	.374	.308
1997 Delmarva	A	36	119	25	1	2	0	—	—	30	10	13	9	0	21	2	2	1	8	5	.62	2	.210	.275	.252
Bluefield	R+	61	240	66	7	3	2	—	—	85	37	35	20	0	36	4	1	1	26	4	.87	5	.275	.340	.354
1998 Delmarva	A	133	503	137	26	6	7	—	—	196	73	62	38	0	90	7	6	7	42	14	.75	9	.272	.328	.390
Bowie	AA	5	19	5	0	0	1	—	—	8	2	3	1	0	1	0	0	0	1	1	.50	0	.263	.300	.421
1999 Frederick	A+	68	273	81	15	1	7	—	—	119	40	41	20	1	35	2	2	5	27	6	.82	6	.297	.343	.436
Bowie	AA	66	283	67	11	1	9	—	—	107	41	36	15	0	39	1	5	6	14	4	.78	6	.237	.272	.378
2000 Rochester	AAA	11	35	6	1	0	0	—	—	7	2	0	3	0	8	1	1	0	2	0	1.00	0	.171	.256	.200
Bowie	AA	50	181	49	7	5	2	—	—	72	26	33	17	0	23	5	1	3	14	8	.64	3	.271	.345	.398
2001 Orioles	R	3	14	4	2	0	0	—	—	6	1	2	0	0	3	0	0	0	0	0	—	0	.286	.286	.429
Frederick	A+	2	7	3	0	0	1	—	—	6	3	2	1	1	3	0	0	0	0	0	—	0	.429	.500	.857
Bowie	AA	13	46	14	5	0	1	—	—	22	6	8	5	1	7	1	0	0	0	1	.00	0	.304	.385	.478
2000 Baltimore	AL	72	182	41	6	3	1	(1	0)	56	21	17	12	0	30	3	2	2	13	4	.76	7	.225	.281	.308
2001 Baltimore	AL	31	98	21	7	0	4	(1	3)	40	16	12	11	0	30	1	2	0	7	0	1.00	1	.214	.300	.408
2 ML YEARS		103	280	62	13	3	5	(2	3)	96	37	29	23	0	60	4	4	2	20	4	.83	8	.221	.288	.343

Troy Mattes

Pitches: Right **Bats:** Right **Pos:** SP-8

Ht: 6'8" **Wt:** 230 **Born:** 8/26/75 **Age:** 26

Year Team	Lg	G	GS	CG	GF	IP	BFP	H	R	ER	HR	SH	SF	HB	TBB	IBB	SO	WP	Bk	W	L	Pct.	ShO	Sv-Op	Hld	ERA
1994 Expos	R	12	11	1	0	55.2	221	35	25	21	2	0	0	3	21	0	51	7	0	3	2	.600	1	0- -	—	3.40
1995 Albany	A	4	4	0	0	19.2	90	21	12	11	0	2	0	0	12	1	15	1	1	0	2	.000	0	0- -	—	5.03
Vermont	A-	10	10	0	0	46	209	51	34	19	3	5	4	5	25	0	23	7	0	3	4	.429	0	0- -	—	3.72
Expos	R	2	2	0	0	12	43	7	0	0	0	0	0	0	3	0	8	0	0	2	0	1.000	0	0- -	—	0.00
1996 Delmarva	A	27	27	5	0	173.1	714	142	77	55	14	6	4	14	50	0	151	17	1	10	9	.526	3	0- -	—	2.86
1997 Wst Plm Bch	A+	20	16	2	3	102	441	123	61	56	8	3	5	5	20	0	61	11	1	6	9	.400	2	1- -	—	4.94
1998 Jupiter	A+	17	10	0	2	73.1	307	73	33	25	4	2	1	3	19	0	42	2	1	7	6	.538	0	0- -	—	3.07
1999 Jupiter	A+	5	5	0	0	24.1	103	27	11	10	2	1	1	3	7	0	12	0	0	3	0	1.000	0	0- -	—	3.70
Harrisburg	AA	20	19	0	0	97.1	433	114	67	58	12	8	4	7	38	0	58	3	0	5	8	.385	0	0- -	—	5.36
2000 Harrisburg	AA	28	28	4	0	174.1	729	170	91	81	20	5	3	4	56	1	109	6	0	11	9	.550	0	0- -	—	4.18
2001 Ottawa	AAA	15	15	0	0	82.1	354	75	38	33	3	3	4	5	33	1	70	4	1	5	5	.500	0	0- -	—	3.61
2001 Montreal	NL	8	8	0	0	45	207	51	33	30	9	2	1	4	21	2	26	6	0	3	3	.500	0	0-0	0	6.00

Mike Matthews

Pitches: Left **Bats:** Left **Pos:** RP-41; SP-10

Ht: 6'2" **Wt:** 175 **Born:** 10/24/73 **Age:** 28

Year Team	Lg	G	GS	CG	GF	IP	BFP	H	R	ER	HR	SH	SF	HB	TBB	IBB	SO	WP	Bk	W	L	Pct.	ShO	Sv-Op	Hld	ERA
1992 Burlington	R+	10	10	0	0	62.1	245	33	13	7	1	2	1	3	27	0	55	3	1	7	0	1.000	0	0- -	—	1.01
Watertown	A-	2	2	0	0	11	47	10	4	4	0	0	1	0	8	0	5	1	0	1	0	1.000	0	0- -	—	3.27
1994 Columbus	A	23	23	0	0	119.2	502	120	53	41	8	3	3	7	44	1	99	7	3	6	8	.429	0	0- -	—	3.08
1995 Canton-Akrn	AA	15	15	1	0	74.1	345	82	62	49	6	2	8	2	43	1	37	8	1	5	8	.385	0	0- -	—	5.93
1996 Canton-Akrn	AA	27	27	3	0	162.1	713	178	96	84	13	6	7	5	74	3	112	6	1	9	11	.450	1	0- -	—	4.66
1997 Buffalo	AAA	5	5	0	0	21	106	32	19	18	7	0	2	0	10	0	17	1	0	0	2	.000	0	0- -	—	7.71
Akron	AA	19	19	3	0	113	492	116	62	48	13	3	0	7	57	0	69	5	4	6	8	.429	1	0- -	—	3.82
1998 Buffalo	AAA	24	23	0	1	130.1	577	137	79	67	19	4	1	5	68	1	86	5	2	9	6	.600	1	0- -	—	4.63

140

		HOW MUCH HE PITCHED						WHAT HE GAVE UP												THE RESULTS						
Year Team	Lg	G	GS	CG	GF	IP	BFP	H	R	ER	HR	SH	SF	HB	TBB	IBB	SO	WP	Bk	W	L	Pct.	ShO	Sv-Op	Hld	ERA
1999 Buffalo	AAA	25	0	0	8	21.1	99	23	18	18	3	1	2	2	18	0	16	0	1	1	2	.333	0	0--	—	7.59
Akron	AA	6	6	0	0	25.2	127	36	30	25	7	0	3	2	15	0	10	0	2	0	5	.000	0	0--	—	8.77
Trenton	AA	3	3	0	0	11.2	52	11	7	6	1	1	1	0	9	0	8	0	0	0	0	—	0	0--	—	4.63
Arkansas	AA	2	2	1	0	12	39	3	0	0	0	0	0	0	1	0	10	0	1	2	0	1.000	1	0--	—	0.00
2000 Memphis	AAA	9	9	0	0	52	216	33	19	18	4	2	0	1	32	1	50	3	0	3	1	.750	0	0--	—	3.12
2000 St. Louis	NL	14	0	0	4	9.1	54	15	12	12	2	0	0	1	10	2	8	0	0	0	0	—	0	0-0	2	11.57
2001 St. Louis	NL	51	10	0	7	89	368	74	32	32	11	4	1	4	33	4	72	4	1	3	4	.429	0	1-3	3	3.24
2 ML YEARS		65	10	0	11	98.1	422	89	44	44	13	4	1	5	43	6	80	4	1	3	4	.429	0	1-3	5	4.03

Gary Matthews Jr.

Bats: B **Throws:** R **Pos:** CF-132; PH/PR-22; LF-20; RF-1 **Ht:** 6'3" **Wt:** 210 **Born:** 8/25/74 **Age:** 27

		BATTING																	BASERUNNING				PERCENTAGES		
Year Team	Lg	G	AB	H	2B	3B	HR	(Hm	Rd)	TB	R	RBI	TBB	IBB	SO	HBP	SH	SF	SB	CS	SB%	GDP	Avg	OBP	SLG
1999 San Diego	NL		36	8	0	0	0	(0	0)	8	4	7	9	0	9	0	0	0	2	0	1.00	1	.222	.378	.222
2000 Chicago	NL	80	158	30	1	2	4	(2	4)	47	24	14	15	1	28	1	1	0	3	0	1.00	2	.190	.264	.297
2001 ChC-Pit	NL	152	405	92	15	2	14	(4	10)	153	63	44	60	2	100	1	5	1	8	5	.62	8	.227	.328	.378
2001 Chicago	NL	106	258	56	9	1	9	(2	7)	94	41	30	38	2	55	1	5	0	5	3	.63	4	.217	.320	.364
Pittsburgh	NL	46	147	36	6	1	5	(2	3)	59	22	14	22	0	45	0	0	1	3	2	.60	4	.245	.341	.401
3 ML YEARS		255	599	130	16	4	18	(6	12)	208	91	65	84	3	137	2	6	1	13	5	.72	11	.217	.315	.347

Dave Maurer

Pitches: Left **Bats:** Right **Pos:** RP-3 **Ht:** 6'2" **Wt:** 205 **Born:** 2/23/75 **Age:** 27

		HOW MUCH HE PITCHED						WHAT HE GAVE UP												THE RESULTS						
Year Team	Lg	G	GS	CG	GF	IP	BFP	H	R	ER	HR	SH	SF	HB	TBB	IBB	SO	WP	Bk	W	L	Pct.	ShO	Sv-Op	Hld	ERA
1997 Clinton	A	25	0	0	10	34.1	142	24	15	11	1	2	1	0	15	0	43	3	1	0	4	.000	0	3--	—	2.88
1998 Rancho Cuc	A+	48	0	0	14	83.1	348	56	27	25	1	5	1	1	46	1	93	8	2	5	2	.714	0	5--	—	2.70
1999 Mobile	AA	54	0	0	33	72	301	59	30	29	7	1	4	3	26	5	59	6	0	4	4	.500	0	3--	—	3.63
2000 Mobile	AA	24	0	0	8	26.2	98	15	8	8	2	3	0	1	3	1	28	1	0	1	2	.333	0	0--	—	2.70
Las Vegas	AAA	35	0	0	10	44.1	193	47	19	16	5	0	0	0	15	1	44	1	0	4	1	.800	0	0--	—	3.25
2001 Portland	AAA	17	0	0	7	18.2	75	11	9	9	4	0	1	1	9	2	21	3	0	0	0	—	0	1--	—	4.34
Louisville	AAA	18	0	0	7	21.2	91	18	11	10	4	1	2	1	7	0	23	0	0	0	1	.000	0	0--	—	4.15
Sacramento	AAA	11	0	0	4	13	60	14	9	8	2	0	0	0	8	0	21	0	0	0	0	—	0	0--	—	5.54
2000 San Diego	NL	14	0	0	1	14.2	64	15	8	6	2	0	0	2	5	1	13	1	0	1	0	1.000	0	0-1	2	3.68
2001 San Diego	NL	3	0	0	1	5	27	8	6	6	1	0	0	0	4	0	4	1	0	0	0	—	0	0-0	0	10.80
2 ML YEARS		17	0	0	2	19.2	91	23	14	12	3	0	0	2	9	1	17	2	0	1	0	1.000	0	0-1	2	5.49

Jason Maxwell

Bats: R **Throws:** R **Pos:** SS-12; 3B-11; 2B-9; PH/PR-8; DH-7 **Ht:** 6'1" **Wt:** 180 **Born:** 3/26/72 **Age:** 30

		BATTING																	BASERUNNING				PERCENTAGES		
Year Team	Lg	G	AB	H	2B	3B	HR	(Hm	Rd)	TB	R	RBI	TBB	IBB	SO	HBP	SH	SF	SB	CS	SB%	GDP	Avg	OBP	SLG
2001 Fort Myers *	A+	2	9	4	1	0	0	—	—	5	1	2	0	0	0	0	0	0	0	0	—	1	.444	.444	.556
Twins *	R	3	10	5	2	0	0	—	—	7	2	0	1	0	2	0	0	0	0	0	—	0	.500	.545	.700
1998 Chicago	NL	7	3	1	0	0	0	(1	0)	4	2	2	0	0	2	0	1	0	0	0	—	0	.333	.333	1.333
2000 Minnesota	AL	64	111	27	6	0	1	(1	0)	36	14	11	9	0	32	1	0	3	2	1	.67	2	.243	.298	.324
2001 Minnesota	AL	39	68	13	4	0	1	(0	1)	20	4	10	9	2	23	0	1	0	2	0	1.00	1	.191	.286	.294
3 ML YEARS		110	182	41	10	0	3	(2	1)	60	20	23	18	2	57	1	2	3	4	1	.80	3	.225	.294	.330

Brent Mayne

Bats: Left **Throws:** Right **Pos:** C-93; PH/PR-9; 1B-1 **Ht:** 6'1" **Wt:** 191 **Born:** 4/19/68 **Age:** 34

		BATTING																	BASERUNNING				PERCENTAGES		
Year Team	Lg	G	AB	H	2B	3B	HR	(Hm	Rd)	TB	R	RBI	TBB	IBB	SO	HBP	SH	SF	SB	CS	SB%	GDP	Avg	OBP	SLG
1990 Kansas City	AL	5	13	3	0	0	0	(0	0)	3	2	1	3	0	3	0	0	0	0	1	.00	0	.231	.375	.231
1991 Kansas City	AL	85	231	58	8	0	3	(2	1)	75	22	31	23	4	42	0	2	3	2	4	.33	6	.251	.315	.325
1992 Kansas City	AL	82	213	48	10	0	0	(0	0)	58	16	18	11	0	26	0	2	3	0	4	.00	5	.225	.260	.272
1993 Kansas City	AL	71	205	52	9	1	2	(0	2)	69	22	22	18	7	31	1	3	0	3	2	.60	6	.254	.317	.337
1994 Kansas City	AL	46	144	37	5	1	2	(1	1)	50	19	20	14	1	27	0	0	0	0	1	.00	3	.257	.323	.347
1995 Kansas City	AL	110	307	77	18	1	1	(1	0)	100	23	27	25	1	41	3	11	1	0	1	.00	16	.251	.313	.326
1996 New York	NL	70	99	26	6	0	1	(1	0)	35	9	6	12	1	22	0	2	0	0	1	.00	6	.263	.342	.354
1997 Oakland	AL	85	256	74	12	0	6	(4	2)	104	29	22	18	1	33	4	2	2	1	0	1.00	6	.289	.343	.406
1998 San Francisco	NL	94	275	75	15	0	3	(0	3)	99	26	32	37	3	47	1	2	2	2	1	.67	8	.273	.359	.360
1999 San Francisco	NL	117	322	97	32	0	2	(1	1)	135	39	39	43	5	65	5	1	3	2	2	.50	16	.301	.389	.419
2000 Colorado	NL	117	335	101	21	0	6	(3	3)	140	36	64	47	13	48	1	4	8	1	3	.25	12	.301	.381	.418
2001 Col-KC	NL	100	326	93	11	1	2	(1	1)	112	28	40	26	5	41	1	0	6	1	2	.33	12	.285	.334	.344
2001 Colorado	NL	49	160	53	7	0	0	(0	0)	60	15	20	16	3	24	0	0	3	0	0	—	4	.331	.385	.375
Kansas City	AL	51	166	40	4	1	2	(1	1)	52	13	20	10	2	17	1	0	3	1	2	.33	8	.241	.283	.313
12 ML YEARS		982	2726	741	147	4	28	(13	15)	980	271	322	277	41	426	16	29	28	13	21	.38	94	.272	.339	.360

Joe Mays

Pitches: Right **Bats:** Both **Pos:** SP-34 **Ht:** 6'1" **Wt:** 185 **Born:** 12/10/75 **Age:** 26

		HOW MUCH HE PITCHED						WHAT HE GAVE UP												THE RESULTS						
Year Team	Lg	G	GS	CG	GF	IP	BFP	H	R	ER	HR	SH	SF	HB	TBB	IBB	SO	WP	Bk	W	L	Pct.	ShO	Sv-Op	Hld	ERA
1999 Minnesota	AL	49	20	2	8	171	746	179	92	83	24	7	6	2	67	2	115	6	0	6	11	.353	1	0-0	2	4.37
2000 Minnesota	AL	31	28	2	1	160.1	723	193	105	99	20	3	5	2	67	1	102	11	0	7	15	.318	0	0-0	0	5.56
2001 Minnesota	AL	34	34	4	0	233.2	957	205	87	82	25	8	8	5	64	2	123	11	0	17	13	.567	2	0-0	1	3.16
3 ML YEARS		114	82	8	9	565	2426	577	284	264	69	18	19	9	198	5	340	28	0	30	39	.435	4	0-0	3	4.21

Dave McCarty

Bats: R Throws: L Pos: 1B-68; PH/PR-30; LF-8; DH-7; RF-1   Ht: 6'5" Wt: 215 Born: 11/23/69 Age: 32

Year Team	Lg	G	AB	H	2B	3B	HR	(Hm	Rd)	TB	R	RBI	TBB	IBB	SO	HBP	SH	SF	SB	CS	SB%	GDP	Avg	OBP	SLG
1993 Minnesota	AL	98	350	75	15	2	2	(2	0)	100	36	21	19	0	80	1	1	0	2	6	.25	13	.214	.257	.286
1994 Minnesota	AL	44	131	34	8	2	1	(1	0)	49	21	12	7	1	32	5	0	0	2	1	.67	3	.260	.322	.374
1995 Min-SF		37	75	17	4	1	0	(0	0)	23	11	6	6	0	22	1	0	1	1	1	.50	1	.227	.289	.307
1996 San Francisco	NL	91	175	38	3	0	6	(5	1)	59	16	24	18	0	43	2	0	2	2	1	.67	5	.217	.294	.337
1998 Seattle	AL	8	18	5	0	0	1	(1	0)	8	1	2	5	0	4	0	0	0	1	0	1.00	0	.278	.435	.444
2000 Kansas City		103	270	75	14	2	12	(6	6)	129	34	53	22	1	68	0	0	3	0	0	—	6	.278	.329	.478
2001 Kansas City	AL	98	200	50	10	0	7	(5	2)	81	26	26	24	1	45	1	1	0	0	0	—	8	.250	.328	.405
1995 Minnesota	AL	25	55	12	3	1	0	(0	0)	17	10	4	4	0	18	1	0	1	0	1	.00	1	.218	.279	.309
San Francisco	NL	12	20	5	1	0	0	(0	0)	6	1	2	2	0	4	0	0	0	1	0	1.00	0	.250	.318	.300
7 ML YEARS		479	1219	294	54	7	29	(20	9)	449	145	144	101	3	294	10	2	10	8	9	.47	36	.241	.302	.368

Quinton McCracken

Bats: B Throws: R Pos: DH-9; PH/PR-8; LF-6; RF-3; CF-2   Ht: 5'7" Wt: 173 Born: 8/16/70 Age: 31

Year Team	Lg	G	AB	H	2B	3B	HR	(Hm	Rd)	TB	R	RBI	TBB	IBB	SO	HBP	SH	SF	SB	CS	SB%	GDP	Avg	OBP	SLG
2001 Edmonton *	AAA	81	361	122	27	4	4	—	—	169	53	45	21	1	54	1	5	2	8	10	.44	5	.338	.374	.468
1995 Colorado	NL	3	1	0	0	0	0	(0	0)	0	0	0	0	0	1	0	0	0	0	0	—	0	.000	.000	.000
1996 Colorado	NL	124	283	82	13	6	3	(2	1)	116	50	40	32	4	62	1	12	1	17	6	.74	5	.290	.363	.410
1997 Colorado	NL	147	325	95	11	1	3	(1	2)	117	69	36	42	0	62	1	6	1	28	11	.72	6	.292	.374	.360
1998 Tampa Bay	AL	155	614	179	38	7	7	(5	2)	252	77	59	41	1	107	3	9	8	19	10	.66	12	.292	.335	.410
1999 Tampa Bay	AL	40	148	37	6	1	1	(1	0)	48	20	18	14	0	23	1	1	1	6	5	.55	7	.250	.317	.324
2000 Tampa Bay	AL	15	31	4	0	0	0	(0	0)	4	5	2	6	0	4	0	0	0	0	1	.00	3	.129	.270	.129
2001 Minnesota	AL	24	64	14	2	2	0	(0	0)	20	7	3	5	0	13	0	1	0	0	1	.00	2	.219	.275	.313
7 ML YEARS		508	1466	411	70	17	14	(9	5)	557	228	158	140	5	272	6	29	11	70	34	.67	35	.280	.343	.380

Allen McDill

Pitches: Left Bats: Left Pos: RP-15   Ht: 6'0" Wt: 170 Born: 8/23/71 Age: 30

Year Team	Lg	G	GS	CG	GF	IP	BFP	H	R	ER	HR	SH	SF	HB	TBB	IBB	SO	WP	Bk	W	L	Pct.	ShO	Sv-Op	Hld	ERA
1992 Kingsport	R+	1	0	0	0	0.1	3	0	0	0	0	0	0	0	2	0	0	0	0	0	0	—	0	0--	—	0.00
Mets	R	10	9	0	0	53.1	216	36	23	16	3	0	0	4	15	0	60	3	0	3	4	.429	0	0--	—	2.70
1993 Kingsport	R+	9	9	0	0	53.1	224	52	19	13	1	1	2	1	14	0	42	2	2	5	2	.714	0	0--	—	2.19
Pittsfield	A-	5	5	0	0	28.1	132	31	22	17	0	2	2	1	15	0	24	3	0	2	3	.400	0	0--	—	5.40
1994 Capital Cty	A	19	19	1	0	111.2	461	101	52	44	11	5	2	4	38	2	102	9	0	9	6	.600	0	0--	—	3.55
1995 St. Lucie	A+	7	7	1	0	49.1	190	36	11	9	2	1	1	0	13	0	28	3	0	4	2	.667	1	0--	—	1.64
Binghamton	AA	12	12	1	0	73	324	69	42	37	5	1	4	3	38	2	44	3	1	3	5	.375	0	0--	—	4.56
Wichita	AA	12	1	0	5	21.1	85	16	7	5	2	0	0	1	5	0	20	1	0	1	0	1.000	0	1--	—	2.11
1996 Omaha	AAA	2	0	0	0	0.1	5	3	2	2	0	0	0	0	1	0	1	2	0	0	1	.000	0	0--	—	54.00
Wichita	AA	54	0	0	30	65	288	79	43	40	10	2	4	4	21	3	62	7	0	1	5	.167	0	11--	—	5.54
1997 Omaha	AAA	23	6	0	5	64.1	295	80	42	42	10	2	1	5	26	2	51	2	0	5	2	.714	0	2--	—	5.88
Wichita	AA	16	0	0	7	17.1	72	18	7	6	0	1	0	0	7	1	14	1	0	0	1	.000	0	3--	—	3.12
1998 Omaha	AAA	61	0	0	22	60.1	246	54	22	16	4	3	0	0	24	3	62	0	0	6	4	.600	0	4--	—	2.39
1999 Oklahoma	AAA	42	0	0	35	48.1	207	45	22	20	6	1	1	2	17	0	46	4	0	1	3	.250	0	18--	—	3.72
2000 Toledo	AAA	16	0	0	5	18.2	82	21	4	2	0	0	0	0	7	0	15	1	0	0	1	1.000	0	0--	—	0.96
Memphis	AAA	23	0	0	5	24.2	114	24	13	12	1	1	0	0	17	0	28	1	0	0	2	.000	0	0--	—	4.38
2001 Pawtucket	AAA	47	0	0	12	71	295	62	27	27	7	6	2	5	19	1	72	4	2	3	3	.500	0	2--	—	3.42
1997 Kansas City	AL	3	0	0	1	4	24	3	6	6	1	1	0	1	8	0	2	0	0	0	0	—	0	0-0	0	13.50
1998 Kansas City	AL	7	0	0	1	6	29	9	7	7	3	0	0	0	2	0	3	0	0	0	0	—	0	0-0	0	10.50
2000 Detroit	AL	13	0	0	1	10	43	13	9	8	2	0	0	1	1	0	7	1	0	0	0	—	0	0-0	0	7.20
2001 Boston	AL	15	0	0	8	14.2	64	13	9	9	1	0	1	1	7	1	16	0	0	0	0	—	0	0-1	0	5.52
4 ML YEARS		38	0	0	11	34.2	160	38	31	30	8	1	1	3	18	1	28	1	0	0	0	—	0	0-1	2	7.79

Donzell McDonald

Bats: Both Throws: Right Pos: PH/PR-4; CF-2; LF-1   Ht: 5'11" Wt: 180 Born: 2/20/75 Age: 27

Year Team	Lg	G	AB	H	2B	3B	HR	(Hm	Rd)	TB	R	RBI	TBB	IBB	SO	HBP	SH	SF	SB	CS	SB%	GDP	Avg	OBP	SLG
1995 Yankees	R	28	110	26	5	1	0	—	—	33	23	9	16	0	24	2	0	1	11	2	.85	1	.236	.341	.300
1996 Oneonta	A-	74	282	78	8	10	2	—	—	112	57	30	43	0	62	2	3	2	54	4	.93	1	.277	.374	.397
1997 Tampa	A+	77	297	88	23	8	3	—	—	136	69	23	48	0	75	4	1	1	39	18	.68	3	.296	.400	.458
1998 Norwich	AA	134	495	125	20	7	6	—	—	177	80	36	55	1	127	4	7	4	35	22	.61	7	.253	.330	.358
Tampa	A+	5	18	6	1	2	0	—	—	11	6	2	2	0	7	1	1	0	2	0	1.00	0	.333	.429	.611
1999 Norwich	AA	137	533	145	19	10	4	—	—	196	95	33	90	0	110	6	11	1	54	20	.73	5	.272	.383	.368
2000 Columbus	AAA	24	77	19	4	4	1	—	—	34	17	6	23	0	11	2	2	0	12	0	1.00	0	.247	.431	.442
Norwich	AA	44	170	41	7	2	2	—	—	58	23	10	35	1	36	0	0	0	13	7	.65	1	.241	.371	.341
2001 Columbus	AAA	105	374	96	11	9	8	—	—	149	59	36	42	1	79	7	1	1	20	4	.83	2	.257	.342	.398
2001 New York	AL	5	3	1	0	0	0	(0	0)	1	0	0	0	0	2	0	1	0	0	0	—	0	.333	.333	.333

John McDonald

Bats: R Throws: R Pos: SS-9; 2B-3; 3B-3; PH/PR-3   Ht: 5'11" Wt: 175 Born: 9/24/74 Age: 27

Year Team	Lg	G	AB	H	2B	3B	HR	(Hm	Rd)	TB	R	RBI	TBB	IBB	SO	HBP	SH	SF	SB	CS	SB%	GDP	Avg	OBP	SLG
1996 Watertown	A-	75	278	75	11	0	2	—	—	92	48	26	32	0	49	5	11	1	11	1	.92	3	.270	.354	.331
1997 Kinston	A+	130	541	140	27	3	5	—	—	188	77	53	51	0	75	2	7	2	6	5	.55	12	.259	.324	.348
1998 Akron	AA	132	514	118	18	2	2	—	—	146	68	43	43	0	61	6	11	6	17	6	.74	7	.230	.293	.284
1999 Akron	AA	55	226	67	12	0	1	—	—	82	31	26	19	0	26	2	2	4	7	3	.70	5	.296	.351	.363
Buffalo	AAA	66	237	75	12	1	0	—	—	89	30	25	11	0	23	2	5	2	6	3	.67	5	.316	.349	.376
2000 Mahoning Vy	A-	5	17	2	1	0	0	—	—	3	1	1	2	0	3	0	0	0	0	0	—	0	.118	.211	.176

Year Team	Lg	G	AB	H	2B	3B	HR	(Hm	Rd)	TB	R	RBI	TBB	IBB	SO	HBP	SH	SF	SB	CS	SB%	GDP	Avg	OBP	SLG
Buffalo	AAA	75	286	77	17	2	1	—	—	101	37	36	21	1	29	1	7	6	4	3	.57	7	.269	.315	.353
Kinston	A+	1	3	1	0	0	0	—	—	1	0	0	0	0	0	0	0	0	0	0	—	0	.333	.333	.333
2001 Buffalo	AAA	116	410	100	17	1	2	—	—	125	52	33	33	0	72	6	9	6	17	10	.63	11	.244	.305	.305
1999 Cleveland	AL	18	21	7	0	0	0	(0	0)	7	2	0	0	0	3	0	0	0	0	1	.00	0	.333	.333	.333
2000 Cleveland	AL	9	9	4	0	0	0	(0	0)	4	0	0	0	0	1	0	0	0	0	0	—	0	.444	.444	.444
2001 Cleveland	AL	17	22	2	1	0	0	(0	0)	3	1	0	1	0	7	1	1	0	0	0	—	0	.091	.167	.136
3 ML YEARS		44	52	13	1	0	0	(0	0)	14	3	0	1	0	11	1	1	0	0	1	.00	2	.250	.278	.269

Keith McDonald

Bats: Right **Throws:** Right **Pos:** C-2; PH/PR-1　　**Ht:** 6'2" **Wt:** 215 **Born:** 2/8/73 **Age:** 29

Year Team	Lg	G	AB	H	2B	3B	HR	(Hm	Rd)	TB	R	RBI	TBB	IBB	SO	HBP	SH	SF	SB	CS	SB%	GDP	Avg	OBP	SLG
1994 Johnson Cty	R+	59	199	49	12	0	6	—	—	79	32	31	27	3	36	5	2	3	3	1	.75	9	.246	.346	.397
1995 Peoria	A	65	179	48	6	0	1	—	—	57	22	20	22	0	38	6	4	0	0	1	.00	2	.268	.367	.318
1996 St. Pete	A+	114	410	111	25	0	2	—	—	142	30	52	34	1	65	5	1	5	1	3	.25	18	.271	.330	.346
1997 Arkansas	AA	79	233	56	16	0	5	—	—	87	32	30	31	0	56	3	1	0	0	0	—	4	.240	.337	.373
1998 Memphis	AAA	58	170	54	8	0	7	—	—	83	21	22	10	2	30	2	2	0	1	1	.50	2	.318	.363	.488
1999 Arkansas	AA	49	163	50	10	0	2	—	—	66	21	14	15	0	35	3	0	2	1	0	1.00	1	.307	.372	.405
Memphis	AAA	39	113	34	7	0	5	—	—	56	20	27	20	0	25	0	1	2	1	0	1.00	1	.301	.400	.496
2000 Memphis	AAA	83	266	70	15	0	5	—	—	100	34	30	28	1	59	3	5	6	1	0	1.00	8	.263	.333	.376
2001 Memphis	AAA	94	333	87	22	1	11	—	—	144	42	42	24	1	60	2	0	3	1	0	1.00	13	.261	.312	.432
2000 St. Louis	NL	6	7	3	0	0	3	(2	1)	12	3	5	2	0	1	0	0	0	0	0	—	1	.429	.556	1.714
2001 St. Louis	NL	2	2	0	0	0	0	—	—	0	0	0	0	0	1	0	0	0	0	0	—	0	.000	.000	.000
2 ML YEARS		8	9	3	0	0	3	(2	1)	12	3	5	2	0	2	0	0	0	0	0	—	1	.333	.455	1.333

Chuck McElroy

Pitches: Left **Bats:** Left **Pos:** RP-44; SP-5　　**Ht:** 6'0" **Wt:** 205 **Born:** 10/1/67 **Age:** 34

Year Team	Lg	G	GS	CG	GF	IP	BFP	H	R	ER	HR	SH	SF	HB	TBB	IBB	SO	WP	Bk	W	L	Pct.	ShO	Sv-Op	Hld	ERA
1989 Philadelphia	NL	11	0	0	4	10.1	46	12	2	2	1	0	0	0	4	1	8	0	0	0	0		0	0-0	0	1.74
1990 Philadelphia	NL	16	0	0	8	14	76	24	13	12	0	0	1	0	10	2	16	0	0	0	1	.000	0	0-0	1	7.71
1991 Chicago	NL	71	0	0	12	101.1	419	73	33	22	7	9	6	0	57	7	92	1	0	6	2	.750	0	3-6	10	1.95
1992 Chicago	NL	72	0	0	30	83.2	369	73	40	33	5	5	5	0	51	10	83	3	0	4	7	.364	0	6-11	3	3.55
1993 Chicago	NL	49	0	0	11	47.1	214	51	30	24	4	5	1	1	25	5	31	3	0	2	2	.500	0	0-0	4	4.56
1994 Cincinnati	NL	52	0	0	13	57.2	230	52	15	15	3	2	0	0	15	2	38	4	0	1	2	.333	0	5-11	10	2.34
1995 Cincinnati	NL	44	0	0	11	40.1	178	46	29	27	5	1	3	1	15	3	27	1	0	3	4	.429	0	0-3	5	6.02
1996 Cin-Cal		52	0	0	12	49	210	45	22	21	4	1	1	2	23	3	45	1	0	7	1	.875	0	0-2	7	3.86
1997 Ana-CWS	AL	61	0	0	16	75	302	73	36	32	5	3	3	2	22	1	62	1	0	1	3	.250	0	1-6	15	3.84
1998 Colorado	NL	78	0	0	27	68.1	281	68	23	22	3	0	3	0	24	0	61	0	0	6	4	.600	0	2-6	19	2.90
1999 Col-NYM	NL	56	0	0	19	54	251	60	34	33	9	1	3	1	36	4	44	5	0	3	1	.750	0	0-3	5	5.50
2000 Baltimore	AL	43	2	0	10	63.1	282	60	36	33	6	0	3	2	34	2	50	6	0	3	0	1.000	0	0-1	2	4.69
2001 Bal-SD	NL	49	5	0	6	75	357	87	53	44	14	1	2	2	46	6	47	6	0	2	3	.400	0	0-3	3	5.28
1996 Cincinnati	NL	12	0	0	1	12.1	59	13	10	9	2	0	0	0	10	1	13	0	0	2	0	1.000	0	0-0	1	6.57
California	AL	40	0	0	11	36.2	151	32	12	12	2	1	1	2	13	2	32	1	0	5	1	.833	0	0-2	6	2.95
1997 Anaheim	AL	13	0	0	3	15.2	66	17	7	6	2	0	0	0	3	0	18	0	0	0	0	—	0	0-2	4	3.45
Chicago	AL	48	0	0	13	59.1	254	56	29	26	3	3	3	2	19	1	44	1	0	1	3	.250	0	1-4	11	3.94
1999 Colorado	NL	41	0	0	12	40.2	192	48	29	28	9	0	2	0	28	3	37	4	0	3	1	.750	0	0-3	5	6.20
New York	NL	15	0	0	7	13.1	59	12	5	5	0	1	1	1	8	1	7	1	0	0	0	—	0	0-0	0	3.38
2001 Baltimore	AL	18	5	0	0	45.1	213	49	29	27	8	0	1	2	28	2	22	3	0	1	2	.333	0	0-0	1	5.36
San Diego	NL	31	0	0	6	29.2	144	38	24	17	6	1	1	0	18	4	25	3	0	1	1	.500	0	0-3	2	5.16
13 ML YEARS		654	7	0	179	739.1	3233	724	366	320	66	28	31	11	362	46	604	31	0	38	30	.559	0	17-52	81	3.90

Joe McEwing

Bats: R **Throws:** R **Pos:** LF-48; PH/PR-36; 3B-25; RF-25; SS-12; 2B-5; 1B-3; CF-2; DH-1　**Ht:** 5'11" **Wt:** 170 **Born:** 10/19/72 **Age:** 29

Year Team	Lg	G	AB	H	2B	3B	HR	(Hm	Rd)	TB	R	RBI	TBB	IBB	SO	HBP	SH	SF	SB	CS	SB%	GDP	Avg	OBP	SLG
1998 St. Louis	NL	10	20	4	1	0	0	(0	0)	5	5	1	1	0	3	1	1	0	0	1	.00	0	.200	.273	.250
1999 St. Louis	NL	152	513	141	28	4	9	(5	4)	204	65	44	41	8	87	6	9	5	7	4	.64	3	.275	.333	.398
2000 New York	NL	87	153	34	14	1	2	(1	1)	56	20	19	5	0	29	1	8	2	3	1	.75	2	.222	.248	.366
2001 New York	NL	116	283	80	17	3	8	(3	5)	127	41	30	17	0	57	10	6	3	8	5	.62	2	.283	.342	.449
4 ML YEARS		365	969	259	60	8	19	(9	10)	392	131	94	64	8	176	18	24	10	18	11	.62	7	.267	.321	.405

Kevin McGlinchy

Pitches: Right **Bats:** Right **2000 Pos:** RP-10　　**Ht:** 6'5" **Wt:** 220 **Born:** 6/28/77 **Age:** 25

Year Team	Lg	G	GS	CG	GF	IP	BFP	H	R	ER	HR	SH	SF	HB	TBB	IBB	SO	WP	Bk	W	L	Pct.	ShO	Sv-Op	Hld	ERA
2001 Braves *	R	2	2	0	0	2	7	1	0	0	0	0	0	0	2	0	2	0	0	0	0	—	0	0--	0	0.00
1999 Atlanta	NL	64	0	0	21	70.1	298	66	25	22	6	4	4	1	30	7	67	1	0	7	3	.700	0	0-2	7	2.82
2000 Atlanta	NL	10	0	0	6	8.1	42	11	4	2	1	1	0	0	6	1	9	1	0	0	0	—	0	0-0	0	2.16
2 ML YEARS		74	0	0	27	78.2	340	77	29	24	7	5	4	1	36	8	76	2	0	7	3	.700	0	0-2	7	2.75

Fred McGriff

Bats: Left **Throws:** Left **Pos:** 1B-123; DH-17; PH/PR-6   **Ht:** 6'3" **Wt:** 215 **Born:** 10/31/63 **Age:** 38

Year Team	Lg	G	AB	H	2B	3B	HR	(Hm	Rd)	TB	R	RBI	TBB	IBB	SO	HBP	SH	SF	SB	CS	SB%	GDP	Avg	OBP	SLG
1986 Toronto	AL	3	5	1	0	0	0	(0	0)	1	1	0	0	0	2	0	0	0	0	0	—	0	.200	.200	.200
1987 Toronto	AL	107	295	73	16	0	20	(7	13)	149	58	43	60	4	104	1	0	0	3	2	.60	3	.247	.376	.505
1988 Toronto	AL	154	536	151	35	4	34	(18	16)	296	100	82	79	3	149	4	0	4	6	1	.86	15	.282	.376	.552
1989 Toronto	AL	161	551	148	27	3	36	(18	18)	289	98	92	119	12	132	4	1	5	7	4	.64	14	.269	.399	.525
1990 Toronto	AL	153	557	167	21	1	35	(14	21)	295	91	88	94	12	108	2	1	4	5	3	.63	7	.300	.400	.530
1991 San Diego	NL	153	528	147	19	1	31	(18	13)	261	84	106	105	26	135	2	0	7	4	1	.80	14	.278	.396	.494
1992 San Diego	NL	152	531	152	30	4	35	(21	14)	295	79	104	96	23	108	1	0	4	8	6	.57	14	.286	.394	.556
1993 SD-Atl	NL	151	557	162	29	2	37	(15	22)	306	111	101	76	6	106	2	0	5	5	3	.63	14	.291	.375	.549
1994 Atlanta	NL	113	424	135	25	1	34	(13	21)	264	81	94	50	8	76	1	0	3	7	3	.70	8	.318	.389	.623
1995 Atlanta	NL	144	528	148	27	1	27	(15	12)	258	85	93	65	6	99	5	0	6	3	6	.33	19	.280	.361	.489
1996 Atlanta	NL	159	617	182	37	1	28	(17	11)	305	81	107	68	12	116	2	0	4	7	3	.70	20	.295	.365	.494
1997 Atlanta	NL	152	564	156	25	1	22	(8	14)	249	77	97	68	4	112	4	0	5	5	0	1.00	22	.277	.356	.441
1998 Tampa Bay	AL	151	564	160	33	0	19	(14	5)	250	73	81	79	9	118	2	0	4	7	2	.78	14	.284	.371	.443
1999 Tampa Bay	AL	144	529	164	30	1	32	(18	14)	292	75	104	86	11	107	1	0	4	1	0	1.00	12	.310	.405	.552
2000 Tampa Bay	AL	158	566	157	18	0	27	(10	17)	256	82	106	91	10	120	0	0	7	2	0	1.00	16	.277	.373	.452
2001 TB-ChC		146	513	157	25	2	31	(17	14)	279	67	102	66	13	106	3	0	4	1	2	.33	13	.306	.386	.544
1993 San Diego	NL	83	302	83	11	1	18	(7	11)	150	52	46	42	4	55	1	0	4	4	3	.57	9	.275	.361	.497
Atlanta	NL	68	255	79	18	1	19	(8	11)	156	59	55	34	2	51	1	0	1	1	0	1.00	5	.310	.392	.612
2001 Tampa Bay	AL	97	343	109	18	0	19	(10	9)	184	40	61	40	9	69	0	0	2	1	1	.50	7	.318	.387	.536
Chicago	NL	49	170	48	7	2	12	(7	5)	95	27	41	26	4	37	3	0	2	0	1	.00	6	.282	.383	.559
16 ML YEARS		2201	7865	2260	397	22	448	(223	225)	4045	1243	1400	1202	159	1698	34	2	66	71	36	.66	205	.287	.381	.514

Ryan McGuire

Bats: Left **Throws:** Left **Pos:** PH/PR-39; RF-9; 1B-4   **Ht:** 6'0" **Wt:** 215 **Born:** 11/23/71 **Age:** 30

Year Team	Lg	G	AB	H	2B	3B	HR	(Hm	Rd)	TB	R	RBI	TBB	IBB	SO	HBP	SH	SF	SB	CS	SB%	GDP	Avg	OBP	SLG
2001 Calgary *	AAA	62	239	72	14	2	8	—	—	114	45	42	26	0	49	1	1	2	0	1	.00	10	.301	.369	.477
1997 Montreal	NL	84	199	51	15	2	3	(2	1)	79	22	17	19	1	34	0	3	1	1	4	.20	3	.256	.320	.397
1998 Montreal	NL	130	210	39	9	0	1	(1	0)	51	17	10	32	0	55	0	1	1	0	0	—	9	.186	.292	.243
1999 Montreal	NL	88	140	31	7	2	2	(1	1)	48	17	18	27	0	33	0	3	0	1	1	.50	9	.221	.347	.343
2000 New York	NL	1	2	0	0	0	0	(0	0)	0	0	0	1	0	0	0	0	0	0	0	—	1	.000	.333	.000
2001 Florida	NL	48	54	10	2	0	1	(1	0)	15	8	8	7	0	15	0	0	2	1	0	1.00	0	.185	.270	.278
5 ML YEARS		351	605	131	33	4	7	(5	2)	193	64	53	86	1	137	0	7	4	3	5	.38	22	.217	.312	.319

Mark McGwire

Bats: Right **Throws:** Right **Pos:** 1B-90; PH/PR-8   **Ht:** 6'5" **Wt:** 250 **Born:** 10/1/63 **Age:** 38

Year Team	Lg	G	AB	H	2B	3B	HR	(Hm	Rd)	TB	R	RBI	TBB	IBB	SO	HBP	SH	SF	SB	CS	SB%	GDP	Avg	OBP	SLG
1986 Oakland	AL	18	53	10	1	0	3	(1	2)	20	10	9	4	0	18	1	0	0	0	1	.00	0	.189	.259	.377
1987 Oakland	AL	151	557	161	28	4	49	(21	28)	344	97	118	71	8	131	5	0	8	1	1	.50	6	.289	.370	.618
1988 Oakland	AL	155	550	143	22	1	32	(12	20)	263	87	99	76	4	117	4	1	4	0	0	—	15	.260	.352	.478
1989 Oakland	AL	143	490	113	17	0	33	(12	21)	229	74	95	83	5	94	3	0	11	1	1	.50	23	.231	.339	.467
1990 Oakland	AL	156	523	123	16	0	39	(14	25)	256	87	108	110	9	116	7	1	9	2	1	.67	13	.235	.370	.489
1991 Oakland	AL	154	483	97	22	0	22	(15	7)	185	62	75	93	3	116	3	1	5	2	1	.67	13	.201	.330	.383
1992 Oakland	AL	139	467	125	22	0	42	(24	18)	273	87	104	90	12	105	5	0	9	0	1	.00	10	.268	.385	.585
1993 Oakland	AL	27	84	28	6	0	9	(5	4)	61	16	24	21	5	19	1	0	1	0	1	.00	0	.333	.467	.726
1994 Oakland	AL	47	135	34	3	0	9	(6	3)	64	26	25	37	3	40	0	0	0	0	0	—	3	.252	.413	.474
1995 Oakland	AL	104	317	87	13	0	39	(15	24)	217	75	90	88	5	77	11	0	6	1	1	.50	9	.274	.441	.685
1996 Oakland	AL	130	423	132	21	0	52	(24	28)	309	104	113	116	16	112	8	0	1	0	0	—	14	.312	.467	.730
1997 Oak-StL		156	540	148	27	0	58	(30	28)	349	86	123	101	16	159	9	0	7	3	0	1.00	9	.274	.393	.646
1998 St. Louis	NL	155	509	152	21	0	70	(38	32)	383	130	147	162	28	155	6	0	4	1	0	1.00	8	.299	.470	.752
1999 St. Louis	NL	153	521	145	21	1	65	(37	28)	363	118	147	133	21	141	2	0	5	0	0	—	12	.278	.424	.697
2000 St. Louis	NL	89	236	72	8	0	32	(18	14)	176	60	73	76	12	78	7	0	2	1	0	1.00	5	.305	.483	.746
2001 St. Louis	NL	97	299	56	4	0	29	(13	16)	147	48	64	56	3	118	3	0	6	0	0	—	7	.187	.316	.492
1997 Oakland	AL	105	366	104	24	0	34	(17	17)	230	48	81	58	8	98	4	0	5	1	0	1.00	9	.284	.383	.628
St. Louis	NL	51	174	44	3	0	24	(13	11)	119	38	42	43	8	61	5	0	2	2	0	1.00	0	.253	.411	.684
16 ML YEARS		1874	6187	1626	252	6	583	(285	298)	3639	1167	1414	1317	150	1596	75	3	78	12	8	.60	147	.263	.394	.588

Tony McKnight

Pitches: Right **Bats:** Left **Pos:** SP-15   **Ht:** 6'5" **Wt:** 205 **Born:** 6/29/77 **Age:** 25

Year Team	Lg	G	GS	CG	GF	IP	BFP	H	R	ER	HR	SH	SF	HB	TBB	IBB	SO	WP	Bk	W	L	Pct.	ShO	Sv-Op	Hld	ERA
1995 Astros	R	3	3	0	0	11.2	48	14	5	5	0	0	2	0	2	0	8	1	0	1	1	.500	0	0--	—	3.86
1996 Astros	R	8	5	0	0	21.2	108	28	21	15	1	0	2	3	7	0	15	3	0	2	1	.667	0	0--	—	6.23
1997 Quad City	A	20	20	0	0	115.1	504	116	71	60	7	6	3	5	55	5	92	6	3	4	9	.308	0	0--	—	4.68
1998 Kissimmee	A+	28	28	0	0	154.1	701	191	101	80	12	4	3	9	50	2	104	12	2	11	13	.458	0	0--	—	4.67
1999 Jackson	AA	24	24	0	0	160.1	653	134	60	49	15	1	0	4	44	0	118	6	1	9	9	.500	0	0--	—	2.75
2000 Round Rock	AA	6	6	0	0	32	141	39	19	17	4	0	1	1	10	1	24	1	0	0	2	.000	0	0--	—	4.78
New Orleans	AAA	19	19	0	0	118.1	511	129	66	60	10	7	3	5	36	3	63	2	2	4	8	.333	0	0--	—	4.56
2001 New Orleans	AAA	18	18	1	0	92.2	396	104	56	49	10	2	4	3	24	0	61	0	0	9	5	.643	0	0--	—	4.76
2000 Houston	NL	6	6	1	0	35	156	35	19	15	4	1	1	2	9	0	23	2	0	4	1	.800	0	0-0	0	3.86
2001 Hou-Pit	NL	15	15	0	0	87.1	396	109	52	48	19	4	3	5	24	4	46	5	0	3	6	.333	0	0-0	0	4.95
2001 Houston	NL	3	3	0	0	18	80	21	8	8	4	1	1	2	3	0	10	1	0	1	0	1.000	0	0-0	0	4.00
Pittsburgh	NL	12	12	0	0	69.1	316	88	44	40	15	3	2	3	21	4	36	4	0	2	6	.250	0	0-0	0	5.19
2 ML YEARS		21	21	1	0	122.1	552	144	71	63	23	5	4	7	33	4	69	7	0	4	7	.500	0	0-0	0	4.63

Mark McLemore

Bats: B **Throws:** R **Pos:** LF-63; 3B-36; SS-35; PH/PR-16; 2B-9; CF-8; DH-2; RF-2   **Ht:** 5'11" **Wt:** 207 **Born:** 10/4/64 **Age:** 37

						BATTING												BASERUNNING				PERCENTAGES		
Year Team	Lg	G	AB	H	2B	3B	HR	(Hm | Rd)	TB	R	RBI	TBB	IBB	SO	HBP	SH	SF	SB	CS	SB%	GDP	Avg	OBP	SLG
1986 California	AL	5	4	0	0	0	0	(0 | 0)	0	0	0	1	0	2	0	1	0	0	1	1.00	0	.000	.200	.000
1987 California	AL	138	433	102	13	3	3	(3 | 0)	130	61	41	48	0	72	0	15	3	25	8	.76	7	.236	.310	.300
1988 California	AL	77	233	56	11	2	2	(1 | 1)	77	38	16	25	0	28	0	5	2	13	7	.65	6	.240	.312	.330
1989 California	AL	32	103	25	3	1	0	(0 | 0)	30	12	14	7	0	19	1	3	1	6	1	.86	2	.243	.295	.291
1990 Cal-Cle	AL	28	60	9	2	0	0	(0 | 0)	11	6	2	4	0	15	0	1	0	1	0	1.00	1	.150	.203	.183
1991 Houston	NL	21	61	9	1	0	0	(0 | 0)	10	6	2	6	0	13	0	0	1	0	1	.00	1	.148	.221	.164
1992 Baltimore	AL	101	228	56	7	2	0	(0 | 0)	67	40	27	21	1	26	0	6	1	11	5	.69	6	.246	.308	.294
1993 Baltimore	AL	148	581	165	27	5	4	(2 | 2)	214	81	72	64	4	92	1	11	6	21	15	.58	21	.284	.353	.368
1994 Baltimore	AL	104	343	88	11	1	3	(2 | 1)	110	44	29	51	3	50	1	4	1	20	5	.80	7	.257	.354	.321
1995 Texas	AL	129	467	122	20	5	5	(3 | 2)	167	73	41	59	6	71	3	10	3	21	11	.66	10	.261	.346	.358
1996 Texas	AL	147	517	150	23	4	5	(3 | 2)	196	84	46	87	5	69	0	2	5	27	10	.73	16	.290	.389	.379
1997 Texas	AL	89	349	91	17	2	1	(0 | 1)	115	47	25	40	1	54	2	6	2	7	5	.58	5	.261	.338	.330
1998 Texas	AL	126	461	114	15	1	5	(4 | 1)	146	79	53	89	1	64	2	12	3	12	4	.75	15	.247	.369	.317
1999 Texas	AL	144	566	155	20	7	6	(2 | 4)	207	105	45	83	2	79	0	9	6	16	8	.67	8	.274	.363	.366
2000 Seattle	AL	138	481	118	23	1	3	(2 | 1)	152	72	46	81	2	78	1	11	4	30	14	.68	12	.245	.353	.316
2001 Seattle	AL	125	409	117	16	9	5	(2 | 3)	166	78	57	69	0	84	0	3	6	39	7	.85	6	.286	.384	.406
1990 California	AL	20	48	7	2	0	0	(0 | 0)	9	4	2	4	0	9	0	1	0	1	0	1.00	1	.146	.212	.188
Cleveland	AL	8	12	2	0	0	0	(0 | 0)	2	2	0	0	0	6	0	0	0	0	0	—	0	.167	.167	.167
16 ML YEARS		1552	5296	1377	209	43	42	(24 | 18)	1798	826	516	735	25	816	11	99	44	249	102	.71	123	.260	.349	.340

Billy McMillon

Bats: L **Throws:** L **Pos:** PH/PR-17; LF-16; RF-8; DH-4   **Ht:** 5'11" **Wt:** 179 **Born:** 11/17/71 **Age:** 30

						BATTING												BASERUNNING				PERCENTAGES		
Year Team	Lg	G	AB	H	2B	3B	HR	(Hm | Rd)	TB	R	RBI	TBB	IBB	SO	HBP	SH	SF	SB	CS	SB%	GDP	Avg	OBP	SLG
1996 Florida	NL	28	51	11	0	0	0	(0 | 0)	11	4	4	5	1	14	0	0	0	0	0	—	1	.216	.286	.216
1997 Fla-Phi	NL	37	90	23	5	1	2	(2 | 0)	36	10	14	6	0	24	0	0	3	2	1	.67	1	.256	.293	.400
2000 Detroit	AL	46	123	37	7	1	4	(3 | 1)	58	20	24	19	0	19	1	2	4	1	0	1.00	2	.301	.388	.472
2001 Det-Oak	AL	40	92	20	8	1	1	(0 | 1)	33	7	14	7	0	25	2	0	1	1	0	1.00	1	.217	.284	.359
1997 Florida	NL	13	18	2	1	0	0	(0 | 0)	3	0	1	0	0	7	0	0	0	0	0	—	0	.111	.111	.167
Philadelphia	NL	24	72	21	4	1	2	(2 | 0)	33	10	13	6	0	17	0	0	3	2	1	.67	1	.292	.333	.458
2001 Detroit	AL	20	34	3	1	0	1	(0 | 1)	7	1	4	2	0	12	1	0	0	0	0	—	1	.088	.162	.206
Oakland	AL	20	58	17	7	1	0	(0 | 0)	26	6	10	5	0	13	1	0	1	1	0	1.00	0	.293	.354	.448
4 ML YEARS		151	356	91	20	3	7	(5 | 2)	138	41	56	37	1	82	3	2	8	4	1	.80	5	.256	.324	.388

Rusty Meacham

Pitches: Right **Bats:** Right **Pos:** RP-24   **Ht:** 6'3" **Wt:** 180 **Born:** 1/27/68 **Age:** 34

		HOW MUCH HE PITCHED						WHAT HE GAVE UP											THE RESULTS					
Year Team		G	GS	CG	GF	IP	BFP	H	R	ER	HR	SH	SF	HB	TBB	IBB	SO	WP	Bk	W	L	Pct.	ShO	Sv-Op	Hld	ERA
2001 Durham *	AAA	27	0	0	26	31	114	17	4	3	2	2	0	1	5	0	30	1	0	2	1	.667	0	15--	—	0.87
1991 Detroit	AL	10	4	0	1	27.2	126	35	17	16	4	1	3	0	11	0	14	0	1	2	1	.667	0	0-0	1	5.20
1992 Kansas City	AL	64	0	0	20	101.2	412	88	39	31	5	3	9	1	21	5	64	4	0	10	4	.714	0	2-6	15	2.74
1993 Kansas City	AL	15	0	0	11	21	104	31	15	13	2	0	1	3	5	1	13	0	0	2	2	.500	0	0-0	1	5.57
1994 Kansas City	AL	36	0	0	15	50.2	213	51	23	21	7	1	4	2	12	1	36	4	0	3	3	.500	0	4-5	7	3.73
1995 Kansas City	AL	49	0	0	26	59.2	262	72	36	33	6	1	4	1	19	5	30	0	0	4	3	.571	0	2-3	7	4.98
1996 Seattle	AL	15	0	0	3	42.1	192	57	28	27	9	0	1	4	13	1	25	1	0	1	1	.500	0	1-1	0	5.74
2000 Houston	NL	5	0	0	2	4.2	23	8	6	6	3	0	0	0	2	0	3	0	0	0	0	—	0	0-0	0	11.57
2001 Tampa Bay	AL	24	0	0	5	35.1	158	39	24	22	3	1	4	2	10	0	13	2	0	1	3	.250	0	0-0	3	5.60
8 ML YEARS		218	9	0	83	343	1490	381	188	169	39	7	26	13	93	13	198	11	1	23	17	.575	0	9-15	34	4.43

Brian Meadows

Pitches: Right **Bats:** Right **Pos:** SP-10   **Ht:** 6'4" **Wt:** 220 **Born:** 11/21/75 **Age:** 26

		HOW MUCH HE PITCHED						WHAT HE GAVE UP											THE RESULTS					
Year Team	Lg	G	GS	CG	GF	IP	BFP	H	R	ER	HR	SH	SF	HB	TBB	IBB	SO	WP	Bk	W	L	Pct.	ShO	Sv-Op	Hld	ERA
2001 Omaha *	AAA	18	18	0	0	105	460	143	73	72	21	1	3	5	20	1	74	1	0	6	5	.545	0	0--	—	6.17
1998 Florida	NL	31	31	1	0	174.1	772	222	106	101	20	14	4	3	46	3	88	5	1	11	13	.458	0	0-0	0	5.21
1999 Florida	NL	31	31	0	0	178.1	795	214	117	111	31	16	8	5	57	5	72	4	1	11	15	.423	0	0-0	0	5.60
2000 SD-KC		33	32	2	0	196.1	869	234	119	112	32	7	5	8	64	6	79	3	0	13	10	.565	0	0-0	0	5.13
2001 Kansas City	AL	10	10	0	0	50.1	224	73	41	39	12	1	2	1	12	2	21	1	0	1	6	.143	0	0-0	0	6.97
2000 San Diego	NL	22	22	0	0	124.2	565	150	80	74	24	7	2	8	50	6	53	3	0	7	8	.467	0	0-0	0	5.34
Kansas City	AL	11	10	2	0	71.2	304	84	39	38	8	0	3	0	14	0	26	0	0	6	2	.750	0	0-0	0	4.77
4 ML YEARS		105	104	3	0	599.1	2660	743	383	363	95	38	19	17	179	16	260	13	2	36	44	.450	0	0-0	0	5.45

Pat Meares

Bats: Right **Throws:** Right **Pos:** 2B-85; PH/PR-3   **Ht:** 6'0" **Wt:** 187 **Born:** 9/6/68 **Age:** 33

						BATTING												BASERUNNING				PERCENTAGES		
Year Team	Lg	G	AB	H	2B	3B	HR	(Hm	Rd)	TB	R	RBI	TBB	IBB	SO	HBP	SH	SF	SB	CS	SB%	GDP	Avg	OBP	SLG
1993 Minnesota	AL	111	346	87	14	3	0	(0	0)	107	33	33	7	0	52	1	4	3	4	5	.44	11	.251	.266	.309
1994 Minnesota	AL	80	229	61	12	1	2	(0	2)	81	29	24	14	0	50	2	6	3	5	1	.83	3	.266	.310	.354
1995 Minnesota	AL	116	390	105	19	4	12	(3	9)	168	57	49	15	0	68	11	4	5	10	4	.71	17	.269	.311	.431
1996 Minnesota	AL	152	517	138	26	7	8	(5	3)	202	66	67	17	1	90	9	4	7	9	4	.69	19	.267	.298	.391
1997 Minnesota	AL	134	439	121	23	3	10	(5	5)	180	63	60	18	0	86	16	3	7	7	7	.50	7	.276	.323	.410
1998 Minnesota	AL	149	543	141	26	3	9	(2	7)	200	56	70	24	1	86	6	3	5	7	4	.64	12	.260	.296	.368
1999 Pittsburgh	NL	21	91	28	4	0	0	(0	0)	32	15	7	9	0	20	2	2	0	0	0	—	1	.308	.382	.352
2000 Pittsburgh	NL	132	462	111	22	2	13	(7	6)	176	55	47	36	6	91	8	5	3	0	1	1.00	13	.240	.305	.381
2001 Pittsburgh	NL	87	270	57	11	1	4	(2	2)	82	27	25	10	3	45	2	1	1	0	2	.00	11	.211	.244	.304
9 ML YEARS		982	3287	849	157	24	58	(22	36)	1228	401	382	150	11	588	57	32	34	43	27	.61	94	.258	.299	.374

Gil Meche

Pitches: Right **Bats:** Right **2000 Pos:** SP-15   **Ht:** 6'3" **Wt:** 200 **Born:** 9/8/78 **Age:** 23

		HOW MUCH HE PITCHED						WHAT HE GAVE UP											THE RESULTS						
Year Team	Lg	G	GS	CG	GF	IP	BFP	H	R	ER	HR	SH	SF	HB	TBB	IBB	SO	WP	Bk	W	L	Pct.	ShO	Sv-Op	Hld	ERA
1999 Seattle	AL	16	15	0	0	85.2	375	73	48	45	9	5	3	2	57	1	47	1	0	8	4	.667	0	0-0	0	4.73
2000 Seattle	AL	15	15	0	0	85.2	363	75	37	36	7	5	4	1	40	0	60	2	0	4	4	.500	1	0-0	0	3.78
2 ML YEARS		31	30	1	0	171.1	738	148	85	81	16	10	7	3	97	1	107	3	0	12	8	.600	1	0-0	0	4.25

Jim Mecir

Pitches: Right **Bats:** Both **Pos:** RP-54   **Ht:** 6'1" **Wt:** 210 **Born:** 5/16/70 **Age:** 32

		HOW MUCH HE PITCHED						WHAT HE GAVE UP											THE RESULTS						
Year Team	Lg	G	GS	CG	GF	IP	BFP	H	R	ER	HR	SH	SF	HB	TBB	IBB	SO	WP	Bk	W	L	Pct.	ShO	Sv-Op	Hld	ERA
2001 Sacramento *	AAA	1	1	0	0	1	4	1	0	0	0	0	0	0	0	0	0	0	0	0	0	—	0	0- -		0.00
1995 Seattle	AL	2	0	0	1	4.2	21	5	1	0	0	0	0	0	2	0	3	0	0	0	0	—	0	0-0	0	0.00
1996 New York	AL	26	0	0	10	40.1	185	42	24	23	6	5	4	0	23	4	38	6	0	1	1	.500	0	0-0	0	5.13
1997 New York	AL	25	0	0	11	33.2	142	36	23	22	5	0	1	2	10	1	25	1	0	0	4	.000	0	0-1	1	5.88
1998 Tampa Bay	AL	68	0	0	23	84	343	68	30	29	6	3	2	3	33	5	77	2	0	7	2	.778	0	0-3	14	3.11
1999 Tampa Bay	AL	17	0	0	3	20.2	91	15	7	6	0	0	2	1	14	0	15	0	0	0	1	.000	0	0-2	6	2.61
2000 TB-Oak	AL	63	0	0	17	85	352	70	31	28	4	1	2	2	36	2	70	2	0	10	3	.769	0	5-13	21	2.96
2001 Oakland	AL	54	0	0	14	63	264	54	25	24	4	3	0	1	26	7	61	2	0	2	8	.200	0	3-8	17	3.43
2000 Tampa Bay	AL	38	0	0	10	49.2	199	35	17	17	2	1	1	1	22	0	33	0	0	7	2	.778	0	1-4	11	3.08
Oakland	AL	25	0	0	7	35.1	153	35	14	11	2	0	1	1	14	2	37	2	0	3	1	.750	0	4-9	10	2.80
7 ML YEARS		255	0	0	79	331.1	1398	290	141	132	25	12	11	9	144	19	289	13	0	20	19	.513	0	8-27	59	3.59

Adam Melhuse

Bats: Both **Throws:** Right **Pos:** C-23; PH/PR-18; 1B-1   **Ht:** 6'2" **Wt:** 185 **Born:** 3/27/72 **Age:** 30

		BATTING																BASERUNNING				PERCENTAGES		
Year Team	Lg	G	AB	H	2B	3B	HR	(Hm	Rd)	TB	R	RBI	TBB	IBB	SO	HBP	SH	SF	SB	CS	SB%	GDP	Avg	OBP	SLG
1993 St.Cathrnes	A-	73	266	68	14	2	5	—	—	101	40	32	45	4	61	0	2	3	4	0	1.00	4	.256	.360	.380
1994 Hagerstown	A	118	422	109	16	3	11	—	—	164	61	58	53	3	77	1	1	6	6	8	.43	13	.258	.338	.389
1995 Dunedin	A+	123	428	92	20	0	4	—	—	124	43	41	61	1	87	1	1	4	6	1	.86	7	.215	.312	.290
1996 Dunedin	A+	97	315	78	23	2	13	—	—	144	50	51	69	2	68	3	0	4	3	1	.75	5	.248	.384	.457
Knoxville	AA	32	94	20	3	0	1	—	—	26	13	6	14	1	29	0	1	1	0	0	1.00	3	.213	.312	.277
1997 Knoxville	AA	31	87	20	3	0	3	—	—	32	14	10	19	1	19	0	1	1	0	0	—	1	.230	.364	.368
Syracuse	AAA	38	118	28	5	1	2	—	—	41	7	9	12	0	18	1	0	1	1	1	.50	2	.237	.311	.347
1998 Syracuse	AAA	12	38	11	3	0	1	—	—	17	4	7	7	0	6	0	0	1	0	0	—	0	.289	.391	.447
Knoxville	AA	76	240	72	22	0	15	—	—	139	56	43	70	1	39	0	0	4	4	4	.50	6	.300	.458	.579
1999 Syracuse	AAA	21	71	20	5	0	2	—	—	31	15	16	10	0	20	0	0	1	1	1	.50	1	.282	.370	.437
Knoxville	AA	107	374	110	25	0	19	—	—	192	79	69	108	7	76	4	0	3	5	6	.45	10	.294	.454	.513
2000 San Antonio	AA	16	58	23	7	0	2	—	—	36	17	9	11	1	9	2	1	1	3	0	1.00	2	.397	.500	.621
Albuquerque	AAA	36	108	37	9	0	1	—	—	49	21	19	22	0	21	0	2	0	4	2	.67	2	.343	.454	.454
Colo Spmgs	AAA	42	140	39	5	1	3	—	—	55	23	18	21	0	35	0	0	0	2	3	.40	4	.279	.373	.393
2001 Colo Spmgs	AAA	54	184	49	10	1	7	—	—	82	26	32	31	1	42	2	1	0	0	1	.00	8	.266	.378	.446
2000 LA-Col	NL	24	24	4	0	1	0	(0	0)	6	3	4	3	0	6	0	0	0	0	0	—	1	.167	.259	.250
2001 Colorado	NL	40	71	13	2	0	1	(0	1)	18	5	8	6	0	18	0	0	2	1	0	1.00	3	.183	.241	.254
2000 Los Angeles	NL	1	1	0	0	0	0	(0	0)	0	0	0	0	0	1	0	0	0	0	0	—	0	.000	.000	.000
Colorado	NL	23	23	4	0	1	0	(0	0)	6	3	4	3	0	5	0	0	0	0	0	—	1	.174	.269	.261
2 ML YEARS		64	95	17	2	1	1	(0	1)	24	8	12	9	0	24	0	0	2	1	0	1.00	4	.179	.245	.253

Mitch Meluskey

Bats: Both **Throws:** Right **2000 Pos:** C-103; PH/PR-23; 3B-1   **Ht:** 6'0" **Wt:** 185 **Born:** 9/18/73 **Age:** 28

		BATTING																BASERUNNING				PERCENTAGES		
Year Team	Lg	G	AB	H	2B	3B	HR	(Hm	Rd)	TB	R	RBI	TBB	IBB	SO	HBP	SH	SF	SB	CS	SB%	GDP	Avg	OBP	SLG
1998 Houston	NL	8	8	2	1	0	0	(0	0)	3	1	0	1	0	4	0	0	0	0	0	—	1	.250	.333	.375
1999 Houston	NL	10	33	7	1	0	1	(0	1)	11	4	3	5	1	6	0	0	0	1	0	1.00	1	.212	.316	.333
2000 Houston	NL	117	337	101	21	0	14	(11	3)	164	47	69	55	10	74	4	1	3	1	0	1.00	7	.300	.401	.487
3 ML YEARS		135	378	110	23	0	15	(11	4)	178	52	72	61	11	84	4	1	3	2	0	1.00	9	.291	.392	.471

Donaldo Mendez

Bats: Right **Throws:** Right **Pos:** SS-46; PH/PR-3   **Ht:** 6'1" **Wt:** 155 **Born:** 6/7/78 **Age:** 24

		BATTING																BASERUNNING				PERCENTAGES		
Year Team	Lg	G	AB	H	2B	3B	HR	(Hm	Rd)	TB	R	RBI	TBB	IBB	SO	HBP	SH	SF	SB	CS	SB%	GDP	Avg	OBP	SLG
1997 Kissimmee	A+	5	16	3	0	0	0	—	—	3	0	0	1	0	4	0	0	0	1	1	.50	0	.188	.235	.188
Astros	R	48	150	29	4	0	1	—	—	36	16	13	13	0	32	2	3	3	9	6	.60	2	.193	.262	.240
1999 Auburn	A-	25	86	18	1	1	0	—	—	21	9	10	2	0	23	4	0	2	10	5	.67	3	.209	.255	.244
2000 Michigan	A	101	370	100	17	0	2	—	—	123	65	51	33	1	68	14	6	3	39	10	.80	3	.270	.351	.332
2001 San Diego	NL	46	118	18	2	1	1	(0	1)	25	11	5	5	2	37	3	1	0	1	2	.33	2	.153	.206	.212

Ramiro Mendoza

Pitches: Right **Bats:** Right **Pos:** RP-54; SP-2   **Ht:** 6'2" **Wt:** 195 **Born:** 6/15/72 **Age:** 30

		HOW MUCH HE PITCHED						WHAT HE GAVE UP											THE RESULTS						
Year Team	Lg	G	GS	CG	GF	IP	BFP	H	R	ER	HR	SH	SF	HB	TBB	IBB	SO	WP	Bk	W	L	Pct.	ShO	Sv-Op	Hld	ERA
1996 New York	AL	12	11	0	0	53	249	80	44	40	5	1	4	4	10	1	34	2	1	4	5	.444	0	0-0	0	6.79
1997 New York	AL	39	15	0	9	133.2	578	157	67	63	15	3	5	5	28	2	82	2	1	8	6	.571	0	2-4	4	4.24
1998 New York	AL	41	14	1	6	130.1	548	131	50	47	9	6	7	9	30	6	56	3	0	10	2	.833	1	1-4	5	3.25
1999 New York	AL	53	6	0	15	123.2	536	141	68	59	13	6	4	3	27	3	80	2	0	9	9	.500	0	3-6	4	4.29
2000 New York	AL	14	9	1	0	65.2	281	66	32	31	9	1	2	4	20	1	30	0	0	7	4	.636	1	0-1	0	4.25
2001 New York	AL	56	2	0	11	100.2	401	89	44	42	9	4	3	2	23	3	70	2	0	8	4	.667	0	6-8	13	3.75
6 ML YEARS		215	57	2	41	607	2593	664	304	282	60	21	22	27	138	16	352	11	2	46	30	.605	2	12-23	26	4.18

Frank Menechino

Bats: R **Throws:** R **Pos:** 2B-136; SS-3; PH/PR-3; DH-1; 3B-1   **Ht:** 5'9" **Wt:** 175 **Born:** 1/7/71 **Age:** 31

								BATTING													BASERUNNING				PERCENTAGES		
Year Team	Lg	G	AB	H	2B	3B	HR	(Hm	Rd)	TB	R	RBI	TBB	IBB	SO	HBP	SH	SF	SB	CS	SB%	GDP	Avg	OBP	SLG
1999 Oakland	AL	9	9	2	0	0	0	(0	0)	2	0	0	0	0	4	0	0	0	0	0	—	0	.222	.222	.222
2000 Oakland	AL	66	145	37	9	1	6	(3	3)	66	31	26	20	0	45	1	1	2	1	4	.20	1	.255	.345	.455
2001 Oakland	AL	139	471	114	22	2	12	(4	8)	176	82	60	79	0	97	19	3	6	2	3	.40	13	.242	.369	.374
3 ML YEARS		214	625	153	31	3	18	(7	11)	244	113	86	99	0	146	20	4	8	3	7	.30	14	.245	.362	.390

Hector Mercado

Pitches: Left **Bats:** Left **Pos:** RP-56   **Ht:** 6'3" **Wt:** 235 **Born:** 4/29/74 **Age:** 28

			HOW MUCH HE PITCHED						WHAT HE GAVE UP											THE RESULTS						
Year Team	Lg	G	GS	CG	GF	IP	BFP	H	R	ER	HR	SH	SF	HB	TBB	IBB	SO	WP	Bk	W	L	Pct.	ShO	Sv-Op	Hld	ERA
1992 Astros	R	13	3	0	4	30	140	22	17	14	0	1	0	3	25	0	36	7	6	1	2	.333	0	0--	—	4.20
1993 Osceola	A+	2	2	0	0	8.2	39	9	7	5	0	0	0	0	6	1	5	0	0	1	1	.500	0	0--	—	5.19
Astros	R	11	11	1	0	67	278	49	26	18	1	0	3	1	29	0	59	10	2	5	4	.556	1	0--	—	2.42
1994 Osceola	A+	25	25	1	0	136.2	601	123	75	60	5	11	4	1	79	4	88	9	3	6	13	.316	1	0--	—	3.95
1995 Kissimmee	A+	19	17	2	0	104	433	96	50	40	2	2	3	3	37	0	75	4	1	6	8	.429	1	0--	—	3.46
Jackson	AA	8	7	0	0	30	157	36	33	26	5	2	1	2	32	1	20	4	0	1	4	.200	0	0--	—	7.80
1996 Kissimmee	A+	56	0	0	18	80	353	78	43	37	4	3	1	4	48	1	68	6	0	3	5	.375	0	3--	—	4.16
1997 Charlotte	AAA	1	1	0	0	5	25	5	5	5	2	0	0	0	5	0	1	1	0	0	1	.000	0	0--	—	9.00
Portland	AA	31	17	1	6	129.2	565	129	66	57	10	6	1	3	54	5	125	16	2	11	3	.786	1	0--	—	3.96
1999 Norfolk	AAA	2	2	0	0	6	22	3	1	1	1	0	0	1	1	0	2	0	0	0	1	.000	0	0--	—	1.50
2000 Louisville	AAA	47	5	0	10	77	339	69	26	26	2	0	6	2	48	2	67	6	0	1	5	.167	0	2--	—	3.04
2001 Louisville	AAA	12	0	0	4	13.1	55	12	2	2	0	0	0	1	6	1	13	1	0	1	0	1.000	0	1--	—	1.35
2000 Cincinnati	NL	12	0	0	4	14	60	12	7	7	2	1	1	0	8	0	13	2	0	0	0	—	0	0-0	1	4.50
2001 Cincinnati	NL	56	0	0	10	53	240	55	27	24	6	1	2	0	30	1	59	4	0	3	2	.600	0	0-2	5	4.08
2 ML YEARS		68	0	0	14	67	300	67	34	31	8	2	3	0	38	1	72	6	0	3	2	.600	0	0-2	6	4.16

Orlando Merced

Bats: L **Throws:** R **Pos:** PH/PR-66; RF-21; LF-11; 3B-2; 1B-1   **Ht:** 6'1" **Wt:** 195 **Born:** 11/2/66 **Age:** 35

								BATTING													BASERUNNING				PERCENTAGES		
Year Team	Lg	G	AB	H	2B	3B	HR	(Hm	Rd)	TB	R	RBI	TBB	IBB	SO	HBP	SH	SF	SB	CS	SB%	GDP	Avg	OBP	SLG
1990 Pittsburgh	NL	25	24	5	1	0	0	(0	0)	6	3	0	1	0	9	0	0	0	0	0	—	1	.208	.240	.250
1991 Pittsburgh	NL	120	411	113	17	2	10	(5	5)	164	83	50	64	4	81	1	1	1	8	4	.67	6	.275	.373	.399
1992 Pittsburgh	NL	134	405	100	28	5	6	(4	2)	156	50	60	52	8	63	2	1	5	5	4	.56	6	.247	.332	.385
1993 Pittsburgh	NL	137	447	140	26	4	8	(3	5)	198	68	70	77	10	64	1	0	2	3	3	.50	9	.313	.414	.443
1994 Pittsburgh	NL	108	386	105	21	3	9	(4	5)	159	48	51	42	5	58	1	0	2	4	1	.80	17	.272	.343	.412
1995 Pittsburgh	NL	132	487	146	29	4	15	(8	7)	228	75	83	52	9	74	1	0	5	7	2	.78	9	.300	.365	.468
1996 Pittsburgh	NL	120	453	130	24	1	17	(9	8)	207	69	80	51	5	74	0	0	3	8	4	.67	9	.287	.357	.457
1997 Toronto	AL	98	368	98	23	2	9	(3	6)	152	45	40	47	1	62	3	0	2	7	3	.70	6	.266	.352	.413
1998 Min-Bos-ChC		84	223	62	12	0	6	(4	2)	92	24	40	20	3	34	1	0	3	1	4	.20	6	.278	.336	.413
1999 Montreal	NL	93	194	52	12	1	8	(3	5)	90	25	26	26	0	27	0	0	1	2	1	.67	5	.268	.353	.464
2001 Houston	NL	94	137	36	6	1	6	(3	3)	62	19	29	14	1	32	1	0	1	5	1	.83	3	.263	.333	.453
1998 Minnesota	AL	63	204	59	12	0	5	(3	2)	86	22	33	17	3	29	1	0	1	1	4	.20	4	.289	.345	.422
Boston	AL	9	9	0	0	0	0	(0	0)	0	0	2	2	0	3	0	0	1	0	0	—	2	.000	.167	.000
Chicago	NL	12	10	3	0	0	1	(1	0)	6	2	5	1	0	2	0	0	1	0	0	—	2	.300	.333	.600
11 ML YEARS		1145	3535	987	199	23	94	(46	48)	1514	509	529	446	46	578	11	2	25	50	27	.65	77	.279	.359	.428

Jose Mercedes

Pitches: Right **Bats:** Right **Pos:** SP-31; RP-2   **Ht:** 6'1" **Wt:** 180 **Born:** 3/5/71 **Age:** 31

			HOW MUCH HE PITCHED						WHAT HE GAVE UP											THE RESULTS						
Year Team	Lg	G	GS	CG	GF	IP	BFP	H	R	ER	HR	SH	SF	HB	TBB	IBB	SO	WP	Bk	W	L	Pct.	ShO	Sv-Op	Hld	ERA
1994 Milwaukee	AL	19	0	0	5	31	120	22	9	8	4	0	0	2	16	1	11	0	1	2	0	1.000	0	0-1	3	2.32
1995 Milwaukee	AL	5	0	0	0	7.1	42	12	9	8	1	0	2	0	8	0	6	1	0	0	1	.000	0	0-2	1	9.82
1996 Milwaukee	AL	11	0	0	4	16.2	74	20	18	17	6	0	1	0	5	0	6	2	0	0	2	.000	0	0-1	2	9.18
1997 Milwaukee	AL	29	23	2	1	159	653	146	76	67	24	3	4	5	53	2	80	1	1	7	10	.412	1	0-0	1	3.79
1998 Milwaukee	NL	7	5	0	0	32	146	42	25	24	5	1	2	1	9	1	11	0	0	2	2	.500	0	0-0	0	6.75
2000 Baltimore	AL	36	20	1	7	145.2	636	150	71	65	15	7	7	3	64	1	70	3	0	14	7	.667	0	0-0	0	4.02
2001 Baltimore	AL	33	31	2	1	184	828	219	125	119	20	2	8	10	63	3	123	5	2	8	17	.320	0	0-0	0	5.82
7 ML YEARS		140	79	5	18	575.2	2499	611	333	308	75	13	24	21	218	8	307	12	4	33	39	.458	1	0-4	7	4.82

Lou Merloni

Bats: R **Throws:** R **Pos:** SS-45; 2B-5; PH/PR-4; 3B-1   **Ht:** 5'10" **Wt:** 194 **Born:** 4/6/71 **Age:** 31

								BATTING													BASERUNNING				PERCENTAGES		
Year Team	Lg	G	AB	H	2B	3B	HR	(Hm	Rd)	TB	R	RBI	TBB	IBB	SO	HBP	SH	SF	SB	CS	SB%	GDP	Avg	OBP	SLG
2001 Pawtucket *	AAA	52	195	51	12	0	4	—	—	75	30	20	15	0	37	5	3	0	2	0	1.00	1	.262	.330	.385
1998 Boston	AL	39	96	27	6	0	1	(1	0)	36	10	15	7	1	20	2	1	0	1	0	1.00	1	.281	.343	.375
1999 Boston	AL	43	126	32	7	0	1	(0	1)	42	18	13	8	0	16	2	3	1	0	0	—	6	.254	.307	.333
2000 Boston	AL	40	128	41	11	2	0	(0	0)	56	10	18	4	1	22	1	4	2	1	0	1.00	8	.320	.341	.438
2001 Boston	AL	52	146	39	10	0	3	(0	3)	58	21	13	6	0	31	3	2	2	2	1	.67	6	.267	.306	.397
4 ML YEARS		174	496	139	34	2	5	(1	4)	192	59	59	25	2	89	8	10	5	4	1	.80	21	.280	.322	.387

Jose Mesa

Pitches: Right **Bats:** Right **Pos:** RP-71   **Ht:** 6'3" **Wt:** 225 **Born:** 5/22/66 **Age:** 36

			HOW MUCH HE PITCHED						WHAT HE GAVE UP											THE RESULTS						
Year Team	Lg	G	GS	CG	GF	IP	BFP	H	R	ER	HR	SH	SF	HB	TBB	IBB	SO	WP	Bk	W	L	Pct.	ShO	Sv-Op	Hld	ERA
1987 Baltimore	AL	6	5	0	0	31.1	143	38	23	21	7	0	0	0	15	0	17	4	0	1	3	.250	0	0-0	1	6.03
1990 Baltimore	AL	7	7	0	0	46.2	202	37	20	20	2	2	2	1	27	2	24	1	1	3	2	.600	0	0-0	0	3.86

Year Team	Lg	G	GS	CG	GF	IP	BFP	H	R	ER	HR	SH	SF	HB	TBB	IBB	SO	WP	Bk	W	L	Pct.	ShO	Sv-Op	Hld	ERA
						HOW MUCH HE PITCHED					**WHAT HE GAVE UP**											**THE RESULTS**				
1991 Baltimore	AL	23	23	2	0	123.2	566	151	86	82	11	5	4	3	62	2	64	3	0	6	11	.353	1	0-0	0	5.97
1992 Bal-Cle	AL	28	27	1	1	160.2	700	169	86	82	14	2	5	4	70	1	62	2	0	7	12	.368	1	0-0	0	4.59
1993 Cleveland	AL	34	33	3	0	208.2	897	232	122	114	21	9	9	7	62	2	118	8	2	10	12	.455	0	0-0	0	4.92
1994 Cleveland	AL	51	0	0	22	73	315	71	33	31	3	3	4	3	26	7	63	3	0	7	5	.583	0	2-6	8	3.82
1995 Cleveland	AL	62	0	0	57	64	250	49	9	8	3	4	2	0	17	2	58	5	0	3	0	1.000	0	46-48	0	1.13
1996 Cleveland	AL	69	0	0	60	72.1	304	69	32	30	6	2	2	3	28	4	64	4	0	2	7	.222	0	39-44	0	3.73
1997 Cleveland	AL	66	0	0	38	82.1	356	83	28	22	7	2	2	3	28	3	69	1	0	4	4	.500	0	16-21	9	2.40
1998 Cle-SF		76	0	0	36	84.2	383	91	50	43	8	6	2	4	38	5	63	10	0	8	7	.533	0	1-4	13	4.57
1999 Seattle	AL	68	0	0	60	68.2	325	84	42	38	11	2	4	4	40	4	42	7	0	3	6	.333	0	33-38	1	4.98
2000 Seattle	AL	66	0	0	29	80.2	372	89	48	48	11	2	6	5	41	0	84	3	0	4	6	.400	0	1-3	11	5.36
2001 Philadelphia	NL	71	0	0	59	69.1	291	65	26	18	4	2	3	2	20	2	59	2	1	3	3	.500	0	42-46	1	2.34
1992 Baltimore	AL	13	12	0	1	67.2	300	77	41	39	9	0	3	2	27	1	22	2	0	3	8	.273	0	0-0	0	5.19
Cleveland		15	15	1	0	93	400	92	45	43	5	2	2	2	43	0	40	0	0	4	5	.500	1	0-0	0	4.16
1998 Cleveland	AL	44	0	0	18	54	244	61	36	31	7	2	4	4	20	3	35	2	0	3	4	.429	0	1-3	7	5.17
San Francisco	NL	32	0	0	18	30.2	139	30	14	12	1	4	0	0	18	2	28	8	0	5	3	.625	0	0-1	6	3.52
13 ML YEARS		627	95	6	362	1166	5104	1228	605	557	108	41	45	39	474	34	787	53	4	61	78	.439	2	180-210	44	4.30

Chad Meyers

Bats: R **Throws:** R **Pos:** PH/PR-12; 2B-4; LF-2; CF-2; 3B-1 **Ht:** 5'11" **Wt:** 185 **Born:** 8/8/75 **Age:** 26

Year Team	Lg	G	AB	H	2B	3B	HR	(Hm	Rd)	TB	R	RBI	TBB	IBB	SO	HBP	SH	SF	SB	CS	SB%	GDP	Avg	OBP	SLG
					BATTING															**BASERUNNING**			**PERCENTAGES**		
2001 Iowa *	AAA	132	446	134	31	5	9	—	—	202	92	54	58	0	72	26	10	5	27	9	.75	9	.300	.407	.453
1999 Chicago	NL	43	142	33	9	0	0	(0	0)	42	17	4	9	1	27	3	2	0	4	2	.67	5	.232	.292	.296
2000 Chicago	NL	36	52	9	2	0	0	(0	0)	11	8	5	3	0	11	1	0	1	1	0	1.00	0	.173	.228	.212
2001 Chicago	NL	18	17	2	0	0	0	(0	0)	2	1	0	2	0	5	4	0	0	0	1	.00	0	.118	.348	.118
3 ML YEARS		97	211	44	11	0	0	(0	0)	55	26	9	14	1	43	8	2	1	5	3	.63	5	.209	.282	.261

Bart Miadich

Pitches: Right **Bats:** Right **Pos:** RP-11 **Ht:** 6'4" **Wt:** 205 **Born:** 2/3/76 **Age:** 26

Year Team	Lg	G	GS	CG	GF	IP	BFP	H	R	ER	HR	SH	SF	HB	TBB	IBB	SO	WP	Bk	W	L	Pct.	ShO	Sv-Op	Hld	ERA
						HOW MUCH HE PITCHED					**WHAT HE GAVE UP**											**THE RESULTS**				
1998 Sarasota	A+	22	0	0	15	48.2	199	40	20	17	1	3	0	1	15	4	64	2	1	3	2	.600	0	7--	—	3.14
Trenton	AA	22	8	0	4	54.1	253	66	39	36	4	1	2	5	26	1	33	3	0	1	6	.143	0	1--	—	5.96
1999 El Paso	AA	12	0	0	2	20	104	37	22	18	3	1	1	2	7	1	16	0	0	0	2	.000	0	1--	—	8.10
High Desert	A+	21	16	0	1	98	448	125	71	59	9	2	4	12	40	0	85	1	1	3	8	.273	0	0--	—	5.42
2000 Erie	AA	28	0	0	17	40.1	171	27	16	15	2	1	2	4	21	0	38	4	0	3	1	.750	0	2--	—	3.35
Edmonton	AAA	10	0	0	3	21.2	101	25	14	11	3	1	0	0	9	0	20	2	0	2	1	.667	0	1--	—	4.57
2001 Salt Lake	AAA	55	0	0	54	59	245	40	20	16	4	3	1	1	29	1	73	5	0	4	4	.500	0	27--	—	2.44
2001 Anaheim	AL	11	0	0	4	10	41	6	5	5	2	0	0	0	8	0	11	1	0	0	0	—	0	0-0	—	4.50

Dan Miceli

Pitches: Right **Bats:** Right **Pos:** RP-51 **Ht:** 6'0" **Wt:** 216 **Born:** 9/9/70 **Age:** 31

Year Team	Lg	G	GS	CG	GF	IP	BFP	H	R	ER	HR	SH	SF	HB	TBB	IBB	SO	WP	Bk	W	L	Pct.	ShO	Sv-Op	Hld	ERA
						HOW MUCH HE PITCHED					**WHAT HE GAVE UP**											**THE RESULTS**				
2001 Colo Sprngs *	AAA	4	0	0	2	3	12	2	2	2	0	1	0	0	1	1	4	3	0	0	2	.000	0	0--	—	6.00
1993 Pittsburgh	NL	9	0	0	1	5.1	25	6	3	3	0	0	0	0	3	0	4	0	1	0	0	—	0	0-0	0	5.06
1994 Pittsburgh	NL	28	0	0	9	27.1	121	28	19	18	5	1	2	2	11	2	27	2	0	2	1	.667	0	2-3	4	5.93
1995 Pittsburgh	NL	58	0	0	51	58	264	61	30	30	7	2	4	4	28	5	56	4	0	4	4	.500	0	21-27	2	4.66
1996 Pittsburgh	NL	44	9	0	17	85.2	398	99	65	55	15	3	7	3	45	5	66	9	0	2	10	.167	0	1-1	4	5.78
1997 Detroit	NL	71	0	0	24	82.2	357	77	49	46	13	5	3	1	38	4	79	3	0	3	2	.600	0	3-8	11	5.01
1998 San Diego	NL	67	0	0	18	72.2	302	64	28	26	6	3	2	1	27	4	70	5	1	10	5	.667	0	2-8	20	3.22
1999 San Diego	NL	66	0	0	28	68.2	296	67	39	34	7	4	2	2	36	5	59	2	0	4	5	.444	0	2-4	9	4.46
2000 Florida	NL	45	0	0	9	48.2	207	45	23	23	4	1	1	1	18	2	40	3	0	6	4	.600	0	0-3	11	4.25
2001 Fla-Col	NL	51	0	0	15	45	199	47	29	24	7	2	2	0	16	2	48	4	0	2	5	.286	0	1-4	8	4.80
2001 Florida	NL	29	0	0	9	24.2	114	29	21	19	5	1	1	0	11	2	31	3	0	0	5	.000	0	0-3	8	6.93
Colorado	NL	22	0	0	6	20.1	85	18	8	5	2	1	1	0	5	0	17	1	0	2	0	1.000	0	1-1	0	2.21
9 ML YEARS		439	9	0	172	494	2169	494	285	259	64	21	23	14	222	29	449	32	2	33	36	.478	0	32-58	69	4.72

Jason Michaels

Bats: Right **Throws:** Right **Pos:** PH/PR-5; LF-1 **Ht:** 6'0" **Wt:** 204 **Born:** 5/4/76 **Age:** 26

Year Team	Lg	G	AB	H	2B	3B	HR	(Hm	Rd)	TB	R	RBI	TBB	IBB	SO	HBP	SH	SF	SB	CS	SB%	GDP	Avg	OBP	SLG
					BATTING															**BASERUNNING**			**PERCENTAGES**		
1998 Batavia	A-	67	235	63	14	3	11	—	—	116	45	49	40	3	69	4	0	2	4	2	.67	5	.268	.381	.494
1999 Clearwater	A+	122	451	138	31	6	14	—	—	223	91	65	68	2	103	3	1	6	10	7	.59	7	.306	.396	.494
2000 Reading	AA	113	437	129	30	4	10	—	—	197	71	74	28	1	87	3	3	7	7	4	.64	9	.295	.337	.451
2001 Scrantn-WB	AAA	109	418	109	19	3	17	—	—	185	58	69	37	2	126	8	0	1	11	3	.79	7	.261	.332	.443
2001 Philadelphia	NL	6	6	1	0	0	0	(0	0)	1	0	1	0	0	2	0	0	0	0	0	—	0	.167	.167	.167

Chris Michalak

Pitches: Left **Bats:** Left **Pos:** SP-18; RP-17 **Ht:** 6'2" **Wt:** 195 **Born:** 1/4/71 **Age:** 31

Year Team	Lg	G	GS	CG	GF	IP	BFP	H	R	ER	HR	SH	SF	HB	TBB	IBB	SO	WP	Bk	W	L	Pct.	ShO	Sv-Op	Hld	ERA
						HOW MUCH HE PITCHED					**WHAT HE GAVE UP**											**THE RESULTS**				
1993 Sou Oregon	A-	16	15	0	0	79	346	77	45	25	2	2	5	6	36	0	57	4	3	7	3	.700	0	0--	—	2.85
1994 W Michigan	A	15	10	0	2	67	291	66	32	29	3	4	2	8	20	0	38	2	3	5	3	.625	0	0--	—	3.90
Modesto	A+	17	10	1	3	77.1	310	67	28	25	13	2	3	3	20	1	46	4	3	5	3	.625	0	2--	—	2.91
1995 Huntsville	AA	7	0	0	4	5.2	32	10	7	7	1	1	0	1	5	0	4	2	0	1	1	.500	0	1--	—	11.12
Modesto	A+	44	0	0	16	65.1	266	56	26	19	3	4	3	4	27	1	49	2	1	3	2	.600	0	2--	—	2.62

Year Team	Lg	G	GS	CG	GF	IP	BFP	H	R	ER	HR	SH	SF	HB	TBB	IBB	SO	WP	Bk	W	L	Pct.	ShO	Sv-Op	Hld	ERA
		HOW MUCH HE PITCHED						**WHAT HE GAVE UP**												**THE RESULTS**						
1996 Modesto	A+	21	0	0	13	38.2	173	37	21	13	4	0	2	2	17	0	39	0	2	2	2	.500	0	4--	—	3.03
Huntsville	AA	21	0	0	4	23.1	123	32	29	20	2	1	1	1	26	4	15	4	0	4	0	1.000	0	0--	—	7.71
1997 High Desert	A+	49	0	0	17	85	362	76	36	25	4	3	0	9	31	1	74	6	1	3	7	.300	0	4--	—	2.65
1998 Tulsa	AA	10	0	0	3	19.2	73	10	4	4	2	2	0	2	2	0	15	0	2	1	2	.333	0	0--	—	1.83
Tucson	AAA	29	9	0	6	73.1	326	91	47	41	11	2	5	4	29	3	50	4	3	3	8	.273	0	0--	—	5.03
1999 Edmonton	AAA	24	0	0	7	28.1	125	28	20	18	3	0	2	1	14	0	25	1	0	1	0	1.000	0	0--	—	5.72
Tucson	AAA	21	6	0	7	64	275	64	30	26	6	2	2	6	26	2	41	1	1	5	0	1.000	0	3--	—	3.66
2000 Durham	AAA	6	0	0	1	6.1	26	6	4	4	1	0	0	0	1	0	7	1	0	0	0	—	0	0--	—	5.68
Albuquerque	AAA	23	21	1	0	133	587	166	72	63	18	6	4	4	55	0	83	4	3	11	3	.786	0	0--	—	4.26
1998 Arizona	NL	5	0	0	2	5.1	29	9	7	7	1	0	1	0	4	0	5	0	0	0	0	—	0	0-0	0	11.81
2001 Tor-Tex	AL	35	18	0	4	136.2	610	157	74	67	19	3	4	13	55	5	67	1	6	8	9	.471	0	1-2	0	4.41
2001 Toronto	AL	24	18	0	2	115	517	133	66	59	14	3	4	12	49	5	57	0	5	6	7	.462	0	0-0	0	4.62
Texas	AL	11	0	0	2	21.2	93	24	8	8	5	0	0	1	6	0	10	1	1	2	2	.500	0	1-2	0	3.32
2 ML YEARS		40	18	0	6	142	639	166	81	74	20	3	5	13	59	5	72	1	6	8	9	.471	0	1-2	0	4.69

Jason Middlebrook

Pitches: Right **Bats:** Right **Pos:** SP-3; RP-1   **Ht:** 6'3" **Wt:** 215 **Born:** 6/26/75 **Age:** 27

Year Team	Lg	G	GS	CG	GF	IP	BFP	H	R	ER	HR	SH	SF	HB	TBB	IBB	SO	WP	Bk	W	L	Pct.	ShO	Sv-Op	Hld	ERA
		HOW MUCH HE PITCHED						**WHAT HE GAVE UP**												**THE RESULTS**						
1997 Rancho Cuc	A+	6	6	0	0	22.1	105	29	15	10	1	1	3	0	12	1	18	2	1	0	2	.000	0	0--	—	4.03
Clinton	A	14	14	2	0	81.1	353	76	46	36	4	3	1	1	39	0	86	6	5	6	4	.600	1	0--	—	3.98
1998 Rancho Cuc	A+	28	28	0	0	150	665	162	99	82	10	1	9	4	63	0	132	17	4	10	12	.455	0	0--	—	4.92
1999 Padres	R	1	1	0	0	5	25	9	5	4	0	0	0	0	1	0	3	0	0	1	0	1.000	0	0--	—	7.20
Mobile	AA	13	13	0	0	63.2	302	78	59	57	9	1	5	8	30	1	38	5	0	4	6	.400	0	0--	—	8.06
2000 Las Vegas	AAA	1	1	0	0	0.1	9	8	8	8	1	0	1	0	0	0	0	0	0	0	1	.000	0	0--	—	216.00
Mobile	AA	24	24	0	0	120	533	133	89	82	15	5	4	4	52	0	75	3	0	5	13	.278	0	0--	—	6.15
2001 Mobile	AA	10	9	0	0	52.2	200	36	10	7	1	0	2	1	9	0	51	0	0	3	0	1.000	0	0--	—	1.20
Portland	AAA	15	15	0	0	90.1	374	86	34	33	5	2	3	2	23	1	66	3	0	7	4	.636	0	0--	—	3.29
2001 San Diego	NL	4	3	0	0	19.1	85	18	11	11	6	1	0	1	10	1	10	0	0	2	1	.667	0	0-0	0	5.12

Doug Mientkiewicz

Bats: Left **Throws:** Right **Pos:** 1B-148; PH/PR-5; DH-2   **Ht:** 6'2" **Wt:** 200 **Born:** 6/19/74 **Age:** 28

Year Team	Lg	G	AB	H	2B	3B	HR	(Hm	Rd)	TB	R	RBI	TBB	IBB	SO	HBP	SH	SF	SB	CS	SB%	GDP	Avg	OBP	SLG
		BATTING																	**BASERUNNING**				**PERCENTAGES**		
1998 Minnesota	AL	8	5	1	0	0	0	(0	0)	1	1	2	4	0	3	0	0	0	1	1	.50	0	.200	.310	.240
1999 Minnesota	AL	118	327	75	21	3	2	(0	2)	108	34	32	43	3	51	4	3	2	1	1	.50	13	.229	.324	.330
2000 Minnesota	AL	3	14	6	0	0	0	(0	0)	6	0	4	0	0	0	0	0	1	0	0	—	1	.429	.400	.429
2001 Minnesota	AL	151	543	166	39	1	15	(11	4)	252	77	74	67	6	92	9	0	7	2	6	.25	10	.306	.387	.464
4 ML YEARS		280	909	252	61	4	17	(11	6)	372	112	112	114	9	146	13	3	10	4	8	.33	24	.277	.362	.409

Kevin Millar

Bats: R **Throws:** R **Pos:** RF-66; PH/PR-28; LF-27; 1B-15; 3B-10; DH-6   **Ht:** 6'0" **Wt:** 210 **Born:** 9/24/71 **Age:** 30

Year Team	Lg	G	AB	H	2B	3B	HR	(Hm	Rd)	TB	R	RBI	TBB	IBB	SO	HBP	SH	SF	SB	CS	SB%	GDP	Avg	OBP	SLG
		BATTING																	**BASERUNNING**				**PERCENTAGES**		
1998 Florida	NL	2	2	1	0	0	0	(0	0)	1	1	0	1	0	0	0	0	0	0	0	—	0	.500	.667	.500
1999 Florida	NL	105	351	100	17	4	9	(3	6)	152	48	67	40	2	64	7	1	8	1	0	1.00	7	.285	.362	.433
2000 Florida	NL	123	259	67	14	3	14	(6	8)	129	36	42	36	0	47	8	0	2	0	0	—	5	.259	.364	.498
2001 Florida	NL	144	449	141	39	5	20	(13	7)	250	62	85	39	2	70	5	0	2	0	1	.00	8	.314	.374	.557
4 ML YEARS		374	1061	309	70	12	43	(22	21)	532	147	194	116	4	181	20	1	12	1	1	.00	20	.291	.368	.501

Corky Miller

Bats: Right **Throws:** Right **Pos:** C-17   **Ht:** 6'1" **Wt:** 220 **Born:** 3/18/76 **Age:** 26

Year Team	Lg	G	AB	H	2B	3B	HR	(Hm	Rd)	TB	R	RBI	TBB	IBB	SO	HBP	SH	SF	SB	CS	SB%	GDP	Avg	OBP	SLG
		BATTING																	**BASERUNNING**				**PERCENTAGES**		
1998 Billings	R+	45	129	35	8	0	5	—	—	58	28	24	24	0	24	21	2	2	1	4	.20	2	.271	.455	.450
1999 Rockford	A	66	195	56	10	1	10	—	—	98	43	40	33	1	42	20	1	1	3	6	.33	5	.287	.438	.503
Chattanooga	AA	33	104	23	10	0	4	—	—	45	20	16	11	0	30	11	0	1	0	0	—	3	.221	.354	.433
2000 Chattanooga	AA	103	317	74	18	0	9	—	—	119	40	44	41	1	51	30	1	1	5	8	.38	12	.233	.373	.375
2001 Chattanooga	AA	59	170	47	12	0	9	—	—	86	25	42	25	1	32	19	1	0	1	2	.33	1	.276	.425	.506
Louisville	AAA	44	144	50	11	0	7	—	—	82	30	28	10	0	19	12	0	1	2	0	1.00	2	.347	.431	.569
2001 Cincinnati	NL	17	49	9	2	0	3	(1	2)	20	5	7	4	0	16	2	0	2	1	0	1.00	1	.184	.263	.408

Damian Miller

Bats: Right **Throws:** Right **Pos:** C-121; PH/PR-4   **Ht:** 6'2" **Wt:** 218 **Born:** 10/13/69 **Age:** 32

Year Team	Lg	G	AB	H	2B	3B	HR	(Hm	Rd)	TB	R	RBI	TBB	IBB	SO	HBP	SH	SF	SB	CS	SB%	GDP	Avg	OBP	SLG
		BATTING																	**BASERUNNING**				**PERCENTAGES**		
1997 Minnesota	AL	25	66	18	1	0	2	(1	1)	25	5	13	2	0	12	0	0	3	0	0	—	2	.273	.282	.379
1998 Arizona	NL	57	168	48	14	2	3	(2	1)	75	17	14	11	2	43	2	2	0	1	0	1.00	6	.286	.337	.446
1999 Arizona	NL	86	296	80	19	0	11	(3	8)	132	35	47	19	3	78	2	0	3	0	0	—	6	.270	.316	.446
2000 Arizona	NL	100	324	89	24	0	10	(6	4)	143	43	44	36	4	74	1	1	2	2	2	.50	6	.275	.347	.441
2001 Arizona	NL	123	380	103	19	0	13	(9	4)	161	45	47	35	9	80	4	4	2	0	1	.00	9	.271	.337	.424
5 ML YEARS		391	1234	338	77	2	39	(21	18)	536	145	165	103	18	287	9	7	10	3	3	.50	25	.274	.332	.434

Matt Miller

Pitches: Left **Bats:** Left **Pos:** RP-13 **Ht:** 6'3" **Wt:** 175 **Born:** 8/2/74 **Age:** 27

Year Team	Lg	G	GS	CG	GF	IP	BFP	H	R	ER	HR	SH	SF	HB	TBB	IBB	SO	WP	Bk	W	L	Pct.	ShO	Sv-Op	Hld	ERA
1996 Jamestown	A-	6	6	0	0	25.1	115	33	16	13	0	1	0	3	13	0	21	6	2	1	3	.250	0	0--	—	4.62
1998 W Michigan	A	14	14	3	0	95	366	59	20	16	1	5	0	4	26	0	102	4	1	7	4	.636	1	0--	—	1.52
Jacksnville	AA	13	13	0	0	61.1	297	70	49	48	6	0	2	2	50	1	49	3	1	3	7	.300	0	0--	—	7.04
1999 Lakeland	A+	19	19	1	0	108.1	473	108	58	50	9	5	2	2	45	0	82	0	1	4	9	.308	0	0--	—	4.15
Jacksnville	AA	7	7	0	0	40.2	176	43	23	20	3	3	1	2	12	0	25	0	0	4	1	.800	0	0--	—	4.43
2000 Jacksnville	AA	20	20	1	0	121.2	513	126	50	43	10	4	3	5	32	1	99	4	0	8	5	.615	0	0--	—	3.18
2001 Toledo	AAA	50	0	0	20	62.2	260	60	26	20	3	5	1	4	18	3	49	1	0	1	2	.333	0	4--	—	2.87
2001 Detroit	AL	13	0	0	5	9.2	48	16	8	8	0	0	0	1	4	0	6	1	0	0	0	—	0	0-0	3	7.45

Travis Miller

Pitches: Left **Bats:** Right **Pos:** RP-45 **Ht:** 6'3" **Wt:** 215 **Born:** 11/2/72 **Age:** 29

Year Team	Lg	G	GS	CG	GF	IP	BFP	H	R	ER	HR	SH	SF	HB	TBB	IBB	SO	WP	Bk	W	L	Pct.	ShO	Sv-Op	Hld	ERA
1996 Minnesota	AL	7	7	0	0	26.1	126	45	29	27	7	1	0	0	9	0	15	0	0	1	2	.333	0	0-0	0	9.23
1997 Minnesota	AL	13	7	0	1	48.1	227	64	49	41	8	1	2	1	23	2	26	5	0	1	5	.167	0	0-0	0	7.63
1998 Minnesota	AL	14	0	0	2	23.1	104	25	10	10	0	0	1	0	11	1	23	2	0	2	0	.000	0	0-0	0	3.86
1999 Minnesota	AL	52	0	0	12	49.2	214	55	19	15	3	2	2	0	16	3	40	6	0	2	2	.500	0	0-2	8	2.72
2000 Minnesota	AL	67	0	0	12	67	316	83	35	29	4	1	3	1	32	2	62	2	0	2	3	.400	0	1-4	10	3.90
2001 Minnesota	AL	45	0	0	14	48.2	216	54	30	26	5	0	4	1	20	1	30	1	0	1	4	.200	0	0-0	5	4.81
6 ML YEARS		198	14	0	41	263.1	1203	326	172	148	27	5	12	3	111	9	196	16	0	7	18	.280	0	1-6	23	5.06

Wade Miller

Pitches: Right **Bats:** Right **Pos:** SP-32 **Ht:** 6'2" **Wt:** 185 **Born:** 9/13/76 **Age:** 25

Year Team	Lg	G	GS	CG	GF	IP	BFP	H	R	ER	HR	SH	SF	HB	TBB	IBB	SO	WP	Bk	W	L	Pct.	ShO	Sv-Op	Hld	ERA
1999 Houston	NL	5	1	2	0	10.1	52	17	11	11	4	0	0	0	5	0	8	0	0	0	1	.000	0	0-0	0	9.58
2000 Houston	NL	16	16	2	0	105	453	104	66	60	14	3	1	3	42	1	89	1	0	6	6	.500	0	0-0	0	5.14
2001 Houston	NL	32	32	1	0	212	873	183	91	80	31	7	5	4	76	3	183	8	0	16	8	.667	0	0-0	0	3.40
3 ML YEARS		53	49	3	2	327.1	1378	304	168	151	49	10	6	7	123	4	280	9	0	22	15	.595	0	0-0	0	4.15

Alan Mills

Pitches: Right **Bats:** Both **Pos:** RP-15 **Ht:** 6'1" **Wt:** 195 **Born:** 10/18/66 **Age:** 35

Year Team	Lg	G	GS	CG	GF	IP	BFP	H	R	ER	HR	SH	SF	HB	TBB	IBB	SO	WP	Bk	W	L	Pct.	ShO	Sv-Op	Hld	ERA
2001 Frederick *	A+	5	0	0	1	5	20	3	4	1	0	0	0	1	0	0	10	0	0	0	0	—	0	1--	—	1.80
Bowie *	AA	7	0	0	2	8	31	5	2	2	0	0	0	0	3	0	10	1	0	0	0	—	0	0--	—	2.25
1990 New York	AL	36	0	0	18	41.2	200	48	21	19	4	4	1	1	33	6	24	3	0	1	5	.167	0	0-2	3	4.10
1991 New York	AL	6	2	0	3	16.1	72	16	9	8	1	0	1	0	8	0	11	2	0	1	1	.500	0	0-0	0	4.41
1992 Baltimore	AL	35	3	0	12	103.1	428	78	33	30	5	6	5	1	54	10	60	2	0	10	4	.714	0	2-3	2	2.61
1993 Baltimore	AL	45	0	0	16	100.1	421	80	39	36	14	4	6	4	51	5	68	3	0	5	4	.556	0	4-7	4	3.23
1994 Baltimore	AL	47	0	0	16	45.1	199	43	26	26	7	1	1	2	24	2	44	2	0	3	3	.500	0	2-4	14	5.16
1995 Baltimore	AL	21	0	0	1	23	118	30	20	19	4	0	1	2	18	4	16	1	0	3	0	1.000	0	0-1	1	7.43
1996 Baltimore	AL	49	0	0	23	54.2	233	40	26	26	10	3	2	1	35	2	50	6	0	3	2	.600	0	3-8	9	4.28
1997 Baltimore	AL	39	0	0	11	38.2	192	41	23	21	5	4	1	1	33	1	32	2	0	2	3	.400	0	0-0	7	4.89
1998 Baltimore	AL	72	0	0	13	77	327	55	32	32	8	2	3	1	50	8	57	4	0	3	4	.429	0	2-5	19	3.74
1999 Los Angeles	NL	68	0	0	18	72.1	322	70	33	30	10	3	4	4	43	4	49	3	0	3	4	.429	0	0-5	18	3.73
2000 LA-Bal		41	0	0	12	49.1	234	56	29	29	9	0	0	2	35	1	36	4	0	4	1	.800	0	2-2	8	5.29
2001 Baltimore	AL	15	0	0	8	14	73	20	15	15	6	0	0	1	11	3	9	0	0	1	1	.500	0	0-0	1	9.64
2000 Los Angeles	NL	18	0	0	9	25.2	119	31	12	12	3	0	0	1	16	0	18	1	0	2	1	.667	0	1-1	2	4.21
Baltimore	AL	23	0	0	3	23.2	115	25	17	17	6	0	0	1	19	1	18	3	0	2	0	1.000	0	1-1	6	6.46
12 ML YEARS		474	5	0	153	636	2819	577	306	291	83	27	25	21	395	46	456	32	0	39	32	.549	0	15-37	87	4.12

Kevin Millwood

Pitches: Right **Bats:** Right **Pos:** SP-21 **Ht:** 6'4" **Wt:** 220 **Born:** 12/24/74 **Age:** 27

Year Team	Lg	G	GS	CG	GF	IP	BFP	H	R	ER	HR	SH	SF	HB	TBB	IBB	SO	WP	Bk	W	L	Pct.	ShO	Sv-Op	Hld	ERA
2001 Macon *	A	1	1	0	0	3	9	0	0	0	0	0	0	0	0	0	5	0	0	0	0	—	0	0--	—	0.00
Greenville *	AA	2	2	0	0	10	42	9	6	5	2	0	2	0	3	0	10	1	0	0	1	.000	0	0--	—	4.50
1997 Atlanta	NL	12	8	0	2	51.1	227	55	26	23	1	3	5	2	21	1	42	1	0	5	3	.625	0	0-0	0	4.03
1998 Atlanta	NL	31	29	3	1	174.1	748	175	86	79	18	8	3	3	56	3	163	6	1	17	8	.680	1	0-0	1	4.08
1999 Atlanta	NL	33	33	2	0	228	906	168	80	68	24	9	3	4	59	2	205	5	0	18	7	.720	0	0-0	0	2.68
2000 Atlanta	NL	36	35	0	0	212.2	903	213	115	110	26	8	5	3	62	2	168	4	0	10	13	.435	0	0-0	0	4.66
2001 Atlanta	NL	21	21	0	0	121	515	121	66	58	20	7	2	1	40	6	84	5	1	7	7	.500	0	0-0	0	4.31
5 ML YEARS		133	126	5	3	787.1	3299	732	373	338	89	35	18	13	238	14	662	21	2	57	38	.600	1	0-0	1	3.86

Eric Milton

Pitches: Left **Bats:** Left **Pos:** SP-34; RP-1 **Ht:** 6'3" **Wt:** 220 **Born:** 8/4/75 **Age:** 26

Year Team	Lg	G	GS	CG	GF	IP	BFP	H	R	ER	HR	SH	SF	HB	TBB	IBB	SO	WP	Bk	W	L	Pct.	ShO	Sv-Op	Hld	ERA
1998 Minnesota	AL	32	32	1	0	172.1	772	195	113	108	25	2	6	2	70	0	107	1	0	8	14	.364	0	0-0	0	5.64
1999 Minnesota	AL	34	34	5	0	206.1	858	190	111	103	28	3	6	3	63	2	163	2	0	7	11	.389	2	0-0	0	4.49
2000 Minnesota	AL	33	33	0	0	200	849	205	123	108	35	4	6	7	44	0	160	5	0	13	10	.565	0	0-0	0	4.86
2001 Minnesota	AL	35	34	2	0	220.2	944	222	109	106	35	8	6	5	61	0	157	2	0	15	7	.682	1	0-0	0	4.32
4 ML YEARS		134	133	8	0	799.1	3423	812	456	425	123	17	24	17	238	2	587	10	0	43	42	.506	3	0-0	0	4.79

Damon Minor

Bats: Left **Throws:** Left **Pos:** 1B-11; PH/PR-8   **Ht:** 6'7" **Wt:** 230 **Born:** 1/5/74 **Age:** 28

Year Team	Lg	G	AB	H	2B	3B	HR	(Hm	Rd)	TB	R	RBI	TBB	IBB	SO	HBP	SH	SF	SB	CS	SB%	GDP	Avg	OBP	SLG
1996 Bellingham	A-	75	269	65	11	1	12	—	—	114	44	55	47	4	86	5	1	1	0	2	.00	5	.242	.363	.424
1997 Bakersfield	A+	140	532	154	34	1	31	—	—	283	98	99	87	8	143	5	0	5	2	1	.67	6	.289	.391	.532
1998 Shreveport	AA	81	289	69	11	1	14	—	—	124	39	52	30	1	51	6	0	2	1	0	1.00	3	.239	.321	.429
San Jose	A+	48	176	50	10	1	7	—	—	83	26	36	28	0	40	2	0	1	0	1	.00	1	.284	.386	.472
1999 Shreveport	AA	136	473	129	33	4	20	—	—	230	76	82	80	6	115	8	0	3	1	0	1.00	10	.273	.385	.486
2000 Fresno	AAA	133	482	140	27	1	30	—	—	259	84	106	87	4	97	1	0	9	0	0	—	11	.290	.394	.537
2001 Fresno	AAA	112	406	125	22	3	24	—	—	225	74	71	44	4	83	5	0	3	1	1	.50	1	.308	.380	.554
2000 San Francisco	NL	10	9	4	0	0	3	(2	1)	13	3	6	2	0	.1	0	0	0	0	0	—	0	.444	.545	1.444
2001 San Francisco	NL	19	45	7	1	0	0	(0	0)	8	3	3	3	1	8	0	0	0	0	0	—	1	.156	.208	.178
2 ML YEARS		29	54	11	1	0	3	(2	1)	21	6	9	5	1	9	0	0	0	0	0	—	1	.204	.271	.389

Ryan Minor

Bats: R **Throws:** R **Pos:** PH/PR-32; 3B-24; DH-3; LF-2; 1B-1   **Ht:** 6'7" **Wt:** 245 **Born:** 1/5/74 **Age:** 28

Year Team	Lg	G	AB	H	2B	3B	HR	(Hm	Rd)	TB	R	RBI	TBB	IBB	SO	HBP	SH	SF	SB	CS	SB%	GDP	Avg	OBP	SLG
2001 Ottawa *	AAA	42	143	35	6	2	5	—	—	60	20	19	16	0	41	6	0	1	0	0		1	.245	.343	.420
1998 Baltimore	AL	9	14	6	1	0	0	(0	0)	7	3	1	0	0	3	0	0	0	0	0	—	0	.429	.429	.500
1999 Baltimore	AL	46	124	24	7	0	3	(3	0)	40	13	10	8	0	43	0	0	1	1	0	1.00	1	.194	.241	.323
2000 Baltimore	AL	32	84	11	1	0	0	(0	0)	12	4	3	3	0	20	1	0	0	0	0	—	0	.131	.170	.143
2001 Montreal	NL	55	95	15	2	0	2	(1	1)	23	10	13	9	0	31	1	0	2	0	1	.00	3	.158	.234	.242
4 ML YEARS		142	317	56	11	0	5	(4	1)	82	30	27	20	0	97	2	0	3	1	1	.50	4	.177	.228	.259

Doug Mirabelli

Bats: Right **Throws:** Right **Pos:** C-75; PH/PR-5; DH-2   **Ht:** 6'1" **Wt:** 218 **Born:** 10/18/70 **Age:** 31

Year Team	Lg	G	AB	H	2B	3B	HR	(Hm	Rd)	TB	R	RBI	TBB	IBB	SO	HBP	SH	SF	SB	CS	SB%	GDP	Avg	OBP	SLG
1996 San Francisco	NL	9	18	4	1	0	0	(0	0)	5	2	1	3	0	4	0	0	0	0	0	—	0	.222	.333	.278
1997 San Francisco	NL	6	7	1	0	0	0	(0	0)	1	0	0	1	0	3	0	0	0	0	0	—	0	.143	.250	.143
1998 San Francisco	NL	10	17	4	2	0	1	(1	0)	9	2	4	2	0	6	0	0	0	0	0	—	0	.235	.316	.529
1999 San Francisco	NL	33	87	22	6	0	1	(1	0)	31	10	10	9	1	25	1	0	1	0	0	—	1	.253	.327	.356
2000 San Francisco	NL	82	230	53	10	2	6	(2	4)	85	23	28	36	2	57	2	3	2	1	0	1.00	6	.230	.337	.370
2001 Tex-Bos	AL	77	190	43	10	0	11	(5	6)	86	20	29	27	2	57	4	1	2	0	0	—	3	.226	.332	.453
2001 Texas	AL	23	49	5	2	0	2	(1	1)	13	4	3	10	0	21	0	0	0	0	0	—	2	.102	.254	.265
Boston	AL	54	141	38	8	0	9	(4	5)	73	16	26	17	2	36	4	1	2	0	0	—	2	.270	.360	.518
6 ML YEARS		217	549	127	29	2	19	(9	10)	217	57	72	78	5	152	7	4	5	1	0	1.00	10	.231	.332	.395

Dave Mlicki

Pitches: Right **Bats:** Right **Pos:** SP-29; RP-5   **Ht:** 6'4" **Wt:** 205 **Born:** 6/8/68 **Age:** 34

Year Team	Lg	G	GS	CG	GF	IP	BFP	H	R	ER	HR	SH	SF	HB	TBB	IBB	SO	WP	Bk	W	L	Pct.	ShO	Sv-Op	Hld	ERA
1992 Cleveland	AL	4	4	0	0	21.2	101	23	14	12	3	2	0	1	16	0	16	1	0	0	2	.000	0	0-0	0	4.98
1993 Cleveland	AL	3	3	0	0	13.1	58	11	6	5	2	0	0	2	6	0	7	2	0	0	0	—	0	0-0	0	3.38
1995 New York	NL	29	25	0	1	160.2	696	160	82	76	23	8	5	4	54	2	123	5	1	9	7	.563	0	0-0	0	4.26
1996 New York	NL	51	2	0	16	90	393	95	46	33	9	8	3	6	33	8	83	7	0	6	7	.462	0	1-3	8	3.30
1997 New York	NL	32	32	1	0	193.2	838	194	89	86	21	3	6	5	76	7	157	5	1	8	12	.400	1	0-0	0	4.00
1998 NYM-LA	NL	30	30	3	0	181.1	789	188	100	92	23	8	7	7	63	5	117	10	0	8	7	.533	1	0-0	0	4.57
1999 LA-Det		33	31	2	0	199	883	219	112	102	25	3	8	12	72	1	120	1	0	14	13	.519	0	0-0	1	4.61
2000 Detroit	AL	24	21	0	1	119.1	547	143	79	74	17	3	6	3	44	1	57	4	0	6	11	.353	0	0-0	0	5.58
2001 Det-Hou		34	29	0	1	167.2	772	203	122	115	37	8	9	15	74	3	97	8	0	11	11	.500	0	0-0	0	6.17
1998 New York	NL	10	10	1	0	57	264	68	38	36	8	2	3	5	25	4	39	4	0	1	4	.200	1	0-0	0	5.68
Los Angeles	NL	20	20	2	0	124.1	525	120	64	56	15	6	4	2	38	1	78	6	0	7	3	.700	0	0-0	0	4.05
1999 Los Angeles	NL	2	0	0	0	7.1	33	10	4	4	1	0	0	0	2	0	1	1	0	0	1	.000	0	0-0	0	4.91
Detroit	AL	31	31	2	0	191.2	850	209	108	98	24	3	8	12	70	1	119	0	0	14	12	.538	0	0-0	0	4.60
2001 Detroit	AL	15	15	0	0	81	391	118	69	66	19	2	3	6	41	2	48	3	0	4	8	.333	0	0-0	0	7.33
Houston	NL	19	14	0	1	86.2	381	85	53	49	18	6	6	9	33	1	49	5	0	7	3	.700	0	0-0	0	5.09
9 ML YEARS		240	177	6	19	1146.2	5077	1236	652	595	160	43	44	55	438	27	777	43	2	62	70	.470	2	1-3	9	4.67

Brian Moehler

Pitches: Right **Bats:** Right **Pos:** SP-1   **Ht:** 6'3" **Wt:** 235 **Born:** 12/31/71 **Age:** 30

Year Team	Lg	G	GS	CG	GF	IP	BFP	H	R	ER	HR	SH	SF	HB	TBB	IBB	SO	WP	Bk	W	L	Pct.	ShO	Sv-Op	Hld	ERA
2001 Toledo *	AAA	2	2	0	0	10.1	45	12	6	5	2	0	0	0	2	0	6	2	0	0	0	.000	0	0- -	—	4.35
1996 Detroit	AL	2	2	0	0	10.1	51	11	10	5	1	1	0	0	8	1	2	1	0	0	1	.000	0	0-0	0	4.35
1997 Detroit	AL	31	31	2	0	175.1	770	198	97	91	22	1	8	5	61	1	97	3	0	11	12	.478	1	0-0	0	4.67
1998 Detroit	AL	33	33	4	0	221.1	912	220	103	96	30	3	3	2	56	1	123	4	0	14	13	.519	3	0-0	0	3.90
1999 Detroit	AL	32	32	2	0	196.1	859	229	116	110	22	8	5	7	59	5	106	4	0	10	16	.385	2	0-0	0	5.04
2000 Detroit	AL	29	29	2	0	178	776	222	99	89	20	3	4	2	40	0	103	2	1	12	9	.571	0	0-0	0	4.50
2001 Detroit	AL	1	1	0	0	8	30	6	3	3	0	0	0	0	1	0	2	0	0	0	0	—	0	0-0	0	3.38
6 ML YEARS		128	128	10	0	789.1	3398	886	428	394	95	16	20	16	225	8	433	14	1	47	51	.480	6	0-0	0	4.49

Chad Moeller

Bats: Right **Throws:** Right **Pos:** C-25; PH/PR-2   **Ht:** 6'3" **Wt:** 210 **Born:** 2/18/75 **Age:** 27

Year Team	Lg	G	AB	H	2B	3B	HR	(Hm	Rd)	TB	R	RBI	TBB	IBB	SO	HBP	SH	SF	SB	CS	SB%	GDP	Avg	OBP	SLG
1996 Elizabethtn	R+	17	59	21	4	0	4	—	—	37	17	13	18	0	9	2	0	0	1	2	.33	3	.356	.519	.627
1997 Fort Wayne	A	108	384	111	18	3	9	—	—	162	58	39	48	0	76	13	2	1	11	8	.58	8	.289	.386	.422
1998 Fort Myers	A+	66	254	83	24	1	6	—	—	127	37	39	31	4	37	3	0	0	2	3	.40	8	.327	.406	.500
New Britain	AA	58	187	44	10	0	6	—	—	72	21	23	24	0	41	3	1	0	2	1	.67	4	.235	.332	.385
1999 New Britain	AA	89	250	62	11	3	4	—	—	91	29	24	21	1	44	6	1	4	0	0	—	7	.248	.317	.364
2000 Salt Lake	AAA	47	167	48	13	1	5	—	—	78	30	20	9	1	45	0	1	1	0	1	.00	6	.287	.322	.467
2001 Tucson	AAA	78	274	75	20	0	8	—	—	119	41	36	25	1	54	2	1	2	1	4	.20	8	.274	.337	.434
2000 Minnesota	AL	48	128	27	3	1	1	(1	0)	35	13	9	9	0	33	0	1	1	1	0	1.00	4	.211	.261	.273
2001 Arizona	NL	25	56	13	0	1	1	(1	0)	18	8	2	6	1	12	0	1	0	0	0	—	2	.232	.306	.321
2 ML YEARS		73	184	40	3	2	2	(2	0)	53	21	11	15	1	45	0	2	1	1	0	1.00	6	.217	.275	.288

Mike Mohler

Pitches: Left **Bats:** Right **Pos:** RP-13   **Ht:** 6'2" **Wt:** 208 **Born:** 7/26/68 **Age:** 33

Year Team	Lg	G	GS	CG	GF	IP	BFP	H	R	ER	HR	SH	SF	HB	TBB	IBB	SO	WP	Bk	W	L	Pct.	ShO	Sv-Op	Hld	ERA
2001 Tucson *	AAA	40	0	0	14	45.1	207	52	28	16	4	2	3	2	14	0	48	4	0	5	0	1.000	0	3--	—	3.18
1993 Oakland	AL	42	9	0	4	64.1	290	57	45	40	10	5	2	2	44	4	42	0	1	1	6	.143	0	0-1	1	5.60
1994 Oakland	AL	1	1	0	0	2.1	14	2	3	2	1	0	0	0	2	0	4	0	0	0	1	.000	0	0-0	0	7.71
1995 Oakland	AL	28	0	0	6	23.2	100	16	8	8	0	1	0	0	18	1	15	1	0	1	1	.500	0	1-2	4	3.04
1996 Oakland	AL	72	0	0	30	81	352	79	36	33	9	6	4	1	41	6	64	9	0	6	3	.667	0	7-13	13	3.67
1997 Oakland	AL	62	10	0	16	101.2	462	116	65	58	11	9	7	7	54	8	66	4	0	1	10	.091	0	1-4	11	5.13
1998 Oakland	AL	57	0	0	16	61	277	70	38	35	6	3	2	4	26	3	42	3	1	3	3	.500	0	0-1	8	5.16
1999 St. Louis	NL	48	0	0	16	49.1	211	47	26	24	3	1	1	1	23	2	31	1	0	1	1	.500	0	1-2	6	4.38
2000 StL-Cle		24	0	0	7	20	102	27	21	20	2	0	0	2	15	1	10	2	0	1	2	.333	0	0-3	4	9.00
2001 Arizona	NL	13	0	0	5	13.2	61	14	11	11	3	2	1	0	9	0	7	1	0	0	0	—	0	0-2	0	7.24
2000 St. Louis	NL	22	0	0	7	19	98	26	20	19	1	0	0	2	15	1	8	2	0	1	1	.500	0	0-2	4	9.00
Cleveland	AL	2	0	0	0	1	4	1	1	1	1	0	0	0	0	0	2	0	0	0	0	1.000	0	0-1	0	9.00
9 ML YEARS		347	20	0	100	417	1869	428	253	231	45	27	17	17	232	25	281	21	2	14	27	.341	0	10-28	47	4.99

Dustan Mohr

Bats: R **Throws:** R **Pos:** RF-15; LF-6; DH-1; PH/PR-1   **Ht:** 6'0" **Wt:** 210 **Born:** 6/19/76 **Age:** 26

Year Team	Lg	G	AB	H	2B	3B	HR	(Hm	Rd)	TB	R	RBI	TBB	IBB	SO	HBP	SH	SF	SB	CS	SB%	GDP	Avg	OBP	SLG
1997 Watertown	A-	74	275	80	20	2	7	—	—	125	52	53	31	1	76	4	0	4	3	6	.33	1	.291	.366	.455
1998 Kinston	A+	134	491	119	23	9	19	—	—	217	60	65	39	3	146	9	2	2	8	4	.67	7	.242	.309	.442
1999 Akron	AA	12	42	7	2	1	0	—	—	11	3	2	5	0	7	0	1	0	0	1	.00	1	.167	.255	.262
Kinston	A+	112	429	120	29	3	8	—	—	179	46	60	26	2	104	1	1	1	6	6	.50	13	.280	.322	.417
2000 Fort Myers	A+	101	370	98	19	2	11	—	—	154	58	75	35	1	65	8	1	4	7	4	.64	11	.265	.338	.416
2001 New Britain	AA	135	518	174	41	3	24	—	—	293	90	91	49	4	111	4	0	3	9	9	.50	6	.336	.395	.566
2001 Minnesota	AL	20	51	12	2	0	0	(0	0)	14	6	4	5	0	17	0	0	1	1	1	.50	0	.235	.298	.275

Ben Molina

Bats: Right **Throws:** Right **Pos:** C-94; PH/PR-5; DH-1   **Ht:** 5'11" **Wt:** 210 **Born:** 7/20/74 **Age:** 27

Year Team	Lg	G	AB	H	2B	3B	HR	(Hm	Rd)	TB	R	RBI	TBB	IBB	SO	HBP	SH	SF	SB	CS	SB%	GDP	Avg	OBP	SLG
2001 Salt Lake *	AAA	5	18	5	1	0	0	—	—	7	2	3	2	0	3	0	0	0	0	0	—	2	.278	.350	.333
Rancho Cuc *	A+	3	11	6	1	0	0	—	—	7	1	2	0	0	1	0	0	0	0	0	—	0	.545	.545	.636
1998 Anaheim	AL	2	1	0	0	0	0	(0	0)	0	0	0	0	0	0	0	0	0	0	0	—	0	.000	.000	.000
1999 Anaheim	AL	31	101	26	5	0	1	(0	1)	34	8	10	6	0	6	2	0	0	0	1	.00	5	.257	.312	.337
2000 Anaheim	AL	130	473	133	20	2	14	(11	3)	199	59	71	23	0	33	6	4	7	1	0	1.00	17	.281	.318	.421
2001 Anaheim	AL	96	325	85	11	0	6	(6	0)	114	31	40	16	3	51	8	2	4	0	1	.00	8	.262	.309	.351
4 ML YEARS		259	900	244	36	2	21	(17	4)	347	98	121	45	3	90	16	6	11	1	2	.33	30	.271	.314	.386

Jose Molina

Bats: Right **Throws:** Right **Pos:** C-15   **Ht:** 6'2" **Wt:** 215 **Born:** 6/3/75 **Age:** 27

Year Team	Lg	G	AB	H	2B	3B	HR	(Hm	Rd)	TB	R	RBI	TBB	IBB	SO	HBP	SH	SF	SB	CS	SB%	GDP	Avg	OBP	SLG
1993 Cubs	R	33	78	17	2	0	0	—	—	19	5	4	12	0	12	0	4	0	3	2	.60	2	.218	.322	.244
Daytona	A+	3	7	1	0	0	0	—	—	1	0	1	2	0	0	0	0	0	0	1	.00	0	.143	.333	.143
1994 Peoria	A	78	253	58	13	1	1	—	—	76	31	33	24	1	61	4	5	4	4	3	.57	5	.229	.302	.300
1995 Daytona	A+	82	233	55	9	1	1	—	—	69	27	19	29	0	53	7	2	2	1	0	1.00	7	.236	.336	.296
1996 Rockford	A	96	305	69	10	1	2	—	—	87	35	27	36	0	71	3	7	4	2	4	.33	8	.226	.310	.285
1997 Iowa	AAA	1	3	1	0	0	0	—	—	1	0	0	1	0	1	0	0	0	0	0	—	1	.333	.500	.333
Daytona	A+	55	179	45	9	1	0	—	—	56	17	23	14	0	25	1	5	2	4	0	1.00	5	.251	.306	.313
Orlando	AA	37	99	17	3	0	1	—	—	23	10	15	12	5	28	2	1	3	0	1	.00	4	.172	.267	.232
1998 West Tenn	AA	109	320	71	10	1	2	—	—	89	33	28	32	1	74	3	10	3	1	5	.17	10	.222	.296	.278
1999 West Tenn	AA	14	35	6	3	0	0	—	—	9	2	5	2	0	14	0	1	1	0	1	.00	1	.171	.211	.257
Iowa	AAA	74	240	63	11	1	4	—	—	88	24	26	20	5	54	4	2	2	0	0	—	3	.263	.327	.367
2000 Iowa	AAA	76	248	58	9	0	1	—	—	70	22	17	23	1	61	0	1	3	1	4	.20	6	.234	.296	.282
2001 Salt Lake	AAA	61	213	64	11	1	5	—	—	92	29	31	14	0	49	2	6	0	1	2	.33	7	.300	.349	.432
1999 Chicago	NL	10	19	5	1	0	0	(0	0)	6	3	1	2	1	4	0	0	0	0	0	—	0	.263	.333	.316
2001 Anaheim	AL	15	37	10	3	0	2	(0	2)	19	8	4	3	0	8	2	0	0	0	0	—	2	.270	.325	.514
2 ML YEARS		25	56	15	4	0	2	(0	2)	25	11	5	5	1	12	2	0	0	0	0	—	2	.268	.328	.446

Raul Mondesi

Bats: Right **Throws:** Right **Pos:** RF-149   **Ht:** 5'11" **Wt:** 215 **Born:** 3/12/71 **Age:** 31

Year Team	Lg	G	AB	H	2B	3B	HR	(Hm	Rd)	TB	R	RBI	TBB	IBB	SO	HBP	SH	SF	SB	CS	SB%	GDP	Avg	OBP	SLG
1993 Los Angeles	NL	42	86	25	3	1	4	(2	2)	42	13	10	4	0	16	0	1	0	4	1	.80	1	.291	.322	.488
1994 Los Angeles	NL	112	434	133	27	8	16	(10	6)	224	63	56	16	5	78	2	0	2	11	8	.58	9	.306	.333	.516
1995 Los Angeles	NL	139	536	153	23	6	26	(13	13)	266	91	88	33	4	96	4	0	7	27	4	.87	7	.285	.328	.496
1996 Los Angeles	NL	157	634	188	40	7	24	(11	13)	314	98	88	32	9	122	5	0	2	14	7	.67	6	.297	.334	.495
1997 Los Angeles	NL	159	616	191	42	5	30	(16	14)	333	95	87	44	7	105	6	1	3	32	15	.68	11	.310	.360	.541
1998 Los Angeles	NL	148	580	162	26	5	30	(13	17)	288	85	90	30	4	112	3	0	4	16	10	.62	8	.279	.316	.497
1999 Los Angeles	NL	159	601	152	29	5	33	(18	15)	290	98	99	71	6	134	3	0	5	36	9	.80	3	.253	.332	.483
2000 Toronto	AL	96	388	105	22	2	24	(10	14)	203	78	67	32	0	73	3	0	3	22	6	.79	8	.271	.329	.523
2001 Toronto	AL	149	572	144	26	4	27	(10	17)	259	88	84	73	3	128	6	0	2	30	11	.73	13	.252	.342	.453
9 ML YEARS		1161	4447	1253	238	43	214	(103	111)	2219	709	669	335	38	864	32	2	28	192	71	.73	66	.282	.335	.499

Craig Monroe

Bats: R **Throws:** R **Pos:** RF-21; LF-6; PH/PR-4; DH-1   **Ht:** 6'1" **Wt:** 195 **Born:** 2/27/77 **Age:** 25

Year Team	Lg	G	AB	H	2B	3B	HR	(Hm	Rd)	TB	R	RBI	TBB	IBB	SO	HBP	SH	SF	SB	CS	SB%	GDP	Avg	OBP	SLG
1995 Rangers	R	54	193	48	6	2	0	—	—	58	22	33	18	0	25	2	1	2	13	2	.87	1	.249	.316	.301
1996 Chston-SC	A	49	153	23	11	1	0	—	—	36	11	9	18	0	48	3	0	0	2	2	.50	3	.150	.253	.235
Hudson Val	A-	67	268	74	16	6	5	—	—	117	53	29	23	0	63	2	0	2	21	7	.75	4	.276	.336	.437
1997 Charlotte	A+	92	328	77	23	1	7	—	—	123	54	41	44	1	80	0	0	6	24	1	.96	5	.235	.320	.375
1998 Charlotte	A+	132	472	114	26	7	17	—	—	205	73	76	66	0	102	3	0	7	50	13	.79	15	.242	.334	.434
1999 Charlotte	A+	130	480	125	21	1	17	—	—	199	77	81	42	2	102	4	3	7	40	16	.71	8	.260	.321	.415
Oklahoma	AAA	6	16	4	1	0	0	—	—	5	2	1	1	0	4	0	1	0	0	0	—	0	.250	.294	.313
2000 Tulsa	AA	120	464	131	34	5	20	—	—	235	89	89	64	4	91	2	1	8	12	13	.48	12	.282	.366	.506
2001 Oklahoma	AAA	114	410	115	25	5	20	—	—	210	60	75	46	2	85	5	1	3	10	8	.56	11	.280	.358	.512
2001 Texas	AL	27	52	11	1	0	2	(1	1)	18	5	6	5	0	18	0	0	0	2	0	1.00	1	.212	.293	.346

Trey Moore

Pitches: Left **Bats:** Left **Pos:** RP-2   **Ht:** 6'0" **Wt:** 190 **Born:** 10/2/72 **Age:** 29

Year Team	Lg	G	GS	CG	GF	IP	BFP	H	R	ER	HR	SH	SF	HB	TBB	IBB	SO	WP	Bk	W	L	Pct.	ShO	Sv-Op	Hld	ERA
2001 Richmond *	AAA	26	25	2	0	163	665	140	64	60	9	8	9	4	41	3	122	6	0	9	8	.529	0	0- -	—	3.31
1998 Montreal	NL	13	11	0	1	61	277	78	37	34	5	1	3	1	17	3	35	2	0	2	5	.286	0	0-0	0	5.02
2000 Montreal	NL	8	8	0	0	35.1	160	55	31	26	7	2	0	4	21	1	24	1	1	1	5	.167	0	0-0	0	6.62
2001 Atlanta	NL	2	0	0	0	4	21	7	5	5	0	0	0	0	2	0	1	1	0	0	0	—	0	0-0	0	11.25
3 ML YEARS		23	19	0	1	100.1	476	140	73	65	12	3	3	5	40	4	60	4	1	3	10	.231	0	0-0	0	5.83

Melvin Mora

Bats: R **Throws:** R **Pos:** CF-88; SS-43; PH/PR-6; 2B-1   **Ht:** 5'11" **Wt:** 180 **Born:** 2/2/72 **Age:** 30

Year Team	Lg	G	AB	H	2B	3B	HR	(Hm	Rd)	TB	R	RBI	TBB	IBB	SO	HBP	SH	SF	SB	CS	SB%	GDP	Avg	OBP	SLG
1999 New York	NL	66	31	5	0	0	0	(0	0)	5	6	1	4	0	7	1	3	0	2	1	.67	0	.161	.278	.161
2000 NYM-Bal		132	414	114	22	5	8	(5	3)	170	60	47	35	3	80	6	4	5	12	11	.52	5	.275	.337	.411
2001 Baltimore	AL	128	436	109	28	0	7	(6	1)	158	49	48	41	2	91	14	5	7	11	4	.73	6	.250	.329	.362
2000 New York	NL	79	215	56	13	2	6	(4	2)	91	35	30	18	3	48	2	2	5	7	3	.70	3	.260	.317	.423
Baltimore	AL	53	199	58	9	3	2	(1	1)	79	25	17	17	0	32	4	2	0	5	8	.38	2	.291	.359	.397
3 ML YEARS		326	881	228	50	5	15	(11	4)	333	115	96	80	5	178	21	12	12	25	16	.61	11	.259	.331	.378

Mike Mordecai

Bats: R **Throws:** R **Pos:** 3B-42; 2B-32; PH/PR-25; SS-4; DH-1; C-1; 1B-1; RF-1   **Ht:** 5'10" **Wt:** 185 **Born:** 12/13/67 **Age:** 34

Year Team	Lg	G	AB	H	2B	3B	HR	(Hm	Rd)	TB	R	RBI	TBB	IBB	SO	HBP	SH	SF	SB	CS	SB%	GDP	Avg	OBP	SLG
1994 Atlanta	NL	4	4	1	0	0	1	(1	0)	4	1	3	1	0	0	0	0	0	0	0	—	0	.250	.400	1.000
1995 Atlanta	NL	69	75	21	6	0	3	(1	2)	36	10	11	9	0	16	0	2	1	0	0	—	0	.280	.353	.480
1996 Atlanta	NL	66	108	26	5	0	2	(0	2)	37	12	8	9	1	24	0	4	1	1	0	1.00	0	.241	.297	.343
1997 Atlanta	NL	61	81	14	2	1	0	(0	0)	18	8	3	6	0	16	0	1	1	0	1	.00	4	.173	.227	.222
1998 Montreal	NL	73	119	24	4	2	3	(1	2)	41	12	10	9	0	20	0	2	0	1	0	1.00	2	.202	.258	.345
1999 Montreal	NL	109	226	53	10	2	5	(4	1)	82	29	25	20	0	31	1	2	1	2	5	.29	1	.235	.297	.363
2000 Montreal	NL	86	169	48	16	0	4	(2	2)	76	20	16	12	0	34	1	1	0	2	2	.50	1	.284	.335	.450
2001 Montreal	NL	96	254	71	17	2	3	(1	2)	101	28	32	19	1	53	1	1	2	2	2	.50	6	.280	.330	.398
8 ML YEARS		564	1036	258	60	7	21	(10	11)	395	120	108	85	2	194	3	12	7	8	10	.44	15	.249	.306	.381

Juan Moreno

Pitches: Left **Bats:** Left **Pos:** RP-45   **Ht:** 6'1" **Wt:** 205 **Born:** 2/28/75 **Age:** 27

Year Team	Lg	G	GS	CG	GF	IP	BFP	H	R	ER	HR	SH	SF	HB	TBB	IBB	SO	WP	Bk	W	L	Pct.	ShO	Sv-Op	Hld	ERA
1995 Athletics	R	20	0	0	8	44.2	181	36	10	6	1	1	1	0	20	0	49	2	5	6	2	.750	0	0- -	—	1.21
1996 W Michigan	A	38	11	0	5	107	475	98	60	52	6	6	6	2	69	5	97	6	2	4	6	.400	0	0- -	—	4.37
1999 Tulsa	AA	42	0	0	27	62.2	255	33	20	16	5	2	3	3	32	2	83	6	0	4	3	.571	0	3- -	—	2.30
2000 Charlotte	A+	1	1	0	0	2	7	0	0	0	0	0	0	0	1	0	0	0	0	0	0	—	0	0- -	—	0.00
Tulsa	AA	5	0	0	3	6.2	30	6	4	4	0	0	1	0	5	0	12	1	0	0	0	—	0	1- -	—	5.40
2001 Tulsa	AA	6	0	0	6	8.2	34	6	1	0	0	3	1	0	3	0	10	1	0	1	1	.500	0	1- -	—	0.00
Oklahoma	AAA	7	0	0	2	9.2	35	4	2	2	1	0	1	0	2	0	13	0	0	0	0	—	0	0- -	—	1.86
2001 Texas	AL	45	0	0	6	41.1	173	22	21	18	6	1	0	0	28	2	36	5	3	3	3	.500	0	0-2	8	3.92

Mike Morgan

Pitches: Right **Bats:** Right **Pos:** RP-30; SP-1 **Ht:** 6'2" **Wt:** 226 **Born:** 10/8/59 **Age:** 42

Year Team	Lg	G	GS	CG	GF	IP	BFP	H	R	ER	HR	SH	SF	HB	TBB	IBB	SO	WP	Bk	W	L	Pct.	ShO	Sv-Op	Hld	ERA
2001 Tucson *	AAA	2	2	0	0	3	14	5	1	1	0	0	0	0	0	0	4	0	0	0	0	—	0	0--	—	3.00
1978 Oakland	AL	3	3	1	0	12.1	60	19	12	10	1	1	0	0	8	0	0	0	0	0	3	.000	0	0-0	0	7.30
1979 Oakland	AL	13	13	2	0	77.1	368	102	57	51	7	4	4	3	50	0	17	7	0	2	10	.167	0	0-0	0	5.94
1982 New York	AL	30	23	2	2	150.1	661	167	77	73	15	2	4	2	67	5	71	6	0	7	11	.389	0	0-0	0	4.37
1983 Toronto	AL	16	4	0	2	45.1	198	48	26	26	6	0	1	0	21	0	22	3	0	0	3	.000	0	0-0	0	5.16
1985 Seattle	AL	2	2	0	0	6	33	11	8	8	2	0	0	0	5	0	2	1	0	1	1	.500	0	0-0	0	12.00
1986 Seattle	AL	37	33	9	2	216.1	951	243	122	109	24	7	3	4	86	3	116	8	1	11	17	.393	1	1-1	0	4.53
1987 Seattle	AL	34	31	8	2	207	898	245	117	107	25	8	5	5	53	3	85	11	0	12	17	.414	2	0-0	0	4.65
1988 Baltimore	AL	22	10	2	6	71.1	299	70	45	43	6	1	0	1	23	1	29	5	0	1	6	.143	0	1-1	0	5.43
1989 Los Angeles	NL	40	19	0	7	152.2	604	130	51	43	6	8	6	2	33	8	72	6	0	8	11	.421	0	0-1	1	2.53
1990 Los Angeles	NL	33	33	6	0	211	891	216	100	88	19	11	4	5	60	5	106	4	1	11	15	.423	4	0-0	0	3.75
1991 Los Angeles	NL	34	33	5	1	236.1	949	197	85	73	12	10	4	3	61	10	140	6	0	14	10	.583	1	1-1	0	2.78
1992 Chicago	NL	34	34	6	0	240	966	203	80	68	14	10	5	3	79	10	123	11	0	16	8	.667	1	0-0	0	2.55
1993 Chicago	NL	32	32	1	0	207.2	883	206	100	93	15	11	5	7	74	8	111	8	2	10	15	.400	1	0-0	0	4.03
1994 Chicago	NL	15	15	1	0	80.2	380	111	65	60	12	7	6	4	35	2	57	5	0	2	10	.167	0	0-0	0	6.69
1995 ChC-StL	NL	21	21	1	0	131.1	548	133	56	52	12	12	5	6	34	2	61	6	0	7	7	.500	0	0-0	0	3.56
1996 StL-Cin	NL	23	23	0	0	130.1	567	146	72	67	16	6	7	1	47	0	74	2	0	6	11	.353	0	0-0	0	4.63
1997 Cincinnati	NL	31	30	1	0	162	688	165	91	86	13	9	2	8	49	6	103	7	0	9	12	.429	0	0-0	1	4.78
1998 Min-ChC	NL	23	22	0	0	120.2	524	138	62	56	21	3	3	8	39	2	60	1	0	4	3	.571	0	0-0	0	4.18
1999 Texas	AL	34	25	1	1	140	632	184	108	97	25	3	5	7	48	2	61	3	1	13	10	.565	0	0-1	0	6.24
2000 Arizona	NL	60	4	0	15	101.2	448	123	55	55	10	7	4	1	40	5	56	0	0	5	5	.500	0	5-6	5	4.87
2001 Arizona	NL	31	1	0	9	38	168	45	20	18	2	2	2	0	17	4	24	2	0	1	0	1.000	0	0-1	5	4.26
1995 Chicago	NL	4	4	0	0	24.2	100	19	8	6	2	2	0	1	9	1	15	0	0	2	1	.667	0	0-0	0	2.19
St. Louis	NL	17	17	1	0	106.2	448	114	48	46	10	10	5	5	25	1	46	6	0	5	6	.455	0	0-0	0	3.88
1996 St. Louis	NL	18	18	0	0	103	452	118	63	60	14	5	6	0	40	0	55	2	0	4	8	.333	0	0-0	0	5.24
Cincinnati	NL	5	5	0	0	27.1	115	28	9	7	2	1	1	1	7	0	19	0	0	2	3	.400	0	0-0	0	2.30
1998 Minnesota	NL	18	17	0	0	98	412	108	41	38	13	0	3	7	24	1	50	1	0	4	2	.667	0	0-0	0	3.49
Chicago	NL	5	5	0	0	22.2	112	30	21	18	8	3	0	1	15	1	10	0	0	0	1	.000	0	0-0	0	7.15
21 ML YEARS		568	411	46	47	2738.1	11716	2902	1409	1283	263	122	75	70	929	76	1390	102	5	140	185	.431	10	8-12	12	4.22

Matt Morris

Pitches: Right **Bats:** Right **Pos:** SP-34 **Ht:** 6'5" **Wt:** 210 **Born:** 8/9/74 **Age:** 27

Year Team	Lg	G	GS	CG	GF	IP	BFP	H	R	ER	HR	SH	SF	HB	TBB	IBB	SO	WP	Bk	W	L	Pct.	ShO	Sv-Op	Hld	ERA
1997 St. Louis	NL	33	33	3	0	217	900	208	88	77	12	11	7	7	69	2	149	5	3	12	9	.571	0	0-0	0	3.19
1998 St. Louis	NL	17	17	2	0	113.2	468	101	37	32	8	6	1	3	42	6	79	3	0	7	5	.583	1	0-0	0	2.53
2000 St. Louis	NL	31	0	0	12	53	226	53	22	21	3	3	1	2	17	1	34	0	0	3	3	.500	0	4-7	7	3.57
2001 St. Louis	NL	34	34	2	0	216.1	909	218	86	76	13	14	5	13	54	3	185	5	1	22	8	.733	1	0-0	0	3.16
4 ML YEARS		115	84	7	12	600	2503	580	233	206	36	34	14	25	182	12	447	13	4	44	25	.638	2	4-7	7	3.09

Warren Morris

Bats: Left **Throws:** Right **Pos:** 2B-29; PH/PR-21; 3B-1 **Ht:** 5'11" **Wt:** 179 **Born:** 1/11/74 **Age:** 28

Year Team	Lg	G	AB	H	2B	3B	HR	(Hm	Rd)	TB	R	RBI	TBB	IBB	SO	HBP	SH	SF	SB	CS	SB%	GDP	Avg	OBP	SLG
2001 Nashville *	AAA	57	223	68	16	2	5	—	—	103	26	40	12	0	21	2	1	3	3	4	.43	5	.305	.342	.462
1999 Pittsburgh	NL	147	511	147	20	3	15	(9	6)	218	65	73	59	3	88	2	4	5	3	7	.30	12	.288	.360	.427
2000 Pittsburgh	NL	144	528	137	31	2	3	(3	0)	181	68	43	65	3	78	2	8	3	7	10	.41	7	.259	.341	.343
2001 Pittsburgh	NL	48	103	21	6	0	2	(2	0)	33	6	11	3	0	9	2	0	1	2	3	.40	2	.204	.239	.320
3 ML YEARS		339	1142	305	57	5	20	(14	6)	432	139	127	127	6	175	6	12	9	12	20	.38	21	.267	.341	.378

Damian Moss

Pitches: Left **Bats:** Right **Pos:** RP-4; SP-1 **Ht:** 6'0" **Wt:** 187 **Born:** 11/24/76 **Age:** 25

Year Team	Lg	G	GS	CG	GF	IP	BFP	H	R	ER	HR	SH	SF	HB	TBB	IBB	SO	WP	Bk	W	L	Pct.	ShO	Sv-Op	Hld	ERA
1994 Danville	R+	12	12	1	0	60.1	265	30	28	24	1	1	0	14	55	0	77	12	3	2	5	.286	1	0--	—	3.58
1995 Macon	A	27	27	0	0	149.1	653	134	73	59	13	0	2	12	70	0	177	14	5	9	10	.474	0	0--	—	3.56
1996 Durham	A+	14	14	0	0	84	333	52	25	21	9	3	3	2	40	0	89	7	2	9	1	.900	0	0--	—	2.25
Greenville	AA	11	10	0	0	58	262	57	41	32	5	0	3	3	35	0	48	12	0	2	5	.286	0	0--	—	4.97
1997 Greenville	AA	21	19	1	0	112.2	498	111	73	67	13	1	8	9	58	0	116	14	2	6	8	.429	0	0--	—	5.35
1999 Macon	A	12	12	0	0	41.2	172	33	20	20	8	1	0	4	15	0	49	2	1	0	3	.000	0	0--	—	4.32
Greenville	AA	7	7	0	0	32.2	171	50	33	31	6	0	3	2	21	0	22	8	0	1	3	.250	0	0--	—	8.54
2000 Richmond	AAA	29	28	0	0	160.2	710	130	67	56	14	8	5	6	106	0	123	10	2	9	6	.600	0	0--	—	3.14
2001 Greenville	AA	3	2	0	1	9	34	7	3	3	0	0	0	0	10	0	10	0	0	1	0	1.000	0	0--	—	3.00
Richmond	AAA	17	16	0	0	88.2	372	75	34	31	10	5	2	3	38	1	94	5	0	5	4	.556	0	0--	—	3.15
2001 Atlanta	NL	5	1	0	2	9	41	3	3	3	1	1	0	0	9	0	8	1	0	0	0	—	0	0-0	0	3.00

Guillermo Mota

Pitches: Right **Bats:** Right **Pos:** RP-53 **Ht:** 6'4" **Wt:** 205 **Born:** 7/25/73 **Age:** 28

Year Team	Lg	G	GS	CG	GF	IP	BFP	H	R	ER	HR	SH	SF	HB	TBB	IBB	SO	WP	Bk	W	L	Pct.	ShO	Sv-Op	Hld	ERA
2001 Ottawa *	AAA	4	0	0	1	4	13	1	1	1	0	0	0	0	4	0	4	0	0	0	0	—	0	0--	—	2.25
1999 Montreal	NL	51	0	0	18	55.1	243	54	24	18	5	3	3	2	25	3	27	1	1	2	4	.333	0	0-1	3	2.93
2000 Montreal	NL	29	0	0	7	30	126	27	21	20	3	1	1	2	12	0	24	1	1	1	1	.500	0	0-0	5	6.00
2001 Montreal	NL	53	0	0	12	49.2	212	51	30	29	9	3	2	1	18	1	31	1	0	1	3	.250	0	0-3	12	5.26
3 ML YEARS		133	0	0	37	135	581	132	75	67	17	7	6	5	55	4	82	3	2	4	8	.333	0	0-4	20	4.47

Chad Mottola

Bats: R **Throws:** R **Pos:** RF-4; LF-2; CF-1; PH/PR-1   **Ht:** 6'3" **Wt:** 215 **Born:** 10/15/71 **Age:** 30

Year Team	Lg	G	AB	H	2B	3B	HR	(Hm	Rd)	TB	R	RBI	TBB	IBB	SO	HBP	SH	SF	SB	CS	SB%	GDP	Avg	OBP	SLG
1992 Billings	R+	57	213	61	8	3	12	—	—	111	53	37	25	0	43	0	0	0	12	3	.80	4	.286	.361	.521
1993 Winston-Sal	A+	137	493	138	25	3	21	—	—	232	76	91	62	2	109	2	0	3	13	7	.65	9	.280	.361	.471
1994 Chattanooga	AA	118	402	97	19	1	7	—	—	139	44	41	30	1	68	1	2	2	9	12	.43	12	.241	.294	.346
1995 Chattanooga	AA	51	181	53	13	1	10	—	—	98	32	39	13	0	32	1	0	1	1	2	.33	2	.293	.342	.541
Indianapolis	AAA	69	239	62	11	1	8	—	—	99	40	37	20	0	50	0	1	1	8	1	.89	6	.259	.315	.414
1996 Indianapolis	AAA	103	362	95	24	3	9	—	—	152	45	47	21	3	93	4	0	4	6	4	.60	10	.262	.307	.420
1997 Chattanooga	AA	46	174	63	9	3	5	—	—	93	35	32	16	1	23	1	1	5	7	1	.88	3	.362	.408	.534
Indianapolis	AAA	83	284	82	10	6	7	—	—	125	33	45	16	2	43	4	0	2	12	4	.75	6	.289	.333	.440
1998 Indianapolis	AAA	5	12	5	0	0	1	—	—	8	2	2	4	0	0	0	0	0	0	2	.00	0	.417	.563	.667
Tulsa	AA	8	26	13	1	0	1	—	—	17	9	7	10	1	1	0	0	0	3	0	1.00	0	.500	.639	.654
Oklahoma	AAA	74	257	68	13	1	2	—	—	89	29	22	18	1	49	1	0	2	8	3	.73	7	.265	.313	.346
1999 Charlotte	AAA	140	511	164	32	4	20	—	—	264	95	94	60	1	83	3	0	7	18	6	.75	7	.321	.391	.517
2000 Syracuse	AAA	134	505	156	25	3	33	—	—	286	85	102	37	2	99	5	0	5	30	15	.67	11	.309	.359	.566
2001 Calgary	AAA	119	457	135	23	2	15	—	—	207	66	66	30	0	85	4	0	1	11	5	.69	5	.295	.343	.453
1996 Cincinnati	NL	35	79	17	3	0	3	(1	2)	29	10	6	6	1	16	0	0	0	2	2	.50	0	.215	.271	.367
2000 Toronto	AL	3	9	2	0	0	0	(0	0)	2	1	2	0	0	4	1	0	0	0	0	—	0	.222	.300	.222
2001 Florida	NL	5	7	0	0	0	0	(0	0)	0	1	1	2	0	2	0	0	1	0	0	—	0	.000	.200	.000
3 ML YEARS		43	95	19	3	0	3	(1	2)	31	12	9	8	1	22	1	0	1	2	2	.50	0	.200	.267	.326

James Mouton

Bats: R **Throws:** R **Pos:** PH/PR-31; CF-28; LF-21; RF-7; DH-1   **Ht:** 5'9" **Wt:** 175 **Born:** 12/29/68 **Age:** 33

Year Team	Lg	G	AB	H	2B	3B	HR	(Hm	Rd)	TB	R	RBI	TBB	IBB	SO	HBP	SH	SF	SB	CS	SB%	GDP	Avg	OBP	SLG
2001 Indianapols *	AAA	2	9	4	2	0	0	—	—	6	0	2	0	0	2	0	0	0	0	0	—	0	.444	.444	.667
1994 Houston	NL	99	310	76	11	0	2	(1	1)	93	43	16	27	0	69	5	2	1	24	5	.83	6	.245	.315	.300
1995 Houston	NL	104	298	78	18	2	4	(2	2)	112	42	27	25	1	59	4	3	1	25	8	.76	5	.262	.326	.376
1996 Houston	NL	122	300	79	15	1	3	(2	1)	105	40	34	38	2	55	0	2	3	21	9	.70	9	.263	.343	.350
1997 Houston	NL	86	180	38	9	1	3	(1	2)	58	24	23	18	0	30	2	2	2	9	7	.56	3	.211	.287	.322
1998 San Diego	NL	55	63	12	2	1	0	(0	0)	16	8	7	7	1	11	0	0	1	4	3	.57	3	.190	.268	.254
1999 Montreal	NL	95	122	32	5	1	2	(1	1)	45	18	13	18	1	31	2	3	1	6	2	.75	2	.262	.364	.369
2000 Milwaukee	NL	87	159	37	7	1	2	(1	1)	52	28	17	30	0	43	3	4	1	13	4	.76	5	.233	.363	.327
2001 Milwaukee	NL	75	138	34	8	0	2	(1	1)	48	20	10	11	0	40	6	3	0	7	3	.70	1	.246	.329	.348
8 ML YEARS		723	1570	386	75	7	18	(9	9)	529	223	147	174	5	338	22	19	10	109	41	.73	34	.246	.328	.337

Lyle Mouton

Bats: Right **Throws:** Right **Pos:** PH/PR-12; LF-6; RF-5   **Ht:** 6'4" **Wt:** 230 **Born:** 5/13/69 **Age:** 33

Year Team	Lg	G	AB	H	2B	3B	HR	(Hm	Rd)	TB	R	RBI	TBB	IBB	SO	HBP	SH	SF	SB	CS	SB%	GDP	Avg	OBP	SLG
2001 Toledo *	AAA	67	262	83	18	2	18	—	—	159	59	49	29	3	66	5	0	1	4	1	.80	12	.317	.394	.607
New Orleans *	AAA	2	9	3	1	0	1	—	—	7	1	1	0	0	3	0	0	0	0	0	—	0	.333	.333	.778
1995 Chicago	AL	58	179	54	16	0	5	(4	1)	85	23	27	19	0	46	2	0	1	1	0	1.00	7	.302	.373	.475
1996 Chicago	AL	87	214	63	8	1	7	(4	3)	94	25	39	22	4	50	2	0	3	3	0	1.00	3	.294	.361	.439
1997 Chicago	AL	88	242	65	9	0	5	(4	1)	89	26	23	14	1	66	1	0	3	4	4	.50	8	.269	.308	.368
1998 Baltimore	AL	18	39	12	2	0	2	(0	2)	20	5	7	4	0	8	0	0	0	0	0	—	0	.308	.372	.513
1999 Milwaukee	NL	14	17	3	1	0	1	(1	0)	7	2	3	2	0	3	0	0	0	0	0	—	0	.176	.263	.412
2000 Milwaukee	NL	42	97	27	7	1	2	(2	0)	42	14	16	10	0	29	1	0	1	1	0	1.00	2	.278	.349	.433
2001 Florida	NL	21	17	1	0	0	0	(0	0)	1	1	1	0	0	7	0	0	0	0	0	—	0	.059	.059	.059
7 ML YEARS		328	805	225	43	2	22	(15	7)	338	96	116	71	5	209	6	0	8	9	4	.69	20	.280	.339	.420

Jamie Moyer

Pitches: Left **Bats:** Left **Pos:** SP-33   **Ht:** 6'0" **Wt:** 175 **Born:** 11/18/62 **Age:** 39

Year Team	Lg	G	GS	CG	GF	IP	BFP	H	R	ER	HR	SH	SF	HB	TBB	IBB	SO	WP	Bk	W	L	Pct.	ShO	Sv-Op	Hld	ERA
1986 Chicago	NL	16	16	1	0	87.1	395	107	52	49	10	3	3	3	42	1	45	3	3	7	4	.636	1	0-0	0	5.05
1987 Chicago	NL	35	33	1	1	201	899	210	127	114	28	14	7	5	97	9	147	11	2	12	15	.444	0	0-0	0	5.10
1988 Chicago	NL	34	30	3	1	202	855	212	84	78	20	14	4	4	55	7	121	4	0	9	15	.375	1	0-2	0	3.48
1989 Texas	AL	15	15	1	0	76	337	84	51	41	10	1	4	2	33	0	44	1	0	4	9	.308	0	0-0	0	4.86
1990 Texas	AL	33	10	1	6	102.1	447	115	59	53	6	1	7	4	39	4	58	1	0	2	6	.250	0	0-0	1	4.66
1991 St. Louis	NL	8	7	0	1	31.1	148	38	21	20	5	-4	2	1	16	0	20	2	1	0	5	.000	0	0-0	0	5.74
1993 Baltimore	AL	25	25	3	0	152	630	154	63	58	11	3	1	6	38	2	90	1	1	12	9	.571	1	0-0	0	3.43
1994 Baltimore	AL	23	23	0	0	149	631	158	81	79	23	5	2	2	38	3	87	1	0	5	7	.417	0	0-0	0	4.77
1995 Baltimore	AL	27	18	0	1	115.2	483	117	70	67	18	5	3	3	30	0	65	0	0	8	6	.571	0	0-0	0	5.21
1996 Bos-Sea	AL	34	21	0	1	160.2	703	177	86	71	23	7	6	2	46	5	79	3	1	13	3	.813	0	0-0	1	3.98
1997 Seattle	AL	30	30	2	0	188.2	787	187	82	81	21	6	1	7	43	2	113	3	0	17	5	.773	0	0-0	0	3.86
1998 Seattle	AL	34	34	4	0	234.1	974	234	99	92	23	4	3	10	42	4	158	3	1	15	9	.625	3	0-0	0	3.53
1999 Seattle	AL	32	32	4	0	228	945	235	108	98	23	6	2	9	48	1	137	3	0	14	8	.636	0	0-0	0	3.87
2000 Seattle	AL	26	26	0	0	154	678	173	103	94	22	3	3	3	53	2	98	4	1	13	10	.565	0	0-0	0	5.49
2001 Seattle	AL	33	33	1	0	209.2	851	187	84	80	24	5	11	10	44	4	119	1	0	20	6	.769	0	0-0	0	3.43
1996 Boston	AL	23	10	0	0	90	405	111	50	45	14	4	3	1	27	2	50	2	1	7	1	.875	0	0-0	0	4.50
Seattle	AL	11	11	0	0	70.2	298	66	36	26	9	3	3	1	19	3	29	1	0	6	2	.750	0	0-0	1	3.31
15 ML YEARS		405	353	21	13	2292	9757	2388	1170	1075	267	81	59	71	664	42	1381	41	10	151	117	.563	6	0-2	2	4.22

Bill Mueller

Bats: Both **Throws:** Right **Pos:** 3B-64; PH/PR-10; 2B-1   **Ht:** 5'10" **Wt:** 180 **Born:** 3/17/71 **Age:** 31

Year Team	Lg	G	AB	H	2B	3B	HR	(Hm	Rd)	TB	R	RBI	TBB	IBB	SO	HBP	SH	SF	SB	CS	SB%	GDP	Avg	OBP	SLG
2001 Iowa *	AAA	8	26	11	3	0	0	—	—	14	3	4	1	0	2	0	0	0	0	0	—	0	.423	.444	.538

155

Year Team	Lg	G	AB	H	2B	3B	HR	(Hm	Rd)	TB	R	RBI	TBB	IBB	SO	HBP	SH	SF	SB	CS	SB%	GDP	Avg	OBP	SLG
								BATTING											**BASERUNNING**				**PERCENTAGES**		
1996 San Francisco	NL	55	200	66	15	1	0	(0	0)	83	31	19	24	0	26	1	1	2	0	0	—	1	.330	.401	.415
1997 San Francisco	NL	128	390	114	26	3	7	(5	2)	167	51	44	48	1	71	3	6	6	4	3	.57	10	.292	.369	.428
1998 San Francisco	NL	145	534	157	27	4	9	(1	8)	211	93	59	79	1	83	1	3	5	3	3	.50	12	.294	.383	.395
1999 San Francisco	NL	116	414	120	24	0	2	(1	1)	150	61	36	65	1	52	3	8	2	4	2	.67	11	.290	.388	.362
2000 San Francisco	NL	153	560	150	29	4	10	(3	7)	217	97	55	52	0	62	6	7	6	4	2	.67	16	.268	.333	.388
2001 Chicago	NL	70	210	62	12	1	6	(3	3)	94	38	23	37	3	19	3	4	3	1	1	.50	4	.295	.403	.448
6 ML YEARS		667	2308	669	133	9	34	(13	21)	922	371	236	305	6	313	17	29	24	16	11	.59	54	.290	.373	.399

Mark Mulder

Pitches: Left **Bats:** Left **Pos:** SP-34

Ht: 6'6" **Wt:** 200 **Born:** 8/5/77 **Age:** 24

Year Team	Lg	G	GS	CG	GF	IP	BFP	H	R	ER	HR	SH	SF	HB	TBB	IBB	SO	WP	Bk	W	L	Pct.	ShO	Sv-Op	Hld	ERA
				HOW MUCH HE PITCHED							**WHAT HE GAVE UP**											**THE RESULTS**			
1999 Vancouver	AAA	22	22	1	0	128.2	549	152	69	58	13	4	5	3	31	0	81	6	0	6	7	.462	0	0--	—	4.06
2000 Sacramento	AAA	2	2	0	0	8.1	44	15	11	5	1	0	0	0	4	0	6	1	0	1	1	.500	0	0--	—	5.40
2000 Oakland	AL	27	27	0	0	154	705	191	106	93	22	3	8	4	69	3	88	6	0	9	10	.474	0	0-0	0	5.44
2001 Oakland	AL	34	34	6	0	229.1	927	214	92	88	16	8	3	5	51	4	153	4	0	21	8	.724	4	0-0	0	3.45
2 ML YEARS		61	61	6	0	383.1	1632	405	198	181	38	11	11	9	120	7	241	10	0	30	18	.625	4	0-0	0	4.25

Terry Mulholland

Pitches: Left **Bats:** Right **Pos:** RP-37; SP-4

Ht: 6'3" **Wt:** 220 **Born:** 3/9/63 **Age:** 39

Year Team	Lg	G	GS	CG	GF	IP	BFP	H	R	ER	HR	SH	SF	HB	TBB	IBB	SO	WP	Bk	W	L	Pct.	ShO	Sv-Op	Hld	ERA
				HOW MUCH HE PITCHED							**WHAT HE GAVE UP**											**THE RESULTS**			
2001 Altoona *	AA	2	2	0	0	2.1	13	5	3	1	0	0	0	0	1	0	3	0	0	0	2	.000	0	0--	0	3.86
1986 San Francisco	NL	15	10	0	1	54.2	245	51	33	30	3	5	1	1	35	2	27	6	0	1	7	.125	0	0--	0	4.94
1988 San Francisco	NL	9	6	2	1	46	191	50	20	19	3	5	0	1	7	0	18	1	0	2	1	.667	1	0--	1	3.72
1989 SF-Phi	NL	25	18	2	4	115.1	513	137	66	63	8	7	1	4	36	3	66	3	0	4	7	.364	1	0-0	1	4.92
1990 Philadelphia	NL	33	26	6	2	180.2	746	172	78	67	15	7	12	2	42	7	75	7	2	9	10	.474	1	0-1	1	3.34
1991 Philadelphia	NL	34	34	8	0	232	956	231	100	93	15	11	6	3	49	2	142	3	0	16	13	.552	3	0-0	0	3.61
1992 Philadelphia	NL	32	32	12	0	229	937	227	101	97	14	10	7	3	46	3	125	3	0	13	11	.542	2	0-0	0	3.81
1993 Philadelphia	NL	29	28	7	0	191	786	177	80	69	20	5	4	3	40	2	116	5	0	12	9	.571	2	0-0	0	3.25
1994 New York	AL	24	19	2	4	120.2	542	150	94	87	24	3	4	3	37	1	72	5	0	6	7	.462	0	0-0	0	6.49
1995 San Francisco	NL	29	24	2	2	149	666	190	112	96	25	11	4	3	38	1	65	4	0	5	13	.278	0	0-0	0	5.80
1996 Phi-Sea		33	33	3	0	202.2	871	232	112	105	22	11	8	5	49	4	86	6	0	13	11	.542	0	0-0	0	4.66
1997 ChC-SF	NL	40	27	1	5	186.2	794	190	100	88	24	17	4	11	51	3	99	3	0	6	13	.316	0	0-0	1	4.24
1998 Chicago	NL	70	6	0	14	112	476	100	49	36	7	5	3	4	39	7	72	4	0	6	5	.545	0	3-5	19	2.89
1999 ChC-Atl	NL	42	24	0	7	170.1	736	201	95	83	21	9	4	1	45	6	83	3	0	10	8	.556	0	1-1	4	4.39
2000 Atlanta	NL	54	20	1	14	156.2	702	198	96	89	24	10	5	4	41	7	78	3	0	9	9	.500	0	1-3	2	5.11
2001 Pit-LA	NL	41	4	0	8	65.2	285	78	35	34	12	1	1	2	17	1	42	1	0	1	1	.500	0	0-0	7	4.66
1989 San Francisco	NL	5	1	0	2	11	51	15	5	5	0	0	0	0	4	0	6	0	0	0	0	—	0	0-0	1	4.09
Philadelphia	NL	20	17	2	2	104.1	462	122	61	58	8	7	1	4	32	3	60	3	0	4	7	.364	1	0-0	0	5.00
1996 Philadelphia	NL	21	21	3	0	133.1	571	157	74	69	17	6	5	3	21	1	52	5	0	8	7	.533	0	0-0	0	4.66
Seattle	AL	12	12	0	0	69.1	300	75	38	36	5	5	3	2	28	3	34	1	0	5	4	.556	0	0-0	0	4.67
1997 Chicago	NL	25	25	1	0	157	668	162	79	71	20	13	3	9	45	2	74	2	0	6	12	.333	0	0-0	0	4.07
San Francisco	NL	15	2	0	5	29.2	126	28	21	17	4	4	1	2	6	1	25	1	0	0	1	.000	0	0-0	1	5.16
1999 Chicago	NL	26	16	0	4	110	485	137	71	63	16	6	3	1	32	4	44	2	0	6	6	.500	0	0-0	0	5.15
Atlanta	NL	16	8	0	3	60.1	251	64	24	20	5	3	1	0	13	2	39	1	0	4	2	.667	0	1-1	4	2.98
2001 Pittsburgh	NL	22	1	0	3	36.1	150	38	15	15	5	1	1	1	10	1	17	1	0	0	0	—	0	0-0	3	3.72
Los Angeles	NL	19	3	0	5	29.1	135	40	20	19	7	0	0	1	7	0	25	0	0	1	1	.500	0	0-0	4	5.83
15 ML YEARS		510	311	46	62	2212.1	9446	2384	1171	1056	237	117	66	51	572	49	1166	57	2	113	125	.475	10	5-10	35	4.30

Scott Mullen

Pitches: Left **Bats:** Right **Pos:** RP-17

Ht: 6'2" **Wt:** 190 **Born:** 1/17/75 **Age:** 27

Year Team	Lg	G	GS	CG	GF	IP	BFP	H	R	ER	HR	SH	SF	HB	TBB	IBB	SO	WP	Bk	W	L	Pct.	ShO	Sv-Op	Hld	ERA
				HOW MUCH HE PITCHED							**WHAT HE GAVE UP**											**THE RESULTS**			
1996 Spokane	A-	15	15	0	0	80.1	352	78	45	35	6	1	2	8	29	0	78	1	0	5	6	.455	0	0--	0	3.92
1997 Lansing	A	16	16	0	0	92.1	391	90	46	38	14	0	3	4	31	0	78	2	1	5	2	.714	0	0--	0	3.70
Wilmington	A+	11	11	0	0	59.1	260	64	35	30	5	1	2	1	26	4	43	5	2	4	4	.500	0	0--	0	4.55
1998 Wilmington	A+	14	14	1	0	85.2	344	68	28	21	4	3	1	7	25	0	56	3	1	8	4	.667	1	0--	0	2.21
Wichita	AA	12	12	0	0	70	289	66	34	32	7	0	3	1	26	0	42	7	0	2	3	.400	0	0--	0	4.11
1999 Wichita	AA	9	9	0	0	49.1	216	47	28	22	2	1	4	1	18	1	30	3	0	4	3	.571	0	0--	0	4.01
Omaha	AAA	20	20	0	0	119.1	543	150	91	83	24	4	6	2	53	2	87	7	1	6	7	.462	0	0--	0	6.26
2000 Wichita	AA	33	1	0	16	73.1	299	65	27	26	5	3	1	1	26	1	61	3	0	3	2	.600	0	7--	0	3.19
Omaha	AAA	16	0	0	5	20.2	85	15	10	7	1	1	2	1	8	0	21	0	0	2	1	.667	0	0--	0	3.05
2001 Omaha	AAA	48	0	0	12	53	240	66	39	39	8	4	2	3	22	2	38	1	0	5	4	.556	0	5--	0	6.62
2000 Kansas City	AL	11	0	0	5	10.1	44	10	5	5	2	0	0	0	3	0	7	0	0	0	0	—	0	0-0	2	4.35
2001 Kansas City	AL	17	0	0	2	10	52	13	6	5	0	0	1	0	9	0	3	0	0	0	0	—	0	0-0	1	4.50
2 ML YEARS		28	0	0	7	20.1	96	23	11	10	2	0	1	0	12	0	10	0	0	0	0	—	0	0-0	3	4.43

Bobby Munoz

Pitches: Right **Bats:** Right **Pos:** RP-8; SP-7

Ht: 6'8" **Wt:** 260 **Born:** 3/3/68 **Age:** 34

Year Team	Lg	G	GS	CG	GF	IP	BFP	H	R	ER	HR	SH	SF	HB	TBB	IBB	SO	WP	Bk	W	L	Pct.	ShO	Sv-Op	Hld	ERA
				HOW MUCH HE PITCHED							**WHAT HE GAVE UP**											**THE RESULTS**			
2001 Ottawa *	AAA	19	18	1	0	110	455	98	47	42	5	8	4	4	39	2	66	4	0	4	6	.400	0	0--	0	3.44
1993 New York	AL	38	0	0	12	45.2	208	48	27	27	1	1	3	0	26	5	33	2	0	3	3	.500	0	0-2	6	5.32
1994 Philadelphia	NL	21	14	1	1	104.1	447	101	40	31	8	5	5	1	35	0	59	5	1	7	5	.583	0	1-2	0	2.67
1995 Philadelphia	NL	3	3	0	0	15.2	70	15	13	10	2	0	2	3	9	0	6	1	0	0	2	.000	0	0-0	0	5.74
1996 Philadelphia	NL	6	6	0	0	25.1	123	42	28	22	5	2	1	2	11	1	7	1	0	0	0	—	0	0-0	0	7.82
1997 Philadelphia	NL	8	7	0	1	33.1	161	47	35	33	4	2	3	2	15	1	20	3	1	1	5	.167	0	0-0	0	8.91
1998 Baltimore	AL	9	1	0	5	12	58	18	13	13	4	1	3	1	6	0	6	0	1	0	0	—	0	0-0	0	9.75
2001 Montreal	NL	15	7	0	4	42	193	53	25	24	6	5	0	2	21	1	21	2	0	0	4	.000	0	0-0	1	5.14
7 ML YEARS		100	38	1	23	278.1	1260	324	181	160	30	16	17	10	119	8	153	12	3	11	22	.333	0	1-4	7	5.17

Eric Munson

Bats: Left Throws: Right Pos: 1B-17   Ht: 6'3" Wt: 220 Born: 10/3/77 Age: 24

Year Team	Lg	G	AB	H	2B	3B	HR	(Hm	Rd)	TB	R	RBI	TBB	IBB	SO	HBP	SH	SF	SB	CS	SB%	GDP	Avg	OBP	SLG
1999 Lakeland	A+	2	6	2	0	0	0	—	—	2	0	1	1	0	1	0	0	0	0	0	—	0	.333	.429	.333
W Michigan	A	67	252	67	16	1	14	—	—	127	42	44	37	3	47	9	0	1	3	1	.75	4	.266	.378	.504
2000 Jacksonville	AA	98	365	92	21	4	15	—	—	166	52	68	39	5	96	18	0	6	5	2	.71	8	.252	.348	.455
2001 Erie	AA	142	519	135	35	1	26	—	—	250	88	102	84	6	141	11	0	6	0	3	.00	6	.260	.371	.482
2000 Detroit	AL	3	5	0	0	0	0	(0	0)	0	0	1	0	0	1	0	0	0	0	0	—	0	.000	.000	.000
2001 Detroit	AL	17	66	10	3	1	1	(1	0)	18	4	6	3	0	21	0	0	0	0	1	.00	2	.152	.188	.273
2 ML YEARS		20	71	10	3	1	1	(1	0)	18	4	7	3	0	22	0	0	0	0	1	.00	2	.141	.176	.254

Calvin Murray

Bats: Right Throws: Right Pos: CF-104; PH/PR-12   Ht: 5'11" Wt: 190 Born: 7/30/71 Age: 30

Year Team	Lg	G	AB	H	2B	3B	HR	(Hm	Rd)	TB	R	RBI	TBB	IBB	SO	HBP	SH	SF	SB	CS	SB%	GDP	Avg	OBP	SLG
2001 Fresno *	AAA	35	138	36	6	1	4	—	—	56	17	12	12	1	33	1	0	1	3	3	.50	2	.261	.322	.406
1999 San Francisco	NL	15	19	5	2	0	0	(0	0)	7	1	5	2	0	4	0	0	0	1	0	1.00	0	.263	.333	.368
2000 San Francisco	NL	108	194	47	12	1	2	(1	1)	67	35	22	29	0	33	3	2	1	9	3	.75	0	.242	.348	.345
2001 San Francisco	NL	106	326	80	14	2	6	(3	3)	116	54	25	32	0	57	3	3	0	8	5	.50	5	.245	.319	.356
3 ML YEARS		229	539	132	28	3	8	(4	4)	190	90	52	63	0	94	6	5	1	18	11	.62	5	.245	.330	.353

Heath Murray

Pitches: Left Bats: Left Pos: RP-36; SP-4   Ht: 6'4" Wt: 210 Born: 4/19/73 Age: 29

Year Team	Lg	G	GS	CG	GF	IP	BFP	H	R	ER	HR	SH	SF	HB	TBB	IBB	SO	WP	Bk	W	L	Pct.	ShO	Sv-Op	Hld	ERA
2001 Toledo *	AAA	11	3	0	1	36	131	22	9	8	5	0	0	0	2	0	44	0	1	1	1	.500	0	1--	—	2.00
1997 San Diego	NL	17	3	0	1	33.1	162	50	25	25	3	3	1	4	21	3	16	1	1	1	2	.333	0	0-0	1	6.75
1999 San Diego	NL	22	8	0	1	50	234	60	33	32	7	3	2	1	26	4	25	1	1	0	4	.000	0	0-0	0	5.76
2001 Detroit	AL	40	4	0	10	63.1	301	82	48	46	11	2	1	3	40	5	42	1	0	1	7	.125	0	0-2	2	6.54
3 ML YEARS		79	15	0	12	146.2	697	192	106	103	21	8	4	8	87	12	83	3	2	2	13	.133	0	0-2	3	6.32

Mike Mussina

Pitches: Right Bats: Both Pos: SP-34   Ht: 6'2" Wt: 185 Born: 12/8/68 Age: 33

Year Team	Lg	G	GS	CG	GF	IP	BFP	H	R	ER	HR	SH	SF	HB	TBB	IBB	SO	WP	Bk	W	L	Pct.	ShO	Sv-Op	Hld	ERA
1991 Baltimore	AL	12	12	2	0	87.2	349	77	31	28	7	3	2	1	21	0	52	3	1	4	5	.444	0	0-0	0	2.87
1992 Baltimore	AL	32	32	8	0	241	957	212	70	68	16	13	6	2	48	2	130	6	0	18	5	.783	4	0-0	0	2.54
1993 Baltimore	AL	25	25	3	0	167.2	693	163	84	83	20	6	4	3	44	2	117	5	0	14	6	.700	2	0-0	0	4.46
1994 Baltimore	AL	24	24	3	0	176.1	712	163	63	60	19	3	9	1	42	1	99	0	0	16	5	.762	0	0-0	0	3.06
1995 Baltimore	AL	32	32	7	0	221.2	882	187	86	81	24	2	2	1	50	4	158	2	0	19	9	.679	4	0-0	0	3.29
1996 Baltimore	AL	36	36	4	0	243.1	1039	264	137	130	31	4	4	3	69	0	204	3	0	19	11	.633	1	0-0	0	4.81
1997 Baltimore	AL	33	33	4	0	224.2	905	197	87	80	27	3	2	3	54	3	218	5	0	15	8	.652	1	0-0	0	3.20
1998 Baltimore	AL	29	29	4	0	206.1	835	189	85	80	22	6	3	4	41	3	175	10	0	13	10	.565	2	0-0	0	3.49
1999 Baltimore	AL	31	31	4	0	203.1	842	207	88	79	16	9	7	1	52	0	172	2	0	18	7	.720	1	0-0	0	3.50
2000 Baltimore	AL	34	34	6	0	237.2	987	236	105	100	28	8	6	3	46	0	210	3	0	11	15	.423	1	0-0	0	3.79
2001 New York	AL	34	34	4	0	228.2	909	202	87	80	20	5	6	4	42	2	214	6	0	17	11	.607	3	0-0	0	3.15
11 ML YEARS		322	322	49	0	2238.1	9110	2097	923	869	230	62	51	26	509	17	1749	45	1	164	92	.641	18	0-0	0	3.49

Greg Myers

Bats: Left Throws: Right Pos: C-36; DH-13; PH/PR-11   Ht: 6'2" Wt: 225 Born: 4/14/66 Age: 36

Year Team	Lg	G	AB	H	2B	3B	HR	(Hm	Rd)	TB	R	RBI	TBB	IBB	SO	HBP	SH	SF	SB	CS	SB%	GDP	Avg	OBP	SLG
2001 Sacramento *	AAA	2	5	0	0	0	0	—	—	0	0	1	3	0	2	0	0	0	0	0	—	1	.000	.375	.000
1987 Toronto	AL	7	9	1	0	0	0	(0	0)	1	1	0	0	0	3	0	0	0	0	0	—	2	.111	.111	.111
1989 Toronto	AL	17	44	5	2	0	0	(0	0)	7	0	1	2	0	9	0	0	0	0	1	.00	2	.114	.152	.159
1990 Toronto	AL	87	250	59	7	1	5	(3	2)	83	33	22	22	0	33	0	1	4	0	1	.00	12	.236	.293	.332
1991 Toronto	AL	107	309	81	22	0	8	(5	3)	127	25	36	21	4	45	0	0	3	0	0	—	13	.262	.306	.411
1992 Tor-Cal	AL	30	78	18	7	0	1	(0	1)	28	4	13	5	0	11	0	1	2	0	0	—	2	.231	.271	.359
1993 California	AL	108	290	74	10	0	7	(4	3)	105	27	40	17	2	47	2	3	3	3	3	.50	8	.255	.298	.362
1994 California	AL	45	126	31	6	0	2	(1	1)	43	10	8	10	3	27	0	5	1	0	2	.00	4	.246	.299	.341
1995 California	AL	85	273	71	12	2	9	(6	3)	114	35	38	17	3	49	1	1	2	0	0	—	4	.260	.304	.418
1996 Minnesota	AL	97	329	94	22	3	6	(3	3)	140	37	47	19	3	52	0	0	5	0	0	—	11	.286	.320	.426
1997 Min-Atl		71	174	45	11	1	5	(3	2)	73	24	29	17	2	32	0	0	0	0	1	.00	4	.259	.321	.420
1998 San Diego	NL	69	171	42	10	0	4	(1	3)	64	19	20	17	1	36	0	0	1	0	0	—	6	.246	.312	.374
1999 SD-Atl	NL	84	200	53	6	0	5	(3	2)	74	19	24	26	4	30	0	0	1	0	0	—	6	.265	.348	.370
2000 Baltimore	AL	43	125	28	6	0	3	(1	2)	43	9	12	8	0	29	1	0	0	0	0	—	7	.224	.271	.344
2001 Bal-Oak	AL	58	161	36	3	0	11	(5	6)	72	24	31	21	1	38	0	0	0	0	0	—	5	.224	.313	.447
1992 Toronto	AL	22	61	14	6	0	1	(0	1)	23	4	13	5	0	5	0	0	2	0	0	—	2	.230	.279	.377
California		8	17	4	1	0	0	(0	0)	5	0	0	0	0	6	0	1	0	0	0	—	4	.235	.235	.294
1997 Minnesota	AL	62	165	44	11	1	5	(3	2)	72	24	28	16	2	29	0	0	0	0	0	—	4	.267	.328	.436
Atlanta	NL	9	9	1	0	0	0	(0	0)	1	0	1	1	0	3	0	0	0	0	0	—	0	.111	.200	.111
1999 San Diego	NL	50	128	37	4	0	3	(2	1)	50	9	15	13	2	14	0	0	0	0	0	—	1	.289	.355	.391
Atlanta	NL	34	72	16	2	0	2	(1	1)	24	10	9	13	2	16	0	0	1	0	0	—	5	.222	.337	.333
2001 Baltimore	AL	25	74	20	2	0	4	(3	1)	34	11	18	8	0	17	0	0	0	0	0	—	2	.270	.341	.459
Oakland	AL	33	87	16	1	0	7	(2	5)	38	13	13	13	1	21	0	0	0	0	0	—	3	.184	.290	.437
14 ML YEARS		908	2539	638	124	7	66	(35	31)	974	267	321	202	23	441	3	12	24	3	9	.25	85	.251	.305	.384

Mike Myers

Pitches: Left Bats: Left Pos: RP-73

Ht: 6'4" Wt: 212 Born: 6/26/69 Age: 33

Year Team	Lg	G	GS	CG	GF	IP	BFP	H	R	ER	HR	SH	SF	HB	TBB	IBB	SO	WP	Bk	W	L	Pct.	ShO	Sv-Op	Hld	ERA
1995 Fla-Det		13	0	0	5	8.1	42	11	7	7	1	0	1	2	7	0	4	0	0	1	0	1.000	0	0-1	1	7.56
1996 Detroit	AL	83	0	0	25	64.2	298	70	41	36	6	2	1	4	34	8	69	2	0	1	5	.167	0	6-8	17	5.01
1997 Detroit	AL	88	0	0	23	53.2	246	58	36	34	12	4	3	2	25	2	50	0	0	0	4	.000	0	2-5	18	5.70
1998 Milwaukee	NL	70	0	0	14	50	211	44	19	15	5	4	2	6	22	1	40	2	1	2	2	.500	0	1-3	23	2.70
1999 Milwaukee	NL	71	0	0	14	41.1	179	46	24	24	7	5	0	3	13	1	35	1	0	2	1	.667	0	0-3	14	5.23
2000 Colorado	NL	78	0	0	22	45.1	177	24	10	10	2	1	0	2	24	3	41	1	0	0	1	.000	0	1-2	15	1.99
2001 Colorado	NL	73	0	0	14	40	169	32	17	16	2	1	1	1	24	7	36	0	0	2	3	.400	0	0-2	10	3.60
1995 Florida	NL	2	0	0	2	2	9	1	0	0	0	0	0	0	3	0	0	0	0	0	0	—	0	0-0	0	0.00
Detroit	AL	11	0	0	3	6.1	33	10	7	7	1	0	1	2	4	0	4	0	0	1	0	1.000	0	0-1	1	9.95
7 ML YEARS		476	0	0	117	303.1	1322	285	154	142	35	17	8	20	149	22	275	6	1	8	16	.333	0	10-24	98	4.21

Rodney Myers

Pitches: Right Bats: Right Pos: RP-37

Ht: 6'1" Wt: 215 Born: 6/26/69 Age: 33

Year Team	Lg	G	GS	CG	GF	IP	BFP	H	R	ER	HR	SH	SF	HB	TBB	IBB	SO	WP	Bk	W	L	Pct.	ShO	Sv-Op	Hld	ERA
2001 Portland *	AAA	8	1	0	1	15	63	13	5	5	1	2	1	2	5	0	14	2	0	1	1	.500	0	0- -	1	3.00
1996 Chicago	NL	45	0	0	8	67.1	298	61	38	35	6	1	5	3	38	3	50	4	1	2	1	.667	0	0-0	1	4.68
1997 Chicago	NL	5	1	0	2	9	44	12	6	6	1	0	0	1	7	1	6	0	0	0	0	—	0	0-0	0	6.00
1998 Chicago	NL	12	0	0	3	18	82	26	14	14	3	0	0	0	6	0	15	1	0	0	0	—	0	0-1	0	7.00
1999 Chicago	NL	46	0	0	5	63.2	278	71	34	31	10	4	2	1	25	2	41	2	0	3	1	.750	0	0-1	8	4.38
2000 San Diego	NL	3	0	0	1	2	8	2	1	1	0	0	0	0	0	0	3	1	0	0	0	—	0	0-0	0	4.50
2001 San Diego	NL	37	0	0	16	47.1	211	53	31	28	6	1	4	4	20	0	29	2	0	1	2	.333	0	1-2	3	5.32
6 ML YEARS		148	1	0	35	207.1	921	225	124	115	26	6	11	9	96	6	144	10	1	6	4	.600	0	1-4	12	4.99

Aaron Myette

Pitches: Right Bats: Right Pos: SP-15; RP-4

Ht: 6'4" Wt: 195 Born: 9/26/77 Age: 24

Year Team	Lg	G	GS	CG	GF	IP	BFP	H	R	ER	HR	SH	SF	HB	TBB	IBB	SO	WP	Bk	W	L	Pct.	ShO	Sv-Op	Hld	ERA
1997 Bristol	R+	9	8	1	0	47.1	215	39	28	19	9	0	0	7	20	0	50	2	1	4	3	.571	0	0- -	—	3.61
Hickory	A	5	5	0	0	31.2	121	19	6	4	1	1	0	2	11	0	27	2	2	3	1	.750	0	0- -	—	1.14
1998 Hickory	A	17	17	0	0	102	421	84	43	28	4	2	3	8	30	0	103	5	2	9	4	.692	0	0- -	—	2.47
Winston-Sal	A+	6	6	1	0	44.2	178	32	14	10	4	1	2	3	14	0	54	0	0	4	2	.667	1	0- -	—	2.01
1999 Birmingham	AA	28	28	0	0	164.2	711	138	76	67	19	3	3	15	77	0	135	6	1	12	7	.632	0	0- -	—	3.66
2000 Birmingham	AA	3	3	0	0	15.1	68	11	7	6	1	0	0	2	8	0	21	1	0	2	0	1.000	0	0- -	—	3.52
Charlotte	AAA	19	18	0	0	111.2	488	103	58	54	18	0	4	7	56	0	85	2	1	5	5	.500	0	0- -	—	4.35
2001 Oklahoma	AAA	12	12	2	0	70	305	64	32	29	5	3	0	5	30	0	76	1	0	4	3	.571	0	0- -	—	3.73
Tulsa	AA	1	1	0	0	6	22	3	0	0	0	0	0	0	1	0	2	0	0	1	0	1.000	0	0- -	—	0.00
1999 Chicago	AL	4	3	0	0	15.2	80	17	11	11	2	0	0	2	14	1	11	2	0	0	2	.000	0	0-0	0	6.32
2000 Chicago	AL	2	0	0	1	2.2	12	0	0	0	0	0	0	0	4	0	1	0	0	0	0	—	0	0-0	0	0.00
2001 Texas	AL	19	15	0	1	80.2	376	94	65	64	12	3	4	11	37	0	67	2	0	4	5	.444	0	0-0	0	7.14
3 ML YEARS		25	18	0	2	99	468	111	76	75	14	3	4	13	55	1	79	4	0	4	7	.364	0	0-0	0	6.82

Charles Nagy

Pitches: Right Bats: Left Pos: SP-13; RP-2

Ht: 6'3" Wt: 200 Born: 5/5/67 Age: 35

Year Team	Lg	G	GS	CG	GF	IP	BFP	H	R	ER	HR	SH	SF	HB	TBB	IBB	SO	WP	Bk	W	L	Pct.	ShO	Sv-Op	Hld	ERA
2001 Buffalo *	AAA	6	6	0	0	38.2	161	40	12	11	0	1	0	1	9	0	18	0	0	5	1	.833	0	0- -	—	2.56
1990 Cleveland	AL	9	8	0	1	45.2	208	58	31	30	7	1	1	1	21	1	26	1	1	2	4	.333	0	0-0	0	5.91
1991 Cleveland	AL	33	33	6	0	211.1	914	228	103	97	15	5	9	6	66	7	109	6	2	10	15	.400	1	0-0	0	4.13
1992 Cleveland	AL	33	33	10	0	252	1018	245	91	83	11	6	9	2	57	1	169	7	0	17	10	.630	3	0-0	0	2.96
1993 Cleveland	AL	9	9	1	0	48.2	223	66	38	34	6	2	1	2	13	1	30	2	0	2	6	.250	0	0-0	0	6.29
1994 Cleveland	AL	23	23	3	0	169.1	717	175	76	65	15	2	2	5	48	1	108	5	1	10	8	.556	0	0-0	0	3.45
1995 Cleveland	AL	29	29	2	0	178	771	194	95	90	20	2	5	6	61	0	139	2	0	16	6	.727	1	0-0	0	4.55
1996 Cleveland	AL	32	32	5	0	222	921	217	89	84	21	2	4	3	61	2	167	7	0	17	5	.773	0	0-0	0	3.41
1997 Cleveland	AL	34	34	1	0	227	991	253	115	108	27	5	6	7	77	4	149	5	0	15	11	.577	1	0-0	0	4.28
1998 Cleveland	AL	33	33	2	0	210.1	930	220	139	122	34	8	6	9	66	12	120	3	0	15	10	.600	0	0-0	0	5.22
1999 Cleveland	AL	33	32	1	0	202	887	238	120	111	26	5	4	6	59	4	126	3	0	17	11	.607	0	0-0	0	4.95
2000 Cleveland	AL	11	11	0	0	57	267	71	53	52	15	5	2	2	21	2	41	1	0	2	7	.222	0	0-0	0	8.21
2001 Cleveland	AL	15	13	0	1	70.1	325	102	53	50	10	3	4	0	20	1	29	2	0	5	6	.455	0	0-0	0	6.40
12 ML YEARS		294	290	31	2	1893.2	8172	2097	1003	926	207	46	53	49	570	36	1213	44	4	128	99	.564	6	0-0	0	4.40

Denny Neagle

Pitches: Left Bats: Left Pos: SP-30

Ht: 6'3" Wt: 225 Born: 9/13/68 Age: 33

Year Team	Lg	G	GS	CG	GF	IP	BFP	H	R	ER	HR	SH	SF	HB	TBB	IBB	SO	WP	Bk	W	L	Pct.	ShO	Sv-Op	Hld	ERA
1991 Minnesota	AL	7	3	0	2	20	92	28	9	9	3	0	0	0	7	2	14	1	0	0	1	.000	0	0-0	0	4.05
1992 Pittsburgh	NL	55	6	0	8	86.1	380	81	46	43	9	4	3	2	43	8	77	3	2	4	6	.400	0	2-4	5	4.48
1993 Pittsburgh	NL	50	7	0	13	81.1	360	82	49	48	10	1	1	3	37	3	73	5	0	3	5	.375	0	1-1	6	5.31
1994 Pittsburgh	NL	24	24	2	0	137	587	135	80	78	18	7	6	3	49	3	122	2	0	9	10	.474	0	0-0	0	5.12
1995 Pittsburgh	NL	31	31	5	0	209.2	876	221	91	80	20	13	6	3	45	3	150	6	0	13	8	.619	1	0-0	0	3.43
1996 Pit-Atl	NL	33	33	2	0	221.1	910	226	93	86	26	10	4	3	48	2	149	3	1	16	9	.640	0	0-0	0	3.50
1997 Atlanta	NL	34	34	4	0	233.1	947	204	87	77	18	12	6	3	49	5	172	3	0	20	5	.800	4	0-0	0	2.97
1998 Atlanta	NL	32	31	5	0	210.1	861	196	91	83	25	7	3	6	60	3	165	4	0	16	11	.593	2	0-0	0	3.55
1999 Cincinnati	NL	20	19	0	0	111.2	492	95	54	53	23	3	5	4	40	3	76	4	0	9	5	.643	0	0-0	0	4.27
2000 Cin-NYY	NL	34	33	1	0	209	906	210	109	105	31	8	6	5	81	4	146	7	1	15	9	.625	0	0-0	0	4.52
2001 Colorado	NL	30	30	0	0	170.2	760	192	107	102	29	8	9	7	60	3	139	2	0	9	8	.529	0	0-0	0	5.38

Year Team	Lg	G	GS	CG	GF	IP	BFP	H	R	ER	HR	SH	SF	HB	TBB	IBB	SO	WP	Bk	W	L	Pct.	ShO	Sv-Op	Hld	ERA
1996 Pittsburgh	NL	27	27	1	0	182.2	745	186	67	62	21	9	3	3	34	2	131	2	1	14	6	.700	0	0-0	0	3.05
Atlanta	NL	6	6	1	0	38.2	165	40	26	24	5	1	1	0	14	0	18	1	0	2	3	.400	0	0-0	0	5.59
2000 Cincinnati	NL	18	18	0	0	117.2	506	111	48	46	15	2	1	3	50	3	88	3	0	8	2	.800	0	0-0	0	3.52
New York	AL	16	15	1	0	91.1	400	99	61	59	16	6	5	2	31	1	58	4	1	7	7	.500	0	0-0	0	5.81
11 ML YEARS		350	251	19	23	1690.2	7146	1670	816	764	212	73	49	42	519	39	1283	42	5	114	77	.597	7	3-5	11	4.07

Blaine Neal

Pitches: Right **Bats:** Left **Pos:** RP-4

Ht: 6'5" Wt: 205 Born: 4/6/78 Age: 24

Year Team	Lg	G	GS	CG	GF	IP	BFP	H	R	ER	HR	SH	SF	HB	TBB	IBB	SO	WP	Bk	W	L	Pct.	ShO	Sv-Op	Hld	ERA
1996 Marlins	R	7	5	0	1	29.1	126	32	18	15	1	0	0	3	6	0	15	3	3	1	1	.500	0	1--	6	4.60
1997 Marlins	R	10	0	0	5	22.1	102	24	11	9	1	0	0	1	11	0	19	2	0	4	1	.800	0	1--		3.63
1999 Kane County	A	26	0	0	18	31	117	21	8	8	2	2	0	0	10	0	31	1	0	4	2	.667	0	6--		2.32
2000 Brevard Cty	A+	41	0	0	34	54.1	231	40	27	13	1	1	2	4	24	3	65	1	0	2	2	.500	0	11--		2.15
2001 Portland	AA	54	0	0	44	53.1	225	43	17	14	1	4	1	2	21	3	45	2	0	2	3	.400	0	21--		2.36
2001 Florida	NL	4	0	0	0	5.1	28	7	4	4	0	0	0	0	5	0	3	1	0	0	0	—	0	0-0	0	6.75

Jeff Nelson

Pitches: Right **Bats:** Right **Pos:** RP-69

Ht: 6'8" Wt: 235 Born: 11/17/66 Age: 35

Year Team	Lg	G	GS	CG	GF	IP	BFP	H	R	ER	HR	SH	SF	HB	TBB	IBB	SO	WP	Bk	W	L	Pct.	ShO	Sv-Op	Hld	ERA
1992 Seattle	AL	66	0	0	27	81	352	71	34	31	7	9	3	6	44	12	46	2	0	1	7	.125	0	6-14	6	3.44
1993 Seattle	AL	71	0	0	13	60	269	57	30	29	5	2	4	8	34	10	61	2	0	5	3	.625	0	1-11	17	4.35
1994 Seattle	AL	28	0	0	7	42.1	185	35	18	13	3	1	1	8	20	4	44	2	0	0	0	—	0	0-0	2	2.76
1995 Seattle	AL	62	0	0	24	78.2	318	58	21	19	4	5	3	6	27	5	96	1	0	7	3	.700	0	2-4	14	2.17
1996 New York	AL	73	0	0	27	74.1	328	75	38	36	6	3	1	2	36	1	91	4	0	4	4	.500	0	2-4	10	4.36
1997 New York	AL	77	0	0	22	78.2	327	53	32	25	7	7	2	4	37	12	81	4	0	3	7	.300	0	2-8	22	2.86
1998 New York	AL	45	0	0	13	40.1	192	44	18	17	1	1	3	8	22	4	35	2	0	5	3	.625	0	3-6	10	3.79
1999 New York	AL	39	0	0	8	30.1	139	27	14	14	2	2	2	3	22	2	35	2	1	8	4	.667	0	1-2	10	4.15
2000 New York	AL	73	0	0	13	69.2	296	44	24	19	2	6	2	2	45	1	71	4	0	8	4	.667	0	0-4	15	2.45
2001 Seattle	AL	69	0	0	16	65.1	273	30	21	20	3	2	0	6	44	1	88	2	0	4	3	.571	0	4-5	26	2.76
10 ML YEARS		603	0	0	170	620.2	2679	494	250	223	40	38	21	53	331	52	648	25	1	39	35	.527	0	21-58	132	3.23

Joe Nelson

Pitches: Right **Bats:** Right **Pos:** RP-2

Ht: 6'2" Wt: 185 Born: 10/25/74 Age: 27

Year Team	Lg	G	GS	CG	GF	IP	BFP	H	R	ER	HR	SH	SF	HB	TBB	IBB	SO	WP	Bk	W	L	Pct.	ShO	Sv-Op	Hld	ERA
1996 Eugene	A-	14	13	0	0	70	309	69	43	34	5	3	1	5	29	1	67	6	0	5	3	.625	0	0--	—	4.37
1997 Durham	A+	25	24	0	0	124.2	543	114	74	66	17	5	4	12	61	1	99	5	0	10	6	.625	0	0--	—	4.76
1998 Greenville	AA	45	12	1	15	108.1	506	124	76	60	9	8	4	5	69	2	74	11	1	6	9	.400	1	2--	—	4.98
1999 Greenville	AA	25	0	0	15	30.1	130	19	15	8	2	2	1	3	14	2	37	0	0	1	1	.500	0	8--	—	2.37
Richmond	AAA	12	3	0	2	33.2	150	33	18	17	2	4	1	0	15	0	31	3	0	2	3	.400	0	1--	—	4.54
2000 Jamestown	A-	3	0	0	1	4	16	3	3	1	0	0	0	0	1	0	7	0	0	0	0	—	0	1--	—	2.25
Braves	R	4	0	0	1	4	18	3	1	1	0	0	0	0	3	0	7	0	0	1	0	1.000	0	1--	—	2.25
2001 Richmond	AAA	29	0	0	12	39.2	152	23	5	5	1	4	0	0	14	2	40	3	0	1	2	.333	0	8--	—	1.13
2001 Atlanta	NL	2	0	0	0	2	16	7	9	8	1	0	1	1	2	0	0	0	0	0	0	—	0	0-0	0	36.00

Robb Nen

Pitches: Right **Bats:** Right **Pos:** RP-79

Ht: 6'5" Wt: 215 Born: 11/28/69 Age: 32

Year Team	Lg	G	GS	CG	GF	IP	BFP	H	R	ER	HR	SH	SF	HB	TBB	IBB	SO	WP	Bk	W	L	Pct.	ShO	Sv-Op	Hld	ERA
1993 Tex-Fla		24	4	0	5	56	272	63	45	42	6	1	2	0	46	0	39	6	1	2	1	.667	0	0-0	0	6.75
1994 Florida	NL	44	0	0	28	58	228	46	20	19	6	3	1	0	17	2	60	3	2	5	5	.500	0	15-15	1	2.95
1995 Florida	NL	62	0	0	54	65.2	279	62	26	24	6	0	1	1	23	3	68	2	0	0	7	.000	0	23-29	0	3.29
1996 Florida	NL	75	0	0	66	83	326	67	21	18	2	5	1	1	21	6	92	4	0	5	1	.833	0	35-42	0	1.95
1997 Florida	NL	73	0	0	65	74	332	72	35	32	7	1	3	1	40	7	81	5	0	9	3	.750	0	35-42	0	3.89
1998 San Francisco	NL	78	0	0	67	88.2	357	59	21	15	4	2	2	1	25	5	110	3	0	7	7	.500	0	40-45	0	1.52
1999 San Francisco	NL	72	0	0	64	72.1	320	79	36	32	8	5	1	0	27	3	77	5	0	3	8	.273	0	37-46	0	3.98
2000 San Francisco	NL	68	0	0	63	66	256	37	15	11	4	4	3	2	19	1	92	5	0	4	3	.571	0	41-46	0	1.50
2001 San Francisco	NL	79	0	0	71	77.2	312	58	28	26	6	0	3	1	22	6	93	2	0	4	5	.444	0	**45-52**	0	3.01
1993 Texas	AL	9	3	0	3	22.2	113	28	17	16	1	0	1	0	26	0	12	2	1	1	1	.500	0	0-0	0	6.35
Florida	NL	15	1	0	2	33.1	159	35	28	26	5	1	1	0	20	0	27	4	0	1	0	1.000	0	0-0	0	7.02
9 ML YEARS		575	4	0	483	641.1	2682	543	247	219	49	21	17	6	240	33	712	35	3	39	40	.494	0	271-317	1	3.07

Nick Neugebauer

Pitches: Right **Bats:** Right **Pos:** SP-2

Ht: 6'3" Wt: 225 Born: 7/15/80 Age: 21

Year Team	Lg	G	GS	CG	GF	IP	BFP	H	R	ER	HR	SH	SF	HB	TBB	IBB	SO	WP	Bk	W	L	Pct.	ShO	Sv-Op	Hld	ERA
1999 Beloit	A	18	18	0	0	80.2	372	50	41	35	4	2	3	6	80	0	125	10	2	7	5	.583	0	0--	—	3.90
2000 Mudville	A+	18	18	0	0	77.1	349	43	40	36	0	0	2	4	87	0	117	10	1	4	4	.500	0	0--	—	4.19
Huntsville	AA	10	10	0	0	50.2	229	35	28	21	2	0	0	3	47	0	57	1	0	1	3	.250	0	0--	—	3.73
2001 Huntsville	AA	21	21	1	0	106.2	453	94	46	41	6	5	3	2	52	0	149	13	0	5	6	.455	1	0--	—	3.46
Indianapolis	AAA	4	4	0	0	24	89	10	5	4	1	1	0	1	9	0	26	1	0	2	1	.667	0	0--	—	1.50
2001 Milwaukee	NL	2	2	0	0	6	30	6	5	5	1	0	0	0	6	0	11	0	0	1	1	.500	0	0-0	0	7.50

Phil Nevin

Bats: Right **Throws:** Right **Pos:** 3B-145; PH/PR-3; DH-1 **Ht:** 6'2" **Wt:** 231 **Born:** 1/19/71 **Age:** 31

Year Team	Lg	G	AB	H	2B	3B	HR	(Hm	Rd)	TB	R	RBI	TBB	IBB	SO	HBP	SH	SF	SB	CS	SB%	GDP	Avg	OBP	SLG
1995 Hou-Det		47	156	28	4	1	2	(2	0)	40	13	13	18	1	40	4	1	0	1	0	1.00	5	.179	.281	.256
1996 Detroit	AL	38	120	35	5	0	8	(3	5)	64	15	19	8	0	39	1	0	1	1	0	1.00	1	.292	.338	.533
1997 Detroit	AL	93	251	59	16	1	9	(4	5)	104	32	35	25	1	68	1	0	1	0	1	.00	5	.235	.306	.414
1998 Anaheim	AL	75	237	54	8	1	8	(3	5)	88	27	27	17	0	67	1	0	2	0	0	—	6	.228	.291	.371
1999 San Diego	NL	128	383	103	27	0	24	(12	12)	202	52	85	51	1	82	1	1	5	1	0	1.00	12	.269	.352	.527
2000 San Diego	NL	143	538	163	34	1	31	(13	18)	292	87	107	59	9	121	4	0	4	2	0	1.00	17	.303	.374	.543
2001 San Diego	NL	149	546	167	31	0	41	(19	22)	321	97	126	71	7	147	4	0	3	4	4	.50	13	.306	.388	.588
1995 Houston	NL	18	60	7	1	0	0	(0	0)	8	4	1	7	1	13	1	1	0	1	0	1.00	1	.117	.221	.133
Detroit	AL	29	96	21	3	1	2	(2	0)	32	9	12	11	0	27	3	0	0	0	0	—	3	.219	.318	.333
7 ML YEARS		673	2231	609	125	4	123	(56	67)	1111	323	412	249	19	564	20	2	16	9	5	.64	54	.273	.349	.498

David Newhan

Bats: Left **Throws:** Right **Pos:** PH/PR-6; 2B-1 **Ht:** 5'10" **Wt:** 180 **Born:** 9/7/73 **Age:** 28

Year Team	Lg	G	AB	H	2B	3B	HR	(Hm	Rd)	TB	R	RBI	TBB	IBB	SO	HBP	SH	SF	SB	CS	SB%	GDP	Avg	OBP	SLG
2001 Scrantn-WB *	AAA	13	55	6	1	0	0	—	—	7	4	2	4	1	11	1	0	0	0	0	—	1	.109	.183	.127
1999 San Diego	NL	32	43	6	1	0	2	(1	1)	13	7	6	1	0	11	0	0	0	2	1	.67	2	.140	.159	.302
2000 SD-Phi	NL	24	37	6	1	0	1	(1	0)	10	8	2	8	1	13	0	0	0	0	0	—	2	.162	.311	.270
2001 Philadelphia	NL	7	6	2	1	0	0	(0	0)	3	2	1	1	0	0	0	0	0	0	0	—	0	.333	.375	.500
2000 San Diego	NL	14	20	3	1	0	1	(1	0)	7	5	2	6	1	7	0	0	0	0	0	—	0	.150	.346	.350
Philadelphia	NL	10	17	3	0	0	0	(0	0)	3	3	0	2	0	6	0	0	0	0	0	—	2	.176	.263	.176
3 ML YEARS		63	86	14	3	0	3	(2	1)	26	17	9	10	1	24	0	0	1	2	1	.67	2	.163	.247	.302

Chris Nichting

Pitches: Right **Bats:** Right **Pos:** RP-43 **Ht:** 6'2" **Wt:** 220 **Born:** 5/13/66 **Age:** 36

Year Team	Lg	G	GS	CG	GF	IP	BFP	H	R	ER	HR	SH	SF	HB	TBB	IBB	SO	WP	Bk	W	L	Pct.	ShO	Sv-Op	Hld	ERA
2001 Louisville *	AAA	27	0	0	23	33.1	135	24	11	11	5	2	1	2	10	0	45	0	0	2	1	.667	0	17--	—	2.97
1995 Texas	AL	13	0	0	3	24.1	122	36	19	19	1	1	2	1	13	1	6	3	0	0	0	—	0	0-0	1	7.03
2000 Cleveland	AL	7	0	0	0	9	46	13	7	7	0	0	1	2	5	1	7	1	0	0	0	—	0	0-1	0	7.00
2001 Cin-Col	NL	43	0	0	11	42.1	189	55	27	21	8	3	2	0	8	1	40	2	0	0	3	.000	0	1-3	4	4.46
2001 Cincinnati	NL	36	0	0	11	36.1	162	46	24	18	6	2	0	0	8	1	33	2	0	0	3	.000	0	1-3	4	4.46
Colorado	NL	7	0	0	0	6	27	9	3	3	2	1	0	0	0	0	7	0	0	0	0	—	0	0-0	0	4.50
3 ML YEARS		63	0	0	15	75.2	357	104	53	47	9	4	5	3	26	3	53	6	0	0	3	.000	0	1-4	5	5.59

Doug Nickle

Pitches: Right **Bats:** Right **Pos:** RP-2 **Ht:** 6'4" **Wt:** 210 **Born:** 10/2/74 **Age:** 27

Year Team	Lg	G	GS	CG	GF	IP	BFP	H	R	ER	HR	SH	SF	HB	TBB	IBB	SO	WP	Bk	W	L	Pct.	ShO	Sv-Op	Hld	ERA
1997 Boise	A-	17	2	0	7	19.2	96	27	17	14	3	0	2	1	8	1	22	0	0	0	1	.000	0	0--	—	6.41
1998 Cedar Rapds	A	20	7	1	3	69	285	66	30	29	2	2	3	4	20	0	59	11	0	8	4	.667	1	0--	—	3.78
Lk Elsinore	A+	11	10	1	0	66.1	285	68	40	33	3	0	1	3	25	0	69	13	1	3	4	.429	0	0--	—	4.48
1999 Clearwater	A+	60	0	0	50	70.2	299	60	25	18	1	1	1	4	23	3	70	6	0	2	4	.333	0	28--	—	2.29
2000 Reading	AA	49	0	0	36	77.1	311	55	25	21	4	4	1	3	22	2	58	4	0	8	3	.727	0	16--	—	2.44
2001 Scrantn-WB	AA	47	1	0	27	85.2	347	62	19	16	2	6	2	1	37	7	60	5	1	9	3	.750	0	7--	—	1.68
2000 Philadelphia	NL	4	0	0	3	2.2	15	5	4	4	0	0	0	1	2	0	0	0	0	0	0	—	0	0-0	0	13.50
2001 Philadelphia	NL	2	0	0	2	2	7	1	0	0	0	0	0	0	0	0	1	0	0	0	0	—	0	0-0	0	0.00
2 ML YEARS		6	0	0	5	4.2	22	6	4	4	0	0	0	1	2	0	1	0	0	0	0	—	0	0-0	0	7.71

Jose Nieves

Bats: R **Throws:** R **Pos:** PH/PR-14; 2B-11; SS-10; DH-4; 3B-2; 1B-1 **Ht:** 6'1" **Wt:** 180 **Born:** 6/16/75 **Age:** 27

Year Team	Lg	G	AB	H	2B	3B	HR	(Hm	Rd)	TB	R	RBI	TBB	IBB	SO	HBP	SH	SF	SB	CS	SB%	GDP	Avg	OBP	SLG
2001 Salt Lake *	AAA	61	258	85	15	4	11	—	—	141	50	37	8	0	36	3	2	2	8	7	.53	3	.329	.354	.547
1998 Chicago	NL	2	1	0	0	0	0	(0	0)	0	0	0	0	0	0	0	0	1	0	0	—	0	.000	.000	.000
1999 Chicago	NL	54	181	45	9	1	2	(2	0)	62	16	18	8	0	25	4	3	3	0	2	.00	5	.249	.291	.343
2000 Chicago	NL	82	198	42	6	3	5	(1	4)	69	17	24	11	1	43	0	2	2	1	1	.50	4	.212	.251	.348
2001 Anaheim	AL	29	53	13	3	1	2	(2	0)	24	5	3	2	0	20	2	2	0	0	1	.00	1	.245	.298	.453
4 ML YEARS		167	433	100	18	5	9	(5	4)	155	38	45	21	1	88	6	8	5	1	4	.20	14	.231	.273	.358

C.J. Nitkowski

Pitches: Left **Bats:** Left **Pos:** RP-61 **Ht:** 6'3" **Wt:** 205 **Born:** 3/9/73 **Age:** 29

Year Team	Lg	G	GS	CG	GF	IP	BFP	H	R	ER	HR	SH	SF	HB	TBB	IBB	SO	WP	Bk	W	L	Pct.	ShO	Sv-Op	Hld	ERA
2001 Toledo *	AAA	1	0	0	1	1	4	1	0	0	0	0	0	0	1	0	0	1	0	0	0	—	0	0--	—	0.00
1995 Cin-Det		20	18	0	0	71.2	338	94	57	53	11	2	4	5	35	3	31	2	2	2	7	.222	0	0-1	—	6.66
1996 Detroit	AL	11	8	0	0	45.2	234	62	44	41	7	0	2	7	38	1	36	2	0	2	3	.400	0	0-0	—	8.08
1998 Houston	NL	43	0	0	11	59.2	250	49	27	25	4	4	2	6	23	2	44	3	1	3	3	.500	0	3-5	8	3.77
1999 Detroit	AL	68	7	0	7	81.2	349	63	44	39	11	1	4	3	45	3	66	4	3	4	5	.444	0	0-0	11	4.30
2000 Detroit	AL	67	11	0	7	109.2	497	124	79	64	13	3	8	4	49	3	81	3	1	4	9	.308	0	0-2	15	5.25
2001 Det-NYM		61	0	0	14	51	241	54	30	28	7	3	1	5	34	8	42	1	0	1	3	.250	0	0-6	6	4.94
1995 Cincinnati	NL	9	7	0	0	32.1	154	41	25	22	4	2	1	2	15	1	18	1	2	1	3	.250	0	0-1	—	6.12
Detroit	AL	11	11	0	0	39.1	184	53	32	31	7	0	3	3	20	2	13	1	0	1	4	.200	0	0-0	—	7.09

	HOW MUCH HE PITCHED				WHAT HE GAVE UP										WP	Bk	THE RESULTS					
Year Team	Lg	G GS CG GF	IP	BFP	H	R	ER	HR SH SF HB	TBB	IBB	SO	WP	Bk	W	L	Pct.	ShO	Sv-Op	Hld	ERA
2001 Detroit	AL	56 0 0 12	45.1	220	51	30	28	7 3 1 5	31	7	38	1	0	0	3	.000	0	0-6	6	5.56
New York	NL	5 0 0 2	5.2	21	3	0	0	0 0 0 0	3	1	4	0	0	1	0	1.000	0	0-0	0	0.00
6 ML YEARS		270 44 0 39	419.1	1909	446	281	250	53 13 21 30	224	20	300	15	7	16	30	.348	0	3-14	40	5.37

Trot Nixon

Bats: L **Throws:** L **Pos:** RF-83; CF-70; PH/PR-6; DH-1   **Ht:** 6'2" **Wt:** 200 **Born:** 4/11/74 **Age:** 28

		BATTING																BASERUNNING				PERCENTAGES		
Year Team	Lg	G	AB	H	2B	3B	HR	(Hm | Rd)	TB	R	RBI	TBB	IBB	SO	HBP	SH	SF	SB	CS	SB%	GDP	Avg	OBP	SLG
1996 Boston	AL	2	4	2	1	0	0	(0 | 0)	3	2	0	0	0	1	0	0	0	1	0	1.00	0	.500	.500	.750
1998 Boston	AL	13	27	7	1	0	0	(0 | 0)	8	3	0	1	0	3	0	0	0	0	0	—	0	.259	.286	.296
1999 Boston	AL	124	381	103	22	5	15	(3 | 12)	180	67	52	53	1	75	3	2	8	3	1	.75	7	.270	.357	.472
2000 Boston	AL	123	427	118	27	8	12	(4 | 8)	197	66	60	63	2	85	2	5	5	8	1	.89	11	.276	.368	.461
2001 Boston	AL	148	535	150	31	4	27	(14 | 13)	270	100	88	79	1	113	7	6	6	7	4	.64	8	.280	.376	.505
5 ML YEARS		410	1374	380	82	17	54	(21 | 33)	658	238	200	196	4	277	12	13	19	19	6	.76	26	.277	.367	.479

Hideo Nomo

Pitches: Right **Bats:** Right **Pos:** SP-33   **Ht:** 6'2" **Wt:** 210 **Born:** 8/31/68 **Age:** 33

		HOW MUCH HE PITCHED			WHAT HE GAVE UP											THE RESULTS					
Year Team	Lg	G GS CG GF	IP	BFP	H	R	ER	HR SH SF HB	TBB	IBB	SO	WP	Bk	W	L	Pct.	ShO	Sv-Op	Hld	ERA
1995 Los Angeles	NL	28 28 4 0	191.1	780	124	63	54	14 11 4 5	78	2	236	19	5	13	6	.684	3	0-0	0	2.54
1996 Los Angeles	NL	33 33 3 0	228.1	932	180	93	81	23 12 6 2	85	6	234	11	3	16	11	.593	2	0-0	0	3.19
1997 Los Angeles	NL	33 33 1 0	207.1	904	193	104	98	23 7 1 9	92	2	233	10	4	14	12	.538	0	0-0	0	4.25
1998 LA-NYM	NL	29 28 3 0	157.1	687	130	86	86	19 8 5 4	94	2	167	13	4	6	12	.333	0	0-0	0	4.92
1999 Milwaukee	NL	28 28 0 0	176.1	767	176	96	89	27 5 5 3	78	2	161	10	1	12	8	.600	0	0-0	0	4.54
2000 Detroit	AL	32 31 1 0	190	828	191	102	100	31 6 3 3	89	1	181	16	0	8	12	.400	0	0-0	0	4.74
2001 Boston	AL	33 33 2 0	198	849	171	105	99	26 4 7 3	96	2	220	6	0	13	10	.565	2	0-0	0	4.50
1998 Arizona	NL	12 12 0 0	67.2	295	57	39	38	8 2 2 3	38	0	73	4	1	2	7	.222	0	0-0	0	5.05
New York	NL	17 16 1 0	89.2	392	73	49	48	11 6 3 1	56	2	94	9	3	4	5	.444	0	0-0	0	4.82
7 ML YEARS		216 214 14 0	1348.2	5747	1162	651	607	163 53 31 29	612	17	1432	85	17	82	71	.536	7	0-0	0	4.05

Greg Norton

Bats: B **Throws:** R **Pos:** PH/PR-72; 3B-24; LF-22; 1B-13; RF-4; DH-1   **Ht:** 6'1" **Wt:** 200 **Born:** 7/6/72 **Age:** 29

		BATTING																BASERUNNING				PERCENTAGES		
Year Team	Lg	G	AB	H	2B	3B	HR	(Hm	Rd)	TB	R	RBI	TBB	IBB	SO	HBP	SH	SF	SB	CS	SB%	GDP	Avg	OBP	SLG
1996 Chicago	AL	11	23	5	0	0	2	(0	2)	11	4	3	4	0	6	0	0	0	0	0	1.00	0	.217	.333	.478
1997 Chicago	AL	18	34	9	2	2	0	(0	0)	15	5	1	2	0	8	0	1	0	0	0	—	0	.265	.306	.441
1998 Chicago	AL	105	299	71	17	2	9	(6	3)	119	38	36	26	1	77	2	1	2	3	3	.50	11	.237	.301	.398
1999 Chicago	AL	132	436	111	26	4	16	(5	11)	185	62	50	69	3	93	2	1	2	4	4	.50	11	.255	.358	.424
2000 Chicago	AL	71	201	49	6	1	6	(4	2)	75	25	28	26	0	47	0	0	2	1	0	1.00	6	.244	.333	.373
2001 Colorado	NL	117	225	60	13	2	13	(7	6)	116	30	40	19	2	65	0	0	2	1	0	1.00	6	.267	.321	.516
6 ML YEARS		454	1218	305	64	7	46	(22	24)	521	164	158	146	6	296	6	3	8	9	8	.53	30	.250	.332	.428

Abraham Nunez

Bats: B **Throws:** R **Pos:** 2B-48; SS-48; PH/PR-36; 3B-1; LF-1   **Ht:** 5'11" **Wt:** 185 **Born:** 3/16/76 **Age:** 26

		BATTING																BASERUNNING				PERCENTAGES		
Year Team	Lg	G	AB	H	2B	3B	HR	(Hm	Rd)	TB	R	RBI	TBB	IBB	SO	HBP	SH	SF	SB	CS	SB%	GDP	Avg	OBP	SLG
1997 Pittsburgh	NL	19	40	9	2	2	0	(0	0)	15	3	6	3	0	10	1	0	1	1	0	1.00	1	.225	.289	.375
1998 Pittsburgh	NL	24	52	10	2	0	1	(0	1)	15	6	2	12	0	14	0	3	0	2	1	.67	1	.192	.344	.288
1999 Pittsburgh	NL	90	259	57	8	0	0	(0	0)	65	25	17	28	0	54	1	13	0	9	1	.90	2	.220	.299	.251
2000 Pittsburgh	NL	40	91	20	1	0	1	(0	1)	24	10	8	8	1	14	0	0	0	0	0	—	3	.220	.283	.264
2001 Pittsburgh	NL	115	301	79	11	4	1	(0	1)	101	30	21	28	1	53	1	4	1	8	2	.80	0	.262	.326	.336
5 ML YEARS		288	743	175	24	6	3	(0	3)	220	74	54	79	2	145	3	20	2	22	5	.81	7	.236	.311	.296

Jose Antonio Nunez

Pitches: Left **Bats:** Left **Pos:** RP-62   **Ht:** 6'2" **Wt:** 165 **Born:** 3/14/79 **Age:** 23

		HOW MUCH HE PITCHED			WHAT HE GAVE UP											THE RESULTS					
Year Team	Lg	G GS CG GF	IP	BFP	H	R	ER	HR SH SF HB	TBB	IBB	SO	WP	Bk	W	L	Pct.	ShO	Sv-Op	Hld	ERA
1998 Mets	R	13 11 1 0	68	267	60	26	18	6 1 3 2	12	0	69	0	1	3	7	.300	0	0-—	—	2.38
1999 Kingsport	R+	13 13 0 0	69.2	296	75	36	29	4 1 4	15	0	63	4	0	3	4	.429	0	0-—	—	3.75
2000 Capital Cty	A	34 5 0 16	95.1	396	82	36	32	6 2 7 10	23	0	112	4	2	3	4	.429	0	8-—	—	3.02
2001 LA-SD	NL	62 0 0 10	59	265	62	35	30	7 2 2 4	25	3	60	5	0	4	2	.667	0	0-2	11	4.58
2001 Los Angeles	NL	6 0 0 2	7.1	42	14	15	11	4 1 0 0	5	0	11	0	0	0	1	.000	0	0-1	0	13.50
San Diego	NL	56 0 0 8	51.2	223	48	20	19	3 1 2 4	20	3	49	5	0	4	1	.800	0	0-1	11	3.31

Vladimir Nunez

Pitches: Right **Bats:** Right **Pos:** RP-49; SP-3   **Ht:** 6'4" **Wt:** 224 **Born:** 3/15/75 **Age:** 27

		HOW MUCH HE PITCHED			WHAT HE GAVE UP											THE RESULTS					
Year Team	Lg	G GS CG GF	IP	BFP	H	R	ER	HR SH SF HB	TBB	IBB	SO	WP	Bk	W	L	Pct.	ShO	Sv-Op	Hld	ERA
2001 Kane County *	A	1 1 0 0	1	5	3	1	1	0 0 0 0	0	0	0	0	0	0	0	—	0	0-0	0	9.00
1998 Arizona	NL	4 0 0 2	5.1	25	7	6	6	0 0 1 0	2	0	2	0	1	0	0	—	0	0-0	0	10.13
1999 Ari-Fla	NL	44 12 0 12	108.2	463	95	63	49	11 7 6 4	54	6	86	8	1	7	10	.412	0	1-3	4	4.06
2000 Florida	NL	17 12 0 0	68.1	322	88	63	60	12 5 5 2	34	2	45	5	0	0	6	.000	0	0-0	0	7.90
2001 Florida	NL	52 3 0 13	92	380	79	33	28	9 2 5 5	30	5	64	1	1	5	4	.444	0	0-1	4	2.74
1999 Arizona	NL	27 0 0 11	34	146	29	15	11	2 2 3 1	20	5	28	3	0	3	2	.600	0	1-2	3	2.91
Florida	NL	17 12 0 0	74.2	317	66	48	38	9 5 3 3	34	1	58	5	1	4	8	.333	0	0-1	1	4.58
4 ML YEARS		117 27 0 30	274.1	1190	269	165	143	32 14 17 11	120	13	197	14	3	11	21	.344	0	1-4	9	4.69

Alex Ochoa

Bats: R **Throws:** R **Pos:** RF-106; LF-36; PH/PR-11; CF-2; DH-1   **Ht:** 6'0"   **Wt:** 200   **Born:** 3/29/72   **Age:** 30

Year Team	Lg	G	AB	H	2B	3B	HR	(Hm	Rd)	TB	R	RBI	TBB	IBB	SO	HBP	SH	SF	SB	CS	SB%	GDP	Avg	OBP	SLG
1995 New York	NL	11	37	11	1	0	0	(0	0)	12	7	0	2	0	10	0	0	0	1	0	1.00	1	.297	.333	.324
1996 New York	NL	82	282	83	19	3	4	(1	3)	120	37	33	17	0	30	2	0	3	4	3	.57	2	.294	.336	.426
1997 New York	NL	113	238	58	14	1	3	(1	2)	83	31	22	18	0	32	2	2	2	3	4	.43	7	.244	.300	.349
1998 Minnesota	AL	94	249	64	14	2	2	(1	1)	88	35	25	10	0	35	1	0	0	6	3	.67	7	.257	.288	.353
1999 Milwaukee	NL	119	277	83	16	3	8	(8	0)	129	47	40	45	2	43	5	0	2	6	4	.60	4	.300	.404	.466
2000 Cincinnati	NL	118	244	77	21	3	13	(9	4)	143	50	58	24	3	27	3	0	4	9	4	.69	7	.316	.378	.586
2001 Cin-Col	NL	148	536	148	30	7	8	(5	3)	216	73	52	45	0	76	4	4	4	17	13	.57	10	.276	.334	.403
2001 Cincinnati	NL	90	349	101	20	4	7	(5	2)	150	48	35	24	0	53	2	2	2	12	9	.57	3	.289	.337	.430
Colorado	NL	58	187	47	10	3	1	(0	1)	66	25	17	21	0	23	2	2	2	5	4	.56	7	.251	.330	.353
7 ML YEARS		685	1863	524	115	19	38	(25	13)	791	280	230	161	5	253	17	6	15	46	31	.60	38	.281	.341	.425

Jose Offerman

Bats: Both   **Throws:** Right   **Pos:** 2B-91; 1B-43; PH/PR-2   **Ht:** 6'0"   **Wt:** 190   **Born:** 11/11/68   **Age:** 33

Year Team	Lg	G	AB	H	2B	3B	HR	(Hm	Rd)	TB	R	RBI	TBB	IBB	SO	HBP	SH	SF	SB	CS	SB%	GDP	Avg	OBP	SLG
1990 Los Angeles	NL	29	58	9	0	0	1	(1	0)	12	7	7	4	1	14	0	1	0	1	0	1.00	1	.155	.210	.207
1991 Los Angeles	NL	52	113	22	2	0	0	(0	0)	24	10	3	25	2	32	1	1	0	3	2	.60	5	.195	.345	.212
1992 Los Angeles	NL	149	534	139	20	8	1	(1	0)	178	67	30	57	4	98	0	5	2	23	16	.59	5	.260	.331	.333
1993 Los Angeles	NL	158	590	159	21	6	1	(1	0)	195	77	62	71	7	75	2	25	8	30	13	.70	12	.269	.346	.331
1994 Los Angeles	NL	72	243	51	8	4	1	(0	1)	70	27	25	38	4	38	0	6	2	2	1	.67	6	.210	.314	.288
1995 Los Angeles	NL	119	429	123	14	6	4	(2	2)	161	69	33	69	0	67	3	10	0	2	7	.22	5	.287	.389	.375
1996 Kansas City	AL	151	561	170	33	8	5	(1	4)	234	85	47	74	3	98	1	7	2	24	10	.71	9	.303	.384	.417
1997 Kansas City	AL	106	424	126	23	6	2	(2	0)	167	59	39	41	3	64	0	6	4	9	10	.47	5	.297	.359	.394
1998 Kansas City	AL	158	607	191	28	13	7	(4	3)	266	102	66	89	1	96	5	2	6	45	12	.79	7	.315	.403	.438
1999 Boston	AL	149	586	172	37	11	8	(5	3)	255	107	69	70	5	79	2	2	7	18	12	.60	11	.294	.391	.435
2000 Boston	AL	116	451	115	14	3	9	(3	6)	162	73	41	70	0	70	1	2	3	0	8	.00	9	.255	.354	.359
2001 Boston	AL	128	524	140	23	3	9	(4	5)	196	76	49	61	2	97	1	3	5	5	2	.71	9	.267	.342	.374
12 ML YEARS		1387	5120	1417	223	68	48	(24	24)	1920	759	471	695	32	828	16	70	35	162	93	.64	83	.277	.363	.375

Tomokazu Ohka

Pitches: Right   **Bats:** Right   **Pos:** SP-21; RP-1   **Ht:** 6'1"   **Wt:** 180   **Born:** 3/18/76   **Age:** 26

Year Team	Lg	G	GS	CG	GF	IP	BFP	H	R	ER	HR	SH	SF	HB	TBB	IBB	SO	WP	Bk	W	L	Pct.	ShO	Sv-Op	Hld	ERA
2001 Pawtucket *	AAA	8	8	1	0	42	188	55	35	26	5	4	3	1	9	0	33	3	0	2	5	.286	0	0--	0	5.57
1999 Boston	AL	8	2	0	3	13	65	21	12	9	2	0	1	0	6	0	8	0	0	1	2	.333	0	0-0	0	6.23
2000 Boston	AL	13	12	0	1	69.1	297	70	25	24	7	1	2	2	26	0	40	3	0	3	6	.333	0	0-0	0	3.12
2001 Bos-Mon		22	21	0	1	107	469	134	70	65	15	2	3	2	29	0	68	2	1	3	9	.250	0	0-0	0	5.47
2001 Boston	AL	12	11	0	1	52.1	241	69	40	36	7	1	1	2	19	0	37	1	1	2	5	.286	0	0-0	0	6.19
Montreal	NL	10	10	0	0	54.2	228	65	30	29	8	1	1	1	10	0	31	1	0	1	4	.200	0	0-0	0	4.77
3 ML YEARS		43	35	0	5	189.1	831	225	107	98	24	3	5	5	61	0	116	5	1	7	17	.292	0	0-0	0	4.66

Will Ohman

Pitches: Left   **Bats:** Left   **Pos:** RP-11   **Ht:** 6'2"   **Wt:** 195   **Born:** 8/13/77   **Age:** 24

Year Team	Lg	G	GS	CG	GF	IP	BFP	H	R	ER	HR	SH	SF	HB	TBB	IBB	SO	WP	Bk	W	L	Pct.	ShO	Sv-Op	Hld	ERA
1998 Williamsprt	A-	10	7	0	0	39	167	39	32	28	6	0	3	1	13	0	35	7	0	4	4	.500	0	0--	—	6.46
Rockford	A	4	4	0	0	24.1	104	25	13	12	3	2	0	2	7	0	21	1	0	1	1	.500	0	0--	—	4.44
1999 Daytona	A+	31	15	2	12	106.2	457	102	59	41	11	2	4	8	41	1	97	6	1	4	7	.364	2	5--	—	3.46
2000 West Tenn	AA	59	0	0	23	71.1	312	55	20	15	3	3	5	3	36	5	85	8	0	6	4	.600	0	3--	—	1.89
2001 Iowa	AAA	40	1	0	11	51	218	51	24	23	9	2	0	1	18	3	66	3	0	5	2	.714	0	4--	—	4.06
2000 Chicago	NL	6	0	0	2	3.1	17	4	3	3	0	0	0	0	4	1	2	1	0	1	0	1.000	0	0-0	1	8.10
2001 Chicago	NL	11	0	0	0	11.2	54	14	10	10	2	0	0	0	6	0	12	2	0	0	1	.000	0	0-0	1	7.71
2 ML YEARS		17	0	0	2	15	71	18	13	13	2	0	0	0	10	1	14	3	0	1	1	.500	0	0-0	2	7.80

Augie Ojeda

Bats: B **Throws:** R **Pos:** 3B-35; SS-31; PH/PR-13; 2B-10   **Ht:** 5'8"   **Wt:** 165   **Born:** 12/20/74   **Age:** 27

Year Team	Lg	G	AB	H	2B	3B	HR	(Hm	Rd)	TB	R	RBI	TBB	IBB	SO	HBP	SH	SF	SB	CS	SB%	GDP	Avg	OBP	SLG
1997 Frederick	A+	34	128	44	11	1	1	—	—	60	25	20	18	1	18	1	4	0	2	5	.29	1	.344	.429	.469
Bowie	AA	58	204	60	9	1	2	—	—	77	33	23	31	1	17	3	4	3	7	0	1.00	6	.294	.390	.377
Rochester	AAA	15	47	11	3	1	0	—	—	16	5	6	8	0	4	0	3	0	1	2	.33	2	.234	.345	.340
1998 Orioles	R	4	15	6	2	0	0	—	—	8	6	2	3	0	1	2	0	0	3	0	1.00	0	.400	.550	.533
Bowie	AA	73	254	65	10	2	1	—	—	82	36	19	36	0	30	3	5	1	0	3	.00	5	.256	.354	.323
1999 Rochester	AAA	1	1	0	0	0	0	—	—	0	1	0	0	0	0	0	0	0	0	0	—	0	.000	.000	.000
Bowie	AA	134	460	123	18	4	10	—	—	179	73	60	57	0	47	11	25	4	6	2	.75	7	.267	.359	.389
2000 Iowa	AAA	113	396	111	23	2	8	—	—	162	56	43	33	1	27	7	3	4	16	6	.73	10	.280	.343	.409
2000 Chicago	NL	28	77	17	3	1	2	(1	1)	28	10	8	10	1	9	0	1	1	0	1	.00	1	.221	.307	.364
2001 Chicago	NL	78	144	29	5	1	1	(1	0)	39	16	12	12	1	20	2	2	2	1	0	1.00	2	.201	.269	.271
2 ML YEARS		106	221	46	8	2	3	(2	1)	67	26	20	22	2	29	2	3	3	1	1	.50	3	.208	.282	.303

Troy O'Leary

Bats: L Throws: L Pos: LF-52; RF-41; PH/PR-14; DH-4   Ht: 6'0" Wt: 200 Born: 8/4/69 Age: 32

Year Team	Lg	G	AB	H	2B	3B	HR	(Hm	Rd)	TB	R	RBI	TBB	IBB	SO	HBP	SH	SF	SB	CS	SB%	GDP	Avg	OBP	SLG
1993 Milwaukee	AL	19	41	12	3	0	0	(0	0)	15	3	3	5	0	9	0	3	0	0	0	—	1	.293	.370	.366
1994 Milwaukee	AL	27	66	18	1	1	2	(0	2)	27	9	7	5	0	12	1	0	1	1	1	.50	0	.273	.329	.409
1995 Boston	AL	112	399	123	31	6	10	(5	5)	196	60	49	29	4	64	1	3	2	5	3	.63	8	.308	.355	.491
1996 Boston	AL	149	497	129	28	5	15	(10	5)	212	68	81	47	3	80	4	1	3	2	2	.60	13	.260	.327	.427
1997 Boston	AL	146	499	154	32	4	15	(5	10)	239	65	80	39	7	70	2	1	4	0	5	.00	13	.309	.358	.479
1998 Boston	AL	156	611	165	36	8	23	(12	11)	286	95	83	36	2	108	5	0	5	2	2	.50	17	.270	.343	.468
1999 Boston	AL	157	596	167	36	4	28	(13	15)	295	84	103	56	5	91	4	0	5	1	2	.33	21	.280	.343	.495
2000 Boston	AL	138	513	134	30	4	13	(7	6)	211	68	70	44	2	76	2	0	4	0	2	.00	12	.261	.320	.411
2001 Boston	AL	104	341	82	16	6	13	(9	4)	149	50	50	25	2	73	5	0	5	1	3	.25	9	.240	.298	.437
9 ML YEARS		1008	3563	984	213	38	119	(61	58)	1630	502	526	286	25	583	24	8	29	13	20	.39	94	.276	.332	.457

John Olerud

Bats: Left Throws: Left Pos: 1B-158; PH/PR-5   Ht: 6'5" Wt: 220 Born: 8/5/68 Age: 33

Year Team	Lg	G	AB	H	2B	3B	HR	(Hm	Rd)	TB	R	RBI	TBB	IBB	SO	HBP	SH	SF	SB	CS	SB%	GDP	Avg	OBP	SLG
1989 Toronto	AL	6	8	3	0	0	0	(0	0)	3	2	0	0	0	1	0	0	0	0	0	—	0	.375	.375	.375
1990 Toronto	AL	111	358	95	15	1	14	(11	3)	154	43	48	57	6	75	1	1	4	0	2	.00	5	.265	.364	.430
1991 Toronto	AL	139	454	116	30	1	17	(7	10)	199	64	68	68	9	84	6	3	10	0	2	.00	12	.256	.353	.438
1992 Toronto	AL	138	458	130	28	0	16	(4	12)	206	68	66	70	11	61	1	1	7	1	0	1.00	15	.284	.375	.450
1993 Toronto	AL	158	551	200	54	2	24	(9	15)	330	109	107	114	33	65	7	0	7	0	2	.00	12	.363	.473	.599
1994 Toronto	AL	108	384	114	29	2	12	(6	6)	183	47	67	61	12	53	3	0	5	1	2	.33	11	.297	.393	.477
1995 Toronto	AL	135	492	143	32	0	8	(1	7)	199	72	54	84	10	54	4	0	1	0	0	—	17	.291	.398	.404
1996 Toronto	AL	125	398	109	25	0	18	(9	9)	188	59	61	60	6	37	10	0	1	1	0	1.00	10	.274	.382	.472
1997 New York	NL	154	524	154	34	1	22	(13	9)	256	90	102	85	5	67	13	0	8	0	0	—	15	.294	.400	.489
1998 New York	NL	160	557	197	36	4	22	(13	9)	307	91	93	96	11	73	4	1	7	2	2	.50	15	.354	.447	.551
1999 New York	NL	162	581	173	39	0	19	(11	8)	269	107	96	125	5	66	11	0	6	3	0	1.00	22	.298	.427	.463
2000 Seattle	AL	159	565	161	45	0	14	(8	6)	248	84	103	102	11	96	4	2	10	2	0	.00	17	.285	.392	.439
2001 Seattle	AL	159	572	173	32	1	21	(15	6)	270	91	95	94	19	70	5	1	7	3	1	.75	21	.302	.401	.472
13 ML YEARS		1714	5902	1768	399	12	207	(107	100)	2812	927	960	1016	138	802	69	9	73	11	13	.46	176	.300	.404	.476

Omar Olivares

Pitches: Right Bats: Right Pos: RP-33; SP-12   Ht: 6'1" Wt: 205 Born: 7/6/67 Age: 34

Year Team	Lg	G	GS	CG	GF	IP	BFP	H	R	ER	HR	SH	SF	HB	TBB	IBB	SO	WP	Bk	W	L	Pct.	ShO	Sv-Op	Hld	ERA
1990 St. Louis	NL	9	6	0	0	49.1	201	45	17	16	2	1	0	2	17	0	20	1	1	1	1	.500	0	0-0	1	2.92
1991 St. Louis	NL	28	24	0	2	167.1	688	148	72	69	13	11	2	5	61	1	91	3	1	11	7	.611	0	1-1	0	3.71
1992 St. Louis	NL	32	30	1	1	197	818	189	84	84	20	8	7	4	63	5	124	2	0	9	9	.500	0	0-0	0	3.84
1993 St. Louis	NL	58	9	0	11	118.2	537	134	60	55	10	4	4	9	54	7	63	4	3	5	3	.625	0	1-5	2	4.17
1994 St. Louis	NL	14	12	1	2	73.2	333	84	53	47	10	3	3	4	37	0	26	5	0	3	4	.429	0	1-1	0	5.74
1995 Col-Phi	NL	16	6	0	4	41.2	195	55	34	32	5	2	2	.3	23	0	22	4	0	1	4	.200	0	0-0	0	6.91
1996 Detroit	AL	25	25	4	0	160	708	169	90	87	16	3	6	9	75	4	81	4	1	7	11	.389	0	0-0	0	4.89
1997 Det-Sea	AL	32	31	3	0	177.1	794	191	109	98	18	2	7	13	81	4	103	5	0	9	9	.500	0	0-0	0	4.03
1998 Anaheim	AL	37	26	1	6	183	805	189	92	82	19	6	4	5	91	1	112	5	0	9	9	.500	0	0-0	0	4.16
1999 Ana-Oak	AL	32	32	4	0	205.2	885	217	105	95	19	3	7	9	81	0	85	6	0	15	11	.577	0	0-0	0	4.16
2000 Oakland	AL	21	16	1	1	108	508	134	86	81	10	0	7	6	60	0	57	4	0	4	8	.333	0	0-0	0	6.75
2001 Pittsburgh	NL	45	12	1	15	110	494	123	87	80	17	3	4	10	42	8	69	3	1	6	9	.400	0	1-2	3	6.55
1995 Colorado	NL	11	6	0	1	31.2	151	44	28	26	4	1	1	2	21	0	15	4	0	1	3	.250	0	0-0	0	7.39
Philadelphia	NL	5	0	0	3	10	44	11	6	6	1	1	1	1	2	0	7	0	0	0	1	.000	0	0-0	0	5.40
1997 Detroit	AL	19	19	3	0	115	502	110	68	60	8	2	4	9	53	1	74	5	0	5	6	.455	2	0-0	0	4.70
Seattle	AL	13	12	0	0	62.1	292	81	41	38	10	0	3	4	28	3	29	0	0	4	3	.571	0	0-0	0	5.49
1999 Anaheim	AL	20	20	3	0	131	558	135	62	59	11	3	5	6	49	0	49	4	0	8	9	.471	0	0-0	0	4.05
Oakland	AL	12	12	1	0	74.2	327	82	43	36	8	0	2	3	32	0	36	2	0	7	2	.778	0	0-0	0	4.34
12 ML YEARS		349	229	16	42	1591.2	6966	1678	889	826	159	46	53	80	685	30	853	46	7	77	86	.472	2	4-9	6	4.67

Darren Oliver

Pitches: Left Bats: Right Pos: SP-28   Ht: 6'2" Wt: 220 Born: 10/6/70 Age: 31

Year Team	Lg	G	GS	CG	GF	IP	BFP	H	R	ER	HR	SH	SF	HB	TBB	IBB	SO	WP	Bk	W	L	Pct.	ShO	Sv-Op	Hld	ERA
2001 Oklahoma *	AAA	1	1	0	0	3	12	0	0	0	0	0	0	0	0	0	3	0	0	0	0	—	0	0- --	—	0.00
Tulsa *	AA	1	1	0	0	5	21	4	3	3	1	1	0	1	2	0	5	0	0	0	1	.000	0	0- --	—	5.40
1993 Texas	AL	2	0	0	0	3.1	14	2	1	1	1	0	0	0	1	1	4	0	0	0	0	—	0	0-0	0	2.70
1994 Texas	AL	43	0	0	10	50	226	40	24	19	4	6	0	.6	35	4	50	2	2	4	0	1.000	0	2-3	9	3.42
1995 Texas	AL	17	7	0	2	49	222	47	25	23	3	5	1	1	32	1	39	4	0	4	2	.667	0	0-0	0	4.22
1996 Texas	AL	30	30	1	0	173.2	777	190	97	90	20	2	7	10	76	3	112	5	1	14	6	.700	1	0-0	0	4.66
1997 Texas	AL	32	32	3	0	201.1	887	213	111	94	29	2	5	11	82	3	104	7	0	13	12	.520	1	0-0	0	4.20
1998 Tex-StL		29	29	2	0	160.1	749	204	115	102	18	8	8	10	66	2	87	7	4	10	11	.476	0	0-0	0	5.73
1999 St. Louis	NL	30	30	2	0	196.1	842	197	96	93	16	11	4	11	74	4	119	6	2	9	9	.500	1	0-0	0	4.26
2000 Texas	AL	21	21	0	0	108	501	151	95	89	16	5	4	4	65	0	104	8	2	11	11	.500	0	0-0	0	6.02
2001 Texas	AL	28	28	1	0	154	696	189	109	103	23	1	9	11	43	1	58	6	1	6	7	.462	0	0-0	0	6.53
1998 Texas	AL	19	19	2	0	103.1	493	140	84	75	11	3	6	10	43	1	58	6	1	6	7	.462	0	0-0	0	6.53
St. Louis	NL	10	10	0	0	57	256	64	31	27	7	5	2	0	23	1	29	1	3	4	4	.500	0	0-0	0	4.26
9 ML YEARS		232	177	9	12	1096	4914	1233	673	614	130	40	34	59	473	21	668	43	12	67	60	.528	3	2-3	9	5.04

163

Joe Oliver

Bats: Right **Throws:** Right **Pos:** C-17   **Ht:** 6'3" **Wt:** 220 **Born:** 7/24/65 **Age:** 36

Year Team	Lg	G	AB	H	2B	3B	HR	(Hm Rd)	TB	R	RBI	TBB	IBB	SO	HBP	SH	SF	SB	CS	SB%	GDP	Avg	OBP	SLG
2001 Red Sox *	R	2	5	5	0	0	1	— —	8	2	1	0	0	0	0	0	0	0	0	—	0	1.000	1.000	1.600
Pawtucket *	AAA	13	41	10	1	0	2	—	17	3	6	0	0	9	0	0	0	1	0	1.00	2	.244	.244	.415
1989 Cincinnati	NL	49	151	41	8	0	3	(1 2)	58	13	23	6	1	28	1	1	2	0	0	—	3	.272	.300	.384
1990 Cincinnati	NL	121	364	84	23	0	8	(3 5)	131	34	52	37	15	75	2	5	1	1	1	.50	6	.231	.304	.360
1991 Cincinnati	NL	94	269	58	11	0	11	(7 4)	102	21	41	18	5	53	0	4	0	0	0	—	14	.216	.265	.379
1992 Cincinnati	NL	143	485	131	25	1	10	(7 3)	188	42	57	35	19	75	1	6	7	2	3	.40	12	.270	.316	.388
1993 Cincinnati	NL	139	482	115	28	0	14	(7 7)	185	40	75	27	2	91	1	2	9	0	0	—	13	.239	.276	.384
1994 Cincinnati	NL	6	19	4	0	0	1	(1 0)	7	1	5	2	1	3	0	0	0	0	0	—	1	.211	.286	.368
1995 Milwaukee	AL	97	337	92	20	0	12	(4 8)	148	43	51	27	1	66	3	2	0	2	4	.33	11	.273	.332	.439
1996 Cincinnati	NL	106	289	70	12	1	11	(6 5)	117	31	46	28	6	54	2	3	3	2	0	1.00	8	.242	.311	.405
1997 Cincinnati	NL	111	349	90	13	0	14	(7 7)	145	28	43	25	1	58	5	2	5	1	3	.25	7	.258	.313	.415
1998 Det-Sea	AL	79	240	54	11	0	6	(3 3)	83	20	32	17	0	48	0	2	4	1	1	.50	8	.225	.272	.346
1999 Pittsburgh	NL	45	134	27	8	0	1	(1 0)	38	10	13	10	0	33	0	0	2	2	0	1.00	4	.201	.253	.284
2000 Seattle	AL	69	200	53	13	1	10	(6 4)	98	33	35	14	1	38	0	5	0	2	1	.67	6	.265	.313	.490
2001 NYY-Bos	AL	17	48	12	2	0	1	(1 0)	17	4	3	2	0	15	0	2	1	0	0	—	0	.250	.275	.354
1998 Detroit	AL	50	155	35	8	0	4	(2 2)	55	8	22	7	0	33	0	0	4	0	1	.00	5	.226	.253	.355
Seattle		29	85	19	3	0	2	(1 1)	28	12	10	10	0	15	0	2	0	1	0	1.00	3	.224	.305	.329
2001 New York	AL	12	36	9	1	0	1	(1 0)	13	3	2	1	0	12	0	2	1	0	0	—	0	.250	.263	.361
Boston		5	12	3	1	0	0	(0 0)	4	1	1	1	0	3	0	0	0	0	0	—	0	.250	.308	.333
13 ML YEARS		1076	3367	831	174	3	102	(54 48)	1317	320	476	248	52	637	15	34	34	13	13	.50	93	.247	.299	.391

Kevin Olsen

Pitches: Right **Bats:** Right **Pos:** SP-2; RP-2   **Ht:** 6'2" **Wt:** 200 **Born:** 7/26/76 **Age:** 25

Year Team	Lg	G	GS	CG	GF	IP	BFP	H	R	ER	HR	SH	SF	HB	TBB	IBB	SO	WP	Bk	W	L	Pct.	ShO	Sv-Op	Hld	ERA
1998 Utica	A-	21	4	0	8	45	181	37	21	13	3	1	0	1	10	1	56	1	1	4	3	.571	0	2--	—	2.60
1999 Brevard Cty	A+	11	11	0	0	57	253	70	37	32	8	1	1	1	13	0	45	3	0	2	5	.286	0	0--	—	5.05
Kane County	A	10	9	0	0	61.1	257	65	25	23	3	0	3	2	16	0	52	2	0	5	2	.714	0	0--	—	3.38
2000 Brevard Cty	A+	18	18	1	0	110	436	93	40	35	2	2	4	6	25	2	77	4	0	4	8	.333	0	0--	—	2.86
Portland		9	9	0	0	54	234	54	30	29	8	1	0	2	21	0	47	3	0	3	4	.429	0	0--	—	4.83
2001 Portland	AA	26	26	2	0	154.2	611	123	56	46	11	2	3	10	21	1	144	0	0	10	3	.769	1	0--	—	2.68
2001 Florida	NL	4	2	0	0	15	56	11	2	2	0	0	0	0	2	1	13	0	0	0	0	—	0	0-0	0	1.20

Gregg Olson

Pitches: Right **Bats:** Right **Pos:** RP-28   **Ht:** 6'4" **Wt:** 208 **Born:** 10/11/66 **Age:** 35

Year Team	Lg	G	GS	CG	GF	IP	BFP	H	R	ER	HR	SH	SF	HB	TBB	IBB	SO	WP	Bk	W	L	Pct.	ShO	Sv-Op	Hld	ERA
1988 Baltimore	AL	10	0	0	4	11	51	10	4	4	1	0	0	0	10	1	9	0	1	1	1	.500	0	1--	1	3.27
1989 Baltimore	AL	64	0	0	52	85	356	57	17	16	1	4	1	1	46	10	90	9	3	5	2	.714	0	27-33	1	1.69
1990 Baltimore	AL	64	0	0	58	74.1	305	57	20	20	3	1	2	3	31	3	74	5	0	6	5	.545	0	37-42	0	2.42
1991 Baltimore	AL	72	0	0	62	73.2	319	74	28	26	1	5	1	1	29	5	72	8	1	4	6	.400	0	31-39	1	3.18
1992 Baltimore	AL	60	0	0	56	61.1	244	46	14	14	3	0	2	0	24	0	58	4	0	1	5	.167	0	36-44	0	2.05
1993 Baltimore	AL	50	0	0	45	45	188	37	9	8	1	2	1	2	18	3	44	5	0	0	2	.000	0	29-35	0	1.60
1994 Atlanta	NL	16	0	0	6	14.2	77	19	15	15	1	2	1	1	13	3	10	0	2	0	2	.000	0	1-1	1	9.20
1995 Cle-KC	AL	23	0	0	12	33	141	28	15	15	4	1	2	0	19	2	21	1	0	3	3	.500	0	3-5	2	4.09
1996 Det-Hou		52	0	0	30	52.1	243	55	30	29	7	1	1	1	35	6	37	6	0	4	0	1.000	0	8-10	1	4.99
1997 Min-KC	AL	45	0	0	18	50	226	58	35	31	3	2	1	1	28	4	34	1	0	4	3	.571	0	1-4	5	5.58
1998 Arizona	NL	64	0	0	49	68.2	281	56	25	23	4	3	1	1	25	1	55	2	0	3	4	.429	0	30-34	0	3.01
1999 Arizona	NL	61	0	0	36	60.2	257	54	28	25	9	1	2	2	25	2	45	1	0	9	4	.692	0	14-23	9	3.71
2000 Los Angeles	NL	13	0	0	9	17.2	81	21	11	10	4	1	1	1	7	0	15	0	0	0	1	.000	0	0-1	0	5.09
2001 Los Angeles	NL	28	0	0	10	24.2	120	26	24	22	4	0	3	0	20	1	24	1	0	0	1	.000	0	0-1	4	8.03
1995 Cleveland	AL	3	0	0	2	2.2	14	5	4	4	1	0	0	0	2	0	0	0	0	0	0	—	0	0-0	0	13.50
Kansas City	AL	20	0	0	10	30.1	127	23	11	11	3	1	2	0	17	2	21	1	0	3	3	.500	0	3-5	2	3.26
1996 Detroit	AL	43	0	0	28	43	196	43	25	24	6	1	0	1	28	4	29	5	0	3	0	1.000	0	8-10	1	5.02
Houston	NL	9	0	0	2	9.1	47	12	5	5	1	0	1	0	7	2	8	1	0	1	0	1.000	0	0-0	0	4.82
1997 Minnesota	AL	11	0	0	5	8.1	55	19	17	17	0	0	0	0	11	1	6	0	0	0	0	—	0	0-0	1	18.36
Kansas City	AL	34	0	0	13	41.2	171	39	18	14	3	2	1	1	17	3	28	1	0	4	3	.571	0	1-4	4	3.02
14 ML YEARS		622	0	0	447	672	2889	598	275	258	46	23	20	12	330	41	588	43	7	40	39	.506	0	217-273	25	3.46

Paul O'Neill

Bats: Left **Throws:** Left **Pos:** RF-130; DH-6; PH/PR-4   **Ht:** 6'4" **Wt:** 215 **Born:** 2/25/63 **Age:** 39

Year Team	Lg	G	AB	H	2B	3B	HR	(Hm Rd)	TB	R	RBI	TBB	IBB	SO	HBP	SH	SF	SB	CS	SB%	GDP	Avg	OBP	SLG
1985 Cincinnati	NL	5	12	4	1	0	0	(0 0)	5	1	1	0	0	2	0	0	0	0	0	—	0	.333	.333	.417
1986 Cincinnati	NL	3	2	0	0	0	0	(0 0)	0	0	0	1	0	1	0	0	0	0	0	—	0	.000	.333	.000
1987 Cincinnati	NL	84	160	41	14	1	7	(4 3)	78	24	28	18	1	29	0	0	0	2	1	.67	3	.256	.331	.488
1988 Cincinnati	NL	145	485	122	25	3	16	(12 4)	201	58	73	38	5	65	2	3	5	8	6	.57	7	.252	.306	.414
1989 Cincinnati	NL	117	428	118	24	2	15	(11 4)	191	49	74	46	8	64	2	0	4	20	5	.80	7	.276	.346	.446
1990 Cincinnati	NL	145	503	136	28	0	16	(10 6)	212	59	78	53	13	103	2	1	5	13	11	.54	12	.270	.339	.421
1991 Cincinnati	NL	152	532	136	36	0	28	(20 8)	256	71	91	73	14	107	1	0	5	12	7	.63	8	.256	.346	.481
1992 Cincinnati	NL	148	496	122	19	1	14	(6 8)	185	59	66	77	15	85	2	3	6	6	3	.67	10	.246	.346	.373
1993 New York	AL	141	498	155	34	1	20	(8 12)	251	71	75	44	5	69	2	0	3	2	4	.33	13	.311	.367	.504
1994 New York	AL	103	368	132	25	1	21	(10 11)	222	68	83	72	13	56	2	0	3	5	4	.56	16	.359	.460	.603
1995 New York	AL	127	460	138	30	4	22	(12 10)	242	82	96	71	8	76	1	0	11	1	2	.33	25	.300	.387	.526
1996 New York	AL	150	546	165	35	1	19	(7 12)	259	89	91	102	8	76	4	0	11	0	1	.00	21	.302	.411	.474
1997 New York	AL	149	553	179	42	0	21	(10 11)	284	89	117	75	8	92	0	0	9	10	7	.59	16	.324	.399	.514
1998 New York	AL	152	602	191	40	2	24	(10 14)	307	95	116	57	2	103	2	0	11	15	1	.94	22	.317	.372	.510
1999 New York	AL	153	597	170	39	4	19	(9 10)	274	70	110	66	1	89	0	0	10	11	9	.55	24	.285	.353	.459
2000 New York	AL	142	566	160	26	0	18	(10 8)	240	79	100	51	0	90	0	0	11	14	9	.61	17	.283	.336	.424

		BATTING										BASERUNNING				PERCENTAGES		
Year Team	Lg	G AB H	2B 3B HR	(Hm Rd)	TB	R RBI	TBB IBB	SO	HBP SH SF	SB CS SB% GDP	Avg OBP SLG
2001 New York	AL	137 510 136	33 1 21	(13 8)	234	77 70	48 4	59	2 0 3	22 3 .88 20	.267 .330 .459
17 ML YEARS		2053 7318 2105	451 21 281	(152 129)	3441	1041 1269	892 107	1166	22 7 90	141 73 .66 221	.288 .363 .470

Luis Ordaz

Bats: R **Throws:** R **Pos:** 2B-19; SS-8; PH/PR-2; DH-1; 3B-1   **Ht:** 5'11" **Wt:** 170 **Born:** 8/12/75 **Age:** 26

		BATTING									BASERUNNING	PERCENTAGES
Year Team	Lg	G AB H	2B 3B HR	(Hm Rd)	TB	R RBI	TBB IBB	SO	HBP SH SF	SB CS SB% GDP	Avg OBP SLG
2001 Omaha *	AAA	14 52 16	1 0 1	— —	20	5 4	2 0	10	3 2 0	3 0 1.00 2	.308 .368 .385
1997 St. Louis	NL	12 22 6	1 0 0	(0 0)	7	3 1	1 0	2	0 0 0	3 0 1.00 0	.273 .304 .318
1998 St. Louis	NL	57 153 31	5 0 0	(0 0)	36	9 8	12 1	18	0 4 0	2 0 1.00 3	.203 .261 .235
1999 St. Louis	NL	10 9 1	0 0 0	(0 0)	1	3 2	1 0	2	0 1 0	1 0 1.00 0	.111 .200 .111
2000 Kansas City	AL	65 104 23	2 0 0	(0 0)	25	17 11	5 0	10	1 4 3	4 2 .67 6	.221 .257 .240
2001 Kansas City	AL	28 56 14	3 0 0	(0 0)	17	8 4	3 0	8	1 2 1	0 0 — 1	.250 .295 .304
5 ML YEARS		172 344 75	11 0 0	(0 0)	86	40 26	22 1	40	2 11 4	10 2 .83 10	.218 .266 .250

Magglio Ordonez

Bats: R **Throws:** R **Pos:** RF-155; PH/PR-4; DH-3; CF-1   **Ht:** 6'0" **Wt:** 210 **Born:** 1/28/74 **Age:** 28

		BATTING									BASERUNNING	PERCENTAGES
Year Team	Lg	G AB H	2B 3B HR	(Hm Rd)	TB	R RBI	TBB IBB	SO	HBP SH SF	SB CS SB% GDP	Avg OBP SLG
1997 Chicago	AL	21 69 22	6 0 4	(2 2)	40	12 11	2 0	8	0 1 0	1 2 .33 1	.319 .338 .580
1998 Chicago	AL	145 535 151	25 2 14	(8 6)	222	70 65	28 1	53	9 2 4	9 7 .56 19	.282 .326 .415
1999 Chicago	AL	157 624 188	34 3 30	(16 14)	318	100 117	47 4	64	1 0 5	13 6 .68 24	.301 .349 .510
2000 Chicago	AL	153 588 185	34 3 32	(21 11)	321	102 126	60 3	64	2 0 15	18 4 .82 28	.315 .371 .546
2001 Chicago	AL	160 593 181	40 1 31	(17 14)	316	97 113	70 7	70	5 0 3	25 7 .78 14	.305 .382 .533
5 ML YEARS		636 2409 727	139 9 111	(64 47)	1217	381 432	207 15	259	17 3 27	66 26 .72 86	.302 .358 .505

Rey Ordonez

Bats: Right **Throws:** Right **Pos:** SS-148; PH/PR-1   **Ht:** 5'9" **Wt:** 159 **Born:** 11/11/72 **Age:** 29

		BATTING									BASERUNNING	PERCENTAGES
Year Team	Lg	G AB H	2B 3B HR	(Hm Rd)	TB	R RBI	TBB IBB	SO	HBP SH SF	SB CS SB% GDP	Avg OBP SLG
1996 New York	NL	151 502 129	12 4 1	(0 1)	152	51 30	22 12	53	1 4 1	1 3 .25 12	.257 .289 .303
1997 New York	NL	120 356 77	5 3 1	(1 0)	91	35 33	18 3	36	1 14 2	11 5 .69 10	.216 .255 .256
1998 New York	NL	153 505 124	20 2 1	(0 1)	151	46 42	23 7	60	1 15 4	3 6 .33 11	.246 .278 .299
1999 New York	NL	154 520 134	24 2 1	(1 0)	165	49 60	49 12	59	1 11 7	8 4 .67 16	.258 .319 .317
2000 New York	NL	45 133 25	5 0 0	(0 0)	30	10 9	17 2	16	0 4 1	0 0 — 4	.188 .278 .226
2001 New York	NL	149 461 114	24 4 3	(0 3)	155	31 44	34 17	43	1 7 2	3 2 .60 17	.247 .299 .336
6 ML YEARS		772 2477 603	90 15 7	(2 5)	744	222 218	163 53	267	5 55 17	26 20 .57 70	.243 .290 .300

Eddie Oropesa

Pitches: Left **Bats:** Left **Pos:** RP-30   **Ht:** 6'3" **Wt:** 215 **Born:** 11/23/71 **Age:** 30

		HOW MUCH HE PITCHED					WHAT HE GAVE UP										THE RESULTS						
Year Team	Lg	G GS CG GF	IP	BFP	H	R	ER	HR SH SF HB	TBB IBB	SO	WP Bk	W	L	Pct.	ShO	Sv-Op	Hld	ERA
1993 St. Paul	IND	4 3 0 0	18.2	—	6	4	4	— — — —	9	19	—	3	1	.750	—	0- —	—	1.93
1994 Vero Beach	A+	19 10 1 3	72	285	54	24	17	2 3 2 4	25 2	67	2 0	4	3	.571	1	0- —	—	2.13
1995 San Antonio	AA	16 0 0 7	17.1	87	22	8	6	2 1 2 3	12 1	16	0 1	1	1	.500	0	1- —	—	3.12
Vero Beach	A+	19 1 0 7	28.1	120	25	12	12	0 1 2 3	10 0	23	4 2	3	1	.750	0	1- —	—	3.81
San Berndno	A+	1 0 0 1	1	3	0	0	0	0 0 0 0	0 0	0	0 0	0	0	—	0	1- —	—	0.00
1996 San Berndno	A+	33 19 0 2	156.1	669	133	74	58	8 1 3 6	77 1	133	8 4	11	6	.647	0	1- —	—	3.34
1997 Shreveport	AA	43 9 1 12	124	531	122	58	54	7 7 4 4	64 0	65	6 6	7	7	.500	0	0- —	—	3.92
1998 Shreveport	AA	32 20 2 3	143	623	143	71	60	6 7 5 7	67 3	104	15 2	7	11	.389	0	0- —	—	3.78
1999 Bakersfield	A+	2 1 0 0	10	41	13	5	4	2 0 0 0	1 0	10	2 0	2	0	1.000	0	0- —	—	3.60
Fresno	AAA	21 18 1 0	102	460	113	69	55	15 3 1 3	49 0	61	13 4	6	5	.545	0	0- —	—	4.85
2000 Shreveport	AA	59 2 0 23	76.1	341	70	38	26	6 3 1 3	40 6	76	3 2	2	4	.333	0	4- —	—	3.07
2001 Scrantn-WB	AAA	14 1 0 3	15.1	61	14	5	4	1 0 0 0	4 1	11	1 0	1	1	.500	0	1- —	—	2.35
Clearwater	A+	2 0 0 0	2	10	2	0	0	0 0 0 1	1 0	3	0 0	0	0	—	0	0- —	—	0.00
2001 Philadelphia	NL	30 0 0 4	19	87	16	10	10	1 1 0 0	17 6	15	1 0	1	0	1.000	0	0-1	6	4.74

Jesse Orosco

Pitches: Left **Bats:** Right **Pos:** RP-35   **Ht:** 6'2" **Wt:** 205 **Born:** 4/21/57 **Age:** 45

		HOW MUCH HE PITCHED					WHAT HE GAVE UP										THE RESULTS						
Year Team	Lg	G GS CG GF	IP	BFP	H	R	ER	HR SH SF HB	TBB IBB	SO	WP Bk	W	L	Pct.	ShO	Sv-Op	Hld	ERA
2001 Las Vegas *	AAA	10 0 0 1	7.1	27	4	0	0	0 0 0 0	2 0	11	1 0	1	0	1.000	0	0- —	—	0.00
1979 New York	NL	18 2 0 6	35	154	33	20	19	4 3 0 2	22 0	22	0 0	1	2	.333	0	0-0	—	4.89
1981 New York	NL	8 0 0 4	17.1	69	13	4	3	2 2 0 0	6 2	18	0 1	0	1	.000	0	1-1	0	1.56
1982 New York	NL	54 2 0 22	109.1	451	92	37	33	7 5 4 2	40 2	89	3 2	4	10	.286	0	4-5	0	2.72
1983 New York	NL	62 0 0 42	110	432	76	27	18	3 4 3 1	38 7	84	1 2	13	7	.650	0	17-22	1	1.47
1984 New York	NL	60 0 0 52	87	355	58	29	25	7 3 3 2	34 6	85	1 1	10	6	.625	0	31-38	0	2.59
1985 New York	NL	54 0 0 39	79	331	66	26	24	6 1 1 0	34 7	68	4 0	8	6	.571	0	17-25	1	2.73
1986 New York	NL	58 0 0 40	81	338	64	23	21	6 2 3 3	35 3	62	2 0	8	6	.571	0	21-29	1	2.33
1987 New York	NL	58 0 0 41	77	335	78	41	38	5 5 4 2	31 9	78	2 0	3	9	.250	0	16-22	4	4.44
1988 Los Angeles	NL	55 0 0 21	53	229	41	18	16	4 3 3 2	30 3	43	1 0	3	2	.600	0	9-15	14	2.72
1989 Cleveland	AL	69 0 0 29	78	312	54	20	18	7 8 3 2	26 4	79	0 0	3	4	.429	0	3-7	12	2.08
1990 Cleveland	AL	55 0 0 28	64.2	289	58	35	28	9 5 3 0	38 7	55	1 0	5	4	.556	0	2-3	2	3.90
1991 Cleveland	AL	47 0 0 20	45.2	202	52	20	19	4 1 3 1	15 8	36	1 1	2	0	1.000	0	0-0	3	3.74
1992 Milwaukee	AL	59 0 0 14	39	174	33	15	14	5 0 2 1	13 1	40	2 0	3	1	.750	0	1-2	11	3.23
1993 Milwaukee	AL	57 0 0 27	56.2	233	47	25	20	2 1 2 3	17 3	67	3 1	3	5	.375	0	8-13	11	3.18
1994 Milwaukee	AL	40 0 0 5	39	174	32	26	22	4 0 2 2	26 2	36	0 0	3	1	.750	0	0-4	8	5.08
1995 Baltimore	AL	65 0 0 23	49.2	200	28	19	18	4 7 5 0	27 7	58	2 1	2	4	.333	0	3-6	15	3.26

165

Year Team	Lg	G	GS	CG	GF	IP	BFP	H	R	ER	HR	SH	SF	HB	TBB	IBB	SO	WP	Bk	W	L	Pct.	ShO	Sv-Op	Hld	ERA
		HOW MUCH HE PITCHED						**WHAT HE GAVE UP**												**THE RESULTS**						
1996 Baltimore	AL	66	0	0	10	55.2	236	42	22	21	5	2	1	2	28	4	52	2	0	3	1	.750	0	0-3	19	3.40
1997 Baltimore	AL	71	0	0	12	50.1	205	29	13	13	6	1	2	0	30	0	46	1	1	6	3	.667	0	0-4	21	2.32
1998 Baltimore	AL	69	0	0	26	56.2	243	46	20	20	6	4	2	1	28	1	50	3	1	4	1	.800	0	7-9	9	3.18
1999 Baltimore	AL	65	0	0	12	32	144	28	21	19	5	2	3	2	20	3	35	2	0	0	2	.000	0	1-4	12	5.34
2000 St. Louis	NL	6	0	0	0	2.1	16	3	3	1	1	0	0	2	3	2	4	0	0	0	0	—	0	0-0	3	3.86
2001 Los Angeles	NL	35	0	0	7	16	69	17	7	7	3	0	1	0	7	1	21	0	0	0	1	.000	0	0-2	10	3.94
22 ML YEARS		1131	4	0	480	1234.1	5175	990	471	417	105	54	49	31	548	82	1128	31	11	84	76	.525	0	141-214	162	3.04

Bill Ortega

Bats: Right **Throws:** Right **Pos:** PH/PR-5 **Ht:** 6'4" **Wt:** 205 **Born:** 7/24/75 **Age:** 26

Year Team	Lg	G	AB	H	2B	3B	HR	(Hm	Rd)	TB	R	RBI	TBB	IBB	SO	HBP	SH	SF	SB	CS	SB%	GDP	Avg	OBP	SLG
				BATTING															**BASERUNNING**				**PERCENTAGES**		
1997 Pr William	A+	73	249	57	14	0	0	—	—	71	23	15	21	1	42	0	1	0	1	2	.33	10	.229	.289	.285
1998 Peoria	A	105	398	110	23	2	2	—	—	143	57	60	39	0	69	5	3	2	4	8	.33	14	.276	.347	.359
1999 Potomac	A+	110	421	129	27	4	9	—	—	191	66	74	38	2	69	4	6	3	7	7	.50	11	.306	.367	.454
Arkansas	AA	20	69	26	9	0	2	—	—	41	10	10	10	0	9	0	1	0	0	0	—	4	.377	.456	.594
2000 Arkansas	AA	86	332	108	18	5	12	—	—	172	51	62	28	4	42	4	0	4	1	5	.17	10	.325	.380	.518
2001 Memphis	AAA	134	495	142	26	4	6	—	—	194	55	62	40	4	74	5	0	3	6	6	.50	17	.287	.344	.392
2001 St. Louis	NL	5	5	1	0	0	0	(0	0)	1	0	0	0	0	0	0	0	0	0	0	—	0	.200	.200	.200

David Ortiz

Bats: Left **Throws:** Left **Pos:** DH-80; 1B-8; PH/PR-7 **Ht:** 6'4" **Wt:** 230 **Born:** 11/18/75 **Age:** 26

Year Team	Lg	G	AB	H	2B	3B	HR	(Hm	Rd)	TB	R	RBI	TBB	IBB	SO	HBP	SH	SF	SB	CS	SB%	GDP	Avg	OBP	SLG
				BATTING															**BASERUNNING**				**PERCENTAGES**		
2001 Twins *	R	4	10	4	0	0	0	—	—	4	3	1	3	1	1	0	0	0	1	0	1.00	0	.400	.538	.400
Fort Myers *	A+	1	3	0	0	0	0	—	—	0	0	0	1	0	0	0	0	0	0	0	—	0	.000	.250	.000
New Britain *	AA	9	37	9	4	0	0	—	—	13	3	1	3	0	9	0	0	1	0	0	—	1	.243	.293	.351
1997 Minnesota	AL	15	49	16	3	0	1	(0	1)	22	10	6	2	0	19	0	0	0	0	0	—	1	.327	.353	.449
1998 Minnesota	AL	86	278	77	20	0	9	(2	7)	124	47	46	39	3	72	5	0	4	1	0	1.00	8	.277	.371	.446
1999 Minnesota	AL	10	20	0	0	0	0	(0	0)	0	1	0	5	0	12	0	0	0	0	0	—	2	.000	.200	.000
2000 Minnesota	AL	130	415	117	36	1	10	(7	3)	185	59	63	57	2	81	0	0	6	1	0	1.00	13	.282	.364	.446
2001 Minnesota	AL	89	303	71	17	1	18	(6	12)	144	46	48	40	8	68	1	1	2	1	0	1.00	6	.234	.324	.475
5 ML YEARS		330	1065	281	76	2	38	(15	23)	475	163	163	143	13	252	6	1	12	3	0	1.00	30	.264	.351	.446

Hector Ortiz

Bats: Right **Throws:** Right **Pos:** C-55; DH-1; PH/PR-1 **Ht:** 6'0" **Wt:** 205 **Born:** 10/14/69 **Age:** 32

Year Team	Lg	G	AB	H	2B	3B	HR	(Hm	Rd)	TB	R	RBI	TBB	IBB	SO	HBP	SH	SF	SB	CS	SB%	GDP	Avg	OBP	SLG
				BATTING															**BASERUNNING**				**PERCENTAGES**		
2001 Omaha *	AAA	42	150	39	7	0	2	—	—	52	19	15	15	0	26	0	1	4	0	3	.00	5	.260	.320	.347
1998 Kansas City	AL	4	4	0	0	0	0	(0	0)	0	1	0	0	0	0	0	0	0	0	0	—	0	.000	.000	.000
2000 Kansas City	AL	26	88	34	6	0	0	(0	0)	40	15	5	8	1	8	1	2	0	0	0	—	0	.386	.443	.455
2001 Kansas City	AL	56	154	38	6	1	0	(0	0)	46	12	11	9	0	24	1	2	0	1	3	.25	5	.247	.293	.299
3 ML YEARS		86	246	72	12	1	0	(0	0)	86	28	16	17	1	32	2	4	0	1	3	.25	5	.293	.343	.350

Jose Ortiz

Bats: Right **Throws:** Right **Pos:** 2B-61; PH/PR-3; DH-1 **Ht:** 5'9" **Wt:** 177 **Born:** 6/13/77 **Age:** 25

Year Team	Lg	G	AB	H	2B	3B	HR	(Hm	Rd)	TB	R	RBI	TBB	IBB	SO	HBP	SH	SF	SB	CS	SB%	GDP	Avg	OBP	SLG
				BATTING															**BASERUNNING**				**PERCENTAGES**		
1996 Athletics	R	52	200	66	12	8	4	—	—	106	43	25	20	2	34	1	1	1	16	5	.76	1	.330	.392	.530
Modesto	A+	1	4	1	0	0	0	—	—	1	0	0	0	0	1	0	0	0	0	0	—	0	.250	.250	.250
1997 Modesto	A+	128	494	122	25	7	16	—	—	209	92	58	60	2	107	6	3	4	22	14	.61	7	.245	.332	.421
1998 Huntsville	AA	94	354	98	24	2	6	—	—	144	70	55	48	0	63	5	6	2	22	8	.73	6	.277	.369	.407
1999 Vancouver	AAA	107	377	107	29	2	9	—	—	167	66	45	29	1	50	9	3	4	13	4	.76	8	.284	.346	.443
2000 Sacramento	AAA	131	518	182	34	5	24	—	—	298	107	108	47	0	64	4	0	2	22	9	.71	21	.351	.408	.575
2001 Sacramento	AAA	65	256	70	16	4	7	—	—	115	41	39	25	0	50	3	1	0	7	4	.64	5	.273	.345	.449
2000 Oakland	AL	7	11	2	0	0	0	(0	0)	2	4	1	2	0	3	0	0	0	0	0	—	0	.182	.308	.182
2001 Oak-Col		64	246	59	8	1	13	(9	4)	108	42	38	17	0	41	4	1	2	4	1	.80	9	.240	.297	.439
2001 Oakland	AL	11	42	7	0	0	0	(0	0)	7	4	3	3	0	5	0	0	1	1	0	1.00	4	.167	.217	.167
Colorado	NL	53	204	52	8	1	13	(9	4)	101	38	35	14	0	36	4	1	1	3	1	.75	5	.255	.314	.495
2 ML YEARS		71	257	61	8	1	13	(9	4)	110	46	39	19	0	44	4	1	2	4	1	.80	9	.237	.298	.428

Ramon Ortiz

Pitches: Right **Bats:** Right **Pos:** SP-32 **Ht:** 6'0" **Wt:** 170 **Born:** 3/23/76 **Age:** 26

Year Team	Lg	G	GS	CG	GF	IP	BFP	H	R	ER	HR	SH	SF	HB	TBB	IBB	SO	WP	Bk	W	L	Pct.	ShO	Sv-Op	Hld	ERA
		HOW MUCH HE PITCHED						**WHAT HE GAVE UP**												**THE RESULTS**						
1999 Anaheim	AL	9	9	0	0	48.1	218	50	35	35	7	0	2	2	25	0	44	2	2	2	3	.400	0	0-0	0	6.52
2000 Anaheim	AL	18	18	2	0	111.1	472	96	69	63	18	4	4	2	55	0	73	7	4	8	6	.571	0	0-0	0	5.09
2001 Anaheim	AL	32	32	2	0	208.2	916	223	114	101	25	9	6	12	76	6	135	7	0	13	11	.542	0	0-0	0	4.36
3 ML YEARS		59	59	4	0	368.1	1606	369	218	199	50	13	12	16	156	6	252	16	6	23	20	.535	0	0-0	0	4.86

Russ Ortiz

Pitches: Right Bats: Right Pos: SP-33   Ht: 6'1" Wt: 210 Born: 6/5/74 Age: 28

			HOW MUCH HE PITCHED				WHAT HE GAVE UP											THE RESULTS					
Year Team	Lg	G	GS	CG	GF	IP	BFP	H	R	ER	HR	SH	SF	HB	TBB	IBB	SO	WP	Bk	W	L	Pct.	ShO	Sv-Op	Hld	ERA
1998 San Francisco	NL	22	13	0	3	88.1	394	90	51	49	11	5	4	4	46	1	75	3	0	4	4	.500	0	0-0	1	4.99
1999 San Francisco	NL	33	33	3	0	207.2	922	189	109	88	24	11	6	6	125	5	164	13	0	18	9	.667	0	0-0	0	3.81
2000 San Francisco	NL	33	32	0	0	195.2	871	192	117	109	28	10	6	7	112	1	167	8	0	14	12	.538	0	0-0	0	5.01
2001 San Francisco	NL	33	33	1	0	218.2	911	187	90	80	13	10	4	0	91	3	169	8	1	17	9	.654	1	0-0	0	3.29
4 ML YEARS		121	111	4	3	710.1	3098	658	367	326	76	36	20	17	374	10	575	32	1	53	34	.609	1	0-0	1	4.13

Keith Osik

Bats: R Throws: R Pos: C-39; PH/PR-9; 1B-5; 3B-3; 2B-2; RF-1   Ht: 6'0" Wt: 192 Born: 10/22/68 Age: 33

						BATTING												BASERUNNING				PERCENTAGES		
Year Team	Lg	G	AB	H	2B	3B	HR	(Hm	Rd)	TB	R	RBI	TBB	IBB	SO	HBP	SH	SF	SB	CS	SB%	GDP	Avg	OBP	SLG
1996 Pittsburgh	NL	48	140	41	14	1	1	(0	1)	60	18	14	14	1	22	1	1	0	1	0	1.00	3	.293	.361	.429
1997 Pittsburgh	NL	49	105	27	9	1	0	(0	0)	38	10	7	9	1	21	1	0	0	1	0	1.00	1	.257	.322	.362
1998 Pittsburgh	NL	39	98	21	4	0	0	(0	0)	25	8	7	13	2	16	2	2	1	1	2	.33	4	.214	.316	.255
1999 Pittsburgh	NL	66	167	31	3	1	2	(1	1)	42	12	13	11	0	30	1	1	1	0	0	—	8	.186	.239	.251
2000 Pittsburgh	NL	46	123	36	6	1	4	(1	3)	56	11	22	14	0	11	5	1	0	3	0	1.00	2	.293	.387	.455
2001 Pittsburgh	NL	56	120	25	4	0	2	(0	2)	35	9	13	13	0	24	3	0	1	1	0	1.00	1	.208	.299	.292
6 ML YEARS		304	753	181	40	4	9	(2	7)	256	68	76	74	4	124	13	7	3	6	3	.67	19	.240	.318	.340

Jimmy Osting

Pitches: Left Bats: Right Pos: RP-3   Ht: 6'5" Wt: 190 Born: 4/7/77 Age: 25

			HOW MUCH HE PITCHED				WHAT HE GAVE UP											THE RESULTS					
Year Team	Lg	G	GS	CG	GF	IP	BFP	H	R	ER	HR	SH	SF	HB	TBB	IBB	SO	WP	Bk	W	L	Pct.	ShO	Sv-Op	Hld	ERA
1995 Danville	R+	11	10	0	0	39	190	46	34	31	1	0	1	0	25	0	43	12	0	2	7	.222	0	0--	—	7.15
1996 Eugene	A-	5	5	0	0	24.1	99	14	11	7	1	0	0	0	13	0	35	1	0	2	1	.667	0	0--	—	2.59
1997 Macon	A	15	15	0	0	57.2	251	54	28	21	3	1	0	2	29	0	62	5	0	2	3	.400	0	0--	—	3.28
1999 Macon	A	27	22	0	5	147	581	130	52	47	13	2	1	5	30	0	131	2	0	14	4	.778	0	2--	—	2.88
2000 Myrtle Bch	A+	4	4	0	0	23	94	25	8	8	0	0	1	0	5	0	17	0	0	2	2	.500	0	0--	—	3.13
Richmond	AAA	3	3	0	0	9.1	52	15	12	12	2	1	1	0	11	1	2	1	0	0	2	.000	0	0--	—	11.57
Greenville	AA	11	11	0	0	71.1	302	67	30	21	6	2	1	0	29	1	52	1	0	2	6	.250	0	0--	—	2.65
Reading	AA	10	9	1	0	56.2	245	53	17	15	1	6	2	4	26	2	31	2	0	4	2	.667	1	0--	—	2.38
2001 Carolina	AA	1	1	0	0	5	22	3	1	1	1	0	0	0	3	0	3	0	0	1	0	1.000	0	0--	—	1.80
Mobile	AA	18	18	0	0	97.2	414	85	41	39	6	4	3	3	42	1	69	7	0	9	4	.692	0	0--	—	3.59
Portland	AAA	5	5	0	0	25.1	124	41	27	27	5	0	0	1	10	0	15	0	0	1	4	.200	0	0--	—	9.59
2001 San Diego	NL	3	0	0	1	2	9	1	0	0	0	0	0	0	2	1	3	0	0	0	0	—	0	0-0	0	0.00

Antonio Osuna

Pitches: Right Bats: Right Pos: RP-4   Ht: 5'11" Wt: 206 Born: 4/12/73 Age: 29

			HOW MUCH HE PITCHED				WHAT HE GAVE UP											THE RESULTS					
Year Team	Lg	G	GS	CG	GF	IP	BFP	H	R	ER	HR	SH	SF	HB	TBB	IBB	SO	WP	Bk	W	L	Pct.	ShO	Sv-Op	Hld	ERA
1995 Los Angeles	NL	39	0	0	8	44.2	186	39	22	22	5	2	1	1	20	2	46	1	0	2	4	.333	0	0-2	11	4.43
1996 Los Angeles	NL	73	0	0	21	84	342	65	33	28	6	7	5	2	32	12	85	3	2	9	6	.600	0	4-9	16	3.00
1997 Los Angeles	NL	48	0	0	18	61.2	245	46	15	15	6	4	1	1	19	2	68	2	0	3	4	.429	0	0-0	10	2.19
1998 Los Angeles	NL	54	0	0	25	64.2	272	50	26	22	8	2	2	2	32	0	72	1	0	7	1	.875	0	6-11	12	3.06
1999 Los Angeles	NL	5	0	0	1	4.2	22	4	5	4	0	0	0	1	3	0	5	1	0	0	0	—	0	0-0	2	7.71
2000 Los Angeles	NL	46	0	0	16	67.1	293	57	30	28	7	4	3	2	35	2	70	1	2	3	6	.333	0	0-3	4	3.74
2001 Chicago	AL	4	0	0	0	4.1	23	8	10	10	3	0	1	1	2	1	6	0	0	0	0	—	0	0-1	0	20.77
7 ML YEARS		269	0	0	89	331.1	1383	269	141	129	35	19	13	10	143	19	352	9	4	24	21	.533	0	10-26	55	3.50

Roy Oswalt

Pitches: Right Bats: Right Pos: SP-20; RP-8   Ht: 6'0" Wt: 170 Born: 8/29/77 Age: 24

			HOW MUCH HE PITCHED				WHAT HE GAVE UP											THE RESULTS					
Year Team	Lg	G	GS	CG	GF	IP	BFP	H	R	ER	HR	SH	SF	HB	TBB	IBB	SO	WP	Bk	W	L	Pct.	ShO	Sv-Op	Hld	ERA
1997 Astros	R	5	5	0	0	28.1	117	25	7	2	2	0	0	0	7	0	28	0	0	1	1	.500	0	0--	—	0.64
Auburn	A-	9	9	1	0	51.2	220	50	29	26	1	0	1	6	15	1	44	3	1	2	4	.333	1	0--	—	4.53
1998 Astros	R	4	4	0	0	16	62	10	6	4	2	1	1	3	1	0	27	0	1	1	1	.500	0	0--	—	2.25
Auburn	A-	11	11	0	0	70.1	289	49	24	17	3	1	2	3	31	0	67	2	1	4	5	.444	0	0--	—	2.18
1999 Michigan	A	22	22	2	0	151.1	643	144	78	75	8	2	5	7	54	0	143	8	4	13	4	.765	0	0--	—	4.46
2000 Kissimmee	A+	8	8	0	0	45.1	191	52	15	15	1	1	1	1	11	0	47	0	1	4	3	.571	0	0--	—	2.98
Round Rock	AA	19	18	2	0	129.2	521	106	37	28	5	4	2	3	22	1	141	4	1	11	4	.733	2	0--	—	1.94
2001 New Orleans	AAA	5	5	0	0	31	128	32	16	15	4	0	0	2	6	0	34	0	1	2	3	.400	0	0--	—	4.35
2001 Houston	NL	28	20	3	4	141.2	575	126	48	43	13	4	4	6	24	2	144	0	0	14	3	.824	1	0-0	0	2.73

Lyle Overbay

Bats: Left Throws: Left Pos: PH/PR-2   Ht: 6'2" Wt: 215 Born: 1/28/77 Age: 25

						BATTING												BASERUNNING				PERCENTAGES		
Year Team	Lg	G	AB	H	2B	3B	HR	(Hm	Rd)	TB	R	RBI	TBB	IBB	SO	HBP	SH	SF	SB	CS	SB%	GDP	Avg	OBP	SLG
1999 Missoula	R+	75	306	105	25	7	12	—	—	180	66	101	40	2	53	2	0	4	10	3	.77	14	.343	.418	.588
2000 South Bend	A	71	259	86	19	3	6	—	—	129	47	47	27	0	36	2	0	2	9	2	.82	2	.332	.397	.498
El Paso	AA	62	244	86	16	2	8	—	—	130	43	49	28	0	39	2	0	2	3	2	.60	6	.352	.420	.533
2001 El Paso	AA	138	532	187	49	3	13	—	—	281	82	100	67	11	92	5	0	8	5	4	.56	6	.352	.423	.528
2001 Arizona	NL	2	2	1	0	0	0	(0	0)	1	0	0	0	0	1	0	0	0	0	0	—	0	.500	.500	.500

Eric Owens

Bats: R **Throws:** R **Pos:** RF-72; CF-37; PH/PR-17; DH-1; LF-1 **Ht:** 6'0" **Wt:** 198 **Born:** 2/3/71 **Age:** 31

Year Team	Lg	G	AB	H	2B	3B	HR	(Hm	Rd)	TB	R	RBI	TBB	IBB	SO	HBP	SH	SF	SB	CS	SB%	GDP	Avg	OBP	SLG
2001 Calgary *	AAA	3	15	4	2	0	0	—	—	6	2	2	0	0	2	0	0	0	1	0	1.00	1	.267	.267	.400
1995 Cincinnati	NL	2	2	2	0	0	0	(0	0)	2	0	1	0	0	0	0	0	0	0	0	—	0	1.000	1.000	1.000
1996 Cincinnati	NL	88	205	41	6	0	0	(0	0)	47	26	9	23	1	38	1	1	2	16	2	.89	2	.200	.281	.229
1997 Cincinnati	NL	27	57	15	0	0	0	(0	0)	15	8	3	4	0	11	0	0	0	3	2	.60	2	.263	.311	.263
1998 Milwaukee	NL	34	40	5	2	0	1	(0	1)	10	5	4	2	0	6	0	1	0	0	3	.000		.125	.167	.250
1999 San Diego	NL	149	440	117	22	3	9	(2	7)	172	55	61	38	2	50	3	2	2	33	7	.83	12	.266	.327	.391
2000 San Diego	NL	145	583	171	19	7	6	(4	2)	222	87	51	45	4	63	4	0	4	29	14	.67	16	.293	.346	.381
2001 Florida	NL	119	400	101	16	5	5	(4	4)	134	51	28	29	2	59	0	4	1	8	6	.57	13	.253	.302	.335
7 ML YEARS		564	1727	452	65	11	21	(10	11)	602	232	157	141	9	227	8	9	9	89	31	.74	48	.262	.319	.349

Vicente Padilla

Pitches: Right **Bats:** Right **Pos:** RP-23 **Ht:** 6'2" **Wt:** 200 **Born:** 9/27/77 **Age:** 24

Year Team	Lg	G	GS	CG	GF	IP	BFP	H	R	ER	HR	SH	SF	HB	TBB	IBB	SO	WP	Bk	W	L	Pct.	ShO	Sv-Op	Hld	ERA
2001 Scrantn-WB *	AAA	16	16	0	0	81.2	313	64	24	22	8	1	3	3	11	0	75	3	1	7	0	1.000	0	0- -		2.42
1999 Arizona	NL	5	0	0	2	2.2	19	7	5	5	1	1	0	0	3	0	0	0	0	0	1	.000	0	0-1	1	16.88
2000 Ari-Phi	NL	55	0	0	16	65.1	291	72	33	27	3	5	3	1	28	7	51	1	0	4	7	.364	0	2-7	15	3.72
2001 Philadelphia	NL	23	0	0	5	34	144	36	18	16	1	0	0	0	12	0	29	1	0	3	1	.750	0	0-3	1	4.24
2000 Arizona	NL	27	0	0	12	35	143	32	10	9	0	0	1	0	10	2	30	0	0	2	1	.667	0	0-1	7	2.31
Philadelphia	NL	28	0	0	4	30.1	148	40	23	18	3	5	2	1	18	5	21	1	0	2	6	.250	0	2-6	8	5.34
3 ML YEARS		83	0	0	23	102	454	115	56	48	5	6	3	1	43	7	80	2	0	7	9	.438	0	2-11	17	4.24

Lance Painter

Pitches: Left **Bats:** Left **Pos:** RP-23 **Ht:** 6'1" **Wt:** 200 **Born:** 7/21/67 **Age:** 34

Year Team	Lg	G	GS	CG	GF	IP	BFP	H	R	ER	HR	SH	SF	HB	TBB	IBB	SO	WP	Bk	W	L	Pct.	ShO	Sv-Op	Hld	ERA
2001 Dunedin *	A+	5	1	0	0	9.1	37	10	1	1	0	2	0	0	1	0	10	1	0	1	1	.500	0	0- -		0.96
Indianapols *	AAA	8	0	0	3	9	43	10	5	3	2	1	0	0	6	0	7	0	0	0	0		0	0- -		5.00
1993 Colorado	NL	10	6	1	2	39	166	52	26	26	5	1	0	0	9	0	16	2	0	2	2	.500	0	0-0	0	6.00
1994 Colorado	NL	15	14	0	1	73.2	336	91	51	50	9	3	5	1	26	2	41	3	1	4	6	.400	0	0-0	0	6.11
1995 Colorado	NL	33	1	0	7	45.1	198	55	23	22	9	0	0	2	10	0	36	4	1	3	0	1.000	0	1-1	4	4.37
1996 Colorado	NL	34	1	0	7	50.2	234	56	37	33	12	3	3	3	25	3	48	1	0	4	2	.667	0	0-1	4	5.86
1997 St. Louis	NL	14	0	0	4	17	69	13	9	9	1	0	0	0	8	2	11	0	0	1	1	.500	0	0-0	3	4.76
1998 St. Louis	NL	65	0	0	9	47.1	207	42	24	21	5	4	2	4	28	3	39	2	0	4	0	1.000	0	1-2	21	3.99
1999 St. Louis	NL	56	4	0	10	63.1	272	63	37	34	6	4	3	2	25	1	56	4	0	4	5	.444	0	1-3	10	4.83
2000 Toronto	AL	42	2	0	11	66.2	285	69	37	35	9	5	1	2	22	1	53	4	0	2	0	1.000	0	0-1	5	4.73
2001 Tor-Mil		23	0	0	7	29	139	38	22	21	7	0	1	2	18	2	20	0	0	1	1	.500	0	0-0		6.52
2001 Toronto	AL	10	0	0	3	18.1	91	27	17	16	4	0	0	1	11	0	14	0	0	0	1	.000	0	0-0	0	7.85
Milwaukee	NL	13	0	0	4	10.2	48	11	5	5	3	0	0	0	7	2	6	0	0	1	0	1.000	0	0-0	0	4.22
9 ML YEARS		292	28	1	55	432	1906	479	266	251	63	20	14	15	171	14	320	20	2	25	17	.595	0	3-8	47	5.23

Orlando Palmeiro

Bats: L **Throws:** L **Pos:** PH/PR-33; DH-30; RF-28; LF-26; CF-7 **Ht:** 5'11" **Wt:** 180 **Born:** 1/19/69 **Age:** 33

Year Team	Lg	G	AB	H	2B	3B	HR	(Hm	Rd)	TB	R	RBI	TBB	IBB	SO	HBP	SH	SF	SB	CS	SB%	GDP	Avg	OBP	SLG
1995 California	AL	15	20	7	0	0	0	(0	0)	7	3	1	1	0	1	0	0	0	0	0	—	0	.350	.381	.350
1996 California	AL	50	87	25	6	1	0	(0	0)	33	6	6	8	1	13	2	1	0	0	1	.00	1	.287	.361	.379
1997 Anaheim	AL	74	134	29	2	2	0	(0	0)	35	19	8	17	1	11	1	3	1	2	2	.50	4	.216	.307	.261
1998 Anaheim	AL	75	165	53	7	2	0	(0	0)	64	28	21	20	1	11	0	7	0	5	4	.56	2	.321	.395	.388
1999 Anaheim	AL	109	317	88	12	1	1	(0	1)	105	46	23	39	1	30	6	6	3	5	5	.50	4	.278	.364	.331
2000 Anaheim	AL	108	243	73	20	2	0	(0	0)	97	38	25	38	0	20	2	10	3	4	1	.80	4	.300	.395	.399
2001 Anaheim	AL	104	230	56	10	1	2	(0	2)	74	29	23	25	2	24	3	7	5	6	6	.50	3	.243	.319	.322
7 ML YEARS		535	1196	331	57	9	3	(0	3)	415	169	107	148	6	110	14	34	12	22	19	.54	18	.277	.360	.347

Rafael Palmeiro

Bats: Left **Throws:** Left **Pos:** 1B-113; DH-46; PH/PR-1 **Ht:** 6'0" **Wt:** 190 **Born:** 9/24/64 **Age:** 37

Year Team	Lg	G	AB	H	2B	3B	HR	(Hm	Rd)	TB	R	RBI	TBB	IBB	SO	HBP	SH	SF	SB	CS	SB%	GDP	Avg	OBP	SLG
1986 Chicago	NL	22	73	18	4	0	3	(1	2)	31	9	12	4	0	6	1	0	0	1	1	.50	4	.247	.295	.425
1987 Chicago	NL	84	221	61	15	1	14	(5	9)	120	32	30	20	1	26	1	0	2	2	2	.50	4	.276	.336	.543
1988 Chicago	NL	152	580	178	41	5	8	(8	0)	253	75	53	38	6	34	3	2	6	12	2	.86	11	.307	.349	.436
1989 Texas	AL	156	559	154	23	4	8	(4	4)	209	76	64	63	3	48	6	2	2	4	3	.57	18	.275	.354	.374
1990 Texas	AL	154	598	191	35	6	14	(9	5)	280	72	89	40	6	59	3	2	8	3	3	.50	24	.319	.361	.468
1991 Texas	AL	159	631	203	49	3	26	(12	14)	336	115	88	68	10	72	6	2	7	4	3	.57	17	.322	.389	.532
1992 Texas	AL	159	608	163	27	4	22	(8	14)	264	84	85	72	8	83	10	5	6	2	3	.40	10	.268	.352	.434
1993 Texas	AL	160	597	176	40	2	37	(22	15)	331	124	105	73	22	85	5	2	9	22	3	.88	8	.295	.371	.554
1994 Baltimore	AL	111	436	139	32	0	23	(11	12)	240	82	76	54	1	63	2	0	6	7	3	.70	11	.319	.392	.550
1995 Baltimore	AL	143	554	172	30	2	39	(21	18)	323	89	104	62	5	65	3	0	5	3	1	.75	12	.310	.380	.583
1996 Baltimore	AL	162	626	181	40	2	39	(21	18)	342	110	142	95	12	96	3	0	8	8	0	1.00	9	.289	.381	.546
1997 Baltimore	AL	158	614	156	24	2	38	(20	18)	296	95	110	79	6	109	5	0	6	5	2	.71	14	.254	.329	.485
1998 Baltimore	AL	162	619	183	36	1	43	(25	18)	350	98	121	79	8	91	7	0	4	11	7	.61	14	.296	.379	.565
1999 Texas	AL	158	565	183	30	1	47	(28	19)	356	96	148	97	14	69	3	0	3	2	4	.33	13	.324	.420	.630
2000 Texas	AL	158	565	163	29	4	39	(26	13)	315	102	120	103	17	77	3	0	7	2	1	.67	14	.288	.397	.558
2001 Texas	AL	160	600	164	33	0	47	(23	24)	338	98	123	101	4	90	7	0	6	1	1	.50	8	.273	.381	.563
16 ML YEARS		2258	8446	2485	488	36	447	(244	203)	4386	1357	1470	1036	128	1073	68	15	91	89	39	.70	191	.294	.372	.519

Dean Palmer

Bats: Right **Throws:** Right **Pos:** DH-57

Ht: 6'1" **Wt:** 210 **Born:** 12/27/68 **Age:** 33

Year Team	Lg	G	AB	H	2B	3B	HR	(Hm	Rd)	TB	R	RBI	TBB	IBB	SO	HBP	SH	SF	SB	CS	SB%	GDP	Avg	OBP	SLG
2001 Toledo *	AAA	1	2	1	0	0	0	—		1	0	0	2	0	0	0	0	1	0	0	—	0	.500	.750	.500
1989 Texas	AL	16	19	2	2	0	0	(0	0)	4	0	1	0	0	12	0	0	1	0	0	—	0	.105	.100	.211
1991 Texas	AL	81	268	50	9	2	15	(6	9)	108	38	37	32	0	98	3	1	0	0	2	.00	4	.187	.281	.403
1992 Texas	AL	152	541	124	25	0	26	(11	15)	227	74	72	62	2	154	4	2	4	10	4	.71	9	.229	.311	.420
1993 Texas	AL	148	519	127	31	2	33	(12	21)	261	88	96	53	4	154	8	0	5	11	10	.52	5	.245	.321	.503
1994 Texas	AL	93	342	84	14	2	19	(11	8)	159	50	59	26	0	89	2	0	1	3	4	.43	7	.246	.302	.465
1995 Texas	AL	36	119	40	6	0	9	(5	4)	73	30	24	21	1	21	4	0	1	1	1	.50	2	.336	.448	.613
1996 Texas	AL	154	582	163	26	2	38	(19	19)	307	98	107	59	4	145	5	0	6	2	0	1.00	15	.280	.348	.527
1997 Tex-KC	AL	143	542	139	31	1	23	(10	13)	241	70	86	41	2	134	3	1	5	2	5	.50	7	.256	.310	.445
1998 Kansas City	AL	152	572	159	27	2	34	(21	13)	292	84	119	48	3	134	6	0	13	8	2	.80	18	.278	.333	.510
1999 Detroit	AL	150	560	147	25	2	38	(24	14)	290	92	100	57	3	153	10	0	4	3	3	.50	12	.263	.339	.518
2000 Detroit	AL	145	524	134	22	2	29	(15	14)	247	73	102	66	2	146	4	0	10	4	1	.80	9	.256	.338	.471
2001 Detroit	AL	57	216	48	11	0	11	(5	6)	92	34	40	27	0	59	3	0	0	1	0	1.00	4	.222	.317	.426
1997 Texas	AL	94	355	87	21	0	14	(6	8)	150	47	55	26	2	84	1	1	3	1	0	1.00	4	.245	.296	.423
Kansas City	AL	49	187	52	10	1	9	(4	5)	91	23	31	15	0	50	2	0	2	1	2	.33	3	.278	.335	.487
12 ML YEARS		1327	4804	1217	229	15	275	(139	136)	2301	731	843	492	21	1299	52	4	50	48	31	.61	91	.253	.326	.479

Jose Paniagua

Pitches: Right **Bats:** Right **Pos:** RP-60

Ht: 6'2" **Wt:** 190 **Born:** 8/20/73 **Age:** 28

Year Team	Lg	G	GS	CG	GF	IP	BFP	H	R	ER	HR	SH	SF	HB	TBB	IBB	SO	WP	Bk	W	L	Pct.	ShO	Sv-Op	Hld	ERA
1996 Montreal	NL	13	11	0	0	51	223	55	24	20	7	1	4	3	23	0	27	2	2	2	4	.333	0	0-0	0	3.53
1997 Montreal	NL	9	3	0	0	18	100	29	24	24	2	1	1	4	16	1	8	1	0	1	2	.333	0	0-0	0	12.00
1998 Seattle	AL	18	0	0	2	22	83	15	5	5	3	0	0	3	5	0	16	2	0	2	0	1.000	0	1-2	6	2.05
1999 Seattle	AL	59	0	0	16	77.2	350	75	37	35	5	4	3	7	52	4	74	6	0	6	11	.353	0	3-12	16	4.06
2000 Seattle	AL	69	0	0	26	80.1	344	68	31	31	6	3	5	7	38	3	71	4	1	3	0	1.000	0	5-8	14	3.47
2001 Seattle	AL	60	0	0	24	66	296	59	35	32	7	0	1	4	38	2	46	3	0	4	3	.571	0	3-4	16	4.36
6 ML YEARS		228	14	0	68	315	1396	301	156	147	30	9	11	28	172	10	242	18	3	18	20	.474	0	12-26	52	4.20

Craig Paquette

Bats: R **Throws:** R **Pos:** 3B-33; LF-33; PH/PR-28; RF-26; 1B-23; 2B-4

Ht: 6'0" **Wt:** 190 **Born:** 3/28/69 **Age:** 33

Year Team	Lg	G	AB	H	2B	3B	HR	(Hm	Rd)	TB	R	RBI	TBB	IBB	SO	HBP	SH	SF	SB	CS	SB%	GDP	Avg	OBP	SLG
1993 Oakland	AL	105	393	86	20	4	12	(8	4)	150	35	46	14	2	108	0	1	1	4	2	.67	7	.219	.245	.382
1994 Oakland	AL	14	49	7	2	0	0	(0	0)	9	0	0	0	0	14	0	1	0	1	0	1.00	0	.143	.143	.184
1995 Oakland	AL	105	283	64	13	1	13	(8	5)	118	42	49	12	0	88	1	3	5	5	2	.71	5	.226	.256	.417
1996 Kansas City	AL	118	429	111	15	1	22	(12	10)	194	61	67	23	2	101	2	3	5	5	3	.63	11	.259	.296	.452
1997 Kansas City	AL	77	252	58	15	1	8	(7	1)	99	26	33	10	0	57	2	1	2	2	2	.50	13	.230	.263	.393
1998 New York	NL	7	19	5	2	0	0			7	3	0	1	0	6	0	0	0	1	0	1.00	3	.263	.263	.368
1999 St. Louis	NL	48	157	45	6	0	10	(7	3)	81	21	37	6	0	38	0	1	2	1	0	1.00	6	.287	.309	.516
2000 St. Louis	NL	134	384	94	24	2	15	(13	2)	167	47	61	27	1	83	2	1	6	4	3	.57	5	.245	.294	.435
2001 St. Louis	NL	123	340	96	17	0	15	(8	7)	158	47	64	18	1	67	5	5	2	3	1	.75	11	.282	.326	.465
9 ML YEARS		731	2306	566	114	9	95	(63	32)	983	282	357	110	6	562	12	16	23	26	13	.67	61	.245	.281	.426

Chan Ho Park

Pitches: Right **Bats:** Right **Pos:** SP-35; RP-1

Ht: 6'2" **Wt:** 204 **Born:** 6/30/73 **Age:** 29

Year Team	Lg	G	GS	CG	GF	IP	BFP	H	R	ER	HR	SH	SF	HB	TBB	IBB	SO	WP	Bk	W	L	Pct.	ShO	Sv-Op	Hld	ERA
1994 Los Angeles	NL	2	0	0	1	4	23	5	5	5	1	0	0	1	5	0	6	0	0	0	0	—	0	0-0	0	11.25
1995 Los Angeles	NL	2	1	0	0	4	16	2	2	2	1	0	0	0	2	0	7	0	0	0	0	—	0	0-0	0	4.50
1996 Los Angeles	NL	48	10	0	7	108.2	477	82	48	44	7	8	1	4	71	3	119	4	3	5	5	.500	0	0-0	0	3.64
1997 Los Angeles	NL	32	29	2	1	192	792	149	80	72	24	9	5	8	70	1	166	4	1	14	8	.636	0	0-0	0	3.38
1998 Los Angeles	NL	34	34	2	0	220.2	946	199	101	91	16	11	10	11	97	1	191	6	2	15	9	.625	0	0-0	0	3.71
1999 Los Angeles	NL	33	33	0	0	194.1	883	208	120	113	31	10	5	14	100	4	174	11	1	13	11	.542	0	0-0	0	5.23
2000 Los Angeles	NL	34	34	3	0	226	963	173	92	82	21	12	5	12	124	4	217	13	0	18	10	.643	1	0-0	0	3.27
2001 Los Angeles	NL	36	35	2	0	234	981	183	98	91	23	16	7	20	91	1	218	3	3	15	11	.577	1	0-0	0	3.50
8 ML YEARS		221	176	9	9	1183.2	5081	1001	546	500	124	66	33	70	560	14	1098	41	11	80	54	.597	2	0-0	4	3.80

Christian Parker

Pitches: Right **Bats:** Right **Pos:** SP-1

Ht: 6'1" **Wt:** 200 **Born:** 7/3/75 **Age:** 26

Year Team	Lg	G	GS	CG	GF	IP	BFP	H	R	ER	HR	SH	SF	HB	TBB	IBB	SO	WP	Bk	W	L	Pct.	ShO	Sv-Op	Hld	ERA
1996 Vermont	A-	14	14	2	0	80	322	63	26	22	1	2	1	4	22	0	61	8	3	7	1	.875	1	0-—	0	2.48
1997 Cape Fear	A	25	25	0	0	153	640	146	72	53	5	9	6	7	49	0	106	9	2	11	10	.524	0	0-—	0	3.12
Wst Plm Bch	A+	3	3	0	0	19	81	22	7	7	0	0	0	0	5	0	10	2	0	1	0	1.000	0	0-—	0	3.32
1998 Harrisburg	AA	36	16	0	8	126.2	550	124	66	49	9	6	2	10	47	3	73	8	0	6	6	.500	0	5-—	0	3.48
1999 Ottawa	AAA	7	0	0	2	10.2	49	10	9	9	0	1	1	2	7	0	5	0	0	0	1	.000	0	0-—	0	7.59
Harrisburg	AA	36	6	0	16	88.2	386	86	39	36	1	5	0	15	37	2	45	10	2	8	5	.615	0	3-—	0	3.65
2000 Norwich	AA	28	28	4	0	204	860	196	86	71	8	11	6	9	58	5	147	8	5	14	6	.700	0	0-—	0	3.13
2001 New York	AL	1	1	0	0	3	18	8	7	7	2	0	0	0	1	0	1	0	0	0	1	.000	0	0-0	0	21.00

Chad Paronto

Pitches: Right **Bats:** Right **Pos:** RP-24

Ht: 6'5" **Wt:** 250 **Born:** 7/28/75 **Age:** 26

Year Team	Lg	G	GS	CG	GF	IP	BFP	H	R	ER	HR	SH	SF	HB	TBB	IBB	SO	WP	Bk	W	L	Pct.	ShO	Sv-Op	Hld	ERA
1996 Frederick	A+	8	1	0	2	15	63	11	9	8	0	2	0	0	8	0	6	2	0	0	1	.000	0	0-—	—	4.80

Year Team	Lg	G	GS	CG	GF	IP	BFP	H	R	ER	HR	SH	SF	HB	TBB	IBB	SO	WP	Bk	W	L	Pct.	ShO	Sv-Op	Hld	ERA
Bluefield	R+	9	2	0	1	21.1	82	16	4	4	0	0	0	0	5	0	24	0	1	1	1	.500	0	1- -	—	1.69
1997 Delmarva	A	28	23	0	2	127.1	569	133	95	67	9	5	5	1	56	1	93	6	0	6	9	.400	0	0- -	—	4.74
1998 Frederick	A+	18	18	0	0	103.2	451	116	44	36	4	3	2	3	39	0	87	8	0	7	6	.538	0	0- -	—	3.13
Bowie	AA	8	7	0	1	35.2	165	38	30	23	1	0	1	3	23	0	28	4	0	1	3	.250	0	0- -	—	5.80
1999 Bowie	AA	15	9	0	0	41	209	59	39	37	3	1	1	4	32	1	27	3	0	0	4	.000	0	0- -	—	8.12
Frederick	A+	13	13	1	0	72.1	323	81	46	38	7	2	1	5	26	1	55	2	0	3	5	.375	0	0- -	—	4.73
2000 Bowie	AA	8	8	1	0	47	183	29	19	15	2	1	2	2	16	0	31	0	0	4	2	.667	0	0- -	—	2.87
Rochester	AAA	12	6	0	2	36	162	40	26	23	5	0	3	1	15	0	18	2	0	1	1	.500	0	0- -	—	5.75
2001 Rochester	AAA	33	0	0	10	43.1	199	44	28	22	5	2	1	4	24	4	39	2	0	3	3	.500	0	1- -	—	4.57
2001 Baltimore	AL	24	0	0	9	27	128	33	24	15	5	1	1	1	11	0	16	1	0	1	3	.250	0	0-1	5	5.00

Jim Parque

Pitches: Left **Bats:** Left **Pos:** SP-5

Ht: 5'11" **Wt:** 170 **Born:** 2/8/76 **Age:** 26

Year Team	Lg	G	GS	CG	GF	IP	BFP	H	R	ER	HR	SH	SF	HB	TBB	IBB	SO	WP	Bk	W	L	Pct.	ShO	Sv-Op	Hld	ERA
1998 Chicago	AL	21	21	0	0	113	507	135	72	64	14	1	0	6	49	0	77	0	3	7	5	.583	0	0-0	0	5.10
1999 Chicago	AL	31	30	1	0	173.2	804	210	111	99	23	5	8	10	79	2	111	3	2	9	15	.375	0	0-0	0	5.13
2000 Chicago	AL	33	32	0	0	187	828	208	105	89	21	5	5	11	71	1	111	2	5	13	6	.684	0	0-0	0	4.28
2001 Chicago	AL	5	5	1	0	28	132	36	26	25	7	2	1	2	10	1	15	0	0	0	3	.000	0	0-0	0	8.04
4 ML YEARS		90	88	2	0	501.2	2271	589	314	277	65	13	14	29	209	4	314	5	10	29	29	.500	0	0-0	0	4.97

Steve Parris

Pitches: Right **Bats:** Right **Pos:** SP-19

Ht: 6'0" **Wt:** 195 **Born:** 12/17/67 **Age:** 34

Year Team	Lg	G	GS	CG	GF	IP	BFP	H	R	ER	HR	SH	SF	HB	TBB	IBB	SO	WP	Bk	W	L	Pct.	ShO	Sv-Op	Hld	ERA
2001 Tennessee *	AA	1	1	0	0	3	12	2	0	0	0	0	0	0	1	0	2	1	0	0	0	—	0	0- -	—	0.00
Syracuse *	AAA	2	2	0	0	7.2	32	6	4	4	1	0	0	1	2	0	8	1	0	0	0	—	0	0- -	—	4.70
1995 Pittsburgh	NL	15	15	1	0	82	360	89	49	49	12	3	2	7	33	1	61	4	0	6	6	.500	1	0-0	0	5.38
1996 Pittsburgh	NL	8	4	0	3	26.1	123	35	22	21	4	1	1	1	11	0	27	2	0	3	0	.000	0	0-0	0	7.18
1998 Cincinnati	NL	18	16	1	0	99	421	89	44	41	9	7	1	4	32	3	77	1	1	6	5	.545	0	0-0	0	3.73
1999 Cincinnati	NL	22	21	2	0	128.2	545	124	59	50	16	7	3	6	52	4	86	3	0	11	4	.733	1	0-0	0	3.50
2000 Cincinnati	NL	33	33	0	0	192.2	861	227	109	103	30	10	3	4	71	5	117	9	1	12	17	.414	0	0-0	0	4.81
2001 Toronto	AL	19	19	1	0	105.2	471	126	60	54	18	4	2	2	41	4	49	3	0	4	6	.400	0	0-0	0	4.60
6 ML YEARS		115	108	5	3	634.1	2781	690	343	318	89	32	12	24	240	17	417	22	2	39	41	.488	3	0-0	0	4.51

John Parrish

Pitches: Left **Bats:** Left **Pos:** RP-15; SP-1

Ht: 5'11" **Wt:** 181 **Born:** 11/26/77 **Age:** 24

Year Team	Lg	G	GS	CG	GF	IP	BFP	H	R	ER	HR	SH	SF	HB	TBB	IBB	SO	WP	Bk	W	L	Pct.	ShO	Sv-Op	Hld	ERA
1996 Orioles	R	11	0	0	6	19.1	83	13	5	4	0	0	0	0	11	0	33	2	0	2	0	1.000	0	2- -	—	1.86
Bluefield	R+	8	0	0	5	13.1	60	11	6	4	0	1	2	0	9	1	18	2	0	2	1	.667	0	1- -	—	2.70
1997 Bowie	AA	1	1	0	0	5	20	3	1	1	0	0	0	0	2	0	3	0	0	1	0	1.000	0	0- -	—	1.80
Frederick	A+	5	5	0	0	22.1	103	23	18	15	3	1	0	2	16	0	17	3	0	1	3	.250	0	0- -	—	6.04
Delmarva	A	23	10	0	5	72.2	315	69	39	31	7	2	3	2	32	3	76	9	0	3	3	.500	0	1- -	—	3.84
1998 Frederick	A+	16	16	1	0	82.2	352	77	39	30	5	3	4	5	27	1	81	9	0	4	4	.500	0	0- -	—	3.27
1999 Delmarva	A	4	0	0	1	10	47	9	8	8	1	0	0	1	6	1	10	3	0	0	1	.000	0	0- -	—	7.20
Frederick	A+	6	6	0	0	36.2	151	34	17	17	4	1	2	0	12	0	44	5	0	2	2	.500	0	0- -	—	4.17
Bowie	AA	12	10	0	2	55.2	248	49	28	25	4	7	5	3	43	1	42	3	1	0	2	.000	0	0- -	—	4.04
2000 Bowie	AA	3	3	0	0	16	64	12	3	3	0	0	1	0	7	0	16	0	0	2	0	1.000	0	0- -	—	1.69
Rochester	AAA	18	18	0	0	104	426	85	54	49	10	3	4	2	56	1	87	6	2	6	7	.462	0	0- -	—	4.24
2001 Rochester	AAA	26	19	1	1	133	565	115	68	52	11	6	5	6	51	4	126	13	0	7	7	.500	0	0- -	—	3.52
2000 Baltimore	AL	8	0	0	0	36.1	180	40	32	29	6	1	4	1	35	0	28	1	0	2	4	.333	0	0-0	0	7.18
2001 Baltimore	AL	16	1	0	7	22	107	22	17	15	5	1	0	3	17	1	20	1	0	1	2	.333	0	0-0	2	6.14
2 ML YEARS		24	9	0	7	58.1	287	62	49	44	11	2	4	4	52	1	48	2	0	3	6	.333	0	0-0	2	6.79

Corey Patterson

Bats: L **Throws:** R **Pos:** CF-45; PH/PR-20; LF-13; RF-1

Ht: 5'9" **Wt:** 180 **Born:** 8/13/79 **Age:** 22

Year Team	Lg	G	AB	H	2B	3B	HR	(Hm	Rd)	TB	R	RBI	TBB	IBB	SO	HBP	SH	SF	SB	CS	SB%	GDP	Avg	OBP	SLG
1999 Lansing	A	112	475	152	35	17	20	—	—	281	94	79	25	1	85	5	0	4	33	9	.79	5	.320	.358	.592
2000 West Tenn	AA	118	444	116	26	5	22	—	—	218	73	82	45	5	115	10	0	7	27	14	.66	7	.261	.338	.491
2001 Iowa	AAA	89	367	93	22	3	7	—	—	142	63	32	29	0	65	1	3	3	19	8	.70	2	.253	.308	.387
2000 Chicago	NL	11	42	7	1	0	2	(1	1)	14	9	2	3	0	14	1	1	0	1	1	.50	0	.167	.239	.333
2001 Chicago	NL	59	131	29	3	0	4	(1	3)	44	26	14	6	0	33	3	2	3	4	0	1.00	1	.221	.266	.336
2 ML YEARS		70	173	36	4	0	6	(2	4)	58	35	16	9	0	47	4	3	3	5	1	.83	1	.208	.259	.335

Danny Patterson

Pitches: Right **Bats:** Right **Pos:** RP-60

Ht: 6'0" **Wt:** 185 **Born:** 2/17/71 **Age:** 31

Year Team	Lg	G	GS	CG	GF	IP	BFP	H	R	ER	HR	SH	SF	HB	TBB	IBB	SO	WP	Bk	W	L	Pct.	ShO	Sv-Op	Hld	ERA
1996 Texas	AL	7	0	0	5	8.2	38	10	4	0	0	0	0	0	3	1	5	0	0	0	0	—	0	0-0	0	0.00
1997 Texas	AL	54	0	0	17	71	296	70	29	27	3	4	3	0	23	4	69	7	1	10	6	.625	0	1-8	9	3.42
1998 Texas	AL	56	0	0	21	60.2	257	64	31	30	11	1	1	2	19	2	33	3	0	2	5	.286	0	2-2	19	4.45
1999 Texas	AL	53	0	0	18	60.1	275	77	38	38	5	0	2	1	19	3	43	2	0	1	0	1.000	0	0-1	4	5.67
2000 Detroit	AL	58	0	0	12	56.2	244	69	26	25	4	3	2	2	14	2	29	1	0	5	1	.833	0	0-2	12	3.97
2001 Detroit	AL	60	0	0	16	64.2	258	64	24	22	4	5	3	4	12	5	27	2	0	6	4	.556	0	1-5	16	3.06
6 ML YEARS		288	0	0	89	322	1368	354	152	142	27	13	11	9	90	17	206	15	1	24	16	.600	0	4-18	60	3.97

Jarrod Patterson

Bats: Left Throws: Right Pos: 3B-13; PH/PR-1   Ht: 6'1" Wt: 195 Born: 9/7/73 Age: 28

								BATTING										BASERUNNING				PERCENTAGES		
Year Team	Lg	G	AB	H	2B	3B	HR	(Hm | Rd)	TB	R	RBI	TBB	IBB	SO	HBP	SH	SF	SB	CS	SB%	GDP	Avg	OBP	SLG
1993 Mets	R	46	166	40	9	1	2	—	—	57	27	25	24	1	28	0	1	4	1	3	.25	5	.241	.330	.343
1994 Kingsport	R+	36	112	29	5	2	5	—	—	53	12	18	12	2	39	1	0	0	2	0	1.00	1	.259	.336	.473
Pittsfield	A-	29	106	19	6	1	1	—	—	30	8	15	10	0	34	0	0	2	0	1	.00	1	.179	.246	.283
1995 Kingsport	R+	64	240	67	17	3	13	—	—	129	45	57	28	2	50	0	0	3	3	1	.75	2	.279	.351	.538
1996 St. Lucie	A+	17	61	11	2	0	1	—	—	16	6	6	3	0	19	1	0	1	1	0	1.00	0	.180	.227	.262
Capital Cty	A	70	213	49	9	1	3	—	—	69	26	37	33	3	65	2	0	4	1	1	.50	3	.230	.333	.324
1997 Regina	IND	65	240	87	24	2	7	—	—	136	52	50	38	2	47	2	2	1	7	3	.70	1	.363	.452	.567
1998 High Desert	A+	131	492	165	34	9	18	—	—	271	89	102	66	4	97	2	0	3	9	2	.82	8	.335	.414	.551
1999 El Paso	AA	67	249	95	27	3	8	—	—	152	63	51	51	6	45	1	0	3	3	2	.60	3	.382	.484	.610
Tucson	AAA	75	274	92	25	3	11	—	—	156	46	47	36	0	37	3	0	3	4	1	.80	9	.336	.415	.569
2000 Altoona	AA	11	36	5	1	0	0	—	—	6	1	4	3	0	11	1	0	1	0	0	—	1	.139	.220	.167
Nashville	AAA	70	198	55	10	0	5	—	—	80	25	30	13	0	40	2	2	2	0	2	.00	2	.278	.326	.404
Ottawa	AAA	25	92	25	6	1	0	—	—	33	9	16	4	0	13	0	0	1	0	0	—	0	.272	.302	.359
2001 Erie	AA	20	70	28	5	1	7	—	—	56	17	18	11	0	11	0	0	1	0	0	—	0	.400	.476	.800
Toledo	AAA	69	213	63	15	2	7	—	—	103	41	25	30	1	47	1	0	3	2	1	.67	2	.296	.381	.484
2001 Detroit	AL	13	41	11	1	1	2	(1 | 1)	20	6	4	0	0	4	2	0	0	0	1	.00	2	.268	.302	.488

Josh Paul

Bats: Right Throws: Right Pos: C-56; PH/PR-7   Ht: 6'1" Wt: 200 Born: 5/19/75 Age: 27

								BATTING										BASERUNNING				PERCENTAGES		
Year Team	Lg	G	AB	H	2B	3B	HR	(Hm | Rd)	TB	R	RBI	TBB	IBB	SO	HBP	SH	SF	SB	CS	SB%	GDP	Avg	OBP	SLG
1996 White Sox	R	1	0	0	0	0	0	—	—	0	0	0	1	0	0	0	0	0	0	0	—	0	—	1.000	—
Hickory	A	59	226	74	16	0	8	—	—	114	41	37	21	3	53	1	3	1	13	4	.76	2	.327	.386	.504
1997 White Sox	R	5	14	6	0	1	0	—	—	8	3	0	1	0	3	0	1	0	1	0	1.00	1	.429	.467	.571
Birmingham	AA	34	115	34	5	0	1	—	—	42	18	16	12	0	25	1	3	0	6	2	.75	4	.296	.367	.365
1998 Winston-Sal	A+	123	444	113	20	7	11	—	—	180	66	63	38	2	91	5	7	2	20	8	.71	11	.255	.319	.405
1999 Birmingham	AA	93	319	89	19	3	4	—	—	126	47	42	29	1	68	5	3	4	6	6	.50	6	.279	.345	.395
2000 Charlotte	AAA	51	168	40	5	1	4	—	—	59	28	19	13	0	38	2	6	1	6	2	.75	3	.238	.299	.351
2001 Charlotte	AAA	22	75	21	4	0	4	—	—	37	11	14	7	0	18	0	1	1	0	0	—	0	.280	.337	.493
1999 Chicago	AL	6	18	4	1	0	0	(0 | 0)	5	2	1	0	0	4	0	0	0	0	0	—	0	.222	.222	.278
2000 Chicago	AL	36	71	20	3	2	1	(1 | 0)	30	15	8	5	0	17	1	2	0	1	0	1.00	0	.282	.338	.423
2001 Chicago	AL	57	139	37	11	0	3	(0 | 3)	57	20	18	13	0	25	0	1	1	6	2	.75	3	.266	.327	.410
3 ML YEARS		99	228	61	15	2	4	(1 | 3)	92	37	27	18	0	46	1	3	1	7	2	.78	6	.268	.323	.404

Carl Pavano

Pitches: Right Bats: Right Pos: SP-8   Ht: 6'5" Wt: 230 Born: 1/8/76 Age: 26

		HOW MUCH HE PITCHED					WHAT HE GAVE UP											THE RESULTS					
Year Team	Lg	G	GS	CG	GF	IP	BFP	H	R	ER	HR	SH	SF	HB	TBB	IBB	SO	WP	Bk	W	L	Pct.	ShO	Sv-Op	Hld	ERA
2001 Jupiter *	A+	3	3	0	0	12.1	51	10	7	3	1	1	0	1	2	0	11	0	0	1	1	.500	0	0--	—	2.19
Ottawa *	AAA	4	4	0	0	27.2	118	27	13	11	4	1	0	3	5	0	19	1	0	2	1	.667	0	0--	—	3.58
1998 Montreal	NL	24	23	0	0	134.2	580	130	70	63	18	5	6	8	43	1	83	1	0	6	9	.400	0	0-0	0	4.21
1999 Montreal	NL	19	18	1	0	104	457	117	66	65	8	5	2	4	35	1	70	1	3	6	8	.429	1	0-0	0	5.63
2000 Montreal	NL	15	15	0	0	97	408	89	40	33	8	4	3	8	34	1	64	1	1	8	4	.667	0	0-0	0	3.06
2001 Montreal	NL	8	8	0	0	42.2	199	59	33	30	7	2	1	2	16	1	36	0	1	1	6	.143	0	0-0	0	6.33
4 ML YEARS		66	64	1	0	378.1	1644	395	209	191	41	16	12	22	128	4	253	3	5	21	27	.438	1	0-0	0	4.54

Jay Payton

Bats: Right Throws: Right Pos: CF-103; PH/PR-4   Ht: 5'10" Wt: 185 Born: 11/22/72 Age: 29

								BATTING										BASERUNNING				PERCENTAGES		
Year Team	Lg	G	AB	H	2B	3B	HR	(Hm | Rd)	TB	R	RBI	TBB	IBB	SO	HBP	SH	SF	SB	CS	SB%	GDP	Avg	OBP	SLG
2001 St. Lucie *	A+	4	16	6	3	0	0	—	—	9	7	0	4	0	1	0	0	0	0	0	—	0	.375	.500	.563
1998 New York	NL	15	22	7	1	0	0	(0 | 0)	8	2	0	1	0	4	0	0	0	0	0	—	0	.318	.348	.364
1999 New York	NL	13	8	2	1	0	0	(0 | 0)	3	1	1	0	0	2	1	0	0	1	2	.33	0	.250	.333	.375
2000 New York	NL	149	488	142	23	1	17	(9 | 8)	218	63	62	30	0	60	3	0	8	5	11	.31	9	.291	.331	.447
2001 New York	NL	104	361	92	16	1	8	(6 | 2)	134	44	34	18	1	52	5	0	2	4	3	.57	11	.255	.298	.371
4 ML YEARS		281	879	243	41	2	25	(15 | 10)	363	110	97	49	1	118	9	0	10	10	16	.38	20	.276	.318	.413

Angel Pena

Bats: Right Throws: Right Pos: C-15; PH/PR-7   Ht: 5'10" Wt: 228 Born: 2/16/75 Age: 27

								BATTING										BASERUNNING				PERCENTAGES		
Year Team	Lg	G	AB	H	2B	3B	HR	(Hm | Rd)	TB	R	RBI	TBB	IBB	SO	HBP	SH	SF	SB	CS	SB%	GDP	Avg	OBP	SLG
2001 Las Vegas *	AAA	53	198	62	8	2	16	—	—	122	39	41	18	1	52	1	0	2	0	1	.00	5	.313	.370	.616
1998 Los Angeles	NL	6	13	3	0	0	0	(0 | 0)	3	1	0	0	0	6	0	0	0	0	0	—	0	.231	.231	.231
1999 Los Angeles	NL	43	120	25	6	0	4	(2 | 2)	43	14	21	12	0	24	0	1	2	0	1	.00	6	.208	.276	.358
2001 Los Angeles	NL	22	54	11	1	0	1	(1 | 0)	15	3	2	1	0	17	0	2	1	0	0	—	0	.204	.214	.278
3 ML YEARS		71	187	39	7	0	5	(3 | 2)	61	18	23	13	0	47	0	3	3	0	1	.00	6	.209	.256	.326

Carlos Pena

Bats: Left Throws: Left Pos: 1B-16; PH/PR-5; DH-1   Ht: 6'2" Wt: 210 Born: 5/17/78 Age: 24

								BATTING										BASERUNNING				PERCENTAGES		
Year Team	Lg	G	AB	H	2B	3B	HR	(Hm | Rd)	TB	R	RBI	TBB	IBB	SO	HBP	SH	SF	SB	CS	SB%	GDP	Avg	OBP	SLG
1998 Rangers	R	2	5	2	0	0	0	—	—	2	1	0	3	0	1	0	0	0	1	1	.50	0	.400	.625	.400
Savannah	A	30	117	38	14	0	6	—	—	70	22	20	8	0	26	4	0	1	3	2	.60	0	.325	.385	.598
Charlotte	A+	7	22	6	1	0	0	—	—	7	1	3	2	0	8	1	0	0	0	1	.00	0	.273	.360	.318
1999 Charlotte	A+	136	501	128	31	8	18	—	—	229	85	103	74	2	135	16	0	6	2	5	.29	7	.255	.365	.457

Year Team	Lg	G	AB	H	2B	3B	HR	(Hm	Rd)	TB	R	RBI	TBB	IBB	SO	HBP	SH	SF	SB	CS	SB%	GDP	Avg	OBP	SLG
2000 Tulsa	AA	138	529	158	36	2	28	—	—	282	117	105	101	10	108	9	1	8	12	0	1.00	7	.299	.414	.533
2001 Oklahoma	AAA	119	431	124	38	3	23	—	—	237	71	74	80	1	127	8	0	0	11	3	.79	6	.288	.408	.550
2001 Texas	AL	22	62	16	4	1	3	(2	1)	31	6	12	10	0	17	0	0	0	0	0	—	1	.258	.361	.500

Elvis Pena

Bats: Both **Throws:** Right **Pos:** 2B-11; PH/PR-5

Ht: 5'11" **Wt:** 155 **Born:** 9/15/76 **Age:** 25

Year Team	Lg	G	AB	H	2B	3B	HR	(Hm	Rd)	TB	R	RBI	TBB	IBB	SO	HBP	SH	SF	SB	CS	SB%	GDP	Avg	OBP	SLG
1994 Rockies	R	49	171	39	5	2	0	—	—	48	31	9	35	0	47	6	1	0	20	12	.63	1	.228	.377	.281
1995 Asheville	A	48	145	33	2	0	0	—	—	35	27	4	28	0	32	4	3	0	23	6	.79	1	.228	.367	.241
Portland	A-	58	215	54	6	3	0	—	—	66	29	18	26	0	45	1	3	0	28	7	.80	2	.251	.335	.307
1996 Salem	A+	102	341	76	9	4	0	—	—	93	48	28	61	2	70	3	13	1	30	16	.65	12	.223	.345	.273
1997 Salem	A+	93	279	62	9	2	1	—	—	78	41	30	37	0	53	2	14	3	16	6	.73	1	.222	.315	.280
1998 Asheville	A	115	428	123	24	4	6	—	—	173	93	48	70	2	85	14	7	2	41	12	.77	5	.287	.403	.404
1999 Colo Sprngs	AAA	13	43	7	1	0	0	—	—	8	5	1	3	0	7	1	0	0	4	1	.80	0	.163	.234	.186
Carolina	AA	110	356	107	24	6	2	—	—	149	57	31	48	2	64	6	8	2	21	6	.78	6	.301	.391	.419
2000 Carolina	AA	126	477	143	16	7	3	—	—	182	92	37	69	2	76	10	4	1	48	13	.79	11	.300	.399	.382
2001 Indianapls	AAA	127	437	105	15	3	1	—	—	129	56	28	30	0	76	8	7	2	12	5	.71	8	.240	.300	.295
2000 Colorado	NL	10	9	3	1	0	0	(0	0)	4	1	1	1	0	1	0	0	0	1	0	1.00	3	.333	.400	.444
2001 Milwaukee	NL	15	40	9	2	0	0	(0	0)	11	5	6	6	0	6	1	0	1	2	0	1.00	3	.225	.333	.275
2 ML YEARS		25	49	12	3	0	0	(0	0)	15	6	7	7	0	7	1	0	1	3	0	1.00	6	.245	.345	.306

Brad Penny

Pitches: Right **Bats:** Right **Pos:** SP-31

Ht: 6'4" **Wt:** 200 **Born:** 5/24/78 **Age:** 24

Year Team	Lg	G	GS	CG	GF	IP	BFP	H	R	ER	HR	SH	SF	HB	TBB	IBB	SO	WP	Bk	W	L	Pct.	ShO	Sv-Op	Hld	ERA
1996 Diamndbcks	R	11	8	0	1	49.2	201	36	18	13	1	0	1	3	14	0	52	3	2	2	2	.500	0	0- -	—	2.36
1997 South Bend	A	25	25	0	0	118.2	489	91	44	36	4	5	0	4	43	2	116	10	2	10	5	.667	0	0- -	—	2.73
1998 High Desert	A+	28	28	1	0	164	661	138	65	54	15	3	2	9	35	2	207	4	0	14	5	.737	0	0- -	—	2.96
1999 El Paso	AA	17	17	0	0	90	391	109	56	48	9	1	2	4	25	0	100	4	2	2	7	.222	0	0- -	—	4.80
Portland	AAA	6	6	0	0	32.1	139	28	15	14	3	0	1	3	14	0	35	3	2	1	0	1.000	0	0- -	—	3.90
2000 Brevard Cty	A+	2	2	0	0	8	33	5	2	1	0	0	0	0	4	0	11	0	1	0	1	.000	0	0- -	—	1.13
Calgary	AAA	3	3	0	0	15	65	8	8	3	1	0	1	3	10	0	16	0	0	2	0	1.000	0	0- -	—	1.80
2000 Florida	NL	23	22	0	0	119.2	529	120	70	64	13	6	2	5	60	4	80	4	1	8	7	.533	0	0-0	0	4.81
2001 Florida	NL	31	31	0	0	205	833	183	92	84	15	8	2	7	54	3	154	2	0	10	10	.500	1	0-0	0	3.69
2 ML YEARS		54	53	1	0	324.2	1362	303	162	148	28	14	4	12	114	7	234	6	1	18	17	.514	1	0-0	0	4.10

Troy Percival

Pitches: Right **Bats:** Right **Pos:** RP-57

Ht: 6'3" **Wt:** 235 **Born:** 8/9/69 **Age:** 32

Year Team	Lg	G	GS	CG	GF	IP	BFP	H	R	ER	HR	SH	SF	HB	TBB	IBB	SO	WP	Bk	W	L	Pct.	ShO	Sv-Op	Hld	ERA
1995 California	AL	62	0	0	16	74	284	37	19	16	6	4	1	4	26	2	94	2	2	3	2	.600	0	3-6	29	1.95
1996 California	AL	62	0	0	52	74	291	38	20	19	8	2	1	2	31	4	100	2	0	0	2	.000	0	36-39	2	2.31
1997 Anaheim	AL	55	0	0	46	52	224	40	20	20	6	1	2	4	22	2	72	5	0	5	5	.500	0	27-31	0	3.46
1998 Anaheim	AL	67	0	0	60	66.2	287	45	31	27	5	3	2	3	37	4	87	3	0	2	7	.222	0	42-48	0	3.65
1999 Anaheim	AL	60	0	0	50	57	230	38	24	24	9	0	1	3	22	0	58	3	0	4	6	.400	0	31-39	0	3.79
2000 Anaheim	AL	54	0	0	45	50	221	42	27	25	7	3	2	2	30	4	49	1	0	5	5	.500	0	32-42	0	4.50
2001 Anaheim	AL	57	0	0	50	57.2	230	39	19	17	3	1	0	2	18	1	71	2	0	4	2	.667	0	39-42	0	2.65
7 ML YEARS		417	0	0	319	431.1	1767	279	160	148	44	14	9	17	186	17	531	18	2	23	29	.442	0	210-247	31	3.09

Eddie Perez

Bats: Right **Throws:** Right **Pos:** C-5; PH/PR-2

Ht: 6'1" **Wt:** 185 **Born:** 5/4/68 **Age:** 34

Year Team	Lg	G	AB	H	2B	3B	HR	(Hm	Rd)	TB	R	RBI	TBB	IBB	SO	HBP	SH	SF	SB	CS	SB%	GDP	Avg	OBP	SLG
2001 Greenville *	AA	10	38	13	2	0	4	—	—	27	7	5	0	0	9	1	0	0	0	0	—	0	.342	.359	.711
1995 Atlanta	NL	7	13	4	1	0	1	(0	1)	8	1	4	0	0	2	0	0	0	0	0	—	0	.308	.308	.615
1996 Atlanta	NL	68	156	40	9	1	4	(2	2)	63	19	17	8	0	19	1	0	2	0	0	—	6	.256	.293	.404
1997 Atlanta	NL	73	191	41	5	0	6	(4	2)	64	20	18	10	0	35	2	1	2	0	1	.00	8	.215	.259	.335
1998 Atlanta	NL	61	149	50	12	0	6	(3	3)	80	18	32	15	0	28	2	1	0	1	1	.50	9	.336	.404	.537
1999 Atlanta	NL	104	309	77	17	0	7	(0	7)	115	30	30	17	4	40	6	4	3	0	1	.00	9	.249	.299	.372
2000 Atlanta	NL	7	22	4	1	0	0	(0	0)	5	0	3	0	0	2	0	0	0	0	0	—	0	.182	.182	.227
2001 Atlanta	NL	5	10	3	0	0	0	(0	0)	3	0	0	0	0	2	0	0	0	0	0	—	0	.300	.300	.300
7 ML YEARS		325	850	219	45	1	24	(9	15)	338	88	104	50	4	128	11	6	7	1	3	.25	26	.258	.305	.398

Neifi Perez

Bats: Both **Throws:** Right **Pos:** SS-133; 2B-4

Ht: 6'0" **Wt:** 177 **Born:** 6/2/75 **Age:** 27

Year Team	Lg	G	AB	H	2B	3B	HR	(Hm	Rd)	TB	R	RBI	TBB	IBB	SO	HBP	SH	SF	SB	CS	SB%	GDP	Avg	OBP	SLG
1996 Colorado	NL	17	45	7	2	0	0	(0	0)	9	4	3	0	0	8	0	1	0	2	2	.50	2	.156	.156	.200
1997 Colorado	NL	83	313	91	18	10	5	(3	2)	139	46	31	21	4	43	1	5	4	4	3	.57	5	.291	.333	.444
1998 Colorado	NL	162	647	177	25	9	9	(6	3)	247	80	59	38	0	70	1	22	4	5	6	.45	8	.274	.313	.382
1999 Colorado	NL	157	690	193	27	11	12	(8	4)	278	108	70	28	0	54	1	9	4	13	5	.72	4	.280	.307	.403
2000 Colorado	NL	162	651	187	39	11	10	(7	3)	278	92	71	30	6	63	0	7	11	3	6	.33	9	.287	.314	.427
2001 Col-KC		136	581	162	26	9	8	(7	1)	230	83	59	26	1	68	1	11	4	6	4	.60	10	.279	.309	.396
2001 Colorado	NL	87	382	114	19	8	7	(7	0)	170	65	47	16	1	49	0	4	4	6	2	.75	6	.298	.326	.445
Kansas City	AL	49	199	48	7	1	1	(0	1)	60	18	12	10	0	19	1	7	3	3	4	.43	2	.241	.277	.302
6 ML YEARS		717	2927	817	132	50	44	(31	13)	1181	413	293	143	11	306	4	55	27	36	28	.56	36	.279	.311	.403

Odalis Perez

Pitches: Left Bats: Left Pos: SP-16; RP-8
Ht: 6'0" Wt: 150 Born: 6/6/78 Age: 24

Year Team	Lg	G	GS	CG	GF	IP	BFP	H	R	ER	HR	SH	SF	HB	TBB	IBB	SO	WP	Bk	W	L	Pct.	ShO	Sv-Op	Hld	ERA
2001 Richmond *	AAA	5	5	0	0	23	92	23	7	7	1	0	0	0	2	0	22	0	0	1	0	1.000	0	0--	—	2.74
1998 Atlanta	NL	10	0	0	0	10.2	45	10	5	5	1	0	0	0	4	0	5	0	0	0	1	.000	0	0-1	5	4.22
1999 Atlanta	NL	18	17	0	0	93	424	100	65	62	12	3	4	1	53	2	82	5	3	4	6	.400	0	0-0	0	6.00
2001 Atlanta	NL	24	16	0	1	95.1	418	108	55	52	7	3	3	1	39	0	71	2	3	7	8	.467	0	0-0	0	4.91
3 ML YEARS		52	33	0	1	199	887	218	125	119	20	6	7	2	96	2	158	7	6	11	15	.423	0	0-1	5	5.38

Robert Perez

Bats: R Throws: R Pos: CF-3; RF-3; DH-1; PH/PR-1
Ht: 6'3" Wt: 195 Born: 6/4/69 Age: 33

Year Team	Lg	G	AB	H	2B	3B	HR	Hm	Rd	TB	R	RBI	TBB	IBB	SO	HBP	SH	SF	SB	CS	SB%	GDP	Avg	OBP	SLG
2001 Columbus *	AAA	36	146	47	7	3	7	—	—	81	20	27	4	1	23	3	0	1	6	5	.55	4	.322	.351	.555
Indianapols *	AAA	20	84	28	9	0	3	—	—	46	13	16	4	1	11	2	0	0	0	1	.00	7	.333	.378	.548
1994 Toronto	AL	4	8	1	0	0	0	0	0	1	0	0	0	0	1	0	0	1	0	0	—	1	.125	.125	.125
1995 Toronto	AL	17	48	9	2	0	1	1	0	14	2	3	0	0	5	0	0	0	0	0	—	1	.188	.188	.292
1996 Toronto	AL	86	202	66	10	0	2	0	2	82	30	21	8	0	17	1	4	1	3	0	1.00	6	.327	.354	.406
1997 Toronto	AL	37	78	15	4	1	2	0	2	27	4	6	0	0	16	0	0	0	0	0	—	2	.192	.192	.346
1998 Sea-Mon		69	141	31	2	0	3	3	0	42	12	14	2	0	28	1	0	1	0	0	—	4	.220	.238	.298
2001 NYY-Mil		8	20	4	1	0	0	0	0	5	1	0	1	0	7	0	0	0	0	1	.00	0	.200	.238	.250
1998 Seattle	AL	17	35	6	1	0	2	2	0	13	3	6	0	0	5	0	0	0	0	0	—	0	.171	.171	.371
Montreal	NL	52	106	25	1	0	1	1	0	29	9	8	2	0	23	1	0	1	0	0	—	4	.236	.255	.274
2001 New York	NL	6	15	4	1	0	0	0	0	5	1	0	1	0	7	0	0	0	0	0	—	0	.267	.313	.333
Milwaukee	NL	2	5	0	0	0	0	0	0	0	0	0	0	0	0	0	0	0	0	0	—	0	.000	.000	.000
6 ML YEARS		221	497	126	19	1	8	4	4	171	49	44	11	0	74	2	4	2	3	1	.75	15	.254	.271	.344

Santiago Perez

Bats: B Throws: R Pos: PH/PR-15; CF-10; LF-9; SS-8; RF-3; 2B-2
Ht: 6'2" Wt: 150 Born: 12/30/75 Age: 26

Year Team	Lg	G	AB	H	2B	3B	HR	Hm	Rd	TB	R	RBI	TBB	IBB	SO	HBP	SH	SF	SB	CS	SB%	GDP	Avg	OBP	SLG
1995 Fayettevlle	A	130	425	101	15	1	4	—	—	130	54	44	30	0	98	1	7	7	10	9	.53	6	.238	.285	.306
1996 Lakeland	A+	122	418	105	18	2	1	—	—	130	33	27	16	1	88	3	7	2	6	5	.55	9	.251	.282	.311
1997 Lakeland	A+	111	445	122	20	12	4	—	—	178	66	46	20	1	98	2	8	5	21	9	.70	6	.274	.305	.400
1998 El Paso	AA	107	454	139	20	13	11	—	—	218	73	64	28	3	70	4	4	5	21	11	.66	7	.306	.348	.480
Louisville	AAA	36	133	36	4	3	3	—	—	55	18	14	6	0	31	0	2	1	6	3	.67	3	.271	.300	.414
1999 Louisville	AAA	108	407	107	23	8	7	—	—	167	57	38	31	1	94	2	2	5	21	4	.84	7	.263	.315	.410
2000 Indianapols	AAA	106	408	112	26	7	5	—	—	167	74	34	44	3	96	1	3	1	31	8	.79	2	.275	.346	.409
2001 Portland	AAA	46	184	50	12	0	5	—	—	77	31	10	15	0	59	2	2	0	18	3	.86	2	.272	.333	.418
2000 Milwaukee	NL	24	52	9	2	0	0	0	0	11	8	2	8	2	9	1	1	1	4	0	1.00	1	.173	.290	.212
2001 San Diego	NL	43	81	16	1	0	0	0	0	17	13	4	15	0	29	0	0	1	5	1	.83	0	.198	.320	.210
2 ML YEARS		67	133	25	3	0	0	0	0	28	21	6	23	2	38	1	1	2	9	1	.90	1	.188	.308	.211

Timo Perez

Bats: L Throws: L Pos: RF-62; PH/PR-18; CF-8; LF-6
Ht: 5'9" Wt: 167 Born: 4/8/77 Age: 25

Year Team	Lg	G	AB	H	2B	3B	HR	Hm	Rd	TB	R	RBI	TBB	IBB	SO	HBP	SH	SF	SB	CS	SB%	GDP	Avg	OBP	SLG
2000 St. Lucie	A+	8	31	11	4	0	1	—	—	18	3	8	2	0	1	1	2	1	3	3	.50	0	.355	.400	.581
Norfolk	AAA	72	291	104	17	5	6	—	—	149	45	37	16	1	25	3	4	4	13	7	.65	4	.357	.392	.512
2001 Norfolk	AAA	48	192	69	10	2	6	—	—	101	37	19	12	2	18	2	2	2	15	2	.88	1	.286	.333	.469
2000 New York	NL	24	49	14	4	1	1	0	1	23	11	3	3	0	5	1	0	1	1	1	.50	0	.247	.287	.356
2001 New York	NL	85	239	59	9	1	5	2	3	85	26	22	12	0	25	2	6	1	1	6	.14	1	.253	.295	.375
2 ML YEARS		109	288	73	13	2	6	2	4	108	37	25	15	0	30	3	6	2	2	7	.22	1	.253	.295	.375

Tomas Perez

Bats: B Throws: R Pos: 2B-29; PH/PR-18; 3B-9; SS-8; RF-1
Ht: 5'11" Wt: 177 Born: 12/29/73 Age: 28

Year Team	Lg	G	AB	H	2B	3B	HR	Hm	Rd	TB	R	RBI	TBB	IBB	SO	HBP	SH	SF	SB	CS	SB%	GDP	Avg	OBP	SLG
1995 Toronto	AL	41	98	24	3	1	1	1	0	32	12	8	7	0	18	0	0	1	0	1	.00	4	.245	.292	.327
1996 Toronto	AL	91	295	74	13	4	1	1	0	98	24	19	25	0	29	1	6	1	1	2	.33	10	.251	.311	.332
1997 Toronto	AL	40	123	24	3	2	0	0	0	31	9	9	11	0	28	1	3	0	1	1	.50	2	.195	.267	.252
1998 Toronto	AL	6	9	1	0	0	0	0	0	1	1	0	1	0	3	0	1	0	0	0	—	1	.111	.200	.111
2000 Philadelphia	NL	45	140	31	7	1	1	0	0	43	17	13	11	2	30	0	1	0	1	1	.50	3	.221	.278	.307
2001 Philadelphia	NL	62	135	41	7	1	3	2	1	59	11	19	7	1	22	2	1	0	0	1	.00	2	.304	.347	.437
6 ML YEARS		285	800	195	33	9	6	4	2	264	74	68	62	3	130	4	12	2	3	6	.33	24	.244	.301	.330

Matt Perisho

Pitches: Left Bats: Left Pos: RP-26; SP-4
Ht: 6'0" Wt: 205 Born: 6/8/75 Age: 27

Year Team	Lg	G	GS	CG	GF	IP	BFP	H	R	ER	HR	SH	SF	HB	TBB	IBB	SO	WP	Bk	W	L	Pct.	ShO	Sv-Op	Hld	ERA
2001 Toledo *	AAA	25	2	0	19	42	173	42	10	8	3	0	1	0	11	0	28	0	0	2	3	.400	0	9--	—	1.71
1997 Anaheim	AL	11	8	0	2	45	217	59	34	30	6	2	2	3	28	0	35	5	2	0	2	.000	0	0-0	0	6.00
1998 Texas	AL	2	2	0	0	5	40	15	14	15	2	0	0	2	8	0	2	0	0	0	0	---	0	0-0	0	27.00
1999 Texas	AL	4	1	0	3	10.1	40	8	3	3	0	0	0	0	2	1	17	1	0	0	0	---	0	0-0	0	2.61
2000 Texas	AL	34	13	0	4	105	515	136	99	86	20	6	5	6	67	3	74	4	0	2	7	.222	0	0-1	0	7.37
2001 Detroit	AL	30	4	0	5	39.1	186	54	29	25	5	2	7	4	14	1	19	0	0	2	3	.400	0	0-2	4	5.72
5 ML YEARS		81	28	0	14	204.2	998	272	182	159	33	10	8	15	119	5	147	10	2	4	14	.222	0	0-3	4	6.99

Herbert Perry

Bats: R **Throws:** R **Pos:** 3B-68; PH/PR-16; 1B-12; DH-10   **Ht:** 6'2" **Wt:** 235 **Born:** 9/15/69 **Age:** 32

								BATTING													BASERUNNING				PERCENTAGES		
Year Team	Lg	G	AB	H	2B	3B	HR	(Hm	Rd)	TB	R	RBI	TBB	IBB	SO	HBP	SH	SF		SB	CS	SB%	GDP	Avg	OBP	SLG
1994 Cleveland	AL	4	9	1	0	0	0	(0	0)	1	1	1	3	1	1	1	0	1		0	0	—	0	.111	.357	.111
1995 Cleveland	AL	52	162	51	13	1	3	(3	0)	75	23	23	13	0	28	4	3	2		1	3	.25	5	.315	.376	.463
1996 Cleveland	AL	7	12	1	1	0	0	(0	0)	2	1	0	1	0	2	0	0	0		0	0	—	0	.083	.154	.167
1999 Tampa Bay	AL	66	209	53	10	1	6	(5	1)	83	29	32	16	1	42	10	0	4		0	0	—	13	.254	.331	.397
2000 TB-CWS	AL	116	411	124	30	1	12	(7	5)	192	71	62	24	1	75	9	2	4		4	1	.80	13	.302	.350	.467
2001 Chicago	AL	92	285	73	21	1	7	(5	2)	117	38	32	23	1	55	7	0	1		2	2	.50	11	.256	.326	.411
2000 Tampa Bay	AL	7	28	6	1	0	0	(0	0)	7	2	1	2	0	7	0	0	0		0	0	—	0	.214	.267	.250
Chicago	AL	109	383	118	29	1	12	(7	5)	185	69	61	22	1	68	9	2	4		4	1	.80	13	.308	.356	.483
6 ML YEARS		337	1088	303	75	4	28	(20	8)	470	163	150	80	4	203	31	5	12		8	6	.57	42	.278	.342	.432

Robert Person

Pitches: Right **Bats:** Right **Pos:** SP-33   **Ht:** 6'0" **Wt:** 194 **Born:** 10/6/69 **Age:** 32

		HOW MUCH HE PITCHED						WHAT HE GAVE UP											THE RESULTS					
Year Team	Lg	G	GS	CG	GF	IP	BFP	H	R	ER	HR	SH	SF	HB	TBB	IBB	SO	WP	Bk	W	L	Pct.	ShO	Sv-Op	Hld	ERA
1995 New York	NL	3	1	0	0	12	44	5	1	1	0	0	0	0	2	0	10	0	0	1	0	1.000	0	0-0	0	0.75
1996 New York	NL	27	13	0	1	89.2	390	86	50	45	16	1	4	2	35	3	76	3	0	4	5	.444	0	0-0	1	4.52
1997 Toronto	AL	23	22	0	0	128.1	566	125	86	80	19	4	6	5	60	2	99	7	0	5	10	.333	0	0-0	0	5.61
1998 Toronto	AL	27	0	0	14	38.1	184	45	31	30	9	2	5	2	22	1	31	0	0	3	1	.750	0	6-8	0	7.04
1999 Tor-Phi		42	22	0	8	148	659	139	84	77	24	7	6	6	85	2	139	5	1	10	7	.588	0	2-2	1	4.68
2000 Philadelphia	NL	28	28	1	0	173.1	743	144	73	70	13	4	9	6	95	1	164	10	1	9	7	.563	1	0-0	0	3.63
2001 Philadelphia	NL	33	33	3	0	208.1	867	179	103	97	34	8	6	8	80	3	183	10	1	15	7	.682	1	0-0	0	4.19
1999 Toronto	AL	11	0	0	7	11	60	9	12	12	1	0	2	4	15	1	12	2	0	0	2	.000	0	2-2	1	9.82
Philadelphia	NL	31	22	0	1	137	599	130	72	65	23	7	4	2	70	1	127	3	1	10	5	.667	0	0-0	0	4.27
7 ML YEARS		183	119	4	23	798	3453	723	428	400	116	26	36	29	379	12	702	35	3	47	37	.560	2	8-10	2	4.51

Chris Peters

Pitches: Left **Bats:** Left **Pos:** RP-7; SP-6   **Ht:** 6'1" **Wt:** 170 **Born:** 1/28/72 **Age:** 30

		HOW MUCH HE PITCHED						WHAT HE GAVE UP											THE RESULTS					
Year Team	Lg	G	GS	CG	GF	IP	BFP	H	R	ER	HR	SH	SF	HB	TBB	IBB	SO	WP	Bk	W	L	Pct.	ShO	Sv-Op	Hld	ERA
2001 Louisville *	AAA	8	6	0	1	31.1	158	46	26	24	2	1	0	5	18	2	16	6	0	3	1	.750	0	0--	—	6.89
Columbus *	AAA	9	8	0	0	52.2	242	56	36	25	7	1	0	4	25	0	29	8	0	2	4	.333	0	0--	—	4.27
1996 Pittsburgh	NL	16	10	0	0	64	283	72	43	40	9	3	3	1	25	0	28	4	0	2	4	.333	0	0-0	2	5.63
1997 Pittsburgh	NL	31	1	0	5	37.1	167	38	23	19	6	5	1	3	21	4	17	4	0	2	2	.500	0	0-1	2	4.58
1998 Pittsburgh	NL	39	21	1	7	148	630	142	63	57	13	4	5	3	55	4	103	4	1	8	10	.444	0	1-1	2	3.47
1999 Pittsburgh	NL	19	11	0	2	71	343	98	59	52	17	4	4	2	27	0	46	2	1	4	5	.556	0	0-0	1	6.59
2000 Pittsburgh	NL	18	0	0	4	28.1	121	23	9	9	2	2	0	1	14	2	16	3	0	1	0	1.000	0	1-1	1	2.86
2001 Montreal	NL	13	6	0	1	31	149	47	26	26	7	2	2	4	15	1	14	4	0	2	4	.333	0	0-1	0	7.55
6 ML YEARS		136	49	1	19	379.2	1693	420	223	203	54	20	15	14	157	11	224	21	2	19	25	.432	0	2-4	8	4.81

Kyle Peterson

Pitches: Right **Bats:** Left **Pos:** SP-2; RP-1   **Ht:** 6'3" **Wt:** 215 **Born:** 4/9/76 **Age:** 26

		HOW MUCH HE PITCHED						WHAT HE GAVE UP											THE RESULTS					
Year Team	Lg	G	GS	CG	GF	IP	BFP	H	R	ER	HR	SH	SF	HB	TBB	IBB	SO	WP	Bk	W	L	Pct.	ShO	Sv-Op	Hld	ERA
1997 Ogden	R+	3	3	0	0	10.1	40	5	2	1	1	0	0	1	4	0	11	0	0	0	0	—	0	0--	—	0.87
1998 Stockton	A+	17	17	0	0	96.1	430	99	54	38	4	6	1	8	33	0	109	5	5	4	7	.364	0	0--	—	3.55
El Paso	AA	7	7	1	0	43	187	41	24	21	2	2	2	1	16	0	33	1	0	3	2	.600	0	0--	—	4.40
Louisville	AAA	1	1	0	0	5.2	27	8	5	5	0	0	0	0	2	0	4	0	0	1	0	1.000	0	0--	—	7.94
1999 Louisville	AAA	18	18	1	0	109	466	90	52	43	13	3	3	6	42	1	95	5	2	7	6	.538	1	0--	—	3.55
2000 Beloit	A	3	3	0	0	15	58	10	4	3	2	0	1	1	4	0	17	0	0	1	1	.500	0	0--	—	1.80
Huntsville	AA	1	1	0	0	4.2	25	6	7	4	1	1	0	0	4	0	1	0	0	1	0	1.000	0	0--	—	7.71
2001 Indianapolis	AAA	21	20	0	0	115	511	143	81	73	17	6	6	7	26	0	73	1	2	2	10	.167	0	0--	—	5.71
1999 Milwaukee	NL	17	12	0	2	77	341	87	46	39	3	4	3	4	25	2	34	1	0	4	7	.364	0	0-1	0	4.56
2001 Milwaukee	NL	3	2	0	0	14.2	68	19	10	9	3	1	0	0	4	2	12	0	0	1	2	.333	0	0-0	0	5.52
2 ML YEARS		20	14	0	2	91.2	409	106	56	48	6	5	3	4	29	4	46	1	0	5	9	.357	0	0-1	0	4.71

Mark Petkovsek

Pitches: Right **Bats:** Right **Pos:** RP-55   **Ht:** 6'0" **Wt:** 198 **Born:** 11/18/65 **Age:** 36

		HOW MUCH HE PITCHED						WHAT HE GAVE UP											THE RESULTS					
Year Team	Lg	G	GS	CG	GF	IP	BFP	H	R	ER	HR	SH	SF	HB	TBB	IBB	SO	WP	Bk	W	L	Pct.	ShO	Sv-Op	Hld	ERA
1991 Texas	AL	4	1	0	1	9.1	53	21	16	15	4	0	1	0	4	0	6	2	0	0	1	.000	0	0-0	0	14.46
1993 Pittsburgh	NL	26	0	0	8	32.1	145	43	25	25	7	4	1	0	9	2	14	4	0	3	0	1.000	0	0-0	0	6.96
1995 St. Louis	NL	26	21	1	1	137.1	569	136	71	61	11	4	4	6	35	3	71	1	1	6	6	.500	1	0-0	0	4.00
1996 St. Louis	NL	48	6	0	7	88.2	377	83	37	35	9	5	1	5	35	2	45	2	0	11	2	.846	0	0-3	10	3.55
1997 St. Louis	NL	55	2	0	19	96	414	109	61	54	14	2	2	6	31	4	51	2	0	4	7	.364	0	2-2	5	5.06
1998 St. Louis	NL	48	10	0	7	105.2	476	131	63	56	9	9	3	8	36	3	55	1	1	7	4	.636	0	0-5	6	4.77
1999 Anaheim	AL	64	0	0	18	83	349	85	37	32	6	5	5	2	21	2	43	3	1	10	4	.714	0	1-4	12	3.47
2000 Anaheim	AL	64	1	0	21	81	341	86	40	39	8	4	1	3	23	6	31	3	0	4	2	.667	0	2-4	16	4.33
2001 Texas	AL	55	0	0	19	76.2	362	103	61	57	14	3	7	5	28	4	42	4	0	1	2	.333	0	0-4	6	6.69
9 ML YEARS		390	41	1	101	710	3086	797	411	374	82	36	25	35	222	26	358	22	4	46	28	.622	1	5-22	55	4.74

Ben Petrick

Bats: Right **Throws:** Right **Pos:** C-77; PH/PR-11; 1B-2 **Ht:** 6'0" **Wt:** 200 **Born:** 4/7/77 **Age:** 25

								BATTING												BASERUNNING				PERCENTAGES		
Year Team	Lg	G	AB	H	2B	3B	HR	(Hm	Rd)	TB	R	RBI	TBB	IBB	SO	HBP	SH	SF	SB	CS	SB%	GDP	Avg	OBP	SLG
2001 Colo Sprngs *	AAA	18	64	16	2	0	1	—	—	21	11	9	13	2	21	0	0	2	1	0	1.00	1	.250	.367	.328
1999 Colorado	NL	19	62	20	3	0	4	(4	0)	35	13	12	10	0	13	0	0	0	1	0	1.00	1	.323	.417	.565
2000 Colorado	NL	52	146	47	10	1	3	(2	1)	68	32	20	20	2	33	2	1	4	1	2	.33	1	.322	.401	.466
2001 Colorado	NL	85	244	58	15	3	11	(7	4)	112	41	39	31	3	67	3	1	3	3	3	.50	5	.238	.327	.459
3 ML YEARS		156	452	125	28	4	18	(13	5)	215	86	71	61	5	113	5	2	7	5	5	.50	7	.277	.364	.476

Andy Pettitte

Pitches: Left **Bats:** Left **Pos:** SP-31 **Ht:** 6'5" **Wt:** 225 **Born:** 6/15/72 **Age:** 30

		HOW MUCH HE PITCHED						WHAT HE GAVE UP												THE RESULTS					
Year Team	Lg	G	GS	CG	GF	IP	BFP	H	R	ER	HR	SH	SF	HB	TBB	IBB	SO	WP	Bk	W	L	Pct.	ShO	Sv-Op	Hld	ERA
1995 New York	AL	31	26	3	1	175	745	183	86	81	15	4	5	1	63	3	114	8	1	12	9	.571	0	0-0	0	4.17
1996 New York	AL	35	34	2	1	221	929	229	105	95	23	7	3	3	72	2	162	6	1	21	8	.724	0	0-0	0	3.87
1997 New York	AL	35	35	4	0	240.1	986	233	86	77	7	6	2	3	65	0	166	7	0	18	7	.720	1	0-0	0	2.88
1998 New York	AL	33	32	5	0	216.1	932	226	110	102	20	6	7	6	87	1	146	5	0	16	11	.593	0	0-0	0	4.24
1999 New York	AL	31	31	0	0	191.2	851	216	105	100	20	6	6	3	89	3	121	3	1	14	11	.560	0	0-0	0	4.70
2000 New York	AL	32	32	3	0	204.2	903	219	111	99	17	7	4	4	80	4	125	2	3	19	9	.679	1	0-0	0	4.35
2001 New York	AL	31	31	2	0	200.2	858	224	103	89	14	8	7	6	41	3	164	2	2	15	10	.600	0	0-0	0	3.99
7 ML YEARS		228	221	19	2	1449.2	6204	1530	706	643	116	44	34	26	497	16	998	33	8	115	65	.639	2	0-0	0	3.99

Adam Pettyjohn

Pitches: Left **Bats:** Right **Pos:** SP-9; RP-7 **Ht:** 6'3" **Wt:** 190 **Born:** 6/11/77 **Age:** 25

		HOW MUCH HE PITCHED						WHAT HE GAVE UP												THE RESULTS					
Year Team	Lg	G	GS	CG	GF	IP	BFP	H	R	ER	HR	SH	SF	HB	TBB	IBB	SO	WP	Bk	W	L	Pct.	ShO	Sv-Op	Hld	ERA
1998 Jamestown	A-	4	4	0	0	22	93	21	10	7	0	1	2	2	4	0	24	1	1	2	2	.500	0	0--	—	2.86
W Michigan	A	8	8	1	0	50.1	210	46	15	11	3	3	0	4	9	0	64	1	0	4	2	.667	1	0--	—	1.97
1999 Lakeland	A+	9	9	2	0	59.2	255	62	35	25	2	2	0	1	11	0	51	2	0	3	4	.429	0	0--	—	3.77
Jacksnville	AA	20	20	0	0	126.2	548	134	75	66	13	3	5	8	35	0	92	4	0	9	5	.643	0	0--	—	4.69
2000 Jacksnville	AA	8	8	0	0	50.1	203	43	20	19	4	1	0	4	12	0	45	2	0	2	2	.500	0	0--	—	3.40
Toledo	AAA	7	7	0	0	39	182	45	34	29	5	2	3	2	22	0	23	1	0	0	4	.000	0	0--	—	6.69
2001 Toledo	AAA	17	17	0	0	107.1	449	107	51	41	9	3	6	4	26	0	78	5	1	5	8	.385	0	0--	—	3.44
2001 Detroit	AL	16	9	0	1	65	293	81	48	42	10	3	3	4	21	2	40	2	0	1	6	.143	0	0-0	1	5.82

Josh Phelps

Bats: Right **Throws:** Right **Pos:** C-7; PH/PR-2 **Ht:** 6'3" **Wt:** 215 **Born:** 5/12/78 **Age:** 24

								BATTING												BASERUNNING				PERCENTAGES		
Year Team	Lg	G	AB	H	2B	3B	HR	(Hm	Rd)	TB	R	RBI	TBB	IBB	SO	HBP	SH	SF	SB	CS	SB%	GDP	Avg	OBP	SLG
1996 Medcine Hat	R+	59	191	46	3	0	5	—	—	64	28	29	27	0	65	6	2	1	5	3	.63	5	.241	.351	.335
1997 Hagerstown	A	68	233	49	9	1	7	—	—	81	26	24	15	0	72	8	0	2	3	2	.60	6	.210	.279	.348
1998 Hagerstown	A	117	385	102	24	1	8	—	—	152	48	44	40	1	80	8	1	5	2	0	1.00	12	.265	.342	.395
1999 Dunedin	A+	110	406	133	27	4	20	—	—	228	72	88	28	0	104	8	2	4	6	3	.67	13	.328	.379	.562
2000 Tennessee	AA	56	184	42	9	1	9	—	—	80	23	28	15	0	66	7	1	2	1	0	1.00	6	.228	.308	.435
Dunedin	A+	30	113	36	7	0	12	—	—	79	26	34	12	0	34	1	0	1	0	0	—	0	.319	.386	.699
2001 Tennessee	AA	136	486	142	36	1	31	—	—	273	95	97	80	4	127	17	0	5	3	3	.50	5	.292	.406	.562
2000 Toronto	AL	1	1	0	0	0	0	(0	0)	0	0	0	0	0	1	0	0	0	0	0	—	0	.000	.000	.000
2001 Toronto	AL	8	12	0	0	0	0	(0	0)	0	3	1	2	0	5	0	0	0	1	0	1.00	1	.000	.143	.000
2 ML YEARS		9	13	0	0	0	0	(0	0)	0	3	1	2	0	6	0	0	0	1	0	1.00	1	.000	.133	.000

Travis Phelps

Pitches: Right **Bats:** Right **Pos:** RP-49 **Ht:** 6'2" **Wt:** 170 **Born:** 7/25/77 **Age:** 24

		HOW MUCH HE PITCHED						WHAT HE GAVE UP												THE RESULTS					
Year Team	Lg	G	GS	CG	GF	IP	BFP	H	R	ER	HR	SH	SF	HB	TBB	IBB	SO	WP	Bk	W	L	Pct.	ShO	Sv-Op	Hld	ERA
1997 Princeton	R+	14	13	1	0	62.2	279	73	42	34	4	3	1	2	23	0	60	4	1	3	5	.571	0	0--	—	4.88
1998 Chston-SC	A	18	18	0	0	91	401	100	54	49	4	1	1	3	35	0	96	7	3	5	8	.385	0	0--	—	4.85
1999 St. Pete	A+	24	23	1	0	133.2	574	148	70	63	6	4	4	11	39	0	101	2	0	10	8	.556	1	0--	—	4.24
2000 Orlando	AA	21	21	2	0	108	448	85	44	36	5	1	1	13	46	0	106	5	0	7	8	.467	0	0--	—	3.00
Durham	AAA	6	6	0	0	29.2	131	29	17	16	6	2	0	0	16	0	21	0	0	3	1	.750	0	0--	—	4.85
2001 Durham	AAA	9	0	0	1	15.2	57	11	0	0	0	1	0	1	1	0	12	1	0	2	0	1.000	0	0--	—	0.00
2001 Tampa Bay	AL	49	0	0	15	62	268	53	30	24	6	2	4	3	24	1	54	2	1	2	2	.500	0	5-6	13	3.48

Jason Phillips

Bats: Right **Throws:** Right **Pos:** C-5; PH/PR-1 **Ht:** 6'1" **Wt:** 171 **Born:** 9/27/76 **Age:** 25

								BATTING												BASERUNNING				PERCENTAGES		
Year Team	Lg	G	AB	H	2B	3B	HR	(Hm	Rd)	TB	R	RBI	TBB	IBB	SO	HBP	SH	SF	SB	CS	SB%	GDP	Avg	OBP	SLG
1997 Pittsfield	A-	48	155	32	9	0	2	—	—	47	15	17	13	0	24	4	1	2	4	0	1.00	2	.206	.282	.303
1998 St. Lucie	A+	8	28	13	2	0	0	—	—	15	4	2	2	0	1	0	1	0	0	0	—	0	.464	.500	.536
Capital Cty	A	69	251	68	15	1	5	—	—	100	36	37	23	1	35	5	1	1	5	2	.71	3	.271	.343	.398
1999 Binghamton	AA	39	141	32	5	0	7	—	—	58	13	23	13	0	20	3	2	1	0	0	—	4	.227	.304	.411
St. Lucie	A+	81	283	73	12	1	9	—	—	114	36	48	23	0	28	8	0	4	0	1	.00	10	.258	.327	.403
2000 St. Lucie	A+	80	297	82	21	0	6	—	—	121	53	41	23	2	19	8	1	1	1	1	.50	12	.276	.343	.407
Binghamton	AA	27	98	38	4	0	0	—	—	42	16	13	7	0	9	2	0	1	0	0	—	3	.388	.435	.429
2001 Binghamton	AA	93	317	93	21	0	11	—	—	147	42	55	31	3	25	5	1	3	0	1	.00	9	.293	.362	.464
Norfolk	AAA	19	66	20	2	0	2	—	—	28	8	14	7	0	8	0	0	1	0	0	—	2	.303	.365	.424
2001 New York	NL	6	7	1	1	0	0	(0	0)	2	2	0	0	0	0	0	0	0	0	0	—	0	.143	.143	.286

Adam Piatt

Bats: Right **Throws:** Right **Pos:** RF-32; PH/PR-6; DH-1   **Ht:** 6'2" **Wt:** 195 **Born:** 2/8/76 **Age:** 26

Year Team	Lg	G	AB	H	2B	3B	HR	(Hm	Rd)	TB	R	RBI	TBB	IBB	SO	HBP	SH	SF	SB	CS	SB%	GDP	Avg	OBP	SLG
1997 Sou Oregon	A-	57	216	63	9	1	13	—	—	113	63	35	35	1	58	1	0	1	19	4	.83	4	.292	.391	.523
1998 Modesto	A+	133	500	144	40	3	20	—	—	250	91	107	80	1	99	0	1	8	20	6	.77	15	.288	.381	.500
1999 Midland	AA	129	476	164	48	3	39	—	—	335	128	135	93	10	101	7	0	9	7	3	.70	11	.345	.451	.704
Vancouver	AAA	6	18	4	1	0	0	—	—	5	1	3	6	0	2	0	0	0	0	0	—	2	.222	.417	.278
2000 Sacramento	AAA	65	254	72	15	0	8	—	—	111	36	42	26	1	57	4	0	3	3	2	.60	3	.283	.355	.437
2001 Modesto	A+	4	15	7	2	0	1	—	—	12	4	2	1	0	5	1	0	0	0	0	—	0	.467	.529	.800
Sacramento	AAA	35	109	28	9	0	1	—	—	40	14	15	11	0	27	3	0	1	2	0	1.00	5	.257	.339	.367
2000 Oakland	AL	60	157	47	5	5	5	(3	2)	77	24	23	23	0	44	1	1	0	0	1	.00	1	.299	.392	.490
2001 Oakland	AL	36	95	20	5	1	0	(0	0)	27	9	6	13	0	26	0	1	2	0	0	—	5	.211	.300	.284
2 ML YEARS		96	252	67	10	6	5	(3	2)	104	33	29	36	0	70	1	2	2	0	1	.00	6	.266	.357	.413

Mike Piazza

Bats: Right **Throws:** Right **Pos:** C-131; PH/PR-7; DH-5   **Ht:** 6'3" **Wt:** 215 **Born:** 9/4/68 **Age:** 33

Year Team	Lg	G	AB	H	2B	3B	HR	(Hm	Rd)	TB	R	RBI	TBB	IBB	SO	HBP	SH	SF	SB	CS	SB%	GDP	Avg	OBP	SLG
1992 Los Angeles	NL	21	69	16	3	0	1	(1	0)	22	5	7	4	0	12	1	0	0	0	0	—	1	.232	.284	.319
1993 Los Angeles	NL	149	547	174	24	2	35	(21	14)	307	81	112	46	6	86	3	0	6	3	4	.43	10	.318	.370	.561
1994 Los Angeles	NL	107	405	129	18	0	24	(13	11)	219	64	92	33	10	65	1	0	2	1	3	.25	11	.319	.370	.541
1995 Los Angeles	NL	112	434	150	17	0	32	(9	23)	263	82	93	39	10	80	1	0	1	1	0	1.00	10	.346	.400	.606
1996 Los Angeles	NL	148	547	184	16	0	36	(14	22)	308	87	105	81	21	93	1	0	2	0	3	.00	21	.336	.422	.563
1997 Los Angeles	NL	152	556	201	32	1	40	(22	18)	355	104	124	69	11	77	3	0	5	5	1	.83	19	.362	.431	.638
1998 LA-Fla-NYM	NL	151	561	184	38	1	32	(15	17)	320	88	111	58	14	80	2	0	5	1	0	1.00	15	.328	.390	.570
1999 New York	NL	141	534	162	25	0	40	(18	22)	307	100	124	51	11	70	1	0	7	2	2	.50	27	.303	.361	.575
2000 New York	NL	136	482	156	26	0	38	(17	21)	296	90	113	58	10	69	3	0	2	4	2	.67	15	.324	.398	.614
2001 New York	NL	141	503	151	29	0	36	(16	20)	288	81	94	67	19	87	2	0	1	0	2	.00	20	.300	.384	.573
1998 Los Angeles	NL	37	149	42	5	0	9	(5	4)	74	20	30	11	4	27	0	0	1	0	0	—	3	.282	.329	.497
Florida	NL	5	18	5	0	1	0	(0	0)	7	1	5	0	0	0	0	0	1	0	0	—	0	.278	.263	.389
New York	NL	109	394	137	33	0	23	(10	13)	239	67	76	47	10	53	2	0	3	1	0	1.00	12	.348	.417	.607
10 ML YEARS		1258	4638	1507	228	4	314	(146	168)	2685	782	975	506	112	719	18	0	31	17	17	.50	149	.325	.391	.579

Hipolito Pichardo

Pitches: Right **Bats:** Right **Pos:** RP-30   **Ht:** 6'1" **Wt:** 195 **Born:** 8/22/69 **Age:** 32

Year Team	Lg	G	GS	CG	GF	IP	BFP	H	R	ER	HR	SH	SF	HB	TBB	IBB	SO	WP	Bk	W	L	Pct.	ShO	Sv-Op	Hld	ERA
2001 Sarasota *	A+	3	3	0	0	6	29	8	3	3	1	0	0	0	2	0	8	0	0	0	0	—	0	0--	—	4.50
Pawtucket *	AAA	3	3	0	0	5	21	3	3	3	0	0	0	0	4	0	2	0	0	0	0	—	0	0--	—	5.40
1992 Kansas City	AL	31	24	1	0	143.2	615	148	71	63	9	4	5	3	49	1	59	3	1	9	6	.600	1	0-0	1	3.95
1993 Kansas City	AL	30	25	2	2	165	720	183	85	74	10	3	8	6	53	2	70	5	3	7	8	.467	0	0-0	1	4.04
1994 Kansas City	AL	45	0	0	19	67.2	303	82	42	37	4	4	2	7	24	5	36	3	0	5	3	.625	0	3-5	6	4.92
1995 Kansas City	AL	44	0	0	16	64	287	66	34	31	4	3	1	4	30	7	43	4	1	8	4	.667	0	1-2	7	4.36
1996 Kansas City	AL	57	0	0	28	68	294	74	44	41	5	3	2	2	26	5	43	4	0	3	5	.375	0	3-5	15	5.43
1997 Kansas City	AL	47	0	0	26	49	215	51	24	23	7	2	0	1	24	8	34	2	1	3	5	.375	0	11-13	4	4.22
1998 Kansas City	AL	27	18	0	2	112.1	503	126	73	64	11	3	3	4	43	2	55	2	0	7	8	.467	0	1-1	2	5.13
2000 Boston	AL	38	1	0	5	65	275	63	29	25	1	2	2	3	26	2	37	2	0	6	3	.667	0	1-2	4	3.46
2001 Boston	AL	30	0	0	5	34.2	159	42	23	19	3	2	2	5	10	3	17	3	0	2	1	.667	0	0-3	4	4.93
9 ML YEARS		349	68	3	103	769.1	3371	835	422	377	54	26	25	35	285	35	394	28	6	50	43	.538	1	20-31	41	4.41

Calvin Pickering

Bats: Left **Throws:** Left **Pos:** 1B-12; PH/PR-8; DH-2   **Ht:** 6'5" **Wt:** 275 **Born:** 9/29/76 **Age:** 25

Year Team	Lg	G	AB	H	2B	3B	HR	(Hm	Rd)	TB	R	RBI	TBB	IBB	SO	HBP	SH	SF	SB	CS	SB%	GDP	Avg	OBP	SLG
1995 Orioles	R	15	60	30	10	0	1	—	—	43	8	22	2	0	6	0	0	1	0	0	—	3	.500	.508	.717
1996 Bluefield	R+	60	200	65	14	1	18	—	—	135	45	66	28	4	64	2	0	1	8	2	.80	4	.325	.411	.675
1997 Delmarva	A	122	444	138	31	1	25	—	—	246	88	79	53	2	139	9	0	1	6	3	.67	14	.311	.394	.554
1998 Bowie	AA	139	488	151	28	2	31	—	—	276	93	114	98	16	119	11	0	4	4	6	.40	20	.309	.434	.566
1999 Rochester	AAA	103	372	106	20	0	16	—	—	174	63	63	60	6	99	11	0	4	1	3	.25	10	.285	.396	.468
2000 Rochester	AAA	60	197	43	10	0	6	—	—	71	20	30	36	2	70	1	0	2	2	2	.50	4	.218	.339	.360
2001 Rochester	AAA	131	461	130	25	0	21	—	—	218	62	98	64	7	149	10	0	3	0	1	.00	16	.282	.379	.473
Louisville	AAA	1	4	1	0	0	0	—	—	4	1	1	1	0	2	0	0	0	0	0	—	0	.250	.400	1.000
1998 Baltimore	AL	9	21	5	0	0	2	(1	1)	11	4	3	3	0	4	0	0	0	0	1	.00	2	.238	.333	.524
1999 Baltimore	AL	23	40	5	1	0	1	(1	0)	9	4	5	11	0	16	0	0	0	0	0	—	1	.125	.314	.225
2001 Cin-Bos	AL	21	54	15	1	0	3	(1	2)	25	4	8	8	0	15	0	0	0	0	0	—	4	.278	.371	.463
2001 Cincinnati	NL	4	4	1	0	0	0	(0	0)	1	0	1	0	0	2	0	0	0	0	0	—	0	.250	.250	.250
Boston	AL	17	50	14	1	0	3	(1	2)	24	4	7	8	0	13	0	0	0	0	0	—	4	.280	.379	.480
3 ML YEARS		53	115	25	2	0	6	(3	3)	45	12	16	22	0	35	0	0	0	0	1	.00	7	.217	.343	.391

Juan Pierre

Bats: Left **Throws:** Left **Pos:** CF-154; PH/PR-7   **Ht:** 6'0" **Wt:** 180 **Born:** 8/14/77 **Age:** 24

Year Team	Lg	G	AB	H	2B	3B	HR	(Hm	Rd)	TB	R	RBI	TBB	IBB	SO	HBP	SH	SF	SB	CS	SB%	GDP	Avg	OBP	SLG
1998 Portland	A-	64	264	93	9	2	0	—	—	106	55	30	19	0	11	2	4	1	38	9	.81	3	.352	.399	.402
1999 Asheville	A	140	585	187	28	5	1	—	—	228	93	55	38	2	37	8	11	6	66	19	.78	12	.320	.366	.390
2000 Carolina	AA	107	439	143	16	4	0	—	—	167	63	32	33	0	26	5	8	4	46	12	.79	4	.326	.376	.380
Colo Sprngs	AAA	4	17	8	0	1	0	—	—	10	3	1	0	0	0	0	0	0	1	1	.50	0	.471	.471	.588
2000 Colorado	NL	51	200	62	2	0	0	(0	0)	64	26	20	13	0	15	1	4	1	7	6	.54	2	.310	.353	.320
2001 Colorado	NL	156	617	202	26	11	2	(0	0)	256	108	55	41	1	29	10	14	1	46	17	.73	6	.327	.378	.415
2 ML YEARS		207	817	264	28	11	2	(0	2)	320	134	75	54	1	44	11	18	2	53	23	.70	8	.323	.372	.392

Chris Piersoll

Pitches: Right **Bats:** Right **Pos:** RP-11   **Ht:** 6'4" **Wt:** 195 **Born:** 9/25/77 **Age:** 24

		HOW MUCH HE PITCHED						WHAT HE GAVE UP												THE RESULTS						
Year Team	Lg	G	GS	CG	GF	IP	BFP	H	R	ER	HR	SH	SF	HB	TBB	IBB	SO	WP	Bk	W	L	Pct.	ShO	Sv-Op	Hld	ERA
1997 Cubs	R	14	0	0	3	31.2	130	21	11	8	0	0	0	2	9	0	35	2	4	4	0	1.000	0	2--	—	2.27
1998 Rockford	A	27	4	1	11	59.2	251	52	28	26	8	1	0	4	20	0	55	3	0	2	0	1.000	0	2--	—	3.92
1999 Daytona	A+	33	0	0	20	67.2	296	68	30	28	7	1	0	7	24	2	74	9	0	7	3	.700	0	5--	—	3.72
West Tenn	AA	8	1	0	4	14.1	57	12	1	1	0	1	0	0	3	0	14	2	0	0	0	—	0	1--	—	0.63
2000 West Tenn	AA	47	0	0	16	60.2	258	51	17	14	4	4	1	2	28	1	54	5	3	3	3	.500	0	2--	—	2.08
2001 Chattanooga	AA	50	0	0	41	56	245	48	24	21	2	1	0	1	30	2	78	3	0	1	4	.200	0	19--	—	3.38
2001 Cincinnati	NL	11	0	0	3	11.1	52	12	4	3	0	0	0	1	6	0	7	0	0	0	0	—	0	0-0	0	2.38

A.J. Pierzynski

Bats: Left **Throws:** Right **Pos:** C-110; PH/PR-10; DH-1   **Ht:** 6'3" **Wt:** 220 **Born:** 12/30/76 **Age:** 25

		BATTING																	BASERUNNING				PERCENTAGES		
Year Team	Lg	G	AB	H	2B	3B	HR	(Hm	Rd)	TB	R	RBI	TBB	IBB	SO	HBP	SH	SF	SB	CS	SB%	GDP	Avg	OBP	SLG
1998 Minnesota	AL	7	10	3	0	0	0	(0	0)	3	1	1	1	0	2	1	0	1	0	0	—	0	.300	.385	.300
1999 Minnesota	AL	9	22	6	2	0	0	(0	0)	8	3	3	1	0	4	1	0	0	0	0	—	0	.273	.333	.364
2000 Minnesota	AL	33	88	27	5	1	2	(1	1)	40	12	11	5	0	14	2	0	1	1	0	1.00	1	.307	.354	.455
2001 Minnesota	AL	114	381	110	33	2	7	(3	4)	168	51	55	16	4	57	4	1	3	1	7	.13	7	.289	.322	.441
4 ML YEARS		163	501	146	40	3	9	(4	5)	219	67	70	23	4	77	8	1	5	2	7	.22	8	.291	.330	.437

Luis Pineda

Pitches: Right **Bats:** Right **Pos:** RP-16   **Ht:** 6'1" **Wt:** 160 **Born:** 6/10/78 **Age:** 24

		HOW MUCH HE PITCHED						WHAT HE GAVE UP												THE RESULTS						
Year Team	Lg	G	GS	CG	GF	IP	BFP	H	R	ER	HR	SH	SF	HB	TBB	IBB	SO	WP	Bk	W	L	Pct.	ShO	Sv-Op	Hld	ERA
1996 Rangers	R	11	11	1	0	71.2	306	67	31	28	6	3	1	3	25	0	66	10	5	3	2	.667	0	0--	—	3.52
1999 W Michigan	A	24	3	0	19	40.1	175	30	18	16	2	2	5	1	26	2	55	5	0	0	2	.000	0	7--	—	3.57
Lakeland	A+	8	0	0	8	8.2	39	6	2	1	0	0	0	0	7	0	8	0	0	1	0	1.000	0	0--	—	1.04
2000 Lakeland	A+	18	0	0	13	26.2	122	23	13	10	3	2	1	1	19	0	42	4	1	1	3	.250	0	4--	—	3.38
2001 Erie	AA	16	12	2	2	85.2	340	68	33	29	8	3	5	2	28	0	92	3	0	6	2	.750	1	0--	—	3.05
Toledo	AAA	2	0	0	0	8	27	3	0	0	0	0	0	0	0	0	6	0	0	1	0	1.000	0	0--	—	0.00
2001 Detroit	AL	16	0	0	4	18.1	82	16	10	10	2	0	1	0	14	2	13	0	0	0	0	.000	0	0-0	2	4.91

Joel Pineiro

Pitches: Right **Bats:** Right **Pos:** SP-11; RP-6   **Ht:** 6'1" **Wt:** 180 **Born:** 9/25/78 **Age:** 23

		HOW MUCH HE PITCHED						WHAT HE GAVE UP												THE RESULTS						
Year Team	Lg	G	GS	CG	GF	IP	BFP	H	R	ER	HR	SH	SF	HB	TBB	IBB	SO	WP	Bk	W	L	Pct.	ShO	Sv-Op	Hld	ERA
1997 Mariners	R	1	0	0	0	3	11	1	0	0	0	0	0	1	0	0	4	0	0	1	0	1.000	0	0--	—	0.00
Everett	A-	18	6	0	9	49	223	54	33	29	2	0	0	3	18	1	59	3	2	4	2	.667	0	2--	—	5.33
1998 Wisconsin	A	16	16	1	0	96	401	92	40	34	8	3	2	3	28	1	84	3	1	8	4	.667	0	0--	—	3.19
Lancaster	A+	9	9	1	0	45	217	58	40	39	6	0	0	6	22	0	48	2	3	2	0	1.000	1	0--	—	7.80
Orlando	AA	1	1	0	0	5	22	7	4	3	0	0	1	0	2	0	2	0	0	1	0	1.000	0	0--	—	5.40
1999 New Haven	AA	28	25	4	0	166	724	190	105	87	18	6	5	5	52	0	116	11	0	10	15	.400	0	0--	—	4.72
2000 New Haven	AA	9	9	0	0	52.1	207	42	25	24	6	0	1	1	12	0	43	0	0	2	1	.667	0	0--	—	4.13
Tacoma	AAA	10	9	2	0	61	256	53	20	19	3	2	1	3	22	1	41	2	0	7	1	.875	2	0--	—	2.80
2001 Tacoma	AAA	18	10	0	2	77	316	68	31	31	8	0	1	1	33	0	64	4	0	6	3	.667	0	0--	—	3.62
2000 Seattle	AL	8	1	0	5	19.1	94	25	13	12	3	0	2	0	13	0	10	0	0	1	0	1.000	0	0-0	0	5.59
2001 Seattle	AL	17	11	0	1	75.1	289	50	24	17	2	1	2	3	21	0	56	2	0	6	2	.750	0	0-0	2	2.03
2 ML YEARS		25	12	0	6	94.2	383	75	37	29	5	1	4	3	34	0	66	2	0	7	2	.778	0	0-0	2	2.76

Dan Plesac

Pitches: Left **Bats:** Left **Pos:** RP-62   **Ht:** 6'5" **Wt:** 217 **Born:** 2/4/62 **Age:** 40

		HOW MUCH HE PITCHED						WHAT HE GAVE UP												THE RESULTS						
Year Team	Lg	G	GS	CG	GF	IP	BFP	H	R	ER	HR	SH	SF	HB	TBB	IBB	SO	WP	Bk	W	L	Pct.	ShO	Sv-Op	Hld	ERA
1986 Milwaukee	AL	51	0	0	33	91	377	81	34	30	5	6	5	0	29	1	75	4	0	10	7	.588	0	14-20	5	2.97
1987 Milwaukee	AL	57	0	0	47	79.1	325	63	30	23	8	1	2	3	23	1	89	6	0	5	6	.455	0	23-36	0	2.61
1988 Milwaukee	AL	50	0	0	48	52.1	211	46	14	14	2	2	0	0	12	2	52	4	6	1	2	.333	0	30-35	0	2.41
1989 Milwaukee	AL	52	0	0	51	61.1	242	47	16	16	6	0	4	0	17	1	52	0	0	3	4	.429	0	33-40	0	2.35
1990 Milwaukee	AL	66	0	0	52	69	299	67	36	34	5	2	2	3	31	6	65	2	0	3	7	.300	0	24-34	2	4.43
1991 Milwaukee	AL	45	10	0	25	92.1	402	92	49	44	12	3	7	3	39	1	61	2	1	2	7	.222	0	8-12	1	4.29
1992 Milwaukee	AL	44	4	0	13	79	330	64	28	26	5	8	4	3	35	5	54	3	1	5	4	.556	0	1-3	1	2.96
1993 Chicago	NL	57	0	0	12	62.2	276	74	37	33	10	4	3	0	21	6	47	5	2	2	1	.667	0	0-2	12	4.74
1994 Chicago	NL	54	0	0	14	54.2	235	61	30	28	9	1	1	1	13	0	53	0	0	2	3	.400	0	1-3	14	4.61
1995 Pittsburgh	NL	58	0	0	16	60.1	259	53	26	24	3	4	3	1	27	7	57	1	0	4	4	.500	0	3-5	11	3.58
1996 Pittsburgh	NL	73	0	0	30	70.1	300	67	35	32	4	2	3	0	24	6	76	4	0	6	5	.545	0	11-17	11	4.09
1997 Toronto	AL	73	0	0	18	50.1	215	47	22	20	8	2	1	0	19	4	61	2	0	2	4	.333	0	1-5	27	3.58
1998 Toronto	AL	78	0	0	16	50	203	41	23	21	4	0	3	1	16	1	55	0	0	4	3	.571	0	4-5	27	3.78
1999 Tor-Ari		64	0	0	11	44.1	198	50	30	29	7	4	1	0	17	2	53	3	0	2	4	.333	0	1-3	15	5.89
2000 Arizona	NL	62	0	0	14	40	182	34	21	14	4	6	1	0	26	2	45	3	0	5	1	.833	0	0-4	9	3.15
2001 Arizona	NL	62	0	0	5	45.1	190	34	18	18	4	0	1	0	24	5	68	1	0	4	5	.444	0	1-2	16	3.57
1999 Toronto	AL	30	0	0	5	22.2	104	28	21	21	4	3	1	0	9	1	26	2	0	0	3	.000	0	0-2	9	8.34
Arizona	NL	34	0	0	6	21.2	94	22	9	8	3	1	0	0	8	1	27	1	0	2	1	.667	0	1-1	6	3.32
16 ML YEARS		946	14	0	405	1002.1	4244	921	449	406	96	45	41	16	373	50	963	40	10	60	67	.472	0	155-226	151	3.65

Scott Podsednik

Bats: L Throws: L Pos: LF-3; PH/PR-2; CF-1; RF-1   Ht: 6'0" Wt: 170 Born: 3/18/76 Age: 26

Year Team	Lg	G	AB	H	2B	3B	HR	(Hm	Rd)	TB	R	RBI	TBB	IBB	SO	HBP	SH	SF	SB	CS	SB%	GDP	Avg	OBP	SLG
1994 Rangers	R	60	211	48	7	1	1	—	—	60	34	17	41	0	34	3	2	3	18	5	.78	1	.227	.357	.284
1995 Hudson Val	A-	65	252	67	3	0	0	—	—	70	42	20	35	3	31	1	1	2	20	6	.77	9	.266	.355	.278
1996 Brevard Cty	A+	108	383	100	9	2	0	—	—	113	39	30	45	0	65	3	7	0	20	10	.67	8	.261	.343	.295
1997 Kane County	A	135	531	147	23	4	3	—	—	187	80	49	60	2	72	3	14	3	28	11	.72	5	.277	.352	.352
1998 Tulsa	AA	17	75	18	4	1	0	—	—	24	9	4	6	0	11	0	0	0	5	2	.71	3	.240	.296	.320
Charlotte	A+	81	302	86	12	4	4	—	—	118	55	39	44	0	32	0	4	6	26	8	.76	2	.285	.369	.391
1999 Rangers	R	5	17	7	2	0	0	—	—	9	6	5	2	0	3	0	0	0	1	0	1.00	1	.412	.474	.529
Tulsa	AA	37	116	18	4	0	0	—	—	22	10	1	5	0	13	0	2	0	6	2	.75	3	.155	.190	.190
2000 Tulsa	AA	49	169	42	7	2	2	—	—	59	20	13	30	1	33	1	1	2	19	4	.83	4	.249	.361	.349
2001 Tacoma	AAA	66	269	78	15	4	3	—	—	110	46	30	13	0	46	2	4	0	12	5	.71	0	.290	.327	.409
2001 Seattle	AL	5	6	1	0	1	0	(0	0)	3	1	3	0	0	1	0	0	0	0	0	—	1	.167	.167	.500

Placido Polanco

Bats: R Throws: R Pos: 3B-103; SS-42; 2B-15; PH/PR-7; DH-1   Ht: 5'10" Wt: 168 Born: 10/10/75 Age: 26

Year Team	Lg	G	AB	H	2B	3B	HR	(Hm	Rd)	TB	R	RBI	TBB	IBB	SO	HBP	SH	SF	SB	CS	SB%	GDP	Avg	OBP	SLG
1998 St. Louis	NL	45	114	29	3	2	1	(0	1)	39	10	11	5	0	9	1	2	0	2	0	1.00	1	.254	.292	.342
1999 St. Louis	NL	88	220	61	9	3	1	(0	1)	79	24	19	15	1	24	0	3	2	1	3	.25	7	.277	.321	.359
2000 St. Louis	NL	118	323	102	12	3	5	(2	3)	135	50	39	16	0	26	1	7	3	4	4	.50	8	.316	.347	.418
2001 St. Louis	NL	144	564	173	26	4	3	(2	1)	216	87	38	25	0	43	6	14	1	12	3	.80	22	.307	.342	.383
4 ML YEARS		395	1221	365	50	12	10	(4	6)	469	171	107	61	1	102	8	26	6	19	10	.66	38	.299	.335	.384

Cliff Politte

Pitches: Right Bats: Right Pos: RP-23   Ht: 5'11" Wt: 185 Born: 2/27/74 Age: 28

Year Team	Lg	G	GS	CG	GF	IP	BFP	H	R	ER	HR	SH	SF	HB	TBB	IBB	SO	WP	Bk	W	L	Pct.	ShO	Sv-Op	Hld	ERA
2001 Clearwater *	A+	7	7	0	0	11	43	8	4	3	0	0	0	0	3	0	15	0	0	0	1	.000	0	0- -	—	2.45
1998 St. Louis	NL	8	8	0	0	37	172	45	32	26	6	3	1	1	18	0	22	2	1	2	3	.400	0	0-0	0	6.32
1999 Philadelphia	NL	13	0	0	0	17.2	85	19	14	14	2	1	0	0	15	0	15	2	0	1	0	1.000	0	0-0	1	7.13
2000 Philadelphia	NL	12	8	0	1	59	251	55	24	24	8	1	1	0	27	1	50	3	0	4	3	.571	0	0-0	0	3.66
2001 Philadelphia	NL	23	0	0	7	26	109	24	8	7	2	1	3	1	8	3	23	1	0	2	3	.400	0	0-0	1	2.42
4 ML YEARS		56	16	0	8	139.2	617	143	78	71	18	6	5	2	68	4	110	8	1	9	9	.500	0	0-0	2	4.58

Sidney Ponson

Pitches: Right Bats: Right Pos: SP-23   Ht: 6'1" Wt: 225 Born: 11/2/76 Age: 25

Year Team	Lg	G	GS	CG	GF	IP	BFP	H	R	ER	HR	SH	SF	HB	TBB	IBB	SO	WP	Bk	W	L	Pct.	ShO	Sv-Op	Hld	ERA
2001 Bowie *	AA	1	1	0	0	4	14	3	0	0	0	0	0	0	1	0	2	0	0	0	0	—	0	0- -	—	0.00
1998 Baltimore	AL	31	20	0	5	135	588	157	82	79	19	3	4	3	42	2	85	4	1	8	9	.471	0	1-2	0	5.27
1999 Baltimore	AL	32	32	6	0	210	897	227	118	110	35	4	7	1	80	2	112	4	0	12	12	.500	1	0-0	0	4.71
2000 Baltimore	AL	32	32	6	0	222	953	223	125	119	30	3	3	6	83	0	152	5	0	9	13	.409	1	0-0	0	4.82
2001 Baltimore	AL	23	23	3	0	138.1	605	161	83	76	21	3	2	6	37	0	84	2	0	5	10	.333	0	0-0	0	4.94
4 ML YEARS		118	107	15	5	705.1	3043	768	408	384	105	13	16	11	242	4	433	15	1	34	44	.436	2	1-2	0	4.90

Bo Porter

Bats: R Throws: R Pos: LF-18; RF-12; CF-10; PH/PR-10; DH-2   Ht: 6'2" Wt: 195 Born: 7/5/72 Age: 29

Year Team	Lg	G	AB	H	2B	3B	HR	(Hm	Rd)	TB	R	RBI	TBB	IBB	SO	HBP	SH	SF	SB	CS	SB%	GDP	Avg	OBP	SLG
1994 Peoria	A	66	221	60	11	2	6	—	—	93	40	29	27	0	59	2	6	4	6	5	.55	5	.271	.350	.421
1995 Daytona	A+	113	336	73	12	2	3	—	—	98	54	19	32	0	104	2	4	3	22	10	.69	5	.217	.287	.292
1996 Daytona	A+	20	63	11	4	1	0	—	—	17	9	6	6	0	24	0	1	0	5	1	.83	0	.175	.239	.270
Rockford	A	105	378	91	22	3	7	—	—	140	83	44	72	1	107	1	3	4	30	14	.68	7	.241	.360	.370
1997 Daytona	A+	122	440	135	20	6	17	—	—	218	87	65	61	1	115	3	1	3	23	13	.64	8	.307	.393	.495
Orlando	AA	8	31	8	1	0	1	—	—	12	4	3	0	0	11	1	0	0	0	1	.00	1	.258	.281	.387
1998 West Tenn	AA	125	464	134	26	11	10	—	—	212	91	68	82	4	117	6	3	5	50	17	.75	9	.289	.399	.457
Iowa	AAA	4	11	4	1	0	0	—	—	5	2	3	4	0	4	0	0	0	1	2	.33	0	.364	.533	.455
1999 Iowa	AAA	111	414	121	24	2	27	—	—	230	86	64	65	0	121	8	1	3	15	17	.47	7	.292	.396	.556
2000 Sacramento	AAA	129	481	131	21	3	14	—	—	200	94	64	88	1	117	5	4	6	39	10	.80	9	.272	.386	.416
2001 Oklahoma	AAA	58	224	55	9	2	13	—	—	107	40	40	26	0	60	3	4	2	10	4	.71	3	.246	.329	.478
1999 Chicago	NL	24	26	5	1	0	0	(0	0)	6	2	0	2	0	13	0	1	0	0	0	—	1	.192	.250	.231
2000 Oakland	AL	17	13	2	0	0	1	(0	1)	5	3	2	2	0	5	0	0	0	0	0	—	0	.154	.267	.385
2001 Texas	AL	48	87	20	4	2	1	(1	0)	31	18	6	9	0	34	0	0	2	3	2	.60	1	.230	.296	.356
3 ML YEARS		89	126	27	5	2	2	(1	1)	42	23	8	13	0	52	0	1	2	3	2	.60	2	.214	.284	.333

Jorge Posada

Bats: B Throws: R Pos: C-131; DH-6; PH/PR-5; 1B-2   Ht: 6'2" Wt: 200 Born: 8/17/71 Age: 30

Year Team	Lg	G	AB	H	2B	3B	HR	(Hm	Rd)	TB	R	RBI	TBB	IBB	SO	HBP	SH	SF	SB	CS	SB%	GDP	Avg	OBP	SLG
1995 New York	AL	1	0	0	0	0	0	(0	0)	0	0	0	0	0	0	0	0	0	0	0	—	0	—	—	—
1996 New York	AL	8	14	1	0	0	0	(0	0)	1	1	0	1	0	6	0	0	0	0	0	—	0	.071	.133	.071
1997 New York	AL	60	188	47	12	0	6	(2	4)	77	29	25	30	2	33	3	1	2	1	2	.33	2	.250	.359	.410
1998 New York	AL	111	358	96	23	0	17	(6	11)	170	56	63	47	7	92	0	0	4	0	1	.00	14	.268	.350	.475
1999 New York	AL	112	379	93	19	2	12	(4	8)	152	50	57	53	2	91	3	0	2	1	0	1.00	9	.245	.341	.401
2000 New York	AL	151	505	145	35	1	28	(18	10)	266	92	86	107	10	151	8	0	4	2	2	.50	11	.287	.417	.527

178

		BATTING																		BASERUNNING				PERCENTAGES		
Year Team	Lg	G	AB	H	2B	3B	HR	(Hm	Rd)	TB	R	RBI	TBB	IBB	SO	HBP	SH	SF	SB	CS	SB%	GDP	Avg	OBP	SLG
2001 New York	AL	138	484	134	28	1	22	(14	8)	230	59	95	62	10	132	6	0	5	2	6	.25	10	.277	.363	.475
7 ML YEARS		581	1928	516	117	4	85	(44	41)	896	287	326	300	31	505	20	1	17	6	11	.35	47	.268	.369	.465

Lou Pote

Pitches: Right **Bats:** Right **Pos:** RP-43; SP-1   **Ht:** 6'3" **Wt:** 200 **Born:** 8/21/71 **Age:** 30

		HOW MUCH HE PITCHED					WHAT HE GAVE UP										THE RESULTS						
Year Team	Lg	G	GS	CG	GF	IP	BFP	H	R	ER	HR	SH	SF	HB	TBB	IBB	SO	WP	Bk	W	L	Pct.	ShO	Sv-Op	Hld	ERA
1999 Anaheim	AL	20	0	0	10	29.1	118	23	9	7	1	1	0	0	12	1	20	1	0	1	1	.500	0	3-3	3	2.15
2000 Anaheim	AL	32	1	0	12	50.1	214	52	23	19	4	1	1	0	17	1	44	3	0	1	1	.500	0	1-1	2	3.40
2001 Anaheim	AL	44	1	0	15	86.2	380	88	41	40	11	1	3	3	32	5	66	3	0	2	0	1.000	0	2-3	0	4.15
3 ML YEARS		96	2	0	37	166.1	712	163	73	66	16	3	4	3	61	7	130	7	0	4	2	.667	0	6-7	5	3.57

Brian Powell

Pitches: Right **Bats:** Right **Pos:** SP-1   **Ht:** 6'2" **Wt:** 205 **Born:** 10/10/73 **Age:** 28

		HOW MUCH HE PITCHED					WHAT HE GAVE UP										THE RESULTS						
Year Team	Lg	G	GS	CG	GF	IP	BFP	H	R	ER	HR	SH	SF	HB	TBB	IBB	SO	WP	Bk	W	L	Pct.	ShO	Sv-Op	Hld	ERA
2001 New Orleans *	AAA	24	23	3	0	144.2	599	142	65	51	13	4	2	6	39	1	96	3	1	9	8	.529	2	0- --	—	3.17
1998 Detroit	AL	18	16	0	1	83.2	383	101	67	59	17	1	1	2	36	2	46	3	0	3	8	.273	0	0-0	0	6.35
2000 Houston	NL	9	5	0	1	31.1	140	34	21	20	8	2	2	1	13	0	14	0	0	2	1	.667	0	0-0	0	5.74
2001 Houston	NL	1	1	0	0	3	17	5	6	6	1	0	0	0	3	0	3	0	0	0	1	.000	0	0-0	0	18.00
3 ML YEARS		28	22	0	2	118	540	140	94	85	26	3	3	3	52	2	63	3	0	5	10	.333	0	0-0	0	6.48

Dante Powell

Bats: R **Throws:** R **Pos:** PH/PR-7; LF-5; RF-3; CF-1   **Ht:** 6'2" **Wt:** 185 **Born:** 8/25/73 **Age:** 28

		BATTING																		BASERUNNING				PERCENTAGES		
Year Team	Lg	G	AB	H	2B	3B	HR	(Hm	Rd)	TB	R	RBI	TBB	IBB	SO	HBP	SH	SF	SB	CS	SB%	GDP	Avg	OBP	SLG
2001 Fresno *	AAA	114	426	120	23	3	22	—	—	215	74	62	34	2	122	4	0	2	25	5	.83	7	.282	.339	.505
1997 San Francisco	NL	27	39	12	1	0	1	(1	0)	16	8	3	4	0	11	0	1	0	1	1	.50	0	.308	.372	.410
1998 San Francisco	NL	8	4	2	0	0	1	(1	0)	5	2	1	3	0	0	0	0	0	0	0	—	0	.500	.714	1.250
1999 Arizona	NL	22	25	4	3	0	0	(0	0)	7	4	1	2	0	6	0	1	0	2	1	.67	0	.160	.222	.280
2001 San Francisco	NL	13	6	2	0	0	0	(0	0)	2	5	0	0	0	0	0	0	0	0	0	—	0	.333	.333	.333
4 ML YEARS		70	74	20	4	0	2	(2	0)	30	19	5	9	0	17	0	2	0	3	2	.60	0	.270	.349	.405

Jay Powell

Pitches: Right **Bats:** Right **Pos:** RP-74   **Ht:** 6'4" **Wt:** 225 **Born:** 1/9/72 **Age:** 30

		HOW MUCH HE PITCHED					WHAT HE GAVE UP										THE RESULTS						
Year Team	Lg	G	GS	CG	GF	IP	BFP	H	R	ER	HR	SH	SF	HB	TBB	IBB	SO	WP	Bk	W	L	Pct.	ShO	Sv-Op	Hld	ERA
1995 Florida	NL	9	0	0	1	8.1	38	7	2	1	0	1	0	2	6	1	4	0	0	0	0	—	0	0-0	2	1.08
1996 Florida	NL	67	0	0	16	71.1	321	71	41	36	5	2	1	4	36	1	52	3	0	4	3	.571	0	2-5	10	4.54
1997 Florida	NL	74	0	0	23	79.2	337	71	35	29	3	6	4	4	30	3	65	3	0	7	2	.778	0	2-4	24	3.28
1998 Fla-Hou	NL	62	0	0	35	70.1	302	58	28	26	6	3	1	3	37	9	62	1	0	7	7	.500	0	7-11	3	3.33
1999 Houston	NL	67	0	0	26	75	341	82	38	36	3	5	2	3	40	4	77	5	0	4	7	.556	0	4-7	16	4.32
2000 Houston	NL	29	0	0	10	27	127	29	18	17	1	1	0	0	19	1	16	0	0	1	1	.500	0	0-0	5	5.67
2001 Hou-Col	NL	74	0	0	20	75	327	75	36	27	9	5	1	2	31	3	54	0	1	5	3	.625	0	7-13	8	3.24
1998 Florida	NL	33	0	0	26	36.1	165	36	19	17	5	3	1	2	22	6	24	1	0	4	4	.500	0	3-6	0	4.21
Houston	NL	29	0	0	9	34	137	22	9	9	1	0	0	1	15	3	38	0	0	3	3	.500	0	4-5	3	2.38
2001 Houston	NL	35	0	0	5	36.1	170	41	18	15	4	1	1	0	19	0	28	0	1	2	2	.500	0	0-5	5	3.72
Colorado	NL	39	0	0	15	38.2	157	34	18	12	5	4	0	2	12	3	26	0	0	3	1	.750	0	7-8	3	2.79
7 ML YEARS		382	0	0	131	406.2	1793	393	198	172	27	23	9	18	199	22	330	12	1	29	20	.592	0	22-40	68	3.81

Todd Pratt

Bats: Right **Throws:** Right **Pos:** C-65; PH/PR-16; 1B-1   **Ht:** 6'3" **Wt:** 230 **Born:** 2/9/67 **Age:** 35

		BATTING																		BASERUNNING				PERCENTAGES		
Year Team	Lg	G	AB	H	2B	3B	HR	(Hm	Rd)	TB	R	RBI	TBB	IBB	SO	HBP	SH	SF	SB	CS	SB%	GDP	Avg	OBP	SLG
1992 Philadelphia	NL	16	46	13	1	0	2	(2	0)	20	6	10	4	0	12	0	0	0	0	0	—	2	.283	.340	.435
1993 Philadelphia	NL	33	87	25	6	0	5	(4	1)	46	8	13	5	0	19	1	1	1	0	0	—	2	.287	.330	.529
1994 Philadelphia	NL	28	102	20	6	1	2	(1	1)	34	10	9	12	0	29	0	0	0	0	1	.00	3	.196	.281	.333
1995 Chicago	NL	25	60	8	2	0	0	(0	0)	10	3	4	6	1	21	0	0	1	0	0	—	1	.133	.209	.167
1997 New York	NL	39	106	30	6	0	2	(1	1)	42	12	19	13	0	32	2	0	0	0	1	.00	1	.283	.372	.396
1998 New York	NL	41	69	19	9	1	2	(1	1)	36	9	18	2	0	20	0	0	0	0	0	—	0	.275	.296	.522
1999 New York	NL	71	140	41	4	0	3	(1	2)	54	18	21	15	0	32	3	0	2	2	0	1.00	1	.293	.369	.386
2000 New York	NL	80	160	44	6	0	8	(2	6)	74	33	25	22	1	31	5	2	1	0	0	—	5	.275	.378	.463
2001 NYM-Phi	NL	80	173	32	8	0	4	(0	4)	52	18	11	34	3	61	3	1	1	1	0	1.00	4	.185	.327	.301
2001 New York	NL	45	80	13	5	0	2	(0	2)	24	6	4	15	1	36	2	0	1	1	0	1.00	4	.163	.306	.300
Philadelphia	NL	35	93	19	3	0	2	(0	2)	28	12	7	19	2	25	1	1	0	0	0	—	2	.204	.345	.301
9 ML YEARS		413	943	232	48	2	28	(12	16)	368	117	130	113	5	257	14	4	6	3	2	.60	21	.246	.334	.390

Curtis Pride

Bats: L **Throws:** R **Pos:** LF-19; PH/PR-16; RF-3; DH-2; CF-1   **Ht:** 6'0" **Wt:** 210 **Born:** 12/17/68 **Age:** 33

		BATTING																		BASERUNNING				PERCENTAGES		
Year Team	Lg	G	AB	H	2B	3B	HR	(Hm	Rd)	TB	R	RBI	TBB	IBB	SO	HBP	SH	SF	SB	CS	SB%	GDP	Avg	OBP	SLG
2001 Jupiter *	A+	6	21	4	1	0	0	—	—	5	3	0	3	0	3	0	0	0	0	1	.00	0	.190	.292	.238
Ottawa *	AAA	22	81	27	4	1	5	—	—	48	14	15	12	2	26	2	0	0	6	1	.86	2	.333	.432	.593
1993 Montreal	NL	10	9	4	1	1	1	(0	1)	10	3	5	0	0	3	0	0	0	1	0	1.00	0	.444	.444	1.111
1995 Montreal	NL	48	63	11	1	0	0	(0	0)	12	10	2	5	0	16	0	1	0	3	2	.60	2	.175	.235	.190
1996 Detroit	AL	95	267	80	17	5	10	(5	5)	137	52	31	31	1	63	0	3	0	11	6	.65	2	.300	.372	.513

179

					BATTING														BASERUNNING				PERCENTAGES		
Year Team	Lg	G	AB	H	2B	3B	HR	(Hm	Rd)	TB	R	RBI	TBB	IBB	SO	HBP	SH	SF	SB	CS	SB%	GDP	Avg	OBP	SLG
1997 Det-Bos	AL	81	164	35	4	4	3	(3	0)	56	22	20	24	1	46	1	2	1	6	4	.60	4	.213	.316	.341
1998 Atlanta	NL	70	107	27	6	1	3	(1	2)	44	19	9	9	0	29	3	1	1	4	0	1.00	2	.252	.325	.411
2000 Boston	AL	9	20	5	1	0	0	(0	0)	6	4	0	1	0	7	0	0	0	0	0	—	0	.250	.286	.300
2001 Montreal	NL	36	76	19	3	1	1	(0	1)	27	8	9	9	0	22	2	0	0	3	2	.60	4	.250	.345	.355
1997 Detroit	AL	79	162	34	4	4	2	(2	0)	52	21	19	24	1	45	1	2	1	6	4	.60	4	.210	.314	.321
Boston	AL	2	2	1	0	0	0	(1	0)	4	1	1	0	0	1	0	0	0	0	0	—	0	.500	.500	2.000
7 ML YEARS		349	706	181	33	12	18	(9	9)	292	118	76	79	2	186	6	7	2	28	14	.67	14	.256	.335	.414

Ariel Prieto

Pitches: Right **Bats:** Right **Pos:** RP-3   **Ht:** 6'2" **Wt:** 247 **Born:** 10/22/69 **Age:** 32

		HOW MUCH HE PITCHED						WHAT HE GAVE UP												THE RESULTS						
Year Team	Lg	G	GS	CG	GF	IP	BFP	H	R	ER	HR	SH	SF	HB	TBB	IBB	SO	WP	Bk	W	L	Pct.	ShO	Sv-Op	Hld	ERA
2001 Durham *	AAA	3	0	0	0	6.2	25	3	2	1	0	0	0	0	2	0	10	0	0	0	0	—	0	0--	—	1.35
1995 Oakland	AL	14	9	1	1	58	258	57	35	32	4	3	2	5	32	1	37	4	1	2	6	.250	0	0-0	0	4.97
1996 Oakland	AL	21	21	2	0	125.2	547	130	66	58	9	5	5	7	54	2	75	6	2	6	7	.462	0	0-0	0	4.15
1997 Oakland	AL	22	22	0	0	125	588	155	84	70	16	3	4	5	70	3	90	7	1	6	8	.429	0	0-0	0	5.04
1998 Oakland	AL	2	2	0	0	8.1	47	17	11	11	2	0	0	1	5	1	5	1	0	0	1	.000	0	0-0	0	11.88
2000 Oakland	AL	8	6	0	2	31.2	148	42	21	18	3	2	1	1	13	0	19	0	0	1	2	.333	0	0-0	0	5.12
2001 Tampa Bay	AL	3	0	0	2	3.2	19	6	1	1	0	0	0	1	2	0	2	0	0	0	0	—	0	0-0	0	2.45
6 ML YEARS		70	60	3	5	352.1	1607	407	218	190	34	13	12	20	176	7	231	17	4	15	24	.385	0	0-0	0	4.85

Tom Prince

Bats: Right **Throws:** Right **Pos:** C-64; PH/PR-1   **Ht:** 5'11" **Wt:** 206 **Born:** 8/13/64 **Age:** 37

					BATTING														BASERUNNING				PERCENTAGES		
Year Team	Lg	G	AB	H	2B	3B	HR	(Hm	Rd)	TB	R	RBI	TBB	IBB	SO	HBP	SH	SF	SB	CS	SB%	GDP	Avg	OBP	SLG
1987 Pittsburgh	NL	4	9	2	1	0	1	(0	1)	6	1	2	0	0	2	0	0	0	0	0	—	0	.222	.222	.667
1988 Pittsburgh	NL	29	74	13	2	0	0	(0	0)	15	3	6	4	0	15	0	2	0	0	0	—	5	.176	.218	.203
1989 Pittsburgh	NL	21	52	7	4	0	0	(0	0)	11	1	5	6	1	12	0	0	1	1	1	.50	1	.135	.220	.212
1990 Pittsburgh	NL	4	10	1	0	0	0	(0	0)	1	1	0	0	0	2	0	0	0	0	1	.00	0	.100	.182	.100
1991 Pittsburgh	NL	26	34	9	3	0	1	(0	1)	15	4	2	7	0	3	1	0	0	0	0	—	3	.265	.405	.441
1992 Pittsburgh	NL	27	44	4	2	0	0	(0	0)	6	1	5	6	0	9	0	0	2	1	1	.50	2	.091	.192	.136
1993 Pittsburgh	NL	66	179	35	14	0	2	(2	0)	55	14	24	13	2	38	7	2	3	1	1	.50	5	.196	.272	.307
1994 Los Angeles	NL	3	6	2	0	0	0	(0	0)	2	2	1	1	0	3	0	0	0	0	0	—	0	.333	.429	.333
1995 Los Angeles	NL	18	40	8	2	1	1	(0	1)	15	3	4	4	0	10	0	0	0	0	0	—	0	.200	.273	.375
1996 Los Angeles	NL	40	64	19	6	0	1	(0	1)	28	6	11	6	2	15	2	3	2	0	0	—	2	.297	.365	.438
1997 Los Angeles	NL	47	100	22	5	0	3	(2	1)	36	17	14	5	0	15	3	4	1	0	0	—	0	.220	.275	.360
1998 Los Angeles	NL	37	81	15	5	1	0	(0	1)	22	7	5	7	1	24	2	2	0	0	0	—	2	.185	.267	.272
1999 Philadelphia	NL	4	6	1	0	0	0	(0	0)	1	1	0	1	0	1	0	0	0	0	0	—	1	.167	.286	.167
2000 Philadelphia	NL	46	122	29	9	0	2	(0	2)	44	14	16	13	0	31	2	3	0	1	0	1.00	5	.238	.321	.361
2001 Minnesota	AL	64	196	43	4	1	7	(3	4)	70	19	23	12	0	39	6	0	1	3	1	.75	5	.219	.284	.357
15 ML YEARS		436	1017	210	57	3	18	(7	11)	327	94	118	86	6	219	23	16	10	7	5	.58	30	.206	.281	.322

Bret Prinz

Pitches: Right **Bats:** Right **Pos:** RP-46   **Ht:** 6'3" **Wt:** 185 **Born:** 6/15/77 **Age:** 25

		HOW MUCH HE PITCHED						WHAT HE GAVE UP												THE RESULTS						
Year Team	Lg	G	GS	CG	GF	IP	BFP	H	R	ER	HR	SH	SF	HB	TBB	IBB	SO	WP	Bk	W	L	Pct.	ShO	Sv-Op	Hld	ERA
1998 Diamndbcks	R	4	0	0	4	5.1	24	7	3	2	0	0	0	1	0	0	3	0	0	0	0	—	0	0--	—	3.38
Lethbridge	R+	11	10	0	0	46.2	204	49	26	16	2	1	0	3	13	0	30	8	0	4	2	.667	0	0--	—	3.09
1999 South Bend	A	30	23	0	3	138.2	594	129	82	69	16	5	7	8	52	0	98	10	4	6	10	.375	0	0--	—	4.48
2000 South Bend	A	6	0	0	5	7.1	26	2	2	0	0	0	0	0	1	0	10	1	0	1	0	1.000	0	1--	—	0.00
El Paso	AA	53	0	0	42	60.2	265	71	24	24	6	1	1	5	16	3	69	3	0	9	1	.900	0	26--	—	3.56
2001 Tucson	AAA	5	0	0	5	5.2	18	1	0	0	0	0	0	0	0	0	6	0	0	0	0	—	0	3--	—	0.00
2001 Arizona	NL	46	0	0	26	41	174	33	13	12	4	3	1	1	19	1	27	1	1	4	1	.800	0	9-12	6	2.63

Luke Prokopec

Pitches: Right **Bats:** Left **Pos:** SP-22; RP-7   **Ht:** 5'11" **Wt:** 166 **Born:** 2/23/78 **Age:** 24

		HOW MUCH HE PITCHED						WHAT HE GAVE UP												THE RESULTS						
Year Team	Lg	G	GS	CG	GF	IP	BFP	H	R	ER	HR	SH	SF	HB	TBB	IBB	SO	WP	Bk	W	L	Pct.	ShO	Sv-Op	Hld	ERA
1997 Savannah	A	13	6	0	5	42	175	37	21	19	8	1	3	1	12	0	45	1	0	3	1	.750	0	0--	—	4.07
1998 San Berndno	A+	20	20	0	0	110.1	460	98	43	33	11	3	2	3	33	1	148	5	1	8	5	.615	0	0--	—	2.69
San Antonio	AA	5	5	0	0	26	106	16	5	4	0	0	1	1	13	0	25	2	1	3	0	1.000	0	0--	—	1.38
1999 San Antonio	AA	27	27	0	0	157.2	685	172	113	95	18	7	8	7	46	0	128	3	1	8	12	.400	0	0--	—	5.42
2000 San Antonio	AA	22	22	1	0	128.2	524	118	40	35	8	4	3	7	23	1	124	0	0	7	3	.700	0	0--	—	2.45
2001 Las Vegas	AAA	1	1	0	0	6	24	3	2	2	0	0	0	0	2	0	8	0	0	1	0	1.000	0	0--	—	3.00
2000 Los Angeles	NL	5	3	0	1	21	88	19	10	7	2	1	1	2	9	0	12	0	0	1	1	.500	0	0-0	0	3.00
2001 Los Angeles	NL	29	22	0	2	138.1	596	146	80	75	27	4	3	4	40	1	91	3	2	8	7	.533	0	0-0	0	4.88
2 ML YEARS		34	25	0	3	159.1	684	165	90	82	29	5	4	6	49	1	103	3	2	9	8	.529	0	0-0	0	4.63

Albert Pujols

Bats: R **Throws:** R **Pos:** 3B-55; 1B-42; LF-39; RF-39; DH-2; PH/PR-2   **Ht:** 6'3" **Wt:** 210 **Born:** 1/16/80 **Age:** 22

					BATTING														BASERUNNING				PERCENTAGES		
Year Team	Lg	G	AB	H	2B	3B	HR	(Hm	Rd)	TB	R	RBI	TBB	IBB	SO	HBP	SH	SF	SB	CS	SB%	GDP	Avg	OBP	SLG
2000 Peoria	A	109	395	128	32	6	17	—	—	223	62	84	38	7	37	5	0	2	2	4	.33	10	.324	.389	.565
Potomac	A+	21	81	23	8	1	2	—	—	39	11	10	7	0	8	0	1	0	1	1	.50	3	.284	.341	.481
Memphis	AAA	3	14	3	1	0	0	—	—	4	1	2	1	0	2	0	0	0	1	0	1.00	0	.214	.267	.286
2001 St. Louis	NL	161	590	194	47	4	37	(18	19)	360	112	130	69	6	93	9	1	7	1	3	.25	21	.329	.403	.610

Bill Pulsipher

Pitches: Left **Bats:** Left **Pos:** RP-37 　　　**Ht:** 6'3" **Wt:** 200 **Born:** 10/9/73 **Age:** 28

		HOW MUCH HE PITCHED						WHAT HE GAVE UP												THE RESULTS						
Year Team	Lg	G	GS	CG	GF	IP	BFP	H	R	ER	HR	SH	SF	HB	TBB	IBB	SO	WP	Bk	W	L	Pct.	ShO	Sv-Op	Hld	ERA
2001 Pawtucket *	AAA	24	0	0	16	31.1	129	27	12	10	1	0	0	1	10	1	23	2	1	1	1	.500	0	10--	—	2.87
1995 New York	NL	17	17	2	0	126.2	530	122	58	56	11	2	1	4	45	0	81	2	1	5	7	.417	0	0-0	0	3.98
1998 NYM-Mil	NL	26	11	0	2	72.1	320	86	41	41	8	4	4	1	31	4	51	2	2	3	4	.429	0	0-1	2	5.10
1999 Milwaukee	NL	19	16	0	1	87.1	398	100	65	58	19	6	4	2	36	2	42	4	0	5	6	.455	0	0-0	0	5.98
2000 New York	NL	2	2	0	0	6.2	39	12	9	9	1	1	0	1	6	0	7	0	0	0	2	.000	0	0-0	0	12.15
2001 Bos-CWS	AL	37	0	0	8	30	146	36	23	20	5	0	2	3	21	0	20	1	0	0	0	—	0	0-0	6	6.00
1998 New York	NL	15	1	0	1	14.1	68	23	11	11	2	1	0	0	5	1	13	0	0	0	0	—	0	0-1	0	6.91
Milwaukee	NL	11	10	0	1	58	252	63	30	30	6	3	4	1	26	3	38	2	2	3	4	.429	0	0-0	0	4.66
2001 Boston	AL	23	0	0	6	22	102	25	15	13	3	0	1	2	14	0	16	1	0	0	0	—	0	0-0	4	5.32
Chicago	AL	14	0	0	2	8	44	11	8	7	2	0	1	1	7	0	4	0	0	0	0	—	0	0-0	2	7.88
5 ML YEARS		101	46	2	11	323	1433	356	196	184	44	13	11	11	139	6	201	9	3	13	19	.406	0	0-1	8	5.13

Nick Punto

Bats: Both **Throws:** Right **Pos:** PH/PR-3; SS-1 　　　**Ht:** 5'9" **Wt:** 170 **Born:** 11/8/77 **Age:** 24

		BATTING																	BASERUNNING				PERCENTAGES		
Year Team	Lg	G	AB	H	2B	3B	HR	(Hm	Rd)	TB	R	RBI	TBB	IBB	SO	HBP	SH	SF	SB	CS	SB%	GDP	Avg	OBP	SLG
1998 Batavia	A-	72	279	69	9	4	1	—	—	89	51	20	42	0	48	1	0	1	19	7	.73	4	.247	.347	.319
1999 Clearwater	A+	106	400	122	18	6	1	—	—	155	65	48	67	3	53	3	3	5	16	7	.70	13	.305	.404	.388
2000 Reading	AA	121	456	116	15	4	5	—	—	154	77	47	69	0	71	2	14	6	33	10	.77	5	.254	.351	.338
2001 Scrantn-WB	AAA	123	463	106	19	5	1	—	—	138	57	39	68	3	114	0	3	1	33	9	.79	15	.229	.327	.298
2001 Philadelphia	NL	4	5	2	0	0	0	(0	0)	2	0	0	0	0	0	0	0	0	0	0	—	0	.400	.400	.400

Paul Quantrill

Pitches: Right **Bats:** Left **Pos:** RP-80 　　　**Ht:** 6'1" **Wt:** 190 **Born:** 11/3/68 **Age:** 33

		HOW MUCH HE PITCHED						WHAT HE GAVE UP												THE RESULTS						
Year Team	Lg	G	GS	CG	GF	IP	BFP	H	R	ER	HR	SH	SF	HB	TBB	IBB	SO	WP	Bk	W	L	Pct.	ShO	Sv-Op	Hld	ERA
1992 Boston	AL	27	0	0	10	49.1	213	55	18	12	1	4	2	1	15	5	24	1	0	2	3	.400	0	1-5	3	2.19
1993 Boston	AL	49	14	1	6	138	594	151	73	60	13	4	2	2	44	14	66	0	1	6	12	.333	1	1-2	3	3.91
1994 Bos-Phi		35	1	0	9	53	236	64	31	29	7	5	3	5	15	4	28	0	2	3	3	.500	0	1-4	3	4.92
1995 Philadelphia	NL	33	29	0	1	179.1	784	212	102	93	20	9	6	6	44	3	103	0	3	11	12	.478	0	0-0	0	4.67
1996 Toronto	AL	38	20	0	7	134.1	609	172	90	81	27	5	7	2	51	3	86	1	1	5	14	.263	0	0-2	1	5.43
1997 Toronto	AL	77	0	0	29	88	373	103	25	19	5	5	3	1	17	3	56	1	0	6	7	.462	0	5-10	16	1.94
1998 Toronto	AL	82	0	0	32	80	345	88	26	23	7	4	3	4	22	6	59	1	0	3	4	.429	0	7-14	27	2.59
1999 Toronto	AL	41	0	0	13	48.2	212	53	19	18	5	1	2	4	17	1	58	1	0	3	2	.600	0	0-4	8	3.33
2000 Toronto	AL	68	0	0	24	83.2	367	100	45	42	7	1	3	2	25	1	47	1	0	2	5	.286	0	1-3	13	4.52
2001 Toronto	AL	80	0	0	20	83	341	86	29	28	6	7	2	6	12	7	58	0	0	11	2	.846	0	2-9	21	3.04
1994 Boston	AL	17	0	0	4	23	101	25	10	9	4	2	2	2	5	1	15	0	0	1	1	.500	0	0-2	3	3.52
Philadelphia	NL	18	1	0	5	30	135	39	21	20	3	3	1	3	10	3	13	0	2	2	2	.500	0	1-2	1	6.00
10 ML YEARS		530	64	1	153	937.1	4074	1084	458	405	96	48	34	32	262	47	555	5	7	52	64	.448	1	18-53	95	3.89

Ruben Quevedo

Pitches: Right **Bats:** Right **Pos:** SP-10 　　　**Ht:** 6'1" **Wt:** 245 **Born:** 1/5/79 **Age:** 23

		HOW MUCH HE PITCHED						WHAT HE GAVE UP												THE RESULTS						
Year Team	Lg	G	GS	CG	GF	IP	BFP	H	R	ER	HR	SH	SF	HB	TBB	IBB	SO	WP	Bk	W	L	Pct.	ShO	Sv-Op	Hld	ERA
1996 Braves	R	10	10	0	0	55	221	50	19	14	1	4	1	1	9	0	49	3	2	2	6	.250	0	0--	—	2.29
1997 Danville	R+	13	11	0	0	68.1	286	46	37	27	6	3	5	4	27	0	78	3	1	1	5	.167	0	0--	—	3.56
1998 Macon	A	25	15	1	0	112	470	114	50	39	13	3	4	1	31	0	117	5	1	11	3	.786	0	0--	—	3.13
Danville	A+	6	6	0	0	32.2	143	28	22	13	2	1	2	3	13	1	35	2	0	2	0	.000	0	0--	—	3.58
1999 Richmond	AAA	21	21	0	0	105.2	444	112	65	63	26	2	2	1	34	0	98	4	0	6	5	.545	0	0--	—	5.37
Iowa	AAA	7	7	1	0	44.1	185	34	18	17	1	2	3	0	21	0	50	0	0	3	1	.750	1	0--	—	3.45
2000 Iowa	AAA	13	13	0	0	74.2	322	68	37	35	7	4	3	3	31	0	77	1	1	7	2	.778	0	0--	—	4.22
2001 Iowa	AAA	22	22	1	0	141.2	588	124	54	47	13	8	6	3	48	3	150	1	0	9	5	.643	1	0--	—	2.99
2000 Chicago	NL	21	15	1	1	88	418	96	81	73	21	4	3	3	54	4	65	2	0	3	10	.231	0	0-0	0	7.47
2001 Milwaukee	NL	10	10	0	0	56.2	253	56	30	29	9	3	2	0	30	4	60	1	0	4	5	.444	0	0-0	0	4.61
2 ML YEARS		31	25	1	1	144.2	671	152	111	102	30	7	5	3	84	8	125	3	0	7	15	.318	0	0-0	0	6.35

Mark Quinn

Bats: R **Throws:** R **Pos:** RF-50; LF-49; DH-18; PH/PR-4 　　　**Ht:** 6'1" **Wt:** 195 **Born:** 5/21/74 **Age:** 28

		BATTING																	BASERUNNING				PERCENTAGES		
Year Team	Lg	G	AB	H	2B	3B	HR	(Hm	Rd)	TB	R	RBI	TBB	IBB	SO	HBP	SH	SF	SB	CS	SB%	GDP	Avg	OBP	SLG
2001 Omaha *	AAA	11	43	8	1	0	2	—	—	15	4	3	0	0	9	0	0	0	0	0	—	0	.186	.186	.349
1999 Kansas City	AL	17	60	20	4	1	6	(2	4)	44	11	18	4	0	11	1	0	0	1	0	1.00	1	.333	.385	.733
2000 Kansas City	AL	135	500	147	33	2	20	(12	8)	244	76	78	35	1	91	3	3	3	5	2	.71	11	.294	.342	.488
2001 Kansas City	AL	118	453	122	31	2	17	(10	7)	208	57	60	12	1	69	7	0	1	9	5	.64	16	.269	.298	.459
3 ML YEARS		270	1013	289	68	5	43	(24	19)	496	144	156	51	2	171	11	3	4	15	7	.68	28	.285	.325	.490

Scott Radinsky

Pitches: Left **Bats:** Left **Pos:** RP-2 　　　**Ht:** 6'3" **Wt:** 215 **Born:** 3/3/68 **Age:** 34

		HOW MUCH HE PITCHED						WHAT HE GAVE UP												THE RESULTS						
Year Team	Lg	G	GS	CG	GF	IP	BFP	H	R	ER	HR	SH	SF	HB	TBB	IBB	SO	WP	Bk	W	L	Pct.	ShO	Sv-Op	Hld	ERA
2001 Akron *	AA	23	0	0	9	23.1	99	30	10	9	1	0	1	1	3	0	19	1	6	2	2	.500	0	3--	—	3.47
Buffalo *	AAA	16	0	0	5	15.1	56	13	7	7	0	2	0	1	7	0	11	0	1	0	1	.000	0	1--	—	4.11
1990 Chicago	AL	62	0	0	18	52.1	237	47	29	28	1	2	2	2	36	1	46	2	1	6	1	.857	0	4-5	10	4.82
1991 Chicago	AL	67	0	0	19	71.1	289	53	18	16	4	4	4	1	23	2	49	0	0	5	5	.500	0	8-15	15	2.02
1992 Chicago	AL	68	0	0	33	59.1	261	54	21	18	3	2	1	2	34	5	48	3	0	3	7	.300	0	15-23	16	2.73

Year Team	Lg	G	GS	CG	GF	IP	BFP	H	R	ER	HR	SH	SF	HB	TBB	IBB	SO	WP	Bk	W	L	Pct.	ShO	Sv-Op	Hld	ERA
						HOW MUCH HE PITCHED					WHAT HE GAVE UP									THE RESULTS						
1993 Chicago	AL	73	0	0	24	54.2	250	61	33	26	3	2	0	1	19	3	44	0	4	8	2	.800	0	4-5	12	4.28
1995 Chicago	AL	46	0	0	10	38	171	46	23	23	7	1	4	0	17	4	14	0	0	2	1	.667	0	1-3	8	5.45
1996 Los Angeles	NL	58	0	0	19	52.1	221	52	19	14	2	4	3	0	17	5	48	0	3	5	1	.833	0	1-4	7	2.41
1997 Los Angeles	NL	75	0	0	14	62.1	258	54	22	20	4	3	4	1	21	5	44	0	0	5	1	.833	0	3-5	26	2.89
1998 Los Angeles	NL	62	0	0	30	61.2	264	63	21	18	5	6	2	4	20	1	45	0	3	6	6	.500	0	13-24	8	2.63
1999 St. Louis	NL	43	0	0	13	27.2	126	27	16	15	2	2	5	1	18	3	17	3	1	2	1	.667	0	3-3	11	4.88
2000 St. Louis	NL	1	0	0	0	0	1	0	0	0	0	0	0	0	1	0	0	0	0	0	0	—	0	0-0	0	—
2001 Cleveland	AL	2	0	0	0	2	13	4	6	6	2	0	0	0	3	0	3	0	0	0	0	—	0	0-0	0	27.00
11 ML YEARS		557	0	0	180	481.2	2091	461	208	184	33	26	25	12	209	29	358	8	12	42	25	.627	0	52-87	113	3.44

Brad Radke

Pitches: Right **Bats:** Right **Pos:** SP-33   **Ht:** 6'2" **Wt:** 188 **Born:** 10/27/72 **Age:** 29

Year Team	Lg	G	GS	CG	GF	IP	BFP	H	R	ER	HR	SH	SF	HB	TBB	IBB	SO	WP	Bk	W	L	Pct.	ShO	Sv-Op	Hld	ERA
						HOW MUCH HE PITCHED					WHAT HE GAVE UP									THE RESULTS						
1995 Minnesota	AL	29	28	2	0	181	772	195	112	107	32	2	9	4	47	0	75	4	0	11	14	.440	1	0-0	0	5.32
1996 Minnesota	AL	35	35	3	0	232	973	231	125	115	40	5	6	4	57	2	148	1	0	11	16	.407	1	0-0	0	4.46
1997 Minnesota	AL	35	35	4	0	239.2	989	238	114	103	28	2	9	3	48	1	174	1	1	20	10	.667	1	0-0	0	3.87
1998 Minnesota	AL	32	32	5	0	213.2	904	238	109	102	23	9	3	4	43	1	146	3	1	12	14	.462	1	0-0	0	4.30
1999 Minnesota	AL	33	33	4	0	218.2	910	239	97	91	28	5	5	1	44	0	121	4	0	12	14	.462	0	0-0	0	3.75
2000 Minnesota	AL	34	34	4	0	226.2	978	261	117	112	27	7	4	5	51	1	141	5	0	12	16	.429	1	0-0	0	4.45
2001 Minnesota	AL	33	33	6	0	226	919	235	105	99	24	10	6	10	26	0	137	4	1	15	11	.577	2	0-0	0	3.94
7 ML YEARS		231	230	28	0	1537.2	6445	1637	781	729	202	40	42	36	316	5	942	22	3	93	95	.495	6	0-0	0	4.27

Tim Raines

Bats: Both **Throws:** Right **Pos:** PH/PR-29; LF-22; DH-1   **Ht:** 5'8" **Wt:** 196 **Born:** 9/16/59 **Age:** 42

Year Team	Lg	G	AB	H	2B	3B	HR	(Hm	Rd)	TB	R	RBI	TBB	IBB	SO	HBP	SH	SF	SB	CS	SB%	GDP	Avg	OBP	SLG
				BATTING															BASERUNNING				PERCENTAGES		
2001 Jupiter *	A+	8	23	8	1	1	1	—	—	14	7	5	5	0	4	0	0	1	1	0	1.00	0	.348	.448	.609
Ottawa *	AAA	2	7	1	1	0	0	—	—	2	1	0	1	0	1	0	0	0	0	0	—	0	.143	.250	.286
1979 Montreal	NL	6	0	0	0	0	0	(0	0)	0	3	0	0	0	0	0	0	0	2	0	1.00	0	—	—	—
1980 Montreal	NL	15	20	1	0	0	0	(0	0)	1	5	0	6	0	3	0	1	0	5	0	1.00	0	.050	.269	.050
1981 Montreal	NL	88	313	95	13	7	5	(3	2)	137	61	37	45	5	31	2	0	3	71	11	.87	7	.304	.391	.438
1982 Montreal	NL	156	647	179	32	8	4	(1	3)	239	90	43	75	9	83	2	6	1	78	16	.83	6	.277	.353	.369
1983 Montreal	NL	156	615	183	32	8	11	(6	6)	264	133	71	97	9	70	2	2	4	90	14	.87	12	.298	.393	.429
1984 Montreal	NL	160	622	192	38	9	8	(2	6)	272	106	60	87	7	69	2	3	4	75	10	.88	7	.309	.393	.437
1985 Montreal	NL	150	575	184	30	13	11	(4	7)	273	115	41	81	13	60	3	3	3	70	9	.89	9	.320	.405	.475
1986 Montreal	NL	151	580	194	35	10	9	(4	5)	276	91	62	78	9	60	2	1	3	70	9	.89	6	.334	.413	.476
1987 Montreal	NL	139	530	175	34	8	18	(9	9)	279	123	68	90	26	52	4	0	3	50	5	.91	9	.330	.429	.526
1988 Montreal	NL	109	429	116	19	7	12	(5	7)	185	66	48	53	14	44	2	0	4	33	7	.83	8	.270	.350	.431
1989 Montreal	NL	145	517	148	29	6	9	(6	3)	216	76	60	93	18	48	3	0	5	41	9	.82	8	.286	.395	.418
1990 Montreal	NL	130	457	131	11	5	9	(6	3)	179	65	62	70	8	43	3	0	8	49	16	.75	9	.287	.379	.392
1991 Chicago	AL	155	609	163	20	6	5	(1	4)	210	102	50	83	9	68	5	9	3	51	15	.77	7	.268	.359	.345
1992 Chicago	AL	144	551	162	22	9	7	(4	3)	223	102	54	81	4	48	0	4	8	45	6	.88	5	.294	.380	.405
1993 Chicago	AL	115	415	127	16	4	16	(7	9)	199	75	54	64	4	35	3	2	2	21	7	.75	7	.306	.401	.480
1994 Chicago	AL	101	384	102	15	5	10	(5	5)	157	80	52	61	3	43	1	4	3	13	0	1.00	10	.266	.365	.409
1995 Chicago	AL	133	502	143	25	4	12	(6	6)	212	81	67	70	3	52	3	3	3	13	2	.87	8	.285	.374	.422
1996 New York	AL	59	201	57	10	0	9	(7	2)	94	45	33	34	1	29	1	0	4	10	1	.91	5	.284	.383	.468
1997 New York	AL	74	271	87	20	2	4	(3	1)	123	56	38	41	0	34	0	0	6	8	5	.62	4	.321	.403	.454
1998 New York	AL	109	321	93	13	1	5	(2	3)	123	53	47	55	1	49	3	0	3	8	3	.73	5	.290	.395	.383
1999 Oakland	AL	58	135	29	5	0	4	(2	2)	46	20	17	26	1	17	0	1	2	4	1	.80	5	.215	.337	.341
2001 Mon-Bal		51	89	27	8	1	1	(1	0)	40	14	9	18	0	9	0	0	2	1	0	1.00	2	.303	.413	.449
2001 Montreal	NL	47	78	24	8	1	0	(0	0)	34	13	4	18	0	6	0	0	1	1	0	1.00	2	.308	.433	.436
Baltimore	AL	4	11	3	0	0	1	(1	0)	6	1	5	0	0	3	0	0	1	0	0	—	0	.273	.250	.545
22 ML YEARS		2404	8783	2588	427	113	169	(83	86)	3748	1562	973	1308	144	947	41	39	74	808	146	.85	139	.295	.386	.427

Tim Raines Jr.

Bats: Both **Throws:** Right **Pos:** CF-7   **Ht:** 5'10" **Wt:** 183 **Born:** 8/31/79 **Age:** 22

Year Team	Lg	G	AB	H	2B	3B	HR	(Hm	Rd)	TB	R	RBI	TBB	IBB	SO	HBP	SH	SF	SB	CS	SB%	GDP	Avg	OBP	SLG
				BATTING															BASERUNNING				PERCENTAGES		
1998 Orioles	R	56	197	48	7	4	1	—	—	66	40	13	30	1	53	12	3	0	37	4	.90	0	.244	.377	.335
1999 Delmarva	A	117	415	103	24	8	2	—	—	149	80	49	71	1	130	3	3	4	49	16	.75	1	.248	.359	.359
2000 Frederick	A+	127	457	108	21	3	2	—	—	141	89	36	67	0	106	13	11	3	81	19	.81	8	.236	.348	.309
2001 Frederick	A+	23	84	21	3	1	3	—	—	35	15	13	13	0	23	0	1	0	14	4	.78	2	.250	.351	.417
Bowie	AA	65	254	74	14	1	4	—	—	102	46	30	34	0	60	3	4	1	29	10	.74	3	.291	.380	.402
Rochester	AAA	40	133	34	5	1	2	—	—	47	19	12	11	0	30	0	2	0	11	3	.79	2	.256	.313	.353
2001 Baltimore	AL	7	23	4	2	0	0	(0	0)	6	6	0	3	0	8	0	1	0	3	0	1.00	0	.174	.269	.261

Aramis Ramirez

Bats: Right **Throws:** Right **Pos:** 3B-157; PH/PR-2   **Ht:** 6'1" **Wt:** 219 **Born:** 6/25/78 **Age:** 24

Year Team	Lg	G	AB	H	2B	3B	HR	(Hm	Rd)	TB	R	RBI	TBB	IBB	SO	HBP	SH	SF	SB	CS	SB%	GDP	Avg	OBP	SLG
				BATTING															BASERUNNING				PERCENTAGES		
1998 Pittsburgh	NL	72	251	59	9	1	6	(3	3)	88	23	24	18	0	72	4	1	1	0	1	.00	3	.235	.296	.351
1999 Pittsburgh	NL	18	56	10	2	1	0	(0	0)	14	2	7	6	0	9	0	1	1	0	0	—	0	.179	.254	.250
2000 Pittsburgh	NL	73	254	65	15	2	6	(4	2)	102	19	35	10	0	36	5	1	4	0	0	—	9	.256	.293	.402
2001 Pittsburgh	NL	158	603	181	40	0	34	(16	18)	323	83	112	40	4	100	8	0	4	5	4	.56	9	.300	.350	.536
4 ML YEARS		321	1164	315	66	4	46	(23	23)	527	127	178	74	4	217	17	3	10	5	5	.50	21	.271	.321	.453

Julio Ramirez

Bats: Right **Throws:** Right **Pos:** CF-21; PH/PR-3; LF-1   **Ht:** 5'11" **Wt:** 170 **Born:** 8/10/77 **Age:** 24

Year Team	Lg	G	AB	H	2B	3B	HR	(Hm	Rd)	TB	R	RBI	TBB	IBB	SO	HBP	SH	SF	SB	CS	SB%	GDP	Avg	OBP	SLG
1995 Marlins	R	48	204	58	9	4	2	—	—	81	35	13	13	0	42	1	1	0	17	6	.74	2	.284	.330	.397
1996 Brevard Cty	A+	17	61	15	0	1	0	—	—	17	11	2	4	0	18	0	0	1	2	3	.40	1	.246	.288	.279
Marlins	R	42	171	49	5	3	0	—	—	60	33	15	14	0	34	3	1	0	25	8	.76	0	.287	.351	.351
1997 Kane County	A	99	376	96	18	7	14	—	—	170	70	53	37	1	122	5	14	2	41	6	.87	1	.255	.329	.452
1998 Brevard Cty	A+	135	559	156	20	12	13	—	—	239	90	58	45	2	147	4	3	2	71	27	.72	3	.279	.336	.428
1999 Portland	AA	138	568	148	30	10	13	—	—	237	87	64	39	1	150	2	5	5	64	14	.82	5	.261	.308	.417
2000 Calgary	AAA	94	350	93	18	3	7	—	—	138	45	52	21	1	86	3	2	4	20	14	.59	5	.266	.310	.394
2001 Charlotte	AAA	88	319	69	11	1	8	—	—	106	36	25	20	0	80	2	2	1	15	6	.71	1	.216	.266	.332
1999 Florida	NL	15	21	3	1	0	0	(0	0)	4	3	2	1	0	6	0	0	0	0	1	.00	0	.143	.182	.190
2001 Chicago	AL	22	37	3	0	0	0	(0	0)	3	2	1	2	0	15	0	0	0	2	0	1.00	0	.081	.128	.081
2 ML YEARS		37	58	6	1	0	0	(0	0)	7	5	3	3	0	21	0	0	0	2	1	.67	0	.103	.148	.121

Manny Ramirez

Bats: Right **Throws:** Right **Pos:** DH-87; LF-55   **Ht:** 6'0" **Wt:** 205 **Born:** 5/30/72 **Age:** 30

Year Team	Lg	G	AB	H	2B	3B	HR	(Hm	Rd)	TB	R	RBI	TBB	IBB	SO	HBP	SH	SF	SB	CS	SB%	GDP	Avg	OBP	SLG
1993 Cleveland	AL	22	53	9	1	0	2	(0	2)	16	5	5	2	0	8	0	0	0	0	0	—	3	.170	.200	.302
1994 Cleveland	AL	91	290	78	22	0	17	(9	8)	151	51	60	42	4	72	0	0	4	4	2	.67	6	.269	.357	.521
1995 Cleveland	AL	137	484	149	26	1	31	(12	19)	270	85	107	75	6	112	5	2	5	6	6	.50	13	.308	.402	.558
1996 Cleveland	AL	152	550	170	45	3	33	(19	14)	320	94	112	85	8	104	3	0	9	8	5	.62	18	.309	.399	.582
1997 Cleveland	AL	150	561	184	40	0	26	(14	12)	302	99	88	79	5	115	7	0	4	2	3	.40	19	.328	.415	.538
1998 Cleveland	AL	150	571	168	35	2	45	(25	20)	342	108	145	76	6	121	6	0	10	5	3	.63	18	.294	.377	.599
1999 Cleveland	AL	147	522	174	34	3	44	(21	23)	346	131	165	96	9	131	13	0	9	2	4	.33	12	.333	.442	.663
2000 Cleveland	AL	118	439	154	34	2	38	(22	16)	306	92	122	86	9	117	3	0	4	1	1	.50	9	.351	.457	.697
2001 Boston	AL	142	529	162	33	2	41	(21	20)	322	93	125	81	25	147	8	0	2	0	1	.00	0	.306	.405	.609
9 ML YEARS		1109	3999	1248	270	13	277	(143	134)	2375	758	929	622	72	927	45	2	47	28	25	.53	107	.312	.406	.594

Joe Randa

Bats: Right **Throws:** Right **Pos:** 3B-137; DH-14; 2B-1   **Ht:** 5'11" **Wt:** 190 **Born:** 12/18/69 **Age:** 32

Year Team	Lg	G	AB	H	2B	3B	HR	(Hm	Rd)	TB	R	RBI	TBB	IBB	SO	HBP	SH	SF	SB	CS	SB%	GDP	Avg	OBP	SLG
1995 Kansas City	AL	34	70	12	2	0	1	(1	0)	17	6	5	6	0	17	0	0	0	0	1	.00	2	.171	.237	.243
1996 Kansas City	AL	110	337	102	24	1	6	(2	4)	146	36	47	26	4	47	1	2	4	13	4	.76	10	.303	.351	.433
1997 Pittsburgh	NL	126	443	134	27	9	7	(5	2)	200	58	60	41	1	64	6	4	5	4	2	.67	10	.302	.366	.451
1998 Detroit	AL	138	460	117	21	2	9	(3	6)	169	56	50	41	1	70	7	3	3	8	7	.53	9	.254	.323	.367
1999 Kansas City	AL	156	628	197	36	8	16	(7	9)	297	92	84	50	4	80	3	1	7	5	4	.56	15	.314	.363	.473
2000 Kansas City	AL	158	612	186	29	4	15	(9	6)	268	88	106	36	3	66	6	1	10	6	3	.67	19	.304	.343	.438
2001 Kansas City	AL	151	581	147	34	2	13	(8	5)	224	59	83	42	2	80	6	1	6	3	2	.60	15	.253	.307	.386
7 ML YEARS		873	3131	895	173	26	67	(35	32)	1321	395	435	242	15	424	29	12	35	39	23	.63	80	.286	.339	.422

Cody Ransom

Bats: Right **Throws:** Right **Pos:** SS-6; PH/PR-6   **Ht:** 6'2" **Wt:** 190 **Born:** 2/17/76 **Age:** 26

Year Team	Lg	G	AB	H	2B	3B	HR	(Hm	Rd)	TB	R	RBI	TBB	IBB	SO	HBP	SH	SF	SB	CS	SB%	GDP	Avg	OBP	SLG
1998 Salem-Keizr	A-	71	236	55	12	7	6	—	—	99	52	27	43	1	56	2	3	4	19	6	.76	4	.233	.351	.419
1999 Bakersfield	A+	99	356	98	12	6	11	—	—	155	69	47	54	0	108	6	1	4	15	8	.65	2	.275	.382	.435
Shreveport	AA	14	41	5	0	0	2	—	—	11	6	4	4	0	22	1	1	2	0	0	—	0	.122	.208	.268
2000 Shreveport	AA	130	459	92	21	2	7	—	—	138	58	47	40	1	141	0	3	3	9	3	.75	9	.200	.263	.301
2001 Fresno	AAA	134	469	113	21	6	23	—	—	215	77	78	44	1	137	0	3	5	17	2	.89	5	.241	.303	.458
2001 San Francisco	NL	9	7	0	0	0	0	(0	0)	0	1	0	0	0	5	0	0	0	0	0	—	0	.000	.000	.000

Pat Rapp

Pitches: Right **Bats:** Right **Pos:** SP-28; RP-3   **Ht:** 6'3" **Wt:** 230 **Born:** 7/13/67 **Age:** 34

Year Team	Lg	G	GS	CG	GF	IP	BFP	H	R	ER	HR	SH	SF	HB	TBB	IBB	SO	WP	Bk	W	L	Pct.	ShO	Sv-Op	Hld	ERA
1992 San Francisco	NL	3	2	0	1	10	43	8	8	8	0	2	0	1	6	1	3	0	0	0	2	.000	0	0-0	0	7.20
1993 Florida	NL	16	16	1	0	94	412	101	49	42	7	8	4	2	39	1	57	6	0	4	6	.400	0	0-0	0	4.02
1994 Florida	NL	24	23	2	1	133.1	584	132	67	57	13	8	4	7	69	3	75	5	1	7	8	.467	1	0-0	0	3.85
1995 Florida	NL	28	28	3	0	167.1	716	158	72	64	10	8	0	7	76	2	102	7	0	14	7	.667	2	0-0	0	3.44
1996 Florida	NL	30	29	0	1	162.1	728	184	95	92	12	15	8	3	91	6	86	13	0	8	16	.333	1	0-0	0	5.10
1997 Fla-SF	NL	27	25	1	0	141.2	638	158	81	76	16	6	6	5	72	4	92	8	0	5	8	.385	1	0-0	0	4.83
1998 Kansas City	AL	32	32	1	0	188.1	855	208	117	111	24	3	6	10	107	7	132	14	0	12	13	.480	1	0-0	0	5.30
1999 Boston	AL	37	26	0	3	146.1	638	147	76	67	13	3	0	7	69	1	90	5	0	6	7	.462	0	0-0	1	4.12
2000 Baltimore	AL	31	30	0	0	174	798	203	125	114	18	1	7	5	83	5	106	8	0	9	12	.429	0	0-0	0	5.90
2001 Anaheim	AL	31	28	1	1	170	731	169	96	90	20	3	7	2	71	2	82	4	0	5	12	.294	0	0-0	0	4.76
1997 Florida	NL	19	19	1	0	108.2	484	121	59	54	11	4	3	3	51	3	64	5	0	4	6	.400	1	0-0	0	4.47
San Francisco		8	6	0	0	33	154	37	24	22	5	2	3	2	21	1	28	3	0	1	2	.333	0	0-0	0	6.00
10 ML YEARS		259	239	9	7	1387.1	6143	1468	790	721	133	57	42	49	683	32	825	70	1	70	91	.435	5	0-0	1	4.68

Britt Reames

Pitches: Right **Bats:** Right **Pos:** RP-28; SP-13   **Ht:** 5'11" **Wt:** 175 **Born:** 8/19/73 **Age:** 28

Year Team	Lg	G	GS	CG	GF	IP	BFP	H	R	ER	HR	SH	SF	HB	TBB	IBB	SO	WP	Bk	W	L	Pct.	ShO	Sv-Op	Hld	ERA
1995 New Jersey	A-	5	5	0	0	29.2	121	19	7	5	1	1	0	3	12	0	42	5	0	2	1	.667	0	0--	—	1.52
Savannah	A	10	10	1	0	54.2	227	41	23	21	7	0	0	5	15	0	63	9	1	3	5	.375	0	0--	—	3.46

Year Team	Lg	G	GS	CG	GF	IP	BFP	H	R	ER	HR	SH	SF	HB	TBB	IBB	SO	WP	Bk	W	L	Pct.	ShO	Sv-Op	Hld	ERA
		HOW MUCH HE PITCHED						**WHAT HE GAVE UP**												**THE RESULTS**						
1996 Peoria	A	25	25	2	0	161	620	97	43	34	5	3	2	4	41	0	167	7	0	15	7	.682	1	0--	--	1.90
1999 Potomac	A+	10	8	0	0	36.2	163	34	21	13	2	2	1	3	21	0	22	4	0	3	2	.600	0	0--	--	3.19
2000 Arkansas	AA	8	8	0	0	39.2	178	46	28	27	4	0	0	2	18	0	39	1	0	2	3	.400	0	0--	--	6.13
Memphis	AAA	13	13	2	0	75	289	55	20	19	2	3	4	2	20	0	77	1	0	6	2	.750	1	0--	--	2.28
2001 Ottawa	AAA	8	8	1	0	54	212	47	24	21	4	3	1	1	13	0	38	1	0	4	3	.571	0	0--	--	3.50
2000 St. Louis	NL	8	7	0	0	40.2	170	30	17	13	4	0	1	1	23	1	31	2	1	2	1	.667	0	0-0	0	2.88
2001 Montreal	NL	41	13	0	3	95	432	101	68	59	16	7	2	5	48	3	86	2	0	4	8	.333	0	0-1	6	5.59
2 ML YEARS		49	20	0	3	135.2	602	131	85	72	20	7	3	6	71	4	117	4	1	6	9	.400	0	0-1	6	4.78

Jeff Reboulet

Bats: R **Throws:** R **Pos:** SS-56; PH/PR-25; 2B-22; 3B-7; LF-2   **Ht:** 6'0" **Wt:** 175 **Born:** 4/30/64 **Age:** 38

Year Team	Lg	G	AB	H	2B	3B	HR	(Hm	Rd)	TB	R	RBI	TBB	IBB	SO	HBP	SH	SF	SB	CS	SB%	GDP	Avg	OBP	SLG
		BATTING																	**BASERUNNING**				**PERCENTAGES**		
1992 Minnesota	AL	73	137	26	7	1	1	(1	0)	38	15	16	23	0	26	1	7	0	3	2	.60	0	.190	.311	.277
1993 Minnesota	AL	109	240	62	8	0	1	(0	1)	73	33	15	35	0	37	2	5	1	5	5	.50	6	.258	.356	.304
1994 Minnesota	AL	74	189	49	11	1	3	(2	1)	71	28	23	18	0	23	1	2	0	0	0	--	6	.259	.327	.376
1995 Minnesota	AL	87	216	63	11	0	4	(1	3)	86	39	23	27	0	34	1	2	0	1	2	.33	3	.292	.373	.398
1996 Minnesota	AL	107	234	52	9	0	0	(0	0)	61	20	23	25	1	34	1	4	2	4	2	.67	10	.222	.298	.261
1997 Baltimore	AL	99	228	54	9	0	4	(2	2)	75	26	27	23	0	44	1	11	2	3	0	1.00	3	.237	.307	.329
1998 Baltimore	AL	79	126	31	6	0	1	(1	0)	40	20	8	19	0	34	2	7	1	0	1	.00	3	.246	.351	.317
1999 Baltimore	AL	99	154	25	4	0	0	(0	0)	29	25	4	33	0	29	2	3	0	1	0	1.00	1	.162	.317	.188
2000 Kansas City	AL	66	182	44	7	0	0	(0	0)	51	29	14	23	0	32	0	6	1	3	1	.75	8	.242	.325	.280
2001 Los Angeles	NL	94	214	57	15	2	3	(3	0)	85	35	22	33	1	48	1	5	0	1	0	1.00	3	.266	.367	.397
10 ML YEARS		887	1920	463	87	4	17	(10	7)	609	270	175	259	2	341	12	52	7	20	14	.59	43	.241	.334	.317

Tim Redding

Pitches: Right **Bats:** Right **Pos:** SP-9; RP-4   **Ht:** 6'0" **Wt:** 180 **Born:** 2/12/78 **Age:** 24

Year Team	Lg	G	GS	CG	GF	IP	BFP	H	R	ER	HR	SH	SF	HB	TBB	IBB	SO	WP	Bk	W	L	Pct.	ShO	Sv-Op	Hld	ERA
		HOW MUCH HE PITCHED						**WHAT HE GAVE UP**												**THE RESULTS**						
1998 Auburn	A-	16	15	0	1	73.2	323	49	44	37	2	2	3	7	50	0	98	10	4	7	3	.700	0	1--	--	4.52
1999 Michigan	A	43	11	0	24	105	470	84	69	58	4	6	5	3	76	1	141	19	2	8	6	.571	0	14--	--	4.97
2000 Kissimmee	A+	24	24	0	0	154.2	649	125	62	46	5	4	6	9	57	1	170	13	0	12	5	.706	0	0--	--	2.68
Round Rock	AA	5	5	0	0	26	111	14	12	10	4	2	1	1	22	0	22	4	0	2	0	1.000	0	0--	--	3.46
2001 Round Rock	AA	14	14	1	0	90.2	364	64	26	22	5	1	0	3	25	0	113	1	0	10	2	.833	1	0--	--	2.18
New Orleans	AAA	6	6	0	0	37.2	153	22	21	19	4	0	1	5	19	0	42	1	0	4	1	.800	0	0--	--	4.54
2001 Houston	NL	13	9	0	1	55.2	249	62	38	34	11	2	3	3	24	0	55	2	0	3	1	.750	0	0-0	0	5.50

Mark Redman

Pitches: Left **Bats:** Left **Pos:** SP-11   **Ht:** 6'5" **Wt:** 220 **Born:** 1/5/74 **Age:** 28

Year Team	Lg	G	GS	CG	GF	IP	BFP	H	R	ER	HR	SH	SF	HB	TBB	IBB	SO	WP	Bk	W	L	Pct.	ShO	Sv-Op	Hld	ERA
		HOW MUCH HE PITCHED						**WHAT HE GAVE UP**												**THE RESULTS**						
2001 Edmonton *	AAA	1	1	0	0	1.1	8	3	2	2	0	0	1	0	1	0	0	0	0	0	0	--	0	0--	--	13.50
Toledo *	AAA	3	3	0	0	13.2	57	14	10	8	3	0	1	1	1	0	12	0	1	0	1	.000	0	0--	--	5.27
1999 Minnesota	AL	5	1	0	0	12.2	65	17	13	12	3	0	1	1	7	0	11	0	0	1	0	1.000	0	0-0	0	8.53
2000 Minnesota	AL	32	24	0	3	151.1	651	168	81	80	22	3	2	3	45	0	117	6	0	12	9	.571	0	0-0	0	4.76
2001 Min-Det	AL	11	11	0	0	58	261	68	32	29	7	2	0	1	23	0	33	6	0	2	6	.250	0	0-0	0	4.50
2001 Minnesota	AL	9	9	0	0	49	219	57	26	23	6	1	0	0	19	0	29	6	0	2	4	.333	0	0-0	0	4.22
Detroit	AL	2	2	0	0	9	42	11	6	6	1	1	0	1	4	0	4	0	0	0	2	.000	0	0-0	0	6.00
3 ML YEARS		48	36	0	3	222	977	253	126	121	32	5	2	5	75	0	161	12	0	15	15	.500	0	0-0	0	4.91

Tike Redman

Bats: Left **Throws:** Left **Pos:** CF-28; RF-7; PH/PR-3   **Ht:** 5'11" **Wt:** 166 **Born:** 3/10/77 **Age:** 25

Year Team	Lg	G	AB	H	2B	3B	HR	(Hm	Rd)	TB	R	RBI	TBB	IBB	SO	HBP	SH	SF	SB	CS	SB%	GDP	Avg	OBP	SLG
		BATTING																	**BASERUNNING**				**PERCENTAGES**		
1996 Pirates	R	26	104	31	4	1	1	(--	--)	40	20	16	12	1	12	0	0	1	15	3	.83	0	.298	.368	.385
Erie	A-	43	170	50	4	6	2	(--	--)	72	31	21	17	0	30	0	2	3	7	3	.70	2	.294	.353	.424
1997 Lynchburg	A+	125	415	104	18	5	4	(--	--)	144	55	45	45	0	82	7	8	1	21	8	.72	8	.251	.333	.347
1998 Lynchburg	A+	131	525	135	26	10	6	(--	--)	199	70	46	32	2	73	1	3	5	36	16	.69	5	.257	.298	.379
1999 Altoona	AA	136	532	143	20	12	3	(--	--)	196	84	60	52	1	52	3	6	10	29	16	.64	6	.269	.332	.368
2000 Nashville	AAA	121	506	132	24	11	4	(--	--)	190	62	51	30	0	73	3	2	4	24	18	.57	4	.261	.306	.375
2001 Nashville	AAA	95	398	121	18	10	3	(--	--)	168	53	42	24	2	37	4	3	3	21	7	.75	6	.304	.347	.422
2000 Pittsburgh	NL	9	18	6	1	0	1	(0	1)	10	2	1	1	0	7	0	0	1	1	0	1.00	0	.333	.368	.556
2001 Pittsburgh	NL	37	125	28	4	1	1	(1	0)	37	8	4	4	0	25	0	0	1	3	5	.38	2	.224	.246	.296
2 ML YEARS		46	143	34	5	1	2	(1	1)	47	10	5	5	0	32	0	0	1	4	5	.44	2	.238	.262	.329

Mike Redmond

Bats: Right **Throws:** Right **Pos:** C-47; PH/PR-1   **Ht:** 6'1" **Wt:** 185 **Born:** 5/5/71 **Age:** 31

Year Team	Lg	G	AB	H	2B	3B	HR	(Hm	Rd)	TB	R	RBI	TBB	IBB	SO	HBP	SH	SF	SB	CS	SB%	GDP	Avg	OBP	SLG
		BATTING																	**BASERUNNING**				**PERCENTAGES**		
1998 Florida	NL	37	118	39	9	0	2	(1	1)	54	10	12	5	2	16	2	4	0	0	0	--	6	.331	.368	.458
1999 Florida	NL	84	242	73	9	0	1	(0	1)	85	22	27	26	2	34	5	5	0	0	0	--	8	.302	.381	.351
2000 Florida	NL	87	210	53	8	1	0	(0	0)	63	17	15	13	3	19	8	1	3	0	0	--	5	.252	.316	.300
2001 Florida	NL	48	141	44	4	0	4	(3	0)	60	19	14	13	4	13	2	1	1	0	0	--	6	.312	.376	.426
4 ML YEARS		256	711	209	30	1	7	(4	3)	262	68	68	57	11	82	17	11	4	0	0	--	25	.294	.359	.368

Rick Reed

Pitches: Right **Bats:** Right **Pos:** SP-32   **Ht:** 6'1" **Wt:** 195 **Born:** 8/16/65 **Age:** 36

		HOW MUCH HE PITCHED					WHAT HE GAVE UP											THE RESULTS					
Year Team	Lg	G	GS	CG	GF	IP	BFP	H	R	ER	HR	SH	SF	HB	TBB	IBB	SO	WP	Bk	W	L	Pct.	ShO	Sv-Op	Hld	ERA
1988 Pittsburgh	NL	2	2	0	0	12	47	10	4	4	1	2	0	0	2	0	6	0	0	1	0	1.000	0	0-0	0	3.00
1989 Pittsburgh	NL	15	7	0	2	54.2	232	62	35	34	5	2	3	2	11	3	34	0	3	1	4	.200	0	0-0	0	5.60
1990 Pittsburgh	NL	13	8	1	2	53.2	238	62	32	26	6	2	1	1	12	6	27	0	0	2	3	.400	0	1-1	1	4.36
1991 Pittsburgh	NL	1	1	0	0	4.1	21	8	6	5	1	0	0	0	1	0	2	0	0	0	0	—	0	0-0	0	10.38
1992 Kansas City	AL	19	18	1	0	100.1	419	105	47	41	10	2	5	5	20	3	49	0	0	3	7	.300	1	0-0	0	3.68
1993 KC-Tex	AL	3	0	0	0	7.2	36	12	5	5	1	0	0	2	2	0	5	0	0	1	0	1.000	0	0-0	0	5.87
1994 Texas	AL	4	3	0	0	16.2	75	17	13	11	3	0	0	1	7	0	12	0	0	1	1	.500	0	0-0	0	5.94
1995 Cincinnati	NL	4	3	0	1	17	70	18	12	11	5	1	0	0	3	0	10	0	0	0	0	—	0	0-0	0	5.82
1997 New York	NL	33	31	2	0	208.1	824	186	76	67	19	7	3	5	31	4	113	0	0	13	9	.591	0	0-0	0	2.89
1998 New York	NL	31	31	2	0	212.1	845	208	84	82	30	8	5	6	29	2	153	1	0	16	11	.593	1	0-0	0	3.48
1999 New York	NL	26	26	1	0	149.1	637	163	77	76	23	6	3	1	47	2	104	1	0	11	5	.688	1	0-0	0	4.58
2000 New York	NL	30	30	0	0	184	768	192	90	84	28	3	5	5	34	3	121	2	1	11	5	.688	0	0-0	0	4.11
2001 NYM-Min		32	32	3	0	202.1	834	211	98	91	28	3	5	3	31	3	142	3	0	12	12	.500	0	0-0	0	4.05
1993 Kansas City	AL	1	0	0	0	3.2	18	6	4	4	0	0	0	1	1	0	3	0	0	0	0	—	0	0-0	0	9.82
Texas		2	0	0	0	4	18	6	1	1	1	0	0	1	1	0	2	0	0	1	0	1.000	0	0-0	0	2.25
2001 New York	NL	20	20	3	0	134.2	531	119	53	52	16	8	1	1	17	3	99	2	0	8	6	.571	0	0-0	0	3.48
Minnesota		12	12	0	0	67.2	303	92	45	39	12	0	2	4	14	0	43	1	0	4	6	.400	0	0-0	0	5.19
13 ML YEARS		213	192	10	5	1222.2	5046	1254	579	537	160	41	28	33	230	26	778	7	4	72	57	.558	5	1-1	1	3.95

Steve Reed

Pitches: Right **Bats:** Right **Pos:** RP-70   **Ht:** 6'2" **Wt:** 212 **Born:** 3/11/66 **Age:** 36

		HOW MUCH HE PITCHED					WHAT HE GAVE UP											THE RESULTS					
Year Team	Lg	G	GS	CG	GF	IP	BFP	H	R	ER	HR	SH	SF	HB	TBB	IBB	SO	WP	Bk	W	L	Pct.	ShO	Sv-Op	Hld	ERA
1992 San Francisco	NL	18	0	0	2	15.2	63	13	5	4	2	0	0	1	3	0	11	0	0	1	0	1.000	0	0-0	1	2.30
1993 Colorado	NL	64	0	0	14	84.1	347	80	47	42	13	2	3	3	30	5	51	1	0	9	5	.643	0	3-6	9	4.48
1994 Colorado	NL	61	0	0	11	64	297	79	33	28	9	0	7	6	26	3	51	1	0	3	2	.600	0	3-10	14	3.94
1995 Colorado	NL	71	0	0	15	84	327	61	24	20	8	3	1	1	21	3	79	0	2	5	2	.714	0	3-6	11	2.14
1996 Colorado	NL	70	0	0	7	75	307	66	38	33	11	2	4	6	19	0	51	1	0	4	3	.571	0	0-6	22	3.96
1997 Colorado	NL	63	0	0	23	62.1	260	49	28	28	10	3	1	5	27	1	43	0	0	4	6	.400	0	6-13	10	4.04
1998 SF-Cle		70	0	0	19	80.1	322	56	29	28	8	2	0	5	27	5	73	0	0	4	3	.571	0	1-6	21	3.14
1999 Cleveland	AL	63	0	0	15	61.2	274	69	33	29	10	4	5	3	20	5	44	2	0	3	2	.600	0	0-3	8	4.23
2000 Cleveland	AL	57	0	0	16	56	243	58	30	27	7	4	1	1	21	4	39	2	1	2	0	1.000	0	0-1	9	4.34
2001 Cle-Atl		70	0	0	14	58.1	250	52	25	23	6	3	1	3	23	5	46	0	0	3	3	.500	0	1-2	11	3.55
1998 San Francisco	NL	50	0	0	14	54.2	213	30	10	9	4	2	0	4	19	5	50	0	0	2	1	.667	0	1-5	13	1.48
Cleveland	AL	20	0	0	5	25.2	109	26	19	19	4	0	0	1	8	0	23	0	0	2	2	.500	0	0-1	8	6.66
2001 Cleveland	AL	31	0	0	8	27.1	116	22	11	11	3	0	0	2	10	2	21	0	0	1	1	.500	0	0-1	6	3.62
Atlanta	NL	39	0	0	6	31	134	30	14	12	3	3	1	1	13	3	25	0	0	2	2	.500	0	1-1	5	3.48
10 ML YEARS		607	0	0	136	641.2	2690	583	292	262	84	23	23	34	217	31	488	7	3	38	26	.594	0	17-53	116	3.67

Pokey Reese

Bats: Right **Throws:** Right **Pos:** SS-78; 2B-51; PH/PR-11   **Ht:** 5'11" **Wt:** 180 **Born:** 6/10/73 **Age:** 29

		BATTING																		BASERUNNING				PERCENTAGES		
Year Team	Lg	G	AB	H	2B	3B	HR	(Hm	Rd)	TB	R	RBI	TBB	IBB	SO	HBP	SH	SF	SB	CS	SB%	GDP	Avg	OBP	SLG
1997 Cincinnati	NL	128	397	87	15	0	4	(3	1)	114	48	26	31	2	82	5	4	0	25	7	.78	1	.219	.284	.287
1998 Cincinnati	NL	59	133	34	2	2	1	(0	1)	43	20	16	14	1	28	0	2	2	3	2	.60	3	.256	.322	.323
1999 Cincinnati	NL	149	585	167	37	5	10	(5	5)	244	85	52	35	3	81	6	5	5	38	7	.84	9	.285	.330	.417
2000 Cincinnati	NL	135	518	132	20	6	12	(3	9)	200	76	46	45	5	86	6	3	5	29	3	.91	8	.255	.319	.386
2001 Cincinnati	NL	133	428	96	20	2	9	(4	5)	147	50	40	34	4	82	3	5	4	25	4	.86	7	.224	.284	.343
5 ML YEARS		604	2061	516	94	15	36	(15	21)	748	279	180	159	15	359	20	19	16	120	23	.84	28	.250	.308	.363

Dan Reichert

Pitches: Right **Bats:** Right **Pos:** SP-19; RP-8   **Ht:** 6'3" **Wt:** 175 **Born:** 7/12/76 **Age:** 25

		HOW MUCH HE PITCHED					WHAT HE GAVE UP											THE RESULTS					
Year Team	Lg	G	GS	CG	GF	IP	BFP	H	R	ER	HR	SH	SF	HB	TBB	IBB	SO	WP	Bk	W	L	Pct.	ShO	Sv-Op	Hld	ERA
2001 Omaha *	AAA	10	5	1	0	32.2	156	45	30	30	4	1	0	4	16	0	30	5	0	1	5	.167	0	0--	—	8.27
1999 Kansas City	AL	12	8	0	0	36.2	183	48	38	37	2	1	1	2	32	1	20	1	0	2	2	.500	0	0-0	0	9.08
2000 Kansas City	AL	44	18	1	11	153.1	690	157	92	80	15	5	7	7	91	1	94	18	0	8	10	.444	1	2-6	4	4.70
2001 Kansas City	AL	27	19	0	4	123	554	131	83	77	14	3	4	8	67	2	77	12	0	8	8	.500	0	0-0	1	5.63
3 ML YEARS		79	45	1	15	313	1427	336	213	194	31	9	12	17	190	4	191	31	0	18	20	.474	1	2-6	5	5.58

Brian Reith

Pitches: Right **Bats:** Right **Pos:** SP-8; RP-1   **Ht:** 6'5" **Wt:** 190 **Born:** 2/28/78 **Age:** 24

		HOW MUCH HE PITCHED					WHAT HE GAVE UP											THE RESULTS					
Year Team	Lg	G	GS	CG	GF	IP	BFP	H	R	ER	HR	SH	SF	HB	TBB	IBB	SO	WP	Bk	W	L	Pct.	ShO	Sv-Op	Hld	ERA
1996 Yankees	R	10	4	0	1	32.2	143	31	16	15	1	2	2	1	16	0	21	3	0	2	3	.400	0	0--	—	4.13
1997 Yankees	R	12	11	1	0	63	270	70	28	20	1	2	2	3	14	0	40	8	0	4	2	.667	0	0--	—	2.86
1998 Greensboro	A	20	20	3	0	118.1	475	86	42	30	7	2	0	3	32	1	116	1	0	6	7	.462	1	0--	—	2.28
1999 Tampa	A+	26	23	0	0	139.2	616	174	87	73	12	7	4	4	35	1	101	4	0	9	9	.500	0	0--	—	4.70
2000 Tampa	A+	18	18	1	0	119.2	487	101	39	29	4	2	3	5	33	0	100	6	1	4	4	.692	1	0--	—	2.18
Dayton	A	5	5	0	0	34.1	139	33	12	11	2	0	0	0	8	0	30	2	0	2	1	.667	0	0--	—	2.88
Chattanooga	AA	5	5	0	0	30	128	31	14	13	3	2	2	1	11	0	29	2	0	1	3	.250	0	0--	—	3.90
2001 Louisville	AAA	1	1	0	0	5	21	7	2	2	0	1	0	0	1	0	6	0	0	0	0	—	0	0--	—	3.60
Chattanooga	AA	18	18	1	0	104.1	448	103	63	46	10	2	5	1	42	1	89	6	0	6	4	.600	0	0--	—	3.97
2001 Cincinnati	NL	9	8	0	0	40.1	192	56	37	35	13	4	2	2	16	0	22	1	0	0	7	.000	0	0-0	0	7.81

185

Chris Reitsma

Pitches: Right **Bats:** Right **Pos:** SP-29; RP-7   **Ht:** 6'5" **Wt:** 214 **Born:** 12/31/77 **Age:** 24

Year Team	Lg	HOW MUCH HE PITCHED						WHAT HE GAVE UP										THE RESULTS					
		G	GS	CG	GF	IP	BFP	H	R	ER	HR	SH	SF	HB	TBB	IBB	SO	WP	Bk	W	L	Pct.	ShO	Sv-Op	Hld	ERA
1996 Red Sox	R	7	6	0	0	26.2	109	24	7	4	0	1	0	2	1	0	32	3	0	3	1	.750	0	0- -	—	1.35
1997 Michigan	A	9	9	0	0	49.2	217	57	23	16	4	0	2	2	13	0	41	3	0	4	1	.800	0	0- -	—	2.90
1998 Sarasota	A+	8	8	0	0	12.2	55	12	6	4	0	0	1	0	5	0	9	0	0	0	0	—	0	0- -	—	2.84
1999 Sarasota	A+	19	19	0	0	96.1	440	116	71	60	11	1	4	10	31	1	79	7	3	4	10	.286	0	0- -	—	5.61
2000 Sarasota	A+	11	11	0	0	64	267	57	29	26	3	4	1	5	17	0	47	0	0	3	4	.429	0	0- -	—	3.66
Trenton	AA	14	14	1	0	90.2	361	78	28	26	7	1	1	2	21	1	58	1	0	7	2	.778	0	0- -	—	2.58
2001 Cincinnati	NL	36	29	0	1	182	800	209	121	107	23	13	8	5	49	6	96	5	0	7	15	.318	0	0-0	1	5.29

Bryan Rekar

Pitches: Right **Bats:** Right **Pos:** SP-25   **Ht:** 6'3" **Wt:** 220 **Born:** 6/3/72 **Age:** 30

Year Team	Lg	HOW MUCH HE PITCHED						WHAT HE GAVE UP										THE RESULTS					
		G	GS	CG	GF	IP	BFP	H	R	ER	HR	SH	SF	HB	TBB	IBB	SO	WP	Bk	W	L	Pct.	ShO	Sv-Op	Hld	ERA
2001 Orlando *	AA	3	3	0	0	12	47	8	3	3	0	0	0	1	1	0	11	2	0	1	0	1.000	0	0- -	—	2.25
1995 Colorado	NL	15	14	1	0	85	375	95	51	47	11	7	4	3	24	2	60	3	2	4	6	.400	0	0-0	1	4.98
1996 Colorado	NL	14	11	0	0	58.1	289	87	61	58	11	3	3	5	26	1	25	4	0	2	4	.333	0	0-i	0	8.95
1997 Colorado	NL	2	2	0	0	9.1	46	11	7	6	3	1	0	0	6	0	4	0	0	1	0	1.000	0	0-0	0	5.79
1998 Tampa Bay	AL	16	15	1	1	86.2	369	95	56	48	16	1	1	8	21	0	55	1	0	2	8	.200	0	0-0	0	4.98
1999 Tampa Bay	AL	27	12	0	2	94.2	437	121	68	61	14	3	2	5	41	2	55	4	0	6	6	.500	0	0-0	1	5.80
2000 Tampa Bay	AL	30	27	2	2	173.1	743	200	92	85	22	3	9	4	39	0	95	5	0	7	10	.412	0	0-0	0	4.41
2001 Tampa Bay	AL	25	25	0	0	140.2	630	167	104	92	21	4	7	6	45	2	87	6	1	3	13	.188	0	0-0	0	5.89
7 ML YEARS		129	106	4	5	648	2889	776	439	397	98	22	33	25	202	7	381	23	3	25	47	.347	0	0-1	2	5.51

Desi Relaford

Bats: B **Throws:** R **Pos:** 2B-54; PH/PR-40; SS-25; 3B-20; P-1   **Ht:** 5'9" **Wt:** 174 **Born:** 9/16/73 **Age:** 28

Year Team	Lg	BATTING																BASERUNNING				PERCENTAGES		
		G	AB	H	2B	3B	HR	(Hm | Rd)	TB	R	RBI	TBB	IBB	SO	HBP	SH	SF	SB	CS	SB%	GDP	Avg	OBP	SLG
1996 Philadelphia	NL	15	40	7	2	0	0	(0 | 0)	9	2	1	3	0	9	0	1	0	1	0	1.00	1	.175	.233	.225
1997 Philadelphia	NL	15	38	7	1	2	0	(0 | 0)	12	3	6	5	0	6	0	1	0	3	0	1.00	0	.184	.279	.316
1998 Philadelphia	NL	142	494	121	25	3	5	(4 | 1)	167	45	41	33	4	87	3	10	6	9	5	.64	9	.245	.293	.338
1999 Philadelphia	NL	65	211	51	11	2	1	(0 | 1)	69	31	26	19	2	54	6	6	0	4	3	.57	5	.242	.322	.327
2000 Phi-SD	NL	128	410	88	14	3	5	(0 | 5)	123	55	46	75	7	71	12	3	2	13	0	1.00	10	.215	.351	.300
2001 New York	NL	120	301	91	27	0	8	(4 | 4)	142	43	36	27	1	65	5	2	5	15	5	.72	4	.302	.364	.472
2000 Philadelphia	NL	83	253	56	12	3	3	(0 | 3)	83	29	30	48	7	45	9	2	1	5	0	1.00	7	.221	.363	.328
San Diego	NL	45	157	32	2	0	2	(0 | 2)	40	26	16	27	0	26	3	1	1	8	0	1.00	3	.204	.330	.255
6 ML YEARS		485	1494	365	80	10	19	(8 | 11)	522	179	156	162	14	272	26	23	13	43	13	.77	29	.244	.326	.349

Mike Remlinger

Pitches: Left **Bats:** Left **Pos:** RP-74   **Ht:** 6'1" **Wt:** 210 **Born:** 3/23/66 **Age:** 36

Year Team	Lg	HOW MUCH HE PITCHED						WHAT HE GAVE UP										THE RESULTS					
		G	GS	CG	GF	IP	BFP	H	R	ER	HR	SH	SF	HB	TBB	IBB	SO	WP	Bk	W	L	Pct.	ShO	Sv-Op	Hld	ERA
1991 San Francisco	NL	8	6	1	1	35	155	36	17	17	5	1	0	0	20	1	19	2	1	2	1	.667	1	0-0	0	4.37
1994 New York	NL	10	9	0	0	54.2	252	55	30	28	9	2	3	1	35	4	33	3	0	1	5	.167	0	0-0	1	4.61
1995 NYM-Cin	NL	7	0	0	4	6.2	34	9	6	5	1	1	0	0	5	0	7	0	0	1	0	1.000	0	0-1	0	6.75
1996 Cincinnati	NL	19	4	0	2	27.1	125	24	17	17	4	3	1	3	19	2	19	2	2	0	1	.000	0	0-0	1	5.60
1997 Cincinnati	NL	69	12	2	10	124	525	100	61	57	11	6	4	7	60	6	145	12	2	8	8	.500	0	2-2	14	4.14
1998 Cincinnati	NL	35	28	1	0	164.1	727	164	96	88	23	12	7	5	87	1	144	11	1	8	15	.348	1	0-0	0	4.82
1999 Atlanta	NL	73	0	0	14	83.2	346	66	24	22	9	2	1	1	35	5	81	5	0	10	1	.909	0	1-3	21	2.37
2000 Atlanta	NL	71	0	0	18	72.2	311	55	29	28	6	3	2	3	37	1	72	3	0	5	3	.625	0	12-16	23	3.47
2001 Atlanta	NL	74	0	0	6	75	313	67	25	23	9	2	0	2	23	4	93	4	0	3	3	.500	0	1-5	31	2.76
1995 New York	NL	5	0	0	4	5.2	27	7	5	4	1	1	0	0	2	0	6	0	0	0	1	.000	0	0-1	0	6.35
Cincinnati	NL	2	0	0	0	1	7	2	1	1	0	0	0	0	3	0	1	0	0	0	0	—	0	0-0	0	9.00
9 ML YEARS		366	59	4	55	643.1	2788	576	305	285	77	32	19	22	321	24	613	42	6	37	38	.493	2	16-27	91	3.99

Edgar Renteria

Bats: R **Throws:** R **Pos:** SS-137; PH/PR-4; DH-1; 1B-1   **Ht:** 6'1" **Wt:** 180 **Born:** 8/7/75 **Age:** 26

Year Team	Lg	BATTING																BASERUNNING				PERCENTAGES		
		G	AB	H	2B	3B	HR	(Hm | Rd)	TB	R	RBI	TBB	IBB	SO	HBP	SH	SF	SB	CS	SB%	GDP	Avg	OBP	SLG
1996 Florida	NL	106	431	133	18	3	5	(2 | 3)	172	68	31	33	0	68	2	2	3	16	2	.89	12	.309	.358	.399
1997 Florida	NL	154	617	171	21	3	4	(3 | 1)	210	90	52	45	1	108	4	19	6	32	15	.68	17	.277	.327	.340
1998 Florida	NL	133	517	146	18	2	3	(2 | 1)	177	79	31	48	1	78	4	9	2	41	22	.65	13	.282	.347	.342
1999 St. Louis	NL	154	585	161	36	2	11	(6 | 5)	234	92	63	53	0	82	2	6	7	37	8	.82	16	.275	.334	.400
2000 St. Louis	NL	150	562	156	32	1	16	(4 | 12)	238	94	76	63	3	77	1	3	6	21	13	.62	19	.278	.346	.423
2001 St. Louis	NL	141	493	128	19	3	10	(3 | 7)	183	54	57	39	4	73	3	8	6	17	4	.81	15	.260	.314	.371
6 ML YEARS		838	3205	895	144	14	49	(20 | 29)	1214	477	310	281	9	486	16	52	33	164	64	.72	92	.279	.337	.379

Al Reyes

Pitches: Right **Bats:** Right **Pos:** RP-19   **Ht:** 6'1" **Wt:** 206 **Born:** 4/10/71 **Age:** 31

Year Team	Lg	HOW MUCH HE PITCHED						WHAT HE GAVE UP										THE RESULTS					
		G	GS	CG	GF	IP	BFP	H	R	ER	HR	SH	SF	HB	TBB	IBB	SO	WP	Bk	W	L	Pct.	ShO	Sv-Op	Hld	ERA
2001 Las Vegas *	AAA	19	0	0	4	29.1	126	24	11	11	3	1	0	5	10	1	37	0	0	0	1	.000	0	0- -	—	3.38
1995 Milwaukee	AL	27	0	0	13	33.1	138	19	9	9	3	1	2	3	18	2	29	0	0	1	1	.500	0	1-1	4	2.43
1996 Milwaukee	AL	5	0	0	2	5.2	29	8	5	5	1	0	0	0	2	0	2	2	0	1	0	1.000	0	0-0	0	7.94
1997 Milwaukee	AL	19	0	0	7	29.2	131	32	19	18	4	2	0	3	9	0	28	1	0	1	2	.333	0	1-1	1	5.46
1998 Milwaukee	NL	50	0	0	13	57	253	55	26	25	9	2	1	2	31	1	58	2	0	5	1	.833	0	0-1	10	3.95
1999 Mil-Bal		53	0	0	12	65.2	287	50	33	33	9	4	3	6	41	3	67	3	0	4	3	.571	0	0-4	6	4.52

Year Team	Lg	G	GS	CG	GF	IP	BFP	H	R	ER	HR	SH	SF	HB	TBB	IBB	SO	WP	Bk	W	L	Pct.	ShO	Sv-Op	Hld	ERA
2000 Bal-LA		19	0	0	6	19.2	86	15	10	10	2	1	2	0	12	1	18	0	0	1	0	1.000	0	0-1	3	4.58
2001 Los Angeles	NL	19	0	0	9	25.2	120	28	13	11	3	0	2	1	13	1	23	0	1	2	1	.667	0	1-2	0	3.86
1999 Milwaukee	NL	26	0	0	6	36	161	27	17	17	5	1	1	3	25	1	39	2	0	2	0	1.000	0	0-1	2	4.25
Baltimore	AL	27	0	0	6	29.2	126	23	16	16	4	3	2	3	16	2	28	1	0	2	3	.400	0	0-3	4	4.85
2000 Baltimore	AL	13	0	0	2	13	62	13	10	10	2	1	2	0	11	1	10	0	0	1	0	1.000	0	0-1	0	6.92
Los Angeles	NL	6	0	0	4	6.2	24	2	0	0	0	0	0	0	1	0	8	0	0	0	0	—	0	0-0	1	0.00
7 ML YEARS		192	0	0	62	236.2	1042	207	115	111	31	10	10	15	126	8	225	8	1	15	8	.652	0	3-10	24	4.22

Dennys Reyes

Pitches: Left **Bats:** Right **Pos:** RP-29; SP-6   Ht: 6'3" **Wt:** 246 **Born:** 4/19/77 **Age:** 25

Year Team	Lg	G	GS	CG	GF	IP	BFP	H	R	ER	HR	SH	SF	HB	TBB	IBB	SO	WP	Bk	W	L	Pct.	ShO	Sv-Op	Hld	ERA
2001 Louisville *	AAA	7	6	0	0	34.1	148	34	15	14	3	0	0	1	16	0	34	3	0	4	2	.667	0	0--	—	3.67
1997 Los Angeles	NL	14	5	0	0	47	207	51	21	20	4	5	1	1	18	3	36	2	1	2	3	.400	0	0-0	0	3.83
1998 LA-Cin	NL	19	10	0	4	67.1	300	62	36	34	3	7	2	1	47	5	77	6	1	3	5	.375	0	0-0	0	4.54
1999 Cincinnati	NL	65	1	0	12	61.2	277	53	30	26	5	4	3	3	39	1	72	5	1	2	2	.500	0	2-3	14	3.79
2000 Cincinnati	NL	62	0	0	15	43.2	200	43	31	22	5	3	3	1	29	0	36	6	0	2	1	.667	0	0-1	10	4.53
2001 Cincinnati	NL	35	6	0	2	53	246	51	35	29	5	2	2	1	35	1	52	5	0	2	6	.250	0	0-0	6	4.92
1998 Los Angeles	NL	11	3	0	4	28.2	130	27	17	15	1	3	1	0	20	4	33	1	1	0	4	.000	0	0-0	0	4.71
Cincinnati	NL	8	7	0	0	38.2	170	35	19	19	2	4	1	1	27	1	44	5	0	3	1	.750	0	0-0	0	4.42
5 ML YEARS		195	22	0	33	272.2	1230	260	153	131	22	21	11	7	168	10	273	24	3	11	17	.393	0	2-4	30	4.32

Shane Reynolds

Pitches: Right **Bats:** Right **Pos:** SP-28   Ht: 6'3" **Wt:** 210 **Born:** 3/26/68 **Age:** 34

Year Team	Lg	G	GS	CG	GF	IP	BFP	H	R	ER	HR	SH	SF	HB	TBB	IBB	SO	WP	Bk	W	L	Pct.	ShO	Sv-Op	Hld	ERA
2001 New Orleans *	AAA	1	1	0	0	7	29	8	0	0	0	0	0	0	0	0	7	0	0	1	0	1.000	0	0--	—	0.00
Round Rock *	AA	1	1	0	0	7	27	5	1	1	0	0	0	0	2	0	5	0	0	1	0	1.000	0	0--	—	1.29
1992 Houston	NL	8	5	0	0	25.1	122	42	22	20	2	6	1	0	6	1	10	1	1	1	3	.250	0	0-0	0	7.11
1993 Houston	NL	5	1	0	0	11	49	11	4	1	0	0	0	0	6	1	10	0	0	0	0	—	0	0-0	0	0.82
1994 Houston	NL	33	14	1	5	124	517	128	46	42	10	4	0	6	21	3	110	3	2	8	5	.615	1	0-0	5	3.05
1995 Houston	NL	30	30	4	0	189.1	792	196	87	73	15	8	0	2	37	6	175	7	1	10	11	.476	2	0-0	0	3.47
1996 Houston	NL	35	35	4	0	239	981	227	103	97	20	11	7	8	44	3	204	5	1	16	10	.615	1	0-0	0	3.65
1997 Houston	NL	30	30	2	0	181	773	189	92	85	19	9	5	3	47	5	152	5	2	9	10	.474	1	0-0	0	4.23
1998 Houston	NL	35	35	3	0	233.1	986	257	99	91	25	5	7	2	53	2	209	5	0	19	8	.704	1	0-0	0	3.51
1999 Houston	NL	35	35	4	0	231.2	963	250	108	99	23	11	5	1	37	0	197	4	0	16	14	.533	2	0-0	0	3.85
2000 Houston	NL	22	22	0	0	131	588	150	86	76	20	6	8	6	45	2	93	5	0	7	8	.467	0	0-0	0	5.22
2001 Houston	NL	28	28	3	0	182.2	772	208	95	88	24	13	2	6	36	2	102	2	0	14	11	.560	0	0-0	0	4.34
10 ML YEARS		261	235	20	5	1548.1	6543	1658	742	672	158	73	35	32	332	25	1262	37	7	100	80	.556	7	0-0	5	3.91

Armando Reynoso

Pitches: Right **Bats:** Right **Pos:** SP-9   Ht: 6'0" **Wt:** 210 **Born:** 5/1/66 **Age:** 36

Year Team	Lg	G	GS	CG	GF	IP	BFP	H	R	ER	HR	SH	SF	HB	TBB	IBB	SO	WP	Bk	W	L	Pct.	ShO	Sv-Op	Hld	ERA
2001 Tucson *	AAA	1	1	0	0	3.2	16	3	0	0	0	0	0	0	2	0	5	0	0	0	0	—	0	0--	—	0.00
1991 Atlanta	NL	6	5	0	1	23.1	103	26	18	16	4	3	0	3	10	1	10	2	0	2	1	.667	0	0-0	0	6.17
1992 Atlanta	NL	3	1	0	1	7.2	32	11	4	4	2	1	0	1	2	1	2	0	0	1	0	1.000	0	1-1	0	4.70
1993 Colorado	NL	30	30	4	0	189	830	206	101	84	22	5	8	9	63	7	117	7	6	12	11	.522	0	0-0	0	4.00
1994 Colorado	NL	9	9	1	0	52.1	226	54	30	28	5	2	2	6	22	1	25	2	2	3	4	.429	0	0-0	0	4.82
1995 Colorado	NL	20	18	0	0	93	418	116	61	55	12	8	2	5	36	3	40	2	0	7	7	.500	0	0-0	0	5.32
1996 Colorado	NL	30	30	0	0	168.2	733	195	97	93	27	3	3	9	49	0	88	4	3	8	9	.471	0	0-0	0	4.96
1997 New York	NL	16	16	1	0	91.1	388	95	47	46	7	3	3	5	29	4	47	4	1	6	3	.667	1	0-0	0	4.53
1998 New York	NL	11	11	0	0	68.1	292	64	31	29	4	4	1	5	32	3	40	2	2	7	3	.700	0	0-0	0	3.82
1999 Arizona	NL	31	27	0	1	167	730	178	90	81	20	6	6	6	67	7	79	7	1	10	6	.625	0	0-0	1	4.37
2000 Arizona	NL	31	30	2	0	170.2	730	179	102	100	22	11	5	6	52	5	89	3	0	11	12	.478	0	0-0	0	5.27
2001 Arizona	NL	9	9	0	0	46.2	207	58	32	31	13	2	2	4	13	2	15	1	0	1	6	.143	0	0-0	0	5.98
11 ML YEARS		196	186	8	3	1078	4689	1182	613	567	138	48	34	60	375	34	552	34	15	68	62	.523	1	1-1	1	4.73

Arthur Rhodes

Pitches: Left **Bats:** Left **Pos:** RP-71   Ht: 6'2" **Wt:** 205 **Born:** 10/24/69 **Age:** 32

Year Team	Lg	G	GS	CG	GF	IP	BFP	H	R	ER	HR	SH	SF	HB	TBB	IBB	SO	WP	Bk	W	L	Pct.	ShO	Sv-Op	Hld	ERA
1991 Baltimore	AL	8	8	0	0	36	174	47	35	32	4	1	3	0	23	0	23	2	0	0	3	.000	0	0-0	0	8.00
1992 Baltimore	AL	15	15	2	0	94.1	394	87	39	38	6	5	1	1	38	2	77	2	1	7	5	.583	1	0-0	0	3.63
1993 Baltimore	AL	17	17	0	0	85.2	387	91	62	62	16	2	3	1	49	1	49	2	0	5	6	.455	0	0-0	0	6.51
1994 Baltimore	AL	10	10	3	0	52.2	238	51	34	34	8	2	3	2	30	1	47	3	0	3	5	.375	2	0-0	0	5.81
1995 Baltimore	AL	19	9	0	3	75.1	336	68	53	52	13	4	0	0	48	1	77	3	1	2	5	.286	0	0-1	0	6.21
1996 Baltimore	AL	28	2	0	5	53	224	48	28	24	6	1	1	0	23	3	62	0	0	9	1	.900	0	1-1	2	4.08
1997 Baltimore	AL	53	0	0	6	95.1	378	75	32	32	9	0	4	4	26	5	102	2	0	10	3	.769	0	1-2	9	3.02
1998 Baltimore	AL	45	0	0	10	77	321	65	30	30	8	2	5	1	34	2	83	1	1	4	4	.500	0	4-8	10	3.51
1999 Baltimore	AL	43	0	0	11	53	244	43	37	32	9	2	2	0	45	6	59	4	0	3	4	.429	0	3-5	5	5.43
2000 Seattle	AL	72	0	0	9	69.1	281	51	34	33	6	1	2	0	29	3	77	4	0	5	8	.385	0	0-7	24	4.28
2001 Seattle	AL	71	0	0	16	68	258	46	14	13	5	1	0	1	12	0	83	3	0	8	0	1.000	0	3-7	32	1.72
11 ML YEARS		381	61	5	60	759.2	3235	672	398	382	90	21	24	10	357	24	739	26	3	56	44	.560	3	12-31	82	4.53

Chris Richard

Bats: L **Throws:** L **Pos:** RF-69; CF-36; DH-20; 1B-18; PH/PR-7 | **Ht:** 6'2" **Wt:** 190 **Born:** 6/7/74 **Age:** 28

Year Team	Lg	G	AB	H	2B	3B	HR	(Hm	Rd)	TB	R	RBI	TBB	IBB	SO	HBP	SH	SF	SB	CS	SB%	GDP	Avg	OBP	SLG
1995 New Jersey	A-	75	284	80	14	3	3	—	—	109	36	43	47	3	31	6	0	2	6	6	.50	3	.282	.392	.384
1996 St. Pete	A+	129	460	130	28	6	14	—	—	212	65	82	57	6	50	9	0	5	7	3	.70	11	.283	.369	.461
1997 Arkansas	AA	113	390	105	24	3	11	—	—	168	62	58	60	1	59	5	0	3	6	4	.60	8	.269	.371	.431
1998 Pr William	A+	8	30	8	2	0	0	—	—	10	5	1	1	0	5	0	0	0	1	0	1.00	2	.267	.290	.333
Arkansas	AA	28	89	18	5	1	2	—	—	31	7	17	9	0	10	1	0	1	0	1	.00	1	.202	.280	.348
1999 Arkansas	AA	133	442	130	26	3	29	—	—	249	78	94	43	5	75	8	0	6	7	7	.50	14	.294	.363	.563
Memphis	AAA	4	17	7	2	0	1	—	—	12	3	4	1	0	2	0	0	0	0	0	—	1	.412	.444	.706
2000 Memphis	AAA	95	375	104	24	0	16	—	—	176	64	75	50	4	70	4	0	3	9	3	.75	5	.277	.366	.469
2000 StL-Bal		62	215	57	14	2	14	(4	10)	117	39	37	17	3	40	4	0	3	7	5	.58	5	.265	.326	.544
2001 Baltimore	AL	136	483	128	31	3	15	(6	9)	210	74	61	45	4	100	8	2	4	11	9	.55	15	.265	.335	.435
2000 St. Louis	NL	6	16	2	0	0	1	(0	1)	5	1	1	2	0	2	0	0	0	0	0	—	0	.125	.222	.313
Baltimore	AL	56	199	55	14	2	13	(4	9)	112	38	36	15	3	38	4	0	3	7	5	.58	5	.276	.335	.563
2 ML YEARS		198	698	185	45	5	29	(10	19)	327	113	98	62	7	140	12	2	7	18	14	.56	20	.265	.332	.468

John Riedling

Pitches: Right **Bats:** Right **Pos:** RP-29 | **Ht:** 5'11" **Wt:** 190 **Born:** 8/29/75 **Age:** 26

Year Team	Lg	G	GS	CG	GF	IP	BFP	H	R	ER	HR	SH	SF	HB	TBB	IBB	SO	WP	Bk	W	L	Pct.	ShO	Sv-Op	Hld	ERA
1994 Billings	R+	15	5	0	2	44.1	221	62	36	27	0	2	2	3	28	0	27	7	0	4	1	.800	0	0--	—	5.48
1995 Billings	R+	13	7	0	2	38.1	192	51	38	30	4	0	3	1	21	2	28	8	0	2	2	.500	0	1--	—	7.04
1996 Chstn-WV	A	26	26	0	0	140	615	135	85	62	2	10	6	10	66	6	90	6	1	6	10	.375	0	0--	—	3.99
1997 Burlington	A	35	16	0	11	102.2	461	101	70	60	8	3	5	7	47	0	104	10	0	7	6	.538	0	0--	—	5.26
1998 Chattanooga	AA	24	20	0	1	102.2	475	112	70	57	10	1	5	4	60	5	86	5	0	3	10	.231	0	0--	—	5.00
1999 Chattanooga	AA	40	0	0	23	42	186	41	23	16	2	1	2	1	20	3	38	7	0	9	5	.643	0	5--	—	3.43
Indianapols	AAA	24	0	0	6	35	142	19	9	6	1	2	0	3	18	2	26	2	0	1	0	1.000	0	1--	—	1.54
2000 Louisville	AAA	53	0	0	18	75	315	63	24	21	7	4	1	1	30	3	75	8	0	6	3	.667	0	5--	—	2.52
2001 Louisville	AAA	1	0	0	0	1	4	0	0	0	0	0	0	0	1	0	1	0	0	0	0	—	0	0--	—	0.00
2000 Cincinnati	NL	13	0	0	5	15.1	63	11	7	4	1	1	0	1	8	0	18	1	0	3	1	.750	0	1-2	2	2.35
2001 Cincinnati	NL	29	0	0	14	33.2	136	22	9	9	1	2	0	2	14	0	23	5	0	1	1	.500	0	1-3	5	2.41
2 ML YEARS		42	0	0	19	49	199	33	16	13	2	3	0	3	22	0	41	6	0	4	2	.667	0	2-5	7	2.39

Paul Rigdon

Pitches: Right **Bats:** Right **Pos:** SP-15 | **Ht:** 6'5" **Wt:** 210 **Born:** 11/2/75 **Age:** 26

Year Team	Lg	G	GS	CG	GF	IP	BFP	H	R	ER	HR	SH	SF	HB	TBB	IBB	SO	WP	Bk	W	L	Pct.	ShO	Sv-Op	Hld	ERA
1996 Watertown	A-	22	0	0	21	39.2	174	41	24	18	4	1	0	2	10	0	46	1	1	2	2	.500	0	6--	—	4.08
1998 Kinston	A+	24	24	0	0	127.1	532	126	65	57	9	2	6	9	35	1	97	3	0	11	7	.611	0	0--	—	4.03
1999 Akron	AA	8	7	0	0	50	177	20	5	5	2	0	1	2	10	0	25	1	0	7	0	1.000	0	0--	—	0.90
Buffalo	AAA	19	19	0	0	103.1	451	114	60	52	11	3	2	1	28	0	60	4	2	7	4	.636	0	0--	—	4.53
2000 Buffalo	AAA	12	12	1	0	71	291	72	27	26	4	2	1	1	18	0	41	1	0	6	1	.857	0	0--	—	3.30
2000 Cle-Mil		17	16	0	0	87.1	381	89	52	50	18	3	5	1	35	5	63	2	0	5	5	.500	0	0-0	0	5.15
2001 Milwaukee	NL	15	15	0	0	79.1	360	86	52	51	13	9	2	3	46	6	49	1	0	3	5	.375	0	0-0	0	5.79
2000 Cleveland	AL	5	4	0	0	17.2	72	21	15	15	4	0	0	0	9	1	15	0	0	1	1	.500	0	0-0	0	7.64
Milwaukee	NL	12	12	0	0	69.2	302	68	37	35	14	3	5	1	26	4	48	2	0	4	4	.500	0	0-0	0	4.52
2 ML YEARS		32	31	0	0	166.2	741	175	104	101	31	12	7	4	81	11	112	3	0	8	10	.444	0	0-0	0	5.45

Jerrod Riggan

Pitches: Right **Bats:** Right **Pos:** RP-35 | **Ht:** 6'4" **Wt:** 185 **Born:** 5/16/74 **Age:** 28

Year Team	Lg	G	GS	CG	GF	IP	BFP	H	R	ER	HR	SH	SF	HB	TBB	IBB	SO	WP	Bk	W	L	Pct.	ShO	Sv-Op	Hld	ERA
1996 Boise	A-	15	15	1	0	89.1	395	90	62	46	10	3	6	5	38	5	80	6	0	3	5	.375	0	0--	—	4.63
1997 Lk Elsinore	A+	8	8	0	0	43	202	60	36	29	1	4	2	4	16	0	31	6	2	2	5	.286	0	0--	—	6.07
Cedar Rapds	A	19	19	3	0	116	506	132	70	63	15	3	7	2	36	2	65	12	2	9	8	.529	1	0--	—	4.89
1998 Capital Cty	A	14	0	0	7	41.1	177	38	21	17	5	3	1	1	14	1	40	2	0	4	1	.800	0	1--	—	3.70
1999 St. Lucie	A+	44	0	0	26	73	305	69	33	27	4	6	1	5	24	5	66	4	0	5	5	.500	0	12--	—	3.33
2000 Binghamton	AA	52	0	0	41	65	252	43	9	8	2	3	2	2	18	0	79	1	0	2	0	1.000	0	28--	—	1.11
2001 Norfolk	AAA	28	0	0	16	32.1	122	26	7	7	4	1	0	0	4	1	37	5	1	2	0	1.000	0	13--	—	1.95
2000 New York	NL	1	0	0	0	2	10	3	2	0	0	0	0	0	0	0	1	0	0	0	0	—	0	0-0	0	0.00
2001 New York	NL	35	0	0	12	47.2	202	42	19	18	5	2	3	0	24	7	41	4	0	3	3	.500	0	0-1	4	3.40
2 ML YEARS		36	0	0	12	49.2	212	45	21	18	5	2	3	0	24	7	42	4	0	3	3	.500	0	0-1	4	3.26

Adam Riggs

Bats: Right **Throws:** Right **Pos:** 2B-11; 3B-1; PH/PR-1 | **Ht:** 6'0" **Wt:** 190 **Born:** 10/4/72 **Age:** 29

Year Team	Lg	G	AB	H	2B	3B	HR	(Hm	Rd)	TB	R	RBI	TBB	IBB	SO	HBP	SH	SF	SB	CS	SB%	GDP	Avg	OBP	SLG
1994 Great Falls	R+	62	234	73	20	3	5	—	—	114	55	44	31	1	38	4	2	2	19	8	.70	2	.312	.399	.487
Yakima	A-	4	7	2	1	0	0	—	—	3	1	0	0	0	1	0	0	0	0	0	—	0	.286	.286	.429
1995 San Berndno	A+	134	542	196	39	5	24	—	—	317	111	106	59	1	93	10	7	4	31	10	.76	9	.362	.431	.585
1996 San Antonio	AA	134	546	143	31	6	14	—	—	228	68	66	37	1	82	9	5	5	16	6	.73	13	.283	.339	.451
1997 Albuquerque	AAA	57	227	69	8	3	13	—	—	122	59	28	29	1	39	3	0	0	12	2	.86	2	.304	.390	.537
1998 Albuquerque	AAA	44	170	63	13	3	4	—	—	94	30	25	21	1	29	3	1	1	12	6	.67	1	.371	.446	.553
1999 Albuquerque	AAA	133	513	150	29	7	13	—	—	232	87	81	54	0	114	10	2	5	25	17	.60	8	.292	.368	.452
2000 Albuquerque	AAA	124	348	109	24	4	12	—	—	177	71	57	35	0	67	2	6	3	11	7	.61	11	.313	.376	.509
2001 Portland	AAA	110	394	103	18	2	21	—	—	188	42	65	12	1	78	0	5	2	8	3	.73	9	.261	.282	.477
1997 Los Angeles	NL	9	20	4	1	0	0	(0	0)	5	3	1	4	1	3	0	0	0	1	0	1.00	1	.200	.333	.250
2001 San Diego	NL	12	36	7	1	0	0	(0	0)	8	2	1	2	0	8	0	0	0	1	1	.50	1	.194	.237	.222
2 ML YEARS		21	56	11	2	0	0	(0	0)	13	5	2	6	1	11	0	0	0	2	1	.67	1	.196	.274	.232

Jose Rijo

Pitches: Right **Bats:** Right **Pos:** RP-13   **Ht:** 6'3" **Wt:** 200 **Born:** 5/13/65 **Age:** 37

		HOW MUCH HE PITCHED					WHAT HE GAVE UP											THE RESULTS						
Year Team	Lg	G	GS	CG	GF	IP	BFP	H	R	ER	HR	SH	SF	HB	TBB	IBB	SO	WP	Bk	W	L	Pct.	ShO	Sv-Op	Hld	ERA
2001 Dayton *	A	1	1	0	0	3	11	3	1	1	0	0	0	0	0	0	1	0	0	0	0	—	0	0--	—	3.00
Chattanooga *	AA	1	1	0	0	3	11	1	0	0	0	0	0	0	1	0	3	1	0	0	0	—	0	0--	—	0.00
Louisville *	AAA	6	4	0	0	14	61	16	9	8	2	2	0	1	5	0	7	1	0	0	0	—	0	0--	—	5.14
1984 New York	AL	24	5	0	8	62.1	289	74	40	33	5	6	1	1	33	1	47	2	1	2	8	.200	0	2--	—	4.76
1985 Oakland	AL	12	9	0	1	63.2	272	57	26	25	6	5	0	0	28	2	65	0	0	6	4	.600	0	0--	—	3.53
1986 Oakland	AL	39	26	4	9	193.2	856	172	116	100	24	10	9	4	108	7	176	6	4	9	11	.450	0	1--	—	4.65
1987 Oakland	AL	21	14	1	3	82.1	394	106	67	54	10	0	3	2	41	1	67	5	2	2	7	.222	0	0-0	—	5.90
1988 Cincinnati	NL	49	19	0	12	162	653	120	47	43	7	8	5	3	63	7	160	1	4	13	8	.619	0	0-2	2	2.39
1989 Cincinnati	NL	19	19	1	0	111	464	101	39	35	6	3	6	2	48	3	86	4	3	7	6	.538	1	0-0	—	2.84
1990 Cincinnati	NL	29	29	7	0	197	801	151	65	59	10	8	1	2	78	1	152	2	5	14	8	.636	1	0-0	—	2.70
1991 Cincinnati	NL	30	30	3	0	204.1	825	165	69	57	8	4	8	3	55	4	172	2	4	15	6	.714	1	0-0	—	2.51
1992 Cincinnati	NL	33	33	2	0	211	836	185	67	60	15	9	4	3	44	1	171	2	1	15	10	.600	0	0-0	—	2.56
1993 Cincinnati	NL	36	36	2	0	257.1	1029	218	76	71	19	13	3	2	62	2	227	0	1	14	9	.609	1	0-0	—	2.48
1994 Cincinnati	NL	26	26	2	0	172.1	733	177	73	59	16	7	2	4	52	1	171	1	2	9	6	.600	0	0-0	—	3.08
1995 Cincinnati	NL	14	14	0	0	69	295	76	33	32	6	3	3	0	22	1	62	3	0	5	4	.556	0	0-0	—	4.17
2001 Cincinnati	NL	13	0	0	4	17	80	19	6	4	2	1	0	0	9	2	12	1	1	0	0	—	0	0-2	2	2.12
13 ML YEARS		345	260	22	37	1803	7527	1621	724	632	134	77	45	27	643	33	1568	29	28	111	87	.561	4	3--	—	3.15

Juan Rincon

Pitches: Right **Bats:** Right **Pos:** RP-4   **Ht:** 5'11" **Wt:** 187 **Born:** 1/23/79 **Age:** 23

		HOW MUCH HE PITCHED					WHAT HE GAVE UP											THE RESULTS						
Year Team	Lg	G	GS	CG	GF	IP	BFP	H	R	ER	HR	SH	SF	HB	TBB	IBB	SO	WP	Bk	W	L	Pct.	ShO	Sv-Op	Hld	ERA
1997 Twins	R	11	10	1	1	58	245	55	21	19	0	2	3	4	24	0	46	7	1	3	3	.500	0	0--	—	2.95
Elizabethtn	R+	2	1	0	0	9.1	41	11	4	4	0	0	0	0	3	0	7	2	0	0	1	.000	0	0--	—	3.86
1998 Fort Wayne	A	37	13	0	17	96.1	427	84	51	41	6	5	1	5	54	1	74	12	0	6	4	.600	0	6--	—	3.83
1999 Quad City	A	28	28	0	0	163.1	683	146	67	53	8	1	3	2	66	3	153	11	0	14	8	.636	0	0--	—	2.92
2000 Fort Myers	A+	13	13	0	0	76.1	309	67	26	18	3	1	0	4	23	2	55	10	0	5	3	.625	0	0--	—	2.12
New Britain	AA	15	15	2	0	89	399	96	55	46	9	0	0	1	39	0	79	9	1	3	9	.250	0	0--	—	4.65
2001 New Britain	AA	29	23	2	0	153.1	645	130	60	49	9	3	3	8	57	5	133	9	1	14	6	.700	1	0--	—	2.88
2001 Minnesota	AL	4	0	0	1	5.2	28	7	5	4	1	1	0	0	5	0	4	0	0	0	0	—	0	0-0	0	6.35

Ricardo Rincon

Pitches: Left **Bats:** Left **Pos:** RP-67   **Ht:** 5'9" **Wt:** 190 **Born:** 4/13/70 **Age:** 32

		HOW MUCH HE PITCHED					WHAT HE GAVE UP											THE RESULTS						
Year Team	Lg	G	GS	CG	GF	IP	BFP	H	R	ER	HR	SH	SF	HB	TBB	IBB	SO	WP	Bk	W	L	Pct.	ShO	Sv-Op	Hld	ERA
1997 Pittsburgh	NL	62	0	0	23	60	254	51	26	23	5	5	1	2	24	6	71	2	3	4	8	.333	0	4-6	18	3.45
1998 Pittsburgh	NL	60	0	0	27	65	272	50	31	21	6	1	2	0	29	2	64	2	0	0	2	.000	0	14-17	11	2.91
1999 Cleveland	AL	59	0	0	14	44.2	193	41	22	22	6	2	1	1	24	5	30	2	1	2	3	.400	0	0-2	11	4.43
2000 Cleveland	AL	35	0	0	4	20	90	17	7	6	1	0	0	1	13	1	20	1	0	2	0	1.000	0	0-0	10	2.70
2001 Cleveland	AL	67	0	0	19	54	223	44	18	17	3	2	3	0	21	5	50	1	0	2	1	.667	0	2-4	12	2.83
5 ML YEARS		283	0	0	87	243.2	1032	203	104	89	21	10	7	4	111	19	235	8	4	10	14	.417	0	20-29	62	3.29

Armando Rios

Bats: L **Throws:** L **Pos:** RF-78; LF-13; PH/PR-11; CF-3   **Ht:** 5'9" **Wt:** 185 **Born:** 9/13/71 **Age:** 30

		BATTING										BASERUNNING									PERCENTAGES		
Year Team	Lg	G	AB	H	2B	3B	HR	(Hm | Rd)	TB	R	RBI	TBB	IBB	SO	HBP	SH	SF	SB	CS	SB%	GDP	Avg	OBP	SLG
1998 San Francisco	NL	12	7	4	0	0	2	(0 | 2)	10	3	3	3	0	2	0	0	0	0	0	—	0	.571	.700	1.429
1999 San Francisco	NL	72	150	49	9	0	7	(4 | 3)	79	32	29	24	1	35	1	1	1	7	4	.64	3	.327	.420	.527
2000 San Francisco	NL	115	233	62	15	5	10	(8 | 2)	117	38	50	31	4	43	0	1	4	3	2	.60	9	.266	.347	.502
2001 SF-Pit	NL	95	319	83	17	3	14	(3 | 11)	148	38	50	36	6	74	0	1	3	3	2	.60	2	.260	.332	.464
2001 San Francisco	NL	93	316	82	17	3	14	(3 | 11)	147	38	49	34	6	73	0	1	2	3	2	.60	2	.259	.330	.465
Pittsburgh	NL	2	3	1	0	0	0	(0 | 0)	1	0	1	2	0	1	0	0	1	0	0	—	1	.333	.500	.333
4 ML YEARS		294	709	198	41	8	33	(9 | 24)	354	111	132	94	11	154	1	3	8	13	8	.62	15	.279	.361	.499

Cal Ripken Jr.

Bats: Right **Throws:** Right **Pos:** 3B-111; DH-14; PH/PR-3   **Ht:** 6'4" **Wt:** 220 **Born:** 8/24/60 **Age:** 41

		BATTING										BASERUNNING									PERCENTAGES		
Year Team	Lg	G	AB	H	2B	3B	HR	(Hm | Rd)	TB	R	RBI	TBB	IBB	SO	HBP	SH	SF	SB	CS	SB%	GDP	Avg	OBP	SLG
1981 Baltimore	AL	23	39	5	0	0	0	(0 | 0)	5	1	0	1	0	8	0	0	0	0	0	—	4	.128	.150	.128
1982 Baltimore	AL	160	598	158	32	5	28	(11 | 17)	284	90	93	46	3	95	3	2	6	3	3	.50	16	.264	.317	.475
1983 Baltimore	AL	162	663	211	47	2	27	(12 | 15)	343	121	102	58	0	97	0	0	5	0	4	.00	24	.318	.371	.517
1984 Baltimore	AL	162	641	195	37	7	27	(16 | 11)	327	103	86	71	1	89	2	0	2	2	1	.67	16	.304	.374	.510
1985 Baltimore	AL	161	642	181	32	5	26	(15 | 11)	301	116	110	67	1	68	1	0	8	2	3	.40	32	.282	.347	.469
1986 Baltimore	AL	162	627	177	35	1	25	(10 | 15)	289	98	81	70	5	60	4	0	6	4	2	.67	19	.282	.355	.461
1987 Baltimore	AL	162	624	157	28	3	27	(10 | 17)	272	97	98	81	0	77	1	0	11	3	5	.38	19	.252	.333	.436
1988 Baltimore	AL	161	575	152	25	1	23	(11 | 12)	248	87	81	102	7	69	2	0	10	2	2	.50	10	.264	.372	.431
1989 Baltimore	AL	162	646	166	30	0	21	(13 | 8)	259	80	93	57	5	72	3	0	6	3	2	.60	22	.257	.317	.401
1990 Baltimore	AL	161	600	150	28	4	21	(8 | 13)	249	78	84	82	18	66	5	1	7	3	1	.75	12	.250	.341	.415
1991 Baltimore	AL	162	650	210	46	5	34	(16 | 18)	368	99	114	53	15	46	5	0	9	6	1	.86	19	.323	.374	.566
1992 Baltimore	AL	162	637	160	29	1	14	(5 | 9)	233	73	72	64	14	50	7	0	7	4	3	.57	13	.251	.323	.366
1993 Baltimore	AL	162	641	165	26	3	24	(14 | 10)	269	87	90	65	19	58	6	0	6	1	4	.20	17	.257	.329	.420
1994 Baltimore	AL	112	444	140	19	3	13	(5 | 8)	204	71	75	32	3	41	4	0	4	1	0	1.00	17	.315	.364	.459
1995 Baltimore	AL	144	550	144	33	2	17	(10 | 7)	232	71	88	52	6	59	2	1	8	0	1	.00	15	.262	.324	.422
1996 Baltimore	AL	163	640	178	40	1	26	(10 | 16)	298	94	102	59	3	78	4	0	4	1	2	.33	28	.278	.341	.466
1997 Baltimore	AL	162	615	166	30	0	17	(10 | 7)	247	79	84	56	3	73	5	0	10	1	0	1.00	19	.270	.331	.402
1998 Baltimore	AL	161	601	163	27	1	14	(8 | 6)	234	65	61	51	0	68	4	1	2	0	0	.00	9	.271	.331	.389
1999 Baltimore	AL	86	332	113	27	0	18	(12 | 6)	194	51	57	13	3	31	3	0	1	0	1	.00	14	.340	.368	.584

189

Year Team	Lg	G	AB	H	2B	3B	HR	(Hm	Rd)	TB	R	RBI	TBB	IBB	SO	HBP	SH	SF	SB	CS	SB%	GDP	Avg	OBP	SLG
								BATTING											BASERUNNING				PERCENTAGES		
2000 Baltimore	AL	83	309	79	16	0	15	(8	7)	140	43	56	23	0	37	3	0	4	0	0	—	10	.256	.310	.453
2001 Baltimore	AL	128	477	114	16	0	14	(3	11)	172	43	68	26	1	63	2	2	9	0	2	.00	15	.239	.276	.361
21 ML YEARS		3001	11551	3184	603	44	431	(214	217)	5168	1647	1695	1129	107	1305	66	10	127	36	39	.48	350	.276	.340	.447

David Riske

Pitches: Right **Bats:** Right **Pos:** RP-26 **Ht:** 6'2" **Wt:** 180 **Born:** 10/23/76 **Age:** 25

Year Team	Lg	G	GS	CG	GF	IP	BFP	H	R	ER	HR	SH	SF	HB	TBB	IBB	SO	WP	Bk	W	L	Pct.	ShO	Sv-Op	Hld	ERA
				HOW MUCH HE PITCHED						WHAT HE GAVE UP												THE RESULTS				
1997 Kinston	A+	39	0	0	23	72	299	58	22	18	3	6	1	2	33	4	90	0	0	4	4	.500	0	2--	—	2.25
1998 Kinston	A+	53	0	0	50	54	218	48	15	14	4	2	1	1	15	0	67	1	0	1	1	.500	0	33--	—	2.33
Akron	AA	2	0	0	1	3	11	1	0	0	0	0	0	0	1	0	5	0	0	0	0	—	0	1--	—	0.00
1999 Akron	AA	23	0	0	22	23.2	90	5	6	5	1	0	2	0	13	0	33	1	0	0	0	—	0	12--	—	1.90
Buffalo	AAA	23	0	0	19	27.2	101	14	3	2	0	1	0	0	7	0	22	0	0	3	0	1.000	0	6--	—	0.65
2000 Buffalo	AAA	2	0	0	3	13	2	1	1	0	0	0	0	2	0	2	2	0	0	0	—	0	0--	—	3.00
Akron	AA	3	1	0	1	4	15	2	0	0	0	0	0	1	0	0	4	0	0	0	0	—	0	1--	—	0.00
2001 Buffalo	AAA	38	0	0	26	53.1	217	45	16	14	2	2	2	2	17	0	72	0	1	2	3	.333	0	15--	—	2.36
1999 Cleveland	AL	12	0	0	3	14	68	20	15	13	2	1	1	0	6	0	16	0	0	1	1	.500	0	0-1	0	8.36
2001 Cleveland	AL	26	0	0	6	27.1	118	20	7	6	3	0	1	2	18	3	29	1	0	2	0	1.000	0	1-1	3	1.98
2 ML YEARS		38	0	0	9	41.1	186	40	22	19	5	1	2	2	24	3	45	1	0	3	1	.750	0	1-2	3	4.14

Todd Ritchie

Pitches: Right **Bats:** Right **Pos:** SP-33 **Ht:** 6'3" **Wt:** 222 **Born:** 11/7/71 **Age:** 30

Year Team	Lg	G	GS	CG	GF	IP	BFP	H	R	ER	HR	SH	SF	HB	TBB	IBB	SO	WP	Bk	W	L	Pct.	ShO	Sv-Op	Hld	ERA
				HOW MUCH HE PITCHED						WHAT HE GAVE UP												THE RESULTS				
1997 Minnesota	AL	42	0	0	19	74.2	331	87	41	38	11	0	1	2	28	0	44	11	0	2	3	.400	0	0-2	3	4.58
1998 Minnesota	AL	15	0	0	7	24	113	30	17	15	1	0	0	0	9	0	21	3	0	0	0	—	0	0-0	0	5.63
1999 Pittsburgh	NL	28	26	2	0	172.1	715	169	79	67	17	3	2	4	54	3	107	7	0	15	9	.625	0	0-0	1	3.50
2000 Pittsburgh	NL	31	31	1	0	187	804	208	111	100	26	8	5	3	51	1	124	5	1	9	8	.529	1	0-0	0	4.81
2001 Pittsburgh	NL	33	33	4	0	207.1	887	211	118	103	23	9	5	7	52	7	124	7	0	11	15	.423	2	0-0	0	4.47
5 ML YEARS		149	90	7	26	665.1	2850	705	366	323	78	20	13	16	194	11	420	33	1	37	35	.514	3	0-2	4	4.37

Luis Rivas

Bats: Right **Throws:** Right **Pos:** 2B-150; PH/PR-4 **Ht:** 5'11" **Wt:** 175 **Born:** 8/30/79 **Age:** 22

Year Team	Lg	G	AB	H	2B	3B	HR	(Hm	Rd)	TB	R	RBI	TBB	IBB	SO	HBP	SH	SF	SB	CS	SB%	GDP	Avg	OBP	SLG
						BATTING													BASERUNNING				PERCENTAGES		
1996 Twins	R	53	201	52	12	1	1	—	—	69	29	13	18	0	37	0	1	0	35	10	.78	2	.259	.320	.343
1997 Fort Wayne	A	121	419	100	20	6	1	—	—	135	61	30	33	1	90	5	6	2	28	18	.61	5	.239	.301	.322
1998 Fort Myers	A+	126	463	130	21	5	4	—	—	173	58	51	14	0	75	3	4	6	34	8	.81	11	.281	.302	.374
1999 New Britain	AA	132	527	134	30	7	7	—	—	199	78	49	41	1	92	2	8	2	31	14	.69	16	.254	.309	.378
2000 New Britain	AA	82	328	82	23	6	3	—	—	126	56	40	36	0	41	4	1	3	11	4	.73	3	.250	.329	.384
Salt Lake	AAA	41	157	50	14	1	3	—	—	75	33	25	13	0	21	2	0	1	7	4	.64	3	.318	.376	.478
2000 Minnesota	AL	16	58	18	4	1	0	(0	0)	24	8	6	2	0	4	0	2	2	2	0	1.00	2	.310	.323	.414
2001 Minnesota	AL	153	563	150	21	6	7	(3	4)	204	70	47	40	0	99	6	5	5	31	11	.74	15	.266	.319	.362
2 ML YEARS		169	621	168	25	7	7	(3	4)	228	78	53	42	0	103	6	7	7	33	11	.75	17	.271	.320	.367

Juan Rivera

Bats: Right **Throws:** Right **Pos:** RF-2; CF-1 **Ht:** 6'2" **Wt:** 170 **Born:** 7/3/78 **Age:** 23

Year Team	Lg	G	AB	H	2B	3B	HR	(Hm	Rd)	TB	R	RBI	TBB	IBB	SO	HBP	SH	SF	SB	CS	SB%	GDP	Avg	OBP	SLG
						BATTING													BASERUNNING				PERCENTAGES		
1998 Yankees	R	57	210	70	9	1	12	—	—	117	43	45	26	2	27	1	0	1	8	5	.62	10	.333	.408	.557
Oneonta	A-	6	18	5	0	0	1	—	—	8	2	3	1	0	4	0	0	0	1	1	.50	0	.278	.316	.444
1999 Yankees	R	5	18	6	0	0	1	—	—	9	7	4	4	0	1	0	0	0	0	0	—	1	.333	.455	.500
Tampa	A+	109	426	112	20	2	14	—	—	178	50	77	26	3	67	5	0	8	5	4	.56	13	.263	.308	.418
2000 Norwich	AA	17	62	14	5	0	2	—	—	25	9	12	6	0	15	0	0	0	0	0	—	2	.226	.294	.403
Tampa	A+	115	409	113	26	1	14	—	—	183	62	69	33	1	56	6	0	5	11	7	.61	9	.276	.336	.447
2001 Norwich	AA	77	316	101	18	3	14	—	—	167	50	58	15	2	50	3	0	3	5	7	.42	10	.320	.353	.528
Columbus	AAA	55	199	65	11	1	14	—	—	120	39	40	15	1	31	1	0	3	4	5	.44	7	.327	.372	.603
2001 New York	AL	3	4	0	0	0	0	(0	0)	0	0	0	0	0	0	0	0	0	0	0	—	0	.000	.000	.000

Mariano Rivera

Pitches: Right **Bats:** Right **Pos:** RP-71 **Ht:** 6'2" **Wt:** 185 **Born:** 11/29/69 **Age:** 32

Year Team	Lg	G	GS	CG	GF	IP	BFP	H	R	ER	HR	SH	SF	HB	TBB	IBB	SO	WP	Bk	W	L	Pct.	ShO	Sv-Op	Hld	ERA
				HOW MUCH HE PITCHED						WHAT HE GAVE UP												THE RESULTS				
1995 New York	AL	19	10	0	2	67	301	71	43	41	11	0	2	2	30	0	51	0	1	5	3	.625	0	0-1	0	5.51
1996 New York	AL	61	0	0	14	107.2	425	73	25	25	1	2	1	2	34	3	130	1	0	8	3	.727	0	5-8	27	2.09
1997 New York	AL	66	0	0	56	71.2	301	65	17	15	5	3	4	0	20	6	68	2	0	6	4	.600	0	43-52	0	1.88
1998 New York	AL	54	0	0	49	61.1	246	48	13	13	3	2	3	1	17	1	36	0	0	3	0	1.000	0	36-41	0	1.91
1999 New York	AL	66	0	0	63	69	268	43	15	14	2	0	2	3	18	3	52	2	1	4	3	.571	0	45-49	0	1.83
2000 New York	AL	66	0	0	61	75.2	311	58	26	24	4	5	2	0	25	3	58	2	0	7	4	.636	0	36-41	0	2.85
2001 New York	AL	71	0	0	66	80.2	310	61	24	21	5	4	1	1	12	2	83	1	0	4	6	.400	0	50-57	0	2.34
7 ML YEARS		403	10	0	311	533	2162	419	163	153	31	16	15	9	156	18	478	8	2	37	23	.617	0	215-249	27	2.58

Mike Rivera

Bats: Right **Throws:** Right **Pos:** C-4

Ht: 6'0" **Wt:** 190 **Born:** 9/8/76 **Age:** 25

Year Team	Lg	G	AB	H	2B	3B	HR	(Hm	Rd)	TB	R	RBI	TBB	IBB	SO	HBP	SH	SF	SB	CS	SB%	GDP	Avg	OBP	SLG
1997 Tigers	R	47	154	44	9	2	10	—	—	87	34	36	18	2	25	3	0	2	0	0	—	2	.286	.367	.565
1998 W Michigan	A	108	403	111	34	3	9	—	—	178	40	67	15	0	68	2	1	5	0	2	.00	0	.275	.301	.442
1999 Jacksnville	AA	7	23	4	1	0	2	—	—	11	3	6	2	0	5	0	0	0	0	0	—	0	.174	.240	.478
Lakeland	A+	104	370	103	20	2	14	—	—	169	44	72	20	0	59	3	0	8	1	1	.50	10	.278	.314	.457
2000 Lakeland	A+	64	243	71	19	4	11	—	—	131	30	53	16	3	45	1	0	2	2	0	1.00	8	.292	.336	.539
Toledo	AAA	4	13	3	3	0	0	—	—	6	0	1	0	0	2	0	0	0	0	0	—	0	.231	.231	.462
Jacksnville	AA	39	150	29	8	1	2	—	—	45	10	9	7	0	30	0	0	1	0	0	—	0	.193	.228	.300
2001 Erie	AA	112	415	120	19	1	33	—	—	240	76	101	44	2	96	10	0	4	2	2	.50	9	.289	.368	.578
2001 Detroit	AL	4	12	4	2	0	0	(0	0)	6	2	1	0	0	2	0	0	0	0	0	—	0	.333	.333	.500

Ruben Rivera

Bats: R **Throws:** R **Pos:** CF-70; PH/PR-38; RF-21; LF-10

Ht: 6'3" **Wt:** 208 **Born:** 11/14/73 **Age:** 28

Year Team	Lg	G	AB	H	2B	3B	HR	(Hm	Rd)	TB	R	RBI	TBB	IBB	SO	HBP	SH	SF	SB	CS	SB%	GDP	Avg	OBP	SLG
1995 New York	AL	5	1	0	0	0	0	(0	0)	0	0	0	0	0	1	0	0	0	0	0	—	0	.000	.000	.000
1996 New York	AL	46	88	25	6	1	2	(0	2)	39	17	16	13	0	26	2	1	2	6	2	.75	1	.284	.381	.443
1997 San Diego	NL	17	20	5	1	0	0	(0	0)	6	2	1	2	0	9	0	0	0	2	1	.67	0	.250	.318	.300
1998 San Diego	NL	95	172	36	7	2	6	(2	4)	65	31	29	28	0	52	2	1	1	5	1	.83	1	.209	.325	.378
1999 San Diego	NL	147	411	80	16	1	23	(10	13)	167	65	48	55	1	143	5	0	4	18	7	.72	9	.195	.295	.406
2000 San Diego	NL	135	423	88	18	6	17	(8	9)	169	62	57	44	1	137	10	0	2	8	4	.67	8	.208	.296	.400
2001 Cincinnati	NL	117	263	67	13	1	10	(6	4)	112	37	34	21	0	83	5	0	1	6	3	.67	7	.255	.321	.426
7 ML YEARS		562	1378	301	61	11	58	(26	32)	558	214	185	163	3	451	24	2	10	45	18	.71	26	.218	.310	.405

Brian Roberts

Bats: B **Throws:** R **Pos:** SS-51; PH/PR-13; 2B-12; DH-7

Ht: 5'9" **Wt:** 170 **Born:** 10/9/77 **Age:** 24

Year Team	Lg	G	AB	H	2B	3B	HR	(Hm	Rd)	TB	R	RBI	TBB	IBB	SO	HBP	SH	SF	SB	CS	SB%	GDP	Avg	OBP	SLG
1999 Delmarva	A	47	167	40	12	1	0	—	—	54	22	21	27	0	42	1	5	1	17	5	.77	0	.240	.347	.323
2000 Orioles	R	9	29	9	1	2	1	—	—	17	8	3	7	0	4	0	0	1	7	1	.88	0	.310	.432	.586
Frederick	A+	48	163	49	6	3	0	—	—	61	27	16	27	1	24	1	7	0	13	10	.57	4	.301	.403	.374
2001 Bowie	AA	22	81	24	7	0	1	—	—	34	12	7	9	0	12	1	2	2	10	0	1.00	2	.296	.366	.420
Rochester	AAA	44	161	43	4	1	1	—	—	52	16	12	28	0	22	0	1	0	23	3	.88	0	.267	.376	.323
2001 Baltimore	AL	75	273	69	12	3	2	(0	2)	93	42	17	13	0	36	0	3	3	12	3	.80	3	.253	.284	.341

Dave Roberts

Bats: L **Throws:** L **Pos:** LF-9; PH/PR-6; DH-2; CF-2; RF-2

Ht: 5'10" **Wt:** 180 **Born:** 5/31/72 **Age:** 30

Year Team	Lg	G	AB	H	2B	3B	HR	(Hm	Rd)	TB	R	RBI	TBB	IBB	SO	HBP	SH	SF	SB	CS	SB%	GDP	Avg	OBP	SLG
2001 Akron *	AA	17	64	13	5	0	0	—	—	18	9	2	9	0	8	1	2	1	4	0	1.00	1	.203	.307	.281
Buffalo *	AAA	62	241	73	12	4	0	—	—	93	34	22	18	0	44	2	8	3	17	6	.74	2	.303	.352	.386
1999 Cleveland	AL	41	143	34	4	0	2	(1	1)	44	26	12	9	0	16	0	3	1	11	3	.79	0	.238	.281	.308
2000 Cleveland	AL	19	10	2	0	0	0	(0	0)	2	1	0	2	0	2	0	1	0	1	1	.50	0	.200	.333	.200
2001 Cleveland	AL	15	12	4	1	0	0	(0	0)	5	3	2	1	0	2	0	0	0	0	1	.00	0	.333	.385	.417
3 ML YEARS		75	165	40	5	0	2	(1	1)	51	30	14	12	0	20	0	4	1	12	5	.71	0	.242	.292	.309

Grant Roberts

Pitches: Right **Bats:** Right **Pos:** RP-16

Ht: 6'3" **Wt:** 205 **Born:** 9/13/77 **Age:** 24

Year Team	Lg	G	GS	CG	GF	IP	BFP	H	R	ER	HR	SH	SF	HB	TBB	IBB	SO	WP	Bk	W	L	Pct.	ShO	Sv-Op	Hld	ERA
1995 Mets	R	11	3	0	4	29.1	121	19	13	7	1	1	1	3	14	1	24	4	1	2	1	.667	0	0- —	—	2.15
1996 Kingsport	R+	13	13	2	0	68.2	285	43	18	16	3	1	0	7	37	1	92	4	0	9	1	.900	2	0- —	—	2.10
1997 Capital Cty	A	22	22	2	0	129.2	530	98	37	34	1	3	3	8	44	0	122	5	0	11	3	.786	1	0- —	—	2.36
1998 St. Lucie	A+	17	17	0	0	72.1	323	72	37	34	11	1	1	5	37	0	70	2	0	4	5	.444	0	0- —	—	4.23
1999 Binghamton	AA	23	23	0	0	131.1	576	135	81	71	9	6	3	12	49	0	94	8	0	7	6	.538	0	0- —	—	4.87
Norfolk	AAA	5	5	0	0	28	122	32	15	14	1	0	1	0	11	2	30	3	0	2	1	.667	0	0- —	—	4.50
2000 Norfolk	AAA	25	25	5	0	157.1	686	154	67	59	6	5	3	8	63	5	115	12	2	7	8	.467	0	0- —	—	3.38
2001 Norfolk	AAA	30	6	0	15	67.2	300	80	38	34	4	3	2	7	19	1	54	2	0	3	5	.375	0	2- —	—	4.52
2000 New York	NL	4	1	0	0	7	38	11	10	9	0	0	2	0	4	1	6	0	0	0	0	—	0	0-0	0	11.57
2001 New York	NL	16	0	0	2	26	110	24	11	11	2	1	1	0	8	1	29	0	1	0	1	1.000	0	0-1	1	3.81
2 ML YEARS		20	1	0	2	33	148	35	21	20	2	1	3	0	12	2	35	0	1	0	1	1.000	0	0-1	1	5.45

Willis Roberts

Pitches: Right **Bats:** Right **Pos:** RP-28; SP-18

Ht: 6'3" **Wt:** 175 **Born:** 6/19/75 **Age:** 27

Year Team	Lg	G	GS	CG	GF	IP	BFP	H	R	ER	HR	SH	SF	HB	TBB	IBB	SO	WP	Bk	W	L	Pct.	ShO	Sv-Op	Hld	ERA
1993 Bristol	R+	10	2	0	2	26	116	24	16	4	0	2	0	1	11	0	23	2	0	2	3	.400	0	1- —	—	1.38
1994 Bristol	R+	4	4	0	0	20.2	81	9	9	9	1	0	2	1	8	0	17	2	0	1	2	.333	0	0- —	—	3.92
1995 Fayettevlle	A	17	15	0	0	80	339	72	33	24	2	1	2	6	40	0	52	15	3	6	3	.667	0	0- —	—	2.70
1996 Lakeland	A+	23	22	2	0	149.1	636	133	60	48	5	8	9	9	69	0	105	13	3	9	7	.563	0	0- —	—	2.89
1997 Jacksnville	AA	26	26	2	0	149	685	181	120	104	18	6	7	6	64	0	86	6	6	6	15	.286	0	0- —	—	6.28
1998 Jacksnville	AA	12	2	0	4	24.2	105	21	10	6	0	2	0	3	10	1	15	1	0	3	1	.750	0	0- —	—	2.19
Toledo	AAA	39	6	0	16	54.2	248	63	33	28	4	3	1	2	28	2	40	4	1	3	3	.500	0	2- —	—	4.61
1999 Toledo	AAA	31	12	0	9	92	433	112	68	64	10	3	3	3	59	3	52	5	4	5	8	.385	0	0- —	—	6.26
2000 Chattanooga	AA	5	5	0	0	32.1	137	33	12	11	0	3	1	2	13	1	28	0	0	4	0	1.000	0	0- —	—	3.06
Louisville	AAA	25	20	2	1	124	550	138	80	78	19	5	4	6	55	0	66	3	1	7	8	.467	0	0- —	—	5.66

Year Team	Lg	G	GS	CG	GF	IP	BFP	H	R	ER	HR	SH	SF	HB	TBB	IBB	SO	WP	Bk	W	L	Pct.	ShO	Sv-Op	Hld	ERA
1999 Detroit	AL	1	0	0	0	1.1	8	3	4	2	0	0	1	1	0	0	0	0	0	0	0	—	0	0-0	0	13.50
2001 Baltimore	AL	46	18	1	20	132	593	142	75	72	15	5	4	11	55	1	95	3	2	9	10	.474	0	6-10	1	4.91
2 ML YEARS		47	18	1	20	133.1	601	145	79	74	15	5	5	12	55	1	95	3	2	9	10	.474	0	6-10	1	5.00

Kerry Robinson

Bats: L Throws: L Pos: PH/PR-55; LF-42; CF-22; RF-17

Ht: 6'0" Wt: 175 Born: 10/3/73 Age: 28

Year Team	Lg	G	AB	H	2B	3B	HR	(Hm	Rd)	TB	R	RBI	TBB	IBB	SO	HBP	SH	SF	SB	CS	SB%	GDP	Avg	OBP	SLG
1995 Johnson Cty	R+	60	250	74	12	8	1	—	—	105	44	26	16	1	30	0	3	2	14	10	.58	3	.296	.336	.420
1996 Peoria	A	123	440	158	17	14	2	—	—	209	98	47	51	5	51	3	4	8	50	26	.66	2	.359	.422	.475
1997 Arkansas	AA	136	523	168	16	3	2	—	—	196	80	62	54	1	64	2	5	2	40	23	.63	7	.321	.386	.375
Louisville	AAA	2	9	1	0	0	0	—	—	1	0	0	0	0	1	0	0	0	0	0	—	0	.111	.111	.111
1998 Orlando	AA	72	309	83	7	5	2	—	—	106	45	26	27	0	28	0	4	2	28	9	.76	6	.269	.325	.343
Durham	AAA	58	242	73	7	4	1	—	—	91	28	28	23	0	30	0	2	1	18	11	.62	1	.302	.361	.376
1999 Tacoma	AAA	79	335	108	16	9	0	—	—	142	53	34	14	0	44	0	3	2	30	7	.81	4	.322	.348	.424
Indianapols	AAA	34	129	34	3	2	1	—	—	44	24	14	4	0	12	1	4	3	14	4	.78	2	.264	.285	.341
2000 Columbus	AAA	119	437	139	17	9	0	—	—	174	71	32	41	0	40	2	10	1	37	18	.67	5	.318	.378	.398
2001 Memphis	AAA	10	40	13	1	0	0	—	—	14	4	3	4	0	10	0	0	0	4	1	.80	1	.325	.386	.350
1998 Tampa Bay	AL	2	3	0	0	0	0	(0	0)	0	0	0	0	0	1	0	0	0	0	0	—	0	.000	.000	.000
1999 Cincinnati	NL	9	1	0	0	0	0	(0	0)	0	0	0	0	0	0	0	0	0	0	1	.00	0	.000	.000	.000
2001 St. Louis	NL	114	186	53	6	1	1	(1	0)	64	34	15	12	0	20	2	4	3	11	2	.85	1	.285	.330	.344
3 ML YEARS		125	190	53	6	1	1	(1	0)	64	38	15	12	0	22	2	4	3	11	3	.79	1	.279	.324	.337

John Rocker

Pitches: Left Bats: Right Pos: RP-68

Ht: 6'4" Wt: 225 Born: 10/17/74 Age: 27

Year Team	Lg	G	GS	CG	GF	IP	BFP	H	R	ER	HR	SH	SF	HB	TBB	IBB	SO	WP	Bk	W	L	Pct.	ShO	Sv-Op	Hld	ERA
1998 Atlanta	NL	47	0	0	16	38	156	22	10	9	4	3	0	3	22	4	42	6	0	1	3	.250	0	2-4	15	2.13
1999 Atlanta	NL	74	0	0	61	72.1	301	47	24	20	5	2	0	1	37	4	104	7	0	4	5	.444	0	38-45	0	2.49
2000 Atlanta	NL	59	0	0	41	53	251	42	25	17	5	1	0	2	48	4	77	5	2	1	2	.333	0	24-27	4	2.89
2001 Atl-Cle		68	0	0	48	66.2	300	58	36	32	4	4	2	5	41	4	79	11	2	5	9	.357	0	23-30	7	4.32
2001 Atlanta	NL	30	0	0	28	32	135	25	13	11	2	0	1	2	16	1	36	5	0	2	2	.500	0	19-23	3	3.09
Cleveland	AL	38	0	0	20	34.2	165	33	23	21	2	4	1	3	25	3	43	6	2	3	7	.300	0	4-7	7	5.45
4 ML YEARS		248	0	0	166	230	1008	169	95	78	18	10	2	11	148	16	302	29	4	11	19	.367	0	87-106	26	3.05

Alex Rodriguez

Bats: Right Throws: Right Pos: SS-161; DH-1

Ht: 6'3" Wt: 215 Born: 7/27/75 Age: 26

Year Team	Lg	G	AB	H	2B	3B	HR	(Hm	Rd)	TB	R	RBI	TBB	IBB	SO	HBP	SH	SF	SB	CS	SB%	GDP	Avg	OBP	SLG
1994 Seattle	AL	17	54	11	0	0	0	(0	0)	11	4	2	3	0	20	0	1	1	3	0	1.00	0	.204	.241	.204
1995 Seattle	AL	48	142	33	6	2	5			59	15	19	6	0	42	0	1	0	4	2	.67	0	.232	.264	.408
1996 Seattle	AL	146	601	215	54	1	36	(18	18)	379	141	123	59	1	104	4	6	7	15	4	.79	15	.358	.414	.631
1997 Seattle	AL	141	587	176	40	3	23	(16	7)	291	100	84	41	1	99	5	4	1	29	6	.83	14	.300	.350	.496
1998 Seattle	AL	161	686	213	35	5	42	(18	24)	384	123	124	45	0	121	10	3	4	46	13	.78	12	.310	.360	.560
1999 Seattle	AL	129	502	143	25	0	42	(20	22)	294	110	111	56	2	109	5	1	8	21	7	.75	12	.285	.357	.586
2000 Seattle	AL	148	554	175	34	2	41	(13	28)	336	134	132	100	5	121	7	0	11	15	4	.79	10	.316	.420	.606
2001 Texas	AL	162	632	201	34	1	52	(26	26)	393	133	135	75	6	131	16	0	9	18	3	.86	17	.318	.399	.622
8 ML YEARS		952	3758	1167	228	14	241	(112	129)	2146	760	730	385	15	747	47	16	41	151	39	.79	80	.311	.378	.571

Felix Rodriguez

Pitches: Right Bats: Right Pos: RP-80

Ht: 6'1" Wt: 190 Born: 12/5/72 Age: 29

Year Team	Lg	G	GS	CG	GF	IP	BFP	H	R	ER	HR	SH	SF	HB	TBB	IBB	SO	WP	Bk	W	L	Pct.	ShO	Sv-Op	Hld	ERA
1995 Los Angeles	NL	11	0	0	5	10.2	45	11	3	3	2	0	0	0	5	0	5	0	0	1	1	.500	0	0-1	0	2.53
1997 Cincinnati	NL	26	1	0	13	46	212	48	23	22	2	0	1	6	28	2	34	4	1	0	0	—	0	0-0	0	4.30
1998 Arizona	NL	43	0	0	23	44	207	44	31	30	5	4	3	1	29	1	36	5	2	0	2	.000	0	5-8	0	6.14
1999 San Francisco	NL	47	0	0	26	66.1	292	52	28	24	6	2	3	2	29	2	55	2	0	2	3	.400	0	0-1	3	3.80
2000 San Francisco	NL	76	0	0	19	81.2	346	65	29	24	5	2	3	3	42	2	95	3	1	4	2	.667	0	3-8	30	2.64
2001 San Francisco	NL	80	0	0	13	80.1	314	53	16	15	5	1	3	1	27	2	91	1	0	9	1	.900	0	0-3	32	1.68
6 ML YEARS		283	1	0	99	329	1416	288	134	122	25	9	13	13	160	9	316	15	4	16	9	.640	0	8-21	65	3.34

Frank Rodriguez

Pitches: Right Bats: Right Pos: RP-7

Ht: 6'0" Wt: 210 Born: 12/11/72 Age: 29

Year Team	Lg	G	GS	CG	GF	IP	BFP	H	R	ER	HR	SH	SF	HB	TBB	IBB	SO	WP	Bk	W	L	Pct.	ShO	Sv-Op	Hld	ERA
2001 Louisville *	AAA	43	0	0	18	80.1	330	67	25	22	5	6	1	5	24	2	56	3	0	8	6	.571	0	5--	—	2.46
1995 Bos-Min	AL	25	18	0	1	105.2	478	114	83	72	11	1	4	5	57	1	59	9	0	5	8	.385	0	0-0	1	6.13
1996 Minnesota	AL	38	33	3	4	206.2	899	218	129	116	27	6	8	5	78	1	110	2	0	13	14	.481	0	2-2	0	5.05
1997 Minnesota	AL	43	15	0	5	142.1	613	147	82	73	12	4	2	4	60	9	65	6	0	3	6	.333	0	0-2	4	4.62
1998 Minnesota	AL	20	11	0	4	70	329	88	58	51	6	1	5	3	30	0	62	6	1	4	6	.400	0	0-0	0	6.56
1999 Seattle	AL	28	5	0	10	73.1	334	94	47	46	11	0	1	4	30	2	47	1	0	2	4	.333	0	3-4	3	5.65
2000 Seattle	AL	23	0	0	5	47.1	214	60	33	33	8	0	3	0	22	2	19	3	0	2	1	.667	0	0-0	2	6.27
2001 Cincinnati	NL	7	0	0	2	8.2	47	16	12	11	1	1	0	0	5	2	9	2	0	0	0	—	0	0-0	0	11.42
1995 Boston	AL	9	2	0	1	15.1	75	21	19	18	3	0	0	1	10	1	14	4	0	0	2	.000	0	0-0	1	10.57
Minnesota	AL	16	16	0	0	90.1	403	93	64	54	8	1	4	5	47	0	45	5	0	5	6	.455	0	0-0	0	5.38
7 ML YEARS		184	82	3	31	654	2914	737	444	402	76	13	24	21	282	17	371	29		29	39	.426	0	5-8	10	5.53

Henry Rodriguez

Bats: Left   Throws: Left   Pos: PH/PR-4; DH-1

Ht: 6'2"   Wt: 225   Born: 11/8/67   Age: 34

		BATTING																	BASERUNNING				PERCENTAGES		
Year Team	Lg	G	AB	H	2B	3B	HR	(Hm	Rd)	TB	R	RBI	TBB	IBB	SO	HBP	SH	SF	SB	CS	SB%	GDP	Avg	OBP	SLG
2001 Columbus *	AAA	18	63	15	2	0	5	—	—	32	9	13	7	0	21	1	0	1	0	0	—	1	.238	.319	.508
1992 Los Angeles	NL	53	146	32	7	0	3	(2	1)	48	11	14	8	0	30	0	1	1	0	0	—	2	.219	.258	.329
1993 Los Angeles	NL	76	176	39	10	0	8	(5	3)	73	20	23	11	2	39	0	0	1	1	0	1.00	1	.222	.266	.415
1994 Los Angeles	NL	104	306	82	14	2	8	(5	3)	124	33	49	17	2	58	2	1	4	0	1	.00	9	.268	.307	.405
1995 LA-Mon	NL	45	138	33	4	1	2	(1	1)	45	13	15	11	2	28	0	1	1	0	1	.00	5	.239	.293	.326
1996 Montreal	NL	145	532	147	42	1	36	(20	16)	299	81	103	37	7	160	3	0	4	2	0	1.00	10	.276	.325	.562
1997 Montreal	NL	132	476	116	28	3	26	(14	12)	228	55	83	42	5	149	2	0	3	3	3	.50	6	.244	.306	.479
1998 Chicago	NL	128	415	104	21	1	31	(16	15)	220	56	85	54	7	113	0	0	4	1	3	.25	6	.251	.334	.530
1999 Chicago	NL	130	447	136	29	0	26	(14	12)	243	72	87	56	6	113	0	0	1	2	4	.33	9	.304	.381	.544
2000 ChC-Fla	NL	112	367	94	21	1	20	(7	13)	177	47	61	36	2	99	4	0	3	1	2	.33	5	.256	.327	.482
2001 New York	AL	5	8	0	0	0	0	(0	0)	0	0	0	0	0	6	0	0	0	0	0	—	0	.000	.000	.000
1995 Los Angeles	NL	21	80	21	4	1	1	(1	0)	30	6	10	5	2	17	0	0	0	0	1	.00	3	.263	.306	.375
Montreal	NL	24	58	12	0	0	1	(1	0)	15	7	5	6	0	11	0	0	1	0	0	—	2	.207	.277	.259
2000 Chicago	NL	76	259	65	15	1	18	(6	12)	136	37	51	22	2	76	3	0	3	1	2	.33	4	.251	.314	.525
Florida	NL	36	108	29	6	0	2	(1	1)	41	10	10	14	0	23	1	0	0	0	0	—	1	.269	.358	.380
10 ML YEARS		930	3011	783	176	9	160	(84	76)	1457	388	520	272	33	795	11	2	22	10	14	.42	53	.260	.321	.484

Ivan Rodriguez

Bats: Right   Throws: Right   Pos: C-106; DH-5; PH/PR-2

Ht: 5'9"   Wt: 205   Born: 11/30/71   Age: 30

		BATTING																	BASERUNNING				PERCENTAGES		
Year Team	Lg	G	AB	H	2B	3B	HR	(Hm	Rd)	TB	R	RBI	TBB	IBB	SO	HBP	SH	SF	SB	CS	SB%	GDP	Avg	OBP	SLG
1991 Texas	AL	88	280	74	16	0	3	(3	0)	99	24	27	5	0	42	0	2	1	0	1	.00	10	.264	.276	.354
1992 Texas	AL	123	420	109	16	1	8	(4	4)	151	39	37	24	2	73	1	7	2	0	0	—	15	.260	.300	.360
1993 Texas	AL	137	473	129	28	4	10	(7	3)	195	56	66	29	3	70	4	5	8	8	7	.53	16	.273	.315	.412
1994 Texas	AL	99	363	108	19	1	16	(7	9)	177	56	57	31	5	42	7	0	4	6	3	.67	10	.298	.360	.488
1995 Texas	AL	130	492	149	32	2	12	(5	7)	221	56	67	16	2	48	4	0	5	0	2	.00	11	.303	.327	.449
1996 Texas	AL	153	639	192	47	3	19	(10	9)	302	116	86	38	7	55	4	0	4	5	0	1.00	15	.300	.342	.473
1997 Texas	AL	150	597	187	34	4	20	(12	8)	289	98	77	38	7	89	8	1	4	7	3	.70	18	.313	.360	.484
1998 Texas	AL	145	579	186	40	4	21	(12	9)	297	88	91	32	4	88	3	0	3	9	0	1.00	18	.321	.358	.513
1999 Texas	AL	144	600	199	29	1	35	(12	23)	335	116	113	24	2	64	1	0	5	25	12	.68	31	.332	.356	.558
2000 Texas	AL	91	363	126	27	4	27	(16	11)	242	66	83	19	5	48	1	0	6	5	5	.50	17	.347	.375	.667
2001 Texas	AL	111	442	136	24	2	25	(16	9)	239	70	65	23	3	73	4	0	1	10	3	.77	13	.308	.347	.541
11 ML YEARS		1371	5248	1595	312	26	196	(104	92)	2547	785	769	279	40	692	37	15	43	75	36	.68	174	.304	.341	.485

Rich Rodriguez

Pitches: Left   Bats: Left   Pos: RP-53

Ht: 6'0"   Wt: 200   Born: 3/1/63   Age: 39

		HOW MUCH HE PITCHED						WHAT HE GAVE UP											THE RESULTS					
Year Team	Lg	G	GS	CG	GF	IP	BFP	H	R	ER	HR	SH	SF	HB	TBB	IBB	SO	WP	Bk	W	L	Pct.	ShO	Sv-Op	Hld	ERA
2001 Akron *	AA	4	0	0	1	5	17	2	0	0	0	0	0	0	0	0	4	0	0	0	0	—	0	1- -		0.00
1990 San Diego	NL	32	0	0	15	47.2	201	52	17	15	2	2	1	1	16	4	22	1	1	1	1	.500	0	1-1	3	2.83
1991 San Diego	NL	64	1	0	19	80	335	66	31	29	8	7	2	0	44	8	40	4	1	3	1	.750	0	0-2	8	3.26
1992 San Diego	NL	61	1	0	15	91	369	77	28	24	4	2	2	0	29	4	64	1	1	6	3	.667	0	0-1	5	2.37
1993 SD-Fla	NL	70	0	0	21	76	331	73	38	32	10	5	0	2	33	8	43	3	0	2	4	.333	0	3-7	10	3.79
1994 St. Louis	NL	56	0	0	15	60.1	260	62	30	27	6	2	1	1	26	4	43	4	0	3	5	.375	0	0-3	15	4.03
1995 St. Louis	NL	1	0	0	0	1.2	4	0	0	0	0	0	0	0	0	0	0	0	0	0	0	—	0	0-0	0	0.00
1997 San Francisco	NL	71	0	0	15	65.1	271	65	24	23	7	3	0	1	21	4	32	0	0	4	3	.571	0	1-5	14	3.17
1998 San Francisco	NL	68	0	0	11	65.2	278	69	28	27	7	2	2	0	20	5	44	3	0	4	0	1.000	0	2-6	22	3.70
1999 San Francisco	NL	62	0	0	8	56.2	255	60	33	33	8	5	2	1	28	5	44	1	0	3	0	1.000	0	0-2	11	5.24
2000 New York	NL	32	0	0	13	37	185	59	40	32	7	0	5	3	15	0	18	2	1	0	1	.000	0	0-0	7	7.78
2001 Cleveland	AL	53	0	0	6	39	174	41	24	18	2	2	1	2	17	3	31	1	1	2	2	.500	0	0-2	8	4.15
1993 San Diego	NL	34	0	0	10	30	133	34	15	11	2	2	0	1	9	3	22	1	0	2	3	.400	0	2-5	8	3.30
Florida	NL	36	0	0	11	46	198	39	23	21	8	3	0	1	24	5	21	2	0	0	1	.000	0	1-2	2	4.11
11 ML YEARS		570	2	0	138	620.1	2663	624	293	260	61	30	16	11	249	45	381	20	5	28	20	.583	0	7-29	96	3.77

Wilfredo Rodriguez

Pitches: Left   Bats: Left   Pos: RP-2

Ht: 6'3"   Wt: 180   Born: 3/20/79   Age: 23

		HOW MUCH HE PITCHED						WHAT HE GAVE UP											THE RESULTS					
Year Team	Lg	G	GS	CG	GF	IP	BFP	H	R	ER	HR	SH	SF	HB	TBB	IBB	SO	WP	Bk	W	L	Pct.	ShO	Sv-Op	Hld	ERA
1997 Astros	R	15	12	1	0	68	279	54	30	23	1	1	1	2	32	0	71	6	4	8	2	.800	1	0- -	—	3.04
1998 Quad City	A	28	27	1	0	165	667	122	70	56	7	4	3	9	62	1	170	8	9	11	5	.688	0	0- -	—	3.05
1999 Kissimmee	A+	25	24	0	1	153.1	624	108	55	49	8	2	5	13	62	0	148	5	1	15	7	.682	0	0- -	—	2.88
2000 Kissimmee	A+	9	9	1	0	53	234	43	29	28	5	1	4	6	30	0	52	4	1	3	5	.375	0	0- -	—	4.75
Round Rock	AA	11	11	0	0	57.2	275	54	42	37	10	4	6	1	52	0	55	2	0	2	4	.333	0	0- -	—	5.77
2001 Round Rock	AA	42	10	0	12	92.1	415	94	61	49	10	6	3	3	56	0	94	13	1	5	9	.357	0	0- -	—	4.78
2001 Houston	NL	2	0	0	1	3	16	6	5	5	2	0	1	0	1	0	3	0	0	0	0	—	0	0-0	0	15.00

Kenny Rogers

Pitches: Left   Bats: Left   Pos: SP-20

Ht: 6'1"   Wt: 217   Born: 11/10/64   Age: 37

		HOW MUCH HE PITCHED						WHAT HE GAVE UP											THE RESULTS					
Year Team	Lg	G	GS	CG	GF	IP	BFP	H	R	ER	HR	SH	SF	HB	TBB	IBB	SO	WP	Bk	W	L	Pct.	ShO	Sv-Op	Hld	ERA
1989 Texas	AL	73	0	0	24	73.2	314	60	28	24	2	6	3	4	42	9	63	6	0	3	4	.429	0	2-5	16	2.93
1990 Texas	AL	69	3	0	46	97.2	428	93	40	34	6	7	4	1	42	5	74	5	0	10	6	.625	0	15-23	6	3.13
1991 Texas	AL	63	9	0	20	109.2	511	121	80	66	14	9	5	6	61	7	73	3	1	10	10	.500	0	5-6	11	5.42
1992 Texas	AL	81	0	0	38	78.2	337	80	32	27	7	4	1	0	26	8	70	4	1	3	6	.333	0	6-10	16	3.09
1993 Texas	AL	35	33	5	0	208.1	885	210	108	95	18	7	5	4	71	2	140	6	5	16	10	.615	0	0-0	1	4.10
1994 Texas	AL	24	24	6	0	167.1	714	169	93	83	24	3	6	3	52	1	120	3	1	11	8	.579	2	0-0	1	4.46
1995 Texas	AL	31	31	3	0	208	877	192	87	78	26	3	5	2	76	1	140	8	1	17	7	.708	1	0-0	0	3.38

193

Year Team	Lg	G	GS	CG	GF	IP	BFP	H	R	ER	HR	SH	SF	HB	TBB	IBB	SO	WP	Bk	W	L	Pct.	ShO	Sv-Op	Hld	ERA
		HOW MUCH HE PITCHED						WHAT HE GAVE UP												THE RESULTS						
1996 New York	AL	30	30	2	0	179	786	179	97	93	16	6	3	8	83	2	92	5	0	12	8	.600	1	0-0	0	4.68
1997 New York	AL	31	22	1	4	145	651	161	100	91	18	2	4	7	62	1	78	2	2	6	7	.462	0	0-0	1	5.65
1998 Oakland	AL	34	34	7	0	238.2	970	215	96	84	19	4	5	7	67	0	138	5	2	16	8	.667	1	0-0	0	3.17
1999 Oak-NYM		31	31	5	0	195.1	845	206	101	91	16	7	7	13	69	1	126	4	1	10	4	.714	1	0-0	0	4.19
2000 Texas	AL	34	34	2	0	227.1	998	257	126	115	20	3	4	11	78	2	127	1	1	13	13	.500	0	0-0	0	4.55
2001 Texas	AL	20	20	0	0	120.2	552	150	88	83	18	1	6	8	49	2	74	4	1	5	7	.417	0	0-0	0	6.19
1999 Oakland	AL	19	19	3	0	119.1	528	135	66	57	8	4	6	9	41	0	68	3	1	5	3	.625	0	0-0	0	4.30
New York	NL	12	12	2	0	76	317	71	35	34	8	3	1	4	28	1	58	1	0	5	1	.833	1	0-0	0	4.03
13 ML YEARS		556	271	31	132	2049.1	8868	2093	1076	964	204	62	58	74	778	41	1315	56	16	132	98	.574	6	28-44	51	4.23

Scott Rolen

Bats: Right **Throws:** Right **Pos:** 3B-151   **Ht:** 6'4" **Wt:** 226 **Born:** 4/4/75 **Age:** 27

Year Team	Lg	G	AB	H	2B	3B	HR	(Hm	Rd)	TB	R	RBI	TBB	IBB	SO	HBP	SH	SF	SB	CS	SB%	GDP	Avg	OBP	SLG
		BATTING																	BASERUNNING				PERCENTAGES		
1996 Philadelphia	NL	37	130	33	7	0	4	(2	2)	52	10	18	13	0	27	1	0	2	0	2	.00	4	.254	.322	.400
1997 Philadelphia	NL	156	561	159	35	3	21	(11	10)	263	93	92	76	4	138	13	0	7	16	6	.73	6	.283	.377	.469
1998 Philadelphia	NL	160	601	174	45	4	31	(19	12)	320	120	110	93	6	141	11	0	6	14	7	.67	10	.290	.391	.532
1999 Philadelphia	NL	112	421	113	28	1	26	(9	17)	221	74	77	67	2	114	3	0	6	12	2	.86	8	.268	.368	.525
2000 Philadelphia	NL	128	483	144	32	6	26	(12	14)	266	88	89	51	9	99	5	0	2	8	1	.89	6	.298	.370	.551
2001 Philadelphia	NL	151	554	160	39	1	25	(12	13)	276	96	107	74	6	127	13	0	12	16	5	.76	6	.289	.378	.498
6 ML YEARS		744	2750	783	186	15	133	(65	68)	1398	481	493	374	27	646	46	0	35	66	23	.74	38	.285	.375	.508

Jimmy Rollins

Bats: Both **Throws:** Right **Pos:** SS-157; PH/PR-1   **Ht:** 5'8" **Wt:** 160 **Born:** 11/27/78 **Age:** 23

Year Team	Lg	G	AB	H	2B	3B	HR	(Hm	Rd)	TB	R	RBI	TBB	IBB	SO	HBP	SH	SF	SB	CS	SB%	GDP	Avg	OBP	SLG
		BATTING																	BASERUNNING				PERCENTAGES		
1996 Martinsvlle	R+	49	172	41	3	1	1	—	—	49	22	16	28	1	20	2	1	0	11	5	.69	2	.238	.351	.285
1997 Piedmont	A	139	560	151	22	8	6	—	—	207	94	59	52	2	80	0	9	3	46	6	.88	4	.270	.330	.370
1998 Clearwater	A+	119	495	121	18	9	6	—	—	175	72	35	41	1	62	4	4	3	23	9	.72	9	.244	.306	.354
1999 Reading	AA	133	532	145	21	8	11	—	—	215	81	56	51	1	47	1	12	2	24	12	.67	8	.273	.336	.404
Scrantn-WB	AAA	4	13	1	1	0	0	—	—	2	0	0	1	0	1	0	1	0	1	0	1.00	0	.077	.143	.154
2000 Scrantn-WB	AAA	133	470	129	28	11	12	—	—	215	67	69	49	1	55	2	5	7	24	7	.77	4	.274	.341	.457
2000 Philadelphia	NL	14	53	17	1	1	0	(0	0)	20	5	5	2	0	7	0	0	0	3	0	1.00	1	.321	.345	.377
2001 Philadelphia	NL	158	656	180	29	12	14	(8	6)	275	97	54	48	2	108	2	9	5	46	8	.85	5	.274	.323	.419
2 ML YEARS		172	709	197	30	13	14	(8	6)	295	102	59	50	2	115	2	9	5	49	8	.86	5	.278	.325	.416

Damian Rolls

Bats: R **Throws:** R **Pos:** 2B-42; PH/PR-19; CF-18; LF-7; DH-6; 3B-1   **Ht:** 6'2" **Wt:** 205 **Born:** 9/15/77 **Age:** 24

Year Team	Lg	G	AB	H	2B	3B	HR	(Hm	Rd)	TB	R	RBI	TBB	IBB	SO	HBP	SH	SF	SB	CS	SB%	GDP	Avg	OBP	SLG
		BATTING																	BASERUNNING				PERCENTAGES		
1996 Yakima	A-	66	257	68	11	1	4	—	—	93	31	27	7	0	46	3	2	1	8	3	.73	5	.265	.291	.362
1997 Savannah	A	130	475	100	17	5	5	—	—	142	57	47	38	0	83	5	3	4	11	3	.79	9	.211	.274	.299
1998 Vero Beach	A+	73	266	65	9	0	0	—	—	74	28	30	23	0	43	2	1	2	13	3	.81	6	.244	.307	.278
San Antonio	AA	50	160	35	6	0	1	—	—	44	18	9	6	0	28	0	1	1	2	0	1.00	9	.219	.246	.275
1999 Vero Beach	A+	127	474	141	26	2	9	—	—	198	68	54	36	2	66	14	4	5	24	13	.65	6	.297	.361	.418
2000 St. Pete	A+	5	16	3	2	0	0	—	—	5	2	0	2	0	3	1	1	0	1	0	1.00	0	.188	.316	.313
Orlando	AA	14	51	13	5	0	0	—	—	18	6	3	7	0	6	1	0	1	1	1	.50	0	.255	.350	.353
2000 Tampa Bay	AL	4	3	1	0	0	0	(0	0)	1	0	0	0	0	1	0	0	0	0	0	—	0	.333	.333	.333
2001 Tampa Bay	AL	81	237	62	11	1	2	(2	0)	81	33	12	10	0	47	0	2	0	12	4	.75	5	.262	.291	.342
2 ML YEARS		85	240	63	11	1	2	(2	0)	82	33	12	10	0	48	0	2	0	12	4	.75	5	.263	.292	.342

J.C. Romero

Pitches: Left **Bats:** Both **Pos:** SP-11; RP-3   **Ht:** 5'11" **Wt:** 195 **Born:** 6/4/76 **Age:** 26

Year Team	Lg	G	GS	CG	GF	IP	BFP	H	R	ER	HR	SH	SF	HB	TBB	IBB	SO	WP	Bk	W	L	Pct.	ShO	Sv-Op	Hld	ERA
		HOW MUCH HE PITCHED						WHAT HE GAVE UP												THE RESULTS						
2001 Edmonton *	AAA	12	10	0	0	63.2	271	67	33	26	4	2	2	0	24	0	55	2	1	3	3	.500	0	0-	—	3.68
1999 Minnesota	AL	5	0	0	3	9.2	39	13	4	4	0	0	0	0	4	0	4	0	0	0	0	—	0	0-0	0	3.72
2000 Minnesota	AL	12	11	0	0	57.2	268	72	51	45	8	4	2	1	30	0	50	2	1	2	7	.222	0	0-0	0	7.02
2001 Minnesota	AL	14	11	0	1	65	286	71	48	45	10	3	2	1	24	1	39	1	0	1	4	.200	0	0-0	0	6.23
3 ML YEARS		31	22	0	4	132.1	593	156	103	94	18	7	4	2	54	1	93	3	1	3	11	.214	0	0-0	0	6.39

Jose Rosado

Pitches: Left **Bats:** Left **2000 Pos:** SP-5   **Ht:** 6'0" **Wt:** 185 **Born:** 11/9/74 **Age:** 27

Year Team	Lg	G	GS	CG	GF	IP	BFP	H	R	ER	HR	SH	SF	HB	TBB	IBB	SO	WP	Bk	W	L	Pct.	ShO	Sv-Op	Hld	ERA
		HOW MUCH HE PITCHED						WHAT HE GAVE UP												THE RESULTS						
1996 Kansas City	AL	16	16	2	0	106.2	441	101	39	38	7	1	4	4	26	1	64	5	1	8	6	.571	0	0-0	0	3.21
1997 Kansas City	AL	33	33	2	0	203.1	881	208	117	106	26	6	11	4	73	3	129	4	2	9	12	.429	0	0-0	0	4.69
1998 Kansas City	AL	38	25	2	1	174.2	757	180	106	91	25	1	3	5	57	2	135	6	1	8	11	.421	1	1-1	2	4.69
1999 Kansas City	AL	33	33	5	0	208	882	197	103	89	24	8	4	5	72	1	141	9	0	10	14	.417	0	0-0	0	3.85
2000 Kansas City	AL	5	5	0	0	27.2	122	29	18	18	4	1	1	4	9	0	15	0	1	2	2	.500	0	0-0	0	5.86
5 ML YEARS		125	112	11		720.1	3083	715	383	342	86	17	23	22	237	7	484	24	5	37	45	.451	2	1-1	2	4.27

194

Brian Rose

Pitches: Right **Bats:** Right **Pos:** RP-7; SP-3

Ht: 6'3" **Wt:** 215 **Born:** 2/13/76 **Age:** 26

		HOW MUCH HE PITCHED						WHAT HE GAVE UP												THE RESULTS						
Year Team	Lg	G	GS	CG	GF	IP	BFP	H	R	ER	HR	SH	SF	HB	TBB	IBB	SO	WP	Bk	W	L	Pct.	ShO	Sv-Op	Hld	ERA
2001 Durham *	AAA	19	15	0	2	98.2	391	88	35	34	11	2	2	3	19	0	88	2	0	9	2	.818	0	1--	—	3.10
1997 Boston	AL	1	1	0	0	3	16	5	4	4	0	0	0	0	2	0	3	0	0	0	0	—	0	0-0	0	12.00
1998 Boston	AL	8	8	0	0	37.2	168	43	32	29	9	0	1	2	14	0	18	0	0	1	4	.200	0	0-0	0	6.93
1999 Boston	AL	22	18	0	1	98	433	112	59	53	19	2	0	2	29	2	51	0	0	7	6	.538	0	0-0	0	4.87
2000 Bos-Col		27	24	0	1	116.2	532	130	78	75	21	3	4	6	51	9	64	4	1	7	10	.412	0	0-0	0	5.79
2001 NYM-TB		10	3	0	2	29	138	41	24	24	7	0	2	0	14	1	15	7	0	0	3	.000	0	0-0	0	7.45
2000 Boston	AL	15	12	0	1	53	239	58	37	36	11	1	2	3	21	3	24	2	0	3	5	.375	0	0-0	0	6.11
Colorado	NL	12	12	0	0	63.2	293	72	41	39	10	2	2	3	30	6	40	2	1	4	5	.444	0	0-0	0	5.51
2001 New York	NL	3	0	0	0	8.2	37	10	4	4	3	0	0	0	2	1	4	0	0	0	1	.000	0	0-0	0	4.15
Tampa Bay	AL	7	3	0	2	20.1	101	31	20	20	4	0	2	0	12	0	11	7	0	0	2	.000	0	0-0	0	8.85
5 ML YEARS		68	54	0	4	284.1	1287	331	197	185	56	5	7	10	110	12	151	11	1	15	23	.395	0	0-0	0	5.86

Aaron Rowand

Bats: R **Throws:** R **Pos:** LF-34; CF-32; RF-11; PH/PR-4

Ht: 6'1" **Wt:** 200 **Born:** 8/29/77 **Age:** 24

		BATTING																		BASERUNNING				PERCENTAGES		
Year Team	Lg	G	AB	H	2B	3B	HR	(Hm	Rd)	TB	R	RBI	TBB	IBB	SO	HBP	SH	SF	SB	CS	SB%	GDP	Avg	OBP	SLG
1998 Hickory	A	61	222	76	13	3	5	—	—	110	42	32	21	0	36	6	5	2	7	3	.70	5	.342	.410	.495
1999 Winston-Sal	A+	133	512	143	37	3	24	—	—	258	96	88	33	2	94	13	2	5	15	10	.60	13	.279	.336	.504
2000 Birmingham	AA	139	532	137	26	5	20	—	—	233	80	98	38	4	117	14	4	4	22	7	.76	12	.258	.321	.438
2001 Charlotte	AAA	82	329	97	28	0	16	—	—	173	54	48	21	3	47	9	2	1	8	2	.80	9	.295	.353	.526
2001 Chicago	AL	63	123	36	5	0	4	(3	1)	53	21	20	15	0	28	4	5	1	5	1	.83	2	.293	.385	.431

Kirk Rueter

Pitches: Left **Bats:** Left **Pos:** SP-34

Ht: 6'2" **Wt:** 205 **Born:** 12/1/70 **Age:** 31

		HOW MUCH HE PITCHED						WHAT HE GAVE UP												THE RESULTS						
Year Team	Lg	G	GS	CG	GF	IP	BFP	H	R	ER	HR	SH	SF	HB	TBB	IBB	SO	WP	Bk	W	L	Pct.	ShO	Sv-Op	Hld	ERA
1993 Montreal	NL	14	14	1	0	85.2	341	85	33	26	5	1	0	0	18	1	31	0	0	8	0	1.000	0	0-0	0	2.73
1994 Montreal	NL	20	20	0	0	92.1	397	106	60	53	11	6	6	2	23	1	50	2	0	7	3	.700	0	0-0	0	5.17
1995 Montreal	NL	9	9	1	0	47.1	184	38	17	17	3	4	0	1	9	0	28	0	0	5	3	.625	1	0-0	0	3.23
1996 Mon-SF	NL	20	19	0	0	102	430	109	50	45	12	4	1	2	27	0	46	2	0	6	8	.429	0	0-0	0	3.97
1997 San Francisco	NL	32	32	0	0	190.2	802	194	83	73	17	10	6	1	51	8	115	3	0	13	6	.684	0	0-0	0	4.36
1998 San Francisco	NL	33	33	1	0	187.2	806	193	100	91	27	5	8	7	57	3	102	6	0	16	9	.640	0	0-0	0	5.41
1999 San Francisco	NL	33	33	1	0	184.2	804	219	118	111	28	6	4	2	55	2	94	2	0	15	10	.600	0	0-0	0	3.96
2000 San Francisco	NL	32	31	0	0	184	799	205	92	81	23	19	9	2	62	5	71	1	0	11	9	.550	0	0-0	0	4.42
2001 San Francisco	NL	34	34	0	0	195.1	840	213	105	96	25	11	6	4	66	4	83	1	0	14	12	.538	0	0-0	0	4.58
1996 Montreal	NL	16	16	0	0	78.2	338	91	44	40	12	4	1	2	22	0	30	0	0	5	6	.455	0	0-0	0	1.93
San Francisco	NL	4	3	0	0	23.1	92	18	6	5	0	0	0	0	5	0	16	2	0	1	2	.333	0	0-0	0	1.93
9 ML YEARS		227	225	4	0	1269.2	5403	1362	658	593	151	66	40	21	368	24	620	17	0	95	60	.613	1	0-0	0	4.20

Johnny Ruffin

Pitches: Right **Bats:** Right **Pos:** RP-3

Ht: 6'3" **Wt:** 170 **Born:** 7/29/71 **Age:** 30

		HOW MUCH HE PITCHED						WHAT HE GAVE UP												THE RESULTS						
Year Team	Lg	G	GS	CG	GF	IP	BFP	H	R	ER	HR	SH	SF	HB	TBB	IBB	SO	WP	Bk	W	L	Pct.	ShO	Sv-Op	Hld	ERA
2001 Calgary *	AAA	37	0	0	32	37.2	148	37	17	16	1	1	2	2	10	3	47	3	0	2	3	.400	0	22--	—	4.36
Louisville *	AAA	9	0	0	8	8.1	33	6	1	0	0	1	0	0	3	0	11	0	0	0	0	—	0	5--	—	0.00
1993 Cincinnati	NL	21	0	0	5	37.2	148	36	16	15	4	1	0	1	11	1	30	2	0	2	1	.667	0	2-3	2	3.58
1994 Cincinnati	NL	51	0	0	13	70	287	57	26	24	7	2	2	0	27	3	44	5	1	7	2	.778	0	1-3	11	3.09
1995 Cincinnati	NL	10	0	0	6	13.1	54	4	3	2	0	0	0	0	11	0	11	3	0	0	0	—	0	0-0	1	1.35
1996 Cincinnati	NL	49	0	0	13	62.1	289	71	42	38	10	4	3	2	37	5	69	8	0	1	3	.250	0	0-1	1	5.49
2000 Arizona	NL	5	0	0	2	9	43	14	9	9	4	0	0	0	3	1	5	0	0	0	0	—	0	0-0	0	9.00
2001 Florida	NL	3	0	0	1	3.2	21	5	4	2	0	0	0	1	4	1	4	0	0	0	0	—	0	0-0	0	4.91
6 ML YEARS		139	0	0	40	196	853	187	100	90	25	7	5	4	93	11	163	18	1	10	6	.625	0	3-7	15	4.13

Ryan Rupe

Pitches: Right **Bats:** Right **Pos:** SP-26; RP-2

Ht: 6'5" **Wt:** 230 **Born:** 3/31/75 **Age:** 27

		HOW MUCH HE PITCHED						WHAT HE GAVE UP												THE RESULTS						
Year Team	Lg	G	GS	CG	GF	IP	BFP	H	R	ER	HR	SH	SF	HB	TBB	IBB	SO	WP	Bk	W	L	Pct.	ShO	Sv-Op	Hld	ERA
2001 Durham *	AAA	2	2	0	0	11	36	3	1	1	0	1	0	0	1	0	17	0	0	0	1	.000	0	0--	—	0.82
1999 Tampa Bay	AL	24	24	0	0	142.1	614	136	81	72	17	1	7	12	57	2	97	4	1	8	9	.471	0	0-0	0	4.55
2000 Tampa Bay	AL	18	18	0	0	91	425	121	75	70	19	2	6	9	31	3	61	4	0	5	6	.455	0	0-0	0	6.92
2001 Tampa Bay	AL	28	26	0	0	143.1	635	161	111	105	30	3	5	11	48	0	123	7	1	5	12	.294	0	0-1	0	6.59
3 ML YEARS		70	68	0	0	376.2	1674	418	267	247	66	6	18	32	136	5	281	15	2	18	27	.400	0	0-1	0	5.90

Glendon Rusch

Pitches: Left **Bats:** Left **Pos:** SP-33

Ht: 6'1" **Wt:** 200 **Born:** 11/7/74 **Age:** 27

		HOW MUCH HE PITCHED						WHAT HE GAVE UP												THE RESULTS						
Year Team	Lg	G	GS	CG	GF	IP	BFP	H	R	ER	HR	SH	SF	HB	TBB	IBB	SO	WP	Bk	W	L	Pct.	ShO	Sv-Op	Hld	ERA
1997 Kansas City	AL	30	27	0	0	170.1	758	206	111	104	28	8	7	7	52	0	116	0	1	6	9	.400	0	0-0	0	5.50
1998 Kansas City	AL	29	24	1	2	154.2	686	191	104	101	22	1	2	4	50	0	94	1	0	6	15	.286	1	1-1	0	5.88
1999 KC-NYM		4	0	0	2	5	26	8	7	7	1	0	0	1	3	0	4	0	0	0	1	.000	0	0-0	0	12.60
2000 New York	NL	31	30	2	0	190.2	802	196	91	85	18	10	7	6	44	2	157	2	0	11	11	.500	0	0-0	0	4.01
2001 New York	NL	33	33	1	0	179	785	216	101	92	23	11	5	7	43	2	156	3	2	8	12	.400	0	0-0	0	4.63
1999 Kansas City	AL	3	0	0	1	4	23	7	7	7	1	0	0	1	3	0	4	0	0	0	1	.000	0	0-0	0	15.75
New York	NL	1	0	0	1	1	3	1	0	0	0	0	0	0	0	0	0	0	0	0	0	—	0	0-0	0	0.00
5 ML YEARS		127	114	5	4	699.2	3057	817	414	389	92	30	21	25	192	4	527	6	3	31	48	.392	1	1-1	0	5.00

B.J. Ryan

Pitches: Left **Bats:** Left **Pos:** RP-61

Ht: 6'6" **Wt:** 230 **Born:** 12/28/75 **Age:** 26

Year Team	Lg	G	GS	CG	GF	IP	BFP	H	R	ER	HR	SH	SF	HB	TBB	IBB	SO	WP	Bk	W	L	Pct.	ShO	Sv-Op	Hld	ERA
1999 Cin-Bal		14	0	0	3	20.1	82	13	7	7	0	0	1	0	13	1	29	1	0	1	0	1.000	0	0-0	0	3.10
2000 Baltimore	AL	42	0	0	9	42.2	193	36	29	28	7	1	1	0	31	1	41	2	1	2	3	.400	0	0-3	7	5.91
2001 Baltimore	AL	61	0	0	9	53	237	47	31	25	6	1	2	2	30	4	54	0	0	2	4	.333	0	2-4	14	4.25
1999 Cincinnati	NL	1	0	0	0	2	9	4	1	1	0	0	0	0	1	0	1	0	0	0	0	—	0	0-0	0	4.50
Baltimore	AL	13	0	0	3	18.1	73	9	6	6	0	0	1	0	12	1	28	1	0	1	0	1.000	0	0-0	0	2.95
3 ML YEARS		117	0	0	21	116	512	96	67	60	13	2	4	2	74	6	124	3	1	5	7	.417	0	2-7	21	4.66

Rob Ryan

Bats: L **Throws:** L **Pos:** PH/PR-6; CF-4; DH-1; RF-1

Ht: 5'11" **Wt:** 192 **Born:** 6/24/73 **Age:** 29

Year Team	Lg	G	AB	H	2B	3B	HR	(Hm	Rd)	TB	R	RBI	TBB	IBB	SO	HBP	SH	SF	SB	CS	SB%	GDP	Avg	OBP	SLG
1996 Lethbridge	R+	59	211	64	8	1	4	—	—	86	55	37	43	1	33	2	5	3	23	6	.79	2	.303	.421	.408
1997 South Bend	A	121	421	132	35	5	8	—	—	201	71	73	89	5	58	2	0	5	12	1	.92	7	.314	.431	.477
1998 Tucson	AAA	116	394	125	18	2	17	—	—	198	71	66	63	3	61	10	0	5	9	3	.75	5	.317	.419	.503
1999 Tucson	AAA	117	414	120	30	5	19	—	—	217	72	88	56	2	70	12	0	5	4	3	.57	13	.290	.386	.524
2000 Tucson	AAA	92	332	102	19	1	8	—	—	147	56	55	45	5	35	11	0	2	1	1	.50	9	.307	.405	.443
2001 Tucson	AAA	63	216	71	17	5	12	—	—	134	45	50	29	3	34	5	0	2	1	3	.25	3	.329	.417	.620
Sacramento	AAA	62	218	49	8	3	7	—	—	84	35	32	39	6	51	3	0	3	1	3	.25	0	.225	.346	.385
1999 Arizona	NL	20	29	7	1	0	2	(1	1)	14	4	5	1	0	8	0	0	0	0	0	—	0	.241	.267	.483
2000 Arizona	NL	27	27	8	1	1	0	(0	0)	11	4	2	4	0	7	1	0	0	0	0	—	0	.296	.406	.407
2001 Ari-Oak		8	8	0	0	0	0	(0	0)	0	0	0	0	0	6	0	0	0	0	0	—	0	.000	.000	.000
2001 Arizona	NL	1	1	0	0	0	0	(0	0)	0	0	0	0	0	1	0	0	0	0	0	—	0	.000	.000	.000
Oakland	AL	7	7	0	0	0	0	(0	0)	0	0	0	0	0	5	0	0	0	0	0	—	0	.000	.000	.000
3 ML YEARS		55	64	15	2	1	2	(1	1)	25	8	7	5	0	21	1	0	0	0	0	—	0	.234	.300	.391

C.C. Sabathia

Pitches: Left **Bats:** Left **Pos:** SP-33

Ht: 6'7" **Wt:** 250 **Born:** 7/21/80 **Age:** 21

Year Team	Lg	G	GS	CG	GF	IP	BFP	H	R	ER	HR	SH	SF	HB	TBB	IBB	SO	WP	Bk	W	L	Pct.	ShO	Sv-Op	Hld	ERA
1998 Burlington	R+	5	5	0	0	18	83	20	14	9	1	0	1	1	8	0	35	1	1	1	0	1.000	0	0--	—	4.50
1999 Mahoning Vy	A-	6	6	0	0	19.2	77	9	5	4	0	0	2	0	12	0	27	0	0	0	0	—	0	0--	—	1.83
Columbus	A	3	3	0	0	16.2	64	8	2	2	1	1	0	1	5	0	20	1	0	2	0	1.000	0	0--	—	1.08
Kinston	A+	7	7	0	0	32	143	30	22	19	3	3	3	1	19	0	29	6	0	3	3	.500	0	0--	—	5.34
2000 Kinston	A+	10	10	2	0	56	232	48	23	22	4	0	1	2	24	0	69	2	1	3	2	.600	2	0--	—	3.54
Akron	AA	17	17	0	0	90.1	394	75	41	36	6	2	1	7	48	0	90	2	1	3	7	.300	0	0--	—	3.59
2001 Cleveland	AL	33	33	0	0	180.1	763	149	93	88	19	3	5	7	95	1	171	7	3	17	5	.773	0	0-0	0	4.39

Erik Sabel

Pitches: Right **Bats:** Right **Pos:** RP-42

Ht: 6'2" **Wt:** 185 **Born:** 10/14/74 **Age:** 27

Year Team	Lg	G	GS	CG	GF	IP	BFP	H	R	ER	HR	SH	SF	HB	TBB	IBB	SO	WP	Bk	W	L	Pct.	ShO	Sv-Op	Hld	ERA
1996 Lethbridge	R+	20	3	0	5	42	184	43	23	13	3	1	3	1	7	0	41	4	0	1	4	.200	0	1--	—	2.79
1997 High Desert	A+	31	22	0	4	143.2	646	174	101	85	21	10	6	10	40	0	86	6	0	11	11	.500	0	1--	—	5.32
1998 High Desert	A+	14	0	0	9	22.2	100	25	8	8	2	1	0	0	4	3	18	0	0	1	0	1.000	0	4--	—	3.18
Tucson	AAA	7	0	0	1	10.1	53	17	10	10	0	2	1	1	5	1	7	1	0	1	0	1.000	0	0--	—	8.71
Tulsa	AA	24	2	0	7	56.1	226	46	24	20	6	0	0	2	13	1	33	6	0	7	0	1.000	0	2--	—	3.20
1999 El Paso	AA	8	1	0	4	10	49	16	9	7	1	0	0	1	4	0	7	0	0	1	0	1.000	0	1--	—	6.30
Tucson	AAA	22	9	0	8	72.2	306	79	36	27	4	5	1	1	24	4	38	3	0	5	2	.714	0	1--	—	3.34
2000 Tucson	AAA	29	15	0	5	98.1	473	149	90	79	16	4	8	5	31	4	61	4	0	4	11	.267	0	1--	—	7.23
2001 Tucson	AAA	18	2	0	7	39.2	162	35	14	13	3	4	1	4	7	1	32	2	0	2	2	.500	0	2--	—	2.95
1999 Arizona	NL	7	0	0	1	9.2	48	12	7	7	1	0	0	2	6	2	6	1	0	0	0	—	0	0-0	0	6.52
2001 Arizona	NL	42	0	0	11	51.1	218	57	26	25	8	1	0	3	12	3	25	1	0	3	2	.600	0	0-0	4	4.38
2 ML YEARS		49	0	0	12	61	266	69	33	32	9	1	0	5	18	5	31	2	0	3	2	.600	0	0-0	4	4.72

Bret Saberhagen

Pitches: Right **Bats:** Right **Pos:** SP-3

Ht: 6'1" **Wt:** 200 **Born:** 4/11/64 **Age:** 38

Year Team	Lg	G	GS	CG	GF	IP	BFP	H	R	ER	HR	SH	SF	HB	TBB	IBB	SO	WP	Bk	W	L	Pct.	ShO	Sv-Op	Hld	ERA
2001 Sarasota *	A+	1	1	0	0	4	17	5	3	3	0	0	0	0	0	0	3	0	0	0	0	—	0	0--	—	6.75
Red Sox *	R	2	2	0	0	5.2	19	3	1	1	0	0	0	0	0	0	2	0	0	0	1	.000	0	0--	—	1.59
Trenton *	AA	1	1	0	0	3.2	14	5	1	1	0	0	0	0	0	0	4	0	0	0	0	—	0	0--	—	2.45
Pawtucket *	AAA	1	1	0	0	6	22	3	2	2	0	0	0	1	1	0	4	1	0	0	0	—	0	0--	—	3.00
1984 Kansas City	AL	38	18	2	9	157.2	634	138	71	61	13	8	5	2	36	4	73	7	1	10	11	.476	1	1-1	1	3.48
1985 Kansas City	AL	32	32	10	0	235.1	931	211	79	75	19	9	7	1	38	1	158	1	3	20	6	.769	1	0-0	0	2.87
1986 Kansas City	AL	30	25	4	0	156	652	165	77	72	15	3	2	2	29	1	112	1	1	7	12	.368	2	0-0	0	4.15
1987 Kansas City	AL	33	33	15	0	257	1048	246	99	96	27	8	5	6	53	2	163	6	1	18	10	.643	4	0-0	0	3.36
1988 Kansas City	AL	35	35	9	0	260.2	1089	271	122	110	18	8	10	4	59	5	171	9	0	14	16	.467	0	0-0	0	3.80
1989 Kansas City	AL	36	35	12	0	262.1	1021	209	74	63	13	9	6	2	43	6	193	8	1	23	6	.793	4	0-0	0	2.16
1990 Kansas City	AL	20	20	5	0	135	561	146	52	49	9	4	4	0	28	1	87	0	1	5	9	.357	0	0-0	0	3.27
1991 Kansas City	AL	28	28	7	0	196.1	789	165	76	67	12	8	3	9	45	5	136	8	1	13	8	.619	2	0-0	0	3.07
1992 New York	NL	17	15	1	0	97.2	397	84	39	38	6	3	3	4	27	1	81	1	1	3	5	.375	1	0-1	0	3.50
1993 New York	NL	19	19	4	0	139.1	556	131	55	51	11	6	6	3	17	4	93	2	2	7	7	.500	1	0-0	0	3.29
1994 New York	NL	24	24	4	0	177.1	696	169	58	54	13	9	6	3	13	0	143	0	0	14	4	.778	0	0-0	0	2.74
1995 NYM-Col	NL	25	25	3	0	153	658	165	78	71	21	7	3	10	33	3	100	1	1	7	6	.538	0	0-0	0	4.18
1997 Boston	AL	6	6	0	0	26	120	30	20	19	5	1	3	2	10	0	14	1	0	0	1	.000	0	0-0	0	6.58
1998 Boston	AL	31	31	0	0	175	725	181	82	77	22	4	8	5	29	1	100	4	0	15	8	.652	0	0-0	0	3.96
1999 Boston	AL	22	22	0	0	119	480	122	43	39	11	4	2	2	11	0	81	1	0	10	6	.625	0	0-0	0	2.95

Year Team	Lg	G	GS	CG	GF	IP	BFP	H	R	ER	HR	SH	SF	HB	TBB	IBB	SO	WP	Bk	W	L	Pct.	ShO	Sv-Op	Hld	ERA
2001 Boston	AL	3	3	0	0	15	64	19	11	10	3	0	0	1	0	0	10	0	0	1	2	.333	0	0-0	0	6.00
1995 New York	NL	16	16	3	0	110	452	105	45	41	13	5	3	5	20	2	71	2	0	5	5	.500	0	0-0	0	3.35
Colorado	NL	9	9	0	0	43	206	60	33	30	8	2	0	5	13	1	29	1	0	2	1	.667	0	0-0	0	6.28
16 ML YEARS		399	371	76	13	2562.2	10421	2452	1036	952	218	89	68	59	471	34	1715	53	12	167	117	.588	16	1-2	1	3.34

Donnie Sadler

Bats: R Throws: R Pos: 2B-28; PH/PR-26; SS-18; 3B-15; LF-11; RF-9; CF-6; DH-2   Ht: 5'6" Wt: 175 Born: 6/17/75 Age: 27

Year Team	Lg	G	AB	H	2B	3B	HR	(Hm	Rd)	TB	R	RBI	TBB	IBB	SO	HBP	SH	SF	SB	CS	SB%	GDP	Avg	OBP	SLG
1998 Boston	AL	58	124	28	4	4	3	(0	3)	49	21	15	6	0	28	3	5	1	4	0	1.00	1	.226	.276	.395
1999 Boston	AL	49	107	30	5	1	0	(0	1)	37	18	4	5	0	20	0	3	0	2	1	.67	1	.280	.313	.346
2000 Boston	AL	49	99	22	5	0	1	(0	1)	30	14	10	5	0	18	1	5	2	3	1	.75	1	.222	.262	.303
2001 Cin-KC		93	185	30	6	0	1	(0	1)	39	28	5	18	0	37	2	5	1	7	4	.64	3	.162	.243	.211
2001 Cincinnati	NL	39	84	17	3	0	1	(0	1)	23	9	3	9	0	20	0	2	0	3	3	.50	3	.202	.280	.274
Kansas City	AL	54	101	13	3	0	0	(0	0)	16	19	2	9	0	17	2	3	1	4	1	.80	0	.129	.212	.158
4 ML YEARS		249	515	110	20	5	5	(0	5)	155	81	34	34	0	103	6	18	4	16	6	.73	6	.214	.268	.301

Olmedo Saenz

Bats: R Throws: R Pos: DH-58; 1B-28; PH/PR-26; 3B-14   Ht: 6'0" Wt: 185 Born: 10/8/70 Age: 31

Year Team	Lg	G	AB	H	2B	3B	HR	(Hm	Rd)	TB	R	RBI	TBB	IBB	SO	HBP	SH	SF	SB	CS	SB%	GDP	Avg	OBP	SLG
1994 Chicago	AL	5	14	2	0	1	0	(0	0)	4	2	0	0	0	5	0	1	0	0	0	—	1	.143	.143	.286
1999 Oakland	AL	97	255	70	18	0	11	(8	3)	121	41	44	22	1	47	15	0	3	1	1	.50	6	.275	.363	.475
2000 Oakland	AL	76	214	67	12	2	9	(3	6)	110	40	33	25	2	40	7	0	1	1	0	1.00	6	.313	.401	.514
2001 Oakland	AL	106	305	67	21	1	9	(6	3)	117	33	32	19	1	64	13	1	3	0	1	.00	9	.220	.291	.384
4 ML YEARS		284	788	206	51	4	29	(17	12)	352	116	106	66	4	156	35	2	7	2	2	.50	22	.261	.343	.447

Tim Salmon

Bats: Right Throws: Right Pos: RF-125; DH-12; PH/PR-1   Ht: 6'3" Wt: 225 Born: 8/24/68 Age: 33

Year Team	Lg	G	AB	H	2B	3B	HR	(Hm	Rd)	TB	R	RBI	TBB	IBB	SO	HBP	SH	SF	SB	CS	SB%	GDP	Avg	OBP	SLG
2001 Rancho Cuc *	A+	2	7	1	0	0	0	—	—	1	1	0	1	0	4	0	0	0	1	1	.50	1	.177	.283	.266
1992 California	AL	23	79	14	1	0	2	(1	1)	21	8	6	11	1	23	1	0	1	1	1	.50	1	.177	.283	.266
1993 California	AL	142	515	146	35	1	31	(23	8)	276	93	95	82	5	135	5	0	8	5	6	.45	6	.283	.382	.536
1994 California	AL	100	373	107	18	2	23	(12	11)	198	67	70	54	2	102	5	0	3	1	3	.25	3	.287	.382	.531
1995 California	AL	143	537	177	34	3	34	(15	19)	319	111	105	91	2	111	6	0	4	5	5	.50	9	.330	.429	.594
1996 California	AL	156	581	166	27	4	30	(18	12)	291	90	98	93	5	125	4	0	3	4	2	.67	8	.286	.386	.501
1997 Anaheim	AL	157	582	172	28	1	33	(17	16)	301	95	129	95	5	142	7	0	11	9	12	.43	7	.296	.394	.517
1998 Anaheim	AL	136	463	139	28	1	26	(13	13)	247	84	88	90	5	100	3	0	10	4	1	.00	6	.300	.410	.533
1999 Anaheim	AL	98	353	94	24	2	17	(7	10)	173	60	69	63	2	82	0	0	6	4	1	.80	7	.266	.372	.490
2000 Anaheim	AL	158	568	165	36	2	34	(17	17)	307	108	97	104	5	139	6	0	2	2	0	.00	14	.290	.404	.540
2001 Anaheim	AL	137	475	108	21	1	17	(11	6)	182	63	49	96	4	121	8	0	2	9	3	.75	11	.227	.365	.383
10 ML YEARS		1250	4526	1288	252	17	247	(134	113)	2315	779	806	779	38	1080	45	0	50	38	36	.51	70	.285	.391	.511

Alex Sanchez

Bats: L Throws: L Pos: PH/PR-17; CF-14; LF-3; RF-3   Ht: 5'10" Wt: 179 Born: 8/26/76 Age: 25

Year Team	Lg	G	AB	H	2B	3B	HR	(Hm	Rd)	TB	R	RBI	TBB	IBB	SO	HBP	SH	SF	SB	CS	SB%	GDP	Avg	OBP	SLG
1996 Devil Rays	R	56	227	64	7	6	1	—	—	86	36	22	10	0	35	6	1	1	20	12	.63	2	.282	.328	.379
1997 Chston-SC	A	131	537	155	15	6	0	—	—	182	73	34	37	2	72	3	12	4	92	40	.70	7	.289	.336	.339
1998 St. Pete	A+	128	545	180	17	9	1	—	—	218	77	50	31	1	70	1	4	12	66	33	.67	5	.330	.360	.400
1999 Orlando	AA	121	500	127	12	4	2	—	—	153	68	29	26	1	88	0	10	2	48	27	.64	8	.254	.290	.306
Durham	AAA	3	10	2	1	0	0	—	—	3	2	0	1	0	0	0	0	0	0	0	—	0	.200	.273	.300
2000 Orlando	AA	20	86	25	2	1	0	—	—	29	12	4	1	0	13	1	1	0	6	2	.25	1	.291	.307	.337
Durham	AAA	107	446	130	18	3	2	—	—	160	76	33	30	1	66	5	3	2	52	20	.72	6	.291	.342	.359
2001 Indianapolis	AAA	83	335	105	14	5	1	—	—	132	52	26	22	1	44	2	2	0	27	8	.77	2	.313	.359	.394
2001 Milwaukee	NL	30	68	14	3	2	0	(0	0)	21	7	4	5	0	13	0	0	0	6	2	.75	0	.206	.260	.309

Jesus Sanchez

Pitches: Left Bats: Left Pos: SP-9; RP-7   Ht: 5'10" Wt: 155 Born: 10/11/74 Age: 27

Year Team	Lg	G	GS	CG	GF	IP	BFP	H	R	ER	HR	SH	SF	HB	TBB	IBB	SO	WP	Bk	W	L	Pct.	ShO	Sv-Op	Hld	ERA
2001 Calgary *	AAA	16	11	0	0	75.2	322	61	32	27	4	1	2	3	33	0	58	2	0	6	1	.857	0		1	3.21
1998 Florida	NL	35	29	0	1	173	765	178	98	86	18	12	4	4	91	2	137	8	5	7	9	.438	0	0-1	0	4.47
1999 Florida	NL	59	10	0	8	76.1	362	84	53	51	16	2	7	4	60	11	62	5	2	5	7	.417	0	0-2	11	6.01
2000 Florida	NL	32	32	2	0	182	805	197	118	108	32	9	12	4	76	4	123	4	0	9	12	.429	2	0-0	0	5.34
2001 Florida	NL	16	9	0	3	62.2	274	61	33	33	7	2	1	2	31	2	46	0	0	2	4	.333	0	0-0	0	4.74
4 ML YEARS		142	80	2	12	494	2206	520	302	278	73	25	24	14	258	19	368	17	7	23	32	.418	2	0-3	11	5.06

Rey Sanchez

Bats: Right Throws: Right Pos: SS-148; PH/PR-1   Ht: 5'9" Wt: 175 Born: 10/5/67 Age: 34

Year Team	Lg	G	AB	H	2B	3B	HR	(Hm	Rd)	TB	R	RBI	TBB	IBB	SO	HBP	SH	SF	SB	CS	SB%	GDP	Avg	OBP	SLG
1991 Chicago	NL	13	23	6	0	0	0	(0	0)	6	1	2	4	0	3	0	0	0	0	0	—	0	.261	.370	.261
1992 Chicago	NL	74	255	64	14	3	1	(1	0)	87	24	19	10	1	17	3	5	2	2	1	.67	7	.251	.285	.341
1993 Chicago	NL	105	344	97	11	2	0	(0	0)	112	35	28	15	7	22	3	9	2	1	1	.50	8	.282	.316	.326

197

Year Team	Lg	G	AB	H	2B	3B	HR	(Hm	Rd)	TB	R	RBI	TBB	IBB	SO	HBP	SH	SF	SB	CS	SB%	GDP	Avg	OBP	SLG
1994 Chicago	NL	96	291	83	13	1	0	(0	0)	98	26	24	20	4	29	7	4	1	2	5	.29	9	.285	.345	.337
1995 Chicago	NL	114	428	119	22	2	3	(0	3)	154	57	27	14	2	48	1	8	2	6	4	.60	9	.278	.301	.360
1996 Chicago	NL	95	289	61	9	0	1	(1	0)	73	28	12	22	6	42	3	8	2	7	1	.88	6	.211	.272	.253
1997 ChC-NYY		135	343	94	21	0	2	(1	1)	121	35	27	16	2	47	1	9	1	4	6	.40	8	.274	.307	.353
1998 San Francisco	NL	109	316	90	14	2	2	(0	2)	114	44	30	16	0	47	4	1	2	0	0	—	11	.285	.325	.361
1999 Kansas City	AL	134	479	141	18	6	2	(1	1)	177	66	56	22	2	48	4	10	3	11	5	.69	14	.294	.329	.370
2000 Kansas City	AL	143	509	139	18	2	1	(1	0)	164	68	38	28	0	55	4	11	3	7	3	.70	17	.273	.314	.322
2001 KC-Atl		149	544	153	18	6	0	(0	0)	183	56	37	15	1	49	2	13	5	11	1	.92	20	.281	.300	.336
1997 Chicago	NL	97	205	51	9	0	1	(1	0)	63	14	12	11	2	26	0	4	0	4	2	.67	7	.249	.287	.307
New York	AL	38	138	43	12	0	1	(0	1)	58	21	15	5	0	21	1	5	1	0	4	.00	1	.312	.338	.420
2001 Kansas City	AL	100	390	118	14	5	0	(0	0)	142	46	28	11	0	34	2	9	4	9	1	.90	11	.303	.322	.364
Atlanta	NL	49	154	35	4	1	0	(0	0)	41	10	9	4	1	15	0	4	1	2	0	1.00	9	.227	.245	.266
11 ML YEARS		1167	3821	1047	158	24	12	(5	7)	1289	440	300	182	25	407	32	78	23	51	27	.65	109	.274	.311	.337

Jared Sandberg

Bats: Right **Throws:** Right **Pos:** 3B-38; 1B-1; PH/PR-1 **Ht:** 6'3" **Wt:** 185 **Born:** 3/2/78 **Age:** 24

Year Team	Lg	G	AB	H	2B	3B	HR	(Hm	Rd)	TB	R	RBI	TBB	IBB	SO	HBP	SH	SF	SB	CS	SB%	GDP	Avg	OBP	SLG
1996 Devil Rays	R	22	77	13	2	1	0	—	—	17	6	7	9	0	26	0	3	0	1	0	1.00	1	.169	.256	.221
1997 St. Pete	A+	2	3	1	0	0	0	—	—	1	1	2	2	0	2	0	0	0	0	0	—	0	.333	.600	.333
Princeton	R+	67	268	81	15	5	17	—	—	157	61	68	42	5	94	2	0	0	12	3	.80	4	.302	.401	.586
1998 Chston-SC	A	56	191	35	11	0	3	—	—	55	31	25	27	0	76	3	0	1	4	0	1.00	6	.183	.293	.288
Hudson Val	A-	73	271	78	15	2	12	—	—	133	49	54	42	1	76	5	0	4	13	3	.81	6	.288	.388	.491
1999 St. Pete	A+	136	504	139	24	1	22	—	—	231	73	96	51	0	133	9	1	5	8	2	.80	12	.276	.350	.458
2000 Orlando	AA	67	244	63	15	1	5	—	—	95	30	35	33	0	55	2	0	3	5	3	.63	6	.258	.348	.389
Durham	AAA	3	15	6	3	0	2	—	—	15	2	7	0	0	6	0	0	0	0	0	—	0	.400	.400	1.000
2001 Orlando	AA	8	28	8	2	0	1	—	—	13	4	4	6	0	10	0	0	0	0	0	—	1	.286	.412	.464
Durham	AAA	93	322	77	16	0	16	—	—	141	39	50	38	0	81	6	2	0	0	0	—	13	.239	.331	.438
2001 Tampa Bay	AL	39	136	28	7	0	1	(1	0)	38	13	15	10	0	45	1	2	0	1	0	1.00	0	.206	.265	.279

Anthony Sanders

Bats: Right **Throws:** Right **Pos:** LF-8; RF-1; PH/PR-1 **Ht:** 6'2" **Wt:** 200 **Born:** 3/2/74 **Age:** 28

Year Team	Lg	G	AB	H	2B	3B	HR	(Hm	Rd)	TB	R	RBI	TBB	IBB	SO	HBP	SH	SF	SB	CS	SB%	GDP	Avg	OBP	SLG
1993 Medcine Hat	R+	63	225	59	9	3	4	—	—	86	44	33	20	0	49	2	3	1	6	5	.55	2	.262	.327	.382
1994 St.Cathrnes	A-	74	258	66	17	3	6	—	—	107	36	45	27	0	53	1	4	2	8	7	.53	2	.256	.326	.415
1995 Hagerstown	A	133	512	119	28	1	8	—	—	173	72	48	52	0	103	1	4	9	26	14	.65	8	.232	.307	.338
1996 Dunedin	A+	102	417	108	25	0	17	—	—	184	75	50	34	0	93	6	0	0	16	12	.57	5	.259	.324	.441
Knoxville	AA	38	133	36	8	0	1	—	—	47	16	18	7	0	33	2	1	0	1	3	.25	0	.271	.317	.353
1997 Dunedin	A+	1	5	1	1	0	0	—	—	2	0	1	1	0	1	0	0	0	0	0	—	0	.200	.333	.400
Knoxville	AA	111	429	114	20	4	26	—	—	220	68	69	44	3	121	3	4	4	20	12	.63	9	.266	.335	.513
1998 Syracuse	AAA	60	209	40	9	2	4	—	—	65	23	19	20	1	65	3	3	1	5	2	.71	3	.191	.270	.311
Knoxville	AA	6	25	10	2	0	2	—	—	24	9	9	2	0	6	0	0	0	1	1	.00	0	.400	.444	.960
1999 Syracuse	AAA	124	496	121	22	5	18	—	—	207	71	59	46	0	111	3	8	5	18	10	.64	9	.244	.309	.417
2000 Tacoma	AAA	114	428	131	21	3	20	—	—	218	72	80	33	2	109	6	2	9	9	8	.53	9	.306	.357	.509
1999 Toronto	AL	3	7	2	1	0	0	(0	0)	3	1	2	0	0	2	0	0	0	0	0	—	1	.286	.286	.429
2000 Seattle	AL	1	1	1	0	0	0	(0	0)	1	1	0	0	0	0	0	0	0	0	0	—	0	1.000	1.000	1.000
2001 Seattle	AL	9	17	3	2	0	0	(0	0)	5	1	2	2	0	3	0	0	0	0	0	—	0	.176	.263	.294
3 ML YEARS		13	25	6	3	0	0	(0	0)	9	3	4	2	0	5	0	0	0	0	0	—	1	.240	.296	.360

Deion Sanders

Bats: L **Throws:** L **Pos:** PH/PR-14; LF-12; CF-4; DH-2; RF-1 **Ht:** 6'1" **Wt:** 195 **Born:** 8/9/67 **Age:** 34

Year Team	Lg	G	AB	H	2B	3B	HR	(Hm	Rd)	TB	R	RBI	TBB	IBB	SO	HBP	SH	SF	SB	CS	SB%	GDP	Avg	OBP	SLG
2001 Louisville *	AAA	19	74	34	4	5	1	—	—	51	12	9	2	0	4	3	2	0	6	3	.67	0	.459	.494	.689
Syracuse *	AAA	25	107	27	7	1	1	—	—	39	15	6	7	0	12	1	2	0	5	4	.56	2	.252	.304	.364
1989 New York	AL	14	47	11	2	0	2	(0	2)	19	7	7	3	1	8	0	0	0	1	0	1.00	0	.234	.280	.404
1990 New York	AL	57	133	21	2	2	3	(1	2)	36	24	9	13	0	27	1	1	1	8	2	.80	2	.158	.236	.271
1991 Atlanta	NL	54	110	21	1	2	4	(2	2)	38	16	13	12	0	23	0	0	0	11	3	.79	1	.191	.270	.345
1992 Atlanta	NL	97	303	92	6	14	8	(5	3)	150	54	28	18	0	52	2	1	1	26	9	.74	5	.304	.346	.495
1993 Atlanta	NL	95	272	75	18	6	6	(1	5)	123	42	28	16	3	42	3	1	2	19	7	.73	3	.276	.321	.452
1994 Atl-Cin	NL	92	375	106	17	4	4	(2	2)	143	58	28	32	1	63	3	2	2	38	16	.70	5	.283	.342	.381
1995 Cin-SF	NL	85	343	92	11	8	6	(3	3)	137	48	28	27	0	60	4	3	2	24	9	.73	1	.268	.327	.399
1997 Cincinnati	NL	115	465	127	13	7	5	(0	5)	169	53	23	34	2	67	6	2	2	56	13	.81	4	.273	.329	.363
2001 Cincinnati	NL	32	75	13	2	0	1	(1	0)	18	6	4	4	0	10	2	2	0	3	4	.43	2	.173	.235	.240
1994 Atlanta	NL	46	191	55	10	0	4	(2	2)	77	32	21	16	1	28	1	1	2	19	7	.73	4	.288	.343	.403
Cincinnati	NL	46	184	51	7	4	0	(0	0)	66	26	7	16	0	35	2	1	0	19	9	.68	1	.277	.342	.359
1995 Cincinnati	NL	33	129	31	2	3	1	(1	0)	42	19	10	9	0	18	2	2	2	16	3	.84	0	.240	.296	.326
San Francisco	NL	52	214	61	9	5	5	(2	3)	95	29	18	18	0	42	2	1	0	8	6	.57	1	.285	.346	.444
9 ML YEARS		641	2123	558	72	43	39	(15	24)	833	308	168	159	7	352	21	12	10	186	63	.75	23	.263	.319	.392

Reggie Sanders

Bats: Right **Throws:** Right **Pos:** RF-119; PH/PR-9 **Ht:** 6'1" **Wt:** 205 **Born:** 12/1/67 **Age:** 34

Year Team	Lg	G	AB	H	2B	3B	HR	(Hm	Rd)	TB	R	RBI	TBB	IBB	SO	HBP	SH	SF	SB	CS	SB%	GDP	Avg	OBP	SLG
2001 Tucson *	AAA	2	6	2	1	0	0	—	—	3	0	1	2	0	0	0	0	0	1	0	1.00	2	.333	.500	.500
1991 Cincinnati	NL	9	40	8	0	1	1	(0	1)	11	6	3	0	0	9	0	0	0	1	1	.50	1	.200	.200	.275
1992 Cincinnati	NL	116	385	104	26	6	12	(6	6)	178	62	36	48	2	98	4	0	1	16	7	.70	6	.270	.356	.462
1993 Cincinnati	NL	138	496	136	16	4	20	(8	12)	220	90	83	51	7	118	5	3	8	27	10	.73	10	.274	.343	.444
1994 Cincinnati	NL	107	400	105	20	8	17	(10	7)	192	66	62	41	1	114	2	1	3	21	9	.70	2	.263	.332	.480

Year Team	Lg	G	AB	H	2B	3B	HR	(Hm	Rd)	TB	R	RBI	TBB	IBB	SO	HBP	SH	SF	SB	CS	SB%	GDP	Avg	OBP	SLG
1995 Cincinnati	NL	133	484	148	36	6	28	(9	19)	280	91	99	69	4	122	8	0	6	36	12	.75	9	.306	.397	.579
1996 Cincinnati	NL	81	287	72	17	1	14	(7	7)	133	49	33	44	4	86	2	0	1	24	8	.75	8	.251	.353	.463
1997 Cincinnati	NL	86	312	79	19	2	19	(11	8)	159	52	56	42	3	93	3	1	0	13	7	.65	9	.253	.347	.510
1998 Cincinnati	NL	135	481	129	18	6	14	(7	7)	201	83	59	51	2	137	7	4	2	20	9	.69	10	.268	.346	.418
1999 San Diego	NL	133	478	136	24	7	26	(11	15)	252	92	72	65	1	108	6	0	1	36	13	.73	10	.285	.376	.527
2000 Atlanta	NL	103	340	79	23	1	11	(4	7)	137	43	37	32	2	78	2	3	0	21	4	.84	9	.232	.302	.403
2001 Arizona	NL	126	441	116	21	3	33	(19	14)	242	84	90	46	7	126	5	1	3	14	10	.58	2	.263	.337	.549
11 ML YEARS		1167	4144	1112	220	44	195	(92	103)	2005	718	630	489	33	1089	44	13	25	229	90	.72	76	.268	.350	.484

Johan Santana

Pitches: Left **Bats:** Left **Pos:** RP-11; SP-4 **Ht:** 6'0" **Wt:** 195 **Born:** 3/13/79 **Age:** 23

Year Team	Lg	G	GS	CG	GF	IP	BFP	H	R	ER	HR	SH	SF	HB	TBB	IBB	SO	WP	Bk	W	L	Pct.	ShO	Sv-Op	Hld	ERA
1997 Auburn	A-	1	1	0	0	4	19	1	1	1	0	0	1	0	6	0	5	0	0	0	0	—	0	0--	—	2.25
Astros	R	9	5	1	0	36.1	176	49	36	32	2	3	1	2	18	0	25	5	1	0	4	.000	0	0--	—	7.93
1998 Quad City	A	2	1	0	0	6.2	36	14	7	7	1	2	0	0	3	0	6	1	0	0	1	.000	0	0--	—	9.45
Auburn	A-	15	15	1	0	86.2	370	81	52	42	9	3	3	10	21	0	88	7	0	7	5	.583	1	0--	—	4.36
1999 Michigan	A	27	26	1	0	160.1	688	162	94	83	14	1	6	10	55	0	150	10	1	8	8	.500	0	0--	—	4.66
2000 Minnesota	AL	30	5	0	0	86	398	102	64	62	11	1	3	2	54	0	64	5	2	2	3	.400	0	0-0	0	6.49
2001 Minnesota	AL	15	4	0	5	43.2	195	50	25	23	6	2	3	3	16	0	28	3	0	1	0	1.000	0	0-0	0	4.74
2 ML YEARS		45	9	0	14	129.2	593	152	89	85	17	3	6	5	70	0	92	8	2	3	3	.500	0	0-0	0	5.90

Pedro Santana

Bats: Right **Throws:** Right **Pos:** 2B-1 **Ht:** 5'11" **Wt:** 160 **Born:** 9/21/76 **Age:** 25

Year Team	Lg	G	AB	H	2B	3B	HR	(Hm	Rd)	TB	R	RBI	TBB	IBB	SO	HBP	SH	SF	SB	CS	SB%	GDP	Avg	OBP	SLG
1996 Astros	R	56	207	56	6	5	1	—	—	75	40	20	21	1	44	4	2	0	33	4	.89	3	.271	.349	.362
1997 W Michigan	A	74	287	75	10	6	3	—	—	106	36	28	14	0	55	6	3	0	20	3	.87	8	.261	.309	.369
1998 W Michigan	A	118	438	115	21	7	4	—	—	162	79	45	28	0	93	9	4	5	64	7	.90	4	.263	.317	.370
1999 Jacksonville	AA	120	512	143	35	6	5	—	—	205	89	49	34	0	98	3	8	5	34	9	.79	8	.279	.325	.400
2000 Jacksonville	AA	112	448	126	20	4	6	—	—	172	61	53	38	1	83	3	4	4	40	8	.83	2	.281	.339	.384
2001 Toledo	AAA	115	432	98	10	3	5	—	—	129	45	30	27	0	97	2	7	3	36	8	.82	4	.227	.274	.299
2001 Detroit	AL	1	0	0	0	0	0	(0	0)	0	0	0	0	0	0	0	0	0	0	0	—	0	—	—	—

F.P. Santangelo

Bats: B **Throws:** R **Pos:** 2B-20; PH/PR-10; CF-5; 3B-3; DH-2; RF-1 **Ht:** 5'10" **Wt:** 165 **Born:** 10/24/67 **Age:** 34

Year Team	Lg	G	AB	H	2B	3B	HR	(Hm	Rd)	TB	R	RBI	TBB	IBB	SO	HBP	SH	SF	SB	CS	SB%	GDP	Avg	OBP	SLG
2001 Sacramento *	AAA	71	188	38	7	1	5			62	32	17	30	0	49	9	8	4	5	4	.56	4	.202	.333	.330
1995 Montreal	NL	35	98	29	5	1	1	(1	0)	39	11	9	12	0	9	2	1	0	1	1	.50	0	.296	.384	.398
1996 Montreal	NL	152	393	109	20	5	7	(5	2)	160	54	56	49	4	61	11	9	5	5	2	.71	6	.277	.369	.407
1997 Montreal	NL	130	350	87	19	5	5	(5	0)	131	56	31	50	1	73	25	12	3	8	5	.62	1	.249	.379	.374
1998 Montreal	NL	122	383	82	18	0	4	(2	2)	112	53	23	44	1	72	23	11	1	7	3	.70	5	.214	.330	.292
1999 San Francisco	NL	113	254	66	17	3	3	(2	1)	98	49	26	53	0	54	11	5	2	12	4	.75	1	.260	.406	.386
2000 Los Angeles	NL	81	142	28	4	0	1	(0	1)	35	19	9	21	0	33	6	6	2	3	2	.60	5	.197	.322	.246
2001 Oakland	AL	32	71	14	4	0	0	(0	0)	18	16	8	11	0	17	5	1	1	1	1	.50	1	.197	.341	.254
7 ML YEARS		665	1691	415	87	14	21	(15	6)	593	258	162	240	6	319	83	45	14	37	18	.67	19	.245	.364	.351

Benito Santiago

Bats: Right **Throws:** Right **Pos:** C-130; PH/PR-3; 1B-2 **Ht:** 6'1" **Wt:** 195 **Born:** 3/9/65 **Age:** 37

Year Team	Lg	G	AB	H	2B	3B	HR	(Hm	Rd)	TB	R	RBI	TBB	IBB	SO	HBP	SH	SF	SB	CS	SB%	GDP	Avg	OBP	SLG
1986 San Diego	NL	17	62	18	2	0	3	(2	1)	29	10	6	2	0	12	0	0	1	0	1	.00	0	.290	.308	.468
1987 San Diego	NL	146	546	164	33	2	18	(11	7)	255	64	79	16	2	112	5	1	4	21	12	.64	12	.300	.324	.467
1988 San Diego	NL	139	492	122	22	2	10	(3	7)	178	49	46	24	2	82	1	5	5	15	7	.68	18	.248	.282	.362
1989 San Diego	NL	129	462	109	16	3	16	(8	8)	179	50	62	26	6	89	1	3	2	11	6	.65	9	.236	.277	.387
1990 San Diego	NL	100	344	93	8	5	11	(5	6)	144	42	53	27	2	55	3	1	7	5	5	.50	4	.270	.323	.419
1991 San Diego	NL	152	580	155	22	3	17	(6	11)	234	60	87	23	5	114	4	0	7	8	10	.44	21	.267	.296	.403
1992 San Diego	NL	106	386	97	21	0	10	(8	2)	148	37	42	21	1	52	0	0	4	2	5	.29	14	.251	.287	.383
1993 Florida	NL	139	469	108	19	6	13	(6	7)	178	49	50	37	2	88	5	0	4	10	7	.59	9	.230	.291	.380
1994 Florida	NL	101	337	92	14	2	11	(4	7)	143	35	41	25	1	57	1	2	4	1	2	.33	11	.273	.322	.424
1995 Cincinnati	NL	81	266	76	20	0	11	(7	4)	129	40	44	24	1	48	4	0	2	2	2	.50	7	.286	.351	.485
1996 Philadelphia	NL	136	481	127	21	2	30	(8	22)	242	71	85	49	7	104	1	0	5	2	2	1.00	10	.264	.332	.503
1997 Toronto	AL	97	341	83	10	0	13	(7	6)	132	31	42	17	1	80	2	1	5	1	0	1.00	10	.243	.279	.387
1998 Toronto	AL	15	29	9	5	0	0	(0	0)	14	3	4	1	0	6	0	0	0	0	0	—	0	.310	.333	.483
1999 Chicago	NL	109	350	87	18	3	7	(2	5)	132	28	36	32	6	71	2	0	2	1	1	.50	12	.249	.313	.377
2000 Cincinnati	NL	89	252	66	11	1	8	(7	1)	103	22	45	19	8	45	1	0	5	2	2	.50	7	.262	.310	.409
2001 San Francisco	NL	133	477	125	25	4	6	(3	3)	176	39	45	23	0	78	2	7	6	5	4	.56	19	.262	.295	.369
16 ML YEARS		1689	5874	1531	267	33	184	(87	97)	2416	630	767	366	44	1093	32	20	60	86	64	.57	162	.261	.305	.411

Jose Santiago

Pitches: Right **Bats:** Right **Pos:** RP-73 **Ht:** 6'3" **Wt:** 215 **Born:** 11/5/74 **Age:** 27

Year Team	Lg	G	GS	CG	GF	IP	BFP	H	R	ER	HR	SH	SF	HB	TBB	IBB	SO	WP	Bk	W	L	Pct.	ShO	Sv-Op	Hld	ERA
1997 Kansas City	AL	4	0	0	3	4.2	24	7	2	1	0	0	0	1	2	1	1	0	0	0	0	—	0	0-0	0	1.93
1998 Kansas City	AL	2	0	0	2	2	9	4	2	2	0	0	0	0	0	0	2	0	0	0	0	—	0	0-0	0	9.00
1999 Kansas City	AL	34	0	0	15	47.1	203	46	23	18	7	1	3	2	14	2	15	2	1	3	4	.429	0	2-3	4	3.42
2000 Kansas City	AL	45	0	0	20	69	302	70	33	30	7	1	3	3	26	3	44	0	0	8	6	.571	0	2-8	5	3.91

Year Team	Lg	G	GS	CG	GF	IP	BFP	H	R	ER	HR	SH	SF	HB	TBB	IBB	SO	WP	Bk	W	L	Pct.	ShO	Sv-Op	Hld	ERA
2001 KC-Phi		73	0	0	11	91.2	397	106	47	47	5	4	5	3	22	2	43	1	0	4	6	.400	0	0-2	9	4.61
2001 Kansas City	AL	20	0	0	6	29.1	136	40	22	22	2	3	3	1	9	1	15	1	0	2	2	.500	0	0-1	0	6.75
Philadelphia	NL	53	0	0	5	62.1	261	66	25	25	3	1	2	2	13	1	28	0	0	2	4	.333	0	0-1	9	3.61
5 ML YEARS		158	0	0	51	214.2	935	233	107	98	19	6	11	9	64	8	105	3	1	15	16	.484	0	4-13	18	4.11

Angel Santos

Bats: Both **Throws:** Right **Pos:** 2B-6; PH/PR-3   **Ht:** 5'11" **Wt:** 185 **Born:** 8/14/79 **Age:** 22

								BATTING											BASERUNNING				PERCENTAGES		
Year Team	Lg	G	AB	H	2B	3B	HR	(Hm	Rd)	TB	R	RBI	TBB	IBB	SO	HBP	SH	SF	SB	CS	SB%	GDP	Avg	OBP	SLG
1997 Red Sox	R	17	60	11	1	0	0	—	—	12	8	7	7	0	11	0	1	2	8	3	.73	0	.183	.261	.200
1998 Red Sox	R	23	77	27	5	1	0	—	—	34	14	13	13	0	10	0	1	2	7	3	.70	1	.351	.435	.442
Lowell	A-	28	102	25	4	1	1	—	—	34	19	12	9	0	12	0	2	0	2	1	.67	4	.245	.306	.333
1999 Augusta	A	130	466	126	30	2	15	—	—	205	83	55	62	4	88	5	2	3	25	10	.71	12	.270	.360	.440
2000 Trenton	AA	80	275	71	17	2	3	—	—	101	32	32	32	0	60	2	1	4	18	8	.69	7	.258	.335	.367
2001 Trenton	AA	129	510	138	32	0	14	—	—	212	75	52	54	2	106	5	3	5	26	9	.74	5	.271	.343	.416
Pawtucket	AAA	4	15	3	1	0	0	—	—	4	1	2	1	0	4	0	0	1	1	0	1.00	0	.200	.235	.267
2001 Boston	AL	9	16	2	1	0	0	(0	0)	3	2	1	2	0	7	0	0	1	0	0	—	2	.125	.211	.188

Victor Santos

Pitches: Right **Bats:** Right **Pos:** RP-26; SP-7   **Ht:** 6'3" **Wt:** 175 **Born:** 10/2/76 **Age:** 25

				HOW MUCH HE PITCHED						WHAT HE GAVE UP										THE RESULTS					
Year Team	Lg	G	GS	CG	GF	IP	BFP	H	R	ER	HR	SH	SF	HB	TBB	IBB	SO	WP	Bk	W	L	Pct.	ShO	Sv-Op	Hld	ERA
1996 Tigers	R	9	9	0	0	50	199	44	12	11	1	3	1	7	13	0	39	3	0	3	2	.600	0	0--	—	1.98
Lakeland	A+	5	4	0	0	28.1	114	19	11	7	2	2	1	4	9	0	25	2	0	2	2	.500	0	0--	—	2.22
1997 Lakeland	A+	26	26	4	0	145	623	136	74	52	10	4	6	6	59	1	108	12	1	10	5	.667	2	0--	—	3.23
1998 Toledo	AAA	5	3	0	1	14.2	80	24	22	18	5	0	0	1	10	0	12	0	0	1	2	.333	0	0--	—	11.05
Lakeland	A+	16	15	0	1	100.1	408	88	38	28	9	5	3	3	24	1	74	3	0	5	2	.714	0	1--	—	2.51
Jacksnville	AA	6	6	0	0	36.2	159	40	20	17	2	1	3	1	15	1	37	1	0	4	2	.667	0	0--	—	4.17
1999 Jacksnville	AA	28	28	2	0	173	722	150	86	67	16	1	5	7	58	2	146	3	0	12	6	.667	1	0--	—	3.49
2000 Tigers	R	1	1	0	0	3	13	2	1	0	0	0	0	0	2	0	5	0	0	0	0	—	0	0--	—	0.00
Lakeland	A+	1	1	0	0	5	20	5	0	0	0	0	0	0	1	0	4	0	0	1	0	1.000	0	0--	—	0.00
Toledo	AAA	2	2	0	0	6.1	33	7	8	8	4	2	0	0	6	0	2	0	0	0	1	.000	0	0--	—	11.37
2001 Toledo	AAA	6	6	0	0	35.1	162	50	27	25	6	1	1	1	12	0	22	0	0	2	1	.667	0	0--	—	6.37
2001 Detroit	AL	33	7	0	6	76.1	335	62	33	28	9	1	3	3	49	4	52	0	0	2	2	.500	0	0-0	2	3.30

Kazuhiro Sasaki

Pitches: Right **Bats:** Right **Pos:** RP-69   **Ht:** 6'4" **Wt:** 209 **Born:** 2/22/68 **Age:** 34

				HOW MUCH HE PITCHED						WHAT HE GAVE UP										THE RESULTS					
Year Team	Lg	G	GS	CG	GF	IP	BFP	H	R	ER	HR	SH	SF	HB	TBB	IBB	SO	WP	Bk	W	L	Pct.	ShO	Sv-Op	Hld	ERA
2000 Seattle	AL	63	0	0	58	62.2	265	42	25	22	10	2	2	2	31	5	78	1	0	2	5	.286	0	37-40	0	3.16
2001 Seattle	AL	69	0	0	63	66.2	261	48	24	24	6	0	0	4	11	2	62	4	0	0	4	.000	0	45-52	0	3.24
2 ML YEARS		132	0	0	121	129.1	526	90	49	46	16	2	2	6	42	7	140	5	0	2	9	.182	0	82-92	0	3.20

Luis Saturria

Bats: R **Throws:** R **Pos:** PH/PR-7; LF-3; CF-3; RF-3   **Ht:** 6'2" **Wt:** 165 **Born:** 7/21/76 **Age:** 25

								BATTING											BASERUNNING				PERCENTAGES		
Year Team	Lg	G	AB	H	2B	3B	HR	(Hm	Rd)	TB	R	RBI	TBB	IBB	SO	HBP	SH	SF	SB	CS	SB%	GDP	Avg	OBP	SLG
1996 Johnson Cty	R+	57	227	58	7	1	5	—	—	82	43	40	24	0	61	7	1	0	12	1	.92	11	.256	.345	.361
1997 Peoria	A	122	445	122	19	5	11	—	—	184	81	51	44	3	95	3	3	3	23	10	.70	5	.274	.341	.413
1998 Pr William	A+	129	462	136	25	9	12	—	—	215	70	73	28	1	104	8	1	7	26	15	.63	12	.294	.341	.465
1999 Arkansas	AA	139	484	118	30	4	16	—	—	204	66	61	35	1	134	5	2	5	16	8	.67	12	.244	.299	.421
2000 Arkansas	AA	129	478	131	25	10	20	—	—	236	78	76	45	5	124	6	2	6	18	11	.62	7	.274	.340	.494
2001 New Haven	AA	8	29	8	3	0	0	—	—	11	5	4	3	2	7	0	0	1	0	0	—	1	.276	.333	.379
Memphis	AAA	119	413	93	16	5	13	—	—	158	63	49	31	0	115	6	3	4	6	8	.43	5	.225	.286	.383
2000 St. Louis	NL	12	5	0	0	0	0	(0	0)	0	1	0	1	0	3	0	0	0	0	0	—	0	.000	.167	.000
2001 St. Louis	NL	13	5	1	1	0	0	(0	0)	2	0	1	0	0	1	0	0	0	1	0	1.00	0	.200	.200	.400
2 ML YEARS		25	10	1	1	0	0	(0	0)	2	1	1	1	0	4	0	0	0	1	0	1.00	0	.100	.182	.200

Scott Sauerbeck

Pitches: Left **Bats:** Right **Pos:** RP-70   **Ht:** 6'3" **Wt:** 197 **Born:** 11/9/71 **Age:** 30

				HOW MUCH HE PITCHED						WHAT HE GAVE UP										THE RESULTS					
Year Team	Lg	G	GS	CG	GF	IP	BFP	H	R	ER	HR	SH	SF	HB	TBB	IBB	SO	WP	Bk	W	L	Pct.	ShO	Sv-Op	Hld	ERA
1999 Pittsburgh	NL	65	0	0	16	67.2	287	53	19	15	6	4	0	4	38	5	55	3	0	4	1	.800	0	2-5	10	2.00
2000 Pittsburgh	NL	75	0	0	13	75.2	349	76	36	34	4	3	3	1	61	8	83	9	2	5	4	.556	0	1-4	13	4.04
2001 Pittsburgh	NL	70	0	0	14	62.2	281	61	41	39	4	2	0	2	40	6	79	3	0	2	2	.500	0	2-4	19	5.60
3 ML YEARS		210	0	0	43	206	917	190	96	88	14	9	3	7	139	19	217	15	2	11	7	.611	0	5-13	42	3.84

Bob Scanlan

Pitches: Right **Bats:** Right **Pos:** RP-18   **Ht:** 6'7" **Wt:** 215 **Born:** 8/9/66 **Age:** 35

				HOW MUCH HE PITCHED						WHAT HE GAVE UP										THE RESULTS					
Year Team	Lg	G	GS	CG	GF	IP	BFP	H	R	ER	HR	SH	SF	HB	TBB	IBB	SO	WP	Bk	W	L	Pct.	ShO	Sv-Op	Hld	ERA
2001 Ottawa *	AAA	32	0	0	31	32.1	151	41	20	14	3	0	3	0	10	0	21	6	0	0	5	.000	0	23--	—	3.90
1991 Chicago	NL	40	13	0	16	111	482	114	60	48	5	8	6	3	40	3	44	5	1	7	8	.467	0	1-2	2	3.89
1992 Chicago	NL	69	0	0	41	87.1	360	76	32	28	4	4	2	1	30	6	42	6	4	3	6	.333	0	14-18	7	2.89
1993 Chicago	NL	70	0	0	13	75.1	323	79	41	38	6	2	6	3	28	7	44	0	2	4	5	.444	0	0-3	25	4.54
1994 Milwaukee	AL	30	12	0	9	103	441	117	53	47	11	1	2	4	28	2	65	3	1	2	6	.250	0	2-3	3	4.11

Year Team	Lg	G	GS	CG	GF	IP	BFP	H	R	ER	HR	SH	SF	HB	TBB	IBB	SO	WP	Bk	W	L	Pct.	ShO	Sv-Op	Hld	ERA
1995 Milwaukee	AL	17	14	0	1	83.1	389	101	66	61	9	0	6	7	44	3	29	3	0	4	7	.364	0	0-0	0	6.59
1996 Det-KC	AL	17	0	0	4	22.1	105	29	19	17	2	1	0	2	12	2	6	1	0	0	1	.000	0	0-1	5	6.85
1998 Houston	NL	27	0	0	9	26.1	118	24	12	9	4	3	3	1	13	0	9	5	0	0	0	.000	0	0-0	3	3.08
2000 Milwaukee	NL	2	0	0	1	1.2	13	6	6	5	0	1	1	1	0	0	1	0	0	0	0	—	0	0-0	0	27.00
2001 Montreal	NL	18	0	0	6	26.1	127	37	23	23	0	3	0	1	14	0	5	1	0	0	0	—	0	0-0	0	7.86
1996 Detroit	AL	8	0	0	2	11	57	16	15	13	1	1	0	1	9	1	3	1	0	0	0	—	0	0-0	0	10.64
Kansas City	AL	9	0	0	2	11.1	48	13	4	4	1	0	0	1	3	1	3	0	0	0	1	.000	0	0-1	5	3.18
9 ML YEARS		290	39	0	100	536.2	2358	583	312	276	41	23	26	23	209	23	245	24	8	20	34	.370	0	17-27	45	4.63

Curt Schilling

Pitches: Right Bats: Right Pos: SP-35   Ht: 6'4" Wt: 231 Born: 11/14/66 Age: 35

Year Team	Lg	G	GS	CG	GF	IP	BFP	H	R	ER	HR	SH	SF	HB	TBB	IBB	SO	WP	Bk	W	L	Pct.	ShO	Sv-Op	Hld	ERA
1988 Baltimore	AL	4	4	0	0	14.2	76	22	19	16	3	0	3	1	10	1	4	2	0	0	3	.000	0	0-0	0	9.82
1989 Baltimore	AL	5	1	0	0	8.2	38	10	6	6	2	0	0	0	3	0	6	1	0	0	1	.000	0	0-0	0	6.23
1990 Baltimore	AL	35	0	0	16	46	191	38	13	13	1	2	4	0	19	0	32	0	0	1	2	.333	0	3-9	5	2.54
1991 Houston	NL	56	0	0	34	75.2	336	79	35	32	2	5	1	0	39	7	71	4	1	3	5	.375	0	8-11	5	3.81
1992 Philadelphia	NL	42	26	10	10	226.1	895	165	67	59	11	7	8	1	59	4	147	4	0	14	11	.560	4	2-3	0	2.35
1993 Philadelphia	NL	34	34	7	0	235.1	982	234	114	105	23	9	7	4	57	6	186	9	3	16	7	.696	2	0-0	0	4.02
1994 Philadelphia	NL	13	13	1	0	82.1	360	87	42	41	10	6	1	3	28	3	58	3	1	2	8	.200	0	0-0	0	4.48
1995 Philadelphia	NL	17	17	1	0	116	473	96	52	46	12	5	2	3	26	2	114	0	1	7	5	.583	0	0-0	0	3.57
1996 Philadelphia	NL	26	26	8	0	183.1	732	149	69	65	16	6	4	3	50	5	182	5	0	9	10	.474	2	0-0	0	3.19
1997 Philadelphia	NL	35	35	7	0	254.1	1009	208	96	84	25	8	8	5	58	3	319	5	1	17	11	.607	2	0-0	0	2.97
1998 Philadelphia	NL	35	35	15	0	268.2	1089	236	101	97	23	14	7	6	61	3	300	12	0	15	14	.517	2	0-0	0	3.25
1999 Philadelphia	NL	24	24	8	0	180.1	735	159	74	71	25	11	3	5	44	0	152	4	0	15	6	.714	1	0-0	0	3.54
2000 Phi-Ari	NL	29	29	8	0	210.1	862	204	90	89	27	11	4	1	45	4	168	4	0	11	12	.478	2	0-0	0	3.81
2001 Arizona	NL	35	35	6	0	256.2	1021	237	86	85	37	8	5	1	39	0	293	4	0	22	6	.786	1	0-0	0	2.98
2000 Philadelphia	NL	16	16	4	0	112.2	474	110	49	49	17	5	1	1	32	4	96	4	0	6	6	.500	1	0-0	0	3.91
Arizona	NL	13	13	4	0	97.2	388	94	41	40	10	6	3	0	13	0	72	0	0	5	6	.455	1	0-0	0	3.69
14 ML YEARS		390	279	71	60	2158.2	8799	1924	864	809	217	92	57	33	538	38	2032	57	7	132	101	.567	16	13-23	10	3.37

Jason Schmidt

Pitches: Right Bats: Right Pos: SP-25   Ht: 6'5" Wt: 213 Born: 1/29/73 Age: 29

Year Team	Lg	G	GS	CG	GF	IP	BFP	H	R	ER	HR	SH	SF	HB	TBB	IBB	SO	WP	Bk	W	L	Pct.	ShO	Sv-Op	Hld	ERA
2001 Altoona *	AA	3	3	0	0	9.1	36	7	1	1	0	0	0	0	1	0	17	0	0	0	1	.000	0	0--	—	0.96
Nashville *	AAA	1	1	0	0	7	25	4	0	0	0	0	0	0	0	0	6	0	0	1	0	1.000	0	0--	—	0.00
1995 Atlanta	NL	9	2	0	1	25	119	27	17	16	2	2	4	1	18	3	19	1	0	2	2	.500	0	0-1	0	5.76
1996 Atl-Pit	NL	19	17	1	0	96.1	445	108	67	61	10	4	9	2	53	0	74	8	1	5	6	.455	0	0-0	0	5.70
1997 Pittsburgh	NL	32	32	2	0	187.2	825	193	106	96	16	10	3	9	76	2	136	8	1	10	9	.526	0	0-0	0	4.60
1998 Pittsburgh	NL	33	33	0	0	214.1	916	228	106	97	24	10	3	4	71	3	158	15	1	11	14	.440	0	0-0	0	4.07
1999 Pittsburgh	NL	33	33	0	0	212.2	937	219	110	99	24	7	7	3	85	4	148	6	4	13	11	.542	0	0-0	0	4.19
2000 Pittsburgh	NL	11	11	0	0	63.1	295	71	43	38	6	1	2	1	41	2	51	1	0	2	5	.286	0	0-0	0	5.40
2001 Pit-SF	NL	25	25	1	0	150.1	641	138	75	68	13	5	3	7	61	3	142	8	1	13	7	.650	0	0-0	0	4.07
1996 Atlanta	NL	13	11	0	0	58.2	274	69	48	44	8	3	6	0	32	0	48	5	1	3	4	.429	0	0-0	0	6.75
Pittsburgh	NL	6	6	1	0	37.2	171	39	19	17	2	1	3	2	21	0	26	3	0	2	2	.500	0	0-0	0	4.06
2001 Pittsburgh	NL	14	14	1	0	84	357	81	46	43	11	3	2	7	28	2	77	3	1	6	6	.500	0	0-0	0	4.61
San Francisco	NL	11	11	0	0	66.1	284	57	29	25	2	2	1	0	33	1	65	5	0	7	1	.875	0	0-0	0	3.39
7 ML YEARS		162	153	6	1	949.2	4178	984	524	475	95	39	31	27	405	17	728	47	7	56	54	.509	0	0-1	0	4.50

Brian Schneider

Bats: Left Throws: Right Pos: C-14; PH/PR-13   Ht: 6'1" Wt: 200 Born: 11/26/76 Age: 25

Year Team	Lg	G	AB	H	2B	3B	HR	Hm	Rd	TB	R	RBI	TBB	IBB	SO	HBP	SH	SF	SB	CS	SB%	GDP	Avg	OBP	SLG
1995 Expos	R	30	97	22	0	0	0	—	—	25	7	4	14	0	23	1	0	0		4	.33	1	.227	.330	.258
1996 Expos	R	52	164	44	5	2	0	—	—	53	26	23	24	3	15	3	2	0	2	3	.40	3	.268	.372	.323
Delmarva	A	5	9	3	0	0	0	—	—	3	0	1	1	0	1	1	0	0	0	0	—	1	.333	.455	.333
1997 Cape Fear	A	113	381	96	20	1	4	—	—	130	46	49	53	2	45	4	6	5	3	6	.33	9	.252	.345	.341
1998 Cape Fear	A	38	134	40	7	2	7	—	—	72	33	30	16	1	9	3	4	2	6	3	.67	3	.299	.381	.537
Jupiter	A+	82	302	82	12	1	3	—	—	105	32	30	22	1	38	1	0	2	4	4	.50	7	.272	.321	.348
1999 Harrisburg	AA	121	421	111	19	1	17	—	—	183	48	66	32	2	56	2	3	1	2	2	.50	6	.264	.318	.435
2000 Ottawa	AAA	67	238	59	22	3	4	—	—	99	22	31	16	1	42	0	2	9	1	0	1.00	5	.248	.285	.416
2001 Ottawa	AAA	97	338	93	27	1	6	—	—	140	33	43	27	4	55	4	0	0	1	0	1.00	1	.275	.336	.414
2000 Montreal	NL	45	115	27	6	0	0	(0	0)	33	6	11	7	2	24	0	0	1	0	1	.00	1	.235	.276	.287
2001 Montreal	NL	27	41	13	3	0	1	(1	0)	19	4	6	6	1	3	0	0	1	0	0	—	0	.317	.396	.463
2 ML YEARS		72	156	40	9	0	1	(1	0)	52	10	17	13	3	27	0	0	2	0	1	.00	1	.256	.310	.333

Scott Schoeneweis

Pitches: Left Bats: Left Pos: SP-32   Ht: 6'0" Wt: 185 Born: 10/2/73 Age: 28

Year Team	Lg	G	GS	CG	GF	IP	BFP	H	R	ER	HR	SH	SF	HB	TBB	IBB	SO	WP	Bk	W	L	Pct.	ShO	Sv-Op	Hld	ERA
1999 Anaheim	AL	31	0	0	6	39.1	175	47	27	24	4	0	1	0	14	1	22	1	0	1	1	.500	0	0-0	3	5.49
2000 Anaheim	AL	27	27	1	0	170	742	183	112	103	21	2	5	6	67	2	78	4	3	7	10	.412	1	0-0	0	5.45
2001 Anaheim	AL	32	32	1	0	205.1	910	227	122	116	21	3	8	14	77	2	104	4	1	10	11	.476	0	0-0	0	5.08
3 ML YEARS		90	59	2	6	414.2	1827	457	261	243	46	5	14	20	158	5	204	9	4	18	22	.450	1	0-0	3	5.27

Pete Schourek

Pitches: Left **Bats:** Left **Pos:** RP-33   **Ht:** 6'5" **Wt:** 220 **Born:** 5/10/69 **Age:** 33

Year Team	Lg	G	GS	CG	GF	IP	BFP	H	R	ER	HR	SH	SF	HB	TBB	IBB	SO	WP	Bk	W	L	Pct.	ShO	Sv-Op	Hld	ERA
2001 Yuma *	IND	6	0	0	3	7	36	8	7	7	0	0	1	1	6	0	10	0	0	0	0	—	0	0--		9.00
1991 New York	NL	35	8	1	7	86.1	385	82	49	41	7	5	4	2	43	4	67	1	0	5	4	.556	1	2-3	3	4.27
1992 New York	NL	22	21	0	0	136	578	137	60	55	9	4	4	2	44	6	60	4	2	6	8	.429	0	0-0	0	3.64
1993 New York	NL	41	18	0	6	128.1	586	168	90	85	13	3	8	3	45	7	72	1	2	5	12	.294	0	0-1	2	5.96
1994 Cincinnati	NL	22	10	0	3	81.1	354	90	39	37	11	6	2	3	29	4	69	0	0	7	2	.778	0	0-0	0	4.09
1995 Cincinnati	NL	29	29	2	0	190.1	754	158	72	68	17	4	4	8	45	3	160	1	1	18	7	.720	0	0-0	0	3.22
1996 Cincinnati	NL	12	12	0	0	67.1	304	79	48	45	7	3	4	3	24	1	54	3	0	4	5	.444	0	0-0	0	6.01
1997 Cincinnati	NL	18	17	0	0	84.2	371	78	59	51	18	4	1	4	38	0	59	2	0	5	8	.385	0	0-0	0	5.42
1998 Hou-Bos		25	23	0	0	124	537	127	64	61	17	5	7	5	50	1	95	7	0	8	9	.471	0	0-0	1	4.43
1999 Pittsburgh	NL	30	17	0	2	113	511	128	75	67	20	3	8	5	49	5	94	0	0	4	7	.364	0	0-0	0	5.34
2000 Boston	AL	21	21	0	0	107.1	464	116	67	61	17	4	1	3	38	2	63	5	0	3	10	.231	0	0-0	0	5.11
2001 Boston	AL	33	0	0	9	30.1	137	35	19	15	4	1	0	1	15	3	20	0	0	1	5	.167	0	0-1	5	4.45
1998 Houston	NL	15	15	0	0	80	354	82	43	40	10	5	4	4	36	0	59	5	0	7	6	.538	0	0-0	0	4.50
Boston	AL	10	8	0	0	44	183	45	21	21	7	0	3	1	14	1	36	2	0	1	3	.250	0	0-0	1	4.30
11 ML YEARS		288	176	3	27	1149	4981	1198	642	586	140	42	43	39	420	36	813	24	5	66	77	.462	1	2-5	11	4.59

Scott Seabol

Bats: Right **Throws:** Right **Pos:** DH-1; PH/PR-1   **Ht:** 6'4" **Wt:** 200 **Born:** 5/17/75 **Age:** 27

Year Team	Lg	G	AB	H	2B	3B	HR	(Hm	Rd)	TB	R	RBI	TBB	IBB	SO	HBP	SH	SF	SB	CS	SB%	GDP	Avg	OBP	SLG
1996 Oneonta	A-	43	142	30	9	1	3	—	—	50	16	10	15	0	30	6	2	0	2	3	.40	1	.211	.313	.352
1997 Greensboro	A	48	136	36	12	2	2	—	—	58	11	15	9	0	26	4	0	2	3	1	.75	1	.265	.325	.426
1998 Greensboro	A	71	210	60	11	0	7	—	—	92	24	33	13	2	40	3	1	2	2	2	.50	4	.286	.333	.438
1999 Greensboro	A	138	543	171	55	6	15	—	—	283	86	89	45	1	91	9	0	11	6	5	.55	9	.315	.370	.521
2000 Norwich	AA	132	493	146	45	2	20	—	—	255	82	78	42	1	108	4	1	2	2	4	.33	11	.296	.355	.517
2001 Columbus	AAA	78	282	75	19	1	10	—	—	126	32	42	14	1	56	4	2	2	3	4	.43	6	.266	.308	.447
Norwich	AA	31	128	32	7	0	4	—	—	51	16	19	5	0	30	3	0	2	1	1	.50	4	.250	.290	.398
2001 New York	AL	1	1	0	0	0	0	(0	0)	0	0	0	0	0	0	0	0	0	0	0	—	0	.000	.000	.000

Rudy Seanez

Pitches: Right **Bats:** Right **Pos:** RP-38   **Ht:** 5'11" **Wt:** 205 **Born:** 10/20/68 **Age:** 33

Year Team	Lg	G	GS	CG	GF	IP	BFP	H	R	ER	HR	SH	SF	HB	TBB	IBB	SO	WP	Bk	W	L	Pct.	ShO	Sv-Op	Hld	ERA
2001 Lk Elsinore *	A+	7	0	0	0	8.2	34	7	3	2	1	0	0	0	2	0	8	0	0	2	0	1.000	0	0--		2.08
1989 Cleveland	AL	5	0	0	2	5	20	1	2	2	0	0	2	0	4	1	7	1	1	0	0	—	0	0-0	0	3.60
1990 Cleveland	AL	24	0	0	12	27.1	127	22	17	17	2	0	1	1	25	1	24	5	0	2	1	.667	0	0-0	3	5.60
1991 Cleveland	AL	5	0	0	0	5	33	10	12	9	2	0	0	0	7	0	7	2	0	0	0	—	0	0-1	0	16.20
1993 San Diego	NL	3	0	0	3	3.1	20	8	6	5	1	1	0	0	2	0	1	0	0	0	0	—	0	0-0	0	13.50
1994 Los Angeles	NL	17	0	0	6	23.2	104	24	7	7	2	4	2	1	9	1	18	3	0	1	1	.500	0	0-1	1	2.66
1995 Los Angeles	NL	37	0	0	12	34.2	159	39	27	26	5	3	0	1	18	3	29	0	0	1	3	.250	0	3-4	6	6.75
1998 Atlanta	NL	34	0	0	8	36	148	25	13	11	2	1	2	1	16	0	50	2	0	4	1	.800	0	2-4	8	2.75
1999 Atlanta	NL	56	0	0	13	53.2	225	47	21	20	3	0	2	1	21	1	41	3	0	6	1	.857	0	3-8	18	3.35
2000 Atlanta	NL	23	0	0	8	21	89	15	11	10	3	1	0	1	9	1	20	0	0	2	4	.333	0	2-3	6	4.29
2001 SD-Atl	NL	38	0	0	8	36	150	23	12	11	4	0	1	1	19	0	41	4	0	0	2	.000	0	1-3	9	2.75
2001 San Diego	NL	26	0	0	8	24	102	15	8	7	3	0	1	1	15	0	24	1	0	0	2	.000	0	1-3	5	2.63
Atlanta	NL	12	0	0	0	12	48	8	4	4	1	0	0	0	4	0	17	3	0	0	0	—	0	0-0	4	3.00
10 ML YEARS		242	0	0	72	245.2	1075	214	128	118	24	10	10	7	130	8	238	20	1	16	13	.552	0	11-24	51	4.32

Bobby Seay

Pitches: Left **Bats:** Left **Pos:** RP-12   **Ht:** 6'2" **Wt:** 221 **Born:** 6/20/78 **Age:** 24

Year Team	Lg	G	GS	CG	GF	IP	BFP	H	R	ER	HR	SH	SF	HB	TBB	IBB	SO	WP	Bk	W	L	Pct.	ShO	Sv-Op	Hld	ERA
1997 Chston-SC	A	13	13	0	0	61.1	269	56	35	31	2	2	2	3	37	0	64	6	0	3	4	.429	0	0--	—	4.55
1998 Chston-SC	A	15	15	0	0	69	289	59	40	33	10	3	2	5	29	0	74	7	2	1	7	.125	0	0--	—	4.30
1999 St. Pete	A+	12	11	0	1	57	238	56	25	19	0	2	4	4	23	0	45	2	0	6	2	.250	0	0--	—	3.00
Orlando	AA	6	6	0	0	17	85	22	15	15	2	0	1	0	15	0	16	4	2	1	2	.333	0	0--	—	7.94
2000 Orlando	AA	24	24	0	0	132.1	568	132	64	57	13	4	5	8	53	1	106	4	0	8	7	.533	0	0--	—	3.88
2001 Orlando	AA	15	13	0	0	64.2	296	81	48	43	9	2	4	3	26	0	49	2	0	2	5	.286	0	0--	—	5.98
2001 Tampa Bay	AL	12	0	0	4	13	58	13	11	9	3	2	0	1	5	1	12	1	0	1	1	.500	0	0-0	0	6.23

Chris Seelbach

Pitches: Right **Bats:** Right **Pos:** RP-5   **Ht:** 6'4" **Wt:** 180 **Born:** 12/18/72 **Age:** 29

Year Team	Lg	G	GS	CG	GF	IP	BFP	H	R	ER	HR	SH	SF	HB	TBB	IBB	SO	WP	Bk	W	L	Pct.	ShO	Sv-Op	Hld	ERA
1991 Braves	R	4	4	0	0	15	65	13	7	7	3	1	0	0	6	0	19	3	1	0	1	.000	0	0--	—	4.20
1992 Macon	A	27	27	1	0	157.1	662	134	65	58	11	3	5	9	68	0	144	5	1	9	11	.450	0	0--	—	3.32
1993 Durham	A+	25	25	0	0	131.1	590	133	85	72	15	4	4	7	74	1	112	10	0	9	9	.500	0	0--	—	4.93
1994 Greenville	AA	15	15	2	0	92.2	363	64	26	24	3	5	4	4	38	2	79	5	0	4	6	.400	0	0--	—	2.33
Richmond	AAA	12	11	0	0	61.1	273	68	37	33	6	2	3	0	36	2	35	3	0	3	5	.375	0	0--	—	4.84
1995 Greenville	AA	9	9	1	0	60.1	249	58	15	11	2	5	3	1	30	0	65	3	1	6	0	1.000	1	0--	—	1.64
Richmond	AAA	14	14	1	0	73.1	314	64	39	38	7	0	3	2	39	0	65	3	0	4	6	.400	0	0--	—	4.66
1996 Charlotte	AAA	25	25	1	0	138.1	650	167	123	113	26	2	5	5	76	3	98	9	1	6	13	.316	0	0--	—	7.35
1997 Charlotte	AAA	16	6	0	1	50.1	241	58	36	35	7	3	3	1	34	2	50	3	0	5	0	1.000	0	0--	—	6.26
1998 Tacoma	AAA	6	6	0	4	11.2	53	13	9	8	5	0	0	0	2	0	10	0	0	1	0	1.000	0	0--	—	6.17
Orlando	AA	23	21	0	0	116	500	103	63	52	5	4	6	4	52	0	106	6	1	8	3	.727	0	0--	—	4.03
1999 Greenville	AA	8	6	1	0	39.1	170	31	18	17	5	1	1	2	19	2	47	2	0	3	2	.600	0	0--	—	3.89
Richmond	AAA	13	8	1	2	57.2	255	51	34	33	4	1	1	2	34	1	48	3	0	6	1	.857	0	0--	—	5.15

		HOW MUCH HE PITCHED						WHAT HE GAVE UP										THE RESULTS						
Year Team	Lg	G	GS	CG	GF	IP	BFP	H	R	ER	HR	SH	SF	HB	TBB	IBB	SO	WP	Bk	W	L	Pct.	ShO	Sv-Op	Hld	ERA
2000 Richmond	AAA	29	22	1	2	118.2	520	118	71	63	12	2	4	5	55	1	96	8	1	5	9	.357	1	2--	—	4.78
2001 Richmond	AAA	22	14	0	3	88.1	380	85	50	50	9	6	3	3	36	4	82	3	0	7	7	.500	0	1--	—	5.09
2000 Atlanta	NL	2	0	0	2	1.2	7	3	2	2	0	0	1	0	0	0	1	0	0	0	1	.000	0	0-0	0	10.80
2001 Atlanta	NL	5	0	0	1	8	38	9	7	7	3	0	0	0	5	1	8	1	0	0	0	—	0	0-0	0	7.88
2 ML YEARS		7	0	0	3	9.2	45	12	9	9	3	0	1	0	5	1	9	1	0	0	1	.000	0	0-0	0	8.38

Kevin Sefcik

Bats: Right **Throws:** Right **Pos:** PH/PR-1   **Ht:** 5'10" **Wt:** 182 **Born:** 2/10/71 **Age:** 31

		BATTING																BASERUNNING				PERCENTAGES		
Year Team	Lg	G	AB	H	2B	3B	HR	(Hm	Rd)	TB	R	RBI	TBB	IBB	SO	HBP	SH	SF	SB	CS	SB%	GDP	Avg	OBP	SLG
2001 Colo Sprngs *	AAA	49	199	62	14	0	2	—	—	82	37	22	24	0	26	3	2	4	5	6	.45	3	.312	.387	.412
Buffalo *	AAA	70	233	46	10	2	5	—	—	75	30	24	18	1	20	2	3	1	4	3	.57	9	.197	.260	.322
1995 Philadelphia	NL	5	4	0	0	0	0	(0	0)	0	1	0	0	0	2	0	0	0	0	0	—	0	.000	.000	.000
1996 Philadelphia	NL	44	116	33	5	3	0	(0	0)	44	10	9	9	3	16	2	1	2	3	0	1.00	4	.284	.341	.379
1997 Philadelphia	NL	61	119	32	3	0	2	(2	0)	41	11	6	4	0	9	1	7	0	1	2	.33	4	.269	.298	.345
1998 Philadelphia	NL	104	169	53	7	2	3	(2	1)	73	27	20	25	0	32	7	3	4	4	2	.67	3	.314	.421	.432
1999 Philadelphia	NL	111	209	58	15	3	1	(1	0)	82	28	11	29	0	24	1	3	0	9	4	.69	4	.278	.368	.392
2000 Philadelphia	NL	99	153	36	6	2	0	(0	0)	46	15	10	13	0	19	2	1	2	4	2	.67	4	.235	.300	.301
2001 Colorado	NL	1	1	0	0	0	0	(0	0)	0	0	0	0	0	0	0	0	0	0	0	—	0	.000	.000	.000
7 ML YEARS		425	771	212	36	10	6	(5	1)	286	92	56	80	3	102	13	15	5	21	10	.68	19	.275	.351	.371

David Segui

Bats: Both **Throws:** Left **Pos:** 1B-65; DH-16; PH/PR-1   **Ht:** 6'1" **Wt:** 202 **Born:** 7/19/66 **Age:** 35

		BATTING																BASERUNNING				PERCENTAGES		
Year Team	Lg	G	AB	H	2B	3B	HR	(Hm	Rd)	TB	R	RBI	TBB	IBB	SO	HBP	SH	SF	SB	CS	SB%	GDP	Avg	OBP	SLG
1990 Baltimore	AL	40	123	30	7	0	2	(1	1)	43	14	15	11	2	15	1	1	0	0	0	—	12	.244	.311	.350
1991 Baltimore	AL	86	212	59	7	0	2	(1	1)	72	15	22	12	2	19	0	3	1	1	1	.50	7	.278	.316	.340
1992 Baltimore	AL	115	189	44	9	0	1	(1	0)	56	21	17	20	3	23	0	2	0	1	0	1.00	4	.233	.306	.296
1993 Baltimore	AL	146	450	123	27	0	10	(6	4)	180	54	60	58	4	53	0	3	8	2	1	.67	18	.273	.351	.400
1994 New York	NL	92	336	81	17	1	10	(5	5)	130	46	43	33	6	43	1	1	3	0	0	—	6	.241	.308	.387
1995 NYM-Mon	NL	130	456	141	25	4	12	(6	6)	210	68	68	40	5	47	3	8	3	2	7	.22	10	.309	.367	.461
1996 Montreal	NL	115	416	119	30	1	11	(6	5)	184	69	58	60	4	54	0	0	1	4	4	.50	8	.286	.375	.442
1997 Montreal	NL	125	459	141	22	3	21	(10	11)	232	75	68	57	12	66	1	0	6	1	0	1.00	9	.307	.380	.505
1998 Seattle	AL	143	522	159	36	1	19	(10	9)	254	79	84	49	4	80	0	0	9	3	1	.75	12	.305	.359	.487
1999 Sea-Tor	AL	121	440	131	27	3	14	(5	9)	206	57	52	40	4	60	1	1	4	1	2	.33	10	.298	.355	.468
2000 Tex-Cle	AL	150	574	192	42	1	19	(8	11)	293	93	103	53	2	84	1	0	6	1	0	1.00	20	.334	.388	.510
2001 Baltimore	AL	82	292	88	18	1	10	(5	5)	138	48	46	49	4	61	4	0	2	1	1	.50	4	.301	.406	.473
1995 New York	NL	33	73	24	3	1	2	(2	0)	35	9	11	12	1	9	1	4	2	1	3	.25	2	.329	.420	.479
Montreal	NL	97	383	117	22	3	10	(4	6)	175	59	57	28	4	38	2	4	1	1	4	.20	8	.305	.355	.457
1999 Seattle	AL	90	345	101	22	3	9	(4	5)	156	43	39	32	4	43	1	1	3	1	2	.33	9	.293	.352	.452
Toronto	AL	31	95	30	5	0	5	(1	4)	50	14	13	8	0	17	0	0	1	0	0	—	1	.316	.365	.526
2000 Texas	AL	93	351	118	29	1	11	(4	7)	182	52	57	34	1	51	0	0	4	1	0	1.00	12	.336	.391	.519
Cleveland	AL	57	223	74	13	0	8	(4	4)	111	41	46	19	1	33	1	0	2	0	0	—	8	.332	.384	.498
12 ML YEARS		1345	4469	1308	267	15	131	(64	67)	1998	639	636	482	53	605	12	19	43	16	18	.47	120	.293	.360	.447

Fernando Seguignol

Bats: B **Throws:** R **Pos:** PH/PR-30; 1B-7; LF-7; RF-7   **Ht:** 6'5" **Wt:** 230 **Born:** 1/19/75 **Age:** 27

		BATTING																BASERUNNING				PERCENTAGES		
Year Team	Lg	G	AB	H	2B	3B	HR	(Hm	Rd)	TB	R	RBI	TBB	IBB	SO	HBP	SH	SF	SB	CS	SB%	GDP	Avg	OBP	SLG
2001 Ottawa *	AAA	60	242	75	12	0	14	—	—	129	36	45	15	2	49	5	0	0	0	1	.00	6	.310	.363	.533
1998 Montreal	NL	16	42	11	4	0	2	(2	0)	21	6	3	3	0	15	0	0	1	0	0	—	1	.262	.304	.500
1999 Montreal	NL	35	105	27	9	0	5	(3	2)	51	14	10	5	1	33	7	0	2	0	0	—	1	.257	.328	.486
2000 Montreal	NL	76	162	45	8	0	10	(1	9)	83	22	22	9	0	46	3	0	1	0	1	.00	5	.278	.326	.512
2001 Montreal	NL	46	50	7	2	0	0	(0	0)	9	0	5	2	1	17	1	0	1	0	0	—	4	.140	.185	.180
4 ML YEARS		173	359	90	23	0	17	(6	11)	164	42	40	19	2	111	11	0	5	0	1	.00	11	.251	.305	.457

Bill Selby

Bats: L **Throws:** R **Pos:** 2B-21; PH/PR-9; 3B-8; 1B-2   **Ht:** 5'10" **Wt:** 195 **Born:** 6/11/70 **Age:** 32

		BATTING																BASERUNNING				PERCENTAGES		
Year Team	Lg	G	AB	H	2B	3B	HR	(Hm	Rd)	TB	R	RBI	TBB	IBB	SO	HBP	SH	SF	SB	CS	SB%	GDP	Avg	OBP	SLG
2001 Louisville *	AAA	88	330	85	19	1	14	—	—	148	47	56	25	3	47	2	1	4	1	0	1.00	6	.258	.310	.448
1996 Boston	AL	40	95	26	4	0	3	(0	3)	39	12	6	9	1	11	0	1	0	1	1	.50	3	.274	.337	.411
2000 Cleveland	AL	30	46	11	1	0	0	(0	0)	12	8	4	1	0	9	1	0	0	0	0	—	1	.239	.271	.261
2001 Cincinnati	NL	36	92	21	7	1	2	(1	1)	36	7	12	5	1	13	1	1	1	0	0	—	1	.228	.273	.391
3 ML YEARS		106	233	58	12	1	5	(1	4)	87	27	22	15	2	33	2	2	1	1	1	.50	5	.249	.299	.373

Aaron Sele

Pitches: Right **Bats:** Right **Pos:** SP-33; RP-1   **Ht:** 6'5" **Wt:** 215 **Born:** 6/25/70 **Age:** 32

		HOW MUCH HE PITCHED						WHAT HE GAVE UP												THE RESULTS						
Year Team	Lg	G	GS	CG	GF	IP	BFP	H	R	ER	HR	SH	SF	HB	TBB	IBB	SO	WP	Bk	W	L	Pct.	ShO	Sv-Op	Hld	ERA
1993 Boston	AL	18	18	0	0	111.2	484	100	42	34	5	2	5	7	48	2	93	5	0	7	2	.778	0	0-0	0	2.74
1994 Boston	AL	22	22	2	0	143.1	615	140	68	61	14	7	5	9	60	2	105	4	0	8	7	.533	0	0-0	0	3.83
1995 Boston	AL	6	6	0	0	32.1	146	32	14	11	3	1	1	3	14	0	21	3	0	3	1	.750	0	0-0	0	3.06
1996 Boston	AL	29	29	1	0	157.1	722	192	110	93	14	6	7	8	67	2	137	2	0	7	11	.389	0	0-0	0	5.32
1997 Boston	AL	33	33	1	0	177.1	810	196	115	106	25	5	7	15	80	4	122	7	0	13	12	.520	0	0-0	0	5.38
1998 Texas	AL	33	33	3	0	212.2	954	239	116	100	14	5	7	13	84	6	167	4	0	19	11	.633	2	0-0	0	4.23
1999 Texas	AL	33	33	2	0	205	920	244	115	109	21	1	3	12	70	3	186	4	0	18	9	.667	2	0-0	0	4.79
2000 Seattle	AL	34	34	2	0	211.2	908	221	110	106	17	5	8	5	74	7	137	5	0	17	10	.630	2	0-0	0	4.51

		HOW MUCH HE PITCHED					WHAT HE GAVE UP										THE RESULTS					
Year Team	Lg	G	GS	CG	GF	IP	BFP	H	R	ER	HR	SH	SF	HB	TBB	IBB	SO	WP	Bk	W	L	Pct.	ShO	Sv-Op	Hld	ERA
2001 Seattle	AL	34	33	2	0	215	899	216	93	86	25	5	9	7	51	2	114	1	0	15	5	.750	1	0-0	0	3.60
9 ML YEARS		242	241	13	0	1466.1	6458	1580	783	706	137	34	52	79	548	28	1082	35	0	107	68	.611	7	0-0	0	4.33

Wascar Serrano

Pitches: Right **Bats:** Right **Pos:** RP-15; SP-5 **Ht:** 6'2" **Wt:** 178 **Born:** 6/2/78 **Age:** 24

		HOW MUCH HE PITCHED						WHAT HE GAVE UP										THE RESULTS						
Year Team	Lg	G	GS	CG	GF	IP	BFP	H	R	ER	HR	SH	SF	HB	TBB	IBB	SO	WP	Bk	W	L	Pct.	ShO	Sv-Op	Hld	ERA
1997 Idaho Falls	R+	2	2	0	0	8.1	43	13	12	11	2	0	0	1	4	0	13	0	0	0	1	.000	0	0--	—	11.88
Padres	R	12	11	0	1	70.2	301	60	43	25	4	0	4	4	22	0	75	8	3	6	3	.667	0	1--	—	3.18
Clinton	A	1	1	1	0	6	24	6	5	4	0	0	0	0	2	1	2	1	0	1	0	1.000	0	0--	—	6.00
1998 Clinton	A	26	26	0	0	156.2	663	150	74	56	6	6	4	6	54	1	143	7	0	9	7	.563	0	0--	—	3.22
1999 Rancho Cuc	A+	21	21	1	0	132.1	537	110	58	49	10	1	5	1	43	0	129	8	5	9	8	.529	1	0--	—	3.33
Mobile	AA	7	7	0	0	42.1	196	48	27	26	5	1	3	6	17	1	29	1	1	2	3	.400	0	0--	—	5.53
2000 Las Vegas	AAA	4	4	0	0	13.1	75	24	23	21	5	0	0	2	10	0	19	4	1	0	1	.000	0	0--	—	14.18
Mobile	AA	20	20	1	0	112.1	471	93	42	35	11	6	1	4	42	0	112	9	0	9	4	.692	0	0--	—	2.80
2001 Portland	AAA	27	13	0	2	93.1	403	98	50	47	10	4	6	5	35	0	73	4	0	6	5	.545	0	0--	—	4.53
2001 San Diego	NL	20	5	0	8	46.2	222	60	37	34	7	5	2	2	21	1	39	6	1	3	3	.500	0	0-0	1	6.56

Scott Servais

Bats: Right **Throws:** Right **Pos:** C-9; PH/PR-2 **Ht:** 6'2" **Wt:** 210 **Born:** 6/4/67 **Age:** 35

		BATTING																BASERUNNING				PERCENTAGES		
Year Team	Lg	G	AB	H	2B	3B	HR	(Hm	Rd)	TB	R	RBI	TBB	IBB	SO	HBP	SH	SF	SB	CS	SB%	GDP	Avg	OBP	SLG
2001 New Orleans *	AAA	44	148	50	10	1	6	—	—	80	22	33	12	1	21	3	1	3	0	0	—	1	.338	.392	.541
1991 Houston	NL	16	37	6	3	0	0	(0	0)	9	0	6	4	0	8	0	1	0	0	0	—	0	.162	.244	.243
1992 Houston	NL	77	205	49	9	0	0	(0	0)	58	12	15	11	2	25	5	6	0	0	0	—	7	.239	.294	.283
1993 Houston	NL	85	258	63	11	0	11	(5	6)	107	24	32	22	2	45	5	3	3	0	0	—	6	.244	.313	.415
1994 Houston	NL	78	251	49	15	1	9	(3	6)	93	27	41	10	0	44	4	7	3	0	0	—	6	.195	.235	.371
1995 Hou-ChC	NL	80	264	70	22	0	13	(8	5)	131	38	47	32	8	52	3	2	3	2	2	.50	9	.265	.348	.496
1996 Chicago	NL	129	445	118	20	0	11	(6	5)	171	42	63	30	1	75	14	3	7	0	2	.00	18	.265	.327	.384
1997 Chicago	NL	122	385	100	21	0	6	(4	2)	139	36	45	24	7	56	6	7	3	0	1	.00	7	.260	.311	.361
1998 Chicago	NL	113	325	72	15	1	7	(5	2)	110	35	36	26	6	51	5	3	1	1	0	1.00	12	.222	.289	.338
1999 San Francisco	NL	69	198	54	10	0	5	(0	5)	79	21	21	13	2	31	3	3	0	0	0	—	9	.273	.327	.399
2000 Col-SF	NL	40	109	24	4	0	1	(1	0)	31	7	13	9	3	17	1	0	1	0	1	.00	1	.220	.283	.284
2001 San Francisco	NL	11	16	6	0	0	0	(0	0)	6	1	0	2	0	3	0	0	0	0	0	—	0	.375	.444	.375
1995 Houston	NL	28	89	20	10	0	1	(1	0)	33	7	12	9	2	15	1	1	1	0	1	.00	4	.225	.300	.371
Chicago	NL	52	175	50	12	0	12	(7	5)	98	31	35	23	6	37	2	1	2	2	1	.67	5	.286	.371	.560
2000 Colorado	NL	33	101	22	4	0	1	(1	0)	29	6	13	7	2	16	1	0	1	0	1	.00	1	.218	.273	.287
San Francisco	NL	7	8	2	0	0	0	(0	0)	2	1	0	2	1	1	0	0	0	0	0	—	0	.250	.400	.250
11 ML YEARS		820	2493	611	130	2	63	(32	31)	934	243	319	183	31	407	46	35	21	3	6	.33	73	.245	.306	.375

Richie Sexson

Bats: Right **Throws:** Right **Pos:** 1B-158 **Ht:** 6'7" **Wt:** 225 **Born:** 12/29/74 **Age:** 27

		BATTING																BASERUNNING			PERCENTAGES		
Year Team	Lg	G	AB	H	2B	3B	HR	(Hm	Rd)	TB	R	RBI	TBB	IBB	SO	HBP	SH	SF	SB	CS	SB%	Avg	OBP	SLG
1997 Cleveland	AL	5	11	3	0	0	0	(0 | 0)	3	1	0	0	0	2	0	0	0	0	0	—	2	.273	.273	.273
1998 Cleveland	AL	49	174	54	14	1	11	(9 | 2)	103	28	35	6	0	42	3	0	0	1	1	.50	3	.310	.344	.592
1999 Cleveland	AL	134	479	122	17	7	31	(18 | 13)	246	72	116	34	0	117	4	0	8	3	3	.50	19	.255	.305	.514
2000 Cle-Mil		148	537	146	30	1	30	(15 | 15)	268	89	91	59	2	159	7	0	4	2	0	1.00	11	.272	.349	.499
2001 Milwaukee	NL	158	598	162	24	0	45	(28 | 17)	327	94	125	60	5	178	6	0	3	2	4	.33	20	.271	.342	.547
2000 Cleveland	AL	91	324	83	16	1	16	(8 | 8)	149	45	44	25	0	96	4	0	3	1	0	1.00	8	.256	.315	.460
Milwaukee	NL	57	213	63	14	0	14	(7 | 7)	119	44	47	34	2	63	3	0	1	1	0	1.00	3	.296	.398	.559
5 ML YEARS		494	1799	487	85	12	117	(70 | 47)	947	284	367	159	7	498	20	0	15	8	8	.50	55	.271	.334	.526

Jeff Shaw

Pitches: Right **Bats:** Right **Pos:** RP-77 **Ht:** 6'2" **Wt:** 200 **Born:** 7/7/66 **Age:** 35

		HOW MUCH HE PITCHED						WHAT HE GAVE UP										THE RESULTS						
Year Team	Lg	G	GS	CG	GF	IP	BFP	H	R	ER	HR	SH	SF	HB	TBB	IBB	SO	WP	Bk	W	L	Pct.	ShO	Sv-Op	Hld	ERA
1990 Cleveland	AL	12	9	0	0	48.2	229	73	38	36	11	1	3	0	20	0	25	3	0	3	4	.429	0	0-0	0	6.66
1991 Cleveland	AL	29	1	0	9	72.1	311	72	34	27	6	1	4	4	27	5	31	6	0	0	5	.000	0	1-4	0	3.36
1992 Cleveland	AL	2	1	0	1	7.2	33	7	7	7	2	2	0	0	4	0	3	0	0	0	1	.000	0	0-0	0	8.22
1993 Montreal	NL	55	8	0	13	95.2	404	91	47	44	12	5	2	7	32	2	50	2	0	2	7	.222	0	0-1	4	4.14
1994 Montreal	NL	46	0	0	15	67.1	287	67	32	29	8	2	4	2	15	2	47	5	0	5	2	.714	0	1-2	10	3.88
1995 Mon-CWS		59	0	0	18	72	309	70	42	39	6	7	1	4	27	4	51	0	0	1	6	.143	0	3-5	6	4.88
1996 Cincinnati	NL	78	0	0	24	104.2	434	99	34	29	8	5	5	2	29	11	69	0	0	8	6	.571	0	4-11	22	2.49
1997 Cincinnati	NL	78	0	0	62	94.2	367	79	26	25	7	3	3	1	12	3	74	1	0	4	2	.667	0	42-49	5	2.38
1998 Cin-LA	NL	73	0	0	69	85	339	75	22	20	8	5	2	1	19	5	55	0	0	3	8	.273	0	48-57	0	2.12
1999 Los Angeles	NL	64	0	0	56	68	284	64	25	21	6	1	2	1	15	1	43	1	0	2	4	.333	0	34-39	0	2.78
2000 Los Angeles	NL	60	0	0	51	57.1	249	61	29	27	7	2	0	1	16	3	39	0	0	3	4	.429	0	27-34	0	4.24
2001 Los Angeles	NL	77	0	0	66	74.2	303	63	32	30	10	3	2	2	18	8	58	0	1	3	5	.375	0	43-52	0	3.62
1995 Montreal	NL	50	0	0	17	62.1	268	58	35	32	4	6	1	3	26	4	45	0	0	1	6	.143	0	3-5	5	4.62
Chicago	AL	9	0	0	1	9.2	41	12	7	7	2	1	0	1	1	0	6	0	0	0	0	—	0	0-0	1	6.52
1998 Cincinnati	NL	39	0	0	35	49.2	192	40	11	10	2	4	2	1	12	4	29	0	0	2	4	.333	0	23-28	0	1.81
Los Angeles	NL	34	0	0	34	35.1	147	35	11	10	6	1	0	0	7	1	26	0	0	1	4	.200	0	25-29	0	2.55
12 ML YEARS		633	19	0	384	848	3549	821	368	334	91	37	28	25	234	44	545	18	1	34	54	.386	0	203-254	47	3.54

Andy Sheets

Bats: Right **Throws:** Right **Pos:** SS-49; PH/PR-1 **Ht:** 6'2" **Wt:** 180 **Born:** 11/19/71 **Age:** 30

				BATTING														BASERUNNING				PERCENTAGES		
Year Team	Lg	G	AB	H	2B	3B	HR	(Hm | Rd)	TB	R	RBI	TBB	IBB	SO	HBP	SH	SF	SB	CS	SB%	GDP	Avg	OBP	SLG
2001 Durham *	AAA	66	225	63	14	2	4	—	—	93	28	22	25	0	45	2	2	1	8	3	.73	6	.280	.356	.413
1996 Seattle	AL	47	110	21	8	0	0	(0 | 0)	29	18	9	10	0	41	1	2	1	2	0	1.00	2	.191	.262	.264
1997 Seattle	AL	32	89	22	3	0	4	(2 | 2)	37	18	9	7	0	34	0	5	1	2	0	1.00	1	.247	.299	.416
1998 San Diego	NL	88	194	47	5	3	7	(2 | 5)	79	31	29	21	3	62	1	2	1	7	2	.78	4	.242	.318	.407
1999 Anaheim	AL	87	244	48	10	0	3	(3 | 0)	67	22	29	14	0	59	0	6	5	1	2	.33	6	.197	.236	.275
2000 Boston	AL	12	21	2	0	0	0	(0 | 0)	2	1	1	0	0	3	0	0	0	0	0	—	1	.095	.095	.095
2001 Tampa Bay	AL	49	153	30	8	0	1	(1 | 0)	41	10	14	12	0	35	0	7	2	2	0	1.00		.196	.251	.268
6 ML YEARS		315	811	170	34	3	15	(8 | 7)	255	100	91	64	3	234	2	22	10	14	4	.78	14	.210	.266	.314

Ben Sheets

Pitches: Right **Bats:** Right **Pos:** SP-25 **Ht:** 6'1" **Wt:** 195 **Born:** 7/18/78 **Age:** 23

		HOW MUCH HE PITCHED						WHAT HE GAVE UP											THE RESULTS						
Year Team	Lg	G	GS	CG	GF	IP	BFP	H	R	ER	HR	SH	SF	HB	TBB	IBB	SO	WP	Bk	W	L	Pct.	ShO	Sv-Op	Hld	ERA
1999 Ogden	R+	2	2	0	0	8	33	8	5	5	2	0	0	1	2	0	12	0	0	0	1	.000	0	0--	—	5.63
Stockton	A+	5	5	0	0	27.2	115	23	11	11	1	0	1	1	14	0	28	1	0	1	0	1.000	0	0--	—	3.58
2000 Huntsville	AA	13	13	0	0	72	288	55	17	15	4	1	4	2	25	0	60	2	0	5	3	.625	0	0--	—	1.88
Indianapolis	AAA	14	13	1	0	81.2	346	77	31	26	4	1	3	4	31	0	59	3	1	3	5	.375	0	0--	—	2.87
2001 Indianapolis	AAA	2	2	0	0	10.2	49	14	5	4	0	2	0	0	3	0	6	0	0	1	1	.500	0	0--	—	3.38
2001 Milwaukee	NL	25	25	1	0	151.1	653	166	89	80	23	8	5	5	48	6	94	3	0	11	10	.524	1	0-0	0	4.76

Gary Sheffield

Bats: Right **Throws:** Right **Pos:** LF-141; DH-2; RF-2 **Ht:** 5'11" **Wt:** 205 **Born:** 11/18/68 **Age:** 33

				BATTING														BASERUNNING				PERCENTAGES		
Year Team	Lg	G	AB	H	2B	3B	HR	(Hm	Rd)	TB	R	RBI	TBB	IBB	SO	HBP	SH	SF	SB	CS	SB%	GDP	Avg	OBP	SLG
1988 Milwaukee	AL	24	80	19	1	0	4	(1	3)	32	12	12	7	0	7	0	1	1	3	1	.75	5	.238	.295	.400
1989 Milwaukee	AL	95	368	91	18	0	5	(2	3)	124	34	32	27	0	33	4	3	3	10	6	.63	4	.247	.303	.337
1990 Milwaukee	AL	125	487	143	30	1	10	(3	7)	205	67	67	44	1	41	3	4	9	25	10	.71	11	.294	.350	.421
1991 Milwaukee	AL	50	175	34	12	2	2	(2	0)	56	25	22	19	1	15	3	1	5	5	5	.50	3	.194	.277	.320
1992 San Diego	NL	146	557	184	34	3	33	(23	10)	323	87	100	48	5	40	6	0	7	5	6	.45	19	.330	.385	.580
1993 SD-Fla	NL	140	494	145	20	5	20	(10	10)	235	67	73	47	6	64	9	0	7	17	5	.77	11	.294	.361	.476
1994 Florida	NL	87	322	89	16	1	27	(15	12)	188	61	78	51	11	50	6	0	5	12	6	.67	10	.276	.380	.584
1995 Florida	NL	63	213	69	8	0	16	(4	12)	125	46	46	55	8	45	4	0	2	19	4	.83	3	.324	.467	.587
1996 Florida	NL	161	519	163	33	1	42	(19	23)	324	118	120	142	19	66	10	0	6	16	9	.64	16	.314	.465	.624
1997 Florida	NL	135	444	111	22	1	21	(13	8)	198	86	71	121	11	79	15	0	2	11	7	.61	7	.250	.424	.446
1998 Fla-LA	NL	130	437	132	27	2	22	(11	11)	229	73	85	95	12	46	8	0	9	22	7	.76	7	.302	.428	.524
1999 Los Angeles	NL	152	549	165	20	0	34	(15	19)	287	103	101	101	4	64	4	0	6	11	5	.69	10	.301	.407	.523
2000 Los Angeles	NL	141	501	163	24	3	43	(23	20)	322	105	109	101	7	71	4	0	6	4	4	.50	12	.325	.438	.643
2001 Los Angeles	NL	143	515	160	28	2	36	(16	20)	300	98	100	94	13	67	4	0	5	10	4	.71	12	.311	.417	.583
1993 San Diego	NL	68	258	76	12	2	10	(6	4)	122	34	36	18	0	30	3	0	3	5	1	.83	9	.295	.344	.473
Florida	NL	72	236	69	8	3	10	(4	6)	113	33	37	29	6	34	6	0	4	12	4	.75	2	.292	.378	.479
1998 Florida	NL	40	136	37	11	1	6	(6	0)	68	21	28	26	1	16	2	0	2	4	2	.67	3	.272	.392	.500
Los Angeles	NL	90	301	95	16	1	16	(5	11)	161	52	57	69	11	30	6	0	7	18	5	.78	4	.316	.444	.535
14 ML YEARS		1592	5661	1668	293	21	315	(157	158)	2948	982	1016	952	98	688	80	9	76	170	81	.68	131	.295	.399	.521

Scott Sheldon

Bats: R **Throws:** R **Pos:** 3B-38; SS-16; PH/PR-9; LF-2; C-1; RF-1 **Ht:** 6'3" **Wt:** 215 **Born:** 11/20/68 **Age:** 33

				BATTING														BASERUNNING				PERCENTAGES		
Year Team	Lg	G	AB	H	2B	3B	HR	(Hm	Rd)	TB	R	RBI	TBB	IBB	SO	HBP	SH	SF	SB	CS	SB%	GDP	Avg	OBP	SLG
1997 Oakland	AL	13	24	6	0	0	1	(1	0)	9	2	2	1	0	6	1	1	0	0	0	—	0	.250	.308	.375
1998 Texas	AL	7	16	2	0	0	0	(0	0)	2	0	1	1	0	6	0	0	0	0	0	—	1	.125	.176	.125
1999 Texas	AL	2	1	0	0	0	0	(0	0)	0	0	0	0	0	0	0	0	0	0	0	—	0	.000	.000	.000
2000 Texas	AL	58	124	35	11	0	4	(1	3)	58	21	19	10	0	37	1	1	2	0	0	—	2	.282	.336	.468
2001 Texas	AL	61	120	24	5	0	3	(1	2)	38	11	11	3	0	35	0	2	2	1	1	.50	2	.200	.216	.317
5 ML YEARS		141	285	67	16	0	8	(3	5)	107	34	33	15	0	84	2	4	4	1	1	.50	5	.235	.275	.375

Scot Shields

Pitches: Right **Bats:** Right **Pos:** RP-8 **Ht:** 6'1" **Wt:** 175 **Born:** 7/22/75 **Age:** 26

		HOW MUCH HE PITCHED						WHAT HE GAVE UP											THE RESULTS						
Year Team	Lg	G	GS	CG	GF	IP	BFP	H	R	ER	HR	SH	SF	HB	TBB	IBB	SO	WP	Bk	W	L	Pct.	ShO	Sv-Op	Hld	ERA
1997 Boise	A-	30	0	0	13	52	225	45	20	17	1	3	2	3	24	4	61	9	1	7	2	.778	0	2--	—	2.94
1998 Cedar Rapds	A	58	0	0	38	74	311	62	33	30	5	5	2	8	29	0	81	9	1	6	5	.545	0	7--	—	3.65
1999 Lk Elsinore	A+	24	9	2	6	107.1	443	91	37	30	1	4	4	5	39	4	113	6	1	10	3	.769	1	1--	—	2.52
Erie	AA	10	10	1	0	74.2	300	57	26	24	10	4	0	6	26	0	81	2	0	4	4	.500	1	0--	—	2.89
2000 Edmonton	AAA	27	27	4	0	163	734	158	104	98	16	1	6	14	82	0	156	7	0	7	13	.350	1	0--	—	5.41
2001 Salt Lake	AAA	21	21	4	0	137.2	578	141	84	76	24	4	4	10	31	0	104	7	1	6	11	.353	0	0--	—	4.97
2001 Anaheim	AL	8	0	0	6	11	48	8	1	0	0	0	0	1	7	0	7	2	0	0	0	—	0	0-0	0	0.00

Tsuyoshi Shinjo

Bats: R **Throws:** R **Pos:** CF-53; LF-46; RF-39; PH/PR-12 **Ht:** 6'1" **Wt:** 185 **Born:** 1/28/72 **Age:** 30

				BATTING														BASERUNNING				PERCENTAGES		
Year Team	Lg	G	AB	H	2B	3B	HR	(Hm	Rd)	TB	R	RBI	TBB	IBB	SO	HBP	SH	SF	SB	CS	SB%	GDP	Avg	OBP	SLG
2001 Brooklyn	A-	2	7	2	0	0	0	—	—	2	0	1	1	0	2	0	0	0	0	0	—		.286	.375	.286
2001 New York	NL	123	400	107	23	1	10	(4	6)	162	46	56	25	3	70	7	4	2	4	5	.44	8	.268	.320	.405

Paul Shuey

Pitches: Right **Bats:** Right **Pos:** RP-47   **Ht:** 6'3" **Wt:** 215 **Born:** 9/16/70 **Age:** 31

Year Team	Lg	G	GS	CG	GF	IP	BFP	H	R	ER	HR	SH	SF	HB	TBB	IBB	SO	WP	Bk	W	L	Pct.	ShO	Sv-Op	Hld	ERA
2001 Akron *	AA	1	1	0	0	1	4	0	0	0	0	0	0	0	1	0	2	0	0	0	0	—	0	0--		0.00
1994 Cleveland	AL	14	0	0	11	11.2	62	14	11	11	1	0	0	0	12	1	16	4	0	0	1	.000	0	5-5	1	8.49
1995 Cleveland	AL	7	0	0	3	6.1	28	5	4	3	0	2	0	0	5	0	5	1	0	0	2	.000	0	0-0	0	4.26
1996 Cleveland	AL	42	0	0	18	53.2	225	45	19	17	6	1	3	0	26	3	44	3	1	5	2	.714	0	4-7	7	2.85
1997 Cleveland	AL	40	0	0	16	45	212	52	31	31	5	4	2	1	28	3	46	2	0	4	2	.667	0	2-3	4	6.20
1998 Cleveland	AL	43	0	0	16	51	222	44	19	17	6	2	0	3	25	5	58	3	0	5	4	.556	0	2-5	12	3.00
1999 Cleveland	AL	72	0	0	28	81.2	351	68	37	32	8	4	1	1	40	7	103	8	0	8	5	.615	0	6-12	19	3.53
2000 Cleveland	AL	57	0	0	12	63.2	270	51	25	24	4	1	3	3	30	3	69	0	0	4	2	.667	0	0-5	28	3.39
2001 Cleveland	AL	47	0	0	11	54.1	244	53	25	17	1	4	2	1	26	5	70	6	0	5	3	.625	0	2-5	9	2.82
8 ML YEARS		322	0	0	115	367.1	1614	332	171	152	31	18	11	9	192	27	411	27	1	31	21	.596	0	21-42	80	3.72

Terry Shumpert

Bats: R **Throws:** R **Pos:** PH/PR-52; 2B-41; LF-24; 3B-12; SS-4   **Ht:** 6'0" **Wt:** 198 **Born:** 8/16/66 **Age:** 35

Year Team	Lg	G	AB	H	2B	3B	HR	(Hm	Rd)	TB	R	RBI	TBB	IBB	SO	HBP	SH	SF	SB	CS	SB%	GDP	Avg	OBP	SLG
1990 Kansas City	AL	32	91	25	6	1	0	(0	0)	33	7	8	2	0	17	1	0	2	3	3	.50	4	.275	.292	.363
1991 Kansas City	AL	144	369	80	16	4	5	(1	4)	119	45	34	30	0	75	5	10	3	17	11	.61	10	.217	.283	.322
1992 Kansas City	AL	36	94	14	5	1	1	(0	1)	24	6	11	3	0	17	0	2	0	2	2	.50	2	.149	.175	.255
1993 Kansas City	AL	8	10	1	0	0	0	(0	0)	1	0	0	2	0	2	0	0	0	1	0	1.00	0	.100	.250	.100
1994 Kansas City	AL	64	160	43	6	2	8	(2	6)	78	28	24	13	0	39	0	5	1	18	3	.86	0	.240	.289	.426
1995 Boston	AL	21	47	11	3	0	0	(0	0)	14	6	3	4	0	13	0	0	1	3	1	.75	0	.234	.294	.298
1996 Chicago	NL	27	31	7	1	0	2	(2	0)	14	5	6	2	0	11	1	0	1	0	1	.00	0	.226	.286	.452
1997 San Diego	NL	13	33	9	3	0	1	(0	1)	15	4	6	3	0	4	0	0	1	0	0	—	1	.273	.324	.455
1998 Colorado	NL	23	26	6	1	0	1	(0	1)	10	3	2	2	0	8	0	0	0	0	0	—	0	.231	.286	.385
1999 Colorado	NL	92	262	91	26	3	10	(8	2)	153	58	37	31	2	41	2	4	5	14	0	1.00	2	.347	.413	.584
2000 Colorado	NL	115	263	68	11	7	9	(7	2)	120	52	40	28	1	40	6	0	3	8	4	.67	3	.259	.340	.456
2001 Colorado	NL	114	242	70	14	5	4	(3	1)	106	37	24	15	2	44	3	4	1	14	3	.82	2	.289	.337	.438
12 ML YEARS		689	1651	426	92	23	41	(23	18)	687	251	195	135	5	311	18	25	17	80	28	.74	24	.258	.318	.416

Ruben Sierra

Bats: B **Throws:** R **Pos:** DH-50; RF-35; PH/PR-11; LF-1   **Ht:** 6'1" **Wt:** 215 **Born:** 10/6/65 **Age:** 36

Year Team	Lg	G	AB	H	2B	3B	HR	(Hm	Rd)	TB	R	RBI	TBB	IBB	SO	HBP	SH	SF	SB	CS	SB%	GDP	Avg	OBP	SLG
2001 Oklahoma *	AAA	24	94	25	2	1	3	(—	—)	38	14	12	10	2	14	0	0	0	2	0	1.00	5	.266	.337	.404
1986 Texas	AL	113	382	101	13	10	16	(8	8)	182	50	55	22	3	65	1	1	5	7	8	.47	8	.264	.302	.476
1987 Texas	AL	158	643	169	35	4	30	(15	15)	302	97	109	39	4	114	2	0	12	16	11	.59	18	.263	.302	.470
1988 Texas	AL	156	615	156	32	2	23	(15	8)	261	77	91	44	10	91	1	0	8	18	4	.82	15	.254	.301	.424
1989 Texas	AL	162	634	194	35	14	29	(21	8)	344	101	119	43	2	82	2	0	10	8	2	.80	7	.306	.347	.543
1990 Texas	AL	159	608	170	37	2	16	(10	6)	259	70	96	49	13	86	1	0	8	9	0	1.00	15	.280	.330	.426
1991 Texas	AL	161	661	203	44	5	25	(12	13)	332	110	116	56	7	91	0	0	9	16	4	.80	17	.307	.357	.502
1992 Tex-Oak	AL	151	601	167	34	7	17	(10	7)	266	83	87	45	12	68	0	0	10	14	4	.78	11	.278	.323	.443
1993 Oakland	AL	158	630	147	23	5	22	(9	13)	246	77	101	52	16	97	0	0	10	25	5	.83	17	.233	.288	.390
1994 Oakland	AL	110	426	114	21	1	23	(11	12)	206	71	92	23	4	64	0	0	11	8	5	.62	15	.268	.298	.484
1995 Oak-NYY	AL	126	479	126	32	0	19	(8	11)	215	73	86	46	4	76	0	0	8	5	4	.56	8	.263	.323	.449
1996 NYY-Det	AL	142	518	128	26	2	12	(4	8)	194	61	72	60	12	83	0	0	9	4	4	.50	12	.247	.320	.375
1997 Cin-Tor	AL	39	138	32	5	3	3	(3	0)	52	10	12	9	2	34	0	0	1	0	0	—	1	.232	.277	.377
1998 Chicago	AL	27	74	16	4	1	4	(0	4)	34	7	11	3	0	11	0	0	0	0	0	—	1	.216	.247	.459
2000 Texas	AL	20	60	14	0	0	1	(0	1)	17	5	7	4	0	9	0	0	0	1	0	1.00	1	.233	.281	.283
2001 Texas	AL	94	344	100	22	1	23	(13	10)	193	55	67	19	0	52	0	0	6	2	0	1.00	13	.291	.322	.561
1992 Texas	AL	124	500	139	30	6	14	(8	6)	223	66	70	31	6	59	0	0	8	12	4	.75	9	.278	.315	.446
Oakland	AL	27	101	28	4	1	3	(2	1)	43	17	17	14	6	9	0	0	2	2	0	1.00	2	.277	.359	.426
1995 Oakland	AL	70	264	70	17	0	12	(3	9)	123	40	42	24	2	42	0	0	3	4	4	.50	2	.265	.323	.466
New York	AL	56	215	56	15	0	7	(5	2)	92	33	44	22	2	34	0	0	5	1	0	1.00	6	.260	.322	.428
1996 New York	AL	96	360	93	17	1	11	(4	7)	145	39	52	40	11	58	0	0	7	1	3	.25	10	.258	.327	.403
Detroit	AL	46	158	35	9	1	1	(0	1)	49	22	20	20	1	25	0	0	2	3	1	.75	2	.222	.306	.310
1997 Cincinnati	AL	25	90	22	5	1	2	(2	0)	35	6	7	6	1	21	0	0	0	0	0	—	1	.244	.292	.389
Toronto	AL	14	48	10	0	2	1	(1	0)	17	4	5	3	1	13	0	0	1	0	0	—	0	.208	.250	.354
15 ML YEARS		1776	6813	1837	363	57	263	(139	124)	3103	947	1121	514	89	1023	7	1	107	135	51	.73	160	.270	.317	.455

Jose Silva

Pitches: Right **Bats:** Right **Pos:** RP-26   **Ht:** 6'5" **Wt:** 235 **Born:** 12/19/73 **Age:** 28

Year Team	Lg	G	GS	CG	GF	IP	BFP	H	R	ER	HR	SH	SF	HB	TBB	IBB	SO	WP	Bk	W	L	Pct.	ShO	Sv-Op	Hld	ERA
2001 Altoona *	AA	2	0	0	0	1.1	7	2	0	0	0	0	0	0	1	0	2	0	0	0	0	—	0	0--	—	0.00
Williamsprt *	A-	2	2	0	0	2	8	2	0	0	0	0	0	0	0	0	2	0	0	0	0	—	0	0--	—	0.00
1996 Toronto	AL	2	0	0	0	2	11	5	3	3	1	0	0	0	0	0	0	0	0	0	0	—	0	0-0	0	13.50
1997 Pittsburgh	NL	11	4	0	0	36.1	174	52	26	24	4	4	3	1	16	3	30	0	1	2	1	.667	0	0-0	0	5.94
1998 Pittsburgh	NL	18	18	1	0	100.1	425	104	55	49	7	5	5	1	30	2	64	2	2	6	7	.462	0	0-0	0	4.40
1999 Pittsburgh	NL	34	12	0	9	97.1	433	100	70	62	10	3	3	3	39	0	77	4	3	2	8	.200	0	4-5	2	5.73
2000 Pittsburgh	NL	51	19	1	12	136	631	178	96	84	16	9	5	5	50	7	98	6	1	11	9	.550	0	0-2	1	5.56
2001 Pittsburgh	NL	26	0	0	10	32	140	35	24	24	6	2	0	5	9	1	23	0	0	3	3	.500	0	0-2	1	6.75
6 ML YEARS		142	53	2	31	404	1814	482	274	246	44	23	16	10	144	13	292	12	7	24	28	.462	0	4-9	5	5.48

Bill Simas

Pitches: Right **Bats:** Left **2000 Pos:** RP-60 **Ht:** 6'3" **Wt:** 235 **Born:** 11/28/71 **Age:** 30

	HOW MUCH HE PITCHED						WHAT HE GAVE UP											THE RESULTS					
Year Team	Lg	G	GS	CG	GF	IP	BFP	H	R	ER	HR	SH	SF	HB	TBB	IBB	SO	WP	Bk	W	L	Pct.	ShO	Sv-Op	Hld	ERA
1995 Chicago	AL	14	0	0	4	14	66	15	5	4	1	0	0	1	10	2	16	1	0	1	1	.500	0	0-0	3	2.57
1996 Chicago	AL	64	0	0	16	72.2	328	75	39	37	6	1	2	3	39	6	65	0	0	2	8	.200	0	2-8	15	4.58
1997 Chicago	AL	40	0	0	11	41.1	193	46	23	19	6	1	1	2	24	3	38	2	0	3	1	.750	0	1-2	3	4.14
1998 Chicago	AL	60	0	0	41	70.2	287	54	29	28	12	2	0	1	22	4	56	1	0	4	3	.571	0	18-24	6	3.57
1999 Chicago	AL	70	0	0	21	72	324	73	36	30	6	4	4	6	32	6	41	4	1	6	3	.667	0	2-5	12	3.75
2000 Chicago	AL	60	0	0	9	67.2	283	69	27	26	9	6	4	1	22	6	49	1	0	2	3	.400	0	0-5	13	3.46
6 ML YEARS		308	0	0	102	338.1	1481	332	159	144	39	14	11	14	149	27	265	9	1	18	19	.486	0	23-44	52	3.83

Brian Simmons

Bats: B **Throws:** R **Pos:** PH/PR-28; LF-19; CF-12; RF-7; DH-2 **Ht:** 6'2" **Wt:** 190 **Born:** 9/4/73 **Age:** 28

	BATTING																BASERUNNING				PERCENTAGES		
Year Team	Lg	G	AB	H	2B	3B	HR	(Hm | Rd)	TB	R	RBI	TBB	IBB	SO	HBP	SH	SF	SB	CS	SB%	GDP	Avg	OBP	SLG
2001 Syracuse *	AAA	52	201	53	10	1	2	—	—	71	24	20	19	0	36	2	2	1	4	5	.44	6	.264	.332	.353
1998 Chicago	AL	5	19	7	0	0	2	(0 | 2)	13	4	6	0	0	2	0	0	0	0	1	.00	0	.368	.368	.684
1999 Chicago	AL	54	126	29	3	3	4	(0 | 4)	50	14	17	9	0	30	0	0	0	1	0	1.00	3	.230	.281	.397
2001 Toronto	AL	60	107	19	5	0	2	(2 | 0)	30	8	8	8	0	26	1	0	1	0	0	1.00	0	.178	.239	.280
3 ML YEARS		119	252	55	8	3	8	(2 | 6)	93	26	31	17	0	58	1	0	1	5	1	.83	3	.218	.269	.369

Randall Simon

Bats: Left **Throws:** Left **Pos:** 1B-43; DH-29; PH/PR-11 **Ht:** 6'0" **Wt:** 180 **Born:** 5/26/75 **Age:** 27

	BATTING																BASERUNNING				PERCENTAGES		
Year Team	Lg	G	AB	H	2B	3B	HR	(Hm | Rd)	TB	R	RBI	TBB	IBB	SO	HBP	SH	SF	SB	CS	SB%	GDP	Avg	OBP	SLG
2001 Toledo *	AAA	59	222	75	13	0	10	—	—	118	27	31	21	2	21	2	0	0	0	3	.00	8	.338	.400	.532
1997 Atlanta	NL	13	14	6	1	0	0	(0 | 0)	7	2	1	1	0	2	0	0	0	0	0	—	1	.429	.467	.500
1998 Atlanta	NL	7	16	3	0	0	0	(0 | 0)	3	2	4	0	0	1	0	0	1	0	0	—	0	.188	.176	.188
1999 Atlanta	NL	90	218	69	16	0	5	(2 | 3)	100	26	25	17	6	25	1	0	1	2	2	.50	10	.317	.367	.459
2001 Detroit	AL	81	256	78	14	2	6	(1 | 5)	114	28	37	15	2	28	0	1	2	0	1	.00	9	.305	.341	.445
4 ML YEARS		191	504	156	31	2	11	(3 | 8)	224	58	67	33	8	56	1	1	4	2	3	.40	20	.310	.351	.444

Chris Singleton

Bats: L **Throws:** L **Pos:** CF-121; LF-19; PH/PR-11; RF-3; DH-2 **Ht:** 6'2" **Wt:** 210 **Born:** 8/15/72 **Age:** 29

	BATTING																BASERUNNING				PERCENTAGES		
Year Team	Lg	G	AB	H	2B	3B	HR	(Hm | Rd)	TB	R	RBI	TBB	IBB	SO	HBP	SH	SF	SB	CS	SB%	GDP	Avg	OBP	SLG
1999 Chicago	AL	133	496	149	31	6	17	(5 | 12)	243	72	72	20	1	45	1	4	6	20	5	.80	10	.300	.328	.490
2000 Chicago	AL	147	511	130	22	5	11	(5 | 6)	195	83	62	35	2	85	1	12	4	22	7	.76	6	.254	.301	.382
2001 Chicago	AL	140	392	117	21	5	7	(4 | 3)	169	57	45	20	2	61	1	14	4	12	11	.52	5	.298	.331	.431
3 ML YEARS		420	1399	396	74	16	35	(14 | 21)	607	212	179	77	5	191	3	30	14	54	23	.70	21	.283	.319	.434

Mike Sirotka

Pitches: Left **Bats:** Left **2000 Pos:** SP-32 **Ht:** 6'1" **Wt:** 200 **Born:** 5/13/71 **Age:** 31

	HOW MUCH HE PITCHED						WHAT HE GAVE UP											THE RESULTS					
Year Team	Lg	G	GS	CG	GF	IP	BFP	H	R	ER	HR	SH	SF	HB	TBB	IBB	SO	WP	Bk	W	L	Pct.	ShO	Sv-Op	Hld	ERA
1995 Chicago	AL	6	6	0	0	34.1	152	39	16	16	2	1	3	0	17	0	19	2	0	1	2	.333	0	0-0	0	4.19
1996 Chicago	AL	15	4	0	2	26.1	122	34	27	21	3	0	2	0	12	0	11	1	0	1	2	.333	0	0-0	0	7.18
1997 Chicago	AL	7	4	0	1	32	130	36	9	8	4	0	0	1	5	1	24	0	0	3	0	1.000	0	0-0	1	2.25
1998 Chicago	AL	33	33	5	0	211.2	911	255	137	119	30	5	7	2	47	0	128	3	1	14	15	.483	0	0-0	0	5.06
1999 Chicago	AL	32	32	3	0	209	909	236	108	93	24	5	9	3	57	2	125	4	0	11	13	.458	1	0-0	0	4.00
2000 Chicago	AL	32	32	1	0	197	832	203	101	83	23	4	3	1	69	1	128	8	2	15	10	.600	0	0-0	0	3.79
6 ML YEARS		125	111	9	3	710.1	3056	803	398	340	86	15	24	7	207	4	435	18	3	45	42	.517	1	0-0	1	4.31

Joe Slusarski

Pitches: Right **Bats:** Right **Pos:** RP-12 **Ht:** 6'4" **Wt:** 195 **Born:** 12/19/66 **Age:** 35

	HOW MUCH HE PITCHED						WHAT HE GAVE UP											THE RESULTS					
Year Team	Lg	G	GS	CG	GF	IP	BFP	H	R	ER	HR	SH	SF	HB	TBB	IBB	SO	WP	Bk	W	L	Pct.	ShO	Sv-Op	Hld	ERA
2001 Richmond *	AAA	6	0	0	4	8	34	9	2	2	0	0	1	0	2	0	5	0	0	0	0	—	0	0--	—	2.25
New Orleans *	AAA	31	0	0	4	40	163	37	17	11	4	2	1	0	8	3	24	0	0	5	2	.714	0	1--	—	2.48
1991 Oakland	AL	20	19	1	0	109.1	486	121	69	64	14	0	3	4	52	1	60	4	0	5	7	.417	0	0-0	0	5.27
1992 Oakland	AL	15	14	0	1	76	338	85	52	46	15	1	5	6	27	0	38	0	1	5	5	.500	0	0-0	0	5.45
1993 Oakland	AL	2	1	0	0	8.2	43	9	5	5	1	2	0	0	11	3	1	0	0	0	0	—	0	0-0	0	5.19
1995 Milwaukee	AL	12	0	0	6	15	73	21	11	9	3	1	1	2	6	1	6	0	0	1	1	.500	0	0-0	0	5.40
1999 Houston	NL	3	0	0	1	3.2	15	1	0	0	0	0	0	0	3	1	3	0	0	0	0	—	0	0-0	0	0.00
2000 Houston	NL	54	0	0	16	77	327	80	36	36	8	2	2	3	22	3	54	6	0	2	7	.222	0	3-4	7	4.21
2001 Atl-Hou	NL	12	0	0	5	16	76	25	16	16	4	1	1	0	4	0	11	0	0	1	0	1.000	0	0-0	0	9.00
2001 Atlanta	NL	4	0	0	1	6	28	9	6	6	2	1	0	0	1	0	5	0	0	0	0	—	0	0-0	0	9.00
Houston	NL	8	0	0	4	10	48	16	10	10	2	0	1	0	3	0	6	0	0	1	0	.000	0	0-0	0	9.00
7 ML YEARS		118	34	1	29	305.2	1358	342	189	176	45	7	12	15	125	9	173	10	1	13	21	.382	0	3-4	7	5.18

J.D. Smart

Pitches: Right **Bats:** Right **Pos:** RP-15 **Ht:** 6'2" **Wt:** 180 **Born:** 11/12/73 **Age:** 28

	HOW MUCH HE PITCHED						WHAT HE GAVE UP											THE RESULTS					
Year Team	Lg	G	GS	CG	GF	IP	BFP	H	R	ER	HR	SH	SF	HB	TBB	IBB	SO	WP	Bk	W	L	Pct.	ShO	Sv-Op	Hld	ERA
1995 Expos	R	2	2	0	0	10.2	43	10	2	2	0	0	1	2	1	0	6	0	0	2	0	1.000	0	0--	—	1.69
Vermont	A-	5	5	0	0	27.2	118	29	9	7	1	1	3	3	7	0	21	0	0	0	1	.000	0	0--	—	2.28

Year Team	Lg	G	GS	CG	GF	IP	BFP	H	R	ER	HR	SH	SF	HB	TBB	IBB	SO	WP	Bk	W	L	Pct.	ShO	Sv-Op	Hld	ERA
1996 Delmarva	A	25	25	3	0	156.2	655	155	75	59	14	2	7	10	31	0	109	8	0	9	8	.529	2	0--	--	3.39
1997 Wst Plm Bch	A+	17	13	1	1	102	422	105	45	37	10	2	3	2	21	0	65	3	0	5	4	.556	0	1--	--	3.26
Harrisburg	AA	12	12	0	0	70.2	308	75	34	29	7	6	3	3	24	0	43	3	0	6	3	.667	0	0--	--	3.69
1998 Cape Fear	A	3	1	0	0	11	39	7	3	3	1	0	0	0	0	0	12	1	0	3	0	1.000	0	0--	--	2.45
Harrisburg	AA	14	11	2	2	77	311	67	23	21	2	3	1	3	18	0	47	3	1	3	5	.375	0	1--	--	2.45
Ottawa	AAA	6	6	0	0	35	149	34	22	19	3	2	2	2	11	0	16	0	0	2	3	.400	0	0--	--	4.89
1999 Ottawa	AAA	6	4	0	0	20.2	90	22	7	6	2	0	0	1	6	0	9	1	1	0	1	.000	0	0--	--	2.61
2000 Ottawa	AAA	4	0	0	2	6.2	34	15	8	8	2	0	0	0	1	0	3	0	0	0	1	.000	0	1--	--	10.80
2001 Oklahoma	AAA	16	0	0	13	23	97	22	9	7	0	2	1	2	6	0	13	2	0	2	2	.500	0	3--	--	2.74
1999 Montreal	NL	29	0	0	6	52	223	56	30	29	4	2	1	0	17	0	21	0	0	0	1	.000	0	0-0	0	5.02
2001 Texas	AL	15	0	0	4	15.1	68	19	11	11	3	0	2	0	4	0	10	1	0	1	2	.333	0	0-2	2	6.46
2 ML YEARS		44	0	0	10	67.1	291	75	41	40	7	2	3	0	21	0	31	1	0	1	3	.250	0	0-2	2	5.35

Bobby Smith

Bats: Right **Throws:** Right **Pos:** 2B-6 | **Ht:** 6'3" **Wt:** 190 **Born:** 5/10/74 **Age:** 28

Year Team	Lg	G	AB	H	2B	3B	HR	(Hm	Rd)	TB	R	RBI	TBB	IBB	SO	HBP	SH	SF	SB	CS	SB%	GDP	Avg	OBP	SLG
2001 Durham *	AAA	107	396	119	25	2	22	--	--	214	67	70	45	1	91	8	0	5	10	2	.83	7	.301	.379	.540
1998 Tampa Bay	AL	117	370	102	15	3	11	(4	7)	156	44	55	34	0	110	6	2	4	5	3	.63	9	.276	.343	.422
1999 Tampa Bay	AL	68	199	36	4	1	3	(1	2)	51	18	19	16	0	64	1	2	1	4	4	.50	8	.181	.244	.256
2000 Tampa Bay	AL	49	175	41	8	0	6	(2	4)	67	21	26	14	1	59	1	0	1	2	2	.50	6	.234	.293	.383
2001 Tampa Bay	AL	6	19	2	0	0	0	(0	0)	2	1	1	3	0	10	0	0	0	0	0	--	1	.105	.227	.105
4 ML YEARS		240	763	181	27	4	20	(7	13)	276	84	101	67	1	243	8	4	6	11	9	.55	24	.237	.303	.362

Bud Smith

Pitches: Left **Bats:** Left **Pos:** SP-14; RP-2 | **Ht:** 6'0" **Wt:** 170 **Born:** 10/23/79 **Age:** 22

Year Team	Lg	G	GS	CG	GF	IP	BFP	H	R	ER	HR	SH	SF	HB	TBB	IBB	SO	WP	Bk	W	L	Pct.	ShO	Sv-Op	Hld	ERA
1998 Johnson Cty	R+	14	14	0	0	64.1	305	85	47	37	9	2	3	2	34	1	65	2	0	3	3	.500	0	0--	--	5.18
1999 Peoria	A	9	9	0	0	54	219	53	20	17	4	1	3	2	16	0	59	2	1	4	1	.800	0	0--	--	2.83
Potomac	A+	18	18	0	0	103.1	433	91	47	34	2	3	2	9	32	0	93	4	0	4	9	.308	0	0--	--	2.96
2000 Arkansas	AA	18	18	3	0	108.2	439	93	32	28	5	2	3	4	27	1	102	5	0	12	1	.923	3	0--	--	2.32
Memphis	AAA	9	8	0	0	54.1	213	40	24	13	4	2	1	1	15	0	34	0	0	5	1	.833	0	0--	--	2.15
2001 Memphis	AAA	17	17	0	0	108	462	114	38	33	6	6	5	4	28	2	78	1	1	8	5	.615	0	0--	--	2.75
2001 St. Louis	NL	16	14	1	1	84.2	351	79	40	36	12	9	1	1	24	5	59	0	0	6	3	.667	1	0-0	0	3.83

Chuck Smith

Pitches: Right **Bats:** Right **Pos:** SP-15 | **Ht:** 6'1" **Wt:** 185 **Born:** 10/21/69 **Age:** 32

Year Team	Lg	G	GS	CG	GF	IP	BFP	H	R	ER	HR	SH	SF	HB	TBB	IBB	SO	WP	Bk	W	L	Pct.	ShO	Sv-Op	Hld	ERA
1991 Astros	R	15	7	1	2	59.1	272	56	36	23	2	3	0	7	37	0	64	7	5	4	3	.571	0	0--	--	3.49
1992 Asheville	A	28	20	1	3	132	596	128	93	76	14	5	4	4	78	1	117	4	7	9	9	.500	0	1--	--	5.18
1993 Quad City	A	22	17	2	3	110.2	488	109	73	57	16	3	2	6	52	0	103	7	4	7	5	.583	0	0--	--	4.64
1994 Jackson	AA	2	0	0	0	6	30	6	6	3	0	2	0	0	5	0	7	0	1	0	0	--	0	0--	--	4.50
Osceola	A+	35	2	0	11	84.2	376	73	41	35	2	2	2	2	49	3	60	7	3	4	4	.500	0	0--	--	3.72
1995 South Bend	A	26	25	4	1	167	688	128	70	50	8	7	2	13	61	0	145	21	11	10	10	.500	2	0--	--	2.69
1996 Pr William	A+	20	20	2	0	123.1	545	125	65	55	7	3	2	10	49	1	99	13	1	6	6	.500	1	0--	--	4.01
Birmingham	AA	7	3	0	2	30.2	124	25	11	9	1	0	0	1	15	2	30	0	1	2	1	.667	0	1--	--	2.64
Nashville	AAA	1	0	0	0	0.2	5	2	2	2	0	0	0	0	1	0	1	0	0	0	0	--	0	0--	--	27.00
1997 Birmingham	AA	25	0	0	6	62.2	280	63	35	22	4	1	2	5	27	5	57	8	3	2	2	.500	0	0--	--	3.16
Nashville	AAA	20	1	0	12	31.2	156	39	33	31	8	2	3	2	23	2	29	8	2	0	3	.000	0	0--	--	8.81
1998 Sioux Falls	IND	8	8	2	0	55	226	44	18	16	1	0	0	3	21	1	70	1	0	5	3	.625	1	0--	--	2.62
1999 Oklahoma	AAA	32	4	2	13	85	341	73	31	28	7	1	3	1	28	0	76	5	0	5	4	.556	0	4--	--	2.96
2000 Oklahoma	AAA	11	11	1	0	66.2	300	73	31	28	3	2	2	2	38	1	73	5	0	5	3	.625	0	0--	--	3.78
2001 Brevard Cty	A+	2	2	0	0	8	31	7	3	3	1	0	0	0	1	0	6	0	0	0	0	--	0	0--	--	3.38
Calgary	AAA	2	2	0	0	12.2	49	12	4	4	0	0	0	0	2	0	9	0	0	2	0	1.000	0	0--	--	2.84
2000 Florida	NL	19	19	1	0	122.2	513	111	50	44	6	4	5	3	54	2	118	6	1	6	6	.500	0	0-0	0	3.23
2001 Florida	NL	15	15	0	0	88	385	89	47	46	10	4	4	6	35	4	71	0	1	5	5	.500	0	0-0	0	4.70
2 ML YEARS		34	34	1	0	210.2	898	200	100	90	16	8	9	9	89	6	189	6	2	11	11	.500	0	0-0	0	3.84

Jason Smith

Bats: Left **Throws:** Right **Pos:** SS-1; PH/PR-1 | **Ht:** 6'3" **Wt:** 195 **Born:** 7/24/77 **Age:** 24

Year Team	Lg	G	AB	H	2B	3B	HR	(Hm	Rd)	TB	R	RBI	TBB	IBB	SO	HBP	SH	SF	SB	CS	SB%	GDP	Avg	OBP	SLG
1997 Williamsprt	A-	51	205	59	5	2	0	--	--	68	25	11	10	0	44	0	0	0	9	2	.82	0	.288	.321	.332
Rockford	A	9	33	6	0	1	0	--	--	8	4	3	2	0	11	0	0	0	1	0	1.00	1	.182	.229	.242
1998 Rockford	A	126	464	111	15	9	7	--	--	165	67	60	31	1	122	1	6	4	23	6	.79	2	.239	.286	.356
1999 Daytona	A+	39	142	37	5	2	5	--	--	61	22	26	12	3	29	3	0	1	9	3	.75	2	.261	.329	.430
2000 West Tenn	AA	119	481	114	22	7	12	--	--	186	55	61	22	3	130	2	2	1	16	10	.62	1	.237	.273	.387
2001 Iowa	AAA	70	240	56	8	6	4	--	--	88	31	15	12	4	71	1	1	2	6	3	.67	4	.233	.271	.367
Durham	AAA	8	31	6	1	0	0	--	--	7	2	3	0	0	11	0	0	0	0	0	--	0	.194	.194	.226
2001 Chicago	NL	2	1	0	0	0	0	(0	0)	0	0	0	0	0	1	0	0	0	0	0	--	0	.000	.000	.000

Mark Smith

Bats: R Throws: R Pos: LF-55; PH/PR-28; CF-6; RF-4; 1B-1   Ht: 6'3" Wt: 225 Born: 5/7/70 Age: 32

		BATTING																	BASERUNNING				PERCENTAGES		
Year Team	Lg	G	AB	H	2B	3B	HR	(Hm	Rd)	TB	R	RBI	TBB	IBB	SO	HBP	SH	SF	SB	CS	SB%	GDP	Avg	OBP	SLG
2001 Ottawa *	AAA	40	145	30	8	0	6	—	—	56	20	17	15	0	38	2	1	0	4	2	.67	1	.207	.290	.386
1994 Baltimore	AL	3	7	1	0	0	0	(0	0)	1	0	2	0	0	2	0	0	0	0	0	—	0	.143	.143	.143
1995 Baltimore	AL	37	104	24	5	0	3	(1	2)	38	11	15	12	2	22	1	2	1	3	0	1.00	4	.231	.314	.365
1996 Baltimore	AL	27	78	19	2	0	4	(3	1)	33	9	10	3	0	20	3	0	0	0	2	.00	0	.244	.298	.423
1997 Pittsburgh	NL	71	193	55	13	1	9	(6	3)	97	29	35	28	1	36	0	0	1	3	1	.75	3	.285	.374	.503
1998 Pittsburgh	NL	59	128	25	6	0	2	(1	1)	37	18	13	10	0	26	3	0	3	7	0	1.00	1	.195	.264	.289
2000 Florida	NL	104	192	47	8	1	5	(2	3)	72	22	27	17	1	54	2	0	2	2	0	1.00	2	.245	.310	.375
2001 Montreal	NL	80	194	47	13	1	6	(3	3)	80	28	18	23	0	38	2	1	2	0	2	.00	3	.242	.326	.412
7 ML YEARS		381	896	218	47	3	29	(16	13)	358	117	120	93	4	198	11	3	9	15	5	.75	13	.243	.319	.400

Roy Smith

Pitches: Right Bats: Right Pos: RP-9   Ht: 6'6" Wt: 235 Born: 5/18/76 Age: 26

		HOW MUCH HE PITCHED						WHAT HE GAVE UP												THE RESULTS						
Year Team	Lg	G	GS	CG	GF	IP	BFP	H	R	ER	HR	SH	SF	HB	TBB	IBB	SO	WP	Bk	W	L	Pct.	ShO	Sv-Op	Hld	ERA
1994 Mariners	R	11	5	0	1	45	164	30	9	8	2	1	1	1	4	0	35	2	0	3	1	.750	0	0--	—	1.60
1995 Wisconsin	A	27	27	1	0	149	669	179	100	89	9	5	2	3	54	2	109	10	2	7	14	.333	0	0--	—	5.38
1996 Wisconsin	A	27	27	0	0	146	679	164	113	83	9	6	4	8	73	3	99	11	2	6	13	.316	0	0--	—	5.12
1997 Memphis	AA	4	0	0	3	4.1	20	6	5	5	0	0	1	0	1	0	6	1	0	0	0	—	0	0--	—	10.38
Wisconsin	A	18	11	0	4	66	304	81	50	41	3	1	2	2	31	0	38	14	2	3	4	.429	0	0--	—	5.59
1998 St. Paul	IND	18	18	1	0	105.2	467	119	75	59	10	3	3	1	36	0	74	6	0	6	7	.462	1	0--	—	5.03
1999 St. Paul	IND	8	7	1	0	42	182	38	18	15	3	1	0	1	23	0	43	1	0	4	2	.667	1	0--	—	3.21
2000 Kinston	A+	21	0	0	9	45	183	35	15	14	0	0	1	3	21	1	45	3	0	2	2	.500	0	2--	—	2.80
Akron	AA	28	0	0	15	55	217	36	14	12	0	4	0	1	22	2	50	6	0	5	1	.833	0	0--	—	1.96
2001 Buffalo	AAA	48	0	0	31	74	307	59	25	18	2	6	1	8	29	4	86	3	0	0	5	.000	0	18--	—	2.19
2001 Cleveland	AL	9	0	0	2	16.1	80	16	14	11	3	0	0	2	13	1	17	0	0	0	0	—	0	0-0	1	6.06

John Smoltz

Pitches: Right Bats: Right Pos: RP-31; SP-5   Ht: 6'3" Wt: 220 Born: 5/15/67 Age: 35

		HOW MUCH HE PITCHED						WHAT HE GAVE UP												THE RESULTS						
Year Team	Lg	G	GS	CG	GF	IP	BFP	H	R	ER	HR	SH	SF	HB	TBB	IBB	SO	WP	Bk	W	L	Pct.	ShO	Sv-Op	Hld	ERA
2001 Macon *	A	1	1	0	0	5	17	4	1	1	0	0	0	0	0	0	5	0	0	0	0	—	0	0--	—	1.80
Greenville *	AA	3	1	0	0	6	20	3	0	0	0	0	0	0	0	0	6	0	0	0	0	—	0	0--	—	0.00
1988 Atlanta	NL	12	12	0	0	64	297	74	40	39	10	2	0	2	33	4	37	2	1	2	7	.222	0	0-0	0	5.48
1989 Atlanta	NL	29	29	5	0	208	847	160	79	68	15	10	7	2	72	2	168	8	3	12	11	.522	0	0-0	0	2.94
1990 Atlanta	NL	34	34	6	0	231.1	966	206	109	99	20	9	8	1	90	3	170	14	3	14	11	.560	2	0-0	0	3.85
1991 Atlanta	NL	36	36	5	0	229.2	947	206	101	97	16	9	9	3	77	1	148	20	2	14	13	.519	0	0-0	0	3.80
1992 Atlanta	NL	35	35	9	0	246.2	1021	206	90	78	17	7	8	5	80	5	215	17	1	15	12	.556	3	0-0	0	2.85
1993 Atlanta	NL	35	35	3	0	243.2	1028	208	104	98	23	13	4	6	100	12	208	13	1	15	11	.577	1	0-0	0	3.62
1994 Atlanta	NL	21	21	1	0	134.2	568	120	69	62	15	7	6	4	48	4	113	7	0	6	10	.375	0	0-0	0	4.14
1995 Atlanta	NL	29	29	2	0	192.2	808	166	76	68	15	13	5	4	72	8	193	13	0	12	7	.632	1	0-0	0	3.18
1996 Atlanta	NL	35	35	6	0	253.2	995	199	93	85	19	10	5	5	55	3	276	10	1	24	8	.750	2	0-0	0	2.94
1997 Atlanta	NL	35	35	7	0	256	1043	234	97	86	21	10	3	1	63	9	241	10	1	15	12	.556	2	0-0	0	3.02
1998 Atlanta	NL	26	26	2	0	167.2	681	145	58	54	10	4	2	4	44	2	173	3	1	17	3	.850	2	0-0	0	2.90
1999 Atlanta	NL	29	29	1	0	186.1	746	168	70	66	14	10	5	4	40	2	156	2	0	11	8	.579	1	0-0	0	3.19
2001 Atlanta	NL	36	5	0	20	59	238	53	24	22	7	1	2	2	10	2	57	0	0	3	3	.500	0	10-11	5	3.36
13 ML YEARS		392	361	47	20	2473.1	10185	2145	1010	920	202	107	63	40	784	57	2155	119	14	160	116	.580	14	10-11	5	3.35

J.T. Snow

Bats: Left Throws: Left Pos: 1B-92; PH/PR-15   Ht: 6'2" Wt: 205 Born: 2/26/68 Age: 34

		BATTING																	BASERUNNING				PERCENTAGES		
Year Team	Lg	G	AB	H	2B	3B	HR	(Hm	Rd)	TB	R	RBI	TBB	IBB	SO	HBP	SH	SF	SB	CS	SB%	GDP	Avg	OBP	SLG
2001 Fresno *	AAA	4	12	0	0	0	0	(0	0)	0	1	0	2	0	7	0	0	0	0	0	—	0	.000	.143	.000
1992 New York	AL	7	14	2	1	0	0	(0	0)	3	1	2	5	1	5	0	0	0	0	0	—	0	.143	.368	.214
1993 California	AL	129	419	101	18	2	16	(10	6)	171	60	57	55	4	88	2	7	6	3	0	1.00	10	.241	.328	.408
1994 California	AL	61	223	49	4	0	8	(7	1)	77	22	30	19	1	48	3	2	1	0	1	.00	2	.220	.289	.345
1995 California	AL	143	544	157	22	1	24	(14	10)	253	80	102	52	4	91	3	5	2	2	1	.67	16	.289	.353	.465
1996 California	AL	155	575	148	20	1	17	(8	9)	221	69	67	56	6	96	5	2	3	1	6	.14	19	.257	.327	.384
1997 San Francisco	NL	157	531	149	36	1	28	(14	14)	271	81	104	96	13	124	1	2	7	6	4	.60	8	.281	.387	.510
1998 San Francisco	NL	138	435	108	29	1	15	(9	6)	184	65	79	58	3	84	0	0	7	1	2	.33	12	.248	.332	.423
1999 San Francisco	NL	161	570	156	25	2	24	(7	17)	257	93	98	86	7	121	5	1	6	0	0	.00	16	.274	.370	.451
2000 San Francisco	NL	155	536	152	33	2	19	(10	9)	246	82	96	66	6	129	11	0	14	1	3	.25	20	.284	.365	.459
2001 San Francisco	NL	101	285	70	12	1	8	(3	5)	108	43	34	55	10	81	4	0	4	0	0	—	2	.246	.371	.379
10 ML YEARS		1207	4132	1092	200	11	159	(82	77)	1791	596	669	548	55	867	34	19	50	14	21	.40	105	.264	.351	.433

Scott Sobkowiak

Pitches: Right Bats: Right Pos: RP-1   Ht: 6'5" Wt: 230 Born: 10/26/77 Age: 24

		HOW MUCH HE PITCHED						WHAT HE GAVE UP												THE RESULTS						
Year Team	Lg	G	GS	CG	GF	IP	BFP	H	R	ER	HR	SH	SF	HB	TBB	IBB	SO	WP	Bk	W	L	Pct.	ShO	Sv-Op	Hld	ERA
1998 Eugene	A-	8	8	0	0	40.2	163	25	12	7	1	0	1	3	13	0	55	4	0	3	2	.600	0	0--	—	1.55
1999 Myrtle Bch	A+	27	26	0	1	139.1	572	100	50	44	10	3	2	2	63	1	161	12	1	9	4	.692	0	0--	—	2.84
2000 Greenville	AA	4	4	0	0	23.1	107	26	16	12	2	0	2	2	15	0	27	0	0	2	1	.667	0	0--	—	4.63
2001 Braves	R	2	2	0	0	7	28	4	2	1	0	1	0	0	1	0	11	1	0	0	0	—	0	0--	—	1.29
Greenville	AA	12	12	0	0	65	305	71	45	40	10	4	2	5	40	0	48	6	1	2	5	.286	0	0--	—	5.54
2001 Atlanta	NL	1	0	0	1	1	5	2	1	1	0	0	0	0	0	0	0	0	0	0	0	—	0	0-0	0	9.00

Luis Sojo

Bats: R **Throws:** R **Pos:** 3B-17; 1B-8; 2B-7; SS-5; PH/PR-5; DH-1 **Ht:** 5'11" **Wt:** 185 **Born:** 1/3/66 **Age:** 36

Year Team	Lg	G	AB	H	2B	3B	HR	(Hm	Rd)	TB	R	RBI	TBB	IBB	SO	HBP	SH	SF	SB	CS	SB%	GDP	Avg	OBP	SLG
1990 Toronto	AL	33	80	18	3	0	1	(0	1)	24	14	9	5	0	5	0	0	0	1	1	.50	1	.225	.271	.300
1991 California	AL	113	364	94	14	1	3	(1	2)	119	38	20	14	0	26	5	19	0	4	2	.67	12	.258	.295	.327
1992 California	AL	106	368	100	12	3	7	(2	5)	139	37	43	14	0	24	1	7	1	7	11	.39	14	.272	.299	.378
1993 Toronto	AL	19	47	8	2	0	0	(0	0)	10	5	6	4	0	2	0	2	1	0	0	—	3	.170	.231	.213
1994 Seattle	AL	63	213	59	9	2	6	(4	2)	90	32	22	8	0	25	2	3	1	2	1	.67	2	.277	.308	.423
1995 Seattle	AL	102	339	98	18	2	7	(4	3)	141	50	39	23	0	19	1	6	1	4	2	.67	9	.289	.335	.416
1996 Sea-NYY	AL	95	287	63	10	1	1	(1	0)	78	23	21	11	0	17	1	8	1	2	2	.50	10	.220	.250	.272
1997 New York	AL	77	215	66	6	1	2	(2	0)	80	27	25	16	0	14	1	5	2	3	1	.75	5	.307	.355	.372
1998 New York	AL	54	147	34	3	1	0	(0	0)	39	16	14	4	0	15	0	1	1	1	0	1.00	5	.231	.250	.265
1999 New York	AL	49	127	32	6	0	2	(1	1)	44	20	16	4	0	17	0	2	0	1	0	1.00	4	.252	.275	.346
2000 Pit-NYY	AL	95	301	86	18	1	7	(4	3)	127	33	37	17	3	22	1	3	1	2	0	1.00	11	.286	.325	.422
2001 New York	AL	39	79	13	2	0	0	(0	0)	15	5	9	4	0	12	1	0	0	1	0	1.00	6	.165	.214	.190
1996 Seattle	AL	77	247	52	8	1	1	(1	0)	65	20	16	10	0	13	1	6	0	2	2	.50	8	.211	.244	.263
New York	AL	18	40	11	2	0	0	(0	0)	13	3	5	1	0	4	0	2	1	0	0	—	2	.275	.286	.325
2000 Pittsburgh	NL	61	176	50	11	0	5	(2	3)	76	14	20	11	3	16	1	0	1	1	0	1.00	6	.284	.328	.432
New York	AL	34	125	36	7	1	2	(2	0)	51	19	17	6	0	6	0	3	0	1	0	1.00	5	.288	.321	.408
12 ML YEARS		845	2567	671	103	12	36	(19	17)	906	300	261	124	3	198	13	56	9	28	20	.58	76	.261	.298	.353

Alfonso Soriano

Bats: Right **Throws:** Right **Pos:** 2B-156; DH-2; PH/PR-1 **Ht:** 6'1" **Wt:** 180 **Born:** 1/7/78 **Age:** 24

Year Team	Lg	G	AB	H	2B	3B	HR	(Hm	Rd)	TB	R	RBI	TBB	IBB	SO	HBP	SH	SF	SB	CS	SB%	GDP	Avg	OBP	SLG
1999 Norwich	AA	89	361	110	20	3	15	—	—	181	57	68	32	1	67	4	0	5	24	16	.60	9	.305	.363	.501
Yankees	R	5	19	5	2	0	1	—	—	10	7	5	1	0	3	1	0	1	0	0	—	1	.263	.318	.526
Columbus	AAA	20	82	15	5	1	2	—	—	28	8	11	5	0	18	0	0	2	1	1	.50	1	.183	.225	.341
2000 Columbus	AAA	111	459	133	32	6	12	—	—	213	90	66	25	1	85	3	2	6	14	7	.67	8	.290	.327	.464
1999 New York	AL	9	8	1	0	0	1	(1	0)	4	2	1	0	0	3	0	0	0	0	1	.00	0	.125	.125	.500
2000 New York	AL	22	50	9	3	0	2	(0	2)	18	5	3	1	0	15	0	2	0	2	0	1.00	0	.180	.196	.360
2001 New York	AL	158	574	154	34	3	18	(8	10)	248	77	73	29	0	125	3	3	5	43	14	.75	7	.268	.304	.432
3 ML YEARS		189	632	164	37	3	21	(9	12)	270	84	77	30	0	143	3	5	5	45	15	.75	7	.259	.294	.427

Juan Sosa

Bats: Right **Throws:** Right **Pos:** 3B-1; PH/PR-1 **Ht:** 6'1" **Wt:** 175 **Born:** 8/19/75 **Age:** 26

Year Team	Lg	G	AB	H	2B	3B	HR	(Hm	Rd)	TB	R	RBI	TBB	IBB	SO	HBP	SH	SF	SB	CS	SB%	GDP	Avg	OBP	SLG
1995 Vero Beach	A+	8	27	6	1	1	1	—	—	12	2	6	0	0	4	0	0	0	2	0	.00	0	.222	.222	.444
Yakima	A-	61	217	51	10	4	3	—	—	78	26	16	15	2	39	1	4	2	8	1	.89	4	.235	.285	.359
1996 Savannah	A	112	370	94	21	2	7	—	—	140	58	38	30	2	64	1	4	1	14	12	.54	9	.254	.311	.378
1997 Vero Beach	A+	92	250	55	5	2	5	—	—	79	32	29	14	0	39	2	3	3	20	8	.71	6	.220	.264	.316
1998 Salem	A+	133	529	147	20	12	8	—	—	215	88	47	43	1	83	4	7	4	64	16	.80	12	.278	.334	.406
1999 Carolina	AA	125	490	135	22	5	7	—	—	188	70	42	31	0	65	2	5	6	38	15	.72	12	.276	.318	.384
Colo Sprngs	AAA	6	28	11	1	1	1	—	—	17	3	5	0	0	1	0	0	0	1	0	1.00	1	.393	.393	.607
2000 Colo Sprngs	AAA	118	449	123	25	9	9	—	—	193	67	69	31	1	54	3	9	2	23	10	.70	16	.274	.324	.430
2001 Colo Sprngs	AAA	14	40	9	1	0	0	—	—	10	2	2	5	0	7	0	1	1	1	1	.50	5	.225	.304	.250
El Paso	AA	29	113	29	5	1	0	—	—	36	14	8	7	0	20	0	1	1	5	2	.71	5	.257	.298	.319
Tucson	AAA	64	182	35	6	1	0	—	—	43	17	12	9	1	22	1	4	2	5	1	.83	11	.192	.232	.236
1999 Colorado	NL	11	9	2	0	0	0	(0	0)	2	3	0	2	0	2	0	0	0	0	0	—	0	.222	.364	.222
2001 Arizona	NL	2	1	0	0	0	0	(0	0)	0	0	0	0	0	1	0	0	0	0	0	—	0	.000	.000	.000
2 ML YEARS		13	10	2	0	0	0	(0	0)	2	3	0	2	0	3	0	0	0	0	0	—	0	.200	.333	.200

Sammy Sosa

Bats: Right **Throws:** Right **Pos:** RF-160 **Ht:** 6'0" **Wt:** 225 **Born:** 11/12/68 **Age:** 33

Year Team	Lg	G	AB	H	2B	3B	HR	(Hm	Rd)	TB	R	RBI	TBB	IBB	SO	HBP	SH	SF	SB	CS	SB%	GDP	Avg	OBP	SLG
1989 Tex-CWS	AL	58	183	47	8	0	4	(1	3)	67	27	13	11	2	47	2	5	2	7	5	.58	6	.257	.303	.366
1990 Chicago	AL	153	532	124	26	10	15	(10	5)	215	72	70	33	4	150	6	2	6	32	16	.67	10	.233	.282	.404
1991 Chicago	AL	116	316	64	10	1	10	(3	7)	106	39	33	14	2	98	2	5	1	13	6	.68	5	.203	.240	.335
1992 Chicago	NL	67	262	68	7	2	8	(4	4)	103	41	25	19	1	63	4	4	2	15	7	.68	4	.260	.317	.393
1993 Chicago	NL	159	598	156	25	5	33	(23	10)	290	92	93	38	6	135	4	0	7	36	11	.77	14	.261	.309	.485
1994 Chicago	NL	105	426	128	17	6	25	(11	14)	232	59	70	25	1	92	2	1	4	22	13	.63	7	.300	.339	.545
1995 Chicago	NL	144	564	151	17	3	36	(19	17)	282	89	119	58	11	134	5	0	2	34	7	.83	8	.268	.340	.500
1996 Chicago	NL	124	498	136	21	2	40	(26	14)	281	84	100	34	6	134	5	0	4	18	5	.78	14	.273	.323	.564
1997 Chicago	NL	162	642	161	31	4	36	(25	11)	308	90	119	45	9	174	2	0	5	22	12	.65	16	.251	.300	.480
1998 Chicago	NL	159	643	198	20	0	66	(35	31)	416	134	158	73	14	171	1	0	5	18	9	.67	20	.308	.377	.647
1999 Chicago	NL	162	625	180	24	2	63	(33	30)	397	114	141	78	8	171	3	0	6	7	8	.47	17	.288	.367	.635
2000 Chicago	NL	156	604	193	38	1	50	(22	28)	383	106	138	91	19	168	2	0	8	7	4	.64	12	.320	.406	.634
2001 Chicago	NL	160	577	189	34	5	64	(34	30)	425	146	160	116	37	153	6	0	12	0	2	.00	6	.328	.437	.737
1989 Texas	AL	25	84	20	3	0	1	(0	1)	26	8	3	0	0	20	0	4	0	0	2	.00	3	.238	.238	.310
Chicago	AL	33	99	27	5	0	3	(1	2)	41	19	10	11	2	27	2	1	2	7	3	.70	3	.273	.351	.414
13 ML YEARS		1725	6470	1795	278	41	450	(246	204)	3505	1093	1239	635	120	1690	44	17	58	231	105	.69	139	.277	.343	.542

Steve Sparks

Pitches: Right **Bats:** Right **Pos:** SP-33; RP-2 **Ht:** 6'0" **Wt:** 180 **Born:** 7/2/65 **Age:** 36

		HOW MUCH HE PITCHED						WHAT HE GAVE UP										THE RESULTS						
Year Team	Lg	G	GS	CG	GF	IP	BFP	H	R	ER	HR	SH	SF	HB	TBB	IBB	SO	WP	Bk	W	L	Pct.	ShO	Sv-Op	Hld	ERA
1995 Milwaukee	AL	33	27	3	2	202	875	210	111	104	17	5	12	5	86	1	96	5	1	9	11	.450	0	0-0	0	4.63
1996 Milwaukee	AL	20	13	1	2	88.2	406	103	66	65	19	3	1	3	52	0	21	6	0	4	7	.364	0	0-0	0	6.60

Year Team	Lg	HOW MUCH HE PITCHED						WHAT HE GAVE UP												THE RESULTS						
		G	GS	CG	GF	IP	BFP	H	R	ER	HR	SH	SF	HB	TBB	IBB	SO	WP	Bk	W	L	Pct.	ShO	Sv-Op	Hld	ERA
1998 Anaheim	AL	22	20	0	1	128.2	562	130	66	62	14	2	3	5	58	0	90	6	0	9	4	.692	0	0-0	0	4.34
1999 Anaheim	AL	28	26	0	1	147.2	688	165	101	89	21	2	8	9	82	0	73	8	0	5	11	.313	0	0-0	0	5.42
2000 Detroit	AL	20	15	1	5	104	446	108	55	47	7	1	1	4	29	0	53	6	0	7	5	.583	1	1-1	0	4.07
2001 Detroit	AL	35	33	8	2	232	982	244	110	94	22	4	9	6	64	1	116	8	2	14	9	.609	1	0-0	0	3.65
6 ML YEARS		158	134	13	13	903	3959	960	509	461	100	17	34	32	371	2	449	39	3	48	47	.505	2	1-1	0	4.59

Justin Speier

Pitches: Right **Bats:** Right **Pos:** RP-54 **Ht:** 6'4" **Wt:** 205 **Born:** 11/6/73 **Age:** 28

Year Team	Lg	HOW MUCH HE PITCHED						WHAT HE GAVE UP												THE RESULTS						
		G	GS	CG	GF	IP	BFP	H	R	ER	HR	SH	SF	HB	TBB	IBB	SO	WP	Bk	W	L	Pct.	ShO	Sv-Op	Hld	ERA
2001 Colo Sprngs *	AAA	11	0	0	4	12.1	54	10	2	2	0	1	1	1	7	0	16	3	1	1	0	1.000	0	2--	—	1.46
1998 ChC-Fla	NL	19	0	0	10	20.2	99	27	20	20	7	2	1	0	13	1	17	3	0	0	3	.000	0	0-1	1	8.71
1999 Atlanta	NL	19	0	0	8	28.2	127	28	18	18	8	0	1	0	13	1	22	0	0	0	0	—	0	0-0	0	5.65
2000 Cleveland	AL	47	0	0	12	68.1	290	57	27	25	9	2	4	4	28	3	69	7	1	5	2	.714	0	0-1	6	3.29
2001 Cle-Col		54	0	0	10	76.2	324	71	40	39	13	2	7	8	20	3	62	6	1	6	3	.667	0	0-1	4	4.58
1998 Chicago	NL	1	0	0	0	1.1	7	2	2	2	0	0	0	0	1	0	2	1	0	0	0	—	0	0-0	0	13.50
Florida	NL	18	0	0	10	19.1	92	25	18	18	7	2	1	0	12	1	15	2	0	0	3	.000	0	0-1	1	8.38
2001 Cleveland	AL	12	0	0	2	20.2	96	24	16	16	5	0	3	3	8	0	15	2	0	2	0	1.000	0	0-0	0	6.97
Colorado	NL	42	0	0	8	56	228	47	24	23	8	2	4	5	12	3	47	4	1	4	3	.571	0	0-1	4	3.70
4 ML YEARS		139	0	0	40	194.1	840	183	105	102	37	6	13	12	74	8	170	16	2	11	8	.579	0	0-3	11	4.72

Shane Spencer

Bats: R **Throws:** R **Pos:** LF-44; RF-28; DH-14; PH/PR-4 **Ht:** 5'11" **Wt:** 225 **Born:** 2/20/72 **Age:** 30

Year Team	Lg	BATTING															BASERUNNING				PERCENTAGES		
		G	AB	H	2B	3B	HR	(Hm | Rd)	TB	R	RBI	TBB	IBB	SO	HBP	SH	SF	SB	CS	SB%	GDP	Avg	OBP	SLG
2001 Columbus *	AAA	49	173	40	10	1	3	—	—	61	17	14	23	0	21	2	0	3	4	1	.80	9	.231	.323	.353
1998 New York	AL	27	67	25	6	0	10	(8 | 2)	61	18	27	5	0	12	0	0	1	0	1	.00	0	.373	.411	.910
1999 New York	AL	71	205	48	8	0	8	(2 | 6)	80	25	20	18	0	51	2	0	1	0	4	.00	1	.234	.301	.390
2000 New York	AL	73	248	70	11	3	9	(4 | 5)	114	33	40	19	0	45	2	0	7	1	2	.33	4	.282	.330	.460
2001 New York	AL	80	283	73	14	2	10	(6 | 4)	121	40	46	21	0	58	4	0	3	4	1	.80	4	.258	.315	.428
4 ML YEARS		251	803	216	39	5	37	(20 | 17)	376	116	133	63	0	166	8	0	12	5	8	.38	9	.269	.324	.468

Bill Spiers

Bats: Left **Throws:** Right **Pos:** PH/PR-4 **Ht:** 6'2" **Wt:** 190 **Born:** 6/5/66 **Age:** 36

Year Team	Lg	BATTING															BASERUNNING				PERCENTAGES		
		G	AB	H	2B	3B	HR	(Hm | Rd)	TB	R	RBI	TBB	IBB	SO	HBP	SH	SF	SB	CS	SB%	GDP	Avg	OBP	SLG
1989 Milwaukee	AL	114	345	88	9	3	4	(1 | 3)	115	44	33	21	1	63	1	4	2	10	2	.83	2	.255	.298	.333
1990 Milwaukee	AL	112	363	88	15	3	2	(2 | 0)	115	44	36	16	0	45	1	6	3	11	6	.65	12	.242	.274	.317
1991 Milwaukee	AL	133	414	117	13	6	8	(1 | 7)	166	71	54	34	0	55	2	10	4	14	8	.64	9	.283	.337	.401
1992 Milwaukee	AL	12	16	5	2	0	0	(0 | 0)	7	2	2	1	0	4	0	1	0	1	1	.50	1	.313	.353	.438
1993 Milwaukee	AL	113	340	81	8	4	2	(2 | 0)	103	43	36	29	2	51	4	9	4	9	8	.53	11	.238	.302	.303
1994 Milwaukee	AL	73	214	54	10	1	0	(0 | 0)	66	27	17	19	1	42	1	3	0	7	1	.88	5	.252	.316	.308
1995 New York	NL	63	72	15	2	1	0	(0 | 0)	19	5	11	12	1	15	0	1	2	0	1	.00	1	.208	.314	.264
1996 Houston	NL	122	218	55	10	1	6	(3 | 3)	85	27	26	20	4	34	2	1	1	7	0	1.00	3	.252	.320	.390
1997 Houston	NL	132	291	93	27	4	4	(0 | 4)	140	51	48	61	6	42	1	1	1	10	5	.67	4	.320	.438	.481
1998 Houston	NL	123	384	105	27	4	4	(1 | 3)	152	66	43	45	0	62	5	1	2	11	2	.85	9	.273	.356	.396
1999 Houston	NL	127	393	113	18	5	4	(1 | 3)	153	56	39	47	2	45	0	3	1	10	5	.67	10	.288	.363	.389
2000 Houston	NL	124	355	107	17	3	3	(2 | 1)	139	41	43	49	3	38	1	2	2	7	4	.64	8	.301	.386	.392
2001 Houston	NL	4	3	1	0	0	0	(0 | 0)	1	0	1	1	0	0	0	0	0	0	0	—	0	.333	.500	.333
13 ML YEARS		1252	3408	922	158	35	37	(13 | 24)	1261	477	388	355	21	496	18	42	22	97	43	.69	73	.271	.341	.370

Scott Spiezio

Bats: B **Throws:** R **Pos:** 1B-105; DH-20; PH/PR-18; 3B-10; LF-10; RF-8 **Ht:** 6'2" **Wt:** 225 **Born:** 9/21/72 **Age:** 29

Year Team	Lg	BATTING															BASERUNNING				PERCENTAGES		
		G	AB	H	2B	3B	HR	(Hm | Rd)	TB	R	RBI	TBB	IBB	SO	HBP	SH	SF	SB	CS	SB%	GDP	Avg	OBP	SLG
1996 Oakland	AL	9	29	9	2	0	2	(1 | 1)	17	6	8	4	1	4	0	2	0	0	1	.00	0	.310	.394	.586
1997 Oakland	AL	147	538	131	28	4	14	(6 | 8)	209	58	65	44	2	75	1	3	4	9	3	.75	13	.243	.300	.388
1998 Oakland	AL	114	406	105	19	1	9	(6 | 3)	153	54	50	44	3	56	2	7	2	1	3	.25	10	.259	.333	.377
1999 Oakland	AL	84	247	60	24	0	8	(3 | 5)	108	31	33	29	3	36	2	1	3	0	0	—	5	.243	.324	.437
2000 Anaheim	AL	123	297	72	11	2	17	(10 | 7)	138	47	49	40	2	56	3	1	4	1	2	.33	5	.242	.334	.465
2001 Anaheim	AL	139	457	124	29	4	13	(8 | 5)	200	57	54	34	4	65	5	3	4	5	2	.71	6	.271	.326	.438
6 ML YEARS		621	1974	501	113	11	63	(34 | 29)	825	253	259	195	15	292	13	17	17	16	11	.59	39	.254	.322	.418

Junior Spivey

Bats: Right **Throws:** Right **Pos:** 2B-66; PH/PR-17; SS-1 **Ht:** 6'0" **Wt:** 185 **Born:** 1/28/75 **Age:** 27

Year Team	Lg	BATTING															BASERUNNING				PERCENTAGES		
		G	AB	H	2B	3B	HR	(Hm | Rd)	TB	R	RBI	TBB	IBB	SO	HBP	SH	SF	SB	CS	SB%	GDP	Avg	OBP	SLG
1996 Diamndbcks	R	20	69	23	0	0	0	—	—	23	13	3	12	0	16	4	1	1	11	2	.85	0	.333	.453	.333
Lethbridge	R+	31	107	36	3	4	2	—	—	53	30	25	23	0	24	3	1	2	8	3	.73	2	.336	.459	.495
1997 High Desert	A+	136	491	134	24	6	6	—	—	188	88	53	69	2	115	11	2	3	14	9	.61	9	.273	.373	.383
1998 High Desert	A+	79	285	80	14	5	5	—	—	119	64	35	64	0	61	3	0	1	34	12	.74	4	.281	.416	.418
Tulsa	AA	34	119	37	10	1	3	—	—	58	26	16	28	1	25	3	1	1	8	4	.67	1	.311	.450	.487
1999 El Paso	AA	44	164	48	10	4	3	—	—	75	40	19	36	0	27	2	1	1	14	10	.58	5	.293	.424	.457
2000 Tucson	AAA	28	117	33	8	4	3	—	—	58	21	16	11	0	17	0	1	1	3	1	.75	4	.282	.341	.496
El Paso	AA	6	19	8	5	0	1	—	—	16	5	2	0	0	5	0	1	0	0	0	—	1	.421	.421	.842
2001 Tucson	AAA	54	194	45	6	0	6	—	—	69	25	27	27	1	32	0	2	0	9	6	.60	4	.232	.326	.356
2001 Arizona	NL	72	163	42	6	3	5	(4 | 1)	69	33	21	23	0	47	2	6	1	3	0	1.00	3	.258	.354	.423

Tim Spooneybarger

Pitches: Right **Bats:** Right **Pos:** RP-4   Ht: 6'3" Wt: 190 Born: 10/21/79 Age: 22

Year Team	Lg	G	GS	CG	GF	IP	BFP	H	R	ER	HR	SH	SF	HB	TBB	IBB	SO	WP	Bk	W	L	Pct.	ShO	Sv-Op	Hld	ERA
1999 Danville	R+	12	0	0	2	24.1	103	15	11	7	0	0	0	2	14	0	36	5	0	3	0	1.000	0	0--	—	2.59
Macon	A	7	0	0	3	10	47	7	4	4	1	1	0	0	10	1	17	2	0	1	0	1.000	0	0--	—	3.60
2000 Myrtle Bch	A+	19	6	0	5	49.2	187	18	7	5	0	4	0	1	19	0	57	6	0	3	0	1.000	0	0--	—	0.91
2001 Greenville	AA	15	0	0	6	21	86	20	12	12	1	1	0	0	4	0	24	5	0	1	1	.500	0	0--	—	5.14
Richmond	AAA	42	0	0	18	50.2	202	33	5	4	1	1	0	2	21	1	58	5	0	3	0	1.000	0	5--	—	0.71
2001 Atlanta	NL	4	0	0	3	4	19	5	1	1	0	1	0	1	2	1	3	0	0	0	1	.000	0	0-0	0	2.25

Ed Sprague

Bats: R **Throws:** R **Pos:** PH/PR-17; 1B-12; DH-9; 3B-8; LF-8; C-1; RF-1   Ht: 6'2" Wt: 205 Born: 7/25/67 Age: 34

Year Team	Lg	G	AB	H	2B	3B	HR	(Hm	Rd)	TB	R	RBI	TBB	IBB	SO	HBP	SH	SF	SB	CS	SB%	GDP	Avg	OBP	SLG
2001 Tacoma *	AAA	5	19	6	2	0	2	—	—	14	6	4	1	0	5	2	0	1	0	0	—	0	.316	.391	.737
1991 Toronto	AL	61	160	44	7	0	4	(3	1)	63	17	20	19	2	43	3	0	1	0	3	.00	2	.275	.361	.394
1992 Toronto	AL	22	47	11	2	0	1	(1	0)	16	6	7	3	0	7	0	0	0	0	0	—	0	.234	.280	.340
1993 Toronto	AL	150	546	142	31	1	12	(8	4)	211	50	73	32	1	85	10	2	6	1	0	1.00	23	.260	.310	.386
1994 Toronto	AL	109	405	97	19	1	11	(6	5)	151	38	44	23	1	95	11	2	4	1	0	1.00	11	.240	.296	.373
1995 Toronto	AL	144	521	127	27	2	18	(12	6)	212	77	74	58	3	96	15	1	7	0	0	—	19	.244	.333	.407
1996 Toronto	AL	159	591	146	35	2	36	(17	19)	293	88	101	60	3	146	12	0	7	0	0	—	7	.247	.325	.496
1997 Toronto	AL	138	504	115	29	4	14	(5	9)	194	63	48	51	0	102	6	0	1	0	1	.00	10	.228	.306	.385
1998 Tor-Oak	AL	132	469	104	25	0	20	(9	11)	189	57	58	26	2	90	13	0	2	1	2	.33	16	.222	.280	.403
1999 Pittsburgh	NL	137	490	131	27	2	22	(10	12)	228	71	81	50	6	93	17	1	6	3	6	.33	12	.267	.352	.465
2000 SD-Bos	NL	106	268	65	16	0	12	(5	7)	117	30	36	25	2	58	3	0	2	0	0	—	3	.243	.312	.437
2001 Seattle	AL	45	94	28	7	0	2	(1	1)	41	9	16	11	1	18	1	0	1	0	0	—	3	.298	.374	.436
1998 Toronto	AL	105	382	91	20	0	17	(6	11)	162	49	51	24	1	73	11	0	2	0	2	.00	15	.238	.301	.424
Oakland	AL	27	87	13	5	0	3	(3	0)	27	8	7	2	1	17	2	0	0	1	0	1.00	1	.149	.187	.310
2000 San Diego	NL	73	157	41	12	0	10	(4	6)	83	19	27	13	2	40	3	0	2	0	0	—	1	.261	.326	.529
Boston	AL	33	111	24	4	0	2	(1	1)	34	11	9	12	0	18	0	0	0	0	0	—	2	.216	.293	.306
11 ML YEARS		1203	4095	1010	225	12	152	(77	75)	1715	506	558	358	21	833	91	6	37	6	12	.33	106	.247	.318	.419

Dennis Springer

Pitches: Right **Bats:** Right **Pos:** SP-3; RP-1   Ht: 5'10" Wt: 185 Born: 2/12/65 Age: 37

Year Team	Lg	G	GS	CG	GF	IP	BFP	H	R	ER	HR	SH	SF	HB	TBB	IBB	SO	WP	Bk	W	L	Pct.	ShO	Sv-Op	Hld	ERA
2001 Las Vegas *	AAA	19	18	2	1	114.1	504	142	74	67	16	6	4	6	28	1	51	4	1	7	7	.500	1	0--	—	5.27
1995 Philadelphia	NL	4	4	0	0	22.1	94	21	15	12	3	2	0	1	9	1	15	1	0	0	3	.000	0	0-0	0	4.84
1996 California	AL	20	15	2	3	94.2	413	91	65	58	24	0	1	6	43	0	64	1	0	5	6	.455	1	0-0	1	5.51
1997 Anaheim	AL	32	28	3	0	194.2	846	199	118	112	32	4	13	10	73	0	75	7	0	9	9	.500	1	0-0	0	5.18
1998 Tampa Bay	AL	29	17	1	8	115.2	517	120	77	70	21	1	2	12	60	1	46	6	0	3	11	.214	0	1-1	0	5.45
1999 Florida	NL	38	29	3	3	196.1	855	231	121	106	23	12	10	7	64	3	83	2	0	6	16	.273	2	1-1	1	4.86
2000 New York	NL	2	2	0	0	11.1	59	20	11	11	2	0	0	1	5	0	5	2	0	1	0	1.000	0	0-0	0	8.74
2001 Los Angeles	NL	4	3	0	1	19	75	19	7	7	3	1	0	3	2	0	7	2	0	1	1	.500	0	0-0	0	3.32
7 ML YEARS		129	98	9	15	654	2859	701	414	376	108	20	26	40	256	5	295	21	0	24	47	.338	4	1-1	2	5.17

Russ Springer

Pitches: Right **Bats:** Right **Pos:** RP-18   Ht: 6'4" Wt: 211 Born: 11/7/68 Age: 33

Year Team	Lg	G	GS	CG	GF	IP	BFP	H	R	ER	HR	SH	SF	HB	TBB	IBB	SO	WP	Bk	W	L	Pct.	ShO	Sv-Op	Hld	ERA
2001 Tucson *	AAA	7	3	0	0	7.1	32	7	4	4	1	0	0	1	3	0	6	0	0	0	0	—	0	0--	—	4.91
1992 New York	AL	14	0	0	5	16	75	18	11	11	0	0	0	0	10	0	12	0	0	0	0	—	0	0-0	2	6.19
1993 California	AL	14	9	1	3	60	278	73	48	48	11	1	1	3	32	1	31	6	0	1	6	.143	0	0-0	0	7.20
1994 California	AL	18	5	0	6	45.2	198	53	28	28	9	1	1	0	14	0	28	2	0	2	2	.500	0	2-3	1	5.52
1995 Cal-Phi		33	6	0	6	78.1	350	82	48	46	16	2	2	7	35	4	70	2	0	1	2	.333	0	1-2	0	5.29
1996 Philadelphia	NL	51	7	0	12	96.2	437	106	60	50	12	5	3	1	38	6	94	5	0	3	10	.231	0	0-3	6	4.66
1997 Houston	NL	54	0	0	13	55.1	241	58	28	26	4	1	2	4	27	2	74	4	0	3	3	.500	0	3-7	9	4.23
1998 Ari-Atl	NL	48	0	0	14	52.2	232	51	26	24	4	2	1	5	30	4	56	5	0	5	4	.556	0	0-4	7	4.10
1999 Atlanta	NL	49	0	0	8	47.1	194	31	20	18	5	0	2	2	22	2	49	0	0	2	1	.667	0	1-1	8	3.42
2000 Arizona	NL	52	0	0	10	62	282	63	36	35	11	2	3	2	34	6	59	3	0	4	3	.333	0	0-2	3	5.08
2001 Arizona	NL	18	0	0	9	17.2	79	20	16	14	5	1	1	0	4	0	12	2	0	0	0	—	0	1-1	2	7.13
1995 California	AL	19	6	0	3	51.2	238	60	37	35	11	1	0	5	25	1	38	1	0	1	2	.333	0	1-2	0	6.10
Philadelphia	NL	14	0	0	3	26.2	112	22	11	11	5	1	2	2	10	3	32	1	0	0	0	—	0	0-0	0	3.71
1998 Arizona	NL	26	0	0	13	32.2	140	29	16	15	4	0	0	1	14	1	37	3	0	4	3	.571	0	0-3	1	4.13
Atlanta	NL	22	0	0	1	20	92	22	10	9	0	2	1	0	16	3	19	2	0	1	1	.500	0	0-1	6	4.05
10 ML YEARS		351	27	1	86	531.2	2366	545	321	300	77	15	16	21	246	25	485	29	0	19	32	.373	0	8-23	38	5.08

Matt Stairs

Bats: L **Throws:** R **Pos:** 1B-89; LF-22; PH/PR-19; DH-2; 2B-1; RF-1   Ht: 5'9" Wt: 225 Born: 2/27/68 Age: 34

Year Team	Lg	G	AB	H	2B	3B	HR	(Hm	Rd)	TB	R	RBI	TBB	IBB	SO	HBP	SH	SF	SB	CS	SB%	GDP	Avg	OBP	SLG
1992 Montreal	NL	13	30	5	2	0	0	(0	0)	7	2	5	7	0	7	0	0	1	0	0	—	0	.167	.316	.233
1993 Montreal	NL	6	8	3	1	0	0	(0	0)	4	1	2	0	0	1	0	0	0	0	0	—	0	.375	.375	.500
1995 Boston	AL	39	88	23	7	1	1	(0	1)	35	8	17	4	0	14	1	1	1	0	1	.00	4	.261	.298	.398
1996 Oakland	AL	61	137	38	5	1	10	(5	5)	75	21	23	19	2	23	1	0	1	1	1	.50	2	.277	.367	.547
1997 Oakland	AL	133	352	105	19	4	27	(20	7)	205	62	73	50	1	60	3	1	4	3	2	.60	6	.298	.386	.582
1998 Oakland	AL	149	523	154	33	1	26	(16	10)	267	88	106	59	4	93	6	1	4	8	3	.73	13	.294	.370	.511
1999 Oakland	AL	146	531	137	26	3	38	(15	23)	283	94	102	89	6	124	2	0	1	2	7	.22	8	.258	.366	.533
2000 Oakland	AL	143	476	108	26	0	21	(9	12)	197	74	81	78	4	122	1	1	6	5	2	.71	7	.227	.333	.414

			BATTING																BASERUNNING				PERCENTAGES		
Year Team	Lg	G	AB	H	2B	3B	HR	(Hm	Rd)	TB	R	RBI	TBB	IBB	SO	HBP	SH	SF	SB	CS	SB%	GDP	Avg	OBP	SLG
2001 Chicago	NL	128	340	85	21	0	17	(5	12)	157	48	61	52	7	76	7	1	3	2	3	.40	4	.250	.358	.462
9 ML YEARS		818	2485	658	140	6	140	(70	70)	1230	398	470	358	24	520	21	5	21	21	19	.53	45	.265	.359	.495

Jason Standridge

Pitches: Right **Bats:** Right **Pos:** RP-8; SP-1   **Ht:** 6'4" **Wt:** 205 **Born:** 11/9/78 **Age:** 23

		HOW MUCH HE PITCHED						WHAT HE GAVE UP												THE RESULTS					
Year Team	Lg	G	GS	CG	GF	IP	BFP	H	R	ER	HR	SH	SF	HB	TBB	IBB	SO	WP	Bk	W	L	Pct.	ShO	Sv-Op	Hld	ERA
1997 Devil Rays	R	13	13	0	0	57.2	246	56	30	23	3	2	5	2	13	1	55	2	2	0	6	.000	0	0- -	—	3.59
1998 Princeton	R+	12	12	0	0	63	298	82	61	49	4	2	4	3	28	0	47	9	0	4	4	.500	0	0- -	—	7.00
1999 Chston-SC	A	18	18	3	0	116	455	80	35	26	5	5	5	7	31	0	84	9	2	9	1	.900	3	0- -	—	2.02
St. Pete	A+	8	8	0	0	48.1	208	49	21	21	0	1	0	4	20	0	26	6	1	4	4	.500	0	0- -	—	3.91
2000 St. Pete	A+	10	10	1	0	56	243	45	28	21	4	0	1	1	31	0	41	6	0	2	4	.333	0	0- -	—	3.38
Orlando	AA	17	17	2	0	97	416	85	46	39	4	2	2	11	43	0	55	4	0	6	8	.429	0	0- -	—	3.62
2001 Durham	AAA	20	20	0	0	102.1	475	130	73	60	13	2	7	3	50	0	48	6	0	5	10	.333	0	0- -	—	5.28
Orlando	AA	2	2	0	0	9.2	44	12	6	6	0	0	0	0	4	0	7	0	0	0	2	.000	0	0- -	—	5.59
2001 Tampa Bay	AL	9	1	0	6	19.1	87	19	10	10	5	0	0	0	14	1	9	0	0	0	0	—	0	0-0	0	4.66

Mike Stanton

Pitches: Left **Bats:** Left **Pos:** RP-76   **Ht:** 6'1" **Wt:** 215 **Born:** 6/2/67 **Age:** 35

		HOW MUCH HE PITCHED						WHAT HE GAVE UP												THE RESULTS					
Year Team	Lg	G	GS	CG	GF	IP	BFP	H	R	ER	HR	SH	SF	HB	TBB	IBB	SO	WP	Bk	W	L	Pct.	ShO	Sv-Op	Hld	ERA
1989 Atlanta	NL	20	0	0	10	24	94	17	4	4	0	4	0	0	8	1	27	1	0	0	1	.000	0	7-8	2	1.50
1990 Atlanta	NL	7	0	0	4	7	42	16	16	14	1	1	0	1	4	2	7	1	0	0	3	.000	0	2-3	0	18.00
1991 Atlanta	NL	74	0	0	20	78	314	62	27	25	6	6	0	1	21	6	54	0	0	5	5	.500	0	7-10	15	2.88
1992 Atlanta	NL	65	0	0	23	63.2	264	59	32	29	6	1	2	2	20	2	44	3	0	5	4	.556	0	8-11	15	4.10
1993 Atlanta	NL	63	0	0	41	52	236	51	35	27	4	5	2	0	29	7	43	1	0	4	6	.400	0	27-33	5	4.67
1994 Atlanta	NL	49	0	0	15	45.2	197	41	18	18	2	2	1	3	26	3	35	1	0	3	1	.750	0	3-4	10	3.55
1995 Atl-Bos		48	0	0	22	40.1	178	48	23	19	6	2	1	1	14	2	23	2	1	2	1	.667	0	1-3	8	4.24
1996 Bos-Tex	AL	81	0	0	28	78.2	327	78	32	32	11	4	2	0	27	5	60	3	2	4	4	.500	0	1-6	22	3.66
1997 New York	AL	64	0	0	15	66.2	283	50	19	19	3	2	0	3	34	2	70	3	2	6	1	.857	0	3-5	26	2.57
1998 New York	AL	67	0	0	26	79	330	71	51	48	13	1	2	4	26	1	69	0	0	4	1	.800	0	6-10	18	5.47
1999 New York	AL	73	1	0	10	62.1	271	71	30	30	5	4	2	1	18	4	59	3	0	2	2	.500	0	0-5	21	4.33
2000 New York	AL	69	0	0	20	68	291	68	32	31	5	2	4	2	24	2	75	1	0	2	3	.400	0	0-4	15	4.10
2001 New York	AL	76	0	0	16	80.1	342	80	25	23	4	2	3	4	29	9	78	3	1	9	4	.692	0	0-1	23	2.58
1995 Atlanta	NL	26	0	0	10	19.1	94	31	14	12	3	2	1	1	6	2	13	1	1	1	1	.500	0	1-2	4	5.59
Boston	AL	22	0	0	12	21	84	17	9	7	3	0	0	0	8	0	10	1	0	1	0	1.000	0	0-1	4	3.00
1996 Boston	AL	59	0	0	19	56.1	239	58	24	24	9	3	2	0	23	4	46	3	2	4	3	.571	0	1-5	15	3.83
Texas	AL	22	0	0	9	22.1	88	20	8	8	2	1	0	0	4	1	14	0	0	1	0	1.000	0	0-1	7	3.22
13 ML YEARS		756	1	0	250	745.2	3169	712	344	319	66	36	19	22	280	46	644	22	6	46	36	.561	0	65-103	180	3.85

Denny Stark

Pitches: Right **Bats:** Right **Pos:** SP-3; RP-1   **Ht:** 6'2" **Wt:** 210 **Born:** 10/27/74 **Age:** 27

		HOW MUCH HE PITCHED						WHAT HE GAVE UP												THE RESULTS					
Year Team	Lg	G	GS	CG	GF	IP	BFP	H	R	ER	HR	SH	SF	HB	TBB	IBB	SO	WP	Bk	W	L	Pct.	ShO	Sv-Op	Hld	ERA
1996 Everett	A-	12	4	0	4	30.1	133	25	19	15	2	3	1	1	17	0	49	5	1	1	3	.250	0	0- -	—	4.45
1997 Wisconsin	A	16	15	1	0	91.1	361	52	27	20	3	4	1	2	33	0	105	5	1	6	3	.667	0	0- -	—	1.97
Lancaster	A+	3	3	0	0	16.2	71	13	7	6	1	1	0	2	10	0	17	0	0	1	1	.500	0	0- -	—	3.24
1998 Lancaster	A+	5	5	0	0	21	100	18	12	10	1	1	0	1	17	0	21	0	0	1	2	.333	0	0- -	—	4.29
Mariners	R	3	1	0	0	8.1	36	9	2	2	0	0	0	0	2	0	13	0	0	0	0	—	0	0- -	—	2.16
1999 New Haven	AA	26	26	2	0	147.1	646	151	82	72	14	6	2	13	62	0	103	7	1	9	11	.450	1	0- -	—	4.40
2000 New Haven	AA	8	8	1	0	49.1	194	31	13	12	1	2	1	3	17	0	42	2	0	4	3	.571	0	0- -	—	2.19
2001 San Antonio	AA	1	1	0	0	6	24	2	0	0	0	0	0	0	2	0	7	0	0	1	0	1.000	0	0- -	—	0.00
Tacoma	AAA	24	24	0	0	151.2	613	124	52	40	12	8	5	7	41	0	130	5	1	14	2	.875	0	0- -	—	2.37
1999 Seattle	AL	5	0	0	2	6.1	31	10	8	7	0	0	0	0	4	0	4	0	0	0	0	0-0	0			9.95
2001 Seattle	AL	4	3	0	0	14.2	68	21	15	15	5	0	1	0	4	0	12	0	0	1	1	.500	0	0-0	0	9.20
2 ML YEARS		9	3	0	2	21	99	31	23	22	5	0	1	0	8	0	16	0	0	1	1	.500	0	0-0	0	9.43

Gene Stechschulte

Pitches: Right **Bats:** Right **Pos:** RP-67   **Ht:** 6'5" **Wt:** 210 **Born:** 8/12/73 **Age:** 28

		HOW MUCH HE PITCHED						WHAT HE GAVE UP												THE RESULTS					
Year Team	Lg	G	GS	CG	GF	IP	BFP	H	R	ER	HR	SH	SF	HB	TBB	IBB	SO	WP	Bk	W	L	Pct.	ShO	Sv-Op	Hld	ERA
1996 New Jersey	A-	20	0	0	6	33	159	41	17	12	0	2	4	2	16	2	27	4	0	1	2	.333	0	0- -	—	3.27
1997 New Jersey	A-	30	0	0	9	36.1	164	45	16	13	2	0	2	1	16	0	28	3	0	1	1	.500	0	1- -	—	3.22
1998 Peoria	A	57	0	0	51	66	279	58	26	19	1	5	2	2	21	2	70	2	0	4	8	.333	0	33- -	—	2.59
1999 Memphis	AAA	2	0	0	0	2.1	14	2	2	2	0	0	1	0	5	0	2	0	0	0	0	—	0	0- -	—	7.71
Arkansas	AA	39	0	0	33	42.1	191	41	26	16	4	4	1	4	20	1	41	3	0	2	6	.250	0	19- -	—	3.40
2000 Memphis	AAA	41	0	0	38	47.2	195	38	13	13	4	5	0	1	18	4	37	1	0	4	1	.800	0	26- -	—	2.45
Arkansas	AA	2	0	0	1	2	8	0	0	0	0	0	0	1	0	0	3	0	0	0	0	—	0	0- -	—	0.00
2000 St. Louis	NL	20	0	0	7	25.2	116	24	22	18	6	0	2	0	17	1	12	2	0	1	0	1.000	0	0-1	3	6.31
2001 St. Louis	NL	67	0	0	18	70	301	71	35	30	10	4	3	4	30	2	51	2	0	1	5	.167	0	6-8	13	3.86
2 ML YEARS		87	0	0	25	95.2	417	95	57	48	16	4	5	4	47	3	63	4	0	2	5	.286	0	6-9	16	4.52

Blake Stein

Pitches: Right **Bats:** Right **Pos:** RP-21; SP-15   **Ht:** 6'7" **Wt:** 240 **Born:** 8/3/73 **Age:** 28

		HOW MUCH HE PITCHED						WHAT HE GAVE UP												THE RESULTS					
Year Team	Lg	G	GS	CG	GF	IP	BFP	H	R	ER	HR	SH	SF	HB	TBB	IBB	SO	WP	Bk	W	L	Pct.	ShO	Sv-Op	Hld	ERA
1998 Oakland	AL	24	20	1	0	117.1	538	117	92	83	22	1	2	5	71	3	89	15	0	5	9	.357	1	0-0	0	6.37
1999 Oak-KC	AL	13	12	0	0	73	327	65	38	37	11	2	1	7	47	1	47	3	0	1	2	.333	0	0-0	0	4.56

Year Team	Lg	HOW MUCH HE PITCHED						WHAT HE GAVE UP												THE RESULTS						
		G	GS	CG	GF	IP	BFP	H	R	ER	HR	SH	SF	HB	TBB	IBB	SO	WP	Bk	W	L	Pct.	ShO	Sv-Op	Hld	ERA
2000 Kansas City	AL	17	17	1	0	107.2	464	98	57	56	19	3	4	3	57	1	78	7	0	8	5	.615	0	0-0	0	4.68
2001 Kansas City	AL	36	15	0	5	131	568	112	73	69	20	1	4	3	79	2	113	10	0	7	8	.467	0	1-2	1	4.74
1999 Oakland	AL	1	1	0	0	2.2	19	6	5	5	1	0	0	0	6	0	4	1	0	0	0	—	0	0-0	0	16.88
Kansas City	AL	12	11	0	0	70.1	308	59	33	32	10	2	1	7	41	1	43	2	0	1	2	.333	0	0-0	0	4.09
4 ML YEARS		90	64	2	5	429	1897	392	260	245	72	7	11	18	254	7	327	35	0	21	24	.467	1	1-2	1	5.14

Garrett Stephenson

Pitches: Right **Bats:** Right 2000 **Pos:** SP-31; RP-1   **Ht:** 6'5" **Wt:** 208 **Born:** 1/2/72 **Age:** 30

Year Team	Lg	HOW MUCH HE PITCHED						WHAT HE GAVE UP												THE RESULTS						
		G	GS	CG	GF	IP	BFP	H	R	ER	HR	SH	SF	HB	TBB	IBB	SO	WP	Bk	W	L	Pct.	ShO	Sv-Op	Hld	ERA
2001 Memphis *	AAA	1	1	0	0	2	8	2	0	0	0	0	0	0	0	0	2	0	0	0	0	—	0	0--	—	0.00
1996 Baltimore	AL	3	0	0	2	6.1	35	13	9	9	1	1	0	1	3	1	3	0	0	0	1	.000	0	0-0	0	12.79
1997 Philadelphia	NL	20	18	2	0	117	474	104	45	41	11	2	5	3	38	0	81	1	0	8	6	.571	0	0-0	0	3.15
1998 Philadelphia	NL	6	6	0	0	23	118	31	24	23	3	1	0	0	19	0	17	0	1	0	2	.000	0	0-0	0	9.00
1999 St. Louis	NL	18	12	0	1	85.1	371	90	43	40	11	5	5	5	29	1	59	0	0	6	3	.667	0	0-0	0	4.22
2000 St. Louis	NL	32	31	3	0	200.1	858	209	105	100	31	6	7	7	63	0	123	2	2	16	9	.640	2	0-0	1	4.49
5 ML YEARS		79	67	5	3	432	1856	447	226	213	57	15	17	16	152	2	283	3	3	30	21	.588	2	0-0	1	4.44

Lee Stevens

Bats: Left **Throws:** Left **Pos:** 1B-152; PH/PR-1   **Ht:** 6'4" **Wt:** 235 **Born:** 7/10/67 **Age:** 34

Year Team	Lg	BATTING																BASERUNNING				PERCENTAGES		
		G	AB	H	2B	3B	HR	(Hm	Rd)	TB	R	RBI	TBB	IBB	SO	HBP	SH	SF	SB	CS	SB%	GDP	Avg	OBP	SLG
1990 California	AL	67	248	53	10	0	7	(4	3)	84	28	32	22	3	75	0	2	3	1	1	.50	8	.214	.275	.339
1991 California	AL	18	58	17	7	0	0	(0	0)	24	8	9	6	2	12	0	1	1	1	2	.33	0	.293	.354	.414
1992 California	AL	106	312	69	19	0	7	(2	5)	109	25	37	29	6	64	1	1	2	1	4	.20	4	.221	.288	.349
1996 Texas	AL	27	78	18	2	3	3	(2	1)	35	6	12	6	0	22	1	0	1	0	0	—	2	.231	.291	.449
1997 Texas	AL	137	426	128	24	2	21	(12	9)	219	58	74	23	2	83	1	1	3	1	3	.25	18	.300	.336	.514
1998 Texas	AL	120	344	91	17	4	20	(13	7)	176	52	59	31	4	93	0	0	1	0	2	.00	6	.265	.324	.512
1999 Texas	AL	146	517	146	31	1	24	(10	14)	251	76	81	52	10	132	0	0	7	2	3	.40	19	.282	.344	.485
2000 Montreal	NL	123	449	119	27	2	22	(14	8)	216	60	75	48	6	105	2	0	2	0	0	—	10	.265	.337	.481
2001 Montreal	NL	152	542	133	35	1	25	(12	13)	245	77	95	74	12	157	5	0	7	2	1	.67	17	.245	.338	.452
9 ML YEARS		896	2974	774	172	13	129	(69	60)	1359	390	474	291	45	743	10	5	27	8	16	.33	84	.260	.326	.457

Scott Stewart

Pitches: Left **Bats:** Right **Pos:** RP-62   **Ht:** 6'2" **Wt:** 225 **Born:** 8/14/75 **Age:** 26

Year Team	Lg	HOW MUCH HE PITCHED						WHAT HE GAVE UP												THE RESULTS						
		G	GS	CG	GF	IP	BFP	H	R	ER	HR	SH	SF	HB	TBB	IBB	SO	WP	Bk	W	L	Pct.	ShO	Sv-Op	Hld	ERA
1994 Rangers	R	14	8	0	3	54.1	221	47	22	17	1	1	0	2	12	0	62	7	9	4	1	.800	0	1--	—	2.82
1995 Chston-SC	A	11	11	1	0	75.2	302	76	38	31	6	1	4	0	14	1	47	3	5	1	7	.125	0	0--	—	3.69
Twins	R	3	1	0	0	5.2	29	7	4	4	0	0	0	1	4	0	9	0	1	0	0	—	0	0--	—	6.35
1996 St. Paul	IND	19	18	0	0	86.1	417	121	70	56	13	5	3	1	42	2	54	14	1	6	8	.429	0	0--	—	5.84
1997 St. Lucie	A+	22	18	4	1	123.1	496	114	62	55	8	3	7	4	18	1	64	4	7	5	10	.333	0	0--	—	4.01
1998 Norfolk	AAA	9	9	0	0	51.2	235	60	43	38	12	3	2	1	22	0	32	0	0	0	6	.000	0	0--	—	6.62
Binghamton	AA	24	13	0	3	90	382	91	44	37	12	4	2	1	29	2	65	2	4	8	5	.615	0	2--	—	3.70
1999 Binghamton	AA	1	1	0	0	5	18	3	0	0	0	0	0	0	0	0	5	0	0	1	0	1.000	0	0--	—	0.00
Norfolk	AAA	35	14	0	3	99.2	442	109	55	49	9	5	2	2	36	1	85	5	3	6	4	.600	0	0--	—	4.42
2000 Norfolk	AAA	53	1	0	18	72	313	80	32	28	3	5	2	3	18	2	57	8	0	3	5	.375	0	5--	—	3.50
2001 Ottawa	AAA	4	0	0	3	5	20	5	1	1	0	1	0	0	1	0	4	0	0	0	0	—	0	0--	—	1.80
2001 Montreal	NL	62	0	0	9	47.2	199	43	20	20	5	2	4	3	13	0	39	2	0	3	1	.750	0	3-4	8	3.78

Shannon Stewart

Bats: Right **Throws:** Right **Pos:** LF-142; DH-13; PH/PR-2   **Ht:** 6'1" **Wt:** 205 **Born:** 2/25/74 **Age:** 28

Year Team	Lg	BATTING																BASERUNNING				PERCENTAGES		
		G	AB	H	2B	3B	HR	(Hm	Rd)	TB	R	RBI	TBB	IBB	SO	HBP	SH	SF	SB	CS	SB%	GDP	Avg	OBP	SLG
1995 Toronto	AL	12	38	8	0	0	0	(0	0)	8	2	1	5	0	5	1	0	0	2	0	1.00	0	.211	.318	.211
1996 Toronto	AL	7	17	3	1	0	0	(0	0)	4	2	2	1	0	4	0	0	0	1	0	1.00	1	.176	.222	.235
1997 Toronto	AL	44	168	48	13	7	0	(0	0)	75	25	22	19	1	24	4	0	2	10	3	.77	3	.286	.368	.446
1998 Toronto	AL	144	516	144	29	3	12	(6	6)	215	90	55	67	1	77	15	6	1	51	18	.74	5	.279	.377	.417
1999 Toronto	AL	145	608	185	28	2	11	(4	7)	250	102	67	59	0	83	8	3	4	37	14	.73	12	.304	.371	.411
2000 Toronto	AL	136	583	186	43	5	21	(12	9)	302	107	69	37	1	79	6	1	4	20	5	.80	12	.319	.363	.518
2001 Toronto	AL	155	640	202	44	7	12	(6	6)	296	103	60	46	1	72	11	0	1	27	10	.73	9	.316	.371	.463
7 ML YEARS		643	2570	776	158	24	56	(28	28)	1150	431	276	234	4	344	45	10	12	148	50	.75	42	.302	.369	.447

Kelly Stinnett

Bats: Right **Throws:** Right **Pos:** C-59; PH/PR-6; DH-1   **Ht:** 5'11" **Wt:** 225 **Born:** 2/4/70 **Age:** 32

Year Team	Lg	BATTING																BASERUNNING				PERCENTAGES		
		G	AB	H	2B	3B	HR	(Hm	Rd)	TB	R	RBI	TBB	IBB	SO	HBP	SH	SF	SB	CS	SB%	GDP	Avg	OBP	SLG
1994 New York	NL	47	150	38	6	2	2	(0	2)	54	20	14	11	1	28	5	0	1	2	0	1.00	3	.253	.323	.360
1995 New York	NL	77	196	43	8	1	4	(1	3)	65	23	18	29	3	65	6	0	0	2	0	1.00	3	.219	.338	.332
1996 Milwaukee	AL	14	26	2	0	0	0	(0	0)	2	1	0	2	0	11	1	0	0	0	0	—	0	.077	.172	.077
1997 Milwaukee	AL	30	36	9	4	0	0	(0	0)	13	2	3	3	0	9	0	0	0	0	0	—	0	.250	.308	.361
1998 Arizona	NL	92	274	71	14	1	11	(5	6)	120	35	34	35	3	74	6	1	2	0	1	.00	9	.259	.353	.438
1999 Arizona	NL	88	284	66	13	0	14	(3	11)	121	36	38	24	2	83	5	2	2	2	1	.67	4	.232	.302	.426
2000 Arizona	NL	76	240	52	7	0	8	(2	6)	83	22	33	19	4	56	6	0	0	0	1	.00	5	.217	.291	.346
2001 Cincinnati	NL	63	187	48	11	0	9	(6	3)	86	27	25	17	3	61	5	1	1	2	2	.50	5	.257	.333	.460
8 ML YEARS		487	1393	329	63	4	48	(17	31)	544	166	165	140	16	387	34	4	6	8	5	.62	29	.236	.320	.391

Ricky Stone

Pitches: Right **Bats:** Right **Pos:** RP-6   **Ht:** 6'1" **Wt:** 168 **Born:** 2/28/75 **Age:** 27

Year Team	Lg	G	GS	CG	GF	IP	BFP	H	R	ER	HR	SH	SF	HB	TBB	IBB	SO	WP	Bk	W	L	Pct.	ShO	Sv-Op	Hld	ERA
1994 Great Falls	R+	13	7	0	4	50.2	232	55	40	25	5	0	1	2	24	0	48	9	0	2	2	.500	0	2--	--	4.44
1995 San Berndno	A+	12	12	0	0	58	273	79	50	42	7	6	3	2	25	0	31	5	0	3	5	.375	0	0--	--	6.52
Yakima	A-	16	6	0	7	48	213	54	31	28	5	2	2	2	20	0	28	4	1	4	4	.500	0	2--	--	5.25
1996 Savannah	A	5	5	0	0	31.2	130	34	15	14	2	2	1	0	9	0	31	5	0	2	1	.667	0	0--	--	3.98
Vero Beach	A+	21	21	1	0	112.2	488	115	58	48	9	4	3	3	46	0	74	10	0	8	6	.571	0	0--	--	3.83
1997 San Antonio	AA	25	5	0	10	52.2	245	63	33	32	4	4	1	3	30	0	46	3	0	0	3	.000	0	3--	--	5.47
San Berndno	A+	8	8	0	0	53.2	206	40	22	20	4	2	1	2	10	0	40	2	0	3	3	.500	0	0--	--	3.35
1998 San Antonio	AA	13	13	1	0	82	336	76	40	35	7	5	1	1	26	0	69	6	0	7	2	.778	1	0--	--	3.84
Albuquerque	AAA	18	16	0	0	105.1	465	120	69	63	13	2	1	3	41	0	85	9	1	5	5	.500	0	0--	--	5.38
1999 Albuquerque	AAA	27	27	2	0	167	764	205	123	102	23	8	7	8	71	4	132	11	1	6	10	.375	0	0--	--	5.50
2000 Albuquerque	AAA	48	7	0	22	120.1	535	146	79	66	9	7	6	7	42	3	75	10	0	9	5	.643	0	5--	--	4.94
2001 New Orleans	AAA	51	8	0	15	95.1	404	98	42	38	8	4	1	8	27	4	78	6	1	6	3	.667	0	2--	--	3.59
2001 Houston	NL	6	0	0	3	7.2	33	8	3	2	1	0	0	0	4	0	4	0	0	0	0	--	0	0-0	0	2.35

Todd Stottlemyre

Pitches: Right **Bats:** Left 2000 **Pos:** SP-18   **Ht:** 6'2" **Wt:** 210 **Born:** 5/20/65 **Age:** 37

Year Team	Lg	G	GS	CG	GF	IP	BFP	H	R	ER	HR	SH	SF	HB	TBB	IBB	SO	WP	Bk	W	L	Pct.	ShO	Sv-Op	Hld	ERA
1988 Toronto	AL	28	16	0	2	98	443	109	70	62	15	5	3	4	46	5	67	2	3	4	8	.333	0	0-1	0	5.69
1989 Toronto	AL	27	18	0	4	127.2	545	137	56	55	11	3	7	5	44	4	63	4	1	7	7	.500	0	0-0	0	3.88
1990 Toronto	AL	33	33	4	0	203	866	214	101	98	18	3	5	8	69	4	115	6	1	13	17	.433	0	0-0	0	4.34
1991 Toronto	AL	34	34	1	0	219	921	194	97	92	21	0	8	12	75	3	116	4	0	15	8	.652	0	0-0	0	3.78
1992 Toronto	AL	28	27	6	0	174	755	175	99	87	20	2	11	10	63	4	98	7	0	12	11	.522	2	0-0	0	4.50
1993 Toronto	AL	30	28	1	0	176.2	786	204	107	95	11	5	11	3	69	5	98	7	1	11	12	.478	1	0-0	0	4.84
1994 Toronto	AL	26	19	3	5	140.2	605	149	67	66	19	4	5	7	48	2	105	0	0	7	7	.500	1	1-3	0	4.22
1995 Oakland	AL	31	31	2	0	209.2	920	228	117	106	26	4	4	6	80	7	205	11	0	14	7	.667	0	0-0	0	4.55
1996 St. Louis	NL	34	33	5	0	223.1	944	191	100	96	30	12	9	4	93	8	194	8	1	14	11	.560	2	0-0	0	3.87
1997 St. Louis	NL	28	28	0	0	181	761	155	86	78	16	8	5	12	65	3	160	6	0	12	9	.571	0	0-0	0	3.88
1998 StL-Tex		33	33	3	0	221.2	949	214	107	92	25	8	6	4	81	1	204	5	2	14	13	.519	0	0-0	0	3.74
1999 Arizona	NL	17	17	0	0	101.1	446	106	51	46	12	3	1	6	40	1	74	2	0	6	3	.667	0	0-0	0	4.09
2000 Arizona	NL	18	18	0	0	95.1	408	98	55	52	18	3	2	2	36	2	76	2	1	9	6	.600	0	0-0	0	4.91
1998 St. Louis	NL	23	23	3	0	161.1	674	146	74	63	20	7	3	4	51	0	147	4	2	9	9	.500	0	0-0	0	3.51
Texas	AL	10	10	0	0	60.1	275	68	33	29	5	1	3	0	30	1	57	1	0	5	4	.556	0	0-0	0	4.33
13 ML YEARS		367	335	25	11	2171.1	9349	2174	1113	1025	242	60	77	83	809	49	1575	64	10	138	119	.537	6	1-4	0	4.25

Scott Strickland

Pitches: Right **Bats:** Right **Pos:** RP-77   **Ht:** 5'11" **Wt:** 180 **Born:** 4/26/76 **Age:** 26

Year Team	Lg	G	GS	CG	GF	IP	BFP	H	R	ER	HR	SH	SF	HB	TBB	IBB	SO	WP	Bk	W	L	Pct.	ShO	Sv-Op	Hld	ERA
1999 Montreal	NL	17	0	0	5	18	78	15	10	9	3	2	0	0	11	0	23	0	0	0	1	.000	0	0-0	2	4.50
2000 Montreal	NL	49	0	0	20	48	200	38	18	16	3	3	3	1	16	2	48	2	0	4	3	.571	0	9-13	6	3.00
2001 Montreal	NL	77	0	0	31	81.1	351	67	36	29	9	3	1	4	41	5	85	4	0	2	6	.250	0	9-12	12	3.21
3 ML YEARS		143	0	0	56	147.1	629	120	64	54	15	8	4	5	68	7	156	6	0	6	10	.375	0	18-25	20	3.30

Joe Strong

Pitches: Right **Bats:** Both **Pos:** RP-5   **Ht:** 6'0" **Wt:** 200 **Born:** 9/9/62 **Age:** 39

Year Team	Lg	G	GS	CG	GF	IP	BFP	H	R	ER	HR	SH	SF	HB	TBB	IBB	SO	WP	Bk	W	L	Pct.	ShO	Sv-Op	Hld	ERA
1984 Medford	A-	20	9	3	10	72	—	64	33	31	2	—	—	2	36	2	66	4	0	5	6	.455	0	2--	--	3.88
1985 Modesto	A+	42	11	2	18	110.1	—	103	79	62	10	—	—	3	60	2	82	10	0	7	7	.500	0	6--	--	5.06
1986 Modesto	A+	36	0	0	30	52.2	—	43	23	20	5	—	—	2	28	4	39	1	0	2	2	.500	0	11--	--	3.42
Huntsville	AA	6	0	0	2	8.1	—	8	5	5	3	—	—	0	7	0	5	0	0	1	1	.500	0	0--	--	5.40
1988 Reno	A+	31	24	2	4	161.2	—	168	114	86	10	—	—	7	96	4	107	13	8	4	13	.235	0	4--	--	4.79
1989 Reno	A+	53	0	0	47	73	—	62	35	29	4	—	—	3	22	2	79	2	1	8	1	.889	0	18--	--	3.58
1993 Las Vegas	AAA	21	0	0	5	27	129	37	23	17	4	1	2	2	10	1	18	0	1	1	3	.250	0	1--	--	5.67
Rancho Cuc	A+	6	0	0	6	10	42	10	3	3	0	0	0	2	2	0	13	2	0	1	0	1.000	0	1--	--	2.70
Wichita	AA	4	3	0	1	14.2	68	13	13	11	2	2	1	0	11	0	13	0	1	1	0	1.000	0	1--	--	6.75
1994 San Berndno	A+	12	11	0	0	53.2	246	60	46	40	11	0	4	3	27	0	43	6	2	2	3	.400	0	0--	--	6.71
1995 Surrey	IND	20	19	9	0	131	555	120	55	40	7	1	1	7	48	1	129	3	1	8	9	.471	0	4--	--	2.75
1999 Orlando	AA	11	7	2	3	38	163	40	24	24	6	1	1	0	18	1	34	0	1	1	4	.200	0	0--	--	5.68
Durham	AAA	6	1	0	1	14.2	71	20	13	13	4	0	0	0	8	0	12	0	0	0	1	.000	0	1--	--	7.98
2000 Calgary	AAA	29	1	0	21	44.2	198	44	21	20	1	1	2	4	20	1	33	7	0	2	1	.667	0	9--	--	4.03
2001 Calgary	AAA	46	0	0	13	59	275	80	45	41	9	3	4	5	18	4	48	6	0	6	3	.667	0	1--	--	6.25
2000 Florida	NL	18	0	0	5	19.2	95	26	16	16	3	1	0	2	12	1	18	2	0	1	1	.500	0	1-2	2	7.32
2001 Florida	NL	5	0	0	2	6.2	25	3	1	1	1	0	0	0	3	0	4	0	0	0	0	--	0	0-0	0	1.35
2 ML YEARS		23	0	0	7	26.1	120	29	17	17	4	1	0	2	15	1	22	2	0	1	1	.500	0	1-2	2	5.81

Tanyon Sturtze

Pitches: Right **Bats:** Right **Pos:** SP-27; RP-12   **Ht:** 6'5" **Wt:** 205 **Born:** 10/12/70 **Age:** 31

Year Team	Lg	G	GS	CG	GF	IP	BFP	H	R	ER	HR	SH	SF	HB	TBB	IBB	SO	WP	Bk	W	L	Pct.	ShO	Sv-Op	Hld	ERA
1995 Chicago	NL	2	0	0	0	2	9	2	2	2	1	0	0	0	1	0	0	0	0	0	0	--	0	0-0	0	9.00
1996 Chicago	NL	6	0	0	3	11	51	16	11	11	3	0	0	0	5	0	7	0	0	1	0	1.000	0	0-0	0	9.00
1997 Texas	AL	9	5	0	1	32.1	155	45	30	30	6	0	1	0	18	0	18	1	1	1	1	.500	0	0-0	0	8.27
1999 Chicago	AL	1	1	0	0	6	22	4	0	0	0	0	0	0	2	0	2	0	0	0	0	--	0	0-0	0	0.00
2000 CWS-TB	AL	29	6	0	9	68.1	300	72	39	36	8	1	2	3	29	1	44	2	0	5	2	.714	0	0-0	0	4.74
2001 Tampa Bay	AL	39	27	0	6	195.1	837	200	98	96	23	2	10	9	79	0	110	11	0	11	12	.478	0	1-3	3	4.42

		HOW MUCH HE PITCHED						WHAT HE GAVE UP											THE RESULTS					
Year Team	Lg	G	GS	CG	GF	IP	BFP	H	R	ER	HR	SH	SF	HB	TBB	IBB	SO	WP	Bk	W	L	Pct.	ShO	Sv-Op	Hld	ERA
2000 Chicago	AL	10	1	0	2	15.2	85	25	23	21	4	0	2	2	15	0	6	1	0	1	2	.333	0	0-0	0	12.06
Tampa Bay	AL	19	5	0	7	52.2	215	47	16	15	4	1	0	1	14	1	38	1	0	4	0	1.000	0	0-0	0	2.56
6 ML YEARS		86	39	0	19	315.1	1374	339	180	175	41	3	16	12	134	1	181	14	1	18	15	.545	0	1-3	3	4.99

Chris Stynes

Bats: R **Throws:** R **Pos:** 3B-46; 2B-43; PH/PR-7; LF-3 — **Ht:** 5'10" **Wt:** 185 **Born:** 1/19/73 **Age:** 29

		BATTING																	BASERUNNING				PERCENTAGES		
Year Team	Lg	G	AB	H	2B	3B	HR	(Hm	Rd)	TB	R	RBI	TBB	IBB	SO	HBP	SH	SF	SB	CS	SB%	GDP	Avg	OBP	SLG
2001 Pawtucket *	AAA	4	15	5	1	0	0	—	—	6	1	1	1	0	2	1	0	0	0	0	—	0	.333	.412	.400
1995 Kansas City	AL	22	35	6	1	0	0	(0	0)	7	7	2	4	0	3	0	0	0	0	0	—	0	.171	.256	.200
1996 Kansas City	AL	36	92	27	6	0	0	(0	0)	33	8	6	2	0	5	0	1	0	5	2	.71	1	.293	.309	.359
1997 Cincinnati	NL	49	198	69	7	1	6	(2	4)	96	31	28	11	1	13	4	2	0	11	2	.85	5	.348	.394	.485
1998 Cincinnati	NL	123	347	88	10	1	6	(3	3)	118	52	27	32	1	36	4	4	1	15	1	.94	5	.254	.323	.340
1999 Cincinnati	NL	73	113	27	1	0	2	(1	1)	34	18	14	12	1	13	0	3	1	5	2	.71	2	.239	.310	.301
2000 Cincinnati	NL	119	380	127	24	1	12	(8	4)	189	71	40	32	2	54	2	3	3	5	2	.71	5	.334	.386	.497
2001 Boston	AL	96	361	101	19	2	8	(3	5)	148	52	33	20	0	56	3	1	1	4	5	.44	12	.280	.322	.410
7 ML YEARS		518	1526	445	68	5	34	(17	17)	625	239	150	113	5	180	13	14	6	45	14	.76	33	.292	.344	.410

Scott Sullivan

Pitches: Right **Bats:** Right **Pos:** RP-79 — **Ht:** 6'3" **Wt:** 210 **Born:** 3/13/71 **Age:** 31

		HOW MUCH HE PITCHED						WHAT HE GAVE UP											THE RESULTS					
Year Team	Lg	G	GS	CG	GF	IP	BFP	H	R	ER	HR	SH	SF	HB	TBB	IBB	SO	WP	Bk	W	L	Pct.	ShO	Sv-Op	Hld	ERA
1995 Cincinnati	NL	3	0	0	1	3.2	17	4	2	2	0	1	0	0	2	0	2	0	0	0	0	—	0	0-0	0	4.91
1996 Cincinnati	NL	7	0	0	4	8	35	7	2	2	0	1	0	1	5	0	3	1	0	0	0	—	0	0-0	0	2.25
1997 Cincinnati	NL	59	0	0	15	97.1	402	79	36	35	12	3	3	7	30	8	96	7	1	5	3	.625	0	1-2	13	3.24
1998 Cincinnati	NL	67	0	0	13	102	440	98	62	59	14	3	4	9	36	4	86	4	0	5	5	.500	0	1-4	5	5.21
1999 Cincinnati	NL	79	0	0	16	113.2	470	88	41	38	10	4	4	8	47	4	78	6	1	5	4	.556	0	3-5	13	3.01
2000 Cincinnati	NL	79	0	0	22	106.1	439	87	44	41	14	2	5	9	38	8	96	7	0	3	6	.333	0	3-6	22	3.47
2001 Cincinnati	NL	79	0	0	16	103.1	437	94	44	38	10	1	5	8	36	8	82	0	0	7	1	.875	0	0-3	20	3.31
7 ML YEARS		373	0	0	87	534.1	2240	457	231	215	60	15	21	42	194	32	443	25	2	25	19	.568	0	8-20	73	3.62

Jeff Suppan

Pitches: Right **Bats:** Right **Pos:** SP-34 — **Ht:** 6'2" **Wt:** 210 **Born:** 1/2/75 **Age:** 27

		HOW MUCH HE PITCHED						WHAT HE GAVE UP											THE RESULTS					
Year Team	Lg	G	GS	CG	GF	IP	BFP	H	R	ER	HR	SH	SF	HB	TBB	IBB	SO	WP	Bk	W	L	Pct.	ShO	Sv-Op	Hld	ERA
1995 Boston	AL	8	3	0	1	22.2	100	29	15	15	4	1	0	0	5	1	19	0	0	1	2	.333	0	0-0	1	5.96
1996 Boston	AL	8	4	0	2	22.2	107	29	19	19	3	1	4	1	13	0	13	3	0	1	1	.500	0	0-0	0	7.54
1997 Boston	AL	23	22	0	1	112.1	503	140	75	71	12	0	4	4	36	1	67	5	0	7	3	.700	0	0-0	0	5.69
1998 Ari-KC		17	14	1	2	78.2	345	91	56	50	13	3	2	1	22	1	51	2	0	1	7	.125	0	0-0	0	5.72
1999 Kansas City	AL	32	32	4	0	208.2	887	222	113	105	28	7	5	3	62	4	103	5	1	10	12	.455	1	0-0	0	4.53
2000 Kansas City	AL	35	33	3	0	217	948	240	121	119	36	5	6	7	84	3	128	7	1	10	9	.526	1	0-0	0	4.94
2001 Kansas City	AL	34	34	1	0	218.1	946	227	120	106	26	5	6	12	74	3	120	6	0	10	14	.417	1	0-0	0	4.37
1998 Arizona	NL	13	13	1	0	66	299	82	55	49	12	3	2	1	21	1	39	2	0	1	7	.125	0	0-0	0	6.68
Kansas City	AL	4	1	0	2	12.2	46	9	1	1	1	0	0	0	1	0	12	0	0	0	0	—	0	0-0	0	0.71
7 ML YEARS		157	142	9	6	880.1	3836	978	519	485	122	22	28	28	296	13	501	28	2	40	48	.455	2	0-0	1	4.96

B.J. Surhoff

Bats: Left **Throws:** Right **Pos:** LF-129; PH/PR-13; DH-3 — **Ht:** 6'1" **Wt:** 200 **Born:** 8/4/64 **Age:** 37

		BATTING																	BASERUNNING				PERCENTAGES		
Year Team	Lg	G	AB	H	2B	3B	HR	(Hm	Rd)	TB	R	RBI	TBB	IBB	SO	HBP	SH	SF	SB	CS	SB%	GDP	Avg	OBP	SLG
1987 Milwaukee	AL	115	395	118	22	3	7	(5	2)	167	50	68	36	1	30	0	5	9	11	10	.52	13	.299	.350	.423
1988 Milwaukee	AL	139	493	121	21	0	5	(3	2)	157	47	38	31	9	49	3	11	3	21	6	.78	12	.245	.292	.318
1989 Milwaukee	AL	126	436	108	17	4	5	(3	2)	148	42	55	25	1	29	3	3	10	14	12	.54	8	.248	.287	.339
1990 Milwaukee	AL	135	474	131	21	4	6	(4	2)	178	55	59	41	5	37	1	7	7	18	7	.72	8	.276	.331	.376
1991 Milwaukee	AL	143	505	146	19	4	5	(3	2)	188	57	68	26	2	33	0	13	6	5	8	.38	11	.289	.319	.372
1992 Milwaukee	AL	139	480	121	19	1	4	(3	1)	154	63	62	46	8	41	2	5	10	14	8	.64	9	.252	.314	.321
1993 Milwaukee	AL	148	552	151	38	3	7	(4	3)	216	66	79	36	5	47	2	4	5	12	9	.57	9	.274	.318	.391
1994 Milwaukee	AL	40	134	35	11	2	5	(2	3)	65	20	22	16	0	14	0	2	2	0	1	.00	5	.261	.336	.485
1995 Milwaukee	AL	117	415	133	26	3	13	(7	6)	204	72	73	37	4	43	4	2	4	7	3	.70	7	.320	.378	.492
1996 Baltimore	AL	143	537	157	27	6	21	(12	9)	259	74	82	47	8	79	3	2	1	0	1	.00	9	.292	.352	.482
1997 Baltimore	AL	147	528	150	30	4	18	(10	8)	242	80	88	49	14	60	5	3	10	1	1	.50	7	.284	.345	.458
1998 Baltimore	AL	162	573	160	34	1	22	(9	13)	262	79	92	49	9	81	1	1	10	9	7	.56	13	.279	.332	.457
1999 Baltimore	AL	162	673	207	38	1	28	(9	19)	331	104	107	43	1	78	2	1	8	5	1	.83	15	.308	.347	.492
2000 Bal-Atl		147	539	157	36	2	14	(7	7)	239	69	68	41	3	58	3	2	2	10	2	.83	10	.291	.344	.443
2001 Atlanta	NL	141	484	131	33	1	10	(5	5)	196	68	58	38	5	48	1	1	7	9	3	.75	5	.271	.321	.405
2000 Baltimore	AL	103	411	120	27	0	13	(6	7)	186	56	57	29	3	46	2	1	0	7	2	.78	5	.292	.341	.453
Atlanta	NL	44	128	37	9	2	1	(1	0)	53	13	11	12	0	12	1	1	2	3	0	1.00	5	.289	.352	.414
15 ML YEARS		2004	7218	2026	392	39	170	(85	85)	3006	946	1019	561	75	727	30	62	97	136	79	.63	149	.281	.331	.416

Larry Sutton

Bats: Left **Throws:** Left **Pos:** PH/PR-25; 1B-11; RF-3 — **Ht:** 6'0" **Wt:** 185 **Born:** 5/14/70 **Age:** 32

		BATTING																	BASERUNNING				PERCENTAGES		
Year Team	Lg	G	AB	H	2B	3B	HR	(Hm	Rd)	TB	R	RBI	TBB	IBB	SO	HBP	SH	SF	SB	CS	SB%	GDP	Avg	OBP	SLG
2001 Memphis *	AAA	29	99	26	5	0	2	—	—	37	12	13	21	0	16	0	0	0	1	1	.50	3	.263	.392	.374
Edmonton *	AAA	45	147	37	7	3	3	—	—	59	23	24	23	2	32	1	0	3	0	1	.00	4	.252	.351	.401
1997 Kansas City	AL	27	69	20	2	0	2	(1	1)	28	9	8	5	0	12	0	1	0	0	0	—	0	.290	.338	.406
1998 Kansas City	AL	111	310	76	14	2	5	(3	2)	109	29	42	29	3	46	3	4	5	3	3	.50	5	.245	.311	.352
1999 Kansas City	AL	43	102	23	6	0	2	(2	0)	35	14	15	13	0	17	0	1	2	1	0	1.00	4	.225	.308	.343

216

Year Team	Lg	G	AB	H	2B	3B	HR	(Hm	Rd)	TB	R	RBI	TBB	IBB	SO	HBP	SH	SF	SB	CS	SB%	GDP	Avg	OBP	SLG
2000 St. Louis	NL	23	25	8	0	0	1	(0	1)	11	5	6	5	0	7	0	1	2	0	0	—	0	.320	.406	.440
2001 St. Louis	NL	33	42	5	1	0	1	(1	0)	9	3	3	1	0	10	0	1	0	0	0	—	1	.119	.140	.214
5 ML YEARS		237	548	132	23	2	11	(7	4)	192	60	74	53	3	92	3	8	9	4	3	.57	10	.241	.307	.350

Ichiro Suzuki

Bats: Left **Throws:** Right **Pos:** RF-152; DH-4; PH/PR-4   **Ht:** 5'11" **Wt:** 157 **Born:** 10/22/73 **Age:** 28

Year Team	Lg	G	AB	H	2B	3B	HR	(Hm	Rd)	TB	R	RBI	TBB	IBB	SO	HBP	SH	SF	SB	CS	SB%	GDP	Avg	OBP	SLG
2001 Seattle	AL	157	692	242	34	8	8	(5	3)	316	127	69	30	10	53	8	4	4	56	14	.80	3	.350	.381	.457

Mac Suzuki

Pitches: Right **Bats:** Right **Pos:** SP-19; RP-14   **Ht:** 6'3" **Wt:** 205 **Born:** 5/31/75 **Age:** 27

		HOW MUCH HE PITCHED						WHAT HE GAVE UP											THE RESULTS						
Year Team	Lg	G	GS	CG	GF	IP	BFP	H	R	ER	HR	SH	SF	HB	TBB	IBB	SO	WP	Bk	W	L	Pct.	ShO	Sv-Op	Hld	ERA
1996 Seattle	AL	1	0	0	0	1.1	8	2	3	3	0	0	0	0	2	1	0	0	0	0	0	—	0	0-0	0	20.25
1998 Seattle	AL	6	5	0	0	26.1	127	34	23	21	3	0	0	0	15	0	19	0	0	1	2	.333	0	0-0	0	7.18
1999 Sea-KC	AL	38	13	0	6	110	510	124	92	83	16	2	3	7	64	3	68	11	0	2	5	.286	0	0-0	0	6.79
2000 Kansas City	AL	32	29	1	0	188.2	839	195	100	91	26	2	3	3	94	6	135	11	0	8	10	.444	1	0-0	0	4.34
2001 KC-Col-Mil		33	19	0	4	118.1	542	122	87	77	20	4	3	8	73	4	89	16	0	5	12	.294	0	0-0	1	5.86
1999 Seattle	AL	16	4	0	3	42	207	47	47	44	7	0	3	4	34	2	32	2	0	0	2	.000	0	0-0	0	9.43
Kansas City	AL	22	9	0	3	68	303	77	45	39	9	2	0	3	30	1	36	9	0	2	3	.400	0	0-0	0	5.16
2001 Kansas City	AL	15	9	0	3	56	251	61	38	33	12	0	3	3	25	1	37	6	0	2	5	.286	0	0-0	0	5.30
Colorado	NL	3	1	0	0	6.1	39	9	12	11	3	0	0	1	11	0	5	2	0	0	2	.000	0	0-0	0	15.63
Milwaukee	NL	15	9	0	1	56	252	52	37	33	5	4	0	4	37	3	47	8	0	3	5	.375	0	0-0	1	5.30
5 ML YEARS		110	66	1	10	444.2	2026	477	305	275	65	8	9	18	248	14	312	38	0	16	29	.356	1	0-0	1	5.57

Mark Sweeney

Bats: L **Throws:** L **Pos:** PH/PR-27; LF-20; RF-3; 1B-2   **Ht:** 6'1" **Wt:** 215 **Born:** 10/26/69 **Age:** 32

		BATTING																	BASERUNNING				PERCENTAGES		
Year Team	Lg	G	AB	H	2B	3B	HR	(Hm	Rd)	TB	R	RBI	TBB	IBB	SO	HBP	SH	SF	SB	CS	SB%	GDP	Avg	OBP	SLG
2001 Indianapols *	AAA	109	404	116	34	1	6			170	65	69	56	6	71	2	0	5	3	1	.75	6	.287	.373	.421
1995 St. Louis	NL	37	77	21	2	0	2	(0	2)	29	5	13	10	0	15	0	1	2	1	1	.50	3	.273	.348	.377
1996 St. Louis	NL	98	170	45	9	0	3	(0	3)	63	32	22	33	2	29	1	5	0	3	0	1.00	4	.265	.387	.371
1997 StL-SD	NL	115	164	46	7	0	2	(2	0)	59	16	23	20	1	32	1	1	1	2	3	.40	3	.280	.358	.360
1998 San Diego	NL	122	192	45	8	3	2	(1	1)	65	17	15	26	0	37	1	0	3	1	2	.33	5	.234	.324	.339
1999 Cincinnati	NL	37	31	11	3	0	2	(1	1)	20	6	7	4	1	9	0	0	0	0	0	—	2	.355	.429	.645
2000 Milwaukee	NL	71	73	16	6	0	1	(0	1)	25	9	6	12	1	18	1	1	0	0	0	—	3	.219	.337	.342
2001 Milwaukee	NL	48	89	23	3	1	3	(1	2)	37	9	11	12	0	23	0	2	0	1	2	.67	0	.258	.347	.416
1997 St. Louis	NL	44	61	13	3	0	0	(0	0)	16	5	4	9	1	14	1	1	1	0	1	.00	2	.213	.319	.262
San Diego	NL	71	103	33	4	0	2	(2	0)	43	11	19	11	0	18	0	0	0	2	2	.50	1	.320	.383	.417
7 ML YEARS		528	796	207	38	4	15	(5	10)	298	94	97	117	5	163	4	10	7	9	7	.56	18	.260	.355	.374

Mike Sweeney

Bats: Right **Throws:** Right **Pos:** 1B-108; DH-38; PH/PR-1   **Ht:** 6'3" **Wt:** 225 **Born:** 7/22/73 **Age:** 28

		BATTING																	BASERUNNING				PERCENTAGES		
Year Team	Lg	G	AB	H	2B	3B	HR	(Hm	Rd)	TB	R	RBI	TBB	IBB	SO	HBP	SH	SF	SB	CS	SB%	GDP	Avg	OBP	SLG
1995 Kansas City	AL	4	4	1	0	0	0	(0	0)	1	1	0	0	0	0	0	0	0	0	0	—	0	.250	.250	.250
1996 Kansas City	AL	50	165	46	10	0	4	(1	3)	68	23	24	18	0	21	4	0	3	1	2	.33	7	.279	.358	.412
1997 Kansas City	AL	84	240	58	8	0	7	(5	2)	87	30	31	17	0	33	6	1	2	3	2	.60	8	.242	.306	.363
1998 Kansas City	AL	92	282	73	18	0	8	(6	2)	115	32	35	24	1	38	2	2	1	2	3	.40	8	.259	.320	.408
1999 Kansas City	AL	150	575	185	44	2	22	(10	12)	299	101	102	54	0	48	10	0	4	6	1	.86	21	.322	.387	.520
2000 Kansas City	AL	159	618	206	30	0	29	(17	12)	323	105	144	71	5	67	15	0	13	8	3	.73	15	.333	.407	.523
2001 Kansas City	AL	147	559	170	46	0	29	(14	15)	303	97	99	64	13	64	2	1	6	10	3	.77	13	.304	.374	.542
7 ML YEARS		686	2443	739	156	2	99	(53	46)	1196	389	435	248	19	271	39	4	29	30	14	.68	71	.302	.372	.490

Greg Swindell

Pitches: Left **Bats:** Right **Pos:** RP-64   **Ht:** 6'3" **Wt:** 230 **Born:** 1/2/65 **Age:** 37

		HOW MUCH HE PITCHED						WHAT HE GAVE UP											THE RESULTS						
Year Team	Lg	G	GS	CG	GF	IP	BFP	H	R	ER	HR	SH	SF	HB	TBB	IBB	SO	WP	Bk	W	L	Pct.	ShO	Sv-Op	Hld	ERA
1986 Cleveland	AL	9	9	1	0	61.2	255	57	35	29	9	3	1	1	15	0	46	3	2	5	2	.714	0	0-0	0	4.23
1987 Cleveland	AL	16	15	4	0	102.1	441	112	62	58	18	4	3	1	37	1	97	0	1	3	8	.273	0	0-0	1	5.10
1988 Cleveland	AL	33	33	12	0	242	988	234	97	86	18	9	5	1	45	3	180	5	0	18	14	.563	4	0-0	0	3.20
1989 Cleveland	AL	28	28	5	0	184.1	749	170	71	69	16	4	4	0	51	1	129	3	1	13	6	.684	2	0-0	0	3.37
1990 Cleveland	AL	34	34	3	0	214.2	912	245	110	105	27	8	6	1	47	2	135	3	2	12	9	.571	0	0-0	0	4.40
1991 Cleveland	AL	33	33	7	0	238	971	241	112	92	21	13	8	3	31	1	169	3	1	9	16	.360	0	0-0	0	3.48
1992 Cincinnati	NL	31	30	5	0	213.2	867	210	72	64	14	9	7	2	41	4	138	3	2	12	8	.600	3	0-0	0	2.70
1993 Houston	NL	31	30	1	0	190.1	818	215	98	88	24	13	3	1	40	3	124	2	2	12	13	.480	1	0-0	0	4.16
1994 Houston	NL	24	24	1	0	148.1	623	175	80	72	20	9	7	1	26	2	74	1	1	8	9	.471	0	0-0	0	4.37
1995 Houston	NL	33	26	1	3	153	659	180	86	76	21	4	8	2	39	2	96	3	0	10	9	.526	1	0-0	0	4.47
1996 Hou-Cle		21	6	0	0	51.2	237	66	46	41	13	1	2	1	19	0	36	0	0	1	4	.200	0	0-2	1	7.14
1997 Minnesota	AL	65	1	0	12	115.2	460	102	46	46	12	2	3	2	25	3	75	0	0	7	4	.636	0	1-7	12	3.58
1998 Min-Bos	AL	81	0	0	15	90.1	385	92	40	36	13	4	2	3	31	3	63	0	0	5	6	.455	0	2-5	24	3.59
1999 Arizona	NL	63	0	0	15	64.2	261	54	19	18	8	4	0	1	21	1	51	0	0	4	0	1.000	0	1-2	19	2.51
2000 Arizona	NL	64	0	0	21	76	318	71	29	27	7	6	3	1	20	5	64	0	0	2	6	.250	0	1-1	9	3.20
2001 Arizona	NL	64	0	0	18	53.2	214	51	27	27	12	1	1	0	12	2	42	1	0	2	6	.250	0	2-5	11	4.53
1996 Houston	NL	8	4	0	3	23	116	35	25	20	5	0	1	1	11	0	15	0	0	0	3	.000	0	0-2	0	7.83
Cleveland	AL	13	2	0	1	28.2	121	31	21	21	8	1	1	0	8	0	21	0	0	1	1	.500	0	0-0	1	6.59

			HOW MUCH HE PITCHED					WHAT HE GAVE UP									THE RESULTS					
Year Team	Lg	G	GS	CG	GF	IP	BFP	H	R	ER	HR	SH	SF	HB	TBB	IBB	SO	WP	Bk	W	L	Pct.	ShO	Sv-Op	Hld	ERA
1998 Minnesota	AL	52	0	0	12	66.1	281	67	27	27	10	3	2	3	18	2	45	3	0	3	3	.500	0	2-4	18	3.66
Boston	AL	29	0	0	3	24	104	25	13	9	3	1	0	0	13	1	18	0	0	2	3	.400	0	0-1	6	3.38
16 ML YEARS		630	269	40	88	2200.1	9158	2275	1030	934	253	94	63	21	496	33	1519	30	12	123	120	.506	12	7-24	77	3.82

Jeff Tabaka

Pitches: Left **Bats:** Right **Pos:** RP-8 **Ht:** 6'2" **Wt:** 201 **Born:** 1/17/64 **Age:** 38

			HOW MUCH HE PITCHED					WHAT HE GAVE UP									THE RESULTS					
Year Team	Lg	G	GS	CG	GF	IP	BFP	H	R	ER	HR	SH	SF	HB	TBB	IBB	SO	WP	Bk	W	L	Pct.	ShO	Sv-Op	Hld	ERA
2001 Memphis *	AAA	32	0	0	14	27.2	116	24	10	8	2	3	3	0	10	2	23	1	0	0	2	.000	0	2- -	—	2.60
1994 Pit-SD	NL	39	0	0	10	41	181	32	29	24	1	3	1	0	27	3	32	1	0	3	1	.750	0	1-1	1	5.27
1995 SD-Hou	NL	34	0	0	6	30.2	128	27	11	11	2	0	0	0	17	1	25	1	0	1	0	1.000	0	0-1	5	3.23
1996 Houston	NL	18	0	0	5	20.1	105	28	18	15	5	1	0	3	14	0	18	3	0	2	2	.000	0	1-1	0	6.64
1997 Cincinnati	NL	3	0	0	1	2	10	1	1	1	1	0	0	2	1	0	1	0	0	0	0	—	0	0-0	0	4.50
1998 Pittsburgh	NL	37	0	0	9	50.2	212	37	19	17	6	2	2	5	22	4	40	1	0	2	2	.500	0	0-0	2	3.02
2001 St. Louis	NL	8	0	0	0	3.2	17	6	3	3	1	0	0	0	1	0	3	0	0	0	0	—	0	0-1	0	7.36
1994 Pittsburgh	NL	5	0	0	2	4	24	4	8	8	1	0	0	0	8	0	2	0	0	0	0	—	0	0-0	0	18.00
San Diego	NL	34	0	0	8	37	157	28	21	16	0	3	1	0	19	3	30	1	0	3	1	.750	0	1-1	1	3.89
1995 San Diego	NL	10	0	0	3	6.1	32	10	5	5	1	0	0	0	5	1	6	1	0	0	0	—	0	0-0	0	7.11
Houston	NL	24	0	0	3	24.1	96	17	6	6	1	0	0	0	12	0	19	0	0	1	0	1.000	0	0-0	5	2.22
6 ML YEARS		139	0	0	31	148.1	653	131	81	71	16	6	3	10	82	8	119	6	0	6	5	.545	0	2-4	8	4.31

Jeff Tam

Pitches: Right **Bats:** Right **Pos:** RP-70 **Ht:** 6'1" **Wt:** 202 **Born:** 8/19/70 **Age:** 31

			HOW MUCH HE PITCHED					WHAT HE GAVE UP									THE RESULTS					
Year Team	Lg	G	GS	CG	GF	IP	BFP	H	R	ER	HR	SH	SF	HB	TBB	IBB	SO	WP	Bk	W	L	Pct.	ShO	Sv-Op	Hld	ERA
1998 New York	NL	15	0	0	5	14.1	60	13	10	10	2	0	0	2	4	1	8	0	0	1	1	.500	0	0-1	1	6.28
1999 Cle-NYM		10	0	0	3	11.2	47	8	7	7	3	1	0	0	4	1	8	0	0	0	0	—	0	0-0	0	5.40
2000 Oakland	AL	72	0	0	23	85.2	351	86	30	25	3	2	4	1	23	8	46	3	0	3	3	.500	0	3-6	19	2.63
2001 Oakland	AL	70	0	0	15	74.2	310	68	27	25	3	3	3	3	29	9	44	0	0	2	4	.333	0	3-6	25	3.01
1999 Cleveland	AL	1	0	0	0	0.1	4	2	3	3	0	1	0	0	1	0	0	0	0	0	0	—	0	0-0	0	81.00
New York	NL	9	0	0	3	11.1	43	6	4	4	3	0	0	0	3	0	8	0	0	0	0	—	0	0-0	0	3.18
4 ML YEARS		167	0	0	46	186.1	768	175	74	67	11	6	7	6	60	19	106	3	0	6	8	.429	0	6-13	45	3.24

Kevin Tapani

Pitches: Right **Bats:** Right **Pos:** SP-29 **Ht:** 6'0" **Wt:** 190 **Born:** 2/18/64 **Age:** 38

			HOW MUCH HE PITCHED					WHAT HE GAVE UP									THE RESULTS					
Year Team	Lg	G	GS	CG	GF	IP	BFP	H	R	ER	HR	SH	SF	HB	TBB	IBB	SO	WP	Bk	W	L	Pct.	ShO	Sv-Op	Hld	ERA
1989 NYM-Min		8	5	0	1	40	169	39	18	17	3	1	2	0	12	1	23	0	1	2	2	.500	0	0-0	0	3.83
1990 Minnesota	AL	28	28	1	0	159.1	659	164	75	72	12	3	4	2	29	2	101	1	0	12	8	.600	1	0-0	0	4.07
1991 Minnesota	AL	34	34	4	0	244	974	225	84	81	23	9	6	2	40	0	135	3	3	16	9	.640	1	0-0	0	2.99
1992 Minnesota	AL	34	34	4	0	220	911	226	103	97	21	8	11	5	48	2	138	4	0	16	11	.593	1	0-0	0	3.97
1993 Minnesota	AL	36	35	3	0	225.2	964	243	123	111	21	3	5	6	57	1	150	4	0	12	15	.444	1	0-0	0	4.43
1994 Min-LA		24	24	4	0	156	672	181	86	80	13	2	5	4	39	0	91	1	0	11	7	.611	0	0-0	0	4.62
1995 Min-LA		33	31	3	0	190.2	834	227	116	105	29	6	5	5	48	4	131	4	0	10	13	.435	1	0-0	0	4.96
1996 Chicago	AL	34	34	1	0	225.1	971	236	123	115	34	6	6	3	76	5	150	13	0	13	10	.565	0	0-0	0	4.59
1997 Chicago	NL	13	13	1	0	85	352	77	33	32	7	7	2	2	23	2	55	0	2	9	3	.750	1	0-0	0	3.39
1998 Chicago	NL	35	34	2	0	219	945	244	120	118	30	11	9	5	62	4	136	7	0	19	9	.679	2	0-0	0	4.85
1999 Chicago	NL	23	23	1	0	136	591	151	81	73	12	8	7	4	33	2	73	3	0	6	12	.333	0	0-0	0	4.83
2000 Chicago	NL	30	30	2	0	195.2	829	208	113	109	35	4	3	8	47	1	150	1	0	8	12	.400	0	0-0	0	5.01
2001 Chicago	NL	29	29	0	0	168.1	729	186	93	84	24	12	3	7	40	6	149	3	0	9	14	.391	0	0-0	0	4.49
1989 New York	NL	3	0	0	1	7.1	31	5	3	3	1	0	1	0	4	0	2	0	1	0	0	—	0	0-0	0	3.68
Minnesota	AL	5	5	0	0	32.2	138	34	15	14	2	1	1	0	8	1	21	0	0	2	2	.500	0	0-0	0	3.86
1995 Minnesota	AL	20	20	3	0	133.2	579	155	79	73	21	3	3	4	34	2	88	3	0	6	11	.353	1	0-0	0	4.92
Los Angeles	NL	13	11	0	0	57	255	72	37	32	8	3	2	1	14	2	43	1	0	4	2	.667	0	0-0	0	5.05
13 ML YEARS		361	354	26	1	2265	9600	2407	1168	1094	260	80	68	53	554	30	1482	44	6	143	125	.534	9	0-0	0	4.35

Fernando Tatis

Bats: Right **Throws:** Right **Pos:** 3B-41; PH/PR-1 **Ht:** 5'10" **Wt:** 170 **Born:** 1/1/75 **Age:** 27

			BATTING																BASERUNNING				PERCENTAGES		
Year Team	Lg	G	AB	H	2B	3B	HR	(Hm	Rd)	TB	R	RBI	TBB	IBB	SO	HBP	SH	SF	SB	CS	SB%	GDP	Avg	OBP	SLG
1997 Texas	AL	60	223	57	9	0	8	(6	2)	90	29	29	14	0	42	0	2	2	3	0	1.00	6	.256	.297	.404
1998 Tex-StL		150	532	147	33	4	11	(6	5)	221	69	58	36	3	123	6	4	1	13	5	.72	16	.276	.329	.415
1999 St. Louis	NL	149	537	160	31	2	34	(16	18)	297	104	107	82	4	128	16	0	4	21	9	.70	11	.298	.404	.553
2000 St. Louis	NL	96	324	82	21	1	18	(11	7)	159	59	64	57	1	94	10	1	2	2	3	.40	12	.253	.379	.491
2001 Montreal	NL	41	145	37	9	0	2	(0	2)	52	20	11	16	0	43	4	0	3	0	0	—	5	.255	.339	.359
1998 Texas	AL	95	330	89	17	2	3	(1	2)	119	41	32	12	2	66	4	4	0	6	2	.75	10	.270	.303	.361
St. Louis	NL	55	202	58	16	2	8	(5	3)	102	28	26	24	1	57	2	0	1	7	3	.70	6	.287	.367	.505
5 ML YEARS		496	1761	483	103	7	73	(39	34)	819	281	269	205	8	430	36	7	12	39	17	.70	51	.274	.359	.465

Eddie Taubensee

Bats: L **Throws:** R **Pos:** C-38; PH/PR-16; DH-5; 2B-1 **Ht:** 6'3" **Wt:** 230 **Born:** 10/31/68 **Age:** 33

			BATTING																BASERUNNING				PERCENTAGES		
Year Team	Lg	G	AB	H	2B	3B	HR	(Hm	Rd)	TB	R	RBI	TBB	IBB	SO	HBP	SH	SF	SB	CS	SB%	GDP	Avg	OBP	SLG
2001 Buffalo *	AAA	7	26	7	1	0	2	—		14	5	7	2	0	6	0	0	0	0	0	—	1	.269	.321	.538
Akron *	AA	2	7	1	0	0	0	—		1	1	1	1	0	1	0	0	0	0	0	—	0	.143	.250	.143
1991 Cleveland	AL	26	66	16	2	1	0	(0	0)	20	5	8	5	1	16	0	0	2	0	0	—	0	.242	.288	.303
1992 Houston	NL	104	297	66	15	0	5	(2	3)	96	23	28	31	3	78	2	0	1	2	1	.67	4	.222	.299	.323
1993 Houston	NL	94	288	72	11	1	9	(4	5)	112	26	42	21	5	44	0	1	2	0	1	1.00	8	.250	.299	.389

218

Year Team	Lg	G	AB	H	2B	3B	HR	(Hm	Rd)	TB	R	RBI	TBB	IBB	SO	HBP	SH	SF	SB	CS	SB%	GDP	Avg	OBP	SLG
1994 Hou-Cin	NL	66	187	53	8	2	8	(2	6)	89	29	21	15	2	31	0	1	2	2	0	1.00	3	.283	.333	.476
1995 Cincinnati	NL	80	218	62	14	2	9	(4	5)	107	32	44	22	2	52	2	1	1	2	2	.50	2	.284	.354	.491
1996 Cincinnati	NL	108	327	95	20	0	12	(6	6)	151	46	48	26	5	64	0	1	5	3	4	.43	4	.291	.338	.462
1997 Cincinnati	NL	108	254	68	18	0	10	(7	3)	116	26	34	22	2	66	1	1	5	0	1	.00	2	.268	.323	.457
1998 Cincinnati	NL	130	431	120	27	0	11	(8	3)	180	61	72	52	6	93	0	2	6	1	0	1.00	12	.278	.352	.418
1999 Cincinnati	NL	126	424	132	22	2	21	(8	13)	221	58	87	30	1	67	1	1	5	0	2	.00	12	.311	.354	.521
2000 Cincinnati	NL	81	266	71	12	0	6	(0	6)	101	29	24	21	1	44	2	1	1	0	0	—	7	.267	.324	.380
2001 Cleveland	AL	52	116	29	2	1	3	(2	1)	42	16	11	10	1	19	1	1	0	0	0	—	3	.250	.315	.362
1994 Houston	NL	5	10	1	0	0	0	(0	0)	1	0	0	0	0	3	0	0	0	0	0	—	1	.100	.100	.100
Cincinnati	NL	61	177	52	8	2	8	(2	6)	88	29	21	15	2	28	0	1	2	2	0	1.00	2	.294	.345	.497
11 ML YEARS		975	2874	784	151	9	94	(43	51)	1235	351	419	255	29	574	9	10	30	11	10	.52	50	.273	.331	.430

Julian Tavarez

Pitches: Right Bats: Left Pos: SP-28; RP-6
Ht: 6'2" Wt: 190 Born: 5/22/73 Age: 29

Year Team	Lg	G	GS	CG	GF	IP	BFP	H	R	ER	HR	SH	SF	HB	TBB	IBB	SO	WP	Bk	W	L	Pct.	ShO	Sv-Op	Hld	ERA
1993 Cleveland	AL	8	7	0	0	37	172	53	29	27	7	0	1	2	13	2	19	3	1	2	2	.500	0	0-0	0	6.57
1994 Cleveland	AL	1	1	0	0	1.2	14	6	8	4	1	0	1	0	1	1	0	0	0	0	0	.000	0	0-0	0	21.60
1995 Cleveland	AL	57	0	0	15	85	350	76	36	23	7	0	2	3	21	1	68	3	2	10	2	.833	0	0-4	19	2.44
1996 Cleveland	AL	51	4	0	13	80.2	353	101	49	48	9	5	4	1	22	5	46	1	0	4	7	.364	0	0-0	13	5.36
1997 San Francisco	NL	89	0	0	13	88.1	378	91	43	38	6	3	8	4	34	5	38	4	0	6	4	.600	0	0-3	26	3.87
1998 San Francisco	NL	60	0	0	12	85.1	374	96	41	36	5	5	3	8	36	11	52	1	1	5	3	.625	0	1-6	10	3.80
1999 San Francisco	NL	47	0	0	12	54.2	258	65	38	36	7	3	2	8	23	5	33	4	1	2	0	1.000	0	0-2	5	5.93
2000 Colorado	NL	51	12	1	8	120	530	124	68	59	11	3	4	7	53	9	62	2	1	11	5	.688	0	1-1	6	4.43
2001 Chicago	NL	34	28	0	1	161.1	712	172	98	81	13	8	4	11	69	4	107	2	1	10	9	.526	0	0-0	2	4.52
9 ML YEARS		398	52	1	74	714	3141	784	410	352	66	27	29	44	274	40	425	20	7	50	33	.602	0	2-16	81	4.44

Billy Taylor

Pitches: Right Bats: Right Pos: RP-1
Ht: 6'8" Wt: 235 Born: 10/16/61 Age: 40

Year Team	Lg	G	GS	CG	GF	IP	BFP	H	R	ER	HR	SH	SF	HB	TBB	IBB	SO	WP	Bk	W	L	Pct.	ShO	Sv-Op	Hld	ERA
2001 Nashville *	AAA	20	0	0	16	20	92	29	17	16	4	2	0	1	3	1	16	0	0	0	3	.000	0	8--	—	7.20
1994 Oakland	AL	41	0	0	11	46.1	195	38	24	18	4	1	1	2	18	5	48	0	0	1	3	.250	0	1-3	2	3.50
1996 Oakland	AL	55	0	0	30	60.1	261	52	30	29	5	4	3	4	25	4	67	1	0	6	3	.667	0	17-19	4	4.33
1997 Oakland	AL	72	0	0	45	73	320	70	32	31	3	1	2	5	36	9	66	0	0	3	4	.429	0	23-30	7	3.82
1998 Oakland	AL	70	0	0	58	73	311	71	37	29	7	3	5	3	22	3	58	0	1	4	9	.308	0	33-37	0	3.58
1999 Oak-NYM		61	0	0	43	56.1	257	68	35	31	5	5	2	2	23	8	52	1	1	1	6	.143	0	26-34	1	4.95
2000 Tampa Bay	AL	17	0	0	7	13.2	62	13	13	13	2	1	0	0	9	2	13	0	0	1	3	.250	0	0-2	0	8.56
2001 Pittsburgh	NL	1	0	0	0	2	8	2	1	1	1	0	0	0	0	0	3	0	0	0	0	—	0	0-0	0	4.50
1999 Oakland	AL	43	0	0	38	43	189	48	23	19	3	4	2	2	14	3	38	1	1	1	5	.167	0	26-33	0	3.98
New York	NL	18	0	0	5	13.1	68	20	12	12	2	1	0	0	9	5	14	0	0	0	1	.000	0	0-1	1	8.10
7 ML YEARS		317	0	0	194	324.2	1414	314	172	152	27	14	13	18	133	32	307	2	2	16	28	.364	0	100-125	16	4.21

Reggie Taylor

Bats: Left Throws: Right Pos: PH/PR-3; CF-2
Ht: 6'1" Wt: 178 Born: 1/12/77 Age: 25

Year Team	Lg	G	AB	H	2B	3B	HR	(Hm	Rd)	TB	R	RBI	TBB	IBB	SO	HBP	SH	SF	SB	CS	SB%	GDP	Avg	OBP	SLG
1995 Martinsvlle	R+	64	239	53	4	6	2	—	—	75	36	32	23	0	58	6	0	4	18	7	.72	5	.222	.301	.314
1996 Piedmont	A	128	499	131	20	6	0	—	—	163	68	31	29	0	136	3	2	3	36	17	.68	10	.263	.305	.327
1997 Clearwater	A+	134	545	133	18	6	12	—	—	199	73	47	30	4	130	4	5	3	40	23	.63	3	.244	.285	.365
1998 Reading	AA	79	337	92	14	6	5	—	—	133	49	22	12	0	73	2	0	2	22	10	.69	2	.273	.300	.395
1999 Reading	AA	127	526	140	17	10	15	—	—	222	75	61	18	1	79	3	3	3	38	20	.66	11	.266	.293	.422
2000 Scrantn-WB	AAA	98	422	116	10	8	15	—	—	187	60	43	21	3	87	2	5	4	23	12	.66	4	.275	.310	.443
2001 Scrantn-WB	AAA	111	464	122	20	9	7	—	—	181	56	50	24	4	94	3	1	4	31	15	.67	10	.263	.301	.390
2000 Philadelphia	NL	9	11	1	0	0	0	(0	0)	1	1	0	0	0	8	0	0	0	1	0	1.00	1	.091	.091	.091
2001 Philadelphia	NL	5	7	0	0	0	0	(0	0)	0	1	0	1	0	1	0	0	0	0	0	—	0	.000	.125	.000
2 ML YEARS		14	18	1	0	0	0	(0	0)	1	2	0	1	0	9	0	0	0	1	0	1.00	1	.056	.105	.056

Miguel Tejada

Bats: Right Throws: Right Pos: SS-162
Ht: 5'9" Wt: 188 Born: 5/25/76 Age: 26

Year Team	Lg	G	AB	H	2B	3B	HR	(Hm	Rd)	TB	R	RBI	TBB	IBB	SO	HBP	SH	SF	SB	CS	SB%	GDP	Avg	OBP	SLG
1997 Oakland	AL	26	99	20	3	2	2	(1	1)	33	10	10	2	0	22	3	0	0	2	0	1.00	3	.202	.240	.333
1998 Oakland	AL	105	365	85	20	1	11	(5	6)	140	53	45	28	0	86	7	4	3	5	6	.45	8	.233	.298	.384
1999 Oakland	AL	159	593	149	33	4	21	(12	9)	253	93	84	57	3	94	10	9	5	8	7	.53	11	.251	.325	.427
2000 Oakland	AL	160	607	167	32	1	30	(16	14)	291	105	115	66	6	102	4	2	2	6	0	1.00	15	.275	.349	.479
2001 Oakland	AL	162	622	166	31	3	31	(17	14)	296	107	113	43	5	89	13	1	4	11	5	.69	14	.267	.326	.476
5 ML YEARS		612	2286	587	119	11	95	(51	44)	1013	368	367	196	14	393	37	16	14	32	18	.64	51	.257	.324	.443

Amaury Telemaco

Pitches: Right Bats: Right Pos: SP-14; RP-10
Ht: 6'3" Wt: 222 Born: 1/19/74 Age: 28

Year Team	Lg	G	GS	CG	GF	IP	BFP	H	R	ER	HR	SH	SF	HB	TBB	IBB	SO	WP	Bk	W	L	Pct.	ShO	Sv-Op	Hld	ERA
2001 Scrantn-WB *	AAA	4	4	0	0	24.2	108	31	11	11	4	1	0	0	6	0	25	0	0	1	2	.333	0	0--	—	4.01
1996 Chicago	NL	25	17	0	2	97.1	427	108	60	59	20	5	3	3	31	2	64	3	0	5	7	.417	0	0-0	0	5.46
1997 Chicago	NL	10	5	0	2	38	169	47	26	26	4	2	1	0	11	0	29	1	0	0	3	.000	0	0-0	0	6.16
1998 ChC-Ari	NL	41	18	0	5	148.2	637	150	75	65	18	8	6	4	46	2	78	7	0	7	10	.412	0	0-0	1	3.93
1999 Ari-Phi	NL	49	0	0	10	53	234	52	34	34	10	4	1	2	26	4	43	5	0	4	0	1.000	0	0-1	3	5.77

Year Team	Lg	HOW MUCH HE PITCHED					WHAT HE GAVE UP											THE RESULTS					
		G	GS	CG	GF	IP	BFP	H	R	ER	HR	SH	SF	HB	TBB	IBB	SO	WP	Bk	W	L	Pct.	ShO	Sv-Op	Hld	ERA
2000 Philadelphia	NL	13	2	0	2	24.1	107	25	22	18	6	0	2	0	14	0	22	1	0	1	3	.250	0	0-1	0	6.66
2001 Philadelphia	NL	24	14	1	2	89.1	388	93	59	55	15	5	2	9	32	3	59	3	0	5	5	.500	0	0-0	1	5.54
1998 Chicago	NL	14	0	0	4	27.2	118	23	12	12	5	0	0	0	13	0	18	3	0	1	1	.500	0	0-0	1	3.90
Arizona	NL	27	18	0	1	121	519	127	63	53	13	8	6	4	33	2	60	4	0	6	9	.400	0	0-0	0	3.94
1999 Arizona	NL	5	0	0	3	6	28	7	5	5	2	1	0	0	6	1	2	0	0	1	0	1.000	0	0-0	0	7.50
Philadelphia	NL	44	0	0	7	47	206	45	29	29	8	3	1	2	20	3	41	5	0	3	0	1.000	0	0-1	0	5.55
6 ML YEARS		162	56	1	23	450.2	1962	475	283	257	73	24	15	18	160	11	295	20	0	22	28	.440	0	0-2	5	5.13

Anthony Telford

Pitches: Right Bats: Right Pos: RP-8
Ht: 6'0" Wt: 195 Born: 3/6/66 Age: 36

Year Team	Lg	HOW MUCH HE PITCHED					WHAT HE GAVE UP											THE RESULTS					
		G	GS	CG	GF	IP	BFP	H	R	ER	HR	SH	SF	HB	TBB	IBB	SO	WP	Bk	W	L	Pct.	ShO	Sv-Op	Hld	ERA
2001 Jupiter *	A+	4	2	0	0	5	25	9	5	4	0	0	0	0	1	0	5	0	0	0	1	.000	0	0--	—	7.20
Ottawa *	AAA	28	8	0	7	76	316	79	42	38	7	2	7	3	17	0	62	0	0	3	5	.375	0	1--	—	4.50
1990 Baltimore	AL	8	8	0	0	36.1	168	43	22	20	4	0	2	1	19	0	20	1	0	3	3	.500	0	0-0	0	4.95
1991 Baltimore	AL	9	1	0	4	26.2	109	27	12	12	3	0	1	0	6	1	24	1	0	0	0	—	0	0-0	0	4.05
1993 Baltimore	AL	3	0	0	2	7.1	34	11	8	8	3	0	0	1	1	0	6	1	0	0	0	—	0	0-0	0	9.82
1997 Montreal	NL	65	0	0	17	89	369	77	34	32	11	4	1	5	33	4	61	6	0	4	6	.400	0	1-5	11	3.24
1998 Montreal	NL	77	0	0	24	91	398	85	45	39	9	10	4	4	36	1	59	8	1	3	6	.333	0	1-5	8	3.86
1999 Montreal	NL	79	0	0	21	96	429	112	52	42	3	3	5	3	38	3	69	3	1	5	4	.556	0	2-9	18	3.94
2000 Montreal	NL	64	0	0	18	78.1	330	76	38	33	10	2	4	5	23	1	68	4	1	5	4	.556	0	3-5	11	3.79
2001 Montreal	NL	8	0	0	0	7	41	14	12	8	2	1	0	1	5	1	5	1	0	0	1	.000	0	0-0	1	10.29
8 ML YEARS		313	9	0	86	431.2	1878	445	223	194	45	20	17	20	161	11	312	25	3	20	24	.455	0	7-24	49	4.04

Brad Thomas

Pitches: Left Bats: Left Pos: SP-5
Ht: 6'3" Wt: 204 Born: 10/22/77 Age: 24

Year Team	Lg	HOW MUCH HE PITCHED					WHAT HE GAVE UP											THE RESULTS					
		G	GS	CG	GF	IP	BFP	H	R	ER	HR	SH	SF	HB	TBB	IBB	SO	WP	Bk	W	L	Pct.	ShO	Sv-Op	Hld	ERA
1996 Great Falls	R+	11	5	0	3	35.2	163	48	27	25	2	1	1	0	11	0	28	5	4	3	2	.600	0	0--	—	6.31
1997 Elizabethtn	R+	14	13	0	0	70.1	307	78	43	35	5	3	0	3	21	0	53	8	2	3	4	.429	0	0--	—	4.48
1998 Fort Wayne	A	27	26	1	1	152.1	650	146	68	50	9	4	5	8	45	1	125	11	3	11	8	.579	0	0--	—	2.95
1999 Fort Myers	A+	27	27	1	0	152.2	666	182	99	81	11	4	5	6	46	0	108	8	1	8	11	.421	1	0--	—	4.78
2000 Fort Myers	A+	12	12	0	0	65	279	62	33	12	3	1	0	3	16	0	57	3	0	6	2	.750	0	0--	—	1.66
New Britain	AA	14	13	1	0	75.1	346	80	47	34	3	3	4	4	46	1	66	9	2	6	6	.500	1	0--	—	4.06
2001 New Britain	AA	19	19	1	0	119.1	474	91	37	26	4	1	2	4	26	0	97	7	0	10	3	.769	1	0--	—	1.96
2001 Minnesota	AL	5	5	0	0	16.1	82	20	17	17	6	1	0	2	14	0	6	2	0	0	2	.000	0	0-0	0	9.37

Frank Thomas

Bats: Right Throws: Right Pos: DH-16; 1B-3; PH/PR-1
Ht: 6'5" Wt: 275 Born: 5/27/68 Age: 34

Year Team	Lg	BATTING																		BASERUNNING				PERCENTAGES		
		G	AB	H	2B	3B	HR	(Hm	Rd)	TB	R	RBI	TBB	IBB	SO	HBP	SH	SF		SB	CS	SB%	GDP	Avg	OBP	SLG
1990 Chicago	AL	60	191	63	11	3	7	(2	5)	101	39	31	44	0	54	2	0	3		0	1	.00	5	.330	.454	.529
1991 Chicago	AL	158	559	178	31	2	32	(24	8)	309	104	109	138	13	112	1	0	2		1	2	.33	20	.318	.453	.553
1992 Chicago	AL	160	573	185	46	2	24	(10	14)	307	108	115	122	6	88	5	0	11		6	3	.67	19	.323	.439	.536
1993 Chicago	AL	153	549	174	36	0	41	(26	15)	333	106	128	112	29	54	2	0	13		4	2	.67	10	.317	.426	.607
1994 Chicago	AL	113	399	141	34	1	38	(22	16)	291	106	101	109	12	61	2	0	7		2	3	.40	15	.353	.487	.729
1995 Chicago	AL	145	493	152	27	0	40	(15	25)	299	102	111	136	29	74	6	0	12		3	2	.60	14	.308	.454	.606
1996 Chicago	AL	141	527	184	26	0	40	(16	24)	330	110	134	109	26	70	5	0	8		1	1	.50	25	.349	.459	.626
1997 Chicago	AL	146	530	184	35	0	35	(16	19)	324	110	125	109	9	69	3	0	7		1	1	.50	15	.347	.456	.611
1998 Chicago	AL	160	585	155	35	2	29	(15	14)	281	109	109	110	2	93	6	0	11		7	0	1.00	14	.265	.381	.480
1999 Chicago	AL	135	486	148	36	0	15	(9	6)	229	74	77	87	13	66	9	0	8		3	3	.50	15	.305	.414	.471
2000 Chicago	AL	159	582	191	44	0	43	(30	13)	364	115	143	112	18	94	5	0	8		1	3	.25	13	.328	.436	.625
2001 Chicago	AL	20	68	15	3	0	4	(2	2)	30	8	10	10	2	12	0	0	1		0	0	—	0	.221	.316	.441
12 ML YEARS		1550	5542	1770	364	10	348	(187	161)	3198	1091	1193	1198	153	847	46	0	91		29	21	.58	165	.319	.438	.577

Jim Thome

Bats: Left Throws: Right Pos: 1B-148; PH/PR-7; DH-6
Ht: 6'4" Wt: 240 Born: 8/27/70 Age: 31

Year Team	Lg	BATTING																		BASERUNNING				PERCENTAGES		
		G	AB	H	2B	3B	HR	(Hm	Rd)	TB	R	RBI	TBB	IBB	SO	HBP	SH	SF		SB	CS	SB%	GDP	Avg	OBP	SLG
1991 Cleveland	AL	27	98	25	4	2	1	(0	1)	36	7	9	5	1	16	1	0	0		1	1	.50	4	.255	.298	.367
1992 Cleveland	AL	40	117	24	3	1	2	(1	1)	35	8	12	10	2	34	2	0	2		2	0	1.00	6	.205	.275	.299
1993 Cleveland	AL	47	154	41	11	0	7	(5	2)	73	28	22	29	1	36	4	0	5		2	1	.67	3	.266	.385	.474
1994 Cleveland	AL	98	321	86	20	1	20	(10	10)	168	58	52	46	5	84	0	1	1		3	3	.50	11	.268	.359	.523
1995 Cleveland	AL	137	452	142	29	3	25	(13	12)	252	92	73	97	3	113	5	0	3		4	3	.57	8	.314	.438	.558
1996 Cleveland	AL	151	505	157	28	5	38	(18	20)	309	122	116	123	8	141	6	0	2		2	2	.50	13	.311	.450	.612
1997 Cleveland	AL	147	496	142	25	0	40	(17	23)	309	104	102	120	9	146	3	0	8		1	1	.50	9	.286	.423	.579
1998 Cleveland	AL	123	440	129	34	2	30	(18	12)	257	89	85	89	8	141	4	0	4		1	0	1.00	7	.293	.413	.584
1999 Cleveland	AL	146	494	137	27	2	33	(19	14)	267	101	108	127	13	171	4	0	0		0	0	—	6	.277	.426	.540
2000 Cleveland	AL	158	557	150	33	1	37	(21	16)	296	106	106	118	4	171	4	0	5		1	0	1.00	9	.269	.398	.531
2001 Cleveland	AL	156	526	153	26	1	49	(30	19)	328	101	124	111	14	185	4	0	3		1	1	.00	9	.291	.416	.624
11 ML YEARS		1230	4160	1186	240	18	282	(152	130)	2406	816	809	875	68	1238	37	1	37		17	12	.59	81	.285	.411	.555

Ryan Thompson

Bats: R Throws: R Pos: RF-12; PH/PR-6; CF-4; LF-1
Ht: 6'3" Wt: 215 Born: 11/4/67 Age: 34

Year Team	Lg	BATTING																		BASERUNNING				PERCENTAGES		
		G	AB	H	2B	3B	HR	(Hm	Rd)	TB	R	RBI	TBB	IBB	SO	HBP	SH	SF		SB	CS	SB%	GDP	Avg	OBP	SLG
2001 Calgary *	AAA	78	300	93	26	0	19	(—	—)	176	53	69	14	1	65	1	1	1		4	3	.57	11	.310	.342	.587
Ottawa *	AAA	21	85	14	4	0	2	(—	—)	24	6	9	3	0	22	1	0	0		0	2	.00	3	.165	.202	.282

BATTING																			BASERUNNING				PERCENTAGES		
Year Team	Lg	G	AB	H	2B	3B	HR	(Hm	Rd)	TB	R	RBI	TBB	IBB	SO	HBP	SH	SF	SB	CS	SB%	GDP	Avg	OBP	SLG		
1992 New York	NL	30	108	24	7	1	3	(3	0)	42	15	10	8	0	24	0	0	1	2	2	.50	2	.222	.274	.389		
1993 New York	NL	80	288	72	19	2	11	(5	6)	128	34	26	19	4	81	3	5	1	2	7	.22	5	.250	.302	.444		
1994 New York	NL	98	334	75	14	1	18	(5	13)	145	39	59	28	7	94	10	3	4	1	1	.50	8	.225	.301	.434		
1995 New York	NL	75	267	67	13	0	7	(3	4)	101	39	31	19	1	77	4	0	4	3	1	.75	12	.251	.306	.378		
1996 Cleveland	AL	8	22	7	0	0	1	(0	1)	10	2	5	1	0	6	0	0	0	0	0	—	1	.318	.348	.455		
1999 Houston	NL	12	20	4	1	0	1	(0	1)	8	2	5	2	0	7	0	0	0	0	0	—	0	.200	.273	.400		
2000 New York	AL	33	50	13	3	0	3	(2	1)	25	12	14	5	0	12	1	0	0	0	1	.00	0	.260	.339	.500		
2001 Florida	NL	18	31	9	5	0	0	(0	0)	14	6	2	1	0	8	0	0	0	0	0	—	2	.290	.313	.452		
8 ML YEARS		354	1120	271	62	4	44	(19	25)	473	149	152	83	12	309	18	8	10	8	12	.40	30	.242	.302	.422		

John Thomson

Pitches: Right Bats: Right Pos: SP-14   Ht: 6'3" Wt: 190 Born: 10/1/73 Age: 28

	HOW MUCH HE PITCHED						WHAT HE GAVE UP											THE RESULTS						
Year Team	Lg	G	GS	CG	GF	IP	BFP	H	R	ER	HR	SH	SF	HB	TBB	IBB	SO	WP	Bk	W	L	Pct.	ShO	Sv-Op	Hld	ERA
2001 Colo Sprngs *	AAA	12	12	0	0	68	285	74	29	25	6	0	1	1	13	0	52	2	0	5	3	.625	0	0--	—	3.31
1997 Colorado	NL	27	27	2	0	166.1	721	193	94	87	15	10	3	5	51	0	106	2	0	7	9	.438	1	0-0	0	4.71
1998 Colorado	NL	26	26	2	0	161	680	174	86	86	21	8	5	2	49	0	106	4	2	8	11	.421	0	0-0	0	4.81
1999 Colorado	NL	14	13	1	1	62.2	305	85	62	56	11	4	2	1	36	1	34	2	0	1	10	.091	0	0-0	0	8.04
2001 Colorado	NL	14	14	1	0	93.2	386	84	46	42	15	3	3	4	25	3	68	1	0	4	5	.444	1	0-0	0	4.04
4 ML YEARS		81	80	6	1	483.2	2092	536	288	271	62	25	13	12	161	4	314	9	2	20	35	.364	2	0-0	—	5.04

Mike Thurman

Pitches: Right Bats: Right Pos: SP-26; RP-2   Ht: 6'5" Wt: 210 Born: 7/22/73 Age: 28

	HOW MUCH HE PITCHED						WHAT HE GAVE UP											THE RESULTS						
Year Team	Lg	G	GS	CG	GF	IP	BFP	H	R	ER	HR	SH	SF	HB	TBB	IBB	SO	WP	Bk	W	L	Pct.	ShO	Sv-Op	Hld	ERA
2001 Jupiter *	A+	1	1	1	0	5	15	2	0	0	0	0	0	0	3	0	3	0	0	1	0	1.000	1	0--	—	0.00
1997 Montreal	NL	5	2	0	1	11.2	48	8	9	7	3	0	0	1	4	0	8	0	0	1	0	1.000	0	0-0	0	5.40
1998 Montreal	NL	14	13	0	1	67	287	60	38	35	7	2	4	3	26	2	32	3	0	4	5	.444	0	0-0	0	4.70
1999 Montreal	NL	29	27	0	1	146.2	622	140	84	66	17	8	3	7	52	4	85	4	1	7	11	.389	0	0-0	0	4.05
2000 Montreal	NL	17	17	0	0	88.1	415	112	69	63	9	5	6	3	46	4	52	2	0	4	9	.308	0	0-0	0	6.42
2001 Montreal	NL	28	26	0	0	147	658	172	90	87	21	8	9	6	50	7	96	8	0	9	11	.450	0	0-0	0	5.33
5 ML YEARS		93	85	0	3	460.2	2035	492	290	258	57	23	22	20	178	17	273	17	1	25	36	.410	0	0-0	0	5.04

Mike Timlin

Pitches: Right Bats: Right Pos: RP-67   Ht: 6'4" Wt: 210 Born: 3/10/66 Age: 36

	HOW MUCH HE PITCHED						WHAT HE GAVE UP											THE RESULTS						
Year Team	Lg	G	GS	CG	GF	IP	BFP	H	R	ER	HR	SH	SF	HB	TBB	IBB	SO	WP	Bk	W	L	Pct.	ShO	Sv-Op	Hld	ERA
1991 Toronto	AL	63	3	0	17	108.1	463	94	43	38	6	6	2	1	50	11	85	5	0	11	6	.647	0	3-8	9	3.16
1992 Toronto	AL	26	0	0	14	43.2	190	45	23	20	0	2	1	1	20	5	35	0	0	0	2	.000	0	1-1	1	4.12
1993 Toronto	AL	54	0	0	27	55.2	254	63	32	29	7	1	3	1	27	3	49	1	0	4	2	.667	0	1-4	9	4.69
1994 Toronto	AL	34	0	0	16	40	179	41	25	23	5	0	0	2	20	0	38	3	0	0	1	.000	0	2-4	5	5.18
1995 Toronto	AL	31	0	0	19	42	179	38	13	10	1	3	0	2	17	5	36	3	1	4	3	.571	0	5-9	4	2.14
1996 Toronto	AL	59	0	0	56	56.2	230	47	25	23	4	2	3	2	18	4	52	3	0	1	6	.143	0	31-38	2	3.65
1997 Tor-Sea	AL	64	0	0	31	72.2	297	69	30	26	8	6	1	1	20	5	45	1	1	6	4	.600	0	10-18	19	3.22
1998 Seattle	AL	70	0	0	40	79.1	321	78	26	26	5	4	2	3	16	2	60	0	0	3	3	.500	0	19-24	5	2.95
1999 Baltimore	AL	62	0	0	52	63	261	51	30	25	9	1	1	5	23	3	50	1	0	3	9	.250	0	27-36	0	3.57
2000 Bal-StL		62	0	0	40	64.2	295	67	33	30	8	7	2	4	35	6	52	0	0	5	4	.556	0	12-18	6	4.18
2001 St. Louis	NL	67	0	0	19	72.2	307	78	35	33	6	1	2	3	19	4	47	3	1	4	5	.444	0	3-7	12	4.09
1997 Toronto	AL	38	0	0	26	47	190	41	17	15	6	4	1	1	14	4	36	1	1	3	2	.600	0	9-13	2	2.87
Seattle	AL	26	0	0	5	25.2	107	28	13	11	2	2	0	0	6	1	9	0	0	3	2	.600	0	1-5	7	3.86
2000 Baltimore	AL	37	0	0	31	35	157	37	22	19	6	5	1	2	15	3	26	0	0	2	3	.400	0	11-15	1	4.89
St. Louis	NL	25	0	0	9	29.2	138	30	11	11	2	2	1	2	20	3	26	0	0	3	1	.750	0	1-3	5	3.34
11 ML YEARS		592	3	0	331	698.2	2976	671	315	283	59	33	17	25	265	48	549	20	3	41	45	.477	0	114-167	63	3.65

Jorge Toca

Bats: Right Throws: Right Pos: PH/PR-9; 1B-3; LF-2   Ht: 6'3" Wt: 220 Born: 1/7/75 Age: 27

BATTING																			BASERUNNING				PERCENTAGES		
Year Team	Lg	G	AB	H	2B	3B	HR	(Hm	Rd)	TB	R	RBI	TBB	IBB	SO	HBP	SH	SF	SB	CS	SB%	GDP	Avg	OBP	SLG		
1999 Binghamton	AA	75	279	86	15	1	20	—	—	163	60	67	32	3	43	5	0	4	5	5	.50	9	.308	.384	.584		
Norfolk	AAA	49	176	59	12	1	5	—	—	88	25	29	6	0	23	1	0	2	0	3	.00	9	.335	.357	.500		
2000 Binghamton	AA	3	11	1	1	0	0	—	—	2	1	0	0	0	0	0	0	0	0	0	—	0	.091	.091	.182		
Norfolk	AAA	120	453	123	25	3	11	—	—	187	58	70	17	3	72	4	0	3	9	8	.53	18	.272	.302	.413		
2001 Norfolk	AAA	111	407	109	13	1	11	—	—	157	53	51	23	1	63	5	0	2	12	2	.86	19	.268	.314	.386		
1999 New York	NL	4	3	1	0	0	0	(0	0)	1	0	0	0	0	2	0	0	0	0	0	—	0	.333	.333	.333		
2000 New York	NL	8	7	3	1	0	0	(0	0)	4	1	4	0	0	1	0	0	0	0	0	—	0	.429	.429	.571		
2001 New York	NL	13	17	3	0	0	0	(0	0)	3	3	1	0	0	8	0	0	0	0	0	—	0	.176	.176	.176		
3 ML YEARS		25	27	7	1	0	0	(0	0)	8	4	5	0	0	11	0	0	0	0	0	—	0	.259	.259	.296		

Kevin Tolar

Pitches: Left Bats: Right Pos: RP-9   Ht: 6'3" Wt: 225 Born: 1/28/71 Age: 31

	HOW MUCH HE PITCHED						WHAT HE GAVE UP											THE RESULTS						
Year Team	Lg	G	GS	CG	GF	IP	BFP	H	R	ER	HR	SH	SF	HB	TBB	IBB	SO	WP	Bk	W	L	Pct.	ShO	Sv-Op	Hld	ERA
1989 White Sox	R	13	12	1	0	60	256	29	16	11	0	1	1	5	54	0	58	10	0	6	2	.750	0	0--	—	1.65
1990 Utica	A-	15	15	1	0	90.1	407	80	44	33	2	1	3	4	61	1	69	9	1	4	6	.400	0	0--	—	3.29
1991 South Bend	A	30	19	0	6	114.2	510	87	54	35	3	5	5	8	85	0	87	6	0	8	5	.615	0	1--	—	2.75
1992 Salinas	A+	14	8	3	3	53.1	255	55	43	36	4	1	7	5	46	0	24	6	0	1	8	.111	0	0--	—	6.08
South Bend	A	18	10	0	6	81.1	339	59	34	26	5	7	4	2	41	0	81	5	1	6	5	.545	0	0--	—	2.88
1993 Sarasota	A+	23	11	0	8	77.1	358	75	55	46	1	5	7	6	51	1	60	8	0	2	6	.250	0	1--	—	5.35

Year Team	Lg	G	GS	CG	GF	IP	BFP	H	R	ER	HR	SH	SF	HB	TBB	IBB	SO	WP	Bk	W	L	Pct.	ShO	Sv-Op	Hld	ERA
1995 Lynchburg	A+	18	0	0	4	19.1	77	13	7	6	1	0	1	1	6	0	19	3	0	2	0	1.000	0	0--	—	2.79
Carolina	AA	12	0	0	3	12.1	59	16	5	5	0	0	2	0	7	0	9	2	0	1	0	1.000	0	0--	—	3.65
1996 Canton-Akrn	AA	50	0	0	15	44.2	201	42	19	13	1	4	2	3	26	2	39	5	0	1	3	.250	0	0--	—	2.62
1997 Binghamton	AA	22	0	0	9	31.2	157	38	20	18	3	4	1	2	22	1	26	6	0	1	1	.500	0	0--	—	5.12
St. Lucie	A+	9	0	0	3	13.1	54	9	3	3	0	0	0	0	6	0	8	1	0	0	0	—	0	1--	—	2.03
1998 Nashville	AAA	1	0	0	0	3	14	2	2	2	0	0	0	0	4	0	1	1	0	0	0	—	0	0--	—	6.00
Carolina	AA	42	0	0	15	48.2	211	35	12	12	1	4	1	2	33	0	48	1	0	1	2	.333	0	1--	—	2.22
Indianapols	AAA	19	0	0	3	14.2	82	21	18	17	3	1	0	0	17	1	19	3	0	1	0	1.000	0	0--	—	10.43
1999 Chattanooga	AA	47	1	0	16	54.1	262	61	32	30	2	2	2	0	45	4	60	4	0	4	4	.500	0	1--	—	4.97
Indianapols	AAA	13	1	0	1	13	53	8	4	3	1	0	1	0	7	1	18	1	0	1	0	1.000	0	0--	—	2.08
2000 Jacksnville	AA	9	0	0	2	17.1	66	7	3	1	0	0	0	0	8	0	19	1	0	2	0	1.000	0	0--	—	0.52
Toledo	AAA	33	0	0	12	46.1	203	37	23	17	4	0	3	0	26	1	42	4	0	4	2	.667	0	2--	—	3.30
2001 Toledo	AAA	44	0	0	32	56	234	49	18	17	3	4	1	1	21	2	73	9	0	3	4	.429	0	7--	—	2.73
2000 Detroit	AL	5	0	0	1	3	12	1	1	1	0	0	0	0	1	0	3	0	0	0	0	—	0	0-0	0	3.00
2001 Detroit	AL	9	0	0	1	10.2	50	7	8	8	0	0	0	0	13	1	11	1	0	0	0	—	0	0-0	0	6.75
2 ML YEARS		14	0	0	2	13.2	62	8	9	9	0	0	0	0	14	1	14	1	0	0	0		0	0-0	0	5.93

Brian Tollberg

Pitches: Right **Bats:** Right **Pos:** SP-19

Ht: 6'3" **Wt:** 195 **Born:** 9/16/72 **Age:** 29

Year Team	Lg	G	GS	CG	GF	IP	BFP	H	R	ER	HR	SH	SF	HB	TBB	IBB	SO	WP	Bk	W	L	Pct.	ShO	Sv-Op	Hld	ERA
1994 Chillicothe	IND	13	13	4	0	94.2	402	90	34	30	5	2	2	8	27	2	69	8	0	7	4	.636	0	0--	—	2.85
1995 Beloit	A	22	22	1	0	132	529	119	59	50	10	2	5	6	27	0	110	5	4	13	4	.765	1	0--	—	3.41
1996 El Paso	AA	26	26	0	0	154.1	663	183	90	84	15	2	3	10	23	0	109	4	1	7	5	.583	0	0--	—	4.90
1997 Mobile	AA	31	13	1	5	123.1	512	123	60	51	15	2	1	4	24	2	108	4	0	6	3	.667	0	0--	—	3.72
1998 Mobile	AA	6	6	1	0	41	152	31	11	11	3	1	0	1	4	0	45	0	1	3	2	.600	0	0--	—	2.41
Las Vegas	AAA	33	15	1	7	110	492	138	85	78	21	2	2	12	27	2	109	0	1	6	6	.500	0	3--	—	6.38
1999 Las Vegas	AAA	5	5	0	0	29.2	123	34	17	16	3	1	0	2	6	0	23	1	0	1	2	.333	0	0--	—	4.85
Padres	R	2	2	0	0	4	16	4	2	2	0	0	0	0	0	0	6	0	0	0	0	—	0	0--	—	4.50
2000 Las Vegas	AAA	13	13	0	0	76.1	311	72	28	24	5	1	2	2	11	0	60	0	0	6	0	1.000	0	0--	—	2.83
2001 Lk Elsinore	A+	2	2	0	0	10	49	18	11	7	1	2	0	0	1	0	9	0	0	2	0	1.000	0	0--	—	6.30
Portland	AAA	4	4	0	0	20	86	24	11	10	3	0	0	0	4	0	10	0	0	1	0	1.000	0	0--	—	4.50
2000 San Diego	NL	19	19	1	0	118	506	126	58	47	13	6	0	5	35	4	76	2	1	4	5	.444	0	0-0	0	3.58
2001 San Diego	NL	19	19	0	0	117.1	503	133	58	56	15	5	7	2	25	3	71	1	0	10	4	.714	0	0-0	0	4.30
2 ML YEARS		38	38	1	0	235.1	1009	259	116	103	28	11	7	7	60	7	147	3	1	14	9	.609	0	0-0	0	3.94

Brett Tomko

Pitches: Right **Bats:** Right **Pos:** RP-7; SP-4

Ht: 6'4" **Wt:** 215 **Born:** 4/7/73 **Age:** 29

Year Team	Lg	G	GS	CG	GF	IP	BFP	H	R	ER	HR	SH	SF	HB	TBB	IBB	SO	WP	Bk	W	L	Pct.	ShO	Sv-Op	Hld	ERA
2001 Tacoma *	AAA	19	18	3	0	127	528	124	64	57	12	7	5	3	25	1	117	2	0	10	6	.625	2	0--	—	4.04
1997 Cincinnati	NL	22	19	0	1	126	519	106	50	48	14	5	9	4	47	4	95	5	0	11	7	.611	0	0-0	0	3.43
1998 Cincinnati	NL	34	34	1	0	210.2	887	198	111	104	22	12	2	7	64	3	162	9	1	13	12	.520	0	0-0	0	4.44
1999 Cincinnati	NL	33	26	1	1	172	744	175	103	94	31	9	5	4	60	10	132	8	0	5	7	.417	0	0-0	1	4.92
2000 Seattle	AL	32	8	0	10	92.1	401	92	53	48	12	5	5	3	40	4	59	1	1	7	5	.583	0	1-2	3	4.68
2001 Seattle	AL	11	4	0	1	34.2	164	42	24	20	9	1	2	0	15	2	22	1	0	3	1	.750	0	0-1	0	5.19
5 ML YEARS		132	91	2	13	635.2	2715	613	341	314	88	32	23	18	226	23	470	24	2	39	32	.549	0	1-3	4	4.45

Steve Torrealba

Bats: Right **Throws:** Right **Pos:** C-2; PH/PR-1

Ht: 6'0" **Wt:** 175 **Born:** 2/24/78 **Age:** 24

Year Team	Lg	G	AB	H	2B	3B	HR	(Hm	Rd)	TB	R	RBI	TBB	IBB	SO	HBP	SH	SF	SB	CS	SB%	GDP	Avg	OBP	SLG
1995 Braves	R	30	92	19	4	0	0	—	—	23	3	10	11	0	20	2	0	1	0	0	—	3	.207	.302	.250
1996 Danville	R+	2	5	1	0	0	0	—	—	1	1	0	0	0	2	0	0	0	0	1	.00	1	.200	.200	.200
Braves	R	52	146	25	2	0	0	—	—	27	9	7	16	0	19	2	5	0	1	2	.33	3	.171	.262	.185
1997 Danville	R+	44	150	34	9	0	2	—	—	49	17	18	15	0	27	2	2	2	0	1	.00	6	.227	.302	.327
1998 Macon	A	67	209	57	10	0	10	—	—	97	28	37	20	0	31	3	1	6	3	0	1.00	7	.273	.336	.464
1999 Myrtle Bch	A+	52	175	37	9	0	6	—	—	64	23	23	13	0	47	2	3	0	1	0	1.00	4	.211	.274	.366
2000 Myrtle Bch	A+	99	334	90	16	0	7	—	—	127	43	35	31	0	79	1	4	6	5	1	.83	12	.269	.328	.380
2001 Greenville	AA	90	295	80	21	0	8	—	—	125	37	34	33	0	54	1	4	0	0	0	—	8	.271	.347	.424
2001 Atlanta	NL	2	2	1	0	0	0	(0	0)	1	0	0	0	0	0	0	0	0	0	0	—	0	.500	.500	.500

Yorvit Torrealba

Bats: Right **Throws:** Right **Pos:** C-3

Ht: 5'11" **Wt:** 190 **Born:** 7/19/78 **Age:** 23

Year Team	Lg	G	AB	H	2B	3B	HR	(Hm	Rd)	TB	R	RBI	TBB	IBB	SO	HBP	SH	SF	SB	CS	SB%	GDP	Avg	OBP	SLG
1995 Bellingham	A-	26	71	11	3	0	0	—	—	14	2	8	2	0	14	1	0	1	0	1	.00	1	.155	.187	.197
1996 San Jose	A+	2	5	0	0	0	0	—	—	0	0	0	1	0	1	0	0	0	0	0	—	0	.000	.167	.000
Burlington	A	1	4	0	0	0	0	—	—	0	0	0	0	0	1	0	0	0	0	0	—	1	.000	.000	.000
Bellingham	A-	48	150	40	4	0	1	—	—	47	23	10	9	0	27	4	4	2	4	1	.80	7	.267	.304	.313
1997 Bakersfield	A+	119	446	122	15	3	4	—	—	155	52	40	31	0	58	5	1	3	4	2	.67	6	.274	.326	.348
1998 San Jose	A+	21	70	20	2	0	0	—	—	22	10	10	1	0	6	0	2	1	2	2	.50	2	.286	.292	.314
Shreveport	AA	59	196	46	7	0	0	—	—	53	18	13	18	3	30	4	3	1	0	5	.00	3	.235	.311	.270
Fresno	AAA	4	11	2	1	0	0	—	—	3	1	1	1	1	4	0	0	0	0	0	—	2	.182	.250	.273
1999 Fresno	AAA	17	63	16	2	0	2	—	—	24	9	10	4	0	11	2	0	0	1	0	1.00	3	.254	.319	.381
Shreveport	AA	65	217	53	10	1	4	—	—	77	25	19	9	0	34	2	2	2	0	2	.00	6	.244	.278	.355
San Jose	A+	19	73	23	3	0	2	—	—	32	10	14	6	0	15	1	0	1	0	0	—	2	.315	.370	.438
2000 Shreveport	AA	108	398	114	21	1	4	—	—	149	50	32	34	2	55	6	10	2	2	3	.40	11	.286	.350	.374
2001 Fresno	AAA	115	394	108	23	3	8	—	—	161	56	36	19	0	65	4	3	2	2	3	.40	11	.274	.313	.409
2001 San Francisco	NL	3	4	2	0	1	0	(0	0)	4	0	2	0	0	0	0	0	0	0	0	—	0	.500	.500	1.000

Josh Towers

Pitches: Right **Bats:** Right **Pos:** SP-20; RP-4

Ht: 6'1" **Wt:** 165 **Born:** 2/26/77 **Age:** 25

Year Team	Lg	G	GS	CG	GF	IP	BFP	H	R	ER	HR	SH	SF	HB	TBB	IBB	SO	WP	Bk	W	L	Pct.	ShO	Sv-Op	Hld	ERA
1996 Bluefield	R+	14	9	0	1	55	234	63	35	32	9	0	1	1	5	0	61	4	1	4	1	.800	0	0--	—	5.24
1997 Delmarva	A	9	1	0	5	18.1	73	18	8	7	1	1	1	0	2	0	16	0	0	0	1	1--	—	3.44
Frederick	A+	25	3	0	8	53.2	252	74	36	29	4	1	1	3	18	0	64	2	1	6	2	.750	0	1--	—	4.86
1998 Frederick	A+	25	20	3	3	145.1	583	137	58	54	11	6	3	11	9	0	122	5	2	8	7	.533	0	1--	—	3.34
Bowie	AA	5	2	0	1	18	80	7	1	0	0	0	2		4	0	7	1	0	2	1	.667	0	1--	—	3.50
1999 Bowie	AA	29	28	5	1	189	786	204	86	79	26	12	4	5	26	1	106	5	3	12	7	.632	2	0--	—	3.76
2000 Rochester	AAA	24	24	5	0	148	618	157	63	57	17	2	4	8	21	0	102	1	1	8	6	.571	1	0--	—	3.47
2001 Rochester	AAA	6	6	1	0	41	168	40	18	16	2	0	1	2	8	2	27	0	0	3	1	.750	0	0--	—	3.51
2001 Baltimore	AL	24	20	1	2	140.1	586	165	74	70	21	3	4	6	16	0	58	1	0	8	10	.444	1	0-0	0	4.49

Steve Trachsel

Pitches: Right **Bats:** Right **Pos:** SP-28

Ht: 6'4" **Wt:** 205 **Born:** 10/31/70 **Age:** 31

Year Team	Lg	G	GS	CG	GF	IP	BFP	H	R	ER	HR	SH	SF	HB	TBB	IBB	SO	WP	Bk	W	L	Pct.	ShO	Sv-Op	Hld	ERA
2001 Norfolk *	AAA	3	3	1	0	19.1	76	13	6	6	0	1	0	0	6	0	12	1	0	2	0	1.000	1	0--	0	2.79
1993 Chicago	NL	3	3	0	0	19.2	78	16	10	10	4	1	1	0	3	0	14	1	0	0	2	.000	0	0-0	0	4.58
1994 Chicago	NL	22	22	1	0	146	612	133	57	52	19	3	3	3	54	4	108	6	0	9	7	.563	0	0-0	0	3.21
1995 Chicago	NL	30	29	2	0	160.2	722	174	104	94	25	12	5	0	76	8	117	2	1	7	13	.350	0	0-0	0	5.15
1996 Chicago	NL	31	31	3	0	205	845	181	82	69	30	3	3	8	62	3	132	5	2	13	9	.591	2	0-0	0	3.03
1997 Chicago	NL	34	34	0	0	201.1	878	225	100	101	32	8	11	5	69	6	160	4	1	8	12	.400	0	0-0	0	4.51
1998 Chicago	NL	33	33	1	0	208	894	204	107	103	27	9	7	8	84	5	149	3	2	15	8	.652	0	0-0	0	4.46
1999 Chicago	NL	34	34	4	0	205.2	894	226	133	127	32	6	14	3	64	4	149	8	3	8	18	.308	0	0-0	0	5.56
2000 TB-Tor	AL	34	34	3	0	200.2	882	232	116	107	26	6	4	6	74	2	110	4	0	8	15	.348	1	0-0	0	4.80
2001 New York	NL	28	28	1	0	173.2	726	168	90	86	28	8	7	3	47	7	144	4	0	11	13	.458	1	0-0	0	4.46
2000 Tampa Bay	AL	23	23	3	0	137.2	606	160	76	70	16	2	5	6	49	1	78	3	0	6	10	.375	1	0-0	0	4.58
Toronto	AL	11	11	0	0	63	276	72	40	37	10	4	1	0	25	1	32	1	0	2	5	.286	0	0-0	0	5.29
9 ML YEARS		249	248	15	0	1520.2	6531	1559	809	747	223	56	57	36	533	39	1083	37	9	79	97	.449	4	0-0	0	4.42

Andy Tracy

Bats: L **Throws:** R **Pos:** PH/PR-22; 3B-11; 1B-3; DH-2

Ht: 6'3" **Wt:** 220 **Born:** 12/11/73 **Age:** 28

Year Team	Lg	G	AB	H	2B	3B	HR	(Hm	Rd)	TB	R	RBI	TBB	IBB	SO	HBP	SH	SF	SB	CS	SB%	GDP	Avg	OBP	SLG
1996 Vermont	A-	57	175	47	11	1	4	—	—	72	26	24	32	2	37	2	1	2	1	1	.50	8	.269	.384	.411
1997 Cape Fear	A	59	210	63	9	2	8	—	—	100	31	43	21	4	47	3	0	2	6	1	.86	4	.300	.369	.476
1998 Jupiter	A+	71	251	67	16	1	11	—	—	118	37	53	39	3	69	3	0	5	6	4	.60	3	.267	.366	.470
Harrisburg	AA	62	211	48	12	3	10	—	—	96	33	33	24	3	62	4	0	3	1	2	.33	5	.227	.314	.455
1999 Harrisburg	AA	134	493	135	26	2	37	—	—	276	96	128	70	4	139	6	1	3	6	1	.86	10	.274	.369	.560
2000 Ottawa	AAA	55	195	60	18	0	10	—	—	108	28	36	34	3	63	2	0	3	2	2	.50	2	.308	.410	.554
2001 Ottawa	AAA	53	190	39	11	1	4	—	—	64	17	19	24	1	72	2	0	1	4	2	.67	2	.205	.300	.337
2000 Montreal	NL	83	192	50	8	1	11	(6	5)	93	29	32	22	1	61	2	0	2	1	0	1.00	3	.260	.339	.484
2001 Montreal	NL	38	55	6	1	0	2	(0	2)	13	4	8	6	0	26	0	0	2	0	0	—	1	.109	.190	.236
2 ML YEARS		121	247	56	9	1	13	(6	7)	106	33	40	28	1	87	2	0	4	1	0	1.00	4	.227	.306	.429

Bubba Trammell

Bats: R **Throws:** R **Pos:** RF-102; LF-34; PH/PR-16; DH-3

Ht: 6'2" **Wt:** 220 **Born:** 11/6/71 **Age:** 30

Year Team	Lg	G	AB	H	2B	3B	HR	(Hm	Rd)	TB	R	RBI	TBB	IBB	SO	HBP	SH	SF	SB	CS	SB%	GDP	Avg	OBP	SLG
1997 Detroit	AL	44	123	28	5	0	4	(2	2)	45	14	13	15	0	35	0	0	2	3	1	.75	2	.228	.307	.366
1998 Tampa Bay	AL	59	199	57	18	1	12	(6	6)	113	28	35	16	0	45	0	0	1	0	2	.00	4	.286	.338	.568
1999 Tampa Bay	AL	82	283	82	19	0	14	(6	8)	143	49	39	43	1	37	1	0	1	0	2	.00	7	.290	.384	.505
2000 TB-NYM	AL	102	245	65	13	2	10	(6	4)	112	28	45	29	0	49	2	0	2	4	0	1.00	4	.265	.345	.457
2001 San Diego	NL	142	490	128	20	3	25	(11	14)	229	66	92	48	2	78	4	0	4	2	2	.50	10	.261	.330	.467
2000 Tampa Bay	AL	66	189	52	11	2	7	(5	2)	88	19	33	21	0	30	2	0	1	3	0	1.00	5	.275	.352	.466
New York	NL	36	56	13	2	0	3	(1	2)	24	9	12	8	0	19	0	0	1	1	0	1.00	3	.232	.323	.429
5 ML YEARS		429	1340	360	75	6	65	(31	34)	642	185	224	151	3	244	7	0	10	9	7	.56	31	.269	.344	.479

Mike Trombley

Pitches: Right **Bats:** Right **Pos:** RP-69

Ht: 6'2" **Wt:** 204 **Born:** 4/14/67 **Age:** 35

Year Team	Lg	G	GS	CG	GF	IP	BFP	H	R	ER	HR	SH	SF	HB	TBB	IBB	SO	WP	Bk	W	L	Pct.	ShO	Sv-Op	Hld	ERA
1992 Minnesota	AL	10	7	0	0	46.1	194	43	20	17	5	2	0	1	17	0	38	0	0	3	2	.600	0	0-0	0	3.30
1993 Minnesota	AL	44	10	0	8	114.1	506	131	72	62	15	3	7	3	41	4	85	5	0	6	6	.500	0	2-5	8	4.88
1994 Minnesota	AL	24	0	0	8	48.1	219	56	36	34	10	1	2	3	18	2	32	3	0	2	0	1.000	0	0-1	1	6.33
1995 Minnesota	AL	20	18	0	0	97.2	442	107	68	61	18	3	2	3	42	1	68	4	0	4	8	.333	0	0-0	0	5.62
1996 Minnesota	AL	43	0	0	19	68.2	292	61	24	23	2	0	3	5	25	8	57	4	0	5	1	.833	0	6-9	4	3.01
1997 Minnesota	AL	67	0	0	21	82.1	349	77	43	40	7	2	3	2	31	4	74	5	0	2	3	.400	0	1-1	11	4.37
1998 Minnesota	AL	77	1	0	17	96.2	413	90	41	39	16	2	1	5	41	3	89	6	1	6	5	.545	0	1-4	23	3.63
1999 Minnesota	AL	75	0	0	56	87.1	377	93	42	42	15	2	3	2	28	2	82	6	0	2	8	.200	0	24-30	3	4.33
2000 Baltimore	AL	75	0	0	32	72	322	67	34	33	15	7	2	4	38	8	72	8	0	4	5	.444	0	4-11	18	4.13
2001 Bal-LA	AL	69	0	0	31	78	334	65	40	38	9	8	4	2	37	5	72	1	0	3	8	.273	0	6-9	13	4.38
2001 Baltimore	AL	50	0	0	21	54.2	226	38	23	21	4	4	3	2	27	2	45	1	0	3	4	.429	0	6-9	11	3.46
Los Angeles	NL	19	0	0	10	23.1	108	27	17	17	5	4	1	0	10	3	27	0	0	0	4	.000	0	0-0	2	6.56
10 ML YEARS		504	36	0	192	791.2	3448	790	420	389	112	30	27	30	318	37	669	42	1	37	46	.446	0	44-70	81	4.42

223

Chris Truby

Bats: Right **Throws:** Right **Pos:** 3B-35; PH/PR-12; 1B-1 **Ht:** 6'2" **Wt:** 190 **Born:** 12/9/73 **Age:** 28

							BATTING												BASERUNNING				PERCENTAGES		
Year Team	Lg	G	AB	H	2B	3B	HR	(Hm	Rd)	TB	R	RBI	TBB	IBB	SO	HBP	SH	SF	SB	CS	SB%	GDP	Avg	OBP	SLG
1993 Astros	R	57	215	49	10	2	1	—	—	66	30	24	22	0	30	1	2	1	16	1	.94	5	.228	.301	.307
Osceola	A+	3	13	0	0	0	0	—	—	0	0	0	0	0	2	0	0	0	0	0	—	0	.000	.000	.000
1994 Quad City	A	36	111	24	4	1	2	—	—	36	12	19	3	0	29	2	0	2	1	1	.50	3	.216	.246	.324
Auburn	A-	73	282	91	17	6	7	—	—	141	56	61	23	0	48	3	1	8	20	4	.83	8	.323	.370	.500
1995 Quad City	A	118	400	93	23	4	9	—	—	151	68	64	41	0	66	3	3	3	27	8	.77	11	.233	.306	.378
1996 Quad City	A	109	362	91	15	3	8	—	—	136	45	37	28	1	74	2	6	5	6	10	.38	8	.251	.305	.376
1997 Quad City	A	68	268	75	14	1	7	—	—	112	34	46	22	0	32	1	1	2	13	4	.76	8	.280	.334	.418
Kissimmee	A+	57	199	49	11	0	2	—	—	66	23	29	8	0	40	2	4	3	8	3	.73	4	.246	.278	.332
1998 Kissimmee	A+	52	212	66	16	1	14	—	—	126	36	48	19	3	30	3	0	2	6	1	.86	2	.311	.373	.594
Jackson	AA	80	308	89	20	5	16	—	—	167	46	63	20	0	50	4	0	5	8	3	.73	5	.289	.335	.542
New Orleans	AAA	5	17	7	1	1	1	—	—	13	6	1	1	0	3	0	0	0	1	0	1.00	0	.412	.444	.765
1999 Jackson	AA	124	465	131	21	3	28	—	—	242	78	87	36	1	88	3	0	12	20	8	.71	11	.282	.329	.520
2000 New Orleans	AAA	64	268	76	11	3	2	—	—	99	31	30	17	2	32	0	0	7	6	2	.75	7	.284	.318	.369
2001 New Orleans	AAA	81	321	100	25	6	12	—	—	173	53	71	24	4	66	4	0	2	10	5	.67	11	.312	.365	.539
2000 Houston	NL	78	258	67	15	4	11	(9	2)	123	28	59	10	1	56	5	1	5	2	1	.67	4	.260	.295	.477
2001 Houston	NL	48	136	28	6	1	8	(4	4)	60	11	23	13	2	38	1	0	2	1	2	.33	1	.206	.276	.441
2 ML YEARS		126	394	95	21	5	19	(13	6)	183	39	82	23	3	94	6	1	7	3	3	.50	5	.241	.288	.464

Michael Tucker

Bats: L **Throws:** R **Pos:** CF-76; LF-75; PH/PR-32; RF-25; 1B-4 **Ht:** 6'2" **Wt:** 185 **Born:** 6/25/71 **Age:** 31

							BATTING												BASERUNNING				PERCENTAGES		
Year Team	Lg	G	AB	H	2B	3B	HR	(Hm	Rd)	TB	R	RBI	TBB	IBB	SO	HBP	SH	SF	SB	CS	SB%	GDP	Avg	OBP	SLG
1995 Kansas City	AL	62	177	46	10	0	4	(1	3)	68	23	17	18	2	51	1	2	0	2	3	.40	3	.260	.332	.384
1996 Kansas City	AL	108	339	88	18	4	12	(2	10)	150	55	53	40	1	69	7	3	4	10	4	.71	7	.260	.346	.442
1997 Atlanta	NL	138	499	141	25	7	14	(5	9)	222	80	56	44	0	116	6	4	1	12	7	.63	7	.283	.347	.445
1998 Atlanta	NL	130	414	101	27	3	13	(10	3)	173	54	46	49	10	112	3	1	2	8	3	.73	4	.244	.327	.418
1999 Cincinnati	NL	133	296	75	8	5	11	(5	6)	126	55	44	37	3	81	3	0	4	11	4	.73	5	.253	.338	.426
2000 Cincinnati	NL	148	270	72	13	4	15	(7	8)	138	55	36	44	1	64	7	0	2	13	6	.68	6	.267	.381	.511
2001 Cin-ChC	NL	149	436	110	19	8	12	(4	8)	181	62	61	46	4	102	2	10	6	16	8	.67	8	.252	.322	.415
2001 Cincinnati	NL	86	231	56	10	1	7	(1	6)	89	31	30	23	1	55	1	5	5	12	5	.71	4	.242	.308	.385
Chicago	NL	63	205	54	9	7	5	(3	2)	92	31	31	23	3	47	1	5	1	4	3	.57	4	.263	.339	.449
7 ML YEARS		868	2431	633	120	31	81	(34	47)	1058	384	313	278	21	595	29	20	19	72	35	.67	40	.260	.341	.435

Jason Tyner

Bats: L **Throws:** L **Pos:** LF-57; CF-47; PH/PR-7; RF-3 **Ht:** 6'1" **Wt:** 170 **Born:** 4/23/77 **Age:** 25

							BATTING												BASERUNNING				PERCENTAGES		
Year Team	Lg	G	AB	H	2B	3B	HR	(Hm	Rd)	TB	R	RBI	TBB	IBB	SO	HBP	SH	SF	SB	CS	SB%	GDP	Avg	OBP	SLG
1998 St. Lucie	A+	50	201	61	2	3	0	—	—	69	30	16	17	0	20	1	3	0	15	11	.58	3	.303	.361	.343
1999 Binghamton	AA	129	518	162	19	5	0	—	—	191	91	33	62	0	46	1	8	1	49	15	.77	8	.313	.387	.369
Norfolk	AAA	3	8	0	0	0	0	—	—	0	0	0	0	0	5	0	0	0	0	0	—	0	.000	.000	.000
2000 Norfolk	AAA	84	327	105	5	2	0	—	—	114	54	28	30	1	32	2	8	2	33	14	.70	3	.321	.380	.349
2001 Durham	AAA	39	157	49	2	1	0	—	—	53	25	12	15	1	10	2	1	1	11	5	.69	1	.312	.371	.338
2000 NYM-TB		50	124	28	4	0	0	(0	0)	32	9	13	5	0	16	2	8	3	7	2	.78	2	.226	.261	.258
2001 Tampa Bay	AL	105	396	111	8	5	0	(0	0)	129	51	21	15	0	42	3	5	1	31	6	.84	6	.280	.311	.326
2000 New York	NL	13	41	8	2	0	0	(0	0)	10	3	5	1	0	4	1	3	2	1	1	.50	1	.195	.222	.244
Tampa Bay	AL	37	83	20	2	0	0	(0	0)	22	6	8	4	0	12	1	5	1	6	1	.86	1	.241	.281	.265
2 ML YEARS		155	520	139	12	5	0	(0	0)	161	60	34	20	0	58	5	13	4	38	8	.83	8	.267	.299	.310

Ugueth Urbina

Pitches: Right **Bats:** Right **Pos:** RP-64 **Ht:** 6'2" **Wt:** 205 **Born:** 2/15/74 **Age:** 28

		HOW MUCH HE PITCHED						WHAT HE GAVE UP											THE RESULTS						
Year Team	Lg	G	GS	CG	GF	IP	BFP	H	R	ER	HR	SH	SF	HB	TBB	IBB	SO	WP	Bk	W	L	Pct.	ShO	Sv-Op	Hld	ERA
1995 Montreal	NL	7	4	0	0	23.1	109	26	17	16	6	2	0	0	14	1	15	2	0	2	2	.500	0	0-0	0	6.17
1996 Montreal	NL	33	17	0	2	114	484	102	54	47	18	1	3	1	44	4	108	3	1	10	5	.667	0	0-1	6	3.71
1997 Montreal	NL	63	0	0	50	64.1	276	52	29	27	9	3	1	0	29	2	84	2	0	5	8	.385	0	27-32	1	3.78
1998 Montreal	NL	64	0	0	59	69.1	272	37	11	10	2	2	1	0	33	2	94	3	2	6	3	.667	0	34-38	1	1.30
1999 Montreal	NL	71	0	0	62	75.2	323	59	35	31	6	1	2	0	36	6	100	6	0	6	6	.500	0	41-50	0	3.69
2000 Montreal	NL	13	0	0	11	13.1	54	11	6	6	1	0	0	0	5	0	22	1	0	1	1	.500	0	8-10	0	4.05
2001 Mon-Bos		64	0	0	53	66.2	278	58	29	27	9	2	1	0	24	1	89	2	1	2	2	.500	0	24-28	3	3.65
2001 Montreal	NL	45	0	0	40	46.2	201	42	24	22	8	1	1	0	21	1	57	2	1	2	1	.667	0	15-18	1	4.24
Boston	AL	19	0	0	13	20	77	16	5	5	1	1	0	0	3	0	32	0	0	0	1	.000	0	9-10	2	2.25
7 ML YEARS		315	21	0	237	426.2	1796	345	181	164	51	11	7	2	185	16	512	19	4	31	27	.534	0	134-159	10	3.46

Juan Uribe

Bats: Right **Throws:** Right **Pos:** SS-69; PH/PR-4 **Ht:** 5'11" **Wt:** 173 **Born:** 7/22/80 **Age:** 21

							BATTING												BASERUNNING				PERCENTAGES		
Year Team	Lg	G	AB	H	2B	3B	HR	(Hm	Rd)	TB	R	RBI	TBB	IBB	SO	HBP	SH	SF	SB	CS	SB%	GDP	Avg	OBP	SLG
1998 Rockies	R	40	148	41	5	3	0	—	—	52	25	17	12	0	25	3	3	2	8	1	.89	1	.277	.339	.351
1999 Asheville	A	125	430	115	28	3	9	—	—	176	57	46	20	0	79	6	11	4	11	7	.61	12	.267	.307	.409
2000 Salem	A+	134	485	124	22	7	13	—	—	199	64	65	38	0	100	4	4	2	22	5	.81	11	.256	.314	.410
2001 Carolina	AA	3	13	3	1	0	0	—	—	4	1	1	0	0	4	0	0	0	1	0	1.00	1	.231	.231	.308
Colo Sprngs	AAA	74	281	87	27	7	7	—	—	149	40	48	12	1	43	2	0	0	11	8	.58	8	.310	.340	.530
2001 Colorado	NL	72	273	82	15	11	8	(3	5)	143	32	53	8	1	55	2	0	0	3	0	1.00	6	.300	.325	.524

Ismael Valdes

Pitches: Right Bats: Right Pos: SP-27 Ht: 6'4" Wt: 225 Born: 8/21/73 Age: 28

		HOW MUCH HE PITCHED					WHAT HE GAVE UP											THE RESULTS						
Year Team	Lg	G	GS	CG	GF	IP	BFP	H	R	ER	HR	SH	SF	HB	TBB	IBB	SO	WP	Bk	W	L	Pct.	ShO	Sv-Op	Hld	ERA
1994 Los Angeles	NL	21	1	0	7	28.1	115	21	10	10	2	3	0	0	10	2	28	1	2	3	1	.750	0	0-0	4	3.18
1995 Los Angeles	NL	33	27	6	1	197.2	804	168	76	67	17	10	5	1	51	5	150	1	3	13	11	.542	2	1-1	2	3.05
1996 Los Angeles	NL	33	33	0	0	225	945	219	94	83	20	7	7	3	54	10	173	1	5	15	7	.682	0	0-0	0	3.32
1997 Los Angeles	NL	30	30	0	0	196.2	795	171	68	58	16	11	3	3	47	1	140	3	2	10	11	.476	0	0-0	0	2.65
1998 Los Angeles	NL	27	27	2	0	174	745	171	82	77	17	5	3	2	66	4	122	4	2	11	10	.524	2	0-0	0	3.98
1999 Los Angeles	NL	32	32	2	0	203.1	871	213	97	90	32	9	8	6	58	2	143	6	0	9	14	.391	1	0-0	0	3.98
2000 ChC-LA	NL	21	20	0	1	107	469	124	69	67	22	0	4	3	40	2	74	0	0	2	7	.222	0	0-0	0	5.64
2001 Anaheim	AL	27	27	1	0	163.2	699	177	82	81	20	3	0	8	50	3	100	3	0	9	13	.409	0	0-0	0	4.45
2000 Chicago	NL	12	12	0	0	67	291	71	40	40	17	0	2	2	27	2	45	0	0	1	3	.250	0	0-0	0	5.37
Los Angeles	NL	9	8	0	1	40	178	53	29	27	5	0	2	1	13	0	29	0	0	1	4	.200	0	0-0	0	6.08
8 ML YEARS		224	197	11	9	1295.2	5443	1264	578	533	146	48	30	26	376	29	930	19	14	72	74	.493	5	1-1	6	3.70

Marc Valdes

Pitches: Right Bats: Right Pos: RP-9 Ht: 6'0" Wt: 188 Born: 12/20/71 Age: 30

		HOW MUCH HE PITCHED					WHAT HE GAVE UP											THE RESULTS						
Year Team	Lg	G	GS	CG	GF	IP	BFP	H	R	ER	HR	SH	SF	HB	TBB	IBB	SO	WP	Bk	W	L	Pct.	ShO	Sv-Op	Hld	ERA
2001 Richmond *	AAA	29	21	0	5	123.2	542	133	67	62	13	9	3	13	41	4	97	2	1	9	11	.450	0	0-0	0	4.51
1995 Florida	NL	3	3	0	0	7	49	17	13	11	1	1	1	1	9	0	2	1	0	0	0	—	0	0-0	0	14.14
1996 Florida	NL	11	8	0	0	48.2	228	63	32	26	3	1	3	1	23	0	13	3	2	1	3	.250	0	0-1	0	4.81
1997 Montreal	NL	48	7	0	9	95	407	84	36	33	2	5	5	8	39	5	54	2	0	4	4	.500	0	2-2	1	3.13
1998 Montreal	NL	20	4	0	3	36.1	169	41	34	30	6	1	2	1	21	2	28	4	0	1	3	.250	0	0-0	1	7.43
2000 Houston	NL	53	0	0	20	56.2	264	69	41	32	3	3	2	5	25	1	35	1	0	5	5	.500	0	2-6	8	5.08
2001 Atlanta	NL	9	0	0	3	7	28	7	6	6	4	0	0	1	1	1	3	0	0	1	0	1.000	0	0-0	3	7.71
6 ML YEARS		144	22	0	35	250.2	1145	281	162	138	21	11	13	16	118	9	135	11	2	12	15	.444	0	4-9	13	4.95

Mario Valdez

Bats: L Throws: R Pos: PH/PR-16; DH-12; LF-7; 1B-6 Ht: 6'2" Wt: 190 Born: 11/19/74 Age: 27

		BATTING																BASERUNNING				PERCENTAGES		
Year Team	Lg	G	AB	H	2B	3B	HR	(Hm	Rd)	TB	R	RBI	TBB	IBB	SO	HBP	SH	SF	SB	CS	SB%	GDP	Avg	OBP	SLG
2001 Modesto *	A+	6	19	8	1	0	2	—	—	15	3	5	2	0	1	1	0	0	0	1	.00	2	.421	.500	.789
1997 Chicago	AL	54	115	28	7	0	1	(0	1)	38	11	13	17	0	39	3	0	2	1	0	1.00	0	.243	.350	.330
2000 Oakland	AL	5	12	0	0	0	0	(0	0)	0	0	0	0	0	3	0	0	0	0	0	—	0	.000	.000	.000
2001 Oakland	AL	32	54	15	1	0	1	(0	1)	19	7	8	12	1	18	1	0	0	1	0	1.00	3	.278	.418	.352
3 ML YEARS		91	181	43	8	0	2	(0	2)	57	18	21	29	1	60	4	0	2	2	0	1.00	3	.238	.352	.315

Eric Valent

Bats: L Throws: L Pos: PH/PR-11; LF-7; DH-4; RF-1 Ht: 6'0" Wt: 191 Born: 4/4/77 Age: 25

		BATTING																	BASERUNNING				PERCENTAGES		
Year Team	Lg	G	AB	H	2B	3B	HR	(Hm	Rd)	TB	R	RBI	TBB	IBB	SO	HBP	SH	SF	SB	CS	SB%	GDP	Avg	OBP	SLG
1998 Piedmont	A	22	89	38	12	0	8	—	—	74	24	28	14	2	19	0	0	1	0	0	—	0	.427	.500	.831
Clearwater	A+	34	125	33	8	1	5	—	—	58	24	25	16	0	29	3	0	1	2	1	.33	4	.264	.359	.464
1999 Clearwater	A+	134	520	150	31	9	20	—	—	259	91	106	58	5	110	5	1	10	5	3	.63	10	.288	.359	.498
2000 Reading	AA	128	469	121	22	5	22	—	—	219	81	90	70	1	89	5	0	6	2	3	.40	7	.258	.356	.467
2001 Scrantn-WB	AAA	117	448	122	30	2	21	—	—	219	65	78	49	4	105	1	0	3	1	0	1.00	13	.272	.352	.489
2001 Philadelphia	NL	22	41	4	2	0	0	(0	0)	6	3	1	4	0	11	1	0	0	0	0	—	0	.098	.196	.146

John Valentin

Bats: Right Throws: Right Pos: SS-18; 3B-3 Ht: 6'0" Wt: 185 Born: 2/18/67 Age: 35

		BATTING																	BASERUNNING				PERCENTAGES		
Year Team	Lg	G	AB	H	2B	3B	HR	(Hm	Rd)	TB	R	RBI	TBB	IBB	SO	HBP	SH	SF	SB	CS	SB%	GDP	Avg	OBP	SLG
2001 Trenton *	AA	3	13	2	1	0	0	—	—	3	1	0	1	0	3	0	0	0	0	0	—	0	.154	.214	.231
Pawtucket *	AAA	10	36	9	1	0	2	—	—	16	7	4	8	0	4	0	0	0	0	0	—	0	.250	.386	.444
1992 Boston	AL	58	185	51	13	0	5	(1	4)	79	21	25	20	0	17	2	4	1	1	0	1.00	5	.276	.351	.427
1993 Boston	AL	144	468	130	40	3	11	(7	4)	209	50	66	49	2	77	2	16	4	3	4	.43	9	.278	.346	.447
1994 Boston	AL	84	301	95	26	2	9	(6	3)	152	53	49	42	1	38	3	5	4	3	1	.75	3	.316	.400	.505
1995 Boston	AL	135	520	155	37	2	27	(11	16)	277	108	102	81	2	67	10	4	6	20	5	.80	7	.298	.399	.533
1996 Boston	AL	131	527	156	29	3	13	(9	4)	230	84	59	63	0	59	7	2	7	9	10	.47	15	.296	.374	.436
1997 Boston	AL	143	575	176	47	5	18	(11	7)	287	95	77	58	5	66	5	1	5	7	4	.64	21	.306	.372	.499
1998 Boston	AL	153	588	145	44	1	23	(11	12)	260	113	73	77	3	82	9	2	5	4	5	.44	9	.247	.340	.442
1999 Boston	AL	113	450	114	27	1	12	(5	7)	179	58	70	40	2	68	4	1	8	0	1	.00	11	.253	.315	.398
2000 Boston	AL	10	35	9	1	0	2	(0	2)	16	6	2	2	0	5	0	1	0	0	0	—	1	.200	.314	.283
2001 Boston	AL	20	60	12	2	0	1	(1	0)	17	8	5	9	0	8	1	0	0	0	1	.00	4	.200	.301	.283
10 ML YEARS		991	3709	1043	266	17	121	(61	60)	1706	596	528	441	15	487	43	36	40	47	31	.60	85	.281	.361	.460

Jose Valentin

Bats: B Throws: R Pos: 3B-66; SS-43; CF-24; PH/PR-12 Ht: 5'10" Wt: 185 Born: 10/12/69 Age: 32

		BATTING																	BASERUNNING				PERCENTAGES		
Year Team	Lg	G	AB	H	2B	3B	HR	(Hm	Rd)	TB	R	RBI	TBB	IBB	SO	HBP	SH	SF	SB	CS	SB%	GDP	Avg	OBP	SLG
1992 Milwaukee	AL	4	3	0	0	0	0	(0	0)	0	1	1	0	0	0	0	0	1	0	0	—	0	.000	.000	.000
1993 Milwaukee	AL	19	53	13	1	2	1	(0	1)	21	10	7	7	1	16	1	2	0	1	0	1.00	1	.245	.344	.396
1994 Milwaukee	AL	97	285	68	19	0	11	(8	3)	120	47	46	38	1	75	2	4	2	12	3	.80	1	.239	.330	.421
1995 Milwaukee	AL	112	338	74	23	3	11	(3	8)	136	62	49	37	0	83	0	7	4	16	8	.67	0	.219	.293	.402
1996 Milwaukee	AL	154	552	143	33	7	24	(10	14)	262	90	95	66	9	145	0	6	4	17	4	.81	0	.259	.336	.475
1997 Milwaukee	AL	136	494	125	23	1	17	(4	13)	201	58	58	39	4	109	4	4	5	19	8	.70	5	.253	.310	.407
1998 Milwaukee	NL	151	428	96	24	0	16	(7	9)	168	65	49	63	8	105	1	2	3	10	7	.59	2	.224	.323	.393

(continued)

Year Team	Lg	G	AB	H	2B	3B	HR	(Hm	Rd)	TB	R	RBI	TBB	IBB	SO	HBP	SH	SF	SB	CS	SB%	GDP	Avg	OBP	SLG
1999 Milwaukee	NL	89	256	58	9	5	10	(3	7)	107	45	38	48	7	52	2	2	5	3	2	.60	3	.227	.347	.418
2000 Chicago	AL	144	568	155	37	6	25	(16	9)	279	107	92	59	1	106	4	13	4	19	2	.90	11	.273	.343	.491
2001 Chicago	AL	124	438	113	22	2	28	(14	14)	223	74	68	50	2	114	3	8	3	9	6	.60	7	.258	.336	.509
10 ML YEARS		1030	3415	845	191	26	143	(66	77)	1517	559	503	407	33	805	17	48	31	106	40	.73	34	.247	.328	.444

John Vander Wal

Bats: L **Throws:** L **Pos:** RF-94; LF-23; PH/PR-19; 1B-14; DH-7   **Ht:** 6'2" **Wt:** 197 **Born:** 4/29/66 **Age:** 36

Year Team	Lg	G	AB	H	2B	3B	HR	(Hm	Rd)	TB	R	RBI	TBB	IBB	SO	HBP	SH	SF	SB	CS	SB%	GDP	Avg	OBP	SLG
1991 Montreal	NL	21	61	13	4	1	1	(0	1)	22	4	8	1	0	18	0	0	1	0	0	—	2	.213	.222	.361
1992 Montreal	NL	105	213	51	8	2	4	(2	2)	75	21	20	24	2	36	0	0	0	3	0	1.00	3	.239	.316	.352
1993 Montreal	NL	106	215	50	7	4	5	(1	4)	80	34	30	27	2	30	1	0	1	6	3	.67	4	.233	.320	.372
1994 Colorado	NL	91	110	27	3	1	5	(1	4)	47	12	15	16	0	31	0	0	1	2	1	.67	4	.245	.339	.427
1995 Colorado	NL	105	101	35	8	1	5	(2	3)	60	15	21	16	5	23	0	0	1	1	1	.50	2	.347	.432	.594
1996 Colorado	NL	104	151	38	6	2	5	(5	0)	63	20	31	19	2	38	1	0	2	2	2	.50	1	.252	.335	.417
1997 Colorado	NL	76	92	16	2	0	1	(0	1)	21	7	11	10	0	33	0	0	0	1	1	.50	2	.174	.255	.228
1998 Col-SD	NL	109	129	36	13	1	5	(3	2)	66	21	20	22	0	34	0	0	1	0	0	—	2	.279	.382	.512
1999 San Diego	NL	132	246	67	18	0	6	(2	4)	103	26	41	37	1	59	2	0	3	2	1	.67	5	.272	.368	.419
2000 Pittsburgh	NL	134	384	115	29	0	24	(13	11)	216	74	94	72	5	92	2	0	3	11	2	.85	7	.299	.410	.563
2001 Pit-SF	NL	146	452	122	28	4	14	(6	8)	200	58	70	68	9	122	1	2	4	8	6	.57	10	.270	.364	.442
1998 Colorado	NL	89	104	30	10	1	5	(3	2)	57	18	20	16	0	29	0	0	1	0	0	—	1	.288	.380	.548
San Diego	NL	20	25	6	3	0	0	(0	0)	9	3	0	6	0	5	0	0	0	0	0	—	1	.240	.387	.360
2001 Pittsburgh	NL	97	313	87	22	3	11	(5	6)	148	39	50	42	6	84	1	0	4	7	4	.64	7	.278	.361	.473
San Francisco	NL	49	139	35	6	1	3	(1	2)	52	19	20	26	3	38	0	2	0	1	2	.33	3	.252	.370	.374
11 ML YEARS		1129	2154	570	126	16	75	(35	40)	953	292	361	312	26	516	7	2	17	36	17	.68	41	.265	.357	.442

Todd Van Poppel

Pitches: Right **Bats:** Right **Pos:** RP-59   **Ht:** 6'5" **Wt:** 235 **Born:** 12/9/71 **Age:** 30

Year Team	Lg	G	GS	CG	GF	IP	BFP	H	R	ER	HR	SH	SF	HB	TBB	IBB	SO	WP	Bk	W	L	Pct.	ShO	Sv-Op	Hld	ERA
1991 Oakland	AL	1	1	0	0	4.2	21	7	5	5	1	0	0	0	2	0	6	0	0	0	0	—	0	0-0	0	9.64
1993 Oakland	AL	16	16	0	0	84	380	76	50	47	10	1	2	2	62	0	47	3	0	6	6	.500	0	0-0	0	5.04
1994 Oakland	AL	23	23	0	0	116.2	532	108	80	79	20	4	4	3	89	2	83	3	1	7	10	.412	0	0-0	0	6.09
1995 Oakland	AL	36	14	1	10	138.1	582	125	77	75	16	3	6	4	56	1	122	4	0	4	8	.333	0	0-0	1	4.88
1996 Oak-Det	AL	37	15	1	8	99.1	491	139	107	100	24	4	7	3	62	3	53	7	0	3	9	.250	1	1-2	0	9.06
1998 Tex-Pit		22	11	0	3	66.1	303	79	52	47	9	3	3	1	28	3	42	7	3	2	4	.333	0	0-0	0	6.38
2000 Chicago	NL	51	2	0	13	86.1	378	80	38	36	10	4	3	2	48	2	77	4	0	4	5	.444	0	2-5	7	3.75
2001 Chicago	NL	59	0	0	18	75	324	63	22	21	9	4	0	0	38	4	90	5	1	4	1	.800	0	0-0	5	2.52
1996 Oakland	AL	28	6	0	8	63	301	86	56	54	13	3	5	2	33	3	37	4	0	1	5	.167	0	1-2	0	7.71
Detroit	AL	9	9	1	0	36.1	190	53	51	46	11	1	2	1	29	0	16	3	0	2	4	.333	1	0-0	0	11.39
1998 Texas	AL	4	4	0	0	19.1	95	26	20	19	5	0	1	0	10	0	10	2	0	1	2	.333	0	0-0	0	8.84
Pittsburgh	NL	18	7	0	3	47	208	53	32	28	4	3	2	0	18	3	32	5	3	1	2	.333	0	0-0	0	5.36
8 ML YEARS		245	82	2	52	670.2	3011	677	431	410	99	23	25	15	385	15	520	33	5	30	43	.411	1	3-7	13	5.50

Jason Varitek

Bats: Both **Throws:** Right **Pos:** C-50; PH/PR-3   **Ht:** 6'2" **Wt:** 220 **Born:** 4/11/72 **Age:** 30

Year Team	Lg	G	AB	H	2B	3B	HR	(Hm	Rd)	TB	R	RBI	TBB	IBB	SO	HBP	SH	SF	SB	CS	SB%	GDP	Avg	OBP	SLG
1997 Boston	AL	1	1	1	0	0	0	(0	0)	1	0	0	0	0	0	0	0	0	0	0	—	0	1.000	1.000	1.000
1998 Boston	AL	86	221	56	13	0	7	(1	6)	90	31	33	17	1	45	2	4	3	2	2	.50	8	.253	.309	.407
1999 Boston	AL	144	483	130	39	2	20	(12	8)	233	70	76	46	2	85	2	5	8	1	2	.33	13	.269	.330	.482
2000 Boston	AL	139	448	111	31	1	10	(2	8)	174	55	65	60	3	84	6	1	4	1	1	.50	16	.248	.342	.388
2001 Boston	AL	51	174	51	11	1	7	(2	5)	85	19	25	21	3	35	1	1	1	0	0	—	6	.293	.371	.489
5 ML YEARS		421	1327	349	94	4	44	(17	27)	583	175	199	144	9	249	11	11	16	4	5	.44	43	.263	.336	.439

Greg Vaughn

Bats: Right **Throws:** Right **Pos:** DH-76; LF-57; PH/PR-3   **Ht:** 6'0" **Wt:** 202 **Born:** 7/3/65 **Age:** 36

Year Team	Lg	G	AB	H	2B	3B	HR	(Hm	Rd)	TB	R	RBI	TBB	IBB	SO	HBP	SH	SF	SB	CS	SB%	GDP	Avg	OBP	SLG
1989 Milwaukee	AL	38	113	30	3	0	5	(1	4)	48	18	23	13	0	23	0	0	2	4	1	.80	0	.265	.336	.425
1990 Milwaukee	AL	120	382	84	26	2	17	(9	8)	165	51	61	33	1	91	1	7	6	7	4	.64	11	.220	.280	.432
1991 Milwaukee	AL	145	542	132	24	5	27	(16	11)	247	81	98	62	2	125	1	2	7	2	2	.50	5	.244	.319	.456
1992 Milwaukee	AL	141	501	114	18	2	23	(11	12)	205	77	78	60	1	123	5	2	5	15	15	.50	8	.228	.313	.409
1993 Milwaukee	AL	154	569	152	28	2	30	(12	18)	274	97	97	89	14	118	5	0	4	10	7	.59	6	.267	.369	.482
1994 Milwaukee	AL	95	370	94	24	1	19	(9	10)	177	59	55	51	6	93	1	0	1	9	5	.64	6	.254	.345	.478
1995 Milwaukee	AL	108	392	88	19	1	17	(8	9)	160	67	59	55	3	89	0	0	4	10	4	.71	10	.224	.317	.408
1996 Mil-SD		145	516	134	19	1	41	(22	19)	278	98	117	82	6	130	6	0	3	9	3	.75	7	.260	.365	.539
1997 San Diego	NL	120	361	78	10	0	18	(11	7)	142	60	57	56	1	110	2	0	3	7	4	.64	7	.216	.322	.393
1998 San Diego	NL	158	573	156	28	4	50	(23	27)	342	112	119	79	6	121	5	0	4	11	4	.73	7	.272	.363	.597
1999 Cincinnati	NL	153	550	135	20	2	45	(20	25)	294	104	118	85	3	137	3	0	5	15	2	.88	9	.245	.347	.535
2000 Tampa Bay	AL	127	461	117	27	1	28	(13	15)	230	83	74	80	3	128	2	0	2	8	1	.89	10	.254	.365	.499
2001 Tampa Bay	AL	136	485	113	25	0	24	(12	12)	210	74	82	71	7	130	3	0	3	11	5	.69	10	.233	.333	.433
1996 Milwaukee	AL	102	375	105	16	0	31	(16	15)	214	78	95	58	4	99	4	0	5	5	2	.71	6	.280	.378	.571
San Diego	NL	43	141	29	3	1	10	(6	4)	64	20	22	24	2	31	2	0	0	4	1	.80	1	.206	.329	.454
13 ML YEARS		1640	5815	1427	271	21	344	(167	177)	2772	981	1038	816	53	1418	34	11	51	118	57	.67	96	.245	.339	.477

Mo Vaughn

Bats: Left **Throws:** Right **2000 Pos:** 1B-147; DH-14; CF-1; PH/PR-1 **Ht:** 6'1" **Wt:** 275 **Born:** 12/15/67 **Age:** 34

Year Team	Lg	G	AB	H	2B	3B	HR	(Hm	Rd)	TB	R	RBI	TBB	IBB	SO	HBP	SH	SF	SB	CS	SB%	GDP	Avg	OBP	SLG
1991 Boston	AL	74	219	57	12	0	4	(1	3)	81	21	32	26	2	43	2	0	4	2	1	.67	7	.260	.339	.370
1992 Boston	AL	113	355	83	16	2	13	(8	5)	142	42	57	47	7	67	3	0	3	3	3	.50	8	.234	.326	.400
1993 Boston	AL	152	539	160	34	1	29	(13	16)	283	86	101	79	23	130	8	0	7	4	3	.57	14	.297	.390	.525
1994 Boston	AL	111	394	122	25	1	26	(15	11)	227	65	82	57	20	112	10	0	2	4	4	.50	7	.310	.408	.576
1995 Boston	AL	140	550	165	28	3	39	(15	24)	316	98	126	68	17	150	14	0	4	11	4	.73	17	.300	.388	.575
1996 Boston	AL	161	635	207	29	1	44	(27	17)	370	118	143	95	19	154	14	0	8	2	0	1.00	17	.326	.420	.583
1997 Boston	AL	141	527	166	24	0	35	(20	15)	295	91	96	86	17	154	12	0	3	2	2	.50	10	.315	.420	.560
1998 Boston	AL	154	609	205	31	2	40	(19	21)	360	107	115	61	13	144	8	0	3	0	0	—	13	.337	.402	.591
1999 Anaheim	AL	139	524	147	20	0	33	(16	17)	266	63	108	54	7	127	11	0	3	0	0	—	11	.281	.358	.508
2000 Anaheim	AL	161	614	167	31	0	36	(18	18)	306	93	117	79	11	181	14	0	5	2	0	1.00	14	.272	.365	.498
10 ML YEARS		1346	4966	1479	250	10	299	(152	147)	2646	784	977	652	136	1262	96	0	42	30	17	.64	118	.298	.387	.533

Javier Vazquez

Pitches: Right **Bats:** Right **Pos:** SP-32 **Ht:** 6'2" **Wt:** 195 **Born:** 7/25/76 **Age:** 25

		HOW MUCH HE PITCHED						WHAT HE GAVE UP											THE RESULTS					
Year Team	Lg	G	GS	CG	GF	IP	BFP	H	R	ER	HR	SH	SF	HB	TBB	IBB	SO	WP	Bk	W	L	Pct.	ShO	Sv-Op	Hld	ERA
1998 Montreal	NL	33	32	0	1	172.1	764	196	121	116	31	9	4	11	68	2	139	2	0	5	15	.250	0	0-0	0	6.06
1999 Montreal	NL	26	26	3	0	154.2	667	154	98	86	20	3	3	4	52	4	113	2	0	9	8	.529	1	0-0	0	5.00
2000 Montreal	NL	33	33	2	0	217.2	945	247	104	98	24	11	3	5	61	10	196	3	0	11	9	.550	1	0-0	0	4.05
2001 Montreal	NL	32	32	5	0	223.2	898	197	92	85	24	9	2	3	44	4	208	3	1	16	11	.593	3	0-0	0	3.42
4 ML YEARS		124	123	10	1	768.1	3274	794	415	385	99	32	12	23	225	20	656	10	1	41	43	.488	5	0-0	0	4.51

Ramon Vazquez

Bats: L **Throws:** R **Pos:** SS-10; 2B-6; PH/PR-5; 3B-2; DH-1 **Ht:** 5'11" **Wt:** 170 **Born:** 8/21/76 **Age:** 25

Year Team	Lg	G	AB	H	2B	3B	HR	(Hm	Rd)	TB	R	RBI	TBB	IBB	SO	HBP	SH	SF	SB	CS	SB%	GDP	Avg	OBP	SLG
1995 Mariners	R	39	141	29	3	1	0	—	—	34	20	11	19	0	27	2	0	1	4	3	.57	2	.206	.309	.241
1996 Everett	A-	33	126	35	5	2	1	—	—	47	25	18	26	0	26	1	2	5	7	2	.78	3	.278	.392	.373
Tacoma	AAA	18	49	11	2	1	0	—	—	15	7	4	4	0	12	1	0	0	0	0	—	2	.224	.296	.306
Wisconsin	A	3	10	3	1	0	0	—	—	4	1	1	2	0	2	0	0	0	0	0	—	1	.300	.417	.400
1997 Wisconsin	A	131	479	129	25	5	8	—	—	188	79	49	78	2	93	3	4	3	16	10	.62	8	.269	.373	.392
1998 Lancaster	A+	121	468	129	26	4	2	—	—	169	77	72	81	5	66	2	4	1	15	11	.58	6	.276	.384	.361
1999 New Haven	AA	127	438	113	27	3	5	—	—	161	58	45	62	4	77	5	6	3	8	1	.89	11	.258	.354	.368
2000 New Haven	AA	124	405	116	25	4	8	—	—	173	58	59	52	4	76	2	8	4	1	6	.14	6	.286	.367	.427
2001 Tacoma	AAA	127	466	140	28	1	10	—	—	200	85	79	76	3	84	1	4	3	9	7	.56	13	.300	.397	.429
2001 Seattle	AL	17	35	8	0	0	0	(0	0)	8	5	4	0	0	3	0	1	1	0	0	—	0	.229	.222	.229

Jorge Velandia

Bats: Right **Throws:** Right **Pos:** SS-8; 3B-1 **Ht:** 5'9" **Wt:** 185 **Born:** 1/12/75 **Age:** 27

Year Team	Lg	G	AB	H	2B	3B	HR	(Hm	Rd)	TB	R	RBI	TBB	IBB	SO	HBP	SH	SF	SB	CS	SB%	GDP	Avg	OBP	SLG
2001 Norfolk *	AAA	67	260	65	21	0	5	—	—	101	25	37	16	0	47	5	10	3	9	4	.69	7	.250	.303	.388
1997 San Diego	NL	14	29	3	2	0	0	(0	0)	5	0	0	1	0	7	0	0	0	0	0	—	0	.103	.133	.172
1998 Oakland	AL	8	4	1	0	0	0	(0	0)	1	0	0	0	0	1	0	0	0	0	0	—	0	.250	.250	.250
1999 Oakland	AL	63	48	9	1	0	0	(0	0)	10	4	2	2	0	13	1	0	0	2	0	1.00	0	.188	.235	.208
2000 Oak-NYM		33	31	3	1	0	0	(0	0)	4	2	2	2	0	8	1	0	0	0	0	—	0	.097	.176	.129
2001 New York	NL	9	9	0	0	0	0	(0	0)	0	0	0	0	0	0	0	0	0	0	0	—	0	.000	.000	.000
2000 Oakland	AL	18	24	3	1	0	0	(0	0)	4	1	2	0	0	6	1	0	0	0	0	—	0	.125	.160	.167
New York	NL	15	7	0	0	0	0	(0	0)	0	1	0	2	0	2	0	0	0	0	0	—	0	.000	.222	.000
5 ML YEARS		127	121	16	4	0	0	(0	0)	20	7	4	7	0	30	2	0	0	2	0	1.00	0	.132	.192	.165

Randy Velarde

Bats: R **Throws:** R **Pos:** 2B-52; 3B-14; DH-11; 1B-10; PH/PR-9; RF-3; LF-2 **Ht:** 6'0" **Wt:** 200 **Born:** 11/24/62 **Age:** 39

Year Team	Lg	G	AB	H	2B	3B	HR	(Hm	Rd)	TB	R	RBI	TBB	IBB	SO	HBP	SH	SF	SB	CS	SB%	GDP	Avg	OBP	SLG
2001 Tulsa *	AA	6	21	8	2	0	0	—	—	10	5	5	1	0	5	0	0	2	0	0	—	1	.381	.375	.476
1987 New York	AL	8	22	4	0	0	0	(0	0)	4	1	1	0	0	6	0	0	0	0	0	—	1	.182	.182	.182
1988 New York	AL	48	115	20	6	0	5	(2	3)	41	18	12	8	0	24	2	0	0	1	1	.50	3	.174	.240	.357
1989 New York	AL	33	100	34	4	2	2	(1	1)	48	12	11	7	0	14	1	3	0	0	3	.00	6	.340	.389	.480
1990 New York	AL	95	229	48	6	2	5	(1	4)	73	21	19	20	0	53	1	2	1	0	3	.00	6	.210	.275	.319
1991 New York	AL	80	184	45	11	1	1	(0	1)	61	19	15	18	0	43	3	5	0	3	1	.75	6	.245	.322	.332
1992 New York	AL	121	412	112	24	1	7	(4	3)	159	57	46	38	1	78	2	4	5	7	2	.78	13	.272	.333	.386
1993 New York	AL	85	226	68	13	2	7	(4	3)	106	28	24	18	2	39	4	3	2	2	2	.50	12	.301	.360	.469
1994 New York	AL	77	280	78	16	1	9	(3	6)	123	47	34	22	0	61	4	2	2	4	2	.67	5	.279	.338	.439
1995 New York	AL	111	367	102	19	1	7	(2	5)	144	60	46	55	0	64	4	3	3	5	1	.83	9	.278	.375	.392
1996 California	AL	136	530	151	27	3	14	(8	6)	226	82	54	70	0	118	5	4	2	7	7	.50	7	.285	.372	.426
1997 Anaheim	AL	1	0	0	0	0	0	(0	0)	0	0	0	0	0	0	0	0	0	0	0	—	0	—	—	—
1998 Anaheim	AL	51	188	49	13	1	4	(1	3)	76	29	26	34	0	42	1	0	1	7	2	.78	4	.261	.375	.404
1999 Ana-Oak	AL	156	631	200	25	7	16	(8	8)	287	105	76	70	2	98	6	4	0	24	8	.75	19	.317	.390	.455
2000 Oakland	AL	122	485	135	23	0	12	(11	1)	194	82	41	54	0	95	3	4	1	9	3	.75	15	.278	.356	.400
2001 Tex-NYY	AL	93	342	95	19	2	9	(3	6)	145	50	32	34	0	86	8	1	1	6	2	.75	8	.278	.356	.424
1999 Anaheim	AL	95	376	115	15	4	9	(4	5)	165	57	48	43	1	56	4	2	0	13	4	.76	8	.306	.383	.439
Oakland	AL	61	255	85	10	3	7	(4	3)	122	48	28	27	1	42	2	2	0	11	4	.73	11	.333	.401	.478
2001 Texas	AL	78	296	88	16	2	9	(3	6)	135	46	31	29	0	73	5	3	1	4	2	.67	8	.297	.369	.456
New York	AL	15	46	7	3	0	0	(0	0)	10	4	1	5	0	13	3	1	0	2	0	1.00	0	.152	.278	.217
15 ML YEARS		1217	4111	1141	206	23	98	(46	52)	1687	611	437	448	5	821	44	37	18	75	37	.67	114	.278	.353	.410

Mike Venafro

Pitches: Left **Bats:** Left **Pos:** RP-70 **Ht:** 5'10" **Wt:** 180 **Born:** 8/2/73 **Age:** 28

Year Team	Lg	G	GS	CG	GF	IP	BFP	H	R	ER	HR	SH	SF	HB	TBB	IBB	SO	WP	Bk	W	L	Pct.	ShO	Sv-Op	Hld	ERA
1999 Texas	AL	65	0	0	11	68.1	283	63	29	25	4	5	2	3	22	0	37	0	0	3	2	.600	0	0-1	19	3.29
2000 Texas	AL	77	0	0	21	56.1	248	64	27	24	2	2	4	4	21	4	32	1	0	3	1	.750	0	1-2	17	3.83
2001 Texas	AL	70	0	0	20	60	266	54	35	32	2	2	4	7	28	4	29	3	0	5	5	.500	0	4-8	21	4.80
3 ML YEARS		212	0	0	52	184.2	797	181	91	81	8	9	10	14	71	8	98	4	0	11	8	.579	0	5-11	57	3.95

Robin Ventura

Bats: Left **Throws:** Right **Pos:** 3B-139; PH/PR-6 **Ht:** 6'1" **Wt:** 198 **Born:** 7/14/67 **Age:** 34

Year Team	Lg	G	AB	H	2B	3B	HR	(Hm	Rd)	TB	R	RBI	TBB	IBB	SO	HBP	SH	SF	SB	CS	SB%	GDP	Avg	OBP	SLG
1989 Chicago	AL	16	45	8	3	0	0	(0	0)	11	5	7	8	0	6	1	0	0	0	0	—	1	.178	.298	.244
1990 Chicago	AL	150	493	123	17	1	5	(2	3)	157	48	54	55	2	53	1	13	3	1	4	.20	5	.249	.324	.318
1991 Chicago	AL	157	606	172	25	1	23	(16	7)	268	92	100	80	3	67	4	8	7	2	4	.33	22	.284	.367	.442
1992 Chicago	AL	157	592	167	38	1	16	(7	9)	255	85	93	93	9	71	0	1	8	2	4	.33	14	.282	.375	.431
1993 Chicago	AL	157	554	145	27	1	22	(12	10)	240	85	94	105	16	82	3	1	6	1	6	.14	18	.262	.379	.433
1994 Chicago	AL	109	401	113	15	1	18	(8	10)	184	57	78	61	15	69	2	2	8	3	1	.75	8	.282	.373	.459
1995 Chicago	AL	135	492	145	22	0	26	(8	18)	245	79	93	75	11	98	1	1	8	4	3	.57	8	.295	.384	.498
1996 Chicago	AL	158	586	168	31	2	34	(13	21)	305	96	105	78	10	81	2	0	8	1	3	.25	18	.287	.368	.520
1997 Chicago	AL	54	183	48	10	1	6	(2	4)	78	27	26	34	5	21	0	0	3	0	0	—	3	.262	.373	.426
1998 Chicago	AL	161	590	155	31	4	21	(15	6)	257	84	91	79	15	111	1	1	3	1	1	.50	10	.263	.349	.436
1999 New York	NL	161	588	177	38	0	32	(13	19)	311	88	120	74	10	109	3	1	5	1	1	.50	14	.301	.379	.529
2000 New York	NL	141	469	109	23	1	24	(12	12)	206	61	84	75	12	91	2	1	4	3	5	.38	14	.232	.338	.439
2001 New York	NL	142	456	108	20	0	21	(9	12)	191	70	61	88	10	101	1	0	4	2	5	.29	13	.237	.359	.419
13 ML YEARS		1698	6055	1638	300	13	248	(117	131)	2708	877	1006	905	118	960	21	30	70	21	37	.36	148	.271	.364	.447

Quilvio Veras

Bats: Both **Throws:** Right **Pos:** 2B-67; PH/PR-7 **Ht:** 5'10" **Wt:** 183 **Born:** 4/3/71 **Age:** 31

Year Team	Lg	G	AB	H	2B	3B	HR	(Hm	Rd)	TB	R	RBI	TBB	IBB	SO	HBP	SH	SF	SB	CS	SB%	GDP	Avg	OBP	SLG
2001 Pawtucket *	AAA	3	10	3	1	0	0	—	—	4	1	0	0	0	3	0	0	0	0	0	—	0	.300	.300	.400
1995 Florida	NL	124	440	115	20	7	5	(2	3)	164	86	32	80	0	68	9	7	2	56	21	.73	7	.261	.384	.373
1996 Florida	NL	73	253	64	8	1	4	(1	3)	86	40	14	51	1	42	2	1	1	8	8	.50	3	.253	.381	.340
1997 San Diego	NL	145	539	143	23	1	3	(3	0)	177	74	45	72	0	84	7	9	4	33	12	.73	9	.265	.357	.328
1998 San Diego	NL	138	517	138	24	2	6	(5	1)	184	79	45	84	2	78	6	1	4	24	9	.73	6	.267	.373	.356
1999 San Diego	NL	132	475	133	25	2	6	(4	2)	180	95	41	65	0	88	2	1	2	30	17	.64	7	.280	.368	.379
2000 Atlanta	NL	84	298	92	15	0	5	(2	3)	122	56	37	51	0	50	5	6	4	25	12	.68	8	.309	.413	.409
2001 Atlanta	NL	71	258	65	14	2	3	(0	3)	92	39	25	24	1	52	7	4	2	7	4	.64	4	.252	.330	.357
7 ML YEARS		767	2780	750	129	15	32	(17	15)	1005	469	239	427	4	462	38	29	19	183	83	.69	44	.270	.372	.362

Dave Veres

Pitches: Right **Bats:** Right **Pos:** RP-71 **Ht:** 6'2" **Wt:** 220 **Born:** 10/19/66 **Age:** 35

Year Team	Lg	G	GS	CG	GF	IP	BFP	H	R	ER	HR	SH	SF	HB	TBB	IBB	SO	WP	Bk	W	L	Pct.	ShO	Sv-Op	Hld	ERA
1994 Houston	NL	32	0	0	7	41	168	39	13	11	4	0	2	1	7	3	28	2	0	3	3	.500	0	1-1	3	2.41
1995 Houston	NL	72	0	0	15	103.1	418	89	29	26	5	6	8	4	30	6	94	4	0	5	1	.833	0	1-3	19	2.26
1996 Montreal	NL	68	0	0	22	77.2	351	85	39	36	10	3	3	6	32	2	81	3	2	6	3	.667	0	4-6	15	4.17
1997 Montreal	NL	53	0	0	11	62	281	68	28	24	5	6	1	2	27	3	47	7	0	2	3	.400	0	1-4	10	3.48
1998 Colorado	NL	63	0	0	26	76.1	319	67	26	24	6	0	2	2	27	2	74	2	2	3	1	.750	0	8-13	8	2.83
1999 Colorado	NL	73	0	0	63	77	349	88	46	44	14	5	2	2	37	7	71	8	1	4	8	.333	0	31-39	0	5.14
2000 St. Louis	NL	71	0	0	61	75.2	310	65	26	24	6	5	2	6	25	2	67	3	1	5	3	.375	0	29-36	1	2.85
2001 St. Louis	NL	71	0	0	44	65.2	279	57	29	27	12	2	1	2	28	1	61	6	0	3	2	.600	0	15-19	8	3.70
8 ML YEARS		503	0	0	249	578.2	2475	558	236	216	62	27	21	25	213	26	523	35	6	29	26	.527	0	90-121	64	3.36

Jose Vidro

Bats: Both **Throws:** Right **Pos:** 2B-121; DH-2; PH/PR-1 **Ht:** 5'11" **Wt:** 190 **Born:** 8/27/74 **Age:** 27

Year Team	Lg	G	AB	H	2B	3B	HR	(Hm	Rd)	TB	R	RBI	TBB	IBB	SO	HBP	SH	SF	SB	CS	SB%	GDP	Avg	OBP	SLG
1997 Montreal	NL	67	169	42	12	1	2	(0	2)	62	19	17	11	0	20	2	0	3	1	0	1.00	1	.249	.297	.367
1998 Montreal	NL	83	205	45	12	0	0	(0	0)	57	24	18	27	0	33	4	6	3	2	2	.50	5	.220	.318	.278
1999 Montreal	NL	140	494	150	45	2	12	(5	7)	235	67	59	29	2	51	4	2	2	0	4	.00	12	.304	.346	.476
2000 Montreal	NL	153	606	200	51	2	24	(11	13)	327	101	97	49	4	69	2	0	6	5	4	.56	17	.330	.379	.540
2001 Montreal	NL	124	486	155	34	1	15	(6	9)	236	82	59	31	2	49	10	2	2	4	1	.80	18	.319	.371	.486
5 ML YEARS		567	1960	592	154	6	53	(22	31)	917	293	250	147	8	222	22	10	16	12	11	.52	53	.302	.355	.468

Brandon Villafuerte

Pitches: Right **Bats:** Right **Pos:** RP-6 **Ht:** 5'11" **Wt:** 180 **Born:** 12/17/75 **Age:** 26

Year Team	Lg	G	GS	CG	GF	IP	BFP	H	R	ER	HR	SH	SF	HB	TBB	IBB	SO	WP	Bk	W	L	Pct.	ShO	Sv-Op	Hld	ERA
1995 Kingsport	R+	20	0	0	6	32	144	28	21	20	0	1	1	1	26	0	42	8	0	5	1	.833	0	0--	—	5.63
1996 Pittsfield	A-	18	7	1	4	62.2	267	53	21	21	5	2	3	6	27	0	59	4	0	8	3	.727	0	1--	—	3.02
1997 Capital City	A	47	3	0	31	75.2	308	58	23	20	6	4	1	4	33	0	88	12	0	3	1	.750	0	7--	—	2.38
1998 Brevard Cty	A+	3	0	0	0	9.2	34	7	3	1	0	0	0	0	1	0	6	0	0	1	0	1.000	0	0--	—	0.93
Portland	AA	30	0	0	11	54.1	262	68	35	30	3	6	0	4	33	2	52	3	0	0	1	.000	0	1--	—	4.97
Charlotte	AAA	10	0	0	1	11.1	55	15	8	8	2	1	0	1	8	0	9	1	0	1	0	1.000	0	0--	—	6.35
1999 Portland	AA	22	12	0	4	100.1	422	97	45	39	11	4	2	5	40	3	85	2	1	6	8	.429	0	0--	—	3.50
Jacksnville	AA	15	0	0	10	24	101	17	6	5	0	4	2	1	12	0	20	1	0	0	2	.000	0	5--	—	1.88

Year Team	Lg	G	GS	CG	GF	IP	BFP	H	R	ER	HR	SH	SF	HB	TBB	IBB	SO	WP	Bk	W	L	Pct.	ShO	Sv-Op	Hld	ERA
2000 Toledo	AAA	46	6	0	21	87.2	417	112	70	65	7	2	3	1	49	1	85	12	1	4	9	.308	0	4--	—	6.67
2001 Oklahoma	AAA	38	0	0	28	63.2	275	63	21	20	4	4	3	6	26	1	65	2	0	5	5	.500	0	10--	—	2.83
2000 Detroit	AL	3	0	0	2	4.1	20	4	5	5	0	0	0	0	4	0	1	1	0	0	0	—	0	0-0	0	10.38
2001 Texas	AL	6	0	0	4	5.2	35	12	9	9	3	0	1	1	4	0	4	1	0	0	0	—	0	0-0	0	14.29
2 ML YEARS		9	0	0	6	10	55	16	14	14	3	0	1	1	8	0	5	2	0	0	0	—	0	0-0	0	12.60

Ron Villone

Pitches: Left Bats: Left Pos: RP-41; SP-12

Ht: 6'4" Wt: 235 Born: 1/16/70 Age: 32

Year Team	Lg	G	GS	CG	GF	IP	BFP	H	R	ER	HR	SH	SF	HB	TBB	IBB	SO	WP	Bk	W	L	Pct.	ShO	Sv-Op	Hld	ERA
1995 Sea-SD		38	0	0	15	45	212	44	31	29	11	3	1	1	34	0	63	3	0	2	3	.400	0	1-5	6	5.80
1996 SD-Mil		44	0	0	19	43	182	31	15	15	6	0	2	5	25	0	38	2	0	1	1	.500	0	2-3	9	3.14
1997 Milwaukee	AL	50	0	0	15	52.2	238	54	23	20	4	2	0	1	36	2	40	3	0	1	0	1.000	0	0-2	8	3.42
1998 Cleveland	AL	25	0	0	6	27	129	30	18	18	3	2	2	2	22	0	15	0	0	0	0	—	0	0-0	1	6.00
1999 Cincinnati	NL	29	22	0	2	142.2	610	114	70	67	8	9	3	5	73	2	97	6	0	9	7	.563	0	2-2	0	4.23
2000 Cincinnati	NL	35	23	0	5	141	643	154	95	85	22	10	8	9	78	3	77	7	0	10	10	.500	0	0-0	1	5.43
2001 Col-Hou	NL	53	12	0	12	114.2	523	133	81	75	18	1	1	5	53	5	113	4	1	6	10	.375	0	0-0	6	5.89
1995 Seattle	AL	19	0	0	7	19.1	101	20	19	17	6	3	0	1	23	0	26	1	0	0	2	.000	0	0-3	3	7.91
San Diego	NL	19	0	0	8	25.2	111	24	12	12	5	0	1	0	11	0	37	2	0	2	1	.667	0	1-2	3	4.21
1996 San Diego	NL	21	0	0	9	18.1	78	17	6	6	2	0	0	1	7	0	19	0	0	1	1	.500	0	0-1	4	2.95
Milwaukee	AL	23	0	0	10	24.2	104	14	9	9	4	0	2	4	18	0	19	2	0	0	0	—	0	2-2	5	3.28
2001 Colorado	NL	22	6	0	6	46.2	222	56	35	33	6	1	1	1	29	4	48	2	0	1	3	.250	0	0-0	4	6.36
Houston	NL	31	6	0	6	68	301	77	46	42	12	0	0	4	24	1	65	2	1	5	7	.417	0	0-0	1	5.56
7 ML YEARS		274	57	2	74	566	2537	560	333	309	72	27	17	28	321	12	443	25	1	29	31	.483	0	5-12	31	4.91

Fernando Vina

Bats: Left Throws: Right Pos: 2B-151; PH/PR-2

Ht: 5'9" Wt: 174 Born: 4/16/69 Age: 33

Year Team	Lg	G	AB	H	2B	3B	HR	(Hm	Rd)	TB	R	RBI	TBB	IBB	SO	HBP	SH	SF	SB	CS	SB%	GDP	Avg	OBP	SLG
1993 Seattle	AL	24	45	10	2	0	0	(0	0)	12	5	2	4	0	3	3	1	0	6	0	1.00	0	.222	.327	.267
1994 New York	NL	79	124	31	6	0	0	(0	0)	37	20	6	12	0	11	12	2	0	3	1	.75	4	.250	.372	.298
1995 Milwaukee	AL	113	288	74	7	7	3	(1	2)	104	46	29	22	0	28	9	4	2	6	3	.67	6	.257	.327	.361
1996 Milwaukee	AL	140	554	157	19	10	7	(4	3)	217	94	46	38	3	35	13	6	4	16	7	.70	15	.283	.342	.392
1997 Milwaukee	AL	79	324	89	12	2	4	(1	3)	117	37	28	12	1	23	7	2	3	8	7	.53	4	.275	.312	.361
1998 Milwaukee	NL	159	637	198	39	7	7	(2	5)	272	101	45	54	2	46	25	5	1	22	16	.58	7	.311	.386	.427
1999 Milwaukee	NL	37	154	41	7	0	1	(0	1)	51	17	16	14	0	6	4	3	2	5	2	.71	1	.266	.339	.331
2000 St. Louis	NL	123	487	146	24	6	4	(1	3)	194	81	31	36	0	36	28	2	1	10	8	.56	5	.300	.380	.398
2001 St. Louis	NL	154	631	191	30	8	9	(5	4)	264	95	56	32	3	35	22	3	2	17	7	.71	7	.303	.357	.418
9 ML YEARS		908	3244	937	146	40	35	(13	22)	1268	496	259	224	9	223	123	28	15	93	51	.65	49	.289	.356	.391

Ken Vining

Pitches: Left Bats: Left Pos: RP-8

Ht: 6'0" Wt: 180 Born: 12/5/74 Age: 27

Year Team	Lg	G	GS	CG	GF	IP	BFP	H	R	ER	HR	SH	SF	HB	TBB	IBB	SO	WP	Bk	W	L	Pct.	ShO	Sv-Op	Hld	ERA
1996 Bellingham	A-	12	11	0	0	60.1	238	45	16	14	4	1	0	1	23	0	69	5	0	4	2	.667	0	0--	—	2.09
1997 San Jose	A+	23	23	1	0	136.2	592	140	77	64	9	1	6	5	60	0	142	3	1	9	6	.600	0	0--	—	4.21
Winston-Sal	A+	5	5	0	0	34.2	153	36	17	11	2	3	0	0	11	0	38	2	0	2	2	.500	0	0--	—	2.86
1998 Birmingham	AA	29	28	1	0	172.2	793	187	103	78	8	5	5	4	91	1	133	16	0	10	12	.455	0	0--	—	4.07
1999 Birmingham	AA	3	3	0	0	11.2	62	20	16	12	1	0	1	1	9	0	8	0	1	0	2	.000	0	0--	—	9.26
2000 Birmingham	AA	43	0	0	13	46.1	188	36	26	21	2	1	1	3	18	4	41	4	0	1	5	.167	0	1--	—	4.08
2001 Charlotte	AAA	41	0	0	9	46	188	35	10	10	2	1	2	1	19	5	47	0	0	2	3	.400	0	4--	—	1.96
2001 Chicago	AL	8	0	0	2	6.2	42	15	13	13	3	0	0	1	7	0	3	0	0	0	0	—	0	0-0	0	17.55

Jose Vizcaino

Bats: B Throws: R Pos: SS-53; PH/PR-53; 2B-18; 3B-7

Ht: 6'1" Wt: 180 Born: 3/26/68 Age: 34

Year Team	Lg	G	AB	H	2B	3B	HR	(Hm	Rd)	TB	R	RBI	TBB	IBB	SO	HBP	SH	SF	SB	CS	SB%	GDP	Avg	OBP	SLG
1989 Los Angeles	NL	7	10	2	0	0	0	(0	0)	2	2	0	0	0	1	0	1	0	0	0	—	0	.200	.200	.200
1990 Los Angeles	NL	37	51	14	1	1	0	(0	0)	17	3	2	4	1	8	0	0	0	1	1	.50	1	.275	.327	.333
1991 Chicago	NL	93	145	38	5	0	0	(0	0)	43	7	10	5	0	18	0	2	2	2	1	.67	1	.262	.283	.297
1992 Chicago	NL	86	285	64	10	4	1	(0	1)	85	25	17	14	2	35	0	5	1	3	0	1.00	4	.225	.260	.298
1993 Chicago	NL	151	551	158	19	4	4	(1	3)	197	74	54	46	2	71	3	8	9	12	9	.57	9	.287	.340	.358
1994 New York	NL	103	410	105	13	3	3	(1	2)	133	47	33	33	3	62	2	5	6	1	11	.08	5	.256	.310	.324
1995 New York	NL	135	509	146	21	5	3	(2	1)	186	66	56	35	4	76	1	13	8	8	3	.73	14	.287	.332	.365
1996 NYM-Cle		144	542	161	17	8	1	(1	0)	197	70	45	35	0	82	3	10	8	15	7	.68	8	.297	.341	.363
1997 San Francisco	NL	151	568	151	19	7	5	(1	4)	199	77	50	48	1	87	0	13	1	8	8	.50	13	.266	.323	.350
1998 Los Angeles	NL	67	237	62	9	0	3	(0	3)	80	30	29	17	0	35	1	10	2	7	3	.70	4	.262	.311	.338
1999 Los Angeles	NL	94	266	67	9	0	1	(1	0)	79	27	29	20	0	23	1	9	2	2	1	.67	9	.252	.304	.297
2000 LA-NYY		113	267	67	10	2	0	(0	0)	81	32	14	22	3	43	1	5	2	6	7	.46	6	.251	.322	.344
2001 Houston	NL	107	256	71	8	3	1	(1	0)	88	38	14	15	0	33	2	9	0	3	2	.60	6	.277	.319	.339
1996 New York	NL	96	363	110	12	6	1	(1	0)	137	47	32	28	0	58	3	6	2	9	5	.64	6	.303	.356	.377
Cleveland	AL	48	179	51	5	2	0	(0	0)	60	23	13	7	0	24	0	4	1	6	2	.75	2	.285	.310	.335
2000 Los Angeles	NL	40	93	19	2	1	0	(0	0)	23	9	4	10	3	15	1	2	0	1	0	1.00	3	.204	.288	.247
New York	AL	73	174	48	8	1	0	(0	0)	58	23	10	12	0	28	0	3	2	5	7	.42	3	.276	.319	.333
13 ML YEARS		1288	4097	1106	141	37	22	(8	14)	1387	498	353	294	16	574	14	90	31	68	53	.56	80	.270	.319	.339

Luis Vizcaino

Pitches: Right **Bats:** Right **Pos:** RP-36 **Ht:** 5'11" **Wt:** 169 **Born:** 6/1/77 **Age:** 25

Year Team	Lg	G	GS	CG	GF	IP	BFP	H	R	ER	HR	SH	SF	HB	TBB	IBB	SO	WP	Bk	W	L	Pct.	ShO	Sv-Op	Hld	ERA
2001 Sacramento *	AAA	27	0	0	19	42	171	35	10	10	5	1	0	1	10	4	56	1	0	2	2	.500	0	7- -	—	2.14
1999 Oakland	AL	1	0	0	1	3.1	16	3	2	2	1	0	0	0	3	0	2	1	0	0	0		0	0-0	0	5.40
2000 Oakland	AL	12	0	0	1	19.1	96	25	17	16	2	0	1	2	11	0	18	1	0	0	1	.000	0	0-0	0	7.45
2001 Oakland	AL	36	0	0	15	36.2	156	38	19	19	8	0	1	0	12	1	31	3	0	2	1	.667	0	1-1	3	4.66
3 ML YEARS		49	0	0	17	59.1	268	66	38	37	11	0	2	2	26	1	51	5	0	2	2	.500	0	1-1	3	5.61

Omar Vizquel

Bats: Both **Throws:** Right **Pos:** SS-154; PH/PR-2 **Ht:** 5'9" **Wt:** 185 **Born:** 4/24/67 **Age:** 35

Year Team	Lg	G	AB	H	2B	3B	HR	(Hm	Rd)	TB	R	RBI	TBB	IBB	SO	HBP	SH	SF	SB	CS	SB%	GDP	Avg	OBP	SLG
1989 Seattle	AL	143	387	85	7	3	1	(1	0)	101	45	20	28	0	40	1	13	2	1	4	.20	6	.220	.273	.261
1990 Seattle	AL	81	255	63	3	2	2	(0	2)	76	19	18	18	0	22	0	10	2	4	1	.80	7	.247	.295	.298
1991 Seattle	AL	142	426	98	16	4	1	(1	0)	125	42	41	45	0	37	0	8	3	7	2	.78	8	.230	.302	.293
1992 Seattle	AL	136	483	142	20	4	0	(0	0)	170	49	21	32	0	38	2	9	1	15	13	.54	14	.294	.340	.352
1993 Seattle	AL	158	560	143	14	2	2	(1	1)	167	68	31	50	2	71	4	13	3	12	14	.46	7	.255	.319	.298
1994 Cleveland	AL	69	286	78	10	1	1	(0	1)	93	39	33	23	0	23	0	11	2	13	4	.76	7	.273	.325	.325
1995 Cleveland	AL	136	542	144	28	0	6	(3	3)	190	87	56	59	0	59	1	10	10	29	11	.73	4	.266	.333	.351
1996 Cleveland	AL	151	542	161	36	1	9	(2	7)	226	98	64	56	0	42	4	12	9	35	9	.80	10	.297	.362	.417
1997 Cleveland	AL	153	565	158	23	6	5	(3	2)	208	89	49	57	1	58	2	16	2	43	12	.78	16	.280	.347	.368
1998 Cleveland	AL	151	576	166	30	6	2	(0	2)	214	86	50	62	1	64	4	12	6	37	12	.76	10	.288	.358	.372
1999 Cleveland	AL	144	574	191	36	4	5	(3	2)	250	112	66	65	0	50	1	17	7	42	9	.82	8	.333	.397	.436
2000 Cleveland	AL	156	613	176	27	3	7	(1	6)	230	101	66	87	0	72	5	7	6	22	10	.69	13	.287	.377	.375
2001 Cleveland	AL	155	611	156	26	8	2	(2	0)	204	84	50	61	0	72	2	15	4	13	9	.59	14	.255	.323	.334
13 ML YEARS		1775	6420	1761	276	44	43	(17	26)	2254	919	565	643	4	648	26	153	56	273	110	.71	121	.274	.340	.351

Ryan Vogelsong

Pitches: Right **Bats:** Right **Pos:** RP-13; SP-2 **Ht:** 6'3" **Wt:** 195 **Born:** 7/22/77 **Age:** 24

Year Team	Lg	G	GS	CG	GF	IP	BFP	H	R	ER	HR	SH	SF	HB	TBB	IBB	SO	WP	Bk	W	L	Pct.	ShO	Sv-Op	Hld	ERA
1998 San Jose	A+	4	4	0	0	19	83	23	16	16	3	1	2	1	4	0	26	2	4	0	0	—	0	0- -	—	7.58
Salem-Keizr	A-	10	10	0	0	56	221	37	15	11	5	3	2	1	16	0	66	2	2	6	1	.857	0	0- -	—	1.77
1999 San Jose	A+	13	13	0	0	69.2	274	37	26	19	3	1	2	3	27	0	86	3	0	4	4	.500	0	0- -	—	2.45
Shreveport	AA	6	6	0	0	28.1	137	40	25	23	7	0	1	2	15	0	23	1	1	0	2	.000	0	0- -	—	7.31
2000 Shreveport	AA	27	27	1	0	155.1	682	153	82	73	15	5	7	13	69	2	147	5	4	6	10	.375	0	0- -	—	4.23
2001 Fresno	AAA	10	10	0	0	58	226	35	18	18	6	0	1	1	18	0	53	1	1	3	3	.500	0	0- -	—	2.79
Nashville	AAA	6	6	0	0	31.2	130	26	15	14	2	0	1	1	15	0	33	1	0	2	3	.400	0	0- -	—	3.98
2000 San Francisco	NL	4	0	0	3	6	24	4	0	0	0	0	0	0	2	0	6	0	0	0	0	—	0	0-0	0	0.00
2001 SF-Pit	NL	15	2	0	8	34.2	164	39	31	26	6	0	1	2	20	1	24	2	0	0	5	.000	0	0-0	1	6.75
2001 San Francisco	NL	13	0	0	8	28.2	130	29	21	18	5	0	1	2	14	0	17	2	0	0	3	.000	0	0-0	1	5.65
Pittsburgh	NL	2	2	0	0	6	34	10	10	8	1	0	0	0	6	1	7	0	0	0	2	.000	0	0-0	0	12.00
2 ML YEARS		19	2	0	11	40.2	188	43	31	26	6	0	1	2	22	1	30	2	0	0	5	.000	0	0-0	1	5.75

Ed Vosberg

Pitches: Left **Bats:** Left **Pos:** RP-18 **Ht:** 6'1" **Wt:** 210 **Born:** 9/28/61 **Age:** 40

Year Team	Lg	G	GS	CG	GF	IP	BFP	H	R	ER	HR	SH	SF	HB	TBB	IBB	SO	WP	Bk	W	L	Pct.	ShO	Sv-Op	Hld	ERA
2001 Scrantn-WB *	AAA	27	0	0	12	27	113	24	9	9	1	2	0	0	13	3	22	2	0	1	0	1.000	0	5- -	—	3.00
1986 San Diego	NL	5	3	0	0	13.2	65	17	11	10	1	0	0	0	9	1	8	0	1	0	1	.000	0	0-0	0	6.59
1990 San Francisco	NL	18	0	0	5	24.1	104	21	16	15	3	2	0	0	12	2	12	0	0	1	1	.500	0	0-0	0	5.55
1994 Oakland	AL	16	0	0	2	13.2	56	16	7	6	2	1	0	0	5	0	12	1	1	0	2	.000	0	0-1	2	3.95
1995 Texas	AL	44	0	0	20	36	154	32	15	12	3	2	3	0	16	1	36	3	2	5	5	.500	0	4-8	5	3.00
1996 Texas	AL	52	0	0	21	44	195	51	17	16	3	2	1	0	21	4	32	1	2	1	1	.500	0	8-9	11	3.27
1997 Tex-Fla		59	0	0	22	53	239	59	30	26	3	2	4	5	21	6	37	2	1	2	3	.400	0	1-3	8	4.42
1999 SD-Ari	NL	19	0	0	3	11	60	22	12	10	1	2	2	2	3	0	8	1	0	1	1	.000	0	0-2	4	8.18
2000 Philadelphia	NL	31	0	0	5	24	106	21	11	11	4	1	0	0	18	0	23	1	0	1	1	.500	0	0-2	11	4.13
2001 Philadelphia	NL	18	0	0	4	12.2	46	8	4	4	0	0	0	0	3	0	11	0	1	0	0	—	0	0-0	0	2.84
1997 Texas	AL	42	0	0	16	41	180	44	23	21	3	1	3	2	15	6	29	1	0	1	2	.333	0	0-1	5	4.61
Florida	NL	17	0	0	6	12	59	15	7	5	0	1	1	3	6	0	8	1	1	1	1	.500	0	1-2	3	3.75
1999 San Diego	NL	15	0	0	3	8.1	47	16	11	9	1	2	2	2	3	0	6	1	0	0	1	.000	0	0-2	4	9.72
Arizona	NL	4	0	0	0	2.2	13	6	1	1	0	0	0	0	0	0	2	0	0	0	0		0	0-0	0	3.38
9 ML YEARS		262	3	0	82	232.1	1025	247	123	110	21	12	10	7	108	14	179	9	8	10	15	.400	0	13-23	41	4.26

Brad Voyles

Pitches: Right **Bats:** Right **Pos:** RP-7 **Ht:** 6'1" **Wt:** 195 **Born:** 12/30/76 **Age:** 25

Year Team	Lg	G	GS	CG	GF	IP	BFP	H	R	ER	HR	SH	SF	HB	TBB	IBB	SO	WP	Bk	W	L	Pct.	ShO	Sv-Op	Hld	ERA
1998 Eugene	A-	7	0	0	4	11.2	57	9	5	4	0	1	1	0	10	1	22	2	0	0	0	—	0	0- -	—	3.09
1999 Macon	A	38	0	0	26	51.1	226	27	21	17	0	1	2	5	39	2	65	7	2	3	3	.500	0	14- -	—	2.98
Myrtle Bch	A+	5	0	0	2	12	50	7	3	3	1	1	0	0	9	1	13	1	0	1	1	.500	0	0- -	—	2.25
2000 Myrtle Bch	A+	39	0	0	36	56.2	212	21	8	7	1	1	3	0	25	2	70	8	0	5	2	.714	0	19- -	—	1.11
2001 Myrtle Bch	A+	2	0	0	2	1.2	6	0	0	0	0	0	0	0	1	0	3	0	0	0	0		0	1- -	—	0.00
Greenville	AA	15	0	0	8	16.2	72	11	3	2	0	2	2	0	10	1	25	6	0	0	0		0	6- -	—	1.08
Wichita	AA	11	0	0	8	15.1	63	8	0	0	0	2	1	1	10	1	19	1	0	1	0	1.000	0	4- -	—	0.00
2001 Kansas City	AL	7	0	0	3	9.1	40	5	4	4	1	0	0	1	8	0	6	0	0	0	0	—	0	0-0	1	3.86

Billy Wagner

Pitches: Left **Bats:** Left **Pos:** RP-64   **Ht:** 5'11" **Wt:** 180 **Born:** 7/25/71 **Age:** 30

Year Team	Lg	G	GS	CG	GF	IP	BFP	H	R	ER	HR	SH	SF	HB	TBB	IBB	SO	WP	Bk	W	L	Pct.	ShO	Sv-Op	Hld	ERA
2001 Round Rock *	AA	1	1	0	0	1	3	0	0	0	0	0	0	0	0	0	2	0	0	0	0	—	0	0--	—	0.00
1995 Houston	NL	1	0	0	0	0.1	1	0	0	0	0	0	0	0	0	0	0	0	0	0	0	—	0	0-0	—	0.00
1996 Houston	NL	37	0	0	20	51.2	212	28	16	14	6	7	2	3	30	2	67	1	0	2	2	.500	0	9-13	3	2.44
1997 Houston	NL	62	0	0	49	66.1	277	49	23	21	5	3	1	3	30	1	106	3	0	7	8	.467	0	23-29	1	2.85
1998 Houston	NL	58	0	0	50	60	247	46	19	18	6	4	0	0	25	1	97	2	0	4	3	.571	0	30-35	1	2.70
1999 Houston	NL	66	0	0	55	74.2	286	35	14	13	5	2	1	1	23	1	124	2	0	4	1	.800	0	39-42	1	1.57
2000 Houston	NL	28	0	0	19	27.2	129	28	19	19	6	0	0	1	18	0	28	7	0	2	4	.333	0	6-15	0	6.18
2001 Houston	NL	64	0	0	58	62.2	251	44	19	19	5	3	1	5	20	0	79	3	0	2	5	.286	0	39-41	0	2.73
7 ML YEARS		316	0	0	251	343.1	1403	230	110	104	33	19	5	13	146	5	501	18	0	21	23	.477	0	146-175	6	2.73

Tim Wakefield

Pitches: Right **Bats:** Right **Pos:** RP-28; SP-17   **Ht:** 6'2" **Wt:** 210 **Born:** 8/2/66 **Age:** 35

Year Team	Lg	G	GS	CG	GF	IP	BFP	H	R	ER	HR	SH	SF	HB	TBB	IBB	SO	WP	Bk	W	L	Pct.	ShO	Sv-Op	Hld	ERA
1992 Pittsburgh	NL	13	13	4	0	92	373	76	26	22	3	6	4	1	35	1	51	3	1	8	1	.889	1	0-0	1	2.15
1993 Pittsburgh	NL	24	20	3	1	128.1	595	145	83	80	14	7	5	9	75	2	59	6	0	6	11	.353	2	0-0	0	5.61
1995 Boston	AL	27	27	6	0	195.1	804	163	76	64	22	3	7	9	68	0	119	11	0	16	8	.667	1	0-0	0	2.95
1996 Boston	AL	32	32	6	0	211.2	963	238	151	121	38	1	9	12	90	0	140	4	1	14	13	.519	0	0-0	0	5.14
1997 Boston	AL	35	29	4	2	201.1	866	193	109	95	24	3	7	16	87	5	151	6	0	12	15	.444	2	0-0	1	4.25
1998 Boston	AL	36	33	2	1	216	932	211	123	110	30	1	8	14	79	1	146	6	1	17	8	.680	0	0-0	0	4.58
1999 Boston	AL	49	17	0	28	140	635	146	93	79	19	1	8	5	72	2	104	1	0	6	11	.353	0	15-18	0	5.08
2000 Boston	AL	51	17	0	13	159.1	706	170	107	97	31	4	8	4	65	3	102	4	0	6	10	.375	0	0-1	3	5.48
2001 Boston	AL	45	17	0	5	168.2	732	156	84	73	13	3	9	18	73	5	148	5	1	9	12	.429	0	3-5	3	3.90
9 ML YEARS		312	205	25	50	1512.2	6613	1498	852	741	194	29	65	88	644	19	1020	46	4	94	89	.514	6	18-24	7	4.41

Chris Wakeland

Bats: Left **Throws:** Left **Pos:** RF-10   **Ht:** 6'0" **Wt:** 185 **Born:** 6/15/74 **Age:** 28

Year Team	Lg	G	AB	H	2B	3B	HR	(Hm	Rd)	TB	R	RBI	TBB	IBB	SO	HBP	SH	SF	SB	CS	SB%	GDP	Avg	OBP	SLG
1996 Jamestown	A-	70	220	68	14	5	10	—	—	122	38	49	43	0	83	4	1	3	8	3	.73	1	.309	.426	.555
1997 W Michigan	A	111	414	118	38	2	7	—	—	181	64	75	43	5	120	4	0	7	20	6	.77	3	.285	.353	.437
1998 Lakeland	A+	131	487	147	26	5	18	—	—	237	82	89	66	4	111	5	4	5	19	13	.59	4	.302	.387	.487
1999 Tigers	R	4	14	1	0	0	0	—	—	1	2	1	0	0	4	0	0	0	0	0	—	0	.071	.071	.071
Lakeland	A+	4	17	7	1	0	0	—	—	8	3	7	0	0	0	0	0	0	1	0	1.00	0	.412	.412	.471
Jacksnville	AA	55	212	68	16	3	13	—	—	129	42	36	35	1	53	4	0	2	6	5	.55	2	.321	.423	.608
2000 Toledo	AAA	141	492	133	25	2	28	—	—	246	65	76	60	6	148	4	0	5	4	5	.44	8	.270	.351	.500
2001 Toledo	AAA	140	547	155	33	3	23	—	—	263	85	84	39	1	126	8	0	4	7	8	.47	9	.283	.338	.481
2001 Detroit	AL	10	36	9	2	0	2	(0	2)	17	5	6	0	0	13	0	0	0	0	0	—	0	.250	.250	.472

Matt Walbeck

Bats: Both **Throws:** Right **Pos:** PH/PR-1   **Ht:** 5'11" **Wt:** 188 **Born:** 10/2/69 **Age:** 32

Year Team	Lg	G	AB	H	2B	3B	HR	(Hm	Rd)	TB	R	RBI	TBB	IBB	SO	HBP	SH	SF	SB	CS	SB%	GDP	Avg	OBP	SLG
2001 Louisville *	AAA	67	197	45	7	0	3	—	—	61	20	25	23	2	26	0	1	0	1	0	1.00	6	.228	.309	.310
Scrantn-WB *	AAA	40	141	42	11	0	2	—	—	59	18	21	11	1	20	2	0	1	0	2	.00	2	.298	.355	.418
1993 Chicago	NL	11	30	6	2	0	1	(1	0)	11	2	6	1	0	6	0	0	0	0	0	—	0	.200	.226	.367
1994 Minnesota	AL	97	338	69	12	0	5	(0	5)	96	31	35	17	1	37	2	1	1	1	1	.50	7	.204	.246	.284
1995 Minnesota	AL	115	393	101	18	1	1	(1	0)	124	40	44	25	2	71	1	1	2	3	1	.75	11	.257	.302	.316
1996 Minnesota	AL	63	215	48	10	0	2	(1	1)	64	25	24	9	0	34	0	1	2	3	1	.75	6	.223	.252	.298
1997 Detroit	AL	47	137	38	3	0	3	(1	2)	50	18	10	12	0	19	0	0	1	3	3	.50	4	.277	.331	.365
1998 Anaheim	AL	108	338	87	15	2	6	(3	3)	124	41	46	30	0	68	2	5	5	1	1	.50	9	.257	.317	.367
1999 Anaheim	AL	107	288	69	8	1	3	(1	2)	88	26	22	26	1	46	3	3	1	2	3	.40	12	.240	.308	.306
2000 Anaheim	AL	47	146	29	5	0	6	(2	4)	52	17	12	7	0	22	1	1	0	0	1	.00	2	.199	.244	.356
2001 Philadelphia	NL	1	1	1	0	0	0	(0	0)	1	0	0	0	0	0	0	0	0	0	0	—	0	1.000	1.000	1.000
9 ML YEARS		596	1886	448	73	4	27	(10	17)	610	200	199	127	4	303	9	12	13	13	11	.54	51	.238	.287	.323

Kevin Walker

Pitches: Left **Bats:** Left **Pos:** RP-16   **Ht:** 6'4" **Wt:** 190 **Born:** 9/20/76 **Age:** 25

Year Team	Lg	G	GS	CG	GF	IP	BFP	H	R	ER	HR	SH	SF	HB	TBB	IBB	SO	WP	Bk	W	L	Pct.	ShO	Sv-Op	Hld	ERA
1995 Padres	R	13	12	0	0	71.2	295	74	34	24	1	1	3	2	12	0	69	1	3	5	5	.500	0	0--	—	3.01
1996 Idaho Falls	R+	1	1	0	0	6	24	4	3	2	1	0	0	0	2	0	4	1	0	1	0	1.000	0	0--	—	3.00
Clinton	A	13	13	0	0	76	339	80	46	40	9	1	6	9	33	0	43	1	0	4	6	.400	0	0--	—	4.74
1997 Clinton	A	19	19	3	0	110.2	495	133	80	60	9	2	5	4	37	0	80	5	2	6	10	.375	1	0--	—	4.88
1998 Clinton	A	2	2	0	0	14.2	59	11	2	2	0	0	0	1	7	0	10	2	0	2	0	1.000	0	0--	—	1.23
Rancho Cuc	A+	22	22	0	0	121.1	514	122	62	56	10	2	3	4	48	0	94	3	0	7	7	.611	0	0--	—	4.15
1999 Rancho Cuc	A+	27	1	0	9	39	169	35	19	15	2	1	2	3	19	3	35	1	0	1	1	.500	0	4--	—	3.46
2000 Mobile	AA	4	0	0	1	4	14	1	1	1	1	0	0	1	0	0	6	0	0	1	0	1.000	0	0--	—	2.25
2000 San Diego	NL	70	0	0	14	66.2	287	49	35	31	5	4	2	5	38	6	56	2	1	7	1	.875	0	0-0	19	4.19
2001 San Diego	NL	16	0	0	5	12	49	5	4	4	0	0	0	0	8	2	17	0	1	0	0	—	0	0-1	4	3.00
2 ML YEARS		86	0	0	19	78.2	336	54	39	35	5	4	2	5	46	8	73	2	2	7	1	.875	0	0-1	23	4.00

Larry Walker

Bats: Left **Throws:** Right **Pos:** RF-129; PH/PR-9; DH-5   **Ht:** 6'3" **Wt:** 233 **Born:** 12/1/66 **Age:** 35

								BATTING											BASERUNNING				PERCENTAGES		
Year Team	Lg	G	AB	H	2B	3B	HR	(Hm Rd)	TB	R	RBI	TBB	IBB	SO	HBP	SH	SF	SB	CS	SB%	GDP	Avg	OBP	SLG
1989 Montreal	NL	20	47	8	0	0	0	(0 0)	8	4	4	5	0	13	1	3	0	1	1	.50	0	.170	.264	.170
1990 Montreal	NL	133	419	101	18	3	19	(9 10)	182	59	51	49	5	112	5	3	2	21	7	.75	8	.241	.326	.434
1991 Montreal	NL	137	487	141	30	2	16	(5 11)	223	59	64	42	2	102	5	1	4	14	9	.61	7	.290	.349	.458
1992 Montreal	NL	143	528	159	31	4	23	(13 10)	267	85	93	41	10	97	6	0	8	18	6	.75	9	.301	.353	.506
1993 Montreal	NL	138	490	130	24	5	22	(13 9)	230	85	86	80	20	76	6	0	6	29	7	.81	8	.265	.371	.469
1994 Montreal	NL	103	395	127	44	2	19	(7 12)	232	76	86	47	5	74	4	0	6	15	5	.75	8	.322	.394	.587
1995 Colorado	NL	131	494	151	31	5	36	(24 12)	300	96	101	49	13	72	14	0	5	16	3	.84	13	.306	.381	.607
1996 Colorado	NL	83	272	75	18	4	18	(12 6)	155	58	58	20	2	58	9	0	3	18	2	.90	7	.276	.342	.570
1997 Colorado	NL	153	568	208	46	4	49	(20 29)	409	143	130	78	14	90	14	0	4	33	8	.80	15	.366	.452	.720
1998 Colorado	NL	130	454	165	46	3	23	(17 6)	286	113	67	64	2	61	4	0	2	14	4	.78	11	.363	.445	.630
1999 Colorado	NL	127	438	166	26	4	37	(26 11)	311	108	115	57	8	52	12	0	6	11	4	.73	12	.379	.458	.710
2000 Colorado	NL	87	314	97	21	7	9	(7 2)	159	64	51	46	4	40	9	0	3	5	5	.50	12	.309	.409	.506
2001 Colorado	NL	142	497	174	35	3	38	(20 18)	329	107	123	82	6	103	14	0	8	14	5	.74	9	.350	.449	.662
13 ML YEARS		1527	5403	1702	370	46	309	(173 136)	3091	1057	1029	660	91	950	103	7	57	209	66	.76	119	.315	.396	.572

Pete Walker

Pitches: Right **Bats:** Right **Pos:** RP-2   **Ht:** 6'2" **Wt:** 195 **Born:** 4/8/69 **Age:** 33

		HOW MUCH HE PITCHED						WHAT HE GAVE UP										THE RESULTS								
Year Team	Lg	G	GS	CG	GF	IP	BFP	H	R	ER	HR	SH	SF	HB	TBB	IBB	SO	WP	Bk	W	L	Pct.	ShO	Sv-Op	Hld	ERA
2001 Norfolk *	AAA	26	26	0	0	168.1	681	145	64	56	12	5	5	0	46	5	106	2	1	13	4	.765	0	0--	1	2.99
1995 New York	NL	13	0	0	10	17.2	79	24	9	9	3	0	1	0	5	0	5	0	0	0	1	.000	0	0-0	1	4.58
1996 San Diego	NL	1	0	0	0	0.2	5	0	0	0	0	0	0	0	3	0	1	0	0	0	0	—	0	0-0	0	0.00
2000 Colorado	NL	3	0	0	1	4.2	27	10	9	9	1	0	0	0	4	0	2	0	0	0	0	—	0	0-0	0	17.36
2001 New York	NL	2	0	0	1	6.2	25	6	2	2	0	0	0	0	0	0	4	0	0	0	0	—	0	0-0	0	2.70
4 ML YEARS		19	0	0	12	29.2	136	40	20	20	4	0	1	0	12	0	12	0	0	1	0	1.000	0	0-0	1	6.07

Todd Walker

Bats: Left **Throws:** Right **Pos:** 2B-142; PH/PR-17; SS-1   **Ht:** 6'0" **Wt:** 185 **Born:** 5/25/73 **Age:** 29

								BATTING											BASERUNNING				PERCENTAGES		
Year Team	Lg	G	AB	H	2B	3B	HR	(Hm Rd)	TB	R	RBI	TBB	IBB	SO	HBP	SH	SF	SB	CS	SB%	GDP	Avg	OBP	SLG
1996 Minnesota	AL	25	82	21	6	0	0	(0 0)	27	8	6	4	0	13	0	0	3	2	0	1.00	4	.256	.281	.329
1997 Minnesota	AL	52	156	37	7	1	3	(1 2)	55	15	16	11	1	30	1	1	2	7	0	1.00	5	.237	.288	.353
1998 Minnesota	AL	143	528	167	41	3	12	(7 5)	250	85	62	47	9	65	2	0	4	19	7	.73	13	.316	.372	.473
1999 Minnesota	AL	143	531	148	37	4	6	(4 2)	211	62	46	52	5	83	1	0	5	18	10	.64	15	.279	.343	.397
2000 Min-Col	AL	80	248	72	11	4	9	(5 4)	118	42	44	27	0	29	1	1	6	7	1	.88	5	.290	.355	.476
2001 Col-Cin	NL	151	551	163	35	2	17	(13 4)	253	93	75	51	1	82	1	4	3	1	8	.11	14	.296	.355	.459
2000 Minnesota	AL	23	77	18	1	0	2	(0 2)	25	14	8	7	0	10	0	0	3	3	0	1.00	3	.234	.287	.325
Colorado	NL	57	171	54	10	4	7	(5 2)	93	28	36	20	0	19	1	1	3	4	1	.80	2	.316	.385	.544
2001 Colorado	NL	85	290	86	18	2	12	(10 2)	144	52	43	25	1	40	0	3	3	1	3	.25	8	.297	.349	.497
Cincinnati	NL	66	261	77	17	0	5	(3 2)	109	41	32	26	0	42	1	1	0	0	5	.00	6	.295	.361	.418
6 ML YEARS		594	2096	608	137	14	47	(30 17)	914	305	249	192	16	302	6	6	20	54	26	.68	56	.290	.348	.436

Donne Wall

Pitches: Right **Bats:** Right **Pos:** RP-32   **Ht:** 6'1" **Wt:** 205 **Born:** 7/11/67 **Age:** 34

		HOW MUCH HE PITCHED						WHAT HE GAVE UP										THE RESULTS								
Year Team	Lg	G	GS	CG	GF	IP	BFP	H	R	ER	HR	SH	SF	HB	TBB	IBB	SO	WP	Bk	W	L	Pct.	ShO	Sv-Op	Hld	ERA
2001 Binghamton *	AA	4	4	0	0	5	16	1	0	0	0	0	0	0	1	0	5	0	0	0	0	—	0	0--	—	0.00
Norfolk *	AAA	4	0	0	1	4.1	26	8	6	5	1	0	1	0	5	0	1	0	0	0	0	—	0	1--	—	10.38
1995 Houston	NL	6	5	0	0	24.1	110	33	19	15	5	0	2	0	5	0	16	1	0	3	1	.750	0	0-0	1	5.55
1996 Houston	NL	26	23	2	1	150	643	170	84	76	17	4	5	6	34	3	99	3	2	9	8	.529	1	0-0	0	4.56
1997 Houston	NL	8	8	0	0	41.2	186	53	31	29	8	0	2	1	16	0	25	2	1	2	5	.286	0	0-0	0	6.26
1998 San Diego	NL	46	1	0	14	70.1	287	50	20	19	6	4	2	1	32	2	56	3	1	5	4	.556	0	1-4	16	2.43
1999 San Diego	NL	55	0	0	12	70.1	290	58	31	24	11	1	1	0	23	3	53	6	0	7	4	.636	0	0-6	18	3.07
2000 San Diego	NL	44	0	0	14	53.2	211	36	20	20	4	3	0	0	21	1	29	1	0	5	2	.714	0	1-5	12	3.35
2001 New York	NL	32	0	0	14	42.2	193	51	24	23	8	3	2	1	17	6	31	1	0	0	4	.000	0	0-0	0	4.85
7 ML YEARS		217	37	2	55	453	1920	451	229	206	59	15	12	10	148	15	309	17	4	31	28	.525	1	2-15	47	4.09

Jeff Wallace

Pitches: Left **Bats:** Left **Pos:** RP-28; SP-1   **Ht:** 6'2" **Wt:** 238 **Born:** 4/12/76 **Age:** 26

		HOW MUCH HE PITCHED						WHAT HE GAVE UP										THE RESULTS								
Year Team	Lg	G	GS	CG	GF	IP	BFP	H	R	ER	HR	SH	SF	HB	TBB	IBB	SO	WP	Bk	W	L	Pct.	ShO	Sv-Op	Hld	ERA
2001 Durham *	AAA	7	0	0	0	9.1	41	6	4	4	1	0	0	1	7	0	11	0	0	0	0	—	0	0--	—	3.86
Orlando *	AA	1	0	0	0	1	5	1	0	0	0	0	0	0	1	0	3	0	0	0	0	—	0	0--	—	0.00
1997 Pittsburgh	NL	11	0	0	1	12	50	8	2	1	0	1	1	0	8	1	14	1	0	0	0	—	0	0-1	3	0.75
1999 Pittsburgh	NL	41	0	0	7	39	176	26	17	16	2	4	1	0	38	1	41	5	0	1	0	1.000	0	0-1	7	3.69
2000 Pittsburgh	NL	38	0	0	6	35.2	185	42	32	28	5	0	2	4	34	1	27	5	0	2	0	1.000	0	0-0	3	7.07
2001 Tampa Bay	AL	29	1	0	9	50.1	225	43	26	19	4	2	0	1	37	0	38	3	1	0	3	.000	0	0-0	1	3.40
4 ML YEARS		119	1	0	23	137	636	119	77	64	11	7	4	5	117	3	120	14	1	3	3	.500	0	0-2	14	4.20

Daryle Ward

Bats: L **Throws:** L **Pos:** PH/PR-46; LF-27; RF-15; 1B-9; DH-3   **Ht:** 6'2" **Wt:** 230 **Born:** 6/27/75 **Age:** 27

								BATTING											BASERUNNING				PERCENTAGES		
Year Team	Lg	G	AB	H	2B	3B	HR	(Hm Rd)	TB	R	RBI	TBB	IBB	SO	HBP	SH	SF	SB	CS	SB%	GDP	Avg	OBP	SLG
1998 Houston	NL	4	3	1	0	0	0	(0 0)	1	1	0	1	0	2	0	0	0	0	0	—	0	.333	.500	.333
1999 Houston	NL	64	150	41	6	0	8	(2 6)	71	11	30	9	0	31	0	0	2	0	0	—	3	.273	.311	.473

					BATTING												BASERUNNING				PERCENTAGES		
Year Team	Lg	G	AB	H	2B	3B	HR	(Hm | Rd)	TB	R	RBI	TBB	IBB	SO	HBP	SH	SF	SB	CS	SB%	GDP	Avg	OBP	SLG
2000 Houston	NL	119	264	68	10	2	20	(13 | 7)	142	36	47	15	2	61	0	0	2	0	0	—	6	.258	.295	.538
2001 Houston	NL	95	213	56	15	0	9	(5 | 4)	98	21	39	19	4	48	1	0	2	0	0	—	3	.263	.323	.460
4 ML YEARS		282	630	166	31	2	37	(20 | 17)	312	69	116	44	6	142	1	0	6	0	0	—	12	.263	.310	.495

Turner Ward

Bats: Both **Throws:** Right **Pos:** PH/PR-17   **Ht:** 6'2" **Wt:** 204 **Born:** 4/11/65 **Age:** 37

					BATTING													BASERUNNING				PERCENTAGES		
Year Team	Lg	G	AB	H	2B	3B	HR	(Hm | Rd)	TB	R	RBI	TBB	IBB	SO	HBP	SH	SF	SB	CS	SB%	GDP	Avg	OBP	SLG
2001 Scrantn-WB *	AAA	70	222	61	22	4	4	—	—	103	28	27	30	4	31	2	0	3	9	0	1.00	5	.275	.362	.464
1990 Cleveland	AL	14	46	16	2	1	1	(0 | 1)	23	10	10	3	0	8	0	0	0	3	0	1.00	1	.348	.388	.500
1991 Cle-Tor	AL	48	113	27	7	0	0	(0 | 0)	34	12	7	11	0	18	0	4	0	1	0	1.00	2	.239	.306	.301
1992 Toronto	AL	18	29	10	3	0	1	(0 | 1)	16	7	3	4	0	4	0	0	0	1	0	1.00	1	.345	.424	.552
1993 Toronto	AL	72	167	32	4	2	4	(2 | 2)	52	20	28	23	2	26	1	3	4	3	3	.50	7	.192	.287	.311
1994 Milwaukee	AL	102	367	85	15	2	9	(3 | 6)	131	55	45	52	4	68	3	0	5	6	2	.75	9	.232	.328	.357
1995 Milwaukee	AL	44	129	34	3	4	1	(3 | 1)	51	19	16	14	1	21	1	1	1	6	1	.86	2	.264	.338	.395
1996 Milwaukee	AL	43	67	12	2	1	2	(0 | 2)	22	7	10	13	0	17	0	1	1	3	0	1.00	3	.179	.309	.328
1997 Pittsburgh	NL	71	167	59	16	1	7	(5 | 2)	98	33	33	18	2	17	2	3	1	4	1	.80	1	.353	.420	.587
1998 Pittsburgh	NL	123	282	74	13	3	9	(6 | 3)	120	33	46	27	1	40	4	4	7	5	4	.56	4	.262	.328	.426
1999 Pit-Ari	NL	59	114	27	3	0	2	(2 | 0)	36	8	15	15	0	15	1	3	2	2	2	.50	2	.237	.326	.316
2000 Arizona	NL	15	52	9	4	0	0	(0 | 0)	13	5	4	5	0	7	0	1	1	1	1	.50	1	.173	.241	.250
2001 Philadelphia	NL	17	15	4	1	0	0	(0 | 0)	5	1	2	1	0	6	1	0	0	0	0	—	1	.267	.353	.333
1991 Cleveland	AL	40	100	23	4	0	0	(0 | 0)	30	11	5	10	0	16	0	4	0	0	0	—	1	.230	.300	.300
Toronto	AL	8	13	4	0	0	0	(0 | 0)	4	1	2	1	0	2	0	0	0	1	0	1.00	1	.308	.357	.308
1999 Pittsburgh	NL	49	91	19	2	0	0	(0 | 0)	21	2	8	13	0	9	1	3	1	2	2	.50	2	.209	.311	.231
Arizona	NL	10	23	8	1	0	2	(2 | 0)	15	6	7	2	0	6	0	0	1	0	0	—	0	.348	.385	.652
12 ML YEARS		626	1548	389	73	11	39	(23 | 16)	601	210	219	186	11	247	13	20	22	33	15	.69	36	.251	.332	.388

John Wasdin

Pitches: Right **Bats:** Right **Pos:** RP-44   **Ht:** 6'2" **Wt:** 196 **Born:** 8/5/72 **Age:** 29

		HOW MUCH HE PITCHED						WHAT HE GAVE UP											THE RESULTS					
Year Team	Lg	G	GS	CG	GF	IP	BFP	H	R	ER	HR	SH	SF	HB	TBB	IBB	SO	WP	Bk	W	L	Pct.	ShO	Sv-Op	Hld	ERA
2001 Rochester *	AAA	5	3	0	2	20.1	91	27	9	9	3	0	2	0	5	0	20	1	0	2	1	.667	0	0--	—	3.98
1995 Oakland	AL	5	2	0	3	17.1	69	14	9	9	4	0	1	0	3	0	6	0	0	1	1	.500	0	0-0	0	4.67
1996 Oakland	AL	25	21	1	2	131.1	575	145	96	87	24	3	6	4	50	5	75	2	2	8	7	.533	0	0-1	0	5.96
1997 Boston	AL	53	7	0	10	124.2	534	121	68	61	18	4	7	3	38	4	84	4	0	4	6	.400	0	0-2	11	4.40
1998 Boston	AL	47	8	0	13	96	424	111	57	56	14	3	6	2	27	8	59	1	0	6	4	.600	0	0-1	4	5.25
1999 Boston	AL	45	0	0	17	74.1	302	66	38	34	14	2	2	0	18	0	57	2	0	8	3	.727	0	2-5	2	4.12
2000 Bos-Col		39	4	1	12	80.1	352	90	48	48	14	1	7	5	24	3	71	3	0	1	6	.143	0	1-2	0	5.38
2001 Col-Bal		44	0	0	7	74	330	86	44	42	11	0	5	6	24	6	64	3	0	3	2	.600	0	0-5	4	5.11
2000 Boston	AL	25	1	0	10	44.2	198	48	25	25	8	0	5	2	15	1	36	1	0	1	3	.250	0	1-2	0	5.04
Colorado	NL	14	3	1	2	35.2	154	42	23	23	6	1	2	3	9	2	35	2	0	0	3	.000	0	0-0	0	5.80
2001 Colorado	NL	18	0	0	2	24.1	110	32	19	19	7	0	1	1	8	2	17	1	0	2	1	.667	0	0-3	0	7.03
Baltimore	AL	26	0	0	5	49.2	220	54	25	23	4	0	4	5	16	4	47	2	0	1	1	.500	0	0-2	4	4.17
7 ML YEARS		258	42	2	64	598	2586	633	360	337	99	13	33	21	184	26	416	15	2	31	29	.517	0	3-16	21	5.07

Jarrod Washburn

Pitches: Left **Bats:** Left **Pos:** SP-30   **Ht:** 6'1" **Wt:** 187 **Born:** 8/13/74 **Age:** 27

		HOW MUCH HE PITCHED						WHAT HE GAVE UP											THE RESULTS					
Year Team	Lg	G	GS	CG	GF	IP	BFP	H	R	ER	HR	SH	SF	HB	TBB	IBB	SO	WP	Bk	W	L	Pct.	ShO	Sv-Op	Hld	ERA
2001 Salt Lake *	AAA	1	1	0	0	7.2	31	9	5	5	1	0	0	0	1	0	5	0	0	0	1	.000	0	0--	—	5.87
1998 Anaheim	AL	15	11	0	0	74	317	70	40	38	11	2	3	3	27	1	48	0	0	6	3	.667	0	0-0	1	4.62
1999 Anaheim	AL	16	10	0	3	61.2	264	61	36	36	6	1	2	1	26	0	39	2	0	4	5	.444	0	0-0	1	5.25
2000 Anaheim	AL	14	14	0	0	84.1	340	64	38	35	16	1	3	1	37	0	49	1	0	7	2	.778	0	0-0	0	3.74
2001 Anaheim	AL	30	30	1	0	193.1	813	196	89	81	25	4	4	7	54	4	126	3	0	11	10	.524	0	0-0	0	3.77
4 ML YEARS		75	65	1	3	413.1	1734	391	203	190	58	8	12	12	144	5	262	6	0	28	20	.583	0	0-0	2	4.14

Dave Weathers

Pitches: Right **Bats:** Right **Pos:** RP-80   **Ht:** 6'3" **Wt:** 230 **Born:** 9/25/69 **Age:** 32

		HOW MUCH HE PITCHED						WHAT HE GAVE UP											THE RESULTS					
Year Team	Lg	G	GS	CG	GF	IP	BFP	H	R	ER	HR	SH	SF	HB	TBB	IBB	SO	WP	Bk	W	L	Pct.	ShO	Sv-Op	Hld	ERA
1991 Toronto	AL	15	0	0	4	14.2	79	15	9	8	1	2	1	2	17	3	13	0	0	1	0	1.000	0	0-0	1	4.91
1992 Toronto	AL	2	0	0	0	3.1	15	5	3	3	1	0	0	0	2	0	3	0	0	0	0	—	0	0-0	0	8.10
1993 Florida	NL	14	6	0	2	45.2	202	57	26	26	3	2	0	1	13	1	34	6	0	2	3	.400	0	0-0	0	5.12
1994 Florida	NL	24	24	0	0	135	621	166	87	79	13	12	4	4	59	9	72	7	1	8	12	.400	0	0-0	0	5.27
1995 Florida	NL	28	15	0	0	90.1	419	104	68	60	8	7	3	5	52	3	60	3	0	4	5	.444	0	0-0	0	5.98
1996 Fla-NYY		42	12	0	9	88.2	409	108	60	54	8	5	2	6	42	5	53	3	0	2	4	.333	0	0-0	3	5.48
1997 NYY-Cle	AL	19	1	0	5	25.2	126	38	24	24	3	2	1	1	15	0	18	3	0	1	3	.250	0	0-1	0	8.42
1998 Cin-Mil	NL	44	9	0	9	110	492	130	69	60	6	6	2	3	41	3	94	7	2	6	5	.545	0	0-1	3	4.91
1999 Milwaukee	NL	63	0	0	14	93	414	102	49	48	14	4	4	2	38	3	74	1	1	7	4	.636	0	2-6	9	4.65
2000 Milwaukee	NL	69	0	0	23	76.1	320	73	29	26	7	4	1	2	32	8	50	0	0	3	5	.375	0	1-7	14	3.07
2001 Mil-ChC	NL	80	0	0	25	86	351	65	24	23	6	10	3	3	34	8	66	0	0	4	5	.444	0	4-10	16	2.41
1996 Florida	NL	31	8	0	8	71.1	319	85	41	36	7	5	1	4	28	4	40	2	0	2	2	.500	0	0-0	3	4.54
New York	AL	11	4	0	1	17.1	90	23	19	18	1	0	1	2	14	1	13	1	0	0	2	.000	0	0-0	0	9.35
1997 New York	AL	10	0	0	3	9	47	15	10	10	1	0	0	0	7	0	4	2	0	0	1	.000	0	0-1	0	10.00
Cleveland	AL	9	1	0	2	16.2	79	23	14	14	2	2	1	1	8	0	14	1	0	1	2	.333	0	0-0	0	7.56
1998 Cincinnati	NL	16	9	0	0	62.1	294	86	47	43	3	4	1	1	27	2	51	5	1	2	4	.333	0	0-0	0	6.21
Milwaukee	NL	28	0	0	9	47.2	198	44	22	17	3	2	1	2	14	1	43	2	1	4	1	.800	0	0-1	3	3.21
2001 Milwaukee	NL	52	0	0	21	57.2	233	37	14	13	3	8	1	2	25	7	46	0	0	3	4	.429	0	4-7	10	2.03
Chicago	NL	28	0	0	4	28.1	118	28	10	10	3	2	1	1	9	1	20	0	0	1	1	.500	0	0-3	6	3.18
11 ML YEARS		400	67	0	91	768.2	3448	863	448	411	70	54	21	29	345	43	537	30	4	38	46	.452	0	7-25	47	4.81

233

Jeff Weaver

Pitches: Right Bats: Right Pos: SP-33 Ht: 6'5" Wt: 200 Born: 8/22/76 Age: 25

			HOW MUCH HE PITCHED				WHAT HE GAVE UP										THE RESULTS					
Year Team	Lg	G	GS	CG	GF	IP	BFP	H	R	ER	HR	SH	SF	HB	TBB	IBB	SO	WP	Bk	W	L	Pct.	ShO	Sv-Op	Hld	ERA
1999 Detroit	AL	30	29	0	1	163.2	717	176	104	101	27	5	5	17	56	2	114	0	0	9	12	.429	0	0-0	0	5.55
2000 Detroit	AL	31	30	2	0	200	849	205	102	96	26	3	9	15	52	2	136	3	2	11	15	.423	0	0-0	0	4.32
2001 Detroit	AL	33	33	5	0	229.1	985	235	116	104	19	12	7	14	68	4	152	3	0	13	16	.448	0	0-0	0	4.08
3 ML YEARS		94	92	7	1	593	2551	616	322	301	72	20	21	46	176	8	402	6	2	33	43	.434	0	0-0	0	4.57

Ben Weber

Pitches: Right Bats: Right Pos: RP-56 Ht: 6'4" Wt: 212 Born: 11/17/69 Age: 32

			HOW MUCH HE PITCHED				WHAT HE GAVE UP										THE RESULTS					
Year Team	Lg	G	GS	CG	GF	IP	BFP	H	R	ER	HR	SH	SF	HB	TBB	IBB	SO	WP	Bk	W	L	Pct.	ShO	Sv-Op	Hld	ERA
1991 St.Cathrnes	A-	16	14	1	2	97.1	417	105	43	35	3	4	2	4	24	2	60	7	2	6	3	.667	0	0- -	—	3.24
1992 Myrtle Bch	A	41	1	0	23	98.2	406	83	27	18	1	2	3	7	29	3	65	7	0	4	7	.364	0	6- -	—	1.64
1993 Dunedin	A+	55	0	0	36	83.1	355	87	36	27	4	9	0	7	25	5	45	7	1	8	3	.727	0	12- -	—	2.92
1994 Dunedin	A+	18	0	0	14	26.1	110	25	8	8	1	6	0	1	5	3	19	1	0	3	2	.600	0	3- -	—	2.73
Knoxville	AA	25	10	0	6	95.2	400	103	49	40	8	3	1	2	16	0	55	4	0	4	3	.571	0	0- -	—	3.76
1995 Knoxville	AA	12	1	0	6	25.1	104	26	12	11	3	0	0	0	6	0	16	0	0	4	1	.800	0	0- -	—	3.91
Syracuse	AAA	25	15	0	3	91.2	403	111	62	55	10	2	1	3	27	1	38	5	0	4	5	.444	0	1- -	—	5.40
1996 Salinas	IND	22	22	2	0	148.1	618	138	68	57	11	11	1	8	42	1	102	15	0	12	6	.667	0	0- -	—	3.46
1999 Fresno	AAA	51	0	0	19	86.1	358	78	34	32	6	3	3	5	28	2	67	9	0	2	4	.333	0	8- -	—	3.34
2000 Fresno	AAA	38	3	0	26	78	328	72	31	21	7	7	4	3	20	0	66	6	2	4	8	.333	0	7- -	—	2.42
Erie	AA	2	0	0	0	1.2	11	3	5	3	1	0	0	0	2	0	2	0	0	1	0	1.000	0	0- -	—	16.20
2000 SF-Ana		19	0	0	3	22.2	103	28	19	16	0	0	1	0	6	1	14	2	0	1	1	.500	0	0-2	2	6.35
2001 Anaheim	AL	56	0	0	19	68.1	299	66	28	26	4	0	0	5	31	8	40	0	1	6	2	.750	0	0-1	6	3.42
2000 San Francisco	NL	9	0	0	2	8	44	16	13	13	0	0	0	0	4	0	6	1	0	0	1	.000	0	0-2	1	14.63
Anaheim	AL	10	0	0	1	14.2	59	12	6	3	0	0	1	0	2	1	8	1	0	1	0	1.000	0	0-0	1	1.84
2 ML YEARS		75	0	0	22	91	402	94	47	42	4	0	1	5	37	9	54	2	1	7	3	.700	0	0-3	8	4.15

John Wehner

Bats: R Throws: R Pos: PH/PR-24; 1B-11; 3B-6; RF-5; LF-3; C-1; 2B-1; CF-1 Ht: 6'3" Wt: 205 Born: 6/29/67 Age: 35

					BATTING														BASERUNNING				PERCENTAGES		
Year Team	Lg	G	AB	H	2B	3B	HR	(Hm	Rd)	TB	R	RBI	TBB	IBB	SO	HBP	SH	SF	SB	CS	SB%	GDP	Avg	OBP	SLG
2001 Altoona *	AA	25	92	21	3	0	0	—		24	10	8	3	0	11	1	0	1	4	0	1.00	0	.228	.258	.261
1991 Pittsburgh	NL	37	106	36	7	0	0	(0	0)	43	15	7	7	0	17	0	0	0	3	0	1.00	0	.340	.381	.406
1992 Pittsburgh	NL	55	123	22	6	0	0	(0	0)	28	11	4	12	2	22	0	2	0	3	0	1.00	4	.179	.252	.228
1993 Pittsburgh	NL	29	35	5	0	0	0	(0	0)	5	3	0	6	1	10	0	2	0	0	0	—	0	.143	.268	.143
1994 Pittsburgh	NL	2	4	1	1	0	0	(0	0)	2	1	3	0	0	1	0	0	0	0	0	—	0	.250	.250	.500
1995 Pittsburgh	NL	52	107	33	0	3	0	(0	0)	39	13	5	10	1	17	0	4	2	3	1	.75	2	.308	.361	.364
1996 Pittsburgh	NL	86	139	36	9	1	2	(1	1)	53	19	13	8	1	22	0	2	0	1	5	.17	3	.259	.299	.381
1997 Florida	NL	44	36	10	2	0	0	(0	0)	12	8	2	2	0	5	1	1	0	1	0	1.00	0	.278	.333	.333
1998 Florida	NL	53	88	20	2	0	0	(0	0)	22	10	5	7	0	12	0	0	1	1	0	1.00	3	.227	.281	.250
1999 Pittsburgh	NL	39	65	12	2	0	1	(0	1)	17	6	4	7	0	12	0	3	0	1	0	1.00	1	.185	.264	.262
2000 Pittsburgh	NL	21	50	15	3	0	1	(1	0)	21	10	9	4	0	6	0	1	0	0	0	—	1	.300	.352	.420
2001 Pittsburgh	NL	43	51	10	1	0	0	(0	0)	11	3	2	10	0	12	0	1	0	2	1	.67	0	.196	.328	.216
11 ML YEARS		461	804	200	33	4	4	(2	2)	253	99	54	73	5	136	1	16	3	15	7	.68	18	.249	.311	.315

Bob Wells

Pitches: Right Bats: Right Pos: RP-65 Ht: 6'0" Wt: 200 Born: 11/1/66 Age: 35

			HOW MUCH HE PITCHED				WHAT HE GAVE UP										THE RESULTS					
Year Team	Lg	G	GS	CG	GF	IP	BFP	H	R	ER	HR	SH	SF	HB	TBB	IBB	SO	WP	Bk	W	L	Pct.	ShO	Sv-Op	Hld	ERA
1994 Phi-Sea		7	0	0	2	9	38	8	2	2	0	0	0	1	4	0	6	0	0	2	0	1.000	0	0-0	0	2.00
1995 Seattle	AL	30	4	0	3	76.2	358	88	51	49	11	4	1	5	39	3	38	1	0	4	3	.571	0	0-1	0	5.75
1996 Seattle	AL	36	16	1	6	130.2	574	141	78	77	25	3	4	6	46	5	94	0	0	12	7	.632	1	0-0	1	5.30
1997 Seattle	AL	46	1	0	19	67.1	304	88	49	43	11	1	2	3	18	1	51	1	0	3	0	1.000	0	2-4	5	5.75
1998 Seattle	AL	30	0	0	4	51.2	228	54	38	35	12	2	1	2	16	1	29	1	0	2	2	.500	0	0-1	1	6.10
1999 Minnesota	AL	76	0	0	18	87.1	364	79	41	37	8	5	3	5	28	4	44	4	0	8	3	.727	0	1-5	17	3.81
2000 Minnesota	AL	76	0	0	25	86.1	351	80	39	35	14	3	5	4	15	2	76	1	0	0	7	.000	0	10-20	11	3.65
2001 Minnesota	AL	65	0	0	18	68.2	299	72	39	39	12	3	4	10	18	2	49	0	0	8	5	.615	0	2-4	16	5.11
1994 Philadelphia	NL	6	0	0	2	5	21	4	1	1	0	0	0	1	3	0	3	0	0	1	0	1.000	0	0-0	0	1.80
Seattle	AL	1	0	0	0	4	17	4	1	1	0	0	0	0	1	0	3	0	0	1	0	1.000	0	0-0	0	2.25
8 ML YEARS		366	21	1	95	577.2	2516	610	337	317	93	18	24	34	184	18	387	8	0	38	27	.585	1	15-35	51	4.94

David Wells

Pitches: Left Bats: Left Pos: SP-16 Ht: 6'4" Wt: 235 Born: 5/20/63 Age: 39

			HOW MUCH HE PITCHED				WHAT HE GAVE UP										THE RESULTS					
Year Team	Lg	G	GS	CG	GF	IP	BFP	H	R	ER	HR	SH	SF	HB	TBB	IBB	SO	WP	Bk	W	L	Pct.	ShO	Sv-Op	Hld	ERA
1987 Toronto	AL	18	0	0	6	29.1	132	37	14	13	0	1	0	0	12	0	32	4	0	4	3	.571	0	1-2	3	3.99
1988 Toronto	AL	41	0	0	15	64.1	279	65	36	33	12	2	2	2	31	9	56	6	2	3	5	.375	0	4-6	9	4.62
1989 Toronto	AL	54	0	0	19	86.1	352	66	25	23	5	3	2	0	28	7	78	6	3	7	4	.636	0	2-9	8	2.40
1990 Toronto	AL	43	25	0	3	189	759	165	72	66	14	9	2	4	45	3	115	7	1	11	6	.647	0	3-3	3	3.14
1991 Toronto	AL	40	28	2	3	198.1	811	188	88	82	24	6	6	2	49	1	106	10	3	15	10	.600	0	1-2	3	3.72
1992 Toronto	AL	41	14	0	14	120	529	138	84	72	16	3	4	8	36	6	62	3	1	7	9	.438	0	2-4	3	5.40
1993 Detroit	AL	32	30	0	0	187	776	183	93	87	26	3	3	7	42	6	139	13	0	11	9	.550	0	0-0	1	4.19
1994 Detroit	AL	16	16	5	0	111.1	464	113	54	49	13	3	1	2	24	6	71	5	0	5	7	.417	1	0-0	0	3.96
1995 Det-Cin		29	29	6	0	203	839	194	88	73	23	7	3	2	53	9	133	7	2	16	8	.667	0	0-0	0	3.24
1996 Baltimore	AL	34	34	3	0	224.1	946	247	132	128	32	8	14	7	51	7	130	4	2	11	14	.440	0	0-0	0	5.14
1997 New York	AL	32	32	5	0	218	922	239	109	102	24	7	7	6	45	0	156	8	0	16	10	.615	2	0-0	0	4.21
1998 New York	AL	30	30	8	0	214.1	851	195	86	83	29	2	2	1	29	0	163	2	0	18	4	.818	5	0-0	0	3.49
1999 Toronto	AL	34	34	7	0	231.2	987	246	132	124	32	6	6	6	62	2	169	1	0	17	10	.630	1	0-0	0	4.82

		HOW MUCH HE PITCHED						WHAT HE GAVE UP												THE RESULTS						
Year Team	Lg	G	GS	CG	GF	IP	BFP	H	R	ER	HR	SH	SF	HB	TBB	IBB	SO	WP	Bk	W	L	Pct.	ShO	Sv-Op	Hld	ERA
2000 Toronto	AL	35	35	9	0	229.2	972	266	115	105	23	6	7	8	31	0	166	9	1	20	8	.714	1	0-0	0	4.11
2001 Chicago	AL	16	16	1	0	100.2	432	120	55	50	12	2	2	3	21	1	59	2	0	5	7	.417	0	0-0	0	4.47
1995 Detroit	AL	18	18	3	0	130.1	539	120	54	44	17	3	2	2	37	5	83	6	1	10	3	.769	0	0-0	0	3.04
Cincinnati	NL	11	11	3	0	72.2	300	74	34	29	6	4	1	0	16	4	50	1	1	6	5	.545	0	0-0	0	3.59
15 ML YEARS		495	325	46	65	2407.1	10051	2462	1183	1090	285	68	57	56	559	57	1635	87	15	166	114	.593	10	13-26	30	4.08

Kip Wells

Pitches: Right **Bats:** Right **Pos:** SP-20; RP-20

Ht: 6'3" **Wt:** 195 **Born:** 4/21/77 **Age:** 25

		HOW MUCH HE PITCHED						WHAT HE GAVE UP												THE RESULTS						
Year Team	Lg	G	GS	CG	GF	IP	BFP	H	R	ER	HR	SH	SF	HB	TBB	IBB	SO	WP	Bk	W	L	Pct.	ShO	Sv-Op	Hld	ERA
2001 Charlotte *	AAA	4	4	0	0	25.1	110	26	11	10	2	1	1	0	8	0	24	2	0	2	1	.667	0	0--	—	3.55
1999 Chicago	AL	7	7	0	0	35.2	153	33	17	16	2	0	2	3	15	0	29	1	2	4	1	.800	0	0-0	0	4.04
2000 Chicago	AL	20	20	0	0	98.2	468	126	76	66	15	1	3	2	58	4	71	7	0	6	9	.400	0	0-0	0	6.02
2001 Chicago	AL	40	20	0	3	133.1	603	145	80	71	14	8	6	12	61	5	99	14	0	10	11	.476	0	0-2	6	4.79
3 ML YEARS		67	47	0	3	267.2	1224	304	173	153	31	9	11	17	134	9	199	22	2	20	21	.488	0	0-2	6	5.14

Vernon Wells

Bats: Right **Throws:** Right **Pos:** CF-27; RF-3

Ht: 6'1" **Wt:** 210 **Born:** 12/8/78 **Age:** 23

		BATTING																	BASERUNNING				PERCENTAGES		
Year Team	Lg	G	AB	H	2B	3B	HR	(Hm	Rd)	TB	R	RBI	TBB	IBB	SO	HBP	SH	SF	SB	CS	SB%	GDP	Avg	OBP	SLG
1997 St.Cathrnes	A-	66	264	81	20	1	10	—	—	133	52	31	30	1	44	1	0	2	8	6	.57	2	.307	.377	.504
1998 Hagerstown	A	134	509	145	35	2	11	—	—	217	86	65	49	1	84	1	1	2	13	8	.62	8	.285	.348	.426
1999 Dunedin	A+	70	265	91	16	2	11	—	—	144	43	43	26	0	34	1	0	1	13	2	.87	6	.343	.403	.543
Knoxville	AA	26	106	36	6	2	3	—	—	55	18	17	12	1	15	0	0	2	6	2	.75	0	.340	.400	.519
Syracuse	AAA	33	129	40	8	1	4	—	—	62	20	21	10	0	22	1	0	3	5	1	.83	3	.310	.357	.481
2000 Syracuse	AAA	127	493	120	31	7	16	—	—	213	76	66	48	1	88	4	1	5	23	4	.85	8	.243	.313	.432
2001 Syracuse	AAA	107	413	116	27	4	12	—	—	187	57	52	29	0	68	4	0	2	15	11	.58	5	.281	.333	.453
1999 Toronto	AL	24	88	23	5	0	1	(1	0)	31	8	8	4	0	18	0	0	0	1	1	.50	6	.261	.293	.352
2000 Toronto	AL	3	2	0	0	0	0	(0	0)	0	0	0	0	0	0	0	0	0	0	0	.00	0	.000	.000	.000
2001 Toronto	AL	30	96	30	8	0	1	(1	0)	41	14	6	5	0	15	1	0	1	5	0	1.00	0	.313	.350	.427
3 ML YEARS		57	186	53	13	0	2	(2	0)	72	22	14	9	0	33	1	0	1	6	1	.86	6	.285	.320	.387

Turk Wendell

Pitches: Right **Bats:** Left **Pos:** RP-70

Ht: 6'2" **Wt:** 205 **Born:** 5/19/67 **Age:** 35

		HOW MUCH HE PITCHED						WHAT HE GAVE UP												THE RESULTS						
Year Team	Lg	G	GS	CG	GF	IP	BFP	H	R	ER	HR	SH	SF	HB	TBB	IBB	SO	WP	Bk	W	L	Pct.	ShO	Sv-Op	Hld	ERA
1993 Chicago	NL	7	4	0	1	22.2	98	24	13	11	0	2	0	0	8	1	15	1	1	1	2	.333	0	0-0	0	4.37
1994 Chicago	NL	6	2	0	1	14.1	76	22	20	19	3	2	1	0	10	1	9	1	0	0	1	.000	0	0-0	0	11.93
1995 Chicago	NL	43	0	0	17	60.1	270	71	35	33	11	3	3	2	24	4	50	1	0	3	1	.750	0	0-0	3	4.92
1996 Chicago	NL	70	0	0	49	79.1	339	58	26	25	8	3	1	3	44	4	75	3	2	4	5	.444	0	18-21	6	2.84
1997 ChC-NYM	NL	65	0	0	21	76.1	345	68	42	37	7	4	3	2	53	6	64	4	0	3	5	.375	0	5-7	2	4.36
1998 New York	NL	66	0	0	17	76.2	319	62	25	25	4	2	1	2	33	9	58	1	0	5	1	.833	0	4-8	11	2.93
1999 New York	NL	80	0	0	14	85.2	369	80	31	29	9	2	1	2	37	8	77	2	1	5	4	.556	0	3-6	21	3.05
2000 New York	NL	77	0	0	17	82.2	346	60	36	33	9	6	3	5	41	7	73	0	1	8	6	.571	0	1-5	16	3.59
2001 NYM-Phi	NL	70	0	0	22	67	297	63	36	33	12	2	4	4	34	9	56	2	0	4	5	.444	0	1-3	8	4.43
1997 New York	NL	52	0	0	18	60	269	53	32	28	4	3	3	1	39	5	54	4	0	3	5	.375	0	4-5	2	4.20
New York	NL	13	0	0	3	16.1	76	15	10	9	3	1	0	1	14	1	10	0	0	0	0	—	0	1-2	0	4.96
2001 New York	NL	49	0	0	14	51.1	218	42	23	20	8	2	3	3	22	6	41	1	0	4	3	.571	0	1-3	6	3.51
Philadelphia	NL	21	0	0	8	15.2	79	21	13	13	4	0	1	1	12	3	15	1	0	0	2	.000	0	0-0	2	7.47
9 ML YEARS		484	6	0	159	565	2459	508	264	245	63	26	17	20	284	49	477	15	5	33	30	.524	0	32-50	67	3.90

Don Wengert

Pitches: Right **Bats:** Right **Pos:** SP-4

Ht: 6'3" **Wt:** 205 **Born:** 11/6/69 **Age:** 32

		HOW MUCH HE PITCHED						WHAT HE GAVE UP												THE RESULTS						
Year Team	Lg	G	GS	CG	GF	IP	BFP	H	R	ER	HR	SH	SF	HB	TBB	IBB	SO	WP	Bk	W	L	Pct.	ShO	Sv-Op	Hld	ERA
2001 Nashville *	AAA	18	18	0	0	112	483	135	60	51	16	3	7	5	20	2	67	3	0	7	7	.500	0	0--	—	4.10
1995 Oakland	AL	19	0	0	10	29.2	129	30	14	11	3	1	1	1	12	2	16	1	0	1	1	.500	0	0-0	1	3.34
1996 Oakland	AL	36	25	1	2	161.1	725	200	102	100	29	3	5	6	60	5	75	4	0	7	11	.389	1	0-0	2	5.58
1997 Oakland	AL	49	12	1	16	134	612	177	96	90	21	5	7	8	41	4	68	2	0	5	11	.313	0	2-3	0	6.04
1998 SD-ChC	NL	31	6	0	9	63.1	288	76	38	37	10	1	0	3	28	0	46	1	0	1	5	.167	0	1-1	0	5.26
1999 Kansas City	AL	11	1	0	2	24.1	116	41	26	25	6	0	2	0	5	0	10	0	0	0	1	.000	0	0-3	1	9.25
2000 Atlanta	NL	10	0	0	6	10	47	12	9	8	2	0	1	0	5	0	7	0	0	0	1	.000	0	0-0	0	7.20
2001 Pittsburgh	NL	4	4	0	0	16	84	33	22	22	2	2	0	0	6	2	4	0	0	0	2	.000	0	0-0	0	12.38
1998 San Diego	NL	10	0	0	3	13.2	64	21	9	9	2	0	0	0	5	0	5	0	0	0	0	—	0	1-1	0	5.93
Chicago	NL	21	6	0	6	49.2	224	55	29	28	8	1	0	3	23	0	41	1	0	1	5	.167	0	0-0	0	5.07
7 ML YEARS		160	48	2	45	438.2	2001	569	307	293	73	11	15	18	157	13	226	8	0	14	32	.304	1	3-7	4	6.01

Jake Westbrook

Pitches: Right **Bats:** Right **Pos:** RP-17; SP-6

Ht: 6'3" **Wt:** 200 **Born:** 9/29/77 **Age:** 24

		HOW MUCH HE PITCHED						WHAT HE GAVE UP												THE RESULTS						
Year Team	Lg	G	GS	CG	GF	IP	BFP	H	R	ER	HR	SH	SF	HB	TBB	IBB	SO	WP	Bk	W	L	Pct.	ShO	Sv-Op	Hld	ERA
1996 Rockies	R	11	11	0	0	62.2	271	66	33	20	0	3	1	8	14	0	57	4	0	4	2	.667	0	0--	—	2.87
Portland	A-	4	4	0	0	24.2	96	22	8	7	1	0	0	1	5	0	19	2	0	1	1	.500	0	0--	—	2.55
1997 Asheville	A	28	27	3	0	170	736	176	93	81	16	5	6	15	55	0	92	3	0	14	11	.560	2	0--	—	4.29
1998 Jupiter	A+	27	27	2	0	171	720	169	70	62	11	5	3	11	60	0	79	4	0	11	6	.647	0	0--	—	3.26
1999 Harrisburg	AA	27	27	2	0	174.2	748	180	88	76	14	12	3	13	63	1	90	2	1	15	5	.688	2	0--	—	3.92
2000 Columbus	AAA	16	15	2	0	89	393	94	53	46	3	4	1	4	38	0	61	2	0	5	7	.417	0	0--	—	4.65
2001 Buffalo	AAA	12	12	0	0	64.2	273	60	27	23	2	1	0	8	23	0	45	0	2	8	1	.889	0	0--	—	3.20

Year Team	Lg	G	GS	CG	GF	IP	BFP	H	R	ER	HR	SH	SF	HB	TBB	IBB	SO	WP	Bk	W	L	Pct.	ShO	Sv-Op	Hld	ERA
2000 New York	AL	3	2	0	1	6.2	38	15	10	10	1	0	2	0	4	1	1	0	0	0	2	.000	0	0- -	0	13.50
2001 Cleveland	AL	23	6	0	3	64.2	290	79	43	42	6	1	5	4	22	4	48	4	0	4	4	.500	0	0-0	5	5.85
2 ML YEARS		26	8	0	4	71.1	328	94	53	52	7	1	7	4	26	5	49	4	0	4	6	.400	0	0-0	5	6.56

Dan Wheeler

Pitches: Right **Bats:** Right **Pos:** RP-13   **Ht:** 6'3" **Wt:** 222 **Born:** 12/10/77 **Age:** 24

		HOW MUCH HE PITCHED						WHAT HE GAVE UP												THE RESULTS						
Year Team	Lg	G	GS	CG	GF	IP	BFP	H	R	ER	HR	SH	SF	HB	TBB	IBB	SO	WP	Bk	W	L	Pct.	ShO	Sv-Op	Hld	ERA
2001 Orlando *	AA	3	3	0	0	16	68	15	5	5	2	0	0	0	6	1	12	0	0	0	1	.000	0	0- -	—	2.81
Durham *	AAA	18	10	0	2	65.1	284	72	51	38	11	1	2	3	11	0	39	1	1	3	5	.375	0	0- -	—	5.23
1999 Tampa Bay	AL	6	6	0	0	30.2	136	35	20	20	7	1	0	0	13	1	32	1	0	0	4	.000	0	0-0	0	5.87
2000 Tampa Bay	AL	11	2	0	6	23	111	29	14	14	2	1	1	2	11	2	17	2	0	1	1	.500	0	0-1	1	5.48
2001 Tampa Bay	AL	13	0	0	3	17.2	87	30	17	17	3	0	2	0	5	0	12	1	1	1	0	1.000	0	0-0	0	8.66
3 ML YEARS		30	8	0	9	71.1	334	94	51	51	12	2	3	2	29	3	61	4	1	2	5	.286	0	0-1	1	6.43

Devon White

Bats: B **Throws:** R **Pos:** CF-86; PH/PR-31; LF-13; RF-2   **Ht:** 6'2" **Wt:** 190 **Born:** 12/29/62 **Age:** 39

		BATTING																	BASERUNNING				PERCENTAGES		
Year Team	Lg	G	AB	H	2B	3B	HR	(Hm	Rd)	TB	R	RBI	TBB	IBB	SO	HBP	SH	SF	SB	CS	SB%	GDP	Avg	OBP	SLG
1985 California	AL	21	7	1	0	0	0	(0	0)	1	7	0	1	0	3	1	0	0	3	1	.75	0	.143	.333	.143
1986 California	AL	29	51	12	1	1	1	(0	1)	18	8	3	6	0	8	0	0	0	6	0	1.00	0	.235	.316	.353
1987 California	AL	159	639	168	33	5	24	(11	13)	283	103	87	39	2	135	2	14	2	32	11	.74	8	.263	.306	.443
1988 California	AL	122	455	118	22	2	11	(3	8)	177	76	51	23	1	84	2	5	1	17	8	.68	5	.259	.297	.389
1989 California	AL	156	636	156	18	13	12	(9	3)	236	86	56	31	3	129	2	7	2	44	16	.73	12	.245	.282	.371
1990 California	AL	125	443	96	17	3	11	(5	6)	152	57	44	44	5	116	3	10	3	21	6	.78	6	.217	.290	.343
1991 Toronto	AL	156	642	181	40	10	17	(9	8)	292	110	60	55	1	135	7	5	6	33	10	.77	7	.282	.342	.455
1992 Toronto	AL	153	641	159	26	7	17	(7	10)	250	98	60	47	0	133	5	0	3	37	4	.90	9	.248	.303	.390
1993 Toronto	AL	146	598	163	42	6	15	(10	5)	262	116	52	57	1	127	7	3	3	34	4	.89	3	.273	.341	.438
1994 Toronto	AL	100	403	109	24	6	13	(5	8)	184	67	49	21	3	80	5	4	2	11	3	.79	4	.270	.313	.457
1995 Toronto	AL	101	427	121	23	5	10	(4	6)	184	61	53	29	1	97	5	1	3	11	2	.85	5	.283	.334	.431
1996 Florida	NL	146	552	151	37	6	17	(5	12)	251	77	84	38	6	99	8	4	9	22	6	.79	8	.274	.325	.455
1997 Florida	NL	74	265	65	13	1	6	(4	2)	98	37	34	32	2	65	7	0	4	13	5	.72	3	.245	.338	.370
1998 Arizona	NL	146	563	157	32	1	22	(11	11)	257	84	85	42	4	102	9	7	6	22	8	.73	9	.279	.335	.456
1999 Los Angeles	NL	134	474	127	20	2	14	(8	6)	193	60	68	39	2	88	11	0	2	19	5	.79	10	.268	.337	.407
2000 Los Angeles	NL	47	158	42	5	1	4	(2	2)	61	26	13	9	0	30	1	0	0	3	6	.33	3	.266	.310	.386
2001 Milwaukee	NL	126	390	108	25	2	14	(6	8)	179	52	47	28	1	95	12	1	1	18	3	.86	6	.277	.343	.459
17 ML YEARS		1941	7344	1934	378	71	208	(99	109)	3078	1125	846	541	32	1526	87	61	47	346	98	.78	98	.263	.319	.419

Gabe White

Pitches: Left **Bats:** Left **Pos:** RP-69   **Ht:** 6'2" **Wt:** 204 **Born:** 11/20/71 **Age:** 30

		HOW MUCH HE PITCHED						WHAT HE GAVE UP												THE RESULTS						
Year Team	Lg	G	GS	CG	GF	IP	BFP	H	R	ER	HR	SH	SF	HB	TBB	IBB	SO	WP	Bk	W	L	Pct.	ShO	Sv-Op	Hld	ERA
1994 Montreal	NL	7	5	0	2	23.2	106	24	16	16	4	1	4	1	11	0	17	0	0	1	1	.500	0	1-1	0	6.08
1995 Montreal	NL	19	1	0	8	25.2	115	26	21	20	7	2	3	1	9	0	25	0	0	1	2	.333	0	0-0	0	7.01
1997 Cincinnati	NL	12	6	0	2	41	168	39	20	20	6	3	2	1	8	1	25	0	0	2	2	.500	0	1-1	3	4.39
1998 Cincinnati	NL	69	3	0	29	98.2	404	86	46	44	17	2	2	1	27	6	83	3	0	5	5	.500	0	9-13	5	4.01
1999 Cincinnati	NL	50	0	0	18	61	261	68	31	30	13	2	1	2	14	1	61	0	0	1	2	.333	0	0-1	3	4.43
2000 Cin-Col	NL	68	0	0	17	84	329	64	23	22	6	2	6	3	15	2	84	1	0	11	2	.846	0	5-9	19	2.36
2001 Colorado	NL	69	0	0	16	67.2	290	70	47	47	18	2	2	1	26	5	47	1	0	1	7	.125	0	0-2	6	6.25
2000 Cincinnati	NL	1	0	0	0	1	6	2	2	2	1	0	0	0	1	0	2	0	0	0	0	—	0	0-0	0	18.00
Colorado	NL	67	0	0	17	83	323	62	21	20	5	2	6	3	14	2	82	1	0	11	2	.846	0	5-9	19	2.17
7 ML YEARS		294	15	0	92	401.2	1673	377	204	199	71	14	17	10	110	15	342	5	0	22	21	.512	0	16-27	39	4.46

Rick White

Pitches: Right **Bats:** Right **Pos:** RP-55   **Ht:** 6'4" **Wt:** 230 **Born:** 12/23/68 **Age:** 33

		HOW MUCH HE PITCHED						WHAT HE GAVE UP												THE RESULTS						
Year Team	Lg	G	GS	CG	GF	IP	BFP	H	R	ER	HR	SH	SF	HB	TBB	IBB	SO	WP	Bk	W	L	Pct.	ShO	Sv-Op	Hld	ERA
1994 Pittsburgh	NL	43	5	0	23	75.1	317	79	35	32	9	7	5	6	17	3	38	2	2	4	5	.444	0	6-9	3	3.82
1995 Pittsburgh	NL	15	9	0	2	55	247	66	33	29	3	3	3	2	18	0	29	2	0	2	3	.400	0	0-0	0	4.75
1998 Tampa Bay	AL	38	3	0	12	68.2	289	66	32	29	8	0	3	2	23	2	39	3	0	2	6	.250	0	0-0	2	3.80
1999 Tampa Bay	AL	63	1	0	11	108	480	132	56	49	8	2	5	1	38	5	81	3	0	5	3	.625	0	0-2	4	4.08
2000 TB-NYM		66	0	0	14	99.2	420	83	44	39	9	1	3	7	38	5	67	3	0	5	9	.357	0	3-7	15	3.52
2001 New York	NL	55	0	0	15	69.2	299	71	38	30	7	2	2	2	17	4	51	1	0	4	5	.444	0	2-4	10	3.88
2000 Tampa Bay	AL	44	0	0	8	71.1	293	57	30	27	7	1	2	5	26	3	47	3	0	3	6	.333	0	2-5	2	3.41
New York	NL	22	0	0	6	28.1	127	26	14	12	2	0	1	2	12	2	20	0	0	2	3	.400	0	1-2	2	3.81
6 ML YEARS		280	18	0	77	476.1	2052	497	238	208	44	15	21	20	151	19	305	14	2	22	31	.415	0	11-22	23	3.93

Rondell White

Bats: Right **Throws:** Right **Pos:** LF-90; PH/PR-5   **Ht:** 6'1" **Wt:** 215 **Born:** 2/23/72 **Age:** 30

		BATTING																	BASERUNNING				PERCENTAGES		
Year Team	Lg	G	AB	H	2B	3B	HR	(Hm	Rd)	TB	R	RBI	TBB	IBB	SO	HBP	SH	SF	SB	CS	SB%	GDP	Avg	OBP	SLG
2001 West Tenn *	AA	9	28	4	1	0	2	—	—	11	2	4	1	0	7	2	0	0	0	0	—	1	.143	.226	.393
1993 Montreal	NL	23	73	19	3	1	2	(1	1)	30	9	15	7	0	16	0	2	1	1	2	.33	2	.260	.321	.411
1994 Montreal	NL	40	97	27	10	1	2	(1	1)	45	16	13	9	0	18	3	0	0	1	1	.50	1	.278	.358	.464
1995 Montreal	NL	130	474	140	33	4	13	(6	7)	220	87	57	41	1	87	6	0	4	25	5	.83	11	.295	.356	.464
1996 Montreal	NL	88	334	98	19	4	6	(2	4)	143	35	41	22	0	53	2	0	1	14	6	.70	11	.293	.340	.428
1997 Montreal	NL	151	592	160	29	5	28	(9	19)	283	84	82	31	3	111	10	1	4	16	8	.67	18	.270	.316	.478
1998 Montreal	NL	97	357	107	21	2	17	(9	8)	183	54	58	30	2	57	7	0	3	16	7	.70	7	.300	.363	.513

Year Team	Lg	G	AB	H	2B	3B	HR	(Hm	Rd)	TB	R	RBI	TBB	IBB	SO	HBP	SH	SF	SB	CS	SB%	GDP	Avg	OBP	SLG
																								BATTING — BASERUNNING — PERCENTAGES	
1999 Montreal	NL	138	539	168	26	6	22	(10	12)	272	83	64	32	2	85	11	0	6	10	6	.63	17	.312	.359	.505
2000 Mon-ChC	NL	94	357	111	26	0	13	(3	10)	176	59	61	33	0	79	4	0	2	5	3	.63	4	.311	.374	.493
2001 Chicago	NL	95	323	99	19	1	17	(7	10)	171	43	50	26	4	56	7	1	0	1	0	1.00	1	.307	.371	.529
2000 Montreal	NL	75	290	89	24	0	11	(3	8)	146	52	54	28	0	67	2	0	2	5	1	.83	4	.307	.370	.503
Chicago		19	67	22	2	0	2	(0	2)	30	7	5	0		12	2	0	0	0	2	.00	0	.328	.392	.448
9 ML YEARS		856	3146	929	186	24	120	(48	72)	1523	470	441	231	12	562	50	4	21	89	38	.70	85	.295	.351	.484

Matt Whiteside

Pitches: Right **Bats:** Right **Pos:** RP-13   **Ht:** 6'0" **Wt:** 200 **Born:** 8/8/67 **Age:** 34

Year Team	Lg	G	GS	CG	GF	IP	BFP	H	R	ER	HR	SH	SF	HB	TBB	IBB	SO	WP	Bk	W	L	Pct.	ShO	Sv-Op	Hld	ERA
2001 Richmond *	AAA	9	0	0	8	10	36	4	0	0	0	0	0	0	1	1	9	0	0	0	0	—	0	4--	—	0.00
1992 Texas	AL	20	0	0	8	28	118	26	8	6	1	0	1	0	11	2	13	2	0	1	1	.500	0	4-4	0	1.93
1993 Texas	AL	60	0	0	10	73	305	78	37	35	7	2	1	1	23	6	39	0	2	2	1	.667	0	1-5	14	4.32
1994 Texas	AL	47	0	0	16	61	272	68	40	34	6	3	2	1	28	3	37	1	0	2	2	.500	0	1-3	7	5.02
1995 Texas	AL	40	0	0	18	53	223	48	24	24	5	2	3	1	19	2	46	4	0	5	4	.556	0	3-4	7	4.08
1996 Texas	AL	14	0	0	7	32.1	148	43	24	24	8	1	2	0	11	1	15	1	0	0	1	.000	0	0-0	1	6.68
1997 Texas	AL	42	1	0	8	72.2	323	85	45	41	4	2	5	3	26	3	44	3	2	4	1	.800	0	0-4	2	5.08
1998 Philadelphia	NL	10	0	0	1	18	85	27	18	17	6	0	0	0	5	0	14	0	1	1	1	.500	0	0-0		8.50
1999 San Diego	NL	10	0	0	4	11	55	19	17	17	1	1	1	0	5	0	9	1	0	1	0	1.000	0	0-0		13.91
2000 San Diego	NL	28	0	0	9	37	159	32	21	17	6	2	1	1	17	3	27	2	1	2	3	.400	0	0-0	6	4.14
2001 Atlanta	AL	13	0	0	8	16.1	81	23	14	13	5	0	1	1	7	1	10	2	0	0	1	.000	0	0-0	1	7.16
10 ML YEARS		284	1	0	89	402.1	1769	449	248	228	49	13	17	8	152	21	254	16	6	18	15	.545	0	9-20	38	5.10

Bob Wickman

Pitches: Right **Bats:** Right **Pos:** RP-70   **Ht:** 6'1" **Wt:** 230 **Born:** 2/6/69 **Age:** 33

Year Team	Lg	G	GS	CG	GF	IP	BFP	H	R	ER	HR	SH	SF	HB	TBB	IBB	SO	WP	Bk	W	L	Pct.	ShO	Sv-Op	Hld	ERA
1992 New York	AL	8	8	0	0	50.1	213	51	25	23	2	1	3	2	20	0	21	3	0	6	1	.857	0	0-0	0	4.11
1993 New York	AL	41	19	1	9	140	629	156	82	72	13	4	1	5	69	7	70	2	0	14	4	.778	1	4-8	2	4.63
1994 New York	AL	53	0	0	19	70	286	54	26	24	3	0	5	1	27	3	56	2	0	5	4	.556	0	6-10	11	3.09
1995 New York	AL	63	1	0	14	80	347	77	38	36	6	4	1	5	33	3	51	2	0	2	4	.333	0	1-10	21	4.05
1996 NYY-Mil	AL	70	0	0	18	95.2	429	106	50	47	10	2	4	5	44	3	75	4	0	7	1	.875	0	0-4	10	4.42
1997 Milwaukee	AL	74	0	0	20	95.2	405	89	32	29	8	6	2	3	41	7	78	8	0	7	6	.538	0	1-5	28	2.73
1998 Milwaukee	NL	72	0	0	51	82.1	357	79	38	34	5	10	3	4	39	2	71	1	0	6	9	.400	0	25-32	9	3.72
1999 Milwaukee	NL	71	0	0	63	74.1	331	75	31	28	6	3	2	2	38	6	60	2	0	3	8	.273	0	37-45	0	3.39
2000 Mil-Cle	NL	69	0	0	60	72.2	309	64	30	25	1	3	1	1	32	5	55	2	0	3	5	.375	0	30-37	0	3.10
2001 Cleveland	AL	70	0	0	56	67.2	270	61	18	18	4	0	0	2	14	2	66	2	0	5	0	1.000	0	32-35	4	2.39
1996 New York	AL	58	0	0	14	79	358	94	41	41	7	1	4	5	34	1	61	3	0	4	1	.800	0	0-3	6	4.67
Milwaukee	AL	12	0	0	4	16.2	71	12	9	6	3	1	0	0	10	2	14	1	0	3	0	1.000	0	0-1	4	3.24
2000 Milwaukee	NL	43	0	0	36	46	194	37	18	15	1	0	1	1	20	2	44	2	0	2	2	.500	0	16-20	0	2.93
Cleveland	AL	26	0	0	24	26.2	115	27	12	10	0	3	0	0	12	3	11	0	0	1	3	.250	0	14-17	0	3.38
10 ML YEARS		591	28	1	310	828.2	3576	812	370	336	58	33	22	30	357	38	603	28	0	58	42	.580	1	136-186	85	3.65

Brad Wilkerson

Bats: Left **Throws:** Left **Pos:** LF-38; PH/PR-11   **Ht:** 6'0" **Wt:** 200 **Born:** 6/1/77 **Age:** 25

Year Team	Lg	G	AB	H	2B	3B	HR	(Hm	Rd)	TB	R	RBI	TBB	IBB	SO	HBP	SH	SF	SB	CS	SB%	GDP	Avg	OBP	SLG
1999 Harrisburg	AA	138	422	99	21	3	8	—	—	150	66	49	88	3	100	7	1	5	3	5	.38	3	.235	.372	.355
2000 Harrisburg	AA	66	229	77	36	2	6	—	—	135	53	44	42	1	38	4	1	3	8	4	.67	4	.336	.442	.590
Ottawa	AAA	63	212	53	11	1	12	—	—	102	40	35	45	1	60	3	0	1	5	4	.56	0	.250	.387	.481
2001 Jupiter	A+	6	26	6	3	0	0	—	—	9	3	1	3	0	10	0	0	0	0		—	0	.231	.310	.346
Ottawa	AAA	69	233	63	10	0	12	—	—	109	43	48	60	0	68	3	2	2	12	5	.71	2	.270	.423	.468
2001 Montreal	NL	47	117	24	7	2	1	(1	0)	38	11	5	17	1	41	0	1	1	2	1	.67	2	.205	.304	.325

Marc Wilkins

Pitches: Right **Bats:** Right **Pos:** RP-14   **Ht:** 5'11" **Wt:** 212 **Born:** 10/21/70 **Age:** 31

Year Team	Lg	G	GS	CG	GF	IP	BFP	H	R	ER	HR	SH	SF	HB	TBB	IBB	SO	WP	Bk	W	L	Pct.	ShO	Sv-Op	Hld	ERA
2001 Nashville *	AAA	32	0	0	10	36	153	38	21	19	2	0	1	3	13	1	24	3	1	4	1	.800	0	1--	—	4.75
1996 Pittsburgh	NL	47	2	0	11	75	331	75	36	32	6	3	4	6	36	6	62	5	0	4	3	.571	0	1-5	4	3.84
1997 Pittsburgh	NL	70	0	0	21	75.2	310	65	33	31	7	4	0	4	33	2	47	5	0	9	5	.643	0	2-4	15	3.69
1998 Pittsburgh	NL	16	0	0	6	15.1	67	13	6	6	1	0	1	2	9	2	17	1	1	0	0	—	0	0-1	4	3.52
1999 Pittsburgh	NL	46	0	0	14	51	227	49	28	24	3	4	2	4	26	1	44	4	1	2	3	.400	0	0-0	8	4.24
2000 Pittsburgh	NL	52	0	0	8	60.1	277	54	34	34	4	3	7	6	43	3	37	3	0	4	2	.667	0	0-0	9	5.07
2001 Pittsburgh	NL	14	0	0	6	17.1	80	22	13	13	2	2	0	1	8	1	11	2	0	0	1	.000	0	0-0	1	6.75
6 ML YEARS		245	2	0	66	294.2	1292	278	150	140	23	16	14	23	155	15	218	20	2	19	14	.576	0	3-10	41	4.28

Rick Wilkins

Bats: Left **Throws:** Right **Pos:** C-7; PH/PR-4; 1B-1   **Ht:** 6'2" **Wt:** 215 **Born:** 6/4/67 **Age:** 35

Year Team	Lg	G	AB	H	2B	3B	HR	(Hm	Rd)	TB	R	RBI	TBB	IBB	SO	HBP	SH	SF	SB	CS	SB%	GDP	Avg	OBP	SLG
2001 Portland *	AAA	68	222	47	15	2	6			84	18	33	15	0	77	1	1	7			.00	3	.212	.257	.378
1991 Chicago	NL	86	203	45	9	0	6	(2	4)	72	21	22	19	2	56	6	7	0	3	3	.50	3	.222	.307	.355
1992 Chicago	NL	83	244	66	9	1	8	(3	5)	101	20	22	28	7	53	0	1	1	0	2	.00	6	.270	.344	.414
1993 Chicago	NL	136	446	135	23	1	30	(10	20)	250	78	73	50	13	99	3	0	4	2	1	.67	6	.303	.376	.561
1994 Chicago	NL	100	313	71	25	2	7	(3	4)	121	44	39	40	5	86	2	1	2	4	3	.57	3	.227	.317	.387
1995 ChC-Hou	NL	65	202	41	3	0	7	(3	4)	65	30	19	46	2	61	1	0	2	0	0	—	9	.203	.351	.322

Year Team	Lg	G	AB	H	2B	3B	HR	(Hm	Rd)	TB	R	RBI	TBB	IBB	SO	HBP	SH	SF	SB	CS	SB%	GDP	Avg	OBP	SLG
						BATTING													**BASERUNNING**				**PERCENTAGES**		
1996 Hou-SF	NL	136	411	100	18	2	14	(6	8)	164	53	59	67	13	121	1	0	10	0	3	.00	5	.243	.344	.399
1997 SF-Sea		71	202	40	6	0	7	(2	5)	67	20	27	18	0	67	0	0	4	0	0	—	0	.198	.259	.332
1998 Sea-NYM		24	56	10	1	1	1	(1	0)	16	8	5	6	0	16	0	0	0	0	0	—	1	.179	.254	.286
1999 Los Angeles	NL	3	4	0	0	0	0	(0	0)	0	0	0	0	0	2	0	0	0	0	0	—	1	.000	.000	.000
2000 St. Louis	NL	4	11	3	0	0	0	(0	0)	3	3	1	2	0	2	0	0	0	0	0	—	0	.273	.385	.273
2001 San Diego	NL	12	22	4	1	0	1	(1	0)	8	3	8	2	0	8	0	0	0	0	0	—	1	.182	.250	.364
1995 Chicago	NL	50	162	31	2	0	6	(3	3)	51	24	14	36	1	51	1	0	1	0	0	—	8	.191	.340	.315
Houston		15	40	10	1	0	1	(0	1)	14	6	5	10	1	10	0	0	1	0	0	—	1	.250	.392	.350
1996 Houston	NL	84	254	54	8	2	6	(3	3)	84	34	23	46	10	81	1	0	5	0	1	.00	1	.213	.330	.331
San Francisco	NL	52	157	46	10	0	8	(3	5)	80	19	36	21	3	40	0	0	5	0	2	.00	4	.293	.366	.510
1997 San Francisco	NL	66	190	37	5	0	6	(1	5)	60	18	23	17	0	65	0	0	3	0	0	—	0	.195	.257	.316
Seattle	AL	5	12	3	1	0	1	(1	0)	7	2	4	1	0	2	0	0	1	0	0	—	0	.250	.286	.583
1998 Seattle	AL	19	41	8	1	1	1	(1	0)	14	5	4	4	0	14	0	0	1	0	0	—	1	.195	.261	.341
New York	NL	5	15	2	0	0	0	(0	0)	2	3	1	2	0	2	0	0	0	0	0	—	0	.133	.235	.133
11 ML YEARS		720	2114	515	95	7	81	(32	49)	867	280	275	278	42	571	13	9	21	9	12	.43	34	.244	.332	.410

Bernie Williams

Bats: Both **Throws:** Right **Pos:** CF-144; DH-1; PH/PR-1 **Ht:** 6'2" **Wt:** 205 **Born:** 9/13/68 **Age:** 33

Year Team	Lg	G	AB	H	2B	3B	HR	(Hm	Rd)	TB	R	RBI	TBB	IBB	SO	HBP	SH	SF	SB	CS	SB%	GDP	Avg	OBP	SLG
1991 New York	AL	85	320	76	19	4	3	(1	2)	112	43	34	48	0	57	1	2	3	10	5	.67	4	.238	.336	.350
1992 New York	AL	62	261	73	14	2	5	(3	2)	106	39	26	29	1	36	1	2	0	7	6	.54	5	.280	.354	.406
1993 New York	AL	139	567	152	31	4	12	(5	7)	227	67	68	53	4	106	4	1	3	9	9	.50	17	.268	.333	.400
1994 New York	AL	108	408	118	29	1	12	(4	8)	185	80	57	61	2	54	3	1	2	16	9	.64	11	.289	.384	.453
1995 New York	AL	144	563	173	29	9	18	(7	11)	274	93	82	75	1	98	5	2	3	8	6	.57	12	.307	.392	.487
1996 New York	AL	143	551	168	26	7	29	(12	17)	295	108	102	82	8	72	0	1	7	17	4	.81	15	.305	.391	.535
1997 New York	AL	129	509	167	35	6	21	(13	8)	277	107	100	73	7	80	1	0	8	15	8	.65	10	.328	.408	.544
1998 New York	AL	128	499	169	30	5	26	(14	12)	287	101	97	74	9	81	1	0	4	15	9	.63	19	.339	.422	.575
1999 New York	AL	158	591	202	28	6	25	(11	14)	317	116	115	100	17	95	1	0	5	9	10	.47	11	.342	.435	.536
2000 New York	AL	141	537	165	37	6	30	(15	15)	304	108	121	71	11	84	5	0	3	13	5	.72	15	.307	.391	.566
2001 New York	AL	146	540	166	38	0	26	(14	12)	282	102	94	78	11	67	6	0	9	11	5	.69	15	.307	.395	.522
11 ML YEARS		1383	5346	1629	316	50	207	(99	108)	2666	964	896	744	71	830	28	9	47	130	76	.63	134	.305	.389	.499

Dave Williams

Pitches: Left **Bats:** Left **Pos:** SP-18; RP-4 **Ht:** 6'2" **Wt:** 205 **Born:** 3/12/79 **Age:** 23

Year Team	Lg	G	GS	CG	GF	IP	BFP	H	R	ER	HR	SH	SF	HB	TBB	IBB	SO	WP	Bk	W	L	Pct.	ShO	Sv-Op	Hld	ERA
						HOW MUCH HE PITCHED					**WHAT HE GAVE UP**											**THE RESULTS**				
1998 Erie	A-	22	2	0	4	47.1	203	45	21	17	6	2	0	3	14	0	38	2	0	2	2	.500	0	0- -	—	3.23
1999 Williamsprt	A-	7	7	1	0	45.2	180	33	17	13	2	0	0	2	11	0	47	0	0	4	2	.667	1	0- -	—	2.56
Hickory	A	9	9	1	0	59	228	42	22	21	5	0	2	6	11	0	46	2	0	3	1	.750	1	0- -	—	3.20
2000 Hickory	A	24	24	1	0	170	687	145	66	56	14	11	2	9	39	2	193	4	0	11	9	.550	1	0- -	—	2.96
Lynchburg	A+	2	2	0	0	11	51	18	8	8	2	1	0	0	3	0	8	2	0	1	0	1.000	0	0- -	—	6.55
2001 Altoona	AA	9	8	1	1	58.2	228	45	17	17	8	1	1	1	12	0	39	0	0	5	2	.714	0	0- -	—	2.61
Nashville	AAA	2	2	0	0	10.2	45	9	5	4	3	0	1	0	5	0	6	0	0	1	1	.500	0	0- -	—	3.38
2001 Pittsburgh	NL	22	18	0	1	114	472	100	53	47	15	3	8	7	45	4	57	0	0	3	7	.300	0	0-0	1	3.71

Gerald Williams

Bats: R **Throws:** R **Pos:** CF-70; PH/PR-26; RF-12; DH-7; LF-6 **Ht:** 6'2" **Wt:** 187 **Born:** 8/10/66 **Age:** 35

Year Team	Lg	G	AB	H	2B	3B	HR	(Hm	Rd)	TB	R	RBI	TBB	IBB	SO	HBP	SH	SF	SB	CS	SB%	GDP	Avg	OBP	SLG
1992 New York	AL	15	27	8	2	0	3	(2	1)	19	7	6	0	0	3	0	0	0	2	0	1.00	0	.296	.296	.704
1993 New York	AL	42	67	10	2	3	0	(0	0)	18	11	6	1	0	14	2	0	1	2	0	1.00	2	.149	.183	.269
1994 New York	AL	57	86	25	8	0	4	(2	2)	45	19	13	4	0	17	0	0	1	1	3	.25	6	.291	.319	.523
1995 New York	AL	100	182	45	18	2	6	(4	2)	85	33	28	22	1	34	1	0	3	4	2	.67	4	.247	.327	.467
1996 NYY-Mil	AL	125	325	82	19	4	5	(3	2)	124	43	34	19	3	57	5	3	3	10	9	.53	8	.252	.299	.382
1997 Milwaukee	AL	155	566	143	32	2	10	(3	7)	209	73	41	19	1	90	6	5	5	23	9	.72	9	.253	.282	.369
1998 Atlanta	NL	129	266	81	19	2	10	(5	5)	134	46	44	17	1	48	3	2	1	11	5	.69	5	.305	.352	.504
1999 Atlanta	NL	143	422	116	24	1	17	(7	10)	193	76	68	33	1	67	6	4	2	19	11	.63	8	.275	.335	.457
2000 Tampa Bay	AL	146	632	173	30	2	21	(6	15)	270	87	89	34	0	103	3	9	4	12	12	.50	5	.274	.312	.427
2001 TB-NYY	AL	100	279	56	18	0	4	(3	1)	86	42	19	18	0	55	5	4	0	13	5	.72	9	.201	.262	.308
1996 New York	AL	99	233	63	15	4	5	(3	2)	101	37	30	15	2	39	4	1	5	7	8	.47	7	.270	.319	.433
Milwaukee		26	92	19	4	0	0	(0	0)	23	6	4	4	1	18	2	2	0	3	1	.75	1	.207	.247	.250
2001 Tampa Bay	AL	62	232	48	17	0	4	(3	1)	77	30	17	13	0	42	4	3	0	10	4	.71	8	.207	.261	.332
New York	AL	38	47	8	1	0	0	(0	0)	9	12	2	5	0	13	1	1	0	3	1	.75	1	.170	.264	.191
10 ML YEARS		1012	2852	739	172	16	80	(35	45)	1183	437	348	167	7	488	31	27	22	97	56	.63	56	.259	.305	.415

Jeff Williams

Pitches: Left **Bats:** Right **Pos:** RP-14; SP-1 **Ht:** 6'0" **Wt:** 185 **Born:** 6/6/72 **Age:** 30

Year Team	Lg	G	GS	CG	GF	IP	BFP	H	R	ER	HR	SH	SF	HB	TBB	IBB	SO	WP	Bk	W	L	Pct.	ShO	Sv-Op	Hld	ERA
						HOW MUCH HE PITCHED					**WHAT HE GAVE UP**											**THE RESULTS**				
1997 San Antonio	AA	5	5	0	0	28.1	119	30	17	17	2	2	0	2	7	0	14	3	1	2	1	.667	0	0- -	—	5.40
San Berndno	A+	18	18	0	0	116	472	101	52	40	8	4	2	2	34	0	72	7	3	10	4	.714	0	0- -	—	3.10
1998 San Antonio	AA	7	7	0	0	41.2	182	43	19	12	3	1	3	0	13	1	35	1	1	3	0	1.000	0	0- -	—	2.59
Albuquerque	AAA	21	21	0	0	121	556	160	87	67	14	3	3	6	49	0	93	6	4	8	8	.500	0	0- -	—	4.98
1999 Albuquerque	AAA	42	14	1	10	125.2	558	151	77	70	14	4	8	9	47	2	86	3	0	9	7	.563	1	4- -	—	5.01
2000 Albuquerque	AAA	12	12	0	0	63.1	266	64	33	30	6	2	1	2	28	0	38	7	0	4	3	.571	0	0- -	—	4.26
2001 Las Vegas	AAA	16	16	1	0	90.2	388	102	49	40	12	4	2	3	24	0	61	0	0	7	5	.583	1	0- -	—	3.97
1999 Los Angeles	NL	5	3	0	1	17.2	73	12	10	8	2	1	0	0	9	0	7	0	0	2	0	1.000	0	0-0	0	4.08
2000 Los Angeles	NL	7	0	0	0	5.2	35	12	11	10	1	0	1	0	8	0	3	0	0	0	0	—	0	0-1	1	15.88

238

Year Team	Lg	G	GS	CG	GF	IP	BFP	H	R	ER	HR	SH	SF	HB	TBB	IBB	SO	WP	Bk	W	L	Pct	ShO	Sv-Op	Hld	ERA
2001 Los Angeles	NL	15	1	0	2	24.1	109	26	18	17	5	1	2	1	17	1	9	1	0	2	1	.667	0	0-0	1	6.29
3 ML YEARS		27	4	0	3	47.2	217	50	39	35	8	2	3	1	34	1	19	1	0	4	1	.800	0	0-1	2	6.61

Matt Williams

Bats: Right **Throws:** Right **Pos:** 3B-102; PH/PR-5; SS-2   **Ht:** 6'2" **Wt:** 219 **Born:** 11/28/65 **Age:** 36

					BATTING																BASERUNNING				PERCENTAGES		
Year Team	Lg	G	AB	H	2B	3B	HR	(Hm	Rd)	TB	R	RBI	TBB	IBB	SO	HBP	SH	SF	SB	CS	SB%	GDP	Avg	OBP	SLG
2001 Tucson *	AAA	5	17	6	2	0	2	—	—	14	4	5	2	1	2	0	0	0	1	0	1.00	0	.353	.421	.824
1987 San Francisco	NL	84	245	46	9	2	8	(5	3)	83	28	21	16	4	68	1	3	1	4	3	.57	5	.188	.240	.339
1988 San Francisco	NL	52	156	32	6	1	8	(7	1)	64	17	19	8	0	41	2	3	1	0	1	.00	7	.205	.251	.410
1989 San Francisco	NL	84	292	59	18	1	18	(10	8)	133	31	50	14	1	72	2	1	2	1	2	.33	5	.202	.242	.455
1990 San Francisco	NL	159	617	171	27	2	33	(20	13)	301	87	122	33	9	138	7	2	5	7	4	.64	13	.277	.319	.488
1991 San Francisco	NL	157	589	158	24	5	34	(17	17)	294	72	98	33	6	128	6	0	7	5	5	.50	11	.268	.310	.499
1992 San Francisco	NL	146	529	120	13	5	20	(9	11)	203	58	66	39	11	109	6	0	2	7	7	.50	15	.227	.286	.384
1993 San Francisco	NL	145	579	170	33	4	38	(19	19)	325	105	110	27	4	80	4	0	9	1	3	.25	12	.294	.325	.561
1994 San Francisco	NL	112	445	119	16	3	43	(20	23)	270	74	96	33	7	87	2	0	3	1	0	1.00	11	.267	.319	.607
1995 San Francisco	NL	76	283	95	17	1	23	(9	14)	183	53	65	30	8	58	2	0	3	2	0	1.00	8	.336	.399	.647
1996 San Francisco	NL	105	404	122	16	1	22	(13	9)	206	69	85	39	9	91	6	0	6	1	2	.33	10	.302	.367	.510
1997 Cleveland	AL	151	596	157	32	3	32	(7	25)	291	86	105	34	4	108	4	0	2	12	4	.75	14	.263	.307	.488
1998 Arizona	NL	135	510	136	26	1	20	(11	9)	224	72	71	43	8	102	3	0	1	5	1	.83	19	.267	.327	.439
1999 Arizona	NL	154	627	190	37	2	35	(17	18)	336	98	142	41	9	93	2	0	8	2	0	1.00	11	.303	.344	.536
2000 Arizona	NL	96	371	102	18	2	12	(5	7)	160	43	47	20	1	51	3	0	3	1	2	.33	11	.275	.315	.431
2001 Arizona	NL	106	408	112	30	0	16	(7	9)	190	58	65	22	3	70	3	0	3	1	0	1.00	15	.275	.314	.466
15 ML YEARS		1762	6651	1789	322	33	362	(176	186)	3263	951	1162	432	84	1296	53	9	56	50	34	.60	173	.269	.316	.491

Mike Williams

Pitches: Right **Bats:** Right **Pos:** RP-65   **Ht:** 6'2" **Wt:** 204 **Born:** 7/29/68 **Age:** 33

Year Team	Lg	G	GS	CG	GF	IP	BFP	H	R	ER	HR	SH	SF	HB	TBB	IBB	SO	WP	Bk	W	L	Pct	ShO	Sv-Op	Hld	ERA
1992 Philadelphia	NL	5	5	1	0	28.2	121	29	20	17	3	1	1	0	7	0	5	0	0	1	1	.500	0	0-0	0	5.34
1993 Philadelphia	NL	17	4	0	2	51	221	50	32	30	5	1	0	0	22	2	33	2	0	1	3	.250	0	0-0	0	5.29
1994 Philadelphia	NL	12	8	0	2	50.1	222	61	31	28	7	2	3	0	20	3	29	0	0	2	4	.333	0	0-0	0	5.01
1995 Philadelphia	NL	33	8	0	7	87.2	367	78	37	32	10	5	3	3	29	2	57	7	0	3	3	.500	0	0-0	1	3.29
1996 Philadelphia	NL	32	29	0	1	167	732	188	107	101	25	6	5	6	67	6	103	16	1	6	14	.300	0	0-0	0	5.44
1997 Kansas City	AL	10	0	0	4	14	70	20	11	10	1	0	1	0	8	1	10	0	0	0	2	.000	0	1-1	0	6.43
1998 Pittsburgh	NL	37	1	0	9	51	204	39	12	11	1	1	2	0	16	4	59	3	0	4	2	.667	0	0-1	7	1.94
1999 Pittsburgh	NL	58	0	0	50	58.1	269	63	36	33	9	2	1	1	37	7	76	4	0	3	4	.429	0	23-28	1	5.09
2000 Pittsburgh	NL	72	0	0	63	72	307	56	34	28	8	2	4	4	40	3	71	1	0	3	4	.429	0	24-29	0	3.50
2001 Pit-Hou	NL	65	0	0	48	64	285	60	28	27	9	3	1	0	35	3	59	2	0	6	4	.600	0	22-25	3	3.80
2001 Pittsburgh	NL	40	0	0	38	41.2	183	39	18	17	6	2	0	0	21	2	43	1	0	2	4	.333	0	22-24	0	3.67
Houston	NL	25	0	0	10	22.1	102	21	10	10	3	1	1	0	14	1	16	1	0	4	0	1.000	0	0-1	3	4.03
10 ML YEARS		341	55	1	186	644	2798	644	348	317	78	23	21	15	281	31	502	35		29	41	.414	0	70-84	13	4.43

Todd Williams

Pitches: Right **Bats:** Right **Pos:** RP-15   **Ht:** 6'3" **Wt:** 210 **Born:** 2/13/71 **Age:** 31

Year Team	Lg	G	GS	CG	GF	IP	BFP	H	R	ER	HR	SH	SF	HB	TBB	IBB	SO	WP	Bk	W	L	Pct	ShO	Sv-Op	Hld	ERA
2001 Yankees *	R	1	1	0	0	2	8	1	0	0	0	0	0	1	0	0	5	0	0	0	0	—	0	0--	—	0.00
Norwich *	AA	6	0	0	1	8	28	4	0	0	0	0	0	1	0	0	5	0	0	1	0	1.000	0	1--	—	0.00
Columbus *	AAA	17	0	0	9	19	100	31	19	15	5	0	0	3	9	3	14	2	0	0	1	.000	0	2--	—	7.11
1995 Los Angeles	NL	16	0	0	5	19.1	83	19	11	11	3	3	1	0	7	2	8	0	0	2	2	.500	0	0-1	0	5.12
1998 Cincinnati	NL	6	0	0	2	9.1	50	15	8	8	1	0	0	0	6	0	4	0	0	0	1	.000	0	0-0	0	7.71
1999 Seattle	AL	13	0	0	7	9.2	47	11	5	5	1	1	0	1	7	0	7	0	0	0	0	—	0	0-0	0	4.66
2001 New York	AL	15	0	0	6	15.1	82	22	9	8	1	0	3	2	9	2	13	0	0	1	0	1.000	0	0-0	1	4.70
4 ML YEARS		50	0	0	20	53.2	262	67	33	32	6	4	4	3	29	4	32	0	0	3	3	.500	0	0-1	1	5.37

Woody Williams

Pitches: Right **Bats:** Right **Pos:** SP-34   **Ht:** 6'0" **Wt:** 195 **Born:** 8/19/66 **Age:** 35

Year Team	Lg	G	GS	CG	GF	IP	BFP	H	R	ER	HR	SH	SF	HB	TBB	IBB	SO	WP	Bk	W	L	Pct	ShO	Sv-Op	Hld	ERA
1993 Toronto	AL	30	0	0	9	37	172	40	18	18	2	2	1	1	22	3	24	2	1	3	1	.750	0	0-2	4	4.38
1994 Toronto	AL	38	0	0	14	59.1	253	44	24	24	5	1	2	2	33	1	56	4	0	1	3	.250	0	0-0	5	3.64
1995 Toronto	AL	23	3	0	10	53.2	232	44	23	22	6	2	0	2	28	1	41	0	0	1	2	.333	0	0-1	1	3.69
1996 Toronto	AL	12	10	1	0	59	255	64	33	31	8	2	1	1	21	1	43	2	0	4	5	.444	0	0-0	0	4.73
1997 Toronto	AL	31	31	0	0	194.2	833	201	99	94	31	8	5	8	66	3	124	7	0	9	14	.391	0	0-0	0	4.35
1998 Toronto	AL	32	32	1	0	209.2	894	196	112	104	36	5	6	2	81	3	151	2	1	10	9	.526	1	0-0	0	4.46
1999 San Diego	NL	33	33	0	0	208.1	887	213	106	102	33	9	9	2	73	5	137	9	0	12	12	.500	1	0-0	0	4.41
2000 San Diego	NL	23	23	0	0	168	700	152	74	70	23	4	3	3	54	2	111	4	0	10	8	.556	0	0-0	0	3.75
2001 SD-StL	NL	34	34	3	0	220	922	224	110	99	35	13	8	6	56	5	154	5	0	15	9	.625	1	0-0	0	4.05
2001 San Diego	NL	23	23	0	0	145	632	170	88	80	28	8	8	5	37	4	102	4	0	8	8	.500	0	0-0	0	4.97
St. Louis	NL	11	11	3	0	75	290	54	22	19	7	5	0	3	19	1	52	1	0	7	1	.875	1	0-0	0	2.28
9 ML YEARS		256	166	9	33	1209.2	5148	1178	598	564	179	44	38	26	434	24	841	35	2	65	63	.508	2	0-3	10	4.20

Scott Williamson

Pitches: Right **Bats:** Right **Pos:** RP-2   **Ht:** 6'0" **Wt:** 185 **Born:** 2/17/76 **Age:** 26

Year Team	Lg	G	GS	CG	GF	IP	BFP	H	R	ER	HR	SH	SF	HB	TBB	IBB	SO	WP	Bk	W	L	Pct.	ShO	Sv-Op	Hld	ERA
1999 Cincinnati	NL	62	0	0	40	93.1	366	54	29	25	8	5	2	1	43	6	107	13	0	12	7	.632	0	19-26	5	2.41
2000 Cincinnati	NL	48	10	0	13	112	495	92	45	41	7	4	2	3	75	7	136	21	1	5	8	.385	0	6-8	6	3.29
2001 Cincinnati	NL	2	0	0	0	0.2	6	1	0	0	0	0	0	1	2	0	0	1	0	0	0	—	0	0-0	1	0.00
3 ML YEARS		112	10	0	53	206	867	147	74	66	15	9	4	5	120	13	243	35	1	17	15	.531	0	25-34	12	2.88

Craig Wilson

Bats: R **Throws:** R **Pos:** PH/PR-43; 1B-26; RF-13; C-10; DH-2; LF-1   **Ht:** 6'2" **Wt:** 217 **Born:** 11/30/76 **Age:** 25

Year Team	Lg	G	AB	H	2B	3B	HR	(Hm	Rd)	TB	R	RBI	TBB	IBB	SO	HBP	SH	SF	SB	CS	SB%	GDP	Avg	OBP	SLG
1995 Medcine Hat	R+	49	184	52	14	1	7	—	—	89	33	35	24	1	41	3	0	4	8	2	.80	1	.283	.367	.484
1996 Hagerstown	A	131	495	129	27	5	11	—	—	199	66	70	32	1	120	10	0	4	17	11	.61	12	.261	.316	.402
1997 Lynchburg	A+	117	401	106	26	1	19	—	—	191	54	69	39	6	98	15	1	2	6	5	.55	3	.264	.350	.476
1998 Lynchburg	A+	61	219	59	12	2	12	—	—	111	26	45	22	1	53	5	0	1	2	1	.67	3	.269	.348	.507
Carolina	AA	45	148	49	11	0	5	—	—	75	20	21	14	0	32	4	0	2	4	1	.80	2	.331	.399	.507
1999 Altoona	AA	111	362	97	21	3	20	—	—	184	57	69	40	0	104	19	1	4	1	3	.25	8	.268	.367	.508
2000 Nashville	AAA	124	396	112	24	2	33	—	—	239	83	86	44	2	121	25	0	7	1	2	.33	7	.283	.383	.604
2001 Nashville	AAA	11	45	13	2	1	1	—	—	20	4	3	2	0	14	1	0	0	0	0	—	1	.289	.333	.444
2001 Pittsburgh	NL	88	158	49	3	1	13	(8	5)	93	27	32	15	1	53	7	1	2	3	1	.75	4	.310	.390	.589

Dan Wilson

Bats: Right **Throws:** Right **Pos:** C-122; PH/PR-8; 1B-2   **Ht:** 6'3" **Wt:** 202 **Born:** 3/25/69 **Age:** 33

Year Team	Lg	G	AB	H	2B	3B	HR	(Hm	Rd)	TB	R	RBI	TBB	IBB	SO	HBP	SH	SF	SB	CS	SB%	GDP	Avg	OBP	SLG
1992 Cincinnati	NL	12	25	9	1	0	0	(0	0)	10	2	3	3	0	8	0	0	0	0	0	—	2	.360	.429	.400
1993 Cincinnati	NL	36	76	17	3	0	0	(0	0)	20	6	8	9	4	16	0	2	1	0	0	—	2	.224	.302	.263
1994 Seattle	AL	91	282	61	14	2	3	(1	2)	88	24	27	10	0	57	1	8	2	1	2	.33	11	.216	.244	.312
1995 Seattle	AL	119	399	111	22	3	9	(5	4)	166	40	51	33	1	63	2	5	1	2	1	.67	12	.278	.336	.416
1996 Seattle	AL	138	491	140	24	0	18	(7	11)	218	51	83	32	2	88	3	9	5	1	2	.33	15	.285	.330	.444
1997 Seattle	AL	146	508	137	31	1	15	(9	6)	215	66	74	39	1	72	5	8	3	7	2	.78	12	.270	.326	.423
1998 Seattle	AL	96	325	82	17	1	9	(6	3)	128	39	44	24	0	56	5	8	6	2	1	.67	6	.252	.308	.394
1999 Seattle	AL	123	414	110	23	2	7	(3	4)	158	46	38	29	4	83	2	10	2	5	0	1.00	10	.266	.315	.382
2000 Seattle	AL	90	268	63	12	0	5	(2	3)	90	31	27	22	0	51	0	11	2	1	2	.33	8	.235	.291	.336
2001 Seattle	AL	123	377	100	20	1	10	(4	6)	152	44	42	20	0	69	2	8	1	3	2	.60	6	.265	.305	.403
10 ML YEARS		974	3165	830	167	10	76	(37	39)	1245	349	397	221	12	563	20	69	23	22	12	.65	84	.262	.312	.393

Enrique Wilson

Bats: B **Throws:** R **Pos:** SS-48; PH/PR-26; 3B-21; 2B-17; DH-1   **Ht:** 5'11" **Wt:** 180 **Born:** 7/27/75 **Age:** 26

Year Team	Lg	G	AB	H	2B	3B	HR	(Hm	Rd)	TB	R	RBI	TBB	IBB	SO	HBP	SH	SF	SB	CS	SB%	GDP	Avg	OBP	SLG
1997 Cleveland	AL	5	15	5	0	0	0	(0	0)	5	2	1	0	0	2	0	0	0	0	0	—	0	.333	.333	.333
1998 Cleveland	AL	32	90	29	6	0	2	(1	1)	41	13	12	4	0	8	1	1	1	2	4	.33	1	.322	.354	.456
1999 Cleveland	AL	113	332	87	22	1	2	(1	1)	117	41	24	25	1	41	1	4	6	5	4	.56	12	.262	.310	.352
2000 Cle-Pit		80	239	70	15	1	5	(3	2)	102	27	27	18	2	24	0	4	2	2	2	.50	6	.293	.340	.427
2001 Pit-NYY		94	228	48	8	1	2	(1	1)	64	17	20	9	0	37	0	2	2	0	5	.00	10	.211	.238	.281
2000 Cleveland	AL	40	117	38	9	0	2	(2	0)	53	16	12	7	0	11	0	2	1	2	1	.67	2	.325	.360	.453
Pittsburgh	NL	40	122	32	6	1	3	(1	2)	49	11	15	11	2	13	0	2	1	0	1	.00	4	.262	.321	.402
2001 Pittsburgh	NL	46	129	24	3	0	1	(0	1)	30	7	8	3	0	23	0	0	1	0	3	.00	7	.186	.203	.233
New York	AL	48	99	24	5	1	1	(1	0)	34	10	12	6	0	14	0	2	1	0	2	.00	3	.242	.283	.343
5 ML YEARS		324	904	239	51	3	11	(6	5)	329	100	84	56	3	112	2	11	11	9	15	.38	29	.264	.305	.364

Jack Wilson

Bats: Right **Throws:** Right **Pos:** SS-107; PH/PR-1   **Ht:** 5'10" **Wt:** 170 **Born:** 12/29/77 **Age:** 24

Year Team	Lg	G	AB	H	2B	3B	HR	(Hm	Rd)	TB	R	RBI	TBB	IBB	SO	HBP	SH	SF	SB	CS	SB%	GDP	Avg	OBP	SLG
1998 Johnson Cty	R+	61	241	90	18	4	4	—	—	128	50	29	18	0	30	3	1	0	22	6	.79	4	.373	.424	.531
1999 Peoria	A	64	251	86	22	4	3	—	—	125	47	28	15	0	23	2	3	0	11	5	.69	2	.343	.384	.498
Potomac	A+	64	257	76	10	1	2	—	—	94	44	18	19	1	31	1	3	1	7	4	.64	2	.296	.345	.366
2000 Potomac	A+	13	47	13	0	1	2	—	—	21	7	7	5	0	10	0	1	1	2	3	.40	1	.277	.340	.447
Arkansas	AA	88	343	101	20	8	6	—	—	155	65	34	36	0	59	5	5	2	2	3	.40	5	.294	.368	.452
Altoona	AA	33	139	35	7	2	1	—	—	49	17	16	14	1	17	2	2	2	1	3	.25	3	.252	.325	.353
2001 Nashville	AAA	27	103	38	6	1	1	—	—	49	20	6	9	0	13	2	1	0	2	2	.50	1	.369	.430	.476
2001 Pittsburgh	NL	108	390	87	17	1	3	(0	3)	115	44	25	16	2	70	1	17	1	1	3	.25	4	.223	.255	.295

Kris Wilson

Pitches: Right **Bats:** Right **Pos:** SP-15; RP-14   **Ht:** 6'4" **Wt:** 225 **Born:** 8/6/76 **Age:** 25

Year Team	Lg	G	GS	CG	GF	IP	BFP	H	R	ER	HR	SH	SF	HB	TBB	IBB	SO	WP	Bk	W	L	Pct.	ShO	Sv-Op	Hld	ERA
1997 Spokane	A-	15	15	0	0	73.2	345	101	50	37	6	0	3	5	21	1	72	1	2	5	3	.625	0	0- -	—	4.52
1998 Wilmington	A+	10	2	0	4	24	96	19	10	10	0	2	2	3	6	1	20	1	0	0	3	.000	0	1- -	—	3.75
Lansing	A	18	18	1	0	117.1	470	119	50	46	7	3	3	3	15	0	74	2	0	10	5	.667	0	0- -	—	3.53
1999 Wilmington	A+	14	4	0	1	48	169	25	7	6	0	0	0	0	11	0	45	1	0	8	1	.889	0	0- -	—	1.13
Omaha	AAA	1	1	0	0	5.1	23	8	5	5	3	0	0	0	0	0	3	0	0	0	1	.000	0	0- -	—	8.44
Wichita	AA	23	10	0	2	74.1	323	91	51	45	11	2	2	3	14	0	45	1	2	5	7	.417	0	0- -	—	5.45
2000 Wichita	AA	21	15	1	1	102.2	425	99	52	40	12	1	4	6	21	0	69	4	1	7	3	.700	0	0- -	—	3.51
2001 Omaha	AAA	6	5	0	0	29	118	31	9	9	2	0	0	1	6	0	18	1	0	2	2	.500	0	0- -	—	2.79

240

Year Team	Lg	G	GS	CG	GF	IP	BFP	H	R	ER	HR	SH	SF	HB	TBB	IBB	SO	WP	Bk	W	L	Pct.	ShO	Sv-Op	Hld	ERA
2000 Kansas City	AL	20	0	0	5	34.1	145	38	16	16	3	1	1	0	11	3	17	0	0	0	1	.000	0	0-1	0	4.19
2001 Kansas City	AL	29	15	0	6	109.1	487	132	78	63	26	1	3	7	32	0	67	1	0	6	5	.545	0	1-1	0	5.19
2 ML YEARS		49	15	0	11	143.2	632	170	94	79	29	2	4	7	43	3	84	1	0	6	6	.500	0	1-2	0	4.95

Paul Wilson

Pitches: Right **Bats:** Right **Pos:** SP-24; RP-13   **Ht:** 6'5" **Wt:** 235 **Born:** 3/28/73 **Age:** 29

Year Team	Lg	G	GS	CG	GF	IP	BFP	H	R	ER	HR	SH	SF	HB	TBB	IBB	SO	WP	Bk	W	L	Pct.	ShO	Sv-Op	Hld	ERA
1996 New York	NL	26	26	1	0	149	677	157	102	89	15	7	3	10	71	11	109	3	3	5	12	.294	0	0-0	0	5.38
2000 Tampa Bay	AL	11	7	0	0	51	206	38	20	19	1	2	4		16	2	40	1	0	1	4	.200	0	0-0	1	3.35
2001 Tampa Bay	AL	37	24	0	6	151.1	674	165	94	82	21	3	12	13	52	2	119	7	0	8	9	.471	0	0-1	0	4.88
3 ML YEARS		74	57	1	6	351.1	1557	360	216	190	37	12	17	23	139	15	268	11	3	14	25	.359	0	0-1	1	4.87

Preston Wilson

Bats: Right **Throws:** Right **Pos:** CF-121; PH/PR-2   **Ht:** 6'2" **Wt:** 193 **Born:** 7/19/74 **Age:** 27

Year Team	Lg	G	AB	H	2B	3B	HR	(Hm	Rd)	TB	R	RBI	TBB	IBB	SO	HBP	SH	SF	SB	CS	SB%	GDP	Avg	OBP	SLG
2001 Calgary *	AAA	4	10	5	2	0	0	—	—	7	3	1	5	0	1	0	0	0	2	0	1.00	0	.500	.667	.700
1998 NYM-Fla	NL	22	51	8	2	0	1	(1	0)	13	7	3	6	0	21	1	2	0	1	1	.50	0	.157	.259	.255
1999 Florida	NL	149	482	135	21	4	26	(8	18)	242	67	71	46	3	156	9	0	6	11	4	.73	15	.280	.350	.502
2000 Florida	NL	161	605	160	35	3	31	(12	19)	294	94	121	55	1	187	8	0	6	36	14	.72	11	.264	.331	.486
2001 Florida	NL	123	468	128	30	2	23	(9	14)	231	70	71	36	2	107	6	0	3	20	8	.71	14	.274	.331	.494
1998 New York	NL	8	20	6	2	0	0	(0	0)	8	3	2	2	0	8	0	0	0	1	1	.50	0	.300	.364	.400
Florida	NL	14	31	2	0	0	1	(1	0)	5	4	1	4	0	13	1	2	0	0	0	—	0	.065	.194	.161
4 ML YEARS		455	1606	431	88	9	81	(30	51)	780	238	266	143	6	471	24	2	15	68	27	.72	40	.268	.334	.486

Tom Wilson

Bats: Right **Throws:** Right **Pos:** C-9   **Ht:** 6'3" **Wt:** 210 **Born:** 12/19/70 **Age:** 31

Year Team	Lg	G	AB	H	2B	3B	HR	(Hm	Rd)	TB	R	RBI	TBB	IBB	SO	HBP	SH	SF	SB	CS	SB%	GDP	Avg	OBP	SLG
1991 Oneonta	A-	70	243	59	12	2	4	—	—	87	38	42	34	2	71	3	0	5	4	4	.50	6	.243	.337	.358
1992 Greensboro	A	117	395	83	22	0	6	—	—	123	50	48	68	0	128	3	1	8	2	1	.67	8	.210	.325	.311
1993 Greensboro	A	120	394	98	20	1	10	—	—	150	55	63	91	0	112	4	3	8	2	5	.29	5	.249	.388	.381
1994 Albany-Col	AA	123	400	100	20	1	7	—	—	143	54	42	58	2	100	6	4	4	4	6	.40	6	.245	.345	.350
1995 Columbus	AAA	22	62	16	3	1	0	—	—	21	11	9	9	0	10	0	2	0	0	0	—	0	.258	.352	.339
Tampa	A+	17	48	8	0	0	0	—	—	8	3	2	11	0	13	0	1	1	1	0	1.00	0	.167	.317	.167
Norwich	AA	28	84	12	4	0	0	—	—	16	6	4	17	0	22	0	0	0	0	0	—	3	.143	.287	.190
1996 Columbus	AAA	1	1	0	0	0	0	—	—	0	0	0	1	0	0	0	0	0	0	0	—	0	.000	.500	.000
Buffalo	AAA	72	208	56	14	2	9	—	—	101	28	30	35	0	66	6	1	0	0	1	.00	6	.269	.390	.486
1997 Columbus	AAA	1	3	0	0	0	0	—	—	0	0	0	0	0	0	0	0	0	0	0	—	0	.000	.250	.000
Norwich	AA	124	419	124	21	4	21	—	—	216	88	80	86	0	126	4	0	5	1	4	.20	8	.296	.416	.516
1998 Tucson	AAA	111	370	112	17	3	12	—	—	171	59	54	41	3	81	7	0	3	3	1	.75	10	.303	.380	.462
1999 Orlando	AA	30	104	30	2	0	7	—	—	53	12	23	18	0	34	3	0	1	0	0	—	2	.288	.405	.510
Durham	AAA	67	215	60	19	0	16	—	—	127	41	44	49	1	59	0	1	1	0	2	.00	9	.279	.411	.591
2000 Columbus	AAA	104	330	91	20	0	20	—	—	171	63	71	73	1	114	3	0	1	2	2	.50	9	.276	.410	.518
2001 Sacramento	AAA	77	259	73	15	1	8	—	—	114	43	48	49	1	62	4	0	8	0	1	.00	5	.282	.394	.440
2001 Oakland	AL	9	21	4	0	0	2	(1	1)	10	4	4	1	0	5	1	0	1	0	0	—	1	.190	.250	.476

Vance Wilson

Bats: Right **Throws:** Right **Pos:** C-27; PH/PR-5   **Ht:** 5'11" **Wt:** 190 **Born:** 3/17/73 **Age:** 29

Year Team	Lg	G	AB	H	2B	3B	HR	(Hm	Rd)	TB	R	RBI	TBB	IBB	SO	HBP	SH	SF	SB	CS	SB%	GDP	Avg	OBP	SLG
1994 Pittsfield	A-	44	166	51	12	0	2	—	—	69	22	20	5	2	27	5	0	2	4	1	.80	1	.307	.343	.416
1995 Capital Cty	A	91	324	81	11	0	6	—	—	110	34	32	19	1	45	8	1	2	4	3	.57	6	.250	.306	.340
1996 St. Lucie	A+	93	311	76	14	2	6	—	—	112	29	44	31	2	41	6	0	4	2	4	.33	7	.244	.321	.360
1997 Binghamton	AA	92	322	89	17	0	15	—	—	151	46	40	20	0	46	5	3	1	2	5	.29	6	.276	.328	.469
1998 Mets	R	10	28	10	5	0	2	—	—	21	5	9	0	0	0	1	0	1	0	1	.00	2	.357	.367	.750
St. Lucie	A+	4	16	1	0	0	0	—	—	1	0	0	0	0	5	0	0	0	0	0	—	0	.063	.063	.063
Norfolk	AAA	46	154	40	3	0	4	—	—	55	18	16	9	0	29	1	3	0	0	3	.00	5	.260	.305	.357
1999 Norfolk	AAA	15	53	14	3	0	3	—	—	26	10	5	4	2	8	1	0	0	1	0	1.00	4	.264	.328	.491
2000 Norfolk	AAA	111	400	104	23	1	16	—	—	177	47	62	24	1	65	12	1	3	11	6	.65	12	.260	.319	.443
2001 Norfolk	AAA	65	228	56	14	0	6	—	—	88	24	31	12	2	34	9	1	3	0	1	.00	7	.246	.306	.386
1999 New York	NL	1	0	0	0	0	0	(0	0)	0	0	0	0	0	0	0	0	0	0	0	—	0	—	—	—
2000 New York	NL	4	4	0	0	0	0	(0	0)	0	0	0	0	0	2	0	0	0	0	0	—	0	.000	.000	.000
2001 New York	NL	32	57	17	3	0	0	(0	0)	20	3	6	2	0	16	2	0	1	0	1	.00	1	.298	.339	.351
3 ML YEARS		37	61	17	3	0	0	(0	0)	20	3	6	2	0	18	2	0	1	0	1	.00	1	.279	.318	.328

Scott Winchester

Pitches: Right **Bats:** Right **Pos:** RP-11; SP-1   **Ht:** 6'2" **Wt:** 210 **Born:** 4/20/73 **Age:** 29

Year Team	Lg	G	GS	CG	GF	IP	BFP	H	R	ER	HR	SH	SF	HB	TBB	IBB	SO	WP	Bk	W	L	Pct.	ShO	Sv-Op	Hld	ERA
2001 Louisville *	AAA	23	6	0	3	53.1	221	50	26	21	5	1	3	3	10	0	37	0	1	6	3	.667	0	0- -	—	3.54
1997 Cincinnati	NL	5	0	0	4	6	30	9	5	4	1	2	0	1	2	0	3	0	0	0	0		0	0-0	0	6.00
1998 Cincinnati	NL	16	16	1	0	79	359	101	56	51	12	2	2	4	27	2	40	3	0	3	6	.333	0	0-0	0	5.81
2000 Cincinnati	NL	5	0	0	3	7.1	35	10	4	3	1	0	1	0	2	0	3	0	0	0	0		0	0-0	0	3.68
2001 Cincinnati	NL	12	1	0	6	24	105	29	19	12	7	3	3	3	4	3	9	0	0	0	2	.000	0	0-0	1	4.50
4 ML YEARS		38	17	1	13	116.1	529	149	84	70	21	7	6	8	35	5	55	3	0	3	8	.273	0	0-0	1	5.42

Randy Winn

Bats: B **Throws:** R **Pos:** RF-62; CF-48; PH/PR-13; LF-9; DH-3   **Ht:** 6'2" **Wt:** 193 **Born:** 6/9/74 **Age:** 28

Year Team	Lg	G	AB	H	2B	3B	HR	(Hm	Rd)	TB	R	RBI	TBB	IBB	SO	HBP	SH	SF	SB	CS	SB%	GDP	Avg	OBP	SLG
1998 Tampa Bay	AL	109	338	94	9	9	1	(0	1)	124	51	17	29	0	69	1	11	0	26	12	.68	2	.278	.337	.367
1999 Tampa Bay	AL	79	303	81	16	4	2	(2	0)	111	44	24	17	0	63	1	4	0	9	9	.50	3	.267	.307	.366
2000 Tampa Bay	AL	51	159	40	5	0	1	(1	0)	48	28	16	26	0	25	2	2	1	6	7	.46	2	.252	.362	.302
2001 Tampa Bay	AL	128	429	117	25	6	6	(3	3)	172	54	50	38	0	81	6	5	2	12	10	.55	10	.273	.339	.401
4 ML YEARS		367	1229	332	55	19	10	(6	4)	455	177	107	110	0	238	10	19	5	53	38	.58	17	.270	.334	.370

Matt Wise

Pitches: Right **Bats:** Right **Pos:** SP-9; RP-2   **Ht:** 6'4" **Wt:** 197 **Born:** 11/18/75 **Age:** 26

Year Team	Lg	G	GS	CG	GF	IP	BFP	H	R	ER	HR	SH	SF	HB	TBB	IBB	SO	WP	Bk	W	L	Pct.	ShO	Sv-Op	Hld	ERA
1997 Boise	A-	15	15	0	0	83	342	62	37	30	5	0	1	2	34	0	86	7	3	9	1	.900	0	0--	—	3.25
1998 Midland	AA	27	27	3	0	167.2	735	195	111	101	23	4	5	6	46	0	131	9	0	9	10	.474	1	0--	—	5.42
1999 Erie	AA	16	16	3	0	98	416	102	48	41	10	4	3	4	24	0	72	1	0	8	5	.615	0	0--	—	3.77
2000 Edmonton	AAA	19	19	2	0	124.1	510	122	54	51	10	2	7	2	26	0	82	0	1	9	6	.600	1	0--	—	3.69
2001 Salt Lake	AAA	21	21	0	0	123.1	527	134	79	69	19	3	1	12	17	0	111	4	1	9	9	.500	0	0--	—	5.04
2000 Anaheim	AL	8	6	0	0	37.1	163	40	23	23	7	0	1	1	13	1	20	1	0	3	3	.500	0	0-0	0	5.54
2001 Anaheim	AL	11	9	0	2	49.1	211	47	27	24	11	2	1	2	18	1	50	0	0	1	4	.200	0	0-0	0	4.38
2 ML YEARS		19	15	0	2	86.2	374	87	50	47	18	2	3	3	31	2	70	1	0	4	7	.364	0	0-0	0	4.88

Jay Witasick

Pitches: Right **Bats:** Right **Pos:** RP-63   **Ht:** 6'4" **Wt:** 235 **Born:** 8/28/72 **Age:** 29

Year Team	Lg	G	GS	CG	GF	IP	BFP	H	R	ER	HR	SH	SF	HB	TBB	IBB	SO	WP	Bk	W	L	Pct.	ShO	Sv-Op	Hld	ERA
1996 Oakland	AL	12	0	0	6	13	55	12	9	9	5	0	1	0	5	0	12	2	0	1	1	.500	0	0-1	0	6.23
1997 Oakland	AL	8	0	0	1	11	53	14	7	7	2	1	0	0	6	0	8	0	0	0	0	—	0	0-0	1	5.73
1998 Oakland	AL	7	3	0	1	27	131	36	24	19	9	0	0	0	15	1	29	2	0	1	3	.250	0	0-0	0	6.33
1999 Kansas City	AL	32	28	1	2	158.1	732	191	108	98	23	4	8	8	83	1	102	5	2	9	12	.429	1	0-0	0	5.57
2000 KC-SD		33	25	2	2	150	697	178	107	97	24	8	4	7	73	5	121	5	1	6	10	.375	0	0-0	0	5.82
2001 SD-NYY		63	0	0	17	79	352	78	41	29	8	3	2	6	33	4	106	4	0	8	2	.800	0	1-4	10	3.30
2000 Kansas City	AL	22	14	2	2	89.1	410	109	65	59	15	3	3	4	38	0	67	3	0	3	8	.273	0	0-0	0	5.94
San Diego	NL	11	11	0	0	60.2	287	69	42	38	9	5	1	3	35	5	54	2	1	3	2	.600	0	0-0	0	5.64
2001 San Diego	NL	31	0	0	9	38.2	164	31	14	8	3	3	0	4	15	3	53	3	0	5	2	.714	0	1-3	5	1.86
New York	AL	32	0	0	8	40.1	188	47	27	21	5	0	2	2	18	1	53	1	0	3	0	1.000	0	0-1	5	4.69
6 ML YEARS		155	56	3	29	438.1	2020	509	296	259	71	16	15	21	215	11	378	18	3	25	28	.472	1	1-5	11	5.32

Bobby Witt

Pitches: Right **Bats:** Right **Pos:** SP-7; RP-7   **Ht:** 6'2" **Wt:** 205 **Born:** 5/11/64 **Age:** 38

Year Team	Lg	G	GS	CG	GF	IP	BFP	H	R	ER	HR	SH	SF	HB	TBB	IBB	SO	WP	Bk	W	L	Pct.	ShO	Sv-Op	Hld	ERA
2001 Tucson *	AAA	5	5	0	0	22.1	92	18	11	9	1	1	2	0	8	1	18	1	0	0	3	.000	0	0--	—	3.63
1986 Texas	AL	31	31	0	0	157.2	741	130	104	96	18	3	9	3	143	2	174	22	3	11	9	.550	0	0-0	0	5.48
1987 Texas	AL	26	25	1	0	143	673	114	82	78	10	5	5	3	140	1	160	7	2	8	10	.444	0	0-0	0	4.91
1988 Texas	AL	22	22	13	0	174.1	736	134	83	76	13	7	6	5	101	2	148	16	8	8	10	.444	2	0-0	0	3.92
1989 Texas	AL	31	31	5	0	194.1	869	182	123	111	14	11	8	2	114	3	166	7	4	12	13	.480	1	0-0	0	5.14
1990 Texas	AL	33	32	7	1	222	954	197	98	83	12	5	6	4	110	3	221	11	2	17	10	.630	1	0-0	0	3.36
1991 Texas	AL	17	16	1	0	88.2	413	84	66	60	4	3	4	1	74	1	82	8	0	3	7	.300	0	0-0	0	6.09
1992 Tex-Oak	AL	31	31	0	0	193	848	183	99	92	16	7	10	2	114	2	125	9	1	10	14	.417	0	0-0	0	4.29
1993 Oakland	AL	35	33	5	0	220	950	226	112	103	16	9	8	3	91	5	131	8	1	14	13	.519	1	0-0	0	4.21
1994 Oakland	AL	24	24	5	0	135.2	618	151	88	76	22	2	7	5	70	4	111	6	1	8	10	.444	3	0-0	0	5.04
1995 Fla-Tex		29	29	2	0	172	748	185	87	79	12	7	5	3	68	2	141	7	0	5	11	.313	0	0-0	0	4.13
1996 Texas	AL	33	32	2	1	199.2	903	235	129	120	28	2	7	2	96	3	157	4	1	16	12	.571	0	0-0	0	5.41
1997 Texas	AL	34	32	3	1	209	919	245	118	112	33	3	7	2	74	4	121	7	0	12	12	.500	0	0-0	0	4.82
1998 Tex-StL		31	18	0	8	116.2	546	150	94	85	21	6	5	2	53	2	58	3	2	7	9	.438	0	0-0	0	6.56
1999 Tampa Bay	AL	32	32	3	0	180.1	815	213	130	117	23	7	8	3	96	1	123	9	1	7	15	.318	2	0-0	0	5.84
2000 Cleveland	AL	7	2	0	2	15.1	77	28	13	13	4	0	0	0	6	2	6	2	0	1	0	1.000	0	0-0	0	7.63
2001 Arizona	NL	14	7	0	0	43.1	193	36	23	23	6	1	2	3	25	1	31	2	0	4	1	.800	0	0-0	3	4.78
1992 Texas	AL	25	25	0	0	161.1	708	152	87	80	14	5	8	2	95	1	100	6	1	9	13	.409	0	0-0	0	4.46
Oakland	AL	6	6	0	0	31.2	140	31	12	12	2	2	2	0	19	1	25	3	0	1	1	.500	0	0-0	0	3.41
1995 Florida	NL	19	19	1	0	110.2	472	104	52	48	8	5	3	2	47	1	95	2	0	2	7	.222	0	0-0	0	3.90
Texas	AL	10	10	1	0	61.1	276	81	35	31	4	2	2	1	21	1	46	5	0	3	4	.429	0	0-0	0	4.55
1998 Texas	AL	14	13	0	0	69.1	329	95	62	59	14	2	4	0	33	1	30	2	1	5	4	.556	0	0-0	0	7.66
St. Louis	NL	17	5	0	8	47.1	217	55	32	26	7	4	1	2	20	1	28	1	1	2	5	.286	0	0-0	0	4.94
16 ML YEARS		430	397	47	13	2465	11003	2493	1449	1324	252	78	97	39	1375	37	1955	128	26	142	157	.475	11	0-0	3	4.83

Kevin Witt

Bats: Left **Throws:** Right **Pos:** 1B-9; PH/PR-5   **Ht:** 6'4" **Wt:** 200 **Born:** 1/5/76 **Age:** 26

Year Team	Lg	G	AB	H	2B	3B	HR	(Hm	Rd)	TB	R	RBI	TBB	IBB	SO	HBP	SH	SF	SB	CS	SB%	GDP	Avg	OBP	SLG
1994 Medcine Hat	R+	60	243	62	10	4	7	—	—	101	37	36	15	0	52	1	1	1	4	1	.80	3	.255	.300	.416
1995 Hagerstown	A	119	479	111	35	1	14	—	—	190	58	50	28	2	148	4	3	0	1	5	.17	5	.232	.280	.397
1996 Dunedin	A+	124	446	121	18	6	13	—	—	190	63	70	39	3	96	6	2	5	9	4	.69	9	.271	.335	.426
1997 Knoxville	AA	127	501	145	27	4	30	—	—	270	76	91	44	7	109	3	1	5	1	0	1.00	13	.289	.349	.539
1998 Syracuse	AAA	126	455	124	20	3	23	—	—	219	71	67	53	6	124	7	1	5	3	3	.50	5	.273	.354	.481
1999 Syracuse	AAA	114	421	117	24	3	24	—	—	219	72	71	64	10	109	3	2	2	0	0	—	11	.278	.376	.520
2000 Syracuse	AAA	135	489	121	24	5	26	—	—	233	58	72	45	6	132	4	1	4	1	1	.50	9	.247	.316	.476
2001 Portland	AAA	129	456	132	28	5	27	—	—	251	66	87	22	0	127	3	0	6	1	1	.50	13	.289	.322	.550
1998 Toronto	AL	5	7	1	0	0	0	(0	0)	1	0	0	0	0	3	0	0	0	0	0	—	0	.143	.143	.143

242

Year Team	Lg	G	AB	H	2B	3B	HR	(Hm	Rd)	TB	R	RBI	TBB	IBB	SO	HBP	SH	SF	SB	CS	SB%	GDP	Avg	OBP	SLG
																		BATTING				**BASERUNNING**		**PERCENTAGES**		
1999 Toronto	AL	15	34	7	1	0	1	(0	1)	11	3	5	2	0	9	0	1	0	0	0	—	0	.206	.250	.324
2001 San Diego	NL	14	27	5	0	0	2	(1	1)	11	5	5	2	0	7	0	0	1	0	0	—	0	.185	.233	.407
3 ML YEARS		34	68	13	1	0	3	(1	2)	23	8	10	4	0	19	0	1	1	0	0	—	0	.191	.233	.338

Mark Wohlers

Pitches: Right **Bats:** Right **Pos:** RP-61 **Ht:** 6'4" **Wt:** 207 **Born:** 1/23/70 **Age:** 32

Year Team	Lg	G	GS	CG	GF	IP	BFP	H	R	ER	HR	SH	SF	HB	TBB	IBB	SO	WP	Bk	W	L	Pct.	ShO	Sv-Op	Hld	ERA
1991 Atlanta	NL	17	0	0	4	19.2	89	17	7	7	1	2	1	2	13	3	13	0	0	3	1	.750	0	2-4	2	3.20
1992 Atlanta	NL	32	0	0	16	35.1	140	28	11	10	0	5	1	1	14	4	17	1	0	1	2	.333	0	4-6	2	2.55
1993 Atlanta	NL	46	0	0	13	48	199	37	25	24	2	5	1	1	22	3	45	0	0	6	2	.750	0	0-0	12	4.50
1994 Atlanta	NL	51	0	0	15	51	236	51	35	26	1	4	6	0	33	9	58	2	0	7	2	.778	0	1-2	7	4.59
1995 Atlanta	NL	65	0	0	49	64.2	269	51	16	15	2	2	0	1	24	3	90	4	0	7	3	.700	0	25-29	2	2.09
1996 Atlanta	NL	77	0	0	64	77.1	323	71	30	26	8	2	2	2	21	3	100	10	0	2	4	.333	0	39-44	0	3.03
1997 Atlanta	NL	71	0	0	55	69.1	300	57	29	27	4	4	4	0	38	0	92	6	0	5	7	.417	0	33-40	1	3.50
1998 Atlanta	NL	27	0	0	17	20.1	113	18	23	23	2	1	0	1	33	0	22	7	0	0	1	.000	0	8-8	0	10.18
1999 Atlanta	NL	2	0	0	0	0.2	10	1	2	2	0	1	0	0	6	0	0	0	0	0	0	—	0	0-0	0	27.00
2000 Cincinnati	NL	20	0	0	7	28	119	19	14	14	3	2	1	0	17	0	20	2	0	1	2	.333	0	0-0	0	4.50
2001 Cin-NYY		61	0	0	25	67.2	298	69	40	32	8	5	3	2	25	2	54	11	0	4	1	.800	0	0-1	13	4.26
2001 Cincinnati	NL	30	0	0	11	32	153	36	20	14	5	4	1	1	7	2	21	4	0	3	1	.750	0	0-1	8	3.94
New York	AL	31	0	0	14	35.2	159	33	20	18	3	1	2	1	18	0	33	7	0	1	0	1.000	0	0-0	5	4.54
11 ML YEARS		469	0	0	265	482	2096	419	232	206	31	33	19	10	246	27	511	43	0	36	25	.590	0	112-134	39	3.85

Randy Wolf

Pitches: Left **Bats:** Left **Pos:** SP-25; RP-3 **Ht:** 6'0" **Wt:** 194 **Born:** 8/22/76 **Age:** 25

Year Team	Lg	G	GS	CG	GF	IP	BFP	H	R	ER	HR	SH	SF	HB	TBB	IBB	SO	WP	Bk	W	L	Pct.	ShO	Sv-Op	Hld	ERA
2001 Scrantn-WB *	AAA	2	2	0	0	9	42	10	6	5	2	1	1	0	5	0	7	0	0	0	1	.000	0	0--		5.00
Reading *	AA	1	1	0	0	6	27	5	3	3	0	0	1	0	2	0	7	0	0	0	0	—	0	0--		4.50
1999 Philadelphia	NL	22	21	0	0	121.2	552	126	78	75	20	5	1	5	67	0	116	4	0	6	9	.400	0	0-0	0	5.55
2000 Philadelphia	NL	32	32	1	0	206.1	889	210	107	100	25	10	8	8	83	2	160	1	0	11	9	.550	0	0-0	0	4.36
2001 Philadelphia	NL	28	25	4	1	163	684	150	74	67	15	11	7	10	51	4	152	1	0	10	11	.476	2	0-0	0	3.70
3 ML YEARS		82	78	5	1	491	2125	486	259	242	60	26	16	23	201	6	428	6	0	27	29	.482	2	0-0	0	4.44

Tony Womack

Bats: Left **Throws:** Right **Pos:** SS-118; PH/PR-9; CF-1 **Ht:** 5'9" **Wt:** 170 **Born:** 9/25/69 **Age:** 32

Year Team	Lg	G	AB	H	2B	3B	HR	(Hm	Rd)	TB	R	RBI	TBB	IBB	SO	HBP	SH	SF	SB	CS	SB%	GDP	Avg	OBP	SLG
2001 Tucson *	AAA	4	13	5	0	1	0			7	1	2	0	0	1	0	0	0	0	1	.00	0	.385	.385	.538
1993 Pittsburgh	NL	15	24	2	0	0	0	(0	0)	2	5	0	3	0	3	0	1	0	2	0	1.00	0	.083	.185	.083
1994 Pittsburgh	NL	5	12	4	0	0	0	(0	0)	4	4	1	2	0	3	0	0	0	0	0	—	0	.333	.429	.333
1996 Pittsburgh	NL	17	30	10	3	1	0	(0	0)	15	11	7	6	0	1	1	3	0	2	0	1.00	0	.333	.459	.500
1997 Pittsburgh	NL	155	641	178	26	9	6	(5	1)	240	85	50	43	2	109	3	2	0	60	7	.90	6	.278	.326	.374
1998 Pittsburgh	NL	159	655	185	26	7	3	(2	1)	234	85	45	38	1	94	0	6	5	58	8	.88	4	.282	.319	.357
1999 Arizona	NL	144	614	170	25	10	4	(1	3)	227	111	41	52	0	68	2	9	7	72	13	.85	4	.277	.332	.370
2000 Arizona	NL	146	617	167	21	**14**	7	(4	3)	237	95	57	30	0	74	5	2	5	45	11	.80	6	.271	.307	.384
2001 Arizona	NL	125	481	128	19	5	3	(2	1)	166	66	30	23	2	54	6	7	1	28	7	.80	4	.266	.307	.345
8 ML YEARS		766	3074	844	120	46	23	(14	9)	1125	462	231	197	5	406	17	30	18	267	46	.85	24	.275	.320	.366

Kerry Wood

Pitches: Right **Bats:** Right **Pos:** SP-28 **Ht:** 6'5" **Wt:** 220 **Born:** 6/16/77 **Age:** 25

Year Team	Lg	G	GS	CG	GF	IP	BFP	H	R	ER	HR	SH	SF	HB	TBB	IBB	SO	WP	Bk	W	L	Pct.	ShO	Sv-Op	Hld	ERA
1998 Chicago	NL	26	26	1	0	166.2	699	117	69	63	14	2	4	11	85	1	233	6	3	13	6	.684	1	0-0	0	3.40
2000 Chicago	NL	23	23	1	0	137	603	112	77	73	17	7	5	9	87	0	132	5	1	8	7	.533	0	0-0	0	4.80
2001 Chicago	NL	28	28	1	0	174.1	740	127	70	65	16	4	5	10	92	3	217	9	0	12	6	.667	1	0-0	0	3.36
3 ML YEARS		77	77	3	0	478	2042	356	216	201	47	13	14	30	264	4	582	20	4	33	19	.635	2	0-0	0	3.78

Steve Woodard

Pitches: Right **Bats:** Left **Pos:** RP-19; SP-10 **Ht:** 6'4" **Wt:** 217 **Born:** 5/15/75 **Age:** 27

Year Team	Lg	G	GS	CG	GF	IP	BFP	H	R	ER	HR	SH	SF	HB	TBB	IBB	SO	WP	Bk	W	L	Pct.	ShO	Sv-Op	Hld	ERA
2001 Akron *	AA	1	1	0	0	3	12	3	1	1	0	0	0	0	1	0	2	1	0	0	0	—	0	0--	—	3.00
Buffalo *	AAA	6	6	1	0	37.2	151	36	11	10	2	2	2	1	1	1	32	1	0	4	2	.667	0	0--	—	2.39
1997 Milwaukee	AL	7	7	0	0	36.2	153	39	25	21	5	0	0	2	6	0	32	0	0	3	3	.500	0	0-0	0	5.15
1998 Milwaukee	NL	34	26	0	2	165.2	692	170	83	77	19	2	4	9	33	4	135	3	2	10	12	.455	0	0-0	0	4.18
1999 Milwaukee	NL	31	29	2	0	185	801	219	101	93	23	9	4	6	36	7	119	4	1	11	8	.579	0	0-0	0	4.52
2000 Mil-Cle		40	22	1	7	147.2	659	182	105	96	26	8	4	6	44	5	100	8	0	4	10	.286	0	0-0	0	5.85
2001 Cleveland	AL	29	10	0	2	97	429	129	59	56	10	7	3	5	17	1	52	4	3	3	3	.500	0	0-0	1	5.20
2000 Milwaukee	NL	27	11	1	6	93.2	432	125	70	62	16	7	3	4	33	4	65	5	0	1	7	.125	0	0-0	0	5.96
Cleveland	AL	13	11	0	1	54	227	57	35	34	10	1	1	2	11	1	35	3	0	3	3	.500	0	0-0	0	5.67
5 ML YEARS		141	94	3	11	632	2734	739	373	343	83	26	15	28	136	17	438	19	6	31	36	.463	0	0-0	1	4.88

Chris Woodward

Bats: R **Throws:** R **Pos:** 2B-17; 3B-10; PH/PR-6; SS-4; 1B-2; DH-1   **Ht:** 6'0" **Wt:** 173 **Born:** 6/27/76 **Age:** 26

							BATTING											BASERUNNING				PERCENTAGES		
Year Team	Lg	G	AB	H	2B	3B	HR	(Hm | Rd)	TB	R	RBI	TBB	IBB	SO	HBP	SH	SF	SB	CS	SB%	GDP	Avg	OBP	SLG
2001 Syracuse *	AAA	51	193	59	14	3	11	—	—	112	29	31	16	0	40	1	2		0	0	—	4	.306	.360	.580
1999 Toronto	AL	14	26	6	1	0	0	(0 | 0)	7	1	2	2	0	6	0	0	1	0	0	—	1	.231	.276	.269
2000 Toronto	AL	37	104	19	7	0	3	(1 | 2)	35	16	14	10	3	28	0	1	0	1	0	1.00	1	.183	.254	.337
2001 Toronto	AL	37	63	12	3	2	2	(2 | 0)	25	9	5	1	0	14	0	2	0	0	1	.00	1	.190	.203	.397
3 ML YEARS		88	193	37	11	2	5	(3 | 2)	67	26	21	13	3	48	0	3	1	1	1	.50	3	.192	.242	.347

Shawn Wooten

Bats: R **Throws:** R **Pos:** DH-27; C-25; 1B-21; PH/PR-11; 3B-1   **Ht:** 5'10" **Wt:** 225 **Born:** 7/24/72 **Age:** 29

							BATTING											BASERUNNING				PERCENTAGES		
Year Team	Lg	G	AB	H	2B	3B	HR	(Hm | Rd)	TB	R	RBI	TBB	IBB	SO	HBP	SH	SF	SB	CS	SB%	GDP	Avg	OBP	SLG
1993 Bristol	R+	52	177	62	12	2	8	—	—	102	26	39	24	2	20	3	0	2	1	2	.33	7	.350	.432	.576
Fayetteville	A	5	16	4	0	0	1	—	—	7	2	5	3	0	3	0	0	0	0	0	—	1	.250	.368	.438
1994 Fayetteville	A	121	439	118	25	1	3	—	—	154	45	61	27	0	84	11	3	4	1	3	.25	11	.269	.324	.351
1995 Jacksnville	AA	20	70	9	1	0	2	—	—	16	4	7	1	0	17	1	0	1	0	0	—	3	.129	.151	.229
Lakeland	A+	38	135	31	10	1	2	—	—	49	11	11	10	0	28	2	0	1	0	1	.00	2	.230	.291	.363
Moose Jaw	IND	52	201	89	17	0	12	—	—	142	38	57	18	0	26	—	0	1	3	2	.60	0	.443	.706	
1996 Moose Jaw	IND	77	292	89	17	0	12	—	—	142	44	57	18	2	46	2	0	1	2	0	1.00	8	.305	.348	.486
1997 Cedar Rapds	A	108	353	102	23	1	15	—	—	172	43	75	49	0	71	6	3	6	0	1	.00	8	.289	.379	.487
1998 Midland	AA	8	28	9	4	0	1	—	—	16	3	6	3	0	4	0	0	0	0	0	—	0	.321	.387	.571
Lk Elsinore	A+	105	395	116	31	0	16	—	—	195	56	74	38	3	82	3	0	4	0	2	.00	9	.294	.357	.494
1999 Erie	AA	137	518	151	27	1	19	—	—	237	70	88	50	1	102	10	1	8	3	1	.75	12	.292	.360	.458
2000 Erie	AA	51	191	56	12	2	9	—	—	99	32	35	17	0	30	2	0	4	4	1	.80	3	.293	.350	.518
Edmonton	AAA	66	252	89	21	3	11	—	—	149	43	42	18	0	38	3	0	1	0	0	—	4	.353	.401	.591
2000 Anaheim	AL	7	9	5	1	0	0	(0 | 0)	6	2	1	0	0	0	0	0	0	0	0	—	0	.556	.556	.667
2001 Anaheim	AL	79	221	69	8	1	8	(3 | 5)	103	24	32	5	0	42	3	0	3	2	0	1.00	5	.312	.332	.466
2 ML YEARS		86	230	74	9	1	8	(3 | 5)	109	26	33	5	0	42	3	0	3	2	0	1.00	5	.322	.340	.474

Tim Worrell

Pitches: Right **Bats:** Right **Pos:** RP-73   **Ht:** 6'4" **Wt:** 231 **Born:** 7/5/67 **Age:** 34

		HOW MUCH HE PITCHED						WHAT HE GAVE UP										THE RESULTS						
Year Team	Lg	G	GS	CG	GF	IP	BFP	H	R	ER	HR	SH	SF	HB	TBB	IBB	SO	WP	Bk	W	L	Pct.	ShO	Sv-Op	Hld	ERA
2001 Giants *	R	1	1	0	0	3	10	1	0	0	0	1	0	0	1	0	2	0	0	0	0	—	0	0--	—	0.00
1993 San Diego	NL	21	16	0	1	100.2	443	104	63	55	11	8	5	0	43	5	52	3	0	2	7	.222	0	0-0	1	4.92
1994 San Diego	NL	3	3	0	0	14.2	59	9	7	6	0	0	1	0	5	0	14	0	0	1	0	1.000	0	0-0	0	3.68
1995 San Diego	NL	9	0	0	4	13.1	63	16	7	7	2	1	0	1	6	0	13	1	0	1	0	1.000	0	0-0	0	4.73
1996 San Diego	NL	50	11	0	8	121	510	109	45	41	9	3	1	6	39	1	99	0	0	9	7	.563	0	1-2	10	3.05
1997 San Diego	NL	60	10	0	14	106.1	483	116	67	61	14	6	6	7	50	2	81	2	1	4	8	.333	0	3-7	16	5.16
1998 Det-Cle-Oak	AL	43	9	0	5	103	440	106	62	60	16	2	3	1	29	3	82	2	0	2	7	.222	0	0-3	6	5.24
1999 Oakland	AL	53	0	0	17	69.1	309	69	38	32	6	1	1	3	34	1	62	1	0	2	2	.500	0	0-5	5	4.15
2000 Bal-ChC		59	0	0	29	69.1	307	72	26	23	10	4	1	1	29	11	57	1	0	5	6	.455	0	3-6	12	2.99
2001 San Francisco	NL	73	0	0	12	78.1	339	71	33	30	4	3	4	3	33	4	63	2	0	2	5	.286	0	0-3	13	3.45
1998 Detroit	AL	15	9	0	0	61.2	265	66	42	41	11	0	1	1	19	2	47	0	0	2	6	.250	0	0-1	0	5.98
Cleveland	AL	3	0	0	1	5.1	24	6	3	3	0	0	2	0	2	0	2	0	0	0	0	—	0	0-0	0	5.06
Oakland	AL	25	0	0	4	36	151	34	17	16	5	2	0	0	8	1	33	2	0	0	1	.000	0	0-2	6	4.00
2000 Baltimore	AL	5	0	0	2	7.1	39	12	6	6	3	0	0	0	5	3	5	0	0	2	2	.500	0	0-0	0	7.36
Chicago	NL	54	0	0	27	62	268	60	20	17	7	4	1	1	24	8	52	1	0	3	4	.429	0	3-6	12	2.47
9 ML YEARS		371	49	0	90	676	2953	672	348	315	72	28	22	22	268	27	523	12	1	27	43	.386	0	7-26	63	4.19

Dan Wright

Pitches: Right **Bats:** Right **Pos:** SP-12; RP-1   **Ht:** 6'5" **Wt:** 225 **Born:** 12/14/77 **Age:** 24

		HOW MUCH HE PITCHED						WHAT HE GAVE UP										THE RESULTS						
Year Team	Lg	G	GS	CG	GF	IP	BFP	H	R	ER	HR	SH	SF	HB	TBB	IBB	SO	WP	Bk	W	L	Pct.	ShO	Sv-Op	Hld	ERA
1999 Bristol	R+	10	0	0	3	18	79	14	8	2	1	0	0	1	9	1	18	3	0	2	0	1.000	0	1--	—	1.00
Burlington	A	2	0	0	0	6	26	5	4	4	1	0	0	1	3	0	3	0	0	0	0	—	0	0--	—	6.00
2000 Winston-Sal	A+	21	21	1	0	132.1	577	135	64	55	4	4	5	10	50	0	106	18	2	9	8	.529	0	0--	—	3.74
Birmingham	AA	7	7	0	0	43.1	175	28	15	12	3	0	0	1	24	0	31	3	0	2	4	.333	0	0--	—	2.49
2001 Birmingham	AA	20	20	0	0	134	548	112	54	42	6	3	7	6	41	0	128	6	2	7	7	.500	0	0--	—	2.82
2001 Chicago	AL	13	12	0	1	66.1	307	78	45	42	12	1	5	2	39	1	36	6	0	3	5	.625	0	0-0	0	5.70

Jamey Wright

Pitches: Right **Bats:** Right **Pos:** SP-33   **Ht:** 6'5" **Wt:** 221 **Born:** 12/24/74 **Age:** 27

		HOW MUCH HE PITCHED						WHAT HE GAVE UP										THE RESULTS						
Year Team	Lg	G	GS	CG	GF	IP	BFP	H	R	ER	HR	SH	SF	HB	TBB	IBB	SO	WP	Bk	W	L	Pct.	ShO	Sv-Op	Hld	ERA
1996 Colorado	NL	16	15	0	0	91.1	406	105	60	50	8	4	2	7	41	1	45	1	2	4	4	.500	0	0-0	1	4.93
1997 Colorado	NL	26	26	1	0	149.2	698	198	113	104	19	8	3	11	71	3	59	6	2	8	12	.400	0	0-0	0	6.25
1998 Colorado	NL	34	34	1	0	206.1	919	235	143	130	24	8	6	11	95	3	86	6	3	9	14	.391	0	0-0	0	5.67
1999 Colorado	NL	16	16	0	0	94.1	423	110	52	51	10	3	4	4	54	3	49	3	0	4	3	.571	0	0-0	0	4.87
2000 Milwaukee	NL	26	25	0	1	164.2	718	157	81	75	12	4	6	18	88	5	96	9	2	7	9	.438	0	0-0	0	4.10
2001 Milwaukee	NL	33	33	1	0	194.2	868	201	115	106	26	7	5	20	98	10	129	6	1	11	12	.478	1	0-0	0	4.90
6 ML YEARS		151	149	3	1	901	4032	1006	564	516	99	34	26	71	447	25	464	31	10	43	54	.443	1	0-0	1	5.15

Jaret Wright

Pitches: Right Bats: Right Pos: SP-7   Ht: 6'2" Wt: 230 Born: 12/29/75 Age: 26

Year Team	Lg	G	GS	CG	GF	IP	BFP	H	R	ER	HR	SH	SF	HB	TBB	IBB	SO	WP	Bk	W	L	Pct.	ShO	Sv-Op	Hld	ERA
2001 Akron *	AA	1	1	0	0	7	23	2	1	1	0	0	0	0	4	0	0	0	0	0	0	—	0	0--	—	1.29
Buffalo *	AAA	7	7	0	0	28.2	124	25	18	15	3	1	0	3	13	0	28	1	0	3	1	.750	0	0--	—	4.71
1997 Cleveland	AL	16	16	0	0	90.1	388	81	45	44	9	3	4	5	35	0	63	1	0	8	3	.727	0	0-0	0	4.38
1998 Cleveland	AL	32	32	1	0	192.2	855	207	109	101	22	4	6	11	87	4	140	6	0	12	10	.545	1	0-0	0	4.72
1999 Cleveland	AL	26	26	0	0	133.2	609	144	99	90	18	3	3	7	77	1	91	4	0	8	10	.444	0	0-0	0	6.06
2000 Cleveland	AL	9	9	1	0	51.2	217	44	27	27	6	0	1	1	28	0	36	2	0	3	4	.429	1	0-0	0	4.70
2001 Cleveland	AL	7	7	0	0	29	140	36	23	21	2	2	1	0	22	0	18	1	1	2	2	.500	0	0-0	0	6.52
5 ML YEARS		90	90	2	0	497.1	2209	512	303	283	57	12	15	24	249	5	348	14	1	33	29	.532	2	0-0	0	5.12

Kelly Wunsch

Pitches: Left Bats: Left Pos: RP-33   Ht: 6'5" Wt: 225 Born: 7/12/72 Age: 29

Year Team	Lg	G	GS	CG	GF	IP	BFP	H	R	ER	HR	SH	SF	HB	TBB	IBB	SO	WP	Bk	W	L	Pct.	ShO	Sv-Op	Hld	ERA
1993 Beloit	A	12	12	0	0	63.1	282	58	39	34	5	4	1	1	39	1	61	5	2	1	5	.167	0	0--	—	4.83
1994 Beloit	A	17	17	0	0	83.1	400	88	69	57	11	4	3	13	47	1	77	6	0	3	10	.231	0	0--	—	6.16
Helena	R+	9	9	1	0	51	238	52	39	29	7	1	2	10	30	0	37	6	1	4	2	.667	0	0--	—	5.12
1995 Beloit	A	14	14	3	0	85.2	364	90	47	40	7	2	0	3	37	0	66	6	0	4	7	.364	1	0--	—	4.20
Stockton	A+	14	13	1	0	74.1	349	89	51	44	4	8	1	7	39	0	62	6	0	5	6	.455	1	0--	—	5.33
1997 Stockton	A+	24	22	2	0	143	627	141	65	55	11	10	4	14	62	0	98	9	2	7	9	.438	2	0--	—	3.46
1998 El Paso	AA	17	17	1	0	101.1	469	127	81	67	11	4	3	9	31	0	70	7	0	5	6	.455	1	0--	—	5.95
Louisville	AAA	9	8	0	0	51.2	220	53	23	22	6	0	1	3	15	0	36	2	0	3	1	.750	0	0--	—	3.83
1999 Huntsville	AA	22	3	0	7	50.2	204	40	13	11	1	1	4	3	23	1	35	0	0	4	1	.800	0	1--	—	1.95
Louisville	AAA	16	2	0	3	41.2	189	52	23	22	4	0	2	6	14	0	20	3	0	2	1	.667	0	0--	—	4.75
2000 Chicago	AL	83	0	0	12	61.1	259	50	22	20	4	0	2	2	29	1	51	0	0	6	3	.667	0	1-5	25	2.93
2001 Chicago	AL	33	0	0	2	22.1	105	21	19	19	4	3	2	6	9	1	16	0	0	2	1	.667	0	0-2	3	7.66
2 ML YEARS		116	0	0	14	83.2	364	71	41	39	8	3	4	8	38	2	67	0	0	8	4	.667	0	1-7	28	4.20

Esteban Yan

Pitches: Right Bats: Right Pos: RP-54   Ht: 6'4" Wt: 230 Born: 6/22/74 Age: 28

Year Team	Lg	G	GS	CG	GF	IP	BFP	H	R	ER	HR	SH	SF	HB	TBB	IBB	SO	WP	Bk	W	L	Pct.	ShO	Sv-Op	Hld	ERA
2001 Orlando *	AA	2	2	0	0	3	12	3	1	1	0	0	0	0	0	0	4	1	0	0	0	—	0	0--	—	3.00
1996 Baltimore	AL	4	0	0	2	9.1	42	13	7	6	3	0	0	0	3	1	7	0	0	0	0	—	0	0-0	0	5.79
1997 Baltimore	AL	3	2	0	0	9.2	58	20	18	17	3	0	1	2	7	0	4	1	0	0	1	.000	0	0-0	0	15.83
1998 Tampa Bay	AL	64	0	0	18	88.2	381	78	41	38	11	1	3	5	41	2	77	6	0	5	4	.556	0	1-5	8	3.86
1999 Tampa Bay	AL	50	1	0	15	61	286	77	41	40	8	6	3	9	32	4	46	2	0	3	4	.429	0	0-3	7	5.90
2000 Tampa Bay	AL	43	20	0	8	137.2	618	158	98	95	26	4	6	11	42	0	111	7	1	7	8	.467	0	0-2	3	6.21
2001 Tampa Bay	AL	54	0	0	51	62.1	264	64	34	27	7	3	1	5	11	1	64	5	0	4	6	.400	0	22-31	0	3.90
6 ML YEARS		218	23	0	94	368.2	1649	410	239	223	58	14	14	32	136	8	309	21	1	19	23	.452	0	23-41	18	5.44

Masato Yoshii

Pitches: Right Bats: Right Pos: RP-31; SP-11   Ht: 6'2" Wt: 210 Born: 4/20/65 Age: 37

Year Team	Lg	G	GS	CG	GF	IP	BFP	H	R	ER	HR	SH	SF	HB	TBB	IBB	SO	WP	Bk	W	L	Pct.	ShO	Sv-Op	Hld	ERA
1998 New York	NL	29	29	1	0	171.2	724	166	79	75	22	9	4	6	53	5	117	5	1	6	8	.429	0	0-0	0	3.93
1999 New York	NL	31	29	1	1	174	723	168	86	85	25	7	6	6	58	3	105	1	0	12	8	.600	0	0-0	0	4.40
2000 Colorado	NL	29	29	0	0	167.1	726	201	112	109	32	8	7	2	53	6	88	2	1	6	15	.286	0	0-0	0	5.86
2001 Montreal	NL	42	11	0	4	113	493	127	65	60	18	4	3	5	26	2	63	4	0	4	7	.364	0	0-0	0	4.78
4 ML YEARS		131	98	2	5	626	2666	662	342	329	97	28	20	19	190	16	373	12	2	28	38	.424	0	0-0	0	4.73

Dmitri Young

Bats: B Throws: R Pos: LF-86; 1B-38; 3B-36; PH/PR-7; RF-1   Ht: 6'2" Wt: 235 Born: 10/11/73 Age: 28

Year Team	Lg	G	AB	H	2B	3B	HR	(Hm	Rd)	TB	R	RBI	TBB	IBB	SO	HBP	SH	SF	SB	CS	SB%	GDP	Avg	OBP	SLG
1996 St. Louis	NL	16	29	7	0	0	0	(0	0)	7	3	2	4	0	5	1	0	0	0	1	.00	1	.241	.353	.241
1997 St. Louis	NL	110	333	86	14	3	5	(2	3)	121	38	34	38	3	63	2	1	3	6	5	.55	8	.258	.335	.363
1998 Cincinnati	NL	144	536	166	48	4	14	(3	11)	258	81	83	47	4	94	2	0	5	2	4	.33	16	.310	.364	.481
1999 Cincinnati	NL	127	373	112	30	2	14	(9	5)	188	63	56	30	1	71	2	0	4	3	1	.75	11	.300	.352	.504
2000 Cincinnati	NL	152	548	166	37	6	18	(6	12)	269	68	88	36	6	80	3	1	5	0	3	.00	16	.303	.346	.491
2001 Cincinnati	NL	142	540	163	28	3	21	(8	13)	260	68	69	37	10	77	5	1	3	8	5	.62	22	.302	.350	.481
6 ML YEARS		691	2359	700	157	15	72	(28	44)	1103	321	332	192	24	390	15	3	20	19	19	.50	74	.297	.351	.468

Eric Young

Bats: Right Throws: Right Pos: 2B-147; PH/PR-3   Ht: 5'8" Wt: 180 Born: 5/18/67 Age: 35

Year Team	Lg	G	AB	H	2B	3B	HR	(Hm	Rd)	TB	R	RBI	TBB	IBB	SO	HBP	SH	SF	SB	CS	SB%	GDP	Avg	OBP	SLG
1992 Los Angeles	NL	49	132	34	1	0	1	(0	1)	38	9	11	8	0	9	0	4	0	6	1	.86	3	.258	.300	.288
1993 Colorado	NL	144	490	132	16	8	3	(3	0)	173	82	42	63	3	41	4	4	4	42	19	.69	9	.269	.355	.353
1994 Colorado	NL	90	228	62	13	1	7	(6	1)	98	37	30	38	1	17	2	5	2	18	7	.72	3	.272	.378	.430
1995 Colorado	NL	120	366	116	21	9	6	(5	1)	173	68	36	49	3	29	5	3	1	35	12	.74	4	.317	.404	.473
1996 Colorado	NL	141	568	184	23	4	8	(7	1)	239	113	74	47	1	31	21	2	5	53	19	.74	9	.324	.393	.421
1997 Col-LA	NL	155	622	174	33	8	8	(2	6)	247	106	61	71	1	54	9	10	6	45	14	.76	18	.280	.359	.397
1998 Los Angeles	NL	117	452	129	24	1	8	(7	1)	179	78	43	45	0	32	5	4	2	42	13	.76	4	.285	.355	.396
1999 Los Angeles	NL	119	456	128	24	2	2	(2	0)	162	73	41	63	0	26	5	6	4	51	22	.70	12	.281	.371	.355
2000 Chicago	NL	153	607	180	40	2	6	(5	1)	242	98	47	63	1	39	8	7	5	54	7	.89	12	.297	.367	.399

245

Year Team	Lg	G	AB	H	2B	3B	HR	(Hm	Rd)	TB	R	RBI	TBB	IBB	SO	HBP	SH	SF	SB	CS	SB%	GDP	Avg	OBP	SLG
						BATTING													**BASERUNNING**				**PERCENTAGES**		
2001 Chicago	NL	149	603	168	43	4	6	(4	2)	237	98	42	42	1	45	9	15	3	31	14	.69	15	.279	.333	.393
1997 Colorado	NL	118	468	132	29	6	6	(2	4)	191	78	45	57	0	37	5	8	5	32	12	.73	16	.282	.363	.408
Los Angeles	NL	37	154	42	4	2	2	(0	2)	56	28	16	14	1	17	4	2	1	13	2	.87	2	.273	.347	.364
10 ML YEARS		1237	4524	1307	238	39	55	(41	14)	1788	762	427	489	11	323	68	65	32	377	128	.75	89	.289	.365	.395

Kevin Young

Bats: Right **Throws:** Right **Pos:** 1B-137; PH/PR-9   **Ht:** 6'3" **Wt:** 222 **Born:** 6/16/69 **Age:** 33

Year Team	Lg	G	AB	H	2B	3B	HR	(Hm	Rd)	TB	R	RBI	TBB	IBB	SO	HBP	SH	SF	SB	CS	SB%	GDP	Avg	OBP	SLG
1992 Pittsburgh	NL	10	7	4	0	0	0	(0	0)	4	2	4	2	0	0	0	0	0	1	0	1.00	0	.571	.667	.571
1993 Pittsburgh	NL	141	449	106	24	3	6	(6	0)	154	38	47	36	3	82	9	5	9	2	2	.50	10	.236	.300	.343
1994 Pittsburgh	NL	59	122	25	7	2	1	(1	0)	39	15	11	8	2	34	1	2	1	0	2	.00	3	.205	.258	.320
1995 Pittsburgh	NL	56	181	42	9	0	6	(5	1)	69	13	22	8	0	53	2	1	3	1	3	.25	5	.232	.268	.381
1996 Kansas City	AL	55	132	32	6	0	8	(4	4)	62	20	23	11	0	32	0	0	0	3	3	.50	2	.242	.301	.470
1997 Pittsburgh	NL	97	333	100	18	3	18	(11	7)	178	59	74	16	1	89	4	1	8	11	2	.85	6	.300	.332	.535
1998 Pittsburgh	NL	159	592	160	40	2	27	(15	12)	285	88	108	44	1	127	11	0	9	15	7	.68	20	.270	.328	.481
1999 Pittsburgh	NL	156	584	174	41	6	26	(16	10)	305	103	106	75	5	124	12	0	4	22	10	.69	13	.298	.387	.522
2000 Pittsburgh	NL	132	496	128	27	0	20	(11	9)	215	77	88	32	1	96	8	0	5	8	3	.73	15	.258	.311	.433
2001 Pittsburgh	NL	142	449	104	33	0	14	(7	7)	179	53	65	42	3	119	11	0	5	15	11	.58	17	.232	.310	.399
10 ML YEARS		1007	3345	875	205	16	126	(76	50)	1490	468	548	274	16	756	58	9	44	78	43	.64	91	.262	.324	.445

Michael Young

Bats: Right **Throws:** Right **Pos:** 2B-104; PH/PR-4   **Ht:** 6'1" **Wt:** 190 **Born:** 10/19/76 **Age:** 25

Year Team	Lg	G	AB	H	2B	3B	HR	(Hm	Rd)	TB	R	RBI	TBB	IBB	SO	HBP	SH	SF	SB	CS	SB%	GDP	Avg	OBP	SLG
1997 St.Cathrnes	A-	74	276	85	18	3	9	—		136	49	48	33	1	59	7	0	3	9	5	.64	6	.308	.392	.493
1998 Hagerstown	A	140	522	147	33	5	16	—		238	86	87	55	1	96	7	7	1	16	8	.67	12	.282	.354	.456
1999 Dunedin	A+	129	495	155	36	3	5	—		212	86	83	61	2	78	4	1	5	30	6	.83	10	.313	.389	.428
2000 Tennessee	AA	91	345	95	24	5	6	—		147	51	47	36	1	72	1	4	6	16	5	.76	5	.275	.340	.426
Tulsa	AA	43	188	60	13	5	1	—		86	30	32	17	1	28	0	3	4	9	3	.75	4	.319	.368	.457
2001 Oklahoma	AAA	47	189	55	8	0	8	—		87	28	28	20	0	34	1	2	2	3	3	.50	6	.291	.358	.460
2000 Texas	AL	2	2	0	0	0	0	(0	0)	0	0	0	0	0	1	0	0	0	0	0	—	0	.000	.000	.000
2001 Texas	AL	106	386	96	18	4	11	(7	4)	155	57	49	26	0	91	3	9	5	3	1	.75	9	.249	.298	.402
2 ML YEARS		108	388	96	18	4	11	(7	4)	155	57	49	26	0	92	3	9	5	3	1	.75	9	.247	.296	.399

Carlos Zambrano

Pitches: Right **Bats:** Both **Pos:** RP-5; SP-1   **Ht:** 6'4" **Wt:** 220 **Born:** 6/1/81 **Age:** 21

Year Team	Lg	G	GS	CG	GF	IP	BFP	H	R	ER	HR	SH	SF	HB	TBB	IBB	SO	WP	Bk	W	L	Pct.	ShO	Sv-Op	Hld	ERA
1998 Cubs	R	14	2	0	4	40	177	39	17	14	0	0	0	0	25	3	36	3	1	0	1	.000	0	1--	—	3.15
1999 Lansing	A	27	24	2	2	153.1	663	150	87	71	9	5	4	10	62	1	98	10	2	13	7	.650	1	0--	—	4.17
2000 West Tenn	AA	9	9	0	0	60.1	241	39	14	9	2	1	0	3	21	0	43	4	0	3	1	.750	0	0--	—	1.34
Iowa	AAA	34	0	0	17	56.2	259	54	30	25	3	5	4	2	40	2	46	3	0	2	5	.286	0	6--	—	3.97
2001 Iowa	AAA	26	25	1	1	150.2	639	124	73	65	9	5	3	14	68	1	155	10	1	10	5	.667	0	0--	—	3.88
2001 Chicago	NL	6	1	0	1	7.2	42	11	13	13	2	1	1	1	8	0	4	1	0	1	2	.333	0	0-1	0	15.26

Victor Zambrano

Pitches: Right **Bats:** Right **Pos:** RP-36   **Ht:** 6'0" **Wt:** 190 **Born:** 8/6/75 **Age:** 26

Year Team	Lg	G	GS	CG	GF	IP	BFP	H	R	ER	HR	SH	SF	HB	TBB	IBB	SO	WP	Bk	W	L	Pct.	ShO	Sv-Op	Hld	ERA
1996 Devil Rays	R	1	0	0	0	3.1	16	4	4	3	0	0	0	0	0	0	6	0	0	0	0	—	0	0--	—	8.10
1997 Devil Rays	R	2	0	0	0	3	10	1	0	0	0	0	0	0	0	0	2	0	0	0	0	—	0	0--	—	0.00
Princeton	R+	20	0	0	6	29.2	126	18	13	6	1	0	0	4	9	1	36	2	1	0	2	.000	0	0--	—	1.82
1998 Chston-SC	A	48	2	0	15	77.1	330	72	32	29	5	5	0	12	20	1	89	7	1	6	4	.600	0	0--	—	3.38
1999 St. Pete	A+	7	0	0	1	9	43	10	6	4	1	0	1	1	5	0	15	1	0	2	0	.000	0	0--	—	4.00
Orlando	AA	40	4	0	12	82.1	379	92	55	42	5	1	2	9	38	2	81	6	1	7	2	.778	0	1--	—	4.59
2000 Durham	AAA	53	0	0	27	62.2	290	72	38	35	9	4	0	4	39	2	55	6	0	6	0	.000	0	0--	—	5.03
2001 Durham	AAA	29	0	0	27	30.1	126	26	10	7	2	0	1	1	12	1	29	4	0	1	2	.333	0	12--	—	2.08
2001 Tampa Bay	AL	36	0	0	19	51.1	212	38	21	18	6	2	0	3	18	0	58	4	0	6	2	.750	0	2-6	5	3.16

Gregg Zaun

Bats: Both **Throws:** Right **Pos:** C-35; PH/PR-6; DH-2   **Ht:** 5'10" **Wt:** 190 **Born:** 4/14/71 **Age:** 31

Year Team	Lg	G	AB	H	2B	3B	HR	(Hm	Rd)	TB	R	RBI	TBB	IBB	SO	HBP	SH	SF	SB	CS	SB%	GDP	Avg	OBP	SLG
2001 Royals *	R	6	18	1	0	0	0	—		1	3	1	7	0	5	0	0	0	0	0	—	1	.056	.320	.056
Omaha *	AAA	11	43	12	4	0	1	—		19	5	8	3	0	3	1	0	1	0	0	—	0	.279	.333	.442
1995 Baltimore	AL	40	104	27	5	0	3	(1	2)	41	18	14	16	0	14	0	2	0	1	1	.50	2	.260	.358	.394
1996 Bal-Fla		60	139	34	9	1	2	(1	1)	51	20	15	14	3	20	2	1	2	1	0	1.00	5	.245	.318	.367
1997 Florida	NL	58	143	43	10	2	2	(0	2)	63	21	20	26	4	18	2	1	0	1		1.00	3	.301	.415	.441
1998 Florida	NL	106	298	56	12	2	5	(2	3)	87	19	29	35	2	52	1	2	2	5	2	.71	7	.188	.274	.292
1999 Texas	AL	43	93	23	2	1	1	(0	1)	30	12	12	10	0	7	0	1	2	1		1.00	3	.247	.314	.323
2000 Kansas City	AL	83	234	64	11	0	7	(2	5)	96	36	33	43	3	34	3	0	2	7	3	.70	4	.274	.390	.410
2001 Kansas City	AL	39	125	40	9	0	6	(1	5)	67	15	18	12	0	16	0	0	1	1	2	.33	2	.320	.377	.536
1996 Baltimore	AL	50	108	25	8	1	1	(1	0)	38	16	13	11	2	15	2	0	2	0	0	—	2	.231	.309	.352
Florida	NL	10	31	9	1	0	1	(0	1)	13	4	2	3	1	5	0	1	0	1	0	1.00	1	.290	.353	.419
7 ML YEARS		429	1136	287	58	6	26	(7	19)	435	141	141	156	12	161	8	7	9	17	8	.68	25	.253	.345	.383

Todd Zeile

Bats: Right **Throws:** Right **Pos:** 1B-149; PH/PR-5   **Ht:** 6'1" **Wt:** 200 **Born:** 9/9/65 **Age:** 36

												BATTING								BASERUNNING				PERCENTAGES		
Year Team	Lg	G	AB	H	2B	3B	HR	(Hm	Rd)	TB	R	RBI	TBB	IBB	SO	HBP	SH	SF	SB	CS	SB%	GDP	Avg	OBP	SLG
1989 St. Louis	NL	28	82	21	3	1	1	(0	1)	29	7	8	9	1	14	0	1	1	0	0	—	1	.256	.326	.354
1990 St. Louis	NL	144	495	121	25	3	15	(8	7)	197	62	57	67	3	77	2	0	6	2	4	.33	11	.244	.333	.398
1991 St. Louis	NL	155	565	158	36	3	11	(7	4)	233	76	81	62	3	94	5	0	6	17	11	.61	15	.280	.353	.412
1992 St. Louis	NL	126	439	113	18	4	7	(4	3)	160	51	48	68	4	70	0	0	7	7	10	.41	11	.257	.352	.364
1993 St. Louis	NL	157	571	158	36	1	17	(8	9)	247	82	103	70	5	76	0	0	6	5	4	.56	15	.277	.352	.433
1994 St. Louis	NL	113	415	111	25	1	19	(9	10)	195	62	75	52	3	56	3	0	7	1	3	.25	13	.267	.348	.470
1995 StL-ChC	NL	113	426	105	22	0	14	(8	6)	169	50	52	34	1	76	4	4	5	1	0	1.00	13	.246	.305	.397
1996 Phi-Bal		163	617	162	32	0	25	(10	15)	269	78	99	82	4	104	1	0	4	1	1	.50	18	.263	.348	.436
1997 Los Angeles	NL	160	575	154	17	0	31	(17	14)	264	89	90	85	7	112	6	0	6	8	7	.53	18	.268	.365	.459
1998 LA-Fla-Tex		158	572	155	32	3	19	(7	12)	250	85	94	69	2	90	4	1	7	4	4	.50	12	.271	.350	.437
1999 Texas	AL	156	588	172	41	1	24	(13	11)	287	80	98	56	3	94	4	1	7	1	2	.33	20	.293	.354	.488
2000 New York	NL	153	544	146	36	3	22	(8	14)	254	67	79	74	4	85	2	0	3	3	4	.43	15	.268	.356	.467
2001 New York	NL	151	531	141	25	1	10	(4	6)	198	66	62	73	3	102	6	0	2	1	0	1.00	15	.266	.359	.373
1995 St. Louis	NL	34	127	37	6	0	5	(2	3)	58	16	22	18	1	23	1	0	2	1	0	1.00	2	.291	.378	.457
Chicago	NL	79	299	68	16	0	9	(6	3)	111	34	30	16	0	53	3	4	3	0	0	—	11	.227	.271	.371
1996 Philadelphia	NL	134	500	134	24	0	20	(9	11)	218	61	80	67	4	88	1	0	4	1	1	.50	16	.268	.353	.436
Baltimore	AL	29	117	28	8	0	5	(1	4)	51	17	19	15	0	16	0	0	0	0	0	—	2	.239	.326	.436
1998 Los Angeles	NL	40	158	40	6	1	7	(1	6)	69	22	27	10	0	24	1	0	1	1	1	.50	5	.253	.300	.437
Florida	NL	66	234	68	12	1	6	(2	4)	100	37	39	31	2	34	2	0	3	2	3	.40	4	.291	.374	.427
Texas	AL	52	180	47	14	1	6	(4	2)	81	26	28	28	0	32	1	1	3	1	0	1.00	3	.261	.358	.450
13 ML YEARS		1777	6420	1717	348	21	215	(103	112)	2752	855	946	801	43	1050	37	7	67	51	50	.50	177	.267	.349	.429

Chad Zerbe

Pitches: Left **Bats:** Left **Pos:** RP-26; SP-1   **Ht:** 6'0" **Wt:** 190 **Born:** 4/27/72 **Age:** 30

		HOW MUCH HE PITCHED						WHAT HE GAVE UP											THE RESULTS						
Year Team	Lg	G	GS	CG	GF	IP	BFP	H	R	ER	HR	SH	SF	HB	TBB	IBB	SO	WP	Bk	W	L	Pct.	ShO	Sv-Op	Hld	ERA
1991 Dodgers	R	16	1	0	4	32.2	145	31	19	8	1	0	3	1	15	0	23	6	3	0	2	.000	0	0--	—	2.20
1992 Great Falls	R+	15	15	1	0	92.1	378	75	27	22	2	1	1	5	26	0	70	5	0	8	3	.727	1	0--	—	2.14
1993 Bakersfield	A+	14	12	1	1	67	326	83	60	44	2	1	2	2	47	0	41	2	2	0	10	.000	0	0--	—	5.91
Vero Beach	A+	10	0	0	1	12.1	64	12	10	9	0	0	2	2	13	1	11	3	1	1	0	1.000	0	0--	—	6.57
1994 Vero Beach	A+	18	18	1	0	98.1	412	88	50	37	6	0	4	2	32	0	68	6	0	5	5	.500	0	0--	—	3.39
1995 San Berndno	A+	28	27	1	0	163.1	718	168	103	83	15	10	5	3	64	0	94	4	0	11	7	.611	0	0--	—	4.57
1996 San Antonio	AA	17	11	1	1	86	384	98	52	43	9	5	2	2	37	0	38	4	0	4	6	.400	0	1--	—	4.50
1997 High Desert	A+	9	8	0	0	36.1	192	61	49	30	7	0	3	1	15	0	26	1	0	1	6	.143	0	0--	—	7.43
Sonoma Cty	IND	14	13	2	0	89.2	417	117	70	54	7	5	4	3	36	1	52	1	0	4	5	.444	0	0--	—	5.42
1998 San Jose	A+	23	0	0	12	37.2	159	37	16	14	3	0	1	3	12	0	28	1	0	2	0	1.000	0	1--	—	3.35
1999 Bakersfield	A+	21	21	0	0	126	533	124	66	51	4	0	5	2	33	0	81	6	0	7	7	.500	0	0--	—	3.64
Shreveport	AA	7	6	0	1	41.1	164	32	13	9	2	1	2	3	10	0	16	0	1	1	3	.250	0	0--	—	1.96
2000 Shreveport	AA	9	9	0	0	38.2	156	37	11	10	1	1	1	1	9	0	34	0	0	2	1	.667	0	0--	—	2.33
Fresno	AAA	17	11	0	1	81.1	347	94	46	39	5	3	2	5	17	0	41	1	1	7	3	.700	0	0--	—	4.32
2001 Fresno	AAA	17	0	0	12	25.1	114	28	13	10	2	1	0	1	9	0	17	0	0	3	4	.429	0	5--	—	3.55
2000 San Francisco	NL	4	0	0	2	6	24	6	3	3	1	1	0	0	1	0	5	0	0	0	0	—	0	0-0	0	4.50
2001 San Francisco	NL	27	1	0	9	39	162	41	21	17	3	3	2	1	10	0	22	2	0	3	0	1.000	0	0-0	0	3.92
2 ML YEARS		31	1	0	11	45	186	47	24	20	4	4	2	1	11	0	27	2	0	3	0	1.000	0	0-0	0	4.00

Jeff Zimmerman

Pitches: Right **Bats:** Right **Pos:** RP-66   **Ht:** 6'1" **Wt:** 200 **Born:** 8/9/72 **Age:** 29

		HOW MUCH HE PITCHED						WHAT HE GAVE UP											THE RESULTS						
Year Team	Lg	G	GS	CG	GF	IP	BFP	H	R	ER	HR	SH	SF	HB	TBB	IBB	SO	WP	Bk	W	L	Pct.	ShO	Sv-Op	Hld	ERA
1999 Texas	AL	65	0	0	14	87.2	336	50	24	23	9	3	6	2	23	1	67	2	0	9	3	.750	0	3-7	24	2.36
2000 Texas	AL	65	0	0	17	69.2	323	80	45	41	10	2	5	2	34	3	74	3	3	5	4	.444	0	1-3	21	5.30
2001 Texas	AL	66	0	0	53	71.1	273	48	19	19	10	2	1	4	16	1	72	0	0	4	4	.500	0	28-31	5	2.40
3 ML YEARS		196	0	0	84	228.2	932	178	88	83	29	7	12	8	73	5	213	5	3	17	12	.586	0	32-41	50	3.27

Barry Zito

Pitches: Left **Bats:** Left **Pos:** SP-35   **Ht:** 6'4" **Wt:** 205 **Born:** 5/13/78 **Age:** 24

		HOW MUCH HE PITCHED						WHAT HE GAVE UP											THE RESULTS						
Year Team	Lg	G	GS	CG	GF	IP	BFP	H	R	ER	HR	SH	SF	HB	TBB	IBB	SO	WP	Bk	W	L	Pct.	ShO	Sv-Op	Hld	ERA
1999 Visalia	A+	8	8	0	0	40.1	157	21	13	11	3	0	1	0	22	0	62	3	0	3	0	1.000	0	0--	—	2.45
Midland	AA	4	4	0	0	22	99	22	15	12	1	0	0	1	11	0	29	2	0	2	1	.667	0	0--	—	4.91
Vancouver	AAA	1	1	0	0	6	24	5	1	1	0	0	0	0	2	0	6	2	0	1	0	1.000	0	0--	—	1.50
2000 Sacramento	AAA	18	18	0	0	101.2	437	88	44	36	4	5	3	2	45	0	91	5	0	8	5	.615	0	0--	—	3.19
2000 Oakland	AL	14	14	1	0	92.2	376	64	30	28	6	1	0	2	45	2	78	2	0	7	4	.636	1	0-0	0	2.72
2001 Oakland	AL	35	35	3	0	214.1	902	184	92	83	18	5	4	13	80	0	205	6	1	17	8	.680	2	0-0	0	3.49
2 ML YEARS		49	49	4	0	307	1278	248	122	111	24	6	4	15	125	2	283	8	1	24	12	.667	3	0-0	0	3.25

Julio Zuleta

Bats: Right **Throws:** Right **Pos:** 1B-35; PH/PR-24 **Ht:** 6'5" **Wt:** 235 **Born:** 3/28/75 **Age:** 27

Year Team	Lg	G	AB	H	2B	3B	HR	(Hm	Rd)	TB	R	RBI	TBB	IBB	SO	HBP	SH	SF	SB	CS	SB%	GDP	Avg	OBP	SLG
1993 Cubs	R	17	53	13	0	1	0	—	—	15	3	6	3	0	12	3	0	0	0	0	—	3	.245	.322	.283
1994 Huntington	R+	6	15	1	0	0	0	—	—	1	0	2	4	0	4	0	0	0	0	0	—	1	.067	.263	.067
Cubs	R	30	100	31	1	0	0	—	—	32	11	8	8	0	18	2	0	0	5	1	.83	0	.310	.373	.320
1995 Williamsprt	A-	30	75	13	3	1	0	—	—	18	9	6	11	1	12	2	0	0	0	1	.00	4	.173	.295	.240
1996 Williamsprt	A-	62	221	57	12	2	1	—	—	76	35	29	19	2	36	8	0	2	7	4	.64	8	.258	.336	.344
1997 Rockford	A	119	430	124	30	5	6	—	—	182	59	77	35	6	88	12	3	8	5	5	.50	7	.288	.353	.423
1998 Daytona	A+	94	366	126	25	1	16	—	—	201	69	86	35	1	59	15	1	5	6	3	.67	12	.344	.418	.549
West Tenn	AA	40	139	41	9	0	2	—	—	56	18	20	10	0	30	3	0	3	0	1	.00	3	.295	.348	.403
1999 West Tenn	AA	133	482	142	37	4	21	—	—	250	75	97	35	6	122	20	0	8	4	3	.57	11	.295	.361	.519
2000 Iowa	AAA	107	392	122	25	1	26	—	—	227	76	94	31	2	77	9	0	4	5	4	.56	14	.311	.372	.579
2001 Iowa	AAA	37	146	45	13	0	7	—	—	79	18	29	7	0	33	3	0	2	3	1	.75	4	.308	.348	.541
2000 Chicago	NL	30	68	20	8	0	3	(1	2)	37	13	12	2	0	19	3	0	0	0	1	.00	2	.294	.342	.544
2001 Chicago	NL	49	106	23	3	0	6	(5	1)	44	11	24	8	1	32	3	0	1	0	1	.00	3	.217	.288	.415
2 ML YEARS		79	174	43	11	0	9	(6	3)	81	24	36	10	1	51	6	0	1	0	2	.00	5	.247	.309	.466

2001 Team Statistics

All the statistics you need to know about your favorite team are here. Final standings, record breakdowns, team batting, pitching and fielding all can be found in this section. Also included here are teams' records against the other league. American League teams have a split vs. NL teams and National League teams have a split vs. AL teams.

Keep in mind that hitting totals in each league will not necessarily mirror hitting totals allowed by that league's pitchers. For example, home runs hit in the American League may not equal the home runs allowed by American League pitchers. The reason is interleague play.

Some of the abbreviations need an explanation. They are:

LD1st = Last date team was in first place; **1st** = number of days team spent in first place (including days tied for the lead); **Lead** = largest first-place lead, if any, during the season; **LHS** = record in games started by opposing lefthanded pitchers; **RHS** = record in games started by opposing righthanded pitchers; **1-R** = record in games decided by one run; **5+R** = record in games decided by five or more runs.

Estadísticas de Equipos del 2001

Todas las estadísticas que necesitas saber de tu equipo favorito están aquí: posición final, desglose final, bateo de equipo, pitcheo y fildeo. Marcas contra cada liga y contra cada equipo.

Percátense que los totales de bateo en cada liga no van a reflejar totales permitidos por los lanzadores de la liga. Por ejemplo, cuadrangulares bateados por la Liga Americana no van a igualar los cuadrangulares permitidos por los lanzadores de la Liga Americana. La razón es que los equipos tienen juegos interliga.

Abreviaciones necesarias:

* represents playoff wild-card berth. = * representa que pasó a la liguilla como el wild-card. **1-R** = Marca en juegos decidido por una carrera; **1st** = días en primer lugar (incluyendo días empatados por el liderato); **5+R** = Marca en juegos decididos por cinco o más carreras; **All-Star** = Pausa del Juego de Estrellas; **At**=En donde; **Central** = División Central; **Conditions**= Condiciones; **Day** = Jugando de Día; **East** = División Este; **GB** = Juegos Detrás; **Grass** = Jugando en grama natural **Home** = Como Local; **LD1st** = Ultima fecha en primer lugar; **Lead** = Ventaja más grande como líder durante la temporada; **LHS** = Marca en juegos confrontando un abridor zurdo; **Monthly** = Desglose mensual; **Night** = Jugando de Noche; **Overall** = Total; **Pct** = Porcentaje de Ganados; **Post** = Después del Juego de Estrellas; **Pre** = Antes del Juego de Estrellas; **RHS** = Marca en juegos confrontando un abridor derecho; **Road** = Como Visitante; **Team vs. Team Breakdown** = Desglose contra cada equipo; **Turf** = Jugando en grama artificial; **W-L** = Ganados-Perdidos; **XInn** = Entradas Extras; **West** = División Oeste.

2001 American League Final Standings

Overall

EAST							CENTRAL							WEST						
Team	W-L	Pct	GB	LD1st	1st	Lead	Team	W-L	Pct	GB	LD1st	1st	Lead	Team	W-L	Pct	GB	LD1st	1st	Lead
New York Yankees	95-65	.594	—	10/7	112	16.5	Cleveland Indians	91-71	.562	—	10/7	92	8.5	Seattle Mariners	116-46	.716	—	10/7	190	21
Boston Red Sox	82-79	.509	13.5	7/21	70	4	Minnesota Twins	85-77	.525	6	8/11	106	5	Oakland Athletics*	102-60	.630	14	4/3	2	0
Toronto Blue Jays	80-82	.494	16	5/7	24	1.5	Chicago White Sox	83-79	.512	8	4/3	3	0.5	Anaheim Angels	75-87	.463	41	4/1	1	0
Baltimore Orioles	63-98	.391	32.5	4/3	2	0	Detroit Tigers	66-96	.407	25	4/8	2	0	Texas Rangers	73-89	.451	43	4/4	2	0
Tampa Bay Devil Rays	62-100	.383	34	4/3	1	0	Kansas City Royals	65-97	.401	26	4/1	1	0							

* represents playoff wild-card berth. Clinch Dates: Seattle 9/19, Oakland 9/23, New York 9/25, Cleveland 9/30.

East Division

Team	AT		VERSUS				LHS	RHS	CONDITIONS					RUNS		MONTHLY						ALL-STAR	
	Home	Road	East	Cent	West	NL	LHS	RHS	Grass	Turf	Day	Night	XInn	1-R	5+R	Apr	May	June	July	Aug	Sep	Pre	Post
New York	51-28	44-37	50-24	23-13	12-20	10-8	19-17	76-48	81-54	14-11	38-22	57-43	8-8	30-18	26-21	14-12	15-10	16-11	19-9	15-14	16-9	52-34	43-31
Boston	41-40	41-39	41-34	16-20	15-17	10-8	15-23	67-56	64-72	18-7	24-21	58-58	6-8	19-23	24-24	16-9	13-17	14-12	11-17	11-17	17-7	51-36	31-43
Toronto	40-42	40-40	37-39	19-13	16-20	8-10	16-20	64-62	29-31	51-51	25-32	55-50	10-6	28-21	27-22	16-9	10-18	12-15	11-16	16-12	15-12	42-46	38-36
Baltimore	30-50	33-48	31-44	16-16	10-26	6-12	13-27	50-71	52-84	11-14	17-30	46-68	5-6	16-27	17-30	12-14	12-14	14-14	6-21	11-16	8-19	40-47	23-51
Tampa Bay	37-44	25-56	29-47	13-19	10-26	10-8	13-23	49-77	18-48	44-52	24-36	38-64	5-5	17-19	14-35	8-18	7-20	9-18	11-15	13-16	14-13	27-61	35-39

Central Division

Team	AT		VERSUS				LHS	RHS	CONDITIONS					RUNS		MONTHLY						ALL-STAR	
	Home	Road	East	Cent	West	NL	LHS	RHS	Grass	Turf	Day	Night	XInn	1-R	5+R	Apr	May	June	July	Aug	Sep	Pre	Post
Cleveland	44-36	47-35	22-14	47-29	15-17	7-11	20-20	71-51	80-65	11-6	23-25	68-46	9-6	25-18	27-21	14-9	19-8	12-15	15-13	16-13	15-13	49-36	42-35
Minnesota	47-34	38-43	13-19	47-29	16-20	9-9	18-21	67-56	37-37	48-40	27-27	58-50	8-7	25-19	18-19	18-6	16-11	14-14	12-15	11-18	14-13	55-32	30-45
Chicago	46-35	37-44	16-16	42-34	13-23	12-6	17-18	66-61	78-69	5-10	26-23	57-56	7-4	22-22	20-21	8-15	12-15	18-9	13-14	17-12	15-14	41-44	42-35
Detroit	37-44	29-52	17-19	24-52	15-17	10-8	19-27	47-69	62-85	4-11	19-36	47-60	3-7	14-21	16-33	8-15	14-13	10-17	14-13	9-20	11-18	36-48	30-48
Kansas City	35-46	30-51	13-19	30-46	14-22	8-10	14-34	51-63	59-86	6-11	19-30	46-67	6-7	11-24	19-32	10-15	10-18	13-13	9-18	12-17	11-16	34-53	31-44

West Division

Team	AT		VERSUS				LHS	RHS	CONDITIONS					RUNS		MONTHLY						ALL-STAR	
	Home	Road	East	Cent	West	NL	LHS	RHS	Grass	Turf	Day	Night	XInn	1-R	5+R	Apr	May	June	July	Aug	Sep	Pre	Post
Seattle	57-24	59-22	33-12	31-10	40-18	12-6	31-14	85-32	106-44	10-2	37-13	79-33	9-4	26-12	34-10	20-5	20-7	18-9	18-9	20-9	20-7	63-24	53-22
Oakland	53-28	49-32	31-14	27-14	32-26	12-6	34-22	68-38	93-54	9-6	36-25	66-35	7-7	21-19	31-9	8-17	18-9	12-15	19-8	22-7	23-4	44-43	58-17
Anaheim	39-42	36-45	24-17	24-21	17-41	10-8	22-27	53-60	68-82	7-5	20-24	55-63	7-8	24-24	19-16	10-15	14-13	14-13	16-11	15-14	6-21	42-45	33-42
Texas	41-41	32-48	21-20	17-28	27-31	8-10	13-28	60-61	66-81	7-8	18-19	55-70	5-8	19-22	23-29	11-14	8-19	12-15	17-10	13-16	12-15	35-52	38-37

Team vs. Team Breakdown

	NYY	Bos	Tor	Bal	TB	Cle	Min	CWS	Det	KC	Sea	Oak	Ana	Tex
New York Yankees	—	13	11	13	13	5	2	5	5	6	3	3	3	3
Boston Red Sox	5	—	12	10	14	3	3	3	4	3	4	3	5	5
Toronto Blue Jays	8	7	—	12	10	4	5	3	4	3	3	3	4	6
Baltimore Orioles	5	9	7	—	10	1	3	3	4	5	1	2	5	2
Tampa Bay Devil Rays	6	5	9	9	—	1	6	2	2	2	2	2	2	4
Cleveland Indians	4	6	2	5	5	—	14	9	13	11	2	4	4	5
Minnesota Twins	4	3	2	3	1	5	—	14	15	13	1	5	6	4
Chicago White Sox	1	3	3	4	5	10	5	—	13	14	2	1	3	7
Detroit Tigers	4	5	2	2	4	6	4	6	—	8	2	1	4	8
Kansas City Royals	0	3	4	2	4	8	6	5	11	—	3	3	4	4
Seattle Mariners	6	6	6	8	7	5	8	7	5	6	—	10	15	15
Oakland Athletics	6	5	6	7	7	3	4	8	6	9	9	—	14	9
Anaheim Angels	4	4	5	4	7	5	3	6	5	5	4	6	—	7
Texas Rangers	4	2	3	7	5	4	5	2	1	5	5	10	12	—

(read wins across and losses down)

2001 National League Final Standings

Overall

EAST Team	W-L	Pct	GB	LD1st	1st	Lead	CENTRAL Team	W-L	Pct	GB	LD1st	1st	Lead	WEST Team	W-L	Pct	GB	LD1st	1st	Lead
Atlanta Braves	88-74	.543	—	10/7	85	3.5	Houston Astros	93-69	.574	—	10/7	67	5.5	Arizona Diamondbacks	92-70	.568	—	10/7	129	6
Philadelphia Phillies	86-76	.531	2	9/24	115	8	St. Louis Cardinals	93-69	.574	—	10/7	23	1.5	San Francisco Giants	90-72	.556	2	5/15	24	1.5
New York Mets	82-80	.506	6	4/1	1	0	Chicago Cubs	88-74	.543	5	8/17	112	6	Los Angeles Dodgers	86-76	.531	6	8/10	43	2
Florida Marlins	76-86	.469	12	4/1	1	0	Milwaukee Brewers	68-94	.420	25	4/1	1	0	San Diego Padres	79-83	.488	13	5/25	4	1
Montreal Expos	68-94	.420	20	4/10	7	1	Cincinnati Reds	66-96	.407	27	5/1	3	0	Colorado Rockies	73-89	.451	19	4/26	10	1
							Pittsburgh Pirates	62-100	.383	31	4/2	2	0							

* represents playoff wild-card berth. Clinch Dates: Arizona 10/5, Atlanta 10/5, Houston 10/7, St. Louis 10/7.

East Division

Team	AT Home	Road	VERSUS East	Cent	West	AL	LHS	RHS	CONDITIONS Grass	Turf	Day	Night	XInn	RUNS 1-R	5+R	MONTHLY Apr	May	June	July	Aug	Sep	ALL-STAR Pre	Post
Atlanta	40-41	48-33	42-34	22-14	15-17	9-9	18-9	70-65	75-64	13-10	29-17	59-57	8-8	19-23	25-21	12-14	14-12	19-9	15-11	12-16	16-12	49-38	39-36
Philadelphia	47-34	39-42	41-35	19-17	19-13	7-11	17-18	69-58	34-34	52-42	25-28	61-48	7-8	27-22	21-17	14-10	20-8	12-16	11-15	14-14	15-13	50-37	36-39
New York	44-37	38-43	43-33	15-21	14-18	10-8	15-17	67-63	70-71	12-9	22-34	60-46	10-10	30-20	17-26	10-15	12-17	13-15	14-11	15-13	18-9	38-51	44-29
Florida	46-34	30-52	34-42	19-17	11-21	12-6	15-23	61-63	67-70	9-16	23-20	53-66	5-11	19-29	28-26	10-14	15-13	16-13	12-12	9-20	14-14	43-45	33-41
Montreal	34-47	34-47	30-46	14-22	16-16	8-10	21-25	47-69	29-40	39-54	24-23	44-71	5-4	13-15	20-32	11-14	10-19	12-15	12-14	13-14	10-18	37-51	31-43

Central Division

Team	AT Home	Road	VERSUS East	Cent	West	AL	LHS	RHS	CONDITIONS Grass	Turf	Day	Night	XInn	RUNS 1-R	5+R	MONTHLY Apr	May	June	July	Aug	Sep	ALL-STAR Pre	Post
Houston	44-37	49-32	18-12	50-34	16-17	9-6	22-12	71-57	87-66	6-3	24-21	69-48	9-7	29-23	28-20	12-12	14-13	15-12	17-11	21-7	14-14	48-38	45-31
St. Louis	54-28	39-41	19-11	49-35	17-16	8-7	16-15	77-54	90-66	3-3	36-23	57-46	2-7	15-21	32-20	12-12	17-11	11-16	13-12	20-10	20-8	43-43	50-26
Chicago	48-33	40-41	16-14	48-36	15-18	9-6	14-22	74-52	84-72	4-2	50-43	38-31	3-6	26-24	24-17	15-9	16-11	15-13	16-10	13-16	13-15	51-35	37-39
Milwaukee	36-45	32-49	15-15	37-47	11-22	5-10	14-20	54-74	64-92	4-2	28-30	40-64	5-7	13-25	25-28	13-11	15-13	11-15	6-20	14-15	9-20	42-44	26-50
Cincinnati	27-54	39-42	16-14	32-52	14-19	4-11	14-23	52-73	62-91	4-5	21-33	45-63	7-5	20-22	18-29	14-10	6-22	12-15	10-16	12-17	12-16	33-54	33-42
Pittsburgh	38-43	24-57	7-23	36-48	11-22	8-7	12-20	50-80	61-92	1-8	18-29	44-71	4-4	22-20	10-36	9-14	8-20	12-15	12-15	8-20	13-16	33-53	29-47

West Division

Team	AT Home	Road	VERSUS East	Cent	West	AL	LHS	RHS	CONDITIONS Grass	Turf	Day	Night	XInn	RUNS 1-R	5+R	MONTHLY Apr	May	June	July	Aug	Sep	ALL-STAR Pre	Post
Arizona	48-33	44-37	18-14	22-17	45-37	7-8	25-16	67-54	88-67	4-3	26-22	66-48	9-6	23-25	34-14	13-12	18-10	18-9	11-15	18-11	14-13	51-36	41-34
San Francisco	49-32	41-40	18-14	21-18	41-35	10-5	21-13	69-59	87-69	3-3	30-26	60-46	6-9	28-22	26-22	12-12	14-15	17-10	15-12	16-12	16-11	46-42	44-30
Los Angeles	44-37	42-39	17-15	23-16	40-36	6-9	25-18	61-58	85-71	1-5	22-23	64-53	7-6	29-29	18-19	15-10	15-13	13-14	18-9	12-16	13-14	48-40	38-36
San Diego	35-46	44-37	17-15	24-15	32-44	6-9	18-26	61-57	76-80	3-3	29-23	50-60	8-1	24-15	23-23	10-15	17-11	10-18	14-11	16-13	12-15	41-47	38-36
Colorado	41-40	32-49	15-17	24-18	32-44	2-10	15-19	58-70	70-85	3-4	28-30	45-59	5-5	18-28	33-25	13-11	13-16	12-15	7-19	14-13	14-15	39-48	34-41

Team vs. Team Breakdown

	Atl	Phi	NYM	Fla	Mon	Hou	StL	ChC	Mil	Cin	Pit	Ari	SF	LA	SD	Col
Atlanta Braves	—	10	10	9	13	3	3	4	3	4	5	2	4	2	3	4
Philadelphia Phillies	9	—	8	14	10	3	2	2	3	4	5	4	3	3	5	4
New York Mets	9	11	—	12	11	3	1	2	3	2	4	3	3	4	1	3
Florida Marlins	10	5	7	—	12	3	3	3	4	2	4	2	2	2	3	2
Montreal Expos	6	9	8	7	—	0	2	3	2	2	5	2	4	3		4
Houston Astros	3	3	3	3	6	—	9	9	12	11	9	4	3	2	3	4
St. Louis Cardinals	3	4	5	3	4	7	—	8	10	10	14	4	2	3	5	3
Chicago Cubs	2	4	4	3	3	8	9	—	8	13	10	3	3	4	2	3
Milwaukee Brewers	3	3	3	2	4	5	7	9	—	10	6	3	5	1	1	1
Cincinnati Reds	2	2	4	4	4	6	7	4	6	—	9	1	4	4	2	3
Pittsburgh Pirates	1	1	2	2	1	8	3	6	11	8	—	2	1	2	2	4
Arizona Diamondbacks	5	3	3	4	3	2	2	6	3	5	4	—	10	10	12	13
San Francisco Giants	2	3	4	4	5	3	4	3	4	2	5	9	—	8	14	10
Los Angeles Dodgers	5	3	2	5	2	4	3	2	5	2	7	9	11	—	9	11
San Diego Padres	3	2	5	4	3	6	1	4	5	4	4	7	5	10	—	10
Colorado Rockies	2	2	4	4	3	2	6	3	5	6	2	6	9	8	9	—

(read wins across and losses down)

American League Batting

Tm	G	AB	H	2B	3B	HR	(Hm	Rd)	TB	R	RBI	TBB	IBB	SO	HBP	SH	SF	ShO	SB	CS	SB%	GDP	LOB	Avg	OBP	SLG
Sea	162	5680	1637	310	38	169	(79	90)	2530	927	881	614	54	989	62	48	70	4	174	42	.81	112	1257	.288	.360	.445
Cle	162	5600	1559	294	37	212	(116	96)	2563	897	868	577	32	1076	69	49	62	7	79	41	.66	126	1136	.278	.350	.458
Tex	162	5685	1566	326	23	246	(124	122)	2676	890	844	548	27	1093	75	25	55	1	97	32	.75	131	1161	.275	.344	.471
Oak	162	5573	1469	334	22	199	(101	98)	2444	884	835	640	57	1021	88	25	59	3	68	29	.70	131	1171	.264	.345	.439
NYY	161	5577	1488	289	20	203	(116	87)	2426	804	774	519	38	1035	64	30	43	5	161	53	.75	119	1123	.267	.334	.435
CWS	162	5464	1463	300	29	214	(114	100)	2463	798	770	520	31	998	52	63	51	4	123	59	.68	128	1054	.268	.334	.451
Bos	161	5605	1493	316	29	198	(97	101)	2461	772	739	520	50	1131	70	28	41	6	46	35	.57	132	1161	.266	.334	.439
Min	162	5560	1514	328	38	164	(76	88)	2410	771	717	495	42	1083	64	25	38	5	146	67	.69	124	1102	.272	.337	.433
Tor	162	5663	1489	287	36	195	(94	101)	2433	767	728	470	47	1094	74	34	43	9	156	55	.74	111	1124	.263	.325	.430
KC	162	5643	1503	277	37	152	(75	77)	2310	729	691	406	31	898	44	36	47	6	100	42	.70	134	1086	.266	.318	.409
Det	162	5537	1439	291	60	139	(58	81)	2267	724	691	466	26	972	51	41	49	6	133	61	.69	120	1093	.260	.320	.409
Ana	162	5551	1447	275	26	158	(86	72)	2248	691	662	494	34	1001	77	46	53	12	116	52	.69	109	1203	.261	.327	.405
Bal	162	5560	1359	262	24	136	(58	78)	2077	687	663	514	26	989	77	38	49	14	133	53	.72	121	1106	.248	.319	.380
TB	162	5524	1426	311	21	121	(60	61)	2142	672	645	456	24	1116	54	45	25	12	115	52	.69	130	1104	.258	.320	.388
AL	1133	78134	20852	4200	440	2506	(1254	1252)	33450	11013	10508	7239	519	14496	921	533	685	94	1647	673	.71	1728	15881	.267	.334	.428

American League Pitching

Tm	G	CG	Rel	IP	BFP	H	R	ER	HR	SH	SF	HB	TBB	IBB	SO	WP	Bk	W	L	Pct.	ShO	Sv-Op	Hld	OAvg	OOBP	OSLG	ERA
Sea	162	8	391	1465	6096	1293	627	576	160	33	44	64	465	28	1051	40	1	116	46	.716	14	56-73	95	.236	.301	.378	3.54
Oak	162	13	416	1463.1	6115	1384	645	583	153	45	33	46	440	49	1117	42	3	102	60	.630	9	44-67	84	.249	.308	.380	3.59
NYY	161	7	361	1451.1	6174	1429	713	649	158	37	47	55	465	29	1266	54	6	95	65	.594	9	57-70	51	.257	.318	.398	4.02
Ana	162	6	384	1437.2	6195	1452	730	671	168	37	39	64	525	47	947	46	2	75	87	.463	1	43-60	50	.263	.331	.412	4.20
Bos	161	3	424	1448	6272	1412	745	667	146	39	45	93	544	50	1259	54	7	82	79	.509	8	48-70	57	.254	.329	.393	4.15
Tor	162	7	471	1462.2	6305	1553	753	696	165	47	43	76	490	60	1041	33	8	80	82	.494	10	41-66	73	.275	.339	.435	4.28
Min	162	12	402	1441.1	6187	1494	766	722	192	55	55	56	445	16	965	58	2	85	77	.525	8	45-64	49	.268	.325	.437	4.51
CWS	162	8	406	1433.1	6200	1465	795	725	181	48	56	88	500	38	921	57	5	83	79	.512	7	51-71	57	.266	.334	.427	4.55
Cle	162	3	483	1446.2	6312	1512	821	746	148	48	50	49	573	44	1218	58	11	91	71	.562	4	42-57	78	.270	.341	.417	4.64
Bal	162	10	392	1432.1	6273	1504	829	744	194	31	41	74	528	28	938	37	5	63	98	.391	6	31-50	65	.269	.337	.439	4.67
KC	162	5	396	1440	6289	1537	858	779	209	33	51	61	576	26	911	73	2	65	97	.401	1	30-50	52	.276	.348	.450	4.87
Det	162	16	388	1429.1	6361	1624	876	795	180	51	52	73	553	56	859	40	4	66	96	.407	2	34-56	48	.289	.357	.461	5.01
TB	162	1	370	1423.2	6288	1513	887	781	207	36	64	75	569	21	1030	75	7	62	100	.383	6	30-52	46	.273	.345	.452	4.94
Tex	162	4	410	1438.1	6469	1670	968	913	222	30	73	63	596	33	951	70	9	73	89	.451	3	37-56	56	.293	.362	.494	5.71
AL	1133	103	5694	20213	87536	20842	11013	10047	2483	570	693	937	7269	525	14474	737	72	1138	1126	.503	89	589-862	861	.267	.334	.427	4.47

American League Fielding

Team	G	PO	Ast	OFAst	E	(Throw	Field)	TC	DP	GDP Opp	GDP	GDP%	PB	OSB	OCS	OSB%	CPkof	PPkof	AVG
Seattle	162	4395	1534	24	83	(33	50)	6012	137	168	115	.685	6	73	29	.72	0	2	.986
Toronto	162	4388	1831	36	97	(45	52)	6316	184	262	159	.607	10	112	47	.70	1	7	.985
Anaheim	162	4313	1690	37	103	(42	61)	6106	142	210	112	.533	16	109	59	.65	1	8	.983
Cleveland	162	4340	1610	33	107	(59	48)	6057	137	196	115	.587	12	128	60	.68	2	3	.982
Minnesota	162	4324	1542	32	108	(54	54)	5974	118	157	93	.592	4	73	43	.63	2	2	.982
New York	161	4354	1529	23	109	(49	60)	5992	132	203	105	.517	21	146	45	.76	1	11	.982
Kansas City	162	4320	1801	38	117	(58	59)	6238	204	261	180	.690	10	105	45	.70	0	9	.981
Boston	161	4344	1558	24	113	(42	71)	6015	129	191	101	.529	23	223	51	.81	1	2	.981
Texas	162	4315	1638	20	114	(45	69)	6067	167	238	146	.613	2	79	66	.54	4	8	.981
Chicago	162	4300	1731	39	118	(56	62)	6149	149	215	130	.605	13	107	40	.73	0	8	.981
Oakland	162	4390	1756	23	125	(56	69)	6271	151	207	119	.575	4	124	55	.69	0	5	.980
Baltimore	162	4297	1598	31	125	(66	59)	6020	137	231	110	.476	15	157	51	.75	3	4	.979
Detroit	162	4288	1775	29	131	(47	84)	6194	164	242	145	.599	30	104	50	.68	1	8	.979
Tampa Bay	162	4271	1531	43	139	(60	79)	5941	144	207	115	.556	8	113	44	.72	4	6	.977
American League	1133	60639	23124	432	1589	(712	877)	85352	2095	2988	1745	.584	174	1653	685	.71	20	83	.981

National League Batting

Tm	G	AB	H	2B	3B	HR	(Hm	Rd)	TB	R	RBI	TBB	IBB	SO	HBP	SH	SF	ShO	SB	CS	SB%	GDP	LOB	Avg	OBP	SLG
Col	162	5690	1663	324	61	213	(124	89)	2748	923	874	511	50	1027	61	81	50	2	132	54	.71	116	1158	.292	.354	.483
Hou	162	5528	1500	313	29	208	(108	100)	2495	847	805	581	52	1119	89	71	56	3	64	49	.57	128	1151	.271	.341	.451
Ari	162	5595	1494	284	35	208	(107	101)	2472	818	776	587	73	1052	57	71	36	7	71	38	.65	105	1183	.267	.341	.442
StL	162	5450	1469	274	32	199	(100	99)	2404	814	768	529	51	1089	65	83	50	5	91	35	.72	125	1095	.270	.339	.441
SF	162	5612	1493	304	40	235	(97	138)	2582	799	775	625	79	1090	50	67	54	4	57	42	.58	108	1242	.266	.342	.460
SD	162	5482	1379	273	26	161	(69	92)	2187	789	753	678	37	1273	41	29	48	16	129	44	.75	121	1160	.252	.336	.399
ChC	162	5406	1409	268	32	194	(95	99)	2323	777	748	577	72	1077	66	117	53	4	67	36	.65	132	1156	.261	.336	.430
LA	162	5493	1399	264	27	206	(94	112)	2335	758	714	519	45	1062	56	57	44	8	89	42	.68	115	1075	.255	.323	.425
Phi	162	5497	1431	295	29	164	(83	81)	2276	746	708	551	52	1125	43	67	61	5	153	47	.77	104	1157	.260	.329	.414
Fla	162	5542	1461	325	30	166	(84	82)	2344	742	713	470	43	1145	67	60	45	9	89	40	.69	118	1117	.264	.326	.423
Mil	162	5488	1378	273	30	209	(107	102)	2338	740	712	488	44	1399	72	65	35	15	66	36	.65	102	1067	.251	.319	.426
Cin	162	5583	1464	304	22	176	(83	93)	2340	735	690	468	47	1172	65	66	40	9	103	54	.66	130	1115	.262	.324	.419
Atl	162	5498	1432	263	24	174	(87	87)	2265	729	696	493	51	1039	45	64	52	8	85	46	.65	132	1095	.260	.324	.412
Mon	162	5379	1361	320	28	131	(68	63)	2130	670	622	478	59	1071	60	64	45	15	101	51	.66	151	1024	.253	.319	.396
Pit	162	5398	1333	256	25	161	(75	86)	2122	657	618	467	51	1106	67	60	35	11	93	73	.56	114	1058	.247	.313	.393
NYM	162	5459	1361	273	18	147	(65	82)	2111	642	608	545	59	1062	65	52	35	12	66	48	.58	124	1181	.249	.323	.387
NL	1296	88100	23027	4613	488	2952	(1446	1506)	37472	12186	11580	8567	865	17908	969	1074	739	133	1456	735	.66	1925	18034	.261	.331	.425

National League Pitching

Tm	G	CG	Rel	IP	BFP	H	R	ER	HR	SH	SF	HB	TBB	IBB	SO	WP	Bk	W	L	Pct.	ShO	Sv-Op	Hld	OAvg	OOBP	OSLG	ERA
Atl	162	5	411	1447.1	6089	1363	643	578	153	53	54	33	499	77	1133	41	8	88	74	.543	13	41-63	61	.250	.314	.384	3.59
Ari	162	12	421	1459.2	6090	1352	677	627	195	64	41	59	461	30	1297	45	6	92	70	.568	13	34-50	58	.247	.311	.404	3.87
StL	162	8	484	1435.1	6121	1389	684	627	196	72	35	72	526	36	1083	45	4	93	69	.574	11	38-55	68	.256	.328	.428	3.93
ChC	162	8	452	1437	6159	1357	701	643	164	60	41	50	550	43	1344	48	5	88	74	.543	6	41-60	88	.249	.321	.398	4.03
NYM	162	6	397	1445.2	6107	1418	713	654	186	63	50	43	438	60	1191	53	7	82	80	.506	14	48-64	46	.257	.314	.419	4.07
Phi	162	8	473	1445.1	6198	1417	719	667	170	73	49	70	527	60	1086	40	6	86	76	.531	7	47-71	69	.259	.329	.424	4.15
Fla	162	3	438	1438	6227	1397	744	691	151	63	44	70	617	53	1119	40	3	76	86	.469	11	32-49	58	.257	.338	.411	4.32
LA	162	3	408	1450.2	6201	1387	744	685	184	69	39	72	524	37	1212	44	11	86	76	.531	5	46-73	63	.252	.323	.411	4.25
SF	162	3	439	1463.1	6294	1437	748	680	145	58	61	33	579	49	1080	50	3	90	72	.556	8	47-63	68	.258	.329	.404	4.18
Hou	162	7	405	1454.2	6236	1453	769	707	221	62	44	70	486	22	1228	42	3	93	69	.574	6	48-65	56	.261	.325	.437	4.37
Mil	162	3	489	1436.1	6338	1452	806	740	197	81	40	72	667	107	1057	58	3	68	94	.420	8	28-45	64	.265	.350	.440	4.64
Mon	162	5	491	1431.1	6250	1509	812	745	190	74	43	61	525	40	1103	55	4	68	94	.420	11	28-46	57	.272	.339	.441	4.68
SD	162	5	422	1440.2	6278	1519	812	724	219	58	47	56	476	54	1088	46	5	79	83	.488	6	46-66	53	.269	.330	.450	4.52
Cin	162	2	461	1442.2	6324	1572	850	765	198	69	50	48	515	46	943	53	4	76	86	.469	2	35-56	58	.279	.341	.455	4.77
Pit	162	8	410	1416.1	6222	1493	858	794	167	58	50	80	549	74	908	49	4	62	100	.383	9	36-51	48	.272	.344	.433	5.05
Col	162	8	476	1430	6306	1522	906	841	239	60	43	64	598	71	1058	38	1	73	89	.451	8	26-50	39	.275	.350	.480	5.29
NL	1296	96	7069	23074.1	99440	23037	12186	11168	2975	1037	731	953	8537	859	17930	747	79	1290	1302	.498	138	621-927	954	.261	.331	.426	4.36

National League Fielding

Team	G	PO	Ast	OFAst	E	(Throw	Field)	TC	DP	GDP Opp	GDP	GDP%	PB	OSB	OCS	OSB%	CPkof	PPkof	AVG
Arizona	162	4379	1559	24	84	(38	46)	6022	148	193	120	.622	12	107	55	.66	1	7	.986
Philadelphia	162	4336	1603	43	91	(41	50)	6030	145	212	120	.566	9	57	32	.64	1	5	.985
Colorado	162	4290	1693	31	96	(40	56)	6079	167	218	135	.619	14	100	36	.74	1	4	.984
Milwaukee	162	4309	1727	32	103	(36	67)	6139	156	201	126	.627	11	93	47	.66	1	5	.983
New York	162	4337	1576	33	101	(40	61)	6014	132	186	105	.565	11	131	40	.77	0	5	.983
Florida	162	4314	1666	32	103	(36	67)	6083	174	203	144	.709	10	75	51	.60	0	5	.983
Atlanta	162	4342	1636	31	103	(55	48)	6081	133	201	107	.532	9	102	50	.67	3	7	.983
Houston	162	4364	1662	32	110	(42	68)	6136	138	199	113	.569	4	66	49	.57	3	1	.982
Montreal	162	4294	1621	36	108	(48	60)	6023	139	198	116	.586	12	128	33	.80	2	6	.982
St. Louis	162	4306	1664	36	110	(54	56)	6080	156	213	136	.638	7	51	37	.58	7	7	.982
Chicago	162	4311	1493	20	109	(50	59)	5913	113	164	91	.555	13	106	46	.70	1	9	.982
Los Angeles	162	4352	1586	32	116	(50	66)	6054	138	176	111	.631	9	82	51	.62	2	4	.981
San Francisco	162	4390	1649	31	118	(32	86)	6157	170	225	136	.604	8	86	45	.66	0	0	.981
Pittsburgh	162	4249	1799	29	133	(53	80)	6181	168	240	141	.588	9	97	37	.72	0	4	.978
Cincinnati	162	4328	1733	36	138	(60	78)	6199	136	182	108	.593	21	75	62	.55	3	5	.978
San Diego	162	4322	1607	26	145	(75	70)	6074	127	215	99	.460	15	94	52	.64	2	1	.976
National League	1296	69223	26274	504	1768	(750	1018)	97265	2340	3226	1908	.591	174	1450	723	.67	27	75	.982

2001 Fielding Statistics

Fielding statistics have come a long way since the days when all we had were games, putouts, assists, errors, fielding percentage and double plays. On the following pages, you'll see that we've added games started and defensive innings, as well as range factor. In the STATS *All-Time Major League Handbook*, range factor is calculated as (putouts plus assists) per game. On the following pages, we've used the formula (putouts plus assists) *per nine innings*, which is a bit more precise. The catchers have an additional section of special stats, where you'll find opponents' stolen base/caught stealing data and team ERA with a particular catcher behind the plate. Although these stats are unofficial, we don't expect that the official ones will be substantially different when they arrive in a few months.

Estadísticas de Fildeo del 2001

Las estadísticas de fildeo han avanzado mucho desde los días cuando los únicos datos que teníamos eran Partidos Jugados, Retirados, Asistencias, Errores, Porcentaje de Fildeo y Doble Plays. En las siguientes páginas verán que hemos añadido Juegos Empezados y Entradas Defensivas, así como el Coeficiente de Alcance. En el *STATS All-Time Major League Handbook*, el Coeficiente de Alcance es calculado de esta manera: (Retiros más Asistencias) dividido por Partidos Jugados. En las siguientes páginas, hemos ocupado la fórmula de: (Retiros más Asistencias) dividido por Entradas Defensivas jugadas, y después multiplicado por nueve. Esto es más preciso. Los receptores tienen una sección adicional de estadísticas especiales, donde podrán encontrar Bases Robadas por Oponentes/Atrapados Robando y la efectividad del equipo cuando un receptor en particular está detrás del plato. Aunque éstas estadísticas son extra-oficiales, las estadísticas oficiales no variarán mucho cuando sean divulgadas en unos cuantos meses.

A = Asistencias; **CERA** = Efectividad de Lanzadores con Receptor Detrás del Plato; **CS%** = Promedio de Atrapados Robando; **CS** = Atrapados Robando; **DP** = Doble Plays; **E** = Errores; **ER** = Carreras Limpias; **G** = Juegos; **GS** = Juegos Empezados; **Inn** = Entradas; **PCS** = Atrapados Robando por Lanzador; **Pct.** = Promedio de Fildeo; **PO** = Retiros; **Regulars** = Regulares; **Rng** = Coeficiente de Alcance; **SBA** = Bases Robadas por Oponente; **Special** = Especial; **The Rest** = El Resto; **Tm** = Equipo.

Catchers = Receptores; **First Basemen** = Primera Bases; **Second Basemen** = Segunda Bases; **Third Basemen** = Tercera Bases; **Shortstops** = Campocortos; **Left Fielders** = Jardineros Izquierdos; **Center Fielders** = Jardineros Centrales; **Right Fielders** = Jardineros Derechos.

First Basemen - Regulars

Player	Tm	G	GS	Inn	PO	A	E	DP	Pct.	Rng
Spiezio, Scott	Ana	105	88	791.2	819	74	1	64	.999	—
Helton, Todd	Col	157	157	1370.0	1303	119	2	139	.999	—
Snow, J.T.	SF	92	80	695.0	659	46	1	76	.999	—
Cox, Steve	TB	78	71	641.0	569	48	1	64	.998	—
Mientkiewicz, Doug	Min	148	143	1269.1	1263	69	4	95	.997	—
Karros, Eric	LA	119	118	1018.1	964	71	4	82	.996	—
Martinez, Tino	NYY	149	146	1293.1	1144	99	5	105	.996	—
Lee, Travis	Phi	156	150	1351.2	1332	75	6	121	.996	—
Clark, Tony	Det	78	75	611.2	647	48	3	69	.996	—
Grace, Mark	Ari	135	127	1111.0	997	62	5	99	.995	—
Sexson, Richie	Mil	158	157	1372.2	1356	129	8	126	.995	—
Delgado, Carlos	Tor	161	161	1438.2	1519	103	9	166	.994	—
McGwire, Mark	StL	90	87	724.2	686	33	4	60	.994	—
Young, Kevin	Pit	137	125	1079.0	1154	70	7	118	.994	—
Lee, Derrek	Fla	156	146	1309.2	1271	114	8	142	.994	—
Conine, Jeff	Bal	80	76	670.2	646	45	4	61	.994	—
Casey, Sean	Cin	136	134	1127.0	1145	63	7	89	.994	—
Konerko, Paul	CWS	144	144	1260.1	1276	90	8	120	.994	—
Olerud, John	Sea	158	149	1347.2	1211	121	9	116	.993	—
Stairs, Matt	ChC	89	74	636.2	516	51	4	38	.993	—
Thome, Jim	Cle	148	144	1280.2	1177	78	10	105	.992	—
Palmeiro, Rafael	Tex	113	113	996.1	906	83	8	112	.992	—
Bagwell, Jeff	Hou	160	159	1414.2	1291	143	12	123	.992	—
Giambi, Jason	Oak	136	136	1176.1	1224	76	11	107	.992	—
Zeile, Todd	NYM	149	145	1273.1	1184	112	11	105	.992	—
Klesko, Ryan	SD	145	143	1240.0	1135	84	11	92	.991	—
Sweeney, Mike	KC	108	108	931.1	945	88	12	124	.989	—
Daubach, Brian	Bos	106	99	905.1	839	75	11	71	.988	—
McGriff, Fred	TOT	123	123	1022.0	924	82	13	82	.987	—
Stevens, Lee	Mon	152	149	1304.0	1287	92	19	113	.986	—
Average	—	129	124	1088.2	1046	81	7	99	.994	

First Basemen - The Rest

Player	Tm	G	GS	Inn	PO	A	E	DP	Pct.	Rng
Abad, Andy	Oak	1	0	1.0	2	0	0	1	1.000	—
Alcantara, Israel	Bos	4	3	20.0	17	2	1	1	.950	—
Arias, Alex	SD	17	11	102.2	91	9	2	6	.980	—
Barkett, Andy	Pit	4	3	26.0	36	3	0	2	1.000	—
Barnes, Larry	Ana	16	10	101.0	86	7	0	5	1.000	—
Bell, David	Sea	2	1	8.0	6	0	0	1	1.000	—
Bellinger, Clay	NYY	6	0	11.0	8	1	0	3	1.000	—
Blake, Casey	Min	3	1	15.2	15	2	0	1	1.000	—
Blake, Casey	Bal	5	3	39.0	29	0	1	3	.967	—
Blum, Geoff	Mon	14	9	84.0	74	9	1	9	.988	—
Bogar, Tim	LA	3	0	9.0	9	0	0	1	1.000	—
Bonilla, Bobby	StL	33	24	223.1	228	10	2	27	.992	—
Brogna, Rico	Atl	67	54	489.1	431	42	3	30	.994	—
Burke, Jamie	Ana	1	0	1.0	2	0	0	1	1.000	—
Burkhart, Morgan	Bos	5	4	36.0	29	2	0	4	1.000	—
Cairo, Miguel	StL	1	0	1.0	0	0	0	0	.000	—
Caminiti, Ken	Atl	33	33	247.2	240	14	6	19	.977	—
Castro, Juan	Cin	1	1	9.0	10	3	0	0	1.000	—
Catalanotto, Frank	Tex	5	0	7.0	6	2	0	0	1.000	—
Chavez, Eric	Oak	1	0	1.0	0	0	0	0	.000	—
Colbrunn, Greg	Ari	14	9	82.0	67	9	1	7	.987	—
Coomer, Ron	ChC	36	14	161.2	136	13	0	19	1.000	—

First Basemen - The Rest

Player	Tm	G	GS	Inn	PO	A	E	DP	Pct.	Rng
Cordero, Wil	Cle	22	18	163.0	161	10	1	17	.994	—
Counsell, Craig	Ari	2	0	3.0	1	1	0	0	1.000	—
Crespo, Felipe	SF	16	9	98.2	101	3	3	10	.972	—
Crespo, Felipe	Phi	2	2	17.0	21	0	0	3	1.000	—
Cromer, D.T.	Cin	8	4	42.0	32	4	1	3	.973	—
Cuddyer, Mike	Min	5	5	40.0	37	2	1	4	.975	—
Davis, Ben	SD	2	1	10.0	9	1	0	0	1.000	—
DeShields, Delino	ChC	1	0	1.0	1	0	0	0	1.000	—
Donnels, Chris	LA	7	4	38.2	40	2	0	4	1.000	—
Dunston, Shawon	SF	1	0	2.0	0	0	0	0	.000	—
Durazo, Erubiel	Ari	38	26	263.2	248	17	2	22	.993	—
Echevarria, Angel	Mil	10	3	48.0	47	2	0	5	1.000	—
Edmonds, Jim	StL	2	2	14.0	14	2	0	2	1.000	—
Erstad, Darin	Ana	12	7	71.1	64	7	0	8	1.000	—
Fernandez, Jose	Ana	2	0	3.0	0	0	1	0	.000	—
Fick, Robert	Det	26	18	156.2	169	12	1	10	.995	—
Franco, Julio	Atl	23	22	188.0	181	16	1	20	.995	—
Fullmer, Brad	Tor	1	1	8.0	12	1	0	1	1.000	—
Galarraga, Andres	Tex	25	25	220.0	195	16	1	26	.995	—
Galarraga, Andres	SF	41	36	322.2	288	13	5	38	.984	—
Garcia, Karim	Cle	2	0	3.0	3	0	0	1	1.000	—
Giambi, Jeremy	Oak	10	8	69.0	74	2	2	6	.974	—
Gibbons, Jay	Bal	7	4	39.0	36	1	0	3	1.000	—
Gil, Benji	Ana	18	9	77.1	69	8	0	7	1.000	—
Graffanino, Tony	CWS	1	0	2.0	3	0	0	1	1.000	—
Green, Shawn	LA	1	1	7.0	5	0	0	1	1.000	—
Guzman, Edwards	SF	7	3	32.0	34	2	1	2	.973	—
Halter, Shane	Det	8	6	55.0	69	7	0	10	1.000	—
Hansen, Dave	LA	25	16	147.0	169	12	3	11	.984	—
Harris, Lenny	NYM	7	5	45.1	33	4	2	1	.949	—
Harvey, Ken	KC	3	3	17.0	11	1	0	1	1.000	—
Hayes, Charlie	Hou	2	0	4.0	7	0	0	1	1.000	—
Helms, Wes	Atl	77	48	467.1	433	31	4	41	.991	—
Hernandez, Alex	Pit	2	0	3.0	4	0	0	1	1.000	—
Hernandez, Ramon	Oak	2	0	4.0	4	0	1	0	.800	—
Hiatt, Phil	LA	6	1	18.0	20	0	1	3	.952	—
Hillenbrand, Shea	Bos	6	5	48.0	50	3	0	4	1.000	—
Hocking, Denny	Min	11	6	55.1	47	6	0	3	1.000	—
Houston, Tyler	Mil	3	2	13.0	12	0	0	0	1.000	—
Huff, Aubrey	TB	19	17	153.0	129	15	5	13	.966	—
Hyzdu, Adam	Pit	4	1	15.1	15	2	0	0	1.000	—
Ibanez, Raul	KC	10	8	63.2	58	8	2	11	.971	—
Jackson, Ryan	Det	35	8	118.0	126	12	0	14	1.000	—
Javier, Stan	Sea	6	5	40.0	26	3	0	4	1.000	—
Jennings, Robin	Oak	6	3	31.0	35	3	0	2	1.000	—
Jennings, Robin	Cin	8	6	60.0	51	6	0	9	1.000	—
Johnson, Mark P.	NYM	21	11	110.1	101	7	1	10	.991	—
Johnson, Nick	NYY	15	10	102.0	90	5	0	4	1.000	—
Jordan, Kevin	Phi	10	9	67.2	53	2	3	4	.948	—
Joyner, Wally	Ana	39	31	267.1	270	18	1	27	.997	—
Kent, Jeff	SF	30	22	213.1	193	14	2	19	.990	—
Kieschnick, Brooks	Col	1	0	1.0	1	0	0	0	1.000	—
Kinkade, Mike	Bal	3	0	5.0	3	0	0	0	1.000	—
LaRue, Jason	Cin	1	0	5.0	5	0	0	0	1.000	—
LeCroy, Matt	Min	2	0	6.0	4	0	0	0	1.000	—
Liefer, Jeff	CWS	15	11	98.0	100	9	3	12	.973	—
Lo Duca, Paul	LA	33	22	212.2	185	17	2	17	.990	—
Lopez, Luis	Tor	5	0	12.0	10	1	0	0	1.000	—

First Basemen - The Rest

Player	Tm	G	GS	Inn	PO	A	E	DP	Pct.	Rng
Mabry, John	StL	2	1	6.0	3	0	0	1	1.000	—
Mabry, John	Fla	1	1	9.0	7	1	0	0	1.000	—
Mackowiak, Rob	Pit	1	0	1.0	0	0	0	0	.000	—
Magadan, Dave	SD	9	1	28.0	24	2	1	2	.963	—
Marrero, Eli	StL	6	1	16.1	19	1	0	4	1.000	—
Martinez, Dave	Atl	10	5	55.0	51	6	0	6	1.000	—
Martinez, Edgar	Sea	1	1	5.0	8	0	0	0	1.000	—
Matheny, Mike	StL	2	0	7.0	7	0	0	2	1.000	—
Mayne, Brent	Col	1	0	1.0	0	0	0	0	.000	—
McCarty, Dave	KC	68	43	428.0	441	45	6	56	.988	—
McEwing, Joe	NYM	3	0	3.2	2	1	1	1	.750	—
McGriff, Fred	TB	74	74	628.2	558	59	9	53	.986	—
McGriff, Fred	ChC	49	49	393.1	366	23	4	29	.990	—
McGuire, Ryan	Fla	4	0	5.0	7	0	0	0	1.000	—
Melhuse, Adam	Col	1	0	1.0	1	0	0	0	1.000	—
Merced, Orlando	Hou	1	0	1.0	1	0	0	0	1.000	—
Millar, Kevin	Fla	15	15	114.1	117	6	0	10	1.000	—
Minor, Damon	SF	11	11	89.2	86	4	1	4	.989	—
Minor, Ryan	Mon	1	1	5.0	3	0	1	0	.750	—
Mordecai, Mike	Mon	1	0	2.0	1	0	0	0	1.000	—
Munson, Eric	Det	17	17	146.0	142	14	1	14	.994	—
Nieves, Jose	Ana	1	0	2.0	2	0	0	0	1.000	—
Norton, Greg	Col	13	5	55.0	66	4	0	6	1.000	—
Offerman, Jose	Bos	43	38	335.2	297	39	3	26	.991	—
Ortiz, David	Min	8	7	55.0	60	2	0	2	1.000	—
Osik, Keith	Pit	5	1	16.0	21	0	0	3	1.000	—
Paquette, Craig	StL	23	13	123.1	125	10	3	17	.978	—
Pena, Carlos	Tex	16	16	142.0	138	15	2	13	.987	—
Perry, Herbert	CWS	12	4	53.1	60	3	0	8	1.000	—
Petrick, Ben	Col	2	0	2.0	3	0	0	1	1.000	—
Pickering, Calvin	Bos	12	12	103.0	90	6	0	8	1.000	—
Posada, Jorge	NYY	2	1	9.0	7	0	0	1	1.000	—
Pratt, Todd	Phi	1	1	9.0	6	1	0	0	1.000	—
Pujols, Albert	StL	42	32	287.0	283	19	5	27	.984	—
Renteria, Edgar	StL	1	0	1.0	2	0	0	1	1.000	—
Richard, Chris	Bal	18	14	132.0	127	9	0	10	1.000	—
Ritchie, Todd	Pit	0	0	0.0	0	0	0	0	.000	—
Saenz, Olmedo	Oak	28	14	167.0	196	16	3	13	.986	—
Sandberg, Jared	TB	1	0	1.0	0	0	0	0	.000	—
Santiago, Benito	SF	2	1	8.0	7	0	0	0	1.000	—
Segui, David	Bal	65	65	546.2	487	33	9	49	.983	—
Seguignol, F.	Mon	3	2	25.1	20	3	2	3	.920	—
Selby, Bill	Cin	2	0	2.0	5	0	0	1	1.000	—
Simon, Randall	Det	43	38	342.0	353	26	3	39	.992	—
Smith, Mark	Mon	1	0	1.0	1	0	0	0	1.000	—
Sojo, Luis	NYY	8	3	30.0	32	3	0	2	1.000	—
Sprague, Ed	Sea	12	6	62.1	52	1	1	4	.981	—
Sutton, Larry	StL	11	2	31.2	38	5	0	3	1.000	—
Sweeney, Mark	Mil	2	0	2.2	3	0	0	2	1.000	—
Thomas, Frank	CWS	3	3	19.2	20	1	1	2	.955	—
Toca, Jorge	NYM	3	1	13.0	14	1	0	1	1.000	—
Tracy, Andy	Mon	3	1	10.0	11	0	0	1	1.000	—
Truby, Chris	Hou	1	0	2.0	1	0	0	0	1.000	—
Tucker, Michael	ChC	4	2	25.1	14	6	2	2	.909	—
Valdez, Mario	Oak	6	1	14.0	15	0	0	2	1.000	—
Vander Wal, John	Pit	13	11	91.1	111	4	1	13	.991	—
Vander Wal, John	SF	1	0	2.0	2	0	0	0	1.000	—
Velarde, Randy	Tex	9	8	73.0	70	2	0	5	1.000	—

First Basemen - The Rest

Player	Tm	G	GS	Inn	PO	A	E	DP	Pct.	Rng
Velarde, Randy	NYY	1	1	6.0	9	2	0	0	1.000	—
Ward, Daryle	Hou	9	3	33.0	19	0	0	2	1.000	—
Wehner, John	Pit	11	3	39.2	51	1	0	2	1.000	—
Wilkins, Rick	SD	1	0	1.0	1	0	0	0	1.000	—
Wilson, Craig A.	Pit	26	17	145.0	166	12	1	16	.994	—
Wilson, Dan	Sea	2	0	2.0	3	0	0	0	1.000	—
Witt, Kevin	SD	9	6	59.0	69	3	0	4	1.000	—
Woodward, Chris	Tor	2	0	4.0	3	0	0	0	1.000	—
Wooten, Shawn	Ana	21	17	123.0	134	11	2	19	.986	—
Young, Dmitri	Cin	38	17	197.2	219	19	0	16	1.000	—
Zuleta, Julio	ChC	35	23	219.0	213	7	2	11	.991	—

Second Basemen - Regulars

Player	Tm	G	GS	Inn	PO	A	E	DP	Pct.	Rng
Bush, Homer	Tor	78	76	660.2	153	254	4	68	.990	5.54
Belliard, Ronnie	Mil	96	93	826.2	213	290	5	66	.990	5.48
Hairston Jr., Jerry	Bal	156	154	1343.1	326	458	19	93	.976	5.25
Easley, Damion	Det	153	153	1329.1	279	496	14	113	.982	5.25
Menechino, Frank	Oak	136	127	1160.2	253	406	15	90	.978	5.11
Walker, Todd	TOT	142	134	1165.1	293	366	11	82	.984	5.09
Jackson, Damian	SD	118	115	1001.2	241	323	8	68	.986	5.07
Kent, Jeff	SF	140	134	1171.0	269	390	9	91	.987	5.06
Meares, Pat	Pit	85	75	645.0	149	213	10	53	.973	5.05
Durham, Ray	CWS	150	148	1294.1	280	446	10	88	.986	5.05
Castillo, Luis	Fla	133	131	1157.0	260	387	13	99	.980	5.03
Kennedy, Adam	Ana	131	123	1102.2	236	376	10	64	.984	5.00
Anderson, Marlon	Phi	140	138	1210.2	270	387	12	86	.982	4.88
Febles, Carlos	KC	78	73	649.1	128	224	7	62	.981	4.88
Young, Michael	Tex	104	102	915.1	212	284	8	79	.984	4.88
Vina, Fernando	StL	151	149	1299.1	313	383	9	100	.987	4.82
Abernathy, Brent	TB	79	78	680.2	150	209	7	56	.981	4.75
Alomar, Roberto	Cle	157	156	1324.0	268	423	5	88	.993	4.70
Grudzielanek, Mark	LA	133	131	1159.1	245	359	10	75	.984	4.69
Offerman, Jose	Bos	91	88	787.0	161	249	11	44	.974	4.69
Boone, Bret	Sea	156	152	1370.0	286	410	10	90	.986	4.57
Young, Eric	ChC	147	145	1244.2	263	366	12	67	.981	4.55
Vidro, Jose	Mon	121	121	1035.1	204	315	9	63	.983	4.51
Alfonzo, Edgardo	NYM	122	119	1026.1	211	301	7	61	.987	4.49
Biggio, Craig	Hou	154	152	1344.2	280	389	11	86	.984	4.48
Soriano, Alfonso	NYY	156	156	1384.1	318	383	19	93	.973	4.35
Bell, Jay	Ari	80	78	664.0	153	168	2	43	.994	4.35
Rivas, Luis	Min	150	148	1304.1	230	335	15	65	.974	3.90
Average	—	126	123	1080.2	237	342	10	76	.983	4.82

Second Basemen - The Rest

Player	Tm	G	GS	Inn	PO	A	E	DP	Pct.	Rng
Abbott, Kurt	Atl	1	1	8.0	1	6	0	0	1.000	7.88
Alicea, Luis	KC	67	58	520.1	105	194	13	47	.958	5.17
Arias, Alex	SD	13	9	78.0	19	19	1	3	.974	4.38
Bellhorn, Mark	Oak	12	9	83.0	15	26	2	4	.953	4.45
Berg, Dave	Fla	34	29	261.2	54	85	5	21	.965	4.78
Blum, Geoff	Mon	25	17	165.2	39	47	1	5	.989	4.67
Bocachica, Hiram	LA	19	14	125.0	23	41	4	8	.941	4.61
Branson, Jeff	LA	6	3	32.0	7	10	0	2	1.000	4.78

Second Basemen - The Rest

Player	Tm	G	GS	Inn	PO	A	E	DP	Pct.	Rng
Butler, Brent	Col	23	19	161.2	44	49	4	14	.959	5.18
Cabrera, Jolbert	Cle	28	6	106.2	20	37	1	5	.983	4.81
Cairo, Miguel	ChC	11	5	55.1	11	19	2	2	.938	4.88
Cairo, Miguel	StL	5	1	13.1	2	4	0	2	1.000	4.05
Castro, Juan	Cin	37	19	199.0	45	59	0	10	1.000	4.70
Catalanotto, Frank	Tex	13	10	89.0	18	23	2	8	.953	4.15
Clapp, Stubby	StL	4	0	10.2	1	6	0	0	1.000	5.91
Cora, Alex	LA	1	1	8.0	1	1	0	0	1.000	2.25
Counsell, Craig	Ari	55	45	403.2	96	133	1	34	.996	5.11
Crespo, Cesar	SD	34	25	242.2	62	67	4	12	.970	4.78
Crespo, Felipe	SF	2	2	11.0	2	3	1	1	.833	4.09
Crespo, Felipe	Phi	1	0	1.0	2	0	0	0	1.000	18.00
Delgado, Wilson	KC	2	2	15.0	2	4	0	0	1.000	3.60
DeRosa, Mark	Atl	5	4	42.0	7	20	0	3	1.000	5.79
DeShields, Delino	ChC	16	8	83.2	28	21	0	1	1.000	5.27
Diaz, Einar	Cle	1	0	2.0	0	1	0	0	1.000	4.50
Eckstein, David	Ana	14	14	116.0	21	34	3	9	.948	4.27
Figueroa, Luis	Pit	3	0	6.0	1	4	0	1	1.000	7.50
Forbes, P.J.	Phi	1	1	9.0	2	2	0	0	1.000	4.00
Fox, Andy	Fla	2	2	19.1	4	4	0	0	1.000	3.72
Freel, Ryan	Tor	7	6	49.0	11	20	1	4	.969	5.69
Frye, Jeff	Tor	47	36	351.1	83	122	1	30	.995	5.25
Garcia, Jesse	Atl	4	0	8.1	3	2	0	1	1.000	5.40
Gil, Benji	Ana	21	16	143.0	30	53	3	14	.965	5.22
Giles, Marcus	Atl	62	59	518.0	104	166	6	31	.978	4.69
Gipson, Charles	Sea	1	0	3.0	0	0	0	0	.000	.00
Gomez, Chris	SD	8	3	34.2	9	11	0	5	1.000	5.19
Graffanino, Tony	CWS	20	14	139.0	32	51	1	13	.988	5.37
Guerrero, Wilton	Cin	11	8	75.0	21	23	0	4	1.000	5.28
Guzman, Edwards	SF	3	0	4.0	3	0	1	0	.750	6.75
Harris, Lenny	NYM	1	0	3.0	1	0	0	0	1.000	3.00
Hocking, Denny	Min	17	8	82.0	23	24	1	6	.979	5.16
Izturis, Cesar	Tor	41	34	306.0	57	110	2	23	.988	4.91
Johnson, Russ	TB	33	31	265.0	60	83	0	21	1.000	4.86
Jordan, Kevin	Phi	10	8	69.2	13	28	2	4	.953	5.30
Lansing, Mike	Bos	31	26	235.2	53	75	4	15	.970	4.89
Lewis, Mark	Cle	3	0	8.0	2	1	0	1	1.000	3.38
Lockhart, Keith	Atl	47	34	313.0	66	84	0	20	1.000	4.31
Lopez, Luis	Mil	15	9	104.1	24	34	0	7	1.000	5.00
Lopez, Mendy	Hou	3	1	14.0	5	2	0	0	1.000	4.50
Lopez, Mendy	Pit	9	7	59.2	14	18	1	4	.970	4.83
Loretta, Mark	Mil	52	52	424.1	115	144	2	31	.992	5.49
Lugo, Julio	Hou	2	0	2.0	0	0	0	0	.000	.00
Macias, Jose	Det	18	9	99.0	25	31	0	3	1.000	5.09
Mackowiak, Rob	Pit	21	19	149.0	34	55	5	8	.947	5.38
Magadan, Dave	SD	1	0	1.0	0	0	0	0	.000	.00
Martinez, Felix	TB	10	8	79.1	15	20	0	3	1.000	3.97
Martinez, Ramon	SF	42	26	277.1	54	98	1	21	.993	4.93
Mateo, Henry	Mon	2	2	18.0	3	6	2	0	.818	4.50
Maxwell, Jason	Min	9	6	55.0	4	17	0	0	1.000	3.44
McDonald, John	Cle	3	0	6.0	2	2	0	1	1.000	6.00
McEwing, Joe	NYM	5	1	16.0	5	6	0	2	1.000	6.19
McLemore, Mark	Sea	9	8	64.0	18	17	2	8	.946	4.92
Merloni, Lou	Bos	5	3	27.1	10	8	1	3	.947	5.93
Meyers, Chad	ChC	4	1	18.1	3	10	0	1	1.000	6.38
Mora, Melvin	Bal	1	1	8.0	0	1	1	0	.500	1.13
Mordecai, Mike	Mon	32	22	212.1	46	58	1	13	.990	4.41
Morris, Warren	Pit	29	23	190.0	41	69	4	15	.965	5.21

Second Basemen - The Rest

Player	Tm	G	GS	Inn	PO	A	E	DP	Pct.	Rng
Mueller, Bill	ChC	1	0	1.0	0	1	0	0	1.000	9.00
Newhan, David	Phi	1	1	7.0	2	0	0	0	1.000	2.57
Nieves, Jose	Ana	11	9	76.0	21	31	0	10	1.000	6.16
Nunez, Abraham	Pit	48	31	302.2	93	103	2	27	.990	5.83
Ojeda, Augie	ChC	10	3	33.0	8	13	0	3	1.000	5.73
Ordaz, Luis	KC	19	13	119.2	21	53	1	16	.987	5.57
Ortiz, Jose	Oak	10	10	87.0	16	23	2	7	.951	4.03
Ortiz, Jose	Col	51	48	422.0	86	137	8	30	.965	4.76
Osik, Keith	Pit	2	0	4.0	1	2	0	0	1.000	6.75
Paquette, Craig	StL	4	1	19.0	3	5	0	0	1.000	3.79
Pena, Elvis	Mil	11	8	81.0	14	36	1	7	.980	5.56
Perez, Neifi	KC	4	4	32.0	9	13	0	1	1.000	6.19
Perez, Santiago	SD	2	1	10.1	4	2	0	0	1.000	5.23
Perez, Tomas	Phi	29	14	148.0	36	49	0	11	1.000	5.17
Polanco, Placido	StL	15	10	93.0	22	36	0	10	1.000	5.61
Randa, Joe	KC	1	0	4.0	3	1	0	1	1.000	9.00
Reboulet, Jeff	LA	22	13	126.1	25	35	1	8	.984	4.27
Reese, Pokey	Cin	51	46	406.2	101	141	5	28	.980	5.36
Relaford, Desi	NYM	54	42	400.1	85	105	6	24	.969	4.27
Riggs, Adam	SD	11	9	72.1	12	20	0	5	1.000	3.98
Roberts, Brian	Bal	12	7	81.0	13	25	2	6	.950	4.22
Rolls, Damian	TB	42	39	347.2	69	113	6	21	.968	4.71
Sadler, Donnie	Cin	15	6	62.2	15	21	2	5	.947	5.17
Sadler, Donnie	KC	13	13	99.2	28	38	0	12	1.000	5.96
Santana, Pedro	Det	1	0	1.0	1	0	0	0	1.000	9.00
Santangelo, F.P.	Oak	20	16	132.2	33	40	0	7	1.000	4.95
Santos, Angel	Bos	6	4	39.0	7	12	2	0	.905	4.38
Selby, Bill	Cin	21	20	156.1	34	49	0	13	1.000	4.78
Shumpert, Terry	Col	41	24	224.0	51	71	4	20	.968	4.90
Smith, Bobby	TB	6	6	51.0	12	11	1	3	.958	4.06
Sojo, Luis	NYY	7	2	26.0	5	8	0	0	1.000	4.50
Spivey, Junior	Ari	66	39	392.0	96	104	3	27	.985	4.59
Stairs, Matt	ChC	1	0	1.0	0	0	0	0	.000	.00
Stynes, Chris	Bos	43	40	359.0	73	116	1	18	.995	4.74
Vazquez, Ramon	Sea	6	2	28.0	3	7	0	0	1.000	3.21
Velarde, Randy	Tex	52	49	434.0	111	135	3	38	.988	5.10
Veras, Quilvio	Atl	67	64	558.0	132	181	3	37	.991	5.05
Vizcaino, Jose	Hou	9	8	94.0	22	26	1	6	.980	4.60
Walker, Todd	Col	77	71	622.1	155	198	7	49	.981	5.10
Walker, Todd	Cin	65	63	543.0	138	168	4	33	.987	5.07
Wehner, John	Pit	1	1	3.1	3	1	0	1	1.000	10.80
Wilson, Enrique	Pit	10	6	56.2	16	19	1	9	.972	5.56
Wilson, Enrique	NYY	7	3	41.0	9	17	0	3	1.000	5.71
Woodward, Chris	Tor	17	10	95.2	22	49	3	10	.959	6.68

Third Basemen - Regulars

Player	Tm	G	GS	Inn	PO	A	E	DP	Pct.	Rng
Macias, Jose	Det	89	83	735.0	68	187	12	23	.955	3.12
Cirillo, Jeff	Col	137	137	1165.0	78	308	7	25	.982	2.98
Chavez, Eric	Oak	149	146	1300.2	100	321	12	27	.972	2.91
Rolen, Scott	Phi	151	151	1329.1	104	325	12	22	.973	2.90
Polanco, Placido	StL	103	93	810.0	60	199	4	16	.985	2.88
Ramirez, Aramis	Pit	157	155	1345.1	92	335	25	33	.945	2.86
Boone, Aaron	Cin	103	101	884.2	72	207	19	17	.936	2.84
Batista, Tony	TOT	101	97	865.2	74	198	15	26	.948	2.83
Ripken Jr., Cal	Bal	111	111	981.2	97	209	14	23	.956	2.81

Third Basemen - Regulars

Player	Tm	G	GS	Inn	PO	A	E	DP	Pct.	Rng
Ventura, Robin	NYM	139	130	1141.1	91	264	16	24	.957	2.80
Bell, David	Sea	134	120	1128.0	92	257	14	21	.961	2.78
Koskie, Corey	Min	150	147	1308.0	95	306	15	19	.964	2.76
Randa, Joe	KC	137	137	1195.2	111	255	13	31	.966	2.75
Castilla, Vinny	TOT	145	143	1263.0	108	275	17	23	.958	2.73
Lamb, Mike	Tex	74	71	634.1	52	139	18	14	.914	2.71
Brosius, Scott	NYY	120	120	1076.2	81	238	22	21	.935	2.67
Lowell, Mike	Fla	144	142	1250.2	108	261	9	35	.976	2.66
Nevin, Phil	SD	145	144	1228.2	96	265	27	26	.930	2.64
Beltre, Adrian	LA	124	121	1080.0	99	215	16	18	.952	2.62
Glaus, Troy	Ana	159	158	1391.2	103	286	19	21	.953	2.52
Williams, Matt	Ari	102	99	852.1	57	177	9	17	.963	2.47
Hillenbrand, Shea	Bos	129	116	1053.0	88	200	18	16	.941	2.46
Huff, Aubrey	TB	73	71	614.0	41	126	15	13	.918	2.45
Fryman, Travis	Cle	96	94	791.0	65	137	12	14	.944	2.30
Jones, Chipper	Atl	149	148	1297.0	75	233	18	12	.945	2.14
Average	—	125	121	1069.0	84	237	15	21	.955	2.70

Third Basemen - The Rest

Player	Tm	G	GS	Inn	PO	A	E	DP	Pct.	Rng
Alicea, Luis	KC	18	15	138.0	12	24	1	3	.973	2.35
Arias, Alex	SD	18	3	62.0	5	17	1	1	.957	3.19
Batista, Tony	Tor	72	68	618.0	56	145	10	21	.953	2.93
Batista, Tony	Bal	29	29	247.2	18	53	5	5	.934	2.58
Bell, Jay	Ari	40	33	303.1	22	56	5	3	.940	2.31
Bellhorn, Mark	Oak	9	5	58.0	3	15	2	0	.900	2.79
Bellinger, Clay	NYY	17	14	115.2	16	30	3	5	.939	3.58
Berg, Dave	Fla	16	5	70.0	1	16	2	2	.895	2.19
Blake, Casey	Min	5	2	16.1	1	3	1	0	.800	2.20
Blum, Geoff	Mon	72	67	570.0	49	120	6	12	.966	2.67
Bocachica, Hiram	LA	8	7	52.0	1	6	2	0	.778	1.21
Bogar, Tim	LA	1	0	3.0	0	0	0	0	.000	.00
Branson, Jeff	LA	1	0	1.0	0	0	0	0	.000	.00
Branyan, Russell	Cle	72	55	511.2	39	108	11	8	.930	2.59
Butler, Brent	Col	9	1	40.0	4	6	0	1	1.000	2.25
Cabrera, Jolbert	Cle	27	10	116.0	9	23	1	2	.970	2.48
Cairo, Miguel	ChC	40	22	218.2	13	32	5	6	.900	1.85
Cairo, Miguel	StL	3	0	4.2	0	0	1	0	.000	.00
Caminiti, Ken	Tex	53	51	441.2	42	99	9	10	.940	2.87
Caminiti, Ken	Atl	13	12	102.0	9	19	2	3	.933	2.47
Castilla, Vinny	TB	24	24	206.1	26	45	5	5	.934	3.10
Castilla, Vinny	Hou	121	119	1056.2	82	230	12	18	.963	2.66
Castro, Juan	Cin	19	8	92.2	3	20	1	3	.958	2.23
Catalanotto, Frank	Tex	11	6	53.0	6	17	1	0	.958	3.91
Colbrunn, Greg	Ari	10	8	63.0	6	8	2	1	.875	2.00
Collier, Lou	Mil	16	13	112.1	8	24	3	2	.914	2.56
Conine, Jeff	Bal	17	16	145.0	15	24	0	0	1.000	2.42
Coolbaugh, Mike	Mil	27	13	125.2	11	23	1	5	.971	2.44
Coomer, Ron	ChC	76	72	552.1	43	101	7	11	.954	2.35
Counsell, Craig	Ari	38	22	240.0	27	58	2	4	.977	3.19
Crede, Joe	CWS	15	13	114.0	17	18	0	3	1.000	2.76
Crespo, Cesar	SD	2	0	2.0	1	0	0	0	1.000	4.50
Cruz, Deivi	Det	7	7	42.0	5	7	0	0	1.000	2.57
Cuddyer, Mike	Min	2	0	3.0	0	0	0	0	.000	.00
Davis, Russ	SF	46	46	374.2	20	61	10	9	.890	1.95
Delgado, Wilson	KC	3	2	17.0	0	7	0	0	1.000	3.71

Third Basemen - The Rest

Player	Tm	G	GS	Inn	PO	A	E	DP	Pct.	Rng
DeRosa, Mark	Atl	1	0	1.0	0	0	0	0	.000	.00
DeShields, Delino	ChC	5	4	34.1	0	4	2	0	.667	1.05
Donnels, Chris	LA	14	12	92.1	6	20	3	2	.897	2.53
Dransfeldt, Kelly	Tex	1	0	1.0	0	0	0	0	.000	.00
Feliz, Pedro	SF	86	51	518.0	40	79	12	6	.908	2.07
Fernandez, Jose	Ana	2	0	1.0	0	0	0	0	.000	.00
Fernandez, Tony	Mil	13	13	111.1	3	25	1	4	.966	2.26
Fox, Andy	Fla	9	4	31.2	6	6	0	1	1.000	3.41
Frye, Jeff	Tor	27	11	121.1	7	22	0	2	1.000	2.15
Gipson, Charles	Sea	9	2	31.0	2	6	1	0	.889	2.32
Graffanino, Tony	CWS	38	14	187.1	16	44	5	1	.923	2.88
Guerrero, Wilton	Cin	4	3	29.0	3	5	1	1	.889	2.48
Gulan, Mike	Fla	1	1	9.0	2	2	0	0	1.000	4.00
Guzman, Edwards	SF	7	2	33.1	4	7	0	1	1.000	2.97
Halter, Shane	Det	74	60	549.1	57	150	17	12	.924	3.39
Hansen, Dave	LA	21	13	119.0	4	34	3	5	.927	2.87
Harris, Lenny	NYM	11	2	33.0	3	4	1	0	.875	1.91
Hayes, Charlie	Hou	11	9	72.1	7	12	0	2	1.000	2.36
Helms, Wes	Atl	17	2	41.0	4	10	0	1	1.000	3.07
Hiatt, Phil	LA	17	7	82.2	9	8	0	1	1.000	1.85
Hocking, Denny	Min	6	5	44.0	1	8	1	0	.900	1.84
Houston, Tyler	Mil	62	55	490.1	30	99	10	11	.928	2.37
Ibanez, Raul	KC	1	0	4.0	0	0	1	0	.000	.00
Johnson, Russ	TB	36	28	254.2	21	50	6	6	.922	2.51
Jordan, Kevin	Phi	10	4	50.0	4	7	0	0	1.000	1.98
Kinkade, Mike	Bal	10	6	58.0	8	11	0	0	1.000	2.95
Larson, Brandon	Cin	9	8	77.2	10	21	2	2	.939	3.59
LaRue, Jason	Cin	3	3	26.0	4	6	1	0	.909	3.46
Lewis, Mark	Cle	4	3	22.0	2	6	1	1	.889	3.27
Liefer, Jeff	CWS	15	14	107.0	7	19	4	2	.867	2.19
Lockhart, Keith	Atl	4	0	6.1	1	0	0	0	1.000	1.42
Lopez, Felipe	Tor	47	47	415.1	26	100	8	6	.940	2.73
Lopez, Luis	Mil	46	33	287.1	30	53	7	9	.922	2.60
Lopez, Luis	Tor	28	28	234.0	17	56	5	4	.936	2.81
Lopez, Mendy	Hou	2	1	9.2	0	1	0	0	1.000	0.93
Lopez, Mendy	Pit	4	1	14.0	2	5	0	0	1.000	4.50
Loretta, Mark	Mil	39	35	309.1	16	54	5	0	.933	2.04
Mackowiak, Rob	Pit	2	0	5.0	0	2	0	1	1.000	3.60
Magadan, Dave	SD	22	14	139.0	15	23	2	2	.950	2.46
Martinez, Ramon	SF	70	63	537.1	44	105	4	7	.974	2.50
Maxwell, Jason	Min	11	8	70.0	8	17	0	1	1.000	3.21
McDonald, John	Cle	3	0	6.0	0	2	0	0	1.000	3.00
McEwing, Joe	NYM	25	17	148.1	15	28	1	5	.977	2.61
McLemore, Mark	Sea	36	32	245.0	25	48	7	3	.913	2.68
Menechino, Frank	Oak	1	0	0.2	0	0	0	0	.000	.00
Merced, Orlando	Hou	2	0	4.0	0	0	0	0	.000	.00
Merloni, Lou	Bos	1	0	2.0	0	0	0	0	.000	.00
Meyers, Chad	ChC	1	0	1.0	0	0	0	0	.000	.00
Millar, Kevin	Fla	10	10	76.2	5	11	0	1	1.000	1.88
Minor, Ryan	Mon	24	15	153.1	12	20	1	0	.970	1.88
Mordecai, Mike	Mon	42	32	301.0	21	53	2	2	.974	2.21
Morris, Warren	Pit	1	1	8.0	0	1	0	1	1.000	1.13
Mueller, Bill	ChC	64	56	495.2	33	96	8	6	.942	2.34
Nieves, Jose	Ana	2	0	4.0	0	3	0	1	1.000	6.75
Norton, Greg	Col	24	20	170.0	8	26	4	2	.895	1.80
Nunez, Abraham	Pit	1	0	1.0	0	0	0	0	.000	.00
Ojeda, Augie	ChC	35	8	135.0	8	34	4	4	.913	2.80
Ordaz, Luis	KC	1	0	2.0	0	0	0	0	.000	.00

Third Basemen - The Rest

Player	Tm	G	GS	Inn	PO	A	E	DP	Pct.	Rng
Osik, Keith	Pit	3	1	11.0	1	3	0	0	1.000	3.27
Paquette, Craig	StL	33	17	189.0	20	35	2	5	.965	2.62
Patterson, Jarrod	Det	13	12	103.0	9	15	2	0	.923	2.10
Perez, Tomas	Phi	9	7	66.0	13	18	1	2	.969	4.23
Perry, Herbert	CWS	68	64	543.1	45	112	10	5	.940	2.60
Pujols, Albert	StL	55	52	431.2	40	111	10	17	.938	3.15
Reboulet, Jeff	LA	7	2	20.2	1	4	2	0	.714	2.18
Relaford, Desi	NYM	20	13	120.0	10	21	2	0	.939	2.33
Riggs, Adam	SD	1	1	9.0	1	4	0	0	1.000	5.00
Rolls, Damian	TB	1	1	9.0	3	3	0	0	1.000	6.00
Sadler, Donnie	KC	15	8	83.1	9	27	0	5	1.000	3.89
Saenz, Olmedo	Oak	14	11	95.2	5	19	2	3	.923	2.26
Sandberg, Jared	TB	38	38	339.2	33	68	6	7	.944	2.68
Santangelo, F.P.	Oak	3	0	8.1	0	0	0	0	.000	.00
Selby, Bill	Cin	8	6	51.2	7	8	2	2	.882	2.61
Sheldon, Scott	Tex	38	29	260.1	37	61	5	1	.951	3.39
Shumpert, Terry	Col	12	4	55.0	2	18	3	1	.870	3.27
Sojo, Luis	NYY	17	9	92.0	7	21	2	2	.933	2.74
Sosa, Juan	Ari	1	0	1.0	0	1	0	0	1.000	9.00
Spiezio, Scott	Ana	10	4	40.0	2	9	1	0	.917	2.47
Sprague, Ed	Sea	8	7	54.0	5	11	1	0	.941	2.67
Stynes, Chris	Bos	46	44	379.0	31	63	5	5	.949	2.23
Tatis, Fernando	Mon	41	40	339.2	18	54	9	2	.889	1.91
Tracy, Andy	Mon	11	8	67.1	5	12	0	0	1.000	2.27
Truby, Chris	Hou	35	33	299.0	17	55	6	4	.923	2.17
Valentin, John	Bos	3	1	14.0	1	1	0	0	1.000	1.29
Valentin, Jose	CWS	66	57	481.2	49	113	13	9	.926	3.03
Vazquez, Ramon	Sea	2	1	7.0	0	1	1	0	.500	1.29
Velandia, Jorge	NYM	1	0	3.0	0	0	0	0	.000	.00
Velarde, Randy	Tex	7	5	48.0	4	9	1	2	.929	2.44
Velarde, Randy	NYY	7	6	52.0	4	16	1	1	.952	3.46
Vizcaino, Jose	Hou	7	0	13.0	0	2	2	0	.500	1.38
Wehner, John	Pit	6	3	22.1	0	6	1	2	.857	2.42
Wilson, Enrique	Pit	2	1	9.2	0	1	0	1	1.000	0.93
Wilson, Enrique	NYY	19	12	115.0	7	29	0	2	1.000	2.82
Woodward, Chris	Tor	10	8	74.0	6	20	5	5	.839	3.16
Wooten, Shawn	Ana	1	0	1.0	0	0	0	0	.000	.00
Young, Dmitri	Cin	36	33	281.0	16	57	9	9	.890	2.34

Shortstops - Regulars

Player	Tm	G	GS	Inn	PO	A	E	DP	Pct.	Rng
Hernandez, Jose	Mil	150	146	1286.0	204	427	18	90	.972	4.42
Ordonez, Rey	NYM	148	140	1226.1	215	385	12	80	.980	4.40
Cruz, Deivi	Det	109	102	920.2	157	292	17	69	.964	4.39
Eckstein, David	Ana	126	118	1051.1	178	332	15	66	.971	4.37
Guzman, Cristian	Min	118	115	1015.0	165	327	21	58	.959	4.36
Vizquel, Omar	Cle	154	152	1320.2	219	414	7	88	.989	4.31
Cora, Alex	LA	132	119	1062.2	178	328	20	63	.962	4.29
Rollins, Jimmy	Phi	157	156	1388.1	216	426	14	99	.979	4.16
Womack, Tony	Ari	118	114	1013.2	151	312	22	74	.955	4.11
Lansing, Mike	Bos	76	71	621.0	108	172	10	37	.966	4.06
Guillen, Carlos	Sea	137	123	1120.0	187	313	10	75	.980	4.02
Gutierrez, Ricky	ChC	144	140	1224.1	173	360	16	67	.971	3.92
Jeter, Derek	NYY	150	150	1312.1	212	343	15	68	.974	3.81
Gomez, Chris	TOT	94	83	731.1	111	189	13	43	.958	3.69
Average	—	130	126	1108.1	191	360	15	79	.973	4.48

Shortstops - The Rest

Player	Tm	G	GS	Inn	PO	A	E	DP	Pct.	Rng
Abbott, Kurt	Atl	1	0	2.0	1	2	0	0	1.000	13.50
Almonte, Erick	NYY	4	0	10.0	4	3	1	1	.875	6.30
Arias, Alex	SD	13	8	74.0	17	16	1	3	.971	4.01
Batista, Tony	Bal	20	19	177.1	33	63	1	11	.990	4.87
Bellhorn, Mark	Oak	5	1	19.0	3	6	1	0	.900	4.26
Bellinger, Clay	NYY	2	0	5.0	0	3	0	0	1.000	5.40
Beltre, Adrian	LA	2	1	9.0	4	3	0	0	1.000	7.00
Berg, Dave	Fla	19	12	115.2	11	29	1	3	.976	3.11
Berroa, Angel	KC	14	12	112.2	21	40	3	9	.953	4.87
Betemit, Wilson	Atl	1	0	1.0	0	0	0	0	.000	.00
Blum, Geoff	Mon	4	0	6.1	2	3	0	1	1.000	7.11
Bogar, Tim	LA	2	2	12.0	1	2	0	0	1.000	2.25
Bordick, Mike	Bal	58	58	508.2	107	146	6	28	.977	4.48
Branson, Jeff	LA	2	0	3.2	0	0	1	0	.000	.00
Butler, Brent	Col	10	6	49.0	5	13	1	3	.947	3.31
Cabrera, Jolbert	Cle	14	7	75.1	11	28	2	4	.951	4.66
Cairo, Miguel	ChC	1	1	8.0	1	1	0	0	1.000	2.25
Cairo, Miguel	StL	1	0	1.0	0	0	0	0	.000	.00
Castilla, Vinny	Hou	3	0	3.2	1	1	0	0	1.000	4.91
Castro, Juan	Cin	46	29	279.2	38	81	7	14	.944	3.83
Chavez, Eric	Oak	1	0	1.0	0	0	0	0	.000	.00
Cintron, Alex	Ari	7	0	15.2	2	6	0	0	1.000	4.60
Coolbaugh, Mike	Mil	3	1	18.0	2	5	0	1	1.000	3.50
Counsell, Craig	Ari	58	46	415.1	70	124	5	31	.975	4.20
Crespo, Cesar	SD	1	0	2.0	1	1	0	0	1.000	9.00
Delgado, Wilson	KC	6	2	24.0	2	10	0	2	1.000	4.50
DeRosa, Mark	Atl	48	38	354.2	51	118	7	21	.960	4.29
Dransfeldt, Kelly	Tex	3	0	7.0	0	4	0	0	1.000	5.14
Everett, Adam	Hou	6	0	7.0	2	2	2	1	.667	5.14
Fox, Andy	Fla	12	11	102.0	14	31	3	9	.938	3.97
Frye, Jeff	Tor	2	0	3.0	0	2	0	0	1.000	6.00
Fryman, Travis	Cle	1	0	2.0	1	2	0	1	1.000	13.50
Garcia, Jesse	Atl	2	0	4.0	0	1	0	0	1.000	2.25
Garciaparra, N.	Bos	21	21	184.0	34	56	3	13	.968	4.40
Gil, Benji	Ana	44	40	339.1	78	110	11	24	.945	4.99
Gipson, Charles	Sea	6	4	33.0	9	11	1	1	.952	5.45
Glaus, Troy	Ana	2	0	4.0	0	1	0	0	1.000	2.25
Gomez, Chris	SD	36	28	245.1	31	58	6	14	.937	3.26

Shortstops - Regulars

Player	Tm	G	GS	Inn	PO	A	E	DP	Pct.	Rng
Sanchez, Rey	TOT	148	143	1242.1	217	479	6	130	.991	5.04
Gonzalez, Alex S.	Tor	154	153	1374.1	249	509	10	120	.987	4.96
Reese, Pokey	Cin	78	70	621.1	117	224	10	34	.972	4.94
Perez, Neifi	TOT	133	132	1159.1	241	395	15	102	.977	4.94
Wilson, Jack	Pit	107	105	883.2	136	342	16	67	.968	4.87
Cabrera, Orlando	Mon	162	160	1406.2	246	514	11	106	.986	4.86
Lugo, Julio	Hou	133	124	1096.0	211	373	22	74	.964	4.80
Rodriguez, Alex	Tex	161	161	1395.1	279	452	18	118	.976	4.72
Jimenez, D'Angelo	SD	85	84	740.2	130	255	21	47	.948	4.68
Renteria, Edgar	StL	137	133	1153.1	207	390	24	85	.961	4.66
Aurilia, Rich	SF	149	146	1313.0	246	423	17	108	.975	4.59
Tejada, Miguel	Oak	162	160	1431.1	256	473	20	93	.973	4.58
Furcal, Rafael	Atl	79	79	694.1	126	224	11	49	.970	4.54
Gonzalez, Alex	Fla	142	139	1220.1	219	396	26	101	.959	4.54
Clayton, Royce	CWS	133	126	1117.1	196	367	7	74	.988	4.53

Shortstops - The Rest

Player	Tm	G	GS	Inn	PO	A	E	DP	Pct.	Rng
Gomez, Chris	TB	58	55	486.0	80	131	7	29	.968	3.91
Graffanino, Tony	CWS	5	0	6.0	2	4	1	2	.857	9.00
Grebeck, Craig	Bos	23	12	118.2	16	32	0	4	1.000	3.64
Guerrero, Wilton	Cin	16	13	114.0	20	31	4	9	.927	4.03
Halter, Shane	Det	62	60	508.2	97	169	9	46	.967	4.71
Hocking, Denny	Min	47	41	368.1	65	111	3	26	.983	4.30
Izturis, Cesar	Tor	6	6	51.0	16	11	1	5	.964	4.76
Jackson, Damian	SD	3	3	27.0	2	6	0	0	1.000	2.67
Johnson, Russ	TB	6	2	23.0	3	3	1	0	.857	2.35
Larkin, Barry	Cin	44	42	341.1	65	108	9	23	.951	4.56
Lofton, James	Bos	7	6	54.0	9	14	2	3	.920	3.83
Lopez, Felipe	Tor	3	2	20.1	6	5	1	1	.917	4.87
Lopez, Luis	Mil	17	9	85.2	16	29	1	5	.978	4.73
Lopez, Mendy	Pit	6	2	29.0	6	12	0	4	1.000	5.59
Loretta, Mark	Mil	9	6	46.2	11	20	1	4	.969	5.98
Magadan, Dave	SD	1	0	1.0	0	0	0	0	.000	.00
Martinez, Felix	TB	67	58	508.2	103	148	15	38	.944	4.44
Martinez, Ramon	SF	24	16	141.1	25	58	3	16	.965	5.29
Maxwell, Jason	Min	12	6	58.0	8	17	3	3	.893	3.88
McDonald, John	Cle	9	3	48.2	8	13	1	2	.955	3.88
McEwing, Joe	NYM	12	6	54.0	7	21	1	1	.966	4.67
McLemore, Mark	Sea	35	30	262.0	41	79	2	20	.984	4.12
Mendez, Donaldo	SD	46	34	300.2	47	91	12	15	.920	4.13
Menechino, Frank	Oak	3	1	12.0	0	1	1	0	.500	0.75
Merloni, Lou	Bos	45	36	332.0	54	100	2	19	.987	4.17
Mora, Melvin	Bal	43	38	333.1	69	125	7	21	.965	5.24
Mordecai, Mike	Mon	4	2	18.1	3	6	0	2	1.000	4.42
Nieves, Jose	Ana	10	4	43.0	10	12	1	2	.957	4.60
Nunez, Abraham	Pit	48	33	309.0	51	131	2	24	.989	5.30
Ojeda, Augie	ChC	31	21	203.2	34	56	2	10	.978	3.98
Ordaz, Luis	KC	8	4	33.0	6	13	2	1	.905	5.18
Perez, Neifi	Col	87	87	763.2	145	264	10	64	.976	4.82
Perez, Neifi	KC	46	45	395.2	96	131	5	38	.978	5.16
Perez, Santiago	SD	8	5	50.0	8	10	2	1	.900	3.24
Perez, Tomas	Phi	8	5	48.0	8	20	0	4	1.000	5.25
Polanco, Placido	StL	42	29	281.0	51	109	0	16	1.000	5.12
Punto, Nick	Phi	1	1	9.0	1	2	0	0	1.000	3.00
Ransom, Cody	SF	6	0	9.0	0	4	0	0	1.000	4.00
Reboulet, Jeff	LA	56	40	363.1	77	96	7	33	.961	4.29
Relaford, Desi	NYM	25	14	134.0	20	48	3	7	.958	4.57
Roberts, Brian	Bal	51	47	413.0	84	131	14	25	.939	4.69
Sadler, Donnie	Cin	12	8	82.1	10	31	0	4	1.000	4.48
Sadler, Donnie	KC	6	2	23.2	7	17	2	3	.923	9.13
Sanchez, Rey	KC	100	98	851.0	155	333	3	99	.994	5.16
Sanchez, Rey	Atl	48	45	391.1	62	146	3	31	.986	4.78
Sheets, Andy	TB	49	47	406.0	80	121	2	29	.990	4.46
Sheldon, Scott	Tex	16	1	36.0	8	16	1	3	.960	6.00
Shumpert, Terry	Col	4	2	22.2	5	1	0	1	1.000	2.38
Smith, Jason	ChC	1	0	1.0	2	0	0	0	1.000	18.00
Sojo, Luis	NYY	5	4	40.0	7	10	0	2	1.000	3.83
Spivey, Junior	Ari	1	0	1.0	0	0	0	0	.000	.00
Uribe, Juan	Col	69	67	594.2	108	184	5	45	.983	4.42
Valentin, John	Bos	18	15	138.1	22	42	2	9	.970	4.16
Valentin, Jose	CWS	43	36	310.0	64	118	9	34	.953	5.28
Vazquez, Ramon	Sea	10	5	50.0	11	9	0	3	1.000	3.60
Velandia, Jorge	NYM	8	2	31.1	2	8	0	2	1.000	2.87
Vizcaino, Jose	Hou	53	38	348.0	50	114	11	21	.937	4.24
Walker, Todd	Cin	1	0	4.0	0	1	0	0	1.000	2.25

Shortstops - The Rest

Player	Tm	G	GS	Inn	PO	A	E	DP	Pct.	Rng
Williams, Matt	Ari	2	2	14.0	3	5	0	1	1.000	5.14
Wilson, Enrique	Pit	28	22	194.2	40	72	3	15	.974	5.18
Wilson, Enrique	NYY	20	7	84.0	13	27	2	4	.952	4.29
Woodward, Chris	Tor	4	1	14.0	3	8	0	2	1.000	7.07

Left Fielders - Regulars

Player	Tm	G	GS	Inn	PO	A	E	DP	Pct.	Rng
Higginson, Bobby	Det	142	142	1215.1	321	10	8	1	.976	2.45
Jones, Jacque	Min	137	121	1076.0	276	8	5	0	.983	2.38
Catalanotto, Frank	Tex	78	72	647.1	168	2	1	0	.994	2.36
Jenkins, Geoff	Mil	104	104	897.1	210	8	3	2	.986	2.19
Anderson, Garret	Ana	144	144	1251.2	294	9	2	2	.993	2.18
Lee, Carlos	CWS	130	129	1048.0	241	9	8	0	.969	2.15
Cordova, Marty	Cle	84	76	632.2	144	6	2	1	.987	2.13
Brown, Dee	KC	77	76	666.0	152	3	1	1	.994	2.09
Young, Dmitri	Cin	86	84	669.0	145	8	7	1	.956	2.06
Floyd, Cliff	Fla	142	140	1212.0	269	8	8	2	.972	2.06
Giles, Brian	Pit	124	102	918.0	199	6	7	2	.967	2.01
Berkman, Lance	Hou	128	111	1013.2	218	5	4	1	.982	1.98
Stewart, Shannon	Tor	142	142	1216.1	257	7	5	0	.981	1.95
Lankford, Ray	TOT	106	96	826.1	167	6	6	1	.966	1.88
DeShields, Delino	TOT	79	72	619.0	126	3	4	0	.970	1.88
Bonds, Barry	SF	143	141	1231.2	246	9	6	1	.977	1.86
Gonzalez, Luis	Ari	161	161	1416.2	280	8	0	1	1.000	1.83
Knoblauch, Chuck	NYY	108	104	890.0	171	8	2	4	.989	1.81
Henderson, Rickey	SD	104	98	812.2	157	5	3	2	.982	1.79
White, Rondell	ChC	90	88	688.0	133	4	3	0	.979	1.79
Surhoff, B.J.	Atl	129	120	1055.0	200	8	3	0	.986	1.77
Agbayani, Benny	NYM	84	82	631.2	123	1	6	0	.954	1.77
Burrell, Pat	Phi	146	143	1250.2	226	18	7	2	.972	1.76
Sheffield, Gary	LA	141	141	1195.0	195	17	6	0	.972	1.60
Average	—	117	112	961.2	205	7	4	1	.979	1.99

Left Fielders - The Rest

Player	Tm	G	GS	Inn	PO	A	E	DP	Pct.	Rng
Abbott, Jeff	Fla	1	0	1.0	0	0	0	0	.000	.00
Alcantara, Israel	Bos	6	5	43.0	4	1	1	0	.833	1.05
Aldridge, Cory	Atl	1	0	1.0	0	0	0	0	.000	.00
Allen, Chad	Min	16	16	131.2	31	1	1	0	.970	2.19
Anderson, Brady	Bal	56	42	383.1	96	1	0	0	1.000	2.28
Aven, Bruce	LA	5	1	22.0	3	0	0	0	1.000	1.23
Barkett, Andy	Pit	9	7	60.2	12	1	0	0	1.000	1.93
Barnes, John	Min	3	3	26.0	8	0	1	0	.889	2.77
Barnes, Larry	Ana	1	1	2.0	0	0	0	0	.000	.00
Bartee, Kimera	Col	9	2	32.2	8	0	1	0	.889	2.20
Bautista, Danny	Ari	3	0	3.0	0	0	0	0	.000	.00
Bell, Derek	Pit	5	5	41.0	6	1	0	0	1.000	1.54
Bellinger, Clay	NYY	13	3	46.0	11	0	0	0	1.000	2.15
Benard, Marvin	SF	15	6	64.2	15	1	1	0	.941	2.23
Berger, Brandon	KC	5	5	41.0	7	0	0	0	1.000	1.54
Bichette, Dante	Bos	37	37	310.2	60	4	2	1	.970	1.85
Bigbie, Larry	Bal	5	2	32.0	9	0	0	0	1.000	2.53
Blum, Geoff	Mon	35	27	250.0	51	1	0	0	1.000	1.87
Bocachica, Hiram	LA	10	3	36.0	7	0	1	0	.875	1.75

Left Fielders - The Rest

Player	Tm	G	GS	Inn	PO	A	E	DP	Pct.	Rng
Bonilla, Bobby	StL	4	2	12.0	1	1	0	0	1.000	1.50
Bradley, Milton	Mon	13	9	79.0	16	0	1	0	.941	1.82
Bragg, Darren	NYM	8	3	34.2	4	0	0	0	1.000	1.04
Branyan, Russell	Cle	31	25	208.0	38	3	3	0	.932	1.77
Brown, Emil	Pit	2	0	2.0	0	0	0	0	.000	.00
Brown, Emil	SD	4	0	7.0	0	0	0	0	.000	.00
Brown, Roosevelt	ChC	21	13	113.2	20	0	0	0	1.000	1.58
Brumbaugh, Cliff	Tex	2	0	5.0	0	0	0	0	.000	.00
Brumbaugh, Cliff	Col	4	2	17.0	2	0	0	0	1.000	1.06
Buchanan, Brian	Min	7	4	40.0	11	0	0	0	1.000	2.47
Buhner, Jay	Sea	10	9	62.0	13	0	0	0	1.000	1.89
Burks, Ellis	Cle	18	17	129.2	21	2	0	0	1.000	1.60
Byrnes, Eric	Oak	8	4	34.0	7	0	1	0	.875	1.85
Cabrera, Jolbert	Cle	36	1	70.0	14	0	0	0	1.000	1.80
Cairo, Miguel	StL	6	2	19.0	7	0	0	0	1.000	3.32
Chavez, Endy	KC	22	13	135.1	31	1	0	0	1.000	2.13
Christensen, M.	LA	3	0	4.1	0	0	0	0	.000	.00
Christenson, Ryan	Oak	1	0	3.0	1	0	0	0	1.000	3.00
Christenson, Ryan	Ari	4	0	6.0	1	0	0	0	1.000	1.50
Clapp, Stubby	StL	4	2	16.0	3	0	0	0	1.000	1.69
Clark, Brady	Cin	26	13	129.1	31	0	1	0	.969	2.16
Colangelo, Mike	SD	25	4	88.0	13	1	0	0	1.000	1.43
Coleman, Michael	NYY	1	0	3.0	0	0	0	0	.000	.00
Collier, Lou	Mil	12	5	57.2	11	0	0	0	1.000	1.72
Conine, Jeff	Bal	22	20	169.0	44	1	0	0	1.000	2.40
Cordero, Wil	Cle	48	35	326.1	59	0	1	0	.983	1.63
Cox, Steve	TB	6	6	48.0	8	0	0	0	1.000	1.50
Crespo, Cesar	SD	6	4	33.0	3	0	0	0	1.000	0.82
Crespo, Felipe	Phi	4	1	18.0	6	1	0	0	1.000	3.50
Cruz, Jacob	Cle	3	2	19.0	4	0	1	0	.800	1.89
Cruz, Jacob	Col	18	14	129.2	21	1	2	0	.917	1.53
Cruz, Jose	Tor	14	9	88.1	16	0	0	0	1.000	1.63
Cummings, Midre	Ari	3	0	6.0	3	0	0	0	1.000	4.50
Curtis, Chad	Tex	10	9	69.2	16	0	1	0	.941	2.07
Cust, Jack	Ari	1	0	2.0	0	0	0	0	.000	.00
Damon, Johnny	Oak	67	64	562.0	131	1	3	1	.978	2.11
Darr, Mike	SD	5	4	32.0	12	0	0	0	1.000	3.38
Daubach, Brian	Bos	6	6	50.0	7	0	0	0	1.000	1.26
Dellucci, David	Ari	8	1	26.0	4	0	0	0	1.000	1.38
DeRosa, Mark	Atl	1	0	2.0	0	0	0	0	.000	.00
DeShields, Delino	Bal	46	44	393.0	86	2	3	0	.967	2.02
DeShields, Delino	ChC	33	28	226.0	40	1	1	0	.976	1.63
Drew, J.D.	StL	1	0	3.0	0	0	0	0	.000	.00
Ducey, Rob	Phi	1	1	5.0	2	0	0	0	1.000	3.60
Ducey, Rob	Mon	8	9	59.1	19	1	0	0	1.000	3.03
Dunn, Adam	Cin	30	25	226.2	50	0	0	0	1.000	1.99
Dunston, Shawon	SF	12	5	50.0	4	0	0	0	1.000	0.72
Dunwoody, Todd	ChC	15	6	68.1	16	1	0	0	1.000	2.24
Echevarria, Angel	Mil	19	15	127.0	19	0	2	0	.905	1.35
Encarnacion, Mario	Col	14	11	107.0	17	1	0	1	1.000	1.51
Fox, Andy	Fla	1	0	3.0	1	0	0	0	1.000	3.00
Freel, Ryan	Tor	1	0	1.0	0	0	0	0	.000	.00
Frye, Jeff	Tor	1	0	1.0	0	0	0	0	.000	.00
Gant, Ron	Col	51	48	388.0	81	2	3	0	.965	1.93
Gant, Ron	Oak	11	8	73.0	4	0	0	0	1.000	0.49
Garcia, Karim	Cle	6	6	43.0	4	1	1	0	.833	1.05
Giambi, Jeremy	Oak	11	9	81.0	9	1	3	0	.769	1.11
Gibbons, Jay	Bal	28	26	224.0	62	3	0	0	1.000	2.61

Left Fielders - The Rest

Player	Tm	G	GS	Inn	PO	A	E	DP	Pct.	Rng
Gilkey, Bernard	Atl	28	17	159.0	31	0	0	0	1.000	1.75
Gipson, Charles	Sea	41	4	92.2	27	0	0	0	1.000	2.62
Gonzalez, Raul	Cin	2	2	17.0	4	0	0	0	1.000	2.12
Goodwin, Tom	LA	8	0	20.0	4	0	0	0	1.000	1.80
Graffanino, Tony	CWS	3	0	5.0	3	0	0	0	1.000	5.40
Greer, Rusty	Tex	60	59	503.0	124	2	5	0	.962	2.25
Grieve, Ben	TB	56	56	471.2	123	4	1	0	.992	2.42
Grissom, Marquis	LA	26	15	145.2	32	0	0	0	1.000	1.98
Guerrero, Wilton	Cin	6	2	24.0	6	0	0	0	1.000	2.25
Guzman, Edwards	SF	2	0	6.0	0	0	0	0	.000	.00
Hamilton, Darryl	NYM	24	18	170.2	42	0	0	0	1.000	2.21
Harris, Lenny	NYM	5	2	18.1	3	0	0	0	1.000	1.47
Helms, Wes	Atl	1	1	8.0	2	0	0	0	1.000	2.25
Hernandez, Jose	Mil	1	0	1.0	0	0	0	0	.000	.00
Hidalgo, Richard	Hou	23	16	147.2	36	4	0	1	1.000	2.44
Hocking, Denny	Min	6	3	31.0	4	0	0	0	1.000	1.16
Hollandsworth, T.	Col	25	17	155.0	32	2	1	0	.971	1.97
Hunter, Brian L.	Phi	22	11	122.2	21	0	0	0	1.000	1.54
Hyzdu, Adam	Pit	8	2	33.0	6	0	0	0	1.000	1.64
Ibanez, Raul	KC	17	15	117.1	27	1	1	0	.966	2.15
Jackson, Ryan	Det	19	7	82.0	18	0	1	0	.947	1.98
Javier, Stan	Sea	62	41	395.2	97	0	1	0	.990	2.21
Jennings, Robin	Oak	3	0	3.0	1	0	0	0	1.000	3.00
Jennings, Robin	Col	1	1	8.0	0	0	1	0	.000	.00
Johnson, Mark P.	NYM	12	8	66.1	7	0	0	0	1.000	0.95
Jones, Chipper	Atl	8	8	65.0	16	0	0	0	1.000	2.22
Jones, Terry	Mon	10	5	52.0	11	0	1	0	.917	1.90
Justice, David	NYY	16	14	122.1	36	4	1	1	.976	2.94
Kendall, Jason	Pit	18	18	147.0	30	0	3	0	.909	1.84
Kielty, Bobby	Min	11	8	69.2	17	0	1	0	.944	2.20
Kieschnick, Brooks	Col	8	2	28.2	5	0	1	0	.833	1.57
Kingsale, Gene	Sea	5	2	25.0	6	0	0	0	1.000	2.16
Kinkade, Mike	Bal	29	24	206.0	49	0	2	0	.961	2.14
Kotsay, Mark	SD	1	1	8.0	5	0	0	0	1.000	5.63
Lankford, Ray	StL	85	76	663.2	135	5	5	1	.966	1.90
Lankford, Ray	SD	21	20	162.2	32	1	1	0	.971	1.83
LaRue, Jason	Cin	2	0	2.0	1	0	0	0	1.000	4.50
Latham, Chris	Tor	15	7	70.0	24	0	0	0	1.000	3.09
Leach, Jalal	SF	1	1	9.0	1	0	0	0	1.000	1.00
Ledee, Ricky	Tex	6	4	38.0	7	0	0	0	1.000	1.66
Lewis, Darren	Bos	27	10	122.0	35	1	0	0	1.000	2.66
Liefer, Jeff	CWS	35	31	280.0	47	2	0	0	1.000	1.58
Little, Mark	Col	13	1	31.2	7	0	0	0	1.000	1.99
Lo Duca, Paul	LA	4	2	25.2	6	0	1	0	.857	2.10
Long, Terrence	Oak	62	60	539.2	109	3	3	2	.974	1.87
Lugo, Julio	Hou	6	1	16.2	2	0	0	0	1.000	1.08
Mabry, John	Fla	3	1	10.2	2	0	0	0	1.000	1.69
Macias, Jose	Det	3	2	17.0	2	0	0	0	1.000	1.06
Mackowiak, Rob	Pit	10	6	61.1	9	1	0	0	1.000	1.47
Magee, Wendell	Det	21	11	110.0	29	1	0	0	1.000	2.45
Magruder, Chris	Tex	8	3	38.1	12	0	0	0	1.000	2.82
Marrero, Eli	StL	8	1	19.0	5	0	1	0	.833	2.37
Martin, Al	Sea	72	71	509.1	131	3	4	2	.971	2.37
Martinez, Dave	Atl	27	16	157.1	32	0	0	0	1.000	1.83
Matos, Luis	Bal	1	1	6.0	0	0	0	0	.000	.00
Matthews Jr., Gary	ChC	20	1	45.1	9	0	0	0	1.000	1.79
McCarty, Dave	KC	8	4	42.0	6	0	2	0	.750	1.29
McCracken, Q.	Min	6	5	44.0	10	0	0	0	1.000	2.05

262

Left Fielders - The Rest

Player	Tm	G	GS	Inn	PO	A	E	DP	Pct.	Rng
McDonald, Donzell	NYY	1	0	1.0	0	0	0	0	.000	.00
McEwing, Joe	NYM	48	20	218.0	42	2	0	1	1.000	1.82
McLemore, Mark	Sea	63	22	286.1	68	2	1	1	.986	2.20
McMillon, Billy	Det	1	0	5.0	1	0	0	0	1.000	1.80
McMillon, Billy	Oak	15	13	122.2	18	1	1	0	.950	1.39
Merced, Orlando	Hou	11	8	68.0	10	1	0	0	1.000	1.46
Meyers, Chad	ChC	2	0	2.0	1	0	0	0	1.000	4.50
Michaels, Jason	Phi	1	0	2.0	0	0	0	0	.000	.00
Millar, Kevin	Fla	27	20	184.0	50	0	0	0	1.000	2.45
Minor, Ryan	Mon	2	1	12.0	0	0	0	0	.000	.00
Mohr, Dustan	Min	6	2	23.0	6	0	0	0	1.000	2.35
Monroe, Craig	Tex	6	1	18.0	8	0	0	0	1.000	4.00
Mottola, Chad	Fla	2	0	4.0	1	0	0	0	1.000	2.25
Mouton, James	Mil	21	5	80.1	23	0	2	0	.920	2.58
Mouton, Lyle	Fla	6	1	19.1	2	0	0	0	1.000	0.93
Norton, Greg	Col	22	13	108.2	14	1	0	0	1.000	1.24
Nunez, Abraham	Pit	1	0	1.0	0	0	0	0	.000	.00
Ochoa, Alex	Cin	3	0	3.1	0	0	0	0	.000	.00
Ochoa, Alex	Col	33	30	271.2	65	3	1	2	.986	2.25
O'Leary, Troy	Bos	52	45	414.1	91	3	1	0	.989	2.04
Owens, Eric	Fla	1	0	2.0	0	0	0	0	.000	.00
Palmeiro, Orlando	Ana	26	13	140.0	36	2	1	1	.974	2.44
Paquette, Craig	StL	33	27	216.1	38	0	0	0	1.000	1.58
Patterson, Corey	ChC	13	2	38.2	11	0	0	0	1.000	2.56
Perez, Santiago	SD	9	4	45.2	12	1	1	0	.929	2.56
Perez, Timo	NYM	6	5	38.0	11	2	0	0	1.000	3.08
Podsednik, Scott	Sea	3	0	6.0	2	0	0	0	1.000	3.00
Porter, Bo	Tex	18	12	101.0	28	1	1	0	.967	2.58
Powell, Dante	SF	5	0	7.0	1	0	0	0	1.000	1.29
Pride, Curtis	Mon	19	13	127.2	30	1	0	0	1.000	2.19
Pujols, Albert	StL	39	37	309.0	72	3	1	0	.987	2.18
Quinn, Mark	KC	49	47	418.1	88	4	2	0	.979	1.98
Raines, Tim	Mon	20	17	138.0	23	0	0	0	1.000	1.50
Raines, Tim	Bal	2	2	19.0	7	0	0	0	1.000	3.32
Ramirez, Julio	CWS	1	0	1.0	0	0	0	0	.000	.00
Ramirez, Manny	Bos	55	55	482.0	98	1	0	0	1.000	1.85
Reboulet, Jeff	LA	2	0	2.0	0	0	0	0	.000	.00
Rios, Armando	SF	13	7	78.0	17	0	0	0	1.000	1.96
Rivera, Ruben	Cin	10	5	53.0	7	1	0	0	1.000	1.36
Roberts, Dave	Cle	9	0	18.0	5	0	0	0	1.000	2.50
Robinson, Kerry	StL	42	15	174.1	40	0	1	0	.976	2.07
Rolls, Damian	TB	7	4	37.0	9	1	0	0	1.000	2.43
Rowand, Aaron	CWS	34	1	60.2	12	0	0	0	1.000	1.78
Sadler, Donnie	Cin	6	2	26.2	3	1	1	0	.800	1.35
Sadler, Donnie	KC	5	2	20.0	5	1	0	0	1.000	2.70
Sanchez, Alex	Mil	3	3	23.0	3	1	0	0	1.000	1.57
Sanders, Anthony	Sea	8	5	39.0	12	0	0	0	1.000	2.77
Sanders, Deion	Cin	12	12	94.1	21	3	0	1	1.000	2.29
Saturria, Luis	StL	3	0	3.0	1	0	0	0	1.000	3.00
Seguignol, F.	Mon	7	3	28.0	7	1	0	0	1.000	2.57
Sheldon, Scott	Tex	2	1	10.0	2	0	0	0	1.000	1.80
Shinjo, Tsuyoshi	NYM	46	24	261.0	68	8	2	3	.974	2.62
Shumpert, Terry	Col	24	21	152.0	38	2	1	0	.976	2.37
Sierra, Ruben	Tex	1	1	8.0	1	0	0	0	1.000	1.13
Simmons, Brian	Tor	19	4	86.0	25	0	0	0	1.000	2.62
Singleton, Chris	CWS	19	1	38.2	11	0	0	0	1.000	2.56
Smith, Mark	Mon	55	44	384.2	88	2	0	1	1.000	2.11
Spencer, Shane	NYY	44	36	341.1	77	5	1	0	.988	2.16

Left Fielders - The Rest

Player	Tm	G	GS	Inn	PO	A	E	DP	Pct.	Rng
Spiezio, Scott	Ana	10	5	44.0	13	0	0	0	1.000	2.66
Sprague, Ed	Sea	8	8	49.0	10	0	0	0	1.000	1.84
Stairs, Matt	ChC	22	19	141.2	31	1	0	0	1.000	2.03
Stynes, Chris	Bos	3	3	26.0	6	0	0	0	1.000	2.08
Sweeney, Mark	Mil	20	19	152.1	29	0	1	0	.967	1.71
Thompson, Ryan	Fla	1	0	2.0	1	0	0	0	1.000	4.50
Toca, Jorge	NYM	2	0	7.0	2	0	0	0	1.000	2.57
Trammell, Bubba	SD	34	27	251.2	56	2	0	0	1.000	2.07
Tucker, Michael	Cin	37	17	197.1	46	0	2	0	.958	2.10
Tucker, Michael	ChC	38	5	113.1	25	0	1	0	.962	1.99
Tyner, Jason	TB	57	39	395.2	102	3	3	0	.972	2.39
Valdez, Mario	Oak	7	4	45.0	10	1	0	1	1.000	2.20
Valent, Eric	Phi	7	6	47.0	20	2	0	0	1.000	4.21
Vander Wal, John	Pit	20	19	137.1	23	0	0	0	1.000	1.51
Vander Wal, John	SF	3	2	17.0	4	0	0	0	1.000	2.12
Vaughn, Greg	TB	57	57	459.0	127	4	3	2	.978	2.57
Velarde, Randy	NYY	2	2	17.0	4	0	0	0	1.000	2.12
Ward, Daryle	Hou	27	26	208.2	42	0	0	0	1.000	1.81
Wehner, John	Pit	3	2	14.0	5	0	0	0	1.000	3.21
White, Devon	Mil	13	11	97.2	28	0	0	0	1.000	2.58
Wilkerson, Brad	Mon	38	34	300.2	62	2	2	0	.970	1.92
Williams, Gerald	NYY	6	2	30.2	9	0	1	0	.900	2.64
Wilson, Craig A.	Pit	1	0	1.0	0	0	0	0	.000	.00
Winn, Randy	TB	9	0	12.1	4	0	0	0	1.000	2.92

Center Fielders - Regulars

Player	Tm	G	GS	Inn	PO	A	E	DP	Pct.	Rng
Hunter, Torii	Min	147	147	1295.1	460	14	4	3	.992	3.29
Singleton, Chris	CWS	121	102	894.1	292	8	3	2	.990	3.02
Murray, Calvin	SF	104	73	710.0	232	4	5	1	.979	2.99
Cameron, Mike	Sea	149	140	1272.1	411	8	6	2	.986	2.96
Jones, Andruw	Atl	161	161	1435.1	461	10	6	6	.987	2.95
Erstad, Darin	Ana	146	146	1269.1	399	10	1	3	.998	2.90
Glanville, Doug	Phi	150	147	1310.2	413	8	4	3	.991	2.89
Kotsay, Mark	SD	106	98	862.0	269	4	4	1	.986	2.85
Beltran, Carlos	KC	152	152	1324.0	404	14	5	6	.988	2.84
Mora, Melvin	Bal	88	80	706.2	218	4	3	1	.987	2.83
Kapler, Gabe	Tex	133	130	1156.1	345	8	1	3	.997	2.75
Payton, Jay	NYM	103	90	825.2	236	6	4	1	.984	2.64
Pierre, Juan	Col	154	140	1257.2	362	4	8	1	.979	2.62
Lofton, Kenny	Cle	130	123	1076.0	310	3	6	0	.981	2.62
Hidalgo, Richard	Hou	128	117	1009.1	279	8	3	3	.990	2.56
Wilson, Preston	Fla	121	120	1049.1	286	12	2	4	.993	2.56
Damon, Johnny	Oak	86	84	744.1	209	4	0	0	1.000	2.55
Williams, Bernie	NYY	144	143	1266.2	338	8	2	1	.994	2.49
Finley, Steve	Ari	131	124	1110.2	300	6	2	3	.994	2.48
Bergeron, Peter	Mon	101	97	846.2	220	6	1	1	.996	2.40
Edmonds, Jim	StL	147	140	1214.2	311	12	6	1	.982	2.39
Matthews Jr., Gary	TOT	132	104	956.1	250	4	7	0	.973	2.39
Griffey Jr., Ken	Cin	90	90	757.0	195	1	3	0	.985	2.33
Grissom, Marquis	LA	95	83	765.1	192	6	0	2	1.000	2.33
Long, Terrence	Oak	74	72	650.0	163	1	3	1	.982	2.27
White, Devon	Mil	86	78	668.1	160	3	0	1	1.000	2.20
Cruz, Jose	Tor	133	132	1168.1	270	5	3	1	.989	2.12
Everett, Carl	Bos	84	83	744.0	168	4	5	1	.972	2.08
Average	—	121	114	1012.1	292	6	3	2	.989	2.65

Center Fielders - The Rest

Center Fielders - The Rest

Player	Tm	G	GS	Inn	PO	A	E	DP	Pct.	Rng
Abbott, Jeff	Fla	9	7	65.0	22	0	1	0	.957	3.05
Aldridge, Cory	Atl	1	1	9.0	2	0	0	0	1.000	2.00
Anderson, Brady	Bal	6	4	42.0	17	0	0	0	1.000	3.64
Anderson, Garret	Ana	12	5	56.0	19	0	0	0	1.000	3.05
Barker, Glen	Hou	60	5	120.0	36	0	0	0	1.000	2.70
Bartee, Kimera	Col	2	1	7.0	0	0	0	0	.000	.00
Bautista, Danny	Ari	28	25	222.0	61	2	0	1	1.000	2.55
Bell, Derek	Pit	1	1	7.0	1	0	0	0	1.000	1.29
Bellinger, Clay	NYY	10	5	55.0	10	0	0	0	1.000	1.64
Benard, Marvin	SF	75	70	590.0	173	3	7	2	.962	2.68
Berkman, Lance	Hou	40	40	325.1	81	2	1	0	.988	2.30
Bigbie, Larry	Bal	19	15	124.2	25	2	0	1	1.000	1.95
Bradley, Milton	Mon	52	50	436.0	137	5	1	1	.993	2.93
Bradley, Milton	Cle	8	3	43.2	12	1	1	0	.929	2.68
Bragg, Darren	NYM	2	1	12.0	5	0	0	0	1.000	3.75
Brosius, Scott	NYY	2	0	4.0	1	0	0	0	1.000	2.25
Brown, Adrian	Pit	7	7	61.0	17	0	0	0	1.000	2.51
Brown, Dee	KC	4	2	23.0	5	0	1	0	.833	1.96
Brown, Emil	Pit	51	26	275.2	78	4	1	1	.988	2.68
Brown, Emil	SD	6	3	27.2	6	0	0	0	1.000	1.95
Brown, Roosevelt	ChC	1	1	7.0	0	0	0	0	.000	.00
Buford, Damon	ChC	33	23	207.1	52	0	0	0	1.000	2.26
Byrnes, Eric	Oak	2	2	15.0	4	0	0	0	1.000	2.40
Cabrera, Jolbert	Cle	35	25	223.0	55	1	2	1	.966	2.26
Cedeno, Roger	Det	67	65	538.0	133	1	5	0	.964	2.24
Chavez, Endy	KC	5	3	33.0	9	1	0	0	1.000	2.73
Christensen, M.	CWS	6	1	18.0	1	0	0	0	1.000	0.50
Christensen, M.	LA	11	10	90.0	22	0	2	0	.917	2.20
Christenson, Ryan	Oak	1	0	1.0	0	0	0	0	.000	.00
Christenson, Ryan	Ari	1	0	1.1	0	0	0	0	.000	.00
Clark, Brady	Cin	7	2	31.0	7	0	0	0	1.000	2.03
Colangelo, Mike	SD	14	11	91.0	29	0	1	0	.967	2.87
Coleman, Michael	NYY	7	6	46.0	7	0	0	0	1.000	1.37
Collier, Lou	Mil	11	10	88.0	29	1	1	0	.968	3.07
Cordova, Marty	Cle	2	0	2.1	1	0	0	0	1.000	3.86
Crespo, Cesar	SD	11	9	88.1	26	1	0	0	1.000	2.75
Cruz, Jacob	Cle	15	10	93.0	26	0	0	0	1.000	2.52
Cruz, Jacob	Col	1	1	5.2	0	0	0	0	.000	.00
Curtis, Chad	Tex	16	16	128.0	52	1	0	1	1.000	3.73
Darr, Mike	SD	29	24	203.0	63	2	0	0	1.000	2.88
DaVanon, Jeff	Ana	13	9	86.0	22	2	1	1	.960	2.51
Dellucci, David	Ari	18	13	124.2	29	0	0	0	1.000	2.09
DeShields, Delino	Bal	1	1	9.0	1	0	0	0	1.000	1.00
Drew, J.D.	StL	20	13	116.1	26	3	1	0	.967	2.24
Ducey, Rob	Phi	1	1	8.0	2	0	0	0	1.000	2.25
Ducey, Rob	Mon	3	2	21.0	4	0	0	0	1.000	1.71
Dunston, Shawon	SF	23	16	132.1	50	0	2	0	.962	3.40
Dunwoody, Todd	ChC	6	5	42.1	14	0	1	0	.933	2.98
Dye, Jermaine	KC	2	2	17.0	3	0	0	0	1.000	1.59
Encarnacion, Juan	Det	56	52	474.1	125	2	4	0	.969	2.41
Escobar, Alex	NYM	9	7	61.2	16	1	1	0	.944	2.48
Fox, Andy	Fla	1	0	1.2	0	0	0	0	.000	.00
Gil, Benji	Ana	1	0	0.1	0	0	0	0	.000	.00
Giles, Brian	Pit	61	57	441.1	108	1	3	0	.973	2.22
Gipson, Charles	Sea	14	2	45.2	10	1	0	0	1.000	2.17
Goodwin, Tom	LA	70	69	590.1	149	1	1	0	.993	2.29
Green, Shawn	LA	2	0	5.0	2	0	0	0	1.000	3.60
Hamilton, Darryl	NYM	11	11	91.2	16	1	0	0	1.000	1.67

Player	Tm	G	GS	Inn	PO	A	E	DP	Pct.	Rng
Hammonds, Jeffrey	Mil	46	46	401.2	107	2	2	0	.982	2.44
Harris, Willie	Bal	8	7	56.0	16	1	0	1	1.000	2.73
Hermansen, Chad	Pit	6	6	47.0	16	0	0	0	1.000	3.06
Hernandez, Jose	Mil	1	1	4.0	2	0	0	0	1.000	4.50
Hocking, Denny	Min	5	3	35.0	13	0	0	0	1.000	3.34
Hollandsworth, T.	Col	12	9	72.0	15	0	0	0	1.000	1.88
Hubbard, Trenidad	KC	2	2	17.0	2	0	0	0	1.000	1.06
Hunter, Brian L.	Phi	18	13	111.2	36	2	0	1	1.000	3.06
Hyzdu, Adam	Pit	1	0	1.0	2	0	0	0	1.000	18.00
Ibanez, Raul	KC	2	0	10.0	1	0	1	0	.500	0.90
Jackson, Damian	SD	2	0	2.0	2	0	0	0	1.000	9.00
Javier, Stan	Sea	13	11	77.0	27	0	0	0	1.000	3.16
Jones, Jacque	Min	2	1	9.0	1	0	0	0	1.000	1.00
Jones, Terry	Mon	13	9	89.0	30	2	0	1	1.000	3.24
Jordan, Brian	Atl	1	0	3.0	2	0	0	0	1.000	6.00
Kielty, Bobby	Min	11	10	91.0	27	1	1	1	.966	2.77
Kingsale, Gene	Bal	1	1	9.0	1	0	0	0	1.000	1.00
Kingsale, Gene	Sea	1	1	8.0	3	0	0	0	1.000	3.38
Lankford, Ray	SD	16	12	112.2	31	0	0	0	1.000	2.48
Latham, Chris	Tor	2	0	5.0	1	0	0	0	1.000	1.80
Ledee, Ricky	Tex	10	9	77.0	20	0	0	0	1.000	2.34
Lewis, Darren	Bos	21	11	112.2	30	0	0	0	1.000	2.40
Little, Mark	Col	14	9	72.2	20	2	0	3	1.000	2.72
Mabry, John	Fla	2	0	1.1	0	0	0	0	.000	.00
Macias, Jose	Det	22	20	174.0	58	1	0	0	1.000	3.05
Magee, Wendell	Det	36	25	243.0	68	3	1	0	.986	2.63
Magruder, Chris	Tex	1	0	2.0	1	0	0	0	1.000	4.50
Martin, Al	Sea	1	0	3.0	1	0	0	0	1.000	3.00
Matos, Luis	Bal	23	17	162.2	46	2	1	2	.980	2.66
Matthews Jr., Gary	ChC	88	64	602.2	150	3	4	0	.975	2.28
Matthews Jr., Gary	Pit	44	40	353.2	100	1	3	0	.971	2.57
McCracken, Q.	Min	2	1	11.0	2	0	0	0	1.000	1.64
McDonald, Donzell	NYY	2	0	7.0	2	0	0	0	1.000	2.57
McEwing, Joe	NYM	2	1	8.0	0	0	0	0	.000	.00
McLemore, Mark	Sea	8	7	49.0	13	1	0	1	1.000	2.57
Meyers, Chad	ChC	2	1	7.0	2	0	0	0	1.000	2.57
Mottola, Chad	Fla	1	1	6.0	1	0	0	0	1.000	1.50
Mouton, James	Mil	28	18	177.1	48	2	1	1	.980	2.54
Nixon, Trot	Bos	70	67	591.1	139	4	3	1	.979	2.18
Ochoa, Alex	Col	2	2	15.0	1	0	0	0	1.000	0.60
Ordonez, Magglio	CWS	1	0	1.0	1	0	0	0	1.000	9.00
Owens, Eric	Fla	37	31	288.1	70	1	1	0	.986	2.22
Palmeiro, Orlando	Ana	7	2	26.0	7	0	0	0	1.000	2.42
Patterson, Corey	ChC	45	24	244.2	70	0	2	0	.972	2.57
Perez, Robert	NYY	3	3	25.1	7	0	0	0	1.000	2.49
Perez, Santiago	SD	10	5	54.0	16	0	0	0	1.000	2.67
Perez, Timo	NYM	8	5	49.0	9	0	0	0	1.000	1.65
Podsednik, Scott	Sea	1	1	10.0	1	0	0	0	1.000	0.90
Porter, Bo	Tex	10	7	75.0	23	0	1	0	.958	2.76
Powell, Dante	SF	1	0	1.0	0	0	0	0	.000	.00
Pride, Curtis	Mon	1	0	3.0	1	0	0	0	1.000	3.00
Raines Jr., Tim	Bal	7	6	56.0	12	0	0	0	1.000	1.93
Ramirez, Julio	CWS	21	12	117.0	43	2	1	0	.978	3.46
Redman, Tike	Pit	28	25	227.2	83	4	2	2	.978	3.44
Richard, Chris	Bal	36	31	266.1	73	1	0	1	1.000	2.50
Rios, Armando	SF	3	3	30.0	10	0	0	0	1.000	3.00
Rivera, Juan	NYY	1	0	3.0	0	0	0	0	.000	.00
Rivera, Ruben	Cin	70	38	405.2	129	3	2	2	.985	2.93

264

Center Fielders - The Rest

Player	Tm	G	GS	Inn	PO	A	E	DP	Pct.	Rng
Roberts, Dave	Cle	2	0	8.0	3	0	0	0	1.000	3.38
Robinson, Kerry	StL	22	9	100.1	39	0	1	0	.975	3.50
Rolls, Damian	TB	18	13	127.1	28	1	0	0	1.000	2.05
Rowand, Aaron	CWS	32	29	237.1	78	2	1	0	.988	3.03
Ryan, Rob	Oak	4	0	9.0	1	0	0	0	1.000	1.00
Sadler, Donnie	Cin	2	1	12.0	2	0	0	0	1.000	1.50
Sadler, Donnie	KC	4	1	16.0	4	0	0	0	1.000	2.25
Sanchez, Alex	Mil	14	9	97.0	21	1	1	0	.957	2.04
Sanders, Deion	Cin	4	4	35.0	13	1	0	0	1.000	3.60
Santangelo, F.P.	Oak	5	4	44.0	10	0	0	0	1.000	2.05
Saturria, Luis	StL	3	0	4.0	0	0	0	0	.000	.00
Shinjo, Tsuyoshi	NYM	53	47	397.2	123	3	0	0	1.000	2.85
Simmons, Brian	Tor	12	9	88.0	23	0	0	0	1.000	2.35
Smith, Mark	Mon	6	4	35.2	9	0	0	0	1.000	2.27
Taylor, Reggie	Phi	2	1	15.0	4	0	0	0	1.000	2.40
Thompson, Ryan	Fla	4	3	26.1	6	1	0	0	1.000	2.39
Tucker, Michael	Cin	32	27	202.0	56	3	0	0	1.000	2.63
Tucker, Michael	ChC	44	44	326.0	86	2	0	0	1.000	2.43
Tyner, Jason	TB	47	47	388.1	113	4	0	1	1.000	2.71
Valentin, Jose	CWS	24	18	165.2	46	3	0	1	1.000	2.66
Wehner, John	Pit	1	0	2.0	0	0	0	0	.000	.00
Wells, Vernon	Tor	27	21	201.1	56	2	2	0	.967	2.59
Williams, Gerald	TB	59	56	493.2	179	5	2	1	.989	3.35
Williams, Gerald	NYY	11	3	44.1	17	0	0	0	1.000	3.45
Winn, Randy	TB	48	46	414.1	134	4	1	0	.993	3.00
Womack, Tony	Ari	1	0	1.0	0	0	0	0	.000	.00

Right Fielders - Regulars

Player	Tm	G	GS	Inn	PO	A	E	DP	Pct.	Rng
Rios, Armando	TOT	78	71	624.0	169	7	6	2	.967	2.54
Jordan, Brian	Atl	144	141	1234.1	319	11	3	2	.991	2.41
Suzuki, Ichiro	Sea	152	148	1313.2	335	8	1	2	.997	2.35
Trammell, Bubba	SD	102	97	821.2	205	3	4	0	.981	2.28
Guerrero, Vladimir	Mon	158	158	1368.1	320	15	12	5	.965	2.20
Salmon, Tim	Ana	125	124	1087.1	253	13	3	5	.989	2.20
Lawton, Matt	TOT	142	136	1210.1	289	3	4	2	.986	2.17
Sosa, Sammy	ChC	160	160	1385.0	326	8	6	1	.982	2.17
Drew, J.D.	StL	97	91	780.1	183	4	5	1	.974	2.16
Ochoa, Alex	TOT	106	99	872.1	200	9	2	3	.991	2.16
Sanders, Reggie	Ari	119	117	1019.2	231	5	1	3	.996	2.08
Burnitz, Jeromy	Mil	153	152	1333.1	294	14	6	4	.981	2.08
Walker, Larry	Col	129	126	1097.0	243	8	4	4	.984	2.06
Gonzalez, Juan	Cle	119	119	981.0	214	10	3	3	.987	2.06
Vander Wal, John	TOT	94	87	722.1	161	3	3	0	.982	2.04
Green, Shawn	LA	159	159	1402.2	310	8	6	0	.981	2.04
Abreu, Bobby	Phi	162	159	1411.1	308	11	8	4	.976	2.03
Ordonez, Magglio	CWS	155	151	1328.1	285	11	5	0	.983	2.01
Nixon, Trot	Bos	83	70	657.0	141	3	5	3	.966	1.97
Mondesi, Raul	Tor	149	149	1318.2	263	19	8	2	.972	1.92
Dye, Jermaine	TOT	153	152	1334.0	271	13	6	1	.979	1.92
O'Neill, Paul	NYY	130	127	1094.1	210	1	4	0	.982	1.74
Alou, Moises	Hou	130	130	1116.2	205	10	2	3	.991	1.73
Average	—	130	127	1109.1	249	9	5	2	.982	2.09

Right Fielders - The Rest

Player	Tm	G	GS	Inn	PO	A	E	DP	Pct.	Rng
Abbott, Jeff	Fla	8	1	19.2	4	0	0	0	1.000	1.83
Alcantara, Israel	Bos	2	1	13.0	4	0	0	0	1.000	2.77
Aldridge, Cory	Atl	2	0	2.0	0	0	0	0	.000	.00
Allen, Chad	Min	15	10	97.0	26	2	1	0	.966	2.60
Anderson, Brady	Bal	66	62	543.0	126	7	3	4	.978	2.20
Aven, Bruce	LA	4	0	8.0	2	0	0	0	1.000	2.25
Barkett, Andy	Pit	2	1	9.0	2	0	0	0	1.000	2.00
Barnes, John	Min	6	3	32.0	8	1	1	0	.900	2.53
Bautista, Danny	Ari	33	17	187.2	41	2	0	1	1.000	2.06
Bell, Derek	Pit	43	36	323.1	71	2	1	1	.986	2.03
Bellhorn, Mark	Oak	1	1	9.0	0	0	0	0	.000	.00
Bellinger, Clay	NYY	2	0	5.0	0	0	0	0	.000	.00
Benard, Marvin	SF	37	9	126.1	25	1	0	0	1.000	1.85
Berkman, Lance	Hou	7	2	29.0	7	0	1	0	.875	2.17
Bichette, Dante	Bos	16	15	117.0	20	0	2	0	.909	1.54
Bigbie, Larry	Bal	17	16	148.0	37	0	0	0	1.000	2.25
Bocachica, Hiram	LA	3	0	3.0	1	0	0	0	1.000	3.00
Bonilla, Bobby	StL	6	5	35.0	10	0	0	0	1.000	2.57
Bradley, Milton	Mon	2	2	16.0	2	0	0	0	1.000	1.13
Bradley, Milton	Cle	1	0	1.0	0	0	0	0	.000	.00
Bragg, Darren	NYM	10	9	73.0	12	1	0	0	1.000	1.60
Bragg, Darren	NYY	3	0	8.0	2	0	0	0	1.000	2.25
Branyan, Russell	Cle	2	1	4.0	1	0	0	0	1.000	2.25
Brown, Dee	KC	3	1	12.0	2	0	0	0	1.000	1.50
Brown, Emil	Pit	2	1	4.0	1	0	0	0	1.000	2.25
Brown, Emil	SD	2	0	7.1	3	0	0	0	1.000	3.68
Brown, Roosevelt	ChC	3	0	8.0	0	0	1	0	.000	.00
Brumbaugh, Cliff	Tex	4	4	26.0	6	0	0	0	1.000	2.08
Brumbaugh, Cliff	Col	8	6	53.0	13	0	0	0	1.000	2.21
Buchanan, Brian	Min	39	32	250.0	59	1	2	0	.968	2.16
Buford, Damon	ChC	1	0	1.0	1	0	0	0	1.000	9.00
Buhner, Jay	Sea	2	1	11.0	2	0	0	0	1.000	1.64
Burks, Ellis	Cle	2	2	15.0	4	0	0	0	1.000	2.40
Byrnes, Eric	Oak	5	2	31.0	3	0	0	0	1.000	0.87
Cabrera, Jolbert	Cle	18	7	96.0	21	0	0	0	1.000	1.97
Canseco, Jose	CWS	2	2	13.0	1	0	0	0	1.000	0.69
Catalanotto, Frank	Tex	15	14	113.0	19	0	0	0	1.000	1.51
Cedeno, Roger	Det	55	55	482.2	103	4	7	1	.939	2.00
Chavez, Endy	KC	2	0	2.0	0	0	0	0	.000	.00
Christenson, Ryan	Oak	3	0	3.0	0	0	0	0	.000	.00
Clark, Brady	Cin	14	3	53.0	14	0	0	0	1.000	2.38
Colangelo, Mike	SD	4	1	13.1	3	0	0	0	1.000	2.03
Coleman, Michael	NYY	3	1	12.0	1	0	0	0	1.000	0.75
Conine, Jeff	Bal	16	14	119.0	41	1	0	0	1.000	3.18
Conti, Jason	Ari	1	0	2.0	0	0	0	0	.000	.00
Cordero, Wil	Cle	5	4	36.0	5	1	0	0	1.000	1.50
Cordova, Marty	Cle	29	21	208.0	55	2	0	0	1.000	2.47
Cox, Steve	TB	2	2	14.0	3	1	0	0	1.000	2.57
Crespo, Cesar	SD	2	1	10.0	0	0	0	0	.000	.00
Crespo, Felipe	SF	1	0	4.0	2	0	0	0	1.000	4.50
Cruz, Jacob	Cle	5	1	23.0	10	0	0	0	1.000	3.91
Cruz, Jacob	Col	6	2	18.0	5	0	0	0	1.000	2.50
Cummings, Midre	Ari	1	0	3.0	1	0	0	0	1.000	3.00
Curtis, Chad	Tex	9	6	55.0	12	1	0	0	1.000	2.13
Damon, Johnny	Oak	5	4	44.0	5	1	0	0	1.000	1.23
Darr, Mike	SD	69	45	437.2	108	4	2	2	.982	2.30
Daubach, Brian	Bos	8	8	68.0	15	0	0	0	1.000	1.99
DaVanon, Jeff	Ana	17	13	117.0	23	1	0	0	1.000	1.85

Right Fielders - The Rest

Player	Tm	G	GS	Inn	PO	A	E	DP	Pct.	Rng
Davis, Eric	SF	48	34	293.1	74	1	3	0	.962	2.30
Dellucci, David	Ari	35	26	233.1	57	0	1	0	.983	2.20
Ducey, Rob	Phi	1	0	2.0	1	0	0	0	1.000	4.50
Ducey, Rob	Mon	3	0	6.0	0	0	0	0	.000	.00
Dunn, Adam	Cin	38	38	312.1	86	3	2	1	.978	2.56
Dunston, Shawon	SF	26	13	128.1	26	4	1	2	.968	2.10
Dunwoody, Todd	ChC	7	2	23.2	5	0	0	0	1.000	1.90
Durazo, Erubiel	Ari	2	2	14.0	4	1	0	0	1.000	3.21
Dye, Jermaine	KC	92	91	796.1	175	6	3	0	.984	2.05
Dye, Jermaine	Oak	61	61	537.2	96	7	3	1	.972	1.72
Echevarria, Angel	Mil	5	3	35.0	8	0	0	0	1.000	2.06
Encarnacion, Juan	Det	63	62	529.0	121	3	2	0	.984	2.11
Encarnacion, Mario	Col	6	5	43.1	16	1	0	1	1.000	3.53
Escobar, Alex	NYM	7	6	56.0	10	2	1	1	.923	1.93
Everett, Carl	Bos	9	9	75.0	17	0	0	0	1.000	2.04
Fick, Robert	Det	8	8	63.0	15	1	0	0	1.000	2.29
Garcia, Karim	Cle	13	6	74.2	11	3	1	0	.933	1.69
Giambi, Jeremy	Oak	37	31	272.2	40	0	0	0	1.000	1.32
Gilkey, Bernard	Atl	8	1	23.1	9	0	0	0	1.000	3.47
Gipson, Charles	Sea	11	2	32.0	3	0	0	0	1.000	0.84
Grieve, Ben	TB	64	62	540.2	117	0	3	0	.975	1.95
Grissom, Marquis	LA	3	3	27.0	2	0	0	0	1.000	0.67
Guillen, Jose	TB	36	35	306.2	86	7	3	3	.969	2.73
Gwynn, Tony	SD	17	16	103.0	17	2	0	0	1.000	1.66
Hamilton, Darryl	NYM	3	3	22.0	8	1	0	0	1.000	3.68
Harris, Lenny	NYM	3	1	9.0	2	0	0	0	1.000	2.00
Hermansen, Chad	Pit	15	5	73.2	14	1	0	1	1.000	1.83
Hernandez, Alex	Pit	4	2	20.0	3	1	0	0	1.000	1.80
Hidalgo, Richard	Hou	37	4	78.0	17	0	0	0	1.000	1.96
Hocking, Denny	Min	5	2	26.2	10	1	0	1	1.000	3.71
Hollandsworth, T.	Col	5	2	21.0	4	0	0	0	1.000	1.71
Hubbard, Trenidad	KC	1	0	1.0	0	0	0	0	.000	.00
Hunter, Brian L.	Phi	5	3	26.0	12	1	0	1	1.000	4.50
Hyzdu, Adam	Pit	18	9	85.2	19	0	0	0	1.000	2.00
Ibanez, Raul	KC	24	14	142.0	28	2	0	0	1.000	1.90
Jackson, Ryan	Det	15	9	88.1	15	0	1	0	.938	1.53
Javier, Stan	Sea	11	9	75.0	15	1	0	1	1.000	1.92
Jennings, Robin	Oak	12	10	84.0	12	1	0	0	1.000	1.39
Jennings, Robin	Cin	15	13	107.1	23	2	3	1	.893	2.10
Johnson, Mark P.	NYM	7	4	36.0	3	0	0	0	1.000	0.75
Jones, Jacque	Min	2	1	10.0	1	0	0	0	1.000	0.90
Jones, Terry	Mon	2	1	10.0	0	0	0	0	.000	.00
Justice, David	NYY	11	8	67.0	13	0	0	0	1.000	1.75
Kendall, Jason	Pit	10	9	67.1	17	1	2	0	.900	2.41
Kielty, Bobby	Min	17	10	100.0	18	1	1	0	.952	1.80
Kieschnick, Brooks	Col	4	1	11.0	4	0	1	0	.800	3.27
Kingsale, Gene	Sea	3	0	9.0	3	0	0	0	1.000	3.00
Kinkade, Mike	Bal	3	1	11.0	1	1	0	0	1.000	1.64
Kotsay, Mark	SD	5	0	8.0	3	0	0	0	1.000	3.38
Lampkin, Tom	Sea	1	0	3.0	0	0	0	0	.000	.00
Lankford, Ray	SD	2	1	9.1	0	0	0	0	.000	.00
Latham, Chris	Tor	14	9	91.0	22	2	0	1	1.000	2.37
Lawton, Matt	Min	94	90	799.2	193	2	4	2	.980	2.19
Lawton, Matt	NYM	48	46	410.2	96	1	0	0	1.000	2.13
Leach, Jalal	SF	2	0	4.0	0	0	0	0	.000	.00
Ledee, Ricky	Tex	60	49	448.1	110	1	3	0	.974	2.23
Lewis, Darren	Bos	29	20	181.2	36	3	0	2	1.000	1.93
Liefer, Jeff	CWS	4	2	21.0	5	0	0	0	1.000	2.14

Right Fielders - The Rest

Player	Tm	G	GS	Inn	PO	A	E	DP	Pct.	Rng
Little, Mark	Col	6	4	37.0	9	1	0	0	1.000	2.43
Lo Duca, Paul	LA	1	0	3.0	3	0	0	0	1.000	9.00
Long, Terrence	Oak	28	26	235.2	60	1	1	0	.984	2.33
Lugo, Julio	Hou	2	0	3.0	0	0	0	0	.000	.00
Mabry, John	StL	2	1	4.2	0	0	0	0	.000	.00
Mabry, John	Fla	34	26	226.2	42	2	2	0	.957	1.75
Macias, Jose	Det	4	4	32.0	12	0	0	0	1.000	3.38
Mackowiak, Rob	Pit	40	31	253.0	61	2	1	1	.984	2.24
Magee, Wendell	Det	19	11	115.2	26	3	0	0	1.000	2.26
Magruder, Chris	Tex	3	2	20.0	8	1	0	0	1.000	4.05
Marrero, Eli	StL	7	3	32.0	6	1	0	0	1.000	1.97
Martin, Al	Sea	1	0	0.1	0	0	0	0	.000	.00
Martinez, Dave	Atl	28	19	187.2	37	2	0	1	1.000	1.87
Mateo, Ruben	Tex	39	37	330.1	70	0	1	0	.986	1.91
Matos, Luis	Bal	10	8	73.0	19	0	0	0	1.000	2.34
Matthews Jr., Gary	ChC	1	0	2.0	0	0	0	0	.000	.00
McCarty, Dave	KC	1	0	2.0	0	0	0	0	.000	.00
McCracken, Q.	Min	3	0	8.0	1	0	0	0	1.000	1.13
McEwing, Joe	NYM	25	21	153.2	30	0	0	0	1.000	1.76
McGuire, Ryan	Fla	9	5	51.0	16	0	0	0	1.000	2.82
McLemore, Mark	Sea	2	1	10.0	0	0	0	0	.000	.00
McMillon, Billy	Det	6	2	33.2	10	0	0	0	1.000	2.67
McMillon, Billy	Oak	2	1	9.0	0	0	0	0	.000	.00
Merced, Orlando	Hou	21	12	110.0	28	0	1	0	.966	2.29
Millar, Kevin	Fla	66	65	515.2	94	2	2	0	.980	1.68
Mohr, Dustan	Min	15	14	118.0	39	0	0	0	1.000	2.97
Monroe, Craig	Tex	21	14	117.0	34	3	0	1	1.000	2.85
Mordecai, Mike	Mon	1	0	2.0	2	0	0	0	1.000	9.00
Mottola, Chad	Fla	4	1	14.0	6	1	0	0	1.000	4.50
Mouton, James	Mil	7	3	29.0	10	0	0	0	1.000	3.10
Mouton, Lyle	Fla	5	1	15.0	2	0	0	0	1.000	1.20
Norton, Greg	Col	4	1	10.0	2	0	0	0	1.000	1.80
Ochoa, Alex	Cin	85	84	732.2	176	6	2	2	.989	2.24
Ochoa, Alex	Col	21	15	139.2	24	3	0	1	1.000	1.74
O'Leary, Troy	Bos	41	38	336.1	72	0	0	0	1.000	1.93
Osik, Keith	Pit	1	0	1.0	2	0	0	0	1.000	18.00
Owens, Eric	Fla	72	60	551.0	110	5	2	1	.983	1.88
Palmeiro, Orlando	Ana	28	21	197.1	43	0	0	0	1.000	1.96
Paquette, Craig	StL	26	21	179.2	32	2	0	1	1.000	1.70
Patterson, Corey	ChC	1	0	3.0	1	0	0	0	1.000	3.00
Perez, Robert	NYY	2	0	3.0	0	0	0	0	.000	.00
Perez, Robert	Mil	1	1	9.0	3	0	0	0	1.000	3.00
Perez, Santiago	SD	8	1	30.1	7	0	1	0	.875	2.08
Perez, Timo	NYM	62	44	427.1	108	3	0	1	1.000	2.34
Perez, Tomas	Phi	1	0	3.0	0	0	0	0	.000	.00
Piatt, Adam	Oak	32	26	234.1	48	3	2	0	.962	1.96
Podsednik, Scott	Sea	1	0	2.0	0	0	0	0	.000	.00
Porter, Bo	Tex	12	3	45.2	10	0	0	0	1.000	1.97
Powell, Dante	SF	3	1	12.1	7	0	0	0	1.000	5.11
Pride, Curtis	Mon	3	0	9.0	1	0	0	0	1.000	1.00
Pujols, Albert	StL	39	33	302.2	56	3	4	0	.937	1.75
Quinn, Mark	KC	50	49	434.2	109	4	3	1	.974	2.34
Redman, Tike	Pit	7	3	32.2	9	0	0	0	1.000	2.48
Richard, Chris	Bal	69	61	538.1	155	5	0	1	1.000	2.67
Rios, Armando	SF	76	69	611.2	169	7	6	2	.967	2.59
Rios, Armando	Pit	2	2	12.1	0	0	0	0	.000	.00
Rivera, Juan	NYY	2	0	9.0	1	0	0	0	1.000	1.00
Rivera, Ruben	Cin	21	13	126.2	34	0	1	0	.971	2.42

Right Fielders - The Rest

Player	Tm	G	GS	Inn	PO	A	E	DP	Pct.	Rng
Roberts, Dave	Cle	2	0	8.0	0	0	0	0	.000	.00
Robinson, Kerry	StL	17	7	83.0	22	2	0	0	1.000	2.60
Rowand, Aaron	CWS	11	4	44.0	13	1	0	0	1.000	2.86
Ryan, Rob	Oak	1	0	1.0	1	0	0	0	1.000	9.00
Sadler, Donnie	Cin	2	0	2.0	0	0	0	0	.000	.00
Sadler, Donnie	KC	7	7	50.0	18	1	0	0	1.000	3.42
Sanchez, Alex	Mil	3	0	6.0	0	0	0	0	.000	.00
Sanders, Anthony	Sea	1	1	7.0	1	0	0	0	1.000	1.29
Sanders, Deion	Cin	1	0	0.1	0	0	0	0	.000	.00
Santangelo, F.P.	Oak	1	0	2.0	0	0	0	0	.000	.00
Saturria, Luis	StL	3	0	4.0	1	0	0	0	1.000	2.25
Seguignol, F.	Mon	7	0	9.0	1	0	0	0	1.000	1.00
Sheffield, Gary	LA	2	0	7.0	1	0	0	0	1.000	1.29
Sheldon, Scott	Tex	1	0	2.0	0	0	0	0	.000	.00
Shinjo, Tsuyoshi	NYM	39	28	258.0	65	1	1	0	.985	2.30
Sierra, Ruben	Tex	35	32	272.0	58	0	4	0	.935	1.92
Simmons, Brian	Tor	7	2	32.0	11	1	0	0	1.000	3.38
Singleton, Chris	CWS	3	3	27.0	8	1	0	0	1.000	3.00
Smith, Mark	Mon	4	0	11.0	2	0	0	0	1.000	1.64
Spencer, Shane	NYY	28	23	215.0	62	2	0	0	1.000	2.68
Spiezio, Scott	Ana	8	4	36.0	7	0	0	0	1.000	1.75
Sprague, Ed	Sea	1	0	2.0	1	0	0	0	1.000	4.50
Stairs, Matt	ChC	1	0	2.1	0	0	0	0	.000	.00
Sutton, Larry	StL	3	1	14.0	1	0	0	0	1.000	0.64
Sweeney, Mark	Mil	3	0	6.0	1	0	0	0	1.000	1.50
Thompson, Ryan	Fla	12	3	45.0	4	0	1	0	.800	0.80
Tucker, Michael	Cin	19	10	100.1	24	4	1	1	.966	2.51
Tucker, Michael	ChC	6	0	12.0	0	0	0	0	.000	.00
Tyner, Jason	TB	3	3	26.0	4	1	2	0	.714	1.73
Valent, Eric	Phi	1	0	3.0	0	0	0	0	.000	.00
Vander Wal, John	Pit	56	51	439.0	83	2	3	0	.966	1.74
Vander Wal, John	SF	38	36	283.1	78	1	0	0	1.000	2.51
Velarde, Randy	Tex	2	1	9.0	2	0	0	0	1.000	2.00
Velarde, Randy	NYY	1	1	8.0	1	0	0	0	1.000	1.13
Wakeland, Chris	Det	10	10	85.0	32	0	2	0	.941	3.39
Ward, Daryle	Hou	15	14	118.0	20	2	1	1	.957	1.68
Wehner, John	Pit	5	1	15.2	2	0	0	0	1.000	1.15
Wells, Vernon	Tor	3	2	21.0	5	0	0	0	1.000	2.14
White, Devon	Mil	2	2	18.0	2	0	0	0	1.000	1.00
Williams, Gerald	NYY	12	1	30.0	3	0	0	0	1.000	0.90
Wilson, Craig A.	Pit	13	11	79.2	17	1	1	0	.947	2.03
Winn, Randy	TB	62	60	536.1	107	8	4	0	.966	1.93
Young, Dmitri	Cin	1	1	8.0	1	0	0	0	1.000	1.13

Catchers - Regulars

Player	Tm	G	GS	Inn	PO	A	E	DP	PB	Pct.
Wilson, Dan	Sea	122	105	941.0	711	32	1	1	3	.999
Ausmus, Brad	Hou	127	120	1056.2	948	62	3	9	1	.997
Johnson, Charles	Fla	125	120	1061.0	846	62	4	15	8	.996
Matheny, Mike	StL	121	117	1002.0	772	69	4	9	6	.995
Mayne, Brent	TOT	93	90	785.1	586	38	3	6	5	.995
Fletcher, Darrin	Tor	129	114	1021.0	720	41	4	8	8	.995
Santiago, Benito	SF	130	119	1080.0	830	62	5	12	8	.994
Miller, Damian	Ari	121	111	978.0	966	81	7	6	10	.993
Estrada, Johnny	Phi	89	80	713.1	543	30	4	4	3	.993
Barrett, Michael	Mon	131	129	1126.0	880	50	7	6	8	.993
Diaz, Einar	Cle	134	126	1114.2	959	93	8	11	7	.992
Blanco, Henry	Mil	102	94	837.1	645	68	6	9	6	.992
Lo Duca, Paul	LA	99	91	801.1	643	53	6	8	4	.991
Molina, Ben	Ana	94	89	781.2	527	36	5	4	4	.991
Piazza, Mike	NYM	131	127	1085.1	919	58	9	5	7	.991
LaRue, Jason	Cin	107	95	841.0	569	75	6	8	15	.991
Davis, Ben	SD	135	122	1076.2	845	60	9	14	8	.990
Rodriguez, Ivan	Tex	106	101	855.1	631	52	7	11	2	.990
Posada, Jorge	NYY	131	126	1093.0	996	52	11	11	18	.990
Hernandez, Ramon	Oak	135	127	1131.2	907	70	11	15	4	.989
Lopez, Javy	Atl	127	115	1026.0	826	50	10	7	5	.989
Flaherty, John	TB	78	69	617.1	458	28	7	4	4	.986
Kendall, Jason	Pit	133	127	1093.0	739	52	12	7	7	.985
Pierzynski, A.J.	Min	110	102	901.2	611	44	10	7	4	.985
Petrick, Ben	Col	77	70	608.2	456	29	8	8	11	.984
Fordyce, Brook	Bal	95	89	768.2	541	30	10	7	8	.983
Average	—	115	107	939.0	734	53	7	8	7	.991

Catchers - The Rest

Player	Tm	G	GS	Inn	PO	A	E	DP	PB	Pct.
Alomar Jr., Sandy	CWS	69	63	545.0	367	19	4	5	5	.990
Bako, Paul	Atl	60	46	397.1	319	29	3	1	4	.991
Barajas, Rod	Ari	50	31	278.1	179	11	1	3	0	.995
Bennett, Gary	Phi	24	21	194.0	151	5	2	2	3	.987
Bennett, Gary	Col	19	15	134.0	96	4	0	1	0	1.000
Borders, Pat	Sea	5	1	19.0	10	2	1	0	0	.923
Brown, Kevin L.	Mil	16	11	96.1	68	6	0	0	2	1.000
Burke, Jamie	Ana	8	0	10.1	10	1	0	0	0	1.000
Cardona, Javier	Det	44	30	270.1	132	15	3	1	8	.980
Casanova, Raul	Mil	56	48	420.2	305	25	3	6	2	.991
Castillo, Alberto	Tor	66	44	404.2	324	25	4	0	2	.989
Castro, Ramon	Fla	4	1	15.1	10	1	0	0	0	1.000
Cota, Humberto	Pit	3	1	10.0	11	0	0	0	0	1.000
Dalesandro, Mark	CWS	1	0	1.0	0	0	0	0	0	.000
DiFelice, Mike	TB	48	46	386.1	293	29	6	4	2	.982
DiFelice, Mike	Ari	12	7	59.2	53	3	1	1	1	.982
Estalella, Bobby	SF	28	28	232.2	185	14	0	5	0	1.000
Estalella, Bobby	NYY	3	1	14.0	14	1	0	0	0	1.000
Eusebio, Tony	Hou	48	40	365.1	300	22	3	4	2	.991
Fabregas, Jorge	Ana	53	42	372.1	267	23	3	3	2	.990
Fasano, Sal	Oak	9	6	56.0	37	3	2	0	0	.952
Fasano, Sal	KC	3	0	5.0	2	0	0	0	1	1.000
Fasano, Sal	Col	25	19	176.1	153	14	3	5	0	.982
Fick, Robert	Det	78	69	595.1	412	26	6	3	12	.986
Gil, Geronimo	Bal	17	17	150.0	121	10	2	1	5	.985
Girardi, Joe	ChC	71	61	552.0	504	33	0	2	6	1.000

Catchers - The Rest

Player	Tm	G	GS	Inn	PO	A	E	DP	PB	Pct.
Gonzalez, Wiki	SD	47	37	330.1	246	21	3	3	6	.989
Greene, Todd	NYY	34	24	227.1	187	14	0	2	1	1.000
Guzman, Edwards	SF	26	14	138.2	86	10	1	1	0	.990
Hall, Toby	TB	46	46	410.0	328	20	5	2	2	.986
Haselman, Bill	Tex	47	35	338.0	234	13	0	2	0	1.000
Hatteberg, Scott	Bos	72	65	581.2	491	29	4	3	13	.992
Hinch, A.J.	KC	43	37	331.2	220	14	3	2	4	.987
Hoover, Paul	TB	2	1	10.0	2	1	0	0	0	1.000
Hubbard, Mike	Tex	5	4	29.1	15	2	0	0	0	1.000
Huckaby, Ken	Ari	1	0	3.0	5	0	0	0	0	1.000
Hundley, Todd	ChC	70	67	558.1	547	25	4	3	6	.993
Inge, Brandon	Det	79	60	537.2	330	40	4	3	10	.989
Jensen, Marcus	Bos	1	1	9.0	12	1	0	0	0	1.000
Jensen, Marcus	Tex	11	6	59.0	35	3	0	0	0	1.000
Johnson, Brian	LA	2	0	4.0	3	0	0	0	0	1.000
Johnson, Mark L.	CWS	61	56	495.1	326	31	3	2	4	.992
Kinkade, Mike	Bal	2	2	16.0	11	1	0	0	0	1.000
Knorr, Randy	Mon	27	24	216.0	168	5	2	0	2	.989
Kreuter, Chad	LA	70	58	526.1	486	29	0	4	5	1.000
Laker, Tim	Cle	14	8	84.1	76	6	1	2	0	.988
Lampkin, Tom	Sea	71	56	504.0	375	23	2	2	3	.995
LeCroy, Matt	Min	3	0	9.0	6	1	0	0	0	1.000
Levis, Jesse	Mil	11	9	82.0	59	3	1	1	1	.984
Lieberthal, Mike	Phi	33	33	283.2	243	9	2	3	0	.992
Lunar, Fernando	Bal	64	46	429.2	267	32	4	3	2	.987
Machado, Robert	ChC	47	34	326.2	317	20	1	3	1	.997
Marrero, Eli	StL	65	45	430.1	352	21	6	2	1	.984
Martinez, Sandy	Mon	1	0	1.1	2	0	0	0	0	1.000
Mayne, Brent	Col	44	42	369.0	317	19	1	4	1	.997
Mayne, Brent	KC	49	48	416.1	269	19	2	2	4	.993
McDonald, Keith	StL	2	0	3.0	1	1	0	0	0	1.000
Melhuse, Adam	Col	23	16	142.0	104	4	1	0	2	.991
Miller, Corky	Cin	17	16	139.0	104	12	1	2	2	.991
Mirabelli, Doug	Tex	23	16	151.2	84	16	1	4	0	.990
Mirabelli, Doug	Bos	52	43	388.2	329	33	2	8	6	.995
Moeller, Chad	Ari	25	13	140.2	111	7	0	0	1	1.000
Molina, Jose	Ana	15	12	103.0	78	6	0	1	2	1.000
Mordecai, Mike	Mon	1	0	1.0	1	0	0	0	0	1.000
Myers, Greg	Bal	8	8	68.0	41	4	0	0	0	1.000
Myers, Greg	Oak	28	23	214.2	152	15	0	2	0	1.000
Oliver, Joe	NYY	12	10	98.1	104	1	1	0	2	.991
Oliver, Joe	Bos	5	5	42.0	33	1	1	0	1	.971
Ortiz, Hector	KC	55	46	410.0	280	28	3	1	1	.990
Osik, Keith	Pit	39	30	264.1	188	12	1	1	1	.995
Paul, Josh	CWS	56	43	392.0	267	24	6	3	4	.980
Pena, Angel	LA	15	13	119.0	125	11	0	0	0	1.000
Perez, Eddie	Atl	5	2	21.0	10	1	0	0	0	1.000
Phelps, Josh	Tor	7	4	37.0	28	2	0	0	0	1.000
Phillips, Jason	NYM	5	0	15.0	15	0	0	0	0	1.000
Pratt, Todd	NYM	31	20	199.2	152	4	1	0	2	.994
Pratt, Todd	Phi	34	28	254.1	190	7	3	1	3	.985
Prince, Tom	Min	64	60	530.2	380	41	0	3	0	1.000
Redmond, Mike	Fla	47	41	361.2	291	23	2	5	2	.994
Rivera, Mike	Det	4	3	26.0	24	2	2	0	0	.929
Schneider, Brian	Mon	14	9	87.0	77	7	0	1	2	1.000
Servais, Scott	Hou	9	2	32.2	38	1	0	0	1	1.000
Sheldon, Scott	Tex	1	0	5.0	4	0	0	0	0	1.000
Sprague, Ed	Sea	1	0	1.0	1	0	0	0	0	1.000

Catchers - The Rest

Player	Tm	G	GS	Inn	PO	A	E	DP	PB	Pct.
Stinnett, Kelly	Cin	59	51	462.2	322	21	12	3	4	.966
Taubensee, Eddie	Cle	38	28	247.2	212	3	3	0	5	.986
Torrealba, Steve	Atl	2	0	3.0	2	0	0	0	0	1.000
Torrealba, Yorvit	SF	3	1	12.0	8	0	0	0	0	1.000
Varitek, Jason	Bos	50	47	426.2	425	32	2	2	3	.996
Wehner, John	Pit	1	0	1.0	1	0	0	0	0	1.000
Wilkins, Rick	SD	7	3	33.2	38	0	0	0	1	1.000
Wilson, Craig A.	Pit	10	4	48.0	22	2	1	0	1	.960
Wilson, Tom	Oak	9	6	61.0	35	3	1	0	0	.974
Wilson, Vance	NYM	27	14	145.2	130	9	1	1	2	.993
Wooten, Shawn	Ana	25	19	170.1	97	11	0	0	8	1.000
Zaun, Gregg	KC	35	31	277.0	181	11	5	4	0	.975

Catchers - Regulars - Special

Player	Tm	G	GS	Inn	SBA	CS	PCS	CS%	ER	CERA
Wilson, Dan	Sea	122	105	941.0	64	18	5	.22	367	3.51
Miller, Damian	Ari	121	111	978.0	107	39	6	.33	384	3.53
Hernandez, R.	Oak	135	127	1131.2	142	44	11	.25	447	3.55
Lopez, Javy	Atl	127	115	1026.0	95	31	6	.28	415	3.64
Posada, Jorge	NYY	131	126	1111.2	131	37	8	.24	466	3.77
Santiago, Benito	SF	130	119	1080.0	101	35	3	.33	461	3.84
Ausmus, Brad	Hou	127	120	1056.2	86	41	11	.40	472	4.02
Matheny, Mike	StL	121	117	1002.0	58	28	3	.45	449	4.03
Piazza, Mike	NYM	131	127	1085.1	147	33	11	.16	488	4.05
Molina, Ben	Ana	94	89	781.2	88	28	9	.24	364	4.19
Blanco, Henry	Mil	102	94	837.1	71	30	0	.42	395	4.25
Lo Duca, Paul	LA	99	91	801.1	79	31	1	.38	379	4.26
Johnson, Charles	Fla	125	120	1061.0	89	37	3	.40	517	4.39
Estrada, Johnny	Phi	89	80	713.1	48	17	3	.31	353	4.45
Pierzynski, A.J.	Min	110	102	901.2	65	21	3	.29	451	4.50
Diaz, Einar	Cle	134	126	1114.2	135	51	5	.35	560	4.52
Davis, Ben	SD	135	122	1076.2	109	39	5	.33	542	4.53
Barrett, Michael	Mon	131	129	1126.0	118	23	6	.15	573	4.58
Fletcher, Darrin	Tor	129	114	1021.0	106	31	7	.24	520	4.58
Fordyce, Brook	Bal	95	89	768.2	121	24	2	.18	397	4.65
Mayne, Brent	TOT	93	90	785.1	79	26	7	.26	414	4.74
Flaherty, John	TB	78	69	617.1	73	16	1	.21	331	4.83
LaRue, Jason	Cin	107	95	841.0	69	42	1	.60	474	5.07
Kendall, Jason	Pit	133	127	1093.0	101	28	13	.17	627	5.16
Rodriguez, Ivan	Tex	106	101	855.1	58	35	12	.50	543	5.71
Petrick, Ben	Col	77	70	608.2	60	14	3	.19	395	5.84
Average	—	115	107	939.0	92	31	6	.34	453	4.34

Catchers - The Rest - Special

Player	Tm	G	GS	Inn	SBA	CS	PCS	CS%	ER	CERA
Alomar Jr., Sandy	CWS	69	63	545.0	45	14	5	.23	272	4.49
Bako, Paul	Atl	60	46	397.1	55	19	1	.33	150	3.40
Barajas, Rod	Ari	50	31	278.1	35	8	4	.13	144	4.66
Bennett, Gary	Phi	24	21	194.0	15	6	2	.31	95	4.41
Bennett, Gary	Col	19	15	134.0	15	2	0	.13	84	5.64
Borders, Pat	Sea	5	1	19.0	2	1	0	.50	9	4.26
Brown, Kevin L.	Mil	16	11	96.1	12	4	0	.33	77	7.19
Burke, Jamie	Ana	8	0	10.1	1	0	0	0	4	3.48
Cardona, Javier	Det	44	30	270.1	21	10	3	.39	118	3.93
Casanova, Raul	Mil	56	48	420.2	50	12	0	.24	219	4.69
Castillo, Alberto	Tor	66	44	404.2	47	14	2	.27	163	3.63
Castro, Ramon	Fla	4	1	15.1	1	0	0	0	12	7.04
Cota, Humberto	Pit	3	1	10.0	0	0	0	0	17	15.30
Dalesandro, Mark	CWS	1	0	1.0	0	0	0	0	0	0.00
DiFelice, Mike	TB	48	46	386.1	44	16	3	.32	248	5.78
DiFelice, Mike	Ari	12	7	59.2	4	3	0	.75	24	3.62
Estalella, Bobby	SF	28	28	232.2	20	6	0	.30	154	5.96
Estalella, Bobby	NYY	3	1	14.0	1	0	0	0	6	3.86
Eusebio, Tony	Hou	48	40	365.1	28	8	0	.29	202	4.98
Fabregas, Jorge	Ana	53	42	372.1	44	15	2	.31	186	4.50
Fasano, Sal	Oak	9	6	56.0	5	2	0	.40	38	6.11
Fasano, Sal	KC	3	0	5.0	0	0	0	0	5	9.00
Fasano, Sal	Col	25	19	176.1	12	6	0	.50	78	3.98
Fick, Robert	Det	78	69	595.1	72	12	5	.10	369	5.58
Gil, Geronimo	Bal	17	17	150.0	18	5	0	.28	64	3.84
Girardi, Joe	ChC	71	61	552.0	47	20	0	.43	278	4.53

Player	Tm	G	GS	Inn	SBA	CS	PCS	CS%	ER	CERA
Gonzalez, Wiki	SD	47	37	330.1	35	13	0	.37	161	4.39
Greene, Todd	NYY	34	24	227.1	45	6	3	.07	122	4.83
Guzman, E.	SF	26	14	138.2	10	4	0	.40	64	4.15
Hall, Toby	TB	46	46	410.0	39	12	2	.27	201	4.41
Haselman, Bill	Tex	47	35	338.0	49	15	6	.21	212	5.64
Hatteberg, Scott	Bos	72	65	581.2	127	12	2	.08	299	4.63
Hinch, A.J.	KC	43	37	331.2	29	7	1	.21	150	4.07
Hoover, Paul	TB	2	1	10.0	1	0	0	0	1	0.90
Hubbard, Mike	Tex	5	4	29.1	7	1	0	.14	21	6.44
Huckaby, Ken	Ari	1	0	3.0	0	0	0	0	1	3.00
Hundley, Todd	ChC	70	67	558.1	66	13	4	.15	226	3.64
Inge, Brandon	Det	79	60	537.2	55	25	3	.42	292	4.89
Jensen, Marcus	Bos	1	1	9.0	1	1	0	1.00	4	4.00
Jensen, Marcus	Tex	11	6	59.0	9	2	1	.13	34	5.19
Johnson, Brian	LA	2	0	4.0	0	0	0	0	1	2.25
Johnson, Mark L.	CWS	61	56	495.1	49	17	2	.32	248	4.51
Kinkade, Mike	Bal	2	2	16.0	2	0	0	0	12	6.75
Knorr, Randy	Mon	27	24	216.0	34	6	5	.03	133	5.54
Kreuter, Chad	LA	70	58	526.1	43	16	4	.31	236	4.04
Laker, Tim	Cle	14	8	84.1	17	2	0	.12	54	5.76
Lampkin, Tom	Sea	71	56	504.0	36	10	0	.28	200	3.57
LeCroy, Matt	Min	3	0	9.0	2	1	0	.50	3	3.00
Levis, Jesse	Mil	11	9	82.0	7	1	0	.14	49	5.38
Lieberthal, Mike	Phi	33	33	283.2	14	5	0	.36	115	3.65
Lunar, Fernando	Bal	64	46	429.2	54	18	1	.32	236	4.94
Machado, Robert	ChC	47	34	326.2	39	13	0	.33	139	3.83
Marrero, Eli	StL	65	45	430.1	30	9	3	.22	178	3.72
Martinez, Sandy	Mon	1	0	1.1	1	0	0	0	0	0.00
Mayne, Brent	Col	44	42	369.0	32	13	5	.30	190	4.63
Mayne, Brent	KC	49	48	416.1	47	13	2	.24	224	4.84
McDonald, Keith	StL	2	0	3.0	0	0	0	0	0	0.00
Melhuse, Adam	Col	23	16	142.0	17	1	0	.06	94	5.96
Miller, Corky	Cin	17	16	139.0	16	8	2	.43	58	3.76
Mirabelli, Doug	Tex	23	16	151.2	21	13	1	.60	101	5.99
Mirabelli, Doug	Bos	52	43	388.2	70	19	0	.27	205	4.75
Moeller, Chad	Ari	25	13	140.2	16	5	4	.08	74	4.73
Molina, Jose	Ana	15	12	103.0	19	8	3	.31	47	4.11
Mordecai, Mike	Mon	1	0	1.0	0	0	0	0	0	0.00
Myers, Greg	Bal	8	8	68.0	13	4	1	.25	35	4.63
Myers, Greg	Oak	28	23	214.2	25	9	3	.27	64	2.68
Oliver, Joe	NYY	12	10	98.1	14	2	1	.08	55	5.03
Oliver, Joe	Bos	5	5	42.0	7	1	0	.14	19	4.07
Ortiz, Hector	KC	55	46	410.0	44	17	1	.37	242	5.31
Osik, Keith	Pit	39	30	264.1	28	8	3	.20	123	4.19
Paul, Josh	CWS	56	43	392.0	53	9	2	.14	205	4.71
Pena, Angel	LA	15	13	119.0	11	4	0	.36	69	5.22
Perez, Eddie	Atl	5	2	21.0	2	0	0	0	11	4.71
Phelps, Josh	Tor	7	4	37.0	6	2	0	.33	13	3.16
Phillips, Jason	NYM	5	0	15.0	1	0	0	0	2	1.20
Pratt, Todd	NYM	31	20	199.2	12	1	0	.08	105	4.73
Pratt, Todd	Phi	34	28	254.1	12	4	1	.27	104	3.68
Prince, Tom	Min	64	60	530.2	49	21	2	.40	268	4.55
Redmond, Mike	Fla	47	41	361.2	36	14	3	.33	162	4.03
Rivera, Mike	Det	4	3	26.0	6	3	1	.40	16	5.54
Schneider, Brian	Mon	14	9	87.0	8	4	1	.43	39	4.03
Servais, Scott	Hou	9	2	32.2	1	0	0	0	33	9.09
Sheldon, Scott	Tex	1	0	5.0	1	0	0	0	2	3.60
Sprague, Ed	Sea	1	0	1.0	0	0	0	0	0	0.00

Catchers - The Rest - Special

Player	Tm	G	GS	Inn	SBA	CS	PCS	CS%	ER	CERA
Stinnett, Kelly	Cin	59	51	462.2	52	12	2	.20	233	4.53
Taubensee, Eddie	Cle	38	28	247.2	36	7	6	.03	132	4.80
Torrealba, Steve	Atl	2	0	3.0	0	0	0	0	2	6.00
Torrealba, Yorvit	SF	3	1	12.0	0	0	0	0	1	0.75
Varitek, Jason	Bos	50	47	426.2	69	18	3	.23	140	2.95
Wehner, John	Pit	1	0	1.0	0	0	0	0	1	9.00
Wilkins, Rick	SD	7	3	33.2	2	0	0	0	21	5.61
Wilson, Craig A.	Pit	10	4	48.0	5	1	0	.20	26	4.88
Wilson, Tom	Oak	9	6	61.0	7	0	0	0	34	5.02
Wilson, Vance	NYM	27	14	145.2	11	6	0	.55	59	3.65
Wooten, Shawn	Ana	25	19	170.1	16	8	3	.38	70	3.70
Zaun, Gregg	KC	35	31	277.0	30	8	2	.21	158	5.13

Pitchers Hitting & Fielding
and Hitters Pitching

The reign of Mike Hampton as the batting champion among major league pitchers is over. Among hurlers with at least 25 at-bats, Hampton had ranked first in batting average in both 1999 and 2000, but that distinction went to teammate Brian Bohanon last summer. Bohanon posted a .323 average in 31 at-bats, and Cincinnati newcomer Jim Brower showed his stick was major league-worthy by finishing second with a .308 mark in 28 plate appearances. Third on the list was San Francisco's Livan Hernandez at .296. Hampton placed fourth with a .291 average, but it's noteworthy that he recorded nearly three times as many plate appearances as Bohanon or Brower. His 23 hits in 79 at-bats were more than any other big league pitcher except Hernandez, who picked up 24 hits in 81 at-bats.

Hampton secured a new title in 2001. His seven homers—the first seven of his major league career—outdistanced the pack for the home-run crown among pitchers. Trailing far behind were teammate Denny Neagle, Jason Schmidt of the Pirates and Giants, and Philadelphia's Robert Person with two each. We understand if you're already thinking that Hampton's just another Coors Field phenomenon. It's true that he batted .400 at Coors and belted four homers there, but he stroked three longballs on the road, as well. No matter how you slice it, Hampton's .582 slugging mark for the 2001 season is impressive.

The pitcher with the best defensive game in 2001 was San Francisco's Kirk Rueter, who handled 61 chances without committing an error. Rueter recorded 11 putouts and 50 assists in compiling his 1.000 fielding percentage, and he participated in a league-best 11 double plays among hurlers. After Rueter, Hampton (perfect in 58 chances) and Hernandez (perfect in 57 chances) weigh in with matching fielding percentages. With no errors in 62 chances, Hernandez was the leader among pitchers during the 2000 season, giving him a perfect record over the past two summers. He committed just one error in 1999, giving him a single miscue in his last 173 chances dating back to the start of the '99 season.

Mr. Hampton also posted the best caught-stealing percentage among pitchers with five or more attempts against them in 2001. His 83-percent success rate on 12 steal attempts included seven catcher assists and three pitcher caught stealings. Rookie Texas southpaw Chris Michalak led the majors with seven successful pickoffs.

Among non-pitchers who took the hill in 2001, Steve Finley, Tim Laker, Mark Loretta and Desi Relaford worked scoreless innings. Loretta was the strikeout king with two whiffs. The ugliest ERAs came courtesy of John Mabry (135.00) and Bobby Bonilla (18.00).

Bateo & Fildeo de Lanzadores
y Bateadores Lanzando

El reino de Mike Hampton como el campeón de bateo de lanzadores ha terminado. Entre lanzadores con 25 o más Veces-al-Bate, Hampton fue el líder en 1999 y 2000. Pero Brian Bohanon ganó el 2001 con un promedio de .323 en 31 Veces-al-Bate, y Jim Brower de Cincinnati terminó segundo con .308 en 28 Veces-al-Bate. Liván Hernández fue tercero con .296. Hampton quedó en cuarto con .291. Sus 23 hits en 79 Veces-al-Bate fueron la segunda marca más alta de hits después de Liván Hernández, quien terminó con 24.

Hampton ganó un título diferente en el 2001. Sus siete cuadrangulares—los primeros siete cuadrangulares de su carrera— lo coronaron el rey de jonrones entre lanzadores. Denny Neagle, Jason Schmidt y Robert Person quedaron empatados en segundo con dos cuadrangulares cada uno. La marca de siete cuadrangulares puede ser explicada por que Hampton jugó en las alturas de Colorado, pero conectó tres jonrones en otros estadios. Su Promedio de Bases Acumuladas de .582 es impresionante, no importa cómo sea analizado.

El lanzador con el mejor guante en el 2001 fue Kirk Rueter, quien tuvo 61 chances sin error. El retiró 11 y asistió en 50 retiros para un Promedio de Fildeo de 1.000. Participó en 11 doble plays—también la mejor marca entre lanzadores. Después de Rueter, Hampton (perfecto en 58 chances) y Hernández (perfecto en 57) tuvieron Promedios de Fildeo de 1.000. Hernández tampoco cometió errores en el 2000, dandole dos años perfectos. El cometió un error al principio de 1999, dandole solo un error en sus últimos 173 chances.

El Señor Hampton también tuvo el mejor Promedio de Bases Robadas contra lanzadores con cinco o más intentos de robar. Corredores que le intentaron robar fueron atrapados 83 por ciento del tiempo. El novato de Texas Chris Michalak fue el líder atrapando corredores tratando de regresar a primera con siete.

Entre los no-lanzadores que tomaron la loma en el 2001: Steve Finley, Tim Laker, Mark Loretta y Desi Relaford trabajaron entradas sin permitir carreras. Loretta fue el rey de los ponches con dos. Las efectividades más feas fueron cortesías de John Mabry (135.00) y Bobby Bonilla (18.00)

2001 Hitting = Bateo del 2001; **A** = Asistencias; **AB** = Veces-al-Bate; **Avg** = Promedio de bateo; **Career hitting** = Estadísticas de toda su carrera; **CS%** = Promedio de Atrapados Robando; **CS** = Atrapados robando; **DP** = Doble plays; **E** = Errores; **Fielding and Holding Runners** = Fildeando y Manejando Corredores en Base; **G** = Juegos; **Inn** = Entradas; **OBP** = Promedio de embasamiento; **PCS** = Atrapados robando por lanzador; **Pct.** = Promedio de fildeo; **PO** = Retiros (Putouts); **PPO** = Corredores retirados tratando de regresar a base; **R** = Carreras; **RBI** = Carreras empujadas; **SBA** = Bases robadas por oponentes; **SB-CS** = Bases robadas - Atrapado robando; **SH** = Sacrificios; **SLG** = Promedio de bases acumuladas; **SO** = Ponches.

Pitchers Hitting

Pitcher, Team	2001 Hitting														Career Hitting													
Pitcher, Team	Avg	OBP	SLG	AB	H	2B	3B	HR	R	RBI	BB	SO	SH	SB-CS	Avg	OBP	SLG	AB	H	2B	3B	HR	R	RBI	BB	SO	SH	SB-CS
Abbott, Paul, Sea	.250	.250	.250	4	1	0	0	0	0	0	0	1	1	0-0	.333	.333	.444	9	3	1	0	0	1	0	0	2	2	0-0
Acevedo, Jose, Cin	.118	.118	.147	34	4	1	0	0	1	1	0	18	2	0-0	.118	.118	.147	34	4	1	0	0	1	1	0	18	2	0-0
Acevedo, Juan, Col-Fla	.333	.333	.667	3	1	1	0	0	1	0	0	0	1	0-0	.092	.132	.123	65	6	2	0	0	4	0	3	33	6	0-0
Adams, Terry, LA	.051	.116	.077	39	2	1	0	0	2	1	3	19	5	0-0	.038	.105	.058	52	2	1	0	0	2	1	4	27	6	0-0
Ainsworth, Kurt, SF	.000	.000	.000	0	0	0	0	0	0	0	0	0	0	0-0	.000	.000	.000	0	0	0	0	0	0	0	0	0	0	0-0
Alfonseca, Antonio, Fla	.000	.000	.000	0	0	0	0	0	0	0	0	0	0	0-0	.000	.000	.000	9	0	0	0	0	0	0	0	7	0	0-0
Almanza, Armando, Fla	.000	.000	.000	0	0	0	0	0	0	0	0	0	0	0-0	.000	.000	.000	4	0	0	0	0	0	0	0	2	1	0-0
Almanzar, Carlos, NYY	.000	.000	.000	0	0	0	0	0	0	0	0	0	0	0-0	.000	.000	.000	4	0	0	0	0	0	0	0	3	0	0-0
Anderson, Brian, Ari	.135	.135	.216	37	5	1	1	0	1	2	0	9	0	0-0	.143	.164	.195	210	30	4	2	1	15	8	6	48	16	2-0
Anderson, Jimmy, Pit	.119	.175	.136	59	7	1	0	0	2	3	4	15	6	0-0	.144	.172	.169	118	17	3	0	0	9	5	4	28	10	0-0
Anderson, Matt, Det	.000	.000	.000	0	0	0	0	0	0	0	0	0	0	0-0	.000	.000	.000	0	0	0	0	0	0	0	0	0	0	0-0
Ankiel, Rick, StL	.000	.111	.000	8	0	0	0	0	1	0	1	5	1	0-0	.209	.253	.314	86	18	1	1	2	9	9	5	28	3	0-0
Appier, Kevin, NYM	.113	.141	.113	62	7	0	0	0	4	4	1	24	3	0-0	.105	.128	.105	76	8	0	0	0	4	4	1	33	3	0-0
Armas Jr., Tony, Mon	.151	.151	.170	53	8	1	0	0	2	4	0	17	6	0-0	.111	.122	.123	81	9	1	0	0	3	5	1	30	9	0-0
Arrojo, Rolando, Bos	.000	.000	.000	4	0	0	0	0	0	0	0	3	0	0-0	.086	.111	.114	35	3	1	0	0	2	3	1	18	3	0-0
Arroyo, Bronson, Pit	.048	.087	.048	21	1	0	0	0	0	1	1	16	0	0-0	.095	.114	.143	42	4	2	0	0	2	1	1	26	2	0-0
Ashby, Andy, LA	.500	.667	.500	2	1	0	0	0	1	1	1	0	2	0-0	.139	.165	.168	459	64	13	0	0	21	22	14	187	74	1-0
Astacio, P., Col-Hou	.094	.094	.094	53	5	0	0	0	2	3	0	17	11	0-0	.130	.139	.144	562	73	6	1	0	24	26	4	210	67	0-1
Atchley, Justin, Cin	.000	.000	.000	1	0	0	0	0	0	0	0	1	0	0-0	.000	.000	.000	1	0	0	0	0	0	0	0	1	0	0-0
Austin, Jeff, KC	.000	.000	.000	0	0	0	0	0	0	0	0	0	0	0-0	.000	.000	.000	0	0	0	0	0	0	0	0	0	0	0-0
Aybar, Manny, ChC	1.000	1.000	1.000	3	3	0	0	0	1	0	0	0	1	0-0	.188	.211	.232	69	13	0	0	1	6	5	2	28	4	0-0
Bacsik, Mike, Cle	.000	.000	.000	0	0	0	0	0	0	0	0	0	0	0-0	.000	.000	.000	0	0	0	0	0	0	0	0	0	0	0-0
Baez, Benito, Fla	.000	.000	.000	1	0	0	0	0	0	0	0	0	0	0-0	.000	.000	.000	1	0	0	0	0	0	0	0	0	0	0-0
Baez, Danys, Cle	.000	.000	.000	0	0	0	0	0	0	0	0	0	0	0-0	.000	.000	.000	0	0	0	0	0	0	0	0	0	0	0-0
Bailey, Cory, KC	.000	.000	.000	0	0	0	0	0	0	0	0	0	0	0-0	.500	.750	.500	2	1	0	0	0	2	0	2	0	1	0-0
Baldwin, J., CWS-LA	.071	.071	.107	28	2	1	0	0	0	1	0	13	1	0-0	.077	.077	.154	39	3	1	1	0	1	2	0	19	3	0-0
Bale, John, Bal	.000	.000	.000	0	0	0	0	0	0	0	0	0	0	0-0	.000	.000	.000	0	0	0	0	0	0	0	0	0	0	0-0
Balfour, Grant, Min	.000	.000	.000	0	0	0	0	0	0	0	0	0	0	0-0	.000	.000	.000	0	0	0	0	0	0	0	0	0	0	0-0
Banks, Willie, Bos	.000	.000	.000	0	0	0	0	0	0	0	0	0	0	0-0	.176	.222	.206	68	12	2	0	0	5	1	2	23	8	0-1
Barcelo, Lorenzo, CWS	.000	.000	.000	0	0	0	0	0	0	0	0	0	0	0-0	.000	.000	.000	0	0	0	0	0	0	0	0	0	0	0-0
Batista, Miguel, Ari	.063	.118	.063	32	2	0	0	0	2	0	2	17	2	0-0	.081	.121	.117	111	9	1	0	1	8	3	5	65	8	0-0
Bauer, Rick, Bal	.000	.000	.000	0	0	0	0	0	0	0	0	0	0	0-0	.000	.000	.000	0	0	0	0	0	0	0	0	0	0	0-0
Beck, Rod, Bos	.000	.000	.000	1	0	0	0	0	0	0	0	1	0	0-0	.211	.211	.211	19	4	0	0	0	0	1	0	10	1	0-0
Beckett, Josh, Fla	.286	.286	.429	7	2	1	0	0	1	0	0	1	2	0-0	.286	.286	.429	7	2	1	0	0	1	0	0	1	2	0-0
Beimel, Joe, Pit	.269	.296	.269	26	7	0	0	0	3	0	1	10	4	0-0	.269	.296	.269	26	7	0	0	0	3	0	1	10	4	0-0
Beirne, Kevin, Tor	.000	.000	.000	0	0	0	0	0	0	0	0	0	0	0-0	.000	.000	.000	0	0	0	0	0	0	0	0	0	0	0-0
Belitz, Todd, Col	.000	.000	.000	1	0	0	0	0	0	0	0	1	0	0-0	.000	.000	.000	1	0	0	0	0	0	0	0	1	0	0-0
Bell, Rob, Cin-Tex	.143	.250	.143	7	1	0	0	0	0	0	1	4	2	0-0	.077	.111	.096	52	4	1	0	0	1	0	2	31	5	0-0
Benes, Alan, StL	.500	.500	.500	2	1	0	0	0	1	0	0	0	0	0-0	.168	.181	.216	125	21	6	0	0	6	8	2	45	9	0-0
Benes, Andy, StL	.156	.182	.250	32	5	3	0	0	1	4	1	15	2	0-0	.140	.184	.198	707	99	20	0	7	45	48	33	298	93	0-0
Benitez, A., NYM	.000	.000	.000	1	0	0	0	0	0	1	0	0	0	0-0	.000	.000	.000	6	0	0	0	0	0	2	0	2	0	0-0
Benoit, Joaquin, Tex	.000	.000	.000	0	0	0	0	0	0	0	0	0	0	0-0	.000	.000	.000	0	0	0	0	0	0	0	0	0	0	0-0
Bere, Jason, ChC	.194	.194	.258	62	12	4	0	0	2	2	0	18	7	0-0	.197	.220	.241	137	27	4	1	0	8	5	3	49	10	0-0
Bernero, Adam, Det	.000	.000	.000	0	0	0	0	0	0	0	0	0	0	0-0	.000	.000	.000	0	0	0	0	0	0	0	0	0	0	0-0
Biddle, Rocky, CWS	.000	.000	.000	1	0	0	0	0	0	0	0	1	1	0-0	.000	.000	.000	1	0	0	0	0	0	0	0	1	1	0-0
Bierbrodt, Nick, Ari-TB	.667	.750	.833	6	4	1	0	0	3	0	2	0	2	0-0	.667	.750	.833	6	4	1	0	0	3	0	2	0	2	0-0
Blair, Willie, Det	.000	.000	.000	2	0	0	0	0	0	0	0	1	0	0-0	.074	.110	.081	148	11	1	0	0	6	5	6	89	12	0-0
Blank, Matt, Mon	.500	.500	.625	8	4	1	0	0	0	1	0	2	0	0-0	.444	.444	.556	9	4	1	0	0	0	1	0	3	0	0-0
Boehringer, B., NYY-SF	.000	.000	.000	3	0	0	0	0	0	0	0	2	0	0-0	.067	.152	.100	30	2	1	0	0	0	2	3	15	3	0-0
Bohanon, Brian, Col	.323	.344	.452	31	10	4	0	0	3	3	1	7	1	0-0	.229	.259	.325	231	53	11	1	3	16	30	10	69	22	0-0
Bones, Ricky, Fla	.500	.333	.500	2	1	0	0	0	0	1	0	1	0	0-0	.100	.200	.100	20	2	0	0	0	3	3	3	6	4	0-0
Borbon, Pedro, Tor	.000	.000	.000	0	0	0	0	0	0	0	0	0	0	0-0	.250	.250	.250	4	1	0	0	0	0	0	0	1	1	0-0
Borkowski, Dave, Det	.000	.000	.000	0	0	0	0	0	0	0	0	0	0	0-0	.000	.000	.000	3	0	0	0	0	0	1	0	2	0	0-0
Borland, Toby, Ana	.000	.000	.000	0	0	0	0	0	0	0	0	0	0	0-0	.083	.077	.083	12	1	0	0	0	1	2	0	3	1	0-0
Borowski, Joe, ChC	.000	.000	.000	0	0	0	0	0	0	0	0	0	0	0-0	.000	.000	.000	2	0	0	0	0	0	0	0	2	1	0-0
Bottalico, Ricky, Phi	.333	.333	.667	3	1	1	0	0	1	1	0	0	0	0-0	.133	.133	.267	15	2	2	0	0	1	1	0	8	1	0-0
Bottenfield, Kent, Hou	.143	.143	.143	14	2	0	0	0	0	0	0	5	1	0-0	.162	.175	.178	191	31	3	0	0	13	10	2	66	26	1-0
Bowles, Brian, Tor	.000	.000	.000	0	0	0	0	0	0	0	0	0	0	0-0	.000	.000	.000	0	0	0	0	0	0	0	0	0	0	0-0
Bradford, Chad, Oak	.000	.000	.000	0	0	0	0	0	0	0	0	0	0	0-0	.000	.000	.000	0	0	0	0	0	0	0	0	0	0	0-0
Brantley, Jeff, Tex	.000	.000	.000	0	0	0	0	0	0	0	0	0	0	0-0	.118	.143	.132	68	8	1	0	0	5	5	2	23	11	0-0
Brea, Leslie, Bal	.000	.000	.000	0	0	0	0	0	0	0	0	0	0	0-0	.000	.000	.000	0	0	0	0	0	0	0	0	0	0	0-0
Brock, Chris, Phi	.333	.333	.333	3	1	0	0	0	0	0	0	0	0	0-0	.197	.234	.262	61	12	1	0	1	5	7	3	12	6	0-0
Brohawn, Troy, Ari	.000	.000	.000	1	0	0	0	0	0	0	0	0	0	0-0	.000	.000	.000	1	0	0	0	0	0	0	0	0	0	0-0
Brower, Jim, Cin	.308	.308	.346	26	8	1	0	0	6	3	0	8	2	0-0	.276	.276	.310	29	8	1	0	0	6	3	0	10	2	0-0
Brown, Kevin, LA	.083	.154	.167	36	3	0	0	1	2	2	0	12	2	0-0	.117	.166	.137	410	48	5	0	1	14	25	19	147	46	0-0
Buddie, Mike, Mil	.250	.250	.250	4	1	0	0	0	1	0	0	3	0	0-0	.250	.250	.250	4	1	0	0	0	1	0	0	3	0	0-0
Buehrle, Mark, CWS	.000	.250	.000	3	0	0	0	0	0	0	1	2	0	0-0	.000	.250	.000	3	0	0	0	0	0	0	1	2	0	0-0
Burba, Dave, Cle	.000	.000	.000	2	0	0	0	0	1	0	0	1	2	0-0	.143	.198	.200	175	25	1	0	3	10	12	10	73	21	0-0
Burkett, John, Atl	.092	.132	.092	65	6	0	0	0	2	1	3	29	7	0-0	.093	.137	.104	536	50	6	0	0	22	18	26	225	60	0-0
Burnett, A.J., Fla	.080	.115	.100	50	4	1	0	0	0	0	1	27	7	0-0	.141	.186	.217	92	13	2	1	1	4	3	4	47	9	0-0
Byrd, Paul, Phi-KC	.167	.167	.167	6	1	0	0	0	0	0	0	2	2	0-0	.147	.212	.147	109	16	0	0	0	9	6	7	28	17	0-0
Cabrera, Jose, Atl	.000	.000	.000	1	0	0	0	0	0	0	0	1	0	0-0	.000	.000	.000	4	0	0	0	0	0	0	0	2	0	0-0
Callaway, Mickey, TB	.000	.000	.000	0	0	0	0	0	0	0	0	0	0	0-0	.667	.667	.667	3	2	0	0	0	0	1	0	0	0	0-0
Carpenter, Chris, Tor	.167	.167	.167	6	1	0	0	0	0	0	0	3	1	0-0	.100	.182	.100	10	1	0	0	0	0	0	1	5	1	0-0
Carrara, Giovanni, LA	.250	.250	.250	12	3	0	0	0	1	0	0	2	0	0-0	.136	.136	.136	22	3	0	0	0	2	0	0	6	2	0-0
Carrasco, Hector, Min	.000	.000	.000	0	0	0	0	0	0	0	0	0	0	0-0	.056	.056	.056	18	1	0	0	0	0	0	0	12	0	0-0
Castillo, Carlos, Bos	.000	.000	.000	0	0	0	0	0	0	0	0	0	0	0-0	.500	.500	.500	2	1	0	0	0	0	0	0	0	0	0-0
Castillo, Frank, Bos	.000	.000	.000	2	0	0	0	0	0	0	0	1	1	0-0	.110	.143	.110	336	37	0	0	0	7	13	13	110	41	0-1
Chacon, Shawn, Col	.043	.063	.043	47	2	0	0	0	2	1	0	22	7	0-0	.043	.063	.043	47	2	0	0	0	2	1	0	22	7	0-0
Charlton, Norm, Sea	.000	.000	.000	0	0	0	0	0	0	0	0	0	0	0-0	.092	.151	.115	87	8	2	0	0	6	1	3	50	10	0-0
Chen, Bruce, Phi-NYM	.128	.128	.128	47	6	0	0	0	1	0	0	19	5	0-0	.084	.094	.084	95	8	0	0	0	1	2	1	49	15	0-0
Chiasson, Scott, ChC	.000	.000	.000	0	0	0	0	0	0	0	0	0	0	0-0	.000	.000	.000	0	0	0	0	0	0	0	0	0	0	0-0
Choate, Randy, NYY	.000	.000	.000	3	0	0	0	0	0	0	0	2	0	0-0	.000	.000	.000	3	0	0	0	0	0	0	0	2	0	0-0
Chouinard, Bobby, Col	.000	.000	.000	0	0	0	0	0	0	0	0	0	0	0-0	.125	.125	.125	8	1	0	0	0	1	0	0	5	1	0-0
Christiansen, J., StL-SF	.000	.000	.000	0	0	0	0	0	0	0	0	0	0	0-0	.100	.100	.100	10	1	0	0	0	0	1	0	7	1	0-0
Christman, Tim, Col	.000	.000	.000	0	0	0	0	0	0	0	0	0	0	0-0	.000	.000	.000	0	0	0	0	0	0	0	0	0	0	0-0
Clemens, Roger, NYY	.000	.000	.000	2	0	0	0	0	0	0	0	2	0	0-0	.125	.222	.188	16	2	1	0	0	1	0	2	6	2	0-0
Clement, Matt, Fla	.080	.132	.080	50	4	0	0	0	2	0	3	18	8	0-0	.073	.131	.085	164	12	0	1	0	12	3	11	81	21	0-0
Coco, Pasqual, Tor	.000	.000	.000	0	0	0	0	0	0	0	0	0	0	0-0	.000	.000	.000	0	0	0	0	0	0	0	0	0	0	0-0

	2001 Hitting														Career Hitting													
Pitcher, Team	Avg	OBP	SLG	AB	H	2B	3B	HR	R	RBI	BB	SO	SH	SB-CS	Avg	OBP	SLG	AB	H	2B	3B	HR	R	RBI	BB	SO	SH	SB-CS
Cogan, Tony, KC	.000	.000	.000	0	0	0	0	0	0	0	0	0	0	0-0	.000	.000	.000	0	0	0	0	0	0	0	0	0	0	0-0
Coggin, Dave, Phi	.061	.114	.091	33	2	1	0	0	1	1	2	13	1	0-0	.050	.095	.075	40	2	1	0	0	1	1	2	17	2	0-0
Colome, Jesus, TB	.000	.000	.000	0	0	0	0	0	0	0	0	0	0	0-0	.000	.000	.000	0	0	0	0	0	0	0	0	0	0	0-0
Colon, Bartolo, Cle	.143	.143	.143	7	1	0	0	0	0	0	0	5	0	0-0	.136	.136	.136	22	3	0	0	0	0	1	0	17	1	0-0
Cone, David, Bos	.000	.000	.000	1	0	0	0	0	0	0	0	1	1	0-0	.154	.192	.176	408	63	9	0	0	28	22	16	90	38	0-1
Cook, Dennis, NYM-Phi	.000	.000	.000	1	0	0	0	0	0	0	0	0	0	0-0	.264	.283	.355	110	29	2	1	2	15	9	3	13	9	0-0
Cooper, Brian, Ana	.000	.000	.000	0	0	0	0	0	0	0	0	0	0	0-0	.000	.000	.000	4	0	0	0	0	0	0	0	3	0	0-0
Coppinger, Rocky, Mil	.000	.000	.000	5	0	0	0	0	0	1	0	1	1	0-0	.125	.125	.125	8	1	0	0	0	0	1	0	3	1	0-0
Cordero, F., Tex	.000	.000	.000	0	0	0	0	0	0	0	0	0	0	0-0	.000	.000	.000	0	0	0	0	0	0	0	0	0	0	0-0
Corey, Mark, NYM	.000	.000	.000	0	0	0	0	0	0	0	0	0	0	0-0	.000	.000	.000	0	0	0	0	0	0	0	0	0	0	0-0
Cormier, Rheal, Phi	.000	.000	.000	1	0	0	0	0	0	0	0	0	0	0-0	.184	.201	.216	185	34	4	1	0	14	12	3	43	28	0-0
Cornejo, Nate, Det	.000	.000	.000	0	0	0	0	0	0	0	0	0	0	0-0	.000	.000	.000	0	0	0	0	0	0	0	0	0	0	0-0
Crabtree, Tim, Tex	.000	.000	.000	0	0	0	0	0	0	0	0	0	0	0-0	.000	.000	.000	1	0	0	0	0	0	0	0	0	0	0-0
Crawford, Paxton, Bos	.000	.000	.000	0	0	0	0	0	0	0	0	0	0	0-0	.000	.000	.000	0	0	0	0	0	0	0	0	0	0	0-0
Creek, Doug, TB	.000	.000	.000	0	0	0	0	0	0	0	0	0	0	0-0	.250	.250	.250	4	1	0	0	0	1	0	0	2	3	0-0
Cressend, Jack, Min	.000	.000	.000	0	0	0	0	0	0	0	0	0	0	0-0	.000	.000	.000	0	0	0	0	0	0	0	0	0	0	0-0
Cruz, Juan, ChC	.125	.125	.125	16	2	0	0	0	0	1	0	5	2	0-0	.125	.125	.125	16	2	0	0	0	0	1	0	5	2	0-0
Cruz, Nelson, Hou	.167	.167	.167	6	1	0	0	0	0	0	0	2	0	0-0	.143	.143	.143	7	1	0	0	0	0	0	0	2	0	0-0
Cubillan, Darwin, Mon	.000	.000	.000	0	0	0	0	0	0	0	0	0	0	0-0	.000	.000	.000	1	0	0	0	0	0	0	0	0	0	0-0
Cunnane, Will, Mil	.000	.000	.000	7	0	0	0	0	0	0	0	1	0	0-0	.194	.242	.290	31	6	1	1	0	4	4	2	9	1	0-0
Daal, Omar, Phi	.236	.250	.255	55	13	1	0	0	7	5	1	10	7	0-0	.203	.246	.242	231	47	6	0	1	21	17	13	50	23	0-0
D'Amico, Jeff, Mil	.067	.176	.200	15	1	0	1	0	0	0	2	5	0	0-0	.079	.145	.175	63	5	1	1	1	2	2	5	27	7	0-0
Darensbourg, Vic, Fla	.000	.000	.000	0	0	0	0	0	0	0	0	0	0	0-0	.125	.222	.125	16	2	0	0	0	0	0	2	5	0	0-0
Davenport, Joe, Col	1.000	1.000	1.000	1	1	0	0	0	0	0	0	0	0	0-0	1.000	1.000	1.000	1	1	0	0	0	0	0	0	0	0	0-0
Davey, Tom, SD	.000	1.000	.000	0	0	0	0	0	0	0	1	0	0	0-0	.000	1.000	.000	0	0	0	0	0	0	0	1	0	0	0-0
Davis, Doug, Tex	.000	.000	.000	3	0	0	0	0	0	0	0	2	1	0-0	.000	.000	.000	3	0	0	0	0	0	0	0	2	1	0-0
Davis, Kane, Col	.000	.000	.000	5	0	0	0	0	0	0	0	5	0	0-0	.000	.000	.000	6	0	0	0	0	0	0	0	6	0	0-0
Davis, Lance, Cin	.121	.121	.152	33	4	1	0	0	3	2	0	15	4	0-0	.121	.121	.152	33	4	1	0	0	3	2	0	15	4	0-0
DeJean, Mike, Mil	.000	.000	.000	3	0	0	0	0	0	0	0	2	0	0-0	.067	.067	.133	15	1	1	0	0	0	0	0	8	1	0-0
de los Santos, V., Mil	.000	.000	.000	0	0	0	0	0	0	0	0	0	0	0-0	.000	.000	.000	6	0	0	0	0	0	0	0	4	0	0-0
Dempster, Ryan, Fla	.049	.065	.066	61	3	1	0	0	1	0	1	29	16	0-0	.070	.084	.090	200	14	4	0	0	9	4	3	88	22	0-0
Dessens, Elmer, Cin	.193	.233	.211	57	11	1	0	0	3	2	3	12	10	0-0	.155	.231	.164	110	17	1	0	0	10	5	11	32	14	0-0
DeWitt, Matt, Tor	.000	.000	.000	0	0	0	0	0	0	0	0	0	0	0-0	.000	.000	.000	0	0	0	0	0	0	0	0	0	0	0-0
Dickey, R.A., Tex	.000	.000	.000	0	0	0	0	0	0	0	0	0	0	0-0	.000	.000	.000	0	0	0	0	0	0	0	0	0	0	0-0
Dingman, Craig, Col	.000	.000	.000	0	0	0	0	0	0	0	0	0	0	0-0	.000	.000	.000	0	0	0	0	0	0	0	0	0	0	0-0
Dotel, Octavio, Hou	.091	.091	.091	11	1	0	0	0	0	0	0	5	1	0-0	.075	.151	.075	67	5	0	0	0	3	1	5	38	9	0-0
Douglass, Sean, Bal	.000	.000	.000	0	0	0	0	0	0	0	0	0	0	0-0	.000	.000	.000	0	0	0	0	0	0	0	0	0	0	0-0
Dreifort, Darren, LA	.152	.176	.303	33	5	2	0	1	4	2	1	20	3	1-0	.188	.216	.309	223	42	9	0	6	26	22	7	97	14	2-0
Drese, Ryan, Cle	.000	.000	.000	0	0	0	0	0	0	0	0	0	0	0-0	.000	.000	.000	0	0	0	0	0	0	0	0	0	0	0-0
Drew, Tim, Cle	.000	.000	.000	0	0	0	0	0	0	0	0	0	0	0-0	.000	.000	.000	0	0	0	0	0	0	0	0	0	0	0-0
Duchscherer, J., Tex	.000	.000	.000	0	0	0	0	0	0	0	0	0	0	0-0	.000	.000	.000	0	0	0	0	0	0	0	0	0	0	0-0
Duckworth, B., Phi	.227	.292	.273	22	5	1	0	0	1	1	2	4	2	0-0	.227	.292	.273	22	5	1	0	0	1	1	2	4	2	0-0
Duncan, C., ChC	.000	.400	.000	3	0	0	0	0	1	1	2	1	0	0-0	.000	.400	.000	3	0	0	0	0	1	1	2	1	0	0-0
Durbin, Chad, KC	.000	.000	.000	1	0	0	0	0	0	0	0	0	1	0-0	.000	.000	.000	1	0	0	0	0	0	0	0	0	1	0-0
Duvall, Mike, Min	.000	.000	.000	0	0	0	0	0	0	0	0	0	0	0-0	.000	1.000	.000	0	0	0	0	0	0	0	1	0	0	0-0
Eaton, Adam, SD	.105	.190	.132	38	4	1	0	0	3	2	4	12	2	1-0	.197	.299	.237	76	15	3	0	0	9	6	10	22	2	3-0
Eischen, Joey, Mon	.000	.000	.000	0	0	0	0	0	0	0	0	0	0	0-0	.000	.000	.000	8	0	0	0	0	0	0	0	3	0	0-0
Elarton, Scott, Hou-Col	.079	.167	.079	38	3	0	0	0	1	2	1	10	5	0-0	.134	.177	.149	134	18	2	0	0	8	3	2	44	21	0-0
Eldred, Cal, CWS	.000	.000	.000	0	0	0	0	0	0	0	0	0	0	0-0	.111	.188	.143	63	7	2	0	0	7	4	6	33	10	0-1
Ellis, Robert, Ari	.154	.185	.154	26	4	0	0	0	2	1	1	12	1	0-0	.154	.185	.154	26	4	0	0	0	2	1	1	12	1	0-0
Embree, Alan, SF-CWS	.000	.000	.000	1	0	0	0	0	0	0	0	0	0	0-0	.000	.333	.000	2	0	0	0	0	0	0	1	1	0	0-0
Erdos, Todd, Bos	.000	.000	.000	0	0	0	0	0	0	0	0	0	0	0-0	.000	.000	.000	3	0	0	0	0	0	0	0	1	0	0-0
Escobar, Kelvim, Tor	.000	.000	.000	0	0	0	0	0	0	0	0	0	0	0-0	.000	.000	.000	8	0	0	0	0	0	0	0	5	0	0-0
Estes, Shawn, SF	.071	.130	.071	42	3	0	0	0	2	1	3	11	6	0-0	.157	.194	.207	305	48	9	0	2	29	20	11	111	48	0-1
Estrada, Horacio, Col	.000	.000	.000	0	0	0	0	0	0	0	0	0	0	0-0	.111	.111	.111	9	1	0	0	0	1	0	0	2	1	0-0
Eyre, Scott, Tor	.000	.000	.000	0	0	0	0	0	0	0	0	0	0	0-0	.200	.200	.200	5	1	0	0	0	0	0	0	3	0	0-0
Farnsworth, Kyle, ChC	.000	.000	.000	2	0	0	0	0	0	0	0	2	0	0-0	.078	.130	.098	51	4	1	0	0	3	2	2	18	8	0-0
Fassero, Jeff, ChC	.000	.000	.000	2	0	0	0	0	0	0	0	2	0	0-0	.075	.139	.093	226	17	2	1	0	16	5	17	129	40	1-0
Fernandez, Jared, Cin	.000	.000	.000	2	0	0	0	0	0	0	0	0	0	0-0	.000	.000	.000	2	0	0	0	0	0	0	0	0	0	0-0
Fernandez, O., Cin	.053	.100	.053	19	1	0	0	0	1	0	1	8	3	0-0	.070	.108	.070	115	8	0	0	0	1	2	4	56	15	0-0
Fetters, Mike, LA-Pit	.000	.000	.000	0	0	0	0	0	0	0	0	0	0	0-0	.000	.000	.000	0	0	0	0	0	0	0	0	0	0	0-0
Figueroa, Nelson, Phi	.250	.280	.292	24	6	1	0	0	4	1	1	11	1	0-0	.259	.286	.296	27	7	1	0	0	5	1	1	12	2	0-0
Fikac, Jeremy, SD	.000	.000	.000	0	0	0	0	0	0	0	0	0	0	0-0	.000	.000	.000	0	0	0	0	0	0	0	0	0	0	0-0
File, Bob, Tor	.000	.000	.000	0	0	0	0	0	0	0	0	0	0	0-0	.000	.000	.000	0	0	0	0	0	0	0	0	0	0	0-0
Finley, Chuck, Cle	.000	.000	.000	0	0	0	0	0	0	0	0	0	0	0-0	.000	.000	.000	21	0	0	0	0	1	0	0	12	1	0-0
Fiore, Tony, TB-Min	.000	.000	.000	0	0	0	0	0	0	0	0	0	0	0-0	.000	.000	.000	0	0	0	0	0	0	0	0	0	0	0-0
Florie, Bryce, Bos	.000	.000	.000	0	0	0	0	0	0	0	0	0	0	0-0	.111	.273	.111	9	1	0	0	0	0	0	2	5	1	0-0
Fogg, Josh, CWS	.000	.000	.000	0	0	0	0	0	0	0	0	0	0	0-0	.000	.000	.000	0	0	0	0	0	0	0	0	0	0	0-0
Fossum, Casey, Bos	.000	.000	.000	0	0	0	0	0	0	0	0	0	0	0-0	.000	.000	.000	0	0	0	0	0	0	0	0	0	0	0-0
Foster, Kevin, Tex	.000	.000	.000	0	0	0	0	0	0	0	0	0	0	0-0	.190	.237	.270	163	31	6	2	1	15	19	9	59	22	2-0
Foster, Kris, Bal	.000	.000	.000	0	0	0	0	0	0	0	0	0	0	0-0	.000	.000	.000	0	0	0	0	0	0	0	0	0	0	0-0
Foulke, Keith, CWS	.000	.000	.000	0	0	0	0	0	0	0	0	0	0	0-0	.133	.133	.133	15	2	0	0	0	0	0	0	5	2	0-0
Fox, Chad, Mil	.000	.000	.000	3	0	0	0	0	0	0	0	1	0	0-0	.000	.000	.000	7	0	0	0	0	0	0	0	3	1	0-0
Franco, John, NYM	.000	.000	.000	0	0	0	0	0	0	0	0	0	0	0-0	.088	.088	.088	34	3	0	0	0	2	1	0	14	3	0-0
Franklin, Ryan, Sea	.000	.000	.000	0	0	0	0	0	0	0	0	0	0	0-0	.000	.000	.000	0	0	0	0	0	0	0	0	0	0	0-0
Franklin, Wayne, Hou	.000	.000	.000	0	0	0	0	0	0	0	0	0	0	0-0	.000	.000	.000	2	0	0	0	0	0	0	0	1	0	0-0
Frascatore, John, Tor	.000	.000	.000	0	0	0	0	0	0	0	0	0	0	0-0	.059	.111	.059	17	1	0	0	0	0	0	1	12	1	0-0
Fuentes, Brian, Sea	.000	.000	.000	0	0	0	0	0	0	0	0	0	0	0-0	.000	.000	.000	0	0	0	0	0	0	0	0	0	0	0-0
Fultz, Aaron, SF	.400	.400	.400	5	2	0	0	0	1	0	0	0	0	0-0	.364	.364	.364	11	4	0	0	0	1	0	0	1	1	0-0
Fyhrie, Mike, ChC-Oak	.000	.000	.000	2	0	0	0	0	0	0	0	0	0	0-0	.000	.000	.000	2	0	0	0	0	0	0	0	0	0	0-0
Gagne, Eric, LA	.136	.156	.295	44	6	2	1	1	3	2	1	13	6	0-1	.146	.157	.232	82	12	2	1	1	5	3	1	21	12	0-1
Gandarillas, Gus, Mil	.000	.000	.000	0	0	0	0	0	0	0	0	0	0	0-0	.000	.000	.000	0	0	0	0	0	0	0	0	0	0	0-0
Garces, Rich, Bos	.000	.000	.000	2	0	0	0	0	0	0	0	1	0	0-0	.000	.000	.000	3	0	0	0	0	0	0	0	1	0	0-0
Garcia, Freddy, Sea	.143	.143	.143	7	1	0	0	0	0	0	0	4	2	0-0	.286	.286	.286	14	4	0	0	0	0	1	0	5	7	0-0
Gardner, Mark, SF	.000	.045	.000	21	0	0	0	0	1	1	1	8	4	0-0	.123	.155	.142	506	62	3	2	1	22	22	16	206	61	0-0
Garland, Jon, CWS	.000	.000	.000	2	0	0	0	0	0	0	0	1	0	0-0	.000	.000	.000	2	0	0	0	0	0	0	0	1	0	0-0
George, Chris, KC	.000	.000	.000	0	0	0	0	0	0	0	0	0	0	0-0	.000	.000	.000	0	0	0	0	0	0	0	0	0	0	0-0
Ginter, Matt, CWS	.000	.000	.000	0	0	0	0	0	0	0	0	0	0	0-0	.000	.000	.000	0	0	0	0	0	0	0	0	0	0	0-0
Glavine, Tom, Atl	.140	.197	.175	57	8	2	0	0	4	2	4	21	17	0-0	.192	.246	.220	956	184	19	2	1	71	66	66	252	155	1-0
Glover, Gary, CWS	.000	.000	.000	0	0	0	0	0	0	0	0	0	0	0-0	.000	.000	.000	0	0	0	0	0	0	0	0	0	0	0-0
Glynn, Ryan, Tex	.000	.000	.000	0	0	0	0	0	0	0	0	0	0	0-0	.000	.000	.000	3	0	0	0	0	0	0	0	1	0	0-0
Gomes, Wayne, Phi-SF	1.000	1.000	1.000	1	1	0	0	0	0	1	1	0	0	0-0	.167	.375	.167	6	1	0	0	0	0	1	2	4	0	0-0

	2001 Hitting														Career Hitting													
Pitcher, Team	Avg	OBP	SLG	AB	H	2B	3B	HR	R	RBI	BB	SO	SH	SB-CS	Avg	OBP	SLG	AB	H	2B	3B	HR	R	RBI	BB	SO	SH	SB-CS
Gonzalez, Dicky, NYM	.100	.143	.100	20	2	0	0	0	1	0	1	4	1	0-0	.100	.143	.100	20	2	0	0	0	1	0	1	4	1	0-0
Gordon, Flash, ChC	.000	.000	.000	0	0	0	0	0	0	0	0	0	0	0-0	.000	.000	.000	0	0	0	0	0	0	0	0	0	0	0-0
Graves, Danny, Cin	.250	.250	1.000	4	1	0	0	1	1	2	0	2	0	0-0	.125	.176	.500	16	2	0	0	2	2	3	1	8	0	0-0
Green, Steve, Ana	.000	.000	.000	0	0	0	0	0	0	0	0	0	0	0-0	.000	.000	.000	0	0	0	0	0	0	0	0	0	0	0-0
Grilli, Jason, Fla	.286	.286	.714	7	2	0	0	1	1	2	0	2	2	0-0	.333	.333	.667	9	3	0	0	1	1	3	0	2	2	0-0
Grimsley, Jason, KC	.000	.000	.000	0	0	0	0	0	0	0	0	0	0	0-0	.103	.205	.103	39	4	0	0	0	3	2	5	11	5	0-0
Groom, Buddy, Bal	.000	.000	.000	0	0	0	0	0	0	0	0	0	0	0-0	.000	.000	.000	0	0	0	0	0	0	0	0	0	0	0-0
Guardado, Eddie, Min	.000	.000	.000	0	0	0	0	0	0	0	0	0	0	0-0	.000	.000	.000	0	0	0	0	0	0	0	0	0	0	0-0
Guthrie, Mark, Oak	.000	.000	.000	0	0	0	0	0	0	0	0	0	0	0-0	.091	.091	.091	11	1	0	0	0	0	0	0	1	1	0-0
Guzman, Geraldo, Ari	.000	.000	.000	1	0	0	0	0	0	0	0	1	0	0-0	.000	.000	.000	20	0	0	0	0	0	0	0	14	3	0-0
Hackman, Luther, StL	.000	.000	.000	1	0	0	0	0	0	0	0	0	2	0-0	.167	.167	.167	6	1	0	0	0	1	0	0	3	2	0-0
Halama, John, Sea	.000	.000	.000	1	0	0	0	0	0	0	0	0	1	0-0	.111	.238	.167	18	2	1	0	0	2	0	3	10	3	0-0
Halladay, Roy, Tor	.000	.000	.000	1	0	0	0	0	0	0	0	0	1	0-0	.000	.000	.000	3	0	0	0	0	0	0	0	2	2	0-0
Hamilton, Joey, Tor-Cin	.125	.125	.250	8	1	1	0	0	0	1	0	5	0	0-0	.117	.138	.179	308	36	5	1	4	16	21	8	157	32	0-0
Hampton, Mike, Col	.291	.309	.582	79	23	2	0	7	20	16	2	21	5	0-1	.242	.298	.330	451	109	11	4	7	62	47	34	118	42	2-3
Harnisch, Pete, Cin	.273	.273	.364	11	3	1	0	0	2	0	0	5	1	0-0	.129	.150	.177	513	66	19	0	2	40	29	12	150	62	0-2
Harper, Travis, TB	.000	.000	.000	0	0	0	0	0	0	0	0	0	0	0-0	.000	.000	.000	0	0	0	0	0	0	0	0	0	0	0-0
Harville, Chad, Oak	.000	.000	.000	0	0	0	0	0	0	0	0	0	0	0-0	.000	.000	.000	0	0	0	0	0	0	0	0	0	0	0-0
Hasegawa, S. Ana	.000	.000	.000	0	0	0	0	0	0	0	0	0	0	0-0	.000	.000	.000	1	0	0	0	0	0	0	0	0	0	0-0
Hawkins, LaTroy, Min	.000	.000	.000	0	0	0	0	0	0	0	0	0	0	0-0	.000	.000	.000	5	0	0	0	0	0	0	0	4	0	0-0
Haynes, Jimmy, Mil	.154	.185	.192	52	8	2	0	0	5	0	2	16	5	0-0	.128	.155	.176	125	16	6	0	0	9	4	4	51	11	0-0
Helling, Rick, Tex	.000	.000	.000	4	0	0	0	0	0	0	0	1	0	0-0	.077	.077	.077	39	3	0	0	0	1	0	0	15	2	0-0
Henry, Doug, KC	.000	.000	.000	0	0	0	0	0	0	0	0	0	0	0-0	.059	.059	.059	17	1	0	0	0	1	0	0	6	2	0-0
Hentgen, Pat, Bal	.000	.000	.000	0	0	0	0	0	0	0	0	0	0	0-0	.115	.159	.115	78	9	0	0	0	4	0	4	25	9	0-0
Heredia, Felix, ChC	.000	.000	.000	1	0	0	0	0	0	0	0	1	0	0-0	.250	.250	.250	12	3	0	0	0	0	1	0	4	1	0-0
Heredia, Gil, Oak	.333	.333	.333	3	1	0	0	0	0	0	0	0	0	0-0	.213	.239	.225	89	19	1	0	0	3	3	3	11	12	0-0
Herges, Matt, LA	.444	.444	.444	9	4	0	0	0	0	1	0	3	1	0-0	.217	.217	.217	23	5	0	0	0	0	1	0	12	2	0-0
Hermanson, D., StL	.081	.109	.097	62	5	1	0	0	2	3	2	30	5	0-0	.096	.156	.135	281	27	5	0	2	12	9	19	143	31	0-0
Hernandez, A., NYY	.000	.000	.000	0	0	0	0	0	0	0	0	0	0	0-0	.000	.000	.000	0	0	0	0	0	0	0	0	0	0	0-0
Hernandez, C., Hou	.200	.200	.200	5	1	0	0	0	0	0	0	2	1	0-0	.200	.200	.200	5	1	0	0	0	0	0	0	2	1	0-0
Hernandez, Livan, SF	.296	.296	.383	81	24	4	0	1	7	8	0	4	4	0-0	.243	.254	.319	345	84	14	0	4	25	33	3	54	24	0-0
Hernandez, O., NYY	.000	.000	.000	0	0	0	0	0	0	0	0	0	0	0-0	.053	.053	.053	19	1	0	0	0	1	0	0	12	2	0-0
Hernandez, R., KC	.000	.000	.000	0	0	0	0	0	0	0	0	0	0	0-0	.500	.500	.500	2	1	0	0	0	0	0	0	1	0	0-0
Herndon, Junior, SD	.000	.000	.000	12	0	0	0	0	0	0	0	11	1	0-0	.000	.000	.000	12	0	0	0	0	0	0	0	11	1	0-0
Hiljus, Erik, Oak	.000	.000	.000	0	0	0	0	0	0	0	0	0	0	0-0	.000	.000	.000	0	0	0	0	0	0	0	0	0	0	0-0
Hill, Ken, TB	.000	.000	.000	0	0	0	0	0	0	0	0	0	0	0-0	.150	.209	.186	333	50	7	1	1	22	21	24	94	67	0-0
Hinchliffe, Brett, NYM	.000	.000	.000	1	0	0	0	0	0	0	0	1	0	0-0	.000	.000	.000	1	0	0	0	0	0	0	0	1	0	0-0
Hitchcock, S., SD-NYY	.125	.125	.125	8	1	0	0	0	1	1	0	6	0	0-0	.094	.126	.094	191	18	0	0	0	14	5	7	103	21	0-1
Hoffman, Trevor, SD	.000	.000	.000	4	0	0	0	0	0	0	0	1	0	0-0	.121	.121	.182	33	4	2	0	0	1	5	0	10	2	0-0
Holt, Chris, Det	.250	.250	.500	4	1	1	0	0	0	0	0	3	0	0-0	.090	.134	.102	177	16	2	0	0	12	6	8	83	21	0-0
Holtz, Mike, Ana	.000	.000	.000	0	0	0	0	0	0	0	0	0	0	0-0	.000	.000	.000	1	0	0	0	0	0	0	0	1	0	0-0
Howry, Bob, CWS	.000	.000	.000	0	0	0	0	0	0	0	0	0	0	0-0	.000	.000	.000	0	0	0	0	0	0	0	0	0	0	0-0
Hudson, Tim, Oak	.000	.000	.000	8	0	0	0	0	1	0	0	3	0	0-0	.067	.125	.067	15	1	0	0	0	1	0	1	6	0	0-0
Hutchinson, Chad, StL	.000	.000	.000	1	0	0	0	0	0	0	0	0	0	0-0	.000	.000	.000	1	0	0	0	0	0	0	0	0	0	0-0
Irabu, Hideki, Mon	.000	.000	.000	3	0	0	0	0	0	0	0	0	0	0-0	.107	.138	.107	28	3	0	0	0	1	1	1	13	5	0-0
Isringhausen, J., Oak	.000	.000	.000	0	0	0	0	0	0	0	0	0	0	0-0	.196	.238	.299	97	19	4	0	2	10	11	5	33	8	0-0
Jackson, Mike, Hou	.000	.000	.000	1	0	0	0	0	0	0	0	0	0	0-0	.179	.207	.250	28	5	2	0	0	3	1	1	4	4	0-0
James, Mike, StL	.000	.000	.000	1	0	0	0	0	0	0	0	0	0	0-0	.000	.000	.000	2	0	0	0	0	1	0	0	0	0	0-0
Jarvis, Kevin, SD	.180	.246	.279	61	11	3	0	1	8	10	5	20	5	0-1	.153	.201	.210	157	24	6	0	1	16	12	7	52	19	0-1
Jennings, Jason, Col	.267	.313	.533	15	4	1	0	1	2	2	1	3	1	0-0	.267	.313	.533	15	4	1	0	1	2	2	1	3	1	0-0
Jensen, Ryan, SF	.167	.231	.167	12	2	0	0	0	0	2	1	3	0	0-0	.167	.231	.167	12	2	0	0	0	0	2	1	3	0	0-0
Jimenez, Jose, Col	.000	.000	.000	1	0	0	0	0	0	0	0	0	0	0-0	.109	.109	.141	64	7	0	1	0	5	4	0	28	5	0-0
Jodie, Brett, NYY-SD	.000	.000	.000	4	0	0	0	0	0	0	0	2	0	0-0	.000	.000	.000	4	0	0	0	0	0	0	0	2	0	0-0
Johnson, Adam, Min	.000	.000	.000	2	0	0	0	0	0	0	0	0	0	0-0	.000	.000	.000	2	0	0	0	0	0	0	0	0	0	0-0
Johnson, Jason, Bal	.333	.500	.333	3	1	0	0	0	0	0	1	2	0	0-0	.091	.167	.091	11	1	0	0	0	0	0	1	8	2	0-0
Johnson, J., Tex	.000	.000	.000	0	0	0	0	0	0	0	0	0	0	0-0	.000	.000	.000	0	0	0	0	0	0	0	0	0	0	0-0
Johnson, Mike, Mon	.000	.000	.000	1	0	0	0	0	0	0	0	1	0	0-0	.163	.182	.163	43	7	0	0	0	3	5	1	16	5	0-0
Johnson, Randy, Ari	.100	.143	.100	80	8	0	0	0	2	2	3	38	7	0-0	.121	.142	.143	315	38	7	0	0	10	18	6	147	24	0-0
Jones, Bobby J., SD	.140	.183	.175	57	8	2	0	0	5	1	3	18	2	0-0	.132	.165	.159	409	54	8	0	1	27	15	15	153	63	0-0
Jones, Todd, Det-Min	.000	.000	.000	0	0	0	0	0	0	0	0	0	0	0-0	.273	.273	.364	11	3	1	0	0	1	0	0	1	0	0-0
Judd, Mike, TB-Tex	.000	.000	.000	1	0	0	0	0	0	0	0	1	0	0-0	.111	.200	.111	9	1	0	0	0	1	0	1	3	4	0-0
Julio, Jorge, Bal	.000	.000	.000	0	0	0	0	0	0	0	0	0	0	0-0	.000	.000	.000	0	0	0	0	0	0	0	0	0	0	0-0
Karnuth, Jason, StL	.000	.000	.000	0	0	0	0	0	0	0	0	0	0	0-0	.000	.000	.000	0	0	0	0	0	0	0	0	0	0	0-0
Karsay, Steve, Cle-Atl	.000	.000	.000	2	0	0	0	0	0	0	0	1	0	0-0	.000	.000	.000	3	0	0	0	0	1	0	0	1	0	0-0
Keisler, Randy, NYY	.000	.000	.000	2	0	0	0	0	0	0	0	0	0	0-0	.000	.000	.000	2	0	0	0	0	0	0	0	0	0	0-0
Kennedy, Joe, TB	.250	.250	.250	4	1	0	0	0	1	0	0	2	0	0-0	.250	.250	.250	4	1	0	0	0	1	0	0	2	0	0-0
Kile, Darryl, StL	.127	.184	.225	71	9	4	0	1	5	4	5	33	5	0-0	.134	.192	.180	635	85	23	0	2	38	40	42	291	78	0-0
Kim, Byung-Hyun, Ari	.167	.167	.167	6	1	0	0	0	0	2	0	2	0	0-0	.100	.182	.100	10	1	0	0	0	0	2	1	4	0	0-0
Kim, Sun-Woo, Bos	.000	.000	.000	0	0	0	0	0	0	0	0	0	0	0-0	.000	.000	.000	0	0	0	0	0	0	0	0	0	0	0-0
King, Ray, Mil	.000	.000	.000	2	0	0	0	0	0	0	0	1	0	0-0	.000	.000	.000	3	0	0	0	0	0	0	0	2	0	0-0
Kline, Steve, StL	.500	.500	.500	2	1	0	0	0	0	0	0	1	0	0-0	.100	.100	.100	10	1	0	0	0	0	0	0	5	2	0-0
Knight, Brandon, NYY	.000	.000	.000	0	0	0	0	0	0	0	0	0	0	0-0	.000	.000	.000	0	0	0	0	0	0	0	0	0	0	0-0
Knott, Eric, Ari	.000	.000	.000	1	0	0	0	0	0	0	0	1	0	0-0	.000	.000	.000	1	0	0	0	0	0	0	0	1	0	0-0
Knotts, Gary, Fla	.500	.500	.500	2	1	0	0	0	0	0	0	0	0	0-0	.500	.500	.500	2	1	0	0	0	0	0	0	0	0	0-0
Koch, Billy, Tor	.000	.000	.000	0	0	0	0	0	0	0	0	0	0	0-0	.000	.000	.000	2	0	0	0	0	0	0	0	2	0	0-0
Kohlmeier, Ryan, Bal	.000	.000	.000	0	0	0	0	0	0	0	0	0	0	0-0	.000	.000	.000	0	0	0	0	0	0	0	0	0	0	0-0
Kolb, Brandon, Mil	.000	.000	.000	1	0	0	0	0	0	0	0	0	0	0-0	.000	.000	.000	2	0	0	0	0	1	0	0	0	0	0-0
Kolb, Danny, Tex	.000	.000	.000	0	0	0	0	0	0	0	0	0	0	0-0	.000	.000	.000	0	0	0	0	0	0	0	0	0	0	0-0
Koplove, Mike, Ari	.000	.000	.000	1	0	0	0	0	0	0	0	1	0	0-0	.000	.000	.000	1	0	0	0	0	0	0	0	1	0	0-0
Lawrence, Brian, SD	.115	.111	.192	26	3	2	0	0	0	3	0	7	2	0-0	.115	.111	.192	26	3	2	0	0	0	3	0	7	2	0-0
Lee, David, SD	.000	.000	.000	1	0	0	0	0	0	0	0	1	0	0-0	.167	.167	.167	6	1	0	0	0	1	0	0	3	0	0-0
Leiter, Al, NYM	.065	.094	.097	62	4	0	1	0	2	3	2	28	0	0-0	.088	.142	.108	352	31	5	1	0	10	14	22	192	34	0-0
Leiter, Mark, Mil	.143	.143	.143	7	1	0	0	0	0	0	0	4	0	0-0	.112	.152	.117	188	21	1	0	0	8	14	9	102	28	0-0
Leskanic, Curtis, Mil	.000	.000	.000	1	0	0	0	0	0	0	0	0	0	0-0	.179	.200	.333	39	7	3	0	1	4	7	1	17	5	0-0
Levine, Al, Ana	.000	.000	.000	0	0	0	0	0	0	0	0	0	0	0-0	.000	.000	.000	0	0	0	0	0	0	0	0	0	0	0-0
Levrault, Allen, Mil	.061	.086	.061	33	2	0	0	0	1	1	1	14	6	0-0	.056	.079	.056	36	2	0	0	0	1	1	1	16	6	0-0
Lidle, Cory, Oak	.000	.000	.000	2	0	0	0	0	0	0	0	2	0	0-0	.000	.100	.000	9	0	0	0	0	1	0	1	7	0	0-0
Lieber, Jon, ChC	.158	.179	.184	76	12	2	0	0	3	2	2	22	9	0-0	.153	.191	.187	418	64	14	0	0	25	20	20	155	40	0-0
Ligtenberg, Kerry, Atl	.000	.000	.000	0	0	0	0	0	0	0	0	0	0	0-0	.000	.000	.000	0	0	0	0	0	0	0	0	0	0	0-0
Lilly, Ted, NYY	.000	.000	.000	1	0	0	0	0	0	0	0	1	2	0-0	.167	.167	.167	6	1	0	0	0	0	0	0	2	3	0-0
Lima, Jose, Hou-Det	.000	.000	.000	17	0	0	0	0	0	0	0	6	1	0-0	.115	.137	.132	234	27	4	0	0	16	8	6	77	33	0-0
Lincoln, Mike, Pit	.250	.250	.250	4	1	0	0	0	0	0	0	0	1	0-0	.200	.200	.200	5	1	0	0	0	0	0	0	0	1	0-0

	2001 Hitting														Career Hitting													
Pitcher, Team	Avg	OBP	SLG	AB	H	2B	3B	HR	R	RBI	BB	SO	SH	SB-CS	Avg	OBP	SLG	AB	H	2B	3B	HR	R	RBI	BB	SO	SH	SB-CS
Linebrink, Scott, Hou	.000	.000	.000	0	0	0	0	0	0	0	0	0	0	0-0	1.000	1.000	1.000	1	1	0	0	0	0	0	0	0	0	0-0
Lira, Felipe, Mon	.000	.000	.000	0	0	0	0	0	0	0	0	0	0	0-0	.211	.200	.526	19	4	0	0	2	3	3	0	13	1	0-0
Lloyd, Graeme, Mon	.000	.333	.000	2	0	0	0	0	0	0	1	0	0	0-0	.000	.333	.000	2	0	0	0	0	0	0	1	0	0	0-0
Loaiza, Esteban, Tor	.000	.000	.000	2	0	0	0	0	0	0	0	0	0	0-0	.178	.192	.202	163	29	2	1	0	11	11	3	35	23	0-0
Loewer, Carlton, SD	.000	.000	.000	0	0	0	0	0	0	0	0	0	0	0-0	.140	.197	.140	57	8	0	0	0	4	2	4	19	7	0-0
Lohse, Kyle, Min	.400	.400	.600	5	2	1	0	0	0	1	0	2	0	0-0	.400	.400	.600	5	2	1	0	0	0	1	0	2	0	0-0
Loiselle, Rich, Pit	.000	.000	.000	0	0	0	0	0	0	0	0	0	0	0-0	.222	.222	.333	9	2	1	0	0	0	2	0	4	2	0-0
Looper, Braden, Fla	.000	.000	.000	2	0	0	0	0	0	0	0	2	0	0-0	.000	.000	.000	4	0	0	0	0	0	0	0	4	0	0-0
Lopez, Albie, TB-Ari	.034	.125	.034	29	1	0	0	0	0	0	2	13	2	0-0	.027	.100	.027	37	1	0	0	0	0	0	2	19	3	0-0
Lowe, Derek, Bos	.000	.000	.000	1	0	0	0	0	0	0	0	1	0	0-0	.000	.100	.000	9	0	0	0	0	0	0	1	7	0	0-0
Lowe, Sean, CWS	.333	.333	.333	3	1	0	0	0	0	0	0	1	0	0-0	.250	.250	.250	8	2	0	0	0	0	0	0	2	0	0-0
Lukasiewicz, Mark, Ana	.000	.000	.000	0	0	0	0	0	0	0	0	0	0	0-0	.000	.000	.000	0	0	0	0	0	0	0	0	0	0	0-0
Lundquist, David, SD	.000	.000	.000	0	0	0	0	0	0	0	0	0	0	0-0	.000	.000	.000	0	0	0	0	0	0	0	0	0	0	0-0
Lyon, Brandon, Tor	.000	.000	.000	0	0	0	0	0	0	0	0	0	0	0-0	.000	.000	.000	0	0	0	0	0	0	0	0	0	0	0-0
MacDougal, Mike, KC	.000	.000	.000	0	0	0	0	0	0	0	0	0	0	0-0	.000	.000	.000	0	0	0	0	0	0	0	0	0	0	0-0
MacRae, Scott, Cin	.000	.000	.000	3	0	0	0	0	0	0	0	1	0	0-0	.000	.000	.000	3	0	0	0	0	0	0	0	1	0	0-0
Maddux, Greg, Atl	.188	.235	.188	64	12	0	0	0	3	3	2	19	13	0-0	.179	.202	.215	1134	203	25	2	4	80	60	28	307	126	4-3
Maduro, Calvin, Bal	.000	.000	.000	0	0	0	0	0	0	0	0	0	0	0-0	.042	.042	.042	24	1	0	0	0	1	0	0	14	1	0-0
Magnante, Mike, Oak	.000	.000	.000	0	0	0	0	0	0	0	0	0	0	0-0	.333	.333	.333	6	2	0	0	0	0	1	0	2	0	0-0
Mahay, Ron, ChC	.000	.000	.000	2	0	0	0	0	0	0	0	1	0	0-0	.231	.286	.462	26	6	3	0	1	3	3	1	8	0	0-0
Mahomes, Pat, Tex	1.000	1.000	1.000	1	1	0	0	0	1	0	0	0	0	0-0	.294	.314	.412	34	10	4	0	0	5	4	1	11	2	0-0
Mann, Jim, Hou	.000	.000	.000	0	0	0	0	0	0	0	0	0	0	0-0	.000	.000	.000	0	0	0	0	0	0	0	0	0	0	0-0
Mantei, Matt, Ari	.000	.000	.000	0	0	0	0	0	0	0	0	0	0	0-0	.200	.200	.200	5	1	0	0	0	0	0	0	2	0	0-0
Manzanillo, Josias, Pit	.000	.000	.000	1	0	0	0	0	0	0	0	0	0	0-0	.091	.091	.091	11	1	0	0	0	0	0	0	5	2	0-0
Marquis, Jason, Atl	.032	.091	.032	31	1	0	0	0	3	0	2	10	2	0-0	.030	.086	.030	33	1	0	0	0	3	0	2	10	2	0-0
Marte, Damaso, Pit	.000	.000	.000	4	0	0	0	0	0	0	0	1	0	0-0	.000	.000	.000	4	0	0	0	0	0	0	0	1	0	0-0
Martin, Tom, NYM	.000	.000	.000	3	0	0	0	0	0	0	0	1	0	0-0	.000	.000	.000	6	0	0	0	0	0	0	0	2	0	0-0
Martinez, Pedro, Bos	.000	.000	.000	0	0	0	0	0	0	0	0	0	0	0-0	.098	.140	.125	255	25	3	2	0	13	11	10	117	37	0-0
Martinez, Ramon, Pit	.000	.000	.000	5	0	0	0	0	0	0	0	2	0	0-0	.153	.163	.181	596	91	12	1	1	33	33	7	200	68	0-2
Mathews, T.J., Oak-StL	.000	.000	.000	3	0	0	0	0	0	0	0	3	0	0-0	.000	.091	.000	10	0	0	0	0	0	0	1	7	0	0-0
Mattes, Troy, Mon	.467	.467	.533	15	7	1	0	0	4	1	0	2	1	0-0	.467	.467	.533	15	7	1	0	0	4	1	0	2	1	0-0
Matthews, Mike, StL	.118	.118	.294	17	2	0	0	1	2	1	0	4	1	0-0	.118	.118	.294	17	2	0	0	1	2	1	0	4	1	0-0
Maurer, Dave, SD	.000	.000	.000	1	0	0	0	0	0	0	0	1	0	0-0	.000	.000	.000	1	0	0	0	0	0	0	0	1	0	0-0
Mays, Joe, Min	.000	.000	.000	1	0	0	0	0	0	0	0	1	1	0-0	.222	.364	.333	9	2	1	0	0	1	0	2	4	2	0-0
McDill, Allen, Bos	.000	.000	.000	0	0	0	0	0	0	0	0	0	0	0-0	.000	.000	.000	0	0	0	0	0	0	0	0	0	0	0-0
McElroy, C., Bal-SD	.000	.000	.000	3	0	0	0	0	0	0	0	1	0	0-0	.214	.214	.333	42	9	3	1	0	4	4	0	13	2	0-1
McKnight, T., Hou-Pit	.000	.077	.000	24	0	0	0	0	0	0	2	10	4	0-0	.000	.051	.000	37	0	0	0	0	1	0	2	16	5	0-0
Meacham, Rusty, TB	.000	.000	.000	0	0	0	0	0	0	0	0	0	0	0-0	.000	.000	.000	0	0	0	0	0	0	0	0	0	0	0-0
Meadows, Brian, KC	.000	.000	.000	0	0	0	0	0	0	0	0	0	0	0-0	.139	.172	.160	144	20	3	0	0	12	6	6	57	13	0-0
Mecir, Jim, Oak	.000	.000	.000	0	0	0	0	0	0	0	0	0	0	0-0	.000	.000	.000	1	0	0	0	0	0	0	0	0	0	0-0
Mendoza, Ramiro, NYY	.000	.000	.000	2	0	0	0	0	0	0	0	2	0	0-0	.000	.000	.000	2	0	0	0	0	0	0	0	2	1	0-0
Mercado, Hector, Cin	.000	.000	.000	2	0	0	0	0	0	0	0	1	0	0-0	.000	.000	.000	3	0	0	0	0	0	0	0	2	0	0-0
Mercedes, Jose, Bal	.000	.000	.000	5	0	0	0	0	0	0	0	4	0	0-0	.053	.100	.053	19	1	0	0	0	0	0	0	12	0	0-0
Mesa, Jose, Phi	.000	.000	.000	0	0	0	0	0	0	0	0	0	0	0-0	.000	1.000	.000	0	0	0	0	0	1	0	1	0	0	0-0
Miadich, Bart, Ana	.000	.000	.000	0	0	0	0	0	0	0	0	0	0	0-0	.000	.000	.000	0	0	0	0	0	0	0	0	0	0	0-0
Miceli, Dan, Fla-Col	.000	.000	.000	0	0	0	0	0	0	0	0	0	0	0-0	.053	.053	.053	19	1	0	0	0	0	0	0	8	0	0-0
Michalak, C., Tor-Tex	.333	.333	1.000	3	1	0	1	0	0	0	0	1	2	0-0	.333	.333	1.000	3	1	0	1	0	0	0	0	1	2	0-0
Middlebrook, Jason, SD	.143	.143	.143	7	1	0	0	0	0	1	0	6	0	0-0	.143	.143	.143	7	1	0	0	0	0	1	0	6	0	0-0
Miller, Matt, Det	.000	.000	.000	0	0	0	0	0	0	0	0	0	0	0-0	.000	.000	.000	0	0	0	0	0	0	0	0	0	0	0-0
Miller, Travis, Min	.000	.000	.000	0	0	0	0	0	0	0	0	0	0	0-0	.000	.000	.000	0	0	0	0	0	0	0	0	0	0	0-0
Miller, Wade, Hou	.167	.191	.197	66	11	2	0	0	6	1	2	20	10	0-0	.140	.156	.168	107	15	3	0	0	7	4	2	37	11	0-0
Mills, Alan, Bal	.000	.000	.000	0	0	0	0	0	0	0	0	0	0	0-0	.000	.167	.000	5	0	0	0	0	0	1	1	3	0	0-0
Millwood, Kevin, Atl	.093	.114	.093	43	4	0	0	0	3	2	1	16	1	0-0	.112	.154	.145	242	27	5	0	1	9	11	12	105	28	0-0
Milton, Eric, Min	.000	.000	.000	2	0	0	0	0	1	0	0	1	0	0-0	.267	.313	.267	15	4	0	0	0	1	1	1	6	0	0-0
Mlicki, Dave, Det-Hou	.111	.111	.111	27	3	0	0	0	2	0	0	11	4	0-0	.116	.195	.138	181	21	4	0	0	11	5	18	67	31	0-0
Moehler, Brian, Det	.000	.000	.000	0	0	0	0	0	0	0	0	0	0	0-0	.000	.077	.000	12	0	0	0	0	1	0	1	6	0	0-0
Mohler, Mike, Ari	.000	.000	.000	0	0	0	0	0	0	0	0	0	0	0-0	.250	.250	.250	4	1	0	0	0	0	0	0	1	0	0-0
Moore, Trey, Atl	1.000	1.000	2.000	1	1	1	0	0	0	0	0	0	0	0-0	.231	.286	.308	26	6	2	0	0	1	0	2	5	3	0-0
Moreno, Juan, Tex	.000	.000	.000	0	0	0	0	0	0	0	0	0	0	0-0	.000	.000	.000	0	0	0	0	0	0	0	0	0	0	0-0
Morgan, Mike, Ari	.000	1.000	.000	0	0	0	0	0	0	0	1	0	0	0-0	.109	.132	.119	497	54	3	1	0	13	15	13	151	59	0-0
Morris, Matt, StL	.139	.162	.167	72	10	2	0	0	5	5	2	33	11	0-0	.158	.212	.186	177	28	5	0	0	10	14	12	86	23	0-1
Moss, Damian, Atl	.000	.500	.000	1	0	0	0	0	0	0	1	1	0	0-0	.000	.500	.000	1	0	0	0	0	0	0	1	1	0	0-0
Mota, Guillermo, Mon	.333	.333	.333	3	1	0	0	0	0	0	0	1	0	0-0	.400	.400	1.000	5	2	0	0	1	1	3	0	1	0	0-0
Moyer, Jamie, Sea	.000	.000	.000	1	0	0	0	0	0	0	0	0	1	0-0	.143	.215	.155	161	23	2	0	0	10	4	15	53	21	0-0
Mulder, Mark, Oak	.200	.200	.200	5	1	0	0	0	0	0	0	1	0	0-0	.111	.111	.111	9	1	0	0	0	0	0	0	4	0	0-0
Mulholland, T., Pit-LA	.000	.000	.000	9	0	0	0	0	0	0	0	5	0	0-0	.112	.132	.146	615	69	13	1	2	26	23	13	279	53	1-1
Mullen, Scott, KC	.000	.000	.000	0	0	0	0	0	0	0	0	0	0	0-0	.000	.000	.000	0	0	0	0	0	0	0	0	0	0	0-0
Munoz, Bobby, Mon	.000	.000	.000	11	0	0	0	0	0	0	0	6	0	0-0	.164	.176	.239	67	11	2	0	1	6	7	1	23	4	0-0
Murray, Heath, Det	.000	.000	.000	0	0	0	0	0	0	0	0	0	0	0-0	.105	.150	.105	19	2	0	0	0	1	0	1	10	1	0-0
Mussina, Mike, NYY	.143	.143	.143	7	1	0	0	0	0	1	0	2	0	0-0	.167	.167	.200	30	5	1	0	0	1	5	0	6	0	0-0
Myers, Mike, Col	.000	.000	.000	0	0	0	0	0	0	0	0	0	0	0-0	.000	.000	.000	1	0	0	0	0	0	0	0	1	0	0-0
Myers, Rodney, SD	.000	.000	.000	2	0	0	0	0	0	0	0	0	0	0-0	.200	.200	.267	15	3	1	0	0	2	1	0	7	0	0-0
Myette, Aaron, Tex	.000	.000	.000	0	0	0	0	0	0	0	0	0	0	0-0	.000	.000	.000	0	0	0	0	0	0	0	0	0	0	0-0
Nagy, Charles, Cle	1.000	1.000	1.000	1	1	0	0	0	1	0	0	0	1	0-0	.118	.118	.118	17	2	0	0	0	2	0	0	10	1	0-0
Neagle, Denny, Col	.196	.233	.375	56	11	4	0	2	6	9	2	12	8	0-0	.158	.191	.217	475	75	13	0	5	26	43	19	140	68	0-1
Neal, Blaine, Fla	.000	.000	.000	0	0	0	0	0	0	0	0	0	0	0-0	.000	.000	.000	0	0	0	0	0	0	0	0	0	0	0-0
Nelson, Jeff, Sea	.000	.000	.000	0	0	0	0	0	0	0	0	0	0	0-0	.000	.000	.000	2	0	0	0	0	0	0	0	0	1	0-0
Nelson, Joe, Atl	.000	.000	.000	0	0	0	0	0	0	0	0	0	0	0-0	.000	.000	.000	0	0	0	0	0	0	0	0	0	0	0-0
Nen, Robb, SF	.000	.000	.000	1	0	0	0	0	0	0	0	0	0	0-0	.000	.000	.000	13	0	0	0	0	0	0	0	3	0	0-0
Neugebauer, Nick, Mil	.000	.000	.000	3	0	0	0	0	0	0	0	1	0	0-0	.000	.000	.000	3	0	0	0	0	0	0	0	1	0	0-0
Nichting, Chris, Cin-Col	.000	.000	.000	1	0	0	0	0	1	0	0	1	1	0-0	.000	.000	.000	1	0	0	0	0	1	0	0	1	1	0-0
Nickle, Doug, Phi	.000	.000	.000	0	0	0	0	0	0	0	0	0	0	0-0	.000	.000	.000	0	0	0	0	0	0	0	0	0	0	0-0
Nitkowski, C., Det-NYM	.000	.000	.000	0	0	0	0	0	0	0	0	0	0	0-0	.133	.133	.133	15	2	0	0	0	1	1	0	10	1	0-0
Nomo, Hideo, Bos	.200	.200	.200	5	1	0	0	0	0	0	0	3	0	0-0	.150	.162	.199	327	49	11	1	1	13	19	5	147	31	0-0
Nunez, Jose A., LA-SD	.000	.000	.000	3	0	0	0	0	0	0	0	2	0	0-0	.000	.000	.000	3	0	0	0	0	0	0	0	2	0	0-0
Nunez, Vladimir, Fla	.111	.200	.111	9	1	0	0	0	1	0	1	4	2	0-0	.130	.145	.185	54	7	0	0	1	3	5	1	15	8	0-0
Ohka, T., Bos-Mon	.167	.167	.167	18	3	0	0	0	1	1	0	8	3	0-0	.167	.167	.167	18	3	0	0	0	1	1	0	8	3	0-0
Ohman, Will, ChC	.000	.000	.000	2	0	0	0	0	0	0	0	1	0	0-0	.000	.000	.000	2	0	0	0	0	0	0	0	1	0	0-0
Olivares, Omar, Pit	.222	.222	.407	27	6	2	0	1	3	6	0	10	0	0-0	.240	.257	.351	242	58	10	1	5	25	29	6	71	14	0-0
Oliver, Darren, Tex	.333	.333	.500	6	2	1	0	0	0	0	0	2	2	0-0	.232	.271	.295	112	26	7	0	0	9	9	4	41	10	0-0
Olsen, Kevin, Fla	.000	.000	.000	3	0	0	0	0	0	0	0	3	1	0-0	.000	.000	.000	3	0	0	0	0	0	0	0	3	1	0-0
Olson, Gregg, LA	.000	.000	.000	0	0	0	0	0	0	0	0	0	0	0-0	.250	.400	1.000	4	1	0	0	1	1	2	1	3	0	0-0

	2001 Hitting														Career Hitting													
Pitcher, Team	Avg	OBP	SLG	AB	H	2B	3B	HR	R	RBI	BB	SO	SH	SB-CS	Avg	OBP	SLG	AB	H	2B	3B	HR	R	RBI	BB	SO	SH	SB-CS
Oropesa, Eddie, Phi	.000	.000	.000	0	0	0	0	0	0	0	0	0	0	0-0	.000	.000	.000	0	0	0	0	0	0	0	0	0	0	0-0
Orosco, Jesse, LA	.000	.000	.000	0	0	0	0	0	0	0	0	0	0	0-0	.169	.250	.169	59	10	0	0	0	2	4	7	25	7	0-0
Ortiz, Ramon, Ana	.000	.000	.000	7	0	0	0	0	0	0	0	2	0	0-0	.000	.000	.000	7	0	0	0	0	0	0	0	2	0	0-0
Ortiz, Russ, SF	.194	.247	.284	67	13	6	0	0	6	6	5	19	8	0-0	.205	.263	.277	224	46	10	0	2	23	21	18	61	26	0-0
Osting, Jimmy, SD	.000	.000	.000	0	0	0	0	0	0	0	0	0	0	0-0	.000	.000	.000	0	0	0	0	0	0	0	0	0	0	0-0
Osuna, Antonio, CWS	.000	.000	.000	0	0	0	0	0	0	0	0	0	0	0-0	.111	.182	.111	9	1	0	0	0	0	1	1	1	0	0-0
Oswalt, Roy, Hou	.191	.208	.213	47	9	1	0	0	3	3	1	12	3	0-0	.191	.208	.213	47	9	1	0	0	3	3	1	12	3	0-0
Padilla, Vicente, Phi	.333	.500	.667	3	1	1	0	0	1	0	1	2	1	0-0	.500	.600	.750	4	2	1	0	0	1	0	1	2	1	0-0
Painter, Lance, Tor-Mil	.000	.000	.000	0	0	0	0	0	0	0	0	0	0	0-0	.156	.176	.219	64	10	2	1	0	6	5	2	33	8	0-0
Paniagua, Jose, Sea	.000	.000	.000	1	0	0	0	0	0	0	0	0	0	0-0	.000	.100	.000	18	0	0	0	0	1	0	2	11	1	0-0
Park, Chan Ho, LA	.145	.203	.188	69	10	3	0	0	6	4	5	22	7	0-0	.170	.206	.238	341	58	15	1	2	23	23	16	125	39	0-0
Parker, Christian, NYY	.000	.000	.000	0	0	0	0	0	0	0	0	0	0	0-0	.000	.000	.000	0	0	0	0	0	0	0	0	0	0	0-0
Paronto, Chad, Bal	.000	.000	.000	0	0	0	0	0	0	0	0	0	0	0-0	.000	.000	.000	0	0	0	0	0	0	0	0	0	0	0-0
Parque, Jim, CWS	.000	.000	.000	0	0	0	0	0	0	0	0	0	0	0-0	.200	.200	.200	10	2	0	0	0	0	0	0	4	3	0-0
Parris, Steve, Tor	.000	.000	.000	1	0	0	0	0	0	0	0	1	1	0-0	.159	.174	.185	157	25	4	0	0	8	15	3	51	16	0-1
Parrish, John, Bal	.000	.000	.000	0	0	0	0	0	0	0	0	0	0	0-0	.000	.000	.000	0	0	0	0	0	0	0	0	0	0	0-0
Patterson, Danny, Det	.000	.000	.000	0	0	0	0	0	0	0	0	0	0	0-0	.000	.000	.000	1	0	0	0	0	0	0	0	0	0	0-0
Pavano, Carl, Mon	.077	.077	.077	13	1	0	0	0	0	0	0	5	1	0-0	.118	.125	.134	119	14	2	0	0	4	5	1	49	15	0-0
Penny, Brad, Fla	.161	.175	.210	62	10	1	1	0	5	1	1	19	3	0-0	.140	.148	.168	107	15	1	1	0	7	3	1	36	4	0-0
Percival, Troy, Ana	.000	.000	.000	0	0	0	0	0	0	0	0	0	0	0-0	.000	.000	.000	1	0	0	0	0	0	0	0	1	0	0-0
Perez, Odalis, Atl	.192	.222	.231	26	5	1	0	0	1	1	0	6	2	0-0	.161	.175	.179	56	9	1	0	0	2	4	0	16	6	0-0
Perisho, Matt, Det	.000	.000	.000	0	0	0	0	0	0	0	0	0	0	0-0	.000	.000	.000	5	0	0	0	0	0	0	0	5	0	0-0
Person, Robert, Phi	.119	.157	.224	67	8	1	0	2	4	6	3	36	5	0-0	.122	.161	.180	189	23	5	0	2	10	9	8	101	22	0-0
Peters, Chris, Mon	.091	.091	.091	11	1	0	0	0	1	0	0	2	0	0-0	.218	.240	.228	101	22	1	0	0	11	7	3	32	6	2-0
Peterson, Kyle, Mil	.200	.200	.400	5	1	1	0	0	1	1	0	1	0	0-0	.148	.179	.185	27	4	1	0	0	3	2	1	10	2	0-0
Petkovsek, Mark, Tex	.000	.000	.000	1	0	0	0	0	0	0	0	0	0	0-0	.161	.229	.172	87	14	1	0	0	10	3	7	18	6	0-0
Pettitte, Andy, NYY	.000	.000	.000	4	0	0	0	0	0	0	0	1	1	0-0	.056	.105	.056	18	1	0	0	0	0	0	1	8	3	0-0
Pettyjohn, Adam, Det	.000	.000	.000	2	0	0	0	0	0	0	0	2	0	0-0	.000	.000	.000	2	0	0	0	0	0	0	0	2	0	0-0
Phelps, Travis, TB	.000	.000	.000	0	0	0	0	0	0	0	0	0	0	0-0	.000	.000	.000	0	0	0	0	0	0	0	0	0	0	0-0
Pichardo, Hipolito, Bos	.000	.000	.000	0	0	0	0	0	0	0	0	0	0	0-0	.000	.000	.000	5	0	0	0	0	0	0	0	3	0	0-0
Piersoll, Chris, Cin	.000	.000	.000	0	0	0	0	0	0	0	0	0	0	0-0	.000	.000	.000	0	0	0	0	0	0	0	0	0	0	0-0
Pineda, Luis, Det	.000	.000	.000	0	0	0	0	0	0	0	0	0	0	0-0	.000	.000	.000	0	0	0	0	0	0	0	0	0	0	0-0
Pineiro, Joel, Sea	.000	.000	.000	0	0	0	0	0	0	0	0	0	0	0-0	.000	.000	.000	0	0	0	0	0	0	0	0	0	0	0-0
Plesac, Dan, Tor	.000	.000	.000	0	0	0	0	0	0	0	0	0	0	0-0	.067	.067	.067	15	1	0	0	0	0	0	0	10	0	0-0
Politte, Cliff, Phi	.000	.333	.000	2	0	0	0	0	1	0	1	1	0	0-0	.097	.171	.129	31	3	1	0	0	2	2	3	13	3	0-0
Ponson, Sidney, Bal	.000	.000	.000	3	0	0	0	0	0	0	0	1	0	0-0	.182	.182	.182	11	2	0	0	0	1	0	0	4	3	0-0
Pote, Lou, Ana	.000	.000	.000	0	0	0	0	0	0	0	0	0	0	0-0	.000	.000	.000	0	0	0	0	0	0	0	0	0	0	0-0
Powell, Brian, Hou	.000	.000	.000	1	0	0	0	0	0	0	0	1	0	0-0	.182	.250	.273	11	2	1	0	0	2	0	1	6	0	0-0
Powell, Jay, Hou-Col	.000	.000	.000	1	0	0	0	0	0	0	0	1	0	0-0	.167	.167	.167	12	2	0	0	0	0	1	0	8	1	0-0
Prieto, Ariel, TB	.000	.000	.000	0	0	0	0	0	0	0	0	0	0	0-0	.000	.000	.000	2	0	0	0	0	0	0	0	1	0	0-0
Prinz, Bret, Ari	.000	.000	.000	0	0	0	0	0	0	0	0	0	0	0-0	.000	.000	.000	0	0	0	0	0	0	0	0	0	0	0-0
Prokopec, Luke, LA	.194	.194	.222	36	7	1	0	0	1	0	0	13	7	0-0	.171	.171	.195	41	7	1	0	0	1	0	0	15	8	0-0
Pulsipher, B., Bos-CWS	.000	.000	.000	0	0	0	0	0	0	0	0	0	0	0-0	.123	.170	.148	81	10	2	0	0	7	4	5	40	13	0-0
Quantrill, Paul, Tor	.000	.000	.000	0	0	0	0	0	0	0	0	0	0	0-0	.098	.154	.098	61	6	0	0	0	5	0	4	26	7	0-0
Quevedo, Ruben, Mil	.250	.250	.250	16	4	0	0	0	1	1	0	8	4	0-0	.174	.174	.174	46	8	0	0	0	2	2	0	18	5	0-0
Radinsky, Scott, Cle	.000	.000	.000	0	0	0	0	0	0	0	0	0	0	0-0	.000	.000	.000	5	0	0	0	0	0	0	0	4	0	0-0
Radke, Brad, Min	.500	.500	.500	4	2	0	0	0	0	0	0	0	0	0-0	.125	.125	.125	16	2	0	0	0	0	0	0	5	1	0-0
Rapp, Pat, Ana	.000	.000	.000	5	0	0	0	0	0	0	0	2	0	0-0	.117	.121	.146	247	29	4	0	1	10	13	1	92	21	0-0
Reames, Britt, Mon	.118	.286	.294	17	2	0	0	1	2	2	4	8	3	0-0	.138	.242	.241	29	4	0	0	1	3	2	4	10	4	0-0
Redding, Tim, Hou	.214	.214	.214	14	3	0	0	0	0	1	0	11	2	0-0	.214	.214	.214	14	3	0	0	0	0	1	0	11	2	0-0
Redman, M., Min-Det	.000	.000	.000	0	0	0	0	0	0	0	0	0	0	0-0	.000	.000	.000	4	0	0	0	0	0	0	0	3	1	0-0
Reed, Rick, NYM-Min	.125	.143	.150	40	5	1	0	0	2	4	1	15	4	0-0	.171	.203	.222	293	50	9	0	2	23	24	12	91	46	0-0
Reed, Steve, Cle-Atl	.000	.000	.000	0	0	0	0	0	0	0	0	0	0	0-0	.143	.143	.143	21	3	0	0	0	0	0	0	6	2	0-0
Reichert, Dan, KC	.000	.000	.000	5	0	0	0	0	0	0	0	4	0	0-0	.111	.111	.111	9	1	0	0	0	0	0	0	6	1	0-0
Reith, Brian, Cin	.250	.250	.250	12	3	0	0	0	0	2	0	4	0	1-0	.250	.250	.250	12	3	0	0	0	0	2	0	4	0	1-0
Reitsma, Chris, Cin	.104	.157	.125	48	5	1	0	0	3	1	2	24	7	0-0	.104	.157	.125	48	5	1	0	0	3	1	2	24	7	0-0
Rekar, Bryan, TB	.000	.000	.000	2	0	0	0	0	0	0	0	1	0	0-0	.145	.203	.182	55	8	2	0	0	4	1	4	25	5	0-1
Remlinger, Mike, Atl	.000	.000	.000	2	0	0	0	0	0	0	0	1	0	0-0	.075	.140	.104	106	8	3	0	0	5	8	8	34	19	0-1
Reyes, Al, LA	.333	.333	.333	3	1	0	0	0	1	0	0	1	1	0-0	.200	.200	.200	10	2	0	0	0	2	0	0	5	1	0-0
Reyes, Dennys, Cin	.182	.182	.182	11	2	0	0	0	0	0	0	6	0	0-0	.070	.111	.093	43	3	1	0	0	2	0	2	20	2	1-0
Reynolds, Shane, Hou	.077	.094	.135	52	4	0	0	1	4	4	1	26	10	0-0	.151	.177	.212	471	71	14	0	5	34	37	13	209	78	0-0
Reynoso, Armando, Ari	.100	.100	.200	10	1	1	0	0	0	2	0	3	3	0-0	.148	.186	.193	337	50	6	0	3	17	13	16	149	38	0-0
Rhodes, Arthur, Sea	.000	.000	.000	1	0	0	0	0	0	0	0	1	0	0-0	.250	.250	.250	4	1	0	0	0	0	0	0	3	0	0-0
Riedling, John, Cin	.000	.000	.000	1	0	0	0	0	0	0	0	1	0	0-0	.000	.000	.000	3	0	0	0	0	0	0	0	3	0	0-0
Rigdon, Paul, Mil	.200	.200	.200	20	4	0	0	0	1	1	0	3	5	0-0	.194	.237	.278	36	7	0	0	1	4	2	2	9	12	0-0
Riggan, Jerrod, NYM	.000	.000	.000	2	0	0	0	0	0	0	0	2	0	0-0	.000	.000	.000	2	0	0	0	0	0	0	0	2	0	0-0
Rijo, Jose, Cin	.000	.000	.000	0	0	0	0	0	0	0	0	0	0	0-0	.193	.208	.238	429	83	13	0	2	25	29	8	94	55	2-1
Rincon, Juan, Min	1.000	1.000	1.000	1	1	0	0	0	0	0	0	0	0	0-0	1.000	1.000	1.000	1	1	0	0	0	0	0	0	0	0	0-0
Rincon, Ricardo, Cle	.000	.000	.000	0	0	0	0	0	0	0	0	0	0	0-0	.000	.000	.000	3	0	0	0	0	0	0	0	1	1	0-0
Riske, David, Cle	.000	.000	.000	0	0	0	0	0	0	0	0	0	0	0-0	.000	.000	.000	0	0	0	0	0	0	0	0	0	0	0-0
Ritchie, Todd, Pit	.153	.194	.186	59	9	2	0	0	1	3	3	27	8	0-0	.172	.200	.201	174	30	5	0	0	8	6	6	66	18	0-0
Rivera, Mariano, NYY	.000	.000	.000	0	0	0	0	0	0	0	0	0	0	0-0	.000	.000	.000	0	0	0	0	0	0	0	0	0	0	0-0
Roberts, Grant, NYM	.000	.000	.000	3	0	0	0	0	0	0	0	3	0	0-0	.000	.000	.000	3	0	0	0	0	0	0	0	3	1	0-0
Roberts, Willis, Bal	.250	.250	.250	4	1	0	0	0	0	0	0	3	1	0-0	.250	.250	.250	4	1	0	0	0	0	0	0	3	1	0-0
Rocker, John, Atl-Cle	.000	.000	.000	0	0	0	0	0	0	0	0	0	0	0-0	.000	.000	.000	0	0	0	0	0	0	0	0	0	0	0-0
Rodriguez, Felix, SF	.000	.000	.000	0	0	0	0	0	0	0	0	0	0	0-0	.154	.214	.462	13	2	1	0	1	3	3	0	4	2	0-0
Rodriguez, Frank, Cin	.000	.000	.000	1	0	0	0	0	0	0	0	1	0	0-0	.167	.167	.167	6	1	0	0	0	1	1	0	2	0	0-0
Rodriguez, Rich, Cle	.000	.000	.000	0	0	0	0	0	0	0	0	0	0	0-0	.107	.194	.107	28	3	0	0	0	3	1	3	9	4	0-0
Rodriguez, W., Hou	.000	.000	.000	0	0	0	0	0	0	0	0	0	0	0-0	.000	.000	.000	0	0	0	0	0	0	0	0	0	0	0-0
Rogers, Kenny, Tex	.000	.000	.000	2	0	0	0	0	0	0	0	2	0	0-0	.122	.163	.122	41	5	0	0	0	3	2	2	16	4	0-0
Romero, J.C., Min	.500	.500	1.000	2	1	1	0	0	1	0	0	0	0	0-0	.500	.500	1.000	2	1	1	0	0	1	0	0	0	0	0-0
Rose, Brian, NYM-TB	.000	.000	.000	1	0	0	0	0	0	0	0	0	0	0-0	.037	.071	.037	27	1	0	0	0	1	0	1	11	4	0-0
Rueter, Kirk, SF	.172	.234	.172	58	10	0	0	0	5	5	5	5	10	0-0	.154	.189	.168	416	64	6	0	0	31	31	19	77	58	0-1
Ruffin, Johnny, Fla	.000	.000	.000	0	0	0	0	0	0	0	0	0	0	0-0	.176	.176	.176	17	3	0	0	0	1	0	0	5	0	1-0
Rupe, Ryan, TB	.333	.333	.667	3	1	1	0	0	1	0	0	1	0	0-0	.125	.125	.250	8	1	1	0	0	1	0	0	2	0	0-0
Rusch, Glendon, NYM	.056	.073	.056	54	3	0	0	0	0	5	1	23	6	0-0	.055	.088	.055	110	6	0	0	0	2	6	4	44	10	0-0
Ryan, B.J., Bal	.000	.000	.000	1	0	0	0	0	0	0	0	0	0	0-0	.000	.000	.000	1	0	0	0	0	0	0	0	0	0	0-0
Sabathia, C.C., Cle	.000	.000	.000	4	0	0	0	0	0	0	0	0	1	0-0	.000	.000	.000	4	0	0	0	0	0	0	0	0	1	0-0
Sabel, Erik, Ari	.000	.000	.000	0	0	0	0	0	0	0	0	0	0	0-0	.000	.000	.000	2	0	0	0	0	0	0	0	2	0	0-0
Saberhagen, Bret, Bos	.000	.000	.000	0	0	0	0	0	0	0	0	0	0	0-0	.121	.177	.142	190	23	4	0	0	13	1	13	49	24	0-0
Sanchez, Jesus, Fla	.235	.235	.235	17	4	0	0	0	2	1	0	3	2	0-0	.182	.200	.197	137	25	0	1	0	10	6	3	38	11	0-0
Santana, Johan, Min	.000	.000	.000	0	0	0	0	0	0	0	0	0	0	0-0	.000	.000	.000	1	0	0	0	0	0	0	0	0	0	0-0

	2001 Hitting														Career Hitting													
Pitcher, Team	Avg	OBP	SLG	AB	H	2B	3B	HR	R	RBI	BB	SO	SH	SB-CS	Avg	OBP	SLG	AB	H	2B	3B	HR	R	RBI	BB	SO	SH	SB-CS
Santiago, Jose, KC-Phi	.000	.250	.000	3	0	0	0	0	0	0	1	3	0	0-0	.000	.250	.000	3	0	0	0	0	0	0	1	3	0	0-0
Santos, Victor, Det	.000	.000	.000	0	0	0	0	0	0	0	0	0	0	0-0	.000	.000	.000	0	0	0	0	0	0	0	0	0	0	0-0
Sasaki, Kazuhiro, Sea	.000	.000	.000	0	0	0	0	0	0	0	0	0	0	0-0	.000	.000	.000	0	0	0	0	0	0	0	0	0	0	0-0
Sauerbeck, Scott, Pit	.000	.000	.000	2	0	0	0	0	0	0	0	1	0	0-0	.000	.000	.000	4	0	0	0	0	0	0	0	2	1	0-0
Scanlan, Bob, Mon	.000	.000	.000	0	0	0	0	0	0	0	0	0	0	0-0	.067	.094	.067	30	2	0	0	0	1	3	1	12	3	0-0
Schilling, Curt, Ari	.133	.143	.145	83	11	1	0	0	4	1	1	28	14	0-0	.154	.177	.178	624	96	13	1	0	28	26	18	219	90	1-1
Schmidt, Jason, Pit-SF	.163	.180	.286	49	8	0	0	2	5	4	1	22	6	0-0	.096	.138	.131	282	27	4	0	2	12	12	14	132	44	0-0
Schoeneweis, S., Ana	.000	1.000	.000	0	0	0	0	0	0	0	2	0	0	0-0	.333	.600	.333	3	1	0	0	0	0	1	2	0	0	0-0
Schourek, Pete, Bos	.000	.000	.000	0	0	0	0	0	0	0	0	0	0	0-0	.164	.192	.201	269	44	4	0	2	15	20	10	81	37	2-0
Seanez, Rudy, SD-Atl	.000	.000	.000	0	0	0	0	0	0	0	0	0	0	0-0	.000	.200	.000	4	0	0	0	0	1	0	1	4	0	0-0
Seay, Bobby, TB	.000	.000	.000	0	0	0	0	0	0	0	0	0	0	0-0	.000	.000	.000	0	0	0	0	0	0	0	0	0	0	0-0
Seelbach, Chris, Atl	.000	.000	.000	0	0	0	0	0	0	0	0	0	0	0-0	.000	.000	.000	0	0	0	0	0	0	0	0	0	0	0-0
Sele, Aaron, Sea	.167	.167	.167	6	1	0	0	0	2	1	0	0	2	0-0	.105	.150	.158	19	2	1	0	0	2	1	1	3	4	0-0
Serrano, Wascar, SD	.111	.111	.111	9	1	0	0	0	0	0	0	4	2	0-0	.111	.111	.111	9	1	0	0	0	0	0	0	4	2	0-0
Shaw, Jeff, LA	.000	.000	.000	0	0	0	0	0	0	0	0	0	0	0-0	.079	.167	.079	38	3	0	0	0	4	0	4	20	3	0-0
Sheets, Ben, Mil	.071	.152	.071	42	3	0	0	0	4	1	4	29	2	0-0	.071	.152	.071	42	3	0	0	0	4	1	4	29	2	0-0
Shields, Scot, Ana	.000	.000	.000	0	0	0	0	0	0	0	0	0	0	0-0	.000	.000	.000	0	0	0	0	0	0	0	0	0	0	0-0
Shuey, Paul, Cle	.000	.000	.000	0	0	0	0	0	0	0	0	0	0	0-0	.000	.000	.000	2	0	0	0	0	0	0	0	1	0	0-0
Silva, Jose, Pit	.000	.000	.000	2	0	0	0	0	0	0	0	2	0	0-0	.111	.158	.122	90	10	1	0	0	1	5	3	38	15	0-0
Slusarski, Joe, Atl-Hou	.000	.000	.000	0	0	0	0	0	0	0	0	0	0	0-0	.111	.111	.111	9	1	0	0	0	1	1	0	5	0	0-0
Smart, J.D., Tex	.000	.000	.000	0	0	0	0	0	0	0	0	0	0	0-0	.000	.000	.000	3	0	0	0	0	0	0	0	0	0	0-0
Smith, Bud, StL	.160	.192	.160	25	4	0	0	0	0	1	1	5	2	0-0	.160	.192	.160	25	4	0	0	0	0	1	1	5	2	0-0
Smith, Chuck, Fla	.192	.222	.192	26	5	0	0	0	1	3	1	8	2	0-0	.136	.149	.136	66	9	0	0	0	3	5	1	27	3	0-0
Smith, Roy, Cle	.000	.000	.000	0	0	0	0	0	0	0	0	0	0	0-0	.000	.000	.000	0	0	0	0	0	0	0	0	0	0	0-0
Smoltz, John, Atl	.000	.125	.000	7	0	0	0	0	0	0	1	3	2	0-0	.173	.248	.223	734	127	20	1	5	69	51	70	281	92	3-2
Sobkowiak, Scott, Atl	.000	.000	.000	0	0	0	0	0	0	0	0	0	0	0-0	.000	.000	.000	0	0	0	0	0	0	0	0	0	0	0-0
Sparks, Steve W., Det	.000	.000	.000	4	0	0	0	0	0	0	0	1	0	0-0	.125	.222	.250	8	1	1	0	0	1	2	1	2	1	0-0
Speier, Justin, Cle-Col	.000	.000	.000	7	0	0	0	0	0	0	0	2	0	0-0	.167	.167	.167	12	2	0	0	0	0	0	0	5	0	0-0
Spooneybarger, T., Atl	.000	.000	.000	0	0	0	0	0	0	0	0	0	0	0-0	.000	.000	.000	0	0	0	0	0	0	0	0	0	0	0-0
Springer, Dennis, LA	.000	.000	.000	6	0	0	0	0	0	0	0	3	1	0-0	.097	.096	.111	72	7	1	0	0	2	2	0	30	4	0-0
Springer, Russ, Ari	.000	.000	.000	0	0	0	0	0	0	0	0	0	0	0-0	.080	.080	.080	25	2	0	0	0	1	0	0	15	3	0-0
Standridge, Jason, TB	.000	.000	.000	0	0	0	0	0	0	0	0	0	0	0-0	.000	.000	.000	0	0	0	0	0	0	0	0	0	0	0-0
Stanton, Mike, NYY	.000	.000	.000	0	0	0	0	0	0	0	0	0	0	0-0	.500	.533	.571	14	7	1	0	0	2	2	1	2	1	0-0
Stark, Denny, Sea	.000	.000	.000	0	0	0	0	0	0	0	0	0	0	0-0	.000	.000	.000	0	0	0	0	0	0	0	0	0	0	0-0
Stechschulte, G., StL	.667	.750	1.667	3	2	0	0	1	1	3	1	1	0	0-0	.667	.750	1.667	3	2	0	0	1	1	3	1	1	0	0-0
Stein, Blake, KC	.000	.000	.000	2	0	0	0	0	0	0	0	0	0	0-0	.000	.000	.000	9	0	0	0	0	0	0	0	6	1	0-0
Stewart, Scott, Mon	.000	.000	.000	0	0	0	0	0	0	0	0	0	0	0-0	.000	.000	.000	0	0	0	0	0	0	0	0	0	0	0-0
Stone, Ricky, Hou	.000	.000	.000	0	0	0	0	0	0	0	0	0	0	0-0	.000	.000	.000	0	0	0	0	0	0	0	0	0	0	0-0
Strickland, Scott, Mon	.000	.000	.000	3	0	0	0	0	0	0	0	2	0	0-0	.000	.000	.000	5	0	0	0	0	0	0	0	4	0	0-0
Strong, Joe, Fla	.000	.000	.000	1	0	0	0	0	0	0	0	1	0	0-0	.000	.000	.000	2	0	0	0	0	0	0	0	2	0	0-0
Sturtze, Tanyon, TB	.125	.125	.125	8	1	0	0	0	0	0	0	3	0	0-0	.111	.111	.111	9	1	0	0	0	0	0	0	3	1	0-0
Sullivan, Scott, Cin	.000	.000	.000	3	0	0	0	0	0	0	0	3	0	0-0	.067	.067	.067	45	3	0	0	0	1	1	0	27	3	0-0
Suppan, Jeff, KC	.400	.400	.400	5	2	0	0	0	0	0	0	2	0	0-0	.243	.263	.243	37	9	0	0	0	1	2	0	9	1	1-0
Suzuki, M., KC-Col-Mil	.000	.053	.000	18	0	0	0	0	0	0	1	10	3	0-0	.043	.083	.043	23	1	0	0	0	1	0	1	12	4	0-0
Swindell, Greg, Ari	.000	.000	.000	0	0	0	0	0	0	0	0	0	0	0-0	.188	.200	.229	245	46	10	0	0	10	13	4	57	36	0-0
Tabaka, Jeff, StL	.000	.000	.000	0	0	0	0	0	0	0	0	0	0	0-0	.250	.400	.500	4	1	1	0	0	1	0	1	2	1	0-0
Tam, Jeff, Oak	.000	.000	.000	0	0	0	0	0	0	0	0	0	0	0-0	.000	.000	.000	1	0	0	0	0	0	0	0	0	0	0-0
Tapani, Kevin, ChC	.240	.255	.240	50	12	0	0	0	1	2	1	14	7	0-0	.153	.201	.199	261	40	6	0	2	14	22	16	105	33	1-1
Tavarez, Julian, ChC	.122	.182	.122	41	5	0	0	0	4	4	3	17	11	0-0	.110	.138	.110	91	10	0	0	0	5	4	3	38	15	0-0
Taylor, Billy, Pit	.000	.000	.000	0	0	0	0	0	0	0	0	0	0	0-0	.000	.000	.000	0	0	0	0	0	0	0	0	0	0	0-0
Telemaco, Amaury, Phi	.095	.174	.095	21	2	0	0	0	2	0	2	8	2	0-0	.102	.152	.133	98	10	1	1	0	5	3	6	46	7	0-0
Telford, Anthony, Mon	.000	.000	.000	0	0	0	0	0	0	0	0	0	0	0-0	.174	.208	.217	23	4	1	0	0	0	3	1	4	4	0-0
Thomas, Brad, Min	.000	.000	.000	0	0	0	0	0	0	0	0	0	0	0-0	.000	.000	.000	0	0	0	0	0	0	0	0	0	0	0-0
Thomson, John, Col	.241	.267	.310	29	7	0	1	0	3	1	1	15	6	0-0	.181	.216	.201	144	26	1	1	0	10	9	7	68	21	0-1
Thurman, Mike, Mon	.024	.068	.024	42	1	0	0	0	0	0	2	27	3	0-0	.031	.086	.031	131	4	0	0	0	6	0	7	93	16	0-0
Timlin, Mike, StL	.000	.000	.000	1	0	0	0	0	0	0	0	0	0	0-0	.000	.000	.000	1	0	0	0	0	0	0	0	0	0	0-0
Tolar, Kevin, Det	.000	.000	.000	0	0	0	0	0	0	0	0	0	0	0-0	.000	.000	.000	0	0	0	0	0	0	0	0	0	0	0-0
Tollberg, Brian, SD	.200	.238	.200	40	8	0	0	0	4	1	2	17	5	0-0	.153	.176	.153	72	11	0	0	0	5	2	2	28	11	0-0
Tomko, Brett, Sea	.000	.000	.000	0	0	0	0	0	0	0	0	0	0	0-0	.149	.191	.176	148	22	4	0	0	9	8	8	60	20	0-0
Towers, Josh, Bal	.000	.000	.000	2	0	0	0	0	0	0	0	0	0	0-0	.000	.000	.000	2	0	0	0	0	0	0	0	0	0	0-0
Trachsel, Steve, NYM	.161	.161	.179	56	9	1	0	0	2	2	0	13	5	0-0	.170	.206	.217	411	70	13	0	2	32	25	18	124	52	1-1
Trombley, Mike, Bal-LA	.000	.000	.000	0	0	0	0	0	0	0	0	0	0	0-0	.000	.000	.000	2	0	0	0	0	0	0	0	2	0	0-0
Urbina, U., Mon-Bos	.000	.000	.000	1	0	0	0	0	0	0	0	1	0	0-0	.094	.127	.094	53	5	0	0	0	3	1	2	32	3	0-0
Valdes, Ismael, Ana	.200	.200	.200	5	1	0	0	0	0	0	0	2	0	1-0	.122	.148	.147	327	40	5	0	1	14	11	10	105	52	4-0
Valdes, Marc, Atl	.000	.000	.000	0	0	0	0	0	0	0	0	0	0	0-0	.093	.152	.093	43	4	0	0	0	1	1	2	15	0	0-0
Van Poppel, Todd, ChC	.286	.286	.286	7	2	0	0	0	1	0	0	3	0	0-0	.167	.194	.200	30	5	1	0	0	4	1	1	11	5	0-0
Vazquez, Javier, Mon	.258	.288	.290	62	16	2	0	0	5	1	2	11	16	0-0	.235	.266	.281	221	52	8	1	0	16	12	9	41	43	0-0
Venafro, Mike, Tex	.000	.000	.000	0	0	0	0	0	0	0	0	0	0	0-0	.000	.000	.000	0	0	0	0	0	0	0	0	0	0	0-0
Veres, Dave, StL	.000	.000	.000	3	0	0	0	0	0	0	0	1	1	0-0	.250	.280	.292	24	6	1	0	0	1	1	1	11	3	0-0
Villafuerte, B., Tex	.000	.000	.000	0	0	0	0	0	0	0	0	0	0	0-0	.000	.000	.000	0	0	0	0	0	0	0	0	0	0	0-0
Villone, Ron, Col-Hou	.045	.045	.091	22	1	1	0	0	2	0	0	9	4	0-0	.100	.108	.118	110	11	2	0	0	4	4	1	29	11	0-0
Vining, Ken, CWS	.000	.000	.000	0	0	0	0	0	0	0	0	0	0	0-0	.000	.000	.000	0	0	0	0	0	0	0	0	0	0	0-0
Vizcaino, Luis, Oak	.000	.000	.000	0	0	0	0	0	0	0	0	0	0	0-0	.000	.000	.000	0	0	0	0	0	0	0	0	0	0	0-0
Vogelsong, R., SF-Pit	.100	.100	.200	10	1	1	0	0	0	0	0	3	0	0-0	.100	.100	.200	10	1	1	0	0	0	0	0	3	0	0-0
Vosberg, Ed, Phi	.000	.000	.000	0	0	0	0	0	0	0	0	0	0	0-0	.000	.000	.000	2	0	0	0	0	0	0	0	1	0	0-0
Voyles, Brad, KC	.000	.000	.000	0	0	0	0	0	0	0	0	0	0	0-0	.000	.000	.000	0	0	0	0	0	0	0	0	0	0	0-0
Wagner, Billy, Hou	.000	.000	.000	0	0	0	0	0	0	0	0	0	0	0-0	.091	.091	.091	11	1	0	0	0	0	0	0	6	0	0-0
Wakefield, Tim, Bos	.333	.333	.333	3	1	0	0	0	0	0	0	2	1	0-0	.122	.143	.183	82	10	2	0	1	3	3	2	29	12	0-0
Walker, Kevin, SD	.000	.000	.000	0	0	0	0	0	0	0	0	0	0	0-0	.250	.250	.250	4	1	0	0	0	0	0	0	1	0	0-0
Walker, Pete, NYM	.000	.000	.000	1	0	0	0	0	0	0	0	1	1	0-0	.000	.000	.000	1	0	0	0	0	0	0	0	1	1	0-0
Wall, Donne, NYM	.000	.000	.000	0	0	0	0	0	1	0	0	0	0	0-0	.176	.211	.191	68	12	1	0	0	6	1	3	22	13	0-0
Wallace, Jeff, TB	.000	.000	.000	0	0	0	0	0	0	0	0	0	0	0-0	.000	.500	.000	1	0	0	0	0	0	0	1	0	0	0-0
Wasdin, John, Col-Bal	.333	.333	.667	3	1	1	0	0	1	1	0	0	0	0-0	.273	.333	.364	11	3	1	0	0	2	1	1	2	1	0-0
Washburn, Jarrod, Ana	.600	.667	.600	5	3	0	0	0	1	0	1	2	0	0-0	.444	.545	.444	9	4	0	0	0	1	2	2	3	4	0-0
Weathers, D., Mil-ChC	.000	.500	.000	1	0	0	0	0	0	0	1	1	0	0-0	.107	.158	.153	131	14	0	0	2	7	4	7	82	16	0-0
Weaver, Jeff, Det	.000	.000	.000	5	0	0	0	0	0	0	0	0	1	0-0	.167	.167	.250	12	2	1	0	0	2	0	0	3	2	0-0
Weber, Ben, Ana	.000	.000	.000	0	0	0	0	0	0	0	0	0	0	0-0	.000	.000	.000	0	0	0	0	0	0	0	0	0	0	0-0
Wells, Bob, Min	.000	.000	.000	0	0	0	0	0	0	0	0	0	0	0-0	.000	1.000	.000	0	0	0	0	0	1	0	1	0	0	0-0
Wells, David, CWS	.000	.000	.000	2	0	0	0	0	0	0	0	1	0	0-0	.130	.130	.130	46	6	0	0	0	2	0	0	9	2	0-0
Wells, Kip, CWS	.167	.167	.167	6	1	0	0	0	1	0	0	5	0	1-0	.125	.125	.125	8	1	0	0	0	1	0	0	7	0	1-0
Wendell, T., NYM-Phi	.000	.000	.000	2	0	0	0	0	0	0	0	1	0	0-0	.077	.182	.077	39	3	0	0	0	1	0	5	17	1	0-0
Wengert, Don, Pit	.000	.250	.000	3	0	0	0	0	0	0	1	2	1	0-0	.000	.095	.000	19	0	0	0	0	0	0	2	5	2	0-0

	2001 Hitting														Career Hitting													
Pitcher, Team	Avg	OBP	SLG	AB	H	2B	3B	HR	R	RBI	BB	SO	SH	SB-CS	Avg	OBP	SLG	AB	H	2B	3B	HR	R	RBI	BB	SO	SH	SB-CS
Westbrook, Jake, Cle	.000	.000	.000	1	0	0	0	0	0	0	0	1	1	0-0	.000	.000	.000	1	0	0	0	0	0	0	0	1	1	0-0
Wheeler, Dan, TB	.000	.000	.000	0	0	0	0	0	0	0	0	0	0	0-0	.000	.000	.000	0	0	0	0	0	0	0	0	0	0	0-0
White, Gabe, Col	.000	.000	.000	3	0	0	0	0	0	0	0	3	0	0-0	.118	.143	.206	34	4	0	0	1	1	3	1	22	9	0-0
White, Rick, NYM	.000	.000	.000	3	0	0	0	0	0	0	0	2	0	0-0	.103	.125	.128	39	4	1	0	0	1	1	0	11	2	0-0
Whiteside, Matt, Atl	.000	.000	.000	0	0	0	0	0	0	0	0	0	0	0-0	.000	.000	.000	2	0	0	0	0	0	0	0	2	0	0-0
Wickman, Bob, Cle	.000	.000	.000	0	0	0	0	0	0	0	0	0	0	0-0	.000	.000	.000	0	0	0	0	0	0	0	0	0	0	0-0
Wilkins, Marc, Pit	.000	.000	.000	0	0	0	0	0	0	0	0	0	0	0-0	.150	.227	.150	20	3	0	0	0	1	2	2	14	1	0-0
Williams, Dave, Pit	.118	.118	.176	34	4	2	0	0	1	2	0	19	3	0-0	.118	.118	.176	34	4	2	0	0	1	2	0	19	3	0-0
Williams, Jeff, LA	.000	.000	.000	4	0	0	0	0	0	0	0	2	0	0-0	.111	.200	.111	9	1	0	0	0	2	0	1	6	1	0-0
Williams, Mike, Pit-Hou	.000	.000	.000	0	0	0	0	0	0	0	0	0	0	0-0	.159	.182	.178	107	17	2	0	0	7	7	3	32	24	1-0
Williams, Todd, NYY	.000	.000	.000	0	0	0	0	0	0	0	0	0	0	0-0	.250	.250	.250	4	1	0	0	0	0	0	0	2	0	0-0
Williams, W., SD-StL	.195	.227	.256	82	16	5	0	0	11	7	3	22	2	0-0	.213	.245	.285	221	47	13	0	1	25	22	9	69	7	0-1
Williamson, Scott, Cin	.000	.000	.000	0	0	0	0	0	0	0	0	0	0	0-0	.043	.154	.043	23	1	0	0	0	1	0	3	14	7	0-0
Wilson, Kris, KC	.333	.333	.333	3	1	0	0	0	1	0	0	1	0	0-0	.333	.333	.333	3	1	0	0	0	1	0	0	1	0	0-0
Wilson, Paul, TB	.000	.000	.000	0	0	0	0	0	0	0	0	0	0	0-0	.080	.115	.140	50	4	0	0	1	3	4	1	32	4	0-0
Winchester, Scott, Cin	.000	.000	.000	3	0	0	0	0	0	0	0	2	0	0-0	.115	.148	.115	26	3	0	0	0	0	1	0	11	2	0-0
Wise, Matt, Ana	.000	.000	.000	0	0	0	0	0	0	0	0	0	0	0-0	.000	.000	.000	0	0	0	0	0	0	0	0	0	0	0-0
Witasick, Jay, SD-NYY	.000	.000	.000	1	0	0	0	0	0	0	0	1	0	0-0	.094	.121	.094	32	3	0	0	0	1	0	3	17	2	0-0
Witt, Bobby, Ari	.250	.250	.250	12	3	0	0	0	0	0	0	7	1	0-0	.141	.164	.234	64	9	3	0	1	2	5	2	25	6	0-0
Wohlers, M., Cin-NYM	.000	.000	.000	0	0	0	0	0	0	0	0	0	0	0-0	.083	.083	.083	12	1	0	0	0	1	0	0	11	1	0-0
Wolf, Randy, Phi	.178	.229	.178	45	8	0	0	0	2	2	3	13	5	0-0	.197	.241	.220	132	26	3	0	0	9	6	8	40	22	0-0
Wood, Kerry, ChC	.188	.204	.208	48	9	1	0	0	3	2	1	15	13	0-0	.183	.205	.254	142	26	1	0	3	12	14	4	41	25	0-0
Woodard, Steve, Cle	.000	.000	.000	1	0	0	0	0	0	0	0	0	0	0-0	.119	.172	.143	126	15	3	0	0	6	6	7	34	14	0-0
Worrell, Tim, SF	.000	.000	.000	2	0	0	0	0	0	0	0	2	1	0-0	.110	.156	.123	73	8	1	0	0	6	4	4	37	10	0-0
Wright, Dan, CWS	.000	.000	.000	0	0	0	0	0	0	0	0	0	0	0-0	.000	.000	.000	0	0	0	0	0	0	0	0	0	0	0-0
Wright, Jamey, Mil	.194	.229	.209	67	13	1	0	0	7	4	3	20	4	0-0	.138	.171	.185	276	38	8	1	1	19	13	11	114	27	0-0
Wright, Jaret, Cle	.500	.500	.500	2	1	0	0	0	0	1	0	0	0	0-0	.286	.286	.286	14	4	0	0	0	2	1	0	6	3	0-0
Wunsch, Kelly, CWS	.000	.000	.000	0	0	0	0	0	0	0	0	0	0	0-0	.000	.000	.000	0	0	0	0	0	0	0	0	0	0	0-0
Yan, Esteban, TB	.000	.000	.000	0	0	0	0	0	0	0	0	0	0	0-0	1.000	1.000	4.000	1	1	0	0	1	1	1	0	1	0	0-0
Yoshii, Masato, Mon	.125	.176	.125	16	2	0	0	0	0	0	1	7	2	0-0	.136	.166	.166	169	23	2	0	1	8	13	6	63	28	1-1
Zambrano, Carlos, ChC	.000	.000	.000	2	0	0	0	0	0	0	0	0	0	0-0	.000	.000	.000	2	0	0	0	0	0	0	0	0	0	0-0
Zambrano, Victor, TB	.000	.000	.000	0	0	0	0	0	0	0	0	0	0	0-0	.000	.000	.000	0	0	0	0	0	0	0	0	0	0	0-0
Zerbe, Chad, SF	.222	.222	.222	9	2	0	0	0	1	1	0	1	2	0-0	.222	.222	.222	9	2	0	0	0	1	1	0	1	2	0-0
Zimmerman, Jeff, Tex	.000	.000	.000	0	0	0	0	0	0	0	0	0	0	0-0	.000	.000	.000	0	0	0	0	0	0	0	0	0	0	0-0
Zito, Barry, Oak	.000	.000	.000	5	0	0	0	0	0	0	0	4	0	0-0	.000	.000	.000	5	0	0	0	0	0	0	0	4	0	0-0

Pitchers Fielding and Holding Runners

2001 Fielding and Holding Runners

Pitcher, Team	G	Inn	PO	A	E	DP	Pct.	SBA	CS	PCS	PPO	CS%
Abbott, Paul, Sea	28	163.0	16	13	0	3	1.000	13	6	0	0	.46
Acevedo, Jose, Cin	18	96.0	4	10	0	1	1.000	10	4	0	0	.40
Acevedo, Juan, Col-Fla	59	60.1	4	6	1	1	.909	5	1	0	0	.20
Adams, Terry, LA	43	166.1	13	31	1	2	.978	15	4	0	0	.27
Ainsworth, Kurt, SF	2	2.0	0	0	0	0	.000	0	0	0	0	.00
Alfonseca, Antonio, Fla	58	61.2	6	8	0	1	1.000	3	0	0	0	.00
Almanza, Armando, Fla	52	41.0	0	3	0	0	1.000	7	3	2	0	.71
Almanzar, Carlos, NYY	10	10.2	1	2	0	0	1.000	0	0	0	0	.00
Anderson, Brian, Ari	29	133.1	8	32	2	2	.952	12	1	4	4	.42
Anderson, Jimmy, Pit	34	206.1	8	37	3	0	.938	37	0	4	0	.11
Anderson, Matt, Det	62	56.0	9	5	0	0	1.000	4	0	0	0	.00
Ankiel, Rick, StL	6	24.0	0	3	0	0	1.000	2	1	0	0	.50
Appier, Kevin, NYM	33	206.2	11	21	2	2	.941	30	8	0	0	.27
Armas Jr., Tony, Mon	34	196.2	14	20	3	1	.919	18	5	1	0	.33
Arrojo, Rolando, Bos	41	103.1	12	17	0	3	1.000	9	1	0	0	.11
Arroyo, Bronson, Pit	24	88.1	3	15	2	1	.900	6	2	0	0	.33
Ashby, Andy, LA	2	11.2	0	1	0	0	1.000	2	1	0	0	.50
Astacio, Pedro, Col-Hou	26	169.2	10	25	1	1	.972	25	8	1	0	.36
Atchley, Justin, Cin	15	10.1	0	0	0	0	.000	0	0	0	0	.00
Austin, Jeff, KC	21	26.0	2	2	2	0	.667	1	1	0	1	1.00
Aybar, Manny, ChC	17	22.2	2	2	1	0	.800	7	1	0	0	.14
Bacsik, Mike, Cle	3	9.0	0	1	0	0	1.000	0	0	0	0	.00
Baez, Benito, Fla	8	9.1	0	1	0	0	1.000	1	0	0	0	.00
Baez, Danys, Cle	43	50.1	4	3	1	0	.875	11	3	0	0	.27
Bailey, Cory, KC	53	67.1	4	6	1	1	.909	5	1	0	0	.20
Baldwin, J., CWS-LA	29	175.0	12	25	1	4	.974	17	7	0	1	.41
Bale, John, Bal	14	26.2	1	2	0	0	1.000	5	2	0	0	.40
Balfour, Grant, Min	2	2.2	0	1	0	0	1.000	0	0	0	0	.00
Banks, Willie, Bos	5	10.2	0	0	0	0	.000	1	0	0	0	.00
Barcelo, Lorenzo, CWS	17	21.0	3	2	0	0	1.000	1	0	0	0	.00
Batista, Miguel, Ari	48	139.1	7	17	1	1	.960	30	5	1	0	.20
Bauer, Rick, Bal	6	33.0	1	2	1	1	.750	5	1	0	0	.20
Beck, Rod, Bos	68	80.2	3	16	0	2	1.000	9	1	2	0	.33
Beckett, Josh, Fla	4	24.0	0	6	0	0	1.000	3	1	0	0	.33
Beimel, Joe, Pit	42	115.1	3	17	2	0	.909	13	1	5	2	.46
Beirne, Kevin, Tor	5	7.0	1	3	0	0	1.000	1	0	0	0	.00
Belitz, Todd, Col	8	9.1	0	1	0	0	1.000	0	0	0	0	.00
Bell, Rob, Cin-Tex	27	149.2	8	15	0	3	1.000	25	10	0	0	.40
Benes, Alan, StL	9	14.2	1	0	0	0	1.000	1	1	0	0	1.00
Benes, Andy, StL	27	107.1	7	9	0	1	1.000	11	5	0	1	.45
Benitez, Armando, NYM	73	76.1	4	4	0	0	1.000	12	1	0	0	.08
Benoit, Joaquin, Tex	1	5.0	0	0	0	0	.000	1	0	0	0	.00
Bere, Jason, ChC	32	188.0	12	15	1	0	.964	17	3	0	1	.18
Bernero, Adam, Det	5	12.1	3	1	0	0	1.000	0	0	0	1	.00
Biddle, Rocky, CWS	30	128.2	6	15	1	0	.955	20	5	0	0	.25
Bierbrodt, Nick, Ari-TB	16	84.1	2	14	0	1	1.000	11	2	2	0	.36
Blair, Willie, Det	9	24.0	3	3	0	0	1.000	3	0	0	0	.00
Blank, Matt, Mon	5	22.2	1	7	0	0	1.000	2	1	0	0	.50
Boehringer, B., NYY-SF	51	69.0	1	2	0	0	1.000	8	0	0	0	.00
Bohanon, Brian, Col	20	97.0	5	12	0	0	1.000	12	4	1	0	.42
Bones, Ricky, Fla	61	64.0	4	16	1	3	.952	2	2	0	0	1.00
Borbon, Pedro, Tor	71	53.1	3	6	0	0	1.000	12	2	0	0	.17
Borkowski, Dave, Det	15	29.2	1	4	1	1	.833	2	0	0	1	.00
Borland, Toby, Ana	2	3.1	1	1	0	0	1.000	0	0	0	0	.00
Borowski, Joe, ChC	1	1.2	0	0	0	0	.000	1	0	0	0	.00
Bottalico, Ricky, Phi	66	67.0	3	10	1	0	.929	4	2	0	0	.50
Bottenfield, Kent, Hou	13	52.0	0	5	0	0	1.000	2	0	0	0	.00
Bowles, Brian, Tor	2	3.2	0	0	0	0	.000	0	0	0	0	.00
Bradford, Chad, Oak	35	36.2	0	8	0	0	1.000	6	1	0	0	.17
Brantley, Jeff, Tex	18	21.0	0	0	0	0	.000	2	1	0	0	.50
Brea, Leslie, Bal	2	2.0	0	0	0	0	.000	0	0	0	0	.00
Brock, Chris, Phi	24	32.2	3	3	1	0	.857	2	1	0	1	.50
Brohawn, Troy, Ari	59	49.1	2	8	0	1	1.000	6	0	1	0	.17
Brower, Jim, Cin	46	129.1	10	29	2	2	.951	9	3	1	0	.44
Brown, Kevin, LA	20	115.2	10	22	2	1	.941	11	2	1	2	.27
Buddie, Mike, Mil	31	41.2	3	13	0	1	1.000	5	4	0	0	.80
Buehrle, Mark, CWS	32	221.1	11	49	3	5	.952	12	3	3	2	.50
Burba, Dave, Cle	32	150.2	17	18	0	1	1.000	19	2	0	1	.11
Burkett, John, Atl	34	219.1	15	26	0	1	1.000	22	7	2	1	.41
Burnett, A.J., Fla	27	173.1	11	27	2	0	.950	25	7	2	3	.36
Byrd, Paul, Phi-KC	19	103.1	8	16	1	0	.960	12	4	0	1	.33
Cabrera, Jose, Atl	55	59.1	2	7	1	1	.900	2	0	0	2	.00
Callaway, Mickey, TB	2	5.0	0	0	0	0	.000	0	0	0	0	.00
Carpenter, Chris, Tor	34	215.2	11	25	0	6	1.000	16	8	0	0	.50
Carrara, Giovanni, LA	47	85.1	5	10	0	1	1.000	6	1	0	0	.17
Carrasco, Hector, Min	56	73.2	0	5	1	0	.833	9	5	0	0	.56
Castillo, Carlos, Bos	2	3.0	1	0	0	0	1.000	3	0	0	0	.00
Castillo, Frank, Bos	26	136.2	16	16	0	1	1.000	33	6	0	0	.18
Chacon, Shawn, Col	27	160.0	8	16	0	0	1.000	18	4	0	2	.22
Charlton, Norm, Sea	44	47.2	6	6	0	0	1.000	5	1	1	0	.40
Chen, Bruce, Phi-NYM	27	146.0	4	21	1	1	.962	17	1	6	1	.41
Chiasson, Scott, ChC	6	6.2	1	2	0	0	1.000	0	0	0	0	.00
Choate, Randy, NYY	37	48.1	2	11	0	1	1.000	3	1	0	0	.33
Chouinard, Bobby, Col	8	7.2	1	1	0	0	1.000	0	0	0	0	.00
Christiansen, J., StL-SF	55	36.1	1	5	0	0	1.000	1	1	0	0	1.00
Christman, Tim, Col	1	2.0	0	0	0	0	.000	0	0	0	0	.00
Clemens, Roger, NYY	33	220.1	11	33	2	3	.957	40	6	0	3	.15
Clement, Matt, Fla	31	169.1	14	20	1	1	.971	11	5	0	0	.45
Coco, Pasqual, Tor	7	14.1	1	3	0	0	1.000	2	0	0	0	.00

2001 Fielding and Holding Runners

Pitcher, Team	G	Inn	PO	A	E	DP	Pct.	SBA	CS	PCS	PPO	CS%
Cogan, Tony, KC	39	24.2	3	3	0	1	1.000	1	0	0	0	.00
Coggin, Dave, Phi	17	95.0	9	12	0	0	1.000	5	3	0	0	.60
Colome, Jesus, TB	30	48.2	4	1	1	0	.833	6	0	0	0	.00
Colon, Bartolo, Cle	34	222.1	12	27	1	4	.975	12	5	0	1	.42
Cone, David, Bos	25	135.2	14	9	2	0	.920	26	7	0	0	.27
Cook, Dennis, NYM-Phi	62	45.2	2	3	1	0	.833	2	0	0	0	.00
Cooper, Brian, Ana	7	13.2	2	0	0	0	1.000	0	0	0	0	.00
Coppinger, Rocky, Mil	8	22.2	1	1	1	1	.667	3	2	0	0	.67
Cordero, Francisco, Tex	3	2.1	0	0	0	0	.000	0	0	0	0	.00
Corey, Mark, NYM	2	1.2	0	0	0	0	.000	0	0	0	0	.00
Cormier, Rheal, Phi	60	51.1	6	10	1	2	.941	4	0	1	0	.25
Cornejo, Nate, Det	10	42.2	3	5	0	1	1.000	5	2	0	0	.40
Crabtree, Tim, Tex	21	23.1	1	5	0	1	1.000	1	1	0	0	1.00
Crawford, Paxton, Bos	8	36.0	3	4	0	0	1.000	3	0	0	0	.00
Creek, Doug, TB	66	62.2	2	5	3	1	.700	10	3	1	0	.40
Cressend, Jack, Min	44	56.1	5	7	0	0	1.000	5	0	0	0	.00
Cruz, Juan, ChC	8	44.2	3	5	0	1	1.000	7	4	0	0	.57
Cruz, Nelson, Hou	66	82.1	8	14	1	0	.957	10	5	1	0	.60
Cubillan, Darwin, Mon	29	26.1	0	1	1	0	.500	2	1	0	1	.50
Cunnane, Will, Mil	31	51.2	4	10	0	0	1.000	5	2	0	0	.40
Daal, Omar, Phi	32	185.2	7	31	1	4	.974	5	1	1	1	.40
D'Amico, Jeff, Mil	10	47.1	2	5	0	0	1.000	3	1	0	0	.33
Darensbourg, Vic, Fla	58	48.2	1	10	1	1	.917	1	0	0	0	.00
Davenport, Joe, Col	7	10.1	0	2	0	0	1.000	0	0	0	0	.00
Davey, Tom, SD	39	38.0	2	6	0	0	1.000	9	2	1	0	.33
Davis, Doug, Tex	30	186.0	5	25	2	2	.938	17	3	8	3	.65
Davis, Kane, Col	57	68.1	1	12	0	1	1.000	6	0	0	0	.00
Davis, Lance, Cin	20	106.1	6	23	1	2	.967	9	1	3	3	.44
DeJean, Mike, Mil	75	84.1	7	16	0	1	1.000	13	3	0	0	.23
de los Santos, V., Mil	1	1.0	0	0	0	0	.000	0	0	0	0	.00
Dempster, Ryan, Fla	34	211.1	16	36	3	7	.945	17	6	1	0	.41
Dessens, Elmer, Cin	34	205.0	6	26	0	3	1.000	28	15	0	0	.54
DeWitt, Matt, Tor	16	19.0	2	3	0	1	1.000	2	0	0	0	.00
Dickey, R.A., Tex	4	12.0	1	1	0	0	1.000	3	2	0	0	.67
Dingman, Craig, Col	7	7.1	0	2	0	0	1.000	2	0	1	0	.50
Dotel, Octavio, Hou	61	105.0	9	14	2	3	.920	9	3	1	0	.44
Douglass, Sean, Bal	4	20.1	0	1	0	0	1.000	1	0	0	0	.00
Dreifort, Darren, LA	16	94.2	4	11	1	2	.938	12	6	0	0	.50
Drese, Ryan, Cle	9	36.2	4	5	1	1	.900	5	3	0	0	.60
Drew, Tim, Cle	8	35.0	3	4	1	1	.875	5	0	1	0	.20
Duchscherer, J., Tex	5	14.2	1	0	0	0	1.000	5	0	0	0	.00
Duckworth, B., Phi	11	69.0	4	7	2	0	.846	3	2	0	0	.67
Duncan, Courtney, ChC	36	42.2	2	2	3	0	.571	9	2	0	0	.22
Durbin, Chad, KC	29	179.0	20	20	1	3	.976	18	6	1	2	.39
Duvall, Mike, Min	8	4.2	0	0	0	0	.000	0	0	0	0	.00
Eaton, Adam, SD	17	116.2	13	18	2	2	.939	6	4	0	0	.67
Eischen, Joey, Mon	24	29.2	3	4	0	0	1.000	3	0	0	0	.00
Elarton, Scott, Hou-Col	24	132.2	9	21	2	2	.938	12	1	2	0	.25
Eldred, Cal, CWS	2	6.0	0	2	0	0	1.000	0	0	0	0	.00
Ellis, Robert, Ari	19	92.0	8	12	0	0	1.000	9	3	0	0	.33
Embree, Alan, SF-CWS	61	54.0	2	4	0	1	1.000	6	1	1	0	.33
Erdos, Todd, Bos	10	16.1	1	1	0	1	1.000	1	1	0	0	1.00
Escobar, Kelvim, Tor	59	126.0	6	8	1	0	.933	19	0	1	0	.05
Estes, Shawn, SF	27	159.0	3	33	3	2	.923	18	2	2	0	.22
Estrada, Horacio, Col	4	4.1	0	1	0	0	1.000	0	0	0	1	.00
Eyre, Scott, Tor	17	15.2	0	2	0	0	1.000	3	3	0	0	1.00
Farnsworth, Kyle, ChC	76	82.0	3	4	0	0	1.000	10	3	0	0	.30
Fassero, Jeff, ChC	82	73.2	3	9	0	2	1.000	4	1	0	0	.25
Fernandez, Jared, Cin	5	12.1	1	4	0	0	1.000	4	2	0	0	.50
Fernandez, O., Cin	20	79.1	2	20	1	2	.957	3	3	0	0	1.00
Fetters, Mike, LA-Pit	54	47.1	1	8	1	0	.900	7	0	0	0	.00
Figueroa, Nelson, Phi	19	89.0	2	6	0	1	1.000	9	2	0	0	.22
Fikac, Jeremy, SD	23	26.1	0	4	0	0	1.000	0	0	0	0	.00
File, Bob, Tor	60	74.1	6	11	1	1	.944	11	2	0	0	.18
Finley, Chuck, Cle	22	113.2	2	11	3	0	.813	14	5	2	0	.50
Fiore, Tony, TB-Min	7	9.2	2	1	0	0	1.000	0	0	0	0	.00
Florie, Bryce, Bos	7	8.2	1	1	0	0	1.000	1	0	0	0	.00
Fogg, Josh, CWS	11	13.1	1	1	0	0	1.000	2	0	1	0	.50
Fossum, Casey, Bos	13	44.1	3	1	0	0	1.000	4	0	0	0	.00
Foster, Kevin, Tex	9	17.2	0	0	0	0	.000	1	1	0	0	1.00
Foster, Kris, Bal	7	10.0	0	4	0	0	1.000	0	0	0	0	.00
Foulke, Keith, CWS	72	81.0	7	11	0	0	1.000	4	0	1	0	.25
Fox, Chad, Mil	65	66.2	4	6	1	0	.909	7	1	0	0	.14
Franco, John, NYM	58	53.1	1	7	1	0	.889	3	1	0	1	.33
Franklin, Ryan, Sea	38	78.1	8	6	0	0	1.000	7	2	0	0	.29
Franklin, Wayne, Hou	11	12.0	0	2	0	0	1.000	0	0	0	0	.00
Frascatore, John, Tor	12	16.1	1	5	0	0	1.000	1	0	1	0	1.00
Fuentes, Brian, Sea	10	11.2	1	3	0	0	1.000	1	0	1	1	1.00
Fultz, Aaron, SF	66	71.0	4	14	0	1	1.000	2	0	0	0	.00
Fyhrie, Mike, ChC-Oak	18	20.0	2	4	0	1	1.000	1	0	0	1	.00
Gagne, Eric, LA	33	151.2	10	11	1	0	.955	16	5	1	0	.38
Gandarillas, Gus, Mil	16	19.2	2	3	0	1	1.000	2	0	0	0	.00
Garces, Rich, Bos	62	67.0	7	11	0	2	1.000	13	0	0	0	.00
Garcia, Freddy, Sea	34	238.2	29	39	1	5	.986	20	2	0	0	.10
Gardner, Mark, SF	23	91.2	2	10	0	0	1.000	13	5	0	0	.38
Garland, Jon, CWS	35	117.0	8	17	1	4	.962	10	5	0	1	.50
George, Chris, KC	13	74.0	7	5	1	0	.923	6	0	1	0	.17
Ginter, Matt, CWS	20	39.2	3	4	0	0	1.000	3	1	0	0	.33
Glavine, Tom, Atl	35	219.1	12	40	0	2	1.000	21	8	3	0	.52

2001 Fielding and Holding Runners

Pitcher, Team	G	Inn	PO	A	E	DP	Pct.	SBA	CS	PCS	PPO	CS%
Glover, Gary, CWS	46	100.1	9	15	1	0	.960	7	3	0	3	.43
Glynn, Ryan, Tex	12	46.0	7	5	0	0	1.000	3	1	0	0	.33
Gomes, Wayne, Phi-SF	55	63.0	2	5	0	0	1.000	4	1	0	0	.25
Gonzalez, Dicky, NYM	16	59.0	4	8	0	0	1.000	13	1	0	0	.08
Gordon, Flash, ChC	47	45.1	1	1	0	0	1.000	6	0	0	0	.00
Graves, Danny, Cin	66	80.1	6	21	0	0	1.000	5	1	0	0	.20
Green, Steve, Ana	1	6.0	0	1	0	1	1.000	0	0	0	0	.00
Grilli, Jason, Fla	6	26.2	1	3	0	0	1.000	1	1	0	0	1.00
Grimsley, Jason, KC	73	80.1	6	12	4	2	.818	14	5	1	0	.43
Groom, Buddy, Bal	70	66.0	4	5	1	1	.900	3	2	0	0	.67
Guardado, Eddie, Min	67	66.2	3	6	0	0	1.000	1	0	0	0	.00
Guthrie, Mark, Oak	54	52.1	0	4	0	0	1.000	7	1	3	0	.57
Guzman, Geraldo, Ari	4	9.1	0	0	0	0	.000	0	0	0	0	.00
Hackman, Luther, StL	35	35.2	1	5	0	0	1.000	1	1	0	0	1.00
Halama, John, Sea	31	110.1	9	21	1	0	.968	5	0	2	1	.40
Halladay, Roy, Tor	17	105.1	7	16	0	0	1.000	17	3	0	0	.18
Hamilton, Joey, Tor-Cin	26	139.2	10	21	2	3	.939	11	6	0	0	.55
Hampton, Mike, Col	32	203.0	12	46	0	5	1.000	12	7	3	0	.83
Harnisch, Pete, Cin	7	35.1	3	1	0	0	1.000	2	1	0	0	.50
Harper, Travis, TB	2	7.0	0	1	0	0	1.000	1	0	0	0	.00
Harville, Chad, Oak	3	3.0	1	1	0	0	1.000	0	0	0	0	.00
Hasegawa, S., Ana	46	55.2	3	6	1	1	.900	1	0	0	0	.00
Hawkins, LaTroy, Min	62	51.1	3	5	0	0	1.000	5	1	0	0	.20
Haynes, Jimmy, Mil	31	172.2	12	24	0	1	1.000	18	6	0	0	.33
Helling, Rick, Tex	34	215.2	15	16	1	1	.969	20	10	3	0	.65
Henry, Doug, KC	53	75.2	4	5	0	1	1.000	8	1	0	0	.13
Hentgen, Pat, Bal	9	62.1	7	10	1	1	.944	7	3	0	0	.43
Heredia, Felix, ChC	48	35.0	3	1	0	0	1.000	8	0	1	0	.13
Heredia, Gil, Oak	24	109.2	16	17	2	0	.943	9	3	0	1	.33
Herges, Matt, LA	75	99.1	5	15	1	1	.952	10	6	1	0	.70
Hermanson, Dustin, StL	33	192.1	4	17	1	0	.955	14	7	0	2	.50
Hernandez, A., NYY	6	22.0	1	3	1	0	.800	3	2	0	1	.67
Hernandez, Carlos, Hou	3	17.2	1	2	0	1	1.000	0	0	0	0	.00
Hernandez, Livan, SF	34	226.2	13	44	0	2	1.000	12	6	0	0	.50
Hernandez, O., NYY	17	94.2	5	12	0	0	1.000	17	2	0	0	.12
Hernandez, R., KC	63	67.2	3	6	0	0	1.000	11	1	0	0	.09
Herndon, Junior, SD	12	42.2	2	10	0	2	1.000	7	2	0	0	.29
Hiljus, Erik, Oak	16	66.0	1	4	0	0	1.000	13	1	0	0	.08
Hill, Ken, TB	5	7.1	2	2	1	0	.800	1	0	0	0	.00
Hinchliffe, Brett, NYM	1	2.0	0	0	0	0	.000	0	0	0	0	.00
Hitchcock, S., SD-NYY	13	70.1	3	7	0	0	1.000	10	0	0	0	.00
Hoffman, Trevor, SD	62	60.1	5	4	0	0	1.000	2	0	0	0	.00
Holt, Chris, Det	30	151.1	9	17	1	1	.963	21	6	0	0	.29
Holtz, Mike, Ana	63	37.0	4	9	1	0	.929	6	0	0	0	.00
Howry, Bob, CWS	69	78.2	2	10	0	0	1.000	6	2	0	0	.33
Hudson, Tim, Oak	35	235.0	21	43	5	3	.928	31	7	0	2	.23
Hutchinson, Chad, StL	3	4.0	0	0	0	0	.000	0	0	0	0	.00
Irabu, Hideki, Mon	3	16.2	0	5	0	0	1.000	5	0	1	0	.20
Isringhausen, J., Oak	65	71.1	1	8	2	0	.818	9	0	0	0	.00
Jackson, Mike, Hou	67	69.0	7	4	0	0	1.000	5	3	0	0	.60
James, Mike, StL	40	38.0	3	4	0	1	1.000	3	0	0	0	.00
Jarvis, Kevin, SD	32	193.1	20	33	1	0	.981	16	7	1	0	.50
Jennings, Jason, Col	7	39.1	4	7	0	3	1.000	2	1	0	0	.50
Jensen, Ryan, SF	10	42.1	5	4	1	1	.900	10	4	0	0	.40
Jimenez, Jose, Col	56	55.0	2	12	0	0	1.000	3	0	0	0	.00
Jodie, Brett, NYY-SD	8	25.1	0	1	0	0	1.000	5	2	0	0	.40
Johnson, Adam, Min	7	25.0	1	3	0	0	1.000	9	3	0	0	.33
Johnson, Jason, Bal	32	196.0	4	16	4	1	.833	53	18	1	0	.36
Johnson, Jonathan, Tex	5	10.1	0	0	0	0	.000	0	0	0	0	.00
Johnson, Mike, Mon	10	11.1	0	0	0	0	.000	0	0	0	0	.00
Johnson, Randy, Ari	35	249.2	2	27	4	1	.879	34	11	4	1	.44
Jones, Bobby J., SD	33	195.0	7	28	0	0	1.000	30	7	1	0	.27
Jones, Todd, Det-Min	69	68.0	7	10	1	0	.944	4	0	0	0	.00
Judd, Mike, TB-Tex	12	29.0	3	1	0	0	1.000	4	1	0	0	.25
Julio, Jorge, Bal	18	21.1	0	2	1	0	.667	5	0	0	0	.00
Karnuth, Jason, StL	4	5.0	0	0	0	0	.000	0	0	0	0	.00
Karsay, Steve, Cle-Atl	74	88.0	7	16	1	1	.958	9	0	1	1	.11
Keisler, Randy, NYY	10	50.2	2	6	2	0	.800	15	1	1	0	.13
Kennedy, Joe, TB	20	117.2	8	14	0	2	1.000	13	3	3	1	.46
Kile, Darryl, StL	34	227.1	11	29	2	2	.952	11	7	0	0	.64
Kim, Byung-Hyun, Ari	78	98.0	3	19	1	0	.957	13	4	0	0	.31
Kim, Sun-Woo, Bos	20	41.2	2	5	0	1	1.000	8	1	0	0	.13
King, Ray, Mil	82	55.0	5	9	1	0	.933	5	0	0	0	.00
Kline, Steve, StL	89	75.0	3	10	0	0	1.000	4	0	0	0	.00
Knight, Brandon, NYY	4	10.2	1	0	0	0	1.000	1	0	0	0	.00
Knott, Eric, Ari	3	4.2	0	0	0	0	.000	0	0	0	0	.00
Knotts, Gary, Fla	2	6.0	1	0	0	0	1.000	0	0	0	0	.00
Koch, Billy, Tor	69	69.1	4	6	1	1	.909	7	0	0	0	.00
Kohlmeier, Ryan, Bal	34	40.2	0	2	0	0	1.000	4	1	0	0	.25
Kolb, Brandon, Mil	10	9.2	0	1	0	0	1.000	1	0	0	0	.00
Kolb, Danny, Tex	17	15.1	0	0	0	0	.000	2	0	0	0	.00
Koplove, Mike, Ari	9	10.0	0	1	0	0	1.000	0	0	0	0	.00
Lawrence, Brian, SD	27	114.2	2	26	4	0	.875	12	4	1	0	.42
Lee, David, SD	41	48.2	2	2	0	0	1.000	6	4	0	0	.67
Leiter, Al, NYM	29	187.1	6	22	2	2	.933	22	2	3	0	.23
Leiter, Mark, Mil	20	36.0	4	7	0	0	1.000	2	1	0	0	.50
Leskanic, Curtis, Mil	70	69.1	7	4	2	0	.846	6	3	0	0	.50
Levine, Al, Ana	64	75.2	3	9	2	1	.857	8	6	0	0	.75
Levrault, Allen, Mil	32	130.2	8	11	2	1	.905	10	2	0	0	.20
Lidle, Cory, Oak	29	188.0	13	30	2	0	.956	25	10	1	1	.44
Lieber, Jon, ChC	34	232.1	16	35	0	4	1.000	9	7	0	0	.78
Ligtenberg, Kerry, Atl	53	59.2	2	1	3	0	.500	15	0	0	0	.00

2001 Fielding and Holding Runners

Pitcher, Team	G	Inn	PO	A	E	DP	Pct.	SBA	CS	PCS	PPO	CS%
Lilly, Ted, NYY	26	120.2	5	22	2	0	.931	31	2	6	0	.26
Lima, Jose, Hou-Det	32	165.2	3	20	2	4	.920	19	4	0	1	.21
Lincoln, Mike, Pit	31	40.1	1	11	1	1	.923	1	0	1	0	1.00
Linebrink, Scott, Hou	9	10.1	0	0	0	0	.000	1	1	0	0	1.00
Lira, Felipe, Mon	4	5.0	1	0	0	0	1.000	3	0	0	0	.00
Lloyd, Graeme, Mon	84	70.1	7	13	1	3	.952	10	0	1	1	.10
Loaiza, Esteban, Tor	36	190.0	15	21	3	0	.923	17	7	0	0	.41
Loewer, Carlton, SD	2	4.1	0	0	0	0	.000	1	0	0	0	.00
Lohse, Kyle, Min	19	90.1	9	12	1	2	.955	12	2	0	0	.17
Loiselle, Rich, Pit	18	18.0	1	4	0	0	1.000	3	0	0	0	.00
Looper, Braden, Fla	71	71.0	4	8	0	1	1.000	11	5	0	0	.45
Lopez, Albie, TB-Ari	33	205.2	7	29	1	1	.973	29	9	0	3	.31
Lowe, Derek, Bos	67	91.2	6	17	1	2	.958	19	2	0	0	.11
Lowe, Sean, CWS	45	127.0	8	21	0	0	1.000	17	2	1	0	.18
Lukasiewicz, Mark, Ana	24	22.1	0	1	0	0	1.000	4	1	0	0	.25
Lundquist, David, SD	17	19.2	1	3	0	0	1.000	2	2	0	0	1.00
Lyon, Brandon, Tor	11	63.0	3	9	0	0	1.000	5	1	0	0	.20
MacDougal, Mike, KC	3	15.1	1	0	0	0	1.000	0	0	0	0	.00
MacRae, Scott, Cin	24	31.1	2	1	0	0	1.000	1	0	0	0	.00
Maddux, Greg, Atl	34	233.0	19	54	1	3	.986	38	14	0	2	.37
Maduro, Calvin, Bal	22	93.2	2	8	0	0	1.000	9	2	0	4	.22
Magnante, Mike, Oak	65	55.1	2	7	1	0	.900	2	1	1	0	1.00
Mahay, Ron, ChC	17	20.2	2	3	0	1	1.000	3	0	1	0	.33
Mahomes, Pat, Tex	56	107.1	15	14	1	2	.967	9	4	0	2	.44
Mann, Jim, Hou	4	5.1	0	1	0	0	1.000	0	0	0	0	.00
Mantei, Matt, Ari	8	7.0	0	0	0	0	.000	0	0	0	0	.00
Manzanillo, Josias, Pit	71	79.2	3	6	1	0	.900	4	0	0	0	.00
Marquis, Jason, Atl	38	129.1	9	21	3	2	.909	6	4	0	1	.67
Marte, Damaso, Pit	23	36.1	1	2	0	0	1.000	3	0	0	0	.00
Martin, Tom, NYM	14	17.0	1	1	0	0	1.000	4	0	1	0	.25
Martinez, Pedro, Bos	18	116.2	5	5	0	0	1.000	12	3	0	0	.25
Martinez, Ramon, Pit	4	15.2	2	2	0	2	1.000	3	0	0	0	.00
Mathews, T.J., Oak-StL	30	37.2	1	6	0	0	1.000	2	2	0	0	1.00
Mattes, Troy, Mon	8	45.0	2	5	1	0	.875	4	2	0	0	.50
Matthews, Mike, StL	51	89.0	4	7	1	0	.917	3	0	1	1	.33
Maurer, Dave, SD	3	5.0	1	1	0	0	1.000	2	0	0	0	.00
Mays, Joe, Min	34	233.2	17	28	1	2	.978	14	5	0	0	.36
McDill, Allen, Bos	15	14.2	0	0	0	0	.000	1	0	0	0	.00
McElroy, Chuck, Bal-SD	49	75.0	4	21	0	1	1.000	13	0	1	0	.08
McKnight, T., Hou-Pit	15	87.1	4	13	1	2	.944	13	2	0	0	.15
Meacham, Rusty, TB	24	35.1	1	7	0	0	1.000	2	0	0	0	.00
Meadows, Brian, KC	10	50.1	4	8	0	1	1.000	10	2	1	2	.30
Mecir, Jim, Oak	54	63.0	3	11	1	1	.933	6	1	1	0	.33
Mendoza, Ramiro, NYY	56	100.2	7	14	0	1	1.000	8	1	0	0	.13
Mercado, Hector, Cin	56	53.0	0	5	1	0	.833	3	0	1	1	.33
Mercedes, Jose, Bal	33	184.0	15	9	0	2	1.000	24	3	0	0	.13
Mesa, Jose, Phi	71	69.1	4	9	0	0	1.000	3	2	1	0	1.00
Miadich, Bart, Ana	11	10.0	1	1	0	0	1.000	0	0	0	0	.00
Miceli, Dan, Fla-Col	51	45.0	2	3	1	0	.833	2	0	0	0	.00
Michalak, C., Tor-Tex	35	136.2	14	30	1	2	.978	10	2	3	7	.50
Middlebrook, Jason, SD	4	19.1	0	2	0	0	1.000	1	0	0	0	.00
Miller, Matt, Det	13	9.2	3	3	0	0	1.000	0	0	0	0	.00
Miller, Travis, Min	45	48.2	1	2	2	0	.600	2	0	0	0	.00
Miller, Wade, Hou	32	212.0	16	36	2	3	.963	23	11	2	0	.57
Mills, Alan, Bal	15	14.0	0	0	0	0	.000	1	0	0	0	.00
Millwood, Kevin, Atl	21	121.0	10	12	0	1	1.000	15	2	0	0	.13
Milton, Eric, Min	35	220.2	7	13	0	1	1.000	7	3	1	0	.57
Mlicki, Dave, Det-Hou	34	167.2	7	20	0	3	1.000	23	7	0	0	.30
Moehler, Brian, Det	1	8.0	0	2	0	0	1.000	0	0	0	0	.00
Mohler, Mike, Ari	13	13.2	0	2	0	0	1.000	1	0	0	0	.00
Moore, Trey, Atl	2	4.0	0	0	0	0	.000	0	0	0	0	.00
Moreno, Juan, Tex	45	41.1	4	0	1	0	.800	3	0	0	0	.00
Morgan, Mike, Ari	31	38.0	0	0	1	0	.000	2	1	0	0	.50
Morris, Matt, StL	34	216.1	8	31	2	0	.951	16	4	1	1	.31
Moss, Damian, Atl	5	9.0	0	1	1	0	.500	2	0	0	0	.00
Mota, Guillermo, Mon	53	49.2	1	10	1	3	.917	9	0	0	0	.00
Moyer, Jamie, Sea	33	209.2	17	27	0	0	1.000	19	6	1	0	.37
Mulder, Mark, Oak	34	229.1	12	40	2	2	.963	26	3	5	1	.31
Mulholland, T., Pit-LA	41	65.2	2	14	0	1	1.000	1	0	0	0	.00
Mullen, Scott, KC	17	10.0	1	1	0	1	1.000	1	0	0	0	.00
Munoz, Bobby, Mon	15	42.0	3	9	1	3	.923	3	1	0	0	.33
Murray, Heath, Det	40	63.1	4	9	0	2	1.000	7	1	2	0	.43
Mussina, Mike, NYY	34	228.2	18	25	1	4	.977	22	12	1	1	.59
Myers, Mike, Col	73	40.0	2	12	0	1	1.000	10	1	0	1	.10
Myers, Rodney, SD	37	47.1	4	7	2	0	.846	1	1	0	1	1.00
Myette, Aaron, Tex	19	80.2	5	7	1	0	.923	14	3	2	0	.36
Nagy, Charles, Cle	15	70.1	9	12	1	1	.955	4	1	0	0	.25
Neagle, Denny, Col	30	170.2	9	17	1	1	.963	13	4	0	0	.31
Neal, Blaine, Fla	4	5.1	0	0	0	0	.000	2	0	0	0	.00
Nelson, Jeff, Sea	69	65.1	2	6	2	1	.800	2	0	0	0	.00
Nelson, Joe, Atl	2	2.0	0	0	0	0	.000	0	0	0	0	.00
Nen, Robb, SF	79	77.2	4	3	0	0	1.000	18	1	0	0	.06
Neugebauer, Nick, Mil	2	6.0	0	0	0	0	.000	2	0	0	0	.00
Nichting, Chris, Cin-Col	43	42.1	3	9	0	0	1.000	3	2	0	0	.67
Nickle, Doug, Phi	2	2.0	0	0	0	0	.000	0	0	0	0	.00
Nitkowski, C., Det-NYM	61	51.0	2	8	0	0	1.000	7	0	1	0	.14
Nomo, Hideo, Bos	33	198.0	17	18	1	2	.972	63	9	2	1	.17
Nunez, Jose A., LA-SD	62	59.0	0	6	2	0	.750	9	0	1	0	.11
Nunez, Vladimir, Fla	52	92.0	7	11	0	1	1.000	6	3	1	0	.67
Ohka, T., Bos-Mon	22	107.0	12	11	1	2	.958	15	4	2	0	.40
Ohman, Will, ChC	11	11.2	1	0	0	0	1.000	0	0	0	0	.00
Olivares, Omar, Pit	45	110.0	4	19	0	1	1.000	6	4	0	1	.67

2001 Fielding and Holding Runners

Pitcher, Team	G	Inn	PO	A	E	DP	Pct.	SBA	CS	PCS	PPO	CS%
Oliver, Darren, Tex	28	154.0	7	26	0	1	1.000	22	5	5	0	.45
Olsen, Kevin, Fla	4	15.0	3	2	0	1	1.000	1	0	0	0	.00
Olson, Gregg, LA	28	24.2	0	3	1	0	.750	3	1	0	0	.33
Oropesa, Eddie, Phi	30	19.0	0	2	0	0	1.000	2	2	0	0	1.00
Orosco, Jesse, LA	35	16.0	1	1	0	0	1.000	5	1	0	0	.20
Ortiz, Ramon, Ana	32	208.2	18	20	6	1	.864	18	8	0	3	.44
Ortiz, Russ, SF	33	218.2	12	34	1	4	.979	12	6	0	0	.50
Osting, Jimmy, SD	3	2.0	0	0	0	0	.000	0	0	0	0	.00
Osuna, Antonio, CWS	4	4.1	0	0	0	0	.000	1	0	0	0	.00
Oswalt, Roy, Hou	28	141.2	19	15	1	1	.971	3	0	1	0	.33
Padilla, Vicente, Phi	23	34.0	4	2	0	1	1.000	0	0	0	0	.00
Painter, Lance, Tor-Mil	23	29.0	5	6	0	2	1.000	2	1	1	0	1.00
Paniagua, Jose, Sea	60	66.0	2	3	1	1	.833	4	0	0	0	.00
Park, Chan Ho, LA	36	234.0	12	40	2	2	.963	17	7	1	0	.47
Parker, Christian, NYY	1	3.0	0	2	0	0	1.000	2	0	0	0	.00
Paronto, Chad, Bal	24	27.0	2	6	0	0	1.000	6	1	0	0	.17
Parque, Jim, CWS	5	28.0	2	8	0	0	1.000	3	0	1	0	.33
Parris, Steve, Tor	19	105.2	4	11	0	0	1.000	8	3	1	1	.50
Parrish, John, Bal	16	22.0	0	2	1	0	.667	0	0	0	0	.00
Patterson, Danny, Det	60	64.2	5	10	0	0	1.000	4	1	2	0	.75
Pavano, Carl, Mon	8	42.2	1	3	0	0	1.000	7	3	0	0	.43
Penny, Brad, Fla	31	205.0	10	27	0	1	1.000	19	7	0	0	.37
Percival, Troy, Ana	57	57.2	3	1	0	0	1.000	15	1	0	0	.07
Perez, Odalis, Atl	24	95.1	5	11	0	0	1.000	9	2	2	0	.44
Perisho, Matt, Det	30	39.1	1	5	0	0	1.000	5	1	2	0	.60
Person, Robert, Phi	33	208.1	5	19	0	1	1.000	20	6	0	1	.30
Peters, Chris, Mon	13	31.0	0	6	0	0	1.000	7	2	1	0	.43
Peterson, Kyle, Mil	3	14.2	1	2	0	0	1.000	1	0	0	0	.00
Petkovsek, Mark, Tex	55	76.2	5	9	0	0	1.000	2	1	0	0	.50
Pettitte, Andy, NYY	31	200.2	9	40	0	2	1.000	16	3	2	5	.31
Pettyjohn, Adam, Det	16	65.0	3	8	0	1	1.000	9	0	2	0	.22
Phelps, Travis, TB	49	62.0	5	11	1	1	.941	3	0	0	0	.00
Pichardo, Hipolito, Bos	30	34.2	3	10	0	1	1.000	3	0	0	0	.00
Piersoll, Chris, Cin	11	11.1	1	0	0	0	1.000	1	0	0	0	.00
Pineda, Luis, Det	16	18.1	0	2	0	0	1.000	3	1	0	0	.33
Pineiro, Joel, Sea	16	75.1	4	4	0	0	1.000	8	4	0	0	.50
Plesac, Dan, Tor	62	45.1	0	4	0	0	1.000	10	1	3	0	.40
Politte, Cliff, Phi	23	26.0	4	4	2	0	.800	3	0	1	1	.33
Ponson, Sidney, Bal	23	138.1	14	19	0	2	1.000	18	4	1	0	.28
Pote, Lou, Ana	44	86.2	11	16	2	2	.931	10	1	1	0	.20
Powell, Brian, Hou	1	3.0	0	0	0	0	.000	0	0	0	0	.00
Powell, Jay, Hou-Col	74	75.0	9	8	1	2	.944	5	1	0	0	.20
Prieto, Ariel, TB	3	3.2	1	0	0	0	1.000	0	0	0	0	.00
Prinz, Bret, Ari	46	41.0	3	6	0	1	1.000	6	2	0	0	.33
Prokopec, Luke, LA	29	138.1	8	15	2	2	.920	11	3	0	1	.27
Pulsipher, B., Bos-CWS	37	30.0	2	6	1	1	.889	4	2	0	0	.50
Quantrill, Paul, Tor	80	83.0	2	12	2	1	.875	9	2	0	0	.22
Quevedo, Ruben, Mil	10	56.2	6	4	0	0	1.000	6	3	0	0	.50
Radinsky, Scott, Cle	2	2.0	0	2	0	0	1.000	0	0	0	0	.00
Radke, Brad, Min	33	226.0	13	44	1	4	.983	26	10	1	1	.42
Rapp, Pat, Ana	31	170.0	19	26	1	1	.978	18	6	0	0	.33
Reames, Britt, Mon	41	95.0	1	23	0	1	1.000	10	1	1	4	.20
Redding, Tim, Hou	13	55.2	4	5	0	1	1.000	5	1	0	1	.20
Redman, Mark, Min-Det	11	58.0	1	10	0	1	1.000	5	1	0	0	.20
Reed, Rick, NYM-Min	32	202.1	17	36	1	1	.981	23	8	1	2	.39
Reed, Steve, Cle-Atl	70	58.1	6	10	1	0	.941	8	3	0	0	.38
Reichert, Dan, KC	27	123.0	17	14	0	3	1.000	10	2	0	0	.20
Reith, Brian, Cin	9	40.1	1	3	0	0	1.000	9	3	0	0	.33
Reitsma, Chris, Cin	36	182.0	13	39	0	1	1.000	12	5	0	0	.42
Rekar, Bryan, TB	25	140.2	18	16	2	2	.944	12	4	0	0	.33
Remlinger, Mike, Atl	74	75.0	1	6	0	0	1.000	3	2	0	0	.67
Reyes, Al, LA	19	25.2	3	3	0	0	1.000	0	0	0	0	.00
Reyes, Dennys, Cin	35	53.0	0	6	2	0	.750	7	3	0	0	.43
Reynolds, Shane, Hou	28	182.2	9	30	0	2	1.000	10	4	0	0	.40
Reynoso, Armando, Ari	9	46.2	1	11	1	2	.923	1	0	0	0	.00
Rhodes, Arthur, Sea	71	68.0	4	9	0	0	1.000	1	0	0	0	.00
Riedling, John, Cin	29	33.2	3	6	0	0	1.000	2	1	0	0	.50
Rigdon, Paul, Mil	15	79.1	10	11	0	1	1.000	11	4	0	0	.36
Riggan, Jerrod, NYM	35	47.2	2	5	0	1	1.000	9	1	1	0	.22
Rijo, Jose, Cin	13	17.0	0	1	1	0	.500	5	0	0	0	.00
Rincon, Juan, Min	4	5.2	0	1	0	0	1.000	1	0	0	0	.00
Rincon, Ricardo, Cle	67	54.0	5	5	1	0	.909	2	1	0	0	.50
Riske, David, Cle	26	27.1	1	5	0	2	1.000	4	3	0	0	.75
Ritchie, Todd, Pit	33	207.1	11	31	2	3	.955	15	4	0	0	.27
Rivera, Mariano, NYY	71	80.2	17	15	1	0	.970	6	3	0	0	.50
Roberts, Grant, NYM	16	26.0	2	1	0	0	1.000	3	1	0	0	.33
Roberts, Willis, Bal	46	132.0	6	21	2	0	.931	11	3	0	0	.27
Rocker, John, Atl-Cle	68	66.2	3	8	4	0	.733	8	0	1	0	.13
Rodriguez, Felix, SF	80	80.1	1	2	1	0	.750	5	2	0	0	.40
Rodriguez, Frank, Cin	7	8.2	0	3	0	0	1.000	1	1	0	0	1.00
Rodriguez, Rich, Cle	53	39.0	0	10	0	1	1.000	3	0	2	0	.67
Rodriguez, W., Hou	2	3.0	0	0	0	0	.000	0	0	0	0	.00
Rogers, Kenny, Tex	20	120.2	6	34	1	3	.976	8	3	1	2	.50
Romero, J.C., Min	14	65.0	9	11	2	0	.909	4	1	2	0	.75
Rose, Brian, NYM-TB	10	29.0	0	6	0	0	1.000	3	1	0	0	.33
Rueter, Kirk, SF	34	195.1	11	50	0	11	1.000	12	8	1	0	.75
Ruffin, Johnny, Fla	3	3.2	0	0	0	0	.000	0	0	0	0	.00
Rupe, Ryan, TB	28	143.1	5	12	2	0	.895	7	3	0	1	.43
Rusch, Glendon, NYM	33	179.0	5	9	2	2	.875	16	3	0	0	.19
Ryan, B.J., Bal	61	53.0	0	4	2	0	.667	11	0	0	0	.00
Sabathia, C.C., Cle	33	180.1	3	21	1	1	.960	42	11	4	0	.36
Sabel, Erik, Ari	42	51.1	3	5	0	1	1.000	3	1	0	0	.33

2001 Fielding and Holding Runners

Pitcher, Team	G	Inn	PO	A	E	DP	Pct.	SBA	CS	PCS	PPO	CS%
Saberhagen, Bret, Bos	3	15.0	1	3	0	0	1.000	4	1	0	0	.25
Sanchez, Jesus, Fla	16	62.2	2	5	1	0	.875	4	1	0	1	.25
Santana, Johan, Min	15	43.2	0	6	2	1	.750	2	1	0	0	.50
Santiago, Jose, KC-Phi	73	91.2	8	11	1	1	.950	7	1	1	0	.29
Santos, Victor, Det	33	76.1	1	11	1	0	.923	12	5	2	0	.58
Sasaki, Kazuhiro, Sea	69	66.2	6	2	1	2	.889	3	0	0	0	.00
Sauerbeck, Scott, Pit	70	62.2	1	5	1	0	.857	1	1	0	0	1.00
Scanlan, Bob, Mon	18	26.1	4	4	1	0	.889	6	0	0	0	.00
Schilling, Curt, Ari	35	256.2	15	21	1	4	.973	13	8	1	1	.69
Schmidt, Jason, Pit-SF	25	150.1	6	9	0	0	1.000	16	6	0	0	.38
Schoeneweis, S., Ana	32	205.1	11	36	0	5	1.000	29	4	5	0	.31
Schourek, Pete, Bos	33	30.1	2	7	1	3	.900	2	0	0	0	.00
Seanez, Rudy, SD-Atl	38	36.0	4	3	0	0	1.000	5	0	0	0	.00
Seay, Bobby, TB	12	13.0	1	2	1	0	.750	2	0	1	0	.50
Seelbach, Chris, Atl	5	8.0	0	0	0	0	.000	1	0	0	0	.00
Sele, Aaron, Sea	34	215.0	15	17	1	1	.970	10	3	0	0	.30
Serrano, Wascar, SD	20	46.2	2	11	0	0	1.000	5	4	0	0	.80
Shaw, Jeff, LA	77	74.2	8	14	0	0	1.000	3	1	0	0	.33
Sheets, Ben, Mil	25	151.1	10	24	2	2	.944	11	4	0	0	.36
Shields, Scot, Ana	8	11.0	1	1	2	1	.500	0	0	0	0	.00
Shuey, Paul, Cle	47	54.1	1	4	4	1	.556	13	1	0	0	.08
Silva, Jose, Pit	26	32.0	1	4	0	0	1.000	1	0	0	0	.00
Slusarski, Joe, Atl-Hou	12	16.0	2	1	0	0	1.000	1	0	0	0	.00
Smart, J.D., Tex	15	15.1	0	1	0	0	1.000	0	0	0	0	.00
Smith, Bud, StL	16	84.2	3	18	0	0	1.000	6	0	1	2	.17
Smith, Chuck, Fla	15	88.0	10	8	1	1	.947	7	3	0	1	.43
Smith, Roy, Cle	9	16.1	0	1	1	1	.500	5	1	0	0	.20
Smoltz, John, Atl	36	59.0	8	7	1	0	.938	2	1	0	0	.50
Sobkowiak, Scott, Atl	1	1.0	0	0	0	0	.000	0	0	0	0	.00
Sparks, Steve W., Det	35	232.0	20	43	1	1	.984	17	7	1	2	.47
Speier, Justin, Cle-Col	54	76.2	2	4	0	0	1.000	6	1	0	0	.17
Spooneybarger, T., Atl	4	4.0	0	0	0	0	.000	0	0	0	0	.00
Springer, Dennis, LA	4	19.0	0	1	0	0	1.000	3	3	0	0	1.00
Springer, Russ, Ari	18	17.2	1	3	1	0	.800	2	0	0	0	.00
Standridge, Jason, TB	9	19.1	1	1	0	0	1.000	2	1	0	0	.50
Stanton, Mike, NYY	76	80.1	6	10	2	1	.889	4	0	2	1	.50
Stark, Denny, Sea	4	14.2	1	0	0	0	1.000	1	0	0	0	.00
Stechschulte, G., StL	67	70.0	7	10	1	1	.944	8	1	2	0	.38
Stein, Blake, KC	36	131.0	6	8	0	0	1.000	20	5	1	1	.30
Stewart, Scott, Mon	62	47.2	0	11	1	1	.917	2	1	1	0	1.00
Stone, Ricky, Hou	6	7.2	0	0	0	0	.000	0	0	0	0	.00
Strickland, Scott, Mon	77	81.1	3	9	2	2	.857	18	0	3	0	.17
Strong, Joe, Fla	5	6.2	0	4	0	0	1.000	1	0	0	0	.00
Sturtze, Tanyon, TB	39	195.1	12	21	0	2	1.000	29	8	1	1	.31
Sullivan, Scott, Cin	79	103.1	6	10	0	0	1.000	5	1	0	1	.20
Suppan, Jeff, KC	34	218.1	18	33	1	1	.981	21	5	1	1	.29
Suzuki, M., KC-Col-Mil	33	118.1	5	16	1	0	.955	17	5	0	1	.29
Swindell, Greg, Ari	64	53.2	1	3	0	1	1.000	6	0	1	0	.17
Tabaka, Jeff, StL	8	3.2	0	2	0	0	1.000	0	0	0	0	.00
Tam, Jeff, Oak	70	74.2	3	11	0	1	1.000	8	2	0	0	.25
Tapani, Kevin, ChC	29	168.1	5	30	1	1	.972	15	8	0	1	.53
Tavarez, Julian, ChC	34	161.1	14	31	3	6	.938	16	6	0	0	.38
Taylor, Billy, Pit	1	2.0	0	0	0	0	.000	0	0	0	0	.00
Telemaco, Amaury, Phi	24	89.1	6	11	1	2	.944	7	3	0	0	.43
Telford, Anthony, Mon	8	7.0	1	1	0	0	1.000	0	0	0	0	.00
Thomas, Brad, Min	5	16.1	0	4	0	0	1.000	0	0	0	0	.00
Thomson, John, Col	14	93.2	17	8	1	3	.962	6	0	0	0	.00
Thurman, Mike, Mon	28	147.0	10	18	1	1	.966	17	0	0	0	.00
Timlin, Mike, StL	67	72.2	6	14	1	2	.952	2	1	0	0	.50
Tolar, Kevin, Det	9	10.2	0	2	0	0	1.000	0	0	0	0	.00
Tollberg, Brian, SD	19	117.1	6	20	2	1	.929	8	4	0	0	.50
Tomko, Brett, Sea	11	34.2	2	3	0	1	1.000	3	0	0	0	.00
Towers, Josh, Bal	24	140.1	10	19	1	2	.967	16	5	1	0	.38
Trachsel, Steve, NYM	28	173.2	15	20	1	3	.972	25	3	0	0	.12
Trombley, Mike, Bal-LA	69	78.0	6	6	0	0	1.000	9	1	0	0	.11
Urbina, U., Mon-Bos	64	66.2	1	7	0	0	1.000	12	1	1	0	.17
Valdes, Ismael, Ana	27	163.2	7	34	0	2	1.000	18	9	0	4	.50
Valdes, Marc, Atl	9	7.0	1	0	0	1	1.000	0	0	0	0	.00
Van Poppel, Todd, ChC	59	75.0	2	8	4	2	.714	9	2	0	1	.22
Vazquez, Javier, Mon	32	223.2	24	32	0	10	1.000	9	1	0	0	.11
Venafro, Mike, Tex	70	60.0	4	13	4	4	.810	2	0	0	0	.00
Veres, Dave, StL	71	65.2	3	7	2	0	.833	1	0	0	0	.00
Villafuerte, B., Tex	6	5.2	0	1	0	0	1.000	0	0	0	0	.00
Villone, Ron, Col-Hou	53	114.2	4	13	0	1	1.000	11	1	3	0	.36
Vining, Ken, CWS	8	6.2	1	1	0	0	1.000	0	0	0	0	.00
Vizcaino, Luis, Oak	36	36.2	0	3	0	0	1.000	1	1	0	0	1.00
Vogelsong, R., SF-Pit	15	34.2	4	6	1	2	.909	5	1	0	0	.20
Vosberg, Ed, Phi	18	12.2	1	1	0	0	1.000	0	0	0	1	.00
Voyles, Brad, KC	7	9.1	0	0	0	0	.000	0	0	0	0	.00
Wagner, Billy, Hou	64	62.2	1	5	1	0	.857	4	1	1	0	.50
Wakefield, Tim, Bos	45	168.2	14	22	2	0	.947	43	10	1	1	.26
Walker, Kevin, SD	16	12.0	0	1	0	0	1.000	0	0	0	0	.00
Walker, Pete, NYM	2	6.2	1	0	0	0	1.000	0	0	0	0	.00
Wall, Donne, NYM	32	42.2	4	7	0	0	1.000	1	0	1	1	1.00
Wallace, Jeff, TB	29	50.1	0	8	0	0	1.000	10	3	0	0	.30
Wasdin, John, Col-Bal	44	74.0	5	6	0	0	1.000	14	1	1	0	.14
Washburn, Jarrod, Ana	30	193.1	6	26	2	0	.941	25	1	11	1	.48
Weathers, D., Mil-ChC	80	86.0	4	14	2	1	.900	2	1	0	0	.50
Weaver, Jeff, Det	33	229.1	21	28	0	4	1.000	25	8	0	3	.32
Weber, Ben, Ana	56	68.1	2	14	2	2	.889	10	4	0	0	.40
Wells, Bob, Min	65	68.2	1	8	0	1	1.000	4	3	0	0	.75
Wells, David, CWS	16	100.2	4	10	4	1	.778	19	1	1	1	.11

2001 Fielding and Holding Runners

Pitcher, Team	G	Inn	PO	A	E	DP	Pct.	SBA	CS	PCS	PPO	CS%
Wells, Kip, CWS	40	133.1	9	19	3	1	.903	17	4	0	0	.24
Wendell, Turk, NYM-Phi	70	67.0	11	7	0	1	1.000	6	1	0	1	.17
Wengert, Don, Pit	4	16.0	0	4	0	0	1.000	1	0	0	0	.00
Westbrook, Jake, Cle	23	64.2	4	15	1	1	.950	9	2	0	1	.22
Wheeler, Dan, TB	13	17.2	3	3	0	1	1.000	1	0	0	0	.00
White, Gabe, Col	69	67.2	3	6	0	1	1.000	9	0	1	0	.11
White, Rick, NYM	55	69.2	3	7	1	1	.909	1	1	0	0	1.00
Whiteside, Matt, Atl	13	16.1	2	1	2	0	.600	3	0	0	0	.00
Wickman, Bob, Cle	70	67.2	8	60	0	0	1.000	5	3	0	0	.60
Wilkins, Marc, Pit	14	17.1	1	3	0	0	1.000	2	0	0	0	.00
Williams, Dave, Pit	22	114.0	6	19	0	1	1.000	12	3	6	1	.75
Williams, Jeff, LA	15	24.1	4	5	0	1	1.000	3	1	1	0	.67
Williams, Mike, Pit-Hou	65	64.0	5	7	1	1	.923	7	0	0	0	.00
Williams, Todd, NYY	15	15.1	1	3	2	0	.667	0	0	0	0	.00
Williams, W., SD-StL	34	220.0	16	23	4	3	.907	21	6	1	0	.33
Williamson, Scott, Cin	2	0.2	0	0	0	0	.000	0	0	0	0	.00
Wilson, Kris, KC	29	109.1	12	11	2	4	.920	4	2	0	0	.50
Wilson, Paul, TB	37	151.1	4	13	1	2	.944	15	4	0	0	.27
Winchester, Scott, Cin	12	24.0	3	4	0	0	1.000	4	3	0	0	.75
Wise, Matt, Ana	11	49.1	1	2	0	0	1.000	6	1	0	0	.17
Witasick, Jay, SD-NYY	63	79.0	1	8	4	1	.692	6	0	0	0	.00
Witt, Bobby, Ari	14	43.1	1	6	0	0	1.000	7	1	0	0	.14
Wohlers, M., Cin-NYY	61	67.2	1	10	3	0	.786	9	1	0	0	.11
Wolf, Randy, Phi	28	163.0	4	19	1	2	.958	6	2	0	0	.33
Wood, Kerry, ChC	28	174.1	11	22	1	1	.971	28	4	2	5	.21
Woodard, Steve, Cle	29	97.0	7	14	2	3	.913	14	3	0	0	.21
Worrell, Tim, SF	73	78.1	4	10	2	1	.875	5	2	0	0	.40
Wright, Dan, CWS	13	66.1	4	11	2	1	.882	11	2	0	1	.18
Wright, Jamey, Mil	33	194.2	17	31	1	4	.980	19	8	0	5	.42
Wright, Jaret, Cle	7	29.0	1	5	0	0	1.000	5	4	0	0	.80
Wunsch, Kelly, CWS	33	22.1	0	5	0	0	1.000	1	0	0	0	.00
Yan, Esteban, TB	54	62.1	9	6	0	0	1.000	8	0	0	0	.00
Yoshii, Masato, Mon	42	113.0	5	18	3	1	.885	13	0	0	0	.00
Zambrano, Carlos, ChC	6	7.2	0	2	0	1	1.000	1	0	0	0	.00
Zambrano, Victor, TB	36	51.1	8	5	0	0	1.000	8	0	0	0	.00
Zerbe, Chad, SF	27	39.0	1	6	1	2	.875	2	1	0	0	.50
Zimmerman, Jeff, Tex	66	71.1	5	4	0	1	1.000	10	6	0	0	.60
Zito, Barry, Oak	35	214.1	9	25	2	3	.944	34	8	3	0	.32

Hitters Pitching

Player	2001 Pitching											Career Pitching										
	G	W	L	Sv	IP	H	R	ER	BB	SO	ERA	G	W	L	Sv	IP	H	R	ER	BB	SO	ERA
Bell, Derek	0	0	0	0	0.0	0	0	0	0	0	0.00	1	0	0	0	1.0	3	5	4	3	0	36.00
Bogar, Tim	0	0	0	0	0.0	0	0	0	0	0	0.00	2	0	0	0	2.0	2	1	1	1	1	4.50
Bonilla, Bobby	1	0	0	0	1.0	3	2	2	1	0	18.00	1	0	0	0	1.0	3	2	2	1	0	18.00
Canseco, Jose	0	0	0	0	0.0	0	0	0	0	0	0.00	1	0	0	0	1.0	2	3	3	3	0	27.00
Donnels, Chris	1	0	0	0	0.1	0	0	0	0	0	0.00	1	0	0	0	0.1	0	0	0	0	0	0.00
Finley, Steve	1	0	0	0	1.0	0	0	0	1	0	0.00	1	0	0	0	1.0	0	0	0	1	0	0.00
Halter, Shane	0	0	0	0	0.0	0	0	0	0	0	0.00	2	0	0	0	1.0	1	0	0	1	0	0.00
Harris, Lenny	0	0	0	0	0.0	0	0	0	0	0	0.00	1	0	0	0	1.0	0	0	0	0	1	0.00
Laker, Tim	1	0	0	0	1.0	1	0	0	1	1	0.00	1	0	0	0	1.0	1	0	0	1	1	0.00
Loretta, Mark	1	0	0	0	1.0	1	0	0	1	2	0.00	1	0	0	0	1.0	1	0	0	1	2	0.00
Mabry, John	1	0	0	0	0.1	3	5	5	3	0	135.00	2	0	0	0	1.0	6	7	7	4	0	63.00
Martinez, Dave	0	0	0	0	0.0	0	0	0	0	0	0.00	2	0	0	0	1.1	2	2	2	4	0	13.50
Mayne, Brent	0	0	0	0	0.0	0	0	0	0	0	0.00	1	1	0	0	1.0	1	0	0	1	0	0.00
Menechino, Frank	0	0	0	0	0.0	0	0	0	0	0	0.00	1	0	0	0	1.0	6	4	4	0	0	36.00
O'Neill, Paul	0	0	0	0	0.0	0	0	0	0	0	0.00	1	0	0	0	2.0	2	3	3	4	2	13.50
Osik, Keith	0	0	0	0	0.0	0	0	0	0	0	0.00	2	0	0	0	2.0	7	9	9	2	2	40.50
Relaford, Desi	1	0	0	0	1.0	0	0	0	0	1	0.00	1	0	0	0	1.0	0	0	0	0	1	0.00
Sheldon, Scott	0	0	0	0	0.0	0	0	0	0	0	0.00	1	0	0	0	0.1	0	0	0	0	1	0.00

Park Data

One of the more remarkable numbers in this section is the low park index (57) that strongly suggests San Francisco's new Pac Bell Park is not conducive to hitting home runs for lefthanded batters. An index so far below 100—the marker for a park's neutrality—is one more statistic to consider in measuring the greatness of Barry Bonds' 2001 season.

The numbers on all of the major league parks for 2001 are here. For each park, we show how the home team and its opponents performed, both at home and on the road, with the exception being that we do not include data from interleague games. The differences in interleague opponents and ballparks would skew the data.

By comparing the per-game averages at the home park and on the road, we can evaluate the park's impact. We simply divide the home average by the road average and multiply the result by 100, generating a park index. If the home and road per-game averages are equal, the index equals 100, and we can conclude that the park had no impact. An index above 100 means that the park favors that particular statistic. The indexes for at-bats, runs, hits, errors, and infield errors are determined on a per-game basis; all other stats are calculated on a per-at-bat basis. "E-infield" denotes infield *fielding* errors. "Alt" is the approximate elevation of the ballpark.

For most parks, data is presented both for 2001 and for the last three years overall. If the park's dimensions have changed over that time, however, we do not combine the data from its old and new configurations. At the end, you'll find a rankings section that shows which parks inflate runs, homers and batting average the most.

Datos de Estadios

Para cada estadio, mostramos como el equipo local y sus oponentes batearon en casa y de visita, con la excepción que no incluímos los juegos interliga. Las diferencias en oponentes de interliga distorsionarían los datos.

Al comparar los promedios por juego en el estadio local y como visitante, podemos evaluar el impacto del estadio. Simplemente dividimos el promedio local por el promedio de visita y lo multiplicamos por 100, creando el índice. Si los promedios de casa y de visita son iguales, el índice es 100, concluyendo que el estadio local es neutral. Un índice sobre 100 significa que el estadio favorece esa estadística. Los índices de at-bats (veces-al-bate), runs (carreras), hits, errors (errores), and infield errors (errores de infielders) son determinados usando promedio de juegos; las otras estadísticas son calculadas usando veces-al-Bate. "E-infield" significa *errores de fildeo* adentro del diamante.

2001 Season = Temporada del 2001; **AB** = Veces-al-bate; **"Alt"** es la elevación apróximada del estadio sobre el nivel de mar en pies; **Avg** = Promedio; **Away Games** = Juegos como visitante; **G** = Partidos Jugados; **Home Games** = Juegos como local; **Index** = Indice; **LHB-Avg** = Promedio de bateadores zurdos; **LHB-HR** = Cuadrangulares de bateadores zurdos; **Opp** = Oponentes; **R** = Carreras; **RHB-Avg** = Promedio de bateadores derechos; **RHB-HR** = Cuadrangulares de bateadores derechos; **SO** = Ponches; **Surface: Grass** = Grama natural; **Surface: Turf** = Grama artificial; **Team** = Equipo.

Ballpark Index Rankings = Rangos; **Runs per Game** = Carreras por Partido; **Home Runs per At-Bat** = Cuadrangulares por Veces-al-Bate; **Batting Average** = Promedio de Bateo.

Anaheim Angels — Edison Int'l Field of Anaheim

Alt: 160 feet **Surface:** Grass

	2001 Season							2000-2001						
	Home Games			Away Games			Index	Home Games			Away Games			Index
	Angels	Opp	Total	Angels	Opp	Total		Angels	Opp	Total	Angels	Opp	Total	
G	72	72	144	72	72	144		144	144	288	144	144	288	
Avg	.265	.267	.266	.251	.258	.254	105	.272	.273	.273	.263	.267	.265	103
AB	2431	2564	4995	2491	2361	4852	103	4849	5106	9955	5057	4806	9863	101
R	319	353	672	290	299	589	114	697	735	1432	667	708	1375	104
H	645	685	1330	626	608	1234	108	1320	1394	2714	1330	1281	2611	104
2B	108	151	259	139	108	247	102	231	277	508	282	227	509	99
3B	11	6	17	14	11	25	66	21	12	33	34	22	56	58
HR	78	75	153	57	73	130	114	193	174	367	150	175	325	112
BB	229	230	459	211	234	445	100	500	515	1015	481	542	1023	98
SO	413	437	850	468	408	876	94	837	812	1649	939	771	1710	96
E	53	49	102	41	55	96	106	117	91	208	99	90	189	110
E-Infield	49	38	87	37	46	83	105	106	71	177	86	73	159	111
LHB-Avg	.275	.262	.269	.241	.256	.248	108	.281	.264	.273	.256	.270	.262	104
LHB-HR	29	30	59	26	28	54	105	86	66	152	78	76	154	98
RHB-Avg	.256	.271	.264	.261	.258	.260	102	.262	.280	.272	.271	.264	.267	102
RHB-HR	49	45	94	31	45	76	121	107	108	215	72	99	171	124

ANAHEIM

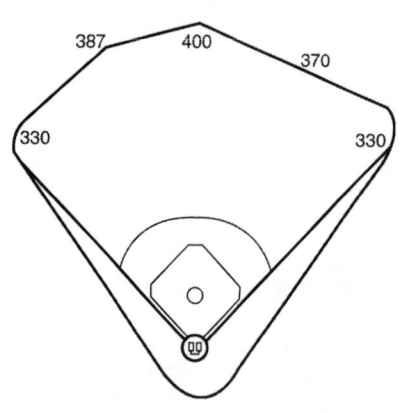

387 400 370
330 330

ARIZONA

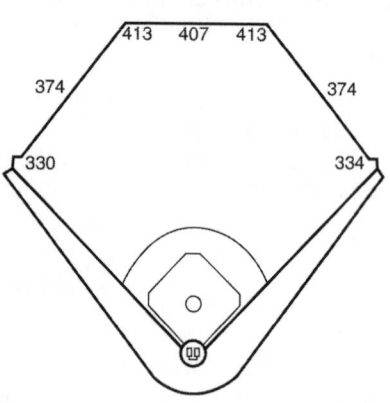

413 407 413
374 374
330 334

Arizona Diamondbacks — Bank One Ballpark

Alt: 1090 feet **Surface:** Grass

	2001 Season							1999-2001						
	Home Games			Away Games			Index	Home Games			Away Games			Index
	D'backs	Opp	Total	D'backs	Opp	Total		D'backs	Opp	Total	D'backs	Opp	Total	
G	75	75	150	72	72	144		222	222	444	219	219	438	
Avg	.283	.258	.270	.253	.233	.243	111	.281	.258	.269	.259	.248	.254	106
AB	2519	2605	5124	2578	2359	4937	100	7478	7715	15193	7745	7285	15030	100
R	408	349	757	350	269	619	117	1185	994	2179	1121	922	2043	105
H	713	672	1385	652	550	1202	111	2101	1987	4088	2007	1808	3815	106
2B	135	114	249	128	96	224	107	394	358	752	381	323	704	106
3B	17	14	31	17	6	23	130	68	52	120	48	28	76	156
HR	102	113	215	89	62	151	137	270	268	538	279	235	514	104
BB	268	211	479	274	222	496	93	778	658	1436	787	709	1496	95
SO	445	589	1034	505	593	1098	91	1303	1648	2951	1487	1724	3211	91
E	39	50	89	39	44	83	103	124	144	268	147	138	285	93
E-Infield	37	38	75	38	39	77	94	112	116	228	131	110	241	93
LHB-Avg	.303	.265	.288	.270	.253	.264	109	.292	.253	.277	.268	.259	.264	105
LHB-HR	51	47	98	51	25	76	128	137	91	228	145	75	220	105
RHB-Avg	.261	.255	.257	.234	.222	.227	113	.268	.260	.263	.250	.243	.246	107
RHB-HR	51	66	117	38	37	75	146	133	177	310	134	160	294	103

Atlanta Braves — Turner Field

Alt: 1050 feet **Surface:** Grass

| | 2001 Season | | | | | | | 1999-2001 | | | | | | |
| | Home Games | | | Away Games | | | | Home Games | | | Away Games | | | |
	Braves	Opp	Total	Braves	Opp	Total	Index	Braves	Opp	Total	Braves	Opp	Total	Index
G	72	72	144	72	72	144		216	216	432	216	216	432	
Avg	.262	.256	.259	.255	.245	.250	104	.268	.248	.258	.263	.253	.258	100
AB	2384	2467	4851	2499	2376	4875	100	7104	7440	14544	7591	7246	14837	98
R	314	302	616	330	260	590	104	1033	848	1881	1074	898	1972	95
H	625	631	1256	637	582	1219	103	1904	1848	3752	1995	1836	3831	98
2B	117	94	211	117	99	216	98	367	295	662	384	327	711	95
3B	10	6	16	11	13	24	67	31	22	53	38	30	68	80
HR	79	68	147	77	67	144	103	232	201	433	261	199	460	96
BB	190	234	424	239	198	437	98	715	631	1346	786	660	1446	95
SO	441	501	942	501	496	997	95	1232	1550	2782	1453	1492	2945	96
E	51	49	100	37	45	82	122	163	198	361	145	166	311	116
E-Infield	47	40	87	29	37	66	132	145	162	307	123	143	266	115
LHB-Avg	.240	.279	.259	.264	.248	.257	101	.262	.262	.262	.263	.260	.261	100
LHB-HR	21	37	58	30	24	54	109	68	87	155	74	70	144	109
RHB-Avg	.279	.242	.259	.248	.243	.245	106	.272	.241	.255	.263	.250	.256	100
RHB-HR	58	31	89	47	43	90	99	164	114	278	187	129	316	90

ATLANTA

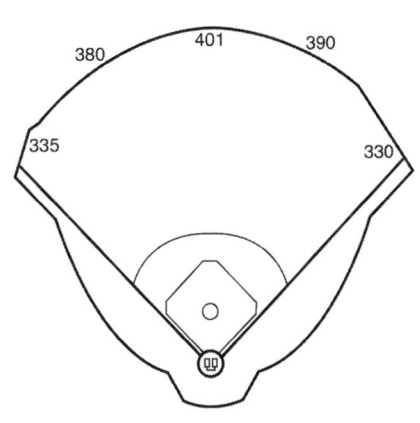

380 401 390 335 330

BALTIMORE

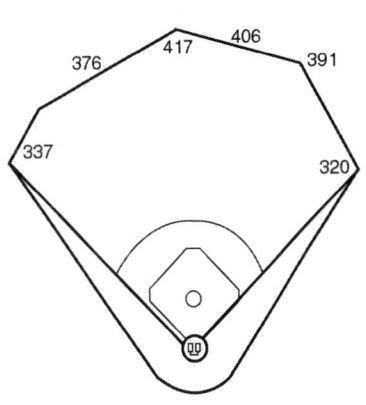

376 417 406 391 337 320

Baltimore Orioles — Oriole Park at Camden Yards

Alt: 20 feet **Surface:** Grass

| | 2001 Season | | | | | | | 1999-2000 | | | | | | |
| | Home Games | | | Away Games | | | | Home Games | | | Away Games | | | |
	Orioles	Opp	Total	Orioles	Opp	Total	Index	Orioles	Opp	Total	Orioles	Opp	Total	Index
G	71	71	142	73	73	146		144	144	288	144	144	288	
Avg	.242	.260	.252	.257	.272	.265	95	.273	.262	.268	.272	.284	.278	96
AB	2306	2505	4811	2567	2464	5031	98	4777	5026	9803	5145	4854	9999	98
R	267	351	618	349	373	722	88	715	731	1446	748	830	1578	92
H	558	652	1210	661	671	1332	93	1306	1318	2624	1400	1377	2777	94
2B	104	128	232	139	152	291	83	244	198	442	300	297	597	76
3B	11	10	21	10	17	27	81	16	27	43	25	36	61	72
HR	50	87	137	63	83	146	98	161	188	349	177	182	359	99
BB	217	221	438	239	233	472	97	548	584	1132	496	595	1091	106
SO	421	432	853	451	409	860	104	786	933	1719	819	842	1661	106
E	47	48	95	56	52	108	90	94	83	177	95	98	193	92
E-Infield	45	42	87	50	43	93	96	82	73	155	84	81	165	94
LHB-Avg	.213	.259	.239	.256	.283	.271	88	.273	.250	.261	.280	.290	.285	91
LHB-HR	24	40	64	23	46	69	96	65	72	137	87	80	167	87
RHB-Avg	.259	.262	.260	.259	.263	.260	100	.274	.273	.273	.266	.278	.272	101
RHB-HR	26	47	73	40	37	77	100	96	116	212	90	102	192	109

Boston Red Sox — Fenway Park

Alt: 21 feet   **Surface:** Grass

| | 2001 Season | | | | | | | 1999-2001 | | | | | | |
| | Home Games | | | Away Games | | | | Home Games | | | Away Games | | | |
	Red Sox	Opp	Total	Red Sox	Opp	Total	Index	Red Sox	Opp	Total	Red Sox	Opp	Total	Index
G	72	72	144	71	71	142		216	216	432	215	215	430	
Avg	.277	.254	.265	.260	.255	.258	103	.281	.260	.270	.266	.248	.257	105
AB	2484	2542	5026	2524	2401	4925	101	7342	7612	14954	7656	7184	14840	100
R	361	342	703	342	323	665	104	1118	1002	2120	1076	951	2027	104
H	687	645	1332	657	612	1269	104	2062	1976	4038	2036	1781	3817	105
2B	150	138	288	135	114	249	113	461	393	854	415	353	768	110
3B	18	9	27	8	16	24	110	53	34	87	39	34	73	118
HR	87	66	153	93	61	154	97	214	196	410	277	220	497	82
BB	246	233	479	223	243	466	101	789	637	1426	769	697	1466	97
SO	495	601	1096	503	535	1038	103	1323	1653	2976	1390	1507	2897	102
E	48	39	87	51	46	97	88	175	141	316	132	123	255	123
E-Infield	40	37	77	42	42	84	90	150	119	269	113	97	210	128
LHB-Avg	.280	.257	.268	.256	.241	.248	108	.281	.263	.272	.259	.245	.252	108
LHB-HR	42	28	70	46	32	78	90	112	72	184	150	101	251	75
RHB-Avg	.274	.251	.262	.264	.268	.266	99	.281	.256	.268	.272	.251	.262	102
RHB-HR	45	38	83	47	29	76	105	102	124	226	127	119	246	89

BOSTON

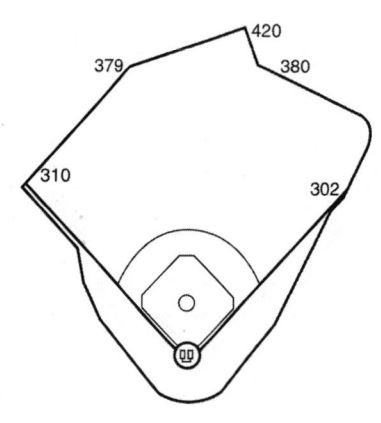

CHICAGO CUBS

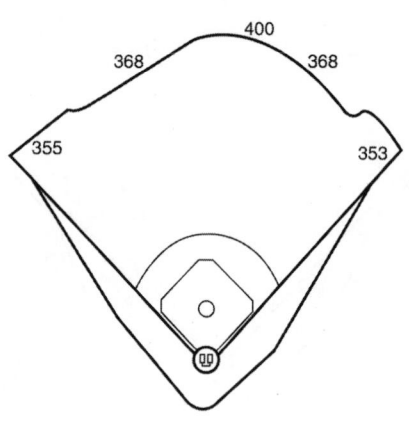

Chicago Cubs — Wrigley Field

Alt: 595 feet   **Surface:** Grass

| | 2001 Season | | | | | | | 1999-2001 | | | | | | |
| | Home Games | | | Away Games | | | | Home Games | | | Away Games | | | |
	Cubs	Opp	Total	Cubs	Opp	Total	Index	Cubs	Opp	Total	Cubs	Opp	Total	Index
G	72	72	144	75	75	150		218	218	436	221	221	442	
Avg	.268	.234	.251	.251	.262	.256	98	.265	.257	.261	.249	.277	.263	99
AB	2333	2432	4765	2573	2512	5085	98	7227	7608	14835	7623	7453	15076	100
R	353	288	641	345	345	690	97	1034	1081	2115	1021	1216	2237	96
H	626	568	1194	646	658	1304	95	1917	1956	3873	1901	2063	3964	99
2B	110	117	227	130	135	265	91	350	358	708	373	402	775	93
3B	15	7	22	15	17	32	73	44	26	70	38	62	100	71
HR	83	69	152	93	84	177	92	246	275	521	265	286	551	96
BB	265	246	511	257	257	514	106	826	784	1610	779	797	1576	104
SO	478	640	1118	503	596	1099	109	1477	1643	3120	1574	1511	3085	103
E	35	57	92	58	50	108	89	142	151	293	163	139	302	98
E-Infield	28	52	80	48	44	92	91	108	127	235	136	120	256	93
LHB-Avg	.261	.236	.248	.216	.289	.254	97	.256	.256	.256	.232	.279	.255	101
LHB-HR	30	26	56	36	43	79	71	71	96	167	99	118	217	78
RHB-Avg	.273	.232	.252	.270	.244	.258	98	.271	.258	.264	.261	.275	.268	99
RHB-HR	53	43	96	57	41	98	109	175	179	354	166	168	334	108

Chicago White Sox — Comiskey Park

Alt: 595 feet Surface: Grass

| | 2001 Season | | | | | | | 1999-2000 | | | | | | |
| | Home Games | | | Away Games | | | Index | Home Games | | | Away Games | | | Index |
	White Sox	Opp	Total	White Sox	Opp	Total		White Sox	Opp	Total	White Sox	Opp	Total	
G	72	72	144	72	72	144		144	144	288	144	144	288	
Avg	.268	.269	.269	.271	.269	.270	99	.281	.275	.278	.279	.279	.279	100
AB	2403	2534	4937	2472	2372	4844	102	4839	5100	9939	5148	4891	10039	99
R	366	377	743	347	345	692	107	789	752	1541	759	748	1507	102
H	645	681	1326	671	638	1309	101	1359	1403	2762	1437	1365	2802	99
2B	129	134	263	145	127	272	95	257	244	501	295	242	537	94
3B	12	10	22	13	17	30	72	36	17	53	25	30	55	97
HR	98	101	199	88	62	150	130	181	181	362	149	170	319	115
BB	261	232	493	205	218	423	114	500	500	1000	459	571	1030	98
SO	433	423	856	446	378	824	102	720	906	1626	840	828	1668	98
E	52	52	104	48	44	92	113	107	94	201	121	121	242	83
E-Infield	46	42	88	38	40	78	113	99	78	177	105	104	209	85
LHB-Avg	.270	.264	.266	.265	.276	.271	98	.261	.274	.268	.266	.290	.278	96
LHB-HR	31	48	79	32	27	59	135	39	83	122	55	77	132	94
RHB-Avg	.268	.273	.270	.275	.263	.269	100	.293	.276	.285	.288	.271	.280	102
RHB-HR	67	53	120	56	35	91	127	142	98	240	94	93	187	129

CHICAGO WHITE SOX

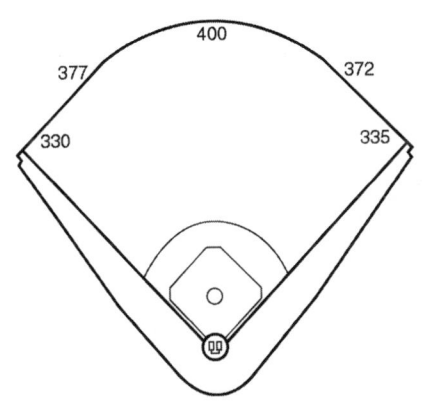

400 · 377 · 372 · 330 · 335

CINCINNATI

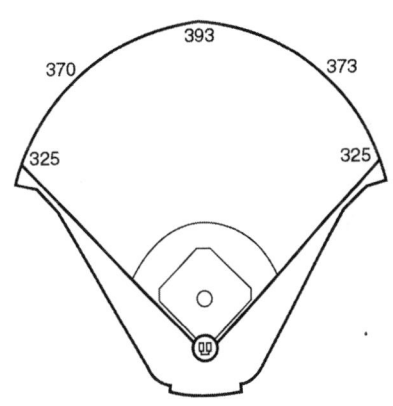

393 · 370 · 373 · 325 · 325

Cincinnati Reds — Cinergy Field

Alt: 550 feet Surface: Grass

| | 2001 Season | | | | | | | 1999-2000 | | | | | | |
| | Home Games | | | Away Games | | | Index | Home Games | | | Away Games | | | Index |
	Reds	Opp	Total	Reds	Opp	Total		Reds	Opp	Total	Reds	Opp	Total	
G	75	75	150	72	72	144		149	149	298	147	147	294	
Avg	.265	.280	.273	.263	.273	.268	102	.274	.255	.265	.270	.243	.257	103
AB	2560	2693	5253	2519	2431	4950	102	4975	5152	10127	5243	4762	10005	100
R	325	409	734	352	360	712	99	758	711	1469	760	609	1369	106
H	678	755	1433	663	663	1326	104	1364	1315	2679	1415	1155	2570	103
2B	153	171	324	124	139	263	116	276	305	581	283	261	544	106
3B	5	10	15	16	15	31	46	29	27	56	41	27	68	81
HR	76	98	174	87	76	163	101	174	201	375	195	139	334	111
BB	209	242	451	215	235	450	94	542	590	1132	474	582	1056	106
SO	499	450	949	568	422	990	90	895	977	1872	1031	926	1957	95
E	64	59	123	64	56	120	98	97	83	180	97	115	212	84
E-Infield	53	49	102	52	50	102	96	77	70	147	77	93	170	85
LHB-Avg	.295	.280	.288	.288	.282	.285	101	.289	.263	.275	.286	.249	.267	103
LHB-HR	37	44	81	53	39	92	84	66	67	133	85	57	142	96
RHB-Avg	.242	.280	.262	.243	.267	.255	103	.266	.251	.259	.261	.239	.251	103
RHB-HR	39	54	93	34	37	71	123	108	134	242	110	82	192	122

Cleveland Indians — Jacobs Field

Alt: 660 feet **Surface:** Grass

	2001 Season							1999-2001						
	Home Games			Away Games			Index	Home Games			Away Games			Index
	Indians	Opp	Total	Indians	Opp	Total		Indians	Opp	Total	Indians	Opp	Total	
G	71	71	142	73	73	146		215	215	430	217	217	434	
Avg	.281	.272	.276	.278	.269	.274	101	.292	.274	.283	.282	.268	.275	103
AB	2405	2518	4923	2563	2457	5020	101	7326	7671	14997	7721	7258	14979	101
R	390	371	761	410	366	776	101	1280	1142	2422	1293	1093	2386	102
H	675	684	1359	712	662	1374	102	2136	2101	4237	2181	1943	4124	104
2B	130	148	278	132	142	274	103	389	447	836	438	387	825	101
3B	10	8	18	23	17	40	46	40	37	77	50	43	93	83
HR	101	75	176	86	59	145	124	303	244	547	259	215	474	115
BB	255	254	509	252	259	511	102	885	827	1712	882	832	1714	100
SO	474	557	1031	481	522	1003	105	1386	1629	3015	1449	1518	2967	101
E	46	38	84	51	57	108	80	137	157	294	114	172	286	104
E-Infield	41	32	73	37	45	82	92	114	126	240	89	139	228	106
LHB-Avg	.281	.275	.278	.277	.295	.286	97	.293	.269	.281	.278	.278	.278	101
LHB-HR	50	29	79	40	24	64	118	152	115	267	121	93	214	120
RHB-Avg	.281	.269	.275	.278	.253	.265	103	.291	.278	.284	.287	.260	.273	104
RHB-HR	51	46	97	46	35	81	128	151	129	280	138	122	260	111

CLEVELAND

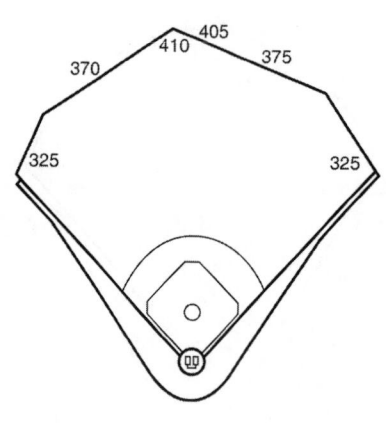

COLORADO

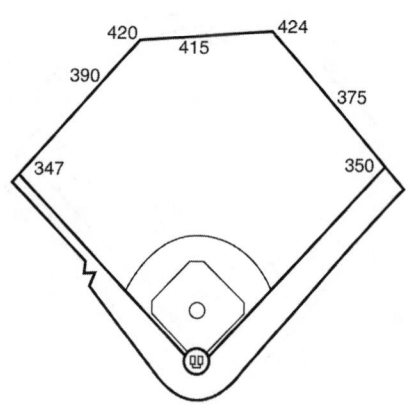

Colorado Rockies — Coors Field

Alt: 5280 feet **Surface:** Grass

	2001 Season							1999-2001						
	Home Games			Away Games			Index	Home Games			Away Games			Index
	Rockies	Opp	Total	Rockies	Opp	Total		Rockies	Opp	Total	Rockies	Opp	Total	
G	75	75	150	75	75	150		225	225	450	225	225	450	
Avg	.337	.287	.312	.255	.257	.256	122	.332	.307	.319	.252	.260	.256	125
AB	2668	2666	5334	2619	2456	5075	105	8053	8177	16230	7767	7331	15098	107
R	525	487	1012	347	343	690	147	1628	1560	3188	973	1043	2016	158
H	898	766	1664	667	630	1297	128	2673	2509	5182	1955	1906	3861	134
2B	181	174	355	124	161	285	119	511	503	1014	375	427	802	118
3B	38	16	54	16	17	33	156	95	57	152	44	48	92	154
HR	118	125	243	85	86	171	135	355	392	747	205	229	434	160
BB	224	305	529	252	252	504	100	777	936	1713	725	840	1565	102
SO	437	495	932	523	491	1014	87	1177	1449	2626	1429	1404	2833	86
E	48	55	103	43	51	94	110	149	205	354	145	162	307	115
E-Infield	33	42	75	35	49	84	89	112	165	277	122	151	273	101
LHB-Avg	.362	.280	.329	.274	.266	.271	122	.347	.299	.326	.269	.272	.270	121
LHB-HR	69	43	112	53	30	83	126	181	144	325	114	86	200	153
RHB-Avg	.308	.291	.298	.234	.252	.244	122	.317	.311	.314	.235	.253	.245	128
RHB-HR	49	82	131	32	56	88	143	174	248	422	91	143	234	166

Detroit Tigers — Comerica Park

Alt: 585 feet **Surface:** Grass

	2001 Season							2000 Season						
	Home Games			Away Games				Home Games			Away Games			
	Tigers	Opp	Total	Tigers	Opp	Total	Index	Tigers	Opp	Total	Tigers	Opp	Total	Index
G	72	72	144	72	72	144		72	72	144	72	72	144	
Avg	.263	.276	.270	.253	.296	.275	98	.280	.281	.280	.275	.281	.278	101
AB	2394	2503	4897	2520	2507	5027	97	2445	2572	5017	2573	2430	5003	100
R	309	357	666	324	414	738	90	350	358	708	396	401	797	89
H	629	692	1321	637	743	1380	96	684	723	1407	708	682	1390	101
2B	118	133	251	141	164	305	84	136	143	279	134	126	260	107
3B	40	27	67	15	18	33	208	20	19	39	16	21	37	105
HR	50	60	110	69	94	163	69	64	58	122	102	98	200	61
BB	210	255	465	201	234	435	110	273	203	476	233	250	483	98
SO	375	359	734	477	388	865	87	388	413	801	476	434	910	88
E	66	57	123	57	59	116	106	50	57	107	46	49	95	113
E-Infield	54	52	106	40	51	91	116	39	46	85	38	41	79	108
LHB-Avg	.279	.295	.287	.260	.284	.272	106	.291	.272	.280	.260	.261	.261	107
LHB-HR	27	43	70	30	44	74	96	27	37	64	33	56	89	72
RHB-Avg	.249	.261	.255	.247	.308	.276	92	.273	.289	.281	.282	.300	.290	97
RHB-HR	23	17	40	39	50	89	46	37	21	58	69	42	111	52

DETROIT

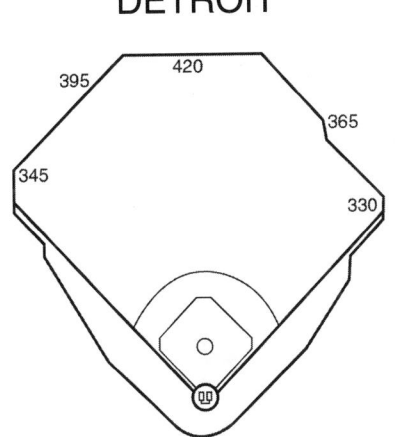

395 / 420 / 365 / 345 / 330

FLORIDA

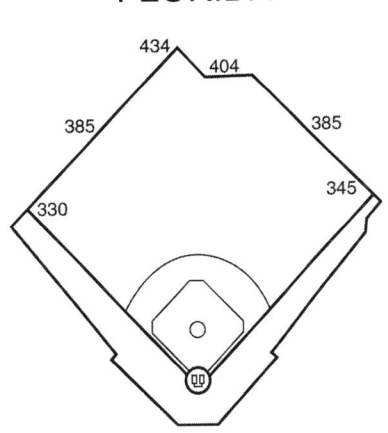

434 / 404 / 385 / 385 / 330 / 345

Florida Marlins — Pro Player Stadium

Alt: 10 feet **Surface:** Grass

	2001 Season							1999-2001						
	Home Games			Away Games				Home Games			Away Games			
	Marlins	Opp	Total	Marlins	Opp	Total	Index	Marlins	Opp	Total	Marlins	Opp	Total	Index
G	71	71	142	73	73	146		214	214	428	218	218	436	
Avg	.261	.245	.253	.259	.275	.267	95	.261	.255	.258	.258	.284	.271	95
AB	2342	2419	4761	2570	2414	4984	98	7182	7406	14588	7593	7243	14836	100
R	312	304	616	321	387	708	89	913	967	1880	944	1191	2135	90
H	612	592	1204	666	665	1331	93	1874	1886	3760	1957	2058	4015	95
2B	132	125	257	154	132	286	94	363	375	738	388	395	783	96
3B	18	24	42	6	20	26	169	56	68	124	33	51	84	150
HR	72	67	139	75	76	151	96	177	203	380	228	240	468	83
BB	220	276	496	197	299	496	105	712	848	1560	614	910	1524	104
SO	482	564	1046	540	427	967	113	1483	1548	3031	1655	1223	2878	107
E	41	39	80	55	42	97	85	148	150	298	170	137	307	99
E-Infield	34	32	66	44	31	75	90	127	122	249	134	110	244	104
LHB-Avg	.261	.253	.255	.267	.281	.276	92	.272	.258	.264	.266	.289	.280	94
LHB-HR	18	26	44	17	33	50	87	46	74	120	50	109	159	74
RHB-Avg	.261	.237	.252	.257	.271	.262	96	.256	.252	.254	.254	.280	.266	96
RHB-HR	54	41	95	58	43	101	102	131	129	260	178	131	309	87

Houston Astros — Enron Field

Alt: 22 feet   **Surface:** Grass

| | 2001 Season | | | | | | | 2000-2001 | | | | | | |
| | Home Games | | | Away Games | | | | Home Games | | | Away Games | | | |
	Astros	Opp	Total	Astros	Opp	Total	Index	Astros	Opp	Total	Astros	Opp	Total	Index
G	75	75	150	72	72	144		147	147	294	147	147	294	
Avg	.276	.257	.266	.261	.260	.261	102	.279	.274	.276	.267	.266	.267	103
AB	2515	2624	5139	2494	2424	4918	100	4937	5241	10178	5138	4972	10110	101
R	408	366	774	351	309	660	113	871	828	1699	754	713	1467	116
H	694	674	1368	651	631	1282	102	1376	1434	2810	1373	1324	2697	104
2B	148	119	267	135	120	255	100	286	273	559	256	254	510	109
3B	19	13	32	10	11	21	146	43	40	83	20	27	47	175
HR	101	115	216	86	83	169	122	224	234	458	190	181	371	123
BB	264	219	483	269	217	486	95	577	492	1069	577	497	1074	99
SO	509	620	1129	506	511	1017	106	987	1112	2099	1053	974	2027	103
E	47	58	105	52	48	100	101	101	99	200	119	104	223	90
E-Infield	41	49	90	47	41	88	98	87	82	169	99	89	188	90
LHB-Avg	.312	.276	.287	.263	.258	.259	111	.295	.299	.298	.281	.273	.276	108
LHB-HR	20	55	75	22	30	52	146	59	113	172	48	76	124	144
RHB-Avg	.268	.243	.257	.261	.262	.261	98	.274	.255	.265	.262	.261	.262	101
RHB-HR	81	60	141	64	53	117	112	165	121	286	142	105	247	113

HOUSTON

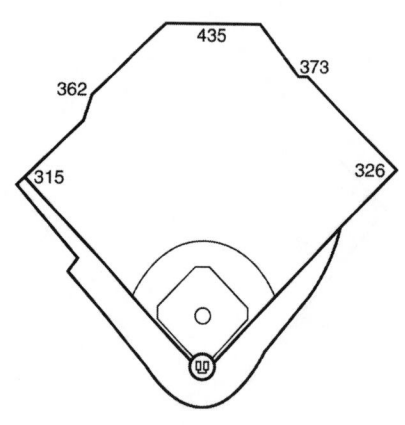

435 373 362 315 326

KANSAS CITY

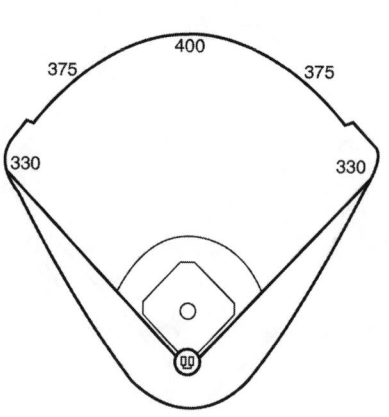

400 375 375 330 330

Kansas City Royals — Ewing M. Kauffman Stadium

Alt: 750 feet   **Surface:** Grass

| | 2001 Season | | | | | | | 1999-2001 | | | | | | |
| | Home Games | | | Away Games | | | | Home Games | | | Away Games | | | |
	Royals	Opp	Total	Royals	Opp	Total	Index	Royals	Opp	Total	Royals	Opp	Total	Index
G	72	72	144	72	72	144		215	215	430	216	216	432	
Avg	.272	.291	.282	.263	.262	.263	107	.288	.289	.288	.270	.271	.270	107
AB	2480	2588	5068	2547	2362	4909	103	7427	7701	15128	7630	7155	14785	103
R	340	421	761	321	347	668	114	1135	1236	2371	1050	1154	2204	108
H	675	752	1427	670	619	1289	111	2140	2224	4364	2057	1939	3996	110
2B	117	134	251	131	103	234	104	360	383	743	388	343	731	99
3B	20	22	42	16	15	31	131	65	53	118	41	38	79	146
HR	65	98	163	70	90	160	99	213	285	498	188	293	481	101
BB	180	243	423	179	275	454	90	623	821	1444	648	888	1536	92
SO	370	425	795	428	369	797	97	1087	1193	2280	1259	1143	2402	93
E	57	57	114	46	60	106	108	152	180	332	150	190	340	98
E-Infield	47	44	91	37	55	92	99	121	146	267	121	167	288	93
LHB-Avg	.273	.293	.285	.263	.263	.263	108	.287	.294	.291	.263	.271	.268	109
LHB-HR	13	49	62	32	46	78	78	44	139	183	56	141	197	89
RHB-Avg	.272	.288	.279	.263	.261	.262	106	.289	.284	.287	.273	.271	.272	105
RHB-HR	52	49	101	38	44	82	118	169	146	315	132	152	284	110

Los Angeles Dodgers — Dodger Stadium

Alt: 340 feet **Surface:** Grass

	2001 Season							1999-2001						
	Home Games			Away Games				Home Games			Away Games			
	Dodgers	Opp	Total	Dodgers	Opp	Total	Index	Dodgers	Opp	Total	Dodgers	Opp	Total	Index
G	72	72	144	75	75	150		219	219	438	222	222	444	
Avg	.248	.239	.243	.264	.260	.262	93	.256	.241	.248	.262	.265	.264	94
AB	2346	2477	4823	2626	2469	5095	99	7187	7529	14716	7806	7428	15234	98
R	299	292	591	401	368	769	80	962	961	1923	1184	1076	2260	86
H	581	592	1173	692	643	1335	92	1837	1818	3655	2049	1969	4018	92
2B	112	107	219	130	135	265	87	314	331	645	396	408	804	83
3B	11	9	20	16	13	29	73	28	24	52	45	42	87	62
HR	86	75	161	104	89	193	88	269	249	518	286	256	542	99
BB	241	238	479	230	227	457	111	775	783	1558	839	755	1594	101
SO	474	562	1036	494	540	1034	106	1392	1593	2985	1489	1524	3013	103
E	51	43	94	56	55	111	88	189	151	340	170	182	352	98
E-Infield	41	33	74	49	46	95	81	157	116	273	146	155	301	92
LHB-Avg	.235	.243	.240	.265	.251	.257	93	.249	.241	.244	.251	.276	.265	92
LHB-HR	26	43	69	36	41	77	95	88	117	205	92	116	208	101
RHB-Avg	.254	.236	.245	.263	.268	.265	93	.259	.242	.251	.268	.257	.263	95
RHB-HR	60	32	92	68	48	116	84	181	132	313	194	140	334	98

LOS ANGELES

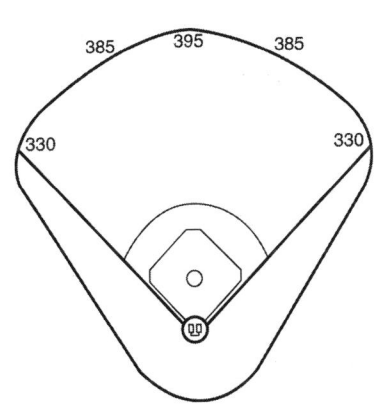

385 395 385
330 330

MILWAUKEE

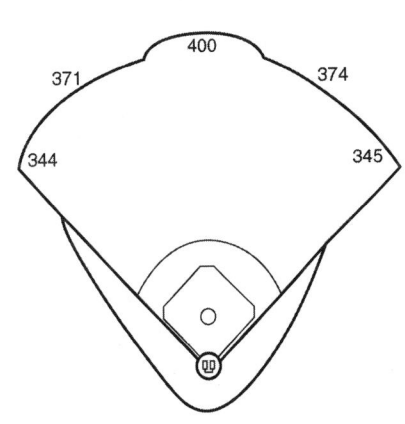

400
371 374
344 345

Milwaukee Brewers — Miller Park

Alt: 635 feet **Surface:** Grass

	2001 Season							1999-2000 (County Stadium)						
	Home Games			Away Games				Home Games			Away Games			
	Brewers	Opp	Total	Brewers	Opp	Total	Index	Brewers	Opp	Total	Brewers	Opp	Total	Index
G	72	72	144	75	75	150		147	147	294	148	148	296	
Avg	.257	.267	.262	.243	.264	.253	104	.247	.275	.262	.265	.276	.270	97
AB	2391	2495	4886	2584	2473	5057	101	4897	5244	10141	5185	4988	10173	100
R	341	357	698	334	372	706	103	655	777	1432	746	773	1519	95
H	615	666	1281	628	652	1280	104	1212	1440	2652	1372	1376	2748	97
2B	117	132	249	137	138	275	94	243	238	481	293	252	545	89
3B	13	14	27	16	21	37	76	26	23	49	24	39	63	78
HR	92	94	186	93	76	169	114	137	163	300	167	189	356	85
BB	213	307	520	238	306	544	99	582	602	1184	584	622	1206	98
SO	614	465	1079	658	488	1146	97	942	872	1814	1136	912	2048	89
E	41	42	83	48	33	81	107	109	114	223	107	101	208	108
E-Infield	36	34	70	38	25	63	116	95	88	183	82	79	161	114
LHB-Avg	.270	.280	.275	.256	.249	.253	109	.245	.273	.260	.274	.276	.275	94
LHB-HR	41	44	85	40	30	70	133	70	62	132	101	57	158	82
RHB-Avg	.250	.259	.254	.235	.274	.253	100	.249	.276	.263	.259	.276	.267	98
RHB-HR	51	50	101	53	46	99	102	67	101	168	66	132	198	86

Minnesota Twins — Hubert H. Humphrey Metrodome   **Alt:** 815 feet   **Surface:** Turf

	2001 Season							1999-2001						
	Home Games			Away Games				Home Games			Away Games			
	Twins	Opp	Total	Twins	Opp	Total	Index	Twins	Opp	Total	Twins	Opp	Total	Index
G	72	72	144	72	72	144		216	216	432	216	216	432	
Avg	.269	.271	.270	.272	.263	.267	101	.271	.282	.277	.263	.275	.269	103
AB	2406	2548	4954	2549	2437	4986	99	7307	7805	15112	7557	7264	14821	102
R	342	344	686	340	335	675	102	1023	1166	2189	930	1063	1993	110
H	648	691	1339	693	640	1333	100	1980	2200	4180	1987	1996	3983	105
2B	146	153	299	147	123	270	111	451	474	925	397	370	767	118
3B	14	20	34	20	11	31	110	62	51	113	42	43	85	130
HR	66	77	143	73	85	158	91	152	271	423	179	261	440	94
BB	230	183	413	223	217	440	94	716	642	1358	677	667	1344	99
SO	478	492	970	496	360	856	114	1343	1443	2786	1411	1155	2566	106
E	47	59	106	56	42	98	108	139	160	299	145	157	302	99
E-Infield	34	47	81	49	37	86	94	109	137	246	124	141	265	93
LHB-Avg	.275	.294	.282	.278	.261	.272	104	.278	.290	.283	.265	.274	.269	105
LHB-HR	39	35	74	47	34	81	93	83	127	210	104	91	195	106
RHB-Avg	.261	.257	.259	.262	.263	.263	98	.262	.277	.271	.260	.276	.269	101
RHB-HR	27	42	69	26	51	77	89	69	144	213	75	170	245	85

MINNESOTA

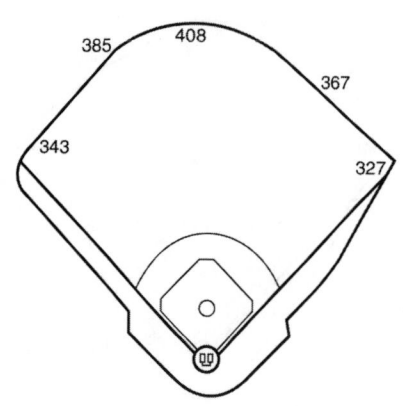

MONTREAL

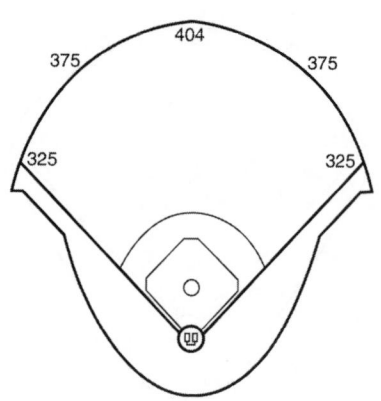

Montreal Expos — Olympic Stadium   **Alt:** 90 feet   **Surface:** Turf

	2001 Season							1999-2001						
	Home Games			Away Games				Home Games			Away Games			
	Expos	Opp	Total	Expos	Opp	Total	Index	Expos	Opp	Total	Expos	Opp	Total	Index
G	72	72	144	72	72	144		216	216	432	216	216	432	
Avg	.258	.267	.263	.242	.271	.256	102	.266	.272	.269	.257	.276	.266	101
AB	2355	2543	4898	2417	2353	4770	103	7191	7628	14819	7478	7214	14692	101
R	308	384	692	273	327	600	115	975	1188	2163	914	1100	2014	107
H	607	679	1286	586	637	1223	105	1910	2078	3988	1920	1991	3911	102
2B	165	152	317	122	121	243	127	469	436	905	377	392	769	117
3B	8	7	15	17	16	33	44	42	41	83	58	45	103	80
HR	54	92	146	55	74	129	110	204	243	447	211	218	429	103
BB	215	225	440	203	232	435	99	618	717	1335	614	750	1364	97
SO	472	511	983	484	486	970	99	1276	1476	2752	1429	1373	2802	97
E	53	47	100	46	50	96	104	190	154	344	179	156	335	103
E-Infield	42	37	79	39	42	81	98	145	127	272	142	128	270	101
LHB-Avg	.235	.293	.264	.238	.281	.259	102	.264	.297	.282	.246	.288	.267	105
LHB-HR	18	32	50	27	35	62	82	62	102	164	80	99	179	93
RHB-Avg	.274	.250	.261	.246	.263	.255	103	.267	.255	.261	.263	.268	.265	98
RHB-HR	36	60	96	28	39	67	136	142	141	283	131	119	250	110

	2001 Season							1999-2001						
	Home Games			Away Games				Home Games			Away Games			
	Mets	Opp	Total	Mets	Opp	Total	Index	Mets	Opp	Total	Mets	Opp	Total	Index
G	72	72	144	72	72	144		215	215	430	216	216	432	
Avg	.244	.253	.249	.254	.271	.262	95	.258	.247	.252	.270	.262	.266	95
AB	2370	2530	4900	2480	2404	4884	100	7062	7436	14498	7534	7175	14709	99
R	267	314	581	302	340	642	90	961	913	1874	1074	1021	2095	90
H	578	641	1219	629	652	1281	95	1819	1840	3659	2036	1880	3916	94
2B	116	119	235	130	131	261	90	346	371	717	418	397	815	89
3B	9	17	26	8	12	20	130	15	50	65	28	59	87	76
HR	57	85	142	71	87	158	90	209	210	419	251	247	498	85
BB	238	197	435	244	191	435	100	821	711	1532	900	704	1604	97
SO	459	575	1034	491	479	970	106	1327	1690	3017	1431	1445	2876	106
E	48	60	108	41	49	90	120	137	164	301	118	156	274	110
E-Infield	40	46	86	34	39	73	118	111	132	243	99	130	229	107
LHB-Avg	.241	.248	.245	.232	.270	.252	97	.260	.245	.252	.259	.267	.263	96
LHB-HR	16	28	44	20	32	52	87	61	60	121	72	88	160	79
RHB-Avg	.245	.256	.251	.264	.272	.268	94	.256	.249	.253	.276	.259	.268	94
RHB-HR	41	57	98	51	55	106	91	148	150	298	179	159	338	88

NEW YORK METS

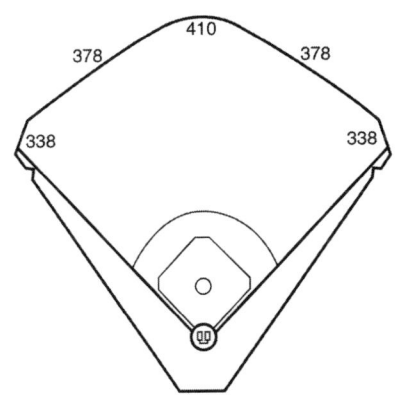

NEW YORK YANKEES

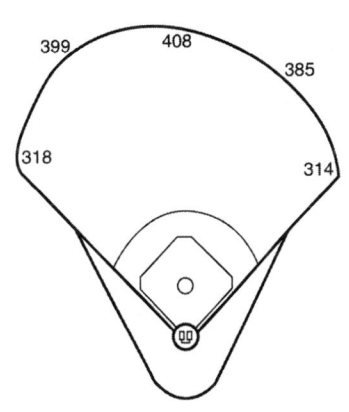

	2001 Season							1999-2001						
	Home Games			Away Games				Home Games			Away Games			
	Yankees	Opp	Total	Yankees	Opp	Total	Index	Yankees	Opp	Total	Yankees	Opp	Total	Index
G	71	71	142	72	72	144		215	215	430	216	216	432	
Avg	.276	.248	.262	.265	.265	.265	99	.275	.250	.262	.277	.267	.273	96
AB	2383	2468	4851	2565	2451	5016	98	7192	7467	14659	7679	7298	14977	98
R	378	295	673	345	332	677	101	1140	936	2076	1155	1054	2209	94
H	657	612	1269	680	649	1329	97	1981	1864	3845	2130	1952	4082	95
2B	138	108	246	128	128	256	99	384	354	738	416	380	796	95
3B	6	6	12	10	16	26	48	29	25	54	42	47	89	62
HR	103	73	176	81	65	146	125	284	214	498	255	216	471	108
BB	217	208	425	226	204	430	102	845	713	1558	787	736	1523	105
SO	406	564	970	503	566	1069	94	1278	1579	2857	1403	1493	2896	101
E	49	61	110	48	47	95	117	153	145	298	143	144	287	104
E-Infield	43	42	85	44	45	89	97	128	110	238	124	123	247	97
LHB-Avg	.290	.242	.267	.254	.253	.254	105	.273	.251	.262	.282	.264	.273	96
LHB-HR	63	31	94	42	32	74	136	157	100	257	128	105	233	113
RHB-Avg	.265	.252	.258	.273	.273	.273	94	.278	.249	.263	.274	.270	.272	97
RHB-HR	40	42	82	39	33	72	115	127	114	241	127	111	238	103

Oakland Athletics — Network Associates Coliseum   Alt: 25 feet   Surface: Grass

	2001 Season							1999-2001						
	Home Games			Away Games				Home Games			Away Games			
	Athletics	Opp	Total	Athletics	Opp	Total	Index	Athletics	Opp	Total	Athletics	Opp	Total	Index
G	72	72	144	72	72	144		216	216	432	215	215	430	
Avg	.257	.243	.250	.274	.268	.271	92	.263	.254	.258	.270	.282	.276	94
AB	2401	2533	4934	2563	2432	4995	99	7159	7583	14742	7670	7339	15009	98
R	376	284	660	434	315	749	88	1195	963	2158	1275	1111	2386	90
H	618	615	1233	702	652	1354	91	1880	1927	3807	2072	2072	4144	91
2B	127	103	230	176	99	275	85	360	376	736	443	389	832	90
3B	7	9	16	12	11	23	70	30	32	62	30	40	70	90
HR	88	69	157	90	72	162	98	290	192	482	304	228	532	92
BB	303	184	487	284	209	493	100	959	691	1650	971	749	1720	98
SO	451	509	960	449	480	929	105	1391	1379	2770	1530	1303	2833	100
E	58	44	102	56	44	100	102	172	145	317	162	146	308	102
E-Infield	47	32	79	47	37	84	94	135	116	251	133	122	255	98
LHB-Avg	.274	.241	.259	.292	.260	.279	93	.271	.258	.265	.282	.276	.280	95
LHB-HR	48	22	70	51	29	80	91	166	74	240	187	95	282	85
RHB-Avg	.239	.244	.242	.250	.273	.263	92	.253	.251	.252	.256	.287	.273	92
RHB-HR	40	47	87	39	43	82	105	124	118	242	117	133	250	100

OAKLAND

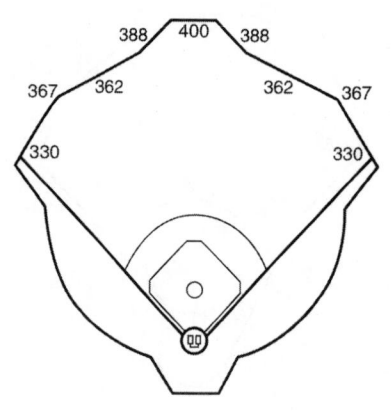

PHILADELPHIA

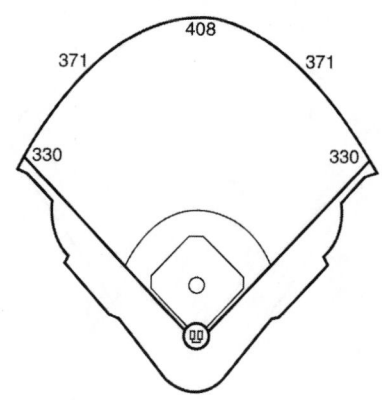

Philadelphia Phillies — Veterans Stadium   Alt: 20 feet   Surface: Turf

	2001 Season							1999-2001						
	Home Games			Away Games				Home Games			Away Games			
	Phillies	Opp	Total	Phillies	Opp	Total	Index	Phillies	Opp	Total	Phillies	Opp	Total	Index
G	72	72	144	72	72	144		216	216	432	216	216	432	
Avg	.253	.249	.251	.268	.270	.269	93	.264	.256	.260	.260	.274	.267	97
AB	2342	2473	4815	2513	2382	4895	98	7205	7492	14697	7473	7134	14607	101
R	319	295	614	337	340	677	91	1030	1050	2080	960	1081	2041	102
H	593	616	1209	673	644	1317	92	1901	1921	3822	1940	1956	3896	98
2B	127	149	276	130	144	274	102	414	468	882	358	394	752	117
3B	15	14	29	12	17	29	102	57	44	101	45	41	86	117
HR	71	69	140	72	75	147	97	199	257	456	205	255	460	99
BB	246	233	479	243	231	474	103	824	842	1666	758	740	1498	111
SO	487	519	1006	511	454	965	106	1500	1617	3117	1452	1295	2747	113
E	30	44	74	52	58	110	67	103	128	231	156	163	319	72
E-Infield	27	39	66	36	47	83	80	90	107	197	119	131	250	79
LHB-Avg	.244	.258	.250	.276	.272	.274	91	.271	.255	.263	.260	.284	.271	97
LHB-HR	35	25	60	31	18	49	117	86	94	180	65	75	140	122
RHB-Avg	.262	.244	.252	.260	.270	.265	95	.259	.257	.258	.259	.269	.264	98
RHB-HR	36	44	80	41	57	98	87	113	163	276	140	180	320	88

Pittsburgh Pirates — PNC Park

Alt: 730 feet **Surface:** Grass

	2001 Season							1999-2000 (Three Rivers Stadium)						
	Home Games			Away Games				Home Games			Away Games			
	Pirates	Opp	Total	Pirates	Opp	Total	Index	Pirates	Opp	Total	Pirates	Opp	Total	Index
G	75	75	150	72	72	144		147	147	294	146	146	292	
Avg	.257	.265	.261	.233	.281	.257	102	.261	.259	.260	.261	.278	.269	97
AB	2489	2626	5115	2408	2363	4771	103	4889	5106	9995	5128	4947	10075	99
R	322	400	722	263	391	654	106	715	731	1446	687	779	1466	98
H	639	697	1336	562	663	1225	105	1277	1325	2602	1338	1377	2715	95
2B	133	149	282	103	139	242	109	292	280	572	254	281	535	108
3B	10	12	22	12	19	31	66	38	25	63	28	37	65	98
HR	70	73	143	76	79	155	86	152	152	304	140	139	279	110
BB	215	265	480	208	244	452	99	509	588	1097	526	629	1155	96
SO	467	432	899	550	399	949	88	1013	1051	2064	1021	901	1922	108
E	69	67	136	54	55	109	120	120	123	243	133	95	228	106
E-Infield	53	59	112	45	47	92	117	102	101	203	108	76	184	110
LHB-Avg	.261	.279	.270	.235	.309	.271	100	.276	.270	.273	.266	.300	.282	97
LHB-HR	29	33	62	25	30	55	100	80	64	144	69	61	130	115
RHB-Avg	.254	.257	.256	.232	.265	.249	103	.251	.253	.252	.257	.266	.261	97
RHB-HR	41	40	81	51	49	100	78	72	88	160	71	78	149	106

PITTSBURGH

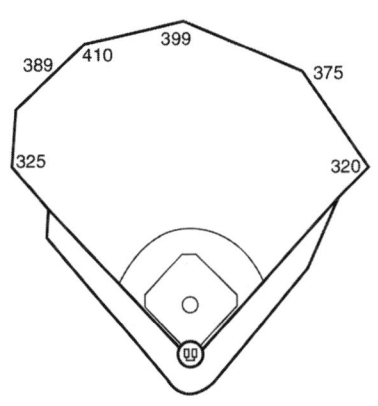

SAN DIEGO

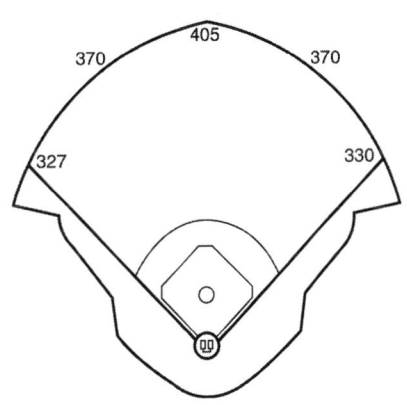

San Diego Padres — Qualcomm Stadium

Alt: 20 feet **Surface:** Grass

	2001 Season							1999-2001						
	Home Games			Away Games				Home Games			Away Games			
	Padres	Opp	Total	Padres	Opp	Total	Index	Padres	Opp	Total	Padres	Opp	Total	Index
G	72	72	144	75	75	150		218	218	436	223	223	446	
Avg	.227	.253	.241	.271	.283	.277	87	.250	.249	.249	.258	.282	.270	92
AB	2334	2535	4869	2645	2576	5221	97	7196	7603	14799	7737	7575	15312	99
R	278	344	622	437	384	821	79	942	994	1936	1135	1214	2349	84
H	530	641	1171	716	728	1444	84	1797	1893	3690	1994	2135	4129	91
2B	102	110	212	152	154	306	74	331	328	659	413	404	817	83
3B	14	14	28	11	17	28	107	42	31	73	36	49	85	89
HR	56	98	154	89	102	191	86	186	259	445	249	291	540	85
BB	292	217	509	325	222	547	100	850	693	1543	864	807	1671	96
SO	581	514	1095	589	469	1058	111	1619	1542	3161	1665	1376	3041	108
E	77	38	115	54	62	116	103	211	143	354	172	163	335	108
E-Infield	72	32	104	43	48	91	119	192	117	309	144	134	278	114
LHB-Avg	.249	.262	.255	.287	.275	.281	91	.267	.251	.258	.274	.291	.283	91
LHB-HR	26	50	76	36	44	80	99	68	105	173	81	118	199	85
RHB-Avg	.209	.246	.229	.258	.288	.273	84	.238	.248	.243	.247	.275	.261	93
RHB-HR	30	48	78	53	58	111	77	118	154	272	168	173	341	86

San Francisco Giants — Pacific Bell Park
Alt: 0 feet **Surface:** Grass

| | 2001 Season | | | | | | | 2000 Season | | | | | | |
| | Home Games | | | Away Games | | | | Home Games | | | Away Games | | | |
	Giants	Opp	Total	Giants	Opp	Total	Index	Giants	Opp	Total	Giants	Opp	Total	Index
G	75	75	150	72	72	144		72	72	144	75	75	150	
Avg	.256	.253	.255	.282	.270	.276	92	.281	.244	.263	.270	.280	.275	95
AB	2523	2642	5165	2600	2425	5025	99	2356	2416	4772	2634	2526	5160	96
R	330	336	666	412	371	783	82	407	265	672	426	405	831	84
H	647	669	1316	732	654	1386	91	663	590	1253	712	707	1419	92
2B	142	140	282	141	124	265	104	127	107	234	142	129	271	93
3B	23	24	47	15	18	33	139	24	11	35	18	26	44	86
HR	90	48	138	129	86	215	62	99	54	153	100	81	181	91
BB	301	260	561	279	276	555	98	304	251	555	353	307	660	91
SO	472	524	996	527	468	995	97	404	475	879	539	507	1046	91
E	52	37	89	54	47	101	85	30	37	67	58	54	112	62
E-Infield	42	32	74	38	38	76	93	28	29	57	42	46	88	67
LHB-Avg	.241	.259	.251	.301	.295	.298	84	.271	.235	.255	.275	.279	.277	92
LHB-HR	48	12	60	66	34	100	57	39	16	55	50	28	78	77
RHB-Avg	.265	.249	.257	.272	.253	.263	98	.290	.249	.267	.267	.280	.274	98
RHB-HR	42	36	78	63	52	115	67	60	38	98	50	53	103	102

SAN FRANCISCO

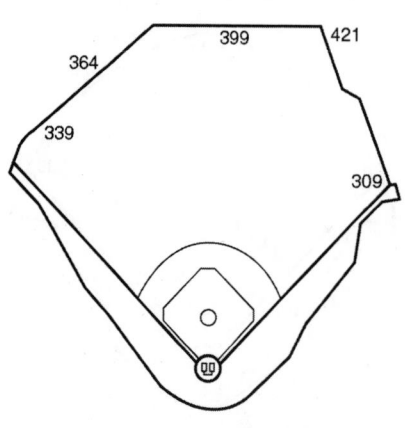

364 — 399 — 421
339
309

SEATTLE

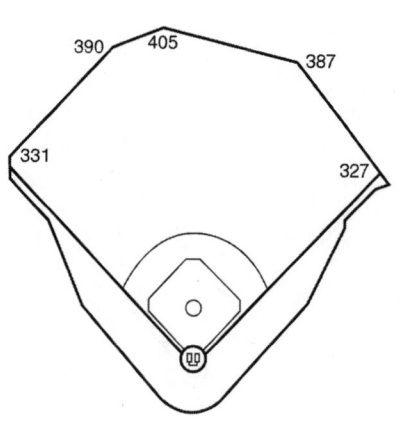

390 — 405 — 387
331
327

Seattle Mariners — Safeco Field
Alt: -2 feet **Surface:** Grass

| | 2001 Season | | | | | | | 1999-2000 (post All-Star 1999) | | | | | | |
| | Home Games | | | Away Games | | | | Home Games | | | Away Games | | | |
	Mariners	Opp	Total	Mariners	Opp	Total	Index	Mariners	Opp	Total	Mariners	Opp	Total	Index
G	72	72	144	72	72	144		108	108	216	105	105	210	
Avg	.286	.224	.255	.292	.249	.271	94	.247	.248	.248	.280	.282	.281	88
AB	2414	2451	4865	2639	2437	5076	96	3496	3735	7231	3717	3519	7236	97
R	395	253	648	421	311	732	89	534	480	1014	599	568	1167	84
H	690	550	1240	770	607	1377	90	864	926	1790	1040	993	2033	86
2B	138	112	250	146	131	277	94	154	192	346	216	206	422	82
3B	13	6	19	19	16	35	57	13	9	22	17	26	43	51
HR	66	60	126	73	82	155	85	124	108	232	146	118	264	88
BB	277	192	469	277	223	500	98	509	413	922	440	426	866	107
SO	415	463	878	460	474	934	98	754	725	1479	726	560	1286	115
E	30	61	91	40	64	104	88	64	64	128	73	75	148	84
E-Infield	26	50	76	33	57	90	84	51	53	104	62	62	124	82
LHB-Avg	.298	.233	.265	.297	.264	.281	94	.238	.240	.239	.279	.285	.282	85
LHB-HR	22	31	53	16	37	53	104	43	38	81	27	60	87	97
RHB-Avg	.275	.218	.246	.288	.237	.263	94	.252	.254	.253	.280	.280	.280	90
RHB-HR	44	29	73	57	45	102	75	81	70	151	119	58	177	84

St. Louis Cardinals — Busch Stadium

Alt: 535 feet **Surface:** Grass

	2001 Season							1999-2001						
	Home Games			Away Games				Home Games			Away Games			
	Cardinals	Opp	Total	Cardinals	Opp	Total	Index	Cardinals	Opp	Total	Cardinals	Opp	Total	Index
G	73	73	146	74	74	148		219	219	438	221	221	442	
Avg	.282	.244	.263	.257	.269	.263	100	.271	.257	.264	.261	.269	.265	100
AB	2389	2459	4848	2561	2443	5004	98	7237	7532	14769	7690	7309	14999	99
R	395	280	675	352	338	690	99	1152	1036	2188	1130	1027	2157	102
H	673	600	1273	659	657	1316	98	1964	1939	3903	2008	1965	3973	99
2B	128	112	240	127	150	277	89	337	404	741	406	407	813	93
3B	18	9	27	12	11	23	121	42	30	72	38	45	83	88
HR	88	86	174	94	93	187	96	300	255	555	273	249	522	108
BB	239	245	484	247	231	478	105	867	855	1722	807	783	1590	110
SO	457	531	988	542	455	997	102	1495	1536	3031	1741	1372	3113	99
E	47	60	107	52	48	100	108	172	166	338	152	171	323	106
E-Infield	37	41	78	40	40	80	99	140	124	264	117	140	257	104
LHB-Avg	.283	.246	.265	.282	.265	.274	97	.283	.259	.271	.275	.268	.272	100
LHB-HR	43	38	81	40	40	80	111	119	102	221	105	96	201	117
RHB-Avg	.281	.243	.261	.240	.272	.256	102	.265	.256	.261	.253	.269	.261	100
RHB-HR	45	48	93	54	53	107	86	181	153	334	168	153	321	103

ST. LOUIS

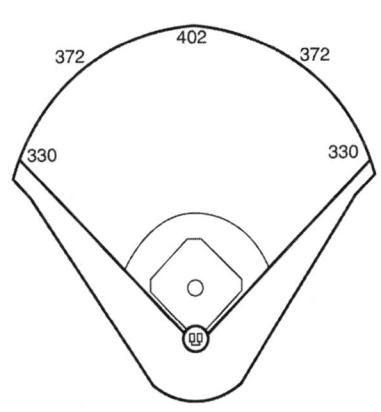

TAMPA BAY

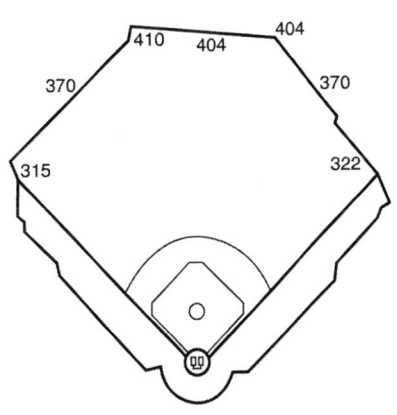

Tampa Bay Devil Rays — Tropicana Field

Alt: 15 feet **Surface:** Turf

	2001 Season							2000-2001						
	Home Games			Away Games				Home Games			Away Games			
	Devil Rays	Opp	Total	Devil Rays	Opp	Total	Index	Devil Rays	Opp	Total	Devil Rays	Opp	Total	Index
G	72	72	144	72	72	144		143	143	286	144	144	288	
Avg	.267	.272	.269	.251	.275	.263	103	.258	.274	.266	.256	.278	.267	100
AB	2433	2548	4981	2480	2390	4870	102	4805	5123	9928	4991	4790	9781	102
R	306	388	694	287	408	695	100	612	773	1385	617	776	1393	100
H	649	693	1342	622	657	1279	105	1241	1403	2644	1276	1332	2608	102
2B	157	154	311	123	132	255	119	272	292	564	220	266	486	114
3B	12	15	27	4	10	14	189	21	32	53	11	25	36	145
HR	50	88	138	54	98	152	89	118	186	304	131	177	308	97
BB	206	236	442	198	286	484	89	467	462	929	417	531	948	97
SO	475	493	968	507	422	929	102	901	946	1847	981	802	1783	102
E	49	43	92	67	40	107	86	108	87	195	113	85	198	99
E-Infield	44	37	81	56	36	92	88	96	78	174	94	74	168	104
LHB-Avg	.268	.270	.269	.268	.281	.274	98	.262	.272	.268	.269	.294	.282	95
LHB-HR	20	36	56	24	38	62	86	40	78	118	46	74	120	95
RHB-Avg	.266	.273	.270	.236	.270	.254	106	.256	.276	.265	.247	.264	.255	104
RHB-HR	30	52	82	30	60	90	91	78	108	186	85	103	188	99

Texas Rangers — The Ballpark in Arlington
Alt: 551 feet **Surface:** Grass

	2001 Season							1999-2001						
	Home Games			Away Games				Home Games			Away Games			
	Rangers	Opp	Total	Rangers	Opp	Total	Index	Rangers	Opp	Total	Rangers	Opp	Total	Index
G	73	73	146	70	70	140		217	217	434	214	214	428	
Avg	.281	.293	.287	.269	.292	.280	102	.294	.292	.293	.277	.292	.284	103
AB	2497	2683	5180	2513	2372	4885	102	7433	7929	15362	7620	7271	14891	102
R	396	442	838	393	415	808	99	1253	1290	2543	1151	1202	2353	107
H	701	787	1488	677	693	1370	104	2187	2313	4500	2108	2123	4231	105
2B	138	191	329	152	159	311	100	420	514	934	439	464	903	100
3B	15	24	39	4	17	21	175	48	54	102	27	50	77	128
HR	109	99	208	111	97	208	94	298	298	596	286	249	535	108
BB	255	262	517	240	262	502	97	820	766	1586	731	795	1526	101
SO	471	427	898	492	394	886	96	1208	1282	2490	1347	1216	2563	94
E	57	55	112	45	48	93	115	179	153	332	146	152	298	110
E-Infield	52	47	99	33	41	74	128	149	133	282	122	132	254	109
LHB-Avg	.279	.295	.287	.283	.304	.293	98	.288	.293	.290	.280	.295	.287	101
LHB-HR	44	50	94	46	40	86	98	141	137	278	126	108	234	116
RHB-Avg	.282	.292	.287	.261	.284	.272	106	.300	.291	.295	.273	.290	.282	105
RHB-HR	65	49	114	65	57	122	91	157	161	318	160	141	301	102

TEXAS

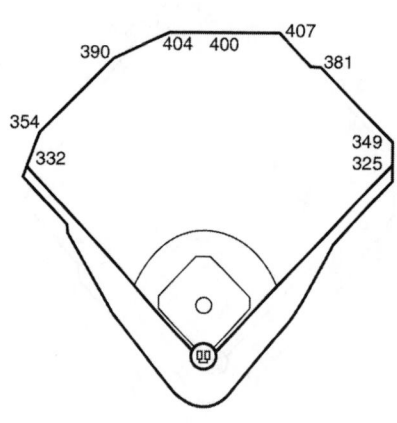

TORONTO

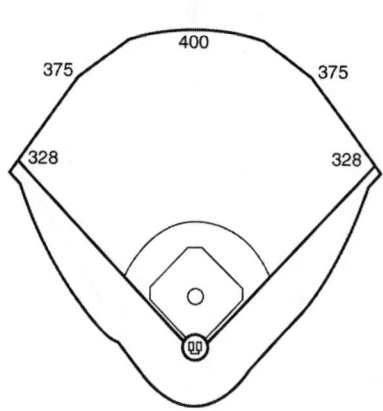

Toronto Blue Jays — SkyDome
Alt: 300 feet **Surface:** Turf

	2001 Season							1999-2001						
	Home Games			Away Games				Home Games			Away Games			
	Blue Jays	Opp	Total	Blue Jays	Opp	Total	Index	Blue Jays	Opp	Total	Blue Jays	Opp	Total	Index
G	72	72	144	71	71	142		216	216	432	215	215	430	
Avg	.265	.272	.268	.257	.276	.267	101	.274	.280	.277	.271	.280	.275	101
AB	2459	2552	5011	2544	2453	4997	99	7340	7716	15056	7716	7342	15058	100
R	348	358	706	333	310	643	108	1110	1184	2294	1110	1063	2173	105
H	652	693	1345	654	678	1332	100	2012	2157	4169	2088	2057	4145	100
2B	120	170	290	123	138	261	111	431	501	932	399	394	793	118
3B	10	14	24	18	7	25	96	24	33	57	37	37	74	77
HR	84	76	160	96	74	170	94	287	244	531	297	255	552	96
BB	218	222	440	197	207	404	109	681	731	1412	694	712	1406	100
SO	477	479	956	500	449	949	100	1364	1389	2753	1475	1294	2769	99
E	43	46	89	47	44	91	96	136	123	259	134	143	277	93
E-Infield	39	36	75	35	32	67	110	123	102	225	108	120	228	98
LHB-Avg	.246	.287	.268	.273	.295	.284	94	.275	.290	.283	.276	.283	.280	101
LHB-HR	38	37	75	54	33	87	88	160	115	275	166	112	278	97
RHB-Avg	.279	.259	.269	.245	.260	.252	107	.273	.271	.272	.266	.278	.272	100
RHB-HR	46	39	85	42	41	83	100	127	129	256	131	143	274	95

1999-2001 Ballpark Index Rankings — Runs per Game

AMERICAN LEAGUE

	Home Games				Away Games				
	Gm	Team	Opp	Total	Gm	Team	Opp	Total	Index
Min	216	1023	1166	2189	216	930	1063	1993	110
KC	215	1135	1236	2371	216	1050	1154	2204	108
CWS**	72	366	377	743	72	347	345	692	107
Tex	217	1253	1290	2543	214	1151	1202	2353	107
Tor	216	1110	1184	2294	215	1110	1063	2173	105
Bos	216	1118	1002	2120	215	1076	951	2027	104
Ana*	144	697	735	1432	144	667	708	1375	104
Cle	215	1280	1142	2422	217	1293	1093	2386	102
TB*	143	612	773	1385	144	617	776	1393	100
NYY	215	1140	936	2076	216	1155	1054	2209	94
Det**	72	309	357	666	72	324	414	738	90
Oak	216	1195	963	2158	215	1275	1111	2386	90
Sea**	72	395	253	648	72	421	311	732	89
Bal**	71	267	351	618	73	349	373	722	88

NATIONAL LEAGUE

	Home Games				Away Games				
	Gm	Team	Opp	Total	Gm	Team	Opp	Total	Index
Col	225	1628	1560	3188	225	973	1043	2016	158
Hou*	147	871	828	1699	147	754	713	1467	116
Mon	216	975	1188	2163	216	914	1100	2014	107
Pit**	75	322	400	722	72	263	391	654	106
Ari	222	1185	994	2179	219	1121	922	2043	105
Mil**	72	341	357	698	75	334	372	706	103
Phi	216	1030	1050	2080	216	960	1081	2041	102
StL	219	1152	1036	2188	221	1130	1027	2157	102
Cin**	75	325	409	734	72	352	360	712	99
ChC	218	1034	1081	2115	221	1021	1216	2237	96
Atl	216	1033	848	1881	216	1074	898	1972	95
NYM	215	961	913	1874	216	1074	1021	2095	90
Fla	214	913	967	1880	218	944	1191	2135	90
LA	219	962	961	1923	222	1184	1076	2260	86
SD	218	942	994	1936	223	1135	1214	2349	84
SF**	75	330	336	666	72	412	371	783	82

*—Current dimensions began 2000; **—Current dimensions began 2001

1999-2001 Ballpark Index Rankings — Home Runs per At-Bat

AMERICAN LEAGUE

	Home Games				Away Games				
	Gm	Team	Opp	Total	Gm	Team	Opp	Total	Index
CWS**	72	98	101	199	72	88	62	150	130
Cle	215	303	244	547	217	259	215	474	115
Ana*	144	193	174	367	144	150	175	325	112
NYY	215	284	214	498	216	255	216	471	108
Tex	217	298	298	596	214	286	249	535	108
KC	215	213	285	498	216	188	293	481	101
Bal**	71	50	87	137	73	63	83	146	98
TB*	143	118	186	304	144	131	177	308	97
Tor	216	287	244	531	215	297	255	552	96
Min	216	152	271	423	216	179	261	440	94
Oak	216	290	192	482	215	304	228	532	92
Sea**	72	66	60	126	72	73	82	155	85
Bos	216	214	196	410	215	277	220	497	82
Det**	72	50	60	110	72	69	94	163	69

NATIONAL LEAGUE

	Home Games				Away Games				
	Gm	Team	Opp	Total	Gm	Team	Opp	Total	Index
Col	225	355	392	747	225	205	229	434	160
Hou*	147	259	215	474	147	190	181	371	123
Mil**	72	92	94	186	75	93	76	169	114
StL	219	300	255	555	221	273	249	522	108
Ari	222	270	268	538	219	279	235	514	104
Mon	216	204	243	447	216	211	218	429	103
Cin**	75	76	98	174	72	87	76	163	101
LA	219	269	249	518	222	286	256	542	99
Phi	216	199	257	456	216	205	255	460	99
ChC	218	246	275	521	221	265	286	551	96
Atl	216	232	201	433	216	261	199	460	96
Pit**	75	70	73	143	72	76	79	155	86
NYM	215	209	210	419	216	251	247	498	85
SD	218	186	259	445	223	249	291	540	85
Fla	214	177	203	380	218	228	240	468	83
SF**	75	90	48	138	72	129	86	215	62

*—Current dimensions began 2000; **—Current dimensions began 2001

1999-2001 Ballpark Index Rankings — Batting Average

AMERICAN LEAGUE

	Home Games				Away Games				
	Gm	Team	Opp	Avg	Gm	Team	Opp	Avg	Index
KC	215	.288	.289	.288	216	.270	.271	.270	107
Bos	216	.281	.260	.270	215	.266	.248	.257	105
Tex	217	.294	.292	.293	214	.277	.292	.284	103
Ana*	144	.272	.273	.273	144	.263	.267	.265	103
Min	216	.271	.282	.277	216	.263	.275	.269	103
Cle	215	.292	.274	.283	217	.282	.268	.275	103
Tor	216	.274	.280	.277	215	.271	.280	.275	101
TB*	143	.258	.274	.266	144	.256	.278	.267	100
CWS**	72	.268	.269	.269	72	.271	.269	.270	99
Det**	72	.263	.276	.270	72	.253	.296	.275	98
NYY	215	.275	.250	.262	216	.277	.267	.273	96
Bal**	71	.242	.260	.252	73	.257	.272	.265	95
Sea**	72	.286	.224	.255	72	.292	.249	.271	94
Oak	216	.263	.254	.258	215	.270	.282	.276	94

NATIONAL LEAGUE

	Home Games				Away Games				
	Gm	Team	Opp	Avg	Gm	Team	Opp	Avg	Index
Col	225	.332	.307	.319	225	.252	.260	.256	125
Ari	222	.281	.258	.269	219	.259	.248	.254	106
Mil**	72	.257	.267	.262	75	.243	.264	.253	104
Hou*	147	.279	.274	.276	147	.267	.266	.267	103
Cin**	75	.265	.280	.273	72	.263	.273	.268	102
Pit**	75	.257	.265	.261	72	.233	.281	.257	102
Mon	216	.266	.272	.269	216	.257	.276	.266	101
Atl	216	.268	.248	.258	216	.263	.253	.258	100
StL	219	.271	.257	.264	221	.261	.269	.265	100
ChC	218	.265	.257	.261	221	.249	.277	.263	99
Phi	216	.264	.256	.260	216	.260	.274	.267	97
Fla	214	.261	.255	.258	218	.258	.284	.271	95
NYM	215	.258	.247	.252	216	.270	.262	.266	95
LA	219	.256	.241	.248	219	.262	.265	.264	94
SD	218	.250	.249	.249	223	.258	.282	.270	92
SF**	75	.256	.253	.255	72	.282	.270	.276	92

*—Current dimensions began 2000; **—Current dimensions began 2001

2001 Lefty/Righty Statistics

These are the numbers that consume managers when they make out lineup cards and when the game is on the line. In the late innings of close contests, managers constantly are making critical platoon decisions regarding pinch-hitters and relief pitchers.

This section reveals the major league hitters who battered lefthanded pitching in 2001. For instance, Bret Boone led American Leaguers by batting .444 and slugging .715 against southpaws. The Dodgers' young catcher Paul Lo Duca ranked first in the National League with a .411 average against lefties, and Sammy Sosa led the circuit with a robust .882 slugging percentage against them. In his 99 at-bats versus southpaws, Moises Alou batted .424 and slugged .657. Dean Palmer batted .340 and slugged at a .755 clip.

These pages also tell you which lefthanded pitchers are effective against lefthanded hitters. Eddie Guardado limited lefty bats to a .167 average and four extra-base hits against 90 lefthanded hitters in 2001. Mike Matthews allowed an even stingier .133 average against lefties, giving up just four extra-base hits in 98 at-bats, producing a .194 slugging mark against. And then there's the secret weapon against lefthanded hitters: San Diego rookie reliever Jeremy Fikac. He held lefties *hitless* in 27 at-bats.

Check out the 2001 stats that assisted big league managers every step of the way last season.

Estadísticas de Zurdo/Derecho del 2001

Estos son los números que torturan los managers cuando crean sus alineaciones, y cuando los juegos están Tardes y Reñidos.

Esta sección muestra los mejores bateadores contra lanzadores zurdos. Por ejemplo, Bret Boone fue el líder de la Liga Americana bateando .444 y un Promedio de Bases Acumuladas (PBA) de .715 contra izquierdos. Paul Lo Duca fue el primero en la Liga Nacional con un promedio de .411 contra zurdos. Sammy Sosa tuvo un PBA de .882 contra zurdos.

Esta sección también muestra cuales lanzadores zurdos son buenos contra bateadores zurdos. Eddie Guardado limitó bateadores zurdos a un promedio de .167, permitiendo solo 4 extra-bases a sus 90 zurdos enfrentados en el 2001. El novato Jeremy Fikac de San Diego no permitió un hit contra zurdos en 27 veces-al-bate.

Revisen las estadísticas del 2001 que los managers de Grandes Ligas consultaron para formar sus estrategias la temporada pasada.

Batters vs. Lefthanded and Righthanded Pitchers

Batter	vs	Avg	AB	H	2B	3B	HR	BI	BB	SO	OBP	SLG
Abad,Andy	L	.000	0	0	0	0	0	0	0	0	.000	.000
Bats Left	R	.000	1	0	0	0	0	0	0	0	.000	.000
Abbott,Jeff	L	.333	12	4	2	0	0	1	0	3	.333	.500
Bats Right	R	.233	30	7	1	0	0	4	3	4	.324	.267
Abbott,Kurt	L	.143	7	1	0	0	0	0	0	2	.143	.143
Bats Right	R	.500	2	1	0	0	0	0	0	1	.500	.500
Abernathy,B	L	.320	75	24	8	1	2	7	6	9	.370	.533
Bats Right	R	.253	229	58	9	0	3	26	21	26	.315	.332
Abreu,Bobby	L	.258	159	41	14	0	1	24	29	41	.366	.365
Bats Left	R	.301	429	129	34	4	30	86	77	96	.404	.608
Agbayani,B	L	.333	72	24	2	2	3	9	12	17	.435	.542
Bats Right	R	.259	224	58	12	0	3	18	24	56	.340	.353
Alcantara,I	L	.091	11	1	1	0	0	1	1	5	.167	.182
Bats Right	R	.333	27	9	0	0	0	2	2	8	.379	.333
Aldridge,Cory	L	.000	0	0	0	0	0	0	0	0	.000	.000
Bats Left	R	.000	5	0	0	0	0	0	0	4	.000	.000
Alfonzo,E	L	.211	90	19	7	0	2	8	8	9	.277	.356
Bats Right	R	.251	367	92	15	0	15	41	43	53	.333	.414
Alicea,Luis	L	.253	83	21	2	0	0	3	4	6	.295	.277
Bats Both	R	.280	304	85	14	4	4	29	19	50	.327	.391
Allen,Chad	L	.269	52	14	5	1	2	9	7	10	.356	.519
Bats Right	R	.260	123	32	8	1	2	11	12	27	.324	.390
Almonte,Erick	L	.000	1	0	0	0	0	0	0	0	.000	.000
Bats Right	R	.667	3	2	1	0	0	0	0	1	.667	1.000
Alomar,R	L	.279	154	43	7	2	7	23	17	28	.351	.487
Bats Both	R	.356	421	150	27	10	13	77	63	43	.437	.561
Alomar Jr.,S	L	.273	44	12	0	0	2	7	1	4	.289	.409
Bats Right	R	.239	176	42	8	1	2	14	11	13	.288	.330
Alou,Moises	L	.424	99	42	6	1	5	21	11	6	.478	.657
Bats Right	R	.309	414	128	25	0	22	87	46	51	.376	.529
Anderson,B	L	.185	81	15	3	0	2	11	13	20	.313	.296
Bats Left	R	.206	349	72	9	3	6	34	47	57	.310	.301
Anderson,G	L	.288	208	60	7	1	6	34	7	31	.312	.418
Bats Left	R	.289	464	134	32	1	22	89	20	69	.315	.504
Anderson,M	L	.327	101	33	9	0	1	13	3	18	.349	.446
Bats Left	R	.285	421	120	21	2	10	48	32	56	.334	.416
Arias,Alex	L	.267	60	16	3	0	0	1	8	12	.362	.317
Bats Right	R	.195	77	15	6	0	2	11	9	10	.273	.351
Aurilia,Rich	L	.322	143	46	7	2	12	26	9	15	.359	.650
Bats Right	R	.325	493	160	30	3	25	71	38	68	.371	.550
Ausmus,Brad	L	.186	70	13	3	0	2	6	12	11	.301	.314
Bats Right	R	.241	352	85	20	4	3	28	18	53	.280	.347
Aven,Bruce	L	.222	9	2	0	0	0	0	0	1	.364	.222
Bats Right	R	.400	15	6	2	0	1	2	0	4	.400	.733
Bagwell,Jeff	L	.296	98	29	8	0	5	22	25	15	.439	.531
Bats Right	R	.287	502	144	35	4	34	108	81	120	.389	.576
Baines,Harold	L	.000	2	0	0	0	0	0	0	0	.000	.000
Bats Left	R	.134	82	11	1	0	0	6	8	16	.207	.146
Bako,Paul	L	.208	24	5	3	0	0	3	2	8	.269	.333
Bats Left	R	.212	113	24	7	1	2	12	18	26	.321	.345
Barajas,Rod	L	.214	28	6	3	0	0	2	1	7	.241	.321
Bats Right	R	.141	78	11	0	0	3	7	3	19	.173	.256
Barker,Glen	L	.167	12	2	0	0	0	0	2	3	.375	.167
Bats Both	R	.000	12	0	0	0	0	1	1	3	.071	.000
Barkett,Andy	L	.250	4	1	0	0	0	0	1	1	.400	.250
Bats Left	R	.310	42	13	2	0	1	3	3	6	.370	.429
Barnes,John	L	.167	6	1	0	0	0	0	1	1	.375	.167
Bats Right	R	.000	15	0	0	0	0	0	0	2	.000	.000
Barnes,Larry	L	.000	5	0	0	0	0	0	0	1	.000	.000
Bats Left	R	.114	35	4	0	0	1	2	1	8	.139	.200
Barrett,M	L	.254	122	31	13	2	0	5	2	10	.266	.393
Bats Right	R	.249	350	87	20	0	6	33	23	44	.296	.357
Bartee,Kimera	L	.000	4	0	0	0	0	1	2	2	.286	.000
Bats Right	R	.000	11	0	0	0	0	0	0	3	.083	.000
Batista,Tony	L	.203	128	26	6	0	5	22	9	22	.257	.367
Bats Right	R	.248	451	112	21	6	20	65	23	91	.286	.455
Bautista,D	L	.239	88	21	3	2	0	8	3	15	.264	.318
Bats Right	R	.343	134	46	8	0	5	18	11	16	.397	.515
Bell,David	L	.256	125	32	6	0	4	17	8	15	.307	.400
Bats Right	R	.261	345	90	22	0	11	47	20	44	.302	.420
Bell,Derek	L	.167	30	5	2	0	1	5	2	4	.219	.333
Bats Right	R	.175	126	22	1	0	4	8	23	34	.302	.278
Bell,Jay	L	.224	116	26	6	0	3	12	18	23	.328	.353
Bats Right	R	.256	312	80	18	1	10	34	47	56	.357	.417
Bellhorn,Mark	L	.118	17	2	0	1	1	1	4	8	.286	.412
Bats Both	R	.140	57	8	1	1	0	3	3	29	.183	.193
Belliard,R	L	.284	67	19	5	0	5	9	7	12	.360	.582
Bats Right	R	.259	297	77	25	3	6	27	28	53	.329	.424
Bellinger,C	L	.261	23	6	0	1	2	6	0	5	.250	.609
Bats Right	R	.121	58	7	1	0	3	6	4	18	.190	.293
Beltran,C	L	.315	168	53	10	2	4	17	15	29	.372	.470
Bats Both	R	.303	449	136	22	10	20	84	37	91	.359	.530
Beltre,Adrian	L	.265	98	26	6	0	3	15	10	13	.330	.418
Bats Right	R	.265	377	100	16	4	10	45	18	69	.304	.408
Benard,Marvin	L	.390	41	16	5	1	1	6	3	10	.422	.634
Bats Left	R	.251	351	88	14	1	14	38	26	56	.308	.416
Bennett,Gary	L	.185	27	5	1	0	1	4	2	6	.233	.333
Bats Right	R	.260	104	27	5	1	1	6	10	18	.328	.356
Berg,Dave	L	.211	57	12	2	0	0	2	3	11	.250	.246
Bats Right	R	.253	158	40	10	1	4	14	11	28	.306	.405
Berger,B	L	.333	9	3	0	0	2	2	0	0	.333	1.000
Bats Right	R	.286	7	2	1	1	0	0	2	2	.444	.714
Bergeron,P	L	.250	80	20	5	2	1	2	8	22	.333	.400
Bats Left	R	.200	295	59	6	2	2	14	20	65	.258	.254
Berkman,L	L	.308	120	37	11	1	2	13	17	21	.400	.467
Bats Both	R	.337	457	154	44	4	32	113	75	100	.438	.661
Berroa,Angel	L	.400	15	6	1	0	0	2	1	1	.438	.467
Bats Right	R	.263	38	10	1	0	0	2	2	9	.300	.289
Betemit,W	L	.000	0	0	0	0	0	0	0	0	.000	.000
Bats Both	R	.000	3	0	0	0	0	0	2	3	.400	.000

Batters vs. Lefthanded and Righthanded Pitchers

Batter	vs	Avg	AB	H	2B	3B	HR	BI	BB	SO	OBP	SLG	Batter	vs	Avg	AB	H	2B	3B	HR	BI	BB	SO	OBP	SLG
Bichette,D	L	.339	112	38	6	0	2	12	10	23	.403	.446	Brumbaugh,C	L	.265	34	9	2	0	1	4	2	9	.306	.412
Bats Right	R	.265	279	74	24	1	10	37	10	53	.292	.466	Bats Right	R	.083	12	1	0	0	0	0	1	5	.154	.083
Bigbie,Larry	L	.185	27	5	1	0	0	2	1	9	.214	.222	Buchanan,B	L	.284	74	21	5	0	6	18	13	21	.404	.595
Bats Left	R	.240	104	25	5	0	2	9	16	33	.342	.346	Bats Right	R	.268	123	33	7	0	4	14	6	37	.300	.423
Biggio,Craig	L	.222	108	24	2	0	6	13	12	21	.331	.407	Buford,Damon	L	.150	20	3	0	0	1	5	1	8	.190	.300
Bats Right	R	.306	509	156	33	3	14	57	54	79	.393	.466	Bats Right	R	.185	65	12	2	0	2	3	3	15	.221	.308
Blake,Casey	L	.444	18	8	1	0	1	4	2	4	.500	.667	Buhner,Jay	L	.136	22	3	1	0	1	1	5	4	.296	.318
Bats Right	R	.053	19	1	0	0	0	0	2	8	.143	.053	Bats Right	R	.304	23	7	1	0	1	4	3	5	.385	.478
Blanco,Henry	L	.164	73	12	3	1	1	10	13	20	.284	.274	Burke,Jamie	L	.500	2	1	0	0	0	0	0	0	.500	.500
Bats Right	R	.224	241	54	15	2	5	21	21	52	.292	.365	Bats Right	R	.000	3	0	0	0	0	0	0	2	.000	.000
Blum,Geoff	L	.263	99	26	6	0	4	11	12	17	.342	.444	Burkhart,M	L	.000	6	0	0	0	0	0	0	2	.000	.000
Bats Both	R	.229	354	81	19	0	5	39	31	77	.305	.325	Bats Both	R	.222	27	6	1	0	1	4	1	9	.250	.370
Bocachica,H	L	.260	50	13	4	0	1	4	5	9	.327	.400	Burks,Ellis	L	.245	110	27	5	0	9	17	14	20	.328	.536
Bats Right	R	.217	83	18	7	1	1	5	4	24	.261	.361	Bats Right	R	.292	329	96	24	1	19	57	48	65	.382	.544
Bogar,Tim	L	.333	9	3	2	0	1	1	1	1	.400	.889	Burnitz,J	L	.224	161	36	8	2	9	29	12	44	.288	.466
Bats Right	R	.333	6	2	0	0	1	1	1	2	.429	.833	Bats Left	R	.262	401	105	24	2	25	71	68	106	.369	.519
Bonds,Barry	L	.312	141	44	9	1	17	34	44	34	.487	.752	Burrell,Pat	L	.265	113	30	7	2	9	25	20	26	.375	.602
Bats Left	R	.334	335	112	23	1	56	103	133	59	.526	.910	Bats Right	R	.256	426	109	22	0	18	64	50	136	.338	.434
Bonilla,Bobby	L	.232	69	16	4	0	3	13	3	19	.264	.420	Bush,Homer	L	.283	60	17	4	0	0	3	2	10	.302	.350
Bats Both	R	.200	105	21	3	0	2	8	20	34	.333	.286	Bats Right	R	.313	211	66	7	1	3	24	6	40	.345	.398
Boone,Aaron	L	.306	98	30	8	0	5	16	14	18	.397	.541	Butler,Brent	L	.205	39	8	2	0	0	4	4	3	.279	.256
Bats Right	R	.290	283	82	18	2	9	46	15	53	.334	.463	Bats Right	R	.263	80	21	5	1	1	10	3	4	.291	.388
Boone,Bret	L	.444	144	64	12	0	9	29	18	17	.497	.715	Byrnes,Eric	L	.269	26	7	1	0	2	3	2	3	.345	.538
Bats Right	R	.296	479	142	25	3	28	112	22	93	.333	.537	Bats Right	R	.167	12	2	0	0	1	2	2	3	.286	.417
Borders,Pat	L	.333	3	1	0	0	0	0	0	0	.333	.333	Cabrera,J	L	.257	109	28	6	2	0	17	4	18	.296	.349
Bats Right	R	.667	3	2	0	0	0	0	0	1	.667	.667	Bats Right	R	.264	178	47	10	1	1	21	12	23	.321	.348
Bordick,Mike	L	.333	63	21	7	0	3	10	2	10	.362	.587	Cabrera,O	L	.268	153	41	8	1	4	26	14	12	.324	.412
Bats Right	R	.217	166	36	6	0	4	20	15	26	.296	.325	Bats Right	R	.279	473	132	33	5	10	70	29	42	.324	.433
Bradley,M	L	.156	64	10	4	2	0	5	6	25	.229	.281	Cairo,Miguel	L	.409	44	18	4	1	1	6	2	6	.435	.614
Bats Both	R	.247	174	43	13	1	1	14	15	40	.311	.351	Bats Right	R	.250	112	28	4	0	2	10	16	17	.341	.339
Bragg,Darren	L	.333	3	1	0	0	0	0	0	2	.333	.333	Cameron,Mike	L	.301	136	41	14	2	6	31	23	26	.388	.566
Bats Left	R	.259	58	15	7	0	0	5	4	22	.317	.379	Bats Right	R	.255	404	103	16	3	19	79	46	129	.340	.450
Branson,Jeff	L	.000	2	0	0	0	0	0	0	0	.000	.000	Caminiti,Ken	L	.267	60	16	5	0	2	8	5	12	.328	.450
Bats Left	R	.316	19	6	0	0	0	0	4	.316	.316	Bats Both	R	.220	296	65	12	1	13	33	38	73	.309	.399
Branyan,R	L	.325	40	13	3	0	5	15	7	16	.451	.775	Canseco,Jose	L	.273	66	18	1	0	9	22	14	18	.395	.697
Bats Left	R	.218	275	60	13	2	15	39	31	116	.294	.444	Bats Right	R	.253	190	48	7	0	7	27	31	57	.356	.400
Brogna,Rico	L	.278	18	5	1	0	1	3	3	6	.381	.500	Cardona,J	L	.167	48	8	3	0	0	4	2	7	.196	.229
Bats Left	R	.245	188	46	8	0	2	18	11	40	.289	.319	Bats Right	R	.354	48	17	5	0	1	6	0	5	.367	.521
Brosius,Scott	L	.256	78	20	2	0	6	13	13	18	.359	.513	Casanova,Raul	L	.333	15	5	0	0	1	4	3	5	.444	.533
Bats Right	R	.294	350	103	23	2	7	36	21	65	.339	.431	Bats Both	R	.254	177	45	10	0	10	29	9	24	.289	.480
Brown,Adrian	L	.000	3	0	0	0	0	0	0	0	.000	.000	Casey,Sean	L	.276	156	43	11	0	2	22	9	23	.327	.385
Bats Both	R	.214	28	6	0	0	1	2	3	3	.290	.321	Bats Left	R	.324	377	122	29	0	11	67	34	40	.386	.488
Brown,Dee	L	.258	89	23	5	0	3	11	4	23	.295	.416	Castilla,V	L	.253	79	20	4	0	4	9	9	17	.330	.456
Bats Left	R	.241	291	70	14	0	4	29	18	58	.284	.330	Bats Right	R	.261	459	120	30	1	21	82	26	91	.304	.468
Brown,Emil	L	.098	41	4	0	0	1	3	8	16	.245	.171	Castillo,A	L	.100	50	5	0	0	0	0	6	10	.196	.100
Bats Right	R	.229	96	22	4	1	2	10	8	33	.302	.354	Bats Right	R	.259	81	21	4	0	1	4	1	20	.294	.346
Brown,K	L	.235	17	4	0	1	1	7	0	8	.235	.529	Castillo,Luis	L	.281	128	36	6	4	2	16	17	18	.361	.438
Bats Right	R	.192	26	5	0	0	3	5	2	10	.276	.538	Bats Both	R	.257	409	105	10	6	0	29	50	72	.338	.311
Brown,R	L	.353	17	6	1	0	2	7	1	2	.389	.765	Castro,Juan	L	.246	57	14	2	0	3	5	10	.306	.281
Bats Left	R	.242	66	16	5	1	2	15	6	10	.311	.439	Bats Right	R	.216	185	40	8	0	3	10	8	40	.246	.308

305

Batters vs. Lefthanded and Righthanded Pitchers

Batter	vs	Avg	AB	H	2B	3B	HR	BI	BB	SO	OBP	SLG
Castro,Ramon	L	1.000	2	2	0	0	0	1	0	0	1.000	1.000
Bats Right	R	.000	9	0	0	0	0	0	1	1	.100	.000
Catalanotto,F	L	.326	46	15	2	1	0	4	5	8	.404	.413
Bats Left	R	.331	417	138	29	4	11	50	34	47	.390	.499
Cedeno,Roger	L	.282	142	40	3	4	3	14	8	31	.320	.423
Bats Both	R	.297	381	113	11	7	3	34	28	52	.344	.386
Chavez,Endy	L	.286	7	2	0	0	0	0	0	1	.286	.286
Bats Left	R	.200	70	14	2	0	0	5	3	7	.233	.229
Chavez,Eric	L	.257	183	47	8	0	7	35	10	39	.299	.415
Bats Left	R	.304	369	112	35	0	25	79	31	60	.356	.602
Christensen,M	L	.667	6	4	1	0	0	4	1	1	.750	.833
Bats Left	R	.277	47	13	1	0	1	3	2	11	.346	.362
Christenson,R	L	.200	5	1	1	0	0	1	1	1	.333	.400
Bats Right	R	.000	3	0	0	0	0	0	0	1	.000	.000
Cintron,Alex	L	.000	1	0	0	0	0	0	0	0	.000	.000
Bats Both	R	.333	6	2	0	1	0	0	0	0	.333	.667
Cirillo,Jeff	L	.264	121	32	6	1	0	13	12	21	.324	.331
Bats Right	R	.327	407	133	20	3	17	70	31	42	.376	.516
Clapp,Stubby	L	.000	2	0	0	0	0	0	0	0	.000	.000
Bats Both	R	.217	23	5	2	0	0	1	1	7	.250	.304
Clark,Brady	L	.279	43	12	1	0	2	5	8	5	.396	.442
Bats Right	R	.256	86	22	2	0	4	13	14	11	.360	.419
Clark,J	L	.000	0	0	0	0	0	0	0	0	.000	.000
Bats Left	R	.000	0	0	0	0	0	0	0	0	.000	.000
Clark,Tony	L	.321	140	45	10	1	7	28	14	27	.376	.557
Bats Both	R	.271	288	78	19	2	9	47	48	81	.374	.444
Clayton,Royce	L	.333	102	34	10	2	2	12	13	19	.409	.529
Bats Right	R	.242	331	80	11	2	7	48	20	53	.285	.350
Colangelo,M	L	.333	57	19	3	2	2	7	3	15	.367	.561
Bats Right	R	.088	34	3	0	1	0	1	5	15	.225	.147
Colbrunn,Greg	L	.235	34	8	4	0	2	4	3	7	.297	.529
Bats Right	R	.317	63	20	4	0	2	14	6	7	.411	.476
Coleman,M	L	.063	16	1	0	0	0	2	0	9	.059	.063
Bats Right	R	.318	22	7	0	0	1	5	0	6	.318	.455
Collier,Lou	L	.326	43	14	6	0	1	6	8	6	.434	.535
Bats Right	R	.214	84	18	2	1	1	8	9	24	.287	.298
Conine,Jeff	L	.376	125	47	9	0	4	31	18	17	.451	.544
Bats Right	R	.291	399	116	14	2	10	66	46	58	.365	.411
Conti,Jason	L	.000	0	0	0	0	0	0	0	0	.000	.000
Bats Left	R	.250	4	1	0	0	0	0	1	2	.400	.250
Coolbaugh,M	L	.294	34	10	5	0	1	6	1	5	.333	.529
Bats Right	R	.111	36	4	1	0	1	1	4	11	.220	.222
Coomer,Ron	L	.292	96	28	5	0	4	17	8	18	.343	.469
Bats Right	R	.249	253	63	14	1	4	36	21	52	.306	.360
Cora,Alex	L	.293	41	12	0	1	1	6	5	6	.383	.415
Bats Left	R	.209	364	76	18	2	3	23	26	52	.273	.294
Cordero,Wil	L	.298	84	25	4	1	1	5	9	19	.381	.405
Bats Right	R	.228	184	42	7	0	3	16	13	31	.280	.315
Cordova,Marty	L	.333	108	36	4	0	7	17	7	19	.379	.565
Bats Right	R	.289	301	87	16	2	13	52	16	62	.337	.485
Cota,Humberto	L	.333	3	1	0	0	0	1	0	1	.333	.333
Bats Right	R	.167	6	1	0	0	0	0	0	4	.167	.167
Counsell,C	L	.337	101	34	7	0	0	5	17	17	.425	.406
Bats Left	R	.258	357	92	15	3	4	33	44	59	.339	.350
Cox,Steve	L	.232	69	16	3	0	0	10	6	21	.313	.275
Bats Left	R	.264	273	72	19	0	12	41	18	54	.326	.465
Crede,Joe	L	.333	15	5	0	1	0	3	1	5	.375	.467
Bats Right	R	.171	35	6	1	0	0	4	2	6	.231	.200
Crespo,Cesar	L	.160	25	4	1	0	0	1	5	9	.300	.200
Bats Both	R	.219	128	28	5	0	4	11	20	41	.324	.352
Crespo,Felipe	L	.176	17	3	1	0	0	2	2	6	.250	.235
Bats Both	R	.189	90	17	3	1	4	13	9	28	.269	.378
Cromer,D.T.	L	.000	0	0	0	0	0	0	0	0	.000	.000
Bats Left	R	.281	57	16	3	0	5	12	3	19	.302	.596
Cruz,Deivi	L	.223	112	25	7	0	2	14	7	10	.267	.339
Bats Right	R	.268	302	81	21	1	5	38	10	36	.300	.394
Cruz,Jacob	L	.300	10	3	0	0	0	2	3	3	.429	.300
Bats Both	R	.209	134	28	5	0	4	16	12	47	.291	.336
Cruz,Jose	L	.290	138	40	11	0	8	23	13	31	.355	.543
Bats Both	R	.269	439	118	27	4	26	65	32	107	.317	.526
Cuddyer,Mike	L	.214	14	3	2	0	0	1	2	5	.313	.357
Bats Right	R	.250	4	1	0	0	0	0	0	1	.250	.250
Cummings,M	L	.000	0	0	0	0	0	0	0	0	.000	.000
Bats Left	R	.300	20	6	0	0	0	1	0	4	.286	.350
Curtis,Chad	L	.191	47	9	1	0	0	2	7	7	.309	.213
Bats Right	R	.294	68	20	2	0	3	8	7	14	.360	.456
Cust,Jack	L	.000	0	0	0	0	0	0	0	0	.000	.000
Bats Left	R	.500	2	1	0	0	0	0	1	0	.667	.500
Dalesandro,M	L	.000	0	0	0	0	0	0	0	0	.000	.000
Bats Right	R	.000	0	0	0	0	0	0	0	0	.000	.000
Damon,Johnny	L	.265	211	56	11	1	3	21	18	25	.325	.370
Bats Left	R	.252	433	109	23	3	6	28	43	45	.323	.360
Darr,Mike	L	.329	73	24	5	0	0	10	9	15	.398	.397
Bats Left	R	.259	216	56	8	1	2	24	30	57	.351	.333
Daubach,Brian	L	.169	59	10	3	0	3	9	7	20	.279	.373
Bats Left	R	.279	348	97	25	3	19	62	46	88	.362	.532
DaVanon,Jeff	L	.280	25	7	0	0	2	2	4	9	.379	.520
Bats Both	R	.159	63	10	2	1	3	7	7	20	.239	.365
Davis,Ben	L	.241	108	26	5	0	5	16	16	31	.344	.426
Bats Both	R	.238	340	81	15	0	6	41	50	81	.335	.335
Davis,Eric	L	.267	75	20	4	1	3	10	6	19	.325	.467
Bats Right	R	.148	81	12	3	2	1	12	7	19	.216	.272
Davis,Russ	L	.293	41	12	2	0	2	3	7	7	.388	.488
Bats Right	R	.246	126	31	11	1	5	14	10	42	.304	.468
de la Rosa,T	L	.000	1	0	0	0	0	0	0	0	.000	.000
Bats Right	R	.000	0	0	0	0	0	0	0	0	.000	.000
Delgado,C	L	.246	171	42	8	0	8	31	22	35	.338	.433
Bats Left	R	.293	403	118	23	1	31	71	89	101	.435	.586
Delgado,W	L	.000	1	0	0	0	0	0	0	0	.000	.000
Bats Both	R	.125	24	3	0	0	0	1	3	10	.222	.125

Batters vs. Lefthanded and Righthanded Pitchers

Batter	vs	Avg	AB	H	2B	3B	HR	BI	BB	SO	OBP	SLG	Batter	vs	Avg	AB	H	2B	3B	HR	BI	BB	SO	OBP	SLG
Dellucci,D	L	.231	26	6	0	0	0	4	0	9	.231	.231	Eusebio,Tony	L	.243	37	9	4	0	1	6	1	7	.263	.432
Bats Left	R	.283	191	54	10	2	10	36	22	43	.363	.513	Bats Right	R	.256	117	30	4	0	4	8	16	27	.360	.393
DeRosa,Mark	L	.417	36	15	3	0	2	5	2	1	.462	.667	Everett,Adam	L	.000	0	0	0	0	0	0	0	0	.000	.000
Bats Right	R	.250	128	32	5	0	1	15	10	18	.319	.313	Bats Right	R	.000	3	0	0	0	0	0	0	1	.000	.000
DeShields,D	L	.183	82	15	3	1	0	6	16	21	.316	.244	Everett,Carl	L	.197	132	26	5	1	3	12	3	32	.237	.318
Bats Left	R	.249	269	67	14	4	5	31	43	56	.352	.387	Bats Both	R	.285	277	79	19	3	11	46	24	72	.361	.495
Diaz,Einar	L	.196	112	22	7	1	0	9	4	12	.244	.277	Fabregas,J	L	.143	7	1	0	0	0	0	0	3	.143	.143
Bats Right	R	.305	325	99	27	0	4	47	13	32	.356	.425	Bats Left	R	.227	141	32	4	2	2	16	3	12	.240	.326
DiFelice,Mike	L	.151	53	8	1	0	0	4	2	14	.190	.170	Fasano,Sal	L	.261	23	6	1	0	1	4	2	10	.370	.435
Bats Right	R	.205	117	24	4	1	2	6	6	35	.262	.308	Bats Right	R	.177	62	11	4	0	2	5	3	21	.239	.339
Donnels,Chris	L	.333	3	1	0	0	0	0	0	1	.333	.333	Febles,Carlos	L	.226	93	21	3	0	2	6	9	19	.294	.333
Bats Left	R	.165	85	14	2	0	3	8	12	24	.276	.294	Bats Left	R	.241	199	48	6	2	6	19	13	39	.290	.382
Dransfeldt,K	L	.000	2	0	0	0	0	0	0	0	.000	.000	Feliz,Pedro	L	.397	58	23	5	1	3	13	3	9	.413	.672
Bats Right	R	.000	1	0	0	0	0	0	0	0	.000	.000	Bats Right	R	.167	162	27	4	0	4	9	7	41	.209	.265
Drew,J.D.	L	.289	83	24	5	3	3	17	10	18	.371	.530	Fernandez,J	L	.056	18	1	1	0	0	0	1	6	.105	.111
Bats Left	R	.332	292	97	13	2	24	56	47	57	.426	.637	Bats Right	R	.143	7	1	0	0	0	0	1	4	.250	.143
Ducey,Rob	L	.000	3	0	0	0	0	0	2	1	.400	.000	Fernandez,T	L	.298	47	14	2	0	2	9	2	5	.327	.468
Bats Left	R	.243	70	17	3	0	3	12	14	24	.372	.414	Bats Both	R	.289	76	22	2	0	0	6	6	12	.345	.316
Dunn,Adam	L	.282	71	20	4	0	6	14	8	23	.370	.592	Fick,Robert	L	.237	76	18	5	0	2	9	9	23	.344	.382
Bats Left	R	.254	173	44	14	1	13	29	30	51	.371	.572	Bats Left	R	.280	325	91	16	2	17	52	30	39	.338	.498
Dunston,S	L	.318	88	28	7	2	6	17	0	11	.326	.648	Figueroa,Luis	L	.000	1	0	0	0	0	0	0	0	.000	.000
Bats Right	R	.245	98	24	3	1	3	8	2	21	.265	.388	Bats Both	R	.000	1	0	0	0	0	0	0	0	.000	.000
Dunwoody,T	L	.250	8	2	1	0	0	0	0	4	.250	.375	Finley,Steve	L	.235	102	24	7	0	2	18	7	16	.288	.363
Bats Left	R	.208	53	11	3	0	1	3	3	10	.250	.321	Bats Left	R	.285	393	112	20	4	12	55	40	51	.349	.448
Durazo,E	L	.188	32	6	2	0	0	2	3	12	.257	.250	Flaherty,John	L	.286	35	10	3	0	1	4	2	4	.324	.457
Bats Left	R	.287	143	41	9	0	12	36	25	37	.395	.601	Bats Right	R	.230	213	49	14	1	3	25	8	29	.260	.347
Durham,Ray	L	.259	143	37	7	4	6	19	14	30	.327	.490	Fletcher,D	L	.162	74	12	3	0	3	8	6	10	.229	.324
Bats Both	R	.269	468	126	35	6	14	46	50	80	.340	.459	Bats Left	R	.240	342	82	17	0	8	48	18	33	.285	.360
Dye,Jermaine	L	.293	164	48	7	0	4	28	23	31	.379	.409	Floyd,Cliff	L	.311	148	46	9	2	9	34	11	32	.376	.581
Bats Right	R	.278	435	121	24	1	22	78	34	81	.332	.490	Bats Left	R	.319	407	130	35	2	22	69	48	69	.394	.577
Easley,Damion	L	.236	148	35	9	4	2	17	17	17	.320	.392	Forbes,P.J.	L	.333	3	1	0	0	0	0	0	0	.333	.333
Bats Right	R	.254	437	111	18	3	9	48	35	73	.324	.371	Bats Right	R	.250	4	1	0	0	0	1	0	2	.250	.250
Echevarria,A	L	.341	44	15	7	0	2	6	3	5	.396	.636	Fordyce,Brook	L	.282	71	20	9	0	1	7	4	6	.320	.451
Bats Right	R	.213	89	19	4	0	3	7	5	24	.268	.360	Bats Right	R	.186	221	41	9	0	4	12	17	50	.252	.281
Eckstein,D	L	.303	165	50	8	0	3	15	13	10	.372	.406	Fox,Andy	L	.000	4	0	0	0	0	0	1	2	.200	.000
Bats Right	R	.278	417	116	18	2	1	26	30	50	.348	.338	Bats Left	R	.195	77	15	0	1	3	7	14	15	.333	.338
Edmonds,Jim	L	.246	122	30	8	0	3	19	22	36	.354	.385	Franco,Julio	L	.400	25	10	0	0	1	5	3	3	.464	.520
Bats Left	R	.323	378	122	30	1	27	91	71	100	.428	.622	Bats Right	R	.262	65	17	4	0	2	6	7	17	.342	.415
Encarnacion,J	L	.259	116	30	6	0	4	14	2	26	.277	.414	Freel,Ryan	L	.250	4	1	0	0	0	0	0	3	.250	.250
Bats Right	R	.236	301	71	13	7	8	38	23	67	.297	.405	Bats Right	R	.278	18	5	1	0	0	3	1	1	.350	.333
Encarnacion,M	L	.364	11	4	0	0	0	0	0	1	.364	.364	Frye,Jeff	L	.278	36	10	2	1	1	1	1	4	.316	.472
Bats Right	R	.196	51	10	1	0	0	3	5	13	.268	.216	Bats Right	R	.237	139	33	4	0	1	14	11	14	.303	.288
Erstad,Darin	L	.204	196	40	11	0	2	20	12	34	.268	.291	Fryman,Travis	L	.257	74	19	2	0	0	3	12	10	.356	.284
Bats Left	R	.283	435	123	24	1	7	43	50	79	.359	.391	Bats Right	R	.265	260	69	13	0	3	35	18	53	.318	.350
Escobar,Alex	L	.167	18	3	0	0	1	1	2	8	.250	.333	Fullmer,Brad	L	.202	119	24	4	0	2	18	3	25	.233	.286
Bats Right	R	.219	32	7	1	0	2	7	1	11	.242	.438	Bats Left	R	.295	403	119	27	2	16	65	35	63	.354	.491
Estalella,B	L	.222	18	4	1	0	0	2	4	3	.364	.278	Furcal,Rafael	L	.349	83	29	6	0	2	9	5	17	.382	.494
Bats Right	R	.190	79	15	4	1	3	8	8	27	.281	.380	Bats Both	R	.249	241	60	13	0	2	21	19	39	.301	.328
Estrada,J	L	.218	55	12	2	0	3	7	1	5	.232	.418	Galarraga,A	L	.268	112	30	9	1	7	24	12	30	.336	.554
Bats Both	R	.230	243	56	13	0	5	30	15	27	.282	.346	Bats Right	R	.251	287	72	19	0	10	45	19	87	.322	.422

Batters vs. Lefthanded and Righthanded Pitchers

Batter	vs	Avg	AB	H	2B	3B	HR	BI	BB	SO	OBP	SLG	Batter	vs	Avg	AB	H	2B	3B	HR	BI	BB	SO	OBP	SLG
Gant,Ron	L	.270	100	27	4	3	4	14	19	32	.380	.490	Grace,Mark	L	.295	149	44	10	1	2	26	17	14	.367	.416
Bats Right	R	.250	152	38	9	0	6	21	16	48	.320	.428	Bats Left	R	.300	327	98	21	1	13	52	50	22	.394	.489
Garcia,Jesse	L	.000	0	0	0	0	0	0	0	0	.000	.000	Graffanino,T	L	.319	47	15	4	0	1	6	8	6	.418	.468
Bats Right	R	.200	5	1	0	0	0	0	0	1	.200	.200	Bats Right	R	.296	98	29	5	0	1	9	8	23	.345	.378
Garcia,Karim	L	.500	4	2	0	0	2	3	0	2	.500	2.000	Grebeck,Craig	L	.125	8	1	1	0	0	0	1	2	.222	.250
Bats Left	R	.293	41	12	3	0	3	6	3	11	.348	.585	Bats Right	R	.030	33	1	0	0	0	2	1	7	.059	.030
Garciaparra,N	L	.313	16	5	1	0	0	0	3	0	.450	.375	Green,Shawn	L	.298	171	51	9	2	10	27	16	33	.360	.550
Bats Right	R	.284	67	19	2	0	4	8	4	9	.324	.493	Bats Left	R	.297	448	133	22	2	39	98	56	74	.377	.616
Giambi,Jason	L	.333	189	63	11	1	11	40	33	31	.451	.577	Greene,Todd	L	.250	16	4	1	0	0	1	3	2	.368	.313
Bats Left	R	.347	331	115	36	1	27	80	96	52	.491	.707	Bats Right	R	.200	80	16	3	0	1	10	0	19	.210	.275
Giambi,Jeremy	L	.250	72	18	3	0	3	10	12	22	.379	.417	Greer,Rusty	L	.233	60	14	5	0	1	10	3	10	.262	.367
Bats Left	R	.291	299	87	23	0	9	47	51	61	.394	.458	Bats Left	R	.286	185	53	18	0	6	19	24	22	.366	.481
Gibbons,Jay	L	.370	27	10	2	0	2	5	2	5	.414	.667	Grieve,Ben	L	.293	150	44	9	2	3	27	22	51	.399	.440
Bats Left	R	.217	198	43	8	0	13	31	15	34	.286	.455	Bats Left	R	.253	392	99	21	0	8	45	65	108	.362	.367
Gil,Benji	L	.294	143	42	7	2	4	15	9	24	.336	.455	Griffey Jr.,K	L	.254	126	32	6	1	5	22	12	24	.326	.437
Bats Right	R	.299	117	35	8	2	4	24	5	33	.323	.504	Bats Left	R	.303	238	72	14	1	17	43	32	48	.386	.584
Gil,Geronimo	L	.571	7	4	1	0	0	3	0	1	.571	.714	Grissom,M	L	.254	134	34	7	1	8	17	2	35	.270	.500
Bats Right	R	.255	51	13	1	0	0	3	5	6	.345	.275	Bats Right	R	.207	314	65	10	0	13	43	14	72	.242	.363
Giles,Brian	L	.267	135	36	9	0	4	16	17	14	.353	.422	Grudzielanek	L	.295	122	36	5	1	6	14	5	18	.326	.500
Bats Left	R	.322	441	142	28	7	33	79	73	53	.419	.642	Bats Right	R	.264	417	110	16	2	7	41	23	65	.315	.362
Giles,Marcus	L	.286	49	14	2	0	2	8	7	10	.375	.449	Guerrero,V	L	.319	135	43	11	2	8	27	25	17	.420	.607
Bats Right	R	.256	195	50	8	2	7	23	21	27	.329	.426	Bats Right	R	.304	464	141	34	2	26	81	35	71	.363	.554
Gilkey,B	L	.268	56	15	2	0	2	9	8	14	.358	.411	Guerrero,W	L	.250	48	12	1	0	1	4	1	6	.265	.333
Bats Right	R	.280	50	14	4	0	0	5	3	17	.315	.360	Bats Both	R	.383	94	36	4	1	0	4	2	11	.396	.447
Ginter,Keith	L	.000	1	0	0	0	0	0	0	0	.000	.000	Guillen,C	L	.295	139	41	5	1	3	16	11	27	.351	.410
Bats Right	R	.000	0	0	0	0	0	0	0	0	.000	.000	Bats Both	R	.243	317	77	16	3	2	37	42	62	.326	.331
Gipson,C	L	.143	35	5	0	2	0	2	3	11	.225	.257	Guillen,Jose	L	.375	24	9	1	0	1	2	1	7	.400	.542
Bats Right	R	.310	29	9	2	0	0	3	1	9	.355	.379	Bats Right	R	.252	111	28	4	0	2	9	5	19	.300	.342
Girardi,Joe	L	.263	57	15	3	1	1	6	9	10	.358	.404	Gulan,Mike	L	.000	3	0	0	0	0	0	0	2	.000	.000
Bats Right	R	.250	172	43	7	0	2	19	12	40	.299	.326	Bats Right	R	.000	3	0	0	0	0	0	2	0	.400	.000
Glanville,D	L	.290	131	38	6	0	5	14	9	15	.340	.450	Gutierrez,R	L	.258	124	32	3	0	2	10	7	10	.306	.331
Bats Right	R	.254	503	128	18	3	9	41	10	76	.270	.356	Bats Right	R	.300	404	121	20	3	8	56	33	46	.356	.423
Glaus,Troy	L	.252	151	38	9	2	9	25	41	32	.407	.517	Guzman,C	L	.312	125	39	10	6	2	9	3	23	.338	.536
Bats Right	R	.249	437	109	29	0	32	83	66	126	.352	.535	Bats Both	R	.299	368	110	18	8	8	42	18	55	.337	.457
Gomez,Chris	L	.243	74	18	5	0	1	5	3	10	.273	.351	Guzman,E	L	.111	9	1	0	0	0	0	0	0	.111	.111
Bats Right	R	.264	227	60	14	0	7	38	14	28	.306	.419	Bats Left	R	.255	106	27	6	0	3	7	5	16	.286	.396
Gonzalez,Alex	L	.235	115	27	9	0	2	11	5	24	.267	.365	Gwynn,Tony	L	.440	25	11	5	0	1	12	5	2	.533	.760
Bats Right	R	.255	400	102	27	1	7	37	25	83	.313	.380	Bats Left	R	.286	77	22	4	1	0	5	5	7	.329	.364
Gonzalez,A	L	.336	122	41	5	0	4	13	11	18	.396	.475	Hairston Jr.,J	L	.290	124	36	7	4	2	14	13	12	.364	.460
Bats Right	R	.233	514	120	20	5	13	63	32	131	.281	.368	Bats Right	R	.216	408	88	18	1	6	33	31	61	.287	.309
Gonzalez,Juan	L	.368	117	43	6	0	10	35	11	18	.417	.675	Hall,Toby	L	.298	47	14	6	0	0	4	1	3	.340	.426
Bats Right	R	.313	415	130	28	1	25	105	30	76	.356	.566	Bats Right	R	.298	141	42	10	0	4	26	3	13	.315	.454
Gonzalez,Luis	L	.312	186	58	13	0	15	42	26	32	.414	.624	Halter,Shane	L	.291	127	37	10	2	3	10	5	24	.318	.472
Bats Left	R	.331	423	140	23	7	42	100	74	51	.435	.716	Bats Right	R	.282	323	91	22	5	9	55	32	76	.353	.464
Gonzalez,Raul	L	.250	8	2	0	0	0	0	0	1	.250	.250	Hamilton,D	L	.267	15	4	0	0	1	1	3	3	.421	.467
Bats Right	R	.167	6	1	0	0	0	0	1	2	.286	.167	Bats Left	R	.207	111	23	7	1	0	4	16	17	.308	.288
Gonzalez,Wiki	L	.345	58	20	4	0	5	16	6	10	.406	.672	Hammonds,J	L	.237	38	9	2	0	0	2	3	7	.293	.289
Bats Right	R	.235	102	24	2	0	3	11	5	18	.295	.343	Bats Right	R	.250	136	34	9	1	6	19	11	35	.320	.463
Goodwin,Tom	L	.250	32	8	2	1	1	4	1	7	.265	.469	Hansen,Dave	L	.100	10	1	0	0	1	3	1	4	.182	.400
Bats Left	R	.228	254	58	6	4	3	18	22	51	.289	.319	Bats Left	R	.246	130	32	10	0	1	17	31	25	.384	.346

Batters vs. Lefthanded and Righthanded Pitchers

Batter	vs	Avg	AB	H	2B	3B	HR	BI	BB	SO	OBP	SLG	Batter	vs	Avg	AB	H	2B	3B	HR	BI	BB	SO	OBP	SLG
Harris,Lenny	L	.000	2	0	0	0	0	0	0	0	.000	.000	Hubbard,T	L	.143	7	1	0	0	0	0	0	1	.143	.143
Bats Left	R	.226	133	30	5	1	0	9	8	9	.270	.278	Bats Right	R	.400	5	2	0	1	0	0	0	1	.400	.800
Harris,Willie	L	.000	2	0	0	0	0	0	0	0	.000	.000	Huckaby,Ken	L	.000	0	0	0	0	0	0	0	0	.000	.000
Bats Left	R	.136	22	3	1	0	0	0	0	7	.136	.182	Bats Right	R	.000	1	0	0	0	0	0	0	1	.000	.000
Harvey,Ken	L	.286	7	2	0	0	0	0	0	2	.286	.286	Huff,Aubrey	L	.172	87	15	1	1	1	14	4	21	.209	.241
Bats Right	R	.200	5	1	1	0	0	2	0	2	.200	.400	Bats Left	R	.269	324	87	24	0	7	31	19	51	.309	.407
Haselman,Bill	L	.318	44	14	2	0	2	7	2	8	.348	.500	Hundley,Todd	L	.292	24	7	3	0	0	5	2	11	.370	.417
Bats Right	R	.267	86	23	4	0	1	18	6	19	.323	.349	Bats Both	R	.176	222	39	7	0	12	26	23	78	.257	.369
Hatteberg,S	L	.176	51	9	2	0	1	4	5	8	.263	.275	Hunter,B	L	.232	56	13	2	0	1	3	5	10	.295	.321
Bats Left	R	.260	227	59	17	0	2	21	28	18	.347	.361	Bats Right	R	.303	89	27	4	0	1	13	11	15	.373	.382
Hayes,Charlie	L	.267	15	4	1	0	0	1	3	2	.389	.333	Hunter,Torii	L	.256	125	32	8	1	6	19	9	38	.316	.480
Bats Right	R	.171	35	6	1	0	0	3	4	14	.250	.200	Bats Right	R	.262	439	115	24	4	21	73	20	87	.303	.478
Helms,Wes	L	.203	79	16	5	1	5	13	6	22	.267	.481	Hyzdu,Adam	L	.167	24	4	0	0	3	6	1	4	.200	.542
Bats Right	R	.234	137	32	5	2	5	23	15	34	.307	.409	Bats Right	R	.229	48	11	1	0	2	3	3	14	.288	.375
Helton,Todd	L	.290	169	49	13	1	7	27	23	37	.378	.503	Ibanez,Raul	L	.200	20	4	0	1	1	5	4	5	.333	.450
Bats Left	R	.354	418	148	41	1	42	119	75	67	.453	.758	Bats Left	R	.286	259	74	11	4	12	49	28	46	.354	.498
Henderson,R	L	.210	124	26	6	0	2	18	33	21	.377	.306	Inge,Brandon	L	.218	55	12	3	0	0	6	5	12	.283	.273
Bats Right	R	.235	255	60	11	3	6	24	48	63	.359	.373	Bats Right	R	.164	134	22	8	0	0	9	4	29	.186	.224
Hermansen,C	L	.167	18	3	0	0	1	1	0	6	.167	.333	Izturis,Cesar	L	.200	30	6	1	0	0	2	0	3	.200	.233
Bats Right	R	.162	37	6	1	0	1	4	1	12	.184	.270	Bats Both	R	.288	104	30	5	2	2	7	2	12	.302	.433
Hernandez,A	L	1.000	1	1	0	0	0	0	0	0	1.000	1.000	Jackson,D	L	.319	113	36	6	1	1	12	15	30	.392	.416
Bats Left	R	.000	0	0	0	0	0	0	0	2	.000	.000	Bats Right	R	.214	327	70	15	5	3	26	29	98	.289	.318
Hernandez,J	L	.339	109	37	7	1	11	26	12	36	.410	.725	Jackson,Ryan	L	.267	15	4	1	0	0	2	1	3	.313	.333
Bats Right	R	.226	433	98	19	1	14	52	27	149	.271	.372	Bats Left	R	.204	103	21	3	2	2	9	4	23	.241	.330
Hernandez,R	L	.241	162	39	8	0	5	16	16	22	.311	.383	Jaha,John	L	.059	17	1	0	0	0	3	2	6	.158	.118
Bats Right	R	.261	291	76	17	0	10	44	21	46	.319	.423	Bats Right	R	.107	28	3	2	0	0	5	4	9	.212	.179
Hiatt,Phil	L	.333	27	9	2	0	1	5	2	10	.379	.519	Javier,Stan	L	.326	89	29	6	0	0	9	14	10	.423	.393
Bats Right	R	.130	23	3	1	0	1	1	1	9	.167	.304	Bats Both	R	.276	192	53	8	1	4	24	22	37	.352	.391
Hidalgo,R	L	.286	105	30	7	1	3	18	10	19	.353	.457	Jenkins,Geoff	L	.316	114	36	8	0	6	21	5	35	.365	.544
Bats Right	R	.273	407	111	22	2	16	62	44	88	.357	.455	Bats Left	R	.244	283	69	13	1	14	42	31	85	.322	.445
Higginson,B	L	.293	164	48	11	3	8	25	29	31	.396	.543	Jennings,R	L	.125	24	3	0	0	1	5	2	5	.192	.250
Bats Left	R	.271	377	102	17	3	9	46	51	34	.354	.403	Bats Left	R	.296	108	32	8	2	2	13	5	13	.325	.463
Hill,G	L	.214	28	6	0	0	1	1	0	7	.214	.321	Jensen,Marcus	L	.167	6	1	0	0	0	0	0	2	.167	.167
Bats Right	R	.079	38	3	0	0	0	1	0	13	.079	.079	Bats Both	R	.174	23	4	1	0	0	2	0	8	.174	.217
Hillenbrand,S	L	.227	132	30	5	1	2	13	4	19	.257	.326	Jeter,Derek	L	.333	123	41	9	0	5	14	12	23	.397	.528
Bats Right	R	.277	336	93	15	1	10	36	9	42	.304	.417	Bats Right	R	.305	491	150	26	3	16	60	44	76	.372	.468
Hinch,A.J.	L	.194	36	7	2	0	1	3	1	3	.237	.333	Jimenez,D	L	.241	87	21	5	0	0	9	10	19	.320	.299
Bats Right	R	.141	85	12	1	0	5	12	7	23	.221	.329	Bats Both	R	.290	221	64	14	0	3	24	29	49	.369	.394
Hocking,Denny	L	.222	81	18	6	0	0	3	9	20	.300	.296	Johnson,Brian	L	.333	3	1	0	0	0	1	0	1	.333	.333
Bats Both	R	.260	246	64	10	2	3	22	20	47	.320	.354	Bats Right	R	.000	1	0	0	0	0	0	0	0	.000	.000
Hollandsworth	L	.158	19	3	0	0	1	3	1	5	.200	.316	Johnson,C	L	.245	53	13	0	0	1	3	9	21	.355	.358
Bats Left	R	.408	98	40	15	1	5	16	7	15	.448	.735	Bats Right	R	.261	398	104	29	0	17	72	29	112	.316	.462
Hollins,Dave	L	.333	3	1	0	0	0	0	0	1	.333	.333	Johnson,M	L	.179	28	5	0	0	0	1	3	10	.250	.179
Bats Both	R	.000	2	0	0	0	0	0	1	1	.333	.000	Bats Left	R	.262	145	38	6	1	5	17	20	21	.355	.421
Hoover,Paul	L	.000	0	0	0	0	0	0	0	0	.000	.000	Johnson,M	L	.000	8	0	0	0	0	0	0	5	.000	.000
Bats Right	R	.250	4	1	0	0	0	0	0	1	.250	.250	Bats Left	R	.273	110	30	6	1	6	23	16	26	.359	.509
Houston,Tyler	L	.280	25	7	0	0	2	5	2	9	.357	.520	Johnson,Nick	L	.389	18	7	2	0	0	4	2	3	.476	.500
Bats Left	R	.290	210	61	7	0	10	33	16	53	.341	.467	Bats Left	R	.122	49	6	0	0	2	4	5	12	.246	.245
Hubbard,Mike	L	.286	7	2	0	0	1	1	0	2	.286	.714	Johnson,Russ	L	.261	69	18	6	0	1	6	14	13	.386	.391
Bats Right	R	.250	4	1	1	0	0	0	0	2	.250	.500	Bats Right	R	.307	179	55	13	2	3	27	20	44	.378	.453

Batters vs. Lefthanded and Righthanded Pitchers

Batter	vs	Avg	AB	H	2B	3B	HR	BI	BB	SO	OBP	SLG
Jones,Andruw	L	.252	111	28	4	0	5	16	8	26	.303	.423
Bats Right	R	.251	514	129	21	2	29	88	48	116	.314	.469
Jones,Chipper	L	.376	109	41	5	2	8	27	19	11	.462	.679
Bats Both	R	.320	463	148	28	3	30	75	79	71	.418	.587
Jones,Jacque	L	.182	55	10	1	0	0	3	2	17	.224	.200
Bats Left	R	.288	420	121	24	0	14	46	37	75	.349	.445
Jones,Terry	L	.276	29	8	3	0	0	2	2	5	.323	.379
Bats Both	R	.250	48	12	2	0	0	0	0	6	.250	.292
Jordan,Brian	L	.292	113	33	8	0	8	31	9	18	.350	.575
Bats Right	R	.295	447	132	24	3	17	66	22	70	.330	.477
Jordan,Kevin	L	.234	47	11	3	0	0	4	5	9	.308	.298
Bats Right	R	.242	66	16	2	0	1	9	9	12	.333	.318
Joyner,Wally	L	.000	11	0	0	0	0	0	1	0	.083	.000
Bats Left	R	.263	137	36	5	1	3	14	12	18	.322	.380
Justice,David	L	.214	112	24	2	0	7	17	10	34	.274	.420
Bats Left	R	.253	269	68	14	1	11	34	44	49	.356	.435
Kapler,Gabe	L	.269	119	32	6	0	7	18	13	13	.336	.496
Bats Right	R	.266	364	97	23	1	10	54	48	57	.352	.418
Karros,Eric	L	.255	94	24	6	0	6	17	9	25	.317	.511
Bats Right	R	.230	344	79	16	0	9	46	32	76	.299	.355
Kendall,Jason	L	.279	111	31	6	2	4	15	6	8	.328	.477
Bats Right	R	.263	495	130	16	0	6	38	38	40	.336	.331
Kennedy,Adam	L	.242	99	24	5	0	0	5	6	16	.309	.293
Bats Left	R	.277	379	105	20	3	6	35	21	55	.320	.393
Kent,Jeff	L	.295	129	38	13	1	3	22	22	23	.401	.481
Bats Right	R	.299	478	143	36	5	19	84	43	73	.360	.515
Kielty,Bobby	L	.333	45	15	6	0	1	5	5	4	.396	.533
Bats Both	R	.186	59	11	2	0	1	9	3	21	.215	.271
Kieschnick,B	L	.000	3	0	0	0	0	0	0	2	.000	.000
Bats Left	R	.256	39	10	2	1	3	9	3	11	.310	.590
Kingsale,Gene	L	.000	5	0	0	0	0	0	1	3	.167	.000
Bats Both	R	.357	14	5	0	0	0	1	1	1	.438	.357
Kinkade,Mike	L	.284	88	25	4	0	3	11	9	18	.364	.432
Bats Right	R	.264	72	19	1	0	1	5	5	13	.321	.319
Klesko,Ryan	L	.256	164	42	13	0	4	20	20	35	.344	.409
Bats Left	R	.299	374	112	21	6	26	93	68	54	.400	.596
Knoblauch,C	L	.253	99	25	3	2	3	11	16	12	.362	.414
Bats Right	R	.249	422	105	17	1	6	33	42	61	.334	.336
Knorr,Randy	L	.103	29	3	1	0	0	2	5	7	.235	.138
Bats Right	R	.274	62	17	1	0	3	8	3	15	.313	.435
Konerko,Paul	L	.297	111	33	11	0	5	21	9	14	.344	.532
Bats Right	R	.278	471	131	24	0	27	78	45	75	.350	.501
Koskie,Corey	L	.242	165	40	10	0	6	25	12	37	.312	.412
Bats Left	R	.290	397	115	27	2	20	78	56	81	.382	.519
Kotsay,Mark	L	.215	107	23	6	0	2	20	13	14	.298	.327
Bats Left	R	.318	299	95	23	1	8	38	35	44	.391	.482
Kreuter,Chad	L	.192	52	10	3	0	3	6	11	11	.333	.423
Bats Both	R	.223	139	31	8	1	3	11	30	41	.363	.360
Laker,Tim	L	.125	8	1	0	0	0	1	1	3	.222	.125
Bats Right	R	.200	25	5	0	0	1	4	5	5	.333	.320

Batter	vs	Avg	AB	H	2B	3B	HR	BI	BB	SO	OBP	SLG
Lamb,Mike	L	.300	50	15	0	0	2	5	2	7	.364	.420
Bats Left	R	.308	234	72	18	0	2	30	12	20	.344	.410
Lampkin,Tom	L	.130	23	3	0	0	0	1	2	7	.259	.130
Bats Left	R	.238	181	43	10	0	5	21	16	34	.315	.376
Lankford,Ray	L	.194	62	12	2	0	3	7	7	31	.275	.371
Bats Left	R	.263	327	86	26	4	16	51	55	114	.373	.514
Lansing,Mike	L	.271	107	29	7	0	2	6	5	16	.307	.393
Bats Right	R	.241	245	59	16	0	6	28	17	34	.288	.380
Larkin,Barry	L	.333	39	13	3	0	1	6	9	10	.458	.487
Bats Right	R	.231	117	27	9	0	1	11	18	15	.343	.333
Larson,B	L	.250	4	1	1	0	0	0	0	1	.250	.500
Bats Right	R	.103	29	3	1	0	0	1	2	9	.161	.138
LaRue,Jason	L	.267	86	23	5	2	1	9	4	17	.312	.407
Bats Right	R	.227	278	63	16	0	11	34	23	89	.301	.403
Latham,Chris	L	.240	25	6	0	0	1	3	7	6	.406	.360
Bats Both	R	.292	48	14	3	1	1	7	3	22	.346	.458
Lawton,Matt	L	.244	123	30	6	0	1	12	14	20	.340	.317
Bats Left	R	.287	436	125	30	1	12	52	71	60	.393	.443
Leach,Jalal	L	.000	0	0	0	0	0	0	0	0	.000	.000
Bats Left	R	.100	10	1	0	0	0	1	2	3	.250	.100
LeCroy,Matt	L	.375	24	9	2	0	3	6	0	6	.375	.833
Bats Right	R	.500	16	8	3	0	0	6	0	2	.500	.688
Ledee,Ricky	L	.267	30	8	4	0	0	10	5	8	.371	.400
Bats Left	R	.226	212	48	17	1	2	26	18	50	.292	.344
Lee,Carlos	L	.243	115	28	6	0	2	12	10	14	.302	.348
Bats Right	R	.275	443	122	27	3	22	72	28	71	.326	.499
Lee,Derrek	L	.310	116	36	11	0	6	14	15	26	.394	.560
Bats Right	R	.274	445	122	26	4	15	61	35	100	.333	.452
Lee,Travis	L	.265	132	35	5	0	6	28	12	30	.324	.439
Bats Left	R	.255	423	108	29	2	14	62	59	79	.346	.433
Levis,Jesse	L	.000	8	0	0	0	0	1	1	0	.111	.000
Bats Left	R	.320	25	8	2	0	0	2	2	7	.370	.400
Lewis,Darren	L	.309	81	25	8	0	0	5	1	9	.317	.407
Bats Right	R	.253	83	21	1	1	1	7	7	16	.333	.325
Lewis,Mark	L	.091	11	1	0	0	0	0	0	3	.091	.091
Bats Right	R	.000	2	0	0	0	0	0	0	1	.000	.000
Lieberthal,M	L	.417	24	10	3	0	0	4	4	2	.500	.542
Bats Right	R	.186	97	18	5	0	2	7	8	19	.269	.299
Liefer,Jeff	L	.105	19	2	1	0	0	0	0	10	.150	.158
Bats Left	R	.268	235	63	12	0	18	39	20	59	.326	.549
Little,Mark	L	.326	43	14	1	0	2	7	1	9	.370	.488
Bats Right	R	.357	42	15	5	0	1	6	0	11	.386	.548
Lockhart,K	L	.111	9	1	0	0	0	0	2	1	.333	.111
Bats Left	R	.225	169	38	6	0	3	12	14	21	.286	.314
Lo Duca,Paul	L	.411	112	46	9	0	7	28	8	7	.437	.679
Bats Right	R	.290	348	101	19	0	18	62	31	23	.353	.500
Lofton,James	L	.000	2	0	0	0	0	0	0	0	.000	.000
Bats Both	R	.208	24	5	1	0	0	1	1	4	.231	.250
Lofton,Kenny	L	.246	118	29	5	0	2	13	8	22	.297	.339
Bats Left	R	.266	399	106	16	4	12	53	39	47	.330	.416

Batters vs. Lefthanded and Righthanded Pitchers

Batter	vs	Avg	AB	H	2B	3B	HR	BI	BB	SO	OBP	SLG	Batter	vs	Avg	AB	H	2B	3B	HR	BI	BB	SO	OBP	SLG
Long,Terrence	L	.278	227	63	10	0	4	30	16	45	.322	.374	Mateo,Henry	L	.500	4	2	0	0	0	0	0	0	.500	.500
Bats Left	R	.286	402	115	27	4	8	55	36	58	.342	.433	Bats Both	R	.200	5	1	1	0	0	0	0	1	.200	.400
Lopez,Felipe	L	.293	58	17	1	2	3	10	1	9	.305	.534	Mateo,Ruben	L	.412	34	14	1	1	1	5	3	10	.459	.588
Bats Both	R	.244	119	29	4	2	2	13	11	30	.303	.361	Bats Right	R	.189	95	18	4	1	0	8	6	18	.275	.253
Lopez,Javy	L	.212	85	18	1	0	5	11	10	23	.299	.400	Matheny,Mike	L	.184	76	14	2	0	4	14	8	18	.262	.368
Bats Right	R	.280	353	99	15	1	12	55	18	59	.328	.431	Bats Right	R	.226	305	69	10	0	3	28	20	58	.280	.289
Lopez,Luis	L	.184	38	7	1	1	0	4	0	8	.184	.263	Matos,Luis	L	.087	23	2	0	0	0	0	0	5	.087	.087
Bats Both	R	.288	184	53	7	2	4	14	14	36	.353	.413	Bats Right	R	.253	75	19	7	0	4	12	11	25	.356	.507
Lopez,Luis	L	.194	36	7	2	0	1	3	2	8	.237	.333	Matthews Jr.,G	L	.241	108	26	4	1	6	18	8	35	.291	.463
Bats Right	R	.265	83	22	2	0	2	7	6	8	.315	.361	Bats Both	R	.222	297	66	11	1	8	26	52	65	.340	.347
Lopez,Mendy	L	.250	24	6	2	1	0	1	1	7	.280	.417	Maxwell,Jason	L	.063	16	1	0	0	0	0	5	9	.286	.063
Bats Right	R	.235	34	8	1	0	1	6	5	13	.341	.353	Bats Right	R	.231	52	12	4	0	1	10	4	14	.286	.365
Loretta,Mark	L	.313	96	30	4	1	0	6	7	9	.362	.375	Mayne,Brent	L	.206	34	7	1	0	0	6	0	7	.229	.235
Bats Right	R	.281	288	81	10	1	2	23	21	37	.341	.344	Bats Left	R	.295	292	86	10	1	2	34	26	34	.346	.356
Lowell,Mike	L	.283	127	36	6	0	4	18	6	16	.313	.425	McCarty,Dave	L	.202	114	23	8	0	1	10	15	27	.290	.298
Bats Right	R	.283	424	120	31	0	14	82	37	63	.348	.455	Bats Right	R	.314	86	27	2	0	6	16	9	18	.378	.547
Lugo,Julio	L	.299	107	32	6	0	1	3	8	19	.348	.383	McCracken,Q	L	.143	14	2	0	0	0	0	2	3	.250	.143
Bats Right	R	.254	406	103	14	3	9	34	38	97	.320	.369	Bats Both	R	.240	50	12	2	2	0	3	3	10	.283	.360
Lunar,F	L	.192	52	10	0	0	0	3	1	8	.204	.192	McDonald,D	L	.000	0	0	0	0	0	0	0	0	.000	.000
Bats Right	R	.270	115	31	7	0	0	13	6	24	.323	.330	Bats Both	R	.333	3	1	0	0	0	0	0	2	.333	.333
Mabry,John	L	.214	14	3	0	0	0	2	2	4	.353	.214	McDonald,J	L	.000	0	0	0	0	0	0	0	0	.000	.000
Bats Left	R	.207	140	29	7	0	6	18	11	42	.280	.386	Bats Right	R	.091	22	2	1	0	0	0	1	7	.167	.136
Machado,R	L	.278	54	15	7	0	1	7	1	10	.304	.463	McDonald,K	L	.000	0	0	0	0	0	0	0	0	.000	.000
Bats Right	R	.185	81	15	3	0	1	6	6	16	.241	.259	Bats Right	R	.000	2	0	0	0	0	0	0	1	.000	.000
Macias,Jose	L	.238	126	30	7	2	0	4	3	7	.262	.325	McEwing,Joe	L	.250	92	23	7	2	4	13	5	18	.311	.500
Bats Both	R	.279	362	101	17	4	8	47	29	47	.333	.414	Bats Right	R	.298	191	57	10	1	4	17	12	39	.357	.424
Mackowiak,R	L	.167	6	1	0	0	0	1	1	3	.286	.167	McGriff,Fred	L	.295	149	44	3	1	11	37	15	33	.364	.550
Bats Left	R	.269	208	56	15	2	4	20	14	49	.320	.418	Bats Left	R	.310	364	113	22	1	20	65	51	73	.394	.541
Magadan,Dave	L	.308	13	4	2	0	0	3	1	1	.357	.462	McGuire,Ryan	L	.143	7	1	1	0	0	3	0	2	.111	.286
Bats Left	R	.243	115	28	5	0	1	9	11	19	.313	.313	Bats Left	R	.191	47	9	1	0	1	5	7	13	.296	.277
Magee,W	L	.237	97	23	5	1	5	12	12	17	.321	.464	McGwire,Mark	L	.167	60	10	1	0	7	16	15	24	.325	.533
Bats Right	R	.191	110	21	6	3	0	5	11	27	.268	.300	Bats Right	R	.192	239	46	3	0	22	48	41	94	.314	.481
Magruder,C	L	.222	18	4	0	0	0	1	1	2	.263	.222	McLemore,M	L	.169	71	12	2	0	1	9	15	12	.307	.239
Bats Both	R	.091	11	1	0	0	0	0	0	3	.167	.091	Bats Both	R	.311	338	105	14	9	4	48	54	72	.402	.441
Marrero,Eli	L	.256	43	11	2	0	2	2	1	7	.273	.442	McMillon,B	L	.250	12	3	1	0	0	1	3	2	.400	.333
Bats Right	R	.269	160	43	9	3	4	21	14	29	.322	.438	Bats Left	R	.213	80	17	7	1	1	13	4	23	.264	.363
Martin,Al	L	.100	10	1	0	1	0	1	1	4	.250	.300	Meares,Pat	L	.197	61	12	4	0	1	6	2	8	.231	.311
Bats Left	R	.245	273	67	15	1	7	41	36	55	.333	.385	Bats Right	R	.215	209	45	7	1	3	19	8	37	.248	.301
Martinez,Dave	L	.257	35	9	2	0	0	3	2	7	.316	.314	Melhuse,Adam	L	.375	8	3	0	0	1	2	0	0	.375	.750
Bats Left	R	.292	202	59	9	3	2	17	19	37	.353	.396	Bats Both	R	.159	63	10	2	0	0	6	6	18	.225	.190
Martinez,E	L	.246	126	31	12	0	5	25	31	17	.399	.460	Mendez,D	L	.231	39	9	0	0	1	2	2	9	.286	.308
Bats Right	R	.328	344	113	28	1	18	91	62	73	.433	.573	Bats Right	R	.114	79	9	2	1	0	3	3	28	.167	.165
Martinez,F	L	.171	35	6	1	0	1	3	2	10	.216	.286	Menechino,F	L	.317	161	51	9	2	4	22	25	29	.431	.472
Bats Both	R	.261	184	48	12	1	0	11	8	36	.308	.337	Bats Right	R	.203	310	63	13	0	8	38	54	68	.337	.323
Martinez,R	L	.293	82	24	6	1	0	6	10	8	.370	.390	Merced,O	L	.600	5	3	0	0	0	2	0	1	.600	.600
Bats Right	R	.243	309	75	12	2	5	31	28	44	.310	.343	Bats Left	R	.250	132	33	6	1	6	27	14	31	.324	.447
Martinez,S	L	.000	1	0	0	0	0	0	0	0	.000	.000	Merloni,Lou	L	.303	33	10	4	0	2	4	2	5	.343	.606
Bats Left	R	.000	0	0	0	0	0	0	0	0	.000	.000	Bats Right	R	.257	113	29	6	0	1	9	4	26	.295	.336
Martinez,Tino	L	.257	175	45	10	0	10	32	9	31	.297	.486	Meyers,Chad	L	.111	9	1	0	0	0	0	2	4	.273	.111
Bats Left	R	.290	414	120	14	2	24	81	33	58	.342	.507	Bats Right	R	.125	8	1	0	0	0	0	0	1	.417	.125

Batters vs. Lefthanded and Righthanded Pitchers

Batter	vs	Avg	AB	H	2B	3B	HR	BI	BB	SO	OBP	SLG	Batter	vs	Avg	AB	H	2B	3B	HR	BI	BB	SO	OBP	SLG
Michaels,J	L	1.000	1	1	0	0	0	1	0	0	1.000	1.000	Newhan,David	L	.000	0	0	0	0	0	0	0	0	.000	.000
Bats Right	R	.000	5	0	0	0	0	0	0	2	.000	.000	Bats Left	R	.333	6	2	1	0	0	1	1	0	.375	.500
Mientkiewicz,D	L	.322	143	46	9	0	3	20	14	31	.409	.448	Nieves,Jose	L	.308	26	8	1	1	2	3	1	10	.333	.654
Bats Left	R	.300	400	120	30	1	12	54	53	61	.379	.470	Bats Right	R	.185	27	5	2	0	0	0	1	10	.267	.259
Millar,Kevin	L	.351	97	34	9	1	3	10	9	9	.407	.557	Nixon,Trot	L	.210	105	22	2	2	1	14	14	30	.309	.295
Bats Right	R	.304	352	107	30	4	17	75	30	61	.364	.557	Bats Left	R	.298	430	128	29	2	26	74	65	83	.393	.556
Miller,Corky	L	.091	11	1	0	0	0	0	1	4	.167	.091	Norton,Greg	L	.271	59	16	2	0	0	4	4	19	.313	.305
Bats Right	R	.211	38	8	2	0	3	7	3	12	.289	.500	Bats Both	R	.265	166	44	11	2	13	36	15	46	.324	.590
Miller,Damian	L	.301	73	22	5	0	1	7	10	19	.381	.411	Nunez,A	L	.297	37	11	1	0	0	3	6	7	.395	.324
Bats Right	R	.264	307	81	14	0	12	40	25	61	.326	.427	Bats Both	R	.258	264	68	10	4	1	18	22	46	.316	.337
Minor,Damon	L	.000	2	0	0	0	0	0	0	1	.000	.000	Ochoa,Alex	L	.308	120	37	8	2	0	10	17	15	.388	.408
Bats Left	R	.163	43	7	1	0	0	3	3	7	.217	.186	Bats Right	R	.267	416	111	22	5	8	42	28	61	.318	.401
Minor,Ryan	L	.143	35	5	2	0	0	6	6	10	.262	.200	Offerman,Jose	L	.217	129	28	7	2	1	12	25	30	.340	.326
Bats Right	R	.167	60	10	0	0	2	7	3	21	.215	.267	Bats Both	R	.284	395	112	16	1	8	37	36	67	.343	.390
Mirabelli,D	L	.283	53	15	2	0	7	18	5	17	.367	.717	Ojeda,Augie	L	.205	39	8	0	0	0	3	0	4	.200	.205
Bats Right	R	.204	137	28	8	0	4	11	22	40	.319	.350	Bats Both	R	.200	105	21	5	1	1	9	12	16	.292	.295
Moeller,Chad	L	.077	13	1	0	0	0	0	3	3	.250	.077	O'Leary,Troy	L	.154	65	10	3	1	0	6	1	20	.164	.231
Bats Right	R	.279	43	12	0	1	1	2	3	9	.326	.395	Bats Left	R	.261	276	72	13	5	13	44	24	53	.327	.486
Mohr,Dustan	L	.353	17	6	0	0	0	1	2	4	.421	.353	Olerud,John	L	.246	142	35	4	0	3	23	20	16	.343	.338
Bats Right	R	.176	34	6	2	0	0	3	3	13	.237	.235	Bats Left	R	.321	430	138	28	1	18	72	74	54	.420	.516
Molina,Ben	L	.218	101	22	4	0	3	14	11	23	.298	.347	Oliver,Joe	L	.200	10	2	0	0	0	0	0	0	.200	.200
Bats Right	R	.281	224	63	7	0	3	26	5	28	.314	.353	Bats Right	R	.263	38	10	2	0	1	3	2	15	.293	.395
Molina,Jose	L	.500	12	6	2	0	1	2	1	3	.538	.917	O'Neill,Paul	L	.244	127	31	11	1	2	12	16	17	.338	.394
Bats Right	R	.160	25	4	1	0	1	2	2	5	.222	.320	Bats Left	R	.274	383	105	22	0	19	58	32	42	.328	.480
Mondesi,Raul	L	.299	107	32	5	0	7	19	26	19	.453	.542	Ordaz,Luis	L	.313	16	5	2	0	0	0	0	1	.313	.438
Bats Right	R	.241	465	112	21	4	20	65	47	109	.312	.432	Bats Right	R	.225	40	9	1	0	0	4	3	7	.289	.250
Monroe,Craig	L	.212	33	7	1	0	2	4	3	10	.278	.424	Ordonez,M	L	.325	117	38	7	1	12	32	15	17	.403	.709
Bats Right	R	.211	19	4	0	0	0	1	3	8	.318	.211	Bats Right	R	.300	476	143	33	0	19	81	55	53	.376	.489
Mora,Melvin	L	.308	107	33	10	0	1	16	16	20	.395	.430	Ordonez,Rey	L	.261	88	23	4	0	1	7	11	5	.347	.341
Bats Right	R	.231	329	76	18	0	6	32	25	71	.307	.340	Bats Right	R	.244	373	91	20	4	2	37	23	38	.287	.335
Mordecai,Mike	L	.313	115	36	7	1	3	20	10	19	.362	.470	Ortega,Bill	L	.000	2	0	0	0	0	0	0	0	.000	.000
Bats Right	R	.252	139	35	10	1	0	12	9	34	.302	.338	Bats Right	R	.333	3	1	0	0	0	0	0	1	.333	.333
Morris,Warren	L	.300	10	3	1	0	0	0	0	2	.300	.400	Ortiz,David	L	.221	86	19	6	1	4	12	8	22	.284	.453
Bats Left	R	.194	93	18	5	0	2	11	3	7	.232	.312	Bats Left	R	.240	217	52	11	0	14	36	32	46	.339	.484
Mottola,Chad	L	.000	3	0	0	0	0	1	1	1	.200	.000	Ortiz,Hector	L	.250	60	15	2	0	0	4	2	8	.274	.283
Bats Right	R	.000	4	0	0	0	0	0	1	1	.200	.000	Bats Right	R	.245	94	23	4	1	0	7	7	16	.304	.309
Mouton,James	L	.162	37	6	1	0	0	3	4	14	.279	.189	Ortiz,Jose	L	.225	71	16	3	1	4	10	6	9	.286	.465
Bats Right	R	.277	101	28	7	0	2	7	7	26	.348	.406	Bats Right	R	.246	175	43	5	0	9	28	11	32	.302	.429
Mouton,Lyle	L	.000	5	0	0	0	0	0	0	0	.000	.000	Osik,Keith	L	.119	42	5	1	0	2	6	4	6	.208	.286
Bats Right	R	.083	12	1	0	0	0	1	0	7	.083	.083	Bats Right	R	.256	78	20	3	0	0	7	9	18	.348	.295
Mueller,Bill	L	.391	46	18	4	0	2	8	7	4	.455	.609	Overbay,Lyle	L	.000	0	0	0	0	0	0	0	0	.000	.000
Bats Both	R	.268	164	44	8	1	4	15	30	15	.389	.402	Bats Left	R	.500	2	1	0	0	0	0	0	1	.500	.500
Munson,Eric	L	.154	13	2	0	0	1	2	0	5	.154	.385	Owens,Eric	L	.274	113	31	6	1	4	7	4	16	.299	.451
Bats Left	R	.151	53	8	3	1	0	4	3	16	.196	.245	Bats Right	R	.244	287	70	10	0	1	21	25	43	.304	.289
Murray,Calvin	L	.238	84	20	6	0	1	6	7	12	.297	.345	Palmeiro,O	L	.067	15	1	0	0	0	0	2	3	.263	.067
Bats Right	R	.248	242	60	8	2	5	19	25	45	.326	.360	Bats Left	R	.256	215	55	10	1	2	23	23	21	.324	.340
Myers,Greg	L	.316	19	6	0	0	2	7	1	5	.350	.632	Palmeiro,R	L	.272	151	41	10	0	12	32	18	33	.362	.576
Bats Left	R	.211	142	30	3	0	9	24	20	33	.309	.423	Bats Left	R	.274	449	123	23	0	35	91	83	57	.387	.559
Nevin,Phil	L	.329	155	51	12	0	9	27	23	40	.416	.581	Palmer,Dean	L	.340	53	18	4	0	6	14	7	10	.417	.755
Bats Right	R	.297	391	116	19	0	32	99	48	107	.377	.591	Bats Right	R	.184	163	30	7	0	5	26	20	49	.285	.319

Batters vs. Lefthanded and Righthanded Pitchers

Batter	vs	Avg	AB	H	2B	3B	HR	BI	BB	SO	OBP	SLG
Paquette,C	L	.312	93	29	3	0	3	16	5	14	.360	.441
Bats Right	R	.271	247	67	14	0	12	48	13	53	.313	.474
Patterson,C	L	.267	30	8	1	0	1	2	1	6	.303	.400
Bats Left	R	.208	101	21	2	0	3	12	5	27	.255	.317
Patterson,J	L	.250	8	2	0	0	0	1	0	0	.250	.250
Bats Left	R	.273	33	9	1	1	2	3	0	4	.314	.545
Paul,Josh	L	.209	43	9	5	0	2	12	5	7	.292	.465
Bats Right	R	.292	96	28	6	0	1	6	8	18	.343	.385
Payton,Jay	L	.261	69	18	2	0	2	7	5	11	.307	.377
Bats Right	R	.253	292	74	14	1	6	27	13	41	.296	.370
Pena,Angel	L	.167	12	2	0	0	0	0	0	5	.167	.167
Bats Right	R	.214	42	9	1	0	1	2	1	12	.227	.310
Pena,Carlos	L	.091	11	1	0	0	0	1	0	5	.091	.091
Bats Left	R	.294	51	15	4	1	3	11	10	12	.410	.588
Pena,Elvis	L	.417	12	5	2	0	0	4	1	1	.429	.583
Bats Both	R	.143	28	4	0	0	0	2	5	5	.294	.143
Perez,Eddie	L	.000	2	0	0	0	0	0	0	1	.000	.000
Bats Right	R	.375	8	3	0	0	0	0	0	1	.375	.375
Perez,Neifi	L	.266	169	45	9	3	3	18	4	28	.283	.408
Bats Both	R	.284	412	117	17	6	5	41	22	40	.319	.391
Perez,Robert	L	.000	3	0	0	0	0	0	0	1	.000	.000
Bats Right	R	.235	17	4	1	0	0	0	1	6	.278	.294
Perez,S	L	.286	14	4	0	0	0	0	1	6	.333	.286
Bats Both	R	.179	67	12	0	0	0	4	14	23	.317	.194
Perez,Timo	L	.154	26	4	0	0	0	3	1	2	.185	.154
Bats Left	R	.258	213	55	9	1	5	19	11	23	.300	.380
Perez,Tomas	L	.354	48	17	1	0	2	7	0	8	.354	.500
Bats Both	R	.276	87	24	6	1	1	12	7	14	.344	.402
Perry,Herbert	L	.256	90	23	6	1	3	13	8	25	.330	.444
Bats Right	R	.256	195	50	15	0	4	19	15	30	.324	.395
Petrick,Ben	L	.213	80	17	6	1	3	13	6	19	.270	.425
Bats Right	R	.250	164	41	9	2	8	26	25	48	.354	.476
Phelps,Josh	L	.000	8	0	0	0	0	1	0	4	.000	.000
Bats Right	R	.000	4	0	0	0	0	0	2	1	.333	.000
Phillips,J	L	.000	1	0	0	0	0	0	0	0	.000	.000
Bats Right	R	.167	6	1	1	0	0	0	0	1	.167	.333
Piatt,Adam	L	.245	53	13	4	0	0	2	7	12	.328	.321
Bats Right	R	.167	42	7	1	1	0	4	6	14	.265	.238
Piazza,Mike	L	.323	99	32	6	0	8	24	23	18	.451	.626
Bats Right	R	.295	404	119	23	0	28	70	44	69	.366	.559
Pickering,C	L	.417	12	5	1	0	0	1	1	4	.462	.500
Bats Left	R	.238	42	10	0	0	3	7	7	11	.347	.452
Pierre,Juan	L	.289	121	35	1	2	0	9	9	7	.360	.331
Bats Left	R	.337	496	167	25	9	2	46	32	22	.383	.435
Pierzynski,A	L	.167	60	10	0	0	0	4	0	11	.177	.167
Bats Left	R	.312	321	100	33	2	7	51	16	46	.348	.492
Podsednik,S	L	.000	0	0	0	0	0	0	0	0	.000	.000
Bats Left	R	.167	6	1	0	1	0	3	0	1	.167	.500
Polanco,P	L	.350	143	50	8	0	0	10	8	15	.384	.406
Bats Right	R	.292	421	123	18	4	3	28	17	28	.328	.375
Porter,Bo	L	.261	46	12	2	1	1	4	3	16	.306	.413
Bats Right	R	.195	41	8	2	1	0	2	6	18	.286	.293
Posada,Jorge	L	.272	147	40	12	0	5	26	24	31	.383	.456
Bats Both	R	.279	337	94	16	1	17	69	38	101	.353	.484
Powell,Dante	L	.000	0	0	0	0	0	0	0	0	.000	.000
Bats Right	R	.333	6	2	0	0	0	0	0	0	.333	.333
Pratt,Todd	L	.250	40	10	2	0	2	7	9	12	.388	.450
Bats Right	R	.165	133	22	6	0	2	4	25	49	.309	.256
Pride,Curtis	L	.111	9	1	0	0	0	0	2	3	.273	.111
Bats Left	R	.269	67	18	3	1	1	9	7	19	.355	.388
Prince,Tom	L	.203	74	15	4	0	2	6	5	18	.268	.338
Bats Right	R	.230	122	28	0	1	5	17	7	21	.293	.369
Pujols,Albert	L	.279	122	34	8	1	8	22	20	22	.386	.557
Bats Right	R	.342	468	160	39	3	29	108	49	71	.408	.624
Punto,Nick	L	.500	2	1	0	0	0	0	0	0	.500	.500
Bats Both	R	.333	3	1	0	0	0	0	0	0	.333	.333
Quinn,Mark	L	.288	125	36	10	1	6	11	5	19	.315	.528
Bats Right	R	.262	328	86	21	1	11	49	7	50	.292	.433
Raines,Tim	L	.278	18	5	1	0	0	1	5	4	.417	.333
Bats Both	R	.310	71	22	7	1	1	8	13	5	.412	.479
Raines Jr.,T	L	.000	0	0	0	0	0	0	0	0	.000	.000
Bats Both	R	.174	23	4	2	0	0	0	3	8	.269	.261
Ramirez,A	L	.297	111	33	9	0	4	19	11	23	.373	.486
Bats Right	R	.301	492	148	31	0	30	93	29	77	.344	.547
Ramirez,Julio	L	.087	23	2	0	0	0	1	2	11	.160	.087
Bats Right	R	.071	14	1	0	0	0	0	0	4	.071	.071
Ramirez,M	L	.342	117	40	6	0	10	25	25	16	.462	.650
Bats Right	R	.296	412	122	27	2	31	100	56	131	.387	.597
Randa,Joe	L	.261	161	42	9	1	2	23	9	20	.298	.366
Bats Right	R	.250	420	105	25	1	11	60	33	60	.310	.393
Ransom,Cody	L	.000	0	0	0	0	0	0	0	0	.000	.000
Bats Right	R	.000	7	0	0	0	0	0	0	5	.000	.000
Reboulet,Jeff	L	.290	100	29	11	2	1	13	16	20	.393	.470
Bats Right	R	.246	114	28	4	0	2	9	17	28	.344	.333
Redman,Tike	L	.083	12	1	0	0	0	0	1	2	.154	.083
Bats Left	R	.239	113	27	4	1	1	4	3	23	.256	.319
Redmond,Mike	L	.375	56	21	2	0	3	7	6	3	.435	.571
Bats Right	R	.271	85	23	2	0	1	7	7	10	.337	.329
Reese,Pokey	L	.226	93	21	4	0	3	11	6	18	.273	.366
Bats Right	R	.224	335	75	16	2	6	29	28	64	.286	.337
Relaford,Desi	L	.240	50	12	0		1	3	5	13	.309	.380
Bats Both	R	.315	251	79	23	0	7	33	22	52	.375	.490
Renteria,E	L	.327	98	32	3	0	3	17	13	14	.398	.449
Bats Right	R	.243	395	96	16	3	7	40	26	59	.292	.352
Richard,Chris	L	.208	106	22	1	0	1	8	4	19	.263	.245
Bats Left	R	.281	377	106	30	3	14	53	41	81	.354	.488
Riggs,Adam	L	.333	6	2	0	0	0	0	0	0	.333	.333
Bats Right	R	.167	30	5	1	0	0	1	2	8	.219	.200
Rios,Armando	L	.326	46	15	3	0	3	7	4	12	.373	.587
Bats Left	R	.249	273	68	14	3	11	43	32	62	.326	.443

Batters vs. Lefthanded and Righthanded Pitchers

Batter	vs	Avg	AB	H	2B	3B	HR	BI	BB	SO	OBP	SLG
Ripken Jr.,C	L	.288	111	32	3	0	2	11	8	8	.328	.369
Bats Right	R	.224	366	82	13	0	12	57	18	55	.260	.358
Rivas,Luis	L	.241	137	33	6	2	2	7	12	27	.307	.358
Bats Right	R	.275	426	117	15	4	5	40	28	72	.323	.364
Rivera,Juan	L	.000	1	0	0	0	0	0	0	0	.000	.000
Bats Right	R	.000	3	0	0	0	0	0	0	0	.000	.000
Rivera,Mike	L	.500	2	1	1	0	0	0	0	0	.500	1.000
Bats Right	R	.300	10	3	1	0	0	1	0	2	.300	.400
Rivera,Ruben	L	.241	79	19	2	0	4	11	10	25	.330	.418
Bats Right	R	.261	184	48	11	1	6	23	11	58	.317	.429
Roberts,Brian	L	.247	81	20	2	2	1	8	3	12	.271	.358
Bats Both	R	.255	192	49	10	1	1	9	10	24	.289	.333
Roberts,Dave	L	.000	1	0	0	0	0	0	0	1	.000	.000
Bats Left	R	.364	11	4	1	0	0	2	1	1	.417	.455
Robinson,K	L	.267	15	4	0	0	1	2	0	2	.267	.467
Bats Left	R	.287	171	49	6	1	0	13	12	18	.335	.333
Rodriguez,A	L	.295	132	39	5	0	12	31	13	34	.369	.606
Bats Right	R	.324	500	162	29	1	40	104	62	97	.407	.626
Rodriguez,H	L	.000	0	0	0	0	0	0	0	0	.000	.000
Bats Left	R	.000	8	0	0	0	0	0	0	6	.000	.000
Rodriguez,I	L	.289	83	24	6	0	5	11	5	14	.326	.542
Bats Right	R	.312	359	112	18	2	20	54	18	59	.352	.540
Rolen,Scott	L	.283	113	32	6	0	4	21	32	27	.458	.442
Bats Right	R	.290	441	128	33	1	21	86	42	100	.354	.512
Rollins,Jimmy	L	.318	148	47	10	4	3	12	17	22	.392	.500
Bats Both	R	.262	508	133	19	8	11	42	31	86	.303	.396
Rolls,Damian	L	.225	80	18	3	0	1	1	6	17	.279	.300
Bats Right	R	.280	157	44	8	1	1	11	4	30	.298	.363
Rowand,Aaron	L	.309	55	17	2	0	2	8	6	14	.377	.455
Bats Right	R	.279	68	19	3	0	2	12	9	14	.390	.412
Ryan,Rob	L	.000	0	0	0	0	0	0	0	0	.000	.000
Bats Left	R	.000	8	0	0	0	0	0	0	6	.000	.000
Sadler,Donnie	L	.088	57	5	2	0	0	1	5	12	.161	.123
Bats Right	R	.195	128	25	4	0	1	4	13	25	.278	.250
Saenz,Olmedo	L	.237	139	33	11	1	4	17	13	27	.305	.417
Bats Right	R	.205	166	34	10	0	5	15	6	37	.280	.355
Salmon,Tim	L	.232	125	29	8	0	4	15	30	23	.385	.392
Bats Right	R	.226	350	79	13	1	13	34	66	98	.358	.380
Sanchez,Alex	L	.200	5	1	1	0	0	0	0	1	.200	.400
Bats Left	R	.206	63	13	2	2	0	4	5	12	.265	.302
Sanchez,Rey	L	.256	133	34	4	2	0	9	3	10	.270	.316
Bats Right	R	.290	411	119	14	4	0	28	12	39	.310	.343
Sandberg,J	L	.195	41	8	1	0	1	5	2	13	.233	.293
Bats Right	R	.211	95	20	6	0	0	10	8	32	.279	.274
Sanders,A	L	.176	17	3	2	0	0	2	2	3	.263	.294
Bats Right	R	.000	0	0	0	0	0	0	0	0	.000	.000
Sanders,Deion	L	.273	11	3	0	0	0	0	0	3	.333	.273
Bats Left	R	.156	64	10	2	0	1	4	4	7	.217	.234
Sanders,R	L	.256	129	33	6	1	14	25	18	35	.351	.643
Bats Right	R	.266	312	83	15	2	19	65	28	91	.331	.510

Batter	vs	Avg	AB	H	2B	3B	HR	BI	BB	SO	OBP	SLG
Santana,Pedro	L	.000	0	0	0	0	0	0	0	0	.000	.000
Bats Right	R	.000	0	0	0	0	0	0	0	0	.000	.000
Santangelo,F	L	.263	19	5	2	0	0	3	1	5	.375	.368
Bats Both	R	.173	52	9	2	0	0	5	10	12	.328	.212
Santiago,B	L	.256	117	30	7	2	1	7	6	15	.288	.376
Bats Right	R	.264	360	95	18	2	5	38	17	63	.298	.367
Santos,Angel	L	.000	0	0	0	0	0	0	0	0	.000	.000
Bats Both	R	.125	16	2	1	0	0	1	2	7	.211	.188
Saturria,Luis	L	.000	0	0	0	0	0	0	0	0	.000	.000
Bats Right	R	.200	5	1	1	0	0	1	0	1	.200	.400
Schneider,B	L	.500	6	3	1	0	0	0	0	1	.500	.667
Bats Left	R	.286	35	10	2	0	1	6	6	2	.381	.429
Seabol,Scott	L	.000	1	0	0	0	0	0	0	0	.000	.000
Bats Right	R	.000	0	0	0	0	0	0	0	0	.000	.000
Sefcik,Kevin	L	.000	1	0	0	0	0	0	0	0	.000	.000
Bats Right	R	.000	0	0	0	0	0	0	0	0	.000	.000
Segui,David	L	.338	77	26	5	0	2	14	13	12	.452	.481
Bats Both	R	.288	215	62	13	1	8	32	36	49	.390	.470
Seguignol,F	L	.125	16	2	1	0	0	2	1	3	.222	.188
Bats Both	R	.147	34	5	1	0	0	3	1	14	.167	.176
Selby,Bill	L	.000	1	0	0	0	0	0	0	0	.000	.000
Bats Left	R	.231	91	21	7	1	2	12	5	13	.276	.396
Servais,Scott	L	.000	1	0	0	0	0	0	0	0	.000	.000
Bats Right	R	.400	15	6	0	0	0	2	2	3	.471	.400
Sexson,Richie	L	.295	139	41	5	1	11	28	19	33	.384	.583
Bats Right	R	.264	459	121	19	2	34	97	41	145	.329	.536
Sheets,Andy	L	.163	43	7	4	0	0	4	6	11	.260	.256
Bats Right	R	.209	110	23	4	0	1	10	6	24	.248	.273
Sheffield,G	L	.374	107	40	5	1	10	27	18	10	.457	.720
Bats Right	R	.294	408	120	23	1	26	73	76	52	.407	.547
Sheldon,Scott	L	.283	60	17	5	0	2	7	1	16	.290	.467
Bats Right	R	.117	60	7	0	0	1	4	2	19	.143	.167
Shinjo,T	L	.305	82	25	1	0	1	8	6	14	.352	.354
Bats Right	R	.258	318	82	22	1	9	48	19	56	.312	.418
Shumpert,T	L	.233	90	21	6	0	1	8	4	17	.271	.333
Bats Right	R	.322	152	49	8	5	3	16	11	27	.376	.500
Sierra,Ruben	L	.321	84	27	8	0	4	17	3	10	.337	.560
Bats Both	R	.281	260	73	14	1	19	50	16	42	.318	.562
Simmons,Brian	L	.250	20	5	2	0	1	3	2	1	.318	.500
Bats Both	R	.161	87	14	3	0	1	5	6	25	.221	.230
Simon,Randall	L	.233	43	10	1	2	2	9	4	5	.292	.488
Bats Left	R	.319	213	68	13	0	4	28	11	23	.351	.437
Singleton,C	L	.300	40	12	1	1	1	2	6	10	.404	.450
Bats Left	R	.298	352	105	20	4	6	43	14	51	.322	.429
Smith,Bobby	L	.000	0	0	0	0	0	0	0	0	.000	.000
Bats Right	R	.105	19	2	0	0	0	1	3	10	.227	.105
Smith,Jason	L	.000	0	0	0	0	0	0	0	0	.000	.000
Bats Left	R	.000	1	0	0	0	0	0	0	1	.000	.000
Smith,Mark	L	.275	91	25	7	1	3	12	14	13	.370	.473
Bats Right	R	.214	103	22	6	0	3	6	9	25	.283	.359

Batters vs. Lefthanded and Righthanded Pitchers

Batter	vs	Avg	AB	H	2B	3B	HR	BI	BB	SO	OBP	SLG
Snow,J.T.	L	.306	49	15	1	0	1	7	6	16	.386	.388
Bats Left	R	.233	236	55	11	1	7	27	49	65	.368	.377
Sojo,Luis	L	.100	20	2	0	0	0	1	1	3	.143	.100
Bats Right	R	.186	59	11	2	0	0	8	3	9	.238	.220
Soriano,A	L	.255	98	25	5	0	3	11	8	22	.312	.398
Bats Right	R	.271	476	129	29	3	15	62	21	103	.303	.439
Sosa,Juan	L	.000	0	0	0	0	0	0	0	0	.000	.000
Bats Right	R	.000	1	0	0	0	0	0	0	1	.000	.000
Sosa,Sammy	L	.387	93	36	5	1	13	30	41	30	.569	.882
Bats Right	R	.316	484	153	29	4	51	130	75	123	.406	.709
Spencer,Shane	L	.313	64	20	4	0	4	19	4	6	.348	.563
Bats Right	R	.242	219	53	10	2	6	27	17	52	.306	.388
Spiers,Bill	L	.000	0	0	0	0	0	0	0	0	.000	.000
Bats Left	R	.333	3	1	0	0	0	0	0	0	.500	.333
Spiezio,Scott	L	.239	109	26	8	0	0	6	11	22	.320	.312
Bats Both	R	.282	348	98	21	4	13	48	23	43	.328	.477
Spivey,Junior	L	.323	65	21	6	1	3	14	11	19	.416	.585
Bats Right	R	.214	98	21	0	2	2	7	12	28	.313	.316
Sprague,Ed	L	.318	66	21	6	0	1	13	6	8	.378	.455
Bats Right	R	.250	28	7	1	0	1	3	5	10	.364	.393
Stairs,Matt	L	.172	29	5	3	0	0	7	3	12	.242	.276
Bats Left	R	.257	311	80	18	0	17	54	49	64	.369	.479
Stevens,Lee	L	.243	152	37	9	1	5	28	16	46	.318	.414
Bats Left	R	.246	390	96	26	0	20	67	58	111	.345	.467
Stewart,S	L	.333	117	39	8	3	1	9	13	12	.397	.479
Bats Right	R	.312	523	163	36	4	11	51	33	60	.365	.459
Stinnett,K	L	.325	40	13	4	0	1	6	3	13	.378	.500
Bats Right	R	.238	147	35	7	0	8	19	14	48	.321	.449
Stynes,Chris	L	.349	106	37	8	0	3	8	6	15	.384	.509
Bats Right	R	.251	255	64	11	2	5	25	14	41	.297	.369
Surhoff,B.J.	L	.219	73	16	6	0	0	10	7	10	.284	.301
Bats Left	R	.280	411	115	27	1	10	48	31	38	.327	.423
Sutton,Larry	L	.000	5	0	0	0	0	0	0	3	.000	.000
Bats Left	R	.135	37	5	1	0	1	3	1	7	.158	.243
Suzuki,Ichiro	L	.318	192	61	6	3	1	23	7	19	.343	.396
Bats Left	R	.362	500	181	28	5	7	46	23	34	.396	.480
Sweeney,Mark	L	.200	5	1	0	0	0	0	2	2	.429	.200
Bats Left	R	.262	84	22	3	1	3	11	10	21	.340	.429
Sweeney,Mike	L	.268	142	38	9	0	6	24	16	23	.338	.458
Bats Right	R	.317	417	132	37	0	23	75	48	41	.386	.571
Tatis,F	L	.235	34	8	3	0	1	4	6	14	.333	.412
Bats Right	R	.261	111	29	6	0	1	7	10	29	.341	.342
Taubensee,E	L	.238	21	5	0	0	0	0	2	10	.304	.238
Bats Left	R	.253	95	24	2	1	3	11	8	9	.317	.389
Taylor,Reggie	L	.000	1	0	0	0	0	0	0	0	.000	.000
Bats Left	R	.000	6	0	0	0	0	0	1	1	.143	.000
Tejada,Miguel	L	.273	187	51	9	2	8	35	19	27	.352	.471
Bats Right	R	.264	435	115	22	1	23	78	24	62	.314	.478
Thomas,Frank	L	.313	16	5	1	0	2	4	3	4	.421	.750
Bats Right	R	.192	52	10	2	0	2	6	7	8	.283	.346
Thome,Jim	L	.232	142	33	8	0	4	22	21	67	.333	.373
Bats Left	R	.313	384	120	18	1	45	102	90	118	.445	.716
Thompson,R	L	.300	10	3	0	0	0	1	0	1	.300	.300
Bats Right	R	.286	21	6	5	0	0	1	1	7	.318	.524
Toca,Jorge	L	.222	9	2	0	0	0	1	0	5	.222	.222
Bats Right	R	.125	8	1	0	0	0	0	0	3	.125	.125
Torrealba,S	L	.000	0	0	0	0	0	0	0	0	.000	.000
Bats Right	R	.500	2	1	0	0	0	0	0	0	.500	.500
Torrealba,Y	L	.000	0	0	0	0	0	0	0	0	.000	.000
Bats Right	R	.500	4	2	0	1	0	2	0	0	.500	1.000
Tracy,Andy	L	.125	8	1	0	0	1	1	0	5	.125	.500
Bats Left	R	.106	47	5	1	0	1	7	6	21	.200	.191
Trammell,B	L	.279	129	36	6	0	4	20	13	25	.354	.419
Bats Right	R	.255	361	92	14	3	21	72	35	53	.321	.485
Truby,Chris	L	.265	34	9	0	0	4	7	4	8	.325	.618
Bats Right	R	.186	102	19	6	1	4	16	9	30	.259	.382
Tucker,M	L	.211	90	19	3	2	3	15	3	29	.245	.389
Bats Left	R	.263	346	91	16	6	9	46	43	73	.341	.422
Tyner,Jason	L	.321	81	26	1	0	0	4	2	10	.345	.333
Bats Left	R	.270	315	85	7	5	0	17	13	32	.302	.324
Uribe,Juan	L	.311	45	14	1	2	2	14	2	8	.340	.556
Bats Right	R	.298	228	68	14	9	6	39	6	47	.322	.518
Valdez,Mario	L	.385	13	5	0	0	0	0	3	2	.529	.385
Bats Left	R	.244	41	10	1	0	1	8	9	16	.380	.341
Valent,Eric	L	.000	2	0	0	0	0	0	0	0	.000	.000
Bats Left	R	.103	39	4	2	0	0	1	4	11	.205	.154
Valentin,John	L	.176	17	3	2	0	0	0	5	0	.391	.294
Bats Right	R	.209	43	9	0	0	1	5	4	8	.277	.279
Valentin,Jose	L	.203	64	13	3	0	3	7	8	15	.292	.391
Bats Both	R	.267	374	100	19	2	25	61	42	99	.344	.529
Vander Wal,J	L	.296	54	16	5	0	0	15	4	16	.345	.389
Bats Left	R	.266	398	106	23	4	14	55	64	106	.366	.450
Varitek,Jason	L	.283	53	15	2	1	1	4	6	10	.350	.415
Bats Both	R	.298	121	36	9	0	6	21	15	25	.380	.521
Vaughn,Greg	L	.192	104	20	7	0	3	12	22	25	.331	.346
Bats Right	R	.244	381	93	18	0	21	70	49	105	.333	.457
Vazquez,R	L	.143	7	1	0	0	0	1	0	0	.125	.143
Bats Left	R	.250	28	7	0	0	0	3	0	3	.250	.250
Velandia,J	L	.000	3	0	0	0	0	0	1	0	.250	.000
Bats Right	R	.000	6	0	0	0	0	0	1	1	.143	.000
Velarde,Randy	L	.297	91	27	6	0	3	13	11	21	.379	.462
Bats Right	R	.271	251	68	13	2	6	19	23	65	.348	.410
Ventura,Robin	L	.271	96	26	8	0	2	15	18	20	.383	.417
Bats Left	R	.228	360	82	12	0	19	46	70	81	.353	.419
Veras,Quilvio	L	.313	64	20	6	0	1	6	3	9	.353	.453
Bats Both	R	.232	194	45	8	2	2	19	21	43	.323	.325
Vidro,Jose	L	.348	135	47	10	1	3	16	6	15	.379	.504
Bats Both	R	.308	351	108	24	0	12	43	25	34	.367	.479
Vina,Fernando	L	.315	130	41	5	1	2	16	8	8	.390	.415
Bats Left	R	.299	501	150	25	7	7	40	24	27	.348	.419

Batters vs. Lefthanded and Righthanded Pitchers

Batter	vs	Avg	AB	H	2B	3B	HR	BI	BB	SO	OBP	SLG
Vizcaino,Jose	L	.250	36	9	0	0	0	3	3	2	.308	.250
Bats Both	R	.282	220	62	8	3	1	11	12	31	.325	.359
Vizquel,Omar	L	.228	171	39	6	0	1	11	12	23	.277	.281
Bats Both	R	.266	440	117	20	8	1	39	49	49	.340	.355
Wakeland,C	L	.000	3	0	0	0	0	0	0	0	.000	.000
Bats Left	R	.273	33	9	2	0	2	6	0	13	.273	.515
Walbeck,Matt	L	.000	0	0	0	0	0	0	0	0	.000	.000
Bats Both	R	1.000	1	1	0	0	0	0	0	0	1.000	1.000
Walker,Larry	L	.378	148	56	13	0	14	52	15	33	.443	.750
Bats Left	R	.338	349	118	22	3	24	71	67	70	.452	.625
Walker,Todd	L	.269	108	29	9	0	2	12	2	16	.288	.407
Bats Left	R	.302	443	134	26	2	15	63	49	66	.370	.472
Ward,Daryle	L	.308	26	8	1	0	4	8	2	5	.357	.808
Bats Left	R	.257	187	48	14	0	5	31	17	43	.319	.412
Ward,Turner	L	.250	4	1	0	0	0	2	0	0	.250	.250
Bats Both	R	.273	11	3	1	0	0	0	1	6	.385	.364
Wehner,John	L	.176	17	3	1	0	0	1	5	5	.364	.235
Bats Right	R	.206	34	7	0	0	0	1	5	7	.308	.206
Wells,Vernon	L	.372	43	16	3	0	1	6	1	5	.378	.512
Bats Right	R	.264	53	14	5	0	0	0	4	10	.328	.358
White,Devon	L	.273	88	24	8	1	2	16	6	20	.319	.455
Bats Both	R	.278	302	84	17	1	12	31	22	75	.350	.460
White,Rondell	L	.268	71	19	4	1	1	8	4	8	.307	.394
Bats Right	R	.317	252	80	15	0	16	42	22	48	.388	.567
Wilkerson,B	L	.125	8	1	0	0	0	0	0	3	.125	.125
Bats Left	R	.211	109	23	7	2	1	5	17	38	.315	.339
Wilkins,Rick	L	.000	0	0	0	0	0	0	0	0	.000	.000
Bats Left	R	.182	22	4	1	0	1	8	2	8	.250	.364
Williams,B	L	.311	151	47	9	0	5	22	26	21	.411	.470
Bats Both	R	.306	389	119	29	0	21	72	52	46	.389	.542
Williams,G	L	.184	38	7	2	0	1	2	6	7	.311	.316
Bats Right	R	.203	241	49	16	0	3	17	12	48	.253	.307
Williams,Matt	L	.313	115	36	8	0	8	28	6	13	.344	.591
Bats Right	R	.259	293	76	22	0	8	37	16	57	.303	.416
Wilson,C	L	.378	45	17	0	0	4	8	5	18	.462	.644
Bats Right	R	.283	113	32	3	1	9	24	10	35	.362	.566
Wilson,Dan	L	.290	131	38	5	0	8	18	5	17	.319	.511
Bats Right	R	.252	246	62	15	1	2	24	15	52	.298	.346
Wilson,E	L	.188	48	9	3	0	0	2	0	7	.184	.250
Bats Both	R	.217	180	39	5	1	2	18	9	30	.253	.289
Wilson,Jack	L	.220	59	13	3	0	0	2	3	10	.258	.271
Bats Right	R	.224	331	74	14	1	3	23	13	60	.254	.299
Wilson,P	L	.208	106	22	4	0	5	11	12	31	.286	.387
Bats Right	R	.293	362	106	26	2	18	60	24	76	.345	.525
Wilson,Tom	L	.000	3	0	0	0	0	0	1	0	.250	.000
Bats Right	R	.222	18	4	0	0	2	4	0	5	.250	.556
Wilson,Vance	L	.286	7	2	0	0	0	0	1	0	.444	.286
Bats Right	R	.300	50	15	3	0	0	6	1	16	.321	.360
Winn,Randy	L	.306	124	38	8	3	0	13	13	11	.386	.419
Bats Both	R	.259	305	79	17	3	6	37	25	70	.319	.393

Batter	vs	Avg	AB	H	2B	3B	HR	BI	BB	SO	OBP	SLG
Witt,Kevin	L	.000	1	0	0	0	0	0	0	1	.000	.000
Bats Left	R	.192	26	5	0	0	2	5	2	6	.241	.423
Womack,Tony	L	.188	96	18	3	1	0	2	4	16	.235	.240
Bats Left	R	.286	385	110	16	4	3	28	19	38	.325	.371
Woodward,C	L	.077	13	1	0	0	1	1	1	2	.143	.308
Bats Right	R	.220	50	11	3	2	1	4	0	12	.220	.420
Wooten,Shawn	L	.304	115	35	6	1	6	18	3	21	.322	.530
Bats Right	R	.321	106	34	2	0	2	14	2	21	.342	.396
Young,Dmitri	L	.280	157	44	6	1	3	17	6	21	.307	.389
Bats Both	R	.311	383	119	22	2	18	52	31	56	.367	.520
Young,Eric	L	.308	120	37	14	1	2	9	9	13	.366	.492
Bats Right	R	.271	483	131	29	3	4	33	33	32	.325	.369
Young,Kevin	L	.270	74	20	7	0	3	9	14	25	.386	.486
Bats Right	R	.224	375	84	26	0	11	56	28	94	.294	.381
Young,Michael	L	.255	98	25	6	2	5	14	8	22	.308	.510
Bats Right	R	.247	288	71	12	2	6	35	18	69	.294	.365
Zaun,Gregg	L	.264	53	14	4	0	2	6	4	5	.316	.453
Bats Both	R	.361	72	26	5	0	4	12	8	11	.420	.597
Zeile,Todd	L	.288	104	30	6	0	5	13	15	13	.378	.490
Bats Right	R	.260	427	111	19	1	5	49	58	89	.355	.344
Zuleta,Julio	L	.256	39	10	1	0	1	8	5	10	.356	.359
Bats Right	R	.194	67	13	2	0	5	16	3	22	.247	.448
AL	L	.263	–	–	–	–	–	–	–	–	.332	.421
	R	.268	–	–	–	–	–	–	–	–	.334	.431
NL	L	.268	–	–	–	–	–	–	–	–	.339	.437
	R	.259	–	–	–	–	–	–	–	–	.329	.422
MLB	L	.266	–	–	–	–	–	–	–	–	.336	.429
	R	.263	–	–	–	–	–	–	–	–	.331	.426

Pitchers vs. Lefthanded and Righthanded Batters

Pitcher	vs	Avg	AB	H	2B	3B	HR	BI	BB	SO	OBP	SLG
Abbott,Paul	L	.243	341	83	15	0	8	38	53	63	.348	.358
Throws Right	R	.232	267	62	23	1	13	35	34	55	.326	.472
Acevedo,Jose	L	.249	169	42	7	1	8	30	21	30	.337	.444
Throws Right	R	.292	202	59	11	1	9	25	13	38	.335	.490
Acevedo,Juan	L	.319	91	29	9	0	1	12	19	15	.441	.451
Throws Right	R	.264	148	39	8	0	5	34	16	32	.333	.419
Adams,Terry	L	.232	289	67	13	0	3	30	24	69	.293	.308
Throws Right	R	.295	356	105	19	2	6	43	30	72	.353	.410
Ainsworth,K	L	.250	4	1	0	0	0	0	0	2	.400	.250
Throws Right	R	.400	5	2	0	0	1	3	2	1	.571	1.000
Alfonseca,A	L	.302	126	38	4	1	5	16	11	14	.355	.468
Throws Right	R	.259	116	30	0	0	1	9	4	26	.312	.284
Almanza,A	L	.210	62	13	3	0	2	8	13	21	.333	.355
Throws Left	R	.244	86	21	6	0	6	17	13	24	.343	.523
Almanzar,C	L	.200	15	3	0	0	1	4	1	0	.250	.400
Throws Right	R	.407	27	11	2	0	1	11	1	6	.414	.593
Anderson,B	L	.272	147	40	7	1	4	19	7	12	.308	.415
Throws Left	R	.304	382	116	26	2	21	60	23	43	.341	.547
Anderson,J	L	.324	142	46	10	1	4	23	20	18	.424	.493
Throws Left	R	.279	666	186	30	3	11	83	63	71	.343	.383
Anderson,Matt	L	.291	110	32	10	4	0	22	8	27	.336	.455
Throws Right	R	.222	108	24	4	0	2	10	10	25	.286	.315
Ankiel,Rick	L	.333	9	3	1	0	0	1	1	3	.400	.444
Throws Left	R	.268	82	22	5	0	7	16	24	24	.438	.585
Appier,Kevin	L	.242	360	87	20	5	14	50	32	68	.312	.442
Throws Right	R	.233	404	94	17	2	8	33	32	104	.300	.344
Armas Jr.,T	L	.273	322	88	20	6	9	39	46	66	.364	.457
Throws Right	R	.226	407	92	19	2	9	51	45	110	.314	.349
Arrojo,R	L	.238	202	48	11	0	4	27	18	28	.311	.351
Throws Right	R	.221	181	40	11	0	4	29	17	50	.314	.348
Arroyo,B	L	.322	152	49	12	0	4	21	21	10	.401	.480
Throws Right	R	.263	190	50	12	2	8	28	13	29	.316	.474
Ashby,Andy	L	.344	32	11	0	0	2	5	0	3	.344	.531
Throws Right	R	.188	16	3	1	0	0	0	1	4	.235	.250
Astacio,Pedro	L	.286	304	87	21	4	10	43	32	62	.364	.480
Throws Right	R	.268	351	94	22	2	12	49	22	82	.321	.444
Atchley,J	L	.350	20	7	1	0	3	10	2	5	.435	.850
Throws Left	R	.227	22	5	0	0	1	3	3	3	.320	.364
Austin,Jeff	L	.273	44	12	2	0	1	4	6	11	.360	.386
Throws Right	R	.273	55	15	2	0	3	15	8	16	.364	.473
Aybar,Manny	L	.268	41	11	1	0	2	10	7	7	.380	.439
Throws Right	R	.333	51	17	2	0	3	5	10	9	.452	.549
Bacsik,Mike	L	.167	12	2	0	1	0	6	1	1	.267	.333
Throws Left	R	.393	28	11	1	0	0	7	2	3	.433	.429
Baez,Benito	L	.471	17	8	1	0	0	3	1	3	.500	.529
Throws Left	R	.438	32	14	3	1	3	14	5	11	.514	.875
Baez,Danys	L	.188	69	13	3	0	1	6	10	21	.291	.275
Throws Right	R	.193	109	21	6	0	4	16	10	31	.276	.358
Bailey,Cory	L	.164	116	19	4	0	0	9	21	34	.290	.198
Throws Right	R	.297	128	38	2	1	3	21	12	27	.352	.398

Pitcher	vs	Avg	AB	H	2B	3B	HR	BI	BB	SO	OBP	SLG
Baldwin,James	L	.260	319	83	16	1	14	49	31	52	.327	.448
Throws Right	R	.299	361	108	16	1	11	40	32	43	.361	.440
Bale,John	L	.138	29	4	0	0	0	2	5	5	.257	.138
Throws Left	R	.219	64	14	4	0	2	11	12	16	.346	.375
Balfour,Grant	L	.667	3	2	0	0	1	2	3	0	.714	1.667
Throws Right	R	.167	6	1	0	0	1	2	0	2	.167	.667
Banks,Willie	L	.000	13	0	0	0	0	0	1	5	.071	.000
Throws Right	R	.200	25	5	3	0	0	1	3	5	.286	.320
Barcelo,L	L	.311	45	14	4	2	0	7	2	7	.333	.489
Throws Right	R	.250	40	10	2	1	1	9	6	8	.362	.425
Batista,M	L	.218	206	45	6	1	4	16	25	38	.306	.316
Throws Right	R	.232	293	68	10	2	9	34	35	52	.329	.372
Bauer,Rick	L	.254	59	15	2	0	4	10	4	4	.297	.492
Throws Right	R	.274	73	20	4	0	3	11	5	12	.329	.452
Beck,Rod	L	.213	141	30	6	0	7	16	20	33	.319	.404
Throws Right	R	.285	165	47	7	1	8	26	8	30	.318	.485
Beckett,Josh	L	.104	48	5	3	0	1	2	8	14	.246	.229
Throws Right	R	.231	39	9	0	0	2	7	3	10	.286	.385
Beimel,Joe	L	.270	122	33	11	0	4	17	10	23	.336	.459
Throws Left	R	.297	330	98	22	0	8	45	39	35	.377	.436
Beirne,Kevin	L	.077	13	1	1	0	0	4	2	4	.200	.154
Throws Right	R	.600	20	12	3	0	1	7	4	1	.667	.900
Belitz,Todd	L	.154	13	2	0	0	2	5	0	3	.154	.615
Throws Left	R	.304	23	7	3	0	0	2	3	2	.385	.435
Bell,Rob	L	.308	315	97	30	2	18	58	43	45	.386	.587
Throws Right	R	.290	272	79	17	1	14	48	21	52	.351	.515
Benes,Alan	L	.389	18	7	1	0	3	5	3	2	.476	.944
Throws Right	R	.184	38	7	1	0	2	6	9	8	.340	.368
Benes,Andy	L	.286	185	53	10	2	13	35	29	36	.381	.573
Throws Right	R	.286	241	69	10	2	17	48	32	42	.379	.556
Benitez,A	L	.212	113	24	5	0	4	11	28	40	.373	.363
Throws Right	R	.215	163	35	3	0	8	21	12	53	.267	.380
Benoit,J	L	.333	12	4	1	0	2	4	2	2	.400	.917
Throws Right	R	.400	10	4	0	0	1	2	1	2	.455	.700
Bere,Jason	L	.289	280	81	27	1	11	47	38	53	.375	.511
Throws Right	R	.209	430	90	20	2	13	41	39	122	.272	.356
Bernero,Adam	L	.348	23	8	3	0	3	9	2	1	.400	.870
Throws Right	R	.185	27	5	2	0	1	4	2	7	.258	.370
Biddle,Rocky	L	.270	274	74	17	0	9	48	24	43	.333	.431
Throws Right	R	.274	230	63	15	1	7	30	28	42	.364	.439
Bierbrodt,N	L	.297	64	19	4	0	4	13	8	15	.375	.547
Throws Left	R	.289	280	81	14	2	13	41	31	58	.366	.493
Blair,Willie	L	.333	45	15	4	0	2	18	6	5	.415	.556
Throws Right	R	.397	58	23	9	1	1	8	5	10	.455	.638
Blank,Matt	L	.267	15	4	0	0	0	1	2	4	.389	.267
Throws Left	R	.268	71	19	3	2	5	13	11	7	.365	.577
Boehringer,B	L	.333	93	31	9	1	4	21	15	17	.418	.581
Throws Right	R	.202	178	36	7	0	3	23	14	43	.276	.292
Bohanon,Brian	L	.296	108	32	4	0	7	23	11	14	.382	.528
Throws Left	R	.333	285	95	22	2	13	48	36	33	.412	.561

Pitchers vs. Lefthanded and Righthanded Batters

Pitcher	vs	Avg	AB	H	2B	3B	HR	BI	BB	SO	OBP	SLG	Pitcher	vs	Avg	AB	H	2B	3B	HR	BI	BB	SO	OBP	SLG
Bones,Ricky	L	.269	104	28	3	2	2	15	15	17	.367	.394	Carrasco,H	L	.318	107	34	5	0	3	22	12	27	.383	.449
Throws Right	R	.299	144	43	9	3	5	31	18	24	.380	.507	Throws Right	R	.251	171	43	12	1	5	25	18	43	.319	.421
Borbon,Pedro	L	.182	99	18	6	2	2	19	6	36	.241	.343	Castillo,C	L	.400	5	2	0	0	1	1	0	0	.400	1.000
Throws Left	R	.306	98	30	6	2	6	17	6	9	.355	.592	Throws Right	R	.167	6	1	0	0	0	1	0	0	.143	.167
Borkowski,D	L	.250	56	14	1	0	3	16	6	16	.323	.429	Castillo,F	L	.249	257	64	15	1	7	28	25	50	.322	.397
Throws Right	R	.271	59	16	2	0	2	7	9	14	.384	.407	Throws Right	R	.270	274	74	17	1	7	35	10	39	.296	.416
Borland,Toby	L	.429	7	3	0	0	1	2	0	0	.429	.857	Chacon,Shawn	L	.261	253	66	13	3	9	38	45	59	.375	.443
Throws Right	R	.500	10	5	1	0	0	3	1	0	.545	.600	Throws Right	R	.259	352	91	24	3	17	51	42	75	.349	.489
Borowski,Joe	L	.667	3	2	1	0	1	3	1	1	.750	2.000	Charlton,Norm	L	.169	71	12	2	0	2	9	5	18	.253	.282
Throws Right	R	.667	6	4	0	0	0	3	2	0	.750	.667	Throws Left	R	.242	99	24	4	0	2	9	6	30	.290	.343
Bottalico,R	L	.282	85	24	7	0	3	12	16	17	.396	.471	Chen,Bruce	L	.278	90	25	6	2	5	12	13	22	.369	.556
Throws Right	R	.218	156	34	8	2	8	32	9	40	.272	.449	Throws Left	R	.256	473	121	31	5	24	69	46	104	.319	.495
Bottenfield,K	L	.333	90	30	6	1	4	16	11	14	.398	.556	Chiasson,S	L	.333	9	3	0	0	2	2	1	2	.400	1.000
Throws Right	R	.254	122	31	5	2	12	28	5	25	.290	.623	Throws Right	R	.125	16	2	0	0	0	0	1	4	.222	.125
Bowles,Brian	L	.200	5	1	0	0	0	0	0	1	.200	.200	Choate,Randy	L	.183	71	13	5	0	0	3	10	24	.318	.254
Throws Right	R	.333	9	3	0	0	0	1	1	3	.400	.333	Throws Left	R	.216	97	21	8	0	0	11	17	11	.358	.299
Bradford,Chad	L	.300	40	12	2	0	3	6	3	7	.349	.575	Chouinard,B	L	.200	15	3	1	0	2	4	1	4	.250	.667
Throws Right	R	.274	106	29	2	1	3	15	3	27	.300	.396	Throws Right	R	.389	18	7	2	0	2	5	0	1	.389	.833
Brantley,Jeff	L	.375	32	12	1	0	3	9	2	4	.412	.688	Christiansen,J	L	.254	59	15	2	0	2	9	11	14	.380	.390
Throws Right	R	.269	52	14	4	0	2	6	7	7	.350	.462	Throws Left	R	.200	70	14	1	0	3	13	4	17	.234	.343
Brea,Leslie	L	.667	6	4	0	0	2	7	2	0	.750	1.667	Christman,Tim	L	.000	3	0	0	0	0	0	0	0	.000	.000
Throws Right	R	.400	5	2	0	0	0	1	1	0	.500	.400	Throws Left	R	.250	4	1	0	0	1	1	0	2	.250	1.000
Brock,Chris	L	.373	51	19	4	0	2	8	6	9	.458	.569	Clemens,R	L	.235	442	104	21	2	10	48	52	123	.315	.360
Throws Right	R	.211	76	16	7	0	4	8	9	17	.291	.461	Throws Right	R	.258	391	101	23	1	9	40	20	90	.300	.391
Brohawn,Troy	L	.386	70	27	6	0	3	13	11	12	.476	.600	Clement,Matt	L	.286	325	93	19	4	6	38	44	45	.379	.425
Throws Left	R	.233	120	28	4	1	2	16	12	18	.294	.333	Throws Right	R	.248	318	79	25	3	9	43	41	89	.350	.431
Brower,Jim	L	.272	206	56	12	0	7	25	32	25	.369	.432	Coco,Pasqual	L	.286	21	6	1	0	0	2	5	2	.423	.333
Throws Right	R	.228	276	63	19	0	10	33	28	69	.307	.406	Throws Right	R	.188	32	6	1	0	0	3	1	7	.250	.219
Brown,Kevin	L	.263	213	56	7	0	6	22	22	41	.335	.380	Cogan,Tony	L	.259	54	14	1	0	5	11	9	14	.403	.556
Throws Right	R	.184	207	38	7	0	2	10	16	63	.246	.246	Throws Left	R	.391	46	18	2	2	2	11	4	3	.442	.652
Buddie,Mike	L	.185	65	12	3	1	1	7	8	5	.280	.308	Coggin,Dave	L	.275	153	42	6	0	1	10	21	13	.373	.333
Throws Right	R	.256	86	22	5	1	1	12	9	17	.343	.372	Throws Right	R	.270	211	57	13	1	6	29	18	49	.329	.427
Buehrle,Mark	L	.213	155	33	6	0	5	23	8	35	.268	.348	Colome,Jesus	L	.186	70	13	4	0	1	7	13	12	.306	.286
Throws Left	R	.234	661	155	34	4	19	54	40	91	.281	.384	Throws Right	R	.222	108	24	5	0	7	19	12	19	.311	.463
Burba,Dave	L	.359	301	108	28	3	10	54	28	53	.408	.571	Colon,Bartolo	L	.278	446	124	20	3	17	58	59	105	.360	.451
Throws Right	R	.255	314	80	19	0	6	48	26	65	.315	.373	Throws Right	R	.242	397	96	21	1	9	37	31	96	.299	.368
Burkett,John	L	.223	367	82	14	3	9	32	39	88	.298	.351	Cone,David	L	.291	282	82	11	1	11	39	33	49	.378	.454
Throws Right	R	.235	446	105	28	1	8	44	31	99	.290	.357	Throws Right	R	.257	257	66	12	0	6	29	24	66	.322	.374
Burnett,A.J.	L	.247	324	80	15	1	5	26	40	63	.332	.346	Cook,Dennis	L	.215	79	17	6	0	3	10	6	14	.276	.405
Throws Right	R	.213	305	65	12	1	15	45	43	65	.315	.407	Throws Left	R	.274	95	26	5	0	5	12	8	24	.337	.484
Byrd,Paul	L	.352	210	74	17	0	7	25	16	12	.396	.533	Cooper,Brian	L	.179	28	5	1	0	1	3	2	2	.233	.321
Throws Right	R	.236	195	46	4	0	5	19	10	40	.273	.333	Throws Right	R	.227	22	5	0	0	1	2	2	5	.280	.364
Cabrera,Jose	L	.247	89	22	5	1	4	20	13	18	.336	.461	Coppinger,R	L	.280	25	7	3	1	0	2	11	3	.500	.480
Throws Right	R	.233	129	30	7	1	1	12	12	25	.299	.326	Throws Right	R	.283	60	17	3	1	5	15	4	12	.333	.617
Callaway,M	L	.125	8	1	0	0	1	1	1	0	.222	.500	Cordero,F	L	.500	4	2	0	0	0	1	2	0	.667	.500
Throws Right	R	.200	10	2	0	0	1	3	1	2	.273	.500	Throws Right	R	.167	6	1	0	0	0	0	0	1	.167	.167
Carpenter,C	L	.288	400	115	30	4	13	45	45	67	.367	.480	Corey,Mark	L	.000	1	0	0	0	0	1	2	0	.667	.000
Throws Right	R	.262	435	114	15	3	16	49	30	90	.325	.421	Throws Right	R	.556	9	5	0	0	0	3	1	3	.600	.556
Carrara,G	L	.259	147	38	6	1	8	19	15	33	.327	.476	Cormier,Rheal	L	.294	68	20	7	0	2	12	5	13	.368	.485
Throws Right	R	.207	169	35	4	1	4	13	9	37	.250	.314	Throws Left	R	.223	130	29	6	1	3	10	12	24	.294	.354

Pitchers vs. Lefthanded and Righthanded Batters

Pitcher	vs	Avg	AB	H	2B	3B	HR	BI	BB	SO	OBP	SLG
Cornejo,Nate	L	.381	97	37	7	1	9	19	20	10	.492	.753
Throws Right	R	.302	86	26	5	1	1	16	8	12	.375	.419
Crabtree,Tim	L	.438	32	14	3	0	0	7	8	5	.524	.531
Throws Right	R	.359	64	23	6	0	3	14	6	11	.417	.594
Crawford,P	L	.286	77	22	3	0	1	8	9	9	.368	.364
Throws Right	R	.265	68	18	1	0	2	11	4	16	.311	.368
Creek,Doug	L	.198	86	17	2	0	2	13	15	25	.327	.291
Throws Left	R	.250	136	34	9	0	5	24	34	41	.402	.426
Cressend,Jack	L	.294	85	25	3	1	4	14	6	16	.333	.494
Throws Right	R	.198	126	25	8	1	2	11	10	24	.263	.325
Cruz,Juan	L	.324	71	23	4	0	3	10	10	16	.415	.507
Throws Right	R	.183	93	17	2	0	1	5	7	23	.248	.237
Cruz,Nelson	L	.273	132	36	4	2	5	22	9	29	.340	.424
Throws Right	R	.209	172	36	9	1	6	23	15	46	.286	.378
Cubillan,D	L	.333	39	13	6	0	1	11	5	4	.383	.564
Throws Right	R	.273	66	18	4	0	0	5	7	15	.342	.333
Cunnane,Will	L	.295	78	23	6	0	2	10	14	20	.409	.449
Throws Right	R	.336	128	43	8	2	4	23	8	17	.377	.523
Daal,Omar	L	.214	126	27	5	2	4	12	11	24	.286	.381
Throws Left	R	.286	602	172	38	6	22	74	45	83	.336	.478
D'Amico,Jeff	L	.333	75	25	7	0	5	15	11	9	.419	.627
Throws Right	R	.289	121	35	10	2	6	21	5	23	.320	.554
Darensbourg,V	L	.294	85	25	10	1	3	23	1	18	.299	.541
Throws Left	R	.262	103	27	3	0	1	7	9	15	.325	.320
Davenport,Joe	L	.211	19	4	0	0	0	5	1	4	.250	.211
Throws Right	R	.235	17	4	0	0	1	2	6	4	.435	.412
Davey,Tom	L	.290	62	18	4	1	0	5	13	11	.413	.387
Throws Right	R	.258	89	23	2	0	3	10	4	26	.298	.382
Davis,Doug	L	.307	166	51	12	2	3	20	12	21	.350	.458
Throws Left	R	.291	580	169	30	6	11	72	57	94	.356	.471
Davis,Kane	L	.337	95	32	8	1	7	15	12	12	.404	.663
Throws Right	R	.204	167	34	7	1	4	18	20	35	.289	.329
Davis,Lance	L	.267	86	23	4	2	3	16	5	8	.308	.465
Throws Left	R	.301	336	101	24	1	9	38	29	45	.358	.458
DeJean,Mike	L	.227	132	30	9	1	1	20	18	34	.329	.333
Throws Right	R	.242	186	45	7	0	3	19	21	34	.335	.328
de los Santos	L	.000	0	0	0	0	0	0	0	0	.000	.000
Throws Left	R	.250	4	1	0	0	0	0	1	1	.400	.250
Dempster,R	L	.270	382	103	27	4	11	51	63	74	.375	.448
Throws Right	R	.269	428	115	23	4	10	57	49	97	.350	.411
Dessens,Elmer	L	.325	369	120	14	0	18	43	24	45	.363	.509
Throws Right	R	.239	422	101	19	0	14	49	32	83	.293	.384
DeWitt,Matt	L	.273	33	9	2	0	1	2	6	6	.385	.424
Throws Right	R	.310	42	13	5	0	1	7	4	7	.383	.500
Dickey,R.A.	L	.158	19	3	1	0	0	2	1	3	.200	.211
Throws Right	R	.370	27	10	5	0	3	9	6	1	.485	.889
Dingman,Craig	L	.273	11	3	2	0	0	3	1	2	.333	.455
Throws Right	R	.400	20	8	0	0	4	10	2	0	.500	1.000
Dotel,Octavio	L	.238	172	41	6	0	1	16	29	67	.347	.291
Throws Right	R	.178	213	38	9	2	4	19	18	78	.248	.296

Pitcher	vs	Avg	AB	H	2B	3B	HR	BI	BB	SO	OBP	SLG
Douglass,Sean	L	.316	38	12	3	0	2	6	8	5	.426	.553
Throws Right	R	.209	43	9	3	0	1	5	3	12	.277	.349
Dreifort,D	L	.294	163	48	11	0	7	36	30	44	.414	.491
Throws Right	R	.215	191	41	6	0	4	24	17	47	.286	.309
Drese,Ryan	L	.288	59	17	4	1	1	7	8	11	.382	.441
Throws Right	R	.205	73	15	3	0	1	5	7	13	.275	.288
Drew,Tim	L	.362	58	21	3	0	4	16	11	4	.472	.621
Throws Right	R	.326	92	30	7	0	5	21	5	11	.370	.565
Duchscherer,J	L	.375	40	15	0	1	4	10	1	6	.432	.725
Throws Right	R	.321	28	9	3	1	1	8	3	5	.406	.607
Duckworth,B	L	.256	90	23	6	1	1	10	16	16	.376	.378
Throws Right	R	.221	154	34	12	0	1	15	13	24	.295	.318
Duncan,C	L	.286	56	16	3	0	2	9	11	15	.414	.446
Throws Right	R	.245	106	26	4	1	3	13	14	34	.328	.387
Durbin,Chad	L	.279	366	102	24	1	7	38	24	49	.327	.407
Throws Right	R	.298	332	99	11	3	19	59	34	46	.371	.521
Duvall,Mike	L	.400	10	4	0	0	1	4	1	4	.417	.700
Throws Left	R	.333	9	3	0	0	0	0	1	0	.400	.333
Eaton,Adam	L	.260	235	61	15	0	9	28	18	53	.320	.438
Throws Right	R	.220	214	47	7	1	11	30	22	56	.295	.416
Eischen,Joey	L	.231	39	9	1	0	1	6	4	11	.302	.333
Throws Left	R	.270	74	20	4	1	3	14	12	8	.379	.473
Elarton,Scott	L	.252	266	67	6	0	17	44	36	57	.339	.466
Throws Right	R	.310	255	79	11	0	17	50	23	30	.380	.553
Eldred,Cal	L	.444	18	8	1	0	1	8	3	6	.583	.667
Throws Right	R	.400	10	4	1	0	0	1	0	0	.400	.500
Ellis,Robert	L	.263	167	44	5	0	6	25	22	15	.345	.401
Throws Right	R	.318	195	62	12	0	6	33	12	26	.362	.472
Embree,Alan	L	.220	91	20	5	1	2	17	8	31	.284	.363
Throws Left	R	.352	128	45	7	1	12	31	9	28	.392	.703
Erdos,Todd	L	.267	30	8	2	0	1	7	2	3	.324	.433
Throws Right	R	.259	27	7	0	0	1	4	6	4	.405	.370
Escobar,K	L	.203	217	44	14	1	6	23	28	57	.293	.359
Throws Right	R	.206	238	49	10	0	2	20	24	64	.282	.273
Estes,Shawn	L	.227	154	35	6	1	2	12	13	33	.288	.318
Throws Left	R	.262	443	116	33	2	9	51	64	76	.355	.406
Estrada,H	L	.300	10	3	1	0	0	3	0	3	.300	.400
Throws Left	R	.500	10	5	2	0	1	4	1	1	.583	1.000
Eyre,Scott	L	.192	26	5	0	0	1	2	3	8	.300	.308
Throws Left	R	.323	31	10	5	0	0	7	4	8	.389	.484
Farnsworth,K	L	.223	121	27	7	0	3	7	13	36	.299	.355
Throws Right	R	.207	184	38	8	1	5	17	16	71	.271	.342
Fassero,Jeff	L	.247	97	24	3	0	3	12	9	30	.308	.371
Throws Left	R	.228	184	42	13	0	3	28	14	49	.285	.348
Fernandez,J	L	.276	29	8	2	0	0	3	3	3	.344	.345
Throws Right	R	.250	20	5	1	0	1	3	2	2	.400	.450
Fernandez,O	L	.310	113	35	11	0	3	19	16	14	.395	.487
Throws Right	R	.319	213	68	18	1	5	37	17	21	.365	.484
Fetters,Mike	L	.247	85	21	2	1	5	17	13	13	.343	.471
Throws Right	R	.269	104	28	6	2	2	17	13	24	.366	.423

Pitchers vs. Lefthanded and Righthanded Batters

Pitcher	vs	Avg	AB	H	2B	3B	HR	BI	BB	SO	OBP	SLG
Figueroa,N	L	.333	129	43	12	0	4	15	19	21	.423	.519
Throws Right	R	.241	216	52	10	3	4	20	18	40	.317	.370
Fikac,Jeremy	L	.000	27	0	0	0	0	0	4	8	.129	.000
Throws Right	R	.234	64	15	1	1	2	8	1	11	.258	.375
File,Bob	L	.242	95	23	3	0	3	12	19	8	.379	.368
Throws Right	R	.207	164	34	7	0	3	21	10	30	.272	.305
Finley,Chuck	L	.250	72	18	8	0	0	6	8	18	.321	.361
Throws Left	R	.299	378	113	26	2	14	60	27	78	.345	.489
Fiore,Tony	L	.176	17	3	1	0	0	2	0	6	.222	.235
Throws Right	R	.300	20	6	2	0	0	4	3	2	.391	.400
Florie,Bryce	L	.278	18	5	1	0	0	3	0	2	.278	.333
Throws Right	R	.350	20	7	2	1	1	6	7	5	.519	.700
Fogg,Josh	L	.214	14	3	2	0	0	2	1	6	.313	.357
Throws Right	R	.206	34	7	2	0	0	2	2	11	.243	.265
Fossum,Casey	L	.188	32	6	1	0	0	3	8	4	.357	.219
Throws Left	R	.275	138	38	8	2	4	19	12	22	.355	.449
Foster,Kevin	L	.290	31	9	0	3	2	6	4	6	.371	.677
Throws Right	R	.324	37	12	0	1	0	8	6	10	.447	.378
Foster,Kris	L	.217	23	5	1	0	1	1	2	5	.280	.391
Throws Right	R	.250	16	4	0	0	0	2	6	3	.455	.250
Foulke,Keith	L	.212	156	33	4	1	3	18	15	42	.283	.308
Throws Right	R	.183	131	24	3	0	0	13	7	33	.262	.206
Fox,Chad	L	.158	101	16	3	1	3	9	15	34	.274	.297
Throws Right	R	.197	142	28	5	0	3	13	21	46	.315	.296
Franco,John	L	.236	55	13	2	0	1	10	2	11	.276	.327
Throws Left	R	.275	153	42	5	1	7	20	17	39	.349	.458
Franklin,Ryan	L	.276	127	35	5	1	8	18	18	19	.366	.520
Throws Right	R	.232	177	41	7	0	5	18	6	41	.270	.356
Franklin,W	L	.412	17	7	0	0	1	2	2	4	.474	.588
Throws Left	R	.294	34	10	1	0	3	7	7	5	.415	.588
Frascatore,J	L	.238	21	5	0	0	0	0	2	3	.304	.238
Throws Right	R	.250	44	11	2	0	4	5	2	6	.283	.568
Fuentes,Brian	L	.111	18	2	0	0	0	3	7	4	.429	.111
Throws Left	R	.235	17	4	1	0	2	7	1	6	.263	.647
Fultz,Aaron	L	.237	114	27	6	0	2	17	5	28	.266	.342
Throws Left	R	.276	156	43	11	1	7	21	16	39	.343	.494
Fyhrie,Mike	L	.310	29	9	0	0	0	1	2	1	.355	.310
Throws Right	R	.205	44	9	0	0	1	3	6	10	.300	.273
Gagne,Eric	L	.256	277	71	22	1	11	46	15	54	.311	.462
Throws Right	R	.247	296	73	15	2	13	45	31	76	.328	.443
Gandarillas,G	L	.343	35	12	0	0	2	10	5	3	.425	.514
Throws Right	R	.302	43	13	2	1	0	6	5	4	.375	.395
Garces,Rich	L	.188	101	19	2	2	1	10	14	19	.291	.277
Throws Right	R	.240	150	36	13	2	5	26	11	32	.305	.453
Garcia,Freddy	L	.242	475	115	33	5	10	37	52	79	.317	.396
Throws Right	R	.205	409	84	14	0	6	42	17	84	.243	.384
Gardner,Mark	L	.290	176	51	11	2	8	25	22	23	.365	.511
Throws Right	R	.237	177	42	8	2	9	27	12	30	.293	.458
Garland,Jon	L	.276	217	60	9	0	6	21	30	22	.369	.401
Throws Right	R	.278	227	63	8	1	10	32	25	39	.348	.454
George,Chris	L	.222	54	12	3	1	3	11	3	5	.254	.481
Throws Left	R	.303	234	71	18	2	11	32	15	27	.343	.538
Ginter,Matt	L	.215	65	14	4	0	0	9	9	9	.321	.277
Throws Right	R	.256	78	20	3	0	2	12	5	15	.337	.372
Glavine,Tom	L	.253	182	46	12	0	5	20	14	27	.303	.401
Throws Left	R	.263	635	167	20	1	19	61	83	89	.347	.387
Glover,Gary	L	.237	207	49	8	1	7	26	20	34	.310	.386
Throws Right	R	.269	182	49	11	1	9	37	12	29	.318	.489
Glynn,Ryan	L	.360	89	32	7	2	1	16	18	6	.463	.517
Throws Right	R	.265	102	27	4	0	6	18	8	9	.315	.480
Gomes,Wayne	L	.319	91	29	3	3	5	26	14	13	.398	.582
Throws Right	R	.279	154	43	10	1	2	13	15	39	.345	.396
Gonzalez,D	L	.365	96	35	4	1	2	18	8	10	.411	.490
Throws Right	R	.266	139	37	8	0	2	17	9	21	.303	.367
Gordon,Flash	L	.188	69	13	3	0	1	5	8	20	.273	.275
Throws Right	R	.188	101	19	5	0	3	13	8	47	.255	.327
Graves,Danny	L	.301	133	40	8	0	5	27	11	18	.363	.474
Throws Right	R	.243	177	43	11	2	2	19	7	31	.277	.362
Green,Steve	L	.273	11	3	0	0	0	0	4	3	.467	.273
Throws Right	R	.100	10	1	0	0	0	1	2	1	.250	.100
Grilli,Jason	L	.276	58	16	2	0	3	7	9	11	.373	.466
Throws Right	R	.326	43	14	1	0	3	7	2	6	.383	.558
Grimsley,J	L	.261	161	42	4	0	4	15	16	21	.328	.360
Throws Right	R	.218	133	29	6	0	4	20	12	40	.291	.353
Groom,Buddy	L	.194	103	20	3	1	3	12	2	27	.208	.330
Throws Left	R	.291	151	44	11	2	1	15	7	27	.327	.411
Guardado,E	L	.167	90	15	3	0	1	8	3	29	.191	.233
Throws Left	R	.216	148	32	8	0	4	19	20	38	.310	.351
Guthrie,Mark	L	.259	85	22	4	1	1	9	11	24	.350	.365
Throws Left	R	.241	112	27	3	0	6	17	9	28	.306	.429
Guzman,G	L	.273	11	3	0	0	1	3	2	1	.385	.545
Throws Right	R	.174	23	4	0	0	1	1	1	3	.208	.304
Hackman,L	L	.308	39	12	5	0	3	5	4	3	.386	.667
Throws Right	R	.172	93	16	6	0	4	10	10	21	.260	.366
Halama,John	L	.357	129	46	5	0	7	17	12	9	.435	.558
Throws Left	R	.271	317	86	13	1	11	42	14	41	.299	.423
Halladay,Roy	L	.228	202	46	11	0	2	23	12	45	.270	.312
Throws Right	R	.255	200	51	15	0	1	13	13	51	.304	.345
Hamilton,Joey	L	.348	287	100	21	1	11	42	23	36	.391	.544
Throws Right	R	.327	284	93	23	3	9	48	21	56	.377	.525
Hampton,Mike	L	.346	159	55	11	1	8	35	16	17	.407	.579
Throws Left	R	.284	638	181	35	5	23	86	69	105	.357	.462
Harnisch,Pete	L	.227	66	15	6	0	2	12	11	3	.329	.409
Throws Right	R	.388	85	33	8	0	7	16	6	14	.430	.729
Harper,Travis	L	.500	20	10	4	0	3	7	2	0	.545	1.150
Throws Right	R	.385	13	5	0	0	2	4	1	2	.429	.846
Harville,Chad	L	.125	8	1	0	0	0	0	0	1	.125	.125
Throws Right	R	.333	3	1	0	0	0	0	0	1	.333	.333
Hasegawa,S	L	.221	95	21	6	1	1	9	13	18	.318	.337
Throws Right	R	.270	115	31	5	0	4	19	7	23	.315	.417

Pitchers vs. Lefthanded and Righthanded Batters

Pitcher	vs	Avg	AB	H	2B	3B	HR	BI	BB	SO	OBP	SLG
Hawkins,L	L	.276	98	27	4	0	1	17	21	25	.402	.347
Throws Right	R	.305	105	32	6	0	2	26	18	11	.400	.419
Haynes,Jimmy	L	.259	247	64	10	3	11	35	38	41	.359	.457
Throws Right	R	.291	405	118	21	4	9	54	40	71	.355	.430
Helling,Rick	L	.296	469	139	32	8	19	64	37	90	.346	.520
Throws Right	R	.298	392	117	36	2	19	58	26	64	.342	.546
Henry,Doug	L	.277	137	38	14	2	8	24	21	22	.371	.584
Throws Right	R	.248	149	37	7	0	6	30	24	35	.360	.416
Hentgen,Pat	L	.178	129	23	5	1	4	13	11	21	.241	.326
Throws Right	R	.275	102	28	5	1	3	12	8	12	.327	.431
Heredia,Felix	L	.292	65	19	5	0	3	16	5	17	.347	.508
Throws Left	R	.333	78	26	5	2	3	15	11	11	.416	.564
Heredia,Gil	L	.291	234	68	15	1	8	23	17	20	.336	.466
Throws Right	R	.344	221	76	8	1	19	43	12	28	.380	.647
Herges,Matt	L	.280	168	47	8	1	6	24	34	31	.403	.446
Throws Right	R	.243	206	50	15	0	2	23	12	45	.302	.345
Hermanson,D	L	.276	304	84	22	2	21	48	36	61	.360	.569
Throws Right	R	.255	436	111	31	1	13	45	37	62	.317	.420
Hernandez,A	L	.205	39	8	0	0	4	5	6	1	.326	.513
Throws Right	R	.175	40	7	1	0	3	4	4	9	.267	.425
Hernandez,C	L	.235	17	4	2	0	1	2	2	1	.316	.529
Throws Left	R	.156	45	7	0	0	0	0	5	16	.240	.156
Hernandez,L	L	.299	425	127	23	7	10	67	56	57	.381	.456
Throws Right	R	.296	470	139	27	3	14	67	29	81	.332	.455
Hernandez,O	L	.278	194	54	8	1	12	28	30	44	.384	.515
Throws Right	R	.213	169	36	7	0	7	18	12	33	.268	.379
Hernandez,R	L	.299	137	41	6	0	4	17	15	31	.368	.431
Throws Right	R	.230	122	28	3	1	3	16	11	15	.299	.344
Herndon,J	L	.383	60	23	7	0	2	12	16	6	.519	.600
Throws Right	R	.288	111	32	8	0	3	15	9	8	.352	.441
Hiljus,Erik	L	.248	145	36	7	1	3	15	12	28	.306	.372
Throws Right	R	.281	121	34	6	0	4	17	9	39	.328	.430
Hill,Ken	L	.333	18	6	2	1	1	6	2	1	.400	.722
Throws Right	R	.333	12	4	0	0	3	5	3	1	.500	1.083
Hinchliffe,B	L	.625	8	5	1	0	1	6	1	2	.700	1.125
Throws Right	R	.667	6	4	0	0	1	1	0	0	.667	1.167
Hitchcock,S	L	.370	73	27	6	0	4	14	7	10	.429	.616
Throws Left	R	.282	220	62	15	2	2	26	14	33	.325	.395
Hoffman,T	L	.214	98	21	1	0	5	9	11	36	.291	.378
Throws Right	R	.218	124	27	5	0	5	22	10	27	.279	.379
Holt,Chris	L	.317	309	98	19	6	12	49	31	38	.384	.534
Throws Right	R	.321	308	99	19	1	6	38	26	42	.378	.448
Holtz,Mike	L	.313	80	25	8	1	2	15	7	20	.378	.513
Throws Left	R	.227	66	15	6	0	3	12	8	18	.311	.455
Howry,Bob	L	.306	147	45	9	3	6	28	14	30	.366	.531
Throws Right	R	.253	158	40	5	1	5	24	16	34	.331	.392
Hudson,Tim	L	.256	461	118	23	1	11	48	37	87	.314	.382
Throws Right	R	.232	422	98	8	0	9	43	34	94	.290	.315
Hutchinson,C	L	.462	13	6	1	1	2	7	1	1	.500	1.154
Throws Right	R	.429	7	3	1	0	1	5	5	1	.692	1.000

Pitcher	vs	Avg	AB	H	2B	3B	HR	BI	BB	SO	OBP	SLG
Irabu,Hideki	L	.333	39	13	2	0	2	6	2	5	.357	.538
Throws Right	R	.290	31	9	2	0	1	2	1	13	.313	.452
Isringhausen,J	L	.240	154	37	8	0	3	13	14	38	.304	.351
Throws Right	R	.152	112	17	7	1	2	15	9	36	.213	.286
Jackson,Mike	L	.294	119	35	5	0	7	18	18	18	.387	.513
Throws Right	R	.231	143	33	4	0	7	20	4	28	.258	.406
James,Mike	L	.268	41	11	2	0	4	13	6	7	.375	.610
Throws Right	R	.302	106	32	8	3	1	19	11	19	.385	.462
Jarvis,Kevin	L	.259	317	82	17	4	19	48	17	51	.298	.517
Throws Right	R	.251	427	107	28	4	18	46	32	82	.307	.461
Jennings,J	L	.310	71	22	6	1	1	7	10	10	.390	.465
Throws Right	R	.247	81	20	8	0	1	9	9	16	.330	.383
Jensen,Ryan	L	.338	68	23	3	1	1	10	18	9	.489	.456
Throws Right	R	.219	96	21	3	1	4	10	7	17	.286	.396
Jimenez,Jose	L	.255	94	24	7	0	4	19	10	16	.327	.457
Throws Right	R	.271	118	32	6	0	2	12	12	21	.336	.373
Jodie,Brett	L	.314	35	11	0	0	4	6	6	6	.415	.657
Throws Right	R	.250	60	15	0	0	6	11	7	7	.328	.550
Johnson,Adam	L	.321	53	17	3	0	4	13	8	10	.419	.604
Throws Right	R	.326	46	15	4	0	2	9	5	7	.429	.543
Johnson,Jason	L	.263	373	98	24	2	16	46	43	57	.341	.466
Throws Right	R	.252	381	96	20	3	12	51	34	57	.327	.415
Johnson,J	L	.235	17	4	0	0	0	3	5	4	.409	.235
Throws Right	R	.375	24	9	5	0	2	8	2	7	.400	.833
Johnson,Mike	L	.286	14	4	2	0	0	0	1	2	.375	.429
Throws Right	R	.300	30	9	2	0	3	5	3	8	.382	.667
Johnson,R	L	.196	107	21	5	0	1	13	9	32	.306	.271
Throws Left	R	.204	783	160	28	2	18	51	62	340	.270	.314
Jones,B	L	.281	310	87	14	2	15	49	22	40	.326	.484
Throws Right	R	.320	510	163	28	4	22	78	16	73	.341	.520
Jones,Todd	L	.325	123	40	7	0	5	24	12	22	.382	.504
Throws Right	R	.301	156	47	8	1	4	19	17	32	.366	.442
Judd,Mike	L	.258	66	17	3	0	4	13	7	10	.324	.485
Throws Right	R	.327	52	17	1	1	0	7	8	6	.413	.385
Julio,Jorge	L	.290	31	9	0	3	1	7	5	3	.405	.581
Throws Right	R	.286	56	16	4	1	1	10	4	19	.333	.446
Karnuth,Jason	L	.429	7	3	0	0	1	1	2	0	.556	.857
Throws Right	R	.250	12	3	2	0	0	1	2	1	.400	.417
Karsay,Steve	L	.257	148	38	6	0	2	8	14	42	.321	.338
Throws Right	R	.203	172	35	6	1	3	18	11	41	.250	.302
Keisler,Randy	L	.250	36	9	2	0	3	7	4	6	.325	.556
Throws Left	R	.261	165	43	3	3	9	24	30	30	.372	.479
Kennedy,Joe	L	.225	89	20	3	0	3	12	8	16	.286	.360
Throws Left	R	.279	365	102	26	3	13	47	26	62	.329	.474
Kile,Darryl	L	.279	380	106	20	1	11	41	30	75	.337	.424
Throws Right	R	.253	482	122	18	3	11	32	35	104	.311	.371
Kim,B	L	.199	156	31	4	0	8	15	20	46	.306	.378
Throws Right	R	.151	179	27	6	1	2	15	24	67	.266	.229
Kim,Sun-Woo	L	.293	92	27	10	0	1	13	10	14	.375	.435
Throws Right	R	.333	81	27	4	1	0	10	11	13	.426	.407

Pitchers vs. Lefthanded and Righthanded Batters

Pitcher	vs	Avg	AB	H	2B	3B	HR	BI	BB	SO	OBP	SLG	Pitcher	vs	Avg	AB	H	2B	3B	HR	BI	BB	SO	OBP	SLG
King,Ray	L	.210	105	22	5	0	1	17	7	25	.257	.286	Lloyd,Graeme	L	.252	103	26	3	2	3	17	10	17	.339	.408
Throws Left	R	.276	98	27	8	3	4	17	18	24	.390	.541	Throws Left	R	.284	169	48	16	0	3	18	11	27	.333	.432
Kline,Steve	L	.149	101	15	0	0	0	10	14	28	.250	.149	Loaiza,E	L	.329	380	125	24	1	9	38	24	46	.379	.468
Throws Left	R	.238	160	38	11	2	3	14	15	26	.313	.388	Throws Right	R	.286	398	114	25	2	18	59	16	64	.315	.495
Knight,B	L	.400	15	6	1	0	2	5	3	2	.500	.867	Loewer,C	L	.500	16	8	4	1	2	9	2	0	.556	1.250
Throws Right	R	.353	34	12	2	0	3	10	0	5	.353	.676	Throws Right	R	.556	9	5	1	0	0	2	1	1	.600	.667
Knott,Eric	L	.333	6	2	0	0	0	2	0	0	.429	.333	Lohse,Kyle	L	.348	181	63	10	4	9	32	17	29	.415	.597
Throws Left	R	.353	17	6	2	0	0	4	0	4	.389	.471	Throws Right	R	.219	178	39	8	1	7	24	12	35	.276	.393
Knotts,Gary	L	.375	8	3	0	0	1	2	0	2	.375	.750	Loiselle,Rich	L	.429	35	15	5	0	3	15	9	3	.565	.829
Throws Right	R	.235	17	4	2	0	0	2	1	7	.350	.353	Throws Right	R	.302	43	13	1	1	0	9	8	6	.434	.372
Koch,Billy	L	.289	121	35	4	0	5	19	20	27	.390	.446	Looper,Braden	L	.250	112	28	3	1	6	15	11	18	.320	.455
Throws Right	R	.245	139	34	8	0	2	20	13	28	.325	.345	Throws Right	R	.236	148	35	6	0	2	19	19	34	.324	.318
Kohlmeier,R	L	.395	81	32	5	0	8	18	9	8	.462	.753	Lopez,Albie	L	.299	365	109	22	1	13	44	51	58	.383	.471
Throws Right	R	.190	84	16	2	1	5	13	10	21	.284	.417	Throws Right	R	.267	439	117	26	1	13	69	24	78	.308	.419
Kolb,Brandon	L	.313	16	5	0	0	2	5	2	6	.368	.688	Lowe,Derek	L	.317	180	57	11	1	3	20	17	37	.380	.439
Throws Right	R	.407	27	11	2	2	4	10	6	2	.500	1.074	Throws Right	R	.250	184	46	5	0	4	19	12	45	.307	.342
Kolb,Danny	L	.261	23	6	0	0	1	6	3	4	.333	.391	Lowe,Sean	L	.281	235	66	13	3	5	26	16	35	.328	.426
Throws Right	R	.257	35	9	1	0	1	3	7	11	.381	.371	Throws Right	R	.233	245	57	12	0	7	27	16	36	.289	.367
Koplove,Mike	L	.250	12	3	0	0	1	4	2	2	.357	.500	Lukasiewicz,M	L	.278	36	10	1	0	1	8	4	9	.350	.389
Throws Right	R	.192	26	5	2	0	0	3	7	12	.400	.269	Throws Left	R	.224	49	11	2	0	5	12	5	16	.316	.571
Lawrence,B	L	.281	196	55	10	3	9	26	17	32	.347	.500	Lundquist,D	L	.241	29	7	2	1	0	4	2	7	.290	.379
Throws Right	R	.215	242	52	6	2	1	23	17	52	.269	.269	Throws Right	R	.271	48	13	4	0	1	8	5	12	.345	.417
Lee,David	L	.222	81	18	6	0	5	14	12	23	.326	.481	Lyon,Brandon	L	.289	128	37	10	1	1	12	11	14	.336	.406
Throws Right	R	.321	106	34	6	0	1	10	15	19	.429	.406	Throws Right	R	.239	109	26	7	0	5	15	4	21	.267	.440
Leiter,Al	L	.254	114	29	9	1	2	11	3	24	.277	.404	MacDougal,M	L	.333	33	11	1	2	1	4	3	2	.405	.576
Throws Left	R	.251	593	149	25	5	16	67	43	118	.303	.391	Throws Right	R	.241	29	7	2	1	1	4	1	5	.267	.483
Leiter,Mark	L	.226	53	12	2	0	2	6	4	10	.293	.377	MacRae,Scott	L	.304	46	14	5	1	0	6	4	7	.360	.457
Throws Right	R	.235	85	20	4	0	4	10	4	16	.278	.424	Throws Right	R	.244	78	19	4	0	0	8	4	11	.291	.295
Leskanic,C	L	.275	102	28	6	1	2	9	17	19	.383	.412	Maddux,Greg	L	.264	401	106	21	2	11	40	13	91	.285	.409
Throws Right	R	.220	159	35	7	0	9	21	14	45	.287	.434	Throws Right	R	.243	469	114	13	2	9	37	14	82	.271	.337
Levine,Al	L	.288	132	38	7	1	5	16	14	12	.358	.470	Maduro,Calvin	L	.261	180	47	7	1	5	22	20	33	.338	.394
Throws Right	R	.229	144	33	4	0	2	22	14	28	.294	.299	Throws Right	R	.217	166	36	5	0	5	19	16	18	.297	.337
Levrault,A	L	.270	222	60	15	1	10	27	34	26	.365	.482	Magnante,Mike	L	.230	87	20	4	0	1	6	6	11	.287	.310
Throws Right	R	.289	298	86	7	3	17	52	25	54	.355	.503	Throws Left	R	.254	118	30	2	0	6	18	7	12	.287	.424
Lidle,Cory	L	.213	380	81	10	2	14	32	29	58	.277	.361	Mahay,Ron	L	.182	22	4	0	1	2	3	4	5	.308	.545
Throws Right	R	.276	322	89	17	2	9	42	18	60	.325	.425	Throws Left	R	.204	49	10	1	0	2	3	11	19	.350	.347
Lieber,Jon	L	.298	403	120	27	2	15	52	25	52	.341	.486	Mahomes,Pat	L	.254	181	46	16	2	9	27	31	25	.358	.514
Throws Right	R	.219	485	106	20	2	10	45	16	96	.247	.330	Throws Right	R	.300	230	69	21	2	8	42	24	36	.360	.513
Ligtenberg,K	L	.241	87	21	4	0	2	7	18	18	.371	.356	Mann,Jim	L	.000	6	0	0	0	0	0	3	1	.333	.000
Throws Right	R	.216	134	29	5	0	2	13	12	38	.277	.299	Throws Right	R	.273	11	3	0	0	0	3	1	4	.429	.273
Lilly,Ted	L	.229	105	24	3	1	2	9	8	28	.303	.333	Mantei,Matt	L	.455	11	5	0	1	2	4	0	5	.455	1.182
Throws Left	R	.278	367	102	26	1	18	61	43	84	.356	.501	Throws Right	R	.063	16	1	0	0	0	0	4	7	.250	.063
Lima,Jose	L	.301	302	91	13	5	20	50	20	28	.347	.576	Manzanillo,J	L	.283	106	30	8	2	2	16	14	23	.371	.453
Throws Right	R	.298	356	106	14	2	15	56	18	56	.337	.475	Throws Right	R	.168	179	30	5	2	2	30	12	57	.225	.251
Lincoln,Mike	L	.196	51	10	4	0	0	7	4	10	.268	.275	Marquis,Jason	L	.220	186	41	9	1	8	23	34	38	.342	.409
Throws Right	R	.240	100	24	7	0	3	12	7	14	.306	.400	Throws Right	R	.243	296	72	14	1	6	32	25	60	.305	.358
Linebrink,S	L	.067	15	1	0	0	0	2	3	4	.211	.067	Marte,Damaso	L	.310	42	13	4	0	1	5	5	10	.396	.476
Throws Right	R	.263	19	5	3	0	0	2	3	5	.417	.421	Throws Left	R	.223	94	21	7	0	4	16	7	29	.286	.426
Lira,Felipe	L	.222	9	2	0	0	0	0	0	1	.222	.222	Martin,Tom	L	.250	32	8	4	0	0	7	3	6	.314	.375
Throws Right	R	.563	16	9	2	0	1	6	2	2	.611	.875	Throws Left	R	.375	40	15	4	1	4	11	7	6	.469	.825

Pitchers vs. Lefthanded and Righthanded Batters

Pitcher	vs	Avg	AB	H	2B	3B	HR	BI	BB	SO	OBP	SLG	Pitcher	vs	Avg	AB	H	2B	3B	HR	BI	BB	SO	OBP	SLG
Martinez,P	L	.216	236	51	7	1	4	19	14	91	.266	.305	Millwood,K	L	.282	195	55	10	0	7	20	25	39	.365	.441
Throws Right	R	.176	187	33	4	2	1	6	11	72	.238	.235	Throws Right	R	.244	270	66	4	1	13	37	15	45	.283	.411
Martinez,R	L	.364	22	8	1	1	2	7	9	2	.548	.773	Milton,Eric	L	.246	142	35	5	0	11	21	13	33	.314	.514
Throws Right	R	.222	36	8	2	0	2	7	7	7	.370	.444	Throws Left	R	.259	722	187	45	4	24	84	48	124	.306	.432
Mathews,T.J.	L	.265	49	13	5	0	0	6	4	8	.315	.367	Mlicki,Dave	L	.321	305	98	23	2	19	54	47	38	.413	.597
Throws Right	R	.260	100	26	6	0	4	12	8	21	.315	.440	Throws Right	R	.291	361	105	20	1	18	56	27	59	.355	.501
Mattes,Troy	L	.309	81	25	3	0	3	8	14	11	.412	.457	Moehler,Brian	L	.217	23	5	1	1	0	2	1	2	.250	.348
Throws Right	R	.265	98	26	7	0	6	22	7	15	.333	.520	Throws Right	R	.167	6	1	0	0	0	1	0	0	.167	.167
Matthews,Mike	L	.133	98	13	3	0	1	9	9	27	.211	.194	Mohler,Mike	L	.375	16	6	1	0	1	3	1	3	.389	.625
Throws Left	R	.268	228	61	15	0	10	27	24	45	.345	.465	Throws Left	R	.242	33	8	2	0	2	5	8	4	.390	.485
Maurer,Dave	L	.364	11	4	1	0	0	1	1	1	.417	.455	Moore,Trey	L	.500	2	1	0	0	0	0	0	0	.500	.500
Throws Left	R	.333	12	4	0	0	1	5	3	3	.467	.583	Throws Left	R	.353	17	6	1	0	0	4	2	1	.421	.412
Mays,Joe	L	.237	460	109	16	5	14	46	30	70	.283	.385	Moreno,Juan	L	.171	70	12	4	0	3	10	17	17	.333	.357
Throws Right	R	.233	412	96	12	0	11	33	34	53	.295	.342	Throws Left	R	.135	74	10	0	0	3	6	11	19	.247	.257
McDill,Allen	L	.233	30	7	0	0	0	7	2	9	.273	.233	Morgan,Mike	L	.208	48	10	2	0	2	8	11	10	.356	.375
Throws Left	R	.240	25	6	1	0	2	6	5	7	.387	.520	Throws Right	R	.354	99	35	9	1	0	20	6	14	.383	.465
McElroy,Chuck	L	.376	109	41	10	0	6	33	18	16	.473	.633	Morris,Matt	L	.237	358	85	17	1	7	29	30	89	.309	.349
Throws Left	R	.234	197	46	6	0	8	28	28	31	.326	.386	Throws Right	R	.286	465	133	28	1	6	50	24	96	.326	.389
McKnight,Tony	L	.276	156	43	3	1	8	20	13	15	.343	.462	Moss,Damian	L	.154	13	2	0	0	1	3	2	4	.267	.385
Throws Right	R	.324	204	66	11	2	11	26	11	31	.359	.559	Throws Left	R	.056	18	1	1	0	0	2	7	4	.320	.111
Meacham,R	L	.270	63	17	4	2	2	16	4	5	.319	.492	Mota,G	L	.310	71	22	3	1	4	11	12	15	.405	.549
Throws Right	R	.282	78	22	10	0	1	12	6	8	.329	.449	Throws Right	R	.248	117	29	6	1	5	23	6	16	.288	.444
Meadows,Brian	L	.350	117	41	7	1	5	19	8	14	.394	.556	Moyer,Jamie	L	.252	214	54	8	0	9	24	11	24	.312	.416
Throws Right	R	.352	91	32	4	0	7	18	4	7	.375	.626	Throws Left	R	.235	567	133	26	3	15	54	33	95	.274	.370
Mecir,Jim	L	.195	118	23	3	2	0	3	15	39	.286	.254	Mulder,Mark	L	.242	198	48	2	1	5	18	7	50	.281	.338
Throws Right	R	.267	116	31	3	1	4	25	11	22	.336	.414	Throws Left	R	.251	662	166	32	1	11	60	44	103	.298	.352
Mendoza,R	L	.248	161	40	9	0	5	20	12	28	.299	.398	Mulholland,T	L	.266	79	21	3	0	3	10	6	12	.330	.418
Throws Right	R	.236	208	49	10	1	4	24	11	42	.278	.351	Throws Left	R	.308	185	57	11	1	9	31	11	30	.347	.524
Mercado,H	L	.287	87	25	5	2	4	22	9	29	.347	.529	Mullen,Scott	L	.389	18	7	2	1	0	4	3	1	.455	.611
Throws Left	R	.252	119	30	3	1	2	8	21	30	.364	.345	Throws Left	R	.250	24	6	1	0	0	3	6	2	.400	.292
Mercedes,Jose	L	.299	374	112	24	3	10	58	36	61	.361	.460	Munoz,Bobby	L	.378	74	28	10	2	2	13	11	6	.465	.649
Throws Right	R	.288	371	107	24	1	10	53	27	62	.345	.439	Throws Right	R	.275	91	25	7	0	4	8	10	15	.353	.484
Mesa,Jose	L	.236	127	30	5	1	1	8	10	22	.300	.315	Murray,Heath	L	.259	81	21	3	0	1	10	17	21	.390	.333
Throws Right	R	.255	137	35	5	0	3	12	10	32	.302	.358	Throws Left	R	.351	174	61	10	2	10	38	23	21	.432	.603
Miadich,Bart	L	.313	16	5	3	0	2	5	3	2	.421	.875	Mussina,Mike	L	.240	421	101	24	1	10	32	21	128	.281	.373
Throws Right	R	.059	17	1	0	0	0	0	5	9	.273	.059	Throws Right	R	.234	431	101	15	1	10	47	21	86	.268	.343
Miceli,Dan	L	.361	72	26	5	0	1	8	10	15	.434	.472	Myers,Mike	L	.231	91	21	6	0	2	12	12	26	.317	.363
Throws Right	R	.196	107	21	5	0	6	18	6	33	.237	.411	Throws Left	R	.216	51	11	3	0	0	4	12	10	.375	.275
Michalak,C	L	.284	141	40	6	0	5	23	13	27	.354	.433	Myers,Rodney	L	.286	77	22	5	0	4	17	7	14	.337	.506
Throws Left	R	.297	394	117	33	2	14	51	42	40	.376	.497	Throws Right	R	.295	105	31	5	0	2	14	13	15	.387	.400
Middlebrook,J	L	.310	29	9	2	0	4	6	6	6	.429	.793	Myette,Aaron	L	.316	174	55	16	0	6	30	18	33	.381	.511
Throws Right	R	.205	44	9	0	0	2	4	4	4	.286	.341	Throws Right	R	.265	147	39	10	1	6	29	19	34	.380	.469
Miller,Matt	L	.222	18	4	1	1	0	4	1	3	.300	.389	Nagy,Charles	L	.293	147	43	10	0	4	27	6	18	.314	.442
Throws Left	R	.480	25	12	4	0	0	3	3	3	.536	.640	Throws Right	R	.391	151	59	15	0	6	19	14	11	.440	.609
Miller,Travis	L	.275	69	19	4	0	1	8	5	15	.324	.377	Neagle,Denny	L	.300	170	51	17	0	5	21	23	32	.399	.488
Throws Left	R	.287	122	35	13	0	4	21	15	15	.359	.492	Throws Left	R	.279	506	141	36	4	24	74	37	107	.325	.508
Miller,Wade	L	.216	365	79	15	1	14	42	35	92	.281	.378	Neal,Blaine	L	.385	13	5	2	1	0	4	2	3	.467	.692
Throws Right	R	.250	416	104	19	0	17	44	41	91	.323	.418	Throws Right	R	.200	10	2	1	0	0	1	3	0	.385	.300
Mills,Alan	L	.455	22	10	2	1	4	13	5	2	.571	1.182	Nelson,Jeff	L	.167	78	13	1	0	1	8	16	29	.316	.218
Throws Right	R	.263	38	10	0	0	2	8	6	7	.378	.421	Throws Right	R	.119	143	17	4	0	2	9	28	59	.284	.189

Pitchers vs. Lefthanded and Righthanded Batters

Pitcher	vs	Avg	AB	H	2B	3B	HR	BI	BB	SO	OBP	SLG	Pitcher	vs	Avg	AB	H	2B	3B	HR	BI	BB	SO	OBP	SLG
Nelson,Joe	L	.500	2	1	0	0	1	6	2	0	.600	2.000	Park,Chan Ho	L	.230	392	90	17	6	16	45	44	81	.319	.426
Throws Right	R	.600	10	6	1	0	0	3	0	0	.636	.700	Throws Right	R	.204	455	93	18	2	7	40	47	137	.292	.299
Nen,Robb	L	.240	150	36	7	1	2	16	12	43	.294	.340	Parker,C	L	.571	7	4	0	0	2	5	1	0	.625	1.429
Throws Right	R	.162	136	22	1	1	4	12	10	50	.221	.272	Throws Right	R	.400	10	4	1	0	0	1	0	1	.400	.500
Neugebauer,N	L	.357	14	5	1	0	1	5	3	6	.471	.643	Paronto,Chad	L	.186	43	8	1	0	0	2	1	6	.205	.209
Throws Right	R	.100	10	1	0	0	0	0	3	5	.308	.100	Throws Right	R	.352	71	25	6	0	5	23	10	10	.434	.648
Nichting,C	L	.408	71	29	7	1	4	14	2	13	.419	.704	Parque,Jim	L	.362	47	17	5	1	4	11	3	8	.423	.766
Throws Right	R	.248	105	26	6	2	4	10	6	27	.286	.457	Throws Left	R	.271	70	19	4	0	3	10	7	7	.333	.457
Nickle,Doug	L	.000	2	0	0	0	0	0	0	1	.000	.000	Parris,Steve	L	.361	230	83	18	3	14	32	25	20	.424	.648
Throws Right	R	.200	5	1	0	0	0	0	0	0	.200	.200	Throws Right	R	.224	192	43	9	0	4	20	16	29	.286	.333
Nitkowski,C	L	.293	82	24	4	0	5	27	11	18	.379	.524	Parrish,John	L	.227	22	5	2	0	0	1	1	8	.292	.318
Throws Left	R	.261	115	30	4	1	2	15	23	24	.401	.365	Throws Left	R	.266	64	17	5	0	5	15	16	12	.427	.578
Nomo,Hideo	L	.222	388	86	13	3	13	47	47	125	.305	.371	Patterson,D	L	.327	104	34	5	0	3	19	6	7	.368	.462
Throws Right	R	.242	351	85	18	2	13	41	49	95	.336	.416	Throws Right	R	.231	130	30	7	0	1	10	6	20	.273	.308
Nunez,J	L	.241	116	28	6	2	4	12	11	31	.315	.431	Pavano,Carl	L	.384	73	28	5	0	3	14	9	12	.446	.575
Throws Left	R	.293	116	34	6	0	3	20	14	29	.376	.422	Throws Right	R	.295	105	31	3	0	4	15	7	24	.351	.438
Nunez,V	L	.213	160	34	5	3	4	16	17	39	.290	.356	Penny,Brad	L	.236	369	87	19	2	5	34	39	70	.312	.339
Throws Right	R	.253	178	45	7	2	5	22	13	25	.313	.399	Throws Right	R	.244	393	96	18	4	10	49	15	84	.280	.387
Ohka,T	L	.303	178	54	14	0	3	23	8	24	.337	.433	Percival,Troy	L	.176	125	22	3	0	2	10	10	45	.237	.248
Throws Right	R	.314	255	80	17	0	12	38	21	44	.368	.522	Throws Right	R	.202	84	17	3	0	1	8	8	26	.287	.274
Ohman,Will	L	.273	22	6	2	0	0	3	1	6	.304	.364	Perez,Odalis	L	.342	73	25	3	0	5	14	6	11	.400	.589
Throws Left	R	.308	26	8	1	0	2	5	5	6	.419	.577	Throws Left	R	.278	299	83	18	0	2	30	33	60	.346	.358
Olivares,Omar	L	.293	184	54	14	3	5	25	24	35	.382	.484	Perisho,Matt	L	.339	62	21	7	0	2	16	4	9	.382	.548
Throws Right	R	.275	251	69	14	1	12	60	18	34	.337	.482	Throws Left	R	.320	103	33	6	1	3	15	10	10	.397	.485
Oliver,Darren	L	.315	162	51	10	3	4	24	11	29	.367	.488	Person,Robert	L	.235	340	80	20	1	17	37	45	86	.332	.450
Throws Left	R	.303	456	138	31	4	19	71	54	75	.377	.513	Throws Right	R	.233	425	99	21	1	17	50	35	97	.293	.407
Olsen,Kevin	L	.148	27	4	2	0	0	0	1	6	.179	.222	Peters,Chris	L	.407	27	11	1	0	2	5	3	5	.452	.667
Throws Right	R	.259	27	7	2	0	0	2	1	7	.286	.333	Throws Left	R	.356	101	36	4	1	5	19	12	9	.431	.564
Olson,Gregg	L	.277	47	13	6	0	3	14	9	13	.386	.596	Peterson,Kyle	L	.448	29	13	3	0	3	8	3	2	.500	.862
Throws Right	R	.260	50	13	0	1	1	11	11	11	.381	.360	Throws Right	R	.176	34	6	2	0	0	1	1	10	.200	.235
Oropesa,Eddie	L	.156	32	5	0	0	1	11	8	10	.325	.250	Petkovsek,M	L	.324	136	44	8	1	5	30	12	19	.381	.507
Throws Left	R	.297	37	11	2	0	0	3	9	5	.435	.351	Throws Right	R	.322	183	59	13	0	9	45	16	23	.377	.541
Orosco,Jesse	L	.275	51	14	1	0	2	12	6	18	.345	.412	Pettitte,Andy	L	.251	167	42	7	0	3	22	6	32	.284	.347
Throws Left	R	.300	10	3	0	0	1	3	1	3	.364	.600	Throws Left	R	.289	629	182	29	7	11	69	35	132	.328	.410
Ortiz,Ramon	L	.285	425	121	26	1	11	54	55	51	.372	.428	Pettyjohn,A	L	.289	38	11	2	0	2	6	5	9	.400	.500
Throws Right	R	.263	388	102	26	4	14	45	21	84	.309	.459	Throws Right	R	.313	224	70	20	2	8	36	16	31	.359	.527
Ortiz,Russ	L	.276	395	109	17	1	7	45	46	71	.351	.377	Phelps,Travis	L	.223	103	23	1	0	1	13	12	18	.305	.262
Throws Right	R	.190	411	78	17	1	6	32	45	98	.268	.280	Throws Right	R	.227	132	30	6	2	5	20	12	36	.297	.417
Osting,Jimmy	L	.333	3	1	1	0	0	1	1	0	.500	.667	Pichardo,H	L	.339	62	21	8	1	2	13	5	5	.382	.597
Throws Left	R	.000	4	0	0	0	0	0	1	3	.200	.000	Throws Right	R	.269	78	21	3	0	1	12	5	12	.348	.346
Osuna,Antonio	L	.500	8	4	0	0	1	6	2	2	.545	.875	Piersoll,C	L	.235	17	4	0	2	0	2	1	2	.278	.471
Throws Right	R	.364	11	4	1	0	2	4	0	4	.417	1.000	Throws Right	R	.286	28	8	2	0	0	3	5	5	.412	.357
Oswalt,Roy	L	.241	274	66	9	2	5	18	15	70	.283	.343	Pineda,Luis	L	.367	30	11	0	1	1	4	6	6	.472	.533
Throws Right	R	.228	263	60	16	0	8	27	9	74	.263	.380	Throws Right	R	.135	37	5	2	1	1	2	8	7	.283	.324
Padilla,V	L	.308	39	12	3	1	1	10	3	8	.357	.513	Pineiro,Joel	L	.230	135	31	10	0	1	13	14	33	.298	.326
Throws Right	R	.258	93	24	7	1	0	13	9	21	.324	.355	Throws Right	R	.150	127	19	3	0	1	6	7	23	.212	.197
Painter,Lance	L	.360	50	18	3	0	5	15	6	8	.439	.720	Plesac,Dan	L	.184	87	16	3	0	3	10	10	47	.268	.322
Throws Left	R	.286	70	20	1	1	2	9	12	12	.390	.414	Throws Left	R	.234	77	18	7	0	1	9	14	21	.355	.364
Paniagua,Jose	L	.257	105	27	6	0	0	15	22	18	.383	.314	Politte,Cliff	L	.231	26	6	0	0	0	2	4	5	.355	.231
Throws Right	R	.216	148	32	5	1	7	26	16	28	.310	.405	Throws Right	R	.257	70	18	3	1	2	8	4	18	.286	.414

Pitchers vs. Lefthanded and Righthanded Batters

Pitcher	vs	Avg	AB	H	2B	3B	HR	BI	BB	SO	OBP	SLG
Ponson,Sidney	L	.321	274	88	26	0	14	43	24	33	.377	.569
Throws Right	R	.258	283	73	17	2	7	33	13	51	.300	.406
Pote,Lou	L	.268	157	42	7	0	7	23	13	29	.324	.446
Throws Right	R	.250	184	46	9	1	4	26	19	37	.325	.375
Powell,Brian	L	.333	3	1	1	0	0	0	1	0	.500	.667
Throws Right	R	.364	11	4	2	0	1	6	2	3	.462	.818
Powell,Jay	L	.296	125	37	7	0	5	24	16	24	.373	.472
Throws Right	R	.233	163	38	8	1	4	23	15	30	.306	.368
Prieto,Ariel	L	.429	7	3	0	0	0	1	0	1	.500	.429
Throws Right	R	.333	9	3	1	0	0	1	2	1	.455	.444
Prinz,Bret	L	.293	58	17	3	0	3	8	12	10	.423	.500
Throws Right	R	.174	92	16	1	0	1	8	7	17	.230	.217
Prokopec,Luke	L	.234	248	58	13	1	14	30	15	36	.278	.464
Throws Right	R	.296	297	88	18	1	13	43	25	55	.356	.495
Pulsipher,B	L	.255	55	14	5	0	3	14	8	13	.364	.509
Throws Left	R	.338	65	22	3	1	2	13	13	7	.450	.508
Quantrill,P	L	.355	107	38	11	0	2	19	6	22	.398	.514
Throws Right	R	.232	207	48	12	1	4	21	6	36	.264	.357
Quevedo,R	L	.275	102	28	11	0	6	17	11	31	.339	.559
Throws Right	R	.241	116	28	10	0	3	11	19	29	.348	.405
Radinsky,S	L	.333	3	1	0	0	1	2	0	1	.333	1.333
Throws Left	R	.429	7	3	1	0	1	4	3	2	.600	1.000
Radke,Brad	L	.271	442	120	27	4	12	48	14	63	.300	.432
Throws Right	R	.271	425	115	20	5	12	53	12	74	.296	.426
Rapp,Pat	L	.267	344	92	17	1	9	46	55	51	.365	.401
Throws Right	R	.254	303	77	11	1	11	44	16	31	.293	.406
Reames,Britt	L	.297	145	43	8	1	5	24	22	27	.391	.469
Throws Right	R	.258	225	58	17	0	11	40	26	59	.344	.480
Redding,Tim	L	.247	85	21	3	0	3	13	17	19	.365	.388
Throws Right	R	.311	132	41	8	2	8	21	7	36	.357	.583
Redman,Mark	L	.333	21	7	3	0	0	1	3	2	.417	.476
Throws Left	R	.285	214	61	7	1	7	27	20	31	.349	.425
Reed,Rick	L	.276	398	110	20	2	15	47	19	78	.309	.450
Throws Right	R	.260	389	101	24	1	13	43	12	64	.289	.427
Reed,Steve	L	.519	52	27	3	1	5	13	14	4	.629	.904
Throws Right	R	.149	168	25	5	2	1	11	9	44	.192	.220
Reichert,Dan	L	.309	246	76	16	3	9	44	38	30	.404	.508
Throws Right	R	.243	226	55	3	1	5	30	29	47	.341	.332
Reith,Brian	L	.324	71	23	6	0	5	14	10	8	.422	.620
Throws Right	R	.340	97	33	9	0	8	18	6	14	.371	.680
Reitsma,Chris	L	.279	330	92	25	3	10	45	25	53	.328	.464
Throws Right	R	.296	395	117	29	1	13	65	24	43	.340	.473
Rekar,Bryan	L	.298	312	93	26	2	9	52	24	40	.348	.481
Throws Right	R	.289	256	74	18	2	12	42	21	47	.349	.516
Remlinger,M	L	.322	90	29	5	2	4	17	4	27	.358	.556
Throws Left	R	.194	196	38	3	1	5	13	19	66	.269	.296
Reyes,Al	L	.292	48	14	3	1	1	7	7	13	.368	.458
Throws Right	R	.250	56	14	2	0	2	7	6	10	.333	.393
Reyes,Dennys	L	.167	54	9	2	0	0	3	10	17	.297	.204
Throws Left	R	.276	152	42	8	2	5	28	25	35	.378	.454
Reynolds,S	L	.303	327	99	16	3	11	40	23	50	.353	.471
Throws Right	R	.279	390	109	20	4	13	45	13	52	.304	.451
Reynoso,A	L	.301	83	25	3	1	5	17	8	6	.381	.542
Throws Right	R	.320	103	33	5	0	8	13	5	9	.352	.602
Rhodes,Arthur	L	.198	121	24	2	0	2	13	7	40	.242	.264
Throws Left	R	.179	123	22	5	0	3	9	5	43	.217	.293
Riedling,John	L	.185	54	10	3	0	1	5	7	9	.279	.296
Throws Right	R	.188	64	12	5	0	0	2	7	14	.288	.266
Rigdon,Paul	L	.234	111	26	6	0	4	12	29	16	.392	.396
Throws Right	R	.317	189	60	10	1	9	33	17	33	.380	.524
Riggan,Jerrod	L	.276	76	21	5	0	2	9	13	12	.378	.421
Throws Right	R	.216	97	21	3	0	3	15	11	29	.291	.340
Rijo,Jose	L	.143	21	3	0	0	2	3	6	2	.333	.429
Throws Right	R	.327	49	16	0	0	0	2	3	10	.365	.367
Rincon,Juan	L	.500	6	3	0	0	0	0	0	0	.500	.500
Throws Right	R	.250	16	4	1	0	1	2	5	4	.429	.500
Rincon,R	L	.213	94	20	3	1	2	12	6	25	.255	.330
Throws Left	R	.233	103	24	5	0	1	9	15	25	.328	.311
Riske,David	L	.143	28	4	2	0	0	3	14	9	.442	.214
Throws Right	R	.232	69	16	1	0	3	11	4	20	.280	.377
Ritchie,Todd	L	.286	378	108	25	4	13	60	28	53	.340	.476
Throws Right	R	.236	436	103	15	3	10	44	24	71	.279	.353
Rivera,M	L	.187	139	26	3	0	0	4	7	33	.226	.209
Throws Right	R	.229	153	35	1	0	5	24	5	50	.256	.333
Roberts,Grant	L	.303	33	10	2	0	1	4	3	6	.361	.455
Throws Right	R	.209	67	14	3	0	1	9	5	23	.260	.299
Roberts,W	L	.264	261	69	20	0	9	35	25	50	.330	.444
Throws Right	R	.284	257	73	14	1	6	34	30	45	.377	.416
Rocker,John	L	.239	46	11	1	0	1	6	15	15	.429	.326
Throws Left	R	.233	202	47	6	1	3	23	26	64	.330	.317
Rodriguez,F	L	.150	113	17	2	0	2	8	15	48	.246	.221
Throws Right	R	.213	169	36	5	2	3	13	12	43	.268	.320
Rodriguez,F	L	.429	14	6	0	0	0	1	3	0	.529	.429
Throws Right	R	.385	26	10	3	0	1	10	2	9	.414	.615
Rodriguez,R	L	.189	74	14	2	0	1	10	4	17	.247	.351
Throws Left	R	.346	78	27	4	2	1	14	13	14	.440	.487
Rodriguez,W	L	.800	5	4	0	1	2	5	0	1	.800	2.400
Throws Left	R	.222	9	2	2	0	0	1	1	2	.273	.444
Rogers,Kenny	L	.323	124	40	10	0	6	26	17	22	.407	.548
Throws Left	R	.302	364	110	23	3	12	46	32	52	.365	.481
Romero,J.C.	L	.286	35	10	3	0	1	3	4	8	.359	.457
Throws Left	R	.276	221	61	20	2	9	39	20	31	.336	.507
Rose,Brian	L	.408	49	20	4	1	2	8	9	8	.492	.653
Throws Right	R	.288	73	21	6	0	5	14	5	7	.329	.575
Rueter,Kirk	L	.283	173	49	9	1	6	22	14	28	.342	.451
Throws Left	R	.283	580	164	39	6	19	70	52	55	.341	.469
Ruffin,Johnny	L	.500	8	4	2	0	0	4	1	2	.556	.750
Throws Right	R	.125	8	1	0	0	0	2	3	2	.417	.125
Rupe,Ryan	L	.294	289	85	15	4	17	55	31	64	.374	.550
Throws Right	R	.272	279	76	15	0	13	48	17	59	.320	.466

Pitchers vs. Lefthanded and Righthanded Batters

Pitcher	vs	Avg	AB	H	2B	3B	HR	BI	BB	SO	OBP	SLG	Pitcher	vs	Avg	AB	H	2B	3B	HR	BI	BB	SO	OBP	SLG
Rusch,Glendon	L	.299	117	35	7	0	3	13	8	18	.354	.436	Silva,Jose	L	.302	43	13	1	0	4	13	4	7	.362	.605
Throws Left	R	.301	601	181	29	4	20	78	35	138	.342	.463	Throws Right	R	.256	86	22	2	0	2	12	5	16	.297	.349
Ryan,B.J.	L	.198	91	18	0	0	2	14	13	37	.298	.264	Slusarski,Joe	L	.393	28	11	2	0	2	11	3	5	.452	.679
Throws Left	R	.261	111	29	4	0	4	14	17	17	.364	.405	Throws Right	R	.333	42	14	2	0	2	7	1	6	.341	.524
Sabathia,C.C.	L	.254	114	29	4	0	1	12	13	16	.351	.316	Smart,J.D.	L	.368	19	7	4	0	1	5	2	4	.409	.737
Throws Left	R	.223	539	120	28	2	18	67	82	155	.326	.382	Throws Right	R	.279	43	12	4	0	2	9	2	6	.304	.512
Sabel,Erik	L	.292	72	21	1	1	3	14	6	12	.346	.458	Smith,Bud	L	.295	78	23	8	0	1	10	6	15	.345	.436
Throws Right	R	.277	130	36	2	1	5	16	6	13	.324	.423	Throws Left	R	.235	238	56	8	1	11	28	18	44	.291	.416
Saberhagen,B	L	.343	35	12	3	0	2	3	0	5	.343	.600	Smith,Chuck	L	.304	158	48	9	3	8	31	17	38	.376	.551
Throws Right	R	.250	28	7	1	0	1	5	0	5	.276	.393	Throws Right	R	.230	178	41	10	1	2	14	18	33	.310	.331
Sanchez,Jesus	L	.204	49	10	2	1	1	3	15	13	.400	.347	Smith,Roy	L	.261	23	6	1	1	1	9	6	9	.414	.522
Throws Left	R	.270	189	51	13	3	6	28	16	33	.329	.466	Throws Right	R	.238	42	10	3	0	2	3	7	8	.373	.452
Santana,Johan	L	.290	31	9	2	0	0	4	2	6	.343	.355	Smoltz,John	L	.263	114	30	8	1	4	12	7	32	.311	.456
Throws Left	R	.293	140	41	5	0	6	19	14	22	.361	.457	Throws Right	R	.211	109	23	1	1	3	12	3	25	.235	.321
Santiago,Jose	L	.352	145	51	10	1	3	26	10	13	.386	.497	Sobkowiak,S	L	1.000	1	1	1	0	0	0	0	0	1.000	2.000
Throws Right	R	.252	218	55	9	1	2	29	12	30	.298	.330	Throws Right	R	.250	4	1	0	0	0	1	0	0	.250	.250
Santos,Victor	L	.254	126	32	6	2	4	17	23	25	.373	.429	Sparks,S	L	.278	468	130	28	3	12	51	35	58	.332	.427
Throws Right	R	.196	153	30	7	1	5	20	26	27	.315	.353	Throws Right	R	.265	431	114	27	1	10	49	29	58	.309	.401
Sasaki,K	L	.218	133	29	8	1	4	17	6	39	.252	.383	Speier,Justin	L	.247	93	23	5	1	4	18	8	21	.302	.452
Throws Right	R	.168	113	19	8	0	2	10	5	23	.230	.292	Throws Right	R	.247	194	48	13	0	9	29	12	41	.310	.454
Sauerbeck,S	L	.272	92	25	5	0	2	15	10	32	.356	.391	Spooneybarger	L	.750	4	3	0	0	0	1	2	1	.714	.750
Throws Left	R	.248	145	36	7	1	2	19	30	47	.377	.352	Throws Right	R	.167	12	2	1	0	0	0	0	2	.167	.250
Scanlan,Bob	L	.378	45	17	1	0	0	9	11	1	.509	.400	Springer,D	L	.353	17	6	1	0	1	1	2	2	.450	.588
Throws Right	R	.313	64	20	5	0	0	13	3	4	.343	.391	Throws Right	R	.250	52	13	1	0	2	6	0	5	.278	.385
Schilling,C	L	.248	448	111	18	0	20	42	23	139	.282	.422	Springer,Russ	L	.357	28	10	0	1	3	6	0	4	.345	.750
Throws Right	R	.242	520	126	21	1	17	42	16	154	.266	.385	Throws Right	R	.222	45	10	1	0	2	8	4	8	.286	.378
Schmidt,Jason	L	.282	238	67	11	2	8	29	31	67	.370	.445	Standridge,J	L	.276	29	8	0	0	1	2	9	3	.447	.379
Throws Right	R	.217	327	71	16	0	5	34	30	75	.289	.312	Throws Right	R	.250	44	11	2	0	4	8	5	6	.327	.568
Schoeneweis,S	L	.209	196	41	7	0	0	18	14	31	.273	.245	Stanton,Mike	L	.283	113	32	6	2	2	15	11	28	.359	.425
Throws Left	R	.304	612	186	34	2	21	87	63	73	.375	.469	Throws Left	R	.251	191	48	9	0	2	14	18	50	.316	.330
Schourek,Pete	L	.250	56	14	5	0	2	9	9	12	.354	.446	Stark,Denny	L	.342	38	13	2	2	3	8	4	6	.395	.737
Throws Left	R	.328	64	21	7	0	2	11	6	8	.394	.531	Throws Right	R	.320	25	8	1	0	2	5	0	6	.320	.600
Seanez,Rudy	L	.151	53	8	1	0	2	8	5	14	.233	.283	Stechschulte,G	L	.275	80	22	5	0	1	5	11	11	.370	.375
Throws Right	R	.197	76	15	2	0	2	8	14	27	.322	.303	Throws Right	R	.272	180	49	10	1	9	34	19	40	.346	.489
Seay,Bobby	L	.350	20	7	1	0	1	5	2	3	.435	.550	Stein,Blake	L	.229	249	57	6	0	13	47	49	55	.355	.410
Throws Left	R	.200	30	6	2	0	2	3	3	9	.273	.467	Throws Right	R	.237	232	55	10	1	7	26	30	58	.327	.379
Seelbach,C	L	.417	12	5	0	0	1	3	2	4	.500	.667	Stewart,Scott	L	.286	70	20	2	0	4	15	4	20	.325	.486
Throws Right	R	.190	21	4	1	0	2	4	3	4	.292	.524	Throws Left	R	.215	107	23	6	0	1	9	9	19	.283	.299
Sele,Aaron	L	.231	438	101	14	4	15	50	36	68	.290	.384	Stone,Ricky	L	.250	16	4	1	0	1	2	2	2	.333	.500
Throws Right	R	.296	389	115	24	2	10	40	15	46	.325	.445	Throws Right	R	.267	15	4	1	0	0	0	0	2	.267	.333
Serrano,W	L	.333	75	25	7	1	2	12	9	17	.400	.533	Strickland,S	L	.274	117	32	4	2	3	15	23	12	.406	.419
Throws Right	R	.299	117	35	6	1	5	20	12	22	.371	.496	Throws Right	R	.189	185	35	5	1	6	17	18	73	.263	.324
Shaw,Jeff	L	.192	130	25	6	1	1	7	11	31	.255	.277	Strong,Joe	L	.200	10	2	0	0	0	0	1	0	.273	.200
Throws Right	R	.257	148	38	8	1	9	25	7	27	.296	.507	Throws Right	R	.083	12	1	0	0	1	4	2	4	.214	.333
Sheets,Ben	L	.324	256	83	14	2	16	47	24	28	.385	.582	Sturtze,T	L	.283	361	102	18	1	7	45	51	46	.368	.396
Throws Right	R	.251	331	83	19	1	7	33	24	66	.304	.378	Throws Right	R	.261	376	98	18	1	16	47	28	64	.321	.441
Shields,Scot	L	.292	24	7	1	0	0	0	4	3	.393	.333	Sullivan,S	L	.252	163	41	7	1	6	16	13	30	.307	.417
Throws Right	R	.063	16	1	0	0	0	0	3	4	.250	.063	Throws Right	R	.237	224	53	18	1	4	29	23	52	.323	.379
Shuey,Paul	L	.280	100	28	5	0	0	12	7	31	.324	.330	Suppan,Jeff	L	.235	460	108	17	4	13	45	34	69	.293	.374
Throws Right	R	.225	111	25	7	0	1	17	19	39	.341	.315	Throws Right	R	.306	389	119	20	5	13	60	40	51	.378	.483

326

Pitchers vs. Lefthanded and Righthanded Batters

Pitcher	vs	Avg	AB	H	2B	3B	HR	BI	BB	SO	OBP	SLG
Suzuki,Mac	L	.281	221	62	12	0	12	44	38	38	.389	.498
Throws Right	R	.258	233	60	14	1	8	25	35	51	.366	.429
Swindell,Greg	L	.259	81	21	4	1	6	11	3	19	.286	.556
Throws Left	R	.244	123	30	8	2	6	19	5	23	.271	.488
Tabaka,Jeff	L	.500	6	3	0	0	0	0	1	1	.571	.500
Throws Left	R	.300	10	3	0	0	1	1	0	2	.300	.600
Tam,Jeff	L	.247	85	21	5	1	1	6	21	12	.398	.365
Throws Right	R	.251	187	47	11	1	2	21	8	32	.286	.353
Tapani,Kevin	L	.229	266	61	12	1	9	36	15	64	.277	.383
Throws Right	R	.312	401	125	24	2	15	49	25	85	.356	.494
Tavarez,J	L	.320	250	80	15	0	6	47	40	31	.416	.452
Throws Right	R	.249	370	92	20	3	7	40	29	76	.316	.376
Taylor,Billy	L	.333	3	1	0	0	0	0	0	0	.333	.333
Throws Right	R	.200	5	1	0	0	1	0	0	3	.200	.800
Telemaco,A	L	.289	173	50	15	1	6	25	15	34	.353	.491
Throws Right	R	.257	167	43	8	1	9	26	17	25	.347	.479
Telford,A	L	.429	14	6	1	1	1	9	0	2	.429	.857
Throws Right	R	.400	20	8	2	0	1	8	5	3	.538	.650
Thomas,Brad	L	.400	15	6	0	0	0	2	2	0	.500	.400
Throws Left	R	.275	51	14	4	0	6	13	12	6	.413	.706
Thomson,John	L	.177	164	29	6	1	7	19	14	38	.244	.354
Throws Right	R	.294	187	55	11	2	8	22	11	30	.340	.503
Thurman,Mike	L	.343	254	87	20	2	11	39	31	25	.408	.567
Throws Right	R	.257	331	85	17	1	10	42	19	71	.304	.405
Timlin,Mike	L	.319	91	29	5	1	4	17	8	15	.366	.527
Throws Right	R	.257	191	49	8	1	2	12	11	32	.307	.340
Tolar,Kevin	L	.231	13	3	0	0	0	0	5	6	.444	.231
Throws Left	R	.167	24	4	1	0	0	3	8	5	.375	.208
Tollberg,B	L	.282	195	55	15	0	7	20	19	31	.343	.467
Throws Right	R	.290	269	78	15	1	8	32	6	40	.305	.442
Tomko,Brett	L	.365	63	23	5	1	4	13	6	9	.420	.667
Throws Right	R	.229	83	19	5	0	5	12	9	13	.298	.470
Towers,Josh	L	.307	257	79	17	2	9	30	13	24	.341	.494
Throws Right	R	.288	299	86	18	1	12	37	3	34	.304	.475
Trachsel,S	L	.232	302	70	11	1	12	33	28	57	.299	.394
Throws Right	R	.273	359	98	21	4	16	47	19	87	.307	.487
Trombley,Mike	L	.230	113	26	3	0	3	17	14	23	.313	.336
Throws Right	R	.229	170	39	10	0	6	23	23	49	.323	.394
Urbina,Ugueth	L	.278	108	30	7	0	5	20	13	36	.355	.481
Throws Right	R	.196	143	28	3	1	4	13	11	53	.252	.315
Valdes,Ismael	L	.294	320	94	19	1	9	35	36	49	.370	.444
Throws Right	R	.261	318	83	15	1	11	35	14	51	.303	.418
Valdes,Marc	L	.333	3	1	0	0	0	0	1	0	.500	.333
Throws Right	R	.250	24	6	0	0	4	13	0	3	.250	.750
Van Poppel,T	L	.281	96	27	8	1	4	11	20	29	.405	.510
Throws Right	R	.194	186	36	8	1	5	15	18	61	.265	.328
Vazquez,J	L	.220	368	81	15	1	14	38	20	106	.264	.380
Throws Right	R	.246	472	116	28	0	10	43	24	102	.283	.369
Venafro,Mike	L	.258	97	25	6	1	0	19	8	19	.330	.340
Throws Left	R	.227	128	29	10	1	2	19	20	10	.342	.367
Veres,Dave	L	.237	93	22	6	0	7	10	12	21	.324	.527
Throws Right	R	.229	153	35	7	0	5	16	16	40	.308	.373
Villafuerte,B	L	.429	14	6	1	0	1	3	2	1	.529	.714
Throws Right	R	.400	15	6	3	0	2	9	2	3	.444	1.000
Villone,Ron	L	.250	120	30	5	0	3	19	19	34	.359	.367
Throws Left	R	.300	343	103	22	3	15	59	34	79	.368	.513
Vining,Ken	L	.385	13	5	1	0	2	4	3	0	.500	.923
Throws Left	R	.476	21	10	1	0	1	6	4	3	.577	.667
Vizcaino,Luis	L	.241	58	14	4	0	4	9	5	12	.302	.517
Throws Right	R	.282	85	24	0	0	4	11	7	19	.333	.424
Vogelsong,R	L	.270	63	17	5	0	2	12	14	14	.405	.444
Throws Right	R	.282	78	22	4	0	4	13	6	10	.341	.487
Vosberg,Ed	L	.231	13	3	1	0	0	6	2	1	.333	.308
Throws Left	R	.167	30	5	0	0	0	1	1	10	.194	.167
Voyles,Brad	L	.133	15	2	0	0	1	3	5	2	.350	.333
Throws Right	R	.188	16	3	3	0	0	3	4	3	.350	.375
Wagner,Billy	L	.261	46	12	2	0	1	8	3	14	.300	.370
Throws Left	R	.182	176	32	11	0	4	14	17	65	.273	.313
Wakefield,Tim	L	.226	266	60	13	1	5	30	35	56	.316	.338
Throws Right	R	.264	363	96	18	2	8	50	38	92	.355	.391
Walker,Kevin	L	.150	20	3	1	0	0	0	3	8	.261	.200
Throws Left	R	.095	21	2	1	1	0	1	5	9	.269	.238
Walker,Pete	L	.250	8	2	1	0	0	1	0	2	.250	.375
Throws Right	R	.235	17	4	1	0	0	1	0	2	.235	.294
Wall,Donne	L	.273	66	18	2	0	3	9	10	10	.364	.439
Throws Right	R	.317	104	33	9	1	5	16	7	21	.363	.567
Wallace,Jeff	L	.161	62	10	2	0	0	5	10	11	.278	.194
Throws Left	R	.268	123	33	10	0	4	17	27	27	.404	.447
Wasdin,John	L	.299	107	32	4	1	6	18	16	14	.397	.523
Throws Right	R	.287	188	54	16	1	5	37	8	50	.324	.463
Washburn,J	L	.287	157	45	3	1	6	18	14	23	.356	.433
Throws Left	R	.257	587	151	41	2	19	66	40	103	.307	.431
Weathers,Dave	L	.213	108	23	4	1	4	7	20	29	.346	.380
Throws Right	R	.218	193	42	11	0	2	19	14	37	.270	.306
Weaver,Jeff	L	.278	472	131	27	8	13	58	49	77	.353	.451
Throws Right	R	.253	411	104	24	1	6	48	19	75	.293	.360
Weber,Ben	L	.210	105	22	4	1	1	12	19	16	.331	.295
Throws Right	R	.278	158	44	8	0	3	15	12	24	.349	.386
Wells,Bob	L	.264	87	23	6	4	4	18	11	16	.333	.563
Throws Right	R	.277	177	49	8	0	8	20	7	33	.340	.458
Wells,David	L	.206	102	21	2	0	3	9	7	16	.270	.314
Throws Left	R	.328	302	99	21	2	9	39	14	43	.357	.500
Wells,Kip	L	.267	247	66	15	0	7	29	34	46	.366	.413
Throws Right	R	.294	269	79	23	0	7	41	27	53	.367	.457
Wendell,Turk	L	.295	95	28	6	1	6	17	19	12	.417	.568
Throws Right	R	.222	158	35	6	1	6	28	15	44	.294	.386
Wengert,Don	L	.378	45	17	3	1	1	8	4	3	.429	.556
Throws Right	R	.500	32	16	3	0	1	8	2	1	.529	.688
Westbrook,J	L	.298	114	34	10	1	3	23	9	20	.339	.482
Throws Right	R	.313	144	45	6	0	3	13	13	28	.383	.417

Pitchers vs. Lefthanded and Righthanded Batters

Pitcher	vs	Avg	AB	H	2B	3B	HR	BI	BB	SO	OBP	SLG
Wheeler,Dan	L	.364	44	16	3	1	2	14	3	3	.396	.614
Throws Right	R	.389	36	14	3	0	1	5	2	9	.410	.556
White,Gabe	L	.269	93	25	4	0	6	20	10	19	.333	.505
Throws Left	R	.271	166	45	9	1	12	23	16	28	.339	.554
White,Rick	L	.271	107	29	6	0	4	16	9	21	.336	.439
Throws Right	R	.249	169	42	7	2	3	23	8	30	.281	.367
Whiteside,M	L	.371	35	13	3	0	2	9	4	4	.425	.629
Throws Right	R	.270	37	10	2	0	3	3	3	6	.341	.568
Wickman,Bob	L	.279	122	34	3	2	2	13	12	38	.348	.385
Throws Right	R	.205	132	27	5	0	2	8	2	28	.222	.288
Wilkins,Marc	L	.333	21	7	3	0	1	6	3	1	.417	.619
Throws Right	R	.313	48	15	2	0	1	9	5	10	.389	.417
Williams,Dave	L	.255	106	27	8	0	2	15	6	14	.299	.387
Throws Left	R	.241	303	73	14	5	13	39	39	43	.332	.449
Williams,Jeff	L	.294	34	10	2	0	2	4	6	3	.405	.529
Throws Left	R	.296	54	16	4	1	3	11	11	6	.409	.574
Williams,Mike	L	.256	117	30	5	2	8	15	19	27	.360	.538
Throws Right	R	.233	129	30	11	1	1	12	16	32	.315	.357
Williams,Todd	L	.444	18	8	1	1	0	6	6	3	.538	.611
Throws Right	R	.280	50	14	6	0	1	9	3	10	.339	.460
Williams,W	L	.251	374	94	20	1	16	47	26	70	.301	.439
Throws Right	R	.281	463	130	29	2	19	53	30	84	.329	.475
Williamson,S	L	.500	2	1	0	0	0	0	1	0	.667	.500
Throws Right	R	.000	1	0	0	0	0	1	1	0	.667	.000
Wilson,Kris	L	.346	217	75	16	4	16	38	20	38	.407	.677
Throws Right	R	.251	227	57	6	2	10	36	12	29	.296	.427
Wilson,Paul	L	.286	294	84	15	0	13	42	35	61	.364	.469
Throws Right	R	.270	300	81	12	0	8	52	17	58	.321	.390
Winchester,S	L	.273	33	9	1	2	5	9	2	4	.316	.879
Throws Right	R	.339	59	20	3	0	2	10	2	5	.375	.492
Wise,Matt	L	.259	108	28	2	0	7	18	9	23	.322	.472
Throws Right	R	.238	80	19	5	0	4	8	9	27	.319	.450
Witasick,Jay	L	.288	111	32	4	1	3	22	17	38	.394	.423
Throws Right	R	.234	197	46	6	0	5	29	16	68	.300	.340
Witt,Bobby	L	.292	65	19	0	1	3	11	12	14	.405	.462
Throws Right	R	.175	97	17	6	0	3	11	13	17	.283	.330
Wohlers,Mark	L	.236	106	25	3	0	7	19	11	26	.303	.462
Throws Right	R	.280	157	44	6	0	1	17	14	28	.345	.338
Wolf,Randy	L	.171	123	21	7	1	2	10	12	46	.250	.293
Throws Left	R	.268	482	129	30	3	13	63	39	106	.330	.423
Wood,Kerry	L	.201	294	59	11	3	7	31	57	96	.338	.330
Throws Right	R	.203	335	68	6	0	9	33	35	121	.286	.301
Woodard,Steve	L	.320	194	62	12	3	5	27	9	26	.351	.490
Throws Right	R	.330	203	67	12	2	5	33	8	26	.364	.483
Worrell,Tim	L	.248	125	31	6	3	2	17	8	23	.294	.392
Throws Right	R	.234	171	40	7	1	2	27	25	40	.335	.322
Wright,Dan	L	.264	140	37	7	2	8	21	24	23	.367	.514
Throws Right	R	.342	120	41	10	0	4	22	15	13	.414	.525
Wright,Jamey	L	.260	312	81	14	0	11	40	45	66	.363	.410
Throws Right	R	.282	426	120	21	6	15	59	53	63	.376	.465
Wright,Jaret	L	.281	64	18	5	0	1	9	14	10	.405	.406
Throws Right	R	.353	51	18	5	0	1	10	8	8	.441	.510
Wunsch,Kelly	L	.262	42	11	2	0	1	8	5	11	.373	.381
Throws Left	R	.233	43	10	0	0	3	11	4	5	.333	.442
Yan,Esteban	L	.272	125	34	3	2	2	15	6	31	.303	.376
Throws Right	R	.252	119	30	5	1	5	20	5	33	.310	.437
Yoshii,Masato	L	.278	194	54	10	2	7	32	10	27	.316	.459
Throws Right	R	.280	261	73	8	1	11	33	16	36	.329	.444
Zambrano,C	L	.455	11	5	2	1	0	2	6	1	.647	.818
Throws Right	R	.300	20	6	0	0	2	9	2	3	.375	.600
Zambrano,V	L	.205	78	16	2	1	3	13	9	24	.287	.372
Throws Right	R	.198	111	22	6	1	3	7	9	34	.276	.351
Zerbe,Chad	L	.396	53	21	3	0	1	13	2	8	.421	.509
Throws Left	R	.215	93	20	4	3	2	12	8	14	.275	.387
Zimmerman,J	L	.220	127	28	5	0	8	14	7	41	.270	.449
Throws Right	R	.163	123	20	3	0	2	12	9	31	.231	.236
Zito,Barry	L	.234	137	32	6	1	3	18	13	31	.346	.358
Throws Left	R	.229	663	152	24	3	15	61	67	174	.301	.342
AL	L	.271	–	–	–	–	–	–	–	–	.343	.436
	R	.264	–	–	–	–	–	–	–	–	.327	.420
NL	L	.269	–	–	–	–	–	–	–	–	.346	.445
	R	.256	–	–	–	–	–	–	–	–	.320	.414
MLB	L	.270	–	–	–	–	–	–	–	–	.345	.440
	R	.260	–	–	–	–	–	–	–	–	.323	.417

Runs Created/
Component Earned Run Average

Four years ago, STATS produced two books that we feel set the standard for encyclopedic information. Ask any question about baseball, and the chances are good you'll find the answer in either our *All-Time Major League Handbook* or *All-Time Baseball Sourcebook*.

Among the mountain of statistics available in each book, it's likely that two of them—Runs Created per 27 Outs (RC/27) and Component ERA (ERC)—are among the most compelling. For a definition of each stat, please consult the Glossary.

The second edition of our *All-Time Handbook* is complete through the 1999 season. The *All-Time Sourcebook* covers historical data through the 1997 campaign. So, for players who are active, this section provides a comprehensive update of these numbers through the 2001 season.

Carreras Creadas/
Efectividad Componente

Hace cuatro años, STATS publicó dos libros que consideramos el estándar de información enciclopédica: nuestros *All-Time Major League Handbook* y el *All-Time Baseball Sourcebook*.

Entre la riqueza de estadísticas en esos libros, Carreras Creadas por 27 Outs (RC/27) y Efectividad Componente (ERC) son las estadísticas más iluminantes. Para el significado de cada estadística, por favor consulten el Glosario.

La segunda edición de nuestro *All-Time Handbook* acapara hasta 1999. Para jugadores que están activos, la sección siguiente actualiza sus números hasta la temporada del 2001.

Career = Durante la carrera del jugador; **ERC** = Efectividad componente; **LERA** = Efectividad de la Liga; **LRC/27** = Promedio de carreras creadas por la liga; **oAvg.** = Promedio de bateo del oponente; **OOB** = Promedio de embasamiento del oponente; **RC/27** = Carreras creadas por 27 outs; **RC** = Carreras creadas.

Runs Created

Player, Team	2001 RC	RC/27	LRC/27	Career RC	RC/27	LRC27
Abad, Andy, Oak	0	0.00	4.86	0	0.00	4.86
Abbott, Jeff, Fla	5	4.19	4.70	71	4.07	5.10
Abbott, Kurt, Atl	0	0.00	4.70	256	4.31	4.74
Abbott, Paul, Sea	0	0.00	4.86	1	3.35	5.08
Abernathy, Brent, TB	44	5.10	4.86	44	5.10	4.86
Abreu, Bobby, Phi	117	6.91	4.70	501	7.54	4.81
Acevedo, Jose, Cin	0	0.00	4.70	0	0.00	4.70
Acevedo, Juan, Col-Fla	1	8.94	4.70	2	0.80	4.75
Adams, Terry, LA	0	0.00	4.70	0	0.00	4.72
Agbayani, Benny, NYM	39	4.51	4.70	147	5.47	4.90
Alcantara, Israel, Bos	5	4.33	4.86	14	5.96	5.08
Aldridge, Cory, Atl	0	0.00	4.70	0	0.00	4.70
Alfonseca, Antonio, Fla	0	—	—	0	0.00	4.69
Alfonzo, Edgardo, NYM	60	4.48	4.70	580	6.10	4.76
Alicea, Luis, KC	41	3.71	4.86	500	4.54	4.74
Allen, Chad, Min	19	3.67	4.86	83	4.07	5.10
Almanza, Armando, Fla	0	—	—	0	0.00	5.00
Almanzar, Carlos, NYY	0	—	—	0	0.00	5.00
Almonte, Erick, NYY	2	26.88	4.86	2	26.88	4.86
Alomar, Roberto, Cle	139	9.00	4.86	1382	6.31	4.72
Alomar Jr., Sandy, CWS	21	3.15	4.86	440	4.16	4.89
Alou, Moises, Hou	98	7.11	4.70	800	6.84	4.59
Anderson, Brady, Bal	52	3.96	4.86	1057	5.62	4.87
Anderson, Brian, Ari	0	0.00	4.70	0	0.00	4.82
Anderson, Garret, Ana	96	5.15	4.86	570	4.88	5.11
Anderson, Jimmy, Pit	1	0.45	4.70	3	0.72	4.84
Anderson, Marlon, Phi	69	4.62	4.70	139	4.08	4.86
Ankiel, Rick, StL	0	0.00	4.70	7	2.61	4.97
Appier, Kevin, NYM	0	0.00	4.70	0	0.00	4.78
Arias, Alex, SD	16	3.83	4.70	207	4.04	4.68
Armas Jr., Tony, Mon	0	0.00	4.70	0	0.00	4.81
Arrojo, Rolando, Bos	0	0.00	4.86	0	0.00	4.99
Arroyo, Bronson, Pit	0	0.00	4.70	0	0.00	4.85
Ashby, Andy, LA	1	8.94	4.70	13	0.74	4.68
Astacio, Pedro, Col-Hou	0	0.00	4.70	9	0.43	4.69
Atchley, Justin, Cin	0	0.00	4.70	0	0.00	4.70
Aurilia, Rich, SF	112	6.63	4.70	368	5.11	4.81
Ausmus, Brad, Hou	34	2.64	4.70	393	3.87	4.85
Aven, Bruce, LA	4	6.71	4.70	90	5.41	4.99
Aybar, Manny, ChC	2	53.66	4.70	3	1.35	4.73
Baez, Benito, Fla	0	0.00	4.70	0	0.00	4.70
Bagwell, Jeff, Hou	137	8.08	4.70	1333	8.06	4.57
Bailey, Cory, KC	0	—	—	2	27.05	4.68
Baines, Harold, CWS	2	0.70	4.86	1570	5.65	4.66
Bako, Paul, Atl	12	2.90	4.70	78	3.03	4.96
Baldwin, James, CWS-LA	0	0.00	4.71	1	0.67	4.83
Banks, Willie, Bos	0	—	—	2	0.83	4.62
Barajas, Rod, Ari	3	0.90	4.70	8	1.92	4.76
Barker, Glen, Hou	0	0.00	4.70	20	3.54	4.95
Barkett, Andy, Pit	5	3.95	4.70	5	3.95	4.70
Barnes, John, Min	0	0.00	4.86	5	2.79	5.11
Barnes, Larry, Ana	0	0.00	4.86	0	0.00	4.86
Barrett, Michael, Mon	40	2.85	4.70	120	3.42	4.88
Bartee, Kimera, Col	0	0.00	4.70	33	2.42	5.22
Batista, Miguel, Ari	0	0.00	4.70	3	0.73	4.77
Batista, Tony, Tor-Bal	71	4.16	4.86	353	5.00	5.05
Bautista, Danny, Ari	32	5.17	4.70	176	3.89	4.92
Beck, Rod, Bos	0	0.00	4.86	1	1.69	4.52
Beckett, Josh, Fla	1	3.83	4.70	1	3.83	4.70
Beimel, Joe, Pit	1	1.17	4.70	1	1.17	4.70
Belitz, Todd, Col	0	0.00	4.70	0	0.00	4.70
Bell, David, Sea	60	4.41	4.86	278	3.99	5.01
Bell, Derek, Pit	11	2.15	4.70	609	4.64	4.69
Bell, Jay, Ari	61	4.76	4.70	1054	4.96	4.52
Bell, Rob, Cin-Tex	0	0.00	4.70	0	0.00	4.96
Bellhorn, Mark, Oak	2	0.81	4.86	31	3.11	4.93
Belliard, Ronnie, Mil	56	5.35	4.70	215	5.32	4.92
Bellinger, Clay, NYY	5	1.82	4.86	26	2.67	5.16
Beltran, Carlos, KC	128	7.78	4.86	289	6.01	5.09
Beltre, Adrian, LA	57	4.14	4.70	249	5.05	4.87
Benard, Marvin, SF	53	4.74	4.70	343	4.96	4.82
Benes, Alan, StL	0	0.00	4.70	2	0.47	4.66
Benes, Andy, StL	1	0.93	4.70	20	0.75	4.50
Benitez, Armando, NYM	0	0.00	4.70	0	0.00	4.95
Bennett, G., Phi-NYM-Col	11	2.84	4.70	39	3.88	4.84
Bere, Jason, ChC	1	0.45	4.70	5	1.08	4.81
Berg, Dave, Fla	21	3.30	4.70	120	4.61	4.85
Berger, Brandon, KC	5	12.22	4.86	5	12.22	4.86

Player, Team	2001 RC	RC/27	LRC/27	Career RC	RC/27	LRC27
Bergeron, Peter, Mon	27	2.29	4.70	85	2.95	4.88
Berkman, Lance, Hou	136	8.92	4.70	213	7.66	4.84
Berroa, Angel, KC	5	3.45	4.86	5	3.45	4.86
Betemit, Wilson, Atl	0	0.00	4.70	0	0.00	4.70
Bichette, Dante, Bos	49	4.46	4.86	1012	5.68	4.65
Biddle, Rocky, CWS	0	0.00	4.86	0	0.00	4.86
Bierbrodt, Nick, Ari-TB	2	13.42	4.70	2	13.42	4.70
Bigbie, Larry, Bal	13	3.33	4.86	13	3.33	4.86
Biggio, Craig, Hou	114	6.68	4.70	1313	6.38	4.48
Blair, Willie, Det	0	0.00	4.86	1	0.18	4.52
Blake, Casey, Min-Bal	6	5.76	4.86	9	3.30	5.08
Blanco, Henry, Mil	25	2.52	4.70	85	3.20	4.89
Blank, Matt, Mon	3	20.12	4.70	3	16.11	4.76
Blum, Geoff, Mon	52	3.76	4.70	117	4.25	4.85
Bocachica, Hiram, LA	15	3.87	4.70	16	3.87	4.72
Boehringer, Brian, NYY-SF	0	0.00	4.70	1	0.82	4.89
Bogar, Tim, LA	2	5.37	4.70	146	3.13	4.76
Bohanon, Brian, Col	4	4.67	4.70	20	2.60	4.84
Bonds, Barry, SF	180	14.64	4.70	1929	8.74	4.42
Bones, Ricky, Fla	0	0.00	4.70	0	0.00	4.34
Bonilla, Bobby, StL	16	3.02	4.70	1178	5.76	4.45
Boone, Aaron, Cin	65	6.01	4.70	212	5.43	4.85
Boone, Bret, Sea	116	6.91	4.86	605	4.55	4.74
Borbon, Pedro, Tor	0	—	—	1	6.74	4.91
Borders, Pat, Sea	1	6.72	4.86	281	3.13	4.66
Bordick, Mike, Bal	29	4.24	4.86	574	3.80	4.97
Borkowski, Dave, Det	0	—	—	0	0.00	5.18
Borland, Toby, Ana	0	—	—	0	0.00	4.64
Borowski, Joe, ChC	0	—	—	0	0.00	4.68
Bottalico, Ricky, Phi	1	13.42	4.70	1	1.80	4.75
Bottenfield, Kent, Hou	0	0.00	4.70	7	1.01	4.73
Bradley, Milton, Mon-Cle	20	2.70	4.71	40	3.31	4.83
Bragg, Darren, NYM-NYY	10	5.59	4.71	278	4.73	5.06
Branson, Jeff, LA	1	1.79	4.70	151	3.26	4.60
Brantley, Jeff, Tex	0	—	—	1	0.37	4.26
Branyan, Russell, Cle	51	5.48	4.86	88	5.44	5.03
Brock, Chris, Phi	0	0.00	4.70	4	1.92	4.90
Brogna, Rico, Atl	20	3.21	4.70	402	4.75	4.73
Brohawn, Troy, Ari	0	0.00	4.70	0	0.00	4.70
Brosius, Scott, NYY	60	4.93	4.86	527	4.60	5.06
Brower, Jim, Cin	4	5.37	4.70	4	4.67	4.78
Brown, Adrian, Pit	3	2.98	4.70	105	4.23	4.84
Brown, Dee, KC	40	3.52	4.86	41	3.13	4.91
Brown, Emil, Pit-SD	12	2.75	4.70	31	2.47	4.77
Brown, Kevin, LA	0	0.00	4.70	8	0.53	4.78
Brown, Kevin L., Mil	8	6.13	4.70	27	4.83	4.95
Brown, Roosevelt, ChC	18	7.43	4.70	38	5.58	4.90
Brumbaugh, Cliff, Tex-Col	3	2.01	4.74	3	2.01	4.74
Buchanan, Brian, Min	29	5.30	4.86	35	4.33	5.00
Buddie, Mike, Mil	0	0.00	4.70	0	0.00	4.70
Buehrle, Mark, CWS	0	0.00	4.86	0	0.00	4.86
Buford, Damon, ChC	3	1.10	4.70	220	3.93	4.99
Buhner, Jay, Sea	4	2.83	4.86	893	6.08	4.85
Burba, Dave, Cle	0	0.00	4.86	8	1.23	4.59
Burke, Jamie, Ana	1	6.72	4.86	1	6.72	4.86
Burkett, John, Atl	0	0.00	4.70	2	0.10	4.46
Burkhart, Morgan, Bos	2	1.92	4.86	17	5.56	5.15
Burks, Ellis, Cle	79	6.21	4.86	1143	6.27	4.62
Burnett, A.J., Fla	0	0.00	4.70	6	1.83	4.82
Burnitz, Jeromy, Mil	95	5.83	4.70	562	5.85	4.83
Burrell, Pat, Phi	85	5.47	4.86	157	5.81	4.83
Bush, Homer, Tor	35	4.70	4.86	135	4.17	5.13
Butler, Brent, Col	11	2.98	4.70	11	2.98	4.70
Byrd, Paul, Phi-KC	0	0.00	4.81	5	1.20	4.90
Byrnes, Eric, Oak	6	5.56	4.86	7	5.08	4.95
Cabrera, Jolbert, Cle	35	4.22	4.86	53	3.61	5.04
Cabrera, Jose, Atl	0	0.00	4.70	0	0.00	4.73
Cabrera, Orlando, Mon	92	5.08	4.70	213	4.24	4.83
Cairo, Miguel, ChC-StL	21	4.58	4.70	187	4.05	5.10
Callaway, Mickey, TB	0	—	—	1	26.71	5.18
Cameron, Mike, Sea	103	6.47	4.86	386	5.29	5.03
Caminiti, Ken, Tex-Atl	44	4.13	4.78	965	5.38	4.43
Canseco, Jose, CWS	47	6.35	4.86	1273	6.19	4.78
Cardona, Javier, Det	7	2.44	4.86	7	1.68	5.00
Carpenter, Chris, Tor	0	0.00	4.86	0	0.00	4.99
Carrara, Giovanni, LA	0	0.00	4.70	0	0.00	4.69
Carrasco, Hector, Min	0	—	—	0	0.00	4.64
Casanova, Raul, Mil	29	5.26	4.70	94	3.68	4.96

Player, Team	2001 RC	RC/27	LRC/27	Career RC	RC/27	LRC27
Casey, Sean, Cin	94	6.50	4.70	353	6.78	4.85
Castilla, Vinny, TB-Hou	70	4.39	4.73	668	5.38	4.73
Castillo, Alberto, Tor	4	0.95	4.86	60	2.55	4.95
Castillo, Carlos, Bos	0	—		1	26.86	5.01
Castillo, Frank, Bos	0	0.00	4.86	1	0.08	4.43
Castillo, Luis, Fla	69	4.36	4.70	271	4.38	4.82
Castro, Juan, Cin	14	1.85	4.70	59	2.07	4.74
Castro, Ramon, Fla	1	2.98	4.70	20	3.09	4.99
Catalanotto, Frank, Tex	85	7.09	4.86	207	5.92	5.06
Cedeno, Roger, Det	79	5.29	4.86	285	5.18	4.83
Chacon, Shawn, Col	0	0.00	4.70	0	0.00	4.70
Charlton, Norm, Sea	0	—		2	0.61	4.07
Chavez, Endy, KC	4	1.63	4.86	4	1.63	4.86
Chavez, Eric, Oak	107	7.03	4.86	250	6.11	5.09
Chen, Bruce, Phi-NYM	0	0.00	4.70	0	0.00	4.83
Choate, Randy, NYY	0	0.00	4.86	0	0.00	4.86
Chouinard, Bobby, Col	0	—		0	0.00	4.87
Christensen, M., CWS-LA	8	5.65	4.71	11	2.89	5.03
Christenson, R., Oak-Ari	1	3.84	4.79	96	4.01	5.12
Christiansen, J., StL-SF	0	—		1	2.70	4.68
Cintron, Alex, Ari	1	5.37	4.70	1	5.37	4.70
Cirillo, Jeff, Col	84	5.78	4.70	674	6.21	4.96
Clapp, Stubby, StL	1	1.34	4.70	1	1.34	4.70
Clark, Brady, Cin	21	5.27	4.70	22	5.13	4.72
Clark, Tony, Det	78	6.43	4.86	490	6.10	5.08
Clayton, Royce, CWS	50	3.75	4.86	514	3.57	4.72
Clemens, Roger, NYY	0	0.00	4.86	2	3.35	5.09
Clement, Matt, Fla	0	0.00	4.70	0	0.00	4.90
Coggin, Dave, Phi	0	0.00	4.70	0	0.00	4.76
Colangelo, Mike, SD	9	3.35	4.70	10	3.68	4.71
Colbrunn, Greg, Ari	17	6.16	4.70	359	5.08	4.67
Coleman, Michael, NYY	3	2.52	4.86	4	1.89	4.91
Collier, Lou, Mil	20	5.42	4.70	77	3.87	4.72
Colon, Bartolo, Cle	0	0.00	4.86	0	0.00	5.09
Cone, David, Bos	0	0.00	4.86	10	0.69	4.08
Conine, Jeff, Bal	107	7.39	4.86	674	5.56	4.78
Conti, Jason, Ari	0	0.00	4.70	13	4.66	4.99
Cook, Dennis, NYM-Phi	0	0.00	4.70	11	3.20	4.14
Coolbaugh, Mike, Mil	4	1.82	4.70	4	1.82	4.70
Coomer, Ron, ChC	39	3.65	4.70	346	4.34	5.07
Cooper, Brian, Ana	0	—		0	0.00	5.30
Coppinger, Rocky, Mil	0	0.00	4.70	1	3.36	4.78
Cora, Alex, LA	33	2.60	4.70	67	2.64	4.83
Cordero, Wil, Cle	21	2.64	4.86	478	4.68	4.82
Cordova, Marty, Cle	62	5.55	4.86	439	5.20	5.10
Cormier, Rheal, Phi	0	0.00	4.70	8	1.20	4.30
Cota, Humberto, Pit	0	0.00	4.70	0	0.00	4.70
Counsell, Craig, Ari	59	4.39	4.70	174	4.63	4.74
Cox, Steve, TB	39	3.90	4.86	89	4.54	5.07
Crabtree, Tim, Tex	0	—		0	0.00	5.01
Crede, Joe, CWS	6	3.93	4.86	8	4.21	4.95
Creek, Doug, TB	0	—		0	0.00	4.63
Crespo, Cesar, SD	16	3.41	4.70	16	3.41	4.70
Crespo, Felipe, SF-Phi	8	2.26	4.70	59	4.33	4.97
Cromer, D.T., Cin	9	5.49	4.70	19	6.63	4.83
Cruz, Deivi, Det	49	4.05	4.86	263	3.71	5.07
Cruz, Jacob, Cle-Col	13	2.82	4.78	41	3.60	4.87
Cruz, Jose, Tor	92	5.67	4.86	352	5.33	5.06
Cruz, Juan, ChC	0	0.00	4.70	0	0.00	4.70
Cruz, Nelson, Hou	0	0.00	4.70	0	0.00	4.80
Cubillan, Darwin, Mon	0	—		0	0.00	5.30
Cuddyer, Mike, Min	2	3.58	4.86	2	3.58	4.86
Cummings, Midre, Ari	1	1.58	4.70	120	3.95	4.81
Cunnane, Will, Mil	0	0.00	4.70	4	4.14	4.77
Curtis, Chad, Tex	18	5.38	4.86	560	4.65	4.97
Cust, Jack, Ari	1	26.83	4.70	1	26.83	4.70
Daal, Omar, Phi	5	2.53	4.70	15	1.87	4.82
Dalesandro, Mark, CWS	0	—		12	3.04	5.10
D'Amico, Jeff, Mil	0	0.00	4.70	0	0.00	4.94
Damon, Johnny, Oak	86	4.56	4.86	580	5.55	5.10
Darensbourg, Vic, Fla	0	—		1	1.80	4.76
Darr, Mike, SD	37	4.49	4.70	72	4.63	4.84
Daubach, Brian, Bos	67	5.68	4.86	217	5.89	5.11
DaVanon, Jeff, Ana	6	2.12	4.86	8	2.31	4.92
Davenport, Joe, Col	1	Inf	—	1	Inf	—
Davey, Tom, SD	0	—		0	—	
Davis, Ben, SD	58	4.25	4.70	94	3.67	4.84
Davis, Doug, Tex	0	0.00	4.86	0	0.00	4.86
Davis, Eric, SF	12	2.48	4.70	963	6.32	4.40
Davis, Kane, Col	0	0.00	4.70	0	0.00	4.80

Player, Team	2001 RC	RC/27	LRC/27	Career RC	RC/27	LRC27
Davis, Lance, Cin	0	0.00	4.70	0	0.00	4.70
Davis, Russ, SF	17	3.43	4.70	254	4.37	5.04
DeJean, Mike, Mil	0	0.00	4.70	0	0.00	4.72
de la Rosa, Tomas, Mon	0	0.00	4.70	11	5.48	5.00
Delgado, Carlos, Tor	118	7.44	4.86	709	7.31	5.11
Delgado, Wilson, KC	0	0.00	4.86	25	3.20	5.07
Dellucci, David, Ari	37	6.20	4.70	124	5.47	4.71
de los Santos, Valerio, Mil	0	—		0	0.00	5.00
Dempster, Ryan, Fla	0	0.00	4.70	0	0.00	4.87
DeRosa, Mark, Atl	24	5.19	4.70	27	5.07	4.74
DeShields, D., Bal-ChC	45	4.24	4.79	811	4.91	4.56
Dessens, Elmer, Cin	2	0.96	4.70	4	1.00	4.79
Diaz, Einar, Cle	58	4.63	4.86	140	4.23	5.07
DiFelice, Mike, TB-Ari	7	1.28	4.84	101	3.11	4.96
Donnels, Chris, LA	5	1.79	4.70	75	3.54	4.48
Dotel, Octavio, Hou	0	0.00	4.70	1	0.38	4.96
Dransfeldt, Kelly, Tex	0	0.00	4.86	1	0.37	5.20
Dreifort, Darren, LA	0	0.00	4.70	13	1.78	4.85
Drew, J.D., StL	92	9.14	4.70	247	7.44	4.90
Ducey, Rob, Phi-Mon	14	6.26	4.70	172	4.51	4.79
Duckworth, Brandon, Phi	1	1.34	4.70	1	1.34	4.70
Duncan, Courtney, ChC	0	0.00	4.70	0	0.00	4.70
Dunn, Adam, Cin	48	6.92	4.70	48	6.92	4.70
Dunston, Shawon, SF	22	4.22	4.70	702	4.22	4.37
Dunwoody, Todd, ChC	1	0.55	4.70	78	2.89	4.84
Durazo, Erubiel, Ari	34	6.96	4.70	107	7.39	4.90
Durbin, Chad, KC	0	0.00	4.86	0	0.00	4.86
Durham, Ray, CWS	94	5.26	4.86	618	5.19	5.10
Duvall, Mike, Min	0	—		0	—	
Dye, Jermaine, KC-Oak	98	5.84	4.86	380	5.23	5.03
Easley, Damion, Det	73	4.25	4.86	518	4.51	5.02
Eaton, Adam, SD	2	1.49	4.70	8	3.36	4.83
Echevarria, Angel, Mil	14	3.65	4.70	62	4.79	4.86
Eckstein, David, Ana	73	4.37	4.86	73	4.37	4.86
Edmonds, Jim, StL	121	8.73	4.70	682	6.72	5.03
Eischen, Joey, Mon	0	—		0	0.00	4.67
Elarton, Scott, Hou-Col	0	0.00	4.70	1	0.19	4.89
Eldred, Cal, CWS	0	—		2	0.79	4.80
Ellis, Robert, Ari	0	0.00	4.70	0	0.00	4.70
Embree, Alan, SF-CWS	0	0.00	4.70	0	0.00	4.65
Encarnacion, Juan, Det	41	3.25	4.86	213	4.36	5.11
Encarnacion, Mario, Col	2	1.03	4.70	2	1.03	4.70
Erdos, Todd, Bos	0	—		0	0.00	4.97
Erstad, Darin, Ana	71	3.86	4.86	495	5.61	5.08
Escobar, Alex, NYM	6	3.93	4.70	6	3.93	4.70
Escobar, Kelvim, Tor	0	—		0	0.00	5.28
Estalella, Bobby, SF-NYY	11	3.69	4.71	89	4.74	4.82
Estes, Shawn, SF	0	0.00	4.70	10	0.86	4.79
Estrada, Horacio, Col	0	—		0	0.00	5.00
Estrada, Johnny, Phi	28	2.99	4.70	28	2.99	4.70
Eusebio, Tony, Hou	21	4.82	4.70	228	4.60	4.74
Everett, Adam, Hou	0	0.00	4.70	0	0.00	4.70
Everett, Carl, Bos	60	5.22	4.86	472	5.91	4.83
Eyre, Scott, Tor	0	—		0	0.00	4.99
Fabregas, Jorge, Ana	8	1.71	4.86	147	2.90	5.03
Farnsworth, Kyle, ChC	0	0.00	4.70	0	0.00	4.99
Fasano, Sal, Oak-KC-Col	11	4.05	4.75	87	4.24	5.12
Fassero, Jeff, ChC	0	0.00	4.70	1	0.11	4.63
Febles, Carlos, KC	32	3.68	4.86	148	4.38	5.13
Feliz, Pedro, SF	15	2.21	4.70	16	2.30	4.71
Fernandez, Jared, Cin	0	0.00	4.70	0	0.00	4.70
Fernandez, Jose, Ana	0	0.00	4.86	0	0.00	4.93
Fernandez, Osvaldo, Cin	0	0.00	4.70	0	0.00	4.74
Fernandez, Tony, Mil-Tor	16	4.52	4.78	1121	4.98	4.56
Fick, Robert, Det	53	4.61	4.86	94	5.18	5.00
Figueroa, Luis, Pit	0	0.00	4.70	0	0.00	4.70
Figueroa, Nelson, Phi	2	2.82	4.70	2	2.44	4.74
Finley, Chuck, Cle	0	—		0	0.00	5.12
Finley, Steve, Ari	71	5.03	4.70	983	5.02	4.54
Flaherty, John, TB	24	3.16	4.86	275	3.38	4.98
Fletcher, Darrin, Tor	36	2.78	4.86	468	4.29	4.74
Florie, Bryce, Bos	0	—		0	0.00	4.84
Floyd, Cliff, Fla	118	8.00	4.70	455	6.21	4.73
Forbes, P.J., Phi	0	0.00	4.70	0	0.00	4.90
Fordyce, Brook, Bal	16	1.76	4.86	141	4.18	5.00
Foster, Kevin, Tex	0	—		14	2.45	4.63
Foulke, Keith, CWS	0	—		0	0.00	4.68
Fox, Andy, Fla	8	3.16	4.70	165	4.25	4.90
Fox, Chad, Mil	0	0.00	4.70	0	0.00	4.69
Franco, John, NYM	0	—		1	0.80	4.25

Player, Team	RC	RC/27	LRC/27	RC	RC/27	LRC27
	2001			**Career**		
Franco, Julio, Atl	15	6.10	4.70	1123	5.43	4.62
Franklin, Wayne, Hou	0	—	—	0	0.00	5.00
Frascatore, John, Tor	0	—	—	0	0.00	4.61
Freel, Ryan, Tor	2	3.16	4.86	2	3.16	4.86
Frye, Jeff, Tor	17	3.29	4.86	294	4.77	5.05
Fryman, Travis, Cle	38	3.94	4.86	937	5.40	4.91
Fullmer, Brad, Tor	71	4.76	4.86	291	5.41	4.92
Fultz, Aaron, SF	0	0.00	4.70	0	0.00	4.91
Furcal, Rafael, Atl	41	4.30	4.70	114	5.07	4.88
Fyhrie, Mike, ChC-Oak	0	0.00	4.70	0	0.00	4.70
Gagne, Eric, LA	0	0.00	4.70	0	0.00	4.84
Galarraga, Andres, Tex-SF	58	4.95	4.80	1243	5.96	4.41
Gant, Ron, Col-Oak	35	4.87	4.75	945	5.34	4.42
Garces, Rich, Bos	0	0.00	4.86	0	0.00	4.80
Garcia, Freddy, Sea	0	0.00	4.86	2	3.15	5.06
Garcia, Jesse, Atl	0	0.00	4.70	1	0.54	5.15
Garcia, Karim, Cle	11	8.96	4.86	80	3.50	4.86
Garciaparra, Nomar, Bos	14	6.17	4.86	510	7.68	5.09
Gardner, Mark, SF	0	0.00	4.70	3	0.16	4.52
Garland, Jon, CWS	0	0.00	4.86	0	0.00	4.86
Giambi, Jason, Oak	156	11.39	4.86	775	8.35	5.11
Giambi, Jeremy, Oak	66	6.22	4.86	153	5.39	5.08
Gibbons, Jay, Bal	26	3.88	4.86	26	3.88	4.86
Gil, Benji, Ana	34	4.64	4.86	127	3.06	5.03
Gil, Geronimo, Bal	9	5.63	4.86	9	5.63	4.86
Giles, Brian, Pit	130	8.34	4.70	557	8.02	4.94
Giles, Marcus, Atl	39	5.39	4.70	39	5.39	4.70
Gilkey, Bernard, Atl	11	3.47	4.70	622	5.26	4.54
Ginter, Keith, Hou	0	0.00	4.70	2	6.72	4.97
Gipson, Charles, Sea	4	1.95	4.86	19	2.69	5.06
Girardi, Joe, ChC	31	4.70	4.70	438	3.83	4.70
Glanville, Doug, Phi	62	3.34	4.70	391	4.42	4.78
Glaus, Troy, Ana	110	6.33	4.86	333	6.10	5.10
Glavine, Tom, Atl	2	0.81	4.70	54	1.56	4.46
Glynn, Ryan, Tex	0	—	—	0	0.00	5.24
Gomes, Wayne, Phi-SF	1	Inf	—	1	5.39	4.68
Gomez, Chris, SD-TB	33	3.65	4.79	315	3.68	4.85
Gonzalez, Alex, Fla	56	3.69	4.86	159	3.46	4.88
Gonzalez, Alex S., Tor	72	3.73	4.86	354	3.57	5.09
Gonzalez, Dicky, NYM	0	0.00	4.70	0	0.00	4.70
Gonzalez, Juan, Cle	108	7.39	4.86	1079	6.67	4.91
Gonzalez, Luis, Ari	163	10.15	4.70	978	6.06	4.64
Gonzalez, Raul, Cin	0	0.00	4.70	0	0.00	4.75
Gonzalez, Wiki, SD	27	6.04	4.70	57	3.70	4.92
Goodwin, Tom, LA	31	3.55	4.70	427	4.20	5.03
Grace, Mark, Ari	84	6.50	4.70	1309	6.29	4.45
Graffanino, Tony, CWS	18	4.28	4.86	120	4.19	4.83
Graves, Danny, Cin	2	17.89	4.70	4	7.69	4.79
Grebeck, Craig, Bos	0	0.00	4.86	249	4.20	4.80
Green, Shawn, LA	135	7.98	4.70	649	6.21	5.03
Greene, Todd, NYY	6	2.04	4.86	76	3.31	5.12
Greer, Rusty, Tex	39	5.49	4.86	688	6.91	5.12
Grieve, Ben, TB	85	5.50	4.86	397	6.06	5.08
Griffey Jr., Ken, Cin	69	6.78	4.70	1381	7.44	4.81
Grilli, Jason, Fla	1	3.83	4.70	1	3.35	4.74
Grimsley, Jason, KC	0	—	—	2	1.35	4.14
Grissom, Marquis, LA	43	3.14	4.70	865	4.52	4.57
Grudzielanek, Mark, LA	72	4.67	4.86	449	4.18	4.75
Guerrero, Vladimir, Mon	115	6.74	4.70	552	7.34	4.79
Guerrero, Wilton, Cin	21	5.69	4.70	178	4.16	4.77
Guillen, Carlos, Sea	57	4.24	4.86	110	4.63	5.03
Guillen, Jose, TB	14	3.62	4.86	203	3.88	4.82
Gulan, Mike, Fla	0	0.00	4.70	0	0.00	4.64
Guthrie, Mark, Oak	0	—	—	0	0.00	4.70
Gutierrez, Ricky, ChC	74	4.74	4.70	361	3.91	4.70
Guzman, Cristian, Min	78	5.73	4.86	179	3.95	5.13
Guzman, Edwards, SF	7	2.09	4.70	7	1.77	4.75
Guzman, Geraldo, Ari	0	0.00	4.70	0	0.00	4.99
Gwynn, Tony, SD	19	7.28	4.70	1611	6.55	4.31
Hackman, Luther, StL	0	0.00	4.70	0	0.00	4.87
Hairston Jr., Jerry, Bal	59	3.57	4.86	104	3.77	5.01
Halama, John, Sea	0	0.00	4.86	1	1.42	4.82
Hall, Toby, TB	25	4.80	4.86	26	4.66	4.89
Halladay, Roy, Tor	0	0.00	4.86	0	0.00	5.05
Halter, Shane, Det	73	5.57	4.86	117	3.83	5.00
Hamilton, Darryl, NYM	12	3.04	4.70	666	5.14	4.78
Hamilton, Joey, Tor-Cin	1	3.83	4.75	5	0.44	4.64
Hammonds, Jeffrey, Mil	25	4.86	4.70	363	5.48	5.01
Hampton, Mike, Col	14	5.96	4.70	48	3.26	4.75
Hansen, Dave, LA	19	4.47	4.70	186	4.81	4.47

Player, Team	RC	RC/27	LRC/27	RC	RC/27	LRC27
	2001			**Career**		
Harnisch, Pete, Cin	1	2.98	4.70	9	0.47	4.53
Harris, Lenny, NYM	9	2.20	4.70	382	3.81	4.40
Harris, Willie, Bal	0	0.00	4.86	0	0.00	4.86
Harvey, Ken, KC	0	0.00	4.86	0	0.00	4.86
Hasegawa, S., Ana	0	—	—	0	0.00	5.30
Haselman, Bill, Tex	18	4.84	4.86	173	4.14	5.07
Hatteberg, Scott, Bos	33	4.05	4.86	178	4.70	5.02
Hawkins, LaTroy, Min	0	0.00	4.70	0	0.00	5.12
Hayes, Charlie, Hou	5	3.19	4.70	631	4.12	4.53
Haynes, Jimmy, Mil	0	0.00	4.70	0	0.00	4.89
Helling, Rick, Tex	0	0.00	4.86	0	0.00	4.85
Helms, Wes, Atl	32	4.96	4.70	34	4.91	4.70
Helton, Todd, Col	150	9.70	4.70	561	9.00	4.82
Henderson, Rickey, SD	61	5.28	4.70	2098	6.80	4.62
Henry, Doug, KC	0	—	—	1	1.42	4.70
Hentgen, Pat, Bal	0	—	—	0	0.00	5.01
Heredia, Felix, ChC	0	0.00	4.70	1	2.69	4.77
Heredia, Gil, Oak	0	0.00	4.86	6	1.98	4.56
Herges, Matt, LA	2	8.94	4.70	2	2.69	4.91
Hermansen, Chad, Pit	1	0.57	4.70	12	1.70	4.93
Hermanson, Dustin, StL	0	0.00	4.70	2	0.19	4.80
Hernandez, Alex, Pit	0	0.00	4.70	0	0.00	4.95
Hernandez, Carlos, Hou	0	0.00	4.70	0	0.00	4.70
Hernandez, Jose, Mil	70	4.38	4.70	367	4.15	4.75
Hernandez, Livan, SF	7	2.89	4.70	22	1.97	4.81
Hernandez, Orlando, NYY	0	—	—	0	0.00	5.17
Hernandez, Ramon, Oak	56	4.16	4.86	138	4.54	5.09
Hernandez, Roberto, KC	0	—	—	0	0.00	4.60
Herndon, Junior, SD	0	0.00	4.70	0	0.00	4.70
Hiatt, Phil, LA	6	4.24	4.70	42	3.22	4.84
Hidalgo, Richard, Hou	77	5.14	4.70	286	5.80	4.85
Higginson, Bobby, Det	90	5.75	4.86	638	6.42	5.09
Hill, Glenallen, Ana	0	0.00	4.86	534	5.02	4.66
Hill, Ken, TB	0	—	—	11	0.84	4.27
Hillenbrand, Shea, Bos	40	2.94	4.86	40	2.94	4.86
Hinch, A.J., KC	5	1.22	4.86	57	2.64	5.04
Hinchliffe, Brett, NYM	0	0.00	4.70	0	0.00	4.70
Hitchcock, S., SD-NYY	1	3.83	4.70	1	0.14	4.78
Hocking, Denny, Min	31	3.23	4.86	200	3.82	5.09
Hoffman, Trevor, SD	0	0.00	4.70	3	2.61	4.65
Hollandsworth, Todd, Col	24	8.59	4.70	260	4.99	4.78
Hollins, Dave, Cle	0	0.00	4.86	515	5.37	4.67
Holt, Chris, Det	0	0.00	4.86	0	0.00	4.85
Holtz, Mike, Ana	0	—	—	0	0.00	4.93
Hoover, Paul, TB	0	0.00	4.86	0	0.00	4.86
Houston, Tyler, Mil	43	6.71	4.70	187	4.65	4.80
Hubbard, Mike, Tex	1	3.36	4.86	2	0.33	4.64
Hubbard, Trenidad, KC	0	0.00	4.86	83	4.56	4.78
Huckaby, Ken, Ari	0	0.00	4.70	0	0.00	4.70
Hudson, Tim, Oak	0	0.00	4.86	1	1.92	5.02
Huff, Aubrey, TB	39	3.18	4.86	57	3.61	4.96
Hundley, Todd, ChC	20	2.57	4.70	497	4.84	4.59
Hunter, Brian L., Phi	22	5.09	4.70	349	3.91	4.91
Hunter, Torii, Min	79	4.86	4.86	164	4.31	5.07
Hutchinson, Chad, StL	0	0.00	4.70	0	0.00	4.70
Hyzdu, Adam, Pit	6	2.73	4.70	12	4.60	4.75
Ibanez, Raul, KC	53	6.78	4.86	104	4.77	5.06
Inge, Brandon, Det	4	0.65	4.86	4	0.65	4.86
Irabu, Hideki, Mon	0	0.00	4.70	0	0.00	5.01
Isringhausen, Jason, Oak	0	—	—	9	2.73	4.70
Izturis, Cesar, Tor	18	4.70	4.86	18	4.70	4.86
Jackson, Damian, SD	52	3.97	4.70	177	4.32	4.89
Jackson, Mike, Hou	0	0.00	4.70	2	2.00	4.50
Jackson, Ryan, Det	11	3.05	4.86	45	3.37	4.76
Jaha, John, Oak	2	1.19	4.86	487	6.05	5.01
James, Mike, StL	0	0.00	4.70	0	0.00	4.85
Jarvis, Kevin, SD	5	2.24	4.70	6	1.02	4.75
Javier, Stan, Sea	46	5.83	4.86	669	4.56	4.67
Jenkins, Geoff, Mil	60	5.19	4.70	260	5.75	4.86
Jennings, Jason, Col	2	4.47	4.70	2	4.47	4.70
Jennings, R., Oak-Col-Cin	18	4.93	4.77	27	4.43	4.73
Jensen, Marcus, Bos-Tex	0	0.00	4.86	25	2.57	4.99
Jensen, Ryan, SF	2	5.37	4.70	2	5.37	4.70
Jeter, Derek, NYY	111	6.70	4.86	659	6.51	5.10
Jimenez, D'Angelo, SD	41	4.64	4.70	46	4.96	4.72
Jimenez, Jose, Col	0	0.00	4.70	1	0.43	4.95
Jodie, Brett, NYY-SD	0	0.00	4.70	0	0.00	4.70
Johnson, Adam, Min	0	0.00	4.86	0	0.00	4.86
Johnson, Brian, LA	1	8.94	4.70	140	3.31	4.75
Johnson, Charles, Fla	64	4.98	4.70	394	4.64	4.81

Player, Team	2001 RC	RC/27	LRC/27	Career RC	RC/27	LRC27
Johnson, Jason, Bal	1	13.44	4.86	1	2.23	5.10
Johnson, Mark L., CWS	22	3.97	4.86	68	3.53	5.12
Johnson, Mark P., NYM	17	4.96	4.70	132	4.79	4.67
Johnson, Mike, Mon	0	0.00	4.70	1	0.64	4.84
Johnson, Nick, NYY	6	2.83	4.86	6	2.83	4.86
Johnson, Randy, Ari	0	0.00	4.70	4	0.35	4.82
Johnson, Russ, TB	47	6.87	4.86	103	4.99	4.99
Jones, Andruw, Atl	93	5.08	4.70	470	5.52	4.79
Jones, Bobby J., SD	2	1.03	4.70	7	0.45	4.69
Jones, Chipper, Atl	131	8.55	4.70	831	7.48	4.74
Jones, Jacque, Min	57	4.20	4.86	176	4.69	5.11
Jones, Terry, Mon	6	2.73	4.70	49	3.03	4.78
Jones, Todd, Det-Min	0	—	—	1	3.38	4.63
Jordan, Brian, Atl	89	5.65	4.70	626	5.66	4.70
Jordan, Kevin, Phi	15	4.63	4.70	137	3.35	4.82
Joyner, Wally, Ana	16	3.71	4.86	1175	5.87	4.64
Judd, Mike, TB-Tex	0	0.00	4.86	1	2.24	4.92
Justice, David, NYY	50	4.46	4.86	998	6.81	4.66
Kapler, Gabe, Tex	76	5.39	4.86	199	5.01	5.10
Karros, Eric, LA	49	3.71	4.70	774	4.90	4.62
Karsay, Steve, Cle-Atl	0	0.00	4.70	0	0.00	4.90
Keisler, Randy, NYY	0	0.00	4.86	0	0.00	4.86
Kendall, Jason, Pit	67	3.75	4.70	477	5.95	4.75
Kennedy, Adam, Ana	49	3.47	4.86	133	3.84	5.09
Kennedy, Joe, TB	1	8.96	4.86	1	8.96	4.86
Kent, Jeff, SF	98	5.77	4.70	830	5.94	4.69
Kielty, Bobby, Min	11	3.48	4.86	11	3.48	4.86
Kieschnick, Brooks, Col	7	5.69	4.70	25	4.88	4.67
Kile, Darryl, StL	1	0.40	4.70	14	0.59	4.63
Kim, Byung-Hyun, Ari	0	0.00	4.70	0	0.00	4.84
King, Ray, Mil	0	0.00	4.70	0	0.00	4.80
Kingsale, Gene, Bal-Sea	3	5.04	4.86	15	2.43	5.20
Kinkade, Mike, Bal	15	3.23	4.86	20	3.14	4.90
Klesko, Ryan, SD	121	7.86	4.70	667	6.84	4.73
Kline, Steve, StL	0	0.00	4.70	0	0.00	4.75
Knoblauch, Chuck, NYY	70	4.51	4.86	1038	6.08	4.93
Knorr, Randy, Mon	10	3.44	4.70	67	3.24	4.89
Knott, Eric, Ari	0	0.00	4.70	0	0.00	4.70
Knotts, Gary, Fla	0	0.00	4.70	0	0.00	4.70
Koch, Billy, Tor	0	—	—	0	0.00	5.24
Kolb, Brandon, Mil	0	0.00	4.70	0	0.00	4.85
Konerko, Paul, CWS	92	5.62	4.86	278	5.28	5.03
Koplove, Mike, Ari	0	0.00	4.70	0	0.00	4.70
Koskie, Corey, Min	100	6.16	4.86	251	6.33	5.08
Kotsay, Mark, SD	69	6.01	4.70	258	4.36	4.82
Kreuter, Chad, LA	24	4.13	4.70	280	3.87	4.86
Laker, Tim, Cle	3	2.78	4.86	28	2.51	4.55
Lamb, Mike, Tex	43	5.58	4.86	96	4.42	5.14
Lampkin, Tom, Sea	22	3.61	4.86	189	4.15	4.74
Lankford, Ray, StL-SD	68	6.02	4.70	937	6.15	4.53
Lansing, Mike, Bos	33	3.16	4.86	523	4.35	4.70
Larkin, Barry, Cin	25	5.59	4.70	1190	6.29	4.43
Larson, Brandon, Cin	0	0.00	4.70	0	0.00	4.70
LaRue, Jason, Cin	39	3.55	4.70	63	3.79	4.80
Latham, Chris, Tor	13	6.35	4.86	19	2.88	4.98
Lawrence, Brian, SD	1	1.03	4.70	1	1.03	4.70
Lawton, Matt, Min-NYM	92	5.75	4.81	496	6.08	5.07
Leach, Jalal, SF	1	2.98	4.70	1	2.98	4.70
LeCroy, Matt, Min	12	12.90	4.86	19	2.94	5.23
Ledee, Ricky, Tex	30	4.11	4.86	150	4.84	5.14
Lee, Carlos, CWS	82	5.09	4.86	236	5.15	5.11
Lee, David, SD	0	0.00	4.70	0	0.00	4.94
Lee, Derrek, Fla	85	5.32	4.70	242	4.74	4.79
Lee, Travis, Phi	79	4.81	4.70	247	4.45	4.80
Leiter, Al, NYM	0	0.00	4.70	1	0.07	4.78
Leiter, Mark, Mil	0	0.00	4.70	3	0.41	4.64
Leskanic, Curtis, Mil	0	0.00	4.70	5	3.55	4.63
Levis, Jesse, Mil	3	3.10	4.70	70	3.61	5.02
Levrault, Allen, Mil	0	0.00	4.70	0	0.00	4.72
Lewis, Darren, Bos	20	4.13	4.86	460	3.78	4.76
Lewis, Mark, Cle	0	0.00	4.86	325	3.98	4.79
Lidle, Cory, Oak	0	0.00	4.86	0	0.00	4.81
Lieber, Jon, ChC	0	0.00	4.70	13	0.86	4.76
Lieberthal, Mike, Phi	12	3.39	4.70	290	4.85	4.78
Liefer, Jeff, CWS	35	4.73	4.86	47	4.24	4.97
Lilly, Ted, NYY	0	0.00	4.86	0	0.00	4.95
Lima, Jose, Hou-Det	0	0.00	4.71	0	0.00	4.84
Lincoln, Mike, Pit	0	0.00	4.70	0	0.00	4.80
Linebrink, Scott, Hou	0	—	—	1	Inf	—
Lira, Felipe, Mon	0	—	—	1	1.58	5.00

Player, Team	2001 RC	RC/27	LRC/27	Career RC	RC/27	LRC27
Little, Mark, Col	16	7.40	4.70	17	6.52	4.68
Lloyd, Graeme, Mon	0	0.00	4.70	0	0.00	4.70
Loaiza, Esteban, Tor	0	0.00	4.86	3	0.50	4.64
Lockhart, Keith, Atl	15	2.78	4.70	239	4.41	4.95
Lo Duca, Paul, LA	94	7.37	4.70	114	6.25	4.78
Loewer, Carlton, SD	0	0.00	4.86	1	0.47	4.73
Lofton, James, Bos	0	0.00	4.86	0	0.00	4.86
Lofton, Kenny, Cle	74	4.87	4.86	938	6.17	4.95
Lohse, Kyle, Min	1	8.96	4.86	1	8.96	4.86
Loiselle, Rich, Pit	0	—	—	1	2.70	4.70
Long, Terrence, Oak	87	4.90	4.86	184	5.38	5.07
Looper, Braden, Fla	0	0.00	4.70	0	0.00	4.85
Lopez, Albie, TB-Ari	0	0.00	4.73	0	0.00	4.84
Lopez, Felipe, Tor	26	5.03	4.86	26	5.03	4.86
Lopez, Javy, Atl	59	4.67	4.70	481	5.30	4.72
Lopez, Luis, Mil	26	3.99	4.70	140	3.36	4.71
Lopez, Luis, Tor	9	2.39	4.86	9	2.39	4.86
Lopez, Mendy, Hou-Pit	7	4.17	4.70	33	3.85	4.96
Loretta, Mark, Mil	47	4.33	4.70	324	4.76	4.90
Lowe, Derek, Bos	0	0.00	4.86	0	0.00	5.00
Lowe, Sean, CWS	0	0.00	4.86	0	0.00	4.69
Lowell, Mike, Fla	88	5.68	4.70	217	5.52	4.89
Lugo, Julio, Hou	53	3.40	4.70	110	3.99	4.83
Lunar, Fernando, Bal	9	1.77	4.86	11	1.49	4.93
Mabry, John, StL-Fla	14	2.89	4.70	281	4.16	4.75
Machado, Robert, ChC	13	3.11	4.70	27	2.89	4.89
Macias, Jose, Det	61	4.30	4.86	87	4.49	4.98
Mackowiak, Rob, Pit	25	3.99	4.70	25	3.99	4.70
MacRae, Scott, Cin	0	0.00	4.70	0	0.00	4.70
Maddux, Greg, Atl	0	0.00	4.70	24	0.61	4.43
Maduro, Calvin, Bal	0	—	—	0	0.00	4.62
Magadan, Dave, SD	10	2.74	4.70	646	5.55	4.42
Magee, Wendell, Det	18	2.80	4.86	76	3.39	4.86
Magnante, Mike, Oak	0	—	—	1	6.72	4.78
Magruder, Chris, Tex	1	1.08	4.86	1	1.08	4.86
Mahay, Ron, ChC	0	0.00	4.70	2	2.68	5.02
Mahomes, Pat, Tex	1	Inf	—	5	5.17	5.00
Mantei, Matt, Ari	0	—	—	1	6.74	4.72
Manzanillo, Josias, Pit	0	0.00	4.70	1	2.24	4.77
Marquis, Jason, Atl	0	0.00	4.70	0	0.00	4.72
Marrero, Eli, StL	26	4.31	4.70	87	3.07	4.81
Marte, Damaso, Pit	0	0.00	4.70	0	0.00	4.70
Martin, Al, Sea	40	4.84	4.86	587	5.21	4.73
Martin, Tom, NYM	0	0.00	4.70	0	0.00	4.65
Martinez, Dave, Atl	24	3.54	4.70	752	4.54	4.61
Martinez, Edgar, Sea	105	8.13	4.86	1259	7.93	4.87
Martinez, Felix, TB	14	2.07	4.86	45	2.19	5.09
Martinez, Pedro, Bos	0	—	—	0	0.00	4.64
Martinez, Ramon, LA	0	0.00	4.70	11	0.51	4.38
Martinez, Ramon E., SF	45	3.81	4.70	97	4.39	4.83
Martinez, Sandy, Mon	0	0.00	4.70	49	2.99	5.12
Martinez, Tino, NYY	94	5.74	4.86	863	5.62	4.99
Mateo, Henry, Mon	1	4.47	4.70	1	4.47	4.70
Mateo, Ruben, Tex	13	3.36	4.86	55	4.20	5.13
Matheny, Mike, StL	31	2.59	4.70	198	3.05	4.96
Mathews, T.J., Oak-StL	0	0.00	4.70	0	0.00	4.67
Matos, Luis, Bal	14	4.70	4.86	28	3.18	5.15
Mattes, Troy, Mon	2	5.37	4.70	2	5.37	4.70
Matthews, Mike, StL	0	0.00	4.70	0	0.00	4.70
Matthews Jr., G., ChC-Pit	54	4.36	4.70	70	3.82	4.80
Maurer, Dave, SD	0	0.00	4.70	0	0.00	4.70
Maxwell, Jason, Min	6	2.83	4.86	20	3.58	5.12
Mayne, Brent, Col-KC	38	4.03	4.79	336	4.19	4.81
Mays, Joe, Min	0	0.00	4.86	1	2.98	5.16
McCarty, Dave, KC	22	3.63	4.86	129	3.53	4.92
McCracken, Quinton, Min	4	1.99	4.86	196	4.53	4.88
McDonald, Donzell, NYY	0	0.00	4.86	0	0.00	4.86
McDonald, John, Cle	0	0.00	4.86	2	1.25	5.04
McDonald, Keith, StL	0	0.00	4.70	3	11.51	4.87
McElroy, Chuck, Bal-SD	0	0.00	4.70	6	4.50	4.47
McEwing, Joe, NYM	37	4.53	4.70	115	4.06	4.91
McGriff, Fred, TB-ChC	102	7.31	4.80	1465	6.67	4.60
McGuire, Ryan, Fla	5	2.92	4.70	57	3.00	4.71
McGwire, Mark, StL	50	5.24	4.70	1441	8.09	4.68
McKnight, Tony, Hou-Pit	0	0.00	4.70	0	0.00	4.80
McLemore, Mark, Sea	70	5.99	4.86	682	4.27	4.95
McMillon, Billy, Det-Oak	12	4.36	4.86	52	4.97	4.91
Meadows, Brian, KC	0	—	—	1	0.19	4.85
Meares, Pat, Pit	17	2.02	4.70	355	3.63	5.02
Mecir, Jim, Oak	0	—	—	0	0.00	5.01

Player, Team	2001			Career		
	RC	RC/27	LRC/27	RC	RC/27	LRC27
Melhuse, Adam, Col	3	1.28	4.70	4	1.28	4.78
Mendez, Donaldo, SD	1	0.26	4.70	1	0.26	4.70
Mendoza, Ramiro, NYY	0	0.00	4.86	0	0.00	4.91
Menechino, Frank, Oak	71	5.00	4.86	96	5.10	4.96
Mercado, Hector, Cin	0	0.00	4.70	0	0.00	4.80
Merced, Orlando, Hou	24	6.07	4.70	565	5.69	4.54
Mercedes, Jose, Bal	0	0.00	4.86	0	0.00	4.75
Merloni, Lou, Bos	11	2.51	4.86	60	4.08	5.08
Mesa, Jose, Phi	0	—		0		
Meyers, Chad, ChC	1	1.68	4.70	13	1.96	4.98
Miceli, Dan, Fla-Col	0	—		1	1.42	4.68
Michaels, Jason, Phi	0	0.00	4.70	0	0.00	4.70
Michalak, Chris, Tor-Tex	1	6.72	4.86	1	6.72	4.86
Middlebrook, Jason, SD	0	0.00	4.70	0	0.00	4.70
Mientkiewicz, Doug, Min	87	5.85	4.86	122	4.66	4.99
Millar, Kevin, Fla	91	7.68	4.70	199	6.81	4.88
Miller, Corky, Cin	5	3.12	4.70	5	3.12	4.70
Miller, Damian, Ari	44	4.03	4.70	160	4.57	4.85
Miller, Wade, Hou	1	0.41	4.70	1	0.26	4.81
Mills, Alan, Bal	0	—		0	0.00	5.00
Millwood, Kevin, Atl	0	0.00	4.70	1	0.11	4.85
Milton, Eric, Min	0	0.00	4.86	2	4.88	5.07
Minor, Damon, SF	2	1.38	4.70	8	4.88	4.74
Minor, Ryan, Mon	3	0.94	4.70	14	1.39	5.05
Mirabelli, Doug, Tex-Bos	26	4.57	4.86	71	4.33	4.93
Mlicki, Dave, Det-Hou	0	0.00	4.71	6	0.84	4.65
Moehler, Brian, Det	0	—		0	0.00	5.10
Moeller, Chad, Ari	1	0.58	4.70	6	1.05	5.12
Mohler, Mike, Ari	0	—		1	8.97	5.00
Mohr, Dustan, Min	3	1.97	4.86	3	1.97	4.86
Molina, Ben, Ana	34	3.58	4.86	98	3.73	5.12
Molina, Jose, Ana	2	1.73	4.86	3	1.79	4.90
Mondesi, Raul, Tor	88	5.21	4.86	712	5.71	4.77
Monroe, Craig, Tex	7	4.48	4.86	7	4.48	4.86
Moore, Trey, Atl	1	Inf		4	4.69	4.76
Mora, Melvin, Bal	53	4.08	4.86	110	4.20	5.00
Mordecai, Mike, Mon	33	4.56	4.70	114	3.73	4.79
Morgan, Mike, Ari	0	—		4	0.21	4.32
Morris, Matt, StL	0	0.00	4.70	5	0.78	4.65
Morris, Warren, Pit	6	1.83	4.70	142	4.25	4.97
Moss, Damian, Atl	0	0.00	4.70	0	0.00	4.70
Mota, Guillermo, Mon	0	0.00	4.70	2	17.90	4.80
Mottola, Chad, Fla	0	0.00	4.70	8	2.73	4.74
Mouton, James, Mil	17	4.11	4.70	175	3.66	4.71
Mouton, Lyle, Fla	0	0.00	4.70	114	5.01	5.08
Moyer, Jamie, Sea	0	0.00	4.86	6	1.00	4.22
Mueller, Bill, ChC	36	6.04	4.70	335	5.13	4.79
Mulder, Mark, Oak	0	0.00	4.86	0	0.00	5.10
Mulholland, Terry, Pit-LA	0	0.00	4.70	7	0.31	4.38
Munoz, Bobby, Mon	0	0.00	4.70	6	2.70	4.64
Munson, Eric, Det	2	0.91	4.86	2	0.84	4.89
Murray, Calvin, SF	37	3.79	4.70	70	4.38	4.82
Murray, Heath, Det	0	—		0	0.00	4.87
Mussina, Mike, NYY	1	4.48	4.86	3	3.22	5.09
Myers, Greg, Bal-Oak	26	5.38	4.86	265	3.51	4.84
Myers, Mike, Col	0	—		0	0.00	5.00
Myers, Rodney, SD	0	0.00	4.70	3	6.74	4.79
Nagy, Charles, Cle	1	26.88	4.86	1	1.68	5.04
Neagle, Denny, Col	6	2.98	4.70	21	1.19	4.67
Nelson, Jeff, Sea	0	—		0	0.00	5.11
Nen, Robb, SF	0	0.00	4.70	0	0.00	4.59
Neugebauer, Nick, Mil	0	0.00	4.70	0	0.00	4.70
Nevin, Phil, SD	115	7.73	4.70	384	6.08	4.94
Newhan, David, Phi	1	5.37	4.70	6	2.12	4.98
Nichting, Chris, Cin-Col	0	0.00	4.70	0	0.00	4.70
Nieves, Jose, Ana	5	3.05	4.86	37	2.73	4.98
Nitkowski, C.J., Det-NYM	0	—		1	1.93	4.66
Nixon, Trot, Bos	96	6.31	4.86	228	5.78	5.09
Nomo, Hideo, Bos	1	6.72	4.86	8	0.69	4.71
Norton, Greg, Col	30	4.65	4.70	151	4.21	5.07
Nunez, Abraham, Pit	32	3.75	4.70	70	3.13	4.83
Nunez, Jose A., LA-SD	0	0.00	4.70	0	0.00	4.70
Nunez, Vladimir, Fla	0	0.00	4.70	1	0.49	4.95
Ochoa, Alex, Cin-Col	63	4.03	4.70	257	4.84	4.81
Offerman, Jose, Bos	71	4.73	4.86	715	4.83	4.80
Ohka, T. Bos-Mon	1	1.49	4.73	1	1.49	4.73
Ohman, Will, ChC	0	0.00	4.70	0	0.00	4.70
Ojeda, Augie, ChC	11	2.44	4.70	20	2.90	4.81
O'Leary, Troy, Bos	41	3.99	4.86	516	5.07	5.11
Olerud, John, Sea	96	6.01	4.86	1098	6.71	4.83

Player, Team	2001			Career		
	RC	RC/27	LRC/27	RC	RC/27	LRC27
Olivares, Omar, Pit	4	5.11	4.70	25	3.38	4.28
Oliver, Darren, Tex	0	0.00	4.86	8	2.22	4.91
Oliver, Joe, NYY-Bos	5	3.45	4.86	393	3.91	4.51
Olsen, Kevin, Fla	0	0.00	4.70	0	0.00	4.70
Olson, Gregg, LA	0	—		2	17.96	4.64
O'Neill, Paul, NYY	72	4.84	4.86	1207	5.80	4.78
Ordaz, Luis, KC	4	2.34	4.86	21	1.91	4.88
Ordonez, Magglio, CWS	115	7.09	4.86	417	6.13	5.09
Ordonez, Rey, NYM	39	2.79	4.70	196	2.59	4.74
Orosco, Jesse, LA	0	—		4	1.84	4.17
Ortega, Bill, StL	0	0.00	4.70	0	0.00	4.70
Ortiz, David, Min	45	5.02	4.86	166	5.39	5.08
Ortiz, Hector, KC	11	2.35	4.86	32	4.62	4.99
Ortiz, Jose, Oak-Col	32	4.29	4.73	33	4.24	4.76
Ortiz, Ramon, Ana	0	0.00	4.86	0	0.00	4.86
Ortiz, Russ, SF	4	1.68	4.70	17	2.19	4.87
Osik, Keith, Pit	11	3.04	4.70	82	3.66	4.79
Osuna, Antonio, CWS	0	—		0	0.00	4.74
Oswalt, Roy, Hou	1	0.65	4.70	1	0.65	4.70
Overbay, Lyle, Ari	0	0.00	4.70	0	0.00	4.70
Owens, Eric, Fla	33	2.74	4.70	195	3.82	4.87
Padilla, Vicente, Phi	1	8.94	4.70	2	17.89	4.70
Painter, Lance, Tor-Mil	0	—		5	2.08	4.66
Palmeiro, Orlando, Ana	28	3.86	4.86	159	4.50	5.10
Palmeiro, Rafael, Tex	124	7.39	4.86	1566	6.69	4.76
Palmer, Dean, Det	35	5.47	4.86	728	5.20	4.96
Paniagua, Jose, Sea	0	0.00	4.86	0	0.00	4.70
Paquette, Craig, StL	57	5.82	4.70	271	3.93	4.98
Park, Chan Ho, LA	2	0.80	4.70	14	1.16	4.77
Parque, Jim, CWS	0	—		1	2.43	5.17
Parris, Steve, Tor	0	0.00	4.86	5	0.90	4.86
Patterson, Corey, ChC	15	3.73	4.70	16	2.96	4.78
Patterson, Danny, Det	0	—		0	0.00	5.18
Patterson, Jarrod, Det	3	2.44	4.86	3	2.44	4.86
Paul, Josh, CWS	18	4.44	4.86	30	4.50	5.02
Pavano, Carl, Mon	0	0.00	4.70	2	0.45	4.84
Payton, Jay, NYM	25	2.35	4.70	90	3.55	4.87
Pena, Angel, LA	1	0.58	4.70	15	2.51	4.89
Pena, Carlos, Tex	12	6.86	4.86	12	6.86	4.86
Pena, Elvis, Mil	4	3.07	4.70	5	3.05	4.76
Penny, Brad, Fla	0	0.00	4.70	0	0.00	4.83
Percival, Troy, Ana	0	—		0	0.00	5.39
Perez, Eddie, Atl	0	0.00	4.70	93	3.72	4.78
Perez, Neifi, Col-KC	68	4.06	4.76	343	4.09	4.82
Perez, Odalis, Atl	0	0.00	4.70	0	0.00	4.87
Perez, Robert, NYY-Mil	1	1.58	4.81	44	3.01	5.05
Perez, Santiago, SD	8	3.20	4.70	13	3.09	4.82
Perez, Timo, NYM	22	3.04	4.70	29	3.37	4.75
Perez, Tomas, Phi	19	5.20	4.70	65	2.69	5.10
Perisho, Matt, Det	0	—		0	0.00	5.22
Perry, Herbert, CWS	36	4.28	4.86	159	5.01	5.12
Person, Robert, Phi	0	0.00	4.70	1	0.14	4.86
Peters, Chris, Mon	0	0.00	4.70	6	1.88	4.73
Peterson, Kyle, Mil	1	6.71	4.70	1	1.08	4.96
Petkovsek, Mark, Tex	0	0.00	4.86	4	1.33	4.63
Petrick, Ben, Col	34	4.61	4.70	71	5.48	4.83
Pettitte, Andy, NYY	0	0.00	4.86	0	0.00	5.08
Pettyjohn, Adam, Det	0	0.00	4.86	0	0.00	4.86
Phelps, Josh, Tor	0	0.00	4.86	0	0.00	4.89
Phillips, Jason, NYM	0	0.00	4.70	0	0.00	4.70
Piatt, Adam, Oak	7	2.27	4.86	39	5.34	5.11
Piazza, Mike, NYM	89	6.37	4.70	932	7.55	4.69
Pichardo, Hipolito, Bos	0	—		0	0.00	5.09
Pickering, Calvin, Cin-Bos	7	4.37	4.85	13	3.59	5.00
Pierre, Juan, Col	100	5.92	4.70	125	5.56	4.78
Pierzynski, A.J., Min	53	4.93	4.86	71	5.07	4.95
Plesac, Dan, Tor	0	—		0	0.00	4.66
Podsednik, Scott, Sea	1	4.48	4.86	1	4.48	4.86
Polanco, Placido, StL	63	3.92	4.70	143	4.11	4.83
Politte, Cliff, Phi	0	0.00	4.70	1	0.82	4.80
Ponson, Sidney, Bal	0	0.00	4.86	1	2.23	5.10
Porter, Bo, Tex	10	3.73	4.86	12	3.04	4.94
Posada, Jorge, NYY	92	6.66	4.86	342	6.16	5.07
Powell, Brian, Hou	0	0.00	4.70	1	2.99	4.97
Powell, Dante, SF	0	0.00	4.70	11	5.10	4.77
Powell, Jay, Hou-Col	0	0.00	4.70	0	0.00	4.68
Pratt, Todd, NYM-Phi	15	2.70	4.70	116	4.20	4.70
Pride, Curtis, Mon	10	4.26	4.70	98	4.70	4.99
Prieto, Ariel, TB	0	—		0	0.00	5.30
Prince, Tom, Min	17	2.86	4.86	94	2.92	4.53

Player, Team	2001 RC	2001 RC/27	2001 LRC/27	Career RC	Career RC/27	Career LRC27
Prokopec, Luke, LA	0	0.00	4.70	0	0.00	4.74
Pujols, Albert, StL	125	7.84	4.70	125	7.84	4.70
Pulsipher, Bill, Bos-CWS	0	—	—	2	0.62	4.75
Punto, Nick, Phi	0	0.00	4.70	0	0.00	4.70
Quantrill, Paul, Tor	0	—	—	0	0.00	4.64
Quevedo, Ruben, Mil	1	1.68	4.70	1	0.61	4.89
Quinn, Mark, KC	51	3.88	4.86	146	5.11	5.09
Radinsky, Scott, Cle	0	—	—	0	0.00	4.62
Radke, Brad, Min	1	13.44	4.86	1	1.79	5.06
Raines, Tim, Mon-Bal	18	7.32	4.72	1581	6.49	4.39
Raines Jr., Tim, Bal	2	2.69	4.86	2	2.69	4.86
Ramirez, Aramis, Pit	119	7.27	4.70	172	5.21	4.76
Ramirez, Julio, CWS	0	0.00	4.86	0	0.00	4.91
Ramirez, Manny, Bos	119	8.44	4.86	900	8.24	5.10
Randa, Joe, KC	76	4.46	4.86	456	5.13	5.05
Ransom, Cody, SF	0	0.00	4.70	0	0.00	4.70
Rapp, Pat, Ana	0	0.00	4.86	1	0.11	4.63
Reames, Britt, Mon	1	1.41	4.70	1	0.90	4.81
Reboulet, Jeff, LA	37	5.98	4.70	224	3.83	4.99
Redding, Tim, Hou	1	2.06	4.70	1	2.06	4.70
Redman, Mark, Min-Det	0	—	—	0	0.00	5.30
Redman, Tike, Pit	5	1.28	4.70	9	2.06	4.73
Redmond, Mike, Fla	19	4.86	4.70	90	4.47	4.88
Reed, Rick, NYM-Min	0	0.00	4.70	12	1.10	4.69
Reed, Steve, Cle-Atl	0	—	—	1	1.35	4.55
Reese, Pokey, Cin	45	3.43	4.70	228	3.76	4.83
Reichert, Dan, KC	0	0.00	4.86	0	0.00	5.04
Reith, Brian, Cin	1	2.98	4.70	1	2.98	4.70
Reitsma, Chris, Cin	0	0.00	4.70	0	0.00	4.70
Rekar, Bryan, TB	0	0.00	4.86	2	0.98	4.71
Relaford, Desi, NYM	48	5.70	4.70	180	4.01	4.79
Remlinger, Mike, Atl	0	0.00	4.70	2	0.45	4.59
Renteria, Edgar, StL	56	3.78	4.70	391	4.13	4.77
Reyes, Al, LA	0	0.00	4.70	0	0.00	4.72
Reyes, Dennys, Cin	0	0.00	4.70	0	0.00	4.68
Reynolds, Shane, Hou	0	0.00	4.70	13	0.72	4.72
Reynoso, Armando, Ari	1	2.24	4.70	6	0.49	4.70
Rhodes, Arthur, Sea	0	0.00	4.86	0	0.00	4.93
Richard, Chris, Bal	64	4.47	4.86	96	4.64	4.99
Riedling, John, Cin	0	0.00	4.70	0	0.00	4.90
Rigdon, Paul, Mil	1	1.28	4.70	1	0.64	4.85
Riggan, Jerrod, NYM	0	0.00	4.70	0	0.00	4.70
Riggs, Adam, SD	0	0.00	4.70	2	1.14	4.67
Rijo, Jose, Cin	0	—	—	18	1.20	4.21
Rincon, Juan, Min	1	Inf	—	1	Inf	—
Rincon, Ricardo, Cle	0	—	—	0	0.00	4.60
Rios, Armando, SF-Pit	46	5.04	4.70	132	6.51	4.87
Ripken Jr., Cal, Bal	53	3.64	4.86	1712	5.18	4.70
Ritchie, Todd, Pit	3	1.36	4.70	3	0.49	4.90
Rivas, Luis, Min	65	3.89	4.86	73	3.96	4.90
Rivera, Juan, NYY	0	0.00	4.86	0	0.00	4.86
Rivera, Mike, Det	2	6.72	4.86	2	6.72	4.86
Rivera, Ruben, Cin	31	4.02	4.70	166	3.94	4.92
Roberts, Brian, Bal	24	2.99	4.86	24	2.99	4.86
Roberts, Dave, Cle	2	5.97	4.86	18	3.56	5.16
Roberts, Grant, NYM	0	0.00	4.70	0	0.00	4.78
Roberts, Willis, Bal	0	0.00	4.86	0	0.00	4.86
Robinson, Kerry, StL	22	4.13	4.70	22	3.99	4.71
Rodriguez, Alex, Tex	149	8.71	4.86	779	7.56	5.10
Rodriguez, Felix, SF	0	—	—	1	2.07	4.88
Rodriguez, Frank, Cin	0	0.00	4.70	1	5.36	5.06
Rodriguez, Henry, NYY	0	0.00	4.86	471	5.48	4.68
Rodriguez, Ivan, Tex	70	5.82	4.86	781	5.35	4.97
Rodriguez, Rich, Cle	0	—	—	3	2.53	4.28
Rogers, Kenny, Tex	0	0.00	4.86	0	0.00	5.03
Rolen, Scott, Phi	112	7.21	4.70	517	6.75	4.76
Rollins, Jimmy, Phi	90	4.80	4.70	98	4.88	4.72
Rolls, Damian, TB	18	2.60	4.86	18	2.57	4.86
Romero, J.C., Min	1	26.88	4.86	1	26.88	4.86
Rose, Brian, NYM-TB	0	0.00	4.70	0	0.00	5.04
Rowand, Aaron, CWS	20	5.60	4.86	20	5.60	4.86
Rueter, Kirk, SF	2	0.91	4.70	8	0.51	4.73
Ruffin, Johnny, Fla	0	—	—	1	1.69	4.61
Rupe, Ryan, TB	1	13.44	4.86	1	3.35	5.11
Rusch, Glendon, NYM	0	0.00	4.70	0	0.00	4.85
Ryan, B.J., Bal	0	0.00	4.86	0	0.00	4.86
Ryan, Rob, Ari-Oak	0	0.00	4.84	8	4.39	4.98
Sabathia, C.C., Cle	0	0.00	4.86	0	0.00	4.86
Sabel, Erik, Ari	0	—	—	0	0.00	5.00
Saberhagen, Bret, Bos	0	—	—	1	0.14	4.51

Player, Team	2001 RC	2001 RC/27	2001 LRC/27	Career RC	Career RC/27	Career LRC27
Sadler, Donnie, Cin-KC	4	0.64	4.79	37	2.26	5.01
Saenz, Olmedo, Oak	24	2.56	4.86	102	4.45	5.08
Salmon, Tim, Ana	63	4.42	4.86	897	7.10	5.05
Sanchez, Alex, Mil	6	2.87	4.70	6	2.87	4.70
Sanchez, Jesus, Fla	1	1.79	4.70	4	0.87	4.81
Sanchez, Rey, KC-Atl	50	3.12	4.81	374	3.34	4.76
Sandberg, Jared, TB	11	2.64	4.86	11	2.64	4.86
Sanders, Anthony, Sea	1	1.92	4.86	3	4.02	4.96
Sanders, Deion, Cin	4	1.53	4.70	279	4.50	4.45
Sanders, Reggie, Ari	72	5.67	4.70	676	5.64	4.62
Santana, Johan, Min	0	—	—	0	0.00	5.30
Santangelo, F.P., Oak	10	4.41	4.86	238	4.68	4.73
Santiago, Benito, SF	41	2.84	4.70	662	3.85	4.42
Santiago, Jose, KC-Phi	0	0.00	4.70	0	0.00	4.70
Santos, Angel, Bos	0	0.00	4.86	0	0.00	4.86
Saturria, Luis, StL	1	6.71	4.70	1	2.99	4.87
Sauerbeck, Scott, Pit	0	0.00	4.70	0	0.00	4.88
Scanlan, Bob, Mon	0	—	—	1	0.77	4.11
Schilling, Curt, Ari	0	0.00	4.70	7	0.30	4.61
Schmidt, Jason, Pit-SF	2	1.12	4.70	2	0.18	4.74
Schneider, Brian, Mon	8	7.40	4.70	16	3.58	4.93
Schoeneweis, Scott, Ana	1	Inf	—	2	26.78	5.30
Schourek, Pete, Bos	0	—	—	9	0.90	4.50
Seabol, Scott, NYY	0	0.00	4.86	0	0.00	4.86
Seanez, Rudy, SD-Atl	0	—	—	0	0.00	4.71
Sefcik, Kevin, Col	0	0.00	4.70	87	3.86	4.80
Segui, David, Bal	61	7.77	4.86	668	5.35	4.80
Seguignol, Fernando, Mon	0	0.00	4.70	35	3.29	4.91
Selby, Bill, Cin	9	3.26	4.70	21	3.07	5.09
Sele, Aaron, Sea	0	0.00	4.86	0	0.00	5.05
Serrano, Wascar, SD	0	0.00	4.70	0	0.00	4.70
Servais, Scott, Hou	2	5.37	4.70	266	3.56	4.59
Sexson, Richie, Mil	103	5.97	4.70	293	5.65	5.00
Shaw, Jeff, LA	0	—	—	0	0.00	4.58
Sheets, Andy, TB	12	2.44	4.86	74	2.88	4.99
Sheets, Ben, Mil	0	0.00	4.70	0	0.00	4.70
Sheffield, Gary, LA	117	8.35	4.70	1159	7.28	4.56
Sheldon, Scott, Tex	5	1.30	4.86	26	3.01	5.05
Shinjo, Tsuyoshi, NYM	48	4.13	4.70	48	4.13	4.70
Shuey, Paul, Cle	0	—	—	0	0.00	4.97
Shumpert, Terry, Col	35	5.16	4.70	217	4.43	4.75
Sierra, Ruben, Tex	46	4.70	4.86	1007	5.12	4.69
Silva, Jose, Pit	0	0.00	4.70	3	0.83	4.83
Simmons, Brian, Tor	8	2.42	4.86	30	3.98	5.03
Simon, Randall, Det	40	5.63	4.86	70	5.01	4.91
Singleton, Chris, CWS	55	4.78	4.86	203	4.98	5.13
Slusarski, Joe, Atl-Hou	0	—	—	0	0.00	5.00
Smart, J.D., Tex	0	—	—	0	0.00	5.00
Smith, Bobby, TB	0	0.00	4.86	82	3.52	5.12
Smith, Bud, StL	0	0.00	4.70	0	0.00	4.70
Smith, Chuck, Fla	1	1.17	4.70	1	0.44	4.89
Smith, Jason, ChC	0	0.00	4.70	0	0.00	4.70
Smith, Mark, Mon	23	3.98	4.70	123	4.67	4.84
Smoltz, John, Atl	0	0.00	4.70	45	1.71	4.39
Snow, J.T., SF	35	4.25	4.70	609	5.06	4.93
Sojo, Luis, NYY	5	2.04	4.86	259	3.39	4.88
Soriano, Alfonso, NYY	73	4.37	4.86	75	4.03	4.90
Sosa, Juan, Ari	0	0.00	4.70	1	3.36	4.97
Sosa, Sammy, ChC	166	10.92	4.70	1152	6.22	4.61
Sparks, Steve W., Det	0	0.00	4.86	1	3.35	4.98
Speier, Justin, Cle-Col	0	0.00	4.70	0	0.00	4.82
Spencer, Shane, NYY	39	4.81	4.86	119	5.18	5.09
Spiers, Bill, Hou	1	13.42	4.70	477	4.82	4.66
Spiezio, Scott, Ana	59	4.56	4.86	255	4.40	5.02
Spivey, Junior, Ari	25	5.12	4.70	25	5.12	4.70
Sprague, Ed, Sea	14	5.38	4.86	502	4.16	5.02
Springer, Dennis, LA	0	0.00	4.70	0	0.00	4.93
Springer, Russ, Ari	0	—	—	0	0.00	4.72
Stairs, Matt, ChC	57	5.75	4.70	442	6.18	5.05
Stanton, Mike, NYY	0	—	—	5	16.86	4.45
Stechschulte, Gene, StL	3	80.49	4.70	3	80.49	4.70
Stein, Blake, KC	0	0.00	4.86	0	0.00	5.04
Stevens, Lee, Mon	84	5.19	4.86	424	4.88	4.83
Stewart, Shannon, Tor	102	5.99	4.86	422	5.93	5.08
Stinnett, Kelly, Cin	24	4.35	4.70	170	4.13	4.80
Strickland, Scott, Mon	0	0.00	4.70	0	0.00	4.82
Strong, Joe, Fla	0	0.00	4.70	0	0.00	4.85
Sturtze, Tanyon, TB	0	0.00	4.86	0	0.00	4.82
Stynes, Chris, Bos	44	4.24	4.86	203	4.76	4.85
Sullivan, Scott, Cin	0	0.00	4.70	0	0.00	4.79

Player, Team	2001 RC	RC/27	LRC/27	Career RC	RC/27	LRC27
Suppan, Jeff, KC	0	0.00	4.86	3	2.78	4.80
Surhoff, B.J., Atl	65	4.73	4.70	1008	4.86	4.79
Sutton, Larry, StL	0	0.00	4.70	72	4.33	5.01
Suzuki, Ichiro, Sea	135	7.64	4.86	135	7.64	4.86
Suzuki, Mac, KC-Col-Mil	0	0.00	4.70	0	0.00	4.81
Sweeney, Mark, Mil	10	3.89	4.70	111	4.74	4.68
Sweeney, Mike, KC	107	6.98	4.86	440	6.48	5.10
Swindell, Greg, Ari	0	—	—	10	1.14	4.37
Tabaka, Jeff, StL	0	—	—	1	6.76	4.64
Tam, Jeff, Oak	0	—	—	0	0.00	4.60
Tapani, Kevin, ChC	3	1.79	4.70	10	1.04	4.77
Tatis, Fernando, Mon	17	3.93	4.70	269	5.30	4.92
Taubensee, Eddie, Cle	11	3.25	4.86	400	4.93	4.63
Tavarez, Julian, ChC	2	1.12	4.70	2	0.55	4.81
Taylor, Reggie, Phi	0	0.00	4.70	0	0.00	4.88
Tejada, Miguel, Oak	103	5.77	4.86	344	5.13	5.08
Telemaco, Amaury, Phi	0	0.00	4.70	1	0.27	4.66
Telford, Anthony, Mon	0	—	—	2	2.34	4.72
Thomas, Frank, CWS	10	4.98	4.86	1362	9.04	4.92
Thome, Jim, Cle	133	9.26	4.86	900	7.78	5.06
Thompson, Ryan, Fla	3	3.35	4.70	130	3.86	4.57
Thomson, John, Col	2	1.92	4.70	4	0.75	4.66
Thurman, Mike, Mon	0	0.00	4.70	0	0.00	4.83
Timlin, Mike, StL	0	0.00	4.70	0	0.00	4.70
Toca, Jorge, NYM	1	1.92	4.70	2	2.69	4.79
Tollberg, Brian, SD	1	0.73	4.70	1	0.37	4.85
Tomko, Brett, Sea	0	—	—	4	0.73	4.72
Torrealba, Steve, Atl	0	0.00	4.70	0	0.00	4.70
Torrealba, Yorvit, SF	2	26.83	4.70	2	26.83	4.70
Towers, Josh, Bal	0	0.00	4.86	0	0.00	4.86
Trachsel, Steve, NYM	0	0.00	4.70	14	0.94	4.70
Tracy, Andy, Mon	1	0.52	4.70	32	4.32	4.93
Trammell, Bubba, SD	80	5.68	4.70	217	5.66	4.96
Trombley, Mike, Bal-LA	0	—	—	0	0.00	5.11
Truby, Chris, Hou	17	4.04	4.70	60	5.12	4.90
Tucker, Michael, Cin-ChC	61	4.57	4.70	351	4.94	4.86
Tyner, Jason, TB	42	3.73	4.86	53	3.44	4.95
Urbina, Ugueth, Mon-Bos	0	0.00	4.70	0	0.00	4.70
Uribe, Juan, Col	45	6.13	4.70	45	6.13	4.70
Valdes, Ismael, Ana	0	0.00	4.86	4	0.31	4.74
Valdes, Marc, Atl	0	—	—	1	0.69	4.66
Valdez, Mario, Oak	10	6.89	4.86	22	4.13	4.94
Valent, Eric, Phi	0	0.00	4.70	0	0.00	4.70
Valentin, John, Bos	6	3.10	4.86	601	5.65	5.02
Valentin, Jose, CWS	73	5.62	4.86	531	5.24	5.05
Vander Wal, John, Pit-SF	68	5.18	4.70	359	5.83	4.65
Van Poppel, Todd, ChC	0	0.00	4.70	2	1.79	4.82
Varitek, Jason, Bos	29	5.95	4.86	176	4.48	5.15
Vaughn, Greg, TB	80	5.51	4.86	989	5.78	4.78
Vazquez, Javier, Mon	5	2.10	4.70	16	1.98	4.82
Vazquez, Ramon, Sea	2	1.85	4.86	2	1.85	4.86
Velandia, Jorge, NYM	0	0.00	4.70	3	0.77	5.00
Velarde, Randy, Tex-NYY	44	4.51	4.86	586	4.96	4.93
Ventura, Robin, NYM	63	4.57	4.70	985	5.64	4.82
Veras, Quilvio, Atl	29	3.76	4.70	391	4.78	4.73
Veres, Dave, StL	0	0.00	4.70	3	3.85	4.69
Vidro, Jose, Mon	83	6.29	4.70	302	5.57	4.85
Villone, Ron, Col-Hou	0	0.00	4.70	1	0.24	4.93
Vina, Fernando, StL	96	5.61	4.70	468	5.14	4.91
Vizcaino, Jose, Hou	27	3.59	4.70	453	3.77	4.63
Vizquel, Omar, Cle	63	3.41	4.86	786	4.14	4.88
Vogelsong, Ryan, SF-Pit	0	0.00	4.70	0	0.00	4.70
Vosberg, Ed, Phi	0	—	—	0	0.00	4.18
Wagner, Billy, Hou	0	—	—	1	2.70	4.72
Wakefield, Tim, Bos	0	0.00	4.86	1	0.32	4.37
Wakeland, Chris, Det	6	5.97	4.86	6	5.97	4.86
Walbeck, Matt, Phi	1	Inf	—	177	3.12	5.14
Walker, Kevin, SD	0	—	—	0	0.00	5.00
Walker, Larry, Col	139	10.81	4.70	1137	7.77	4.50
Walker, Pete, NYM	0	0.00	4.70	0	0.00	4.70
Walker, Todd, Col-Cin	77	4.95	4.70	290	4.87	4.99
Wall, Donne, NYM	0	—	—	1	0.39	4.67
Wallace, Jeff, TB	0	—	—	0	0.00	5.00
Ward, Daryle, Hou	31	5.13	4.70	86	4.80	4.90
Ward, Turner, Phi	0	0.00	4.70	215	4.62	4.86
Wasdin, John, Col-Bal	1	13.42	4.70	1	2.99	4.94
Washburn, Jarrod, Ana	2	26.88	4.86	3	8.94	5.10
Weathers, Dave, Mil-ChC	0	0.00	4.70	1	0.20	4.64
Weaver, Jeff, Det	0	0.00	4.86	1	2.23	5.05
Wehner, John, Pit	4	2.38	4.70	62	2.58	4.51

Player, Team	2001 RC	RC/27	LRC/27	Career RC	RC/27	LRC27
Wells, Bob, Min	0	—	—	0	—	—
Wells, David, CWS	0	0.00	4.86	0	0.00	4.84
Wells, Kip, CWS	0	0.00	4.86	0	0.00	4.98
Wells, Vernon, Tor	14	5.62	4.86	22	4.18	5.03
Wendell, Turk, NYM-Phi	0	0.00	4.70	1	0.73	4.70
Wengert, Don, Pit	0	0.00	4.70	0	0.00	4.62
Westbrook, Jake, Cle	0	0.00	4.86	0	0.00	4.86
White, Devon, Mil	60	5.49	4.70	994	4.68	4.64
White, Gabe, Col	0	0.00	4.70	2	1.38	4.70
White, Rick, NYM	0	0.00	4.70	1	0.71	4.70
White, Rondell, ChC	58	6.51	4.70	480	5.47	4.73
Whiteside, Matt, Ari	0	—	—	0	0.00	4.60
Wickman, Bob, Cle	0	—	—	0	0.00	4.80
Wilkerson, Brad, Mon	8	2.19	4.70	8	2.19	4.70
Wilkins, Marc, Pit	0	—	—	1	1.50	4.77
Wilkins, Rick, SD	3	4.24	4.70	269	4.34	4.48
Williams, Bernie, NYY	100	6.67	4.86	1000	6.75	4.99
Williams, Dave, Pit	0	0.00	4.70	0	0.00	4.70
Williams, Gerald, TB-NYY	16	1.78	4.86	346	4.09	5.04
Williams, Jeff, LA	0	0.00	4.70	0	0.00	4.87
Williams, Matt, Ari	57	4.87	4.70	984	5.18	4.50
Williams, Mike, Pit-Hou	0	—	—	5	1.18	4.60
Williams, Todd, NYY	0	—	—	0	0.00	4.61
Williams, Woody, SD-StL	2	0.77	4.70	15	2.14	4.89
Williamson, Scott, Cin	0	—	—	0	0.00	5.00
Wilson, Craig A., Pit	36	8.26	4.70	36	8.26	4.70
Wilson, Dan, Sea	46	4.21	4.86	388	4.13	5.09
Wilson, Enrique, Pit-NYY	8	1.08	4.77	82	3.01	5.04
Wilson, Jack, Pit	29	2.37	4.70	29	2.37	4.70
Wilson, Kris, KC	0	0.00	4.86	0	0.00	4.86
Wilson, Paul, TB	0	—	—	0	0.00	4.68
Wilson, Preston, Fla	56	4.12	4.70	222	4.74	4.90
Wilson, Tom, Oak	1	1.41	4.86	1	1.41	4.86
Wilson, Vance, NYM	6	3.74	4.70	6	3.43	4.73
Winchester, Scott, Cin	0	0.00	4.70	0	0.00	4.61
Winn, Randy, TB	55	4.36	4.86	139	3.82	5.04
Witasick, Jay, SD-NYY	0	0.00	4.70	0	0.00	5.06
Witt, Bobby, Ari	0	0.00	4.70	3	1.31	4.69
Witt, Kevin, SD	4	4.67	4.70	6	2.82	4.97
Wohlers, Mark, Cin-NYY	0	—	—	1	2.25	4.47
Wolf, Randy, Phi	0	0.00	4.70	5	1.03	4.90
Womack, Tony, Ari	51	3.68	4.70	397	4.55	4.78
Wood, Kerry, ChC	1	0.52	4.70	12	2.29	4.73
Woodard, Steve, Cle	0	0.00	4.86	1	0.21	4.86
Woodward, Chris, Tor	3	1.47	4.86	17	2.78	5.13
Wooten, Shawn, Ana	32	5.38	4.86	34	5.57	4.87
Worrell, Tim, SF	0	0.00	4.70	4	1.44	4.59
Wright, Jamey, Mil	4	1.85	4.70	8	0.81	4.75
Wright, Jaret, Cle	0	0.00	4.86	2	4.13	5.03
Yan, Esteban, TB	0	—	—	2	53.57	5.30
Yoshii, Masato, Mon	1	1.68	4.70	3	0.45	4.86
Young, Dmitri, Cin	77	5.06	4.70	344	5.21	4.78
Young, Eric, ChC	76	4.23	4.70	674	5.15	4.69
Young, Kevin, Pit	52	3.69	4.70	453	4.59	4.76
Young, Michael, Tex	46	3.94	4.86	46	3.91	4.86
Zambrano, Carlos, ChC	0	0.00	4.70	0	0.00	4.70
Zaun, Gregg, KC	21	6.27	4.86	156	4.67	4.93
Zeile, Todd, NYM	77	5.08	4.70	918	4.95	4.59
Zerbe, Chad, SF	1	2.68	4.70	1	2.68	4.70
Zito, Barry, Oak	0	0.00	4.86	0	0.00	4.86
Zuleta, Julio, ChC	11	3.35	4.70	22	4.25	4.81

Component Earned Run Average

	2001				Career			
Pitcher, Team	OAvg	OOB	ERC	LERA	OAvg	OOB	ERC	LERA
Abbott, Paul, Sea	.238	.338	4.33	4.47	.239	.334	4.16	4.59
Acevedo, Jose, Cin	.272	.336	4.84	4.36	.272	.336	4.84	4.36
Acevedo, Juan, Col-Fla	.285	.376	5.34	4.36	.274	.348	4.75	4.38
Adams, Terry, LA	.267	.326	3.74	4.36	.260	.337	4.03	4.35
Ainsworth, Kurt, SF	.333	.500	16.26	4.36	.333	.500	16.26	4.36
Alfonseca, Antonio, Fla	.281	.335	4.24	4.36	.286	.351	4.64	4.43
Almanza, Armando, Fla	.230	.339	4.73	4.36	.218	.355	4.34	4.51
Almanzar, Carlos, NYY	.333	.356	5.63	4.47	.284	.346	5.21	4.60
Anderson, Brian, Ari	.295	.332	5.00	4.36	.283	.320	4.51	4.54
Anderson, Jimmy, Pit	.287	.358	4.69	4.36	.286	.359	4.80	4.48
Anderson, Matt, Det	.257	.311	3.19	4.47	.241	.348	4.26	4.73
Ankiel, Rick, StL	.275	.434	9.17	4.36	.225	.332	4.03	4.59
Appier, Kevin, NYM	.237	.306	3.38	4.36	.244	.313	3.45	4.49
Armas Jr., Tony, Mon	.247	.336	3.95	4.36	.239	.332	3.81	4.45
Arrojo, Rolando, Bos	.230	.313	3.25	4.47	.267	.345	4.64	4.69
Arroyo, Bronson, Pit	.289	.355	5.09	4.36	.295	.369	5.57	4.48
Ashby, Andy, LA	.292	.306	4.42	4.36	.266	.322	3.97	4.27
Astacio, Pedro, Col-Hou	.276	.341	4.68	4.36	.269	.332	4.34	4.27
Atchley, Justin, Cin	.286	.375	7.74	4.36	.286	.375	7.74	4.36
Austin, Jeff, KC	.273	.362	5.31	4.47	.273	.362	5.31	4.47
Aybar, Manny, ChC	.304	.420	8.38	4.36	.268	.349	4.79	4.42
Bacsik, Mike, Cle	.325	.378	5.56	4.47	.325	.378	5.56	4.47
Baez, Benito, Fla	.449	.509	16.75	4.36	.449	.509	16.75	4.36
Baez, Danys, Cle	.191	.282	2.51	4.47	.191	.282	2.51	4.47
Bailey, Cory, KC	.234	.321	3.20	4.47	.259	.349	3.99	4.35
Baldwin, James, CWS-LA	.281	.345	4.94	4.42	.274	.341	4.88	4.73
Bale, John, Bal	.194	.319	3.21	4.47	.214	.345	4.40	4.55
Balfour, Grant, Min	.333	.462	13.78	4.47	.333	.462	13.78	4.47
Banks, Willie, Bos	.132	.214	1.06	4.47	.271	.356	4.85	4.23
Barcelo, Lorenzo, CWS	.282	.347	4.33	4.47	.250	.302	3.40	4.76
Batista, Miguel, Ari	.226	.320	3.43	4.36	.269	.355	4.78	4.42
Bauer, Rick, Bal	.265	.315	4.74	4.47	.265	.315	4.74	4.47
Beck, Rod, Bos	.252	.319	4.25	4.47	.243	.291	3.18	4.16
Beckett, Josh, Fla	.161	.263	2.36	4.36	.161	.263	2.36	4.36
Beimel, Joe, Pit	.290	.366	5.24	4.36	.290	.366	5.24	4.36
Beirne, Kevin, Tor	.394	.487	11.51	4.47	.283	.360	5.72	4.86
Belitz, Todd, Col	.250	.308	4.25	4.36	.255	.345	5.06	4.50
Bell, Rob, Cin-Tex	.300	.370	6.40	4.44	.273	.353	5.69	4.53
Benes, Alan, StL	.250	.382	7.55	4.36	.255	.337	4.34	4.26
Benes, Andy, StL	.286	.380	7.27	4.36	.251	.316	3.81	4.10
Benitez, Armando, NYM	.214	.314	3.67	4.36	.183	.297	2.94	4.59
Benoit, Joaquin, Tex	.364	.423	13.11	4.47	.364	.423	13.11	4.47
Bere, Jason, ChC	.241	.314	3.75	4.36	.256	.356	4.94	4.57
Bernero, Adam, Det	.260	.321	5.79	4.47	.267	.333	4.44	4.80
Biddle, Rocky, CWS	.272	.347	4.85	4.47	.280	.351	5.16	4.54
Bierbrodt, Nick, Ari-TB	.291	.368	6.37	4.44	.291	.368	6.37	4.44
Blair, Willie, Det	.369	.437	8.45	4.47	.286	.342	4.85	4.34
Blank, Matt, Mon	.267	.369	6.08	4.36	.252	.344	4.74	4.46
Boehringer, Brian, NYY-SF	.247	.327	4.02	4.42	.259	.350	4.73	4.53
Bohanon, Brian, Col	.323	.404	7.52	4.36	.282	.359	5.21	4.42
Bones, Ricky, Fla	.286	.374	5.27	4.36	.283	.346	4.92	4.52
Bonilla, Bobby, StL	.600	.667	37.56	4.36	.600	.667	37.56	4.36
Borbon, Pedro, Tor	.244	.298	3.44	4.47	.238	.331	3.85	4.48
Borkowski, Dave, Det	.261	.356	5.28	4.47	.285	.378	6.12	4.76
Borland, Toby, Ana	.471	.500	14.71	4.47	.259	.357	4.54	4.21
Borowski, Joe, ChC	.667	.750	39.91	4.36	.303	.401	5.99	4.33
Bottalico, Ricky, Phi	.241	.318	3.88	4.36	.237	.333	4.03	4.38
Bottenfield, Kent, Hou	.288	.338	6.27	4.36	.271	.345	4.74	4.36
Bowles, Brian, Tor	.286	.333	3.55	4.47	.286	.333	3.55	4.47
Bradford, Chad, Oak	.281	.314	4.36	4.47	.269	.311	3.66	4.62
Brantley, Jeff, Tex	.310	.372	6.74	4.47	.237	.319	3.69	3.95
Brea, Leslie, Bal	.545	.643	37.82	4.47	.375	.508	14.10	4.83
Brock, Chris, Phi	.276	.359	5.50	4.36	.272	.345	5.11	4.49
Brohawn, Troy, Ari	.289	.362	5.07	4.36	.289	.362	5.07	4.36
Brower, Jim, Cin	.247	.335	4.21	4.36	.269	.351	5.16	4.57
Brown, Kevin, LA	.224	.291	2.71	4.36	.247	.304	3.14	4.28
Buddie, Mike, Mil	.225	.316	3.09	4.36	.263	.333	4.01	4.52
Buehrle, Mark, CWS	.230	.279	2.79	4.47	.239	.292	3.11	4.56
Burba, Dave, Cle	.306	.361	5.43	4.47	.261	.338	4.40	4.43
Burkett, John, Atl	.230	.294	2.86	4.36	.276	.324	4.00	4.22
Burnett, A.J., Fla	.231	.323	3.76	4.36	.240	.334	3.99	4.46
Byrd, Paul, Phi-KC	.296	.337	4.62	4.46	.262	.331	4.48	4.44
Cabrera, Jose, Atl	.239	.315	3.38	4.36	.254	.315	3.72	4.47
Callaway, Mickey, TB	.167	.250	3.65	4.47	.324	.412	7.82	4.78
Carpenter, Chris, Tor	.274	.345	4.82	4.47	.285	.353	5.09	4.69
Carrara, Giovanni, LA	.231	.287	3.10	4.36	.291	.368	6.18	4.49
Carrasco, Hector, Min	.277	.344	4.42	4.47	.258	.344	4.15	4.46
Castillo, Carlos, Bos	.273	.250	3.79	4.47	.258	.326	4.60	4.66

	2001				Career			
Pitcher, Team	OAvg	OOB	ERC	LERA	OAvg	OOB	ERC	LERA
Castillo, Frank, Bos	.260	.308	3.68	4.47	.268	.326	4.18	4.17
Chacon, Shawn, Col	.260	.360	5.22	4.36	.260	.360	5.22	4.36
Charlton, Norm, Sea	.212	.274	2.41	4.47	.240	.327	3.61	4.08
Chen, Bruce, Phi-NYM	.259	.327	4.75	4.36	.244	.317	4.15	4.48
Chiasson, Scott, ChC	.200	.286	4.13	4.36	.200	.286	4.13	4.36
Choate, Randy, NYY	.202	.341	3.03	4.47	.206	.332	3.30	4.59
Chouinard, Bobby, Col	.303	.324	7.39	4.36	.280	.340	4.71	4.63
Christiansen, J., StL-SF	.225	.304	3.41	4.36	.241	.334	3.74	4.33
Christman, Tim, Col	.143	.143	1.73	4.36	.143	.143	1.73	4.36
Clemens, Roger, NYY	.246	.309	3.43	4.47	.229	.295	2.92	4.37
Clement, Matt, Fla	.267	.365	4.84	4.36	.263	.361	4.85	4.52
Coco, Pasqual, Tor	.226	.323	3.00	4.47	.243	.365	4.62	4.57
Cogan, Tony, KC	.320	.420	9.09	4.47	.320	.420	9.09	4.47
Coggin, Dave, Phi	.272	.348	4.30	4.36	.282	.357	4.65	4.42
Colome, Jesus, TB	.208	.309	3.62	4.47	.208	.309	3.62	4.47
Colon, Bartolo, Cle	.261	.332	4.24	4.47	.253	.331	4.10	4.70
Cone, David, Bos	.275	.351	5.06	4.47	.232	.309	3.33	4.22
Cook, Dennis, NYM-Phi	.247	.309	3.93	4.36	.250	.322	3.95	4.15
Cooper, Brian, Ana	.200	.255	2.51	4.47	.275	.353	5.45	4.85
Coppinger, Rocky, Mil	.282	.392	6.77	4.36	.265	.361	5.74	4.80
Cordero, Francisco, Tex	.300	.417	5.73	4.47	.285	.390	6.16	4.89
Corey, Mark, NYM	.500	.615	21.72	4.36	.500	.615	21.72	4.36
Cormier, Rheal, Phi	.247	.320	3.67	4.36	.273	.316	3.85	4.17
Cornejo, Nate, Det	.344	.439	9.48	4.47	.344	.439	9.48	4.47
Crabtree, Tim, Tex	.385	.456	9.03	4.47	.281	.346	4.45	4.78
Crawford, Paxton, Bos	.276	.342	4.60	4.47	.261	.335	3.87	4.67
Creek, Doug, TB	.230	.374	4.84	4.47	.229	.361	4.96	4.52
Cressend, Jack, Min	.237	.291	3.13	4.47	.263	.320	3.75	4.56
Cruz, Juan, ChC	.244	.322	3.59	4.36	.244	.322	3.59	4.36
Cruz, Nelson, Hou	.237	.310	3.59	4.36	.259	.324	4.25	4.64
Cubillan, Darwin, Mon	.295	.358	4.69	4.36	.335	.414	8.03	4.67
Cunnane, Will, Mil	.320	.390	5.93	4.36	.296	.377	5.79	4.37
Daal, Omar, Phi	.273	.327	4.45	4.36	.269	.336	4.37	4.40
D'Amico, Jeff, Mil	.306	.360	6.30	4.36	.260	.320	4.27	4.65
Darensbourg, Vic, Fla	.277	.313	3.52	4.36	.262	.335	4.02	4.43
Davenport, Joe, Col	.222	.349	3.98	4.36	.220	.360	4.08	4.43
Davey, Tom, SD	.272	.349	4.53	4.36	.257	.353	4.46	4.67
Davis, Doug, Tex	.295	.354	4.90	4.47	.298	.368	5.49	4.63
Davis, Kane, Col	.252	.331	4.50	4.36	.280	.367	5.96	4.44
Davis, Lance, Cin	.294	.348	4.91	4.36	.294	.348	4.91	4.36
DeJean, Mike, Mil	.236	.332	3.56	4.36	.279	.356	4.74	4.38
de los Santos, Valerio, Mil	.250	.400	5.48	4.36	.243	.320	4.29	4.54
Dempster, Ryan, Fla	.269	.362	4.91	4.36	.264	.358	4.98	4.49
Dessens, Elmer, Cin	.279	.325	4.49	4.36	.293	.339	4.64	4.41
DeWitt, Matt, Tor	.293	.384	5.34	4.47	.318	.416	7.53	4.66
Dickey, R.A., Tex	.283	.377	6.57	4.47	.283	.377	6.57	4.47
Dingman, Craig, Col	.355	.444	12.04	4.36	.367	.425	9.34	4.69
Donnels, Chris, LA	.000	.000	0.00	4.36	.000	.000	0.00	4.36
Dotel, Octavio, Hou	.205	.294	2.62	4.36	.235	.329	4.15	4.52
Douglass, Sean, Bal	.259	.351	5.27	4.47	.259	.351	5.27	4.47
Dreifort, Darren, LA	.251	.348	4.50	4.36	.252	.336	4.14	4.42
Drese, Ryan, Cle	.242	.324	3.27	4.47	.242	.324	3.27	4.47
Drew, Tim, Cle	.340	.413	8.95	4.47	.358	.435	9.77	4.56
Duchscherer, Justin, Tex	.353	.421	10.68	4.47	.353	.421	10.68	4.47
Duckworth, Brandon, Phi	.234	.326	2.98	4.36	.234	.326	2.98	4.36
Duncan, Courtney, ChC	.259	.359	4.91	4.36	.259	.359	4.91	4.36
Durbin, Chad, KC	.288	.349	5.15	4.47	.291	.359	5.63	4.60
Duvall, Mike, Min	.368	.409	8.42	4.47	.307	.403	6.70	4.81
Eaton, Adam, SD	.241	.308	4.01	4.36	.251	.325	4.19	4.50
Eischen, Joey, Mon	.257	.354	4.89	4.36	.273	.366	5.08	4.40
Elarton, Scott, Hou-Col	.280	.359	6.21	4.36	.255	.329	4.44	4.50
Eldred, Cal, CWS	.429	.529	14.25	4.47	.256	.334	4.39	4.52
Ellis, Robert, Ari	.293	.354	5.17	4.36	.281	.347	4.85	4.39
Embree, Alan, SF-CWS	.297	.347	6.20	4.43	.256	.336	4.41	4.47
Erdos, Todd, Bos	.263	.366	4.94	4.47	.283	.372	5.74	4.63
Escobar, Kelvim, Tor	.204	.287	2.54	4.47	.257	.338	4.30	4.75
Estes, Shawn, SF	.253	.339	3.96	4.36	.256	.350	4.25	4.39
Estrada, Horacio, Col	.400	.455	11.24	4.36	.316	.420	9.04	4.58
Eyre, Scott, Tor	.263	.348	3.96	4.47	.287	.377	6.44	4.66
Farnsworth, Kyle, ChC	.213	.282	2.76	4.36	.261	.340	4.93	4.52
Fassero, Jeff, ChC	.235	.293	2.97	4.36	.258	.320	3.84	4.37
Fernandez, Jared, Cin	.265	.368	5.21	4.36	.265	.368	5.21	4.36
Fernandez, Osvaldo, Cin	.316	.376	5.82	4.36	.287	.348	4.81	4.33
Fetters, Mike, LA-Pit	.259	.356	5.37	4.36	.260	.345	4.24	4.45
Figueroa, Nelson, Phi	.275	.357	4.76	4.36	.277	.353	4.85	4.40
Fikac, Jeremy, SD	.165	.216	1.33	4.36	.165	.216	1.33	4.36
File, Bob, Tor	.220	.314	2.98	4.47	.220	.314	2.98	4.47
Finley, Chuck, Cle	.291	.341	4.85	4.47	.255	.331	4.02	4.43

	2001				Career			
Pitcher, Team	OAvg	OOB	ERC	LERA	OAvg	OOB	ERC	LERA
Finley, Steve, Ari	.000	.500	4.48	4.36	.000	.500	4.48	4.36
Fiore, Tony, TB-Min	.243	.317	3.07	4.47	.300	.391	6.31	4.74
Florie, Bryce, Bos	.316	.422	7.37	4.47	.265	.352	4.54	4.59
Fogg, Josh, CWS	.208	.264	1.73	4.47	.208	.264	1.73	4.47
Fossum, Casey, Bos	.259	.355	4.70	4.47	.259	.355	4.70	4.47
Foster, Kevin, Tex	.309	.415	6.96	4.47	.259	.336	4.72	4.21
Foster, Kris, Bal	.231	.362	4.97	4.47	.231	.362	4.97	4.47
Foulke, Keith, CWS	.199	.274	2.06	4.47	.219	.279	2.74	4.67
Fox, Chad, Mil	.181	.298	2.75	4.36	.228	.322	3.62	4.29
Franco, John, NYM	.264	.330	4.50	4.36	.247	.319	3.31	3.92
Franklin, Ryan, Sea	.250	.311	4.08	4.47	.249	.319	4.26	4.52
Franklin, Wayne, Hou	.333	.433	10.43	4.36	.301	.405	7.52	4.53
Frascatore, John, Tor	.246	.290	4.12	4.47	.272	.344	4.73	4.46
Fuentes, Brian, Sea	.171	.362	4.39	4.47	.171	.362	4.39	4.47
Fultz, Aaron, SF	.259	.311	3.75	4.36	.261	.323	3.97	4.49
Fyhrie, Mike, ChC-Oak	.247	.321	3.34	4.39	.275	.335	4.39	4.79
Gagne, Eric, LA	.251	.320	4.22	4.36	.251	.334	4.62	4.48
Gandarillas, Gus, Mil	.321	.398	5.90	4.36	.321	.398	5.90	4.36
Garces, Rich, Bos	.219	.299	3.09	4.47	.224	.313	3.37	4.69
Garcia, Freddy, Sea	.225	.283	2.61	4.47	.242	.318	3.59	4.71
Gardner, Mark, SF	.263	.330	4.71	4.36	.261	.327	4.24	4.12
Garland, Jon, CWS	.277	.358	5.16	4.47	.283	.367	5.57	4.64
George, Chris, KC	.288	.326	4.82	4.47	.288	.326	4.82	4.47
Ginter, Matt, CWS	.238	.329	3.44	4.47	.278	.365	5.46	4.56
Glavine, Tom, Atl	.261	.338	4.21	4.36	.252	.314	3.40	4.05
Glover, Gary, CWS	.252	.314	4.12	4.47	.251	.314	4.09	4.48
Glynn, Ryan, Tex	.309	.388	6.81	4.47	.303	.385	6.75	4.79
Gomes, Wayne, Phi-SF	.294	.366	5.11	4.36	.267	.356	4.59	4.40
Gonzalez, Dicky, NYM	.306	.347	4.63	4.36	.306	.347	4.63	4.36
Gordon, Flash, ChC	.188	.262	2.27	4.36	.243	.329	3.83	4.40
Graves, Danny, Cin	.268	.314	3.59	4.36	.255	.328	3.75	4.49
Green, Steve, Ana	.190	.370	3.79	4.47	.190	.370	3.79	4.47
Grilli, Jason, Fla	.297	.377	6.44	4.36	.315	.395	6.75	4.41
Grimsley, Jason, KC	.241	.311	3.34	4.47	.264	.362	4.84	4.56
Groom, Buddy, Bal	.252	.279	2.75	4.47	.288	.352	4.78	4.64
Guardado, Eddie, Min	.197	.268	2.13	4.47	.261	.333	4.42	4.67
Guthrie, Mark, Oak	.249	.326	4.17	4.47	.269	.336	4.22	4.27
Guzman, Geraldo, Ari	.206	.270	3.04	4.36	.275	.341	4.70	4.59
Hackman, Luther, StL	.212	.297	3.71	4.36	.274	.371	6.19	4.43
Halama, John, Sea	.296	.340	5.21	4.47	.295	.348	4.95	4.75
Halladay, Roy, Tor	.241	.287	2.61	4.47	.277	.351	4.96	4.74
Hamilton, Joey, Tor-Cin	.338	.384	6.57	4.46	.271	.338	4.30	4.31
Hampton, Mike, Col	.296	.367	5.69	4.36	.265	.335	4.05	4.35
Harnisch, Pete, Cin	.318	.384	7.81	4.36	.245	.313	3.70	4.08
Harper, Travis, TB	.455	.500	19.14	4.47	.288	.364	6.56	4.83
Harville, Chad, Oak	.182	.182	0.91	4.47	.290	.375	5.72	4.79
Hasegawa, S., Ana	.248	.316	3.50	4.47	.262	.331	4.23	4.70
Hawkins, LaTroy, Min	.291	.401	6.02	4.47	.307	.368	5.95	4.73
Haynes, Jimmy, Mil	.279	.356	4.69	4.36	.288	.371	5.49	4.65
Helling, Rick, Tex	.297	.344	5.39	4.47	.264	.333	4.66	4.68
Henry, Doug, KC	.262	.365	5.59	4.47	.245	.337	4.22	4.31
Hentgen, Pat, Bal	.221	.279	2.77	4.47	.264	.330	4.28	4.66
Heredia, Felix, ChC	.315	.384	6.75	4.36	.260	.354	4.63	4.39
Heredia, Gil, Oak	.316	.357	6.50	4.47	.285	.327	4.38	4.54
Herges, Matt, LA	.259	.350	4.20	4.36	.254	.335	3.84	4.51
Hermanson, Dustin, StL	.264	.335	4.80	4.36	.263	.329	4.21	4.40
Hernandez, Adrian, NYY	.190	.297	4.30	4.47	.190	.297	4.30	4.47
Hernandez, Carlos, Hou	.177	.261	1.88	4.36	.177	.261	1.88	4.36
Hernandez, Livan, SF	.297	.356	5.03	4.36	.281	.344	4.66	4.42
Hernandez, Orlando, NYY	.248	.333	4.87	4.47	.237	.308	3.71	4.77
Hernandez, Roberto, KC	.266	.336	4.23	4.47	.235	.313	3.34	4.59
Herndon, Junior, SD	.322	.417	6.98	4.36	.322	.417	6.98	4.36
Hiljus, Erik, Oak	.263	.316	4.00	4.47	.265	.322	4.24	4.54
Hill, Ken, TB	.333	.444	11.42	4.47	.260	.337	4.06	4.22
Hinchliffe, Brett, NYM	.643	.688	46.20	4.36	.347	.451	11.37	4.83
Hitchcock, S. SD-NYY	.304	.352	5.15	4.44	.272	.337	4.67	4.55
Hoffman, Trevor, SD	.216	.285	3.20	4.36	.202	.263	2.28	4.28
Holt, Chris, Det	.319	.381	6.11	4.47	.295	.355	4.91	4.46
Holtz, Mike, Ana	.274	.348	4.77	4.47	.259	.348	4.39	4.72
Howry, Bob, CWS	.279	.348	4.78	4.47	.234	.319	3.65	4.72
Hudson, Tim, Oak	.245	.303	3.22	4.47	.236	.309	3.36	4.72
Hutchinson, Chad, StL	.450	.593	27.84	4.36	.450	.593	27.84	4.36
Irabu, Hideki, Mon	.314	.338	5.57	4.36	.271	.333	4.84	4.70
Isringhausen, Jason, Oak	.203	.266	2.18	4.47	.263	.340	4.20	4.40
Jackson, Mike, Hou	.260	.319	4.45	4.36	.220	.303	3.11	4.19
James, Mike, StL	.293	.382	5.80	4.36	.244	.342	4.04	4.69
Jarvis, Kevin, SD	.254	.303	4.05	4.36	.293	.348	5.61	4.38
Jennings, Jason, Col	.276	.358	4.58	4.36	.276	.358	4.58	4.36
Jensen, Ryan, SF	.268	.378	5.68	4.36	.268	.378	5.68	4.36
Jimenez, Jose, Col	.264	.332	4.14	4.36	.264	.341	4.20	4.52

	2001				Career			
Pitcher, Team	OAvg	OOB	ERC	LERA	OAvg	OOB	ERC	LERA
Jodie, Brett, NYY-SD	.274	.361	7.09	4.37	.274	.361	7.09	4.37
Johnson, Adam, Min	.323	.424	8.59	4.47	.323	.424	8.59	4.47
Johnson, Jason, Bal	.257	.334	4.53	4.47	.272	.352	5.27	4.68
Johnson, Jonathan, Tex	.317	.404	7.49	4.47	.319	.427	7.77	4.79
Johnson, Mike, Mon	.295	.380	7.05	4.36	.290	.371	6.45	4.49
Johnson, Randy, Ari	.203	.274	2.35	4.36	.212	.301	3.02	4.37
Jones, Bobby J., SD	.305	.335	5.41	4.36	.274	.324	4.19	4.28
Jones, Todd, Det-Min	.312	.373	6.03	4.47	.252	.338	4.01	4.46
Judd, Mike, TB-Tex	.288	.365	5.86	4.47	.300	.384	6.74	4.47
Julio, Jorge, Bal	.287	.361	5.17	4.47	.287	.361	5.17	4.47
Karnuth, Jason, StL	.316	.458	9.29	4.36	.316	.458	9.29	4.36
Karsay, Steve, Cle-Atl	.228	.283	2.36	4.41	.269	.330	4.05	4.63
Keisler, Randy, NYY	.259	.364	6.33	4.47	.278	.382	6.80	4.55
Kennedy, Joe, TB	.269	.321	4.23	4.47	.269	.321	4.23	4.47
Kile, Darryl, StL	.265	.322	3.84	4.36	.261	.341	4.29	4.21
Kim, Byung-Hyun, Ari	.173	.284	2.45	4.36	.188	.318	3.26	4.48
Kim, Sun-Woo, Bos	.312	.399	5.72	4.47	.312	.399	5.72	4.47
King, Ray, Mil	.241	.325	3.51	4.36	.229	.320	3.32	4.46
Kline, Steve, StL	.203	.288	2.20	4.36	.251	.333	3.93	4.44
Knight, Brandon, NYY	.367	.404	11.03	4.47	.367	.404	11.03	4.47
Knott, Eric, Ari	.348	.400	7.20	4.36	.348	.400	7.20	4.36
Knotts, Gary, Fla	.280	.357	5.84	4.36	.280	.357	5.84	4.36
Koch, Billy, Tor	.265	.356	4.54	4.47	.254	.329	3.75	4.75
Kohlmeier, Ryan, Bal	.291	.371	7.24	4.47	.291	.374	6.36	4.65
Kolb, Brandon, Mil	.372	.453	15.04	4.36	.330	.429	9.30	4.52
Kolb, Danny, Tex	.259	.362	5.03	4.47	.283	.373	5.42	4.73
Koplove, Mike, Ari	.211	.388	5.25	4.36	.211	.388	5.25	4.36
Laker, Tim, Cle	.250	.400	5.48	4.47	.250	.400	5.48	4.47
Lawrence, Brian, SD	.244	.304	3.30	4.36	.244	.304	3.30	4.36
Lee, David, SD	.278	.385	5.86	4.36	.270	.383	5.68	4.47
Leiter, Al, NYM	.252	.299	3.26	4.36	.238	.331	3.73	4.41
Leiter, Mark, Mil	.232	.284	3.31	4.36	.265	.334	4.41	4.22
Leskanic, Curtis, Mil	.241	.327	4.18	4.36	.255	.342	4.39	4.31
Levine, Al, Ana	.257	.325	3.66	4.47	.270	.339	4.43	4.74
Levrault, Allen, Mil	.281	.359	5.89	4.36	.278	.358	5.66	4.38
Lidle, Cory, Oak	.242	.299	3.35	4.47	.265	.318	3.91	4.53
Lieber, Jon, ChC	.255	.290	3.19	4.36	.271	.310	3.90	4.36
Ligtenberg, Kerry, Atl	.226	.316	3.14	4.36	.213	.291	2.86	4.37
Lilly, Ted, NYY	.267	.344	5.10	4.47	.272	.349	5.47	4.51
Lima, Jose, Hou-Det	.299	.342	5.53	4.44	.282	.323	4.61	4.50
Lincoln, Mike, Pit	.225	.293	2.94	4.36	.306	.365	6.17	4.72
Linebrink, Scott, Hou	.176	.326	2.54	4.36	.279	.406	7.09	4.50
Lira, Felipe, Mon	.440	.481	12.69	4.36	.286	.352	5.26	4.76
Lloyd, Graeme, Mon	.272	.336	4.19	4.36	.260	.318	3.72	4.64
Loaiza, Esteban, Tor	.307	.347	5.30	4.47	.292	.344	4.91	4.48
Loewer, Carlton, SD	.520	.571	23.60	4.36	.308	.355	5.39	4.37
Lohse, Kyle, Min	.284	.347	5.43	4.47	.284	.347	5.43	4.47
Loiselle, Rich, Pit	.359	.495	11.11	4.36	.274	.370	5.09	4.33
Looper, Braden, Fla	.242	.322	3.77	4.36	.271	.347	4.40	4.51
Lopez, Albie, TB-Ari	.281	.343	4.78	4.43	.279	.348	4.95	4.67
Loretta, Mark, Mil	.250	.400	5.48	4.36	.250	.400	5.48	4.36
Lowe, Derek, Bos	.283	.343	4.31	4.47	.257	.314	3.48	4.70
Lowe, Sean, CWS	.256	.308	3.51	4.47	.275	.350	4.72	4.67
Lukasiewicz, Mark, Ana	.247	.330	5.12	4.47	.247	.330	5.12	4.47
Lundquist, David, SD	.260	.326	3.72	4.36	.289	.363	5.23	4.62
Lyon, Brandon, Tor	.266	.305	3.50	4.47	.266	.305	3.50	4.47
Mabry, John, Fla	.750	.857	115.9	4.36	.667	.769	61.34	4.73
MacDougal, Mike, KC	.290	.343	5.04	4.47	.290	.343	5.04	4.47
MacRae, Scott, Cin	.266	.316	3.30	4.36	.266	.316	3.30	4.36
Maddux, Greg, Atl	.253	.278	2.70	4.36	.241	.286	2.63	4.03
Maduro, Calvin, Bal	.240	.319	3.71	4.47	.268	.354	5.14	4.41
Magnante, Mike, Oak	.244	.287	3.13	4.47	.278	.343	4.23	4.47
Mahay, Ron, ChC	.197	.337	4.32	4.36	.248	.339	4.67	4.65
Mahomes, Pat, Tex	.280	.359	5.31	4.47	.273	.364	5.57	4.58
Mann, Jim, Hou	.176	.391	3.87	4.36	.290	.421	7.22	4.45
Mantei, Matt, Ari	.222	.323	5.18	4.36	.199	.338	3.59	4.42
Manzanillo, Josias, Pit	.211	.281	2.33	4.36	.238	.324	3.66	4.41
Marquis, Jason, Atl	.234	.320	3.70	4.36	.239	.325	3.91	4.40
Marte, Damaso, Pit	.250	.320	3.93	4.36	.282	.355	5.48	4.45
Martin, Tom, NYM	.319	.405	8.02	4.36	.290	.368	5.29	4.50
Martinez, Pedro, Bos	.199	.253	1.84	4.47	.206	.269	2.31	4.44
Martinez, Ramon, Pit	.276	.442	9.01	4.36	.239	.319	3.59	4.02
Mathews, T.J., Oak-StL	.262	.315	3.78	4.43	.245	.316	3.67	4.52
Mattes, Troy, Mon	.285	.371	6.18	4.36	.285	.371	6.18	4.36
Matthews, Mike, StL	.227	.305	3.34	4.36	.241	.328	4.04	4.38
Maurer, Dave, SD	.348	.444	10.33	4.36	.288	.374	6.04	4.56
Mays, Joe, Min	.235	.289	3.05	4.47	.264	.326	4.21	4.71
McDill, Allen, Bos	.236	.328	4.14	4.47	.277	.371	6.45	4.64
McElroy, Chuck, Bal-SD	.284	.379	6.47	4.43	.258	.342	4.20	4.21
McKnight, Tony, Hou-Pit	.303	.352	5.98	4.36	.286	.336	5.26	4.43

	2001				Career			
Pitcher, Team	OAvg	OOB	ERC	LERA	OAvg	OOB	ERC	LERA
Meacham, Rusty, TB	.277	.325	4.18	4.47	.282	.328	4.35	4.43
Meadows, Brian, KC	.351	.386	7.47	4.47	.309	.358	5.60	4.51
Mecir, Jim, Oak	.231	.310	3.00	4.47	.238	.320	3.40	4.73
Mendoza, Ramiro, NYY	.241	.287	2.84	4.47	.278	.322	4.05	4.70
Mercado, Hector, Cin	.267	.357	4.99	4.36	.262	.354	4.85	4.41
Mercedes, Jose, Bal	.294	.354	5.18	4.47	.275	.342	4.73	4.63
Mesa, Jose, Phi	.246	.301	3.07	4.36	.273	.344	4.45	4.43
Miadich, Bart, Ana	.182	.341	4.38	4.47	.182	.341	4.38	4.47
Miceli, Dan, Fla-Col	.263	.320	4.34	4.36	.262	.340	4.49	4.37
Michalak, Chris, Tor-Tex	.293	.371	5.68	4.47	.297	.374	5.86	4.46
Middlebrook, Jason, SD	.247	.345	5.85	4.36	.247	.345	5.85	4.36
Miller, Matt, Det	.372	.438	7.86	4.47	.372	.438	7.86	4.47
Miller, Travis, Min	.283	.347	4.82	4.47	.304	.367	5.55	4.74
Miller, Wade, Hou	.234	.304	3.57	4.36	.247	.317	4.03	4.45
Mills, Alan, Bal	.333	.452	11.82	4.47	.246	.356	4.70	4.45
Millwood, Kevin, Atl	.260	.319	4.20	4.36	.244	.301	3.42	4.45
Milton, Eric, Min	.257	.308	4.05	4.47	.260	.313	4.18	4.72
Mlicki, Dave, Det-Hou	.305	.382	6.86	4.41	.275	.343	4.87	4.42
Moehler, Brian, Det	.207	.233	1.43	4.47	.284	.333	4.55	4.74
Mohler, Mike, Ari	.286	.390	6.39	4.36	.272	.368	5.02	4.63
Moore, Trey, Atl	.368	.429	8.06	4.36	.329	.391	6.71	4.38
Moreno, Juan, Tex	.153	.291	2.83	4.47	.153	.291	2.83	4.47
Morgan, Mike, Ari	.306	.373	4.90	4.36	.276	.336	4.26	4.08
Morris, Matt, StL	.265	.318	3.50	4.36	.258	.319	3.43	4.30
Moss, Damian, Atl	.097	.300	2.61	4.36	.097	.300	2.61	4.36
Mota, Guillermo, Mon	.271	.335	4.77	4.36	.260	.334	4.29	4.50
Moyer, Jamie, Sea	.239	.285	3.03	4.47	.269	.323	4.10	4.42
Mulder, Mark, Oak	.249	.294	2.95	4.47	.273	.329	4.15	4.65
Mulholland, Terry, Pit-LA	.295	.342	5.34	4.36	.276	.322	4.05	4.08
Mullen, Scott, KC	.310	.423	6.89	4.47	.277	.365	5.46	4.70
Munoz, Bobby, Mon	.321	.404	6.71	4.36	.295	.364	5.29	4.27
Murray, Heath, Det	.322	.418	7.69	4.47	.325	.417	7.33	4.44
Mussina, Mike, NYY	.237	.274	2.65	4.47	.248	.291	3.15	4.60
Myers, Mike, Col	.225	.339	3.29	4.36	.253	.348	4.39	4.58
Myers, Rodney, SD	.291	.367	5.50	4.36	.282	.361	5.20	4.36
Myette, Aaron, Tex	.293	.381	6.23	4.47	.282	.385	6.24	4.55
Nagy, Charles, Cle	.342	.379	6.60	4.47	.281	.334	4.45	4.54
Neagle, Denny, Col	.284	.344	5.21	4.36	.258	.315	3.89	4.27
Neal, Blaine, Fla	.304	.429	7.12	4.36	.304	.429	7.12	4.36
Nelson, Jeff, Sea	.136	.295	2.20	4.47	.221	.332	3.41	4.59
Nelson, Joe, Atl	.583	.625	33.03	4.36	.583	.625	33.03	4.36
Nen, Robb, SF	.203	.260	2.12	4.36	.226	.297	2.93	4.30
Neugebauer, Nick, Mil	.250	.400	6.94	4.36	.250	.400	6.94	4.36
Nichting, Chris, Cin-Col	.313	.339	5.46	4.36	.326	.377	6.21	4.54
Nickle, Doug, Phi	.143	.143	0.54	4.36	.316	.409	6.05	4.51
Nitkowski, C.J., Det-NYM	.274	.392	5.89	4.46	.275	.369	5.41	4.68
Nomo, Hideo, Bos	.231	.320	3.90	4.47	.231	.317	3.72	4.39
Nunez, Jose A. LA-SD	.267	.346	4.73	4.36	.267	.346	4.73	4.36
Nunez, Vladimir, Fla	.234	.302	3.17	4.36	.262	.340	4.34	4.50
Ohka, T., Bos-Mon	.309	.355	5.52	4.41	.297	.351	5.21	4.63
Ohman, Will, ChC	.292	.370	6.26	4.36	.295	.394	6.55	4.42
Olivares, Omar, Pit	.283	.356	5.34	4.36	.275	.353	4.74	4.35
Oliver, Darren, Tex	.306	.375	6.14	4.47	.286	.362	5.28	4.66
Olsen, Kevin, Fla	.204	.232	1.34	4.36	.204	.232	1.34	4.36
Olson, Gregg, LA	.268	.383	6.36	4.36	.239	.328	3.57	4.25
Oropesa, Eddie, Phi	.232	.384	4.20	4.36	.232	.384	4.20	4.36
Orosco, Jesse, LA	.279	.348	5.25	4.36	.220	.306	3.07	4.01
Ortiz, Ramon, Ana	.274	.343	4.65	4.47	.262	.340	4.60	4.66
Ortiz, Russ, SF	.232	.309	3.08	4.36	.248	.343	4.30	4.48
Osting, Jimmy, SD	.143	.333	1.96	4.36	.143	.333	1.96	4.36
Osuna, Antonio, CWS	.421	.478	16.71	4.47	.225	.309	3.26	4.30
Oswalt, Roy, Hou	.235	.273	2.68	4.36	.235	.273	2.68	4.36
Padilla, Vicente, Phi	.273	.333	3.80	4.36	.287	.355	4.43	4.54
Painter, Lance, Tor-Mil	.317	.410	8.23	4.43	.284	.353	5.15	4.37
Paniagua, Jose, Sea	.233	.341	4.34	4.47	.256	.361	4.73	4.63
Park, Chan Ho, LA	.216	.305	3.15	4.36	.230	.325	3.75	4.38
Parker, Christian, NYY	.471	.500	21.01	4.47	.471	.500	21.01	4.47
Paronto, Chad, Bal	.289	.354	5.98	4.47	.289	.354	5.98	4.47
Parque, Jim, CWS	.308	.369	6.86	4.47	.294	.366	5.63	4.81
Parris, Steve, Tor	.299	.362	5.75	4.47	.279	.347	4.92	4.45
Parrish, John, Bal	.256	.396	7.06	4.47	.276	.414	7.49	4.75
Patterson, Danny, Det	.274	.316	3.21	4.47	.284	.334	4.14	4.69
Pavano, Carl, Mon	.331	.391	6.99	4.36	.269	.335	4.35	4.44
Penny, Brad, Fla	.240	.296	2.96	4.36	.249	.318	3.57	4.46
Percival, Troy, Ana	.187	.258	1.90	4.47	.181	.275	2.42	4.74
Perez, Odalis, Atl	.290	.357	4.79	4.36	.281	.359	5.02	4.45
Perisho, Matt, Det	.327	.391	6.71	4.47	.322	.411	7.61	4.74
Person, Robert, Phi	.234	.311	3.84	4.36	.242	.330	4.29	4.49
Peters, Chris, Mon	.367	.435	9.24	4.36	.282	.353	5.16	4.33
Peterson, Kyle, Mil	.302	.343	5.60	4.36	.288	.344	4.42	4.53

	2001				Career			
Pitcher, Team	OAvg	OOB	ERC	LERA	OAvg	OOB	ERC	LERA
Petkovsek, Mark, Tex	.323	.379	6.74	4.47	.288	.346	4.72	4.38
Pettitte, Andy, NYY	.281	.319	3.82	4.47	.273	.333	4.12	4.73
Pettyjohn, Adam, Det	.309	.366	5.84	4.47	.309	.366	5.84	4.47
Phelps, Travis, TB	.226	.301	3.27	4.47	.226	.301	3.27	4.47
Pichardo, Hipolito, Bos	.300	.363	5.11	4.47	.279	.345	4.35	4.50
Piersoll, Chris, Cin	.267	.365	4.47	4.36	.267	.365	4.47	4.36
Pineda, Luis, Det	.239	.366	4.73	4.47	.239	.366	4.73	4.47
Pineiro, Joel, Sea	.191	.257	1.71	4.47	.220	.293	2.68	4.56
Plesac, Dan, Tor	.207	.311	3.07	4.47	.244	.312	3.47	4.22
Politte, Cliff, Phi	.250	.306	3.11	4.36	.267	.349	4.79	4.46
Ponson, Sidney, Bal	.289	.339	5.04	4.47	.278	.337	4.81	4.76
Pote, Lou, Ana	.258	.325	4.21	4.47	.254	.320	3.81	4.67
Powell, Brian, Hou	.357	.471	13.15	4.36	.292	.363	6.31	4.64
Powell, Jay, Hou-Col	.260	.335	4.30	4.36	.255	.345	4.06	4.33
Prieto, Ariel, TB	.375	.474	9.19	4.47	.294	.378	5.61	4.77
Prinz, Bret, Ari	.220	.310	3.27	4.36	.220	.310	3.27	4.36
Prokopec, Luke, LA	.268	.321	4.69	4.36	.266	.324	4.62	4.39
Pulsipher, Bill, Bos-CWS	.300	.411	7.56	4.47	.283	.357	5.20	4.33
Quantrill, Paul, Tor	.274	.311	3.31	4.47	.293	.342	4.58	4.52
Quevedo, Ruben, Mil	.257	.344	4.79	4.36	.266	.360	5.81	4.52
Radinsky, Scott, Cle	.400	.538	26.18	4.47	.253	.330	3.72	4.20
Radke, Brad, Min	.271	.298	3.45	4.47	.272	.311	3.99	4.74
Rapp, Pat, Ana	.261	.333	4.30	4.47	.277	.362	4.92	4.44
Reames, Britt, Mon	.273	.362	5.52	4.36	.254	.350	4.85	4.44
Redding, Tim, Hou	.286	.360	5.87	4.36	.286	.360	5.87	4.36
Redman, Mark, Min-Det	.289	.355	5.26	4.47	.284	.343	5.04	4.79
Reed, Rick, NYM-Min	.268	.299	3.69	4.40	.266	.303	3.70	4.27
Reed, Steve, Cle-Atl	.236	.316	3.51	4.41	.244	.313	3.70	4.33
Reichert, Dan, KC	.278	.374	5.46	4.47	.280	.383	5.62	4.73
Reith, Brian, Cin	.333	.394	8.42	4.36	.333	.394	8.42	4.36
Reitsma, Chris, Cin	.288	.334	4.59	4.36	.288	.334	4.59	4.36
Rekar, Bryan, TB	.294	.348	5.31	4.47	.298	.350	5.37	4.60
Relaford, Desi, NYM	.000	.000	0.00	4.36	.000	.000	0.00	4.36
Remlinger, Mike, Atl	.234	.296	3.27	4.36	.241	.334	4.10	4.29
Reyes, Al, LA	.269	.350	5.07	4.36	.235	.338	4.28	4.55
Reyes, Dennys, Cin	.248	.357	4.77	4.36	.254	.360	4.54	4.39
Reynolds, Shane, Hou	.290	.327	4.38	4.36	.273	.313	3.80	4.30
Reynoso, Armando, Ari	.312	.366	6.77	4.36	.283	.348	4.86	4.29
Rhodes, Arthur, Sea	.189	.230	1.61	4.47	.238	.323	3.86	4.55
Riedling, John, Cin	.186	.284	2.13	4.36	.193	.296	2.42	4.44
Rigdon, Paul, Mil	.287	.385	5.90	4.36	.275	.357	5.36	4.53
Riggan, Jerrod, NYM	.243	.330	3.67	4.36	.246	.329	3.69	4.37
Rijo, Jose, Cin	.271	.354	5.00	4.36	.241	.308	3.23	3.88
Rincon, Juan, Min	.318	.444	8.33	4.47	.318	.444	8.33	4.47
Rincon, Ricardo, Cle	.223	.294	2.62	4.47	.226	.311	3.22	4.45
Riske, David, Cle	.206	.339	3.81	4.47	.255	.357	4.83	4.60
Ritchie, Todd, Pit	.259	.308	3.68	4.36	.270	.323	4.17	4.52
Rivera, Mariano, NYY	.209	.242	1.74	4.47	.213	.272	2.30	4.75
Roberts, Grant, NYM	.240	.294	3.03	4.36	.265	.320	3.73	4.41
Roberts, Willis, Bal	.274	.354	4.98	4.47	.277	.356	5.05	4.48
Rocker, John, Atl-Cle	.234	.351	4.03	4.42	.202	.329	3.42	4.48
Rodriguez, Felix, SF	.188	.259	1.92	4.36	.236	.328	3.67	4.42
Rodriguez, Frank, Cin	.400	.457	9.65	4.36	.286	.358	5.18	4.79
Rodriguez, Rich, Cle	.270	.349	4.19	4.47	.265	.336	4.09	4.06
Rodriguez, Wilfredo, Hou	.429	.438	15.38	4.36	.429	.438	15.38	4.36
Rogers, Kenny, Tex	.307	.376	6.22	4.47	.265	.334	4.24	4.57
Romero, J.C., Min	.277	.339	4.89	4.47	.297	.362	5.49	4.69
Rose, Brian, NYM-TB	.336	.399	8.12	4.44	.287	.352	5.73	4.74
Rueter, Kirk, SF	.283	.341	4.65	4.36	.278	.328	4.25	4.33
Ruffin, Johnny, Fla	.313	.476	8.59	4.36	.251	.336	4.30	4.20
Rupe, Ryan, TB	.283	.348	5.67	4.47	.282	.351	5.46	4.72
Rusch, Glendon, NYM	.301	.344	4.97	4.36	.293	.342	4.91	4.55
Ryan, B.J., Bal	.233	.335	4.13	4.47	.223	.337	4.08	4.70
Sabathia, C.C., Cle	.228	.330	3.86	4.47	.228	.330	3.86	4.47
Sabel, Erik, Ari	.282	.332	4.65	4.36	.285	.347	5.01	4.39
Saberhagen, Bret, Bos	.302	.313	4.90	4.47	.252	.289	3.01	4.16
Sanchez, Jesus, Fla	.256	.346	4.49	4.36	.276	.363	5.33	4.44
Santana, Johan, Min	.292	.358	5.36	4.47	.299	.385	6.17	4.76
Santiago, Jose, KC-Phi	.292	.333	4.09	4.39	.276	.329	4.15	4.67
Santos, Victor, Det	.222	.341	4.18	4.47	.222	.341	4.18	4.47
Sasaki, Kazuhiro, Sea	.195	.241	1.90	4.47	.190	.263	2.41	4.69
Sauerbeck, Scott, Pit	.257	.369	4.60	4.36	.250	.370	4.52	4.52
Scanlan, Bob, Mon	.339	.419	6.40	4.36	.281	.349	4.47	4.20
Schilling, Curt, Ari	.245	.273	3.03	4.36	.238	.287	2.96	4.18
Schmidt, Jason, Pit-SF	.244	.324	3.72	4.36	.268	.342	4.46	4.34
Schoeneweis, Scott, Ana	.281	.351	4.87	4.47	.280	.349	4.87	4.69
Schourek, Pete, Bos	.292	.375	5.64	4.47	.270	.335	4.44	4.19
Seanez, Rudy, SD-Atl	.178	.287	2.78	4.36	.233	.330	3.86	4.30
Seay, Bobby, TB	.260	.339	5.03	4.47	.260	.339	5.03	4.47
Seelbach, Chris, Atl	.273	.368	7.57	4.36	.308	.378	7.52	4.40

Pitcher, Team	2001				Career			
	OAvg	OOB	ERC	LERA	OAvg	OOB	ERC	LERA
Sele, Aaron, Sea	.261	.306	3.70	4.47	.275	.344	4.55	4.71
Serrano, Wascar, SD	.313	.382	6.39	4.36	.313	.382	6.39	4.36
Shaw, Jeff, LA	.227	.277	2.79	4.36	.255	.308	3.51	4.24
Sheets, Ben, Mil	.283	.340	4.78	4.36	.283	.340	4.78	4.36
Shields, Scot, Ana	.200	.333	3.10	4.47	.200	.333	3.10	4.47
Shuey, Paul, Cle	.251	.333	3.46	4.47	.240	.334	3.84	4.76
Silva, Jose, Pit	.271	.319	4.59	4.36	.297	.355	5.10	4.46
Slusarski, Joe, Atl-Hou	.357	.387	8.01	4.36	.285	.357	5.35	4.25
Smart, J.D., Tex	.306	.338	5.55	4.47	.283	.332	4.41	4.54
Smith, Bud, StL	.250	.304	3.50	4.36	.250	.304	3.50	4.36
Smith, Chuck, Fla	.265	.341	4.43	4.36	.255	.335	3.89	4.51
Smith, Roy, Cle	.246	.388	6.49	4.47	.246	.388	6.49	4.47
Smoltz, John, Atl	.238	.274	2.85	4.36	.233	.295	2.96	3.98
Sobkowiak, Scott, Atl	.400	.400	7.48	4.36	.400	.400	7.48	4.36
Sparks, Steve W., Det	.271	.321	3.97	4.47	.274	.346	4.73	4.72
Speier, Justin, Cle-Col	.247	.307	3.93	4.39	.249	.323	4.46	4.58
Spooneybarger, Tim, Atl	.313	.368	4.53	4.36	.313	.368	4.53	4.36
Springer, Dennis, LA	.275	.324	4.19	4.36	.279	.351	5.25	4.62
Springer, Russ, Ari	.274	.308	5.13	4.36	.264	.345	4.86	4.40
Standridge, Jason, TB	.260	.379	6.63	4.47	.260	.379	6.63	4.47
Stanton, Mike, NYY	.263	.332	3.61	4.47	.253	.324	3.69	4.38
Stark, Denny, Sea	.333	.368	7.99	4.47	.344	.390	8.10	4.59
Stechschulte, Gene, StL	.273	.354	4.90	4.36	.266	.354	5.11	4.43
Stein, Blake, KC	.233	.342	4.57	4.47	.244	.351	5.04	4.70
Stewart, Scott, Mon	.243	.299	3.31	4.36	.243	.299	3.31	4.36
Stone, Ricky, Hou	.258	.303	3.69	4.36	.258	.303	3.69	4.36
Strickland, Scott, Mon	.222	.322	3.65	4.36	.221	.311	3.33	4.47
Strong, Joe, Fla	.136	.240	1.86	4.36	.284	.387	6.14	4.56
Sturtze, Tanyon, TB	.271	.345	4.65	4.47	.280	.354	5.08	4.57
Sullivan, Scott, Cin	.243	.317	3.55	4.36	.232	.312	3.46	4.40
Suppan, Jeff, KC	.267	.333	4.40	4.47	.282	.341	4.87	4.69
Suzuki, Mac, KC-Col-Mil	.269	.377	5.94	4.41	.274	.368	5.62	4.75
Swindell, Greg, Ari	.250	.277	3.58	4.36	.268	.308	3.72	4.11
Tabaka, Jeff, StL	.375	.412	9.25	4.36	.237	.345	4.26	4.21
Tam, Jeff, Oak	.250	.326	3.18	4.47	.254	.316	3.21	4.66
Tapani, Kevin, ChC	.279	.325	4.38	4.36	.272	.317	3.99	4.37
Tavarez, Julian, ChC	.277	.358	4.70	4.36	.283	.354	4.71	4.50
Taylor, Billy, Pit	.250	.250	4.70	4.36	.254	.332	3.85	4.75
Telemaco, Amaury, Phi	.274	.350	5.07	4.36	.272	.337	4.77	4.31
Telford, Anthony, Mon	.412	.500	14.07	4.36	.268	.337	4.32	4.34
Thomas, Brad, Min	.303	.432	10.12	4.47	.303	.432	10.12	4.47
Thomson, John, Col	.239	.295	3.52	4.36	.285	.343	4.77	4.29
Thurman, Mike, Mon	.294	.351	5.19	4.36	.275	.343	4.67	4.45
Timlin, Mike, StL	.277	.327	3.95	4.36	.255	.327	3.72	4.52
Tolar, Kevin, Det	.189	.400	4.35	4.47	.167	.355	3.23	4.57
Tollberg, Brian, SD	.287	.321	4.29	4.36	.280	.327	4.27	4.49
Tomko, Brett, Sea	.288	.350	6.31	4.47	.254	.320	4.01	4.43
Towers, Josh, Bal	.297	.321	4.51	4.47	.297	.321	4.51	4.47
Trachsel, Steve, NYM	.254	.304	3.80	4.36	.267	.329	4.42	4.36
Trombley, Mike, Bal-LA	.230	.319	3.52	4.44	.260	.333	4.43	4.62
Urbina, Ugueth, Mon-Bos	.231	.297	3.41	4.39	.217	.298	3.22	4.31
Valdes, Ismael, Ana	.277	.338	4.57	4.47	.255	.309	3.64	4.33
Valdes, Marc, Atl	.259	.286	5.90	4.36	.285	.366	5.10	4.31
Van Poppel, Todd, ChC	.223	.316	3.61	4.36	.264	.360	5.27	4.63
Vazquez, Javier, Mon	.235	.274	2.75	4.36	.266	.321	4.12	4.45
Venafro, Mike, Tex	.240	.337	3.58	4.47	.261	.338	3.75	4.75
Veres, Dave, StL	.232	.314	4.11	4.36	.255	.325	3.91	4.32
Villafuerte, Brandon, Tex	.414	.486	17.59	4.47	.356	.455	11.81	4.66
Villone, Ron, Col-Hou	.287	.366	5.81	4.36	.261	.362	5.08	4.54
Vining, Ken, CWS	.441	.548	20.56	4.47	.441	.548	20.56	4.47
Vizcaino, Luis, Oak	.266	.321	4.80	4.47	.277	.351	5.60	4.64
Vogelsong, Ryan, SF-Pit	.277	.372	6.20	4.36	.264	.356	5.40	4.40
Vosberg, Ed, Phi	.186	.239	1.35	4.36	.278	.357	4.69	4.53
Voyles, Brad, KC	.161	.350	3.85	4.47	.161	.350	3.85	4.47
Wagner, Billy, Hou	.198	.278	2.42	4.36	.189	.281	2.52	4.35
Wakefield, Tim, Bos	.248	.339	4.02	4.47	.259	.339	4.55	4.60
Walker, Kevin, SD	.122	.265	1.33	4.36	.194	.316	2.89	4.59
Walker, Pete, NYM	.240	.240	1.63	4.36	.325	.382	6.54	4.29
Wall, Donne, NYM	.300	.363	5.72	4.36	.260	.320	4.03	4.33
Wallace, Jeff, TB	.232	.363	4.53	4.47	.237	.383	5.08	4.51
Wasdin, John, Col-Bal	.292	.352	5.27	4.43	.271	.326	4.56	4.73
Washburn, Jarrod, Ana	.263	.318	4.03	4.47	.251	.317	3.99	4.65
Weathers, Dave, Mil-ChC	.216	.299	2.59	4.36	.288	.364	4.99	4.33
Weaver, Jeff, Det	.266	.326	3.89	4.47	.269	.331	4.34	4.73
Weber, Ben, Ana	.251	.341	3.90	4.47	.262	.338	3.90	4.56
Wells, Bob, Min	.273	.338	4.89	4.47	.270	.331	4.67	4.77
Wells, David, CWS	.297	.335	4.69	4.36	.264	.308	3.74	4.49
Wells, Kip, CWS	.281	.366	5.16	4.47	.289	.374	5.62	4.69
Wendell, Turk, NYM-Phi	.249	.342	4.74	4.36	.241	.334	3.99	4.33
Wengert, Don, Pit	.429	.470	10.93	4.36	.316	.374	6.34	4.69

Pitcher, Team	2001				Career			
	OAvg	OOB	ERC	LERA	OAvg	OOB	ERC	LERA
Westbrook, Jake, Cle	.306	.363	5.25	4.47	.324	.379	5.93	4.51
Wheeler, Dan, TB	.375	.402	8.38	4.47	.315	.377	6.52	4.78
White, Gabe, Col	.270	.337	5.42	4.36	.248	.300	3.79	4.38
White, Rick, NYM	.257	.303	3.52	4.36	.269	.328	4.04	4.57
Whiteside, Matt, Atl	.319	.383	8.26	4.36	.284	.347	4.82	4.55
Wickman, Bob, Cle	.240	.285	2.69	4.47	.259	.338	3.97	4.54
Wilkins, Marc, Pit	.319	.397	6.27	4.36	.256	.357	4.38	4.36
Williams, Dave, Pit	.244	.324	3.89	4.36	.244	.324	3.89	4.36
Williams, Jeff, LA	.295	.407	7.02	4.36	.282	.395	6.42	4.46
Williams, Mike, Pit-Hou	.244	.337	4.45	4.36	.262	.339	4.41	4.26
Williams, Todd, NYY	.324	.402	7.01	4.47	.302	.384	6.10	4.39
Williams, Woody, SD-StL	.268	.317	4.15	4.36	.256	.321	4.17	4.58
Williamson, Scott, Cin	.333	.667	24.61	4.36	.202	.317	3.05	4.60
Wilson, Kris, KC	.297	.352	6.17	4.47	.295	.349	5.70	4.58
Wilson, Paul, TB	.278	.343	4.94	4.47	.264	.340	4.43	4.43
Winchester, Scott, Cin	.315	.353	6.09	4.36	.315	.368	6.15	4.28
Wise, Matt, Ana	.250	.321	4.65	4.47	.260	.325	4.78	4.66
Witasick, Jay, SD-NYY	.253	.335	4.22	4.42	.290	.372	6.01	4.74
Witt, Bobby, Ari	.222	.333	4.26	4.36	.265	.358	4.85	4.34
Wohlers, Mark, Cin-NYY	.262	.328	4.18	4.42	.234	.327	3.48	4.17
Wolf, Randy, Phi	.248	.314	3.46	4.36	.261	.338	4.41	4.52
Wood, Kerry, ChC	.202	.311	3.22	4.36	.207	.320	3.48	4.39
Woodard, Steve, Cle	.325	.358	5.33	4.47	.292	.333	4.66	4.50
Worrell, Tim, SF	.240	.318	3.32	4.36	.257	.329	4.10	4.38
Wright, Dan, CWS	.300	.389	6.74	4.47	.300	.389	6.74	4.47
Wright, Jamey, Mil	.272	.370	5.36	4.36	.291	.381	5.64	4.36
Wright, Jaret, Cle	.313	.420	6.82	4.47	.268	.357	4.98	4.71
Wunsch, Kelly, CWS	.247	.353	5.11	4.47	.228	.324	3.71	4.79
Yan, Esteban, TB	.262	.307	3.68	4.47	.282	.354	5.34	4.76
Yoshii, Masato, Mon	.279	.323	4.60	4.36	.275	.330	4.53	4.45
Zambrano, Carlos, ChC	.355	.488	11.86	4.36	.355	.488	11.86	4.36
Zambrano, Victor, TB	.201	.281	2.80	4.47	.201	.281	2.80	4.47
Zerbe, Chad, SF	.281	.327	3.83	4.36	.280	.324	3.82	4.39
Zimmerman, Jeff, Tex	.192	.251	2.23	4.47	.214	.280	2.86	4.75
Zito, Barry, Oak	.230	.309	3.33	4.47	.220	.305	3.12	4.61

2001 Leader Boards

Our extensive leader boards provide plenty of fodder for analysis and debate. Let's take a look at a few of the many interesting stats featured in this year's leader boards:

Not only did Arizona aces Curt Schilling and Randy Johnson finish No. 1 and 2 in all of baseball in innings pitched. The 38-year-old Johnson averaged 116.6 pitches per start to lead all of baseball, and the 35-year-old Schilling ranked fourth in the National League at 106.0. Schilling faced more batters than any major league hurler (1,021), while Johnson finished third in the category (994). Already qualifying as the workhorse of the American League is the 25-year-old anchor of Detroit's pitching staff, Jeff Weaver. He ranked first in the circuit in both batters faced (985) and pitches per start (109.7).

In the American League, a quartet of young hurlers with star potential allowed the lowest number of hits per nine innings among starters. Leading the way was 21-year-old rookie southpaw C.C. Sabathia at 7.44. The only righthander in the group, 25-year-old Freddy Garcia, followed with 7.50 hits allowed per nine. Trailing Garcia was 22-year-old Mark Buehrle (7.64) and 23-year-old Barry Zito (7.73). All of these guys will become *less* hittable.

Bret Boone didn't have much trouble against Buehrle or Zito, but then again, he battered southpaws all season. The Seattle second baseman led the American League in all three hitting percentages against lefties: .444/.497/.715. Of course, he also led the circuit in RBI with 141.

It probably isn't much of a surprise that Barry Bonds led all major leaguers with just 6.5 at-bats per home run in 2001, considering he also set the single-season record for walks. Amazingly, though, Bonds didn't lead the National League in percentage of pitches taken. That honor goes to another future Hall of Famer who is known for his plate patience and his ability to get on base. Rickey Henderson, who batted .227 but produced a .366 on-base percentage, took 66.6 percent of the pitches he faced, compared to 65.7 percent for Bonds.

There's plenty more of these kinds of stats. Check out the leader boards that follow.

Sección de Líderes del 2001

Unas notas interesantes de nuestra Sección de Líderes:

Curt Schilling y Randy Johnson no solo terminaron 1 y 2 en entradas lanzadas, Johnson de 38 años de edad, tuvo un promedio de 116.6 lanzamientos por juego abierto y Schilling, 35, un promedio de 106.0. Schilling se enfrentó a más bateadores que cualquier otro lanzador en las Grandes Ligas (1,021). Johnson terminó tercero (994). Jeff Weaver, 25, fue el líder de la Liga Americana en bateadores enfrentados (985) y lanzamientos por juego (109.7).

En la Liga Americana, cuatro lanzadores jóvenes pueden volverse estrellas por qué no permiten muchos hits por nueve entradas lanzadas. El primero es el novato zurdo de 21 años C.C. Sabathia con 7.44. El único derecho es Freddy García con 7.50. Mark Buehrle sigue a García con 7.64 y después Barry Zito con 7.73. Bret Boone no tuvo muchos problemas contra Buehrle o Zito, después de todo él acribilló a zurdos toda la temporada. Boone bateó .444/.497/.715 contra zurdos y por supuesto fue el líder de la Liga Americana con 141 carreras empujadas.

No sorprende que Bonds fue el líder de cuadrangulares por veces-al-bate con 6.5 en el 2001, considerando que también estableció un nuevo record de bases por bolas. Pero, sorprendentemente, Bonds no fue el líder en lanzamientos observados. Ese honor es de Ricky Henderson, quien es conocido por ser paciente sobre el plato. Henderson bateó solo .227, pero tuvo un promedio de embasamiento de .366 y observó 66.6 por ciento de los lanzamientos que le tiraron, comparado a 65.7 para Bonds.

Traducciones (para más traducciones ver el Glosario): **%CS by Catchers** = Promedio de AR por Receptor; **%Pitches Taken** = Lanzamientos no Tirados por Bateador; **AB per HR** = VB por HR; **Allowed** = Permitido; **At-Bats** = Veces-al-Bate **(VB)**; **Avg at Home** = Pro como Local; **Avg on the Road** = Pro como Visitante; **Avg vs LHP** = Pro vs Lanz. Zurdos; **Avg vs RHP** = Pro vs Lanz. Derechos; **Baserunners per 9 IP** = Embasados por 9 EL; **Bases Loaded** = Bases Llenas; **Batters Faced** = Bateadores Enfrentados; **Batting Average** = Promedio de bateo **(Pro)**; **Caught Stealing** = Atrapados Robando(**AR**); **Cleanup Hitter Slg** = PBA del Cuarto Bate; **Complete Games** = Juegos Completos; **Doubles Allowed** = Dobles Permitidos; **ERA** = Efectividad; **Games Finished** = Juegos Cerrados; **Games Started** = Juegos Abiertos; **Games** = Juegos; **GDP/GDP Opp** = ADP/Op ADP; **GDP** = Arranques para Doble Play **(ADP)**; **Ground/Fly Ratio** = Proporción de Arranques/Elevados; **Hit Batsmen** = Bateadores Golpeados; **Hit by Pitch** = Golpeado por Lanz.; **Hits Allowed** = Hits Permitidos; **Home Runs Allowed** = HR Permitidos; **Innings Pitched** = Entradas Lanzadas **(EL)**; **Late & Close** = Tarde y Reñido; **Leadoff Hitters OBP** = PE del Primer Bate; **Losses** = Derrotas; **Minimum** = Mínimo requerido; **OBP vs LHP** = PE vs Lanz. Zurdos; **OBP vs RHP** = PE de Embasamiento vs Lanz. Derechos; **On-Base Percentage** = Promedio de Embasamiento **(PE)**; **Opposition** = de Oponente; **Pitcher per PA** = Lanzamientos por Veces al Plato; **Pitches Seen** = Lanzamientos Observados; **Plate Appearances** = Veces al Plato; **Relief** = Relevo; **Run Support per 9 IP** = Carreras de Soporte por 9 EL; **Runs Allowed** = Carreras Permitidas; **Runs Batted In** = Carreras Empujadas; **Runs Scored** = Carreras Anotadas; **Sacrifice Flies** = Elevados de Sacrificio; **Sacrifice Hits** = Toques de Sacrificio; **Saves** = Salvados; **SB Success %** = Promedio de BR; **Scoring Position Average** = Pro con Corredores en Posición de Anotar; **Shutouts** = Blanqueadas; **Singles** = Sencillos; **SLG vs LHP** = PBA vs lanz. zurdos; **SLG vs RHP** = PBA vs lanz. derechos; **Slugging Percentage** = Promedio de Bases Acumuladas **(PBA)**; **Special Batting Leaders** = Lideratos Especiales; **Strikeouts per 9 IP** = K por 9 EL; **Times on Base** = Veces en Base; **Total Bases** = Bases Acumuladas; **Walks** = BB; **Wild Pitches** = Lanzamientos Salvajes; **Wins** = Victorias.

2001 American League Batting Leaders

Batting Average
minimum 502 PA

Player, Team	AB	H	AVG
I Suzuki, Sea	**692**	**242**	**.350**
J Giambi, Oak	520	178	.342
R Alomar, Cle	575	193	.336
B Boone, Sea	623	206	.331
F Catalanotto, Tex	463	153	.330
J Gonzalez, Cle	532	173	.325
A Rodriguez, Tex	632	201	.318
S Stewart, Tor	640	202	.316
D Jeter, NYY	614	191	.311
J Conine, Bal	524	163	.311

On-Base Percentage
minimum 502 PA

Player, Team	PA*	OB	OBP
J Giambi, Oak	**671**	**320**	**.477**
E Martinez, Sea	581	246	.423
J Thome, Cle	644	268	.416
R Alomar, Cle	668	277	.415
C Delgado, Tor	704	287	.408
M Ramirez, Bos	620	251	.405
J Olerud, Sea	678	272	.401
A Rodriguez, Tex	732	292	.399
B Williams, NYY	633	250	.395
F Catalanotto, Tex	511	200	.391

* AB + BB + HBP + SF

Slugging Percentage
minimum 502 PA

Player, Team	AB	TB	SLG
J Giambi, Oak	**520**	**343**	**.660**
J Thome, Cle	526	328	.624
A Rodriguez, Tex	632	393	.622
M Ramirez, Bos	529	322	.609
J Gonzalez, Cle	532	314	.590
B Boone, Sea	623	360	.578
R Palmeiro, Tex	600	338	.563
E Martinez, Sea	470	255	.543
E Burks, Cle	439	238	.542
M Sweeney, KC	559	303	.542

Games

C Delgado, Tor	**162**
T Long, Oak	**162**
A Rodriguez, Tex	**162**
M Tejada, Oak	**162**
2 tied with	161

Plate Appearances

I Suzuki, Sea	**738**
A Rodriguez, Tex	732
J Damon, Oak	719
D Erstad, Ana	716
R Palmeiro, Tex	714

At-Bats

I Suzuki, Sea	**692**
G Anderson, Ana	672
J Damon, Oak	644
S Stewart, Tor	640
A Gonzalez, Tor	636

Hits

I Suzuki, Sea	**242**
B Boone, Sea	206
S Stewart, Tor	202
A Rodriguez, Tex	201
G Anderson, Ana	194

Singles

I Suzuki, Sea	**192**
S Stewart, Tor	139
D Eckstein, Ana	134
D Jeter, NYY	132
B Boone, Sea	129

Doubles

J Giambi, Oak	**47**
M Sweeney, KC	46
S Stewart, Tor	44
E Chavez, Oak	43
R Durham, CWS	42

Triples

C Guzman, Min	**14**
R Alomar, Cle	12
C Beltran, KC	12
R Cedeno, Det	11
R Durham, CWS	10

Home Runs

A Rodriguez, Tex	**52**
J Thome, Cle	49
R Palmeiro, Tex	47
T Glaus, Ana	41
M Ramirez, Bos	41

Total Bases

A Rodriguez, Tex	**393**
B Boone, Sea	360
J Giambi, Oak	343
R Palmeiro, Tex	338
J Thome, Cle	328

Runs Scored

A Rodriguez, Tex	**133**
I Suzuki, Sea	127
B Boone, Sea	118
R Alomar, Cle	113
D Jeter, NYY	110

Runs Batted In

B Boone, Sea	**141**
J Gonzalez, Cle	140
A Rodriguez, Tex	135
M Ramirez, Bos	125
J Thome, Cle	124

GDP

J Olerud, Sea	**21**
P O'Neill, NYY	20
D Fletcher, Tor	18
J Gonzalez, Cle	18
A Huff, TB	18

Sacrifice Hits

D Eckstein, Ana	**16**
O Vizquel, Cle	15
C Singleton, CWS	14
M Johnson, CWS	10
6 tied with	9

Sacrifice Flies

J Gonzalez, Cle	**16**
B Boone, Sea	13
M Cameron, Sea	13
J Dye, KC-Oak	11
A Gonzalez, Tor	10

Stolen Bases

I Suzuki, Sea	**56**
R Cedeno, Det	55
A Soriano, NYY	43
M McLemore, Sea	39
C Knoblauch, NYY	38

Caught Stealing

R Cedeno, Det	**15**
A Soriano, NYY	14
I Suzuki, Sea	14
J Damon, Oak	12
B Higginson, Det	12

Walks

J Giambi, Oak	**129**
C Delgado, Tor	111
J Thome, Cle	111
T Glaus, Ana	107
R Palmeiro, Tex	101

Intentional Walks

M Ramirez, Bos	**25**
J Giambi, Oak	24
C Delgado, Tor	22
J Olerud, Sea	19
J Thome, Cle	14

Hit by Pitch

D Eckstein, Ana	**21**
F Menechino, Oak	19
C Delgado, Tor	16
E Diaz, Cle	16
A Rodriguez, Tex	16

Strikeouts

J Thome, Cle	**185**
B Grieve, TB	159
T Glaus, Ana	158
M Cameron, Sea	155
A Gonzalez, Tor	149

2001 National League Batting Leaders

Batting Average
minimum 502 PA

Player, Team	AB	H	AVG
L Walker, Col	**497**	**174**	**.350**
T Helton, Col	587	197	.336
M Alou, Hou	513	170	.331
L Berkman, Hou	577	191	.331
C Jones, Atl	572	189	.330
A Pujols, StL	590	194	.329
B Bonds, SF	476	156	.328
S Sosa, ChC	577	189	.328
J Pierre, Col	617	202	.327
L Gonzalez, Ari	609	198	.325

On-Base Percentage
minimum 502 PA

Player, Team	PA*	OB	OBP
B Bonds, SF	**664**	**342**	**.515**
L Walker, Col	601	270	.449
S Sosa, ChC	711	311	.437
T Helton, Col	695	300	.432
L Berkman, Hou	688	296	.430
L Gonzalez, Ari	728	312	.429
C Jones, Atl	677	289	.427
G Sheffield, LA	618	258	.417
J Edmonds, StL	607	249	.410
B Giles, Pit	674	272	.404

* AB + BB + HBP + SF

Slugging Percentage
minimum 502 PA

Player, Team	AB	TB	SLG
B Bonds, SF	**476**	**411**	**.863**
S Sosa, ChC	577	425	.737
L Gonzalez, Ari	609	419	.688
T Helton, Col	587	402	.685
L Walker, Col	497	329	.662
L Berkman, Hou	577	358	.620
A Pujols, StL	590	360	.610
C Jones, Atl	572	346	.605
S Green, LA	619	370	.598
B Giles, Pit	576	340	.590

Games

B Abreu, Phi	**162**
O Cabrera, Mon	**162**
L Gonzalez, Ari	**162**
4 tied with	161

Plate Appearances

L Gonzalez, Ari	**728**
J Rollins, Phi	720
J Bagwell, Hou	717
C Biggio, Hou	717
S Sosa, ChC	711

At-Bats

J Rollins, Phi	**656**
R Aurilia, SF	636
D Glanville, Phi	634
F Vina, StL	631
O Cabrera, Mon	626

Hits

R Aurilia, SF	**206**
J Pierre, Col	202
L Gonzalez, Ari	198
T Helton, Col	197
A Pujols, StL	194

Singles

J Pierre, Col	**163**
F Vina, StL	144
P Polanco, StL	140
R Aurilia, SF	127
J Kendall, Pit	127

Doubles

L Berkman, Hou	**55**
T Helton, Col	54
J Kent, SF	49
B Abreu, Phi	48
A Pujols, StL	47

Triples

J Rollins, Phi	**12**
J Pierre, Col	11
J Uribe, Col	11
L Castillo, Fla	10
3 tied with	8

Home Runs

B Bonds, SF	**73**
S Sosa, ChC	64
L Gonzalez, Ari	57
S Green, LA	49
T Helton, Col	49

Total Bases

S Sosa, ChC	**425**
L Gonzalez, Ari	419
B Bonds, SF	411
T Helton, Col	402
S Green, LA	370

Runs Scored

S Sosa, ChC	**146**
T Helton, Col	132
B Bonds, SF	129
L Gonzalez, Ari	128
J Bagwell, Hou	126

Runs Batted In

S Sosa, ChC	**160**
T Helton, Col	146
L Gonzalez, Ari	142
B Bonds, SF	137
2 tied with	130

GDP

V Guerrero, Mon	**24**
R Coomer, ChC	23
P Polanco, StL	22
D Young, Cin	22
A Pujols, StL	21

Sacrifice Hits

T Glavine, Atl	**17**
R Gutierrez, ChC	**17**
J Wilson, Pit	**17**
R Dempster, Fla	16
J Vazquez, Mon	16

Sacrifice Flies

J Kent, SF	**13**
S Rolen, Phi	12
S Sosa, ChC	12
R Gutierrez, ChC	11
R Hidalgo, Hou	11

Stolen Bases

J Pierre, Col	**46**
J Rollins, Phi	**46**
V Guerrero, Mon	37
B Abreu, Phi	36
L Castillo, Fla	33

Caught Stealing

J Pierre, Col	**17**
L Castillo, Fla	16
V Guerrero, Mon	16
3 tied with	14

Walks

B Bonds, SF	**177**
S Sosa, ChC	116
B Abreu, Phi	106
J Bagwell, Hou	106
L Gonzalez, Ari	100

Intentional Walks

S Sosa, ChC	**37**
B Bonds, SF	35
L Gonzalez, Ari	24
V Guerrero, Mon	24
C Jones, Atl	20

Hit by Pitch

C Biggio, Hou	**28**
F Vina, StL	22
J Kendall, Pit	20
R Hidalgo, Hou	16
2 tied with	14

Strikeouts

J Hernandez, Mil	**185**
R Sexson, Mil	178
P Burrell, Phi	162
L Stevens, Mon	157
S Sosa, ChC	153

2001 American League Pitching Leaders

Earned Run Average
minimum 162 IP

Pitcher, Team	IP	ER	ERA
F Garcia, Sea	**238.2**	**81**	**3.05**
M Mussina, NYY	228.2	80	3.15
J Mays, Min	233.2	82	3.16
M Buehrle, CWS	221.1	81	3.29
T Hudson, Oak	235.0	88	3.37
J Moyer, Sea	209.2	80	3.43
M Mulder, Oak	229.1	88	3.45
B Zito, Oak	214.1	83	3.49
R Clemens, NYY	220.1	86	3.51
C Lidle, Oak	188.0	75	3.59

Won-Lost Percentage
minimum 15 decisions

Pitcher, Team	W	L	Pct
R Clemens, NYY	**20**	**3**	**.870**
P Abbott, Sea	17	4	.810
C Sabathia, Cle	17	5	.773
J Moyer, Sea	20	6	.769
F Garcia, Sea	18	6	.750
A Sele, Sea	15	5	.750
M Mulder, Oak	21	8	.724
C Lidle, Oak	13	6	.684
E Milton, Min	15	7	.682
B Zito, Oak	17	8	.680

Opposition AVG
minimum 162 IP

Pitcher, Team	AB	H	AVG
F Garcia, Sea	**884**	**199**	**.225**
C Sabathia, Cle	653	149	.228
B Zito, Oak	800	184	.230
M Buehrle, CWS	816	188	.230
H Nomo, Bos	739	171	.231
J Mays, Min	872	205	.235
M Mussina, NYY	852	202	.237
P Abbott, Sea	608	145	.238
J Moyer, Sea	781	187	.239
C Lidle, Oak	702	170	.242

Games

P Quantrill, Tor	**80**
M Stanton, NYY	76
J Grimsley, KC	73
K Foulke, CWS	72
3 tied with	71

Games Started

T Hudson, Oak	**35**
B Zito, Oak	**35**
9 tied with	34

Complete Games

S Sparks, Det	**8**
M Mulder, Oak	6
B Radke, Min	6
J Weaver, Det	5
4 tied with	4

Games Finished

K Foulke, CWS	**69**
M Rivera, NYY	66
K Sasaki, Sea	63
B Koch, Tor	56
B Wickman, Cle	56

Wins

M Mulder, Oak	**21**
R Clemens, NYY	20
J Moyer, Sea	20
F Garcia, Sea	18
T Hudson, Oak	18

Losses

J Mercedes, Bal	**17**
C Durbin, KC	16
J Weaver, Det	16
J Suppan, KC	14
3 tied with	13

Saves

M Rivera, NYY	**50**
K Sasaki, Sea	45
K Foulke, CWS	42
T Percival, Ana	39
B Koch, Tor	36

Shutouts

M Mulder, Oak	**4**
F Garcia, Sea	3
M Mussina, NYY	3
6 tied with	2

Hits Allowed

R Helling, Tex	**256**
S Sparks, Det	244
E Loaiza, Tor	239
B Radke, Min	235
J Weaver, Det	235

Doubles Allowed

R Helling, Tex	**68**
S Sparks, Det	55
R Ortiz, Ana	52
J Weaver, Det	51
E Milton, Min	50

Triples Allowed

R Helling, Tex	**10**
B Radke, Min	9
J Suppan, KC	9
J Weaver, Det	9
D Davis, Tex	8

Home Runs Allowed

R Helling, Tex	**38**
E Milton, Min	35
R Rupe, TB	30
C Carpenter, Tor	29
J Johnson, Bal	28

Batters Faced

J Weaver, Det	**985**
S Sparks, Det	982
T Hudson, Oak	980
F Garcia, Sea	971
J Mays, Min	957

Innings Pitched

F Garcia, Sea	**238.2**
T Hudson, Oak	235.0
J Mays, Min	233.2
S Sparks, Det	232.0
2 tied with	229.1

Runs Allowed

R Helling, Tex	**134**
J Mercedes, Bal	125
S Schoeneweis, Ana	122
J Suppan, KC	120
J Weaver, Det	116

Strikeouts

H Nomo, Bos	**220**
M Mussina, NYY	214
R Clemens, NYY	213
B Zito, Oak	205
B Colon, Cle	201

Walks Allowed

H Nomo, Bos	**96**
C Sabathia, Cle	95
B Colon, Cle	90
P Abbott, Sea	87
B Zito, Oak	80

Hit Batsmen

T Wakefield, Bos	**18**
C Carpenter, Tor	16
S Schoeneweis, Ana	14
J Weaver, Det	14
4 tied with	13

Wild Pitches

R Clemens, NYY	**14**
K Wells, CWS	**14**
D Reichert, KC	12
3 tied with	11

Balks

C Michalak, Tor-Tex	**6**
M Buehrle, CWS	5
J Moreno, Tex	3
C Sabathia, Cle	3
S Woodard, Cle	3

2001 National League Pitching Leaders

Earned Run Average
minimum 162 IP

Pitcher, Team	IP	ER	ERA
R Johnson, Ari	**249.2**	**69**	**2.49**
C Schilling, Ari	256.2	85	2.98
J Burkett, Atl	219.1	74	3.04
G Maddux, Atl	233.0	79	3.05
D Kile, StL	227.1	78	3.09
M Morris, StL	216.1	76	3.16
R Ortiz, SF	218.2	80	3.29
A Leiter, NYM	187.1	69	3.31
K Wood, ChC	174.1	65	3.36
W Miller, Hou	212.0	80	3.40

Won-Lost Percentage
minimum 15 decisions

Pitcher, Team	W	L	Pct
R Oswalt, Hou	**14**	**3**	**.824**
C Schilling, Ari	22	6	.786
R Johnson, Ari	21	6	.778
J Lieber, ChC	20	6	.769
M Morris, StL	22	8	.733
T Glavine, Atl	16	7	.696
R Person, Phi	15	7	.682
W Miller, Hou	16	8	.667
K Wood, ChC	12	6	.667
R Ortiz, SF	17	9	.654

Opposition AVG
minimum 162 IP

Pitcher, Team	AB	H	AVG
K Wood, ChC	**629**	**127**	**.202**
R Johnson, Ari	890	181	.203
C Park, LA	847	183	.216
J Burkett, Atl	813	187	.230
A Burnett, Fla	629	145	.231
R Ortiz, SF	806	187	.232
R Person, Phi	765	179	.234
W Miller, Hou	781	183	.234
J Vazquez, Mon	840	197	.235
K Appier, NYM	764	181	.237

Games

S Kline, StL	**89**
G Lloyd, Mon	84
J Fassero, ChC	82
R King, Mil	82
2 tied with	80

Games Started

T Glavine, Atl	**35**
C Park, LA	**35**
C Schilling, Ari	**35**
13 tied with	34

Complete Games

C Schilling, Ari	**6**
J Lieber, ChC	5
J Vazquez, Mon	5
3 tied with	4

Games Finished

R Nen, SF	**71**
J Shaw, LA	66
A Benitez, NYM	64
J Mesa, Phi	59
2 tied with	58

Wins

M Morris, StL	**22**
C Schilling, Ari	**22**
R Johnson, Ari	21
J Lieber, ChC	20
2 tied with	17

Losses

B Jones, SD	**19**
J Anderson, Pit	17
J Haynes, Mil	17
3 tied with	15

Saves

R Nen, SF	**45**
A Benitez, NYM	43
T Hoffman, SD	43
J Shaw, LA	43
J Mesa, Phi	42

Shutouts

G Maddux, Atl	**3**
J Vazquez, Mon	**3**
4 tied with	2

Hits Allowed

L Hernandez, SF	**266**
B Jones, SD	250
C Schilling, Ari	237
M Hampton, Col	236
J Anderson, Pit	232

Doubles Allowed

C Reitsma, Cin	**54**
D Hermanson, StL	53
D Neagle, Col	53
R Dempster, Fla	50
L Hernandez, SF	50

Triples Allowed

L Hernandez, SF	**10**
5 tied with	8

Home Runs Allowed

K Jarvis, SD	**37**
B Jones, SD	**37**
C Schilling, Ari	**37**
W Williams, SD-StL	35
3 tied with	34

Batters Faced

C Schilling, Ari	**1021**
L Hernandez, SF	1008
R Johnson, Ari	994
C Park, LA	981
J Lieber, ChC	958

Innings Pitched

C Schilling, Ari	**256.2**
R Johnson, Ari	249.2
C Park, LA	234.0
G Maddux, Atl	233.0
J Lieber, ChC	232.1

Runs Allowed

L Hernandez, SF	**143**
M Hampton, Col	138
B Jones, SD	137
J Anderson, Pit	123
R Dempster, Fla	123

Strikeouts

R Johnson, Ari	**372**
C Schilling, Ari	293
C Park, LA	218
K Wood, ChC	217
J Vazquez, Mon	208

Walks Allowed

R Dempster, Fla	**112**
J Wright, Mil	98
T Glavine, Atl	97
K Wood, ChC	92
3 tied with	91

Hit Batsmen

C Park, LA	**20**
J Wright, Mil	**20**
R Johnson, Ari	18
E Gagne, LA	16
2 tied with	15

Wild Pitches

M Clement, Fla	**15**
K Appier, NYM	12
4 tied with	10

Balks

O Daal, Phi	**3**
C Park, LA	**3**
O Perez, Atl	**3**
8 tied with	2

2001 American League Special Batting Leaders

Scoring Position AVG
minimum 100 PA

Player, Team	AB	H	AVG
I Suzuki, Sea	**136**	**61**	**.449**
R Alomar, Cle	132	56	.424
J Conine, Bal	140	56	.400
C Beltran, KC	142	55	.387
J Giambi, Oak	113	40	.354
J Posada, NYY	132	45	.341
C Singleton, CWS	86	29	.337
J Gonzalez, Cle	158	53	.335
J Thome, Cle	148	49	.331
E Diaz, Cle	113	37	.327

Leadoff OBP
minimum 150 PA

Player, Team	PA*	OB	OBP
F Catalanotto, Tex	**367**	**146**	**.398**
L Rivas, Min	176	69	.392
I Suzuki, Sea	726	277	.382
S Stewart, Tor	465	172	.370
D Eckstein, Ana	496	177	.357
R Greer, Tex	275	95	.345
R Cedeno, Det	562	190	.338
C Knoblauch, NYY	575	193	.336
R Durham, CWS	574	191	.333
J Macias, Det	152	50	.329

* AB + BB + HBP + SF

Cleanup SLG
minimum 150 PA

Player, Team	AB	TB	SLG
M Ramirez, Bos	**511**	**310**	**.607**
J Gonzalez, Cle	532	314	.590
R Palmeiro, Tex	595	338	.568
C Delgado, Tor	520	295	.567
B Williams, NYY	231	122	.528
F McGriff, TB	282	147	.521
M Sweeney, KC	252	131	.520
T Martinez, NYY	313	160	.511
M Ordonez, CWS	338	172	.509
C Koskie, Min	400	199	.498

Avg vs. LHP
minimum 125 PA

B Boone, Sea	**.444**
J Conine, Bal	.376
J Gonzalez, Cle	.368
M Ramirez, Bos	.342
A Gonzalez, Tor	.336

Avg vs. RHP
minimum 377 PA

I Suzuki, Sea	**.362**
R Alomar, Cle	.356
J Giambi, Oak	.347
F Catalanotto, Tex	.331
E Martinez, Sea	.328

AVG at Home
minimum 251 PA

A Rodriguez, Tex	**.361**
S Stewart, Tor	.351
J Giambi, Oak	.349
I Suzuki, Sea	.343
C Beltran, KC	.342

AVG on the Road
minimum 251 PA

I Suzuki, Sea	**.356**
M Ordonez, CWS	.349
R Alomar, Cle	.345
B Boone, Sea	.339
J Giambi, Oak	.336

OBP vs. LHP
minimum 125 PA

B Boone, Sea	**.497**
M Ramirez, Bos	.462
R Mondesi, Tor	.453
J Conine, Bal	.451
J Giambi, Oak	.451

OBP vs. RHP
minimum 377 PA

J Giambi, Oak	**.491**
J Thome, Cle	.445
R Alomar, Cle	.437
C Delgado, Tor	.435
E Martinez, Sea	.433

Late & Close
minimum 50 PA

C Guzman, Min	**.467**
J Jones, Min	.423
I Suzuki, Sea	.400
J Encarnacion, Det	.391
B Molina, Ana	.387

Bases Loaded
minimum 10 PA

S Halter, Det	**.714**
C Koskie, Min	.636
B Grieve, TB	.583
R Palmeiro, Tex	.583
2 tied with	.571

SLG vs. LHP
minimum 125 PA

B Boone, Sea	**.715**
M Ordonez, CWS	.709
J Gonzalez, Cle	.675
M Ramirez, Bos	.650
A Rodriguez, Tex	.606

SLG vs. RHP
minimum 377 PA

J Thome, Cle	**.716**
J Giambi, Oak	.707
A Rodriguez, Tex	.626
E Chavez, Oak	.602
M Ramirez, Bos	.597

AB per HR
minimum 502 PA

J Thome, Cle	**10.7**
A Rodriguez, Tex	12.2
R Palmeiro, Tex	12.8
M Ramirez, Bos	12.9
J Giambi, Oak	13.7

Times on Base

J Giambi, Oak	**320**
A Rodriguez, Tex	292
C Delgado, Tor	287
I Suzuki, Sea	280
R Alomar, Cle	277

Pitches Seen

A Rodriguez, Tex	**2881**
T Glaus, Ana	2853
R Durham, CWS	2822
J Damon, Oak	2801
C Delgado, Tor	2801

Pitches per PA
minimum 502 PA

J Thome, Cle	**4.16**
J Valentin, CWS	4.14
T Nixon, Bos	4.14
E Martinez, Sea	4.13
M Cameron, Sea	4.09

% Pitches Taken
minimum 1500 pitches

F Menechino, Oak	**65.9**
M McLemore, Sea	65.5
E Martinez, Sea	65.3
J Giambi, Oak	63.9
T Nixon, Bos	63.7

Ground/Fly Ratio
minimum 502 PA

I Suzuki, Sea	**2.63**
R Cedeno, Det	2.52
B Grieve, TB	2.13
J Jones, Min	2.12
D Jeter, NYY	1.96

GDP/GDP Opp
minimum 50 PA

R Branyan, Cle	**0.02**
C Everett, Bos	0.03
A Martin, Sea	0.03
I Suzuki, Sea	0.03
B Anderson, Bal	0.04

SB Success %
minimum 20 SB attempts

C Beltran, KC	**96.9**
D Jeter, NYY	90.0
P O'Neill, NYY	88.0
D Eckstein, Ana	87.9
M Cameron, Sea	87.2

Steals of Third

I Suzuki, Sea	**14**
A Soriano, NYY	11
R Alomar, Cle	8
C Knoblauch, NYY	7
R Mondesi, Tor	7

% CS by Catchers
minimum 70 SB attempts

E Diaz, Cle	**35.4**
D Mirabelli, Tex-Bos	34.4
R Hernandez, Oak	25.2
D Fletcher, Tor	24.2
B Molina, Ana	24.1

2001 National League Special Batting Leaders

Scoring Position AVG
minimum 100 PA

Player, Team	AB	H	AVG
C Biggio, Hou	98	38	**.388**
B Bonds, SF	89	34	.382
A Ramirez, Pit	145	55	.379
L Walker, Col	124	47	.379
P Lo Duca, LA	103	39	.379
C Paquette, StL	94	35	.372
K Millar, Fla	106	39	.368
T Helton, Col	172	62	.360
S Casey, Cin	146	52	.356
S Rolen, Phi	157	55	.350

Leadoff OBP
minimum 150 PA

Player, Team	PA*	OB	OBP
C Biggio, Hou	510	193	**.378**
P Lo Duca, LA	209	79	.378
C Counsell, Ari	273	103	.377
J Pierre, Col	638	238	.373
T Walker, Col-Cin	256	94	.367
R Henderson, SD	443	162	.366
D White, Mil	255	93	.365
F Vina, StL	685	244	.356
Q Veras, Atl	177	63	.356
R Belliard, Mil	184	64	.348

* AB + BB + HBP + SF

Cleanup SLG
minimum 150 PA

Player, Team	AB	TB	SLG
T Helton, Col	435	314	**.722**
S Green, LA	291	180	.619
C Jones, Atl	236	145	.614
G Sheffield, LA	240	145	.604
L Berkman, Hou	533	319	.598
A Pujols, StL	358	213	.595
P Nevin, SD	517	307	.594
B Giles, Pit	332	194	.584
F McGriff, ChC	170	95	.559
R Sexson, Mil	446	249	.558

Avg vs. LHP
minimum 125 PA

P Lo Duca, LA	**.411**
S Sosa, ChC	.387
L Walker, Col	.378
C Jones, Atl	.376
G Sheffield, LA	.374

Avg vs. RHP
minimum 377 PA

T Helton, Col	**.354**
A Pujols, StL	.342
L Walker, Col	.338
L Berkman, Hou	.337
J Pierre, Col	.337

AVG at Home
minimum 251 PA

L Walker, Col	**.406**
T Helton, Col	.384
J Cirillo, Col	.362
K Millar, Fla	.355
A Pujols, StL	.354

AVG on the Road
minimum 251 PA

C Jones, Atl	**.349**
S Casey, Cin	.339
L Berkman, Hou	.327
R Klesko, SD	.326
A Ramirez, Pit	.325

OBP vs. LHP
minimum 125 PA

S Sosa, ChC	**.569**
B Bonds, SF	.487
C Jones, Atl	.462
S Rolen, Phi	.458
G Sheffield, LA	.457

OBP vs. RHP
minimum 377 PA

B Bonds, SF	**.526**
T Helton, Col	.453
L Walker, Col	.452
L Berkman, Hou	.438
L Gonzalez, Ari	.435

Late & Close
minimum 50 PA

J Vidro, Mon	**.471**
M Williams, Ari	.419
M Alou, Hou	.395
D Martinez, Atl	.391
J Pierre, Col	.367

Bases Loaded
minimum 10 PA

D White, Mil	**.700**
S Sosa, ChC	.667
T Shinjo, NYM	.583
E Owens, Fla	.545
J Kent, SF	.526

SLG vs. LHP
minimum 125 PA

S Sosa, ChC	**.882**
B Bonds, SF	.752
L Walker, Col	.750
G Sheffield, LA	.720
C Jones, Atl	.679

SLG vs. RHP
minimum 377 PA

B Bonds, SF	**.910**
T Helton, Col	.758
L Gonzalez, Ari	.716
S Sosa, ChC	.709
L Berkman, Hou	.661

AB per HR
minimum 502 PA

B Bonds, SF	**6.5**
S Sosa, ChC	9.0
L Gonzalez, Ari	10.7
T Helton, Col	12.0
S Green, LA	12.6

Times on Base

B Bonds, SF	**342**
L Gonzalez, Ari	312
S Sosa, ChC	311
T Helton, Col	300
L Berkman, Hou	296

Pitches Seen

B Abreu, Phi	**2896**
J Bagwell, Hou	2890
T Helton, Col	2824
S Sosa, ChC	2732
A Pujols, StL	2716

Pitches per PA
minimum 502 PA

J Bell, Ari	**4.27**
T Zeile, NYM	4.18
L Castillo, Fla	4.13
K Young, Pit	4.11
B Abreu, Phi	4.11

% Pitches Taken
minimum 1500 pitches

R Henderson, SD	**66.6**
B Bonds, SF	65.7
T Zeile, NYM	63.7
B Abreu, Phi	63.1
L Castillo, Fla	61.9

Ground/Fly Ratio
minimum 502 PA

J Pierre, Col	**2.77**
L Castillo, Fla	2.59
P Polanco, StL	2.31
R Ordonez, NYM	2.15
R Gutierrez, ChC	2.13

GDP/GDP Opp
minimum 50 PA

E Durazo, Ari	**0.02**
R Sanders, Ari	0.02
B Bonds, SF	0.03
S Sosa, ChC	0.04
J Rollins, Phi	0.05

SB Success %
minimum 20 SB attempts

P Reese, Cin	**86.2**
C Floyd, Fla	85.7
D White, Mil	85.7
J Rollins, Phi	85.2
R Klesko, SD	85.2

Steals of Third

J Pierre, Col	**14**
V Guerrero, Mon	9
J Rollins, Phi	8
D Glanville, Phi	7
2 tied with	6

% CS by Catchers
minimum 70 SB attempts

H Blanco, Mil	**42.3**
B Ausmus, Hou	40.0
C Johnson, Fla	39.5
P Lo Duca, LA	38.5
B Davis, SD	32.7

2001 American League Special Pitching Leaders

Baserunners per 9 IP
minimum 162 IP

Player, Team	IP	BR	BR/9
M Mussina, NYY	228.2	248	9.76
M Buehrle, CWS	221.1	244	9.92
F Garcia, Sea	238.2	273	10.29
J Moyer, Sea	209.2	241	10.35
J Mays, Min	233.2	274	10.55
M Mulder, Oak	229.1	270	10.60
B Radke, Min	226.0	271	10.79
C Lidle, Oak	188.0	227	10.87
T Hudson, Oak	235.0	293	11.22
A Sele, Sea	215.0	274	11.47

Strikeouts per 9 IP
minimum 162 IP

Player, Team	IP	SO	SO/9
H Nomo, Bos	198.0	220	10.00
R Clemens, NYY	220.1	213	8.70
B Zito, Oak	214.1	205	8.61
C Sabathia, Cle	180.1	171	8.53
M Mussina, NYY	228.2	214	8.42
B Colon, Cle	222.1	201	8.14
T Wakefield, Bos	168.2	148	7.90
A Pettitte, NYY	200.2	164	7.36
T Hudson, Oak	235.0	181	6.93
C Carpenter, Tor	215.2	157	6.55

Run Support per 9 IP
minimum 162 IP

Player, Team	IP	R	R/9
P Abbott, Sea	163.0	141	7.79
R Clemens, NYY	220.1	161	6.58
A Sele, Sea	215.0	157	6.57
A Pettitte, NYY	200.2	144	6.46
R Helling, Tex	215.2	145	6.05
E Loaiza, Tor	190.0	127	6.02
J Moyer, Sea	209.2	140	6.01
D Davis, Tex	186.0	124	6.00
M Mulder, Oak	229.1	148	5.81
C Lidle, Oak	188.0	119	5.70

Opposition OBP
minimum 162 IP

M Mussina, NYY	.274
M Buehrle, CWS	.279
F Garcia, Sea	.283
J Moyer, Sea	.285
J Mays, Min	.289

Opposition SLG
minimum 162 IP

F Garcia, Sea	.344
B Zito, Oak	.345
M Mulder, Oak	.349
T Hudson, Oak	.350
M Mussina, NYY	.358

Hits per 9 IP
minimum 162 IP

C Sabathia, Cle	7.44
F Garcia, Sea	7.50
M Buehrle, CWS	7.64
B Zito, Oak	7.73
H Nomo, Bos	7.77

Home Runs per 9 IP
minimum 162 IP

F Garcia, Sea	0.60
M Mulder, Oak	0.63
A Pettitte, NYY	0.63
D Davis, Tex	0.68
T Wakefield, Bos	0.69

AVG vs. LHB
minimum 125 BFP

C Bailey, KC	.164
T Percival, Ana	.176
P Hentgen, Bal	.178
M Rivera, NYY	.187
J Mecir, Oak	.195

AVG vs. RHB
minimum 225 BFP

F Garcia, Sea	.205
K Escobar, Tor	.206
C Sabathia, Cle	.223
B Zito, Oak	.229
P Abbott, Sea	.232

AVG Allowed ScPos
minimum 125 BFP

J Mays, Min	.202
K Escobar, Tor	.204
J Kennedy, TB	.214
F Garcia, Sea	.216
M Buehrle, CWS	.219

OBP Lead Off Inn
minimum 150 BFP

M Mussina, NYY	.225
J Moyer, Sea	.255
T Hudson, Oak	.267
J Mays, Min	.271
F Garcia, Sea	.276

K/BB Ratio
minimum 162 IP

B Radke, Min	5.27
M Mussina, NYY	5.10
A Pettitte, NYY	4.00
M Mulder, Oak	3.00
R Clemens, NYY	2.96

Grd/Fly Ratio Off
minimum 162 IP

T Hudson, Oak	2.26
M Mulder, Oak	1.93
S Schoeneweis, Ana	1.84
C Lidle, Oak	1.81
C Carpenter, Tor	1.65

Pitches per Start
minimum 30 games started

J Weaver, Det	109.7
R Clemens, NYY	109.2
B Colon, Cle	107.4
S Sparks, Det	107.2
R Helling, Tex	106.0

Pitches per Batter
minimum 162 IP

B Radke, Min	3.45
R Ortiz, Ana	3.46
S Schoeneweis, Ana	3.49
C Carpenter, Tor	3.55
C Lidle, Oak	3.56

Steals Allowed

H Nomo, Bos	52
R Clemens, NYY	34
J Johnson, Bal	34
T Wakefield, Bos	32
2 tied with	27

Caught Stealing Off

J Johnson, Bal	19
C Sabathia, Cle	15
R Helling, Tex	13
M Mussina, NYY	13
J Washburn, Ana	12

SB% Allowed
minimum 162 IP

R Helling, Tex	35.0
D Davis, Tex	35.3
M Mussina, NYY	40.9
E Milton, Min	42.9
3 tied with	50.0

Pickoffs

J Washburn, Ana	12
D Davis, Tex	11
C Michalak, Tor-Tex	10
A Pettitte, NYY	7
2 tied with	6

PkOf Throw/Runner
minimum 162 IP

C Lidle, Oak	0.81
M Mulder, Oak	0.79
J Washburn, Ana	0.78
M Buehrle, CWS	0.76
T Hudson, Oak	0.74

GDP Induced

M Mulder, Oak	26
C Carpenter, Tor	25
D Reichert, KC	25
S Schoeneweis, Ana	25
3 tied with	23

GDP per 9 IP
minimum 162 IP

C Durbin, KC	1.2
S Schoeneweis, Ana	1.1
C Carpenter, Tor	1.0
M Mulder, Oak	1.0
T Sturtze, TB	1.0

Quality Starts

T Hudson, Oak	25
F Garcia, Sea	24
M Mussina, NYY	24
B Zito, Oak	24
M Mulder, Oak	22

2001 National League Special Pitching Leaders

Baserunners per 9 IP
minimum 162 IP

Player, Team	IP	BR	BR/9
C Schilling, Ari	256.2	277	9.71
R Johnson, Ari	249.2	270	9.73
G Maddux, Atl	233.0	254	9.81
J Vazquez, Mon	223.2	244	9.82
J Lieber, ChC	232.1	274	10.61
B Penny, Fla	205.0	244	10.71
J Burkett, Atl	219.1	263	10.79
A Leiter, NYM	187.1	228	10.95
W Miller, Hou	212.0	263	11.17
S Trachsel, NYM	173.2	218	11.30

Strikeouts per 9 IP
minimum 162 IP

Player, Team	IP	SO	SO/9
R Johnson, Ari	249.2	372	13.41
K Wood, ChC	174.1	217	11.20
C Schilling, Ari	256.2	293	10.27
R Wolf, Phi	163.0	152	8.39
C Park, LA	234.0	218	8.38
J Bere, ChC	188.0	175	8.38
J Vazquez, Mon	223.2	208	8.37
T Armas Jr., Mon	196.2	176	8.05
K Tapani, ChC	168.1	149	7.97
R Person, Phi	208.1	183	7.91

Run Support per 9 IP
minimum 162 IP

Player, Team	IP	R	R/9
M Hampton, Col	203.0	160	7.09
D Neagle, Col	170.2	131	6.91
M Morris, StL	216.1	154	6.41
Williams, SD-StL	220.0	146	5.97
R Dempster, Fla	211.1	139	5.92
P Astacio, Col-Hou	169.2	111	5.89
J Lieber, ChC	232.1	150	5.81
K Jarvis, SD	193.1	124	5.77
O Daal, Phi	185.2	119	5.77
J Wright, Mil	194.2	124	5.73

Opposition OBP
minimum 162 IP

C Schilling, Ari	.273
R Johnson, Ari	.274
J Vazquez, Mon	.274
G Maddux, Atl	.278
J Lieber, ChC	.290

Opposition SLG
minimum 162 IP

R Johnson, Ari	.309
K Wood, ChC	.315
R Ortiz, SF	.328
J Burkett, Atl	.354
C Park, LA	.358

Hits per 9 IP
minimum 162 IP

R Johnson, Ari	6.52
K Wood, ChC	6.56
C Park, LA	7.04
A Burnett, Fla	7.53
J Burkett, Atl	7.67

Home Runs per 9 IP
minimum 162 IP

T Adams, LA	0.49
R Ortiz, SF	0.54
M Morris, StL	0.54
J Anderson, Pit	0.65
B Penny, Fla	0.66

AVG vs. LHB
minimum 125 BFP

F Rodriguez, SF	.150
R Wolf, Phi	.171
J Thomson, Col	.177
J Shaw, LA	.192
R Johnson, Ari	.196

AVG vs. RHB
minimum 225 BFP

O Dotel, Hou	.178
K Brown, LA	.184
R Ortiz, SF	.190
K Wood, ChC	.203
R Johnson, Ari	.204

AVG Allowed ScPos
minimum 125 BFP

R Johnson, Ari	.178
S Sullivan, Cin	.185
C Park, LA	.197
M DeJean, Mil	.200
D Kile, StL	.210

OBP Lead Off Inn
minimum 150 BFP

J Vazquez, Mon	.237
A Leiter, NYM	.247
B Penny, Fla	.256
J Bere, ChC	.256
K Jarvis, SD	.259

K/BB Ratio
minimum 162 IP

C Schilling, Ari	7.51
G Maddux, Atl	6.41
R Johnson, Ari	5.24
J Vazquez, Mon	4.73
K Tapani, ChC	3.72

Grd/Fly Ratio Off
minimum 162 IP

J Anderson, Pit	2.53
T Adams, LA	2.29
M Morris, StL	2.01
J Wright, Mil	1.90
S Reynolds, Hou	1.86

Pitches per Start
minimum 30 games started

R Johnson, Ari	116.6
L Hernandez, SF	108.4
R Ortiz, SF	106.6
C Schilling, Ari	106.0
J Vazquez, Mon	105.4

Pitches per Batter
minimum 162 IP

G Maddux, Atl	3.18
S Reynolds, Hou	3.30
T Ritchie, Pit	3.39
J Anderson, Pit	3.39
J Lieber, ChC	3.40

Steals Allowed

J Anderson, Pit	33
M Batista, Ari	24
G Maddux, Atl	24
4 tied with	22

Caught Stealing Off

E Dessens, Cin	15
R Johnson, Ari	15
G Maddux, Atl	14
W Miller, Hou	13
T Glavine, Atl	11

SB% Allowed
minimum 162 IP

M Hampton, Col	16.7
J Lieber, ChC	22.2
K Rueter, SF	25.0
C Schilling, Ari	30.8
D Kile, StL	36.4

Pickoffs

B Anderson, Ari	8
J Beimel, Pit	7
B Chen, Phi-NYM	7
D Williams, Pit	7
K Wood, ChC	7

PkOf Throw/Runner
minimum 162 IP

J Burkett, Atl	1.22
A Leiter, NYM	1.04
S Trachsel, NYM	0.84
A Burnett, Fla	0.67
J Anderson, Pit	0.67

GDP Induced

J Anderson, Pit	29
M Hampton, Col	29
K Rueter, SF	28
J Wright, Mil	26
2 tied with	24

GDP per 9 IP
minimum 162 IP

K Rueter, SF	1.3
M Hampton, Col	1.3
J Anderson, Pit	1.3
J Wright, Mil	1.2
O Daal, Phi	1.1

Quality Starts

R Johnson, Ari	27
C Schilling, Ari	27
C Park, LA	26
G Maddux, Atl	24
M Morris, StL	24

2001 American League Relief Pitching Leaders

Saves

Player, Team	Saves
M Rivera, NYY	**50**
K Sasaki, Sea	45
K Foulke, CWS	42
T Percival, Ana	39
B Koch, Tor	36
J Isringhausen, Oak	34
B Wickman, Cle	32
L Hawkins, Min	28
R Hernandez, KC	28
J Zimmerman, Tex	28

Save Percentage
minimum 20 SvOp

Player, Team	Op	Sv	Pct
K Foulke, CWS	**45**	**42**	**93.3**
T Percival, Ana	42	39	92.9
M Anderson, Det	24	22	91.7
B Wickman, Cle	35	32	91.4
J Zimmerman, Tex	31	28	90.3
M Rivera, NYY	57	50	87.7
K Sasaki, Sea	52	45	86.5
R Hernandez, KC	34	28	82.4
B Koch, Tor	44	36	81.8
D Lowe, Bos	30	24	80.0

Relief ERA
minimum 50 relief IP

Player, Team	IP	ER	ERA
A Rhodes, Sea	**68.0**	**13**	**1.72**
A Levine, Ana	72.2	17	2.11
K Foulke, CWS	81.0	21	2.33
M Rivera, NYY	80.2	21	2.34
B Wickman, Cle	67.2	18	2.39
J Zimmerman, Tex	71.1	19	2.40
D Baez, Cle	50.1	14	2.50
M Stanton, NYY	80.1	23	2.58
J Isringhausen, Oak	71.1	21	2.65
T Percival, Ana	57.2	17	2.65

Relief Wins

P Quantrill, Tor	**11**
M Stanton, NYY	9
4 tied with	8

Relief Losses

A Levine, Ana	**10**
D Lowe, Bos	**10**
K Foulke, CWS	9
J Mecir, Oak	8
J Rocker, Cle	7

Holds

A Rhodes, Sea	**32**
J Grimsley, KC	26
J Nelson, Sea	26
J Tam, Oak	25
M Stanton, NYY	23

Blown Saves

L Hawkins, Min	**9**
Isringhausen, Oak	**9**
E Yan, TB	**9**
T Jones, Det-Min	8
B Koch, Tor	8

Relief Games

P Quantrill, Tor	**80**
M Stanton, NYY	76
J Grimsley, KC	73
K Foulke, CWS	72
3 tied with	71

Games Finished

K Foulke, CWS	**69**
M Rivera, NYY	66
K Sasaki, Sea	63
B Koch, Tor	56
B Wickman, Cle	56

Relief Innings

P Mahomes, Tex	**92.1**
R Mendoza, NYY	91.0
P Quantrill, Tor	83.0
L Pote, Ana	81.2
K Foulke, CWS	81.0

% Inherited Scored
min 30 inherited runners

J Nelson, Sea	**13.2**
R Mendoza, NYY	15.2
D Patterson, Det	16.1
M Guthrie, Oak	16.3
A Rhodes, Sea	17.2

Opposition AVG
minimum 50 relief IP

J Nelson, Sea	**.136**
T Percival, Ana	.187
A Rhodes, Sea	.189
D Baez, Cle	.191
J Zimmerman, Tex	.192

Opposition OBP
minimum 50 relief IP

A Rhodes, Sea	**.230**
K Sasaki, Sea	.241
M Rivera, NYY	.242
J Zimmerman, Tex	.251
T Percival, Ana	.258

Opposition SLG
minimum 50 relief IP

J Nelson, Sea	**.199**
T Percival, Ana	.258
K Foulke, CWS	.261
M Rivera, NYY	.274
A Rhodes, Sea	.279

1st Batter AVG
minimum 40 first BFP

D Baez, Cle	**.103**
J Nelson, Sea	.107
K Foulke, CWS	.136
E Guardado, Min	.143
A Rhodes, Sea	.143

Avg vs. LHB
minimum 50 relief IP

C Bailey, KC	**.164**
E Guardado, Min	.167
J Nelson, Sea	.167
K Escobar, Tor	.170
T Percival, Ana	.176

Avg vs. RHB
minimum 50 relief IP

J Nelson, Sea	**.119**
J Isringhausen, Oak	.152
J Zimmerman, Tex	.163
K Sasaki, Sea	.168
A Rhodes, Sea	.179

AVG Runners On
minimum 50 relief IP

J Nelson, Sea	**.153**
K Escobar, Tor	.163
S Lowe, CWS	.163
V Zambrano, TB	.167
R Rincon, Cle	.172

AVG Allowed ScPos
minimum 50 relief IP

V Zambrano, TB	**.113**
S Lowe, CWS	.123
E Guardado, Min	.145
J Nelson, Sea	.148
K Escobar, Tor	.160

Easy Saves

T Percival, Ana	**26**
K Sasaki, Sea	**26**
J Isringhausen, Oak	24
M Rivera, NYY	22
B Wickman, Cle	22

Regular Saves

M Rivera, NYY	**25**
K Foulke, CWS	18
K Sasaki, Sea	15
B Koch, Tor	13
3 tied with	10

Tough Saves

B Groom, Bal	**5**
T Percival, Ana	**5**
K Foulke, CWS	4
K Sasaki, Sea	4
3 tied with	3

Pitches per Batter
minimum 50 relief IP

D Patterson, Det	**3.25**
R Mendoza, NYY	3.29
J Tam, Oak	3.37
M Petkovsek, Tex	3.48
V Zambrano, TB	3.49

2001 National League Relief Pitching Leaders

Saves

Player, Team	Saves
R Nen, SF	45
A Benitez, NYM	43
T Hoffman, SD	43
J Shaw, LA	43
J Mesa, Phi	42
B Wagner, Hou	39
D Graves, Cin	32
A Alfonseca, Fla	28
F Gordon, ChC	27
M Williams, Pit-Hou	22

Save Percentage
minimum 20 SvOp

Player, Team	Op	Sv	Pct
B Wagner, Hou	41	39	95.1
T Hoffman, SD	46	43	93.5
A Benitez, NYM	46	43	93.5
J Mesa, Phi	46	42	91.3
M Williams, Pit-Hou	25	22	88.0
F Gordon, ChC	31	27	87.1
R Nen, SF	52	45	86.5
J Shaw, LA	52	43	82.7
J Rocker, Atl	23	19	82.6
B Kim, Ari	23	19	82.6

Relief ERA
minimum 50 relief IP

Player, Team	IP	ER	ERA
F Rodriguez, SF	80.1	15	1.68
S Kline, StL	75.0	15	1.80
C Fox, Mil	66.2	14	1.89
O Dotel, Hou	84.0	18	1.93
J Mesa, Phi	69.1	18	2.34
D Weathers, Mil-ChC	86.0	23	2.41
V Nunez, Fla	74.1	20	2.42
T Van Poppel, ChC	75.0	21	2.52
J Brower, Cin	80.0	24	2.70
B Wagner, Hou	62.2	19	2.73

Relief Wins

M Herges, LA	9
G Lloyd, Mon	9
F Rodriguez, SF	9
J Cabrera, Atl	7
S Sullivan, Cin	7

Relief Losses

M Herges, LA	8
J Brower, Cin	7
G White, Col	7
6 tied with	6

Holds

F Rodriguez, SF	32
M Remlinger, Atl	31
J Fassero, ChC	25
K Farnsworth, ChC	24
R Bottalico, Phi	22

Blown Saves

J Shaw, LA	9
D Graves, Cin	7
M Herges, LA	7
C Leskanic, Mil	7
R Nen, SF	7

Relief Games

S Kline, StL	89
G Lloyd, Mon	84
J Fassero, ChC	82
R King, Mil	82
2 tied with	80

Games Finished

R Nen, SF	71
J Shaw, LA	66
A Benitez, NYM	64
J Mesa, Phi	59
2 tied with	58

Relief Innings

S Sullivan, Cin	103.1
M Herges, LA	99.1
B Kim, Ari	98.0
Weathers, Mil-ChC	86.0
M DeJean, Mil	84.1

% Inherited Scored
min 30 inherited runners

D Cook, NYM-Phi	18.2
Weathers, Mil-ChC	18.2
A Fultz, SF	18.6
3 tied with	20.6

Opposition AVG
minimum 50 relief IP

B Kim, Ari	.173
C Fox, Mil	.181
O Dotel, Hou	.182
F Rodriguez, SF	.188
B Wagner, Hou	.198

Opposition OBP
minimum 50 relief IP

F Rodriguez, SF	.259
R Nen, SF	.260
O Dotel, Hou	.266
J Shaw, LA	.277
G Swindell, Ari	.277

Opposition SLG
minimum 50 relief IP

O Dotel, Hou	.251
F Rodriguez, SF	.280
S Kline, StL	.295
C Fox, Mil	.296
B Kim, Ari	.299

1st Batter AVG
minimum 40 first BFP

A Benitez, NYM	.123
S Sullivan, Cin	.125
B Wagner, Hou	.138
G Carrara, LA	.146
M Matthews, StL	.147

Avg vs. LHB
minimum 50 relief IP

S Kline, StL	.149
F Rodriguez, SF	.150
C Fox, Mil	.158
J Shaw, LA	.192
B Kim, Ari	.199

Avg vs. RHB
minimum 50 relief IP

B Kim, Ari	.151
O Dotel, Hou	.159
R Nen, SF	.162
J Manzanillo, Pit	.168
2 tied with	.182

AVG Runners On
minimum 50 relief IP

Weathers, Mil-ChC	.144
T Van Poppel, ChC	.158
F Rodriguez, SF	.172
C Fox, Mil	.176
J Mesa, Phi	.180

AVG Allowed ScPos
minimum 50 relief IP

Farnsworth, ChC	.110
T Van Poppel, ChC	.114
C Fox, Mil	.129
C Leskanic, Mil	.157
Weathers, Mil-ChC	.161

Easy Saves

R Nen, SF	28
T Hoffman, SD	27
J Shaw, LA	27
A Benitez, NYM	26
J Mesa, Phi	24

Regular Saves

B Wagner, Hou	20
J Mesa, Phi	18
R Nen, SF	15
J Shaw, LA	15
A Benitez, NYM	14

Tough Saves

T Hoffman, SD	7
D Graves, Cin	5
B Kim, Ari	4
J Rocker, Atl	4
2 tied with	3

Pitches per Batter
minimum 50 relief IP

A Alfonseca, Fla	3.24
E Sabel, Ari	3.31
M Yoshii, Mon	3.38
D Graves, Cin	3.41
M Jackson, Hou	3.42

2001 American League Bill James Leaders

Top Game Scores of the Year

Pitcher	Date	Opp	IP	H	R	ER	BB	K	SC
H Nomo, Bos	5/25	Tor	9.0	1	0	0	0	14	99
M Mussina, NYY	9/2	Bos	9.0	1	0	0	0	13	98
H Nomo, Bos	4/4	Bal	9.0	0	0	0	3	11	95
M Mulder, Oak	7/6	Ari	9.0	1	0	0	0	9	94
M Mussina, NYY	9/28	Bal	9.0	3	0	0	0	13	94
R Halladay, Tor	10/5	Cle	9.0	2	0	0	0	8	91
M Mussina, NYY	5/1	Min	9.0	3	0	0	0	10	91
P Martinez, Bos	4/8	TB	8.0	3	0	0	3	16	89
3 tied with									88

Worst Game Scores of the Year

Pitcher	Date	Opp	IP	H	R	ER	BB	K	SC
S Schoeneweis, Ana	5/23	Bal	4.0	12	11	11	3	0	-9
W Roberts, Bal	6/15	Phi	3.0	10	9	9	2	0	1
S Schoeneweis, Ana	6/29	Sea	2.2	11	9	9	2	3	1
A Lopez, TB	5/30	Oak	4.1	12	9	9	3	2	2
C Finley, Cle	5/28	Det	1.0	8	8	8	2	1	4
B Rekar, TB	5/11	Cle	4.0	13	10	8	0	4	4
C Finley, Cle	5/17	Tex	1.0	9	8	8	0	2	5
D Wright, CWS	8/22	KC	0.2	9	7	7	1	0	5
3 tied with									6

Runs Created

J Giambi, Oak	156
A Rodriguez, Tex	149
R Alomar, Cle	139
I Suzuki, Sea	135
J Thome, Cle	133
C Beltran, KC	128
R Palmeiro, Tex	124
M Ramirez, Bos	119
C Delgado, Tor	118
B Boone, Sea	116

Runs Created per 27 Outs
minimum 502 PA

J Giambi, Oak	11.4
J Thome, Cle	9.3
R Alomar, Cle	9.0
A Rodriguez, Tex	8.7
M Ramirez, Bos	8.4
E Martinez, Sea	8.1
C Beltran, KC	7.8
I Suzuki, Sea	7.6
C Delgado, Tor	7.4
J Conine, Bal	7.4

Offensive Winning Pct
minimum 502 PA

J Giambi, Oak	.846
J Thome, Cle	.784
R Alomar, Cle	.774
A Rodriguez, Tex	.762
M Ramirez, Bos	.751
E Martinez, Sea	.737
C Beltran, KC	.719
I Suzuki, Sea	.712
C Delgado, Tor	.701
J Conine, Bal	.698

Secondary Average
minimum 502 PA

J Giambi, Oak	.569
J Thome, Cle	.542
T Glaus, Ana	.474
C Delgado, Tor	.460
R Palmeiro, Tex	.458
M Ramirez, Bos	.454
A Rodriguez, Tex	.446
E Martinez, Sea	.440
E Burks, Cle	.412
M Cameron, Sea	.394

Isolated Power
minimum 502 PA

J Thome, Cle	.333
J Giambi, Oak	.317
A Rodriguez, Tex	.304
M Ramirez, Bos	.302
R Palmeiro, Tex	.290
T Glaus, Ana	.281
J Gonzalez, Cle	.265
E Burks, Cle	.262
C Delgado, Tor	.261
J Cruz, Tor	.256

Power/Speed Number

J Cruz, Tor	33.0
M Cameron, Sea	28.8
R Mondesi, Tor	28.4
M Ordonez, CWS	27.7
C Beltran, KC	27.1
A Rodriguez, Tex	26.7
C Koskie, Min	26.5
A Soriano, NYY	25.4
R Alomar, Cle	24.0
D Jeter, NYY	23.6

Speed Scores
minimum 800 AB over last two years

C Guzman, Min	8.10
C Beltran, KC	8.01
J Damon, Oak	7.75
C Singleton, CWS	7.74
M Cameron, Sea	7.14
K Lofton, Cle	7.13
M McLemore, Sea	7.01
R Alomar, Cle	6.98
R Durham, CWS	6.95
D Erstad, Ana	6.95

Cheap Wins

J Moyer, Sea	6
P Abbott, Sea	5
D Davis, Tex	5
R Clemens, NYY	4
F Garcia, Sea	4
M Mulder, Oak	4
D Oliver, Tex	4
J Suppan, KC	4
12 tied with	3

Tough Losses

J Mays, Min	5
10 tied with	4

2001 National League Bill James Leaders

Top Game Scores of the Year

Pitcher	Date	Opp	IP	H	R	ER	BB	K	SC
R Johnson, Ari	5/8	Cin	9.0	3	1	1	0	20	97
K Wood, ChC	5/25	Mil	9.0	1	0	0	2	14	97
G Maddux, Atl	5/2	Mil	9.0	2	0	0	1	14	96
C Schilling, Ari	4/10	LA	9.0	2	0	0	0	10	93
C Park, LA	7/18	Mil	9.0	2	0	0	0	9	92
B Penny, Fla	6/26	Mon	8.0	1	0	0	1	13	92
J Vazquez, Mon	5/15	LA	9.0	2	0	0	0	9	92
R Wolf, Phi	9/26	Cin	9.0	1	0	0	1	8	92
T Ritchie, Pit	7/13	KC	9.0	1	0	0	0	6	91
B Smith, StL	9/3	SD	9.0	0	0	0	4	7	90

Worst Game Scores of the Year

Pitcher	Date	Opp	IP	H	R	ER	BB	K	SC
J Anderson, Pit	8/3	Col	2.1	11	11	11	3	3	-9
J Herndon, SD	8/30	StL	3.0	9	11	11	4	1	-6
K Tapani, ChC	4/24	Col	3.1	11	10	10	3	1	-4
A Benes, StL	4/4	Col	2.2	9	10	10	2	2	0
M Hampton, Col	7/28	LA	2.1	9	9	9	2	1	2
C Pavano, Mon	8/15	LA	3.0	12	8	8	2	1	2
J Sanchez, Fla	8/14	SF	2.1	10	8	8	3	0	2
S Chacon, Col	7/8	Ana	5.0	12	11	11	1	5	3
5 tied with									5

Runs Created

B Bonds, SF	180
S Sosa, ChC	166
L Gonzalez, Ari	163
T Helton, Col	150
L Walker, Col	139
J Bagwell, Hou	137
L Berkman, Hou	136
S Green, LA	135
C Jones, Atl	131
B Giles, Pit	130

Runs Created per 27 Outs
minimum 502 PA

B Bonds, SF	14.6
S Sosa, ChC	10.9
L Walker, Col	10.8
L Gonzalez, Ari	10.1
T Helton, Col	9.7
L Berkman, Hou	8.9
J Edmonds, StL	8.7
C Jones, Atl	8.6
G Sheffield, LA	8.3
B Giles, Pit	8.3

Offensive Winning Pct
minimum 502 PA

B Bonds, SF	.906
S Sosa, ChC	.844
L Walker, Col	.841
L Gonzalez, Ari	.823
T Helton, Col	.810
L Berkman, Hou	.783
J Edmonds, StL	.775
C Jones, Atl	.768
G Sheffield, LA	.759
B Giles, Pit	.759

Secondary Average
minimum 502 PA

B Bonds, SF	.929
S Sosa, ChC	.607
L Gonzalez, Ari	.527
T Helton, Col	.520
L Walker, Col	.495
B Abreu, Phi	.471
J Bagwell, Hou	.470
G Sheffield, LA	.466
R Klesko, SD	.452
B Giles, Pit	.450

Isolated Power
minimum 502 PA

B Bonds, SF	.536
S Sosa, ChC	.409
L Gonzalez, Ari	.363
T Helton, Col	.349
L Walker, Col	.312
S Green, LA	.300
L Berkman, Hou	.289
P Nevin, SD	.282
A Pujols, StL	.281
B Giles, Pit	.281

Power/Speed Number

V Guerrero, Mon	35.4
B Abreu, Phi	33.3
S Green, LA	28.4
R Klesko, SD	26.0
C Floyd, Fla	22.8
B Bonds, SF	22.1
J Rollins, Phi	21.5
P Wilson, Fla	21.4
L Walker, Col	20.5
R Sanders, Ari	19.7

Speed Scores
minimum 800 AB over last two years

T Goodwin, LA	8.52
T Womack, Ari	8.35
J Pierre, Col	7.74
D Glanville, Phi	7.48
P Bergeron, Mon	7.41
M Benard, SF	7.40
P Reese, Cin	7.21
D Jackson, SD	7.21
N Perez, Col	7.15
L Castillo, Fla	7.07

Cheap Wins

M Hampton, Col	5
L Hernandez, SF	5
B Tollberg, SD	5
9 tied with	4

Tough Losses

J Haynes, Mil	6
G Maddux, Atl	6
P Astacio, Col-Hou	5
J Burkett, Atl	5
A Burnett, Fla	5
W Miller, Hou	5
C Park, LA	5
7 tied with	4

2001 Active Career Batting Leaders

Batting Average
minimum 1000 PA

Player, Team	AB	H	AVG
1 Tony Gwynn	9288	3141	.338
2 Todd Helton	2368	791	.334
3 Nomar Garciaparra	2519	836	.332
4 Mike Piazza	4638	1507	.325
5 Derek Jeter	3744	1199	.320
6 Frank Thomas	5542	1770	.319
7 Vladimir Guerrero	2755	879	.319
8 Edgar Martinez	5902	1882	.319
9 Larry Walker	5403	1702	.315
10 Manny Ramirez	3999	1248	.312
11 Sean Casey	1919	597	.311
12 Jeff Cirillo	3937	1224	.311
13 Lance Berkman	1023	318	.311
14 Alex Rodriguez	3758	1167	.311
15 Jason Giambi	3398	1048	.308
16 Mark Grace	7632	2343	.307
17 Bobby Abreu	2417	742	.307
18 Chipper Jones	4041	1240	.307
19 Roberto Alomar	7796	2389	.306
20 Moises Alou	4238	1297	.306
21 Rusty Greer	3630	1107	.305
22 Bernie Williams	5346	1629	.305
23 Ivan Rodriguez	5248	1595	.304
24 Jason Kendall	2900	881	.304
25 Jeff Bagwell	5949	1803	.303

On-Base Percentage
minimum 1000 PA

Player, Team	PA*	OB	OBP
1 Frank Thomas	6877	3014	.438
2 Edgar Martinez	7103	3022	.425
3 Barry Bonds	9801	4102	.419
4 Todd Helton	2743	1142	.416
5 Jeff Bagwell	7233	3004	.415
6 Jason Giambi	4081	1682	.412
7 Jim Thome	5109	2098	.411
8 Brian Giles	3018	1233	.409
9 Bobby Abreu	2865	1170	.408
10 Manny Ramirez	4713	1915	.406
11 Lance Berkman	1211	492	.406
12 John Olerud	7060	2853	.404
13 Rickey Henderson	13010	5234	.402
14 Chipper Jones	4746	1899	.400
15 Gary Sheffield	6769	2700	.399
16 Larry Walker	6223	2465	.396
17 Mark McGwire	7657	3018	.394
18 Derek Jeter	4223	1654	.392
19 Tim Salmon	5400	2112	.391
20 Mike Piazza	5193	2031	.391
21 Dave Magadan	4939	1927	.390
22 Bernie Williams	6165	2401	.389
23 Jason Kendall	3347	1301	.389
24 Rusty Greer	4195	1629	.388
25 Tony Gwynn	10187	3955	.388

* AB + BB + HBP + SF

Slugging Percentage
minimum 1000 PA

Player, Team	AB	TB	SLG
1 Todd Helton	2368	1472	.622
2 Manny Ramirez	3999	2375	.594
3 Mark McGwire	6187	3639	.588
4 Vladimir Guerrero	2755	1616	.587
5 Barry Bonds	7932	4639	.585
6 Mike Piazza	4638	2685	.579
7 Lance Berkman	1023	592	.579
8 Frank Thomas	5542	3198	.577
9 Larry Walker	5403	3091	.572
10 Alex Rodriguez	3758	2146	.571
11 Nomar Garciaparra	2519	1436	.570
12 Juan Gonzalez	5824	3308	.568
13 Ken Griffey Jr.	6716	3799	.566
14 Brian Giles	2513	1408	.560
15 Jim Thome	4160	2308	.555
16 Carlos Delgado	3475	1926	.554
17 Jeff Bagwell	5949	3296	.554
18 Chipper Jones	4041	2204	.545
19 Jason Giambi	3398	1851	.545
20 Sammy Sosa	6470	3505	.542
21 Edgar Martinez	5902	3129	.530
22 Richie Sexson	1799	947	.526
23 Ryan Klesko	3463	1822	.526
24 Moises Alou	4238	2221	.524
25 Bobby Abreu	2417	1261	.522

Hits

Cal Ripken Jr.	3184
Tony Gwynn	3141
Rickey Henderson	3000
Harold Baines	2866
Tim Raines	2588
Rafael Palmeiro	2485
Roberto Alomar	2389
Mark Grace	2343
Barry Bonds	2313
Tony Fernandez	2276
Fred McGriff	2260
Julio Franco	2204
Andres Galarraga	2172
Craig Biggio	2149
Paul O'Neill	2105
Wally Joyner	2060
Barry Larkin	2048
B.J. Surhoff	2026
Bobby Bonilla	2010
Ken Griffey Jr.	1987

Home Runs

Mark McGwire	583
Barry Bonds	567
Jose Canseco	462
Ken Griffey Jr.	460
Sammy Sosa	450
Fred McGriff	448
Rafael Palmeiro	447
Cal Ripken Jr.	431
Juan Gonzalez	397
Harold Baines	384
Andres Galarraga	377
Matt Williams	362
Jeff Bagwell	349
Frank Thomas	348
Greg Vaughn	344
Gary Sheffield	315
Mike Piazza	314
Ellis Burks	313
Jay Buhner	310
Larry Walker	309

Runs Batted In

Cal Ripken Jr.	1695
Harold Baines	1628
Barry Bonds	1542
Rafael Palmeiro	1470
Mark McGwire	1414
Jose Canseco	1407
Fred McGriff	1400
Andres Galarraga	1341
Ken Griffey Jr.	1335
Juan Gonzalez	1282
Paul O'Neill	1269
Sammy Sosa	1239
Jeff Bagwell	1223
Frank Thomas	1193
Bobby Bonilla	1173
Matt Williams	1162
Dante Bichette	1141
Tony Gwynn	1138
Ruben Sierra	1121
Wally Joyner	1106

Stolen Bases

Rickey Henderson	1395
Tim Raines	808
Barry Bonds	484
Kenny Lofton	479
Delino DeShields	453
Roberto Alomar	446
Marquis Grissom	409
Chuck Knoblauch	388
Eric Young	377
Craig Biggio	365
Barry Larkin	362
Eric Davis	349
Devon White	346
Tom Goodwin	329
Tony Gwynn	319
Brady Anderson	311
Omar Vizquel	273
Tony Womack	267
Steve Finley	265
Julio Franco	260

Seasons Played

Rickey Henderson	23
Harold Baines	22
Jesse Orosco	22
Tim Raines	22
Cal Ripken Jr.	21
Mike Morgan	21
Tony Gwynn	20
John Franco	18
Roger Clemens	18
8 tied with	17

Games

Cal Ripken Jr.	3001
Rickey Henderson	2979
Harold Baines	2830
Tony Gwynn	2440
Tim Raines	2404
Barry Bonds	2296
Rafael Palmeiro	2258
Fred McGriff	2201
Tony Fernandez	2158
Bobby Bonilla	2113

At-Bats

Cal Ripken Jr.	11551
Rickey Henderson	10710
Harold Baines	9908
Tony Gwynn	9288
Tim Raines	8783
Rafael Palmeiro	8446
Barry Bonds	7932
Tony Fernandez	7911
Fred McGriff	7865
Roberto Alomar	7796

Runs Scored

Rickey Henderson	2248
Barry Bonds	1713
Cal Ripken Jr.	1647
Tim Raines	1562
Tony Gwynn	1383
Rafael Palmeiro	1357
Roberto Alomar	1341
Craig Biggio	1305
Harold Baines	1299
Fred McGriff	1243

Doubles

Cal Ripken Jr.	603
Tony Gwynn	543
Rickey Henderson	503
Harold Baines	488
Rafael Palmeiro	488
Mark Grace	487
Barry Bonds	483
Paul O'Neill	451
Roberto Alomar	446
Edgar Martinez	443

Triples

Tim Raines	113
Steve Finley	94
Tony Fernandez	92
Tony Gwynn	85
Delino DeShields	73
Roberto Alomar	72
Dave Martinez	72
Barry Bonds	71
Devon White	71
Barry Larkin	70

AB per HR
minimum 1000 AB

Mark McGwire	10.6
Barry Bonds	14.0
Sammy Sosa	14.4
Manny Ramirez	14.4
Ken Griffey Jr.	14.6
Juan Gonzalez	14.7
Jim Thome	14.8
Mike Piazza	14.8
Carlos Delgado	15.2
Todd Helton	15.2

AB per RBI
minimum 1000 AB

Manny Ramirez	4.3
Mark McGwire	4.4
Juan Gonzalez	4.5
Todd Helton	4.6
Frank Thomas	4.6
Mike Piazza	4.8
Jeff Bagwell	4.9
Richie Sexson	4.9
Lance Berkman	4.9
Carlos Delgado	4.9

Total Bases

Cal Ripken Jr.	5168
Barry Bonds	4639
Harold Baines	4604
Rickey Henderson	4503
Rafael Palmeiro	4386
Tony Gwynn	4259
Fred McGriff	4045
Ken Griffey Jr.	3799
Andres Galarraga	3784
Tim Raines	3748

Walks

Rickey Henderson	2141
Barry Bonds	1724
Mark McGwire	1317
Tim Raines	1308
Fred McGriff	1202
Frank Thomas	1198
Cal Ripken Jr.	1129
Jeff Bagwell	1098
Edgar Martinez	1066
Harold Baines	1062

Intentional Walks

Barry Bonds	355
Tony Gwynn	203
Ken Griffey Jr.	193
Harold Baines	187
Fred McGriff	159
Frank Thomas	153
Mark McGwire	150
Tim Raines	144
John Olerud	138
Jeff Bagwell	137

Hit by Pitch

Craig Biggio	197
Andres Galarraga	166
Brady Anderson	152
Chuck Knoblauch	135
Jason Kendall	124
Fernando Vina	123
Jeff Bagwell	103
Larry Walker	103
Rickey Henderson	93
Damion Easley	92

Strikeouts

Jose Canseco	1942
Andres Galarraga	1858
Fred McGriff	1698
Sammy Sosa	1690
Rickey Henderson	1631
Mark McGwire	1596
Devon White	1526
Harold Baines	1441
Ray Lankford	1434
Greg Vaughn	1418

K/BB Ratio
minimum 1000 AB

Tony Gwynn	.549
Mark Grace	.589
Eric Young	.661
Frank Thomas	.707
Gary Sheffield	.723
Tim Raines	.724
Orlando Palmeiro	.743
Barry Bonds	.744
Dave Magadan	.760
Rickey Henderson	.762

Sacrifice Hits

Jay Bell	158
Omar Vizquel	153
Roberto Alomar	127
Greg Maddux	126
Darren Lewis	99
Mark McLemore	99
Mike Bordick	91
Jose Vizcaino	90
Rey Sanchez	78
Steve Finley	77

Sacrifice Flies

Cal Ripken Jr.	127
Ruben Sierra	107
Harold Baines	99
Bobby Bonilla	97
B.J. Surhoff	97
Mark Grace	93
Wally Joyner	91
Rafael Palmeiro	91
Frank Thomas	91
Paul O'Neill	90

SB Success %
minimum 100 SB attempts

Tony Womack	85.3
Tim Raines	84.7
Eric Davis	84.1
Pokey Reese	83.9
Barry Larkin	83.2
Stan Javier	82.8
Roberto Alomar	80.8
Rickey Henderson	80.7
Brian L. Hunter	80.7
Doug Glanville	80.6

Caught Stealing

Rickey Henderson	333
Delino DeShields	146
Tim Raines	146
Barry Bonds	138
Tony Fernandez	138
Eric Young	128
Tony Gwynn	125
Kenny Lofton	122
Chuck Knoblauch	114
Ray Lankford	113

GDP

Cal Ripken Jr.	350
Harold Baines	298
Tony Gwynn	260
Julio Franco	258
Paul O'Neill	221
Fred McGriff	205
Rafael Palmeiro	191
Mark Grace	181
Jose Canseco	178
Todd Zeile	177

AB per GDP
minimum 1000 AB

Greg Maddux	162.0
Tony Womack	128.1
Brady Anderson	107.0
Andy Fox	102.1
Roger Cedeno	101.2
Jose Valentin	100.4
Cristian Guzman	96.5
Marvin Benard	93.7
Johnny Damon	92.5
Tom Goodwin	92.3

2001 Active Career Pitching Leaders

Wins

Roger Clemens	**280**
Greg Maddux	257
Tom Glavine	224
Randy Johnson	200
David Cone	193
Chuck Finley	189
Kevin Brown	180
Bret Saberhagen	167
David Wells	166
Mike Mussina	164

Losses

Mike Morgan	**185**
Chuck Finley	158
Bobby Witt	157
Greg Maddux	146
Roger Clemens	145
Andy Benes	135
Tom Glavine	132
Terry Mulholland	125
Kevin Tapani	125
David Cone	123

Winning Percentage
minimum 100 decisions

Pedro Martinez	**.691**
Randy Johnson	.664
Roger Clemens	.659
Mike Mussina	.641
Andy Pettitte	.639
Greg Maddux	.638
Tom Glavine	.629
Bartolo Colon	.613
Kirk Rueter	.613
Aaron Sele	.611

ERA
minimum 750 IP

Pedro Martinez	**2.66**
John Franco	2.75
Greg Maddux	2.84
Jesse Orosco	3.04
Roger Clemens	3.10
Randy Johnson	3.13
Jose Rijo	3.15
Kevin Brown	3.18
Bret Saberhagen	3.34
John Smoltz	3.35

Games

Jesse Orosco	**1131**
John Franco	998
Dan Plesac	946
Mike Jackson	902
Mike Stanton	756
Chuck McElroy	654
Roberto Hernandez	643
Rod Beck	642
Jeff Shaw	633
Mark Guthrie	632

Games Started

Roger Clemens	**544**
Greg Maddux	501
Tom Glavine	469
Chuck Finley	435
David Cone	415
Mike Morgan	411
Kevin Brown	399
Bobby Witt	397
Randy Johnson	391
Bret Saberhagen	371

Innings Pitched

Roger Clemens	**3887.0**
Greg Maddux	3551.0
Tom Glavine	3120.0
Chuck Finley	3006.2
David Cone	2880.2
Kevin Brown	2776.1
Randy Johnson	2748.1
Mike Morgan	2738.1
Bret Saberhagen	2562.2
John Smoltz	2473.1

Batters Faced

Roger Clemens	**16007**
Greg Maddux	14396
Tom Glavine	13094
Chuck Finley	12829
David Cone	12099
Mike Morgan	11716
Kevin Brown	11511
Randy Johnson	11376
Bobby Witt	11003
Bret Saberhagen	10421

Complete Games

Roger Clemens	**116**
Greg Maddux	102
Randy Johnson	79
Bret Saberhagen	76
Kevin Brown	72
Curt Schilling	71
Chuck Finley	61
David Cone	56
Tom Glavine	50
Mike Mussina	49

Complete Game %
minimum 100 GS

Curt Schilling	**0.25**
Roger Clemens	0.21
Bret Saberhagen	0.20
Greg Maddux	0.20
Randy Johnson	0.20
Kevin Brown	0.18
Pedro Martinez	0.16
Mike Mussina	0.15
Greg Swindell	0.15
Terry Mulholland	0.15

Shutouts

Roger Clemens	**45**
Greg Maddux	34
Randy Johnson	30
David Cone	22
Tom Glavine	21
Ramon Martinez	20
Mike Mussina	18
Kevin Brown	17
Bret Saberhagen	16
Curt Schilling	16

Quality Start %*
minimum 100 GS

Pedro Martinez	**70.7**
Greg Maddux	70.2
Randy Johnson	68.5
Kevin Brown	67.6
Roger Clemens	67.2
Curt Schilling	67.0
Tom Glavine	64.6
Jose Rijo	64.5
Mike Mussina	64.3
Chan Ho Park	63.1

*since 1987

Strikeouts

Roger Clemens	**3717**
Randy Johnson	3412
David Cone	2655
Greg Maddux	2523
Chuck Finley	2436
John Smoltz	2155
Curt Schilling	2032
Kevin Brown	2021
Pedro Martinez	1981
Bobby Witt	1955

Walks Allowed

Bobby Witt	**1375**
Roger Clemens	1258
Chuck Finley	1254
Randy Johnson	1160
David Cone	1124
Tom Glavine	1062
Mike Morgan	929
Darryl Kile	890
Andy Benes	858
Ken Hill	852

Strikeouts/9 IP
minimum 750 IP

Randy Johnson	**11.17**
Pedro Martinez	10.53
Hideo Nomo	9.56
Arthur Rhodes	8.76
Dan Plesac	8.65
Roger Clemens	8.61
Curt Schilling	8.47
Chan Ho Park	8.35
David Cone	8.29
Jesse Orosco	8.22

Walks per 9 Innings
minimum 750 IP

Bret Saberhagen	**1.65**
Rick Reed	1.69
Brad Radke	1.85
Brian Anderson	1.85
Greg Maddux	1.93
Shane Reynolds	1.93
Jon Lieber	1.97
Rheal Cormier	2.01
Jose Lima	2.03
Greg Swindell	2.03

K/BB Ratio	
minimum 750 IP	
Pedro Martinez	4.24
Shane Reynolds	3.80
Curt Schilling	3.78
Bret Saberhagen	3.64
Jon Lieber	3.46
Mike Mussina	3.44
Rick Reed	3.38
Greg Maddux	3.32
Greg Swindell	3.06
Jose Lima	3.03

Hits per 9 Innings	
Pedro Martinez	6.71
Randy Johnson	6.92
Mike Jackson	7.20
Jesse Orosco	7.22
Chan Ho Park	7.61
Roger Clemens	7.65
Hideo Nomo	7.75
David Cone	7.76
John Smoltz	7.81
Jeff Brantley	7.90

Baserunners/9 IP	
minimum 750 IP	
Pedro Martinez	9.59
Greg Maddux	10.30
Curt Schilling	10.40
Bret Saberhagen	10.47
Mike Mussina	10.58
John Smoltz	10.80
Roger Clemens	10.87
Randy Johnson	11.13
Rick Reed	11.17
Mike Jackson	11.21

Home Runs/9 IP	
minimum 750 IP	
Greg Maddux	0.50
John Franco	0.55
Kevin Brown	0.55
Bob Wickman	0.63
Hipolito Pichardo	0.63
Roger Clemens	0.65
Tom Glavine	0.65
Jose Rijo	0.67
Shawn Estes	0.67
Pedro Martinez	0.69

Opposition AVG*	
minimum 750 IP	
Pedro Martinez	.206
Randy Johnson	.212
Mike Jackson	.219
Roger Clemens	.229
Chan Ho Park	.230
David Cone	.231
Hideo Nomo	.231
John Smoltz	.233
Jeff Brantley	.237
Arthur Rhodes	.238
*since 1987	

Opposition OBP*	
minimum 750 IP	
Pedro Martinez	.269
Greg Maddux	.285
Curt Schilling	.287
Bret Saberhagen	.290
Mike Mussina	.291
John Smoltz	.295
Roger Clemens	.297
Jose Rijo	.300
Randy Johnson	.301
Kevin Millwood	.301
*since 1987	

Opposition SLG*	
minimum 750 IP	
Pedro Martinez	.316
Greg Maddux	.332
Randy Johnson	.332
John Franco	.339
Roger Clemens	.339
Kevin Brown	.342
Jose Rijo	.346
Mike Jackson	.349
Norm Charlton	.355
John Smoltz	.355
*since 1987	

Home Runs Allowed	
Chuck Finley	291
David Wells	285
Andy Benes	279
Roger Clemens	279
Jamie Moyer	267
Mike Morgan	263
Kevin Tapani	260
David Cone	254
Greg Swindell	253
Bobby Witt	252

Hit Batsmen	
Roger Clemens	129
Randy Johnson	125
Kevin Brown	119
Darryl Kile	109
David Cone	106
Greg Maddux	97
Pedro Astacio	89
Tim Wakefield	88
Omar Olivares	80
Aaron Sele	79

Wild Pitches	
David Cone	149
Bobby Witt	128
Chuck Finley	127
John Smoltz	119
Roger Clemens	106
Mike Morgan	102
Darryl Kile	97
Flash Gordon	93
Kevin Appier	91
Kevin Brown	89

GDP Induced*	
Greg Maddux	291
Tom Glavine	291
Chuck Finley	285
Kevin Brown	280
Mike Morgan	258
Roger Clemens	242
Bobby Witt	209
Terry Mulholland	208
Kenny Rogers	205
Omar Olivares	195
*since 1987	

GDP/9 IP*	
minimum 750 IP	
Jamey Wright	1.25
Bob Wickman	1.18
Mike Hampton	1.16
Shawn Estes	1.15
Andy Pettitte	1.11
Omar Olivares	1.10
Hipolito Pichardo	1.10
Mike Morgan	1.04
Pat Rapp	1.01
Joey Hamilton	0.99
*since 1987	

Saves	
John Franco	422
Trevor Hoffman	314
Roberto Hernandez	294
Robb Nen	271
Rod Beck	266
Gregg Olson	217
Mariano Rivera	215
Troy Percival	210
Jeff Shaw	203
Todd Jones	183

Save %	
minimum 50 SvOp	
Kazuhiro Sasaki	89.1
Trevor Hoffman	88.5
Mariano Rivera	86.3
Kerry Ligtenberg	86.3
Armando Benitez	86.1
Jose Mesa	85.7
Robb Nen	85.5
Billy Koch	85.5
Troy Percival	85.0
Keith Foulke	84.8

Games Finished	
John Franco	741
Roberto Hernandez	543
Robb Nen	483
Jesse Orosco	480
Rod Beck	479
Trevor Hoffman	468
Gregg Olson	447
Dan Plesac	405
Mike Jackson	393
Jeff Shaw	384

SB % Allowed*	
minimum 750 IP	
Kirk Rueter	35.0
Terry Mulholland	37.3
Omar Daal	41.1
Kenny Rogers	41.7
Chris Carpenter	41.8
Chan Ho Park	47.5
Greg Swindell	52.0
Rick Helling	53.2
Curt Schilling	53.3
Livan Hernandez	53.4
*since 1987	

Player Profiles

Breaking down great seasons is an entertaining way to pass some of the offseason. Three of the top performers during the 2001 campaign were a trio of southpaws: Barry Bonds, Jason Giambi and Randy Johnson. The player profiles that follow come directly from the *Major League Handbook's* companion volume, *STATS Player Profiles*, which contains breakdowns like these for every 2001 major leaguer. Below are just a few of the breakdowns that our profiles feature.

For starters, Bonds and Giambi had a lot more in common than their handedness and their pending free agency last summer. When they put the ball in play while ahead in the count, both were .400 hitters. Giambi posted a .629 on-base percentage in those situations; Bonds slugged at a scalding 1.099 clip when the count was in his favor.

Both hitters were outstanding second-half performers. Giambi batted .367 in the second half—45 points higher than he did before the All-Star break—as he led Oakland during its incredible second-half surge to the American League wild-card berth. He also slugged nearly 100 points higher during the second half, further establishing himself as a tremendous hitter who takes his game to another level down the stretch. His five-year splits prove it.

Bonds was Superman in the final weeks of the season. And while National League pitchers were working around him and issuing loads of free passes, Bonds still finished with a fantastic flurry. His best monthly hitting percentages over the entire season were generated in September/October: a .403 average, .600 OBP and 1.078 slugging mark. It's incredible to see his profile littered with slugging percentages in the .800s and .900s.

If you asked Giambi and Bonds for a short list of pitchers they would prefer to never face, both might include Johnson. The Big Unit was strong from start to finish in 2001, consistently working 40-45 innings and fanning 60 or more batters each month as he chased Nolan Ryan's single-season record for strikeouts. Johnson's 372 strikeouts fell short of Ryan's mark by 11, but the southpaw sure turned up the heat as the season wore on. He went 10-1 in the second half, posting a 2.23 ERA that nearly was a half-run lower than his 2.71 ERA before the All-Star break.

Another impressive number in Johnson's profile is his stingy .203 average allowed to opponents. Hitters batted an even .200 against him in the second half, and he has several breakdowns for which the average against him was below .200. His opponents could do no better than .192 against him in his first 75 pitches of the night. They batted .194 through the first six innings. When hitters put the ball in play when they were behind in the count, they batted .143. With runners in scoring position, the mark was .178. Lefties have hit .192 against him over the last five years.

Perfiles de Jugadores

Los tres mejores ejecutantes de la temporada del 2001 fueron los zurdos Barry Bonds, Jason Giambi y Randy Johnson. Los Perfiles de Jugadores proveen más datos sobre éstos jugadores. Aquí continuan unos perfiles. El libro compañero del *Major League Handbook's*, *STATS Player Profiles*, tiene los perfiles de todos los peloteros que jugaron en las Grandes Ligas en el 2001.

Por ejemplo, Bonds y Giambi tienen mucho en común. Cuando batearon cuando la cuenta les favorecía, los dos tuvieron un promedio de .400. Giambi tuvo un promedio de embasamiento de .629 en esa situación; Bonds tuvo un promedio de bases acumuladas de 1.099 cuando la cuenta estaba en su favor.

Los dos bateadores fueron impresionantes en la segunda mitad de la temporada. Giambi bateó .367—45 puntos más que en la primera mitad—empujando a Oakland a los playoffs. Y Giambi ha hecho lo mismo las últimas cinco temporadas.

Si le preguntan a Giambi y a Bonds que lanzadores les dan problemas, los dos pueden incluir Randy Johnson. Johnson tuvo 372 ponches, faltandole 11 ponches para igualar el record de ponches en una temporada por Nolan Ryan. Johnson terminó 10-1 en la segunda mitad con una efectividad de 2.23.

Otro número mortífero en el perfil de Johnson es el .203 promedio de bateo que le permitió a sus oponentes. Peloteros batearon solo .192 en contra sus primeros 75 lanzamientos de cada juego abierto. Cuando la cuenta le favorecía a Johnson, le bateaban solo .143. Con corredores en posición de anotar, le batearon .178. Zurdos batearon .192 contra Johnson en los últimos cinco años.

#P/PA = Lanzamientos/Veces-al-Bate; **#P/S** = Lanzamientos por Juego Abierto; **#Pit** = Lanzamientos Observados; **...Days Rest** = Días de Descanso (abridores); **1st Inning Pitched** = 1ra Entrada Lanzada; **Ahead in Count** = Ventaja en la Cuenta; **As...** = Jugando como...; **Away** = Visita; **Batting #...** = Bateando #... en la alineación; **Behind in Count** = Detrás en la Cuenta; **By Position** = Desglose por Posición; **Career** = Carrera; **CG** = J.Completos; **Close & Late** = Tarde & Reñido; **Day** = Día; **FB** = Elevados; **First 75 Pitches** = 1eros 75 Lanzamientos; **First Pitch** = 1er Lanzamiento; **Flyball** = Elevado; **G/F** = Arranque/Elevados; **GB** = Arranques; **Grass** = Grama Natural; **Groundball** = de Arranque; **Home** = Local; **Inning** = Entrada; **L** = Derr.; **Last Five Years** = Ultimos 5 Años; **Night** = Noche; **None on/out** = Sin Embasados/Outs; **None on** = Sin Embasados; **Other** = Otro; **Post-All Star** = Después del Juego de Estrellas; **Pre-All Star** = Antes del Juego de Estrellas; **QS** = Abiertos de Calidad; **Reliever** = Relevista; **Runners on** = Con Embasados; **Scoring Posn** = Embasados en Posición de Anotar; **Season** = Temporada; **ShO** = Blanqueadas; **Starter** = Abridor; **Sup** = Carreras de Soporte; **Turf** = Grama Artificial; **Two Strikes** = 2 Strikes; **vs 1st Batr (relief)** = Contra 1er Bateador (relevo); **vs Left** = vs Zurdo; **vs Right** = vs Derecho; **W** = Vict.

Barry Bonds — Giants
Age 37 – Bats Left (flyball hitter)

	Avg	G	AB	R	H	2B	3B	HR	RBI	BB	SO	HBP	GDP	SB	CS	OBP	SLG	IBB	SH	SF	#Pit	#P/PA	GB	FB	G/F
2001 Season	.328	153	476	129	156	32	2	73	137	177	93	9	5	13	3	.515	.863	35	0	2	2552	3.84	115	207	0.56
Last Five Years	.300	713	2395	592	718	150	20	233	549	642	411	31	45	104	28	.450	.671	129	1	23	11655	3.77	642	1020	0.63

2001 Season

	Avg	AB	H	2B	3B	HR	RBI	BB	SO	OBP	SLG		Avg	AB	H	2B	3B	HR	RBI	BB	SO	OBP	SLG
vs. Left	.312	141	44	9	1	17	34	44	34	.487	.752	First Pitch	.385	78	30	5	0	11	28	28	0	.542	.872
vs. Right	.334	335	112	23	1	56	103	133	59	.526	.910	Ahead in Count	.401	152	61	12	2	30	47	88	0	.627	1.099
Home	.335	224	75	19	0	37	71	80	46	.516	.915	Behind in Count	.233	133	31	7	0	15	30	0	61	.255	.624
Away	.321	252	81	13	2	36	66	97	47	.514	.817	Two Strikes	.200	180	36	6	0	16	33	61	93	.407	.500
Day	.320	153	49	15	0	26	48	42	32	.472	.928	Batting #3	.325	440	143	32	2	66	124	163	82	.513	.857
Night	.331	323	107	17	2	47	89	135	61	.533	.833	Batting #4	.344	32	11	0	0	6	12	13	10	.532	.906
Grass	.329	465	153	32	2	71	134	169	88	.512	.865	Other	.500	4	2	0	0	1	1	1	1	.600	1.250
Turf	.273	11	3	0	0	2	3	8	5	.600	.818	April	.240	75	18	5	0	11	22	13	15	.363	.747
Pre-All Star	.305	259	79	18	0	39	73	88	55	.487	.826	May	.369	84	31	5	0	17	30	31	24	.547	1.036
Post-All Star	.355	217	77	14	2	34	64	89	38	.547	.908	June	.297	74	22	3	0	11	19	34	15	.514	.784
Inning 1-6	.343	327	112	24	2	53	102	128	60	.530	.914	July	.302	86	26	10	1	6	15	30	11	.492	.651
Inning 7+	.295	149	44	8	0	20	35	49	33	.480	.752	August	.350	80	28	5	1	12	26	31	17	.536	.888
Scoring Posn	.382	89	34	11	0	13	59	71	20	.650	.944	Sept/Oct	.403	77	31	4	0	16	25	38	11	.600	1.078
Close & Late	.314	70	22	6	0	10	14	33	21	.547	.829	vs. AL	.271	48	13	2	0	5	6	16	10	.453	.625
None on/out	.340	94	32	7	1	17	17	20	15	.461	.979	vs. NL	.334	428	143	30	2	68	131	161	83	.522	.890

2001 By Position

Position	Avg	AB	H	2B	3B	HR	RBI	BB	SO	OBP	SLG	G	GS	Innings	PO	A	E	DP	Fld Pct	Rng Fctr	In Zone	Outs	Zone Rtg	MLB Zone
As lf	.333	454	151	31	2	71	135	168	86	.518	.879	143	141	1231.2	246	9	6	1	.977	1.86	267	244	.914	.880

Last Five Years

	Avg	AB	H	2B	3B	HR	RBI	BB	SO	OBP	SLG		Avg	AB	H	2B	3B	HR	RBI	BB	SO	OBP	SLG
vs. Left	.277	751	208	41	4	61	154	164	142	.412	.586	First Pitch	.377	371	140	29	3	40	108	97	0	.515	.795
vs. Right	.310	1644	510	109	16	172	395	478	269	.467	.710	Ahead in Count	.383	708	271	57	7	92	211	336	0	.580	.873
Home	.315	1151	362	77	11	123	297	300	201	.460	.721	Behind in Count	.205	774	159	37	6	47	119	0	294	.214	.451
Away	.286	1244	356	73	9	110	252	342	210	.441	.625	Two Strikes	.185	949	176	36	7	56	130	208	411	.335	.415
Day	.283	969	274	65	9	91	224	227	187	.422	.650	Batting #3	.300	2045	614	135	17	200	461	557	347	.452	.676
Night	.311	1426	444	85	11	142	325	415	224	.468	.685	Batting #4	.298	326	97	13	3	30	77	76	61	.434	.632
Grass	.301	2152	648	133	16	213	496	558	359	.447	.675	Other	.292	24	7	2	0	3	11	9	3	.485	.750
Turf	.288	243	70	17	4	20	53	84	52	.478	.638	March/April	.270	370	100	24	2	33	79	89	52	.415	.614
Pre-All Star	.290	1207	350	72	8	114	262	317	204	.441	.646	May	.341	349	119	23	2	41	95	96	72	.481	.771
Post-All Star	.310	1188	368	78	12	119	287	325	207	.459	.696	June	.275	404	111	18	2	35	75	111	68	.436	.589
Inning 1-6	.308	1702	524	108	17	177	427	441	274	.451	.703	July	.275	397	109	31	4	31	90	97	78	.423	.607
Inning 7+	.280	693	194	42	3	56	122	201	137	.447	.592	August	.316	459	145	28	3	47	112	128	82	.466	.697
Scoring Posn	.295	572	169	39	5	43	294	265	113	.510	.607	Sept/Oct	.322	416	134	26	7	46	98	121	59	.473	.750
Close & Late	.290	348	101	23	2	25	63	129	73	.485	.583	vs. AL	.284	229	65	13	1	21	39	60	45	.441	.624
None on/out	.274	467	128	36	4	49	49	81	77	.386	.683	vs. NL	.301	2166	653	137	19	212	510	582	366	.451	.676

Jason Giambi — Athletics
Age 31 – Bats Left (flyball hitter)

	Avg	G	AB	R	H	2B	3B	HR	RBI	BB	SO	HBP	GDP	SB	CS	OBP	SLG	IBB	SH	SF	#Pit	#P/PA	GB	FB	G/F
2001 Season	.342	154	520	109	178	47	2	38	120	129	83	13	17	2	0	.477	.660	24	0	9	2643	3.94	147	198	0.74
Last Five Years	.315	759	2686	490	847	181	6	161	571	507	476	40	64	7	4	.426	.567	46	0	42	13084	4.00	757	988	0.77

2001 Season

	Avg	AB	H	2B	3B	HR	RBI	BB	SO	OBP	SLG		Avg	AB	H	2B	3B	HR	RBI	BB	SO	OBP	SLG
vs. Left	.333	189	63	11	1	11	40	33	31	.451	.577	First Pitch	.500	50	25	6	0	7	16	20	0	.649	1.040
vs. Right	.347	331	115	36	1	27	80	96	52	.491	.707	Ahead in Count	.404	114	46	13	1	11	39	74	0	.629	.825
Home	.349	258	90	17	0	27	61	57	37	.474	.729	Behind in Count	.278	241	67	15	1	12	39	0	66	.291	.498
Away	.336	262	88	30	2	11	59	72	46	.480	.592	Two Strikes	.271	255	69	17	1	14	42	35	83	.361	.510
Day	.317	199	63	15	0	18	42	36	31	.426	.663	Batting #3	.352	455	160	43	1	36	112	123	71	.492	.688
Night	.358	321	115	32	2	20	78	93	52	.505	.657	Batting #4	.277	65	18	4	1	2	8	6	12	.356	.462
Grass	.335	463	155	39	2	37	111	117	75	.475	.667	Other	.000	0	0	0	0	0	0	0	0	.000	.000
Turf	.404	57	23	8	0	1	9	12	8	.493	.596	April	.350	80	28	7	0	6	19	26	15	.518	.663
Pre-All Star	.322	283	91	25	1	19	60	71	49	.463	.618	May	.384	99	38	11	0	7	25	24	15	.504	.707
Post-All Star	.367	237	87	22	1	19	60	58	34	.493	.709	June	.262	84	22	6	1	6	16	21	15	.420	.571
Inning 1-6	.345	368	127	30	2	28	96	93	54	.480	.666	July	.300	90	27	6	1	5	16	10	14	.382	.556
Inning 7+	.336	152	51	17	0	10	24	36	29	.469	.645	August	.370	92	34	8	0	8	25	29	12	.520	.717
Scoring Posn	.354	113	40	12	0	7	72	51	14	.531	.646	Sept/Oct	.387	75	29	9	0	6	19	19	12	.505	.747
Close & Late	.355	76	27	8	0	5	15	16	18	.443	.658	vs. AL	.349	458	160	44	1	33	108	122	69	.491	.666
None on/out	.310	100	31	9	1	7	7	11	13	.389	.630	vs. NL	.290	62	18	3	1	5	12	7	14	.361	.613

2001 By Position

Position	Avg	AB	H	2B	3B	HR	RBI	BB	SO	OBP	SLG	G	GS	Innings	PO	A	E	DP	Fld Pct	Rng Fctr	In Zone	Outs	Zone Rtg	MLB Zone
As DH	.316	57	18	6	0	6	12	12	9	.443	.737	17	17	—	—	—	—	—	—	—	—	—	—	—
As 1b	.346	462	160	41	2	32	108	117	74	.482	.652	136	136	1176.1	1224	76	11	107	.992	—	232	203	.875	.850

Last Five Years

	Avg	AB	H	2B	3B	HR	RBI	BB	SO	OBP	SLG
vs. Left	.298	878	262	49	1	40	165	133	164	.401	.493
vs. Right	.324	1808	585	132	5	121	406	374	312	.437	.603
Home	.329	1324	435	81	3	93	287	246	232	.438	.605
Away	.302	1362	412	100	3	68	284	261	244	.413	.530
Day	.320	1054	337	72	2	74	233	178	176	.418	.602
Night	.313	1632	510	109	4	87	338	329	300	.431	.544
Grass	.312	2365	738	154	6	144	497	452	426	.425	.565
Turf	.340	321	109	27	0	17	74	55	50	.430	.583
Pre-All Star	.303	1438	435	96	3	78	284	266	260	.413	.536
Post-All Star	.330	1248	412	85	3	83	287	241	216	.440	.603
Inning 1-6	.318	1904	605	136	5	119	435	344	330	.423	.582
Inning 7+	.309	782	242	45	1	42	136	163	146	.432	.531
Scoring Posn	.319	686	219	47	0	48	396	185	147	.450	.598
Close & Late	.319	345	110	13	0	18	63	72	66	.443	.513
None on/out	.311	562	175	38	1	34	34	71	80	.393	.564

	Avg	AB	H	2B	3B	HR	RBI	BB	SO	OBP	SLG
First Pitch	.420	286	120	24	0	25	81	37	0	.493	.766
Ahead in Count	.396	626	248	61	1	54	183	286	0	.577	.756
Behind in Count	.244	1181	288	47	3	45	176	0	381	.252	.403
Two Strikes	.231	1297	300	56	4	54	192	184	476	.330	.406
Batting #3	.326	1651	539	110	4	110	375	375	298	.453	.598
Batting #5	.288	545	157	33	0	29	105	72	101	.371	.508
Other	.308	490	151	38	2	29	61	60	77	.386	.529
March/April	.305	439	134	21	1	29	98	72	81	.402	.556
May	.304	474	144	35	1	21	92	97	80	.423	.515
June	.314	408	128	37	1	24	82	82	76	.435	.586
July	.300	456	137	27	2	24	84	74	80	.399	.526
August	.318	453	144	34	0	27	103	99	72	.444	.572
Sept/Oct	.351	456	160	27	1	36	112	83	87	.447	.651
vs. AL	.318	2387	760	157	5	144	511	455	423	.429	.569
vs. NL	.291	299	87	24	1	17	60	52	53	.396	.548

Randy Johnson — Diamondbacks

Age 38 – Pitches Left

	ERA	W	L	Sv	G	GS	IP	BB	SO	Avg	H	2B	3B	HR	RBI	OBP	SLG	CG	ShO	Sup	QS	#P/S	SB	CS	GB	FB	G/F
2001 Season	2.49	21	6	0	35	34	249.2	71	372	.203	181	33	2	19	64	.274	.309	3	2	5.34	27	117	19	15	223	188	1.19
Last Five Years	2.64	96	37	0	169	167	1227.1	380	1703	.211	940	176	10	115	371	.281	.333	38	15	5.04	125	118	131	83	1198	1004	1.19

2001 Season

	ERA	W	L	Sv	G	GS	IP	H	HR	BB	SO
Home	2.54				18	18	131.1	99	10	31	192
Away	2.43	9	3	0	17	16	118.1	82	9	40	180
Day	2.92	5	2	0	11	11	74.0	58	7	29	115
Night	2.31	16	4	0	24	23	175.2	123	12	42	257
Grass	2.52	21	6	0	34	33	242.2	179	18	67	361
Turf	1.29	0	0	0	1	1	7.0	2	1	4	11
April	4.03	3	3	0	6	6	44.2	38	7	11	61
May	1.54	2	1	0	6	6	41.0	21	1	16	62
June	2.41	5	1	0	6	6	41.0	35	4	13	66
July	2.04	3	0	0	5	4	35.1	20	3	8	62
August	1.81	5	1	0	6	6	44.2	33	1	10	61
Sept/Oct	2.93	3	0	0	6	6	43.0	34	3	13	60
Starter	2.56	20	6	0	34	34	242.2	180	19	70	356
Reliever	0.00	1	0	0	1	0	7.0	1	0	1	16
0-3 Days Rest (Start)	0.00	0	0	0	0	0	0.0	0	0	0	0
4 Days Rest	2.61	15	6	0	28	28	200.1	147	17	57	294
5+ Days Rest	2.34	5	0	0	6	6	42.1	33	2	13	62
vs. AL	3.21	1	0	0	2	2	14.0	14	1	3	18
vs. NL	2.44	20	6	0	33	32	235.2	167	18	68	354
Pre-All Star	2.71	11	5	0	19	19	132.2	98	13	42	202
Post-All Star	2.23	10	1	0	16	15	117.0	83	6	29	170

	Avg	AB	H	2B	3B	HR	RBI	BB	SO	OBP	SLG
vs. Left	.196	107	21	5	0	1	13	9	32	.306	.271
vs. Right	.204	783	160	28	2	18	51	62	340	.270	.314
Inning 1-6	.194	726	141	28	2	14	49	56	309	.265	.296
Inning 7+	.244	164	40	5	0	5	15	15	63	.315	.366
None on	.202	555	112	17	2	14		43	237	.275	.315
Runners on	.206	335	69	16	0	5	50	28	135	.273	.299
Scoring Posn	.178	180	32	10	0	2	43	20	90	.264	.267
Close & Late	.214	84	18	2	0	4	11	9	36	.299	.384
None on/out	.205	239	49	9	1	8	8	19	107	.278	.351
vs. 1st Batr (relief)	.000	1	0	0	0	0	0	0	1	.000	.000
1st Inning Pitched	.242	128	31	8	0	2	7	14	47	.324	.352
First 75 Pitches	.192	558	107	22	1	12	32	41	238	.258	.299
Pitch 76-90	.221	113	25	4	0	0	8	6	48	.273	.257
Pitch 91-105	.223	103	23	4	1	3	9	12	36	.319	.369
Pitch 106+	.224	116	26	3	0	4	15	12	50	.311	.353
First Pitch	.330	91	30	5	0	3	9	1	0	.361	.484
Ahead in Count	.143	526	75	11	1	6	26	0	316	.158	.202
Behind in Count	.336	122	41	6	0	6	16	33	0	.478	.533
Two Strikes	.139	575	80	15	2	7	26	37	372	.203	.209
Pre-All Star	.206	476	98	16	0	13	38	42	202	.284	.321
Post-All Star	.200	414	83	17	2	6	26	29	170	.264	.295

Last Five Years

	ERA	W	L	Sv	G	GS	IP	H	HR	BB	SO
Home	2.59	52	17	0	86	85	635.1	490	55	182	900
Away	2.69	44	20	0	83	82	592.0	450	60	198	803
Day	2.93	27	8	0	53	52	378.0	280	34	149	558
Night	2.51	69	29	0	116	115	849.1	660	81	231	1145
Grass	2.79	68	28	0	121	120	870.2	681	89	272	1200
Turf	2.27	28	9	0	48	47	356.2	259	26	108	503
March/April	3.26	15	5	0	29	29	204.1	153	24	70	275
May	2.77	17	6	0	30	30	218.0	165	19	67	293
June	2.55	17	10	0	29	29	215.2	167	21	61	308
July	2.64	13	8	0	27	26	204.1	152	20	67	297
August	1.89	18	6	0	28	28	204.2	151	12	59	245
Sept/Oct	2.74	16	2	0	26	25	180.1	152	19	56	250
Starter	2.66	94	37	0	167	167	1218.1	937	115	379	1684
Reliever	0.00	2	0	0	2	0	9.0	3	0	1	19
0-3 Days Rest (Start)	0.00	0	0	0	0	0	0.0	0	0	0	0
4 Days Rest	2.60	72	27	0	126	126	921.2	708	81	287	1269
5+ Days Rest	2.85	22	10	0	41	41	296.2	229	34	92	415
vs. AL	3.13	29	13	0	55	54	385.1	305	38	141	529
vs. NL	2.42	67	24	0	114	113	842.0	635	77	239	1174
Pre-All Star	2.91	53	24	0	95	95	687.0	520	73	219	949
Post-All Star	2.30	43	13	0	74	72	540.1	420	42	161	754

	Avg	AB	H	2B	3B	HR	RBI	BB	SO	OBP	SLG
vs. Left	.192	437	84	13	1	5	32	41	166	.290	.261
vs. Right	.213	4011	856	163	9	110	339	339	1537	.280	.341
Inning 1-6	.207	3537	731	152	7	92	299	302	1385	.277	.332
Inning 7+	.229	911	209	24	3	23	72	78	318	.298	.338
None on	.212	2754	583	107	5	72	72	242	1059	.283	.333
Runners on	.211	1694	357	69	5	43	299	138	644	.278	.334
Scoring Posn	.200	942	188	42	3	26	251	78	399	.269	.333
Close & Late	.239	524	125	17	2	14	48	43	192	.304	.359
None on/out	.206	1167	240	52	1	32	32	100	440	.276	.334
vs. 1st Batr (relief)	.000	2	0	0	0	0	0	0	2	.000	.000
1st Inning Pitched	.219	612	134	35	1	18	50	61	245	.294	.368
First 75 Pitches	.200	2706	540	116	5	63	192	225	1071	.267	.316
Pitch 76-90	.216	550	119	23	1	13	48	42	209	.283	.333
Pitch 91-105	.243	527	128	20	1	19	61	51	177	.319	.393
Pitch 106+	.230	665	153	17	3	20	70	62	246	.306	.355
First Pitch	.345	449	155	28	3	20	66	7	0	.368	.555
Ahead in Count	.145	2587	374	70	4	41	143	0	1463	.155	.222
Behind in Count	.338	707	239	51	1	37	105	206	0	.487	.570
Two Strikes	.134	2723	366	70	5	39	138	167	1703	.192	.207
Pre-All Star	.210	2477	520	97	5	73	224	219	949	.283	.342
Post-All Star	.213	1971	420	79	5	42	147	161	754	.278	.322

2001 Manager Tendencies

One of the things about baseball which appeals to many of us is the game's endless opportunity for analysis. . . and few things are analyzed more than managerial decisions. Major league skippers may not have batting averages and slugging percentages to point to at the end of the season, but when it comes time to judge their performance and production, there's no reason we can't take a look at their statistics.

Which manager posted the best stolen-base success rate?

Which skippers were constantly tinkering with their lineups?

Which managers wore out a path to the pitching mound?

It's questions like these that get our second-guessing juices going, and it's questions like these that inspired the following pages, which look at managerial tendencies in a number of situations. Once again, the skippers are compared based on offense, defense, lineups and pitching use. We don't rank the managers; there is plenty of room for argument on whether certain moves are good or bad. We are simply providing fodder for the discussion.

Offensively, managers have control over bunting, stealing and the timing of hit-and-runs. The *Handbook* looks at the quantity, timing and success of these moves.

Defensively, the *Handbook* looks at the success of pitchouts, the frequency of intentional walks, and the pattern of defensive substitutions.

Most managers spend large amounts of their time devising lineups. The *Handbook* shows the number of lineups used, as well as the platoon percentage. The use of pinch-hitters and pinch-runners also is explored.

Finally, how does the manager use pitchers? For starters, the *Handbook* shows slow and quick hooks, along with the number of times a starter was allowed to throw more than 120 and 140 pitches. For relievers, we look at the number of relief appearances, mid-inning changes and how often a pitcher gets a save going more than one inning (a rare occurrence these days).

For the purposes of this section, it is assumed that a coach filling in for his manager will make his decisions based on what the manager would do in a given situation.

The categories include:

Stolen Base Success Percentage: Stolen bases divided by attempts.

Pitchout Runners Moving: The number of times the opposition is running when a manager calls a pitchout.

Double Steals: The number of double steals attempted in 2001.

Out Percentage: The proportion of stolen bases with that number of outs.

Sacrifice Bunt Attempts: A bunt is considered a sac attempt if no runner is on third, there are no outs, or the pitcher attempts a bunt.

Sacrifice Bunt Success%: A bunt that results in a sacrifice or a hit, divided by the number of attempts.

Favorite Inning: The most common inning in which an event occurred.

Hit-and-Run Success: The hit-and-run results in baserunner advancement with no double play.

Intentional Walk Situation: Runners on base, first base open, and anyone but the pitcher up. The teams must be within two runs of each other, or the tying run must be on base, at bat or on deck.

Defensive Substitutions: Straight defensive substitutions, with the team leading by four runs or less.

Number of Lineups: Based on batting order, 1-8 for National Leaguers, 1-9 for American Leaguers.

Percent LHB vs. RHSP and RHB vs. LHSP: A measure of platooning. A batter is considered to always have the platoon advantage if he is a switch-hitter.

Percent PH platoon: Frequency the manager gets his pinch-hitter the platoon advantage. Switch-hitters always have the advantage.

Score Diff: The most common score differential on which an intentional walk is called for.

Slow and Quick Hooks: See the glossary for complete information. This measures how often a pitcher is left in longer than is standard practice, or pulled earlier than normal.

Mid-Inning Change: The number of times a manager changed pitchers in the middle of an inning.

1-Batter Appearances: The number of times a pitcher was brought in to face only one batter. Called the "Tony La Russa special" because of his penchant for trying to orchestrate specific matchups for specific situations.

3 Pitchers (2 runs or less): The club gives up two runs or less in a game, but uses at least three pitchers.

Tendencias de los Managers del 2001

Una de las atracciones del beisbol son las infinitas oportunidades de analizar el juego . . . y pocas cosas son más analizadas que las decisiones de los managers. Ellos no tienen dobles o ponches, pero sí podemos estudiar sus propias estadísticas.

¿Cuál es el manager con la mejor proporción de éxito en bases robadas? ¿Cuáles managers alteran más sus alineaciones? ¿Cuáles managers mataron la grama encaminados a la loma? Estas son el tipo de preguntas que inspiraron las siguientes páginas.

En el ataque, managers tienen control sobre toques, robar bases y cuando hacer el correr-y-batear (*hit and run*). El *Handbook* reporta la cantidad y el éxito de éstas decisiones. En la defensa, el *Handbook* reporta el éxito de las bolas malas intencionadas, de la frequencia de bases por bolas intencionales, y las tendencias de substituciones defensivas.

Muchos managers dedican gran cantidad de tiempo eligiendo sus alineaciones. El *Handbook* muestra cambios en alineaciones, así como el porcentaje de alternar entre bateadores derechos y zurdos. El uso de bateadores y corredores emergentes es también estudiado.

Finalmente, como usan sus lanzadores. Quien tiene un gatillo rápido para sacar sus lanzadores y quien tiene un gatillo lento, así como cuantas veces los abridores fueron permitidos tirar más de 120 y 140 lanzamientos. Para relevistas, estudiamos el número de relevos, cambios a media entrada y el número de salvados de más de una entrada.

Nosotros asumimos que un entrenador trabajando en vez del manager toma las mismas decisiones que su jefe tomaría en esa situación.

SB% = Éxito de Bases Robadas: Bases robadas divididas por intentos.

Pitchout Rn Mvg = Bola Intencional con Corredor en Movimiento: Número de veces que la oposición corría cuando el manager ordenó una bola mala intencional.

2nd SB-CS = Robando 2da base; SB = bases robadas; CS = atrapado robando. **3rd SB-CS = ** Robando 3ra base; SB = bases robadas; CS = atrapado robando. **Home SB-CS =** Robando Home; SB = bases robadas; CS = atrapado robando. **Double Steals = Doble Robos:** El número de intentos de doble robos en el 2001. **Out Percentage = Desglose por Outs:** Proporción de bases robadas por número de outs.

Sacrifice Bunts = Sacrificios de Toques Intentados: Un toque es considerado de sacrificio cuando no hay corredor en tercera, no hay outs, o cuando un lanzador intenta un toque.

G = Juegos; **Att =** Intentos.

Suc. % = Promedio de Éxito de Toques de Sacrificio: Un toque que resulta en sacrificio o imparable, dividido por el número de intentos.

Fav. Inning = Entrada Favorita: La entrada más común en que un evento ocurre.

Sqz = Toque Suicida: Toque con embasado en 3ra corriendo a home antes del lanzamiento.

Hit & Run = Éxito de Correr-y-Batear: El número de Correr-y-Batear que resultó en corredores avanzando sin un doble play.

Pitchout = Bola Mala Intencional: Bola mala a propósito para tratar de anticipar un robo de base y tratar de atrapar al corredor tratando de robar.

Runners Moving = Corredores en Movimiento: Veces que una bola mal intencionada ocurrió cuando los corredores si estaban en movimiento.

% CS = Porcentaje de atrapados de robo de base cuando se ocuparon bolas malas intencionales.

Non-PO CS% = El porcentaje de atrapados robando base sin ocupar bolas malas intencionales.

IBB = Situación de Bases por Bola Intencionales: Corredores en base, pero nadie en primera, y sin un lanzador bateando. Los equipos tienen que estar separados por dos carreras o menos, o la carrera del empate está embasada, al bate, o esperando turno a batear.

Pct of Situations = Porcentaje de Situación.

Favorite Score Diff. = Diferencia de marcador favorito para base por bola intencional.

Defensive Subs = Substituciones Defensivas: Substituciones defensivas directas, con el equipo en la delantera por cuatro carreras o menos.

Favorite Inning = Entrada favorita.

Pos. 1 = 1era posición que el manager prefiere hacer substitución defensiva. **Pos. 2 =** 2da posición que el manager prefiere hacer substitución defensiva. **Pos. 3 =** 3ra posición que el manager prefiere hacer substitución defensiva.

Número de Alineaciones (Lineups Used): Basado en orden de bateo, 1-8 para la Liga Nacional, 1-9 para la Liga Americana.

%LHB vs. RHSP = Porcentaje de Bateadores Zurdos contra Lanzadores Derechos; %RHB vs. LHSP = Bateadores Derechos contra Lanzadores Zurdos: Una medida de alternar. Bateadores ambidiestros son considerados de tener la ventaja de alternación.

#PH = Número de veces que ocupó un bateador emergente. **PH BA** = Promedio realizados por los bateadores emergentes. **PH HR** = Cuadrangulares por bateadores emergentes. **#PR** = Número de corredores emergentes. **PR SB - CS** = Bases Robadas - Atrapado Robando base por corredores emergentes.

Percent PH Platoon = Porcentaje de Alternar Emergentes: Frecuencia que el manager le da a su bateador emergente la ventaja de alternación. Bateadores ambidiestros son considerados de tener la ventaja de alternación.

Gatillo Lento o Rápido: Miren el glosario para información completa. Esto mide que tan a menudo un lanzador es permitido continuar más o menos de lo normal.

Slow Hooks = Gatillo lento para sacar un lanzador; **Quick Hooks** = Gatillo rápido

>120 Pitches = Permitido lanzar más de 120 veces; **>140 Pitches** = Más de 140 lanzamientos

3 Days Rest = Veces que lanzador abrió un juego con 3 días de descanso.

Relief App = Relevos; **Mid-Inning Change** = Número cambios a media entrada

Save 1 IP = Juegos Salvados de más de una entrada

1st Platoon Pct = Porcentaje que el manager le intentó dar a su lanzador la ventaja de alternar (derecho contra derecho, izquierdo contra izquierdo).

1-Batter App = Enfrentando solo un Bateador: El número de veces el manager metió un relevista para enfrentarse solo un bateador.

3 Pitchers (2 runs) = 3 Lazadores (2 carreras o menos): El equipo permite dos carreras o menos en un juego, pero ocupa por lo menos tres lanzadores.

366

OFFENSE

	G	Att	SB%	Ptchout Rn Mvg	Stolen Bases 2nd SB-CS	3rd SB-CS	Home SB-CS	Double Steals	Out Pct 0	1	2	Sac Bunts Att	Suc. %	Fav. Inning	Sqz	Hit & Run Att	Suc. %
AL Managers																	
Garner, Phil, Det	162	194	68.6	8	123-56	10-5	0-0	3	28.4	29.4	42.3	58	77.6	7	7	67	28.4
Hargrove, Mike, Bal	162	186	71.5	4	112-47	20-5	1-1	5	19.9	36.0	44.1	57	80.7	3	3	92	30.4
Howe, Art, Oak	162	97	70.1	2	54-24	14-4	0-1	3	26.8	38.1	35.1	40	72.5	7	1	43	27.9
Kelly, Tom, Min	162	213	68.5	7	125-58	19-4	2-5	8	16.0	37.1	46.9	36	80.6	8	5	136	38.2
Kerrigan, Joe, Bos	43	33	48.5	0	14-13	2-4	0-0	1	30.3	30.3	39.4	9	77.8	5	0	16	18.8
Manuel, Charlie, Cle	162	120	65.8	2	64-36	15-5	0-0	2	14.2	35.0	50.8	67	89.6	1	2	55	32.7
Manuel, Jerry, CWS	162	182	67.6	3	98-50	25-9	0-0	8	18.7	40.1	41.2	95	83.2	1	4	107	35.5
Martinez, Buck, Tor	162	211	73.9	10	135-48	20-6	1-1	3	20.4	37.9	41.7	47	72.3	7	1	110	34.5
McRae, Hal, TB	148	157	68.8	9	94-44	14-3	0-2	4	20.4	29.9	49.7	61	83.6	7	3	83	47.0
Muser, Tony, KC	162	142	70.4	5	86-38	14-4	0-0	3	12.7	40.1	47.2	50	78.0	3	0	100	33.0
Narron, Jerry, Tex	134	106	76.4	2	66-22	13-2	2-1	7	12.3	42.5	45.3	29	72.4	5	1	50	24.0
Oates, Johnny, Tex	28	23	69.6	0	14-7	2-0	0-0	0	17.4	39.1	43.5	6	100.0	6	0	4	25.0
Piniella, Lou, Sea	162	216	80.6	7	149-33	25-7	0-2	11	24.1	43.5	32.4	62	82.3	7	4	93	41.9
Rothschild, Larry, TB	14	10	70.0	1	6-2	1-1	0-0	0	10.0	40.0	50.0	1	100.0	8	1	3	0.0
Scioscia, Mike, Ana	162	168	69.0	6	95-45	20-3	1-4	4	15.5	33.9	50.6	66	80.3	5	2	116	36.2
Torre, Joe, NYY	161	214	75.2	6	132-46	28-7	1-0	5	19.2	32.7	48.1	41	80.5	1	0	102	35.3
Williams, Jimy, Bos	118	48	62.5	4	29-16	1-1	0-1	1	18.8	25.0	56.3	31	83.9	3	1	35	40.0
NL Managers																	
Alou, Felipe, Mon	53	39	71.8	1	24-8	3-1	1-2	3	28.2	46.2	25.6	28	85.7	3	2	18	44.4
Baker, Dusty, SF	162	99	57.6	3	53-35	4-7	0-0	1	25.3	42.4	32.3	95	73.7	5	4	49	46.9
Baylor, Don, ChC	162	103	65.0	3	61-31	5-5	1-0	2	24.3	34.0	41.7	140	89.3	3	5	63	33.3
Bell, Buddy, Col	162	186	71.0	2	106-46	25-7	1-1	8	21.5	36.0	42.5	108	78.7	2	9	108	28.7
Bochy, Bruce, SD	162	173	74.6	5	111-35	18-3	0-6	10	18.5	39.3	42.2	43	74.4	6	3	83	36.1
Boles, John, Fla	48	56	75.0	2	40-14	1-0	1-0	0	28.6	35.7	35.7	22	95.5	4	0	12	25.0
Boone, Bob, Cin	162	157	65.6	3	88-45	13-4	2-5	4	17.8	28.0	54.1	88	78.4	3	1	69	31.9
Bowa, Larry, Phi	162	200	76.5	6	123-42	30-3	0-2	11	21.0	32.5	46.5	87	85.1	3	5	82	29.3
Brenly, Bob, Ari	162	109	65.1	5	66-36	5-0	0-2	2	30.3	30.3	39.4	89	83.1	3	12	98	43.9
Cox, Bobby, Atl	162	131	64.9	2	74-40	11-6	0-0	4	20.6	35.1	44.3	84	82.1	3	4	85	35.3
Dierker, Larry, Hou	162	113	56.6	3	59-40	4-7	1-2	0	12.4	38.1	49.6	95	78.9	3	5	52	23.1
La Russa, Tony, StL	162	126	72.2	2	81-27	9-7	1-1	5	20.6	32.5	46.8	102	88.2	7	9	118	55.1
Lopes, Davey, Mil	162	102	64.7	7	60-34	6-0	0-2	2	23.5	37.3	39.2	82	79.3	3	2	82	35.4
McClendon, Lloyd, Pit	162	166	56.0	9	79-60	14-9	0-4	5	16.9	44.6	38.6	83	74.7	6	7	148	28.4
Perez, Tony, Fla	114	73	64.4	4	42-23	5-3	0-0	1	26.0	34.2	39.7	54	75.9	3	4	33	42.4
Torborg, Jeff, Mon	109	113	64.6	4	55-32	18-7	0-1	3	16.8	32.7	50.4	52	80.8	3	6	60	25.0
Tracy, Jim, LA	162	131	67.9	2	78-36	10-4	1-2	0	21.4	29.8	48.9	81	74.1	3	7	54	27.8
Valentine, Bobby, NYM	162	114	57.9	2	59-36	7-6	0-6	1	21.9	36.8	41.2	66	89.4	2	12	128	34.4

DEFENSE

	G	Pitchout Total	Runners Moving	CS%	Non-PO CS%	Intentional BB IBB	Pct. of Situations	Favorite Score Diff.	Def. Subs Total	Favorite Inning	Pos. 1	Pos. 2	Pos. 3
AL Managers													
Garner, Phil, Det	162	36	9	55.6	31.0	29	4.2	-2	14	9	c-5	1b-4	rf-3
Hargrove, Mike, Bal	162	71	19	52.6	21.7	17	2.3	-2	20	9	c-6	lf-5	2b-3
Howe, Art, Oak	162	43	11	27.3	31.0	41	6.5	0	18	9	c-4	3b-3	ss-3
Kelly, Tom, Min	162	22	7	28.6	37.6	14	2.1	-2	6	8	lf-2	rf-2	2b-1
Kerrigan, Joe, Bos	43	16	5	40.0	22.1	4	2.0	-1	6	8	lf-3	c-2	rf-1
Manuel, Charlie, Cle	162	43	10	50.0	30.9	34	4.9	0	49	8	lf-19	3b-10	rf-5
Manuel, Jerry, CWS	162	41	10	50.0	25.5	30	4.5	-2	50	8	cf-23	lf-18	3b-4
Martinez, Buck, Tor	162	42	12	66.7	26.5	47	6.4	0	28	9	lf-11	cf-5	2b-4
McRae, Hal, TB	148	28	6	50.0	25.2	12	1.9	-2	15	9	lf-7	cf-3	rf-2
Muser, Tony, KC	162	47	16	68.8	25.4	18	3.0	0	23	9	1b-12	lf-6	2b-2
Narron, Jerry, Tex	134	5	2	100.0	43.7	16	2.8	-2	19	9	rf-11	lf-4	c-3
Oates, Johnny, Tex	28	2	0	–	52.9	7	6.6	2	5	7	cf-2	c-1	2b-1
Piniella, Lou, Sea	162	33	4	75.0	26.5	23	4.2	-1	64	8	lf-23	3b-12	cf-8
Rothschild, Larry, TB	14	0	0	–	62.5	1	2.0	0	1	8	lf-1	ph-0	ph-0
Scioscia, Mike, Ana	162	50	9	66.7	33.3	33	5.0	-2	8	8	c-3	1b-3	lf-1
Torre, Joe, NYY	161	21	5	60.0	22.6	22	3.3	0	14	9	lf-5	c-2	2b-2
Williams, Jimy, Bos	118	106	29	27.6	15.1	29	4.8	-2	26	8	3b-8	ss-8	rf-4
NL Managers													
Alou, Felipe, Mon	53	7	1	0.0	22.4	10	4.7	4	5	8	lf-2	c-1	3b-1
Baker, Dusty, SF	162	45	12	75.0	30.3	32	5.2	-2	19	9	c-4	rf-4	3b-3
Baylor, Don, ChC	162	45	14	64.3	26.8	32	5.2	-2	42	8	cf-14	3b-12	lf-8
Bell, Buddy, Col	162	43	6	50.0	25.4	43	6.9	-2	14	7	lf-7	cf-2	c-1
Bochy, Bruce, SD	162	23	6	66.7	34.3	40	6.8	-2	27	7	rf-9	lf-5	ss-4
Boles, John, Fla	48	14	3	66.7	40.5	7	3.8	-2	8	6	3b-4	lf-2	2b-1
Boone, Bob, Cin	162	25	8	50.0	45.0	27	4.2	-1	19	8	3b-5	2b-4	cf-4
Bowa, Larry, Phi	162	38	10	70.0	31.6	43	6.9	0	5	7	1b-2	lf-1	cf-1
Brenly, Bob, Ari	162	43	10	50.0	32.9	23	4.1	0	20	8	1b-5	c-4	2b-4
Cox, Bobby, Atl	162	90	18	38.9	28.0	55	9.9	-2	23	8	lf-13	3b-3	ss-3
Dierker, Larry, Hou	162	12	0	–	42.6	13	2.4	1	20	8	cf-15	3b-2	c-1
La Russa, Tony, StL	162	25	3	133.3	38.8	31	5.2	0	13	7	lf-6	rf-4	cf-2
Lopes, Davey, Mil	162	51	9	77.8	30.5	71	11.5	-1	14	9	c-4	lf-4	1b-2
McClendon, Lloyd, Pit	162	52	4	25.0	27.7	49	7.9	-2	32	8	2b-10	cf-7	rf-7
Perez, Tony, Fla	114	12	2	50.0	39.3	28	6.9	-1	8	7	rf-5	cf-2	ss-4
Torborg, Jeff, Mon	109	13	4	0.0	20.4	21	4.8	0	3	9	c-1	3b-1	cf-1
Tracy, Jim, LA	162	10	2	50.0	38.2	25	4.0	4	20	8	lf-9	3b-5	2b-2
Valentine, Bobby, NYM	162	76	18	33.3	22.2	36	5.9	-1	34	8	rf-11	cf-8	ss-6

LINEUPS

	Starting Lineup				Substitutions					
	G	Lineups Used	%LHB vs. RHSP	%RHB vs. LHSP	#PH	Percent PH Platoon	PH BA	PH HR	#PR	PR SB-CS
AL Managers										
Garner, Phil, Det	162	116	55.8	85.3	93	87.1	.221	1	40	1-0
Hargrove, Mike, Bal	162	139	41.9	85.0	82	78.0	.275	2	27	2-1
Howe, Art, Oak	162	116	61.5	56.0	131	82.4	.204	2	30	1-0
Kelly, Tom, Min	162	126	68.6	68.7	128	78.9	.236	5	14	1-0
Kerrigan, Joe, Bos	43	42	49.5	83.3	29	86.2	.280	2	8	0-0
Manuel, Charlie, Cle	162	114	53.6	82.5	105	80.0	.244	4	30	3-3
Manuel, Jerry, CWS	162	115	41.0	97.8	104	70.2	.170	1	34	7-2
Martinez, Buck, Tor	162	100	48.6	79.6	129	91.5	.268	2	23	2-1
McRae, Hal, TB	148	121	49.8	71.1	76	59.2	.190	0	27	3-1
Muser, Tony, KC	162	130	43.8	95.4	108	75.9	.175	3	23	1-0
Narron, Jerry, Tex	134	94	50.5	81.2	92	68.5	.232	2	14	0-0
Oates, Johnny, Tex	28	14	34.3	85.2	16	81.3	.143	0	3	0-0
Piniella, Lou, Sea	162	115	56.7	82.0	121	87.6	.320	4	44	3-2
Rothschild, Larry, TB	14	8	47.0	66.7	6	33.3	.250	1	2	1-0
Scioscia, Mike, Ana	162	130	57.3	73.2	118	84.7	.245	4	30	0-0
Torre, Joe, NYY	161	94	50.2	76.2	76	67.1	.217	3	33	3-1
Williams, Jimy, Bos	118	93	55.6	88.5	69	78.3	.095	0	22	3-0
AL Managers										
Alou, Felipe, Mon	53	40	47.5	84.6	84	90.5	.143	1	4	1-0
Baker, Dusty, SF	162	122	39.1	82.7	261	65.1	.246	14	22	0-0
Baylor, Don, ChC	162	140	42.2	83.3	230	73.0	.231	6	31	0-0
Bell, Buddy, Col	162	118	58.1	71.6	314	65.6	.214	5	27	3-0
Bochy, Bruce, SD	162	116	52.2	81.1	255	73.3	.226	2	54	4-1
Boles, John, Fla	48	17	23.1	89.9	74	51.4	.206	1	5	0-0
Boone, Bob, Cin	162	132	46.1	76.9	313	65.8	.235	6	46	0-2
Bowa, Larry, Phi	162	81	56.1	70.8	232	69.0	.242	6	15	3-1
Brenly, Bob, Ari	162	123	52.7	60.7	321	70.7	.278	14	35	1-0
Cox, Bobby, Atl	162	113	50.5	89.3	278	81.7	.253	2	50	5-2
Dierker, Larry, Hou	162	80	20.1	97.7	248	80.2	.209	8	42	4-4
La Russa, Tony, StL	162	117	41.0	72.8	256	73.4	.222	6	26	2-0
Lopes, Davey, Mil	162	116	42.1	83.0	252	72.6	.192	4	25	2-1
McClendon, Lloyd, Pit	162	131	43.8	82.3	255	60.8	.174	10	17	4-1
Perez, Tony, Fla	114	68	24.6	90.5	158	64.6	.158	3	24	1-0
Torborg, Jeff, Mon	109	73	51.9	85.5	167	71.9	.197	0	12	0-0
Tracy, Jim, LA	162	111	38.0	84.5	264	68.6	.197	6	34	4-1
Valentine, Bobby, NYM	162	144	33.5	83.3	298	82.6	.236	1	33	1-3

PITCHING

	Starters						Relievers					
	G	Slow Hooks	Quick Hooks	>120 Pitches	>140 Pitches	3 Days Rest	Relief App	Mid-Inning Change	Save >1 IP	1st Batter Platoon Pct	1-Batter App	3 Pitchers (<=2 runs)
AL Managers												
Garner, Phil, Det	162	23	12	9	0	0	391	205	3	63.7	41	16
Hargrove, Mike, Bal	162	17	13	3	0	0	392	178	10	60.9	37	25
Howe, Art, Oak	162	11	19	4	0	0	416	187	5	63.2	41	39
Kelly, Tom, Min	162	5	10	4	0	5	402	182	5	61.9	37	18
Kerrigan, Joe, Bos	43	2	10	0	0	0	109	37	1	62.4	3	7
Manuel, Charlie, Cle	162	17	28	10	0	3	484	202	3	67.1	41	31
Manuel, Jerry, CWS	162	19	26	5	0	3	406	181	16	61.8	30	23
Martinez, Buck, Tor	162	15	25	2	0	1	471	221	3	68.6	57	26
McRae, Hal, TB	148	28	16	5	0	0	342	134	12	56.7	16	24
Muser, Tony, KC	162	11	11	8	0	1	396	161	5	53.5	23	19
Narron, Jerry, Tex	134	18	9	6	0	0	340	143	5	60.9	20	17
Oates, Johnny, Tex	28	8	1	3	0	0	70	44	2	62.9	8	3
Piniella, Lou, Sea	162	11	22	5	0	3	392	168	9	65.2	28	44
Rothschild, Larry, TB	14	4	3	0	0	0	28	13	0	71.4	0	0
Scioscia, Mike, Ana	162	12	18	5	0	0	384	163	9	65.6	38	24
Torre, Joe, NYY	161	13	16	10	1	3	362	158	17	68.7	22	32
Williams, Jimy, Bos	118	4	26	5	0	0	315	109	11	59.4	18	17
NL Managers												
Alou, Felipe, Mon	53	3	11	1	0	1	171	50	1	65.5	10	12
Baker, Dusty, SF	162	15	19	10	0	3	439	137	4	61.7	32	34
Baylor, Don, ChC	162	12	22	5	0	1	452	151	0	62.2	42	36
Bell, Buddy, Col	162	30	18	8	0	1	476	179	6	64.9	49	19
Bochy, Bruce, SD	162	15	14	6	0	0	422	164	10	65.6	42	25
Boles, John, Fla	48	5	6	3	0	0	128	42	0	57.8	13	9
Boone, Bob, Cin	162	11	24	1	0	0	461	178	9	63.1	30	23
Bowa, Larry, Phi	162	12	21	6	0	0	473	182	2	66.9	57	29
Brenly, Bob, Ari	162	10	21	22	1	4	421	136	7	66.7	37	35
Cox, Bobby, Atl	162	9	12	4	0	0	412	99	8	52.3	21	39
Dierker, Larry, Hou	162	14	20	9	0	2	405	106	4	47.4	18	26
La Russa, Tony, StL	162	13	21	7	0	0	485	209	7	68.0	60	46
Lopes, Davey, Mil	162	14	25	3	0	2	489	164	7	63.2	37	27
McClendon, Lloyd, Pit	162	19	27	2	0	0	410	150	5	60.0	20	20
Perez, Tony, Fla	114	8	7	5	0	0	302	97	1	59.6	22	19
Torborg, Jeff, Mon	109	10	19	5	0	2	320	114	4	64.1	31	21
Tracy, Jim, LA	162	13	15	8	0	2	409	121	4	63.0	35	30
Valentine, Bobby, NYM	162	11	9	7	0	0	397	108	6	59.2	17	31

2002 Batter Projections

Every baseball season contains its share of surprises. We enter April carrying some degree of confidence in regards to how we think the new campaign will transpire. But by the end of May, much of that confidence has been ripped assunder and lies scattered in pieces in our mind's eye.

Well, thank God for that. Why play the season if performance can be predicted with absolute certainty? It can't, of course, which permits us the sweet consolation of continual surprise. For instance, had last spring's conventional wisdom prevailed, we would have been denied the spectacular achievements of the Seattle Mariners. After losing Ken Griffey Jr. and Alex Rodriguez in consecutive years, the Mariners looked like they might have difficulty breaking .500, much less challenging for a playoff spot. Instead, they broke .700 and made a mockery of the playoff chase by setting an American League record with 116 wins.

That's not to say we aren't interested in predictions, nor in making them ourselves. It's only human nature to attempt to peer into the crystal ball, hoping to gain some insight into future events. And that's what this annual exercise is all about.

It's also true that not all predictions are the equivalent of tossing darts at the wall. We happen to think that the batter projections you'll find in this section arguably are the finest available. Need convincing? Check out some of last year's bullseyes:

Bernie Williams

	Avg	G	AB	R	H	2B	3B	HR	RBI	BB	SO	SB	CS
Actual 2001	.307	146	540	102	166	38	0	26	94	78	67	11	5
Projected 2001	.305	143	541	105	165	32	4	25	104	83	88	11	7

Manny Ramirez

	Avg	G	AB	R	H	2B	3B	HR	RBI	BB	SO	SB	CS
Actual 2001	.306	142	529	93	162	33	2	41	125	81	147	0	1
Projected 2001	.310	149	532	111	165	37	1	41	132	96	128	2	2

Magglio Ordonez

	Avg	G	AB	R	H	2B	3B	HR	RBI	BB	SO	SB	CS
Actual 2001	.305	160	593	97	181	40	1	31	113	70	70	25	7
Projected 2001	.301	156	599	94	180	37	2	30	114	49	61	12	7

Matt Lawton

	Avg	G	AB	R	H	2B	3B	HR	RBI	BB	SO	SB	CS
Actual 2001	.277	151	559	95	155	36	1	13	64	85	80	29	8
Projected 2001	.281	152	555	86	156	33	2	14	77	90	62	18	7

While these projections were by no means perfect, we have a feeling Miss Cleo now would be crowing had she made them. In fact, each of these projections wound up scoring between 978 and 980 in the similarity system we designed. Those are exceptionally high scores, marks more than worthy of bragging.

At times, our projections are so accurate they're scary. Not Nostradamus scary, though at least they're authentic. For example, we projected Moises Alou to hit 28 home runs and drive in 108 runs. He wound up with 27 homers and 108 RBI. For Andruw Jones, we projected 34 homers and 103 RBI. He nailed the 34 homers, but drove in one extra run (104). Meanwhile, Einar Diaz matched our projected homers (4) and batting average (.277), but played more than we expected and drove in considerably more runs (56) than predicted (35).

Those are the kinds of successes we aren't reluctant to describe. At the other end of the spectrum are our "failures," those cases where our projections swung and missed. Actually, we aren't reluctant to divulge the whiffs, either, since they can be fairly illuminating.

Most of the worst similarity scores have to do with guys for whom we made projections but who then didn't play in the majors. Either they retired (Albert Belle), got injured (Mo Vaughn) or returned to the minors (Wilton Veras). Of the 445 projections we made last year, 32 fell into one of these categories. Of the other 413, only six produced a similarity score below 700. Frank Thomas registered the lowest mark:

Frank Thomas

	Avg	G	AB	R	H	2B	3B	HR	RBI	BB	SO	SB	CS
Actual 2001	.221	20	68	8	15	3	0	4	10	10	12	0	0
Projected 2001	.318	148	537	98	171	34	1	35	122	102	85	2	2

Although Thomas had gotten off to a slow start in terms of batting average, this is clearly a sub-category of the injury excuse. Thomas tore his triceps in April and played in just 20 games. The injury bug also destroyed Nomar Garciaparra's projection:

Nomar Garciaparra

	Avg	G	AB	R	H	2B	3B	HR	RBI	BB	SO	SB	CS
Actual 2001	.289	21	83	13	24	3	0	4	8	7	9	0	1
Projected 2001	.343	147	583	114	200	45	6	29	109	53	52	13	5

However, while Derek Bell's season ended due to a hamstring injury, something tells us the Pirates wish he could have suffered the injury even earlier:

Derek Bell

	Avg	G	AB	R	H	2B	3B	HR	RBI	BB	SO	SB	CS
Actual 2001	.173	46	156	14	27	3	0	5	13	25	38	0	2
Projected 2001	.269	143	561	83	151	28	1	17	79	56	129	12	6

We thought Adam Piatt would seize the right-field job in Oakland and have a breakthrough campaign. Instead he struggled, contracted viral meningitis and spent some time in the minors:

Adam Piatt

	Avg	G	AB	R	H	2B	3B	HR	RBI	BB	SO	SB	CS
Actual 2001	.211	36	95	9	20	5	1	0	6	13	26	0	0
Projected 2001	.297	151	543	97	161	38	4	25	102	69	120	4	3

These were the kind of players for whom playing time was the primary factor in ruining their projection. Obviously, there were other poor projections for guys who played either far better or far worse than we had anticipated. The most high-profile example of the former is Barry Bonds. Sure he had blasted 49 homers in 2000. But he had hit 37 and 34 the previous two years.

370

We thus expected Bonds to launch a respectable total of 40 homers in 2001:

Barry Bonds

	Avg	G	AB	R	H	2B	3B	HR	RBI	BB	SO	SB	CS
Actual 2001	.328	153	476	129	156	32	2	73	137	177	93	13	3
Projected 2001	.280	144	492	112	138	29	3	40	102	112	85	18	6

At age 36, Bonds broke records and demolished our projection. More power to him. Two other players who displayed sudden power surges included Bret Boone and Luis Gonzalez:

Bret Boone

	Avg	G	AB	R	H	2B	3B	HR	RBI	BB	SO	SB	CS
Actual 2001	.331	158	623	118	206	37	3	37	141	40	110	5	5
Projected 2001	.254	145	548	74	139	29	2	20	75	49	106	8	6

Luis Gonzalez

	Avg	G	AB	R	H	2B	3B	HR	RBI	BB	SO	SB	CS
Actual 2001	.325	162	609	128	198	36	7	57	142	100	83	1	1
Projected 2001	.302	151	573	92	173	35	4	25	101	66	70	7	5

Bonds, Boone and Gonzalez all rate between 788 and 790 on the similarity score scale. But they're exceptional cases. The only other hitter who managed at least 400 plate appearances last season but scored under 800 was Shane Halter (782). Compare that to the 47 hitters who scored between 800 and 899, and a whopping 162 whose similarity score was at least 900 (minimum 400 PA).

Those numbers allow us to point with pride to the accuracy of our projections. And we continue to spend considerable time trying to fine-tune them. Our goal is to make them as precise as possible. We believe they'll be very useful as you prepare your fantasy draft lists or simply anticipate the upcoming season.

Sure, some of the projections you'll find over the following pages might look foolish this time next year. Of course, we'd probably be alarmed and somewhat disappointed if there weren't any clanks off the glove. After all, we enjoy an occasional surprise ourselves.

—Jim Henzler

Prognóstico de Bateadores del 2002

Cada temporadas trae sus sorpresas. En abril tenemos confianza de que sabemos cómo el año se va a desarrollar. Pero para finales de mayo, esa confianza ha sufrido.

Pero disfrutamos la diferencia. ¿Para qué jugar si los resultados se podrían prognosticar perfectamente? Por ejemplo, el marzo pasado los Marineros aparentaban ser un equipo mediocre, especialmente sin Ken Griffey Jr. y sin Alex Rodríguez. Sin embargo ganaron más del 70 por ciento de sus juegos y establecieron una nueva marca de victorias en la Liga Americana con 116.

Eso no significa que no es divertido tratar de prognosticar, y de esto se trata la próxima sección.

Los prognósticos en esta sección son unos de los mejores. ¿Necesitan pruebas? Miren estos que les dimos en el blanco:

Bernie Williams

	Pro	J	VB	C	H	2B	3B	HR	CE	BB	K	BR	AR
Actual 2001	.307	146	540	102	166	38	0	26	94	78	67	11	5
Prognóstico 2001	.305	143	541	105	165	32	4	25	104	83	88	11	7

Manny Ramírez

	Pro	J	VB	C	H	2B	3B	HR	CE	BB	K	BR	AR
Actual 2001	.306	142	529	93	162	33	2	41	125	81	147	0	1
Prognóstico 2001	.310	149	532	111	165	37	1	41	132	96	128	2	2

Magglio Ordóñez

	Pro	J	VB	C	H	2B	3B	HR	CE	BB	K	BR	AR
Actual 2001	.305	160	593	97	181	40	1	31	113	70	70	25	7
Prognóstico 2001	.301	156	599	94	180	37	2	30	114	49	61	12	7

Matt Lawton

	Pro	J	VB	C	H	2B	3B	HR	CE	BB	K	BR	AR
Actual 2001	.277	151	559	95	155	36	1	13	64	85	80	29	8
Prognóstico 2001	.281	152	555	86	156	33	2	14	77	90	62	18	7

Aunques estos prognósticos no fueron perfectos, están buenos. Cada uno de ellos tiene una marca entre 978 y 980 en el sistema de similaridad que hemos diseñado.

Pero a veces nuestros prognósticos son tan exactos que dan miedo. Por ejemplo nuestra predicción de Moisés Alou fue de 28 cuadrangulares y empujar 108 carreras. El terminó con 27 cuadrangulares y 108 empujadas. Para Andruw Jones, nuestro prognóstico fue de 34 cuadrangulares y 103 empujadas. Terminó con 34 y 104. Mientras Einar Díaz igualó nuestro prognóstico de cuadrangulares (4) y promedio (.277), pero jugó más de lo esperado y superó nuestra predicción de carreras empujadas (35) llegando hasta 56.

Tenemos nuestros fracasos, pero también son divertidos estudiarlos.

Las peores Marcas de Similaridad son los prognósticos para jugadores que ni siquiera jugaron el año pasado: retiros (Albert Belle), lesiones (Mo Vaughn) o regresado a las menores (Wilton Veras). De los 445 prognósticos que hicimos el año pasado, 32 de ellos fracasaron por estas razones. De los otros 413, solo seis resultaron en Marcas de Similaridad menores de 700. Frank Thomas fue el peor:

Frank Thomas

	Pro	J	VB	C	H	2B	3B	HR	CE	BB	K	BR	AR
Actual 2001	.221	20	68	8	15	3	0	4	10	10	12	0	0
Prognóstico 2001	.318	148	537	98	171	34	1	35	122	102	85	2	2

Aunque Thomas empezó con un mal promedio de bateo, realmente fue su lesión que arruinó su prognóstico. Una lesión tambien condenó el prognóstico de Nomar Garciaparra:

Nomar Garciaparra

	Pro	J	VB	C	H	2B	3B	HR	CE	BB	K	BR	AR
Actual 2001	.289	21	83	13	24	3	0	4	8	7	9	0	1
Prognóstico 2001	.343	147	583	114	200	45	6	29	109	53	52	13	5

Aunque una ruptura del tendón de la corva terminó la temporada de Derek Bell, a lo mejor los Piratas hubieran querido que la lesión hubiera llegado más temprano:

Derek Bell

	Pro	J	VB	C	H	2B	3B	HR	CE	BB	K	BR	AR
Actual 2001	.173	46	156	14	27	3	0	5	13	25	38	0	2
Prognóstico 2001	.269	143	561	83	151	28	1	17	79	56	129	12	6

Nosotros opinamos que Adam Piatt iba a ser una estrella en el jardín derecho para Oakland, se enfermó con meningitis y se pasó recuperando en las menores:

Adam Piatt

	Pro	J	VB	C	H	2B	3B	HR	CE	BB	K	BR	AR
Actual 2001	.211	36	95	9	20	5	1	0	6	13	26	0	0
Prognóstico 2001	.297	151	543	97	161	38	4	25	102	69	120	4	3

Pero no solo fallamos por lesiones. Ciertos prognósticos erraron por que peloteros jugaron mejor o peor que era esperado. El mejor ejemplo es Barry Bonds. Aunque el se había volado la cerca 49 en el 2000, solo había conectado 37 y 34 jonrones las dos temporadas anteriores.

Nosotros esperabamos unos 40 cuadrangulares de su bate en el 2001:

Barry Bonds

	Pro	J	VB	C	H	2B	3B	HR	CE	BB	K	BR	AR
Actual 2001	.328	153	476	129	156	32	2	73	137	177	93	13	3
Prognóstico 2001	.280	144	492	112	138	29	3	40	102	112	85	18	6

A los 36 años, Bonds rompió el record y se burló de nuestro prognóstico.

Otros dos jugadores que comieron espinaca fueron Bret Boone y Luis González:

Bret Boone

	Pro	J	VB	C	H	2B	3B	HR	CE	BB	K	BR	AR
Actual 2001	.331	158	623	118	206	37	3	37	141	40	110	5	5
Prognóstico 2001	.254	145	548	74	139	29	2	20	75	49	106	8	6

Luis Gonzalez

	Pro	J	VB	C	H	2B	3B	HR	CE	BB	K	BR	AR
Actual 2001	.325	162	609	128	198	36	7	57	142	100	83	1	1
Prognóstico 2001	.302	151	573	92	173	35	4	25	101	66	70	7	5

Bonds, Boone y González dieron Marcas de Similaridad entre 788 y 790. Pero fueron la excepción. Solo un jugador más (con 400 veces al bate) tuvo una Marca de Similaridad menor de 800: Shane Halter (782). Comparado con 47 bateadores entre 800 and 899, y una marca impresionante de 162 con mós de 900 (un mínimo de 400 VB).

Estos números nos dan orgullo, y aun así continuamos refinando nuestras fórmulas.

Por supuesto que alguna de los prognósticos que siguen se verán ridículos al final de la próxima temporada. Pero sería una temporada aburrida si no hubieran sorpresas.

—Jim Henzler

Projections for 2002 Batters

Batter	Age	Avg	G	AB	R	H	2B	3B	HR	RBI	BB	SO	SB	CS	OBP	SLG
Abbott,Jeff, Fla	29	.284	84	169	22	48	11	0	5	23	11	26	1	1	.328	.438
Abernathy,Brent, TB	24	.276	120	384	57	106	26	0	5	39	29	37	15	7	.327	.383
Abreu,Bobby, Phi	28	.312	160	584	112	182	40	7	27	103	113	124	28	11	.423	.543
Agbayani,Benny, NYM	30	.283	116	343	46	97	20	2	12	51	46	74	7	6	.368	.458
Alfonzo,Edgardo, NYM	28	.290	140	525	97	152	29	2	22	81	78	69	5	2	.381	.478
Alicea,Luis, KC	36	.260	92	304	43	79	14	3	3	30	30	47	3	2	.326	.355
Allen,Chad, Min	27	.265	73	245	32	65	15	2	4	31	20	48	5	3	.321	.392
Alomar,Roberto, Cle	34	.296	154	571	105	169	32	4	18	84	81	85	25	6	.383	.461
Alomar Jr.,Sandy, CWS	36	.270	77	244	29	66	13	0	5	31	12	28	1	1	.305	.385
Alou,Moises, Hou	35	.314	132	481	74	151	28	2	26	101	54	53	4	2	.383	.543
Anderson,Brady, Bal	38	.242	96	327	52	79	16	2	10	36	53	65	10	4	.347	.394
Anderson,Garret, Ana	30	.294	161	653	85	192	39	2	28	104	29	91	7	5	.324	.489
Anderson,Marlon, Phi	28	.275	154	557	72	153	31	5	10	67	41	73	15	6	.324	.402
Arias,Alex, SD	34	.258	66	128	16	33	5	0	2	14	14	17	1	0	.331	.344
Aurilia,Rich, SF	30	.287	154	582	85	167	28	2	26	85	50	84	2	2	.343	.476
Ausmus,Brad, Hou	33	.258	131	449	58	116	20	2	6	44	49	71	7	4	.331	.352
Bagwell,Jeff, Hou	34	.286	158	559	127	160	36	2	38	118	118	125	13	6	.411	.562
Bako,Paul, Atl	30	.237	74	198	17	47	10	0	2	18	24	52	1	0	.320	.318
Barajas,Rod, Ari	26	.247	67	219	23	54	14	0	6	32	7	37	1	1	.270	.393
Barrett,Michael, Mon	25	.276	142	468	57	129	33	2	7	56	34	48	2	2	.325	.400
Batista,Tony, Bal	28	.260	157	596	85	155	30	2	34	101	38	113	4	2	.304	.488
Bautista,Danny, Ari	30	.276	111	232	31	64	11	2	6	31	13	34	3	2	.314	.418
Bell,David, Sea	29	.256	141	503	67	129	26	2	15	61	44	71	3	3	.316	.406
Bell,Derek, Pit	33	.251	89	275	40	69	13	1	8	37	32	69	5	2	.329	.393
Bell,Jay, Ari	36	.260	120	415	65	108	22	2	16	55	56	82	3	2	.348	.439
Belliard,Ronnie, Mil	27	.273	149	521	85	142	35	4	11	59	70	75	11	6	.359	.418
Beltran,Carlos, KC	25	.294	151	606	107	178	30	9	22	98	51	111	23	4	.349	.482
Beltre,Adrian, LA	23	.279	148	530	78	148	30	3	19	80	54	89	16	6	.346	.455
Benard,Marvin, SF	32	.269	131	412	70	111	22	2	11	44	41	72	13	7	.336	.413
Bennett,Gary, Col	30	.259	71	201	22	52	12	0	5	26	21	32	0	0	.329	.393
Berg,Dave, Fla	31	.271	90	236	28	64	14	1	3	22	22	45	2	1	.333	.377
Bergeron,Peter, Mon	24	.255	135	471	75	120	21	5	4	35	50	94	19	12	.326	.346
Berkman,Lance, Hou	26	.315	152	565	110	178	43	2	34	117	99	115	10	7	.417	.579
Berroa,Angel, KC	22	.280	48	164	28	46	9	1	3	18	7	31	6	2	.310	.402
Bichette,Dante, Bos	38	.289	106	398	55	115	23	1	15	65	31	67	4	2	.340	.465
Bigbie,Larry, Bal	24	.252	64	202	26	51	10	1	3	20	23	51	5	3	.329	.356
Biggio,Craig, Hou	36	.278	149	551	98	153	32	2	14	60	72	98	19	7	.361	.419
Blanco,Henry, Mil	30	.238	114	341	37	81	21	1	8	38	39	66	2	2	.316	.375
Blum,Geoff, Mon	29	.250	135	404	52	101	25	1	11	49	42	74	4	3	.321	.399
Bocachica,Hiram, LA	26	.259	80	243	36	63	14	2	6	28	18	49	8	5	.310	.407
Bonds,Barry, SF	37	.298	154	484	127	144	28	2	58	125	148	89	14	5	.446	.702
Bonilla,Bobby, StL	39	.250	75	140	15	35	7	1	4	19	20	32	0	0	.344	.400
Boone,Aaron, Cin	29	.279	124	430	61	120	26	2	14	64	32	75	11	4	.329	.447
Boone,Bret, Sea	33	.297	144	555	89	165	29	2	26	101	46	108	7	5	.351	.497
Bordick,Mike, Bal	36	.247	125	474	61	117	17	1	11	52	39	81	8	5	.304	.357
Bradley,Milton, Cle	24	.271	132	420	60	114	26	3	7	44	46	89	15	10	.343	.398
Branyan,Russell, Cle	26	.232	114	358	58	83	15	2	29	73	45	156	2	1	.318	.528
Brosius,Scott, NYY	35	.251	129	451	57	113	22	1	14	62	38	79	4	3	.309	.397
Brown,Dee, KC	24	.267	131	439	64	117	21	3	14	61	34	94	10	6	.319	.424
Brown,Emil, SD	27	.269	62	171	28	46	9	1	4	20	17	39	7	3	.335	.404

Projections for 2002 Batters

Batter	Age	Avg	G	AB	R	H	2B	3B	HR	RBI	BB	SO	SB	CS	OBP	SLG
Buchanan,Brian, Min	28	.252	83	262	36	66	15	0	10	39	20	66	3	2	.305	.424
Buhner,Jay, Sea	37	.230	63	148	19	34	6	0	9	27	29	48	0	0	.356	.453
Burks,Ellis, Cle	37	.284	121	398	67	113	23	2	23	75	60	74	5	3	.378	.525
Burnitz,Jeromy, Mil	33	.250	146	520	88	130	27	2	31	100	90	133	4	3	.361	.488
Burrell,Pat, Phi	25	.276	152	554	88	153	36	2	28	101	84	163	1	1	.371	.500
Bush,Homer, Tor	29	.284	99	359	50	102	14	1	3	34	17	64	16	6	.316	.354
Butler,Brent, Col	24	.281	76	171	22	48	10	0	4	18	10	16	1	1	.320	.409
Byrnes,Eric, Oak	26	.265	68	204	36	54	14	0	6	26	18	33	9	4	.324	.422
Cabrera,Jolbert, Cle	29	.271	114	262	41	71	15	2	2	27	17	36	8	4	.315	.366
Cabrera,Orlando, Mon	27	.260	153	557	68	145	34	5	13	71	35	46	12	6	.304	.409
Cairo,Miguel, StL	28	.274	70	164	20	45	8	1	2	15	12	17	7	3	.324	.372
Cameron,Mike, Sea	29	.258	154	555	99	143	27	5	22	98	81	148	32	10	.352	.443
Caminiti,Ken, Atl	39	.252	77	234	36	59	14	0	12	39	36	51	2	1	.352	.466
Canseco,Jose, CWS	37	.243	78	304	47	74	14	0	18	52	50	97	6	3	.350	.467
Casanova,Raul, Mil	29	.234	98	278	27	65	12	1	11	39	22	48	1	1	.290	.403
Casey,Sean, Cin	27	.321	151	564	86	181	42	1	20	100	57	79	1	1	.383	.505
Castilla,Vinny, Hou	34	.273	131	494	62	135	23	1	23	86	34	78	2	3	.320	.464
Castillo,Alberto, Tor	32	.220	59	118	10	26	3	0	1	10	11	23	0	0	.287	.271
Castillo,Luis, Fla	26	.297	142	552	93	164	18	4	2	35	79	89	47	18	.385	.355
Castro,Juan, Cin	30	.223	84	220	22	49	9	1	3	19	14	41	0	1	.269	.314
Catalanotto,Frank, Tex	28	.302	133	434	68	131	27	3	13	58	38	59	8	4	.358	.468
Cedeno,Roger, Det	27	.291	141	494	88	144	19	6	7	47	58	91	48	15	.366	.397
Chavez,Eric, Oak	24	.285	154	551	99	157	38	2	31	109	62	93	6	4	.357	.530
Cintron,Alex, Ari	23	.267	75	217	25	58	11	2	1	19	7	25	3	3	.290	.350
Cirillo,Jeff, Col	32	.309	149	569	88	176	37	2	14	85	62	73	6	3	.377	.455
Clark,Brady, Cin	29	.285	76	221	37	63	15	1	6	28	30	25	6	3	.371	.443
Clark,Tony, Det	30	.276	139	503	70	139	28	1	24	84	64	124	1	1	.358	.479
Clayton,Royce, CWS	32	.254	140	473	68	120	24	3	11	52	39	91	11	7	.311	.387
Colbrunn,Greg, Ari	32	.295	79	129	17	38	7	0	5	20	15	19	1	1	.368	.465
Collier,Lou, Mil	28	.259	69	185	26	48	11	1	4	23	21	41	3	2	.335	.395
Conine,Jeff, Bal	36	.301	130	445	56	134	23	1	12	70	42	57	4	3	.361	.438
Coomer,Ron, ChC	35	.263	101	315	32	83	15	1	8	44	22	46	1	1	.312	.394
Cora,Alex, LA	26	.234	126	397	43	93	17	4	4	36	24	54	5	5	.278	.327
Cordero,Wil, Cle	30	.277	93	282	40	78	18	1	8	38	21	49	1	1	.327	.433
Cordova,Marty, Cle	32	.276	114	373	51	103	23	2	13	61	33	78	4	3	.335	.453
Cota,Humberto, Pit	23	.261	59	134	16	35	7	0	3	17	6	27	2	1	.293	.381
Counsell,Craig, Ari	31	.280	123	346	53	97	21	3	3	33	40	50	3	3	.355	.384
Cox,Steve, TB	27	.281	139	449	65	126	32	1	17	73	49	74	2	2	.351	.470
Crede,Joe, CWS	24	.279	102	308	45	86	19	0	10	48	27	62	2	2	.337	.438
Crespo,Cesar, SD	23	.235	68	183	33	43	8	1	4	20	25	51	11	4	.327	.355
Crespo,Felipe, Phi	29	.265	59	117	18	31	7	1	4	19	16	25	3	2	.353	.444
Cruz,Deivi, Det	26	.282	153	535	63	151	37	2	10	68	15	50	3	3	.302	.415
Cruz,Jacob, Col	29	.269	66	156	22	42	8	1	6	25	13	37	2	2	.325	.449
Cruz,Jose, Tor	28	.254	154	563	93	143	33	3	29	80	74	129	19	6	.341	.478
Curtis,Chad, Tex	33	.248	49	105	17	26	7	0	2	14	15	21	3	1	.342	.371
Damon,Johnny, Oak	28	.294	158	646	115	190	33	7	14	72	70	61	34	11	.363	.432
Darr,Mike, SD	26	.278	108	302	46	84	19	2	4	42	34	72	9	4	.351	.394
Daubach,Brian, Bos	30	.268	137	467	65	125	36	2	23	85	50	122	2	1	.338	.501
Davis,Ben, SD	25	.244	138	435	56	106	24	0	11	61	55	105	4	3	.329	.375
Davis,Russ, SF	32	.254	87	248	32	63	15	1	11	36	19	61	1	1	.307	.456

Projections for 2002 Batters

Batter	Age	Avg	G	AB	R	H	2B	3B	HR	RBI	BB	SO	SB	CS	OBP	SLG
Delgado,Carlos, Tor	30	.293	162	584	110	171	41	1	41	124	111	131	1	1	.406	.577
Dellucci,David, Ari	28	.284	107	208	30	59	16	4	6	31	20	42	2	2	.346	.486
DeRosa,Mark, Atl	27	.261	63	188	25	49	10	0	2	18	13	22	3	3	.308	.346
DeShields,Delino, ChC	33	.269	117	308	46	83	13	3	5	35	42	54	15	6	.357	.380
Diaz,Einar, Cle	29	.277	136	452	54	125	27	1	5	52	22	48	5	3	.310	.374
DiSarcina,Gary, Ana	34	.251	83	247	28	62	12	1	1	24	11	26	3	3	.283	.320
Drew,J.D., StL	26	.293	138	454	92	133	23	4	25	74	70	98	16	7	.387	.526
Dunn,Adam, Cin	22	.291	143	512	101	149	33	1	35	99	77	140	10	4	.384	.564
Dunston,Shawon, SF	39	.254	97	201	28	51	14	2	8	30	3	38	4	2	.265	.463
Durazo,Erubiel, Ari	28	.317	103	281	54	89	17	1	17	54	43	62	1	1	.407	.566
Durham,Ray, CWS	30	.276	154	620	114	171	35	6	18	67	73	109	25	11	.352	.439
Dye,Jermaine, Oak	28	.294	159	606	98	178	34	2	29	110	65	110	5	2	.362	.500
Easley,Damion, Det	32	.251	144	530	74	133	27	2	15	65	54	99	10	5	.320	.394
Echevarria,Angel, Mil	31	.300	60	110	14	33	10	0	4	17	9	20	0	0	.353	.500
Eckstein,David, Ana	27	.286	155	590	84	169	28	2	4	51	46	59	25	7	.338	.361
Edmonds,Jim, StL	32	.272	142	493	101	134	30	1	28	86	92	142	7	5	.386	.507
Encarnacion,Juan, Det	26	.277	138	512	72	142	28	6	17	70	25	100	20	8	.311	.455
Encarnacion,Mario, Col	24	.263	80	213	33	56	9	1	8	33	18	63	5	5	.320	.427
Erstad,Darin, Ana	28	.293	158	656	101	192	37	3	17	81	63	102	22	9	.355	.436
Escobar,Alex, NYM	23	.253	84	253	35	64	12	2	7	33	22	86	9	3	.313	.399
Estalella,Bobby, NYY	27	.229	64	175	24	40	11	1	8	28	26	51	1	0	.328	.440
Estrada,Johnny, Phi	26	.256	58	199	19	51	12	0	5	23	7	15	0	0	.282	.392
Eusebio,Tony, Hou	35	.258	73	194	18	50	10	0	4	26	23	43	0	0	.336	.371
Everett,Adam, Hou	25	.248	48	137	22	34	6	1	2	13	16	28	5	2	.327	.350
Everett,Carl, Bos	31	.283	128	480	76	136	27	2	23	87	46	110	14	7	.346	.492
Fabregas,Jorge, Ana	32	.245	45	102	8	25	4	0	1	12	8	10	0	0	.300	.314
Febles,Carlos, KC	26	.266	125	444	78	118	22	5	9	45	45	79	21	8	.333	.399
Feliz,Pedro, SF	25	.249	74	233	28	58	13	1	9	35	9	47	1	1	.277	.429
Fick,Robert, Det	28	.268	121	384	62	103	25	2	15	66	44	65	3	2	.343	.461
Finley,Steve, Ari	37	.261	140	506	79	132	24	4	21	72	54	80	8	5	.332	.449
Flaherty,John, TB	34	.249	83	281	25	70	13	0	6	33	13	41	1	1	.282	.359
Fletcher,Darrin, Tor	35	.262	120	404	37	106	22	1	13	58	22	46	0	0	.300	.418
Floyd,Cliff, Fla	29	.296	148	544	98	161	34	2	27	98	64	103	21	8	.370	.515
Fordyce,Brook, Bal	32	.260	111	334	36	87	21	0	10	41	23	55	1	1	.308	.413
Frye,Jeff, Tor	35	.280	65	157	21	44	12	1	1	12	16	22	2	1	.347	.389
Fryman,Travis, Cle	33	.283	138	492	64	139	27	2	14	76	52	97	3	3	.351	.431
Fullmer,Brad, Tor	27	.283	151	552	78	156	41	2	25	97	39	75	4	3	.330	.500
Furcal,Rafael, Atl	21	.288	135	493	83	142	26	2	6	49	64	83	39	14	.370	.385
Galarraga,Andres, SF	41	.258	105	345	40	89	19	1	15	59	26	98	2	2	.310	.449
Gant,Ron, Oak	37	.240	89	288	48	69	13	1	13	39	42	71	5	2	.336	.427
Garciaparra,N., Bos	28	.339	138	540	103	183	40	5	25	101	58	46	9	4	.403	.570
Giambi,Jason, Oak	31	.314	153	529	106	166	38	1	35	122	125	95	1	1	.445	.588
Giambi,Jeremy, Oak	27	.288	138	434	70	125	24	1	16	69	69	99	2	2	.386	.459
Gil,Benji, Ana	29	.244	96	271	33	66	13	1	7	31	19	64	6	4	.293	.376
Giles,Brian, Pit	31	.308	152	548	106	169	32	3	35	109	101	72	8	4	.416	.569
Giles,Marcus, Atl	24	.281	133	488	75	137	28	2	15	66	54	82	16	9	.352	.439
Gilkey,Bernard, Atl	35	.250	77	128	14	32	7	0	3	16	15	28	1	1	.329	.375
Girardi,Joe, ChC	37	.251	92	279	31	70	13	1	4	30	22	50	1	1	.306	.348
Glanville,Doug, Phi	31	.285	146	606	87	173	27	4	11	54	32	80	23	6	.321	.398
Glaus,Troy, Ana	25	.265	161	577	111	153	37	1	43	107	103	151	9	5	.376	.556

Projections for 2002 Batters

Batter	Age	Avg	G	AB	R	H	2B	3B	HR	RBI	BB	SO	SB	CS	OBP	SLG
Gomez,Chris, TB	31	.263	122	388	45	102	20	1	7	41	33	57	2	1	.321	.374
Gonzalez,Alex, Fla	25	.251	154	574	74	144	29	5	12	62	24	112	5	4	.281	.382
Gonzalez,Alex S., Tor	29	.252	153	603	79	152	31	3	16	69	49	131	14	7	.308	.393
Gonzalez,Juan, Cle	32	.298	136	526	89	157	31	2	31	112	43	98	2	1	.351	.542
Gonzalez,Luis, Ari	34	.308	152	585	103	180	34	3	45	123	79	76	5	4	.390	.607
Gonzalez,Wiki, SD	28	.264	96	242	29	64	13	1	9	38	20	30	1	1	.321	.438
Goodwin,Tom, LA	33	.256	106	312	53	80	9	2	3	26	34	62	21	8	.329	.327
Grace,Mark, Ari	38	.298	139	486	74	145	31	2	13	74	75	35	2	2	.392	.451
Graffanino,Tony, CWS	30	.281	95	267	42	75	14	2	4	31	28	45	6	5	.349	.393
Green,Shawn, LA	29	.290	162	625	121	181	39	3	40	116	81	117	23	7	.371	.554
Greer,Rusty, Tex	33	.300	114	424	75	127	29	2	12	71	63	60	2	2	.390	.462
Grieve,Ben, TB	26	.282	157	553	88	156	38	1	22	93	80	131	3	1	.373	.474
Griffey Jr.,Ken, Cin	32	.282	147	531	99	150	29	2	39	115	83	108	11	5	.379	.565
Grissom,Marquis, LA	35	.246	118	439	54	108	20	2	14	55	27	88	10	5	.290	.396
Grudzielanek,Mark, LA	32	.281	137	555	79	156	29	3	10	53	36	79	8	5	.325	.398
Guerrero,Vladimir, Mon	26	.326	159	596	110	194	39	6	42	123	61	73	18	11	.388	.622
Guerrero,Wilton, Cin	27	.287	74	188	22	54	7	3	1	16	9	24	5	2	.320	.372
Guillen,Carlos, Sea	26	.262	133	431	70	113	20	3	8	52	49	82	4	3	.338	.378
Guillen,Jose, TB	26	.275	84	269	38	74	16	2	9	41	16	52	2	1	.316	.450
Gutierrez,Ricky, ChC	32	.274	139	474	67	130	18	3	8	53	56	63	6	5	.351	.376
Guzman,Cristian, Min	24	.267	154	562	82	150	27	11	8	51	34	94	22	9	.309	.397
Guzman,Edwards, SF	25	.255	71	212	23	54	9	0	3	23	7	26	1	1	.279	.340
Hairston Jr.,Jerry, Bal	26	.263	128	445	69	117	24	3	8	49	41	60	17	10	.325	.384
Hall,Toby, TB	26	.304	132	434	57	132	30	0	16	76	18	34	2	1	.332	.484
Halter,Shane, Det	32	.258	110	380	47	98	20	2	7	38	34	83	7	7	.319	.376
Hammonds,Jeffrey, Mil	31	.281	116	402	68	113	23	2	16	70	39	86	9	6	.345	.468
Harris,Lenny, NYM	37	.269	90	108	11	29	4	0	1	10	7	8	3	1	.313	.333
Haselman,Bill, Tex	36	.248	51	125	11	31	7	0	3	15	8	26	0	0	.293	.376
Hatteberg,Scott, Bos	32	.263	92	236	28	62	17	0	5	29	36	32	0	0	.360	.398
Helms,Wes, Atl	26	.259	78	232	28	60	12	1	9	36	13	50	1	1	.298	.435
Helton,Todd, Col	28	.337	160	584	125	197	49	2	43	134	95	80	6	4	.430	.649
Henderson,Rickey, SD	43	.247	88	283	47	70	13	1	5	26	55	58	19	6	.370	.353
Hernandez,Jose, Mil	32	.242	142	500	66	121	18	3	19	65	45	155	5	5	.305	.404
Hernandez,R., Oak	26	.253	144	467	63	118	23	0	16	76	42	64	2	2	.314	.405
Hidalgo,Richard, Hou	26	.279	152	545	92	152	39	3	30	99	65	106	9	6	.356	.527
Higginson,Bobby, Det	31	.282	154	542	86	153	33	3	21	79	80	83	10	6	.375	.470
Hillenbrand,Shea, Bos	26	.275	105	378	47	104	21	1	8	46	11	39	3	3	.296	.399
Hinch,A.J., KC	28	.246	42	130	16	32	5	0	4	15	9	24	1	1	.295	.377
Hocking,Denny, Min	32	.257	108	311	39	80	15	2	4	30	29	58	5	3	.321	.357
Hollandsworth,T., Col	29	.279	114	358	61	100	20	2	15	45	34	80	10	5	.342	.472
Houston,Tyler, Mil	31	.249	110	293	34	73	12	0	14	41	25	79	1	1	.308	.433
Huff,Aubrey, TB	25	.284	140	525	76	149	41	2	19	77	47	89	2	2	.343	.478
Hundley,Todd, ChC	33	.220	97	295	35	65	13	0	17	49	36	92	1	1	.305	.437
Hunter,Brian L., Phi	31	.259	85	174	26	45	7	1	1	12	15	30	12	4	.317	.328
Hunter,Torii, Min	26	.271	154	560	85	152	31	4	21	80	32	108	12	9	.311	.454
Ibanez,Raul, KC	30	.254	116	264	35	67	15	2	10	40	24	47	1	1	.316	.439
Inge,Brandon, Det	25	.222	119	279	30	62	20	1	3	34	18	69	4	3	.269	.333
Izturis,Cesar, Tor	22	.247	101	295	33	73	13	3	1	24	10	26	14	5	.272	.322
Jackson,Damian, SD	28	.242	136	446	69	108	28	4	6	41	58	115	24	8	.329	.363
Jackson,Ryan, Det	30	.279	40	104	12	29	6	0	2	14	8	23	1	1	.330	.394

Projections for 2002 Batters

Batter	Age	Avg	G	AB	R	H	2B	3B	HR	RBI	BB	SO	SB	CS	OBP	SLG
Javier,Stan, Sea	38	.261	100	303	43	79	12	1	3	29	34	54	7	3	.335	.337
Jenkins,Geoff, Mil	27	.283	142	516	87	146	35	3	29	92	42	128	5	2	.337	.531
Jennings,Robin, Cin	30	.266	65	184	25	49	12	1	5	26	12	29	2	2	.311	.424
Jeter,Derek, NYY	28	.327	153	612	123	200	33	5	20	84	75	104	23	6	.400	.495
Jimenez,D'Angelo, SD	24	.278	120	436	65	121	23	2	7	55	48	74	9	7	.349	.388
Johnson,Charles, Fla	30	.253	137	450	58	114	24	0	21	70	51	121	1	0	.329	.447
Johnson,Mark L., CWS	26	.247	90	259	36	64	11	1	6	31	40	53	2	1	.348	.367
Johnson,Mark P., NYM	34	.254	69	138	19	35	8	0	6	23	23	29	1	1	.360	.442
Johnson,Russ, TB	29	.279	108	258	41	72	17	1	4	31	36	51	4	4	.367	.399
Jones,Andruw, Atl	25	.280	161	624	113	175	32	4	36	102	67	110	21	8	.350	.518
Jones,Chipper, Atl	30	.313	159	578	116	181	36	3	37	106	110	82	14	7	.423	.578
Jones,Jacque, Min	27	.285	154	547	75	156	34	2	18	75	34	108	11	8	.327	.453
Jordan,Brian, Atl	35	.278	140	522	79	145	26	3	20	86	38	84	8	4	.327	.454
Jordan,Kevin, Phi	32	.252	62	107	10	27	5	0	1	13	8	13	0	0	.304	.327
Justice,David, NYY	36	.267	135	449	74	120	22	1	25	81	75	92	3	2	.372	.488
Kapler,Gabe, Tex	26	.284	149	510	86	145	36	3	20	89	59	75	12	6	.359	.484
Karros,Eric, LA	34	.252	116	428	49	108	21	0	19	70	43	95	3	2	.321	.435
Kendall,Jason, Pit	28	.302	147	553	97	167	34	4	12	65	64	59	21	9	.374	.443
Kennedy,Adam, Ana	26	.277	148	541	72	150	33	6	9	65	30	65	17	8	.315	.410
Kent,Jeff, SF	34	.286	154	574	90	164	37	2	24	107	74	110	9	6	.367	.483
Kielty,Bobby, Min	25	.257	109	343	50	88	25	1	9	44	50	87	3	2	.351	.414
Kinkade,Mike, Bal	29	.301	71	206	32	62	14	2	5	31	16	31	4	2	.351	.461
Klesko,Ryan, SD	31	.291	144	532	93	155	33	3	29	104	88	89	14	5	.392	.528
Knoblauch,Chuck, NYY	33	.285	133	492	87	140	25	4	11	49	62	58	22	9	.365	.419
Konerko,Paul, CWS	26	.290	154	565	88	164	31	1	29	102	54	78	1	0	.352	.503
Koskie,Corey, Min	29	.289	154	551	88	159	33	3	20	89	78	118	13	6	.377	.468
Kotsay,Mark, SD	26	.288	138	468	71	135	27	4	11	58	41	49	11	6	.346	.434
Kreuter,Chad, LA	37	.225	80	204	23	46	9	0	4	23	36	48	0	0	.342	.328
Lamb,Mike, Tex	26	.297	148	538	78	160	39	2	12	73	36	62	2	2	.341	.444
Lampkin,Tom, Sea	38	.225	65	151	18	34	6	0	5	19	12	28	1	1	.282	.364
Lankford,Ray, SD	35	.242	128	397	60	96	27	3	18	61	59	140	9	4	.340	.461
Lansing,Mike, Bos	34	.256	84	254	33	65	15	1	6	28	17	39	3	1	.303	.394
Larkin,Barry, Cin	38	.288	116	403	68	116	21	2	9	45	59	42	13	5	.379	.417
LaRue,Jason, Cin	28	.246	120	382	51	94	27	2	14	52	27	89	3	2	.296	.437
Lawton,Matt, NYM	30	.279	155	556	85	155	34	2	13	74	87	68	22	8	.376	.417
Ledee,Ricky, Tex	28	.256	98	309	46	79	18	2	8	43	37	73	6	4	.335	.405
Lee,Carlos, CWS	26	.294	154	579	91	170	35	2	25	102	34	87	10	5	.333	.491
Lee,Derrek, Fla	26	.267	159	550	80	147	29	2	25	83	55	141	4	3	.334	.464
Lee,Travis, Phi	27	.255	151	548	77	140	28	2	18	78	82	96	9	3	.352	.412
Lewis,Darren, Bos	34	.248	82	218	29	54	8	2	2	18	18	28	7	4	.305	.330
Lieberthal,Mike, Phi	30	.268	123	406	60	109	25	1	16	65	39	64	1	1	.333	.453
Liefer,Jeff, CWS	27	.271	83	269	46	73	18	2	17	52	30	67	1	1	.344	.543
Lockhart,Keith, Atl	37	.253	79	166	20	42	8	1	2	17	17	21	1	1	.322	.349
Lo Duca,Paul, LA	30	.291	135	491	67	143	30	1	17	72	43	32	7	7	.348	.460
Lofton,Kenny, Cle	35	.285	130	501	96	143	24	4	12	59	67	78	24	8	.370	.421
Long,Terrence, Oak	26	.291	156	612	91	178	34	5	15	84	47	90	12	7	.341	.436
Lopez,Felipe, Tor	22	.255	108	384	53	98	17	4	11	42	26	98	10	8	.302	.406
Lopez,Javy, Atl	31	.286	133	462	57	132	22	1	22	84	34	81	2	1	.335	.481
Lopez,Luis, Mil	31	.256	98	203	24	52	13	1	4	22	14	44	1	1	.304	.389
Lopez,Luis, Tor	28	.307	82	238	32	73	15	0	4	36	21	23	0	0	.363	.420

Projections for 2002 Batters

Batter	Age	Avg	G	AB	R	H	2B	3B	HR	RBI	BB	SO	SB	CS	OBP	SLG
Loretta,Mark, Mil	30	.287	114	425	56	122	19	2	4	45	37	47	3	3	.344	.369
Lowell,Mike, Fla	28	.275	148	542	69	149	34	0	21	90	50	90	2	1	.336	.454
Lugo,Julio, Hou	26	.277	140	513	93	142	25	4	12	48	45	98	17	10	.335	.411
Lunar,Fernando, Bal	25	.214	71	201	15	43	8	0	0	17	8	37	0	0	.244	.254
Mabry,John, Fla	31	.242	49	91	11	22	7	0	3	13	7	25	0	0	.296	.418
Machado,Robert, ChC	29	.244	69	197	21	48	12	0	5	24	12	35	1	1	.287	.381
Macias,Jose, Det	28	.251	101	338	42	85	15	4	4	35	27	42	6	4	.307	.355
Mackowiak,Rob, Pit	26	.269	72	193	26	52	12	1	4	26	8	41	3	2	.299	.404
Magadan,Dave, SD	39	.270	82	115	10	31	5	0	1	13	20	19	0	0	.378	.339
Magee,Wendell, Det	29	.258	86	240	34	62	13	1	8	30	22	51	2	2	.321	.421
Marrero,Eli, StL	28	.226	97	230	30	52	14	2	6	27	16	39	6	2	.276	.383
Martin,Al, Sea	34	.270	98	322	51	87	16	2	11	35	31	68	9	4	.334	.435
Martinez,Dave, Atl	37	.266	116	278	35	74	11	2	3	26	30	46	5	4	.338	.353
Martinez,Edgar, Sea	39	.311	133	470	73	146	33	1	23	104	87	91	2	1	.418	.532
Martinez,Felix, TB	28	.234	64	188	24	44	9	2	1	15	14	35	5	3	.287	.319
Martinez,Ramon E., SF	29	.277	122	408	53	113	24	2	9	49	38	53	2	2	.339	.412
Martinez,Tino, NYY	34	.268	150	557	81	149	29	1	25	104	53	83	2	2	.331	.458
Mateo,Ruben, Cin	24	.275	75	171	25	47	10	1	5	24	9	30	3	1	.311	.433
Matheny,Mike, StL	31	.233	102	309	30	72	13	1	5	32	24	68	0	0	.288	.330
Matos,Luis, Bal	23	.230	62	196	25	45	8	1	3	23	13	33	10	5	.278	.327
Matthews Jr.,Gary, Pit	27	.226	136	442	66	100	17	2	12	53	54	105	9	4	.310	.355
Mayne,Brent, KC	34	.269	118	338	32	91	17	0	3	43	41	55	2	2	.348	.346
McCarty,Dave, KC	32	.253	100	261	37	66	15	1	10	37	30	65	2	2	.330	.433
McEwing,Joe, NYM	29	.262	120	332	45	87	22	3	7	36	24	62	6	4	.312	.410
McGriff,Fred, ChC	38	.281	146	520	68	146	25	1	26	91	78	112	2	1	.375	.483
McGwire,Mark, StL	38	.230	102	304	58	70	13	0	32	72	76	101	0	0	.384	.589
McLemore,Mark, Sea	37	.251	131	463	75	116	17	2	4	45	73	80	18	8	.353	.322
Meares,Pat, Pit	33	.246	67	207	24	51	10	1	4	23	14	40	1	1	.294	.362
Meluskey,Mitch, Det	28	.319	104	342	58	109	27	0	15	61	63	59	1	1	.425	.529
Menechino,Frank, Oak	31	.260	138	423	74	110	22	3	11	56	61	94	3	5	.353	.404
Merced,Orlando, Hou	35	.278	59	90	11	25	9	1	3	18	9	15	1	1	.343	.500
Merloni,Lou, Bos	31	.278	57	158	20	44	11	0	2	19	11	27	1	1	.325	.386
Mientkiewicz,Doug, Min	28	.280	149	546	74	153	37	1	13	73	65	87	5	4	.357	.423
Millar,Kevin, Fla	30	.286	143	416	58	119	29	3	17	75	43	71	0	0	.353	.493
Miller,Corky, Cin	26	.245	68	196	27	48	13	0	8	30	18	38	2	2	.308	.434
Miller,Damian, Ari	32	.275	114	360	45	99	23	1	12	48	33	81	1	1	.336	.444
Minor,Damon, SF	28	.254	51	122	17	31	6	0	5	19	15	28	0	0	.336	.426
Mirabelli,Doug, Bos	31	.245	55	143	18	35	8	0	5	20	19	34	1	0	.333	.406
Molina,Ben, Ana	27	.269	109	357	37	96	16	0	8	49	19	33	1	1	.306	.381
Mondesi,Raul, Tor	31	.271	154	569	97	154	32	4	31	95	65	123	25	11	.345	.504
Mora,Melvin, Bal	30	.257	136	389	53	100	21	2	7	42	39	78	11	7	.325	.375
Mordecai,Mike, Mon	34	.249	108	229	25	57	12	1	4	22	18	43	2	2	.304	.362
Morris,Warren, Pit	28	.277	96	321	40	89	18	2	6	42	34	46	4	5	.346	.402
Mouton,James, Mil	33	.231	62	78	11	18	6	0	1	8	11	22	3	1	.326	.346
Mueller,Bill, ChC	31	.293	134	460	78	135	27	1	8	50	59	51	3	2	.374	.409
Munson,Eric, Det	24	.239	61	197	29	47	12	1	8	33	21	55	1	1	.312	.431
Murray,Calvin, SF	30	.263	106	315	49	83	18	2	6	31	29	58	12	6	.326	.390
Myers,Greg, Oak	36	.234	58	128	14	30	7	0	5	18	15	27	0	0	.315	.406
Nevin,Phil, SD	31	.282	143	522	81	147	30	1	35	113	65	126	2	1	.361	.544
Nixon,Trot, Bos	28	.271	150	549	94	149	29	4	22	76	84	110	10	4	.368	.459

Projections for 2002 Batters

Batter	Age	Avg	G	AB	R	H	2B	3B	HR	RBI	BB	SO	SB	CS	OBP	SLG
Norton,Greg, Col	29	.258	101	244	36	63	13	1	11	35	37	58	2	1	.356	.455
Nunez,Abraham, Pit	26	.253	131	387	45	98	13	2	2	30	38	63	12	5	.320	.313
Ochoa,Alex, Col	30	.284	144	395	63	112	25	3	9	53	43	55	10	7	.354	.430
Offerman,Jose, Bos	33	.273	119	469	75	128	20	5	8	47	70	76	12	7	.367	.388
Ojeda,Augie, ChC	27	.241	73	145	19	35	6	1	2	14	13	15	2	1	.304	.338
O'Leary,Troy, Bos	32	.267	109	390	57	104	23	3	14	58	34	66	1	1	.325	.449
Olerud,John, Sea	33	.294	154	551	87	162	36	1	18	90	105	77	2	1	.407	.461
O'Neill,Paul, NYY	39	.281	134	513	69	144	27	1	18	85	50	76	11	5	.345	.442
Ordonez,Magglio, CWS	28	.305	159	609	102	186	36	2	31	114	63	66	16	7	.371	.524
Ordonez,Rey, NYM	29	.245	148	498	44	122	19	2	2	47	47	53	4	3	.310	.303
Ortiz,David, Min	26	.276	143	486	75	134	36	1	22	82	65	109	1	1	.361	.490
Ortiz,Jose, Col	25	.275	142	530	95	146	32	2	18	81	40	81	15	7	.326	.445
Osik,Keith, Pit	33	.234	61	128	10	30	6	0	2	15	12	20	1	1	.300	.328
Owens,Eric, Fla	31	.272	113	382	51	104	14	2	5	38	30	47	16	7	.325	.359
Palmeiro,Orlando, Ana	33	.269	98	219	31	59	11	1	1	22	29	21	4	3	.355	.342
Palmeiro,Rafael, Tex	37	.282	157	561	90	158	31	1	40	117	97	80	3	3	.388	.554
Palmer,Dean, Det	33	.245	121	444	64	109	21	1	25	82	53	126	3	2	.326	.466
Paquette,Craig, StL	33	.254	112	335	42	85	18	1	14	58	17	71	2	1	.290	.439
Patterson,Corey, ChC	22	.238	106	336	55	80	17	2	11	42	25	81	14	6	.291	.399
Paul,Josh, CWS	27	.264	78	220	35	58	12	1	5	29	18	48	4	3	.319	.395
Payton,Jay, NYM	29	.282	125	404	54	114	20	2	12	49	25	50	6	6	.324	.431
Perez,Eddie, Atl	34	.255	61	161	15	41	8	0	5	20	7	22	0	0	.286	.398
Perez,Neifi, KC	27	.287	149	628	91	180	32	9	10	68	29	59	7	5	.318	.414
Perez,Timo, NYM	25	.306	89	284	42	87	14	2	6	31	15	28	8	6	.341	.433
Perez,Tomas, Phi	28	.245	73	192	20	47	9	1	3	23	11	34	1	1	.286	.349
Perry,Herbert, CWS	32	.278	85	263	39	73	18	1	7	37	18	50	1	1	.324	.433
Petrick,Ben, Col	25	.301	118	382	65	115	25	3	20	65	50	80	6	5	.382	.539
Piatt,Adam, Oak	26	.278	115	331	53	92	22	2	12	55	41	81	2	2	.358	.465
Piazza,Mike, NYM	33	.318	139	503	88	160	25	0	37	110	59	77	2	1	.390	.588
Pierre,Juan, Col	24	.338	158	606	99	205	23	7	1	57	42	32	44	19	.381	.404
Pierzynski,A.J., Min	25	.276	121	406	51	112	26	1	6	48	16	56	2	2	.303	.389
Polanco,Placido, StL	26	.292	142	456	64	133	20	3	3	41	23	38	7	4	.326	.368
Posada,Jorge, NYY	30	.265	147	501	74	133	31	1	23	86	83	138	2	2	.370	.469
Pratt,Todd, Phi	35	.242	56	124	16	30	5	0	4	17	18	34	0	0	.338	.379
Pujols,Albert, StL	22	.334	157	574	115	192	48	4	39	130	71	88	2	2	.408	.636
Quinn,Mark, KC	28	.304	145	536	78	163	37	2	24	90	27	89	6	4	.337	.515
Ramirez,Aramis, Pit	24	.294	150	591	81	174	34	1	30	102	51	85	3	3	.350	.508
Ramirez,Manny, Bos	30	.305	151	531	106	162	37	1	41	137	97	142	2	2	.412	.610
Randa,Joe, KC	32	.287	146	571	74	164	29	3	14	82	41	72	5	4	.335	.422
Reboulet,Jeff, LA	38	.222	96	189	29	42	8	0	1	13	30	39	1	1	.329	.280
Redman,Tike, Pit	25	.253	54	194	23	49	8	3	1	18	12	25	7	3	.296	.340
Redmond,Mike, Fla	31	.284	82	204	20	58	10	0	2	21	18	22	0	0	.342	.363
Reese,Pokey, Cin	29	.255	141	514	72	131	22	3	11	49	40	84	26	6	.309	.374
Relaford,Desi, NYM	28	.247	106	235	31	58	14	1	4	26	32	43	6	3	.337	.366
Renteria,Edgar, StL	26	.282	149	546	88	154	27	2	13	63	54	75	29	12	.347	.410
Richard,Chris, Bal	28	.257	140	505	73	130	31	2	21	78	46	98	9	7	.319	.451
Rios,Armando, Pit	30	.265	117	340	53	90	19	2	14	60	43	74	6	4	.347	.456
Rivas,Luis, Min	22	.258	148	561	79	145	33	6	6	56	39	92	24	10	.307	.371
Rivera,Ruben, Cin	28	.215	101	274	40	59	12	2	12	36	31	90	7	3	.295	.405
Roberts,Brian, Bal	24	.252	67	246	32	62	10	1	1	16	21	35	17	5	.311	.313

Projections for 2002 Batters

Batter	Age	Avg	G	AB	R	H	2B	3B	HR	RBI	BB	SO	SB	CS	OBP	SLG
Robinson,Kerry, StL	28	.280	90	175	25	49	5	2	0	15	11	21	11	5	.323	.331
Rodriguez,Alex, Tex	26	.310	159	609	141	189	39	2	50	138	88	126	25	8	.397	.627
Rodriguez,Ivan, Tex	30	.307	128	498	82	153	30	2	28	86	24	66	10	5	.339	.544
Rolen,Scott, Phi	27	.287	152	567	105	163	40	3	31	107	78	130	12	4	.374	.533
Rollins,Jimmy, Phi	23	.268	154	590	82	158	30	10	13	63	48	77	29	8	.323	.419
Rolls,Damian, TB	24	.249	80	225	30	56	11	1	1	17	12	41	7	3	.287	.320
Rowand,Aaron, CWS	24	.273	126	337	54	92	20	1	15	57	24	68	9	4	.321	.472
Sadler,Donnie, KC	27	.213	61	150	21	32	6	1	1	11	14	30	4	2	.280	.287
Saenz,Olmedo, Oak	31	.265	87	226	32	60	14	1	9	33	19	43	1	1	.322	.456
Salmon,Tim, Ana	33	.273	129	454	76	124	25	1	23	74	87	115	3	2	.390	.485
Sanchez,Rey, Atl	34	.271	140	499	59	135	18	2	1	41	22	52	6	3	.301	.321
Sandberg,Jared, TB	24	.235	48	153	17	36	9	0	4	21	16	42	1	0	.308	.373
Sanders,Reggie, Ari	34	.264	124	425	76	112	22	3	23	66	49	109	18	8	.340	.492
Santiago,Benito, SF	37	.251	122	386	30	97	17	1	7	41	26	72	2	2	.299	.355
Sequi,David, Bal	35	.283	133	484	66	137	28	1	14	68	52	80	1	1	.353	.432
Sexson,Richie, Mil	27	.265	157	573	93	152	29	3	40	120	57	158	2	2	.332	.536
Sheets,Andy, TB	30	.226	67	195	20	44	8	1	3	21	16	42	2	2	.284	.323
Sheffield,Gary, LA	33	.292	144	513	92	150	26	1	34	102	99	68	9	5	.407	.546
Shinjo,Tsuyoshi, NYM	30	.268	118	384	44	103	23	1	10	52	24	66	4	4	.311	.411
Shumpert,Terry, Col	35	.275	114	265	41	73	17	2	7	29	24	44	8	4	.336	.434
Sierra,Ruben, Tex	36	.267	86	303	40	81	16	2	13	49	27	47	2	1	.327	.462
Simon,Randall, Det	27	.279	81	251	28	70	16	0	7	37	18	28	2	2	.327	.426
Singleton,Chris, CWS	29	.279	121	408	60	114	21	4	9	51	24	56	12	6	.319	.417
Smith,Mark, Mon	32	.236	72	148	20	35	10	0	5	20	15	36	2	1	.307	.405
Snow,J.T., SF	34	.248	115	375	54	93	18	1	12	58	57	94	1	1	.347	.397
Soriano,Alfonso, NYY	24	.266	155	563	85	150	34	3	18	79	31	117	28	12	.305	.433
Sosa,Sammy, ChC	33	.297	154	579	126	172	28	3	57	140	93	163	6	5	.394	.651
Spencer,Shane, NYY	30	.260	81	258	35	67	16	1	9	37	23	50	1	2	.320	.434
Spiezio,Scott, Ana	29	.259	110	305	43	79	18	1	11	43	33	48	1	1	.331	.433
Spivey,Junior, Ari	27	.246	77	228	37	56	12	2	5	26	28	45	7	6	.328	.382
Stairs,Matt, ChC	34	.244	108	316	49	77	17	0	16	56	52	79	3	2	.351	.449
Stevens,Lee, Mon	34	.249	135	481	65	120	25	1	22	75	57	131	1	1	.329	.443
Stewart,Shannon, Tor	28	.309	152	637	108	197	39	4	16	72	52	81	33	12	.361	.458
Stinnett,Kelly, Cin	32	.230	61	178	20	41	8	1	7	23	15	51	1	1	.290	.404
Stynes,Chris, Bos	29	.283	118	346	54	98	18	1	8	35	27	50	7	3	.335	.410
Surhoff,B.J., Atl	37	.272	125	463	58	126	23	1	12	60	33	52	5	3	.321	.404
Suzuki,Ichiro, Sea	28	.335	155	669	123	224	35	7	8	74	30	50	48	15	.363	.444
Sweeney,Mike, KC	28	.308	154	590	99	182	37	0	27	110	67	60	7	3	.379	.508
Tatis,Fernando, Mon	27	.271	128	436	78	118	27	1	21	70	70	113	10	5	.372	.482
Taubensee,Eddie, Cle	33	.279	57	154	19	43	8	0	5	25	12	26	0	0	.331	.429
Tejada,Miguel, Oak	26	.270	162	612	110	165	32	3	30	107	59	93	8	5	.334	.479
Thomas,Frank, CWS	34	.309	146	528	97	163	34	1	31	110	99	83	3	2	.418	.553
Thome,Jim, Cle	31	.271	152	521	101	141	31	2	39	108	120	176	0	0	.407	.562
Trammell,Bubba, SD	30	.269	144	501	70	135	28	1	24	84	56	85	3	2	.343	.473
Truby,Chris, Hou	28	.272	67	228	29	62	13	2	9	38	14	45	4	2	.314	.465
Tucker,Michael, ChC	31	.259	135	336	54	87	17	3	12	45	43	84	10	5	.343	.435
Tyner,Jason, TB	25	.283	88	311	43	88	7	2	0	22	21	31	21	8	.328	.318
Uribe,Juan, Col	21	.304	144	546	62	166	40	16	14	89	16	95	11	8	.324	.513
Valentin,Javier, Min	26	.231	65	182	18	42	9	1	4	21	14	31	1	1	.286	.357
Valentin,John, Bos	35	.262	75	225	35	59	15	1	7	31	21	35	1	1	.325	.431

Projections for 2002 Batters

Batter	Age	Avg	G	AB	R	H	2B	3B	HR	RBI	BB	SO	SB	CS	OBP	SLG
Valentin,Jose, CWS	32	.253	126	438	76	111	24	2	22	65	56	96	9	5	.338	.468
Vander Wal,John, SF	36	.262	133	393	53	103	22	2	14	67	64	103	5	3	.365	.435
Varitek,Jason, Bos	30	.261	126	403	53	105	27	1	13	59	47	75	1	1	.338	.429
Vaughn,Greg, TB	36	.233	130	464	74	108	21	1	27	78	72	127	8	3	.336	.457
Vaughn,Mo, Ana	34	.288	143	527	77	152	25	1	33	100	59	140	1	0	.360	.528
Vazquez,Ramon, Sea	25	.267	59	210	32	56	11	1	3	28	27	40	2	2	.350	.371
Velarde,Randy, NYY	39	.273	108	414	61	113	19	1	9	41	44	83	8	4	.343	.389
Ventura,Robin, NYM	34	.250	144	488	69	122	25	1	23	81	78	101	2	2	.353	.447
Veras,Quilvio, Bos	31	.266	87	304	50	81	14	1	4	28	42	57	14	8	.355	.359
Vidro,Jose, Mon	27	.310	141	533	85	165	39	1	17	74	38	56	4	3	.356	.482
Vina,Fernando, StL	33	.290	134	542	78	157	24	5	6	40	36	34	12	8	.334	.386
Vizcaino,Jose, Hou	34	.266	113	274	34	73	13	2	1	25	20	36	4	3	.316	.339
Vizquel,Omar, Cle	35	.270	153	575	86	155	24	2	4	51	67	65	22	9	.346	.339
Wakeland,Chris, Det	28	.265	70	204	27	54	11	1	8	28	19	55	2	2	.327	.446
Walker,Larry, Col	35	.335	137	451	94	151	30	2	32	103	66	74	9	4	.420	.623
Walker,Todd, Cin	29	.289	147	540	83	156	34	2	13	66	55	79	12	7	.355	.431
Ward,Daryle, Hou	27	.294	129	367	56	108	22	0	27	76	29	77	0	0	.346	.575
Wells,Vernon, Tor	23	.269	137	438	62	118	30	3	11	55	34	75	15	8	.322	.427
White,Devon, Mil	39	.254	106	339	43	86	19	2	10	43	25	74	9	4	.305	.410
White,Rondell, ChC	30	.295	112	407	59	120	24	2	17	60	30	75	7	4	.343	.489
Wilkerson,Brad, Mon	25	.251	127	351	58	88	25	1	10	49	63	92	6	4	.365	.413
Williams,Bernie, NYY	33	.305	146	544	102	166	33	4	26	103	83	83	9	6	.397	.524
Williams,Gerald, NYY	35	.254	94	244	35	62	14	1	7	32	15	43	7	4	.297	.406
Williams,Matt, Ari	36	.276	120	464	61	128	21	1	18	74	27	73	2	1	.316	.442
Wilson,Craig A., Pit	25	.269	110	275	45	74	15	1	17	50	25	86	2	1	.330	.516
Wilson,Dan, Sea	33	.253	120	368	41	93	20	1	8	40	25	73	2	1	.300	.378
Wilson,Enrique, NYY	26	.270	86	230	29	62	14	1	3	24	16	28	3	3	.317	.378
Wilson,Jack, Pit	24	.253	89	320	44	81	16	2	2	27	20	53	2	3	.297	.334
Wilson,Preston, Fla	27	.275	142	506	82	139	29	2	28	90	48	143	19	9	.338	.506
Wilson,Vance, NYM	29	.240	64	125	12	30	6	0	3	14	6	22	1	1	.275	.360
Winn,Randy, TB	28	.287	117	418	67	120	23	5	5	43	42	76	17	11	.352	.402
Womack,Tony, Ari	32	.273	126	490	73	134	19	6	4	36	30	57	36	9	.315	.361
Wooten,Shawn, Ana	29	.291	82	268	33	78	15	1	9	40	16	50	1	1	.331	.455
Young,Dmitri, Cin	28	.300	150	517	73	155	36	3	19	78	38	80	3	3	.348	.491
Young,Eric, ChC	35	.282	137	539	85	152	25	3	5	42	54	37	38	14	.347	.367
Young,Kevin, Pit	33	.259	107	367	53	95	21	1	14	60	37	84	9	5	.327	.436
Young,Michael, Tex	25	.271	117	439	66	119	25	4	11	61	35	90	9	4	.325	.421
Zaun,Gregg, KC	31	.265	103	234	29	62	13	1	6	32	32	27	4	2	.353	.406
Zeile,Todd, NYM	36	.259	126	448	55	116	23	1	13	61	54	79	2	2	.339	.402
Zuleta,Julio, ChC	27	.277	62	191	29	53	13	0	10	37	12	47	1	1	.320	.503

These Guys Can Play Too and Might Get A Shot

Predicting major league playing time in 2002 for young minor leaguers is a difficult task. We are confident, however, that if the players listed below were to get a big league shot in the upcoming season, their numbers would resemble the stats you'll find in the chart. These players generally fit into one of two categories: they either have a decent chance to play in the majors in 2002, or we think they deserve a chance. Listed below are the players' Major League Equivalencies (or MLEs) for their 2001 seasons. An MLE is not a prediction of what a player will do in the future; it's an interpretation of what he did in the minors last year. The MLE adjusts a player's minor league stats and re-expresses them in major league terms. In short, an MLE shows you what a player would have hit if he'd been playing in the majors. It has just as much predictive value as a major leaguer's 2001 numbers, but no more. Ages are as of June 30, 2002.

Batter	Age	Avg	G	AB	R	H	2B	3B	HR	RBI	BB	SO	SB	CS	OBP	SLG
Berger,Brandon	27	.288	120	441	82	127	25	2	34	98	30	93	10	5	.333	.585
Blalock,Hank	21	.312	68	266	44	83	16	3	10	53	29	39	2	2	.380	.508
Borchard,Joe	23	.284	133	507	89	144	25	0	26	92	54	169	3	4	.353	.487
Broussard,Ben	25	.300	100	343	68	103	26	0	19	58	44	73	7	2	.380	.542
Brown,Roosevelt	26	.314	88	347	54	109	29	0	17	61	11	70	2	5	.335	.545
Burroughs,Sean	21	.297	104	380	54	113	24	0	7	49	32	57	6	2	.352	.416
Byrd,Marlon	24	.289	137	491	87	142	21	6	22	72	36	101	22	8	.338	.491
Castro,Ramon	26	.281	108	360	53	101	25	0	16	59	25	79	0	1	.327	.483
Chen,Chin-Feng	24	.284	66	215	41	61	13	1	14	44	30	69	3	4	.371	.549
Choi,Hee Seop	23	.205	77	258	30	53	9	0	10	36	27	70	3	1	.281	.357
Conti,Jason	27	.292	130	496	70	145	31	4	10	53	31	88	3	5	.334	.431
Crede,Joe	24	.272	124	460	66	125	33	0	17	64	46	92	1	1	.338	.454
Cuddyer,Mike	23	.284	141	497	83	141	35	2	25	76	56	115	3	9	.356	.513
Cust,Jack	23	.246	135	423	61	104	20	1	20	59	77	168	4	3	.362	.440
Diaz,Juan	26	.247	74	271	37	67	16	0	16	42	14	90	0	0	.284	.483
Ensberg,Morgan	26	.306	87	314	62	96	20	0	23	58	43	63	4	3	.389	.589
German,Esteban	23	.274	130	460	91	126	23	2	7	34	54	89	32	10	.350	.378
Ginter,Keith	26	.266	132	455	72	121	31	4	16	66	58	155	6	6	.349	.457
Grabowski,Jason	26	.269	114	379	51	102	28	2	7	50	53	99	5	3	.359	.409
Hafner,Travis	25	.268	88	317	52	85	23	0	18	65	44	86	2	0	.357	.511
Hart,Jason	24	.218	134	476	56	104	22	0	14	59	44	106	2	3	.285	.353
Harvey,Ken	24	.316	79	304	45	96	17	2	7	52	12	61	2	0	.342	.454
Hinske,Eric	24	.249	121	417	56	104	23	0	18	62	42	117	14	5	.318	.434
Hudson,Orlando	24	.292	139	490	73	143	36	8	6	71	49	79	15	6	.356	.435
Johnson,Nick	23	.235	110	349	57	82	18	0	15	41	68	110	6	2	.360	.415
Kelton,Dave	22	.300	58	220	30	66	8	3	11	41	19	58	0	3	.356	.514
Lane,Jason	25	.306	137	519	93	159	35	1	36	112	46	106	10	2	.363	.586
LeCroy,Matt	26	.294	101	377	40	111	15	0	14	61	27	101	0	2	.342	.446
Magruder,Chris	25	.270	127	474	73	128	24	6	11	51	43	93	5	5	.331	.416
Matranga,Dave	25	.290	107	396	72	115	34	1	10	56	34	103	12	7	.347	.457
Mohr,Dustan	26	.319	135	505	79	161	40	2	20	80	36	121	6	9	.364	.525
Overbay,Lyle	25	.313	138	502	60	157	42	2	9	73	41	98	3	4	.365	.458
Pena,Carlos	24	.279	119	426	66	119	36	2	22	69	74	130	8	2	.386	.528
Phelps,Josh	24	.277	136	476	85	132	35	0	27	86	60	134	2	3	.358	.521
Rivera,Juan	23	.299	132	498	77	149	25	2	23	85	23	85	6	12	.330	.496
Rivera,Mike	25	.259	112	398	64	103	17	0	23	86	32	99	1	2	.314	.475
Romano,Jason	23	.264	87	330	45	87	13	0	3	28	30	60	7	5	.325	.330
Thames,Marcus	25	.301	139	505	102	152	39	2	27	87	55	108	7	4	.370	.547
Valent,Eric	25	.262	117	442	58	116	30	1	19	70	45	112	0	0	.331	.464

Estos Jugadores Pueden Jugar si se les da un Chance

Prognosticar quienes en las ligas menores van a jugar en las Grandes Ligas en el 2002 es difícil. Pero nosotros tenemos confianza en decir que si estos jugadores le dan una oportunidad de jugar, sus números serían similares a los que presentamos. Estos jugadores pertenecen a dos categorías: tienen un buen chance de jugar en las Grandes Ligas en el 2002, o nosotros pensamos que merecen el chance. Los números que presentamos son sus Equivalente de Grades Ligas del 2001. El Equivalente de Grades Ligas no es un prognóstico, si no una interpretación de sus temporadas en las ligas menores del 2001. Las edades mostradas son las edades de los jugadores el 30 de junio del 2002.

Bateador	Edad	Avg	J	VB	C	H	2B	3B	HR	CE	BB	K	BR	AR	PE	PBA
Berger,Brandon	27	.288	120	441	82	127	25	2	34	98	30	93	10	5	.333	.585
Blalock,Hank	21	.312	68	266	44	83	16	3	10	53	29	39	2	2	.380	.508
Borchard,Joe	23	.284	133	507	89	144	25	0	26	92	54	169	3	4	.353	.487
Broussard,Ben	25	.300	100	343	68	103	26	0	19	58	44	73	7	2	.380	.542
Brown,Roosevelt	26	.314	88	347	54	109	29	0	17	61	11	70	2	5	.335	.545
Burroughs,Sean	21	.297	104	380	54	113	24	0	7	49	32	57	6	2	.352	.416
Byrd,Marlon	24	.289	137	491	87	142	21	6	22	72	36	101	22	8	.338	.491
Castro,Ramon	26	.281	108	360	53	101	25	0	16	59	25	79	0	1	.327	.483
Chen,Chin-Feng	24	.284	66	215	41	61	13	1	14	44	30	69	3	4	.371	.549
Choi,Hee Seop	23	.205	77	258	30	53	9	0	10	36	27	70	3	1	.281	.357
Conti,Jason	27	.292	130	496	70	145	31	4	10	53	31	88	3	5	.334	.431
Crede,Joe	24	.272	124	460	66	125	33	0	17	64	46	92	1	1	.338	.454
Cuddyer,Mike	23	.284	141	497	83	141	35	2	25	76	56	115	3	9	.356	.513
Cust,Jack	23	.246	135	423	61	104	20	1	20	59	77	168	4	3	.362	.440
Diaz,Juan	26	.247	74	271	37	67	16	0	16	42	14	90	0	0	.284	.483
Ensberg,Morgan	26	.306	87	314	62	96	20	0	23	58	43	63	4	3	.389	.589
German,Esteban	23	.274	130	460	91	126	23	2	7	34	54	89	32	10	.350	.378
Ginter,Keith	26	.266	132	455	72	121	31	4	16	66	58	155	6	6	.349	.457
Grabowski,Jason	26	.269	114	379	51	102	28	2	7	50	53	99	5	3	.359	.409
Hafner,Travis	25	.268	88	317	52	85	23	0	18	65	44	86	2	0	.357	.511
Hart,Jason	24	.218	134	476	56	104	22	0	14	59	44	106	2	3	.285	.353
Harvey,Ken	24	.316	79	304	45	96	17	2	7	52	12	61	2	0	.342	.454
Hinske,Eric	24	.249	121	417	56	104	23	0	18	62	42	117	14	5	.318	.434
Hudson,Orlando	24	.292	139	490	73	143	36	8	6	71	49	79	15	6	.356	.435
Johnson,Nick	23	.235	110	349	57	82	18	0	15	41	68	110	6	2	.360	.415
Kelton,Dave	22	.300	58	220	30	66	8	3	11	41	19	58	0	3	.356	.514
Lane,Jason	25	.306	137	519	93	159	35	1	36	112	46	106	10	2	.363	.586
LeCroy,Matt	26	.294	101	377	40	111	15	0	14	61	27	101	0	2	.342	.446
Magruder,Chris	25	.270	127	474	73	128	24	6	11	51	43	93	5	5	.331	.416
Matranga,Dave	25	.290	107	396	72	115	34	1	10	56	34	103	12	7	.347	.457
Mohr,Dustan	26	.319	135	505	79	161	40	2	20	80	36	121	6	9	.364	.525
Overbay,Lyle	25	.313	138	502	60	157	42	2	9	73	41	98	3	4	.365	.458
Pena,Carlos	24	.279	119	426	66	119	36	2	22	69	74	130	8	2	.386	.528
Phelps,Josh	24	.277	136	476	85	132	35	0	27	86	60	134	2	3	.358	.521
Rivera,Juan	23	.299	132	498	77	149	25	2	23	85	23	85	6	12	.330	.496
Rivera,Mike	25	.259	112	398	64	103	17	0	23	86	32	99	1	2	.314	.475
Romano,Jason	23	.264	87	330	45	87	13	0	3	28	30	60	7	5	.325	.330
Thames,Marcus	25	.301	139	505	102	152	39	2	27	87	55	108	7	4	.370	.547
Valent,Eric	25	.262	117	442	58	116	30	1	19	70	45	112	0	0	.331	.464

2002 Pitcher Projections

The only thing that might be more difficult than projecting pitching performance is actually throwing an assortment of pitches for strikes. The best pitchers manage to maintain consistent mechanics and pitch command from year to year, but for everyone else, predictable performance can be elusive and making accurate projections can be maddening.

Despite all of the variables that can go wrong for a pitcher, STATS devised a formula we use, which considers only hurlers who have worked 150 games or 500 innings in the big leagues.

Examples of success in our projections of a year ago include Mets southpaw Glendon Rusch and Atlanta ace Greg Maddux:

Glendon Rusch

	W	L	ERA	G	IP	H	BB	SO	BR/9
Actual 2001	8	12	4.63	33	179	216	43	156	13.0
Projected 2001	11	12	4.43	30	187	206	43	154	12.0

Greg Maddux

	W	L	ERA	G	IP	H	BB	SO	BR/9
Actual 2001	17	11	3.05	34	233	220	27	173	9.5
Projected 2001	19	9	2.94	34	239	227	40	166	10.1

In case there's any doubt about how difficult it is to project pitchers' performances, we supply a couple of cases of projections gone wrong. Early in the season, Philadelphia manager Larry Bowa said a healthy Jose Mesa in spring training looked like a different pitcher than the one in Seattle's camp the year before. Hardly anyone else anticipated Mesa's resurgence. Likewise with Atlanta's John Burkett:

Jose Mesa

	W	L	ERA	SV	IP	H	BB	SO	BR/9
Actual 2001	3	3	2.34	42	69	65	20	59	11.0
Projected 2001	4	5	5.14	0	77	86	39	62	14.6

John Burkett

	W	L	ERA	G	IP	H	BB	SO	BR/9
Actual 2001	12	12	3.04	34	219	187	70	187	10.5
Projected 2001	7	9	5.24	31	139	168	53	101	14.3

We'll try again with our projections for 2002, which you'll find on the pages that follow.

—Thom Henninger

Prognóstico de Lanzadores del 2002

Prognosticas lanzadores es difícil. Solamente los mejores lanzadores son consistentes. El resto de los lanzadores te hacen perder el pelo.

Sin embargo, STATS trata de prognosticar usando una fórmula que considera solo los lanzadores que han trabajado 150 juegos o 500 entradas en las Grandes Ligas.

Como ejemplos de nuestros buenos Prognósticos pueden ver Glendon Rusch de los Mets y Greg Maddux de Atlanta:

Glendon Rusch

	V	D	Efe	J	EL	H	BB	K	Em/9
Actual 2001	8	12	4.63	33	179	216	43	156	13.0
Prognóstico 2001	11	12	4.43	30	187	206	43	154	12.0

Greg Maddux

	V	D	Efe	J	EL	H	BB	K	Em/9
Actual 2001	17	11	3.05	34	233	220	27	173	9.5
Prognóstico 2001	19	9	2.94	34	239	227	40	166	10.1

En caso que dudan que los prognósticos son dificiles, aquí pueden ver unos ejempls. Larry Bowa dijó en marzo que un José Mesa sano era un lanzador diferente al José Mesa lesionado del año pasado con Seattle. Casi nadie anticipaba que Mesa iba a renacer. Lo mismo con John Burkett de Atlanta:

Jose Mesa

	V	D	Efe	J	EL	H	BB	K	Em/9
Actual 2001	3	3	2.34	42	69	65	20	59	11.0
Prognóstico 2001	4	5	5.14	0	77	86	39	62	14.6

John Burkett

	V	D	Efe	J	EL	H	BB	K	Em/9
Actual 2001	12	12	3.04	34	219	187	70	187	10.5
Prognóstico 2001	7	9	5.24	31	139	168	53	101	14.3

Vamos a tratar prognosticar de nuevo en el 2002. El resultado continua.

—Thom Henninger

Projections for 2002 Pitchers

Pitcher	Age	ERA	W	L	Sv	G	GS	IP	H	HR	BB	SO	BR/9
Abbott,Paul, Sea	34	4.13	11	9	0	30	27	168	147	21	80	107	12.2
Acevedo,Juan, Fla	32	4.37	4	4	0	60	0	68	68	8	31	41	13.1
Adams,Terry, LA	29	3.92	11	10	0	28	28	179	182	14	58	141	12.1
Alfonseca,Antonio, Fla	30	4.22	2	4	27	61	0	64	69	6	21	41	12.7
Anderson,Brian, Ari	30	4.72	9	10	0	30	25	160	175	28	36	73	11.9
Anderson,Matt, Det	25	4.06	2	4	38	64	0	62	55	6	36	57	13.2
Appier,Kevin, NYM	34	4.17	12	12	0	32	32	203	205	24	63	152	11.9
Arrojo,Rolando, Bos	33	4.29	5	4	0	38	17	126	129	16	49	94	12.7
Ashby,Andy, LA	34	4.05	11	10	0	28	28	180	184	22	45	96	11.4
Astacio,Pedro, Hou	32	4.82	12	12	0	32	32	198	212	32	63	182	12.5
Aybar,Manny, TB	27	4.71	2	2	0	29	1	42	44	5	18	28	13.3
Baldwin,James, LA	30	4.86	9	12	0	29	28	176	186	27	63	105	12.7
Batista,Miguel, Ari	31	4.45	9	9	0	34	24	164	168	19	75	107	13.3
Benes,Andy, StL	34	5.67	6	9	0	45	18	127	132	21	72	100	14.5
Benitez,Armando, NYM	29	2.84	3	3	46	74	0	76	47	9	39	108	10.2
Bere,Jason, ChC	31	4.75	10	12	0	32	32	182	187	25	74	161	12.9
Blair,Willie, Det	36	5.43	2	3	0	22	8	68	85	11	20	37	13.9
Boehringer,Brian, SF	32	4.24	3	3	0	41	1	51	51	6	21	38	12.7
Bohanon,Brian, Col	33	5.24	9	10	0	28	25	165	176	23	80	87	14.0
Bones,Ricky, Fla	33	4.76	3	4	0	59	0	68	78	7	29	47	14.2
Borbon,Pedro, Tor	34	4.22	4	3	0	67	0	49	45	6	27	36	13.2
Bottalico,Ricky, Phi	32	4.43	4	4	7	65	0	69	64	10	34	58	12.8
Bottenfield,Kent, Hou	33	4.50	8	7	0	35	20	138	144	20	42	89	12.1
Brantley,Jeff, Tex	38	6.19	2	2	0	30	0	32	38	7	16	29	15.2
Brown,Kevin, LA	37	2.91	17	9	0	33	33	235	187	20	77	218	10.1
Burba,Dave, Cle	35	4.55	11	10	0	32	29	164	175	19	59	143	12.8
Burkett,John, Atl	37	3.96	12	11	0	33	30	191	194	16	61	160	12.0
Byrd,Paul, KC	31	4.36	6	6	0	18	16	97	100	15	24	54	11.5
Carpenter,Chris, Tor	27	4.54	12	12	0	34	32	202	212	25	70	140	12.6
Carrasco,Hector, Min	32	4.44	4	4	0	60	0	75	83	7	32	63	13.8
Castillo,Frank, Bos	33	4.07	10	7	0	26	25	137	140	17	35	96	11.5
Charlton,Norm, Sea	39	3.55	2	1	0	30	0	33	30	3	11	32	11.2
Christiansen,Jason, SF	32	3.15	4	2	0	58	0	40	32	3	21	39	11.9
Clemens,Roger, NYY	39	3.68	15	10	0	33	33	215	197	23	70	203	11.2
Clement,Matt, Fla	27	4.62	10	12	0	32	32	181	182	18	91	147	13.6
Colon,Bartolo, Cle	27	4.05	14	10	0	33	33	211	199	22	85	212	12.1
Cone,David, Bos	39	5.51	8	10	0	27	26	142	166	21	60	115	14.3
Cook,Dennis, Phi	39	4.68	3	4	0	64	0	50	51	8	22	44	13.1
Cormier,Rheal, Phi	35	3.63	4	3	0	61	0	57	57	5	16	37	11.5
Crabtree,Tim, Tex	32	4.07	3	2	0	37	0	42	47	3	16	31	13.5
Creek,Doug, TB	33	4.50	4	4	0	59	0	62	51	9	46	70	14.1
Daal,Omar, Phi	30	4.22	11	11	0	32	31	179	186	21	54	103	12.1
Darensbourg,Vic, Fla	31	3.91	4	3	0	57	0	53	53	5	22	39	12.7
DeJean,Mike, Mil	31	3.89	5	4	0	68	0	74	69	6	38	50	13.0
Dempster,Ryan, Fla	25	4.79	11	14	0	34	34	216	219	24	108	188	13.6
Dreifort,Darren, LA	30	4.43	4	4	0	11	11	65	62	7	32	58	13.0
Elarton,Scott, Col	26	5.47	8	10	0	26	26	153	164	28	68	102	13.6
Eldred,Cal, CWS	34	5.49	5	6	0	16	16	82	92	11	41	72	14.6
Embree,Alan, CWS	32	4.34	4	3	0	62	0	56	56	8	22	52	12.5
Escobar,Kelvim, Tor	26	3.75	7	5	0	54	15	144	133	13	65	128	12.4

Projections for 2002 Pitchers

Pitcher	Age	ERA	W	L	Sv	G	GS	IP	H	HR	BB	SO	BR/9
Estes,Shawn, SF	29	4.42	10	10	0	28	28	169	170	14	82	119	13.4
Fassero,Jeff, ChC	39	3.76	5	4	10	75	0	67	64	7	24	58	11.8
Fetters,Mike, Pit	37	4.50	3	3	18	53	0	48	45	7	25	38	13.1
Finley,Chuck, Cle	39	4.20	10	8	0	26	26	148	153	17	46	128	12.1
Foulke,Keith, CWS	29	2.28	4	2	46	72	0	83	60	8	20	88	8.7
Fox,Chad, Mil	31	3.63	5	4	10	65	0	67	57	6	36	84	12.5
Franco,John, NYM	41	4.17	3	4	2	59	0	54	53	7	22	53	12.5
Frascatore,John, Tor	32	4.63	2	2	0	28	0	35	37	6	13	17	12.9
Garces,Rich, Bos	31	2.96	6	2	3	63	0	70	55	6	25	59	10.3
Garcia,Freddy, Sea	25	3.40	15	8	0	30	29	201	183	18	58	134	10.8
Gardner,Mark, SF	40	4.62	6	7	0	25	17	111	114	15	41	67	12.6
Glavine,Tom, Atl	36	4.40	12	13	0	34	34	221	221	21	98	129	13.0
Gomes,Wayne, SF	29	4.43	4	4	0	58	0	67	67	6	38	50	14.1
Gordon,Flash, ChC	34	2.95	2	2	30	58	0	55	40	5	24	79	10.5
Graves,Danny, Cin	28	3.43	3	4	35	66	0	84	76	7	32	51	11.6
Grimsley,Jason, KC	34	3.87	5	4	0	70	1	86	81	9	37	55	12.3
Groom,Buddy, Bal	36	3.52	5	4	5	70	0	64	65	4	18	49	11.7
Guardado,Eddie, Min	31	3.74	2	4	29	68	0	65	55	9	27	62	11.4
Guthrie,Mark, Oak	36	4.58	4	3	0	61	0	59	60	8	26	51	13.1
Hamilton,Joey, Cin	31	4.71	9	10	0	25	25	151	173	16	48	94	13.2
Hampton,Mike, Col	29	4.76	13	12	0	32	32	208	221	24	87	135	13.3
Harnisch,Pete, Cin	35	5.14	6	7	0	18	18	105	107	16	51	56	13.5
Hasegawa,S., Ana	33	4.30	4	4	2	53	0	69	67	9	28	44	12.4
Hawkins,LaTroy, Min	29	5.29	3	5	7	63	0	63	76	8	26	40	14.6
Haynes,Jimmy, Mil	29	5.24	9	13	0	32	30	182	204	22	82	98	14.1
Helling,Rick, Tex	31	4.54	15	11	0	34	34	216	225	34	63	150	12.0
Henry,Doug, KC	38	4.56	4	4	0	59	0	77	66	13	47	59	13.2
Hentgen,Pat, Bal	33	4.70	9	12	0	29	29	180	195	26	55	106	12.5
Heredia,Felix, ChC	26	4.60	3	3	0	57	0	43	46	4	22	38	14.2
Heredia,Gil, Oak	36	4.86	9	8	0	27	23	139	161	20	37	67	12.8
Herges,Matt, LA	32	3.67	6	5	0	70	1	103	97	9	41	74	12.1
Hermanson,Dustin, StL	29	4.50	12	12	0	35	32	194	198	25	74	108	12.6
Hernandez,Livan, SF	27	4.91	12	15	0	34	34	231	260	27	87	150	13.5
Hernandez,O., NYY	32	4.20	12	10	0	29	29	193	172	26	86	145	12.0
Hernandez,R., KC	37	4.11	2	4	33	65	0	70	72	8	24	53	12.3
Hitchcock,Sterling, NYY	31	4.38	12	10	0	30	30	189	193	28	56	145	11.9
Hoffman,Trevor, SD	34	2.25	3	2	45	65	0	64	47	6	15	71	8.7
Holt,Chris, Det	30	5.24	8	11	0	31	25	170	207	17	64	102	14.3
Holtz,Mike, Ana	29	4.50	3	3	0	62	0	38	41	4	18	36	14.0
Howry,Bob, CWS	28	3.43	6	3	0	68	0	76	66	7	34	71	11.8
Hudson,Tim, Oak	26	3.29	17	8	0	33	33	219	193	20	66	175	10.6
Isringhausen,J., Oak	29	3.68	3	3	44	65	0	71	64	7	31	63	12.0
Jackson,Mike, Hou	37	4.57	4	4	0	67	0	69	68	14	22	46	11.7
James,Mike, StL	34	3.86	3	2	0	44	0	42	38	5	19	32	12.2
Jarvis,Kevin, SD	32	5.17	8	12	0	29	28	167	184	36	42	105	12.2
Jimenez,Jose, Col	28	4.05	4	3	14	61	0	60	61	5	25	40	12.9
Johnson,Randy, Ari	38	2.64	20	8	0	35	34	249	192	21	71	360	9.5
Jones,Bobby J., SD	32	4.85	10	12	0	31	31	182	210	30	35	103	12.1
Jones,Todd, Min	34	4.57	4	4	4	68	0	67	71	7	30	62	13.6
Karsay,Steve, Atl	30	3.43	6	4	4	73	0	84	80	6	28	75	11.6

Projections for 2002 Pitchers

Pitcher	Age	ERA	W	L	Sv	G	GS	IP	H	HR	BB	SO	BR/9
Kile,Darryl, StL	33	4.09	14	12	0	34	34	229	231	28	65	185	11.6
Kim,Byung-Hyun, Ari	23	3.03	3	3	34	72	0	89	59	10	50	116	11.0
Kline,Steve, StL	29	3.27	3	4	20	87	0	77	67	6	30	63	11.3
Koch,Billy, Tor	27	3.63	3	4	38	69	0	72	69	6	28	59	12.1
Leiter,Al, NYM	36	3.29	14	9	0	30	30	194	180	18	48	168	10.6
Leiter,Mark, Mil	39	3.50	2	1	0	20	3	36	32	6	8	26	10.0
Leskanic,Curtis, Mil	34	4.00	5	4	20	71	0	72	66	6	41	67	13.4
Levine,Al, Ana	34	4.17	5	4	2	60	2	82	82	9	34	38	12.7
Lieber,Jon, ChC	32	3.88	15	12	0	34	34	239	245	31	42	168	10.8
Ligtenberg,Kerry, Atl	31	3.16	4	3	0	55	0	57	45	5	28	55	11.5
Lima,Jose, Det	29	4.81	10	11	0	32	29	176	195	31	40	101	12.0
Lira,Felipe, Phi	30	5.84	1	2	0	20	2	37	50	6	14	19	15.6
Lloyd,Graeme, Mon	35	3.99	5	4	0	84	0	70	70	8	22	45	11.8
Loaiza,Esteban, Tor	30	4.71	11	12	0	35	30	193	225	27	41	123	12.4
Looper,Braden, Fla	27	3.99	5	4	5	72	0	70	69	6	31	41	12.9
Lopez,Albie, Ari	30	4.61	11	12	0	37	30	199	210	24	73	118	12.8
Lowe,Derek, Bos	29	3.23	7	3	8	69	2	92	89	6	24	76	11.1
Lowe,Sean, CWS	31	4.17	5	4	3	47	9	108	109	12	43	68	12.7
Maddux,Greg, Atl	36	3.10	17	10	0	34	34	238	239	19	28	179	10.1
Magnante,Mike, Oak	37	4.14	4	3	0	62	0	50	53	5	17	21	12.6
Mahomes,Pat, Tex	31	4.81	5	4	0	55	4	103	99	15	61	73	14.0
Manzanillo,Josias, Pit	34	3.21	5	3	6	62	0	73	60	7	29	67	11.0
Martinez,Pedro, Bos	30	2.06	20	4	0	31	31	214	154	16	46	287	8.4
Mathews,T.J., StL	32	4.20	3	2	0	37	0	45	45	6	16	33	12.2
Mays,Joe, Min	26	4.09	13	12	0	33	32	209	214	26	57	119	11.7
McElroy,Chuck, SD	34	5.07	3	4	0	47	4	71	75	9	43	52	15.0
Meadows,Brian, KC	26	5.27	5	7	0	18	17	99	123	16	24	40	13.4
Mecir,Jim, Oak	32	2.96	6	2	2	57	0	70	57	4	32	61	11.4
Mendoza,Ramiro, NYY	30	3.64	5	3	6	42	4	89	90	8	21	55	11.2
Mercedes,Jose, Bal	31	4.79	8	12	0	34	27	171	195	19	59	100	13.4
Mesa,Jose, Phi	36	3.95	2	4	37	69	0	73	69	7	34	62	12.7
Miceli,Dan, Col	31	4.70	3	3	0	49	0	46	49	7	20	42	13.5
Miller,Travis, Min	29	4.42	3	3	0	52	0	55	63	3	23	44	14.1
Millwood,Kevin, Atl	27	4.09	9	9	0	26	26	152	145	20	50	114	11.5
Milton,Eric, Min	26	4.35	12	13	0	33	33	209	212	32	58	157	11.6
Mlicki,Dave, Hou	34	5.45	8	10	0	31	26	152	171	23	67	81	14.1
Moehler,Brian, Det	30	4.07	6	5	0	15	15	95	107	11	12	54	11.3
Morgan,Mike, Ari	42	4.88	3	3	0	41	2	59	71	5	24	34	14.5
Morris,Matt, StL	27	3.30	16	9	0	33	33	210	204	13	52	171	11.0
Moyer,Jamie, Sea	39	3.77	13	9	0	31	31	191	189	24	40	114	10.8
Mulholland,Terry, LA	39	5.25	3	5	0	45	9	96	119	16	25	52	13.5
Mussina,Mike, NYY	33	3.28	17	9	0	33	33	225	214	22	41	205	10.2
Myers,Mike, Col	33	3.43	5	2	0	75	0	42	35	4	20	37	11.8
Nagy,Charles, Cle	35	5.45	4	5	0	14	12	66	82	10	19	36	13.8
Neagle,Denny, Col	33	5.02	11	11	0	31	31	183	200	29	64	138	13.0
Nelson,Jeff, Sea	35	2.55	6	2	0	70	0	67	41	3	45	78	11.6
Nen,Robb, SF	32	2.55	3	2	40	75	0	74	56	5	23	89	9.6
Nitkowski,C.J., NYM	29	4.56	4	4	0	63	4	71	68	10	37	55	13.3
Nomo,Hideo, Bos	33	4.57	12	11	0	33	32	195	180	28	95	202	12.7
Olivares,Omar, Pit	34	4.62	4	5	6	37	13	109	119	12	47	54	13.7

Projections for 2002 Pitchers

Pitcher	Age	ERA	W	L	Sv	G	GS	IP	H	HR	BB	SO	BR/9
Oliver,Darren, Tex	31	5.44	9	9	0	26	26	139	166	16	59	81	14.6
Ortiz,Russ, SF	28	4.05	13	11	0	33	33	211	195	23	88	171	12.1
Painter,Lance, Mil	34	4.50	2	2	0	29	1	42	43	5	17	34	12.9
Paniagua,Jose, Sea	28	3.93	5	4	0	63	0	71	62	6	40	60	12.9
Park,Chan Ho, LA	29	3.67	14	11	0	33	33	223	194	23	87	211	11.3
Parque,Jim, CWS	26	5.21	11	12	0	30	30	202	237	26	72	118	13.8
Parris,Steve, Tor	34	4.93	8	9	0	24	24	135	145	19	52	75	13.1
Patterson,Danny, Det	31	4.21	4	4	0	59	0	62	70	6	15	34	12.3
Percival,Troy, Ana	32	2.78	2	2	41	56	0	55	39	6	23	59	10.1
Person,Robert, Phi	32	4.07	12	11	0	31	31	197	176	28	76	179	11.5
Petkovsek,Mark, Tex	36	4.50	5	4	0	58	0	78	89	9	23	38	12.9
Pettitte,Andy, NYY	30	3.92	14	10	0	31	31	202	220	18	41	144	11.6
Plesac,Dan, Tor	40	3.68	4	3	2	62	0	44	35	4	26	58	12.5
Ponson,Sidney, Bal	25	4.63	10	14	0	30	30	210	229	31	56	138	12.2
Powell,Jay, Col	30	4.12	4	3	14	59	0	59	58	5	30	49	13.4
Quantrill,Paul, Tor	33	3.90	6	4	2	76	0	83	92	6	21	51	12.3
Radke,Brad, Min	29	3.86	14	12	0	33	33	226	249	26	26	139	11.0
Rapp,Pat, Ana	34	4.79	10	11	0	31	29	171	184	19	72	94	13.5
Reed,Rick, Min	36	4.32	12	12	0	31	31	196	217	29	30	134	11.3
Reed,Steve, Atl	36	4.34	4	4	0	66	0	58	59	8	21	42	12.4
Rekar,Bryan, TB	30	5.21	7	11	0	27	26	152	178	22	48	88	13.4
Remlinger,Mike, Atl	36	3.28	6	4	2	73	0	74	60	8	30	79	10.9
Reyes,Dennys, Cin	25	4.32	3	3	0	44	4	50	46	4	32	50	14.0
Reynolds,Shane, Hou	34	4.25	13	10	0	29	29	195	217	23	38	121	11.8
Reynoso,Armando, Ari	36	4.81	5	6	0	16	16	88	99	13	25	42	12.7
Rhodes,Arthur, Sea	32	3.18	6	3	0	71	0	68	52	7	31	79	11.0
Rincon,Ricardo, Cle	32	3.35	4	2	0	56	0	43	35	4	21	36	11.7
Ritchie,Todd, Pit	30	4.07	12	12	0	32	32	201	210	23	50	126	11.6
Rivera,Mariano, NYY	32	2.05	4	2	49	69	0	79	58	4	19	68	8.8
Rocker,John, Cle	27	3.34	5	3	17	65	0	62	46	5	41	84	12.6
Rodriguez,Felix, SF	29	2.78	7	3	2	79	0	81	64	5	30	85	10.4
Rodriguez,Rich, Cle	39	4.50	3	2	0	46	0	38	40	5	16	25	13.3
Rogers,Kenny, Tex	37	5.19	10	9	0	25	25	156	183	17	63	90	14.2
Rosado,Jose, KC	27	4.28	7	8	0	20	20	122	130	16	40	81	12.5
Rueter,Kirk, SF	31	4.88	11	13	0	33	33	192	212	26	65	78	13.0
Rusch,Glendon, NYM	27	4.48	10	12	0	32	32	183	206	22	44	155	12.3
Santiago,Jose, Phi	27	4.07	5	4	0	64	0	84	91	8	25	41	12.4
Sauerbeck,Scott, Pit	30	4.16	4	4	6	72	0	67	62	5	45	71	14.4
Schilling,Curt, Ari	35	3.36	17	10	0	33	33	241	224	33	37	238	9.7
Schmidt,Jason, SF	29	4.45	11	11	0	30	30	188	192	20	76	170	12.8
Schourek,Pete, Bos	33	4.82	2	2	0	29	7	56	61	9	23	40	13.5
Seanez,Rudy, Atl	33	2.90	3	1	0	33	0	31	23	3	14	29	10.7
Sele,Aaron, Sea	32	4.04	14	11	0	34	33	214	233	20	51	126	11.9
Shaw,Jeff, LA	35	3.52	3	4	43	71	0	69	65	8	17	48	10.7
Shuey,Paul, Cle	31	3.47	4	2	0	50	0	57	50	4	28	70	12.3
Simas,Bill, CWS	30	4.04	5	3	0	63	0	69	66	9	25	48	11.9
Sirotka,Mike, Tor	31	4.65	10	8	0	24	24	151	162	19	53	94	12.8
Smoltz,John, Atl	35	2.92	3	3	35	66	0	71	64	6	14	62	9.9
Sparks,Steve W., Det	36	4.18	10	9	0	27	24	168	180	17	46	85	12.1
Springer,Russ, Ari	33	4.22	2	2	0	29	0	32	30	5	15	31	12.7

Projections for 2002 Pitchers

Pitcher	Age	ERA	W	L	Sv	G	GS	IP	H	HR	BB	SO	BR/9
Stanton,Mike, NYY	35	3.79	6	4	0	74	0	76	79	5	26	77	12.4
Stottlemyre,Todd, Ari	37	4.44	5	5	0	13	13	71	71	10	27	54	12.4
Sullivan,Scott, Cin	31	3.46	7	4	0	79	0	104	90	12	39	83	11.2
Suppan,Jeff, KC	27	4.81	11	13	0	32	32	206	222	29	70	117	12.8
Swindell,Greg, Ari	37	3.69	5	3	0	64	0	61	57	9	13	50	10.3
Tam,Jeff, Oak	31	3.23	6	3	0	71	0	78	74	5	26	45	11.5
Tapani,Kevin, ChC	38	4.58	10	11	0	29	29	177	192	29	42	146	11.9
Tavarez,Julian, ChC	29	4.68	8	9	0	40	23	148	160	13	63	89	13.6
Telemaco,Amaury, Phi	28	4.63	4	4	0	20	10	68	69	11	24	48	12.3
Telford,Anthony, Mon	36	4.32	3	3	0	45	0	50	56	4	18	39	13.3
Timlin,Mike, StL	36	3.99	5	4	4	65	0	70	68	8	27	52	12.2
Tomko,Brett, Sea	29	4.57	3	3	0	25	5	65	68	9	25	46	12.9
Trachsel,Steve, NYM	31	4.43	10	12	0	30	30	183	192	26	49	124	11.9
Trombley,Mike, LA	35	4.38	4	5	2	71	0	76	72	12	33	72	12.4
Urbina,Uqueth, Bos	28	2.78	3	2	43	66	0	68	50	5	28	92	10.3
Valdes,Ismael, Ana	28	4.53	9	9	0	25	25	145	153	20	44	93	12.2
Van Poppel,Todd, ChC	30	4.10	4	4	0	56	1	79	71	10	42	82	12.9
Vazquez,Javier, Mon	25	3.65	14	11	0	32	32	222	221	26	44	203	10.7
Venafro,Mike, Tex	28	3.51	6	3	0	72	0	59	58	3	23	31	12.4
Veres,Dave, StL	35	4.17	5	4	13	71	0	69	64	10	28	63	12.0
Villone,Ron, Hou	32	4.60	5	4	0	56	3	88	89	11	45	63	13.7
Wagner,Billy, Hou	30	2.49	3	2	42	61	0	65	44	6	24	91	9.4
Wakefield,Tim, Bos	35	4.50	7	6	0	47	17	166	167	22	74	126	13.1
Wall,Donne, NYM	34	3.72	3	2	0	36	0	46	42	6	17	31	11.5
Wasdin,John, Bal	29	4.62	3	4	0	42	1	76	83	12	22	64	12.4
Watson,Allen, NYY	31	5.40	2	2	0	24	1	40	46	7	18	31	14.4
Weathers,Dave, ChC	32	3.80	5	4	0	76	0	83	79	7	34	62	12.3
Weaver,Jeff, Det	25	4.25	13	12	0	32	32	220	228	27	65	147	12.0
Wells,Bob, Min	35	4.08	5	4	4	69	0	75	76	11	19	52	11.4
Wells,David, CWS	39	4.44	13	11	0	31	31	219	256	23	46	149	12.4
Wendell,Turk, Phi	35	3.88	5	4	2	72	0	72	62	9	34	63	12.0
White,Gabe, Col	30	3.95	5	3	0	69	0	73	68	13	19	66	10.7
White,Rick, NYM	33	3.94	5	4	0	59	0	80	81	7	27	57	12.1
Wickman,Bob, Cle	33	3.39	3	3	32	70	0	69	65	4	27	58	12.0
Wilkins,Marc, Pit	31	4.78	2	2	0	27	0	32	32	3	19	23	14.3
Williams,Mike, Hou	33	4.16	5	4	5	67	0	67	60	7	39	71	13.3
Williams,Woody, StL	35	4.12	13	11	0	30	30	203	200	31	52	138	11.2
Witasick,Jay, NYY	29	5.52	3	4	0	53	0	75	87	12	37	79	14.9
Witt,Bobby, Ari	38	5.29	1	2	0	12	5	34	37	6	18	21	14.6
Wohlers,Mark, NYY	32	4.00	4	3	0	47	0	54	50	6	27	42	12.8
Woodard,Steve, Cle	27	4.58	4	4	0	33	14	114	134	15	26	72	12.6
Worrell,Tim, SF	34	4.20	5	4	0	68	0	75	75	8	33	63	13.0
Wright,Jamey, Mil	27	5.01	9	13	0	31	30	185	197	20	93	116	14.1
Yan,Esteban, TB	28	4.35	2	4	26	55	0	60	63	8	20	51	12.4
Yoshii,Masato, Mon	37	5.15	4	6	0	38	17	131	153	23	37	71	13.1
Zimmerman,Jeff, Tex	29	3.04	3	2	35	66	0	71	55	9	23	66	9.9

Career Assessments

Barry Bonds' assault on the single-season home-run record deservedly commanded the baseball world's attention last summer. But while Bonds raced to immortality in the span of six months, another slugger maintained his steady progress toward another cherished mark. And over the next few years, we'll find out if the drama that Bonds generated in 2001 will be matched by Sammy Sosa.

Sosa continued to blast homers with remarkable consistency last season, topping 60 for the third time in the last four years. As a result, we now figure Sosa's odds of surpassing Henry Aaron's career-record total of 755 home runs at 47 percent. At his current rate of production, Sosa could be as close as five years away from overtaking Hammerin' Hank. Of course, don't overlook Bonds. He's obviously shown the ability to handle the pressure associated with the pursuit of a high-profile record. And nobody improved their chances of reaching 756 more than Bonds did in 2001, as his odds kangarooed from six to 43 percent.

All told, there are currently 10 players who have established at least a one-percent shot at Aaron's mark. That's two more than there were last year at this time. While Carlos Delgado's chances have fallen below one percent (perhaps temporarily), Troy Glaus, Todd Helton and Jim Thome have joined the group. Alex Rodriguez is another surger, improving his chances from 16 to 27 percent. However, Ken Griffey Jr.'s odds dropped again, plummeting from 36 to 10 percent. And Mark McGwire's poor season leaves him clinging to only the scantest hope of reaching 756.

Now that Rickey Henderson has become the latest player to crack the 3,000-hit barrier, it looks like it may be a few years before someone else joins the club. Roberto Alomar matched his career high with 193 hits last season. While he isn't a lock to reach 3,000, it will be an upset if he doesn't eventually get there. Alomar will begin the 2001 campaign at age 34. Even though he's about 100 hits behind Rafael Palmeiro, he's also more than three years younger, making Alomar's odds (90 percent) roughly twice as high as Palmeiro's (47 percent). Alomar, Rodriguez, Derek Jeter and Vladimir Guerrero are the only players boasting at least a one-percent shot at 4,000 hits.

Rodgriguez did nothing last year to hurt his odds in any category. He also boasts a 37-percent chance of driving in 2,000 runs. In fact, he joins Sosa as the only players who have established at least a 20-percent chance of reaching 2,298 RBI, a sum that would shatter another Aaron record. Having just turned 26 this past July, Rodriguez figures to maintain his charge up the career charts for quite some time. His pursuit of the various milestones, as well as that by many other players, may not elicit the daily updates that Bonds' quest generated last season. Still, the drama continues to unfold nevertheless.

—Jim Henzler

Estudio de Carreras

El asalto de Barry Bonds al récord de jonrones en una temporada correctamente comandó la atención del público. Pero al mismo tiempo otro pelotero continuaba su asalto callado a otro record. Y en los próximos años nos daremos cuenta si Sammy Sosa igualará la atención recibida por Bonds esta temporada.

Sosa sobrepasó 60 cuadrangulares el año pasado por la tercera vez en las últimas cuatro campañas. Y como resultado, nosotros hemos estimados los chances de que Sosa pase los 755 jonrones de Henry Aaron en un 47 por ciento. Si continua al mismo paso, Sosa podría sobrepasar la marca de vida de cuadrangulares en cinco años. Por supuesto no hay que olvidarse de Bonds. Nadie mejoró sus chances el año pasado como Bonds, subiendo de seis a 43 por ciento.

En éste momento hay 10 jugadores que tienen un chance de por lo menos un por ciento de pasar la marca de Aaron. Dos peloteros más que habían después del 2000. Mientras el chance de Carlos Delgado bajó a menos de un por ciento (a lo mejor solo por el momento), Troy Glaus, Todd Helton y Jim Thome se han sumado a este grupo. Alex Rodríguez mejoró sus chances de 16 a 27 por ciento. Pero Ken Griffey Jr. bajo de nuevo de 36 a 10 por ciento. Y Mark McGwire tuvo una mala temporada, dejandolo con una pequeña esperanza.

Ahora que Rickey Henderson ha llegado a 3,000 hits, parece que van a ser a ser años hasta que alquien más se sume al club. Roberto Alomar igualó su mejor marca de hits la temporada pasada con 193. Aunque no hay garantías que el llegue a 3,000, sería una desilución si no llegara a la marca. Alomar va a tener 34 años al principio de la próxima temporada. Aunque él está 100 hits detrás de Rafael Palmeiro, Alomar es tres años más joven, dándole a Alomar un chance de 90 por ciento de llegar a la marca, casí el doble de los chances de que Palmeiro llegue a 3,000 (47 por ciento). Alomar, Rodríguez, Derek Jeter y Vladimir Guerrero son los únicos jugadores con por lo menos un chance de un por ciento de llegar a 4,000 hits.

Rodríguez mejoró en varias categorías. El tiene un chance de 37 por ciento de llegar a 2,000 carreras empujadas. El y Sosa son los únicos jugadores que tienen por lo menos un chance de 20 por ciento de llegar a 2,298 CE, otro de los records de Aaron. Teniendo solo 26 años, Rodríguez va a mantener su marcha hacia ciertas marcas por muchos años. Su busqueda de éstas marcas, así como el trabajo de otros jugadores, no generaron la atención diaria de Bonds, pero éste guión sigue siendo escrito de todos modos.

—Jim Henzler

Player	Age	Current			Home Runs					Hits			RBI	
		H	HR	RBI	500	600	700	756	800	3000	4000	4257	2000	2298
Mark McGwire	37	1626	583	1414	8/5/99	99%	27%	2%	—	—	—	—	—	—
Barry Bonds	36	2313	567	1542	4/17/01	98%	82%	43%	25%	12%	—	—	27%	—
Sammy Sosa	32	1795	450	1239	97%	93%	68%	47%	35%	28%	—	—	48%	21%
Ken Griffey Jr.	31	1987	460	1335	96%	77%	24%	10%	2%	19%	—	—	28%	4%
Rafael Palmeiro	36	2485	447	1470	96%	37%	3%	—	—	47%	—	—	21%	—
Jose Canseco	36	1877	462	1407	94%	—	—	—	—	—	—	—	—	—
Fred McGriff	37	2260	448	1400	93%	—	—	—	—	3%	—	—	—	—
Juan Gonzalez	31	1727	397	1282	90%	35%	7%	—	—	20%	—	—	37%	12%
Alex Rodriguez	25	1167	241	730	84%	60%	36%	27%	21%	35%	5%	—	37%	20%
Jeff Bagwell	33	1803	349	1223	76%	26%	4%	—	—	16%	—	—	25%	4%
Manny Ramirez	29	1248	277	929	68%	32%	12%	5%	—	10%	—	—	29%	12%
Jim Thome	30	1186	282	809	67%	30%	11%	4%	—	—	—	—	8%	—
Gary Sheffield	32	1668	315	1016	53%	17%	—	—	—	11%	—	—	2%	—
Vladimir Guerrero	25	879	170	512	50%	26%	12%	6%	2%	26%	2%	—	17%	6%
Troy Glaus	24	475	118	312	47%	27%	13%	8%	4%	3%	—	—	4%	—
Todd Helton	27	791	156	514	47%	25%	11%	5%	2%	18%	—	—	21%	9%
Carlos Delgado	29	978	229	706	47%	21%	6%	—	—	5%	—	—	10%	—
Chipper Jones	29	1240	227	737	42%	17%	3%	—	—	18%	—	—	5%	—
Shawn Green	28	1066	192	600	40%	18%	4%	—	—	15%	—	—	8%	—
Andruw Jones	24	792	150	465	36%	17%	5%	—	—	20%	—	—	9%	—
Richie Sexson	26	487	117	367	29%	12%	2%	—	—	—	—	—	5%	—
Jason Giambi	30	1048	187	675	24%	6%	—	—	—	4%	—	—	7%	—
Luis Gonzalez	33	1632	221	917	20%	1%	—	—	—	15%	—	—	3%	—
Mike Piazza	32	1507	314	975	20%	—	—	—	—	—	—	—	—	—
Greg Vaughn	35	1427	344	1038	15%	—	—	—	—	—	—	—	—	—
Albert Pujols	21	194	37	130	13%	2%	—	—	—	4%	—	—	5%	—
Brian Giles	30	761	150	490	13%	—	—	—	—	—	—	—	—	—
Tony Batista	27	634	125	385	13%	—	—	—	—	—	—	—	—	—
Miguel Tejada	25	587	95	367	11%	—	—	—	—	8%	—	—	7%	—
Magglio Ordonez	27	727	111	432	10%	—	—	—	—	11%	—	—	6%	—
Larry Walker	34	1702	309	1029	10%	—	—	—	—	—	—	—	—	—
Eric Chavez	23	400	71	256	9%	—	—	—	—	1%	—	—	1%	—
Jose Cruz	27	575	116	319	8%	—	—	—	—	—	—	—	—	—
Raul Mondesi	30	1253	214	669	7%	—	—	—	—	—	—	—	—	—
Scott Rolen	26	783	133	493	6%	—	—	—	—	3%	—	—	1%	—
Frank Thomas	33	1770	348	1193	6%	—	—	—	—	—	—	—	—	—
Jermaine Dye	27	735	110	425	5%	—	—	—	—	9%	—	—	3%	—
Paul Konerko	25	519	84	306	5%	—	—	—	—	5%	—	—	—	—
Phil Nevin	30	609	123	412	5%	—	—	—	—	—	—	—	—	—
Richard Hidalgo	25	486	87	299	5%	—	—	—	—	—	—	—	—	—
Ryan Klesko	30	978	195	655	3%	—	—	—	—	—	—	—	—	—
Jeromy Burnitz	32	852	188	604	3%	—	—	—	—	—	—	—	—	—
Jim Edmonds	31	1075	193	626	3%	—	—	—	—	—	—	—	—	—
Aramis Ramirez	23	315	46	178	3%	—	—	—	—	—	—	—	—	—
Garret Anderson	29	1237	135	633	2%	—	—	—	—	20%	—	—	4%	—
Mike Sweeney	27	739	99	435	2%	—	—	—	—	11%	—	—	5%	—
Tino Martinez	33	1468	263	1002	1%	—	—	—	—	—	—	—	—	—
Rickey Henderson	42	3000	290	1094	—	—	—	—	—	10/7/01	—	—	—	—
Roberto Alomar	33	2389	190	1018	—	—	—	—	—	90%	3%	—	—	—
Derek Jeter	27	1199	99	488	—	—	—	—	—	33%	3%	—	—	—

397

Player	Age	Current			Home Runs					Hits			RBI	
		H	HR	RBI	500	600	700	756	800	3000	4000	4257	2000	2298
Johnny Damon	27	1059	74	401	—	—	—	—	—	21%	—	—	—	—
John Olerud	32	1768	207	960	—	—	—	—	—	19%	—	—	—	—
Darin Erstad	27	930	86	395	—	—	—	—	—	17%	—	—	—	—
Shannon Stewart	27	776	56	276	—	—	—	—	—	15%	—	—	—	—
Craig Biggio	35	2149	180	811	—	—	—	—	—	14%	—	—	—	—
Neifi Perez	26	817	44	293	—	—	—	—	—	14%	—	—	—	—
Bernie Williams	32	1629	207	896	—	—	—	—	—	13%	—	—	—	—
Ray Durham	29	1143	97	436	—	—	—	—	—	9%	—	—	—	—
Bobby Abreu	27	742	96	383	—	—	—	—	—	9%	—	—	—	—
Edgar Renteria	25	895	49	310	—	—	—	—	—	8%	—	—	—	—
Mark Grace	37	2343	163	1082	—	—	—	—	—	7%	—	—	—	—
Jeff Cirillo	31	1224	94	570	—	—	—	—	—	6%	—	—	—	—
Jose Vidro	26	592	53	250	—	—	—	—	—	6%	—	—	—	—
Carlos Beltran	24	491	53	260	—	—	—	—	—	6%	—	—	—	—
Luis Castillo	25	605	6	116	—	—	—	—	—	5%	—	—	—	—
Sean Casey	26	597	65	326	—	—	—	—	—	5%	—	—	—	—
Omar Vizquel	34	1761	43	565	—	—	—	—	—	4%	—	—	—	—
Chuck Knoblauch	32	1776	92	593	—	—	—	—	—	4%	—	—	—	—
Edgardo Alfonzo	27	985	104	482	—	—	—	—	—	4%	—	—	—	—
Adrian Beltre	22	464	55	234	—	—	—	—	—	4%	—	—	—	—
Ben Grieve	25	635	87	375	—	—	—	—	—	3%	—	—	—	—
Juan Pierre	23	264	2	75	—	—	—	—	—	3%	—	—	—	—
Carlos Lee	25	466	64	260	—	—	—	—	—	2%	—	—	—	—
Cristian Guzman	23	400	19	131	—	—	—	—	—	2%	—	—	—	—
Jeff Kent	33	1409	216	899	—	—	—	—	—	1%	—	—	—	—
Dmitri Young	27	700	72	332	—	—	—	—	—	1%	—	—	—	—

Note: A date in place of a percentage indicates the date on which the player achieved the specific milestone.

Glossary

% Inherited Scored

A Relief Pitching statistic indicating the percentage of runners on base at the time a relief pitcher enters a game that he allows to score.

% Pitches Taken

The number of pitches a batter does not swing at divided by the total number of pitches he sees.

1st Batter Average

The batting average allowed by a relief pitcher to the first batter he faces in a game.

1st Batter OBP

The On-Base Percentage allowed by a relief pitcher to the first batter he faces in a game.

Active Career Batting Leaders

Minimum of 1,000 At-Bats required for Batting Average, On-Base Percentage, Slugging Percentage, At-Bats Per HR, At-Bats Per GDP, At-Bats Per RBI, and Strikeout-to-Walk Ratio. One hundred (100) Stolen Base Attempts required for Stolen Base Success %. Any player who appeared in 2001 is eligible for inclusion provided he meets the category's minimum requirements.

Active Career Pitching Leaders

Minimum of 750 Innings Pitched required for Earned Run Average, Opponent Batting Average, all of the "Per 9 Innings" categories, and Strikeout-to-Walk Ratio. Two hundred fifty (250) Games Started required for Complete Game Frequency. One hundred (100) decisions required for Win-Loss Percentage. Any player who appeared in 2001 is eligible for inclusion provided he meets the category's minimum requirements.

AVG Allowed ScPos

Batting Average Allowed with Runners in Scoring Position.

AVG Bases Loaded

Batting Average with the Bases Loaded.

Batting Average

Hits divided by At-Bats.

Blown Save

Entering a game in a Save Situation (see Save Situation in Glossary) and allowing the tying or go-ahead run to score.

Career Assessments

Once known as the Favorite Toy, this method is used to estimate a player's chance of achieving a specific goal. In the following example, we'll say 3,000 hits. Four things are considered:

1. Need Hits, the number of hits needed to reach the goal. (Of course, this also could be Need Home Runs, Need Doubles, etc.)

2. Years Remaining. The number of years remaining to meet the goal is estimated by (42 minus Age) divided by two. This formula assigns a 20-year-old player 11.0 remaining seasons, a 25-year-old player 8.5 remaining seasons, a 30-year-old player 6.0 remaining seasons, and a 35-year-old player 3.5 remaining seasons. For catchers, the estimated remaining seasons is multiplied by 0.70. Any active player is assumed to have at least half a season remaining, regardless of his age. Additionally, if a player is coming off a year with at least 100 hits *and* an offensive winning percentage of at least .500, he's assumed to have at least 1.5 remaining seasons. And if a player is coming off a year with at least 100 hits *or* an offensive winning percentage of at least .500, he's assumed to have at least 1.0 remaining seasons.

3. Established Hit Level. For 2001, the established hit level would be found by adding 1999 Hits, (2000 Hits multiplied by two) and (2001 Hits multiplied by three), then dividing by six. A player can't have an established performance level that is less than 75 percent of his most recent performance. In other words, a player who had 200 hits in 2001 can't have an established hit level less than 150.

4. Projected Remaining Hits. This is found by multiplying Years Remaining by the Established Hit Level.

Once you get the projected remaining hits, the chance of getting to the goal is figured by dividing Projected Remaining Hits by Need Hits, then subtracting .5. Thus if Need Hits and Projected Remaining Hits are the same, the chance of reaching the goal is 50 percent. A player's chance of continuing to progress toward a goal can't be more than .97 raised to the power of Years Remaining. This prevents a player from figuring to have a 148 percent chance of reaching a goal.

Catcher's ERA

The Earned Run Average of a club's pitchers with a particular catcher behind the plate. To figure this for a catcher, multiply the Earned Runs Allowed by pitchers while he was catching times nine and divide that by his number of Innings Caught.

Cheap Win

To determine the starting pitcher's Game Score: (1) Start with 50. (2) Add 1 point for each out recorded by the starting pitcher. (3) Add 2 points for each inning the pitcher completes after the fourth inning. (4) Add 1 point for each strikeout. (5) Subtract 2 points for each hit allowed. (6) Subtract 4 points for each earned run allowed. (7) Subtract 2 points for an unearned run. (8) Subtract 1 point for each walk.

If he wins with a game score under 50, it's a Cheap Win. The 2001 leaders in Cheap Wins are listed in the Leader Board section.

Cleanup Slugging%

The Slugging Percentage of a player when batting fourth in the batting order.

Complete Game Frequency

Complete Games divided by Games Started.

Component ERA (ERC)

A statistic that estimates what a pitcher's ERA should have been, based on his pitching performance. The steps in calculating an ERC are:

1. Subtract the pitcher's Home Runs Allowed from his Hits Allowed.

2. Multiply Step 1 by 1.255.

3. Multiply his Home Runs allowed by four.

4. Add Steps 2 and 3 together.

5. Multiply Step 4 by .89.

6. Add his Walks and Hit Batsmen.

7. Multiply Step 6 by .475.

8. Add Steps 5 and 7 together.

This yields the pitcher's total base estimate (PTB), which is:

$$(((H\text{-}HR) * 1.255) + (HR * 4)) * .89) + ((BB + HB) * .475)$$

For those pitchers for whom there is intentional walk data, use this formula instead:

$$(((H\text{-}HR) * 1.255) + (HR * 4)) * .89) + ((BB + HB - IBB) * .56)$$

9. Add Hits and Walks and Hit Batsmen.

10. Multiply Step 9 by PTB.

11. Divide Step 10 by Batters Facing Pitcher. If BFP data is unavailable, approximate it by multiplying Innings Pitched by 2.9, then adding Step 9.

12. Multiply Step 11 by 9.

13. Divide Step 12 by Innings Pitched.

14. Subtract .56 from Step 13.

This is the pitcher's ERC, which is:

$$(((((H + BB + HB) * PTB) / BFP) * 9) / IP) - .56$$

If the result after Step 13 is less than 2.24, adjust the formula as follows:

$$(((((H + BB + HB) * PTB) / BFP) * 9) / IP) * .75$$

Earned Run Average

(Earned Runs * 9) divided by Innings Pitched.

Easy Save

This distinction is made to gauge the difficulty of a save. An Easy Save occurs when the first batter faced doesn't represent the tying run and the reliever pitches one inning or less.

Fielding Percentage

(Putouts plus Assists) divided by (Putouts plus Assists plus Errors).

Games Finished

The last relief pitcher for either team in any given game is credited with a Game Finished.

Game Scores

To determine the starting pitcher's Game Score: (1) Start with 50. (2) Add 1 point for each out recorded by the starting pitcher. (3) Add 2 points for each inning the pitcher completes after the fourth inning. (4) Add 1 point for each strikeout. (5) Subtract 2 points for each hit allowed. (6) Subtract 4 points for each earned run allowed. (7) Subtract 2 points for an unearned run. (8) Subtract 1 point for each walk.

The top Game Scores of 2001 are listed in the Leader Board section.

GDP

Ground into Double Play.

GDP Opportunity

Any situation with a runner on first and less than two out.

Ground/Fly Ratio (Grd/Fly)

For batters, groundballs hit divided by flyballs hit. For pitchers, groundballs allowed divided by flyballs allowed. All batted balls except line drives and bunts are included.

Hold

A hold is credited any time a relief pitcher enters a game in a Save Situation (see definition, except for point 3c.), records at least one out and leaves the game never having relinquished the lead. Note: a pitcher cannot finish the game and receive credit for a hold, nor can he earn a hold and a save in the same game.

Inherited Runners

Any runner on base when a reliever enters a game is considered inherited by that pitcher.

Isolated Power

Slugging Percentage minus Batting Average.

K/BB Ratio

Strikeouts divided by Walks.

Late & Close

A Late & Close situation meets the following requirements: (1) the game is in the seventh inning or later, and (2) the batting team is either leading by one run, tied, or has the potential tying run on base, at bat, or on deck. Note: this situation is very similar to the characteristics of a Save Situation.

Leadoff On Base%

The On-Base Percentage of a player when batting first in the batting order.

LHS

Lefthanded Starting Pitcher.

Major League Equivalency (MLE)

A translation of a Double-A or Triple-A hitter's statistics into a big league equivalent. The formula considers the player's level of competition, league, home ballpark and parent club's ballpark.

Offensive Winning Percentage

A player's offensive winning percentage (OWP) equals the percentage of games a team would win with nine of that player in its lineup, given average pitching and defense. The formula is the square of Runs Created per 27 Outs, divided by the sum of the square of Runs Created per 27 Outs and the square of the league average of runs per game.

On-Base Percentage

(Hits plus Walks plus Hit by Pitcher) divided by (At-Bats plus Walks plus Hit by Pitcher plus Sacrifice Flies).

Opponent Batting Average

Hits Allowed divided by (Batters Faced minus Walks minus Hit Batsmen minus Sacrifice Hits minus Sacrifice Flies minus Catcher's Interference).

PA*

The divisor for On-Base Percentage: At-Bats plus walks plus Hit By Pitcher plus Sacrifice Flies; or Plate Appearances minus Sacrifice Hits and Times Reached Base on Defensive Interference.

Park Index

A method of measuring the extent to which a given ballpark influences a given statistic. Using home runs as an example, here's how the index is calculated:

1. Add Home Runs and Opponent Home Runs in home games.

2. Add At-Bats and Opponent At-Bats in home games. (If At-Bats are unavailable, use home games.)

3. Divide Step 1 by Step 2.

4. Add Home Runs and Opponent Home Runs in road games.

5. Add At-Bats and Opponent At-Bats in road games. (If At-Bats are unavailable, use road games.)

6. Divide Step 4 by Step 5.

7. Divide Step 3 by Step 6.

8. Multiply Step 7 by 100.

An index of 100 means the park is completely neutral. A park index of 118 for home runs indicates that games played in the park feature 18 percent more home runs than the average park.

PCS (Pitchers Caught Stealing)

The number of runners retired when the pitcher, not the catcher, throws to a base to keep the runner close and the runner breaks to the next base before he is tagged out. Note: such plays are often referred to as pickoffs, but appear in official records as Caught Stealing. The most common scoring for a Pitcher Caught Stealing is a 1-3-6 play. The runner is officially charged with a Caught Stealing because he broke for the next base. A pickoff (with a fielding play of 1-3 being the most common) is not an official statistic.

Pitches per PA

For a hitter, the total number of pitches seen divided by total number of Plate Appearances.

PkOf Throw/Runner

The number of Pickoff Throws made by a pitcher divided by the number of runners on first base.

Plate Appearances

At-Bats plus Total Walks plus Hit By Pitcher plus Sacrifice Hits plus Sacrifice Flies plus Times Reached on Defensive Interference.

Power/Speed Number

A way to look at power and speed in one number. A player must score high in both areas to earn a high Power/Speed Number. The formula: (HR * SB * 2) divided by (HR + SB).

PPO (Pitcher Pickoff)

The number of runners retired when the pitcher throws to a base to keep the runner close and the runner is out trying to return to that base. A Pitcher Pickoff is not an official stat and does not count as a Caught Stealing.

Quality Start

A Quality Start is an outing in which a starting pitcher works at least six innings and allows three earned runs or less.

Quality Start Percentage

Quality Starts divided by Games Started.

Quick Hooks and Slow Hooks

A quick Hook is the removal of a pitcher who has pitched less than six innings and given up three runs or less. A Slow Hook occurs when a pitcher pitches more than nine innings, or allows seven or more runs, or whose combined innings pitched and runs allowed totals 13 or more.

Range Factor

The number of Successful Chances (Putouts plus Assists) times nine divided by the number of Defensive Innings Played. The average for a player at each position in 2001:

Second Base:	4.86		Left Field:	2.02
Third Base:	2.64		Center Field:	2.63
Shortstop:	4.48		Right Field:	2.10

RHS

Righthanded Starting Pitcher.

Run Support Per 9 IP

The number of runs scored by a pitcher's team while he was still in the game times nine divided by his Innings Pitched.

Runs Created

Bill James has devised 24 different Runs Created formulas, depending on the statistics available in a given year. The current method is as follows:

1. Add hits plus walks plus hit by pitcher.

2. Subtract caught stealings and grounded into double plays from Step 1. This is the A Factor.

3. Add unintentional walks plus hit by pitcher.

4. Multiply Step 3 by .24.

5. Multiply stolen bases by .62.

6. Add sacrifice hits plus sacrifice flies.

7. Multiply Step 6 by .5.

8. Add total bases plus Step 4 plus Step 5 plus Step 7.

9. Multiply strikeouts by .03.

10. Subtract Step 9 from Step 8. This is the B Factor.

11. Add at-bats plus walks plus hit by pitcher plus sacrifice hits plus sacrifice flies. This is the C Factor.

To summarize:

$$A = H + BB + HBP - CS - GDP$$

$$B = ((BB - IBB + HBP) * .24) + (SB * .62) + ((SH + SF) * .5) + TB - (SO * .03)$$

$$C = AB + BB + HBP + SH + SF$$

Each player's runs created is determined as if he were operating in a context of eight other players of average skill. The final steps are:

12. Multiply C by 2.4.

13. Add A plus Step 12.

14. Multiply C by 3.

15. Add B plus Step 14.

16. Multiply Step 13 by Step 15.

17. Multiply C by 9.

18. Divide Step 16 by Step 17.

19. Multiply C by .9.

20. Subtract Step 19 from Step 18.

Expressed as an equation, that's:

$$((((C * 2.4) + A) * ((C * 3) + B)) / (C * 9)) - (C * .9)$$

Where home runs with men on base and batting average with runners in scoring position are available, we make further adjustments. First, figure out the player's home run percentage by dividing his home runs by his at-bats. Then multiply that number by his at-bats with men on base to find his expected home runs in that situation. Subtract the expected total from the real total, and add the result to his runs created. For example, a player with 20 homers in 600 overall at-bats who hit 10 homers in 150 at-bats with men on base would get an extra five runs created because he would have been expected to hit five. If he hit three homers in 150 at-bats with men on base, he would lose two runs created.

The runners-in-scoring-position adjustment works in similar fashion. Multiply a player's batting average by his at-bats with runners in scoring position to determine his expected hits in that situation. Subtract the expected number from the real number, and again add the result to his runs created. A .300 hitter who batted .350 in 200 at-bats with runners in scoring position would get 10 extra runs created (70 hits minus 60 expected hits). If he batted .280 in that situation, he would lose four runs created (56 hits minus 60 expected hits).

The second-to-last step is to round a player's runs created to the nearest integer. Finally, once all of a team's individual players' runs created have been calculated, compare their total to the team's runs scored and reconcile the difference proportionally. For instance, if a team's players created 700 runs and the club scored 728 runs, increase each player's runs created by 4 percent (728 / 700 = 1.04) and round each off to the nearest integer once again. Repeat if necessary until the two are equal.

Runs Created per 27 Outs (RC/27)

This statistic estimates how many runs per game a team made up of nine of the same player would score. The name is actually a misnomer, however, because Bill James has based his revised formula on the number of league outs per team game rather than 27. The calculation is runs created multiplied by league outs per team game, divided by outs made (the sum of a player's at-bats plus sacrifice hits plus sacrifice flies plus caught stealings plus grounded into double plays, less his hits), or:

$$((RC * ((3 * LgIP) / (2 * LgG))) / (AB - H + SH + SF + CS + GDP)$$

Save Percentage

Saves (SV) divided by Save Opportunities (OP).

Save Situation

Credit a pitcher with a save when he meets all three of the following conditions:

1. He is the finishing pitcher in a game won by his club.

2. He is not the winning pitcher.

3. He qualifies under one of the following conditions:

a. He enters the game with a lead of no more than three runs and pitches for at least one inning.

b. He enters the game, regardless of the count, with the potential tying run either on base, or at-bat, or on deck (that is, the potential tying run is either already on base or is one of the first two batsmen he faces).

c. He pitches effectively for at least three innings.

No more than one save may be credited in each game.

SB Success%

Stolen Bases divided by (Stolen Bases plus Caught Stealing).

Secondary Average

A way to look at a player's extra bases gained, independent of Batting Average. The formula:

$$(TB - H + BB + SB - CS) / AB$$

Similarity Score

A method of measuring the degree of similarity of two statistical lines for a player or a team. Two identical stat lines would generate a score of 1,000.

Slugging Percentage

Total Bases divided by At-Bats.

Speed Score

To figure speed scores, start with the player's record over the last two seasons combined. With that record, you figure six elements of the speed score:

1. The stolen base percentage. Figure the score here as $((SB + 3) / (SB + CS + 7) - .4) * 20$.

2. The frequency of stolen base attempts. Figure the score here as $(SB + CS) / (Singles + BB + HBP)$. Take the square root of that, and divide that by .07. If a player attempts to steal one-tenth of the time when he is on first base, you take the square root of .10 (.316) and divide that by .07, yielding a speed score of 4.52.

3. Triples. Figure the player's triples as a percentage of balls in play (3B) / (AB - HR - SO). From this assign an integer from 0 to 10, based on the following chart:

Less than .001	0
.001-.0023	1
.0023-.0039	2
.0039-.0058	3
.0058-.0080	4
.0080-.0105	5
.0105-.013	6
.013-.0158	7
.0158-.0189	8
.0189-.0223	9
.0223 or higher	10

4. The number of runs scored as a percentage of times on base. Figure first the percentage as (R - HR) / (H + HBP + BB - HR). From this subtract .1, and then divide by .04. Thus, if a player has 150 hits, five hit by pitcher and 95 walks, hits 30 home runs and scores 100 runs, you would figure (100 - 30) / (150 + 5 + 95 - 30), or $^{70}/_{220}$, which is .318. Subtract .1, and you have .218. Divide by .04, and his speed score on this point would be 5.45.

5. The frequency of grounding into double play. The formula here is ((.055 - (GDP / (AB - HR - SO)) / .005).

6. Range factor. If the player is a catcher, his speed score on this point is 1; if a first baseman, 2; if a designated hitter, 1.5. If he plays second base, then his speed score element six is 1.25 times his range factor; if third base, 1.51 times his range factor; if shortstop, 1.52 times his range factor; if the outfield, 3 times his range factor. Remember to figure range factors over a two-year period.

If any speed score is over 10.00, then move it down to 10; if it is less than zero, move it up to zero. No element can be outside the 0 to 10 range. When you have the six elements of the speed score, throw out the lowest one. The player's speed score is the average of the other five.

Times on Base
Hits plus Bases on Balls plus times Hit by Pitches.

Total Bases
Hits plus Doubles plus (2 * Triples) plus (3 * Home Runs).

Tough Loss
To determine the starting pitcher's Game Score: (1) Start with 50. (2) Add 1 point for each out recorded by the starting pitcher. (3) Add 2 points for each inning the pitcher completes after the fourth inning. (4) Add 1 point for each strikeout. (5) Subtract 2 points for each hit allowed. (6) Subtract 4 points for each earned run allowed. (7) Subtract 2 points for an unearned run. (8) Subtract 1 point for each walk.

If the starting pitcher scores over 50 and loses, it's a Tough Loss. The 2001 leaders in Tough Losses are listed in the Leader Board section.

Tough Save
This distinction is made to gauge the difficulty of a save. A Tough Save occurs if the reliever enters with the tying run anywhere on base.

Win-Loss Percentage or Winning Percentage
Wins divided by (Wins plus Losses).

Glosario en Español

% Inherited Scored (%Heredado que Anotó)

Estadística de Relevo que indica el porcentaje de corredores embasados (cuando el relevista entró al juego) que el relevista permitió que anotaran.

% Pitches Taken (% de Lanzamientos Observados)

Número de lanzamientos que el bateador no le tiró dividido por todos los lanzamientos que le enviaron.

1st Batter Average (Promedio del 1er Bateador)

El promedio de bateo permitido por un relevista al primer bateador enfrentado en un juego.

1st Batter OBP (Promedio de Embasamiento del 1er Bateador)

Promedio de Embasamiento permitido por un relevista al primer bateador enfrentado en un juego.

Active Career Batting Leaders

Un mínimo de 1,000 Veces-al-Bate requerido para Promedio de Bateo, Promedio de Enbasamiento, Promedio de Bases Acumuladas, Veces-al-Bate por Cuadrangular, Veces-al-Bate por Arranques para Doble Play, Veces-al-Bate para Empujadas, y la Relación de Ponches-a-Bases por Bolas. Cien (100) Intentos de Robar Bases son requeridos para calificar para el liderato de Exito de Bases Robadas. Cualquier pelotero que jugó en el 2001 es elegible para los liderato si cumplen estos requisitos.

Active Career Pitching Leaders

Un mínimo de 750 Entradas Lanzadas son requeridas para Efectividad, Promedio de Oponente, todos las categorías de "Por 9 Entradas", y la Relación de Ponches-a-Bases por Bolas. 250 juegos abiertos son requeridos para la Frecuencia de Juegos Completos. 100 Decisiones requeridas para el Porcentaje de Ganados-Perdidos. Cualquier lanzador que jugó en el 2001 es elegible para los liderato si cumplen estos requisitos.

AVG Allowed ScPos

Promedio de Bateo Permitido con Corredores en Posición de Anotar.

AVG Bases Loaded

Promedio de Bateo con las bases llenas.

Batting Average (Promedio de Bateo)

Imparables divididos por Veces-al-Bate.

Blown Save (Salvado Fallado)

Entrando en Situación de Salvamiento y permitiendo que anote la carrera del empate o de ventaja.

Career Assessments (Evaluación de Carrera).

Método para estimar la posibilidad de un jugador llegando a una marca especial. Por ejemplo, para los chances de llegar a 3,000 hits consideramos lo siguiente:

1. Hits Restantes para llegar a la marca (por supuesto, también puede ser cuadrangulares o dobles restantes),

2. Los Años Restante para llegar a la marca son estimados de esta manera: (42 menos la edad del jugador) dividido por dos. Esta fórmula asigna a un jugador de 20 años que va a jugar 11 temporadas más, a un jugador de 25 años 8.5 temporadas más, a un jugador de 35 años, 3.5 temporadas más. Adicionalmente, si un jugador tuvo 100 hits en la temporada pasada, asumimos que va a jugar por lo menos un año más, y en ciertas situaciones 1.5 años más. Para receptores, se les anticipa que jueguen solo el 70% de peloteros normales.

3. Nivel de Imparables Establecido. Para el 2001, el nivel tiene una fórmula de: [(Hits del 2001)x3] + [(Hits del 2000)x2] + [Hits del 1999], todo dividido por 6. Un jugador no puede tener un Nivel de Imparables Establecido de menos del 75% del número de hits en su última campaña. Por ejemplo, un jugador que tuvo 200 hits en el 2001, no puede tener un Nivel de Imparables Establecido menor de 150 hits.

4. Prógnostico de Hits. Esto es calculado al multiplicar los Años Restante por el Nivel de Imparables Establecido.

Ya cuando el Prognóstico de Hits es calculado, el chance de llegar a una marca se obtiene: [(Prognóstico de Hits) / (Hits Restantes)] - 0.5. Si el (Prognóstico de Hits) = (Hits Restantes), el chance de llegar a la marca es 50%. Jugadores no pueden tener un chance más de 148% de llegar a una marca.

Catcher's ERA (Efectividad de Pitcheo de Receptores)

La Efectividad de Pitcheo de un equipo con un receptor en particular detrás del plato: Multiplica las carreras limpias permitidas mientras el receptor jugaba por nueve, y divide el resultado por las entradas jugadas detrás del plato.

Cheap Win (Victoria Barata)

Una victoria con una Valoración de Juego (Game Score) de menos de 50.

Cleanup Slugging% (Promedio de Bases Acumuladas de Cuarto Bates)

El Promedio de Bases Acumuladas de un jugador cuando batea 4to en su alineación.

Complete Game % (Frecuencia de Juegos Completos)

Juegos Completos divididos por Juegos Abiertos.

Component ERA o ERC (Efectividad Componente)

Una estadística que analiza la Efectividad que un lanzador debió de haber tenido basado en como pitchó. Las partes para calcular la Efectividad Componente son:

1. (Hits Permitidos) menos (Cuadrangulares Permitidos)

2. Multiplicar el resultado de la Primera Parte por 1.255

3. Multiplicar Cuadrangulares Permitidos por Cuatro.

4. (Parte 2) sumada a (Parte 3).

5. Multiplicar el resultado de Parte 4 por 0.89.

6. Sumar (Bases por Bolas) a (Bateadores Golpeados).

7. Multiplicar Parte 6 por 0.475.

8. Sumar Parte 5 y Parte 7.

Esto resulta en la Base de la Efectividad Componente (BEC) de un lanzador:

$$(((H-HR) * 1.255) + (HR * 4)) * 0.89) + ((BB + BG) * 0.475)$$

Para lanzadores que tienen Bases por Bolas Intencionales (BBI), se ocupa la siguiente fórmula:

$$(((H-HR) * 1.255) + (HR * 4)) * .89) + ((BB + HB - BBI) * .56)$$

9. Sumar Hits más Bases por Bolas más Bateadores Golpeados.

10. Multiplicar Parte 9 por BEC.

11. Dividir Parte 10 por el número de Bateadores Enfrentado (BE) por el lanzador. Si no se puede encontrar los BE, aproximar por multiplicar entradas lanzadas por 2.9, y después sumar a Parte 9.

12. Multiplicar Parte 11 por Parte 9.

13. Dividir Parte 12 por Entradas Lanzadas (EL).

14. Restar 0.56 de Parte 13.

Esta es la Efectividad Componente de un lanzador:

$$(((((H + BB + BG) * BEC) / BE) * 9) / EL) - .56$$

Si el resultado después de Parte 13 es menos de 2.24, ajustar la fórmula de esta manera:

$$(((((H + BB + BG) * BEC) / BE) * 9) / EL) * .75$$

Earned Run Average (Efectividad)

(Carreras Limpias * 9) dividido por Entradas Lanzadas.

Easy Save (Salvado Fácil)

Un juego Salvado Fácil ocurre cuando el primer bateador enfrentado no representa la carrera del empate y el cerrador lanza una entrada o menos.

Fielding Percentage (Promedio de Fildeo)

(Bateadores Retirados más Asistencias) Dividido por (Bateadores Retirados más Asistencias más Errores)

Games Finished (Juego Cerrado)

El último relevista durante un juego se le da un Juego Cerrado.

Game Scores (Valoración de Juego)

Para determinar la Valoración de Juego de un abridor: Se empieza con 50. (2) Sumar 1 punto por cada out sacado por el lanzador. (3) Sumar 2 puntos por cada entrada completa después de la cuarta entrada. (4) Sumar 1 punto por cada ponche. (5) Restar 2 puntos por cada hit permitido. (6) Restar 4 puntos por cada Carrera Limpia permitida. (7) Restar 2 puntos por cada Carrera Sucia. (8) Restar 1 punto por cada Base por Bolas.

Las Valoraciones de Juego más altas en el 2001 están en la Sección de Líderes.

GDP (Arranque para Doble Play (ADP))

Bola de Arranque Bateada a un Doble Play.

GDP Opportunity (Oportunidad para ADP)

Cualquier situación con un corredor en primera base y menos de dos outs.

Ground/Fly Ratio (Grd/Fly) (Proporción de Arranques/Elevados (Arr/Ele))

Para bateadores, Arranques divididos por Elevados. Para lanzadores, Arranques permitidos dividido por Elevados permitidos. Todas bolas bateados son incluidas menos líneas o toques.

Hold (Sujetón)

A un relevista se le da un Sujetón cuando el relevista entra en una situación de Salvar, saca por lo menos un Out, y sale de juego sin rendir la delantera. Nota: Un lanzador no puede Cerrar un juego y recibir un Sujetón, ni puede ganarse un Sujetón y un Salvado en el mismo juego.

Inherited Runners (Corredores Heredados)

Cualquier corredor embasado cuando el relevista entra al juego es considerado Heredado por ese relevista.

Isolated Power (Poder Aislado)

Promedio de Bases Acumuladas (PBA) menos Promedio de Bateo (Pro).

K/BB Ratio (Proporción de K/BB)

Ponches (K) divididos por Bases por Bolas (BB).

Late & Close (Tarde y Reñido)

Una situación Tarde y Reñida es definida de esta manera: (1) el juego está en la séptima entrada o más avanzado, y (2) el equipo bateando tiene la ventaja por una carrera, está empatado, o tiene la carrera de un posible empate embasada

Leadoff On Base% (Promedio de Embasamiento del Primer Bate)

El Promedio de Embasamiento de un jugador cuando batea primero en la alineación.

LHS (AZ)

Abridor Zurdo.

Major League Equivalency (MLE) (Equivalente de Grades Ligas)

Una interpretación del valor en Grandes Ligas de las estadísticas de un jugador en las ligas menores de Doble-A o Triple-A. La fórmula considera el nivel de compentencia, la liga, el estadio local, y el estadio del equipo de Grandes Ligas de la organización a quien le pertenece el jugador.

Offensive Winning Percentage (OWP) (Promedio Ofensivo de Victorias)

El Promedio Ofensivo de Victorias (POV) iguala el promedio de juegos que el equipo hubiera ganado si el jugador hubiera bateado en las nueve posiciones de la alineación, considerando pitcheo y defensa normal. La fórmula es (Carreras Creadas por 27 Outs cuadradas), dividida por la suma de (Carreras Creadas por 27 Outs cuadradas) + (el Average de Carreras por Juego de la Liga cuadrado).

On-Base Percentage (Promedio de Embasamiento (PE))

(Hits + BB + Golpeado por Lanzador) dividido por (Veces-al-Bate + BB + Golpeado por Lanzador + Sacrificios).

Opponent Batting Average (Promedio de Oponente)

Hits Permitidos dividido por (Bateadores Enfrentados menos Bases por Bolas menos Bateadores Golpeados menos Toques de Sacrificio menos Elevados de Sacrificio menos Interferencias del Receptor).

PA*

Veces-al-Bate (VB) más Golpeado por Lanzador más Elevados de Sacrificio; o Apariciones al Plato menos Sacrificios y Embasamientos por Interferencia Defensiva.

Park Index (Indice de Estadio)

El método para medir las influencias de los estadios a una estadística. Usando Cuadrangulares como ejemplo:

1. Sumar Cuadrangulares de Locales y Cuadrangulares de Rivales en casa.

2. Sumar Veces-al-Bate de locales y Veces-al-Bate de Rivales en casa. (Usar juegos en casa si no se pueden encontrar VB.)

3. Dividir Parte 1 por Parte 2.

4. Sumar Cuadrangulares de Locales y Cuadrangulares de Rivales como visitante.

5. Sumar Veces-al-Bate y Veces-al-Bate de Rivales como visitante. (Usar juegos en como visitante si no se pueden encontrar VB.)

6. Dividir Parte 4 por Parte 5.

7. Dividir Parte 3 por Parte 6.

8. Multiplicar Parte 7 por 100.

Un índice de 100 significa que el estadio es neutral. Un índice de 118 para cuadrangulares significa que el estadio favorece cuadrangulares por un 18% que en un parque normal.

PCS (Pitchers Caught Stealing) Atrapados Robando por Lanzador

El número de corredor retirados por el lanzador, no el receptor, tirando a una base para mantener al corredor cerca de la base, y el corredor trata de avanzar a la próxima base cuando es tocado para out. La jugada más común es del lanzador al inicialista al campocorto (1-3-6). Al corredor se le da un Atrapado Robando porque trató de avanzar a la base siguiente.

Pitches per PA (Lanzamientos por Turnos al Plato)

Para un bateador, el número de lanzamientos recibidos divididos por el número total de Veces al Plato.

PkOf Throw/Runner (Tiros a Primera/Corredor)

El número de Tiros a Primera por un lanzador dividido por el número de embasados en primera base.

Plate Appearances (Veces a Caja de Bateo)

Veces-al-Bate más total de Bases por Bolas más Golpeado por Lanzador más Toques y Elevados de Sacrificio más Embasamientos por Interferencia Defensiva.

Power/Speed Number (Poder/Velocidad)

Una manera de ver Poder y Velocidad en un número. Un jugador tienen que tener muchos cuadrangulares y bases robadas para tener un número de Poder/Velocidad. La fórmula es (HR * BR* 2) dividido por (HR + BR).

PPO (Pitcher Pickoff) (Pickoffs de Lanzador)

El número de embasados retirados cuando un lanzador tira a una base para mantener los corredores cerca a la base y el corredor es out tratando de regresar a la base. Pickoffs no es una estadística oficial y no cuenta como un Atrapado Robando.

Quality Start (Inicio de Calidad)

Un juego iniciado de calidad es cuando un abridor trabaja por lo menos seis entradas y permite tres carreras limpias o menos.

Quality Start Percentage (Porcentaje de Inicios de Calidad)

Inicios de Calidad dividido por Juegos Iniciados.

Quick Hooks and Slow Hooks (Gatillo Rápido y Gatillo Lento)

Un Gatillo Rápido es cuando un Abridor es sacado de un juego y ha trabajado menos de 6 entradas y ha permitido 3 carreras o menos. Un Gatillo Lento es cuando un pitcher lanza más de nueve entradas, o permite 7 o más carreras, o la combinación de entradas lanzadas y carreras permitidas suman 13 o más.

Range Factor (Coeficiente de Alcance)

El número de Chances Exitosos (Retirados más Asistencias) multiplicado por 9 y dividido por el número de Entradas Defensivas Jugadas. El averaje para cada posición en el 2001:

Segunda Base:	4.86	J. Izquierdo:	2.02
Tercera Base:	2.64	J. Central:	2.63
Campocorto:	4.48	J. Derecho:	2.10

RHS (AD)

Abridor Derecho.

Run Support Per 9 IP (Carreras de Soporte por 9 Entradas Lanzadas)

El número de carreras anotadas por el equipo del lanzador mientras él estaba en el juego, multiplicadas por nueve, y dividido por sus Entradas Lanzadas.

Runs Created (Carreras Creadas)

Bill James ha creado 24 diferentes fórmulas para calcular Carreras Creadas. La fórmula actual es:

1. Sumar Hits + Bases por Bolas + Golpeados por Lanzador.

2. Restar Atrapado Robando y Arranques para Doble Plays de Parte 1. Este es el Factor A.

3. Sumar Bases por Bolas (no intencionales) + Golpeados por Lanzador.

4. Multiplicar Parte 3 por 0.24.

5. Multiplicar Bases Robadas por 0.62.

6. Sumar Toques de Sacrificio + Elevados de Sacrificio.

7. Multiplicar Parte 6 by 0.5.

8. Sumar Bases Acumuladas + Parte 4 + Parte 5 + Parte 7.

9. Multiplicar Ponches por 0.03.

10. Restar Parte 9 de Parte 8. Esto es el Factor B.

11. Sumar Veces-al-Bate + Bases por Bolas + Golpeados por Lanzador + Toques de Sacrificio + Elevados de Sacrificio. Esto es el Factor C.

Resumen:

$$A = H + BB + GPL - AR - ADP$$

$$B = ((BB - BBI + GPL) * .24) + (BR * .62) + ((TS + ES) * .5) + BA - (K * .03)$$

$$C = VB + BB + GPL + TS + ES$$

Las Carreras Creadas por cada jugador son determinadas como si él jugara con otros ocho jugadores con abilidades normales. Las últimas partes son:

12. Multiplicar C por 2.4.

13. Sumar A + Parte 12.

14. Multiplicar C por 3.

15. Sumar B + Parte 14.

16. Multiplicar Parte 13 por Parte 15.

17. Multiplicar C por 9.

18. Dividir Parte 16 por Parte 17.

19. Multiplicar C por 0.9.

20. Restar Parte 19 de Parte 18.

Escrito como fórmula:

$$((((C * 2.4) + A) * ((C * 3) + B)) / (C * 9)) - (C * .9)$$

Cuando se pueden encontrar las estadísticas de Cuadrangulares con Embasados y Promedio de Bateo con corredores en Posición de Anotar, la fórmula se puede refinar. Primero, dividir Cuadrangulares por Veces-al-Bate. Después multiplicar ese número por las Veces-al-Bate con Embasados para encontrar el número de cuadrangulares esperados en esa situación. Restar el total esperado por el total actual, y sumar el resultado a sus Carreras Creadas. Por ejemplo, un jugador con 20 cuadrangulares en 600 Veces-al-Bate que conectó 10 cuadrangulares en 150 Veces-al-Bate con Embasados, recibiría cinco Carreras Creadas extras. Si hubiera conectado solo tres cuadrangulares en 150 Veces-al-Bate, hubiera perdido dos Carreras Creadas.

El ajustamiento de Embasados-en-Posición-de-Anotar funciona similarmente. Multiplicar Promedio de Bateo en las Veces-al-Bate con Embasados en Posición de Anotar para determinar el número de hits esperados en esa situación. Restar el número esperado por el número actual, y sumar el resultado a sus Carreras Creadas. Un jugador de .300 que bateó .350 en 200 Veces-al-Bate con Embasados en Posición de Anotar recibiría 10 Carreras Creadas extras (70 hits menos 60 hits esperados). Si él bateara .280 en esa situación, él perdería cuatro Carreras Creadas (56 hits menos 60 hits esperados).

La penúltima parte es apróximar las Carreras Creadas al número entero más cercano. Finalmente, después de haber calculado Carreras Creadas para todos los jugadores en un equipo, se comparan sus totales al total de Carreras anotadas por el equipo y ajustar las diferencias proporcionalmente. Por ejemplo, si los jugadores de un equipo crearon 700 carreras y el equipo anotó 728 carreras, se le añade a cada jugador un 4 por ciento (728 / 700 = 1.04) y de nuevo apróximar cada Carrera Creada al número entero más cercano. Repitan esto hasta que los dos números sean iguales.

Runs Created per 27 Outs (RC/27); (Carreras Creadas por 27 Outs; CC/27)

Esta estadística estima cuantas carreras por partido anotaría un equipo integrado de nueve del mismo jugador. (La fórmula un poco mal nombrada por que Bill James basa la fórmula en outs por equipo, no por 27.) La calculación es Carreras Creadas multiplicadas por Outs por Equipo en la liga, dividido por Outs (la suma de las Veces-al-Bate del jugador menos sus Hits más Toques de Sacrificio más Elevados de Sacrificios más Atrapados Robando más Arranques para Doble Plays):

$$((CC * (3 * \text{Entradas Lanzadas de la Liga} / (2 * \text{Juegos de la Liga}))) / (VB - H + TS + ES + AR + ADP)$$

Save Percentage (Promedio de Salvados)

Salvados (SV) divididos by Oportunidades de Salvar (OP).

Save Situation (Situación de Salvar)

Se le da a un relevista un Salvado cuando cumple éstas tres condiciones:

1. El es el último lanzador en un juego ganado por su equipo.

2. El no fue el lanzador ganador.

3. Y una de las siguientes condiciones:

a. Entra al juego con tres carreras o menos de ventaja y lanza por lo menos una entrada.

b. Entra al juego con la posible carrera del empate en base, o bateando, o en el círculo de espera.

c. Lanza bien en tres o más entradas.

No se puede otorgar más de un Salvado por cada juego.

SB Success% (Promedio de Bases Robadas)

Bases Robadas divididas por (Bases Robadas más Atrapados Robando).

Secondary Average (Promedio Secundario)

Extra bases acumuladas independientemente de Promedio de Bateo:

$$(BA - H + BB + BR - AR) / VB$$

Similarity Score (Marca de Similaridad)

Método para medir la similaridad de dos estadísticas para un jugador o para un equipo. Dos líneas identicas tienen una Marca de Similaridad de 1,000.

Slugging Percentage (Promedio de Bases Acumuladas)

Bases Acumuladas divididas por Veces-al-Bate.

Speed Score (Marca de Velocidad)

La Marca de Velocidad se calcula ocupando las estadísticas de un jugador en sus últimas dos temporadas:

1. Promedio de Bases Robadas. Calcula la marca así: $((BR + 3) / (BR + AR + 7) - .4) * 20$.

2. La frecuencia de Intentos de Robar Bases. Calcula la marca así: $(BR + AR) / (\text{Sencillos} + BB + GPL)$. Saquen la raíz cuadrada del resultado, y dividanlo por 0.07. Si un jugador intenta robar un décimo de veces que está en primera, le sacan la raíz cuadrada de 0.10 (0.316) y dividanlo por 0.07, resultando en una Marca de Velocidad de 4.52 en esta categoría.

3. Triples. Calculen triples como el porcentaje de pelotas en juego (3B)/(VB-HR-K). Con este resultado, asignenle al jugador un número redondo de 0 a 10 basado en lo siguiente:

Menos de .001	0
.001-.0023	1
.0023-.0039	2
.0039-.0058	3
.0058-.0080	4
.0080-.0105	5
.0105-.013	6
.013-.0158	7
.0158-.0189	8
.0189-.0223	9
.0223 para arriba	10

4. El número de carreras anotadas como un porcentaje de veces en base. Calculen el porcentaje: (C - HR)/(H + GPL + BB - HR). Resten 0.1 del resultado y dividanlo por 0.04. Así que si un jugador tiene 150 Hits, 5 Golpeados por Lanzador y 95 Bases por Bolas, 30 Cuadrangulares y anota 100 carreras, uno calcularía: (100 - 30) / (150 + 5 + 95 - 30), o $^{70}/_{220}$, que es 0.318. Restenle 0.1 y tienen 0.218. Dividanlo por 0.04 y la Marca de Velocidad en esta categoría es 5.45.

5. Frecuencia de Arrancar para Doble Plays: ((.055 - (ADP / (VB - HR - SO)) / .005).

6. Coeficiente de Alcance. Si el jugador es un receptor, su Marca de Velocidad de esta categoría es 1; si es un primera Base, 2; si es un bateador designado, 1.5. Si juega segunda base, la marca de su sexta categoría es su Coeficiente de Alcance multiplicado por 1.25; si es un tercera base, su Coeficiente de Alcance multiplicado por 1.51; si es un campocorto, su Coeficiente de Alcance multiplicado por 1.52; si es un jardinero, su coeficiente de alcance multiplicado por 3. (Recuerdense de ocupar números de sus últimas dos temporadas.

Si el resultado de cualquiera de estas categorías fue más de 10, bajenlo a 10; si un resultado fue menos de cero, subanlo a cero. Ninguna categoría debe de estar afuera de 0 a 10. Ya cuando tengan los resultados de las seis categorías, eliminen la marca más baja. La Marca de Velocidad de un jugador es el averaje de las otras cinco.

Times on Base (Veces en Base)
Hits + Bases por Bolas + Golpeados por Lanzador.

Total Bases (Bases Acumuladas)
Hits + Dobles + (2 * Triples) + (3 * Cuadrangulares).

Tough Loss (Derrota Difícil)
Para determinar la Valoración de Juego de un abridor: (1) Se empieza con 50. (2) Sumar 1 punto por cada out sacado por el lanzador. (3) Sumar 2 puntos por cada entrada completa después de la cuarta entrada. (4) Sumar 1 punto por cada ponche. (5) Restar 2 puntos por cada hit permitido. (6) Restar 4 puntos por cada Carrera Limpia permitida. (7) Restar 2 puntos por cada Carrera Sucia. (8) Restar 1 punto por cada Base por Bolas.

Si el abridor tiene una Valoración de Juego más alta de 50 y pierde, entonces fue una Derrota Dura. Los abridores con más Derrotas Duras están en la Sección de Líderes.

Tough Save (Salvado Difícil)
Un Salvado Difícil ocurre cuando un relevista entra al juego con la posible carrera del empate en base.

Win-Loss Percentage or Winning Percentage (Promedio de Ganado-Perdidos o Porcentaje de Ganados)
Ganados divididos por (Victorias más Derrotas).

About STATS, Inc.

STATS, Inc., a News Corporation company, is affiliated with, and the official statistics provider to FOX Sports. STATS collects and disseminates most, if not all, of the information found within these pages, in addition to the statistics you might find on your favorite web site. STATS, Inc. is the nation's leading sports information and statistical analysis company, providing detailed sports services for a wide array of consumer and commercial clients.

As one of the elite companies in sports, STATS provides the most detailed, up-to-the-minute sports information to professional teams, print and broadcast media, software developers and interactive service providers around the country. STATS' network of trained sports reporters records the details of more than 3,800 sporting events across the four major sports annually. Some of our major clients include FOX Sports, the Associated Press, Lycos, *The Sporting News*, ESPN.com, Yahoo!, Electronic Arts, MSNBC, SONY and Topps.

STATS Publishing, a division of STATS, Inc., produces 10 pro sports annuals, including the *Major League Handbook*, *The Scouting Notebook*, the *Pro Football Handbook*, the *Pro Basketball Handbook* and the *Hockey Handbook*. The annuals now are available in an e-book format on our website (www.stats.com), as well as the traditional book form. In 1998, we introduced two baseball encyclopedias, the *All-Time Major League Handbook* (second edition updated through 1999) and the *All-Time Baseball Sourcebook*. Together they combine for more than 5,000 pages of baseball history. We added the *Pro Football Sourcebook* as an annual in 2000. Also, original articles by STATS authors appear three times per week in the Insider section of ESPN.com. All of our publications and additional editorial content deliver STATS' expertise to fans, scouts, general managers and media across the country.

In addition, STATS Fantasy Sports is at the forefront of the fantasy sports industry. We develop fantasy baseball, football, basketball, hockey, golf and auto racing games for a host of sites. We also feature the first historical baseball simulation game created specifically for the Internet—Diamond Legends. No matter what time of year, STATS Fantasy Sports has a fantasy game to keep even the most passionate sports fan satisfied.

Information technology has grown by leaps and bounds in the last decade. STATS will continue to be at the forefront as a supplier of the most up-to-date, in-depth sports information available.

For more information on our products, or on joining our reporter network, contact us via:

Internet — www.stats.com
      http://biz.stats.com

Toll Free in the USA at 1-800-63-STATS (1-800-637-8287)

Outside the USA at 1-847-470-8798

Or write to:

STATS, Inc.
8130 Lehigh Ave.
Morton Grove, IL 60053

Acerca de STATS, Inc.

STATS, Inc., una compañía de la News Corporation, es afiliada, y es la proveedora oficial de estadísticas para Fox Sports. STATS recauda y distribuye la información en este libro, así como las estadísticas en tus sitios de internet favoritos. STATS, Inc. es la compañía vanguardia de información y análisis estadístico en Norte América, abasteciendo servicios deportivos a una numerosa colección de clientes.

Como una compañía vanguardia en deportes, STATS distribuye la información más detallada al instante a equipos profesionales, periódicos, televisión, compañías desarrolladoras de videojuegos y de servicios interactivos. La red de reporteros de STATS cubren los detalles de más de 10,000 eventos deportivos. Nuestra lista de clientes incluyen Fox Sports, la AP, Univisión, Lycos, *The Sporting News*, ESPN.com, ESPNDeportes, Yahoo!, Electronic Arts, MSNBC, SONY y Topps.

STATS Publishing, una división de STATS, Inc., produce 10 libros anuales, incluyendo este *Major League Handbook*, *The Scouting Notebook*, el *Pro Football Handbook*, el *Pro Basketball Handbook* y el *Hockey Handbook*. En 1998, introducimos dos enciclopedias de beisbol, el *All-Time Major League Handbook* (la segunda edición actualizada en el 2000) y el *All-Time Baseball Sourcebook*. Juntas, las enciclopedias tienen más de 5,000 páginas de la historia del beisbol. Incorporamos el *Pro Football Sourcebook* como un libro anual en el 2000. También, artículos escritos por STATS aparecen tres veces a la semana en la sección *Insider* de ESPN.com.

Además, STATS Fantasy Sports está en la delantera de la industria de juegos de deportes de fantasía. Nosotros desarrollamos juegos de fantasía de beisbol, fútbol, fútbol americano, basquetbol, hockey, golf y de carreras para sitios de internet. Nosotros tambien brindamos el único juego de beisbol histórico creado específico para el internet—Diamond Legends (Leyendas del Diamante). No importa que fecha del año, STATS Fantasy Sports tiene un juego de fantasía para satisfacer los aficionados del deporte.

Las telecomunicaciones han crecido increíblemente en la última década. STATS continuará como la compañía vanguardia de abastecimiento de datos de deportes al instante.

Para más información sobre nuestros productos, contáctenos de las siguientes maneras:

Internet — www.stats.com
        http://biz.stats.com

Para llamar gratis en los Estados Unidos: 1-800-63-STATS (1-800-637-8287)

1-847-470-8798

Escribanos a:

STATS, Inc.
8130 Lehigh Ave.
Morton Grove, IL 60053
Estados Unidos

Notes

Notes

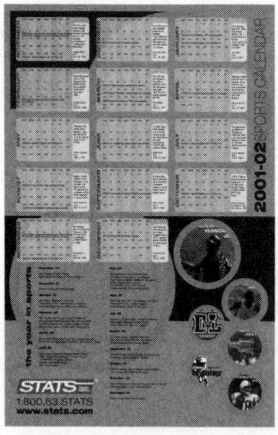

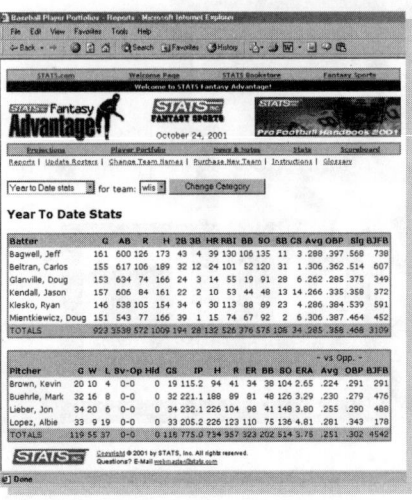
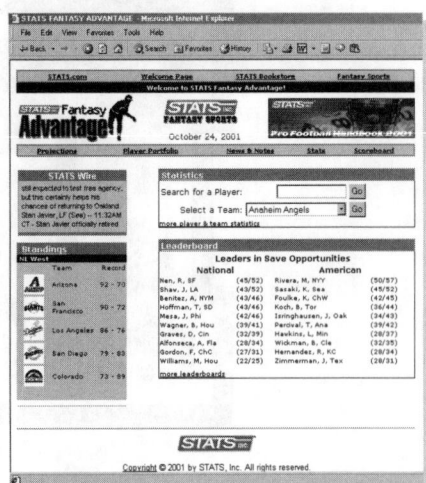